UNIT V: GENETIC ANALYSIS OF POPULATIONS

21   Genetic Analysis of Quantitative Traits   713

22   Population Genetics and Evolution at the Population, Species, and Molecular Levels   742

19   Cancer and Regulation of the Cell Cycle*   *469*

21   Genomics, Bioinformatics, and Proteomics*   *522*

SPECIAL TOPICS IN MODERN GENETICS

3   DNA Forensics*   *701*

4   Genomics and Personalized Medicine*   *712*

5   Genetically Modified Foods*   *724*

6   Gene Therapy*   *738*

Integrated and Improved Problem-Solving Strategy

Genetic Analysis worked examples provide unparalleled support for problem-solving instruction.

A consistent approach to problem solving is used throughout the book to help students understand the logic and purpose of each step in the problem-solving process. Genetic Analysis is integrated throughout each chapter, following discussions of important content, to help students immediately apply concepts in a problem-solving context.

Each Genetic Analysis example guides students with a unique, consistent, three-step approach that trains them to **Evaluate, Deduce,** and then **Solve** problems.

Every Genetic Analysis example is presented in a clear, **two-column format** that helps students see the Solution Strategy in one column and its corresponding execution in a separate Solution Step column.

NEW! A new **"Break it Down"** component has been added to help students get started with formulating an approach to solving a problem.

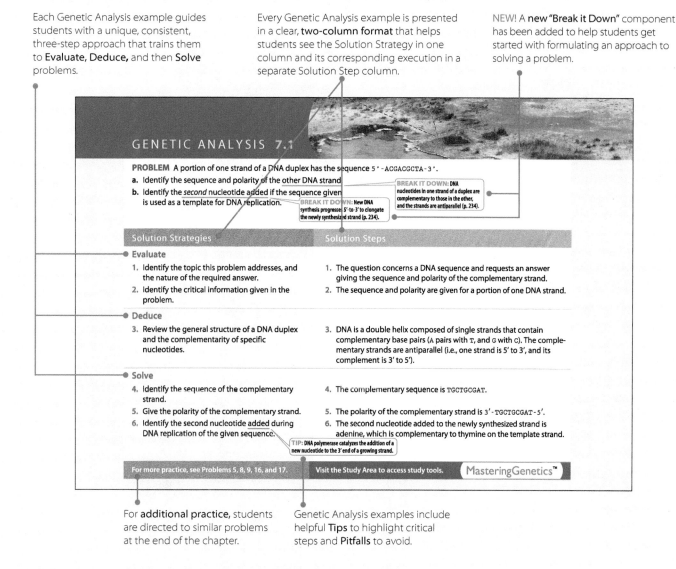

GENETIC ANALYSIS 7.1

PROBLEM A portion of one strand of a DNA duplex has the sequence 5'-ACGACGCTA-3'.
a. Identify the sequence and polarity of the other DNA strand.
b. Identify the *second* nucleotide added if the sequence given is used as a template for DNA replication.

BREAK IT DOWN: New DNA synthesis progresses 5'-to-3' to elongate the newly synthesized strand (p. 234).

BREAK IT DOWN: DNA nucleotides in one strand of a duplex are complementary to those in the other, and the strands are antiparallel (p. 234).

Solution Strategies	Solution Steps
Evaluate	
1. Identify the topic this problem addresses, and the nature of the required answer.	1. The question concerns a DNA sequence and requests an answer giving the sequence and polarity of the complementary strand.
2. Identify the critical information given in the problem.	2. The sequence and polarity are given for a portion of one DNA strand.
Deduce	
3. Review the general structure of a DNA duplex and the complementarity of specific nucleotides.	3. DNA is a double helix composed of single strands that contain complementary base pairs (A pairs with T, and G with C). The complementary strands are antiparallel (i.e., one strand is 5' to 3', and its complement is 3' to 5').
Solve	
4. Identify the sequence of the complementary strand.	4. The complementary sequence is TGCTGCGAT.
5. Give the polarity of the complementary strand.	5. The polarity of the complementary strand is 3'-TGCTGCGAT-5'.
6. Identify the second nucleotide added during DNA replication of the given sequence.	6. The second nucleotide added to the newly synthesized strand is adenine, which is complementary to thymine on the template strand.

TIP: DNA polymerase catalyzes the addition of a new nucleotide to the 3' end of a growing strand.

For more practice, see Problems 5, 8, 9, 16, and 17.   Visit the Study Area to access study tools.   MasteringGenetics™

For **additional practice**, students are directed to similar problems at the end of the chapter.

Genetic Analysis examples include helpful **Tips** to highlight critical steps and **Pitfalls** to avoid.

The accompanying **Student Solutions Manual and Study Guide** (ISBN 10: 0-13-379558-6) provides additional worked problems along with tips for solving problems. It also presents solutions to all of the textbook problems in a consistent *Evaluate, Deduce,* and *Solve* format to complement the approach modeled in the Genetic Analysis examples.

MasteringGenetics Provides 24/7 Coaching in Solving Genetics Problems

In-depth tutorials, focused on key genetics concepts, reinforce problem-solving skills by coaching students with hints and feedback specific to their misconceptions.

Transcription and RNA Processing

During transcription, RNA polymerase synthesizes RNA from a DNA template with the help of accessory proteins. In this tutorial, you will review the steps of transcription in eukaryotes and bacteria and investigate splicing of mRNAs in eukaryotes.

Part A - Transcription in bacteria

The diagram below shows a length of DNA containing a bacterial gene.

Drag the labels to their appropriate locations in the diagram to describe the function or characteristics of each part of the gene. Not all labels will be used.

If an incorrect answer is submitted, MasteringGenetics gives **instant feedback specific to the error made,** helping students overcome misconceptions and strengthen problem-solving skills.

Submit Hints My Answers Give Up Review Part

Incorrect; Try Again; 5 attempts remaining

You labeled 2 of 5 targets incorrectly. For (b), recall that transcription of inverted repeats produces an RNA transcript containing complementary segments. What three-dimensional arrangement results when those segments base-pair with each other?

If students working on a tutorial get stuck, they can access hints to get back on track.

MasteringGenetics: Transcription and RNA Processing - Google Chrome

session.masteringgenetics.com/myct/itemView?assignmentProblemID=2791894&hintID=1

Hint 1. Specific sequences in bacterial genes (click to open)

Hint 2. How are the two DNA strands of a gene used during transcription?

A short stretch of a coding strand has the sequence 5'-CGGCTAGAAT-3'. What are the sequences of the template strand and the RNA transcript?

Complete the table by dragging the correct label to the appropriate location. Labels may be used once, more than once, or not at all.

Coding strand	5'-CGGCTAGAAT-3'
Template strand	
RNA transcript	

Submit My Answers Give Up

Tutorial Topics include:

- Pedigree Analysis
- Recombination and Linkage Mapping
- Sex Linkage
- Gene Interactions
- DNA Replication
- Transcription and RNA Processing
- Translation
- Quantitative Genetics
- Genomics: Sequencing and Genome Databases

…and more!

NEW! A **bank of approximately 140 new practice problems** is now available for assignments. These questions, only available in MasteringGenetics, include coaching and feedback and are not duplicated elsewhere in the end-of-chapter problem sets, test bank, Study Area, or solutions manual.

A wide variety of question types helps engage students with different types of activities, including labeling, sorting, multiple-choice, short-answer, and figure questions. **About 90 percent of the book's end-of-chapter problems are now assignable** in the MasteringGenetics item library.

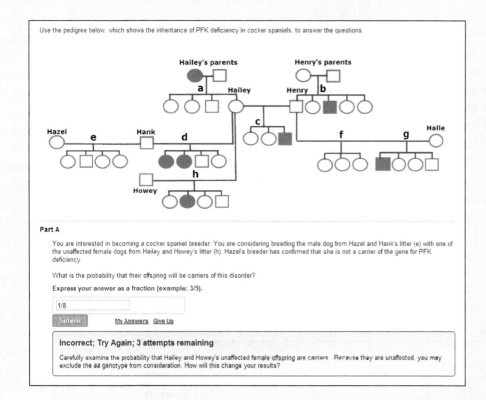

Use the pedigree below, which shows the inheritance of PFK deficiency in cocker spaniels, to answer the questions.

Part A

You are interested in becoming a cocker spaniel breeder. You are considering breeding the male dog from Hazel and Hank's litter (e) with one of the unaffected female dogs from Hailey and Howey's litter (h). Hazel's breeder has confirmed that she is not a carrier of the gene for PFK deficiency.

What is the probability that their offspring will be carriers of this disorder?

Express your answer as a fraction (example: 3/5).

1/8

Submit   My Answers   Give Up

Incorrect; Try Again; 3 attempts remaining

Carefully examine the probability that Hailey and Howey's unaffected female offspring are carriers. Because they are unaffected, you may exclude the aa genotype from consideration. How will this change your results?

Pre-built assignments help instructors easily assign questions focused on the key ideas of each chapter. Curated by experienced MasteringGenetics users, these "best of" homework assignments contain the most frequently assigned questions from the library.

NEW! Learning Catalytics is a "bring your own device" assessment and classroom activity system that expands the possibilities for student engagement. Using Learning Catalytics, you can deliver a wide range of auto-gradable or open-ended questions that test content knowledge and build critical thinking skills. Eighteen different answer types provide great flexibility, including graphical, numerical, textual input, and more.

MasteringGenetics users may select from Pearson's new library of question clusters that explore challenging genetics topics through a series of 2–5 questions that focus on a single scenario or data set, build in difficulty, and require higher-level thinking.

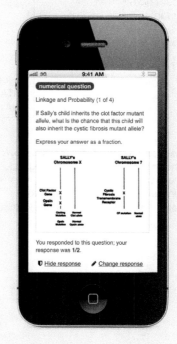

New, Up-to-Date Discussions on Genomics, Epigenetics and More

Genomic investigations are rapidly expanding and changing what we know about genetics. **Coverage of important techniques and findings are integrated throughout the text.**

New coverage includes a discussion of the impact of lateral gene transfer on bacterial genomes in Chapter 6; a new Experimental Insight of cancer genomics in Chapter 12; discussions of new genome methods and analyses in Chapter 18; and updated coverage of the human genome, including data on interaction with Neandertals and Denisovans in Chapter 22.

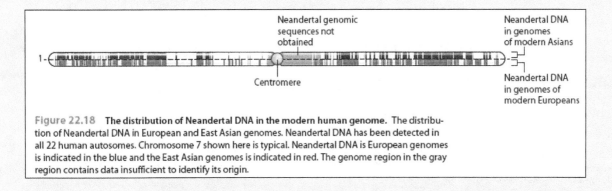

Figure 22.18 **The distribution of Neandertal DNA in the modern human genome.** The distribution of Neandertal DNA in European and East Asian genomes. Neandertal DNA has been detected in all 22 human autosomes. Chromosome 7 shown here is typical. Neandertal DNA is European genomes is indicated in the blue and the East Asian genomes is indicated in red. The genome region in the gray region contains data insufficient to identify its origin.

NEW! **Expanded coverage of archaea molecular biology** is presented in Chapters 7, 8, 9, 11, 12, and 14. These recent advancements in understanding the genetics and molecular biology of archaea allow insightful comparisons to the genetics of bacteria and eukaryotes, particularly in relation to molecular genetic processes and to evolution.

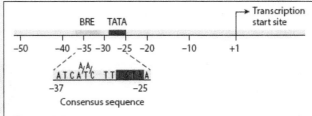

Figure 8.16 **Archaea promoter consensus sequences.** The TATA box and BRE box sequences bind TBP and TFB along with RNA polymerase to initiate transcription.

NEW! **Revised and expanded coverage of epigenetics** shows how epigenetics is at the heart of the evolution and regulation of gene expression in eukaryotes. Enhanced coverage appears in Chapters 11 and 15, including discussions of the histone code and chromatin states, and on epigenetic readers, writers, and erasers.

Epigenetic Heritability

Activating the transcription of an individual gene requires a confluence of regulatory proteins that remodel or modify chromatin to provide enhancer and promoter access to transcription factors that initiate and carry out transcript synthesis, as we saw above in the detailed description of *PHO5* transcription. Mechanisms controlling differential chromatin state formation and maintenance produce patterns of gene expression in different types of cells that are required for the growth and development of complex organisms. In a broad sense, these regulatory processes are the reason a single fertilized egg can develop and produce many distinct types of cells (liver cells, muscle cells, brain cells, and so on) that look and act differently even though they carry the same genetic information.

Among the trillions of somatic cells in your body are scores of different cell types, and yet all these cells contain the same genetic information. The differences of morphology and function between cell types are genetically controlled, as evidenced by the fact that daughter cells have the same structures and functions as parental cells, but DNA sequence variability *is not* the reason for those

Unique, Carefully-Crafted Figures Illustrate and Clarify Complex Processes

Nine Foundation Figures combine visuals and words to help students grasp pivotal genetics concepts in a concise, easy-to-follow format.

Three new Foundation Figures have been added to the Second Edition.

Fig. 4.22 Epistatic Ratios
NEW! Fig. 7.14 DNA Replication
Fig. 7.22 The Trombone Model of DNA Replication
NEW! Fig. 8.6 Bacterial Transcription
Fig. 8.22 The Gene Expression Machine Model for Coupling Transcription with pre-mRNA Processing
NEW! Fig. 9.9 Bacterial Translation Elongation
Fig. 11.6 Condensing the Nuclear Material
Fig. 12.25 Molecular Model of Meiotic Recombination
Fig.14.23 Regulation of Bacteriophage Entry into the Lytic or Lysogenic Cycle

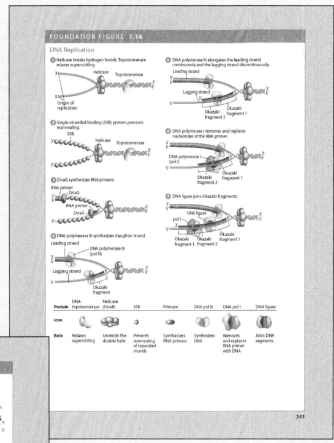

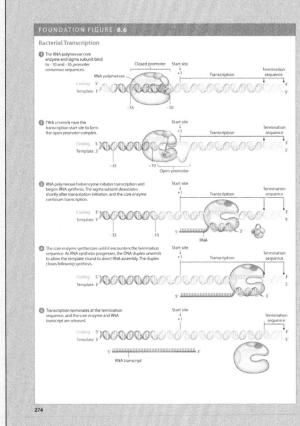

An Integrated Approach to Mendelian and Molecular Genetics

Within a traditional chapter organization, Sanders and Bowman integrate transmission genetics and molecular genetics in the text, tables, and figures. This approach helps in demonstrating how today's geneticists think.

Table 2.6 identifies the molecular characterization of four of the pea plant traits Mendel studied. It provides a synopsis of the wild-type and mutant functions of the four known genes.

Table 2.6	Identification and Molecular Characterization of Four of Mendel's Traits			
Trait	Gene and Gene Product	Wild-Type Allele and Function	Mutant Allele and Function	Reference
Seed shape (round and wrinkled seeds)	The gene is *Sbe1*, producing starch-branching enzyme.	The dominant wild-type allele (*R*) produces starch-branching enzyme that converts amylase, a linear starch, into amylopectin, a complex branched starch.	The recessive mutant allele (*r*) contains an inserted segment about 800 base pairs in length. The transcript of the mutant allele does not produce an enzyme product, resulting in a loss of function.	Bhattacharyya, M. K., et al. 1990. *Cell* 60: 115–122.
Stem length (tall and short plants)	The gene is *Le*, producing gibberellin 3β-hydroxylase (G3βH).	G3βH produced by the dominant allele *Le* converts a precursor in the synthesis of the plant growth hormone gibberellin that causes plants to grow tall.	The recessive mutant *le* allele contains a base substitution that results in an amino acid change. The mutant G3βH has less than 5% the activity of the wild-type product and produces little gibberellin, leading to short plants.	Lester, D. R., et al. 1997. *Plant Cell* 9: 1435–1443. Martin, D. N., et al. 1997. *Proc. Natl. Acad. Sci., USA* 94: 8907–8911.

Experimental Insight essays discuss influential experiments, summarize real data derived from the experiments, and explain conclusions drawn from the analysis of results. NEW! Experimental Insight 12.1 describes the base substitutions or deletions responsible for mutations of three of the Mendel genes, and NEW! Experimental Insight 13.2 describes the transposition event that is the cause of mutation of the fourth gene.

Experimental Insight 12.1

Mendel's Mutations

Table 2.6 on page 000 and the accompanying text briefly describe the wild-type and mutant alleles of the four genes of Mendel that h[...] described in this [...] tions and are de[...] described in Sect[...]

STEM LENGTH: A[...]

The *Le* gene va[...] groups led by D[...] mined that the l[...] produces an enz[...] produces the gr[...] effect of the dom[...] of growth hormo[...] long stems that [...] mutant allele (*le*[...] reduces the bios[...] 5% of the wild-ty[...] short plants.

The *le* allele [...] changes an alani[...] of the gene. This [...] to A-T transition[...] It is an example [...] function of the a[...] sequence of the [...] synthesis of a gro[...]

POD COLOR: AN[...]

The 2007 studie[...] groups led by la[...] molecular basis [...] and the recessiv[...] ele produces an [...] of chlorophyll c[...] normally occurs [...] results in mature[...]

produces a very poorly functioning enzyme, largely disabling a critical step of chlorophyll breakdown. Consequently, chlo-

Experimental Insight 13.2

Mendel's Peas Are Shaped by Transposition

Gregor Mendel left good descriptions, data, and analyses of the crosses he used for establishing the law of segregation and the law of independent assortment, but he did not leave any seeds to give geneticists direct access to the genes themselves. Experimental Insight 12.1 identifies three of the genes studied by Mendel that have now been identified and analyzed. Details of the discovery in 1990 of a fourth gene are described here. It is the gene responsible for the round and wrinkled seed shapes described by Mendel, now known as *SBE1*, the starch branching enzyme 1 gene.

The gene was identified and shown to be responsible for the seed shape variation Mendel reported by a laboratory group led by Cathie Martin (Bhattacharyya et al., 1990). In its paper, the group reports western blot, northern blot, and Southern blot evidence that the recessive mutant allele, *r*, is altered by the insertion of approximately 800 bp of DNA. The insertion is of transposable DNA, and its effect is insertional inactivation of the ability to produce a starch branching enzyme that is the normal gene product. The researchers also provide a physiological explanation for the appearance of wrinkled seed shape.

WESTERN BLOT ANALYSIS

Prior to the start of this study, considerable evidence already suggested that seed shape variation was due to differences in starch synthesis. Among candidate enzymes known to be important in starch synthesis was SBE1. The researchers used *RR* (pure-breeding round) plants as a source of SBE1 to raise an antibody against the enzyme. They used protein gel electrophoresis and western blot analysis to test for reactivity between the anti-SBE1 antibody and proteins extracted from *RR* and *rr* (pure-breeding wrinkled) plants. The antibody detected the enzyme in *RR* plant protein gels but not in *rr* plant protein gels ❶. This indicates that *RR* plants produce SBE1 but that *rr* plants do not.

Northern blot

than in *RR* plants and that it is produced at just a fraction of the percentage present in *RR* plants.

SOUTHERN BLOT ANALYSIS

The *SBE1* gene contains several restriction sequences, including two for the restriction enzyme *EcoRI*. The researchers took DNA isolated from *RR* and *rr* plants, digested it with *EcoRI*, and performed DNA gel electrophoresis and Southern blot analysis with the *SBE1* molecular probe. They found that the probe hybridized a DNA fragment approximately 3.5 kb in length from *RR* plants and a fragment of about 4.3 kb from *rr* plants ❸. This result could indicate either the insertion of approximately 800 bp of DNA into the *r* allele or the presence of a mutation that changes an *EcoRI* restriction sequence and alters the size of the restriction fragment (see Section 10.2). Analysis of the DNA sequence of the *r* allele revealed that the larger restriction fragment was created by insertion of DNA into one of the exons of the *SBE1* gene ❹. This event caused insertional inactivation of the *r* allele of *SBE1*. Additional examination of the DNA insert found it to be very similar to the *Ac* transposable genetic element identified by McClintock. The transposable DNA element identified by this work is named *Ips-r* (insertion *Pisum sativum-r*).

Western blot

Southern blot

NORTHERN BLOT ANALYSIS

The researchers next derived a molecular probe for the *SBE1* gene and tested mRNA from *RR* and *rr* plants in northern blot analysis. They found that the molecular probe hybridized with a 3300-nucleotide mRNA derived from *RR* plants and with a 4100-nucleotide mRNA from *rr* plants. They found as well that the larger transcript from *rr* plants was about tenfold less abundant than the smaller transcript from *RR* plants ❷. These results indicate that the transcript of *SBE1* in *rr* plants is longer

WRINKLED SEED DEVELOPMENT

The physiological explanation of wrinkled seed development is tied to the loss of function of SBE1. In mature round peas, almost half the dry weight is starch. About 35% of the starch is in a simple linear form known as amylose. The remainder is in complexly branched forms, most commonly a form known as amylopectin. Free molecules of sucrose make up about 5% of the dry weight. Amylose is actively converted to amylopectin by SBE1 in round seeds. In wrinkled seeds, about 30% of starch is amylopectin, and about 70% is amylose. Amylose readily

10 The Integration of Genetic Approaches: Understanding Sickle Cell Disease

Unique Chapter 10: **The Integration of Genetic Approaches** explores the hereditary and molecular basis of sickle cell disease in humans, integrating discussions of many research techniques.

Thorough Coverage of Experiments and Research Techniques

Research Technique boxes explore important research methods and visually illustrate the results and interpretations of the techniques. NEW! A new Research Technique box on microbial genotyping using growth characteristics has been added to Chapter 6.

Genotyping Using Microbial Growth

The results of experiments on microbes described in this chapter have shaped our understanding of how genes work, including how they are organized and how they are expressed. A basic set of common laboratory techniques and analyses assessing growth or failure to grow in liquid or semisolid media made up of different components can be used to determine the genetic makeup of microorganisms. Proper interpretation of the genotype of a microbe based on its pattern of growth on different media is an essential skill of genetic analysis that is easy to master once you understand a few key concepts.

ANABOLIC AND CATABOLIC PATHWAYS Compounds that influence the growth of microbes on growth media fall into two broad categories. In the first are compounds synthesized by prototrophic (wild-type) microbes in biosynthetic pathways that are often described as *anabolic pathways*. In anabolic pathways, *energy is used to synthesize* complex compounds from simpler ones through sequential reaction steps. Figure 4.17 and the accompanying discussion of the anabolic pathway that synthesizes the amino acid methionine (pages 121–123) provide an example. In contrast, *catabolic pathways* are pathways through which *energy is produced by the breakdown* of complex compounds into simpler ones. Catabolic pathways also follow sequential steps. Our discussion of phenylketonuria (PKU) (pages 121–123) highlights the catabolic pathway that breaks down the amino acid phenylalanine. Similarly, compounds such as polysaccharide sugars like lactose and other carbohydrates are broken down in catabolic pathways.

VISUALIZING MICROBIAL GROWTH When microbial growth occurs on a semisolid growth plate in a petri dish, individual *colonies* may appear on the plate. Each colony is actually hundreds of thousands to millions of individual microbes that are all descendant from a single microbial cell among those originally spread on the plate in a very dilute solution. Depending on microbe genotypes and the composition of the growth medium, it is possible that more than one microbial genotype is growing on a particular plate, but what is certain is that the cells in each colony are genetically identical. In a liquid growth medium, microbial growth produces cloudiness—the result of there being so many living cells in the growth vessel that the passage of light through the medium is impeded by the cells. There are no colonies in liquid media.

Identifying the genotype of a microbe often requires assessing the growth of a particular colony on different growth media. This is accomplished by replica plating. One method of replica plating is to simply touch a colony growing on one growth medium with a sterile toothpick or a similar instrument to gather some cells of the colony and then touch a spot on a different growth plate. Systematic use of a grid pattern on the new plate and care in the recording of growth results permit comparison of growth results on different plates so as to identify colony genotypes. An alternative replica plating method involves transferring all the colonies growing on one plate to a new growth plate all at once. A round wooden or plastic block slightly smaller in diameter than a petri dish and covered with a piece of sterilized velvet is used for this. The velvet-covered block is gently pressed onto the colonies of one plate to pick up some cells from each colony and then is used to stamp one or more fresh growth-medium plates. Growth results can be compared between plates, and genotypes of colonies can be identified because all the colonies are in the same relative positions on both the original and the new plate.

ALLELIC IDENTIFICATION Distinguishing between compounds produced by anabolic pathways and those broken down in catabolic pathways is a critical aspect of interpreting microbial growth and identifying microbial genotype that requires knowledge of growth media and their constituents. As defined in Experimental Insight 4.1, a *minimal medium* contains glucose as the carbon source, since glycolysis is the fundamental energy-producing reaction in many organisms, including humans and many microbes. The minimal medium also contains nitrogen, some inorganic salts, and water. In order to grow on a minimal medium, a microbe must synthesize every compound it needs for metabolism, DNA replication, transcription, and translation. The compounds required to carry out these essential functions are the products of anabolic pathways. Only *prototrophs* (wild-types) can synthesize all the products required for growth on a minimal medium. The ability to synthesize an essential compound by completion of an anabolic pathway is indicated in genetic notation by a "+" (plus) symbol and identifies a wild-type allele; thus, a microbe capable of biosynthesizing the amino acid methionine is identified as met^+ (spoken "met plus"). In contrast, the "−" (minus) symbol indicates the organism in an *auxotroph* (mutant) that is unable to synthesize a particular compound due to mutation. The control prototroph shown in Figure 4.19 (p. 127) is met^+, whereas the four other strains are each met^-. Auxotrophs can also grow on *supplemented minimal medium*, which is a minimal medium supplemented with just the specific compound or compounds an auxotroph is unable to produce on its own.

In the case of catabolic pathways—allelic symbols identify the ability of a strain to complete a catabolic pathway with a superscript "+" and the inability to complete a catabolic pathway with the "−" symbol. For example, microbes that are able to grow on a medium that contains the milk sugar lactose instead of glucose are lac^+. The ability to grow on lactose requires production of the enzymes that breakdown lactose into simpler compounds. In contrast, microbes that are unable to grow on lactose-containing media are lac^-. These strains are unable to produce one or more of the enzymes required for lactose metabolism.

The accompanying figure guides you through the identification of prototrophs and auxotrophs among 10 microbial colonies for the amino acids alanine (ala) and proline (pro) and for the ability of the colonies to break down lactose. Genotype identification is accomplished by comparing growth on plates of media containing different constituents. The accompanying table summarizes the genotype of each colony and the reasoning used to identify the genotype.

(continued)

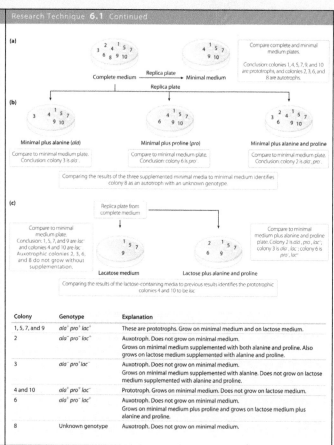

Colony	Genotype	Explanation
1, 5, 7, and 9	$ala^+ pro^+ lac^+$	These are prototrophs. Grow on minimal medium and on lactose medium.
2	$ala^- pro^- lac^+$	Auxotroph. Does not grow on minimal medium. Grows on minimal medium supplemented with both alanine and proline. Also grows on lactose medium supplemented with alanine and proline.
3	$ala^- pro^+ lac^-$	Auxotroph. Does not grow on minimal medium. Grows on minimal medium supplemented with alanine. Does not grow on lactose medium supplemented with alanine and proline.
4 and 10	$ala^+ pro^+ lac^-$	Prototroph. Grows on minimal medium. Does not grow on lactose medium.
6	$ala^+ pro^- lac^-$	Auxotroph. Does not grow on minimal medium. Grows on minimal medium plus proline and grows on lactose medium plus alanine and proline.
8	Unknown genotype	Auxotroph. Does not grow on minimal medium.

Case Studies are short, real-world examples that appear at the end of every chapter and highlight central ideas or concepts of the chapter to remind students of some of the practical applications of genetics. NEW! New Case Studies have been added to Chapters 1, 3, 5, 21, and 22.

CASE STUDY

GWAS and Crohn's Disease

Yasunori Ogura and colleagues used GWAS to identify several chromosome regions associated with Crohn's disease (CD), an inflammatory bowel disease that affects humans at a prevalence of 150 to 200 cases per 100,000 people. The etiology of CD is unknown, but one prominent hypothesis proposes that it is an inflammatory response to intestinal bacteria and other microflora.

CD clusters in families: Susceptibility to the disease is inherited but is influenced by multiple genes. The severity of CD is highly variable, from relatively mild to potentially fatal. Clinicians describe CD severity using a scale that captures the quantitative nature of the trait, making CD a candidate disease for QTL analysis. In the study by Ogura and colleagues, the strongest statistical evidence of association of a genetic marker with a susceptibility gene came from chromosome region 16q12. A gene initially identified as *NOD2* and subsequently renamed *CARD15* (caspase recruitment domain, member 15), is a candidate for a gene influencing susceptibility to CD.

GENE STRUCTURE AND MUTATION *CARD15* encodes 12 exons that direct the production of a 1040–amino acid protein. Ogura and colleagues sequenced the exons and introns

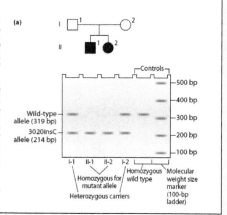

Genetic Analysis
An Integrated Approach

Second Custom Edition for University of California, Irvine

Taken from:
Genetic Analysis: An Integrated Approach
by Mark F. Sanders and John L. Bowman

Concept of Genetics, Eleventh Edition
by William S. Klug, Michael R. Cummings, Charlotte A. Spencer,
and Michael A. Palladino, with contributions by Darrell Killian

Cover Art: Courtesy of Stephen Dixon.

Taken from:

Genetic Analysis: An Integrated Approach
by Mark F. Sanders and John L. Bowman
Copyright © 2015 by Pearson Education, Inc.
Hoboken, New Jersey 07030

Concept of Genetics, Eleventh Edition
by William S. Klug, Michael R. Cummings, Charlotte A. Spencer, and Michael A. Palladino,
with contributions by Darrell Killian
Copyright © 2015, 2012, 2009 by Pearson Education, Inc.

Copyright © 2015, 2013 by Pearson Learning Solutions
All rights reserved.

Pearson Learning Solutions, 330 Hudson Street, New York, New York 10013
A Pearson Education Company
www.pearsoned.com

Printed in the United States of America

3 17

000200010271975581

EEB/BC

ISBN 10: 1-323-14280-0
ISBN 13: 978-1-323-14280-6

About the Authors

 **Mark F. Sanders** has been a faculty member in the Department of Molecular and Cellular Biology at the University of California, Davis since 1985. In that time, he has taught more than 150 genetics courses to nearly 35,000 undergraduate students. Specializing in teaching the genetics course for which this book is written, his genetics teaching experience also includes a genetics laboratory course, an advanced human genetics course for biology majors, and a human heredity course for nonscience majors, as well as introductory biology and courses in population genetics and evolution. He has also been active in undergraduate student advising, undergraduate education administration, and he has directed several undergraduate education programs.

Dr. Sanders received his B.A. degree in Anthropology from San Francisco State University, his M.A. and Ph.D. degrees in Biological Anthropology from the University of California, Los Angeles, and he received 4 years of training as a postdoctoral researcher studying inherited susceptibility to human breast and ovarian cancer at the University of California, Berkeley.

 **John L. Bowman** is a professor in the School of Biological Sciences at Monash University in Melbourne, Australia, and an adjunct professor in the Department of Plant Biology at the University of California, Davis in the United States. He received a B.S. in Biochemistry at the University of Illinois at Urbana-Champaign in 1986 and a Ph.D. in Biology from the California Institute of Technology in Pasadena, California. His Ph.D. research focused on how the identities of floral organs are specified in *Arabidopsis* (described in Chapter 20). He conducted postdoctoral research at Monash University on the regulation of floral development. From 1996 to 2006, his laboratory at UC Davis focused on developmental genetics of plants, focusing on how leaves are patterned. From 2006 to 2011, he was a Federation Fellow at Monash University, where his laboratory is studying land plant evolution using a developmental genetics approach. He was elected a Fellow of the Australian Academy of Science in 2014. At UC Davis he taught genetics, "from Mendel to cancer," to undergraduate students, and he continues to teach genetics courses at Monash University.

Dedication

Preface

For genetics researchers, genetics instructors, and the students who choose to study genetics, these are wonderful times to be practicing our craft. The first years of the 21st century have seen unprecedented expansion of our knowledge in genetics. Data on topics that were seemingly impenetrable just a few years ago are now abundant. Novel approaches to old problems have provided profound insights on the development and evolution of members of all three domains of life. And advancements in genomics, proteomics, transcriptomics, and other enterprises of the "omic" world have opened avenues for research that were unimaginable in years past. The dawn of the 21st century was something of a milestone for genetics—it inaugurated the second century of genetics. One hundred years after the foundational genetic principles of Gregor Mendel were rediscovered the genomics era accomplished the major feat of completing the human genome sequence. Genetics barely seemed to pause to acknowledge this triumph, and the field has been "full speed ahead" in its second century. New genome sequences are published weekly, and we now have not just complete genome sequences of ourselves and thousands of other living organisms, but also the genome sequences of two archaic human ancestors, Neandertals and Denisovans, both of which died out more than 30,000 years ago. These are great times to be a geneticist or a student studying genetics!

Our Integrated Approach

Both the first edition of our textbook and this second edition carry the unique subtitle *An Integrated Approach*. This phrase embodies our pedagogical approach that has three principles: (1) integrating problem solving throughout the text—not relegating it to the end of the chapter—and consistently modeling a powerful, three-step problem-solving approach (Evaluate, Deduce, and Solve) in every worked example; (2) integrating an evolutionary perspective and evolutionary evaluation throughout the book; and (3) integrating descriptions of Mendelian genetic and molecular genetic analysis designed to make it clear that these approaches are two sides of the same coin—different approaches to investigating the same basic sets of observations. In our second edition, we adhere to and strengthen the integrated approach that has resonated strongly with instructors and students.

New to This Edition

The overarching goals that have driven our revision are improving student learning, making the job of learning genetics easier and more effective for students, and incorporating the new information in genetics that is helping to define its future growth. To that end, we highlight key new features and information designed to accomplish our revision goals.

- **Enhanced problem solving** Because so many students struggle with formulating an approach to solving genetics problems, we have added a new "Break It Down" component to each of the Genetic Analysis worked examples throughout the text. "Break It Down" models the concept of breaking down problem solving by deciphering the essential information needed to start solving the problem.

- **Enhanced integration of Mendelian and molecular genetics** Strong coverage of Mendel's principles of segregation and independent assortment using Mendel's own data is maintained, and more discussion of the molecular basis of four identified genes Mendel studied has been added. For instance, Table 2.6 provides a synopsis of the wild-type and mutant functions of the four known genes; Experimental Insight 12.1 describes the base substitutions or deletions responsible for mutations of three of the genes; and Experimental Insight 13.2 describes the transposition event that is the cause of mutation of the fourth gene.

- **New and expanded Foundation Figures** These one- or two-page figures combine visuals and words to help students master key concepts. These figures were well received in the first edition, and we have modified and expanded some Foundation Figures and we added three new ones to this edition: Foundation Figure 7.14 DNA Replication; Foundation Figure 8.6 Bacterial Transcription; and Foundation Figure 9.9 Bacterial Translation Elongation.

- **Expanded coverage of archaea molecular biology** Recent advancements in understanding the genetics and molecular biology of archaea—one of three domains of life—are described. These recent findings allow insightful comparisons to the genetics of bacteria and eukaryotes, particularly in relation to molecular genetic processes and to evolution. New archaea discussions and descriptions appear in Chapters 7, 8, 9, 11, 12, and 14.

- **Extending the integration of evolution throughout the text** The evolutionary perspective takes an even more prominent role in several discussions throughout the book, including in discussions of the archaea where evolutionary comparisons to bacteria and to eukaryotes is a significant component of the discussion. In addition, Chapter 22 (Population Genetics and

Evolution at the Population, Species and Molecular Levels) has been substantially modified to feature additional discussion of natural selection in Darwin's finches, broader discussion of molecular genetic support for natural selection, new discussion of the evolution of the vertebrate steroid receptor family, and new discussion of the Neandertal genome and its contributions to the modern human genome.

▌ **Revised epigenetic coverage** It is abundantly clear that epigenetics is at the heart of the evolution and regulation of gene expression in eukaryotes. Coverage of epigenetics has been revised in Chapter 11 (Chromosome Structure), and Chapter 15 (Regulation of Gene Expression in Eukaryotes) has been substantially rewritten to expand coverage of epigenetics and to describe new information. Chapter 15's discussion focuses on the histone code and chromatin states and on epigenetic readers, writers, and erasers.

▌ **Integrating coverage of genomics throughout** Genomic investigations are rapidly expanding and changing what we know about genetics. Coverage of important techniques and findings is integrated throughout the text, such as a new discussion of the impact of lateral gene transfer on bacterial genomes in Chapter 6 (Genetic Analysis and Mapping in Bacteria and Bacteriophages); a new Experimental Insight of cancer genomics in Chapter 12 (Gene Mutation, DNA Repair, and Homologous Recombination); discussions of new genome methods and analyses in Chapter 18 (Genomics: Genetics from a Whole-Genome Perspective); and updated coverage of the human genome, including data on interaction with Neandertals and Denisovans in Chapter 22 (Population Genetics and Evolution at the Population, Species, and Molecular Levels).

▌ **Enhanced coverage of molecular evolution** The text's focus on evolution in genetics now includes more coverage of molecular evolution integrated into appropriate chapters. Chapters 7 (DNA Structure and Replication), 8 (Molecular Biology of Transcription and RNA Processing), and 9 (The Molecular Biology of Translation) have expanded discussions of the evolution of these molecular processes. Chapter 11 (Chromosome Structure) discusses the evolution of histone proteins in archaea and eukaryotes. Chapter 14 (Regulation of Gene Expression in Bacteria and Bacteriophage) describes evolutionary comparisons of regulatory mechanisms in archaea and bacteria. Chapter 15 (Regulation of Gene Expression in Eukaryotes) contains expanded coverage of the evolution of regulatory functions. Chapter 22 (Population Genetics and Evolution at the Population, Species, and Molecular Levels) contains new discussions of evolution at the population, species, and molecular levels.

▌ **New Case Studies** Case Studies at the end each chapter connect examples of research to central ideas and concepts in the chapter, reminding students of the practical applications of genetics. New Case Studies include: The Modern Human Family Mystery (Chapter 1); The (Degenerative) Evolution of the Mammalian Y Chromosome (Chapter 3); Mapping the Gene for Cystic Fibrosis (Chapter 5); and Detecting the Major Gene Influencing Crohn's Disease (Chapter 21).

New and Updated Coverage

We revisited each chapter with fresh eyes and helpful feedback from users and reviewers of the text. Here are some of the highlights of chapter-by-chapter changes in the second edition.

Chapter 1: The Molecular Basis of Heredity, Variation, and Evolution

▌ New discussion of the role of genomics, proteomics, and other "omic" investigative strategies

▌ New Case Study on the Neandertal genome and human–Neandertal genome comparison

Chapter 2: Transmission Genetics

▌ New Experimental Insight on plant breeding and evolution

▌ Additional end-of-chapter problems

▌ Revised and updated coverage of the molecular basis of Mendel's traits

Chapter 3: Cell Division and Chromosome Heredity

▌ New Genetic Analysis worked example on X-linked inheritance

▌ New Case Study of the evolution of the mammalian Y chromosome

▌ Additional end-of-chapter problems

Chapter 4: Inheritance Patterns of Single Genes and Gene Interaction

▌ New section on the dominant mutant pattern of mouse coat color and recessive lethality of the yellow allele

▌ Revised discussion of gene interactions in metabolic pathways

Chapter 5: Genetic Linkage and Mapping in Eukaryotes

▌ New section on hotspots and cold spots of recombination in genomes

- Revisions to sections on correction of map distances and the evolutionary favorability of recombination
- New Case Study of the mapping of the human cystic fibrosis (*CFTR*) gene

Chapter 6: Genetic Analysis and Mapping in Bacteria and Bacteriophage

- New Research Technique box on microbial genotyping using growth characteristics
- New section on lateral gene transfer and evolution
- New section on identification and assessment of lateral gene transfer in genomes
- New end-of-chapter problems

Chapter 7: DNA Structure and Replication

- New Foundation Figure featuring an overview of DNA replication
- New material on DNA replication in archaea and comparison of archaeal replication components to those in bacteria and eukaryotes
- New Genetic Analysis worked example on the function of critical proteins in DNA replication
- Discussion of PCR and dideoxy sequencing is retained and a new section introducing next generation sequencing has been added

Chapter 8: Molecular Biology of Transcription and RNA Processing

- New Foundation Figure on bacterial transcription
- New material on transcription in archaea and comparisons of archaeal, bacterial, and eukaryotic transcription processes and molecules
- New section on archaea promoters
- New discussion of the torpedo model of transcription termination in eukaryotes
- New end-of-chapter problems

Chapter 9: The Molecular Biology of Translation

- New section on amino acids and polypeptide structures
- New material on archaeal ribosomes and comparison with bacterial and eukaryotic ribosomes
- New material on archaeal translation initiation and comparison with the processes in bacteria and eukaryotes
- New Foundation Figure on bacterial translation
- New Genetic Analysis worked example on translation
- Additional end-of-chapter problems

Chapter 10: The Integration of Genetic Approaches: Understanding Sickle Cell Disease

- New material on the pathophysiology of sickle cell disease and on the identification of the molecular basis for the condition
- Additional end-of-chapter problems

Chapter 11: Chromosome Structure

- New section on viral structure and viral genomes
- New Genetic Analysis worked example on detecting chromosome variation
- New section on archaeal chromosomes, the role of chromatin in archaea, and the evolutionary implications of this new information
- Additional end-of-chapter problems

Chapter 12: Gene Mutation, DNA Repair, and Homologous Recombination

- New Experimental Insight describing the molecular basis of mutations produced by three of genes studied by Mendel—pod color, stem length, and flower color—whose mutations result from base substitutions
- New Experimental Insight on the BROCA system, a genome sequence–based assessment of risk for inherited susceptibility to breast and ovarian cancer
- Updated discussion of DNA damage repair in bacteria and eukaryotes
- New discussion of DNA damage repair and homologous recombination in archaea species
- New discussion of the bacterial RecBCD system
- Additional end-of-chapter problems on DNA damage repair systems
- A revised Foundation Figure more clearly explains processes at work in meiotic recombination

Chapter 13: Chromosome Aberrations and Transposition

- New Experimental Insight discussing the molecular basis and molecular genetic analysis of Mendel's round and wrinkled seed trait that is caused by transposition
- Updated discussion of transposition in eukaryotes and bacteria

Chapter 14: Regulation of Gene Expression in Bacteria and Bacteriophage

- New section on transcriptional regulation in archaeal species

New discussion comparing and contrasting bacterial and archaeal transcription regulation and its evolutionary implications

Chapter 15: Regulation of Gene Expression in Eukaryotes

An integrated view of chromatin modification, with a focus on how readers, writers, and erasers modulate and maintain chromatin architecture

A discussion of the roles of long noncoding RNAs in gene regulation, using Xist and X-chromosome inactivation as an example

Chapter 16: Analysis of Gene Function by Forward Genetics and Reverse Genetics

A reorganized discussion of how genes and their function are identified via forward and reverse genetics

A discussion of using genomics approaches to clone genes identified via forward genetics

Chapter 17: Recombinant DNA Technology and Its Applications

Reorganized presentation of the nuts and bolts of recombinant DNA technology and how to construct transgenic organisms

A discussion of genome editing as a future direction of genetics

Chapter 18: Genomics: Genetics from a Whole-Genome Perspective

Expanded coverage of copy number variants and their origins

New Experimental Insight on the human microbiome

New Genetic Analysis problem on the determination of homology, paralogy, and orthology based on interpreting phylogenetic trees

Chapter 19: Organelle Inheritance and the Evolution of Organelle Genomes

Provides an up-to-date account of the diversity in organelle inheritance in several lineages of eukaryotes

Chapter 20: Developmental Genetics

Provides in-depth coverage of the genetics of animal development and a vignette of how plants are both similar but also differ

Chapter 21: Genetic Analysis of Quantitative Traits

New discussion of human GWAS analysis, including an introduction to Manhattan plot assessment

New Case Study on GWAS analysis of Crohn's disease

Chapter 22: Population Genetics and Evolution at the Population, Species, and Molecular Levels

New discussion of convergent evolution of lactase persistence in humans

New Genetic Analysis worked example on determination of relative fitness and the operation of natural selection in *Drosophila*

A new section on contemporary evolution in Darwin's finches

A new section on gene and genome evolution focusing on the vertebrate steroid receptor gene family

New discussion of the variability and evolution of the human genome

A new Case Study on the evidence for interbreeding between Neandertals and modern humans

New end-of-chapter problems

A Problem-Solving Approach

To help train students to become more effective problem solvers, we employ a unique problem-solving feature called Genetic Analysis that gives students a consistent, repeatable method to help them learn and practice problem solving. Genetic Analysis teaches how to start thinking about a problem, what the end goal is, and what kind of analysis is required to get there. The three steps of this problem-solving framework are *Evaluate, Deduce,* and *Solve.*

Evaluate: Students learn to identify the topic of the problem, specify the nature or format of the answer, and identify critical information given in the problem.

Deduce: Students learn how to use conceptual knowledge to analyze data, make connections, and infer additional information or next steps.

Solve: Students learn how to accurately apply analytical tools and to execute their plan to solve a given problem.

Irrespective of the type of problem a student faces, this framework guides students through the stages of problem solving and gives them the confidence to undertake new problems.

Each Genetic Analysis is organized in a two-column format to help students easily follow each enumerated step of the Solution Strategy in the left-hand column along with its corresponding enumerated execution event of the Solution Step in the right-hand column. We enhanced the Genetic Analysis examples by adding *Break It Down* callouts to the problem statement of each example. This new element is designed to aid students who often struggle with identifying the concepts and information contained in a problem that are critical to starting the problem-solving process. We also include problem-solving Tips to highlight critical steps and Pitfalls to avoid, gathered from our teaching experience. It is also important to note that Genetic Analysis examples are integrated throughout each chapter, right after discussions of important content, to help students immediately apply concepts they are learning to the context of problem solving. Each chapter includes two or three Genetic Analysis features, and the book contains 50 in all.

We pair Genetic Analysis with strong end-of-chapter problems that are divided into two groups. Chapter Concept problems come first and review the critical information, principles, and analytical tools discussed in the chapter. These are followed by Application and Integration problems that are more challenging and give students practice in solving problems that are broader in scope. All solutions to the end-of-chapter problems in the *Study Guide and Solutions Manual* use the evaluate-deduce-solve model to reinforce the approach.

An Evolutionary Perspective

Geneticists are acutely aware of evolutionary relationships between genes, genomes, and organisms. Evolutionary processes at the organismal level discovered through comparative biology can also shed light on the function of genes and organization of genomes at the molecular level. Likewise, the function of genes and organization of genomes informs the evolutionary model. The integration of evolution and the evolutionary perspective remains a central organizing theme of the second edition, and this approach has been greatly enhanced through coverage of the molecular biology of archaeal species. Details of archaeal processes are described in a context that compares and contrasts archaea with bacteria and eukaryotes.

Connecting Transmission and Molecular Genetics

Experiments that shed light on principles of transmission genetics preceded the discovery of the structure and function of DNA and its role in inherited molecular variation by several decades. Yet biologists recognize that DNA variation is the basis of inherited morphological variation observed in transmission genetics. Understanding how these two approaches to genetics are connected is vital to thinking like a geneticist. We have retained the integration of transmission genetics and molecular genetics in

the text and have enhanced this feature in two ways: first, through additional discussion of the molecular basis of hereditary variation, including the mutations that underlie the four identified genes examined by Mendel, and second, with a much more robust genomic approach.

Pathways Through the Book

This book is written with a Mendel-first approach that many instructors find offers the most effective pedagogical approach for teaching genetics. We are cognizant, however, that the scope of information covered in genetics courses varies and that instructor preferences differ. We have kept differences and alternative approaches in mind while writing the book. Thus, we provide *five pathways* through the book that instructors can use to meet their varying course goals and objectives. Each pathway features integration of problem solving through the inclusion of Genetic Analysis features in each chapter.

1. Mendel-First Approach

Ch 1–22
This pathway provides a traditional approach that begins with Mendelian genetics and integrates it with evolutionary concepts and connects it to molecular genetics. As examples, we discuss genes responsible for four of Mendel's traits (Chapter 2), Chapter 12 and Chapter 13, as well as gene structure in relation to dominance and functional level (Chapter 5). We draw together hereditary variation, molecular variation, and evolution in the discussion of sickle cell disease (Chapter 10).

2. Molecular-First Approach

Ch 1 → Ch 7–10 → Ch 2–6 → Ch 11–22
This pathway provides a molecular-first approach to develop a clear understanding of the molecular basis of heredity and variation before delving into the analysis of hereditary transmission.

3. Integration of Molecular Analysis

Ch 1 → Ch 10 → Ch 2–15 → Ch 16–22
This pathway focuses on the parallels of transmission and molecular genetic analyses right from the start, and it best reflects the way a geneticist would approach study of the field. We recommend this pathway for students who already have a strong genetics background and are familiar with some common molecular techniques.

4. Quantitative Genetics Focus

Ch 1–2 → Ch 21 → Ch 3–20 → Ch 22
This pathway incorporates quantitative genetics early in the course by introducing polygenic inheritance (Chapter 2) and following it up with a comprehensive discussion of quantitative genetics (Chapter 21).

5. Population Genetics Focus

Ch 1–2 → Ch 22 → Ch 3–21

This pathway incorporates population genetics early in the course. Instructors can use the introduction to evolutionary principles and processes (Chapter 1) and the role of genes and alleles in transmission (Chapter 2) and then address evolution at the population level and at higher levels (Chapter 22).

Chapter Features

A principal goal of our writing style and chapter organization is to engage the reader both intellectually and visually to invite continuous reading, all the while clearly explaining complex and difficult ideas. Our conversational tone encourages student reading and comprehension, and our attractive design and realistic art program visually engage students and put them at ease. Experienced instructors of genetics know that students are more engaged when they can relate concepts to the real world. To that end, we use real experimental data to illustrate genetic principles and analysis as well as to familiarize students with exciting research and creative researchers in the field. We also discuss a broad array of organisms—such as humans, bacteria, yeast, plants, fruit flies, nematodes, vertebrates, and viruses—to exemplify genetic principles.

Careful thought has been given to our chapter features; each one serves to improve student learning. The following features illustrate how we highlight central ideas, problems, and methods that are important for understanding genetics.

- **Genetic Analysis:** This is our key problem-solving feature that guides students through the problem-solving process by using the *evaluate-deduce-solve* framework.
- **Foundation Figures:** Highly detailed illustrations of pivotal concepts in genetics.
- **Experimental Insights:** Discuss critical or illustrative experiments, the data derived from the experiments, and the conclusions drawn from analysis of experimental results.
- **Research Techniques:** Explore important research methods and visually illustrate the results and interpretations.
- **Case Studies:** Short, real-world examples, at the end of every chapter, highlight central ideas or concepts of the chapter with interesting examples that remind students of some practical applications of genetics.

MasteringGenetics

A key reviewing and testing tool is MasteringGenetics, the most powerful online homework and assessment system available. Tutorials follow the Socratic method,

coaching students to the correct answer by offering feedback specific to a student's misconceptions as well as providing hints students can access if they get stuck. The interactive approach of the tutorials provides a unique way for students to learn genetics concepts while developing and honing their problem-solving skills. In addition to tutorials, MasteringGenetics includes animations, quizzes, and end-of-chapter problems from the textbook. This exclusive product of Pearson greatly enhances learning genetics through problem solving, and new features include:

- A new category of Practice Problems are like end-of-chapter questions in scope and level of difficulty and are found only in MasteringGenetics. Solutions are not available in the Study Guide and Solutions Manual, and the bank of questions extends your options for assigning challenging problems. Each problem includes specific wrong answer feedback to help students learn from their mistakes and to guide them toward the correct answer.
- Nearly 90% of the end-of-chapter questions are now included in the item library for assignments. The questions use a broad range of answer types in addition to multiple choice, such as sorting, labeling, numerical, and ranking.
- LearningCatalytics is a "bring your own device" (smartphone, tablet, or laptop) assessment and active classroom system that expands the possibilities for student engagement. Instructors can create their own questions, draw from community content shared by colleagues, or access Pearson's new library of question clusters that explore challenging topics through a series of two to five questions that focus on a single scenario or data set, build in difficulty, and require higher-level thinking.

Student Supplements

MasteringGenetics

ISBN: 0133983501 / 9780133983500

Study Guide and Solutions Manual

ISBN: 0133795586 / 9780133795585

Heavily updated and accuracy-checked by Peter Mirabito from the University of Kentucky, the *Study Guide and Solutions Manual* is divided into four sections: Genetics Problem-Solving Toolkit, Types of Genetics Problems, Solutions to End-of-Chapter Problems, and Test Yourself. In the "toolkit," students are reminded of key terms and concepts and key relationships that are needed to solve the types of problems in a chapter. This is followed by a breakdown of the types of problems students will encounter in the end-of-chapter problems for a particular chapter; they learn the key strategies to solve each type, variations on a problem type that they may encounter, and a worked example modeled after the Genetic Analysis feature of the main textbook. The solutions also reflect the *evaluate-deduce-solve* strategy of the Genetic Analysis feature. Finally, for more practice, we've included five to 10 Test Yourself problems and accompanying solutions.

Instructor Supplements

MasteringGenetics

ISBN: 0133983501 / 9780133983500

MasteringGenetics engages and motivates students to learn and allows you to easily assign automatically graded activities. Tutorials provide students with personalized coaching and feedback. Using the gradebook, you can quickly monitor and display student results. MasteringGenetics easily captures data to demonstrate assessment outcomes. Resources include:

- In-depth tutorials that coach students with hints and feedback specific to their misconceptions.
- An item library of thousands of assignable questions including reading quizzes and end-of-chapter problems. You can use publisher-created prebuilt assignments to get started quickly. Each question can be easily edited to match the precise language you use.
- A gradebook that provides you with quick results and easy-to-interpret insights into student performance.

TestGen TestBank

ISBN: 0133999696 / 9780133999693

Test questions are available as part of the TestGen EQ Testing Software, a text-specific testing program that is networkable for administering tests. It also allows instructors to view and edit questions, export the questions as tests, and print them out in a variety of formats.

Instructor Resource DVD

ISBN: 0134005856 / 9780134005850

The Instructor Resource DVD offers adopters of the text convenient access to the most comprehensive and innovative set of lecture presentation and teaching tools offered by any genetics textbook. Developed to meet the needs of veteran and newer instructors alike, these resources include:

- The JPEG files of all text line drawings with labels individually enhanced for optimal projection results (as well as unlabeled versions) and all text tables.
- Most of the text photos, including all photos with pedagogical significance, as JPEG files.
- A set of PowerPoint® presentations consisting of a thorough lecture outline for each chapter augmented by key text illustrations and animations.
- PowerPoint® presentations containing a comprehensive set of in-class Classroom Response System (CRS) questions for each chapter.
- In Word and PDF files, a complete set of the assessment materials and study questions and answers from the test bank.

We Welcome Your Comments and Suggestions

Genetics is continuously changing, and textbooks must also change continuously to keep pace with the field and to meet the needs of instructors and students. Communication with our talented and dedicated users is a critical driver of change. We welcome all suggestions and comments and invite you to communicate with us directly. Please send comments or questions about the book to us at mfsanders@ucdavis.edu or john.bowman@ monash.edu.

Acknowledgments

In our first edition, we described the adage that begins with the words "It takes a village..." as aptly applying to the development and assembly of the first edition of our textbook. As was the case in the first edition, this second edition has been a true team effort, and we are grateful to all of our teammates. We particularly wish to thank our editorial team led by our executive editor Michael Gillespie, our developmental editor Moira Lerner Nelson, and our project coordinator Crystal Clifton for their guidance and assistance in bringing this new edition to life. We also thank our compatriot Peter Mirabito, author of the Study Guide and Solutions Manual, for his work assembling an exceptionally useful supplement. Beth Wilbur, Paul Corey, and Deborah Gale have also been essential supporters that have made this new edition a reality.

On the production side, we thank the fine artists at Precision who have managed to turn our rudimentary cartoons into instructive pieces of art. We thank the production team at Pearson Education led by Margaret Young.

The Pearson Education marketing team led by Lauren Harp has provided expert guidance in bringing our textbook to the attention of genetics instructors throughout North America and indeed around the world.

Finally, and perhaps most importantly, we thank the scores of gifted genetics instructors and the thousands of genetics students who used the first edition of our book and the many reviewers and accuracy checkers whose contributions have been invaluable. Many of our users and all of our reviewers have provided comments and feedback that have immeasurably improved this second edition. We are humbled and gratified by their praise and encouraged by their support and the generosity with which they apply their expertise.

Reviewers

Nancy Bachman, *SUNY Oneonta*
John Belote, *Syracuse University*
Laura Hill Bermingham, *University of Vermont*
Aimee Bernard, *University of Colorado–Denver*
Michelle Bell Boissiere, *Xavier University*
Ginger Brininstool, *Louisiana State University*
Mirjana Brockett, *Georgia Institute of Technology*
Mary Bryk, *Texas A&M University*
David Camerini, *University of California at Irvine*
Aaron Cassill, *University of Texas–San Antonio*
Robert S. Dotson, *Tulane University*
Michelle Gaudette, *Tufts University*
Patricia Geppert, *University of Texas–San Antonio*
Michael Gilchrist, *University of Tennessee*
Matthew Gilg, *University of North Florida*
Kelly Hogan, *University of North Carolina at Chapel Hill*
Oliver Kerscher, *College of William and Mary*
Emily Larson, *University of Vermont*
Chin-Yo Lin, *University of Houston*
Hsiu-Ping Liu, *Metropolitan State University of Denver*
Martha Lundell, *University of Texas–San Antonio*
Fordyce Lux III, *Metropolitan State University of Denver*
Craig Miller, *University of California, Berkeley*
Ray Neubauer, *University of Texas at Austin*
Todd Nickle, *Mount Royal University*
Richard D. Noyes, *University of Central Arkansas*
Joanne Odden, *Metropolitan State University of Denver*
Robin E. Owen, *Mount Royal University*
Fiona Rawle, *University of Toronto Mississauga*
Nick Robinson, *University of Cambridge*
Chris Rock, *Texas Tech University*
Pamela Sandstrom, *University of Nevada at Reno*
Inder Saxena, *University of Texas at Austin*
Ron Siu, *UCLA*
Fernando Tenjo-Fernandez, *Virginia Commonwealth University*
Pattie Thompson, *University of Texas–San Antonio*
Kevin Thornton, *University of California at Irvine*
Douglas Thrower, *University of California, Santa Barbara*
Meena Vijayaraghavan, *Tulane University*
Alyson Zeamer, *University of Texas–San Antonio*

Reviewers and Class Testers of the First Edition

Bert Abbott, *Clemson University*
Mary Alleman, *Duquesne University*
Ancha Baranova, *George Mason University*
Daron Barnard, *Worcester State University*
Mary Bedell, *University of Georgia*
Timothy Bloom, *Campbell University*
Indrani Bose, *Western Carolina University*
James Bradley, *Auburn University*
Mirjana Brockett, *Georgia Institute of Technology*
Gerald Buldak, *Loyola University Chicago*
Carol Burdsal, *Tulane University*
Patrick Burton, *Wabash College*
Pat Calie, *Eastern Kentucky University*
Vicki Cameron, *Ithaca College*
Kimberly Carlson, *University of Nebraska at Kearney*
Steven M. Carr, *Memorial University of Newfoundland*

Aaron Cassill, *University of Texas–San Antonio*
Clarissa Cheney, *Pomona College*
Francis Choy, *University of Victoria*
Hui Min Chung, *University of West Florida*
Craig Coleman, *Brigham Young University*
Beth Conway, *Lipscomb University*
Cynthia Cooper, *Washington State University Vancouver*
Kirsten Crossgrove, *University of Wisconsin–Whitewater*
Kenneth Curr, *California State University, East Bay*
Kenyon Daniel, *University of South Florida*
Kim Dej, *McMaster University*
Chunguang Du, *Montclair State University*
John Elder, *Valdosta State University*
Victoria Finnerty, *Emory University*
Robert Fowler, *San Jose State University*
Rick Gaber, *Northwestern University*
Anne Galbraith, *University of Wisconsin–La Crosse*
Susan Godfrey, *University of Pittsburgh*
Michael Goodisman, *Georgia Tech University*
Nels Granholm, *South Dakota State University*
Jody Hall, *Brown University*
John Hamlin, *Louisiana State University, Eunice*
Pam Hanratty, *Indiana University*
Mike Harrington, *University of Alberta*
Patrick Hayes, *Oregon State University*
Jutta Heller, *Loyola University*
Jerald Hendrix, *Kennesaw State University*
Kathleen Hill, *University of Western Ontario*
Kelly Hogan, *University of North Carolina at Chapel Hill*
Barbara Hollar, *University of Detroit Mercy*
Nancy Huang, *Colorado College*
Rick Jellen, *Brigham Young University*
David Johnson, *Samford University*
Diana Johnson, *George Washington University*
Erik Johnson, *Wake Forest University*
Hope Johnson, *California State University, Fullerton*
Christopher Jones, *Moravian College*
Cheryl Jorcyk, *Boise State University*
David Kass, *Eastern Michigan University*
Cliff Keil, *University of Delaware*
Todd Kelson, *Brigham Young University, Idaho*
Steven Kempf, *Auburn University*
Oliver Kerscher, *College of William & Mary*
Joomyeong Kim, *Louisiana State University*
Elliot Krause, *Seton Hall University*
Jocelyn Krebs, *University of Alaska*
Melanie Lee-Brown, *Guilford College*
Alan Leonard, *Florida International University*
Min-Ken Liao, *Furman University*
Alan Lloyd, *University of Texas at Austin*
Kirill Lobachev, *Georgia Tech University*
Heather Lorimer, *Youngstown State University*
Fordyce Lux, *Metropolitan State College of Denver*
Clint Magill, *Texas A&M University*
Jeffrey Marcus, *Western Kentucky University*
Phillip McClean, *North Dakota State University*
Philip Meneely, *Haverford College*
John Merriam, *UCLA*
Scott Michaels, *Indiana University*
Peter Mirabito, *University of Kentucky*
Paul Morris, *Bowling Green State University*

Marlene Murray-Nsuela, *Andrews University*
Nikolas Nikolaidis, *California State University, Fullerton*
Margaret A. Olney, *St. Martin's University*
Kavita Oomen, *Georgia State University*
Greg Orloff, *Emory University*
John C. Osterman, *University of Nebraska–Lincoln*
John N. Owens, *retired*
J. S. Parkinson, University of Utah
Bernie Possidente, *Skidmore College*
Chara J. Ragland, *Texas A&M University*
Rebekah Rampey, *Harding University*
Dennis Ray, *University of Arizona*
Rosie Redfield, *University of British Columbia*
John Rinehart, *Eastern Oregon University*
Mike Robinson, *Miami University, Ohio*
Melissa Rowland-Goldsmith, *Chapman University*
John Scales, *Midwestern State University*
Malcolm Schug, *University of North Carolina at Greensboro*
Rodney Scott, *Wheaton College*
Lillie Searles, *University of North Carolina*
Marty Shankland, *University of Texas, Austin*
Patricia Shields, *University of Maryland*
Bin Shuai, *Wichita State University*
Linda Sigismondi, *University of Rio Grande*
Leslie Slusher, *West Chester University of Pennsylvania*
Tom Snyder, *Michigan Technical College*
Jeff Stuart, *Purdue University*
Susan Sullivan, *Louisiana State University, Alexandria*
Christine Terry, *Augusta State University*
Tin Tin Su, *University of Colorado–Boulder*
Martin Tracey, *Florida International University*
Jimmy Triplett, *Jacksonville State University*
Tara Turley-Stoulig, *Louisiana State University*
Fyodor Umov, *University of California, Berkeley*
Virginia Vandergon, *California State University, Northridge*
Sarah VanVickle-Chavez, *Washington University in St. Louis*
Dennis Venema, *Trinity Western University*
David Waddell, *University of North Florida*
Dunkan Walker, *private business*

Clifford Weil, *Purdue University*
Karen Weiler, *West Virginia University*
Dan Wells, *University of Houston*
David Westenberg, *Missouri University of Science & Technology*
Bruce Wightman, *Muhlenberg College*
Diana Wolf, *University of Alaska Fairbanks*
Andrew J. Wood, *Southern Illinois University*
Craig Woodard, *Mt. Holyoke College*
Joanna Wysocka-Diller, *Auburn University*
Lev Yampolsky, *East Tennessee State University*
Ann Yezerski, *King's College*
Roger Young, *Drury University*
Janey Youngblom, *California State University, Stanislaus*
Chaoyang Zeng, *University of Wisconsin–Milwaukee*

Supplements and Media Contributors

Laura Hill Bermingham, *University of Vermont*
Aimee Bernard, *University of Colorado–Denver*
Pat Calie, *Eastern Kentucky University*
Christy Fillman, *University of Colorado–Boulder*
Kathleen Fitzpatrick, *Simon Fraser University*
Michelle Gaudette, *Tufts University*
Christopher Halweg, *North Carolina State University*
Jutta Heller, *Loyola University*
David Kass, *Eastern Michigan University*
Fordyce Lux III, *Metropolitan State College*
Peter Mirabito, *University of Kentucky*
Pam Osenkowski, *Loyola University*
Jennifer Osterhage, *University of Kentucky*
Louise Paquin, *McDaniel College*
Fiona Rawle, *University of Toronto Mississauga*
Tara Stoulig, *Southeastern Louisiana State*
Kevin Thornton, *University of California at Irvine*
Douglas Thrower, *University of California, Santa Barbara*
Sarah Van Vickle-Chavez, *Washington University in St. Louis*
Dennis Venema, *Trinity Western University*
Andrew J. Wood, *Southern Illinois University*

The Molecular Basis of Heredity, Variation, and Evolution

CHAPTER OUTLINE

1.1 Modern Genetics Is in Its Second Century

1.2 The Structure of DNA Suggests a Mechanism for Replication

1.3 DNA Transcription and Messenger RNA Translation Express Genes

1.4 Evolution Has a Molecular Basis

This sculpture of DNA stands in the garden of Clare College Memorial Court at the University of Cambridge, England. It was erected to honor the discovery of DNA structure by Francis Crick and James Watson working at the University of Cambridge (Watson lived in Clare College Memorial Court during his time in Cambridge), as well as to honor the contributions of Rosalind Franklin and Maurice Wilkins working at Kings College, London.

ESSENTIAL IDEAS

- Modern genetics developed during the 20th century and is a prominent discipline of the biological sciences.

- DNA replication produces exact copies of the original molecule.

- The "central dogma of biology" describing the relationship between DNA, RNA, and protein is a foundation of molecular biology.

- Gene expression is a two-step process that first produces an RNA transcript of a gene and then synthesizes an amino acid string by translation of RNA.

- Evolution is a foundation of modern genetics that occurs through four processes.

Life is astounding, both in the richness of its history and in its diversity. From the single-celled organisms that evolved billions of years ago have descended millions of species of microorganisms, plants, and animals. These species are connected by a shared evolutionary past that is revealed by the study of genetics, the science that explores genome composition and organization and the transmission, expression, variation, and evolution of hereditary characteristics of organisms.

Genetics is a dynamic discipline that finds applications everywhere humans interact with one another and with other organisms. In research laboratories, on farms, in grocery stores, and in medical offices, courtrooms, and other settings, genetics plays a prominent and expanding role in our lives. Modern genetics is an increasingly gene- and genome-based discipline—that is, it is increasingly focused on the entirety of the hereditary information carried by organisms and on the molecular circumstances that express genes. Yet despite its increasingly gene-focused emphasis, genetics retains a strong interest in traditional areas of inquiry and investigation—heredity, variation, and evolution. Welcome to the fascinating discipline of genetics; you are in for an exciting and rewarding journey.

In this chapter, we survey the scope of modern genetics and present some basic information about deoxyribonucleic acid—DNA, the carrier of genetic information. We begin with a brief overview of the origins and contemporary range of genetic science. Next we retrace some of the fundamentals of *DNA replication,* and of *transcription* and *translation* (the two main components of gene expression), by reviewing what you learned about these processes in previous biology courses, and we introduce the most prominent of the modern-day "-omic" avenues of research and investigation in genetics. In the final section, we describe the central position of evolution in genetics and discuss the roles of heredity and variation in evolution.

1.1 Modern Genetics Is in Its Second Century

Humans have been implicitly aware of genetics for more than 10,000 years (**Figure 1.1**). From the time of the domestication of rice in Asia, maize in Central America, and wheat in the Middle East, humans have recognized that desirable traits found in plants and animals can be reproduced and enhanced in succeeding generations through selective mating. On the other hand, explicit exploration and understanding of the hereditary principles of genetics—what we might think of as the science of modern genetics—is a much more recent development.

The First Century of Modern Genetics

In 1900, three botanists working independently of one another—Carl Correns in Germany, Hugo de Vries in Holland, and Erich von Tschermak in Austria—reached strikingly similar conclusions about the pattern of transmission of hereditary traits in plants (**Figure 1.2**). Each reported that his results mirrored those published in 1866 by an obscure amateur botanist and Augustinian monk named Gregor Mendel. (Mendel's work is discussed in Chapter 2.) Although Correns, de Vries, and Tschermak had actually *rediscovered* an explanation of hereditary transmission that Mendel had published 34 years earlier, their announcement of the identification of principles of hereditary transmission gave modern genetics its start.

Biologists immediately began testing, verifying, and expanding on the newly appreciated explanation of heredity. In 1901, William Bateson, an early and vigorous proponent of "Mendelism," read a publication by a British physician-scientist named Archibald Garrod describing the appearance of the hereditary disease alkaptonuria in multiple members of unrelated families. Bateson immediately realized that Garrod's description depicted "exactly the conditions most likely to enable a rare, usually recessive character to show itself." Garrod, with Bateson's interpretive assistance, had produced the first documented example of a human hereditary disorder.

Localizing the Genetic Material Shortly thereafter, Walter Sutton and Theodore Boveri independently used microscopy to observe chromosome movement during cell division in reproductive cells. They each noted that the patterns of chromosome movement mirrored the transmission of the newly rediscovered Mendelian hereditary units. This work implied that the hereditary units, or *genes,* posited by Mendel are located on *chromosomes.* We now know that **genes**—the physical units of heredity—are composed of defined DNA sequences that collectively control gene *transcription* (described later in the chapter) and contain the information to produce RNA molecules, one category of which is called messenger RNA or mRNA and is used to produce proteins by *translation* (described later in the chapter). **Chromosomes** consist of single long molecules of double-stranded DNA that in plants and animals are bound by many different kinds of protein that give chromosomes their structure and can affect the transcription of genes the chromosomes carry. The chromosomes of sexually reproducing organisms typically occur in pairs known as **homologous pairs** or, more simply, as **homologs.** Each chromosome carries many genes, and homologs carry genes for the same traits in the same order on each member of the pair.

Figure 1.1 Ancient applications of genetics. **(a)** An early record of human genetic manipulation is this Assyrian relief from 882–859 BCE. It shows priests in bird masks artificially pollinating date palms. **(b)** Modern maize (left) is thought to have developed through human domestication of its wild ancestor teosinte (right).

Bacteria and archaea are single-celled organisms that do not have a true nucleus. In almost all cases, species of bacteria and archaea have a single, usually circular chromosome. As a consequence, in the genome of these organisms, there is just one copy of each gene, a condition described as **haploid.** Bacterial and archaeal chromosomes are bound by a relatively small amount of protein. Limited amounts of proteins help localize bacterial chromosomes to a region of the cell known as the **nucleoid.** Some archaeal species have chromosomes that have associated proteins that make them appear to be similar to bacterial chromosomes, but other species appear to have a more eukaryote-like chromosome organization.

In contrast, bacteria and archaea, the cells of eukaryotes—a classification that includes all single-celled and multicellular plants and animals—contain a true nucleus that permanently sequesters multiple sets of chromosomes. Almost all eukaryotes have haploid and **diploid** stages in their lifecycles. For example, sperm and eggs produced in animals are haploid, having one copy of each chromosome pair in the genome. In the diploid state, the eukaryotic genome contains two copies—a homologous pair—of each gene. (Although, even in a diploid state, genes located on eukaryotic sex chromosomes might not be present in two copies, as we describe in Chapter 4.) Numerous eukaryotic genomes, particularly those of plants, contain more than two copies of each chromosome—a genome composition known as **polyploidy.**

In addition to the chromosomes carried in their nuclei—the so-called nuclear chromosomes—plant and animal cells also contain genetic material in specialized organelles called **mitochondria,** and plant cells contain a third type of gene-containing organelle called **chloroplasts.** Many of these organelles are present by the dozens in each cell, and each mitochondrion or chloroplast carries one or more copies of its own chromosome. Mitochondrial and chloroplast genes produce proteins that work with protein produced by nuclear genes to perform essential functions in cells—mitochondria are essential for the production of adenosine triphosphate (ATP) that is the principal source of cellular energy, and chloroplasts are necessary for photosynthesis. Mitochondria and chloroplasts are transmitted in the cytoplasm during cell division, and

(a) Carl Correns

(b) Hugo de Vries

(c) Erich von Tschermak

Figure 1.2 Early 20th century genetic theorists. **(a)** Carl Correns, **(b)** Hugo de Vries, and **(c)** Erich von Tschermak simultaneously rediscovered the experiments and principles of Gregor Mendel in 1900.

the term **cytoplasmic inheritance** is used to identify the random distribution of mitochondria and chloroplasts among daughter cells.

Mitochondria and chloroplasts have an evolutionary history, having descended from ancient parasitic bacterial invasion of eukaryotic cells. Since the time of their acquisition by eukaryotes, mitochondria and chloroplasts have evolved an endosymbiotic relationship with their eukaryotic hosts, and the precise genetic content of mitochondria and chloroplasts varies by eukaryotic host species (see Chapter 19).

A complete set of nuclear chromosomes are transmitted during the cell-division process called **mitosis** to produce genetically identical daughter cells. In contrast, sexual reproduction to produce offspring occurs by the cell-division process called **meiosis** that produces reproductive or sex cells, often identified as **gametes**—sperm and egg in animals and pollen and egg in plants. The gametes of a diploid species are haploid and contain one chromosome from each of the homologous pairs of chromosomes in the genome. The union of haploid gametes at fertilization produces a diploid fertilized egg that begins mitotic division to produce the zygote.

Predictable patterns of gene transmission during sexual reproduction are a focus of later chapters that discuss hereditary transmission and the analysis of transmission ratios (Chapter 2), cell division and chromosome heredity (Chapter 3), gene action and interaction of genes in producing variation of physical appearance (Chapter 4), and the analysis of genetic linkage between genes (Chapter 5).

Genetic experiments taking place in roughly the first half of the 20th century developed the concept of the gene as the physical unit of heredity and revealed the relationship between **phenotype,** meaning the observable traits of an organism, and **genotype,** meaning the genetic constitution of an organism. Biologists also described how hereditary variation is attributable to alternative forms of a gene, called **alleles.** The alleles of a gene have differences in DNA sequence that alter the product of the gene.

During the early decades of the 20th century, the study of gene transmission was established as a foundation of genetics. The concepts of gene action and gene interaction in producing phenotype variation were described, as was the concept of mapping genes along chromosomes. It was also during this period that evolutionary biologists developed gene-based models of evolution. These, too, are integral to genetic analysis, and their use continues to the present day.

Identifying the Genetic Material An experiment conducted in 1944 by Oswald Avery, Colin MacLeod, and Maclyn McCarty identified *deoxyribonucleic acid (DNA)* as the hereditary material and is commonly credited with inaugurating the "molecular era" in genetics (see Chapter 7).

This new era, which spanned the second half of the 20th century and continues to the present day, began an effort to discover the molecular structure of DNA. This research reached a milestone in 1953, when the experimental work of many biologists, including, most famously, James Watson, Francis Crick, Maurice Wilkins, and Rosalind Franklin, led to the identification of the double-helical structure of DNA. A few years later, in 1958, the common mechanism of DNA replication was ascertained. By the mid-1960s, the basic mechanisms of DNA transcription and messenger RNA (mRNA) translation were laid out, and the genetic code by which mRNA is translated into proteins was deciphered. Gene cloning and the development of recombinant DNA technologies developed and progressed rapidly during the 1970s. By the early 1980s, biologists realized that to properly understand the unity and complexity of life, they would have to study and compare the **genomes** of species, the complete sets of DNA sequences, including all genes and regions controlling genes. This realization launched the "genomics era" in genetics, which continues to expand rapidly today.

Since the inception of genome sequencing, biologists deciphered thousands of genomes that range in size from a few tens of thousands of DNA base pairs in the simplest viral genomes to tens of billions of base pairs in the largest plant and animal genomes. Fittingly, in 2001, a century after Garrod and Bateson's historic identification of alkaptonuria as a human hereditary disease, collaborative scientific groups from around the world published the completed "first draft" of the human genome. Collective efforts like the Human Genome Project and the other genome sequencing projects that have been and will be undertaken promise to provide databases that will make the second century of genetics every bit as remarkable as its first century.

Genetics—Central to Modern Biology

One of the foundations of modern biology is the demonstration that all life on Earth shares a common origin in the form of the "*l*ast *u*niversal *c*ommon *a*ncestor," or **LUCA** (Figure 1.3). All life is descended from this common ancestor and is most commonly divided into three major domains. These three domains of life are **Eukarya, Bacteria,** and **Archaea.**

The three-domain model of life is originally derived from the research of Carl Woese and colleagues in the mid-1970s. In contrast to earlier models, which were based on morphology alone, Woese used molecular sequences to determine phylogenetic relationships between existing organisms and thus to trace the evolution of life. Woese used the sequence of ribosomal RNA (rRNA), a small molecule produced directly from DNA in all organisms, as his basis for comparison. His premise was simple—evolutionary theory predicts that closely related species will have more similarity in their

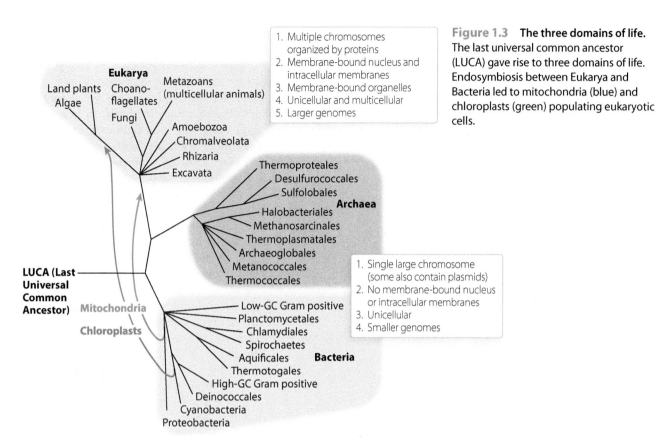

1. Multiple chromosomes organized by proteins
2. Membrane-bound nucleus and intracellular membranes
3. Membrane-bound organelles
4. Unicellular and multicellular
5. Larger genomes

1. Single large chromosome (some also contain plasmids)
2. No membrane-bound nucleus or intracellular membranes
3. Unicellular
4. Smaller genomes

Figure 1.3 **The three domains of life.** The last universal common ancestor (LUCA) gave rise to three domains of life. Endosymbiosis between Eukarya and Bacteria led to mitochondria (blue) and chloroplasts (green) populating eukaryotic cells.

rRNA sequences than will species that are less closely related. Furthermore, species that are members of the same evolutionary lineage will share certain rRNA sequence changes that are not shared with species outside the lineage. Since Woese's work, many researchers have used other molecules to refine and propose additional details to the three-domain model. The tree of life remains a work in progress, but the three-domain model is well established. We use this model in subsequent chapters to compare and contrast molecular features, activities, and processes to shed additional light on the evolutionary relationships between the three domains.

A second foundation of biology is the recognition that the hereditary material—the molecular substance that conveys and stores genetic information—is **deoxyribonucleic acid (DNA)** in all organisms. Certain viruses use **ribonucleic acid (RNA)** as their hereditary material. Most biologists argue that viruses are not alive. Rather, they are obligate intracellular parasites that are noncellular and must invade host cells where they reproduce at the expense of the host cell. In living organisms, DNA has a double-stranded structure described as a **DNA double helix,** or as a **DNA duplex,** consisting of two strands joined together in accordance with specific biochemical rules. Certain viral genomes consist of a small single-stranded DNA molecule that replicates to form a DNA duplex in a host cell.

Eukarya, Bacteria, and Archaea share general mechanisms of **DNA replication,** the process that precisely duplicates the DNA duplex prior to cell division, and they also share general mechanisms of gene expression, the processes through which the genetic information guides development and functioning of an organism. All organisms express their genetic information by a two-step process that begins with **transcription,** a process in which one strand of DNA is used to direct the synthesis of a single strand of RNA. Transcription produces various forms of RNA, including **messenger RNA (mRNA),** which in all organisms undergoes **translation** to produce proteins at structures called **ribosomes.**

As the biological discipline devoted to the examination of all aspects of heredity and variation between generations and through evolutionary time, genetics is central to modern biology. Modern genetics has three major branches. **Transmission genetics,** also known as **Mendelian genetics,** is the study of the transmission of traits and characteristics in successive generations. **Evolutionary genetics** studies the origins of and genetic relationships between organisms and examines the evolution of genes and genomes. **Molecular genetics** studies inheritance and variation in nucleic acids (DNA and RNA), proteins, and genomes and tries to connect them to inherited variation and evolution in organisms.

These branches of genetics are not rigidly differentiated. There is substantial cross-communication among them, and it is rare to find a geneticist today who doesn't use analytical approaches from all three. Similarly, not only are most biological scientists, to a greater or lesser extent, also geneticists, but many of the methods and techniques of genetic experimentation and analysis are shared by all biological scientists. After all, genetic analysis interprets the common language of life by integrating information from all three branches.

1.2 The Structure of DNA Suggests a Mechanism for Replication

At its core, hereditary transmission is the process of dispersing genetic information from parents to offspring. In sexually reproducing organisms, this process is accomplished by the generation of reproductive sex cells in males (the sperm or pollen) and females (the egg), followed by the union of egg and sperm (animals) or pollen (plants) or spores (yeast) at fertilization, with the subsequent development of an organism. DNA is the hereditary molecule in reproductive cells. Similarly, in somatic (body) cells of plants and animals and in organisms that reproduce by asexual processes, DNA is the hereditary molecule that ensures that successive generations of cells are identical.

Experiments and research on cells taking place from the late 1800s through the mid-1900s culminated in the identification of DNA as the hereditary material (see Section 7.1). This identification was of monumental importance to biologists and biochemists and was the foundation of new molecular-focused approaches in biological science research. Understanding the molecular structure of DNA was key to two fundamental areas of inquiry: (1) how DNA could carry the diverse array of genetic information present in the various genomes of animals and plants and (2) how the molecule replicated. In this section, we review basic concepts of DNA structure and DNA replication. The molecular details of DNA structure and replication are provided in Chapter 7.

The Discovery of DNA Structure

In the early 1950s, James Watson, an American in his mid-20s who had recently completed a doctoral degree, and Francis Crick, a British biochemist in his mid-30s, began working together at the University of Cambridge, England, to solve the puzzle of DNA structure. Their now-legendary collaboration culminated in a 1953 publication that ignited the molecular era in genetics.

Watson and Crick's paper accurately described the molecular structure of DNA as a double helix composed of two strands of DNA with an invariant sugar-phosphate backbone on the outside and nucleotide bases—adenine, thymine, guanine, and cytosine—arrayed in complementary base pairs that orient themselves toward the center of the molecule. This discovery was of enormous importance because with the structure of DNA unveiled, the "gene"

had a physical form and was no longer just a conceptual entity. In this physical form, genes could be examined and sequenced, compared with other genes in the genome, and compared with similar genes in other species.

Watson and Crick's description of DNA structure was not the product of their work exclusively. In fact, unlike others who made significant contributions to the discovery of DNA structure, Watson and Crick were not actively engaged in laboratory research. Outside of their salaries, they had very little financial support available to conduct research. In lieu of laboratory research, Watson and Crick put their efforts into DNA-model building, basing their interpretations on experimental data gathered by others.

Rosalind Franklin, a biophysicist working with Maurice Wilkins at King's College in London, was one of the principal sources of information used by Watson and Crick. Franklin used an early form of X-ray diffraction imagery to examine the crystal structure of DNA. In Franklin's method, X-rays bombarding crystalline preparations of DNA were diffracted as they encountered the atoms in the crystals (Figure 1.4). The pattern of diffracted X-rays was recorded on X-ray film, and the structure of the molecules in the crystal was deduced from that pattern. Franklin's most famous X-ray diffraction photograph clearly shows (to the well-trained eye) that DNA is a duplex, consisting of two strands twisted around one another in a double helix.

In devising their DNA model, Watson and Crick combined Franklin's X-ray diffraction data with information published a few years earlier by Erwin Chargaff. Chargaff had determined the percentages of the four DNA nucleotide bases in the genomes of a wide array of organisms and had concluded that the percentages of adenine and thymine are approximately equal to one another and that the percentages of cytosine and guanine are equal to one another as well (Table 1.1). Known as **Chargaff's rule,** this information helped Watson and Crick formulate the hypothesis that DNA nucleotides are arranged in **complementary base pairs.** Adenine, on one strand of the double

(a)   (b)

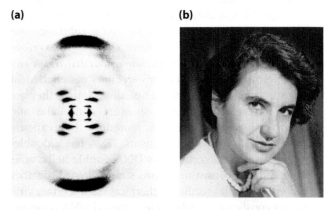

Figure 1.4 X-ray diffraction evidence of DNA structure.
(a) This X-shaped pattern is consistent with the diffraction of X-ray beams by a helical molecule composed of two strands.
(b) Rosalind Franklin obtained this X-ray diffraction result.

Table 1.1	Nucleotide-Base Composition of Various Genomes					
Source Genome	Percentage of Each Nucleotide Base				Ratios	
	Adenine (A)	Guanine (G)	Cytosine (C)	Thymine (T)	G + C	G/C
Bacteria						
E. coli (B)	23.8	26.8	26.3	23.1	53.1	1.02
Yeast						
S. cerevisiae	31.3	18.7	17.1	32.9	35.8	1.09
Fungi						
N. crassa	23.0	27.1	26.6	23.3	53.7	1.02
Invertebrate						
C. elegans	31.2	19.3	20.5	29.1	39.8	0.94
D. melanogaster	27.3	22.5	22.5	27.6	45.0	1.00
Plant						
A. thaliana	29.1	20.5	20.7	29.7	41.2	0.99
Vertebrate						
M. musculus	29.2	21.7	19.7	29.4	41.4	1.10
H. sapiens	30.6	19.7	19.8	30.3	39.5	0.99

helix, pairs only with thymine on the other DNA strand, and cytosine pairs only with guanine to form the other base pair. With these data, their own knowledge of biochemistry, and their analysis of incorrect models of DNA structure, Watson and Crick built a table-top model of DNA out of implements and materials scattered around their largely inactive research laboratory space—wire, tin, tape, and paper, supported by ring stands and clamps (Figure 1.5).

Figure 1.5   James Watson (left) and Francis Crick (right) in 1953 with their cardboard-and-wire model of DNA.

DNA Nucleotides

Each strand of the double helix is composed of **DNA nucleotides** that have three principal components: a five-carbon deoxyribose sugar, a phosphate group, and one of four nitrogen-containing nucleotide bases, designated **adenine (A), guanine (G), thymine (T), and cytosine (C)** (Figure 1.6). The nucleotides forming a strand are linked together by a covalent **phosphodiester bond** between the 5′ phosphate group of one nucleotide and the 3′ hydroxyl (OH) group of the adjacent nucleotide. Phosphodiester bonding leads to alternation of deoxyribose sugars and phosphate groups along the strand and gives the molecule a sugar-phosphate backbone.

The nucleotide bases are hydrophobic (water-avoiding) and naturally orient toward the water-free interior of the duplex. The bases can occur in any order along one strand of the molecule, but DNA is most stable as a duplex of two strands that have complementary base sequences, so that an A on one strand faces a T on the second strand and a G on one strand faces a C on the other. This complementary base pairing is the basis of Chargaff's rule and produces equal percentages of A and T and of C and G in double-stranded DNA molecules. **Hydrogen bonds,** noncovalent bonds consisting of weak electrostatic attractions, form between complementary base pairs to join the two DNA strands into a double helix. Each strand of DNA has a 5′ end and a 3′ end. These designations refer to the phosphate group (5′) and hydroxyl group (3′) at the opposite ends of each strand of DNA and establish **strand polarity,** that is, the 5′-to-3′ orientation of each strand. Complementary strands of DNA are **antiparallel,**

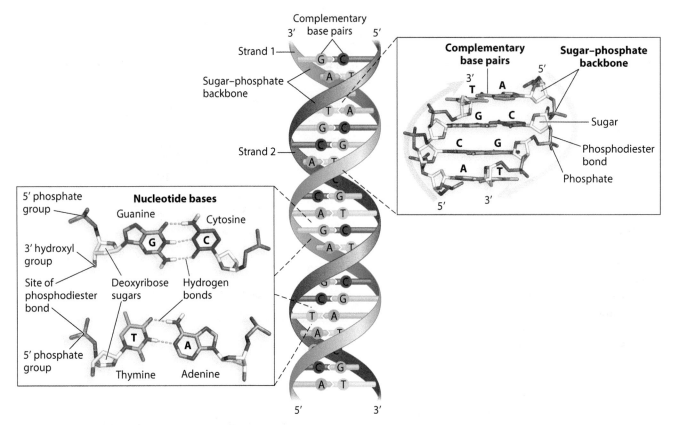

Figure 1.6   DNA composition and structure. DNA nucleotides contain a deoxyribose sugar, a phosphate group, and a nucleotide base (A, T, G, or C). Phosphodiester bonds join adjacent nucleotides in each strand, and hydrogen bonds join complementary nucleotides of strands that have antiparallel orientation.

meaning that the polarities of the complementary strands run in opposite directions—one strand is oriented 5′ to 3′ and the complementary strand is oriented 3′ to 5′. **Genetic Analysis 1.1** guides you through a problem that tests your understanding of base-pair complementation and complementary strand polarity.

If you are like many biology students, you have probably wondered from time to time what DNA actually looks like, both on the macroscopic and microscopic level. Even today's best microscopes have difficulty capturing high-resolution images of DNA, although computer-aided techniques for analyzing molecular structure can produce an interpretation of its microscopic appearance, as you'll see in Chapters 7, 8, and 9, for example. However, you do not need sophisticated instrumentation to produce a sample of DNA that you can hold in your hand. **Experimental Insight 1.1** presents a simple recipe for DNA isolation you can do at home with common and safe household compounds.

DNA Replication

The identification of the double-helical structure of DNA established a starting point for a new set of questions about heredity. The first of these questions concerned how DNA

replicates. After correctly describing DNA structure in their 1953 paper, Watson and Crick closed with a directive for future research on the question of DNA replication: "It has not escaped our notice that the specific base-pairing we have proposed immediately suggests a possible copying mechanism for the genetic material."

Indeed, as a consequence of the A-T and G-C complementary base-pairing rules, it was evident that each single strand of DNA contains the information necessary to generate the second strand of DNA and that DNA replication generates two identical DNA duplexes from the original parental duplex during each replication cycle. At the time Watson and Crick described the structure of DNA, however, the mechanism of replication was not known. It would take another 5 years for Matthew Meselson and Franklin Stahl, in an ingenious experiment of simple design, to prove that DNA replicates by a *semiconservative* mechanism (see Chapter 7).

In **semiconservative replication,** the mechanism by which DNA usually replicates, the two complementary strands of original DNA separate from one another, and each strand acts as a template to direct the synthesis of a new, complementary strand of DNA with antiparallel polarity. The mechanism is termed "semiconservative" because after the completion of DNA replication, each

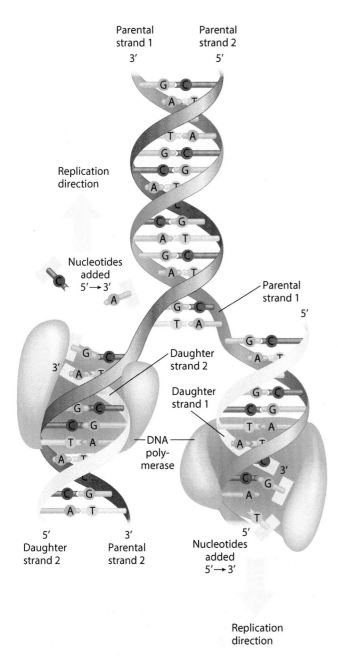

Figure 1.7 **Semiconservative DNA replication.** Each parental DNA strand serves as the template for synthesis of its daughter strand. DNA polymerase synthesizes daughter strands one nucleotide at a time.

phosphodiester bond to join the new nucleotide to the previous nucleotide in the nascent (growing) daughter strand.

The biochemistry of nucleic acids and DNA polymerases dictates that DNA strands elongate only in the 5′-to-3′ direction. In other words, nucleotides are added exclusively to the 3′ end of the nascent strand, leading to 5′-to-3′ growth. Like the parental duplex, each new DNA duplex contains antiparallel strands. Each parental strand–daughter strand combination forms a new double helix of DNA that is an exact replica of the original parental duplex.

1.3 DNA Transcription and Messenger RNA Translation Express Genes

The **central dogma of biology** is a statement describing the flow of hereditary information. It summarizes the critical relationships between DNA, RNA, and protein; the functional role that DNA plays in maintaining, directing, and regulating the expression of genetic information; and the roles played by RNA and proteins in gene function. Francis Crick proposed the original version of the central dogma, shown in Figure 1.8a, in 1956 to encapsulate the role DNA plays in directing transcription of RNA and, in turn, the role messenger RNA plays in translation of proteins. As Crick told the story years later, he wrote this concept as "DNA → RNA → protein" (spoken as "DNA to RNA to protein") on a slip of paper and taped it to the wall above his desk to remind himself of the direction of information transfer during the expression of genetic information. The most important idea it conveys is that DNA does not code directly for protein. Rather, DNA makes up the genome of an organism and is a permanent repository of genetic information in each cell, directing gene expression by the transcription of DNA to RNA and, ultimately, the production of proteins.

Over the decades since Crick first introduced the central dogma, biologists have developed a clear understanding of the role of DNA in maintaining and expressing genetic information. Most of the details of the two-stage process by which genetic information in sequences of DNA is transcribed to RNA and then translated to protein are known, as described in later chapters (transcription in Chapter 8 and translation in Chapter 9). For example, biologists now know that several forms of RNA are found in cells, and all these RNA molecules are transcribed and play a variety of roles in cells, but only mRNA is translated.

Two important categories of RNA that are not translated but nonetheless play critical roles in translation are ribosomal RNA and transfer RNA. **Ribosomal RNA (rRNA)** forms part of the ribosomes, the plentiful cellular structures where protein assembly takes place. **Transfer RNA (tRNA)** carries **amino acids,** the building blocks of proteins, to ribosomes. An updated central

new duplex is composed of one **parental strand** (conserved from the original DNA) and one newly synthesized **daughter strand** (Figure 1.7).

DNA replication begins at an origin of replication, with the breaking of hydrogen bonds that hold the strands together. (This process is much like what happens when a zipper comes undone.) DNA polymerases are the enzymes active in DNA replication. Using each parental DNA strand as a template, these enzymes identify the nucleotide that is complementary to the first unpaired nucleotide on the parental strand and then catalyze formation of a

PROBLEM Determine the sequence and polarity of the DNA strand complementary to the strand shown below.

> **BREAK IT DOWN:** A DNA sequence is a string of A, G, T, and C nucleotides that is 5′ on one end and 3′ on the other (p. 7)

3 ′-...ACGGATCCTCCCTAGTGCGTAATACG...-5 ′

> **BREAK IT DOWN:** Complementarity of DNA nucleotides pairs A with T and G with C (p. 6)

Solution Strategies	Solution Steps
Evaluate	
1. Identify the topic of this problem and the kind of information the answer should contain.	1. This problem concerns nucleotide complementarity in a DNA duplex and the polarity of complementary strands. The answer should contain the nucleotide sequence and polarity of a strand complementary to the given one.
2. Identify the critical information given in the problem.	2. The problem provides the nucleotide sequence and polarity of one strand of a DNA duplex.
Deduce	
3. Recall the base-pairing relationships of DNA nucleotides in complementary strands.	3. In complementary DNA strands, base pairing joins adenine with thymine and guanine with cytosine to form a DNA duplex.

> **TIP:** Complementary DNA strands are antiparallel, with one strand 3′ → 5′ and the other 5′ → 3′.

> **PITFALL:** Always check the polarity of a strand you are given; don't assume it's written with either the 5′ or 3′ end facing a certain way.

4. Recall the polarity relationship of complementary DNA strands.	4. The second strand of this duplex will be oriented with its 5′ end to the left and its 3′ end to the right.
Solve	
5. Give the sequence and polarity of the complementary DNA strand.	5. By the rules of complementary base pairing and antiparallel strand orientation, the second DNA strand is

5 ′-TGCCTAGGAGGGATCACGCATTATGC-3 ′

For more practice, see Problems 11, 12, and 14.   Visit the Study Area to access study tools.   **MasteringGenetics™**

---

dogma of biology is shown in **Figure 1.8b**. In addition to mRNA, rRNA, and tRNA, the figure identifies **reverse transcription,** a form of information flow that synthesizes DNA from an RNA template in RNA-containing viruses (retroviruses) by using an enzyme called reverse transcriptase. It also identifies micro-RNA (miRNA), the focus of a rapidly emerging new area of RNA investigation that studies the role of these small RNA molecules in the regulation of gene expression in plants and animals (see Chapter 15).

Transcription

Transcription is the process by which information in DNA sequence is converted into RNA sequence. Transcription uses one strand of the DNA making up a gene to direct synthesis of a single-stranded RNA transcript. The DNA strand from which the transcript is synthesized is called the **template strand.** The RNA-synthesizing enzyme RNA polymerase pairs template-strand nucleotides with complementary RNA nucleotides to synthesize new transcript

Figure 1.8 The central dogma of biology. (a) Francis Crick's original central dogma of biology. (b) The updated central dogma of biology.

(a)

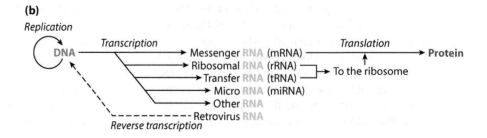

(b)

Experimental Insight 1.1

Countertop DNA Isolation—Try This at Home!

For all the abundance of DNA in cells, its molecular structure is too small to see without the aid of the most powerful electron microscopes. However, that doesn't mean DNA must remain invisible to the naked eye. The key to seeing it is simply a question of volume. If enough DNA is collected together, it can be seen—although not, of course, in its molecular detail. Using a rich source of DNA (such as onions, which are available year-round, or strawberries, whose nuclei contain eight copies of each chromosome) and a few familiar household items, you can collect a visible sample of DNA in about 30 minutes.

INGREDIENTS

1 small peeled onion (about 1 cup) or about 1 cup strawberries with leaves removed

1 to 2 cups water with 1 teaspoon of dissolved salt per cup

2 tablespoons dishwashing liquid

1 tablespoon meat tenderizer (containing "papain" from papaya)

4 to 6 ounces isopropyl ("rubbing") alcohol (95% is best, but 70% is sufficient)

EQUIPMENT

Food processor (for onion) or a potato masher or ricer (for strawberries)

Small bowl

Clear glass jar or container with vertical sides

Cheesecloth to layer over the top of the glass container with a few inches to spare all around

1 rubber band to go around the glass container

1 chopstick or a similar wooden implement

DIRECTIONS

1. Peel onion and finely chop in food processor or thoroughly mash strawberries in bowl.

2. Add 1 to 2 cups water to onion and process into a fine slurry. Pour slurry into small bowl. If using strawberries, add about 1 cup water and mash into a fine slurry.

3. Add 2 tablespoons liquid dishwashing soap to slurry and stir gently. Be careful not to let the soap get foamy. Let mixture stand at least 10 to 15 minutes (longer is fine) while the soap breaks down the cell and nuclear membranes.

4. Add 1 tablespoon meat tenderizer to mixture, stir gently, and let stand at least 10 to 15 minutes (longer is fine). The papain will digest much of the protein released by the ruptured cells and also the proteins attached to DNA.

5. Place 2 to 3 layers cheesecloth loosely over the opening of the glass container, allowing the cloth to form a small "bowl" inside the opening. Use the rubber band to hold the cheesecloth in place. Pour the slurry mixture through the cheesecloth, scooping out the onion or strawberry debris as it fills the cheesecloth bowl. Approximately 8 to 12 ounces of "juice" will collect at the bottom of the container. Discard the cheesecloth and its contents.

6. Pour the alcohol into the juice and stir very briefly. Let the juice mixture stand for at least 5 to 10 minutes. As the juice settles, the alcohol rises to the top, and the large mass of floating cottony material in it is DNA.

7. When the alcohol has completely separated from the juice, you can "spool" the DNA onto a chopstick by slowly twirling the stick in the cottony DNA.

---

in the 5′-to-3′ direction; the transcript is antiparallel to the DNA template strand (Figure 1.9).

The complementary partner of the DNA template strand is known as the **coding strand.** In the past, the coding strand has also been identified as the "nontemplate

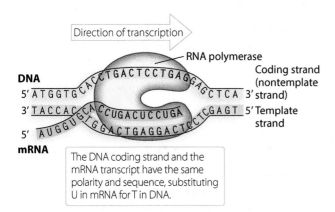

Direction of transcription

RNA polymerase

Coding strand (nontemplate strand)

DNA

5′ ATGGTGCAC TGACTCCTGAGG AGCTCA 3′

3′ TACCAC CCUGACUCCUGA CGAGT 5′ Template strand

5′ AUGGUGCA GGACTGAGGACT TCGAGT

mRNA

The DNA coding strand and the mRNA transcript have the same polarity and sequence, substituting U in mRNA for T in DNA.

Figure 1.9   **The correspondence of RNA to DNA template and coding strands.**

strand," but that term is rarely used anymore. Because the coding strand is both complementary and antiparallel to the DNA template strand, it has the same $5' \to 3'$ polarity as the RNA transcript synthesized from the template strand; moreover, the RNA transcript and the DNA coding strand are identical in nucleotide sequence, except for the appearance of U in the place of T. Our descriptions in this textbook will refer to this DNA strand as the "coding strand," but it is also correct to identify the strand as the nontemplate strand.

RNA is composed of four nucleotides that are chemically very similar to DNA. RNA nucleotides consist of a ribose sugar (as opposed to deoxyribose found in DNA), a phosphate group, and one of four nitrogenous bases. Three of the RNA nucleotide bases are adenine, cytosine, and guanine. They are identical to the same nucleotide bases found in DNA. The fourth RNA base is **uracil (U)**. It is chemically closely related to thymine; thus, in DNA–RNA and in RNA–RNA complementary base pairing, uracil pairs with adenine. All other complementary base-pair arrangements are as we described them previously.

Transcription is the process in which the enzyme RNA polymerase uses the template strand of DNA to synthesize RNA transcripts. To begin transcription, RNA polymerase, and any other proteins necessary for transcription, must locate a gene and gain access to the template DNA strand by interacting with DNA sequences that control transcription. Once the coding sequence of the gene has been transcribed, the RNA polymerase must stop transcription and release the transcript.

Promoters are the most common type of DNA sequences controlling transcription. Promoters are recognized by RNA polymerase, and they direct RNA polymerase to a nearby gene. Promoters themselves are regulatory sequences and are not transcribed. Instead, the transcription of a gene begins near the promoter at the **start of transcription,** the DNA location where transcription of a sequence begins. Transcription ends at the **termination sequence,** where another DNA sequence facilitates the cessation of transcription (Figure 1.10a). In bacteria and archaea, protein-producing genes are transcribed into mRNA that is quickly translated to produce the protein. Eukaryotic genes have a different structure than do bacterial and most archaeal genes. Nearly all eukaryotic genes are subdivided into **exons,** which contain the coding information that will be used during translation, and **introns,** which intervene between exons and are removed from the transcript before translation (Figure 1.10b). Bacterial genes do not contain introns, and only a tiny number of archaeal genes are suspected to contain introns. The removal of introns from eukaryotic mRNA and other modifications before translation occurs in the nucleus (see Chapter 8).

Translation

Translation converts the genetic message of mRNA into sequences of amino acids using the *genetic code.* The amino acids are joined to one another by a covalent bond called a **peptide bond.** The resulting string of amino acids is a **polypeptide,** which upon folding makes up all or part of a **protein.**

Translation of mRNA occurs at ribosomes, where sets of three consecutive nucleotides, each set called a **codon,** specify the amino acid at each position of a polypeptide. Each mRNA codon is a triplet of RNA nucleotides coded by three complementary DNA nucleotides on the template strand. The DNA nuceotides complementary to codon nucleotides are known as the DNA triplet (Figure 1.11a). Translation begins with mRNA attaching to a ribosome in a manner that places the **start codon,** the codon specifying the first amino acid of a polypeptide, in the necessary location (Figure 1.11b). The start codon is most commonly AUG and is the codon at which translation begins. The start codon is read by the ribosome in the 5′ → 3′ direction, A then U then G. To read each subsequent codon, the ribosome moves 5′ → 3′ along the mRNA to assemble the amino acid string.

Amino acids are transported to ribosomes by transfer RNAs (tRNAs). At each codon, complementary base pairing occurs between codon nucleotides and a three-nucleotide sequence of tRNA called an **anticodon.** This interaction assembles amino acids in the order dictated by the mRNA sequence. Ribosomal proteins power the continuous progression of the ribosome along mRNA and catalyze peptide bond formation in the growing polypeptide chain. Translation continues until the ribosome encounters a **stop codon,** thus bringing translation to a halt.

The **genetic code,** through which mRNA codons specify amino acids, was deciphered by a series of experiments that took place during the early 1960s. The experiments revealed that the genetic code contains 64 codons; every codon consists of three positions that are each filled by one of the four RNA nucleotides. An mRNA codon is read in the 5′-to-3′ direction: The first base of the codon is at its 5′ end, the third base is at its 3′ end, and the second base is in the middle.

Figure 1.10 Gene structure in bacteria, archaea, and eukaryotes. Coding sequences contain information to be transcribed into RNA. Promoter sequences regulate the initiation of transcription, and termination sequences control the cessation of transcription. **(a)** Bacterial and most, but not all, archaeal genes contain a single coding sequence that carries the information of the gene. **(b)** The coding sequence of eukaryotic genes is split up into exons, which are separated by introns.

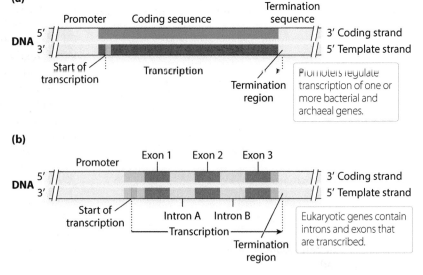

(a)

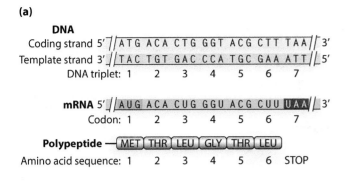

(b)

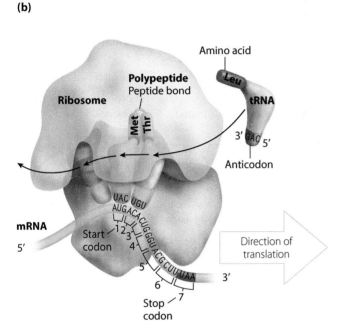

Figure 1.11   Overview of translation. (a) Messenger RNA codons are complementary and antiparallel to DNA triplets of the template strand. **(b)** Ribosomes initiate translation of mRNA at the start codon and move along the mRNA in the 3′ direction, adding a new amino acid to the nascent polypeptide by reading each codon. Transfer RNA molecules carry amino acids to ribosomes, where the tRNA anticodon sequences interact with codon sequences of mRNA. Translation terminates when the ribosome encounters a stop codon.

A total of 61 of the 64 codons specify amino acids, and the other 3 are the stop codons. The 64 codons are displayed in **Table A** (inside the book front cover) using the three-letter and one-letter abbreviations. **Table B** (also inside the book front cover) lists the names and abbreviations of each amino acid, along with their codons. The genetic code is redundant, with individual amino acids encoded by as many as six codons and as few as one codon.

Genetic Analysis 1.2 allows you to work through the transcription and translation of the DNA sequence assessed in Genetic Analysis 1.1.

Genomes, Proteomes, and "-omic" Approaches

Genomics is the field that focuses on the sequencing, interpretation, and comparison of genomes of different organisms. Genomic data collection and analysis involve an array of molecular techniques and analytical strategies that aid in identification and examination of the totality of the DNA in a cell, nucleus, or organelle (mitochondria and chloroplasts) carried by a species. Indeed, genomics has made critical contributions to many areas of biological investigation. From medicine to the study of hereditary variation to the study of evolution, genomic data are proving critically important.

Much has changed in DNA sequencing since it began in the 1980s. Genome sequencing is accomplished today by automated high-throughput methods, so-called next-generation sequencing that is thousands of times faster, and far cheaper, than the original genome sequencing methods (see Chapters 7, 18, and 22 for details and applications).

To date, thousands of genome sequences have been compiled. Among the smallest genomes are those of viruses, mitochondria, and chloroplasts, which generally contain tens of thousands to a few hundred thousand base pairs. In contrast, the largest sequenced genomes are those of some plant species that carry multiple sets of chromosomes from their progenitors and have billions of base pairs. Genome sizes are usually identified in terms of **megabases (Mb)**, with 1 Mb equal to 1 million base pairs.

Certain selected species known as "model organisms" are commonly used in genetics and genomics experiments. They are selected because their biology is well known, they are easy to work with and propagate, and they can be investigated through multiple experiments and thus be seen from a more complete perspective. A reference table inside the book back cover provides genomic and other critical information about nine model organisms, including the bacterium *E. coli*, the plant *Arabidopsis thaliana*, the yeast *Saccharomyces cerevisiae*, the fruit fly *Drosophila melanogaster*, and humans (*Homo sapiens*).

Genomics has a seemingly limitless array of applications. For example, genomic techniques and analyses can be used to identify specific genes, to identify allelic variants producing hereditary diseases, to map genes, to identify regions of genomes that increase or decrease the likelihood of an organism expressing a particular trait, to compare gene sequences within and among species, to trace the evolution of genes, and to identify the evolutionary relationships between related organisms.

The Human Genome Project, completed in 2000, was a landmark achievement that, by producing the nucleotide sequence of an entire representative human genome, set a new course for the genetic investigation of humans. In so doing, it made some striking discoveries. For example, 45% of the human genome consists of transposable genetic elements. These are mobile DNA sequences that can move throughout the genome

PROBLEM The DNA duplex identified in Genetic Analysis 1.1 is

$$3'-...ACGGATCCTCCCTAGTGCGTAATACG...-5'$$
$$5'-...TGCCTAGGAGGGATCACGCATTATGC...-3'$$

> **BREAK IT DOWN:** The coding strand has the same $5' \rightarrow 3'$ polarity as the mRNA and also the same base sequence except for the presence of uracil (U) instead of thymine (T) (p. 12).

One strand of the double-stranded DNA sequence serves as the coding strand and the other as the template strand that is transcribed to produce an mRNA. The mRNA is translated into a polypeptide containing five amino acids, the first of which is methionine (Met), encoded by the start codon AUG. The mRNA also contains a stop codon.

> **BREAK IT DOWN:** Translation uses mRNA codons (three consecutive mRNA nucleotides) to direct the assembly of polypeptides (strings of amino acids) (p. 12).

a. Identify the DNA coding strand and the nucleotides corresponding to the start codon, amino acid codons, and the stop codon.

> **BREAK IT DOWN:** The start codon is AUG, and it is followed by four more codons and then a stop codon (p. 12).

b. Write the sequence and polarity of the mRNA transcript, showing the codons for the five amino acids and the stop codon.

> **BREAK IT DOWN:** Messenger RNA codons are written and translated 5' to 3' using the genetic code, which contains three stop codons, UAA, UAG, and UGA (inside front cover).

c. Write the amino acid sequence of the polypeptide produced, using both the three-letter and one-letter codes for the sequence. (See the genetic code tables inside the front cover).

Solution Strategies	Solution Steps
Evaluate	
1. Identify the topic of this problem and the kind of information the answer should contain.	1. The problem concerns identification of the coding strand of DNA and the sequence of mRNA encoding five amino acids in a polypeptide. The amino acid sequence is also required.
2. Identify the critical information given in the problem.	2. The double-stranded DNA sequence is given. It contains a sequence corresponding to the start codon (AUG), encodes five amino acids, and contains a stop codon.
Deduce	
3. Scan the double-stranded DNA sequence to identify possible DNA coding-strand triplets and triplets that might be a start codon.	3. The double-stranded DNA sequence contains two possible triplets corresponding to start codons (5'-ATG-3'), one on each strand. Each is highlighted here in bold:

$$5'-TGCCTAGGAGGGATCACGCATTATGC-3'$$
$$3'-ACGGATCCTCCCTAGTGCGTAATACG-5'$$

> **PITFALL:** Don't simply read left to right. Instead, identify strand polarity and read $5' \rightarrow 3'$.

> **TIP:** The start codon in mRNA is 5'-AUG-3' (methionine), coded by the template–DNA strand triplet 5'-ATG-3'.

4. Scan the double-stranded DNA to identify possible DNA coding-strand triplets corresponding to possible stop codons.	4. Four DNA triplets potentially correspond to a stop codon. Each corresponding stop codon is shown in bold type below.

$$3'-ACGGATCCTCCCTAGTGCGTAAATCG-5'$$
$$5'-...TGCCTAGGAGGGATCACGCATTATGC...-3'$$

> **TIP:** There are three stop codons, UAA, UAG, and UGA, corresponding to DNA coding-strand triplets TAA, TAG, and TGA, respectively.

Solve	
	Answer a
5. Determine which 5'-ATG-3' DNA triplet that is followed by four additional codons (12 nucleotides) encoding amino acids and then by a stop codon corresponds to the authentic start codon.	5. The potential start codon in the upper strand to the right (5'-ATG-3') corresponds to the authentic start codon (AUG). The following 12 nucleotides correspond to the amino acid codons and the stop codon (5'-TAG-3', which corresponds to the UAG stop codon of mRNA).

> **TIP:** The total length of this region would be 18 nucleotides.

	Answer b
6. Determine the mRNA sequence and polarity, showing the codons.	6. The mRNA sequence is

$$5'-AUG\ CGU\ GAU\ CCC\ UCC\ UAG-3'$$
$$\text{Start} \qquad\qquad\qquad\qquad \text{Stop}$$

	Answer c
7. Determine the amino acid sequence of the polypeptide encoded by this mRNA.	7. The polypeptide encoded by this mRNA is Met-Arg-Asp-Pro-Ser, or M-R-D-P-S.

For more practice, see Problems 15, 16, and 19. Visit the Study Area to access study tools. **MasteringGenetics™**

(see Section 13.7). It also showed that almost 26% of the genome consists of noncoding introns, and only 1.5% of the genome consists of protein-coding exons. Section 18.1 provides additional details of the content and genetic annotation of the human genome.

Genome sequencing and analysis are not limited to living species. Several extinct species have recently had their genomes sequenced for comparison to those of living relatives. These species include the mastodon (for comparison to the elephant), the quagga (for comparison to the zebra), and two extinct lineages of early humans, Neandertals and Denisovans (for comparison to the modern human genome). We look at the interesting results of the Neandertal–Denisovan–*Homo sapiens* genome comparisons in the Case Study that concludes the chapter.

On the heels of genomic sequencing, additional arenas of "-omic" investigations and analyses have developed. **Transcriptomics,** the study of the **transcriptome,** the complete set of genes that undergo transcription in a given cell, allows researchers to investigate and compare different cell types to identify differences in the genes that are transcribed there, to characterize changes in the levels of gene transcription within a single cell type, or to see how biological changes affect transcription. Such studies can make important contributions to the understanding of biological abnormalities in cancer by identifying the genes whose transcription is either increased or decreased in cancer cells versus normal cells (see the Case Study in Chapter 12). Along the same lines, **metabolomics,** the study of chemical processes involving metabolites**,** examines metabolic processes and outcomes in specific cells, tissues, organs, and organisms. Metabolomic comparisons of related organisms ties directly to genomics through shared genetic ancestry, and it can also reveal new genetic adaptations that have altered metabolism is organisms.

Proteomics, the study of the **proteome,** the complete set of proteins encoded in a genome, examines the functions of proteins, their localization, their regulation, and their interactions in a comprehensive way. In other words, rather than analyzing the structure and function of individual proteins and looking one by one for interacting partners, proteomics is a methodology for examining large numbers of proteins at once. Multiple techniques are used to collect and analyze the proteomes of organisms. Among the numerous applications for proteomics are the use of proteomic analysis to decipher complex networks of protein–protein interaction in cells to find the number and types of such interactions there (see Section 18.1).

Each of these "-omic" approaches has its own goals, but collectively they also share a common goal—to contribute to the comprehensive understanding of complex biological systems. Called **systems biology,** this comprehensive approach to understanding biological complexity has become possible through the development and the incorporation of genomics, proteomics, transcriptomics, and metabolomics. One overarching goal of the biological sciences—to which genetics is a principal contributing discipline—is to understand the normal and abnormal biology of organisms in a comprehensive way through systems biology.

Applied to humans, for example, systems biology aims to understand how cells work in health and disease, to explain the details of how a single cell develops into a complete organism, and even to explain phenomena as complex as learning, memory, personality, and the development of personality disorders. These enormously complex attributes of organisms result in part from networks of interactions between genes, proteins, metabolites, and environmental influences. They are the most challenging aspects of modern biology, requiring both the understanding of genetic principles and analysis and the use and application of new tools and technologies for data collection and assessment. This is the exciting and dynamic world in which modern genetics operates.

1.4 Evolution Has a Molecular Basis

As biologists survey varieties of life, assess the genetic similarities and differences between species, and explore the relationship of modern organisms to one another and to their extinct ancestors, it becomes apparent that all life is connected through DNA. Richard Dawkins, a biologist and author of several books on evolution, made note of this molecular connection, observing that life "is a river of DNA, flowing and branching through geologic time." Dawkins's "river through time" connecting all organisms is DNA. This shared DNA is a basis for identifying and studying relationships between organisms and tracing their evolutionary histories.

Life is not static or uniform, of course; it evolves as DNA diverges into separate "branches" whose metaphorical forking leads to new species. The Dawkins quote suggests that for heredity to maintain genetic continuity across generations and for variation to develop between organisms and evolve new species, the biochemical processes that replicate DNA and express the genetic information must also be universal. From this perspective the universality of DNA as the hereditary molecule of life, the shared processes of DNA replication and transcription, and the use of the same genetic code by all life are consistent with the idea of a single origin of life that has evolved into the millions of species inhabiting Earth today as well as other millions that preceded them but are now extinct.

Life on Earth originated from a single source during the Archaean Eon that lasted from 4 billion to 2.5 billion years ago. In 2011, an international group of scientists led by David Wacey discovered fossils of a sulphur-metabolizing single-celled organism in 3.49-billion-year-old rocks from Western Australia (**Figure 1.12**). At that time in Earth's history there was very little oxygen present, and the first living organisms, likely not much different from those identified in fossil form, metabolized sulphur-containing compounds for growth. Organisms with similar metabolism exist today around hot springs and thermal vents.

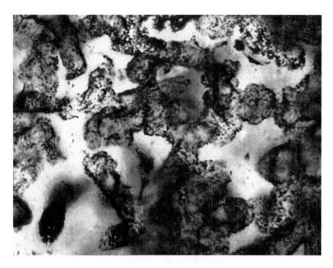

Figure 1.12 **The earliest fossils on Earth.** These single-celled sulphur-metabolizing organisms are fossilized in 3.49-billion-year-old rocks in Western Australia.

These early life-forms have given rise to a dazzling array of species, most now extinct. Some of those extinct ancestors, however, gave rise to modern species that inhabit every conceivable ecological niche on Earth, from the most temperate to the most extreme.

Darwin's Theory of Evolution

Over the millennia since life originated, untold millions of species have come and gone, through the operation of shared processes that faithfully replicated their DNA and passed it on to the next generation while also allowing for the accumulation of variation that drives diversification. This variation, the changes life has undergone, is explained by the theory of **evolution,** which says that all organisms are related by common ancestry and have diversified over time. The four widely recognized evolutionary processes are described below, but first some general comments on Charles Darwin's theory of *evolution by natural selection.*

This view of evolution was proposed separately and independently by both Charles Darwin and Alfred Wallace in the late 1850s. Both authors based their proposals on firsthand observations of the distribution and diversity of life across the globe. Each author described higher rates of survival and reproduction of certain forms of a species over alternative forms through the process of natural selection that favors the survival and reproduction of the most fit individuals in each generation. Unlike the other processes we describe in this overview of evolution, natural selection works at the phenotypic level, but like all evolutionary processes, its effectiveness is based on underlying genetic variation. Natural selection operating to favor one morphological form over others increases the frequency of the favored form in the population and, by doing so, increases the frequencies of the alleles controlling the favored form. Over many generations, forms that produce more offspring also leave more copies of the alleles that control the

phenotype, creating the hallmark of evolutionary change—change in the genetic makeup of the population.

Charles Darwin's theory of evolution by natural selection is now a firmly established scientific fact incorporating three principles of population genetics that were obvious to many naturalists in Darwin's day but were not assembled into a coherent model until Darwin articulated their connection in his 1859 publication *The Origin of Species by Means of Natural Selection.* Darwin's union of observation and principles into an evolutionary theory had a revolutionary effect on biology and laid the foundation of the modern biological sciences. Darwin's principles of populations are

1. Variation exists among the individual members of populations with regard to the expression of traits.
2. Hereditary transmission allows the variation in traits to be passed from one generation to the next.
3. Certain variant forms of traits give the individuals that carry them a higher rate of survival and reproduction in particular environmental conditions. These organisms leave more offspring and increase the frequency of the variant form in the population.

Yet while Darwin laid out the general process by which species evolved, he never understood the underlying hereditary mechanisms that allowed the process to occur. Today, however, more than 150 years after Darwin introduced his revolutionary proposal, biologists fully understand the role of genetics in evolution. With regard to Darwin's evolutionary principles, biology has established that

1. Phenotypic variation of expressed traits reflects inherited genetic variation. DNA-sequence differences (allelic variation) must be the cause of phenotypic variation if evolution is to occur.
2. Hereditary transmission of phenotypic variation requires that offspring inherit and express the alleles that were responsible for the variation in parental organisms.
3. Organisms carrying alleles that are favored by natural selection have a reproductive advantage over organisms that do not carry favored alleles. The former group therefore leaves more copies of their alleles in the next generation, causing the population to evolve through a change in allele frequency.

In other words, progressive phenotypic change in a population is paralleled by genetic changes.

In this particular process of evolution—evolution by natural selection—one form reproduces in greater numbers than others in a population because of being better adapted to the conditions driving natural selection. This process, also known as adaptive evolution, is common; but many examples of so-called nonadaptive evolution (or neutral evolution), the evolution of characteristics that are reproductively or functionally equivalent to other forms in the population, are also observed. Nonadaptive traits are neutral with respect to natural selection, conferring neither a selective advantage nor a selective disadvantage to their bearer, yet their evolutionary basis is fundamentally the same as that of adaptive evolution, as the following paragraphs attest.

Four Evolutionary Processes

The foundations of evolutionary genetics (which, you will recall, studies and compares genetic changes in populations and species over time) were established in the first four decades of the 20th century by several notable evolutionary biologists and innumerable lesser-known individuals. Interestingly, this work took place before DNA was identified as the hereditary material and before the chemical structure of genes was defined and understood. Ronald Fisher, Sewall Wright, J. B. S. Haldane, and many others devised mathematical and statistical models of gene frequency distribution and evolution in populations and species, leading to evolutionary hypotheses that have been tested and verified countless times in laboratory and natural populations.

Through this massive body of work, evolutionary biology has confirmed Darwin's model of the evolution of species by natural selection and expanded the description of evolution to include three additional processes. Thus, biologists identify four processes of evolution, each leading to *changes in the frequencies of alleles in a population over time,* a hallmark characteristic of evolutionary change. The four evolutionary processes are

1. **Natural selection**—the differential survival and reproduction of members of a population owing to possession of favored traits. Population members with the best-adapted morphological form are best able to survive and reproduce, and they leave more offspring than those possessing less-adaptive forms. Over time, the frequency of the best-adapted form and the alleles that produce it increase in the population.

2. **Migration**—the movement of individual organisms from one population to another. This migratory movement transfers alleles from one population to another, and if the allele frequencies between the populations are different and if the number of migrating individuals is large enough, migration can rapidly alter allele frequencies.

3. **Mutation**—the slow acquisition of inherited variation that increases the diversity of populations and serves as the "raw material" of evolutionary change. Mutation, occurring in many different ways in genomes, provides the genetic diversity that is essential for evolution.

4. **Genetic drift**—the random change of allele frequencies due to chance in randomly mating populations. Genetic drift occurs in all populations, but it is most pronounced in very small populations, where statistically significant fluctuations in allele frequencies can occur from one generation to the next.

By the middle of the 20th century, the **modern synthesis of evolution**—the name given to the merging of evolutionary theory with the results of experimental, mathematical, and molecular population biology—emerged as a unified view of evolution. The modern synthesis tells the story of morphological and molecular evolution of plant and animal species using experimentally verified processes and mechanisms.

Among the best-known principal architects of the modern synthesis are Theodosius Dobzhansky and Ernst Mayr, who drew together ideas from Darwin, Fisher, Wright, Haldane, and others to demonstrate how evolution operates in real populations. Dobzhansky and Mayr profoundly influenced the thinking and research of generations of biologists by demonstrating that evolutionary events revealed by laboratory investigations and in natural populations are consistent with the predictions made by Fisher, Wright, and Haldane. In simple terms, Dobzhansky and Mayr showed that evolution in populations and evolution in species occur as predicted by evolutionary theory. Today, having been fleshed out by the work of countless researchers, the modern synthesis gives a clear and virtually complete picture of the factors that produce the evolutionary changes in populations and of the mechanisms that produce the evolution of species. We incorporate evolutionary examples into many chapters and also have a chapter devoted specifically to evolution in species and in populations (see Chapter 22).

Tracing Evolutionary Relationships

Evolutionary biologists investigate evolution by studying morphological (physical) and molecular (DNA, RNA, and protein) evolution of populations and organisms. Both morphological and molecular comparisons can be used to identify relationships between living species and to reveal ancestor–descendant relationships. These similarities and differences can be depicted in a diagram called a **phylogenetic tree,** a branching diagram that describes the ancestor–descendant relationships among species or other taxa. The tree of life shown in Figure 1.3 is one type of phylogenetic tree. These trees summarize the evolutionary histories of species by using branching points in the tree to represent the common ancestors of descendant organisms.

The most commonly used approach to phylogenetic tree construction is the **cladistic** approach, which depicts species' evolutionary relationships by sorting the species into groups called **clades,** or **monophyletic groups,** based on **shared derived characteristics,** or **synaptomorphies,** either morphological or molecular. Synaptomorphies are shared by organisms that are members of a clade. Such sharing of traits is interpreted to indicate that the common ancestor shared by clade members also possessed the trait. Synaptomorphies, whether they are of body morphology, proteins, or nucleic acid sequence, occur through **homology,** the presence of the trait or sequence in a common ancestor. An example morphological homology is limb structure in vertebrates. The limbs of humans, horses, bats, and seals have different functions, but they share the same underlying structure in terms of the number and arrangement of bones in the limbs. These similarities are due to the common ancestry of vertebrates.

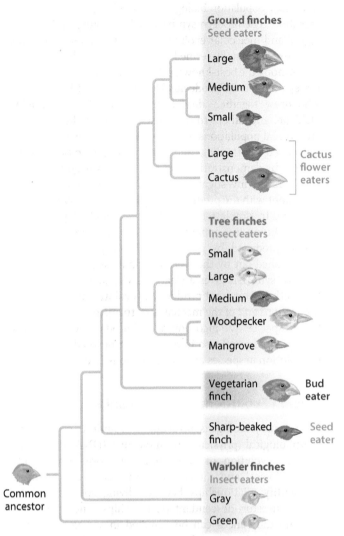

Figure 1.13   Morphological evolution. A phylogenetic tree based on morphological and other characteristics shows the apparent evolutionary relationships between 14 species of finches inhabiting the Galápagos Islands.

presence of wings in birds and bats. These wings—despite the similarities brought about by convergent evolution—have independent origins.

Figure 1.13 shows a phylogenetic tree for 14 finch species that inhabit the Galápagos Islands. These finch species were one of the groups studied by Darwin as he formulated his evolutionary theory. The tree shown here is based on a variety of morphological and behavioral characteristics, including the beak shape, beak size, feeding habits, and habitat of each species, as well as its degree of isolation or separation from other species in the Galápagos Islands.

Constructing Phylogenetic Trees Using Morphology and Anatomy Consider the features shared by various animals listed in **Figure 1.14**. One common morphological feature common to all these animals is the presence of a backbone. This feature unites these animals into a clade we know as vertebrates that all share a common vertebrate ancestor. A second morphological feature, the presence of four legs, unites all the tetrapod animals and excludes salmon. Thus, all the animals except the salmon can be united into a clade we call tetrapods. Because fish are not within the clade of tetrapods, they form an *outgroup* to tetrapods. An **outgroup** is a taxon or group of taxa that is related to, but not included within, the clade in question. The species within the clade of interest are called the **ingroup.** In our example, each successive clade is identified by grouping species based on other shared characteristics.

After a phylogenetic tree has been constructed, it may be used to infer the characters of ancestral species. For example, we can infer that the common ancestor of all the taxa in Figure 1.15 had a backbone, which would therefore be an ancestral character; but it did not

In some instances, closely related taxa *fail* to share a particular trait even though they have a close common ancestor. The branch of a phylogenetic tree missing a particular trait or sequence is identified as a **paraphyletic group.** Paraphyletic groups include some but not all the descendants of a single common ancestor. Paraphyletic groups frequently occur when one lineage of a related group of taxa loses a trait that is retained by descendants or when one lineage develops a new trait not found in other descendants of the common ancestor.

In some apparent cases of synaptomorphy, the similarities are not a result of sharing a close common ancestor. Instead, convergent evolution has led unrelated organisms to display similar-looking traits. Such instances are known as **homoplasmy.** One example of homoplasmy is the

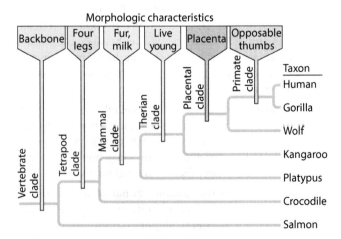

Figure 1.14   The identification of clades based on morphological characters. Organisms are assessed for the presence or absence of a series of morphological characters and those that share derived characteristics form clades. The origins of specific traits can be traced on the phylogenetic tree.

have four legs, which in this case would be a derived character that evolved later, in the common ancestry of tetrapods.

Constructing Phylogenetic Trees Using Molecules Phylogenetic trees based on molecular characteristics are constructed in the same manner as those based on morphological characteristics, except the shared features are DNA sequences or the amino acid sequences of proteins. Descendant groups have nucleic acid or amino acid sequences that are derived from ancient sequences possessed by their common ancestors (i.e., homology). As a consequence of DNA sequence homology, the most closely related molecular sequences are those that have the smallest number of differences between them, and they are carried by the most closely related species.

Figure 1.15 examines the DNA sequences containing the first 15 nucleotides of the β-globin gene from seven

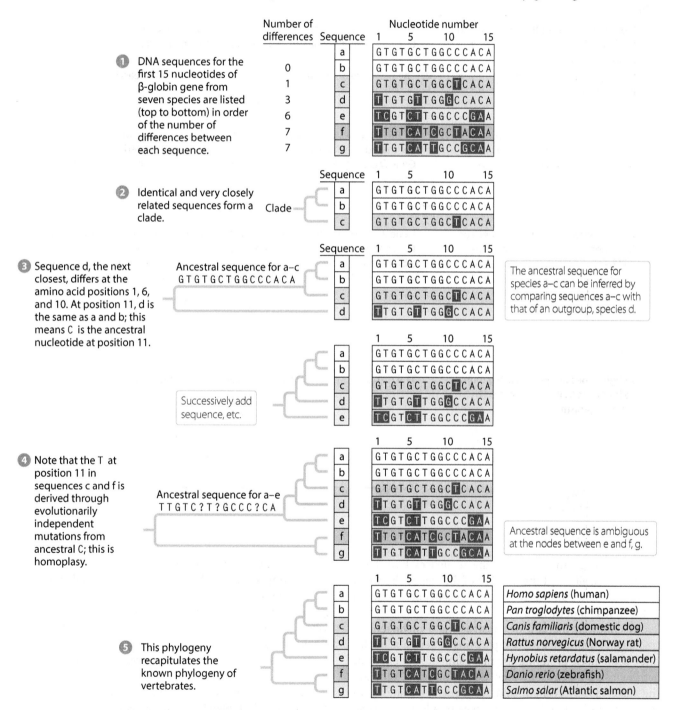

Figure 1.15 **Construction of a phylogenetic tree based on molecular characters, using the principle of homology.**

PROBLEM Evolutionary biologists have searched the genomes of pigs, whales, and cows to identify the presence or absence of six genes, labeled *A* to *F* in the table at right. A gene is marked with a plus symbol (+) if it is found in a genome, or by a minus symbol (−) if it is not found. Use the information in the table to construct the most likely phylogenetic tree relating cow, whale, and pig.

> **BREAK IT DOWN:** Correlation of the presence or absence of certain genes is due to shared ancestry and the number of similarities and differences between related organisms (p. 19)

Organism	Gene					
	A	*B*	*C*	*D*	*E*	*F*
Pig	+	−	−	+	−	−
Whale	+	+	+	−	+	−
Cow	+	+	+	−	−	+

Solution Strategies	Solution Steps

Evaluate

1. Identify the topic of this problem and the kind of information the answer should contain.

2. Identify the critical information given in the problem.

1. This problem uses genetic characteristics in order to construct a phylogenetic tree depicting the relationships between three mammals.

2. The presence or absence of each of six genes is given for each type of mammal.

Deduce

3. Identify genes shared by all three groups, genes shared by two of the groups, and genes unique to one group.

3. Of the six genes tested, gene *A* is found in all three organisms. Genes *B* and *C* are shared by whale and cow genomes but are not detected in the pig genome. Gene *D* is unique to pigs, *E* is unique to whales, and *F* is unique to cows.

Solve

> **TIP:** Genes shared by organisms are likely to have been present in their common ancestor.

4. Assign shared genes to phylogenetic branches that in the completed tree will be shared by the corresponding organisms.

4. Gene *A* is assigned to the base of the phylogenetic tree, which ascends from the common ancestor of the three organisms. Genes *B* and *C* are assigned to a branch shared by whale and cow. Genes *D*, *E*, and *F* are unique to separate groups and therefore are placed on separate branches.

5. Assign genes unique to each genome to branches that are not shared by other organisms.

5. The complete phylogenetic tree containing all genes is shown below.

For more practice, see Problem 18. Visit the Study Area to access study tools. **Mastering**Genetics™

---

species (**a** to **g**). In the figure, the sequences have been aligned vertically, and the number of differences between the top sequence and each of the other sequences is noted in the first step of the figure.

A common method of constructing a phylogenetic tree begins with pairwise comparisons of genes or nucleotide sequences, grouping the most similar sequences or genes closest together (on the assumption that they are the most closely related) and subsequently bringing in the more distantly related sequences to add to the tree. Analysis in this example begins with sequences **a** and **b**, since they are identical, and then successively attaches

more distantly related sequences to the tree. Sequence information from **c,** which differs from **a** and **b** at one nucleotide, is appended next, followed by the other sequences. A completed phylogenetic tree constructed by following these steps recapitulates the known phylogeny of vertebrates.

Genetic Analysis 1.3 guides you in constructing a simple phylogenetic tree.

The availability of DNA sequence data and genomic data has revolutionized how we construct and view phylogenies. Some groups that were traditionally grouped together, such as mammals, birds, and amphibians, do prove, from DNA sequence and genomic data, to form monophyletic groups. However, analyses have indicated that reptiles and fish do not form monophyletic groups and are, instead, paraphyletic. For example, crocodiles are now known to be more closely related to birds than to other reptiles. Similarly, morphological and molecular analyses of dinosaurs (recall it is sometimes possible to obtain some molecular information from extinct species) suggest they are the sister group of birds, implying that extant birds are a kind of modern-day descendant of dinosaurs.

In addition to sequence changes that alter expressed genes, molecular evolution also occurs to regulatory sequences. These sequences are essential for gene transcription and usually operate by binding proteins that activate or repress transcription or by blocking the binding of transcriptionally active proteins. Numerous evolutionary analyses and genome sequence comparisons have identified the important role of such evolution in the diversification of organisms.

CASE STUDY

The Modern Human Family

Modern humans and their early ancestors—an evolutionary group known collectively as hominins—evolved in Africa and moved out of Africa to Europe, Asia, and beyond in an undetermined number of successive migrations that began nearly 2 million years ago. The original migrants were most likely the common ancestors of *Homo erectus* and other hominins. The most recent migrants, migrating out of Africa about 80,000 to 100,000 years ago, were ourselves—anatomically modern humans who constitute all of the world's populations today. The story of how the modern human genome came to be in its present state is the subject of deeply interesting and rapidly changing research in evolutionary anthropology that derives much of its information for analysis from the sequencing of the genomes of long-extinct ancestors of modern humans.

HOMININ EVOLUTION MODELS Prior to the late 1990s, only fossil evidence was available to model hominin evolution. Two principal hypotheses, the Multiregional (MRE) hypothesis and the Recent African Origin (RAO) hypothesis, emerged to explain the evolution of modern humans from our fossilized ancestors. The models agree that the genus *Homo* evolved in Africa and that multiple waves of early hominins had migrated out of Africa to populate Europe and Asia. The MRE hypothesis proposes that local development of modern humans occurred in several locales at about the same time. Under this model, all humans share a deep, common origin, but humans have been in many global locations for a long time and they have diversified locally to produce the populations we observe today. In contrast, the RAO hypothesis proposes that anatomically modern humans migrated out of Africa in a single wave about 80,000 to 100,000 years ago, supplanting the descendants of earlier hominin migrations they encountered and establishing modern-day human populations.

Since the late 1990s, increasingly more efficient methods have been developed to isolate and sequence DNA derived from fossilized bones. First demonstrated on bones from Neandertals in 1997, these methods have now produced extensive "archaic" genomic DNA sequences on multiple hominins that are now extinct. These data have offered general support for the RAO hypothesis, but they also provided evidence that encounters with archaic hominins took place and occurred with different consequences for the modern human genome in locales.

ARCHAIC GENOME SEQUENCES Genomics has undergone amazingly rapid development of methods and applications in recent years, and genome experts such as Svante Paabo have used new methods to decipher the genomes of extinct, so-called "archaic" hominins. The archaic genomes are derived from DNA isolated from bone fragments that are 30,000 or more years old. Using highly specialized techniques, Paabo and his colleagues have assembled genomic sequence data on two archaic hominins that rival the genome data for modern humans in depth and accuracy of genome coverage. One archaic genome is from Neandertals, the hominin that was widely dispersed in Europe and Asia from 400,000 years ago or more until about 30,000 years ago. The second archaic genome is from Denisovans, a more recently identified hominin named for Denisova cave in Siberia where its bones were first discovered. Denisovans were closely related to and contemporaneous with Neandertals. Paabo's group has sequenced both nuclear DNA (the DNA from chromosomes contained in the nucleus) and mitochondrial DNA (the DNA contained in mitochondria that populated the cytoplasm of cells) of Neandertals and Denisovans to compare with the modern human genome.

THE MODERN HUMAN GENOME The genomic information analyzed to date tells us that once modern humans migrated out of Africa, they met and mated with Neandertals and with Denisovans in Europe and Asia. The nuclear genomic data indicated that 2% to 4% of genomic DNA of humans living outside Africa is of Neandertal origin. The data also reveal that Denisovan DNA comprises about 4% of the genomes of Australian aboriginals and those descendants from Papua New Guinea and other Pacific Islands. Figure 1.16 depicts the current view of hominin migrations.

THE GENOMIC STORY OF HOMININS While there is much more to learn about the evolutionary history of hominins, some basic elements are in place. *Homo erectus*, modern humans, Neandertals, Denisovans, and one or more unknown lineages all share common African ancestry. *Homo erectus*

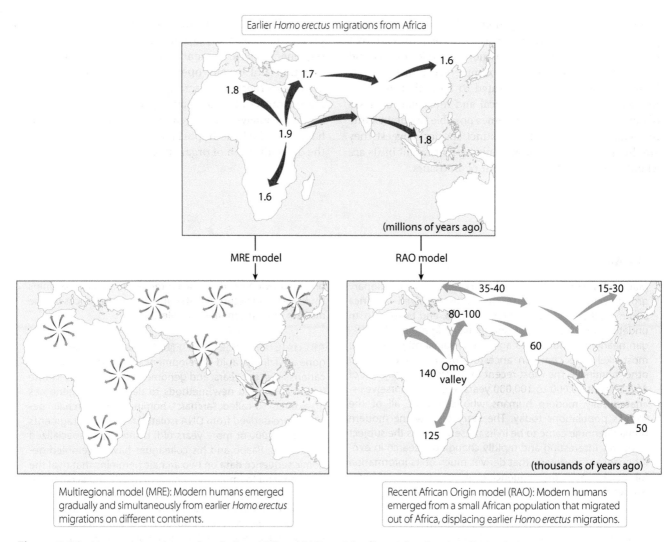

Figure 1.16   Human migration and evolution. MRE and RAO models of hominin migration. Genomic evidence indicates multiple migrations with replacement of archaic hominins by modern humans accompanied by interbreeding.

migrated out of Africa nearly 2 million years ago and left descendants in Europe and Asia that were the common ancestor of Neandertals and Denisovans. Neandertals and Denisovans subsequently diversified but may have maintained a very low level of interbreeding. Once modern humans migrated out of Africa they quickly encountered and mated with Neandertals and with Denisovans. Both archaic groups were eventually eliminated by modern humans, but they left genetic evidence of their interbreeding in the modern human genome in the form of DNA sequences and specific genes.

The exploration of the evolution and origins of the modern human genome is a rapidly changing new arena of investigation. We explore this topic further in Chapter 22, but stay tuned—there is surely much more to come soon.

SUMMARY

MasteringGenetics™   For activities, animations, and review quizzes, go to the Study Area.

1.1   Modern Genetics Is in Its Second Century

▮ Genetic principles first outlined by Gregor Mendel in 1865 were "rediscovered" in 1900 and so made modern genetics a 20th-century scientific discipline.

▮ Study of the transmission of morphological variation during the first half of the 20th century established transmission genetics as a central focus of genetic analysis.

▮ The analysis of DNA, RNA, and protein beginning in the second half of the 20th century established genetics as a molecular discipline.

▮ Life on Earth has three domains—Bacteria, Archaea, and Eukarya—that share a common evolutionary history.

1.2 The Structure of DNA Suggests a Mechanism for Replication

- Deoxyribonucleic acid (DNA) is the genetic material. DNA is a double helix containing two strands of nucleotides that are composed of a five-carbon deoxyribose sugar, a phosphate group, and one of four nucleotide bases: adenine (A), thymine (T), cytosine (C), or guanine (G).

- Nucleotides in a DNA strand are joined by covalent phosphodiester bonds between the 5′ phosphate of one nucleotide and the 3′ OH of the adjoining nucleotide.

- DNA strands are joined by hydrogen bonds that form between complementary base pairs. A pairs with T and C pairs with G.

- Strands of the DNA duplex are antiparallel; one strand is oriented $5′ \rightarrow 3′$, and the complementary strand is oriented $3′ \rightarrow 5′$.

- DNA replicates by a semiconservative process that produces exact copies of the original DNA double helix.

- DNA polymerase uses one strand of DNA as a template to synthesize a complementary daughter strand one nucleotide at a time in the 5′-to-3′ direction.

1.3 DNA Transcription and Messenger RNA Translation Express Genes

- The central dogma of biology (DNA → RNA → protein) identifies DNA as an information repository and describes how DNA dictates protein structure through a messenger RNA intermediary that in turn directs polypeptide synthesis.

- Transcription is the process that synthesizes single-stranded RNA from a template DNA strand.

- RNA transcripts have the same $5′ \rightarrow 3′$ polarity and sequence as the coding strand of DNA; they differ only in the presence of U rather than T.

- Certain DNA sequences, most commonly promoters, bind RNA polymerase and other transcriptional proteins.

- Translation is the process that uses messenger RNA (mRNA) sequences to synthesize proteins.

- Messenger RNA codons base-pair with tRNA anticodons at the ribosome.

- Each tRNA carries a specific amino acid that is added to the growing polypeptide chain.

- The genetic code contains 61 codons that specify amino acids and 3 that are stop codons.

- Genomics, proteomics, transcriptomics, and metabolomics are new investigative strategies that can help decipher complex problems of systems biology.

1.4 Evolution Has a Molecular Basis

- Four processes—natural selection, migration, mutation, and genetic drift—drive the evolution of populations and species.

- The evolution of adaptive morphological characters occurs through natural selection pressures exerted on species by their environments. Nonadaptive characters that are neutral with respect to natural selection evolve by other evolutionary processes.

- The modern synthesis of evolution is the name applied to the union of transmission genetics, molecular genetics, Darwinian evolution, and modern evolutionary genetics.

- Phylogenetic trees describe the evolutionary relationships among modern species and trace their descent from common ancestors to identify the most likely pattern of evolution.

- Shared derived characteristics are molecular or morphological attributes that evolve in descendant species from ancient characters found in a common ancestor.

- Molecular phylogenies trace the evolution of nucleic acid or protein sequences from common ancestors to modern species.

KEYWORDS

allele *(p. 4)*
amino acid *(p. 9)*
anticodon *(p. 12)*
antiparallel *(p. 8)*
Archaea *(p. 4)*
Bacteria *(p. 4)*
central dogma of biology *(p. 9)*
Chargaff's rule *(p. 6)*
chloroplasts *(p. 3)*
chromosome *(p. 2)*
cladistics (clade; monophyletic group) *(p. 17)*
coding strand (nontemplate strand) *(p. 11)*
codon *(p. 12)*
complementary base pair *(p. 6)*

cytoplasmic inheritance *(p. 4)*
daughter strand *(p. 9)*
deoxyribonucleic acid (DNA) *(p. 5)*
diploid *(p. 3)*
DNA double helix (DNA duplex) *(p. 5)*
DNA nucleotide: adenine (A), guanine (G), thymine (T), cytosine (C) *(p. 7)*
DNA replication (semiconservative replication) *(p. 5)*
Eukarya (eukaryote) *(p. 4)*
evolution *(p. 16)*
evolutionary genetics *(p. 5)*
exon *(p. 12)*
gamete *(p. 4)*
gene *(p. 2)*
genetic code *(p. 12)*

genetic drift *(p. 17)*
genome (genomics) *(p. 4)*
genomics *(p. 13)*
genotype *(p. 4)*
haploid *(p. 3)*
homologous chromosomes (homologous pair, homologs) *(p. 2)*
homology *(p. 17)*
homoplasmy *(p. 18)*
hydrogen bond *(p. 7)*
ingroup *(p. 18)*
intron *(p. 12)*
megabase (Mb) *(p. 13)*
meiosis *(p. 4)*
messenger RNA (mRNA) *(p. 5)*
metabolomics *(p. 15)*

migration *(p. 17)*
mitochondria *(p. 3)*
mitosis *(p. 4)*
modern synthesis of evolution
    (p. 17)
molecular genetics *(p. 5)*
mutation *(p. 17)*
natural selection *(p. 17)*
nucleoid *(p. 3)*
outgroup *(p. 18)*
paraphyletic group *(p. 18)*
parental strand *(p. 9)*
peptide bond *(p. 12)*
phenotype *(p. 4)*

phosphodiester bond *(p. 7)*
phylogenetic tree *(p. 17)*
polyploidy *(p. 3)*
promoter *(p. 12)*
protein (polypeptide) *(p. 12)*
proteomics (proteome) *(p. 15)*
reverse transcription *(p. 10)*
ribonucleic acid (RNA) *(p. 5)*
ribosomal RNA (rRNA) *(p. 9)*
ribosome *(p. 5)*
semiconservative replication *(p. 8)*
shared derived characteristic
    (synaptomorphy) *(p. 17)*
start codon *(p. 12)*

start of transcription *(p. 12)*
stop codon *(p. 12)*
strand polarity (5′ and 3′) *(p. 7)*
systems biology *(p. 15)*
template strand *(p. 10)*
termination sequence (transcription
    termination) *(p. 12)*
transcription *(p. 5)*
transcriptomics (transcriptome) *(p. 15)*
transfer RNA (tRNA) *(p. 9)*
translation *(p. 5)*
transmission genetics (Mendelian
    genetics) *(p. 5)*
uracil (U) *(p. 11)*

PROBLEMS   (MasteringGenetics™   Visit for instructor-assigned tutorials and problems.

Chapter Concepts

1. Genetics affects many aspects of our lives. Identify three ways genetics affects your life or the life of a family member or friend. The effects can be regularly encountered or can be one time only or occasional.

2. How do you think the determination that DNA is the hereditary material affected the direction of biological research?

3. A commentator once described genetics as "the queen of the biological sciences." The statement was meant to imply that genetics is of overarching importance in the biological sciences. Do you agree with this statement? In what ways do you think the statement is accurate?

4. All life shares DNA as the hereditary material. From an evolutionary perspective, why do you think this is the case?

5. Define the terms *allele, chromosome,* and *gene* and explain how they relate to one another. Develop an analogy between these terms and the process of using a street map to locate a new apartment to live in next year (i.e., consider which term is analogous to a street, which to a type of building, and which to an apartment floor plan).

6. Define the terms *genotype* and *phenotype,* and relate them to one another.

7. Define *natural selection,* and describe how natural selection operates as a mechanism of evolutionary change.

Application and Integration

13. If thymine makes up 21% of the DNA nucleotides in the genome of a plant species, what are the percentages of the other nucleotides in the genome?

14. What reactive chemical groups are found at the 5′ and 3′ carbons of nucleotides? What is the name of the bond formed when nucleotides are joined in a single strand? Is this bond covalent or noncovalent?

For answers to selected even-numbered problems, see Appendix: Answers.

8. Describe the modern synthesis of evolution, and explain how it connects Darwinian evolution to molecular evolution.

9. What are the four processes of evolution? Briefly describe each process.

10. Define each of the following terms:
    a. transcription
    b. allele
    c. central dogma of biology
    d. translation
    e. DNA replication
    f. gene
    g. chromosome
    h. antiparallel
    i. phenotype
    j. complementary base pair
    k. nucleic acid strand polarity
    l. genotype
    m. natural selection
    n. mutation
    o. modern synthesis of evolution

11. Compare and contrast the genome, the proteome, and the transcriptome of an organism.

12. With respect to transcription describe the relationship and sequence correspondence of the RNA transcript and the DNA template strand. Describe the relationship and sequence correspondence of the mRNA transcript to the DNA coding strand.

For answers to selected even-numbered problems, see Appendix: Answers.

15. Identify two differences in chemical composition that distinguish DNA from RNA.

16. What is the central dogma of biology? Identify and describe the molecular processes that accomplish the flow of genetic information described in the central dogma.

17. A portion of a polypeptide contains the amino acids Trp-Lys-Met-Ala-Val. Write the possible mRNA and template-strand DNA sequences. (Hint: Use A/G and T/C to indicate that either adenine/guanine or thymine/cytosine could occur in a particular position, and use N to indicate that any DNA nucleotide could appear.)

18. The following segment of DNA is the template strand transcribed into mRNA:

    5'-...GACATGGAA...-3'

    a. What is the sequence of mRNA created from this sequence?
    b. What is the amino acid sequence produced by translation?

19. Consider the following segment of DNA:

    5'-...ATGCCAGTCACTGACTTG...-3'
    3'-...TACGGTCAGTGACTGAAC...-5'

    a. How many phosphodiester bonds are required to form this segment of double-stranded DNA?
    b. How many hydrogen bonds are present in this DNA segment?
    c. If the lower strand of DNA serves as the template transcribed into mRNA, how many peptide bonds are present in the polypeptide fragment into which the mRNA is translated?

20. Examine Figure 1.14 and answer the following questions.
    a. How many clades are shown in the figure?
    b. What characteristic is shared by all clades in the figure?
    c. What characteristics are shared by the mammalian clade and the human clade? What characteristics distinguish these two clades?

21. Fill in the missing nucleotides so there are three per block and the missing amino acid abbreviations in the graphic shown

DNA

Coding 5'	| | | GGC | GA | | | T | | 3'
Template 3'	| | | | C | | | G | | 5'

mRNA codon

5' \| \| UAC \| \| \| A \| A \| 3'

tRNA anticodon

3' \| \| UUA \| \| 5'

Amino acid

3-letter	MET | | | | | |
1-letter	| | | | E | S |

22. Four nucleic-acid samples are analyzed to determine the percentages of the nucleotides they contain. Survey the data in the table below, determine which samples are DNA and which are RNA, and specify whether each sample is double-stranded or single-stranded. Justify each answer.

	A	G	T	U	C
Sample 1	22%	28%	22%	0	28%
Sample 2	30%	30%	0	20%	20%
Sample 3	18%	32%	0	18%	32%
Sample 4	29%	29%	21%	0	21%

23. Are seed-eating finches among Darwin's finches monophyletic or paraphyletic? What about cactus flower–eating finches?

24. If one is constructing a phylogeny of reptiles using DNA sequence data, which taxon (birds, mammals, amphibians, or fish) might be suitable to use as an outgroup?

25. Using the following amino acid sequences obtained from different species of apes, construct a phylogenetic tree of the apes.

Pongo pygmaeus	G G P H Y R L I A V E D
Pongo abelii	G G P H Y R L I A V E D
Pan paniscus	G A P H F R L L A V E E
Pan troglodytes	G A P H F R L L A V E E
Gorilla gorilla	G A P H F R L I A V E E
Gorilla beringei	G A P H F R L I A V E E
Homo sapiens	G A P H F N L L A V E E
Hylobates lar	G G P H Y R L I S V E D
Hoolock hoolock	G G P H Y R L I S V D D
Common ancestor	G G P H Y R L I S V D D

2

Transmission Genetics

CHAPTER OUTLINE

2.1 Gregor Mendel Discovered the Basic Principles of Genetic Transmission

2.2 Monohybrid Crosses Reveal the Segregation of Alleles

2.3 Dihybrid and Trihybrid Crosses Reveal the Independent Assortment of Alleles

2.4 Probability Theory Predicts Mendelian Ratios

2.5 Chi-Square Analysis Tests the Fit between Observed Values and Expected Outcomes

2.6 Autosomal Inheritance and Molecular Genetics Parallel the Predictions of Mendel's Hereditary Principles

ESSENTIAL IDEAS

■ Mendel's hereditary experiments with pea plants identified two laws of heredity known as segregation and independent assortment.

■ Consistent and predictable phenotype ratios in generations descending from two parents differing for a single trait support the law of segregation.

■ The inheritance of two or more traits is predicted by the law of independent assortment.

■ The rules of probability predict genetic inheritance.

■ The statistical method known as chi-square analysis is used to evaluate how closely the predicted outcomes of genetic crosses match experimental observations.

■ The inheritance of certain traits in human families follows the hereditary laws of segregation and independent assortment.

■ Genes controlling four traits described by Mendel have been identified and the activity of their alleles characterized.

This statue of Gregor Mendel stands in the garden of the St. Thomas monastery in Brno, Czech Republic just a few feet from where his greenhouse once stood. You can take a virtual tour of the museum and see additional interactive features at www.mendel-museum.com.

When Gregor Mendel identified and described two fundamental laws of hereditary transmission, he ush ered in a new era of understanding in biology. The terms *Mendelian genetics* and *Mendelism* were coined to recognize this contribution, and they are used as synonyms for **transmission genetics,** the field that describes and investigates the patterns of transmission of genes and traits from parents to offspring. Like his contemporary Charles Darwin, who elegantly described the process of evolution by natural selection, Mendel articulated a new way to view the world.

Mendel was by no stretch of the imagination the first person to examine the transmission of hereditary traits in plants.

Many amateur botanists of the 18th and early 19th centuries conducted what were then called studies of "plant hybridization" on many species, including the edible pea plant (*Pisum sativum*) that was the subject of Mendel's experiments. Others before him had even carried out crosses similar to Mendel's, some made observations like those on which Mendel based his two principles of heredity, and some even came close to articulating a description of the hereditary principles Mendel described. But no one described hereditary transmission as precisely as Mendel did. Mendel succeeded because of his superior experimental design and his quantification of results. His approach allowed him to formulate and test genetic hypotheses with a level of rigor that no one had achieved before him or would achieve for another 35 years.

In this chapter, we examine how Mendel used experimental designs and results to identify two pivotal principles of hereditary transmission. We see (1) how Mendel's unprecedented experimental designs enabled him to detect genetic phenomena that escaped identification by his predecessors and (2) how the transmission of traits can be predicted using random probability theory. The chapter concludes with a description of the molecular genetics of four of the genes controlling traits described by Mendel. To date, the other three genes remain unidentified, although their effects on phenotypic variation are well known. We begin, however, with a short biography of Gregor Mendel that reveals how his educational experiences profoundly influenced his approach to scientific exploration.

2.1 Gregor Mendel Discovered the Basic Principles of Genetic Transmission

Born in 1822 to a farming family of modest means in the village of Hynčice that is now part of the Czech Republic, Johann (later known by his clerical name, Gregor) Mendel completed the equivalent of high school at age 18 with a certificate attesting to exceptional academic abilities. He began his higher education at the Olomouc Philosophical Institute in 1840, but these studies took a severe toll on his mental and physical health, and he gave them up after the first year. In 1843, after attempting unsuccessfully to restart his education at

Olomouc, he decided to pursue higher learning by entering the priesthood instead. Based on its strong reputation in teacher training and a recommendation from a former teacher at Olomouc, he selected St. Thomas monastery in the Czech city of Brno. Mendel's duties at St. Thomas included temporary teaching of natural science at a middle school in Brno. His keen interest in teaching science and his desire to become a permanent teacher led monastery administrators to send Mendel to the University of Vienna in 1851 to study natural science as preparation for a teaching examination.

In Vienna, Mendel studied plant physiology and plant biology with Professor Franz Unger and physics with Professor Christian Doppler as well as Doppler's successor, Professor Andreas von Ettinghausen. From Professor Unger, Mendel learned to think critically about prevailing theories of plant reproduction and hybridization. Doppler, an experimental physicist famous for describing the Doppler effect, espoused a "particulate" view of physics and taught Mendel how to study individual characteristics separately in experiments. Professor Ettinghausen taught Mendel the mathematics of combinatorial analysis. Mendel would apply these lessons to his later research. In 1853, Mendel returned to Brno, where he took and passed the written portion of the permanent teachers' examination but apparently never completed the oral portion, remaining a "temporary" teacher at the school in Brno until he became abbot of the monastery in 1868.

In the summer of 1856, after a 3-year period during which he pondered how he might pursue his interest in natural science, Mendel began his work on trait heredity in the edible pea plant *Pisum sativum*. Mendel began his studies by gathering 34 different varieties of peas collected from local suppliers. Over the next 2 years, he tested each variety for its ability to uniformly reproduce identical characteristics from one generation to the next. Ultimately, he settled on 14 strains of *Pisum* representing seven individual traits, each of which had two easily distinguished forms of expression in a seed or plant (Figure 2.1). Mendel worked with these 14 strains for the next 5 years, concluding his experiments in 1863.

On February 8 and March 8, 1865, Mendel discussed his work on peas at two meetings of the Natural History Society of Brunn (Brno). The society published his report in its *Proceedings* the following year, 1866. After publication of his work, Mendel corresponded with several prominent botanists in Europe, most notably Karl Naegeli. Mendel's letters to Naegeli have scientific significance because they clearly lay out his experiments, his results, and his conclusions. Unfortunately, neither Naegeli nor any of his contemporaries seemed to grasp the importance of Mendel's work.

After becoming abbot of the monastery in 1868, Mendel gave up his work in genetics but continued to pursue his interests in bee keeping and meteorology. As abbot, he became involved in business activities such as holding a seat on the board of directors of a local

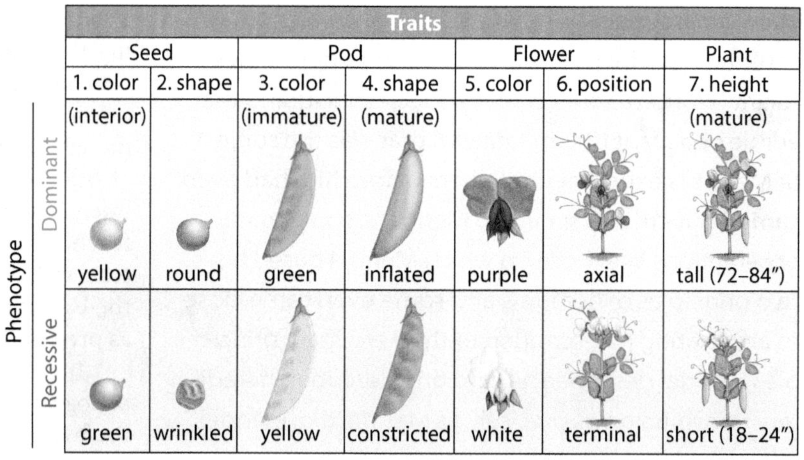

Figure 2.1 The seven dichotomous traits of *Pisum sativum* studied by Mendel. Each trait has a dominant phenotype and a recessive phenotype that are easily distinguished.

Traits						
Seed		Pod		Flower		Plant
1. color	2. shape	3. color	4. shape	5. color	6. position	7. height
(interior) yellow	round	(immature) green	(mature) inflated	purple	axial	(mature) tall (72–84″)
green	wrinkled	yellow	constricted	white	terminal	short (18–24″)

Phenotype: Dominant / Recessive

bank and running a brewery that generated income for St. Thomas. He faithfully served the monastery until his death in 1884. Mendel died in scientific obscurity, never having had the importance of his experiments understood or appreciated. Sixteen years after his death, in 1900, biologists would replicate and rediscover his experiments and launch a revolution in biology.

Mendel's Modern Experimental Approach

Mendel successfully identified principles of hereditary transmission that eluded investigators who preceded him and continued to elude investigators for many years after his death. Was Mendel more insightful? Did he make fortuitous choices by selecting *Pisum sativum* as his experimental organism and in selecting his seven characteristics? Did he have a superior approach to genetic experimentation and analysis? The answer to each of these questions is yes.

Mendel's superior insight came principally from his familiarity with quantitative thinking and his understanding of the particulate nature of matter, learned through the study of physics with Doppler. Central to Mendel's experimental success was counting the number of progeny with specific phenotypes. This logical and now routine component of data gathering was the key to Mendel's ability to formulate the hypotheses that explained his results. Under Doppler and Ettinghausen, Mendel had learned to isolate individual properties of matter he wished to study and to think in quantitative terms about combinations of outcomes.

Mendel made a fortuitous choice in selecting the pea plant as his experimental organism. Peas were commonly used for hybridization studies in Mendel's time, so a large number of strains displaying different phenotypic characteristics were available. The pea plant is hardy and was easy for a skilled botanist like Mendel to manipulate and crossbreed.

In choosing to study individual traits of the pea plant, Mendel designed his experiments to test the **blending theory** of heredity that was the predominant hereditary theory at the time. The blending theory viewed the traits of progeny as a mixture of the characteristics possessed by the two parental forms. Under this theory, progeny were believed to display characteristics that were approximately intermediate between those of the parents. For example, the blending theory would predict that crossing a black cat and a white cat would produce gray kittens, and that the original black or white colors would never reappear if the gray kittens were bred to one another. Mendel reasoned that if the blending theory were true, he would see evidence of it in each trait. If no blending were seen in individual traits, the blending theory would be disproved.

As crucial as his quantitative approach and choice of *Pisum* were to his ultimate success, Mendel's radically new experimental design was his most important innovation. Mendel was ahead of his time in that his scientific experiments were hypothesis driven. In other words, following an initial observation, he devised a hypothesis to explain the observation and then carried out an independent experiment to test the hypothesis. It is for experimental innovations and his analysis that *Mendelian genetics* is the term used to identify this field of genetics. An experimenter employing this approach, known today as the *scientific method*, will follow these steps:

1. Make initial observations about a phenomenon or process.
2. Formulate a testable hypothesis to explain observations.
3. Design a controlled experiment to test the hypothesis.
4. Collect data from the controlled experiment.
5. Interpret experimental results, comparing the observed results to those expected under assumptions of the hypothesis.
6. Draw reasonable conclusions, reformulating or retesting the hypothesis if necessary.

Mendel followed these steps to collect data on individual traits of the pea plant, formulate hypotheses to explain his phenotypic observations, and conduct independent experiments to test his predictions.

Five Critical Experimental Innovations

Five features of Mendel's breeding experiments distinguish them from those of his contemporaries and were critical to his success: (1) controlled crosses between plants; (2) use of pure-breeding strains to begin the experimental controlled crosses; (3) selection of dichotomous traits; (4) quantification of results; and (5) use of replicate, reciprocal, and test crosses.

Controlled Crosses between Plants In nature, pea plant flowers contain both a pollen-producing anther and an egg-containing ovule and usually self-fertilize (**Figure 2.2**). Self-fertilization occurs when sperm-containing pollen from the anther fertilizes an egg within the ovule. Fertilized ovules develop in the ovary, which matures into fruit (seed pod) as seeds (peas) develop inside. A mature seed pod usually contains five to seven peas, each of which results from a different fertilization event. In genetic experiments, peas can be collected and scored for their phenotypes or can be planted to produce pea plants that are scored for their traits.

Pea plants are also capable of cross-pollination, if pollen from one plant is used to fertilize the ovules of another. In nature, plants are cross-pollinated by insects, birds, mammals, and wind. Mendel used his familiarity with plants to carry out **artificial cross-fertilization** (**Figure 2.3**). First, he emasculated developing pea flowers by cutting off the nascent anthers. This modification made the plants incapable of self-pollination, but the

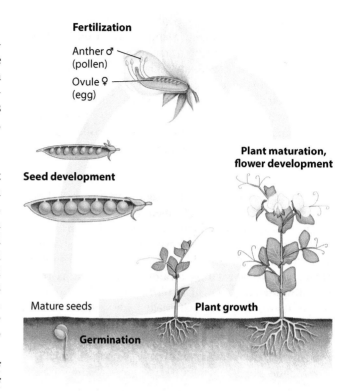

Figure 2.2 **Life cycle of *Pisum sativum*.** Seeds (peas) are planted and germinate, growing into mature flowering plants. Eggs in the flower ovule are fertilized by pollen produced from anthers. Immature seeds arise from individual fertilized eggs in the pod that forms as seeds develop. After seeds mature, they are dispersed to renew the cycle.

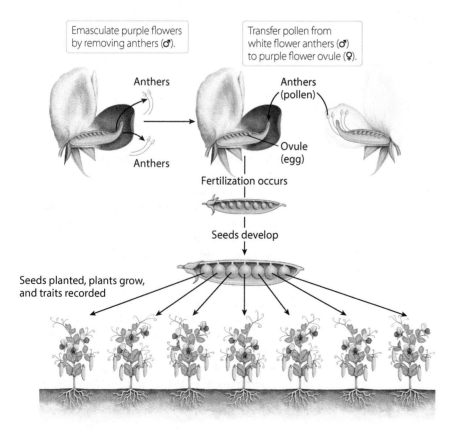

Figure 2.3 **Artificial cross-fertilization of pea plants.**

ovules could still be fertilized by cross-fertilization with pollen from another plant. Mendel carried out artificial cross-fertilization by using a small paintbrush to lift mature pollen from a non-emasculated flower and brush it onto an emasculated flower. With this manipulation Mendel restricted reproduction to those plants he identified beforehand as likely to yield informative results, thus performing what is now known as a **controlled genetic cross** between selected organisms.

Pure-Breeding Strains to Begin Experimental Crosses

During the 2 years before beginning his hereditary experiments, Mendel performed numerous controlled genetic crosses to obtain strains that consistently produced a single phenotype without variation. Strains of this kind that consistently produce the same phenotype are called **pure-breeding strains,** also known as **true-breeding strains.** The self-fertilization of a pure-breeding purple-flowered plant will yield only purple flowers among progeny plants. Two plants from a pure-breeding line can be crossed to one another and will produce progeny with the same phenotype.

Mendel's work generated 14 pure-breeding strains for his 7 traits, and he used two different pure-breeding strains to begin each of his hereditary experiments. For example, Mendel crossed pure-breeding purple-flowered plants with pure-breeding white-flowered plants. By artificial cross-fertilization of these **parental generation** (**P generation**) plants, Mendel produced seeds that were grown into the **first filial generation** (**F$_1$ generation**) of plants (**Figure 2.4**). The F$_1$ plants were then used as the sources of pollen and egg to produce the seeds that were grown into the **second filial generation** (**F$_2$ generation**). The **third filial generation** (**F$_3$ generation**) was produced by crossing plants from the F$_2$ generation, and so on for as many generations as needed.

Selection of Single Traits with Dichotomous Phenotypes

Each of the seven traits that Mendel chose is found in just two dichotomous forms. The two phenotypes are readily distinguished from one another, so there can be no ambiguity of assignment, and there are no intermediate phenotypes. For example, one trait was seed color; every seed was either yellow or green.

The alternative forms of the seven traits Mendel studied are illustrated in Figure 2.1. The 14 pure-breeding strains were bred for (1) seed color (yellow or green), (2) seed shape (round or wrinkled), (3) pod color (green or yellow), (4) pod shape (inflated or constricted), (5) flower color (purple or white), (6) flower position (axial or terminal), and (7) plant height (tall or short).

It is interesting to note that Mendel initially had selected an eighth trait producing either gray or white exterior seed coats. Early in his analysis, however, he found that plants with purple flowers *always* had gray seed coats and that those with white flowers *always* had white seed

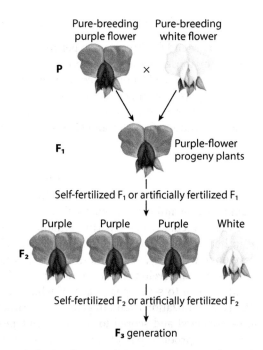

Figure 2.4   Production of three generations of pea plants. Plants of the P generation are artificially cross-fertilized to produce the F$_1$ generation. Self-fertilization or crossing of F$_1$-generation plants produces the F$_2$ generation. F$_2$ plants either self-fertilize or are crossed to one another to produce the F$_3$ generation.

coats. He correctly speculated that flower color and seed-coat color were determined by the same genetic mechanism. The pigment anthocyanin is responsible for plants that have purple flower color and gray seed coats, but a mutation eliminates anthocyanin production in plants with white flowers and white seed coats.

Quantification of Results

Each time Mendel made a controlled cross, he carefully counted the number of progeny plants of each phenotype. This seemingly simple act—now standard in scientific data gathering—was revolutionary in Mendel's day. By obtaining large numbers of offspring from each cross, as was possible when using peas, and by expressing his results numerically, Mendel could more easily analyze them for revealing patterns such as the occurrence of consistent ratios between phenotypes. These ratios were critically important to Mendel's discovery of the rules by which he could predict transmission of alleles during reproduction, and they are the foundation of Mendel's two laws of heredity.

Replicate-, Reciprocal-, and Test-Cross Analysis

The final features that distinguished Mendel's experiments are his use of three genetic-cross strategies that have become tried-and-true approaches to genetic analysis. Rather than simply counting the results of a single cross, for example, Mendel made many **replicate crosses,** producing hundreds of F$_1$ plants and several thousand F$_2$ plants by repeating the same cross several times.

Mendel also performed **reciprocal crosses,** in which the same genotypes are crossed but the sexes of the donating parents are switched. The plant providing the egg in the first cross is used as a source of pollen in the reciprocal cross. An example of a reciprocal cross is shown in Figure 2.5a. First, pollen from a strain producing yellow peas (*GG*) is used to fertilize the egg of plants from a strain producing green peas (*gg*). Then a reciprocal cross is performed using pollen from the green-pea–producing plant to fertilize eggs of the yellow-pea–producing plant. Note that both these reciprocal crosses produce F_1 with yellow peas. We discuss the importance of this result in the following section.

Finally, Mendel performed **test crosses** (Figure 2.5b). Here, *R* and *r* represent alleles of the rugose gene, meaning "full of wrinkles." We examine the results and significance of this kind of controlled genetic cross below. In Figure 2.5b, we introduce a bit of genotype shorthand with the designation *R_* to identify the round seeded plant in the test cross that is either *RR* or *Rr*. Spoken "are

blank," the designation means either that the second allele is unknown (that's the case here) or that it is not relevant (as shown in Figure 2.6).

2.2 Monohybrid Crosses Reveal the Segregation of Alleles

In this section we illustrate the results and interpretation of Mendel's crosses by studying the transmission of two of Mendel's traits, pea color (yellow or green) and, in separate crosses, the transmission of pea shape (round or wrinkled). The results and interpretations we describe apply equally well to the five other traits Mendel examined. The uniformity of the experimental results and interpretations are due to Mendel's decision to conduct experiments on each trait in the same way. He began hereditary experiments on each trait by artificial cross-fertilization of pure-breeding parental plants to produce an F_1 generation, and he then self-fertilized or intercrossed F_1 plants to produce the F_2 generation.

Identifying Dominant and Recessive Traits

By crossing pure-breeding yellow-pea–producing plants and pure-breeding green-pea producers in replicate and reciprocal crosses, Mendel consistently found that all of the F_1 plants produced yellow peas and none produced green peas (Figure 2.6). Mendel identified yellow as the **dominant phenotype** on the basis of its presence in the F_1, and he identified green as the **recessive phenotype** since it is not seen among F_1 progeny. Mendel next crossed F_1 yellow plants to produce the F_2 and observed reemergence of the recessive green phenotype. Among the F_2, Mendel found that approximately three-fourths (75%) of the peas were yellow and the remaining one-fourth (25%) were green. The yellow : green ratio in the F_2 is $\frac{3}{4}:\frac{1}{4}$, or roughly 3:1. Mendel correctly interpreted these results to indicate that F_2 offspring with the dominant trait were a mixture of two genotypes—*GG* and *Gg*, in this case—and that plants with the recessive trait were homozygous recessive—*gg* in this instance. In general terms, the dominant F_2 can be classified as being *G_* ("*G* blank"). In this context, the second allele, whether *G* or *g*, is not important in determining the phenotype; thus *G_* is a kind of shorthand for indicating that the genotype is either *GG* or *Gg*. Mendel made similar observations for his experiments testing inheritance of pea shape. Replicate and reciprocal crosses of pure-breeding round-pea–producing plants with pure-breeding wrinkled-pea–producing plants produced F_1 plants bearing exclusively round peas. This result identifies round as the dominant phenotype and wrinkled as the recessive phenotype. His F_1 cross produced F_2 peas in the ratio 75% round to 25% wrinkled—once again a roughly 3:1 ratio.

(a) Reciprocal crosses

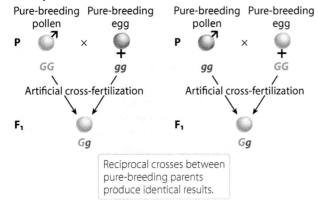

Reciprocal crosses between pure-breeding parents produce identical results.

(b) Test cross

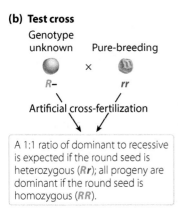

A 1:1 ratio of dominant to recessive is expected if the round seed is heterozygous (*Rr*); all progeny are dominant if the round seed is homozygous (*RR*).

Figure 2.5   Reciprocal crosses and test cross. (a) Two reciprocal crosses between different pure-breeding yellow (*GG*) and green (*gg*) parents produce F_1 plants with yellow seeds (*Gg*). **(b)** A test cross is made between an F_1 with the dominant phenotype that is possibly heterozygous (as indicated by *R–*) and a pure-breeding (*rr*) plant with the recessive phenotype. See Section 2.2 for definitions of these terms.

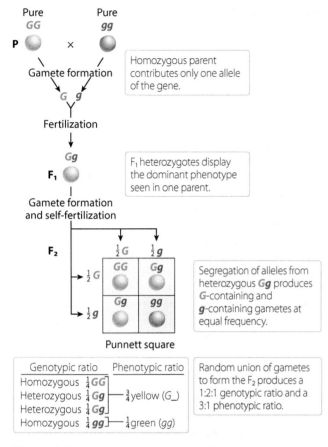

Figure 2.6 Segregation of alleles for seed color. In the cross between yellow-seeded and green-seeded pure-breeding parental plants, F₁ progeny display the dominant yellow phenotype. Note that the 3:1 phenotypic ratio and 1:2:1 genotypic ratio displayed in the F₂ generation result from crossing the F₁.

Tabulating results over several growing seasons for all seven traits, Mendel counted more than 20,000 F_2 peas or plants. **Table 2.1** displays Mendel's results revealing three consistent features: (1) dominance of one phenotype over the other in the F_1 generation, (2) reemergence of the recessive phenotype in the F_2 generation, and (3) a ratio of approximately 3:1 (dominant: recessive) among F_2 phenotypes. Mendel determined that yellow is dominant to green and round is dominant to wrinkled based on F_1 results. Green pea color and wrinkled pea shape reemerge in the F_2, which displays a consistent 3:1 ratio between the dominant and recessive phenotypes. For example, Mendel classified 8023 F_2 peas by their color and 7324 F_2 peas by their shape. Among the F_2 peas classified by color, he found 6022 yellow seeds and 2001 green seeds, a ratio of almost exactly three to one. Of the F_2 seeds classified for pea shape, 5474 were round and 1850 were wrinkled, again a ratio of very nearly three to one. Data for each of the other five characteristics revealed the same 3:1 ratio of dominant to recessive in the F_2.

Evidence of Particulate Inheritance and Rejection of the Blending Theory

Mendel's F_1 experimental results reject the blending theory of heredity. Specifically, the observation that all F_1 progeny have the same phenotype (i.e., the dominant phenotype) that is indistinguishable from the phenotype of one of the pure-breeding parents contradicts the blending theory prediction that the F_1 would display a phenotype that is a blend of the two parental phenotypes.

Table 2.1	Mendel's Observations for Seven Monohybrid Traits in the F₁ and F₂ Generations			
Crosses between Pure-Breeding Parental Phenotypes	**F₁ Phenotype**	**F₂ Phenotypes**		**F₂ Phenotype Ratio**
		Dominant	**Recessive**	
Round × wrinkled seeds[a]	All round seeds	5474 round	1850 wrinkled	2.96:1
Yellow × green seeds (interior seed color)	All yellow seeds	6022 yellow	2001 green	3.01:1
Purple × white flowers[b] (gray × white seed coat, or exterior seed color)	All purple flowers (gray seed coat)	705 purple	224 white	3.15:1
Axial × terminal flowers	All axial flowers	651 axial	207 terminal	3.14:1
Green × yellow pods	All green pods	428 green	152 yellow	2.82:1
Inflated × constricted pods	All inflated pods	882 inflated	299 constricted	2.95:1
Tall × short plants	All tall plants	787 tall	277 short	2.84:1
TOTAL		14,949	5010	2.98:1

[a] The dominant phenotype is written first and always appears as the F₁ phenotype.
[b] A single gene controls both flower color and seed-coat color. Mendel discussed both traits but recognized they were controlled by the same gene.

The persistence of the dominant phenotype and the re-emergence of the recessive phenotype in the F_2 also run counter to the predictions of the blending theory.

Having rejected the blending theory, however, Mendel went on to propose a new hereditary hypothesis. Taking advantage of the analytical superiority of his quantitative approach to data analysis, Mendel proposed that each trait is determined by two "particles of heredity." Mendel used the German word *elemente*, a term meaning "unit or element," to describe the two discrete units of hereditary information for each trait. This idea is the basis of Mendel's theory of **particulate inheritance,** which proposes that each plant carries two particles of heredity for each trait. A plant receives one unit of heredity in the egg and the second unit in pollen. Each parental plant passes one of its two particles to offspring during reproduction.

The hereditary particles that are passed from one generation to the next are called *alleles* in modern terminology. This term had not been invented in Mendel's time (nor had the term *gene*, for that matter), but he correctly surmised that two *elementen* (alleles) were present for each trait in a plant and together determined the phenotype of the trait. Mendel used letters as symbols to represent the alleles for each trait, and he proposed a pattern of allele transmission from parents to offspring that explained his phenotypic observations in the F_1 and the F_2. Mendel proposed that pure-breeding lines contain two identical copies of the same allele.

Pure-breeding organisms have a **homozygous genotype,** a term meaning that the two alleles (i.e., the two copies of the gene) carried by an organism are identical. If a homozygous plant is self-fertilized or if two organisms pure-breeding for the same trait are crossed, the progeny receive identical alleles from each parent and have the same homozygous genotype as the parents as well as the same phenotype. In contrast, if a genetic cross is made between pure-breeding parents with different traits, each parent is homozygous for a different allele. The progeny receive a distinct allele from each parent and have a **heterozygous genotype,** a term meaning that two different alleles make up the genotype. Heterozygous organisms can have a dominant phenotype if they carry a copy of the dominant allele.

Geneticists now know that inheritance of the seven traits Mendel described is controlled by pairs of alleles of seven different genes. Thus, while Mendel did not use the words *gene* or *allele*, he understood the concept embodied by each term. Contemporary genetics describes inheritance of Mendel's traits in terms of genes and alleles and continues to use letters to represent alleles. Different notational schemes and gene-naming conventions have been adopted for different species. (A table describing gene naming, gene nomenclature, and other information about the genes and genomes of model genetic organisms is located inside the book back cover.)

Central to understanding the inheritance of the seven traits Mendel studied is the concept that pure-breeding organisms have homozygous genotypes. In Figure 2.6, for example, the pure-breeding yellow parent has the *GG* homozygous genotype, and the pure-breeding green parent has the *gg* homozygous genotype. Crosses of pure-breeding parents of different homozygous genotypes produce heterozygous (*Gg*) F_1 progeny that all have the dominant yellow phenotype. According to Mendel's hypothesis, each pure-breeding parent passes one allele to the F_1, making it heterozygous. One allele, *G* in this case, is dominant and produces the dominant phenotype in all the F_1.

The heterozygous F_1 are then crossed with one another or are self-fertilized in a **monohybrid cross,** a term referring to a cross between two organisms that have the same heterozygous genotype for one gene. With a dominant and a recessive allele in the heterozygous genotype of plants undergoing a monohybrid cross, a 3:1 **phenotypic ratio** is predicted for the F_2. At the same time, F_2 organisms are predicted to have three genotypes: The two homozygous genotypes (the same genotypes present in the original pure-breeding parents) are each expected to occur in one-fourth of the F_2 progeny, and the heterozygous genotype is predicted in the remaining one-half of the F_2 progeny. Therefore, among the F_2, a 1:2:1 **genotypic ratio** is predicted. The one-fourth of the F_2 that are homozygous *GG* plus the one-half of F_2 progeny that are heterozygous *Gg* are the three-fourths of the F_2 with the dominant (yellow) phenotype. The remaining one-fourth of the F_2 contain the homozygous *gg* genotype and have the recessive (green) phenotype. The same inheritance pattern occurs for all the other traits studied by Mendel.

Segregation of Alleles

Figure 2.6 uses letters as symbols to represent alleles and genotypes in parental, F_1, and F_2 organisms and introduces a simple and functional tool of genetic analysis—the Punnett square. The **Punnett square** method of diagramming the genetic content of gametes and their union to form offspring is named in honor of Sir Reginald Punnett, a famous geneticist of the early 20th century. The Punnett square separates the two alleles carried by each reproducing organism, placing those from one parent along the vertical margin of the square and those from the other parent along the horizontal margin. These separated alleles represent the **gametes** of reproducing organisms, the sperm (or pollen) and egg cells, each of which carries only one copy of each gene. The squares in the body of the Punnett diagram show the results expected from random uniting of the gametes, identifying the genotype of offspring produced by each possible combination of parental gametes. In Figure 2.6, the gametes of the F_1 parents are placed at the margins of the Punnett square, and gamete union produces the F_2 generation in the genotype proportions shown in the body of the Punnett square.

Mendel used the concept of particulate inheritance to analyze his experiments and to formulate a hypothesis to explain his results. Mendel's first hypothesis is known as the **law of segregation,** sometimes also known as **Mendel's first law.** This hypothesis describes the particulate nature of inheritance, identifies the segregation (separation) of alleles during gamete formation, and proposes the random union of gametes to produce progeny in predictable proportions:

The law of segregation *The two alleles for each trait will separate (segregate) from one another during gamete formation, and each allele will have an equal probability* $\left(\frac{1}{2}\right)$ *of inclusion in a gamete. Random union of gametes at fertilization will unite one gamete from each parent to produce progeny in ratios that are determined by chance.*

The law of segregation applies to each of the seven traits Mendel examined, and each experiment produces similar results. We can take flower color as an example and use the law of segregation to explain the events shown in Figure 2.4, from the parental cross through the production of F_2 progeny. Gametes formed by pure-breeding purple (*PP*) parents all contain *P*. Similarly, gametes from pure-breeding white (*pp*) parents all contain *p*. The F_1 all have the dominant purple phenotype and have a heterozygous (*Pp*) genotype. Segregation of alleles is more easily visualized among gametes produced by the heterozygous F_1 plants: One-half of the gametes from those plants are expected to contain *P* and one-half to contain *p*. The random union of gametes from the heterozygous F_1 plants leads to the combinations and frequencies shown in the Punnett square of Figure 2.6, leading to the 1:2:1 genotypic ratio and the 3:1 phenotypic ratio.

Hypothesis Testing by Test-Cross Analysis

Mendel proposed the law of segregation to explain the phenotype proportions he observed in the F_1 and F_2 generations of his breeding experiments. Consistent with good scientific method, he considered the law of segregation to be a hypothesis that made testable predictions about cross progeny. Mendel's proposal that F_1 progeny are heterozygous is critical to the proposal that the gametes that produce the F_2 will have an equal chance of containing one or the other of the alleles. Based on his segregation hypothesis, Mendel expected one-half of the gametes derived from the heterozygous F_1 to carry the dominant allele and the remaining one-half to carry the recessive allele.

To test this prediction, Mendel performed test-cross analysis, by mating a suspected heterozygous F_1 plant with a pure-breeding recessive plant (**Figure 2.7**). Based on the segregation hypothesis, Mendel predicted that test-cross progeny phenotypes would be 50% dominant and 50% recessive. The test cross diagrammed in Figure 2.7 is performed between a plant grown from a round F_1 seed and a pure-breeding wrinkled-seed plant. In this test, the wrinkled-seed plant is homozygous *rr* and produces only *r*-containing gametes. Therefore, if the F_1 plant is heterozygous, it should produce *R* gametes and *r* gametes

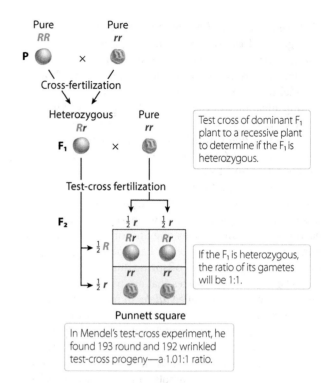

In Mendel's test-cross experiment, he found 193 round and 192 wrinkled test-cross progeny—a 1.01:1 ratio.

Figure 2.7 Test-cross analysis of F₁ plants. A test cross between an F_1 plant and one that is homozygous recessive produces progeny with a 1:1 ratio of the dominant to the recessive phenotype if the F_1 plant is heterozygous.

at a frequency of $\frac{1}{2}$ each. Consequently, the progeny of the cross would be $\frac{1}{2}$ *Rr* and $\frac{1}{2}$ *rr*, resulting in a 1:1 ratio of round: wrinkled. As the figure indicates, Mendel performed this cross and observed 193 round peas and 192 wrinkled peas in test-cross progeny. Mendel performed this kind of test-cross analysis for several of his traits and consistently observed a 1:1 ratio in test-cross progeny (**Table 2.2**).

Table 2.2	Test-Cross Results from Mendel's Experiments		
Test Cross	**Test-Cross Progeny**		**Ratio**
	Dominant	**Recessive**	
Round seed (*Rr*) × wrinkled seed (*rr*)	193 round (*Rr*)	192 wrinkled (*rr*)	1.01:1
Yellow seed (*Gg*) × green seed (*gg*)	196 yellow (*Gg*)	189 green (*gg*)	1.04:1
Purple flower (*Pp*) × white flower (*pp*)	85 purple (*Pp*)	81 white (*pp*)	1.05:1
Tall plants (*Tt*) × short plants (*tt*)	87 tall (*Tt*)	79 short (*tt*)	1.10:1
TOTAL	561	541	1.04:1

Mendel's test-cross results validate two components of his segregation hypothesis. First, the results show that F_1 plants with the dominant phenotype have a heterozygous genotype. Second, the results validate the proposal that chance determines the frequency of gametes containing each allele. Had Mendel been incorrect about the heterozygous genotype of the F_1, or incorrect about the role of chance in producing the frequency of alleles in gametes, the result of the test cross would be different. If the round-seed plant were homozygous RR rather than Rr, all of the progeny of the cross would have the Rr genotype and would produce round peas. If the placement of alleles into gametes was not random, the phenotypes of test-cross progeny would not display a 1:1 ratio.

Hypothesis Testing by F_2 Self-Fertilization

A second pivotal component of Mendel's segregation hypothesis concerns the genotypes of F_2 progeny. Specifically, Mendel's hypothesis predicts that F_2 plants with the dominant phenotype can be either homozygous or heterozygous. His hypothesis further predicts that the plants are twice as likely to be heterozygous as homozygous. Look at Figure 2.6, for example, and notice that one-half of the F_2 progeny are heterozygous, whereas one-quarter of the F_2 progeny are homozygous for the dominant allele. Thus, among F_2 plants with the dominant phenotype (i.e., excluding F_2 plants with the recessive phenotype), two-thirds of the plants are heterozygous and one-third are homozygous for the dominant allele.

Mendel used a self-fertilization experiment to test the validity of his proposal that heterozygotes and homozygotes occur at a 2:1 ratio among dominant F_2 plants (**Figure 2.8**). He reasoned that self-fertilized F_2 plants could be identified as homozygous if they produced only progeny with the same phenotype. In contrast, self-fertilization of heterozygous F_2 plants with the dominant phenotype would produce some progeny with the dominant phenotype and a smaller number with the recessive phenotype, in a 3:1 ratio.

Mendel tested his segregation hypothesis by self-fertilizing F_2 plants of the *dominant phenotype*, examining the progeny of each of these self-fertilizations to determine whether they exhibited the dominant phenotype only or both phenotypes. The results of his seven F_2 dominant self-fertilization experiments are shown in **Table 2.3**. Mendel's largest sample was for seed shape; he self-fertilized 565 round-seeded F_2 plants. In this experiment he found that 193 of the plants (34.2%) produced only round peas in progeny, demonstrating that these plants are homozygous for the dominant allele (RR). Self-fertilization of the other 372 round-pea–producing F_2 plants (65.8%) produced both round peas and wrinkled peas in progeny plants. The ratio 372:193 is very close to the 2:1 ratio of heterozygous to homozygous genotypes

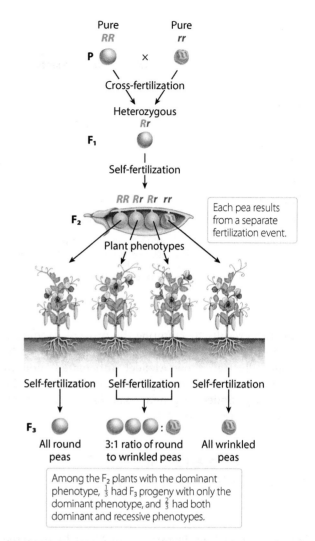

Figure 2.8   Determination of the genotype of F_2 plants by the production of F_3 progeny. F_2 plants are self-fertilized and their seeds are scored. Among the dominant (round) F_2, approximately one-third are expected to be homozygous for the dominant allele (RR). These plants produce progeny that have only round peas. The remaining two-thirds of the dominant F_2 are expected to be heterozygous, and produce both round and wrinkled peas in progeny. All F_2 wrinkled peas are homozygous recessive (rr) and produce only wrinkled peas as progeny.

that Mendel predicted would constitute the dominant, round-pea–producing F_2 plants.

Mendel's self-fertilization results consistently show a 2:1 ratio among dominant F_2 plants for each of the seven traits examined. These results validate the proposal that gametes unite at random to produce progeny. Taken together, the test-cross experiments and the dominant F_2 self-fertilization experiments represent successfully designed and executed independent experiments for testing components of Mendel's segregation hypothesis. In these tests, Mendel made predictions about the experimental outcomes and then

Table 2.3	Results of Mendel's Experiments to Identify F$_2$-Plant Genotypes by Their F$_3$ Progeny		
Trait[a]	Heterozygous F$_2$ Plants[b]	Homozygous F$_2$ Plants[c]	Ratio[d]
Seed shape	372	193	1.93:1
Seed color	353	166	2.13:1
Flower color	64	36	1.78:1
Pod shape	71	29	2.45:1
Pod color	125	75	1.67:1
Flower position	67	33	2.03:1
Plant height	72	28	2.57:1
TOTAL	1124	560	2.01:1

[a] Mendel self-fertilized only F$_2$ plants with the dominant phenotype in this experiment.
[b] F$_2$ plants were heterozygous if the F$_3$ progeny they produced by self-fertilization had both dominant and recessive phenotypes.
[c] F$_2$ plants were homozygous if the F$_3$ progeny they produced by self-fertilization had only the dominant phenotype.
[d] The expected ratio of heterozygous to homozygous F$_2$ plants was 2.00:1.

verified the results by counting the progeny produced. The resulting data supported his segregation hypothesis and illustrate how Mendel anticipated modern scientific methods, using approaches that would not be consistently applied to genetic experiments for several decades (**Genetic Analysis 2.1**).

2.3 Dihybrid and Trihybrid Crosses Reveal the Independent Assortment of Alleles

Each of the seven traits investigated by Mendel showed the same pattern of hereditary transmission that is explained by the law of segregation. The uniformity of phenotype proportions in F$_1$, F$_2$, test-cross, and self-fertilization progeny suggests that the same mechanism is responsible for allelic segregation in each one of the selected traits, but what about the inheritance of two or more traits simultaneously? Is there a pattern or ratio of phenotypes that allowed Mendel to propose a transmission mechanism when two or more genes are examined at the same time?

Dihybrid-Cross Analysis of Two Genes

To test the simultaneous transmission of two traits in the pea plant, Mendel performed a series of **dihybrid crosses**, crosses between organisms that differ for two traits. These tests followed an experimental strategy that paralleled his investigation of allelic segregation of single traits.

As **Figure 2.9** illustrates, Mendel began each dihybrid cross with pure-breeding lines. Having determined, for example, that round pea shape is dominant to wrinkled shape and that yellow pea color is dominant to green color, Mendel proposed that pure-breeding plants producing round, yellow peas have the genotype *RRGG* and that

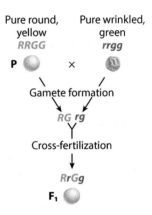

Figure 2.9 Dihybrid-cross analysis. Parental plants that are pure-breeding for two traits are cross-fertilized to produce F$_1$ progeny that are dihybrid and display the two dominant phenotypes round and yellow.

pure-breeding plants for the recessive phenotypes wrinkled and green have the genotype *rrgg*. Gametes produced by the round, yellow plant contain one allele for each type of gene and are *RG*. In contrast, gametes from the wrinkled, green plant are *rg*. Mendel's model predicts that all of the F$_1$ progeny will therefore have the dihybrid genotype *RrGg*. These F$_1$ are heterozygous for two traits and display the dominant parental phenotypes round and yellow.

Heterozygous F$_1$ dihybrids (*RrGg*) have received alleles *R* and *G* from the round, yellow pure-breeding parent and alleles *r* and *g* from the pure-breeding wrinkled, green parent. If the assortment of alleles for each type of gene is independent, gametes produced by these F$_1$ plants are equally likely to contain *any* combination of one allele for seed shape and one allele for seed color. Probabilities of each combination of alleles for each type of gene are predicted by recognizing that four combinations of alleles will be found in the gametes—*RG*, *Rg*, *rG*, and *rg*—and that each combination is expected to occur with a frequency of $\frac{1}{4}$.

PROBLEM The presence of short hairs on the leaves of tomato plants is a dominant trait controlled by the allele *H*. The corresponding recessive trait, smooth leaf, is found in plants with the genotype *hh*. The table at right shows the progeny of three independent crosses of parental plants with genotypes and phenotypes that are unknown.

Cross	Number of Progeny	
	Hairy Leaf	Smooth Leaf
1	32	11
2	42	45
3	0	24

> **BREAK IT DOWN:** Dominant and recessive alleles dictate that hairy-leaf plants are *HH* or *Hh*; smooth-leaf plants are *hh* (p. 31)

Examine the distributions of phenotypes in the progeny of each cross, and determine the parental genotypes for each cross. Use a Punnett square to diagram Cross 1.

> **BREAK IT DOWN:** Phenotype ratios among progeny identify the genotypes of parents in a cross (p. 33)

> **BREAK IT DOWN:** Use a Punnett square to accurately organize gamete production and gamete union (p. 34)

Solution Strategies	Solution Steps

Evaluate

1. Identify the topic this problem addresses and the kind of information the answer should contain.

2. Identify the critical information given in the problem.

1. The problem presents the leaf-form phenotypes of progeny produced by three separate crosses of parental plants with unknown genotypes and phenotypes. The answer must identify parental genotypes and phenotypes for each cross and use a Punnett square to diagram Cross 1.

2. The information given for each cross is the number of progeny with hairy (dominant) and smooth (recessive) leaves. Interpretation of the phenotype ratio of progeny is required to determine parental genotypes and phenotypes.

> **TIP:** The numbers of progeny with each phenotype can be expressed as a ratio.

Deduce

3. Examine the progeny of Cross 1, and determine the approximate ratio of progeny phenotypes.

> **PITFALL:** Genetics experiments produce finite numbers of progeny, so phenotypes may vary from expected ratios. Don't expect to see precise ratios in real data.

3. Ratio of phenotypes in Cross 1 progeny:

$$\frac{32}{11} = 2.91:1$$

This is an approximate 3:1 ratio. The recessive phenotype appears in about $\frac{1}{4}$ of the progeny $\left(\frac{11}{43}\right)$, and the remaining $\frac{3}{4}$ $\left(\frac{32}{43}\right)$ have the dominant phenotype.

4. Examine the progeny of Cross 2, and determine the approximate ratio of progeny phenotypes.

4. Ratio of phenotypes for Cross 2:

$$\frac{42}{45} = 0.93:1$$

This is an approximate 1:1 ratio in which the dominant phenotype is seen in about one-half of the progeny $\left(\frac{42}{97}\right)$ and the recessive phenotype is seen in the other half of the progeny $\left(\frac{45}{97}\right)$.

5. Examine the progeny of Cross 3, and determine the approximate ratio of progeny phenotypes.

5. Cross 3 produced only the recessive phenotype, so the ratio is 0:1.

Solve

6. Based on the results of Cross 1, identify the genotypes and phenotypes of the parental plants in the cross. Construct a Punnett square to illustrate this cross.

> **TIP:** There are two alleles for this gene, and three genotypes are possible. The recessive phenotype is found in plants with the *hh* genotype, whereas the dominant phenotype will be found in plants that are *Hh* and *HH*.

6. The recessive progeny in this cross have the genotype *hh*, so each parent in Cross 1 must carry a copy of *h*. The dominant progeny are either *HH* or *Hh*. The 3:1 progeny phenotype ratio is consistent with a parental cross *Hh* × *Hh*. The Punnett square for this cross is consistent with the observed 3:1 ratio:

	H	*h*
H	*HH*	*Hh*
h	*Hh*	*hh*

7. Based on the results of Cross 2, identify the genotypes and phenotypes of the parents.

7. Both parental plants in Cross 2 carry at least one copy of *h*. The 1:1 progeny ratio is consistent with the ratio expected for a test cross of a heterozygous organism to one that is homozygous recessive. This cross is *Hh* × *hh*.

8. Based on the results of Cross 3, identify the parental genotypes and phenotypes.

8. Cross 3 produces only *hh* progeny. This is expected for a pure-breeding cross between two homozygous organisms. This cross is *hh* × *hh*.

For more practice, see Problems 10, 14, and 29. Visit the Study Area to access study tools. **MasteringGenetics**™

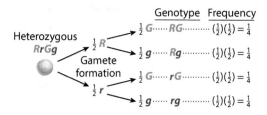

Genotype Frequency

Figure 2.10   The forked-line method for determining gamete genotype frequency. Chance is responsible for the independent assortment of alleles included in four genetically different gametes.

Figure 2.10 shows a diagrammatic aid called the **forked-line diagram** that is used to determine gamete genotypes and frequencies. The forked-line diagram illustrates that one-half of all gametes produced by an $RrGg$ plant will contain R and one-half will contain r. If the segregation of G and g is independent of the R and r alleles, then one-half of the gametes containing R will also carry G and the other half will carry g. The same is true for r-bearing gametes; one-half will carry G and the remaining half will carry g. The frequency of each of the four gamete genotypes is $\left(\frac{1}{2}\right)\left(\frac{1}{2}\right) = \frac{1}{4}$.

A Punnett square can be used to illustrate the random union of these four different gametes to produce F_2 progeny (**Figure 2.11**). Each gamete has a predicted frequency of $\frac{1}{4}$, and each cell of the Punnett square has a predicted frequency of $\left(\frac{1}{4}\right)\left(\frac{1}{4}\right) = \frac{1}{16}$. Among F_2 progeny, four phenotypes are observed, displaying either (1) both dominant phenotypes, (2) the dominant phenotype for one trait and the recessive phenotype for the other (there are two versions of this), or (3) both recessive phenotypes. The F_2 phenotypes appear in the ratio $\frac{9}{16}:\frac{3}{16}:\frac{3}{16}:\frac{1}{16}$.

By examining the F_2 phenotype proportions, we can see the relationship between the 3:1 ratio for each trait

and the 9:3:3:1 ratio when the two traits are considered simultaneously. When pea shape and pea color are considered individually, monohybrid crosses produce F_2 that are $\frac{3}{4}$ dominant and $\frac{1}{4}$ recessive. The cross of two dihybrids also yields proportions of $\frac{3}{4}$ dominant to $\frac{1}{4}$ recessive for each trait, making the prediction of phenotypic ratios among the F_2 for both traits combined a problem of combinatorial arithmetic. Figure 2.11 reminds us that genotypes falling into the $R-$ and the $G-$ classes each occur in $\frac{3}{4}$ of the progeny, while rr and gg genotype classes each occur in $\frac{1}{4}$ of the progeny. The dash in the genotypes $R-$ and $G-$ is a "blank" that could be filled by either a second copy of the dominant allele or a copy of the recessive allele. In either case, the resulting genotype—for example, RR or Rr—produces the dominant phenotype. The co-occurrence of the two dominant phenotypes (round, yellow) is therefore expected to have a frequency of $\left(\frac{3}{4}\right)\left(\frac{3}{4}\right) = \frac{9}{16}$, the two recessive phenotypes (wrinkled, green) will occur with a frequency of $\left(\frac{1}{4}\right)\left(\frac{1}{4}\right) = \frac{1}{16}$, and the two phenotypic classes that display one dominant and one recessive trait (round, green and wrinkled, yellow) will each be found in a frequency of $\left(\frac{3}{4}\right)\left(\frac{1}{4}\right) = \frac{3}{16}$.

This outcome illustrates **Mendel's law of independent assortment,** also known as **Mendel's second law.**

The law of independent assortment *During gamete formation, the segregation of alleles at one gene is independent of the segregation of alleles at another gene.*

Mendel reached his conclusions regarding independent assortment on the basis of numerous dihybrid crosses. The cross of pure-breeding round, yellow plants with pure-breeding wrinkled, green plants was an instrumental one. After crossing the pure-breeding parents and allowing self-fertilization of the F_1, Mendel counted the phenotypes among the F_2 and found that both of the parental phenotypes (round, yellow and wrinkled, green) were present along with two *nonparental* phenotypes: round, green and wrinkled, yellow. Among the F_2 produced in his experiment, Mendel found 315 round, yellow plants; 108 round, green plants; 101 wrinkled, yellow plants; and 32 wrinkled, green plants (**Figure 2.12a**).

This F_2 observation contains two features of pivotal importance to Mendel's hypothesis. First, parental and nonparental phenotypes are seen at frequencies that differ from one another. The most numerous class of F_2 progeny display the dominant parental phenotypes for each trait, round and yellow. The smallest class of F_2 progeny have the two recessive parental phenotypes, wrinkled and green; and the two nonparental F_2 classes (round, green and wrinkled, yellow) are intermediate and approximately equal in number. From these numbers, Mendel recognized that the ratios between the dominant and recessive forms of each trait followed the familiar 3:1 pattern. In looking at pea shape, for example, Mendel found that 423 (315 + 108) plants were round and that 133 (101 + 32) plants were wrinkled. The ratio 423:133 reduces to 3.18:1. Similarly, for pea color he found a ratio of 416 (315 + 101) yellow to 140 (108 + 32) green—a

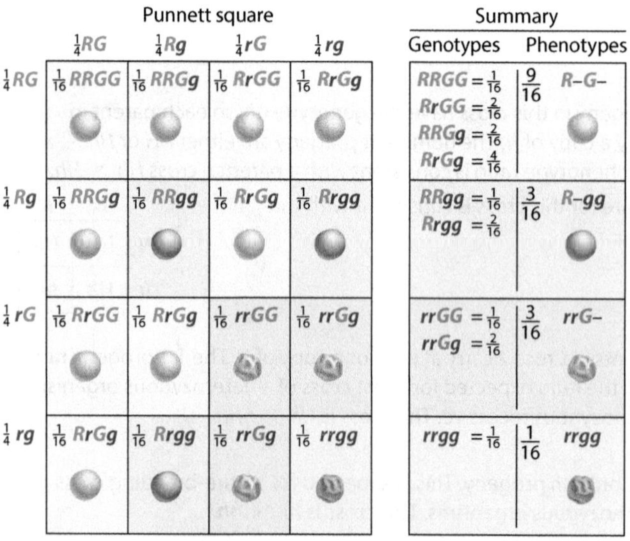

Punnett square

	$\frac{1}{4}RG$	$\frac{1}{4}Rg$	$\frac{1}{4}rG$	$\frac{1}{4}rg$
$\frac{1}{4}RG$	$\frac{1}{16}$ *RRGG*	$\frac{1}{16}$ *RRGg*	$\frac{1}{16}$ *RrGG*	$\frac{1}{16}$ *RrGg*
$\frac{1}{4}Rg$	$\frac{1}{16}$ *RRGg*	$\frac{1}{16}$ *RRgg*	$\frac{1}{16}$ *RrGg*	$\frac{1}{16}$ *Rrgg*
$\frac{1}{4}rG$	$\frac{1}{16}$ *RrGG*	$\frac{1}{16}$ *RrGg*	$\frac{1}{16}$ *rrGG*	$\frac{1}{16}$ *rrGg*
$\frac{1}{4}rg$	$\frac{1}{16}$ *RrGg*	$\frac{1}{16}$ *Rrgg*	$\frac{1}{16}$ *rrGg*	$\frac{1}{16}$ *rrgg*

Summary

Genotypes		Phenotypes
$RRGG = \frac{1}{16}$ $RrGG = \frac{2}{16}$ $RRGg = \frac{2}{16}$ $RrGg = \frac{4}{16}$	$\frac{9}{16}$	$R-G-$
$RRgg = \frac{1}{16}$ $Rrgg = \frac{2}{16}$	$\frac{3}{16}$	$R-gg$
$rrGG = \frac{1}{16}$ $rrGg = \frac{2}{16}$	$\frac{3}{16}$	$rrG-$
$rrgg = \frac{1}{16}$	$\frac{1}{16}$	$rrgg$

Figure 2.11   Independent assortment of alleles at two loci. Self-fertilization or crossing of dihybrid F_1 ($RrGg$) to one another produces nine genotypes distributed in a 9:3:3:1 phenotypic ratio among F_2 progeny.

(a)

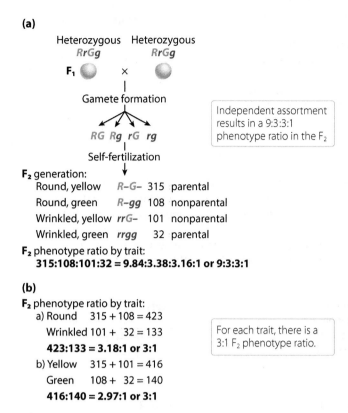

(b)

F₂ phenotype ratio by trait:
a) Round   315 + 108 = 423

Wrinkled 101 + 32 = 133

423:133 = 3.18:1 or 3:1

b) Yellow   315 + 101 = 416

Green   108 + 32 = 140

416:140 = 2.97:1 or 3:1

> For each trait, there is a 3:1 F₂ phenotype ratio.

Figure 2.12   Phenotype proportions in the progeny of a dihybrid cross performed by Mendel. (a) When the two traits are considered simultaneously, a phenotypic ratio of 9:3:3:1 is expected. (b) For each trait considered individually, progeny display an approximate 3:1 ratio of the dominant to the recessive phenotype.

ratio of 2.97:1 (**Figure 2.12b**). Considering each trait individually, the cross of heterozygous F₁ plants has produced an F₂ generation in which $\frac{3}{4}$ of the progeny have the dominant phenotype and $\frac{1}{4}$ have the recessive phenotype.

Second, Mendel predicted that if alleles at each gene unite at random to produce the F₂, then the expected F₂-plant phenotypes will occur in predictable frequencies. He hypothesized that F₂ progeny displaying the two dominant traits (round and yellow) will occur at a frequency of $\left(\frac{3}{4}\right)\left(\frac{3}{4}\right) = \frac{9}{16}$. Similarly, progeny carrying the two recessive traits (wrinkled and green) are expected at a frequency of $\left(\frac{1}{4}\right)\left(\frac{1}{4}\right) = \frac{1}{16}$, and each of the nonparental phenotypes is expected at a frequency of $\left(\frac{3}{4}\right)\left(\frac{1}{4}\right) = \frac{3}{16}$. Independent assortment of alleles at the two genes therefore leads to an expected distribution among the F₂ of

round, yellow	R–G–	$\frac{9}{16}$
round, green	R–gg	$\frac{3}{16}$
wrinkled, yellow	rrG–	$\frac{3}{16}$
wrinkled, green	$rrgg$	$\frac{1}{16}$

Mendel's count of 315 round, yellow; 108 round, green; 101 wrinkled, yellow; and 32 wrinkled, green (see Figure 2.12) can be converted to a ratio by dividing each number by 32, the value of the smallest class. The division by 32 reduces Mendel's observed ratio to 9.84:3.38:3.16:1, which is a close fit to the 9:3:3:1 ratio

predicted by his model. From this result, Mendel hypothesized that independent assortment in a dihybrid organism produces four different gamete genotypes at equal frequencies. Random union of the gametes then produces four phenotypic classes as a result of dominance relationships at each locus, and the ratio of these F₂ phenotypic classes is expected to be 9:3:3:1 (**Genetic Analysis 2.2**).

Testing Independent Assortment by Test-Cross Analysis

To test his hypothesis that combinations of pea shape and color are determined by the independent assortment of alleles, Mendel once again turned to test-cross analysis. Having proposed that the F₁ plants with round, yellow seeds were dihybrid and had the genotype $RrGg$, he predicted that the test cross of a dihybrid ($RrGg$) to a pure-breeding wrinkled, green plant ($rrgg$) would produce four offspring phenotypes at a frequency of $\frac{1}{4}$ each. **Figure 2.13** shows that the dihybrid F₁ plant was expected to produce

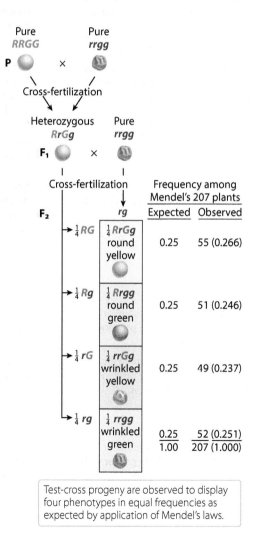

> Test-cross progeny are observed to display four phenotypes in equal frequencies as expected by application of Mendel's laws.

Figure 2.13   Mendel's test cross to verify independent assortment. Mendel predicted and observed an approximate 1:1:1:1 ratio among progeny, supporting his hypothesis of independent assortment.

PROBLEM In a certain mammalian species, long fur and the appearance of white spots are produced by dominant alleles F and S, respectively, which assort independently. The genotype ff produces short fur, and the genotype ss produces solid fur color. Given the parental genotypes for each of the following crosses, determine the expected proportions of all progeny phenotypes.

	Male		**Female**
Cross 1:	$FF\,Ss$	$\times$	$Ff\,ss$
Cross 2:	$ff\,Ss$	$\times$	$Ff\,Ss$
Cross 3:	$Ff\,Ss$	$\times$	$Ff\,Ss$

BREAK IT DOWN: If genes assort independently, fur length will be independent of the presence or absence of spots (p. 38).

BREAK IT DOWN: Use a Punnett square or a forked-line diagram to accurately predict cross outcomes (p. 39).

Solution Strategies	Solution Steps

Evaluate

1. Identify the topic of this problem and the kind of information the answer should contain.

1. This is a transmission genetic problem in which parental genotypes are given. Answers must predict the phenotypes of progeny and their expected proportions. These are predicted by determining the parental gametes and their proportions.

2. Identify the critical information given in the problem.

2. Genotypes of parents are given for each cross. The genotypes are used to predict the genotypes of parental gametes and the gamete proportions.

Deduce

3. For Cross 1, identify the genetically different gametes that can be produced by each parent and calculate the predicted proportion of each gamete.

TIP: A forked-line diagram is a useful tool for predicting the alleles in gametes and gamete frequencies.

3. Each of the parents can produce two genetically different gametes at predicted frequencies of $\frac{1}{2}$ each.

Cross 1

Male

$1F \left\langle \begin{array}{l} \frac{1}{2}\,S \cdots FS \cdots (1)(\frac{1}{2}) = \frac{1}{2} \\ \frac{1}{2}\,s \cdots Fs \cdots (1)(\frac{1}{2}) = \frac{1}{2} \end{array} \right.$

Female

$\frac{1}{2}F \longrightarrow 1s \cdots Fs \cdots (\frac{1}{2})(1) = \frac{1}{2}$
$\frac{1}{2}f \longrightarrow 1s \cdots fs \cdots (\frac{1}{2})(1) = \frac{1}{2}$

4. Identify the content and frequency of the genetically different gametes produced by the parents in Cross 2.

PITFALL: Carefully identify the genotype of each parent to avoid errors.

4. The male produces two types of gametes at a predicted frequency of $\frac{1}{2}$ each. The female produces four genetically different gametes at frequencies of $\frac{1}{4}$ each.

Cross 2

Male

$1f \left\langle \begin{array}{l} \frac{1}{2}\,S \cdots fS \cdots (1)(\frac{1}{2}) = \frac{1}{2} \\ \frac{1}{2}\,s \cdots fs \cdots (1)(\frac{1}{2}) = \frac{1}{2} \end{array} \right.$

Female

$\frac{1}{2}F \left\langle \begin{array}{l} \frac{1}{2}\,S \cdots FS \cdots (\frac{1}{2})(\frac{1}{2}) = \frac{1}{4} \\ \frac{1}{2}\,s \cdots Fs \cdots (\frac{1}{2})(\frac{1}{2}) = \frac{1}{4} \end{array} \right.$

$\frac{1}{2}f \left\langle \begin{array}{l} \frac{1}{2}\,S \cdots fS \cdots (\frac{1}{2})(\frac{1}{2}) = \frac{1}{4} \\ \frac{1}{2}\,s \cdots fs \cdots (\frac{1}{2})(\frac{1}{2}) = \frac{1}{4} \end{array} \right.$

5. Predict the gamete content and frequencies for the parents in Cross 3.

5. Both parents are dihybrids that produce four genetically different gametes at frequencies of $\frac{1}{4}$ each.

Cross 3

Male

$\frac{1}{2}F \left\langle \begin{array}{l} \frac{1}{2}\,S \cdots FS \cdots (\frac{1}{2})(\frac{1}{2}) = \frac{1}{4} \\ \frac{1}{2}\,s \cdots Fs \cdots (\frac{1}{2})(\frac{1}{2}) = \frac{1}{4} \end{array} \right.$

$\frac{1}{2}f \left\langle \begin{array}{l} \frac{1}{2}\,S \cdots fS \cdots (\frac{1}{2})(\frac{1}{2}) = \frac{1}{4} \\ \frac{1}{2}\,s \cdots fs \cdots (\frac{1}{2})(\frac{1}{2}) = \frac{1}{4} \end{array} \right.$

Female

$\frac{1}{2}F \left\langle \begin{array}{l} \frac{1}{2}\,S \cdots FS \cdots (\frac{1}{2})(\frac{1}{2}) = \frac{1}{4} \\ \frac{1}{2}\,s \cdots Fs \cdots (\frac{1}{2})(\frac{1}{2}) = \frac{1}{4} \end{array} \right.$

$\frac{1}{2}f \left\langle \begin{array}{l} \frac{1}{2}\,S \cdots fS \cdots (\frac{1}{2})(\frac{1}{2}) = \frac{1}{4} \\ \frac{1}{2}\,s \cdots fs \cdots (\frac{1}{2})(\frac{1}{2}) = \frac{1}{4} \end{array} \right.$

Solve

6. Construct a Punnett square for Cross 1 and predict the progeny phenotypes and proportions.

6. The predicted Cross 1 progeny are $\frac{1}{2}$ long, spotted and $\frac{1}{2}$ long, solid.

♂ / ♀

	FS	Fs
Fs	FFSs	FFss
fs	FfSs	Ffss

7. Construct a Punnett square for Cross 2 and predict the progeny phenotypes and proportions.

7. The progeny predicted from Cross 2 are $\frac{3}{8}$ long, spotted; $\frac{1}{8}$ long, solid, $\frac{3}{8}$ short, spotted, and $\frac{1}{8}$ short, solid.

♂ / ♀

	fS	fs
FS	FfSS	FfSs
Fs	FfSs	Ffss
fS	ffSS	ffSs
fs	ffSs	ffss

8. Construct a Punnett square for Cross 3 and predict the progeny phenotypes and proportions.

8. The progeny produced by Cross 3 are predicted to be $\frac{9}{16}$ long, spotted; $\frac{3}{16}$ long, solid; $\frac{3}{16}$ short, spotted; and $\frac{1}{16}$ short, solid.

♀ / ♂

	FS	Fs	fS	fs
FS	FFSS	FFSs	FfSS	FfSs
Fs	FFSs	FFss	FfSs	Ffss
fS	FfSS	FfSs	ffSS	ffSs
fs	FfSs	Ffss	ffSs	ffss

For more practice, see Problems 6, 12, and 27

Visit the Study Area to access study tools.

MasteringGenetics™

four different gamete genotypes. Recalling the logic of the forked-line diagram, remember that one-half of the gametes are expected to contain R and one-half to contain r. Gametes carry G and g independently of R or r, meaning that four different combinations of these alleles are possible in gametes: RG, rG, Rg, and rg, each occurring at an expected frequency of $\left(\frac{1}{2}\right)\left(\frac{1}{2}\right) = \frac{1}{4}$. In contrast, the homozygous recessive green, wrinkled ($rrgg$) plant can produce only an rg gamete. In the figure, we see that the test-cross progeny are expected to have four genotypes, each corresponding to a different phenotype. The predicted progeny are expected to be $\frac{1}{4}$ $RrGg$ (round, yellow), $\frac{1}{4}$ $Rrgg$ (round, green), $\frac{1}{4}$ $rrGg$ (wrinkled, yellow), and $\frac{1}{4}$ $rrgg$ (wrinkled, green).

Mendel performed this cross, and his results almost exactly matched expectation. He found that the 207 test-cross progeny were composed of 55 round, yellow; 51 round, green; 49 wrinkled, yellow; and 52 wrinkled, green plants. This result confirmed the dihybrid genotype of the F_1 plant and supported the hypothesis that alleles for pea shape assort independently of those for pea color during gamete formation and that gametes unite at random to form offspring.

Testing Independent Assortment by Trihybrid-Cross Analysis

Mendel further tested the hypothesis of independent assortment by examining the results of a **trihybrid cross,** a cross involving three traits—in this case, seed shape, seed color, and flower color. He began this experiment by crossing a pure-breeding round, yellow, purple-flowered parental plant ($RRGGWW$) to a pure-breeding wrinkled, green, white-flowered plant ($rrggww$). **Figure 2.14** illustrates the cross of pure-breeding parental strains and the resulting F_1 progeny, which display the dominant phenotypes round, yellow, and purple. The F_1 are presumed to be trihybrid ($RrGgWw$). The presumptive trihybrid F_1 plants were then crossed to produce F_2 plants, and the results were compared to expectations.

The forked-line diagram in Figure 2.14 shows the number and expected frequency of gamete genotypes. In the general case, for example, assuming there are two alleles for each gene, the number of different gamete genotypes is expressed as 2^n, where n = the number of genes involved. In this example, there are three genes ($n = 3$), and $2^3 = 8$ different combinations of alleles possible for

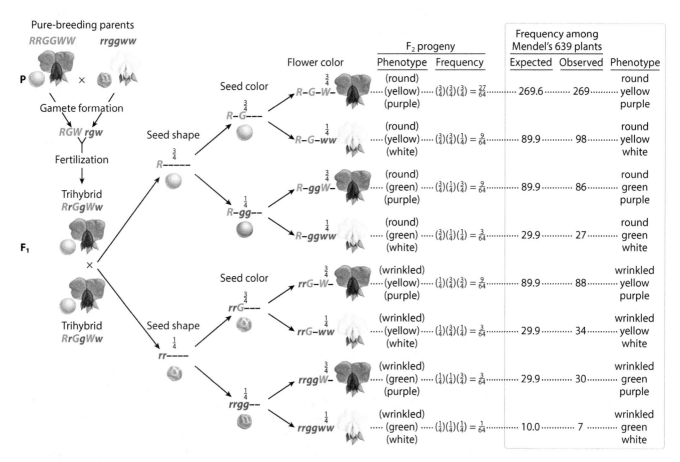

Figure 2.14 **Trihybrid cross to verify independent assortment.** The forked-line method can be used to determine the expected phenotype frequencies produced by a trihybrid cross. Expected and observed results for the F_2 generation of Mendel's trihybrid-cross experiment supported his hypothesis of independent assortment.

the three traits in gametes from the trihybrid plant. The frequency of each gamete genotype is determined as $\left(\frac{1}{2}\right)^n$, or $\left(\frac{1}{2}\right)^3 = \frac{1}{8}$. To predict the number of genetically different gametes and their frequencies, the exponent 3 is used because there are three genes being examined in the experiment. In arithmetic computations like these, the exponent value usually indicates the number of genes.

Figure 2.14 illustrates a way of using the forked-line method to predict the expected frequency of the eight phenotypic classes of this trihybrid cross. For the general case where there are two phenotypes (dominant and recessive) for each trait, there are 2^n phenotypes in the F_2. Once again, n = the number of genes. In this example, there are $2^3 = 8$ phenotypes in the F_2 progeny. Computation of each expected phenotype frequency is based on the expected frequencies of $\frac{3}{4}$ dominant and $\frac{1}{4}$ recessive for each trait. The expected frequency of each trihybrid class is the product of three fractions representing the predicted probabilities of the dominant or recessive form for each trait. For the eight F_2 phenotypes from a trihybrid cross, the expected phenotype ratio is $\frac{27}{64}:\frac{9}{64}:\frac{9}{64}:\frac{3}{64}:\frac{9}{64}:\frac{3}{64}:\frac{3}{64}:\frac{1}{64}$.

Mendel used this combinatorial thinking to predict the outcome of an experimental trihybrid cross. His experimental results for this test are given in Figure 2.14 for 639 F_2 progeny from the cross of round, yellow, purple-flowered F_1 plants. Mendel predicted the number of progeny expected in each phenotype class by multiplying the expected proportion times the sample size, 639. His results were remarkably close to expectation. The close match of these observed and expected values provides a second piece of independent evidence supporting the law of independent assortment.

Taken together, Mendel's analyses of the transmission of single traits and the joint transmission of two or three independent traits represented a major advance in the scientific understanding of hereditary transmission. The law of segregation and the law of independent assortment are the most fundamental principles of genetic transmission in diploid organisms, and they form the foundation of our understanding of transmission, molecular, and population and evolutionary genetics.

Probability Calculations in Genetics Problem Solving

The predicted F_2-phenotype ratio from a trihybrid cross seems complicated, and at first you might not see clearly why that is the expected distribution. The key to understanding the calculation demonstrated in Figure 2.14 is to realize that each independently assorting locus truly can be treated independently of others.

Let's look at the progeny-phenotype distribution for a dihybrid cross. We expect that for each trait individually, $\frac{3}{4}$ of the progeny will display the dominant phenotype and $\frac{1}{4}$ the recessive phenotype. We could use a Punnett square to determine the phenotypic distribution

of the two traits in combination as we did in Figure 2.11, but the independence of each gene gives us a quicker way to calculate the distribution of phenotypes: by their probability. In this case, the expected progeny phenotype proportions can be obtained by multiplying the two ratios—$\left(\frac{3}{4}:\frac{1}{4}\right)\left(\frac{3}{4}:\frac{1}{4}\right)$—to yield the expected ratio of $\frac{9}{16}:\frac{3}{16}:\frac{3}{16}:\frac{1}{16}$, or 9:3:3:1. We can use the same approach to predict the ratio among F_2 progeny of a trihybrid cross as well. Taking an example from Figure 2.14, notice that the expected proportion of any F_2 phenotype class can be predicted by the probability method. For the round, yellow, purple class, the predicted proportion is $\frac{3}{4} \times \frac{3}{4} \times \frac{3}{4} = \frac{27}{64}$, and for round, yellow, white it is $\frac{3}{4} \times \frac{3}{4} \times \frac{1}{4} = \frac{9}{64}$. Using the probability method can save time and reduce the chance of an error in predicting outcomes for more complex crosses.

Another advantage to using probability for solving genetic problems is its easy adaptability to different sorts of questions. For example, what proportion of progeny produced by self-fertilization of a trihybrid yellow, round, purple plant (*GgRrWw*) will have the same *genotype* as the parental plant? To determine the answer, we identify the probability of the genotype for each individual trait and then multiply those three probabilities together. At each locus the cross is heterozygous by heterozygous, so one-half of the progeny are expected to be heterozygous. The probability that offspring of a trihybrid self-fertilization will be trihybrid is therefore $\left(\frac{1}{2}\right)\left(\frac{1}{2}\right)\left(\frac{1}{2}\right) = \frac{1}{8}$. If we wanted to determine the proportion of progeny from the trihybrid cross that are *rrGGWw*, we again treat the loci independently and calculate the probability as $\left(\frac{1}{4}\right)\left(\frac{1}{4}\right)\left(\frac{1}{2}\right) = \frac{1}{32}$.

The problems at the end of this chapter, as well as **Genetic Analysis 2.3**, provide a number of opportunities for you to practice using the principles of transmission genetics. As **Experimental Insight 2.1** points out, however, opportunities to collect evidence of Mendel's laws of heredity may be as close as the produce aisle of your local grocery store.

The Rediscovery of Mendel's Work

In 1900, after remaining virtually unknown for 34 years, Mendel's experimental results and interpretations were rediscovered almost simultaneously by three botanists working independently of one another. Carl Correns and Erich von Tschermak both worked on *Pisum sativum*, the same plant Mendel had used, and Hugo de Vries worked on a different plant species. Each of the three identified the hereditary principles Mendel had first described in 1865. With support from the contemporaneous discoveries of the behavior of chromosomes during meiotic cell division, followed quickly by confirming evidence from other species of plants and animals, the basic principles of segregation and independent assortment were widely and rapidly disseminated in the first decade of the 20th century.

PROBLEM For the same mammalian species and the same traits described in Genetic Analysis 2.2 which described dominance relationships between the alleles of each gene, a cross between a male that has long, solid-colored fur and a female that has short, spotted fur produces eight offspring. The offspring are 2 long, spotted; 2 short, solid; 2 long, solid; and 2 short, spotted. Given the phenotypes of the parents and the distribution of offspring phenotypes, determine the genotypes of parents and offspring.

> **BREAK IT DOWN:** Review the dominance relationships between alleles of each gene (p. 39).

> **BREAK IT DOWN:** The phenotype ratio among of a cross identifies parental genotypes (p. 39).

Solution Strategies	Solution Steps

Evaluate

1. Identify the topic of this problem and the kind of information the answer should contain.

2. Identify the critical information given in the problem.

1. The problem requires the determination of parental genotypes and progeny genotypes based on the phenotypes of parents and the proportions of progeny with different phenotypes.

2. In this mammalian species, long fur is dominant to short fur and spotted fur color is dominant to solid fur color. Each parent is homozygous recessive for one trait and is dominant for the other trait. The progeny display a 1:1:1:1 ratio of phenotypes.

Deduce

> **TIP:** Use the known and placeholder genotypes for parents and progeny phenotype ratios to completely identify parental genotypes.

3. Record what is known about the parental genotypes by writing homozygous recessive alleles for the recessive trait and writing a dominant allele and a "blank" as a placeholder for the dominant trait.

3. The long, solid parent is *F–ss*, carrying at least one dominant (*F–*) allele for long fur and homozygous recessive alleles (*ss*) for solid coat. The short, spotted parent is *ffS–*, carrying homozygous recessive alleles (*ff*) for fur length and at least one dominant allele (*S–*) for spotted coat.

> **PITFALL:** You cannot presume to know the genotype of an organism with the dominant phenotype without segregation information. Use general genotype forms *F–* and *S–* as placeholders for the homozygous dominant or heterozygous genotypes.

4. Infer what is known about progeny genotypes by writing homozygous recessive alleles or dominant alleles with a "blank" placeholder.

4. The inferred progeny genotypes are

   F–S– long, spotted
   ffss short, solid
   F–ss long, solid
   ffS– short, spotted

5. Determine the phenotype ratio of long fur to short fur among the progeny of the cross.

5. Four long fur and four short, a 1:1 ratio of dominant and recessive phenotypes.

> **TIP:** Traits assorting independently can be analyzed individually. Assess segregation based on progeny phenotype ratios for one trait at a time.

6. Determine the phenotype ratio of spotted fur to solid fur among the progeny.

6. Four progeny have spotted fur and four have solid fur, a 1:1 ratio of phenotypes.

Solve

7. Determine the parental genotypes necessary to produce progeny with the observed ratio of long to short fur.

7. To produce the recessive short fur phenotype, each parent must contribute a recessive (*f*) allele. The female parent with short fur is *ff*, and the male parent with long fur must be heterozygous (*Ff*) for this gene. The genotype of the male parent with long, solid-colored fur is *Ffss*.

♀\♂	*Fs*	*fs*
fS	*FfSs* Long, spotted	*ffSs* Short, spotted
fs	*Ffss* Long, solid	*ffss* Short, solid

8. Determine the parental genotypes necessary to produce the observed ratio of spotted to solid coat.

8. The male parent with the recessive phenotype solid coat contributes a recessive (*s*) allele. The female parent with spotted coat must be heterozygous (*Ss*). The short, spotted female has the genotype *ffSs*.

9. Verify the parental genotypes in this cross by using a Punnett square analysis and the forked-line method to predict phenotype probabilities.

> **PITFALL:** To avoid errors, use a Punnett square or a forked-line diagram to verify that the parental genotypes you assign will produce progeny in the observed ratio.

9. For the cross *Ffss* × *ffSs*, each parent produces two genetically different gametes at frequencies of $\frac{1}{2}$ each. For each gene, a heterozygous genotype is crossed with a homozygous recessive genotype, resulting in a 1:1 ratio of dominant to recessive phenotype for each trait. The Punnett square predicts four different progeny genotypes and phenotypes in a 1:1:1:1 ratio, and the forked-line method gives the same result.

$\frac{1}{2}$ *fS* $\begin{cases} \frac{1}{2}\ Fs = \frac{1}{4}\ FfSs \text{ Long spotted} \\ \frac{1}{2}\ fs = \frac{1}{4}\ ffSs \text{ Short spotted} \end{cases}$

$\frac{1}{2}$ *fs* $\begin{cases} \frac{1}{2}\ Fs = \frac{1}{4}\ Ffss \text{ Long solid} \\ \frac{1}{2}\ fs = \frac{1}{4}\ ffss \text{ Short solid} \end{cases}$

For more practice, see Problems 3, 16, and 40. | Visit the Study Area to access study tools. | **MasteringGenetics™**

Experimental Insight 2.1

Mendelism in the Produce Aisle

Many of the appealing characteristics of fruits and vegetables available in grocery stores and at farmer's markets are the result of intensive selective breeding, a form of natural selection generated by breeders, who select which organisms are to reproduce and determine the crosses that will occur. For example, in recent years many new vegetable varieties have been introduced into the marketplace. Among these is a variety of corn that goes by several names, including "bicolor," "peaches and cream," and "yellow and white." Most of the kernels on a cob of bicolored corn are yellow, but a sizable number are white. With close inspection and a little quantitative analysis, you should be able to identify the genetic mechanism that produces this variation in color.

An ear of corn is a mini-genetic experiment: Each kernel on the ear, like each pea in a pod, is a separate seed, produced by a fertilization event independent of the events that produced

adjacent kernels. This means that each mature ear of corn carries hundreds of progeny for analysis.

Bicolor corn originates with the cross of two pure-breeding corn lines, one producing yellow kernels and the other producing white kernels. The yellow plant is WW, and the white plant is ww. When seed company geneticists cross these parental stocks, the kernels on the F_1 plants are yellow and have the heterozygous Ww genotype. This F_1 seed is allowed to mature and is packaged for sale to farmers and home gardeners, who plant it to produce a crop. The seed is commonly labeled "hybrid," meaning "monohybrid," to reflect the heterozygosity at the kernel-color locus. Owing to segregation of alleles at the kernel-color locus, the plants that grow from this F_1 seed produce both yellow (W—) and white (ww) kernels on each ear.

If you saw some of this corn in your grocery store, how would you verify that the genetic basis of its yellow and white kernels is the segregation of two alleles at a single locus? The answer is that you would count the number of yellow kernels and the number of white kernels on ears of bicolor corn with the expectation of a ratio of approximately 3:1 between the yellow and white kernels.

Recent genetics classes of one of the authors have examined several dozen ears of bicolor corn and counted 9304 yellow kernels and 3052 white kernels. Among the total of 12,356 kernels there are 75.3% yellow and 24.7% white, a ratio of 3.05:1. You will use these data in Problem 20 at the end of the chapter to do a statistical test to see if the observed data fit the hypothesis that this trait is the product of the segregation of alleles at a single gene. The next time you shop for fruits and vegetables, keep in mind that you are looking at Mendelian genetics in action!

The approach to genetic analysis we describe in this chapter is often dubbed Mendelian genetics for the obvious reason that Gregor Mendel was the first scientist to offer a mechanism to explain the hereditary patterns he observed. However Mendel was not the first person to make these observations. **Experimental Insight 2.2** shows why, but for a failure to quantify the results of his own crosses of pea plants, Charles Naudin, a contemporary of Mendel's, might have been the first scientist to succeed at explaining heredity. And, you can be an experimental geneticist too! **Experimental Insight 2.3** describes a genetics breeding program you could start right in your own community.

2.4 Probability Theory Predicts Mendelian Ratios

Mendel recognized that chance (or random probability, the same process that determines the outcome of coin flips and rolls of the dice) is the arithmetic principle underlying the segregation of alleles for a given gene and

governing the independent assortment of alleles for different genes. The preceding discussions have demonstrated that the basic rules of Mendelian inheritance are actually those of random probability theory. The Mendelian probabilities we have discussed to this point are most clearly expressed by four rules of probability theory—the *product rule*, the *sum rule, conditional probability*, and *binomial probability*. In this section, we look more closely at these rules that describe and predict the outcome of genetic events governed by the rules of chance.

The Product Rule

If two or more events are independent of one another, their joint probability, the likelihood of their simultaneous or consecutive occurrence, is the product of the probabilities of each one individually. The **product rule,** also called the **multiplication rule,** describes these circumstances.

You have already used the product rule several times in determining the outcomes of genetic crosses. For example, in Figures 2.6 and 2.7 the product rule is used to

Experimental Insight 2.2

Naudinian Genetics, Anyone?

Before Mendel, many "plant hybridists" experimented with pea plants and other plants, attempting to discern the mechanisms of plant reproduction and the process of hereditary transmission of traits. Mendel cited the work of several early hybridists in his 1866 paper.

Several of these plant hybridists came close to discovering the hereditary principles that today bear Mendel's name; none succeeded fully. For example, in 1823, Thomas Andrew Knight determined that gray seed coat is dominant to white and that self-fertilization of certain gray-seeded plants produces both gray and white seed in progeny plants. In 1822, John Goss, working with a pea variety that had blue and white seeds, reported that crossing a pure-breeding white-seeded plant with a pure-breeding blue-seeded plant produced only blue seeds in first-generation plants, and that self-fertilization then produced a second generation with a mixture of white and blue seeds in plants. Carl Friedrich Gaertner came tantalizingly close to explaining segregation in 1827 when he reported results of a cross between pure-breeding gold-kernel maize and pure-breeding red-striped maize. All the F_1 had gold kernels, and among the F_2, 328 plants had only gold kernels and 103 had red-striped kernels. If Gaertner had been able to correctly interpret his data, he would have identified a 3.18:1 ratio in the F_2. Alas, he never did and missed his "golden" opportunity to explain simple heredity.

Similar fates befell other plant hybridists, but arguably the one who came closest to explaining heredity prior to Mendel was Charles Naudin, who in 1863 seemed poised to beat Mendel to the punch by 2 years. In that year, Naudin reported the following:

- The results of reciprocal crosses are identical. (Similar observations by Mendel were important in his identification of the particulate nature of hereditary factors.)
- F_1 progeny display a single phenotype (as Mendel reported 2 years later).
- F_2 progeny display two phenotypes. (These observations are the result of the segregation of alleles.)
- The hereditary units for traits are separated in pollen and egg formation. (This concept was fundamental to the segregation observation of Mendel.)
- Nonparental combinations of phenotypes appear in the F_2 generation. (This is identical to Mendel's independent assortment observation.)

After making these observations, why wasn't Naudin able to propose a hereditary mechanism to explain them? The answer is that Naudin, like his predecessors and others who would follow, failed to quantify his results. Naudin did not report the number of plants falling into different phenotypic categories, and he was therefore unable to recognize the ratios between phenotypic classes that are the key to interpreting hereditary transmission. Without quantitative data, Naudin was unable to formulate a testable hypothesis.

Alas, poor Naudin! Were it not for his failure to see the necessity of quantifying experimental results, we might well be discussing Naudinian genetics in this chapter instead of Mendelian genetics!

---

determine that the chance of producing an F_2 plant with the recessive phenotype by the cross of heterozygous F_1 plants that are Gg or Rr. The probability of producing the recessive phenotype is $\left(\frac{1}{2}\right)\left(\frac{1}{2}\right) = \frac{1}{4}$ in each case. Similarly, in Figure 2.10, the probability of a dihybrid organism producing gametes with each of the four different genotypes is predicted by applying the product rule in the forked-line diagram. Likewise, in Figure 2.11, the probability that F_2 offspring will be homozygous recessive for both traits from a cross of F_1 dihybrid plants with the genotype $RrGg$ is predicted by applying the product rule.

The Sum Rule

The **sum rule,** also called the **addition rule,** defines the joint probability of occurrence of any of two or more mutually exclusive events by summing the probabilities of each event. This rule is applied when more than one outcome satisfies the conditions of the probability question. Mutually exclusive events in this context are alternative outcomes, only one of which can occur to the exclusion of the other outcomes.

You applied the sum rule to several genetic calculations in the preceding section. For example, in

Figure 2.6 the probability that F_2 progeny of the cross $Gg \times Gg$ will be heterozygous is determined by adding the chance of obtaining either of the two possible ways of obtaining offspring with the dominant phenotype: $\left(\frac{1}{4}\right) + \left(\frac{1}{4}\right) + \left(\frac{1}{4}\right) = \frac{3}{4}$. Similarly, in Figure 2.11, the probability that the F_2 progeny of the cross of dihybrid heterozygotes ($RrGg$) have the two dominant phenotypes is obtained by applying the sum rule. This probability is $\left(\frac{1}{16}\right) + \left(\frac{2}{16}\right) + \left(\frac{2}{16}\right) + \left(\frac{4}{16}\right) = \left(\frac{9}{16}\right)$.

Conditional Probability

Probability questions in genetic experiments can be asked before a cross is made, as when the product rule and the sum rule are used to predict the likelihood of obtaining a certain genotype or phenotype from a cross. Certain other probability questions are asked *after* a cross has been made, such as questions about the probability that an organism has a particular genotype given that the organism has a particular phenotype. This kind of probability is called **conditional probability,** and it is applied when specific information about the outcome modifies, or "conditions," the probability calculation.

Experimental Insight 2.3

Genetics and Evolution at a Library near You?

The Central Rocky Mountain Permaculture Institute (CRMPI) (www.crmpi.org) in cooperation with the Basalt Regional Library (www.basaltlibrary.org) in Basalt, Colorado, established an unusual vegetable-seed–lending program in early 2013. The vegetable seeds available to library patrons through the Basalt Seed Lending Library were collected by CRMPI Director Stephanie Syson through donations from seed companies across the United States. The seeds are all from "heirloom" or "open pollinating" vegetable varieties, pure-breeding plants that only produce progeny with the specific traits characteristic of the vegetable variety. If, for example, the seeds are for a bean plant that has bush (short) growth and green bean pods containing white seeds, then the plants resulting from those seeds and from seeds harvested for planting in successive years will all have bush growth, green pods, and white seeds.

Seeds for beets, broccoli, melons, squashes, peas, tomatoes, various greens, and other vegetables available in the lending library offer a potentially bountiful harvest, but the Basalt Seed Lending Library is about more than just providing free seeds. Library patrons who use the seeds are also asked to save seeds from plants that grow and produce well. Good vegetable-plant growth and production can be a challenge in the Basalt area. Located at approximately 6300 feet of elevation in the shadows of the Rocky Mountains, Basalt has poor soil and a short growing season. CRMPI Director Syson and Basalt Regional Library Director Barbara Milnor run workshops to teach patrons how to properly save seeds for use the following year. According to Syson and Milnor, the ultimate goals of the lending program are (1) to identify vegetable varieties that grow well in the Basalt area and (2) to produce strains of vegetables that are better adapted to conditions in the Basalt area by collecting and replanting seeds from the best-growing and best-producing plants each year.

Only a few dozen libraries around the country have seed-lending programs like this one. Maybe a library near you will start one soon, or maybe you can help set one up. These programs operate on a sound genetic and evolutionary basis, as you will discover in the process of answering Problem 49 at the end of this chapter.

A genetic example of conditional probability would be to ask of the F_2 progeny of a cross like $Gg \times Gg$, "What is the probability that yellow-seeded progeny plants are heterozygous Gg like the parents?" (Mendel asked this question in seeking to test his hypothesis of segregation; see Figure 2.6). Yellow seed is present in $\frac{3}{4}$ of the progeny, but this phenotypic class contains two genotypes, GG and Gg, that are not equally frequent. In this case, the genotype Gg is found in $\frac{2}{3}$ of the yellow F_2 progeny. The other yellow F_2 are GG. Under the conditional criterion that the only progeny phenotype considered is yellow seeds, the answer to the question posed earlier is that the yellow-seeded progeny of the cross have a $\frac{2}{3}$ probability of being Gg.

Another application of conditional probability is the question, "If the yellow-seeded F_2 are allowed to self-fertilize, what proportion of them are expected to breed true?" This question is similar to the one Mendel asked as he devised an independent test of his segregation hypothesis (see Table 2.3). True-breeding F_2 progeny must be homozygous, and in his seed-color experiment, only those progeny with the genotype GG meet this conditional contingency. Since the genotype GG is found in one-third of the yellow-seeded F_2, the same proportion of true-breeding plants is expected as a result of self-fertilization.

Binomial Probability

In determining the outcomes of certain genetic events, just one event need be predicted. An example is the question, "What is the chance a couple produces a daughter?" The answer is obtained by assuming that the father has a $\frac{1}{2}$ chance of donating an X chromosome and producing a daughter and an equal $\frac{1}{2}$ chance of donating a Y chromosome to produce a son, and that male and female offspring are equally likely. In contrast, other questions concerning genetic outcomes require that we assess the probability of a combination or sequence of such events (events for which there are two or more possible outcomes each time). For example, determining the probabilities of different combinations of boys and girls in sets of siblings or the risk of the recessive phenotype in one or more children of a couple who are each heterozygous carriers of a recessive disease requires computation of a particular combination of events that each have two alternative outcomes. To make these determinations, we use **binomial probability** calculations, expanding the binomial expression to reflect the number of outcome combinations and the probability of each combination.

Construction of a Binomial Expansion Formula A binomial expression contains two variables, each representing the frequency of one of two alternative outcomes. We can express the likelihood of one outcome as having a frequency p and the alternative outcome as having a frequency q. Since the events p and q are the only outcomes possible, the sum of the two frequencies is $(p + q) = 1$. If we are examining the probabilities of the outcomes for a series of two alternative events, such as multiple flips of a coin or several successive children born to a couple, we can expand the binomial to the power of the number of successive events (n) to calculate the probabilities. The binomial expansion formula is written as $(p + q)^n$.

In some kinds of probability problems, the values of the binomial variables p and q will be equal; that is,

$p = q = \frac{1}{2}$, as in the probability of producing a boy or a girl. In other cases, the two binomial values will not be equal, as in the probability that heterozygous parents will produce a child with a recessive trait $\left(\frac{1}{4}\right)$ versus a child with the dominant trait $\left(\frac{3}{4}\right)$. Let's use combinatorial probability to predict the likelihood of different numbers of boys and girls produced when a couple has three children. A combinatorial approach allows us to list all the possible birth orders of boys and girls and to group them according to the total numbers of boys and girls in each set of three siblings. The following table shows that there are 2^3 or eight different birth orders of boys and girls. This conclusion is determined based on two possible outcomes (a boy or a girl) for three successive events. Assuming the probabilities of having a boy or having a girl are $\frac{1}{2}$, each different order has a probability of $\left(\frac{1}{2}\right)^3 = \frac{1}{8}$. The outcomes can be grouped into four sets that each contain a different total number of boys and girls.

	0 Boys 3 Girls	1 Boy 2 Girls	2 Boys 1 Girl	3 Boys 0 Girls
	GGG	GGB	GBB	BBB
		GBG	BGB	
		BGG	BBG	
Probability:	$\frac{1}{8}$	$\frac{3}{8}$	$\frac{3}{8}$	$\frac{1}{8}$

We can see that there is only one order in which to get either three boys (BBB) or three girls (GGG), and each has a probability of $\frac{1}{8}$. Notice that we use the product rule to obtain each probability. But what about the cases of 2 boys and 1 girl or 2 girls and 1 boy, where there are three different birth orders (the orders of boys and girls among the siblings) for each outcome? Here we recognize that *each* birth order has a probability of $\left(\frac{1}{2}\right)^3 = \frac{1}{8}$ and that we must sum up all similar outcomes to determine the probability of 1 or 2 boys or girls in three consecutive siblings. In each of these cases, using the sum rule, the probability is $\left(\frac{1}{8}\right) + \left(\frac{1}{8}\right) + \left(\frac{1}{8}\right) = \frac{3}{8}$.

Arithmetically, we use the binomial expansion to the third power $\left[(p + q)^3\right]$ to represent the three successive siblings. Assuming that the probability of one outcome is

p and the probability of the other outcome is q, then the general case for the binomial expands as follows:

$$(p + q)^3 = p^3 + 3p^2q + 3pq^2 + q^3$$

The values being added on the right side of the equality are the frequencies of the four sets of outcomes p and q.

Application of Binomial Probability to Progeny Phenotypes Binomial probability and the binomial expansion can be used whenever a probability question addresses a repeating series of events that have two alternative outcomes. Let's look at the production of yellow and green peas in pods with six peas each. In this example, the dominant allele G determines yellow color and the recessive allele g determines green color. The cross producing progeny peas is a self-fertilization of a yellow-seeded heterozygous (Gg) plant. The probability that a seed is yellow is $\frac{3}{4}$, since the genotype would be either GG or Gg, and the probability that the seed is green, and therefore has the gg genotype, is $\frac{1}{4}$. We will use the variable p to represent the probability of yellow seeds and the variable q to represent the probability of green seeds.

In our example of pea pods with six seeds that are produced by crossing heterozygous (Gg) parental plants, there are two possible color outcomes for each pea and six peas per pod, for a total of 2^6 or 64 combinations. Counting the total number of yellow and green peas in each pod, there are seven categories that each have a different number of yellow and green peas per pod, as we discuss momentarily.

The application of binomial expansion to complex genetic calculations requires repetition and precision in the use of the product rule and the sum rule. However, a convenient shortcut called **Pascal's triangle** eliminates the repetitive calculations required for multiple expansions of the binomial probability equation and can be used for any number of expansions between 0 and the nth power to yield the size of each possible class and the total number of classes possible (**Figure 2.15**). Let's return to our pea pod example of binomial probability to see how Pascal's triangle is used.

Figure 2.16 makes use of the values taken from the $n = 6$ line of Pascal's triangle (highlighted in Figure 2.15).

n (number of events)						Binomial coefficients								Total number of combinations
0							1							1
1							1	1						2
2						1	2	1						4
3					1	3	3	1						8
4				1	4	6	4	1						16
5			1	5	10	10	5	1						32
6		1	6	15	20	15	6	1						64
7	1	7	21	35	35	21	7	1						128
8	1	8	28	56	70	56	28	8	1					256
9	1	9	36	84	126	126	84	36	9	1				512
10	1	10	45	120	210	252	210	120	45	10	1			1024
11	1	11	55	165	330	462	462	330	165	55	11	1		2048
12	1	12	66	220	495	792	924	792	495	220	66	12	1	4096

Figure 2.15 Pascal's triangle of binomial coefficients $(p + q)$ raised to the nth power. Each line of the table shows the distribution of the total number of combinations for a given value of n (number of events). For example, for $(p+q)^2$, use the $n=2$ line, which predicts a total of four outcome combinations distributed in a 1:2:1 or $\frac{1}{4} : \frac{1}{2} : \frac{1}{4}$ ratio. Applications using the highlighted lines, $n=4$ and $n=6$, are discussed in the text.

Figure 2.16 Binomial-probability calculation of seed-color phenotype in six-seeded pods. Pascal's triangle has been used to find the coefficients for the binomial equation expanded to $n=6$. The 64 different outcomes are displayed in seven classes, and the equation is used to compute the expected frequency of each class.

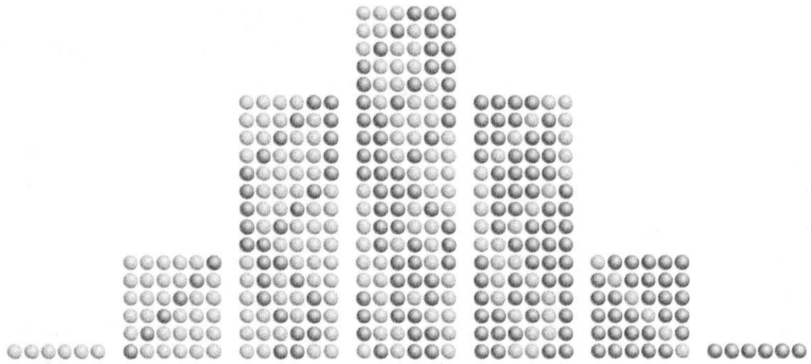

Seed-color outcome class	6 yellow 0 green	5 yellow 1 green	4 yellow 2 green	3 yellow 3 green	2 yellow 4 green	1 yellow 5 green	0 yellow 6 green	
Number of combinations leading to occurrence	1	6	15	20	15	6	1	$= 64$
Probability of occurrence for outcome class	p^6	$6p^5q$	$15p^4q^2$	$20p^3q^3$	$15p^2q^4$	$6pq^5$	q^6	$= 1.00$
Frequency of occurrence for outcome class ($p=\frac{3}{4}, q=\frac{1}{4}$)	0.178	0.356	0.297	0.132	0.033	0.004	0.0002	$= 1.00$

These coefficients of the binomial expansion for $n = 6$ give the proportions of each of the seven outcome classes for this example. The coefficients are 1, 6, 15, 20, 15, 6, and 1, and they add up to a total of 64 different combinations. The coefficients are used to multiply the binomial probability of each outcome class. For this case where $p = \frac{3}{4}$ and $q = \frac{1}{4}$, the expected frequency of obtaining six yellow peas in a pod, for example, is calculated as $1(p^6)$, or $\left(\frac{3}{4}\right)^6 = 0.178$; for pods containing 3 yellow and 3 green peas, the frequency is $20\left[\left(\frac{3}{4}\right)^3\left(\frac{1}{4}\right)^3\right] = 0.132$; the proportion of pods containing 2 yellow and 4 green peas is $15\left[\left(\frac{3}{4}\right)^2\left(\frac{1}{4}\right)^4\right] = 0.033$; and so on. The complete set of expected frequencies for different combinations of seed color is shown at the bottom of Figure 2.16. Notice that the sum of category probabilities and the sum of category frequencies are each 1.00. This correspondence verifies that all possible outcomes have been taken into account.

2.5 Chi-Square Analysis Tests the Fit between Observed Values and Expected Outcomes

Sections 2.1 through 2.4 contain numerous examples of how the principles of probability can be used to predict the likelihood of different outcomes of genetic crosses. Genetic experiments like the ones described, and like the ones Mendel conducted, make predictions based on the hypothesis that chance (i.e., probability) determines the transmission of traits. To assess the validity of this hypothesis, however, geneticists must be able to compare the outcomes they obtain in their experiments to the outcomes that might be expected to occur. For example, are Mendel's F_2 results in Table 2.1 compatible with his segregation hypothesis predicting a 3:1 phenotype ratio?

Scientists must be able to make objective comparisons of observed and expected results to test genetic hypotheses. Qualitative statements such as "the observed results seem to be close to the results we expected" are unacceptable for scientific work. Instead, a quantitative approach, or in this case a statistical approach, is necessary to objectively compare the results obtained from a cross with the results that are predicted by probability. Mendel did not have appropriate statistical tools available to him. But in the early 1900s, the *chi-square test* was derived as a statistical test for comparison of observed experimental results with the results that may be expected when chance is generating the outcome. This section describes the chi-square test and its application to the analysis of genetic data, including some of Mendel's F_2 results. We begin, however, with a brief discussion of a *normal*, or *Gaussian*, distribution, on which chi-square analysis is based.

The Normal Distribution

In large samples, outcomes that are predicted by chance have a **normal (Gaussian) distribution.** A normal distribution is a binomial distribution that is often called a "bell-shaped curve" because of the general shape of the curve the data form when they are graphed (**Figure 2.17**).

A normal distribution contains all the possible experimental outcomes. The **mean (μ)** is the average outcome,

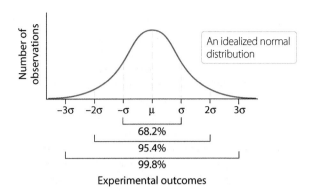

Figure 2.17 **Graphing the distribution of chance outcomes produces a normal distribution.** The standard deviation (σ) is used to characterize the scatter of possible outcomes around the mean (μ).

and other outcomes are distributed around the mean. The tall central segment of the curve nearest the mean represents the outcomes with the highest probability of occurrence. The probability of experimental outcomes gets smaller toward the farthest left and right portions of the curve. The probability of a particular experimental outcome is quantified by a measurement called the **standard deviation (σ).** In a normal distribution, approximately 68.2% of all outcome values fall within one standard deviation of the mean, 95.4% of outcomes fall within two standard deviations of the mean, and 99.8% of outcomes fall within three standard deviations of the mean (Figure 2.17). The observed result of a particular experiment can be compared to the normal distribution to determine the probability of that particular experimental observation compared to all possible outcomes in the distribution, using σ, the standard deviation, as a guide.

By convention, observed experimental outcomes that have a probability of less than 5% (<0.05)—that is, a probability that is more than two standard deviations away from the mean—are often considered to show *statistically significant* difference between the observed outcome and the expected outcome. Chi-square analysis tests for statistically significant deviation in genetic experimental results.

Chi-Square Analysis

The **chi-square (χ^2) test** is the most common statistical method used in genetics experiments for comparing observed experimental outcomes to the results expected based on the probability hypothesis. Chi-square testing quantifies how closely an experimental observation matches the expected outcome by determining the probability of the observed outcome. The chi-square test is appropriate for this task when the experimental hypothesis used to predict the outcome depends on chance, as Mendelian ratios do. Thus, when a chi-square test is conducted, the test is measuring how well the experimental

observations match experimental predictions. The chi-square test has proven flexible and accurate in measuring the fit between observed and expected experimental results across a wide range of experiments.

The chi-square value for the analysis of a given experiment is obtained in two steps. First, the difference between the number observed and number expected in each outcome category is squared and divided by the number expected in the category; and second, the values obtained for each outcome class are summed. The χ^2 formula is

$$\chi^2 = \sum \frac{(O - E)^2}{E}$$

where O is the observed number of offspring in each outcome class, E is the number expected for each class, and the summation (Σ) is taken over all possible outcome classes.

The size of the chi-square value for an experiment is dependent on the three parameters of experimental sample size, number of outcome classes, and the number of observations in each outcome class, so it stands to reason that experiments with large numbers of outcome classes or more experimental observations recorded for each outcome class tend to have larger chi-square values than those found in experiments with lower numbers in each class. Simply stated, the addition of more or larger values to obtain a chi-square value leads to greater sums. Consequently, chi-square values are not directly comparable from one experiment to the next. Instead, each experimental chi-square value is interpreted in terms of the normal distribution of expected results for an experiment *of that size.*

The interpretation is done by means of a **probability value (P value),** which is a quantitative expression of the probability that the results of another experiment of the same size and structure will *deviate as much or more from expected results by chance.* P values in chi-square analysis are directly related to the probability of experimental outcomes in a normal distribution. High values for P (values close to 1) are associated with low χ^2 values. Low chi-square values occur when the observed and expected results are very similar. A high P value indicates that chance alone is likely to explain the deviations of experimental observations from expected values. Thus, an experiment producing a P value of 0.90 means that observed and expected results are close together and that 90% of all possible χ^2 values are equal to or greater than the value obtained in the experiment. On the other hand, low P values correspond to high chi-square values. They indicate substantial difference between observed and expected outcomes. The greater the difference between observed and expected results of an experiment, the greater the χ^2 value and the lower the P value.

The statistical interpretation of a chi-square value is obtained by identifying the P value for each experiment, and the P value is dependent on the number of

degrees of freedom (*df*) in the experiment being examined. For each experiment, the *df* value is most often equal to the number of outcome classes (*n*) minus 1, or (*n* − 1). In a statistical sense, *df* is equal to the number of independent variables in an experiment. For example, suppose we were conducting a chi-square test of 100 coin flips. There are two outcome classes, heads and tails, each of which we expect to see 50 times. However, once we record the number of events in one class, say 54 heads, the number of events in the second class becomes dependent on that first number. In our coin flip example, if we flip a coin 100 times and there are 54 heads recorded, the other 46 flips must be tails. Here the number of degrees of freedom is one because, while there are two possible outcomes, the value of one is always dependent on the value of the other.

Table 2.4 is a chi-square table, containing chi-square values for different degrees of freedom in the body of the table, along the left-hand margin of the table. The corresponding *P* values are listed along the top margin. To determine the *P* value for the chi-square value from an experiment, the first step is to determine the number of degrees of freedom. The second step is to locate the chi-square value on the line corresponding to the degrees of freedom. The *P* value for the result of the experiment in question is then found at the top of the column containing the chi-square value.

Interpretation of chi-square results is based on the corresponding *P* value. A statistically significant result from chi-square analysis is defined as one for which the *P* value is *less than 0.05*. This means that there is less than a 5% chance (<0.05) of obtaining the experimental observation by chance. By convention, when any experimental result has less than a 5% probability, the hypothesis of chance is *rejected*. In other words, if the *P* value is less than 0.05, the difference between the observed and expected results is considered statistically significant, and the experimental hypothesis is rejected. Conversely, *P* values greater than 0.05 indicate a nonsignificant deviation between observed and expected values. These values result in *failure to reject* the chance hypothesis.

Chi-Square Analysis of Mendel's Data

Modern statistical methods allow us to do something Mendel could not do—test his experimental data for its compatibility with the predictions of the laws of segregation and independent assortment. Table 2.1 contains data from Mendel for F_2 segregation of the seven traits he tested. In the first row of the table, we see that Mendel scored 7324 F_2 seeds for round or wrinkled phenotypes. Among these, he counted 5474 round and 1850 wrinkled. Based on the predictions of his segregation hypothesis, Mendel expected that 75% of the F_2 would be round and the remaining 25% wrinkled. That means he expected $(7324)(0.75) = 5493$ round seeds

Table 2.4	The Chi-Square Table									
	Probability (*P*) Value									
df	0.95	0.90	0.70	0.50	0.30	0.20	0.10	0.05	0.01	0.001
1	0.004	0.016	0.15	0.46	1.07	1.64	2.17	3.84	6.64	10.83
2	0.10	0.21	0.71	1.39	2.41	3.22	4.61	5.99	9.21	13.82
3	0.35	0.58	1.42	2.37	3.67	4.64	6.25	7.82	11.35	16.27
4	0.71	1.06	2.20	3.36	4.88	5.99	7.78	9.49	13.28	18.47
5	1.15	1.61	3.00	4.35	6.06	7.29	9.24	11.07	15.09	20.52
6	1.64	2.20	3.83	5.35	7.23	8.56	10.65	12.59	16.81	22.46
7	2.17	2.83	4.67	6.35	8.38	9.80	12.02	14.07	18.48	24.32
8	2.73	3.49	5.53	7.34	9.52	11.03	13.36	15.51	20.09	26.13
9	3.33	4.17	6.39	8.34	10.66	12.24	14.68	16.92	21.67	27.88
10	3.94	4.87	7.27	9.34	11.78	13.44	15.99	18.31	23.21	29.59
11	4.58	5.58	8.15	10.34	12.90	14.63	17.28	19.68	24.73	31.26
12	5.23	6.30	9.03	11.34	14.01	15.81	18.55	21.03	26.22	32.91
13	5.89	7.04	9.93	12.34	15.12	16.99	19.81	22.36	27.69	34.53
14	6.57	7.79	10.82	13.34	16.22	18.15	21.06	23.69	29.14	36.12
15	7.26	8.55	11.72	14.34	17.32	19.31	22.31	25.00	30.58	37.70

Fail to reject chance hypothesis	Reject chance hypothesis

Note: Chi-square values are in the body of the table, degrees of freedom are at the far-left side, and probability values are at the top of each column of chi-square values.

and $(7324)(0.25) = 1831$ wrinkled seeds. There is 1 degree of freedom in the experiment, and the chi-square is calculated as

$$\chi^2 = (5474 - 5493)^2/5493 + (1850 - 1831)^2/1831$$
$$= 0.066 + 0.197 = 0.263$$

For $df = 1$, the P value falls between 0.50 and 0.70 (see Table 2.4). This is well above the cutoff value of 0.05 and consequently represents a nonsignificant deviation between the observed outcome and the values expected for an experiment of this size. We fail to reject the hypothesis that chance is responsible for the observed outcome, and we can say, therefore, that Mendel's F_2 data for seed shape are consistent with the predictions of the law of segregation.

Figure 2.12 provides data Mendel collected on seed shape and seed color that we can use to test whether his results were consistent with his predictions of independent assortment. Based on the predicted $\frac{9}{16}:\frac{3}{16}:\frac{3}{16}:\frac{1}{16}$, or 9:3:3:1 ratio, the 556 F_2 produced by Mendel would be expected to have the following distribution, where $\frac{9}{16} = 0.5625$, $\frac{3}{16} = 0.1875$, and $\frac{1}{16} = 0.0625$.

Round, yellow	$(556)(0.5625) =$	312.75
Round, green	$(556)(0.1875) =$	104.25
Wrinkled, yellow	$(556)(0.1875) =$	104.25
Wrinkled, green	$(556)(0.0625) =$	34.75
		556.00

The chi-square value is calculated as

$$\chi^2 = (315 - 312.75)^2/312.75 + (108 - 104.25)^2/104.25$$
$$+ (101 - 104.25)^2/104.25 + (32 - 34.75)^2/34.75$$
$$= 0.016 + 0.135 + 0.101 + 0.218 = 0.470$$

In this case, $df = 3$, and the P value falls between 0.90 and 0.95. This indicates a nonsignificant deviation because the P value is above the 0.05 cutoff value. Mendel's F_2 data for seed color and seed shape are therefore also consistent with the predictions of independent assortment. A third example of chi-square analysis, using trihybrid-cross results from one of Mendel's experiments, is shown in Table 2.5. From statistical analysis of these data we conclude that Mendel's results are consistent with the predictions of segregation and independent assortment.

2.6 Autosomal Inheritance and Molecular Genetics Parallel the Predictions of Mendel's Hereditary Principles

During the first decade of the 20th century, immediately after the rediscovery of Mendel's rules of hereditary transmission, biologists began to extend Mendel's findings to species other than pea plants. They also identified

Table 2.5	Chi-Square Analysis of Mendel's Trihybrid-Cross Data	
Mendel's Observation[a]		**Number Expected**
Phenotype	**Number**	
Round, yellow, purple	269	269.58
Round, yellow, white	98	89.86
Round, green, purple	86	89.86
Round, green, white	27	29.95
Wrinkled, yellow, purple	88	89.86
Wrinkled, yellow, white	34	29.95
Wrinkled, green, purple	30	29.95
Wrinkled, green, white	7	9.98
Total	639	638.99

Chi-square calculation $[(O - E)^2/E]$
$$\chi^2 = (269 - 269.58)^2/269.58 + (98 - 89.86)^2/89.86$$
$$+ (86 - 89.86)^2/89.86 + (27 - 29.95)^2/29.95$$
$$+ (88 - 89.86)^2/89.86 + (34 - 29.95)^2/29.95$$
$$+ (30 - 29.95)^2/29.95 + (7 - 9.98)^2/9.98$$
$$= 2.67$$
$df = 7$
P value > 0.90

[a] Data are taken from Figure 2.14.

exceptions to Mendelian hereditary principles (Chapter 4). In this final section, we apply Mendelian principles to the transmission of certain traits in humans. In addition, we consider the correspondence of molecular genetics findings to Mendelian inheritance and explore the underlying causes of four of the traits that Mendel studied.

Autosomal inheritance refers to the transmission of genes that are carried on autosomes, the chromosomes (22 pairs in humans) that are not sex chromosomes (X and Y chromosomes). Autosomal pairs of chromosomes are found in both males and females. Because of the two copies of each autosome in our genome, we, like all diploid organisms, carry two copies (alleles) of each autosomal gene. The alleles on homologous chromosomes can be identical, in which case a person has a homozygous genotype; or the alleles can be different, producing a heterozygous genotype. Autosomal inheritance allows us to see Mendel's law of segregation and law of independent assortment in action. Autosomes are distinct from the sex chromosomes and autosomal inheritance follows different patterns than does the inheritance of genes on sex chromosomes (see Chapter 3).

Pedigrees, or family trees, are a kind of symbolic shorthand used to trace the inheritance of traits in humans and in animals such as horses, dogs, cats, cattle, and others. In standard pedigree notation, males are represented by squares and females by circles (Figure 2.18). A filled circle or square indicates that the phenotype of interest is present. A line through a symbol indicates the person is

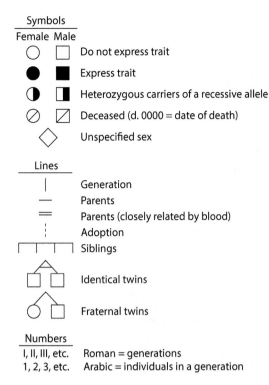

Symbols
Female Male
○ □ Do not express trait
● ■ Express trait
◐ ◨ Heterozygous carriers of a recessive allele
⊘ ◿ Deceased (d. 0000 = date of death)
◇ Unspecified sex

Lines
| Generation
— Parents
= Parents (closely related by blood)
⋮ Adoption
⌐⊤⌐ Siblings
△ Identical twins
○○ Fraternal twins

Numbers
I, II, III, etc.   Roman = generations
1, 2, 3, etc.   Arabic = individuals in a generation

Figure 2.18 Common pedigree symbols.

deceased. Parents are connected to each other by a horizontal line from which a vertical line descends to their progeny. Individuals in a pedigree are numbered by a Roman numeral (I, II, III, etc.) to indicate their generation combined with an Arabic numeral (1, 2, 3, etc.) that identifies each organism in a generation. Identifying an individual by a Roman numeral followed by an Arabic numeral, as in I-2 or III-6, is an efficient way to ensure clarity in referring to particular organisms and, in the case of humans, allows protection of privacy by not requiring the use of names.

Autosomal Dominant Inheritance

The pedigree in **Figure 2.19** shows characteristics commonly observed for **autosomal dominant inheritance** of a disease. Notice the following six characteristics:

1. **Each individual who has the disease has at least one affected parent.** Anyone carrying at least one

copy of a dominant allele will display the dominant phenotype. Therefore, any disease or disorder caused by a dominant allele is seen in successive generations (this characteristic is described as a vertical pattern of transmission). In Figure 2.19, all 13 affected children in generations II, III, and IV have at least one affected parent. The only exceptions to this general rule are (1) the occurrence of a new mutation in a child and (2) a person with the dominant mutation entering the family through marriage. The pedigree shows no evidence of a new mutation, but individual III-16 marries into the family and has the dominant mutation.

2. **Males and females are affected in equal numbers.** Mutations carried on an autosome are equally likely to occur in either sex. Among the total of 15 affected individuals in the figure, 7 are male and 8 are female.

3. **Either sex can transmit the disease allele.** Seven parents in Figure 2.19 with the mutant phenotype have transmitted the disease to one or more children. Three of the transmitting parents are male and four are female.

4. **In crosses in which one parent is affected and the other is not, approximately half the offspring express the disease.** Diseases caused by dominant mutations are usually rare in populations, and most affected individuals are heterozygous. A cross between one affected parent and one unaffected parent can most often be genetically interpreted as a heterozygous-by-homozygous cross, expected to produce a 1:1 ratio between phenotypes. In this family, there are six crosses between an affected person who is heterozygous and an unaffected person who is homozygous for the recessive allele. Among the 19 children produced by these crosses, 9 of the children are affected and 10 are unaffected. The children of the cross between III-14 and III-15 are excluded from this count because both parents have the dominant mutant phenotype.

5. **Two unaffected parents will not have any children with the disease.** Dominant phenotypes require the presence of at least one copy of the dominant allele. If each parent has the recessive ("normal") phenotype, they must each be homozygous for the

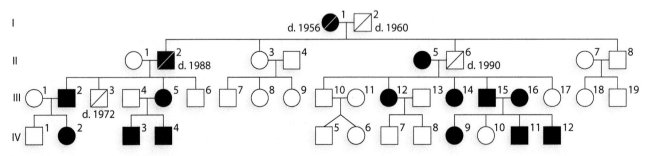

Figure 2.19 Autosomal dominant inheritance.

recessive allele, and all their offspring should also be homozygous. Three crosses of this kind are shown in the pedigree, and all seven resulting children have the normal phenotype. New mutation is an exception to this rule, but it is not seen in this family.

6. **Two affected parents may produce unaffected children.**   If each parent is heterozygous, the expected ratio between affected and unaffected children is 3:1. The mating between III-15 and III-16 produces four children of whom three are affected. The mating of two heterozygous affected parents presents a one-in-four chance of producing a child homozygous for the mutant allele and a one-in-four chance of producing a child homozygous for the recessive allele. The homozygous recessive child (IV-10) is unaffected.

Autosomal Recessive Inheritance

Figure 2.20 shows a human pedigree displaying the characteristics commonly observed for **autosomal recessive inheritance** of a disease. There are six key features to notice:

1. **Individuals who have the disease are often born to parents who do not.**   A child with the disease (the recessive phenotype) must have inherited one copy of the recessive allele from each parent. Moreover, it is common for children with the disease to have been produced by parents with the dominant (normal) phenotype who are heterozygous. Four affected family members, IV-5, IV-6, IV-10, and V-3, are the children of heterozygous carrier parents. That is, III-2 and III-3 are heterozygous carriers, as are III-4 and III-5 and IV-1 and IV-2.

2. **If only one parent has the disorder, the risk that a child has the disorder depends on the genotype of the other parent.**   The affected parent is homozygous recessive and must pass a copy of the recessive allele to each child. If the unaffected parent is heterozygous, the risk that a given child will be affected is $\frac{1}{2}$. If the unaffected parent is homozygous for the dominant allele, all children will be unaffected heterozygotes.

3. **If both parents have the disorder, all children will have the disorder.**   If both parents are homozygous recessive, all their offspring will have the same homozygous genotype. The four affected siblings in the last generation of the idealized pedigree inherit their disorder in this way.

4. **The sex ratio of affected offspring is expected to be equal.**   Males and females are equally likely to be homozygous for the recessive allele. The sex of a child is independent of the likelihood that the homozygous recessive genotype occurs at the autosomal gene. In the example pedigree there are a total of eight affected individuals—four males and four females.

5. **The disease is usually not seen in each generation; but if an affected child is produced by unaffected parents, the risk to subsequent children of the couple is $\frac{1}{4}$.**   If both parents have the dominant phenotype, they can produce a child with the recessive phenotype only if they are each heterozygous. This is usually rare in a population, so production of affected children is rare. If an affected child is born to a healthy couple, however, each parent is a heterozygous carrier of the recessive disease allele, and the disease risk to each additional child is $\frac{1}{4}$. In the example pedigree, the recessive condition is confined to the fourth and fifth generations.

6. **If the disease or disorder is rare in the population, unaffected parents of an affected child are more likely to be related to one another.**   Individuals who are related to one another can carry identical alleles as a result of their shared ancestry. If the recessive allele is present in the family, the sharing of alleles through common ancestry increases the probability that related individuals might both be carriers of the recessive allele in comparison to the population at large. In Figure 2.20, the two affected parents of the four affected siblings are related to one another. When a disease is rare, the assumption is that a person who married into the family does not carry the disease allele (i.e., is homozygous dominant) unless there is contradicting evidence from the pedigree (i.e., one of the offspring has the recessive phenotype).

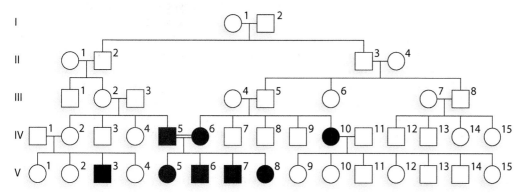

Figure 2.20   **Autosomal recessive inheritance.**

Molecular Genetics of Mendel's Traits

The discovery of the basis of Mendel's traits continues to the present day using methods of molecular genetics to identify the genes responsible for the phenotypic variation Mendel studied. These molecular analyses, the first of which was published in 1990, describe the nucleic acid (DNA and RNA) variation and the polypeptide (protein and enzyme) variation responsible for Mendel's traits. A cornerstone of modern genetics is the seamless integration of the principles of transmission genetics with those of molecular genetic analysis, and the molecular genetic analysis of Mendel's traits reveals that the molecular genetic and the transmission genetic analyses are—two sides of the same coin. The pattern of transmission of morphologic variants is traceable through examination of the hereditary molecules DNA, RNA, and protein.

Identifying these genes and determining how molecular variation in them produces morphologic variation in pea plants requires the demonstration that (1) allelic variation coincides with morphologic variation, (2) DNA variation in the alleles produces different protein products, (3) the protein products from each allele have different structures that lead to different functional capabilities, and (4) the functional differences between the protein products of different alleles account for the observed morphological variation in pea plants. The molecular differences between the alleles also usually clarify why the alleles are dominant or recessive relative to one another.

Mendel did not leave any neatly labeled packets of seeds for later researchers to analyze, so the process of pinpointing the exact traits he examined and the genes and proteins responsible for them has been complicated. Table 2.6 identifies the researchers and the genes responsible for four of Mendel's seven traits. For each gene, the wild-type DNA, RNA, and protein sequences have been identified, and the specific mutations producing the mutant alleles have been determined. In each case, the mutations significantly reduce or entirely eliminate production or function of the wild-type polypeptide, thus each of the mutations is recessive. These mutations are discussed briefly here, and in further detail in Experimental Insight 12.1 and in Experimental Insight 13.2.

Seed Shape (Round and Wrinkled, Gene *Sbe1*) In 1990, research published by Madan Bhattacharyya and colleagues described the identification and molecular analysis of a gene responsible for round and wrinkled seed shape. The *Sbe1* gene produces the starch-branching enzyme that helps convert a linear form of starch called amylose into a complex branched form of starch called amylopectin. As a consequence of the action of fully functional starch-branching enzyme, round seeds have a much higher percentage of amylopectin and a much lower percentage of amylose than do wrinkled seeds, which do not have functional starch-branching enzyme. Amylose readily loses sugar molecules, and in developing wrinkled seeds, the high concentration of free sugar leads the seeds to excessive water uptake that swells the developing seeds. As seeds mature they naturally dehydrate. The maturing wrinkled seeds lose much more water than do maturing round seeds, resulting in a partial collapse of the wrinkled seed membranes that does not occur in round seeds. See Experimental Insight 13.2 for more details.

Stem Length (Tall and Short, Gene *Le*) In 1997, two research groups, one led by David Martin and the other by Diane Lester, determined that a gene called *Le* produces the variation in stem length that Mendel saw as tall and short plants by controlling growth of the main stem of the plant. This *Le* gene produces giberellin 3β-hydroxylase, an enzyme that catalyzes one step of the multistep biochemical pathway synthesizing the plant growth hormone giberellin. Wild-type plants are able to produce giberellin and can grow tall, but a base substitution mutation in the mutant allele results in a very low level of giberellin and poor growth. See Experimental Insight 13.2 for more details.

Seed Color (Yellow and Green, Gene *Sgr*) Two studies published in 2007, one by Ian Armstead and colleagues and the other by Sylvain Aubry and colleagues, identified the *Sgr* gene, known as "stay-green," that produces mutant green seeds rather than wild-type yellow seeds in plants that are homozygous for a mutation of the gene. In this case, the polypeptide product of *Sgr* is an enzyme that catalyzes a step in the breakdown of chlorophyll, a green-colored compound. Chlorophyll breakdown normally occurs as seeds mature, and results in the yellow color of wild-type seeds. A mutation prevents production of a functional enzyme, and the absence of its activity in the chlorophyll-breakdown pathway results in the retention of green color in mutant seeds. See Experimental Insight 12.1 for more details.

Flower Color (Purple and White, Gene *bHLH*) In 2010, the gene responsible for the white-flower mutation in Mendel's pea plants was identified. A research group led by Roger Hellens determined that mutation of the *bHLH* gene in pea plants produces mutant white flowers rather than wild-type purple flowers. The protein product of *bHLH* is a transcription factor protein that interacts with other proteins to activate the transcription of certain genes. In this case, the genes targeted for transcription activation are active in the pathway that normally produces the purple-colored plant pigment anthocyanin. Wild-type plants produce enough of the gene product (the transcription factor protein) to activate transcription of anthocyanin-producing genes. Plants that are homozygous for mutations of this gene, however, are unable to activate transcription of the pigment-producing genes. These plants lack the purple anthocyanin pigment, and so their flowers are white. See Experimental Insight 12.1 for more details.

Table 2.6 Identification and Molecular Characterization of Four of Mendel's Traits

Trait	Gene and Gene Product	Wild-Type Allele and Function	Mutant Allele and Function	Reference
Seed shape (round and wrinkled seeds)	The gene is *Sbe1*, producing starch-branching enzyme.	The dominant wild-type allele (*R*) produces starch-branching enzyme that converts amylase, a linear starch, into amylopectin, a complex branched starch.	The recessive mutant allele (*r*) contains an inserted segment about 800 base pairs in length. The transcript of the mutant allele does not produce an enzyme product, resulting in a loss of function.	Bhattacharyya, M. K., et al. 1990. *Cell* 60: 115–122.
Stem length (tall and short plants)	The gene is *Le*, producing gibberellin 3β-hydroxylase (G3βH).	G3βH produced by the dominant allele *Le* converts a precursor in the synthesis of the plant growth hormone gibberellin that causes plants to grow tall.	The recessive mutant *le* allele contains a base substitution that results in an amino acid change. The mutant G3βH has less than 5% the activity of the wild-type product and produces little gibberellin, leading to short plants.	Lester, D. R., et al. 1997. *Plant Cell* 9: 1435–1443. Martin, D. N., et al. 1997. *Proc. Natl. Acad. Sci., USA* 94: 8907–8911.
Seed color (yellow seed and green seed)	The gene was originally named *I* gene and was later renamed *Sgr* (called "stay green"). The gene produces an enzyme that helps break down chlorophyll.	The dominant wild-type allele (*I*) produces an enzyme that catalyzes one step in the chlorophyll breakdown pathway, which turns wild-type seeds yellow as they mature.	The recessive mutant allele (*i*) contains two base substitutions and a base pair insertion. The resulting mutant polypeptide has no function, leading to a blockage of the chlorophyll breakdown pathway and causing mutant seeds to retain their immature green color.	Armstead, I., et al. 2007. *Science* 315: 73. Aubry, S., et al. 2008. *Plant Mol. Biol.* 67: 243–256.
Flower color (purple flower and white flower)	Originally named gene *A* and renamed *bHLH*, the gene produces a protein that activates transcription of target genes.	The dominant wild-type allele (*A*) produces a protein that activates transcription of genes required to synthesize the purple-colored plant pigment called anthocyanin.	The recessive mutant allele (*a*) contains a base substitution that results in production of abnormal mRNA. The mutant mRNA does not produce the transcription-activating protein, thus blocking anthocyanin production and resulting in the development of white flowers.	Hellens, R. P., et al. 2010. *PLoS One* 5: 1–8.

Note: For a comprehensive review, see Reid, J. B., and J. J. Ross. 2011. *Genetics* 189: 3–10.

A common feature of each of the genes controlling Mendel's traits is that the wild-type alleles are dominant to mutant alleles that are recessive. This is a consequence of the loss of function on the part of the mutant alleles. For each gene, one or two copies of the wild-type allele results in the wild-type phenotype, whereas the mutant phenotype is produced in plants that are homozygous for the mutant allele. We discuss the relationship between alleles and explore other kinds of dominance relationships in Section 4.1.

In broader terms, the conclusions from molecular studies identifying genes Mendel examined in his crosses are that (1) the inheritance of allelic variants precisely parallels the pattern of transmission of morphological variation and (2) morphological variation in pea plants results from differences in the structure and function of the proteins produced by the alleles. Molecular genetic analysis has led to (3) identification of the DNA-sequence differences between alleles, determination of the impact of those differences on mRNA, and description of the alteration of protein structures resulting from each mRNA; and (4) functional analysis of the protein product of each allele to describe the role it plays in producing the phenotype.

CASE STUDY

Inheritance of Sickle Cell Disease in Humans

The Online Mendelian Index of Man (OMIM) is a continuously updated public information catalog providing up-to-date information on more than 18,000 human hereditary traits. OMIM can be accessed at www.ncbi.nlm.nih.gov/omim. Each trait listed in the OMIM catalog has a unique identifier number. One trait, named sickle cell disease (SCD), OMIM number 603903, is the subject of a later discussion (see Chapter 10) that introduces several important research techniques and uses them to describe the discovery and analysis of the molecular basis of SCD and the evolution of the mutant allele. Here we examine the hereditary transmission of SCD, which is caused by a base substitution mutation in the β-globin gene. The base substitution alters the β-globin protein and results in the inheritance of SCD as an autosomal recessive condition. The inheritance of the β^S variant and SCD can be traced by identifying the phenotypes of family members and displaying them in a pedigree, or family tree.

PEDIGREE ANALYSIS The pedigrees shown in **Figure 2.21** identify females with circles and males with squares, and are typical of a family in which SCD is inherited. Blue circles and squares indicate family members who do not have the trait being traced; a pink circle or square indicates a person with the trait (in this case, SCD). In **Figure 2.21a**, the father and mother are identified as I-1 and I-2. Their daughter II-4 is affected by SCD, as indicated by a pink circle. Her siblings, individuals II-1, II-2, and II-3, are healthy.

The pedigree in Figure 2.21a identifies the genotype for the β-globin gene in each member of a certain family. Each person carries two copies of the gene. Note that person II-1 is homozygous for β^A, the wild-type allele. Alternatively, siblings II-2 and II-3 and the parents in the pedigree, I-1 and I-2, are heterozygous and carry alleles β^A and the mutant allele β^S.

The child II-4 is homozygous for β^S and has SCD. This disorder is a recessive trait because the phenotype is displayed only in a person who is homozygous for the allele that produces it. In contrast, the dominant, wild-type phenotype is produced by the presence of either one or two copies of β^A. In this family, each parent has the dominant, wild-type phenotype, but the appearance of a child with the recessive trait means that each parent must be a heterozygous carrier of a recessive allele.

PUNNETT SQUARE ANALYSIS Figure 2.21b illustrates the idealized transmission of alleles from heterozygous parents to offspring in generation II using a Punnett square. Each of the two alleles carried by a heterozygote has a chance of being transmitted to an offspring. Chance dictates that four different combinations of alleles can be transmitted from these parents

(a)

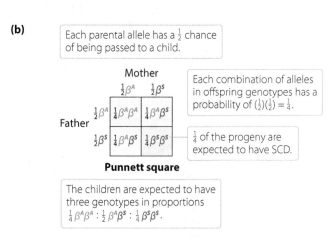

The offspring of two heterozygous carrier parents are expected to be $\frac{3}{4}$ dominant and $\frac{1}{4}$ recessive.

(b)

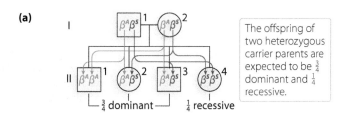

Each parental allele has a $\frac{1}{2}$ chance of being passed to a child.

Each combination of alleles in offspring genotypes has a probability of $(\frac{1}{2})(\frac{1}{2}) = \frac{1}{4}$.

$\frac{1}{4}$ of the progeny are expected to have SCD.

The children are expected to have three genotypes in proportions $\frac{1}{4}\beta^A\beta^A : \frac{1}{2}\beta^A\beta^S : \frac{1}{4}\beta^S\beta^S$.

Figure 2.21 Hereditary transmission of sickle cell disease. **(a)** Each parent passes one allele to each child. **(b)** Three genotypes are expected to occur among the children in the proportions shown.

to their children. The arrows in the figure indicate the parental origin of alleles in the homozygous and heterozygous children of this couple. Notice that three of the four children have the dominant phenotype, being either homozygous for the dominant allele ($\beta^A\beta^A$) or heterozygous ($\beta^A\beta^S$), and that one of the four children has the homozygous $\beta^S\beta^S$ genotype and therefore suffers from SCD.

The ratio of $\frac{3}{4}$ dominant to $\frac{1}{4}$ recessive is the 3:1 ratio of phenotypes that, as we saw repeatedly in this chapter, is the expected statistical outcome of crosses between two heterozygous organisms. Each allele transmitted from a heterozygote has a $\frac{1}{2}$ chance of being passed to a child. Any one of the four combinations of alleles transmitted to a child is expected to occur with a frequency of $(\frac{1}{2})(\frac{1}{2}) = \frac{1}{4}$; thus, the frequency of children with SCD produced by heterozygous carrier parents is $\frac{1}{4}$. The three genotypes in the children are expected to occur in the ratio $\frac{1}{4}\beta^A\beta^A : \frac{1}{2}\beta^A\beta^S : \frac{1}{4}\beta^S\beta^S$. These genotypes can be distinctly identified using DNA- and protein-based analysis. (We describe these molecular techniques and explore other details of SCD in Chapter 10.)

2.1 Gregor Mendel Discovered the Basic Principles of Genetic Transmission

▪ A broad education in science and mathematics prepared Gregor Mendel to design hybridization experiments that could reveal the principles of hereditary transmission.

2.2 Monohybrid Crosses Reveal the Segregation of Alleles

▪ Mendel's experimental design had five important features: controlled crosses, use of pure-breeding parental strains, examination of discreet traits, quantification of results, and the use of replicate and reciprocal crosses.

▪ Crosses between pure-breeding parental plants with different phenotypes produce monohybrid F_1 progeny with the dominant phenotype.

▪ Monohybrid crosses produce a 3:1 ratio of the dominant to the recessive phenotype among F_2 progeny and demonstrate the operation of the law of segregation.

▪ The law of segregation states that two alleles at a gene will separate from one another during gamete formation, each allele has an equal probability of inclusion in a gamete, and gametes unite at random during reproduction.

▪ Mendel used test-cross analysis to demonstrate that F_1 plants are monohybrid, and he used the self-fertilization of F_2 plants with the dominant phenotype to demonstrate that the latter have a 2:1 ratio of heterozygotes to homozygotes.

2.3 Dihybrid and Trihybrid Crosses Reveal the Independent Assortment of Alleles

▪ The F_2 progeny of dihybrid F_1 plants display a 9:3:3:1 phenotype ratio that demonstrates the operation of the law of independent assortment.

▪ Mendel used trihybrid-cross analysis to demonstrate that alleles of multiple genes are transmitted in accordance with the predictions of the law of independent assortment.

2.4 Probability Theory Predicts Mendelian Ratios

▪ The product rule of probability is used to determine the likelihood of two or more independent events occurring simultaneously or consecutively. The joint probability is determined by multiplying the probabilities of the independent events.

▪ The sum rule of probability is applied when two or more outcomes are possible. The individual probabilities of the outcomes are added together to determine the joint probability.

▪ Conditional probability is the probability of outcomes that are contingent on particular conditions.

▪ Binomial probability theory describes the distribution of outcomes of an experiment in terms of the number of outcome classes and the frequency of each class. Pascal's triangle is a convenient tool for determining the distribution of binomial outcomes.

2.5 Chi-Square Analysis Tests the Fit between Observed Values and Expected Outcomes

▪ The chi-square test (χ^2) compares observed results with the results predicted by a genetic hypothesis that is based on chance.

▪ The result of the chi-square test determines how closely predictions match results.

▪ The significance of a chi-square value is determined by the P (probability) value corresponding to the number of degrees of freedom in the experiment.

2.6 Autosomal Inheritance and Molecular Genetics Parallel the Predictions of Mendel's Hereditary Principles

▪ Traits transmitted by autosomal inheritance are equally likely in males and females.

▪ Autosomal dominant inheritance produces a vertical pattern of transmission in which each organism with the dominant trait has at least one parent with the trait.

▪ Traits transmitted in an autosomal recessive pattern are usually distributed in a horizontal pattern in which offspring with the recessive trait frequently descend from parents that are heterozygous and have the dominant phenotype.

▪ Molecular analysis of four of Mendel's traits illustrates how transmission genetic analysis and molecular genetic analysis characterize the same hereditary processes at different levels.

KEYWORDS

artificial cross-fertilization *(p. 29)*
autosomal dominant inheritance *(p. 52)*
autosomal inheritance *(p. 51)*
autosomal recessive inheritance *(p. 53)*
binomial probability *(p. 46)*

blending theory *(p. 28)*
chi-square test (χ^2 test) *(p. 49)*
conditional probability *(p. 45)*
controlled genetic cross *(p. 30)*
degrees of freedom (*df*) *(p. 50)*

dihybrid cross *(p. 36)*
dominant phenotype *(p. 31)*
F_1, F_2, F_3 generation *(p. 30)*
forked-line diagram *(p. 38)*
gamete *(p. 33)*

genotypic ratio *(p. 33)*

heterozygous genotype (heterozygote)
    (p. 33)

homozygous genotype (homozygote)
    (p. 33)

law of independent assortment (Mendel's
    second law) *(p. 38)*

law of segregation (Mendel's first law)
    (p. 34)

mean (μ) *(p. 48)*

monohybrid cross *(p. 33)*

normal (Gaussian) distribution *(p. 48)*

parental generation (P generation)
    (p. 30)

particulate inheritance *(p. 33)*

Pascal's triangle *(p. 47)*

pedigree *(p. 51)*

phenotypic ratio *(p. 33)*

product rule (multiplication rule) *(p. 44)*

Punnett square *(p. 33)*

pure-breeding (true-breeding) *(p. 30)*

P value (probability value) *(p. 49)*

recessive phenotype *(p. 31)*

reciprocal cross *(p. 31)*

replicate cross *(p. 30)*

standard deviation (σ) *(p. 49)*

sum rule (addition rule) *(p. 45)*

test cross (test-cross analysis) *(p. 31)*

transmission genetics *(p. 26)*

trihybrid cross *(p. 41)*

PROBLEMS

(MasteringGenetics™) **Visit for instructor-assigned tutorials and problems.**

Chapter Concepts

1. Compare and contrast the following terms:
   a. dominant and recessive
   b. genotype and phenotype
   c. homozygous and heterozygous
   d. monohybrid cross and test cross
   e. dihybrid cross and trihybrid cross

2. For the cross $BB \times Bb$, what is the expected genotype ratio? What is the expected phenotype ratio?

3. For the cross $Aabb \times aaBb$, what is the expected genotype ratio? What is the expected phenotype ratio?

4. In mice, black coat color is dominant to white coat color. In the pedigree below, mice with a black coat are represented by darkened symbols, and those with white coats are shown as open symbols. Using allele symbols B and b, determine the genotypes for each mouse.

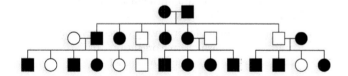

5. Two parents plan to have three children. What is the probability that the children will be two girls and one boy?

6. Consider the cross $AaBbCC \times AABbCc$.
   a. How many different gamete genotypes can each organism produce?
   b. Use a Punnett square to predict the expected ratio of offspring phenotypes.
   c. Use the forked-line method to predict the expected ratio of offspring phenotypes.

7. If a chi-square test produces a chi-square value of 7.83 with 4 degrees of freedom,
   a. in what interval range does the P value fall?
   b. is the result sufficient to reject the chance hypothesis?
   c. above what chi-square value would you reject the chance hypothesis for an experiment with 7 degrees of freedom?

For answers to selected even-numbered problems, see Appendix: Answers.

8. Determine whether the statements below are true or false. If a statement is false, provide the correct information or revise the statement to make it correct.
   a. If a dihybrid cross is performed, the expected genotypic ratio is 9:3:3:1.
   b. A student uses the product rule to predict that the probability of flipping a coin twice and getting a head and then a tail is $\frac{1}{4}$.
   c. A test cross between a heterozygous parent and a homozygous recessive parent is expected to produce a 1:1 genotypic and phenotypic ratio.
   d. The outcome of a trihybrid cross is predicted by the law of segregation.
   e. Reciprocal crosses that produce identical results demonstrate that a strain is pure-breeding.
   f. If a woman is heterozygous for albinism, an autosomal recessive condition that results in the absence of skin pigment, the proportion of her gametes carrying the allele that allows pigment expression is expected to be 75%.
   g. The progeny of a trihybrid cross are expected to have one of 27 different genotypes.
   h. If a dihybrid F_1 plant is self-fertilized,
      (1) $\frac{9}{16}$ of the progeny will have the same phenotype as the F_1 parent.
      (2) $\frac{1}{16}$ of the progeny will be true-breeding.
      (3) $\frac{1}{2}$ of the progeny will be heterozygous at one or both loci.

9. In the datura plant, purple flower color is controlled by a dominant allele P. White flowers are found in plants homozygous for the recessive allele p. Suppose that a purple-flowered datura plant with an unknown genotype is self-fertilized and that its progeny are 28 purple-flowered plants and 10 white-flowered plants.
   a. Use the results of the self-fertilization to determine the genotype of the original purple-flowered plant.
   b. If one of the purple-flowered progeny plants is selected at random and self-fertilized, what is the probability it will breed true?

10. The dorsal pigment pattern of frogs can be either "leopard" (white pigment between dark spots) or "mottled" (pigment between spots appears mottled). The trait is controlled by an autosomal gene. Males and females are selected from pure-breeding populations, and a pair of reciprocal crosses is performed. The cross results are shown below.

    Cross 1:   P: Male leopard × female mottled

    F_1: All mottled

    F_2: 70 mottled, 22 leopard

    Cross 2:   P: Male mottled × female leopard

    F_1: All mottled

    F_2: 50 mottled, 18 leopard

    a. Which of the phenotypes is dominant? Explain your answer.
    b. Compare and contrast the results of the reciprocal crosses in the context of autosomal gene inheritance.
    c. In the F_2 progeny from both crosses, what proportion is expected to be homozygous? What proportion is expected to be heterozygous?
    d. Propose two different genetic crosses that would allow you to determine the genotype of one mottled frog from the F_2 generation.

11. Black skin color is dominant to pink skin color in pigs. Two heterozygous black pigs are crossed.

    a. What is the probability that their offspring will have pink skin?
    b. What is the probability that the first and second offspring will have black skin?
    c. If these pigs produce a total of three piglets, what is the probability that two will be pink and one will be black?

12. A male mouse with brown fur color is mated to two different female mice with black fur. Black female 1 produces a litter of 9 black and 7 brown pups. Black female 2 produces 14 black pups.

    a. What is the mode of inheritance of black and brown fur color in mice?
    b. Choose symbols for each allele, and identify the genotypes of the brown male and the two black females.

13. Figure 2.13 shows the results of Mendel's test-cross analysis of independent assortment. In this experiment, he first crossed pure-breeding round, yellow plants to pure-breeding wrinkled, green plants. The round yellow F_1 are crossed to pure-breeding wrinkled, green plants. Use chi-square analysis to show that Mendel's results do not differ significantly from those expected.

14. An experienced goldfish breeder receives two unusual male goldfish. One is black rather than gold, and the other has a single tail fin rather than a split tail fin. The breeder crosses the black male to a female that is gold. All the F_1 are gold. She also crosses the single-finned male to a female with a split tail fin. All the F_1 have a split tail fin. She then crosses the black male to F_1 gold females and, separately, crosses the single-finned male to F_1 split-finned females. The results of the crosses are shown below.

    Black male × F_1 gold female:

Gold	32
Black	34

    Single-finned male × F_1 split-finned female:

Split fin	41
Single fin	39

    a. What do the results of these crosses suggest about the inheritance of color and tail fin shape in goldfish?
    b. Is black color dominant or recessive? Explain. Is single tail dominant or recessive? Explain.
    c. Use chi-square analysis to test your hereditary hypothesis for each trait.

15. The pedigree below shows the transmission of albinism (absence of skin pigment) in a human family.

    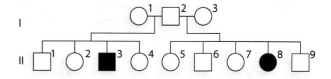

    a. What is the most likely mode of transmission of albinism in this family?
    b. Using allelic symbols of your choice, identify the genotypes of the male and his two mates in generation I.
    c. The female I-1 and her mate, male I-2, had four children, one of whom has albinism. What is the probability that they could have had a total of four children with *any other outcome* except one child with albinism and three with normal pigmentation?
    d. What is the probability that female I-3 is a heterozygous carrier of the allele for albinism?
    e. One child of female I-3 has albinism. What is the probability that any of the other four children are carriers of the allele for albinism?

16. A geneticist crosses a pure-breeding strain of peas producing yellow, wrinkled seeds with one that is pure-breeding for green, round seeds.

    a. Use a Punnett square to predict the F_2 progeny that would be expected if the F_1 are allowed to self-fertilize.
    b. What proportion of the F_2 progeny are expected to have yellow seeds? Wrinkled seeds? Green seeds? Round seeds?
    c. What is the expected phenotype distribution among the F_2 progeny?

17. Suppose an F_1 plant from Problem 16 is crossed to the pure-breeding green, round parental strain. Use a forked-line diagram to predict the phenotypic distribution of the resulting progeny.

18. In pea plants, the appearance of flowers along the main stem is a dominant phenotype called "axial" and is controlled by an allele T. The recessive phenotype, produced by an allele t, has flowers only at the end of the stem and is called "terminal." Pod form displays a dominant phenotype "inflated," controlled by an allele C, and a recessive

"constricted" form, produced by the *c* allele. A cross is made between a pure-breeding axial, constricted plant and a plant that is pure-breeding terminal, inflated.

a. The F_1 progeny of this cross are allowed to self-fertilize. What is the expected phenotypic distribution among the F_2 progeny?

b. Suppose that all of the F_2 progeny with terminal flowers, i.e., plants with terminal flowers and inflated pods and plants with terminal flowers and constricted pods, are saved and allowed to self-fertilize to produce a partial F_3 generation. What is the expected phenotypic distribution among these F_3 plants?

Application and Integration

20. Experimental Insight 2.1 describes data on the kernel color distribution of bicolor corn, collected by a genetics class like yours. To test the hypothesis that the kernel color of bicolor corn is the result of the segregation of two alleles at a single genetic locus, the class counted 12,356 kernels and found that 9304 were yellow and 3052 were white. Use chi-square analysis to evaluate the fit between the segregation hypothesis and the class results.

21. The pedigree below shows the transmission of a phenotypic character.

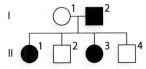

Using *B* to represent a dominant allele and *b* to represent a recessive allele,

a. give the genotype(s) possible for each member of the family, assuming the trait is autosomal dominant.

b. give the genotype(s) possible for each member of the family, assuming the trait is autosomal recessive.

22. The seeds in bush bean pods are each the product of an independent fertilization event. Green seed color is dominant to white seed color in bush beans. If a heterozygous plant with green seeds self-fertilizes, what is the probability that 6 seeds in a single pod of the progeny plant will consist of

a. 3 green and 3 white seeds?

b. all green seeds?

c. at least 1 white seed?

23. List all the different gametes that are possible from the following genotypes.

a. *AABbCcDd*

b. *AabbCcDD*

c. *AaBbCcDd*

d. *AabbCCdd*

24. Organisms with the genotypes *AABbCcDd* and *AaBbCcDd* are crossed. What are the expected proportions of the following progeny?

a. *A–B–C–D–*

b. *AabbCcDd*

c. a phenotype identical to either parent

d. *A–B–ccdd*

c. If an F_1 plant from the initial cross described above is crossed to a plant that is terminal, constricted, what is the expected distribution among the resulting progeny?

d. If the plants with terminal flowers produced by the cross in part (c) are saved and allowed to self-fertilize, what is the expected phenotypic distribution among the progeny?

19. If two six-sided dice are rolled, what is the probability that the total number of spots showing is

a. 4?

b. 7?

c. greater than 5?

d. an odd number?

For answers to selected even-numbered problems, see Appendix: Answers.

25. In humans, the ability to bend the thumb back beyond vertical is called hitchhiker's thumb and is recessive to the inability to do so (OMIM 274200). Also, the presence of attached earlobes is recessive to unattached earlobes (OMIM 128900). In the pedigree shown, the left half of the circle or square is filled if the person has the dominant non-hitchhiker's thumb and empty if hitchhiker's thumb is present. The right half of the symbol is filled if the person has unattached earlobes and is empty if earlobes are attached. Use allelic symbols *H* and *h* for the thumb and *E* and *e* for earlobes, and identify the genotypes for each family member.

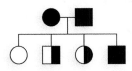

26. In the fruit fly *Drosophila*, a rudimentary wing called "vestigial" and dark body color called "ebony" are inherited at independently assorting genes and are recessive to their dominant wild-type counterparts, full wing and gray body color. Dihybrid wild-type males and females are crossed, and 3200 progeny are produced. How many progeny flies are expected to be found in each phenotypic class?

27. In pea plants, plant height, seed shape, and seed color are governed by three independently assorting genes. The three genes have dominant and recessive alleles, with tall (*T*) dominant to short (*t*), round (*R*) dominant to wrinkled (*r*), and yellow (*G*) dominant to green (*g*).

a. If a true-breeding tall, wrinkled, yellow plant is crossed to a true-breeding short, round, green plant, what phenotypic ratios are expected in the F_1 and F_2?

b. What proportion of the F_2 are expected to be tall, wrinkled, yellow? *ttRRGg*?

c. What proportion of the F_2 that produce round, green seeds (regardless of the height of the plant) are expected to breed true?

28. A variety of pea plant called Blue Persian produces a tall plant with blue seeds. A second variety of pea plant called Spanish Dwarf produces a short plant with white seed. The two varieties are crossed, and the resulting seeds are collected. All of the seeds are white; and when planted, they produce all tall plants. These tall F_1 plants are allowed

to self-fertilize. The results for seed color and plant stature in the F$_2$ generation are as follows:

F$_2$ Plant Phenotype	Number
Blue seed, tall plant	97
White seed, tall plant	270
Blue seed, short plant	33
White seed, short plant	100
TOTAL	500

a. Which phenotypes are dominant, and which are recessive? Why?
b. What is the expected distribution of phenotypes in the F$_2$ generation?
c. State the hypothesis being tested in this experiment.
d. Examine the data in the table by the chi-square test, and determine whether they conform to expectations of the hypothesis.

29. In tomato plants, the production of red fruit color is under the control of an allele *R*. Yellow tomatoes are *rr*. The dominant phenotype for fruit shape is under the control of an allele *T*, which produces two lobes. Multilobed fruit, the recessive phenotype, have the genotype *tt*. Two different crosses are made between parental plants of unknown genotype and phenotype. Use the progeny phenotype ratios to determine the genotypes and phenotypes of each parent.

Cross 1 progeny:	$\frac{3}{8}$	two-lobed, red
	$\frac{3}{8}$	two-lobed, yellow
	$\frac{1}{8}$	multilobed, red
	$\frac{1}{8}$	multilobed, yellow
Cross 2 progeny:	$\frac{1}{4}$	two-lobed, red
	$\frac{1}{4}$	two-lobed, yellow
	$\frac{1}{4}$	multilobed, red
	$\frac{1}{4}$	multilobed, yellow

30. A male and a female are each heterozygous for both cystic fibrosis (CF) and phenylketonuria (PKU). Both conditions are autosomal recessive, and they assort independently.
a. What proportion of the children of this couple will have neither condition?
b. What proportion of the children will have either PKU or CF but not both?
c. What proportion of the children will be carriers of one or both conditions?

31. In a sample of 640 families with 6 children each, the distribution of boys and girls is as shown in the following table:

Number of families	9	63	147	204	151	56	10
Number of girls	0	1	2	3	4	5	6
Number of boys	6	5	4	3	2	1	0

a. Are the numbers of boys to girls in these families consistent with the expected 1:1 ratio? Support your answer by chi-square analysis.
b. Is the distribution of the numbers of boys and girls in the families consistent with the expectations of binomial probability? Support your answer.

32. A sample of 120 families with 4 children each in which both parents are carriers of an autosomal recessive mutation for cystic fibrosis (CF) produces the following distribution of children with and without cystic fibrosis:

Number of families	16	52	32	18	2
Children with CF	0	1	2	3	4
Children free of CF	4	3	2	1	0

a. Is the total number of children with CF in these families consistent with the expected ratio? Support your answer.
b. What is the expected distribution of the number of families with 0 through 4 children with CF in this sample under the assumptions of binomial probability?
c. Is the distribution of families with 0 through 4 children with CF consistent with the ratios expected under binomial probability? Support your answer.

33. A woman expressing a dominant phenotype is heterozygous (*Dd*) at the gene.
a. What is the probability that the dominant allele carried by the woman will be inherited by a grandchild?
b. What is the probability that two grandchildren of the woman who are first cousins to one another will each inherit the dominant allele?
c. Draw a pedigree that illustrates the transmission of the dominant trait from the grandmother to two of her grandchildren who are first cousins.

34. Two parents who are each known to be carriers of an autosomal recessive allele have four children. None of the children has the recessive condition. What is the probability that one or more of the children is a carrier of the recessive allele?

35. An organism having the genotype *AaBbCcDdEe* is self-fertilized. Assuming the loci assort independently, determine the following proportions:
a. gametes that are expected to carry only dominant alleles
b. progeny that are expected to have a genotype identical to that of the parent
c. progeny that are expected to have a phenotype identical to that of the parent
d. gametes that are expected to be *ABcde*
e. progeny that are expected to have the genotype *AabbCcDdE–*

36. A man and a woman are each heterozygous carriers of an autosomal recessive mutation of a disorder that is fatal in infancy. They both want to have multiple children, but they are concerned about the risk of the disorder appearing in one or more of their children. In separate calculations, determine the probabilities of the couple having five children with 0, 1, 2, 3, 4, and all 5 children being affected by the disorder.

37. For a single dice roll, there is a $\frac{1}{6}$ chance that any particular number will appear. For a pair of dice, each specific combination of numbers has a probability of $\frac{1}{36}$ of occurring. Most total values of two dice can occur more than

one way. As a test of random probability theory, a student decides to roll a pair of six-sided dice 300 times and tabulate the results. She tabulates the number of times each different total value of the two dice occurs. Her results are the following:

Total Value of Two Dice	Number of Times Rolled
2	7
3	11
4	23
5	36
6	42
7	53
8	40
9	38
10	30
11	12
12	8
TOTAL	300

The student tells you that her results fail to prove that random chance is the explanation for the outcome of this experiment. Is she correct or incorrect? Support your answer.

38. You have four guinea pigs for a genetic study. One male and one female are from a strain that is pure-breeding for short brown fur. A second male and female are from a strain that is pure-breeding for long white fur. You are asked to perform two *different* experiments to test the proposal that short fur is dominant to long fur and that brown is dominant to white. You may use any of the four original pure-breeding guinea pigs or any of their offspring in experimental matings. Design two different experiments (crossing different animals and using different combinations of phenotypes) to test the dominance relationships of alleles for fur length and color, and make predictions for each cross based on the proposed relationships. Anticipate that the litter size will be 12 for each mating and that female guinea pigs can produce three litters in their lifetime.

39. Galactosemia is an autosomal recessive disorder caused by the inability to metabolize galactose, a component of the lactose found in mammalian milk. Galactosemia can be partially managed by eliminating dietary intake of lactose and galactose. Amanda is healthy, as are her parents, but her brother Alonzo has galactosemia. Brice has a similar family history. He and his parents are healthy, but his sister Brianna has galactosemia. Amanda and Brice are planning a family and seek genetic counseling. Based on the information provided, complete the following activities and answer the questions.

a. Draw a pedigree that includes Amanda, Brice, their siblings, and parents. Identify the genotype of each person, using G and g to represent the dominant and recessive alleles, respectively.

b. What is the probability that Amanda is a carrier of the allele for galactosemia? What is the probability that Brice is a carrier? Explain your reasoning for each answer.

c. What is the probability that the first child of Amanda and Brice will have galactosemia? Show your work.

d. If the first child has galactosemia, what is the probability that the second child will have galactosemia? Explain the reasoning for your answer.

40. Sweet yellow tomatoes with a pear shape bring a high price per basket to growers. Pear shape, yellow color, and terminal flower position are recessive traits produced by alleles f, r, and t, respectively. The dominant phenotypes for each trait—full shape, red color, and axial flower position—are the product of dominant alleles F, R, and T. A farmer has two pure-breeding tomato lines. One is full, yellow, terminal and the other is pear, red, axial. Design a breeding experiment that will produce a line of tomato that is pure-breeding for pear shape, yellow color, and axial flower position.

41. A cross between a spicy variety of *Capsicum annum* pepper and a sweet (nonspicy) variety produces F_1 progeny plants that all have spicy peppers. The F_1 are crossed, and among the F_2 plants are 56 that produce spicy peppers and 20 that produce sweet peppers. Dr. Ara B. Dopsis, an expert on pepper plants, discovers a gene designated *Pun1* that he believes is responsible for spicy versus sweet flavor of peppers. Dr. Dopsis proposes that a dominant allele P produces spicy peppers and that a recessive mutant allele p results in sweet peppers.

a. Are the data on the parental cross and the F_1 and F_2 consistent with the proposal made by Dr. Dopsis? Explain why or why not, using P and p to indicate probable genotypes of pepper plants.

b. Assuming the proposal is correct, what proportion of the spicy F_2 pepper plants do you expect will be pure-breeding? Explain your answer.

42. Alkaptonuria is an infrequent autosomal recessive condition. It is first noticed in newborns when the urine in their diapers turns black upon exposure to air. The condition is caused by the defective transport of the amino acid phenylalanine through the intestinal walls during digestion. About 4 people per 1000 are carriers of alkaptonuria.

Sara and James had never heard of alkaptonuria and were shocked to discover that their first child had the condition. Sara's sister Mary and her husband Frank are planning to have a family and are concerned about the possibility of alkaptonuria in one of their children.

The four adults (Sara, James, Mary, and Frank) seek information from a neighbor who is a retired physician. After discussing their family histories, the neighbor says, "I never took genetics, but I know from my many years in practice that Sara and James are both carriers of this recessive condition. Since their first child had the condition, there is a very low chance that the next child will also have it, because the odds of having two children with a recessive condition are very low. Mary and Frank have no chance of having a child with alkaptonuria because Frank has no family history of the condition." The two couples each have babies and *both* babies have alkaptonuria.

a. What are the genotypes of the four adults?

b. What was incorrect about the information given to Sara and James? What is incorrect about the information given to Mary and Frank?

c. What is the probability that the second child of Mary and Frank will have alkaptonuria?

d. What is the chance that the third child of Sara and James will be free of the condition?

e. The couples are worried that one of their grandchildren will inherit alkaptonuria. How would you assess the risk that one of the offspring of a child with alkaptonuria will inherit the condition?

43. Humans vary in many ways from one another. Among many minor phenotypic differences are the following five independently assorting traits that have a dominant and a recessive phenotype: (1) forearm hair (alleles *F* and *f*)—the presence of hair on the forearm is dominant to the absence of hair on the forearm; (2) earlobe form (alleles *E* and *e*)—unattached earlobes are dominant to attached earlobes; (3) widow's peak (alleles *W* and *w*)—a distinct "V" shape to the hairline at the top of the forehead is dominant to a straight hairline; (4) hitchhiker's thumb (alleles *H* and *h*)—the ability to bend the thumb back beyond vertical is dominant and the inability to do so is recessive; and (5) freckling (alleles *D* and *d*)—the appearance of freckles is dominant to the absence of freckles.

If a couple with the genotypes *Ff Ee Ww Hh Dd* and *Ff Ee Ww Hh Dd* have children, what is the chance the children will inherit the following characteristics?

a. the same phenotype as the parents

b. four dominant traits and one recessive trait

c. all recessive traits

d. the genotype *Ff EE Ww hh dd*

44. In chickens, the presence of feathers on the legs is due to a dominant allele (*F*), and the absence of leg feathers is due to a recessive allele (*f*). The comb on the top of the head can be either pea-shaped, a phenotype that is controlled by a dominant allele (*P*), or a single comb controlled by a recessive allele (*p*). The two genes assort independently. Assume that a pure-breeding rooster that has feathered legs and a single comb is crossed with a pure-breeding hen that has no leg feathers and a pea-shaped comb. The F_1 are crossed to produce the F_2. Among the resulting F_2, however, only birds with a single comb and feathered legs are allowed to mate. These chickens mate at random to produce F_3 progeny. What are the expected genotypic and phenotypic ratios among the resulting F_3 progeny?

45. A pure-breeding fruit fly with the recessive mutation cut wing, caused by the homozygous *cc* genotype, is crossed to a pure-breeding fly with normal wings, genotype *CC*. Their F_1 progeny all have normal wings. F_1 flies are crossed, and the F_2 progeny have a 3:1 ratio of normal wing to cut wing. One male F_2 fly with normal wings is selected at random and mated to an F_2 female with normal wings. Using all possible genotypes of the F_2 flies selected for this cross, list all possible crosses between the two flies involved in this mating, and determine the probability of each cross.

46. Situs inversus is a congenital condition in which the major visceral organs are reversed from their normal positions. Investigations into the genetics of this abnormality revealed that individuals with at least one dominant allele (*SI*) of an autosomal gene are normal but, surprisingly, of individuals that are homozygous for a recessive allele (*si*), $\frac{1}{2}$ are situs inversus and $\frac{1}{2}$ are normal.

a. What genotypes and phenotypes are expected in progeny from a cross of two *si si* individuals?

b. What genotypes and phenotypes are expected in progeny from a cross of two *SI si* individuals?

47. Domestic dogs evolved from ancestral grey wolves. Wolves have coats of short, straight hair and lack "furnishings," a growth pattern marked by eyebrows and a mustache found in domestic dogs. In domestic dogs, coat variation is controlled by allelic variation in three genes. Recessive mutant alleles in the *FGF5* gene result in long hair, while dogs carrying the dominant ancestral allele have short hair. Likewise, recessive mutant alleles in the *KRT71* gene result in curly hair, whereas dogs with an ancestral dominant allele have straight hair. Dominant mutant alleles in the *RSPO2* gene cause the presence of furnishings, while dogs homozygous for the ancestral recessive allele have no furnishings.

A pure breeding curly- and long-haired poodle with furnishings was crossed to a pure-breeding short- and straight-haired border collie lacking furnishings.

a. What are the genotypes and phenotypes of the puppies?

b. If dogs of the F_1 generation are interbred, what proportions of genotypes and phenotypes are expected in the F_2?

48. Alleles at the *IGF-1* locus in dogs, encoding insulin-like growth factor, largely determine whether a domestic dog will be large or small. Dogs with an ancestral dominant allele are large, whereas dogs homozygous for the mutant recessive allele are small. Chondrodysplasia, a short-legged phenotype (as in dachshunds and basset hounds), is caused by a dominant gain-of-function allele of the *FGF4* gene. The *MSTN* gene encodes myostatin, a negative regulator of muscle development. Dogs with a dominant ancestral allele of the *MTSN* gene have normal muscle development, while dogs homozygous for recessive mutants in the *MTSN* gene are "double muscled" and have trouble running quickly. However, dogs heterozygous for the mutant allele run faster than either of the homozygotes.

You breed a pure-breeding small basset hound of normal musculature with a pure-breeding "bully" whippet, a double-muscled large dog with normal legs.

a. What are the genotypes and phenotypes of the F_1 puppies?

b. If the F_1 of this cross is interbred, what proportion of the F_2 are expected to be fast runners and what proportion normal-speed runners?

49. The Basalt Seed Lending Library run by the Central Rocky Mountain Permaculture Institute and the Basalt (Colorado) Regional Library (see Experimental Insight 2.3) loans heirloom vegetable seeds to patrons.

a. The many different types of seed produce plants and vegetables that consistently have specific traits. Give a genetic explanation for the consistent production of the same traits from plants grown from heirloom seeds.

b. A goal of the seed-lending program over time is to generate seeds and plants that thrive and yield better harvests. From an evolutionary perspective, explain how saving and replanting seeds from the most productive plants each year contributes to this goal.

3 Cell Division and Chromosome Heredity

CHAPTER OUTLINE

3.1 Mitosis Divides Somatic Cells

3.2 Meiosis Produces Gametes for Sexual Reproduction

3.3 The Chromosome Theory of Heredity Proposes That Genes Are Carried on Chromosomes

3.4 Sex Determination Is Chromosomal and Genetic

3.5 Human Sex-Linked Transmission Follows Distinct Patterns

3.6 Dosage Compensation Equalizes the Expression of Sex-Linked Genes

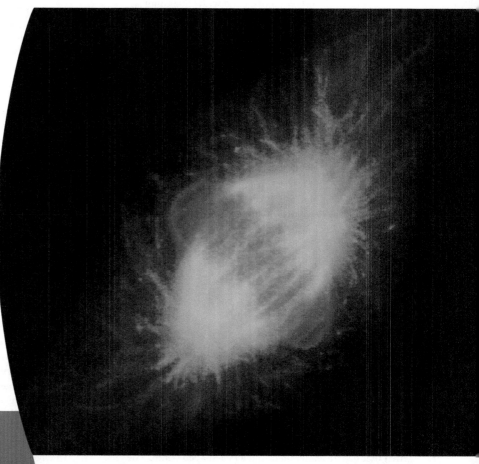

ESSENTIAL IDEAS

- The cell cycle consists of interphase, during which cells carry out regular functions and replicate their DNA, and M phase, the cell-division segment of the cycle.

- Mitosis divides somatic cells and produces two genetically identical daughter cells.

- Meiosis occurs in germ-line cells and produces four genetically different haploid cells that form gametes for reproduction.

- The separation of chromosomes and sister chromatids during meiosis is the mechanical basis of Mendel's law of segregation and law of independent assortment.

- The chromosome theory of heredity identified chromosomes as the cell structures containing genes.

- Sex determination is controlled by chromosomal and genetic factors that vary among species.

- Dosage compensation equalizes the expression of sex-linked genes of males and females of animal species.

Cell division is a complex but carefully controlled process. Chromosomes, stained in blue, are ready to separate in anaphase. Different kinds of microtubules, shown in green, help drive the chromosome segregation process.

A couple of decades or so ago, at the moment of conception that culminated in your birth, two gametes united to form the single fertilized cell—the zygote—from which you developed. Your sex was determined in that instant by the sex chromosome carried by the fertilizing sperm—an X chromosome if you are female or a Y chromosome if you are male. Shortly after fertilization, cell division began that over the next few hours increased the tiny zygote to two cells, then four cells, then eight cells, and so on, as it moved down the fallopian tube toward the uterus. Over several days, these cell divisions produced hundreds of exact genetic replicas of the original fertilized egg. About 1 week after fertilization, these cells, now called a blastocyst, were implanted into the uterine wall, and within 2 weeks of conception, genetically controlled processes of cell differentiation and cell specialization began to form the first embryonic organs and structures. These processes eventually determined the structure and function of each cell in your body (see Chapter 20).

Since then, your body has produced thousands of generations of cells. The mechanism of cell division that produced most of them, **mitosis,** is an ongoing process that with each division creates two identical **daughter cells** that are exact genetic replicas of the parental cell they are derived from. Mitosis produces somatic cells, the structural cells of the body. Therefore, mitosis is responsible for the growth and maintenance of your body, its organs, and its various structures; it repairs the damage and injury your body sustains, and it produces new cells to replace those that undergo programmed cell death (apoptosis). While you have been reading this passage, approximately 200 cells in your body have undergone mitotic division.

There are trillions of somatic cells in your body, and nearly all of them contain a nucleus that encloses two sets of chromosomes. The somatic cells of most other eukaryotes also contain multiple sets of chromosomes. The most common multiple of chromosome sets in animal nuclei is two, and the number of chromosomes present as homologous pairs in such nuclei is called the **diploid number.** Your somatic cell nuclei contain 46 chromosomes each, in 23 homologous pairs, so your diploid number is 46. The diploid number varies among species (each species having its characteristic number of pairs) and so is identified nonspecifically as 2*n*. The value *n* represents the **haploid number** of chromosomes, a value that is one-half the diploid number and is the number of chromosomes contained in the nuclei of gametes, the nonsomatic cells.

Gametes, produced from **germ-line cells,** are the germinal, or reproductive, cells: sperm and egg in animals or pollen and egg in plants. Germ-line cells divide by **meiosis,** which is different in several ways from mitosis.

In this chapter, we examine both mitosis and meiosis, and we look closely at the connection between meiotic cell division and Mendel's laws of heredity. We also explore patterns of sex determination in eukaryotes and look at processes that equalize the expression of genes carried on **sex chromosomes,** the chromosomes that determine sex. In addition, we study the special patterns of inheritance of genes on the X chromosome, and we describe how the discovery of genes on the X chromosome supported the **chromosome theory of heredity,** the theory that chromosomes are the cell structures that carry genes.

3.1 Mitosis Divides Somatic Cells

Mitosis, the cell-division process that produces two genetically identical daughter cells from a single original parental cell, is among the most fundamental and important processes occurring in eukaryotes. It is a genetically controlled process that follows a precise script to enable organisms to grow and develop normally and to maintain the structures and functions of their organs, tissues, and other bodily components. Life depends on the orderly progression and proper regulation of mitosis. If too little cell division takes place or cell division occurs too slowly, an organism may fail to develop at all, or it may have morphologic abnormalities. On the other hand, too much cell division can lead to growth of structures beyond their normal boundaries, likewise producing morphologic abnormality and possible death.

Stages of the Cell Cycle

Cell division is regulated by genetic control of the **cell cycle,** the life cycle cells must pass through in order to replicate their DNA and divide. Since well-regulated cell division is such an integral part of life, it will not surprise you to learn that the cell cycles of all eukaryotes are similar and that much of the molecular machinery that controls the cell cycle is evolutionarily conserved in plants and animals. The striking similarity of cell cycle control genes and processes in plants and animals, and the sharing of many of these genes with Bacteria and Archaea, is powerful evidence that all life evolved from a single common ancestor.

The eukaryotic cell cycle is divided into two principal phases—**M phase,** a short segment of the cell cycle during which cells divide, and **interphase,** the longer period between one M phase and the next (**Figure 3.1a**). Interphase consists of three successive stages, G_1, S, and G_2. During these stages, respectively, the cell expresses its genetic information, replicates its chromosomes, and prepares for entry into M phase. M phase is divided into substages that correspond to the progress of the cell during its division.

When viewed under a light microscope, somatic cells in interphase may appear rather placid, but their outward

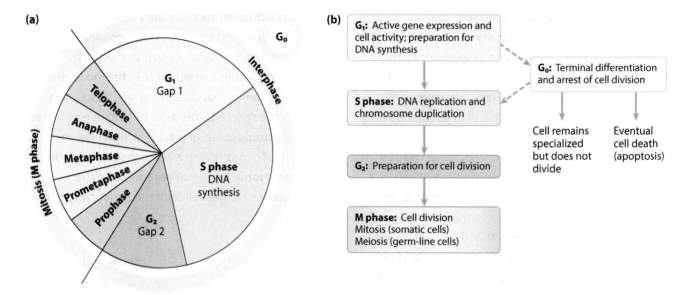

Figure 3.1   The cell cycle. (a) The cell cycle is divided into interphase and M phase, which are each further subdivided. The cycles are not drawn to scale. **(b)** An overview of cell cycle activities.

appearance gives little indication of the complex activity taking place inside. Gene transcription occurs continuously throughout the cell cycle, but during the **G_1 (or Gap 1) phase** of interphase, cells rates of transcription and translation are particularly high. (**Figure 3.1b**). Cells of different types vary in how many genes they express, in how they function in the body, and in how they interact with other cells. Consequently, the duration of G_1 varies. Some types of cells are rapidly dividing and spend only a short time, perhaps as little as a few hours, in G_1. Other cells linger in G_1 for periods of days, weeks, or more.

As they approach the end of G_1, cells follow one of two alternative paths. Most cells enter the **S phase,** or **synthesis phase,** during which DNA replication (DNA synthesis) takes place. On the other hand, a small subset of specialized cells transition from G_1 into a nondividing state called **G_0** ("G zero"), a kind of semiperpetual G_1-like state in which cells express their genetic information and carry out normal functions but do not progress through the cell cycle (see Figure 3.1b). Several kinds of cells in your body, including certain cells in your eyes and bones, reach a mature state of differentiation, enter G_0, and rarely if ever divide again. Most G_0 cells maintain their specialized functions until they enter programmed cell death (apoptosis) and die. Cells only rarely leave G_0 and resume the cell cycle.

DNA replication takes place during S phase and results in a doubling of the amount of DNA in each nucleus and the creation of two *sister chromatids* for each chromosome. Entry into the S phase almost always commits the cell to proceeding through the remainder of the cycle and then dividing. The completion of S phase brings about the transition to the **G_2,** or **Gap 2,** phase of the cell cycle, during which cells prepare for division. Interphase ends when cells enter M phase, from which two identical daughter cells emerge.

The successive generations of cells produced through mitosis as one cell cycle follows the next are known as cell lines or cell lineages. Each cell line or cell lineage contains identical cells (i.e., clones) that are all descended from a single founder cell. Mitosis ensures that the genetic information in cells is faithfully passed to successive generations of cell lineages. Occasional mutations occur in individual cells, however, and these are also perpetuated during the proliferation of the cell line.

Substages of M Phase

M phase follows interphase and is divided into five substages—**prophase, prometaphase, metaphase, anaphase,** and **telophase**—whose principal features are described in **Figure 3.2**. These five substages accomplish two important functions of cell division—karyokinesis and cytokinesis. **Karyokinesis** is the equal partitioning of the chromosomal material in the nucleus of the parental cell between the nuclei of the two daughter cells. This process requires first that each of the chromosomes in the nucleus be fully and accurately duplicated and then that the duplicate copies of each chromosome be separated so that one copy goes to the nucleus of one daughter cell and the second copy goes to the other daughter nucleus. Karyokinesis is followed by **cytokinesis,** the partitioning of the cytoplasmic contents of the parental cell into the daughter cells. Cytokinesis does not demand the same degree of equivalency required in karyokinesis. The cytoplasm of the parental cells contains an abundance of the proteins and organelles that the daughter cells require in order to function, so the division of this material need not be equal. Cells entering mitosis are diploid (2*n*), and they are diploid at the end of mitosis as well.

The chromosomes are so diffuse during interphase that they cannot be clearly seen by light microscopy. Chromosome condensation begins in early prophase and progressively condenses chromosomes, which are visible by mid-prophase. Chromosome condensation continues until chromosomes reach their maximum level of condensation in metaphase. Nuclear envelope breakdown also occurs in prophase, and chromosome centromeres become visible as do the sister chromatids of each chromosome. The **centromere** is a specialized DNA sequence on each chromosome, and its location is identified as a constriction where the **sister chromatids**—the two copies that were duplicated in S phase—are joined together. Centromeric DNA sequence binds a specialized protein complex called the **kinetochore** that facilitates chromosome division later in M phase.

The definition and usage of the terms *chromosome*, *chromatid*, and *sister chromatid* sometimes cause confusion, and this is a good time to present the definitions we will use in the remaining discussion of cell division. The term *chromosome* is used throughout the cell cycle to identify each DNA-containing structure that has a centromere. At the end of G_1, a chromosome consists of a single DNA duplex with associated proteins. After the completion of S phase, a chromosome consists of two replicated DNA duplexes with associated proteins. The two DNA molecules making up this chromosome are identical. Individually, these DNA molecules are identified as chromatids, and together they are identified as the sister chromatids.

Chromosome Distribution

In addition to visible changes to chromosomes, cellular changes are also apparent in prophase. In animal cells, although not in most plants, fungi, or algae, two organelles called **centrosomes** appear that migrate during M phase to form the two opposite poles of the dividing cell. Each centrosome contains a pair of subunits called centrioles (**Figure 3.3**). Centrosomes are the source of **spindle fiber microtubules** that emanate from each centrosome. Spindle fiber microtubules are polymers of tubulin protein subunits that elongate by the addition of tubulin subunits and shorten by the removal of tubulin subunits. Microtubules are polar; they have a "minus" (−) end anchored at the centrosome and a "plus" (+) end that grows away from the centrosome. Specialized proteins called motor proteins are associated with microtubules. Motor proteins move chromosomes and other cell structures along microtubules.

Three kinds of spindle fibers emanate from centrosomes in a 360° pattern identified as the **aster:**

1. **Kinetochore microtubules** embed in the protein complex called the kinetochore (described shortly) that assembles at the centromere of each chromatid. Kinetochore microtubules are responsible for chromosome movement during cell division.

2. **Polar microtubules,** also called **nonkinetochore microtubules,** extend toward the opposite pole of their centrosome and overlap with polar microtubules from that pole. These microtubules contribute to the elongation of the cell and to cell stability during division.

3. **Astral microtubules** grow toward the membrane of the cell, where they attach and contribute to cell stability.

The kinetochore, a protein complex with an outer plate and an inner plate, assembles on the centromere and is bound by the plus ends of kinetochore microtubules. By the end of prometaphase, kinetochore microtubules from each centrosome are attached to the kinetochore of each chromatid of the sister chromatid pair (see Figure 3.3).

Metaphase chromosomes condense more than 10,000-fold in comparison to the beginning of prophase. This makes them easily visible under the microscope and allows them to be easily moved within the cell. Because they are tethered to kinetochore microtubules from opposite centrosomes, the sister chromatids experience opposing forces that are critical to the positioning of chromosomes along an imaginary midline at the equator of the cell. This imaginary line is called the **metaphase plate.**

The tension created by the pull of kinetochore microtubules is balanced by a companion process known as **sister chromatid cohesion.** Sister chromatid cohesion is produced by the protein cohesin that localizes between the sister chromatids and holds them together to resist the pull of kinetochore microtubules (**Figure 3.4**). Cohesin is a 4-subunit protein; its central component is a polypeptide produced by the gene Scc 1, for "sister chromatid cohesion." Cohesin coats sister chromatids along their entire length but is most concentrated near centromeres, where the pull of microtubules is greatest. As microtubules move chromosomes toward the midline of the cell, cohesin helps keep the sister chromatids together, to ensure proper chromosome positioning and to prevent their premature separation.

Anaphase is the part of M phase during which sister chromatids separate and begin moving to opposite poles in the cell. Anaphase includes two distinct events tied to microtubule action: anaphase A, characterized by the separation of sister chromatids, and anaphase B, characterized by the elongation of the cell into an oblong shape.

Anaphase A begins abruptly with two simultaneous events. First, the enzyme separase initiates cleavage of polypeptides in cohesin, thus breaking down the connection between sister chromatids. Second, kinetochore microtubules begin to depolymerize at their (+) ends to initiate chromosome movement toward the centrioles. The separation of sister chromatids in anaphase A is called chromosome **disjunction.** As anaphase progresses, sister chromatids complete their disjunction and eventually congregate around the centrosomes at the cell poles.

The next part of anaphase, anaphase B, is characterized by the polymerization of polar microtubules that extends their length and causes the cell to take on an

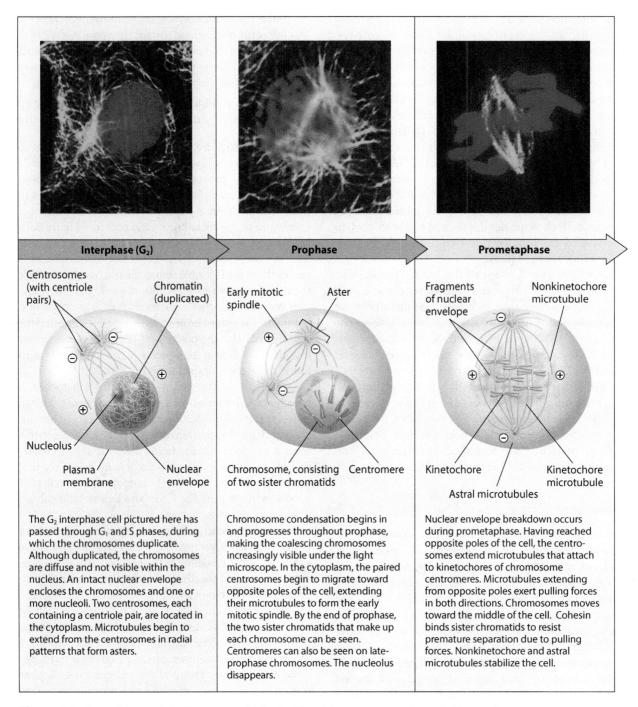

Interphase (G₂)

Centrosomes (with centriole pairs)
Chromatin (duplicated)

Nucleolus

Plasma membrane
Nuclear envelope

The G₂ interphase cell pictured here has passed through G₁ and S phases, during which the chromosomes duplicate. Although duplicated, the chromosomes are diffuse and not visible within the nucleus. An intact nuclear envelope encloses the chromosomes and one or more nucleoli. Two centrosomes, each containing a centriole pair, are located in the cytoplasm. Microtubules begin to extend from the centrosomes in radial patterns that form asters.

Prophase

Early mitotic spindle
Aster

Chromosome, consisting of two sister chromatids
Centromere

Chromosome condensation begins in and progresses throughout prophase, making the coalescing chromosomes increasingly visible under the light microscope. In the cytoplasm, the paired centrosomes begin to migrate toward opposite poles of the cell, extending their microtubules to form the early mitotic spindle. By the end of prophase, the two sister chromatids that make up each chromosome can be seen. Centromeres can also be seen on late-prophase chromosomes. The nucleolus disappears.

Prometaphase

Fragments of nuclear envelope
Nonkinetochore microtubule

Kinetochore
Astral microtubules
Kinetochore microtubule

Nuclear envelope breakdown occurs during prometaphase. Having reached opposite poles of the cell, the centrosomes extend microtubules that attach to kinetochores of chromosome centromeres. Microtubules extending from opposite poles exert pulling forces in both directions. Chromosomes moves toward the middle of the cell. Cohesin binds sister chromatids to resist premature separation due to pulling forces. Nonkinetochore and astral microtubules stabilize the cell.

Figure 3.2 **Interphase and the five stages of mitosis.** The chromosomes are shown in blue, and the centrosomes, asters, and spindle fibers are shown in green.

oblong shape. The oblong shape facilitates cytokinesis at the end of telophase, which leads to the formation of two daughter cells.

Completion of Cell Division

In telophase, nuclear membranes begin to reassemble around the chromosomes gathered at each pole, eventually enclosing the chromosomes in nuclear envelopes. Chromosome decondensation begins and ultimately returns chromosomes to their diffuse interphase state. At the same time, microtubules disassemble. As telophase comes to an end, two identical nuclei are observed within a single elongated cell that is about to be divided into two daughter cells by the process of cytokinesis.

In animal cells, a contractile ring composed of actin microfilaments creates a cleavage furrow around the circumference of the cell; the contractile ring pinches the cell in two (**Figure 3.5**). In plant cells, cytokinesis entails the construction of new cell walls near the cellular midline. In both plant and animal cells, cytokinesis divides the cytoplasmic fluid and organelles.

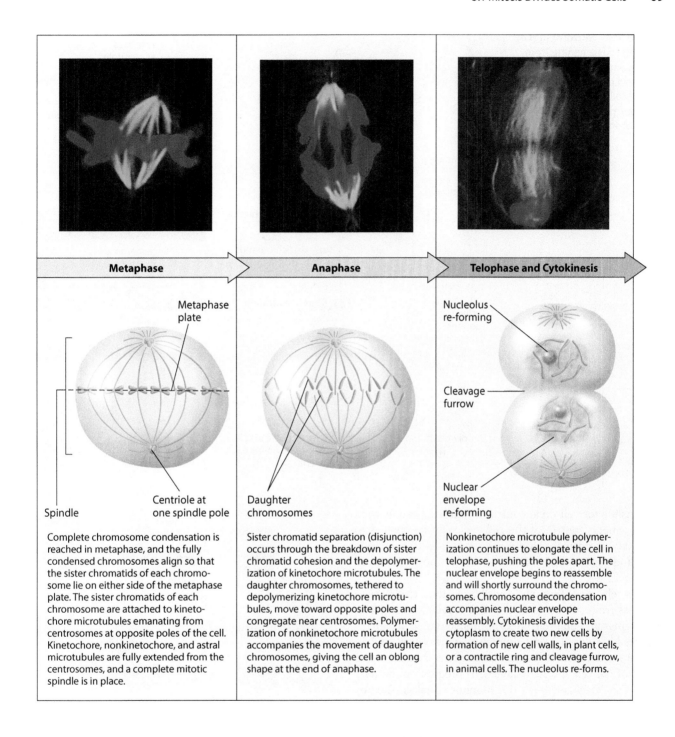

Metaphase	Anaphase	Telophase and Cytokinesis

Metaphase plate

Spindle

Centriole at one spindle pole

Daughter chromosomes

Nucleolus re-forming

Cleavage furrow

Nuclear envelope re-forming

Complete chromosome condensation is reached in metaphase, and the fully condensed chromosomes align so that the sister chromatids of each chromosome lie on either side of the metaphase plate. The sister chromatids of each chromosome are attached to kinetochore microtubules emanating from centrosomes at opposite poles of the cell. Kinetochore, nonkinetochore, and astral microtubules are fully extended from the centrosomes, and a complete mitotic spindle is in place.

Sister chromatid separation (disjunction) occurs through the breakdown of sister chromatid cohesion and the depolymerization of kinetochore microtubules. The daughter chromosomes, tethered to depolymerizing kinetochore microtubules, move toward opposite poles and congregate near centrosomes. Polymerization of nonkinetochore microtubules accompanies the movement of daughter chromosomes, giving the cell an oblong shape at the end of anaphase.

Nonkinetochore microtubule polymerization continues to elongate the cell in telophase, pushing the poles apart. The nuclear envelope begins to reassemble and will shortly surround the chromosomes. Chromosome decondensation accompanies nuclear envelope reassembly. Cytokinesis divides the cytoplasm to create two new cells by formation of new cell walls, in plant cells, or a contractile ring and cleavage furrow, in animal cells. The nucleolus re-forms.

Mitosis separates the members of each pair of sister chromatids into identical nuclei, thus forming two genetically identical daughter cells. **Figure 3.6** shows four chromosomes in a cell of an organism that is dihybrid (*AaBb*) for genes on the chromosomes shown. The figure follows major events of the cell cycle, showing the generation of sister chromatids in S phase, chromosome alignment on the metaphase plate in metaphase, and the production of two identical (*AaBb*) daughter cells at the end of telophase. Notice that the diploid (2*n*) number of chromosomes is maintained throughout the cell cycle.

Cell Cycle Checkpoints

Cell biologists find that no matter what the duration of the cell cycle, most cells follow the same basic program; this suggests that common, genetically controlled signals drive the cell cycle. Knowledge of the genes and proteins controlling the cell cycle comes not from normal cells but from the study of cell lineages possessing mutations that affect their progression through the cell cycle. These studies have produced important insights into genetic control of the cell cycle, and in recent decades, biologists have discovered the identities and functions of many genes

Figure 3.3 Microtubules in dividing cells emanate from centrosomes. Astral microtubules and polar microtubules control cell shape, and kinetochore microtubules attach to chromosome kinetochores.

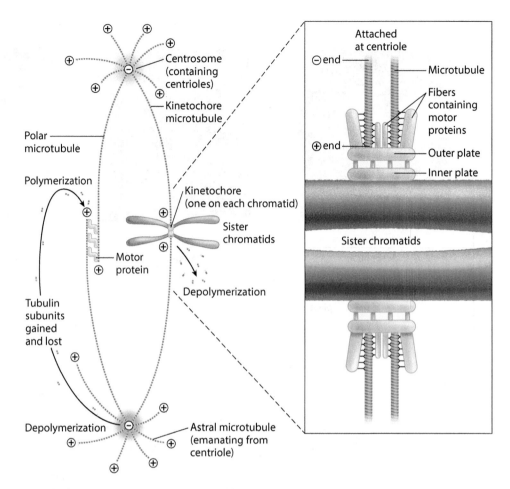

responsible for cell cycle control. What has been learned about genetic control of the cell cycle can be applied to the study of normal cell division as well as to the study of cell division abnormalities such as those displayed in cancer.

As cells move through the cell cycle, their readiness to progress from one stage to the next is regularly assessed. The numerous **cell cycle checkpoints,** four of which are illustrated in **Figure 3.7a,** are times during the cell cycle when cells are monitored by protein interactions that assess the status of the cell and its readiness to progress to the next stage. One mechanism for this monitoring takes place by means of protein complexes that join a protein kinase with a second protein known as a cyclin protein. Protein kinases catalyze protein phosphorylation—the addition of a phosphate group transferred from a nucleotide triphosphate such as ATP or GTP to a target protein. Phosphorylation changes the conformation of target proteins and can either activate or inactivate the target protein. Protein kinases are usually present continuously in cells at relatively steady concentrations. **Cyclin proteins,** however, are so named because their concentrations are cyclic and linked to cell cycle stage. Cyclin protein production is stimulated by growth factor proteins that are produced by other cells. The protein kinase components of these complexes are activated only when they associate with a cyclin; thus, the protein kinases are called **cyclin-dependent kinases,** abbreviated

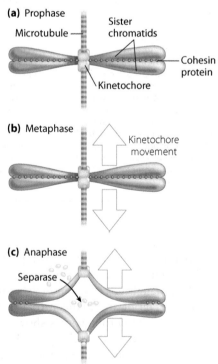

Figure 3.4 Sister chromatid cohesion during mitosis. Cohesin protein generates cohesion between sister chromatids **(a)** and **(b)**. At anaphase **(c)**, separase protein digests cohesin and allows sister chromatids to separate.

(a)

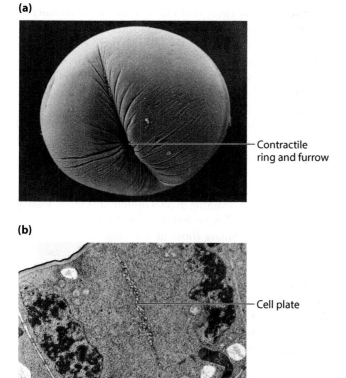

Contractile ring and furrow

(b)

Cell plate

Figure 3.5   Cytokinesis in animal cells (a) and plant cells (b).

Cdk. In their activated state, cyclin–Cdk complexes phosphorylate numerous target proteins and regulate cell cycle progression at various checkpoints.

Changes in the production of cyclin proteins changes through the cell cycle (**Figure 3.7b**). For example, Cdk4 joins with cyclin D2, forming cyclin D2–Cdk4 that is active at the G_1-S checkpoint. Separately, Cdk4 pairs with cyclin D1 to form cyclin D1–Cdk4 that is active later in the cell cycle.

One prominent target of cyclin D1–Cdk4 is the retinoblastoma protein (pRB) that is produced by the retinoblastoma 1 (*RB1*) gene. In normal cells, pRB binds a transcription activator protein known as E2F, and together the pRB–E2F complex blocks cell cycle progression from G_1 to S phase (**Figure 3.8**). The cyclin D1–Cdk4 complex phosphorylates pRB, causing it to release E2F. Free E2F binds to DNA and activates the transcription of several genes that produce proteins essential in S phase. In other words, active cyclin D1–Cdk4 allows the cell to pass through the G_1 checkpoint and enter S phase by releasing E2F that is otherwise bound to unphosphorylated RB.

The presence of unphosphorylated pRB in a cell acts as a brake on the cell cycle, halting it at the G_1 checkpoint and preventing progression to S phase. The *RB1* gene that produces pRB and known as a **tumor suppressor gene** because the protein product of this and other genes of the same type block progression of the cell cycle. In contrast, the production of cyclin D1, from expression of the *cyclin D1* gene, leads

to formation of the cyclin D1–Cdk4 complex that *stimulates* cell cycle progression from G_1 to S phase. Cyclin D1 is one of many examples of proteins produced by genes known as **proto-oncogenes.** When expressed, proto-oncogenes stimulate cell cycle progression. Mutated proto-oncogenes, designated **oncogenes,** are associated with cancer development.

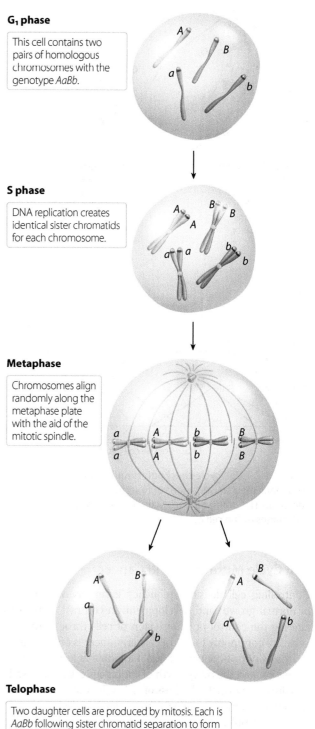

G_1 phase

This cell contains two pairs of homologous chromosomes with the genotype *AaBb*.

S phase

DNA replication creates identical sister chromatids for each chromosome.

Metaphase

Chromosomes align randomly along the metaphase plate with the aid of the mitotic spindle.

Telophase

Two daughter cells are produced by mitosis. Each is *AaBb* following sister chromatid separation to form daughter chromosomes.

Figure 3.6   **An overview of mitosis.**

(a)

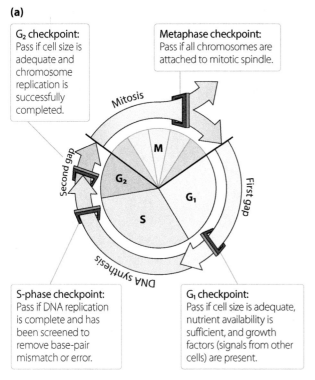

G₂ checkpoint:
Pass if cell size is adequate and chromosome replication is successfully completed.

Metaphase checkpoint:
Pass if all chromosomes are attached to mitotic spindle.

S-phase checkpoint:
Pass if DNA replication is complete and has been screened to remove base-pair mismatch or error.

G₁ checkpoint:
Pass if cell size is adequate, nutrient availability is sufficient, and growth factors (signals from other cells) are present.

(b)

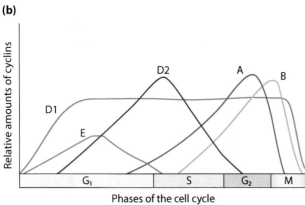

Figure 3.7 **Cell cycle checkpoints and cyclin proteins.** (a) Genetic mechanisms monitor four major cell cycle checkpoints. (b) The production of cyclin proteins varies coincident with stages of the cell cycle.

Cell Cycle Mutations and Cancer

Controlling cell division frequency is an essential activity of normal growth and development. In contrast, mutations altering the control or progression of cells through the cell cycle are commonly found in cancer. Cancer is often characterized by out-of-control cell proliferation that leads to tumor formation and the overgrowth of cancerous cells that invade and displace normal cells. Loss of cell cycle control is a fundamental mechanism leading to cancer development.

As examples of the loss of cell cycle control in cancer, let's consider two kinds of mutations that alter the normal interaction of cyclin D1–Cdk4 and pRB. The first category

of mutations are those that either increase the number of copies of cyclin D1 by duplicating the *cyclin D1* gene, or significantly increase the level of transcription of *cyclin D1*. These mutations lead to higher-than-normal levels of cyclin D1. Since Cdk4 is continuously available in cells, over-production of cyclin D1 causes uncontrolled entry into S phase by continuous phosphorylation of pRB and release of E2F to stimulate S-phase–related gene transcription. Mutations of this kind occur in parathyroid tumors, B-cell lymphomas, and certain other cancers in humans.

Mutation of the *RB1* gene and the production of abnormal pRB drives a different kind of abnormal growth. Mutation of *RB1* resulting in pRB protein that binds weakly or not at all to E2F contributes to the development of several cancers, including those of the lung, bladder, breast, and bone, by allowing uncontrolled entry into S phase.

Mutation of *RB1* is also the cause of a cancer of light-sensitive cells of the retina in the eye. The cancer, called retinoblastoma, occurs in early childhood and forms tumors of rapidly proliferating cells in the retina. Retinoblastoma is rare, occurring in 1 in 15,000 children. It occurs in two forms: a hereditary type, meaning that a child inherits a mutation of *RB1* from a parent, and a sporadic type in which *RB1* mutations are not inherited. Retinoblastoma occurs only when *both copies* of *RB1* are mutated; thus, the development of retinoblastoma is an example of a recessive cancer phenotype.

In hereditary retinoblastoma, one *RB1* mutation is inherited; this means that all cells of the body, including retinal cells, carry one mutant gene. The acquisition of the second mutation of the wild-type copy of *RB1* occurs at a somatic level: The wild-type *RB1* gene could undergo mutation in any of the millions of cells in either retina. This second mutation produces the recessive genotype that leads to retinoblastoma development.

Sporadic retinoblastoma also requires that both *RB1* genes undergo mutation; however, both copies of the gene are wild type at fertilization, meaning that mutation must alter the two copies of the gene *in the same retinal cell*.

3.2 Meiosis Produces Gametes for Sexual Reproduction

Reproduction is a basic requirement of living organisms. In more than three centuries of observation, biologists have identified a dizzying array of reproductive methods, mechanisms, and behaviors in animals, plants, and microbes. Even so, reproduction can be divided into two broad categories: (1) asexual reproduction, in which organisms reproduce without mating, giving rise to progeny that are genetically identical to their parent; and (2) sexual reproduction, in which cells called reproductive cells or gametes are produced by cell division and unite during fertilization.

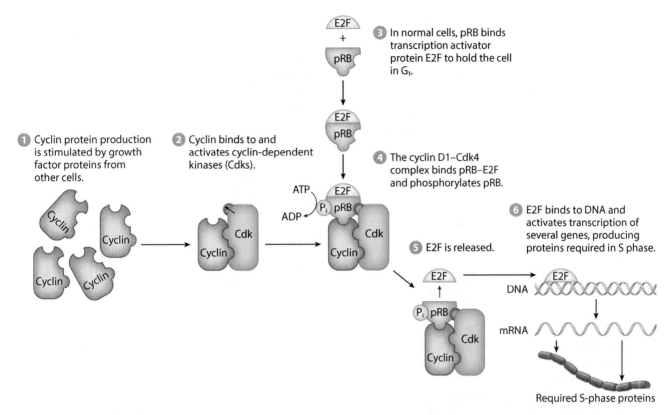

Figure 3.8   Cyclin–Cdk complexes regulate the cell cycle. Cyclin D1–Cdk4 specifically interacts with pRB–E2F to regulate entry into S phase.

Bacteria and archaea reproduce exclusively by asexual reproduction. These organisms are haploid; they usually have just a single chromosome. Cell division follows shortly after the completion of chromosome replication; each cell produces two genetically identical daughter cells.

Single-celled eukaryotes, such as yeast, can reproduce either sexually or asexually. Asexual reproduction in yeast is similar to cell division in bacteria. A haploid yeast cell undergoes DNA replication and distributes a copy of each chromosome to identical daughter cells. While yeast spend most of their life cycle in a haploid state and actively reproduce as haploids, it is also common for two haploid yeast cells to fuse and form a diploid cell that produces gametes (called spores) by meiosis. The spores produced by each completed meiotic division are usually contained in a structure called an ascus. The individual haploid spores of an ascus can be removed and grown on plates, as we will see illustrated later in the chapter.

In contrast to single-celled eukaryotes, multicellular eukaryotes reproduce predominantly by sexual means. In most animal species and dioecious plants, males and females carry distinct reproductive tissues and structures. Mating requires the production of haploid gametes from both male structures and female structures. The union of haploid gametes produces diploid progeny. In monoecious plant species, including the *Pisum sativum* that Mendel

worked with, male and female reproductive tissues are present in each plant, and self-fertilization is the common mode of reproduction, although fertilization involving pollen from one plant fertilizing the flower of another also occurs.

In sexually reproducing animals, specialized germ-line cells undertake meiosis to produce haploid gametes, or reproductive cells. Female gametes are produced by the ovary in female animals or by the ovule in plants. Male germ-line cells are located in testes in animals, where they produce sperm. In the anthers of flowering plants, pollen containing two sperm cells is produced. These descriptions are broadly true for most plants and animals, but there are many exceptions, including the observation of asexual reproduction in several species of fish, rotifers (small aquatic organisms), and salamanders. In addition, male ants, bees, and wasps have haploid somatic cells, and their processes of gamete production are distinctive.

Meiosis versus Mitosis

Meiosis shares numerous features that are similar or identical to events in mitosis. For example, interphase of all cells is the same. Interphase of the germ-line cell cycle contains stages G_1, S, and G_2 that are indistinguishable from those in somatic cells. Similarly, the actions and functions of

Table 3.1	Comparison of Mitosis and Meiosis	
Characteristic	**Mitosis**	**Meiosis**
Purpose	Produce genetically identical cells for growth and maintenance	Produce gametes for sexual reproduction that are genetically different
Location	Somatic cells	Germ-line cells
Mechanics	One round of division following one round of DNA replication	Two rounds of division (meiosis I and meiosis II) following a single round of DNA replication The mechanical basis of Mendel's laws of heredity
Homologous chromosomes	Do not pair Rarely undergo recombination	Synapsis during prophase I Crossing over during prophase I Separate at anaphase I
Sister chromatids	Attach to spindle fibers from opposite poles in metaphase Separate and migrate to opposite poles at anaphase	Attach to spindle fibers from the same pole in metaphase I Migrate to the same pole in anaphase I Attach to spindle fibers from opposite poles in metaphase II Separate and migrate to opposite poles in anaphase II
Product	Two genetically identical diploid daughter cells that continue to divide by mitosis	Four genetically different haploid cells that mature to form gametes and unite to form diploid zygotes

subcellular structures such as centrosomes and the microtubules they produce are the same in all cells. Nor is mitosis exclusive to somatic cells. Germ-line cells of plants and animals are created and maintained by mitotic division. These cells undertake meiosis solely for the purpose of producing gametes. Meiosis is distinguished from mitosis by the activities taking place during meiotic M phase and by the production of four haploid gametes. **Table 3.1** compares and contrasts numerous differences in the processes and outcomes of mitosis and meiosis that are described in the following sections.

Meiotic interphase is followed by two successive cell-division stages known as **meiosis I** and **meiosis II**. There is no DNA replication between these meiotic cell divisions, so the result of meiosis is the production of four haploid daughter cells (**Figure 3.9**). In meiosis I,

Figure 3.9   An overview of meiosis.

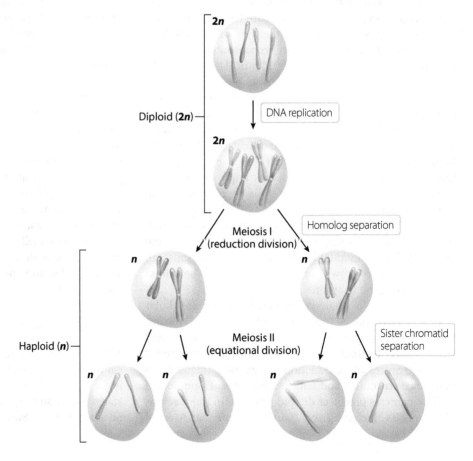

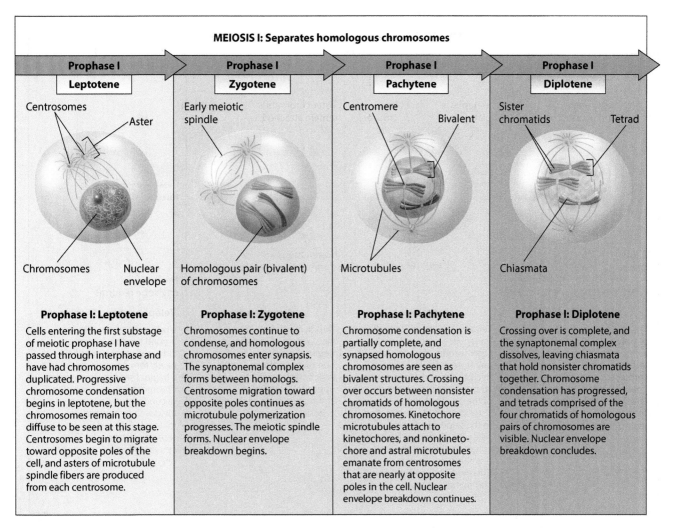

MEIOSIS I: Separates homologous chromosomes

Prophase I	Prophase I	Prophase I	Prophase I
Leptotene	**Zygotene**	**Pachytene**	**Diplotene**

Prophase I: Leptotene

Cells entering the first substage of meiotic prophase I have passed through interphase and have had chromosomes duplicated. Progressive chromosome condensation begins in leptotene, but the chromosomes remain too diffuse to be seen at this stage. Centrosomes begin to migrate toward opposite poles of the cell, and asters of microtubule spindle fibers are produced from each centrosome.

Prophase I: Zygotene

Chromosomes continue to condense, and homologous chromosomes enter synapsis. The synaptonemal complex forms between homologs. Centrosome migration toward opposite poles continues as microtubule polymerization progresses. The meiotic spindle forms. Nuclear envelope breakdown begins.

Prophase I: Pachytene

Chromosome condensation is partially complete, and synapsed homologous chromosomes are seen as bivalent structures. Crossing over occurs between nonsister chromatids of homologous chromosomes. Kinetochore microtubules attach to kinetochores, and nonkinetochore and astral microtubules emanate from centrosomes that are nearly at opposite poles in the cell. Nuclear envelope breakdown continues.

Prophase I: Diplotene

Crossing over is complete, and the synaptonemal complex dissolves, leaving chiasmata that hold nonsister chromatids together. Chromosome condensation has progressed, and tetrads comprised of the four chromatids of homologous pairs of chromosomes are visible. Nuclear envelope breakdown concludes.

Figure 3.10   **The stages of meiosis** (*continued on p. 76*).

homologous chromosomes separate from one another, reducing the diploid number of chromosomes ($2n$) to the haploid number (n). In meiosis II, sister chromatids separate to produce four haploid gametes, each with one chromosome of every diploid pair.

Following the completion of meiosis, each gamete contains a single nucleus holding a haploid chromosome set. The gametes of the two sexes are often dramatically different in size and morphology, however. Female gametes are generally much larger than male gametes and have a haploid nucleus, a large amount of cytoplasm, and a full array of organelles. In contrast, male gametes contain a haploid nucleus but very little cytoplasm and virtually no organelles. As the fertilized ovum begins mitotic division, the organelles and cytoplasmic structures provided by the maternal gamete support its early zygotic growth.

Meiosis I

Three hallmark events take place during meiosis I:

1. Homologous chromosome pairing

2. Crossing over between homologous chromosomes

3. Segregation (separation) of the homologous chromosomes that reduces chromosomes to the haploid number

Meiosis I is divided into four stages: prophase I, metaphase I, anaphase I, and telophase I. Homologous chromosome pairing, called chromosome synapsis, and recombination take place in prophase I; thus, this stage is subdivided into five substages—leptotene stage, zygotene stage, pachytene stage, diplotene stage, and diakinesis stage—to more accurately trace the interactions and recombination of homologous chromosomes. Figure 3.10 describes these stages and prophase I substages in detail.

Chromosome condensation begins during leptotene, when the meiotic spindle is formed by microtubules emanating from the centrosomes, which are moving to positions at opposite ends of the cell. The nuclear membrane begins to break down in zygotene, and the first hallmark feature of meiosis occurs—homologous chromosome **synapsis,** the alignment of homologous chromosome pairs. Synapsis initiates formation of a protein bridge called the **synaptonemal complex,** a tri-layer

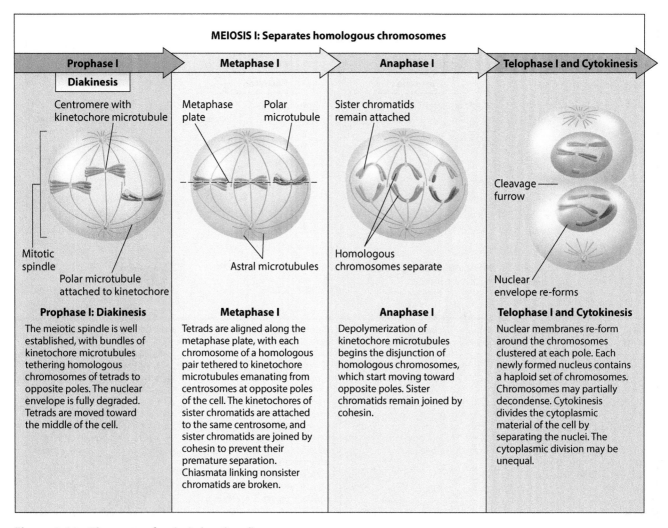

MEIOSIS I: Separates homologous chromosomes

Prophase I	Metaphase I	Anaphase I	Telophase I and Cytokinesis

Prophase I: Diakinesis

The meiotic spindle is well established, with bundles of kinetochore microtubules tethering homologous chromosomes of tetrads to opposite poles. The nuclear envelope is fully degraded. Tetrads are moved toward the middle of the cell.

Metaphase I

Tetrads are aligned along the metaphase plate, with each chromosome of a homologous pair tethered to kinetochore microtubules emanating from centrosomes at opposite poles of the cell. The kinetochores of sister chromatids are attached to the same centrosome, and sister chromatids are joined by cohesin to prevent their premature separation. Chiasmata linking nonsister chromatids are broken.

Anaphase I

Depolymerization of kinetochore microtubules begins the disjunction of homologous chromosomes, which start moving toward opposite poles. Sister chromatids remain joined by cohesin.

Telophase I and Cytokinesis

Nuclear membranes re-form around the chromosomes clustered at each pole. Each newly formed nucleus contains a haploid set of chromosomes. Chromosomes may partially decondense. Cytokinesis divides the cytoplasmic material of the cell by separating the nuclei. The cytoplasmic division may be unequal.

Figure 3.10   The stages of meiosis (continued).

protein structure that maintains synapsis by tightly binding *nonsister chromatids* of homologous chromosomes to one another (Figure 3.11).

Nonsister chromatids are chromatids belonging to different members of a homologous pair of chromosomes. The binding of nonsister chromatids by a synaptonemal complex draws the homologs into close contact (synapsis). The synaptonemal complex contains two lateral elements, each consisting of proteins adhered to a chromatid from a different member of a pair of homologous chromosomes as well as a central element that joins the lateral elements. The function of the synaptonemal complex is to properly align homologous chromosomes before their separation and then to facilitate recombination between homologous chromosomes.

Chromosome condensation continues in pachytene, and sister chromatids of each chromosome can be visually distinguished by light microscopy. At this stage, the paired homologs are called a tetrad in recognition of the four chromatids that are microscopically visible in each homologous pair. Within the central element of the synaptonemal complex, new structures called **recombination nodules** appear at intervals.

Recombination nodules play a pivotal role in **crossing over** of genetic material between nonsister chromatids of homologous chromosomes. The number of recombination nodules correlates closely with the average number of crossover events along each homologous chromosome arm. Two important observations have been made about recombination nodules. First, their appearance and location within the synaptonemal complex is coincident with the timing and location of crossing over; and second, recombination nodules seem to be present in organisms that undergo crossing over and absent in those that do not. Cell biologists have concluded that recombination nodules are aggregations of enzymes and proteins that are required to carry out genetic exchange between the nonsister chromatids of homologous chromosomes during pachytene. Later chapters discuss the genetic consequences of crossing over (Chapter 5) and the molecular processes of crossing over (Chapter 12).

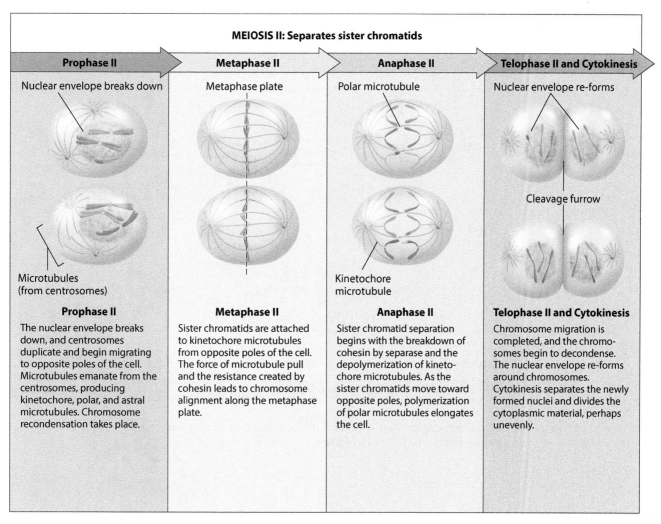

MEIOSIS II: Separates sister chromatids

| Prophase II | Metaphase II | Anaphase II | Telophase II and Cytokinesis |

Nuclear envelope breaks down

Metaphase plate

Polar microtubule

Nuclear envelope re-forms

Cleavage furrow

Microtubules (from centrosomes)

Kinetochore microtubule

Prophase II

The nuclear envelope breaks down, and centrosomes duplicate and begin migrating to opposite poles of the cell. Microtubules emanate from the centrosomes, producing kinetochore, polar, and astral microtubules. Chromosome recondensation takes place.

Metaphase II

Sister chromatids are attached to kinetochore microtubules from opposite poles of the cell. The force of microtubule pull and the resistance created by cohesin leads to chromosome alignment along the metaphase plate.

Anaphase II

Sister chromatid separation begins with the breakdown of cohesin by separase and the depolymerization of kinetochore microtubules. As the sister chromatids move toward opposite poles, polymerization of polar microtubules elongates the cell.

Telophase II and Cytokinesis

Chromosome migration is completed, and the chromosomes begin to decondense. The nuclear envelope re-forms around chromosomes. Cytokinesis separates the newly formed nuclei and divides the cytoplasmic material, perhaps unevenly.

Figure 3.10   The stages of meiosis.

The chromosomes continue to condense in diplotene as the synaptonemal complex begins to dissolve. The dissolution allows homologs to pull apart slightly, revealing contact points between nonsister chromatids. These contact points are called **chiasmata** (singular: **chiasma**), and they are located along chromosomes where crossing over has occurred. Chiasmata mark the locations of DNA-strand exchange between nonsister chromatids of homologous chromosomes.

Cohesin protein is present between sister chromatids to resist the pulling forces of kinetochore microtubules (Figure 3.12). In diakinesis, kinetochore microtubules actively move synapsed chromosome pairs toward the metaphase plate, where the homologs will align side by side.

The chiasmata between homologous chromosomes are resolved in late prophase I so that the homologs can be aligned in metaphase I. This process of resolving the contacts between homologs is critical as to the completion of recombination between homologous chromosomes.

Homologous chromosomes align on opposite sides of the metaphase plate in metaphase I. Kinetochore microtubules from one centrosome attach to the kinetochores of *both* sister chromatids of one chromosome. Meanwhile, kinetochore microtubules from the other centrosome attach to the kinetochores of the sister chromatids of the homolog. Karyokinesis takes place in anaphase I as homologous chromosomes separate from one another and are dragged to opposite poles of the cell (see Figure 3.10). The sister chromatids of each chromosome remain firmly joined by cohesin. Nuclear membrane reformation takes place in telophase I, when a haploid set of chromosomes are enclosed at each pole of the cell. Cytokinesis follows the completion of telophase I.

Homologous chromosome disjunction (separation) in meiosis I reduces the number of chromosomes at each pole to the haploid number, so that one representative of each homologous pair of chromosomes is present. The first meiotic division is known as the *reduction division,* to signify the reduction of chromosome number from diploid to haploid.

Recall that sex chromosomes differ from their autosomal counterparts in that the X chromosome and Y

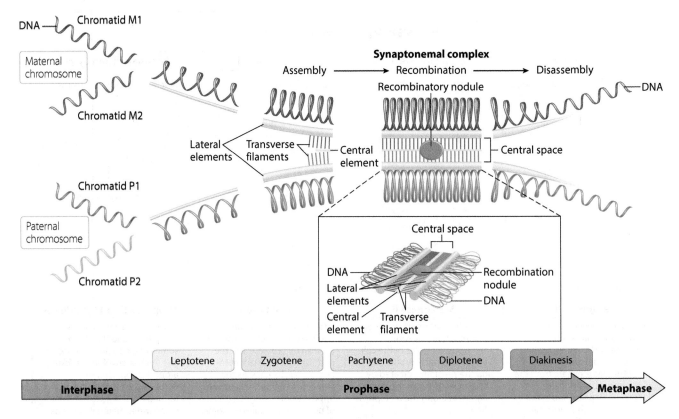

Figure 3.11 The synaptonemal complex. A detailed line drawing of the synaptonemal complex and associated recombination nodules based on electron micrographs.

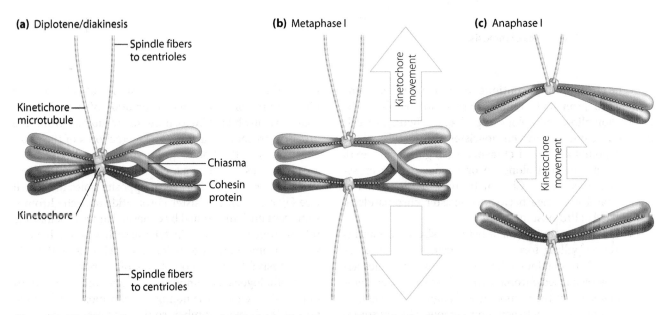

Figure 3.12 Homolog separation in meiosis I. (a) In diplotene and diakinesis of prophase I, crossing over between homologs is complete and contacts between homologs (chiasmata) are resolved. **(b)** Spindle fibers pull chromosomes to align them on the metaphase plate. Cohesin protein adheres sister chromatids against the pull of spindle fibers. **(c)** Homologous chromosomes separate at anaphase I.

chromosome have very few genes in common. Even so, the X and Y chromosomes of males align as homologs in prophase I. This synapsis is accomplished with the aid of **pseudoautosomal regions (PARs)** on the two types of sex chromosomes. The term *pseudoautosomal* means "false autosomal"; a PAR is a segment of homology between otherwise different chromosomes. PARs are like homologous sequences carried on authentic autosomes. The pattern of inheritance of a pseudoautosomal region would be indistinguishable from the pattern of autosomal inheritance, as a consequence of the homology.

Human X and Y chromosomes each contain two pseudoautosomal regions, PAR1 and PAR2, that are located at opposite ends of the chromosomes (Figure 3.13). PAR1 is located on the short arms of the X and Y chromosomes and contains about 2.7 Mb (millions of base pairs) of DNA. PAR2 is located on the long arms of the chromosomes and is shorter than PAR1—about 300,000 base pairs. Crossing over during chromosome synapsis occurs regularly between PAR1 regions. Studies estimate the rate of recombination to be as much as twentyfold higher than for an equivalently sized region in autosomes.

Meiosis II

The second meiotic division divides each haploid product of meiosis I by separating sister chromatids from one another in a process that is reminiscent of mitosis, except that the number of chromosomes in each cell is one-half the number observed in mitosis. The products of meiosis II mature to form the gametes that contain a haploid set of chromosomes. The four stages of meiosis II—prophase II, metaphase II, anaphase II, and telophase II—are shown and described in Figure 3.10.

Meiosis II bears a general resemblance to mitosis in that kinetochore microtubules from opposite centrosomes attach to the kinetochores of sister chromatids. Also, as in mitosis, in meiosis II the chromosomes align randomly along the metaphase plate. Furthermore, sister

chromatid separation is accompanied by cohesin breakdown, the action of motor proteins, and depolymerization of microtubules. Cytokinesis takes place at the end of telophase II. There are, however, only a haploid number of chromosomes present in each cell during meiosis II. Four genetically distinct haploid cells, each carrying one chromosome that represents each homologous pair, are the products of meiosis II.

The Mechanistic Basis of Mendelian Ratios

The separation of homologous chromosomes and sister chromatids in meiosis constitutes the mechanical basis of Mendel's laws of segregation and independent assortment. The connection between meiosis and Mendelian hereditary principles was first suggested, independently, by Walter Sutton and Theodor Boveri in 1903. Based on microscopic observations of chromosomes during meiosis, Sutton and Boveri proposed two important ideas. First, meiosis was the process generating Mendel's rules of heredity; and second, genes were located on chromosomes. Over the next 2 decades, work on numerous species proved these hypotheses to be correct.

We can understand segregation by following a pair of homologous chromosomes through meiosis in a heterozygous organism. The organism in Figure 3.14, for example, has the *Aa* heterozygous genotype. DNA replication in S phase creates identical sister chromatids for each chromosome. At metaphase I, the homologs align on opposite sides of the metaphase plate; and at

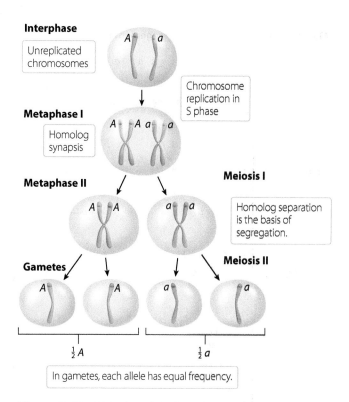

Figure 3.14 **Meiosis and the law of segregation.**

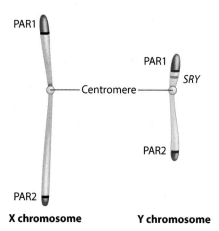

Figure 3.13 **The pseudoautosomal regions of the X and Y chromosomes.**

anaphase I, the homologs separate from one another. This movement segregates the chromosome composed of two *A*-bearing chromatids from the chromosome bearing the two *a*-containing chromatids. Following these cells through to the separation of sister chromatids in meiosis II, we find that among the four gametes are two containing the *A* allele and two containing *a*. This outcome explains the 1:1 ratio of alleles that the law of segregation predicts for gametes of a heterozygous organism.

The independent assortment of alleles is illustrated by the behavior of two pairs of homologs during meiotic division in an organism, as demonstrated in Figure 3.15 using the *AaBb* dihybrid genotype. Once again, S phase creates two identical sister chromatids for each chromosome. In metaphase I, however, two equally likely arrangements of the two homologous

pairs can occur. In each arrangement, the homologous chromosomes are on opposite sides of the metaphase plate. Obviously, when a cell undergoes meiosis, only one or the other of these alternative arrangements will occur; thus, each cell undergoing metaphase I of meiosis will have either "arrangement I" or "arrangement II." Over a large number of meiotic divisions, arrangement I and arrangement II are equally frequent. Arrangement I has chromosomes carrying dominant alleles on one side of the metaphase plate, and chromosomes carrying recessives on the opposite side. Arrangement II has a dominant-bearing and a recessive-bearing chromosome on each side of the metaphase plate. The first meiotic division segregates *A* from *a* and *B* from *b* to create the haploid products of meiosis I division.

If we now follow each haploid product of meiosis I through the meiosis II division, we see that the four

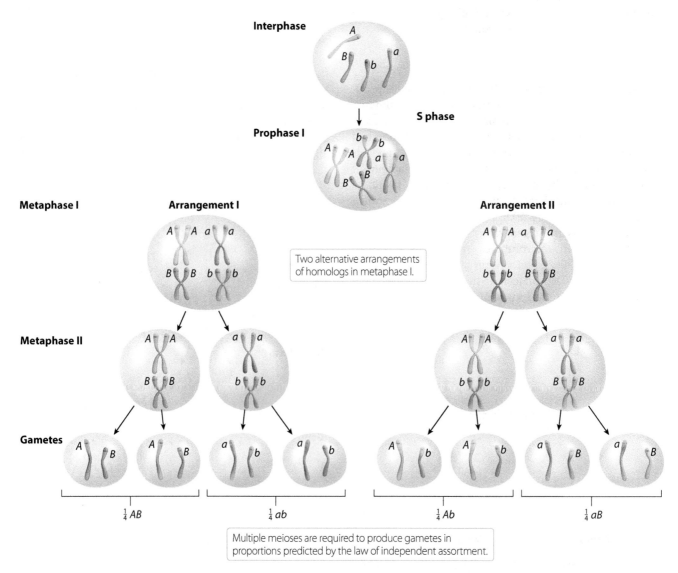

Figure 3.15 **Meiosis and the law of independent assortment.**

gametes produced by arrangement I have the genotypes *AB* and *ab* in equal frequency. In contrast, the four gametes produced by arrangement II have the genotypes *Ab* and *aB* in equal frequency. Taking both possible arrangements of homologous chromosomes at metaphase I into account, eight gametes are generated with four equally frequent genotypes. Each of the gamete genotypes—*AB, Ab, aB,* and *ab*—is produced in a frequency of 25%. The result of a large number of meiotic divisions in an *AaBb* dihybrid is a 1:1:1:1 ratio among gametes, as expected by Mendel's law of independent assortment.

Segregation in Single-Celled Diploids

We have seen that in sexually reproducing plants and animals, (1) the segregation of alleles can be explained by the disjunction of homologous chromosomes in meiosis I, and (2) independent assortment results from the different combinations of alleles to be found among the many gametes produced by an organism. Direct support of these conclusions is observed in the sexual reproduction of single-celled organisms such as yeast, which form diploid genomes for the purpose of sexual reproduction.

The yeast species *Saccharomyces cerevisiae* (also known as baker's yeast) can live and reproduce as a haploid but that can also form a diploid genome and produce gametes. Meiosis in *S. cerevisiae* produces four haploid gametes, called spores, that are contained in a sac-like structure called an **ascus.** The spores can be removed from the ascus and grown individually to reveal the alleles they contain.

S. cerevisiae, like all yeast, can reproduce by either sexual or asexual means. Asexual reproduction takes place in haploid cells by a process called budding, in which a haploid daughter cell grows out of the progenitor (parental) cell. Following DNA replication, sister chromatids separate and move into separate nuclei. One nucleus moves into a small bud that forms the daughter cell and is pinched off from the progenitor cell by cytokinesis. The newly formed bud has the same haploid genotype as its progenitor cell.

Sexual reproduction in *S. cerevisiae* is induced by starvation conditions and involves the union of two haploid yeast cells that are of different *mating types.* The mating types, called MATa and MATα, result from a difference in gene expression. Only the cross MATa × MATα produces a diploid strain, and meiosis in diploids produces the ascus containing four gametes.

To demonstrate these events, let us look at a visible marker of allelic variation in yeast (**Figure 3.16**). The wild-type allele (ADE^+) for synthesis of the nucleotide base adenine leads to the growth of a white yeast colony. In contrast, mutant alleles (ade^-) that partially block adenine synthesis produce the growth of red-colored colonies. The red color appears in ade^- mutants due to the buildup of an intermediate product in the adenine synthesis pathway.

When the haploid cross MATa ADE^+ × MATα ade^- is made, the resulting diploid has the heterozygous genotype ADE^+/ade^-. Meiosis in this heterozygous strain produces an ascus containing four haploid spores that can be separated and grown independently to form colonies. The plate illustrated in Figure 3.16 shows two red yeast colonies and two white colonies, directly illustrating the 1:1 ratio expected for allelic segregation during meiosis in the heterozygous organism.

Genetic Analysis 3.1 gives you practice identifying the principles of Mendelian transmission in meiotic cell division.

3.3 The Chromosome Theory of Heredity Proposes That Genes Are Carried on Chromosomes

The early 20th century was a time of rapid expansion of genetic knowledge, fueled in large part by the rediscovery of Mendel's hereditary principles in 1900 and, to a somewhat lesser extent, by Sutton and Boveri's proposal that chromosome behavior in meiosis mirrors hereditary transmission of genes. Biologists were hard at work testing the new "gene hypotheses" of segregation and independent assortment in an array of organisms.

Thomas Hunt Morgan, initially skeptical of the gene hypothesis, began working on the tiny fruit fly *Drosophila melanogaster.* Morgan intended to rigorously test Mendel's rules in a natural species, not a domesticated one like *Pisum sativum.* Unlike Mendel, however, Morgan had no readily available phenotypic variants to examine. So, he and his students set out from their laboratory at Columbia University in New York City to the then-rural landscape of Long Island to attract fruit flies by hanging buckets of rotting fruit on trees. Once captured and transported back to the laboratory, the flies were examined under the microscope to identify phenotypic variants. Flies captured from the wild were almost invariably of the same phenotype for each trait examined, and Morgan's group referred to these phenotypes as the "wild type." We use the term *wild-type* today to signify the phenotype that is the most common in a population.

Morgan found *Drosophila* an easy organism to maintain and reproduce in small glass bottles filled with a semisolid mixture of cornmeal, sugar, and water. The life cycle of *Drosophila* is between 12 and 14 days depending on growth conditions, so 25 to 30 generations could be raised in a year. Morgan took advantage of this rapid reproduction to raise large numbers of flies over many generations, searching for occasional de novo (i.e., newly occurring) mutant phenotypes in his laboratory-reared populations and also in flies captured in the wild. Over several years, he found many phenotypic variants that he used for performing and analyzing controlled genetic crosses between selected male and female fruit flies.

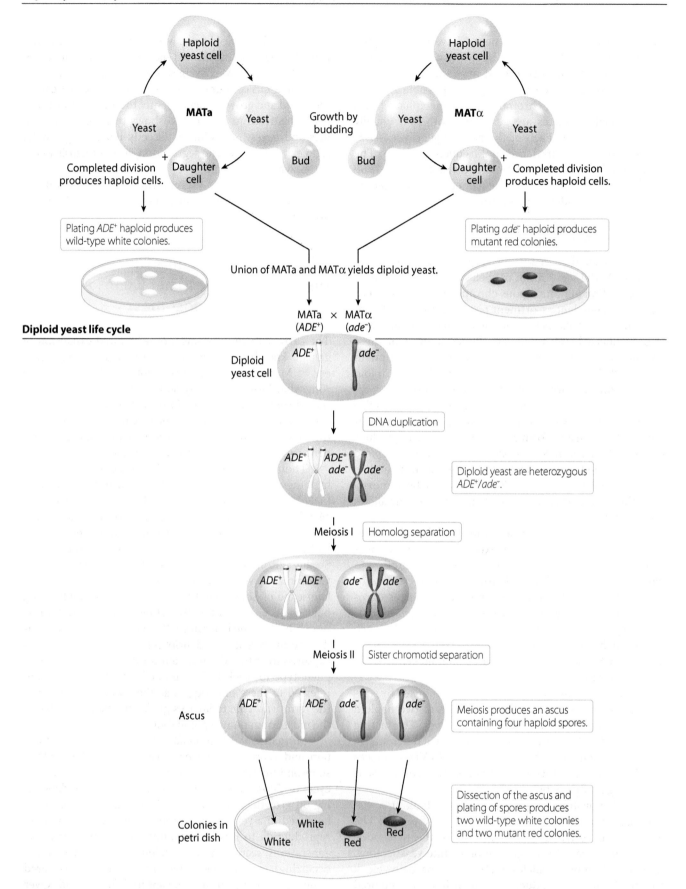

Figure 3.16 **Direct observation of the chromosomal basis of allelic segregation in the haploid–diploid life cycle of yeast.**

PROBLEM A diploid organism has the genotype $D_1D_2E_1E_2$. Gene *D* and gene *E* are on different chromosomes. In the diagrams requested, illustrate only these two pairs of chromosomes and label each copy of each allele on chromosomes and sister chromatids.

> **BREAK IT DOWN:** This organism is a dihybrid (heterozygous for two genes). A total of four chromosomes—two homologous pairs—must be illustrated (p. 81).

a. Diagram *any correct* mitotic metaphase, illustrate these two pairs of chromosomes, and label the alleles.

b. Diagram *any correct* meiotic metaphase I, illustrate these two pairs of chromosomes, and label the alleles.

> **BREAK IT DOWN:** There is more than one correct way to answer this and other questions posed in this problem. Follow the rules of segregation and independent assortment (p. 81).

c. Describe the differences between the diagrams with respect to homolog and chromosome alignment.

d. Compare the outcome of mitosis with the outcome of meiosis in terms of the number of chromosomes and the genotype of the cells produced.

> **BREAK IT DOWN:** Figures 3.6 and 3.9 provide overviews of mitosis and meiosis in terms of chromosome division (p. 71 and 74).

Solution Strategies	Solution Steps
Evaluate	
1. Identify the topic of this problem and the kind of information the answer should contain.	1. This problem concerns comparisons of mitosis and meiosis. Parts (a) and (b) require illustration of chromosome alignments at metaphase in mitosis and in meiosis I. Part (c) requires an explanation of the differences in those alignments, and part (d) requires comparison of the outcomes of mitosis and meiosis.
2. Identify the critical information given in the problem.	2. The organism is identified as a dihybrid for a pair of autosomal genes on different chromosomes.

> **TIP:** Heterozygous organisms carry different alleles on homologous chromosomes, but the alleles on sister chromatids are identical.

Deduce	
3. DNA duplicates in S phase. Identify the distribution of the different alleles on homologous chromosomes following completion of S phase.	3. Sister chromatids carry identical alleles as a result of DNA replication in S phase. Thus, for example, sister chromatids of a single chromosome each carry a copy of *D1*. Likewise, identical alleles are carried on each set of sister chromatids.
4. Review the overall patterns of chromosome alignment along the metaphase plate during mitotic and meiotic divisions.	4. During mitotic metaphase, chromosomes align in single file and in an arbitrary order along the metaphase plate. In meiotic metaphase I, homologs align opposite one another along the metaphase plate.

Solve

Answer a

5. Diagram chromosome alignment during mitotic metaphase.

5. Any order of the four chromosomes in single file along the metaphase plate is a correct order. One example is shown.

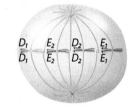

Answer b

6. Diagram any correct chromosome alignment during meiotic metaphase I.

6. Homologous chromosomes align opposite one another along the metaphase plate in meiotic metaphase I. The two correct arrangements of order of homologous chromosomes are shown.

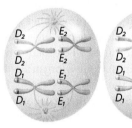

Answer c

7. Describe the diagram differences with respect to homologs.

7. Homologous chromosomes synapse in meiosis, but not in mitosis. The consequence of synapsis is that homologs align next to one another and on opposite sides of the metaphase plate in metaphase I. The absence of synapsis in mitosis leads chromosomes to align in any order along the metaphase plate in mitotic metaphase.

Answer d

8. Describe the different outcomes of mitosis and meiosis.

8. Mitosis produces two diploid daughter cells that are genetically identical to one another and to the parental cell they are derived from. Meiosis produces four haploid daughter cells that are genetically different.

X-Linked Inheritance

While Sutton and Boveri were observing chromosome movements during meiosis, a researcher named Nettie Stevens was beginning a microscopic study to determine whether differences in chromosomes were evident between males and females of a species of beetles, *Tenebrio molitor*. In *T. molitor*, Stevens found that diploid cells of female beetles contained 20 large chromosomes, but diploid cells of males contained only 19 large chromosomes and 1 small chromosome. When examining the chromosomes in *T. molitor* eggs and sperm, Stevens observed that all eggs contain 10 large chromosomes. Her examination of sperm, however, showed that about half the sperm she examined contained 10 large chromosomes while the other half contained 9 large chromosomes and 1 small chromosome.

Stevens went on to study the chromosomes in somatic cells and gametes of other insects, and she concluded that sex-dependent hereditary differences are due to the presence of two large X chromosomes in females and one X chromosome and a much smaller Y chromosome in males. **Sex-linked inheritance** refers to the hereditary transmission of genes on the sex chromosomes. Stevens proposed that sex chromosomes in ova of *T. molitor* are always of the same type—each ovum contains a copy of every autosomal chromosome and one X chromosome. On the other hand, sperm can carry one copy of every autosome and either an X chromosome or a Y chromosome. Stevens suggested that the presence of either an X or a Y chromosome in sperm determines the sex of offspring and that the equal frequency of X- and Y-bearing sperm accounts for the equal proportions of male and female offspring seen in crosses. Stevens was one of the first biologists to examine the transmission of sex-linked traits, and her studies of *T. molitor* were the first to propose a chromosomal basis for sex determination.

In 1910, Thomas Hunt Morgan began a series of experiments in *Drosophila* that would validate Stevens's proposal that X and Y chromosomes help determine sex and would also provide evidence suggesting that genes are carried on chromosomes. The experiments began when Lilian Morgan, Thomas Hunt Morgan's wife and an important contributor to the laboratory group, found a mutant male *Drosophila* with white eyes in a bottle of wild-type flies that had been maintained in the lab for about a year. This white-eyed male stood out as a mutant because in *Drosophila*, wild-type flies have eyes the color of red bricks (**Figure 3.17**).

The mutant white-eyed male was crossed to a wild-type, red-eyed female. The cross produced 1237 F_1 flies, all with red eyes—a result indicating dominance of the wild type over the mutant. Subsequently, the F_1 were crossed to one another to produce an F_2 that were expected to have a 3:1 ratio of red eyes to white eyes. Among the F_2 were 2459 red-eyed females, 1011 red-eyed males, and 782 white-eyed males (Cross A in **Figure 3.18**). No white-eyed females appeared in the F_2. Clearly, the F_2 result differed significantly from expectation, and white eyes seemed to be linked to male sex.

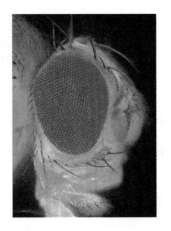

Figure 3.17 **X-linked eye-color phenotypes in *Drosophila melanogaster*.** Red eyes (left) are produced by a dominant wild-type allele. White eyes (right) are produced by a recessive mutant allele.

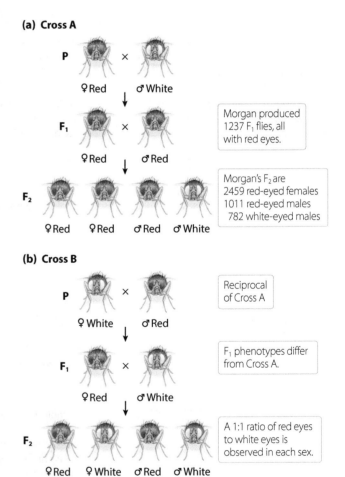

(a) Cross A

P — ♀ Red × ♂ White

Morgan produced 1237 F_1 flies, all with red eyes.

F_1 — ♀ Red × ♂ Red

Morgan's F_2 are
2459 red-eyed females
1011 red-eyed males
782 white-eyed males

F_2 — ♀ Red   ♀ Red   ♂ Red   ♂ White

(b) Cross B

P — ♀ White × ♂ Red

Reciprocal of Cross A

F_1 — ♀ Red × ♂ White

F_1 phenotypes differ from Cross A.

F_2 — ♀ Red   ♀ White   ♂ Red   ♂ White

A 1:1 ratio of red eyes to white eyes is observed in each sex.

Figure 3.18 **Two reciprocal *Drosophila* crosses performed by Morgan to determine X-linkage of the gene for eye color.** (a) Cross A determines that all F_1 flies and all female F_2 flies have red (wild-type) eye color. One-half of F_2 males have red eyes and one-half have white eyes. (b) Cross B is the reciprocal of Cross A, producing a different result in the F_1 and F_2 generations.

The unexpected result from this cross prompted a closer look at transmission of white eyes to a white-eyed female with a wild-type, red-eyed male. The F_1 of the reciprocal cross were red-eyed females and white-eyed males (Cross B in Figure 3.18). The F_2 contained equal proportions of red-eyed and white-eyed males and females.

Diagrams of the crosses in Figure 3.18 are illustrated in **Figure 3.19**, where w represents the recessive allele for white eye and w^+ the dominant allele for red

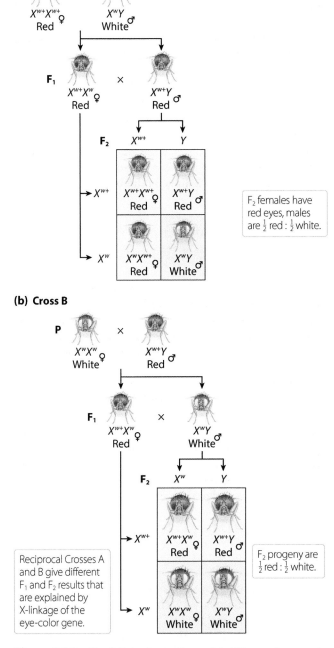

(a) Cross A

F$_2$ females have red eyes, males are $\frac{1}{2}$ red : $\frac{1}{2}$ white.

(b) Cross B

Reciprocal Crosses A and B give different F_1 and F_2 results that are explained by X-linkage of the eye-color gene.

F$_2$ progeny are $\frac{1}{2}$ red : $\frac{1}{2}$ white.

Figure 3.19   The X-linked genetic model of Morgan's eye-color inheritance experiments in *Drosophila*. X and Y chromosome segregation in **(a)** Cross A and **(b)** Cross B from Figure 3.18.

eye. The differences between reciprocal crosses observed by Morgan are not anticipated by Mendel's laws of heredity. In fact, recall that Mendel performed many reciprocal crosses and found no differences in the phenotype proportions. Morgan realized that transmission of X chromosomes in *Drosophila* could account for the appearance of white and red eyes in his crosses if the X chromosome carried a gene for eye color. In Cross A, the single X chromosome of a white-eyed male carries a recessive allele designated w. The X chromosome is present along with a Y chromosome in the genome of the male fruit fly. X chromosomes of females each carry a dominant allele w^+ that produces red eye color. The F_1 of this cross are red-eyed males that are w^+Y and red-eyed females that are w^+w. The F_2 of this cross contain equal proportions of white-eyed (wY) and red-eyed (w^+Y) males and red-eyed females that are, in equal proportions, w^+w^+ and w^+w. Cross B between a white-eyed female and a red-eyed male produces red-eyed female and white-eyed male F_1 progeny as well as equal proportions of red- and white-eyed males and females in the F_2.

Morgan's analysis of these experiments describes **X-linked inheritance,** a term identifying the transmission of genes carried on the X chromosome. Morgan proposed X-linked inheritance as the mode of transmission of eye color in *Drosophila*. Morgan's X-linked inheritance hypothesis requires some new terminology in reference to male genotypes for X-linked genes. We use the term **hemizygous,** a word meaning "half zygous," to refer to male genotypes for X-linked genes. This term is used because males have a single X chromosome; therefore, unlike females, males cannot be homozygous or heterozygous for X-linked genes. Hemizygous males inherit their X chromosome from their mother; moreover, they express any allele on their X chromosome, since the Y chromosome does not carry genes that are homologous to those on the X chromosome. In contrast to males, females have two X chromosomes and can display heterozygous and homozygous genotypes for X-linked genes, just as they can for autosomal genes. Note also that males can transmit either the X chromosome or the Y chromosome, but that the X chromosome is passed exclusively to female progeny and the Y chromosome exclusively to male progeny. In contrast, females can transmit either X chromosome to any of their offspring.

Testing the Chromosome Theory of Heredity

Morgan's observations on the inheritance pattern of *Drosophila* eye color led him to propose the chromosome theory of heredity, hypothesizing that genes are carried on chromosomes. Calvin Bridges, a student of Morgan, studied fruit flies with unexpected eye-color phenotypes and abnormal chromosome numbers and provided proof of the chromosome theory of heredity.

Bridges focused his study on Cross B (see Figures 3.18 and 3.19), between a white-eyed female (ww) and a red-eyed male (w^+Y). Nearly all the progeny from this cross had the expected phenotype and were either red-eyed females (w^+w) or white-eyed males (wY), but about 1 in every 2000 F_1 flies had an "exceptional phenotype"—a term used to identify progeny with unexpected characteristics. Specifically, the exceptional flies were either white-eyed *females* or red-eyed *males*. Bridges's detection of exceptional progeny left him with two questions to answer: (1) how could the exceptional progeny be explained, and (2) did the appearance of exceptional progeny provide the information necessary to test the hypothesis that genes are on chromosomes?

The answer to the first question came when Bridges looked at chromosomes of the exceptional progeny under the microscope. He saw the exceptional females had three sex chromosomes—two X chromosomes and one Y chromosome (XXY) (**Figure 3.20**). As we discuss in the next section, fruit flies with two X chromosomes are females, even if there happens to be a Y chromosome as well, as there is in this case. Bridges also observed an abnormal number of chromosomes in exceptional males. They carried a single X chromosome but no Y chromosome (XO). Fruit flies with one X chromosome are male, regardless of whether they carry a Y chromosome.

Based on his observations, Bridges proposed that the Y chromosome carried by exceptional females came from the male parent, the only source of a Y chromosome in the cross, and that both X chromosomes in these exceptional females came from the mother, giving the exceptional females two copies of the w allele and white eye color. Bridges used similar logic to suggest that the single X chromosome in exceptional males came from the male parent that passed the w^+ allele. The exceptional males with a single X chromosome expressed the w^+ allele as red eyes.

According to Bridges's proposal, the exceptional phenotypes and abnormal numbers of chromosomes were the result of rare mistakes in meiosis caused by the failure of X chromosomes to separate properly in either the first or second meiotic division in females. Failed chromosome separation is called **nondisjunction.** Notice in Figure 3.20 that nondisjunction also produces XXX or YO progeny. Bridges never saw these progeny, however, because YO progeny fail to develop, and XXX is usually lethal. Bridges's observations provide conclusive proof of the chromosome theory of heredity by showing that the white (w) allele segregates with the X chromosome during normal meiosis and during nondisjunction. **Genetic Analysis 3.2** gives you some practice spotting X-linked inheritance.

3.4 Sex Determination Is Chromosomal and Genetic

The term **sex determination** encompasses the genetic and biological processes that produce the male and female characteristics of a species. The sex of most organisms is identified on two levels: chromosomal sex, the presence of sex chromosomes associated with male and female sex in a species; and phenotypic sex, the internal and external morphology found in each sex. Chromosomal sex is determined at the moment of fertilization and is controlled by the sex chromosome contributed by the heterogametic parent. In contrast, phenotypic sex is a matter of appropriate gene expression and the development of sex characteristics during gestation or growth. In this section, we examine the patterns and processes of chromosomal and phenotypic sex determination in several organisms.

Sex Determination in *Drosophila*

Bridges's study of X-chromosome nondisjunction and his proof of the chromosome theory of heredity also provided information about sex determination in *Drosophila*. In *Drosophila*, the number of X chromosomes and their relation to the number of haploid sets of autosomal chromosomes are a critical component in determining sex, and the number of Y chromosomes, or even the absence of a second sex chromosome, seems not to disrupt the pattern of sex determination. Thus, in *Drosophila*, flies with the

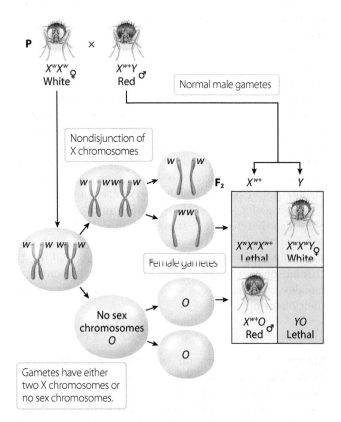

Figure 3.20 Exceptional progeny observed by Calvin Bridges result from X-chromosome nondisjunction during female meiosis.

PROBLEM A female fruit fly from a pure-breeding stock with yellow body color and full wing size is crossed to a male from a pure-breeding stock with gray body and vestigial wings. The cross progeny consists of males with yellow body color and full-sized wings and females with gray body color and full-sized wings.

> **BREAK IT DOWN:** Pure-breeding females and males are homozygous for autosomal alleles. Pure-breeding females are homozygous for X-linked alleles, but males are hemizygous (pp. 89 and 89).

a. Determine the mode of inheritance of each trait.

b. Give genotypes for parental flies and the male and female progeny using clearly defined allele designations of your choice.

> **BREAK IT DOWN:** All male and female progeny have full-sized wings, but they differ in body color, suggesting possible sex-linkage for that trait (p. 87).

Solution Strategies	Solution Steps
Evaluate	
1. Identify the topic of this problem and the kind of information the answer should contain.	1. The patterns of transmission of two *Drosophila* traits and the genotypes of organisms are to be determined based on the number and proportions of male and female F_1 progeny with the traits.
2. Identify the critical information given in the problem.	2. Pure-breeding parental phenotypes are given along with the phenotypes of male and female progeny in the F_1.
Deduce	
3. Consider the F_1 phenotype results in light of the parental phenotypes.	3. All F_1 progeny have full-sized wings and none have vestigial wings, suggesting that full-sized wing is dominant. The F_1 males are exclusively yellow-bodied, whereas F_1 females are exclusively gray-bodied. The F_1 male body color is identical to that of the parental female, whereas the F_1 females' body color is identical to that in the male parent.

TIP: Cross results that appear equally in both sexes are consistent with autosomal inheritance. Sex-dependent differences in a cross suggest sex-linked inheritance.

4. Hypothesize the modes of inheritance of body color and wing form from the F_1 data.	4. The observation of one body color in F_1 males and another in females suggests this is an X-linked trait. Since hemizygous males have yellow body and females have gray body, it is likely that gray body is dominant and yellow body is recessive. The F_1 results for wing form are the same for both sexes, suggesting that this trait is autosomal.

TIP: Test the hypothesized mode of inheritance by comparing the predicted and observed F_1 progeny ratios.

Solve	Answer a
5. Test the proposed mode of transmission of wing form.	5. The F_1 of both sexes have full-sized wings, consistent with an autosomal trait. The pure-breeding full-winged parent transmits the dominant alleles to all progeny, and the pure-breeding vestigial parent transmits the recessive allele. The F_1 are predicted to be heterozygous and display the dominant trait.
6. Test the mode of transmission of body color.	6. The sex-dependent difference in body color among F_1 males and females strongly suggests this trait is X-linked. The F_1 males inherit the maternal recessive allele for yellow body color and express the trait because they are hemizygous. F_1 females inherit a recessive allele on the maternal X chromosome and a dominant allele on the paternal X and are heterozygous, thus displaying the dominant phenotype.

TIP: Compare observed and expected F_2 progeny to test the hypothesized mode of inheritance.

	Answer b
7. Determine genotypes for parental and F_1 flies. Use X^{y^+} for yellow body, X^y for gray body, v^+ for full wing, and v for vestigial wing.	7. The genotypes of pure-breeding parents are X^y/X^y; v^+/v^+ for yellow-bodied, full-winged females and X^{y^+}/Y; v/v for gray-bodied, vestigial-winged males. The F_1 females are X^y/X^{y^+}; v^+/v and F_1 males are X^y/Y; v^+/v.

PITFALL: Remember that males are hemizygous for X-linked traits. Giving their genotype as homozygous or heterozygous is incorrect.

sex-chromosome constitutions XY, XYY, and XO are all male, whereas flies that are XX or XXY are female.

Bridges's *Drosophila* data identified the ratio of X chromosomes to the number of haploid sets of autosomes as 1X:2A in males and as 2X:2A in females. Bridges called this the **X/A ratio,** or the **X/autosome ratio.** In reality, the X/A ratio is too simplistic to explain *Drosophila* sex determination. *Drosophila* sex is determined by regulatory proteins that relay the number of X chromosomes present in nuclei of cells in *Drosophila* embryos. These proteins control expression of the *sex-lethal (Sxl)* gene in XX flies. As we discuss in the Case Study at the end of Chapter 8, Sxl protein controls the expression of additional genes that drive sex development.

Mammalian Sex Determination

Like *Drosophila,* placental mammals have two kinds of sex chromosomes, identified as X and Y. Unlike *Drosophila,* however, sex determination in placental mammals depends on the presence or absence of the Y chromosome. A single gene on the Y chromosome, abbreviated *SRY* (sex-determining region of Y, and also known as the testis determining factor), initiates a series of events that lead to male sex-phenotype development in the embryo. Consequently, mammalian embryos that have one or more Y chromosomes (XY, XXY, and XYY, for example) and therefore express *SRY* will develop as males. Conversely, embryos carrying only X chromosomes (XX, XO, and XXX, for example) and lacking *SRY* expression will develop as females.

SRY expression produces the transcription factor protein testis-determining factor (TDF) that elicits a cascade of gene transcription and developmental events that ultimately produce male internal and external structures. Early mammalian embryos contain twin clusters of tissue identified as undifferentiated gonads that can develop into either ovaries or testes. Connected to the undifferentiated gonads are two sets of tissues called the Wolffian ducts and the Müllerian ducts. The undifferentiated gonads develop, but just one of the ductal tissues develops. Wolffian ducts can develop to form male sexual and reproductive structures. Alternatively, Müllerian ducts can develop to form female sexual and reproductive structures. In male embryos, TDF initiates testicular development by stimulating interstitial cells in the gonadal tissue to synthesize two male androgenic hormones, testosterone and dihydrotestosterone (DHT). These hormones help drive Wolffian duct development that leads to formation of internal and external male sexual and reproductive structures. Separately, in specialized cells called sustentacular cells, TDF stimulates production of Müllerian-inhibitory factor (MIF) that degrades Müllerian ducts to prevent development of female sexual structures (**Figure 3.21**).

Female embryos do not carry a Y chromosome and therefore lack production of TDF. The current model suggests that the absence of TDF suppresses the expression of genes that lead to male development and, instead, leads to

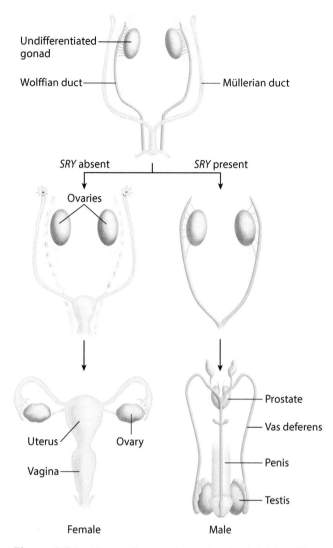

Figure 3.21   Mammalian sex determination is initiated by the Y-linked *SRY* gene.

expression of genes that stimulate the undifferentiated gonad tissue to develop into ovaries and cause Müllerian ducts to develop into female sexual and reproductive structures.

While *SRY* is a necessary gene in mammalian sex development, it is not sufficient by itself to direct sexual development. For example, mutations of X-linked and autosomal genes mentioned in **Experimental Insight 3.1** on page 89 have been identified as causes of abnormalities of human sexual development.

Diversity of Sex Determination

You are now familiar with the XX and XY chromosome designation signifying that females carry two X chromosomes (XX) and males carry an X chromosome and a Y chromosome (XY). In many bird species, some reptiles, certain fish, and moths and butterflies, however, females carry two different sex chromosomes, and males carry two sex chromosomes that are the same. To avoid confusion with the XX/XY system, a different lettering system called

Experimental Insight **3.1**

Mutations Altering Human Sex Development

Many genes in addition to *SRY* direct human sexual development. Here we identify three other genes whose mutation affects the production or cell-signaling capacity of the male androgenic hormones testosterone and DHT (dihydrotestosterone) and results in abnormal sexual development. These conditions have different causes and distinctive consequences. From a medical perspective, ambiguous gender identification is a consequence of the conditions. In personal terms, significant psychosocial issues of self and of gender identity confront individuals with each of these conditions.

ANDROGEN INSENSITIVITY SYNDROME (AIS)

AIS (OMIM 300068) (see the Case Study in Chapter 2, p. 56, for a discussion of OMIM) is caused by mutations of the X-linked *AR* (androgen receptor) gene. *AR* is pivotal in producing androgen receptors on androgen-sensitive cells. AIS individuals are XY, have a fully functional *SRY* gene, and produce normal amounts of testosterone and DHT. In the absence of androgen receptors, however, testosterone and DHT cannot bind to cells, which therefore do not initiate the gene expression that accompanies male sexual development. Due to this deficit, individuals with AIS have an external phenotype that appears to be female (i.e., sex reversal); but internal reproductive structures do not develop as either male or female, thus rendering AIS individuals sterile. Androgen insensitivity prevents development of male sexual structures, whereas *SRY*-initiated MIF production degrades the Müllerian ducts and blocks the development of female sexual structures.

PSEUDOHERMAPHRODITISM

When genes operating in the biochemical pathway controlling testosterone and DHT are mutated, improper androgen levels occur, and individuals can exhibit *pseudohermaphroditism*—a term referring to the appearance of nonfunctional forms of both male and female structures in a single person. Pseudohermaphrodites are sterile. The autosomal recessive disorder 5-alpha-reductase deficiency (OMIM 607306) produces a form of pseudohermaphroditism due to mutation of the steroid 5-alpha-reductase-2 (*SRD5A2*) gene. *SRD5A2* produces 5-alpha-reductase enzyme that helps convert testosterone to DHT. Individuals with 5-alpha-reductase deficiency are XY, have a wild-type *SRY* gene, undergo Wolffian duct development, and express MIF. Wolffian duct development produces male internal structures, but the inability to convert testosterone to DHT results in the absence of external male structures. At birth, individuals with 5-alpha-reductase deficiency appear to be female. At puberty, however, the adrenal glands begin testosterone production that leads to secondary male sexual characteristics such as deepening of the voice, facial hair growth, and development of a masculine physique.

CONGENITAL ADRENAL HYPERPLASIA (CAH)

Mutation of *CYP21*, a gene producing the enzyme 21-hydroxylase, causes the most common form of autosomal recessive congenital adrenal hyperplasia (CAH) (OMIM 201910). Functional 21-hydroxylase participates in depletion of testosterone and DHT; thus, its mutation leads to accumulation of testosterone and DHT. *CYP21* mutation produces pseudohermaphroditism in males and females due to high androgen levels. Boys with CAH enter puberty as early as 3 years of age and display male musculature, enlarged penis, and testes growth. Girls with CAH are born with an enlarged clitoris that can be mistaken for a small penis. While normal internal female reproductive anatomy is present, CAH females experience male-like facial hair growth and deepening voice at puberty. Menstruation does not occur, due to excessive androgen levels.

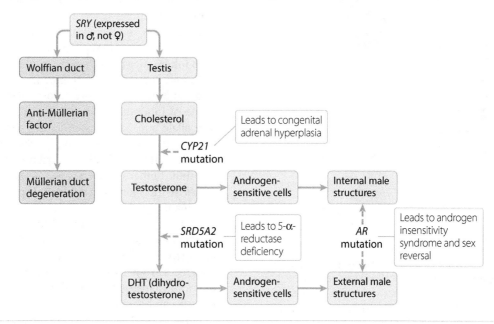

the **Z/W system** is used in these cases. In the Z/W system, males are identified as having two Z sex chromosomes, or a sex chromosome composition of ZZ. In contrast, females have two different sex chromosomes and are identified as ZW. The letters Z and W are used to highlight the different sex-chromosome compositions associated with each sex. In such species, males are designated ZZ and females ZW.

The sex-chromosome differences in the Z/W system produce different results from reciprocal crosses involving Z-linked genes, just as there are reciprocal cross differences for X-linked genes. Figure 3.22 shows reciprocal crosses between pure-breeding hens (female) and roosters (male) involving a Z-linked dominant allele for barred

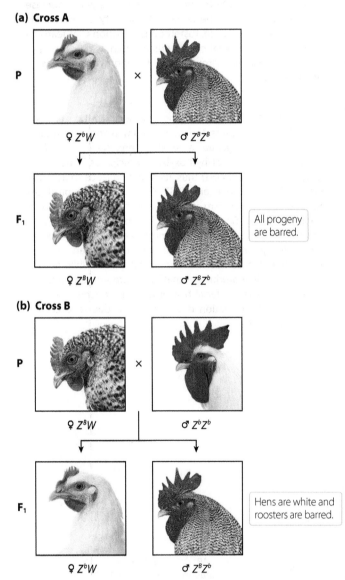

(a) Cross A

P

$♀ Z^bW$ × $♂ Z^BZ^B$

F₁

All progeny are barred.

$♀ Z^BW$ $♂ Z^BZ^b$

(b) Cross B

P

$♀ Z^BW$ × $♂ Z^bZ^b$

F₁

Hens are white and roosters are barred.

$♀ Z^bW$ $♂ Z^BZ^b$

Figure 3.22 **ZW inheritance of feather form in poultry is revealed by analysis of reciprocal crosses.** **(a)** A hemizygous female (hen) with recessive nonbarred (white) feathers crossed to a pure-breeding male (rooster) with dominant barred feathers produces F₁ progeny that are all barred. **(b)** The reciprocal cross produces barred roosters and nonbarred (white) hens.

feathers (Z^B) and its recessive counterpart, nonbarred feathers (Z^b). The F₁ results of the reciprocal crosses reveal differences consistent with sex-linked inheritance. Cross A produces barred hens (Z^BW) and barred roosters (Z^BZ^b) in the F₁, whereas Cross B produces nonbarred hens (Z^bW) and barred roosters (Z^BZ^b). The F₂ results of these crosses also yield differences consistent with sex-linked inheritance. We can conclude that the mechanism of transmission of Z-linked genes in the Z/W system is analogous to that in the XX/XY system except that the patterns are the reverse of those in placental mammals.

Sex chromosome content is even more unusual in monotremes like the platypus, an egg-laying mammal that is native to Australia. Male platypus sex chromosomes are represented as $X_1Y_1X_2Y_2X_3Y_3X_4Y_4X_5Y_5$ and female platypus sex chromosomes as $X_1X_1X_2X_2X_3X_3X_4X_4X_5X_5$. Multiple sets of sex chromosomes have also been documented in some plant species, termites, and spiders. In dioecious plants (those with male plants and female plants), sex chromosomes are often not obvious at all, and they are therefore difficult to study. And, in certain reptiles and fishes, sex is dependent on environmental variables such as temperature. In other words, the sex of an individual can change during its lifetime, even though its chromosomes do not.

3.5 Human Sex-Linked Transmission Follows Distinct Patterns

Sex chromosomes typically differ between males and females of a species and in most animal species, for example, females have two copies of the X chromosome and, therefore, two copies of each gene on the chromosome. In contrast, males typically have one X chromosome and one Y chromosome and, thus, just one copy of each X chromosome gene and one copy of each Y chromosome gene. The inheritance of sex-linked mutant alleles on the X chromosome produces mutant phenotypes in distinctive patterns. Two inheritance patterns of sex-linked genes are common. **X-linked recessive** inheritance is the hereditary pattern that determines white eye color in *Drosophila*. With this mode of inheritance, females homozygous for the recessive allele and hemizygous males whose X chromosome carries the recessive allele display the recessive phenotype. The alternative mode of X-linked transmission is **X-linked dominant** inheritance, in which heterozygous females and males hemizygous for the dominant allele express the dominant phenotype.

Three features of X-linked dominant and X-linked recessive inheritance present a contrast to our description of inheritance of autosomal traits. First, autosomal dominant and recessive alleles generally have the same patterns in males and females, but when the traits are X-linked, the terms *recessive* and *dominant* refer specifically to their expression in females. For X-linked alleles, females can be homozygous or heterozygous, but males are hemizygous and express the

Table 3.2	A Short List of Human X-Linked Dominant and X-Linked Recessive Traits[a]
Disease	**Symptom**
X-Linked Dominant Disorders	
Amelogenesis imperfecta (OMIM 301200)	Abnormal tooth-enamel development and distribution
Congenital generalized hypertrichosis (OMIM 307150)	Extensive hair distribution on the face and body
Hypophosphatemia (OMIM 307800)	Phosphate deficiency causing rickets (bowleggedness)
Rett syndrome (OMIM 312750)	Mental retardation and neurodevelopmental defects
X-Linked Recessive Disorders	
Anhidrotic ectodermal dysplasia (OMIM 305100)	Absence of teeth, hair, and sweat glands
Color blindness (red–green) (OMIM 303800)	Color-perception deficiency
Fragile X syndrome (OMIM 300624)	Mental retardation and neurodevelopmental defects
Hemophilia A (OMIM 306700)	Blood-clotting abnormality
Lesch-Nyhan syndrome (OMIM 300322)	Mental retardation with self-mutilation and spastic cerebral palsy
Muscular dystrophy (Becker type, OMIM 300376) and Duchenne type (OMIM 310200)	Progressive muscle weakness
Ornithine transcarbamylase deficiency (OMIM 311250)	Mental deterioration due to ammonia accumulation with protein ingestion
Retinitis pigmentosa (OMIM 300029)	Night blindness, constricted visual field

[a] OMIM = Online Mendelian Inheritance of Man (see Chapter 2 Case Study for discussion).

allele on their X chromosome, regardless of the hereditary pattern in females. Second, the probability of transmission of X-linked alleles to offspring is not the same for the two sexes as it is for autosomal alleles. Female X-linked transmission is identical to autosomal transmission, but hemizygous males always transmit their X chromosome to female offspring and their Y chromosome to male offspring. Lastly, whereas females receive one copy of X-linked alleles from each parent, males receive their X-linked alleles from their mother and their Y-linked alleles from their father.

Expression of X-Linked Recessive Traits

X-linked recessive traits are expressed in hemizygous males who carry the recessive allele and in females who are homozygous for the recessive allele. Because hemizygous males express the single copy of a recessive X-linked allele in their phenotype, one of the hallmarks of X-linked recessive inheritance is the observation that many more males than females express the traits. Table 3.2 lists several X-linked disorders, including color blindness that affects perception of red and green color and hemophilia A, a blood-clotting disorder that we discuss in more detail just ahead. Four features characterizing X-linked recessive inheritance are illustrated in Figure 3.23.

1. As a result of male hemizygosity, more males than females have the recessive phenotype. There are 10 recessive males and 2 recessive females.

2. If a recessive male mates with a homozygous dominant female, all progeny have the dominant phenotype. All female offspring are heterozygous carriers,

Figure 3.23   An idealized example of X-linked recessive inheritance.

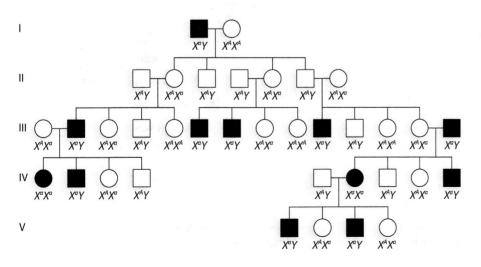

and all male offspring are hemizygous for the dominant allele. See the progeny resulting from the cross I-1 × I-2.

3. Matings of recessive males and carrier females produce the recessive phenotype in half the offspring and the dominant phenotype in the other half. See the results of the crosses III-13 × III-4 and III-1 × III-2.

4. Mating of a homozygous recessive female and a hemizygous dominant male produces male progeny with the recessive phenotype, and female offspring who have the dominant phenotype and are carriers of the recessive allele. See the results of the cross IV-5 × IV-6.

Hemophilia A, a serious blood-clotting disorder, is caused by mutation of an X-linked gene called *factor VIII (F8)* that produces a blood-clotting protein called factor VIII protein. Hemophilia A is transmitted in an X-linked recessive manner, most often by a carrier mother who passes the mutant allele to an affected son. In typical X-linked recessive fashion, approximately half the sons of carrier mothers have the disease. In these families, the disease often appears to "skip" a generation because the mutant allele is passed from affected father to carrier daughter and on to an affected grandson.

In some families, a de novo (newly occurring) mutation of the *F8* gene is responsible for the appearance of hemophilia. An example occurred in the royal families of England and Europe: An apparent de novo mutation of the *F8* gene affected Queen Victoria of England (**Figure 3.24**). Victoria had four sons, one of whom had hemophilia, along with five daughters, two of whom were known carriers. Victoria's carrier daughters had normal blood clotting but introduced the mutation to the royal families of Russia, Germany, and Spain through intermarriage. These daughters passed the mutation to their sons who had hemophilia and to their daughters who were carriers like their mothers. **Genetic Analysis 3.3** analyzes the hereditary transmission of hemophilia A.

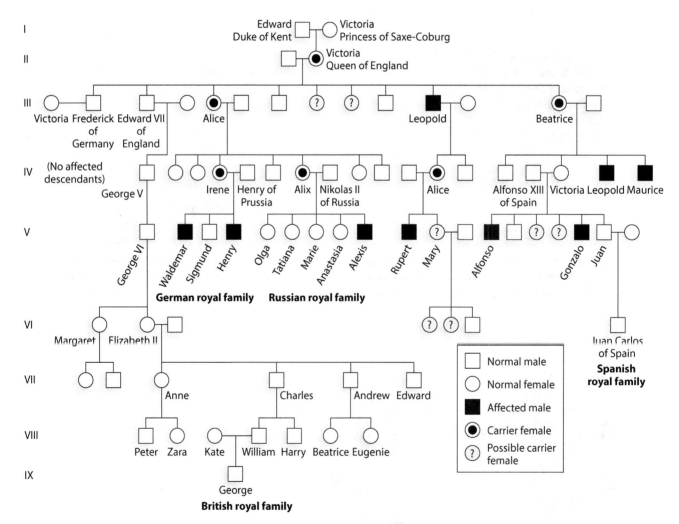

Figure 3.24 Hemophilia in the royal families of Europe. Note that some parents are omitted from the pedigree for clarity. In all cases, these individuals carry and contribute wild-type alleles.

PROBLEM Hemophilia A is an X-linked recessive blood-clotting disorder caused by mutation of the *factor VIII* gene. Suppose a heterozygous woman with normal blood clotting has children with a man who also has normal blood clotting. Determine the probability of each of the following outcomes.

a. The probability of a son having hemophilia A.

b. The probability of a child of either sex having normal blood clotting.

c. The probability of having three children, each of whom has hemophilia A.

d. The probability of having four children, two of whom have hemophilia A and two of whom have normal blood clotting.

> **BREAK IT DOWN:** The woman can transmit the recessive allele to a child of either sex, but the man transmits his X-linked allele to daughters and his Y chromosome to sons (p. 90).

> **BREAK IT DOWN:** The information given about the pattern of inheritance of hemophilia A and the status of the woman and the man allows identification of their genotypes (p. 92).

> **BREAK IT DOWN:** Parts (a) and (b) can be predicted using a Punnett square (p. 33); parts (c) and (d) are applications of binomial probability (p. 91).

Solution Strategies	Solution Steps

Evaluate

1. Identify the topic this problem addresses and describe the nature of the required answers.

2. Identify the critical information given in the problem.

1. This problem addresses inheritance probabilities of an X-linked recessive trait for the parental genotypes given. The answers should be stated as fraction, decimal, or percentage probabilities.

2. The inheritance pattern of the trait in question is identified as X-linked recessive, the phenotype of each parent is given, and the woman is identified as a heterozygote.

Deduce

3. Deduce the genotypes of the woman and the man.

> **TIP:** Remember that males are hemizygous for X-linked traits.

> **TIP:** Use a Punnett square to assist you in accurately predicting the possible outcomes of mating.

4. Determine the possible phenotypes and phenotype probabilities for children of this couple.

3. The woman is identified as being heterozygous and so her genotype is $X^H X^h$, where the uppercase and lowercase superscripts represent the dominant and recessive alleles, respectively. The man has normal blood clotting and is hemizygous for the wild-type allele. His genotype is $X^H Y$.

4. The Punnett square predicts four different genotypes among the possible children of this couple.

	X^H	Y
X^H	$X^H X^H$ Healthy	$X^H Y$ Healthy
X^h	$X^H X^h$ Healthy	$X^h Y$ Hemophilia A

Solve

5. Determine the probability of a child of this couple having hemophilia A.

Answer a

5. From the Punnett square, we see that one of the four possible offspring genotypes is a male with hemophilia A. The probability of having a child with hemophilia A is 0.25, or 25%.

6. Determine the probability of a child with normal blood clotting being produced by this couple.

Answer b

6. The Punnett square also shows that the remaining 3 in 4 possible offspring genotypes would produce normal blood clotting. The probability that a child of this couple has normal blood clotting is 0.75, or 75%.

7. Calculate the probability that if the couple has three children, each of them will have hemophilia A.

Answer c

7. The risk that each child will have hemophilia A is 25%. For three children with hemophilia A, the probability is $(.25)(.25)(.25) = 0.0156$, or $\left(\frac{1}{4}\right)\left(\frac{1}{4}\right)\left(\frac{1}{4}\right) = \frac{1}{64}$.

> **TIP:** Use binomial probability to calculate the likelihood of consecutive outcomes.

8. Calculate the probability that if the couple has four children, two will have hemophilia A and two will have normal blood clotting.

Answer d

8. The chance the couple has four children, two of whom have hemophilia A and two of whom are healthy, is predicted by the binomial expansion. There are six different ways (birth orders) to produce two healthy and two affected children. The probabilities are ¾ for a healthy child and ¼ for a child with hemophilia A, so the requested probability is $6\left[\left(\frac{3}{4}\right)\left(\frac{3}{4}\right)\left(\frac{1}{4}\right)\left(\frac{1}{4}\right)\right] = \left(\frac{54}{256}\right)$, or 0.2109.

For more practice, see Problems 12, 13, and 25.   Visit the Study Area to access study tools.   **MasteringGenetics**™

X-Linked Dominant Trait Transmission

Transmission of traits controlled by X-linked dominant alleles has three distinctive characteristics:

1. Heterozygous females mated to wild-type males transmit the dominant allele to half their progeny of each sex.

2. Because daughters receive their X chromosome from their father, dominant hemizygous males mated to homozygous recessive females transmit the dominant trait to *all* their daughters, but to *none* of their sons.

3. Since just a single copy of the allele is necessary to produce the dominant phenotype, the dominant phenotype is about equally frequent in males and females.

Congenital generalized hypertrichosis (CGH) is a rare and dramatic X-linked dominant disorder in humans that displays each of these characteristics. The condition substantially increases the number of hair follicles on the body and produces much more body hair than normal, both in males and females (Figure 3.25a). Females with CGH have a recognizable phenotype, but face and body hair is less extensive and tends to be present in patches, for reasons we discuss later in the chapter. A partial pedigree of a family with CGH illustrates the transmission of the dominant alleles by the woman III-1 to about half her children and transmission of the allele by the man II-2 to all his daughters but none of his sons (Figure 3.25b).

Y-Linked Inheritance

The Y chromosome is found only in males, and **Y-linked** genes are transmitted in a male-to-male pattern. In mammals, fewer than 50 genes are found on the Y chromosome; and like *SRY*, those genes are likely to play a role in male sex determination or development. Many of the genes on the human Y chromosome have counterparts on the X chromosome, but they are located in regions that do not recombine with the X chromosome. Overall, only about 5% of the length of the Y chromosome is composed of pseudoautosomal regions, and recombination between X and Y is limited to these regions.

Females never carry a Y chromosome; so from an evolutionary perspective, it makes sense that the genes carried on a Y chromosome should be male-specific, having either to do with male sex determination or reproduction. Indeed, the most recent genomic evidence suggests that the mammalian Y chromosome has rapidly evolved over the past 300 million to 350 million years, undergoing

(a)

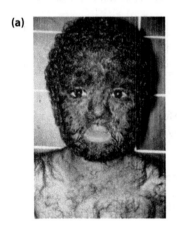

(b)

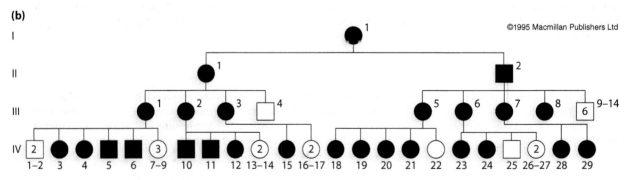

Figure 3.25 **Congenital generalized hypertrichosis (CGH), an X-linked dominant trait in humans.** **(a)** A boy with CGH. **(b)** A large family with CGH. In the single instance of transmission from an affected male (II-2), notice that all daughters (III-5 to III-8) have CGH. The 6-year-old boy in panel **(a)** is IV-5. Some individuals have been omitted from the pedigree for clarity.

multiple changes in structure but preserving a handful of genes that are essential to male fertility and survival. The fascinating evolution of the mammalian Y chromosome is the subject of the Case Study at the end of this chapter.

3.6 Dosage Compensation Equalizes the Expression of Sex-Linked Genes

In organisms with sex chromosomes, there is an imbalance between the sexes in the copy number of genes on the sex chromosomes. In *Drosophila* and placental mammals, females have two copies of each X-linked gene, one on each X chromosome, whereas males have just a single copy of each X-linked gene. In animals, gene dosage balance is essential for normal embryonic development and normal biological processes. Any mechanism that compensates for differences in the number of copies of genes due to the different chromosome constitutions of males and females is called **dosage compensation.** There are at least three dosage compensation mechanisms that equalize X-linked gene expression between male and female animals. Table 3.3 shows dosage compensation mechanisms in animals. In this section, we focus attention on dosage compensation in placental mammals.

Placental mammals, including humans, use *random X inactivation* as their dosage compensation mechanism. Early in mammalian gestational development, about 2 weeks after fertilization in humans, when the female early embryo consists of a few hundred cells, one of the two X chromosomes in each somatic cell of a female is randomly inactivated. This idea was first proposed in 1961 by Mary Lyon in her **random X inactivation hypothesis,** also known as the **Lyon hypothesis.** In approximately half the somatic cells in a female embryo, the maternally derived X chromosome is inactivated; and in the other half of somatic cells, inactivation silences the paternally derived X

chromosome. At the end of this process, each somatic cell of a female has one active X chromosome that is equally likely to be the maternal X or the paternal X.

Random X inactivation takes place in every cell with two or more X chromosomes. Following inactivation, the inactive chromosome can be seen as a tightly condensed mass adhering to the nuclear wall. The inactive X chromosome is known as a **Barr body,** having first been visualized by Murray Barr in 1949.

X inactivation is a permanent feature of somatic cells of placental mammalian females. Since some cells have an active maternal X chromosome and an inactive paternal X chromosome and other cells have the opposite pattern, normal placental mammalian females are, in terms of X chromosomes, a mosaic of two kinds of cells. One cell type (pink) expresses the maternally derived X chromosome, and the other (blue) expresses the paternally derived X chromosome (Figure 3.26). Each individual cell expresses the allelic information of only one of those chromosomes, with all descendant cells maintaining the same inactivation pattern as to original ancestral cell.

In most cases, the silencing of one X chromosome in each cell of a female has no detectable effect on the function of a tissue or on the phenotype. Occasionally, however, female carriers of X-linked recessive traits display a phenotypic manifestation of the recessive allele. Calico and tortoiseshell coat-color patterning in female cats is a product of mosaicism created by random X inactivation (Figure 3.27). Females with an allele for black coat color on one X chromosome and yellow coat color on the homologous X chromosome have black and yellow patches of fur corresponding to portions of skin where each X chromosome is active. The sizes and the distribution of the orange and black sectors of these cats reflect the locations of the clonal descendants of the cells in which each X chromosome was originally inactivated. The specific pattern of X inactivation is unique to each female cat embryo, and the patterns

Table 3.3	Mechanisms of Dosage Compensation in Animals		
Animal	**Sex Chromosomes**		**Dosage Compensation Mechanism**
	Males	**Females**	
Fruit fly	XY	XX	Expression of X-linked genes in males is doubled relative to female X-linked gene expression.
Roundworm	XO	XX[a]	Gene expression of each X chromosome in the hermaphrodite ("female") is decreased to one-half that of the X chromosome in the male.
Marsupial mammals	XY	XX	The paternally derived X chromosome is inactivated in all female somatic cells.
Placental mammals	XY	XX	One X chromosome is randomly inactivated in each female somatic cell.

[a] XX worms are hermaphrodites.

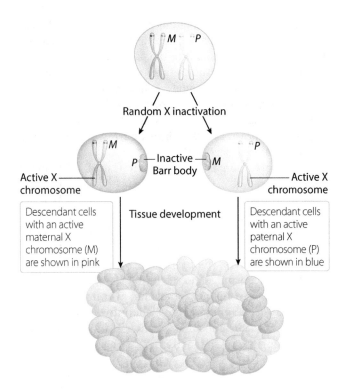

Figure 3.26   Random X inactivation in female placental mammals. M represents the maternally derived X chromosome and P the paternally derived X chromosome.

Figure 3.27   Calico coat, produced by X inactivation in female cats.

of cellular migration are variable as well. As a result, each adult female calico or tortoiseshell cat has a unique pattern of black and orange sectors marking its coat.

Not all genes on the "inactivated" X chromosome are transcriptionally silent. A 2005 study of 624 X-linked genes showed that about 15% of the genes escape complete silencing. On average, transcription of the X-linked genes that remain active is reduced by about 50–85% in comparison to transcription on the active X chromosome. The genes that escape inactivation are largely clustered on the short arm of the chromosome near PAR1.

Random X inactivation requires a gene on the X chromosome called the *X-inactivation–specific transcript (XIST)* that encodes a large RNA molecule. *XIST* RNA spreads out from the gene, "painting" the X chromosome as it accumulates. X chromosomes that are painted with *XIST* RNA have all, or nearly all, of their genes silenced. The *XIST* RNA accumulates only on the one chromosome transcribing the gene and does not spread to the homologous X chromosome. In other words, *XIST* acts only in cis (on the same chromosome) but not in trans (on the homologous chromosome). Examination of inactivated chromosomes in the nucleus detects *XIST* RNA coating the Barr body in a nucleus.

CASE STUDY

The (Degenerative) Evolution of the Mammalian Y Chromosome

Mammalian X and Y chromosomes are the "odd couple" of homologous chromosomes for several reasons. First, they are very different from each other in size. The human Y chromosome is less than one-third the size of the X chromosome. Second, they aren't really all that homologous. The human X chromosome contains several 2000–3000 genes, but the Y chromosome contains just a few dozen genes. Third, the small pseudoautosomal regions they share at their ends make up just a few percent of the total sequence of either chromosome. The pseudoautosomal regions are sufficient for synapsis in prophase I, and recombination between X and Y is frequent in these regions, but only about 5% of the

Y chromosome participates in recombination. The other 95% of the chromosome experiences no crossing over. Finally, and perhaps most significantly, the mammalian Y chromosome has evolved very rapidly over the past 300 million years or so, shrinking in size and genetic content as essential genes have been shifted to other chromosomes, leaving just a handful of genes behind.

A STORY OF DEGENERATION Beginning with the work of Bruce Lahn and David Page in 1999, the composition and evolution of the mammalian Y chromosome have been subjects of active investigation. The view of Y chromosome evolution first proposed by Lahn and Page has been supported and verified by additional studies and by genome sequencing, and it tells the story of an evolutionary pathway that features progressive degeneration.

In 1999, Lahn and Page studied the human X and Y chromosomes and identified 19 genes that are present on both chromosomes, called X–Y shared genes. These genes are left over from a time when the chromosomes were much more similar and regularly recombined. Lahn and Page reasoned that they could trace the evolution of the genes by studying differences between the DNA sequences of the X–Y shared genes—more differences accrue the longer genes have been separated. What they found was quite surprising: The differences between the X–Y shared genes followed a distinct and suggestive pattern. X–Y shared genes nearest each other on the X chromosome short arm were most similar to their Y-chromosome counterparts, but X–Y shared genes on the long arm of the X chromosome were the most different from their Y-chromosome counterparts. In all, Lahn and Page identified four well-defined "strata" among the X–Y shared genes, each stratum having its own distinct level of sequence similarity. Within each of the strata, the level of X–Y shared-gene similarity was remarkably consistent, but there were substantial differences in gene similarity between strata. This suggested four major evolutionary events that reshaped the Y chromosome, resulting in structural changes that progressively restricted recombination between the X and the Y chromosomes.

MAJOR RESTRUCTURING EVENTS By comparing DNA sequences across species, Lahn and Page determined that the autosomal precursors of X and Y were very similar at the time reptiles diverged from mammals, about 350 million years ago (mya). The monotremes (such as the platypus and echidna) separated from the placental mammals 240–320 mya, but not before the *SRY* gene evolved in their common ancestor. Both monotremes and mammals have *SRY*, but reptiles do not. This implies that *SRY* developed about 350 mya (**Figure 3.28**). The *SRY* gene produces TDF, the protein that initiates a cascade of events that produces males. With the acquisition of *SRY*, the Y chromosome became different from the X chromosome, and the region surrounding *SRY*—the first of Lahn and Page's four strata—became the first region of the Y chromosome to be unable to recombine with the X chromosome. This event also contributed to the shrinkage of the Y chromosome.

About 130–170 mya, a structural change altered the Y chromosome and produced a second stratum that was unable to recombine with the X chromosome. Marsupials (such as kangaroos) retain the old Y-chromosome structure, so the generation of the second stratum demarcates the separation of marsupial and placental mammals. Another structural change to the Y chromosome, between 80 and 130 mya, created a third stratum of divergence, further restricting recombination with the X chromosome and shrinking the Y chromosome. This change marks the separation of the monkeys from nonsimian placental mammals. Most recently, about 30–50 mya, the fourth stratum was created by another structural change to the Y chromosome. This change—present in the human lineage that includes our great ape relatives but not present in monkeys—limited recombination to the end of the Y chromosome and reduced its size. In humans, recombination between X and Y chromosomes is limited to PAR1, the largest of the remaining regions of X–Y homology. Little if any recombination occurs in PAR2.

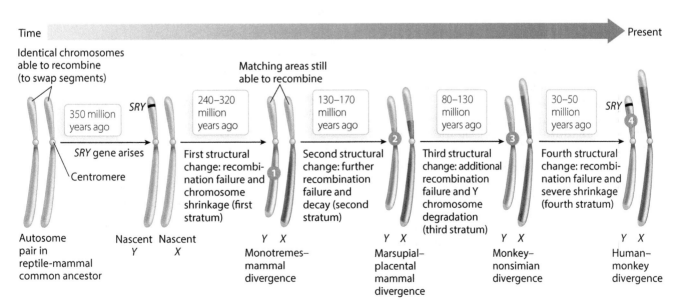

Figure 3.28 The proposed evolutionary development of the mammalian Y chromosome through four major structural rearrangements.

The functioning of genes remaining on the Y chromosome was directly affected by the events that prevented X–Y recombination. Without recombination, Y-linked genes were subject to mutational degradation that would eventually render them nonfunctional. To prevent this, strong natural selection operated to move essential genes off the Y chromosome to other chromosomes. The genes that remain on the human Y chromosome are almost exclusively important in male development or sperm production, but even these remain subject to mutational degradation.

What will be the ultimate fate of the human Y chromosome? Is it destined to be lost? Scientists don't know what will happen, but recent genomic data may provide a clue. The Y chromosome, it seems, has backup copies of its genes. These duplicated copies are also on the Y chromosome, and they may serve to protect the Y chromosome from the loss of critical information.

SUMMARY   (MasteringGenetics™   For activities, animations, and review quizzes, go to the Study Area.

3.1 Mitosis Divides Somatic Cells

▮ The cell cycle has two principal phases: interphase, whose stages are G_1, S, and G_2; and M phase, during which cell division occurs.

▮ Mitosis is the process of division for somatic cells. Mitosis contains five substages: prophase, prometaphase, metaphase, anaphase, and telophase.

▮ Mitosis contains a single cell division and separates sister chromatids into diploid daughter cells that are genetically identical to one another and to the parental cell they are derived from.

▮ The cell cycle is under tight genetic control. Regulatory molecules control the transition from one stage of the cycle to the next by acting at genetically controlled checkpoints to monitor cell cycle transitions.

▮ Mutation of cell cycle control genes is associated with cancer development.

3.2 Meiosis Produces Gametes for Sexual Reproduction

▮ Meiosis contains two cell divisions, designated meiosis I and meiosis II.

▮ During meiosis I (the "reduction division"), homologous chromosomes are separated to produce haploid daughter cells that carry one chromosome from each homologous pair of chromosomes.

▮ The meiosis II division separates sister chromatids and produces four genetically different haploid daughter cells that form gametes.

▮ During prophase I, homologous chromosomes synapse with the aid of the synaptonemal complex. Homologous chromosomes can cross over to exchange genetic material during this substage.

▮ Mendel's laws of segregation and independent assortment find their mechanical basis in the patterns of separation of chromosomes and sister chromatids during meiosis.

3.3 The Chromosome Theory of Heredity Proposes That Genes Are Carried on Chromosomes

▮ The chromosome theory of heredity proposes that genes are carried on chromosomes and are faithfully transmitted through gametes to successive generations.

▮ Thomas Hunt Morgan's identification of X-linked transmission of white eye color in *Drosophila* and Calvin Bridges's analysis of exceptional phenotypes produced by X-chromosome nondisjunction demonstrated the validity of the chromosome theory of heredity.

3.4 Sex Determination Is Chromosomal and Genetic

▮ Mechanisms of sex determination take many forms in animals. *Drosophila* sex is determined by the ratio of expression of X-linked and autosomal genes, whereas human sex is determined by the presence of *SRY* on the Y chromosome.

▮ Sex-chromosome patterns are diverse among organisms. Birds, fishes, and some insects have Z and W sex chromosomes, and monotremes have multiple sets of sex chromosomes.

3.5 Human Sex-Linked Transmission Follows Distinct Patterns

▮ Human X-linked dominant inheritance and X-linked recessive inheritance are identifiable, respectively, by the pattern of male transmission and the pattern of male expression of traits.

▮ Genes on the Y chromosome are transmitted exclusively from male to male.

3.6 Dosage Compensation Equalizes the Expression of Sex-Linked Genes

▮ Dosage compensation balances the level of expression of sex-linked genes and is critical for normal animal development. Mechanisms for achieving dosage compensation vary among species.

▮ Random inactivation of one X chromosome in each cell of placental mammalian females is controlled by an X-inactivation center on the X chromosome.

KEYWORDS

ascus *(p. 81)*
aster *(p. 67)*
Barr body *(p. 95)*
Cdk (cyclin-dependent kinase) *(pp. 70–71)*
cell cycle (cell cycle checkpoint) *(pp. 65–70)*
centromere *(p. 67)*
centrosome *(p. 67)*
chiasma (chiasmata) *(p. 77)*
chromosome theory of heredity *(p. 65)*
crossing over *(p. 76)*
cyclin protein *(p. 70)*
cytokinesis *(p. 66)*
daughter cell *(p. 65)*
diploid number *(p. 65)*
disjunction *(p. 67)*
dosage compensation *(p. 95)*
gamete (germ-line cell) *(p. 65)*
haploid number *(p. 65)*

hemizygous *(p. 85)*
interphase (G_1 phase, S phase, G_2 phase) *(p. 65–66)*
karyokinesis *(p. 66)*
kinetochore *(p. 67)*
M phase (prophase, prometaphase, metaphase, anaphase, telophase) *(pp. 65, 66)*
meiosis (meiosis I, meiosis II) *(pp. 65, 74)*
metaphase plate *(p. 67)*
mitosis *(p. 65)*
nondisjunction *(p. 86)*
nonsister chromatid *(p. 76)*
oncogene *(p. 71)*
proto-oncogene *(p. 71)*
pseudoautosomal region (PAR) *(p. 79)*
random X-inactivation (Lyon hypothesis) *(p. 95)*

recombination nodule *(p. 76)*
sex chromosome *(p. 65)*
sex determination *(p. 86)*
sex-linked inheritance (X-linked inheritance, Y-linked inheritance) *(pp. 84, 85, 94)*
sister chromatid *(p. 67)*
spindle fiber microtubule (kinetochore, polar, and astral microtubule) *(p. 67)*
synapsis *(p. 75)*
synaptonemal complex *(p. 75)*
tumor suppressor gene *(p. 71)*
X/autosome ratio (X/A ratio) *(p. 88)*
X-linked dominant *(p. 90)*
X-linked inheritance *(p. 85)*
X-linked recessive *(p. 90)*
Z/W system *(p. 90)*

PROBLEMS

MasteringGenetics™   Visit for instructor-assigned tutorials and problems.

Chapter Concepts

1. Examine the following diagrams of cells from an organism with diploid number $2n = 6$, and identify what stage of M phase is represented.

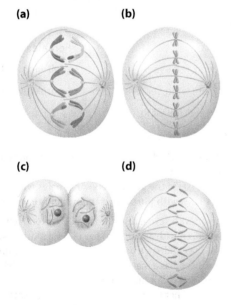

(a)   **(b)**

(c)   **(d)**

2. Our closest primate relative, the chimpanzee, has a diploid number of $2n = 48$. For each of the following stages of M phase, identify the number of chromosomes present in each cell.
   a. end of mitotic telophase
   b. meiotic metaphase I
   c. end of meiotic anaphase II
   d. early mitotic prophase
   e. mitotic metaphase
   f. early prophase I

For answers to selected even-numbered problems, see Appendix: Answers.

3. In a test of his chromosome theory of heredity, Morgan crossed an F_1 female *Drosophila* with red eyes to a male with white eyes. The F_1 females were produced from Cross A shown in Figure 3.19. Predict the offspring Morgan would have expected under his hypothesis that the gene for eye color is on the X chromosome in fruit flies.

4. Tension between sister chromatids is essential to ensure their efficient separation at mitotic anaphase or in meiotic anaphase II. Explain why sister chromatid cohesion is important, and discuss the role of the proteins cohesin and separase in sister chromatid separation.

5. The diploid number of the hypothetical animal *Geneticus introductus* is $2n = 36$. Each diploid nucleus contains 3 ng of DNA in G_1.
   a. What amount of DNA is contained in each nucleus at the end of S phase?
   b. Explain why a somatic cell of *Geneticus introductus* has the same number of chromosomes and the same amount of DNA at the beginning of mitotic prophase as one of these cells does at the beginning of prophase I of meiosis.
   c. Complete the following table by entering the number of chromosomes and amount of DNA present per cell at the end of each stage listed.

End of Cell Cycle Stage	Number of Chromosomes	Amount of DNA
Telophase I		
Mitotic anaphase		
Telophase II		

6. An organism has alleles R_1 and R_2 on one pair of homologous chromosomes, and it has alleles T_1 and T_2 on another pair. Diagram these pairs of homologs at the end of metaphase I, the end of telophase I, and the end of telophase II, and show how meiosis in this organism produces gametes in expected Mendelian proportions. Assume no crossover between homologous chromosomes.

7. Explain how the behavior of homologous chromosomes in meiosis parallels Mendel's law of segregation for autosomal alleles D and d. During which stage of M phase do these two alleles segregate from one another?

8. Suppose crossover occurs between the homologous chromosomes in the previous problem. At what stage of M phase do alleles D and d segregate?

9. Alleles A and a are on one pair of autosomes, and alleles B and b are on a separate pair of autosomes. Does crossover between one pair of homologs affect the expected proportions of gamete genotypes? Why or why not? Does crossover between both pairs of chromosomes affect the expected gamete proportions? Why or why not?

10. How many Barr bodies are found in a normal human female nucleus? In a normal male nucleus?

11. Describe the role of the following structures or proteins in cell division:
    a. microtubules   b. cyclin-dependent kinases
    c. kinetochores   d. synaptonemal complex

Application and Integration

For answers to selected even-numbered problems, see Appendix: Answers.

12. A woman's father has ornithine transcarbamylase deficiency (OTD), an X-linked recessive disorder producing mental deterioration if not properly treated. The woman's mother is homozygous for the wild-type allele.
    a. What is the woman's genotype? (Use D to represent the dominant allele and d to represent the recessive allele.)
    b. If the woman has a son with a normal man, what is the chance the son will have OTD?
    c. If the woman has a daughter with a man who does not have OTD, what is the chance the daughter will be a heterozygous carrier of OTD? What is the chance the daughter will have OTD?
    d. Identify a male with whom the woman could produce a daughter with OTD.
    e. For the instance you identified in part (d), what proportion of daughters produced by the woman and the man are expected to have OTD? What proportion of sons of the woman and the man are expected to have OTD?

13. In humans, hemophilia (OMIM 306700) is an X-linked recessive disorder that affects the gene for factor VIII protein, which is essential for blood clotting. The dominant and recessive alleles for the *factor VIII* gene are represented by H and h. Albinism is an autosomal recessive condition that results from mutation of the gene producing tyrosinase, an enzyme in the melanin synthesis pathway. A and a represent the tyrosinase alleles. A healthy woman named Clara (II-2), whose father (I-1) has hemophilia and whose brother (II-1) has albinism, is married to a healthy man named Charles (II-3), whose parents are healthy. Charles's brother (II-5) has hemophilia, and his sister (II-4) has albinism. The pedigree is shown below.

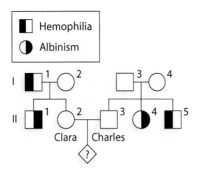

a. What are the genotypes of the four parents (I-1 to I-4) in this pedigree?
b. Determine the probability that the first child of Clara and Charles will be a
   i. boy with hemophilia
   ii. girl with albinism
   iii. healthy girl
   iv. boy with both albinism and hemophilia
   v. boy with albinism
   vi. girl with hemophilia
c. If Clara and Charles's first child has albinism, what is the chance the second child has albinism? Explain why this probability is higher than the probability you calculated in part (b).

14. A wild-type male and a wild-type female *Drosophila* with red eyes and full wings are crossed. Their progeny are shown below.

Males	Females
$\frac{3}{8}$ full wing, red eye	$\frac{3}{4}$ full wing, red eye
$\frac{3}{8}$ miniature wing, red eye	$\frac{1}{4}$ purple eye, full wing
$\frac{1}{8}$ purple eye, full wing	
$\frac{1}{8}$ miniature wing, purple eye	

a. Using clearly defined allele symbols of your choice, give the genotype of each parent.
b. What is/are the genotype(s) of females with purple eye? Of males with purple eye and miniature wing?

15. A woman with severe discoloration of her tooth enamel has four children with a man who has normal tooth enamel. Two of the children, a boy (B) and a girl (G), have discolored enamel. Each has a mate with normal tooth enamel and produces several children. G has six children, four boys and two girls. Two of her boys and one of her girls have discolored enamel. B has seven children, four girls and three boys. All four of his daughters have discolored enamel, but all his boys have normal enamel. Explain the inheritance of this condition.

16. In a large metropolitan hospital, cells from newborn babies are collected and examined microscopically over a 5-year period. Among approximately 7500 newborn males, six have one Barr body in the nuclei of their somatic cells. All

other newborn males have no Barr bodies. Among 7500 female infants, four have two Barr bodies in each nucleus, two have no Barr bodies, and the rest have one. What is the cause of the unusual number of Barr bodies in a small number of male and female infants?

17. In cats, tortoiseshell coat color appears in females. A tortoiseshell coat has patches of dark brown fur and patches of orange fur that each in total cover about half the body but have a unique pattern in each female. Male cats can be either dark brown or orange, but a male cat with tortoiseshell coat is rarely produced. Two sample crosses between males and females from pure-breeding lines produced the tortoiseshell females shown.

Cross I   P: dark brown male × orange female

F₁: orange males and tortoiseshell females

Cross II   P: orange male × dark brown female

F₁: dark brown males and tortoiseshell females

a. Explain the inheritance of dark brown, orange, and tortoiseshell coat colors in cats.
b. Why are tortoiseshell cats female?
c. The genetics service of a large veterinary hospital gets referrals for three or four male tortoiseshell cats every year. These cats are invariably sterile and have underdeveloped testes. How are these tortoiseshell male cats produced? Why do you think they are sterile?

18. The gene causing Coffin-Lowry syndrome (OMIM 303600) was recently identified and mapped on the human X chromosome. Coffin-Lowry syndrome is a rare disorder affecting brain morphology and development. It also produces skeletal and growth abnormalities, as well as abnormalities of motor control. Coffin-Lowry syndrome affects males who inherit a mutation of the X-linked gene. Most carrier females show no symptoms of the disease but a few carriers do. These carrier females are always less severely affected than males. Offer an explanation for this finding.

19. Four eye-color mutants in *Drosophila*—apricot, brown, carnation, and purple—are inherited as recessive traits. Red is the dominant wild-type color of fruit-fly eyes. Eight crosses (A to H) are made between parents from pure-breeding lines.

Cross	Parents		F₁ Progeny	
	Female	**Male**	**Female**	**Male**
A	Apricot	Red	Red	Apricot
B	Brown	Red	Red	Red
C	Red	Purple	Red	Red
D	Red	Apricot	Red	Red
E	Carnation	Red	Red	Carnation
F	Purple	Red	Red	Red
G	Red	Brown	Red	Red
H	Red	Carnation	Red	Red

a. Which of these eye-color mutants are X-linked recessive and which are autosomal recessive? Explain how you distinguish X-linked from autosomal heredity.
b. Predict F₂ phenotype ratios of Crosses A, B, D, and G.

20. For each pedigree shown,
a. Identify which simple pattern of hereditary transmission (autosomal dominant, autosomal recessive, X-linked dominant, or X-linked recessive) is most likely to have occurred. Give genotypes for individuals involved in transmitting the trait.
b. Determine which other pattern(s) of transmission is/are possible. For each possible mode of transmission, specify the genotypes necessary for transmission to occur.
c. Identify which pattern(s) of transmission is/are impossible. Specify why transmission is impossible.

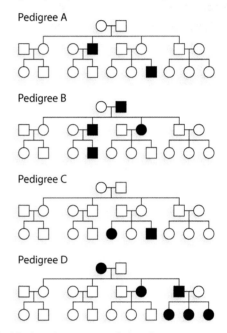

21. Use the blank pedigrees provided to depict transmission of (a) an X-linked recessive trait and (b) an X-linked dominant trait, by filling in circles and squares to represent individuals with the trait of interest. Give genotypes for each person in each pedigree. Carefully design each transmission pattern so that pedigree (a) cannot be confused with autosomal recessive transmission and pedigree (b) cannot be confused with autosomal dominant transmission. Identify the transmission events that eliminate the possibility of autosomal transmission for each pedigree.

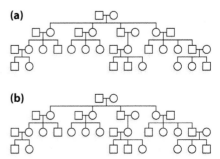

22. Figure 3.22 (page 90) illustrates reciprocal crosses involving chickens with sex-linked dominant barred mutation. For Cross A and for Cross B, cross the F_1 roosters and hens and predict the feather patterns of roosters and hens in the F_2.

23. In fruit flies, yellow body (y) is recessive to gray body (y^+), and the trait of body color is inherited on the X chromosome. Vestigial wing (v) is recessive to full-sized wing (v^+), and the trait has autosomal inheritance. A cross of a male with yellow body and full wings to a female with gray body and full wings is made. Based on an analysis of the progeny of the cross shown below, determine the genotypes of parental and progeny flies.

Phenotype	Number of Males	Number of Females
Yellow body, full wing	296	301
Yellow body, vestigial wing	101	98
Gray body, full wing	302	298
Gray body, vestigial wing	101	103
	800	800

24. In a species of fish, a black spot on the dorsal fin is observed in males and females. A fish breeder carries out a pair of reciprocal crosses and observes the following results.

    Cross I   Parents: black-spot male × nonspotted female

    Progeny: 22 black-spot males

    24 black-spot females

    25 nonspotted males

    21 nonspotted females

    Cross II   Parents: nonspotted male × black-spot female

    Progeny: 45 black-spot males

    53 nonspotted females

    a. Why does this evidence support the hypothesis that a black spot is sex linked?
    b. Identify which sex is homogametic and which is heterogametic. Give genotypes for the parents in each cross, and explain the progeny proportions in each cross.

25. Lesch-Nyhan syndrome (OMIM 300322) is a rare X-linked recessive disorder that produces severe mental retardation, spastic cerebral palsy, and self-mutilation.
    a. What is the probability that the first son of a woman whose brother has Lesch-Nyhan syndrome will be affected?
    b. If the first son of the woman described in (a) is affected, what is the probability that her second son is affected?
    c. What is the probability that the first son of a man whose brother has Lesch-Nyhan syndrome will be affected?

26. In humans, *SRY* is located near a pseudoautosomal region (PAR) of the Y chromosome, a region of homology between the X and Y chromosomes that allows them to synapse during meiosis in males and is a region of crossover between the chromosomes. The diagram below shows *SRY* in relation to the pseudoautosomal region.

About 1 in every 25,000 newborn infants is born with sex reversal; the infant is either an apparent male, but with two X chromosomes, or an apparent female, but with an X and a Y chromosome. Explain the origin of sex reversal in human males and females involving the *SRY* gene. (*Hint*: See Experimental Insight 3.1 for a clue about the mutational mechanism.)

27. In an 1889 book titled *Natural Inheritance* (Macmillan, New York), Francis Galton, who investigated the inheritance of measurable (quantitative) traits, formulated a law of "ancestral inheritance." The law stated that each person inherits approximately one-half of his or her genetic traits from each parent, about one-quarter of the traits from each grandparent, one-eighth from each great grandparent, and so on. In light of the chromosome theory of heredity, argue either in favor of Galton's law or against it.

28. *Drosophila* has a diploid chromosome number of $2n = 8$, which includes one pair of sex chromosomes (XX in females and XY in males) and three pairs of autosomes. Consider a *Drosophila* male that has a copy of the A_1 allele on its X chromosome (the Y chromosome is the homolog) and is heterozygous for alleles B_1 and B_2, C_1 and C_2, and D_1 and D_2 of genes that are each on a different autosomal pair. In the diagrams requested below, indicate the alleles carried on each chromosome and sister chromatid. Assume that no crossover occurs between homologous chromosomes.

    a. What is the genotype of cells produced by mitotic division in this male?
    b. Diagram *any correct* alignment of chromosomes at mitotic metaphase.
    c. Diagram *any correct* alignment of chromosomes at metaphase I of meiosis.
    d. For the metaphase I alignment shown in (c), what gamete genotypes are produced at the end of meiosis?
    e. How many different metaphase I chromosome alignments are possible in this male? How many genetically different gametes can this male produce? Explain your reasoning for each answer.

29. A wild-type *Drosophila* male and a female with wild-type phenotype are crossed, producing 324 female progeny and 161 male progeny. All their progeny are wild type.

    a. Propose a genetic hypothesis to explain these data.
    b. Design an experiment that will test your hypothesis, using the wild-type progeny identified above. Describe the results you expect if your hypothesis is true.

30. In *Drosophila,* the X-linked echinus eye phenotype disrupts formation of facets and is recessive to wild-type eye. Autosomal recessive traits vestigial wing and ebony body assort independently of one another. Examine the progeny from the three crosses shown below, and identify the genotype of parents in each cross.

Parental Phenotype		Progeny Phenotype	Proportion	
Female	**Male**		**Female**	**Male**
a. Wild type	Echinus	Wild type	$\frac{3}{8}$	$\frac{3}{8}$
		Echinus	$\frac{3}{8}$	$\frac{3}{8}$
		Vestigial	$\frac{1}{8}$	$\frac{1}{8}$
		Echinus, vestigial	$\frac{1}{8}$	$\frac{1}{8}$
b. Wild type	Wild type	Vestigial, ebony	$\frac{2}{32}$	$\frac{1}{32}$
		Vestigial	$\frac{6}{32}$	$\frac{3}{32}$
		Ebony	$\frac{6}{32}$	$\frac{3}{32}$
		Wild type	$\frac{18}{32}$	$\frac{9}{32}$
		Echinus, vestigial, ebony	0	$\frac{1}{32}$
		Echinus, vestigial	0	$\frac{3}{32}$
		Echinus, ebony	0	$\frac{3}{32}$
		Echinus	0	$\frac{9}{32}$
c. Ebony	Echinus	Echinus, vestigial, ebony	$\frac{1}{32}$	$\frac{1}{32}$
		Echinus, vestigial	$\frac{3}{32}$	$\frac{3}{32}$
		Echinus, ebony	$\frac{3}{32}$	$\frac{3}{32}$
		Echinus	$\frac{9}{32}$	$\frac{9}{32}$
		Vestigial, ebony	$\frac{1}{32}$	$\frac{1}{32}$
		Vestigial	$\frac{3}{32}$	$\frac{3}{32}$
		Ebony	$\frac{3}{32}$	$\frac{3}{32}$
		Wild type	$\frac{9}{32}$	$\frac{9}{32}$

31. While examining a young tortoiseshell cat, you and the veterinarian you are interning with get a surprise—the cat is male, not female! From your undergraduate genetics course, you recall that tortoiseshell coats are produced by the random X-inactivation that takes place in mammalian females. The veterinarian orders a chromosome analysis of the cat and finds that he is XXY: He has two X chromosomes and one Y chromosome. Help the veterinarian figure out how a tortoiseshell cat could be male. (*Hint:* Think about X-inactivation in mammals with two X chromosomes.)

32. Red-green color blindness in humans is inherited as an X-linked recessive condition. Consider reciprocal crosses between a color-blind parent and a parent with normal color vision in which the dominant allele is identified as C and the recessive allele as c. Cross 1 is $Cc \times c$Y, and Cross 2 is $cc \times C$Y. Determine the phenotypes and their proportions in progeny produced by each cross. Explain why the reciprocal cross results are consistent with an X-linked recessive inheritance but not with an autosomal recessive inheritance of color blindness.

4

Inheritance Patterns of Single Genes and Gene Interaction

CHAPTER OUTLINE

4.1 Interactions between Alleles Produce Dominance Relationships

4.2 Some Genes Produce Variable Phenotypes

4.3 Gene Interaction Modifies Mendelian Ratios

4.4 Complementation Analysis Distinguishes Mutations in the Same Gene from Mutations in Different Genes

ESSENTIAL IDEAS

■ Dominance relationships between alleles have a molecular basis. The biological effects of gene products determine what type of dominance is observed.

■ Gene expression can be affected by nongenetic (environmental) factors and also as a consequence of factors related to sex.

■ Gene expression can be affected by interactions with other genes, causing characteristic changes in Mendelian ratios.

■ Mutation of different genes can produce the same effect on phenotype. The number of genes causing mutation of a phenotype is discovered by genetic complementation analysis.

The shape and the color of summer squash are traits that are determined by gene interaction.

Mendel's laws of segregation and independent assortment encapsulate the basic rules of genetic transmission in diploid organisms. We see the results of these rules in the relative proportions of progeny with different phenotypes from crosses. By assessing the molecular basis for the phenotypic variation, we can also glimpse the connection between hereditary transmission of phenotypic traits and DNA, RNA, or protein sequence variability. Lastly, on the mechanical level explored in Chapter 3, we find the physical basis of these rules in the movement and segregation of homologous chromosomes and sister chromatids during meiosis.

Mendel's success in identifying and describing these two hereditary laws was partly due to his use of traits whose phenotypic characteristics are determined exclusively by inheritance of alleles for single genes. In interpreting the inheritance of these traits, he did not have to contend with phenotypic variation introduced by other genes or by environmental (nongenetic) factors.

In Mendel's experiments, each trait was decided by a single pair of alleles, one fully dominant and one fully recessive, at each of seven genes. Furthermore, environmental factors played a minimal role in the phenotypic variation Mendel observed. The simple case in which just two alleles influence a trait and environment plays no meaningful role is, however, quite rare in nature. Although a diploid organism can have no more than two alleles at a locus (because such individuals have just two copies of each chromosome), there may be many alleles for a single locus within a population.

In most cases, phenotype determination is more complex than portrayed by Mendel's examples because one or more additional circumstances affect the phenotypic outcome. Together, these circumstances are thought of as "extensions of Mendelian inheritance," a phrase that includes two distinct kinds of influences on the phenotype ratios produced by crosses. The first category that extends Mendel's hereditary concepts are relationships between alleles of a single gene that are other than completely dominant and completely recessive. The second category of extended Mendelian inheritance is heredity of traits that are influenced by alleles of two or more genes. Categorized as *gene interactions,* this phrase refers to any of several ways different genes can collaborate or interact with one another or with nongenetic (environmental) factors to influence the expression of a phenotypic character. In this chapter, we examine several examples of allele interactions with patterns of dominance that are different from those described by Mendel, as well as examples of interactions between genes and between genes and environmental factors that include the following:

▌ There may be more than two alleles for a given locus within the population.

▌ Dominance of one allele over another may not be complete.

▌ Two or more genes may affect a single trait.

▌ The expression of a trait may be dependent on the interaction of two or more genes, on the interaction of genes with nongenetic factors, or both.

Our examination of these extensions of Mendelian inheritance focuses on patterns of phenotypic variation that result from the occurrence of allelic, gene-gene, or gene-environment interaction. Our discussions demonstrate that while traits arising through these interactions do not always exhibit the classic Mendelian ratios (described in Chapter 2), the observed ratios can nevertheless be explained by the operation of Mendelian principles, overlaid by patterns of interaction between alleles or between genes that are different from those encountered by Mendel.

4.1 Interactions between Alleles Produce Dominance Relationships

Mendel wisely chose to examine traits presenting in one of two alternative forms. One form of each trait he studied displayed complete dominance over the other form. Complete dominance makes the phenotype of a heterozygous organism indistinguishable from that of an organism homozygous for the dominant allele; thus, only organisms homozygous for the recessive allele display the recessive phenotype. The complete dominance of one allele also results in the exclusive expression of the dominant phenotype among the heterozygous F_1 progeny of a cross between pure-breeding homozygous parents, while the F_2 progeny display a 3:1 ratio of dominant to recessive phenotypes. We now know that the phenotypes of the seven traits that Mendel studied are controlled by two alternative alleles at seven different genes. In the cases that have been examined at the molecular level, the dominant alleles reflect the wild-type function of the gene, while the recessive alleles encode gene products with reduced or no functional activity.

Questions concerning the molecular basis of dominant and recessive alleles drove genetic research in the early and mid-20th century, including questions of how dominance of an allele could be ascertained, why certain mutations are recessive whereas others are dominant, and whether mutations always cause genes to lose function or whether mutations can impart new or additional functions to alleles.

The Molecular Basis of Dominance

A character is called dominant if it is seen in organisms with the homozygous and heterozygous genotypes, and it is called recessive if it is observed only in a single homozygous genotype. In this sense, dominance and recessiveness have a phenotypic basis. The phenotypes are, however, a consequence of the activities of proteins produced by the alleles of a gene. In this sense, dominance and recessiveness also have a molecular basis. The dominance of one allele over another is determined by the activity of the protein products of the allele—by the manner in which the protein products of alleles work to produce the phenotype.

Let's compare two examples to illustrate the molecular basis of dominance and recessiveness. In both examples, a wild-type allele produces an active enzyme and a mutant allele produces either very little enzyme or none at all. In the first example the mutant allele is recessive, but in the second example the mutant allele is dominant.

Haplosufficient Wild-Type Allele Is Dominant In the first example, gene R has a dominant wild-type allele R^+ and a recessive mutant allele r. Gene R produces an enzyme that must generate 40 or more units of catalytic activity to drive a critical reaction step. Successful completion of this step produces the wild-type phenotype, whereas failure to complete the step generates a mutant phenotype. Each copy of allele R^+ produces 50 units of enzyme activity. The mutant allele r produces no functional enzyme and has 0 units of activity. Homozygous R^+R^+ organisms produce 100 units of enzyme activity (50 units from each copy of R^+), far exceeding the minimum required to achieve the wild-type phenotype. Heterozygous organisms (R^+r) produce a total of 50 units of enzyme activity, which is sufficient to produce the wild-type phenotype. Homozygous rr organisms produce no enzymatic action, however, and display the mutant phenotype. Based on its ability to catalyze the critical reaction step and produce the wild-type phenotype in either a homozygous (R^+R^+) or heterozygous (R^+r) genotype, R^+ is dominant over r. Dominant wild-type alleles of this kind are identified as **haplosufficient** since one (haplo) copy is sufficient to produce the wild-type phenotype in the heterozygous genotype.

Haploinsufficient Wild-Type Allele Is Recessive The second example involves gene T, for which the wild-type allele is recessive to a mutant allele. Gene T produces an enzyme required to catalyze a critical reaction step that produces a wild-type phenotype if it is completed. The inability to complete the reaction step results in a mutant phenotype. For the reaction step in question, 18 units of enzyme activity are required. The wild-type allele T_1 produces 10 units of activity. A mutant allele, T_2, generates 5 units of enzyme activity. Homozygous T_1T_1 organisms generate 20 units of catalytic enzyme activity, enough to catalyze the critical reaction step and produce the wild-type phenotype. Heterozygous organisms, on the other hand, produce only 15 units of enzymatic activity and have the mutant phenotype because they fall short

of the 18 units required to catalyze the reaction step. Similarly, homozygous T_2T_2 organisms, which produce 10 units of enzyme activity, also have a mutant phenotype. In this case, the mutant allele T_2 is dominant over the wild-type allele T_1 since both the heterozygous (T_1T_2) and homozygous (T_2T_2) organisms have a mutant phenotype. In cases like this, the wild-type allele is identified as **haploinsufficient** because a single copy is not sufficient to produce the wild-type phenotype in the heterozygous genotype.

Functional Effects of Mutation

Genetic analysis often focuses on rare mutations and other infrequent phenomena. In many instances, the study of these rare events provides clues to the underlying causes of commonly occurring events that are not yet understood. In the case of any genetic mutation, a central question concerns the precise mechanism through which the mutation disrupts normal gene function.

From a functional perspective, organisms with two copies of the wild-type allele have the wild-type phenotype (**Figure 4.1a**). The same would be true if an organism had a single copy of a fully dominant wild-type allele. Using the level of activity of the protein products of the wild-type allele as the basis for comparison, mutant alleles can often be placed into either a *loss-of-function* or a *gain-of-function* category. A **loss-of-function mutation** results in a significant decrease or in the complete loss of the functional activity of a gene product. This common mutational category contains mutations like those described in the R-gene and T-gene examples. Loss-of-function mutant alleles are usually recessive, but under certain circumstances, they may be dominant, depending on whether the wild-type allele is haplosufficient or haploinsufficient.

Gain-of-function mutations identify alleles that have acquired a new function or have their expression altered in a way that gives them substantially more activity than the wild-type allele. Gain-of-function mutations are almost always dominant and usually produce dominant mutant phenotypes in heterozygous organisms. As a consequence of their newly acquired functions, certain gain-of-function mutations are lethal in a homozygous state.

Loss-of-Function Mutations As the previous discussion suggests, mutations resulting in a loss of function vary in the extent of loss of normal activity of the gene product. A loss-of-function mutation that results in a complete loss of gene function in comparison to the wild-type gene product is identified as a **null mutation,** also known as an **amorphic mutation** (**Figure 4.1b**). The word *null* means "zero" or "nothing," and the word *amorphic* means "without form." These mutant alleles produce no functional gene product and are often lethal in a homozygous genotype. The elimination of functional

(a) Wild type

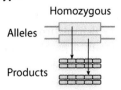

The expression of the products of wild-type alleles produces wild-type phenotype. See Figure 4.5 for an example.

(b) Loss of function: Null/amorphic mutation

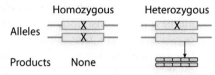

Null alleles produce no functional product. Homozygous null organisms have mutant (amorphic) phenotype due to absence of the gene product. See Figure 4.5 for an example.

(c) Loss of function: Leaky/hypomorphic mutation

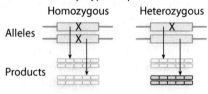

Leaky mutant alleles produce a small amount of wild-type gene product. Homozygous organisms have a mutant (hypomorphic) phenotype. See Figure 4.5 for an example.

(d) Loss of function: Dominant negative mutation

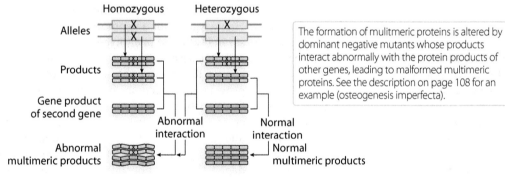

The formation of mulitmeric proteins is altered by dominant negative mutants whose products interact abnormally with the protein products of other genes, leading to malformed multimeric proteins. See the description on page 108 for an example (osteogenesis imperfecta).

(e) Gain of function: Hypermorphic mutation

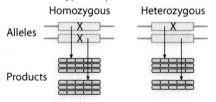

Excessive expression of the gene product leads to excessive gene action. The mutant phenotype may be more severe or lethal in the homozygous genotype than in the heterozygous genotype. See Figure 4.10 for an example.

(f) Gain of function: Neomorphic mutation

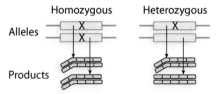

The mutant allele has novel function that produces a mutant phenotype in homozygous and heterozygous organisms, and may be more severe in homozygous organisms. See Figure 16.20 for an example.

Figure 4.1   The functional consequences of mutation.   (a) Wild type. **(b)**, **(c)**, and **(d)** Loss-of-function mutations. **(e)** and **(f)** Gain-of-function mutations.

gene products can result from various types of mutational events, including those that block transcription, produce a gene product that lacks activity, or result in deletion of all or part of the gene.

Alternatively, a mutation resulting in partial loss of gene function may be identified as a **leaky mutation,** also known as a **hypomorphic mutation** (Figure 4.1c). *Hypomorphic* means "reduced form"; like the term *leaky,* it implies that a small percentage of normal functional capability is retained by the mutant allele but at a lower level than is found for the wild-type allele. The severity of the phenotypic abnormality depends on the residual level of activity from the leaky mutant allele. A greater percentage of activity from a leaky allele results in a less severely affected phenotype than when the mutation incurs a more substantial loss of function. Both null and hypomorphic loss-of-function mutations are often recessive and homozygous lethal. Dominant loss-of-function mutations are also known to occur.

Certain loss-of-function mutations produce dominant mutant phenotypes through alterations in the function of a multimeric protein of which the mutant polypeptide forms a part (Figure 4.1d). Multimeric proteins, composed of two or more polypeptides that join together to form a functional protein, are particularly subject to **dominant negative mutations** as a consequence of some change that prevents the polypeptides from interacting normally to produce a functional protein. A multimeric protein that contains an abnormal polypeptide may suffer a reduction or total loss of functional capacity. Mutations of this kind are dominant due to the substantial loss of function of the multimeric protein. These mutations are characterized as "negative" due to the spoiler effect of the abnormal polypeptide on the multimeric protein.

An example of dominant negative mutation is seen in the human hereditary disorder osteogenesis imperfecta (OMIM 116200, 116210, and 116220), which is caused by defects in the bone protein collagen and has multiple forms with different severity. Collagen protein is composed of three interwoven polypeptide strands—two polypeptides from the *COL1A1* gene and one polypeptide from the *COL1A2* gene. The trimeric collagen protein is subject to dominant negative mutation as a consequence of *COL1A1* mutations that produce a defective polypeptide. The trimeric structure of collagen and the 2:1 ratio of incorporation of COL1A1 polypeptide over COL1A2 polypeptide means that in individuals who are homozygous wild type for *COL1A2* and heterozygous for *COL1A1* mutation, most collagen protein contains one or two mutant COL1A1 proteins. As a result, most collagen protein is defective, and osteogenesis imperfecta develops.

Gain-of-Function Mutations Mutations resulting in a gain of function fall into two categories that depend on the functional behavior of the new mutation. **Hypermorphic** ("greater than wild-type form") **mutations** produce more gene activity per allele than the wild type (Figure 4.1e) and are usually dominant. The gene product of a hypermorphic allele is indistinguishable from that of the wild-type allele, but it is present in a greater amount and thus induces a higher level of activity. The excess concentration is the functional equivalent of overdrive, pushing processes forward more rapidly, at the wrong time, in the wrong place, or for a longer time than normal. Hypermorphic mutants often result from regulatory mutations that increase gene transcription, block the normal response to regulatory signals that silence transcription, or increase the number of gene copies by gene duplication. The severity of phenotypic effect may coincide with the genotype such that mutation homozygotes display a more severely affected phenotype than is observed in heterozygotes.

Gain-of-function mutations resulting from **neomorphic** ("new form") **mutations** acquire novel gene activities not found in the wild type (Figure 4.1f) and are usually dominant. The gene products of neomorphic mutants are functional, but have structures that differ from the wild-type gene product. The altered structures lead the mutant protein to function differently than the wild-type protein. Homozygotes for a neomorphic allele may exhibit a more severely affected phenotype than do heterozygotes.

Our description of the molecular basis of dominance and of loss-of-function and gain-of-function mutations provides a conceptual basis for understanding how different patterns of dominance relationships can develop among alleles of a gene. These concepts apply to all diploid organisms, but the various notational systems used to identify genes and alleles in different species do not all depict these relationships in the same ways. These different notational systems developed in the early years of genetics research when genetic experiments were carried out by experts in widely divergent fields of biology with little intercommunication. Geneticists studying fruit flies developed one notation system for identifying wild-type and mutant alleles, geneticists studying yeast developed another, and geneticists studying plants developed another. As the table inside the front cover illustrates, each model organism has its own unique style of gene description and nomenclature. The different notation systems cause confusion for students of genetics because they follow different rules for naming and identifying genes and alleles. The table inside the back cover contains the rule systems we follow throughout this book.

Incomplete Dominance

Mendel's description of inheritance of traits controlled by a dominant and a recessive allele of single genes is a simple hereditary process that is relatively rare in nature. More commonly with single-gene traits, the dominance of one allele over another is not complete. **Incomplete dominance,** also known as **partial dominance,** identifies such circumstances. When incomplete dominance exists among alleles, the phenotype of the heterozygous organism is distinctive; it falls between the phenotypes of the homozygotes on a continuum of some kind and is typically more similar to one homozygous phenotype than the other. When traits display incomplete dominance, two pure-breeding parents with different phenotypes produce F_1 heterozygotes having a phenotype different from that of either parent. The F_1 phenotype is intermediate between the parental forms, although it may more closely resemble one parental phenotype than the other.

In previous discussions we used a notational system in which an uppercase letter—for example, *A*—indicates a dominant allele, and the same letter in lowercase—*a*—designates a recessive allele. In incomplete dominance systems, the relationship between alleles is different, so a different notational system—one that avoids implying dominance or recessiveness—is used. In the nomenclature system for incomplete dominance, alleles are symbolized with either upper- or lowercase letters plus a suffix that may be a number or a letter. Examples of how pairs of alleles with incomplete dominance can be designated are $A1$ and $A2$, B^1 and B^2, d_1 and d_2, and w^a and w^b.

Genetic research has identified innumerable examples of incomplete dominance in animals and plants; one example is the trait described as flowering time in Mendel's pea plants (*Pisum sativum*). In peas, the first appearance of flowers is under the genetic control of a locus that we will call *T* (for flowering *time*). The earliest-flowering strain of pea plants has the homozygous genotype T_1T_1; the flowering time of this strain is described as day 0.0. The latest-flowering strain is homozygous T_2T_2, and it flowers 5.2 days later on average than T_1T_1 plants. A cross of pure-breeding early-flowering and late-flowering strains produces T_1T_2 heterozygous progeny that begin to flower 3.7 days later on average than the earliest-flowering strain (**Figure 4.2a**).

Genetic crosses show that flowering time is controlled by a single locus. Self-fertilization of T_1T_2 plants produces a 1:2:1 ratio of early-, intermediate-, and late-flowering progeny (**Figure 4.2b**). We say the T_2 allele is partially dominant, but not completely dominant, to T_1 because the heterozygous phenotype is distinct from either homozygous phenotype but more closely resembles the late-flowering strain.

Codominance

Codominance, like incomplete dominance, leads to a heterozygous phenotype different from the phenotype of either homozygous parent. Unlike incomplete dominance, however, codominance is characterized by the detectable expression of both alleles in heterozygotes. Codominance is most clearly identified when the protein products of both alleles are detectable in heterozygous organisms, typically by means of some sort of molecular analysis such as gel electrophoresis or a biochemical assay that can distinguish between the different proteins. We explore the details of these types of molecular analysis in a later discussion (see Chapter 10).

Dominance Relationships of ABO Alleles

More than one pattern of dominance between the alleles of a gene can occur under certain circumstances. Here we examine the codominance of two alleles and the recessiveness of a third allele of the gene determining human blood type.

One physiological attribute many of us know about ourselves is our blood type, which is type A, type B, type AB, or type O. All of us have one of these four common blood types that result from alleles at the ABO blood group gene located on chromosome 9 (OMIM 110300). There are three alleles in all human populations, and combinations of the alleles can occur. Most combinations of different ABO alleles result in complete dominance of one allele, but one combination results in codominance.

The three alleles of the ABO gene are identified as I^A, I^B, and i, and the four blood groups are phenotypes produced by different combinations of these alleles. On the basis of genotype–phenotype (i.e., blood type) correlation, geneticists have concluded that I^A and I^B have complete dominance over i, and that I^A and I^B are codominant to one another. The complete dominance of I^A and I^B to i is indicated by the identification of blood type A in individuals whose genotype is I^AI^A or I^Ai, and of blood type B in individuals whose genotype is I^BI^B or I^Bi. The completely recessive nature of the i allele is confirmed by the observation that only ii homozygotes have blood type O. Lastly, codominance of I^A and I^B to one another is confirmed by the observation that blood type AB occurs only in individuals who have the heterozygous genotype I^AI^B.

(a)

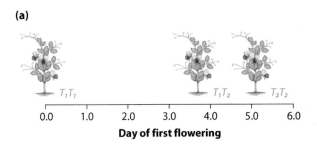

(b)

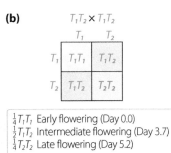

Figure 4.2 Incomplete dominance in flowering time of pea plants. (a) Allele T_2 is incompletely dominant over allele T_1 as indicated by the late flowering time of T_1T_2 plants. **(b)** Segregation of alleles T_1 and T_2.

Testing for ABO Blood Type Blood typing for ABO blood type makes use of an antigen–antibody reaction to determine if a specific antigen—identified by a sugar moiety embedded on the surface of red blood cells—is present in a given person's blood. An antibody is a molecule, produced by the immune system, that binds to a specific antigen. A positive reaction occurs when the antibody detects its antigen target. The antibody binds the antigen and also attaches to other antigen-bound antibodies, causing red blood cells to form visible clumps. Clumping indicates that the antibody has detected its antigen target, whereas an absence of clumping indicates that blood does not contain the antigen target of the antibody.

To test for ABO blood type, two antisera—one called "anti-A antiserum" and containing purified anti-A antibody, the other called "anti-B antiserum" and containing purified anti-B antibody—are placed in separate depressions on a microscope slide, and a drop of the blood to be typed is added to each depression. A person with blood type A shows clumping with anti-A antiserum but not with anti-B (Figure 4.3). Conversely, blood type B is identified when clumping occurs with anti-B but not with anti-A. If clumping occurs with both antisera, the blood type is AB. Clumping with neither antiserum identifies blood type O.

Proper cross-matching of blood type is essential for safe blood transfusion. In reality, several antigens produced by different genes determine the suitability of donor and recipient blood for transfusion, and hospitals and clinics must carefully compare donor and recipient blood to identify the possibility of adverse reactions before transfusion takes place. The general rule for safe blood transfusion is that the recipient blood must not contain an antibody that reacts with an antigen in the donated blood. When such a reaction occurs, hemolysis can occur and blood clots produced by clumping blood cells form at the site of transfusion. These adverse reactions can potentially cause life-threatening complications.

The antibodies anti-A and anti-B develop in humans from birth, but people do not carry an antibody if they also carry the corresponding antigen. Thus people with blood type A, who have the A antigen, also carry the anti-B antibody. People with blood type B have the B antigen and the anti-A antibody. Those with blood type AB have both antigens and neither anti-A nor anti-B antibody. Finally, people with blood type O have neither A nor B antigen and have both anti-A and anti-B antibody.

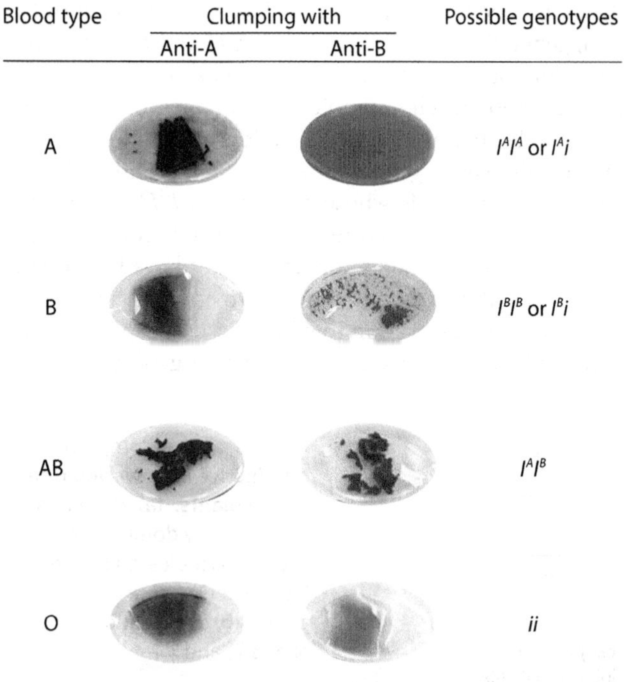

The Molecular Basis of Dominance and Codominance of ABO Alleles The two ABO blood group antigens on the surfaces of red blood cells each have a slightly different molecular structure. The antigens are glycolipids that contain a lipid component and an oligosaccharide component. The lipid portion of the antigen is anchored in the red blood cell membrane, and the segment protruding outside the cell contains the oligosaccharide. Initially, the oligosaccharide is composed of five sugar molecules and is called the H antigen. It results from the activity of an enzyme produced by the *H* gene (Figure 4.4). The H antigen is present on the surfaces of all red blood cells; it can be further modified, in two alternative ways, by the addition of a sixth sugar, or it can be left unmodified. The final modification of the H antigen depends on the enzymatic activity of the protein product of the ABO blood group locus.

Two alternative sugars can be added to the H antigen by the gene products of the I^A or I^B alleles, respectively. If the I^A allele is present in the genotype, it produces the gene product α-3-N-acetyl-D-galactosaminyltransferase, or simply, "A-transferase." A-transferase catalyzes the addition of the sugar N-acetylgalactosamine to the H antigen, producing a six-sugar oligosaccharide known as the A antigen. The I^B allele, on the other hand, produces α-3-D-galactosyltransferase, commonly called "B-transferase," which catalyzes the addition of a different sugar, galactose, and produces a six-sugar oligosaccharide known as the B antigen. The molecular basis of the differences between the A and B alleles is several nucleotide differences that change four amino acids of the resulting transferase enzymes and alter enzymatic activity. In contrast, the *i* allele is due to a single base-pair deletion and is a null allele that does not produce a functional gene product capable of adding a sixth sugar to the H antigen.

At the cellular level, anti-A antibody recognizes the N-acetylgalactosamine addition mediated by I^A, and anti-B antibody identifies the galactose addition produced by the action of I^B. Neither of these antibodies has any reactivity with the unmodified H antigen, so unmodified H antigen, present in individuals with blood type O, is not recognized by either

Blood type	Clumping with		Possible genotypes
	Anti-A	Anti-B	
A			I^AI^A or I^Ai
B			I^BI^B or I^Bi
AB			I^AI^B
O			*ii*

Figure 4.3 **ABO blood type.** Blood type is determined by mixing a drop of blood with a drop of anti-A or anti-B antiserum.

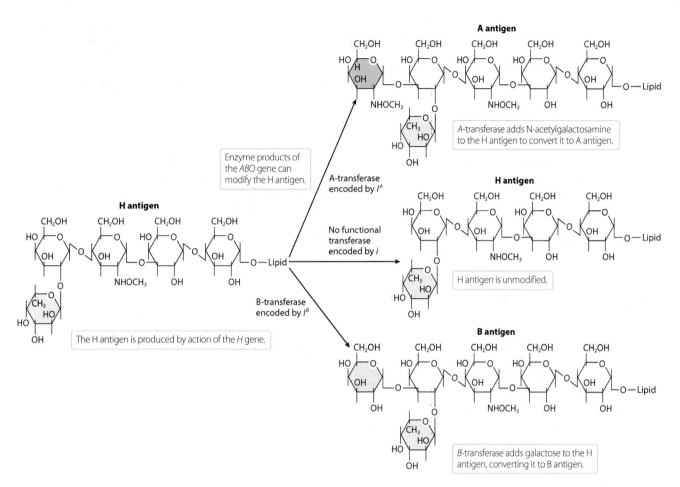

Figure 4.4   Production of ABO blood group antigens.

antibody. Either one or two copies of the I^A or the I^B allele in a genotype is sufficient to produce an ABO antigen detectable by anti-A or anti-B antibodies. Both I^A and I^B are dominant to i, since I^A and I^B produce enzymes that modify the H antigen but i does not. On the other hand, the $I^A I^B$ genotype leads to production of both A-transferase and B-transferase, resulting in the addition of N-acetylgalactosamine to some H antigens and the addition of galactose to other H antigens. In the $I^A I^B$ genotype, all red blood cells carry both types of H-antigen modifications; about half of the red cell surface antigens are A antigens, and the rest are B antigens. In the heterozygous $I^A I^B$ genotype, therefore, the action of both alleles is detected in the phenotype, leading to the conclusion that I^A and I^B are codominant to one another.

Many nonhuman primates have a blood group system that is essentially identical to the human ABO blood group system. ABO blood groups have been identified in the great apes (chimpanzee, gorilla, and orangutan) as well as in numerous Old World monkey species, including macaques (genus *Macaca*) and baboons (genus *Papio*). Two important evolutionary observations derive from this finding. First, the ABO blood group is a long-standing feature of the immune system genetics in primates, one that evolved early in the ancestral history of primates and was retained over tens of millions of years as primates diversified. Second, the retention of the ABO

blood group system in primates demonstrates the importance of this immune system response in protecting primates from infectious and foreign antigens. Natural selection has played a preeminent role in maintaining this system. The ABO blood group genes are one example of the shared evolutionary history that can be identified through the examination of the taxonomic distribution of genes in lineages. **Genetic Analysis 4.1** examines the inheritance of blood group phenotypes, where alleles have a variety of dominance relationships.

Allelic Series

Diploid genomes contain pairs of homologous chromosomes; thus, each individual organism can possess at most two alleles at a locus. In populations, however, the number of alleles is theoretically unlimited, and some genes have scores of alleles. At the population level, a locus possessing three or more alleles is said to have multiple alleles. The ABO blood group locus, with its three alleles, is one example of multiple alleles. Like the *ABO* gene, other multiple-allelic loci display a variety of dominance relationships among the alleles. Commonly, an order of dominance emerges among the alleles, based on the activity of each allele's protein product, forming a sequential series known as an **allelic series.** Alleles in an allelic series can be completely dominant or

PROBLEM The MN blood group in humans is an autosomal codominant system with two alleles, *M* and *N*. Its three blood group phenotypes, M, MN, and N, correspond to the genotypes *MM*, *MN*, and *NN*. The ABO blood group assorts independently of the MN blood group.

> **BREAK IT DOWN:** The discussion on page 110 about the relationships among ABO alleles will help you to identify the parental genotypes from the phenotypes given here.

A male with blood type O and blood type MN has a female partner with blood type AB and blood type N. Identify the blood types that might be found in their children, and state the proportion for each type.

> **BREAK IT DOWN:** Alleles of the ABO system have both dominant-recessive and codominant relationships (p. 113).

Solution Strategies	Solution Steps
Evaluate	
1. Identify the topic of this problem and the kind of information the answer should contain.	1. The problem concerns the inheritance of two blood types. The gene determining ABO blood type carries three alleles: I^A and I^B are codominant to one another and dominant to *i*. The MN blood group gene carries two alleles that are codominant. The answer requires finding the possible blood types, and their expected proportions, of the children of parents whose blood types are given.
2. Identify the critical information given in the problem.	2. The blood types of the parents are given.

> **TIP:** Blood type O is the recessive phenotype, and blood type MN is due to codominance of alleles.

Deduce	
3. Deduce the blood group genotypes of the male parent.	3. The male has blood types O and MN. Type O results from homozygosity for the recessive *i* allele, whereas MN is produced in heterozygotes carrying both alleles. The male genotype is *ii MN*.
4. Deduce the blood group genotypes of the female parent.	4. The female has blood groups AB and N. The AB blood type is found in heterozygotes, and blood type N in homozygotes. The female blood group genotype is $I^A I^B$ *NN*.

> **TIP:** Blood type AB is due to codominance, and blood type N is due to homozygosity.

Solve	
5. Identify the gamete genotypes and their frequencies for the male.	5. Independent assortment predicts two gamete genotypes for the male: All gametes contain *i*, half carry *M*, and half carry *N*.
6. Identify the female gamete genotypes and their frequencies.	6. Independent assortment predicts two gamete genotypes for the female: All gametes contain *N*, half contain I^A, and half contain I^B.
7. Predict the progeny genotypes and phenotypes.	7.

> **TIP:** Use a Punnett square to evaluate this cross.

♂ ♀	*Mi*	*Ni*
NI^A	$MNI^A i$ Blood types: *MN* and *A*	$NNI^A i$ Blood types: *N* and *A*
NI^B	$MNI^B i$ Blood types: *MN* and *B*	$NNI^B i$ Blood types: *N* and *B*

For more practice, see Problems 6, 9, and 31.
Visit the Study Area to access study tools.   **MasteringGenetics™**

---

completely recessive, or they can display various forms of incomplete dominance or codominance.

The C-Gene System for Mammalian Coat Color   Genetic analysis of coat color in mammals reveals that many genes are required to produce and distribute pigment to the hair follicles or skin cells, where they are displayed as coat color or skin color. While various interactions among these genes can modify color expression, we focus here on just one gene, the *C* (color) gene that is responsible for coat color in mammals such as cats, rabbits, and mice. This gene has dozens of alleles that have been identified in more than 80 years of genetic analysis, but we limit our discussion to just four alleles that form an allelic series. The *C* gene produces the enzyme tyrosinase, which is active in the first two steps of a multistep biochemical pathway that synthesizes the pigment melanin, which imparts coat color in furred mammals and skin color in humans. In the initial melanin pathway steps, tyrosinase is responsible for the breakdown (catabolism) of the amino acid tyrosine.

The *C*-gene alleles form an allelic series that is revealed by the phenotypes of offspring of various matings. Allele *C* is dominant to all other alleles of the gene, and any genotype with at least one copy of *C* produces wild-type coat color. These genotypes are written as *C–* to indicate that regardless of the second allele in the genotype, the phenotype is dominant. Three other alleles, producing tyrosinase enzymes with reduced or no tyrosinase activity, form an allelic series with *C* (**Figure 4.5**). The allele c^{ch} produces a phenotype called chinchilla, a diluted coat color. This allele is hypomorphic and generates reduced coat color as a result of the reduced level of activity of the gene product. The c^h

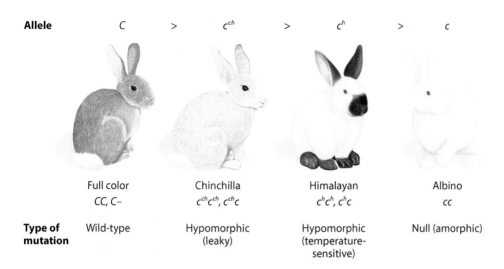

Allele	C	>	c^{ch}	>	c^h	>	c

Full color
$CC, C–$

Chinchilla
$c^{ch}c^{ch}, c^{ch}c$

Himalayan
c^hc^h, c^hc

Albino
cc

Type of mutation   Wild-type   Hypomorphic (leaky)   Hypomorphic (temperature-sensitive)   Null (amorphic)

Figure 4.5 **Allelic series for coat-color determination in mammals.**

allele produces the Himalayan phenotype, characterized by fully pigmented extremities (paws, tail, nose, and ears) but virtually absent pigmentation on other parts of the body. The Himalayan phenotype is the "Siamese" coat-color pattern often seen in cats, rabbits, and mice. This allele is temperature sensitive, as we describe momentarily. Finally, the c allele produces a protein product with no enzymatic activity. This is a fully recessive null (amorphic) allele that does not produce a functional gene product. Homozygosity for this allele produces an albino phenotype.

Crosses between animals with different genotypes at the C gene indicate the dominance relations of the alleles. For example, in Crosses A, B, and C in **Figure 4.6**, complete dominance of C over other alleles in the series is demonstrated by the finding that all of the progeny of an animal with the genotype CC have full color, regardless of the genotype of the mate. The dominance order of alleles in the series is revealed by the pattern of 3:1 ratios obtained from crosses of various heterozygous genotypes shown in Figure 4.6. In Cross D, chinchilla is shown to be partially dominant over Himalayan. Most of the coat of these animals has diluted (chinchilla) color, and the Himalayan pattern has darker color of paws, face, and tail. Cross E shows that chinchilla is completely dominant over albino. Himalayan, too, is completely dominant over albino (Cross F). The dominance relationships within this allelic series locus can be expressed as $C > c^{ch} > c^h > c$.

The Molecular Basis of the C-Gene Allelic Series
Tyrosinase enzymes produced by different C-gene alleles have distinctive levels of catabolic activity that are the basis for the dominance relationships between the alleles. The allele C is a dominant wild-type allele producing fully active tyrosinase that is defined as 100% activity. The percentage of wild-type tyrosinase activity produced by each allele explains the order observed for the allelic series. Biochemical examination reveals that the enzyme produced by the c^{ch} hypomorphic allele has less than 20% of the activity of the wild-type enzyme. In the homozygous $c^{ch}c^{ch}$ genotype or

heterozygous genotypes $c^{ch}c^h$ or $c^{ch}c$, only a small amount of melanin is synthesized. This leads to a decreased amount of pigment, and it has the effect of muting the coat color.

The tyrosinase enzyme produced by the hypomorphic c^h (Himalayan) allele is unstable and is inactivated at a temperature very near the normal body temperature of most mammals. This type of gene product is an example of a **temperature-sensitive allele.** Cats with the Siamese coat-color pattern are familiar examples of the action of this temperature-sensitive allele. The parts of cats that are farthest away from the core of the body (the paws, ears, tail, and tip of the nose) at most times tend to be slightly cooler than the trunk. At these cooler extremities, the temperature-sensitive tyrosinase produced by the c^h allele remains active, producing pigment in the hairs there. However, in the warmer central portion of the body, the slightly higher temperature is enough to cause the tyrosinase produced by the c^h allele to denature, or unravel. This inactivates the enzyme and leads to an absence of pigment in the central portion of the body. Animals that are c^hc^h or c^hc have the Himalayan phenotype. The final allele in the series, c, is a null allele that does not produce functional tyrosinase. Homozygotes for this allele are unable to initiate the catabolism of tyrosine. This leads to an absence of melanin and produces the condition known as albinism.

Lethal Alleles

Certain single-gene mutations are so detrimental that they cause death early in life or terminate gestational development. These life-ending mutations affect genes whose products are essential to life. Homozygosity for mutation of these essential genes is lethal, and the mutations are identified as **lethal alleles.** As a rule, recessive lethal alleles have low frequencies in populations, although they may persist in some populations over a long period of time. Natural selection can eliminate copies of the allele when they occur in homozygous genotypes; however, recessive lethal alleles are "hidden" by dominant

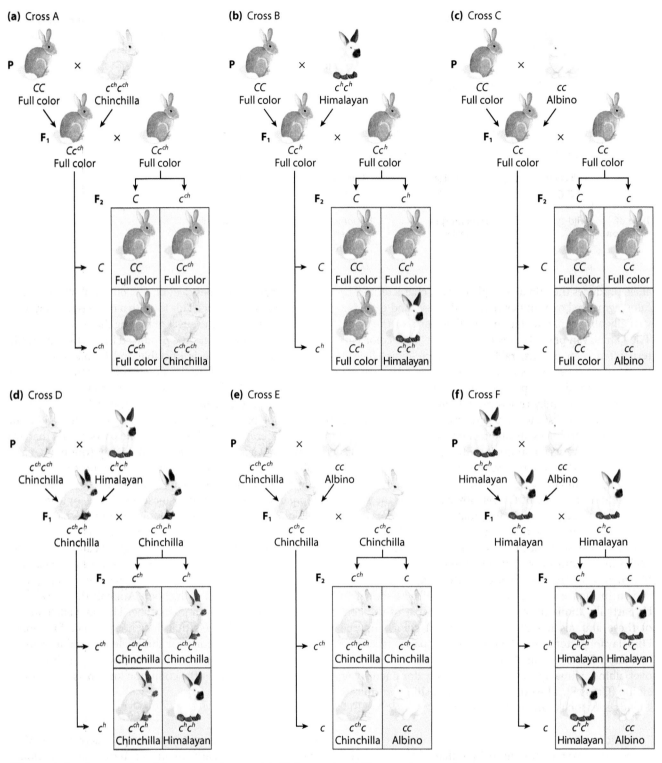

Figure 4.6 **The genetics of *C*-gene dominance.** (a)–(f) Crosses A to F illustrate the complete dominance of *c* and the complete recessiveness of *c*, and establish the allelic series as $C > c^{ch} > c^h > c$.

wild-type alleles in heterozygous genotypes, thus evading natural selection. Under certain circumstances, heterozygous carriers of a recessive lethal allele have a natural selection advantage (see Chapter 10).

Lethal alleles are often detected as distortions in segregation ratios, where one or more classes of expected progeny are missing. For example, in plant and animal crosses between two organisms heterozygous for a recessive lethal allele, the phenotype of the progeny is 3:1 (viable:dead). The dead offspring are homozygous for a recessive lethal mutation. These progeny might not be seen at all, due to embryonic lethality, or they may be

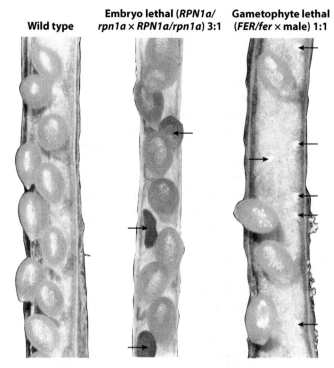

Figure 4.7   Evidence of lethal mutations in plants. Gametophytic lethality is detected by observing a 1:1 ratio of living to dead seeds. Arrows indicate undeveloped seeds.

stillborn or die very young. Of the viable offspring, two-thirds are expected to be heterozygous for the lethal allele and one-third are expected to be homozygous for the dominant wild-type allele (Figure 4.7).

Detection in Plants   In flowering plants, the effects of lethal alleles can be observed directly. For example, mutation of the *RPN1a* gene that encodes a subunit of the 26S proteosome, a multi-protein complex involved in protein degradation, is an example of a loss-of-function null mutation (*rpn1a*) that results in embryonic lethality in *Arabidopsis thaliana* and other plant species. In an *RPN1a/rpn1a* × *RPN1a/rpn1a* cross, a 3:1 segregation ratio of living seeds (*RPN1a*) to dead seeds (*rpn1a/rpn1a*) can be observed in the fruit. When the living seeds are planted, approximately two-thirds are heterozygous for the lethal allele (*RPN1a/rpn1a*) and one-third are homozygous for the wild-type allele (*RPN1a/RPN1a*).

Lethal mutations that result in female gametophytic lethality are also detectable in flowering plants. Consider a plant heterozygous for a female gametophytic allele, *FER/fer*, in which the wild-type *FER* allele was derived from its mother, and the mutant *fer* allele came from its father. During megasporogenesis, half of all megaspores will inherit the *FER* allele and the other half will inherit the *fer* allele. Embryo sacs derived from megaspores inheriting the *fer* allele will die, so that only half of all ovules develop into seeds. The alleles segregate in a 1:1 ratio that is observed among the developing seeds in a fruit. Note that the 1:1 ratio is a

direct observation of Mendelian ratios in the gametes of a heterozygous organism. Thus a 1:1 ratio distinguishes female gametophytic lethality from embryonic lethality, which results in a 3:1 ratio among seeds. Plants usually produce pollen in excess, similar to the excess of sperm production relative to egg production in animals; thus, male gametophytic lethality is not observable by looking at developing seeds in the fruit. It can be detected, however, by looking for plants in which half of all the pollen grains are dead.

Detection in Animals   In contrast, lethal alleles in animals are usually detected by a distortion in segregation ratios. The first case of a lethal allele was identified in 1905 by Lucien Cuenot, who studied a lethal mutation in mice carrying a dominant mutation for yellow coat color. In mice, wild-type coat color is a brown color, called "agouti" (*a-GOO-tee*), produced by the presence of yellow and black pigments in each hair shaft (Figure 4.8a). Agouti hairs are black at the base and tip, with yellow pigment in the central portion of the shaft. Yellow coat color is seen when yellow pigment is deposited along the entire length of the hair shaft, not just in the middle portion as it is in agouti (Figure 4.8b). The *Agouti* gene is one of the pigment-producing genes found in mammals with furry coats. It produces a yellow pigment called pheomelanin that is found in the hairs of mammalian coats. An independently assorting gene produces the black pigment that is part of

(a) Agouti coat color

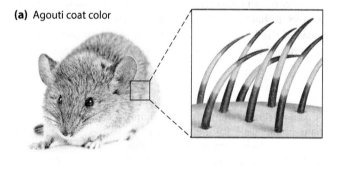

(b) Yellow coat color

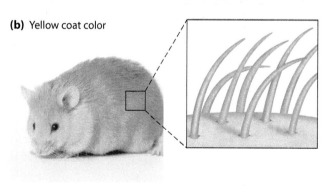

Figure 4.8   Coat color in mice. (a) Wild-type agouti coat color is a mixture of black and yellow pigment in hair shafts. **(b)** Yellow coat occurs when yellow pigment produced by the overly active mutant allele A^Y displaces black pigment.

this example. The wild-type allele for agouti coat color is designated A, and its normal activity leads to the production of a moderate amount of yellow pigment. The mutant allele, designated A^Y, is a hypermorphic allele. It is a dominant gain-of-function mutation that produces substantially more yellow pigment than does the wild-type allele.

The A^Y mutation is dominant, but true-breeding yellow mice cannot be produced. From a genetic perspective, this means that mice with yellow coat color are heterozygous (AA^Y) and that the A^YA^Y genotype is lethal in embryonic development due to its interference with an essential gene, as we explain momentarily. From this information, two important observations about the genetics of the yellow allele can be made. First, mating an agouti mouse and a yellow mouse will *always* result in a 1:1 ratio of agouti and yellow among progeny (Figure 4.9a). Second, crosses between two yellow mice (both of which are necessarily heterozygous) produce evidence of the recessive lethal nature of the A^Y allele (Figure 4.9b). The outcome of these crosses is a 2:1 ratio of yellow to agouti, rather than the 3:1 ratio that is anticipated when heterozygotes expressing a dominant allele are crossed. The genetic interpretation of this observation is that alleles of heterozygous yellow mice segregate normally in gamete formation and unite at random to produce a 1:2:1 ratio at conception, but that A^YA^Y zygotes do not survive gestation. Recessive lethality of A^Y prevents embryonic development of homozygotes, eliminating that class among progeny and resulting in the 2:1 ratio seen among progeny of heterozygous parents.

Nearly a century after Cuenot first identified homozygous lethality of the mutant A^Y allele, the molecular basis of the lethality was identified. Much to the surprise of geneticists, the lethality had little to do with yellow coat color itself; instead, yellow coat was an almost inadvertent consequence of a mutation that deleted part of a gene near the coat-color gene.

The mutation producing the A^Y allele results from a deletion that affects two genes, the *Agouti* gene and a neighboring gene identified as *Raly*. *Raly* produces a protein that is essential for mouse embryo development. Each gene has its own promoter. The wild-type *Raly* promoter drives a high level of transcription, whereas the *Agouti* gene promoter is considerably less actively transcribed (Figure 4.10). The dominant mutation producing yellow coat color comes about by a deletion of approximately 120,000 bp that deletes the entire *Raly* gene and the *Agouti* gene promoter, thus bringing the *Agouti* gene under the control of the *Raly* promoter, leading to a mutant hypermorphic agouti allele. The *Raly* promoter drives a high level of *Agouti* gene transcription that results in excess yellow pigment that displaces black pigment in hair shafts and leads to the mutant yellow phenotype. In reality, however, this deletion mutation affects both the *Agouti* and *Raly* genes that happen to be side by side on the mouse chromosome. By this deletion, *Agouti* transcription is substantially increased and the *Raly* gene is deleted. Heterozygotes with the AA^Y genotype have yellow coats and survive due to haplosufficiency of the single copy of *Raly*. Homozygous A^YA^Y mice are unable to produce the essential protein product from the *Raly* gene and fail to develop, resulting in the skewed 2:1 Mendelian ratio that characterizes the progeny of two heterozygous yellow-coated mice.

An Allele That Is Both Dominant and Recessive The A^Y allele is a rare example of an allele that can be classified as both dominant and recessive. This may sound confusing

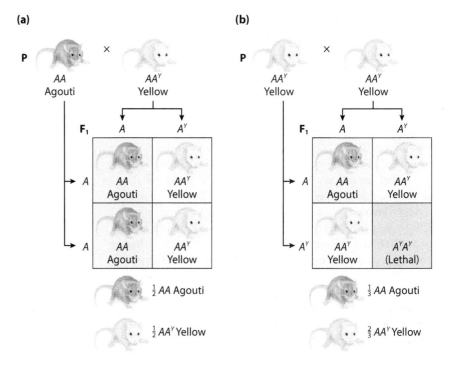

Figure 4.9   Dominance and lethality of A^Y. (a) A 1:1 ratio identifies A^Y as a dominant mutant allele. **(b)** The lethality of A^Y in the homozygous genotype results in a 2:1 ratio of yellow to agouti in the cross of yellow-coated heterozygous mice.

(a)

P AA × AA^Y
Agouti   Yellow

F_1 A A^Y

A AA AA^Y
        Agouti   Yellow

A AA AA^Y
        Agouti   Yellow

$\frac{1}{2} AA$ Agouti

$\frac{1}{2} AA^Y$ Yellow

(b)

P AA^Y × AA^Y
Yellow   Yellow

F_1 A A^Y

A AA AA^Y
        Agouti   Yellow

A^Y AA^Y A^YA^Y
        Yellow   (Lethal)

$\frac{1}{3} AA$ Agouti

$\frac{2}{3} AA^Y$ Yellow

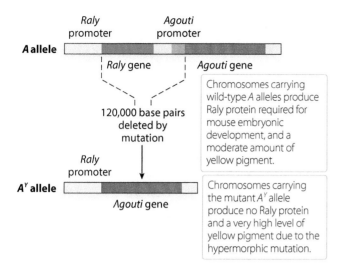

Figure 4.10 **Mutation of *Raly* and *Agouti* producing yellow coat.**

and contradictory, but it is based on the phenotypes produced by genotypes of the *Agouti* gene. We refer to the mutant allele as dominant or as recessive depending on the particular phenotype we happen to be examining.

When we look at the ratio of agouti versus yellow coat color among the progeny produced by a yellow mouse mating with an agouti mouse, we see a 1:1 ratio that indicates dominance of the mutant allele over the wild-type allele. Dominance in this instance is due to the gain-of-function of yellow pigment by the mutant allele. If, on the other hand, we look at the ratio of progeny with yellow versus agouti coat color in the cross of two yellow mice, we see a 2:1 ratio that is the result of the homozygous lethality of the mutant allele. In this context, lethality only affects homozygotes, and the mutant allele is recessive to the wild-type. This relationship is due to the loss of function of the *Raly* gene caused by its deletion. We have, therefore, the odd circumstance of one mutant allele that is both dominant and recessive, depending on how its phenotypic effect is examined.

Sex-Limited Traits

The sex of an organism can exert an influence on its gene expression. This effect is often due to the hormonal environment (i.e., in a male or in a female) in which the gene is located. As such, the differential expression of a gene is sex-dependent. One consequence of such influence is the potential limitation of gene expression to one sex but not the other in a pattern called **sex-limited gene expression.** Differences in gene expression between the sexes can result in the appearance of these **sex-limited traits.** Both sexes typically carry the genes for sex-limited traits, but the genes are expressed in just one sex.

In mammals, for example, the development of breasts and the ability to produce milk are traits limited to females. Horn development is a trait limited to males in

some species of sheep, cows, and other hoofed animals. Behavioral traits in some species, particularly traits related to mating, are also strongly influenced by sex. For example, the courtship behavior of crowned cranes includes an elaborate display of body positioning, neck intertwining, and vocalization that is performed differently by males and females of the species.

The mechanism that limits the expression of a trait to just one sex is most often the differential influence of hormones acting as intercellular regulators of gene expression. In the case of male canary vocalization, for example, changes in male singing patterns are initiated in late winter by an increase in male hormones released by the brain in response to increased day length and warmer temperatures. These hormones stimulate enlargement of the testes and increased production of testosterone, which in turn stimulates the development of neurons in the brain that elaborate the song center, induce the development of muscles in the vocalization area of the throat, and allow males to produce sex-limited vocalization to attract mates.

Sex-Influenced Traits

Sex-influenced traits are those in which the phenotype corresponding to a particular genotype differs depending on the sex of the organism carrying the genotype. Hormones are thought to influence the differential expression of genotypes in the sexes.

The appearance of a chin beard versus the absence of a beard, the beardless phenotype, in certain goat breeds is an example of a sex-influenced trait. Bearding is inherited as an autosomal trait determined by two alleles, B_1 and B_2, which are present in three genotypes in each sex. In both sexes, B_1B_1 homozygotes are beardless, and homozygotes of either sex with the B_2B_2 genotype are bearded. It is thought that androgenic hormones are a principal factor influencing the bearded phenotype. The effect of different levels of androgenic hormones on bearding in the sexes is seen by comparing females and males with the heterozygous genotype (B_1B_2). Heterozygous males have a beard, whereas heterozygous females are beardless. Figure 4.11 illustrates the results of a cross between two heterozygotes that produces different ratios of bearded to beardless males and females. Mendelian inheritance occurs, but as a consequence of sex-influenced expression, the cross yields a 3:1 ratio of bearded to beardless males and a 3:1 ratio of beardless to bearded females. The dominance relationship of these alleles varies with sex. Allele B_1 is dominant to B_2 in females since females that are heterozygous B_1B_2 have the same beardless phenotype as do B_1B_1 females. On the other hand, allele B_2 is dominant over B_1 in males since heterozygotes are bearded just like B_2B_2 homozygotes. Analogous to the classification of the A^Y allele we discussed earlier, the B_1 and B_2 alleles exhibit flexibility of dominance, in this case depending on the sex of the bearer.

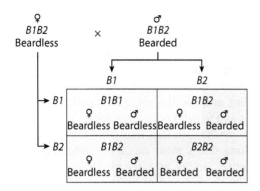

Figure 4.11 **Sex-influenced inheritance of beard appearance in goats.** Dominance of the B_1 and B_2 alleles is expressed differently in males and females.

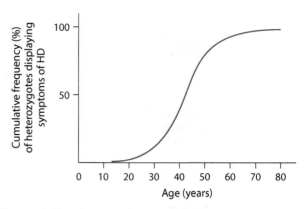

Figure 4.12 **The age-of-onset curve for Huntington disease (HD).**

Delayed Age of Onset

From an evolutionary perspective, it is easy to understand that a dominant lethal allele can be efficiently eliminated by the action of natural selection. Even so, there are numerous examples of dominant lethal hereditary conditions, and a pertinent evolutionary genetic question concerns how these mutations persist in populations. One answer is that some dominant lethal alleles sidestep natural selection by having a **delayed age of onset;** the abnormalities they produce do not appear until after affected organisms have had an opportunity to reproduce and transmit the mutation to the next generation.

One well-characterized example of delayed age of onset of a dominant lethal allele in humans is the condition called Huntington disease (HD). This progressive neuromuscular disorder, usually fatal within 10 to 15 years of diagnosis, is caused by mutation of a gene near one end of chromosome 4. (We have more to say about the symptoms and progression of HD in Chapter 5, where we also discuss the mapping of the HD gene, and in Chapter 16, where we discuss the cloning of the HD gene.) The HD mutant allele persists in the population because symptoms do not begin in about half of all cases until the person's late thirties or early forties, well after most people have begun having children (**Figure 4.12**).

Functionally, the onset of symptoms of HD is delayed because the symptoms are due to neuron death, which usually takes place over an extended period of time that often stretches over several decades.

4.2 Some Genes Produce Variable Phenotypes

To interpret phenotype ratios and identify the distribution of genotypes among phenotypic classes, geneticists make the assumption that phenotypes differ because their underlying genotypes differ. This assumption is valid only to the extent that a particular genotype always produces the same phenotype. If the correspondence between genotype and phenotype holds true in every case, the trait is identified as having **complete penetrance** If the correspondence between genotype and phenotype does not consistently hold true—if instead the same genotype can produce different phenotypes—the usual reasons are gene–environment interaction or interactions with alleles of other genes in the genome.

In this section, we describe two phenomena, referred to as *incomplete penetrance* and *variable expressivity*, in which phenotypic variation occurs among organisms with the same genotype. In addition, we look at specific instances of environmental influence on gene expression that is often associated with incomplete penetrance or variable expressivity.

Incomplete Penetrance

When the phenotype of an organism is consistent with the organism's genotype, the organism is said to be **penetrant** for the trait. In such a case, if the organism carries a dominant allele for the trait in question, the dominant phenotype is displayed. Sometimes an organism with a particular genotype fails to produce the corresponding phenotype, in which case the organism is **nonpenetrant** for the trait.

Traits for which nonpenetrant individuals occasionally or routinely occur are identified as displaying **incomplete penetrance.** The human condition known as polydactyly ("many digits") is an autosomal dominant condition that displays incomplete penetrance. Individuals with polydactyly have more than five fingers and toes—the most common alternative number is six (**Figure 4.13**). Polydactyly occurs in hundreds of families around the world, and in these families the dominant allele is nonpenetrant in about 25–30% of individuals who carry it. Most people who carry the dominant mutant polydactyly allele have extra digits; but at least one in four people with the mutant allele do not have extra digits and instead express the normal five digits. The gene mutated to produce polydactyly was recently identified (see Chapter 20).

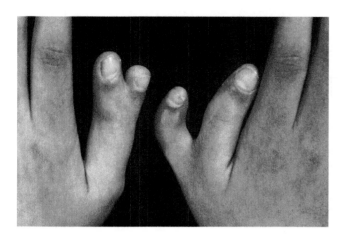

Figure 4.13   Polydactyly, an autosomal dominant trait with incomplete penetrance.

Figure 4.14 shows a family in which polydactyly segregates as a dominant mutation. Nine individuals in the family carry a copy of the polydactyly allele. Six of them are penetrant for the phenotype (meaning that they express the phenotype), but at least three family members—II-6, II-10, and III-10—are nonpenetrant. Each of these individuals has a child or grandchild with polydactyly; thus, each carries the dominant allele for polydactyly but is nonpenetrant for the condition. When nonpenetrant individuals are relatively common, the magnitude of frequency of penetrance can be quantified. Penetrance values vary among different families, but for the family shown in Figure 4.14, the penetrance of polydactyly is $\frac{6}{9}$, or 66.7%, which is about the average seen worldwide among hundreds of families with polydactyly.

Variable Expressivity

Sometimes the discrepancy between genotype and phenotype is a matter of the degree or specific manifestation of expression of a trait rather than presence or absence of the trait altogether. In the phenomenon of **variable**

expressivity, the same genotype produces phenotypes that vary in the degree or form of expression of the allele of interest.

Waardenburg syndrome is a human autosomal dominant disorder displaying variable expressivity. Individuals with Waardenburg syndrome may have any or all of four principal features of the syndrome: (1) hearing loss, (2) differently colored eyes, (3) a white forelock of hair, and (4) premature graying of hair. In the Waardenburg pedigree shown in Figure 4.15, notice that the circles and squares representing family members with Waardenburg syndrome may be entirely or only partly colored. Each quadrant of the symbols represents one of the principal features of the syndrome. The diversity of symbol darkening demonstrates the variation in expressivity of Waardenburg syndrome in this family. Molecular genetic analysis tells us that each family member with Waardenburg syndrome carries exactly the same dominant allele, yet among the eight affected members of the family, there are six different patterns of phenotypic expression.

It is often difficult to pinpoint the cause of incomplete penetrance or variable expressivity. Three kinds of interactions may be responsible: (1) other genes that act in ways that modify the expression of the mutant allele, (2) environmental or developmental (i.e., nongenetic) factors that interact with the mutant allele to modify its expression, or (3) some combination of other genes and environmental factors interacting to modify expression of the mutation. In inbred laboratory strains of model genetic organisms, variation in genetic factors can be eliminated experimentally to allow separation of gene–gene and gene–environment variability, something that cannot be done in organisms such as humans.

Gene–Environment Interactions

Genes control virtually all of the differences observed between species. The genome of an organism lays out the body plan and biochemical pathways of the organism, and it controls the progress of development from conception to

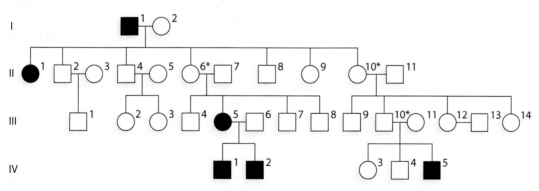

* Nonpenetrant individual

Figure 4.14   Incomplete penetrance for polydactyly. Three nonpenetrant individuals (II-6, II-10, and III-10) are seen in this family.

Figure 4.15 Variable expressivity of Waardenburg syndrome.

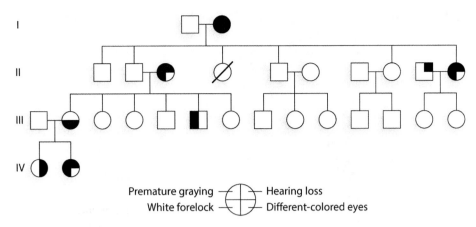

Premature graying ⎯ Hearing loss
White forelock ⎯ Different-colored eyes

death. But genes alone are not responsible for all the variation seen between organisms. The environment, the myriad of physical substances, events, and conditions an organism encounters at different stages of life, is the other essential contributor to observable variation between organisms. **Gene–environment interaction** is the result of the influence of environmental factors (i.e., nongenetic factors) on the expression of genes and on the phenotypes of organisms.

As an example, consider the tall and short pure-breeding lines of pea plants studied by Mendel. Inherited genetic variation dictates that one line will produce tall plants and the other line will produce short plants, but the environment in which the individual plants are grown also has a significant influence on plant height. Environmental factors such as variations in water, light, soil nutrients, and temperature each influence plant growth. It is not hard to imagine that genetically identical plants of a type adapted to temperate zones might grow to different heights if one plant has an ideal growth environment while the other faces a hot, arid environment with poor soil.

Phenotypic expression of genotypes can also depend on the interaction of genetically controlled developmental programs and external factors operating on organisms. For example, the seasonal change in coat color observed in arctic mammals that are nearly white in winter but have darker coats in spring and summer results from an interaction between numerous genes and external environmental cues such as day length and temperature. Similarly, environmental cues that induce plants to bloom in the spring trigger changes in gene expression that stimulate the growth and development of multiple plant structures, including flowers and reproductive structures. Such capacities to make seasonal changes evolved by aiding the survival of these organisms, and they suggest that gene–environment interaction is pivotal in understanding and interpreting phenotypic variation.

Environmental Modification to Prevent Hereditary Disease A prime example of gene–environment interaction in humans is actually a case of environmental intervention that is commonly practiced to prevent the development of the human autosomal recessive condition

known as phenylketonuria (PKU). This case illustrates that the same alleles may produce different phenotypes in different environments. PKU is caused by the absence of the enzyme phenylalanine hydroxylase, which catalyzes the first step of the pathway that breaks down the amino acid phenylalanine, a common component of dietary protein.

At one time, PKU accounted for thousands of cases of severe mental retardation every year. PKU occurred in 1 out of 10,000 to 1 out of 20,000 newborns in most populations around the world. Infants with PKU are normal at birth, but over the first several months of life the body's inability to carry out the normal breakdown of phenylalanine leads to the buildup of a compound that is toxic to developing neurons. As neurons die, mental and motor capacities are irretrievably lost, making full manifestation of PKU inevitable. In the 1960s, a simple blood test became available to detect PKU in the first days of life. The test identifies the disease before the disease has had a chance to manifest itself and begin to damage the body. PKU was among the first, and is now one of dozens of rare hereditary disorders for which newborn infants are routinely screened in U.S. hospitals.

Given early detection, the key to preventing PKU, is the severe restriction of phenylalanine in the diet. Because phenylalanine is an amino acid and is a component of almost all proteins, babies with PKU are given a diet consisting of specially selected and processed proteins that have had phenylalanine removed. An infant who is started on the phenylalanine-free diet soon after birth and kept on it through adolescence avoids the complications of PKU and will develop and function normally despite having PKU. Thousands of people with PKU are living fully normal and productive lives today, thanks to this simple environmental modification that prevents the expression of the devastating PKU phenotype. In this case, people who are homozygous recessive for the mutant PKU allele do not express the trait if they are raised in a largely phenylalanine-free environment.

Dietary hazards abound for children and young adults with PKU, particularly in the form of the artificial sweetener known as aspartame. This sweetener is made by a chemical reaction that fuses the amino acids phenylalanine and aspartic acid to form a compound we perceive to taste sweet. Once consumed, aspartame is quickly broken down into its two constituent amino acids, and phenylalanine is released. Regular intake of aspartame is dangerous for those with PKU; for this reason, a dietary caution reading "Phenylketonurics: Contains phenylalanine" appears on the packaging of food products containing aspartame. Look for it on the next artificially sweetened product you pick up!

Pleiotropic Genes

Pleiotropy is the alteration of multiple, distinct traits of an organism by a mutation in a single gene. The impact of such mutations is, in reality, a reflection of the fact that all genes interact in one way or another with other genes. No gene acts alone in producing a phenotype. Rather, genes act in concert, each producing its own product and having its own effect, to produce a phenotype. Since all genes interact, it comes as no surprise that mutation of one gene has consequences for the expression of other genes and that the mutation of a single gene can have a large impact on phenotype. Most mutations displaying pleiotropy do so either by altering the development of phenotypic features through the direct action of the mutant protein or as a secondary result of a cascade of problems stemming from the mutation.

Mendel unknowingly encountered a case of pleiotropy in his examination of pea plants. Two of the traits he considered for his studies were the inheritance of purple versus white flower color (see Table 2.1) and the inheritance of a gray versus a white seed coat. Upon noticing that plants with white flowers invariably also have white seed coats, whereas purple-flowered plants always have gray seed coats, he correctly surmised that the inheritance of these traits had the same genetic basis. Today we know that flower color, seed-coat color, and the appearance of color at leaf axils (where the leaf attaches to the stem) result from the production of the purple pigment anthocyanin. Mutations that block anthocyanin production are pleiotropic because they leave several plant structures without color and produce mutant white phenotypes for multiple traits.

Pleiotropy through the direct action of a mutant protein product is frequently encountered in studies of development. One example is the activity of the *Drosophila* hormone called juvenile hormone (JH), which is active throughout the *Drosophila* life cycle and influences numerous attributes of development and reproduction. Increased production or increased activity of JH has been shown to prolong developmental time, decrease adult body size, promote early sexual maturity, raise fecundity (the ability to produce offspring), and decrease life span. An evolutionary tradeoff is associated with changes in JH level or activity. On the one hand, producing more JH can lead to production of more offspring through earlier sexual maturity and higher fecundity. On the other hand, body size decreases and life span is shortened by increased JH activity.

Pleiotropy in sickle cell disease (SCD) is an example of the phenotypically diverse secondary effects that can occur due to a mutant allele. SCD (OMIM 603903) is an autosomal recessive condition caused by mutation of the β-globin gene that, in turn, affects the structure and function of hemoglobin, the main oxygen-carrying molecule in red blood cells (see Chapter 10). Many of the red blood cells of people with SCD take on a sickle shape and cause numerous physical problems and complications (**Figure 4.16**).

4.3 Gene Interaction Modifies Mendelian Ratios

No gene operates alone to produce a phenotypic trait. Rather, genes work together to build the complex structures and organ systems of plants and animals. What we see as a phenotype is the physical manifestation of the action of many genes that have each played a role and have worked in complex but coordinated ways to produce a trait or structure. At the cellular and molecular levels, the mutual reliance of genes on one another requires each gene to carry out its activity in the right place, at the right time, and at the appropriate level.

Think of this process as analogous to a symphony orchestra playing a piece of classical music. The orchestra has many instruments and players, each with their own notes, tones, keys, and volume. If the players use their instruments as directed by the sheet music, the result will be smooth and harmonious. If, however, one player is off time or off key, the error might disrupt the entire performance. The same can be said of genes: Each must play its part correctly—that is, give a wild-type performance—or the integrity of the trait will be at risk. For example, the products of several genes interact in biosynthetic pathways to produce pigments that are responsible for flower color. Similarly, a complex phenotypic attribute like the ability to hear requires many genes to produce the various structures of the ear that convert acoustical vibrations into the electrical impulses that are transmitted to the brain and converted into what we perceive as sound.

In this section, we look in detail at **gene interaction,** the collaboration of multiple genes in the production of a single phenotypic character or a group of related characteristics. First, however, let's examine the genetic control of phenotypes from a perspective we have not yet explored.

Gene Interaction in Pathways

Genes commonly work together in pathways, multistep biochemical processes that operate either as biosynthetic pathways, synthesizing complex compounds such as amino acids, or as degradation pathways, breaking complex compounds down into simpler or elemental constituents. Biosynthetic pathways result from the expression of genes whose products help build complex compounds or molecules that are the end product of the pathway. Through successive reaction steps that produce

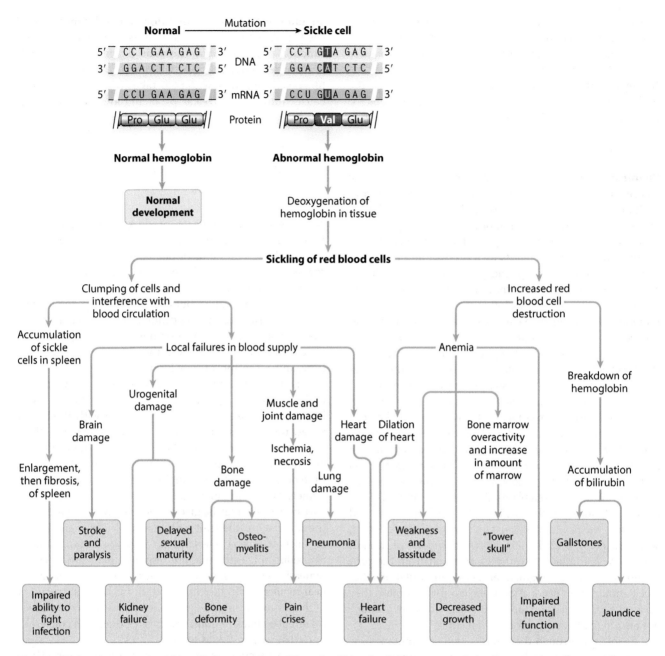

Figure 4.16 Pleiotropy in sickle cell disease. The sickling of red blood cells has a range of phenotypic consequences.

a series of intermediate compounds, these pathways—known broadly as anabolic pathways—lead ultimately to the production of an end product such as a pigment, amino acid, hormone, or nucleotide. The opposite process, the breakdown of compounds into intermediate compounds and often into elemental constituents, is undertaken by catabolic pathways.

Figure 4.17 gives an example of each type of pathway and shows that the expression of multiple genes is required for the completion of any pathway. The anabolic pathway that synthesizes the amino acid methionine is shown in Figure 4.17a. Completion of this pathway, and thus the production of methionine, requires the expression of four genes that each produce an enzyme catalyzing a distinct step of the pathway. Homozygosity for a mutant

allele of any of these genes can block the pathway and would prevent methionine synthesis.

The catabolic pathway that breaks down the amino acid phenylalanine is shown in Figure 4.17b. It, too, utilizes the enzymes produced by multiple genes. The figure identifies several steps of the pathway that are blocked by mutations of certain genes. Each of these mutations causes a distinct human hereditary disorder, including PKU that we just described.

It is common for biologists to describe phenotypic characters or hereditary disorders such as those identified in Figure 4.17b as single-gene traits. This designation means that different forms of a trait can be transmitted to offspring by the segregation of alleles of a single gene. Phenotypic characteristics such as pea flower color and pea shape are

(a) In anabolic pathways the sequential action of gene products catalyzes steps of a biosynthetic pathway.

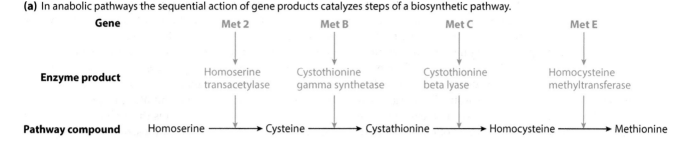

(b) The action of gene products in catabolic pathways breaks down complex compounds into simpler compounds.

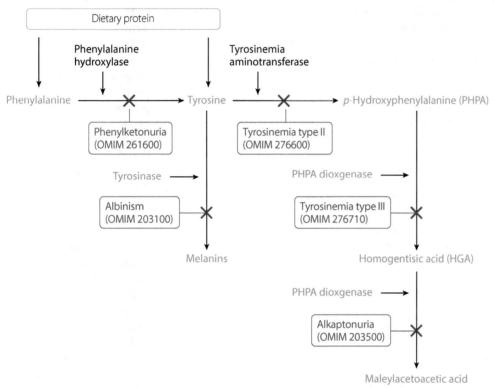

Figure 4.17   Gene action in pathways.   (a) In anabolic pathways the sequential action of gene products catalyzes steps of a biosynthetic pathway. **(b)** The action of gene products in catabolic pathways breaks down complex compounds into simpler compounds

examples of single-gene traits inherited as the result of allelic variation of a single gene, just as PKU is caused by inherited variation of the gene producing phenylalanine hydroxylase.

The term *single-gene trait* conveniently summarizes the observation that inherited variation for one gene can produce a mutant phenotype rather than a wild-type phenotype. The term is not, however, an accurate depiction of genetic reality. The anabolic and catabolic pathways illustrated in Figure 4.17 are representative of common forms of gene interaction. They reveal the necessity for several genes to work together to produce the wild-type phenotype for a trait. At the same time, they also show that the mutation of any of the participating genes could block or alter the wild-type phenotype. The mutant and wild-type phenotypes would segregate as single-gene traits, despite the involvement of multiple genes in producing those phenotypes. Similarly, the

following example of *Drosophila* eye color illustrates that genes with a variety of functions contribute to production of the wild-type red eye color of *Drosophila*.

Geneticists have identified many distinct mutant eye-color phenotypes in fruit flies, and these variants have been mapped to different genes. We will consider just three of these genes, two that produce different eye-color pigments, and a third that transports pigments to eye cells. The *brown* gene produces an enzyme that operates in a pathway synthesizing a vermilion-colored (bright red) pigment. The gene carries a dominant wild-type allele bw^+ and a recessive null mutant allele bw, and flies that are $bwbw$ have brown-colored eyes. The gene is named after the mutant phenotype it is associated with. The *vermilion* gene produces an enzyme that is active in a pathway synthesizing a brown pigment. The wild-type allele v^+ is dominant over the null mutant allele v. Flies that are *vv* have vermilion-colored eyes. The *white* gene produces a pigment-transporting protein from the dominant allele w^+ that carries pigments to the eye. A mutant protein from the *w* allele is incapable of pigment transportation, and flies that do not produce the protein have white eyes. This is the X-linked *w* gene we discussed in Section 3.3.

Production of wild-type proteins from all three genes is necessary to produce wild-type eye color, and hereditary eye color mutations result from the mutation of one or more of the genes (**Figure 4.18**). Wild-type eye color is the result of synthesis of brown and vermilion pigments and the transportation of both pigments to eye cells, where they are blended. Mutation of any one or more of these genes results in a mutant phenotype. This example demonstrates that multiple genes are active in pathways determining different biological properties. Inherited variation of one gene can block a segment of a pathway and produce a mutation attributable to a single gene, but such a finding does not negate the importance of the action of multiple genes affecting each trait.

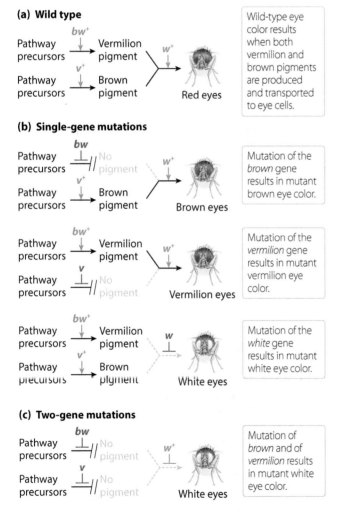

(a) Wild type

Wild-type eye color results when both vermilion and brown pigments are produced and transported to eye cells.

(b) Single-gene mutations

Mutation of the *brown* gene results in mutant brown eye color.

Mutation of the *vermilion* gene results in mutant vermilion eye color.

Mutation of the *white* gene results in mutant white eye color.

(c) Two-gene mutations

Mutation of *brown* and of *vermilion* results in mutant white eye color.

Figure 4.18 Interacting genes control eye color in *Drosophila*. (a) Wild-type (red) eye color requires activity of three genes. **(b)** Mutation of any gene produces a distinctive mutant phenotype. **(c)** Double mutation of *brown* and *vermilion* produces white eyes.

In addition to biosynthetic (anabolic) pathways and catabolic pathways, two additional types of pathways are frequently cited as examples featuring the interaction of multiple genes in the production of a trait or characteristic. *Signal transduction pathways* are responsible for reception of chemical signals, such as hormones, that are generated outside a cell and initiate a response inside a cell. Signal transduction operates through the release of a signaling molecule that is part of a sequence of steps culminating in the activation or repression of gene expression in response to an intracellular or extracellular signal.

Second, genes whose products make up *developmental pathways* to direct normal growth, development, and differentiation of body parts and structures. Numerous developmental pathways have been identified in organisms, and the functions of their genes have been determined by experimental analyses of mutant phenotypes. Geneticists use this analytic approach, known as *genetic dissection*, to identify the step-by-step events making up a genetic pathway. The use of genetic dissection to analyze a biosynthetic pathway is explored in the next section. Examples of signal transduction and developmental pathways are presented in later discussions (see Chapter 20).

The One Gene–One Enzyme Hypothesis

The concept of pathways requiring gene action originated with Archibald Garrod's suggestion in 1908 that the inability to produce the enzyme homogentisic acid oxidase is the cause of the human hereditary condition known as alkaptonuria (see Figure 4.17b). It was not until the middle of the 20th century, however, that comprehensive details of specific genetic pathways began to emerge. George Beadle and Edward Tatum were among the first to investigate biosynthetic pathways, in research that laid the groundwork for the later definition and examination of signal transduction and developmental pathways.

Beadle and Tatum's experiment studied growth variants of the fungus *Neurospora crassa*, and its details are described in **Experimental Insight 4.1**. The idea behind their experiments was simple—to generate single-gene growth mutations in *Neurospora* and interpret the normal function of genes by observing the phenotypic consequences of their mutation. The famous hereditary proposal known as the **one gene–one enzyme hypothesis** came out of these experiments. It says that each gene produces an enzyme, and each enzyme has a specific functional role in a biosynthetic pathway. Beadle and Tatum observed that single-gene mutations block the completion of biosynthetic pathways and lead to the production of mutant fungi that are deficient in their ability to grow without specific nutritional supplementation. Their hypothesis proposed that each mutant phenotype was attributable to the loss or defective function of a specific enzyme. The consequence of these mutants was the blockage of a biosynthetic pathway and the absence of the end product of the pathway. Since each enzyme defect was inherited as a single-gene defect, the one gene–one enzyme hypothesis identifies the direct connection between genes, proteins, and phenotypes. Two new terms that are used multiple times in this section are introduced in Experimental Insight 4.1. The term **prototroph** or **protrophic** means "wild-type." The word's meaning derives from *prototype*, meaning "the original version." In contrast, the term **auxotroph** or **auxotrophic** means "mutant."

The one gene–one enzyme concept has undergone adjustments since its proposal, to account for three observations: (1) Some protein-producing genes do not produce enzymes, but produce transport proteins, structural proteins, regulatory proteins, or other nonenzyme proteins; (2) some genes produce RNAs rather than proteins; and (3) some proteins (e.g., β-globin) must join with other proteins to acquire a function. Despite these modifications, Beadle and Tatum's fundamental conclusion linking each gene to a particular product is valid and forms the basis for understanding of gene function.

Genetic Dissection to Investigate Gene Action

Beadle and Tatum's experiments opened the way to investigation of the roles of individual-gene mutations in biosynthetic pathways. These investigations began with three assumptions about biosynthetic pathways that have proven to be correct: (1) Biosynthetic pathways consist of sequential steps, (2) completion of one step generates the substrate for the next step in the pathway, and (3) completion of every step is necessary for production of the end product of the pathway. These assumptions support the conclusion that wild-type strains are able to complete each pathway step, and that mutant strains are unable to complete a pathway because one or more pathway steps are blocked by mutation.

Genetic dissection in this context is an experimental approach that separately tests the ability of a mutant to execute each step of a biosynthetic pathway and assembles the steps of a pathway by determining the point

---

Experimental Insight 4.1

The One Gene–One Enzyme Hypothesis

George Beadle and Edward Tatum's experiments had the goal of describing gene function. Their work took place at about the time DNA was being identified as the hereditary molecule, and more than a decade before DNA structure was identified. To provide information for analysis, Beadle and Tatum devised an experiment that would induce single-gene mutations in the filamentous fungus *Neurospora crassa* and then studied the mutants to determine how mutations altered *Neurospora* growth. Recall that *Neurospora* can grow as a haploid, or two haploid cells can fuse to form and grow as diploids that undergo meiosis (see Chapter 2).

MUTATION PREPARATION

To begin, Beadle and Tatum grew numerous genetically identical cultures of haploid wild-type fungi that were irradiated to induce random mutations ❶. The irradiated conidia (asexually produced fungal spores) were mated with wild-type haploids. The resulting diploids underwent meiosis to produce haploid spores that were grown in a two-step process to identify mutants. The diploids could also be tested to confirm the presence of a single-gene mutation by observation of a 3:1 ratio in their progeny. Irradiated haploid spores were grown first on a *complete growth medium* that contains a rich mixture of nutrients and supplements and is capable of supporting the growth of wild-type and mutant fungi ❷. Next, growing fungi were picked from colonies on the complete medium and transferred to a *minimal growth medium* that supplies only the minimal constituents needed to support the growth of wild-type fungi ❸. Mutant fungi are identified because they grow on complete medium containing many nutritional and other supplements that support the growth of wild-type as well as mutant fungi, but they are unable to grow on a minimal growth medium, which supplies only elemental constituents and supports the growth of wild-type fungi only.

MUTATION ANALYSIS

With numerous mutants in hand, Beadle and Tatum were able to address questions of which genes were mutated by

first identifying the chemical category of the compound that cannot be produced and then determining the specific missing compound. An example of this analysis is illustrated in steps ❹ and ❺, where growth analysis tests a mutant for its ability to grow on various kinds of *supplemented minimal media*. These are growth media that have had one or more compounds added to them to support the growth of specific kinds of mutants. Step ❹ shows one mutant that grows only on medium that has been supplemented with all 20 of the common amino acids; this result indicates that the strain lacks the ability to synthesize one or more amino acids. The specific defect in this mutant strain is tested in step ❺ using 20 different supplemented minimal media, each supplemented with one amino acid. One mutant grows on minimal medium supplemented with methionine (met), thus identifying the strain as one that is unable to synthesize methionine. This strain is described as being *met−* ("met minus" or "methionine minus"), to identify the defective pathway as the one synthesizing methionine. The wild type is able to synthesize methionine and is identified as *met+* ("met plus" or "methionine plus").

HYPOTHESIS OF GENE FUNCTION

By testing hundreds of independent mutants in this way, Beadle and Tatum discovered that most mutants carried single mutations that could be overcome by supplementing minimal growth media with one particular compound. In the above case, supplementing a minimal medium with methionine supports the growth of *met−* fungi. This finding led them to propose that single mutations prevented mutants from completing a specific step of a biochemical pathway. Based on this outcome, they proposed that single-gene mutations altered the ability of mutants to produce one enzyme critical in a particular biosynthetic pathway. The correlation between single-gene mutations and single defects in biosynthetic pathways is the basis of the one gene–one enzyme hypothesis.

(Continued)

Experimental Insight 4.1 Continued

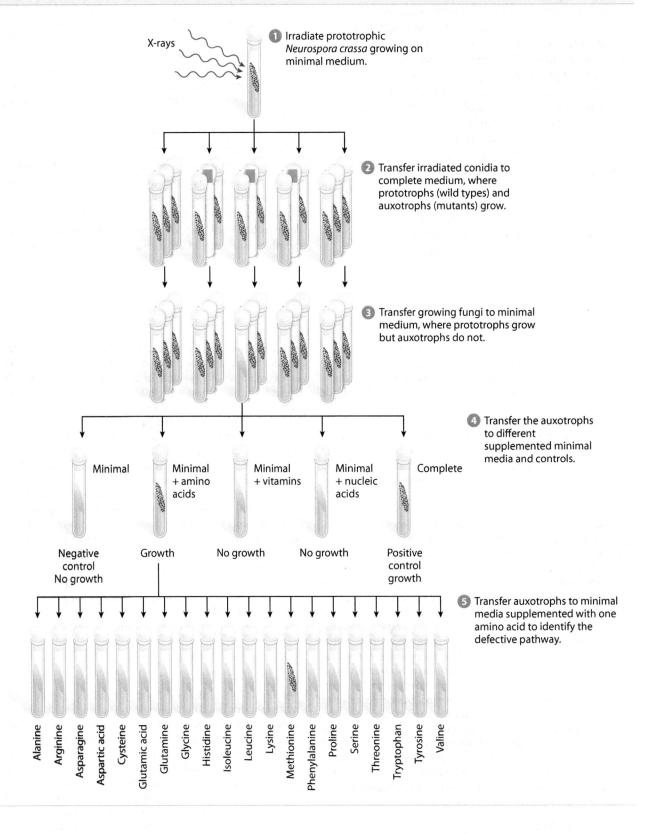

X-rays

1 Irradiate prototrophic *Neurospora crassa* growing on minimal medium.

2 Transfer irradiated conidia to complete medium, where prototrophs (wild types) and auxotrophs (mutants) grow.

3 Transfer growing fungi to minimal medium, where prototrophs grow but auxotrophs do not.

4 Transfer the auxotrophs to different supplemented minimal media and controls.

Minimal

Minimal + amino acids

Minimal + vitamins

Minimal + nucleic acids

Complete

Negative control No growth

Growth

No growth

No growth

Positive control growth

5 Transfer auxotrophs to minimal media supplemented with one amino acid to identify the defective pathway.

Alanine · Arginine · Asparagine · Aspartic acid · Cysteine · Glutamic acid · Glutamine · Glycine · Histidine · Isoleucine · Leucine · Lysine · Methionine · Phenylalanine · Proline · Serine · Threonine · Tryptophan · Tyrosine · Valine

at which the pathway is blocked in each mutant. The strategy of genetic dissection is illustrated for a *met–* strain in Figure 4.19 using experimental data collected in 1947 by Norman Horowitz on four independently isolated *Neurospora crassa met–* mutants.

The goals of Horowitz's genetic dissection analysis were to (1) determine the number of intermediate steps within the methionine biosynthetic pathway, (2) determine the order of steps in the pathway, and (3) identify the step affected by each mutation. In designing his experiment, Horowitz relied on previous biochemical work identifying homoserine as the first compound in the methionine biosynthetic pathway and identifying cysteine, homocysteine, and cystathionine as later intermediates in the pathway. Horowitz tested the control prototroph (*met+*) and four methionine-requiring auxotrophs (Met 1 to Met 4) for their ability to grow on (1) minimal medium, (2) minimal medium plus cysteine only, (3) minimal medium plus cystathionine only, (4) minimal medium plus homocysteine only, and (5) minimal medium plus methionine only. Figure 4.19a shows growth (+) or no growth (–) of the four *met–* mutants and the wild-type strain (*met+*) on each of the experimental media. The wild-type strain grows on all media, since supplementation of minimal medium with any of the intermediates has no effect on its growth. Each methionine mutant grows on minimal medium plus methionine, the end product of the biosynthetic pathway, but they show different growth patterns with other supplemented media. The following is an analysis of each mutant:

1. Met 1 grows only on minimal medium plus methionine, thus indicating that a mutation in the last step of the pathway prevents conversion of the final intermediate product to methionine. Only the addition of methionine to minimal medium bypasses the pathway block.

2. Met 2 exhibits growth with supplementation by either methionine or homocysteine, thus indicating a block at the step that produces homocysteine. This result also tells us that homocysteine is the substrate converted to methionine in the biosynthetic pathway.

3. Met 3 grows on minimal medium supplemented with either methionine, homocysteine, or cystathionine, but not on minimal medium plus cysteine. This tells us that Met 3 is blocked at the step that produces cystathionine and that cystathionine precedes homocysteine in the pathway.

4. Met 4 grows with any supplementation of minimal medium. This tells us that Met 4 is defective at a step that precedes the production of cysteine.

Figure 4.19b shows the steps of the biosynthetic pathway for methionine as determined by analysis of these mutants. The pathway step that is blocked in the mutant is identified based on the logic that supplementation by a compound needed *after* the blockage will permit growth, whereas adding a compound used *before* the blockage will not aid growth. The blocked step is also identified by the substance that accumulates in the auxotroph: In each mutant, a different intermediate substance builds up because the step that would convert it to the next intermediate in the pathway is defective. Accumulation of cysteine by Met 3, cystathionine by Met 2, and homocysteine by Met 1 supports the assignment of these mutants to specific steps in the pathway. Genetic Analysis 4.2 illustrates genetic dissection of a biosynthetic pathway by assessment of the growth habits of auxotrophs.

Epistasis and Its Results

Genes contributing to different steps of a multistep anabolic or catabolic pathway or to a signal transduction or developmental pathway work together to produce the end product or outcome of the pathway. Because of this interaction, mutation of one gene may prevent completion of the pathway and production of the end product. In other words, gene interaction can result in one gene influencing whether and how other pathway genes are expressed or how they function.

In this section, we describe simple gene interactions that occur in various ways to produce distinctive progeny phenotype ratios as a result of the specific interaction mechanisms. These altered ratios of wild-type and mutant phenotypes are caused by **epistasis** or **epistatic interactions,** the name

(a) Experimental data

| Mutant strain | Growth Medium | | | | | Compound accumulating in mutant |
	Minimal medium	Minimal + cysteine	Minimal + cystathionine	Minimal + homocysteine	Minimal + methionine	
Control prototroph	+	+	+	+	+	None
Met 1	–	–	–	–	+	Homocysteine
Met 2	–	–	–	+	+	Cystathionine
Met 3	–	–	+	+	+	Cysteine
Met 4	–	+	+	+	+	Homoserine

(b) Order of intermediates in pathway

Figure 4.19 **Genetic dissection of methionine biosynthesis pathway.** **(a)** Growth of a wild-type strain and four independent *met–* mutant strains on minimal medium and various supplemented minimal media. For each mutant, the compound that accumulates is the one that immediately precedes the point of blockage. **(b)** The order of intermediate compounds in the methionine biosynthesis pathway and the step blocked in each *met–* mutant strain.

Met 4   Met 3   Met 2   Met 1

Homoserine → Cysteine → Cystathionine → Homocysteine → Methionine

PROBLEM Four zmt⁻ bacterial mutants (zmt-1 to zmt-4), each with a single-gene mutation, are available for study.

BREAK IT DOWN: zmt is the pathway end product, and compounds D, F, M, R, S are intermediate compounds that precede zmt (p. 127).

Five intermediates in the zmt-synthesis pathway have been identified (D, F, M, R, and S), but their order in the pathway is not known. Each mutant is tested for its ability to grow on minimal medium supplemented with one of the intermediate compounds. All mutants grow when zmt is added to minimal medium, and the wild-type strain grows under all growth conditions tested. Find the order of intermediates in the zmt-synthesis pathway, and identify the step that is blocked in each mutant strain. In the growth table at right, "+" indicates growth and "−" indicates no growth.

Mutant Strain	Added to Minimal Medium						
	D	F	M	R	S	Nothing	zmt
Wild type	+	+	+	+	+	+	+
zmt-1	−	−	−	−	+	−	+
zmt-2	−	+	+	+	+	−	+
zmt-3	−	+	−	−	+	−	+
zmt-4	−	+	+	−	+	−	+

BREAK IT DOWN: Growth on a supplemented minimal medium occurs if the medium provides a compound the mutant is unable to produce (p. 127).

Solution Strategies	Solution Steps

Evaluate

1. Identify the topic of this problem and the kind of information the answer should contain.

1. This problem deals with mutants of the zmt-synthesis pathway and requires an analysis of the defect in each mutant as well as ordering of the intermediates in the zmt-synthesis pathway.

2. Identify the critical information given in the problem.

2. The problem provides growth information for wild-type zmt⁺ bacteria as well as four zmt⁻ mutant strains when plated on minimal medium and media individually supplemented with zmt or one of five intermediates in the zmt-synthesis pathway.

Deduce

3. Compare and evaluate the patterns of growth supported by the supplements.

TIP: A supplement that supports growth of all or most mutants is likely to be near the end of the pathway.

3. All mutants grow with zmt supplementation and with supplementation by compound S. None grows without any supplementation, and none obtains growth support from compound D. Compounds F, M, and R each support growth of one or more mutants.

4. Identify the final product of the pathway and next-latest pathway intermediate compound.

4. zmt is the last compound synthesized. Compound S also supports the growth of all mutants and is likely the immediate precursor of zmt.

TIP: A supplement supporting growth of the fewest mutants is likely at the beginning of the pathway.

Solve

5. Identify the first compound synthesized in the pathway.

5. Compound D does not support growth of any of the zmt⁻ mutants and likely occurs before any of the synthesis steps affected by mutations. Compound D is the first compound shown in the pathway.

6. Identify the second, third, and fourth compounds synthesized in the pathway.

TIP: Medium supplemented with an intermediate compound that occurs after the pathway step that is blocked by a mutation will support growth.

6. Compound R supports the growth of only one mutant, zmt-2, indicating the compound bypasses the step blocked in zmt-2. Compound R likely follows compound D in the pathway, and zmt-2 is defective in its ability to convert D to R. zmt-2 grows on intermediate compounds that occur after its point of pathway blockage, but not on compound D that comes before the zmt-2 blockage.

Compound M supports growth of zmt-2 and zmt-4, bypassing the blockage in both mutants. Growth of zmt-4 is not supported by compounds D or R that occur before the conversion step blocked in zmt-4. The conclusion is that compound M follows R and that zmt-4 is unable to convert R to M. Compounds F, M, and S each support growth of zmt-4, so each bypasses the blockage.

Compound F supports growth of zmt-3 and follows compound M in the pathway. zmt-3 is unable to convert M to F. Compound S supports new growth of zmt-1, indicating that it follows compound F in the pathway and that zmt-1 fails to convert compound F to S.

TIP: To confirm this solution, verify that growth of each mutant is supported by supplementation with compounds that follow the blockage but not by supplementation with compounds that precede the blockage.

7. Assemble the zmt-synthesis pathway, and identify the mutants at each pathway step.

7.
$$zmt\text{-}2 \quad\ zmt\text{-}4 \quad\ zmt\text{-}3 \quad\ zmt\text{-}1$$
$$D \longrightarrow R \longrightarrow M \longrightarrow F \longrightarrow S \longrightarrow zmt$$

Gene interaction:	None 9:3:3:1	Complementary 9:7	Duplicate 15:1	Dominant 9:6:1	Recessive epistasis 9:3:4	Dominant epistasis 12:3:1	Dominant supression 13:3
Genotype ratio $\frac{1}{16}$ AABB $\frac{2}{16}$ AaBB $\frac{2}{16}$ AABb $\frac{4}{16}$ AaBb	$\frac{9}{16}$ A–B–	$\frac{9}{16}$ A–B–	A–B–	$\frac{9}{16}$ A–B–	$\frac{9}{16}$ A–B–	A–B– $\frac{12}{16}$	$\frac{9}{16}$ A–B–
$\frac{1}{16}$ AAbb $\frac{2}{16}$ Aabb	$\frac{3}{16}$ A–bb	A–bb	$\frac{15}{16}$ A–bb	A–bb $\frac{6}{16}$	$\frac{3}{16}$ A–bb	A–bb	$\frac{3}{16}$ A–bb
$\frac{1}{16}$ aaBB $\frac{2}{16}$ aaBb	$\frac{3}{16}$ aaB–	$\frac{7}{16}$ aaB–	aaB–	aaB–	aaB– $\frac{4}{16}$	$\frac{3}{16}$ aaB–	aaB– $\frac{4}{16}$
$\frac{1}{16}$ aabb	$\frac{1}{16}$ aabb	aabb	$\frac{1}{16}$ aabb	$\frac{1}{16}$ aabb	aabb	$\frac{1}{16}$ aabb	aabb

Figure 4.20   Patterns resulting from epistatic gene interaction.

given to gene interactions in which an allele of one gene modifies or prevents the expression of alleles at another gene. A minimum of two genes are required for epistasis, and for the sake of simplicity, we limit the descriptions in this discussion to epistatic interactions between two genes. The genes that interact through epistasis are involved in producing a particular phenotypic characteristic, and they participate in the same pathway. For two interacting genes, epistasis is most readily detected among progeny of dihybrid crosses where both genes carry dominant and recessive alleles. In these cases, independent assortment predicts a 9:3:3:1 ratio of four phenotypes in the F_2 progeny, but epistasis results in fewer than four phenotypes. This reduction in the number of F_2 phenotype classes occurs because different genotype classes have the same phenotype. In other words, the hallmark of epistatic interaction in a dihybrid cross is modification of the 9:3:3:1 ratio due to the combining of two or more genotype classes into a single phenotypic class.

Epistasis results from mutation in pathways that require a specific activity from every gene in the pathway for the wild-type phenotype to be produced. Given the possible outcomes of dihybrid crosses, there are six ways the F_2 phenotype proportions can be rearranged by epistasis. All six altered ratios have been seen in plants or animals. Figure 4.20 gives an overview of these patterns, showing the modification of dihybrid ratios that characterizes each form of epistasis. The remainder of this discussion provides a brief description and example of each of the epistatic patterns. First, however, we describe a dihybrid cross involving two genes contributing to feather color in budgerigar parakeets, popularly known as "budgies," in which there is *no interaction* between the genes to alter the resulting 9:3:3:1 phenotypic ratio.

No Interaction (9:3:3:1 ratio) Epistasis is most easily identified through specific deviations from the expected 9:3:3:1 ratio among the F_2 progeny of a dihybrid cross involving dominant and recessive alleles. This expected F_2 ratio results from the action of two independently assorting genes *in the absence of epistasis*—that is, when the genes do not interact to change the expression of one or the other.

The analysis begins with the mating of a pure-breeding blue budgie (*BByy*) to a pure-breeding yellow budgie (*bbYY*). The F_1 progeny have wild-type green feather color and are dihybrid (*BbYy*), and they are shown at the left in Figure 4.21. Progeny in the F2 generation shown in Figure 4.21 have four feather-color phenotypes, as predicted by independent assortment. Green feather color (wild type) is observed in $\frac{9}{16}$ of the progeny, blue feathers and yellow feathers are each seen in $\frac{3}{16}$ of the F_2, and the white-feather phenotype appears in $\frac{1}{16}$ of the F_2 progeny. The 9:3:3:1 phenotypic ratio provides evidence that two independently assorting genes contribute to the feather-color phenotype. This ratio indicates that the genes *are not* undergoing epistatic interaction with one another.

Six examples of epistatic interactions between two genes, each with a dominant and a recessive allele are shown in Foundation Figure 4.22. As we describe these patterns here, and as you examine Figure 4.22, notice that

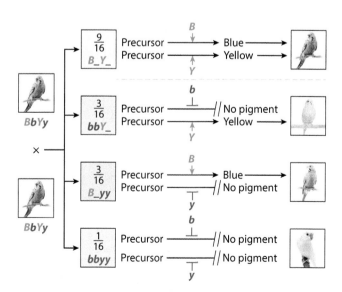

Figure 4.21   No gene interaction in the production of feather color in budgerigar parakeets. A 9:3:3:1 ratio results from the independent assortment of alleles in a dihybrid cross of green-feathered budgies with the dihybrid genotype *BbYy*.

Epistatic Ratios

1 Complementary gene interaction

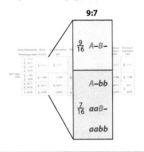

Example: sweet pea flower color

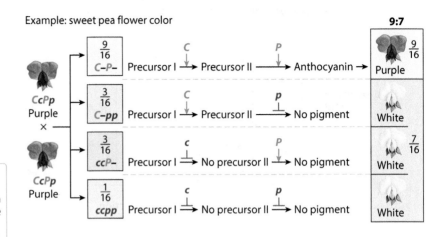

Complementary gene interaction occurs when genes must act in tandem to produce a phenotype. The wild-type action from both genes is required to produce the wild-type phenotype. Mutation of one or both genes produces a mutant phenotype.

2 Duplicate gene action

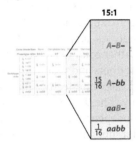

Example: bean flower color

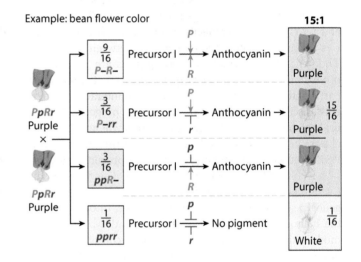

Duplicate gene action allows dominant alleles of either duplicate gene to produce the wild-type phenotype. Only organisms with homozygous mutations of both genes have a mutant phenotype.

3 Dominant gene interaction

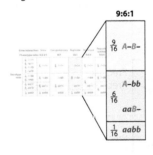

Example: squash fruit shape

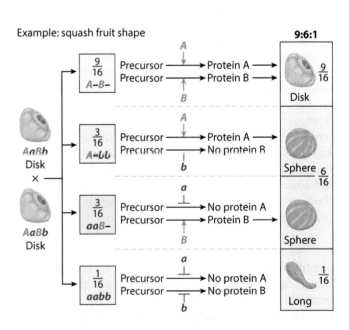

Dominant gene interaction occurs between genes that each contribute to a phenotype, producing one phenotype if dominant alleles are present at each gene, a second phenotype if recessive alleles are homozygous for either gene, and a third phenotype if recessive homozygosity occurs at both genes.

❹ Recessive epistasis

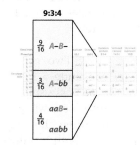

Recessive epistasis occurs when recessive alleles at one gene mask or reduce the expression of alleles at the interacting locus.

Example: labrador retriever coat color

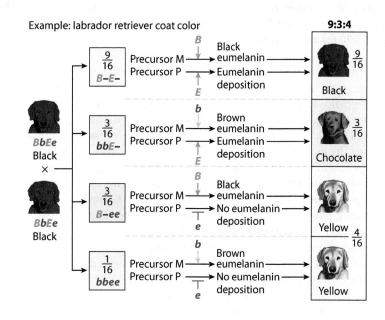

❺ Dominant epistasis

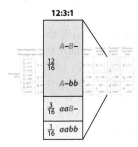

In dominant epistasis, a dominant allele of one gene masks or reduces the expression of alleles of a second gene.

Example: summer squash color

❻ Dominant suppression

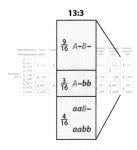

Dominant suppression occurs when the dominant allele of one gene suppresses the expression of a dominant allele of a second gene.

Example: chicken feather color

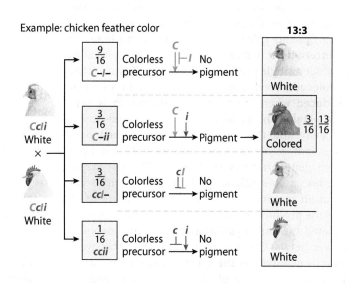

the phenotypic ratios observed for each trait result from the combining of the 9:3:3:1 genotype categories. (Refer to Figure 4.20 for an overview of these epistatic patterns.)

Complementary Gene Interaction (9:7 ratio) William Bateson (the enthusiastic proponent of Mendelism) and Reginald Punnett (of Punnett square fame) were the first biologists to document a deviation from the expected 9:3:3:1 F_2 progeny ratio of a dihybrid cross resulting from the epistatic interaction of two genes. In experiments conducted on sweet peas (*Lathyrus odoratus*), an ornamental plant different from Mendel's edible pea (*Pisum sativum*), Bateson and Punnett began by crossing two pure-breeding white-flowered lines. The F_1 generation yielded a surprise—all of the progeny plants had purple flowers. When Bateson and Punnett crossed F_1 plants, the F_2 produced a ratio of $\frac{9}{16}$ purple-flowered plants to $\frac{7}{16}$ white-flowered plants.

Bateson and Punnett recognized that their results could be explained if two genes interacted with one another to produce sweet pea flower color. Assuming two genes are responsible for a single pigment that gives the sweet pea flower its purple color, each parental line—represented by the genotypes *ccPP* and *CCpp*—is pure-breeding for white flowers as a result of homozygosity for recessive alleles at one of the genes. The cross of these two lines of pure-breeding white parents produces dihybrid purple-flowered F_1 plants—genotype *CcPp*—because the dominant allele at each locus enables completion of each step of the pathway leading to the synthesis of purple pigment. Independent assortment of alleles results in four genotypic classes, *C–P–*, *ccP–*, *C–pp*, and *ccpp*, produced in the 9:3:3:1 ratio that is expected from a dihybrid cross. Among the F_2, however, only the $\frac{9}{16}$ carry the *C–P–* genotype that confers the ability to produce purple pigment. The remaining $\frac{7}{16}$ of the F_2 are homozygous either for one of the recessive alleles *c* and *p* or for both sets of alleles. None of these plants are able to synthesize pigment, due to the absence of functional gene products from one or both loci, and they all have the same mutant phenotype.

A 9:7 phenotypic ratio results from **complementary gene interaction** that requires genes to work in tandem to produce a single product. Figure 4.22 ❶ shows that at the molecular level, purple flower color in sweet peas is produced when the pigment anthocyanin is deposited in petals. The production of the purple-flowered F_1 progeny and the 9:7 F_2 ratio is explained by the independent assortment of two genes, *C* and *P*, that produce gene products controlling different steps of the anthocyanin-synthesis pathway. Since anthocyanin production requires the action of the product of *C* as well as the product of *P*, both steps must be successfully completed for anthocyanin production and deposition in flower petals. On the other hand, any recessive homozygous genotype at the *C* locus, the *P* locus, or both loci results in blockage of the pathway and production of white flowers containing no pigment.

The ability of two mutants with the same mutant phenotype to produce progeny with the wild-type phenotype is called *genetic complementation,* and it indicates that more than one gene is involved in determining the phenotype. We discuss the details of genetic complementation in the last section of this chapter.

Duplicate Gene Action (15:1 ratio) Two genes that duplicate one another's activity constitute a redundant genetic system in which any genotype possessing at least one copy of a dominant allele at *either* locus will produce the dominant phenotype. Only when homozygous recessive mutant alleles are present at both loci does the recessive phenotype appear. The genes in a redundant system are said to have **duplicate gene action;** they either encode the same gene product, or they encode gene products that have the same effect in a single pathway or compensatory pathways.

Figure 4.22 ❷ provides an illustration and explanation of duplicate gene action identified inadvertently by Gregor Mendel in an experiment involving flower color in bean plants. Near the end of his famous 1866 paper describing inheritance in peas, Mendel described an experiment with beans that began with the cross of a pure-breeding purple-flowered bean plant to a pure-breeding white-flowered bean plant. The F_1 plants all had purple flowers, and Mendel probably assumed that flower color determination in beans would follow the same pattern as in peas. Among the 32 F_2 plants Mendel produced, however, 31 had purple flowers and only 1 had white flowers. Among the F_2 plants, $\frac{15}{16}$ have a genotype containing at least one copy of either *P* or *R*, and only $\frac{1}{16}$ have the genotype *pprr* and the white-flowered phenotype.

Figure 4.22 ❷ shows that a dominant allele at either locus is capable of catalyzing the conversion of a precursor to anthocyanin and producing the dominant phenotype. Conversely, if homozygous recessive alleles are present at both loci, no functional gene product is produced, and the synthesis pathway is not completed. White flowers result from the absence of pigment in the $\frac{1}{16}$ of the F_2 progeny that are homozygous recessive for alleles of both genes.

Dominant Gene Interaction (9:6:1 ratio) Fruit shape in summer squash is classified as either long, spherical, or disk shaped. Plants that bear long fruit are consistently pure-breeding, indicating that these plants are homozygous for genes controlling fruit shape. On the other hand, plants producing disk-shaped fruit or spherical fruit are sometimes pure-breeding and sometimes not, indicating that plants producing disk-shaped or spherical fruit can be either homozygous or heterozygous for the genes controlling the trait. Figure 4.22 ❸ illustrates and describes **dominant interaction** between two genes controlling squash fruit shape. Dominant interaction is characterized by a 9:6:1 ratio of phenotypes in the progeny of a dihybrid cross.

A cross of two pure-breeding plants producing spherical fruit can generate F_1 that have disk-shaped fruit. This result indicates an interaction between genes controlling fruit shape and suggests that the F_1 disk-shape–producing plants are dihybrid. The F_2 progeny, which display the phenotypic proportions $\frac{9}{16}$ disk, $\frac{6}{16}$ spherical, and $\frac{1}{16}$ long, confirm that hypothesis. Which of the three phenotypes occurs depends on whether a dominant allele is present for both genes, one gene, or neither gene. In the F_2 generation, plants with at least one dominant allele at each locus ($A–B–$) have disk-shaped fruit, plants with recessive alleles at each locus ($aabb$) produce long fruit, and plants that are homozygous recessive at either of the loci ($A–bb$ or $aaB–$) produce spherical fruit.

The molecular model of the events underlying dominant interaction assumes that each gene produces a different protein that contributes to fruit shape. When dominant allelic action produces both proteins, disk-shaped fruit is generated. If only one of the proteins is produced, spherical fruit results, as for the genotypic classes $aaB–$ and $A–bb$. Plants that are homozygous for recessive alleles of both genes ($aabb$) produce neither protein, and long fruit is the result.

Recessive Epistasis (9:3:4 ratio) Black, chocolate, and yellow coat colors in Labrador retrievers result from the interaction of two genes, one that produces pigment and another that distributes the pigment to hair follicles. This form of gene interaction, in which homozygosity for a recessive allele at one locus can mask the phenotypic expression of a second gene, is called **recessive epistasis** and has the characteristic 9:3:4 ratio of phenotypes illustrated by Figure 4.22 **④**.

Crossing pure-breeding chocolate parents to pure-breeding yellow ones produces F_1 progeny with black coats. That the F_1 progeny are dihybrid is revealed by the F_2 generation, in which $\frac{9}{16}$ of the progeny carry the genotypes in the $B–E–$ class and have black coats, $\frac{3}{16}$ have a genotype that is $bbE–$, resulting in chocolate-colored coats, and $\frac{4}{16}$ carry genotypes that are either $B–ee$ or $bbee$ and have yellow coats.

The molecular explanation for this genetic system is tied to production of the hair pigment melanin. Dogs can produce eumelanin that gives hair a black or brown color and pheomelanin that gives hair a reddish or yellowish tone. The E gene is *TYRP1* that controls eumelanin distribution. The wild-type allele E yields full eumelanin deposition, but allele e blocks deposition. Gene B is *MC1R* that controls eumelanin synthesis, with B producing a large amount of eumelanin that overwhelms the pheomelanin present to produce a black coat color. The alternative allele b produces a reduced amount of eumelanin. When mixed with pheomelanin in the coat, the resulting color is brown, sometimes called "chocolate." Dogs that are $B–E–$ produce, transport, and deposit large amounts of eumelanin and have black coats. Dogs that are $bbE\_$ produce less eumelanin due to their bb genotype and have chocolate (brown) coats. Dogs that are homozygous ee are unable to transport and deposit eumelanin and instead deposit only pheomelanin. These dogs have yellow coat color.

Dominant Epistasis (12:3:1 ratio) Determination of fruit color in summer squashes provides an example of **dominant epistasis,** where a dominant allele of one gene blocks the expression of an allele of a second gene. Summer squash occur in three colors: white, yellow, and green. In Figure 4.22 **⑤**, the cross of dihybrid $WwYy$ (white) plants yields a 12:3:1 ratio of white:yellow:green plants. Plants with one or two copies of W—that is, $W–Y–$ (9/16) and $W–yy$ (3/16)—produce white squash due to the inhibition of conversion of the colorless precursor compound to green pigment. Plants that are homozygous ww are able to convert the colorless precursor to green pigment, and the dominant allele of the Y gene produces an enzyme that converts green pigment to yellow pigment. Homozygosity for the recessive allele (yy) leaves the green pigment unaltered and green squash are produced. Notice that in ww plants, segregation of Y-gene alleles in a cross of Yy monohybrids produces a 3:1 ratio of $Y–$ (yellow) and yy (green) squash. This ratio can be seen by looking at plants that are $wwY–\left(\frac{3}{16}\right)$ and $wwyy\left(\frac{1}{16}\right)$.

At the molecular level, summer squash color production is a two-step biochemical process in which a colorless precursor is converted to a green intermediate by an enzyme produced in plants that are ww. In plants that are $W–$, however, the enzyme is not produced, and conversion of the precursor is blocked. Plants that are $Y–$ produce a second enzyme to convert green pigment to yellow pigment, but those that are yy do not produce the enzyme. If no green pigment is available, the squashes remain white, regardless of the genotype of the Y gene.

Dominant Suppression (13:3 ratio) Our final example of epistatic gene interaction is **dominant suppression,** illustrated in Figure 4.22 **⑥**. Dominant suppression is similar to dominant epistasis but occurs when a dominant allele of one gene completely suppresses the phenotypic expression of alleles of another gene. In chickens, for example, feather color requires a dominant allele C. Chickens that are homozygous for a recessive allele c have white feathers. The C allele can have its color-producing action suppressed by a dominant suppressor allele, I. The recessive allele i does not exert suppression. Crosses between pure-breeding colored chickens ($CCii$) and pure-breeding white chickens ($ccII$) produce white-feathered F_1 that are dihybrid ($CcIi$). Production of the F_2 results in a 13:3 ratio that is characteristic of dominant suppression. Chickens carrying a cc genotype are unable to produce feather color, and those carrying $C–$ along with $I–$ have feather color production suppressed. Only chickens with the *C–ii* genotype are able to produce colored feathers.

Figure 4.22 ⑥ shows that the product of allele *C* converts a colorless precursor into pigment, whereas the allele *c* product is inactive and fails to convert the precursor, resulting in white feather color for *cc* genotypes. Dominant suppression of *C* by the product of *I* prevents pigment production in chickens with the *C–I–* genotype. The homozygous genotype *ii* is unable to suppress color in the *C–*. **Genetic Analysis 4.3** tests your ability to analyze crosses involving epistatic gene interaction.

4.4 Complementation Analysis Distinguishes Mutations in the Same Gene from Mutations in Different Genes

Suppose you are a geneticist working in California, and you have identified a recessive mutation causing petunia flowers to be white rather than the wild-type purple color. A friend of yours, also a geneticist, is working on petunias in the Netherlands and contacts you because she has also identified a recessive mutation resulting in white-flowered petunias. Since there has been no contact between California petunias and Netherland petunias, the mutations have arisen independently. When geneticists encounter organisms with the same mutant phenotype, two initial questions are (1) do these organisms have mutations of the same gene or of different genes, and (2) how many genes are responsible for the mutations observed?

We have already seen that mutations of different genes can produce the same, or very similar, abnormal phenotypes. This phenomenon is known as **genetic heterogeneity.** We have also seen that a mating of two organisms with the same or a similar abnormal phenotype can sometimes produce offspring with the wild-type phenotype. This phenomenon is called **genetic complementation,** and it occurs when mutant organisms carry mutations of different genes that produce the same abnormal phenotype. In contrast, if the two mutations are in the same gene, offspring of a cross between the two mutants will have a mutant phenotype. This is the way pure-breeding mutants are perpetuated, since the parents and the offspring are all homozygous for a mutant allele of a gene. In the context of our discussion in this section, however, crossing two mutants and producing only mutant progeny is identified as a failure of genetic complementation. In this section, we describe how to distinguish whether two independent mutations are in the same gene or in different genes.

An analytic approach called genetic complementation testing examines the relation between two or more recessive mutations affecting one phenotypic attribute. Researchers use it to determine whether two recessive mutations are in the same gene or in different genes. It also provides information on the number of different genes that can produce the mutant phenotype. Here we limit our discussion to testing eukaryotic genomes, using eye color in *Drosophila* as an example. Strategies for complementation testing in bacteria and bacterial viruses (bacteriophage) differ somewhat from those used in plants and animals (see discussion in Section 6.6).

Genetic complementation testing crosses pure-breeding mutants for a recessive mutation and examines the phenotype of cross progeny. The heterozygous F_1 progeny of these crosses are then examined for the wild-type or mutant phenotypes. If wild-type progeny are produced, genetic complementation has occurred, and the conclusion is that the mutant alleles are of different genes. On the other hand, if the mutant alleles are of the same gene, the progeny of two pure-breeding mutants will have a mutant phenotype. This result indicates that no genetic complementation has taken place.

As an example, we examine genetic complementation testing using two genes affecting *Drosophila* eye color, both of which we have discussed previously: the *vermilion* gene, whose product produces eye-color pigment, and the *white* gene, whose product produces the eye-color pigment transport protein. Both genes are located on the X chromosome in *Drosophila*. The sequential action of the gene products in eye-color production is illustrated in **Figure 4.23a.** Genetic complementation is illustrated by the production of wild-type (red) female progeny from the cross of a pure-breeding female with vermilion eyes to a pure-breeding male with white eyes. No genetic complementation occurs when a pure-breeding apricot female and a pure-breeding buff male are crossed. All progeny have mutant eye colors.

Genetic complementation analysis utilizes numerous crosses of different pure-breeding mutants to one another to determine if the progeny are mutant (no genetic complementation) or wild type (genetic complementation). A table of genetic complementation testing data shown in **Figure 4.23b** indicates whether the cross of parental mutant phenotypes produces wild-type progeny (indicated in the table by plus symbols: +), or mutant progeny (indicated in the table by minus symbols: −). Any given pair of mutants that *complement* one another by producing wild-type progeny are mutations of *different genes*. (Recall the results of complementary gene action illustrated in Figure 4.22 ①.) In contrast, the cross of mutant parents produces only the mutant phenotype in progeny when the mutations *fail to complement* one another and are mutations of the *same gene*.

PROBLEM Dr. Ara B. Dopsis, a famous plant geneticist, decides to try his hand at iris propagation. He selects two pure-breeding irises, one red and the other blue, and crosses them. To his surprise, all F_1 plants have purple flowers. He decides to create more purple irises by self-fertilizing the F_1 irises. Dr. Dopsis produces 320 F_2 plants consisting of 182 with purple flowers, 59 with blue flowers, and 79 with red flowers.

BREAK IT DOWN: Neither red nor blue is dominant (p. 134).

BREAK IT DOWN: Examine the ratio of progeny phenotypes carefully to propose a mechanism of inheritance (p. 133).

a. From the information available, describe the genetic phenomenon that produces the phenotypic ratio observed in the F_2 plants. Identify the number of genes that are involved in this trait.

b. Using clearly defined symbols of your own choosing, identify the genotypes of parental and F_1 plants.

Solution Strategies	Solution Steps
Evaluate	
1. Identify the topic this problem addresses and describe the nature of the required answer.	1. This problem concerns the interpretation of F_1 and F_2 result; it requires identification of the genetic mechanism responsible for the observed results, and the assignment of genotypes to parental and F_1 plants in a manner consistent with the genetic mechanism.
2. Identify the critical information given in the problem.	2. The problem states that the blue- and red-flowered parents are pure-breeding and that their F_1 are exclusively purple flowered. Among the F_2, purple is predominant, but red and, to a lesser extent, blue are also observed.
Deduce	
3. Deduce the potential genetic mechanisms that could account for producing purple-flowered F_1 plants from the pure-breeding red and blue parental plants.	3. Two potential mechanisms are suggested by these data. First, a single gene with incomplete dominance might generate a phenotype in F_1 heterozygous plants that is different from that of either homozygous parent. Second, two genes displaying an epistatic interaction might account for a phenotype in an F_1 dihybrid that is distinct from either pure-breeding parent.
4. Determine the relative phenotype proportions predicted by the possible genetic mechanisms and compare them to the observed phenotype ratio. TIP: Compare the relative percentages of each phenotype to see which genetic model most closely predicts the observed percentages.	4. A single-gene model predicts that the self-fertilization of an F_1 heterozygote will result in a 1:2:1 (25%:50%:25%) ratio in the F_2. A two-gene epistasis model producing three F_2 phenotypes could be dominant gene interaction (9:6:1 ratio), dominant epistasis (12:3:1 ratio), or recessive epistasis (9:4:3 ratio). Recessive epistasis predictions are a closer match to the observations than dominant epistasis predictions. Recessive epistasis predicts phenotype percentages of approximately 56%:25%: 19%. The observed ratio of F_2 phenotypes is $\frac{182}{320} = 56.8\%$ purple, $\frac{79}{320} = 24.7\%$ red, and $\frac{59}{320} = 18.4\%$ blue.
Solve	Answer a
5. Identify the genetic mechanism most likely to account for the outcomes of these crosses. TIP: See Foundation Figure 4.22 for the phenotype ratios characteristic of each type of epistatic interaction.	5. Comparison of the F_2 predictions of the single-gene incomplete dominance model and the two-gene recessive epistasis model determines that recessive epistasis is a better match with the relative progeny proportions. The likely genetic model explaining these data is recessive epistasis. (Note that the number of F_2 observed in each category can be compared to the number expected by chi-square analysis.)
6. Assign genotypes to parental and F_1 plants. TIP: Foundation Figure 4.22 identifies genotypes associated with each phenotype.	6. Using symbols A and a for one gene and B and b for the second gene, the genotypes of plants are Parents: $aaBB$ (red) and $AAbb$ (blue) F_1: $AaBb$ (purple)

Figure 4.23 Genetic complementation and no genetic complementation involving the *Drosophila* eye color genes *vermilion* and *white*. (a) The cross of pure-breeding vermilion to pure-breeding white shows genetic complementation by production of wild-type eye color in the F$_1$. The cross between pure-breeding apricot and pure-breeding buff produces no genetic complementation in the F$_1$ that have mutant eye color. (b) Genetic complementation testing among nine distinct *Drosophila* eye color mutants reveals five complementation groups corresponding to five genes. Five mutant alleles of *white* mutually fail to complement and are assigned to the same gene. The other four mutants each complement one another, and the *white* gene mutants and are assigned to their own gene.

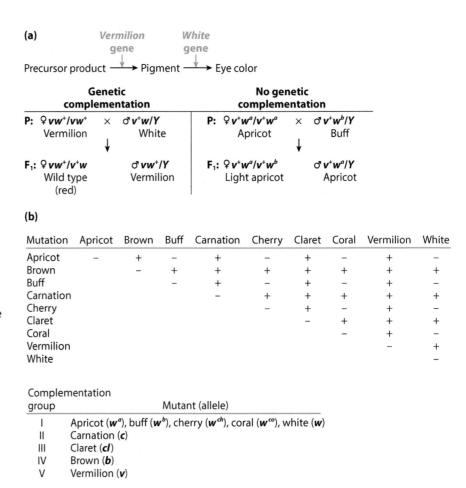

Complementation analysis of the *Drosophila* eye-color mutation results displayed in Figure 4.23b focuses on crosses that *fail to complement* as these are the result of mutations that are in the same gene. Mutations that mutually fail to complement one another are identified as a **complementation group,** consisting of one or more mutant alleles of a single gene. A complementation group consists of mutants whose phenotypes consistently fail to complement one another and that complement mutants in other complementation groups. In the genetic context, a "complementation group" is synonymous with a "gene" because the mutant alleles of each complementation group all affect the same phenotypic characteristic. Thus, in genetic complementation analysis, the number of complementation groups equals the number of genes.

In the complementation testing data in Figure 4.23b, apricot, buff, cherry, coral, and white all exhibit a mutual failure to complement. This result identifies the five mutants as occurring in the same gene. (Historically, white was the first mutation identified and is the name the gene has become known by.) Geneticists conclude that apricot, buff, cherry, coral, and white are mutant alleles of the *white* (*w*) gene in *Drosophila*. These mutations form complementation group I. In contrast, the mutations brown, carnation, claret, and vermilion each complement all other mutants. This observation tells investigators that they are not alleles of another mutant, but that instead each mutant represents a separate gene. Each of these mutants forms its own complementation group (i.e., complementation groups II through V). Therefore, among the nine *Drosophila* eye-color mutants examined, five genes (five complementation groups) are identified. One gene is represented by five mutants, and the other four genes are represented by one mutation each.

Genetic complementation analysis is an important tool of genetic analysis. The rare human cancer-prone disorder xeroderma pigmentosum (various OMIM designations) can result from the inheritance of mutations from any seven genes that were originally identified by genetic complementation analysis. The following Case Study outlines this analysis.

CASE STUDY

Complementation Groups in a Human Cancer-Prone Disorder

In this case study, we examine the use of genetic complementation analysis to identify the number of genes involved in a rare but genetically heterogeneous human condition called xeroderma pigmentosum (XP). XP is characterized by severe sensitivity to ultraviolet (UV) irradiation from sunlight and by up to a thousandfold increase in the rate of sun-induced skin cancer. While the experimental approaches to complementation testing in humans are necessarily different from those employed for laboratory organisms, the interpretations of "crosses" follow the same processes.

People with XP are deficient in a type of DNA repair called nucleotide excision repair (NER) that would otherwise protect their skin from the UV-induced damage that leads to cancer. In NER, a short section of DNA containing a UV-induced lesion is removed, and the gap is filled by new DNA (see Section 12.5).

COMPLEMENTATION GROUPS   Research work that began in the late 1970s identified seven complementation groups representing seven different genes (each has its own OMIM designation) that are mutated in different forms of XP. Two approaches were successful in revealing some or all of these groups. Anthony Andrews and his colleagues obtained cultured skin cells from XP patients and from normal controls and tested the ability of the cells to grow after exposure to measured doses of UV irradiation (**Figure 4.24**). The cells were exposed to UV light at a wavelength of 254 nm for different amounts of time, and their growth was measured as the percentage of original cells able to form colonies after UV exposure. These researchers identified five distinct patterns of response to UV exposure that are designated as complementation groups A to E.

Other researchers measured the response of cultured XP cells to UV exposure by determining the level of NER taking place in XP cell cultures taken from different XP individuals in comparison to normal cells. The results showed that XP cell lines vary in their levels of NER from less than 5% of normal to about 50% of normal. These results could be due to the mutations being in different genes or, alternatively, to different hypomorphic alleles of the same gene.

Genetic complementation analysis was used in the study of XP cell cultures with low NER to identify cell lineages carrying different XP gene mutations. To do this, two cells from lineages with low NER were fused to form a heterokaryon, a hybrid cell with two nuclei. A heterokaryon contains all the genetic information from both contributing cells. The experimental rationale is that if the two cells contain mutations of *different* genes, the heterokaryon will experience genetic complementation that would be detected as normal or near normal levels of NER; but if the mutations are in the same gene, NER will be about the same in the heterokaryon as in the individual cell lines. This analysis of NER levels in XP heterokaryons ultimately indicated seven complementation groups of XP genes.

ASSOCIATED GENE FUNCTIONS   Each of the seven XP-associated genes has had its function identified and its position mapped in the human genome in the last decade or so. Four of the genes produce proteins that are required to remove a segment of the strand of DNA damaged by UV irradiation as part of the DNA repair process. Proteins from two other XP-associated genes are required to recognize UV-induced DNA damage, and the seventh gene produces a protein that binds to the DNA lesion once it is located. The knowledge of the identity of the seven XP-associated genes has led to the finding that other cancer-associated hereditary diseases also involve mutations of one or another of the XP-associated genes.

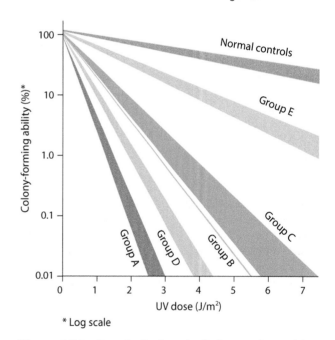

* Log scale

Figure 4.24   Growth of cultured cells from patients with xeroderma pigmentosum (XP). Five XP complementation groups are identified based on growth ability.

SUMMARY   ⟨ MasteringGenetics™ ⟩   For activities, animations, and review quizzes, go to the Study Area.

4.1 Interactions between Alleles Produce Dominance Relationships

▯ Loss-of-function mutations decrease or eliminate gene activity. Gain-of-function mutations can cause over-expression or result in new functions.

▯ Incomplete dominance produces heterozygotes with phenotypes that differ from those of either homozygote but are closer to one homozygous phenotype than the other.

▯ Codominant alleles are both equally detected in the Heterozygous phenotype.

▌ The interaction of allelic products determines the dominance relationship between alleles.

▌ ABO blood types are produced by alleles whose protein products produce dominance or codominance depending on the genotype.

▌ Multiple alleles of a single gene can display a variety of dominance relationships that establish an allelic series.

▌ Lethal alleles can kill gametes, can prevent the gestational development of certain classes of progeny, or can have their lethal effect later in life.

▌ In sex-limited and sex-influenced traits, alleles are manifested differently in each sex.

4.2 Some Genes Produce Variable Phenotypes

▌ In incomplete penetrance, an allele does not always have the expected effect on the phenotype.

▌ In variable expressivity, organisms with the same genotype have different degrees of phenotypic expression.

▌ Pleiotropic mutations affect two or more distinct and seemingly independent attributes of the phenotype.

4.3 Gene Interaction Modifies Mendelian Ratios

▌ Epistasis is revealed by six alternative ratios that are modifications of the 9:3:3:1 ratio expected among the progeny of a dihybrid cross.

▌ Epistasis types and their ratios are complementary gene interaction (9:7), duplicate gene action (15:1), dominant gene interaction (9:6:1), recessive epistasis (9:3:4), dominant epistasis (12:3:1), and dominant suppression (13:3).

4.4 Complementation Analysis Distinguishes Mutations in the Same Gene from Mutations in Different Genes

▌ In genetic heterogeneity, mutations in different genes can produce the same phenotype.

▌ Genetic complementation produces progeny with the wild-type phenotype from parents that are pure-breeding for similar mutant phenotypes. The detection of genetic complementation means the mutations occur in different genes.

▌ The failure to detect genetic complementation from the cross of two similar mutant organisms identifies the mutant alleles as being carried by the same gene.

KEYWORDS

allelic series *(p. 111)*
auxotroph (auxotrophic) *(p. 125)*
codominance *(p. 109)*
complementary gene interaction
     (9:7 ratio) *(p. 132)*
complete penetrance *(p. 118)*
complementation group *(p. 136)*
delayed age of onset *(p. 118)*
dominant epistasis (12:3:1 ratio) *(p. 133)*
dominant interaction (9:6:1 ratio)
     (p. 132)
dominant negative mutation *(p. 108)*
dominant suppression (13:3 ratio) *(p. 133)*
duplicate gene action (15:1 ratio) *(p. 132)*
epistatic interaction (epistasis) *(p. 127)*

gain-of-function mutation *(p. 106)*
gene–environment interaction *(p. 120)*
gene interaction *(p. 121)*
genetic complementation *(p. 134)*
genetic dissection *(p. 125)*
genetic heterogeneity *(p. 134)*
haploinsufficient *(p. 106)*
haplosufficient *(p. 106)*
hypermorphic mutation *(p. 108)*
incomplete dominance (partial
     dominance) *(p. 108)*
incomplete penetrance (nonpenetrant,
     penetrant) *(p. 118)*
leaky mutation (hypomorphic mutation)
     (p. 108)

lethal allele *(p. 113)*
loss-of-function mutation *(p. 106)*
neomorphic mutation *(p. 108)*
null mutation (amorphic mutation) *(p. 106)*
one gene–one enzyme hypothesis *(p. 124)*
pleiotropy *(p. 121)*
prototroph (prototrophic) *(p. 125)*
recessive epistasis (9:3:4 ratio) *(p. 133)*
sex-influenced trait (sex-influenced
     expression) *(p. 117)*
sex-limited trait (sex-limited gene
     expression) *(p. 117)*
temperature-sensitive allele *(p. 113)*
variable expressivity *(p. 119)*

PROBLEMS

(MasteringGenetics™) **Visit for instructor-assigned tutorials and problems.**

Chapter Concepts

For answers to selected even-numbered problems, see Appendix: Answers.

1. Define and distinguish *incomplete penetrance* and *variable expressivity*.

2. Define and distinguish *epistasis* and *pleiotropy*.

3. When working on barley plants, two researchers independently identify a short-plant mutation and develop homozygous recessive lines of short plants. Careful measurements of the height of mutant short plants versus normal tall plants indicate that the two mutant lines have the same

height. How would you determine if these two mutant lines carry mutation of the same gene or of different genes?

4. Fifteen bacterial colonies growing on a complete medium are replica-plated to a minimal medium. Twelve of the colonies grow on minimal medium.

   a. Using terminology from the chapter, characterize the 12 colonies that grow on minimal medium and the 3 colonies that do not.

b. The three colonies that do not grow on minimal medium are replica-plated to minimal medium plus the amino acid serine (min + Ser), and all three colonies grow. Characterize these three colonies.

c. The serine biosynthetic pathway is a three-step pathway in which each step is catalyzed by the enzyme product of a different gene, identified as enzymes A, B, and C in the diagram below.

3-Phosphoglycerate $\xrightarrow{\text{Enzyme A}}$ 3-Phospho-hydroxypyruvate $\xrightarrow{\text{Enzyme B}}$
(3-PHP)
3-Phosphoserine $\xrightarrow{\text{Enzyme C}}$ Serine
(3-PS) (Ser)

Mutant 1 grows only on min + Ser. In addition to growth on min + Ser, mutant 2 also grows on min + 3-PHP and min + 3-PS. Mutant 3 grows on min + 3-PS and min + Ser. Identify the step of the serine biosynthesis pathway at which each mutant is defective.

5. In a type of parakeet known as a "budgie," feather color is controlled by two genes. A yellow pigment is synthesized under the control of a dominant allele Y. Budgies that are homozygous for the recessive y allele do not synthesize yellow pigment. At an independently assorting gene, the dominant allele B directs synthesis of a blue pigment. Recessive homozygotes with the bb genotype do not produce blue pigment. Budgies that produce both yellow and blue pigments have green feathers; those that produce only yellow pigment or only blue pigment have yellow or blue feathers, respectively; and budgies that produce neither pigment are white (albino).

a. List the genotypes for green, yellow, blue, and albino budgies.

b. A cross is made between a pure-breeding green budgie and a pure-breeding albino budgie. What are the genotypes of the parent birds?

c. What are the genotype(s) and phenotype(s) of the F_1 progeny of the cross described in part (b)?

d. If F_1 males and females are mated, what phenotypes are expected in the F_2, and in what proportions?

e. The cross of a green budgie and a yellow budgie produces offspring that are 12 green, 4 blue, 13 yellow, and 3 albino. What are the genotypes of the parents?

6. The ABO and MN blood groups are given below for four sets of parents (1 to 4) and four children (a to d). Recall that the ABO blood group has three alleles: I^A, I^B, and i. The MN blood group has two codominant alleles, M and N. Using your knowledge of these genetic systems, match each child with every set of parents who might have conceived the child, and exclude any parental set that could not have conceived the child.

	Mother		Father	
	ABO	MN	ABO	MN
1	O	M	B	M
2	B	N	B	N
3	AB	MN	B	MN
4	A	N	B	MN

	Children	
	ABO	MN
a	B	M
b	O	M
c	AB	MN
d	B	N

7. The wild-type color of horned beetles is black, although other colors are known. A black horned beetle from a pure-breeding strain is crossed to a pure-breeding green female beetle. All of their F_1 progeny are black. These F_1 are allowed to mate at random with one another, and 320 F_2 beetles are produced. The F_2 consists of 179 black, 81 green, and 60 brown. Use these data to explain the genetics of horned beetle color.

8. Two genes interact to produce various phenotypic ratios among F_2 progeny of a dihybrid cross. Design a different pathway explaining each of the F_2 ratios below, using hypothetical genes R and T and assuming that the dominant allele at each locus catalyzes a different reaction or performs an action leading to pigment production. The recessive allele at each locus is null (loss-of-function). Begin each pathway with a colorless precursor that produces a white or albino phenotype if it is unmodified. The ratios are for F_2 progeny produced by crossing wild-type F_1 organisms with the genotype $RrTt$.

a. $\frac{9}{16}$ dark blue : $\frac{6}{16}$ light blue : $\frac{1}{16}$ white

b. $\frac{12}{16}$ white : $\frac{3}{16}$ green : $\frac{1}{16}$ yellow

c. $\frac{9}{16}$ green : $\frac{3}{16}$ yellow : $\frac{3}{16}$ blue : $\frac{1}{16}$ white

d. $\frac{9}{16}$ red : $\frac{7}{16}$ white

e. $\frac{15}{16}$ black : $\frac{1}{16}$ white

f. $\frac{9}{16}$ black : $\frac{3}{16}$ gray : $\frac{4}{16}$ albino

g. $\frac{13}{16}$ white : $\frac{3}{16}$ green

9. The ABO blood group assorts independently of the Rhesus (Rh) blood group and the MN blood group. Three alleles, I^A, I^B, and i, occur at the *ABO* locus. Two alleles, R, a dominant allele producing Rh+, and r, a recessive allele for Rh−, are found at the *Rh* locus, and codominant alleles M and N occur at the *MN* locus. Each gene is autosomal.

a. A child with blood types A, Rh−, and M is born to a woman who has blood types O, Rh−, and MN and a man who has blood types A, Rh+, and M. Determine the genotypes of each parent.

b. What proportion of children born to a man with genotype $I^A I^B Rr MN$ and a woman who is $I^A i Rr NN$ will have blood types B, Rh−, and MN? Show your work.

c. A man with blood types B, Rh+, and N says he could not be the father of a child with blood types O, Rh−, and MN. The mother of the child has blood types A, Rh+, and MN. Is the man correct? Explain.

10. In rats, gene B produces black coat color if the genotype is $B-$, but black pigment is not produced if the genotype is bb. At an independent locus, gene D produces yellow pigment if the genotype is $D-$, but no pigment is produced when the genotype is dd. Production of both pigments results in brown coat color. If neither pigment is produced,

coat color is cream. Determine the genotypes of parents of litters with the following phenotype distributions.

   a. 4 brown, 4 black, 4 yellow, 4 cream

   b. 3 brown, 3 yellow, 1 black, 1 cream

   c. 9 black, 7 brown

11. In the rats identified in Problem 10, a third independently assorting gene involved in determination of coat color in rats is the C gene. At this locus, the genotype $C-$ permits expression of pigment from genes B and D. The cc genotype, however, prevents expression of coat color and results in albino rats. For each of the following crosses, determine the expected phenotype ratio of progeny.

   a. $BbDDCc \times BbDdCc$

   b. $BBDdcc \times BbddCc$

   c. $bbDDCc \times BBddCc$

   d. $BbDdCC \times BbDdCC$

12. Using the information provided in Problems 10 and 11, determine the genotype and phenotype of parents that produce the following progeny:

   a. $\frac{9}{16}$ brown : $\frac{3}{16}$ black : $\frac{4}{16}$ albino

   b. $\frac{3}{8}$ black : $\frac{3}{8}$ cream : $\frac{2}{8}$ albino

   c. $\frac{27}{64}$ brown : $\frac{16}{64}$ albino : $\frac{9}{64}$ yellow : $\frac{9}{64}$ black : $\frac{3}{64}$ cream

   d. $\frac{3}{4}$ brown : $\frac{1}{4}$ yellow

13. Total cholesterol in blood is reported as the number of milligrams (mg) of cholesterol per 100 milliliters (mL) of blood. The normal range is 180–220 mg/100 mL. A gene mutation altering the function of cell-surface cholesterol receptors restricts the ability of cells to collect cholesterol from blood and draw it into cells. This defect results in elevated blood cholesterol levels. Individuals who are heterozygous for a mutant allele and a wild-type allele have levels of 300–600 mg/100 mL, and those who are homozygous for the mutation have levels of 800–1000 mg/100 mL. Identify the genetic term that best describes the inheritance of this form of elevated cholesterol level, and justify your choice.

14. Flower color in snapdragons results from the amount of the pigment anthocyanin in the petals. Red flowers are produced by plants that have full anthocyanin production, and ivory-colored flowers are produced by plants that lack the ability to produce anthocyanin. The allele $An1$ has full activity in anthocyanin production, and the allele $An2$ is a null allele. Dr. Ara B. Dopsis, a famous genetic researcher, crosses pure-breeding red snapdragons to pure-breeding ivory snapdragons and produces F_1 progeny plants that have pink flowers. He proposes that this outcome is the result of incomplete dominance, and he crosses the F_1 to test his hypothesis. What phenotypes does Dr. Dopsis predict will be found in the F_2, and in what proportions?

15. A plant line with reduced fertility comes to the attention of a plant breeder who observes that seed pods often contain a mixture of viable seeds that can be planted to produce new plants, and withered seeds that cannot be sprouted. The breeder examines numerous seed pods in the reduced fertility line and counts 622 viable seeds and 204 nonviable seeds.

   a. What single-gene mechanism best explains the breeder's observation?

   b. Propose an additional experiment to test the genetic mechanism you propose. If your hypothesis is correct, what experimental outcome do you predict?

16. In cattle, an autosomal mutation called *Dexter* produces calves with short stature and short limbs. Embryos that are homozygous for the *Dexter* mutation have severely stunted development and either spontaneously abort or are stillborn. What progeny phenotypes do you expect from the cross of two *Dexter* cows? What are the expected proportions of the expected phenotypes?

Application and Integration

17. The coat color in mink is controlled by two codominant alleles at a single locus. Red coat color is produced by the genotype R_1R_1, silver coat by the genotype R_1R_2, and platinum color by R_2R_2. White spotting of the coat is a recessive trait found with the genotype ss. Solid coat color is found with the $S-$ genotype.

   a. What are the expected progeny phenotypes and proportions for the cross $SsR_1R_2 \times ssR_2R_2$?

   b. If the cross $SsR_1R_2 \times SsR_1R_1$ is made, what are the progeny phenotypes, and in what proportions are they expected to occur?

   c. Two crosses are made between mink. Cross 1 is the cross of a solid, silver mink to one that is solid, platinum. Cross 2 is between a spotted, silver mink and one that is solid, silver. The progeny are described in the table below. Use these data to determine the genotypes of the parents in each cross.

Cross	Offspring					
	Spotted, platinum	Spotted, silver	Spotted, red	Solid, platinum	Solid, silver	Solid, red
1	2	3	0	6	5	0
2	3	7	2	4	5	3

For answers to selected even-numbered problems, see Appendix: Answers.

18. Strains of petunias come in four pure-breeding colors: white, blue, red, and purple. White petunias are produced when plants synthesize no flower pigment. Blue petunias and red petunias are produced when plants synthesize blue or red pigment only. Purple petunias are produced in plants that synthesize both red *and* blue pigment. The mixture of red and blue makes purple. Flower-color pigments are synthesized by gene action in two separate pigment-producing biochemical pathways. Pathway I contains gene A that produces an enzyme to catalyze conversion of a colorless pigment designated white$_1$ to blue pigment. In Pathway II, the enzymatic product of gene B converts the colorless pigment designated white$_2$ to red pigment. The two genes assort independently.

$$\text{Pathway I:} \quad \text{White}_1 \xrightarrow{\text{gene } A} \text{Blue}$$
$$+ \quad = \quad \text{Purple}$$
$$\text{Pathway II:} \quad \text{White}_2 \xrightarrow[\text{gene } B]{} \text{Red}$$

   a. What are the possible genotype(s) for pure-breeding red petunias?

   b. What are the possible genotype(s) for true-breeding blue petunias?

c. True-breeding red petunias are crossed to pure-breeding blue petunias, and all the F_1 progeny have purple flowers. If the F_1 are allowed to self-fertilize and produce the F_2, what is the expected phenotypic distribution of the F_2 progeny? Show your work.

19. Feather color in parakeets is produced by the blending of pigments produced from two biosynthetic pathways shown below. Four independently assorting genes (*A, B, C,* and *D*) produce enzymes that catalyze separate steps of the pathways. For the questions below, use an uppercase letter to indicate a dominant allele producing full enzymatic activity and a lowercase letter to indicate a recessive allele producing no functional enzyme. Feather colors produced by mixing pigments are green (yellow + blue) and purple (red + blue). Red, yellow, and blue feathers result from production of one colored pigment, and white results from absence of pigment production.

Enzyme A   Enzyme B
Pathway I: Compound I ⟶ Compound II ⟶ Compound III
             (colorless)   (red)   (yellow)
Enzyme C   Enzyme D
Pathway II: Compound X ⟶ Compound Y ⟶ Compound Z
             (colorless)   (colorless)   (blue)

a. What is the genotype of a pure-breeding purple parakeet strain?
b. What is the genotype of a pure-breeding yellow strain of parakeet?
c. If a pure-breeding blue strain of parakeet (*aa BB CC DD*) is crossed to one that is pure-breeding purple, predict the genotype(s) and phenotype(s) of the F_1. Show your work.
d. If F_1 birds identified in part (c) are mated at random, what phenotypes do you expect in the F_2 generation? What are the ratios among phenotypes? Show your work.

20. Brachydactyly type D is a human autosomal dominant condition in which the thumbs are abnormally short and broad. In most cases, both thumbs are affected, but occasionally just one thumb is involved. The accompanying pedigree shows a family in which brachydactyly type D is segregating. Filled circles and squares represent females and males who have involvement of both thumbs. Half-filled symbols represent family members with just one thumb affected.

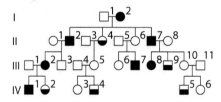

a. Is there any evidence of variable expressivity in this family? Explain.
b. Is there evidence of incomplete penetrance in this family? Explain.

21. A male and a female mouse are each from pure-breeding albino strains. They have a litter of 10 pups, all of which have normal pigmentation. The F_1 pups are crossed to one another to produce 56 F_2 mice, of which 31 are normally pigmented and 25 are albino.

a. Using clearly defined allele symbols of your own choosing, give the genotypes of parental and F_1 mice. What genetic phenomenon explains these parental and F_1 phenotypes?
b. What genetic phenomenon explains the F_2 results? Use your allelic symbols to explain the F_2 results.

22. Xeroderma pigmentosum (XP) is an autosomal recessive condition characterized by moderate to severe sensitivity to ultraviolet (UV) light. Patients develop multiple skin lesions on UV-exposed skin, and skin cancers often develop as a result. XP is caused by deficient repair of DNA damage from UV exposure.

a. Many genes are known to be involved in repair of UV-induced DNA damage, and several of these genes are implicated in XP. What genetic phenomenon is illustrated by XP?
b. A series of 10 skin-cell lines was grown from different XP patients. Cells from these lines were fused, and the heterokaryons were tested for genetic complementation by assaying their ability to repair DNA damage caused by a moderate amount of UV exposure. In the table below, + indicates that the fusion cell line performs normal DNA damage mutation repair, and − indicates defective DNA repair. Use this information to determine how many DNA-repair genes are mutated in the 10 cell lines, and identify which cell lines share the same mutated genes.

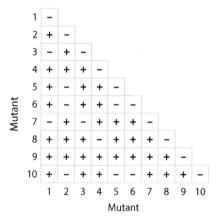

23. Three strains of green-seeded lentil plants appear to have the same phenotype. The strains are designated G_1, G_2, and G_3. Each green-seeded strain is crossed to a pure-breeding yellow-seeded strain designated Y. The F_1 of each cross are yellow; however, self-fertilization of F_1 plants produces F_2 with different proportions of yellow- and green-seeded plants as shown below.

Parental Strain		F_1 Phenotype	F_2 Phenotype	
Green	Yellow		Green	Yellow
G_1	Y	All yellow	$\frac{1}{4}$	$\frac{3}{4}$
G_2	Y	All yellow	$\frac{7}{16}$	$\frac{9}{16}$
G_3	Y	All yellow	$\frac{37}{64}$	$\frac{27}{64}$

a. For what number of genes are variable alleles segregating in the $G_1 \times Y$ cross? The $G_2 \times Y$ cross? In the $G_3 \times Y$ cross? Explain your rationale for each answer.
b. Using the allele symbols *A* and *a*, *B* and *b*, and *D* and *d* to represent alleles at segregating genes, give the genotypes of parental and F_1 plants in each cross.

c. For each set of F_2 progeny, provide a genetic explanation for the yellow : green ratio. What are the genotypes of yellow and green F_2 lentil plants in the $G_2 \times Y$ cross?

d. If green-seeded strains G_1 and G_3 are crossed, what are the phenotype and the genotype of F_1 progeny?

e. What proportion of the F_2 are expected to be green? Show your work.

f. If strains G_2 and G_3 are crossed, what will be the phenotype of the F_1?

g. What proportion of the F_2 will have yellow seeds? Show your work.

24. Blue flower color is produced in a species of morning glories when dominant alleles are present at two gene loci, A and B. (Plants with the genotype $A–B–$ have blue flowers.) Purple flowers result when a dominant allele is present at only one of the two gene loci, A or B. (Plants with the genotypes $A–bb$ and $aaB–$ are purple.) Flowers are red when the plant is homozygous recessive for each gene (i.e., $aabb$).

a. Two pure-breeding purple strains are crossed, and all the F_1 plants have blue flowers. What are the genotypes of the parental plants?

b. If two F_1 plants are crossed, what are the expected phenotypes and frequencies in the F_2?

c. If an F_1 plant is backcrossed to one of the pure-breeding parental plants, what is the expected ratio of phenotypes among progeny? Why is the phenotype ratio the same regardless of which parental strain is selected for the backcross?

25. The following crosses are performed between morning glories whose flower color is determined as described in Problem 24. Use the segregation data to determine the genotype of each parental plant.

Parental Phenotypes	Offspring Phenotypes
a. blue × blue	$\frac{3}{4}$ blue : $\frac{1}{4}$ purple
b. purple × purple	$\frac{1}{4}$ blue : $\frac{1}{2}$ purple : $\frac{1}{4}$ red
c. blue × red	$\frac{1}{4}$ blue : $\frac{1}{2}$ purple : $\frac{1}{4}$ red
d. purple × red	$\frac{1}{2}$ purple : $\frac{1}{2}$ red
e. blue × purple	$\frac{3}{8}$ blue : $\frac{1}{2}$ purple : $\frac{1}{8}$ red

26. Two pure-breeding strains of summer squash producing yellow fruit, Y_1 and Y_2, are each crossed to a pure-breeding strain of summer squash producing green fruit, G_1, and to one another. The following results are obtained:

Cross	P	F_1	F_2
I	Y_1 (yellow) × G_1 (green)	All yellow	$\frac{3}{4}$ yellow : $\frac{1}{4}$ green
II	Y_2 (yellow) × G_1 (green)	All green	$\frac{3}{4}$ green : $\frac{1}{4}$ yellow
III	Y_1 (yellow) × Y_2 (yellow)	All yellow	$\frac{13}{16}$ yellow : $\frac{3}{16}$ green

a. Examine the results of each cross and predict how many genes are responsible for fruit-color determination in summer squash. Justify your answer.

b. Using clearly defined symbols of your choice, give the genotypes of parental, F_1, and F_2 plants in each cross.

c. If the F_1 of Crosses I and II are mated, predict the phenotype ratio of the progeny.

27. Marfan syndrome is an autosomal dominant disorder in humans. It results from mutation of the gene on chromosome 15, that produces the connective tissue protein fibrillin. In its wild-type form, fibrillin gives connective tissues, such as cartilage, elasticity. When mutated, however, fibrillin is rigid and produces a range of phenotypic complications, including excessive growth of the long bones of the leg and arm, sunken chest, dislocation of the lens of the eye, and susceptibility to aortic aneurysm, which can lead to sudden death in some cases.

Different sets of symptoms are seen among various family members, as shown in the pedigree below. Each quadrant of the circles and squares represents a different symptom, as the key indicates.

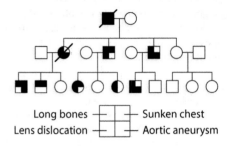

Long bones ┬ Sunken chest
Lens dislocation ┴ Aortic aneurysm

Since all cases of Marfan syndrome are caused by mutation of the fibrillin gene, and all family members with Marfan syndrome carry the same mutant allele, how do you explain the differences shown in the pedigree?

28. Yeast are single-celled eukaryotic organisms that grow in culture as either haploids or diploids. Diploid yeast are generated when two haploid strains fuse together. Seven haploid strains of yeast exhibit similar growth habit: At 25°C, each strain grows normally, but at 37°C, they show different growth capabilities. The table below displays the growth pattern.

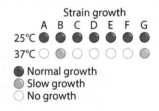

a. Describe the nature of the mutation affecting each of these mutant yeast strains. Explain why strains B and G display different growth habit at 37°C than the other strains.

b. Each of the mutant pairs of haploid yeast is fused, and the resulting diploids are tested for their ability to grow at 37°C. The results of the growth experiment are shown below.

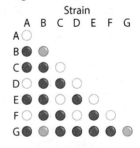

How many different genes are mutated among these seven yeast strains? Identify the strains that represent each gene mutation.

29. During your work as a laboratory assistant in the research facilities of Dr. O. Sophila, a world-famous geneticist, you come across an unusual bottle of fruit flies. All the flies in the bottle appear normal when they are in an incubator set at 22°C. When they are moved to a 30°C incubator, however, a few of the flies slowly become paralyzed; and after about 20 to 30 minutes, they are unable to move. Returning the flies to 22°C restores their ability to move after about 30 to 45 minutes.

   With Dr. Sophila's encouragement, you set up 10 individual crosses between single male and female flies that exhibit the unusual behavior. Among 812 progeny, 598 exhibit the unusual behavior and 214 do not. When you leave one of the test bottles in the 30°C incubator too long, you discover that more than 2 hours at high temperature kills the paralyzed flies. When you tell this to Dr. Sophila, he says, "Ah ha! I know the genetic explanation for this condition." What is his explanation?

30. Dr. Ara B. Dopsis and Dr. C. Ellie Gans are performing genetic crosses on daisy plants. They self-fertilize a blue-flowered daisy and grow 100 progeny plants that consist of 55 blue-flowered plants, 22 purple-flowered plants, and 23 white-flowered plants. Dr. Dopsis believes this is the result of segregation of two alleles at one locus and that the progeny ratio is 1:2:1. Dr. Gans thinks the progeny phenotypes are the result of two epistatic genes and that the ratio is 9:3:4.

   The two scientists ask you to resolve their conflict by performing chi-square analysis on the data for *both* proposed genetic mechanisms. For each proposed mechanism, fill in the values requested on the form the researchers have provided for your analysis.

   a. Use the form below to calculate chi square for the 1:2:1 hypothesis of Dr. Sophila.

Phenotype	Observed	Expected
Blue	55	_____
Purple	22	_____
White	23	_____
Chi-square value: _____ df: _____ p value > _____		

   b. Use the form below to calculate chi square for the 9:3:4 hypothesis of Dr. Gans.

Phenotype	Observed	Expected
Blue	55	_____
Purple	22	_____
White	23	_____
Chi-square value: _____ df: _____ p value > _____		

   c. What is your conclusion regarding these two genetic hypotheses?

   d. Using any of the 100 progeny plants, propose a cross that will verify the conclusion you proposed in part (c). Plants may be self-fertilized, or one plant can be crossed to another. What result will be consistent with the 1:2:1 hypothesis? What result will be consistent with the 9:3:4 hypothesis?

31. Human ABO blood type is determined by three alleles, two of which (I^A and I^B) produce gene products that modify the H antigen produced by protein activity of an independently

assorting H gene. A rare abnormality known as the "Bombay phenotype" is the result of epistatic interaction between the gene for the ABO blood group and the H gene. Individuals with the Bombay phenotype appear to have blood type O based on the inability of both anti-A antibody and anti-B antibody to detect an antigen. The apparent blood type O in Bombay phenotype is due to the absence of H antigen as a result of homozygous recessive mutations of the H gene. Individuals with the Bombay phenotype have the hh genotype. Use the information above to make predictions about the outcome of the cross shown below.

$$I^A I^B Hh \times I^A I^B Hh$$

32. In rabbits, albinism is an autosomal recessive condition caused by the absence of the pigment melanin from skin and fur. Pigmentation is a dominant wild-type trait. Three pure-breeding strains of albino rabbits, identified as strains 1, 2, and 3, are crossed to one another. In the table below, F_1 and F_2 progeny are shown for each cross. Based on the available data, propose a genetic explanation for the results. As part of your answer, create genotypes for each albino strain using clearly defined symbols of your own choosing. Use your symbols to diagram each cross, giving the F_1 and F_2 genotypes.

	Cross	F_1 Progeny	F_2 Progeny
Cross A	strain 1 × strain 2	56 albino	192 albino
Cross B	strain 1 × strain 3	72 pigmented	181 pigmented, 139 albino
Cross C	strain 2 × strain 3	34 pigmented	89 pigmented, 72 albino

33. Dr. O. Sophila, a close friend of Dr. Ara B. Dopsis, reviews the F_2 results Dr. Dopsis obtained in his experiment with iris plants described in Genetic Analysis 4.3. Dr. Sophila thinks the F_2 progeny demonstrate that a single gene with incomplete dominance has produced a 1:2:1 ratio. Dr. Dopsis insists his proposal of recessive epistasis producing a 9:4:3 ratio in the F_2 is correct. To test his proposal, Dr. Dopsis examines the F_2 data under the assumptions of the single-gene incomplete dominance model using chi-square analysis. Calculate and interpret this chi-square value. Can Dr. Dopsis reject the single-gene incomplete dominance model on the basis of this analysis? Explain why or why not.

34. In a breed of domestic cattle, horns can appear on males and on females. Males and females can also be hornless. The following crosses are performed with parents from pure-breeding lines.

Cross I	Cross II
Parents: horned male × hornless female	Parents: hornless male × horned female
F_1: males horned, females hornless	F_1: males horned, females hornless
F_2: males are $\frac{3}{4}$ horned, $\frac{1}{4}$ hornless	F_2: males are $\frac{3}{4}$ horned, $\frac{1}{4}$ hornless
females are $\frac{1}{4}$ horned, $\frac{3}{4}$ hornless	females are $\frac{1}{4}$ horned, $\frac{3}{4}$ hornless

Explain the inheritance of this phenotype in cattle, and assign genotypes to all cattle in Cross I.

5

Genetic Linkage and Mapping in Eukaryotes

CHAPTER OUTLINE

5.1 Linked Genes Do Not Assort Independently

5.2 Genetic Linkage Mapping Is Based on Recombination Frequency between Genes

5.3 Three-Point Test-Cross Analysis Maps Genes

5.4 Recombination Results from Crossing Over

5.5 Linked Human Genes Are Mapped Using Lod Score Analysis

5.6 Recombination Affects Evolution and Genetic Diversity

5.7 Genetic Linkage in Haploid Eukaryotes Is Identified by Tetrad Analysis

5.8 Mitotic Crossover Produces Distinctive Phenotypes

ESSENTIAL IDEAS

▌ Genetic linkage occurs between genes that lie so close to one another on a chromosome that alleles are unable to assort independently.

▌ Genetic linkage produces significantly more progeny with parental phenotypes and significantly fewer progeny with nonparental phenotypes than are expected by chance.

▌ Crossing over between homologous chromosomes results in recombination of alleles on chromosomes in gametes.

▌ Geneticists use the frequency of recombination between genes to construct gene maps identifying the relative order of and distance between genes on chromosomes.

▌ Cytological evidence demonstrates that recombination results from crossing over between homologous chromosomes.

▌ Specialized statistical methods aid in mapping human genes.

▌ Recombination creates substantial new genetic diversity that is favored by evolution. It also randomizes the arrangements of alleles of linked genes on chromosomes.

▌ Mitotic crossover is rare and can result in the localized appearance of distinctive phenotypes.

Thomas Hunt Morgan, Nobel laureate (1933), discovered sex-linked inheritance, identified genetic linkage, proposed crossing over between homologous chromosomes, and developed the concept of gene mapping by recombination analysis.

In 1933, Thomas Hunt Morgan won the Nobel Prize for Physiology or Medicine—partly for his work establishing sex-linked inheritance and the chromosome theory of heredity (see Section 3.3) and partly for his role in identifying and explaining *genetic linkage and recombination* and their application to *genetic linkage mapping*, which we discuss in this chapter. Morgan, like all successful scientists, was assisted by dedicated colleagues who included many exceptional students and other scientists. Among them were Calvin Bridges, whose work we discussed in connection with the chromosome theory of heredity, and Alfred Sturtevant, who as an undergraduate researcher in Morgan's laboratory became the first person to use genetic linkage data to assemble a genetic map. A number of less well-remembered researchers, including Morgan's wife Lilian, were also important members of the research enterprise.

The work of Morgan, his colleagues, and numerous others led to the validation of three foundational theories in genetics. First, the work validated the chromosome theory of heredity, and it expanded the theory by showing that each chromosome carries multiple genes in a specific order. Second, the research validated the concept of the gene as a physical entity that is an integral part of a chromosome, and it led to work that expanded understanding of gene structure and demonstrated that genes are composed of nucleotides between which recombination may occur. Third, the work validated evolutionary theory by confirming that closely related species have a similar number of chromosomes and a similar arrangement of genes on chromosomes. The work led to an expansion of evolutionary theory that showed that recombination provides a mechanism by which variation in chromosome number and the arrangement of genes on chromosomes can accrue as species diverge from a common ancestor.

The observations and analysis of genetic linkage, recombination, and genetic linkage mapping are the focus of this chapter, which also touches on the connection between gene mapping and the investigation of chromosome evolution.

5.1 Linked Genes Do Not Assort Independently

Genes that are located on the same chromosome are called **syntenic genes.** When two syntenic genes are so close to one another that their alleles are unable to assort independently, the genes are said to be linked to one another. This **genetic linkage** produces a distinctive pattern of gamete genotypes that can be quantified and analyzed to map the locations of genes on chromosomes. The alleles of syntenic genes can be reshuffled by crossing over between homologous chromosomes to produce **recombinant chromosomes.** In studies of linked genes, chromosomes that do not undergo crossing over to reshuffle the alleles under study are identified as **parental chromosomes,** or

nonrecombinant chromosomes. The discovery of genetic linkage, made more than a century ago, opened the door to the development of **genetic linkage mapping,** which plots the positions of genes on chromosomes. Over the last century, new methods for identifying and mapping genes have been added to the analytical arsenal of genetics, but the importance of genetic linkage and its mapping applications remains undiminished.

Mendelian genetic ratios such as 3:1 and 9:3:3:1 are the products of segregation and independent assortment of alleles of genes for which chance determines the probabilities of gamete genotypes and the results of gamete union. Even when these independently assorting genes are subject to epistatic interactions, the rules of probability describe the distribution of the contributing alleles and can be used to interpret the resulting ratios (see Section 4.3).

Often, two genes assort independently because they are located on separate chromosomes, but syntenic genes can also assort independently, if they are far apart on a chromosome. In this situation, crossing over occurs frequently enough between the genes to randomize the combinations of alleles produced during meiosis. Syntenic genes that are in close proximity to one another do not cross over frequently enough to randomize the combinations of alleles in gametes. As a result, the genes do not assort independently. Instead, the alleles on each of the original chromosomes (the parental chromosomes) continue to reside on the same chromosome as it segregates from its homolog during cell division.

To repeat, the connection that causes alleles of linked genes to segregate together during meiosis can be broken by crossing over. Recall that homologous chromosomes synapse and form the synaptonemal complex in prophase I (see Figure 3.11). The recombination nodules, consisting of proteins and enzymes, that form part of this complex can generate crossing over by facilitating the breakage, exchange, and reunion of segments of homologous chromosomes. This recombination of chromosome segments reshuffles the alleles carried at linked genes, resulting in haploid gametes that contain different combinations of alleles of syntenic genes than were present in the diploid cell that began meiosis.

The following observations and conclusions about genetic linkage are essential to understanding the phenomenon. We discuss them in the following paragraphs and then expand on the same fundamental ideas throughout the remainder of the chapter.

1. Linked genes are always syntenic, and they are always located near one another on a chromosome. When syntenic genes are so far apart on the chromosome that crossing over between them generates independent assortment of the alleles, the genes are not linked.

2. Genetic linkage leads to the production of a significantly greater number of gametes containing chromosomes with parental combinations of alleles than would be expected under assumptions

of independent assortment and to a significantly smaller number of gametes containing chromosomes with alleles that are different from the parental combinations.

3. Crossing over is less likely to occur between linked genes that are close to one another than between genes that are farther apart on a chromosome. The frequency of crossing over is roughly proportionate to the distance between genes, a relationship that allows genes to be mapped.

Indications of Genetic Linkage

Genetic linkage can be recognized by comparing the observed frequencies of gamete genotypes, or progeny phenotypes, with the frequencies expected under the assumptions of independent assortment. If genes are linked, parental gametes—also known as nonrecombinant gametes—that contain parental combinations of the alleles will be produced significantly more often than predicted by chance. The excess parental gametes will also result in progeny in which *parental* phenotypes for the genes occur significantly

more often than predicted by chance. Here "significantly" is used in the sense of statistical significance as determined by chi-square analysis (see Section 2.5).

Figure 5.1 demonstrates the identification of genetic linkage by comparing the frequencies of gamete genotypes for two crosses, one illustrating independent assortment and the other genetic linkage. In Figure 5.1a, gene *A* and gene *B* are on different chromosomes, and alleles of the genes assort independently. The parental organisms are *AABB* and *aabb*, and their gametes *AB* and *ab* are the parental gametes. The F$_1$ progeny are dihybrid (*AaBb*), and independent assortment predicts these dihybrids will produce four genetically different gametes in a ratio of 1:1:1:1. Notice that the frequency of parental gametes (*AB* and *ab*) is 50%, and that the frequency of nonparental gametes (*Ab* and *aB*) is also 50%.

Figure 5.1b illustrates gamete-genotype production for syntenic genes *D* and *E* that are linked. The *DDee* parent produces parental gametes that are *De*, and the *ddEE* parent produces *dE* gametes. The dihybrid F$_1$ progeny are *DdEe*, carrying alleles *D* and *e* on one chromosome and *d* and *E* on the homolog. This arrangement of alleles can be written *DeE*, with the slash ("/") separating

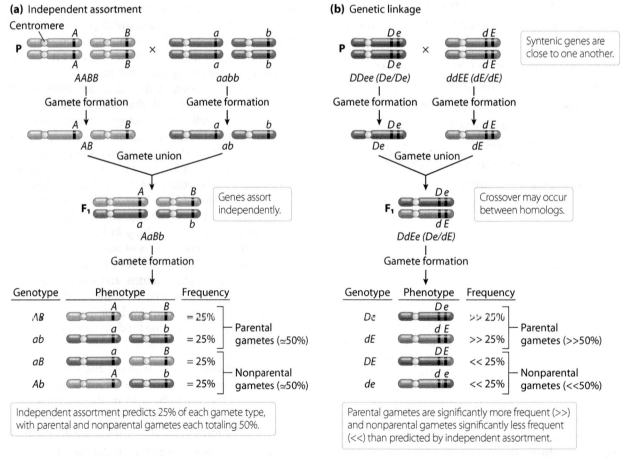

(a) Independent assortment

(b) Genetic linkage

Syntenic genes are close to one another.

Genes assort independently.

Crossover may occur between homologs.

Genotype	Phenotype	Frequency	
AB	A B	= 25%	Parental gametes (≈50%)
ab	a b	= 25%	
aB	a B	= 25%	Nonparental gametes (≈50%)
Ab	A b	= 25%	

Genotype	Phenotype	Frequency	
De	De	>> 25%	Parental gametes (>>50%)
dE	dE	>> 25%	
DE	DE	<< 25%	Nonparental gametes (<<50%)
de	de	<< 25%	

Independent assortment predicts 25% of each gamete type, with parental and nonparental gametes each totaling 50%.

Parental gametes are significantly more frequent (>>) and nonparental gametes significantly less frequent (<<) than predicted by independent assortment.

Figure 5.1   Independent assortment versus genetic linkage. (a) For this dihybrid, four genetically different gametes are expected at 25% each when the genes assort independently. **(b)** When genes are linked, parental gametes are much more frequent than expected by chance and are more frequent than nonparental gametes.

(a) Complete genetic linkage (no crossover)

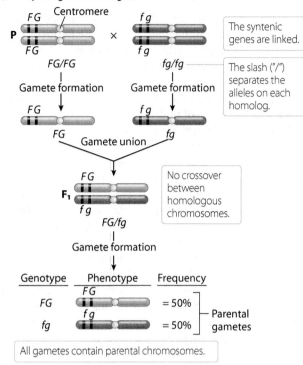

The syntenic genes are linked.

The slash ("/") separates the alleles on each homolog.

No crossover between homologous chromosomes.

Genotype	Phenotype	Frequency	
FG	*F G*	= 50%	Parental gametes
fg	*f g*	= 50%	

All gametes contain parental chromosomes.

(c) Incomplete genetic linkage (crossover in 40% of gametes)

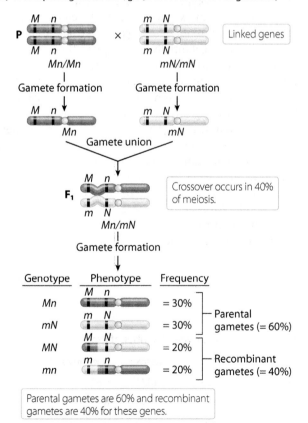

Linked genes

Crossover occurs in 40% of meiosis.

Genotype	Phenotype	Frequency	
Mn	*M n*	= 30%	Parental gametes (= 60%)
mN	*m N*	= 30%	
MN	*M N*	= 20%	Recombinant gametes (= 40%)
mn	*m n*	= 20%	

Parental gametes are 60% and recombinant gametes are 40% for these genes.

(b) Incomplete genetic linkage (crossover in 20% of gametes)

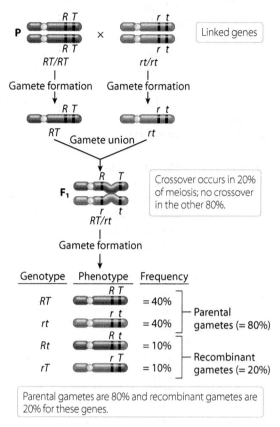

Linked genes

Crossover occurs in 20% of meiosis; no crossover in the other 80%.

Genotype	Phenotype	Frequency	
RT	*R T*	= 40%	Parental gametes (= 80%)
rt	*r t*	= 40%	
Rt	*R t*	= 10%	Recombinant gametes (= 20%)
rT	*r T*	= 10%	

Parental gametes are 80% and recombinant gametes are 20% for these genes.

Figure 5.2 Complete versus incomplete genetic linkage. (a) Genes exhibiting complete genetic linkage do not recombine and all gametes are parental. (b) Linked genes with a recombination frequency of 20% produce 20% nonparental gametes and 80% parental gametes. (c) Linked genes with a recombination frequency of 40% produce 60% parental gametes and 40% nonparental gametes.

the alleles carried on each member of the homologous chromosome pair. With genetic linkage, the rate of recombination among the alleles is low, and parental allele combinations usually stay together during meiosis, leading to the production of parental gametes (*De* and *dE*) at a combined frequency that is significantly greater than 50%. The low frequency of crossing over between closely linked genes results in the production of recombinant, or nonparental, gametes (*DE* and *de*) at a combined frequency that is significantly less than 50%.

Complete genetic linkage is observed when no recombination at all occurs between linked genes. Complete genetic linkage can be identified, for example, in cases where a dihybrid produces two equally frequent gametes containing only parental allele combinations and no recombinant gametes (**Figure 5.2a**). The absence of recombination between homologs usually has a specific biological basis. Certain organisms, including *Drosophila* males and other males in the insect order *Diptera* (of which *Drosophila* is a member), exhibit complete genetic linkage. There is no recombination between homologous chromosomes in these male flies. The biological basis of the absence of recombination in these organisms remains unknown.

Incomplete genetic linkage is far more common for linked genes. The resulting recombination between the homologs produces a mixture of parental and nonparental gametes. In the F_1 dihybrid shown in **Figure 5.2b**, recombination produces four genetically different gametes, of which two are parental and two are nonparental (recombinant). The two parental gametes each have approximately the same frequency, and their total is significantly greater than 50% of all gametes. In this example, the frequency of each parental gamete (RT and rt) is 40%, and the total frequency of parental gametes is 80%. Recombinant gametes, which have nonparental combinations of alleles, are approximately equal in frequency to one another and constitute significantly less than 50% of all gametes. In this case, a total of 20% of gametes are recombinant: 10% of the gametes are Rt and 10% are rT. Since the relative proportions of parental and recombinant gametes depend on the frequency of crossing over between linked genes, the proportions differ among pairs of linked genes. Note that the percentages of different gametes obtained for the cross in **Figure 5.2c** are different from those in Figure 5.2b, and also notice that the parental alleles on chromosomes in Figure 5.2c are a dominant and a recessive allele—Mn/mN. Parental chromosomes do not necessarily always contain all dominant and all recessive alleles. Rather, parental chromosomes are defined by whatever combination of alleles are originally present on the homologs.

The **recombination frequency,** expressed as the variable r, identifies the rate of recombination for a given pair of linked genes. The value of r is expressed as

$$r = \frac{\text{number of recombinants}}{\text{total number of progeny}}$$

Recombination frequency varies between different pairs of syntenic genes, depending roughly on the distance separating the genes on the chromosome. Comparing Figure 5.2b and Figure 5.2c, for example, we see that recombination frequency is 20% ($r = 0.20$) in Figure 5.2b and 40% ($r = 0.40$) in Figure 5.2c. The greater recombination frequency in Figure 5.2c compared to Figure 5.2b is most likely the consequence of a greater distance between genes N and M than between genes T and R. The correlation between recombination frequency and gene distance can be expressed in two equivalent ways: (1) crossing over occurs at a higher rate between genes that are separated by a greater distance, and at a lower rate for genes that are closer together; and (2) linked genes with higher recombination frequencies are more distant from one another than linked genes with lower recombination frequencies. There are some caveats to this generalization, however, as we discuss in later sections.

The Discovery of Genetic Linkage

William Bateson, an early champion of Mendelian genetics, and Reginald Punnett, after whom the Punnett square is named, reported a series of experiments on sweet peas in 1905, 1906, and 1908. Those experiments opened a new chapter in genetics by drawing attention to genetic linkage. Bateson and Punnett studied the traits of flower color and the shape of pollen grains in sweet peas, first as independent traits and then together in the same plants.

When the traits were studied separately, the genes for flower color and pollen shape obeyed the rules of segregation—generating 3:1 phenotypic ratios among the F_2, for example. But Bateson and Punnett went on to study both traits in the same plants, intending to test the law of independent assortment. They crossed pure-breeding purple-flowered, long-pollen plants ($PPLL$) to pure-breeding red-flowered, round-pollen plants ($ppll$). As expected, the F_1 consisted exclusively of purple-flowered, long-pollen plants, and these plants were crossed to obtain the F_2. But then, instead of the 9:3:3:1 ratio predicted by the independent assortment hypothesis, a far larger than expected portion of F_2 progeny showed parental combinations of phenotypes, and many fewer showed nonparental combinations (**Table 5.1**).

In the F_2, Bateson and Punnett observed that the two parental phenotypes—purple, long and red, round—were substantially in excess of expected frequencies, and that the two nonparental phenotypes—purple, round and red, long—were substantially less frequent than expected. This observation led Bateson and Punnett to suggest that the two combinations of alleles carried in the parents—PL and pl—remained together very frequently when they were passed through gametes to subsequent generations by an unknown mechanism. Bateson and Punnett described these alleles as exhibiting "coupling." They described the appearance of new, nonparental phenotypes in the F_2 as indicating "repulsion" of the parental alleles, to produce nonparental phenotypes in progeny.

In 1911, Morgan performed the first of many crosses that confirmed and explained the observation of coupling and repulsion identified by Bateson and

Table 5.1	Bateson and Punnett's Observed and Expected Phenotypes in F_2 Sweet Peas		
Phenotype	**Genotype**	**Number of Progeny**	
		Observed	Expected (9:3:3:1 ratio)
Purple, long	$P-L-$	4831	(6952)(9/16) = 3910.5
Purple, round	$P-ll$	390	(6952)(3/16) = 1303.5
Red, long	$ppL-$	393	(6952)(3/16) = 1303.5
Red, round	$ppll$	1338	(6952)(1/16) = 434.5
		6952	6952.0

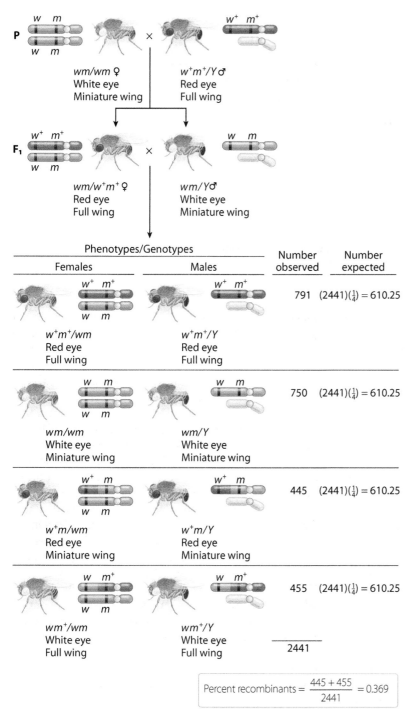

Figure 5.3 **Morgan's analysis of genetic linkage of X-linked genes for eye color (*w*) and wing form (*m*).** The number of test-cross progeny with each phenotype are compared to expected values that are determined assuming independent assortment of the genes.

Punnett. Morgan had by this time identified several genes on the X chromosome of the fruit fly, including *w* (white eye) and *m* (miniature wing). **Figure 5.3** illustrates that Morgan crossed a female pure-breeding for white eyes and miniature wings (*wm/wm*) with hemizygous wild-type males displaying red eye and full wing (*w⁺m⁺/Y*). The F₁ progeny were dihybrid wild-type females (*w⁺m⁺/wm*) and white, miniature (*wm/Y*) hemizygous males.

Morgan then produced an F₂ generation, predicting a 1:1:1:1 ratio based on the assumption of independent

assortment of the genes. Instead, Morgan found substantial deviation from expectations. As in the Bateson and Punnett experiment, Morgan observed that parental phenotypes predominated (791 + 750 = 1541, or 63.1%) and that fewer than the expected number of nonparental phenotypes were produced. The recombination frequency for this experiment is $r = 445 + 455/2441 = 0.369$, or 36.9%. Notice that the two parental phenotypes are observed in an approximate 1:1 ratio (791:750), as are the nonparental phenotypes (455:445), as expected from segregation.

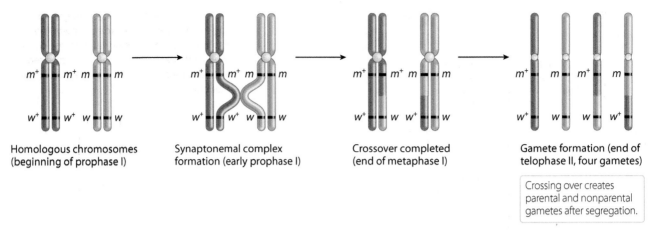

Homologous chromosomes
(beginning of prophase I)

Synaptonemal complex
formation (early prophase I)

Crossover completed
(end of metaphase I)

Gamete formation (end of
telophase II, four gametes)

Crossing over creates
parental and nonparental
gametes after segregation.

Figure 5.4   Morgan's crossing-over hypothesis. Each homolog initially contains identical sister chromatids. A single crossover produces two recombinant chromatids. Completion of meiosis produces two parental gametes and two recombinant gametes.

Based on this result, Morgan proposed that parental phenotypes are produced when the gametes of the F_1 female carry chromosomes with the same sets of alleles as in the parents, in this case w^+m^+ and wm. Eggs containing parental alleles unite with sperm carrying w and m on the X chromosome or carrying the Y chromosome, and parental phenotypes (the same phenotypes as in the P generation flies) are produced. Conversely, nonparental phenotypes are the result of recombination between homologous X chromosomes during F_1 female meiosis (**Figure 5.4**). The production of recombinant chromosomes carrying either w^+m or wm^+ required the physical rearrangement (recombination) of homologous X chromosomes. The union of eggs containing recombinant X chromosomes with sperm produced F_2 with nonparental phenotypes. Morgan confirmed this explanation through the examination of many other pairs of linked genes on the fruit fly X chromosome.

Detecting Autosomal Genetic Linkage through Test-Cross Analysis

Turning his attention to autosomal genes and employing 20/20 hindsight, Morgan realized that Bateson and Punnett had detected genetic linkage but were unable to explain it because, with respect to experimental design, *they had performed the wrong cross.* The F_2 progeny in the Bateson and Punnett experiment fell into four phenotypic classes, but three of those classes contained multiple genotypes, owing to the dominance relationships among the alleles (see Figure 2.11). Bateson and Punnett were unable to determine which alleles in the progeny derived from each F_1 parent because they had no way of ascertaining the high frequency of parental combinations of alleles and the low frequency of recombinants in F_1 gametes.

Morgan realized that the linkage of autosomal genes in *Drosophila* could be fully interpreted through the use of **two-point test-cross analysis** in which a dihybrid F_1 fly is crossed to a pure-breeding mate with the recessive

phenotypes. The "two points" in these analyses are the two genes being tested. In two-point test-cross analysis, the homozygous recessive fly contributes only recessive alleles to test-cross progeny. In contrast, the dihybrid fly can contribute either a dominant allele of a gene, in which case the progeny display the dominant phenotype, or the recessive allele, thus producing the recessive form of the trait.

In one experiment, Morgan used test-cross analysis to examine genetic linkage of autosomal genes affecting eye color and wing shape. *Drosophila* eye color is red if an autosomal dominant allele pr^+ is present, whereas the recessive purple eye color is produced when the only allele present is pr. Full-sized wing is the product of an autosomal dominant allele vg^+, and its recessive counterpart, vestigial wing, is determined by the allele vg. Morgan crossed fruit flies that are pure-breeding for red eyes and full wing with pure-breeding purple-eyed, vestigial-winged flies (**Figure 5.5a**). The F_1 were uniformly red eyed and full winged ($pr^+ vg^+/pr$ vg). Morgan then test-crossed dihybrid F_1 females to purple-eyed, vestigial-winged males (pr vg/pr vg). In this cross, males contributed only recessive alleles (pr and vg), but females could produce any one of four gamete genotypes. The alleles of the female gamete thus controlled the phenotype of test-cross progeny. If the female contributed a dominant allele to progeny, the phenotype for that trait was dominant; and conversely, if the donated female allele was recessive, the phenotype was recessive. Test-cross progeny phenotypes corresponded directly to the alleles contributed by F_1 females, thus making it possible to unambiguously identify the allelic content of chromosomes in female gametes.

Under the assumption of independent assortment, dihybrid females should produce four equally frequent gametes, and test-cross progeny are expected to have four phenotypes distributed in a 1:1:1:1 ratio (see Figure 2.13). With genetic linkage however, parental combinations of alleles occur preferentially in gametes, producing test-cross progeny with a significant excess of parental phenotypes and a significant deficit of nonparental phenotypes.

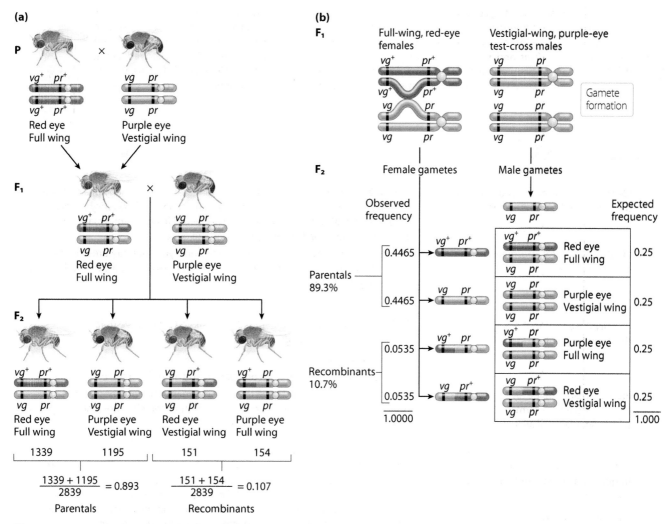

Figure 5.5 **Morgan's test-cross analysis of genetic linkage between autosomal genes.** (a) Dihybrid F₁ females (*pr⁺vg⁺/pr vg*) are test-crossed to males homozygous for recessive mutant purple eye color and vestigial wing (*pr vg/pr vg*), permitting identification of progeny as carrying either a parental or a recombinant chromosome. (b) Single crossover during female meiosis leads to parental and recombinant gametes at frequencies specified by recombination or by chance, and gamete union produces test-cross progeny.

Morgan's test-cross progeny displayed the four expected phenotypes, but in numbers that deviated dramatically from expected Mendelian proportions. Among test-cross progeny, 89.3% were parental, and just 10.7% were recombinant. The nonrecombinant progeny classes were found in approximately a 1:1 ratio (1339:1195), as were the recombinant classes (154:151); thus, the two parental chromosomes were transmitted equally frequently, as were the two recombinant chromosomes. Figure 5.5b shows that among the 89.3% of parental female gametes, one-half, or 44.65%, are predicted to be of each parental type. Similarly, among the 10.7% of gametes that are recombinant, each recombinant type is predicted with a frequency of 5.35%.

In the years immediately following Morgan's explanation of genetic linkage, other biologists, working on plant species and animal species, used test-cross analysis to verify Morgan's hypothesis. The collective results of these experimental observations can be summarized as follows:

1. Genetic linkage is a physical relationship between genes that are located near one another on a chromosome.

2. Recombination occurs between linked genes on homologous chromosomes in significantly less than 50% of meiotic divisions. Significantly more than 50% of gametes contain parental combinations of alleles.

3. The recombination frequency varies among linked genes and is roughly proportionate to the distance between genes on a chromosome.

Genetic Analysis 5.1 takes you through the identification of parental and recombinant progeny and the determination of recombination frequency.

PROBLEM In tomato plants (*Lycopersicon esculentum*), red fruit color (*T*–) is dominant to tangerine color (*tt*), and smooth leaf (*H*–) is dominant to hairy leaf (*hh*). Both genes are located on chromosome 7, and they have a recombination frequency of 20%. A pure-breeding plant producing tangerine-colored fruit and smooth leaves is crossed to a pure-breeding red-fruited, hairy-leaved plant. The F$_1$ are test-crossed to a pure-breeding tangerine-fruited, hairy plant. What are the expected genotypes, phenotypes, and phenotype proportions among test-cross progeny?

> **BREAK IT DOWN:** A recombination frequency of 20% means that 80% of gametes are parental and 20% are recombinant.

> **BREAK IT DOWN:** Pure-breed tangerine, smooth is *ttHH* and pure-breeding red, hairy is *TThh*.

> **BREAK IT DOWN:** The F$_1$ are *TtHh* and they are test-crossed to *tthh*.

Solution Strategies	Solution Steps
Evaluate	
1. Identify the topic of this problem and the nature of the required answer.	1. This problem concerns the prediction of inheritance in progeny of a test cross for linked genes. The answer requires that the expected frequency of each possible category of test-cross progeny be predicted from the information given about recombination frequency between the genes.
2. Identify the critical information given in the problem.	2. Dominant and recessive phenotypes, the phenotypes of two pure-breeding parental plants, and the recombination frequency between genes controlling two traits are given in the problem.
Deduce	
3. Identify the alleles in the gametes of the parental plants.	3. Each parent is pure-breeding for a dominant and a recessive trait: Tangerine, smooth = *ttHH* Red, hairy = *TThh* Parental gametes = all *tH* from one parent and all *Th* from the other
4. Identify the genotype and phenotype of F$_1$ plants, and determine the parental arrangements of alleles.	4. F$_1$ are dihybrid (*tH/Th*) and have the two dominant phenotypes (red and smooth). The pure-breeding parents have contributed chromosomes carrying *tH* and *Th*.
Solve	
5. Determine the number and frequency of F$_1$ gametes, given the recombination frequency of 20%.	5. Four genetically different gametes are possible: *tH, Th, TH,* and *th*. Among these gametes, 20% will be recombinants and 80% parentals (100% − 20% = 80%). Chance predicts that the two parental gametes (*tH* and *Th*) are produced at equal frequency. Likewise, the two recombinant gametes (*TH* and *th*) are produced at equal frequency. The expected gamete frequencies are

> **TIP:** With genetic linkage, parental combinations of alleles are significantly greater than 50% of the gametes.

$$\text{Parentals: } tH = (0.80)(1/2) = 0.40$$
$$Th = (0.80)(1/2) = 0.40$$
$$\text{Recombinants: } TH = (0.20)(1/2) = 0.10$$
$$th = (0.20)(1/2) = 0.10$$

6. Determine the expected outcome of the test cross.	6. Test-cross progeny are expected to be 40% each tangerine, smooth and red, hairy; and 20% each red, smooth and tangerine, hairy.

> **TIP:** There are two equally likely parental gametes and two equally likely recombinant gametes.

				th	(1.0)	Test-cross progeny	
Parental	0.40	*tH*	*tH/th*	0.40		Tangerine, smooth	40%
	0.40	*Th*	*Th/th*	0.40		Red, hairy	40%
Recombinant	0.10	*TH*	*TH/th*	0.10		Red, smooth	10%
	0.10	*th*	*th/th*	0.10		Tangerine, hairy	10%

5.2 Genetic Linkage Mapping Is Based on Recombination Frequency between Genes

An important outcome of Morgan's studies of linked genes in *Drosophila* was his recognition that significantly more parental than recombinant progeny occurred and that the proportion of recombinants varied considerably from one pair of linked genes to another. Morgan summarized this idea in 1911, stating, "The proportions that result are not so much the expression of a numerical system as of the relative location of the factors (genes) in the chromosome." Morgan was saying that independent assortment was not determining the relative proportions of gametes produced by an organism. Instead, the close proximity of linked genes on a chromosome overrode the expected influence of independent assortment. The linkage of genes preferentially retained parental combinations of alleles and led to a much higher proportion of parental gametes and a much lower proportion of nonparental gametes than were expected by chance. Morgan's intuition was correct, and his insight profoundly changed views of hereditary transmission and of the location and organization of genes on chromosomes. In this section, we examine methods for constructing genetic maps from recombination data for two linked genes, and in the next section, we'll move on to consider the mapping of three linked genes.

The First Genetic Linkage Map

In the context of early 20th-century biology, Morgan's idea that genes were on chromosomes was not novel. For example, Sutton, Boveri, and others had noted the parallel between hereditary transmission and chromosome division. But biologists at the time did not know either the structure of genes or how they were encoded on chromosomes (see Section 3.4). Morgan was the first to demonstrate that genes are on chromosomes, however, and his proposal that the recombination frequency for a linked pair of genes might correspond to the *distance* between those genes on a chromosome was a novel idea.

Morgan viewed genes as inhabiting fixed locations on chromosomes. Like cities along a road, the order of genes could be determined, the locations of genes on a chromosome could be specified, and the distances between genes could be quantified. If his hypothesis were correct, he reasoned, then recombination frequencies could be used to produce a genetic linkage map depicting gene order along a chromosome and to calculate a quantitative index of linear distances between genes. As Morgan discussed his ideas about recombination frequency and gene distances, Alfred Sturtevant, then an undergraduate student

Table 5.2	Sturtevant's Recombination Data for Five X-Linked Genes in *Drosophila*
Gene Pairs	**Recombination Frequency**
Yellow (*y*) and white (*w*)	214/21,736 = 0.010
Yellow (*y*) and vermilion (*v*)	1464/4551 = 0.322
Vermilion (*v*) and white (*w*)	471/1584 = 0.297
Vermilion (*v*) and miniature (*m*)	17/573 = 0.030
Miniature (*m*) and white (*w*)	2062/6116 = 0.337
White (*w*) and rudimentary (*r*)	406/898 = 0.452
Rudimentary (*r*) and vermilion (*v*)	109/405 = 0.269

working in Morgan's laboratory, had an epiphany. In a 1965 book, Sturtevant recalled the moment:

> In the latter part of 1911, in a conversation with Morgan, I suddenly realized that the variations in strength of linkage, already attributed by Morgan to differences in the spatial separation of genes, offered the possibility of determining sequences in the linear dimension of a chromosome. I went home and spent most of the night (to the neglect of my other undergraduate homework) in producing the first chromosome map.

Sturtevant used the results of numerous two-point test-cross experiments on five X-linked genes in *Drosophila* to create the first genetic linkage map. He based his map-building approach on the idea that smaller recombination frequencies indicated genes residing closer to each other on the chromosome, and larger recombination frequencies indicated greater distances between genes on the chromosome. To construct his genetic map, Sturtevant used the data in Table 5.2. His finished recombination map is illustrated in Figure 5.6. In the century since Sturtevant first compiled his map, millions of progeny fruit flies have been analyzed for X-chromosome recombination. The accumulated data have led to slight modifications in Sturtevant's

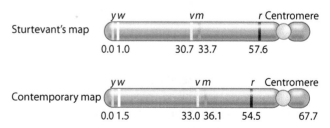

Figure 5.6 The first linkage map. The original *Drosophila* X chromosome map of five genes assembled by Alfred Sturtevant (top) and the contemporary X-chromosome map for *Drosophila* based on current data (bottom). Sturtevant's map is based in part on the recombination frequencies given in Table 5.2.

estimated recombination frequencies but have not necessitated any changes in gene order. Sturtevant assembled his map using logic of the kind demonstrated in the following four steps:

1. Of the genes tested, the pair with the smallest recombination frequency, and therefore in closest proximity, are the gene producing white eye (*w*) and the gene carrying yellow (*y*) body. With their recombination frequency of just 1%, they must be at almost the same spot on the chromosome.

2. Vermilion (*v*) is more distant from yellow (32.2% recombination) than it is from white (29.7% recombination), suggesting the order *y–w–v*.

3. Miniature (*m*) is close to vermilion (3% recombination) but is more distant from white (33.7% recombination) than is vermilion. Adding miniature to the gene map produces the order *y–w–v–m*.

4. Rudimentary (*r*) is very distant from white (45.2% recombination) and also fairly distant from vermilion (26.9% recombination). This information places rudimentary on the opposite side of the map from white, yielding the final map *y–w–v–m–r*.

Map Units

As we examine our map of the *Drosophila* X chromosome (Figure 5.6), the correlation between recombination frequency and physical distance on chromosomes becomes easier to understand. The recombination frequencies between genes on a chromosome can even be converted into units of physical distance, using the concept of a **map unit (m.u.)**. A map unit is also known as a **centiMorgan (cM)** in honor of Thomas Hunt Morgan's contribution to recombination mapping. It is common (at least in introductory genetics courses) to use the equivalency:

1% recombination = 1 m.u. or 1 cM of distance between linked genes

This is an approximation, and not a very good one for certain regions of particular genomes, as we discuss in a later section. Despite its shortcomings, however, it is accurate enough for our instructional purposes in this textbook.

Chi-Square Analysis of Genetic Linkage Data

In our discussion of genetic linkage data, we have noted that when genes are linked, *significantly* more parental phenotypes than recombinant phenotypes are found among progeny. But how can we tell whether the observed data constitute evidence of genetic linkage rather than a simple case of chance variation from expected values? The question is settled by the use of chi-square analysis of observed and expected values to identify statistically significant differences. (Section 2.5 describes the chi-square test and demonstrates the calculation and interpretation of chi-square *p*, or probability, values.)

As an example, let's revisit the data obtained by Morgan on the *w* gene affecting eye color and the *m* gene controlling wing form in *Drosophila*, presented in Figure 5.3. The cross of F_1 dihybrid females (wm/w^+m^+) to white-eyed, miniature-winged males (wm/Y) produces an F_2 generation that would have been expected to display a 1:1:1:1 phenotypic ratio. This ratio is based on the assumption that independent assortment determines the alleles contained in female gametes. Using the observed and expected values, we calculate the chi-square value as follows:

$$\chi^2 = \frac{(791 - 610.25)^2}{610.25} + \frac{(750 - 610.25)^2}{610.25}$$
$$+ \frac{(445 - 610.25)^2}{610.25} + \frac{(455 - 610.25)^2}{610.25} = 169.79$$

There are 3 degrees of freedom (df = 3) in this problem, and the corresponding *p* value is $p < 0.005$ (see Table 2.4). This observed result indicates a significant deviation from expected results, suggesting that chance is not responsible for the observed distribution. Combined with the observation that the two phenotypes that exceed the expected number are parental, these data are consistent with the presence of genetic linkage between the genes.

5.3 Three-Point Test-Cross Analysis Maps Genes

Two-point test-cross analysis is an effective way to calculate the recombination frequency between two linked genes and to infer the distance between the genes, but it is not the most effective way to build genetic maps containing multiple genes. By expanding the idea of test-cross analysis to **three-point test-cross analysis,** however, geneticists can efficiently map three linked genes simultaneously.

Finding the Relative Order of Genes by Three-Point Mapping

Let's consider a three-point test cross between a trihybrid organism ($a^+ab^+bc^+c$) and an organism that is homozygous recessive for the three traits (*aabbcc*). The configuration of alleles in the trihybrid does not have to be known at the start, since the three-point analysis will deduce the configuration of alleles on parental chromosomes as part of the process.

Incomplete genetic linkage of three genes in a trihybrid produces eight genetically different gamete genotypes. This is the same number of genetically different gametes expected if we assume independent assortment; but, unlike the expectations for independent assortment, the gamete frequencies are unequal if the genes are linked. Among the eight gamete genotypes are two parental genotypes that are significantly more frequent than expected by chance as well as six recombinant genotypes, each detected less often than expected. Assuming, for the purposes of this example, that the three linked genes are in the order $a-b-c$, we can identify parental and recombinant gametes by the relative frequencies of the corresponding test-cross progeny classes.

Imagine that Test cross 1 mates a trihybrid organism with the genotype $a^+b^+c^+/abc$ to one that is abc/abc (**Figure 5.7a**). Test cross 2 shows an alternative arrangement of alleles on parental chromosomes, mating the trihybrid a^+bc^+/ab^+c to an organism with genotype abc/abc (**Figure 5.7b**). In Test cross 1, parental gametes ($a^+b^+c^+$ and abc) are produced when no crossovers occur between the genes, and the resulting

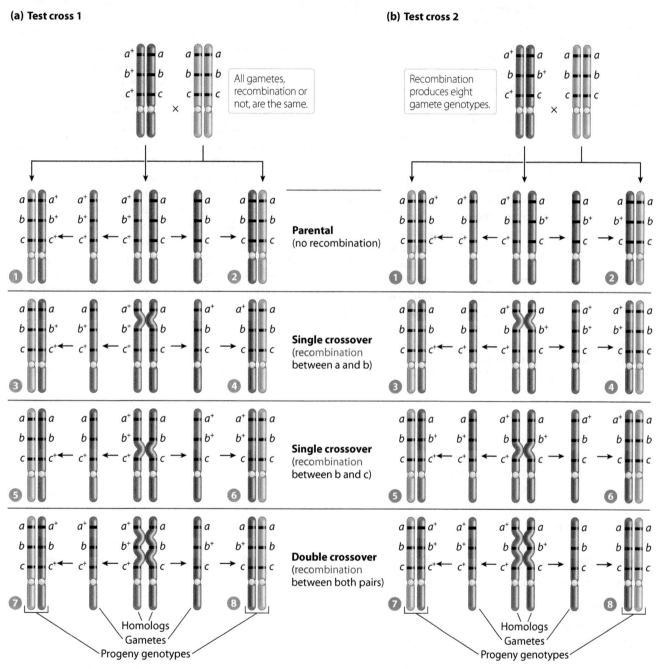

(a) Test cross 1

(b) Test cross 2

Figure 5.7   Three-point test crosses for different allele configurations in a trihybrid parent crossed to a triple recessive parent. **(a)** In Test cross 1, parental chromosomes carry the three wild-type and the three recessive alleles. Gametes with these alleles are parental and produce progeny with parental phenotypes. Single- and double-recombinant gametes lead to test-cross progeny displaying recombination. Test-cross progeny with eight genotypes (❶ to ❽) are produced. **(b)** In Test cross 2, a different configuration of alleles on parental chromosomes produces parental and recombinant progeny that are different from those in Test cross 1. Eight test-cross progeny genotypes (❶ to ❽) are produced.

progeny have either the three wild-type or three recessive phenotypes. A single crossover occurring between genes *a* and *b* produces two recombinant gametes, a^+bc and ab^+c^+, and progeny with the corresponding patterns of phenotypes. Likewise, single crossover between genes *b* and *c* also produces two recombinant gametes, a^+b^+c and abc^+, and corresponding progeny. A double-crossover event that causes crossing over both between *a* and *b* and between *b* and *c* will produce a pair of double-crossover gametes, a^+bc^+ and ab^+c, and progeny with the corresponding mixtures of wild-type and recessive traits.

Test cross 2 produces the same eight gamete genotypes obtained from Test cross 1, but the alleles start out arranged differently on the parental chromosomes. Thus, the parental and recombinant gamete genotypes in this test cross are different from those in the first test cross. In this test cross, the parental gametes are a^+bc^+ and ab^+c. The single-crossover gametes are a^+b^+c and abc^+ for crossover between genes *a* and *b*. Single crossover between genes *b* and *c* produces gametes a^+bc and ab^+c^+. A double-crossover causing recombination between each pair of genes produces double-crossover gametes $a^+b^+c^+$ and abc.

As expected when genes are linked, each of the six recombinant gametes is observed at a frequency that is significantly less than predicted by chance. Single-crossover gametes form at frequencies determined by the relative distances between gene pairs. Within each single-crossover class, the two gametes will be equally frequent. Double-crossover gametes will be the least frequent class because *both* crossover events must occur. As within each single-crossover class, the two kinds of double-crossover gametes are produced at equal frequency.

Constructing a Three-Point Recombination Map

To illustrate the use of three-point test-cross data for constructing a genetic map, we will now analyze the data from a 1935 study by Rollins Emerson of genetic linkage in maize (*Zea mays*). Emerson tested three genes: the gene producing the phenotypes green seedling (*V–*) and yellow seedling (*vv*), the gene producing rough leaf (*Gl–*) and glossy leaf (*gl gl*), and the gene for normal fertility (*Va–*) and variable fertility (*va va*).

Maize was an important genetic experimental organism in the first half of the 20th century because of the large number of variable genetic traits it possesses, the ease with which large numbers of plants can be grown in a single season, the ability of researchers to control matings in a manner similar to Mendel's, and the production of large numbers of seeds from each cross. On an ear of corn, each kernel is a seed produced by the union of gametes; thus, a single ear can carry hundreds of progeny seeds, each the product of independent fertilization, and a small number of plants can yield tens of thousands of progeny seeds for analysis.

Emerson crossed pure-breeding wild-type plants having the dominant phenotypes green seedling, rough leaves, and normal fertility (*V Gl Va/V Gl Va*) to pure-breeding plants having the recessive phenotypes yellow seedling, glossy leaves, and variable fertility (*v gl va/v gl va*). The cross produced F_1 trihybrid plants with the dominant phenotypes and the genotype *V Gl Va/v gl va* that carries three dominant alleles on one chromosome and three recessive alleles on the homolog. The F_1 were then test-crossed to pure-breeding yellow, glossy, variable plants (*v gl va/v gl va*). The test-cross progeny are shown in Table 5.3. To create a genetic map that

Table 5.3	Emerson's Three-Point Test-Cross Analysis		
Parental cross:	*V Gl Va/V Gl Va* Green, rough, normal	×	*v gl va/ v gl va* yellow, glossy, variable
Test cross:	*V Gl Va/v gl va* Green, rough, normal	×	*v gl va/v gl va* yellow, glossy, variable

Test-cross progeny:

Phenotype	Number Observed	Number Expected	Genotype (♀ gamete/♂ gamete)
1. Yellow, rough, normal	60	90.75	*v Gl Va/v gl va*
2. Yellow, glossy, normal	48	90.75	*v gl Va/v gl va*
3. Yellow, rough, variable	4	90.75	*v Gl va/v gl va*
4. Yellow, glossy, variable	270	90.75	*v gl va/v gl va*
5. Green, rough, normal	235	90.75	*V Gl Va/v gl va*
6. Green, glossy, normal	7	90.75	*V gl Va/v gl va*
7. Green, rough, variable	40	90.75	*V Gl va/v gl va*
8. Green, glossy, variable	62	90.75	*V gl va/v gl va*
	726	726	

places the three genes in correct relative order and to calculate recombination frequencies between gene pairs, we ask and answer five questions about these data:

1. Are the data consistent with the proposal of genetic linkage?
2. What alleles are on each parental chromosome?
3. What is the gene order on the chromosome?
4. What are the recombination frequencies of the gene pairs?
5. Is the frequency of double crossovers consistent with independence of the single crossovers?

Question 1: Are the Data Consistent with the Proposal of Genetic Linkage? Under the assumptions of independent assortment, trihybrid plants produce eight genetically different gametes at a frequency of 0.125, or 1/8, each, and test-cross progeny are expected in eight equally frequent phenotypic classes. In this experiment, with 726 test-cross progeny, the expected number of progeny in each class would be $(726)(0.125) = 90.75$. Chi-square analysis comparing observed and expected numbers of progeny in each class yields a chi-square value in excess of 800. There are $(8 - 1) = 7$ degrees of freedom, and the corresponding p value is $p < 0.005$. From this result, we conclude that the observed distribution of test-cross progeny deviates significantly from expectation, and we reject the independent assortment hypothesis as the explanation of these data.

If the deviation in this experiment is due to genetic linkage, then we would expect the numbers of progeny having parental phenotypes to be excessively high. Comparing the observed and expected values in each test-cross class shows that only two phenotype classes exceed expected numbers: the green, rough, normal class and the yellow, glossy, variable class. These are the two parental phenotypes. From this analysis, we conclude that the data are consistent with genetic linkage: the distribution of test-cross progeny deviates significantly from what would be expected from independent assortment, and only parental phenotypes are seen more often than expected by chance.

Question 2: What Alleles Are on Each Parental Chromosome? We can answer this question in two ways. The simpler approach is to use the phenotype information available about pure-breeding parental plants in the cross. The parent plants were pure-breeding dominant and pure-breeding recessive. From this information, we know that trihybrid F_1 plants have the dominant alleles on one chromosome and the recessive alleles on the homologous chromosome. The genetic structure of the test cross is $V\ Gl\ Va/v\ gl\ va \times v\ gl\ va/v\ gl\ va$, and so the alleles on parental chromosomes must be $V\ Gl\ Va$ and $v\ gl\ va$. Test-cross progeny Classes 4 and 5 in Table 5.3 are parentals.

The second approach is necessary when we do not know the phenotypes of parents or when the alleles on each chromosome are not known. In this approach, test-cross

data are used to determine parental chromosomes. The data in Table 5.3 indicate that the test-cross progeny in Class 5—green, rough, normal ($V\ Gl\ Va/v\ gl\ va$)—and in Class 4—yellow, glossy, variable ($v\ gl\ va/v\ gl\ va$)—exceed expected frequency and are therefore the parental classes. Both approaches tell us the same story: The parental chromosomes carry alleles $V\ Gl\ Va$ and $v\ gl\ va$.

Question 3: What Is the Gene Order on the Chromosome? With parental chromosomes identified, the six remaining classes must be recombinants: four are single-crossover classes, and two are double crossovers. Double-crossover progeny will be the least frequent of all classes, because *both* crossover events must occur simultaneously to produce **double recombinants,** or **double crossovers.** From progeny numbers, we may presume that the smallest classes, Class 3—yellow, rough, variable—and Class 6—green, glossy, normal—are the probable double recombinants. We can use these predictions to test possible gene orders on parental chromosomes.

For these three genes there are only three possible gene orders: (1) va–v–gl, (2) v–va–gl, or (3) va–gl–v. There are no data to assist us in determining the left-to-right orientation of the chromosome, so the difference between these gene orders is defined entirely by which gene is in the *middle*—v, va, or gl—and which two genes flank the middle gene. Each gene order could be written in the opposite direction, since each is a *relative* order of the three genes. For example, va–v–gl and gl–v–va are equivalent gene orders because each has v as the middle gene.

There are two ways to determine the gene order. One procedure is to list each gene order possible for the parental chromosomes, draw the corresponding double crossover chromosomes, and then determine whether the double crossover gametes produced by this activity match the predicted double crossover progeny. If a match is not seen, the gene order is incorrect, but if a match is found, the correct gene order has been identified.

1. Possible gene order va–v–gl

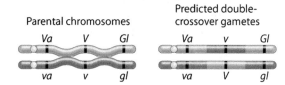

Result: Double-crossover gametes obtained from this gene order are not those predicted from the data.

Conclusion: The proposed gene order is incorrect; v is not the middle gene.

2. Possible gene order v–va–gl

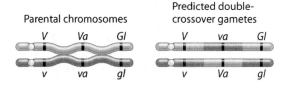

Result: Double-crossover gametes obtained from this gene order are not those predicted from the data.

Conclusion: The proposed gene order is incorrect; *va* is not the middle gene.

3. Possible gene order *v–gl–va*

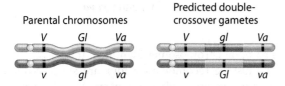

Parental chromosomes   Predicted double-crossover gametes

Result: Double-crossover gametes obtained from this gene order match those predicted from the data.

Conclusion: This proposed gene order is correct: *gl* is the middle gene, and the gene order may be written as either *v–gl–va* or *va–gl–v*. This analysis confirms that test-cross progeny Classes 3 and 6 are double-crossover progeny.

The second method for determining gene order is a shortcut approach that requires some familiarity with recombination. Looking back at Figure 5.7, note that if we compare parental and double-crossover chromosomes, the alleles of the outside genes appear to remain the same while the middle allele appears to switch. In other words, when we compare one parental chromosome with one double-recombinant chromosome, two alleles match and one does not. The odd one out is the allele in the middle. If a trihybrid parent has alleles arranged as $a^+b^+c^+/abc$, then double crossover produces gametes that are a^+bc^+/ab^+c. Parental alleles a^+ and c^+ match one double recombinant, and alleles b and b^+ are switched. Similarly, the second parental gamete has alleles a and c that match the other double recombinant. Alleles of the middle gene, b and b^+, have switched in the double recombinant compared to the parental chromosome.

Remember, we have already identified the parental and double-crossover phenotypic groups by their numbers. We now look at the double crossovers to see which two alleles match parental phenotypes and to see which allele changes and is therefore the middle gene. In our data set, double-recombinant chromosomes are *V gl Va* and *v Gl va*. In this case, alleles of the *gl* gene have switched, indicating that *gl* is the middle gene. Based on this approach, the gene orders and alleles on parental chromosomes are *V Gl Va* and *v gl va*.

Question 4: What Are the Recombination Frequencies of the Gene Pairs? Taking the gene pairs one at a time, we calculate the recombination frequencies by counting the total number of crossovers that occur between the genes of that pair. Every crossover event between the two genes is counted, whether the event occurs by itself (a single crossover) or simultaneously with another event (a double crossover). In this case, there are 11 double recombinants, each with one crossover between *v* and *gl* and one crossover between *gl* and *va*, for a total of 22 crossover events between *v* and *va*. Single-crossover progeny are

predicted on the basis of parental chromosomes having the gene order *v–gl–va*. Between *v* and *gl*, a single crossover produces the following.

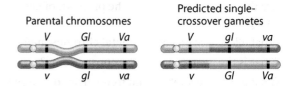

Parental chromosomes   Predicted single-crossover gametes

Test-cross progeny carrying these recombinant chromosomes have the phenotypes yellow, rough, normal (Class 1) and green, glossy, variable (Class 8). The recombination frequency is calculated as the sum of all single and double recombinants for this gene pair divided by the total number of progeny: 60 + 62 + 4 + 7/726 = 0.183, or 18.3%. Therefore, the distance between these genes is approximately 18.3 cM.

Single crossover between *gl* and *va* produces the following.

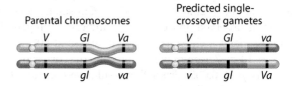

Parental chromosomes   Predicted single-crossover gametes

Test-cross progeny carrying these chromosomes are found in Class 2 (yellow, glossy, normal) and Class 7 (green, rough, variable). Recombination frequency r = 48 + 40 + 4 + 7/726 = 0.136, or 13.6%. The intergenic distance is approximately 13.6 cM.

Recombination between the flanking markers, *va* and *v*, is calculated by counting all crossovers between those genes. Recombination between *v* and *va* is r = 60 + 62 + 48 + 40 + 22/726 = 0.320, or 32%.

Question 5: Is the Frequency of Double Crossovers Consistent with Independence of the Single Crossovers? Asking and answering questions 1 through 4 identifies the alleles on each parental chromosome, and determines the gene order and recombination frequencies between genes. But in most tests of genetic linkage, the number of double crossovers is *less* than the number expected, and question 5 allows this common observation to be quantified. The reduction in the observed number of double crossovers is caused by an effect called **interference** (*I*), which limits the number of crossovers that can occur in a short length of chromosome. Interference, which we discuss further in Section 5.4, is quantified by comparing the number or frequency of observed double-crossover events to the number or frequency expected assuming each crossover event occurs independently. In Emerson's data set, there are 11 double crossovers among test-cross progeny, or (11/726) = 0.015 (1.5%). If each crossover were independent, expected double-crossover frequency would be the product of the two single-crossover frequencies, $(0.183)(0.136) = 0.025$ (2.5%). The expected number of double-crossover progeny would therefore be $(0.025)(726) = 18.2$. Observed double recombinants are divided by expected double recombinants, producing a value known as the **coefficient of coincidence** (*c*). Either the numbers or the frequencies of observed and expected double recombinants can be used to determine *c*:

$$c = \frac{\text{observed double recombinants}}{\text{expected double recombinants}}$$

$$= 11/18.2 = 0.60 \,(\text{using numbers})$$

or

$$= 0.015/0.025 = 0.60 \,(\text{using frequencies})$$

Interference is defined as $I = 1 - c$, so for this data set $I = 1 - 0.60 = 0.40$. Interference identifies the proportion of double recombinants that are expected but *are not produced* in the experiment (the difference between expectation and actuality). In this case, the number of double recombinants was 40% lower than expected. Interference is a very common observation in most regions of most genomes. On occasion, however, certain regions of some genomes generate *more* double recombinants than expected. In these cases $I < 0$, a situation called **negative interference.** Interference will be $I = 0$ when the observed and expected double crossovers are equal. The molecular basis of interference is not well understood, although current research shows that there is a mechanical limit that restricts the number of recombination events in a particular region of a chromosome.

Determining Gamete Frequencies from Genetic Maps

The same principle used to construct genetic linkage maps—the relation between relative distances and recombination frequency—can be used to make predictions in the opposite direction, that is, to determine the expected frequencies of recombinant gametes on the basis of completed genetic linkage maps.

In **Figure 5.8a**, two linked genes have a recombination frequency of 10%. For the dihybrid organism *AB/ab*, two gametes (*AB* and *ab*) are parental, and two (*Ab* and *aB*) are recombinant. Recombinant gametes equal 10% of total gametes, and each recombinant is expected to occur with the same frequency. The probability is calculated as $(1/2)(0.010) = 0.05$ for each recombinant gamete. In this calculation, 1/2 is the probability of each recombinant chromosome appearing in a gamete, and 0.010 is the probability of recombination between the genes. Conversely, parental gametes *AB* and *ab* are formed at a frequency equal to 100% minus 10%, or 90% of total gametes. Parental gametes are also expected at equal frequency—in this case $(1/2)(0.90)$, or 45% each.

Gamete frequencies for three linked genes are predicted in a similar manner. In **Figure 5.8b**, genes *a* and *b* are shown along with a third gene, *c*, located 20 cM from gene *b*. To predict gamete frequencies, we make the assumption that interference is $I = 0$ to simplify the calculation of the number of recombinants. For the trihybrid *ABC/abc*, parental gametes are produced when

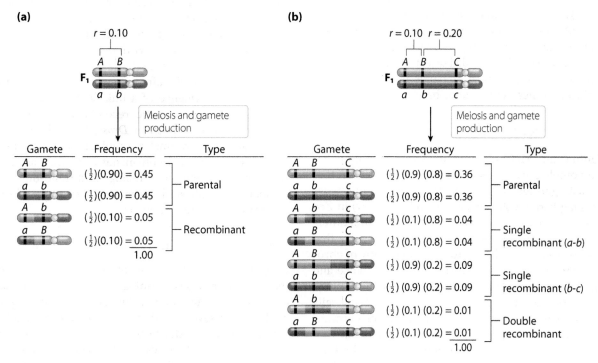

Figure 5.8 **Gamete genotype frequencies calculated from genetic linkage data.** (a) Gamete frequencies predicted from a map of two linked genes. (b) Gametes predicted from a map of three linked genes assuming interference is zero ($I = 0$).

crossover does not occur in either gene interval. The probability of *no crossovers* between genes *a* and *b* is 90% (0.9), and between *b* and *c* it is 80% (0.8). Considering both gene pairs, the proportion of nonrecombinant gametes is $(0.9)(0.8) = 0.72$. There are two equally frequent parental gametes, each with an expected frequency of $(0.72)(0.5) = 0.36$. Recombination frequency is 10% (0.1) between *a* and *b*. Two single recombinants between genes *a* and *b* have an expected frequency of $(0.1)(0.8)(0.5) = 0.04$ each. Similarly, single recombinants between genes *b* and *c* have expected frequencies of $(0.9)(0.2)(0.5) = 0.09$ each. Each of the double-recombinant gametes, *AbC* and *aBc*, are expected with a frequency of $(0.1)(0.2)(0.5) = 0.01$. The sum of frequencies of the eight predicted gamete genotypes is 1.0, indicating that all gametes have been counted.

5.4 Recombination Results from Crossing Over

Morgan's hypothesis of recombination by crossing over between homologous chromosomes has stood the test of time and is now universally accepted. When he proposed it, Morgan's model fit nicely with a 1909 observation by F. A. Janssens, who captured a view of meiotic chromosomes under the microscope and suggested that the chiasmata seen between homologous chromosomes might be points of recombination. Clear proof of the hypothesis of gene recombination by chromosome exchange was not obtained, however, until 20 years after Morgan proposed it. In 1931, research published by Harriet Creighton and Barbara McClintock on crossing over in corn (*Zea mays*), and a nearly simultaneous report by Curt Stern on crossing over in *Drosophila*, provided direct evidence that gene recombination and physical exchange between homologous chromosomes went hand-in-hand.

Cytological Evidence of Recombination

Creighton and McClintock studied recombination between homologous copies of chromosome 9 in corn that were distinguished by two genetic markers—the genes controlling kernel color (*c1*) and starch type (*wx*) In *Zea mays*—and by two cytological markers—structural differences in the homologous copies of chromosome 9 that were observed under the microscope. One copy of chromosome 9 had the normal microscopic appearance and carried alleles *c1* and *Wx*. The homologous copy of chromosome 9 carried alleles *C1* and *wx* and was cytologically altered in two ways. On the end nearer *C1*, the chromosome had a darkly staining region called a "knob"; on the other end, near *wx*, the chromosome carried a fragment of chromosome 8 that had been transferred by a chromosome-rearrangement event called *translocation* (we explore this event in Section 13.4). Creighton and

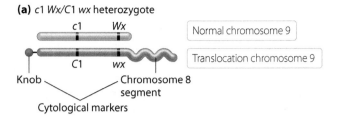

(a) c1 Wx/C1 wx heterozygote

Normal chromosome 9

Translocation chromosome 9

Knob — Chromosome 8 segment

Cytological markers

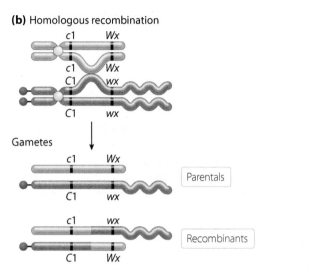

(b) Homologous recombination

Gametes

Parentals

Recombinants

Figure 5.9 **Cytological proof from *Zea mays* that recombination results from crossing over.** Progeny displaying recombinant phenotypes are also seen to carry physically rearranged chromosomes.

McClintock obtained cytological evidence that recombination involved the physical exchange between homologous chromosomes by detecting genetic recombinants (chromosomes carrying the alleles *C1* and *Wx* or carrying the alleles *c1* and *wx*) that were also cytologically rearranged chromosomes (**Figure 5.9**).

Just a few weeks after Creighton and McClintock reported their evidence of a link between chromosome rearrangement and genetic recombination, Curt Stern reported similar findings in *Drosophila*. The combined genetic and chromosomal recombination analyses in corn and fruit fly provided convincing evidence that genetic recombination between homologous chromosomes is accompanied by physical exchange between the chromosomes in plants and in animals.

Limits of Recombination along Chromosomes

Creighton, McClintock, and Stern showed convincingly that crossover is accompanied by chromosome breakage and rejoining. Morgan and Sturtevant's work, supported by data from several of their contemporaries, established that the relative distance between two linked genes on a chromosome influences the frequency of recombination between them. Two important questions about the likelihood and frequency of crossing over derive from these observations. First, why does distance between genes influence recombination frequency? And second, is there an upper limit to the frequency of recombinant gametes for a pair of linked genes?

The answer to the first question is that in early prophase I, points of crossing over are established at recombination nodules that occur along the synaptonemal complex (see Section 3.2). Two genes that are close to one another are less likely to have a recombination nodule between them and are less likely to recombine than are a pair of genes separated by a greater distance on a chromosome.

Recombination occurs after DNA replication has been completed, when each member of a homologous chromosome pair is composed of two sister chromatids. This is the four-strand stage. Single crossovers involve one chromatid from each homolog. There are four equivalent ways this process can occur, and all four events produce the same outcome—two parental gametes and two recombinant gametes (Figure 5.10a). Crossovers that occur between nonsister chromatids but not between the loci tested will not leave genetic evidence of recombination (Figure 5.10b).

There are three patterns of double crossover between two genes. The outcomes of each pattern are unique with respect to the number of recombinant gametes produced. **Two-strand double crossover** produces no recombinants, because two recombination events between a pair of genes do not produce genetic evidence of recombination in the form of a recombinant gamete (Figure 5.11a). A **three-strand double crossover,** involving three of the sister chromatids, can happen in two ways that each produce

the same genetic outcome—two parental and two recombinant chromosomes in gametes (Figure 5.11b). When a **four-strand double crossover** occurs, all four chromosomes in gametes are recombinant (Figure 5.11c).

In answer to the second question we posed earlier, recombination between a pair of linked genes is limited to 50% of the gametes. As we have seen, of the four gametes produced by single crossover, two are recombinant gametes (have the nonparental genotype) and so result in a total of 50% recombinant. Likewise, summing the outcomes of the example two-, three-, and four-strand double crossovers shown in Figure 5.11 gives a total of 8/16 (50%) recombinant gametes. This establishes an upper limit of 50% as the frequency of both parental and nonparental genotypes in gametes. Most instances of genetic linkage produce substantially more than 50% parental chromosomes and substantially less than 50% nonparental. The smallest proportions of recombinant chromosomes are associated with the most tightly linked genes (i.e., the genes that are closest together), and the recombinant proportions increase as the distance between genes becomes greater. Recombination frequencies between *linked* genes can increase *up to* 50% as the distance between genes gets larger, and the corresponding frequency of parental chromosomes *decreases* to 50%. Thus, frequencies of recombination between linked genes are always less than 50%. Once there is sufficient distance between syntenic genes, however, crossover randomizes the combinations of alleles on chromosomes, and the pattern becomes that of independent assortment. In other words, syntenic genes that are far apart assort independently.

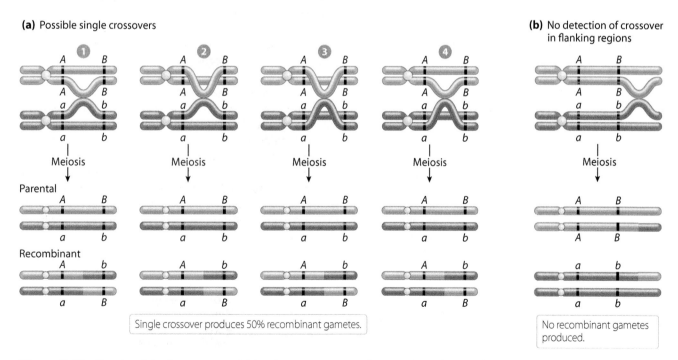

(a) Possible single crossovers

(b) No detection of crossover in flanking regions

Single crossover produces 50% recombinant gametes.

No recombinant gametes produced.

Figure 5.10 Results of single crossover. (a) Single crossovers occur between homologous chromosomes in multiple ways. Each meiosis produces two parental chromosomes and two recombinant chromosomes, thus 50% of gametes can carry recombinant chromosomes. **(b)** Single crossover taking place outside the chromosome region being tested does not reveal recombinant chromosomes.

(a) Two-strand double crossover
(three equivalent ways, one position held constant)

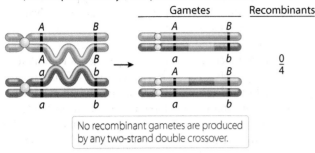

No recombinant gametes are produced by any two-strand double crossover.

(b) Three-strand double crossover (one position held constant)

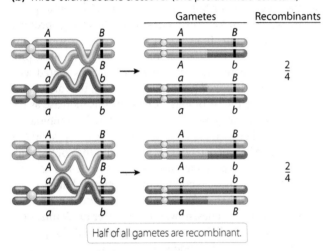

Half of all gametes are recombinant.

(c) Four-strand double crossover (one position held constant)

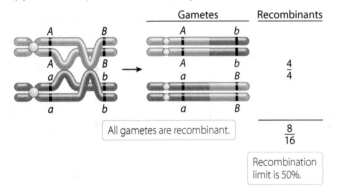

All gametes are recombinant.

$$\frac{8}{16}$$

Recombination limit is 50%.

Figure 5.11 Results of double crossover. Double crossovers between two genes involving two, three, or all four chromatids result collectively in a maximum of 50% recombinant gametes.

Genetic Analysis 5.2 presents the results of test crosses involving three linked genes and takes you through the determination of recombination frequencies between the genes.

Recombination within Genes

Our discussion thus far describes how the linear order of genes along chromosomes can be determined based on crossover *between* genes. Does crossover ever occur *within* genes? The answer is yes.

Crossing over within genes, called **intragenic recombination,** is an infrequent event that is detected through the examination of large numbers of progeny, usually for evidence of recombination between homologs carrying different mutant alleles of the same gene. Since the site of mutation within the gene is different for each allele, intragenic recombination produces one wild-type recombinant chromosome and one double-mutant chromosome.

Melvin Green and Kathleen Green were the first to report intragenic recombination in a 1949 study of the *Drosophila* gene for an X-linked recessive mutant eye phenotype called "lozenge," which disrupts the number and pattern of facets on the eye of the fly. Several different mutations of the lozenge gene each produce a distinctive lozenge phenotype. The Greens (a husband and wife team), following up on work begun a few years earlier by Clarence Oliver, used lozenge-eyed females, each carrying two different lozenge-producing alleles, lz^{BS} and lz^g, on the homologous copies of their X chromosomes (**Figure 5.12**). The lozenge mutations are located at different positions within the lozenge gene; each mutant allele has mutant DNA sequence at the site of mutation but has wild-type DNA sequence in the rest of the gene. Rare intragenic recombination leads to one double-mutant X chromosome carrying both lozenge mutations in a single gene, and a wild-type X chromosome with a lozenge gene that contains neither mutation. The double-mutant chromosomes produce a phenotype that is distinct from either of the mutations alone. The Greens detected fewer than 20 double-mutant X chromosomes and the wild-type X chromosome in more than 16,000 progeny of the lozenge-eyed females, but the result was sufficient to verify intragenic recombination.

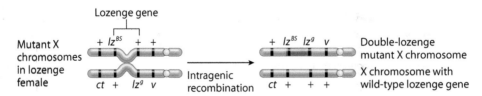

Figure 5.12 Intragenic recombination in the lozenge eye gene of *Drosophila*. Progeny resulting from intragenic recombination can be detected by a distinct lozenge phenotype produced by the double-mutant chromosome or by having wild-type eyes. The genes *ct* and *v* are used to verify intragenic recombination.

PROBLEM Dr. O. Sophila, a famous geneticist, is evaluating genetic linkage among three X-linked genes in *Drosophila*. At these genes, red eye (v^+) is dominant to vermilion eye (v); full wing (r^+) is dominant to rudimentary wing (r); and gray body color (y^+) is dominant to yellow (y). Dr. Sophila has the results of three test crosses. Help Dr. Sophila identify which pairs of genes are linked, and calculate the recombination frequency between linked genes.

> **BREAK IT DOWN:** Test-cross progeny allow each allele to be assigned to a chromosome (p. 154).

> **BREAK IT DOWN:** If genes are linked, the frequency of progeny with parental phenotypes will be significantly greater than expected by chance (p. 155).

Test Cross I:

♀ *yv/++* (gray body, red eye) ×
♂ *yv/Y* (yellow body, vermilion eye)

Progeny	Number
Yellow, vermilion	338
Gray, red	332
Yellow, red	160
Gray, vermilion	170
	1000

Test Cross II:

♀ *vr/++* (red eye, full wing) ×
♂ *vr/Y* (vermilion eye, rudimentary wing)

Progeny	Number
Vermilion, rudimentary	396
Red, full	389
Vermilion, full	110
Red, rudimentary	105
	1000

Test Cross III:

♀ *yr/++* (gray body, full wing) ×
♂ *yr/Y* (yellow body, rudimentary wing)

Progeny	Number
Yellow, rudimentary	246
Gray, full	252
Yellow, full	259
Gray, rudimentary	243
	1000

Solution Strategies	Solution Steps

Evaluate

1. Identify the topic of this problem and the nature of the required answer.

1. This problem involves the assessment of three test crosses involving X-linked genes. The answer requires determination of genetic linkage versus independent assortment for each gene pair and, for linked genes, the calculation of recombination frequency.

2. Identify the critical information given in the problem.

2. The genotypes and phenotypes of test-cross flies are given, and the number of test-cross progeny in each phenotypic category is also given.

Deduce

3. Determine the test-cross results expected under the assumption of independent assortment.

3. In each cross, the dihybrid female would be expected to produce four genetically different gametes at frequencies of 25% each and the progeny would be expected to display four phenotypes in a 1:1:1:1 ratio (250 each). In Test cross I, for example, the following results would be expected, and expected results would be similar for the other test crosses as well.

Phenotype	Female	Male	Number
Yellow, vermilion	*yv/yv*	*yv/Y*	250
Gray, red	*yv/y⁺v⁺*	*y⁺v⁺/y*	250
Yellow, red	*yv/yv⁺*	*yv⁺/Y*	250
Gray, vermilion	*yv/y⁺v*	*y⁺v/Y*	250

> **TIP:** Chi-square analysis could be used to test the statistical significance of deviations between observed and expected outcomes.

Solve

4. Examine each cross and determine if there is evidence of genetic linkage between the gene pairs.

4. Test cross I and Test cross II show clear deviation from the predicted ratio, with parental categories substantially greater than 250 each and nonparental categories substantially less than 250 each. The progeny of Test cross III are distributed in numbers consistent with the independent assortment prediction. These statements are based on chi-squared analysis that is not shown.

5. Calculate the recombination frequencies between linked pairs of genes.

5. In Test cross I, the recombinant progeny are yellow, red and gray, vermilion. $r = 160 + 170/1000 = 0.330$, indicating that these genes are linked and are separated by 33 m.u.

In Test cross II, the recombinant phenotypes are vermilion, full and red, rudimentary. The recombination frequency is $r = 110 + 105/1000 = 0.215$, or approximately 21.5 m.u.

For more practice, see Problems 2, 4, and 28.   Visit the Study Area to access study tools.   **Mastering**Genetics™

Biological Factors Affecting Accuracy of Genetic Maps

Inherent in the use of recombination frequency as a measure of approximate distance between genes along a chromosome is the assumption that genetic distance and physical distance are proportional throughout the genome and that recombination frequencies for given genes are constant among all members of a species. However, studies in numerous species indicate that age, environment, sex, and other, as yet undetermined, factors may affect recombination frequency and may affect the relationship between the genetic recombination map and the physical map of a chromosome. For example, advancing age of female fruit flies decreases the frequency of crossover between gene pairs; more crossovers between a specific pair of genes are seen in younger females than in older. Female *Drosophila* crossover frequency is also affected by temperature. Growth of a fruit-fly colony at 22°C is optimal for recombination, and increases or decreases of temperature from optimum can change crossover frequency. Restricting dietary levels of calcium and magnesium, important cofactors for enzymes that interact with DNA, also decreases crossover frequency in fruit flies.

The most dramatic impact on recombination frequency in animals, however, is connected to sex. Recombination frequency differs for males and females of most animal species and follows a general pattern in which the heterogametic sex, the sex with two different sex chromosomes (most often males), has a lower rate of recombination than the homogametic sex, the sex with two fully homologous sex chromosomes (most often females). The higher recombination frequency in the homogametic sex is a genome-wide phenomenon and *is not* limited to the sex chromosomes. Fruit flies display an extreme version of this phenomenon— female fruit flies undergo homologous recombination while male fruit flies undergo no recombination at all!

These observations are seen across the taxonomic spectrum, including in humans. Human females experience more crossing over than human males, resulting in a larger recombination map in females. A detailed recombination and genome sequencing analysis of human chromosome 19 exemplifies this phenomenon. Chromosome 19 is composed of about 65 megabases (Mb), or 65 million base pairs, in both male and female genomes (**Figure 5.13**). However, the length of the chromosome as determined by adding the estimated recombination distances along the entire length of the chromosome is a larger number of map units in females than in males. Also notice that recombination frequencies are greater in regions at the ends of the chromosome in males but are greater in females in central chromosome regions. For the human genome as a whole, the female genetic map contains about 4400 cM, and the male map about 2700 cM. Geneticists studying the human genome usually produce a "sex averaged" human genetic map that is slightly larger than 3500 cM.

Among different species, the number of nucleotide base pairs per map unit varies. For example, the human

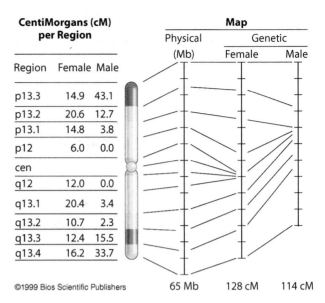

| CentiMorgans (cM) per Region | | |
Region	Female	Male
p13.3	14.9	43.1
p13.2	20.6	12.7
p13.1	14.8	3.8
p12	6.0	0.0
cen		
q12	12.0	0.0
q13.1	20.4	3.4
q13.2	10.7	2.3
q13.3	12.4	15.5
q13.4	16.2	33.7

©1999 Bios Scientific Publishers

65 Mb   128 cM   114 cM

Figure 5.13   Physical distance versus recombination distance on human male and female chromosome 19. In most sexually reproducing organisms, the heterogametic sex has fewer recombination events and a shorter recombination map than does the homogametic sex. Data adapted from J. L. Weber et al. (1993).

genome consists of a little less than 3 billion base pairs of DNA and the sex-averaged genome contains about 830,000 bp/cM. In contrast, the *Arabidopsis* genome contains about 200,000 bp/cM; thus, recombination is about four times as frequent in *Arabidopsis* as it is in humans.

Recombination Is Dominated by Hotspots

Estimates of average numbers of base pairs per centiMorgan, of the average recombination frequency for a species, and of distances in a sex-averaged recombination map such as the one described for humans are just that: averaged estimates. In contrast, genome-based information on organisms has led to the creation of fine-scale genetic maps of species that identify the distribution of recombination across the genome with much greater precision. Detailed assessment of recombination in human, mouse, and yeast genomes reveals a highly variable pattern of recombination within each genome that has led to the identification of **recombination hotspots** and **recombination coldspots** although in most cases, genetic recombination maps reveal proportionality between recombination frequencies and the physical maps of chromosomes.

Genetic recombination maps are generated by analysis of recombination information and recombination frequency data. Physical maps of chromosomes, on the other hand, are based on genomic sequence data that identify specific genes within DNA sequence. The proportionality between genetic recombination maps and physical maps of a chromosome makes it possible to generate maps that locate the position and approximate distance between genes along a chromosome. This proportionality exists because almost all regions of DNA are about equally likely to initiate recombination.

Nevertheless, as noted above, many genomes do contain hotspots and coldspots of recombination—segments of chromosomes that undergo substantially more or substantially less recombination than the average for a species.

Studies in yeast have examined this phenomenon in detail, and one study of yeast chromosomes has identified hotspots and coldspots side by side. In Figure 5.14, the coldspot of recombination between *spo7* and *cdc15* results in mapping data that appear to place the genes closer to one another than they are in the physical map. In contrast, the hotspot between *cdc15* and *FLO1* makes them appear to be farther apart on the genetic recombination map than on the physical map of the chromosome. The other genes in this chromosome region have generally good proportionality between recombination and physical distances.

The reason for the existence of hotspots and coldspots of recombination may have to do with the ability of DNA regions near specific genes to initiate the molecular events associated with the first steps of crossing over. In the case

of the coldspot between *spo7* and *cdc15* in yeast, the chromosome centromere is between the genes, which may be an additional factor contributing to the relatively low recombination between those genes. We discuss more about the molecular process of recombination in Section 12.7.

Correction of Genetic Map Distances

Many factors affect crossing over and recombination in eukaryotic genomes. Different genetic recombination maps for the two sexes of a species, age- and temperature-dependent variation in recombination in *Drosophila* females, and hotspots and coldspots of recombination scattered within the genome are examples of the influence of various factors on recombination. Given these diverse and sometimes species-specific effects, it is reasonable to ask whether recombination frequencies and map distances calculated on the basis of observed recombination between gene pairs are in fact fully accurate representations of the actual numbers of recombination events. The answer is no. Experimental evidence indicates that the map distances calculated between two randomly selected genes usually *underestimate* the physical distance between the genes, largely because of undetected crossovers between them. The farther apart two syntenic genes are, the greater the inaccuracy, because double crossovers between a pair of genes are not detected as recombinant for flanking markers.

A single crossover between genes *A* and *B* in a dihybrid (*AB/ab*) produces two parental gametes (*AB* and *ab*) and two recombinant gametes (*Ab* and *aB*). As illustrated in Figure 5.11, however, a double crossover between the same genes produces crossover gametes that are not recombinant for flanking markers and are indistinguishable from parentals. These crossover-nonrecombinant gametes are not counted when recombination frequency between genes is calculated, because they are not observed. Larger distances between genes provide greater opportunity for double crossover and thus greater likelihood of crossover-nonrecombinant gametes.

In theory, the relationship between recombination frequency and map distance is linear, but this is not the case in reality. Line ❶ in Figure 5.15 depicts a linear relationship between recombination frequency and the distance in map units (cM). In contrast, line ❷ illustrates that relationship as actually measured in organisms. The lines diverge at about 8 cM, indicating that the relationship between recombination frequency and map distance is linear only for linked genes that are separated by less than 8 cM, and that observed recombination frequencies usually underestimate the physical distance between genes.

The central problem in correlating recombination frequency with the number of recombination events is the difficulty of identifying the number of meioses that produce each possible number of crossovers—zero, one, two, three, four, and so on. In an attempt to correctly model different recombination classes and to accurately assess the correlation between recombination

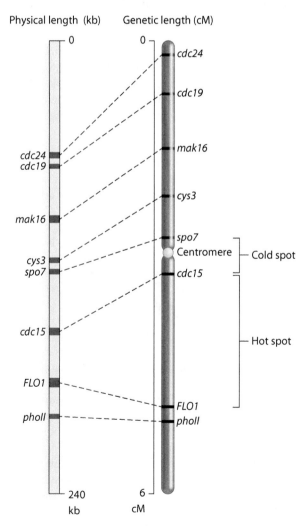

Figure 5.14 Comparison of the physical map and recombination map of yeast chromosome 1. A hotspot of recombination is detected between *cdc15* and *FLO1*. A coldspot of recombination occurs between *spo7* and *cdc15*.

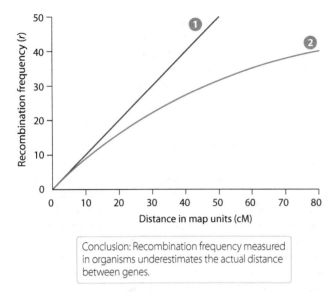

Conclusion: Recombination frequency measured in organisms underestimates the actual distance between genes.

Figure 5.15   The relationship between recombination frequency and physical distance between genes. Line **1** traces a linear relationship between recombination frequency and the physical distance separating linked genes. Line **2** traces the observed correspondence between recombination frequency and physical distance.

frequency and crossover, J. B. S. Haldane developed a **mapping function** in 1919 that correlates map distance and recombination frequency between gene pairs. The Haldane mapping function has limitations, and several researchers proposed modifications of it to account for specific conditions affecting recombination in different species.

One consistent concern raised about Haldane's mapping function is that it may overestimate the actual recombination frequency when interference occurs. Damodar Kosambi developed a modified mapping function to correct map distance in species with interference, and it has become one of the most widely applied improvements.

Mapping functions are a quantitative solution to the issue of variability of recombination frequencies across the genome and between species. Meanwhile, the advent of genomic sequence analysis, and the ability to precisely compare recombination maps and physical maps, will continue to generate insight into recombination. Genetic maps are continually subject to refinement, and while the most accurate maps are constructed by summing many small intervals between genes, the precision in gene mapping keeps evolving more than 100 years after Alfred Sturtevant deduced the first genetic map.

5.5 Linked Human Genes Are Mapped Using Lod Score Analysis

Until relatively recently, the human genetic map was rather sparse. Humans cannot be studied through controlled matings and in any case produce much smaller

numbers of offspring than do organisms like *Drosophila* and *Zea mays*. Consequently, gene-mapping methods developed and used successfully to map genes in model organisms are difficult to apply to human gene mapping. Historically, X-linked genes, by virtue of their unique patterns of transmission, were the first and easiest human genes to map, whereas progress in mapping human autosomal genes was hampered by a scarcity of known polymorphic genetic markers, such as blood group antigens and blood proteins.

Human genome mapping changed significantly in the mid-1980s, facilitated both by the emergence of molecular genetic methods to identify polymorphic DNA markers and by advances in gene-mapping software. Different types of polymorphic DNA markers, including restriction fragment length polymorphisms (RFLPs) and single nucleotide polymorphisms (SNPs) (described in Section 10.2), ultimately made thousands of new human genetic markers available for study in linkage analysis. Combined with sophisticated statistical techniques and modern computer power, the use of polymorphic DNA markers has given geneticists the ability to effectively map human genes by genetic linkage analysis.

The availability of large numbers of DNA markers on each chromosome led first to the identification of **linkage groups**, clusters of syntenic genes that are linked to one another, and then to assignment of chromosomal locations to linkage groups. The discovery of genetic linkage between a genetic marker with a known chromosome location and any member of a linkage group assigns the linkage group to a chromosome location near the genetic marker. Different linkage groups on the same chromosome can then be organized into maps of chromosome segments and whole chromosomes.

Allelic Phase

Efforts to map human genes often focus on finding the chromosomal locations of disease-causing genes. This is a common first step toward the eventual cloning and sequencing of a gene that may be the cause of hereditary disease. A strategy known as *functional cloning*, or *reverse genetics* (see Section 16.2), can be used to map a gene whose function is not known. Once the location of the gene is identified, the gene can be cloned and sequenced, and the sequence can be examined for clues to the normal function of the gene and to the mechanisms by which gene mutation produces inherited abnormalities.

To map genes, parental and recombinant chromosomes must be identified, and one of the first obstacles researchers encounter in the effort to map human genes is the difficulty of determining **allelic phase,** a term referring to which alleles of linked genes are on each parental chromosome. Knowing allelic phase improves the statistical power of genetic linkage estimates. **Figure 5.16** illustrates how allelic phase is identified in a family, and it points to

(a)

Family A

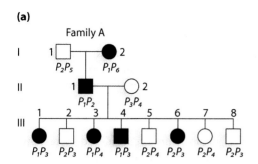

Figure 5.16 **Allelic phase analysis in human families A and B.**

(b)

Family B

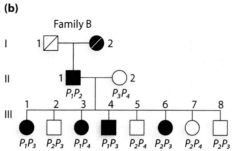

Allelic phase is known in family A by tracing the transmission of the disease allele (D) and the P_1 genetic marker allele from I-2 to II-1 and to III-1, III-3 and III-4; III-6 is a probable recombinant.

Allelic phase is not known in family B because the disease allele carried by II-1 could be on either the chromosome carrying genetic marker allele P_1 or the chromosome carrying P_2.

the importance of key individuals in determining allelic phase. The two pedigrees in the figure are identical in structure and in the distribution of an autosomal dominant hereditary disease indicated by shaded symbols. Notice, however, that individuals I-1 and I-2 are alive and are genotyped for the genetic marker in Family A but not in Family B. The alleles of the gene determining the disease phenotype are D and d. In addition to allelic information for the disease locus, the pedigrees show allelic information for a closely linked polymorphic DNA marker that has six alleles identified as P_1 to P_6.

Allelic phase is known to be $P_1 D$ in Family A because the affected woman in generation I (I-2) transmits marker allele P_1 along with the dominant disease allele (D) to her son, II-1. The unaffected man in generation I (I-1) is homozygous for the recessive wild-type allele (dd) at the disease locus and heterozygous for DNA marker alleles P_2 and P_5. Allelic phase in II-1 is $P_1 D/P_2 d$; the chromosome on the left of the solidus (/) is maternal, the chromosome on the right paternal. Considering that his mate (II-2) is $P_3 d/P_4 d$, we can identify the transmission of parental and recombinant gametes from II-1 to his children in generation III. Children III-1, III-3, and III-4 inherited a paternal chromosome carrying P_1D to produce their disease and either the P_3 or P_4 allele along with d on their maternal chromosome. On the other hand, III-2, III-5, III-7, and III-8 inherited alleles P_2 and d on their paternal chromosome and either P_3 or P_4 along with d on their maternal chromosome. Child III-6 has apparently inherited a recombinant chromosome carrying alleles P_2 and D from her father along with P_3 and d on the maternal chromosome.

The pedigree for Family B does not allow identification of allelic phase. In this family, there is no marker information for generation I, and thus allelic phase for II-1 is unknown. He could either be $P_1 D/P_2 d$ or $P_1 d/P_2 D$. For the purposes of genetic linkage analysis, each possible phase must be treated as equally likely. With allelic phase in II-1 unknown, we cannot be certain which of his children have inherited parental chromosomes and

which carry recombinants. If II-1 is $P_1 D/P_2 d$, his children III-1 to III-5, and III-7 and III-8 are parental, and III-6 is recombinant. Alternatively, if he is $P_1 d/P_2 D$, then III-1 to III-5 and III-7 and III-8 are recombinant and III-6 is parental.

Lod Score Analysis

Although it is not possible to unambiguously identify and count recombinants in pedigrees like Family B, a statistical method developed by Newton Morton in 1955, and refined and expanded since then, allows geneticists to calculate the overall probability of genetic linkage. Morton's method determines whether genetic linkage exists between genes for which allelic phase is unknown by comparing the likelihood of obtaining the genotypes and phenotypes observed in a pedigree if two genes are linked versus the likelihood of getting the same pedigree outcomes if the genes assort independently. The ratio of these two likelihoods gives the "odds" of genetic linkage, and the logarithm of the odds ratio generates the **lod score,** a statistical value representing the probability of genetic linkage between the genes.

The numerator of the odds ratio that yields the lod score is the likelihood that the distribution of phenotypes and genotypes in the pedigree is produced by genetic linkage between the genes. The denominator is the likelihood of the same pedigree outcomes assuming independent assortment between the genes (i.e., no genetic linkage). Lod score analysis evaluates each pedigree and determines the likelihood of genetic linkage for many different recombination frequencies, each expressed as a variable called the θ **value** ("theta value"). Using input data on each family member that identifies presence or absence of the disease and the genotype at a potentially linked marker gene, software programs calculate the likelihoods of genetic linkage versus no linkage between the genes and compute lod scores for each θ value specified by the investigator. The θ values are any recombination frequency between $\theta = 0$ (complete genetic linkage) and $\theta = 0.50$ (independent assortment). The programs determine lod scores, and because they are log values, the lod scores for a given θ value in different families can be added together. After analyzing all available family data, the lod scores for each θ value are summed and the highest lod score value obtained in a study is designated $\mathbf{Z_{max}}$. The Z_{max} corresponds to the θ value that is the most likely recombination frequency between the genes tested.

For each θ value tested, the lod score will be positive if the likelihood of genetic linkage is greater than the likelihood of independent assortment, because in that case, the numerator value (likelihood assuming genetic linkage) is greater than the denominator value (likelihood assuming independent assortment). Conversely, if the pedigree is more likely to be produced by independent assortment than by genetic linkage, the independent assortment likelihood will be larger than the genetic linkage likelihood, and the lod score will be negative.

Lod scores are calculated using the assumption that if two genes have a recombination frequency equal to θ, the probability that a particular gamete is recombinant is also equal to θ, and the probability that a gamete is nonrecombinant is 1 − θ. **Table 5.4** shows calculated lod score values for the two families shown in Figure 5.16. Notice that the lod scores are higher for Family A than for Family B. This is because with allelic phase known in Family A, the likelihood estimate for genetic linkage between the disease gene and the marker gene is more accurate and leads to a higher probability of genetic linkage in this case. For each child in generation III, the probability that the gamete from the mother is parental is 1 − θ, and the probability that a recombinant gamete is transmitted from mother to child is θ. Since allelic phase is known for Family A, only the known phase is tested. In contrast, Family B does not have a known allelic phase; thus, each possible phase is assumed to be equally likely. In the Family B lod score computation, each phase is tested and is part of the numerator. Because a known allelic phase produces more genetic linkage information, the lod scores for Family A are greater than the lod scores for Family B. In the context of lod score analysis, Family A is identified as the more informative of the two pedigrees.

A lod score is a statistic that can argue in favor of genetic linkage, if the probability of genetic linkage is sufficiently greater than the probability of independent assortment, or it can argue against genetic linkage, if the probability of independent assortment is sufficiently greater than the linkage probability. Lod scores can be interpreted for individual families, or they can be added together for as many families as are analyzed. In either case, lod score significance is interpreted by the following parameters:

1. A lod score of 3.0 or greater is considered significant evidence *in favor* of genetic linkage. Such a score indicates significant odds of genetic linkage at each θ value at which it occurs. The θ values identified as significant indicate the most likely number of centiMorgans between linked genes.

2. Lod score values of less than −2.0 represent significant evidence *against* genetic linkage. Any lod score values for single or multiple families less than −2.0 reject genetic linkage at each θ value with that result.

3. Lod score values between 3.0 and −2.0 are inconclusive, neither affirming nor rejecting genetic linkage between the genes examined. Inconclusive results can be revised as additional data are collected.

The three lod score curves shown in **Figure 5.17** illustrate that lod score results may produce different

Table 5.4	Lod Score Values for the Families in Figure 5.16				
Family A (Phase Known)					
θ value	0	0.1	0.2	0.3	0.4	0.5
Lod score	−∞	1.09	1.03	0.80	0.46	0.0
Family B (Phase Unknown)					
θ value	0	0.1	0.2	0.3	0.4	0.5
Lod score	−∞	0.79	0.73	0.50	0.19	0.0

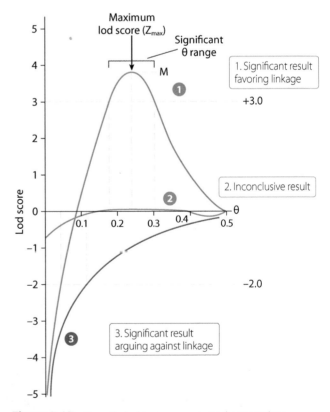

Figure 5.17 **Sample lod score curves.** Lod score values (vertical axis) are plotted against recombination fractions (θ values, horizontal axis) for three hypothetical lod score analyses.

Mapping a Gene for Breast and Ovarian Cancer Susceptibility

Most cases of cancer develop through the acquisition of multiple mutations in somatic cells, meaning that there is no inherited mutation that increases the likelihood of cancer development. In some families, however, the frequent occurrence of a particular kind of cancer in a pattern consistent with single-gene inheritance can suggest the hereditary transmission of a mutant allele that increases the susceptibility of individuals to the cancer. The identity, indeed the very existence of these genes, is not known until they are conclusively shown to contribute to cancer development. One research strategy to identify cancer-susceptibility genes seeks genetic linkage of susceptibility genes to genetic markers that have a known chromosome location.

In the late 1970s, Mary Claire King and several collaborators devised a strategy in a search for a gene whose mutation could increase susceptibility to breast and ovarian cancer in families. King and her colleagues sought to maximize the chance of finding such a cancer-susceptibility gene by carefully selecting families in which multiple cases of breast and ovarian cancers appeared at young ages, and in which occasional cases of bilateral cancer occurred (affecting both breasts or both ovaries in a single patient) in patterns consistent with an autosomal dominant inheritance of disease susceptibility.

King initially looked for genetic linkage between inherited cancer susceptibility and biochemical markers such as polymorphic blood proteins and enzymes. None of the dozens of biochemical markers screened produced significant evidence of genetic linkage to a breast and ovarian cancer susceptibility gene. In the early 1990s, however, King and her colleagues turned to the use of DNA genetic markers. Then, in 1994, they identified genetic linkage between a group of tightly clustered DNA markers on human chromosome 17 and a gene named *Breast Cancer 1* (*BRCA1*). Lod score analysis of chromosome 17, as summarized in the following table, revealed that the candidate gene has a Z_{max} value of 21.68 at $\theta = 0.13$.

Five genetic markers that are part of a multipoint linkage analysis are shown. *BRCA1* is most likely close to the middle of this linkage group, near the DNA marker gene *D17S588*.

Subsequent studies have identified and cloned the *BRCA1* gene and determined that it participates with a second gene called *BRCA2* in DNA mutation repair. A large number of mutations of *BRCA1* have been identified, and some of them dramatically increase the likelihood that a woman will develop breast or ovarian cancer. Other mutations of *BRCA1* do not appear to significantly increase breast or ovarian cancer risk. A good deal of work remains to be done to clarify the role of this gene in breast and ovarian cancer development, but the research strategy designed by King demonstrates the power of genetic linkage analysis for locating genes of interest. (We discuss more about *BRCA1* and *BRCA2* in Chapter 12).

Lod Score Data for Linkage of *BRCA1* to Chromosome 17q in Humans

Genetic Marker	Lod Scores at Recombination (θ) Values							
	0.001	0.01	0.05	0.10	0.20	0.30	Z_{max}	θ_{max}
D17S250	−11.98	−8.96	−1.20	3.81	7.30	6.65	7.42	0.23
D17S579	−1.43	1.62	8.55	12.08	12.55	9.17	13.02	0.16
D17S588	8.23	11.39	18.35	21.33	20.15	14.79	21.68	0.13
NME1	−1.41	0.75	6.01	8.70	9.13	6.76	9.45	0.16
D17S74	−39.15	−31.73	−13.34	−2.73	6.32	7.50	7.67	0.27

Source: Data from J. Hall et al. (1994).

patterns depending on the level of information available for the pedigree and on the actual relationship between the genes tested. Curve ❶ displays data with a maximum lod score value (Z_{max}) of about 4.0 at $\theta = 0.23$, suggesting the two genes are separated by 23 cM. The lod scores are significantly positive in the range of 18 to 30 map units. The curve provides significant evidence against genetic linkage at $\theta < 0.5$. Curve ❷ results from there being very little genetic linkage information, and its lod scores are inconclusive at all distances. Curve ❸ rejects genetic linkage at θ values less than 0.12 but is inconclusive through the rest of the linkage range.

A number of more comprehensive software programs permitting multipoint linkage analysis have been developed to simultaneously analyze genetic linkage data for multiple genes and genetic markers. Multipoint linkage analysis tests all possible gene orders to identify the most likely order of linked genes. **Experimental Insight 5.1** discusses the application of lod score analysis in the mapping of *BRCA1*, a gene whose mutation can increase susceptibility to breast and ovarian cancer in women. **Genetic Analysis 5.3** guides you through the interpretation of lod score values for linkage between a disease-causing gene and a linked DNA genetic marker.

PROBLEM In a study of human families with an autosomal dominant disease caused by a gene whose location is unknown, geneticists use lod score analysis to test linkage between the disease gene and a variable DNA genetic marker. Provide a complete interpretation of the lod score data displayed in the following table, and identify the most likely distance between the marker gene and the disease gene.

> **BREAK IT DOWN:** The lod score is a statistical value that allows identification of the most likely recombination distance between genes and, by extension, rejection of linkage (pp. 167–168).

> **BREAK IT DOWN:** Lod score values greater than +3.0 indicate statistically significant evidence in favor of genetic linkage, and values less than −2.0 significant evidence against linkage at specified θ values (p. 168).

θ Value													
0.0	0.01	0.02	0.03	0.04	0.05	0.06	0.08	0.10	0.15	0.20	0.30	0.40	0.50
$-\infty$	−6.95	−1.10	0.20	1.22	2.25	7.23	7.02	5.11	4.23	−2.01	−6.84	−9.91	0.0

Solution Strategies	Solution Steps

Evaluate

1. Identify the topic of this problem and the nature of the required answer.

1. This problem concerns lod score analysis assessing genetic linkage between a variable DNA genetic marker and a gene carrying a dominant mutation producing a disease. The answer requires interpretation of the lod score values, identification of potential genetic linkage, and determination of the most likely distance between the DNA marker gene and the disease gene.

2. Identify the critical information given in the problem.

2. Lod score values are given for 14 θ values (map units between genes).

> **TIP:** Survey the entire lod score table to identify significant and nonsignificant lod score values.

Deduce

3. Identify significant lod score values in the lod score table and locate Z_{max}.

3. Significant evidence against genetic linkage occurs at $\theta \leq 0.01$ and at $\theta \geq 0.20$. Conversely, significant results in favor of genetic linkage are seen at $\theta = 0.06$ to $\theta = 0.15$. The Z_{max} value is 7.23 and corresponds to $\theta = 0.06$ (6 m.u.).

Solve

4. Interpret the meaning of the lod scores for genetic linkage.

4. The data support genetic linkage between the marker gene and the disease gene at recombination distances of between 6 m.u. and 15 m.u. Linkage between the genes is rejected at less than 2 m.u. and at more than 20 m.u. The lod score results between 2 m.u. and 5 m.u. are inconclusive.

> **TIP:** Note the θ values corresponding to significant lod score values.

5. Identify the most likely distance between the DNA marker gene and the disease gene.

5. The Z_{max} value is 7.23 at $\theta = 0.06$, thus identifying the most likely distance between the disease gene and the marker gene as 6 m.u.

> **TIP:** The maximum lod score value corresponds to a specific distance between genes that is identified by its θ value.

For more practice, see Problems 18, 28, and 29.   Visit the Study Area to access study tools.   MasteringGenetics™

5.6 Recombination Affects Evolution and Genetic Diversity

Recombination between homologous chromosomes is a potent evolutionary factor. It is so strongly favored by evolution that it is essentially ubiquitous in eukaryotes. Recombination is a companion of sexual reproduction as an evolutionary hallmark in eukaryotes because it provides a mechanism for generating genetic diversity among offspring. From an evolutionary perspective, genetic diversity increases the chance that organisms will survive and reproduce in changing environments, and it enhances the ability of organisms to adapt to new environmental niches previously unoccupied by the species.

In comparison to vegetative propagation, such as that seen in yeast, independent assortment during sexual reproduction provides one mechanism for genetic diversification. Recall, for example, that independent assortment of your 23 pairs of homologous chromosomes can generate well over 8 million genetically different gametes. Recombination between homologous chromosomes adds substantially to this number by reshuffling the alleles carried on parental chromosomes, thus producing much more genetic diversity than would be possible by independent assortment alone.

Experimental evidence supports the idea that homologous recombination is a potent factor in evolution and that recombination is favored by natural selection. A meta-analysis study by Sarah Otto and Thomas

Lenormand in 2002 examined recombination rates in a large number of artificial selection experiments conducted by other researchers who were studying the evolution of traits that were unrelated to sex or recombination. Otto and Lenormand determined that in the majority of cases, the rate of recombination had increased significantly as a result of the application of artificial selection to a trait. This result indicates that evolution is enhanced by the occurrence of recombination and that recombination rates increase in response to evolution.

Recombination has a second evolutionary effect, this one operating at the level of populations. As populations age, one would expect recombination to randomize the combinations of alleles on chromosomes. When this expected randomization does not occur, evolution is frequently the cause. The specific array of alleles in a set of linked genes on a single chromosome is called a **haplotype** (a contraction of "**haplo**id geno**type**"). Because the alleles in a haplotype belong to linked genes, they tend to be passed together during meiosis. Homologous chromosomes carried by an organism can contain different haplotypes. Haplotypes can consist of any combination of linked genes producing molecular genetic variation—SNPs, for example—or morphological variation. Haplotypes that are defined by SNP loci usually span regions of 10,000 to 100,000 base pairs, whereas haplotypes for genes producing morphological variation tend to be much larger, spanning up to several million base pairs. Using letters A through F to specify linked SNP loci, and primed (′) and unprimed letters to distinguish the alleles of these sequences, we can specify two sample haplotypes for the same region on homologous chromosomes as

$$...A'\ B\ C'\ D\ E\ F'...$$
$$...A\ B'\ C\ D'\ E'\ F...$$

Over multiple generations, crossing over is expected to occur between the original haplotypes to produce new haplotypes that occur at frequencies determined by chance. In other words, for genes in a population, the genotype for a chromosome at one gene is expected to be independent of its genotypes for other genes. When this occurs, the chromosome region is said to be in **linkage equilibrium.** This means that knowing the alleles at one gene does not help predict the alleles present at other genes on the chromosome.

As an example, let's consider two SNP genes A and B in the haplotypes above. Assuming that the frequencies of alleles at SNP A are $A = 0.70$ and $A' = 0.30$ and at SNP B are $B = 0.20$ and $B' = 0.80$, we can use chance to predict haplotypes. For the A SNP and the B SNP, the predicted haplotypes and frequencies are

$$A'B' = (0.30)(0.80) = 0.24$$
$$A'B = (0.30)(0.20) = 0.06$$
$$A\ B' = (0.70)(0.80) = 0.56$$
$$A\ B = (0.70)(0.20) = \underline{0.14}$$
$$= 1.00$$

When linkage equilibrium is not observed, the frequencies of certain haplotypes in a population deviate significantly from the frequencies expected. This situation is identified as **linkage disequilibrium,** and it frequently occurs as a consequence of evolutionary processes operating on a population. Two different evolutionary processes are common causes of linkage disequilibrium. (1) Migration can produce linkage disequilibrium if haplotypes have been recently introduced into a population and there has not been a sufficient number of generations for crossing over to randomize alleles. (2) If one specific allele in a haplotype is favored by natural selection, the allele will increase in frequency in the population. The other alleles in the haplotype will also be favored because of their close proximity to the favored allele. Recombination is constantly reshuffling the alleles on chromosomes so that over multiple generations an allele favored by natural selection will be part of different multilocus genotypes, but in the short term, linkage disequilibrium can be observed as the result of natural selection on one allele in a haplotype. Recombination eventually randomizes the alleles in haplotypes containing an allele favored by natural selection to eliminate linkage disequilibrium, but the number of generations required is determined by the strength of natural selection and the distances between linked genes.

5.7 Genetic Linkage in Haploid Eukaryotes Is Identified by Tetrad Analysis

The genetic mapping experiments conducted in maize, *Drosophila*, humans, and other diploid organisms have allowed biologists to develop extensive genetic maps for many species. They are a triumph of scientific reasoning and the careful execution of experimental design. As successful as these experiments have been, however, certain other organisms have life cycles that allow the genotypes of individual gametes to be studied more directly, without requiring interpretation of the expression of traits among the progeny of controlled crosses. For this research, geneticists depend on eukaryotic microorganisms such as the class *Ascomycetes* that includes bread mold (*Neurospora crassa*) and yeast (*Saccharomyces cerevisiae*).

Ascomycetes species spend most of their life cycle in a haploid state, dividing by mitosis to produce new cells. For example, haploid yeast cells of *Saccharomyces cerevisiae* undergo mitotic division during the vegetative portion of the life cycle, reproducing new haploid cells that bud off from parental cells (**Figure 5.18**). Diploid yeast form by the union of two genetically different haploid *mating types*. The diploid yeast cells undergo meiosis, producing four haploid **ascospores** contained within a saclike structure called an **ascus.** The four ascospores in an ascus are called a **tetrad.** In yeast, the ascospores are not arranged in any particular order, so the structure

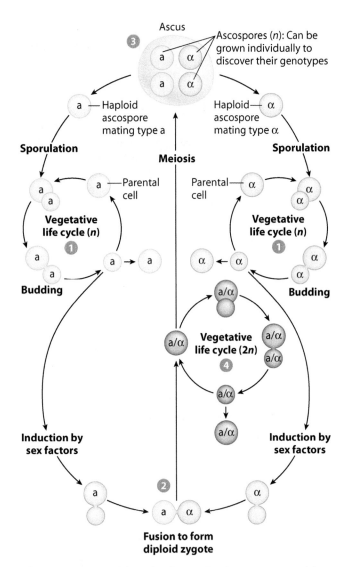

Figure 5.18 **The life cycle of yeast *Saccharomyces cerevisiae.*** ❶ Haploid yeast grow by vegetative propagation. ❷ Yeast of different mating types can fuse to produce diploids. ❸ Haploid ascospores are produced by meiosis in diploid yeast. ❹ Diploid strains propagate by vegetative growth.

is called an **unordered tetrad.** Within each tetrad, two of the ascospores are of the **a** mating type and two are of the α mating type. At maturity, the ascus ruptures in an event known as sporulation, and spores are released to grow as haploids. In laboratory studies, mature ascospores can be removed from their ascus and grown as haploids in culture to discover their genotypes. This process is called **tetrad analysis.**

Analysis of Unordered Tetrads

Suppose a dihybrid yeast cell with the genotype a^+ab^+b is produced by fusing two haploid cells with genotypes a^+b^+ and ab. If the genes are on different chromosomes, two equally likely arrangements of chromosomes occur in metaphase I, labeled "Alternative I" and "Alternative

II" in **Figure 5.19a.** If no crossover occurs between homologs, each tetrad contains ascospores with two genotypes. Ascospores produced by the Alternative I arrangement of metaphase chromosomes contain the same alleles as were found in the parental haploids (a^+b^+ and ab, in this case). Tetrads with these two ascospore genotypes are known as **parental ditypes (PD).** Tetrads that undergo the Alternative II metaphase chromosome arrangement produce ascospores that have different genotypes than the parents. These tetrads are called **nonparental ditypes (NPD).** If crossing over occurs between either of the homologous chromosome pairs, the tetrad contains ascospores with four different genotypes and is known as a **tetratype (TT)** (**Figure 5.19b**).

Now let's consider what is observed when the genes are linked. In Figures 5.10 and 5.11, we saw that several types of single and double crossover can occur between homologous chromosomes in diploids; **Figure 5.20** illustrates the tetrad combinations that result from no crossover and from single and various double crossovers between a pair of homologous chromosomes carrying alleles a^+b^+/ab at linked loci. The figure illustrates that for these linked genes, all three tetrad types form, but PD and TT tetrads are each more frequent than NPD. PD tetrads are most common, being produced when no crossover occurs between genes and when two-strand double crossover takes place. TT tetrads are less frequent than PD, occurring when single crossovers or three-strand double crossovers take place. NPD tetrads are least frequent, forming only when four-strand double crossover occurs. Genetic linkage produces the tetrad expectation PD > TT > NPD.

Genetic linkage analysis in tetrads is based on the relative frequencies of different tetrad types rather than an assessment of individual progeny. The formula used to determine recombination frequency in tetrad analysis (familiar from our previous assessments of genetic linkage) is

$$r = \frac{\text{number of recombinants} \times (100)}{\text{total number of progeny}}$$

An example of this analysis comes from a study that examined tetrads produced by fusion of haploid strains $pdx\ pan^+ \times pdx^+pan$. The data in **Table 5.5** show that among 49 tetrads analyzed, 28 are PD, 20 are TT, and 1 is NPD. A close examination of Figure 5.20 reveals that in tetrads, recombinant chromosomes are found in one-half the ascospores of TT tetrads and all the ascospores of NPD tetrads. On this basis, tetrad recombination frequency is determined using

$$r = \frac{\left(\frac{1}{2}\text{TT}\right) + \text{NPD}}{\text{total tetrads}}$$

Recombination frequency for this example is therefore

$$r = \frac{\left[\left(\frac{1}{2}\right)(20) + 1\right]}{49} = 0.224\,(22.4\%)$$

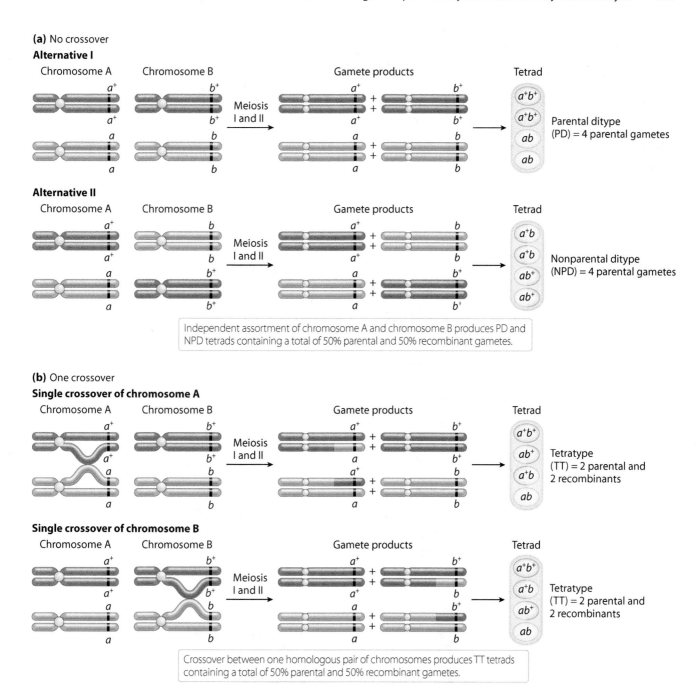

Figure 5.19   Tetrad results for unlinked genes. **(a)** Parental ditype (PD) and nonparental ditype (NPD) tetrads are the products of segregation and independent assortment. Each ascus contains two genetically different types of ascospore. **(b)** Single crossovers between either homologous pair of chromosomes produce tetratype (TT) tetrads that contain four genetically different ascospores.

Ordered Ascus Analysis

Fungi such as *Neurospora crassa* follow the same basic haploid–diploid life cycle as yeast but produce an ascus with eight haploid ascospores rather than four. In *Neurospora*, the fusion of two haploid fungi forms a diploid meiocyte that undergoes meiotic divisions to generate four haploid products aligned in a tetrad ascus. Mitotic division of the ascospores immediately follows completion of meiosis, forming an eight-member

ascus (Figure 5.21). The two members of each mitotically produced pair of daughter spores are adjacent to one another in the *Neurospora* octad, and the octad is called an **ordered ascus.** Consequently, the arrangement of daughter spores reflects the identity and orientation of the alleles carried by each chromatid in metaphase I. An ordered ascus can be dissected before sporulation, and haploid spores can be removed one by one to determine their genotype. In this way, each product of meiosis is

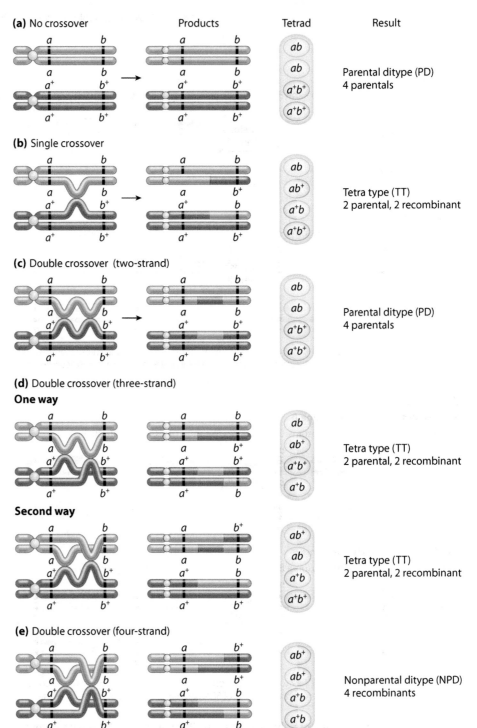

Figure 5.20 **Tetrad formation with linked genes is determined by the occurrence or type of crossover.** (a) No crossing over produces the parental ditype. (b) Single crossover produces the tetratype. (c) Two-strand double crossover produces the parental ditype. (d) Three-strand double crossover produces the tetratype. (e) Four-strand double crossover produces the nonparental ditype.

(a) No crossover · Products · Tetrad · Result

ab / *ab* / *a⁺b⁺* / *a⁺b⁺* — Parental ditype (PD) 4 parentals

(b) Single crossover

ab / *ab⁺* / *a⁺b* / *a⁺b⁺* — Tetra type (TT) 2 parental, 2 recombinant

(c) Double crossover (two-strand)

ab / *ab* / *a⁺b⁺* / *a⁺b⁺* — Parental ditype (PD) 4 parentals

(d) Double crossover (three-strand)
One way

ab / *ab⁺* / *a⁺b⁺* / *a⁺b* — Tetra type (TT) 2 parental, 2 recombinant

Second way

ab⁺ / *ab* / *a⁺b* / *a⁺b⁺* — Tetra type (TT) 2 parental, 2 recombinant

(e) Double crossover (four-strand)

ab⁺ / *ab⁺* / *a⁺b* / *a⁺b* — Nonparental ditype (NPD) 4 recombinants

Table 5.5	**Recombination Calculation in Tetrads**	

Genotype: *pdx pan⁺/pdx⁺ pan*

	Tetrad Types		
	PD	**TT**	**NPD**
Ascospore genotypes	*pdx pan⁺*	*pdx pan⁺*	*pdx pan*
	pdx pan⁺	*pdx pan*	*pdx pan*
	pdx⁺ pan	*pdx⁺ pan⁺*	*pdx⁺ pan⁺*
	pdx⁺ pan	*pdx⁺ pan*	*pdx⁺ pan⁺*
Number	28	20	1 = 49

identified, and its spatial relationship to other meiotic products is determined.

Ordered ascus analysis can be used to map the distance between linked genes and the position of a gene relative to the centromere of its chromosome. Gene-to-centromere distance is calculated based on the segregation of homologous chromosomes in meiosis I and of sister chromatids in meiosis II. In an *a⁺a* meiocyte in which no crossover occurs between the gene and the centromere, alleles segregate in meiosis I. Completion of meiosis and the mitotic division produces an ordered ascus with four spores of one type grouped in the top half

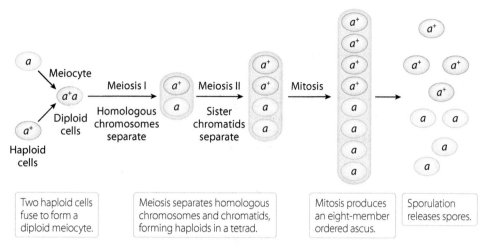

Figure 5.21   Ordered ascus production in the fungus *Neurospora crassa*.

Two haploid cells fuse to form a diploid meiocyte.	Meiosis separates homologous chromosomes and chromatids, forming haploids in a tetrad.	Mitosis produces an eight-member ordered ascus.	Sporulation releases spores.

of the ascus and spores of the other type filling the bottom half (Figure 5.22). This pattern of segregation is called **first-division segregation,** to signify the separation of alleles a^+ and a in the first meiotic division. In the absence of crossover, none of the spores in first-division segregation asci are recombinant.

If crossover takes place, alleles a^+ and a are not separated until the second meiotic division, a pattern called **second-division segregation.** If crossover occurs between the gene and centromere, a single crossover produces one of four different octad patterns, depending on the orientation of chromatids during meiosis. One example is illustrated in Figure 5.23a where the ordered ascus has a 2:2:2:2 ratio. Alternative chromosome orientations accompanied by single crossover produce three additional ordered ascus patterns that group identical mitotic products next to one another (Figure 5.23b). In each case, the overall 1:1 ratio of the two alleles is seen among the eight ascospores—only the order of spores differs. The relative proportion of second-division segregation asci is used to calculate the map distance (in centiMorgans) between a gene and the centromere via the formula

$$x \text{ cM} = \frac{\frac{1}{2}(\text{number of second-division segregation asci})}{\text{total number of asci}} \times 100$$

This calculation is equivalent to counting the number of recombinant spores and dividing by the total number of progeny, because one-half the spores in second-division segregation asci are recombinant. Figure 5.24 provides an example using *Neurospora crassa*. Wild-type fungi that grow as buff-colored colonies with normal growth habit are mated to mutants that grow as orange colonies with fluffy growth habit. As computed in the figure, the distance from the centromere to the color gene is 16.5 cM, and the distance from the centromere to the growth-habit gene is 30.7 cM.

5.8 Mitotic Crossover Produces Distinctive Phenotypes

Our discussion of crossing over and recombination has been limited to events that occur during meiosis. You may have wondered whether crossing over occurs during mitosis, and if so, what its consequences are. Synapsis of homologous chromosomes during mitosis occurs only occasionally in animals; thus, there is little opportunity for recombination to occur. In certain cases, however, homologous recombination does occur during mitosis. The

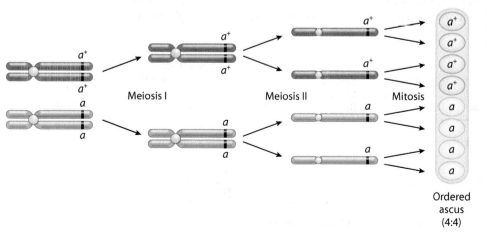

Figure 5.22   First-division segregation in ordered ascus formation.

Ordered ascus (4:4)

(a)   **(b)**

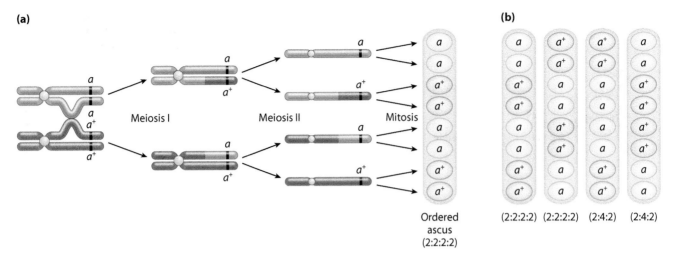

Figure 5.23 **Second-division segregation in ordered ascus formation.** **(a)** This single crossover produces a 2:2:2:2 ordered ascus. **(b)** Different outcomes of second-division segregation can occur, depending on the chromatids involved in crossing over.

rate of **mitotic crossover** varies considerably among organisms, but its consequences have been revealed through some fascinating examples.

The first well-documented example of mitotic crossover came in 1936, when Curt Stern studied *Drosophila* crosses of two X-linked recessive traits, yellow body color (*y*) and short, twisted bristles called singed (*sn*). Stern crossed females homozygous for wild-type (gray) body color and singed bristles ($y^+ sn/y^+ sn$) with yellow-bodied, normal-bristled males ($y sn^+/Y$) and obtained dihybrid F₁ females that had wild-type body color and bristle form ($y^+ sn/y sn^+$). Close examination of a small number of F₁ females revealed an unexpected phenotype. These females had wild-type body color and wild-type bristles over most of the body but had small patches of either yellow body color or singed bristles. Even more surprising, some females had a patch of yellow body *and* a patch of singed bristles, and when they did, the patches were always *adjacent* to one another in a pattern called a twin spot (**Figure 5.25**). Among these three unusual spotting patterns, twin spot was about twice as common as single yellow spotting and single yellow spotting was much more common than single singed spotting.

In formulating an explanation for the odd patches and their different frequencies, Stern reasoned that since the twin spots were always side by side, they must result from reciprocal events. He realized that rare crossover between homologous chromosomes during mitosis could explain twin spots, and it could also be a source of both kinds of single spots as well. Stern proposed that mitotic crossover events like those illustrated in Figure 5.25 were responsible for single and twin spots in *Drosophila*. Twin spotting is explained by mitotic crossover between *sn* and the centromere if the particular pattern of chromosome segregation illustrated in Figure 5.25 takes place. Mitotic crossover between *y* and *sn* followed by the chromosome segregation shown produces single yellow spots. The double crossover and chromosome segregation pattern shown are required to produce single singed spot. Twin spotting is the most common observation because the map distance between *sn* and the centromere is 45 cM. In contrast, the distance between *y* and *sn* is 21 cM, so twin spotting is about twice as common as single yellow spot. The double crossover producing single singed spot is less frequent than either single crossover, thus single singed spot is the least frequent phenotype.

P (genotype)	F1 (genotype)	Trait	First Division (D1)	Second Division (D2)	Combined (D1 + D2)	Distance from Centromere to Trait $\dfrac{\left[\frac{D2}{2}\right]}{[D1 + D2]} \times 100 = cM$	Gene Map
C^+g^+	C^+g^+/cg	Color (c)	73	36	109	$\dfrac{\left[\frac{36}{2}\right]}{[109]} \times 100 = 16.5$	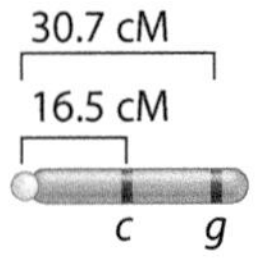 30.7 cM 16.5 cM
cg		Growth (g)	42	67	109	$\dfrac{\left[\frac{67}{2}\right]}{[109]} \times 100 = 30.7$	c g

Figure 5.24 **Calculation of centromere-to-gene distance in *Neurospora crassa*.**

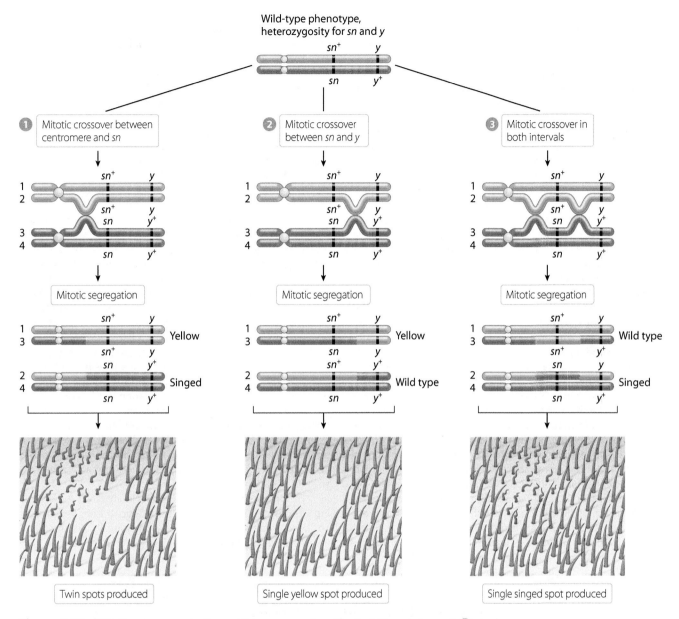

Figure 5.25   Mitotic crossover. In *Drosophila* crosses analyzed by Curt Stern, twin spots ❶, single yellow spot ❷, and single singed spot ❸ were produced by mitotic crossing over followed by a particular segregation pattern during mitotic cell division. In each set of diagrams, the chromatids and their centromeres are first numbered prior to crossing over. The numbers used after crossing over show the segregation patterns that produce the identified mitotic crossover phenotypes.

CASE STUDY

Mapping the Gene for Cystic Fibrosis

Cystic fibrosis (CF) (OMIM 219700) is an autosomal recessive disorder caused by a defect in the *cystic fibrosis transmembrane conductance regulator* (*CFTR*) gene that is located on chromosome 7 in humans. The protein product of *CFTR* spans the membrane of cells, regulating the flow of chloride ions in and out of the cell. Mutations of *CFTR* primarily affect glands producing mucus, digestive enzymes, and sweat.

First identified in the late 1930s, CF proved to be a relatively common disorder, particularly in Caucasian populations, where it occurs at a frequency of 1 in 2500 infants, according to the American Lung Association. It is much less common in Hispanics (1 in 15,000), African Americans (1 in 30,000), and Native Pacific Islanders (1 in 100,000). In Caucasians, the frequency of heterozygous carriers of the recessive allele is approximately 4%. Numerous family studies identified CF as being caused by mutation of a single gene, although the gene was not identified until the 1980s. Many mutant alleles of the gene are known, although one mutation is very common.

The principal clinical difficulty in CF is very thick mucus that clogs the airways in the lungs and in the ducts that transport digestive enzymes from the pancreas to the small intestine. Chronic and severe respiratory infections are a hallmark of CF, as are digestive difficulties that can result in chronic malnutrition, even with adequate food intake. Awareness of the principal complications of CF has led to better management and improved survival. In the 1950s, CF patients rarely survived long enough to enter elementary school. By 1985, the average age of survival stood at about 25 years. By 2007, mean survival had improved to approximately 28 years. CF patients with less severe forms of the disease survive even longer.

With family studies indicating that a single autosomal gene was responsible for CF, researchers used genetic linkage mapping and lod score analysis to locate the CF gene. All 22 autosomes were studied, and initially a great deal of negative genetic linkage information was obtained. These data identified chromosomes where the gene *was not* located. The first important piece of positive gene mapping evidence came in 1985 when Hans Eiberg and colleagues identified the close linkage of the CF gene to the *PON* gene that produces the blood serum enzyme paraoxonase. Unfortunately, *PON* did not have a known chromosome location at the time, so despite the finding that the CF gene was near *PON*, the identity of the chromosome carrying the genes remained a mystery.

A few months later, however, Lap-Chee Tsui and colleagues identified a DNA RFLP marker known as *D7S15* that was linked to both the CF gene and to *PON* (see Section 5.5). *D7S15* was known to reside near the middle of the long arm of chromosome 7. Like almost all RFLPs, *D7S15* is not part of an expressed gene, and it has nothing to do with causing CF. It is merely a DNA sequence variant that is detected in a noncoding segment of chromosome 7. As Table 5.6 shows, however, lod score values for *D7S15*–CF and *D7S15*–*PON* linkage as reported by Tsui et al. (1985) for 39 families with CF clearly demonstrated close genetic linkage between the genes and the RFLP. Lod score values greater than +3.0 are seen for *D7S15*–CF linkage

in the range $\theta = 0.10$ to 0.20, with a_{max} value of 3.96 at $\theta = 0.14$. For the *D7S15*–*PON* analysis, significantly positive lod scores are seen in the range $\theta = 0.01$ to 0.20, with a Z_{max} value of 5.01 at $\theta = 0.05$. Taken together, the lod score analysis indicated the order *D7S15*-*PON*-CF with a distance of approximately 5 cM from *D7S15* to *PON* and 14 cM from *PON* to CF.

With the segment of chromosome 7 containing the CF gene identified, researchers examined the chromosome 7 region and quickly found additional DNA genetic markers that were linked even more closely to the CF gene. Using these markers, they identified a segment of about 500,000 bp of DNA as the likely location of the CF gene. By examining DNA sequences for the probable presence of expressed genes and by testing for the presence of genes that were known to be expressed in sweat glands, a group of investigators led by Tsui and Francis Collins cloned and sequenced the CF gene in 1989. Investigators quickly determined that the protein product of the CF gene is a transmembrane conductance regulatory protein, at which point the gene acquired its *CFTR* designation.

One mutation known to delete three consecutive DNA base pairs and alter one amino acid of the CFTR protein accounts for almost 50% of the known *CFTR* mutant alleles. Numerous other *CFTR* mutant alleles have also been identified, but none of these has a frequency of more than a few percent. The various *CFTR* mutant alleles produce different levels of functionality in the transmembrane protein, to some extent allowing clinical variation in CF patients to be attributed to particular mutant alleles. Knowing the frequency of the one common mutation and having identified many other *CFTR* mutations, medical geneticists are able to offer prenatal genetic testing to CF families and are able to accurately identify the mutant alleles and probable disease severity in patients.

The process of first mapping, then cloning, then sequencing *CFTR* to identify its function is a genetic strategy known as *positional cloning* or *reverse genetic analysis*. We discuss this investigative strategy more completely in Chapter 16.

Table 5.6	Linkage Data from 39 Families with Cystic Fibrosis								
	Lod Scores at Various Recombination Distances (θ)								
Marker–Gene	0.01	0.05	0.10	0.15	0.20	0.25	0.30	0.35	0.40
D7S15–CF	−5.88	1.67	3.63	3.95	3.62	2.97	2.18	1.38	0.67
D7S15–*PON*	4.27	5.01	4.78	4.28	3.66	2.97	2.25	1.51	0.81

SUMMARY   (MasteringGenetics™   For activities, animations, and review quizzes, go to the Study Area.

5.1 Linked Genes Do Not Assort Independently

▊ Genetic linkage identifies genes that are so close to one another on a chromosome that their alleles do not assort independently.

▊ With genetic linkage, parental combinations occur at frequencies that are significantly greater than those predicted by chance, and nonparental combinations are much less frequent than expected.

▊ William Bateson and Reginald Punnett first observed genetic linkage when they noticed high numbers of parental phenotypes in F_2 progeny.

▊ Thomas Hunt Morgan performed test-cross analysis of linked genes to demonstrate that linkage violates independent assortment and that crossover between homologous chromosomes is responsible for the production of recombinant gametes.

- Crossover frequency between linked genes is correlated with the distance between genes on a chromosome. Crossover occurs less often between genes that are close together than between genes that are farther apart.

- In crosses involving linked genes, the two parental phenotypes are observed in progeny in approximately equal frequencies. The two recombinant phenotypes also occur at approximately equal frequency.

5.2 Genetic Linkage Mapping Is Based on Recombination Frequency between Genes

- The correlation between physical map distance and recombination frequency permits gene mapping based on recombination frequency.

5.3 Three-Point Test-Cross Analysis Maps Genes

- Three or more genes can be mapped by test-cross analysis. In a three-point cross, parental phenotypes are most frequent, double recombinants are least frequent, and the four phenotypes resulting from two single-recombination events are of intermediate frequency that depends on the actual distance between genes.

- Genetic linkage maps are constructed in five steps:

  1. Find significantly higher proportions of parental phenotypes than predicted by chance.
  2. Identify the alleles on parental chromosomes (the most common classes).
  3. Identify double recombinants (the least frequent classes), comparing them to parental chromosomes to determine gene order.
  4. Calculate recombination frequencies between genes.
  5. Calculate interference with the occurrence of double crossovers.

- Recombination frequency usually underestimates the physical distance between genes. Mapping functions are used to correct these estimates.

- Hotspots and coldspots of recombination are found in many genomes, reflecting the uneven distribution of homologous recombination.

5.4 Recombination Results from Crossing Over

- Studies correlating genetic recombination with the visible recombination of distinctive physical structures on chromosomes support the idea that crossing over causes recombination.

- Crossing over occurs at the four-strand stage in prophase I of meiosis, after completion of DNA replication. Two nonsister chromatids of homologous chromosomes exchange parts in two-strand single crossovers. Two, three, or all four chromatids can be involved in double crossovers.

- Recombination occurs within genes as well as between genes. Several biological properties of organisms affect recombination. In animals, the heterogametic sex experiences less recombination genome-wide than the homogametic sex.

5.5 Linked Human Genes Are Mapped Using Lod Score Analysis

- Statistical approaches such as lod score analysis detect evidence of linkage in small families.

- Lod score analysis determines the likelihood of genetic linkage between genes at specified recombination values (θ values). A cumulative lod score of +3.0 or more is statistically significant evidence in favor of genetic linkage between two genes. Lod scores of −2.0 or less represent significant evidence against genetic linkage.

5.6 Recombination Affects Evolution and Genetic Diversity

- Recombination between homologs adds substantially to the genetic diversity produced through sexual reproduction.

- Homologous recombination helps break down linkage disequilibrium to randomize the alleles of linked genes.

5.7 Genetic Linkage in Haploid Eukaryotes Is Identified by Tetrad Analysis

- In certain eukaryotic microorganisms, the products of individual meiotic cell divisions are contained within an ascus. Parental and recombinant gametes contained in an ascus can be analyzed to map genes.

5.8 Mitotic Crossover Produces Distinctive Phenotypes

- Mitotic crossing over is a rare event that produces patches of tissue with unusual phenotype.

KEYWORDS

allelic phase *(p. 166)*

ascus (ascospore) *(p. 171)*

coefficient of coincidence (c) *(p. 159)*

double recombinant (double crossover), two-, three-, or four-stranded *(pp. 157, 161)*

first-division segregation *(p. 175)*

genetic linkage (genetic linkage mapping), complete and incomplete *(p. 145)*

haplotype *(p. 171)*

interference (*I*), *(p. 158)*

intragenic recombination *(p. 162)*

linkage equilibrium and disequilibrium *(p. 171)*

linkage group *(p. 166)*

lod score (log of the odds ratio) *(p. 167)*

mapping function *(p. 166)*

map unit (m.u.), centiMorgan (cM) *(p. 154)*

mitotic crossover *(p. 176)*

negative interference *(p. 159)*

nonparental ditype (NPD) *(p. 172)*

ordered ascus *(p. 173)*

parental (nonrecombinant) chromosome or gamete *(p. 145)*

parental ditype (PD) *(p. 172)*

recombinant (nonparental) chromosome or gamete *(p. 145)*

recombination coldspot (recombination hotspot) *(p. 164)*

recombination frequency (r) *(p. 148)*

second-division segregation *(p. 175)*

syntenic gene *(p. 145)*

tetrad *(p. 171)*

tetrad analysis *(p. 172)*

tetratype (TT) *(p. 172)*

theta value (θ value) *(p. 167)*

three-point test-cross analysis *(p. 154)*

two-point test-cross analysis *(p. 150)*

unordered tetrad *(p. 172)*

Z_{max} *(p. 168)*

PROBLEMS

MasteringGenetics™ Visit for instructor-assigned tutorials and problems.

Chapter Concepts

For answers to selected even-numbered problems, see Appendix: Answers.

1. For parts a, b, and c, draw a diagram illustrating the alleles on homologous chromosomes for the following genotypes, assuming in each case that the genes reside on the same chromosome in the order written. For parts d and e, give the information requested.

   a. *AB/ab*

   b. *aBc/abC*

   c. *DFg/DFG*

   d. the gametes produced by an organism with the genotype *Rt/rT*

   e. progeny of the cross *Rt/rT × rt/rt*

2. In a diploid species of plant, the genes for plant height and fruit shape are syntenic and separated by 18 m.u. Allele *D* produces tall plants and is dominant to *d* for short plants, and allele *R* produces round fruit and is dominant to *r* for oval fruit.

   a. A plant with the genotype *DR/dr* produces gametes. Identify gamete genotypes, label parental and recombinant gametes, and give the frequency of each gamete genotype.

   b. Give the same information for a plant with the genotype *Dr/dR*.

3. A pure-breeding tall plant producing oval fruit as described in Problem 2 is crossed to a pure-breeding short plant producing round fruit.

   a. The F₁ are crossed to short plants producing oval fruit. What are the expected proportions of progeny phenotypes?

   b. If the F₁ identified in part (a) are crossed to one another, what proportion of the F₂ are expected to be short and produce round fruit? What proportion are expected to be tall and produce round fruit?

4. Genes *E* and *H* are syntenic in an experimental organism with the genotype *EH/eh*. Assume that during each meiosis, one crossover occurs between these genes. No homologous chromosomes escape crossover, and none undergo double crossover. Are genes *E* and *H* genetically linked? Why or why not? What is the proportion of parental gametes produced by meiosis?

5. In tomato plants, purple leaf color is controlled by a dominant allele *A*, and green leaf by a recessive allele *a*. At another locus, hairy leaf *H* is dominant to hairless leaf *h*. The genes for leaf color and leaf texture are separated by 16 m.u. on chromosome 5. On chromosome 4, a gene controlling leaf shape has two alleles: a dominant allele *C*

that produces cut-leaf shape and a recessive allele *c* that produces potato-shaped leaf.

   a. The cross of a purple, hairy, cut plant heterozygous at each gene to a green, hairless, potato plant produces the following progeny:

Phenotype	Frequency, %
Purple, hairy, cut	21
Purple, hairy, potato	21
Green, hairless, cut	21
Green, hairless, potato	21
Purple, hairless, cut	4
Purple, hairless, potato	4
Green, hairy, cut	4
Green, hairy, potato	4
	100

   Give the genotypes of parental and progeny plants in this experiment.

   b. Fully explain the number and frequency of each phenotype class.

6. In *Drosophila*, the map positions of genes are given in map units numbering from one end of a chromosome to the other. The X chromosome of *Drosophila* is 66 m.u. long. The X-linked gene for body color—with two alleles, y^+ for gray body and *y* for yellow body—resides at one end of the chromosome at map position 0.0. A nearby locus for eye color, with alleles w^+ for red eye and *w* for white eye, is located at map position 1.5. A third X-linked gene, controlling bristle form, with f^+ for normal bristles and *f* for forked bristles, is located at map position 56.7. Each gene resides on the X chromosome, and at each locus the wild-type allele is dominant over the mutant allele.

   a. In a cross involving these three X-linked genes, do you expect any gene pair(s) to show genetic linkage? Explain your reasoning.

   b. Do you expect any of these gene pair(s) to assort independently? Explain your reasoning.

   c. A wild-type female fruit fly with the genotype y^+w^+f/ywf^+ is crossed to a male fruit fly that has yellow body, white eye, and forked bristles. Predict the frequency of each progeny phenotype class produced by this mating.

   d. Explain how each of the predicted progeny classes is produced.

7. Genes *A*, *B*, and *C* are linked on a chromosome and found in the order *A-B-C*. Genes *A* and *B* recombine with a frequency of 8%, and genes *B* and *C* recombine at a frequency of 24%. For the cross $a^+b^+c/abc^+ \times abc/abc$, predict the frequency of progeny genotypes. Assume interference is zero.

8. Gene *G* recombines with gene *T* at a frequency of 7%, and gene *G* recombines with gene *R* at a frequency of 4%.
   a. Draw two possible genetic maps for these three genes, and identify the recombination frequencies predicted for each map.
   b. Assuming any desired genotype is available, propose a genetic cross whose result could be used to determine which of the proposed genetic maps is correct.

9. Genes *A*, *B*, *C*, *D*, and *E* are linked on a chromosome and occur in the order given. The test cross *Ae/aE* × *ae/ae* indicates the genes recombine with a frequency of 28%.
   a. If 1000 progeny are produced by the test cross, determine the number of progeny in each outcome class.
   b. Previous genetic linkage crosses have determined that recombination frequencies for these genes are 6% for genes *A* and *B*, 4% for genes *B* and *C*, 10% for genes *C* and *D*, and 11% for genes *D* and *E*. The sum of these frequencies between genes *A* and *E* is 31%. Why does the recombination distance between these genes, determined by adding the intervals between adjacent linked genes, differ from the distance determined by the test cross?

10. Syntenic genes can assort independently. Explain this observation.

11. The recombination frequency between linked genes is less than 50%. Why is 50% recombination the maximum value?

12. On the *Drosophila* X chromosome, the dominant allele y^+ produces gray body color and the recessive allele *y* produces yellow body. This gene is linked to one controlling full eye shape by a dominant allele lz^+ and lozenge eye shape with a recessive allele *lz*. These genes recombine with a frequency of approximately 28%. The *Lz* gene is linked to gene *F* controlling bristle form, where the dominant is long bristles and the recessive is forked bristles. The *Lz* and *F* genes recombine with a frequency of approximately 32%.
   a. Using any genotypes you choose, design two separate crosses, one to test recombination between genes *Y* and *Lz* and the second between genes *Lz* and *F*. Assume 1000 progeny are produced by each cross, and give the number of progeny in each outcome category. (In setting up your crosses, remember that *Drosophila* males do not undergo recombination.)
   b. Can any cross reveal genetic linkage between gene *Y* and gene *F*? Why or why not?
   c. Why is "independent assortment" the genetic term that best describes the observations of a genetic cross between gene *Y* and gene *F*?

Application and Integration

13. Researchers cross a corn plant that is pure-breeding for the dominant traits colored aleurone (*C1*), full kernel (*Sh*), and waxy endosperm (*Wx*) to a pure-breeding plant with the recessive traits colorless aleurone (*c1*), shrunken kernel (*sh*), and starchy (*wx*). The resulting F$_1$ plants were crossed to pure-breeding colorless, shrunken, starchy plants. Counting the kernels from about 30 ears of corn yields the following data.

Kernel Phenotype	Number
Colored, shrunken, starchy	116
Colored, full, starchy	601
Colored, full, waxy	2538
Colored, shrunken, waxy	4
Colorless, shrunken, starchy	2708
Colorless, full, starchy	2
Colorless, full, waxy	113
Colorless, shrunken, waxy	626
	6708

   a. Why are these data consistent with genetic linkage among the three genes?
   b. Perform a chi-square test to determine if these data show significant deviation from the expected phenotype distribution.
   c. What is the order of these genes in corn?

For answers to selected even-numbered problems, see Appendix: Answers.

   d. Calculate the recombination fraction between the gene pairs.
   e. What is the interference value for this data set?

14. Nail–patella syndrome is an autosomal disorder affecting the shape of nails on fingers and toes as well as the structure of kneecaps. The pedigree below shows the transmission of nail–patella syndrome in a family along with ABO blood type.

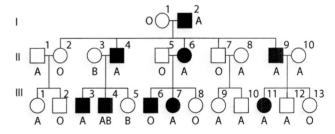

   a. Is nail–patella syndrome a dominant or a recessive condition? Explain your reasoning.
   b. Does this family give evidence of genetic linkage between nail–patella syndrome and ABO blood group? Why or why not?
   c. Using *N* and *n* to represent alleles at the nail–patella locus and I^A, I^B, and *i* to represent ABO alleles, write the genotypes of I-1 and I-2 as well as their five children in generation II.
   d. Explain why III-6 has nail–patella syndrome and III-8 does not. Give genotypes for these two individuals.
   e. Explain why III-11 has nail–patella syndrome and III-12 does not. Give genotypes for these two individuals.

15. Three dominant traits of corn seedlings, tunicate seed (*T–*), glossy appearance (*G–*), and liguled stem (*L–*), are studied along with their recessive counterparts, nontunicate (*tt*), nonglossy (*gg*), and liguleless (*ll*). A trihybrid plant with the three dominant traits is crossed to a nontunicate, nonglossy, liguleless plant. Kernels on ears of progeny plants are scored for the traits, with the following results:

Phenotype	Number
Tunicate, glossy, liguled	102
Tunicate, glossy, liguleless	106
Tunicate, nonglossy, liguled	18
Tunicate, nonglossy, liguleless	20
Nontunicate, glossy, liguled	22
Nontunicate, glossy, liguleless	23
Nontunicate, nonglossy, liguled	99
Nontunicate, nonglossy, liguleless	110
	500

a. Is there evidence of genetic linkage among any of these gene pairs? If so, identify the evidence.
b. Is there evidence of independent assortment among any of these gene pairs? If so, identify the evidence.
c. Using the gene symbols given above, write the genotypes of F_1 and F_2 plants.
d. If evidence of linkage is present, calculate the recombination fraction(s) from the data presented.
e. Could all three genes be carried on the same chromosome? Discuss why or why not.

16. In a diploid plant species, an F_1 with the genotype *Gg Ll Tt* is test-crossed to a pure-breeding recessive plant with the genotype *gg ll tt*. The offspring genotypes are as follow

Genotype	Number
Gg Ll Tt	621
Gg Ll tt	3
Gg ll Tt	64
Gg ll tt	109
gg Ll Tt	103
gg Ll tt	67
gg ll Tt	7
gg ll tt	626
	1600

a. What is the order of these three linked genes?
b. Calculate the recombination fractions between each pair of genes.
c. Why is the recombination fraction for the outside pair of genes not equal to the sum of recombination fractions between the adjacent gene pairs?
d. What is the interference value for this data set?
e. Explain the meaning of this *I* value.

17. The table given lists the arrangement of alleles of linked genes in dihybrid organisms, the recombination frequency between the genes, and specific gamete genotypes. Using the information provided, determine the expected frequency of gametes given. Assume one map unit equals 1% recombination and, when three genes are involved, interference is zero.

Dihybrid Genotype	Recombination Frequency	Gamete Genotype
A. *DE/de*	8%	*De*
B. *AD/ad*	28%	*ad*
C. *DEF/def*	E-F 24%	*dEf*
	D-E 8%	
D. *BdE/bDe*	B-D 18%	*Bde*
	D-E 8%	

18. The Rh blood group in humans is determined by a gene on chromosome 1. A dominant allele produces Rh+ blood type, and a recessive allele generates Rh−. Elliptocytosis is an autosomal dominant disorder that produces abnormally shaped red blood cells that have a short life span resulting in hereditary anemia. A large family with elliptocytosis is tested for genetic linkage of Rh blood group and the disease. The lod score data below are obtained for the family.

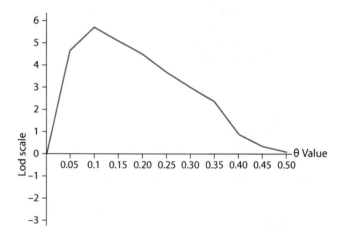

a. From these data, can you conclude that Rh and elliptocytosis loci are genetically linked in this family? Why or why not?
b. What is Z_{max} for this family?
c. Over what range of θ do lod scores indicate significant evidence in favor of genetic linkage?

19. Genetic linkage mapping for a large number of families identifies 4% recombination between the genes for Rh blood type and elliptocytosis. At the Rh locus, alleles *R* and *r* control Rh+ and Rh− blood types. Allele *E* producing elliptocytosis is dominant to the wild-type recessive allele *e*. Tom and Terri each have elliptocytosis, and each is Rh+. Tom's mother has elliptocytosis and is Rh− while his father is healthy and has Rh+. Terri's father is Rh+ and has elliptocytosis; Terri's mother is Rh− and is healthy.

a. What is the probability that the first child of Tom and Terri will be Rh− and have elliptocytosis?
b. What is the probability that a child of Tom and Terri who is Rh+ will have elliptocytosis?

20. *Neurospora* with the genotype $a^+ a$ form tetrads in the following frequencies:

Tetrad	Number
$a^+ a^+ a\, a$	192
$a\, a\, a^+ a^+$	208
$a\, a^+ a\, a^+$	23
$a\, a^+ a^+ a$	27
$a^+ a\, a^+ a$	29
$a^+ a\, a\, a^+$	21
	500

   a. What is the distance between the gene and the centromere?

   b. Diagram the meiosis producing the tetrad class $a\, a\, a^+ a^+$.

   c. Diagram the meiosis producing the tetrad class $a^+ a\, a\, a^+$.

21. Gene *R* and gene *T* are genetically linked. Answer the following questions concerning a dihybrid organism with the genotype *Rt/rT*:

   a. If *r* = 0.20, give the expected frequencies of gametes produced by the dihybrid.

   b. Determine the gamete frequencies if a two-strand double crossover occurs between the genes.

   c. Determine the genotypes of gametes produced by a three-strand double crossover in this dihybrid organism.

   d. Determine the genotypes of gametes produced by a four-strand double crossover in this dihybrid.

22. T. H. Morgan's data on eye color and wing form, shown in Figures 5.3 and 5.5, reveal genetic linkage between the two genes. Test this genetic linkage data with chi-square analysis, and show that the results are significantly different from the expectation under the assumption of independent assortment.

23. A wild-type trihybrid soybean plant is crossed to a pure-breeding soybean plant with the recessive phenotypes pale leaf (*l*), oval seed (*r*), and short height (*t*). The results of the three-point test cross are shown below. Traits not listed are wild type.

Phenotype	Number
Pale	648
Pale, oval	64
Pale, short	10
Pale, oval, short	102
Oval	6
Oval, short	618
Short	84
Wild type	98
	1630

   a. What are the alleles on each homologous chromosome of the parental wild-type trihybrid soybean plant? Place the alleles in their correct gene order. Use *L*, *R*, and *T* to represent dominant alleles and *l*, *r*, and *t* for recessive alleles.

   b. Calculate the recombination fraction between the adjacent genes.

   c. Calculate the interference value for these data.

24. The boss in your laboratory has just heard of a proposal by another laboratory that genes for eye color and the length of body bristles may be linked in *Drosophila*. Your lab has numerous pure-breeding stocks of *Drosophila* that could be used to verify or refute genetic linkage. In *Drosophila*, red eyes (c^+) are dominant to brown eyes (*c*), and long bristles (d^+) are dominant to short bristles (*d*). Your lab boss asks you to design an experiment to test the genetic linkage of eye color and bristle-length genes, and to begin by crossing a pure-breeding line homozygous for red eyes and short bristles to a pure-breeding line that has brown eyes and long bristles.

   a. Give the genotypes of the pure-breeding parental flies, and the genotype(s) and phenotype(s) of the F_1 progeny they produce.

   b. In your experimental design, what is the genotype and phenotype of the line you propose to cross to the F_1 to obtain the most useful information about genetic linkage between the eye color and bristle-length genes? Explain why you make this choice.

   c. Assume the eye color and bristle-length genes are separated by 28 m.u. What are the approximate frequencies of phenotypes expected from the cross you proposed in part (b)?

   d. How would the results of the cross differ if the genes are not linked?

25. In rabbits, chocolate-colored fur (w^+) is dominant to white fur (*w*), straight fur (c^+) is dominant to curly fur (*c*), and long ear (s^+) is dominant to short ear (*s*). The cross of a trihybrid rabbit with straight, chocolate-colored fur and long ears to a rabbit that has white, curly fur and short ears produces the following results:

Phenotype	Number
White, short, straight	13
Chocolate, long, straight	165
Chocolate, long, curly	13
White, long, straight	82
Chocolate, short, straight	436
Chocolate, short, curly	79
White, short, curly	162
White, long, curly	450
	1400

   a. Determine the order of the genes on the chromosome, and identify the alleles that are present on each of the homologous chromosomes in the trihybrid rabbits.

   b. Calculate the recombination frequencies between each of the adjacent pairs of genes.

   c. Determine the interference value for this cross.

26. The following progeny are obtained from a test cross of a trihybrid wild-type plant to a plant with the recessive phenotypes compound leaves (*c*), intercalary leaflets (*i*),

and green fruits (*g*). (Traits not listed are wild type.) The test-cross progeny are as follows:

Phenotype	Number
Compound leaves	324
Compound leaves, intercalary leaflets	32
Compound leaves, green fruits	5
Compound leaves, intercalary leaflets, green fruits	51
Intercalary leaflets	3
Intercalary leaflets, green fruits	309
Green fruits	42
Wild type	49
	815

a. Determine the order of the three genes, and construct a genetic map that identifies the correct order and the alleles carried on each chromosome in the trihybrid parental plant.

b. Calculate the frequency of recombination between the adjacent genes in the map.

c. How many double-crossover progeny are expected among the test-cross progeny? Calculate the interference for this cross.

27. In tomatoes, the allele *T* for tall plant height is dominant to dwarf allele *t*, the *P* allele for smooth skin is dominant to the *p* allele for peach fuzz skin, and the allele *R* for round fruit is dominant to the recessive *r* allele for oblong fruit. The genes controlling these traits are linked on chromosome 1 in the tomato genome, and the genes are arranged in the order and with the recombination frequencies shown.

Gene	*T*	*P*	*R*

| Recombination frequency | 0.04 | 0.18 | |

a. A pure-breeding tall, peach fuzz, round plant is crossed to a pure-breeding plant that is dwarf, smooth, oblong. What are the gamete genotypes produced by each of these plants?

b. What are the genotype and phenotype of the F_1 progeny of this cross?

c. What are the genotypes of gametes produced by the F_1, and what is the predicted frequency of each gamete?

d. The F_1 are test-crossed to dwarf, peach fuzz, oblong plants, and 1000 test-cross progeny are produced. What are the phenotypes of test-cross progeny, and what number of progeny is expected in each class?

28. Neurofibromatosis 1 (NF1) is an autosomal dominant disorder inherited on human chromosome 17. Part of the analysis mapping the *NF1* gene to chromosome 17 came from genetic linkage studies testing segregation of *NF1* and

DNA genetic markers on various chromosomes. A DNA marker with two alleles, designated *1* and *2*, is linked to *NF1*. The pedigree below shows segregation of *NF1* (darkened symbols) and gives genotypes for the DNA marker for each family member.

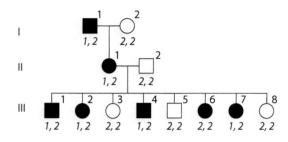

a. Determine the alleles for the *NF1* gene and the DNA marker gene on each chromosome carried by the four family members in generation I and generation II. Use *N* for the dominant *NF1* allele and *n* for the recessive allele and assume I-1 is heterozygous for the disease allele (*Nn*).

b. Based on the phase of alleles on chromosomes in generation II, is there any evidence of recombination among the eight offspring in generation III? Explain.

c. What is the estimated recombination frequency between the *NF1* gene and the DNA marker?

29. A 2006 genetic study of a large American family (Ikeda et al., 2006) identified genetic linkage between DNA markers on chromosome 11 and the gene producing the autosomal dominant neuromuscular disorder spinocerebellar ataxia type 5 (*SCA5*). The following lod score data are taken from the 2006 study:

	Theta (θ) Value					
	0.01	0.05	0.10	0.20	0.30	0.40
SCA5 and DNA marker *A*	11.02	12.26	11.94	10.04	7.26	3.77
SCA5 and DNA marker *B*	0.35	0.94	1.07	0.99	0.75	0.43

a. Does either group of lod scores indicate statistically significant odds in favor of genetic linkage? Explain your answer.

b. What is the maximum value for each set of lod scores?

c. Based on the available information, is DNA marker *A* linked to the gene producing SCA5? Explain your answer.

d. Based on available information, is DNA marker *B* linked to the gene for SCA5? Explain your answer.

30. A *Drosophila* experiment examining potential genetic linkage of X-linked genes studies a recessive eye mutant (echinus), a recessive wing-vein mutation (crossveinless), and a recessive bristle mutation (scute). The wild-type phenotypes are dominant. Trihybrid wild-type females (all have the same genotype) are crossed to hemizygous males displaying the three recessive phenotypes. Among the

20,765 progeny produced from these crosses are the phenotypes and numbers listed in the table. Any phenotype not given is wild type.

Phenotype	Number
1. Echinus	8576
2. Scute	977
3. Crossveinless	716
4. Echinus, scute	681
5. Scute, crossveinless	8808
6. Scute, crossveinless, echinus	4
7. Echinus, crossveinless	1002
8. Wild type	1
	20,765

a. Determine the gene order and identify the alleles on the homologous X chromosomes in the trihybrid females.
b. Calculate the recombination frequencies between each of the gene pairs.
c. Compare the recombination frequencies and speculate about the source of any apparent discrepancies in the recombination data.
d. Use chi-square analysis to demonstrate that the data in this experiment are not the result of independent assortment.

31. As part of their analysis of intragenic recombination, Melvin Green and Kathleen Green studied lozenge-eyed females with the mutation lz^{46} on one X chromosome and the mutation lz^g on the homologous X chromosome. The lz^g-bearing X chromosome also carried recessive mutations for cut wing (ct) and vermilion-colored eye (v). These females were mated to cut wing males that had vermilion-colored, lozenge-shaped eyes. The chromosomes of these flies are depicted in the following drawing.

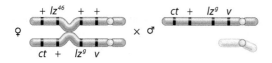

a. Diagram the recombination event within the lz gene and draw the resulting recombinant X chromosomes, illustrating the lz alleles and the flanking markers on each chromosome.
b. What are the phenotypes of progeny male flies carrying lz intragenic recombinants? (A double-mutant

X chromosome carrying both lz^g and lz^{46} produces a compound lozenge eye that has a different appearance than either the lz^g- or lz^{46}-derived eye.)

32. In experiments published in 1918 that sought to verify and expand the genetic linkage and recombination theory proposed by Morgan, Thomas Bregger studied potential genetic linkage in corn (*Zea mays*) for genes controlling kernel color (colored is dominant to colorless) and starch content (starchy is dominant to waxy). Bregger performed two crosses. In Cross 1, pure-breeding colored, starchy-kernel plants (*C1 Wx/C1 Wx*) were crossed to plants pure-breeding for colorless, waxy kernels (*c1 wx/c1 wx*). The F_1 of this cross were test-crossed to colorless, waxy plants. The test-cross progeny are as follows:

Phenotype	Number
Colored, waxy	310
Colored, starchy	858
Colorless, waxy	781
Colorless, starchy	311
	2260

In Cross 2, plants pure-breeding for colored, waxy kernels (*C1 wx/C1 wx*) and colorless, starchy kernels (*c1 Wx/c1 Wx*) were mated, and their F_1 were test-crossed to colorless, waxy plants. The test-cross progeny are as follows:

Phenotype	Number
Colored, waxy	340
Colored, starchy	115
Colorless, waxy	92
Colorless, starchy	298
	845

a. For each set of test-cross progeny, determine whether genetic linkage or independent assortment is more strongly supported by the data. Explain the rationale for your answer.
b. Calculate the recombination frequency for each of the progeny groups.
c. Are the results of these two experiments mutually compatible with the hypothesis of genetic linkage? Explain why or why not.
d. Merge the two sets of progeny data and determine the combined recombination frequency.

6

Genetic Analysis and Mapping in Bacteria and Bacteriophages

CHAPTER OUTLINE

6.1 Bacteria Transfer Genes by Conjugation

6.2 Interrupted Mating Analysis Produces Time-of-Entry Maps

6.3 Conjugation with F′ Strains Produces Partial Diploids

6.4 Bacterial Transformation Produces Genetic Recombination

6.5 Bacterial Transduction Is Mediated by Bacteriophages

6.6 Bacteriophage Chromosomes Are Mapped by Fine-Structure Analysis

6.7 Lateral Gene Transfer Alters Genomes

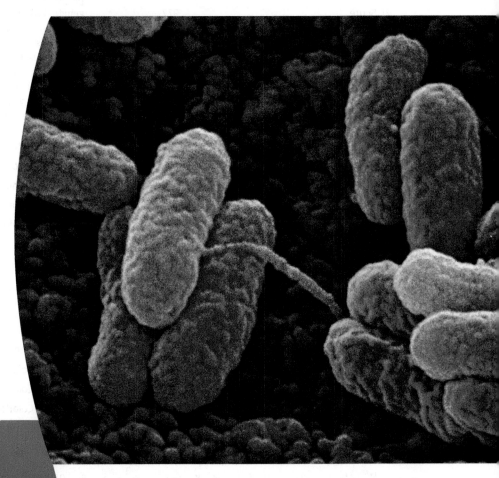

ESSENTIAL IDEAS

- Bacterial conjugation is a one-way transfer of genetic material from a donor cell to a recipient cell. Three types of donor cells can conjugate with recipient cells to transfer donor DNA.

- Donor bacterial genetic maps are derived from conjugation analysis.

- A particular type of bacterial conjugation can produce bacteria with genomes that are partially diploid.

- Transformation is the absorption of extracellular DNA across the cell wall and membrane of a recipient bacterial cell, and its analysis leads to mapping of donor bacterial genes.

- Transduction, mediated by bacteriophages, is the transfer of DNA from a donor bacterial cell to a recipient cell, and its analysis leads to mapping of donor bacterial genes.

- Fine-structure genetic analysis of a bacteriophage genome demonstrated that DNA nucleotide base pairs are the fundamental units of mutation and recombination.

- Lateral gene transfer is a prevalent mechanism for the exchange of genes among bacteria and for the evolution of genomes.

Bacteria transfer DNA to one another by multiple mechanisms, including the process of gene transfer called conjugation, shown here. The bacterial "donor" (center left) transfers DNA through a tube that connects it to a bacterial "recipient" (lower right).

Here's a disturbing little secret of human life: Your body contains approximately 100 trillion cells, but only about 10 trillion of them are yours! The other 90% of the cells you carry around are bacteria, fungi, and other forms of microscopic life. Many of these biological hitchhikers perform useful, even essential, functions. For example, you carry hundreds of species of bacteria in your gut that collectively have a mass of more than 3 pounds. Without these intestinal bacteria, your digestion of carbohydrates would be impaired, and your ability to manufacture essential nutrients such as vitamin B_{12} and vitamin K would be disabled. The bacteria teeming in your digestive tract also help keep potentially harmful bacteria at bay by vigorously competing for available nutrients. Similarly, the millions of bacteria that currently reside on your skin (yes, even though you showered recently!) help keep your skin healthy by competing with infectious bacteria. Despite this normal and healthy competition, harmful bacteria can gain access to our bodies. Occasionally even our normally helpful microbial passengers turn against us and cause illness, infection, or, in extreme cases, death.

Given the biological, medical, and technological importance of bacteria and other microorganisms, it is no wonder they are studied intensively in modern genetics, using the bacterium *Escherichia coli* and yeast *Saccharomyces cerevisiae* as model genetic organisms. The relative ease of studying microorganisms fueled revolutionary change in genetics in the latter half of the 20th century. Much of the initial information in molecular genetics and many of the methods of genetic analysis pioneered in the study of bacteria have proven valuable in the study of more complex organisms.

In this chapter, our focus is on investigating and understanding how genetic analysis is applied to the study of gene transfer and mapping in bacterial and bacteriophage genomes. We take a historical genetic approach in our discussion, focusing on the applications of genetic analysis that were used to map genes in bacterial genomes in the decades before genome sequencing was developed. Genome sequences of thousands of bacterial species are now published, and their analysis verifies the accuracy and validity of the conclusions reached through use of the approaches we describe in this chapter.

We begin by looking at three mechanisms by which DNA can be transferred from one bacterium to another. After showing how analysis of these processes helps microbial geneticists locate the positions of genes on the bacterial chromosome, the chapter turns to a discussion of bacteriophages, the viruses that infect bacterial cells. It describes experiments that led to a fine-structure map of a bacteriophage genome and provided an essential bridge between transmission genetics and modern molecular genetics.

6.1 Bacteria Transfer Genes by Conjugation

Bacteria propagate by binary fission, a process in which the bacterial chromosome replicates, and a copy is distributed to each of the progeny cells along with a share of the contents of the dividing cell. In a matter of hours, this form of clonal propagation can generate a "colony" containing thousands of genetically identical bacteria cells. The ability of bacteria to produce colonies of clones, however, does not mean that bacteria never recombine genetically. A series of studies in the 1940s and 1950s identified and described the three mechanisms of gene transfer and recombination between bacteria that are a focus of this chapter.

Bacteria are a highly diverse taxonomic group, and they are essential for genetic study. Among the features that make bacteria so useful to geneticists are the following:

- **Genomic simplicity.** Most bacterial genomes contain fewer genes and fewer base pairs in their haploid genomes than do other organisms.
- **Uncomplicated genotypes.** The haploid genomes of most bacteria allow all mutations to be observed directly, without interference from dominance interactions between alleles.
- **Short generation times.** Bacteria reproduce rapidly; their generation times can be measured in minutes.
- **Large numbers of progeny.** Enormous numbers of clonal progeny can be examined, increasing the likelihood that statistically rare events will be observed.
- **Ease of propagation.** Microbes may be grown either in liquid culture or on culture plates. The cultures are easy and inexpensive to maintain, and they require little laboratory space.
- **Numerous heritable differences.** Mutants are easily created, identified, isolated, and manipulated for examination.

A central characteristic of interest in this chapter is the propensity of bacteria to transfer genetic material from one individual bacterium to another. Transfer occurs by three processes: *conjugation*, the transfer of replicated DNA from a donor bacterium to a recipient bacterium; *transformation*, the uptake of DNA from the environment by a recipient bacterium; and *transduction*, the transfer of DNA from a donor bacterium to a recipient bacterium by way of a viral vector. Each of these mechanisms involves a *one-way transfer* of genetic material from a bacterial *donor* cell to a *recipient* cell. The transferred DNA is either an extrachromosomal *plasmid* or a portion of the donor bacterial chromosome. Often, the plasmids transferred into recipient cells bring new genes that change the growth behavior of recipient cells. Alternatively, plasmids may carry a *second copy* of genes already on the bacterial chromosome. When bacterial chromosome DNA from the donor cell is transferred to a recipient bacterium, the homologous parts of the donor and recipient DNA molecules can undergo recombination that leads to a change in the genotype of the recipient cell.

Regardless of the nature of the DNA transferred from donor cells to recipient cells, a key to understanding the process is to remember that it is a one-way street: Genetic material moves from donor to recipient.

Each of these processes is an example of *lateral gene transfer,* a nonreproductive process through which bacteria and archaea actively exchange genetic material. Lateral gene transfer also takes place between bacteria and eukaryotes. The impact of these events on genomes and on the evolution of life are topics for later discussion in this chapter.

Characteristics of Bacterial Genomes

Bacterial genomes are usually composed of a *single* chromosome that carries primarily essential genes—those necessary for the species' metabolic and growth activities. The **bacterial chromosome** is usually a covalently closed, *circular* molecule of double-stranded DNA. In keeping with the small size of the genome—from a few hundred thousand to several million base pairs—the bacterial chromosome, too, is usually quite *small,* likewise varying from a few hundred thousand to several million base pairs.

In addition to the main bacterial chromosome, most bacteria also carry multiple copies of **plasmids,** small double-stranded circular DNA molecules containing nonessential genes that are used infrequently or under specialized conditions not ordinarily encountered by the species (**Figure 6.1**). Plasmids vary widely in their

number of genes and their total number of base pairs, but they are always considerably smaller than bacterial chromosomes. Plasmids are described as extrachromosomal DNA, meaning they are generally separate from the bacterial chromosome, although we will encounter some exceptions as the chapter proceeds.

Many different kinds of naturally occurring plasmids are found in bacteria, and each contains several genes. One plasmid we are about to discuss, called an **F (fertility) plasmid,** contains genes that promote its own transfer from a donor bacterium to a recipient. Another type of plasmid we discuss, known as an **R (resistance) plasmid,** carries **antibiotic resistance** genes that can be transferred from donors to recipients. Plasmids are easily modified in the laboratory to produce specific characteristics or to carry particular genes that are useful in a wide range of recombinant DNA applications (see Chapters 16 and 17). For purposes of most of our discussion in this chapter, we will only consider antibiotic resistance genes that are carried on an R plasmid. Consequently, a strain that is resistant to an antibiotic carries an R plasmid with the gene, and an antibiotic susceptible strain does not carry an R plasmid. This approach simplifies our discussion and understanding of experimental results, but in reality, numerous bacterial strains carry antibiotic resistance genes on the bacterial chromosome. The transfer of both plasmid-borne and chromosome-borne antibiotic resistance genes among bacterial strains is a major contributing factor to the rapid spread of antibiotic resistant strains of infectious bacteria.

Plasmids generally replicate autonomously. Consequently, up to several dozen copies of a plasmid can be found in a single bacterial cell. Such plasmids are identified as "high-copy-number" plasmids. Alternatively, low-copy-number plasmids are generally unable to replicate on their own because their replication is tied to that of the bacterial chromosome. These plasmids are present in 1 or 2 copies per bacterial cell. As you will soon see, high-copy-number plasmids play a pivotal role in conjugation and in the analysis of bacterial gene transfer and gene mapping.

A key to identifying the genotypes of bacterial strains is to assess their growth on media having different constituents. This is a procedure that is easy to master by understanding a few principles of microbial growth. **Research Technique 6.1** introduces you to the interpretation of microbial-growth results and the identification of microbial genotype.

Conjugation Identified

Bacterial DNA transfer was first identified by Joshua Lederberg and Edward Tatum in 1946. They used two triple-auxotrophic strains of *E. coli* that had different nutritional requirements for growth (see Experimental Insight 4.1, pages 125–126, for a review of prototrophy and auxotrophy). The researchers first established three

Ruptured
E. coli cell

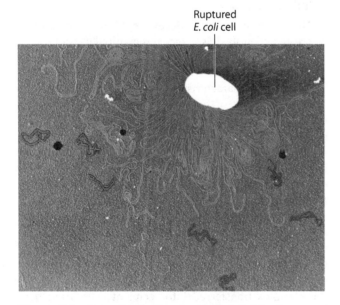

Figure 6.1 Bacterial chromosome and plasmids. A ruptured *E. coli* cell has released its chromosomal DNA along with multiple plasmids (red).

Research Technique 6.1

Genotyping Using Microbial Growth

The results of experiments on microbes described in this chapter have shaped our understanding of how genes work, including how they are organized and how they are expressed. A basic set of common laboratory techniques and analyses assessing growth or failure to grow in liquid or semisolid media made up of different components can be used to determine the genetic makeup of microorganisms. Proper interpretation of the genotype of a microbe based on its pattern of growth on different media is an essential skill of genetic analysis that is easy to master once you understand a few key concepts.

ANABOLIC AND CATABOLIC PATHWAYS Compounds that influence the growth of microbes on growth media fall into two broad categories. In the first are compounds synthesized by prototrophic (wild-type) microbes in biosynthetic pathways that are often described as *anabolic pathways*. In anabolic pathways, *energy is used* to *synthesize* complex compounds from simpler ones through sequential reaction steps. Figure 4.17 and the accompanying discussion of the anabolic pathway that synthesizes the amino acid methionine (pages 121–123) provide an example. In contrast, *catabolic pathways* are pathways through which *energy is produced* by the *breakdown* of complex compounds into simpler ones. Catabolic pathways also follow sequential steps. Our discussion of phenylketonuria (PKU) (pages 121–123) highlights the catabolic pathway that breaks down the amino acid phenylalanine. Similarly, compounds such as polysaccharide sugars like lactose and other carbohydrates are broken down in catabolic pathways.

VISUALIZING MICROBIAL GROWTH When microbial growth occurs on a semisolid growth plate in a petri dish, individual *colonies* may appear on the plate. Each colony is actually hundreds of thousands to millions of individual microbes that are all descendant from a single microbial cell among those originally spread on the plate in a very dilute solution. Depending on microbe genotypes and the composition of the growth medium, it is possible that more than one microbial genotype is growing on a particular plate, but what is certain is that the cells in each colony are genetically identical. In a liquid growth medium, microbial growth produces cloudiness—the result of there being so many living cells in the growth vessel that the passage of light through the medium is impeded by the cells. There are no colonies in liquid media.

Identifying the genotype of a microbe often requires assessing the growth of a particular colony on different growth media. This is accomplished by *replica plating*. One method of replica plating is to simply touch a colony growing on one growth medium with a sterile toothpick or a similar instrument to gather some cells of the colony and then touch a spot on a different growth plate. Systematic use of a grid pattern on the new plate and care in the recording of growth results permit comparison of growth results on different plates so as to identify colony genotypes. An alternative replica plating method involves transferring all the colonies growing on one plate to a new growth plate all at once. A round wooden or plastic block slightly smaller in diameter than a petri dish and covered with a piece of sterilized velvet is used for this. The velvet-covered block is gently pressed onto the colonies of one plate to pick up some cells from each colony and then is used to stamp one or more fresh growth-medium plates. Growth results can be compared between plates, and genotypes of colonies can be identified because all the colonies are in the same relative positions on both the original and the new plate.

ALLELIC IDENTIFICATION Distinguishing between compounds produced by anabolic pathways and those broken down in catabolic pathways is a critical aspect of interpreting microbial growth and identifying microbial genotype that requires knowledge of growth media and their constituents. As defined in Experimental Insight 4.1, a *minimal medium* contains glucose as the carbon source, since glycolysis is the fundamental energy-producing reaction in many organisms, including humans and many microbes. The minimal medium also contains nitrogen, some inorganic salts, and water. In order to grow on minimal medium, a microbe must synthesize every compound it needs for metabolism, DNA replication, transcription, and translation. The compounds required to carry out these essential functions are the products of anabolic pathways. Only *prototrophs* (wild-types) can synthesize all the products required for growth on a minimal medium. The ability to synthesize an essential compound by completion of an anabolic pathway is indicated in genetic notation by a "+" (plus) symbol and identifies a wild-type allele; thus, a microbe capable of biosynthesizing the amino acid methionine is identified as met^+ (spoken "met plus"). In contrast, the "−" (minus) symbol indicates the organism in an *auxotroph* (mutant) that is unable to synthesize a particular compound due to mutation. The control prototroph shown in Figure 4.19 (p. 127) is met^+, whereas the four other strains are each met^-. Auxotrophs can also grow on *supplemented minimal medium*, which is a minimal medium supplemented with just the specific compound or compounds an auxotroph is unable to produce on its own.

In the case of catabolic pathways—allelic symbols identify the ability of a strain to complete a catabolic pathway with a superscript "+" and the inability to complete a catabolic pathway with the "−" symbol. For example, microbes that are able to grow on a medium that contains the milk sugar lactose instead of glucose are lac^+. The ability to grow on lactose requires production of the enzymes that breakdown lactose into simpler compounds. In contrast, microbes that are unable to grow on lactose-containing media are lac^-. These strains are unable to produce one or more of the enzymes required for lactose metabolism.

The accompanying figure guides you through the identification of prototrophs and auxotrophs among 10 microbial colonies for the amino acids alanine (ala) and proline (pro) and for the ability of the colonies to break down lactose. Genotype identification is accomplished by comparing growth on plates of media containing different constituents. The accompanying table summarizes the genotype of each colony and the reasoning used to identify the genotype.

(continued)

Research Technique 6.1 Continued

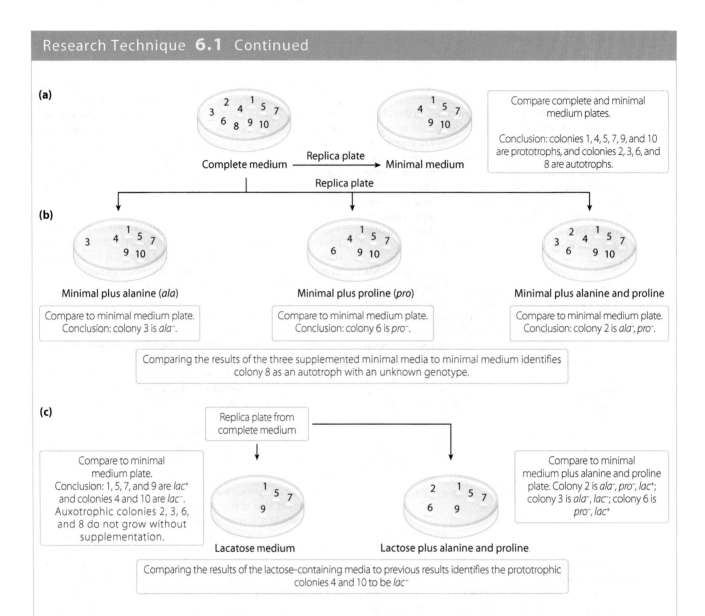

Colony	Genotype	Explanation
1, 5, 7, and 9	$ala^+ pro^+ lac^+$	These are prototrophs. Grow on minimal medium and on lactose medium.
2	$ala^- pro^- lac^+$	Auxotroph. Does not grow on minimal medium. Grows on minimal medium supplemented with both alanine and proline. Also grows on lactose medium supplemented with alanine and proline.
3	$ala^- pro^+ lac^-$	Auxotroph. Does not grow on minimal medium. Grows on minimal medium supplemented with alanine. Does not grow on lactose medium supplemented with alanine and proline.
4 and 10	$ala^+ pro^+ lac^-$	Prototroph. Grows on minimal medium. Does not grow on lactose medium.
6	$ala^+ pro^- lac^+$	Auxotroph. Does not grow on minimal medium. Grows on minimal medium plus proline and grows on lactose medium plus alanine and proline.
8	Unknown genotype	Auxotroph. Does not grow on minimal medium.

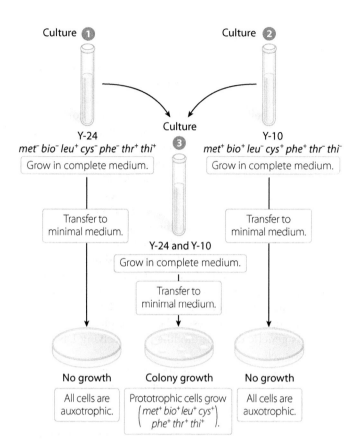

Culture ❶   Culture ❷

Culture ❸

Y-24
met⁻ bio⁻ leu⁺ cys⁻ phe⁻ thr⁺ thi⁺

Grow in complete medium.

Transfer to minimal medium.

Y-10
met⁺ bio⁺ leu⁻ cys⁺ phe⁺ thr⁻ thi⁻

Grow in complete medium.

Transfer to minimal medium.

Y-24 and Y-10

Grow in complete medium.

Transfer to minimal medium.

No growth

All cells are auxotrophs.

Colony growth

Prototrophic cells grow (*met⁺ bio⁺ leu⁺ cys⁺ phe⁺ thr⁺ thi⁺*).

No growth

All cells are auxotrophs.

Figure 6.2 Lederberg and Tatum's detection of recombination between auxotrophic *E. coli* cells. Auxotrophic bacterial strains ❶ (Y-24) and ❷ (Y-10) each contain multiple mutations and grow on complete medium, but not on minimal medium. ❸ Mixing the strains leads to the formation of prototrophic bacteria that grow on minimal medium.

separate bacterial cultures growing, initially, in a complete medium (**Figure 6.2**). In culture ❶, they grew an auxotrophic strain called Y-24, which has the genotype *bio⁻ leu⁺ cys⁻ phe⁻ thr⁺ thi⁺*. Because of its genotype, the Y-24 strain requires addition of the vitamin biotin (*bio*) and the amino acids cysteine (*cys*) and phenylalanine (*phe*) to a minimal medium for growth. In culture ❷, they placed an auxotrophic strain called Y-10, which has the genotype *bio⁺ leu⁻ cys⁺ phe⁺ thr⁻ thi⁻*. The Y-10 strain requires addition of the vitamin thiamine (*thi*) and the amino acids leucine (*leu*) and threonine (*thr*) for growth. Culture ❸ contained an equal mixture of both Y-10 and Y-24.

Each culture was allowed to grow. Then approximately 10^9 cells from each culture were plated onto dishes of minimal medium, where a prototrophic (wild-type) genotype is required for growth. Lederberg and Tatum saw no growth on Plates 1 and 2, which contained cells transferred from culture ❶ and culture ❷, respectively. These results were consistent with the nutritional requirements of Y-24 and Y-10, and indicated that all the

cells transferred to those plates were auxotrophs. Plate 3, however, developed about 100 growing colonies! These colonies grew from bacterial cells that had somehow acquired the prototrophic genotype (*met⁺ bio⁺ leu⁺ cys⁺ phe⁺ thr⁺ thi⁺*).

Lederberg and Tatum were certain that this outcome did not result from the reversion (reverse mutation) of auxotrophs to prototrophs (reversion is mutation that produces a wild-type allele from a mutant allele). First, the odds of that many genes reverting at once are prohibitively small. Second, plates 1 and 2 served as "negative control" plates. If reversion were responsible, these plates would show colony growth. Instead of reversion, the researchers claimed there had been a transfer of genetic information. More specifically, they proposed that one auxotrophic strain was transferring some of its prototrophic alleles to the other auxotrophic strain when the two strains were mixed, and that the second strain was replacing its auxotrophic alleles by incorporating the prototrophic information from the first strain.

Lederberg and Tatum hypothesized that physical contact between bacteria was necessary for gene transfer, but their original experiment did not provide direct evidence that this might be so. Four years later, Bernard Davis replicated the work and showed the necessity of contact between bacterial cells for gene transfer to take place. For his experiment, Davis constructed a U-tube with a fine glass filter separating one arm from the other (**Figure 6.3**). The filter was a glass disk with very small pores that allowed passage of small molecules such as nutrients but not bacterial cells. A cotton ball plugging one end of the U-tube and a rubber stopper connected to an air line at the other allowed Davis to move the material in the tube by alternating suction and pressure. The tube contained a culture of *E. coli* strain Y-10 on one side of the glass disk and a culture of strain 58-161, auxotrophic for methionine synthesis (*met⁻*), on the other side of the disk, and the glass disk prevented direct contact between the two bacterial strains.

Based on Lederberg and Tatum's experiments, Davis hypothesized that direct contact between the auxotrophic strains was needed to produce prototrophic bacteria. After alternating suction and pressure for several hours, Davis plated bacterial samples from each side of the U-tube onto minimal medium and found no growth from either side of the U-tube. This lack of growth was an indication that cells on either side of the disk retained their auxotrophy. Davis concluded that physical contact between bacterial cells is required for gene transfer to take place.

Microscopic studies have confirmed the physical union between bacteria hypothesized by Lederberg and Tatum and supported by Davis. This process of gene transfer is called **conjugation.** One of the participating bacteria, known as a **donor cell,** transfers some of its

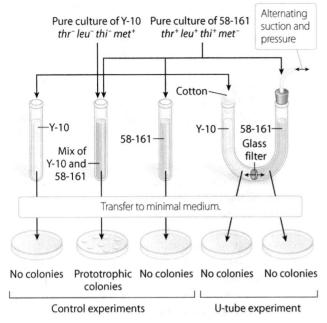

Figure 6.3   Davis's U-tube experiment, showing that genetic recombination requires cell-to-cell contact. Auxotrophic bacterial strains Y-10 and 58-161 are unable to grow on minimal medium, but produce some prototrophs that grow on minimal medium when they make contact following mixing. Prototrophs are not produced when the auxotrophs are placed in a U-tube, indicating that direct contact is required to generate prototrophic bacteria.

genetic information to the other cell, known as a **recipient cell.** The genetic information is conveyed by way of a hollow tube known as a **conjugation pilus** or **conjugation tube** that physically connects donor and recipient. Conjugation is pictured in the chapter-opening photo on page 186. In the photo, the conjugation pilus is the thread-like structure in the middle connecting the donor and recipient bacterial cells.

Transfer of the F Factor

In 1953, William Hayes discovered that the bacteria interacting in Lederberg and Tatum's and in Davis's experiments did not contribute equally to the genetic outcome, as they do in a genetic cross between eukaryotes. Instead, the process was unequal, leading Hayes to conclude that a one-way transfer of genetic information takes place between donors and recipients.

Hayes further proposed that the ability to act as a donor was hereditary and was determined by a "fertility factor" (F factor) that was transferable from donors to recipients. Donors are designated as F^+(F^+cells) to indicate their possession of an F factor, and recipients are identified as F^-(F^-cells) and lack the F factor. An F^- is also known as a **recipient cell.** In the years after Hayes proposed the existence of the F factor,

microbiologists identified the F factor as the F plasmid (fertility plasmid).

Microbiologists today know that conjugation is controlled by genes carried on the F plasmid. As a consequence, only donor cells initiate conjugation. Recipient cells (F^- cells) are unable to initiate conjugation. Conjugation occurs between a donor cell and a recipient, but not between two donor cells. F factor genes direct the construction of hair-like pili (the plural of *pilus*) that have sensory functions. One pilus becomes specialized to serve as the conjugation pilus that connects donor and recipient, forming the conduit across which DNA from the donor cell is transferred (see the chapter-opening photo). Ultimately, three kinds of cells are seen in conjugation: a donor cell that contains an F plasmid and donates genetic information, a recipient cell that receives DNA from a donor cell but does not contain a functional F factor, and the **exconjugant cell** that is produced by conjugation. An exconjugant cell is essentially a recipient cell that has had its genetic content modified by receiving DNA from a donor cell.

The F factor is some 100 kb in length, and about 35% of its sequence is devoted to about 40 genes that control conjugation (**Figure 6.4**). The F plasmid genes that play a role in *E. coli* conjugation are given four-letter designations consisting of the prefix *tra* or *trb* followed by a capital letter. Much of the remainder of the F factor consists of four insertion sequence (IS) elements: one copy of IS2, two copies of IS3, and one copy of the very large IS1000. **Insertion sequence (IS) elements** are mobile segments of bacterial DNA that are capable of transposing themselves throughout the bacterial genome and have an important functional role in bacterial gene transfer Section 13.6.

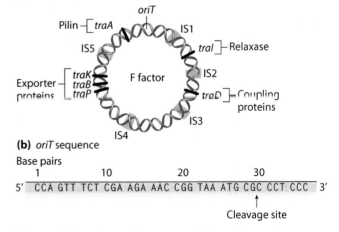

Figure 6.4   F plasmid structure. (a) Several genes important in F factor transfer are shown along with the origin of transfer (*oriT*) and several insertion sequence (IS) locations. **(b)** The 38-bp sequence of *oriT*, including the cleavage site.

Conjugation between an F$^+$ donor and an F$^-$ recipient transfers a copy of the F factor and produces exconjugants that are F$^+$ donors, as illustrated in Figure 6.5. Conjugation begins with contact between the F$^+$ and the F$^-$ cell, initiated by the formation of a conjugation pilus. Conjugation pili are composed of pilin protein, produced by the *traA* gene on the F factor (see Figure 6.4). Circular DNA elements like the F factor that can replicate independently of the bacterial chromosome or, as we discuss in the following section, can integrate into the bacterial

chromosome and replicate as part of the chromosome, are also termed **episomes**.

Shortly after contact is established by the conjugation pilus, gene expression from the F factor produces a protein complex called the relaxosome. This protein complex binds to a specialized F factor sequence called the **origin of transfer (*oriT*)**. At *oriT*, the relaxosome catalyzes cleavage of one phosphodiester bond on one DNA strand, called the **T strand,** to signify that this is the strand transferred to the recipient cell. DNA cleavage at *oriT* defines

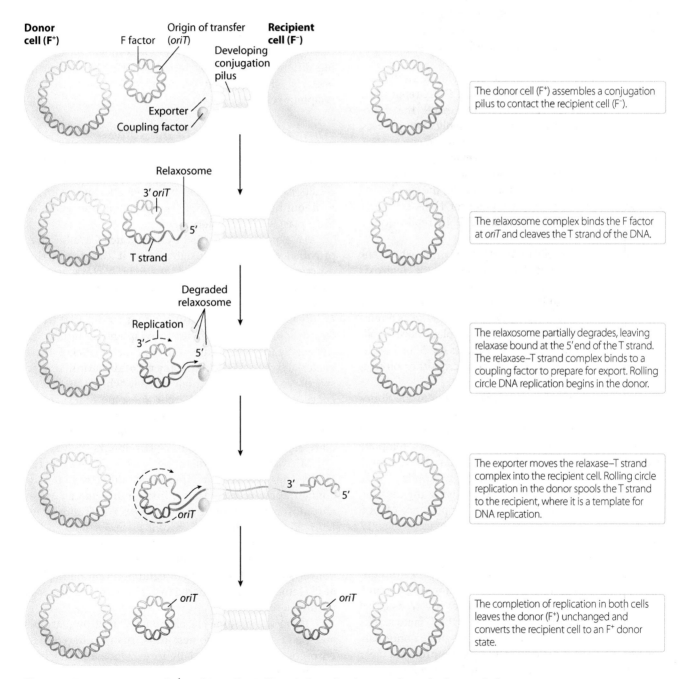

Figure 6.5   Conjugation of F$^+$ and F$^-$ cells. Rolling circle replication transfers a single strand of the F factor, beginning at *oriT*, from a donor cell to a recipient cell, where it is replicated to convert the recipient cell (F$^-$) to an F$^+$ donor.

a 3′ end and a 5′ end on the T strand and initiates some unwinding of the DNA duplex in the vicinity of *oriT*.

T strand unwinding releases most of the components of the relaxosome, but one protein, called relaxase, the product of the *traI* gene, binds to the free 5′ end of the T strand DNA to form a nucleoprotein complex. The nucleoprotein complex at the 5′ end of the T strand provides a critical recognition signal for a protein called the coupling protein, the product of the *traD* gene, which takes a position near the entry of the conjugation pilus. The nucleoprotein complex binds briefly to the coupling protein and then affiliates with several proteins of the exporter complex that move the nucleoprotein complex and the T strand across the conjugation pilus and into the recipient cell.

T strand transfer across the conjugation pilus is accompanied by a specialized process of DNA replication, known as **rolling circle replication,** inside the donor cell. In this specialized unidirectional replication process, one strand of DNA is spooled off across the conjugation pilus while, within the donor, the remaining DNA strand serves as the template for unidirectional synthesis of a replacement DNA strand. In the recipient, the spooled-off DNA strand also acts as a template for DNA synthesis. We discuss the molecular details of DNA replication in Chapter 7.

Rolling circle replication begins at *oriT*, where the single-stranded break in DNA exposed the 3′ hydroxyl end of the T strand. At this exposed 3′ hydroxyl end, DNA polymerase adds new nucleotides, utilizing the complementary, intact (unbroken) DNA strand as a template. The new DNA replication taking place during rolling circle replication eventually displaces the 5′ end of the T strand, freeing it to be transferred across the conjugation pilus into the recipient cell.

Completion of rolling circle replication in the donor cell restores the donor's double-stranded F factor, leaving that cell's F^+ donor state intact. Meanwhile, inside the recipient cell, the imported T strand acts as a template directing the synthesis of a complementary DNA strand. At the conclusion of this process, the two ends of *oriT* join to circularize the molecule, completing the creation of an F factor in the recipient. With the presence of an F factor, the formerly F^- recipient cell is converted to an F^+ donor cell.

Table 6.1 identifies two pivotal outcomes of $F^+ \times F^-$ conjugation. First, complete transfer of the F factor converts the F^- recipient cell to an F^+ donor cell. Second, no donor bacterial chromosomal genes are transferred during this conjugation process. Only the F factor DNA is transferred to an F^- recipient cell by an F^+ donor cell. You will recall that Lederberg and Tatum provided clear evidence of chromosomal gene transfer from one bacterial strain to another, and Davis showed that conjugation was required for the transfer to occur. However, $F^+ \times F^-$ conjugation *is not responsible* for the observations of

Table 6.1	Outcomes of Bacterial Conjugation	
Conjugation	Outcome	
	Exconjugant Converted to Donor State?	Donor Bacterial Genes Transferred to Exconjugant?
$F^+ \times F^-$	Yes, $F^- \rightarrow F^+$	No
Hfr $\times F^-$	No	Yes
$F' \times F^-$	Yes, $F^- \rightarrow F'$	Yes

Lederberg and Tatum; the logical conclusion is that there must be some other type of conjugation, involving different kinds of bacterial donor cells, to transfer bacterial chromosomal genes from a donor cell to a recipient cell.

Formation of an Hfr Chromosome

Contact between the donor and the recipient bacteria is required for gene transfer, but the Lederberg and Tatum results cannot be explained by conjugation involving an F^+ donor because in $F^+ \times F^-$ conjugation, only genes on the F plasmid are transferred.

An experiment in 1953 by Luigi Luca Cavalli-Sforza provided critical new insight when it was found that a previously unknown form of donor bacteria was responsible for the gene transfers observed by Lederberg, Tatum, and Davis. Working with mutagenized donor *E. coli*, Cavalli-Sforza identified donor strains that transferred donor bacterial genes to recipient bacteria at an extraordinarily high rate. Cavalli-Sforza labeled these bacterial strains **high-frequency recombination,** or **Hfr,** strains to indicate the high rate at which Hfr donor genes recombined with the chromosome of F^- recipients. Cavalli-Sforza also determined that conjugation involving Hfr donors and F^- recipients virtually never converted the recipients to F^+ or Hfr donors.

Microscopic examination of Cavalli-Sforza's Hfr strain revealed an important difference in the configuration of the F factor. Instead of being an extra-chromosomal plasmid, the F factor in Hfr strains is integrated into the bacterial chromosome, forming an **Hfr chromosome** (Figure 6.6). The formation of Hfr chromosomes is rare: Only about 1 in every 100,000 F^+ cells converts to an Hfr cell. The integration event takes place at IS elements that are shared by F plasmids and bacterial chromosomes.

There are multiple IS elements shared by plasmids and bacterial chromosomes; thus, many different Hfr chromosomes can potentially form. Once an Hfr chromosome forms, it is stable and does not change to an alternative Hfr form. Two attributes of the F factors in Hfr chromosomes distinguish one Hfr from another. First, the *location* of F factor integration varies between

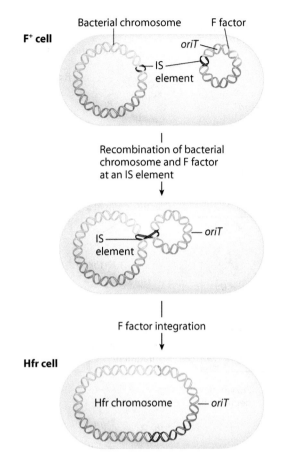

F⁺ cell

Bacterial chromosome   F factor

oriT

IS element

|

Recombination of bacterial chromosome and F factor at an IS element

↓

IS element   *oriT*

|

F factor integration

↓

Hfr cell

Hfr chromosome   *oriT*

Figure 6.6   Hfr chromosomes. Hfr cells carry an Hfr chromosome that is created when an F factor integrates into an insertion sequence (IS) in the bacterial chromosome.

Hfr strains: It can occur at any of the IS sites present on the bacterial chromosome. Second, the integrated F factor can have one of two different *orientations* at each integration location. The integration of an F factor to form a new Hfr chromosome occurs just once, establishing an Hfr strain with a site of F factor insertion and an orientation of the F factor that are fixed characteristics of all bacteria of the resulting Hfr lineage. Both location and orientation of the F factor are important to consider in mapping bacterial genes in Hfr chromosomes, as we discuss in Section 6.2.

Hfr Gene Transfer

Hfr bacteria transfer genetic material to recipient cells by the same rolling circle replication process seen in $F^+ \times F^-$ conjugation. As in $F^+ \times F^-$ conjugation, the relaxosome binds to *oriT* and cuts the T strand to initiate unwinding and transfer of the T strand to the recipient. A portion of the integrated F factor is transferred first, followed by the bacterial chromosomes and finally by the remainder of the integrated F factor. In theory the entire Hfr chromosome could be transferred during Hfr $\times$ F⁻ conjugation, but in reality this is impossible.

The normal movement of bacteria will break the conjugation pilus long before Hfr transfer is completed. Thus, only a portion of the F factor sequence is transferred from the donor to the recipient, along with a portion of the donor bacterial chromosome containing genes located near the IS site of insertion. In conjugation experiments, the duration of conjugation is variable in duration. Some conjugation events are very short, others quite long, and others of intermediate duration.

The segment of T strand DNA that is successfully transferred into the recipient cell is used as template DNA to generate a double-stranded linear fragment. At whatever point the conjugation pilus ruptures, conjugation is interrupted, and T strand transfer and replication cease. **Figure 6.7** illustrates conjugation between an Hfr with the genotype $thr^+ \ leu^- \ str^S$ and an F⁻ with the genotype $thr^- \ leu^+ \ str^R$ (the function of str^R and str^S is explained momentarily). Within the recipient cell, the donor DNA is a linear double-stranded DNA fragment containing a portion of the F factor and a segment of donor bacterial DNA that was adjacent to *oriT*. Without the complete *oriT* sequence, the linear DNA cannot circularize; and since only a portion of the F factor is transferred, Hfr donors cannot convert F⁻ recipient cells to a donor state (see Table 6.1). However, before the linear segment of donated donor DNA undergoes enzymatic degradation in the recipient cell, it can undergo homologous recombination with the recipient chromosome. The new exconjugant cell, formerly the recipient cell, may thus acquire one or more genes from the donor bacterial chromosome.

Conjugation experiments mix one strain of donor bacteria in a culture vessel with a different strain of recipient bacteria. Exconjugants produced within the vessel can be identified by their acquisition of donor genes. Exconjugants are identified by their genotypes that are distinct from those of either the donor strain or the recipient strain. Exconjugants are identified by their growth on a **selective growth medium,** a medium containing compounds that permit only exconjugants with specific genotypes to grow and that also prevent the growth of donor cells and recipient cells.

In experiments of this kind, antibiotic sensitivity and resistance is used as a tool to control growth of bacteria. In the recipient cells, resistance to the antibiotic streptomycin (str^R) comes from a gene carried on an extrachromosomal R plasmid (see Figure 6.7). The donor cell is streptomycin sensitive (str^S), but this is due to the *absence of an R plasmid,* not to the presence of an allele for streptomycin sensitivity. Streptomycin resistance is therefore a genotypic attribute of recipient and exconjugant cells but not of donor cells, and the presence of streptomycin in the selective growth medium will kill donor cells so they do not grow and potentially confuse the analysis.

Figure 6.7 Hfr conjugation and exconjugant detection. An Hfr chromosome fragment transferred during interrupted mating between an Hfr donor cell to an F⁻ recipient cell can undergo homologous recombination with the recipient chromosome. Exconjugants are detected on selective growth media, such as the minimal medium shown here.

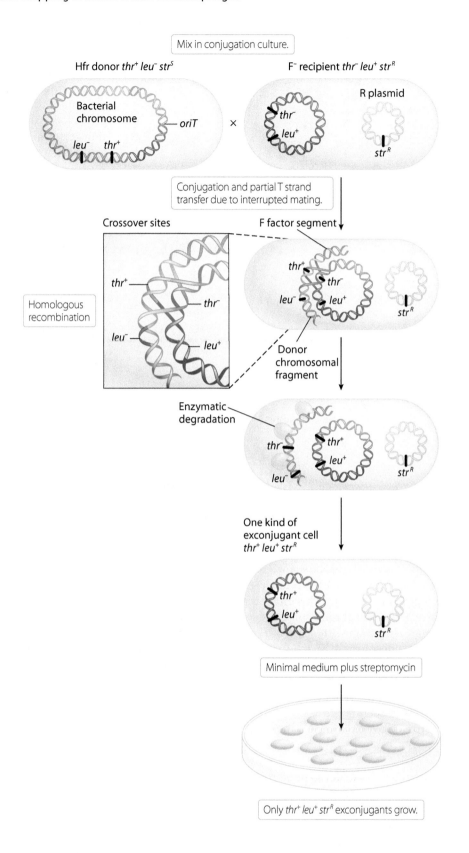

As an example, consider again a conjugation experiment involving an Hfr strain that is susceptible to streptomycin (str^S) and carries the alleles thr^+ and leu^- (for biosynthesis of the amino acid threonine and the inability to synthesize leucine). Imagine that the F⁻ strain is unable to synthesize threonine (thr^-) but capable of leucine synthesis (leu^+) and resistant to streptomycin (str^R). The selective medium necessary to grow and isolate exconjugants in this case is a minimal medium plate with added streptomycin. The streptomycin in the selective medium kills str^S donor cells, and the absence of threonine prevents growth of nonrecombinant recipient cells. All growing cells on the selection plate are $thr^+ leu^+ str^R$, a genotype that could occur only in exconjugants.

In Figure 6.7, a segment of donor DNA containing $thr^+ leu^-$ is shown aligning with its homologous counterpart in the recipient bacterial chromosome, containing $thr^- leu^+$. Homologous recombination can replace a segment of the recipient chromosome with a homologous segment of DNA from the donor chromosome. In the case shown here, two crossovers transfer thr^+ from the donor DNA into the recipient chromosome, so that exconjugants have the genotype $thr^+ leu^+ str^R$. This recombination is produced by the activity of a group of recombination proteins and enzymes in bacteria that operate in the *RecBCD pathway*. We discuss this pathway, and its counterpart used during meiotic recombination in eukaryotes, in Sections 12.6 and 12.7.

With or without homologous recombination to form an exconjugant, the ultimate fate of linear DNA in bacteria cells is enzymatic degradation through the action of nuclease enzymes. If nucleases reach the donated DNA before it can pair and recombine with the recipient chromosome, exconjugant formation is blocked. If recombination does take place, an exconjugant chromosome forms, and the segment of the recipient chromosome that was spliced out during recombination is degraded along with the remainder of the donated DNA.

For our purposes, conjugation between an Hfr donor cell and an F⁻ recipient cell has two key outcomes. First, the transfer of one or more donor alleles into the recipient chromosome by homologous recombination forms an exconjugant chromosome. Second, the F factor is not transferred in full during conjugation, and therefore the F⁻ recipient cell is not converted to a donor state (see Table 6.1).

6.2 Interrupted Mating Analysis Produces Time-of-Entry Maps

We have noted that Hfr chromosomes are too long to be fully transferred from a donor cell to a recipient cell. As a consequence, **interrupted mating,** the cessation of conjugation caused by breakage of the conjugation tube, takes place during naturally occurring conjugation. Interrupted matings stop conjugation before the Hfr chromosome can be completely transferred from the donor to the recipient. Several decades ago, researchers realized that if experimental conjugation was tested for gene transfer at timed intervals, it would be possible

to map the order of donor genes, and to determine the distances between genes. This experimental strategy is called **time-of-entry mapping.**

Each Hfr strain used in time-of-entry mapping experiments will transfer genes in a specific order that is a characteristic of the strain. The *order* of gene transfer and the *time* of the first appearance of recombinants for each gene are functions of the gene's proximity to the origin of transfer (*oriT*). As a result, genes that are closest to the 5′ end of the T strand cross the conjugation pilus shortly after conjugation begins, while genes that are more distant from the 5′ end of the T strand will cross the conjugation pilus later in time. Genes closest to *oriT* are also more frequently transferred than are genes that are more distant from *oriT*. The result is that genes that are closest to *oriT* recombine into exconjugant chromosomes at earlier times and in greater numbers than genes that are distant from *oriT*. The number of minutes between the beginning of conjugation and the appearance of a particular recombinant is identified as the "time of entry" of the gene of interest. This measure, reported as minutes of conjugation, can be used to determine the order of genes on the Hfr chromosome in a time-of-entry map.

Time-of-Entry Mapping Experiments

In 1956, Ellie Wollman, Francois Jacob, and William Hayes used conjugation data from the F⁻ strain P678 and the Hfr strain HfrH to demonstrate the utility of interrupted mating for time-of-entry mapping. In this experiment, P678 is str^R, resistant to the antibiotic streptomycin, and HfrH is str^S, streptomycin sensitive. The donor and recipient genotypes for six genes studied are given in Table 6.2. Two of these genes had known locations: the genes for threonine and leucine synthesis

Table 6.2	Genotypes of *E. coli* Strains F⁻ P678 and HfrH
HfrH	**F⁻ P678**
thr⁺ (prototrophic for threonine)	*thr⁻* (auxotrophic for threonine)
leu⁺ (prototrophic for leucine)	*leu⁻* (auxotrophic for leucine)
azi^R (resistant to sodium azide)	*azi^S* (susceptible to sodium azide)
tonA^R (resistant to phage T1 infection)	*tonA^S* (sensitive to phage T1 infection)
lac⁺ (able to utilize lactose)	*lac⁻* (unable to utilize lactose)
galB⁺ (able to utilize galactose)	*galB⁻* (unable to utilize galactose)

Figure 6.8 **Time-of-entry mapping.** **(a)** Recombinants are identified by screening exconjugants for donor allele acquisition at regular intervals and plotting their time of entry into the exconjugant chromosome. **(b)** Donor alleles leu^+ and thr^+ appear in exconjugants within 4 minutes of conjugation initiation. Other donor alleles follow according to their order on the chromosome. **(c)** The Hfr chromosome time-of-entry map is assembled from the recombinant data.

(a) Donor allele appearance

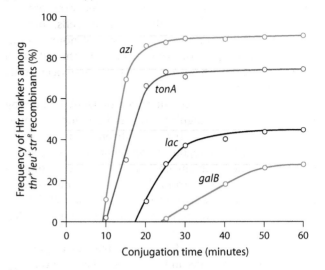

(b) Conjugation progression

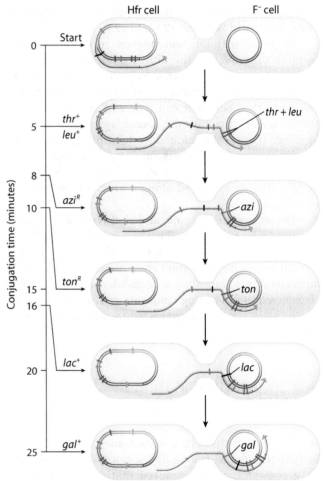

(c) Hfr chromosome map

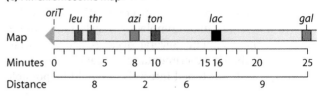

(*thr* and *leu*), which are closer to the origin of transfer in HfrH than any of the other genes tested. The goal of this experiment was to map the positions of *azi, tonA, lac,* and *galB* relative to *thr* and *leu* and to determine the distance between genes in minutes of conjugation.

The experiment begins by mixing of donor and recipient bacterial strains to initiate conjugation. Every few minutes, a small sample of the culture is removed and agitated to break any conjugation pili, interrupt the mating, and stop the process of DNA transfer. The sample bacteria are plated on growth plates containing different supplemental compounds in the medium to determine if exconjugants have formed by recombination between the recipient chromosome and homologous donated DNA. The first recombinant alleles in exconjugants are, as expected, thr^+ and leu^+. The researchers select for these exconjugants by plating cells on a medium that lacks leucine and threonine but contains streptomycin and therefore will permit the growth of only leu^+ thr^+ str^R exconjugants. The order of the other four genes is determined using these leu^+ thr^+ str^R exconjugants.

Samples from the conjugation mixture are taken every few minutes and plated on the selective medium that identifies those with the leu^+ thr^+ str^R genotype. Exconjugants with this genotype are then placed on a second plate to determine which other donor alleles have undergone recombination.

Figure 6.8a shows the results of this experiment, which are interpreted in **Figure 6.8b**: Exconjugants carrying the donor *azi* allele appear 8 minutes after conjugation begins, *tonA* recombinants appear at 10 minutes, *lac* recombinants appear at 16 minutes, and *galB* recombinants are the last to appear, at 25 minutes. The order of these four genes and the distances in minutes between them are combined to produce the time-of-entry genetic map for HfrH (**Figure 6.8c**).

Time-of-entry mapping is an effective approach for mapping genes near the 5′ end of the T strand. However, the genetic mapping information obtainable from a single Hfr strain is limited. First, because the conjugation pilus is broken and mating is interrupted, the likelihood of gene transfer drops off quickly with distance from *oriT*. Second, an Hfr strain can transfer genes in just one direction.

To obtain experimental information about gene order and distances between genes on the bacterial chromosome of a given species, multiple Hfr strains with different sites of episome insertion and different orientations of the episome are examined. Each IS element on the bacterial chromosome constitutes a different *location* of F factor integration, and each integration location transfers a different gene first. The donor chromosome shown in Figure 6.9a illustrates six genes and six IS elements. Each IS element is a potential site for F factor integration, and the first gene to transfer will be different for each integration

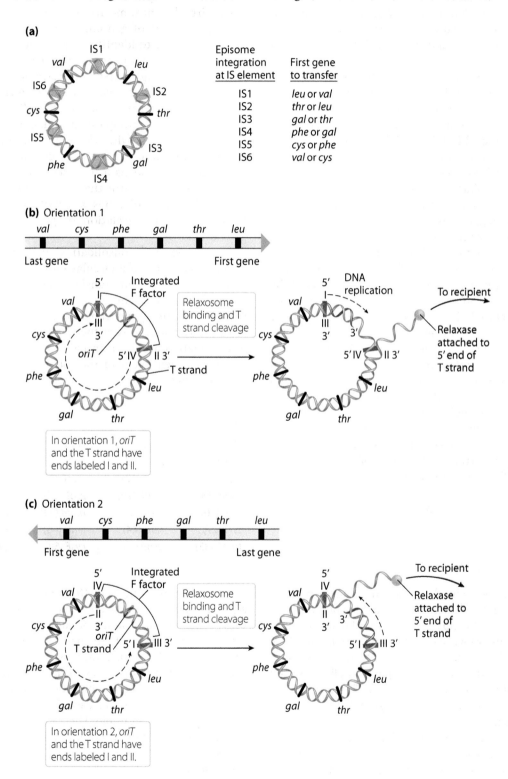

Figure 6.9 **F factors integrate at IS sites in one of two orientations.** (a) A model bacterial chromosome with six insertion sequences (IS1 to IS6) and six nearby marker genes. (b) One F factor orientation into IS1 transfers the *leu* gene first. (c) The alternative F factor orientation at IS1 transfers the *val* gene first. Relaxase attaches to the free end of *oriT* at the beginning of transfer.

site. In addition, at each IS element, the episome can be oriented in either of two directions (Figure 6.9b). Thus, F factor *orientation* is a second factor determining the order of gene transfer for an Hfr strain. Once F factor insertion location and orientation occur, they are fixed characteristics of the Hfr strain that do not change. This gives each Hfr strain a consistent and determinable order of gene transfer.

Figure 6.9b illustrates F factor integration and gene transfer from IS1 in orientation 1. In this orientation, the gene transfer order will be *leu-thr-gal-phe-cys-val.* In the figure, the four ends of the double-stranded episomes are labeled I, II, III, and IV; the 5'-to-3' polarity of strands is also indicated. Recall that relaxosome binding to *oriT* leads to cleavage of the T strand, which in Figure 6.9b is illustrated with ends I and II. The 5' end of the T strand (with relaxase attached) moves across the conjugation pilus with *leu* as the first gene following the episome fragment. The T strand acts as a template strand for DNA replication in the recipient cell, and the 3' end of the T strand (highlighted in red) is the start point for rolling circle replication of the plasmid in the donor cell. Figure 6.9c shows the same simplified bacterial chromosome with insertion at IS1 in orientation. As with orientation 1, the T strand carries *oriT* and has ends labeled I and II. Orientation 2 is the opposite of orientation 1, and it transfers genes in the opposite order. When the T strand is cleaved and its 5' end moves across the conjugation pilus, the first marker gene to transfer will be *val,* followed by *cys-phe-gal-thr-leu.* Once again, the T strand transfers 5' end first into the recipient cell and the strand is a replication template strand. The 3' end of the T strand in the donor cell (highlighted in red) is the start point for rolling circle replication. Genetic Analysis 6.1 guides you through time-of-entry mapping for an Hfr conjugation experiment.

Consolidation of Hfr Maps

In Hfr maps, an arrowhead is used to indicate the orientation of the integrated F factor. You can think of the arrowhead as indicating the tip of a DNA strand that is the first part to enter and move across the conjugation pilus. The first gene to follow the arrowhead into the recipient is closest to *oriT* and crosses the conjugation pilus first and most frequently among all donor genes. This leads it to be the first gene to recombine and the gene that recombines in the highest frequency.

Using this method, more than 4300 genes were mapped in the *E. coli* genome before genomic sequencing became a reality. The time-of-entry map of the chromosome of the model genetic organism *E. coli* is shown with selected genes in Figure 6.10a. The chromosome is measured as 100 minutes in length, the approximate length of time it would take to transfer the entire chromosome from a donor to a recipient. With the advent of genomic sequencing, however, it became possible to identify every nucleotide base pair, and every gene, in a genome. The accuracy and validity of Hfr mapping can be demonstrated by comparing a small segment of *E. coli* genomic sequence with the corresponding segment of the *E. coli* time-of-entry map. Figure 6.10b compares a segment of the *E. coli* time-of-entry map with the corresponding segment of the chromosome produced by genomic sequencing. The comparison spans a little less than 3 minutes of conjugation time, more than 2 million base pairs of DNA, and dozens of genes, a few of which are shown. It reveals exact correlation of gene placement and gene order.

Let's practice consolidating time-of-entry maps into a larger map of a circular chromosome using the following data on gene transfer from four different Hfr strains. For each strain, the genes are listed in order of transfer. The first gene transferred is at the top and the last gene transferred is at the bottom, and the minutes of conjugation are given in parentheses for each gene. The genes mentioned in the following discussion are presented in color.

Hfr Strain

Hfr1	Hfr2	Hfr3	Hfr4
serR (2)	*nadB* (8)	*tyrT* (4)	*serR* (4)
leuY (10)	*proL* (17)	*fumC* (12)	*pheR* (12)
asnB (15)	*fumC* (29)	*proL* (24)	*cysE* (25)
serC (20)	*tyrT* (37)	*nadB* (33)	*leuU* (37)
tyrT (27)	*serC* (44)	*leuU* (46)	*nadB* (50)
fumC (35)	*asnB* (49)	*cysE* (58)	*proL* (59)

The data set from each Hfr strain is used to generate a partial map showing gene order, the distance in minutes between genes, and the orientation of the integrated F factor. The individual Hfr maps are then consolidated to show each F factor integration site, its orientation, and the gene order and distances in minutes. We anticipate that the minutes of conjugation between a given pair of genes will be the same in each Hfr strain transferring the gene pair. For example, Hfr strains 1, 2, and 3 each transfer the gene pair *tyrT-fumC*, and in each strain the genes are 8 minutes apart, no matter the orientation of the episome.

(a) Data collected from Hfr strains for construction of time-of-entry map

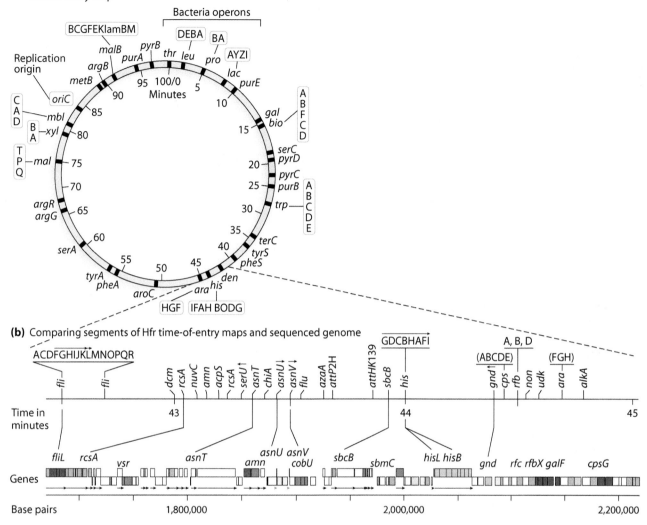

(b) Comparing segments of Hfr time-of-entry maps and sequenced genome

Figure 6.10   Consolidated Hfr map of *E. coli*.   (a) The 100-minute genetic map of *E. coli*. Genes of bacterial operons (see Section 14.2) are boxed. The origin of replication (*oriC*) is seen at 84 minutes. **(b)** Comparison of a segment of an Hfr time-of-entry map with a genomic sequence map. A 2.5-minute segment (minutes 42.5–45) of the *E. coli* time-of-entry map is shown in comparison to a segment of approximately 500,000 base pairs of the *E. coli* genome derived from *E. coli* genomic sequencing. Selected genes between 42.5 minutes and 45 minutes on the time-of-entry map (upper) are aligned with their positions in the genome sequence map (lower) to illustrate the compatibility of the two mapping approaches.

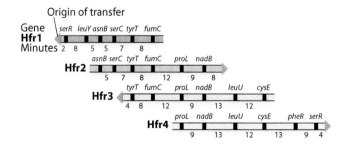

Continuation of the overlap process leads eventually to closure of the circle and completion of the chromosome map. In the above table, for example, notice that Hfr1 and Hfr4 share *serR* as the gene nearest the site of insertion. This is the connection that allows us to close the circular map. To begin construction of the circular map, we will assume that Hfr1 transfers genes in a clockwise direction, in other words, *serR* is first and *fumC* is last.

PROBLEM An interrupted mating experiment is carried out in *E. coli* to map genes for biosynthesis of the amino acids threonine (*thr*), leucine (*leu*), glutamic acid (*glu*), and alanine (*ala*). An Hfr strain that is *his⁺ thr⁺ leu⁺ glu⁺ ala⁺ str^S* transfers his very early and is sensitive to the antibiotic streptomycin. It is mated to an F⁻ strain with the genotype *his⁻ thr⁻ leu⁻ glu⁻ ala⁻ str^R*. A time-of-entry profile for *thr, leu, glu,* and *ala* is shown at right.

> **BREAK IT DOWN:** A time-of-entry map gives the order of genes on the donor chromosome based on their successive appearance in exconjugants. The gene closest to the origin of transfer appears first and is followed, in order, by additional genes (p. 198).

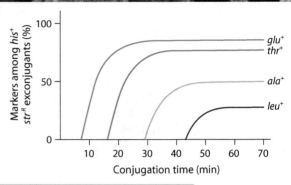

a. Exconjugants that are *his⁺* and *str^R* are initially selected for additional experimental analysis. What compounds must be present or absent in growth plates to allow exconjugants containing these selected markers to grow?

> **BREAK IT DOWN:** These initial exconjugants must be able to biosynthesize histidine and must be resistant to streptomycin. Genotypes for the other genes are not tested in initial screening, but they are tested in the time-of-entry experiment (p. 198).

b. Use the data provided to deduce the order of genes transferred in this Hfr strain and to identify the distances in minutes. Identify the order of genes on the donor chromosome and indicate the approximate location of the *his* gene.

Solution Strategies	Solution Steps
Evaluate	
1. Determine the topic this problem addresses and the nature of the required answer.	1. The problem concerns conjugation between an Hfr donor and an F⁻ recipient. Answer (a) requires identification of growth medium constituents for a *his⁺, str^R* exconjugant; answer (b) requires a map of the donor genes based on their time of entry.
2. Identify the critical information given in the problem.	2. Donor and recipient genotypes are given. A time-of-entry profile identifies the minutes of conjugation needed to transfer each donor gene to the recipient.
Deduce	
3. Determine the significance of the very early transfer of *his⁺* in the context of developing a time-of-entry map.	3. Very early transfer of *his⁺* indicates the gene is close to *oriT* and will be the first gene to cross the conjugation tube.

> **TIP:** Genes that are closer to *oriT* have earlier and more frequent opportunities to transfer to the recipient and to appear as recombinants in exconjugants than do genes that are distant from *oriT*.

Solve

4. Identify the compounds needed to allow growth of exconjugants with the selected markers *his⁺* and *str^R*, irrespective of the genotypes for the other genes.

> **TIP:** To select exconjugants that are *his⁺* and *str^R*, growth plates must provide conditions in which only the exconjugants that are resistant to streptomycin and able to synthesize histidine can grow.

Answer a

4. The growth plate used to select these markers would contain streptomycin and the amino acids threonine, leucine, glutamic acid, and alanine. The plate would lack histidine, thus requiring the growing strain to be *his⁺*.

Answer b

5. Construct a time-of-entry map based on the conjugation data.

5. Given that *his* transfers first, and that gene order and distances are identified by the time at which recombinants appear in exconjugants, the Hfr map for this strain is as follows:

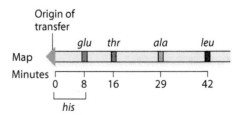

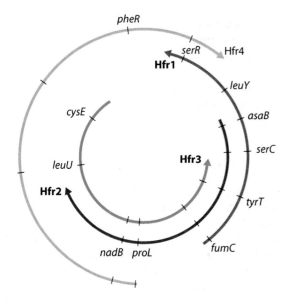

Once completed, the consolidated Hfr map identifies gene order, the cumulative number of minutes, the site of each F factor integration, and orientation:

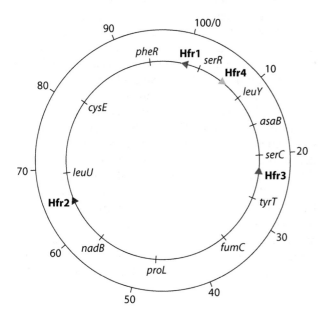

While conjugation mapping is an accurate way to determine gene order and to approximate the distance between genes, it is not precise enough to accurately map closely linked genes, since the differences in the time of entry of closely linked genes may be only a few seconds. Two other mechanisms of DNA transfer between bacteria, transformation and transduction, were devised to allow more detailed determination of the order of closely linked genes. Section 6.4 discusses gene mapping by transformation, and Section 6.5 describes gene mapping by transduction. First, however, we describe the final type of donor configuration for the F factor.

6.3 Conjugation with F′ Strains Produces Partial Diploids

Table 6.1 lists a third configuration of the F factor in donor bacteria, that of the so-called **F′** ("F prime") **donor,** which contains a functional but altered F factor derived from imperfect excision of the F factor out of the Hfr chromosome. The integration event that creates an Hfr chromosome depends on interactions between matching IS elements of the F factor and of the bacterial chromosome, and when this process is reversed, the F factor can once again become an extrachromosomal F^+ factor. Occasionally, however, the excision event is imprecise, and the excised F factor—in this case called an **F′ factor**—contains all of its own DNA plus a segment of bacterial chromosomal DNA from the region adjacent to the integration site (**Figure 6.11a**). An F′ factor can carry a variable length of bacterial DNA. Donor cells carrying an F′ factor are called **F′ cells.**

Like the other forms of conjugation described above, conjugation between an F′ donor and an F^- recipient follows the by-now-familiar process of relaxosome complex binding to *oriT*, cleavage of the T strand, and movement of the T strand across the conjugation pilus with its 5′ end leading the way. Cells with small F′ factors are more likely to transfer the entire F′ factor than are cells with large bacterial chromosome inclusions. Consequently, small inclusions are usually transferred in their entirety.

If the entire F′ chromosome is transferred, both parts of *oriT* are transferred, allowing the F′ factor to circularize in the recipient cell. At the completion of F′ factor transfer in such cases, the recipient cell, now containing a complete F′ factor, is converted to an F′ donor (see Table 6.1). It has acquired copies of all the donor chromosomal genes carried on the F′ factor. Because the newly received chromosomal genes are homologs of genes already present on the recipient bacterial chromosome, the resulting exconjugants are **partial diploids.** The diploid portion of the genome is limited to the genes present in two copies, one on the exconjugant chromosome and the second on the F′ factor. No homologous recombination is necessary to produce these partially diploid genotypes, and partial diploidy is retained as a characteristic of these exconjugants and their descendants.

Figure 6.11b illustrates the creation of a partial diploid exconjugant carrying two alleles of the *lac* gene. The *lac*$^+$ allele on the F′ factor enables the cell to use lactose for growth, whereas the mutant *lac*$^-$ allele on the exconjugant chromosome is unable to function in lactose utilization. In this partial diploid, the *lac*$^+$ allele is dominant over the *lac*$^-$ allele. Partial diploids of this type have been used in genetic studies to examine the mode of action of

(a)

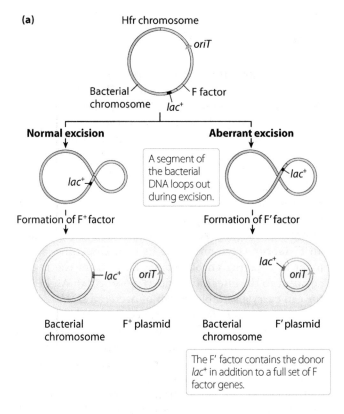

(b)

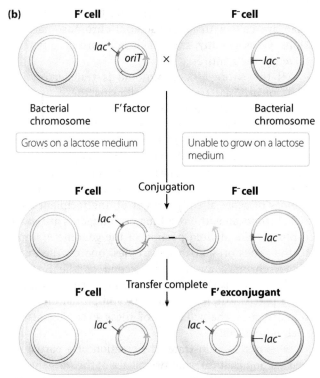

The exconjugant is a *lac⁺/lac⁻* partial diploid and has acquired the ability to grow on a lactose medium. Because F′plasmid transfer was complete, the exconjugant can act as an F′donor.

Figure 6.11   F factor excision from Hfr integration. (a) Normal excision (left) restores an Hfr to an F⁺, whereas aberrant excision (right) forms an F′ plasmid in an F′ donor cell. (b) F′ × F⁻ conjugation produces an exconjugant that is a partial diploid *lac⁺/lac⁻*.

genes in bacteria and to dissect the regulation of coordinated gene action in bacterial metabolism and growth (see Section 14.3).

Genetic Analysis 6.2 guides you through an analysis of donor and recipient bacterial strains and the identification of donor types through the analysis of three conjugation experiments.

Plasmids and Conjugation in Archaea

Research on archaea species is still in its infancy in comparison to the many decades of research that exist on bacteria. Despite this short research history, a number of significant observations have been made with regard to archaeal plasmids and conjugation among archaeal cells.

Like bacteria, archaea are single-celled haploid organisms. All of the genes that are essential for the normal metabolic and physiologic activities of the cell are carried on the archaeal chromosome. Ongoing research on archaea plasmids that began in the early 1990s has identified dozens of different plasmids among archaeal species. While much more study is needed, the information available at present indicates that most archaeal plasmids replicate by rolling circle replication. The data further identify numerous instances of plasmid-driven conjugation between archaeal donor and recipient cells. The genetic composition of archaeal conjugative plasmids has not been well characterized, nor is there enough information to be able to describe the details of the archaeal conjugation apparatus. To date there is evidence of some similarities to bacterial conjugation, but there is also evidence that some aspects of archaeal conjugation may be substantially different from bacterial conjugation.

In following chapters, we compare and contrast selected molecular processes and structures in archaea with their counterparts in bacteria and eukaryotes. Like the apparent circumstance with conjugation, archaea share some attributes with bacteria, but we will see that they also commonly share features with eukaryotes as well.

6.4 Bacterial Transformation Produces Genetic Recombination

Transformation occurs when a recipient cell takes up a fragment of donor cell DNA from the surrounding growth medium. The DNA fragment passes through the wall and membrane of the recipient cell and is incorporated into the recipient cell chromosome by homologous recombination. Transformation is a naturally occurring mechanism that can be used to produce accurate maps of bacterial genes, including those that are closely linked and not readily mapped by conjugation experiments. The recipient cell taking up transforming DNA is identified as competent, meaning able to internalize exogenous

PROBLEM In *E. coli,* the abilities to utilize the sugar lactose, synthesize the amino acid methionine, and resist the antibiotic streptomycin are conferred by alleles *lac*⁺ and *met*⁺ and the R plasmid carrying. Bacteria without the R plasmid are susceptible to streptomycin (*str*ˢ), and mutant alleles *lac*⁻ and *met*⁻ produce bacteria that are unable to grow on media containing lactose and require methionine supplementation for growth. *E. coli* strains are identified as donors or recipients in the first table, which also contains information on their ability to grow under various conditions. The second table contains growth information for the exconjugants of mating between donor and recipient strains. In each table, "+" indicates growth and "−" indicates no growth. "Min" signifies a minimal medium, and supplemented minimal medium plates are indicated by, for example, "Min+met" (minimal medium plus methionine). "Lac" indicates a plate containing only lactose as the sugar.

Strain	Type	Strain Growth				
		Min	Lac	Min+met	Min+met+str	Lac+met+str
A	Donor	+	+	+	−	−
B	Donor	+	+	+	−	−
C	Donor	+	+	+	−	−
D	Recipient	−	−	+	+	−

a. Use the growth information in the first table to determine the genotype of each strain at the *lac* and met genes and for resistance or susceptibility to streptomycin loci.

> **BREAK IT DOWN:** Anabolic and catabolic pathways and the determination of genotypes for alleles in these pathways are described in Research Technique 6.1, pp. 189–190.

b. Use the growth information in the second table to determine the genotypes of exconjugants produced by each mating.

c. Compare the genotypes and mating behavior of donors, recipient, and exconjugants to determine whether each donor is F⁺, Hfr, or F′. Explain your rationale for each donor identification.

Mating	Exconjugant Growth				Are the Exconjugants Donors?
	Min+str	Min+met+str	Lac+str	Lac+met+str	
A × D	+	+	−	−	Yes
B × D	−	+	−	−	Yes
C × D	−	+	−	+	No

> **BREAK IT DOWN:** Table 6.1, p. 194, summarizes the potential conversion of and bacterial gene transfer to exconjugants by donors.

Solution Strategies | Solution Steps

Evaluate

1. Identify the topic this problem addresses and the nature of the required answer.

1. This is a conjugation problem in which genotypes of donors and a recipient are determined by growth characteristics. Donor types (F⁺, Hfr, F′) are identified by growth characteristics of exconjugants. The answers require identifying genotypes for *lac, met,* and *str* for each donor, recipient, and exconjugant.

2. Identify the critical information given in the problem.

2. The two tables identify growth characteristics. The first table contains growth information on three donors (A, B, and C) and a recipient (D). The second table contains growth information on the exconjugants of mating between each donor and the recipient.

Deduce

3. Compare the growth characteristics of donors and the recipient in the first table, and deduce which genotypes are likely the same.

3. The growth characteristics of the three donor strains (A, B, and C) are identical on each kind of medium. These three strains have the same genotype. The recipient, strain D, has a different set of growth characteristics and therefore a different genotype.

4. Examine the exconjugants in the second table and determine which have been converted from recipients to donors.

> TIP: When an exconjugant has been converted to a donor state, we know it has received a complete copy of the F factor.

4. Donor A and donor B transfer a complete F sequence to the recipient and convert the exconjugant to a donor. Donor C does not transfer the complete F sequence, so the C × D exconjugant is not converted to a donor.

Solve

5. Determine the genotypes of the donor and recipient strains from growth information in the first table.

Answer a

5. The genotype shared by donor strains A, B, and C is *met*⁺ *lac*⁺ *str*ˢ. The minimal medium contains glucose. Growth of donor strains in this medium indicates their prototrophy for methionine (*met*⁺). Growth in the lactose–containing medium indicates they are *lac*⁺. The inability of donors to grow in media containing streptomycin indicates they are *str*ˢ.

The recipient genotype is *met*⁻ *lac*⁻ *str*ᴿ. It is unable to grow on the minimal (glucose-containing) medium, but it can grow on glucose plus methionine, indicating it is *met*⁻. It also grows on the minimal medium plus methionine and streptomycin, indicating that it is *str*ᴿ. Lactose utilization is tested on the medium containing lactose plus methionine and streptomycin. Here it fails to grow, indicating it is *lac*⁻.

205

6. Determine the genotypes of exconjugants from growth information in the second table.

> TIP: Compare the genotypes of exconjugants to the recipient genotype to determine if one or more donor alleles have been transferred during conjugation. Use Table 6.1 for help in categorizing each donor.

7. Identify each donor by donor type and explain the rationale for each identification.

Answer b

6. Using analysis similar to that employed above, we conclude that the exconjugant genotypes are

A × D met^+ lac^- str^R, conversion to donor
B × D met^- lac^- str^R, conversion to donor
C × D met^- lac^+ str^R, no conversion

Answer c

7. A × D exconjugants have acquired met^+ and have undergone conversion to a donor state. F′ donors can transfer an allele and convert the recipient, so we conclude that strain A is an F′ donor. Exconjugants of the B × D mating retain the recipient genotype, but they are converted to a donor state. F$^+$ donors produce this result, so strain B is an F$^+$ donor. The C × D conjugation produces exconjugants that have acquired lac^+ but have not undergone conversion. This is a characteristic of Hfr donors, so we conclude that strain C is Hfr.

For more practice, see Problems 19 and 23.

Visit the Study Area to access study tools.

MasteringGenetics™

(donor) DNA. Transformation is also used as a laboratory technique by molecular biologists seeking to introduce DNA into microbial cells, plant cells, and animal cells as part of the process of creating recombinant DNA or transgenic organisms (see Sections 16.2 and 16.4).

Steps in Transformation

Transformation is a four-step process, as illustrated in Figure 6.12. It is preceded by the **lysis,** or breakage, of a donor cell and the release of fragmented DNA from the donor chromosome. The transforming DNA is double stranded and can be taken up by a recipient bacterial cell.

The passage of double-stranded transforming DNA across the recipient cell wall and cell membrane is accompanied by degradation of one of the strands (step ❶ of Figure 6.12). The remaining strand of transforming DNA aligns with, or "invades," a complementary region of the recipient chromosome ❷. The alignment triggers the action of several enzymes that excise one strand of the recipient chromosome and replace it with the transforming strand. This recombination event forms heteroduplex DNA: One strand is derived from the recipient cell, and the approximately complementary transforming strand is derived from the bacterial donor ❸. After the subsequent DNA replication and cell-division cycle ❹, one daughter cell is a transformed cell, also called the **transformant.** It contains a chromosome carrying the transforming strand and its newly synthesized complementary strand. The other daughter cell retains the recipient chromosome and is not genetically altered.

Mapping by Transformation

Transforming DNA is usually shorter than about 100,000 bp (100 kb) in length. For a bacterial species like *E. coli,* which has a genome of 4×10^6 bp of DNA

and approximately 5000 genes, the transforming DNA may have 1, 2, or as many as 50 genes. Even at maximum lengths, transforming DNA from the donor cell represents only 1 to 2% of the total genome of the recipient cell. Consequently, transformation is useful for mapping genes that are closely linked. To be mapped by transformation, two or more genes must be transferred into the recipient on the same fragment of transforming DNA. Thus, genetic analysis focuses on **cotransformation,** the simultaneous transformation of two or more genes. For cotransformation to occur, the crossover events must incorporate closely linked genes on a single fragment of transforming DNA.

6.5 Bacterial Transduction Is Mediated by Bacteriophages

Transduction is the transfer of genetic material from a donor bacterial cell and the integration of that material into a recipient bacterial cell by way of a bacteriophage acting as a vector. To accomplish this transfer, a bacteriophage must infect the donor cell, and a few of the progeny phages must errantly package a fragment of the donor bacterial chromosome rather than a complete copy of the phage chromosome.

Following lysis of the original bacterial host cell, phages carrying the mispackaged bacterial DNA attach to a new host cell (the recipient cell) and inject the donor chromosome fragment. Inside the recipient, homologous recombination can take place between the donated fragment and the recipient chromosome. In this section, we review the life cycles of bacteriophages (*phages,* for short) that infect *E. coli.* We then consider *cotransduction mapping,* a powerful technique for mapping bacterial genomes and the role of *generalized transduction* in this process. We conclude the section with a discussion of *specialized transduction.*

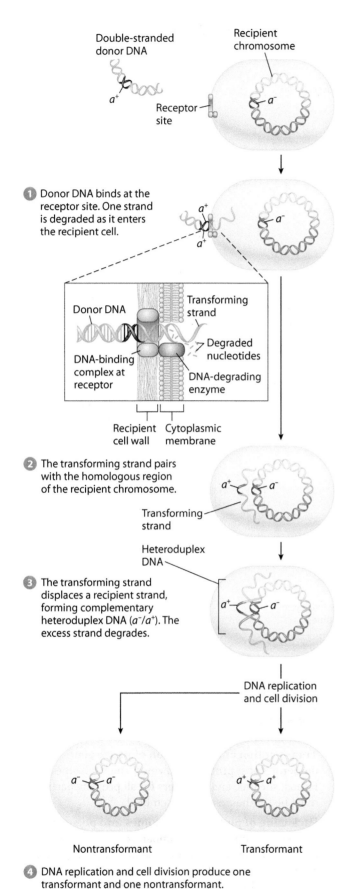

① Donor DNA binds at the receptor site. One strand is degraded as it enters the recipient cell.

② The transforming strand pairs with the homologous region of the recipient chromosome.

③ The transforming strand displaces a recipient strand, forming complementary heteroduplex DNA (a^-/a^+). The excess strand degrades.

④ DNA replication and cell division produce one transformant and one nontransformant.

Figure 6.12   Transformation of a competent bacterium (a^-) by donor DNA (a^+).

Bacteriophage Life Cycles

Bacteriophage particles are generally less than 1% the size of the bacterial cells they attack. Their outer structure is a protein coat composed of an icosahedral head, a hollow protein sheath, and in some phages, a set of appendages called tail fibers (**Figure 6.13**). The phage's head houses its rudimentary genome, composed of a single chromosome ranging in size from about 5000 to 100,000 base pairs. The replication of phage DNA, the transcription of phage genes, and the translation that produces phage proteins are dependent on numerous proteins and enzymes found in the host bacterial cells, which the phages must infect in order to reproduce.

Bacteriophages employ a variety of mechanisms to attack bacteria. All of the mechanisms make use of bacterial proteins that evolved in the bacteria for other purposes than as a means of phage entry. For example, λ phage uses the maltose-binding protein of *E. coli* as a site of attachment. Maltose-binding protein studs the surface of *E. coli* cells, which use it to sense the presence of the sugar maltose in the growth medium. Thus, when studying the infection of *E. coli* by λ phage, microbiologists add maltose to the growth medium as a means of enhancing the phage infection rate.

Bacteriophages actively seek out and attach to host cells, commencing a six-step process called the **lytic cycle,** that leads to the lysis of the host cell. Lysis releases up to 200 progeny phage particles. The steps composing the lytic cycle are depicted in **Figure 6.14**.

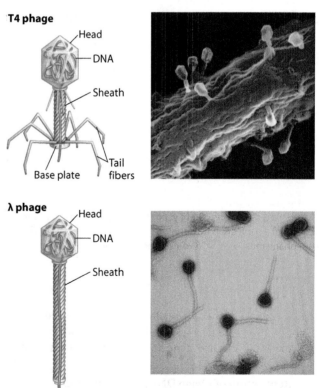

Figure 6.13   T4 bacteriophage and λ phage structures. Bacteriophages consist of a proteinaceous head filled with DNA, a sheath, and, in some phages, tail fibers.

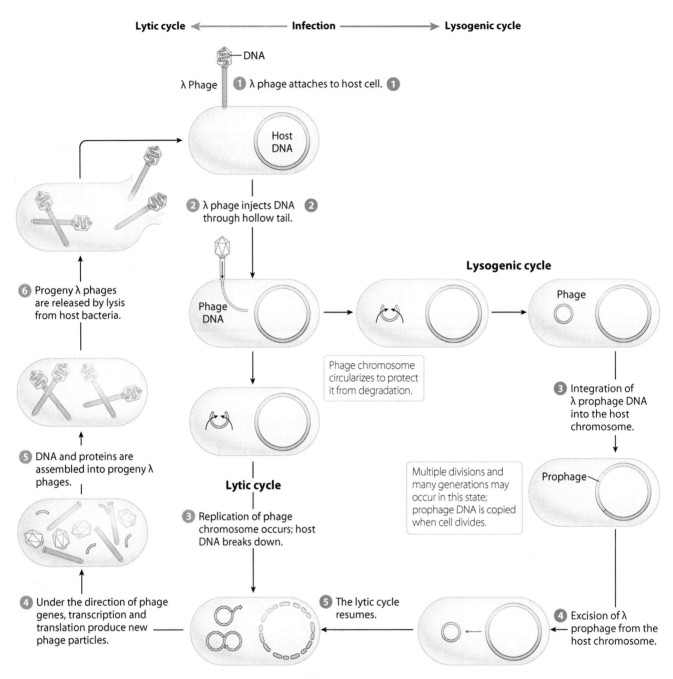

Figure 6.14   The lytic and lysogenic life cycles of a temperate bacteriophage. The lytic cycle progresses directly from infection through phage reproduction to lysis. The lysogenic cycle features the integration of the phage into the host chromosome where it resides until excision and resumption of the lytic cycle.

① **Attachment of the phage particle to the host cell.**

② **Injection of the phage chromosome into the host cell.** Injection is quickly followed by circularization of the phage chromosome, to protect it from enzymatic degradation.

③ **Replication of phage DNA,** using numerous host proteins and enzymes. A copy of the phage chromosome is required for each of the eventual progeny phage particles, which generally number between 50 and 200.

④ **Transcription and translation of phage genes,** using numerous host proteins, enzymes, and ribosomes. Heads, sheaths, and tail fibers for all progeny particles must be synthesized and assembled.

⑤ **Packaging of phage chromosomes into phage heads.** This step is commonly accompanied by fragmentation of the host chromosome. Occasional mispackaging of a fragment of the host chromosome into a phage head can follow chromosome fragmentation.

⑥ **Lysis of the host cell,** resulting in the death of the host and the release of progeny phage particles.

Certain bacteriophages—classified as **temperate phages,** of which λ phage is the best-known example—are capable of a temporary, alternative life cycle that leads to the integration of the phage chromosome into the bacterial host chromosome. The integration process is termed **lysogeny.** Environmental and growth conditions are largely what initiate a **lysogenic cycle.** Lysogeny can persist for many bacterial replication and division cycles, but it eventually comes to an end, and the lytic cycle resumes. (We discuss the details and genetic regulation of this alternation between life cycles in Section 14.6.) Five steps characterizing the lysogenic cycle are shown in Figure 6.14.

1 **Attachment of the phage particle to the host cell.**

2 **Injection of the phage chromosome into the host cell,** followed by phage-chromosome circularization.

3 **Integration of the phage chromosome into the host chromosome.** This process is site specific, meaning that it occurs at a specific DNA sequence found in both the phage and bacterial chromosomes. Once integrated into the host chromosome, the phage DNA is termed the **prophage.** The prophage remains stably integrated at the same location for multiple cycles of bacterial chromosome replication and cell division.

4 **Excision of the prophage.** In response to an environmental signal, such as a high dose of ultraviolet irradiation, the prophage reverses its integration and is excised intact. This event is usually an exact reversal of the site-specific integration, but rare mistakes in prophage excision lead to a specific kind of abnormal phage that may contain host genetic material.

5 **Resumption of the lytic cycle,** beginning with phage-chromosome replication.

Generalized Transduction

In the decades since the 1952 discovery and description of discovered generalized transduction by Norman Zinder and Joshua Lederberg, numerous kinds of generalized transducing phages have been identified. **Generalized transducing phages** are formed when a random piece of donor bacterial DNA of the appropriate length is mistakenly packed into the phage head instead of a similarly sized length of phage DNA. This occasional error in DNA packaging occurs because the packing mechanism that inserts DNA into the phage head discriminates DNA by its length (in base pairs) rather than by sequence. Generalized transducing phages can carry any segment of donor DNA, since the process of mistaken packaging is random.

The phage P1 is a well-studied bacteriophage that infects *E. coli* and is a prolific producer of generalized transducing phages. This phage was initially chosen for

intensive study of its transduction ability because it has a large genome of nearly 100,000 bp (100 kb). To produce progeny generalized transducing phages, P1 must capture segments of donor bacterial DNA that are almost exactly 100 kb, a length that is nearly 2% of the *E. coli* chromosome. Analysis of P1 infections tells us that about 1 in 50 progeny of a P1 infection are generalized transducing phages.

Figure 6.15 illustrates generalized transduction in seven steps (combining attachment and injection into a single first step). The outcome of transduction is the production of a **transductant,** a bacterium that has acquired one or more donor genes through transduction:

1 A normal P1 phage attaches to a donor bacterial cell and injects its chromosome into the cell.

2 Replication of the phage chromosome is followed by transcription and translation to produce phage proteins. Fragmentation of the bacterial chromosome precedes the packaging of phage chromosomes into phage heads.

3 Assembly of progeny phage, including packing of phage heads, is largely normal, but a few progeny phages receive a random fragment of the donor bacterial chromosome that is approximately the same length as the phage chromosome. These abnormal progeny phages are *generalized transducing phages.*

4 Host-cell lysis releases normal and generalized transducing phages.

5 Generalized transducing phages attach to new recipient cells and inject the fragment of donor DNA.

6 In each recipient cell, homologous recombination occurs between the fragment of donor DNA and the recipient chromosome. Pairs of crossover events are required to splice the donor fragment into the recipient chromosome and excise a homologous segment of the chromosome. The excised chromosome fragment is degraded by enzymes.

7 A stable transductant strain results.

Cotransduction

The donor cell in the transduction experiment shown in Figure 6.16 has the genotype *met*+ *his*+, and the recipient is *met*− *his*−. The bacterial culture in which this experiment takes place will contain millions of bacteria, most of which are not transduced. In addition, many cells may be transduced with donor alleles that are not tested for in the experiment. The transductants detected in this particular experiment are those in which either one or both of the *met*+ or *his*+ alleles are transduced.

Transductants having either the genotype *met*+ *his*− or the genotype *met*− *his*+ offer evidence that each allele can be individually transduced. In addition, a certain number of transductants will undergo simultaneous

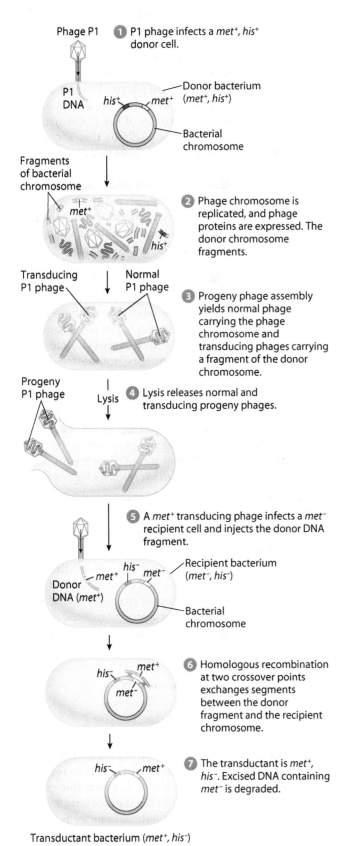

Phage P1

1 P1 phage infects a *met⁺*, *his⁺* donor cell.

P1 DNA

his⁺ *met⁺*

Donor bacterium (*met⁺*, *his⁺*)

Bacterial chromosome

Fragments of bacterial chromosome

met⁺

his⁺

2 Phage chromosome is replicated, and phage proteins are expressed. The donor chromosome fragments.

Transducing P1 phage

Normal P1 phage

3 Progeny phage assembly yields normal phage carrying the phage chromosome and transducing phages carrying a fragment of the donor chromosome.

Progeny P1 phage

Lysis

4 Lysis releases normal and transducing progeny phages.

5 A *met⁺* transducing phage infects a *met⁻* recipient cell and injects the donor DNA fragment.

met⁺ *his⁻* *met⁻*

Donor DNA (*met⁺*)

Recipient bacterium (*met⁻*, *his⁻*)

Bacterial chromosome

his⁻ *met⁺*

met⁻

6 Homologous recombination at two crossover points exchanges segments between the donor fragment and the recipient chromosome.

his⁻ *met⁺*

7 The transductant is *met⁺*, *his⁻*. Excised DNA containing *met⁻* is degraded.

Transductant bacterium (*met⁺*, *his⁻*)

Figure 6.15 **Transduction by P1 phage.** Transducing phages are generated by the mistaken packaging of a fragment of the donor bacterium's DNA into a phage head (**3**). Transductant bacteria are produced by homologous recombination between the introduced fragment of donor DNA and the recipient bacterial chromosome (**6**) and (**7**).

transduction of both genes to produce *met⁺ his⁺* transductants. These cells have undergone **cotransduction** of both donor alleles. The frequency of cotransduction, called **cotransduction frequency,** depends on how close the two genes are to one another on the donor chromosome. The closer the genes are, the higher the probability of cotransduction (thus, the higher the cotransduction frequency), and the farther apart the genes are, the lower the cotransduction probability. If, for example, an experimenter carried out the transduction cross in Figure 6.16 and identified 200 transductants for *met⁺*, the experimenter could determine the frequency of cotransduction by then identifying how many of those *met⁺* transductants were also transduced (i.e., were cotransduced) for *his⁺*. If the analysis determined that 28 of the 200 *met⁺* transductants were also transduced for *his⁺*, the cotransduction frequency for those genes is $14\%\left(\frac{28}{200}\right)$.

To succeed in finding cotransductants in an experiment, researchers may have to genotype large numbers of colonies. To reduce the number of colonies that must be genotyped in such experiments, a two-step strategy is used that first identifies cells transduced with one donor allele and then screens those transductants for the acquisition of additional donor alleles. The first step employs a **selected marker screen** to identify transductants for one of the donor alleles of interest. Transductants for the selected marker are then screened a second time, for a second donor allele, in an **unselected marker screen.** The goal is to determine the percentage of transductants for the selected marker that are also transduced for the unselected marker, while reducing unnecessary colony genotyping.

Cotransduction Mapping

Genetic map construction in bacteria uses cotransduction frequencies to determine the relative order of three or more genes. In **cotransduction mapping,** the frequency of cotransduction is greater for genes that are close together and is lower for genes that are farther apart. The reason is that any two genes on the donor chromosome have two chances to be separated by a chromosomal event. The first separation chance comes when the donor chromosome fragments. Genes that are close together are more likely to be on the same donor chromosome fragment than genes that are far apart. The second chance for separation comes during homologous recombination. Once again, genes that are close together on the donor fragment are less likely to be separated by a crossover event than genes that are far apart on the fragment.

Let's look at two studies that test the order of the same four genes in *E. coli.* Figure 6.16 provides cotransduction data for experiments performed in 1959 by Charles Yanofsky on genes that are part of the *tryptophan operon,* a cluster of genes involved in the synthesis of the amino acid tryptophan that share a single promoter.

(a) Cotransduction frequencies

Donor genotype	Recipient genotype	Selected marker	Unselected marker	Percent cotransduction of unselected marker with cys^+
$cys^+ trpE^+$	$cys^- trpE^-$	cys^+	$trpE^+$	63
$cys^+ trpC^+$	$cys^- trpC^-$	cys^+	$trpC^+$	53
$cys^+ trpB^+$	$cys^- trpB^-$	cys^+	$trpB^+$	47
$cys^+ trpA^+$	$cys^- trpA^-$	cys^+	$trpA^+$	46

(b) *trp* operon map

cys   trpE trpC trpB trpA

Figure 6.16   Yanofsky's cotransduction frequency analysis and mapping of *trp* operon genes in *E. coli*.
(a) Cotransduction frequencies of cys^+ and a gene of the *trp* operon are determined in separate selected marker-unselected marker experiments. (b) Yanofsky's proposed map of the *trp* operon.

Table 6.3	Test of Yanofsky's Proposed *trp* Operon Gene Order	
Transductant Class	**Transductant Genotype**	**Number**
1	$cys^+ trpC^- trpB^-$	139
2	$cys^+ trpC^- trpB^+$	18
3	$cys^+ trpC^+ trpB^+$	141
4	$cys^+ trpC^+ trpB^-$	4
TOTAL		302

(We discuss this operon in detail in Section 14.4). For the current discussion, you only need to know that genes in an operon are transcribed under the control of a single promoter and are much closer to one another than genes that have their own promoters.

Yanofsky used the selected–unselected marker approach to determine cotransduction frequencies for each of four genes in the tryptophan operon (*trpA*, *trpB*, *trpC*, and *trpE*) and a gene outside the operon, *cys*. Yanofsky performed four crosses, each with a donor strain that was cys^+ and prototrophic for one *trp* gene. His recipient strains were each cys^- and auxotrophic for the *trp* gene being tested. At the time he began his experiments, Yanofsky knew that *cys* lies outside the tryptophan operon, and he constructed his experiments to measure the cotransduction frequency between *cys* and the *trp* gene of interest. In each experiment, cys^+ was the selected marker used to identify informative transductants. The unselected marker was the *trp* allele from the donor. Yanofsky acquired data to determine the cotransduction frequency of cys^+ and the unselected *trp* marker.

In his first experiment, he determined that among cys^+ transductants, 63% are cotransduced for $trpE^+$. In his second experiment, he found 53% cotransduction between cys^+ and $trpC^+$. Yanofsky concluded that *trpE* is closer to *cys* than is *trpC* based on the higher cotransduction frequencies for *cys* and *trpE* than for *cys* and *trpC*. Cotransduction frequencies for *cys* and *trpB* and for *cys* and *trpA* are not sufficiently different to determine gene order, but based on cotransduction frequencies, *trpA* and *trpB* are each more distant from *cys* than are *trpE* and *trpC*. Yanofsky proposed a genetic map of the tryptophan operon with the order *cys-trpE-trpC-trpB-trpA*.

The second study was conducted to test the order of these genes and either corroborate or refute Yanofsky's

proposed gene map. In this study the donor bacterial genotype is $cys^+ trpC^- trpB^-$ and the recipient genotype is $cys^- trpC^+ trpB^+$. Transductants are selected for cys^+ transduction, and the transductants are then screened to determine their genotypes for *trpC* and *trpB*. The genotypes of 302 cys^+ transductants are shown in Table 6.3. Cotransductants for the donor *cys* and *trpC* alleles havethe genotype $cys^+ trpC^-$ and are found in Class 1, which has 139 cotransductants, and Class 2, which has 18. The *cys–trpC* cotransduction frequency is therefore $\frac{139}{302} + \frac{18}{302} = 0.52$, or 52%. Similarly, cotransduction of *cys* and *trpB* is identified by the genotype $cys^+ trpB^-$. Transductant Classes 1 and 4 have this cotransductant genotype, and the cotransduction frequency is $\frac{139}{302} + \frac{4}{302} = 0.47$, or 47%.

To test Yanofsky's proposed *trp* operon map, the crossover events required to produce each cotransductant class are identified. Figure 6.17 illustrates the locations of four crossover points used in different combinations for each cotransductant class. Transductants acquiring cys^+ must undergo crossover at point 1 plus atleast one additional point. The precise location of crossover point 1 can vary over a large expanse of the chromosome to the left of *cys*. The second crossover point must occur to the right of *cys* in any of three locations: at location 2, within a relatively large distance between *cys*, which is outside the operon, and *trpC* within the operon; at point 3, a very small space in the operon between *trpC* and *trpB*; or at point 4, a large region to the right of *trpB*. Three different double-crossover combinations generate transductant Classes 1, 2, and 3, and transductant Class 4 is produced by a quadruple recombination requiring crossover at all four points. The quadruple crossover is expected to be the least frequent of the combinations producing cotransductants. This study verifies Yanofsky's proposed *trp* operon map for two reasons. First, cotransduction frequencies for *cys–trpC* and for *cys–trpB* are almost identical in the two studies (53% versus 52% for *cys–trpC*, and 46 versus 47% for *cys–trpB*), placing *trpC* closest to *cys* in both. Second, the quadruple recombination event is expected to occur less frequently than any of the double crossover events.

Crossover analysis of cotransduction data

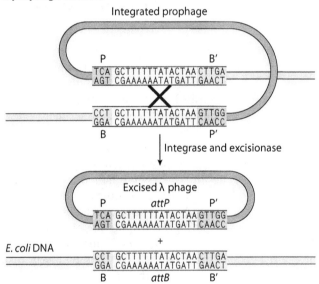

Figure 6.17 **A test of Yanofsky's proposed *trp* operon gene map.** The approximate locations of possible crossovers are numbered 1 through 4. For each cotransductant genotype, the required crossover sites are identified.

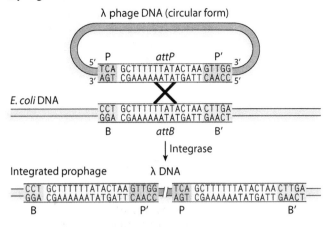

Figure 6.18 **Bacteriophage λ site-specific integration and excision.** Integration occurs at identical *attB* and *attP* DNA sequences on the bacterial chromosome and in phage DNA, respectively. Excision of the prophage exactly reverses integration.

Specialized Transduction

As described above, temperate bacteriophages, such as lambda (λ) phage, have the ability to lysogenize their host by integrating into the host chromosome to create a prophage. The site of integration is a DNA sequence called the ***att* site** (for "attachment") that is identical in the bacterial chromosome and the phage chromosome. The 15-bp sequence is called *attP* in lambda phage (the *P* stands for phage) and *attB* (*B* for bacteria) in its host *E. coli* bacterium (**Figure 6.18**). A specialized phage enzyme recognizes the *att* sites and makes a staggered cut there. The complementary single-stranded ends of cleaved *att* DNA reanneal as the prophage integrates, to create an *att* sequence at each end of the integrated prophage. Sequences P and P′ flanking *attP* and B and B′ flanking *attB* are added to allow you to more

easily follow the integration and excision processes of the prophage.

Because the *attB* and *attP* sequences are identical, the excision of a prophage is almost always the exact reversal of prophage integration. Occasionally, however, excision is inaccurate: It removes only a portion of the prophage and, along with it, a portion of the adjacent bacterial chromosome. Aberrant excision of a prophage forms a **specialized transducing phage** (**Figure 6.19**). In *E. coli*, *attB* is located between the genes *galK* and *bioA*; thus, aberrant prophage excision occurring in one direction will capture the bacterial *gal*+ gene to form the λ*dgal*+ specialized transducing phage (d is for defective), and in the other direction will capture the bacterial *bioA* gene, to form the λ*dbio*+ specialized transducing phage.

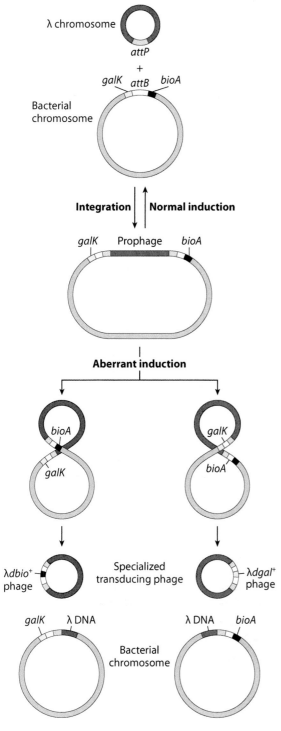

Figure 6.19 **Patterns of λ prophage induction.** The λ phage integrates into the host bacterial chromosome to form the prophage by site-specific recombination between the *attP* and *attB* sites (upper). Normal prophage induction precisely reverses integration and restores *attB* and *attP* sequences (middle). Aberrant induction (lower) produces specialized transducing phage λ*dbio*⁺ or λ*dgal*⁺, depending on the direction of aberrant induction.

Both kinds of specialized transducing phages are defective for certain attributes of phage growth and behavior. The λ*dgal*⁺ phage is missing several essential genes, so while it can infect host cells, it cannot complete either the lytic or lysogenic cycle. In contrast, λ*dbio*⁺ phages are not missing any essential genes, but they lack genes necessary for lysogeny. Thus, λ*dbio*⁺ phages are exclusively lytic.

Genetic Analysis 6.3 guides you through an analysis of a transduction to determine gene order in a donor strain.

6.6 Bacteriophage Chromosomes Are Mapped by Fine-Structure Analysis

Before DNA was identified as the hereditary material, many biologists regarded genes as indivisible units of heredity that could not be subdivided by recombination. This idea derives from Mendel's original description of "particulate inheritance" of traits. Before knowing the molecular structure of DNA, biologists had difficulty describing how recombination within a gene could occur. Geneticists knew that different mutations could affect a single gene, and had data from the 1949 study of intragenic recombination of the *Drosophila* lozenge eye mutation by Melvin and Kathleen Green showing that different mutations can occupy unique locations within a gene (see Figure 5.12). But what remained lacking was a refined understanding of the internal structure, or fine structure, of genes.

Beginning in the early 1950s, Seymour Benzer helped define how biologists view the structure of genes with a series of experiments that revealed the existence of a **genetic fine structure,** a phrase referring to the composition of genes at the level of their molecular building blocks. Benzer demonstrated that the building blocks of genes were responsible for both mutation and recombination. The publication of his principal conclusions coincided with the identification of the molecular structure of DNA. When the functional subunits of DNA were revealed to be nucleotides, it was impossible to miss the connection between them and Benzer's fine structure.

Benzer focused on two questions. First, was the gene the fundamental unit of mutation, or could components of genes be mutated? Second, was recombination a process occurring only between genes, or did recombination also occur between the components of genes? Benzer studied these questions using the *rII* region of the T4 bacteriophage. Genes in the *rII* region determine whether and how the phage will lyse its *E. coli* host. Lysis is examined using a bacterial lawn, a solid coating of bacteria on the surface of a growth medium. If the growing bacteria are exposed to a bacteriophage, infected cells lyse and

PROBLEM In *E. coli*, *thr*⁺ and *leu*⁺ are prototrophic alleles that control synthesis of the amino acids threonine and leucine. The auxotrophic alleles are defective in their ability to synthesize these amino acids. Bacteria carrying the *azi*ᴿ allele are resistant to the effects of the compound azide that inhibits protein transport, and those carrying *azi*ˢ are susceptible to the inhibitory effects of azide. *E. coli* with the genotype *thr*⁺ *leu*⁺ *azi*ᴿ are infected with the P1 phage. Progeny phages are collected and used to infect bacteria with the genotype *thr*⁻ *leu*⁻ *azi*ˢ, and the cells are then placed on media selective for one or two of the donor markers in a transduction experiment. The table at right identifies the selected markers and gives the frequency of cotransduction of unselected markers for each experiment. From the information provided, determine the order of the three genes on the donor chromosome.

> **BREAK IT DOWN:** Carefully note the genotypes of the donor and recipient strains and remember that transductant genotypes are the former recipient genotypes that have acquired one or more donor genes (p. 211).

Experiment	Selected Marker(s)	Unselected Marker(s)
1	*leu*⁺	*azi*ᴿ = 50%, *thr*⁺ = 4%
2	*thr*⁺	*azi*ᴿ = 0%, *leu*⁺ = 4%
3	*leu*⁺ and *thr*⁺	*azi*ᴿ = 2%

Solution Strategies	Solution Steps

Evaluate

1. Identify the topic this problem addresses and the nature of the required answer.

1. This is a cotransduction problem in which cotransduction frequencies are to be used to determine the order of three genes in the donor.

2. Identify the critical information given in the problem.

2. The results of three transduction experiments are given. Each experiment has a different gene as the selected marker.

Deduce

3. Be aware of the advantage of using the selected–unselected marker experimental approach.

3. Selecting for transduction of one of the genes of interest and then evaluating transductants for the other gene(s) reduces the number of plates that must be evaluated and simplifies the experimental analysis.

4. Interpret the results of each experiment.

> **TIP:** Cotransduction frequencies are highest for genes that are closest together on the bacterial chromosome.

4. Experiment 1 indicates close proximity of *leu* and *azi*, and a greater distance between *leu* and *thr*. Experiment 2 suggests the same more distant relationship between *thr* and *leu*, but also shows no cotransduction between *thr* and *azi*. Experiment 3 informs us that cotransduction of all three donor alleles occurs, though at a low frequency. We can interpret this to mean that the segment of chromosome containing these genes is small enough to form a single fragment for transduction.

Solve

5. Combine your observations to identify the order of these three genes.

> **TIP:** Crossovers occur in pairs during the homologous recombination that accompanies transduction. When three genes are involved, a quadruple crossover is less frequent than any of the double crossovers.

5. Putting the results of these experiments together, we can identify cotransduction of *thr* and *azi* (shown at 0% in experiment 2) as the quadruple-crossover cotransductant. All other events are a result of double crossover. The quadruple crossover event is expected to be least frequent among the cotransductants. On this basis, *leu* can be identified as the middle gene of the three tested. The gene map is shown below, and the four crossover intervals are identified.

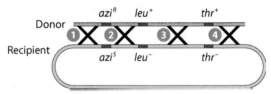

The crossover events accounting for each cotransduction detected in the experiments are shown below.

Cotransduction	Crossovers
*azi*ᴿ and *leu*⁺	1 and 3
leu⁺ and *thr*⁺	2 and 4
*azi*ᴿ, *leu*⁺, and *thr*⁺	1 and 4

For more practice, see Problems 9, 20, and 24.   Visit the Study Area for a VideoTutor solution.   MasteringGenetics™

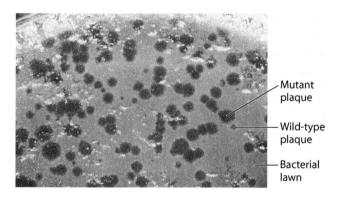

Figure 6.20   Plaque formation by *rII* wild types and mutants. On a bacterial lawn of *E. coli* B strain, small, circular wild-type plaques are formed by T4 phages with a wild-type *rII* region. Large, irregular mutant plaques are formed by T4 phages with *rII* mutations.

progeny phages are released. Progeny phages infect new host cells, and as the infection–lysis–infection cycle continues, a bacteria-free spot called a plaque—a hole in the bacterial lawn—appears on the growth medium.

Benzer showed that two genes, *rIIA* and *rIIB*, control the ability of T4 phages to lyse *E. coli* host cells. Those T4 phages carrying wild-type copies of *rIIA* and *rIIB* lyse multiple strains of *E. coli*, leading to the production of small plaques (Figure 6.20). On the other hand, phages with mutation of either *rIIA* or *rIIB* form large, irregularly shaped plaques on *E. coli* strain B, but they are unable to form any plaques on *E. coli* K12 (λ).

Benzer used several different mutagens to produce almost 20,000 *rII* mutants that he studied in three ways. First, he used *genetic complementation analysis*, which showed that there are two genes in the *rII* region. Second, he mapped different mutations of *rIIA* and different mutations of *rIIB*, thus showing that *intragenic recombination* was possible and could be used to establish the locations of different mutations in each gene. Finally, Benzer developed *deletion mapping* to refine the genetic map. The following discussions examine each of these achievements individually.

Genetic Complementation Analysis

To identify the number of genes in the *rII* region, Benzer performed genetic complementation analysis, coinfecting K12 (λ) bacteria with different pairs of *rII* mutants. When two *rII* mutants exhibiting genetic complementation coinfect K12 (λ) bacteria, plaques form on the bacterial lawn, indicating that wild-type lysis has been restored. This result identifies the mutants as mutations of different genes. Coinfections by *rII* mutants that did not lead to plaque formation on K12 (λ) represented a failure to complement, and these pairs were identified as mutations of the same gene. These mutants of a single gene are alleles of one another. Benzer identified two genetic complementation

groups, which he designated A and B, and these led him to identify two genes in the *rII* region: *rIIA* and *rIIB*.

Subsequent analysis revealed that each gene produces a protein and that both proteins are required for lysis. Figure 6.21a illustrates genetic complementation for

(a) Complementation of mutations in different genes

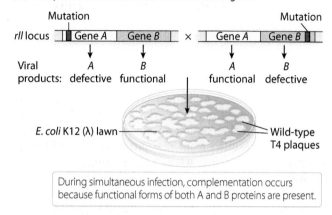

During simultaneous infection, complementation occurs because functional forms of both A and B proteins are present.

(b) No complementation of mutations in the same genes

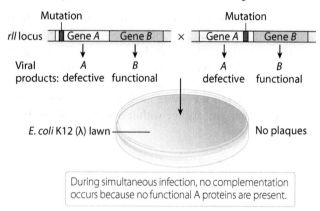

During simultaneous infection, no complementation occurs because no functional A proteins are present.

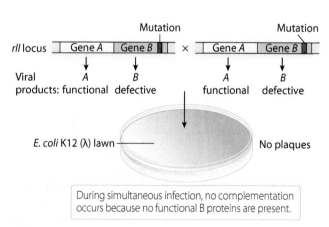

During simultaneous infection, no complementation occurs because no functional B proteins are present.

Figure 6.21   Genetic complementation analysis for *rII* lysis. (a) Genetic complementation of two lysis-defective phage mutants occurs when the mutants carry mutations of different genes. Genetic complementation is revealed by the formation of many wild-type plaques on K12 (λ) bacteria. (b) No complementation occurs in lysis-defective mutants that carry mutations of the same gene.

one pair of *rII* mutants. One mutant produces functional A protein and the other produces functional B protein, thus providing all the protein components necessary to carry out lysis. Genetic complementation produces a large number of plaques in infected bacterial lawns, but the individual progeny phages released following lysis remain mutant. **Figure 6.21b** illustrates a failure of mutants to complement. In this example, both mutants carry a mutation of *rIIB*.

Intragenic Recombination Analysis

On rare occasions, Benzer observed that two lysis mutants that fail to complement (i.e., mutants of the same gene) nonetheless produce a few plaques of K12 (λ). He proposed that these plaques were produced by wild-type phage that resulted from rare intragenic recombination between two mutants whose chromosomes carry mutations in different locations in a single gene (**Figure 6.22**). One of the resulting recombinant chromosomes carries a double mutation, and the other is wild type. Wild-type chromosomes are found in progeny phages, that carry out wild-type lysis.

Based on a determination of the number of cells in an experimental flask and counting the number of K12 (λ) plaques subsequently produced, Benzer was able to calculate the intragenic recombination frequency within the *rII* gene for a given pair of mutations. Reasoning that reciprocal recombination was more likely to occur between two mutations that are distant within a gene, and less likely

between mutations that are closer within a gene, Benzer was able to convert the observed number of plaques into a frequency of recombination with which he mapped *rII* mutations. The detected recombination frequencies were very small, but because of the large number of observations he made, Benzer was able to conclude that if no wild-type recombinants were obtained, the mutations occurred in the same nucleotide.

Deletion-Mapping Analysis

Benzer's mutagenesis of *rII* generated two types of mutants: **revertible mutants,** which could undergo spontaneous reversion back to wild type, and **nonrevertible mutants,** which *never* reverted. Revertible mutations are caused by DNA base-sequence substitutions (point mutations), which can be changed back to wild-type sequence by reversion. On the other hand, nonrevertible mutations are partial deletion mutations, in which part of the gene sequence is lost. A deleted DNA sequence cannot be restored by reversion.

Using a technique called **deletion mapping,** Benzer took advantage of this difference between revertible and nonrevertible mutants to map the position of individual *rII* mutations. Deletion mapping relies on the production of wild-type phage by intragenic recombination between a revertible mutant and nonrevertible mutant. When one mutant is revertible and the other is nonrevertible, the ability to form wild-type intragenic recombinants depends on the locations of the mutations. **Figure 6.23a** illustrates reversion to wild type through intragenic recombination between a point mutation and a deletion mutation whose locations *do not overlap.* In contrast, **Figure 6.23b** shows that if the locations of the point mutation and the deletion mutation *overlap* one another, the production of wild-type intragenic recombinants is impossible. Wild-type recombinants are not formed in this case, because the deletion mutant cannot provide the wild-type sequence to replace the mutated sequence in the point mutant.

In research published between 1955 and 1962, Benzer conducted deletion mapping of almost 20,000 *rII* mutants. He infected bacteria with phage carrying individual revertible mutations (point mutations), paired one at a time with phage carrying different nonrevertible mutations (deletion mutations).

In 1961, Benzer published a fine-structure map containing 1612 point mutations of *rIIA* and *rIIB* (**Figure 6.24**). Two features of this map are of interest. First, the mutations are scattered throughout *rIIA* and *rIIB*, suggesting the genes are composed of subunits that are individually mutable. Second, the distribution of the mutations is nonrandom. More than 100 point mutations aggregate in region A6c, and region B4 is the site of more than 500 independent point mutations. These sites are *mutational hotspots* that can be brought about by several circumstances (see Section 12.1).

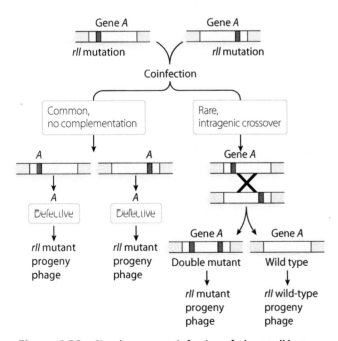

Figure 6.22 Simultaneous coinfection of a host cell by two noncomplementing *rIIA* mutants. No complementation (left) is the common and expected outcome. Rarely, however, intragenic recombination (right) produces wild-type and double-mutant progeny phage.

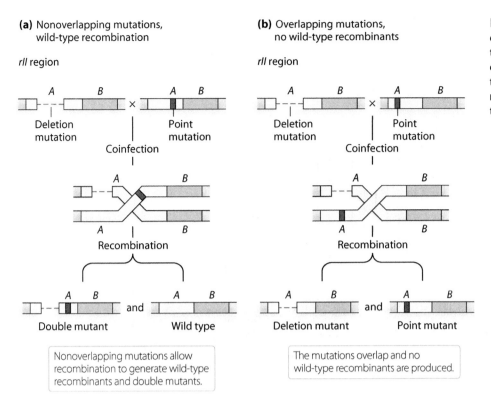

(a) Nonoverlapping mutations, wild-type recombination

(b) Overlapping mutations, no wild-type recombinants

Nonoverlapping mutations allow recombination to generate wild-type recombinants and double mutants.

The mutations overlap and no wild-type recombinants are produced.

Figure 6.23   Deletion mapping of mutants in the *rII* region. Wild-type recombinants form if the site of point mutation does not overlap the site of deletion, but if the two mutation sites overlap, no wild-type recombinants are possible.

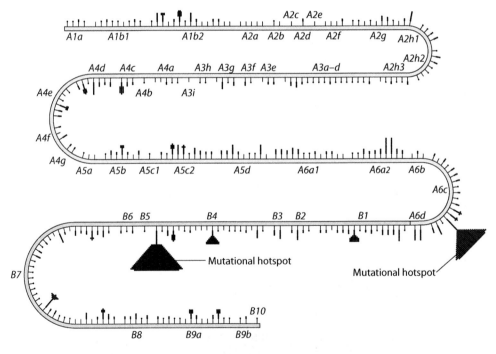

Figure 6.24   A genetic map showing the location of revertible (point) mutants of the *rII* region. This mutational map assembled by Benzer places more than 1600 mutants in the *rII* region and identifies hotspots where mutations are particularly common.

Several of Benzer's deletions are shown, and his mapping strategy is outlined, in **Figure 6.25**. Thirty-two deletion mutants in two groups called Series I and Series II are shown in Figure 6.25a. In Figure 6.25b, an *rIIA* point mutant is tested for its ability to form wild-type recombinants with the seven Series I deletion mutants and a subset of three Series II deletion mutants. Series I mutants are

used first, to determine which of the six segments of *rIIA* (A1 to A6) contains the point mutant. The point mutant in this example forms wild-type recombinants with deletion mutant *638* but not with any of the six other mutants tested. The only *rIIA* region present in *638* that is absent in the other mutants is segment A6, leading to the conclusion that the point mutation occurs in the A6 segment of

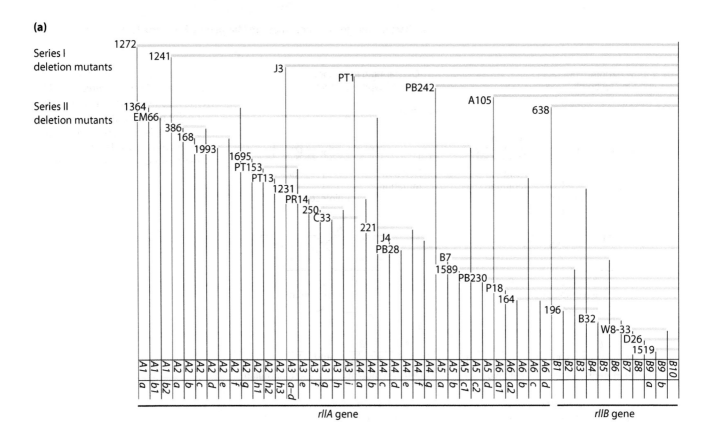

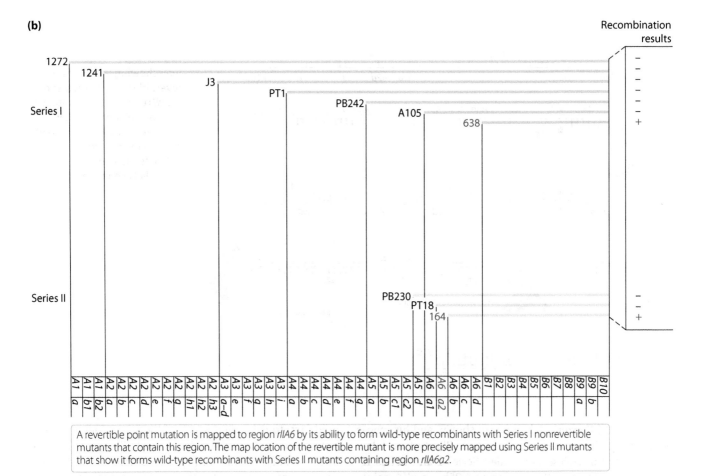

A revertible point mutation is mapped to region *rIIA6* by its ability to form wild-type recombinants with Series I nonrevertible mutants that contain this region. The map location of the revertible mutant is more precisely mapped using Series II mutants that show it forms wild-type recombinants with Series II mutants containing region *rIIA6a2*.

Figure 6.25   Deletion mapping in the *rII* region.   (a) Seven Series I partial-deletion mutants of the *rII* region and 25 Series II partial-deletion mutants subdivide the *rII* region into 47 segments. **(b)** Deletion-mapping analysis of an *rIIA* point (revertible) mutant to region *rIIA6a2* by its ability to form wild-type recombinants (+) and its inability to form wild-type recombinants (−) with partial-deletion mutants of Series I and Series II.

rIIA. The A6 region is subdivided into four segments (A6a to A6d). The three partial-deletion mutants of Series II are then selected for the final step in the mapping. In the Series II analysis, we see that the point mutant does not form wild-type recombinants with *PB230* and *P18* but is able to do so with *164*. The smallest interval that is missing from *PB230* and *P18* but present in *164* is the a2 region of *rIIA6*. This point mutation therefore maps to *rIIA6a2*.

6.7 Lateral Gene Transfer Alters Genomes

The genetic maps created by analysis of data from conjugation, transduction, and transformation experiments were extraordinarily important for understanding the content and organization of bacterial genomes. Contemporaneous with the identification of DNA structure (the early 1950s) and with descriptions of the molecular basis of DNA replication, transcription, and translation (the late 1950s and early 1960s), these genetic maps served as the foundation for DNA-sequence–based maps of bacterial and archaeal genomes that have been produced by the thousands since the late 1990s. The earlier genetic maps gave a precise outline of the order and relative positions of most genes in commonly investigated genomes such as that of *E. coli*, and they made it possible to jump-start the process of identifying the functions of genes in bacterial and archaeal genomes, a process known as *annotation*. Chapter 18 contains a detailed discussion of genome sequencing strategies, genome structures, evolutionary genomics, and genome annotation. Here we provide a brief overview of *lateral gene transfer* that has contributed substantially to the content of many genomes.

Lateral Gene Transfer and Genome Evolution

Lateral gene transfer (LGT), also known as horizontal gene transfer (HGT), is the transfer of genetic material between individual bacteria or archaea and other organisms. The participating organisms are sometimes members of the same species, but they can also be members of different species or even distinct taxonomic groups. Common examples of LGT are the three bacterial transfer processes discussed in this chapter: conjugation, transformation, and transduction. Each of these processes occurs readily in and between species. Extensive studies of LGT across a wide range of bacterial and archaeal species find that on average more than 12% of the genes in a genome are the result of LGT. The range in the amount acquired by LGT is quite wide, from a high of more than 25% in the genome of the archaeal organism *Methanosarcina acetivorans* to less than 2% of the genome in the bacterium *Mycoplasma genitalium*. *E. coli* is relatively high on the LGT percentage-transfer list, with about 17% of the genome transferred by LGT. Studies of LGT detect a substantial bias in the biological function of laterally transferred genes. Genes whose protein products are expressed at the cell surface, genes encoding DNA-binding proteins, and genes whose products have pathogenicity-related functions are much more likely to undergo LGT.

LGT between bacteria is prevalent, but in addition, there has long been evidence of limited LGT between bacteria and eukaryotes. Prior to the availability of genome sequence information, LGT between bacteria and eukaryotes was thought to be limited to the transfer of a very small number of genes. From an evolutionary perspective, the most prominent example of bacteria–eukaryote LGT is the presence of mitochondria in plant and animal cells and the presence of chloroplasts in plant cells. Mitochondria and chloroplasts are essential organelles in eukaryotic cells. Millennia ago, ancient bacteria invaded ancient eukaryotic cells and, through a process of coevolution on the part of both cells, mitochondria and chloroplasts established endosymbiotic relationships with eukaryotic cells. Both organelles carry their own chromosomes that contain unique genetic information. Mitochondrial gene products work with nuclear gene products to produce adenosine triphosphate (ATP) in animal cells, and chloroplast gene products are responsible for photosynthesis in plant cells. The inheritance of mitochondrial and chloroplast genes differs from that of nuclear genes because the organelles are cytoplasmic, not nuclear. We discuss the details of cytoplasmic heredity and the evolution of mitochondria and chloroplasts in Chapter 19.

A second well-known example of bacteria–eukaryote LGT is the transfer of DNA from the bacterium *Agrobacterium tumefaciens* to plants. *Agrobacterium* transfers about 10,000 to 30,000 base pairs of DNA from its much larger tumor-inducing (Ti) plasmid to plant cells. In plants, this DNA causes crown gall disease, a type of cancerous tumor. The natural propensity of Ti plasmid to transfer into plant cells is utilized in the research laboratory in the production of transgenic plants, as we discuss in Chapter 17.

In 2007, genome sequencing information demonstrated extensive LGT between the bacterium *Wolbachia* and a large number of insects. The data indicate that roughly one-third of all arthropod genomes contain *Wolbachia* DNA transferred by LGT. Researchers speculate that LGT between bacteria and animals may be much more common than previously thought. Only some of the transferred genes appear to actually enter the germ line where they can be transmitted during reproduction. There is, however, recent speculation that DNA transferred by LGT from bacteria could become inserted into the genomes of somatic cells, where it could induce mutations. If such insertional mutagenesis were to occur, it could possibly cause abnormalities, including the development of cancer. More information will emerge about this topic in the near future.

Identifying Lateral Gene Transfer in Genomes

LGT is identified by the presence of DNA-sequence features that make certain portions of a genome distinct from the rest of the genome. These distinctive genome regions are called **genomic islands** because they occur within a confined portion of the genome. Genomic islands typically are large segments that span 10–200 kb and often include multiple genes that may have related functions. Two common ways to identify a genomic island acquired by LGT are (1) by determining that a group of genes are much more similar to genes of a distantly related species than to those of a closely related species and (2) by detecting a region of genome that has a ratio of G–C base pairs to A–T base pairs that is substantially higher or lower than the average in the rest of the genome.

Recent evidence points to a significant role for LGT in the evolution of genomes. Moreover, in two particular ways, some LGT-driven events are of profound medical importance to humans. First, LGT has allowed many organisms to adapt rapidly to changing environmental conditions by acquiring the ability to resist one or more antibiotic compounds. The capacity to resist the effects of antibiotics can allow drug-resistant bacteria to proliferate in the presence of the antibiotics. LGT within and between bacterial species is a common route for the rapid dissemination of antibiotic resistance.

Medical practitioners today routinely encounter patients with infections produced by bacterial strains that are resistant to one or more of the commonly used anibiotics. The U.S. Centers for Disease Control and Prevention (CDC) issued a report in late 2013 highlighting the seriousness of antibiotic resistance as a prevalent medical problem. The report stated that each year in the United States more than 2 million people are infected with antibiotic-resistant bacteria and that the annual death rate from these infections is nearly 25,000.

Antibiotic resistance is readily transferred among bacteria by LGT, and the presence of resistance genes is increased by the extensive use, and misuse, of antibiotics. The 2013 CDC report attributes a substantial portion of the increase in antibiotic-resistant strains to the pervasive use of antibiotics in animal agriculture where they are often used to promote growth in animals with no signs of infection. These circumstances and the impact of this phenomenon on the practice of medicine are the subject of the Case Study in this chapter.

The second medically-relevant consequence of LGT in bacteria is the acquisition of **pathogenicity islands,** a subtype of genomic islands, containing multiple genes producing proteins that promote the ability of the bacteria to invade the body of a host and also containing genes that produce toxic compounds.

The common, and usually friendly, intestinal bacterium *E. coli* exists in a number of different strains, some of which are pathogenic. The most common strains of *E. coli* are commensal bacteria that inhabit our intestinal tract and provide benefits without doing harm. Some strains, however, have acquired pathogenicity islands and cause illnesses such as diarrhea and meningitis. The recently identified pathogenic strain of *E. coli* O157:H7 contains a pathogenicity island acquired by transduction. *E. coli* O157:H7 is found in some contaminated beef and on some fresh produce, including lettuce. Thorough rinsing can, but does not always, remove the pathogen from lettuce, and undercooking contaminated beef does not raise its temperature high enough to kill pathogens that may be present. The pathogenicity island in *E. coli* O157:H7 contains genes that promote the adhesion of the pathogen to intestinal cells and a toxin gene that acts similarly, although not as dramatically, as the *Vibrio cholera* toxin. Infection with *E. coli* O157:H7 produces diarrhea that can be severe in immune-compromised individuals or in infants and the elderly. The island also contains a gene producing a toxin that blocks translation in cells. This toxin particularly affects kidney and intestinal cells and contributes to bloody diarrhea.

CASE STUDY

The Evolution of Antibiotic Resistance and Change in Medical Practice

Alexander Fleming got a little sloppy with his sterile technique one day in 1929 and made a mistake that has since saved millions of lives. Fleming was working with *Staphylococcus,* a common bacterial strain that causes a serious and potentially fatal "staph" infection when it enters the body through a cut or abrasion. On the fateful day, Fleming unknowingly contaminated his *Staphylococcus* culture with a fungus.

Normally, fungal cells reproduce in culture along with bacterial cells and are noticed when the culture is spread on plates. Fleming's contaminating fungus was different, however, because when Fleming spread his contaminated culture on plates, only fungal colonies grew—there were no bacterial colonies! The fungus had killed the bacterial cells in the culture. Recognizing this as an important, if inadvertent, discovery, Fleming quickly identified the fungus as *Penicillium* and gave the compound that killed *Staphylococcus* the name penicillin.

In the 1930s, Howard Florey showed that penicillin was an effective antibiotic against a broad spectrum of infectious bacteria. At the beginning of World War II, Florey directed a major "scale-up" project to put penicillin into mass production. Penicillin proved tremendously effective at preventing what otherwise might have been fatal bacterial infections.

Today, although penicillin and other antibiotics continue to save lives, antibiotic-resistant strains of bacteria are increasingly the cause of difficult-to-treat infections and even death. This is quickly becoming an acute problem in modern medicine. For example, at present more than 95% of *Staphylococcus* strains found in hospitals are resistant to penicillin, and some strains carry resistance alleles to multiple antibiotics. Examples include methicillin-resistant *Staphylococcus aureus* (MRSA) and other infectious organisms that have acquired resistance to multiple antibiotic compounds. Antibiotic resistance is a rapidly growing problem that has already changed practices in medical treatment of infectious disease. The future holds more changes, both in patient treatment and the broader use of antibiotics.

What happened to bring about this shift? The answer has two parts. One component we have already mentioned—the evolution of antibiotic resistance and the acquisition of pathogenicity by bacteria through lateral gene transfer. Antibiotic resistance can be readily transferred within a species and between bacterial species by conjugation, transduction or transformation.

The second factor is the use and misuse of antibiotics themselves that establishes an environment in which resistant strains proliferate at the expense of sensitive strains. Exposing bacteria to antibiotics generally leads to killing antibiotic-sensitive bacteria and can allow the survival of antibiotic-resistant bacteria. Even when they are properly used, antibiotics can act as an agent of artificial selection that facilitates the survival of resistant strains at the expense of sensitive strains. When antibiotics are misused, such as when they are used pervasively in animal agriculture to increase growth even though no infection is present, are not taken for the prescribed period of time by a patient, and are used to treat non-bacterial infections, they eliminate great numbers of antibiotic-sensitive bacteria and promote the proliferation of resistant bacteria.

Resistance and sensitivity to antibiotics are not absolute characteristics. A "resistant" strain is just that—resistant to an antibiotic but not necessarily impervious to it. It takes more antibiotic to kill a resistant strain than to kill a sensitive strain. With regard to treating an infected person or animal, however, the medical question is: At what dosage is the benefit of the antibiotic outweighed by the harm to the patient?

At present, and increasingly in the future, physicians will have to be acutely aware of the events and behaviors that can lead to bacterial infection, be hypervigilant in spotting potential infections by resistant strains, and be prepared to quickly adapt medical treatments and protocols to manage resistant strains of bacteria. Future physicians must understand how and why antibiotic resistance has evolved if they are going to be successful in dealing with its ramifications for their patients.

SUMMARY (MasteringGenetics™ For activities, animations, and review quizzes, go to the Study Area.

6.1 Bacteria Transfer Genes by Conjugation

- Bacteria transfer genetic material in a unidirectional process (donor cell to recipient cell) called conjugation. Experimental analysis determined that conjugation requires direct contact between donor and recipient.

- Conjugation is controlled by genes on a plasmid known as an F factor. Donor bacteria that carry an extrachromosomal F factor are F⁺ cells, and bacteria without an F factor are F⁻, or recipient, cells.

- F factor transfer begins with the binding of a relaxosome protein complex at the transfer origin (*oriT*) and cleavage of one strand of F factor DNA, the T strand. Rolling circle DNA replication transfers the F factor from the donor cell to the recipient cell across a conjugation pilus.

- Conjugation between an F⁺ donor and an F⁻ recipient transfers the F factor only. The F⁻ cell is converted to an F⁺ cell but receives no genetic material from the donor bacterial chromosome.

- F factor integration into the donor chromosome takes place by recombination at insertion sequences (IS) found in both the F factor and the donor chromosome. F factor integration creates an Hfr (high-frequency recombination) chromosome.

- Many different kinds of Hfr chromosomes can occur in a single bacterial species. Each Hfr has a particular orientation and site of integration.

- Conjugation between an Hfr donor and an F⁻ recipient transfers a portion of the F factor and a segment of donor DNA. The donor segment undergoes homologous recombination with the recipient chromosome. Exconjugants

receive donor bacterial genes but are not converted to a donor state.

6.2 Interrupted Mating Analysis Produces Time-of-Entry Maps

- Time-of-entry maps are created for each Hfr strain by interrupted mating studies that identify the order of entry of donor genes and determine the distance (in minutes) between transferred genes.

- Hfr maps for a given bacterium are consolidated to form a genetic map of the donor chromosome as a whole.

6.3 Conjugation with F′ Strains Produces Partial Diploids

- F′ donor strains are created when excision of an F factor from Hfr integration removes F factor DNA along with adjacent donor chromosome DNA.

- Conjugation between an F′ donor and an F⁻ recipient generates partial diploidy in exconjugants.

6.4 Bacterial Transformation Produces Genetic Recombination

- Extracellular fragments of DNA released when a donor bacterial cell lyses can be absorbed across the cell membrane of a competent recipient cell as transforming DNA.

- Transforming DNA undergoes homologous recombination with the recipient chromosome to produce transformants that have acquired donor DNA.

6.5 Bacterial Transduction Is Mediated by Bacteriophages

▮ Bacteriophage infection of a host bacterial cell can lead to lysis of the host cell.

▮ Temperate bacteriophages can undergo site-specific integration into the host chromosome by lysogeny.

▮ Generalized transducing phages are created when a phage particle mistakenly packages a segment of a bacterial chromosome during lysis of the host cell.

▮ Recipient cells undergo generalized transduction when donor DNA introduced by a generalized transducing phage recombines with the recipient chromosome. Any donor genes can be transduced during generalized transduction.

▮ Cotransduction mapping determines the order of genes on the donor chromosome.

▮ Specialized transducing phages are produced by the aberrant excision of a lysogenic prophage that removes a portion of the prophage and an adjacent segment of host DNA. Specialized transduction is limited to transduction of genes adjacent to the site of prophage integration.

6.6 Bacteriophage Chromosomes Are Mapped by Fine-Structure Analysis

▮ Seymour Benzer used genetic complementation analysis to determine that two genes make up the *rII* region controlling T4 bacteriophage lysis of *E. coli*.

▮ Analysis of intragenic recombination, and deletion mapping of more than 1600 *rIIA* and *rIIB* mutants, led to the conclusion that DNA nucleotides are the fundamental unit of recombination.

6.7 Lateral Gene Transfer Alters Genomes

▮ LGT is common within species and among diverse species.

▮ LGT usually involves multiple genes in genomic islands.

▮ Bacteria commonly acquire pathogenicity and antibiotic resistance through LGT.

▮ LGT between bacterial and eukaryotic genomes is well documented and may be more common than was previously thought.

KEYWORDS

antibiotic resistance *(p. 188)*
attachment site (*att* site) *(p. 212)*
bacterial chromosome *(p. 188)*
conjugation *(p. 191)*
conjugation pilus (conjugation tube) *(p. 192)*
cotransduction (cotransduction frequency, cotransduction mapping) *(p. 210)*
cotransformation *(p. 206)*
deletion mapping *(p. 216)*
donor cell (bacterial donor) *(p. 191)*
episome *(p. 193)*
exconjugant cell *(p. 192)*
F (fertility) factor (F plasmid) *(p. 188)*
F⁺ cell (F⁺ donor) *(p. 192)*
F⁻ (F⁻ cells) *(p. 192)*
F′ cell (F′ donor) *(p. 203)*

F′ factor *(p. 203)*
generalized transduction (generalized transducing phage) *(p. 209)*
genetic fine structure *(p. 213)*
genomic island *(p. 220)*
Hfr (high-frequency recombination) cell (Hfr donor) (Hfr chromosome) *(p. 194)*
interrupted mating *(p. 197)*
IS (insertion sequence) element *(p. 192)*
lateral gene transfer (LGT) *(p. 219)*
lysogenic cycle (lysogeny) *(p. 209)*
lytic cycle (lysis) *(p. 207)*
nonrevertible mutants *(p. 216)*
origin of transfer (*oriT*) *(p. 193)*
partial diploid *(p. 203)*
pathogenicity island *(p. 220)*
plasmid *(p. 188)*

prophage *(p. 209)*
R (resistance) plasmid *(p. 188)*
recipient cell (F⁻ cell) *(p. 192)*
revertible mutant *(p. 216)*
rolling circle replication *(p. 194)*
selected marker screen *(p. 210)*
selective growth medium *(p. 195)*
specialized transduction (specialized transducing phage) *(p. 212)*
T strand *(p. 193)*
temperate phage *(p. 209)*
time-of-entry mapping *(p. 197)*
transductant *(p. 209)*
transduction *(p. 206)*
transformant *(p. 206)*
transformation *(p. 204)*
unselected marker screen *(p. 210)*

PROBLEMS

(MasteringGenetics™   Visit for instructor-assigned tutorials and problems.)

Chapter Concepts

1. For bacteria that are F⁺, Hfr, F′, and F⁻, perform or answer the following.
   a. Describe the state of the F factor.
   b. Which of these cells are donors? Which is the recipient?
   c. Which of these donors can convert exconjugants to a donor state?

For answers to even-numbered problems, see Appendix: Answers.

   d. Which of these donors can transfer a donor gene to exconjugants?
   e. Describe the results of conjugation (i.e., changes in the recipient and the exconjugant) that allow detection of the state of the F factor in a donor strain.
   f. Describe a "partial diploid" and how it originates.

2. The flow diagram shown below identifies possible relationships between bacterial strains in various F factor states. For each of the four links in the diagram, provide a description of the events involved in the transition.

$$F^- \xrightarrow{1} F^+ \underset{3}{\overset{2}{\rightleftarrows}} Hfr \xrightarrow{4} F'$$

3. Conjugation between an Hfr cell and an F⁻ cell does not usually result in conversion of exconjugants to the donor state. Occasionally however, the result of this conjugation is two Hfr cells. Explain how this occurs.

4. Bacteria transfer genes by conjugation, transduction, and transformation. Compare and contrast these mechanisms. In your answer, identify which if any processes involve homologous recombination and which if any do not.

5. Explain the importance of the following features in conjugating donor bacteria:
   a. the origin of transfer
   b. the conjugation pilus
   c. homologous recombination
   d. the relaxosome
   e. relaxase
   f. T strand DNA
   g. pilin protein

Application and Integration

12. What is lateral gene transfer? How might it take place between two bacterial cells?

13. Lateral gene transfer is thought to have played a major role in the evolution of bacterial genomes. Describe the impact of LGT on bacterial genome evolution.

14. Seven deletion mutations (1 to 7 in the table below) are tested for their ability to form wild-type recombinants with five point mutations (a to e). The symbol "+" indicates that wild-type recombination occurs, and "–" indicates that wild types are not formed. Use the data to construct a genetic map of the order of point mutations, and indicate the segment deleted by each deletion mutation.

| | Deletion Mutation | | | | | | |
Point Mutation	1	2	3	4	5	6	7
a	–	+	–	–	+	+	–
b	+	+	+	–	+	–	–
c	+	+	+	+	–	–	–
d	–	+	+	–	+	–	–
e	+	–	–	–	+	+	–

15. An *rII* lysis mutation caused by a point mutation is tested against several deletion mutations shown in Figure 6.25 for its ability to form wild-type recombinants. The deletion mutants are divided into two groups, Series I and Series II. In the "result" column of the table below, "+" indicates the formation of wild-type recombinants and "–" indicates that wild types do not form. In the first part of your answer, use the Series I data exclusively to identify the segment

6. Describe the difference between the bacteriophage lytic cycle and lysogenic cycle.

7. Describe what is meant by the term *site-specific recombination* as used in identifying the processes that lead to the integration of temperate bacteriophages into host bacterial chromosomes during lysogeny or to the formation of specialized transducing phage.

8. What is a prophage, and how is a prophage formed?

9. How is the frequency of cotransduction related to the relative positions of genes on a bacterial chromosome? Draw a map of three genes and describe the expected relationship of cotransduction frequencies to the map.

10. Describe the differences between genetic complementation and recombination as they relate to the detection of wild-type lysis by a mutant bacteriophage.

11. Among the mechanisms of gene transfer in bacteria, which one is capable of transferring the largest chromosome segment from donor to recipient? Which process generally transfers the smallest donor segments to the recipient? Explain your reasoning for both answers.

For answers to even-numbered problems, see Appendix: Answers.

of the *rII* region containing the lysis mutant tested. In the second part of your answer, use the Series II data to refine the point mutation location. Explain your rationale for mutation location assignments for both the Series I and the Series II data.

Series I		Series II	
Deletion Mutation	Result	Deletion Mutation	Result
1272	–	1364	+
1241	–	EM66	–
J3	–	386	+
PT1	+	168	+
PB242	+	1993	–
A105	+	1695	–
638	+	PT153	+
		1231	–
		C33	+
		250	–

16. Suppose you have an *rII* lysis mutant that maps to segment *A2h2*. Use the Series I and Series II deletion mutants identified in the problem above, and fill out the "results" columns with the "+" and "–" designations expected for the *A2h2* mutant.

17. Five Hfr strains from the same bacterial species are analyzed for their ability to transfer genes to F⁻ recipient bacteria. The data shown below list the origin of transfer (*oriT*) for each strain and give the order of genes, with the

first gene on the left and the last gene on the right. Use the data to construct a circular map of the bacterium.

Hfr Strain	Genes Transferred
Hfr 1	oriT met ala lac gal
Hfr 2	oriT met leu thr azi
Hfr 3	oriT gal pro trp azi
Hfr 4	oriT leu met ala lac
Hfr 5	oriT trp azi thr leu met

18. An interrupted mating study is carried out on Hfr strains 1, 2, and 3 identified in the problem above. After conjugation is established, a small sample of the mixture is collected every minute for 20 minutes to determine the distance between genes on the chromosome. Results for each of the three Hfr strains are shown below. The total duration of conjugation (in minutes) is given for each transferred gene.

Hfr strain 1	oriT	met	ala	lac	gal
Duration (min)	0	2	8	13	17
Hfr strain 2	oriT	met	leu	thr	azi
Duration (min)	0	2	7	10	17
Hfr strain 3	oriT	gal	pro	trp	azi
Duration (min)	0	3	8	14	19

a. For each Hfr strain, draw a time-of-entry profile like the one in Figure 6.8a.
b. Using the chromosome map you prepared in answer to Problem 15, determine the distance in minutes between each gene on the map.
c. Explain why azi is the last gene of strain 2 to transfer in the 20 minutes of conjugation time. How many minutes of conjugation time would be needed to allow the next gene on the map to transfer from Hfr strain 2?
d. Write out the interrupted mating results you would expect after 20 minutes of conjugation for Hfr strains 4 and 5. Use the format shown at the beginning of this problem.
e. In minutes, what is the total length of the chromosome in the donor species?

19. An Hfr strain with the genotype $cys^+ leu^+ met^+ str^S$ is mated with an F$^-$ strain carrying the genotype $cys^- leu^- met^- str^R$. In an interrupted mating experiment, small samples of the conjugating bacteria are withdrawn every 3 minutes for 30 minutes. The withdrawn cells are shaken vigorously to stop conjugation and then placed on three different selection media, composed as follows:

Medium 1: Minimal medium plus leucine, methionine, and streptomycin

Medium 2: Minimal medium plus cysteine, methionine, and streptomycin

Medium 3: Minimal medium plus cysteine, leucine, and streptomycin

a. What donor gene is the selected marker in each medium?
b. List all possible bacterial genotypes growing on each medium.
c. What is the purpose of adding streptomycin to each selection medium?

The table on next page shows the number of colonies growing on each selection medium. The sampling time indicates how many minutes have passed since conjugation began.

Sampling Time (minutes)	Number of Colonies		
	Plate 1	Plate 2	Plate 3
3	0	0	0
6	0	0	0
9	0	62	0
12	0	87	0
15	51	124	0
18	79	210	62
21	109	250	85
24	144	250	111
27	152	250	122
30	152	250	122

d. Determine the order of donor genes cys, leu, and met from the interrupted mating data.
e. Suppose a fourth selection medium containing leucine and streptomycin is prepared. At what sampling time do you expect the first-growing colonies to appear? Explain your reasoning.

20. A triple-auxotrophic strain of E. coli having the genotype $phe^- met^- ara^-$ is used as a recipient strain in a transduction experiment. The strain is unable to synthesize its own phenylalanine or methionine, and it carries a mutation that leaves it unable to utilize the sugar arabinose for growth. The recipient is crossed to a prototrophic strain with the genotype $phe^+ met^+ ara^+$. The table below shows the selected marker and gives cotransduction frequencies for the unselected markers.

Selected Marker	Selected Colonies Containing the Unselected Marker (%)		
	phe^+	met^+	ara^+
met^+	4	–	7
phe^+	–	2	51
met^+, phe^+	–	–	79
ara^+	68	5	–

a. Identify the compounds present in each of the selective media.
b. Use the cotransduction data to determine the order of these genes.

21. Penicillin was first used in the 1940s to treat gonorrhea infections produced by the bacterium Neisseria gonorrhoeae. According to the CDC, in 1984, fewer than 1% of gonorrhea infections was caused by penicillin-resistant N. gonorrhoeae. By 1990, more than 10% of cases were penicillin-resistant, and a few years later the level of resistance was at greater than 95%. Almost every year the CDC issues new treatment guidelines for gonorrhea that identify the recommended antibiotic drugs and dosages.

a. Why is the CDC so active in making these recommendations?

b. What are the short-term implications of these frequent changes for physicians and clinics that treat sexually transmitted diseases like gonorrhea and for individuals infected with gonorrhea?

c. What are the long-term implications of these frequent changes in treatment recommendations for the patient population?

22. An attribute of growth behavior of eight bacteriophage mutants (1 to 8) is investigated in experiments that establish coinfection by pairs of mutants. The experiments determine whether the mutants complement one another (+) or fail to complement (−). These eight mutants are known to result from point mutation. The results of the complementation tests are shown below.

Mutations

	1	2	3	4	5	6	7	8
1	−	+	+	+	−	+	+	−
2		−	+	+	+	+	+	+
3			−	+	+	+	−	+
4				−	+	−	+	+
5					−	+	+	−
6						−	+	+
7							−	+
8								−

a. How many genes are represented by these mutations?

b. Identify the mutants of each gene.

c. In each coinfection above that is identified as a failure to complement (−), researchers see evidence of recombination producing wild-type growth. How do the researchers distinguish between wild-type growth resulting from complementation and wild-type growth that is due to recombination?

d. A new mutation, designated 9, fails to complement mutants 1, 3, 5, 7, and 8. Wild-type recombinants form between mutant 9 and mutations 3, 5, and 8; however, no wild-type recombinants form between mutant 9 and mutations 1 and 7. What kind of mutation is mutant 9? Explain your reasoning.

e. New mutation 10 fails to complement mutants 1, 4, 5, 6, 8, and 9. Mutant 10 forms wild-type recombinants with mutants 1, 5, and 6, but not with mutants 4 and 8. Mutant 9 and mutant 10 form wild-type recombinants. What kind of mutation is mutant 10? Explain your reasoning.

f. Gene mapping information identifies mutations 2 and 3 as the flanking markers in this group of genes. Assuming these mutations are on opposite ends of the gene map, determine the order of mutations in the region of the chromosome.

23. Synthesis of the amino acid histidine is a multistep anabolic pathway that uses the products of 13 genes (*hisA* to *hisM*) in *E. coli.* Two independently isolated *his⁻ E. coli* mutants, designated *his1⁻* and *his2⁻*, are studied in a conjugation experiment. A *his⁺* F′ donor strain that carries a copy of the *hisJ* gene on the plasmid is mated with a *his1⁻* recipient strain in experiment 1 and with a *his2⁻* recipient in experiment 2. The exconjugants are grown on plates lacking histidine. Growth is observed among the exconjugants of experiment 2 but not among those of experiment 1.

a. Why is growth observed in experiment 2 but not in experiment 1?

b. What is the genotype of exconjugants in experiment 2?

24. The phage P1 is used as a generalized transducing phage in an experiment combining a donor strain of *E. coli* of genotype *leu⁺ phe⁺ ala⁺* and a recipient strain that is *leu⁻ phe⁻ ala⁻*. In separate experiments, transductants are selected for *leu⁺* (experiment A), for *phe⁺* (experiment B), and for *ala⁺* (experiment C). Following selection, transductant genotypes for the unselected markers are identified.

a. What compound or compounds are added to the minimal medium to select for transductants in experiments A, B, and C?

Selection experiment results below show the frequency of each genotype.

Experiment A		Experiment B		Experiment C	
phe⁻ ala⁻	26%	*leu⁻ ala⁻*	65%	*leu⁻ phe⁻*	71%
phe⁺ ala⁻	50%	*leu⁺ ala⁻*	48%	*leu⁺ phe⁻*	21%
phe⁻ ala⁺	19%	*leu⁻ ala⁺*	0%	*leu⁻ phe⁺*	0%
phe⁺ ala⁺	3%	*leu⁺ ala⁺*	4%	*leu⁺ phe⁺*	3%

b. Determine the order of genes on the donor chromosome.

c. Diagram the crossover events that form each of the transductants in experiment A.

d. In experiment B, why are there no transductants with the genotype *leu⁻ ala⁺*?

25. A series of seven point mutations are mapped along the *rIIA* gene and then tested for their ability to form wild-type recombinants with *rII* partial-deletion mutants. In the table, "+" indicates the formation of wild-type recombinants, and "−" indicates that wild types do not form. Use the data to show the length and endpoints of each deletion as accurately as you can.

rIIA point mutants	37	46	21	19	34	27	12
Mutant map:							

Deletion Mutants	Point Mutants						
	12	19	21	27	34	37	46
B622	+	+	−	+	+	+	−
CT48	−	+	+	−	−	+	+
MB101	+	+	+	+	+	−	−
VG14	+	−	+	+	+	+	+
N220	+	−	−	+	−	+	+

26. Five *rII* partial-deletion mutants are mapped and then tested for their ability to form wild-type recombinants

with six point mutants. The extent and endpoints of deletion mutants are shown below the *rII* region of the chromosome.

a. Use the data in Table A to place each point mutation as precisely as you can along the chromosome.

Table A

	Deletion Mutants				
Point Mutants	**C19**	**L36**	**M12**	**R22**	**W42**
55	+	+	−	+	+
67	+	−	+	−	−
74	+	+	+	−	−
82	−	+	−	+	+
85	+	+	+	−	+
91	−	−	+	+	+

b. Use the complementation data in Table B to determine where the division between *rIIA* and *rIIB* is located on the *rII* region.

Table B

	Complemented by	
Deletion Mutant	***rIIA***	***rIIB***
C19	+	−
L36	−	−
M12	+	−
R22	−	+
W42	−	+

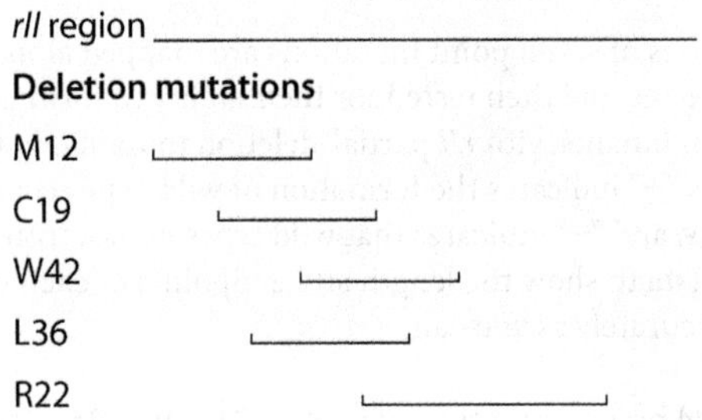

c. Based on the data and on your analysis, draw a complementation table for the five point mutants 55, 67, 74, 82, and 85. (Skip mutant 91 for this problem.)

d. Add mutant 91 to your complementation table (assume it maps to *rIIA*).

27. A 2013 CDC report identified the practice of routinely adding antibiotic compounds to animal feed as a major culprit in the rapid increase in the number of antibiotic-resistant strains. Agricultural practice in recent decades has encouraged the addition of antibiotics to the animal feed to promote growth rather than to treat disease.

a. Speculate about the process by which feeding antibiotics to animals such as cattle might lead to an increase in the number of antibiotic-resistant strains of bacteria.

b. How might the increase in antibiotic-resistant strains of bacteria in cattle be a threat to human health?

28. Hfr strains that differ in integrated F factor orientation and site of integration are used to construct consolidated bacterial chromosome maps. The data below show the order of gene transfer for five strains.

Hfr Strain	**Order of Gene Transfer (first → last)**
Hfr A	*oriT* – *thr* – *leu* – *azi* – *ton* – *pro* – *lac* – *ade*
Hfr B	*oriT* – *mtl* – *xyl* – *mal* – *str* – *his*
Hfr C	*oriT* – *ile* – *met* – *thi* – *thr* – *leu* – *azi* – *ton*
Hfr D	*oriT* – *his* – *trp* – *gal* – *ade* – *lac* – *pro* – *ton*
Hfr E	*oriT* – *thi* – *met* – *ile* – *mtl* – *xyl* – *mal* – *str*

a. Identify the overlaps between Hfr strains. Identify the orientations of F factors relative to one another.

b. Draw a consolidated map of the bacterial chromosome. (*Hint:* Begin by placing the insertion site for Hfr A at the 2 o'clock position and arranging the genes *thr-leu-azi-* . . . in clockwise order.)

DNA Structure and Replication

The laboratory method known as polymerase chain reaction (PCR) is made possible by *Taq* polymerase that was first isolated from *Thermus aquaticus* bacteria living in near-boiling conditions in Yellowstone National Park. The inset photo (upper left) shows growing *T. aquaticus*.

CHAPTER OUTLINE

7.1 DNA Is the Hereditary Molecule of Life

7.2 The DNA Double Helix Consists of Two Complementary and Antiparallel Strands

7.3 DNA Replication Is Semiconservative and Bidirectional

7.4 DNA Replication Precisely Duplicates the Genetic Material

7.5 Molecular Genetic Analytical Methods Make Use of DNA Replication Processes

ESSENTIAL IDEAS

■ Seventy-five years of observations and analysis culminated in the identification of DNA as the hereditary molecule.

■ DNA is a double-stranded molecule consisting of four kinds of nucleotides, abbreviated A, T, C, and G, that are held together by a mechanism of complementary base pairing.

■ DNA replication faithfully duplicates the genome by a semiconservative process that progresses bidirectionally from each origin of replication.

■ Origins of replication are defined by their nucleotide sequence. Numerous proteins and enzymes act in concert to produce two identical DNA duplexes.

■ Laboratory techniques based on a molecular understanding of DNA replication perform targeted replication of short DNA sequences and sequence DNA.

The central dogma of biology identifies DNA as the repository of genomic information for organisms and describes its central role in the production of RNA transcripts of genes and of polypeptides produced by translation of mRNA (see Figure 1.8, p. 10). DNA's ongoing role in these processes requires its faithful replication in each cell cycle, and that is the subject of this chapter.

In Chapter 1, we reviewed the primary and secondary structures of DNA and RNA and the fundamentals of DNA replication. In this chapter, we discuss the structure of DNA in greater detail and extend the earlier description to include the molecular processes occurring in DNA replication. We also examine two analytical methodologies—polymerase chain reaction (PCR) and DNA sequencing—that were developed as an outcome of the understanding of replication. The Case Study at the end of the chapter describes the use of PCR and DNA sequencing to identify and analyze the mutation associated with Huntington disease (OMIM 143100), an autosomal dominant disorder in humans.

7.1 DNA Is the Hereditary Molecule of Life

When scientists speak of the "hereditary molecule" of a species, they mean the molecular substance that carries and conveys the species' genetic information. Our contemporary understanding of hereditary transmission and the evolution of species is rooted in the knowledge that DNA is the hereditary molecule of all organisms. Long before the hereditary role of DNA was established, however, research had identified five essential characteristics of hereditary material. The hereditary material must be

1. Localized to the nucleus and a component of chromosomes
2. Present in a stable form in cells
3. Sufficiently complex to contain the genetic information required to direct the structure, function, development, and reproduction of organisms
4. Able to accurately replicate itself so that daughter cells contain the same information as parental cells
5. Mutable, undergoing mutation at a low rate that introduces genetic variation and serves as a foundation for evolutionary change

Chromosomes Contain DNA

The weakly acidic substance known today as DNA was first noticed in 1869, when Friedrich Miescher isolated it from the nuclei of white blood cells in a mixture of nucleic acids and proteins he called "nuclein." Miescher made little progress in determining the composition of nuclein, however, and the substance was little studied over the next several decades.

In the 1870s, microscopic studies identified the fusion of male and female nuclei during reproduction. Shortly thereafter, chromosomes were observed in cell nuclei. This was followed by the observation that the nuclei of different species contain different numbers of chromosomes, as well as by descriptions of the equal chromosome contributions of males and females to reproduction. The

earliest suggestion that DNA was the hereditary material was based on these tantalizing bits of information. It came from Edmund Wilson in 1895. After accurately documenting that sperm and egg cells contribute the same number of chromosomes during reproduction, Wilson speculated,

> The precise equivalence of the chromosomes contributed by the sexes is a physical correlative of the fact that the two sexes play, on the whole, equal parts in hereditary transmission, and it seems to show that the chromosomal substance, the chromatin, is to be regarded as the physical basis of inheritance. Now, chromatin is known to be closely similar to, if not identical with a substance known as nuclein ($C_{29} H_{49} N_9 P_3 O_{22}$, according to Miescher), which analysis shows to be a tolerably definite chemical composed of nucleic acid (a complex organic acid rich in phosphorus) and albumin. And thus we reach the remarkable conclusion that inheritance may, perhaps, be effected by the physical transmission of a particular chemical compound from parent to offspring.

In 1900, Mendel's hereditary principles were rediscovered, and their predictions were widely disseminated in biology (see Section 1.1). Shortly thereafter, in 1903, Wilson's student Walter Sutton and, independently, Theodor Boveri accurately described the parallels between homologous chromosome and sister-chromatid separation during meiotic cell division and the inheritance of genes.

Over the next 20 years, the nucleus and chromosomes were a focus of biological investigations of heredity. By 1920, the principal constituent of nuclein was identified as DNA, and the basic chemistry of DNA was deciphered. The molecule was determined to be a polynucleotide consisting of four repeating subunits—the four DNA nucleotides—held together by covalent bonds. The four DNA nucleotides are adenine (A), thymine (T), cytosine (C), and guanine (G).

In 1923, DNA was localized to chromosomes. This discovery made DNA a candidate for the hereditary material, but DNA is not the sole constituent of chromosomes. Proteins are in high concentration in chromosomes; RNA is present in the nucleus and around chromosomes; and other compounds, including lipids and carbohydrates, were also considered as potential candidates for the hereditary material at one time or another. In fact, some early researchers, including, eventually, Edmund Wilson, thought protein was potentially a better candidate for the hereditary material than DNA. They noted that protein is composed of 20 different amino acids, whereas DNA has only 4 kinds of nucleotides. The protein proponents suggested that the "20-letter alphabet" of protein could contain more information than the "4-letter alphabet" of DNA. It was against this backdrop that the results of three experiments conducted between 1928 and 1952 combined to identify DNA—not RNA, protein, or another chemical constituent of cells—as the hereditary material of organisms.

A Transformation Factor Responsible for Heredity

Frederick Griffith, a British physician with an interest in epidemiology, studied pneumonia infection in mice and published a lengthy research report in 1928 describing his findings. Modern biology focuses on just the few pages of Griffith's long report that provided indirect evidence that DNA is the molecule responsible for conveying hereditary characteristics in bacteria.

Griffith studied strains of the bacterium *Pneumococcus*, which causes fatal pneumonia in mice. He found that strains of the bacterium that cause pneumonia in mice grow in colonies that have a smooth (S) appearance, whereas those *Pneumococcus* strains that do not cause disease are identifiable by their rough (R) appearance (**Figure 7.1**). It was later determined that rough bacterial strains have a mutant allele of the polysaccharide gene, which results in a weakened and easily broken capsule. This single gene mutation thus leaves R bacteria vulnerable to attack by mouse immune system antibodies.

The S and R forms of *Pneumococcus* occur in four antigenic types of the bacteria, identified as I, II, III, and IV. Each antigenic type elicits a different immune response from the mouse immune system as a result of the presence of several genetic differences. A single mutation of the polysaccharide gene can convert an S strain to an R strain *of the same antigenic type*—for example, converting an SII strain to an RII strain—but the antigenic type cannot be changed by a single mutation. In other words, mutation alone cannot change RII bacteria into SIII.

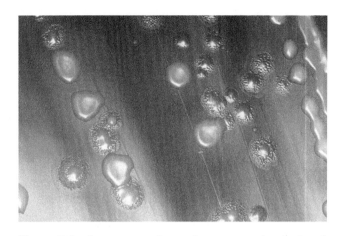

Figure 7.1   Appearance of smooth versus rough colonies of *Pneumococcus*.

Griffith's most important observations are derived from four injection tests he performed using S and R bacterial strains of different antigenic types (**Figure 7.2**). Following each injection test, he was able to draw blood from injected mice and culture the blood to identify the type of bacterium growing, if any, in the mouse. Griffith's first three injection results show that ❶ injecting mice with S-strain bacteria produces illness and death, ❷ injection of "heat-killed" S-strain bacteria (the bacteria are killed using high heat and pressure) does not induce illness, and ❸ injection of an R strain does not produce illness. Griffith's most significant result ❹ came when he injected a mixture of heat-killed SIII strain and living RII strain. He found that most of the

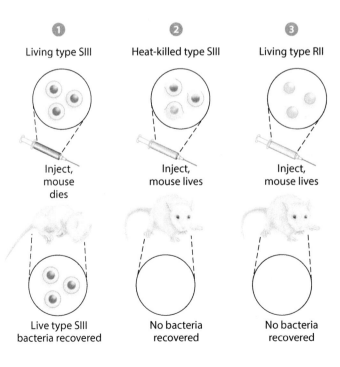

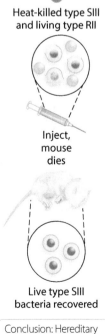

Figure 7.2   Frederick Griffith's experiment identifying a "transformation factor" responsible for heredity. ❶ Injection of living SIII bacteria kills mice. ❷ Heat-killed SIII do not kill mice, nor do living RII bacteria ❸. ❹ Coinjection of a mixture of heat-killed SIII and living RII bacteria results in mouse death by SIII infection.

mice became ill and died from pneumonia. His tests of blood cultures from the dead mice revealed living SIII bacteria. Knowing that this outcome could not have been the result of a simple mutational event, Griffith proposed that a molecular component he called the transformation factor was responsible for transforming RII into SIII.

In Griffith's proposal, the transforming factor was a molecule that carried hereditary information. He was unable to identify this molecule, but of course today we know it to be DNA. Today biologists also know that the process identified by Griffith is a naturally occurring process called *transformation,* which is used by bacteria to transfer DNA (see Section 6.4).

DNA Is the Transformation Factor

Shortly after Griffith published his report on the transformation factor, Martin Dawson, working with Oswald Avery, developed an in vitro transformation procedure to mix living R cells with a purified extract of cellular material derived from heat-killed SIII cells containing the transformation factor. Biochemical assays indicated that the SIII extract consisted mostly of DNA, along with a small amount of RNA and trace amounts of proteins, lipids, and polysaccharides.

The most direct evidence that DNA was the transformation factor came from an experiment performed by Avery and his colleagues Colin MacLeod and Maclyn McCarty in 1944 (**Figure 7.3**). This experiment identified the role of DNA in transformation by eliminating lipids, polysaccharides, protein, RNA, and DNA one at a time from the SIII extract. In each experimental trial, the SIII extract was treated to remove one component at a time, and the treated extract was mixed with RII cells. The in vitro transformation reaction was allowed to take place, and the occurrence or prevention of transformation was assessed.

Figure 7.3 shows that in vitro transformation takes place in the control experiment ❶, and when lipids and polysaccharides ❷, proteins ❸, or RNA ❹ are removed from the extract. In contrast to the other results, experiment ❺, which uses DNase to specifically degrade DNA, does not result in transformation—a clear indication that transformation is blocked by the destruction of DNA. Based on these observations, Avery, MacLeod, and McCarty correctly concluded that DNA is the transformation factor and the probable hereditary material.

DNA Is the Hereditary Molecule

Avery, MacLeod, and McCarty's work convinced many biologists that DNA was the long-sought hereditary material, and a great deal of research in the late 1940s and early

Figure 7.3 Avery, MacLeod, and McCarty's use of in vitro transformation to identify DNA as the most likely hereditary molecule. A purified extract from heat-killed SIII bacteria successfully transforms RII cells in the control experiment ❶. Destruction of lipids and polysaccharides ❷, proteins ❸, or RNA ❹ does not affect transformation; however, destruction of DNA ❺ prevents transformation.

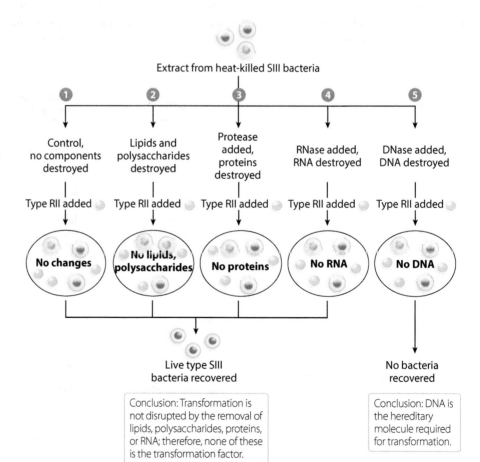

1950s was devoted to deducing the physical structure of DNA. Biologists realized that once the structure of DNA was known, the chemical nature of genes would be identified, and biological research would move into the realm of genetic molecular biology. As clear and convincing as the work of Avery and his colleagues seems in retrospect, however, there were several unanswered questions about the role of DNA in heredity. There was also a need to demonstrate directly that the presence of a specific DNA molecule induces the appearance of a particular phenotype. That evidence came in a 1952 report by Alfred Hershey and Martha Chase, who showed that DNA, but not protein, is responsible for bacteriophage infection of bacterial cells.

Bacteriophages, also known as **phages,** are viruses that infect bacteria. Phages such as T2, for example, consist of a protein shell with a tail segment that attaches to a host bacterial cell and a head segment that contains DNA. T2 phages are among the many bacteriophages that do not carry any RNA. Like other phages, T2 must infect host bacterial cells

in order to reproduce. Infection by a phage proceeds as illustrated in Figure 6.15 (p. 210) and culminates in the lysis of the host cell and the release of dozens of progeny phages.

In their experiment, Hershey and Chase took advantage of an essential difference between the chemical composition of DNA and protein to confirm the hereditary role of DNA (**Figure 7.4**). Proteins contain large amounts of sulfur but almost no phosphorus; conversely, DNA contains a large amount of phosphorus but no sulfur. Hershey and Chase initially grew phage cultures in different growth media. One growth medium contained ^{35}S, the radioactive form of sulfur, to label protein ❶; the other contained radioactive phosphorus, ^{32}P, to label DNA ❶. The researchers used radioactively labeled phages from each medium to infect unlabeled host bacterial cells in parallel experiments ❷ ❷.

After a short time, each mixture was agitated in a blender to separate bacterial cells from the now empty phage shells. Such empty phage shells are called "ghosts" ❸ ❸. The relatively large bacterial cells were easily separated from the

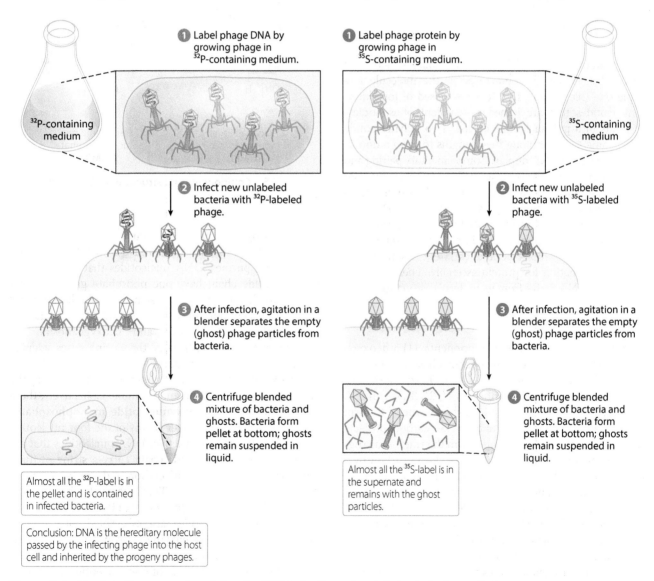

Figure 7.4   Hershey-Chase experiment showing DNA to be the molecule in bacteriophages that causes lysis of infected bacterial cells.

ghosts by centrifugation. The heavier bacteria collect in a pellet at the bottom of the centrifuge tube, while the lighter ghosts remain suspended in the supernatant. Testing each fraction for radioactivity revealed that virtually all the ^{32}P label was associated with newly infected bacterial cells and almost none with ghost particles ❹. On the other hand, the ^{35}S label was found in the ghost-particle fraction, and only trace amounts were found associated with the bacterial pellet ❹. This result demonstrates that phage DNA, but not phage protein, is transferred to host bacterial cells and directs the synthesis of phage DNA and proteins, the assembly of progeny phage particles, and ultimately the lysis of infected cells. The experiment demonstrated that the transformation factor identified previously by Griffith was DNA; it also showed that Avery, MacLeod, and McCarty were correct in concluding that DNA is the hereditary material.

7.2 The DNA Double Helix Consists of Two Complementary and Antiparallel Strands

Watson and Crick's model of the secondary structure of DNA indicates that in some respects, the molecule is a simple one (see Section 1.2). It is composed of four kinds of nucleotides that are joined by covalent phosphodiester bonds into polynucleotide chains. Two polynucleotide chains come together along their lengths to form a double helix, also called a DNA duplex. Complementary pairing and hydrogen bonding between the nucleotide base pairs join the two strands in the double helix. Yet for all its simplicity—being composed of just four types of nucleotides—DNA is a complex informational molecule that serves as a permanent repository of genetic information in cells, and it directs the production of RNA molecules that carry out actions in cells or carry information for protein assembly. These essential functions of DNA derive from its molecular structure.

DNA Nucleotides

A DNA nucleotide has three components: (1) a deoxyribose sugar, (2) one of four nitrogenous bases, and (3) up to three phosphate groups (**Figure 7.5**). Deoxyribose contains 5 carbons that are identified as 1′, 2′, 3′, 4′, and 5′. An oxygen atom connects the 1′ carbon to the 4′ to form a five-sided (pentose) ring, and the 5′ carbon projects outward from the 4′ carbon (and from the ring). A nitrogenous (nucleotide) base is attached to the 1′ carbon by a covalent bond; a hydroxyl group (OH) is attached to the 3′ carbon; and a single phosphate molecule, or a chain of phosphates up to three molecules long, is attached at the 5′ carbon. Deoxyribose has hydrogen atoms bound at the 2′ carbon instead of a hydroxyl (OH) group. This is the basis for naming the sugar *deoxy*ribose.

The four nitrogenous bases in DNA are of two structural types—a single-ringed form called a pyrimidine, and

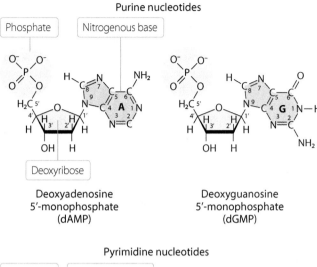

Purine nucleotides

Deoxyadenosine
5′-monophosphate
(dAMP)

Deoxyguanosine
5′-monophosphate
(dGMP)

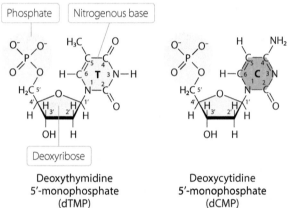

Pyrimidine nucleotides

Deoxythymidine
5′-monophosphate
(dTMP)

Deoxycytidine
5′-monophosphate
(dCMP)

Figure 7.5 **Components and structures of DNA nucleotide monophosphates.**

a double-ringed form called a purine. Cytosine (C) and thymine (T) are pyrimidines, and adenine (A) and guanine (G) are purines. DNA nucleotides that are part of a polynucleotide chain have one phosphate group at their 5′ carbon that forms the covalent phosphodiester bond with the adjacent nucleotide in the strand. Deoxyadenosine 5′-monophosphate (dAMP) and deoxyguanosine 5′-monophosphate (dGMP) carry the purine bases adenine and guanine, and deoxycytidine 5′-monophosphate (dCMP) and deoxythymidine 5′-monophosphate (dTMP) carry the pyrimidine bases cytosine and thymine. Collectively, these are identified as the **deoxynucleotide monophosphates (dNMPs),** where *N* can refer to any of the four nucleotide bases. In contrast, free (reactive) DNA nucleotides that are not part of a polynucleotide chain carry a string of three phosphate groups at the 5′ carbon and are identified as dATP, dGTP, dCTP, and dTTP. Collectively, these are the **deoxynucleotide triphosphates (dNTPs).**

Individual nucleotides are assembled into a polynucleotide chain by the enzyme DNA polymerase, which catalyzes the formation of a phosphodiester bond between the 3′ hydroxyl group of one nucleotide and the 5′ phosphate group of an adjacent nucleotide (**Figure 7.6**).

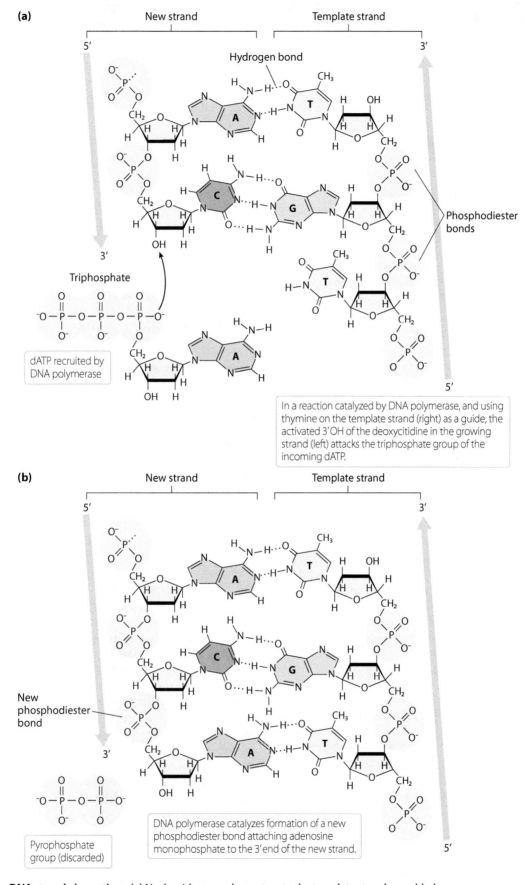

(a)

Hydrogen bond

Triphosphate

dATP recruited by DNA polymerase

In a reaction catalyzed by DNA polymerase, and using thymine on the template strand (right) as a guide, the activated 3'OH of the deoxycitidine in the growing strand (left) attacks the triphosphate group of the incoming dATP.

(b)

New phosphodiester bond

Pyrophosphate group (discarded)

DNA polymerase catalyzes formation of a new phosphodiester bond attaching adenosine monophosphate to the 3'end of the new strand.

Figure 7.6   DNA strand elongation. (a) Nucleotides complementary to the template strand are added to the 3' end of the new strand by DNA polymerase. **(b)** DNA nucleotide triphosphates are recruited by DNA polymerase, which uses catalytic action to remove two phosphates (the pyrophosphate group) and form a new phosphodiester bond.

PROBLEM A portion of one strand of a DNA duplex has the sequence 5'-ACGACGCTA-3'.

a. Identify the sequence and polarity of the other DNA strand.

b. Identify the *second* nucleotide added if the sequence given is used as a template for DNA replication.

> **BREAK IT DOWN:** DNA nucleotides in one strand of a duplex are complementary to those in the other, and the strands are antiparallel (p. 234).

> **BREAK IT DOWN:** New DNA synthesis progresses 5'-to-3' to elongate the newly synthesized strand (p. 234).

Solution Strategies	Solution Steps
Evaluate	
1. Identify the topic this problem addresses, and the nature of the required answer.	1. The question concerns a DNA sequence and requests an answer giving the sequence and polarity of the complementary strand.
2. Identify the critical information given in the problem.	2. The sequence and polarity are given for a portion of one DNA strand.
Deduce	
3. Review the general structure of a DNA duplex and the complementarity of specific nucleotides.	3. DNA is a double helix composed of single strands that contain complementary base pairs (A pairs with T, and G with C). The complementary strands are antiparallel (i.e., one strand is 5' to 3', and its complement is 3' to 5').
Solve	
4. Identify the sequence of the complementary strand.	4. The complementary sequence is TGCTGCGAT.
5. Give the polarity of the complementary strand.	5. The polarity of the complementary strand is 3'-TGCTGCGAT-5'.
6. Identify the second nucleotide added during DNA replication of the given sequence.	6. The second nucleotide added to the newly synthesized strand is adenine, which is complementary to thymine on the template strand.

> **TIP:** DNA polymerase catalyzes the addition of a new nucleotide to the 3' end of a growing strand.

For more practice, see Problems 5, 8, 9, 16, and 17. Visit the Study Area to access study tools. **MasteringGenetics**™

Two of the three phosphates of a dNTP are removed (as a pyrophosphate group) during phosphodiester bond formation, leaving the nucleotides of a polynucleotide chain in their monophosphate form. Each polynucleotide chain has a **sugar-phosphate backbone** consisting of alternating sugar and phosphate groups throughout its length.

Complementary DNA Nucleotide Pairing

DNA is most stable as a double helix, and the two polynucleotide strands that make up the duplex have a specific relationship that follows two rules: (1) the arrangement of the nucleotides is such that the nucleotide bases of one strand are *complementary* to the corresponding nucleotide bases on the second strand (A pairs with T and G pairs with C), and (2) the two strands are *antiparallel* in orientation (if one strand is, for example 5'-ATCG-3', then the complementary strand is 3'-TAGC-5').

Complementary base pairing joins a purine nucleotide on one strand to a pyrimidine nucleotide on the other. The chemical basis of such pairing is the formation of a stable number of hydrogen (H) bonds between the bases of the different strands. Hydrogen bonds are noncovalent bonds that form between the partial charges that are associated with the hydrogen, oxygen, and nitrogen

atoms of nucleotide bases. As Figure 7.6 shows, two stable hydrogen bonds form for each A-T base pair, and three hydrogen bonds are formed by each G-C base pair (see also Figure 1.6, p. 8).

Antiparallel strand orientation is essential to the formation of stable hydrogen bonds. In Figure 7.6, notice that the nucleotides in one strand are oriented with their 5' carbon toward the top and their 3' carbon toward the bottom. The complementary nucleotides in the other strand are antiparallel; that is, their 5'-to-3' orientations run in the *opposite* direction. Antiparallel orientation of complementary strands brings the partial charges of complementary nucleotides into alignment to form hydrogen bonds. If complementary strands were to align in parallel (i.e., with their 5' and 3' carbons facing in the same direction), the charges of complementary nucleotides would repel, and no hydrogen bonds would form. **Genetic Analysis 7.1** explores relationships between complementary DNA strands.

The Twisting Double Helix

The DNA double helix has an axis of helical symmetry, an imaginary line that passes lengthwise through the core of the double helix and marks the center of the molecule.

The molecular dimensions of DNA are measured using the unit called an angstrom (Å) or in nanometers (nm). One angstrom is equal to 10^{-10} meters, or 1 ten-billionth of a meter, and 1 nm equals one-billionth of a meter, or 10^{-9} meters. In DNA, the distance from the axis of symmetry to the outer edge of the sugar-phosphate backbone is 10 Å (1 nm), and the molecular diameter is 20 Å (2 nm) at any point along the length of the helix (Figure 7.7a). The 20-Å molecular diameter results from complementary pairing of each purine with the complementary pyrimidine (A with T, G with C) and gives each base pair the same dimension.

Nucleotide base pairs are spaced at intervals of 3.4 Å along DNA duplexes. This tight packing of DNA bases in the duplex leads to **base stacking,** the offsetting of adjacent base pairs so that their planes are parallel, and imparts a twist to the double helix. Figure 7.7a shows that one complete helical turn spans 34 Å. This span is occupied by approximately 10.5 base pairs. Figure 7.7b is a space-filling model that illustrates base-pair stacking and the twisting of the sugar-phosphate backbones. Figure 7.7c is a ball-and-stick model illustrating how base pairs twist around the axis of symmetry to create the helical spiral.

Base-pair stacking creates two grooves in the double helix, gaps between the spiraling sugar-phosphate backbones that partially expose the nucleotides. The alternating grooves, known as the **major groove** and **minor groove,** are highlighted in Figures 7.7b and 7.7c. The major groove is approximately 12 Å wide, and the minor groove is approximately 6 Å wide. The major and minor grooves are regions where DNA-binding proteins can most easily make direct contact with nucleotides along one or both strands of the double helix. In this chapter and in later chapters, we discuss many of the important functions DNA-binding proteins perform, such as regulating the initiation of transcription and controlling the onset and progression of DNA replication. Most of these functions depend on the presence of characteristic sequences of DNA nucleotides. DNA-binding proteins gain access to DNA nucleotides in major and minor grooves of the molecule.

The models of the DNA double helix presented in Figure 7.7 illustrate the most common and most stable form of DNA, known as B-form DNA, which has a right-handed twisting of the sugar-phosphate backbone. B-form DNA is overwhelmingly the most common DNA structure in organisms. Two other rarer and less stable forms of the DNA double helix have also been identified. A-form DNA is more compact than B-form DNA, with about 11 base pairs per complete helical twist and a higher degree of tilt of the base pairs relative to the

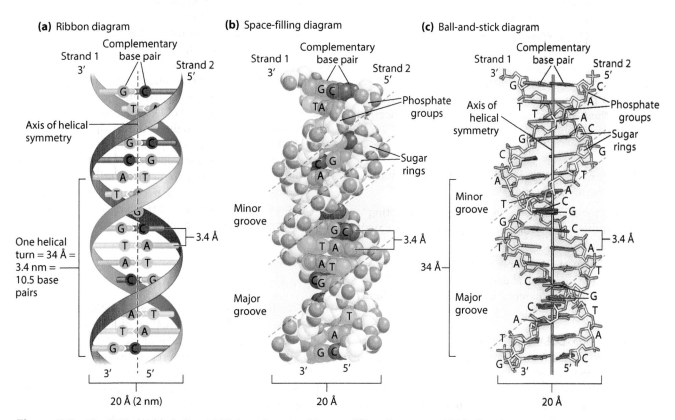

Figure 7.7   The DNA double helix. (a) Ribbon diagram, (b) space-filling diagram, and (c) ball-and-stick diagram show the sugar-phosphate backbones, base pairs, major and minor grooves, and dimensions of the DNA duplex.

backbone. A-form DNA is occasionally detected in cells. The third form of DNA, Z-form DNA, is quite different from A-form and B-form DNA. Z-form DNA has a left-handed twist that gives the sugar-phosphate backbone a zigzag appearance—hence the name Z-form. Z-form DNA occurs in the presence of a high concentration of positively charged ions. Only a tiny portion of total cellular DNA is ever in the Z form, and its physiological significance in cells is not known.

7.3 DNA Replication Is Semiconservative and Bidirectional

Given the role of DNA as an information repository and an information transmitter, the integrity of the nucleotide sequence of DNA is of paramount importance. Each time DNA is copied, the new version must be a precise duplicate of the original version. The high fidelity of DNA replication is essential to reproduction and to the normal development of biological structures and functions. Without faithful DNA replication, the information of life would become hopelessly garbled by rapidly accumulating mutations that would threaten survival.

Considering the importance of DNA throughout the biological world, it was no surprise to discover that the general mechanism of DNA replication is the same in all organisms. This universal process evolved in the earliest life-forms and has been retained for billions of years. As organisms diverged and became more complex, however, an array of differences did develop among DNA replication proteins and enzymes. Despite the diversification of these specific components of DNA replication, three attributes of DNA replication are shared by all organisms:

1. Each strand of the parental DNA molecule remains intact during replication.

2. Each parental strand serves as a template directing the synthesis of a complementary, antiparallel daughter strand.

3. Completion of DNA replication results in the formation of two identical daughter duplexes, each composed of one parental strand and one daughter strand.

As we describe DNA replication in bacteria, archaea, and eukaryotes in following sections, we will point out similarities and differences among the domains. The shared features of DNA replication are present because all life evolved from a common origin. At the same time, the differences in DNA replication between the domains are also the result of evolution, which favored specific adaptations.

Three Competing Models of Replication

In their famous 1953 paper describing the structure of DNA, Watson and Crick concluded with the observation

> It has not escaped our notice that the specific base-pairing we have proposed immediately suggests a possible copying mechanism for the genetic material.

Specifically, Watson and Crick recognized that a consequence of complementary base pairing was that nucleotides on one strand of the duplex could be used to identify the nucleotides of the other strand. Watson and Crick presumed that DNA replication used the nucleotide sequence of each strand to form a new pair of DNA duplexes, hypothesizing that each DNA strand of the original duplex would act as a template for the synthesis of a new daughter strand. Watson and Crick did not know the precise mechanism by which template-based replication took place, however, raising the crucial question of what the exact mechanism of replication might be.

Almost immediately after the DNA structure was identified, three competing models of DNA replication emerged (**Figure 7.8**). The models shared the idea that the two original strands (the parental strands) of the duplex act as templates to direct the assembly of newly synthesized DNA by complementary base pairing. The models also predicted that the completion of DNA replication produced two identical DNA duplexes (daughter duplexes). The models differed, however, in describing the makeup of the daughter duplexes. The ❶ **semiconservative DNA replication** model—which proved to be correct—proposed that each daughter duplex contains one original parental strand of DNA and one complementary, newly synthesized daughter strand. The ❷ **conservative DNA replication** model predicts that one daughter duplex contains the two strands of the parental molecule and the other contains two newly synthesized daughter strands. Lastly, the ❸ **dispersive DNA replication** model predicts that each daughter duplex is a composite of interspersed parental duplex segments and daughter duplex segments.

The Meselson-Stahl Experiment

In 1958, Matthew Meselson and Franklin Stahl took advantage of the newly developed method of high-speed cesium chloride (CsCl) density gradient ultracentrifugation to decipher the mechanism of DNA replication in an experiment of beautiful simplicity. In this analytical method, a tube filled with a CsCl mixture is subjected to high ultracentrifuge speeds that exert thousands of gravities of separating force, creating a graded variation in density—a density gradient—throughout the CsCl mixture. When substances are placed in the CsCl gradient and ultracentrifugation

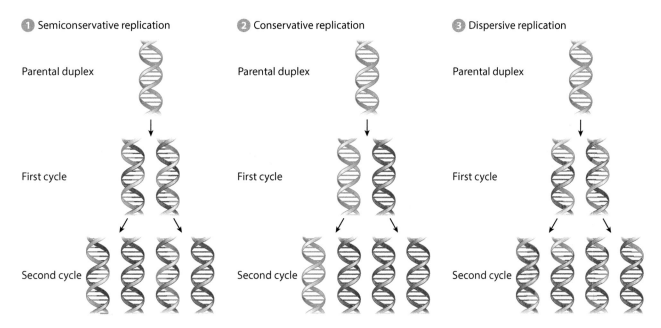

1 Semiconservative replication   **2** Conservative replication   **3** Dispersive replication

Parental duplex   Parental duplex   Parental duplex

First cycle   First cycle   First cycle

Second cycle   Second cycle   Second cycle

Figure 7.8   Three proposed mechanisms of DNA replication tested by Meselson and Stahl. The results expected for two cycles of DNA replication are shown for each model.

takes place, the substances migrate until they reach the point in the density gradient where their molecular density is matched by that of the gradient. Migration stops at that point. This technique is capable of separating molecules that have only slightly different molecular weights.

Meselson and Stahl began their experiment by growing *Escherichia coli* in a growth medium containing the rare heavy isotope of nitrogen, ^{15}N, for many generations. Under these growth conditions, parental DNA is fully saturated with heavy-isotope-containing nitrogen. All the DNA duplexes contain only the heavy nitrogen isotope, and they are designated $^{15}N/^{15}N$ to signify the incorporation of ^{15}N in both strands of the duplex. (By the same token, a DNA duplex composed of two strands containing only ^{14}N, the normal isotope of nitrogen, is designated $^{14}N/^{14}N$, and a duplex with one strand containing each isotope is designated $^{15}N/^{14}N$.) DNA collected for CsCl gradient analysis from this starting generation, designated generation 0, was exclusively $^{15}N/^{15}N$. Next, some of these ^{15}N-labeled *E. coli* were transferred to a new growth medium containing only the normal light isotope of nitrogen, ^{14}N. At the end of each successive DNA replication cycle, DNA was collected from a few cells on the ^{14}N medium for CsCl analysis. Growth in this medium leads to the incorporation of DNA nucleotides containing the light isotope into newly synthesized strands.

Figure 7.9 shows the results of CsCl gradient analysis of DNA collected from three replication cycles, beginning with generation 0. The experimental results are consistent with the semiconservative model only. The conservative model predicted DNA molecules with two distinct densities after generation 1 ($^{15}N/^{15}N$ and $^{14}N/^{14}N$). The results reject this model. Similarly, the dispersive model predicted a single DNA density in all generations. The

generation 2 results reject this replication model. The data are consistent with the predictions of the semiconservative model of DNA replication through generation 3 shown and beyond. Within a few years of Meselson and Stahl's identification of semiconservative replication in bacteria, the mechanism was identified experimentally in eukaryotes as well, solidifying the idea that all life shares the same general process of DNA replication, as a consequence of life's single origin and the evolutionary connections among living things.

Origin and Directionality of Replication in Bacterial DNA

Solving the riddle of the basic mechanism of DNA replication introduced new questions about how replication is initiated and how it progresses. Does replication commence at specific points on each chromosome? If so, how many such points does a chromosome have? Does DNA replication progress in one direction or in both directions from a replication origin? Experimental evidence clearly demonstrates that DNA replication is most often **bidirectional,** progressing in both directions from a single **origin of replication** in bacterial chromosomes and from multiple origins of replication in eukaryotic chromosomes.

In 1963, John Cairns reported the first evidence of a single origin of DNA replication in *E. coli*. Based on Cairn's evidence, it appeared that once replication gets underway in bacteria, there is expansion around the origin of replication, forming a **replication bubble,** as seen in **Figure 7.10**. The image shown in the figure is similar to the type of result Cairns obtained, but by itself, it did not allow a determination as to whether replication takes place in one direction away from the origin (unidirectional) or

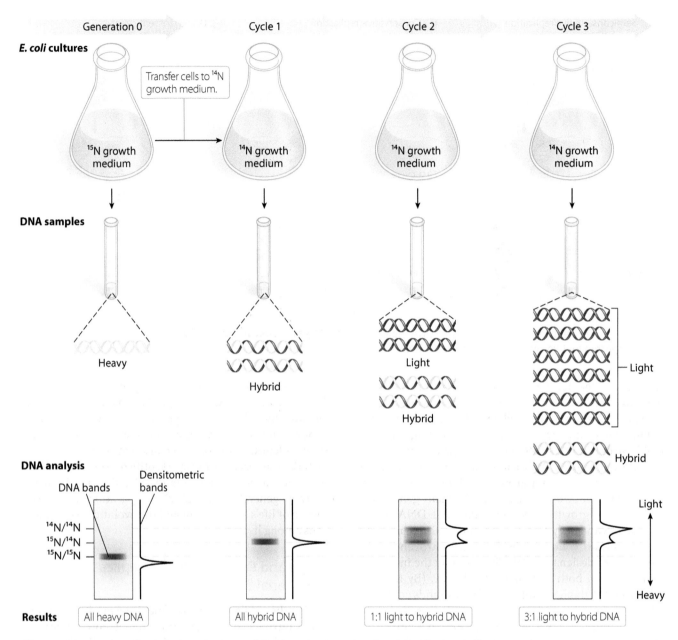

Figure 7.9   The Meselson-Stahl experimental results. Photographs of DNA bands in centrifuge tubes and densitometry scans (lower) identify the duplex DNA composition at each stage and are consistent only with semiconservative DNA replication. The semiconservative replication process is interpreted for each replication cycle.

in both directions (bidirectional). The resolution of this uncertainty held important implications. If DNA replicated bidirectionally, the time required to replicate a bacterial chromosome would be, give or take, about half that required if replication were unidirectional.

The replication bubble is where active DNA replication takes place. If replication were unidirectional, the origin of replication would eventually also serve as the terminus of replication, once the process was completed around the circumference of the circular bacterial chromosome. If, on the other hand, replication were bidirectional. Bidirectionality of replication would also mean that each end of the replication bubble would contain a **replication fork** where

new DNA nucleotides are added to elongating daughter strands. Furthermore, bidirectional replication would also mean that because the growth of the replication bubble progresses in both directions from the origin of replication, the terminus of replication would be halfway around the chromosome from the origin of replication. In contrast, unidirectional replication would mean that the origin and the terminus were at the same location.

In 1968, Joel Huberman and Arthur Riggs used a technique called pulse-chase labeling to produce the first experimental evidence of bidirectional replication in mammalian chromosomes (**Figure 7.11**). In pulse-chase labeling experiments, cells are exposed alternately to high levels of a

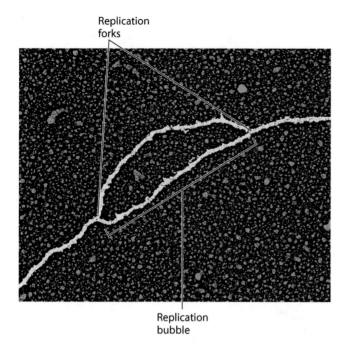

Replication forks

Replication bubble

Figure 7.10   DNA replication bubble and replication forks. A replication bubble expands bidirectionally from an origin of replication and active DNA synthesis takes place at each replication fork.

radioactive compound that they then incorporate into the DNA they are synthesizing. This is the "pulse." Following each pulse, the radioactive compound is temporarily removed to allow replication to proceed without radioactive labeling of newly synthesized DNA. This is the "chase." The result of the alternation between the presence and absence of the radioactive compound can be examined by autoradiography of newly replicated DNA. Autoradiography shows dark tracks where high levels of radioactive tracer are present and light tracks where levels are low. The bidirectional replication model predicts alternating dark and light tracks in *both directions* from replication origins during a pulse-chase labeling experiment that will be symmetrical around an origin of replication. With bidirectional replication, the alternating pattern of bands occurs because the expanding replication fork incorporates radioactivity in both directions away from the replication origin during the pulse in a symmetrical manner. The same concept applies to the absence of radioactivity in regions replicated during the chase. The pattern of symmetrical, alternating regions around each eukaryotic origin of replication obtained by Huberman and Riggs is consistent only with bidirectional replication.

Additional support for the bidirectionality of DNA replication comes from biochemical studies of the DNA polymerase responsible for most *E. coli* DNA replication. This DNA polymerase is capable of incorporating about 1000 nucleotides per second into a newly synthesized strand. At this rate of synthesis, the 4×10^6 nucleotides of the genome can be replicated in approximately 2000 seconds (33 minutes). This is close to the minimum generation time of *E. coli*. The enzymatic rate of the molecule

would have to be twice as fast if replication was unidirectional to complete replication within the generation time. In contrast to bacteria, the rate of catalytic activity of eukaryotic DNA polymerase is approximately 2000 to 4000 nucleotides per minute, less than a tenth the rate in *E. coli*. Eukaryotes have genomes many times larger than *E. coli*, and multiple chromosomes to replicate, so one can logically conclude they replicate their genomes from multiple origins of replication on each chromosome.

In bacteria, the matter of the directionality of replication was at last conclusively resolved in 1973, when Raymond Rodriguez and his colleagues provided definitive evidence of bidirectional replication by showing that the origin of replication and the terminus of replication are on opposite sides of the chromosome and are separated by almost exactly 180 degrees of circumference around the circular chromosome. In the image shown in Figure 7.12a, the origin of replication is labeled by radioactivity on one side of the chromosome, while the replication terminus is labeled on the opposite side of the chromosome. The only possible interpretation is that DNA replication in bacteria is bidirectional. Figure 7.12b illustrates the progression of bidirectional replication from its origin to its completion.

Multiple Replication Origins in Eukaryotes

Autoradiograph analysis reveals multiple origins of replication on eukaryotic chromosomes, and direct observation by electron microscopy confirms it (Figure 7.13a). Most

(a) Result of pulse-labeling experiment

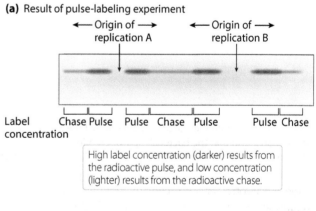

←— Origin of —→ replication A   ←— Origin of —→ replication B

Label concentration

Chase Pulse   Pulse Chase Pulse   Pulse Chase

High label concentration (darker) results from the radioactive pulse, and low concentration (lighter) results from the radioactive chase.

(b) Interpretation according to bidirectional model

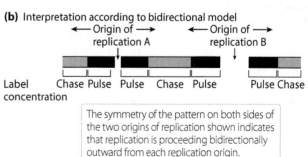

←— Origin of —→ replication A   ←— Origin of —→ replication B

Label concentration

Chase Pulse   Pulse Chase Pulse   Pulse Chase

The symmetry of the pattern on both sides of the two origins of replication shown indicates that replication is proceeding bidirectionally outward from each replication origin.

Figure 7.11   Pulse-chase labeling evidence of bidirectional DNA replication. (a) Huberman and Riggs results of pulse-chase labeling in mammalian chromosomes. **(b)** Interpretation of pulse-chase results according to the bidirectional model.

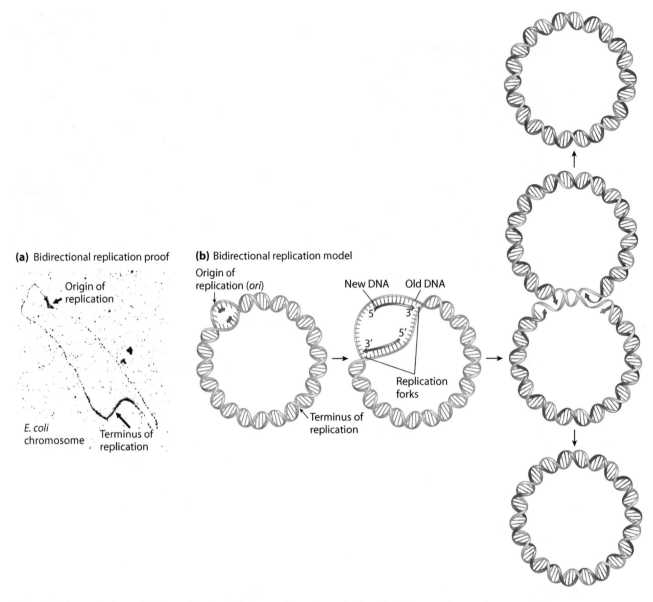

(a) Bidirectional replication proof

Origin of replication

E. coli chromosome

Terminus of replication

(b) Bidirectional replication model

Origin of replication (*ori*)

New DNA   Old DNA

5′   3′

3′   5′

Replication forks

Terminus of replication

Figure 7.12   Bidirectional DNA replication. (a) Autoradiograph results from Rodriguez and coworkers in 1973, showing that the bacterial replication origin and replication terminus are on opposite sides of the chromosome. **(b)** The model of bidirectional replication of a circular bacterial chromosome.

large eukaryotic genomes contain thousands of origins of replication, separated on average, on each chromosome, by 40,000 to 50,000 base pairs (bp). Current estimates indicate that the human genome contains more than 10,000 origins of replication that are spaced 30 to 300 kilobases (kb) apart. Eukaryotic replication origins are not all initiated at the same moment. Notice, for example, that in Figure 7.13, the replication bubbles shown are of different sizes, indicating that replication was initiated in them at different times. Among different types of cells, the length of S phase is variable, meaning that the rate of progression of DNA replication varies among cells of different types. Rapidly dividing cells replicate their DNA more quickly (i.e., have shorter S phase) than do slowly dividing cells. In addition, experimental evidence identifies "early-replicating" (i.e., early in S phase) and "late-replicating" (late in S phase) segments of large eukaryotic

genomes. Early-replicating genome segments appear to contain many expressed genes, whereas late-replicating regions contain many fewer expressed genes. In *Drosophila*, for example, late-replicating regions include chromosome segments immediately surrounding centromeres, where few expressed genes are located.

Regardless of differences in the timing of initiation of the multiple origins of replication on a eukaryotic chromosome, each of the replication bubbles emanating from an origin of replication expands toward the others to eventually merge, resulting in the replication of all of the DNA in each eukaryotic nucleus by the end of S phase (Figure 7.13b). The end products of replication of each eukaryotic chromosome are a pair of identical DNA duplexes that are sister chromatids. The sister chromatids will remain joined through G₂ and will be separated at anaphase of the upcoming M phase.

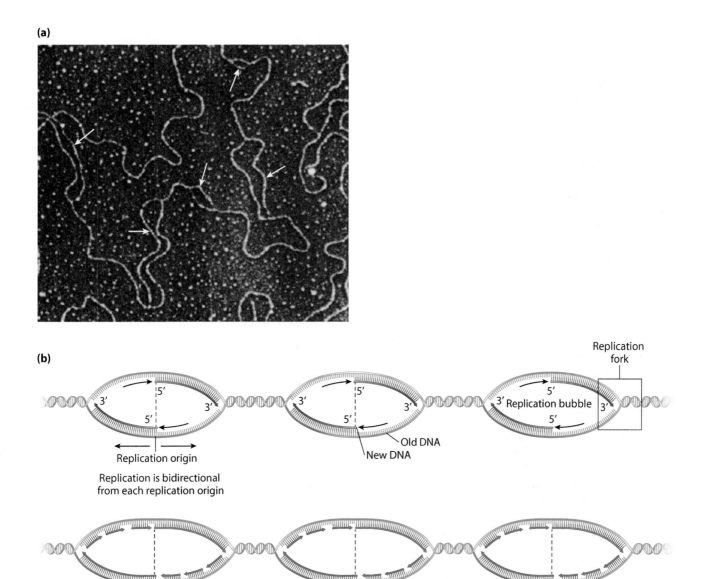

Figure 7.13 **Multiple origins of replication on a single chromosome from *Drosophila melanogaster*.** **(a)** The arrows point to replication bubbles, which are expanding bidirectionally. Different replication-bubble sizes indicate different start times. **(b)** Structures of multiple origins of replication in eukaryotic chromosomes.

7.4 DNA Replication Precisely Duplicates the Genetic Material

A great deal of what molecular biologists know about DNA replication comes from the study of bacteria, particularly *E. coli.* Chapter 1 presents a general overview of some of the basic steps of DNA replication. This section provides additional details of the process. Much remains to be learned about the mechanisms of DNA replication in the three domains of life; however, the information available to date

and the availability of genome sequences have revealed that eukaryotes and archaea possess strikingly similar DNA replication machinery that is evolutionarily distinct from the replication machinery in bacteria. The archeael process is, in many ways, a simpler version, and likely an ancestral version, of eukaryotic DNA replication. The evolutionary history of the development of DNA replication is the subject of active investigation, but what is clear is that during the evolution of life, two distinctly different sets of DNA replication machinery developed, one in bacteria and the other in archaea and eukaryotes. We will highlight similarities and differences between these processes as we move through this chapter section, comparing and contrasting the events and molecular activities that accompany DNA replication in species of the three domains.

To begin, we offer a cautionary note about discussions of DNA replication. Although parts of our replication discussion identify individual enzymes and proteins, do not be misled into thinking of these proteins as solo actors that enter and leave the replication fork at will. Instead, they are part of large, complex aggregations of proteins and enzymes called *replisomes* that assemble at each replication fork. In *E. coli*, for example, the replisomes active in DNA replication contain more than 30 distinct proteins and enzymes. Later in the section, we describe how one replisome at each replication fork carries out the nearly simultaneous replication of both template strands.

We begin this section with Foundation Figure 7.14, which provides a step-by-step overview of bacterial DNA replication. At each step, the activities of the principal molecular players are identified. You can refer back to this Foundation Figure as you make your way through the following pages.

DNA Sequences at Replication Origins

Origins of DNA replication contain sequences that attract replication enzymes. The best-characterized origin-of-replication sequence is from *E. coli* and is designated *oriC*. This sequence, which contains approximately 245 bp of DNA, is AT-rich (i.e., has a preponderance of adenine and thymine base pairs). DNA regions containing A-T richness require less energy for their denaturation, a process we will see happening at *oriC* early in the initiation of replication.

OriC is subdivided by three 13-bp sequences, so-called 13-mers, followed by four 9-bp sequences, called 9-mers (Figure 7.15a). Other bacterial species have origin-of-replication sequences that are similar to *oriC*. This similarity is a product of evolutionary conservation of DNA sequences and the functionality of those sequences. Natural selection has acted to maintain sequence similarity because the function of the conserved sequence region is essential to the survival of the organism. In other words, natural selection maintains sequences of DNA within a region that performs an essential function. Comparisons of evolutionarily conserved sequences within and among related species often leads to the identification of **consensus sequences.** These sequences have a generally similar pattern of base pairs, although they are not identical. Rather, consensus sequences are described by the nucleotides found *most often* at each position of DNA in the conserved region. In this context a consensus sequence is a conserved nucleotide sequence that acts as the binding site for proteins that initiate replication. Consensus sequences are plentiful in nucleic acids and generally function as conserved recognition sequences for protein binding in regulatory processes.

The 13-mer and 9-mer consensus sequences that are part of *oriC* have been maintained by natural selection because they have essential functional roles in replication initiation. Beyond the presence of the consensus sequences themselves, natural selection may also act to maintain specific spacing between different segments of a consensus sequence region. Spacing can be important to the function of the sequence because DNA-binding proteins must assemble at consensus sequence sites. Different proteins may be attracted to different regions of consensus sequences, and each protein requires physical space to bind to DNA and to interact with the other proteins bound to the consensus sequence region.

Among eukaryotic organisms, the yeast *Saccharomyces cerevisiae* has the most fully characterized origin-of-replication sequences. In yeast, the multiple origins of replication are known as autonomously replicating sequence (ARS). There is overall conservation of DNA sequence in ARSs, and their organization is similar throughout the yeast genome. ARS1 in yeast has been fully sequenced (Figure 7.15b). Within the 95 bp of ARS1 is an 11-bp consensus sequence and three other regions (B_1, B_2, and B_3) of conserved DNA sequences that differ somewhat from one another and from the 11-bp consensus sequence region.

Much less is known about the DNA sequences at replication origins in other eukaryotic species, particularly in multicellular species. What is known is that there are thousands of origins of replication distributed among the multiple chromosomes of eukaryotes. These origins initiate replication at various times during S phase of the cell cycle, leading to the identification of early- and late-replicating segments of chromosomes. Genome sequence data do not identify any sequence consistent with a replication of origin sequence in multicellular eukaryotes; thus it seems likely that DNA is selected for replication in multicellular eukaryotes based on chromatin modification rather than by the presence of specific DNA sequence.

Archaeal species fall somewhere in between the alternatives represented by the single, sequence-specific origin of replication in bacteria, the multiple and sequence-specific origins in yeast, and the numerous, non-sequence-specific origins in multicellular eukaryotes. Since the archaea possess homologs of the eukaryotic replication proteins, but also have small, circular chromosomes like bacteria, it was initially unclear whether archaeal cells would utilize single or multiple origins of replication. The first archaeal species to have its origin of replication mapped was *Pyrococcus abyssi*. It has a single origin of replication. Subsequently it was found that the archaeal species *Sulfolobus solfataricus* uses three origins of replication. Multiple origins of replication have been found in a variety of other archaeal species, although others with a single replication origin have also been identified.

In addition, many archaeal species possess an ORB (origin recognition box) sequence at the sites of replication origin. These sequences bind replication-initiating proteins that are homologous to those in eukaryotes, indicating that the molecular processes that initiate replication in archaea are more similar to those of eukaryotes than those of bacteria.

DNA Replication

1 Helicase breaks hydrogen bonds. Topoisomerase relaxes super-coiling.

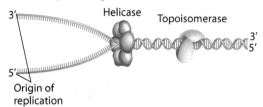

3′
Helicase
Topoisomerase
3′
5′
5′
Origin of replication

2 Single-stranded binding (SSB) protein prevents reannealing.

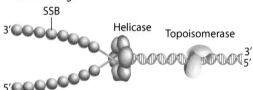

SSB
3′
Helicase
Topoisomerase
3′
5′
5′

3 DnaG synthesizes RNA primers.

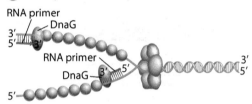

RNA primer
DnaG
3′
5′
3′
RNA primer
DnaG
3′
5′
3′
5′
5′

4 DNA polymerase III synthesizes daughter strand.

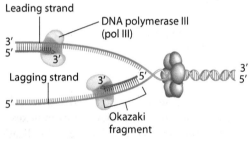

Leading strand
DNA polymerase III (pol III)
3′
5′
3′
Lagging strand
3′
5′
3′
5′
5′
Okazaki fragment

5 DNA polymerase III elongates the leading strand continuously and the lagging strand discontinuously.

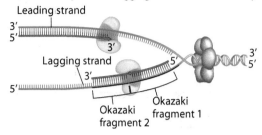

Leading strand
3′
5′
3′
3′
5′
Lagging strand
3′
5′
5′
Okazaki fragment 2
Okazaki fragment 1

6 DNA polymerase I removes and replaces nucleotides of the RNA primer.

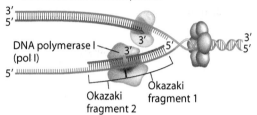

3′
5′
3′
3′
5′
DNA polymerase I (pol I)
3′
5′
5′
Okazaki fragment 2
Okazaki fragment 1

7 DNA ligase joins Okazaki fragments.

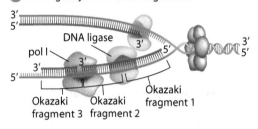

3′
5′
DNA ligase
3′
pol I
3′
5′
3′
3′
5′
5′
Okazaki fragment 3
Okazaki fragment 2
Okazaki fragment 1

Protein	DNA topoisomerase	Helicase (DnaB)	SSB	Primase	DNA pol III	DNA pol I	DNA ligase
Icon							
Role	Relaxes supercoiling	Unwinds the double helix	Prevents reannealing of separated strands	Synthesizes RNA primers	Synthesizes DNA	Removes and replaces RNA primer with DNA	Joins DNA segments

(a) *E. coli oriC*

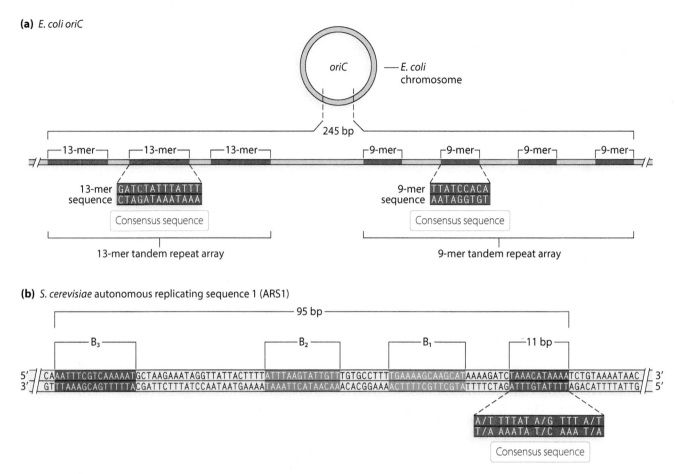

(b) *S. cerevisiae* autonomous replicating sequence 1 (ARS1)

Figure 7.15 **Origin of replication sequences in *E. coli* and yeast.** (a) *OriC* in *E. coli* contains three 13-mer and four 9-mer consensus sequences in a region of 245 base pairs of conserved sequence. (b) The yeast ARS1 origin of replication contains a consensus 11-bp segment and regions B_1, B_2, and B_3, spanning 95 base pairs of conserved sequence. A solidus (/) between nucleotides of consensus sequences (e.g., A/T) indicates that the two nucleotides are equally common at this position.

Replication Initiation

DNA replication in *E. coli* requires that replication-initiating enzymes locate and bind to the consensus sequences in *oriC*. In *E. coli*, three enzymes, DnaA, DnaB, and DnaC, bind at *oriC* and initiate DNA replication (**Figure 7.16** and **Table 7.1**). The first to bind is DnaA, attaching to the 9-mer components of *oriC*. The DnaA bends DNA and breaks (hydrolyzes) hydrogen bonds in the A-T–rich 13-mer region of *oriC*, creating an open complex, a short region where strands of the duplex are separated. Then DnaB, carried to *oriC* by DnaC, attaches to both strands in the open complex. The DnaB is a **helicase** protein that uses ATP energy to hydrolyze hydrogen bonds joining complementary nucleotides. This hydrolysis separates the DNA strands and unwinds the double helix. The unwound strands of DNA would seek maximum stability by reannealing, re-forming complementary double-stranded DNA, except for the presence of **single-stranded binding protein (SSB).** Single-stranded binding protein prevents reannealing of the separated strands, keeping them available to serve as templates for new DNA synthesis (see Figure 7.14, step ①).

In eukaryotes, helicase recruitment and activity is best understood in yeast, where four protein subcomplexes are involved. At eukaryotic replication origins, a prereplication complex (preRC) of 14 proteins assembles. Six proteins of the preRC, Orc1 through Orc6 (Orc1–6), form a subunit identified as the origin replication complex (ORC) that acts as the initiator of eukaryotic DNA replication by identifying the origin site. ORC is then bound by the proteins Cdc6 and Cdt1 and by a double hexamer of the replicative helicase MCM. Each hexamer is made up of six subunit of the protein Mcm2–7. The paired Mcm2–7 hexameric rings encircle both strands of the DNA duplex. As S phase commences, two additional proteins Cdc45 and a multisubunit GINS protein, join with Mcm2–7. Collectively, they form the CMG complex (Cdc45–Mcm2–7–GINS). The CMG complex is the fully actives DNA unwinding, leading to breakage of hydrogen bonds between the DNA strands ahead of DNA polymerase activity.

In archaea, it is thought that helicase recruitment is similar to events in yeast. An initiator protein complex identified as Orc1/Cdc6 binds to ORB sequences at the origin

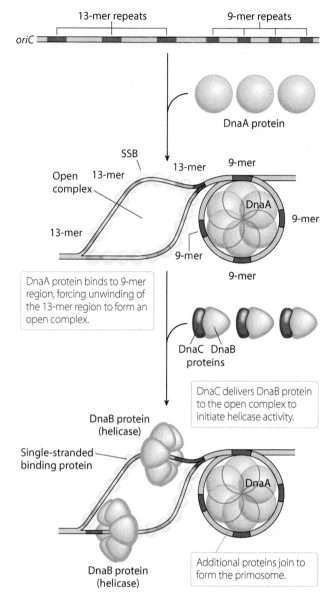

Figure 7.16 **Replication initiation at *oriC*, requiring DnaA, DnaB, and DnaC proteins.**

	Domain			
Bacteria	**Eukarya**	**Archaea**	**Role in Replication**	
DnaA	Orc1–6	Orc1/Cdc6	Replication-origin recognition	
DnaB, DnaC	Cdc6/Cdt1	Orc1/Cdc6	Helicase activity	
	Mcm2–7	Mcm		
	GINS	GINS	Helicase recruitment	
DnaG	Primase/pol α	Primase	Primer synthesis	
DNA Pol III	DNA pol δ	Pol B	DNA synthesis	
	DNA pol ε	Pol D		
DNA pol I	RPA	RPA	DNA synthesis	
RnaseH	FEN1/DNA2	FEN1/DNA2	Primer removal	
β (sliding) clamp	PCNA	PCNA	DNA polymerase progression	
Tau protein	RFC	RFC	Replication fork progression	

Table 7.1 **DNA Replication Proteins and Enzymes**

new DNA nucleotide can be added by DNA polymerase. To satisfy the requirement for a primer, DNA replication is initiated by a specialized RNA polymerase, DnaG, also, called **primase,** that synthesizes a short **RNA primer.**

In *E. coli* DNA replication, the DnaG complex joins DnaA, DnaB, and DnaC at *oriC*, where DnaG synthesizes the RNA primer. Measuring just one dozen to two dozen nucleotides in length, RNA primers provide the 3′ OH needed for DNA polymerase activity. RNA primers contain the nucleotide base uracil (U), in place of thymine. Consequently, RNA primers cannot remain as part of fully replicated DNA. Thus, while they are essential for allowing DNA polymerase to begin its DNA synthesis, RNA primers are temporary and are removed from newly synthesized DNA strands by a process we describe in the following section.

In eukaryotic DNA replication, the RNA-synthesizing enzyme primase synthesizes the RNA primer at replication origins. Eukaryotic primase activity is delivered by a four protein complex known as the polymerase α complex. Two of these subunits are the catalytic and regulatory subunits of primase, and the other two are catalytic subunits of a DNA polymerase α. After the RNA primer has been synthesized, polymerase α synthesizes DNA for a short distance. It is soon replaced by the main DNA polymerase, polymerase δ or ε.

The archaeal equivalent, also called primase, consists of two protein subunits. These subunits are homologs of the eukaryotic primase subunits. There are no archaeal homologs of DNA polymerase α, which appearntly evolved in eukaryotes. Although the archaeal primase is distinct from bacterial DnaG it should be noted that

of replication. This complex contains at least one protein, and possibly as many as three proteins, that are homologous to the eukaryotic ORC1 and CDC6 proteins. These events initiate replication, although several of the details of the complete mechanism are not yet known (see Table 7.1).

In all organisms, the DNA polymerase enzymes that are responsible for synthesizing new DNA strands use the template strand to direct the addition of nucleotides to daughter strands in a complementary and antiparallel manner. These new nucleotides are added to the 3′ end of the growing daughter strand, and the overall direction of daughter strand elongation is 5′ to 3′. Curiously, however, DNA polymerases are unable to *initiate* DNA strand synthesis on their own. To perform its catalytic activity, a DNA polymerase requires the presence of a primer sequence, a short single-stranded segment that begins a daughter strand and provides a 3′-OH end to which a archaea possess homologs of DnaG. The archaeal DnaG homologs are, however, involved in RNA processing events rather than functioning in DNA replication.

During DNA replication, all DNA molecules undergo some level of superhelical twisting that imparts torsional twisting to the molecule beyond that of the spiraling double helix. Linear DNA found in eukaryotes manages this extra twisting relatively easily, since the ends of chromosomes are free to twist to uncoil. Circular chromosomes are a different matter. Since they are closed by covalent bonds (phosphodiester bonds), superhelical twisting that accompanies DNA replication creates torsional stress that would shear the molecule if it were left uncontrolled. As replication progresses, unwinding of the double helix causes superhelical twisting to accumulate, producing **supercoiled DNA** that resembles an over-twisted rubber band (**Figure 7.17a**). To avoid random breakage in the molecule that could lead to a breakdown of DNA replication, enzymes known as **topoisomerases,** also called DNA gyrases, catalyze a controlled cleavage and rejoining of DNA to allow over-wound DNA strands to unwind (**Figure 7.17b**). Relief of supercoiling is accomplished by cutting either one or both strands of DNA (various topoisomerases operate differently), allowing DNA to unwind and then resealing the strands.

Continuous and Discontinuous Strand Replication

Each strand of parental DNA acts as a template for the synthesis of a new daughter strand of DNA. In *E. coli,* daughter DNA strands are synthesized at the replication fork by the **DNA polymerase III (pol III) holoenzyme,** the principal DNA-synthesizing enzyme (see **Figure 7.14,** step 4). *Holoenzyme* is the general term used for multiprotein

complexes in which a core enzyme is associated with additional protein components that complete its structure and lead to its function. The pol III holoenzyme begins its work at the 3'-OH end of an RNA primer and rapidly synthesizes new DNA with a sequence complementary to the template-strand nucleotides. Pol III adds new nucleotides to a daughter strand as long as there are complementary nucleotides on the template strand to direct nucleotide addition to the daughter strand.

Experimental evidence indicates that most of the enzymes we are describing as participating in DNA replication are part of a single large protein complex at each replication fork called the **replisome.** There is one replisome at each replication fork, and each contains, among other components, two complete pol III holoenzymes. In each replisome, one pol III holoenzyme carries out the 5'-to-3' synthesis of one daughter strand *continuously,* in the *same* direction in which the replication fork progresses. The second pol III enzyme in a replisome carries out synthesis of the other daughter strand. The continuously elongated daughter strand is called the **leading strand** (**Figure 7.18**). Notice that Figure 7.18 divides the replication bubble into four quadrants. The upper right and lower left quadrants contain leading strands.

The daughter strands in the upper left and lower right quadrants shown in Figure 7.18 have a 5'-to-3' direction of elongation that runs *opposite* to the direction of movement of the replication fork. These daughter strands are elongated *discontinuously,* in short segments, each of which is initiated by an RNA primer. The discontinuously synthesized daughter strand is called the **lagging strand.** Thus in Figure 7.18, the lower right and upper left quadrants of the replication bubble contain lagging strands.

Reiji Okazaki detected the synthesis of short fragments of DNA in the replication of the lagging strand.

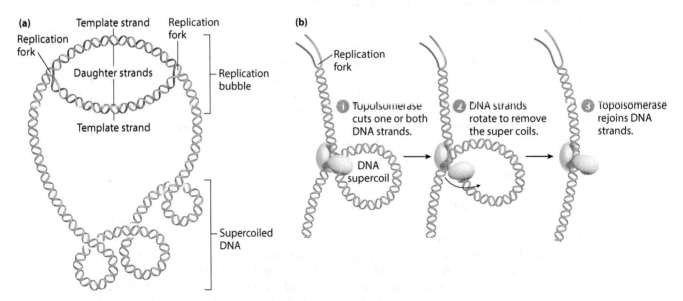

Figure 7.17 **DNA supercoiling in bacteria (a) and its cutting and release by topoisomerase (b).**

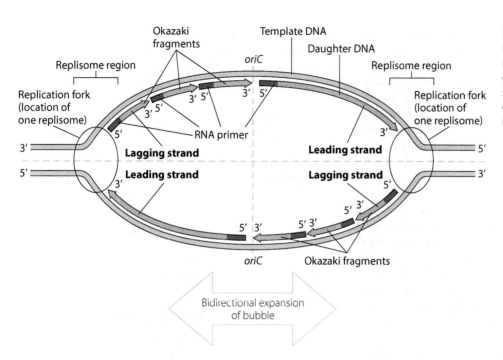

He observed that early in bacterial replication, newly synthesized DNA segments on one strand are 1000 to 2000 nucleotides long, while later in replication the newly synthesized segments are much longer. Okazaki's discovery suggested that short segments of DNA are synthesized and that these short segments are joined together as replication progresses. The short segments of newly replicated DNA are called **Okazaki fragments,** and they are the result of discontinuous synthesis of DNA on the lagging strand. Okazaki fragments in eukaryotes are much shorter than those in bacteria, 100 to 200 nucleotides in length. Similarly, archaeal Okazaki fragments are short.

In Figure 7.18, notice that each daughter strand contains a segment characterized as leading strand that adjoins a segment characterized as lagging strand. All daughter strands are composed of adjoining leading and lagging segments, and they will ultimately be structurally identical.

Overall, the pattern of DNA replication involving a leading strand and a lagging strand is similar in bacteria, eukaryotes, and archaea. Three DNA polymerases are recruited to eukaryotic origins of replication sites. All three are part of the large replisome complex that assembles at each replication fork to carry out leading and lagging strand synthesis. DNA polymerase ε is responsible for leading strand synthesis, while DNA polymerase δ is responsible for lagging strand synthesis. DNA polymerase α, which begins the DNA synthesis following RNA primer synthesis and extends a few nucleotides before being replaced by the main DNA replication enzyme, is more active on the lagging strand due to multiple priming events.

It is less clear how archaeal leading and lagging strand repliction is accomplished and regulated. Archaea generally possess at least one, and often multiple, homologs of eukaryotic replication polymerases. This has led to speculation that the polymerases in archaea function in about the same way as do those in eukaryotes. See Table 7.2 for a comparison of selected DNA polymerases in the three domains of life.

RNA Primer Removal and Okazaki Fragment Ligation

To complete DNA replication, RNA primers must be removed and replaced with DNA, and Okazaki fragments must be joined together to form complete DNA strands.

Table 7.2	Properties of Selected Bacterial, Eukaryotic, and Archaeal DNA Polymerases
Polymerase	**Functions**
Bacterial polymerases	
DnaG	RNA primer synthesis
I	RNA primer removal, proofreading, mutation repair
III	DNA replication, proofreading
Eukaryotic polymerases	
Primase/α	Primer synthesis and lagging strand synthesis
δ	Lagging strand synthesis, proofreading, DNA mutation repair
ε	Leading strand synthesis, proofreading, DNA mutation repair
Archaea polymerases	
Primase	Primer synthesis
PolB	DNA synthesis
PolD	DNA synthesis

In *E. coli* these tasks are accomplished by the enzymes *DNA polymerase I* and *DNA ligase* that are each part of the replisome complex at each replication fork.

When DNA pol III on the lagging strand reaches an RNA primer, thus running out of template, it leaves a single-stranded gap between the last DNA nucleotide of the newly synthesized daughter strand and the first nucleotide of the RNA primer (**Figure 7.19**). The pol III, having very low affinity for these DNA–RNA single-stranded gaps, is then replaced by **DNA polymerase I (pol I),** which has high affinity for such gaps (Figure 7.19, ①). The DNA pol I removes nucleotides of the RNA primer one by one and replaces them with DNA nucleotides, beginning with the 5′ nucleotide of the RNA primer and progressing in the 3′ direction until all the RNA nucleotides in the primer have been replaced by DNA nucleotides complementary to the template strand.

The pol I enzyme possesses two activities that accomplish the removal of RNA nucleotides and their replacement by DNA nucleotides. DNA pol I first uses its **5′-to-3′ exonuclease activity** to remove the 5′-most nucleotide from the RNA primer. This creates one open space opposite the template, which is then filled with the correct DNA nucleotide by the **5′-to-3′ polymerase activity** of DNA pol I. The pol I removes each RNA primer nucleotide and replaces each with a DNA nucleotide. In so doing, pol I continually pushes the single-stranded gap in the 3′ direction, eventually replacing all of the RNA primer nucleotides with DNA nucleotides.

Once the entire RNA primer is replaced, a remaining single-stranded gap sits between two DNA nucleotides. At this point, **DNA ligase,** having exclusive and very high affinity for DNA–DNA single-stranded gaps, is attracted to the gap and there performs its single task of forming a phosphodiester bond between the two DNA nucleotides that joins two Okazaki fragments. Both pol I and DNA ligase are active on leading *and* lagging strands. The level of activity is greater on lagging strands, however, where every 1000 to 2000 nucleotides, they are needed to join Okazaki fragments during replication of *E. coli* DNA.

In eukarya and archaea, RNA primers are removed and DNA segments are ligated together to finish replication. The principal enzymes that accomplish these tasks are very similar. Replication protein A (RPA) and two nuclease enzymes, Fen1 and Dna2, accomplish primer removal and replacement in eukaryotes and archaea. DNA ligase operates to seal single-stranded nicks to complete the assembly of new DNA strands.

Simultaneous Synthesis of Leading and Lagging Strands

As we have seen, the replisome components in *E. coli* include two DNA pol III holoenzymes, one of which synthesizes the leading strand and the other the lagging strand. As we describe momentarily, a similar organization exists during eukaryotic and archaeal DNA replication as well. Each

replisome complex carries out replication of the leading strand and the lagging strand simultaneously. The replisome also includes pol I and ligase, as well as numerous other components that collectively carry out DNA replication.

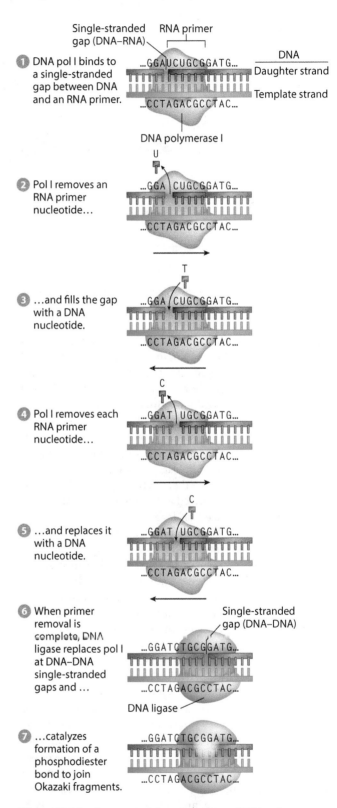

Figure 7.19   Removal and replacement of RNA primer nucleotides and ligation of Okazaki fragments in *E. coli*.

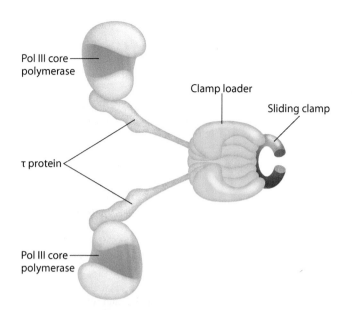

Pol III core polymerase

Clamp loader

Sliding clamp

τ protein

Pol III core polymerase

Figure 7.20 **DNA polymerase III holoenzyme.** The complex contains two DNA polymerase core enzymes attached to τ (tau) arms, and the clamp loader, shown holding a sliding clamp.

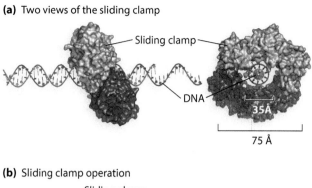

(a) Two views of the sliding clamp

Sliding clamp

DNA

35Å

75 Å

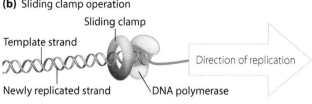

(b) Sliding clamp operation

Sliding clamp

Template strand

Direction of replication

Newly replicated strand

DNA polymerase

Figure 7.21 **The DNA sliding clamp.** **(a)** Two views of the sliding clamp, one showing the clamp and DNA polymerase on DNA in profile (left) and the other showing DNA through the "doughnut hole" of the sliding clamp (right). **(b)** The sliding clamp–DNA polymerase complex has high processivity during replication.

The "processivity" of DNA polymerases alone—that is, the ability of DNA polymerases to drive their own movement along template strands during replication—is comparatively low. This means that, by themselves, they are unable to provide the momentum required to both synthesize new DNA and progress along the template strand. To enhance the processivity of these polymerases, they associate with an auxiliary protein complex known as a **sliding clamp.**

The two *E. coli* DNA pol III holoenzymes each contains 11 protein subunits. The two pol III core polymerases are each tethered to a different copy of the τ (tau) protein (**Figure 7.20**). The τ proteins are joined to a five-protein complex known as the **clamp loader.** Two additional proteins form the sliding clamp, a protein structure that can close around double-stranded DNA during replication. The sliding clamp, with its diameter of approximately 50 Å, has a "doughnut hole" of about 35 Å that encircles the DNA (**Figure 7.21a**).

Each sliding clamp locks onto a DNA template strand and there affiliates with DNA pol III core enzyme, firmly anchoring the enzyme to the template to carry out the bulk of replication (**Figure 7.21b**). The clamp is the key to the enzyme's high level of activity. Pol III on DNA without a sliding clamp has very low processivity. When no more template is available, the DNA pol III is dropped by the sliding clamp and replaced by DNA pol I, which as we have seen removes RNA primers and replaces them with DNA.

Foundation Figure 7.22 presents a model of how the DNA pol III holoenzyme coordinates the simultaneous synthesis of leading and lagging strands at a replication fork. The outline of this model was proposed in the early 1960s by Arthur Kornberg to explain the experimental observation that a single large protein complex at each replication fork carries out replication of both strands of DNA. Known both as the Kornberg model and as the "trombone" model, it has been revised and updated in the decades since it was first proposed. The trombone model depicts the activity of the clamp loader in providing a mechanism for the continuous synthesis of leading strand regions and for the grasping, synthesis, and release of lagging strand regions by DNA pol III–sliding clamp complexes affiliated with each arm of the clamp loader. This model provides a mechanism by which a single replisome can advance with the replication fork and synthesize both daughter strands as it proceeds. In summary, replisomes contain multiple DNA polymerase enzymes and a large number of accessory proteins that operate in a rapid and highly coordinated manner to carry out DNA synthesis.

In archaea and eukaryotes, homologous proteins provide processivity to DNA polymerases. The **proliferating cell nuclear antigen (PCNA)** protein functions as the sliding clamp in archaeal and eukaryotic replication, encircling the DNA template strand. In these domains, the replication factor C (RFC) complex fills the role of the bacterial τ protein by connecting the DNA polymerases to the clamp loader and sliding clamp.

DNA Proofreading

Accurate replication of DNA is essential for the survival of organisms. The introduction of errors into a DNA sequence during replication could create potentially lethal mutations. While this occasionally happens, DNA replication is remarkably accurate and is not a major source of mutation, largely because DNA polymerases are generally able to undertake **DNA proofreading** to be sure

The Trombone Model of DNA Replication

Lagging strand

Okazaki fragment

Daughter duplex

RNA primer

5′
3′

Lagging strand DNA polymerase

3′ OH

Okazaki fragment

SSB bound to DNA

5′

5′

Parental duplex

DNA helicase

Sliding clamp

Clamp loader

τ proteins

Leading strand DNA polymerase

3′ OH

Leading strand

Daughter duplex

3′
5′

① DNA helicase denatures the parental duplex, and SSB coats leading strand and lagging strand templates. The leading strand DNA pol III–sliding clamp complex synthesizes the leading strand continuously. The lagging strand pol III–sliding clamp complex synthesizes an Okazaki fragment.

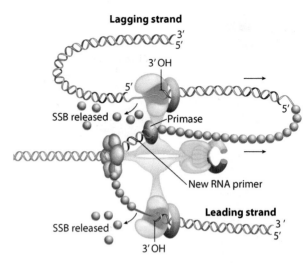

Lagging strand

3′
5′

3′ OH

SSB released

Primase

5′

5′

New RNA primer

SSB released

3′ OH

Leading strand

3′
5′

② Primase binds the lagging strand template and synthesizes a new RNA primer. SSB is released ahead of leading strand and lagging strand synthesis, and ahead of RNA primer synthesis.

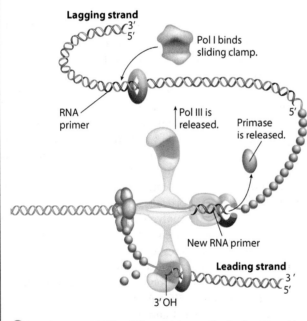

Lagging strand

3′
5′

Pol I binds sliding clamp.

RNA primer

Pol III is released.

Primase is released.

5′

New RNA primer

3′ OH

Leading strand

3′
5′

③ Lagging strand DNA pol III completes synthesis of an Okazaki fragment and is released by the sliding clamp. A DNA pol I replaces pol III to begin removal of the RNA primer and replacement of RNA nucleotides by DNA nucleotides.

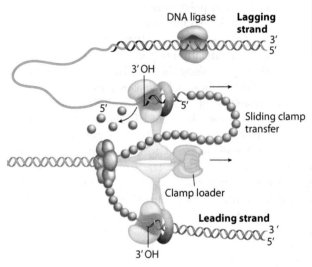

DNA ligase

Lagging strand

3′
5′

3′ OH

5′

5′

Sliding clamp transfer

Clamp loader

3′ OH

Leading strand

3′
5′

④ DNA ligase joins Okazaki fragments. The clamp loader places a new sliding clamp near the 3′ end of the RNA primer on the newly primed lagging strand. Lagging strand DNA pol III binds the sliding clamp and initiates synthesis of a new Okazaki fragment.

replication is accurate. As a result of DNA proofreading, mutations due to DNA replication errors occur about once every billion (10^9) nucleotides in wild-type *E. coli*. To put this number into perspective, consider this textbook as an analogy. It contains about 800 pages, each holding about 5000 "bits" of information (letters, punctuation marks, spaces, etc.) for a total of 4×10^6 bits per book. It would take 250 books, each the size of this one, to equal 10^9 bits of information. If each bit were equal to a DNA nucleotide, the error rate for DNA replication would be like having *one* typographical error in all 250 books!

This extraordinary accuracy is the work of the multifunctional DNA polymerases that have the ability not only to synthesize DNA (5′-to-3′ polymerase activity) but also to "proofread" newly synthesized DNA for accuracy and remove erroneous nucleotides (see Table 7.2). This proofreading ability resides in the **3′-to-5′ exonuclease activity** of DNA polymerases capable of removing some of the newly laid daughter strand sequence.

Polymerases like pol III and pol I have a structure somewhat like an open hand: A "thumb" and "fingers" hold the template and daughter strands in the "palm," where 5′-to-3′ polymerase activity is centered (**Figure 7.23**). When a replication error occurs, the mismatched DNA bases of the template and daughter strands are unable to hydrogen bond properly. As a result, the 3′-OH end of the daughter strand becomes displaced, blocking the further addition of nucleotides and inducing rotation of the daughter strand into the 3′-to-5′ exonuclease site at the "heel" of the hand. Several nucleotides, including the mismatched one, are then removed from the 3′ end of the daughter strand, after which the daughter strand rotates back to the polymerase site in the palm and replication resumes. Like their counterparts in bacteria, the principal DNA replication polymerases in eukaryotes and archaea also have proofreading ability to help ensure the accuracy of DNA replication.

Genetic Analysis 7.2 checks your understanding and analysis of molecular events at the replication fork.

Finishing Replication

Once bacterial DNA replication has completed the synthesis of new DNA and the replacement of RNA primer nucleotides with DNA nucleotides, separation of the daughter chromosomes must occur. This is accomplished by topoisomerase enzymes that break one of the double-stranded chromosomes, pass the other chromosome through the gap, and then reseal the double-stranded break. A similar event may occur at the end of archaeal replication to separate the daughter chromosomes. Linear chromosomes, such as those in the nuclei of your cells, present a unique and different problem with regard to DNA replication—they cannot be replicated all the way to their ends! Instead, eukaryotic chromosomes get progressively shorter with each replication cycle.

(a) DNA polymerase error

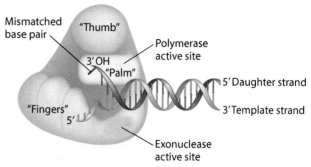

(b) Exonuclease removal of mismatched base pair

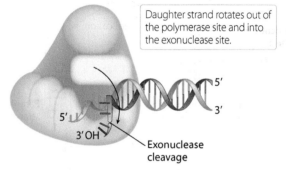

Daughter strand rotates out of the polymerase site and into the exonuclease site.

(c) Daughter strand resumes DNA synthesis

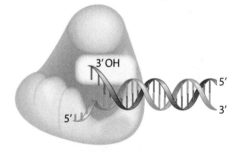

Figure 7.23   DNA polymerase proofreading activity.
(a) A replication error by polymerase. **(b)** Polymerase shifts on newly synthesized DNA to utilize its 3′-to-5′ exonuclease activity. **(c)** The polymerase resumes 5′-to-3′ synthesis.

This apparent deficiency in the replication process is a consequence of an RNA primer being located at one end of the lagging strand and thus not able to be replaced by DNA. In consequence, the resulting lagging strand is shorter than its template strand, causing the chromosome to become shorter with each replication cycle (**Figure 7.24**).

The loss of DNA with each replication cycle sounds ominous, but the problem is solved by the presence at chromosome ends of repetitive DNA sequences called **telomeres.** Telomeres do not contain protein-coding genes, but instead are made up of repeats that are most often 6-bp sequences repeated hundreds or thousands of times to give the telomere a length of 2 to 20 kb, depending on the species. Since its sequences are repetitive and contain no genetic information, portions of the telomere can

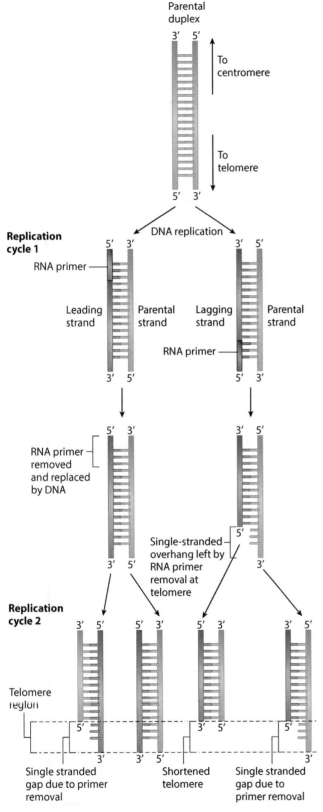

Figure 7.24 Loss of DNA at telomeres. Leading strands are synthesized to the ends of linear chromosomes, but lagging strands are shortened each replication cycle, when RNA primer sequence at the telomere end of the template strand is removed but not replaced with DNA nucleotides.

safely be lost in each replication cycle, without consequence to the organism. Gel electrophoresis of telomeric DNA has documented the progressive shortening of telomere length during cell culture.

Telomeres are synthesized by the ribonucleoprotein **telomerase,** consisting of several proteins and a molecule of RNA. The telomerase RNA molecule is encoded by a distinct gene and acts as the template for the telomeric DNA repeat sequence. Elizabeth Blackburn and Carol Greider discovered both telomeres and telomerase in 1987 and along with Jack Szostak were awarded the 2009 Nobel Prize in Physiology or Medicine for their work.

Figure 7.25 depicts the mechanism of telomerase action deduced from the study of the ciliated protozoan *Tetrahymena*. The repetitive sequence 5'-TTGGGG-3' is the characteristic telomeric repeat sequence of *Tetrahymena*. The template RNA in the *Tetrahymena* telomerase contains the repeat AACCCC that is used to

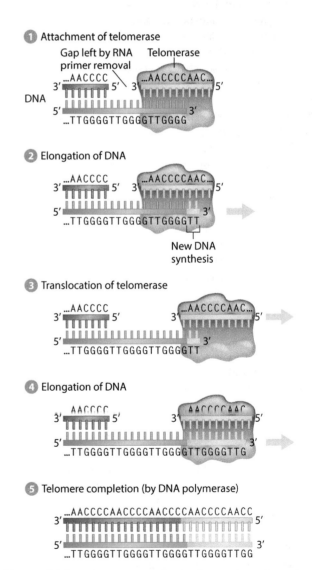

Figure 7.25 Telomerase synthesis of repeating telomeric sequence.

PROBLEM Two strains of *E. coli* have temperature-sensitive mutations that hamper their ability to complete DNA replication. At 25°C, both strains are able to complete replication, but neither is able to complete replication at 40°C. At 40°C, temperature-sensitive mutant 1 is able to synthesize DNA by DNA polymerase III activity, and it is able to remove RNA primers and replace them with DNA, but it accumulates many short segments of DNA (Okazaki fragments) that are not joined together. At 40°C, temperature-sensitive mutant 2 also synthesizes DNA by polymerase III activity, but it is unable to remove RNA primers and replace them with DNA. For each of these mutants, use the information provided here to identify the molecule that is most likely carrying the temperature-sensitive mutation. Identify which normal major events of DNA replication each mutant can complete at 40°C and which normal events are altered in each mutant.

> **BREAK IT DOWN:** Temperature-sensitive mutations are the result of proteins that have full function at a lower temperature but denature and lose function at higher temperatures (see Section 4.1)

Solution Strategies	Solution Steps
Evaluate	
1. Identify the topic area addressed by this problem.	1. This problem addresses DNA replication and asks you to identify the function of particular proteins and enzymes that are active at different stages of replication.
2. Identify the critical information given in the problem and the nature of the required answer.	2. Two *E. coli* strains with different temperature-sensitive mutations of DNA replication are described. Mutant strain 1 accumulates Okazaki fragments that cannot be joined together, and mutant strain 2 is unable to remove RNA primers.
Deduce	
3. Review the molecular events and principal molecules that are involved in RNA primer removal and RNA primer replacement. TIP: The function of principal proteins and enzymes in *E. coli* DNA replication is discussed in Section 7.4	3. A review of Foundation Figure 7.14 (p. 243) and of Section 7.4 shows that in *E. coli*, DNA polymerase I is responsible for the removal of RNA primer nucleotides and their replacement with DNA nucleotides, and that DNA ligase joins Okazaki fragments together.
Solve	
4. Identify the molecule affected by mutation in mutant 1.	4. Mutant 1 is most likely to have a defect in DNA ligase.
5. Identify the molecule affected by mutation in mutant 2.	5. Mutant 2 is most likely to have a defect in DNA polymerase I.
6. Identify which parts of DNA replication are completed at 40°C and which are affected by each mutation.	6. Mutant 1 is able to synthesize RNA primers by DnaG activity and is able to synthesize DNA with polymerase III activity. It is also able to remove RNA primers and replace the RNA nucleotides with DNA through polymerase I activity. However, mutant 1 is defective in its ability to ligate Okazaki fragments together by DNA ligase activity, and these fragments remain unconnected. Mutant 2 has fully functional DnaG and polymerase III to synthesize RNA primers and most DNA. It lacks active DNA pol I, however, and is therefore unable to remove RNA primers and replace them with DNA.

For more practice, see Problems 14, 15, and 18.   Visit the Study Area to access study tools.   **Mastering**Genetics™

---

elongate the telomere of one strand enough to allow new DNA replication to fill out the chromosome ends.

In the decades since Blackburn and Greider identified telomere structure and this mechanism for their maintenance, similar repeating telomeric sequences have been detected in all eukaryotes. For example, the human telomeric repeat sequence is 5′-TTAGGG-3′, and it is encoded by a telomeric RNA molecule with the complementary repetitive sequence 3′-AAUCCC-5′. In humans, telomeric sequence is repeated 250 to 1500 times at chromosome ends. The same telomeric sequence and template DNA sequence are found in vertebrates, protozoans (*Trypanosoma*),

yeast (*Saccharomyces*), fungus (*Neurospora*), and plants (*Arabidopsis*). This represents an example of convergent evolution of DNA sequences. Convergent evolution is a mechanism producing similar traits or, in this case, DNA sequences among distantly related organisms due to allow similar adaptation or natural selection pressure.

The importance of telomerase activity in germ-line cells has been demonstrated in experimental mouse lines that are mutated to be homozygous for loss-of-function mutations of the *TERT* (*telomerase reverse transcriptase*) gene, the gene that encodes telomerase. These homozygous mutant mice are relatively normal when interbred for up to three generations, but severe developmental and fertility defects are detected in the fourth and fifth inbred generations. *TERT* loss-of-function homozygosity is lethal by the seventh generation, meaning that no inbred *TERT*-deficient mice can be maintained by inbreeding for more than six generations.

The molecular explanation for the delayed phenotypic effect of *TERT* inactivation is that each successive generation of inbreeding in the homozygous mutant line leads to the loss of telomeric DNA. It is now evident that genetic mechanisms monitor telomere length, and that telomere length is a kind of chronometer that keeps track of the age of a cell. Once the shortening reaches a critical point, the cell is directed into the apoptotic pathway, the mechanism of programmed cell death that removes old or damaged cells from an organism. This phenomenon is thought to be the explanation for a long-standing observation in cell biology that most normal cells survive in culture for between about 30 to 50 cell divisions before entering a crisis phase, where their division first slows and then stops altogether, and the cells die.

Telomeres, Aging, and Cancer

Considering the importance of telomere length to chromosome stability, cell longevity, and reproductive success, it may surprise you to learn that telomerase activity is limited to only a few kinds of cells in eukaryotes. Telomerase is active in germ-line cells, where it functions to ensure that gametes pass on full-length chromosomes. Telo merase activity is also detected in some stem cells, thus enabling the cells that differentiate from those stem cells to have full-length chromosomes. In contrast, telomerase activity is virtually nonexistent in differentiated somatic cells, the kinds of cells that have finite life spans and make up nearly all the cells of most body organs and tissues. In somatic cells, genes responsible for producing telomerase are turned off, and almost no telomerase activity is detectable. This accounts for the finite life span of somatic cells in cell culture first observed in 1965 by Leonard Hayflick, who found that the number of cell divisions of cultured cells is dependent on the source of the cells. This limitation on the growth of most cells in culture is known as the Hayflick limit.

The connection between telomerase inactivity and normal aging of cells prompted geneticists to look at human premature aging conditions for evidence of mutations affecting telomere formation or telomerase activity. In the rare human condition dyskeratosis congenita (OMIM 305000), patients have abnormalities of skin and nails, occasional loss of vision and hearing, and abnormalities of blood cell production that are a frequent cause of death. The *DKC1* gene responsible for dyskeratosis congenita affects the activity of genes responsible for normal telomerase function. Defective telomerase activity and shortened telomeres are thought to be at the root of dyskeratosis congenita.

In contrast to the importance of telomerase activity for maintaining normal telomere length as chromosomes are passed through the germ line, what is the consequence of abnormal *reactivation* of telomerase activity in somatic cells? Such an event can lead aging cells to continue to proliferate, allowing them to escape programmed cell death by apoptosis. This is exactly what seems to happen in many kinds of cancer, where mutations reactivate the expression of *TERT* and reintroduce telomerase activity into cells where *TERT* is normally silent.

Recent studies of gene expression in human cancer cells find that mutations reactivating *TERT* are among the most frequent mutations in cancers of all types. In cancers of the internal organs, including lung, breast, stomach, ovary, kidney, bladder, uterus, testis, and prostate, 78% to 100% of advanced-cancer cells show evidence of reactivation of telomerase activity. This is a highly significant increase over the 0% to 3% rate of telomerase reactivation in normal somatic cells. In the cancer cells, the reactivation of telomerase activity appears to stabilize telomere length, disrupting the normal program of progressive telomere shortening that would lead to apoptosis. This extended life span may allow affected cells to acquire additional mutations associated with cancer development and cancer advancement.

7.5 Molecular Genetic Analytical Methods Make Use of DNA Replication Processes

Molecular biologists have used their understanding of the enzymes and processes of DNA replication to develop new laboratory methods of molecular genetic analysis. Two widely used methods that developed directly from this knowledge are the *polymerase chain reaction* (*PCR*) and *dideoxyribonucleotide DNA sequencing*. In this section, we look at both of these methods and at their use in deciphering DNA variation.

The Polymerase Chain Reaction

The **polymerase chain reaction (PCR)** is an automated version of DNA replication that takes place in a test tube containing a total reaction volume of 20 to 50 microliters. (One microliter is one-millionth of a liter.) Despite its very small total reaction volume, a typical PCR reaction produces millions of copies of a short, targeted segment of DNA from the original DNA molecule. The almost limitless uses of PCR in modern biological research include the collection of DNA from extinct species for evolutionary study; comparison of DNA among living species; forensic genetic applications such as paternity testing, crime scene analysis, and individual identification; and production of DNA segments for genome sequencing projects.

Polymerase chain reactions are in vitro DNA-replication reactions performed using double-stranded DNA containing the target sequence that is to be copied, a supply of the four DNA nucleotides, a heat-stable DNA polymerase, and two different single-stranded DNA primers (described below). These PCR components are mixed with a buffer solution at the beginning of the reaction, and the reaction is repeated through a series of 30 to 35 "cycles." During each cycle, the number of copies of the target DNA sequence region doubles. This doubling process is known as "amplification," and it is common to speak of "PCR amplification" in reference to the process and of "amplified DNA" as the product of the reaction.

The DNA polymerase most often used in PCR is called *Taq* polymerase, named after the thermophilic bacterial species *Thermus aquaticus* that was first collected in Yellowstone National Park. This bacterium lives in hot springs at near-boiling conditions, having evolved heat-stable proteins that remain active at these temperatures. The heat stability of *Taq* DNA polymerase is important to the efficiency of PCR. The first sample of *Thermus aquiticus* was collected from hot springs in Yellowstone national Park by Thomas Brock and Louise Brock in 1965. Brock was a microbiologist and his attention was drawn to some brown scum in the hot spring that looked something like the inset image in the opener photo for this chapter. Brock thought the scum looked like bacteria that live in other bodies of water, so he transported a sample back to his laboratory and managed to grow it. What he discovered was a new bacterial species and in the process he opened new avenues of research on "extremophiles"—organisms that live in extreme environments—and he helped pave the way for the use of *Taq* polymerase in PCR.

As useful as Taq polymerase has been, there are now even more efficient polymerases for PCR derived from thermophilic (heat-loving) archaeal species. DNA polymerases from *Pyrococcus furiosus* and *Thermococcus kodakaraensis* are more efficient than Tao polymerase, having about 20-fold lower error rates due to their superior proofreading capabilities.

The PCR reaction itself closely resembles DNA replication as we describe it in this chapter. It does, however, differ somewhat from cellular DNA replication by using two different, short, single-stranded DNA sequences called PCR primers to provide start points for *Taq* polymerase synthesis. PCR primers, like RNA primers in cellular replication, are generally 12 to 24 nucleotides in length. One single-stranded primer binds to each of the DNA strands that serve as templates in PCR amplification. Importantly, the primers also bind on *opposite sides* of the region of DNA to be copied in PCR. The primer binding sites are at the 5′ and 3′ boundaries of most of the replication products that will eventually be produced in the PCR reaction.

Each polymerase chain reaction cycle is a three-step DNA replication reaction (**Figure 7.26**). Each step of a PCR cycle lasts from 30 seconds to several minutes, and 30 to 36 is a typical number of cycles. Each complete PCR cycle doubles the number of copies of the target DNA sequence, so beginning with a single copy of double-stranded target sequence, completing the first PCR cycle produces 2 copies of the target sequence, two cycles produces 4 copies, three

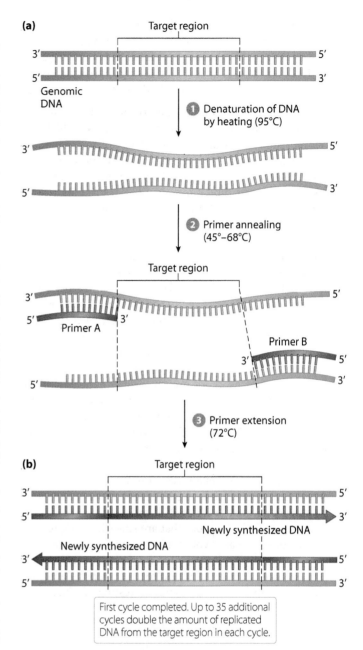

Figure 7.26   Polymerase chain reaction (PCR). (a) The three-step cycle of PCR. **(b)** Amplification doubles the number of copies of the targeted DNA sequence each cycle.

cycles 8 copies, and so on. After completing 30 PCR cycles the yield is 2^{30}, or more than 1 billion copies of the target sequence, and completion of 36 cycles can yield more than 68 billion copies of the target sequence. The steps of each PCR cycle are as follows:

1 *Denaturation.* The reaction mixture is heated to approximately 95°C, causing double-stranded DNA to *denature* into single strands as the hydrogen bonds between complementary strands break down.

2 *Primer annealing.* The reaction temperature is reduced to between about 45°C and 68°C to allow *primer annealing*, the hybridization of the two primers to complementary sequences that bracket the target sequence.

③ *Primer extension.* Raising the temperature of the reaction to 72°C allows *primer extension*, during which *Taq* DNA polymerase synthesizes DNA, beginning at the 3' end of each primer and taking approximately 1 minute for every 1000 bp synthesized.

PCR has an enormous variety of applications, but it also has limitations, the most important of which are (1) the requirement of some knowledge of the sequences needed for primers and (2) that amplification products longer than 10 to 15 kb are difficult to produce. In most cases, the length limitations on PCR restrict its use to the study of selected DNA segments or individual genes. The requirement for primer sequence information can be satisfied by informed guesses about the sequences likely to occur at primer binding sites or by using primers from one species to amplify similar sequences in another species. For example, a biologist wanting to study DNA-sequence similarity between species could use a pair of primers that amplify a *Drosophila* gene to examine the human genome for a related gene. There may be one or more base-pair mismatches between the *Drosophila* primers and the human DNA sequences they bind to, but the mismatches need not prevent primer annealing if the temperature of the PCR reaction is lowered during step 2 of the reaction. The lower temperature can increase the stability of hybridization of the primers and their target sequences enough to allow the former to prime the PCR amplification.

The polymerase chain reaction makes it practical to obtain large quantities of DNA from a particular gene for molecular analysis. The PCR procedure usually takes place in small plastic tubes that are specially designed for this purpose. It has revolutionized many aspects of biology, such as molecular genetics, recombinant DNA analysis, evolutionary genetics, and forensic genetic analysis, including crime scene and paternity testing of DNA.

Separation of PCR Products

The PCR process selectively amplifies only the fragment of DNA bounded by the two primers, and the fragment or fragments of DNA produced by amplification are highly concentrated. Gel electrophoresis is then used to separate those amplified fragments from the rest of the reaction mixture (see Chapter 10), after which they are easily visualized by staining with EtBr (ethidium bromide) due to their high concentration in the gel. The size of PCR products is measured in base pairs, and any variability in their length results from differences in the number of nucleotides between the two primer binding sites. These differences can be exploited in genetic analysis to identify alleles of amplified genes, particularly if alleles differ from one another by containing different numbers of base pairs. As an example, let's look at an analysis of short repeating sequences of DNA that are frequently used as one kind of genetic marker. Known as a variable

number tandem repeat (VNTR) and also known as short tandem repeats (STRs), this type of marker contains end-to-end repeating DNA sequences that are each up to 20 bp in length. These types of genetic markers are the kind used in forensic genetic analysis where the goal is to match a crime scene DNA sample with that of a suspect or to identify paternity.

Figure 7.27a shows four hypothetical VNTR alleles of a gene (V_1 to V_4) that might be found in a population. The alleles differ in the number of repeats of the DNA sequence they carry. The repeats are consecutively numbered in the figure. The PCR primers bind to the same sequences for each allele. The primers bind outside the repeat region, so amplification of each allele produces a DNA fragment of a characteristic length that is determined by the number of DNA repeats the allele contains.

Because here are four alleles for this VNTR gene, there are 10 possible genotypes. In Figure 7.27b, gel electrophoresis of PCR-amplified DNA fragment bands shows that each genotype has a distinctive band number and composition. Each homozygous genotype has a single band and each heterozygous genotype has two bands. The bands are identified by their repeat number.

The inheritance of the VNTR alleles follows a codominant pattern in which both alleles are detected in heterozygous genotypes. In the family represented in Figure 7.27c, each parent transmits one allele to each child and as a consequence of the different heterozygous genotypes of the parents, each allele in a child can be traced to one of the parents. Notice that there are two DNA bands for each each homozygous person and two bands for each heterozygous person. VNTRs and other similar DNA genetic markers display codominant inheritance (see Section 4.1).

Dideoxynucleotide DNA Sequencing

The ultimate description of any DNA molecule is its sequence of bases. Applied at the genome level, DNA sequence information can include the whole genome—that is, all coding and regulatory sequences of genes, as well as all the other DNA sequence, including repetitive sequences, that make up the genome. Genomic sequence information can also be more limited, most commonly including only those portions of the genome that are transcribed into RNA. We discuss approaches to creating and analyzing genomic sequence data in Chapters 17 and 18.

DNA sequencing technology has also found broad application in agriculture, medicine, and evolutionary biology. DNA sequencing technologies have changed rapidly as laboratory and computer technology have combined to make sequencing faster and cheaper by orders of magnitude.

The first DNA-sequencing protocols were developed in 1977, one by Allan Maxam and Walter Gilbert and another by Fred Sanger. Of the two methods, Sanger's was more amenable to automation, and it is the basis for the high-throughput approach to genome sequencing that is the

(a) Each allele produces a PCR fragment of a different length.

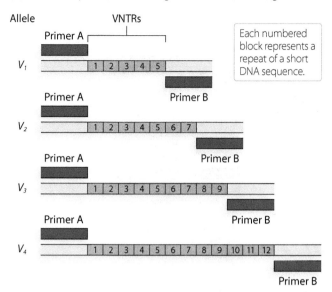

(b) VNTR band patterns

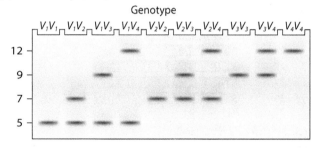

(c) Inheritance of VNTR variation

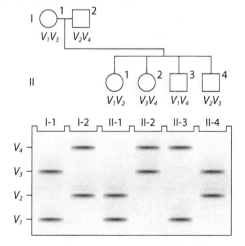

Figure 7.27 PCR amplification of variable number tandem repeat (VNTR) alleles. **(a)** Four VNTR alleles (V_1 to V_4) are characterized by different numbers of identical DNA repeat sequences. **(b)** Ten genotypes are possible for the VNTR gene, each having a unique pattern of PCR-fragment sizes. One band is seen for each homozygous genotype and two bands for each heterozygous genotype. **(c)** Hereditary transmission of VNTR alleles follows a codominant pattern.

method of choice today. Here we first describe Sanger's dideoxynucleotide DNA sequencing method, and then we describe the newest generation of automated DNA sequencing, commonly identified as next-generation DNA sequencing.

Dideoxynucleotide DNA sequencing—also called **dideoxy DNA sequencing,** or Sanger sequencing—is Sanger's DNA sequencing method. Based on cellular DNA replication reactions, dideoxy sequencing uses DNA polymerase to replicate new DNA from a single-stranded template (the strand to be sequenced) beginning at a primer sequence attached to the template strand. In dideoxy sequencing reactions, the four standard deoxynucleotide (dNTP) components of DNA, in large amounts, are mixed with smaller amounts of a **dideoxynucleotide triphosphate (ddNTP).**

Dideoxynucleotides differ from deoxynucleotides in lacking two oxygen atoms (*dideoxy* means "two deoxygenated sites") rather than the usual one deoxygenated site. Whereas dNTPs are deoxygenated at the 2′ carbon and have a hydroxyl group (OH) at the 3′ carbon, ddNTPs have hydrogen (H) atoms rather than hydroxyl groups at the 2′ *and* 3′ carbons (**Figure 7.28a**). The absence of a hydroxyl group at the 3′ carbon in ddNTP prevents the ddNTP from forming a phosphodiester bond to elongate a DNA strand. Incorporation of a ddNTP by DNA polymerase into a growing strand is a chain-terminating event that blocks further strand elongation (**Figure 7.28b**). Dideoxy sequencing therefore produces a large number of partial replication products, each terminated by incorporation of a ddNTP at a different site in the sequence.

In preparation for dideoxy sequencing, many copies of the DNA fragment to be sequenced are obtained in single-stranded form, usually by denaturing double-stranded DNA. Samples of the fragment are then placed in four parallel replication reactions. Each reaction mixture contains the DNA strand to be sequenced, a single-stranded DNA primer, DNA polymerase, large amounts of each of the four standard nucleotides (dATP, dGTP, dCTP, and dTTP), and a small amount of *one* dideoxynucleotide, either that of adenine (ddATP), thymine (ddTTP), cytosine (ddCTP), or guanine (ddGTP).

The four parallel DNA-sequencing reactions shown in **Figure 7.29** are used to sequence the DNA fragment shown at the top of the figure. As each reaction begins, a single-stranded 18-mer primer binds to template DNA. Using the five nucleotides available in each reaction, DNA polymerase replicates the DNA fragment by adding nucleotides beginning at the 3′-OH end of the primer. The primers used in dideoxy sequencing are labeled with either radioactive phosphorus (^{32}P) or with a fluorescent label on their 5′ ends to facilitate detection of the DNA fragments produced in the sequencing reaction. In Figure 7.29a, showing the ddCTP-containing reaction, DNA synthesis from a template strand progresses until it reaches the first guanine on the template strand. At this point, the reaction can incorporate one of two different kinds of cytosine. If the normal dCTP is incorporated, as it is in most cases due to its high

(a)

Chemical structure

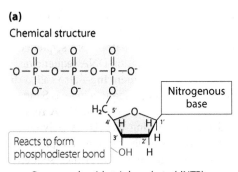

Deoxynucleotide triphosphate (dNTP)

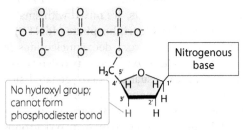

Dideoxynucleotide triphosphate (ddNTP)

(b)

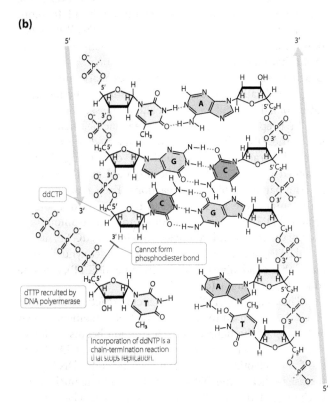

Figure 7.28 Nucleotides used in DNA sequencing reactions. (a) Dideoxynucleotides (ddNTPs) are deoxygenated at both the 2′ and 3′ carbons and cannot be used to elongate DNA. **(b)** The incorporation of a dideoxynucleotide of cytosine (ddCTP) terminates the replication reaction.

concentration, the replication reaction will proceed. If, on the other hand, the reaction incorporates ddCTP, which will happen in fewer cases due to its lower concentration, the replication reaction terminates. Each time the template strand nucleotide is a guanine, a few replicating fragments

(a) ddCTP reaction ("C" lane)

Incorporation of dCTP allows the chain to continue growing, but incorporation of ddCTP terminates chain elongation.

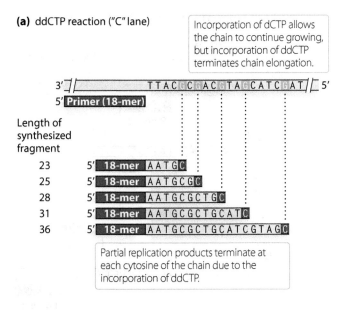

Partial replication products terminate at each cytosine of the chain due to the incorporation of ddCTP.

(b) ddGTP reaction ("G" lane)

Length of synthesized fragment	Partial replication products
22	5′ 18-mer A A T G
24	5′ 18-mer A A T G C G
27	5′ 18-mer A A T G C G C T G
32	5′ 18-mer A A T G C G C T G C A T C G
35	5′ 18-mer A A T G C G C T G C A T C G T A G

(c) ddTTP reaction ("T" lane)

Length of synthesized fragment	Partial replication products
21	5′ 18-mer A A T
26	5′ 18-mer A A T G C G C T
30	5′ 18-mer A A T G C G C T G C A T
33	5′ 18-mer A A T G C G C T G C A T C G T
38	5′ 18-mer A A T G C G C T G C A T C G T A G C T

(d) ddATP reaction ("A" lane)

Length of synthesized fragment	Partial replication products
19	5′ 18-mer A
20	5′ 18-mer A A
29	5′ 18-mer A A T G C G C T G C A
34	5′ 18-mer A A T G C G C T G C A T C G T A
38	5′ 18-mer A A T G C G C T G C A T C G T A G C T A

Figure 7.29 DNA sequencing reactions. (a) A target region of DNA is located by binding a single-stranded primer of 18 nucleotides (an "18-mer") that carries a 5′ label. Replication products terminated by ddCTP each have a different length. **(b)** Replication products terminated by ddGTP. **(c)** Termination products generated by ddTTP. **(d)** Termination products generated by ddATP.

incorporate ddCTP and terminate the reaction. Most reactions incorporate dCTP and continue replication. Some of these longer fragments will incorporate ddCTP at the next opportunity and stop replicating, while most others incorporate dCTP and continue replication. Replication proceeds this way, halting in a few fragments each time a G appears on the template strand and a C is incorporated into the newly synthesized fragment. The result from this reaction is a series of partially replicated fragments whose replication is halted at each site of C incorporation.

The three other reaction mixtures, containing ddGTP, ddTTP, and ddATP, likewise produce a series of partial replication products that all end with their particular ddNTP (Figure 7.29b–d). Upon the completion of the four parallel sequencing reactions, partial replication DNA products will occur for every nucleotide in the template.

After the replication reactions are complete, the contents of each reaction are loaded into separate lanes of a DNA electrophoresis gel. Following completion of gel electrophoresis, the DNA sequence can be determined by examining the different-sized replication products spread across the four gel lanes. The bands shown in Figure 7.30a are visible in an autoradiograph because the primers that begin each fragment are end-labeled with ^{32}P. The shortest fragment seen is in the A lane at the bottom, indicating that the first ddNTP nucleotide added to the 3′ end of the primer was ddATP. The second-shortest fragment is also in the A lane, indicating that chains to which ddATP was added in the second position terminated elongation there. The

third-shortest fragment in the gel is in the T lane, and the fourth-shortest in this example is in the G lane. So far, the sequence of nucleotides in the synthesized DNA is AATG.

By continuation of this analytical process, the DNA sequence of the synthesized strand is "read" from the gel in the 5′-to-3′ direction (the direction in which a replicating strand elongates), as demonstrated in Figure 7.30a. The "inferred strand" is the template strand, which is complementary and antiparallel to the sequenced strand. Figure 7.30b shows an autoradiograph of a dideoxysequencing gel and shows a portion of the sequence read near the middle of the gel at the left.

Manual dideoxy sequencing, as described above, is a labor-intensive process that today has been largely supplanted by high-throughput, automated DNA sequencing and powerful computational software and hardware that can run 24 hours a day, 365 days a year, and assemble genomic sequence at the rate of 10,000 to 20,000 bp per hour! Genetic Analysis 7.3 tests your skills at interpreting dideoxy sequencing results.

New DNA-Sequencing Technologies: Next Generation and Third Generation

New generations of DNA-sequencing technologies are continuing to be developed. So-called **next-generation sequencing** technology ascertains the sequence of a single strand of DNA by synthesizing a complementary strand and detecting which nucleotide is added at each step.

To begin the procedure, the sample to be sequenced is broken into double-stranded fragments, and then the fragments are denatured and their individual single strands of DNA are captured and immobilized on beads. The beads, each bearing a single DNA strand, are placed in wells of an electrophoretic gel, where single-stranded DNA linkers are added and bind to one end of the DNA fragments. Next, PCR primers complementary to the linkers are added to serve as the starting points of PCR amplification.

PCR amplification is accomplished by sequentially flooding the wells with solutions containing the four nucleotides A, T, C, and G. The nucleotides are tagged with a molecule that emits light at a specific wavelength, furnishing a means of indicating that the nucleotide has been added to a new strand in the PCR reaction. A photo receptor detects the light and sends a signal through computer software to generate a profile of the order in which nucleotides are incorporated during synthesis (Figure 7.31). In this manner,

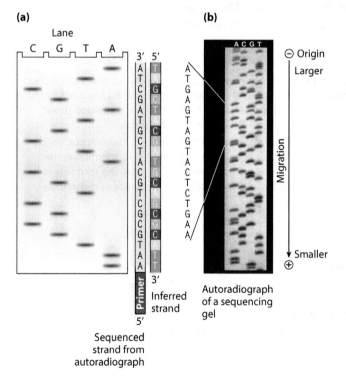

Figure 7.30   Interpretation of a DNA sequencing gel.
(**a**) Replication of each fragment terminates with the addition of a ddNTP. Nucleotides of the newly synthesized "sequenced strand" are read off the autoradiograph, and the 5′-to-3′ polarity of the strand corresponds to the smaller-to-larger fragment-length direction. The "inferred strand" is the template strand, and it is complementary and antiparallel to the "sequenced strand." (**b**) A photograph of a dideoxy sequencing gel.

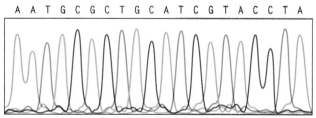

Figure 7.31   Next-generation sequencing output. Labels on nucleotides incorporated into newly synthesized DNA are excited and their emissions captured in next-generation sequencing.

PROBLEM From the dideoxy DNA sequencing gel shown below, deduce the sequence and strand polarities of the DNA duplex fragment.

> **BREAK IT DOWN:** Chain termination, caused by the incorporation of a dideoxynucleotide, produces the partially replicated DNA fragments detected in a DNA sequencing gel (p. 259).

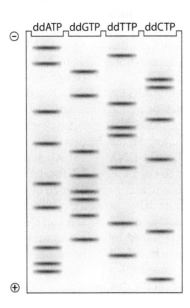

Solution Strategies	Solution Steps

Evaluate

1. Identify the topic this problem addresses and the nature of the required answer.

2. Identify the critical information given in the problem.

1. This question concerns dideoxynucleotide DNA sequencing. The answer requires interpretation of a DNA sequencing gel to determine the double-stranded sequence of a fragment of DNA, including strand polarities.

2. A dideoxynucleotide DNA sequencing gel is shown.

Deduce

3. Review the essential steps of dideoxy-nucleotide DNA sequencing.

4. Examine the gel and identify the "beginning" of DNA synthesis.

> **TIP:** DNA fragments toward the bottom of the gel (nearer the positive pole) are shorter than fragments higher up in the gel. The sequence of the synthesized strand shown in the gel is 5′ at the bottom and 3′ at the top.

3. DNA polymerase incorporates nucleotides in four parallel reactions. Each reaction mixture includes the four normal DNA nucleotides (dNTPs) and one labeled dideoxynucleotide (ddNTP). Incorporation of a dNTP allows continued strand synthesis, but incorporation of a ddNTP terminates synthesis.

4. The 3′ end of the primer is used to initiate DNA synthesis. The first nucleotide incorporated during synthesis is cytosine, as determined by identifying the location of the smallest synthesized fragment: the "C" lane. The second and third nucleotides are both adenine. The first three nucleotides are therefore 5′-CAA-3′.

Solve

5. Write the rest of the sequence (along with the polarity) of the synthesized strand shown in the gel.

6. Determine the sequence and polarity of the template strand used for DNA synthesis.

5. The synthesized strand is

   5′-[primer] CAATACGTCAGCAGTCGATTCATCGCGATA 3′.

6. The template DNA strand is

   3′-GTTATCGACTCCTCAGCTAAGTACGGCTAT-5′.

next-generation sequencing identifies the sequence of a DNA strand "by synthesis" rather than by chain termination, as is the case with dideoxy sequencing.

One major advance of next-generation sequencing technologies is that thousands to millions of sequencing reactions are run simultaneously, producing orders of magnitude more sequence information than dideoxy sequencing. As a result, next-generation sequencing is often referred to as being "massively parallel" or "high throughput" in its approach. Another advantage of next-generation sequencing over dideoxy sequencing is that DNA can be present as a single copy rather than the large number of copies of the strand to be sequenced that is needed for dideoxy sequencing.

Eliminating the need to have large numbers of copies in order to sequence the DNA has two significant advantages. First, it facilitates the sequencing of DNA samples that are found in only trace amounts, such as the small amounts of DNA obtained from the Neandertal and Denisovan bone samples described in the Case Study in Chapter 1 (pp. 21–22) and in Chapter 22 or the scant DNA samples obtained from the frozen remains of a wooly mammoth preserved in permafrost in Siberia. Next-generation sequencing is powerful enough to distinguish mammoth DNA from DNA of environmental contaminants, such as grasses in existence at the time the mammoth died that are also preserved in the permafrost. The second advantage of next-generation sequencing is that it excels over the earlier methods at sequencing DNA that is highly repetitive. On the other hand, next-generation methods have the disadvantage of producing sequence segments of only 20 to 500 bases versus the 800 to 1000 bases sequenced by dideoxy sequencing methods.

Currently being developed are newer procedures described as "third-generation" DNA sequencing technologies. These offer the possibility of sequencing millions of *single copies* of DNA molecules *directly* and in *parallel*. The combination of next-generation and third-generation sequencing technologies is causing, and will continue to cause, the price of sequencing to plummet. In 2001, when the final draft of the human genome was completed, the cost of sequencing 1 million base pairs by dideoxy sequencing was approximately $10,000. By 2005, the cost had been cut to approximately $1000 per million base pairs. By 2010, using third-generation sequencing, the cost of sequencing 1 million bases pairs was approximately $1.

The reduction in the cost of sequencing has led to an explosion of sequences available in public databases. Consider, for example, that about 10 billion base pairs were available in public databases in 2000, but by 2010 the number was more than 300 billion base pairs. A stated goal of modern genomic science is to produce the complete genome sequence of a person for less than $1000—the so-called "thousand-dollar genome"—by 2020. When this becomes feasible, it may be routine for your own genome sequence to be part of your medical file and for decisions about your personal disease treatment, disease prevention, and health monitoring to be made on the basis of your individual genome.

These new medical possibilities raise some unprecedented social and ethical questions. From the earliest days of the development of recombinant DNA technologies in the early 1970s through to the present day, the potential social, ethical, environmental, and economic issues engendered by the technology have been the subject of intense debate. In 1975, following a self-imposed moratorium on recombinant DNA research, scientists met at the Asilomar Institute in California to draw up a set of guidelines addressing many of the safety concerns expressed by scientists and members of the public. A new array of issues raised by the dawn of the era of personal genome sequencing, including questions of confidentiality, potential bias, and personal choice, will need to be addressed by similar public debates.

CASE STUDY

Use of PCR and DNA Sequencing to Analyze Huntington Disease Mutations

Both PCR and DNA sequencing analysis have been used to study the gene identified as *HD* that is mutated in Huntington disease (OMIM 143100). *HD* encodes the huntingtin protein that is expressed in brain cells and in other cells of the body. The normal function of wild-type huntingtin is not known, but it interacts with dozens of other proteins. In mutant form, huntingtin appears to aggregate with itself and other proteins, hastening the death of neurons in the brain that lead to the motor abnormalities—progressive loss of motor control by unintentional and uncontrollable movement—that are characteristic of the disease.

TRINUCLEOTIDE REPEAT EXPANSION Huntington disease is one of several human trinucleotide repeat expansion disorders that are caused by increases in the length of gene sections containing end-to-end repeats of three nucleotides. A CAG trinucleotide region of *HD* that encodes the amino acid glutamine produces a polyglutamine tract in the wild-type allele. The length of the polyglutamine tract is increased in mutant huntingtin protein as a result of an increased number of CAG repeats in mutant alleles.

Regions of repeating DNA sequence, such as those containing many repeats of DNA triplets, are known as "hotspots"

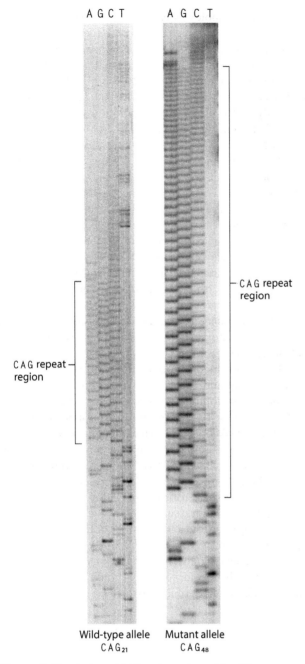

A G C T   A G C T

CAG repeat region

CAG repeat region

Wild-type allele
CAG₂₁

Mutant allele
CAG₄₈

Figure 7.32 **Dideoxy DNA sequencing of the *HD* gene.**
Gel electrophoresis results of dideoxy sequencing of a wild-type
HD allele with 21 CAG repeats is compared to the results for an
HD allele with 48 CAG repeats.

of mutation, regions that undergo a greater than average
number of mutations. One common mechanism of mutation
in regions of repeating DNA sequence is so-called strand slippage. We discuss this mutational process in more detail in
Section 12.3. For now, simply know that DNA polymerase can
occasionally slip backward during the replication of repetitive
DNA, so that it erroneously copies a segment of sequence

twice. The result of this slippage is an increase in the number
of nucleotides in a region of repeating DNA sequence. While
this happens occasionally, it rarely causes a problem because
most repetitive DNA is not transcribed and no abnormal RNAs
are produced. A few regions of repetitive DNA sequence, like
this CAG repeat region, are transcribed, however, and their
expansion can cause a mutation.

**CAG REPEAT NUMBERS IN WILD-TYPE AND MUTANT
HD ALLELES** Wild-type *HD* genes vary in the number of
CAG repeats, ranging from 6 to 28 repeats in the general
population. *HD* alleles with 28 to 35 CAG repeats do not cause
disease, but as a consequence of the increased CAG number,
the alleles are unstable and prone to further expansion. Alleles
that have 36 to 40 CAG repeats have expanded beyond the
normal range, and the huntingtin protein produced by these
alleles can behave abnormally and can result in disease symptoms that show reduced penetrance. Individuals who carry
36 to 40 CAG repeats might or might not develop HD. If they
do, disease symptoms have a late age of onset and progress
slowly. Individuals with *HD* alleles containing more than 40
CAG repeats have HD that can develop at any time from the
late teens onward. **Figure 7.32** shows dideoxy DNA sequencing analysis of the CAG repeat segment of the *HD* gene for a
wild-type allele with 21 CAG repeats and for a mutant allele
with 48 CAG repeats.

**POLYMERASE CHAIN REACTION DETECTS THE NUM-
BER OF REPEATS** The polymerase chain reaction provides
another way of visualizing the CAG triplet repeat expansion
and of following the transmission of alleles in the families of
people with HD. Employing primers that bind on opposite
sides of the CAG repeat region, researchers amplify fragments of DNA by PCR and separate them by gel electrophoresis. The binding sites of the PCR primers are identical for all
alleles, but differences are seen in the lengths of amplified
PCR products because of different numbers of CAG repeats
between the primer binding sites. Amplified DNA fragments
containing the primers are shorter if they are generated from
wild-type DNA sequences than from mutant alleles, because
wild-type alleles have a smaller number of repeats than do
mutant alleles. In the Huntington disease family shown in
Figure 7.33, each person with HD is heterozygous and carries one wild-type allele with fewer than 36 repeats of the
CAG sequence and one expanded allele with more than
36 repeats. In contrast, family members shown here who do
not have HD carry two alleles that each contain fewer than
36 CAG repeats.

PRESYMPTOMATIC MOLECULAR DIAGNOSIS OF HD
These and similar molecular methods are used to assess the
number of CAG repeats in *HD* for presymptomatic genetic testing of people at risk for inheriting Huntington disease. At-risk
individuals can be tested before disease symptoms appear and
can be told whether they carry an expanded *HD* allele. These
methods can also be used to identify the presence of a CAG
expansion of *HD* in individuals diagnosed with Huntington disease by clinicians.

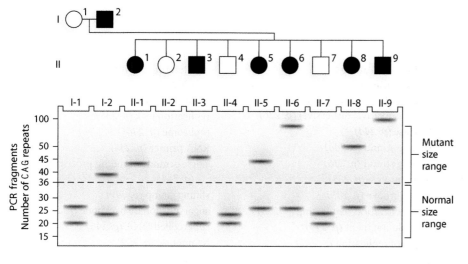

Figure 7.33 CAG **expansion of the** *HD* **gene detected by Southern blot analysis of PCR-amplified DNA.** Each family member represented by a filled circle or square has Huntington disease. PCR analysis of the *HD* gene reveals each such person to be heterozygous for HD and to carry one disease-producing allele with more than 36 CAG repeats.

SUMMARY   **(MasteringGenetics™**)   For activities, animations, and review quizzes, go to the Study Area.

7.1 DNA Is the Hereditary Molecule of Life

▯ F. Griffith determined in 1928 that a molecular transformation factor was responsible for transformation of living R bacteria into an S form.

▯ In 1944, O. Avery, C. MacLeod, and M. McCarty's study of in vitro transformation caused by an S-cell extract identified DNA as the transformation factor and strongly suggested it is the hereditary material.

▯ A. Hershey and M. Chase determined in 1952 that bacteriophage T2 uses DNA, not protein, to reproduce within host *E. coli* cells.

7.2 The DNA Double Helix Consists of Two Complementary and Antiparallel Strands

▯ The DNA nucleotides consist of the five-carbon sugar deoxyribose, a phosphate group, and one of four nitrogen-containing nucleotide bases.

▯ The DNA nucleotide bases are the purines adenine and guanine, and the pyrimidines cytosine and thymine.

▯ Phosphodiester bonds form between 5′ phosphate and 3′ OH groups to join nucleotides into polynucleotide chains.

▯ Complementary base pairs consist of a purine and a pyrimidine. In DNA, A and T form two stable hydrogen bonds, whereas G and C form three stable hydrogen bonds.

▯ Complementary nucleic acid strands are antiparallel.

▯ The stacking of base pairs in DNA imparts helical twisting that creates major grooves and minor grooves in the duplex.

7.3 DNA Replication Is Semiconservative and Bidirectional

▯ Experimental evidence demonstrates that DNA replication is semiconservative, meaning each daughter molecule receives one parental strand and one newly synthesized strand that was produced using the parental strand as a template.

▯ Most DNA replication is bidirectional. A replication bubble with replication forks at each end expands as replication progresses.

▯ Bacterial genomes have a single replication origin, whereas eukaryotic genomes have many origins of replication.

▯ Eukaryotic replication origins initiate asynchronously during S phase.

▯ Eukaryotic DNA replication produces sister chromatids.

7.4 DNA Replication Precisely Duplicates the Genetic Material

▯ Bacterial, archaeal and yeast DNA replication begins at specific locations that bind replication initiation proteins. Specific conserved sequences are found in bacteria, but replication initiation is directed by chromatin state in eukaryotes.

▯ DNA replication begins with the synthesis of an RNA primer by primase, followed by synthesis of leading and lagging DNA strands by DNA polymerase.

▯ To complete replication, RNA primers are removed by DNA polymerase, and DNA segments are joined by DNA ligase.

▯ DNA polymerases not only replicate DNA but also proofread newly synthesized DNA for accuracy.

▯ Eukaryotic and archaeal DNA replication proteins have a high degree of homology reflecting a shared common ancestry. Bacteria have analogous proteins, but are ancestrally more distant.

▯ Eukaryotic chromosomes have repetitive sequences called telomeres at their ends that shorten with each replication in somatic cell cycles.

▯ Telomerase is a ribonucleoprotein that synthesizes telomeric repeat sequences to maintain telomere length in germ-line and stem cells.

7.5 Molecular Genetic Analytical Methods Make Use of DNA Replication Processes

▯ The polymerase chain reaction (PCR) is used to produce large numbers of copies of target DNA sequences.

▯ Dideoxynucleotide DNA sequencing is used to determine the sequence of DNA fragments.

▯ Next-generation and third-generation DNA sequencing are much faster and far cheaper methods that have paved the way for large numbers of genome sequencing projects and personal human genome sequencing.

KEYWORDS

bacteriophage (phage) *(p. 231)*
base stacking *(p. 235)*
bidirectional DNA replication *(p. 237)*
clamp loader *(p. 249)*
consensus sequence *(p. 242)*
deoxynucleotide 5′-monophosphate (dNMP) *(p. 232)*
deoxynucleotide 5′-triphosphate (dNTP) *(p. 232)*
dideoxy DNA sequencing *(p. 257)*
dideoxynucleotide triphosphate (ddNTP) *(p. 257)*
DNA ligase *(p. 248)*
DNA polymerase (pol I, pol III, 5′-to-3′ polymerase activity) *(pp. 246–248)*

DNA proofreading (3′-to-5′ exonuclease activity) *(pp. 249–251)*
DNA replication (semiconservative, conservative, dispersive) *(p. 236)*
helicase *(p. 244)*
lagging strand *(p. 246)*
leading strand *(p. 246)*
major groove *(p. 235)*
minor groove *(p. 235)*
next-generation sequencing *(p. 259)*
Okazaki fragment *(p. 247)*
origin of replication *(p. 237)*
polymerase chain reaction (PCR) *(p. 254)*
primase (DnaG) *(p. 245)*

proliferating cell nuclear antigen (PCNA) *(p. 249)*
replication bubble *(p. 237)*
replication fork *(p. 238)*
replisome *(p. 246)*
RNA primer *(p. 245)*
single-stranded binding protein (SSB) *(p. 244)*
sliding clamp *(p. 249)*
sugar-phosphate backbone *(p. 234)*
supercoiled DNA *(p. 246)*
telomerase *(p. 252)*
telomere *(p. 251)*
topoisomerase *(p. 246)*

PROBLEMS

MasteringGenetics™ Visit for instructor-assigned tutorials and problems.

Chapter Concepts

For answers to selected even-numbered problems, see Appendix: Answers.

1. What results from the experiments of Frederick Griffith provided the strongest support for his conclusion that a transformation factor is responsible for heredity?

2. Explain why Avery, MacLeod, and McCarty's in vitro transformation experiment showed that DNA, but not RNA or protein, is the hereditary molecule.

3. Hershey and Chase selected the bacteriophage T2 for their experiment assessing the role of DNA in heredity because T2 contains protein and DNA, but not RNA. Explain why T2 was a good choice for this experiment.

4. Explain how the Hershey and Chase experiment identified DNA as the hereditary molecule.

5. One strand of a fragment of duplex DNA has the sequence 5′-ATCGACCTGATC-3′.
   a. What is the sequence of the other strand in the duplex?
   b. What is the name of the bond that joins one nucleotide to another in the DNA strand?
   c. Is the bond in part (b) a covalent or a noncovalent bond?
   d. Which chemical groups of nucleotides react to form the bond in part (b)?
   e. What enzymes catalyze the reaction in part (d)?
   f. Identify the bond that joins one strand of a DNA duplex to the other strand.
   g. Is the bond in part (f) a covalent or a noncovalent bond?
   h. What term is used to describe the pattern of base pairing between one DNA strand and its partner in a duplex?
   i. What term is used to describe the polarity of two DNA strands in a duplex?

6. The principles of complementary base pairing and antiparallel polarity of nucleic acid strands in a duplex are universal for the formation of nucleic acid duplexes. What is the chemical basis for this universality?

7. For the following fragment of DNA, determine the number of hydrogen bonds and the number of phosphodiester bonds present:

   5′-ACGTAGAGTGCTC-3′
   3′-TGCATCTCACGAG-5′

8. Figures 1.6 and 1.7 present simplified depictions of nucleotides containing deoxyribose, a nucleotide base, and a phosphate group (see pages 8 and 9). Use this simplified method of representation to illustrate the sequence 3′-AGTCGAT-5′ and its complementary partner in a DNA duplex.
   a. What kind of bond joins the C to the G within a single strand?
   b. What kind of bonds join the C in one strand to the G in the complementary strand?
   c. How many phosphodiester bonds are present in this DNA duplex?
   d. How many hydrogen bonds are present in this DNA duplex?

9. Consider the sequence 3′-ACGGTAGGTG-5′.
   a. What is the double-stranded sequence?
   b. What is the total number of covalent bonds joining the nucleotides in each strand?
   c. What is the total number of noncovalent bonds joining the nucleotides of the complementary strands?

10. DNA polymerase III is the main DNA-synthesizing enzyme in bacteria. Describe how it carries out its role of elongating a strand of DNA.

11. You are participating in a study group preparing for an upcoming genetics exam, and one member of the group proposes that each of you draw the structure of two DNA nucleotides joined in a single strand. The figures are drawn

and exchanged for correction. You receive the drawing below to correct.

a. Identify and correct at least five things that are wrong in the depiction of each nucleotide.

b. What is wrong with the way the nucleotides are joined?

c. Draw this single-stranded segment correctly.

12. Explain how RNA participates in DNA replication.

13. A sample of double-stranded DNA is found to contain 20% cytosine. Determine the percentage of the three other DNA nucleotides in the sample.

14. Bacterial DNA polymerase I and DNA polymerase III perform different functions during DNA replication.

a. Identify the principal functions of each molecule.

b. If mutation inactivated DNA polymerase I in a strain of *E. coli*, would the cell be able to replicate its DNA? If so, what kind of abnormalities would you expect to find in the cell?

c. If a strain of *E. coli* acquired a mutation that inactivated DNA polymerase III function, would the cell be able to replicate its DNA? Why or why not?

Application and Integration

20. Matthew Meselson and Franklin Stahl demonstrated that DNA replication is semiconservative in bacteria. Briefly outline their experiment and its results for two DNA replication cycles, and identify how the alternative models of DNA replication were excluded by the data.

21. Raymond Rodriguez and colleagues demonstrated conclusively that DNA replication in *E. coli* is bidirectional. Explain why locating the origin of replication on one side of the circular chromosomes and the terminus of replication on the opposite side of the chromosome supported this conclusion.

22. Joel Huberman and Arthur Riggs used pulse labeling to examine the replication of DNA in mam malian cells. Briefly describe the Huberman-Riggs experiment, and identify how the results exclude a unidirectional model of DNA replication.

23. Why do the genomes of eukaryotes, such as *Drosophila*, need to have multiple origins of replication, whereas bacterial genomes, such as that of *E. coli*, have only a single origin?

24. Bloom syndrome (OMIM 210900) is an autosomal recessive disorder caused by mutation of a DNA helicase. Among the principal symptoms of the disease are chromosome

15. Diagram a replication fork in bacterial DNA and label the following structures or molecules.

a. DNA pol III
b. helicase
c. RNA primer
d. origin of replication
e. leading strand (label its polarity)
f. DNA pol I
g. topoisomerase
h. SSB protein
i. lagging strand (label its polarity)
j. primase
k. Okazaki fragment

16. Which of the following equations are true for the percentages of nucleotides in double-stranded DNA?

a. $(A + G)/(C + T) = 1.0$
b. $(A + T)/(G + C) = 1.0$
c. $(A)/(T) = (G)/(C)$
d. $(A)/(C) = (G)/(T)$
e. $(A)/(G) = (T)(C)$

17. Which of the following equalities is not true for double-stranded DNA?

a. $(G + T) = (A + C)$
b. $(G + C) = (A + T)$
c. $(G + A) = (C + T)$

18. List the order in which the following proteins and enzymes are active in *E. coli* DNA replication: DNA pol I, SSB, ligase, helicase, DNA pol III, and primase.

19. Two viral genomes are sequenced, and the following percentages of nucleotides are identified:

Genome 1: A = 28%, C = 22%, G = 28%, T = 22%
Genome 2: A = 22%, C = 28%, G = 28%, T = 22%

What is the structure of DNA in each genome?

For answers to selected even-numbered problems, see Appendix: Answers.

instability and a propensity to develop cancer. Explain these symptoms on the basis of the helicase mutation.

25. How does rolling circle replication (see Section 6.1) differ from bidirectional replication?

26. Telomeres are found at the ends of eukaryotic chromosomes.

a. What is the sequence composition of telomeres?
b. How does telomerase assemble telomeres?
c. What is the functional role of telomeres?
d. Why is telomerase usually active in germ-line cells but not in somatic cells?

27. A family consisting of a mother (I-1), a father (I-2), and three children (II-1, II-2, and II-3) are genotyped by PCR for a region of an autosome containing repeats of a 10-bp sequence. The mother carries 16 repeats on one chromosome and 21 on the homologous chromosome. The father carries repeat numbers of 18 and 26.

a. Following the illustration style of Figure 7.27c, which aligns members of a pedigree with their DNA fragments in a gel, draw a DNA gel containing the PCR fragments generated by amplification of DNA from the parents (I-1 and I-2). Label the size of each fragment.

b. Identify all the possible genotypes of children of this couple by specifying PCR fragment lengths in each genotype.

c. What genetic term best describes the pattern of inheritance of this DNA marker? Explain your choice.

28. In a dideoxy DNA sequencing experiment, four separate reactions are carried out to provide the replicated material for DNA sequencing gels. Reaction products are usually run in gel lanes labeled A, T, C, and G.

a. Identify the nucleotides used in the dideoxy DNA sequencing reaction that produces molecules for the A lane of the sequencing gel.

b. How does PCR play a role in dideoxy DNA sequencing?

c. Why is incorporation of a dideoxynucleotide during DNA sequencing identified as a "replication-terminating" event?

29. The following dideoxy DNA sequencing gel is produced in a laboratory.

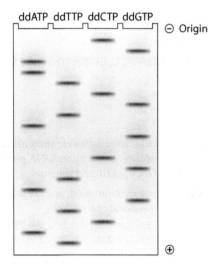

What is the double-stranded DNA sequence of this molecule? Label the polarity of each strand.

30. Using an illustration style and labeling similar to that in Problem 29, draw the electrophoresis gel containing dideoxy sequencing fragments for the DNA template strand 3'-AGACGATAGCAT-5'.

31. A PCR reaction begins with one double-stranded segment of DNA. How many double-stranded copies of DNA are present after the completion of 10 amplification cycles? After 20 cycles? After 30 cycles?

32. DNA replication in early *Drosophila* embryos occurs about every 5 minutes. The *Drosophila* genome contains approximately 1.8×10^8 base pairs. Eukaryotic DNA polymerases synthesize DNA at a rate of approximately 40 nucleotides per second. Approximately how many origins of replication are required for this rate of replication?

33. Three independently assorting VNTR markers are used to assess the paternity of a colt (C) recently born to a quarter horse mare (M). Blood samples are drawn from the mare, her colt, and three possible male sires (S_1, S_2, and S_3). DNA at each marker locus is amplified by PCR, and a DNA electrophoresis gel is run for each marker. Amplified DNA bands are visualized in each gel by ethidium bromide staining. Gel results are shown below for each marker.

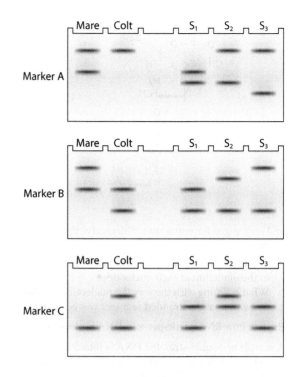

Evaluate the data and determine if any of the potential sires can be excluded. Explain the basis of exclusion, if any, in each case.

34. A sufficient amount of a small DNA fragment is available for dideoxy sequencing. The fragment to be sequenced contains 20 nucleotides following the site of primer binding:

5'-ATCGCTCGACAGTGACTAGC-[primer site]-3'

Dideoxy sequencing is carried out, and the products of the four sequencing reactions are separated by gel electrophoresis. Draw the bands you expect will appear on the gel from each of the sequencing reactions.

35. Suppose that future exploration of polar ice on Mars identifies a living microbe and that analysis indicates the organism carries double-stranded DNA as its genetic material. Suppose further that DNA replication analysis is performed by first growing the microbe in a growth medium containing the heavy isotope of nitrogen (^{15}N), that the organism is then transferred to a growth medium containing the light isotope of nitrogen (^{14}N), and that the nitrogen composition of the DNA is examined by CsCl ultracentrifugation and densitometry after the first, second, and third replication cycles in the ^{14}N-containing medium. The results of the experiment are illustrated for each cycle. The control shows the positioning of the three possible DNA densities. Based on the results shown, what can you conclude about the mechanism of DNA replication in this organism? (Hint: See the description of the Meselson and Stahl experiment on pp. 236–237.)

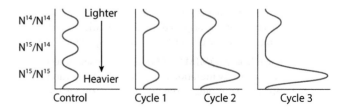

Molecular Biology of Transcription and RNA Processing

8

CHAPTER OUTLINE

8.1 RNA Transcripts Carry the Messages of Genes

8.2 Bacterial Transcription Is a Four-Stage Process

8.3 Archaeal and Eukaryotic Transcription Displays Structural Homology and Common Ancestry

8.4 Post-Transcriptional Processing Modifies RNA Molecules

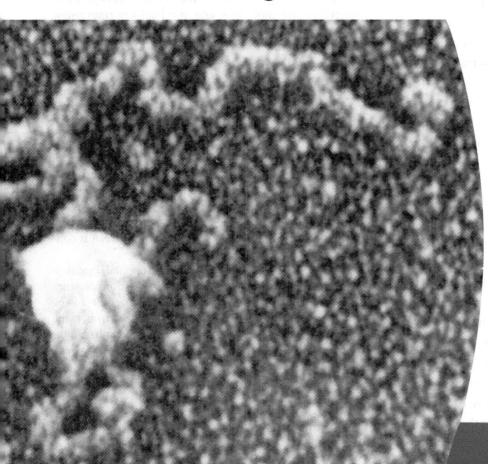

An electron micrograph of a spliceosome engaged in intron splicing.

Wilhelm Johansson introduced the term *gene* in 1909 to describe "the fundamental unit of inheritance." Johansson's definition encompasses the understanding that genes contain genetic information and are passed from one generation to the next and that genes are the basis of the fundamental structural, functional, developmental, reproductive, and evolutionary properties of organisms. This basic definition of the gene remains valid today, more than a century after being coined, but our knowledge of molecular genetics has expanded enormously, refining our understanding of the structure and function of genes and clarifying the roles genes play in producing traits.

ESSENTIAL IDEAS

■ Ribonucleic acid (RNA) molecules are transcribed from genes and are classified either as messenger RNA or as one of several types of functional RNA.

■ Bacterial transcription is a four-step process that begins with promoter recognition by RNA polymerase and ends with the completion of transcript synthesis.

■ Eukaryotes and archaea have homologous transcription proteins and processes. Eukaryotes use different RNA polymerases to transcribe different kinds of RNA. Each type of polymerase initiates transcription at a different type of promoter.

■ Eukaryotic RNAs undergo three processing steps after transcription. Alternative events during and after transcription allow different transcripts and proteins to be produced from the same DNA sequence.

The central dogma of biology describes the flow of genetic information from DNA to RNA to protein (see Figure 1.8). It conveys that DNA is the repository of genetic information, which is converted through *transcription* into RNA, one type of which is then *translated* into protein. Transcription is the process by which RNA polymerase enzymes and other transcriptional proteins and enzymes use the template strand of DNA to synthesize a complementary RNA strand. Translation is the process by which *messenger RNA* is used to direct protein synthesis.

This chapter describes the mechanisms of RNA transcription in the three domains of life: bacteria, archaea, and eukaryotes. We will also examine the events that modify the precursor messenger RNA (mRNA) to yield the mature mRNA that subsequently undergoes translation to produce proteins. We will see that these transcriptional events are closely tied to the process of translation, the subject of the following chapter.

This chapter also discusses the shared evolutionary history and common ancestry of bacteria, archaea, and eukaryotes. We will see that, bacteria have a number of general features of transcription in common with archaea and eukaryotes. At the same time, we see that, differences among the members of these domains, including differences in cell structure, gene structure, and genome organization, lead to significant differences in how their genes are transcribed and translated.

Multiple types of RNA are introduced and described here, but the principal focus of discussion is mRNA. The discovery of mRNA and of its function raised numerous questions: How is a gene recognized by the transcription machinery? Where does transcription begin? Which strand of DNA is transcribed? Where does transcription end? How much transcript is made? How is RNA modified after transcription? We answer these questions in the chapter and set the answers in a context that compares and contrasts the process of transcription in bacterial, archaeal, and eukaryotic genomes.

8.1 RNA Transcripts Carry the Messages of Genes

In the late 1950s, with the structure of DNA in hand, molecular biology researchers focused on identifying and describing the molecules and mechanisms responsible for conveying the genetic message of DNA. RNA was known to be chemically similar to DNA and present in abundance in all cells, but its diversity and biological roles remained to be discovered. Some roles were strongly suggested by cell structure. For example, in eukaryotic cells, DNA is located in the nucleus, whereas protein synthesis takes place in the cytoplasm, suggesting that DNA could not code directly for proteins but RNA perhaps could. Bacteria, however, lack a nucleus, so an open research question was whether bacteria and eukaryotes used similar mechanisms and similar molecules to convey the genetic message for protein synthesis. The search was on to identify the types of RNA in cells and to identify the mechanisms by which the genetic message of DNA is conveyed for protein synthesis.

It is worth noting that the experimental evidence identifying archaea as occupying a separate domain from bacteria and eukaryotes was obtained after some of the fundamental information about transcription became known. We introduce transcription in archaea in a later section. These microbes, which like bacteria also lack a nucleus, reveal an intriguing blend of bacterial and eukaryotic features. The archaeal core transcriptional proteins are clearly homologous to the eukaryotic apparatus, while the regulation of these processes is more bacteria-like in nature.

RNA Nucleotides and Structure

Both DNA and RNA are polynucleotide molecules composed of nucleotide building blocks. One principal difference between the molecules is the single-stranded structure of RNA versus the double-stranded structure of DNA. Despite their single-stranded structure, however, RNA molecules can, and frequently do, adopt folded secondary structures by complementary base pairing of segments of the molecule. In certain instances, folded secondary structures are essential to RNA function, as we discuss in the following section.

The RNA nucleotides, like those of DNA, are composed of a five-carbon sugar, a nucleotide base, and one or more phosphate groups. Each RNA nucleotide carries one of four possible nucleotide bases. At the same time, RNA nucleotides have two critical chemical differences in comparison to DNA nucleotides. The first difference concerns the identity of the RNA nucleotide bases. The purines adenine and guanine in RNA are identical to the purines in DNA. Likewise, the pyrimidine cytosine is identical in RNA and DNA. In RNA, however, the second pyrimidine

Purine nucleotides

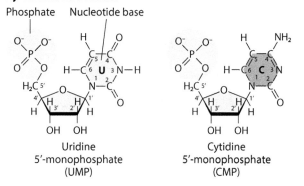

Pyrimidine nucleotides

Figure 8.1 **The four RNA ribonucleotides.** Shown in their monophosphate forms, each ribonucleotide consists of the sugar ribose, one phosphate group, and one of the nucleotide bases adenine, guanine, cytosine, and uracil.

is **uracil** (U) rather than the thymine carried by DNA. The four RNA **ribonucleotides** (A, U, G, C) are shown in Figure 8.1. The structure of uracil is similar to that of thymine, but notice, by comparing the structure of uracil in Figure 8.1 with that of thymine in Figure 7.5, that thymine has a methyl group (CH_3) at the 5 carbon of the pyrimidine ring, whereas uracil does not. In all other respects, uracil is similar to thymine, and when uracil undergoes base pairing, its complementary partner is adenine.

The second chemical difference between RNA and DNA nucleotides is the presence of the sugar **ribose** in RNA rather than the deoxyribose occurring in DNA. The ribose gives RNA its name (ribonucleic acid). Compare the ribose molecules shown in Figure 8.1 to deoxyribose in Figure 7.5, and notice that ribose carries a hydroxyl group (OH) not found in deoxyribose at the 2′ carbon of the ring. Except for this difference, ribose and deoxyribose are identical, having a nucleotide base attached to the 1′ carbon and a hydroxyl group at the 3′ carbon.

The similarity of the sugars of RNA and DNA leads to the formation of essentially identical sugar-phosphate backbones in the molecules. RNA strands are assembled by formation of phosphodiester bonds, between the 5′ phosphate of one nucleotide and the 3′ hydroxyl of the

adjacent nucleotide, that are identical to those found in DNA (Figure 8.2). RNA is synthesized from a DNA template strand using the same purine-pyrimidine complementary base pairing described for DNA except for the pairing between adenine of DNA with uracil of RNA. **RNA polymerase** enzymes catalyze the addition of each ribonucleotide to the 3′ end of the nascent strand and form phosphodiester bonds between a triphosphate group at the 5′ carbon of one nucleotide and the hydroxyl group at the 3′ carbon of the adjacent nucleotide, eliminating two phosphates (the pyrophosphate group), just as in DNA synthesis. Compare Figure 8.2 to Figure 7.6 to see the similarity of these nucleic acid synthesis processes.

Identification of Messenger RNA

In their search for the RNA molecule responsible for transmitting the genetic information content of DNA to the ribosome for protein production, researchers utilized many techniques. Among the methods used was the pulse-chase technique (see Section 7.3) to follow the trail of newly synthesized RNA in cells. The "pulse" step of this technique exposes cells to radioactive nucleotides that become incorporated into newly synthesized nucleic acids (see Chapter 7). After a short incubation period to incorporate the labeled nucleotides, a "chase" step replaces any remaining unincorporated radioactive nucleotides by introducing an excess of unlabeled nucleotides. An experimenter can then observe the location and movement of the labeled nucleic acid to determine the pattern of its movement and its ultimate destination and fate.

In 1957, microbiologist Elliot Volkin and geneticist Lazarus Astrachan used the pulse-chase method to examine transcription in bacteria immediately following infection by a bacteriophage. Exposing newly infected bacteria to radioactive uracil, they observed rapid incorporation of the label, indicating a burst of transcriptional activity. In the chase phase of the experiment, when radioactive uracil was removed, Volkin and Astrachan found that the radioactivity quickly dissipated, indicating that the newly synthesized RNA broke down rapidly. They concluded that the synthesis of a type of RNA with a very short life span is responsible for the production of phage proteins that drive progression of the infection.

Similar pulse-chase experiments were soon conducted with eukaryotic cells. In these experiments, cells were pulsed with radioactive uracil that was then chased with nonradioactive uracil. Immediately after the pulse, radioactivity was concentrated in the nucleus, indicating that newly synthesized RNA has a nuclear location. Over a short period, radioactivity migrated to the cytoplasm, where translation takes place. The radioactivity dissipated after lingering in the cytoplasm for a period of time. These experiments led researchers to conclude that the RNA synthesized in the nucleus was likely to act as an

(a)

(b)

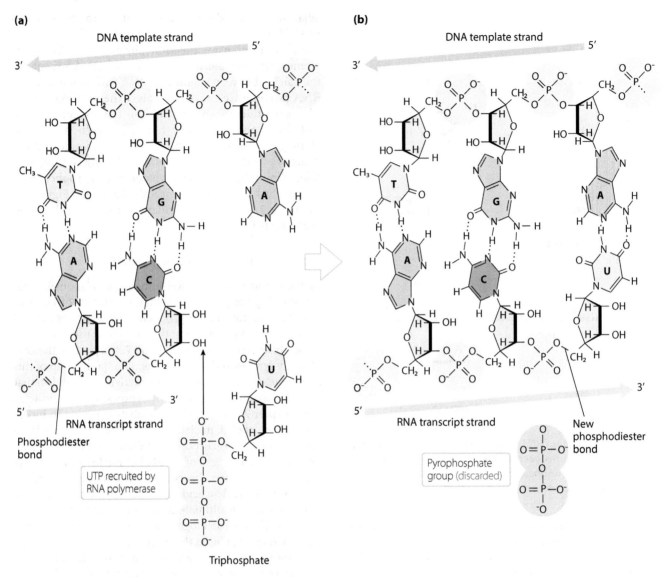

Figure 8.2 **RNA synthesis.**

intermediary carrying the genetic message of DNA to the cytoplasm for translation into proteins.

The discovery of mRNA was capped in 1961 when an experiment by the biologists Sydney Brenner, Francois Jacob, and Matthew Meselson identified an unstable form of RNA as the genetic messenger. Brenner and his colleagues designed an experiment using the bacteriophage T2 and *Escherichia coli* to investigate whether phage protein synthesis requires newly constructed ribosomes, or whether phage proteins could be produced using existing bacterial ribosomes and a messenger molecule to encode the proteins. The experiment found that newly synthesized phage RNA associates with bacterial ribosomes to produce phage proteins. The RNA that directed the protein synthesis formed and degraded quickly, leading the experimenters to conclude that a phage "messenger" RNA with a short half-life is responsible for protein synthesis during infection.

RNA Classification

A large variety of different RNA species exist within any cell. The most essential types of RNA are found in all cells in all three domains, but several others are specific to eukaryotic cells. Table 8.1 identifies and briefly describes the most important types of RNA found in cells, although it is not an exhaustive list, as there are too many varieties of RNA to describe all of them here.

All RNAs are transcribed from RNA-encoding genes. The various types of RNA are constructed from the same building blocks but perform different roles in the cell. In light of these different roles, RNAs are divided into two general categories—*messenger RNA* and *functional RNA*.

Genes transcribing **messenger RNA (mRNA)** are protein-producing genes, and their transcripts direct protein synthesis by the process of translation. Messenger RNA is the short-lived intermediary form of RNA that

Table 8.1	Major RNA Molecules

Type of RNA	Function
Messenger RNA (mRNA)	Used to encode the sequence of amino acids in a polypeptide. May be polycistronic (encoding two or more polypeptides) in bacteria and archaea. Encodes single polypeptides in nearly all eukaryotes (see Section 8.2).
Ribosomal RNA (rRNA)	Along with numerous proteins, helps form the large and small ribosomal subunits that unite for translation of mRNA (see Sections 8.4 and 9.2).
Transfer RNA (tRNA)	Carries amino acids to ribosomes and binds there to mRNA by complementary base pairing in order to deposit the amino acids to elongate the polypeptide (see Sections 8.4 and 9.3).
Small nuclear RNA (snRNA)	Found in eukaryotic nuclei, where multiple snRNAs join with numerous proteins to form spliceosomes that remove introns from precursor mRNA (see Section 8.4).
MicroRNA (miRNA) and small interfering RNA (siRNA)	Eukaryotic regulatory RNAs that have different origins. Involved in eukaryotic regulation of gene expression (see Section 15.3).
Telomerase RNA	Along with several proteins, forms telomerase, the ribonucleoprotein complex essential for maintaining and elongating telomere length of eukaryotic chromosomes (see Section 7.4).

conveys the genetic message of DNA to ribosomes for translation. Messenger RNA is the only form of RNA that undergoes translation. Transcription of mRNA and post-transcriptional processing of mRNA are principal areas of focus in this chapter.

Functional RNAs perform a variety of specialized roles in the cell. The functional RNAs carry out their activities in nucleic acid form and are not translated. Two major categories of functional RNA are active in bacterial and eukaryotic translation. **Transfer RNA (tRNA)** is encoded in dozens of different forms in all genomes. Each tRNA is responsible for binding a particular amino acid that it carries to the ribosome. There the tRNA interacts with mRNA and deposits its amino acid for inclusion in the growing protein chain. **Ribosomal RNA (rRNA)** combines with numerous proteins to form the ribosome, the molecular machine responsible for translation. Certain bacterial rRNA molecules interact with mRNA to initiate translation.

Three additional types of functional RNA perform specialized functions in eukaryotic cells only. **Small nuclear RNA (snRNA)** of various types is found in the nucleus of eukaryotic cells, where it participates in mRNA processing. Certain snRNAs unite with nuclear proteins to form ribonucleoprotein complexes that are responsible for intron removal. We discuss these activities in later sections of this chapter. **Micro RNA (miRNA)** and **small interfering RNA (siRNA)** are recently recognized types of regulatory RNA that are particularly active in plant and animal cells. Micro RNAs and siRNAs have a widespread and important role in the post-transcriptional regulation of mRNA, regulating protein production through a process called *RNA interference*. Their transcription and activities are beyond the scope of this chapter, but they are central to the discussion of the regulation of gene expression in eukaryotes in Chapter 15.

Lastly, certain RNAs in eukaryotic cells have catalytic activity. In contrast to DNA, which is exclusively a repository of genetic information, catalytically active RNA molecules can catalyze biological reactions. Called **ribozymes,** catalytically active RNAs can activate cellular reactions, including the removal of introns in a process identified as *self-splicing,* described later in the chapter.

8.2 Bacterial Transcription Is a Four-Stage Process

Transcription is the synthesis of a single-stranded RNA molecule by RNA polymerase. It is most clearly understood and described in bacteria, and *E. coli* is the model experimental organism from which the majority of our knowledge of bacterial transcription has been derived. In this section, we examine the four stages of transcription in bacteria: (1) promoter recognition and identification, (2) the initiation of transcript synthesis, (3) transcript elongation, and (4) transcription termination.

Like all RNA polymerases, bacterial RNA polymerase uses one strand of DNA, the **template strand,** to assemble the transcript by complementary and antiparallel base pairing of RNA nucleotides with DNA nucleotides of the template strand (see Figure 1.9 for a review). The **coding strand** of DNA, also known as the **nontemplate strand,** is complementary to the template strand. The gene—that is, the stretch of DNA regions that produces an RNA transcript—contains several segments with distinct functions (**Figure 8.3**). The **promoter** of the gene is immediately **upstream**—that is, immediately 5′ to the start of transcription, which is identified as corresponding to the +1 nucleotide. The promoter is not transcribed. Instead, the promoter sequence is a transcription-regulating DNA

Figure 8.3   A general diagram of gene structure and associated nomenclature.

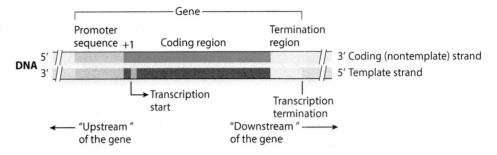

sequence that controls the access of RNA polymerase to the gene. The **coding region** is the portion of the gene that is transcribed into mRNA and contains the information needed to synthesize the protein product of the gene. The **termination region** is the portion of the gene that regulates the cessation of transcription. The termination region is located immediately **downstream**—that is, immediately 3' to the coding segment of the gene.

Bacterial RNA Polymerase

A single type of *E. coli* RNA polymerase catalyzes transcription of all RNAs. The initial experimental evidence supporting this conclusion came from analysis of the effect of the antibiotic rifampicin on bacterial RNA synthesis. Rifampicin inhibits RNA synthesis by preventing RNA polymerase from catalyzing the formation of the first phosphodiester bond in the RNA chain. In rifampicin-sensitive (rif^S) bacterial strains, synthesis of all three major types of RNA (mRNA, tRNA, and rRNA) is inhibited in the presence of rifampicin. In contrast, rifampicin-resistant (rif^R) bacteria actively transcribe DNA into the three major RNAs when rifampicin is present. Molecular analysis identifies a single mutation of RNA polymerase in rif^R strains that allows it to remain catalytically active when exposed to rifampicin, and subsequent molecular studies have confirmed the presence of a single bacterial RNA polymerase.

Bacterial RNA polymerase is composed of a pentameric (five-polypeptide) **RNA polymerase core** that binds to a sixth polypeptide, called the **sigma subunit (σ),** which induces a conformational change in the core enzyme that switches it to its active form. In its active form, the RNA polymerase is described as a holoenzyme, a term meaning an intact complex of multiple subunits, with full enzymatic capacity. **Figure 8.4** shows a common type of sigma subunit known as σ^{70}, but there are also other sigma subunits in *E. coli*.

The RNA polymerase core consists of two α subunits, designated αI and αII, two β subunits, and an ω (omega) subunit. The molecular weight of the five-subunit core RNA polymerase is approximately 390 kD (kiloDaltons), and with the sigma subunit added, the holoenzyme has a molecular weight of 430 kD. Each of these subunits have been evolutionarily conserved in archaea and in eukaryotes, as we discuss in the following section.

By itself, the core RNA polymerase can transcribe DNA template-strand sequence into RNA sequence, but the core is unable to efficiently bind to a promoter or initiate RNA synthesis without a sigma subunit. The joining of the sigma subunit to the core enzyme to form a holoenzyme induces a conformational shift in the core segment that enables it to bind specifically to particular promoter consensus sequences. The addition of the sigma subunit to the core RNA polymerase, with its five subunits and approximately 390-kD molecular weight, produces a holoenzyme having a molecular weight of approximately 430 kD. Each of the subunits has been evolutionarily conserved in archaea and in eukaryotes, as we discuss in a following section.

This single RNA polymerase is responsible for all bacterial transcription. Thus, the bacterial RNA polymerase must recognize promoters for protein-coding genes as well as for genes that produce functional RNAs, such as tRNA and rRNA. However, not all promoters of bacterial genes are identical. There is great diversity among bacterial promoter sequences, permitting certain genes to be expressed only under special circumstances. Bacteria manage the recognition of the promoters of these specialized genes by producing several different types of sigma subunits that can join the core polymerase. These so-called **alternative sigma subunits** alter the specificity of the holoenzymes for promoter regions by imparting

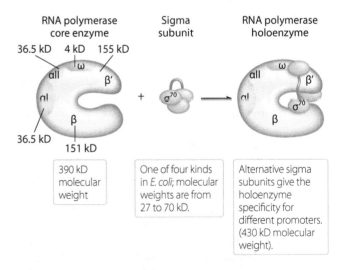

Figure 8.4   Bacterial RNA polymerase core plus a sigma (σ) subunit forms the fully active holoenzyme.

distinct conformational changes to the core. These differences enable transcription of specific genes under the appropriate conditions, or at the correct time.

Bacterial Promoters

A promoter is a double-stranded DNA sequence that is the binding site for RNA polymerase. Promoters are regulatory DNA sequences that bind transcription proteins, and their presence usually indicates that a gene is nearby. Bacterial promoters are located a short distance upstream of the coding sequence, typically within a few nucleotides of the start of transcription, represented by the +1 nucleotide. RNA polymerase is attracted to promoters by the presence of **consensus sequences,** short regions of DNA sequences that are highly similar, though not necessarily identical, to one another and are located in the same position relative to the start of transcription of different genes.

Although promoters are double stranded, promoter consensus sequences are usually written in a single-stranded shorthand form that gives the 5'-to-3' sequence of the coding (non-template) strand of DNA (Figure 8.5). The most commonly occurring bacterial promoter contains two consensus sequence regions that each play an important functional role in recognition by RNA polymerase and the subsequent initiation of transcription. These consensus sequences are located upstream from the +1 nucleotide (the start of transcription) in a region flanking the gene where the nucleotides are denoted by negative numbers and are not transcribed. At the −10 position of the *E. coli* promoter is the **Pribnow box sequence,** or the **−10 consensus sequence,** consisting of 6 bp having the consensus sequence 5'-TATAAT-3'. The Pribnow box is separated by about 25 bp from another 6-bp region, the **−35 consensus sequence,** identified by the nucleotides 5'-TTGACA-3'. The nucleotide sequences that occur upstream, downstream, and between these consensus sequences are highly variable and contain no other consensus sequences. Thus, in a functional sense,

the −10 (Pribnow) and −35 consensus sequences are important because of their nucleotide content, their location relative to one another, and their location relative to the start of transcription. In contrast to the consensus sequences themselves, the nucleotides between −10 and −35 are important as spacers between the consensus elements, but their specific sequences are not critical.

Natural selection has operated to retain strong sequence similarity in consensus regions and to retain the position of the consensus regions relative to the start of transcription. The effectiveness of evolution in maintaining promoter consensus sequences is illustrated by comparison with the sequences between and around −10 and −35, which are not conserved and which exhibit considerable variation. In addition, the spacing between the sequences and their placement relative to the +1 nucleotide is stable. RNA polymerase is a large molecule that binds to −10 and −35 consensus sequences and occupies the space between and immediately around the sites. Crystal structure models show that the enzyme spans enough DNA to allow it to contact promoter consensus regions and reach the +1 nucleotide. Once bound at a promoter in this fashion, RNA polymerase can initiate transcription. Genetic Analysis 8.1 guides you through the identification of promoter consensus regions.

Transcription Initiation

RNA polymerase holoenzyme initiates transcription through a process involving two steps. In the first step, the holoenzyme makes an initial loose attachment to the double-stranded promoter sequence and then binds tightly to it to form the **closed promoter complex** (❶ in Foundation Figure 8.6). In the second step, the bound holoenzyme unwinds approximately 18 bp of DNA around the −10 consensus sequence to form the **open promoter complex** (❷). Following formation of the open promoter complex, the holoenzyme progresses downstream to initiate RNA synthesis at the +1 nucleotide on the template strand of DNA (❸).

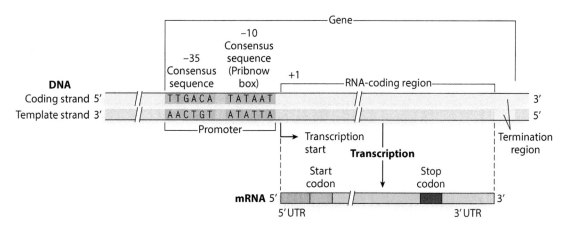

Figure 8.5 **Bacterial promoter structure.** Two promoter consensus sequences—the Pribnow box at −10 and the −35 sequence—are essential promoter regulatory elements.

Bacterial Transcription

1 The RNA polymerase core enzyme and sigma subunit bind to −10 and −35 promoter consensus sequences.

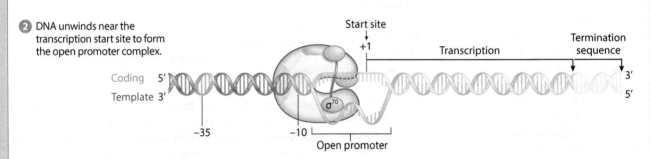

Closed promoter
Start site
+1
Transcription
Termination sequence
RNA polymerase
Coding 5′
Template 3′
σ⁷⁰
3′
5′
−35
−10

2 DNA unwinds near the transcription start site to form the open promoter complex.

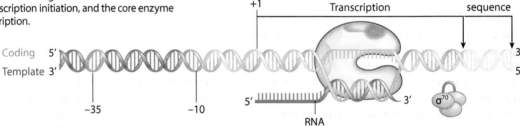

Start site
+1
Transcription
Termination sequence
Coding 5′
Template 3′
σ⁷⁰
3′
5′
−35
−10
Open promoter

3 RNA polymerase holoenzyme initiates transcription and begins RNA synthesis. The sigma subunit dissociates shortly after transcription initiation, and the core enzyme continues transcription.

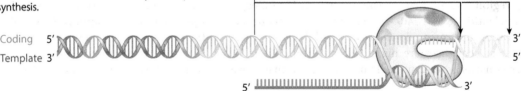

Start site
+1
Transcription
Termination sequence
Coding 5′
Template 3′
−35
−10
5′
3′
σ⁷⁰
RNA

4 The core enzyme synthesizes until it encounters the termination sequence. As RNA synthesis progresses, the DNA duplex unwinds to allow the template strand to direct RNA assembly. The duplex closes following synthesis.

Start site
+1
Transcription
Termination sequence
Coding 5′
Template 3′
3′
5′
5′
3′

5 Transcription terminates at the termination sequence, and the core enzyme and RNA transcript are released.

Start site
+1
Termination sequence
Coding 5′
Template 3′
3′
5′
5′
RNA transcript
3′

PROBLEM DNA sequences in the promoter region of 10 *E. coli* genes are shown. Sequences at the −35 and −10 sites are boxed.

a. Use the sequence information provided to deduce the −35 and −10 consensus sequences.

b. Speculate on the relative effects on transcription of a mutation in a promoter consensus region versus a mutation in the sequence between consensus regions.

> **BREAK IT DOWN:** Promoter consensus sequences are similar in different genes and bind transcriptionally active proteins (p. 273).

> **BREAK IT DOWN:** Research methods directed at detecting promoters and assessing their functionality are described in Research Technique 8.1 and Figure 8.11.

Gene	−35 region		−10 region	+1
A2	AATGC TTGACT CTGTAGCGGGAAGGCG--	TATAAT GCACACC-	C CGC
bio	AAAAC GTGTTT TTTGTTGTTAATTCGGTG	TAGACT TGT---AA	A CCT
his	AGTTC TTGCTT TCTAACGTGAAAGTGGTT	TAGGTT AAAAGAC-	A TCA
lac	CAGGC TTTACA CTTTATGCTTCCGGCTCG	TATGTT GTG-TGG-	A ATT
lacI	GAATG GCGCAA AACTTTTCGCGGTATGG-	CATGAT AGCGCCC-	G GAA
leu	AAAAG TTGACA TCCGTTTTTGTATCCAG-	TAACTC TAAAAGC-	A TAT
recA	AACAC TTGATA CTGTATGAGCATACAG--	TATAAT TGCTTC--	A ACA
trp	AGCTG TTGACA ATTAATCATCGAACTAG-	TTAACT AGTACGC-	A AGT
tRNA	AACAC TTTACA GCGGGCCGTCATTTGA--	TATGAT GCGCCCC-	G CTT
X1	TCCGC TTGTCT TCCTAGGCCGACTCCC--	TATAAT GCGCCTCCA	T CG

Solution Strategies	Solution Steps

Evaluate

1. Identify the topic this problem addresses and the nature of the required answer.

2. Identify the critical information provided in the problem.

1. This question concerns bacterial promoters. The answer requires identification of consensus sequences for −35 and −10 regions of promoters and speculation about the consequences of promoter mutations.

2. The problem provides promoter sequence information for 10 *E. coli* genes and identifies the segment of each promoter containing the −10 and −35 regions.

Deduce

3. Examine the −10 and −35 sequences of these promoters, and look for common patterns.

> **TIP:** A consensus sequence identifies the most common nucleotide at each position in a DNA segment.

3. The −10 and −35 sites are the location of RNA polymerase binding during transcription initiation. Count the numbers of A, T, C, and G in each position in the boxed regions.

Solve

4. Determine the consensus sequence at the −10 and −35 regions.

> **TIP:** Identify the most commonly occurring nucleotide in each position of the 6-nucleotide consensus region of these genes.

Answer a

4. At the −10 site, and moving left to right (toward +1), the most common nucleotides in each position in the consensus region, and the number of times they occur in that position, are

$$\text{T A T A A T}$$
$$(9)\ (9)\ (6)\ (5)\ (5)\ (9)$$

At the −35 site, also moving left to right (toward the +1), the most common nucleotides in each position, and the number of times they occur in that position, are

$$\text{T T G A C A}$$
$$(8)\ (9)\ (8)\ (6)\ (6)\ (6)$$

Answer b

5. Compare and contrast the likely effects of consensus sequence mutations with those of mutations occurring between consensus regions.

5. Mutation in a consensus sequence is likely to alter the efficiency with which a protein binds to the promoter and to decrease the amount of gene transcription. In contrast, mutations between consensus sequences are unlikely to alter gene transcription because the sequences in these intervening regions do not bind tightly to RNA polymerase.

Table 8.2	*Escherichia coli* RNA Polymerase Sigma Subunits			
Subunit	Molecular Weight (Daltons)	Consensus Sequence		Function
		−35	−10	
σ^{28}	28	TAAA	GCCGATAA	Flagellar synthesis and chemotaxis
σ^{32}	32	CTTGAA	CCCCATTA	Heat shock genes
σ^{54}	54	CTGGPyAPyPu	TTGCA	Nitrogen metabolism
σ^{70}	70	TTGACA	TATAAT	Housekeeping genes

Bacterial promoters often differ from the consensus sequence by one or more nucleotides, and some are different at several nucleotides. Since considerable DNA-sequence variation occurs among promoters, it is reasonable to ask how RNA polymerase is able to recognize promoters and reliably initiate RNA synthesis. For an answer, we turn to the sigma subunits that confer promoter recognition and chain-initiation ability on RNA polymerase.

Four alternative sigma subunits identified in *E. coli* are named according to their molecular weight (Table 8.2). Each alternative sigma subunit leads to recognition of a different set of −10 and −35 consensus sequences by the holoenzyme. These different consensus sequence elements are found in promoters of different types of genes; thus, the sigma subunit that it becomes attached to determines the specific gene promoters a holoenzyme will recognize.

The sigma subunit σ^{70} is the most common in bacteria. It recognizes promoters of "housekeeping genes," the genes whose protein products are continuously needed by cells. Because of the constant need for their products, housekeeping genes are continuously expressed. Subunits σ^{54} and σ^{32} recognize promoters of genes involved in nitrogen metabolism and genes expressed in response to environmental stress such as heat shock and are utilized when the action of these genes is required. The fourth sigma subunit, σ^{28}, recognizes promoters for genes required for bacterial chemotaxis (chemical sensing and motility).

The specificity of each type of sigma subunit for different promoter consensus sequences produces RNA polymerase holoenzymes that have different DNA-binding specificities. Microbial geneticists estimate that each *E. coli* cell contains about 3000 RNA polymerase holoenzymes at any given time and that each of the four kinds of sigma subunits is represented to a differing degree among them. Because sigma subunits readily attach and detach from core enzymes in response to changes in environmental conditions, the organism is able to change its transcription patterns to adjust to different conditions.

Transcription Elongation and Termination

Upon reaching the +1 nucleotide, the holoenzyme begins RNA synthesis by using the template strand to direct RNA assembly. The holoenzyme remains intact until the first 8 to 10 RNA nucleotides have been joined. At that point, the sigma subunit dissociates from the core enzyme, which continues its downstream progression (❸ in Foundation Figure 8.6). The sigma subunit itself remains intact and can associate with another core enzyme to transcribe another gene.

Downstream progression of the RNA polymerase core is accompanied by DNA unwinding ahead of the enzyme to maintain approximately 18 bp of unwound DNA (❹). As the RNA polymerase passes, progressing at a rate of approximately 40 nucleotides per second, the DNA double helix reforms in its wake. When transcription of the gene is completed, the 5' end of the RNA trails off the core enzyme (❺).

The end product of transcription is a single-stranded RNA that is complementary and antiparallel to the template DNA strand. The transcript has the same 5'-to-3' polarity as the coding strand of DNA, the strand complementary to the template strand. The coding strand and the newly formed transcript also have identical nucleotide sequences, except for the presence of uracil in the transcript in place of thymine in the coding strand. For this reason, gene sequences are written in 5'-to-3' orientation as single-stranded sequences based on the coding strand of DNA. This allows easy identification of the mRNA sequence of a gene by simply substituting U for T.

Gene transcription is not a one-time event, and shortly after one round of transcription is initiated, a second round begins with new RNA polymerase–promoter interaction. Following sigma subunit dissociation and core enzyme synthesis of 50 to 60 RNA nucleotides, a new holoenzyme can bind to the promoter and initiate a new round of transcription while the first core enzyme continues along the gene. In addition, if the transcript under construction is mRNA, the 5' end is immediately available to begin translation. In contrast, transcripts that are functional RNAs, such as transfer and ribosomal RNA, must await the completion of transcription before undergoing the folding into secondary structures that readies them for cellular action.

Transcription Termination Mechanisms

Termination of transcription in bacterial cells is signaled by a DNA termination sequence that usually contains a repeating sequence producing distinctive 3' RNA sequences.

Termination sequences are downstream of the stop codon; thus, they are transcribed after the coding region of the mRNA and so are not translated. Two transcription termination mechanisms occur in bacteria. The most common is **intrinsic termination,** a mechanism dependent only on the occurrence of specialized repeat sequences in DNA that induce the formation in RNA of a secondary structure leading to transcription termination. Less frequently, bacterial gene transcription terminates by **rho-dependent termination,** a mechanism characterized by a different terminator sequence and requiring the action of a specialized protein called the **rho protein.**

Intrinsic Termination Most bacterial transcription termination occurs exclusively as a consequence of termination sequences encoded in DNA—that is, by intrinsic termination. Intrinsic termination sequences have two features. First, they are encoded by a DNA sequence containing an **inverted repeat,** a DNA sequence repeated in opposite directions but with the same 5′-to-3′ polarity. **Figure 8.7** shows the inverted repeats ("repeat 1" and "repeat 2") in a termination sequence, separated by a short spacer sequence that is not part of either repeat. The second feature of intrinsic termination sequences is a string of adenines on the template DNA strand that begins at the 5′ end of the repeat 2 region. Transcription of inverted repeats produces mRNA with complementary segments that are able to fold into a short double-stranded stem ending with a single-stranded loop. This secondary structure is a **stem-loop structure,** also known as a **hairpin.** A string of uracils complementary to the adenines on the template strand immediately follows the stem-loop structure at the 3′ end of the RNA.

The formation of a stem-loop structure followed immediately by a poly-U sequence near the 3′ end of RNA causes the RNA polymerase to slow down and destabilize. In addition, the 3′ U-A region of the RNA–DNA duplex contains the least stable of the complementary base pairs. Together, the instability created by RNA polymerase slowing and the U-A base pairs induces RNA polymerase to release the transcript and separate from the DNA. The behavior of RNA polymerase during intrinsic termination of transcription is like that of a bicycle rider at slow speed. Slow forward momentum creates instability and eventually the rider loses balance. In a similar way, RNA polymerase is destabilized as it slows while transcribing inverted repeat sequences, and it falls off DNA when the transcript is released where A-U base pairs form.

Rho-Dependent Termination In contrast to the more common intrinsic termination, certain bacterial genes require the action of rho protein to bind to nascent mRNA and catalyze separation of mRNA from RNA polymerase to terminate transcription. Genes whose transcription is rho-dependent have termination sequences that are

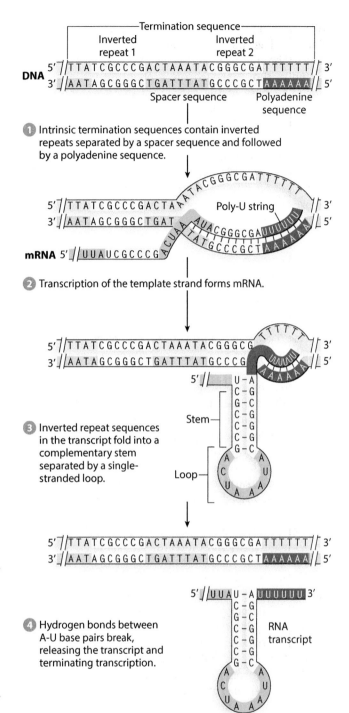

Figure 8.7 Intrinsic termination of transcription is driven by the presence of inverted repeat DNA sequences.

distinct from those in genes utilizing intrinsic termination. Stem-loop structures often form as part of rho-dependent termination, but rho-dependent terminator sequences do not have a string of uracil residues. Instead, the sequences contain a **rho utilization site,** or **rut site,** which is a stretch of approximately 50 nucleotides that is rich in cytosine and poor in guanine.

Rho protein is composed of six identical polypeptides and has two functional domains, both of which are utilized during the two-step process of transcription termination. The first step is initiated when rho protein is activated by an ATP molecule that binds to one functional domain of rho. Activated rho protein utilizes its second domain to bind to the rut site of the RNA transcript. Using ATP-derived energy, rho then moves along the mRNA in the 3′ direction, eventually catching up to RNA polymerase that has slowed near a terminator sequence. As the rho travels, it catalyzes the breakage of hydrogen bonds between mRNA and the DNA template strand. The bond breakage releases the transcript from the RNA polymerase and induces the polymerase to release the DNA.

8.3 Archaeal and Eukaryotic Transcription Displays Structural Homology and Common Ancestry

Bacteria use a single RNA polymerase core enzyme and several alternative sigma subunits to transcribe all genes. Similarly, archaea have a single type of RNA polymerase. Eukaryotes, by contrast, each have multiple RNA polymerases that are specialized for the transcription of different genes. The archaeal and eukaryotic RNA polymerases responsible for the transcription of most polypeptide-producing genes share a common structure that is divergent from the bacterial RNA polymerase. Transcription in archaea and eukaryotes progresses through the same four stages we described for bacteria: promoter recognition, transcription initiation, transcript elongation, and transcription termination. Several structural and functional factors make transcription more complex in archaea and eukaryotes. First, eukaryotic promoters and consensus sequences are considerably more diverse than in *E. coli*, and eukaryotes have three different RNA polymerases that recognize different promoters, transcribe different genes, and produce different RNAs. Promoter consensus sequences in archaea are considerably less complicated than those in eukaryotes, but they appear to be more diverse than bacterial promoter sequences. Second, the molecular apparatus assembled at promoters to initiate and elongate transcription is more complex in eukaryotes and in archaea. Third, eukaryotic genes contain introns and exons, requiring extensive post-transcriptional processing of mRNA. Archaeal genes generally do not contain introns, although there is RNA splicing of archaeal pre-tRNAs in a similar manner to eukaryotic pre-tRNA splicing. We describe these details in a later section. Finally, eukaryotic DNA is permanently associated with a large amount of protein to form a compound known as *chromatin*.

Chromatin plays a central role in regulating eukaryotic transcription. Chromatin structure is a permanent feature and a dynamic feature of eukaryotic genomes. Its state controls the accessibility of DNA to transcription, either permitting or blocking RNA polymerase and transcription factor access to promoters. In later chapters, we discuss chromatin structure (Chapter 11) and explore the functional role of chromatin in the regulation of gene expression in eukaryotes (Chapter 15).

Eukaryotic and Archaeal RNA Polymerases

Three different RNA polymerases transcribe distinct classes of RNA coded by eukaryotic genomes: **RNA polymerase I (RNA pol I)** transcribes three ribosomal RNA genes, **RNA polymerase II (RNA pol II)** is responsible for transcribing messenger RNAs that encode polypeptides as well as for transcribing most small nuclear RNA genes, and **RNA polymerase III (RNA pol III)** transcribes all transfer RNA genes as well as one small nuclear RNA gene and one ribosomal RNA gene. RNA pol II and RNA pol III are responsible for miRNA and siRNA synthesis.

The RNA polymerases of members of all three domains of life share similarities of sequence and function. The *E. coli* RNA polymerase core enzyme has five units. Each of these subunits has a homolog in the 10 to 13 subunit (depending on the species) archaeal RNA polymerase and in the 10 to 12 subunit (depending on the species) eukaryotic RNA polymerase II (Table 8.3).

Despite differences in sizes and molecular complexity, the RNA polymerases have a similar overall structure, forming a characteristic shape one reminiscent of DNA polymerase (see Figure 7.23), with a "hand" composed of protein "fingers" to help RNA polymerase grasp DNA, and a "palm" in which polymerization takes place. These similarities of RNA polymerase structure and function are a direct result of the shared evolutionary history of bacteria, archaea, and eukaryotes.

Table 8.3	RNA Polymerase Composition	
Bacteria	**Archaea**	**Eukarya**
Escherichia coli 5 subunits	*Sulfolobus solfataricus* 10 subunits	*Saccaromyces cerevisiae* (RNA pol II) 12 subunits
Homologous proteins:		
β′	RpoA′/A″	Rpb1
β	RpoB	Rpb2
αI	RpoD	Rpb3
ω	RpoK	Rpb6
αII	RpoL	Rpb11
Additional proteins:		
	RpoE, RpoF, RpoH,	Rpb4, Rpb5, Rpb7, Rpb8,
	RpoN and RpoP	Rpb9, Rpb10, Rpb12

Consensus Sequences for Eukaryotic RNA Polymerase II Transcription

RNA polymerase II transcribes eukaryotic polypeptide-coding genes into mRNA. The promoters for these genes are numerous and highly diverse, with different overall lengths and differences in the number and type of consensus sequences prominent among the sources of promoter variation. Given these characteristics, it is reasonable to ask how RNA polymerases locate promoter DNA for different genes.

Three lines of investigation help researchers to identify and characterize promoters of different polypeptide-coding genes: (1) promoters are identified by determining which DNA sequences are bound by proteins associated with RNA pol II during transcription, (2) putative promoter sequences from different genes are compared to evaluate their similarities, and (3) mutations that alter gene transcription are examined to identify how DNA base-pair changes affect transcription. **Research Technique 8.1** discusses the experimental identification and analysis of promoters.

Research Technique 8.1

Band Shift Assay to Identify Promoters

PURPOSE The functional action of promoters in transcription depends on consensus DNA sequences that bind RNA polymerase and transcription factor proteins. To locate promoters, molecular biologists first scan DNA for potential promoter consensus sequences and then determine that the sequence binds transcriptionally active proteins.

MATERIALS AND PROCEDURES Fragments of DNA containing suspected promoter consensus sequence are examined by two experimental methods. The first, called *band shift assay*, verifies that the sequence of interest binds proteins. The second, called *DNA footprint protection assay*, identifies the exact location of the protein-binding sequence.

In band shift assay, two identical samples of DNA fragments that contain suspected consensus sequence are analyzed. One DNA sample is a control to which no transcriptional proteins are added. The experimental DNA sample, on the other hand, has transcriptional proteins added. Both the control and the experimental DNA samples are subjected to electrophoresis.

DNA footprint protection also begins with two identical samples of DNA fragments containing suspected consensus sequences. All fragments are end-labeled with ^{32}P. The experimental DNA is mixed with transcriptional proteins, but the control sample is not. Both samples are exposed to DNase I that randomly cuts DNA that is not protected by protein. The samples are run in separate lanes of an electrophoresis gel, and each end-labeled fragment produced is identified by autoradiography.

DESCRIPTION In the band shift assay result, notice that the electrophoretic mobility of experimental DNA is slower than that of control DNA. This is the anticipated result if the experimental sample contains consensus sequence that is bound by transcriptional proteins. The bound protein increases the molecular weight of the experimental sample and slows its migration relative to the same DNA without bound protein. In the DNA footprint protection assay, notice that the experimental DNA lane contains a gap in which no DNA fragments appear. The gap represents "footprint protection" for the portion of the fragment that is protected from DNase I digestion

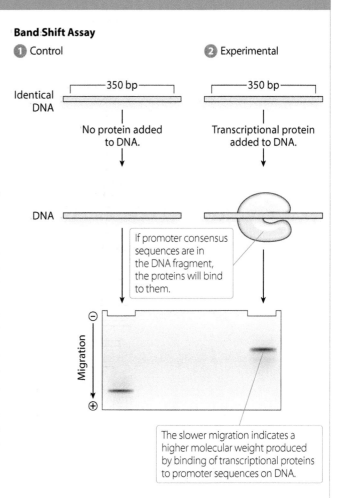

Band Shift Assay

1 Control   **2** Experimental

Identical DNA

|← 350 bp →| |← 350 bp →|

No protein added to DNA.   Transcriptional protein added to DNA.

DNA

If promoter consensus sequences are in the DNA fragment, the proteins will bind to them.

Migration

The slower migration indicates a higher molecular weight produced by binding of transcriptional proteins to promoter sequences on DNA.

by bound transcriptional proteins. No such protection occurs for the control fragment that is randomly cleaved.

CONCLUSION Evidence from these two methods constitutes necessary but not sufficient evidence that the DNA fragment contains a promoter. The final piece of evidence that a DNA fragment contains a promoter rests on mutational analysis that identifies functional changes caused by mutations of specific nucleotides of promoter consensus sequences (see Figure 8.11).

(continued)

Research Technique 8.1 Continued

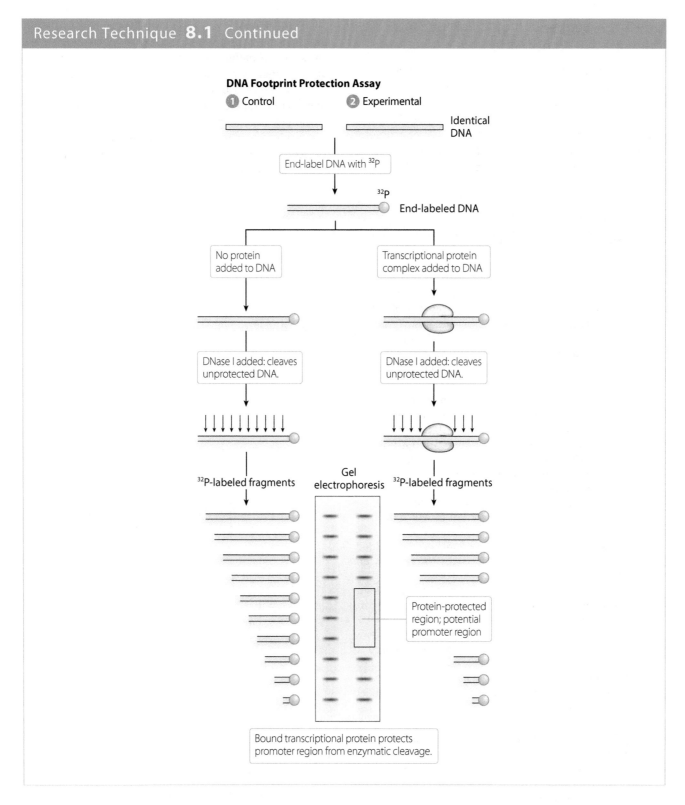

DNA Footprint Protection Assay

① Control   ② Experimental

Identical DNA

End-label DNA with ³²P

³²P
End-labeled DNA

No protein added to DNA

Transcriptional protein complex added to DNA

DNase I added: cleaves unprotected DNA.

DNase I added: cleaves unprotected DNA.

³²P-labeled fragments

Gel electrophoresis

³²P-labeled fragments

Protein-protected region; potential promoter region

Bound transcriptional protein protects promoter region from enzymatic cleavage.

The most common eukaryotic promoter consensus sequence, the *TATA box*, is shown in Figure 8.8 as part of a set of three consensus segments that were the first eukaryotic promoter elements to be identified. A **TATA box,** also known as a **Goldberg-Hogness box,** is located approximately at position −25 relative to the beginning of the transcriptional start site. Consisting of 6 bp with the consensus sequence TATAAA, it is the most strongly conserved promoter element in eukaryotes. The figure shows two additional consensus sequence elements that are more variable in their frequency in promoters. A 4-bp consensus sequence identified as the **CAAT box** is most commonly located near −80 when it is present in the promoter. An upstream GC-rich region called the **GC-rich box,** with

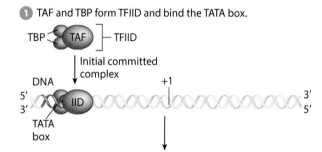

	GC-rich box	CAAT box		TATA box	
DNA 5′	GGGCGG	CAAT		TATAAA	3′
3′	CCCGCC	GTTA		ATATTT	5′
	−90	−80		−25	+1

Figure 8.8   Three eukaryotic promoter consensus sequence elements. The TATA box and the CAAT box are common; the presence of the upstream GC-rich box is more variable.

a consensus sequence GGGCGG located −90 or more upstream of the transcription start, has a frequency that is less than that of CAAT box sequences.

Comparison of eukaryotic promoters reveals a high degree of variability in the type, number, and location of consensus sequence elements (**Figure 8.9**). Some promoters contain all three of the consensus sequences identified above, others contain one or two of these consensus elements, some contain none at all, and many contain other types of consensus sequence elements altogether. For example, the thymidine kinase gene contains TATA, CAAT, and GC-rich boxes along with an octamer (OCT) sequence, called an OCT box. The histone *H2B* gene contains two OCT boxes in addition to a TATA box and a pair of CAAT boxes. All of these consensus sequence elements play important roles in the binding of *transcription factors,* a group of transcriptional proteins described below.

Promoter Recognition

RNA polymerase II recognizes and binds to promoter consensus sequences in eukaryotes with the aid of proteins called **transcription factors (TF).** The TF proteins bind to promoter regulatory sequences and influence transcription initiation by interacting, directly or indirectly, with RNA polymerase. Transcription factors that influence mRNA transcription, and therefore interact with RNA pol II, are given the designation TFII. Individual TFII proteins also carry a letter designation, such as A, B, or C.

In most eukaryotic promoters, the TATA box is the principal binding site for transcription factors during

promoter recognition. At the TATA box, a protein called TFIID, a multisubunit protein containing **TATA-binding protein (TBP)** and subunits of a protein called **TBP-associated factor (TAF),** binds the TATA box sequence. The assembled TFIID binds to the TATA box region to form the **initial committed complex** (**Figure 8.10**). Next, TFIIA, TFIIB, TFIIF, and RNA polymerase II join the

① TAF and TBP form TFIID and bind the TATA box.

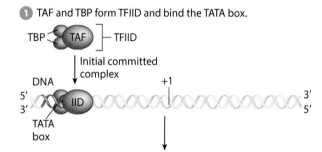

② The addition of TFIIA, TFIIB, RNA polymerase II, and TFIIF forms the minimal initiation complex.

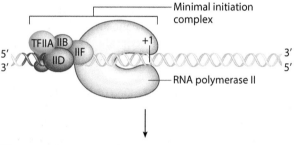

③ TFIIE and TFIIH join to form the preinitiation complex. RNA polymerase II is poised to begin transcription.

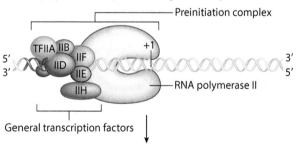

④ RNA polymerase II is released from the GTPs in the preinitiation complex to begin transcription.

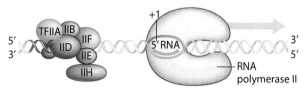

Figure 8.10   Six general transcription factor proteins bind the promoter region to set the stage for eukaryotic transcription by RNA polymerase II.

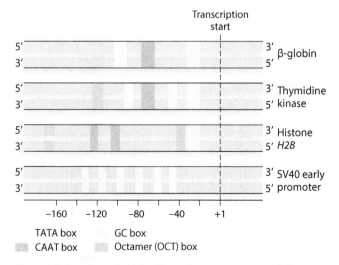

Figure 8.9   Examples of eukaryotic promoter variability.

initial committed complex to form the **minimal initiation complex**, which in turn is joined by TFIIE and TFIIH to form the **preinitiation complex (PIC)**. The complete **initiation complex** contains six proteins that are commonly identified as **general transcription factors (GTFs)**. Once assembled, the complete initiation complex directs RNA polymerase II to the +1 nucleotide on the template strand, where it begins the assembly of messenger RNA.

While most of the eukaryotic genes that have been examined have a TATA box and undergo TBP binding, there is evidence that some metazoan genes may use a related factor called TLF (*TBP-like factor*). The complexity of TBP, TLF, and associated proteins is analogous to the different sigma factors in prokaryotic systems, thus allowing differential recognition of promoters in eukaryotes.

Detecting Promoter Consensus Elements

The diversity of eukaryotic promoters begs an important question: How do researchers verify that a segment of DNA is a functionally important component of a promoter? The research has two components; the first, outlined in Research Technique 8.1, is discovering the presence and location of DNA sequences that transcription factor proteins will bind to. The second component involves mutational analysis to confirm the functionality of the sequence. Researchers produce many different point mutations in the DNA sequence under study and then compare the level of transcription generated by each mutant promoter sequence with transcription generated by the wild-type sequence.

Figure 8.11 shows a synopsis of promoter mutation analysis from an experiment performed by the molecular biologist Richard Myers and colleagues on a mammalian β-globin gene promoter. These researchers produced mutations of individual base pairs in TATA box, CAAT box, and GC-rich sequences, and of nucleotides between the consensus sequences, to identify the effect of each individual mutation on the relative transcription level of the gene. They found that most base-pair mutations in each of the three consensus regions significantly decreased the transcription level of the gene and found two base substitutions in the CAAT box region that significantly increased transcription. In contrast, mutations outside the consensus regions had nonsignificant effects on transcription level. Such results show the functional importance of specific DNA sequences in promoting transcription and confirm a functional role in transcription for TATA box, CAAT box, and GC-rich sequences.

Enhancers and Silencers

Promoters alone are often not sufficient to initiate transcription of eukaryotic genes, and other regulatory sequences are needed to drive transcription. This is particularly the case for multicellular eukaryotes that have different numbers and patterns of expressed genes in different cells and tissues, and that change their patterns of gene expression as the organisms grow and develop. These *tissue-specific* or *developmental* types of transcriptional regulation are fully discussed in later chapters (Chapters 15 and 20), but here we highlight two categories of DNA transcription-regulating sequences that lead to differential expression of genes.

Enhancer sequences are one important group of DNA regulatory sequences that increase the level of transcription of specific genes. Enhancer sequences bind specific proteins that interact with the proteins bound at gene promoters, and together promoters and enhancers drive transcription of certain genes. In many situations, enhancers are located upstream of the genes they regulate; but enhancers can be located downstream as well. Some enhancers are relatively close to the genes they regulate, but others are thousands to tens of thousands of base pairs away from their target genes. Thus, important questions for molecular biologists are: What proteins are

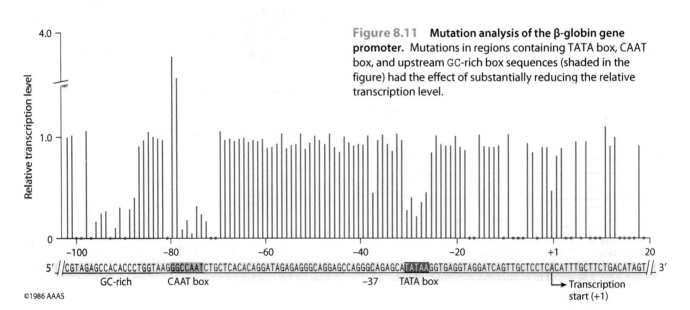

Figure 8.11 Mutation analysis of the β-globin gene promoter. Mutations in regions containing TATA box, CAAT box, and upstream GC-rich box sequences (shaded in the figure) had the effect of substantially reducing the relative transcription level.

©1986 AAAS

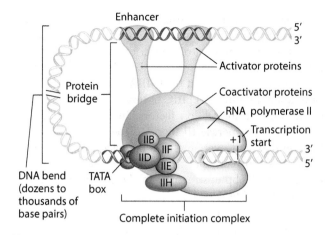

Figure 8.12 Enhancers activate transcription in cooperation with promoters. A protein bridge composed of transcriptional proteins forms between enhancer and promoter sequences, which may be separated by thousands of nucleotides.

bound to enhancers, and how do enhancer sequences regulate transcription of the gene given their different distances from the start of transcription?

The answers are that enhancers bind activator proteins and associated coactivator proteins to form a protein "bridge" that bends the DNA and links the complete initiation complex at the promoter to the activator–coactivator complex at the enhancer (Figure 8.12). The bend produced in the DNA may contain dozens to thousands of base pairs. The action of enhancers and the proteins they bind dramatically increases the efficiency of RNA pol II in initiating transcription, and as a result increases the level of transcription of genes regulated by enhancers.

At the other end of the transcription-regulating spectrum are **silencer sequences,** DNA elements that can act at a great distance to repress transcription of their target genes. Silencers bind transcription factors called repressor proteins, inducing bends in DNA that are similar to what is seen when activators and coactivators bind to enhancers—except with the consequence of reducing the transcription of targeted genes. Like enhancers, silencers can be located upstream or downstream of a target gene and can reside up to several thousand base pairs away from it. Thus enhancers and silencers may operate by similar general mechanisms but with opposite effects on transcription. We discuss these and other eukaryotic regulatory DNA sequences in more detail in Chapter 15.

RNA Polymerase I Promoters

The genes for rRNA are transcribed by RNA polymerase I, utilizing a transcription initiation mechanism similar to that used by RNA pol II. RNA polymerase I is the most specialized eukaryotic RNA polymerase, as it transcribes a limited number of genes. It is recruited to upstream promoter elements following the initial binding of transcription factors, and it transcribes ribosomal RNA genes found in the **nucleolus** (plural, **nucleoli**), a nuclear

organelle containing rRNA and multiple tandem copies of the genes encoding rRNAs (tandem means "end to end"). In *Arabidopsis,* for example, each nucleolus contains about 700 copies of rRNA genes. Nucleoli play a key role in the manufacture of ribosomes. At nucleoli, transcribed ribosomal RNA genes are packaged with proteins to form the large and small ribosomal subunits.

Promoters recognized by RNA pol I contain two similar functional sequences near the start of transcription. The first is the **core element,** stretching from −45 to +20 and bridging the start of transcription, and the second is the **upstream control element,** spanning nucleotides −100 to −150 (Figure 8.13). The core element is essential for transcription initiation, and the upstream control element increases the level of gene transcription. Both of these elements are rich in guanine and cytosine; DNA sequence comparisons show that all upstream control elements have the same base pairs at approximately 85 percent of nucleotide positions, and the same is true of all core elements. Two upstream binding factor 1 (UBF1) proteins bind the upstream control element. A second protein complex, known as sigma-like factor 1 (SL1) protein, binds the core

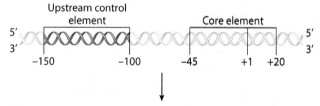

① The core element initiates transcription, and the upstream control element increases transcription efficiency.

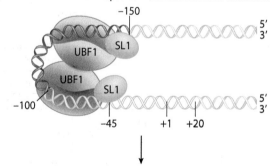

② UBF1 and SL1 bind to upstream control and core elements.

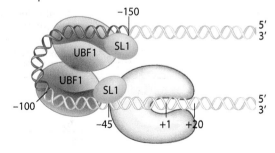

③ RNA pol I is recruited to the core element to initiate transcription.

Figure 8.13 Promoter consensus sequences for transcription initiation by RNA polymerase I.

element. This complex recruits RNA pol I to the core element, to initiate transcription of rRNA genes.

RNA Polymerase III Promoters

The remaining eukaryotic RNA polymerase, RNA polymerase III, is primarily responsible for transcription of tRNA genes. However, it also transcribes one rRNA and other RNA-encoding genes. Each of these genes has a promoter structure that differs significantly from the structure of promoters recognized by RNA pol I or RNA pol II. Small nuclear RNA genes have three upstream elements, whereas the genes for 5S ribosomal RNA and transfer RNA each contain two **internal promoter elements** that are *downstream* of the start of transcription.

The upstream elements of small nuclear RNA genes are a TATA box, a **promoter-specific element (PSE)**, and an octamer (OCT) (Figure 8.14a). A small number of transcription factors—TFIIIs, in this case—bind to these elements and recruit RNA polymerase III, which initiates transcription in a manner similar to that of the other polymerases.

The genes for 5S ribosomal RNA and transfer RNA have internal promoter elements called **internal control regions (ICRs)**; see Figure 8.14b and c. The ICRs are two

short DNA sequences—designated box A and box B in some genes and box A and box C in other genes—located downstream of the start of transcription, between nucleotides +55 and +80 (Figure 8.15). To initiate transcription, box B or box C is bound by TFIIIA, which facilitates the subsequent binding of TFIIIC to box A. TFIIIB then binds to the other transcription factors. In the final initiation step, RNA polymerase III binds to the transcription factor complex and overlaps the +1 nucleotide. With RNA polymerase correctly positioned, transcription begins approximately 55 bp upstream of the beginning of box A, at the +1 nucleotide.

Termination in RNA Polymerase I or III Transcription

Each of the eukaryotic RNA polymerases utilizes a different mechanism to terminate transcription. Here we briefly describe termination in transcription by RNA pol I and RNA pol III, leaving termination of RNA pol II transcription for more extensive discussion in Section 8.4. Transcription by RNA polymerase III is terminated in a manner reminiscent of *E. coli* transcription termination. The RNA pol III transcribes a terminator sequence that creates a string of uracils in the transcript. The poly-U string is similar to the string that occurs in bacterial intrinsic termination (see Section 8.2). The RNA pol III

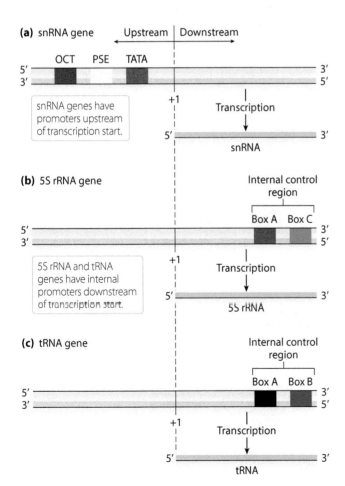

Figure 8.14   Promoter variation in genes transcribed by RNA polymerase III.

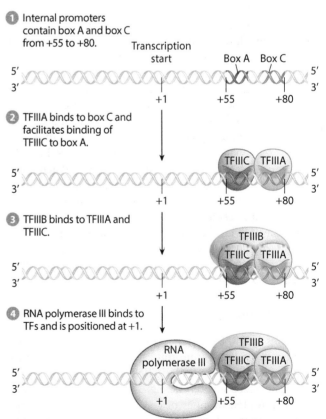

Figure 8.15   Promoter internal control regions for transcription by RNA polymerase III.

terminator sequence does not contain an inverted repeat, however, so no stem-loop structure forms near the 3′ end of RNA.

Transcription by RNA pol I is terminated at a 17-bp consensus sequence that binds **transcription-terminating factor I (TTFI).** The binding site for TTFI is the DNA consensus sequence

$$\text{AGGTCGACCAG}^A/_T^A/_T\text{NTCG}$$

In this sequence, adenine and thymine are equally likely to appear at two adjacent sites, as indicated by the diagonal lines; N signifies a location at which all four nucleotides are more or less equally frequent. A large rRNA precursor transcript is cleaved about 18 nucleotides upstream of the TTFI binding site, so the consensus sequence does not appear in the mature transcript.

Archaeal Transcription

The transcription machinery of archaea is distinct from that of bacteria and represents a simplified and ancestrally related version of the eukaryotic apparatus that is most similar to the RNA pol II holoenzyme. While bacterial transcription utilizes different sigma subunits to alter core polymerase specificity for distinct promoters, eukaryotes use a group of general transcription factors to facilitate the recognition of promoter consensus sequences. In the case of the eukaryotic RNA polymerase II holoenzyme, six general transcription factors are recruited to the promoter. Archaeal transcription follows the eukaryotic model, using three proteins homologous to eukaryotic transcription factors to identify two promoter consensus regions.

Studies examining archaeal promoters and transcription initiation in the thermophilic archaeal species *Sulfolobus shibatae* have identified a TATA-binding protein (TBP, a subunit of TFIID) and transcription factor B (TFB), a homolog of eukaryotic TFIIB, as the only proteins required for interaction with RNA polymerase in the initiation of archaeal transcription (**Figure 8.16**). TBP binds to a TATA box in the archaeal promoter, and TFB binds a BRE box (TFB-recognition element) that is immediately upstream of the TATA box. With TBP and TFB bound to their promoter elements, RNA polymerase is directed approximately 25 base pairs downstream to the transcription start site. A third component, TFIIE[α], a homolog of the eukaryotic GTP TFIIE, is not always required for transcription, but it enhances TATA box binding, thereby stimulating transcription.

8.4 Post-Transcriptional Processing Modifies RNA Molecules

Bacterial, archaeal, and eukaryotic transcripts differ in several ways. For example, eukaryotic transcripts are more stable than bacterial and archaeal transcripts. The half-life of a typical eukaryotic mRNA is measured in hours to days, whereas bacterial mRNAs have an average half-life measured in seconds to minutes. A second difference is the separation, in time and in location, between transcription and translation. Recall that in bacteria the lack of a nucleus leads to coupling of transcription and translation. Similarly, archaea lack a nucleus, leading to the possibility of synchrony between transcription and translation. In eukaryotic cells, on the other hand, transcription takes place in the nucleus, and translation occurs later at free ribosomes or at those attached to the rough endoplasmic reticulum in the cytoplasm. A third difference is the presence of introns in eukaryotic genes that are absent from most bacterial and archaeal genes. Each of these differences comes into play as we consider post-transcriptional modifications of mRNA in eukaryotic cells, which is the focus of this section.

In discussing post-transcriptional processing, we highlight three processing steps that are coordinated during transcription to modify the initial eukaryotic gene mRNA transcript, called **pre-mRNA,** into **mature mRNA,** the fully processed mRNA that migrates out of the nucleus to the cytoplasm for translation. These modification steps are (1) **5′ capping,** the addition of a modified nucleotide to the 5′ end of mRNA; (2) **3′ polyadenylation,** cleavage at the 3′ end of mRNA and addition of a tail of multiple adenines to form the **poly-A tail**; and (3) **intron splicing,** RNA splicing to remove introns and ligate exons. We conclude the section with a discussion of the mechanisms directing alternative splicing and self-splicing RNAs.

Capping 5′ mRNA

After RNA pol II has synthesized the first 20 to 30 nucleotides of the mRNA transcript, a specialized enzyme, guanylyl transferase, adds a guanine to the 5′ end of the pre-mRNA, producing an unusual 5′-to-5′ bond that forms a triphosphate linkage. Additional enzymatic action then methylates the newly added guanine and may also methylate the next one or more nucleotides of the transcript. This addition of guanine to the transcript and the subsequent methylation is known as 5′ capping.

Guanylyl transferase initiates 5′ capping in three steps depicted in **Figure 8.17**. Before capping, the terminal 5′ nucleotide of mRNA contains three phosphate groups,

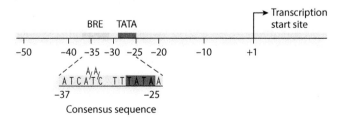

Figure 8.16 Archaea promoter consensus sequences. The TATA box and BRE box sequences bind TBP and TFB along with RNA polymerase to initiate transcription.

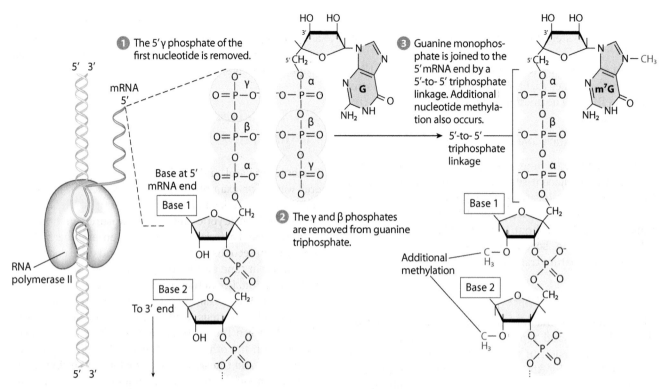

Figure 8.17 **Capping the 5′ end of eukaryotic pre-mRNA.**

labeled α, β, and γ in Figure 8.17. Guanylyl transferase first removes the γ phosphate, leaving two phosphates on the 5′ terminal nucleotide ❶. The guanine triphosphate containing the guanine that is to be added loses two phosphates (γ and β) to form a guanine monophosphate ❷. Then, guanylyl transferase joins the guanine monophosphate to the mRNA terminal nucleotide to form the 5′-to-5′ triphosphate linkage ❸. Methyl transferase enzyme then adds a methyl (CH₃) group to the 7-nitrogen of the new guanine, forming 7-methylguanosine (m⁷G). Methyl transferase may also add methyl groups to 2′–OH of nearby nucleotides of mRNA.

The 5′ cap has several functions, including (1) protecting mRNA from rapid degradation, (2) facilitating mRNA transport across the nuclear membrane, (3) facilitating subsequent intron splicing, and (4) enhancing translation efficiency by orienting the ribosome on mRNA.

Polyadenylation of 3′ Pre-mRNA

Termination of transcription by RNA pol II is not fully understood, but it appears likely to be tied to the processing and polyadenylation of the 3′ end of pre-mRNA. It is clear that the 3′ end of mRNA is not generated by transcriptional termination. Rather, the 3′ end of the pre-mRNA is created by enzymatic action that removes a segment from the 3′ end of the transcript and replaces it with a string of adenine nucleotides, the poly-A tail. This step of pre-mRNA processing is thought to be associated with subsequent termination of transcription.

Figure 8.18 illustrates these steps. Polyadenylation begins with the binding of a factor called cleavage and polyadenylation specificity factor (CPSF) near a six-nucleotide mRNA sequence, AAUAAA, that is downstream of the stop codon and thus not part of the coding sequence of the gene. This six-nucleotide sequence is known as the **polyadenylation signal sequence.** The binding of cleavage-stimulating factor (CStF) to a uracil-rich sequence several dozen nucleotides downstream of the polyadenylation signal sequence quickly follows, and the binding of two other cleavage factors, CFI and CFII, and polyadenylate polymerase (PAP) enlarges the complex ❶. The pre-mRNA is then cleaved 15 to 30 nucleotides downstream of the polyadenylation signal sequence ❷. The cleavage releases a transcript fragment bound by CFI, CFII, and CStF, which is later degraded ❸. The 3′ end of the cut pre-mRNA then undergoes the enzymatic addition of 20 to 200 adenine nucleotides that form the 3′ poly-A tail through the action of CPSF and PAP ❹. After addition of the first 10 adenines, molecules of poly-A-binding protein II (PABII) join the elongating poly-A tail and increase the rate of adenine addition ❺. The 3′ poly-A tail has several functions, including (1) facilitating transport of mature mRNA across the nuclear membrane, (2) protecting mRNA from degradation, and (3) enhancing translation by enabling ribosomal recognition of messenger RNA.

Certain eukaryotic mRNA transcripts do not undergo polyadenylation. The most prominent of these are transcripts of genes producing *histone proteins*, which are key components of *chromatin*, the DNA–protein complex

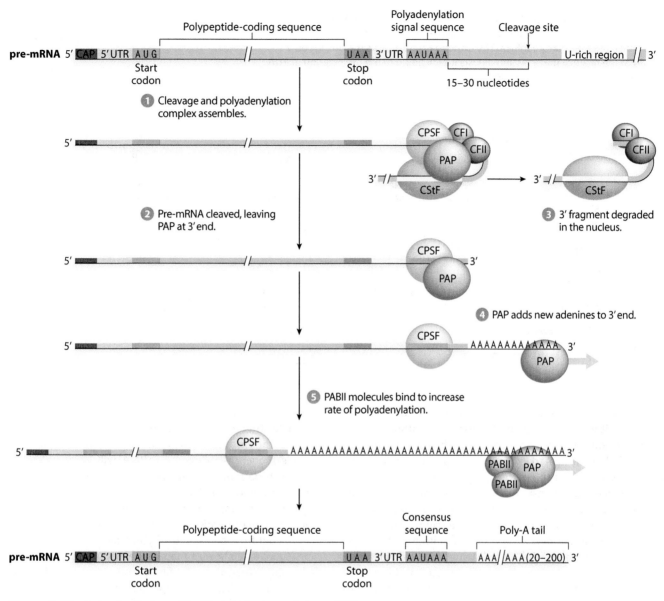

Figure 8.18 **Polyadenylation of the 3′ end of eukaryotic pre-mRNA.**

that makes up eukaryotic chromosomes (see Chapter 11). On these and other "tailless" mRNAs, the 3′ end contains a short stem-loop structure reminiscent of the ones seen in the intrinsic transcription termination mechanism of bacteria. There may be an evolutionary connection between bacterial transcription termination and stem-loop formation on "tailless" eukaryotic mRNAs.

The Torpedo Model of Transcription Termination

The connection between polyadenylation and transcription termination lies in the activity of a specialized RNase (an RNA-destroying enzyme) that attacks and digests the residual RNA transcript attached to RNA pol II after 3′ transcript cleavage (Figure 8.19). Following polyadenylation and 3′

cleavage, the residual segment of the transcript still attached to RNA pol II is not capped at its 5′ end. This end is attacked by the specialized RNase that rapidly digests the remaining transcript. The RNase is thought of as a "torpedo" aimed at the residual mRNA attached to RNA pol II. Studies have shown that the torpedo RNase is a highly processive enzyme, meaning that it rapidly carries out its enzymatic action. Once the RNase destroys the residual mRNA and catches up to RNA pol II, it triggers dissociation of the polymerase from template strand DNA to terminate transcription.

Pre-mRNA Intron Splicing

The third step of pre-mRNA processing is intron splicing, which consists of removing intron segments from pre-mRNA and ligating the exons. Intron splicing requires

Figure 8.19   The torpedo model of eukaryotic transcription termination.
Eukaryotic transcription ❶ leads to 3′ cleavage near the poly-A signal sequence
❷ which releases mature mRNA. The torpedo RNase attacks the uncapped 5′
end of the residual mRNA ❸ and digests it ❹, leading to the dissociation of RNA
polymerase II and the torpedo RNase ❺.

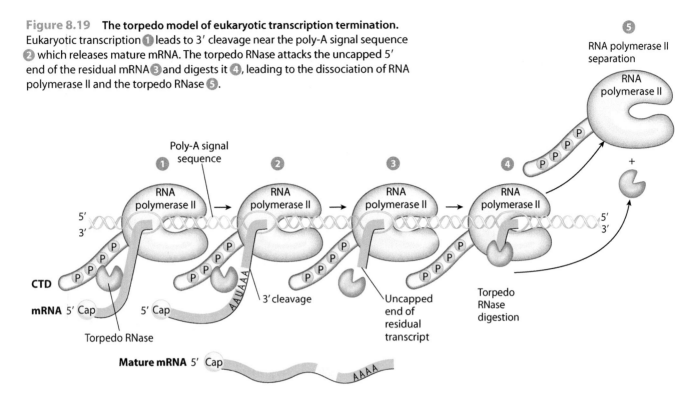

exquisite precision to remove all intron nucleotides accurately without intruding on the exons, and without leaving behind additional nucleotides, so that the mRNA sequence encoded by the ligated exons will completely and faithfully direct synthesis of the correct polypeptide. As an example of the need for precision in intron removal, consider the following "precursor string" made up of exon-like blocks of letters forming three-letter words interrupted by unintelligible intron-like blocks of letters. If editing removes the "introns" accurately, the "edited string" can be divided into its three-letter words to form a "sentence." If an error in editing were to remove too many or too few letters, a nonsense sentence would result.

The finding that introns interrupt the genetically informative segments of eukaryotic genes was a stunning discovery reported independently by the molecular biologists Richard Roberts and Phillip Sharp in 1977. Nothing known about eukaryotic gene structure at the time suggested that most eukaryotic genes are subdivided into intron and exon elements. Roberts and Sharp shared the 1993 Nobel Prize in Physiology or Medicine for their codiscovery of "split genes" in the eukaryotic genome.

Sharp's research group discovered the split nature of eukaryotic genes by using a technique known as R-looping.

In this method, DNA encoding a gene is isolated, denatured to single-stranded form, and then mixed with the mature mRNA transcript from the gene. Regions of the gene that encode sequences in mature mRNA will be complementary to those sequences in the mRNA and will hybridize with them to form a DNA–mRNA duplex. However, DNA segments encoding introns will not find complementary sequences in mature mRNA and will remain single-stranded, looping out from between the hybridized sequences.

Figure 8.20 shows a map of the *hexon* gene studied in R-looping experiments by Sharp and colleagues. The experimental results, photographed by electron microscopy, reveal four DNA–mRNA hybrid regions where exon DNA sequence pairs with mature mRNA sequence. Three single-stranded R-loop sequences are introns which do not pair with mRNA.

Splicing Signal Sequences

Eukaryotic pre-mRNA contains specific short sequences that define the 5′ and 3′ junctions between introns and their neighboring exons. In addition, there is a consensus sequence near each intron end to assist in its accurate identification. The **5′ splice site** is located at the 5′ intron end, where it abuts an exon (**Figure 8.21**). This site

	intron	intron	intron
Precursor string:	youmaynoxpghrcyeomtp	wtipthepfxwubijrdlzmcolz	otandsipthetea
Edited string:	youmaynowtipthepotandsipthetea		
Sentence:	you may now tip the pot and sip the tea		

(a)

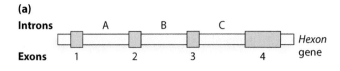

(b)

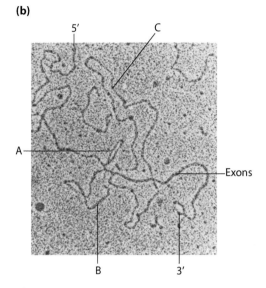

Figure 8.20   R-loop experimental analysis. (a) The *hexon* gene contains four exons (1 to 4) and three introns (A to C). **(b)** Electron micrographs show hybridization of mature mRNA with exon sequences of denatured *hexon* DNA. Intron sequences are not hybridized and remain single stranded.

contains a consensus sequence with a nearly invariant GU dinucleotide forming the 5′-most end of the intron. The consensus sequence includes the last three nucleotides of the adjoining exon, as well as the four or five nucleotides that follow the GU in the intron. At the **3′ splice site** on the opposite end of the intron, a consensus sequence of 11 nucleotides contains a pyrimidine-rich region and a nearly invariant AG dinucleotide at the 3′-most end of the intron. The third consensus sequence, called the branch site, is located 20 to 40 nucleotides upstream of the 3′ splice site. This consensus sequence is pyrimidine-rich and contains an invariant adenine, called the **branch point adenine,** near the 3′ end.

Mutation analysis shows that these consensus sequences are critical for accurate intron removal. Mutations altering nucleotides in any of the three consensus regions can produce abnormally spliced mature mRNA. The abnormal mRNAs—too short if exon sequence is mistakenly removed, too long if intron sequence is left behind, or altered in other ways that result in improper reading of mRNA sequence—produce proteins with incorrect sequences of amino acids (see Chapter 12).

Introns are removed from pre-mRNA by an snRNA–protein complex called the **spliceosome.** The spliceosome is something like a molecular workbench to which pre-mRNA is attached while spliceosome subunit components cut and splice it in a four-step process that, first, cleaves

the 5′ splice site; second, forms a **lariat intron structure** that binds the 5′ intron end to the branch point adenine; third, cleaves the 3′ splice site; and finally, ligates exons and releases the lariat intron to be degraded to its nucleotide components. An electron micrograph of a spliceosome in action is seen in the opener photo for this chapter.

Figure 8.21 illustrates the steps of nuclear pre-mRNA splicing, beginning with the aggregation of five small nuclear ribonucleoproteins (snRNPs; pronounced "snurps") to form a spliceosome. The snRNPs are snRNA–protein subunits designated U1 to U6. The spliceosome is a large complex made up of multiple snRNPs, but its composition is dynamic; it changes throughout the different stages of splicing when individual snRNPs come and go as particular reaction steps are carried out.

Coupling of Pre-mRNA Processing Steps

Each intron–exon junction is subjected to the same spliceosome reactions, raising the question of whether there is a particular order in which introns are removed from pre-mRNA—or whether U1 and U2 search more or less randomly for 5′ splice-site and branch-site consensus sequences, inducing spliceosome formation when they happen to encounter an intron. The answer is that introns appear to be removed one by one, but not necessarily in order along the pre-mRNA. For example, a study of intron splicing of the mammalian *ovomucoid* gene demonstrates the successive steps of intron removal. The *ovomucoid* gene contains eight exons and seven introns. The pre-mRNA transcript is approximately 5.6 kb, and the mature mRNA is reduced to 1.1 kb. Northern blot analysis of *ovomucoid* pre-mRNAs at various stages of intron removal illustrates that each intron is removed separately, rather than all introns being removed at once. The order of intron removal does not precisely match their 5′-to-3′ order in pre-mRNA.

The three steps of pre-mRNA processing are tightly coupled. In comprehensive models developed over the last decade or so, the carboxyl terminal domain (CTD) of RNA polymerase II plays an important role in this coupling by functioning as an assembly platform and regulator of pre-mRNA processing machinery. The CTD is located at the site of emergence of mRNA from the polymerase and contains multiple heptad (seven-member) repeats of amino acids that can be phosphorylated. Binding of processing proteins to the CTD allows the mRNA to be modified as it is transcribed.

Current models propose that "gene expression machines" consisting of RNA polymerase II and an array of pre-mRNA-processing proteins are responsible for the coupling of transcription and pre-mRNA processing. **Foundation Figure 8.22** illustrates this gene expression machine model. The CTD of RNA polymerase II associates with multiple proteins that carry out capping (CAP), intron splicing (SF), and polyadenylation (pA) so that the processes of transcription and pre-mRNA processing occur simultaneously. At the initiation of transcription, phosphorylation (P) along

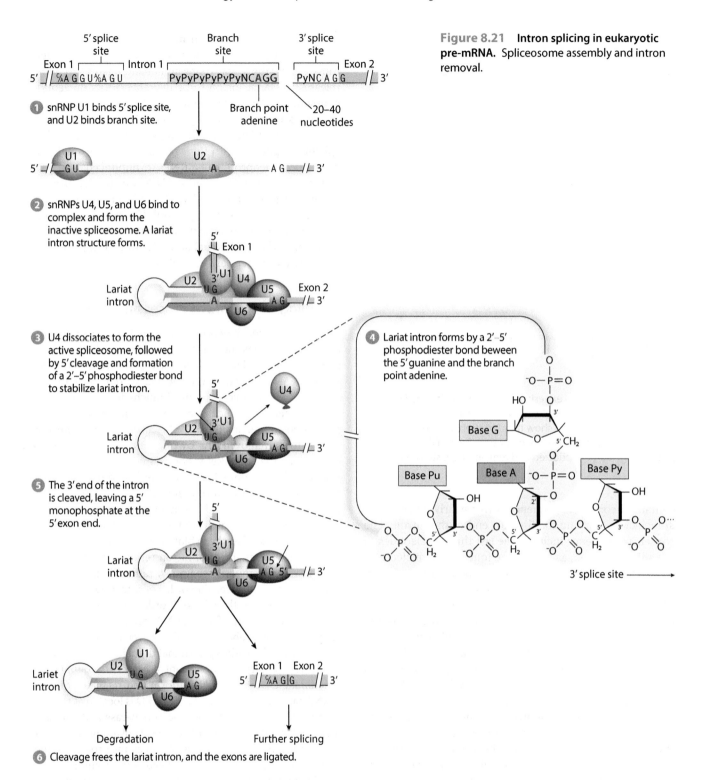

Figure 8.21   Intron splicing in eukaryotic pre-mRNA. Spliceosome assembly and intron removal.

① snRNP U1 binds 5′ splice site, and U2 binds branch site.

② snRNPs U4, U5, and U6 bind to complex and form the inactive spliceosome. A lariat intron structure forms.

③ U4 dissociates to form the active spliceosome, followed by 5′ cleavage and formation of a 2′–5′ phosphodiester bond to stabilize lariat intron.

④ Lariat intron forms by a 2′–5′ phosphodiester bond beween the 5′ guanine and the branch point adenine.

⑤ The 3′ end of the intron is cleaved, leaving a 5′ monophosphate at the 5′ exon end.

⑥ Cleavage frees the lariat intron, and the exons are ligated.

the CTD assists the binding of 5′-capping enzymes, which carry out their capping function and then dissociate. During transcription elongation, specific transcription elongation factors bind the CTD and facilitate splicing-factor binding. The CTD also contains the torpedo RNase responsible for digestion of the residual transcript left attached to RNA pol II by 3′ cleavage linked to polyadenylation. The torpedo RNase is loaded onto the transcript from the CTD to quickly trigger transcription termination.

Alternative Transcripts of Single Genes

Before the complete sequencing of the human genome in the early 2000s, estimates of the number of human genes varied, having been as high as 80,000 to 100,000 genes 20 years or so earlier. A principal reason for this prediction was that human cells produce well over 100,000 distinct polypeptides. It came as something of a surprise, then, when gene annotation of the human genome revealed a total

The Gene Expression Machine Model for Coupling Transcription with pre-mRNA Processing

1 At the initiation of transcription the carboxyl terminal domain (CTD) of RNA polymerase II affiliates with capping (CAP), polyadenylation (pA), splicing factor (SF), and torpedo RNase (RNase).

2 RNA pol II initiates transcription after dissociation of the general transcription factors (GTPs). The pre-mRNA processing proteins on the CTD begin their work, starting with the CAP proteins carrying out 5' capping.

3 Capping proteins dissociate and pre-mRNA elongates.

4 Spliceosome complexes affiliate with pre-mRNA with the aid of SF proteins. Intron splicing takes place as RNA pol continues elongation of mRNA.

5 Polyadenylation proteins identify the pA signal sequence and carry out polyadenylation. Transcription terminates. Splicing continues to completion. Torpedo RNase digests the residual mRNA.

6 Fully processed mature mRNA dissociates from RNA pol II and is transported to cytoplasm for translation. The torpedo RNase digest residual transcript and triggers RNA pol II dissociation to terminate transcription.

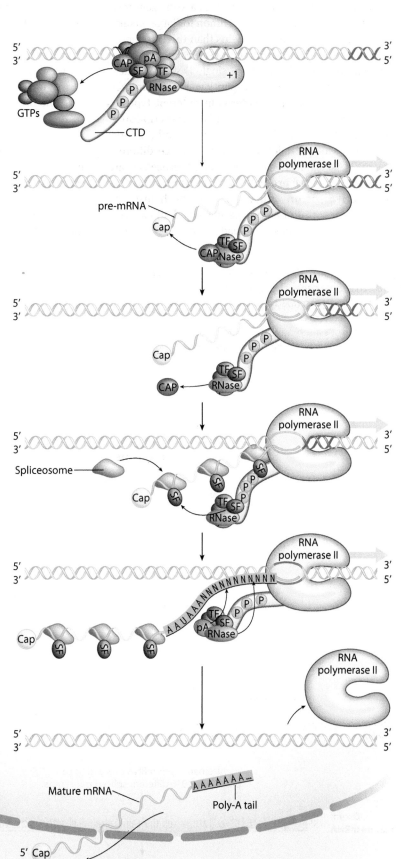

content of approximately 22,800 genes. The difference between the number of genes and the number of polypeptides is mirrored by similar findings in other eukaryotic genomes, especially those of mammals. It is common for large eukaryotic genomes to express more proteins than there are genes in the genomes. Three transcription-associated mechanisms can account for the ability of single DNA sequences to produce more than one polypeptide: (1) pre-mRNA can be spliced in alternative patterns in different types of cells; (2) alternative promoters can initiate transcription at distinct +1 start points in different cell types; and (3) alternative locations of polyadenylation can produce different mature mRNAs. Collectively, these varied processes are identified as **alternative pre-mRNA processing.**

Alternative intron splicing is the mechanism by which post-transcriptional processing of identical pre-mRNAs in different cells can lead to mature mRNAs with different combinations of exons. These alternative mature mRNAs produce different polypeptides. In other words, alternative splicing is a mechanism by which a single DNA sequence can produce more than one specific protein. Alternative splicing is common in mammals—approximately 70 percent of human genes are thought to undergo alternative splicing—but it is less common in other animals, and it is rare in plants.

The products of the human *calcitonin/calcitonin gene-related peptide* (*CT/CGRP*) gene exemplify the process of alternative splicing (Figure 8.23a). The *CT/CGRP* gene produces the same pre-mRNA transcript in many cells, including thyroid cells and neuronal cells. The transcript contains six exons and five introns and includes two alternative polyadenylation sites, one in exon 4 and the other following exon 6. In thyroid cells, *CT/CGRP* pre-mRNA is spliced to form mature mRNA containing exons 1 through 4, using the first

Figure 8.23   Alternative splicing. (a) The *calcitonin/calcitonin gene-related protein* (*CT/CGRP*) gene is transcribed into either calcitonin or CGRP. **(b)** *Dscam* pre-mRNA contains numerous alternatives for exons 4, 6, 9, and 17. Combinatorial splicing could generate as many as 38,016 different mature mRNAs.

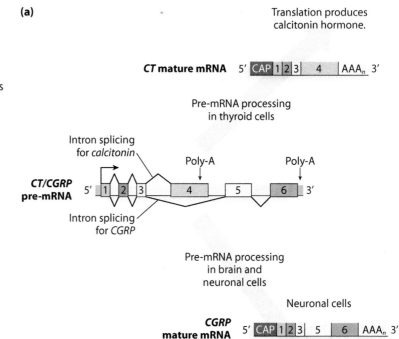

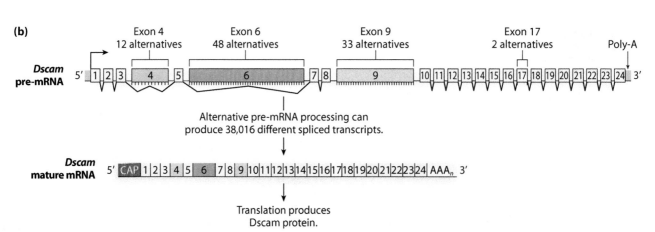

poly-A site for polyadenylation. Translation produces calcitonin, a hormone that helps regulate calcium. In neuronal cells, the same pre-mRNA is spliced to form mature mRNA containing exons 1, 2, 3, 5, and 6. Polyadenylation takes place at the site that follows exon 6, since exon 4 is spliced out as though it were an intron. Translation in neuronal cells produces the hormone CGRP.

One of the most complex patterns of alternative splicing occurs in the *Drosophila Dscam* gene, which produces a protein directing axon growth in *Drosophila* larvae. Mature mRNA from *Dscam* contains 24 exons, but as shown in Figure 8.23b, numerous alternative sequences can be used as exons 4, 6, 9, and 17. In total, more than 38,000 different alternative splicing arrangements of *Dscam* are possible, although not all are observed in the organism.

The use of **alternative promoters** occurs when more than one sequence upstream of a gene can bind transcription factors and initiate transcription. Similarly, **alternative polyadenylation** is possible when genes contain more than one polyadenylation signal sequence that can activate 3′ pre-mRNA cleavage and polyadenylation. Alternative promoters and alternative polyadenylation are driven by the variable expression of transcriptional or polyadenylation proteins in a cell-type-specific manner. The variable expression of transcriptional and polyadenylation proteins generates characteristic mature mRNAs from specific genes in particular cells. The result

is that transcription of a single gene may lead to the production of several different mature mRNAs in different types of cells, and to their translation into distinct proteins in each of those cell types.

A comprehensive example of a single gene for which all three alternative mechanisms operate to produce distinct polypeptides in different cells is that of the rat α-tropomyosin (α-*Tm*) gene that produces nine different mature mRNAs and, correspondingly, nine different tropomyosin proteins from a single gene. Figure 8.24a shows a map of α-*Tm*. The gene contains 14 exons, including alternatives for exons 1, 2, 6, and 9. The gene has two promoters (identified as P_1 and P_2) as well as five alternative polyadenylation sites (identified as A_1 to A_5). The nine distinct mature mRNAs from α-*Tm* are produced in muscle cells (two forms), brain cells (three forms), and fibroblast cells (four forms); see Figure 8.24b. Each different mature mRNA illustrates a unique pattern of promoter selection, intron splicing, and choice of polyadenylation site. All mature mRNAs, and their corresponding tropomyosin proteins, contain the genetic information of exons 3, 4, 5, 7, and 8; however, they may contain distinct information in the alternative exons that depends largely on the cell-type-specific selection of promoter and polyadenylation site.

In striated muscle cells, for example, promoter P_1 and polyadenylation site A_2 are used. The mature mRNA includes the alternative exons 1a, 2b, 6b, 9a, and 9b. In contrast,

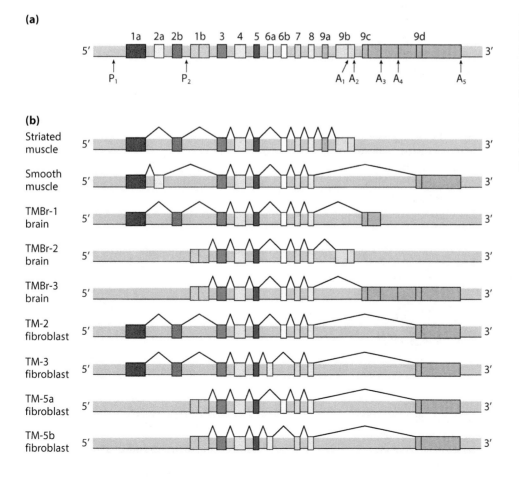

(a)

(b)
Striated muscle
Smooth muscle
TMBr-1 brain
TMBr-2 brain
TMBr-3 brain
TM-2 fibroblast
TM-3 fibroblast
TM-5a fibroblast
TM-5b fibroblast

Figure 8.24 Alternative pre-mRNA processing of the rat α-tropomyosin gene. Alternative splicing patterns are indicated by the arched lines connecting exons. Nine distinct mature mRNAs produced by different types of muscle, brain, and fibroblast cells each produce a different tropomyosin protein.

tropomyosin in smooth muscle cells utilizes promoter P_1 and polyadenylation site A_5, and its mature mRNA contains exons 1a, 2a, 6b, and 9d. Brain cells produce three different tropomyosin proteins, each of which are translated from differentially spliced pre-mRNAs that also utilize different polyadenylation sites. In addition, two forms of the brain cell tropomyosin proteins are translated from mRNAs that utilize promoter P_2, and one from an mRNA utilizing P_1. Among the four different tropomyosin proteins produced in fibroblasts, the mRNAs all use polyadenylation site A_5, but they differ in selection of P_1 versus P_2, and alternative splicing occurs as well. **Genetic Analysis 8.2** guides you through analysis of the results of alternative mRNA processing.

Control of Alternative Splicing

We have seen that specific RNA sequences at 5' and 3' splice sites are crucial to accurate pre-mRNA splicing and that alternative splicing is widespread in many genomes, with some genes having a large number of alternative protein products from different splicing patterns of pre-mRNA.

Obviously, alternative splicing is carefully controlled in cells, but what mechanisms are involved in that control? The answer appears to be specific sequences in exons and in introns that bind splicing proteins to either enhance or suppress splicing at nearby splice sites. The sequences are identified as **exonic** or **intronic splicing enhancers (ESE or ISE)** and **exonic** or **intronic splicing silencers (ESS or ISS)**. ESE and ISE sequences, for example, attract protein rich in serine and arginine (one-letter abbreviations S and R, respectively) called SR proteins (**Figure 8.25**). SR proteins direct spliceosome activity to nearby splice sites. These proteins are the products of a large and diverse family of genes, and differential gene transcription in cells is key to SR-protein control of different splicing patterns.

ESS and ISS sequences seem to work in a manner similar to that of splice enhancer sequences, attracting splice repressor proteins that prevent splicing using nearby splice sites. Current evidence indicates that these splice repressor proteins are members of a diverse group of heterogeneous nuclear ribonucleoproteins (hnRNPs). Binding of hnRNPs to ESS or ISS sequences blocks the action of the spliceosome at nearby splice sites.

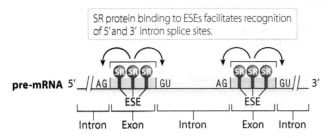

Figure 8.25 **SR-protein recruitment to ESEs, directing spliceosome components to nearby splice sites.** Binding of SR protein to ISEs has a similar result. In contrast, protein binding to ESS and ISS elements blocks nearby spliceosome binding.

Intron Self-Splicing

In addition to introns that are spliced by spliceosomes, certain other RNAs can contain introns that self-catalyze their own removal. Three categories of self-splicing introns, designated group I, group II, and group III introns, have been identified. The molecular biologist Thomas Cech and his colleagues discovered group I introns in 1981, when they observed that a 413-nucleotide precursor mRNA of an rRNA gene from the protozoan *Tetrahymena* could splice itself without the presence of any protein. Following up on this initial observation, Cech and others have shown that group I introns are large, self-splicing ribozymes (catalytically active RNAs) that catalyze their own excision from certain mRNAs and also from tRNA and rRNA precursors in bacteria, simple eukaryotes, and plants. **Intron self-splicing** takes place by way of two transesterification reactions (**Figure 8.26** ❶, ❷) that excise

❶ Exon-intron base pairing. The G-binding site nucleotide attacks the UpA bond, bonding to the adenine and cleaving exon A.

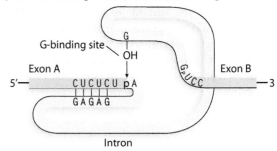

❷ The 3' end of exon A attacks the GpU bond at the intron–exon junction.

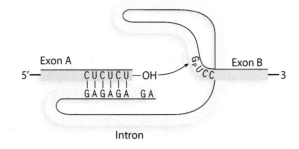

❸ The intron is released, and exons ligate.

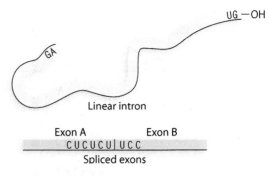

Figure 8.26 **Self-splicing of group I introns.**

PROBLEM The *JLB-1* gene, expressed in several human organs, contains seven exons (1 to 7) and six introns (A to F). Three oligonucleotide probes (I to III), hybridizing to exons 2, 4, and 7, respectively, are indicated by asterisks below the gene map:

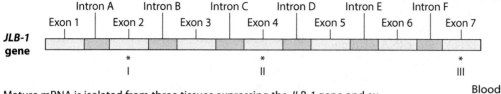

Mature mRNA is isolated from three tissues expressing the *JLB-1* gene and examined by northern blotting using the three oligonucleotide probes indicated above. The probes bind to complementary sequences in mRNA. Northern blot patterns of hybridization between each probe and mRNA isolated from blood, liver, and kidney cells are shown. For each northern blot:

a. Explain the meaning of the hybridization result.

b. Identify the biological process or processes accounting for the observed patterns of hybridization in the northern blots.

> **BREAK IT DOWN:** Molecular probes bind only to their target sequences. A band appears in the northern blot only if the exon target of a probe is present in the mRNA (p. 289, See also p. 349).

> **BREAK IT DOWN:** Differences in the results for different tissues indicate the presence of alternative transcripts of the gene (p. 289, see also p. 349).

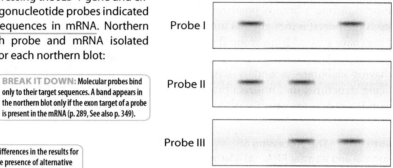

Solution Strategies	Solution Steps

Evaluate

1. Identify the topic this problem addresses and the nature of the required answer.

1. This problem concerns the production of mature mRNAs from a single human gene expressed in different organs. The answer requires identification of the specific mechanisms responsible for the data obtained from each organ.

2. Identify the critical information provided in the problem.

2. The problem gives gene structure, the binding location of each of three molecular probes hybridizing the gene, and the results of three northern blot analyses of mature mRNA from different organs.

Deduce

3. Identify the regions of *JLB-1* that are anticipated to be part of the pre-mRNA.

3. Pre-mRNA from this gene is anticipated to include all intron and exon sequences.

4. Identify the regions expected to be found in mature mRNA.

4. Exon segments are expected in mature mRNA, along with modification at the 5′ mRNA end (capping) and the 3′ end (poly-A tailing).

Solve

5. Determine the hybridization pattern of molecular probes in each tissue.

> **TIP:** Hybridization of a probe occurs when the probe finds its target sequence. The absence of hybridization indicates that the target sequence for a probe is not present.

Answer a

5. Blood: Probes I and II hybridize, but probe III does not. This result indicates that exons 2 and 4 are present in the mature mRNA of blood, but exon 7 is not.

Liver: Probe I fails to hybridize to mRNA from liver, indicating that exon 1 is missing from liver mRNA. Probes II and III hybridize liver mRNA, indicating that exons 4 and 7 are included in the mature transcript.

Kidney: Probe II does not hybridize kidney mRNA, indicating that exon 4 is missing from it. Probes I and III find hybridization targets, indicating that exons 2 and 7 are present in the transcript.

Answer b

6. Interpret the hybridization patterns in each tissue and identify the process or processes that reasonably account for the observed patterns.

> **TIP:** Alternative promoters, alternative polyadenylation sites, and alternative splicing are three mechanisms that lead eukaryotic genomes to generate distinct proteins from the same gene.

6. Blood: The absence of exon 7 is most likely due to either the use of an alternative polyadenylation site that generates 3′ cleavage of pre-mRNA ahead of exon 7 or to differential splicing that removes exon 7 from pre-mRNA during intron splicing.

Liver: The absence of exon 2 is most likely due either to use of an alternative promoter that initiates transcription at a point past exon 2 or to differential splicing of liver pre-mRNA.

Kidney: The absence of exon 4 is most likely the result of differential splicing of pre-mRNA.

For more practice, see Problems 2, 3, and 8.   Visit the Study Area to access study tools.   MasteringGenetics™

the intron and allow exons to ligate ❸. Cech and Sidney Altman shared the 1989 Nobel Prize in Physiology or Medicine for their contributions to the discovery and description of the catalytic properties of RNA.

Group II introns, which are also self-splicing ribozymes, are found in mRNA, tRNA, and rRNA of fungi, plants, protists, and bacteria. Group II introns form highly complex secondary structures containing many stem-loop arrangements. Their self-splicing takes place in a lariat-like manner utilizing a branch point nucleotide that in many cases is adenine. It is thought that nuclear pre-mRNA splicing may have evolved from group II self-splicing introns.

Group III introns and group II introns are similar in having elaborate secondary structures and lariat-like splicing structures that utilize a branch point nucleotide. Group III introns are much shorter than group II introns,

however, and their secondary structures are different from those of group II introns.

Ribosomal RNA Processing

In bacteria, archaea, and eukaryotes, rRNAs are transcribed as large precursor molecules that are cleaved into smaller RNA molecules by removal and discarding of spacer sequences intervening between the sequences of the different RNAs. The *E. coli* genome, for example, contains seven copies of an rRNA gene. Each gene copy is transcribed into a single 30S precursor RNA that is processed by the removal of intervening sequences to yield 5S, 16S, and 23S rRNAs, along with several tRNA molecules (**Figure 8.27a**). All seven gene copies produce the same three rRNAs, but each gene generates a different

Figure 8.27 The processing of ribosomal and transfer RNA. (a) A large transcript is cleaved to produce rRNA and tRNA in *E. coli*. **(b)** Human rRNA genes are part of a 40-kb repeating sequence that produces three rRNAs.

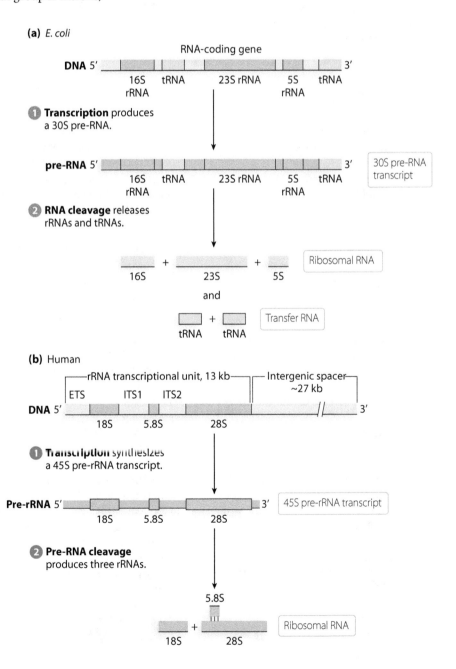

set of tRNAs. There is evidence that archaea use a similar process to produce some rRNA molecules.

Eukaryotic genomes have hundreds of rRNA genes clustered in regions of repeated genes on various chromosomes. Each gene produces a 45S precursor rRNA that contains an external transcription sequence (ETS) and two internal transcription sequences (ITS1 and ITS2) that are removed by processing. The transcript is processed in multiple steps to yield three rRNA molecules weighing 5.8S, 18S, and 28S (Figure 8.27b). Eukaryotic genomes differ somewhat in the steps that process the 45S pre-rRNA transcript. In general, however, the 45S transcript is cleaved to a 41S intermediate from which the 18S transcript is then removed, followed by cleavage that produces the 28S and 5.8S transcripts. The 5.8S and 28S products pair with one another and become part of the same ribosomal subunit. After processing, the resulting rRNAs fold into complex secondary structures and are joined by proteins to form ribosomal subunits. Some

chemical modifications of rRNA, particularly methylation of selected nucleotide bases, occur after completion of transcription.

Transfer RNA Processing

The production of tRNA, whether in bacteria, archaea, or eukaryotes, also requires post-transcriptional processing. Each type of tRNA has distinctive nucleotides and a specific pattern of folding, but all tRNAs have similar structures and functions (Figure 8.28). Some bacterial transfer RNA molecules are produced simultaneously with rRNAs, as described above (see Figure 8.27a). Other tRNAs are transcribed as part of a large pre-tRNA transcript that is then cleaved to yield multiple tRNA molecules. In eukaryotes, tRNA genes occur in clusters on specific chromosomes. Each eukaryotic tRNA gene is individually transcribed by RNA polymerase III, and a single pre-tRNA is produced from each gene.

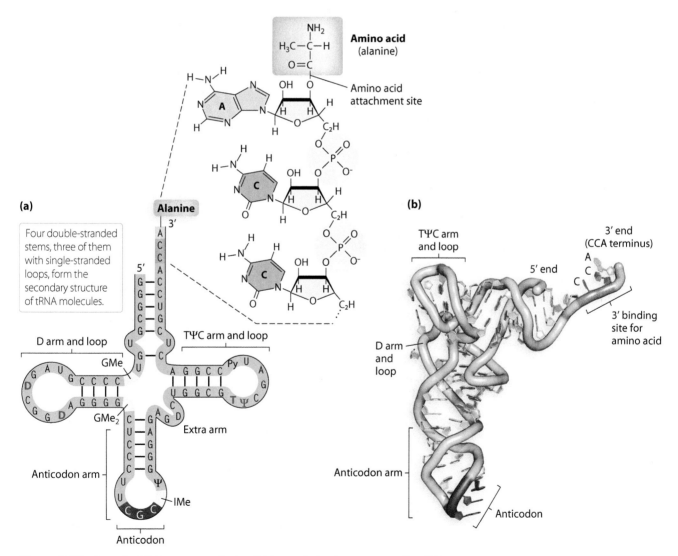

Figure 8.28   Transfer RNA structure. Each tRNA has a distinctive structure. The tRNA carrying alanine is illustrated in two-dimensions (**a**) and three-dimensions (**b**).

The number of different tRNAs produced depends on the type of organism. In bacteria, the exact number of different tRNAs varies, but it is usually substantially *less than* 61, the number of codons found in mRNA. At a minimum, each species must have at least 20 different tRNAs, one for each amino acid, but most produce at least 30 to 40 different tRNAs. The low number of different tRNAs (compared to number of codons) results from a phenomenon called *third-base wobble*, a relaxation of the "rules" of complementary base pairing at the third base of codons (see Chapter 9). Although third-base wobble plays a role in reducing the number of distinct tRNA genes needed in eukaryotic genomes, eukaryotes nevertheless produce a larger number of different tRNAs than bacteria do. Some eukaryotic genomes contain a full complement of 61 different tRNA genes, one corresponding to each codon of the genetic code.

Bacterial tRNAs require processing before they are ready to assume their functional role of transporting amino acids to the ribosome. The precise processing events differ somewhat among tRNAs, but several features are common. First, many tRNAs are cleaved from large precursor tRNA transcripts to produce several individual tRNA molecules. Second, nucleotides are trimmed off the 5′ and 3′ ends of tRNA transcripts to prepare the mature molecule. Third, certain individual nucleotides in different tRNAs are chemically modified to produce a distinctive molecule. Fourth, tRNAs fold into a precise three-dimensional structure that includes four double-stranded stems, three of which are capped by single-stranded loops; each stem and loop constitutes an "arm" of the tRNA molecule. Fifth, tRNAs undergo post-transcriptional addition of bases. The most common addition is three nucleotides, CCA, at the 3′ end of the molecule. This region is the binding site for the amino acid the tRNA molecule transports to the ribosome. Figure 8.28 shows tRNA$_{Ala}$, which carries alanine. The CCA terminus is indicated, along with chemically modified nucleotides in each arm that are characteristic of this tRNA. Both a two-dimensional and a three-dimensional representation are shown.

Eukaryotic and archaeal tRNAs undergo processing modifications similar to those of bacterial tRNAs. In addition, however, eukaryotic pre-tRNAs may contain small introns that are removed during processing. For example, an intron 14 nucleotides in length is removed from the precursor molecule by a specialized nuclease enzyme that cleaves the 5′ and 3′ splice sites of tRNA introns. The cleaved tRNA then refolds to form the anticodon stem, and the enzyme RNA ligase joins the 5′ and 3′ ends of the tRNA.

Post-Transcriptional RNA Editing

A firmly established tenet in the central dogma of biology is the role of DNA as the repository and purveyor of genetic information. Notwithstanding the modifications made to precursor RNA transcripts after transcription, a fundamental principle of biology is that DNA dictates the sequence of mRNA nucleotides and controls the order of amino acids in proteins. And yet, in the mid-1980s, a phenomenon called **RNA editing** was uncovered that is responsible for post-transcriptional modifications that change the genetic information carried by mRNA.

Two kinds of RNA editing occur. In one kind of RNA editing, uracils are inserted into edited mRNA with the assistance of a specialized RNA called **guide RNA (gRNA)**. A guide RNA, transcribed from a separate RNA-encoding gene, contains a sequence complementary to the region of mRNA that it edits. With the aid of a protein complex, a portion of guide RNA pairs with complementary nucleotides of pre-edited mRNA and acts as a template to direct the insertion (and occasionally the deletion) of uracil (**Figure 8.29**). Guide RNA releases edited mRNA after editing is complete. The protein translated from edited mRNA may differ from the protein produced from unedited transcript.

The second kind of RNA editing is by base substitution, and frequently consists of the replacement of cytosine with uracil (C-to-U editing) in mRNA by removal of the amino group from cytosines. We describe the details of this process, known as deamination, in Section 12.3 and here simply examine the consequences of the event. This type of RNA editing has been identified in mammals, most land plants, and several single-celled eukaryotes.

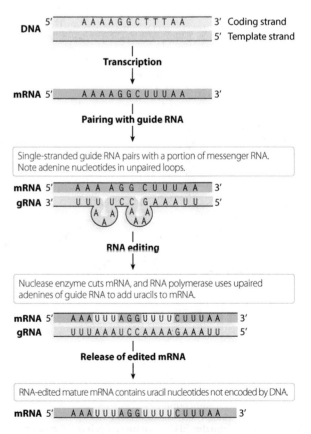

Figure 8.29 Guide RNA (gRNA) directs RNA editing.

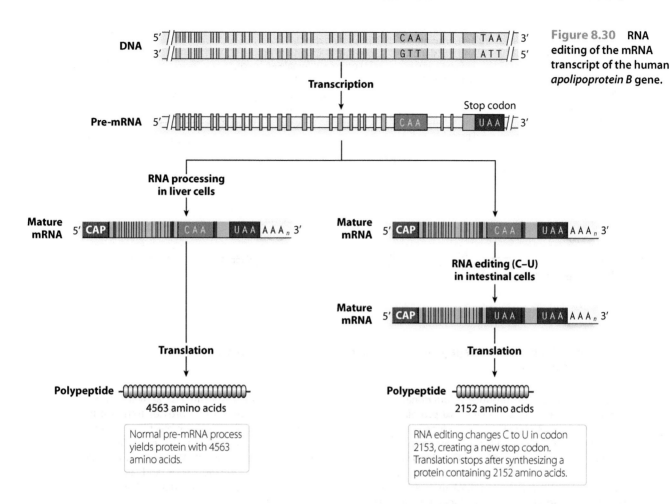

Figure 8.30 RNA editing of the mRNA transcript of the human *apolipoprotein B* gene.

Normal pre-mRNA process yields protein with 4563 amino acids.

RNA editing changes C to U in codon 2153, creating a new stop codon. Translation stops after synthesizing a protein containing 2152 amino acids.

The consequence of C-to-U RNA editing is demonstrated by the protein products of the mammalian *apolipoprotein B* gene (Figure 8.30). An identical gene containing 29 exons is found in all mammalian cells, and the same mRNA is transcribed in all tissues. Part of this messenger RNA sequence includes codon number 2153 that has the sequence CAA and is translated as glutamine in liver apolipoprotein B, a protein consisting of 4563 amino acids. In intestinal cells, however, RNA editing changes the cytosine in codon 2153 to a uracil, converting the codon to UAA. This C-to-U change produced by RNA editing creates a "stop" codon that halts translation after the assembly of the first 2152 amino acids of intestinal apolipoprotein B.

CASE STUDY

Sexy Splicing: Alternative mRNA Splicing and Sex Determination in *Drosophila*

The number of X chromosomes in the nuclei of *Drosophila* embryos is critical in sex determination, but the X/autosome (X/A) ratio proposed by Calvin Bridges (X/A = 1.0 in females and X/A = 0.5 in males) as the underlying cause is not the entire story (see Section 3.4). In fact, the process involves differential gene expression and pre-mRNA splicing. The molecular basis of *Drosophila* sex determination depends on a series of steps that begins with the transcription activation of the *sex-lethal* (*Sxl*) gene, includes alternative splicing of the pre-mRNA transcript of the *transformer* (*Tra*) gene, and culminates with one of two alternative splicing variants of the pre-mRNA transcripts of the *double-sex* (*Dsx*) gene. The Dsx protein directs further transcription activation and repression, leading to female or to male development.

The X/A ratio in fly embryos initially influences the transcription and translation of two X-linked activator proteins called SisA and SisB, and an autosomal gene producing a transcription repressor protein called Deadpan (Figure 8.31). Since the genes producing SisA and SisB are X-linked, early female embryos produce twice as much of each activator as do early male embryos, and the ratio of SisA + SisB to Deadpan differs between female and male embryos. In early female embryos, the ratio of SisA + SisB protein to Deadpan protein leads to transcription of the *Sxl* gene and to the production of Sxl protein. *Sxl* transcription is repressed in male embryos and no Sxl protein is produced.

Sxl protein is a splicing regulator that operates on the pre-mRNA transcript of the *Tra* gene. In female embryos,

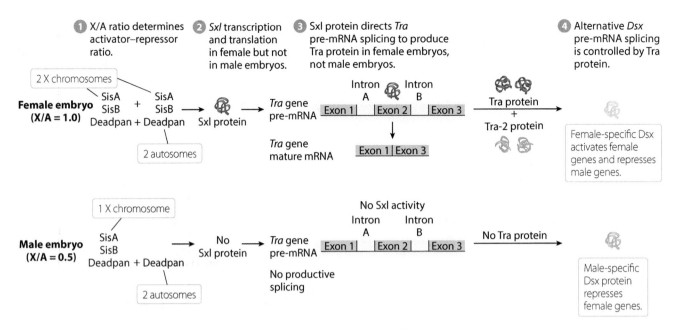

Figure 8.31   The X/A ratio determines gene transcription and transcript splicing pattern to determine sex in fruit flies.

Tra pre-mRNA is spliced to produce a functional Tra protein. In male embryos, the absence of Sxl protein leads to alternative *Tra* pre-mRNA splicing that does not produce functional Tra protein. The Tra protein is also a splicing regulator; it operates on the pre-mRNA of *Dsx* along with a second protein known as Tra-2. In female embryos, Tra protein and Tra-2 protein splice *Dsx* pre-mRNA in one alternative variant, which when translated produces female-specific Dsx protein. Female-specific Dsx activates transcription of female-specific genes and represses transcription of male-specific genes to produce female flies. Tra protein is absent in male embryos, and *Dsx* pre-mRNA is spliced in another alternative variant. Dsx protein in male embryos represses female-specific genes and allows transcription of unrepressed male-specific genes, leading to male sex development.

8.1 RNA Transcripts Carry the Messages of Genes

- RNA molecules are synthesized by RNA polymerases using as building blocks the RNA nucleotides A, G, C, and U to form single-stranded sequences complementary to DNA template strands.

- Messenger RNA is the transcript that undergoes translation to produce proteins. Five other major forms of functional RNA are transcribed, and may undergo modification, but are not translated.

8.2 Bacterial Transcription Is a Four-Stage Process

- Transcription has four stages: promoter recognition, chain initiation, chain elongation, and chain termination.

- A single RNA polymerase transcribes all bacterial genes. This polymerase is a holoenzyme composed of a five-subunit core enzyme and a sigma subunit that aids the recognition of different forms of bacterial promoters.

- Bacterial promoters have two consensus sequence regions located upstream of the transcription start at approximately −10 and −35.

- The core enzyme of bacterial RNA polymerase carries out RNA synthesis following chain initiation by the holoenzyme.

- Transcription of most bacterial genes terminates by an intrinsic mechanism that depends only on DNA terminator sequences. Certain bacterial genes have a rho-dependent mechanism of transcription termination.

8.3 Archaeal and Eukaryotic Transcription Displays Structural Homology and Common Ancestry

- Eukaryotic cells contain three types of RNA polymerases that transcribe mRNA and the various classes of functional RNA.

- RNA polymerase II transcribes mRNA by interaction with numerous transcription factors that lead the enzyme to recognize promoters controlling transcription of polypeptide-coding genes.

- Promoters recognized by RNA polymerase II have a TATA box and additional regulatory elements that bind transcription factors and RNA pol II during transcription initiation. Transcription shows similarities among all three domains of life due to the sharing of a common ancestor and the essential nature of transcription.

- Archaeal transcription is a simplified version of eukaryotic transcription and is dissimilar from bacterial transcription.

- Three archaeal transcription proteins, TBP, TFB, and less often TFIIE α, share homology with bacterial and eukaryotic proteins and initiate transcription by interacting with RNA polymerase.

- Eukaryotic promoter regulatory elements are recognized by their consensus sequences.

- Tissue-specific and developmental modifications in transcription are regulated by enhancer and silencer sequences.

- RNA polymerase I uses exclusive transcription factors to recognize upstream consensus sequences of ribosomal RNA genes.

- RNA polymerase III recognizes promoter consensus sequences that are upstream and downstream of the start of transcription.

8.4 Post-Transcriptional Processing Modifies RNA Molecules

- 5′ capping of eukaryotic messenger RNA adds a methylated guanine through the action of guanylyl transferase shortly after transcription is initiated.

- Polyadenylation at the 3′ end of eukaryotic messenger RNA is signaled by an AAUAAA sequence and is accomplished by a complex of enzymes.

- Intron splicing is controlled by cellular proteins that identify introns and exons and form spliceosome complexes that remove introns and ligate exons.

- Consensus sequences at the 5′ splice site, the 3′ splice site, and the branch point serve as guides during intron splicing.

- Alternative splicing is regulated by cell-type-specific variation of proteins that identify introns and exons.

- Some RNA molecules have catalytic activity and are able to self-splice introns without the aid of proteins.

- Ribosomal and transfer RNA molecules are generated by cleavage of large precursor molecules transcribed in bacterial, archaeal, and eukaryotic genomes.

- RNA editing is a post-transcriptional altering of nucleotide sequence, causing the transcripts to differ from the corresponding template DNA sequence.

KEYWORDS

3′ polyadenylation (3′ poly-A tailing) *(p. 285)*

3′ splice site *(p. 289)*

5′ capping *(p. 285)*

5′ splice site *(p. 288)*

−35 consensus sequence *(p. 273)*

alternative pre-mRNA processing (alternative intron splicing, promoter, polyadenylation) *(pp. 292, 293)*

branch point adenine *(p. 289)*

CAAT box *(p. 280)*

closed promoter complex *(p. 273)*

coding region *(p. 272)*

coding strand (nontemplate strand) *(p. 271)*

consensus sequence *(p. 273)*

core element *(p. 283)*

downstream *(p. 272)*

enhancer sequence *(p. 282)*

exonic and intronic splicing enhancers (ESEs and ISE) *(p. 294)*

exonic and intronic splicing silencers (ESS and ISS) *(p. 294)*

functional RNA (tRNA, rRNA, snRNA, miRNA, siRNA, ribozyme) *(p. 271)*

GC-rich box *(p. 280)*

general transcription factors (GTFs) *(p. 282)*

guide RNA (gRNA) *(p. 298)*

initial committed complex *(p. 281)*

initiation complex *(p. 282)*

internal control region (ICR) *(p. 284)*

internal promoter element *(p. 284)*

intrinsic termination *(p. 277)*

intron self-splicing *(p. 294)*

intron splicing *(p. 285)*

intronic splicing enhancer, suppressor (ISE, ISS) *(p. 294)*

inverted repeat *(p. 277)*

lariat intron structure *(p. 289)*

mature mRNA *(p. 285)*

messenger RNA (mRNA) *(p. 270)*

micro RNA (miRNA) *(p. 271)*

minimal initiation complex *(p. 282)*

nucleolus (nucleoli) *(p. 283)*

open promoter complex *(p. 273)*

polyadenylation signal sequence *(p. 286)*

precursor mRNA (pre-mRNA) *(p. 285)*

preinitiation complex (PIC) *(p. 282)*

Pribnow box (−10 consensus sequence) *(p. 273)*

promoter *(p. 271)*

promoter-specific element (PSE) *(p. 284)*

rho-dependent termination (rho protein) *(p. 277)*

rho utilization site (rut site) *(p. 277)*

ribonucleotide (A,U,G,C) *(p. 269)*

ribose *(p. 269)*

ribosomal RNA (rRNA) *(p. 271)*

ribozymes *(p. 271)*

RNA editing *(p. 298)*

RNA polymerase core *(p. 272)*

RNA polymerase *(p. 269)*

RNA polymerase I, II, III (RNA pol I, II, III) *(p. 278)*

sigma (σ) subunit (alternative sigma subunit) *(p. 272)*

silencer sequence *(p. 283)*

small interfering RNA (siRNA) *(p. 271)*

small nuclear RNA (snRNA) *(p. 271)*

spliceosome *(p. 289)*

stem-loop (hairpin structure) *(p. 277)*

TATA box (Goldberg-Hogness box) *(p. 280)*

TATA-binding protein (TBP) *(p. 281)*

TBP-associated factor (TAF) *(p. 281)*

template strand *(p. 271)*

termination region *(p. 272)*

transcription factors (TF) *(p. 281)*

transcription-terminating factor I (TTFI) *(p. 285)*

transfer RNA (tRNA) *(p. 271)*

upstream *(p. 271)*

upstream control element *(p. 283)*

uracil (U) *(p. 269)*

PROBLEMS — MasteringGenetics™ — Visit for instructor-assigned tutorials and problems.

Chapter Concepts

For answers to selected even-numbered problems, see Appendix: Answers.

1. Based on discussion in this chapter,
   a. What is a gene?
   b. Why are genes for rRNA and tRNA considered to be genes even though they do not produce polypeptides?

2. In one to two sentences each, describe the three processes that commonly modify eukaryotic pre-mRNA.

3. Answer these questions concerning promoters.
   a. What role do promoters play in transcription?
   b. What is the common structure of a bacterial promoter with respect to consensus sequences?
   c. What consensus sequences are detected in the mammalian β-globin gene promoter?
   d. Eukaryotic promoters are more variable than bacterial promoters. Explain why.
   e. What is the meaning of the term *alternative promoter*? How does the use of alternative promoters affect transcription?

4. The diagram below shows a DNA duplex. The template strand is identified, as is the location of the +1 nucleotide.

   +1

   5′ _____|_____ 3′ template strand
   3′ _____ 5′ coding strand

   a. Assume this region contains a gene transcribed in a bacterium. Identify the location of promoter consensus sequences and of the transcription termination sequence.
   b. Assume this region contains a gene transcribed to form mRNA in a eukaryote. Identify the location of the most common promoter consensus sequences.
   c. If this region is a eukaryotic gene transcribed by RNA polymerase III, where are the promoter consensus sequences located?

5. The following is a portion of an mRNA sequence:

   3′-AUCGUCAUGCAGA-5′

   a. During transcription, was the adenine at the left-hand side of the sequence the first or the last nucleotide added to the portion of mRNA shown? Explain how you know.
   b. Write out the sequence and polarity of the DNA duplex that encodes this mRNA segment. Label the template and coding DNA strands.
   c. Identify the direction in which the promoter region for this gene will be located.

6. Compare and contrast the properties of DNA polymerase and RNA polymerase, listing at least three similarities and at least three differences between the molecules.

7. The DNA sequences shown below are from the promoter regions of six bacterial genes. In each case, the last nucleotide in the sequence (highlighted in blue) is the +1 nucleotide that initiates transcription.
   a. Examine these sequences and identify the Pribnow box sequence at approximately −10 for each promoter.
   b. Determine the consensus sequence for the Pribnow box from these sequences.

Gene 1	. . .	TTCCGGCTCGTATGTTGTGTGG A	. . .
Gene 2	. . .	CGTCATTTGATATGATGCGCCCC G	. . .
Gene 3	. . .	CCACTGGCGGTGATACTGAGCAC A	. . .
Gene 4	. . .	TTTATTGCAGCTTATAATGGTTAC A	. . .
Gene 5	. . .	TGCTTCTGACTATAATAGACAGG G	. . .
Gene 6	. . .	AAGTAAACACGGTACGATGTACCAC A	. . .

8. Bacterial and eukaryotic gene transcripts can differ, in the transcripts themselves, in whether the transcripts are modified before translation, and in how the transcripts are modified. For each of these three areas of contrast, describe what the differences are and why the differences exist.

9. Describe the two types of transcription termination found in bacterial genes. How does transcription termination differ for eukaryotic genes?

10. What is the role of enhancer sequences in transcription of eukaryotic genes? Speculate about why enhancers are not part of transcription of bacterial genes.

11. Describe the difference between intron sequences and spacer sequences, such as the spacer sequence depicted in Figure 8.27b.

12. Draw a bacterial promoter and label its consensus sequences. How does this promoter differ from a eukaryotic promoter transcribed by RNA polymerase II? By RNA polymerase I? By RNA polymerase III?

13. How do SR proteins help guide pre-mRNA intron splicing? What is meant by the term *alternative splicing*, and how does variation in SR protein production play a role?

14. Three genes identified in the diagram as *A*, *B*, and *C* are transcribed from a region of DNA. The 5′-to-3′ transcription of genes *A* and *C* elongates mRNA in the right-to-left direction, and transcription of gene *B* elongates mRNA in the left-to-right direction. For each gene, identify the coding strand by designating it as an "upper strand" or "lower strand in the diagram."

Application and Integration

For answers to selected even-numbered problems, see Appendix: Answers.

15. The eukaryotic gene *Gen-100* contains four introns labeled A to D. Imagine that *Gen-100* has been isolated and its DNA has been denatured and mixed with polyadenylated mRNA from the gene.

    a. Illustrate the R-loop structure that would be seen with electron microscopy.
    b. Label the introns.
    c. Are intron regions single stranded or double stranded? Why?

16. The segment of the bacterial *TrpA* gene involved in intrinsic termination of transcription is shown below.

    ```
    3'-TGGGTCGGGGCGGATTACTGCCCCGAAAAAAAAACTTG-5'
    5'-ACCCAGCCCCGCCTAATGACGGGGCTTTTTTTTTGAAC-3'
    ```

    a. Draw the mRNA structure that forms during transcription of this segment of the *TrpA* gene.
    b. Label the template and coding DNA strands.
    c. Explain how a sequence of this type leads to intrinsic termination of transcription.

17. A 2-kb fragment of *E. coli* DNA contains the complete sequence of a gene for which transcription is terminated by the rho protein. The fragment contains the complete promoter sequence as well as the terminator region of the gene. The cloned fragment is examined by band shift assay (see Research Technique 8.1). Each lane of a single electrophoresis gel contains the 2-kb cloned fragment under the following conditions:

    Lane 1: 2-kb fragment alone

    Lane 2: 2-kb fragment plus the core enzyme

    Lane 3: 2-kb fragment plus the RNA polymerase holoenzyme

    Lane 4: 2-kb fragment plus rho protein

    a. Diagram the relative positions expected for the DNA fragments in this gel retardation analysis.
    b. Explain the relative positions of bands in lanes 1 and 3.
    c. Explain the relative positions of bands in lanes 1 and 4.

18. A 3.5-kb segment of DNA containing the complete sequence of a mouse gene is available. The DNA segment contains the promoter sequence and extends beyond the polyadenylation site of the gene. The DNA is studied by band shift assay (see Research Technique 8.1), and the following gel bands are observed.

    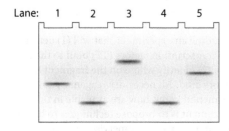

    Match these conditions to a specific lane of the gel.

    a. 3.5-kb fragment plus TFIIB and TFIID
    b. 3.5-kb fragment plus TFIIB, TFIID, TFIIF, and RNA polymerase II

    c. 3.5-kb fragment alone
    d. 3.5-kb fragment plus RNA polymerase II
    e. 3.5-kb fragment plus TFIIB

19. A 1.0-kb DNA fragment from the 5′ end of the mouse gene described in the previous problem is examined by DNA footprint protection analysis (see Research Technique 8.1). Two samples are end-labeled with ^{32}P, and one of the two is mixed with TFIIB, TFIID, and RNA polymerase II. The DNA exposed to these proteins is run in the right-hand lane of the gel shown below and the control DNA is run in the left-hand. Both DNA samples are treated with DNase I before running the samples on the electrophoresis gel.

    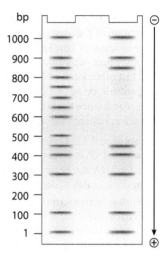

    a. What length of DNA is bound by the transcriptional proteins? Explain how the gel results support this interpretation.
    b. Draw a diagram of this DNA fragment bound by the transcriptional proteins, showing the approximate position of proteins along the fragment. Use the illustration style seen in Research Technique 8.1 as a model.
    c. Explain the role of DNase I.

20. Wild-type *E. coli* grow best at 37°C but can grow efficiently up to 42°C. An *E. coli* strain has a mutation of the sigma subunit that results in an RNA polymerase holoenzyme that is stable and transcribes at wild-type levels at 37°C. The mutant holoenzyme is progressively destabilized as the temperature is raised, and it completely denatures and ceases to carry out transcription at 42°C. Relative to wild-type growth, characterize the ability of the mutant strain to carry out transcription at

    a. 37°C   b. 40°C   c. 42°C
    d. What term best characterizes the type of mutation exhibited by the mutant bacterial strain? (*Hint*: The term was used in Chapter 4 to describe the Himalayan allele of the mammalian *C* gene.)

21. A mutant strain of *Salmonella* bacteria carries a mutation of the rho protein that has full activity at 37°C but is completely inactivated when the mutant strain is grown at 40°C.

    a. Speculate about the kind of differences you would expect to see if you compared a broad spectrum of mRNAs from the mutant strain grown at 37°C and the same spectrum of mRNAs from the strain when grown at 40°C.

b. Are all mRNAs affected by the rho protein mutation in the same way? Why or why not?

22. The human β-globin wild-type allele and a certain mutant allele are identical in sequence except for a single base-pair substitution that changes one nucleotide at the end of intron 2. The wild-type and mutant sequences of the affected portion of pre-mRNA are

	Intron 2	Exon 3
wild type	5'-CCUCCCACAG	CUCCUG-3'
mutant	5'-CCUCCCACUG	CUCCUG-3'

a. Speculate about the way in which this base substitution causes mutation of β-globin protein.

b. This is one example of how DNA sequence change occurring somewhere other than in an exon can produce mutation. List other kinds of DNA sequence changes occurring outside exons that can produce mutation. In each case, characterize the kind of change you would expect to see in mutant mRNA or mutant protein.

23. Microbiologists describe the processes of transcription and translation as "coupled" in bacteria. This term indicates that a bacterial mRNA can be undergoing transcription at the same moment it is also undergoing translation.

a. How is coupling of transcription and translation possible in bacteria?

b. Is coupling of transcription and translation possible in single-celled eukaryotes such as yeast? Why or why not?

24. A full-length eukaryotic gene is inserted into a bacterial chromosome. The gene contains a complete promoter sequence and a functional polyadenylation sequence, and it has wild-type nucleotides throughout the transcribed region. However, the gene fails to produce a functional protein.

a. List at least three possible reasons why this eukaryotic gene is not expressed in bacteria.

b. What changes would you recommend to permit expression of this eukaryotic gene in a bacterial cell?

25. The accompanying illustration shows a portion of a gene undergoing transcription. The template and coding strands for the gene are labeled, and a segment of DNA sequence is given. For this gene segment:

a. Superimpose a drawing of RNA polymerase as it nears the end of transcription of the DNA sequence.

b. Indicate the direction in which RNA polymerase moves as it transcribes this gene.

c. Write the polarity and sequence of the RNA transcript from the DNA sequence given.

d. Identify the direction in which the promoter for this gene is located.

Coding strand 5' XXXX ATCGCATTAACGATCGATC XXXX 5'
Template strand 3' XXXX TAGCGTAATTGCTAGCTAG XXXX 3'

26. DNA footprint protection (described in Research Technique 8.1) is a method that determines whether proteins bind to a specific sample of DNA and thus protect part of the DNA from random enzymatic cleavage by DNase I. A 400-bp segment of cloned DNA is thought to contain a promoter. The cloned DNA is analyzed by DNA footprinting to determine if it has the capacity to act as a promoter sequence. The gel shown below has two lanes, each containing the cloned 400-bp DNA fragment treated with DNase I to randomly cleave unprotected DNA. Lane 1 is cloned DNA that was mixed with RNA polymerase II and several TFII transcription factors before exposure to DNase I. Lane 2 contains cloned DNA that was exposed only to DNase I. RNA pol II and TFIIs were not mixed with DNA before adding DNase I.

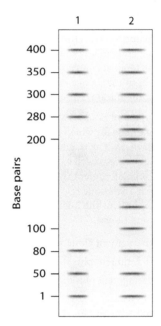

a. Explain why this gel provides evidence that the cloned DNA may act as a promoter sequence.

b. Approximately what length is the DNA region protected by RNA pol II and TFIIs?

c. What additional genetic experiments would you suggest to verify that this region of cloned DNA contains a functional promoter?

27. Suppose you have a 1-kb segment of cloned DNA that is suspected to contain a eukaryotic promoter including a TATA box, a CAAT box, and an upstream GC-rich sequence. The clone also contains a gene whose transcript is readily detectable. Your laboratory supervisor asks you to outline an experiment that will (1) determine if eukaryotic transcription factors (TF) bind to the fragment and, if so, (2) identify where on the fragment the transcription factors bind. All necessary reagents, equipment, and experimental know-how are available in the laboratory. Your assignment is to propose techniques to be used to address the three items your supervisor has listed and to describe the kind of results that would indicate binding of TF to the DNA, the location of the binding. (*Hint:* The techniques and general results are discussed in this chapter.)

The Molecular Biology of Translation

9

CHAPTER OUTLINE

9.1 Polypeptides Are Composed of Amino Acid Chains That Are Assembled at Ribosomes

9.2 Translation Occurs in Three Phases

9.3 Translation Is Fast and Efficient

9.4 The Genetic Code Translates Messenger RNA into Polypeptide

9.5 Experiments Deciphered the Genetic Code

9.6 Translation Is Followed by Polypeptide Folding, Processing, and Protein Sorting

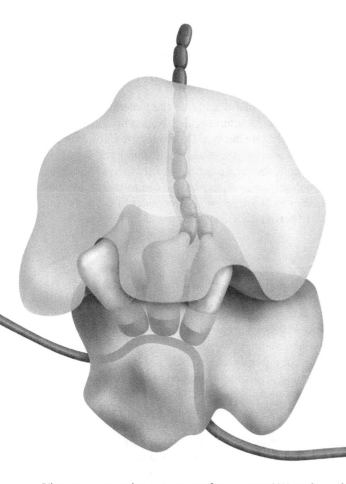

Ribosomes use codon sequences of messenger RNA to direct the assembly of polypeptides during translation. This rendering of a ribosome engaged in translation is based on recent crystal structure analysis and accurately shows the large subunit (top) and small subunit (bottom), the track of mRNA through the small subunit, the spaces for E, P, and A sites into which tRNAs fit, and the egress of the polypeptide through the large subunit.

ESSENTIAL IDEAS

▪ Translation is the cellular process of polypeptide production carried out by ribosomes under the direction of mRNA.

▪ Ribosomes assemble on mRNA and initiate translation at the start codon.

▪ Polypeptide elongation and termination are similar in bacteria and eukaryotes.

▪ Transfer RNA molecules carry amino acids to ribosomes, which assemble polypeptides with the aid of ribosomal proteins.

▪ A virtually universal genetic code comprising 64 mRNA codons directs polypeptide assembly.

▪ Polypeptides undergo posttranslational folding and processing, and in eukaryotes are sorted into vesicles for transport to cellular destinations or for secretion.

Long before the discovery that DNA is the hereditary molecule, biologists had established the relationship between genes and proteins. In 1902, Archibald Garrod was the first to explicitly draw this connection when he proposed that the human hereditary disorder alkaptonuria was caused by an inherited defect in the enzyme homogentisic acid oxidase (see Section 4.3 and Figure 4.17b). As Garrod and other biologists expanded their exploration of the gene–protein connection, they found evidence that hereditary variation was closely tied to variations in proteins. Principal

305

among the biologists who developed this connection were George Beadle and Edward Tatum, whose research established the "one gene–one enzyme" hypothesis (Chapter 5).

This chapter discusses translation, the mechanism by which the messenger RNA (mRNA) transcripts of genes are used to assemble amino acids into polypeptide strings that form proteins. Translation is carried out by ribosomes that bring together mRNA transcripts and transfer RNA (tRNA) molecules that carry amino acids and facilitate the assembly of polypeptides, strings of amino acids.

Polypeptides form the enzymes (catalytic proteins), structural proteins, transport proteins, signaling proteins, hormones, and other components that are assembled into cell structures and that perform biological activities in cells. Your body is composed of trillions of cells that collectively express and utilize tens of thousands of different polypeptides, all synthesized by translation.

The story of how polypeptides are produced by translation, and the story of how scientists came to understand the process, offers intriguing insight into the design of molecular genetic experiments. In this chapter, we describe some of these experiments and examine the molecular biology of translation. We look at the homology of proteins that are active in translation in organisms from the three domains of life and describe how this and other features of translation are evidence of a single origin of life and of the evolutionary relationships between bacteria, archaea, and eukaryotes. In the final chapter section, we discuss posttranslational processes that are instrumental in producing functional proteins and guiding them to their appropriate destinations in cells. The chapter concludes with a case study describing the action of commonly used antibiotics that interfere with bacterial translation.

9.1 Polypeptides Are Composed of Amino Acid Chains That Are Assembled at Ribosomes

Twenty different amino acids are the basic building blocks of polypeptides. All amino acids have features in common and features that are distinct. The distinctive features impart specific characteristics that allow the amino acid to participate in certain chemical reactions or behave in a hydrophilic or hydrophobic manner. In part, the common features allow amino acids to be joined into polypeptides by covalent bond formation between adjacent amino acids in the chain.

Amino Acid Structure

The shared features of amino acids are a central carbon molecule known as the α-carbon, an amino (NH_3) group, and a carboxyl (COOH) group (Figure 9.1). Each amino and carboxyl group is joined to the α-carbon. During polypeptide assembly, an enzyme in the ribosome catalyzes the formation of a **peptide bond** between the carboxyl group of one amino acid and the amino group of the next amino acid in the chain. Each amino acid added in this way becomes a new monomer in the growing polymer that is the elongating polypeptide. The term **polypeptide** identifies a string of amino acids that are joined by peptide bonds. Each *protein* has a unique sequence of amino acids, may be composed of one or more polypeptide chains, and generally have a characteristic three-dimensional structure.

The distinctive portion of each amino acid is its side chain, known as an **R-group,** that is joined to the α-carbon. The R-groups range in complexity from a single hydrogen atom to ringed structures that in themselves contain multiple carbon atoms. Each R-group imparts specific characteristics as shown in Table 9.1. Ten of the amino acids have nonpolar R-groups, meaning that they have no charged atoms that can participate in formation of hydrogen bonds with other amino acids. Five other amino acids have polar R-groups that can carry partial

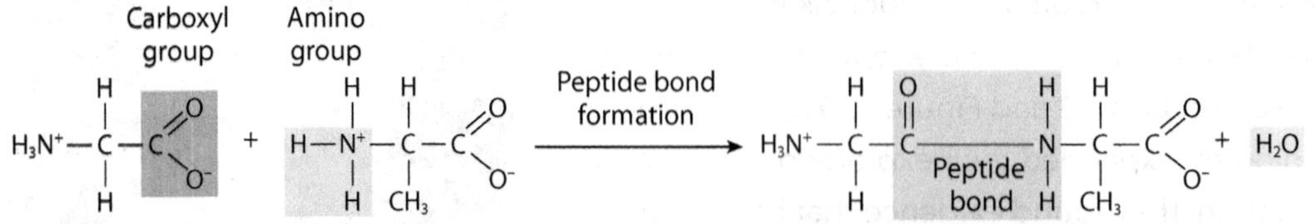

Figure 9.1 Peptide bond formation. The carboxyl group of one amino acid reacts with the amino group of a second amino acid to form a covalent peptide bond that joins amino acids in a polypeptide.

Table 9.1	Amino Acids Grouped by Their Side Chain Properties
Nonpolar side chains: Have no charged or electronegative atoms at pH 7.0 to form hydrogen bonds.	
Alanine (Ala or A)	Methionine (Met or M)
Cysteine (Cys or C)	Phenylalanine (Phe or F)
Glycine (Gly or G)	Proline (Pro or P)
Isoleucine (Ile or I)	Tryptophan (Trp or W)
Leucine (Leu or L)	Valine (Val or V)
Polar side chains: Have partial charges at pH 7.0 and can form hydrogen bonds.	
Asparagine (Asp or N)	Threonine (Thr or T)
Glutamine (Glu or Q)	Tyrosine (Tyr or Y)
Serine (Ser or S)	
Electrically charged side chains: At pH 7.0, can form hydrogen and ionic bonds.	
Basic Side Chains	**Acidic Side Chains**
Arginine (Arg or R)	Aspartate (Asp or D)
Histidine (His or H)	Glutamate (Glu or E)
Lysine (Lys or K)	

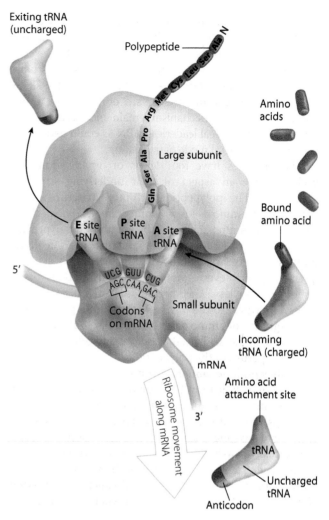

Figure 9.2   **Translation overview.**

charges and can participate in hydrogen bond formation with other amino acids. The five remaining amino acids have electrically charged R-groups: Three are basic and two are acidic. Electrically charged R-groups allow these amino acids to form ionic bonds and hydrogen bonds.

Polypeptide and Transcript Structure

Polypeptide assembly is orchestrated by ribosomes, which are ribonucleoprotein "machines" containing multiple molecules of ribosomal RNA (rRNA) and dozens of proteins. Ribosomes of all organisms are composed of two subunits that assemble into a ribosome as translation begins. Ribosomes bind mRNA and provide an environment for complementary base pairing between mRNA codon sequences and the anticodon sequences of tRNA. (In Chapter 1 and Figure 1.11, we review these basic mechanical features of translation.) **Figure 9.2** encapsulates the essential elements of translation. Ribosomes translate mRNA in the 5′ → to 3′ direction, beginning with the start codon and ending with a stop codon. At each triplet codon, complementary base pairing between mRNA and tRNA determines which amino acid is added to the nascent (growing) polypeptide. The start codon and stop codon define the boundaries of the translated segment of mRNA. The resulting polypeptides have an N-terminal (amino-terminal) end corresponding to the 5′ end of mRNA and a C-terminal (carboxyl-terminal) end that corresponds to the 3′ end of mRNA (**Figure 9.3**).

Figure 9.3 identifies two segments of the mRNA transcript that do not undergo translation. Between the 5′ end of mRNA and the start codon is a segment known as the

5′ untranslated region, abbreviated **5′ UTR.** The region between the stop codon and the 3′ end of the molecule is the **3′ untranslated region,** or **3′ UTR.** The 5′ UTR contains sequences that help initiate translation and the 3′ UTR contains sequences associated with transcription termination in almost all bacterial and eukaryotic mRNAs. By comparison,

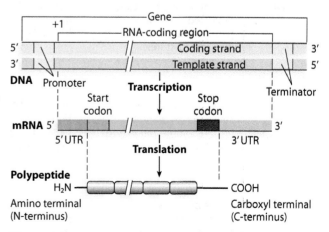

Figure 9.3   **Alignment of DNA, mRNA, and polypeptide.**

relatively little is known about the roles of archaeal 5′ and 3′ UTRs. Many archaeal mRNAs have a 5′ UTR that functions similarly to those of bacteria and eukaryotes. However, a substantial proportion of archaeal mRNAs—some studies suggest 50% or more of them—do not have a 5′ UTR. These so-called "leaderless" mRNAs are still efficiently translated, but the details of the mechanism remain unclear. It has been proposed that archaeal leaderless mRNAs could perhaps be a relic of an ancestral mode of translation.

Polypeptides have four levels of organization that each describe an aspect of their underlying structure (Table 9.2). The polypeptide **primary structure** is the sequence of amino acids contained in the polypeptide. The order of amino acids and the length of a polypeptide (the number of amino acids it contains) are effectively limitless. There are billions of possible amino acid sequence options even among short polypeptides of 20 amino acids or less. The specific order of amino acids is, however, critical to the proper function of a polypeptide. The R-groups of amino acids affect the solubility and reactivity of amino acids, and therefore they affect the functional properties of the polypeptide.

Polypeptide **secondary structure** is generated by hydrogen bonds that form between amino acids. Hydrogen bond formation requires that amino acids with polar R-groups align with one another. This is accomplished by bending or twisting the polypeptide in one of two possible structures. An **α-helix (alpha helix)** is a twisted coil of amino acids stabilized by hydrogen bonds between partially charged R-groups. A **β-pleated sheet (beta-pleated sheet)** is a 180-degree bend created when a segment of a polypeptide folds. The primary structure is critical to determining which, if either, of these secondary structures forms in a polypeptide.

A polypeptide's **tertiary structure** is the result of a variety of interactions involving the R-groups. Interactions such as hydrogen bonding, covalent bonding, ionic interactions, and hydrophobic interactions produce the overall shape of the protein. Tertiary structure is dependent on primary and secondary structure, and it should come as no surprise that protein shapes vary widely. These shapes form the binding, interaction, and catalytic domains that are responsible for the protein's action in the body. The tertiary structure of a protein may change in response to the presence of other chemical substances, including other protein molecules. For example, an enzyme may have a catalytically active tertiary structure under some circumstances and have an alternative, nonactive tertiary structure under others.

Primary, secondary, and tertiary structures describe different levels of organization of individual polypeptides. But some proteins contain two or more polypeptides, an organization described as **quaternary structure.** Proteins that have a quaternary structure contain distinct polypeptides that each have their own primary, secondary, and tertiary structures. Such proteins are often described as *multimers*. The individual polypeptides of a multimer may be identical or may be different. For example, a protein composed of four identical polypeptides can be called a *homotetramer*, and a four-polypeptide protein that contains two or more different polypeptides can be identified as a *heterotetramer*. Table 9.2 summarizes these four levels of polypeptide structure and illustrates the red blood cell

Table 9.2	Polypeptide Structure		
Level	**Description**	**Stabilized by**	**Example: Hemoglobin**
Primary	The sequence of amino acids in a polypeptide	Peptide bonds	Gly — Ser — Asp — Cys
Secondary	Formation of α-helices and β-pleated sheets in a polypeptide (thus, depends on primary structures)	Hydrogen bonding between groups along the peptide-bonded backbone.	One α-helix
Tertiary	Overall three-dimensional shape of a polypeptide (includes contribution from secondary structures)	Bonds and other interactions between R-groups, or between R-groups and the peptide-bonded backbone.	One of hemoglobin's subunits
Quaternary	Shape produced by combinations of polypeptides (each with its own tertiary structure)	Bonds and other interactions between R-groups, and between peptide backbones of different polypeptides.	Hemoglobin consists of four polypeptide subunits

protein hemoglobin—a heterotetramer—as an example of a protein with a quaternary structure. Hemoglobin and a specific variant of one of the polypeptides in this heterotetramer are the focus of discussion in Chapter 10.

Ribosome Structures

The specific molecules composing bacterial, archaeal, and eukaryotic ribosomes differ, but the overall structures and functions of the ribosomes are similar, reflecting the fundamental nature of the translation process in all forms of life. In all three domains, ribosomes perform three essential tasks:

1. Bind messenger RNA and identify the start codon where translation begins.
2. Facilitate the complementary base pairing of mRNA codons and tRNA anticodons that determines amino acid order in the polypeptide.
3. Catalyze peptide bond formation between amino acids during polypeptide formation.

Differences in ribosomal composition between bacteria, archaea, and eukaryotes include the number and sequence of rRNA molecules and the number and type of ribosomal proteins. Although the archaeal and bacterial ribosomes are similar in size, and somewhat smaller than the eukaryotic ribosomes, most of the archaeal ribosomal proteins (and the tRNAs and protein factors involved in translation) display homology to their eukaryotic counterparts. In all three domains, ribosomes display key structural similarities that are divided into two main subunits, called the **large ribosomal subunit** and the **small ribosomal subunit.** By convention, subunit size is measured in Svedberg

units (S), which describe the velocity of their sedimentation when subjected to a centrifugal force. Named in honor of Theodor Svedberg, a 1926 Nobel Laureate in Chemistry and inventor of the ultracentrifuge, higher S values indicate faster sedimentation rates and larger molecules. It should be noted that Svedberg units are not additive when ribosomal subunits are combined because sedimentation is a composite property that is affected by multiple molecular factors, including size, shape, and hydration state.

The ribosomes of *E. coli* are the most thoroughly studied bacterial ribosomes and serve as a model for general ribosome structure (**Figure 9.4a**). The small subunit of bacterial ribosomes has a Svedberg value of 30S. It contains 21 proteins and a single 16S rRNA composed of 1541 nucleotides. The large subunit of the bacterial ribosome is a 50S particle composed of 32 proteins, a small 5S rRNA containing 120 nucleotides, and a large 23S rRNA containing 2904 nucleotides. When fully assembled, the intact bacterial ribosome has a Svedberg value of 70S.

Both the large and small subunits contribute to the formation of three regions that play important functional roles during translation: the **peptidyl site, or P site,** the **aminoacyl site, or A site** and, the **exit site, or E site.** The P site holds a tRNA to which the nascent polypeptide is attached. The A site binds a new tRNA molecule carrying the next amino acid to be added to the polypeptide. The E site provides an avenue of egress for tRNAs as they leave the ribosome after their amino acid has been added to the polypeptide chain. Ribosomes also form a channel through which the polypeptide emerges. In addition, there is a channel in the large subunit through which the nascent polypeptide is extruded from the ribosome (see Figure 9.2).

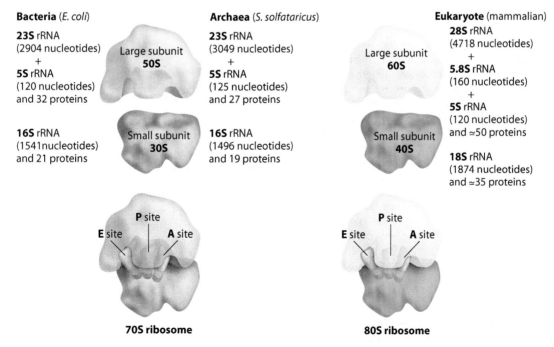

Bacteria (*E. coli*)	Archaea (*S. solfataricus*)	Eukaryote (mammalian)
23S rRNA (2904 nucleotides) + **5S** rRNA (120 nucleotides) and 32 proteins — Large subunit **50S**	**23S** rRNA (3049 nucleotides) + **5S** rRNA (125 nucleotides) and 27 proteins — Large subunit **60S**	**28S** rRNA (4718 nucleotides) + **5.8S** rRNA (160 nucleotides) + **5S** rRNA (120 nucleotides) and ≈50 proteins — Large subunit **60S**
16S rRNA (1541nucleotides) and 21 proteins — Small subunit **30S**	**16S** rRNA (1496 nucleotides) and 19 proteins — Small subunit **40S**	**18S** rRNA (1874 nucleotides) and ≈35 proteins — Small subunit **40S**

P site   E site   A site
70S ribosome

P site   E site   A site
80S ribosome

Figure 9.4   Ribosomes of bacteria, archaea, and eukaryotes. (a) The best-studied bacteria ribosome is that of *E. coli*, and the best-described archaeal ribosome is that of *Haloarcula marismortui*. **(b)** The best-studied eukaryotic ribosomes are mammalian.

Among eukaryotes, mammalian ribosomes are the most fully characterized (**Figure 9.4b**). The small 40S ribosomal subunit contains approximately 35 proteins and a single 18S rRNA composed of 1874 nucleotides. The large mammalian ribosomal subunit has a Svedberg value of 60S and contains 45 to 50 proteins, along with three molecules of rRNA. The rRNA molecules have values of 5S (120 nucleotides), 5.8S (160 nucleotides), and 28S (4718 nucleotides). The intact mammalian ribosome has a Svedberg value of 80S. Like the bacterial ribosome, the intact mammalian ribosome possesses a P site, an A site, an E site, and a channel for polypeptide egress.

The ribosomes of archaeal species have not been studied nearly as fully as those of bacterial and eukaryotes, but some information is available. The first atomic crystal structure of the large ribosomal subunit of an archaeon was that of *Haloarcula marismortui*. This structure included a 23S and a 5S rRNA and 27 proteins. Follow-up analysis of the small subunit structure revealed a 16S rRNA and 19 proteins. This is the basis for the conclusion that archaeal ribosomes have an overall size and structure similar to that of the 70S bacterial ribosome. As we discuss later, however, archaeal tRNAs and translation proteins are similar to those in eukaryotes.

The proteins contained in ribosomal subunits can be separated from one another by a specialized type of electrophoresis called two-dimensional gel electrophoresis. The 21 proteins that are part of the small ribosomal subunit in *E. coli* and the 31 proteins found in the large ribosomal subunit are efficiently separated by this method. **Research Technique 9.1** describes how two-dimensional

---

Research Technique 9.1

Two-Dimensional Gel Electrophoresis and the Identification of Ribosomal Proteins

PURPOSE All ribosomes are composed of two subunits that are each a complex mixture of rRNA and dozens of proteins. One approach to determining the number of proteins contained in each ribosomal subunit uses a method of electrophoresis known as two-dimensional gel electrophoresis to separate the proteins by their charge in the first dimension and then by their mass in the second dimension. Two-dimensional gel electrophoresis produces a distinctive "protein fingerprint" that distributes each ribosomal protein to a different location in the two-dimensional gel.

MATERIALS AND PROCEDURES Ribosomes are isolated from cells, the subunits are separated, and the subunits are treated to dissociate the proteins they contain. The mixture containing liberated ribosomal proteins is then separated in the first dimension by a version of gel electrophoresis known as isoelectric focusing. In this procedure, proteins are separated exclusively by their charge. In contrast to conventional gel electrophoresis, which uses a buffered solution to maintain constant pH throughout the gel, isoelectric focusing gels contain a pH gradient. A protein's pH environment affects its charge, and every protein has a pH—called the isoelectric point—at which it has neutral charge and cannot move in an electrical field. In isoelectric focusing, proteins migrate through the pH gradient to their isoelectric point, where they stop.

Once isoelectric focusing is complete, protein separation takes place in the second dimension, which uses SDS (sodium dodecyl sulfate) gel electrophoresis. SDS is a strong anionic detergent that denatures proteins by disrupting the interactions that keep them folded. Denatured proteins migrate through the gel at a rate determined by their mass, that is, by the number of amino acids they contain. In the SDS gel dimension of two-dimensional gel electrophoresis, each protein has a unique starting point corresponding to

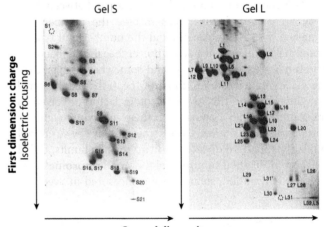

First dimension: charge
Isoelectric focusing

Second dimension: mass
SDS gel electrophoresis

its isoelectric point. Proteins with large mass (more amino acids) migrate a short distance in the second dimension, whereas proteins with small mass (fewer amino acids) migrate a greater distance.

DESCRIPTION A pair of two-dimensional electrophoresis gels, one containing proteins of the small subunit of the *E. coli* ribosome (gel S) and the other containing proteins of the large subunit (gel L), reveal protein spots (the protein fingerprint) corresponding to the positions of proteins that make up each ribosomal subunit. Each spot identifies the location of a unique protein that differs from the other proteins in the gel by a combination of charge and mass. The proteins in gel S are identified as S1 to S21, and in gel L as L1 to L32.

CONCLUSION Two-dimensional gel electrophoresis identifies 21 proteins in the small subunit of the *E. coli* ribosome and 32 proteins in the large ribosomal subunit. Each protein obtained by two-dimensional electrophoresis can be subjected to additional biochemical examination to specifically identify the protein and investigate its role in translation.

gel electrophoresis is used to characterize the proteins found in *E. coli* ribosomal subunits.

A Three-Dimensional View of the Ribosome

Ribosomes are so small—a mere 25 nanometers (nm) in diameter—that almost 10,000 of them can fit in the same space as the period at the end of this sentence. No one has ever "seen" a ribosome, but powerful molecular imaging techniques can resolve the three-dimensional configuration of ribosomes and ribosomal subunits, at levels of resolution that are measured in ångströms (Å). These structural analyses have clarified how ribosomal subunits fit together, and have produced a detailed understanding of ribosomal interactions with mRNA and tRNA.

Structural analysis of ribosomes and other molecular complexes in cells is made possible by a technique known as cryo-electron microscopy (cryo-EM), pioneered by Robert Glaeser in the 1970s and perfected by Jacques Dubochet in the 1980s. Cryo-EM uses liquid nitrogen or liquid ethane, with temperatures nearly −200°C, to instantaneously freeze macromolecules and thus preserve them in their native state. A frozen macromolecule is then placed on a microcaliper and scanned from various angles by electron beams that collect data analyzed by specialized software to create a three-dimensional picture of molecular structure. Cryo-EM creates exquisitely precise three-dimensional images of ribosome structure—much like CAT-scan imaging of the human body—revealing atomic-level details of ribosome structure (**Figure 9.5**). These images have identified the location and dimensions of the E, A, and P sites, for example, and have clarified the mechanical activities of ribosomes during translation. This work was recognized with the 2009 Nobel Prize in Chemistry awarded to Ada Yonath, Thomas Steitz, and Venki Ramakrishnan.

9.2 Translation Occurs in Three Phases

Translation occurs in three phases: initiation, elongation, and termination. The three phases are generally similar in bacteria, archaea, and eukaryotes, and yet they differ in several ways, particularly during translation initiation, where distinct mechanisms are used to identify the start codon.

Translation Initiation

Translation initiation in all organisms begins when the small ribosomal subunit binds near the 5′ end of mRNA and identifies the start codon sequence. In the next stage, the **initiator tRNA,** the tRNA carrying the first amino acid of the polypeptide, binds to the start codon. In the final stage of initiation, the large subunit joins the small subunit to form an intact ribosome, and translation begins. During these stages, *initiation factor proteins* help control ribosome formation and binding of the initiator tRNA, and guanosine triphosphate (GTP) provides energy. The tRNAs used during translation each carry a specific amino acid and are identified as **charged tRNAs.** In contrast, a tRNA without an amino acid is **uncharged.** Specialized enzymes discussed in a later section are responsible for recognizing different tRNAs and charging each one with the correct amino acid.

Starting translation at the authentic (correct) start codon is essential for translation of the correct polypeptide.

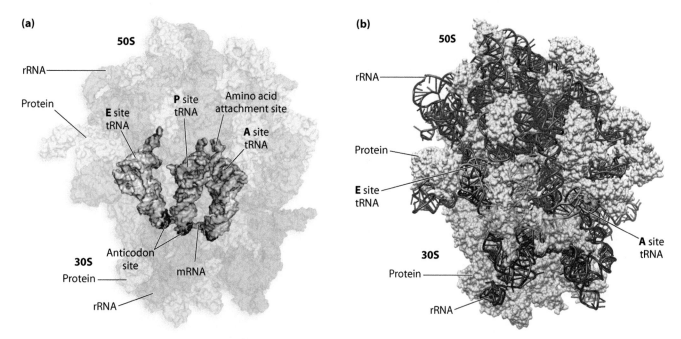

Figure 9.5 **Three-dimensional computer interpretations of cryo-EM–generated data depict ribosome structure.**

Errant translation starting at the wrong codon, or even at the wrong nucleotide of the start codon, may produce an abnormal polypeptide and result in a nonfunctional protein. Thus, critical questions for biologists studying translation initiation were these: How does the ribosome locate the authentic start codon? And if more than one AUG (start codon) sequence occurs near the 5′ end of the mRNA, how is the authentic start codon identified? Bacteria and eukaryotes use different mechanisms to identify the authentic start codon.

Bacterial Translation Initiation In *E. coli*, six critical molecular components come together to initiate the translation process: (1) mRNA, (2) the small ribosomal subunit, (3) the large ribosomal subunit, (4) the initiator tRNA, (5) three essential initiation factor proteins, and (6) GTP.

For most of translation initiation in bacteria, the 30S ribosomal subunit is affiliated with an **initiation factor (IF)** protein called IF3, which facilitates binding between the mRNA and the 30S subunit. IF3 also prevents the 30S subunit from binding to the 50S subunit (**Figure 9.6**).

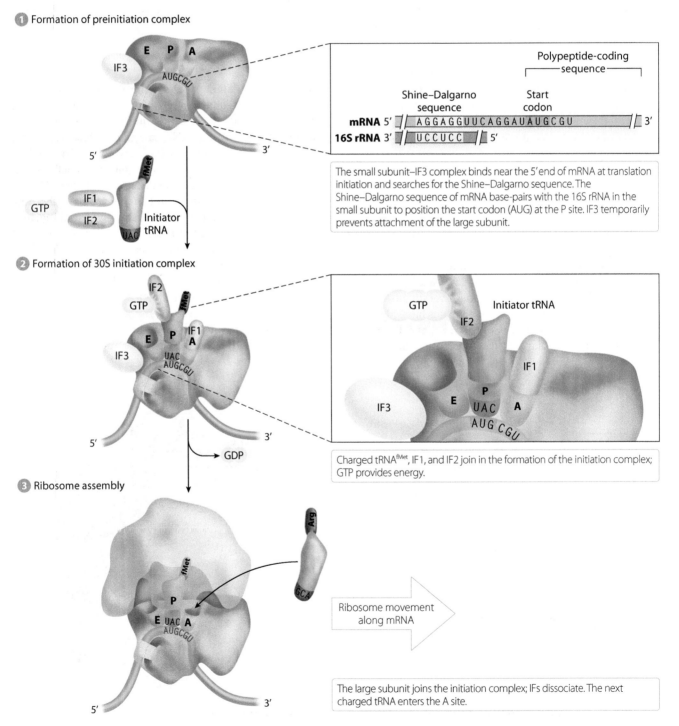

① Formation of preinitiation complex

The small subunit–IF3 complex binds near the 5′ end of mRNA at translation initiation and searches for the Shine–Dalgarno sequence. The Shine–Dalgarno sequence of mRNA base-pairs with the 16S rRNA in the small subunit to position the start codon (AUG) at the P site. IF3 temporarily prevents attachment of the large subunit.

② Formation of 30S initiation complex

Charged tRNA^fMet, IF1, and IF2 join in the formation of the initiation complex; GTP provides energy.

③ Ribosome assembly

Ribosome movement along mRNA

The large subunit joins the initiation complex; IFs dissociate. The next charged tRNA enters the A site.

Figure 9.6 **Initiation of bacterial translation.**

The small subunit–IF3 complex binds near the 5′ end of mRNA, searching for the AUG sequence that serves as the start codon. The **preinitiation complex** forms when the authentic start codon sequence is identified by base pairing that occurs between the 16S rRNA in the 30S ribosome and a short mRNA sequence located a few nucleotides upstream of the start codon in the 5′ UTR of mRNA (Figure 9.6, ❶). John Shine and Lynn Dalgarno identified the location and sequence of this region in 1974, and it is named the **Shine–Dalgarno sequence** in recognition of their work.

The Shine–Dalgarno sequence is a purine-rich sequence of about six nucleotides located three to nine nucleotides upstream of the start codon. A complementary pyrimidine-rich segment containing the sequence UCCUCC is found near the 3′ end of 16S rRNA, and it pairs with the Shine–Dalgarno sequence to position the mRNA on the 30S subunit (see Figure 9.6). The Shine–Dalgarno sequence is another example of a consensus sequence. Like the consensus sequences we describe for promoters (Chapter 8) the Shine–Dalgarno sequence has a characteristic nucleotide composition and a precise position relative to the start codon, but its exact nucleotide sequence varies slightly from one mRNA to another (Figure 9.7).

In the next step of translation initiation (Figure 9.6, ❷), the initiator tRNA binds to the start codon at what will be part of the P site after ribosome assembly. The amino acid on the initiator tRNA is a modified methionine called **N-formylmethionine (fMet);** thus, the charged initiator tRNA is abbreviated **tRNA^fMet.** This tRNA has a 3′-UAC-5′ anticodon sequence that is a complementary mate to the start codon sequence. An initiation factor (IF) protein designated IF2 and a molecule of GTP are bound at the P site to facilitate binding of tRNA^fMet. Initiation factor 1 (IF1) also joins the complex to forestall attachment of the 50S subunit. At this point, the **30S initiation complex,** consisting of mRNA bound to the 30S subunit,

tRNA^fMet located at the start codon, three initiation factors, and a molecule of GTP, has been formed.

In the final step of initiation (Figure 9.6, ❸), the 50S subunit joins the 30S subunit to form the intact ribosome. The energy for the union of the two subunits is derived from hydrolysis of GTP to GDP (guanosine diphosphate). The dissociation of IF1, IF2, and IF3 accompanies the joining of subunits that creates the **70S initiation complex.** This complex is a fully active ribosome with a P site, an A site, an E site, and a channel for exit of the polypeptide. The first tRNA (tRNA^fMet) is already paired with mRNA at the P site, and the open A site contains the second codon and is awaiting the next charged tRNA.

Eukaryotic Translation Initiation The eukaryotic 40S ribosomal subunit complexes with three **eukaryotic initiation factor (eIF)** proteins eIF1, eIF1A, and eIF3 to form the preinitiation complex (Figure 9.8, ❶). In step ❷ the preinitiation complex joins with the initiator tRNA and eIF5.

The **initiation complex** is formed by binding of the mRNA. This initiates the process called **scanning** (Figure 9.8, ❸), in which the small ribosomal subunit moves along the 5′ UTR in search of the start codon. About 90% of eukaryotic mRNAs use the first AUG encountered by the initiation complex as the start codon, but the remaining 10% use the second or, in some cases, the third AUG as the start codon. The initiation complex is able to accurately locate the authentic start codon because the codon is embedded in a consensus sequence that reads

$$5′\text{-}ACCAUGG\text{-}3′$$

(the start codon itself is shown in bold). This consensus sequence is called the **Kozak sequence** after Marilyn Kozak, who discovered it in 1978.

Locating the start codon leads to recruitment of the 60S subunit to the complex, using energy derived from GTP hydrolysis. This final step ❹ in the formation of the 80S ribosome is accompanied by joining of the two subunits and dissociation of the eIF proteins. In the 80S ribosome, the initiator tRNA^Met is located at the P site; the A site is vacant, awaiting arrival of the second tRNA (Genetic Analysis 9.1).

Archaeal Translation Initiation and Its Implications for Evolution Archaeal ribosome subunits are composed of rRNAs that are more similar in size to those of bacteria than of eukaryotes. However, the ribosomal RNAs that make up the central structure of the subunits are distinct in each domain. Indeed the archaeal domain was only discovered after Carl Woese sequenced and compared rRNAs from many organisms and found that their sequences clustered into the three domains of life depicted in Figure 1.3.

Despite the similarity in size of archaeal and bacterial ribosomes, the process of translation initiation

Figure 9.7 The Shine–Dalgarno consensus binding sequence. The AUG start codon sequence (orange) is near the Shine–Dalgarno region (gold), which binds to the 3′ end of 16S rRNA.

	Shine–Dalgarno sequence	Start codon
E. coli araB	UUUGGAUGGAGUGAAACGAUGGCGAUUGCA 3′	
E. coli lacI	CAAUUCAGGGUGGUGAAUAUGAAACCAGUA	
E. coli lacZ	UUCACACAGGAAACAGCUAUGACCAUGAUU	
E. coli thrA	GGUAACCAGGUAACAAGGAUGCGAGUGUUG	
E. coli trpA	AGCACGAGGGGAAAUCUGAUGGAACGCUAC	
E. coli trpB	AUAUGAAGGAAAGGAACAAUGACAACAUUA	
λ phage cro	AUGUACUAAGGAGGUUGUAUGGAACAACGC	
R17 phage A protein	UCCUAGGAGGUUUGACCUAUGCGAGCUUUU	
Qβ phage A replicase	UAACUAAGGAUGAAAUGCAUGUCUAAGACA	
φX174 phage A protein	AAUCUUGGAGGCUUUUUUAUGGUUCGUUCU	
E. coli RNA polymerase B	AGCGAGCUGAGGAACCCUAUGGUUUACUCC	
Consensus sequence	AGGAGG	

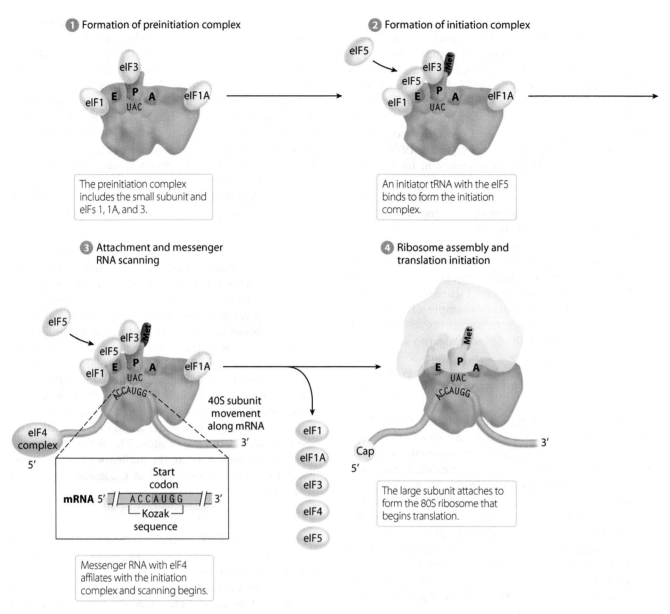

1 Formation of preinitiation complex

The preinitiation complex includes the small subunit and eIFs 1, 1A, and 3.

2 Formation of initiation complex

An initiator tRNA with the eIF5 binds to form the initiation complex.

3 Attachment and messenger RNA scanning

40S subunit movement along mRNA

Start codon

mRNA 5' ┤ A C C A U G G ├ 3'
└── Kozak ──┘
sequence

Messenger RNA with eIF4 affilates with the initiation complex and scanning begins.

4 Ribosome assembly and translation initiation

The large subunit attaches to form the 80S ribosome that begins translation.

Figure 9.8 **Initiation of eukaryotic translation.**

in archaea is decidedly eukaryote-like. One example of this similarity is the archaeal use of methionine as the common first amino acid of polypeptide chains. This is like eukaryotes and unlike bacteria, which use N-tromyl-methionine. A second aspect of archaeal translation initiation concerns the presence of Shine–Dalgarno sequences. These are relatively common in archaeal species that either do not produce leaderless mRNAs or produce very few. In contrast, archaeal species that produce a high proportion of leaderless mRNA, Shine–Dalgarno sequences are not as common, although they have been detected.

More significantly from an evolutionary perspective, **Table 9.3** lists archaeal translation initiation factor proteins and identifies their homologies to eukaryotic and bacterial proteins. Recall from our discussion in Section 1.4

that amino acid or nucleic acid sequences (proteins, DNA, or RNA) that are homologous have a common ancestral origin. As a consequence, proteins that have greater degrees of homology have more recent common ancestral history than do proteins with lower levels of homology. If proteins do not share a common ancestral history, they will not reveal homology.

Based on the homologous protein information in Table 9.3, it is clear that translation initiation in archaea is more complex than in bacteria and that known **archaeal initiation factor** proteins (**aIFs**) are homologous in structure and function to eIFs. This comparison of critical translational proteins also indicates striking similarity of translation initiation across the three domains of life. Translation in all forms of life has a common origin. Evolution has acted to conserve the key protein

Table 9.3	Translation Initiation Factor Homologs		
Function	Bacterial Homolog[a]	Archaeal Homolog[b]	Eukaryotic Homolog[c]
mRNA binding; start codon fidelity	IF3 (in some phyla only)	aIF1	eIF1
mRNA binding	IF1	aIF1a	eIF1A/eIF4
tRNA P site binding	IF2	aIF2/5	eIF5
tRNA^Met binding	No homolog	aIF3	eIF3

[a] The absence of a homologous protein is identified as "No homolog."
[b] Archaeal proteins are identified by the letter *a*.
[c] Eukaryotic proteins are identified by the letter *e*.

components of translation, with each domain acquiring its own specific features of translation.

The archaea have multiple mechanisms of mRNA–ribosome interaction at translation initiation. This is most apparent at the 5′ mRNA end where certain archaeal species have a large percentage—some studies say more than 50% of their mRNAs—that appear not to have a 5′ UTR. Those mRNAs lacking a 5′ UTR are said to be leaderless mRNAs and are apparently missing all or most of the translation initiating segments, including the Shine–Dalgarno sequence in some cases. The mechanism through which leaderless mRNA translation is initiated is not yet known. Archaeal species producing mRNAs with 5′ UTRs typically have Shine–Dalgarno sequences to aid translation intiation.

Analysis of experimental in vitro translation (translation in a test tube using ribosomes and translationally active proteins) testing the ability of bacterial and eukaryotic ribosomes and translational proteins to translate leaderless mRNAs from archaea finds that translation works efficiently in both in vitro systems. Leaderless mRNAs are very rare in bacteria or in eukaryotes, yet they are efficiently translated in vitro. This finding does not suggest a translational mechanism, but it has led to speculation that the leaderless mRNA state may be ancestral to the state featuring 5′ UTRs. In other words, it is possible that the last universal common ancestor (LUCA) of bacteria, archaea, and eukaryotes produced leaderless mRNAs and that the mRNAs with 5′ UTRs are a more recent development. In this context, archaeal translation may be something of a relic reminiscent of the situation in the LUCA.

Polypeptide Elongation

Elongation, the second phase of translation, begins with the recruitment of **elongation factor (EF)** proteins into the initiation complex. Elongation factors facilitate three steps of polypeptide synthesis:

1. Recruitment of charged tRNAs to the A site

2. Formation of a peptide bond between sequential amino acids

3. Translocation of the ribosome in the 3′ direction along mRNA

GTP cleavage provides the energy for each step of elongation in bacteria, archaea, and eukaryotes (Foundation Figure 9.9). Moreover, the steps in the elongation process are the same in all three types of organisms: although the elongation factors differ, the ribosomal P, A, and E sites of all three organisms serve nearly identical functions. The rates of elongation are also similar; bacteria add about 20 new amino acids per second to a nascent polypeptide chain, and eukaryotes elongate the polypeptide at a rate of 15 amino acids per second. The elongation rate in archaea has not been established. Lastly, numerous studies indicate high fidelity of translation in all organisms. An error rate of approximately one amino acid in each 10,000 added to polypeptides is estimated for bacteria.

Polypeptide Elongation in Bacteria Different elongation factor proteins (EFs) and other ribosomal proteins carry out elongation in a series of steps depicted in Foundation Figure 9.9, while specifically describing translation in bacteria, is generally accurate for all organisms. The energy required for these steps is generated by hydrolysis, the cleavage of one phosphate molecules from guanosine triphosphate molecules (GTP). Hydrolysis releases energy and converts nucleotide triphosphates to nucleotide diphosphates (i.e., GTP → GDP). In step ❶ a charged tRNAs is bound by the elongation factor EF-Tu and GTP. In step ❷, the tRNA affiliates with the correct anticodon sequence enters the A site. In step ❸ tRNA pairs with the mRNA codon and hydrolysis of GTP releases EF-Tu-GDP from tRNA. In step ❹, the enzyme peptidyl transferase catalyzes peptide bond formation between the amino acid at the P site and the newly recruited amino acid at the A site. This elongates the polypeptide and transfers the polypeptide to the tRNA at the A site. The tRNA at the P site departs the ribosome through

Bacterial Translation Elongation

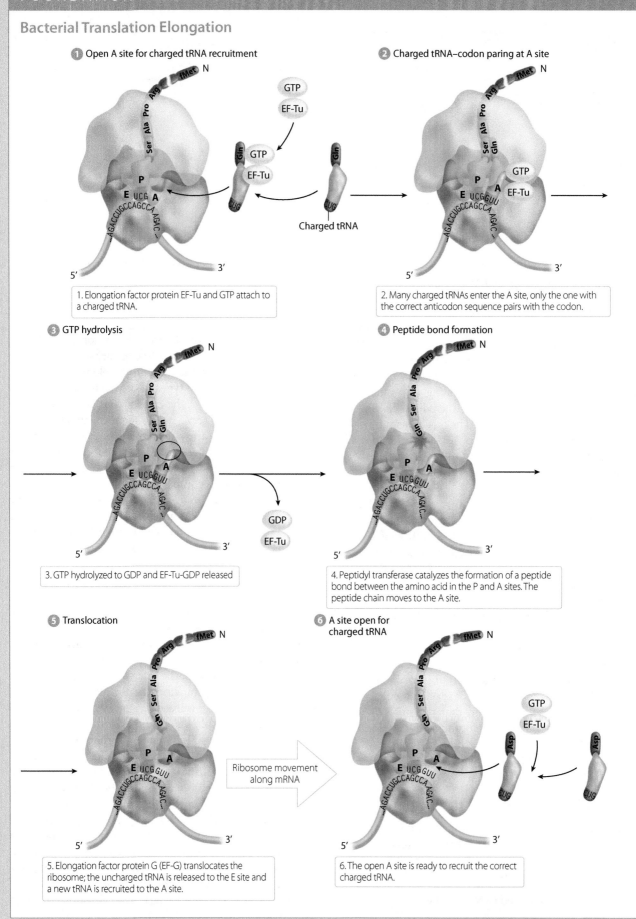

1 Open A site for charged tRNA recruitment

1. Elongation factor protein EF-Tu and GTP attach to a charged tRNA.

2 Charged tRNA–codon paring at A site

2. Many charged tRNAs enter the A site, only the one with the correct anticodon sequence pairs with the codon.

3 GTP hydrolysis

3. GTP hydrolyzed to GDP and EF-Tu-GDP released

4 Peptide bond formation

4. Peptidyl transferase catalyzes the formation of a peptide bond between the amino acid in the P and A sites. The peptide chain moves to the A site.

5 Translocation

Ribosome movement along mRNA

5. Elongation factor protein G (EF-G) translocates the ribosome; the uncharged tRNA is released to the E site and a new tRNA is recruited to the A site.

6 A site open for charged tRNA

6. The open A site is ready to recruit the correct charged tRNA.

PROBLEM In an investigation designed to identify the consensus sequence containing the AUG codon that initiates translation of eukaryotic mRNA, Marilyn Kozak (1986) compared the amounts of protein produced from 10 mutant mRNA molecules having different single-base substitutions flanking the AUG. Protein production was gauged by the optical density (OD) of protein bands in electrophoretic gels. Higher OD values indicated more protein produced. In the two tables shown, AUG, the start codon, is highlighted and its adenine (A) is labeled the +1 nucleotide of the translated region. Kozak examined six single-base mutants at nucleotide −3 and +4. These are identified by number (1 to 6) in Table A. She also examined four single-base mutants of positions −2 and −1. These are numbered 7 to 10 in Table B. The OD for protein production by each mutant was measured and is given below the mutant in the table. Use the OD values to determine answers to the problem questions.

> **BREAK IT DOWN:** The Kozak consensus sequence, 5'-ACCAUGG-3', includes the AUG start codon sequence and several surrounding mRNA nucleotides and is critical to ribosome recognition of the authentic start codon (p. 313).

> **BREAK IT DOWN:** Efficient translation of mRNA produces more protein and is indicated by higher OD values for mutants possessing that capability (p. 313).

Table A — Six Position −3 and +4 Mutants

Mutant number	1	2	3	4	5	6
−3	G	A	U	C	G	A
−2	C	C	C	C	C	C
−1	C	C	C	C	C	C
+1	A	A	A	A	A	A
+2	U	U	U	U	U	U
+3	G	G	G	G	G	G
+4	U	U	G	G	G	G
OD	0.7	2.6	0.9	0.9	3.1	5.0

Table B — Four Position −2 and −1 Mutants

Mutant number	7	8	9	10
−3	A	A	A	A
−2	C	C	G	G
−1	A	A	A	A
+1	A	A	A	A
+2	U	U	U	U
+3	G	G	G	G
OD	3.3	1.8	1.9	2.0

a. Looking just at the nucleotides in positions −3 and +4 for the six mutants in Table A, decide which nucleotides give the highest level of protein production.

b. Describe the impact of each nucleotide (A, T, C, and G) in the −3 position.

c. Looking just at nucleotides at position −2 and −1 for the four mutants in Table B, decide which nucleotides give the highest level of protein production.

d. Why did Kozak use only A in the −3 position to test the effects of nucleotides at positions −2 and −1?

e. Putting together data from both Table A and Table B, give the sequence of the mRNA region from −3 to +4 that produces the highest level of translation.

Solution Strategies	Solution Steps
Evaluate	
1. Identify the topic this problem addresses and the nature of the requested answer.	1. This problem involves examination and interpretation of the effects that sequence differences surrounding the mRNA start codon have on translation. The answer requires identifying the effects of base substitutions on translation and identifying the mRNA sequence corresponding to the highest translation level.
2. Identify the critical information given in the problem.	2. Two tables provide mRNA sequence for different sequence variants. For each variant, an OD value describes the approximate level of protein produced by translation of the sequence. Higher OD values correspond to more protein production.

> **TIP:** Notice that AUG is the start codon sequence in all mutants tested. As a consequence, differences in OD result from differences among the surrounding nucleotides.

Deduce	
3. Identify the constant and variable nucleotides displayed in Table A.	3. In Table A, the nucleotide C is constant at positions −1 and −2, and position +3 is always G. Nucleotide variability is limited to positions −3 and +4.
4. Identify the constant and variable nucleotides shown in Table B.	4. In Table B, only the nucleotide at the −2 position varies; all other nucleotides are constant.

Solve

5. Specify the nucleotides in the −3 and +4 positions (Table A) that give the highest OD.

6. Assess how each nucleotide in the −3 position affects OD.

7. Evaluate how nucleotide differences at the −1 and −2 positions (Table B) affect OD.

8. Explain the decision to base Table B evaluations only on sequences with A in the −3 position.

> **TIP:** Compare OD values and nucleotide differences from both tables to determine the most efficient consensus sequence.

9. Identify the start codon consensus sequence that results in the highest level of translation.

Answer a

5. In Table A, the presence of A in position −3 and G in position +4 produces the highest OD value. At the +4 position, G produces two high OD values and two low ODs, and T produces one high and one low OD.

Answer b

6. At position −3, A produces the highest and the third-highest OD values; G produces the second-highest and the lowest OD; T and C produce the same low OD value.

Answer c

7. In Table B, a C in position −2 and an A in position −1 produce the highest OD. Considering only the variable position −2, C produces higher OD values than does G.

Answer d

8. Adenine is selected as the nucleotide in position −3 for Table B evaluations based on the high average OD value for this nucleotide in comparison to other nucleotides. The average OD for A in the −3 position is $\frac{(5.0\ +\ 2.6)}{2} = 3.8$ versus the next-highest average of $\frac{(3.1\ +\ 0.7)}{2} = 1.9$ for G in the −3 position.

Answer e

9. Data from the two tables combined identify the sequence ACCAUGG (start codon in bold) as the most efficient consensus sequence for the start codon. For the nucleotide positions immediately surrounding the start codon, A is most efficient at −3, C is more efficient than G at −2, C is more efficient than A at −1, and G is more efficient than U at +4.

For more practice, see Problems 32, 33, and 34.

Visit the Study Area to access study tools.

MasteringGenetics™

---

the E site. In step ❺ elongation factor EF-G uses GTP hydrolysis to, EFs translocate the ribosome by moving it in the 3′ direction on mRNA. This translocation step is exactly one codon in length, that is, three nucleotides. Translocation moves the tRNA formerly at the A site to the P site, and opens the A site for binding by a charged tRNA with the correct anticodon sequence. In step ❻ the next charged tRNA is ready to enter the A site.

Elongation of Eukaryotic and Archaeal Polypeptides

Evolution has acted to strongly conserve the basic biochemistry of polypeptide elongation in all three domains of life. The elongation factors that carry out polypeptide elongation in eukaryotes and archaea are shown in **Table 9.4**. All organisms use two elongation factors to carry out polypeptide elongation, and the illustration of polypeptide elongation in Figure 9.9 is an equally accurate portrayal of the process in eukaryotes and archaea. Based on sequence comparisons, the archaeal and eukaryotic elongation factor homologs are more alike than are archaeal and bacterial EFs. This sequence analysis supports the initial assessment of Carl Woese that eukaryotes and archaea are more closely related to one another than either is to bacteria (see Section 1.1).

Translation Termination

The elongation cycle continues until one of the three stop codons, UAG, UGA, or UAA, enters the A site of the ribosome. There are no tRNAs with anticodons complementary to stop codons, so the entry of a stop codon into the A site is a translation-terminating event. All organisms use **release factors (RF)** to bind a stop codon in the A site (**Figure 9.10**). The catalytic activity of RFs releases the polypeptide bound to tRNA at the P site. Polypeptide release causes ejection of the RF from the P site and leads to the separation of the ribosomal subunits.

In bacteria, two release factors, RF1 and RF2, recognize stop codons. RF1 recognizes UAG and UAA, and

Table 9.4	Translation Elongation Factor Homologs		
Function	**Bacterial Homolog**	**Archaeal Homolog**	**Eukaryotic Homolog**
Adjusts tRNA in A site	EFT	aEF1	eEF1
Promotes translocation	EFG	aEF2	eEF2

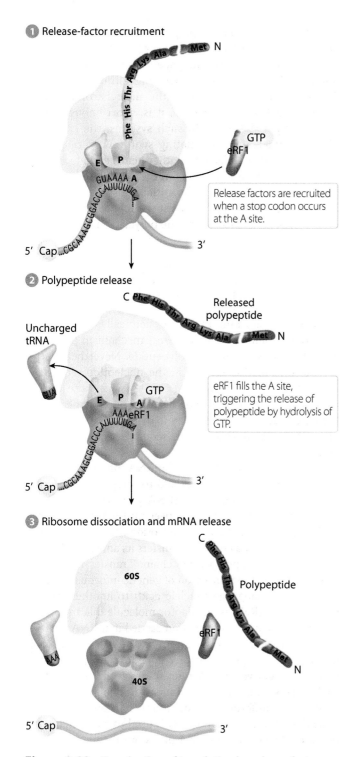

1 Release-factor recruitment

Release factors are recruited when a stop codon occurs at the A site.

2 Polypeptide release

Released polypeptide

Uncharged tRNA

eRF1 fills the A site, triggering the release of polypeptide by hydrolysis of GTP.

3 Ribosome dissociation and mRNA release

60S

Polypeptide

eRF1

40S

5′ Cap _____ 3′

Figure 9.10 **Termination of translation by release factor (eRF) proteins.** A similar process terminates bacterial and archaeal translation.

RF2 recognizes UAA and UGA. A third bacterial release factor, RF3, is active in recycling RF1. Eukaryotic and archaeal translation are terminated by the action of a single release factor, identified as eRF1 in eukaryotes and aRF1 in archaea, that recognizes all three stop codons in organisms of both of these domains. Eukaryotes

Function	Bacterial Homolog	Archaeal Homolog	Eukaryotic Homolog
Stop codon recognition	RF1 and RF2	aRF1	eRF1
Recycling RF1 and eRF1	RF3	No homolog	eRF3
Ribosome recycling	RRF	No homolog	No homolog

Table 9.5 Translation Termination Factor Homologs

have a second RF that, like RF3 of bacteria, participates in recycling eRF1. The currently available information on sequence and function of RFs suggests that archaea and eukaryotes have RFs that are more like one another than either is to bacterial RFs (Table 9.5).

9.3 Translation Is Fast and Efficient

With mRNA transcripts of hundreds to thousands of genes in cells, translation is an active and ongoing process that must efficiently initiate, elongate, and terminate polypeptide synthesis. In recent decades, research has uncovered several aspects of the translation machinery that help explain the speed, accuracy, and efficiency of polypeptide production.

The Translational Complex

Cell biologists estimate that each bacterial cell contains about 20,000 ribosomes, collectively constituting nearly one-quarter of the mass of the cell. The number of ribosomes per eukaryotic cell is variable, but it too is in the tens of thousands. Given these numbers, it is not surprising that translation is almost never a matter of a solitary ribosome translating a single mRNA. Rather, electron micrographs reveal structures called **polyribosomes,** a busy translational complex containing multiple ribosomes that are each actively translating the same mRNA (Figure 9.11). Each ribosome in the polyribosome structure independently synthesizes a polypeptide, markedly increasing the efficiency of utilization of an mRNA.

In bacteria, the coupling of transcription and translation (Chapter 8) allows ribosomes to engage in translation of the 5′ region of mRNAs whose 3′ end is still under construction by RNA polymerase. This coupling is observed in Figure 9.11. Transcription occurs along DNA in the left-hand to right-hand direction. Translation of the mRNA transcripts begins before transcription is complete. In eukaryotes, however, transcription and translation are uncoupled. Transcription takes place in the nucleus, where pre-mRNA is processed to form mature mRNA. Translation occurs in the cytoplasm after release of mature mRNA.

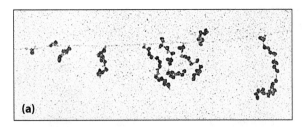

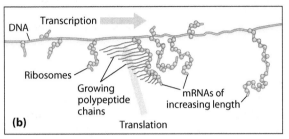

Figure 9.11   Polyribosomes. (a) Electron micrograph of a poly-ribosome shows multiple ribosomes simultaneously translating a single mRNA molecule. Ribosomes that are closest to the stop codon have the longest polypeptides. (b) Artist rendition of the polyribosome electron micrograph. Transcription and translation are coupled in bacteria, and the translation direction is indicated.

Translation of Polycistronic mRNA

Each polypeptide-producing gene in eukaryotes produces monocistronic mRNA, meaning mRNA that directs the synthesis of a single kind of polypeptide. The scanning model for translation described earlier for eukaryotes implies that a single start codon is identified in eukaryotic mRNA to initiate synthesis of one kind of polypeptide chain. In contrast, groups of bacterial and archaeal genes often share a single promoter, and the resulting mRNA transcript contains information that synthesizes several different polypeptides. These **polycistronic mRNAs** are produced as part of operon systems that regulate the transcription of sets of bacterial genes functioning in the same metabolic pathway (a form of regulation we discuss in Chapter 15).

Polycistronic mRNAs consist of multiple polypeptide-producing segments—multiple cistrons—that each contain sequence information for translation initiation. In the case of bacteria, and in all but the leaderless mRNAs in archaea, the translation-initiating region contains a Shine–Dalgarno sequence and start and stop codons. An intercistronic spacer sequence that is not translated separates the cistrons of polycistronic mRNA and contains the Shine–Dalgarno sequences (Figure 9.12).

Bacterial intercistronic spacers are variable in length: Some are just a few nucleotides long, although most are 30 to 40 nucleotides long. If the intercistronic spacer is a few nucleotides in length, it is, short enough to be spanned by a ribosome. In such systems, the ribosome remains intact after completing synthesis of one polypeptide, and it translates the other genes encoded in the polycistronic mRNA as well. On the other hand, for longer intercistronic spacers, the initial ribosome dissociates and new translation initiation must occur to translate the next polypeptide encoded by the polycistronic mRNA.

9.4 The Genetic Code Translates Messenger RNA into Polypeptide

Nucleic acids and amino acids are chemically very different compounds, and there is no *direct* mechanism by which mRNA could synthesize a polypeptide. Nevertheless, the genetic information carried in the nucleotide sequences of mRNA does provide a means by which the amino acid sequences of polypeptides can be specified. The "genetic code" is the name used to describe the correspondence between mRNA codon sequences and individual amino acids.

Converting the sequence of mRNA into a polypeptide depends on transfer RNA (tRNA) to carry amino acids to the ribosome. At ribosomes, tRNA pairs with mRNA by complementary base pairing between mRNA codon nucleotides and tRNA anticodon nucleotides. Once the correct tRNA is bound by a codon, it transfers its amino acid to the end of a growing polypeptide chain. Transfer RNA molecules facilitate the translation of genetic information from one chemical language (nucleic acid) to another (amino acid). That is, tRNA is an adaptor molecule that interprets and then acts on the information carried in mRNA.

Our review of translation and the genetic code in Chapter 1 depicts a triplet genetic code: Groups of three consecutive mRNA nucleotides form codons that each correspond to one amino acid. The genetic code contains 64 different codons, more than enough to encode the 20 common amino acids used to construct polypeptides. The greater number of codons than amino acids

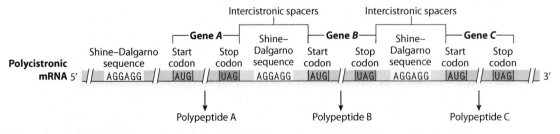

Figure 9.12   Polycistronic mRNA. A polycistronic mRNA is a transcript of multiple genes and will produce a polypeptide from each gene.

leads to *redundancy* of the genetic code, as evidenced by the observation that single amino acids are specified by from one to as many as six different codons. This redundancy is explained by aspects of the base-pairing interactions between tRNA anticodons and mRNA codons.

The Genetic Code Displays Third-Base Wobble

The triplet genetic code is a biological example of Ockham's razor, the principle that the simplest hypothesis is the most likely to be correct: During the late 1950s, arithmetic logic led many researchers to conclude that the genetic code was most likely triplet. This simple solution to the question of how amino acid sequences could be coded by nucleic acid sequences posits that a doublet genetic code (two nucleotides per codon) could produce just 16 (4^2) combinations of codons, which is not enough different combinations to specify 20 amino acids. On the other hand, a quadruplet genetic code would generate 4^4, or 256, different combinations of codons—far too many for the needs of genomes. In contrast, a triplet genetic code, yielding 4^3, or 64, different codons, provides enough variety to encode 20 amino acids with some, but not excessive, redundancy (**Figure 9.13** and genetic code information inside the front cover of the book). Among the 64 codons, 61 specify amino acids, and the remaining

3 are the stop codons that terminate translation. Only two amino acids, methionine (Met)—with the codon AUG—and tryptophan (Trp)—with the codon UGG—are encoded by single codons. The other 18 amino acids are specified by two to six codons. Codons that specify the same amino acid are called **synonymous codons.**

Each transfer RNA molecule carries a particular amino acid to the ribosome, where complementary base pairing between each mRNA codon sequence and the corresponding anticodon sequence of a correct tRNA takes place. Note that this complementary base pairing requires antiparallel alignment of the mRNA and tRNA strands. Consider the codon sequence for aspartic acid (Asp), 5'-GAC-3'. Base-pairing rules predict that the tRNA anticodon sequence is 3'-CUG-5' (**Figure 9.14**). Asp is also specified by a synonymous codon, 5'-GAU-3', that pairs with tRNA carrying the anticodon sequence 5'-CUA-3'. Transfer RNA molecules with different anticodon sequences for the same amino acid are called **isoaccepting tRNAs.**

Does the presence of synonymous codons and isoaccepting tRNAs mean that a genome must provide 61 different tRNA genes and transcribe a tRNA molecule to match each codon? The answer is no. In fact, most genomes have 30 to 50 different tRNA genes. How does a genome that encodes fewer than 61 different tRNA molecules recognize all 61 functional codons? The answer lies in relaxation of the strict complementary base-pairing rules at the third base of the codon. The mechanics of translation provide for flexibility in the pairing of the third base, the 3'-most nucleotide, of the codon. **Third-base wobble** is the name given to the mechanism that relaxes the requirement for complementary base pairing between the third base of a codon and the corresponding nucleotide of its anticodon.

How does third-base wobble work? The answer is found in the chemical structures of nucleotides that hydrogen bond in base-pairing reactions. A careful look at synonymous codons reveals a pattern to the chemical structure of the third bases in cases of wobble. With the exception of the AUA codon for isoleucine (Ile) and the UGG codon for tryptophan (Trp), synonymous codons can be grouped into pairs that have the same two nucleotides in the first and second positions and differ only at the third base, where

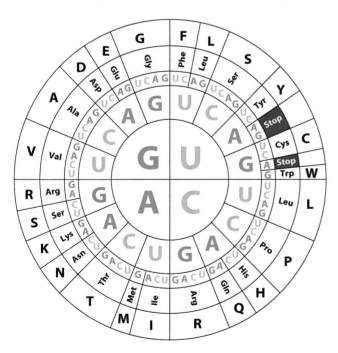

Figure 9.13 The genetic code. To read this circular table of the genetic code, start with the inner ring, which contains the nucleotide in the first position (5' nucleotide) of a codon. The second-position nucleotide is in the second ring, and the third-position nucleotide is in the third ring. Three-letter and one-letter abbreviations for the corresponding amino acids occupy the outermost rings.

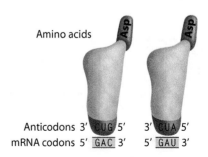

Figure 9.14 Codon–anticodon pairing. A pair of isoaccepting aspartic acid tRNAs illustrates complementary antiparallel base-pairing of codon and anticodon sequences.

the synonymous codons either both carry a purine (A or G) or both carry a pyrimidine (C or U). For example, consider the synonymous pairs of codons for histidine (His) and glutamine (Gln; see Figure 9.13). The first two bases of each of these codons are C and A. Both His codons have a pyrimidine at the third position, whereas the Gln codons have a purine in the third position. As you look at other pairs of synonymous codons in the genetic code information inside the book front cover, notice that they also differ only by carrying the alternative purine or pyrimidine nucleotide at the third position.

Amino acids specified by four synonymous codons, such as alanine (Ala), valine (Val), and glycine (Gly), display an analogous pattern: Each amino acid is represented by two pairs of synonymous codons, and the members of each pair differ in the third position only, by carrying the alternate purine or pyrimidine. The pattern continues in arginine (Arg), serine (Ser), and leucine (Leu), each of which is specified by six synonymous codons. These sets of codons each consist of three pairs, each pair having the same nucleotides in the first two positions and differing by having the alternate purine or pyrimidine in the third position.

Third-base wobble occurs through flexible base pairing between the wobble nucleotide—that is, the 3′ nucleotide of a codon—and the 5′ nucleotide of an anticodon. At the wobble position, base pairing between the nucleotides of the codon and the anticodon need not be complementary. They must, however, involve a purine and a pyrimidine. Third-base wobble pairings are summarized in Table 9.6. The wobble nucleotides in different anticodons include all the RNA nucleotides and also the modified nucleotide **inosine (I).** Inosine is structurally similar to G but lacks the amino group attached to guanine's 2 carbon. Because of this difference, inosine base-pairs with either purines or pyrimidines. Figure 9.15 shows three examples of third-base wobble, in which three tRNA molecules collectively recognize seven different codons.

Charging tRNA Molecules

Transfer RNA molecules are transcribed from tRNA genes. Recall the three-dimensional structure of tRNAs (see Figure 8.28) and the CCA terminus at the 3′ end of tRNA molecules as the site of attachment of an amino

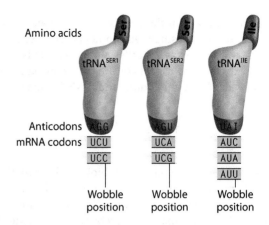

Figure 9.15   Effect of wobble. Wobble base pairing reduces the number of different tRNAs required during translation. In this example, two different tRNAs, each carrying serine, each use wobble to recognize a different pair of serine codons. A single isoleucine-carrying tRNA uses wobble to recognize three isoleucine codons.

acid. Each tRNA carries only one of the 20 amino acids, and correct charging of each tRNA is crucial for the integrity of the genetic code.

The charging of tRNAs is catalyzed by enzymes called **aminoacyl-tRNA synthetases** or, more simply, **tRNA synthetases.** There are 20 different tRNA synthetases, one for each of the amino acids. To charge an uncharged tRNA, a tRNA synthetase catalyzes a two-step reaction that forms a bond between the carboxyl group of the amino acid and the 3′ hydroxyl group of adenine in the CCA terminus. Experimental analysis reveals that the recognition of isoaccepting tRNAs by tRNA synthetase is a complex process that does not follow a single set of rules. Mutations in any of the four arms of tRNA, or in the anticodon sequence itself, render a tRNA unrecognizable to its tRNA synthetase.

Studies of structural interactions between tRNA synthetases and their tRNAs show tRNA synthetase to be a large molecule that contacts several parts of a tRNA as part of the recognition process. These contact points can include the anticodon sequence and the other arms and loops of the tRNA (Figure 9.16). Once in contact with tRNA synthetase, the tRNA acceptor stem fits into an active site of tRNA synthetase. The active site contains the amino acid that will be added to the tRNA acceptor stem and ATP that provides energy for amino acid attachment.

Familiarize yourself with Figure 9.13 and the genetic code information inside the front cover by using them to decipher the mutations shown in Genetic Analysis 9.2.

9.5 Experiments Deciphered the Genetic Code

A remarkable set of experiments performed over less than 4 years in the early 1960s deciphered the genetic code and opened the way for biologists to understand

Table 9.6	Third-Base Wobble Pairing between Codon and Anticodon Nucleotides
3′ Nucleotide *of Codon*	**5′ Nucleotide** *of Anticodon*
A or G	U
G	C
U	A
U or C	G
U, C, or A	I

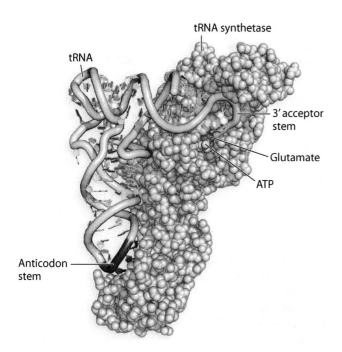

Figure 9.16 **Interaction of aminoacyl-tRNA synthetase with tRNA.** Aminoacyl-tRNA synthetase contacts multiple points on tRNA. ATP and the 3′ acceptor stem of tRNA fit in a cleft that also accommodates the amino acid.

the molecular processes that convert a messenger RNA nucleotide sequence into a polypeptide. At the time, biologists knew *what* the hereditary material was (DNA), and they knew *what* molecule conveyed the genetic message to ribosomes for translation (mRNA), but they did not know *how* the protein-coding information carried by messenger RNA was deciphered during the assembly of polypeptides. Several questions had to be answered about the structural nature of the genetic code before the code itself could be deciphered. The three most important questions, listed here, are examined in the sections below:

1. Do neighboring codons overlap one another, or is each codon a separate sequence?

2. How many nucleotides make up a messenger RNA codon?

3. Is the polypeptide-coding information of messenger RNA continuous, or is coding information interrupted by gaps?

No Overlap in the Genetic Code

Consider the partial messenger RNA sequence

...ACUAAG...

If the genetic code is triplet and nonoverlapping (recall that a doublet code does not provide enough codons to specify 20 amino acids, and a quadruplet code provides

far too many), this partial sequence produces two codons, each specifying an amino acid:

codon	1	2
	...ACU	AAG...
amino acid	1	2

In an overlapping triplet genetic code, on the other hand, these six nucleotides would spell out four complete codons and two partial codons. The sequence would fully encode four amino acids and contribute to the coding of two others:

...ACUAAG...

amino acid 1	ACU
2	CUA
3	UAA
4	AAG
5	AG...
6	G...

In 1957, based on his analysis of the available information on amino acid sequences of proteins, Sidney Brenner became convinced that an overlapping triplet genetic code was impossible because it was too restrictive. To test his hypothesis, Brenner examined the upstream neighbor of each AAG lysine in a large number of proteins and found 17 different amino acids in that position. He concluded that an overlapping genetic code restricted evolutionary flexibility and was unsupported by biochemical observations.

Conclusive evidence of a nonoverlapping genetic code came from a 1960 study of single-nucleotide substitutions induced by the mutation-producing compound nitrous oxide. Heinz Fraenkel-Conrat and his colleagues studied the effect of nitrous oxide on the coat protein of tobacco mosaic virus (TMV). Nitrous oxide causes mutations by inducing single base-pair substitutions in DNA that lead to mutant mRNA molecules with one nucleotide base change compared to wild-type mRNA. A single base change in mRNA would alter *three consecutive codons* if the genetic code were overlapping, but just a *single codon* if the genetic code were nonoverlapping (Figure 9.17a). Fraenkel-Conrat's mutation analysis revealed that only single amino acid changes occurred as a result of mutation by nitrous oxide. This result is consistent with that predicted for a nonoverlapping genetic code, and it is inconsistent with the prediction for an overlapping genetic code.

A Triplet Genetic Code

Proof of a triplet genetic code came in 1961 when Francis Crick, Leslie Barnett, Sidney Brenner, and R. J. Watts-Tobin used the compound proflavin to create mutations in a gene called *rII* in T4 bacteriophage. Proflavin causes mutations by inserting or deleting single base pairs from DNA. This deletion leads to the absence of single nucleotides from

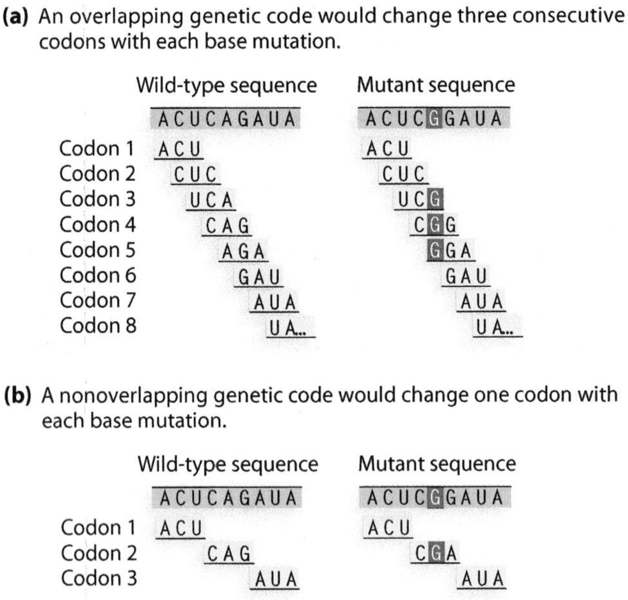

(a) An overlapping genetic code would change three consecutive codons with each base mutation.

	Wild-type sequence	Mutant sequence
	A C U C A G A U A	A C U C G G A U A
Codon 1	A C U	A C U
Codon 2	C U C	C U C
Codon 3	U C A	U C G
Codon 4	C A G	C G G
Codon 5	A G A	G G A
Codon 6	G A U	G A U
Codon 7	A U A	A U A
Codon 8	U A..	U A..

(b) A nonoverlapping genetic code would change one codon with each base mutation.

	Wild-type sequence	Mutant sequence
	A C U C A G A U A	A C U C G G A U A
Codon 1	A C U	A C U
Codon 2	C A G	C G A
Codon 3	A U A	A U A

Figure 9.17 Proof that the genetic code is nonoverlapping. The sequence of the last 10 amino acids at the C-terminal end of a TMV protein contained a single amino acid change following the induction of base-substitution mutation. This result conforms to the prediction of the nonoverlapping model of the genetic code.

mRNA, thus changing the reading frame of the mRNA. **Reading frame** refers to the specific codon sequence as determined by the point at which the grouping of nucleotides into triplets begins. The addition or deletion of nucleotides changes the reading frame and produces a mutation called a **frameshift mutation.**

The following analogy illustrates the impact of frameshift mutations. Single-letter additions or deletions garble the translated message by changing the reading frame:

wild-type: YOUMAYNOWSIPTHETEA ("you may now sip the tea")
mutant (addition): YOUMA C YNOWSIPTHETEA ("you ma c yno wsi pth ete a")
mutant (deletion): YOUMAYNO | | SIPTHETEA ("you may nos ipt het ea")

Frameshift mutations can be reverted (i.e., the correct reading frame can be restored) if a second mutation in a different location within the same gene restores the reading frame. This second mutation, called a **reversion mutation,** counteracts ("reverses") the reading frame disruption by inserting a nucleotide, if the initial mutation was a deletion, or by deleting a nucleotide, if the initial mutation was an insertion. For example, here is how the two frameshift mutations shown above might be reverted:

mutant (addition): YOUMA C YNOWSIPTHETEA (you mac yno wsi pth ete a)
reversion mutant (deletion): YOUMA C YNO | | SIPTHETEA ("you mac yno sip the tea")

mutant (deletion): YOUMAYNO | | SIPTHETEA ("you may nos ipt het ea")
reversion (addition): YOUMAYNOSIP R THE TEA ("you may nos ipr the tea")

Crick and his colleagues analyzed numerous bacteriophage proflavin-induced *rII*-gene mutants, designating each addition mutant as a (+) and each deletion mutation as a (−). They *guessed* that the first *rII*-gene mutant they examined, a mutation designated FC 0, resulted from insertion ("FC" stands for Francis Crick). Designating FC 0 as a (+) mutation turned out to be a correct guess. Based on their assumptions that (1) the genetic code is a nonoverlapping triplet and (2) FC 0 is an insertion (+) mutation, the data reported by Crick and colleagues supported the notion that the genetic code is based on nucleotide triplets.

Data on several mutants is displayed in Table 9.7. Each mutant is designated either (+) or (−). Any combination of a (+) mutant and a (−) mutant generates a wild-type revertant. In each case, the initial mutation causes a frameshift mutation, and the reversion mutation restores the reading frame. The triplet structure of the genetic code is demonstrated by the observation that the reading frame is restored by the presence of *three* (+) mutations or *three* (−) mutations. For example, the total of three insertions restores the reading frame in the following sentence after the position of the third insertion:

triple mutant (addition):
YOUMA C YNOW T S L IPTHETEA ("you ma c yno w t s l ip the tea")

No Gaps in the Genetic Code

In their 1961 research, Crick and colleagues also suggested that the genetic code is read as a continuous string of mRNA nucleotides uninterrupted by any kind of gap,

Table 9.7	Phenotypes Resulting from Various Combinations of Proflavin-Induced Base-Pair Insertion (+) and Deletion (−) Mutations at the *rII* Locus of Bacteriophage T4

Combined Mutations	+/− Designations	Result
FC 0, FC 1	+ −	Wild-type revertant
FC 0, FC 21	+ −	Wild-type revertant
FC 40, FC 1	+ −	Wild-type revertant
FC 58, FC 1	+ −	Wild-type revertant
FC 0, FC 40, FC 58	+ + +	Wild-type revertant
FC 1, FC 21, FC 23	− − −	Wild-type revertant
FC 0, FC 40	+ +	*rII* mutant
FC 0, FC 58	+ +	*rII* mutant
FC 1, FC 21	− −	*rII* mutant
FC 1, FC 23	− −	*rII* mutant

PROBLEM A portion of an mRNA encoding C-terminal amino acids and the stop codon of a wild-type polypeptide is

5'-...CAACUGCCUGACCCACACUUAUCACUAAGUAGCCUAGCAGUCUGA...-3'

The wild-type amino acid sequence encoded by this portion of mRNA contains the amino acid Asn encoded by the codon 5'-CAA-3'. The remainder of the amino acids are encoded in the same reading frame.

> **BREAK IT DOWN:** The mRNA sequence is complementary to the DNA template strand and differs from the DNA coding strand only by having uracil instead of thymine (p. 270).

N...Asn-Cys-Leu-Thr-His-Thr-Tyr-His-C

The C-terminal ends of three independently obtained mutant proteins produced by this gene are as follows.

Mutant 1:   N...Asn-Cys-Leu-Thr-His-Thr-C
Mutant 2:   N...Asn-Cys-Leu-Thr-His-Thr-Tyr-His-Lys-C
Mutant 3:   N...Asn-Cys-Leu-Thr-His-Thr-Tyr-His-Tyr-Ser-Ser-Leu-Ala-Val-C

Identify the mutational events that produce each of the mutant proteins.

> **BREAK IT DOWN:** Mutations occur at the level of DNA. Comparison of each mutant DNA and amino acid sequences with the wild-type sequence will reveal how the DNA sequence is changed (p. 321).

Solution Strategies	Solution Steps
Evaluate	
1. Identify the topic this problem addresses and the nature of the requested answer.	1. This problem concerns evaluation of the C-terminal end of a wild-type protein sequence and the mRNA segment that encodes it and comparison of the wild-type protein to three mutant proteins to determine the alteration producing each mutant. The answers require the identification of specific mRNA sequence changes leading to each mutant protein.
2. Identify the critical information given in the problem.	2. In this problem the C-terminal end of a wild-type protein and the mRNA sequence that encodes it are given. Also given are the C-terminal sequences of three mutant proteins encoded by mutant mRNA sequences derived by alteration of the wild-type sequence.
Deduce	
3. Use the genetic code to identify the codons corresponding to wild-type amino acids and to identify the stop codon.	3. Two codons, AAC and AAU, encode asparagine (Asn). If we skip the 5'-most nucleotide of the mRNA sequence and begin reading at the A in the second position, the first codon is AAC followed by UGC-CUG-ACC-CAC-ACU-UAU-CAC-UAA. These codons encode the wild-type amino acids, and UAA is the stop codon.
4. Compare each mutant polypeptide to the wild type and determine which codon contains the mutation. **TIP:** Any of three stop codons (UAG, UGA, or UAA) terminates translation immediately after the codon specifying the amino acid at the C terminus of a polypeptide.	4. Mutant 1—The polypeptide sequence is truncated two amino acids short of the normal stop codon. The Tyr codon (UAU) appears to have changed to a stop codon. Mutant 2—The wild-type sequence is extended by the addition of lysine (Lys), indicating that mutation changed the stop codon to a codon specifying Lys and is now followed immediately by a new stop codon. Mutant 3—The wild-type sequence is extended by six amino acids. This suggests another mutation affected the stop codon.
Solve	
5. Identify the mutation and its consequence for translation in Mutant 1.	5. Two different base substitutions altering the tyrosine (Tyr) codon UAU to a stop codon could cause Mutant 1. The wild-type UAU codon was most likely altered by base substitution to form either a UAA or a UAG stop codon.
6. Identify the mutation and its consequence in Mutant 2.	6. Lysine (Lys), which was added to the mutant polypeptide, is encoded by AAA or AAG. Deletion of the U from the wild-type stop codon would produce an AAG codon followed by UAG, a stop codon.
7. Identify the mutation and its consequence in Mutant 3. **TIP:** Examine the wild-type nucleotide sequence at the place where mutation is expected to have occurred, and identify ways in which base substitution, insertion, or deletion could have had the observed effect on the amino acid sequence.	7. Tyrosine, specified by codons UAU and UAC, is found in place of the normal stop codon. This is followed by a serine codon (UCN or AGU/C), rather than the GUA (Val) that follows the "in-frame" stop codon in the wild type. A base-pair insertion that adds a U or a C into the third position of the normal UAA stop codon forms a UAU or a UAC tyrosine (Tyr) codon. The altered reading frame from that point would then read AGU (Ser), followed by AGC (Ser), CUA (Leu), GCA (Ala), GUC (Val), and UGA (stop).

space, or pause. If a gap or spacer were present between mRNA codons, the mRNA transcript might be represented as follows (*x* indicates the gap between codons):

YOUxMAYxNOWxSIPxTHExTEAx ("you may now sip the tea")

If the genetic code were structured in some such way, with each codon set off from its neighbors, insertion or deletion of a nucleotide would not cause the kind of frameshift mutation that Crick and colleagues had observed. Instead, insertion or deletion of nucleotides could be expected to alter the affected codon but not the identity of adjoining codons. For example, consider the following insertion mutation, where the separation between codons confines the alteration to a single word:

YOUx,MA T Yx,NOWx,SIPx,THEx,TEAx, ("you ma t y now sip the tea")

Deciphering the Genetic Code

The genetic code was deciphered in a series of experiments performed between 1961 and 1965. This remarkable 4-year period in biology was highlighted by extensive collaborative and competitive international research that culminated in the assembly of a simple table containing the instructions shared by all organisms for translating mRNA nucleotide sequences into polypeptide sequences. Deciphering the genetic code was a milestone in establishing the mechanism of the central dogma of biology (DNA → RNA → protein) and laying the molecular foundation for modern genetic research. This triumph of deductive reasoning was instantly recognized for its profound significance, and it resulted in the awarding of a Nobel Prize in Physiology or Medicine to Har Gobind Khorana and Marshall Nirenberg in 1968.

Once it had been established that the genetic code consists of triplets, researchers sprang to the task of establishing which triplets are associated with each amino acid in the process of translation. Nirenberg and Johann Heinrich Matthaei performed a simple experiment in 1961 that laid the groundwork for later experiments in deciphering the genetic code. Their experimental design was straightforward: Construct synthetic strings of repeating nucleotides, and use an in vitro translation system to translate the sequence into a polypeptide. For example, Nirenberg and Matthaei synthesized an artificial mRNA containing only uracils, known as a poly(U). They devised an in vitro translation system composed of the known cellular components of bacterial translation—ribosomes, charged transfer RNA molecules, and essential translational proteins. Regardless of where translation might begin along the poly(U) mRNA, the only possible codon it contained was UUU. The researchers were therefore hoping to determine which amino acid corresponds to the UUU codon.

Twenty separate in vitro translations of poly(U) mRNA were carried out, each time using a pool of 19 unlabeled amino acids and one amino acid labeled with radioactive carbon (C^{14}). To determine which amino acid is encoded by poly(U) mRNA, Nirenberg and Matthaei used a different radioactive amino acid in each translation. They detected production of a highly radioactive polypeptide after conducting translation in a system containing radioactively labeled phenylalanine (**Figure 9.18**). The radioactive polypeptide was poly-phenylalanine (poly-Phe). Since the only possible triplet codon in the mRNA was UUU, Nirenberg and Matthaei reasoned that 5'-UUU-3' codes for phenylalanine. They went on to construct poly(A), poly(C), and poly(G) synthetic mRNAs and identified 5'-AAA-3' as a codon for lysine (Lys), 5'-CCC-3' as a proline (Pro) codon, and 5'-GGG-3' as a codon for glycine (Gly) (**Table 9.8**).

Khorana adapted the experimental strategy of Nirenberg and Matthaei to synthesize mRNA molecules that contained di-, tri-, and tetranucleotide repeats. His construction of repeat-sequence mRNAs allowed him to define many additional codons (see Table 9.8). For example, Khorana used the dinucleotide repeat UC to form a synthetic mRNA with the sequence

5'-UCUCUCUCUCUCUCUCUC-3'

This mRNA can be translated in either a reading frame that begins with uracil or a reading frame that begins with cytosine. In both cases, the reading frame produces

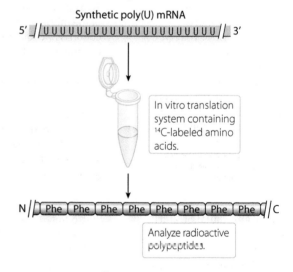

(a) In vitro translation of synthetic mRNA

Synthetic poly(U) mRNA

In vitro translation system containing ^{14}C-labeled amino acids.

Analyze radioactive polypeptides.

(b) Incorporation of ^{14}C-labeled phenylalanine into polypeptides

Synthetic mRNA	Radioactivity (counts/min)
None	44
Poly(U)	39,800
Poly(A)	50
Poly(C)	38

Figure 9.18 **Use of synthetic mRNAs to determine genetic code possibilities.** **(a)** Synthetic poly(U) mRNA is translated in vitro in the presence of individual ^{14}C-labeled amino acids. A polypeptide consisting of phenylalanine is formed. **(b)** These radioactivity counts demonstrate that only poly(U) synthetic mRNA incorporates radioactive phenylalanine into a polypeptide.

Table 9.8	Example Polypeptide Production from Synthetic mRNAs		
Synthetic mRNA	**mRNA Sequence**	**Polypeptides Synthesized**	**Observation**
Repeating nucleotides	Poly-U UUUU...	Phe- Phe- Phe...	Polypeptides have one amino acid.
	Poly-C CCCC...	Pro- Pro- Pro	
Repeating dinucleotides	Poly-UC UCUC...	Ser-Leu-Ser-Leu	Polypeptides have two alternating amino acids.
	Poly-AG AGAG...	Arg-Glu-Arg-Glu	
Repeating trinucleotides	Poly-UUC UUCUUCUUC...	Phe-Phe...and Ser-Ser...and Leu-Leu...	Three polypeptides have one amino acid each.
	Poly-AAG AAGAAGAAG...	Lys-Lys...and Arg-Arg... and Glu-Glu	
Repeating tetranucleotides	Poly-UAUC UAUCUAUC...	Tyr-Leu-Ser-Ile-Tyr-Leu-Ser-Ile	Some polypeptides have four repeating amino acids. Others identify stop codons.
	Poly-GUAA GUAAGUAA...	None (UAA stop codon)	

Note: Data adapted from Khorana (1967).

alternating UCU-CUC codons. Khorana identified the amino acids of the resulting polypeptide and found it contained alternating serine (Ser) and leucine (Leu).

When Khorana used mRNA containing trinucleotide repeats, most of these mRNAs produced three different polypeptides that each consisted of only one kind of amino acid. For example, the reading frame for poly-UUC can begin with either of the uracils or with cytosine. Messenger RNA is read as consecutive UUC codons if the first uracil initiates the reading frame, as UCU if the second uracil begins the reading frame, or as CUU if cytosine is at the start of the reading frame. Although the different reading frames each produced a polypeptide containing one amino acid, Khorana was again unsure which codon specified which amino acid.

Nirenberg and Philip Leder contributed the final piece of the genetic code puzzle in 1964 when they devised an experiment to resolve the ambiguities of codon identity remaining from Khorana's experiments. They synthesized many different mini-mRNAs that were each just three nucleotides in length (**Figure 9.19**). The tiny mRNAs were added individually to in vitro translation systems containing ribosomes, along with 19 unlabeled amino acids and 1 ^{14}C-labeled amino acid, all attached to different transfer RNA molecules. The mRNA formed a complex with the ribosome and the tRNA charged with the corresponding amino acid. Each in vitro mixture was then poured through a filter that captured the large ribosome–mRNA–tRNA complexes but permitted noncomplexed molecules of mRNA or tRNA to pass through. The filter was subsequently tested to determine if the three-nucleotide mRNA sequence bound a transfer RNA with the radioactive amino acid. Nirenberg and Leder tested all 64 combinations of nucleotides with their tiny mRNA system and were able to identify codon–amino acid correspondences for the entire genetic code. In addition, they identified the

nucleotide composition of the three stop codons, UAA, UAG, and (Use **Genetic Analysis 9.3** to test your skill at interpreting the genetic code).

The (Almost) Universal Genetic Code

In astonishing testimony to a single origin of life on Earth and to the power of evolution to maintain virtually complete uniformity over hundreds of millions of years, every living organism uses the same genetic code to synthesize polypeptides. In all living things, from bacteria to humans, the hereditary script carried by any given mRNA is translated by a similar mechanism and produces the same polypeptide. The universality of the genetic code makes it possible to use bacterial systems to express biologically important protein products found in plants or animals. The production of human insulin to treat diabetes and of factor VIII protein to treat hemophilia are two of numerous examples of recombinant human gene cloning that are possible in part because bacteria and humans use the same genetic code for translation.

As with most general rules, however, there are a few exceptions to the universality of the genetic code; thus, biologists characterize the genetic code as *almost* universal. The exceptions are found principally in mitochondria, which are specially adapted to life within plant and animal cells, but two exceptions occur in free-living organisms as well (**Table 9.9**). The near universality of the genetic code presents two important evolutionary questions. First, why has the genetic code remained essentially unchanged in living organisms; and second, why have changes evolved mostly in mitochondria? The answer to the first question is that natural selection pressure against codon change is intense. A single codon change would dramatically alter the composition of almost every polypeptide an organism produces.

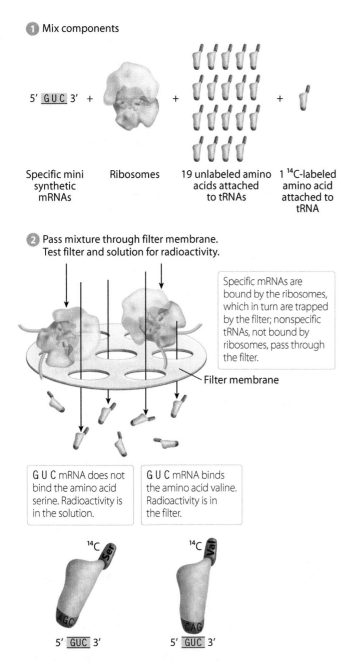

1 Mix components

5′ G U C 3′ + Ribosomes + (tRNAs) + (tRNA)

Specific mini synthetic mRNAs | Ribosomes | 19 unlabeled amino acids attached to tRNAs | 1 ¹⁴C-labeled amino acid attached to tRNA

2 Pass mixture through filter membrane. Test filter and solution for radioactivity.

Specific mRNAs are bound by the ribosomes, which in turn are trapped by the filter; nonspecific tRNAs, not bound by ribosomes, pass through the filter.

Filter membrane

G U C mRNA does not bind the amino acid serine. Radioactivity is in the solution.

G U C mRNA binds the amino acid valine. Radioactivity is in the filter.

¹⁴C Ser | ¹⁴C Val

AGC | CAG

5′ GUC 3′ | 5′ GUC 3′

Figure 9.19 Deciphering the genetic code with synthetic mini mRNAs. For the synthetic mini mRNA GUC, a ¹⁴C-labeled serine tRNA does not hybridize within the ribosome to form a complex, and radioactivity is located in the pass-through solution. ¹⁴C-labeled valine tRNA does hybridize to the GUC mini mRNA within the ribosome. The mRNA–ribosome–tRNA complex is caught by the filter membrane, where radioactivity is detected.

	Table 9.9	Genomes Using Modifications of the Universal Genetic Code	
Codon	**Universal Code**	**Unusual Code**	**Genome**
AGA, AGG	Arg	Stop	Mitochondria in plants, animals, and yeast
AUA, AUU	Ile	Met	Mitochondria in plants, animals, and yeast
UGA	Stop	Trp	Mitochondria in plants, animals, and yeast, and in *Mycoplasma* species
CUN^a	Leu	Thr	Mitochondria in yeast
UAA, UAG	Stop	Gln	Green algae, protozoa
UGA	Stop	Cys	Protozoa

N^a = any third-position nucleotide.

animal cells are small compared to nuclear genomes, and any disruption caused by a change in the mitochondrial genetic code is likely to be limited, since the number of genes affected is so small. In addition, there are many mitochondria per cell, providing "backup copies" of the mitochondrial genome. If a change in the genetic code severely disrupts the function of one mitochondrion, others are present in the cell to carry out normal activities.

Transfer RNAs and Genetic Code Specificity

In our discussion of the genetic code and polypeptide assembly at the ribosome, we describe the specific base-pair interaction between the anticodon sequence of charged tRNA and the codon sequence of mRNA as the key to incorporating the correct amino acid into the polypeptide. But how did biologists determine that the specificity of the genetic code resides in the tRNA–mRNA interaction and not in the recognition of the amino acid carried by tRNA?

The answer came from a simple and clever experiment by Francois Chapeville and several colleagues in 1962. The researchers began by preparing normal cysteine-charged tRNAs. This complex is designated Cys-tRNA^{Cys}. The researchers then treated Cys-tRNA^{Cys} with the compound Raney nickel that removes an SH group from cysteine and converts it to alanine. This treatment produces Ala-tRNA^{Cys} in which alanine rather than cysteine is attached to tRNA^{Cys}. When Chapeville and colleagues used Ala-tRNA^{Cys} in an in vitro translation reaction, the polypeptide contained alanine rather than cysteine in amino acid positions that would normally carry cysteine. In other words, Ala-tRNA^{Cys} efficiently paired with mRNA codons specifying cysteine and deposited alanine in the nascent polypeptide, even though the mRNA sequence specified cysteine.

Countless evolutionary examples tell us that nearly all of the changes that occur would be deleterious, and many would be lethal. Simply stated, a change in the genetic code would alter the rules of the game of life, and natural selection prevents such changes.

The answer to the second question is that natural selection appears to be less intensive on the mitochondrial genetic code than on the genetic code for nuclear genes. The genomes of mitochondria found in plant and

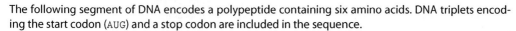

The following segment of DNA encodes a polypeptide containing six amino acids. DNA triplets encoding the start codon (AUG) and a stop codon are included in the sequence.

BREAK IT DOWN: The DNA coding strand differs from mRNA by the presence of T in DNA in place of the U in RNA (p. 270).

5'-...CCCAGCCTAGCCTTTGCAAGAGGCCATATCGAC...-3'
3'-...GGGTCGGATCGGAAACGTTCTCCGGTATAGCTG...-5'

a. Identify the sequence and polarity of the mRNA encoded by this gene.

b. Determine the amino acid sequence of the polypeptide, and identify the N- and C-terminal ends of the polypeptide.

BREAK IT DOWN: The genetic code (see inside the front cover or Figure 9.13) is used for translation (p. 321).

c. Base-substitution mutation changes the first transcribed G of the template strand to an A. How does this alter the polypeptide?

BREAK IT DOWN: A base substitution on the template DNA strand also requires that the nucleotide on the coding strand be changed to the complementary nucleotide (p. 321).

Solution Strategies	Solution steps
Evaluate	
1. Identify the topic this problem addresses and the nature of the requested answer.	1. This problem concerns the identification of DNA coding and template strands, the protein encoded by DNA, and an evaluation of a mutation of the DNA sequence. The answer requires identification of the DNA strands, identification of start and stop codons, and determination of the amino acid sequence of wild-type and mutant proteins.
2. Identify the critical information given in the problem.	2. DNA sequence that includes a start (AUG) codon and a stop codon is given.
Deduce	
3. Identify the start codon by inspecting both DNA strands for 3'-TAC-5' that potentially encodes a start (AUG) codon on the template strand. TIP: The AUG start codon is the most common codon for translation initiation and is encoded by the DNA triplet 3'-TAC-5'.	3. Scanning both DNA strands in their 3' to 5' direction identifies a single 3'-TAC-5' sequence. The sequence is on the upper strand of the sequence beginning with the seventh nucleotide from the right.
4. Survey the putative template strand identified in the previous step and determine if DNA triplets 3'-ATC-5', 3'-ACT-5', and 3'-ATT-5' encoding possible stop codons occur as the seventh codon of an mRNA sequence. TIP: The stop codons UAG, UGA, and UAA are encoded by DNA triplets 3'-ATC-5', 3'-ACT-5', and 3'-ATT-5'.	4. Since just one DNA triplet encoding a start codon is present, a scan of the strand at the correct distance from the start codon does find a 3'-ATC-5' triplet sequence encoding a UAG stop codon: 5'-CCCAGC CTA GCCTTTGCAAGAGGC CAT ATCGAC-3' TIP: Substituting U for T on the coding strand produces mRNA sequence. Alternatively, arranging RNA nucleotides complementary to the template strand and assigning antiparallel polarity produces mRNA.
Solve	
5. Identify the mRNA sequence encoding the six amino acids of the polypeptide. TIP: The mRNA sequence can be determined from either the coding strand or the template strand of DNA.	Answer a 5. The mRNA sequence is 5'-AUG GCC UCU UGC AAA GGC UAG-3'
6. List the amino acid sequence of the polypeptide.	Answer b 6. The polypeptide sequence is N-Met-Ala-Ser-Cys-Lys-Gly-C
7. Identify the effect of the G → A base substitution on the polypeptide.	Answer c 7. Substituting the first transcribed G → A alters the second codon of mRNA by changing GCC → GUC and substitutes valine (Val) for alanine (Ala) in the second position of the polypeptide sequence.

For more practice, see Problems 1, 28, 30, and 31.   Visit the Study Area to access study tools.   MasteringGenetics™

329

Two important conclusions come from this experiment. First, the genetic code derives its specificity through the complementary base-pair interaction of tRNA and mRNA. The amino acid carried by charged tRNA does not play a role in determining which amino acids are incorporated into polypeptides. Rather, tRNA alone—acting through the base-pairing interaction of its anticodon with the codon of mRNA—gives specificity to the genetic code. Second, these findings show the importance of the fidelity with which aminoacyl-tRNA synthetases correctly recognize their cognate tRNAs and charge them with the proper amino acid.

9.6 Translation Is Followed by Polypeptide Folding, Processing, and Protein Sorting

Translation produces polypeptides, but the production of functional proteins is not complete until the polypeptides are folded into their functional tertiary or quaternary structures. Recall from Section 9.1 that these steps involve the formation of ionic or covalent bonds, and they may also involve specific chemical modifications of amino acids in polypeptides. In addition, two other categories of posttranslational events provide further modifications and sort the proteins for transport to their destinations.

Posttranslational Polypeptide Processing

The removal of one or more amino acids from a polypeptide is a common form of **posttranslational polypeptide processing.** Earlier in the chapter, we identified AUG as the usual start codon and noted that it encodes the modified amino acid N-formylmethionine (fMet) in bacterial cells and methionine in eukaryotes. Yet fMet is never found in functional bacterial proteins, and amino acids other than methionine are frequently the first amino acid of polypeptides in eukaryotes. The absence of fMet from functional bacterial proteins is the result of posttranslational cleavage of fMet from each bacterial polypeptide (**Figure 9.20a**). Similarly, methionine is usually removed as part of posttranslational processing in eukaryotes, and the new N-terminal amino acid is acetylated as part of the process.

In addition to N-terminal amino acids, other amino acid residues can be chemically modified as well. One of the most common modifications of individual amino acids is performed by enzymes known as kinases that carry out phosphorylation of proteins by adding a phosphate group to individual amino acids (**Figure 9.20b**). This is an important regulatory process that can switch a protein from an inactive to an active form, or vice versa. Other enzymes may add methyl groups, hydroxyl groups, or acetyl groups to individual amino acids of polypeptides. The addition of carbohydrate side chains to polypeptides to form a glycoprotein is another important kind of posttranslational modification. For example, in one kind of

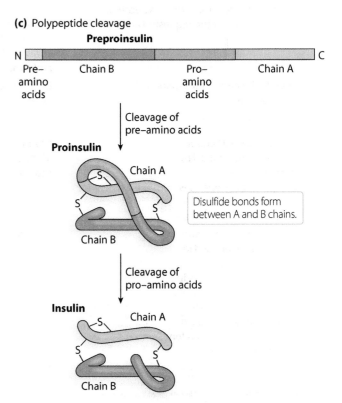

(a) Cleavage of N-terminal amino acids

(b) Chemical modification of internal amino acids

(c) Polypeptide cleavage

Figure 9.20 Examples of posttranslational processing.

posttranslational modification, the H substance is altered by the protein products of the I^A and I^B alleles of the ABO blood group gene (see Section 4.1).

Posttranslational processing may also include the cleavage of a polypeptide into multiple segments that each form functional proteins or that aggregate after elimination of one or more segments to form a functional protein. Production of the hormone insulin, which facilitates transport of glucose into cells, includes two posttranslational modification steps that remove segments of the original polypeptide (**Figure 9.20c**). The polypeptide product translated from the insulin gene is called preproinsulin. It is an inactive protein that contains a leader segment, called the pre–amino acid segment, at the N-terminal end and a connecting segment, called the pro–amino acid segment, that separates the A-chain segment and the B-chain segment, the two functional pieces of the polypeptide. During posttranslational processing of preproinsulin, the pre–amino acids of the signal sequence are removed, after the polypeptide is transported through the cell membrane, to form proinsulin. Three disulfide bonds form within and between the A-chain and B-chain segments, followed by polypeptide cleavage that removes the pro–amino acid segment. What results is a functional insulin molecule consisting of 20 amino acids in the A-chain segment and 31 amino acids in the B-chain segment.

The Signal Hypothesis

Like the passengers in a busy airline terminal, the proteins produced in a cell have different destinations, to which they travel with the aid of a "ticket" that tells the cell where to transport them. The destination is often an organelle or the cell membrane; in certain cases, the polypeptide is destined for transport out of the cell. The ticket that communicates the destination of a polypeptide is a **signal sequence** of 15 to 20 or so amino acids at the N-terminal end.

First articulated in the early 1970s by Gunther Blobel, the **signal hypothesis** proposes that the first 15 to 20 amino acids of many polypeptides contain an "address label" in the form of a signal sequence that designates the protein's destination in the cell. Blobel's hypothesis proposed that the signal sequence directs proteins to the endoplasmic reticulum (ER), where they are sorted for their cellular destinations.

Blobel's signal hypothesis is now a widely accepted model for the identification of the cellular destinations of proteins. In fact, follow-up research has identified the mechanism by which proteins are processed and packaged for export from a cell. While proteins destined to remain in a cell are typically translated at "free" ribosomes (ribosomes that float freely in the cytoplasm), large numbers of ribosomes are attached to the rough endoplasmic reticulum (rough ER) where proteins destined for intercellular transport are translated. **Figure 9.21** illustrates the translation of polypeptides

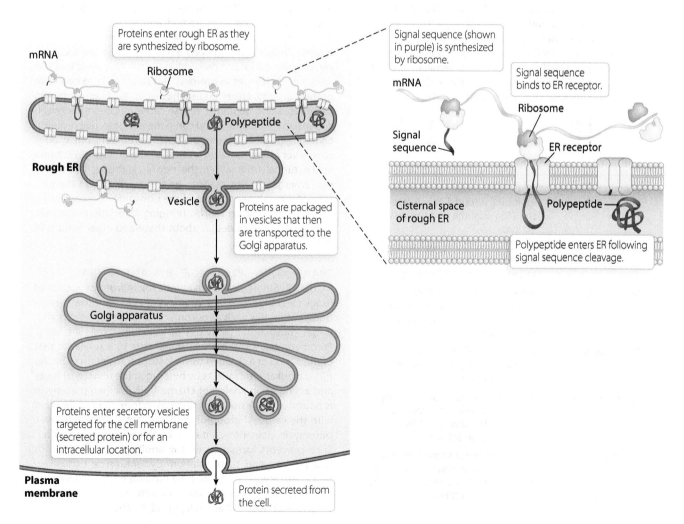

Figure 9.21   Proteins enter the endoplasmic reticulum (ER). Translated proteins enter the cisternal space of the ER through receptors that cleave the signal sequences to begin the protein-sorting process.

into the cisternal space of the rough ER where the polypeptides are processed and packaged for transport to the Golgi apparatus. In the Golgi apparatus additional protein processing takes place and the proteins are packaged into vesicles for transport to the intercellular destinations.

CASE STUDY

Antibiotics and Translation Interference

We have all taken antibiotics at various times during our lives to counteract a painful or persistent microbial infection. As a result of the efficiency of these compounds, we have experienced rapid relief of symptoms and elimination of the infection. These beneficial effects are accomplished by selective cell death or through blocking cell proliferation. Specifically, the antibiotic kills microorganisms without harming our own cells in the process or they act to prevent further microbial cell growth. What is the biochemical basis of antibiotic action? How do antibiotic compounds specifically target microbial cells for destruction?

PROTEIN SYNTHESIS INHIBITION BY ANTIBIOTIC COMPOUNDS You will probably not be surprised to learn that different antibiotics target different aspects of microbe biology to inhibit. But you may be surprised to learn that many different antibiotics target microbial translation as their mode of action (Table 9.10). Familiar antibiotics such as tetracycline, streptomycin, and chloramphenicol target different stages of microbial translation, as do less

familiar antibiotics such as erythromycin, puromycin, and cycloheximide. Each antibiotic contains a different active compound that takes advantage of unique features of bacterial translation to disrupt the production of bacterial proteins while not interfering with the translation of proteins in our cells.

TRANSLATION DISRUPTION BY AMINOGLYCOSIDES *Streptomycin* is one of several antibiotics in a class of biochemical compounds called *aminoglycosides*. Streptomycin inhibits bacterial translation by interfering with binding of N-formylmethionine tRNA to the ribosome, thus preventing the initiation of translation. Streptomycin can also cause misreading of mRNA during translation by generating mispairing between codons and anticodons. For example, the codon UUU normally specifies phenylalanine, but streptomycin induces pairing between a UUU codon and the tRNA carrying isoleucine, whose codon is AUU. This error leads to amino acid changes in proteins and potentially to defective protein activity. Other aminoglycosides, such as neomycin, kanamycin, and gentamycin, also cause mispairing between codons and anticodons and can generate defective proteins. *Erythromycin* also impairs bacterial translation, but it does so in a very different way. It binds to the 50S (large) subunit in the tunnel from which the newly synthesized polypeptide emerges. In this manner, erythromycin blocks the passage of the polypeptide out of the ribosome. This causes the ribosome to stall on mRNA, bringing translation to a halt. Table 9.10 provides details about these and other actions of antibacterial agents.

TRANSLATION BLOCKAGE BY ANTIFUNGAL COMPOUNDS Single-celled eukaryotic microorganisms, such as fungi, can also cause human infections. To fight these infections, antibiotics such as puromycin and cycloheximide that target translational activities of eukaryotic cells are used. *Puromycin* has a three-dimensional structure similar to that of the 3′ end of a charged tRNA. It stops translation of bacterial and eukaryotic mRNAs by binding at the ribosomal A site and acting as an analog of charged tRNA. When puromycin is bound at the A site, its amino group forms a peptide bond with the carboxyl group of the P-site amino acid. However, puromycin does not contain a carboxyl group. This difference prevents formation of any additional peptide bonds and puts an end to translation. *Cycloheximide* exclusively blocks eukaryotic translation by binding to the 60S subunit and inhibiting peptidyl transferase activity, much like chloramphenicol does to bacterial peptidyl transferase.

Table 9.10	Antibiotic Inhibitors of Protein Synthesis
Antibiotic	**Inhibitory Action**
Chloramphenicol	Blocks polypeptide formation by inhibiting peptidyl transferase in the 70S ribosome (antibacterial action)
Erythromycin	Blocks translation by binding to 50S subunit and inhibiting polypeptide release (antibacterial action)
Streptomycin	Inhibits translation initiation and causes misreading of mRNA by binding to the 30S subunit (antibacterial action)
Tetracycline	Binds to the 30S subunit and inhibits binding of charged tRNAs (antibacterial action)
Cycloheximide	Blocks polypeptide formation by inhibiting peptidyl transferase activity in the 80S ribosome (antieukaryote action)
Puromycin	Causes premature termination of translation by acting as an analog of charged tRNA (antibacterial and antieukaryote action)

9.1 Polypeptides Are Composed of Amino Acid Chains That Are Assembled at Ribosomes

- Polypeptides contain 20 kinds of amino acids that carry side chains, giving them specific properties.

- Translation takes place at the ribosome, where mRNA codons are coupled to transfer RNA anticodons by complementary base pairing.

- Polypeptides have four structural levels: the amino acid order (primary), intrachain folding (secondary), three-dimensional functional folding (tertiary), and multimeric protein structure (quaternary).

- Polypeptides have an N-terminal (amino) end and a C-terminal (carboxyl) end.

- Ribosomes are composed of two subunits that each consist of ribosomal RNA and numerous proteins.

- Ribosomes have three functional sites of action: the P site, where the polypeptide is held; the A site, where tRNA molecules bind to add their amino acid to the end of the polypeptide; and the E site, which provides an exit point for uncharged tRNAs.

9.2 Translation Occurs in Three Phases

- Bacterial translation is initiated with the binding of the Shine–Dalgarno sequence on the 5′ mRNA end to a complementary sequence of nucleotides on the 3′ end of the 16S rRNA in the small ribosomal subunit. The nearby start codon is the site where translation commences.

- In eukaryotic mRNA, the 5′ cap is the binding site for eukaryotic initiation factors that cause the small ribosomal subunit to begin scanning in search of the start codon, which is part of the Kozak sequence.

- Archaea carry multiple translation-initiation factors that are homologous to eukaryotic initiation factors, but they also produce a high proportion of leaderless mRNAs that have an unknown translation-initiation mechanism.

- During polypeptide synthesis, charged tRNAs enter the A site, and peptidyl transferase catalyzes peptide bond formation, transferring the polypeptide from the A-site tRNA to the P-site tRNA. Elongation factor proteins translocate the ribosome, shifting the tRNA–polypeptide complex from the A site to the P site and opening the A site for the next charged tRNA.

- Translation terminates when a stop codon enters the A site. Release factor proteins, rather than tRNA, bind to stop codons. Release factors cause release of the polypeptide and lead to the dissociation of the ribosome from mRNA.

9.3 Translation Is Fast and Efficient

- An mRNA undergoes simultaneous translation by several ribosomes that attach to it sequentially to form a polyribosome.

- Usually, a ribosome will dissociate from mRNA upon encountering a stop codon, but the small size of some intercistronic spacers in bacterial polycistronic mRNAs permits a ribosome to translate two or more polypeptides sequentially from the mRNA before dissociating.

- The evolutionary evidence derived from homologies among translationally active proteins of members of the three domains of life suggests that archaea are more closely related to eukaryotes than they are to bacteria.

9.4 The Genetic Code Translates Messenger RNA into Polypeptide

- The genetic code is redundant, meaning that most amino acids are specified by more than one codon. Redundancy of the genetic code is made possible by third-base wobble that relaxes the strict complementary base-pairing requirements at the third base of the codon.

- Specialized enzymes called aminoacyl-tRNA synthetases catalyze the addition of a specific amino acid to each tRNA.

9.5 Experiments Deciphered the Genetic Code

- In vitro experimental analysis demonstrates that the genetic code is triplet and does not contain gaps or overlaps.

- Each mRNA codon is composed of three consecutive nucleotides. Of the 64 codons contained in the genetic code, 61 specify amino acids and 3 are stop codons.

- The genetic code was deciphered by analysis of in vitro translation of synthetic messenger RNA.

- The genetic code is essentially universal among living organisms. The few exceptions to the genetic code are found mainly in mitochondria.

- Properly charged tRNAs play the central role in converting mRNA sequence into polypeptide sequence.

9.6 Translation Is Followed by Polypeptide Folding, Processing, and Protein Sorting

- Formation of functional proteins occurs after translation is completed and may be aided by ribosome-associated proteins or by separate protein complexes.

- Proteins in eukaryotic cells are sorted to their cellular destinations by signal sequences at their N-terminal ends. Signal sequences are removed from polypeptides in the ER, and polypeptides destined for different sites in the cell are differentially glycosylated before being packaged for transport to the Golgi apparatus.

- In the Golgi apparatus, polypeptides are packaged into transport vesicles for shipment to their cellular destinations.

KEYWORDS

3' untranslated region (3' UTR) *(p. 307)*
5' untranslated region (5' UTR) *(p. 307)*
30S initiation complex *(p. 313)*
70S initiation complex *(p. 313)*
aminoacyl site (A site) *(p. 309)*
α-helix (alpha helix) *(p. 308)*
aminoacyl-tRNA synthetase (tRNA synthetase) *(p. 322)*
archaeal initiation factor (aIF) *(p. 314)*
β-pleated sheet (beta-pleated sheet) *(p. 308)*
charged tRNA *(p. 311)*
elongation factor (EF) *(p. 315)*
eukaryotic initiation factor (eIF) *(p. 313)*
exit site (E site) *(p. 309)*
frameshift mutation *(p. 324)*
initiation complex *(p. 313)*

initiation factor (IF) *(p. 312)*
initiator tRNA *(p. 311)*
inosine (I) *(p. 322)*
isoaccepting tRNA *(p. 321)*
Kozak sequence *(p. 313)*
large ribosomal subunit *(p. 309)*
N-formylmethionine (fMet; tRNA^{fMet}) *(p. 313)*
peptide bond *(p. 306)*
peptidyl site (P site) *(p. 309)*
polypeptide *(p. 306)*
polycistronic mRNA *(p. 320)*
polyribosome *(p. 319)*
posttranslational polypeptide processing *(p. 330)*
preinitiation complex *(p. 313)*
primary structure *(p. 308)*

quaternary structure *(p. 308)*
R-group *(p. 306)*
release factor (RF) *(p. 318)*
reading frame *(p. 324)*
reversion mutation *(p. 324)*
scanning *(p. 313)*
secondary structure *(p. 308)*
Shine–Dalgarno sequence *(p. 313)*
signal hypothesis *(p. 331)*
signal sequence (leader sequence) *(p. 331)*
small ribosomal subunit *(p. 309)*
synonymous codon *(p. 321)*
tertiary structure *(p. 308)*
third-base wobble *(p. 321)*
uncharged tRNA *(p. 311)*

PROBLEMS

MasteringGenetics™ Visit for instructor-assigned tutorials and problems.

Chapter Concepts

For answers to selected even-numbered problems, see Appendix: Answers.

1. Some proteins are composed of two or more polypeptides. Suppose the DNA template strand sequence 3'-TACGTAGGCTAACGGAGTAAGCTAACT-5' produces a polypeptide that joins in pairs to form a functional protein.
   a. What is the amino acid sequence of the polypeptide produced from this sequence?
   b. What term is used to identify a functional protein like this one formed when two identical polypeptides join together?

2. In the experiments that deciphered the genetic code, many different synthetic mRNA sequences were tested.
   a. Describe how the codon for phenylalanine was identified.
   b. What was the result of studies of synthetic mRNAs composed exclusively of cytosine?
   c. What result was obtained for synthetic mRNAs containing AG repeats, that is,

      AGAGAGAG...?

   d. Predict the results of experiments examining GCUA repeats.

3. Several lines of experimental evidence pointed to a triplet genetic code. Identify three pieces of information that supported the triplet hypothesis of genetic code structure.

4. Outline the events that occur during initiation of translation in *E. coli*.

5. A portion of a DNA template strand has the base sequence

   5'-...ACGCGATGCGTGATGTATAGAGCT...-3'

   a. Identify the sequence and polarity of the mRNA transcribed from this fragmentary template strand sequence.
   b. Determine the amino acid sequence encoded by this fragment. Identify the N- and C-terminal directions of the polypeptide.
   c. Which is the third amino acid added to the polypeptide chain?

6. Describe three features of tRNA molecules that lead to their correct charging by tRNA synthetase enzymes.

7. Identify the amino acid carried by tRNAs with the following anticodon sequences.
   a. 5'-UAG-3'
   b. 5'-AAA-3'
   c. 5'-CUC-3'
   d. 5'-AUG-3'
   e. 5'-GAU-3'

8. For each of the anticodon sequences given in the previous problem, identify the other codon sequence to which it could potentially pair using third base wobble.

9. What is the role of codons UAA, UGA, and UAG in translation? What events occur when one of these codons appears at the A site of the ribosome?

10. Compare and contrast the composition and structure of bacterial and eukaryotic ribosomes, identifying at least three features that are the same and three features that are unique to each type of ribosome.

11. Consider translation of the following mRNA sequence:

    5′-...AUGCAGAUCCAUGCCUAUUGA...-3′

    a. Diagram translation at the moment the fourth amino acid is added to the polypeptide chain. Show the ribosome; label its A, P, and E sites; show its direction of movement; and indicate the position and anticodon triplet sequence of tRNAs that are currently interacting with mRNA codons.

    b. What is the anticodon triplet sequence of the next tRNA to interact with mRNA?

    c. What events occur to permit the next tRNA to interact with mRNA?

12. The diagram of a eukaryotic ribosome shown below contains several errors.

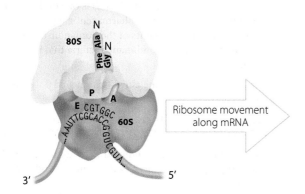

    a. Examine the diagram carefully, and identify each error.

    b. Redraw the diagram, and correct each error using the mRNA sequence shown.

13. Third-base wobble allows some tRNAs to recognize more than one mRNA codon. Based on this chapter's discussion of wobble, what is the *minimal* number of tRNA molecules necessary to recognize the following amino acids?

    a. leucine

    b. arginine

    c. isoleucine

    d. lysine

14. The genetic code contains 61 codons to specify the 20 common amino acids. Many organisms carry fewer than 61 different tRNA genes in their genomes. These genomes take advantage of isoaccepting tRNAs and the rules governing third-base wobble to encode fewer than 61 tRNA genes. Use these rules to calculate the *minimal* number of tRNA genes required to specify all 20 of the common amino acids.

15. The three major forms of RNA (mRNA, tRNA, and rRNA) interact during translation.

    a. Describe the role each form of RNA performs during translation.

    b. Which of the three types of RNA might you expect to be the least stable? Why?

    c. Which form of RNA is least stable in eukaryotes? Why is this form least stable?

    d. Compared to the average stability of mRNA in *E. coli*, is mRNA in a typical human cell more stable or less stable? Why?

16. The figure below contains sufficient information to fill in every row. Use the information provided to complete the figure.

DNA

Coding 5′	A	G G C	T A A	3′
Template 3′	A	T	C	5′

mRNA codon

5′	C		A C	3′

tRNA anticodon

3′	U A	C U C U		5′

Amino acid

3-letter	Cys	Glu		
1-letter	N	E		

17. The line below represents a mature eukaryotic mRNA. The accompanying list contains many sequences or structures that are part of eukaryotic mRNA. A few of the items in the list, however, are not found in eukaryotic mRNA. As accurately as you can, show the location, on the line, of the sequences or structures that belong on eukaryotic mRNA; then, separately, list the items that are not part of eukaryotic mRNA.

    5′ _____ 3′

    a. stop codon

    b. poly-A tail

    c. intron

    d. 3′ UTR

    e. promoter

    f. start codon

    g. AAUAAA

    h. 5′ UTR

    i. 5′ cap

    j. termination sequence

18. After completing Problem 17, carefully draw a line below the mRNA to represent its polypeptide product in accurate alignment with the mRNA. Label the N-terminal and C-terminal ends of the polypeptide. Carefully draw two lines above and parallel to the mRNA, and label them "coding strand" and "template strand." Locate the DNA promoter sequence. Identify the locations of the +1 nucleotide and of a transcription termination sequence.

19. Define and describe the differences in the primary, secondary and tertiary structures of a protein.

20. Describe the roles and relationships between

    a. tRNA synthetases and tRNA molecules.

    b. tRNA anticodon sequences and mRNA codon sequences.

Application and Integration

For answers to selected even-numbered problems, see Appendix: Answers.

21. In an experiment to decipher the genetic code, a poly-AC mRNA (ACACACAC...) is synthesized. What pattern of amino acids would appear if this sequence were to be translated by a mechanism that reads the genetic code as
    a. a doublet without overlaps?
    b. a doublet with overlaps?
    c. a triplet without overlaps?
    d. a triplet with overlaps?
    e. a quadruplet without overlaps?
    f. a quadruplet with overlaps?

22. Identify and describe the steps that lead to the secretion of proteins from eukaryotic cells.

23. The amino acid sequence of a portion of a polypeptide is

    N...Cys-Pro-Ala-Met-Gly-His-Lys...C.

    a. What is the mRNA sequence encoding this polypeptide fragment? Use N to represent any nucleotide, Pu to represent a purine, and Py to represent a pyrimidine. Label the 5′ and 3′ ends of the mRNA.
    b. Give the DNA template and coding strand sequences corresponding to the mRNA. Use the N, Pu, and Py symbols as placeholders.

24. Har Gobind Khorana and his colleagues performed numerous experiments translating synthetic mRNAs. In one experiment, an mRNA molecule with a repeating UG dinucleotide sequence was assembled and translated.
    a. Write the sequence of this mRNA and give its polarity.
    b. What is the sequence of the resulting polypeptide?
    c. How did the polypeptide composition help confirm the triplet nature of the genetic code?
    d. If the genetic code were a doublet code instead of a triplet code, how would the result of this experiment be different?
    e. If the genetic code was overlapping rather than non-overlapping, how would the result of this experiment be different?

25. An experiment by Khorana and his colleagues translated a synthetic mRNA containing repeats of the trinucelotide UUG.
    a. How many reading frames are possible in this mRNA?
    b. What is the result obtained from each reading frame?
    c. How does the result of this experiment help confirm the triplet nature of the genetic code?

26. The human β-globin polypeptide contains 146 amino acids. How many mRNA nucleotides are required to encode this polypeptide?

27. The mature mRNA transcribed from the human β-globin gene is considerably longer than the sequence needed to encode the 146–amino acid polypeptide. Give the names of three sequences located on the mature β-globin mRNA but not translated.

28. Figure 9.7 contains several examples of the Shine–Dalgarno sequence. Using the seven Shine–Dalgarno sequences from *E. coli*, determine the consensus sequence and identify its location relative to the start codon.

29. Figure 9.20 shows three posttranslational steps required to produce the sugar-regulating hormone insulin from the starting polypeptide product preproinsulin.
    a. A research scientist is interested in producing human insulin in the bacterial species *E. coli*. Will the genetic code allow the production of human proteins from bacterial cells? Explain why or why not.
    b. Explain why it is not feasible to insert the entire human insulin gene into *E. coli* and anticipate the production of insulin.
    c. Recombinant human insulin (made by inserting human DNA encoding insulin into *E. coli*) is one of the most widely used recombinant pharmaceutical products in the world. What segments of the human insulin gene are used to create recombinant bacteria that produce human insulin?

30. A DNA sequence encoding a five–amino acid polypeptide is given below.

    ...ACGGCAAGATCCCACCCTAATCAGACCGTACCATTCACCTCCT...
    ...TGCCGTTCTAGGGTGGGATTAGTCTGGCATGGTAAGTGGAGGA...

    a. Locate the sequence encoding the five amino acids of the polypeptide, and identify the template and coding strands of DNA.
    b. Give the sequence and polarity of the mRNA encoding the polypeptide.
    c. Give the polypeptide sequence, and identify the N-terminus and C-terminus.
    d. Assuming the sequence above is a bacterial gene, identify the region encoding the Shine–Dalgarno sequence.
    e. What is the function of the Shine–Dalgarno sequence?

31. A portion of the coding strand of DNA for a gene has the sequence

    5′-...GGAGAGAATGAATCT...-3′

    a. Write out the template DNA strand sequence and polarity as well as the mRNA sequence and polarity for this gene segment.
    b. Assuming the mRNA is in the correct reading frame, write the amino acid sequence of the polypeptide using three-letter abbreviations and, separately, the amino acid sequence using one-letter abbreviations.

32. A eukaryotic mRNA has the following sequence. The 5′ cap is indicated in italics (*CAP*), and the 3′ poly(A) tail is indicated by italicized adenines.

    5′-*CAP*CCAAGCGUUACAUGUAUGGAGAGAAUGAAACUG-
    AGGCUUGCCACGUUUGUUAAGCACCUAUGCUACCG*AAAAAAA*
    AAAAAAAAAAAAAAAAA-3′

    a. Locate the start codon and stop codon in this sequence.
    b. Determine the amino acid sequence of the polypeptide produced from this mRNA. Write the sequence using the three-letter and one-letter abbreviations for amino acids.

33. Diagram a eukaryotic gene containing three exons and two introns, the pre-mRNA and mature mRNA transcript of the gene, and a partial polypeptide that contains the following sequences and features. Carefully align the nucleic acids, and locate each sequence or feature on the appropriate molecule.

    a. the AG and GU dinucleotides corresponding to intron–exon junctions
    b. the +1 nucleotide
    c. the 5′ UTR and the 3′ UTR
    d. the start codon sequence
    e. a stop codon sequence
    f. a codon sequence for the amino acids Gly-His-Arg at the end of exon 1 and a codon sequence for the amino acids Leu-Trp-Ala at the beginning of exon 2

34. The following table contains DNA-sequence information compiled by Marilyn Kozak (1987). The data consist of the percentage of A, C, G, and T at each position among the 12 nucleotides preceding the start codon in 699 genes from various vertebrate species, and as the first nucleotide after the start codon. The start codon occupies positions +1 to +3, and the +4 nucleotide occurs immediately after the start codon. Use the data to determine the consensus sequence for the 13 nucleotides (−12 to −1 and +4) surrounding the start codon in vertebrate genes.

Position	−12	−11	−10	−9	−8	−7	−6	−5	−4	−3	−2	−1	[start]	+4
Percent A	23	26	25	23	19	23	17	18	25	61	27	15	[AUG]	23
Percent C	35	35	35	26	39	37	19	39	53	2	49	55	[AUG]	16
Percent G	23	21	22	33	23	20	44	23	15	36	13	21	[AUG]	46
Percent T	19	18	18	18	19	20	20	20	7	1	11	9	[AUG]	15

35. The following table lists α-globin and β-globin gene sequences for the 12 nucleotides preceding the start codon and the first nucleotide following the start codon. The data are for 16 vertebrate globin genes reported by Kozak (1987). The sequences are written from −12 to +4 with the start codon sequence in capital letters.

	Gene Sequence	
	−12	**start +4**
α-Globin Family		
Human adult	agagaacccaccATGg	
Human embryonic	caccctgccgccATGt	
Baboon	ccagcgcgggcATGg	
Mouse adult	caggaagaaaccATGg	
Rabbit adult	gaaggaaccaccATGg	
Goat embryonic	tcagctgccaccATGt	
Duck adult	ggagctgcaaccATGg	
Chicken embryonic	ctctcctgcacaATGg	
β-Globin Family		
Human fetal	agtccagacgccATGg	
Human embryonic	aggcctggcatcATGg	
Rabbit adult	aaacagacagaATGg	
Rabbit embryonic	agaccagacatcATGg	
Chicken adult	ccaaccgccgccATGg	
Chicken embryonic	cccgctgccaccATGg	
Xenopus adult	tcaactttggccATGg	
Xenopus larval	tctacagccaccATGg	

Use the data in this table to

a. Determine the consensus sequence for the 16 selected α-globin and β-globin genes.
b. Compare the consensus sequence for these globin genes to the consensus sequence derived from the larger study of 699 vertebrate genes in Problem 34.

36. The six nucleotides preceding the start codon and the first nucleotide after the start codon in eukaryotes exhibit strong sequence preference as determined by the percentages of nucleotides in the −6 to −1 positions and the +4 position. Use the data given in the table for Problem 35 to determine the seven nucleotides that most commonly surround the start in vertebrates.

37. In terms of the polycistronic composition of mRNAs and the presence or absence of Shine–Dalgarno sequences, compare and contrast bacterial, archaeal, and eukaryotic mRNAs.

38. Organisms of all three domains of life usually use the mRNA codon AUG as the start codon.

    a. Do organisms of the three domains use the same amino acid as the initial amino acid in translation? Identify similarities and differences.
    b. Despite AUG being the most common start codon sequence, very few proteins have methionine as the first amino acid. Why is this the case?

10

The Integration of Genetic Approaches: Understanding Sickle Cell Disease

CHAPTER OUTLINE

10.1 An Inherited Hemoglobin Variant Causes Sickle Cell Disease

10.2 Genetic Variation Can Be Detected by Examining DNA, RNA, and Proteins

10.3 Sickle Cell Disease Evolved by Natural Selection in Human Populations

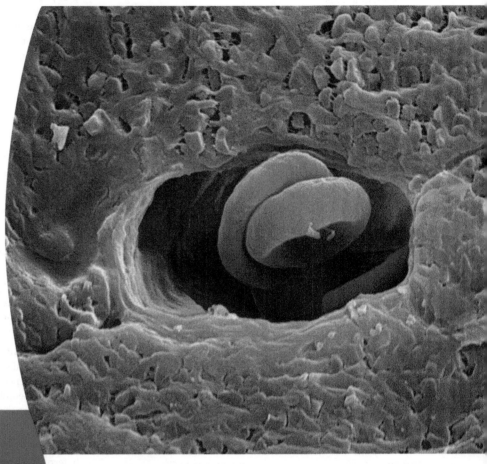

Normal red blood cells barely squeeze through narrow capillaries, but sickle-shaped red blood cells can block blood flow in capillaries.

ESSENTIAL IDEAS

▪ Progress in understanding the human hereditary anemia called sickle cell disease shows the power of combining analytical approaches from transmission genetics, molecular genetics, and evolutionary genetics.

▪ A mutant allele of one of the two genes forming the red blood cell protein hemoglobin causes abnormalities that lead to sickle cell disease.

▪ The transmission of sickle cell disease in families parallels molecular genetic analysis of globin gene and protein variation.

▪ The geographic distribution of the mutation producing sickle cell disease is attributable to natural selection pressure exerted in malaria-rich environments.

In previous chapters, we described gene transmission and function, the structure and function of DNA, the processes of gene expression, and the role of evolution in genetics. Each of these aspects of modern genetics contributes to the broad explanatory power of the science, a power achieved specifically through the integration of these principles and approaches. This chapter is designed to bring the integration of these genetic analysis approaches into focus using the human hereditary disorder sickle cell disease as an example.

The chapter has a second purpose as well. In the course of illustrating how analyses of hereditary transmission, molecular genetic variation, and evolution contribute to a comprehensive understanding of sickle cell disease, it also describes gel electrophoresis and related experimental methods that are commonly applied to the analysis of DNA, RNA, and protein variation. These methods are part of the basic "toolkit" of genetic analysis and can be used to obtain substantial information about nucleic acid and protein variation.

10.1 An Inherited Hemoglobin Variant Causes Sickle Cell Disease

Sickle cell disease (SCD), also known as sickle cell anemia, has been intensively investigated for more than a century, and its study has generated a revolution in genetics. Not only was SCD among the first genetic disorders shown to be caused by an inherited defect in a protein molecule, but the discovery of its cause—several years before DNA was identified as the hereditary molecule—helped pave the way for the molecular era in genetics. In fact, sickle cell disease has the distinction of being the first hereditary disorder to be designated as a "molecular disease." It demonstrates that inherited diseases have a molecular basis, and it played a key role in establishing the molecular nature of mutations. Investigation of SCD and the description of the molecular basis of the disease led ultimately to an explanation of the role natural selection plays in the evolution and maintenance of the disease-causing allele in populations.

SCD is a potentially fatal autosomal recessive disorder caused by an abnormality in the structure and function of **hemoglobin (Hb),** the main oxygen-carrying protein in red blood cells. The hemoglobin defect producing SCD shortens the life span of red blood cells from an average of about 120 days for normal red blood cells to an average of 10 to 20 days for red blood cells in individuals with SCD. As a result of the greatly shortened life span of red blood cells, individuals with SCD have, severe anemia (an abnormally low number of red blood cells) that reduces the ability of blood to deliver oxygen to tissues. Oxygen deprivation causes tissue damage and tissue death throughout the body, accompanied by significant muscle pain and accumulated damage to organs.

The hemoglobin variant causing SCD is one of hundreds of different variant hemoglobin alleles occurring in people around the world, and inherited variations in hemoglobin are the most common type of hereditary abnormality found in humans. Hundreds of millions of people carry mutant alleles that alter the structure or function of hemoglobin molecules. Most of these alleles are rare. But a few, such as the mutant allele causing SCD, are common in certain populations. The SCD allele is common in multiple populations around the Mediterranean region, in the Middle East, and in Africa, and the mutant allele has formed and evolved independently in each of these regions.

The First Patient with Sickle Cell Disease

Several principles of molecular genetics have their origin in the study of hemoglobin and the genes that produce it, including the concept of a molecular disease—a designation bestowed on SCD by Linus Pauling in 1954. A good place to begin our discussion, however, is with an event that occurred more than a century ago—December 1904, to be precise—when Walter Noel, a 20-year-old man of African origin, was admitted to Presbyterian Hospital in New York City suffering from severe anemia and debilitating muscle pain. Noel had arrived in New York City a year or so earlier from the Caribbean island of Grenada, and he had just begun the first year of a dentistry training program when he was admitted to the hospital.

The physician in charge of Noel's case was an intern named Ernest Irons, who was supervised by a more experienced physician named James Herrick. Irons drew blood from Noel, examined it under a microscope, and was shocked to see that many of Noel's red blood cells had a peculiar elongated and sickled shape that contrasted starkly with the circular, biconcave shape of normal red blood cells (**Figure 10.1**).

With intensive treatment of his symptoms, Noel recovered from this initial bout with the illness. Over the

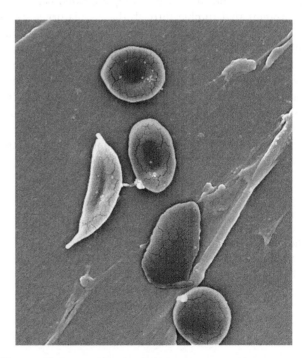

Figure 10.1   Red blood cell shape. Normal red blood cells have a biconcave shape (top), whereas sickle-shaped red blood cells are elongated (left). Other partially deformed red blood cells are also seen in this image.

next two and a half years, he was to be readmitted several times and treated for the same symptoms. After completing his dentistry training, he returned to Grenada, where he practiced dentistry until he died 9 years later at the age of 32. In 1910, Herrick published a paper describing Walter Noel's case. The paper was the first clinical description of SCD, although the disorder had no name at the time Herrick described it. Its original name, "sickle cell anemia," was created several years later by combining *sickle,* for the characteristic deformity of the red blood cells, and *anemia,* for the chronic shortage of red blood cells in most patients.

During periodic events known as "sickle crises," sickle cell disease patients experience severe muscle pain. The pain is due to oxygen deprivation in organs and tissues that is brought about by the presence of large numbers of sickle-shaped red blood cells in their circulation. As seen in Figure 10.1, sickle-shaped red blood cells are longer than the normal, biconcave red blood cells, and they are large enough to impede blood flow in small blood vessels and capillaries. These blood vessels and capillaries are barely wide enough for normal, biconcave red blood cells to move through in single file (see the chapter opener photo). The reduced blood flow deprives the surrounding tissues of oxygen, causing immediate pain as well as potential long-term damage to organs and tissues.

Red blood cells are oxygen transportation and delivery specialists. They are pumped from the heart to the lungs, where they pick up oxygen, and then through the circulatory system to carry oxygen and other molecules throughout the body. Red blood cells do not contain nuclei and cannot divide; thus they are essentially sacks of proteins that tumble through the circulatory systems to pick up and deliver their molecular cargo. They circulate until they are damaged and removed from circulation—about 100 to 120 days on average for normal red blood cells. Red blood cells that undergo sickling are damaged more quickly than normal and have a life span. Unfortunately, the body's red blood cell production capacity is limited. The accelerated rate of loss of red blood cells in SCD results in chronic anemia as one of the symptoms of the disorder.

Hemoglobin Structure

Hemoglobin molecules are tetramers, protein structures consisting of four proteins joined together. They are an example of a protein with a quaternary structure (see Table 9.2, p. 308). The hemoglobin tetramer contains two protein chains from each of two different **globin genes** that are encoded on separate chromosomes in the human genome. Each molecule of the most common form of hemoglobin consists of two **α-globin** (pronounced *AL-fa GLOBE-in*) **proteins,** produced by the **α-globin gene,** and two **β-globin** (*BAY-ta GLOBE-in*) **proteins,** produced by the **β-globin gene.** This particular composition, denoted $\alpha_2\beta_2$, is identified as hemoglobin A, or HbA, where *Hb* is an abbreviation for *hemoglobin* and *A* designates the most common form. Each of the four globin proteins in hemoglobin has a specific tertiary structure, and each carries one iron-containing molecule of heme that undergoes reversible binding with a molecule of oxygen. Thus, each globin tetramer can bind and transport four oxygen molecules.

The α-globin and β-globin genes are members of a family of closely related globin genes that evolved from a common ancestral gene. Due to their common origin, α-globin and β-globin genes have similar composition, and their protein products have strong structural and functional similarities. The organization of the two genes is also very similar (**Figure 10.2**). Both genes contain three exons and two introns. The α-globin gene encodes a polypeptide containing 141 amino acids, and the polypeptide encoded by the β-globin gene contains 146 amino acids.

Globin Gene Mutations

The globin genes may be the most intensively studied genes in the human genome, and the existence and distribution of α-globin and β-globin gene variants are well documented in most human populations. At present, nearly 500 different allelic variants of the α-globin and β-globin genes are known. Nearly all of these globin gene variants are rare. Some are so rare that they exist

Figure 10.2 Globin proteins and their genes. The α-globin and β-globin genes each contain three exons and two introns. The amino acids encoded by each exon are indicated by the numbers describing their places in the final polypeptide chain.

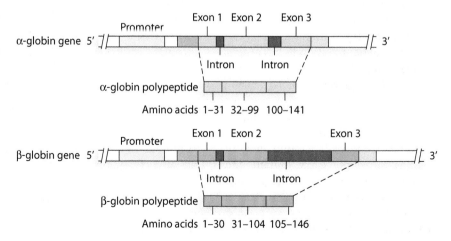

only in a single family. There are a few notable exceptions, however, and these more common variants provide well-researched examples of some hereditary and evolutionary processes that you are likely to have studied in previous biology courses. They also give us the chance to explore how globin gene variants affect hemoglobin structure and function.

In a century of research since Herrick's description of Walter Noel's SCD, physicians and human biologists have fully explored the heredity, molecular basis, and evolution of the disorder. Today biologists know that SCD is a common autosomal recessive hereditary anemia caused by a single base-pair substitution in the β-globin gene sequence (Figure 10.3). This type of mutation is known as a point mutation. The mutant allele, designated β^S, produces a β-globin protein that contains the amino acid valine (Val) in the sixth position of the 146 amino acids of the protein. In comparison, the wild-type $\boldsymbol{\beta^A}$ **allele** encodes glutamic acid (Glu) at the sixth amino acid position. Individuals with SCD carry two $\boldsymbol{\beta^S}$ **alleles** and do not have the β^A allele; this form of hemoglobin is identified as HbS. Such individuals have the genotype $\beta^S\beta^S$ and produce only mutant β-globin chains.

When two mutant β-globin proteins join two normal α-globin proteins, the hemoglobin molecules

(a) β^A **allele**

(b) β^S **allele**

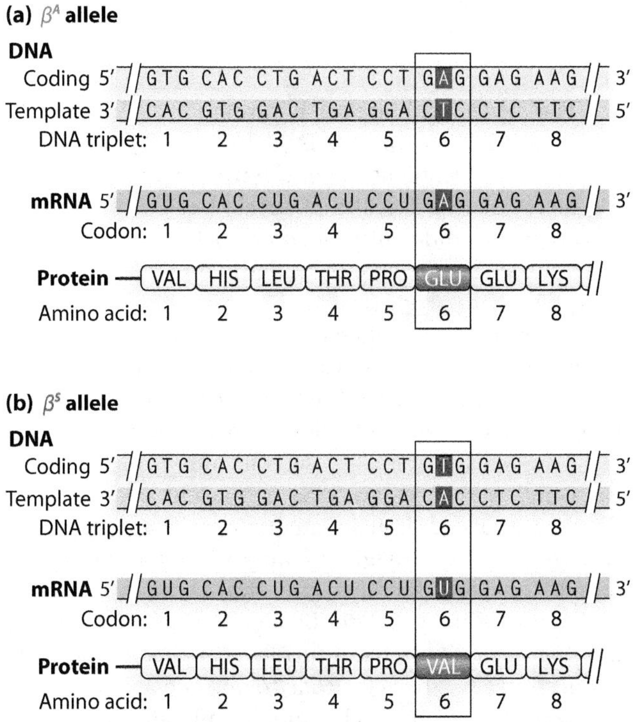

Figure 10.3   SCD mutation in the DNA sequence of the β-globin gene. DNA, mRNA, and amino acid sequences spanning the first eight amino acids of **(a)** the wild-type β^A allele and **(b)** the β^S allele are shown. A single nucleotide polymorphism occurs in DNA triplet 6 (boxed), causing a change in the sixth codon of mRNA and a change in the sixth amino acid of the polypeptide from Glu to Val.

formed are structurally abnormal. Glutamic acid (Glu) has an electrically charged side chain that allows it to interact with other amino acids in ways that valine (Val), which has a nonpolar side chain, cannot (see Figure 9.1, p. 306). The presence of Val in β-globin alters the secondary and tertiary structure of the β^S protein so that it forms a hydrophobic cleft not seen in the β^A protein (Figure 10.4). When tetrameric hemoglobin protein forms, the hydrophobic clefts of β^S proteins enable the attachment of hemoglobin molecules in long chains. These chains are particularly likely to form when oxygen concentration in red blood cells drops. Chain formation distorts the shape of affected red blood cells, producing their characteristic sickle shape first seen by Ernest Irons. This deformation also damages red blood cells and shortens their lifespan relative to normal red blood cells.

Individuals who are heterozygous carriers of SCD have the genotype $\beta^A\beta^S$. All their hemoglobin tetramers contain two normal α-globin proteins, but some contain two β^A proteins, some contain two β^S proteins, and others contain one of each type of β-globin protein. Consequently, a small percentage of the red blood cells of heterozygous individuals can acquire a sickle-shaped form when oxygen level is low, as it is when red blood cells are returning to the heart. This condition shortens the average life span of red blood cells in heterozygotes, but not nearly as severely as in those with SCD. Furthermore, since only a small percentage of red blood cells are affected in heterozygotes, they do not develop, the anemia seen in those with SCD. Heterozygous carriers are sometimes identified as having "sickle cell trait," while their symptoms are generally mild, severe complications can occur under circumstances in which the availability of oxygen is reduced or the need for oxygen is high. Potential health consequences for athletes who are heterozygous carriers of sickle cell trait are one area of concern. For example, in 2010, following the deaths of ten student athletes with sickle cell trait over the previous decade, the National Collegiate Athletic Association (NCAA) implemented a policy offering student athletes the option of being tested for sickle cell trait.

10.2 Genetic Variation Can Be Detected by Examining DNA, RNA, and Proteins

We now turn our attention to widely used molecular genetics techniques that have been crucial for analyzing the β^S and β^A alleles as well as the mRNA and proteins that are produced by the alleles. We consider them here along with techniques used to identify certain specific types of DNA sequence variation. We do this in historical context, describing techniques and research results

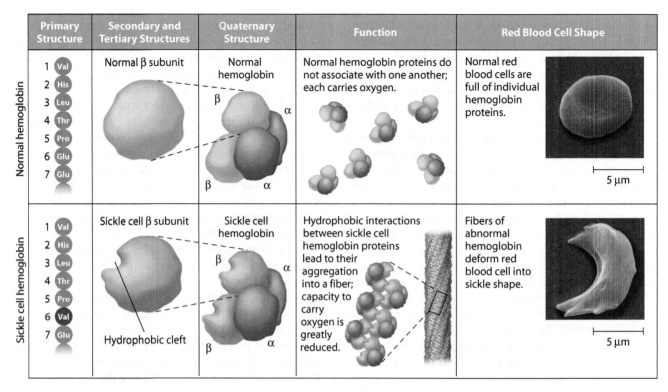

Primary Structure	Secondary and Tertiary Structures	Quaternary Structure	Function	Red Blood Cell Shape
Normal hemoglobin 1 Val, 2 His, 3 Leu, 4 Thr, 5 Pro, 6 Glu, 7 Glu	Normal β subunit	Normal hemoglobin β α β α	Normal hemoglobin proteins do not associate with one another; each carries oxygen.	Normal red blood cells are full of individual hemoglobin proteins. 5 μm
Sickle cell hemoglobin 1 Val, 2 His, 3 Leu, 4 Thr, 5 Pro, 6 Val, 7 Glu	Sickle cell β subunit — Hydrophobic cleft	Sickle cell hemoglobin β α β α	Hydrophobic interactions between sickle cell hemoglobin proteins lead to their aggregation into a fiber; capacity to carry oxygen is greatly reduced.	Fibers of abnormal hemoglobin deform red blood cell into sickle shape. 5 μm

Figure 10.4 **Hemoglobin structural change in sickle cell disease.** (a) The substitution of valine for glutamic acid in the polypeptide product of the β^S creates a hydrophobic pocket not present in the polypeptide of the β^A allele. (b) Mutant hemoglobin tetramers aggregate by the hydrophobic regions adhering to one another. Long strands of aggregated hemoglobin protein crystalize, leading to red blood cell deformation (sickling).

in the order they occurred in the study of SCD and discussing how new information contributed to understanding of the condition at each step. The molecular methods discussed in this section are useful in a wide range of genetic analyses, although some of the specific techniques have been replaced with more modern methods. Understanding how the original techniques work and how their results are interpreted makes it much easier to understand how the modern methods work, the data they produce, and how those data are interpreted.

Gel Electrophoresis

In 1949, James Neel used transmission genetic analysis to demonstrate that SCD is an autosomal recessive disorder.

Neel examined red blood cells of 42 parents who had a child with SCD but who did not have SCD themselves. He found that a small proportion of the red blood cells of each of the parents tested were sickle shaped. The number of sickle-shaped red blood cells was consistent with each parent being a heterozygous carrier (β^A β^S) and demonstrated that SCD is an autosomal recessive trait. That same year, Linus Pauling and his colleagues published the first description of the molecular basis of SCD and coined the term *molecular disease* to describe it. They used the term to denote a disease caused by a variation in the molecular structure of a protein.

Pauling isolated hemoglobin from people having each of the various genotypes ($\beta^A\beta^A$, $\beta^A\beta^S$, and $\beta^S\beta^S$) and used the analytical technique of **gel electrophoresis** to separate the hemoglobin molecules of each type. Gel electrophoresis separates different protein or nucleic acid molecules from one another in an electrical field on the basis of their charge, size, and shape (**Figure 10.5**). A gel support matrix is created by molding a liquid inside a form, typically a plastic casting tray. A "comb" is placed in the liquid as it is poured into the form, to produce "wells," or depressions, in the gel. In the form, the liquid solidifies into a flexible semisolid.

The wells are small reservoirs into which biological samples, such as proteins or nucleic acid (DNA or RNA), are loaded. Usually, multiple wells are employed, each marking the **origin of migration** for one of the samples and thus serving as the starting point for one of the "lanes" of the gel. After biological samples are loaded into the wells, an electrical current is applied to the gel by connecting a positive electrode to one end and a negative electrode to the other. The samples migrate through the matrix of tiny pores and passageways created by the solidification of the gel. Molecules make their way from the origin of migration near the negatively charged end of the gel toward the positive charge at the opposite end.

The materials most commonly used to form electrophoresis gels are **agarose,** a form of cellulose, and **polyacrylamide,** a synthetic material made by a polymerization

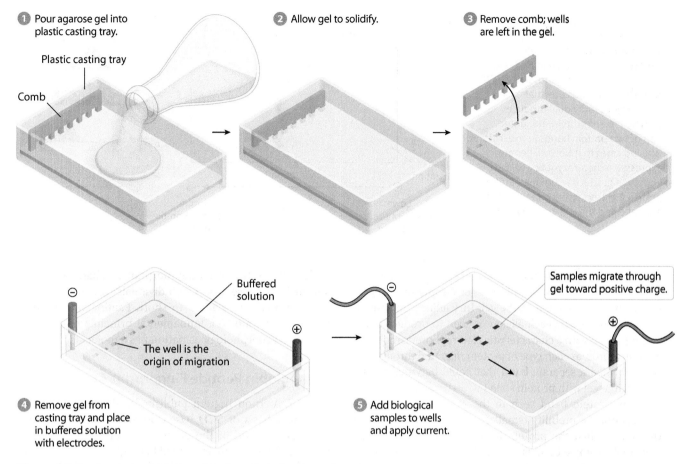

Figure 10.5 **Apparatus and procedure for gel electrophoresis.**

reaction between chemical compounds. Neither of these substances interacts with proteins or nucleic acids as they move through the gel, so the rates of migration of different protein or nucleic acid molecules are determined entirely by the characteristics of the molecules in each sample.

In gel electrophoresis, biological molecules that have electric charge migrate toward the end having the opposite charge. Most biological molecules, including DNA, RNA, and, at pH 7.0, most proteins, have negative charge and migrate toward the positive end. Therefore, the origin of migration is usually placed near the negative end. Proteins with positive charge migrate toward the negative end, so when they are being studied, the origin of migration will be placed near the positive end.

Molecular movement through the electrophoresis gel is driven by the flow of electricity. Molecules migrate continuously and at a steady rate when electricity flows, and they stop moving when current flow is turned off. In electrophoretic gels, the migratory rate of molecules depends on three parameters of molecular structure. Each of these parameters individually is important in determining how a particular molecule migrates, but they can also interact with one another to produce a characteristic migration rate for each molecule. The parameters are as follows.

■ **Molecular weight**—Smaller molecules (i.e., proteins with fewer amino acids or nucleic acids with fewer

nucleotides) migrate more quickly than larger molecules. This characteristic is an important determinant of electrophoretic migration of all biological molecules, and it is the main parameter in DNA and RNA migration.

■ **Molecular charge**—Molecules with greater negative charge migrate toward the positive pole more rapidly than molecules with less negative charge. Variation in molecular charge of proteins is imparted by amino acid composition and is an important characteristic influencing protein migration. In contrast, nucleic acids have negative charge that derives from the sugar-phosphate backbone. This negative charge is proportionate to mass and thus does not contribute to differences in migration rate among nucleic acid molecules of different lengths.

■ **Molecular shape (molecular conformation)**— Tightly condensed, globular molecules migrate more quickly than linear molecules. Protein migration can be strongly influenced by conformation; however, when nucleic acids are being compared, the only migration differences caused by molecular shape occur in comparisons of linear and circular DNA.

Pauling's electrophoretic analysis of hemoglobin proteins purified from red blood cells showed that proteins produced by individuals with different β-globin genotypes

Figure 10.6 Gel electrophoresis of hemoglobin proteins.
(a) Individuals with the three genotypes $\beta^S\beta^S$, $\beta^A\beta^S$, and $\beta^A\beta^A$ are analyzed. The single bands in the $\beta^S\beta^S$ and $\beta^A\beta^A$ lanes indicate that each homozygous individual produces a single type of protein. The detection of two protein bands in the $\beta^A\beta^S$ lane indicates that both alleles are expressed in heterozygotes. (b) Each genotype produces a unique pattern of protein electrophoretic mobility that is also reflected by densitometry results.

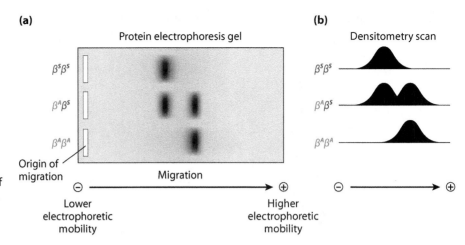

have different **electrophoretic mobility,** a term that describes either the rate of a molecule's electrophoretic migration or its final position in the gel. In Pauling's analysis of hemoglobin protein, each allele was seen to produce a different protein with a characteristic electrophoretic mobility; in other words, as each type of protein migrated through the gel, it formed a separate **band** that could be visualized by staining the gel with protein stain (Figure 10.6a).

The protein band seen in the $\beta^S\beta^S$ lane had lower electrophoretic mobility (smaller distance migrated from the origin) than the protein band detected in the $\beta^A\beta^A$ lane. Only a single band is detected in each of these lanes, suggesting that all the protein in the lane is identical. In contrast, when an electrophoresis lane contains protein from a heterozygous ($\beta^A\beta^S$) individual, the protein in that lane separates into two bands, each corresponding to the electrophoretic mobility of the protein bands in the lanes containing protein from a homozygote. The lower electrophoretic mobility of β^S, versus β^A, is due to the replacement of glutamic acid (with a charged side chain) by valine (with a nonpolar side chain) in the β^S, protein.

Pauling then used a technique called densitometry to show that a single kind of β-globin protein is present in lanes containing protein from a homozygous individual, and that two kinds of protein are present in lanes containing protein taken from heterozygotes (Figure 10.6b). Densitometry quantifies the amount of protein present in a gel lane by measuring how much light is blocked from passing through the gel by the presence of a band of protein. The densitometry curve peaks when light passage is obscured by the presence of a band of material in the electrophoresis gel.

The importance of Pauling's work is twofold. First, it introduced laboratory methods for the detection of distinct forms of globin protein; and second, it demonstrated that hemoglobin variation explains the inheritance of SCD as a molecular disease. Pauling's study was the first to show that the inheritance patterns of disorders in pedigrees parallel those of the transmission of molecular variation. His work also illustrates that among heterozygous carriers, molecular evidence often supports the expression of both

alleles, even if the abnormal morphology characteristic of a disorder is present only in individuals who are homozygous for a recessive allele. In short, Pauling was the first to draw attention to a fundamental principle of genetics: Hereditary morphologic variation has a molecular basis.

Hemoglobin Peptide Fingerprint Analysis

In 1957, Vernon Ingram published a description of the molecular basis of SCD based on analysis of the amino acid composition of the hemoglobin proteins produced by each allele. Ingram examined hemoglobin protein variation with a two-step approach called **peptide fingerprint analysis** (Figure 10.7). To prepare for fingerprint analysis, the hemoglobin protein is first broken into many fragments by chemical treatment. The peptide fragments generated contain different segments of the protein, and some peptide fragments overlap others. The protein fragments are then subjected to electrophoresis to separate the fragments in one direction, or dimension, on a gel. Next the hemoglobin fragments are separated in a second dimension, perpendicular to the first, by **chromatography,** which uses a solvent to carry fragments with different amino acid composition to different final positions. At the end of these two separations, the locations of numerous short peptide fragments on the chromatography paper form a pattern of "spots" that serve as a kind of "fingerprint" of the protein. Ingram deduced the amino acid sequence of each spot and compared the fingerprint pattern of β^A protein to that of β^S protein.

Ingram found that just a single amino acid in the hemoglobin of people with SCD (genotype $\beta^S\beta^S$) was different in the hemoglobin of people who were homozygous for the wild-type allele (genotype $\beta^A\beta^A$). In those with SCD, the amino acid valine (single-letter abbreviation V) substitutes for glutamic acid (single-letter abbreviation E) in amino acid position number 6 of the 146 amino acids in the β-globin protein chain. As confirmation of his conclusion, Ingram examined the hemoglobin peptide fingerprints for heterozygous carriers of SCD (genotype $\beta^A\beta^S$). He found that they had spots corresponding to both the glutamic-acid-containing portion of wild-type hemoglobin

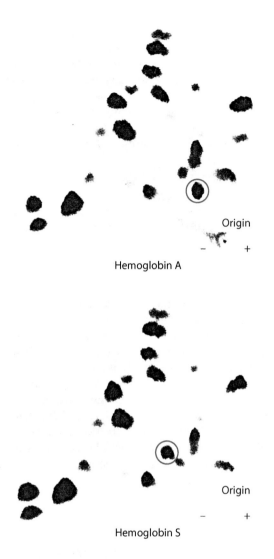

Figure 10.7   Hemoglobin protein peptide fragment analysis. Comparison of hemoglobin protein peptide fragments identified the glutamic acid (E) to valine (V) amino acid change. Different positions of the two circled peptide fragments are due to the amino acid change.

(the product of the β^A allele) and the valine-containing portion of mutant hemoglobin (the product of the β^S allele). **Genetic Analysis 10.1** guides you through genotype identification by protein gel electrophoresis.

Identification of DNA Sequence Variation

With the identification of hemoglobin protein structure and the amino acid sequences of the α-globin and β-globin chains, scientists were ready to combine the analysis of hemoglobin variation with analysis of DNA and mRNA sequences to explain how nucleic acid variation produces SCD. Before we can examine this research, however, some additional description of nucleic acid and of protein electrophoretic analysis is required. This subsection and the next present some background information on the identification of DNA sequence variability using DNA-digesting enzymes and gel electrophoresis. These techniques are

tools with many applications in DNA analysis. After discussing them, we return to the analysis of SCD.

DNA sequences are linear strings of the nucleotides adenine (A), guanine (G), cytosine (C), and thymine (T). Scientists compare genome sequences from different organisms by aligning them side by side and noting the number, location, and type of nucleotide sequence differences. Genomic analysis has determined that the most common kind of DNA sequence difference between organisms of the same species is variation of single nucleotides, a type of difference called a **single nucleotide polymorphism** (**SNP**; pronounced *snip*). SNPs originate as point mutations, that is, base-pair substitution mutations of the type that changed β^A, DNA sequence into β^S, sequence. SNPs are prevalent in the genomes of all organisms. The human genome, for example, contains millions of SNPs scattered among the approximately 3 billion base pairs (bp) that constitute our genome. By their prevalence, SNPs have become an important category of genetic marker that can be used for gene mapping (see Section 5.5), and they can also be used to identify so-called DNA fingerprints that are used for crime scene DNA analysis and in paternity testing (see Chapter 22). SNPs usually occur in unexpressed regions of genomes and have no detectable effect on phenotype. Occasionally, however, SNPs occur in expressed regions of genes, where the variation can affect the phenotype, as occurs in SCD.

Whether or not the sequence variation at a SNP locus affects a phenotypic character, the allelic sequence is transmitted from one generation to the next. **Figure 10.8** shows two DNA sequences representing two SNP alleles that are identical except for the highlighted base pairs. An A-T base pair is found in allele S_1, and a G-C pair specifies allele S_2. Individual organisms in a population can be homozygous (S_1S_1 or S_2S_2) or heterozygous (S_1S_2) for these SNP alleles. The pattern of hereditary transmission of SNP alleles follows the same pattern as alleles of expressed genes, with each parent contributing one allele to offspring.

The complete sequencing and surveying of a genome in search of SNP variation is accomplished by genome sequencing techniques (see Section 18.2). For certain genetic analyses involving SNPs, however, it is not necessary to examine complete genome sequences. For these analyses, SNP variation can be detected using a special class of DNA-digesting enzymes that act only on specific DNA sequences. Known as **restriction endonucleases**—or, more commonly, **restriction enzymes**—these enzymes act like precise molecular scissors. Restriction enzymes bind to exact DNA nucleotide sequence of a few base pairs, called the **restriction sequence** of the enzyme. Following binding, the restriction enzyme cuts each strand of DNA by cleaving a precise phosphodiester bond on each strand of the molecule. When long DNA molecules containing multiple restriction sequences are treated with a restriction enzyme, many fragments of DNA are produced. The number of restriction fragments produced by a given restriction enzyme is characteristic for a given sequence of

(a)

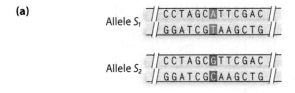

(b)

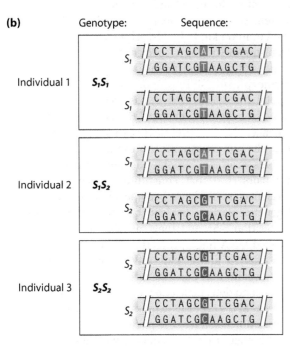

Figure 10.8   Single nucleotide polymorphism (SNP). **(a)** At a SNP locus, two alleles differ by one base pair. Allele S_1 contains an A-T base pair (green), and allele S_2 contains a G-C base pair (purple). **(b)** Three genotypes result from these two alleles.

DNA. When SNPs are present, they can alter one or more restriction sequences. If this occurs, DNA samples from two individuals that are exposed to the same restriction enzyme will produce a different number or a difference in length (in base pairs) of restriction fragments. These inherited DNA sequence variations are called **restriction fragment length polymorphisms (RFLPs),** and they are a common consequence of the presence of SNPs.

Hundreds of different restriction enzymes have been identified since they were first discovered in the 1960s. They are naturally occurring molecules found in microorganisms, particularly bacteria. In these organisms, restriction enzymes act to protect the organism from foreign DNA that might invade the cell. Recall from Chapter 6 that conjugation, transduction, and transformation all introduce DNA from one bacterium (the donor) into another (the recipient) and that infection of bacteria by bacteriophage begins with the transfer of phage DNA into the host cell. Restriction enzymes are a part of the molecular mechanism that can destroy invading foreign DNA. Restriction enzymes share three general properties:

1. Each enzyme exclusively recognizes its own restriction sequence, consisting of a precise 5′-to-3′ nucleotide order on each DNA strand. For example, the restriction enzyme *Eco*RI exclusively recognizes the restriction sequence 5′-GAATTC-3′. Because the restriction sequence for each restriction endonuclease is precise, any variation blocks the ability of the restriction enzyme to recognize the sequence.

2. Restriction sequences are usually palindromes, meaning that each strand of the double-stranded restriction sequence has the same nucleotide order (running from 5′ to 3′). The double-stranded *Eco*RI restriction sequence is

   5′-GAATTC-3′

   3′-CTTAAG-5′

3. A restriction enzyme cuts each strand of its restriction sequence in the same way. For example, *Eco*RI cuts each strand of DNA between the G and the A of the restriction sequence (**Figure 10.9**). Some restriction enzymes, like *Eco*RI, cut the DNA strands in a staggered, or offset, manner and produce short single-stranded ends called **sticky ends.** Other restriction enzymes, such as *Sma*I and *Pvu*II, do not generate staggered cuts on the two DNA strands. Instead, they cut through both DNA strands at a single place, resulting in restriction fragments that have **blunt ends.**

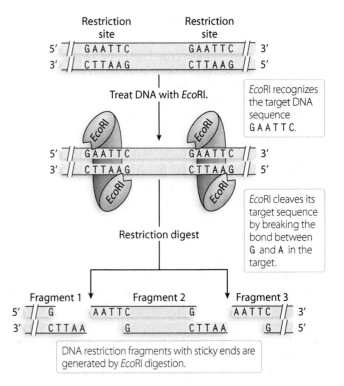

Figure 10.9   Restriction digestion by *Eco*RI.

PROBLEM Individuals homozygous for the β^A or β^S, hemoglobin alleles produce single protein bands with different electrophoretic mobility on gels. A second β-globin gene mutation designated β^C differs by a single DNA base-pair substitution from the β^A, allele. Individuals who are homozygous for this allele have the genotype $\beta^C\beta^C$ and produce a single protein band with an electrophoretic mobility that is distinct from either of the other two protein bands.

> **BREAK IT DOWN:** The electrophoretic mobility of a protein is a composite property of the size, charge, and shape of that protein. Single amino acid changes resulting from base-substitution mutations can produce mobility differences (p. 344).

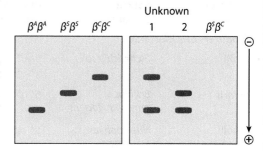

The first gel diagram to the right illustrates the electrophoretic mobility of hemoglobin protein from individuals with the $\beta^A\beta^A$, $\beta^S\beta^S$, and $\beta^C\beta^C$ genotypes. The second gel diagram on the right illustrates bands for two individuals with unknown genotypes and has space to fill in the bands for the $\beta^S\beta^C$ genotype.

a. Interpret the hemoglobin or heterozygous genotypes if the corresponding homozygous geneotypes have proteins with distinct mobilities protein band patterns for Unknown 1 and Unknown 2, and identify the genotype of each person.

b. Draw the hemoglobin protein band pattern expected for an individual who is $\beta^S\beta^C$.

> **BREAK IT DOWN:** Two protein electrophoretic bands are produced for heterozygous genotypes if the corresponding homozygous genotypes have proteins with distinct mobilities (p. 344).

Solution Strategies	Solution Steps
Evaluate	
1. Identify the topic this problem addresses and the nature of the required answer.	1. This problem concerns the interpretation of hemoglobin protein migration in gel electrophoresis. The problem requires identification of genotypes based on protein band migration. It also requires prediction of the band pattern for a certain genotype.
2. Identify the critical information given in the problem.	2. The problem gives examples of hemoglobin protein migration for three genotypes that are the basis for determining the genotypes of unknown samples.
Deduce	
3. Identify the possible genotypes involving alleles β^A, β^S, and β^C.	3. For a gene with three alleles, three of the possible genotypes are homozygous ($\beta^A\beta^A$, $\beta^S\beta^S$, and $\beta^C\beta^C$) and three are heterozygous ($\beta^A\beta^S$, $\beta^A\beta^C$, and $\beta^S\beta^C$).
4. Determine the hemoglobin protein band pattern associated with each genotype.	4. Homozygous genotypes produce one protein band, and heterozygous genotypes produce two protein bands on an electrophoretic gel:

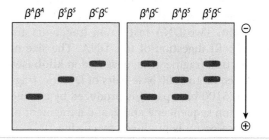

> **TIP:** Match the bands in the Unknown lanes with bands corresponding to alleles of identified genotypes.

Solve

Answer a

5. Identify the genotypes producing the hemoglobin protein band patterns for Unknown 1 and Unknown 2.

5. Unknown 1 has one protein band that matches the electrophoretic mobility of β^A and a second protein band that matches β^C. Unknown 1 is $\beta^A\beta^C$. Unknown 2 has protein bands that match β^A and β^S. Unknown 2 is $\beta^A\beta^S$.

> **TIP:** Use the bands of identified alleles to predict the band pattern for a new genotype.

Answer b

6. Draw the band pattern for an individual with the $\beta^S\beta^C$ genotype.

6. The protein band pattern expected for $\beta^S\beta^C$ will have two bands, one for β^S and the other for β^C.

Table 10.1	Examples of Restriction Enzymes	
Restriction Endonuclease	**Source Organism**	**Restriction Sequence**
Producers of sticky ends		
EcoRI	*Escherichia coli*	5′-GA͟ATTC-3′ 3′-CTTAAG-5′
BamHI	*Bacillus amyloliquifaciens*	5′-GGATCC-3′ 3′-CCTAGG-5′
HindIII	*Haemophilus influenzae*	5′-AAGCTT-3′ 3′-TTCGAA-5′
DdeI	*Desulfovibrio desulfuricans*	5′-CTNAG-3′ 3′-GANTC-5′
Producers of blunt ends		
PvuII	*Proteus vulgaris*	5′-CAGCTG-3′ 3′-GTCGAC-5′
SmaI	*Serratia marcescens*	5′-CCCGGG-3′ 3′-GGGCCC-5′

Note: N = any nucleotide (A, T, C, or G); ∧ and ∨ indicate cleavage locations.

Restriction sequences are listed in Table 10.1, which groups them according to whether they produce sticky ends or blunt ends. Restriction enzymes have a wide variety of uses in laboratory experimentation. Among these is their use in the creation of recombinant DNA molecules (see Chapters 16 and 17).

SNP variation is one kind of DNA-sequence change that can destroy or create a restriction sequence by substituting one DNA base pair for another. **Research Technique 10.1** illustrates one mechanism for the generation of an RFLP. There, allele R^1 represents a portion of a chromosome containing three *Eco*RI restriction sequences, labeled as restriction sequences 1, 2, and 3, from left to right. Two DNA restriction fragments are generated by *Eco*RI digestion of this DNA. The size of the DNA restriction fragments is measured in **kilobases (kb)**, with 1 kb equal to 1000 base pairs of DNA. A fragment of 5.1 kb (5100 base pairs) is produced by cutting DNA at restriction sequences 1 and 2, and a fragment of 4.2 kb (4200 base pairs) is produced by cutting DNA at restriction sequences 2 and 3. Allele R^2 represents the same region of DNA as shown for R^1 but with a single base-pair substitution in restriction sequence 2 that is highlighted in red. Notice that restriction sequences 1 and 3 are the same in both alleles and that the only difference between them is the base pair substitution in restriction sequence 2. The mutation of restriction sequence 2 makes it unrecognizable by *Eco*RI as the sequence is no longer the 5′-GAATTC-3′ sequence used by *Eco*RI. Restriction sequence 2 is destroyed by base-pair substitution and no longer exists on chromosomes carrying allele R^2. Treating DNA containing R^2 with *Eco*RI will result in digestion at restriction sites 1 and 3,

but since restriction sequence 2 has been destroyed by mutation, DNA is not cut in this region. The result will be a single DNA restriction fragment of 9.3 kb, the sum of the lengths of the two restriction fragments produced from allele R^1. Research Technique 10.1 also shows the variation in the number and length of DNA restriction fragments generated for the three genotypes at this RFLP. In this case, a molecular probe (see Research Technique 10.2 for details) identifies DNA on both sides of the location of restriction site 2.

The hereditary transmission of these alleles follows an autosomal codominant pattern. In the pedigree shown, the parents are each heterozygous and their offspring could have any of the three potential genotypes.

Analogous results producing RFLP variation would be obtained in cases where base substitution mutation creates a new restriction sequence where one did not exist previously. This circumstance is illustrated for a globin gene mutation in this chapter's Case Study. RFLP variation can also be generated by mutations that insert or delete DNA between two existing restriction sequences. In such cases, neither of the restriction sequences flanking the insertion or deletion is mutated, it is just the number of base pairs between the restriction sequence that is changed. We see an example of this kind of mutation in Section 13.7, where we discuss DNA transposition. Interestingly, the mutation discussed there affects one of the genes Gregor Mendel studied in his analysis of heredity in pea plants.

Molecular Probes

The use of electrophoretic analysis for detecting DNA RFLPs, variation in mRNA transcripts from expressed genes, or variation in the polypeptide products of genes can be straightforward if a small number of different molecules are present in the electrophoretic sample. Alternatively, analysis can be complicated by the sheer number of restriction fragments, mRNA molecules, or protein molecules in a sample under analysis. Treating human genomic DNA with a restriction enzyme like *Eco*RI, whose restriction sequence is common in the genome, can produce hundreds of thousands of restriction fragments. Similarly, isolating mRNA molecules or protein molecules from cells yields a large number of different products. Without methods for identifying specific substances—whether specific DNA sequences, mRNA transcripts, or protein products—electrophoretic analysis would be hopelessly complex.

When a small number of different molecules are present in an electrophoretic sample of DNA or mRNA, a compound called **ethidium bromide (EtBr)** can be used as a chemical tag all the DNA fragments or RNA molecules in electrophoresis gels. EtBr attaches to all DNA or RNA in a gel by binding to the sugar-phosphate backbone. EtBr is not specific to any nucleotide sequence and will attach to any DNA or RNA fragment regardless of the length or sequence of the fragment. EtBr will be concentrated where nucleic acid bands are located, and

(a)

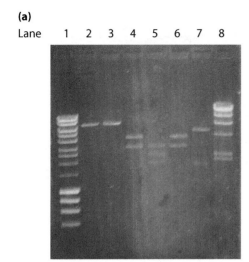

(b)

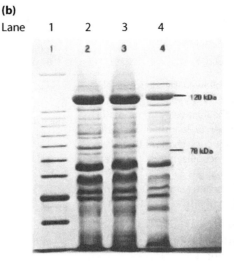

Figure 10.10   **Visualization of nucleic acids and proteins in gels.** **(a)** Nucleic acid molecules (DNA and RNA) are visualized by binding ethidium bromide (EtBr) to them. EtBr fluoresces when excited by ultraviolet light, revealing bands of DNA in the gel. Molecular weight size markers are in lanes 1 and 8, and experimental samples are in lanes 2 through 7. **(b)** General protein stains (such as coomassie blue, shown here) bind to proteins in electrophoretic gels to reveal the locations of protein bands. Protein standards are in lane 1, and experimental samples are in lanes 2 through 4.

more molecules of EtBr will attach to larger nucleic acid fragments than to smaller nucleic acid fragments. The exposure of gels containing EtBr-stained nucleic acids to ultraviolet light excites the EtBr and causes it to emit fluorescent light, so that bands in EtBr-stained DNA or RNA gels can be visualized and photographed (Figure 10.10a). Molecular weight size markers, DNA fragments of known length, that serve as control samples for this gel are in lanes 1 and 8 of Figure 10.10a. Experimental samples are in lanes 2 through 7. For protein electrophoresis gels, general protein stains—stains that bind to any protein— can be used to discover the location of each protein run through the gel (Figure 10.10b).

Protein standards, proteins with known electrophoretic mobilities that serve as controls for the protein electrophoresis gel, are in lane 1. Experimental samples are in lanes 2 through 5. EtBr staining of nucleic acid gels and general protein staining of protein electrophoresis gels have many uses, but neither of these methods detects a specific nucleic acid sequence or a specific protein.

Two innovations in gel electrophoresis methods have made the identification of specific proteins and the detection of specific sequences in mRNAs and DNA fragments possible. The first is the development of methods for "blotting," a general name for the transfer of nucleic acids or proteins from an electrophoresis gel to a membrane that can withstand rigorous treatment and analysis. The membrane is most often a durable synthetic material that can serve as a permanent record of gel results. **Southern blotting** (named after its inventor, Edwin Southern) is the term applied to DNA transfer; **northern blotting** (named by tongue-in-cheek analogy with Southern blotting) identifies the transfer of mRNA from a gel to a membrane; and **western blotting** is the term identifying the gel-to-membrane transfer of proteins.

The second innovation is the development of **molecular probes.** These are antibodies, if the target is the identification of a specific protein, or single-stranded nucleic acids, for the identification of a specific DNA or RNA sequence. Molecular probes are essential for identifying a particular nucleic acid sequence or a specific protein from a heterogeneous pool of molecules in an electrophoresis gel. In a way, the process of searching for a DNA or RNA fragment containing a specific string of nucleotides or of searching through a large number of proteins for a specific protein is analogous to trying to find a specific word or phrase in a text document. Scanning each block of letters for the correct string is almost impossible without a tool for targeting the desired sequence. Just as word processing programs locate a desired word or phrase by searching for a specific string of letters using a "find" command, biologists use molecular probes to identify target nucleic acid sequences or target proteins following electrophoresis.

In the search for a target DNA molecule in a Southern blot, the molecular probe is a short, single-stranded DNA fragment, and the target molecule is a region of DNA that contains a sequence complementary to the probe sequence. Similarly, single-stranded molecular probes detect target mRNAs in northern blots by the complementary base pairing of probe and a segment of the target nucleotide sequence. The pairing of complementary nucleic acid strands of the probe and the target sequence is called **hybridization.** In contrast to the nucleic acid probes used to detect DNA or RNA target sequences, molecular probes used to detect target proteins in western blots are, as mentioned earlier, antibodies—immune system proteins that bind only to specific target proteins. Descriptions of Southern, northern, and western blotting, and the use of different kinds of molecular probes to identify specific nucleic acids or proteins on the blots, are provided in **Research Technique 10.2.**

Electrophoretic Analysis of Sickle Cell Disease

Like the hundreds of other mutations of the α-globin and β-globin genes that affect humans, the mutation producing SCD is a DNA sequence change that leads to an mRNA transcript differing from the wild type

Research Technique 10.1

The Production and Detection of DNA Restriction Fragment Length Polymorphisms

PURPOSE Restriction digestion followed by DNA gel electrophoresis is one method for detecting variation of DNA sequence that alters the number or the relative positions of RFLP sequences. Variation in the number or length of restriction fragments can result from DNA sequence changes that alter a restriction sequence, making it unrecognizable, or that create a new restriction sequence. RFLP changes can also result from the insertion or deletion of DNA between restriction sequences that increase or decrease the length of restriction fragments.

MATERIALS AND PROCEDURES DNA is isolated from cells and treated with one or more restriction enzymes to produce DNA restriction fragments. The restriction fragments are then separated by DNA gel electrophoresis, causing the fragments to be visualized as "bands" on the gel. Laboratory methods described in Research Technique 10.2 can also aid in the identification of specific restriction fragments.

DESCRIPTION DNA sequence variation altering the number or length of restriction fragments (RFLPs) produces distinctive restriction fragments for each allele. Organisms that are homozygous for DNA sequence at a restriction site shown in the diagram produce the same restriction fragments from homologous chromosomes. Heterozygous organisms have different DNA sequences on the two homologous chromosomes and, as the diagram shows, they, produce a total of three different restriction fragments from the chromosome regions shown. Detection of any or all of these fragments on a DNA gel is dictated by which molecular probe is used.

Transmission of the RFLP alleles follows an autosomal co-dominant pattern in which DNA bands from both alleles are observed in heterozygous (R^1R^2) individuals.

CONCLUSION DNA base substitution changes that alter a restriction sequence and the insertion or deletion of DNA between two restriction sequences are the principal ways DNA sequence alterations can produce RFLPs. RFLP alleles form genotypes whose DNA restriction fragments produce distinctive patterns in gel electrophoresis. Each genotype has a distinctive combination of band number and band size on the gel.

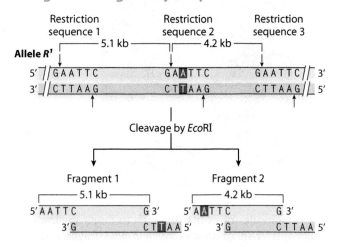

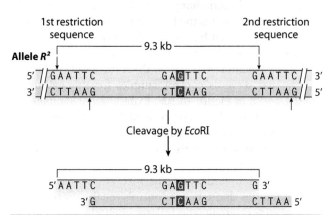

RFLP Variation. Two homologous regions of DNA are identical except for a SNP that produces a base-pair substitution (highlighted) in restriction site 2 of one chromosome. DNA treated with *Eco*RI cuts allele R^1 at three restriction sites (1, 2, and 3) and forms two small DNA restriction fragments of 5.1 and 4.2 kb. The base substitution in the DNA sequence of the R^2 allele eliminates restriction site 2, and the DNA is cut only at sites 1 and 3, resulting in a single DNA restriction fragment of 9.3 kb.

and, ultimately, to the production of a mutant form of β-globin protein. Specifically, through genetic studies spanning a period of 50 years, scientists discovered that a change in a single DNA base leads to a single-base difference in mRNA transcripts and to β-globin proteins that differ at just one of the 146 amino acids that comprise them.

The key portion of the DNA, mRNA, and amino acid sequences of the wild-type ($β^A$) and mutant ($β^S$) alleles is shown in Figure 10.4 (see p. 342). The single-nucleotide difference between the alleles is the result of a SNP of the type we described above. In comparison to the wild-type allele, the mutant $β^S$ allele contains a single DNA base-pair substitution in the sixth DNA triplet of the coding

sequence. This substitution leads to a single-nucleotide change in codon 6 of mRNA and to a protein with valine (Val) rather than glutamic acid (Glu) as the sixth amino acid in the β-globin polypeptide chain.

Southern Blot Analysis of β-Globin Gene Variation The $β^S$ SNP is unusual in that it occurs in the coding sequence of the gene, whereas most SNPs occur in noncoding segments of the genome. We can detect the SNP in the $β^S$ allele because it destroys a restriction sequence, leading to an RFLP that is revealed by Southern blot analysis.

Either two or three restriction sequences for the restriction endonuclease *Dde*I can occur near the

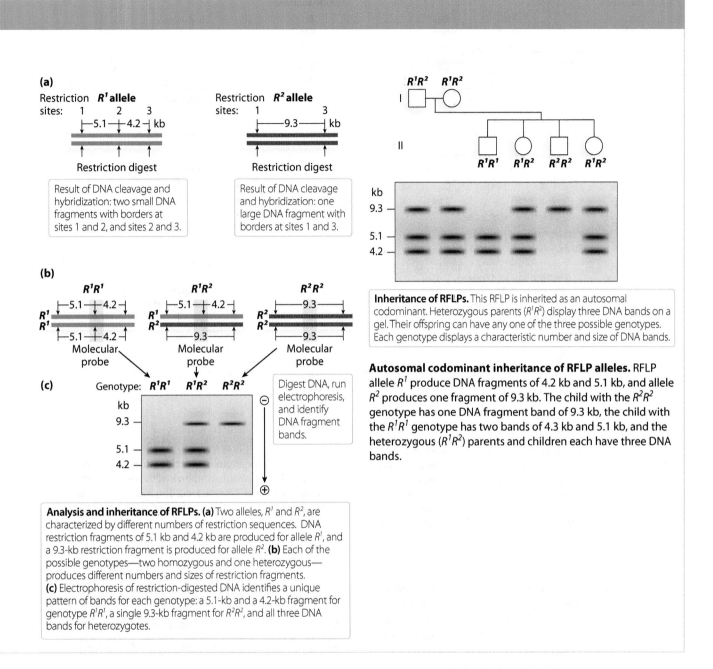

Inheritance of RFLPs. This RFLP is inherited as an autosomal codominant. Heterozygous parents (R^1R^2) display three DNA bands on a gel. Their offspring can have any one of the three possible genotypes. Each genotype displays a characteristic number and size of DNA bands.

Autosomal codominant inheritance of RFLP alleles. RFLP allele R^1 produce DNA fragments of 4.2 kb and 5.1 kb, and allele R^2 produces one fragment of 9.3 kb. The child with the R^2R^2 genotype has one DNA fragment band of 9.3 kb, the child with the R^1R^1 genotype has two bands of 4.3 kb and 5.1 kb, and the heterozygous (R^1R^2) parents and children each have three DNA bands.

Analysis and inheritance of RFLPs. (a) Two alleles, R^1 and R^2, are characterized by different numbers of restriction sequences. DNA restriction fragments of 5.1 kb and 4.2 kb are produced for allele R^1, and a 9.3-kb restriction fragment is produced for allele R^2. **(b)** Each of the possible genotypes—two homozygous and one heterozygous—produces different numbers and sizes of restriction fragments. **(c)** Electrophoresis of restriction-digested DNA identifies a unique pattern of bands for each genotype: a 5.1-kb and a 4.2-kb fragment for genotype R^1R^1, a single 9.3-kb fragment for R^2R^2, and all three DNA bands for heterozygotes.

β-globin gene, depending on the allele. *Dde*I recognizes the double-stranded restriction sequence 5′-CTNAG-3′, where N indicates that any of the four nucleotides (A, T, C, or G) can occur in the middle of the 5-bp sequence as long as the variable nucleotide is flanked by CT and AG dinucleotide combinations.

Figure 10.11 shows three *Dde*I restriction sites, labeled 1, 2, and 3, in the β^A allele. All three *Dde*I restriction sequences are cleaved, producing two DNA fragments of 1150 bp and 200 bp for the DNA region shown. Southern blotting of DNA from the β^A allele produces two DNA bands corresponding to fragment lengths of 1150 bp and 200 bp. The target sequence for the molecular probe is split between two restriction fragments by DNA cleavage

at *Dde*I site 2, and the probe hybridizes to both the 1150-bp and the 200-bp restriction fragments from β^A alleles.

In contrast, in Figure 10.12, the β^S allele is shown to contain two *Dde*I restriction sequences, labeled sites 1 and 3. The middle restriction sequence, labeled 2 in Figure 10.11, is missing from the β^S allele as a result of the base-pair substitution that produces the SNP. Only *Dde*I restriction sites 1 and 3 are cleaved in DNA carrying the β^S allele; site 2 is not recognized by *Dde*I because of the SNP variation. This cleavage produces a single restriction fragment of 1350 bp in DNA carrying the β^S sequence. The length of this fragment is the sum of the lengths of the two restriction fragments detected from the β^A allele (i.e., 1150 bp + 200 bp). Southern blot

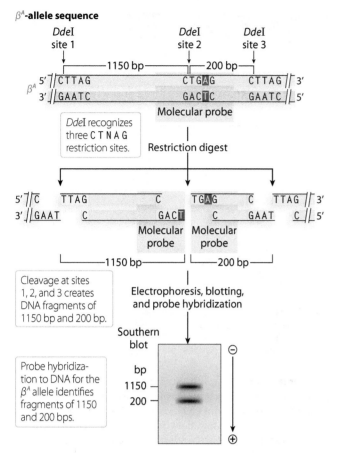

Figure 10.11 *Dde*I **restriction digestion and Southern blotting of wild-type β-globin gene.** Restriction digestion and Southern blot analysis of βᴬ-allele DNA sequence identifies two DNA fragments that are hybridized by the molecular probe. A restriction fragment of 1150 bp (1.15 kb) is produced by cleavage at sites 1 and 2, and the 200-bp fragment is produced by cleavage at sites 2 and 3.

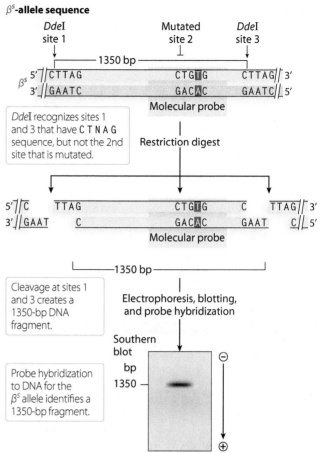

Figure 10.12 **The single-nucleotide polymorphism in the βˢ allele.** Base-pair substitution inactivates *Dde*I site 2, and only sites 1 and 3 are cleaved. The molecular probe detects a single 1350-bp (1.35-kb) fragment in Southern blot analysis.

analysis of βˢ-allele DNA produces a single DNA restriction fragment, measuring 1350 bp (1.35 kb) in length. Because *Dde*I site 2 is altered by SNP variation, the entire molecular probe target sequence is contained on a single 1350-bp (1.35-kb) restriction fragment (Figure 10.13). People who are βᴬβᴬ have bands of 1150 bp (1.15 kb) and 200 bp (0.20 kb) detected by the probe. Those who are βˢβˢ have a single band of 1350 bp (1.35 kb), and those who have βᴬβˢ produce all three bands because they carry both alleles.

The mutation that creates the βˢ allele by base-pair substitution of the βᴬ allele is the kind of mutation described in Research Technique 10.1 as creating an RFLP. **Genetic Analysis 10.2** guides your interpretation of Southern blot analysis.

Northern and Western Blot Analysis of the β-Globin Gene Transcript and Protein The DNA sequences of the βᴬ and βˢ alleles are identical except for the SNP that distinguishes the sequence of one from the other. Upon

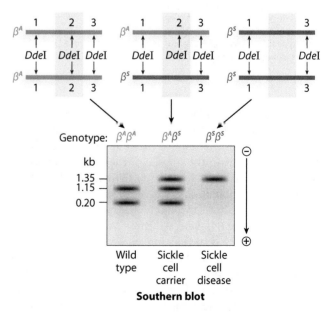

Figure 10.13 RFLP results for β-globin genotypes.

transcription, each allele produces an mRNA molecule containing 664 nucleotides. The single-nucleotide substitution that differentiates the two alleles does not alter the *length* of the mRNA transcript. Considering that the molecular attribute producing electrophoretic mobility differences among mRNAs is total length of the molecule, it is not surprising that in this instance there is *no difference* in the electrophoretic mobilities of the mRNA transcripts of these two alleles, because the lengths of their mRNAs are identical. A northern blot analysis performed on mRNA from individuals with the three β-globin genotypes detects the same single-mRNA band for each genotype (**Figure 10.14**). Consequently, northern analysis is not useful in detecting variation in this case.

Although the sequence difference between these two mRNAs is not detectable by northern blot analysis, a difference in the electrophoretic mobility of the polypeptides for which they code is detectable using western blot analysis, because the resulting proteins differ in amino acid content. Recall from Figure 10.3 that the polypeptides produced by the β^A and β^S alleles differ at the sixth amino acid position of their respective 146-member amino acid strings. The amino acid change results in a small charge difference that produces distinctive electrophoretic mobilities for the proteins. Western blots reveal hemoglobin protein bands for the three genotypes in patterns that are essentially identical to the band patterns Pauling first detected (**Figure 10.15**). Individuals with homozygous genotypes $\beta^A\beta^A$ and $\beta^S\beta^S$ each produce a single protein band with different electrophoretic

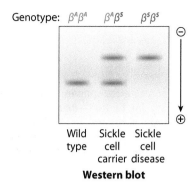

Figure 10.15   Western blot analysis of human β-globin protein. Single protein bands are seen in western blot analysis of $\beta^A\beta^A$ and $\beta^S\beta^S$ homozygotes; two protein bands are detected for heterozygotes.

mobility, and heterozygous individuals ($\beta^A\beta^S$) have two protein bands, each corresponding to the polypeptide product of a different allele.

10.3 Sickle Cell Disease Evolved by Natural Selection in Human Populations

Dozens of variant alleles of hemoglobin genes produce one form or another of hereditary anemia. According to the World Health Organization, hereditary anemias are the most common of all human genetic diseases; they occur in an estimated 250 to 300 million people around the world. Most of the globin-gene mutations causing hereditary anemia are rare, but a few are found in high frequency in certain populations. The β^S allele occurs in frequencies as high as 15% in several indigenous populations of Africa, the Middle East, and the Indian subcontinent. Population and evolutionary genetic analysis verifies that the allele arose independently in each region and has risen to high frequency by the same evolutionary process in each locality. Examples of other β-globin alleles found in high frequency are β^C, primarily in populations from West Africa, and β^E, in populations from Southeast Asia and the Pacific Islands.

The high frequencies of β^S, β^C, and β^E are consistent with the conclusion that natural selection is working to increase the occurrence of these alleles. Population studies over the last 50 years have firmly established malaria as the agent of natural selection leading to a high frequency of these β-globin gene alleles in certain populations. An environment where malaria is endemic favors the survival and reproduction of individuals who are heterozygous for β^A and one of the mutant alleles over the other genotypes. In other words, individuals who are $\beta^A\beta^S$, $\beta^A\beta^C$, or $\beta^A\beta^E$ have a survival and reproductive advantage over individuals who are homozygous $\beta^A\beta^A$ (and therefore succumb more easily to malaria) and over those who are homozygous for the mutant alleles (and therefore suffer from hereditary anemia).

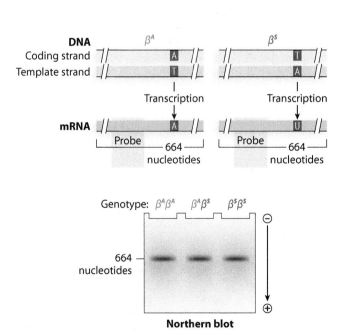

Figure 10.14   Northern blot analysis of human β-globin mRNA. Transcription produces an mRNA that is 664 nucleotides in length for both alleles. The results of northern blot analysis are therefore identical for the three genotypes.

Research Technique 10.2

Blotting and Probing Nucleic Acid and Protein Molecules

PURPOSE After gel electrophoresis, the separated nucleic acids or proteins are blotted—that is, transferred—onto a membrane that can withstand the vigorous manipulation that accompanies analysis. Molecular probes are applied to blots to detect sequences carried in DNA or RNA, and to detect specific proteins.

MATERIALS AND PROCEDURES Restriction-digested DNA, isolated mRNA, or isolated proteins are first subjected to gel electrophoresis. Known standards and molecular weight size markers are run alongside experimental samples as controls to identify the length of nucleic acids or to identify the electrophoretic mobility of proteins. If the gel contains DNA,

the DNA must be denatured after electrophoresis is completed to allow molecular probes to locate their target sequence in a later step. Denaturation of DNA is accomplished by bathing the gel in a sodium hydroxide (NaOH) solution that breaks the hydrogen bonds between the strands. The gel is then blotted with a nucleic-acid-binding or protein-binding membrane that will absorb sample molecules from the gel. Next, single-stranded nucleic acid molecular probes tagged with either radioactivity or fluorescent or chemiluminescent labels are applied to the prepared membrane in a solution. The probes have sequences complementary to a specific target sequence. Probes that hybridize to their targets label the location of the band containing the target sequence via their chemical tags.

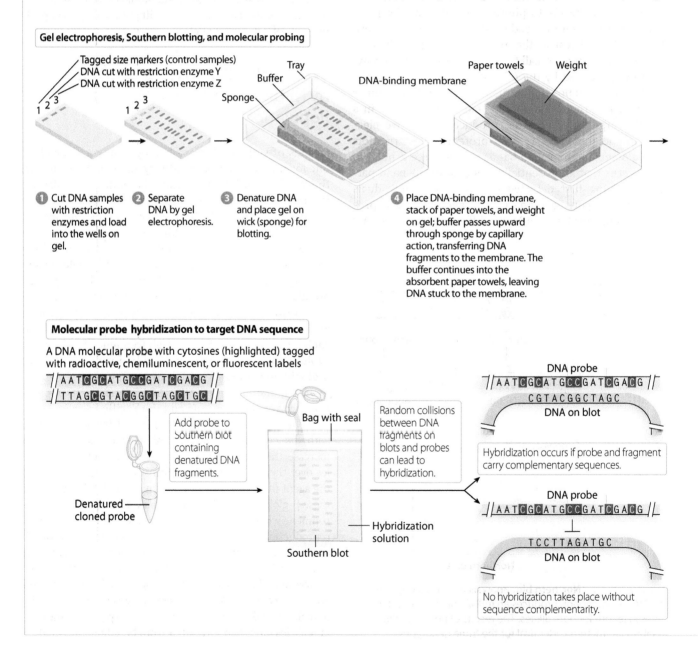

Molecular probe molecules that are not bound to a target molecule on the blot are washed away. Subsequently, for radioactively labeled molecular probes, autoradiography using X-ray film captures the location of any bound molecular probe by detecting the radiation. Different detection methods are used if molecular probes are tagged with fluorescent or chemiluminescent labels. Similar methods are used to prepare Southern blots of restriction-digested DNA, northern blots of mRNA, and western blots of protein, except that neither RNA nor protein is denatured before blotting.

DESCRIPTION Southern blotting is named after its developer, Edwin Southern, and uses single-stranded molecular probes

to detect denatured DNA on the blot by complementary base pairing. Northern blotting detects membrane-bound mRNAs using single-stranded molecular probes in a manner similar to that of Southern blotting. Western blotting detects proteins with the use of antibodies that specifically bind to target proteins.

CONCLUSION Southern, northern, and western blots are produced by similar methods and use molecular probes to detect sample molecules or sequences of interest. Labeled molecular probes bind to specific target sequences or molecules and are detected in autoradiographs or other analyses of blots that serve as a permanent record of the results of gel electrophoresis.

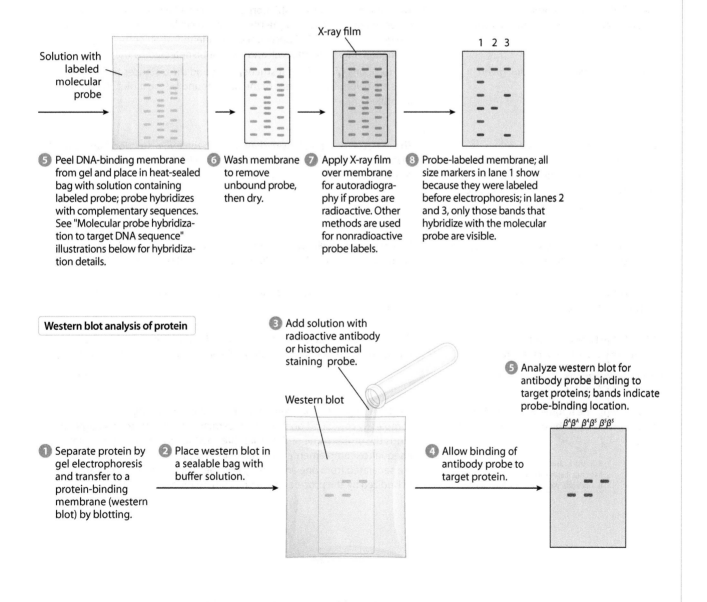

5 Peel DNA-binding membrane from gel and place in heat-sealed bag with solution containing labeled probe; probe hybridizes with complementary sequences. See "Molecular probe hybridization to target DNA sequence" illustrations below for hybridization details.

6 Wash membrane to remove unbound probe, then dry.

7 Apply X-ray film over membrane for autoradiography if probes are radioactive. Other methods are used for nonradioactive probe labels.

8 Probe-labeled membrane; all size markers in lane 1 show because they were labeled before electrophoresis; in lanes 2 and 3, only those bands that hybridize with the molecular probe are visible.

Western blot analysis of protein

1 Separate protein by gel electrophoresis and transfer to a protein-binding membrane (western blot) by blotting.

2 Place western blot in a sealable bag with buffer solution.

3 Add solution with radioactive antibody or histochemical staining probe.

4 Allow binding of antibody probe to target protein.

5 Analyze western blot for antibody probe binding to target proteins; bands indicate probe-binding location.

PROBLEM The 6-kb segment of DNA shown contains the *Bca* gene. The hybridization location for a <u>molecular probe</u> complementary to a portion of the gene is indicated. The locations of five *Eco*RI restriction sequences are also indicated, and the distances (in kilobases) between restriction sites are given.

> **BREAK IT DOWN:** A nucleic acid molecular probe will hybridize to any-sized fragment containing complementary base sequence (p. 354).

a. If this 6-kb region is digested with *Eco*RI, how many DNA fragments are generated? How many nucleotide base pairs are expected in each of the resulting <u>restriction fragments</u>?

> **BREAK IT DOWN:** Each restriction fragment has an *Eco*RI restriction site at each end (p. 352).

b. Which restriction fragment(s) will contain all or part of the *Bca* gene?

c. DNA from the 6-kb segment is digested with *Eco*RI, and the resulting fragments are separated by DNA gel electrophoresis. Which of the restriction fragments will be bound by the molecular probe and seen as bands in the Southern blot? Which fragments will not be detected by Southern blotting? Explain your answer.

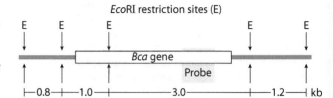

Solution Strategies	Solution Steps
Evaluate	
1. Identify the topic this problem addresses and the nature of the required answer.	1. This problem concerns restriction digestion of a fragment of a gene and detection of restriction fragments with a molecular probe for a portion of the gene of interest. The answer requires identification of the length of restriction fragments that will and will not be detected by the probe.
2. Identify the critical information given in the problem.	2. The locations of five *Eco*RI restriction sites and the distances between the sites are given. The segment of the gene bound by the molecular probe is identified.
Deduce	
3. Examine the diagram to assess the relationship of the molecular probe to the gene, and assess the kilobase scale in relation to the *Eco*RI restriction sites and restriction fragments.	3. The molecular probe binds to the longer of the two restriction fragments that contain part of the *Bca* gene. The sum of kilobase pairs in all the *Eco*RI restriction fragments equals 6.0 kb.
Solve	Answer a
4. Determine the number and length (in base pairs) of restriction fragments.	4. Digestion with *Eco*RI produces four restriction fragments with lengths that are 0.8 kb (800 bp), 1.0 kb (1000 bp), 3.0 kb (3000 bp), and 1.2 kb (1200 bp).
	Answer b
5. Identify the DNA fragments that contain portions of the *Bca* gene.	5. The 1.0- and the 3.0-kb restriction fragments contain segments of the *Bca* gene.
	Answer c
6. Identify the DNA fragment that will <u>hybridize</u> with the molecular probe.	6. Only the 3.0-kb restriction fragment contains the sequence hybridized by the molecular probe. This fragment will be seen on the Southern blot.
TIP: Molecular probes hybridize to target regions that contain complementary base sequences.	
7. Explain why one fragment is hybridized by the probe and why <u>other fragments</u> are not.	7. The DNA sequence complementary to the molecular probe sequence is completely contained on the 3.0-kb restriction fragment, so this fragment binds the probe. None of the other three restriction fragments contains a sequence complementary to the molecular probe, so although they are separated from one another by DNA gel electrophoresis, they are not hybridized by the probe and are not seen on the Southern blot.
PITFALL: Avoid confusion by remembering that DNA fragments that do not contain sequences complementary to a molecular probe cannot hybridize with the probe.	

For more practice, see Problems 15, 23, and 25.   Visit the Study Area to access study tools.   MasteringGenetics™

356

Malaria Infection

Malaria is a potentially fatal infectious disease caused by protozoans. One of the most common and most serious forms of malaria is caused by *Plasmodium falciparum*. This protozoan is carried by the mosquito vector *Anopheles gambeii,* which transfers the protozoan to animals, including humans, when it bites them. The symptoms of malaria include high fever and other problems that can cause death if not effectively treated. Once infected with *P. falciparum,* a person can suffer recurrences of malaria throughout life. As a consequence, victims of the disease are less healthy than their uninfected counterparts and are susceptible to other diseases as well. Overall, malaria victims experience higher morbidity (illness) and mortality (death) and produce fewer children than do the rest of the population.

Plasmodium falciparum and the mosquito that carries it flourish in tropical environments, and therefore malaria is endemic to the tropics. *P. falciparum* embryos live in their mosquito hosts, but they do not begin larval development until they are transferred to a mammalian host. Once inside a mammalian host, the plasmodium begins to mature, first in the liver of the host animal and later in the red blood cells.

Heterozygous Advantage

One of the best-documented examples of natural selection in the evolution of human populations has been the relationship observed between malaria and the β^S allele (**Figure 10.16**). Numerous anthropological and epidemiological studies have recorded the effects of malaria on the evolution of β^S and SCD in African populations, and in other populations in Southern Europe and Asia. The central finding of these studies is that heterozygotes with the genotype $\beta^A\beta^S$ survive and reproduce more dependably than other genotypes in environments where malaria is common.

The improved survival and reproduction of heterozygotes can be explained at a cellular level by the selective advantage that heterozygotes derive from the shortened average life span of their red blood cells. The average red cell life span in these individuals is shortened due to the presence of a certain amount of mutant β-globin protein and the consequent formation of a small number of sickle-shaped red blood cells. The shorter red cell life spans interrupt the developmental cycle of *Plasmodium* larvae by preventing many of the immature parasites from reaching maturity. As a result, heterozygotes suffer fewer cases of malaria than are experienced by $\beta^A\beta^A$ homozygotes, and when they do get malaria, their disease is less severe.

On a population level, individuals with SCD (homozygous for the mutant gene) survive and reproduce very poorly due to their hemoglobin disorder. Those who are $\beta^A\beta^A$ also have lower reproductive fitness than do

(a)

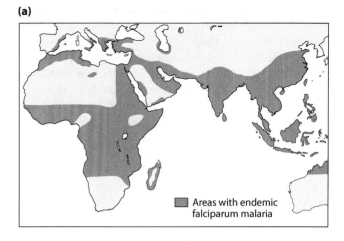

Areas with endemic falciparum malaria

(b)

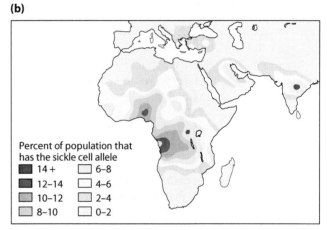

Percent of population that has the sickle cell allele
14+   6–8
12–14   4–6
10–12   2–4
8–10   0–2

(c)

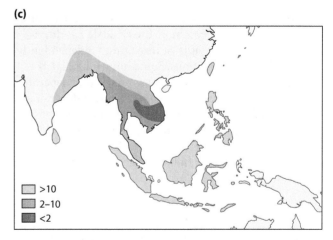

>10
2–10
<2

Figure 10.16   The distribution of malaria and sickle cell disease. **(a)** Colored areas indicate the regions of the world where malaria is an endemic disease. Epidemic disease is periodic or seasonal. Endemicity ranges from hypoendemic, where disease is always present but at low frequency, to holoendemicity, where disease is always present at extremely high frequency. **(b)** Frequency distribution of the β^S allele in some of the human populations occupying the malarial belt. **(c)** The distribution of the β^E allele in Southeast Asia.

heterozygous carriers, because of the ravages of malaria. The result is that natural selection favors heterozygous carriers and causes populations to evolve a gene pool that includes large proportions of both alleles. This **heterozygous advantage** seen for $\beta^A\beta^S$ individuals is balanced by the disadvantage to those with SCD. This mechanism of natural selection is called **balancing selection.** The action of the conflicting forces in balancing selection that favor the β^S allele in heterozygous genotypes and act against it in the homozygous genotype produce an overall increase in the β^S allele until it reaches a stable **equilibrium frequency,** where the gain and loss of β^S alleles is equal. The term **balanced polymorphism** is used to describe the end result of balancing selection, a result in which the loss of an allele because of selection against one of its phenotypes is balanced by natural selection in favor of the allele for another phenotype.

In research concerning heterozygous advantage in the evolution of β^S, three findings are particularly important:

1. The frequency of SCD carriers rises with increasing age in the population. Studies of genotype frequencies in malaria-afflicted populations find the frequency of $\beta^A\beta^S$ heterozygotes to be lower in children than in adolescents, and to be lower in adolescents than in adults. In other words, individuals with $\beta^S\beta^S$ and $\beta^A\beta^A$ genotypes are being lost from these populations at younger ages than are heterozygotes.

2. Heterozygous women produce a greater average number of children than do women who are $\beta^A\beta^A$. This is an indication that the overall health of heterozygotes is better, leading them to reproduce more efficiently.

3. Across the "malaria belt," the portion of the tropics where malaria is common, the β^S allele has developed and evolved at least three times independently in different populations. Some human biologists believe the genetic evidence supports four separate mutation and evolution events. These independent evolutionary events account for the presence of β^S in high frequency in populations in the Middle East, the region surrounding the Mediterranean Ocean, parts of the Indian subcontinent, and parts of Africa.

Evolution of β^C and β^E

Additional support for the role of balancing selection in the evolution of globin genes comes from the study of two other β-globin gene alleles that are present at high frequencies in other populations in the malaria belt. Mutant β-globin alleles β^C and β^E have evolved due to the natural selection pressure of malaria in much the same way β^S has evolved.

The mutation known as β^C likely occurred thousands of years ago on the west coast of Africa. This mutation is a

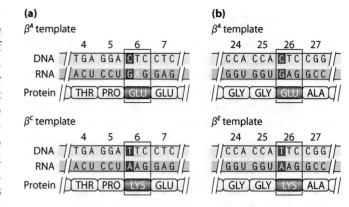

Figure 10.17 Sequence comparisons of β^A (the wild type) and mutant β-globin alleles β^C and β^E. **(a)** β^S and β^C are base-substitution mutants that alter amino acid position 6, changing glutamic acid (Glu) to lysine (Lys) in β^C. **(b)** The base substitution mutant β^E changes amino acid 26 from glutamic acid (Glu) to lysine (Lys).

base substitution of a nucleotide immediately adjacent to the site of the β^S mutation in the sixth DNA triplet of the β-globin gene (**Figure 10.17a**). The effect of the mutation is to change the sixth amino acid of the β-globin protein from glutamic acid to lysine.

Although the mutation affects the same amino acid position altered in β^S, the complications of the mutation are not as severe as those seen in SCD. Homozygosity for the β^C mutation does not produce severe anemia and is rarely fatal. Like SCD carriers, however, heterozygotes with the genotype $\beta^A\beta^C$ are more resistant to malaria than are $\beta^A\beta^A$ homozygotes. This situation leads to the spread of the β^C mutation by a process of natural selection parallel to that seen for β^S.

On the other side of the malaria belt, in Southeast Asia and the adjacent Pacific Islands, another β-globin gene mutation, β^E, is prevalent. β^E is a base substitution mutation that alters amino acid 26 of the β-globin protein, changing it from glutamic acid to lysine (**Figure 10.17b**). The anemia seen in $\beta^E\beta^E$ homozygotes is severe, but the selection it exerts against β^E is balanced by the greater resistance of heterozygous carriers of the allele to malaria.

Like the β^S variant that has been our focus throughout this chapter, the β^C and β^E variants are distributed across the malarial belt that spans much of the tropical regions surrounding the equator. Clinical and epidemiological studies confirm that all three β-globin gene variants are advantageous in the heterozygous state because they reduce the incidence and intensity of malarial disease in carriers. The incidence of hereditary disease produced by homozygosity is balanced by the improved odds of survival and reproduction for carriers of these globin gene variants.

CASE STUDY

Transmission and Molecular Genetic Analysis of Thalassemia

Autosomal recessive forms of a hereditary anemia called thalassemia result from mutations of globin genes that create an imbalance in the ratio of the α-globin to β-globin polypeptides. The imbalance reduces the amount of hemoglobin that can form and generates anemia. Owing to differences between mutant alleles, **thalassemias** exhibit varying levels of severity, from mild to fatal. One particular form of thalassemia is common on the Mediterranean island of Sardinia.

The Sardinian thalassemia mutation (OMIM 141900) is a DNA nucleotide base substitution (GC → AT) in the 39th codon (corresponding to the 39th amino acid) of the β-globin gene (Figure 10.18a). The mutation changes the 39th codon of the transcript from 5'-CAG-3', coding for the amino acid glutamine (Gln), to the sequence 5'-UAG-3', which is a stop codon. This change results in the premature termination of translation of β-globin protein after the first 38 amino acids. The truncated protein is not functional. Consequently, individuals who are homozygous for the mutant allele have no β-globin protein. Their ability to form hemoglobin is greatly diminished, causing severe anemia. Heterozygotes also have diminished capacity to produce hemoglobin, and they suffer from chronic anemia. Since heterozygotes have one wild-type β-globin allele, however, their anemia is less severe than in homozygotes.

Wild-type β-globin alleles have two recognition sites for restriction endonuclease *Mae*I (restriction sequence 5'-CTAG-3') in the vicinity of the gene (Figure 10.18b). The base-substitution mutation in DNA triplet 39 creates a new *Mae*I restriction site that is not found in the wild-type sequence. As we identified in Research Technique 10.1, the creation of a new restriction sequence by a base-pair substitution mutation is a second mutational mechanism for the creation of RFLPs. In this case, whereas the wild-type allele contains two *Mae*I restriction sites separated by approximately 1500 base pairs (1.5 kb), the mutant allele sequence contains a third *Mae*I restriction site that cleaves the 1.5-kb region into two DNA fragments of 0.5 kb and 1.0 kb. Southern blot analysis of *Mae*I–digested β-globin DNA utilizes a molecular probe that binds near one end of the β-globin gene. The probe binds a 1.5-kb DNA fragment produced by *Mae*I treatment of the wild-type allele and a 1.0-kb DNA fragment produced by *Mae*I treatment of the mutant allele. The 0.5-kb DNA fragment is also produced by *Mae*I digestion of the mutant allele, but that fragment is not detected in Southern blot analysis because it is not bound by the molecular probe.

(a) DNA sequence variation of β-globin alleles

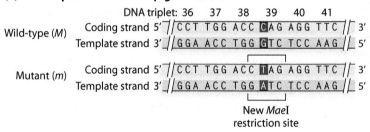

(b) Restriction digestion of β-globin alleles

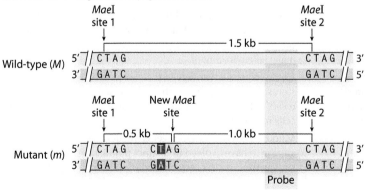

(c) Southern blot analysis of β-globin allele variation

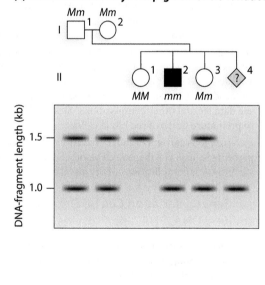

Figure 10.18   **Molecular genetic analysis of variation at DNA triplet 39 of the β-globin gene in Sardinian β-thalassemia. (a)** DNA sequences of the wild-type (*M*) and mutant (*m*) β-globin alleles from triplet 36 through 41. **(b)** Restriction maps of wild-type and triplet-39 mutant alleles show a new *Mae*I restriction site in the mutant allele. The location of molecular probe binding identifies a 1.5-kb DNA fragment for the wild-type allele (*M*) and a 1.0-kb fragment for the mutant allele (*m*). **(c)** Southern-blot analysis of a family showing segregation of wild-type and triplet-39 mutant alleles. Heterozygous (*Mm*) parents produce children with all three genotypes. The genotype of II-4 is discussed in the text.

In terms of the presence or absence of the Sardinian mutant allele, three genotypes are possible at this locus, each having a unique restriction fragment banding pattern detectable by Southern blotting. Homozygotes for the wild-type allele (*MM*) produce a single Southern blot band of 1.5 kb. Homozygotes with severe anemia have the *mm* genotype and produce a single DNA band of 1.0 kb. Heterozygotes (*Mm*) produce both bands, since they carry both alleles.

Figure 10.18c shows a nuclear family pedigree that is consistent with an autosomal pattern of inheritance of

thalassemia. The pedigree symbols for each family member are located directly above the Southern blot lane containing that person's DNA. The Southern blot detects a different pattern of DNA bands for each genotype. The figure also illustrates Southern blot results for DNA obtained from a fetus (the diamond-shaped symbol identified as II-4) being carried by I-2. This analysis is a prenatal molecular diagnostic test for Sardinian thalassemia that is based on the Southern blot band differences among the three possible genotypes.

SUMMARY   (MasteringGenetics™)   For activities, animations, and review quizzes, go to the Study Area.

10.1 An Inherited Hemoglobin Variant Causes Sickle Cell Disease

▌ Hemoglobin is an abundant protein in red blood cells, transporting oxygen throughout the body. Its structure is tetrameric, composed of two polypeptides encoded by the α-globin gene and two polypeptides encoded by the β-globin gene.

▌ Mutation of genes frequently leads to abnormal structure and function of proteins. Mutations of α-globin or β-globin genes often produce hereditary anemia, the most common category of hereditary disease known in humans.

▌ Sickle cell disease (SCD) is a common hereditary anemia in humans caused by homozygosity for the β^S allele of the β-globin gene. Individuals with SCD have the genotype $\beta^S\beta^S$. The globin protein produced by β^S differs from the normal β-globin gene product (β^A) by a single amino acid substitution.

▌ Hemoglobin in people with SCD is unstable and linearizes at low oxygen concentration, distorting the red blood cell into a sickle shape. The distorted cells can block narrow capillaries, producing oxygen starvation in tissues that leads to tissue damage and other complications. Sickle cell disease leads to premature death of red blood cells.

▌ Heterozygous carriers of the β^S mutation ($\beta^A\beta^S$) have a small percentage of sickle-shaped red blood cells but do not suffer symptoms or complications of the disease.

10.2 Genetic Variation Can Be Detected by Examining DNA, RNA, and Proteins

▌ Gel electrophoresis demonstrates the molecular basis of SCD by revealing that the protein products of the β^A and β^S alleles have different electrophoretic mobilities. Distinctive electrophoretic band patterns are detected for many genotypes of the β-globin locus.

▌ The single amino acid substitution caused by the β^S allele is a valine in place of a glutamine in the β-globin protein.

▌ DNA analysis identifies the β^S mutation as a base-pair substitution in the β-globin gene that produces a single nucleotide polymorphism (SNP) and eliminates a *Dde*I restriction site.

▌ An RFLP distinguishes the β^A and β^S alleles.

▌ The pattern of inheritance of RFLPs parallels that of alleles at the β-globin gene.

▌ DNA restriction fragments are detected by transferring denatured DNA fragments from electrophoresis gels to a permanent membrane in the Southern blotting process.

▌ In Southern blots, single-stranded nucleic acid probes labeled with radioactive or chemical markers hybridize with complementary target sequences in DNA fragments.

▌ The presence and size of one or more DNA fragments hybridized by a molecular probe are revealed by the appearance of bands in Southern blot analysis.

▌ Northern blotting is similar to Southern blotting but examines mRNA for differences in length.

▌ Western blotting uses antibodies with radioactive or chemical labels to detect protein electrophoretic mobility variation.

10.3 Sickle Cell Disease Evolved by Natural Selection in Human Populations

▌ The β^S allele has evolved to high frequency in many populations in the malaria belt as a consequence of natural selection, which favors $\beta^A\beta^S$ heterozygotes as the most fit in the malarial environment.

▌ Heterozygous advantage in the case of β^A and β^S alleles stems from disruption of the malarial parasite life cycle, a result of the somewhat shorter average life span of red blood cells in heterozygotes.

▌ Mutations of the β-globin gene, including β^C and β^E, appear to have evolved in distinct populations by processes similar to those that established β^S in human populations.

KEYWORDS

α-globin gene and protein *(p. 340)*
β-globin gene and protein *(p. 340)*
β^A allele *(p. 341)*
β^S allele *(p. 341)*

agarose (agarose gel) *(p. 342)*
balanced polymorphism *(p. 358)*
balancing selection *(p. 358)*
band (in electrophoresis gel) *(p. 344)*

blunt end *(p. 346)*
chromatography *(p. 344)*
electrophoretic mobility *(p. 344)*
equilibrium frequency *(p. 358)*

ethidium bromide (EtBr) *(p. 348)*
gel electrophoresis *(p. 342)*
hemoglobin (Hb) *(p. 339)*
heterozygous advantage *(p. 358)*
hybridization (of molecular probe) *(p. 349)*
kilobase (kb) *(p. 348)*
molecular probe (probe) *(p. 349)*
northern blotting *(p. 349)*

origin of migration *(p. 342)*
peptide fingerprint analysis *(p. 344)*
polyacrylamide (polyacrylamide gel) *(p. 342)*
restriction endonuclease (restriction enzyme) *(p. 345)*
restriction fragment length polymorphism (RFLP) *(p. 346)*

restriction sequence *(p. 345)*
sickle cell disease (SCD) *(p. 339)*
single nucleotide polymorphism (SNP) *(p. 345)*
Southern blotting *(p. 349)*
sticky end *(p. 346)*
thalassemias *(p. 359)*
western blotting *(p. 349)*

PROBLEMS   (MasteringGenetics™) Visit for instructor-assigned tutorials and problems.

Chapter Concepts

1. Define the following terms as described in this chapter:
   a. balanced polymorphism
   b. heterozygous advantage
   c. balancing selection
   d. intron
   e. hemoglobin tetramer
   f. hereditary anemia
   g. exon
   h. heterozygous
   i. recessive
   j. molecular disease
   k. restriction endonuclease
   l. homozygous
   m. gel electrophoresis
   n. restriction fragment length polymorphism (RFLP)
   o. SNP
   p. electrophoretic mobility
   q. Southern blot
   r. molecular probe
   s. northern blot
   t. antibody probe
   u. western blot

2. Using sickle cell disease as an example, describe the similarities and differences between the terms *genetic disease* and *molecular disease*. How are molecular or genetic diseases different from diseases that are caused by an infectious organism such as a bacterium?

3. Compare and contrast the contributions of Neel, Pauling, and Ingram to our understanding of the genetic and molecular bases of sickle cell disease.

4. Why do differences in protein electrophoretic mobility often result from changes to protein amino acid sequences? How can electrophoretic mobility differences arise between the protein products of different alleles?

5. Electrophoretic analysis of hemoglobin from a person with normal HbA and a person with hereditary anemia reveals no difference in the electrophoretic mobility. How can this occur?

6. Many types of hereditary anemia result from single amino acid substitutions affecting one of the hemoglobin protein chains. For example, the wild-type β-globin allele has the template DNA sequence CTC at triplet 6, which encodes the amino acid glutamic acid (Glu) at position 6 of the β-globin protein (see Figure 10.3). The mutant allele

For answers to selected even-numbered problems, see Appendix: Answers.

producing β^S contains the DNA sequence CAC and encodes valine (Val) at β-globin position 6, and the β^C mutation contains TTC in DNA and encodes lysine (Lys) at position 6. The table below shows several other β-globin gene mutants that are the result of single amino acid substitutions. Use the information provided and Table A inside the front cover to determine the wild-type template DNA sequence and the template sequence for each mutant.

β-Globin Form	Position	Amino Acid
β^A (wild type)	7	Glu
Siriraj	7	Lys
San Jose	7	Gly
β^A (wild type)	58	Pro
Ziguinchor	58	Arg
β^A (wild type)	145	Tyr
Bethesda	145	His
Fort Gordon	145	Asp

7. A single base substitution creates the α-globin gene mutant Hb Constant Spring (Hb^{CS}), whose product contains 172 amino acids. Wild-type α-globin protein contains 141 amino acids. The wild-type mRNA carries the codon CGU to encode arginine (Arg) as the final amino acid of the chain, followed by the stop codon UAA. The Hb^{CS} mutant produces mRNA that has the sequence CGUCAA in this region. Explain how the single DNA base substitution in Hb^{CS} can lead to production of a protein that contains 31 more amino acids than the wild type has.

8. Wild-type β-globin protein is composed of 146 amino acids. A β-globin gene mutant known as Hb Cranston contains 157 amino acids. Partial mRNA sequences of β^A and Hb Cranston (β^{Cr}) are shown. The numbers indicate amino acid positions. Identify the mutation that causes β^{Cr}, and describe how the mutation leads to a longer than normal β-globin protein chain.

```
        144 145 146 Stop
βᴬ  AAG UAU CAC UAA GCU CGC UUU CUU GCU GUC
    CAA UUU CUA UUA A
        144 145 146 147         150
βᶜʳ AAG AGU AUC ACU AAG CUC GCU UUC UUG
                155 156 157 Stop
    CUG UCC AAU UUC UAU UAA
```

9. Describe why sickle cell disease is considered to be a recessive genetic disorder.

10. What molecular parameter causes DNA fragments to have different electrophoretic mobility? What parameter causes different mobilities in mRNA? What parameters cause different mobilities in proteins?

11. How is an autoradiograph produced from a Southern blot?

12. Both Southern blotting and northern blotting can reveal information about the DNA fragments or RNA molecules being examined, but the positions of nucleic acid bands in one kind of blot cannot be directly compared with those in the other. Why?

13. The target sequence on a fragment of DNA is 3'-ATATCGCACGGACT-5'. What is the sequence and polarity of an equivalent-length molecular probe used to detect this target sequence? Explain why the molecular probe you have proposed will detect the targeted sequence.

14. The β^S allele occurs in a central West African population at a frequency of 15%. The same allele occurs in a population from the southern tip of Africa at a frequency of less than 1%. Speculate about the reason for the different frequencies of the allele in these two African populations.

Application and Integration

15. The family represented in the pedigree and Southern blot below has been evaluated for the presence and distribution of the β^S allele. Use the information in the Southern blot and the explanation provided in the chapter to identify the phenotype and determine the genotype of each person tested.

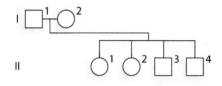

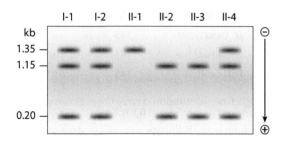

16. Suppose the mating couple (I-1 and I-2) shown in Problem 15 are expecting a fifth child.

    a. Is it possible that their fetus could have sickle cell disease? If so, what is the probability? If not, explain why not.

    b. Fetal DNA is collected and analyzed by Southern blotting. The fetus has a single DNA band that is 1.35 kb in length. What is your interpretation of this result? Explain your answer.

17. What are restriction endonucleases, and why are they useful in identifying DNA sequence variation?

18. Following restriction digestion, DNA fragments produced by digestion with certain enzymes have "sticky ends," while fragments produced by digestion using other enzymes have "blunt ends." Distinguish the meaning of these two terms.

19. The double-stranded DNA sequence below is part of a restriction fragment you wish to detect by autoradiography.

For answers to selected even-numbered problems, see Appendix: Answers.

5'-...ATTCATGACGGACTATTCGAGAGCTGATGCAT...-3'
3'-...TAAGTACTGCCTGATAAGATCTCGACTACGTA...-5'

Identify which of the following molecular probes is the best choice for achieving the desired hybridization reaction. Indicate where on the upper or lower strand the probe will hybridize.

    a. 3'-TGATATCGTACCGAA-5'
    b. 5'-TGCCTGATAAGATCT-3'
    c. 3'-ACAGCCTAGTAAGAT-5'
    d. 3'-ACTGCCTGATAAGCT-5'

20. Restriction enzymes recognize specific double-stranded DNA sequences that have the same sequence on both strands. For example, the restriction sequence for *Bam*HI is 5'-GGATCC-3' on each DNA strand and for *Sma*I is 5'-CCCGGG-3' on each strand. A single phosphodiester bond on each strand is cut at the same place in the sequence on each strand. Explain how restriction enzymes are able to recognize the same sequence and cut the sequence in the same place on each DNA strand.

21. Four alleles of a variable DNA marker gene produce differentsized DNA fragments as follows: $R^1 = 4$ kb, $R^2 = 13$ kb, $R^3 = 10$ kb, $R^4 = 7$ kb.

    a. Identify the genotypes of individuals depicted in lanes 1, 2, and 3 in the gel shown.

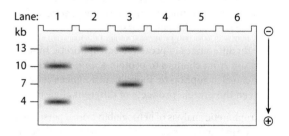

    b. In lanes 4, 5, and 6, draw the band patterns expected for individuals with, respectively, genotypes R^1R^3, R^3R^4, and R^1R^1.

22. Consider this DNA sequence:

5'-TTCGAATTCGACTCAGGATCCTACAAGTTTCAT-3'
3'-AAGCTTAAGCTGAGTCCTAGGATGTTCAAACTA-5'

Which of the following restriction sites are present in this sequence? Draw a box around each restriction sequence.

a. *Eco*RI (5'-GAATTC-3')
b. *Bam*HI (5'-GGATCC-3')
c. *Hin*III (5'-AAGCTT-3')

23. Two probes designated probe A and probe B hybridize very near one another in a region of DNA that contains DNA fragment length variation when digested with the restriction enzyme *Hin*III. Four maps show the location and intervening distances in kilobases of *Hin*III restriction sites and the binding locations of probes A and B. The maps correspond to alleles H^1 to H^4.

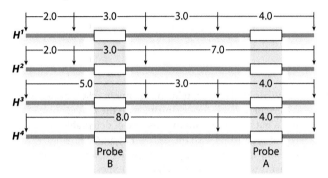

a. For the genotype H^1H^3, what DNA bands are expected in an autoradiogram using probe A? Using probe B? Using both probes together?
b. For the genotype H^2H^4, what band pattern is expected using probe A? Probe B? Using both probes together?
c. Suppose a woman with the genotype H^1H^3 has a child with a man whose genotype is H^2H^4. What are the four possible genotypes for a child of this couple?
d. What are the sizes of bands produced by each possible child of this couple using probe A? Using probe B?

24. Plants of a particular species can either have the dominant wild-type phenotype, tall (T), or the recessive phenotype called dwarf (D). Genetic analysis has identified the stature gene, and DNA analysis of tall plants yields a DNA fragment of 7.5 kb corresponding to a portion of the gene. The wild-type gene map is illustrated, along with an autoradiograph showing DNA restriction fragments from a normal parental plant (T; lane 1), a tall plant that carries a copy of the mutant allele (T; lane 2), the two DNA fragment patterns observed in tall progeny plants (T; lanes 3 and 4), and the DNA fragment pattern seen in dwarf plants (D; lane 5).

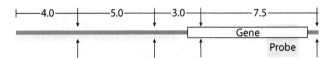

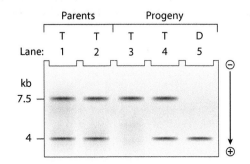

a. Purpose two mutational events that could cause the small DNA fragment that represents the mutant allele.
b. In northern blot analysis of mRNA, what mRNA differences would you anticipate for your two proposed mutational mechanisms?

25. A second strain of dwarf plants has a different mutation of the same gene identified in Problem 24. In the second strain, plants carrying a copy of the mutant allele produce a DNA restriction fragment of 10.5 kb, rather than the 7.5-kb fragment. DNA fragments produced by digestion of DNA from tall carrier plants are shown below in lanes 1 and 2, fragments from tall progeny of carriers are shown in lanes 3 and 4, and DNA from dwarf plants is shown in lane 5.

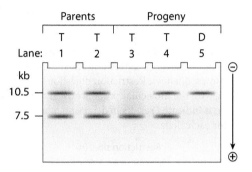

a. What mutational mechanism is most likely responsible for the production of abnormal DNA fragment length corresponding to this mutant allele? Explain your reasoning.
b. In comparison to the length of mRNA from the normal allele, will the mRNA from this mutant allele most likely be longer, shorter, or about the same length? Explain your answer.

26. During gel electrophoresis of linear DNA molecules, why do longer molecules move more slowly than shorter molecules? What determines the difference in electrophoretic mobility of mRNA molecules?

27. What three features of proteins are most important in determining their electrophoretic mobility? Based on your answer, describe how single amino acid substitutions can change the electrophoretic mobility of a protein.

28. In molecular biology, restriction endonucleases isolated from bacteria are used to cleave DNA into fragments. What functional role do restriction endonucleases serve in the bacteria from which they are derived?

29. A complete plant gene containing four introns and five exons is carried on a 6.0-kb DNA fragment. DNA sequencing analysis finds that this fragment contains 1000 base pairs that flank the transcribed region of the gene and 5000 base pairs that are transcribed. Four introns contain 3500 base pairs, and five exons contain 1500 base pairs. Northern blot analysis is performed on mRNA of this gene using a probe that binds to a portion of one of the exons. mRNA isolated from the cytoplasm of cells is compared to mRNA isolated from cell nuclei on the northern blot. Do you expect that all the mRNAs will be a uniform length, or will mRNA molecules of multiple lengths be detected on the northern blot?

30. Two male hounds, identified in the figure as ♂1 and ♂2, got loose one night at Wet Noses Puppy Farm. A female (♀A in the figure) got pregnant and had a litter of three

puppies (P1, P2, and P3). The owner of Wet Noses is desperate to know which male is the father and has electrophoretic analysis of a variable DNA genetic marker (shown in the figure) to guide in the identification. The owner thinks ♂1 is the father of the three puppies. Is the owner correct? Explain your answer.

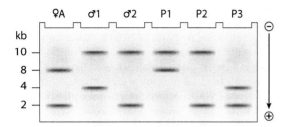

31. The map below illustrates three alleles in a genome segment. The alleles differ in the number and location of restriction sequences. Restriction digestion and Southern blotting with the molecular probe whose hybridization location is indicated results in detection of a single DNA band for each allele.

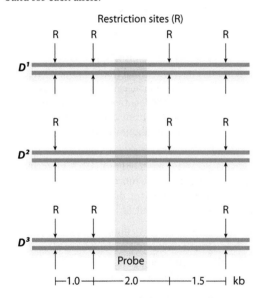

a. List the size (in kilobases) of DNA bands detected by Southern blotting of restriction-digested DNA from organisms with the genotypes D^2D^2, D^2D^3, and D^3D^3.
b. Restriction-digested DNA from two organisms is analyzed by Southern blotting. Restriction fragments of 2.0 and 3.5 kb are observed on the Southern blot of one organism, and bands of 2.0 and 3.0 kb are observed for the other. What are the genotypes of these organisms?
c. Organisms with the genotype D^1D^1 are identified by the detection of a 2.0-kb DNA band on a Southern blot.

Why does this genotype produce a single detectable band, and why are the 1.0- and 1.5-kb restriction fragments not detected in Southern blotting?

32. A dominant wild-type allele D produces full enzyme function, but a recessive allele d_1 produces no functional enzymatic action, and a recessive allele d_2 produces reduced enzyme function. Western blot analysis of the proteins produced by organisms with different genotypes for this gene gives the results shown.

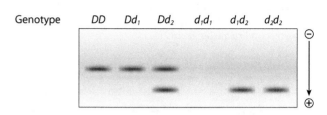

a. What kind of a protein change might result in two western blot bands for organisms with the Dd_2 genotype?
b. What might explain the absence of detectable protein for organisms with the d_1d_1 genotype?
c. Why might there be just one protein band for organisms with the d_1d_2 and d_2d_2 genotypes?
d. Based on your assessment of the western blot analysis, speculate about the nature of the mutations producing d_1 and d_2. In other words, what has happened at the DNA level to produce these mutations?

33. Northern blot analysis is performed on mRNA produced by transcription of a gene in organisms with different genotypes. Three alleles occur at the gene: N is a dominant wild-type allele, and alleles n_1 and n_2 are each recessive alleles. Results of northern blot analysis of organisms with six different genotypes are shown.

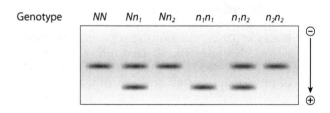

a. Organisms with the genotypes NN, Nn_2, and n_2n_2 each have single bands with the same electrophoretic mobility. Thinking about the composition of mRNA, explain this observation.
b. Organisms that are n_1n_1 have a single mRNA band with higher electrophoretic mobility. Thinking about the composition of mRNA, explain this observation.
c. Two mRNA bands are detected for organisms with the Nn_1 and the n_1n_2 genotypes. Explain this observation.

Chromosome Structure

11

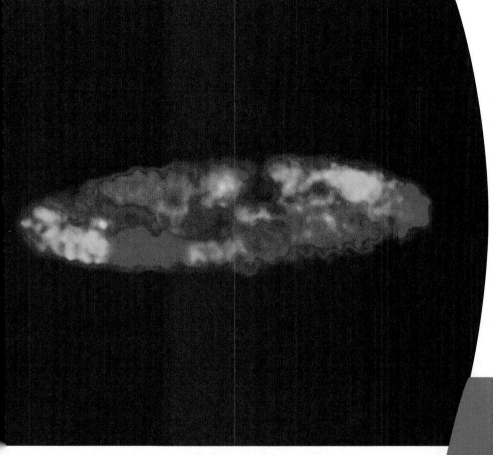

Interphase chromosome territories in a chicken cell nucleus. Different fluorescent in situ hybridization probes label each chromosome that lays in its own well-defined territory.

CHAPTER OUTLINE

11.1 Viruses Are Infectious Particles Containing Nucleic Acid Genomes

11.2 Bacterial Chromosomes Are Organized by Proteins

11.3 Eukaryotic Chromosomes Are Organized into Chromatin

11.4 Chromatin Compaction Varies along the Chromosome

11.5 Chromatin Organizes Archaeal Chromosomes

ESSENTIAL IDEAS

■ Viruses are noncellular, infectious particles with nucleic acid genomes that are packaged in protein capsules.

■ DNA supercoiling and DNA-associated proteins compress the bacterial chromosome into a nucleoid region within the cell.

■ Large amounts of protein organize and condense eukaryotic chromosomes.

■ Chromosome bands uniquely identify each chromosome but vary with chromosome condensation level.

■ Different degrees of eukaryotic chromosome condensation are associated with differential transcription.

■ Archaeal chromosomes are organized and compacted by proteins.

The genome of a species is the total amount of hereditary information in an entire set of its chromosomes. Chromosomes consist largely of DNA, and we describe the molecular structure of DNA and the importance of its nucleotide sequence in Chapter 7. But the structure and sequence of DNA are only a partial description of the genome. Arguably even more important to the genome story is the way the DNA is organized in chromosomes.

Every chromosome carries a single, long DNA molecule. The chromosome may be singular, as in bacterial and archaeal species; it may be a member of a homologous pair of chromosomes, as in diploid eukaryotic species; or it may be one of multiple chromosomes in a polyploid set, as in certain plant species. Whatever their number and regardless of whether they belong to archaea, bacteria, or eukarya, all chromosomes are composed of DNA that is organized by proteins of different types and in different amounts.

The combination of protein and DNA in chromosomes is critical in accomplishing four essential functions. First, protein helps compact the DNA so that chromosomes will fit efficiently into the bacterial or archaeal cell or into the eukaryotic nucleus. Second, protein helps stabilize DNA and protects it from damage. Third, protein promotes chromosome condensation required for cell division. Finally, the packaging of chromosomes with proteins helps regulate DNA replication and gene transcription, particularly in eukaryotic genomes.

This chapter describes chromosome structure and the composition of the genetic material in viruses, bacteria, eukaryotes, and archaea. The association of proteins of various types with DNA and the ways in which this association aids in accomplishing the four essential functions identified above are central to the discussion. We begin with a discussion of virus structure, viral genomes, and the variability of the genetic material carried by viruses.

11.1 Viruses Are Infectious Particles Containing Nucleic Acid Genomes

A **virus** is a noncellular infectious particle containing nucleic acid in a small genome that encodes a limited number of genes. The nucleic acid can be either single-stranded or double-stranded DNA or RNA. Viral genomes do not contain all of the genetic information required for the virus to replicate and express its genetic material. As a consequence, viruses are obligate parasites, meaning that they must infect a **host cell**—which, depending on the virus, may be a bacterial, archaeal, plant, or animal cell—in order to express the genetic information contained in the genome and produce the proteins required to generate new viral progeny. Each type of virus has a limited "host range," meaning that a particular type of virus can infect only cells of a certain host or group of hosts.

Viruses are not cellular; they lack most of the features belonging to a cell. Instead, they are particles consisting of a protein structure with genetic material contained inside. Other proteins encasing the viral particle recognize binding sites on the surface of potential host cells. Once bound to the outside of a host cell, the virus may enter the cell or inject its genetic material into the host cell to begin the infection cycle. Viral infections of host cells proceed by one of two mechanisms. Some viruses spread their progeny by budding new progeny viral particles from an infected host cell. Many chronic viral infections in eukaryotes are sustained by budding. Infection by the human immunodeficiency virus (HIV) is maintained in this manner. Alternatively, an infected host cell my undergo lysis (rupture) that releases a large number of progeny viral particles. Section 6.5 describes details of lysis following viral (bacteriophage) infection of bacterial cells. Whether released by budding or by lysis, progeny viral particles seek out new host cells to infect. Certain viruses have a third option as well: entry into the lysogenic life cycle. Viruses capable of lysogeny integrate into a host chromosome, replicating along with the host DNA, until conditions are right for the virus to excise itself and undertake host cell lysis.

Viral Genomes

The content of viral genomes, the structural configuration of the nucleic acid, and the genome size all vary from one kind of virus to another (Table 11.1). Regardless of whether DNA or RNA is the genetic material of a viral particle, and irrespective of whether the nucleic acid is double-stranded or single-stranded, the nucleic acid is associated with no additional proteins.

Viral genomes range in size from a few thousand bases of single-stranded DNA or RNA (or base pairs, in the case of double-stranded RNA) to more than 200,000 base pairs of double-stranded DNA, and they range in content from 5 genes to nearly 300 genes. Viruses with a small number of genes typically express all their genes shortly after infection. Viruses with larger genomes and more genes, such as bacteriophage λ (lambda), cytomegalovirus, and herpes simplex virus, express their genes in a regulated manner at different times following infection.

Despite their diverse genome structures, viruses follow the central dogma of molecular biology (DNA → RNA → protein) outlined in Figure 1.8, meaning that regardless of the type of nucleic acid comprising the genome, mRNA is generated by transcription of viral genes for translation. These processes, along with viral genome replication, utilize host cell proteins and host cell structures such as ribosomes.

Viral Protein Packaging

The viral genetic material is enclosed in a protein coat known as a **capsid.** Some viral genomes are packaged in a capsid that is a protein shell. These viruses, called

Table 11.1	Composition and Organization of Selected Viral Genomes				
Virus	**Nucleic Acid**[a]	**Genome Size**	**Number of Genes**[b]	**Chromosome**	**Form Host**
Parvovirus	ssDNA	5176 bases	5	Linear	Animals
øX174	ssDNA	5386 bases	11	Circular	Bacteria
fd	ssDNA	6400 bases	10	Linear	Bacteria
Simian virus 40	dsDNA	5243 bp	5	Circular	Animals
Cauliflower mosaic virus	dsDNA	8025 bp	7	Circular	Plants
Bacteriophage lambda	dsDNA	48,514 bp	71	Linear	Bacteria
Bacteriophage T4	dsDNA	168,903 bp	288	Linear	Bacteria
Herpes simplex virus	dsDNA	158,400 bp	77	Linear	Animals
Human cytomegalovirus	dsDNA	229,351 bp	162	Linear	Animals
Poliovirus	ssRNA	7433 bases	13	Linear	Animals
Tobacco mosaic virus	ssRNA	6400 bases	6	Linear	Plants
Human immunodeficiency virus (HIV)	ssRNA	9700 bases	9	Linear	Animals
Influenza virus	ssRNA	13,500 bases	11	Linear	Animals
Reovirus	dsRNA	23,549 bp	10	Linear	Animals

[a] ss = single-stranded; ds = double-stranded
[b] If linear

nonenveloped viruses, are sometimes identified as "naked viruses," since they consist of nothing but a protein shell enclosing viral genetic material. In other viruses, called **enveloped viruses,** the capsid is surrounded by an envelope of host cell cytoplasmic membrane that is acquired as the viral progeny escape the host cell (Figure 11.1).

Non-enveloped viruses undergo capsid self-assembly. In this assembly process the capsid incorporates a copy of the viral genomes that, once fully assembled, is ready for release from the host cell. Figure 11.2a shows the self-assembly of the tobacco mosaic virus capsid and packaging of the single-stranded linear RNA genome of the virus. Figure 11.2b is an electron micrograph of tobacco mosaic virus.

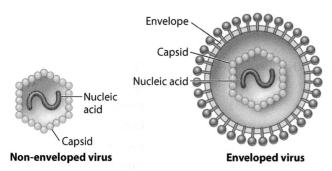

Figure 11.1 Enveloped and non-enveloped viruses. A protein capsid encloses the viral chromosome. An enveloped virus acquires its covering of host cell cytoplasmic membrane as it is released from the cell.

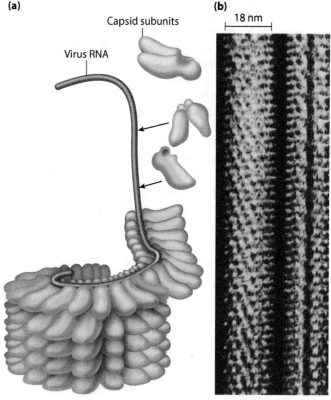

Figure 11.2 Viral structure and assembly. (a) Assembly of the tobacco mosaic virus and packaging of its genetic material. **(b)** Electronmicrograph showing the rod-shaped tobacco mosaic virus.

More complex viral particles, such as bacteriophage T4 and bacteriophage λ are assembled by a process known as **directed assembly.** The non-capsid proteins catalyze the assembly of capsid components but dissociate as the process nears its end, leaving the finished viral particle composed of its specific components. Directed assembly also includes the incorporation of the viral genome into the capsid.

11.2 Bacterial Chromosomes Are Organized by Proteins

Bacterial genomes are haploid and generally contain a single chromosome composed of double-stranded DNA. Depending on the species and the growth conditions, certain bacteria will sometimes carry two or more copies of the bacterial chromosome. The genetic information carried on each chromosome copy is identical, so each gene is represented by a single DNA sequence. In this section, we describe properties of bacterial genomes and the structure of bacterial chromosomes.

Bacterial Genome Content

Most bacterial species, including widely studied bacterial species such as *Escherichia coli* and *Bacillus subtilis*, have circular chromosomes. There are, however, numerous examples of bacterial species that contain a linear chromosome. Table 11.2 illustrates some of the chromosome diversity found among bacterial species.

Most bacterial genomes encode several thousand genes that are densely packed throughout the chromosome. These so-called **structural genes** contain the DNA sequences that encode bacterial proteins. These are considered to be genes that are essential for normal bacterial functions and metabolism, and they populate the majority of the chromosome. These regions include the regulatory sequences that promote and terminate transcription, as we discuss in Chapter 8. Interspersed between genes are short intergenic regions. These regions are not transcribed and serve to separate one gene from the next gene on the chromosome. Bacterial chromosomes contain small amounts of repetitive DNA sequence that are found in multiple copies in the chromosome, and are located in intergenic regions. These repetitive sequences are rarely transcribed, but they may play important roles in DNA replication, in recombination between chromosomes, or in regulating gene transcription.

Bacterial Chromosome Compaction

The chromosomes of bacteria are densely compacted into a series of tight loops, which makes the **nucleoid,** the region in which they are contained, remarkably small (Figure 11.3). If the 4.6 Mb of the *E. coli* chromosome were to be unpacked from the nucleoid and laid out along a ruler, it would measure about 1200 μm, nearly 1000 times longer than the *E. coli* cell itself. To get a sense of this size difference, imagine trying to stuff a 62-foot-long thread into the kind of gelatin-based capsule you might take for allergies or a headache!

How does *E. coli* package a chromosome 1000 times longer than itself and leave room for molecular activities such as replication, transcription, and translation? The

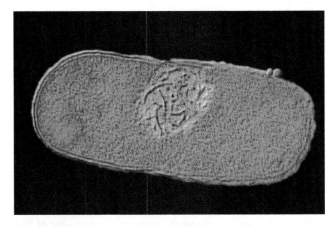

Figure 11.3 **The nucleoid of *E. coli*.** Supercoiling condenses the *E. coli* chromosome, and proteins help organize it in the nucleoid region.

Table 11.2	Chromosome Diversity among Bacteria		
Species	**Genome Size (in Mb)**	**Number of Chromosomes**	**Chromosome Form(s)**
Mycoplasma genitalium	0.58	1	Circular
Borrelia burgdorferi	1.4	2	One circular, one linear
Haemophilus influenzae	1.83	1	Circular
Vibrio cholerae	4.0	2	Both circular
Escherichia coli	4.2	1	Circular
Agrobacterium tumefaciens	5.7	4	Three circular, one linear
Sinorhizobium meliloti	6.7	3	All circular

answer is twofold. First, proteins help organize the chromosome into the loops that efficiently pack the nucleoid, and second, the circular DNA of the chromosome undergoes additional, superhelical twisting known as *DNA supercoiling.*

Bacterial DNA is associated with two major groups of proteins: **small nucleoid-associated proteins** and **structural maintenance of chromosomes (SMC) proteins.** Several different proteins belong to the small nucleoid-associated group of proteins, and all appear to participate in DNA bending that contributes to folding and condensation of the chromosome. The small nucleoid-associated proteins whose functions are best characterized are H-NS protein and HU protein. Figure 11.4 illustrates a possible general arrangement for H-NS and HU in securing loops of chromosomal DNA within the nucleoid. It also shows that the role of the SMC proteins is to hold the DNA in coils, or perhaps in V-shaped configurations. In addition to HU, H-NS, and SMC proteins, other proteins interact in the nucleoid to compact DNA. The precise identity and individual roles of these proteins is still a subject of active investigation.

The second mechanism facilitating chromosome compaction in the nucleoid is **DNA supercoiling,** which twists the duplex around on itself much like the twisting of a rubber band. Covalently closed circular chromosomes like those of bacteria exist in various coiled forms. The least twisted form of these is the relaxed-circle form that can be visualized as an undistorted rubber band lying flat on a plane in an open *O* shape. When the DNA duplex is in its standard coiled form with approximately 10 base pairs per helical turn (see Figure 7.7), it is in a relaxed circle form. In contrast, DNA molecules can be compacted by supercoiling as a response to over- or under-rotation of helical twisting. A portion of a DNA molecule that has its helix *over-rotated* has approximately 12.5 bp per helical twist, and will exhibit **positive supercoiling.** In contrast, a helix that is *under-rotated* has approximately 8.3 bp per helical twist and will exhibit **negative supercoiling.** Over-rotated

and under-rotated DNA structures are unstable and are stabilized by supercoiling.

Visualized by electron microscopy, supercoiled DNA looks something like a rubber band that as a result of extensive twisting has become convoluted, overlaps itself, and will not lie flat on a plane. Multiple intermediate supercoiled forms occur in large circular chromosomes.

DNA supercoiling and the relaxation of supercoiling are enzymatically controlled processes. **DNA gyrase,** also known as **topoisomerase II,** is responsible for introducing negative supercoiling. DNA gyrase contains four protein subunits that form two protein "jaws" that grasp the DNA duplex in different locations and twist the helix around itself to form negative supercoils. A second enzyme, **topoisomerase I,** is responsible for unwinding negative supercoils in four steps. Topoisomerase I first binds negatively supercoiled DNA and then catalyzes the breakage of one strand of the duplex. Remaining bound to the DNA, the enzyme then allows the broken strand to rotate around the intact strand to relieve tension. Lastly, it religates the broken strand. These same enzymes also operate on linear bacterial DNA, which can also be supercoiled. Homologous enzymes are found in eukaryotic cells, where they perform similar tasks.

Figure 11.5 shows supercoiling and the effect of topoisomerase I on highly supercoiled DNA. The electron micrographs in Figure 11.5a show two circular chromosomes from the same bacterial species, one highly supercoiled and the other in a relaxed-circle structure. Figure 11.5b shows gel electrophoresis results for highly supercoiled DNA after 5 minutes of exposure to topoisomerase I (lane 2) and 30 minutes of exposure to topoisomerase I (lane 3), using relaxed-circle DNA and highly supercoiled DNA (both without having been exposed to the enzyme) in lane 1 as controls. Notice in comparing lanes that with exposure to topoisomerase I and with the passage of time there is more relaxed-circle DNA (darker electrophoretic bands indicating more DNA) and less highly supercoiled DNA (lighter electrophoretic bands indicating less DNA).

Negative supercoiling has a critical role in bacterial cells beyond its role in chromosome compaction. Negative supercoiling promotes DNA strand separation associated with DNA replication and transcription. As a consequence, the role of DNA gyrase in controlling negative supercoiling is of considerable interest in medical research as a potential target for drugs with antibacterial activity. Two categories of drugs—coumarins and quinolones—have broad inhibitory effects on bacterial topoisomerases, including DNA gyrase. These compounds do not affect eukaryotic topoisomerases, which are different enough from bacterial topoisomerases to avoid the inhibitory effects. The antibiotic compound ciprofloxacin (more commonly known as Cipro) is one example of a broad-spectrum antibiotic that inhibits bacterial DNA gyrase activity and thus inhibits the growth and reproduction of bacteria.

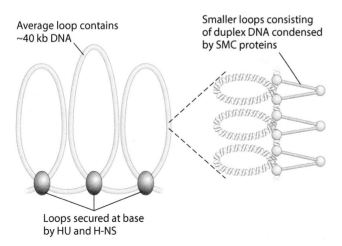

Average loop contains ~40 kb DNA

Smaller loops consisting of duplex DNA condensed by SMC proteins

Loops secured at base by HU and H-NS

Figure 11.4   Bacterial chromosome condensation by proteins.

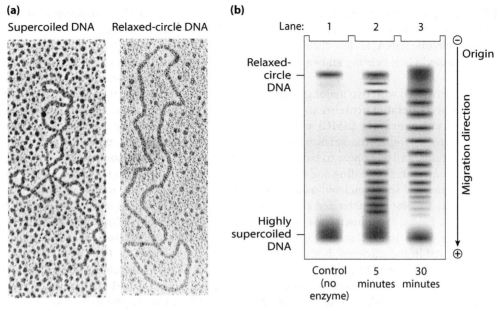

Figure 11.5 **Circular DNA of bacteria in multiple forms.** (a) Electron micrographs show supercoiled and relaxed-circle chromosomes. (b) The coiling of circular bacterial DNA determines its electrophoretic mobility. In lane 1, highly supercoiled DNA has a much higher electrophoretic mobility than the same DNA in a relaxed-circle state. In lane 2, 5 minutes of treatment with topoisomerase I to relax supercoiling produces many different coiled forms of the chromosome. In lane 3, 30 minutes of topoisomerase I treatment converts much of the DNA to relaxed circle.

11.3 Eukaryotic Chromosomes Are Organized into Chromatin

With regard to their number, structure, and organization, eukaryotic chromosomes differ from bacterial and archaeal chromosomes in numerous ways. For example, eukaryotes possess multiple chromosomes, which in diploids occur in homologous pairs. Also, the chromosomes are permanently localized to the nucleus, where replication, transcription, and mRNA processing take place. In addition, eukaryotic chromosomes undergo cyclic condensation for cell division. The total amount of DNA in eukaryotic genomes is tens to thousands of times greater than in bacterial or archaeal genomes.

To manage the massive amount of DNA and the multiple chromosomes and need for periodic chromosome condensation, eukaryotic chromosomes are organized by a nucleoprotein complex known as **chromatin** that is a mixture of the DNA that makes up the chromosomes along with an array of proteins that organize and compact the DNA. In this section, we describe the organizational role of chromatin by identifying the essential proteins that participate in this compaction process and looking at the mechanisms that promote it. There is, in addition, a second critical function for chromatin in eukaryotes that we take up in the following section: the generation of different chromatin states that vary in their degree of chromosome compaction and participate

in the regulation of gene expression by controlling access of transcription-initiating proteins to regulatory DNA sequences. A more detailed discussion of chromatin function in regulating eukaryotic gene expression is then presented in Chapter 15.

Chromatin Compaction

Why is chromosome compaction by chromatin important? Simply stated, eukaryotic chromosomes would not fit into the nucleus without compaction, and chromosome segregation during cell division would be impossible. Each one of your chromosomes contains one long DNA double helix that is incorporated with large amounts of protein into the complex known as chromatin. Each of your somatic cell nuclei contains more than 6 billion base pairs of DNA divided among 46 chromosomes, and all that DNA fits in the nucleus and still allows space for DNA replication, transcription, and mRNA processing, thanks to a remarkable feat of biomolecular engineering brought about by chromatin. If all the chromosomes were taken from one of your somatic cell nuclei and the 46 chromosomes were stripped of their proteins and unwound to a relaxed state, the DNA molecules laid end to end would span 1.8 meters—nearly 6 feet. This is more than 260,000 times the diameter of the nucleus! The DNA from your shortest chromosome alone would be almost 15,000 times longer than the nuclear diameter. Returning to the analogy of the medicinal capsule mentioned in the previous section in connection with the *E. coli* chromosome, a capsule representing a human nucleus would contain 46 pieces of thread, representing the 46 human chromosomes, with a combined length of 625 feet.

Histone Proteins and Nucleosomes

By weight, each eukaryotic chromosome is approximately half DNA and half proteins, and about one-half of the protein content of chromatin is **histone protein.** The histones are five small, basic proteins that are positively charged and bind tightly to negatively charged DNA. Equally abundant, but more diverse, is an array of hundreds of types of other DNA-binding proteins named, by default, **nonhistone proteins.** This large array of proteins performs a variety of tasks in the nucleus, not all of which are defined.

The five types of histone proteins in chromatin are designated **H1, H2A, H2B, H3,** and **H4** (Table 11.3). H1 is the largest and most variable histone protein, containing 215 to 244 amino acids, depending on the species. The other four histones are considerably smaller and more uniform in size, containing between 102 and 129 amino acids.

Among eukaryotes, there is very strong evolutionary conservation of the amino acid sequences of histone proteins. This consistency among eukaryotes suggests that there is significant evolutionary pressure to retain the structure and function of each histone protein. A comparison of the amino acid sequences of H4 in cows and pea plants, for example, demonstrates this high degree of evolutionarily retained identity. Cows and pea plants last shared a common ancestor more than 500 million years ago, when the animal and land plant lineages diverged. Over those hundreds of millions of years of evolutionary change, there are just two amino acid differences among the 102 amino acids in the protein. The comparison tells us that since the time when plants and animals last shared a common ancestor, extraordinarily strong evolutionary pressure has maintained H4 DNA and its amino acid sequence identity in organisms. This example of evolutionary conservation speaks to the importance of histones in eukaryotic chromosome organization.

Table 11.3	Histone Protein Characteristics			
Ratio of Histone[a]	Basic/Acidic Amino Acids	Molecular Weight (D)	Number of Amino Acids	Location
H1	5.4	23,000	224	Linker DNA
H2A	1.4	13,960	129	Nucleosome
H2B	1.7	13,774	125	Nucleosome
H3	1.8	15,273	135	Nucleosome
H4	2.5	11,236	102	Nucleosome

[a] Histone proteins from calf thymus gland.

Histones are the principal agents in chromatin packaging, and the fundamental unit of histone protein organization is the **nucleosome core particle.** The nucleosome core particle is a heterooctameric protein complex that contains two molecules each of four histones—H2A, H2B, H3, and H4 (Foundation Figure 11.6). These proteins are continuously transcribed and translated in eukaryotic cells, and histone genes are one family of genes that are present in multiple copies in eukaryotic genomes.

Nucleosome core particles self-assemble. The histone proteins first self-assemble into dimers containing two different histones each: H2A-H2B dimers contain one molecule each of histone 2A and histone 2B, and H3-H4 dimers contain one molecule each of histone 3 and histone 4. Current evidence indicates that nucleosome core particles are formed in steps that begin with two H3-H4 dimers assembling to form a histone tetramer. The tetramer is then joined by two H2A-H2B dimers to form the octameric nucleosome core particle.

Nucleosome core particles are flat-ended structures approximately 11 nm in diameter by 5.7 nm thick (see Figure 11.6a). Each nucleosome core particle is wrapped by approximately 146 base pairs of DNA that twist one and two-thirds turns around the core particle. This wrapping is the first level of DNA condensation, and it condenses the DNA approximately sevenfold.

The 146 bp of DNA wrapped around a nucleosome core particle is called **core DNA,** and the combination of a nucleosome core particle wrapped with core DNA is identified as a **nucleosome.** Electron micrographs of chromatin fibers in a highly decondensed state show a regular series of circular structures strung together by connecting filaments (see Figure 11.6b). This form of chromatin is identified as the "beads on a string" morphology of chromatin. The "beads" are nucleosomes that are a little more than 11 nm in diameter, and the "string" is called **linker DNA.** Linker DNA is the DNA between regions of core DNA.

The length of linker DNA segments varies among organisms, although in each species it is a consistent length, and, thus, nucleosomes occur at regular intervals. In the yeast *Saccharomyces cerevisiae*, linker DNA is 13 to 18 bp in length. Linker DNA is about 35 bp long in the fruit fly *Drosophila*. In humans and other mammals, linker DNA spans about 40 to 50 bp; in sea urchins, linker DNA is very long—approximately 110 bp. If the 146 bp in length of core DNA is added to the length of linker DNA, the nucleosome repeat distance of the beads-on-a-string structure is approximately 160 to 260 bp. This beads-on-a-string form of chromatin is identified as the **10-nm fiber,** since the diameter of nucleosomes is approximately 10 nm.

This nucleosome-based model of chromatin was proposed by Roger Kornberg in 1974. Kornberg based his model on biochemical observations that chromatin contains a ratio of one molecule of each of the four core histone proteins (H2, H2A, H3, and H4) to each 100 base pairs and one molecule of the histone H1 to each 200 base pairs.

Condensing the Nuclear Material

The hierarchy of chromatin organization and chromosome condensation.

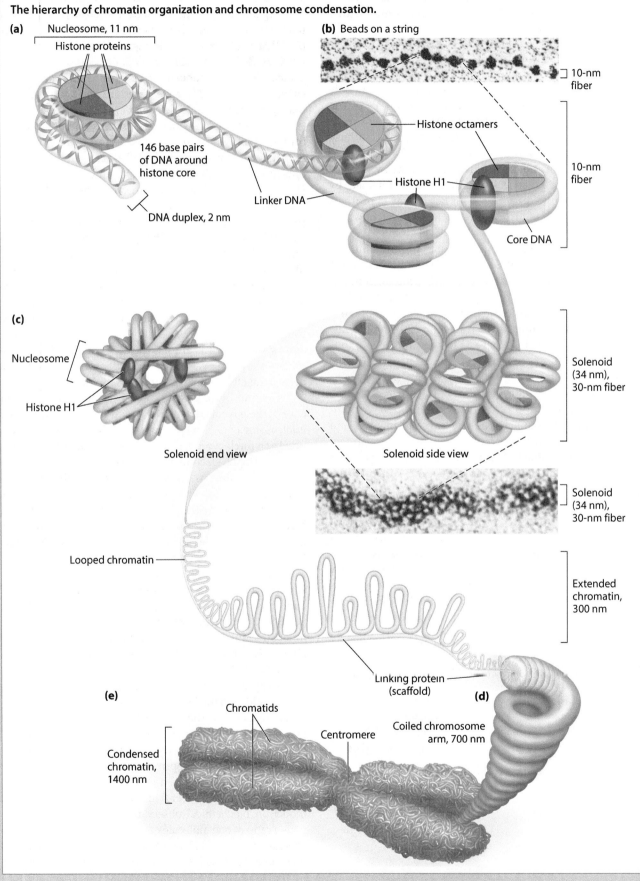

(a) Nucleosome, 11 nm

Histone proteins

146 base pairs of DNA around histone core

DNA duplex, 2 nm

(b) Beads on a string

10-nm fiber

Histone octamers

Histone H1

10-nm fiber

Core DNA

(c)

Nucleosome

Histone H1

Solenoid end view

Solenoid side view

Solenoid (34 nm), 30-nm fiber

Solenoid (34 nm), 30-nm fiber

Looped chromatin

Extended chromatin, 300 nm

Linking protein (scaffold)

(d) Coiled chromosome arm, 700 nm

(e)

Chromatids

Centromere

Condensed chromatin, 1400 nm

Structural protein–imaging described momentarily supported Kornberg's model, but the molecular proof of the model's validity came from research by Markus Noll who treated eukaryotic chromatin with different concentrations of the enzyme DNaseI to cut DNA where it is not protected by bound proteins. Recall from Research Technique 8.1 (pp. 279–280) and discussion in Section 8.3 in connection with DNA footprint-protection analysis that DNaseI cuts DNA that is not protein-protected but is unable to cut DNA in regions bound by protein. Noll's most important result was obtained by mixing mammalian chromatin with a high concentration of DNaseI and using gel electrophoresis to determine that the length of DNA fragments produced by DNaseI digestion measured approximately 200 bp in length. This is precisely the length Kornberg predicted, as it is the sum of the approximately 145 bp of DNA wrapping a nucleosome core particle and the 55 bp of linked DNA between nucleosomes.

Kornberg's model was supported by structural protein studies, X-ray diffraction imaging, and cryogenic electron microscopy (cryo-EM). The latter has produced detailed images of nucleosome structure and revealed the likely points of interaction between the octameric nucleosome core particle and core DNA. Timothy Richmond and his colleagues have described the crystal structure of the nucleosome using cryo-EM at 2.8-Å resolution (Figure 11.7). Richmond's analysis indicates that there are 1.65 turns of core DNA around each nucleosome core particle. The analysis identifies additional molecular interactions between the N-terminal (amino terminal) tails of histone proteins and core and linker DNA. These interactions are critically important to the type of chromatin structure present in regions of eukaryotic chromosomes. Different chromatin states play major roles in the regulation of eukaryotic gene expression, as we discuss in Chapter 15.

The 10-nm fiber is an unnatural state for chromatin. To achieve it, chromatin must be chemically treated and held in conditions that are not found in cells. Under normal cellular conditions, chromatin forms the **30-nm fiber,** which is six times more condensed than the 10-nm fiber (see Figure 11.6c). Electron micrographs and molecular modeling help us visualize how the 30-nm fiber is assembled. If we consider the 10-nm fiber to be a kind of primary structure for chromatin, then the 30-nm fiber is a secondary structure. It is produced by coalescence of the 10-nm fiber into a cylindrical filament of coiled nucleosomes that is hollow in the middle. Due to its coiled structure and open middle, the 30-nm fiber is often also called the **solenoid structure** (like the coil of wire in the starter of a car). Each turn of the solenoid structure contains six to eight nucleosomes. The diameter of the solenoid is approximately 34 nm.

The histone protein H1 plays a key role in stabilizing the solenoid structure. The long N-terminal and C-terminal ends of the H1 protein attach to adjacent nucleosome core particles. H1 protein pulls the nucleosomes into an orderly solenoid array and lines the inside of the structure. Experimental analysis shows that chromatin from which H1 has been removed can form 10-nm fibers but not 30-nm fibers. Chromatin exists in a 30-nm-fiber state or a more condensed state during interphase. Genetic Analysis 11.1 guides you through an interpretation of chromatin organization.

Higher Order Chromatin Organization and Chromosome Structure

Beyond the 30-nm stage, chromatin compaction and the presence of nonhistone proteins are integral to the structure of chromosomes and the process of chromosome condensation that initiates with the onset of prophase in the M phase of the cell cycle. Nonhistone proteins perform multiple roles in influencing chromosome structure and in facilitating M phase chromosome

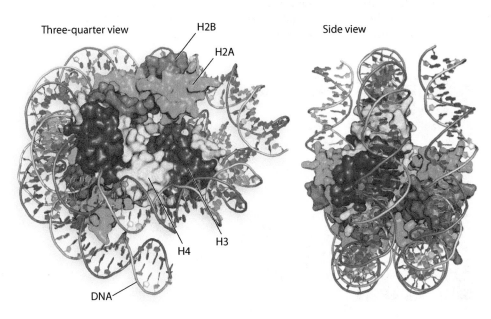

Figure 11.7 Nucleosome structure. A computer-generated rendering of the X-ray crystal structure of the nucleosome at 2.8-Å resolution by cryo-electron microscopy shows the eight histone protein molecules in the color-coded nucleosome core particle. DNA wraps one and two-thirds turns around the core particle, a span of approximately 146 bp.

Three-quarter view   H2B   H2A   Side view

H4   H3

DNA

condensation. Interphase chromosome structure results from the formation of looped domains of chromatin similar to supercoiled bacterial DNA (see Figure 11.6d). The loops are variable in size, containing from tens to hundreds of kilobase pairs and consisting of 30-nm-fiber DNA looped on a category of nonhistone proteins that are the foundation of chromosome shape. The diameter of looped chromatin is approximately 300 nm, so looped chromatin is called the **300-nm fiber.** With continued condensation, the chromatin loops form the sister chromatids. In metaphase, chromosome condensation reaches its zenith, resulting in chromosomes that are easily visualized by microscopy (see Figure 11.6e).

The **chromosome scaffold** is a filamentous nonhistone protein framework that gives chromosomes their shape. This scaffold is in some ways like the steel superstructure that provides the shape, strength, and support for a building. Figure 11.8a shows a fully condensed chromosome at metaphase, and Figure 11.8b shows the protein scaffold of a metaphase chromosome after being stripped of DNA. The shape of the chromosome scaffold is clearly reminiscent of the metaphase chromosome structure, consisting of sister chromatids joined at the centromere, which is visible as a constriction near the midpoint of the scaffold. The stringy material surrounding the scaffold is DNA.

Chromatin loops containing 20,000 to 100,000 bp are anchored to the chromosome scaffold by other nonhistone proteins at sites called **matrix attachment regions (MARs)** (Figure 11.9). The **radial loop–scaffold model** predicts that the chromatin loops gather into rosette-like structures and are further compressed by nonhistone proteins. The total compaction of chromatin achieved by metaphase is approximately a 250-fold compaction of the already condensed 300-nm fiber.

Higher order chromosome condensation plays a critical role in two distinctive features of eukaryotic genetics. First, the general process of chromosome condensation compacts chromosomes to a degree that allows them to be efficiently separated at anaphase. Second,

the chromatin loops formed during condensation play a role in regulating gene expression. Recent analysis of DNA binding to the chromosome scaffold indicates that certain repetitive DNA sequences are common at MARs. These sequences, called ATC sequences, are rich in A-T base pairs and have a high concentration of C in one strand. ATC sequences are found throughout the genome. Consequently, they can attach to the MARs in different patterns in different tissues. Experimental evidence indicates that active transcription takes place in chromatin loops, particularly in segments of loops that are distant from MARs. Thus, larger loops tend to have more active transcription than small loops.

The positioning of ATC sequences throughout the genome appears to play a role in cell-type-dependent patterns of chromatin looping in given chromosomes that can lead to expression of certain genes in one type of cell but not in another. For example, if gene *A* is designated for expression in a certain type of cell but gene *B* is not, gene *A* will be found far away from an MAR, whereas gene *B* will be close to an MAR. The molecular details of this model are clearer for single-celled eukaryotes than for mammals, but it appears that the position of a gene within the nucleus is a factor in its transcription. We discuss this observation in more detail in Chapter 15.

Nucleosome Distribution and Synthesis during Replication

Our discussion of DNA replication in Chapter 7 described the enzymatic processes necessary for the synthesis of new daughter DNA strands. This process doubles the total amount of DNA in a nucleus and results in each chromosome containing two identical sister chromatids. All of this newly synthesized DNA must be organized by nucleosome core particles. Having described the structure and function of nucleosomes in chromatin, we now take a moment to describe the process of managing existing nucleosome core particles

Figure 11.8 The chromosome scaffold of a metaphase chromosome. (a) A metaphase chromosome. (b) Stripped of chromatin, the chromosome scaffold is composed of nonhistone proteins that form a superstructure to anchor DNA loops and gives the chromosome its shape.

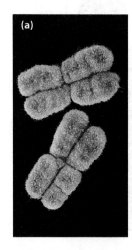

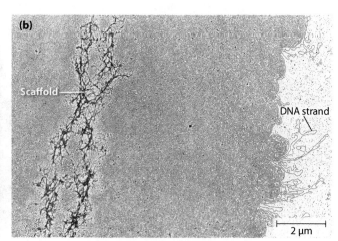

Scaffold

DNA strand

2 μm

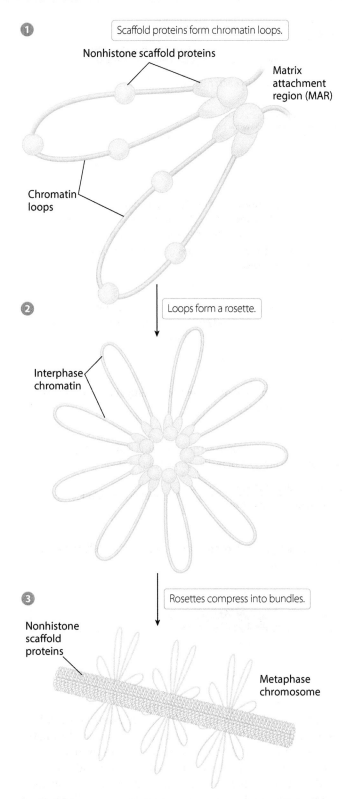

Figure 11.9 **The radial loop–scaffold model of chromatin condensation.** ❶ Chromatin is anchored at matrix attachment regions (MARs). ❷ Nonhistone proteins organize chromatin loops into rosettes. ❸ Rosettes are compressed in metaphase chromosomes.

during replication and the process of adding these and new nucleosome core particles to DNA after the replication fork passes.

The ubiquitous presence of nucleosomes raises several questions about their management and synthesis in connection to DNA replication. Are old nucleosomes recycled during replication? Are new nucleosome proteins synthesized during replication? Do old nucleosome core particles remain intact, so that nucleosomes are composed of either old histone proteins or newly synthesized histone proteins, or are old and newly synthesized histone protein mixed? And how are nucleosome core particles, whatever their composition, distributed to the sister chromatids during replication?

Experimental research has answered these questions. Evidence collected by numerous investigators finds that the assembly of nucleosome core particles in connection with replication is driven by the partial denaturing of old core particles into either dimers or tetramers. These old core particle components are randomly joined with other dimers and tetramers after replication to form complete nucleosome core particles. There is a great deal of new histone protein synthesis during DNA replication, and the newly synthesized proteins form dimers and tetramers. This mixture of old and newly synthesized core particle components is the pool from which post-replication nucleosome core particles are assembled. The experimental evidence indicates that most nucleosome core particles present after replication are a mixture of some old nucleosome core particle dimers or tetramers and some newly synthesized core particle dimers or tetramers. In addition, a few histone core particles are composed of entirely newly synthesized histone proteins, and some are composed of entirely old core particle components.

The current model proposes that as the replication fork passes, nucleosomes break down into protein subassemblies—specifically, H3-H4 tetramers and H2A-H2B dimers. The H3-H4 tetramers immediately reaffiliate, more or less at random, with one of the sister chromatid products of replication. In contrast, many H2A-H2B dimers apparently become disassembled into individual histone proteins and then quickly reform into dimers with either old or newly synthesized protein partners.

Enough new synthesis of all four proteins takes place to double the number of nucleosomes. In this process, new H2A-H2B dimers and H3-H4 tetramers assemble. Some new H2A-H2B dimers join old H3-H4 tetramers already on DNA, while other new H2A-H2B dimers join new H3-H4 tetramers to form nucleosomes. Thus, about half of the nucleosomes assembled during replication are composed of old H3-H4 tetramers that are randomly distributed to the sister chromatids and combined with

PROBLEM The plant species *Arabidopsis thaliana* has a genome containing approximately 100 million bp of DNA. For this problem, assume *Arabidopsis* has a core-DNA length of 145 bp and a linker-DNA length of 55 bp.

a. Determine the approximate number of nucleosomes in each nucleus.

> BREAK IT DOWN: The nucleosome is wrapped by core DNA, and the spans between nucleosomes consist of linker DNA (p. 371).

b. Determine approximately how many molecules of histone protein H4 are found in each nucleus.

> BREAK IT DOWN: Histone core particles are heterooctamers containing two molecules each of four histone proteins (p. 371).

Solution Strategies	Solution Steps
Evaluate	
1. Identify the topic this problem addresses and the nature of the required answer.	1. This problem asks about the number of nucleosomes per nucleus and about the histone composition of nucleosomes. The answer requires approximate numbers of nucleosomes and of histone H4 molecules per nucleus.
2. Identify the critical information given in the problem.	2. The approximate genome size of *A. thaliana* is given in base pairs, as are the lengths of its core and linker DNA.
Deduce	
3. Describe the number of DNA base pairs that wrap around each nucleosome, and state the approximate number in the span between nucleosomes. TIP: The combined length of core plus linker DNA affiliated with each nucleosome is 145 bp + 55 bp = 200 bp	3. The core DNA wrapping a nucleosome is 145 bp in length. Linker DNA between nucleosomes is approximately 55 bp in length. In total, there is one nucleosome for about every 200 bp of DNA.
4. Describe nucleosome composition.	4. Nucleosomes are octamers of histone protein consisting of two molecules each of H2A, H2B, H3, and H4.
Solve	Answer a
5. Calculate the number of nucleosomes in each *A. thaliana* nucleus.	5. If we estimate that a new nucleosome associates with DNA about every 200 bp, the approximate number of nucleosomes per nucleus is $$\frac{1 \times 10^8 \text{ nucleotides/nucleus}}{2 \times 10^2 \text{ nucleotides/nucleosome}} = 5 \times 10^5 \text{ nucleosomes/nucleus}$$
	Answer b
6. Calculate the number of molecules of H4 in the nucleosomes of an *Arabidopsis* nucleus.	6. There are 2 H4 molecules per nucleosome, thus $(2)(5 \times 10^5) = 10^6$, or 1 million H4 molecules, per nucleus.

For more practice, see Problems 4, 7, and 18. | Visit the Study Area to access study tools. | MasteringGenetics™

---

either new or old H2A-H2B dimers. The remaining nucleosomes contain new H3-H4 and either new or old H2A-H2B components (**Figure 11.10**).

11.4 Chromatin Compaction Varies along the Chromosome

In the previous section, we described the role of chromatin in chromosome compaction. In this section, we discuss differences in chromosome compaction along chromosomes, consider the consequences of this variability for visualizing chromosome structure, and take a first look at the functional consequence of variation in chromatin state for differential gene transcription.

Chromosome Shape and Chromosome Karyotypes

During prophase of the cell cycle, chromosome condensation prepares the chromosomes for sister chromatid segregation. As chromosome condensation reaches its zenith in late prophase, the sister chromatids become individually visible with the aid of microscopy, and each chromosome takes on a characteristic shape. Condensed chromosomes are divided by their centromere into segments known as **chromosome arms** that are almost invariably of unequal lengths.

One chromosome arm, called the **short arm,** also known as the **p arm,** is shorter than the other arm that

(a)   Nucleosome

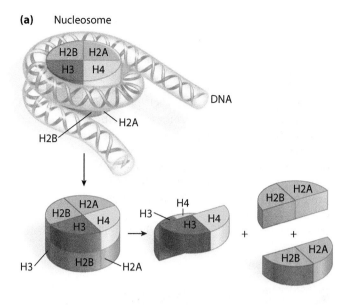

(b)

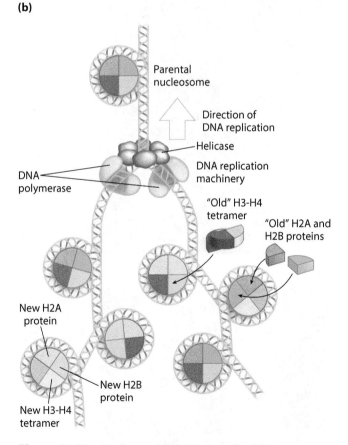

Parental nucleosome

Direction of DNA replication

Helicase

DNA replication machinery

DNA polymerase

"Old" H3-H4 tetramer

"Old" H2A and H2B proteins

New H2A protein

New H2B protein

New H3-H4 tetramer

Figure 11.10 **Nucleosome inheritance after DNA replication.** Following the passage of the replication fork, "old" H3-H4 tetramers are randomly assigned to daughter strands, and newly synthesized H3-H4 tetramers inhabit strands not bound by old tetramers. Old and new H2A-H2B dimers join the tetramers to form complete nucleosomes.

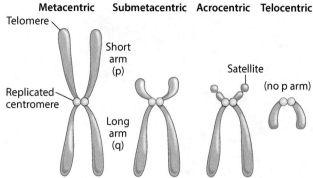

Figure 11.11 **Chromosome shape.** The position of the centromere and the ratio of the lengths of the long arm (q arm) and short arm (p arm) at metaphase determine chromosome shape.

is known as the **long arm,** or the **q arm** (Figure 11.11). The position of the centromere determines the relative lengths of the short and long arms, leading to descriptive terms for the shapes of metaphase chromosomes. A **metacentric chromosome** has a more or less centrally located centromere and chromosome arms of similar lengths. **Submetacentric chromosomes** have a centromere nearer one end, producing one arm that is distinctly shorter than the other. The centromere of **acrocentric chromosomes** is nearly at the end of the chromosome. The "short arm" of acrocentric chromosomes is often composed of highly repetitive DNA. These repetitive regions are known as "satellites" in part because secondary chromosome constrictions appear to partially pinch off the repetitive segment of the short arm. **Telocentric chromosomes** have a terminal centromere and no short arm.

Chromosome number differs among species, but each species has a characteristic chromosome number. In eukaryotes, like humans, the **karyotype** is a visual display of chromosomes seen by microscopy. A karyotype displays all the chromosomes in a nucleus. In the case of a human karyotype, it contains 22 pairs of autosomes and one pair of sex chromosomes. The human karyotype is arranged and numbered with the largest autosomal pair as chromosome 1 and the rest of the autosomes following in order of descending length. The sex chromosomes are identified separately.

The chromosomes in a karyotype may be stained with various dyes to produce the *chromosome banding* pattern that is distinct for each pair or type of chromosomes in the set. A normal human male karyotype contains 22 pairs of autosomes (numbered 1 through 22) and one X and one Y chromosome, and a normal human female karyotype contains 22 autosomal pairs of chromosomes along with a pair of X chromosomes.

In Situ Hybridization

The contemporary approach to examining chromosome number, structure, and genetic content is the use of *in situ hybridization* methods. These methods visualize karyotypes through the use of chromosome-specific

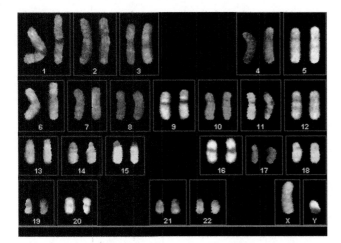

Figure 11.12   A human karyotype. With distinct fluorophores labeling 24 chromosome-specific FISH probes, this normal human male karyotype displays a different color pattern for each chromosome. Autosomal pairs are numbered 1 to 22, and the X and Y chromosomes are labeled.

molecular probes that are tagged with fluorescent compounds to facilitate detection (Figure 11.12). Using microscopy and computer-enhanced imaging, these methods allow chromosome inspection with great precision.

The karyotype in Figure 11.12 uses molecular probes that are specific to each of the 24 chromosomes in a human male karyotype (22 autosomes, an X chromosome, and a Y chromosome) pictured in the karyotype. Each of the chromosome-specific molecular probes is tagged with a different fluorescent compound. When excited, each of these compounds emits light of a different wavelength, allowing a computer-driven photoreceptor to capture the emissions and convert them into an image with the different colors seen in the karyotype.

The hybridization of the chromosome-specific molecular probes is similar to the hybridization of the probes described in Research Technique 10.2. Rather than being specific to a single gene, however, these probes label an entire chromosome. Furthermore, unlike the preparation for gel electrophoresis and Southern blot methods described in Chapter 10, chromosomal DNA need not be fragmented for a chromosome-specific target sequence to be detected by the molecular probe. Instead, the chromosomes are fixed on a microscope slide, the DNA is denatured (i.e., separated into single strands), and the probe is applied. This technique is known as **in situ hybridization** because, unlike other hybridization methods, it labels intact chromosomes.

The first generation of in situ hybridization methods used radioactive nucleic acid probes that produced autoradiographs when a small piece of photographic film was placed on top of a chromosome spread on a microscope slide. Decay of ^{32}P radioactive label in the probe exposed the photographic film, which was then developed in the same way as an autoradiograph of an electrophoresis gel. In chromosome autoradiographs, dark regions

corresponded to the chromosome locations of a DNA sequence hybridized by the probe.

Today, most in situ hybridization applications use fluorescent compounds, commonly known as fluorophores, to label molecular probes. This is known as **fluorescent in situ hybridization (FISH).** Using FISH, fluorophores can be attached to chromosome-specific probes that label certain chromosome sequences but not others or to gene-specific molecular probes. Figure 11.13a illustrates the use of two gene-specific FISH probes, one with a fluorophore producing red color and the other with a fluorophore producing green color, to identify two genes on the same human chromosome. Figure 11.13b utilizes multiple FISH probes to individually label each human chromosome. In

(a)

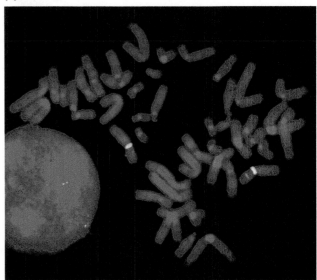

(b)

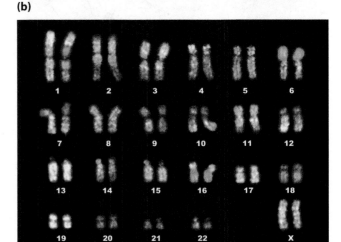

Figure 11.13   Fluorescent in situ hybridization (FISH). (a) Two FISH probes hybridizing with target sequences on a human chromosome are detected by production of differently colored fluorophore emissions. (b) Multiple probes and fluorescent compounds make each chromosome distinctive.

this instance, the probes are segments of chromosomes that differ in their sequenced content. The probes are labeled with distinct fluorophores, leading to some chromosomes having multiple colors in the image.

Imaging Chromosome Territory during Interphase

Early observers of chromosomes in the nucleus, including Edmund Wilson, Walter Sutton, and Theodore Boveri, hypothesized that chromosomes contained the genetic material and noticed that interphase chromosomes are not uniformly arrayed within a nucleus. They suggested that this variation might be related to chromosome activity. Recent research using FISH techniques to study chromosome positioning in the interphase nucleus indicates that these early suggestions are valid.

Cell biologists Thomas Cremer and Christoph Cremer have used FISH methods to investigate the arrangement of chromosomes in the nucleus during interphase and found that chromosomes are partitioned into their own chromosome territories (see the chapter-opening photo (p. 365) and Figure 11.14. A **chromosome territory** is a small region of the nucleus that is the domain of a single chromosome. It is not bounded by any sort of membrane, nor is it demarcated in any distinctive manner. Chromosomes do not occupy exactly the same territory in each nucleus (the nucleus does not have reserved seating for each chromosome), but once confined to a territory, a chromosome does not stray from it until the initiation of M phase of the cell cycle. Chromosomes are, however, dynamically active within their territories during interphase and can be seen to move, twist, and turn during transcription and DNA replication. The chromosomes appear to be anchored by their centromeres and perhaps to take positions that allow, for each chromosome, characteristic patterns of gene expression and other activities during interphase.

Adjacent chromosome territories are separated by an **interchromosomal domain** that contains no chromatin. These domains are channels for the movement of proteins, enzymes, and RNA molecules within the nucleus and among chromosome territories. The distribution of chromosome territories places the largest and most gene-rich chromosomes toward the center of the nucleus, while the territories of smaller chromosomes containing fewer genes are located toward the outer edges of the nucleus.

The positioning of a chromosome within its territory corresponds to the activities in which the parts of the chromosome are engaged at particular stages of interphase. For example, chromosome regions that replicate early in S phase are generally found further away from the nuclear membrane. The regions closer to the center of the nucleus are the locales of so-called early-replicating chromosome segments. In contrast, late-replicating chromosome segments, portions of chromosomes that replicate late in S phase, are found nearer to the nuclear membrane. Also, the most transcriptionally active chromosome regions are found closest to the border between a chromosome territory and an interchromosomal domain, presumably because of (1) greater access to proteins and enzymes needed for transcription and (2) faster dispersal of RNA transcripts after transcription is completed. While transcription occurs throughout each chromosome territory, experimental evidence suggests that transcription is most intense bordering on interchromosomal domains.

Recently, C. Anthony Blau and several colleagues have extended the Cremers's findings by developing a three-dimensional model of the 16 chromosomes in yeast haploid nuclei (Figure 11.15). Employing a method that differentially identifies each chromosome, the researchers were able to precisely map the location of each chromosome within the nucleus. The resulting three-dimensional map of chromosome positioning reveals that chromosome centromeres are clustered together and that the

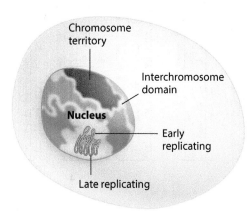

Figure 11.14 **Chromosome territories in the eukaryotic nucleus.** Chromosomes occupy discrete territories separated by interchromosome domains during interphase of the cell cycle.

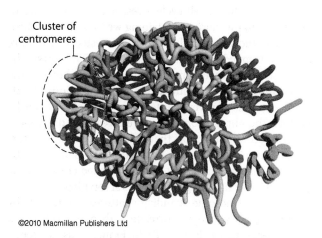

©2010 Macmillan Publishers Ltd

Figure 11.15 **A three-dimensional model of chromosomes in the yeast nucleus.** Yeast-chromosome centromeres are clustered toward one end of the nucleus; chromosome arms radiate from the centromere cluster.

chromosome arms project away from the centromere cluster. Knowledge of the positioning of chromosomes within the nucleus will make it possible to determine how DNA sequences influence chromosome positioning and, in turn, how chromosome positioning influences the transcription and replication of sequences.

FISH techniques have numerous applications in the analysis of chromosomes in humans and other species. One important and practical use of these methods is the identification of the complex chromosome rearrangements often found in cancer cells, which we discuss in the Case Study that ends the chapter.

Chromosome Banding

Chromosome condensation, driven by chromatin compaction, reaches its maximum at the end of metaphase, when chromosomes are in their most condensed state. Using chromosome staining methods and microscopy, cytogeneticists can distinguish each chromosome by its overall size and shape and by the patterns of light and dark **chromosome banding** that are produced along the length of chromosomes by treatment with specific dyes and stains. These are the methods that were originally used to produce karyotypes, and their legacy is essential to both basic chromosome nomenclature and to the foundations of our understanding of the role of chromatin state in gene expression.

During the late 1960s and early 1970s, several techniques for chromosome banding were developed, primarily by experimentation with human and other mammalian chromosomes. Chromosome banding allows cytogeneticists to accurately identify each chromosome and chromosome segment in a karyotype according to internationally agreed upon standard banding patterns for each chromosome.

Generating a karyotype and banding the chromosomes is a multistep process that begins with the growing of cells in culture followed by the use of a chemical treatment to stop the cell cycle in, or just before, metaphase. Chemically induced cell cycle arrest maximizes the number of cells in the culture containing well-condensed chromosomes. Individual cells from the arrested cell culture are then dropped onto a microscope slide. This bursts the cells and ruptures the nuclear membrane, allowing the chromosomes to spill out. After some additional treatment, any one of several different dyes or stains can be used on the chromosomes to reveal regional differences in chromatin compaction that produce a series of alternating chromosome bands. Banded chromosomes can be examined using microscopy, and the banded chromosome spreads are often photographed for karyotyping.

The chromosome banding patterns produced by different stains and dyes correlate with one another. An international symposium in Paris, France, was convened in 1971 to agree on the standard banding pattern for each human chromosome as well as on a standardized nomenclature for identifying chromosome banding patterns based on karyotypes of metaphase chromosomes. This nomenclature

remains in use today to ensure accuracy in identifying each chromosome and in describing any chromosome variants or abnormalities. The standardized banding is based on the highly reproducible patterns of some 300 or so lightly and darkly stained bands in chromosome-specific patterns seen on human chromosomes. The banding method is known as **G (Giemsa) banding,** and it is named after the staining compound called Giemsa stain that is used to generate the chromosome bands.

The standardized G banding nomenclature uses letters and numbers to identify the major and minor band regions of each chromosome. The numbering begins at each chromosome centromere and progresses outward along each arm toward the telomere (**Figure 11.16**). Major regions are subdivided to permit a designation for each light- and dark-band region of a chromosome. Each band is given a designation that specifies the chromosome number, chromosome arm, and band location. An

Standard banding patterns and landmark designations for human chromosomes 1 through 5

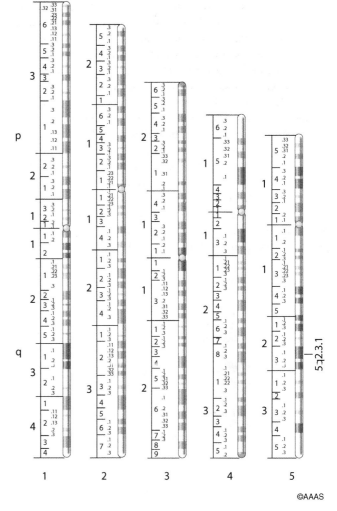

©AAAS

Figure 11.16 **Standardized human chromosome banding patterns.** Human chromosomes 1 to 5 in late prophase. Heterochromatic regions are shown as gray and black bands, euchromatic regions as white bands.

example is 5q2.3.1, which is the dark band on the long arm of chromosome 5 indicated in Figure 11.16.

Chromosome banding by G banding and other techniques was at one time limited to chromosomes in metaphase. Recently, however, advanced techniques have allowed cytogeneticists to stain chromosomes earlier in the cell cycle. Chromosome banding in prometaphase chromosome spreads produces as many as 2000 chromosome bands. Like the bands seen in metaphase chromosomes, these bands are highly reproducible, and chromosome-specific prometaphase banding patterns are now standardized. We discuss more about the applications of chromosome banding in Chapter 13.

Heterochromatin and Euchromatin

Each chromosome band, whether in a metaphase chromosome spread or a prometaphase spread, contains many chromatin loops, thus holding between 1 million and 10 million base pairs of DNA. Multiple genes can be contained in each chromosome band.

The basis of chromosome banding is chromatin state. Chromatin condensation varies throughout the cell cycle but also varies from one part of a chromosome to another. G banding and other chromosome banding methods detect these differences in chromatin compaction by their ability to differentially stain regions of greater or lesser chromatin compaction.

There is clear evidence that chromatin state is directly related to the ability of transcriptionally active proteins to initiate gene transcription. This means that chromosome banding patterns are associated with the distribution of expressed genes. During interphase, chromosome regions containing genes that are actively expressed generally have a lesser degree of chromatin condensation than chromosome regions that do not contain expressed genes. These regions of active expression are identified as **euchromatin,** or as **euchromatic regions.** Most expressed genes are located in euchromatic regions, where condensation is variable during the cell cycle. Euchromatic chromosome regions are lightly staining regions of G-banded chromosomes. Conversely, chromosome regions in which chromatin is tightly condensed are said to contain **heterochromatin** and are called **heterochromatic regions.** Heterochromatic regions contain many fewer expressed genes than do euchromatic regions. With fewer expressed gene sequences, heterochromatic DNA is more likely than euchromatic DNA to contain repetitive DNA sequences. Heterochromatin is identified as darkly staining chromosome regions in G-banded chromosomes.

Two distinct classes of heterochromatin are detected. **Facultative heterochromatin** exhibits variable levels of condensation. At times, facultative heterochromatin is highly condensed, while at other times it is less so. The transcription of genes in regions of facultative heterochromatin usually correlates with periods of less compaction. **Constitutive heterochromatin,** on the other hand,

is in a permanent heterochromatic state and contains very few expressed genes. Constitutive heterochromatin is predominantly composed of repetitive DNA sequences. It is particularly prominent in chromosome telomeres and in the centromeric regions of chromosomes, and, correspondingly, neither telomeric nor centromeric constitutive heterochromatin contains expressed genes.

Genetic Analysis 11.2 gives you practice with these concepts as you interpret the results of a hypothetical experiment involving the use of FISH probes that have unknown sequence targets within chromosomes.

Centromere Structure

The observation that expressed genes are common in euchromatic regions and uncommon in heterochromatic regions suggested to researchers that there might be a connection between chromatin state and gene expression. Understanding of the connection between chromatin state and gene expression came initially from studies of an unusual circumstance in the fruit fly *Drosophila* involving a chromosome translocation and heterochromatic DNA near the centromere.

Centromeres are specialized DNA sequence regions that are not found elsewhere in the genome. Centromeres bind kinetochore proteins and spindle fiber microtubules and in this way play an essential role in the division of homologous chromosomes and sister chromatids during cell division (see Figures 3.4 and 3.6).

In the early 1980s, John Carbon and Louis Clarke described centromeric DNA, or CEN sequences, in the yeast *Saccharomyces cerevisiae* with an analysis of the sequences of 16 yeast centromeres. Each centromere was found to have a slightly different CEN sequence. Yeast CEN sequences span 112 to 120 bp and are divided into three domains, designated centromeric DNA elements (CDE) I, II, and III. Figure 11.17a shows four examples of yeast CEN sequences that illustrate the overall similarity but subtle variation in centromere sequences. The centromeric consensus sequences revealed in Carbon and Clarke's analysis are shown in Figure 11.17b. That of CDE I is an 8-bp sequence RTCACRTG, where R is either of the purines adenine or guanine. That of CDE III contains 26 bp rich in A-T. Between these elements is CDE II, varying in length from 78 to 86 bp and having more than 90% of its sequence composed of A-T base pairs. A single microtubule attaches to the kinetochore in yeast, but multiple microtubules attach to the kinetochores of other species (Figure 11.17c).

The highly repetitive centromeric DNA sequences of eukaryotes are a region of constitutive heterochromatin. A specialized form of the histone H3 protein known as centromere protein A (CENP-A) binds centromeric DNA. CENP-A is similar to H3 from its C-terminal end through much of its length but has a very different N-terminal tail that is much longer than the one found in other H3 molecules. The extended CENP-A N-terminal tail is critical to the binding of kinetochore proteins.

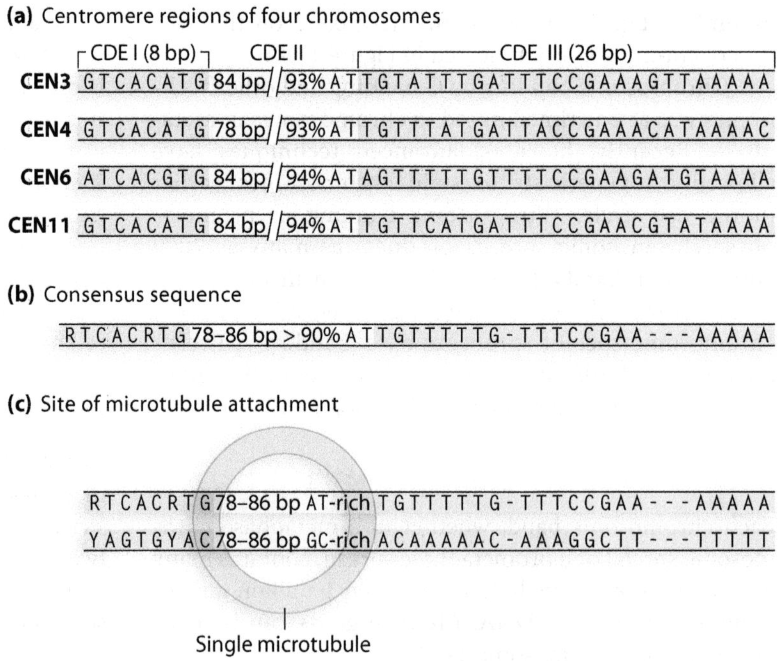

Figure 11.17   Conserved nucleotide sequence at the yeast centromere. (a) Centromeric sequence variation. **(b)** The centromeric consensus sequence. **(c)** Microtubule attachment to the centromere region. (Abbreviations: R = purine, Y = pyrimidine.)

(a) Centromere regions of four chromosomes

┌CDE I (8 bp)┐   CDE II   ┌───────────── CDE III (26 bp) ─────────────┐

CEN3   GTCACATG 84 bp // 93% ATTGTATTTGATTTCCGAAAGTTAAAAA

CEN4   GTCACATG 78 bp // 93% ATTGTTTATGATTACCGAAACATAAAAC

CEN6   ATCACGTG 84 bp // 94% ATAGTTTTTGTTTTCCGAAGATGTAAAA

CEN11 GTCACATG 84 bp // 94% ATTGTTCATGATTTCCGAACGTATAAAA

(b) Consensus sequence

RTCACRTG 78–86 bp > 90% ATTGTTTTTG-TTTCCGAA---AAAAA

(c) Site of microtubule attachment

RTCACRTG 78–86 bp AT-rich TGTTTTTG-TTTCCGAA---AAAAA
YAGTGYAC 78–86 bp GC-rich ACAAAAAC-AAAGGCTT---TTTTT

Single microtubule

Position Effect Variegation: Effect of Chromatin State on Transcription

Cell and molecular biologists now know that chromatin state is a critical component of the opportunity to transcribe genes in eukaryotes. Most expressed genes are located in euchromatic regions of chromosomes where DNA is not as tightly affiliated with histones. In contrast, relatively few expressed genes are found in heterochromatic regions where histones and other protein tightly bind DNA. Thus differences in chromatin state play an important role in regulating eukaryotic gene expression, as we discuss in Chapter 15.

The constitutive heterochromatin in centromeric regions is present in all but the S phase of the cell cycle when DNA replicates. During S phase, histones and other proteins that otherwise bind to DNA release their grip to allow replication. We have seen that nucleosome core particles dissociate from DNA and partially disassemble ahead of the replication fork during S phase and that they are then reconstituted after the replication fork passes. Once the replication fork passes, new and original histone dimers and tetramers reassemble, and heterochromatic compaction is reestablished in the centromeric region. In the case of replication of centromeres, however, the borders for reestablishing boundaries on each arm of the chromosome are somewhat variable. The reason for the variability is that there are no expressed genes in the immediate vicinity of centromeres, and a little more or a little less spread of centromeric heterochromatin after the completion of replication normally has no impact on gene expression.

Study of the reacquisition of centromeric heterochromatin following replication provided the circumstances for the first observation of the role of chromatin state in controlling gene expression. The first experimental evidence connecting chromatin structure to gene expression came from the observation of **position effect variegation (PEV),** a mutation affecting eye color in *Drosophila*. During the 1920s and 1930s, in tests of the effect of X-rays on *Drosophila* development, Hermann Muller identified X-ray–exposed fruit flies with a variegated pattern of eye color. Whereas the wild-type *Drosophila* eye is red, flies with variegated eye color had red and white patches of eye tissue. Furthermore, the variegation differed from one fly to the next and was even different between the eyes of a single fly. Muller presumed that the red patches resulted from expression of the wild-type w^+ allele for red color. White patches of fly eyes have no color, as the result of absence of w^+ expression.

In Muller's most important variegation experiments, he began with flies that were pure-breeding for red eye, that is, males were w^+/Y and females were w^+/w^+. Recall that the w^+ gene is located near the telomere of the X chromosome (see Figure 5.6). After exposing these flies to X-rays and producing progeny with variegated eye color, he noticed that the X chromosomes of flies with variegated eye color had an abnormal structure. These X chromosomes had been broken by the damaging effects of X-rays very near the centromere, and the acentric chromosome pieces had then rejoined the remainder of the X chromosome, except that now they were inverted 180 degrees relative to their normal position. He realized that, as a result of this X chromosome inversion, w^+ had moved from its normal location near the telomere of the X chromosome to a new position near the centromere of the chromosome.

At the time, Muller speculated that the new position of w^+ near the centromere altered its expression. By a

PROBLEM Suppose Dr. O. Sophila receives three new FISH probes from a colleague with the request that Dr. Sophila's laboratory determine the likely hybridization targets of the probes on human chromosomes. Each FISH probe contains a single specific sequence. Chromosome spreads are prepared, and FISH probes labeled with distinct fluorophores are added. The following results are obtained: Probe A is several dozen nucleotides in length, and it labels each chromosome centromere but no other parts of any chromosome; probe B is about a dozen nucleotides in length, and it labels the telomeres on every chromosome but no other parts of any chromosome; probe C is about a dozen nucleotides in length, and it labels a single spot on each copy of chromosome 4 at band position 4q3.2. Dr. Sophila asks you to interpret these experimental results and to help his colleague by identifying the likely sequence-binding target of each probe.

BREAK IT DOWN: Review the discussion of FISH on pp. 377–378.

Solution Strategies	Solution Steps
Evaluate	
1. Identify the topic of this problem and the nature of the requested answer.	1. This problem concerns the interpretation of hybridization results of FISH (fluorescent in situ hybridization) in human chromosomes.
2. Identify the critical information given in the problem.	2. The answer must identify the likely target sequences detected by each of the three FISH probes based on the described hybridization patterns.
Deduce	
3. Review the meaning and interpretation of probe hybridization to DNA	3. Centromeres contain a specialized DNA sequence that is bound by kinetochore proteins rather than histone proteins. Telomeres are composed of hundreds of copies of short, repetitive DNA sequences generated by telomerase.
TIP: FISH probes hybridize by complementary base pairing. Probes longer than about 20 base pairs may hybridize even if there are a few mismatches.	
4. Recall the makeup of eukaryotic chromosomes in terms of their content of protein-coding genes and other types of DNA sequences.	4. Heterochromatic DNA contains few expressed genes, and heterochromatic DNA sequences are more likely to be repetitive.
Solve	
5. Provide an interpretation of the DNA sequence targeted by probe A.	5. By hybridizing exclusively to centromeric regions, probe A is likely to be targeting the specialized DNA sequences that attract kinetochore proteins. These sequences are somewhat variable from centromere to centromere, but they are similar, and probe A is long enough to hybridize to multiple similar but not identical target sequences.
6. Provide an interpretation of the DNA sequence targeted by probe B.	6. Hybridization exclusively to telomeres indicates that probe B is targeting the short repetitive DNA sequences of telomeres.
7. Provide an interpretation of the DNA sequence targeted by probe C.	7. Probe C hybridizes to a single location on homologous copies of chromosome 4 that is most likely to be a protein-coding gene. The band 4q3.2 is a euchromatic region of the chromosome, where many expressed genes are located. The identity of the gene cannot be determined, however, without additional information.

For more practice, see Problems 13 and 25. Visit the Study Area to access study tools. **Mastering**Genetics™

mechanism he could not explain, the new position of w^+ near the centromere led to the allele being expressed in some cells but not in others. Those cells in which the allele was expressed had pigment deposition and were red, and those in which expression did not occur were white. The pattern of positioning of w^+-expressing and w^+-nonexpressing cells differed from fly to fly and between the eyes of a single fly; hence the variegation patterns differed.

Follow-up research has determined that Muller's general explanation for PEV was correct—with inversion,

the expression of w^+ varies from cell to cell. The molecular basis for PEV was discovered several decades later, and it is the result of the extent of centromeric heterochromatin spread following replication in inverted chromosomes. **Figure 11.18** illustrates this occurrence. If centromeric heterochromatin distribution after replication does not reach the new location of w^+, the gene will be in a euchromatic region and can be actively transcribed. This allows pigment deposition and can constitute a patch of red eye color. On the other hand, in cells in which centromeric

Figure 11.18 Position effect variegation of eye color in *Drosophila*. The w^+ allele is expressed in wild-type X chromosomes and in inverted X chromosomes when the latter contain centromeric heterochromatin that does not spread to cover the gene. If the spread of centromeric heterochromatin covers the new gene location in inverted X chromosomes, w^+ is silenced. The CH_3 (methyl) groups indicate the locations of heterochromatin.

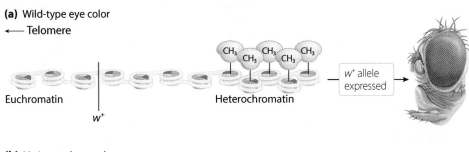

(a) Wild-type eye color

← Telomere

Euchromatin

w^+

Heterochromatin

w^+ allele expressed

(b) Variegated eye color

Inversion moves w^+ near the centromere.

w^+

w^+ allele expressed

w^+ allele silenced

Heterochromatin spread is variable.

heterochromatin spreads across the new location of w^+, the allele is in a heterochromatic region and is not expressed. Pigment is lacking in these cells, which therefore can constitute a white patch of eye color. The formation of heterochromatin is usually associated with the methylation (addition of CH_3 groups) to amino acids of histone proteins. The CH_3 groups in Figure 11.18 indicate the presence of heterochromatin. We discuss this phenomenon in Chapter 15.

The key to variegation in this case is the extent of the spread of centromeric heterochromatin in X chromosomes having the inversion that places w^+ near the centromere. If centromeric heterochromatin spreads across the new location of w^+, the allele is transcriptionally silenced because transcriptional proteins are unable to access regulatory DNA sequences that are in a tightly bound chromatin state. If, on the other hand, centromeric heterochromatin does not spread as far as the new location of w^1, the allele is in a euchromatic region where DNA is in a less tightly compacted chromatin state, and transcription can take place.

Since Muller first described position effect variegation and since its molecular basis was identified, geneticists and cell biologists have come to understand that chromatin structure is a critical component of gene expression in eukaryotic genomes. Research on PEV establishing the direct role of chromatin state on w^+ expression, and extensive follow-up research establishing the central role of chromatin state in eukaryotic gene expression, has led to two central conclusions: (1) Gene expression can be controlled by the state of

the chromatin in which a gene is located, and (2) gene expression or gene silencing can be dictated by chromatin structure that is transmissible from one cell generation to the next. We discuss these and other topics related to the regulation of eukaryotic gene expression in Chapter 15.

11.5 Chromatin Organizes Archaeal Chromosomes

In chapters discussing DNA replication, transcription, and translation, we have compared and contrasted important functional proteins and activities in archaeal cells with similar proteins and activities in bacterial and eukaryotic cells. In this section, we turn our attention to the structure of the chromosome in archaea—specifically, to the issue of protein-based organization of the chromosome by histone proteins and to the evolutionary implications of the presence of archaeal histone proteins. Through this discussion, we will see the shared ancestry of archaea and eukaryotes.

Archaeal Chromosome and Genome Characteristics

The genetics of bacteria and eukaryotes have been studied over many decades, in species too numerous to accurately count. In contrast, the domain Archaea is relatively newly discovered, having been first identified through the work of Carl Woese on ribosomal RNA genes in the mid-1970s (see Chapter 1), a proposal that only achieved wide acceptance in biology in the 1980s.

Despite the relatively recent start to investigations of archaeal species, some general chromosome and genome characteristics are clear. For example, archaeal cells, like bacterial cells, have no nucleus. Archaea are haploids and, like bacteria, have a genome usually consisting of a single chromosome that is usually circular. The total size of archaeal chromosomes varies over more than a tenfold range. The smallest archaeal chromosome sequenced to date is that of *Nanoarchaeum equitani*, with 490,885 bp, and the largest chromosome is in *Methanosarcina acetivorans*, with 5,791,492 bp. Like bacterial genomes, a high percentage of the archaeal genome encodes proteins. On average, of any archaeal total genome sequence, 87% consists of protein-coding sequences. This value is equivalent to the bacterial genome average and is far greater than the percentages of protein coding sequences found in eukaryotic genomes. Also as in bacterial genomes, some repetitive DNA sequences, as well as intergenic regions between genes, are found. In addition, many archaeal genes share promoters and other transcription-regulating DNA sequences, as do many bacterial genes. (We discuss the coordinated transcription of multiple bacterial genes in Chapter 14.) Lastly, like bacterial cells, archaeal cells often contain plasmids as extrachromosomal DNA, and there are numerous examples of gene transfer between archaeal cells by conjugation. These circumstances are described for bacteria in Chapter 6.

Archaeal Histones

In sharp contrast to the above list of general similarities between archaeal genomes and chromosomes and those of bacteria, many, perhaps most, archaea have histone proteins that are homologous to the histone proteins forming nucleosome core particles in eukaryotes. As of early 2014, histone protein amino acid sequence data were limited to about 90 species, but these data indicate that archaeal histone proteins form a family of proteins with strong homology to eukaryotic histones. On average, archaeal histones contain 65 to 75 amino acids. Three-dimensional protein structure studies have determined that these histone proteins self-assemble into multimeric complexes with other histone proteins and that the resulting structures resemble those seen in eukaryotes.

For the most thoroughly studied type of archaeal histone protein, strong homology is identified with eukaryotic histones H3 and H4. This homology results in identical amino acid sequences in protein segments critical to folding. As in eukaryotes, archaeal histone complexes affiliate with DNA that wraps the complex. A span of approximately 90 bp of archaeal DNA is required to wrap the histone protein complex (Figure 11.19).

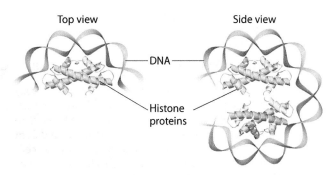

Figure 11.19   Archaeal DNA wrapping of histone proteins. A span of approximately 90 bp of DNA wraps a histone protein complex in archaea. The archaeal histones shown are homologs of eukaryotic H3 and H4.

What is the functional role of histones in archaeal cells? The answer is not currently known, but the question is under active research investigation. At the moment, the available evidence indicates a role for archaeal histone proteins in DNA compaction, but there is as yet little evidence that archaeal histones play a role in regulating gene transcription. This makes sense in terms of the single-celled, haploid character of archaea. Like bacteria, archaea must be capable of accessing and transcribing any gene at any time. The situation is very different for multicellular eukaryotes, in which each type of specialized cell is incapable of expressing most genes and instead expresses only its own specific limited number of genes. On one hand, homology of eukaryotic and archaeal histone proteins suggests that they have similar composition and might share some functional similarity. On the other hand, separate evolution of archaeal and eukaryotic histones may have led to different functional capabilities.

Phylogenetic Origins of Histone Proteins

Histone proteins are not found in bacteria, they are present in all eukaryotes, and they are found in most archaea. This suggests that histone proteins were not present in the LUCA (last universal common ancestor) and arose after the bacterial split off but before diversification of archaea and eukaryotes. With the divergence of archaeal and eukaryotic lineages, separate evolution has shaped the composition and function of histone proteins in each.

The implications of the evidence from the study of histone proteins in archaea and eukaryotes are in keeping with the evolutionary discussions of earlier chapters. Three distinct domains have evolved from their last universal common ancestor. The bacterial lineage was the first to split from the common ancestral root of eukaryotes and archaea. The result of the subsequent archaea–eukarya split is that both domains are seen to share features with bacteria while having more in common with one another.

CASE STUDY

Fishing for Chromosome Abnormalities in Cancer Cells

The genomes of cancer cells are highly abnormal and typically contain numerous gene mutations that disrupt many fundamental cell activities, such as cell cycle control, cell-to-cell interactions and communication, rate of cell division, and DNA damage repair. In addition, the chromosomes of cancer cells commonly display multiple abnormalities, including deletions or duplications of all or parts of chromosomes, and various structural abnormalities, such as translocations in which part of one chromosome is transferred and attached to a nonhomologous chromosome.

At one time, G banding was used as a way of identifying chromosome abnormalities in cancer cells. This process has been largely replaced by the development of multicolor FISH techniques and the use of distinct probes and fluorophores for each chromosome. The new methodology permits more accurate detection and identification of chromosome abnormalities. Figure 11.20a shows the chromosomes of a cancer cell in which FISH has revealed multiple chromosomal abnormalities. Notice that several chromosomes contain more than one color. Normal chromosomes would have a single, solid color. The presence of multiple colors on a chromosome indicates that the chromosome is actually composed of pieces from two or more nonhomologous chromosomes. This occurrence reflects the general instability and high mutation rate of the genomes of cancer cells.

While these features are common in cancer cells, they are usually a consequence, not a cause, of cancer. On the other hand, a few rare cancers appear to be caused by specific chromosome rearrangements that occur so frequently in the cancer that they are effectively diagnostic for that particular type of cancer. Figures 11.20b and 11.20c show two examples. One, in Figure 11.20b, shows a specific reciprocal

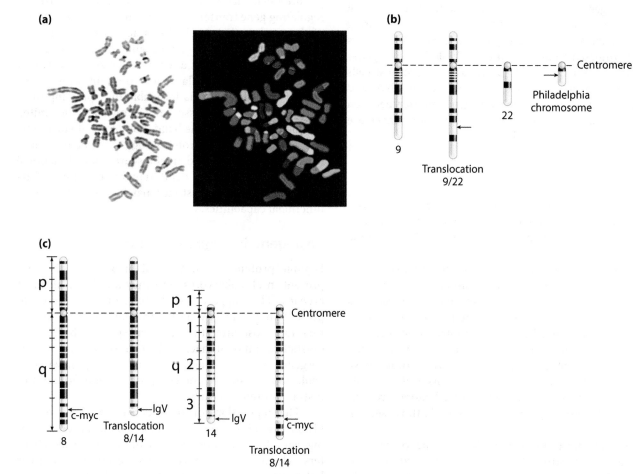

Figure 11.20   **FISH detection of chromosome rearrangements in human cancer cells.** (a) General chromosome instability leads to the frequent observation of multiple chromosome abnormalities in cancer cells, abnormalities that are readily observed using FISH methods (right). (b) A reciprocal translocation between chromosome 9 and chromosome 22 is very common in chronic myelogenous leukemia (CML). (c) Translocation between chromosome 8 and chromosome 14 is frequently detected in Burkitt's lymphoma cells.

translocation between one copy of chromosome 9 and one copy of chromosome 22 that is seen in most cases of chronic myelogenous leukemia (CML). One copy of chromosome 9 and one copy of chromosome 22 undergo chromosome breaks at the locations indicated by the arrows and exchange pieces in a reciprocal translocation mutation. The other copies of chromosome 9 and of chromosome 22 are intact. The result of the translocation is a dramatic overexpression of a growth-stimulating protein that triggers the leukemia. Overexpression occurs because the growth protein gene has been moved from its normal location to a new location where a very active promoter overdrives its transcription. This is a classic dominant gain-of-function mutation (see Chapter 4). Translocation also results in a characteristically small chromosome 22 called the Philadelphia chromosome. Since it was first identified in the 1960s, the Philadelphia chromosome has been a hallmark of CML.

The second cancer resulting directly from chromosome rearrangement is Burkitt's lymphoma, shown in Figure 11.20c. In Burkitt's lymphoma, a reciprocal translocation between chromosomes 8 and 14 is very frequently observed. As in CML, chromosome translocation puts a growth-stimulating gene in a new location where it is overexpressed.

G banding pattern differences between normal chromosomes and the translocation chromosomes of Burkitt's lymphoma and CML were the original methods used to identify these characteristic chromosome rearrangements. In recent years, the use of FISH, with its chromosome-specific fluorophores, has made the task of identifying these and other specific chromosome rearrangements in cancer considerably simpler. FISH has become an important diagnostic tool in the identification of other chromosome abnormalities as well. We describe some of these abnormalities in more detail in Chapter 13.

SUMMARY   (MasteringGenetics™   For activities, animations, and review quizzes, go to the Study Area.

11.1 Viruses Are Infectious Particles Containing Nucleic Acid Genomes

- Viruses are noncellular infectious particles that contain single- or double-stranded DNA or RNA as their genetic material.

- Viral genomes do not contain the genes required to support replication of the genetic material or transcription and translation of viral genes. Viruses are therefore obligate parasites of host cells.

- Viral genomes are contained in protein capsids that in some viral species are enveloped by host cell cytoplasmic membranes and in some species are unenveloped.

11.2 Bacterial Chromosomes Are Organized by Proteins

- Bacterial genomes are haploid and usually contain a single, circular chromosome. The genomes of certain bacterial species contain more than one chromosome.

- Bacterial chromosomes are 1000 or more times longer than the cells they reside in and are localized to the nucleoid region.

- Proteins associate with bacterial chromosomes to aid compaction.

- Supercoiling of circular bacterial chromosomes is the principal mechanism for compaction of the chromosome into bacterial cells.

11.3 Eukaryotic Chromosomes Are Organized into Chromatin

- Eukaryotic nuclei contain multiple chromosomes that are highly compacted.

- Eukaryotic chromosomes are composed of chromatin—a mixture of DNA, histone proteins, and other nonhistone proteins.

- Eight histone protein molecules form nucleosomes around which 146 bp of DNA wraps to form the 10-nm fiber.

- The 10-nm fiber condenses to form the 30-nm fiber.

- Nonhistone proteins form the chromosome scaffold that gives structure to chromatids and aids in additional chromosome compaction during prophase of the cell cycle.

- Chromatin loops form with the aid of proteins that help form the chromosome scaffold. In each different type of cell, expressed genes are more distant from anchor points on the scaffold than unexpressed genes.

11.4 Chromatin Compaction Varies along the Chromosome

- Chromosomes are categorized by structure on the basis of the centromere position and the ratio of long arm (q arm) length to short arm (p arm) length.

- Specialized molecular probes are used for in situ hybridization to locate specific genes or chromosome-specific DNA sequences. These probes often utilize fluorescent labels for detection.

- During interphase, each chromosome inhabits a territory of its own in the nucleus. Chromosome positioning within the territory is tied to replication and transcription.

- Each chromosome has a distinctive banding pattern created by applying stains or dyes to condensed chromosome spreads.

- Heterochromatic DNA forms darkly staining bands that contain relatively few expressed genes.

- Euchromatic DNA forms lightly staining bands that contain the majority of expressed genes.

- The centromere consists of specialized DNA sequences that bind kinetochore proteins.

- Studies of position effect variegation (PEV) have determined that the structure of chromatin surrounding a gene directly influences transcription.

11.5 Chromatin Organizes Archaeal Chromosomes

▊ Archaea are haploids with a single chromosome that is associated with histone proteins in most species.

▊ Archaeal histones are homologous to eukaryotic histones and function to compact the chromosome by wrapping of DNA around histone protein complexes.

▊ Phylogenetic analysis comparing histone proteins has determined that histones developed after the branching off of the bacterial lineage and before the divergence of the eukarya and archaea lineages.

KEYWORDS

10-nm fiber *(p. 371)*
30-nm fiber (solenoid) *(p. 373)*
300-nm fiber *(p. 374)*
acrocentric chromosome *(p. 377)*
capsid *(p. 366)*
chromatin *(p. 370)*
chromosome arm [long arm (q arm), short arm (p arm)] *(p. 376)*
chromosome banding (Giemsa banding, G banding) *(p. 380)*
chromosome scaffold *(p. 374)*
chromosome territory *(p. 379)*
constitutive heterochromatin *(p. 381)*
core DNA *(p. 371)*
directed assembly *(p. 368)*
DNA gyrase (topoisomerase II) *(p. 369)*
DNA supercoiling (negative supercoiling, positive supercoiling) *(p. 369)*

enveloped virus *(p. 367)*
euchromatin (euchromatic region) *(p. 381)*
facultative heterochromatin *(p. 381)*
fluorescent in situ hybridization (FISH) *(p. 378)*
heterochromatin (heterochromatic region) *(p. 381)*
histone protein (H1, H2A, H2B, H3, H4) *(p. 371)*
host cell *(p. 366)*
in situ hybridization *(p. 378)*
interchromosomal domain *(p. 379)*
karyotype *(p. 377)*
linker DNA *(p. 371)*
matrix attachment region (MAR) *(p. 374)*
metacentric chromosome *(p. 377)*

nonenveloped virus *(p. 367)*
nonhistone protein *(p. 371)*
nucleoid *(p. 368)*
nucleosome *(p. 371)*
nucleosome core particle *(p. 371)*
position effect variegation (PEV) *(p. 382)*
radial loop–scaffold model *(p. 374)*
small nucleoid-associated protein *(p. 369)*
solenoid structure *(p. 373)*
structural gene *(p. 368)*
structural maintenance of chromosomes (SMC) protein *(p. 369)*
submetacentric chromosome *(p. 377)*
telocentric chromosome *(p. 377)*
topoisomerase I *(p. 369)*
virus *(p. 366)*

PROBLEMS

MasteringGenetics™ Visit for instructor-assigned tutorials and problems.

Chapter Concepts

For answers to selected even-numbered problems, see Appendix: Answers.

1. Describe the structure and composition of a bacterial chromosome. Describe the same features of a bacterial plasmid. How are these structures similar, and how do they differ?

2. Biologists typically define bacterial and archaeal genomes as "haploid," but some bacterial genomes contain more than one chromosome in the genome, and some archaeal cells have more than one copy of the chromosome. Does the term "haploid" conflict with the occurrence of more than one chromosome in bacterial genomes or of multiple copies of the chromosome in archaeal genomes? Why or why not?

3. Bacterial DNA is compacted by two principal mechanisms. Identify and briefly describe each mechanism.

4. The human genome contains 2.9×10^9 base pairs. Approximately how many nucleosomes are required to organize the 10-nm–fiber structure of the human genome? Show the calculation you use to determine the answer.

5. Give descriptions for the following terms:
   a. histone proteins
   b. nucleosome core particle
   c. CEN sequences
   d. G bands
   e. euchromatin
   f. heterochromatin
   g. nucleosome
   h. chromosome territory
   i. nucleoid

6. Describe the importance of light and dark G bands that appear along chromosomes.

7. In eukaryotic DNA,
   a. Where are you most likely to find histone protein H4?
   b. Where are you most likely to find histone protein H1?
   c. Along a 6000-bp segment of DNA, approximately how many molecules of each kind of histone protein do you expect to find? Explain your answer.
   d. How does the role of H1 differ from the role of H3 in chromatin formation?

8. Describe the relative differences you expect between the levels of chromosome condensation in interphase and in metaphase.

9. Human late prophase karyotypes have about 2000 visible G bands. The human genome contains approximately 22,000 genes. Consider the region 5p1.5 through the end of the short arm of chromosome 5 that is identified on the late prophase chromosome in Figure 11.16, and assume the entire region is deleted. Approximately how many genes will be lost as a result of the deletion?

10. What are the two or three most essential components of a bacterial chromosome sequence? Of a eukaryotic chromosome sequence? Thinking in an evolutionary context, devise an argument to explain why these components are present.

11. Explain why viruses are described as "particles" and not as "cells" and why they are characterized as "obligate parasites" of host cells.

12. Do bacterial chromosomes have centromeres? Do they have telomeres? Devise an argument for each answer to explain why or why not from an evolutionary perspective.

13. A researcher interested in studying a human gene on chromosome 21 and another gene on the X chromosome uses FISH probes to locate each gene. The chromosome 21 probe produces green fluorescent color, and the X chromosome probe produces red fluorescent color.
    a. If the subject studied is female, how many green and red spots will be detected? Explain your answer.
    b. If the subject studied is male, how many green and red spots will be detected? Explain your answer.

14. Describe how DNA sequence will change with distance from the telomere.

15. In what way does position effect variegation (PEV) of *Drosophila* eye color indicate that chromatin state can affect gene transcription?

16. What are chromosome territories, and what significance do these regions have for gene expression?

17. Identify two important differences that distinguish heterochromatic regions of chromosomes from euchromatic regions.

Application and Integration

18. As a follow-up to Genetic Analysis 11.1, in which you determined the approximate number of nucleosomes per nucleus in *Arabidopsis thaliana*, answer these questions:
    a. If the number of nucleosomes given in answer to part (a) of Genetic Analysis 11.1 is for the nucleus of a cell in G_1 of the cell cycle, how many nucleosomes do you expect in the nucleus after completion of S phase? Explain your answer.
    b. Are all of the additional nucleosomes that are present after completion of S phase of the cell cycle composed of newly synthesized histone proteins? Explain your answer.

19. A survey of organisms living deep in the ocean reveals two new species whose DNA is isolated for analysis. DNA samples from both species are treated to remove nonhistone proteins. Each DNA sample is then treated with DNaseI that cuts DNA not protected by proteins but is unable to cut DNA bound by histone proteins. Following DNaseI treatment, DNA samples are subjected to gel electrophoresis, and the gels are stained with ethidium bromide to stain all DNA bands in the gel. The ethidium bromide staining patterns of DNA from each species are shown in the figure. The number of base pairs in small DNA fragments is shown at the left of the gel. Interpret the gel results in terms of chromatin organization and the spacing of nucleosomes in the chromatin of each species.

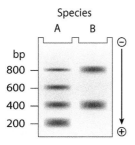

For answers to selected even-numbered problems, see Appendix: Answers.

20. A eukaryote with a diploid number of $2n = 6$ carries the chromosomes shown below and labeled A to F

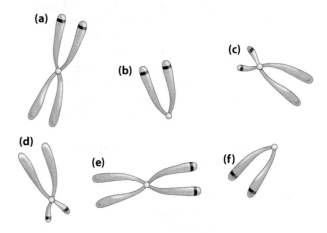

    a. Carefully examine and redraw these chromosomes in any valid metaphase I alignment. Draw and label the metaphase plate, and label each chromosome by its assigned letter.
    b. Explain how you determined the correct alignment of homologous chromosomes on opposite sides of the metaphase plate.

21. The chromosome diagram shown below represents a eukaryotic chromosome stained by G (Giemsa) banding. Indicate the heterochromatic and euchromatic regions of the chromosome, and label the chromosome's centromeric and telomeric regions.

Centromere

    a. What term best describes the shape of this chromosome?
    b. Do you expect the centromeric region to contain facultative heterochromatin? Why or why not?

c. Describe the features of general sequence composition and protein binding that differentiate the centromeric region from other regions of the chromosome.

d. Why are expressed genes not found in the telomeric region of chromosomes?

e. Are you more likely to find the DNA sequence encoding the digestive enzyme amylase in a heterochromatic, euchromatic, centromeric, or telomeric region? Explain your reasoning.

22. Suppose the genome of a bacterium contains a circular chromosome composed of 1.6×10^6 bp. A geometric calculation tells us that the diameter of the circular chromosome is about 10 times the diameter of the cell.

a. How is this chromosome packaged inside the cell?

b. Describe how this chromosome is packaged in the bacterial nucleoid.

c. Why is this chromosome supercoiled?

23. DNaseI cuts DNA that is not directly associated with nucleosomes. Markus Noll's treatment of human DNA with DNaseI produced DNA fragments that are consistently about 200 bp in length. Why does this result indicate that nucleosomes are evenly spaced on human DNA? What result would be obtained if nucleosomes were randomly spaced along DNA?

24. Histone protein H4 isolated from pea plants and cow thymus glands contains 102 amino acids in both cases. A total of 100 of the amino acids are identical between the two species. Give an evolutionary explanation for this strong amino acid sequence identity based on what you know about the functions of histones and nucleosomes.

25. The molecular probes used in FISH can detect repetitive DNA sequences or unique sequences that are parts of genes.

a. How are the binding locations of FISH probes on chromosomes identified?

b. Distinguish the detection of a FISH probe from the detection of a molecular probe in a Southern blot.

26. Experimental evidence demonstrates that the nucleosomes present in a cell after the completion of S phase are composed of some "old" histone dimers and some newly synthesized histone dimers. Describe the general design for an experiment that uses a protein label such as ^{35}S to show that nucleosomes are often a mixture of old and new histone dimers following DNA replication.

27. DNaseI cuts DNA that is not protected by bound proteins but is unable to cut DNA that is complexed with proteins. Human DNA is isolated, stripped of its nonhistone proteins, and mixed with DNaseI. Samples are removed after 30 minutes, 1 hour, and 4 hours and run separately in gel electrophoresis. The resulting gel is stained with ethidium bromide, and the results are shown in the figure. DNA fragment sizes in base pairs (bp) are estimated by the scale to the left of the gel.

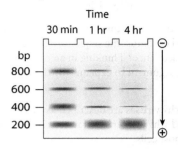

a. Examine the gel results and speculate why longer DNaseI treatment produces different results.

b. Draw a conclusion about the organization of chromatin in the human genome from this gel.

28. Genomic DNA from the nematode worm *Caenorhabditis elegans* is organized by nucleosomes in the manner typical of eukaryotic genomes, with 145 bp encircling each nucleosome and approximately 55 bp in linker DNA. When *C. elegans* chromatin is carefully isolated, stripped of nonhistone proteins, and placed in an appropriate buffer, the chromatin decondenses to the 10-nm fiber structure. Suppose researchers mix a sample of 10-nm-fiber chromatin with a large amount of the enzyme DNase I that randomly cleaves DNA in regions not protected by bound protein. Next, they remove the nucleosomes, separate the DNA fragments by gel electrophoresis, and stain the fragments by ethidium bromide.

a. Approximately what range of DNA fragment sizes do you expect to see in the stained electrophoresis gel? How many bands will be visible on the gel?

b. Explain the origin of DNA fragments seen in the gel.

c. How do the expected results support the 10-nm-fiber model of chromatin?

29. What function do histone proteins perform in archaeal chromosomes? How is this function accomplished? What function is performed by histones in eukaryotes that is apparently not performed by archaeal histones?

30. Based on discussions of specific proteins and structures in bacteria, archaea, and eukaryotes in this and other chapters, briefly describe your view of the evolutionary relationship between the three domains of life.

Gene Mutation, DNA Repair, and Homologous Recombination

CHAPTER OUTLINE

- 12.1 Mutations Are Rare and Occur at Random
- 12.2 Gene Mutations Modify DNA Sequence
- 12.3 Gene Mutations May Arise from Spontaneous Events
- 12.4 Mutations May Be Induced by Chemicals or Ionizing Radiation
- 12.5 Repair Systems Correct Some DNA Damage
- 12.6 Proteins Control Translesion DNA Synthesis and the Repair of Double-Strand Breaks
- 12.7 DNA Double-Strand Breaks Initiate Homologous Recombination
- 12.8 Gene Conversion Is Directed Mismatch Repair in Heteroduplex DNA

The baby kangaroo peeking out of its mother's pouch has autosomal recessive albinism, a condition that occurs in about 1 in 20,000 births.

ESSENTIAL IDEAS

- Gene mutations are rare and random.
- Mutations change DNA sequence, alter polypeptide composition and function, and cause phenotypic variation.
- Spontaneous nucleotide changes can lead to mutation.
- Chemical mutagens and radiation can damage DNA and produce mutations.
- DNA repair systems can directly repair DNA damage or can remove and replace damaged segments.
- Specialized enzymes can bypass a blockage of DNA replication caused by unrepaired damage.
- Controlled DNA double-strand breaks initiate homologous recombination and also recombination between homologous chromosomes in meiosis.
- Gene conversion is a directed DNA-sequence change associated with homologous recombination.

Mutation can be defined most simply as a heritable change in DNA sequence, a definition that covers an enormous range of changes. Mutation is indispensable in two ways. From an evolutionary perspective, mutations generate new hereditary variety. Variant alleles can cause organisms to differ from one another, enabling the organisms to evolve through any of the four evolutionary processes we identified in Section 1.4. Mutation is also indispensable from the perspective of genetic analysis. Whether for studying the effects of variant alleles on organisms, the processes that damage or repair DNA, or some other aspect of gene properties and function, mutation analysis is at the heart of genetics.

Within the cell, mutations can derive from spontaneous changes or through the action of DNA-damaging agents. Some changes to DNA that lead to mutation are the result of spontaneous alterations of the structure of nucleotide bases. On rare occasions, errors made during DNA replication can lead to mutation. Also, damage done to DNA by chemical, physical, or biological agents can affect DNA nucleotide bases and lead to mutation. Through whatever mechanism they occur, however, mutations are random, occurring in different species at different average rates, and affecting some genes more often than others as a consequence of the gene's composition.

In this chapter, we focus on mutation at the level of the individual gene—that is, gene mutation. We describe spontaneous changes to DNA nucleotide base structure and the occasional DNA replication errors that can generate gene mutations. We also examine the DNA-damaging actions of chemical and physical agents and the role this damage plays in producing gene mutation. We postpone discussion of the biological agents of mutation to the following chapter, which describes mutations at the chromosome level. (Among the mutations described in connection with chromosomes in Chapter 13 are processes involving the transposition of mobile elements of DNA that can move from place to place in the genome.)

We end the current chapter with a discussion of DNA damage repair mechanisms and the connection between mechanisms of DNA double-strand break repair and crossing over. In the process, we examine bacterial systems of crossing over and also the crossing over between homologous chromosomes in eukaryotes that is observed during meiosis.

12.1 Mutations Are Rare and Occur at Random

Gene mutations are random and their occurrence is rare. The random nature of mutations was first experimentally demonstrated by Salvador Luria and Max Delbrück in 1943. This preceded by just a few months the identification of DNA as the hereditary material by Avery, MacLeod, and McCarty (see Section 7.1), and it came a decade before the molecular structure of DNA would be described. In the 70 years since this observation, the understanding of the causes, consequences, and occurrence of mutations has been a staple of genetic research.

The decades of study of gene mutations have produced several general conclusions. First, mutation rates are low in all genomes, meaning that genome stability is paramount and mutations contribute slowly to inherited diversity. Second, gene mutations are usually deleterious to the organism, meaning that they impair the function of the gene or gene product and potentially harm the fitness of the organism. Third, despite their typically deleterious nature, mutations are essential for the generation of inherited genetic diversity that fuels evolutionary change. Fourth, gene mutation rates differ considerably among organisms, and they are more common in larger genomes than in smaller genomes. Genomes appear to have different levels of tolerance for mutations, and mutation repair efficiency may vary among organisms. Lastly, mutation rates among different genes of a single species show variation, suggesting that there are intrinsic DNA sequence variables that lead to different mutation rates among the genes in a genome.

Mutation Rates

In bacteria and other haploid microorganisms, the **mutation rate** is measured as the number of times mutation alters a particular gene per replication cycle or per generation. Mutations in these organisms are most often studied by screening for auxotrophic nutritional deficiencies that impair the organisms' ability to grow on a minimal medium.

Mutation rate in sexually reproducing diploids is the number of mutational events in a given gene per generation. Recessive mutations can be identified particularly through the use of genome sequencing analysis and other molecular methods that can detect variation at the DNA sequence level. Mutations detected at the morphological level or affecting enzymes in a metabolic or biochemical pathway are more likely to be dominant mutations. Dominant mutations are easier to detect, since a single copy of a dominant mutant allele will manifest in the phenotype. In contrast, a recessive mutation affecting morphology or a biochemical pathway will not be detectable if the organism is heterozygous because the recessive allele will have its effect masked by the dominant allele. Mutation rates differ among organisms, and they differ between genes carried by a single species. Table 12.1 lists average mutation rates for selected organisms. Mutation rates as low as 1×10^{-9} to rates as high as 1×10^{-4} are reported. Several biological factors intrinsic to organisms, including genome size and the organism's life cycle, influence the average mutation rate in an organism.

Mutation rates are variable among genes in an organism's genome, and gene structure or composition is frequently a component of these differences. Factors including the composition of certain genes or genome regions

Table 12.1	Mutation Rate Ranges for Selected Taxonomic Groups
Organism	**Range**
Bacteria (*Escherichia coli*)	1×10^{-7} to 1×10^{-9}
Algae (*Chlamydomonas reinhardii*)	1×10^{-7} to 1×10^{-8}
Fungi (*Neurospora crassa*)	1×10^{-7} to 1×10^{-8}
Plant (*Zea mays*)	1×10^{-6} to 1×10^{-7}
Insect (*Drosophila melanogaster*)	1×10^{-5} to 1×10^{-6}
Mammal (*Homo sapiens*)	1×10^{-4} to 1×10^{-6}

Table 12.2	Mutation Rates in Five Mouse Coat Color Genes[a]		
Gene	**Number of Gametes Tested**	**Number of Mutations Detected**	**Mutation Rate (1×10^{-6})**
A (agouti)	67,395	3	44.5
B (brown)	919,699	3	3.3
C (nonagouti)	150,391	5	33.2
D (dilute)	839,447	10	11.9
Ln (leaden)	243,444	4	16.4
Totals and average	2,220,376	25	11.2 (average)

[a] = Mutations are wild-type dominant to recessive mutant in germ cells (sperm and egg). Data adapted from G. Schlager and M. M. Dicke (1971).

make them more likely than other genes to be affected by mutation. In the human genome, for example, the average mutation rate for the average gene is on the order of 1 to 10 per million gametes, or about 1×10^{-6}. But in specific genes, such as *DYS*, which produces the human X-linked recessive disorder Duchenne muscular dystrophy, and *NF1*, which produces autosomal dominant neurofibromatosis, substantially elevated mutation rates are observed. Genes like these are identified as being **hotspots of mutation,** individual genes or regions of genomes where mutations occur much more often than average.

DYS and *NF1* have mutation rates that are about 1×10^{-4}, which is one to two orders of magnitude greater than the average human gene. Their high mutation rate is due to their size. These genes are the two largest genes known in the human genome. *DYS*, spanning approximately 2.5 million bp on the X chromosome, is the largest. *NF1* is also very large, spanning well over 1 million bp.

Similar gene-to-gene variation in mutation rates is observed in other mammals. A 1971 report by Gunther Schlager and Margaret Dicke examined long-term data on mutation rates of five mouse coat color genes. The data, collected over many generations of mouse production at a commercial facility, yielded mutation rates that ranged from 2 to 12×10^{-6} per gene per generation (Table 12.2).

Determination of Mutation Rate from Genome Sequence Analysis

In methods that detect mutations in multicelled eukaryotes by analyzing expressed genes, only a relatively small subset of the genome can be sampled. In contrast, whole genome sequencing (described in Chapter 18) allows assessment of mutation rates throughout the genome. In a 2010 study of mutation rate and types of mutations in the plant *Arabidopsis thaliana*, Michael Lynch and his colleagues reported genome sequence analysis of five plants derived by 30 generations of single-seed descent from a common ancestral plant. The researchers detected a total of 116 mutations, 99 base-pair substitution mutations, and 17 insertion or deletion mutations, so-called indel mutations. The overall mutation rate for the genome was

5.9×10^{-9} per site per generation. Most of the base-pair substitution mutations were G-C to A-T changes, and most of the indel mutations were 1- to 3-bp changes in the number of repeats of AT dinucleotides. The researchers speculated that the large number of G-C to A-T base-substitution mutations was due to mutation at hotspots or via DNA damage induced by ultraviolet light. We discuss these mechanisms later in the chapter.

Mutation rate data on the human genome have also recently been published. In 2011, a large research group led by Philip Awadalla examined the human genome for evidence of mutation rate variation within and among families. Their data are based on assessment of the genome sequences of two parent–child trios, each consisting of a child and both parents. After complete genome sequencing and comparison of sequences, Awadalla and his colleagues calculated a mutation rate of 1.17×10^{-8} for one parent–child trio and 0.87×10^{-8} for the other parent–child trio. The researchers found that somatic-cell mutations occurred at a much higher rate than germ-cell (sperm and egg) mutations. Looking at germ-cell mutations, the researchers were able to determine the parent of origin of each mutation. They found that for one family, 92% of the mutations were paternal in origin, whereas in the other family only 36% of mutations were paternal in origin. These findings indicate that there may be substantial variation in mutation rates in families, and they point to the need for a much more detailed analysis of mutations to determine how factors such as age, genetic background, and environmental exposures affect mutation rate in humans.

12.2 Gene Mutations Modify DNA Sequence

Gene mutations most often characterized by a change in DNA sequence that occurs by substituting, adding, or deleting one or more DNA base pairs. These kinds of localized mutations occur at a specific or identifiable location in a gene and are called **point mutations.** In this section, we describe an overview of gene mutation occurrence, and then describe several types of point mutations that have characteristic consequences depending on the type of sequence change and the location of sequence change in a gene.

Base-Pair Substitution Mutations

The replacement of one nucleotide base pair by another is a **base-pair substitution mutation.** Two types of base-pair substitutions occur: **transition mutations,** in which one purine replaces the other (i.e., A replaces G, or vice versa) or one pyrimidine replaces the other (i.e., C replaces T, or vice versa); and **transversion mutations,** in which a purine is replaced by a pyrimidine, or vice versa.

When base-pair substitution mutations occur in the coding-sequence of a gene, they are further categorized at the molecular level by the manner in which they alter the informational content of the gene. Such base-pair mutations may be silent mutations, missense mutations, or nonsense mutations. **Table 12.3** summarizes these mutations.

Silent Mutation A base-pair substitution producing an mRNA codon specifying the same amino acid as the wild-type mRNA is known as a **silent mutation.** **Figures 12.1a** and **12.1b** illustrate a silent mutation in which an A-T to G-C transition mutation changes the wild-type leucine codon (5'-UUA-3') to a mutant codon (5'-UUG-3') that also encodes leucine. Silent mutations are possible because the genetic code is redundant, having 2 to 6 codons for most amino acids (see Table B inside the front cover).

Missense Mutation A base-pair substitution that results in an amino acid change to the protein is a **missense**

Table 12.3 Point Mutations

Type	Consequence
Coding-Sequence Mutations	
Silent	No amino acid sequence change
Missense	Changes one amino acid
Nonsense	Creates stop codon and terminates translation
Frameshift	Wrong sequence of amino acids
Regulatory Mutations	
Promoter	Changes timing or amount of transcription
Polyadenylation	Alters sequence of mRNA
Splice site	Improperly retains an intron or excludes exon
DNA replication mutation, e.g., triplet-repeat expansion	Increases (or less often, decreases) number of short repeats of DNA

(a) Wild-type sequence

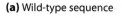

(b) Silent mutation

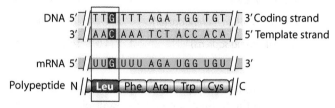

(c) Missense mutation

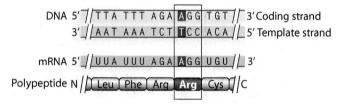

(d) Nonsense mutation

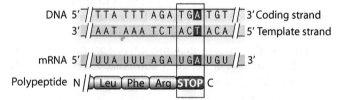

Figure 12.1 The consequences of base-pair substitutions.

mutation. Figure 12.1c shows a T-A to A-T transversion mutation that alters the wild-type 5'-UGG-3' codon to 5'-AGG-3', changing the amino acid from tryptophan to arginine. Protein function may be altered by a missense mutation. The specific consequence of the protein change (i.e., whether it results in complete or only partial loss of protein function) depends on what kind of amino acid change takes place and where in the polypeptide chain the change occurs. The tall versus short stature of pea plants studied by Mendel is caused by a missense mutation. See **Experimental Insight 12.1** for a discussion.

Nonsense Mutation A base-pair substitution that creates a stop codon in place of a codon specifying an amino acid is a **nonsense mutation.** The GC-to-AT base-pair substitution shown in **Figure 12.1d** that changes the UGG (Trp) codon to a UGA (stop) codon is an example of a nonsense mutation.

Experimental Insight **12.1**

Mendel's Mutations

Table 2.6 on page 55 and the accompanying text briefly describe the wild-type and mutant alleles of the four genes of Mendel that have been identified to date. The three genes described in this Experimental Insight result from point mutations and are described here. The fourth gene of Mendel is described in Section 13.7.

STEM LENGTH: A MISSENSE MUTATION

The *Le* gene variation was identified in 1997 by research groups led by Diane Lester and David Martin, who determined that the wild-type dominant allele of this gene (*Le*) produces an enzyme active in the biosynthetic pathway that produces the growth hormone giberillin-3-β-hydroxylase. The effect of the dominant allele is to generate the wild-type level of growth hormone production, which, in turn, produces the long stems that characterize tall pea plants. The recessive mutant allele (*le*) is unable to produce the enzyme, and this reduces the biosynthesis of the growth hormone to about 5% of the wild-type level. The result is poor stem growth and short plants.

The *le* allele is the result of a missense mutation that changes an alanine to a threonine in the polypeptide product of the gene. This missense change is brought about by a G-C to A-T transition mutation in the *le* allele's DNA sequence. It is an example of a missense mutation that inactivates the function of the allele's protein product. In this case, the consequence of the mutation is the significant reduction of the synthesis of a growth hormone.

POD COLOR: AN INSERTION MUTATION

The 2007 studies of the *Sgr* ("stay green") gene by research groups led by Ian Armstead and Sylvain Aubry identified the molecular basis for the dominant wild-type yellow seed pod and the recessive mutant green seed pod. The wild-type allele produces an enzyme that participates in the breakdown of chlorophyll contained in the seed pod. This breakdown normally occurs in conjunction with pod maturation, and it results in mature seed pods that are yellow. The mutant allele produces a very poorly functioning enzyme, largely disabling a critical step of chlorophyll breakdown. Consequently, chlorophyll is retained in mature pods, making them green.

The mutant allele contains a 6-bp insertion that changes the enzyme product by adding two additional codons to mRNA and two amino acids to the protein. This insertion of 6 bp, being a multiple of three nucleotides as found in a codon, does not change the reading frame. Thus, in the mutant protein, the amino acid sequence is normal except for the presence of the two additional amino acids. Since the mutant protein is largely normal, it is able to retain partial function, albeit significantly reduced in comparison to wild-type.

FLOWER COLOR: AN mRNA-SPLICING MUTATION

Purple flower color is dominant in pea plants, and it results from the production of the pigment anthocyanin. The recessive mutant phenotype is white flower color, and in these plants there is no anthocyanin production. A research group led by Roger Hellens identified the *bHLH* gene as the source of the white flower mutation in pea plants. This gene produces a transcription factor protein that helps activate the transcription of several genes, including some in the anthocyanin-production pathway. In the absence of a functioning protein product from the *bHLH* gene, anthocyanin production does not take place.

The mutation in the recessive allele is a G-C to A-T base-pair substitution that alters the guanine at the 5' splice site of one of the introns of the allele. Recall that 5' splice sites have an invariant GU dinucleotide in mRNA. The base substitution identified by Hellens changes the 5' sequence to an AU dinucleotide that is not recognized as a splice site. An alternative splice site (known as a cryptic splice site; see the text for discussion) is used instead to process the mutant mRNA transcript. The aberrant splicing elongates the mature mRNA by eight nucleotides. This addition of mRNA nucleotides results in a frameshift during translation, and the protein product is nonfunctional.

Frameshift Mutations

Insertion or deletion of one or more base pairs in the coding sequence of a gene leads to addition or deletion of mRNA nucleotides. This can alter the reading frame of the codon sequence, beginning at the point of mutation. The result would be a **frameshift mutation,** in which the mutant polypeptide contains an altered amino acid sequence from the point of mutation to the end of the polypeptide (**Figure 12.2**). In addition to producing the wrong amino acids in a portion of the polypeptide, frameshift mutations also commonly generate premature stop codons that result in a truncated polypeptide. For these reasons, frameshift mutations usually result in the complete loss of protein function and thus produce null alleles. The yellow versus green seed pod trait studied by Mendel is caused by an insertion of six base pairs of DNA. Since the insertion is a multiple of three nucleotides, it adds two codons to the mutant allele mRNA. Thus, this particular mutant is not the result of a frameshift mutation, but the insertion of DNA base pairs is a common mechanism producing such mutations. See Experimental Insight 12.1 for a discussion.

Regulatory Mutations

Some point mutations have the effect of reducing or increasing the amount of wild-type gene transcript and the amount of wild-type polypeptide without affecting the

(a) Wild-type sequence

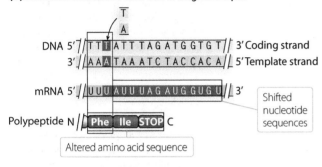

(b) Frameshift mutation: Insertion of single base pair

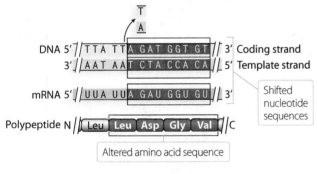

(c) Frameshift mutation: Deletion of single base pair

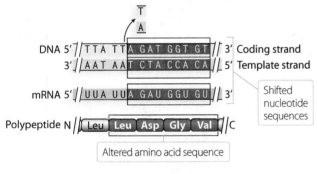

Figure 12.2   Frameshift mutation.

transcript and polypeptide sequences. These mutations, classified as **regulatory mutations,** occur in noncoding regions of genes, such as promoters, introns, and regions coding 5′-UTR and 3′-UTR segments of mRNA. None of these regions directly encodes amino acids, but mutations in these regions can lead to the production of abnormal mRNAs that, in turn, produce mutant proteins. Three types of regulatory mutations are commonly recognized: promoter mutations, splicing mutations, and cryptic splice sites.

Promoter Mutations Promoter consensus sequences recognized by RNA polymerase II and its associated transcription factors direct the efficient initiation of transcription. Mutations that alter consensus sequence nucleotides and interfere with efficient transcription initiation are **promoter mutations.** The human β-globin gene offers multiple examples of promoter mutations, with various consequences for transcription. **Figure 12.3a** lists mutations at six positions of the human β-globin gene

promoter that each result in a moderate reduction in the amount of β-globin gene transcript and in a reduced amount of β-globin protein. Each of the six promoter mutations shown here reduces transcription, but none eliminates transcription entirely. Some promoter mutations of other genes result in the complete elimination of transcription.

Splicing Mutations The DNA dinucleotide GT, on the coding strand, occurs invariably at the 5′ splice site of the intron to demarcate the boundary between the 5′ intron end and the 3′ end of an exon (the GT of coding strand DNA corresponds to the GU dinucleotide of mRNA; see Figure 8.21). In the human β-globin gene, an AG dinucleotide occurs at the 3′ end of exon 1. Each of these dinucleotides is part of the consensus sequence at which the spliceosome forms. Mutations of either of these dinucleotide sequences or of nearby nucleotides in the consensus sequence within the intron can result in splicing errors that inaccurately remove intron sequences from pre-mRNA.

In intron 1 of the β-globin gene, two separate mutations that substitute the guanine of the GT dinucleotide abolish normal splicing entirely in mutations

(a) Mutations in promoter

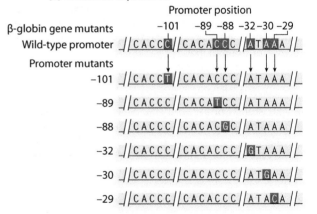

(b) Mutations in intron 1

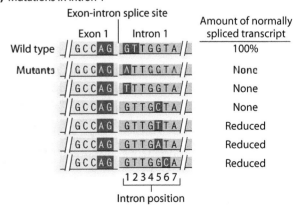

Figure 12.3   Regulatory mutations of the human β-globin gene. (a) These base-pair substitution mutations in the promoter reduce transcription of the gene. **(b)** These base-pair substitutions in intron 1 reduce or eliminate normal pre-mRNA splicing.

that are known as **splicing mutations** (Figure 12.3b). Additionally, one base-pair substitution mutation of position 5 of intron 1 by itself also prevents the production of normally spliced mRNA. The translation of the abnormally spliced transcripts does not produce wild-type β-globin protein. Other base-pair substitution mutations in intron 1 result in production of a mixture of normally and abnormally spliced transcript and produce some wild-type β-globin protein. One of Mendel's traits, the purple versus white flower phenotype, is caused by a splicing mutation. See Experimental Insight 12.1 for discussion.

Cryptic Splice Sites Certain base-pair substitution mutations produce new splice sites that replace or compete with authentic splice sites during pre-mRNA processing. These newly formed splice sites are known as **cryptic splice sites.** Intron 1 of the human β-globin gene is 130 nucleotides in length. A base-pair substitution mutation that changes G to A at position 110 of intron 1 creates an AG dinucleotide that is a cryptic splice site (Figure 12.4). The cryptic splice site is spliced in about 90% of the intron 1 3′ splicing events. This aberrant splicing leaves 19 additional nucleotides in the mature mRNA; these nucleotides have been removed in the other 10% of mature transcripts, which are spliced at the authentic 3′ splice site for intron 1. In Genetic Analysis 12.1, you can practice identifying types of mutations by the alterations they produce in polypeptides.

Polyadenylation Mutations Processing of the 3′ end of eukaryotic mRNAs is initiated by the presence of a 5′ AAUAAA 3′ polyadenylation signal sequence (see Section 8.4), and mutation of this sequence can block proper 3′ processing of mRNA. One example of this mutation is found in a rare variant of the human α globin gene in which the DNA coding strand sequence is mutated from 5′ AATAAA 3′ to 5′ AATAAG 3′. The A-T to G-C base substitution blocks recognition of the polyadenylation signal sequence, generates abnormal mRNA, and leads to a severe reduction in the amount of function α globin protein.

Forward Mutation and Reversion

Forward mutation, often identified simply as "mutation," converts a wild-type allele to a mutant allele. In contrast, mutations identified as **reverse mutations,** or, more commonly, as **reversions,** convert a mutation to a wild-type or near wild-type state. The mechanisms of base-pair substitution described earlier are examples of processes that create mutation. Reversions can be caused by similar mechanisms. In one type of reversion, called a **true reversion,** the wild-type DNA sequence is restored to encode its original message by a second mutation at the same site or within the same codon (Figure 12.5a). Alternatively, reversion can occur by a second mutation elsewhere in the gene. Figure 12.5b illustrates an example of one such reversion— an **intragenic reversion,** which is a reversion that occurs through mutation elsewhere in the same gene. Here the initial mutation was caused by deletion of two base pairs, and the intragenic reversion is a compensatory insertion of two base pairs near the site of the initial mutation, restoring the allele to a near wild-type form. Figure 12.5c illustrates an example of a **second-site reversion,** produced by mutation in a different gene. In this case, the original mutation inactivates gene *A* and results in the loss of function of the major pigment-transporting protein in a flower. A minor pigment-transporting gene, *B*, remains active, transporting a small amount of blue pigment from gene *C*. The initial mutation produces a light-blue flower. The second-site reversion is a mutation of gene *B* that increases gene transcription and thus increases production of the pigment-transporting protein. The mutation of gene *B* compensates for the mutation of gene *A* and restores the wild-type dark-blue flower phenotype. Second-site mutations are also known as **suppressor mutations** because the second mutation, by restoring wild-type appearance, can be said to "suppress" the mutant phenotype generated by the first mutation.

12.3 Gene Mutations May Arise from Spontaneous Events

Spontaneous mutations arise in cells without being induced by exposure of DNA to a physical, chemical, or biological agent capable of creating DNA damage. Spontaneous mutations arise primarily through errors during DNA replication and through spontaneous changes in the chemical structure of nucleotide bases.

DNA Replication Errors

DNA replication has extraordinarily high fidelity. Replication errors resulting in base-pair mismatches between a template strand and a newly synthesized

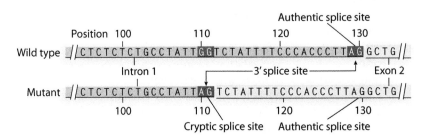

Figure 12.4 **Cryptic splicing.** Base-pair substitution of G-C to A-T at position 110 of intron 1 of the human β-globin gene creates a cryptic 3′ splice site.

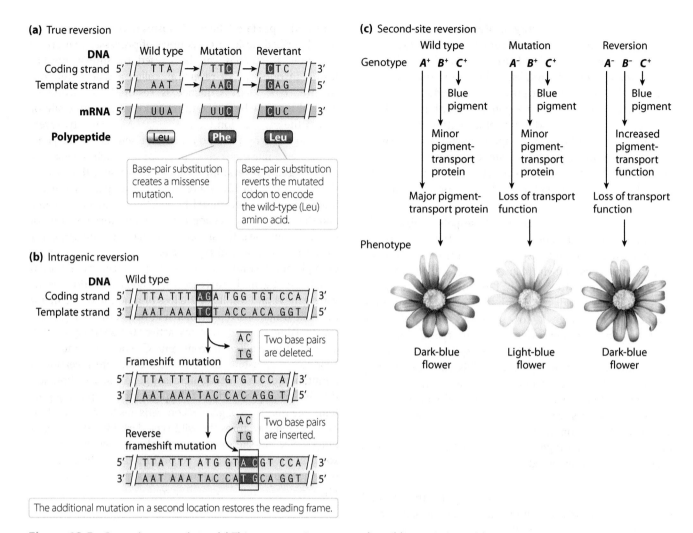

Figure 12.5 **Reversion mutations.** **(a)** This true reversion restores the wild-type amino acid sequence to the polypeptide. **(b)** This intragenic reversion reverts a frameshift mutation caused by a 2-bp deletion by insertion of 2 bp at a nearby site in the gene. **(c)** Second-site reversion restores a near wild-type phenotype through a compensatory mutation of a second gene.

strand of DNA occur at an approximate rate of 1×10^{-9} in wild-type *Escherichia coli*, and a similar accuracy rate is found in eukaryotic DNA replication. The overall efficiency of DNA replication is attributable to the proofreading capabilities of DNA polymerases and to the operation of DNA base-pair mismatch repair systems (see Section 12.5).

An exception to the general accuracy of replication, however, is observed in genomic regions containing short repetitive sequences whose number can be either increased or decreased by replication errors. Replication errors in such regions are another source of hotspots of mutation. The repeating DNA sequences are commonly short, end-to-end repeats consisting of repeating sequences of the same two nucleotides (dinucleotide repeats), of the same three nucleotides (trinucleotide repeats), or of longer repeating units.

Mutations altering the number of DNA repeats occur by a process called **strand slippage**. In the mid-1960s,

George Streisinger and his colleagues described the first known example of strand slippage, which generated frameshift mutations caused by adding nucleotides in a gene of the bacteriophage T4. Streisinger proposed that strand slippage occurs when the DNA polymerase of the replisome temporarily dissociates from the template strand as it moves across a region of repeating DNA sequence (Figure 12.6). He suggested that, during dissociation, a portion of newly replicated DNA forms a temporary double-stranded hairpin structure induced by the complementary base pairing of nucleotides in the loop. Reassociation of DNA polymerase and resumption of replication leads to re-replication of a portion of the repeat region, increasing the length of the repeat region in the daughter strand.

In the past two decades, a number of strand slippage mutations have been identified as the causes of various hereditary diseases in humans and other organisms. The human diseases are classified as **trinucleotide repeat disorders** (Table 12.4). The wild-type

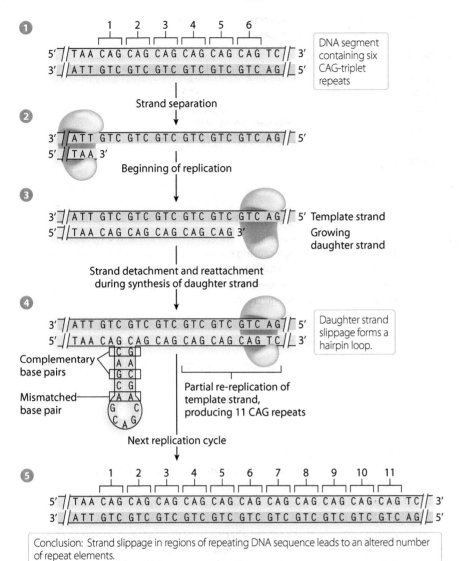

Figure 12.6   Strand slippage during DNA replication.

alleles of the genes in question normally contain a variable number of DNA trinucleotide repeats. On rare occasions, these gene regions undergo mutations through strand slippage that cause the number of trinucleotide repeats to increase. For each of these disorders, expansion of the number of trinucleotide repeats beyond the wild-type range results in a hereditary disorder. Most often the mutations block the production of wild-type mRNA and reduce or eliminate the production of wild-type protein.

Table 12.4	Human Trinucleotide Repeat Disorders					
Disease	**OMIM Number**	**Repeat Sequence**	**Repeat Range**		**Principal Disease Phenotype**
			Normal	**Disease**	
Fragile X syndrome	309550	CGG	6–50	200–2000	Mental retardation
Friedreich ataxia	229300	GAA	6–29	200–900	Loss of coordination
Huntington disease	143100	CAG	10–34	40–200	Uncontrolled movement
Jacobsen syndrome	147791	CGG	11	100–1000	Growth retardation
Myotonic dystrophy (type I)	160900	CTG	5–37	80–1000	Muscle weakness
Spinal and bulbar muscular atrophy	313200	CAG	14–32	40–55	Muscle wasting
Spinocerebellar ataxia (multiple forms)	271245	CAG	4–44	45–140	Loss of coordination

PROBLEM In a mutant analysis a goal is often to identify the type of mutation that has occurred. In this problem, a fragment of a polypeptide with the wild-type amino acid sequence is given:

Met–His–Ala–Trp–Asn–Gly–Glu–His–Arg

The amino acid sequences of three mutants are shown below. For each mutant, identify the type of mutation that has occurred and specify how the mRNA sequence has been changed.

> **BREAK IT DOWN:** Use the wild-type amino acid sequence to determine the mRNA sequence, including all possible redundancies, as the starting point for mutant analysis. (Use the genetic code, p. 321; see also inside the front cover)

> **BREAK IT DOWN:** Identification of the mutations requires deducing each mutant mRNA sequence and comparing it to the wild-type mRNA sequence. (pp. 394–395)

Mutation 1: Met–His–Ala–Trp–Lys–Gly–Glu–His–Arg

Mutation 2: Met–His–Ala

Mutation 3: Met–Met–Leu–Gly–Met–Ala–Glu–His–Arg

Solution Strategies	Solution Steps
Evaluate	
1. Identify the topic this problem addresses and the nature of the required answer.	1. This problem concerns mutations affecting the amino acid sequence of a gene. The type of change causing each mutation must be identified, and the effect of the mutation on mRNA must be described.
2. Identify the critical information given in the problem.	2. The wild-type amino acid sequence and the corresponding portions of the mutant polypeptides are given.
Deduce	
3. Determine the sequence of wild-type mRNA.	3. The sequence of wild-type mRNA is,

> **TIP:** Use N if the position could be occupied by any nucleotide, $^A/_G$ for the alternative purines, and $^U/_C$ for alternative pyrimidines.

$$5'\text{-AUG } CA^U/_C \text{ GCN UGG } AA^U/_C \text{ GGN } GA^A/_G \text{ } CA^U/_C{}^A/_C GN\text{-}3'$$

> **TIP:** Use the genetic code in Figure 9.13 or in Table B inside the front cover.

Solve

4. Compare each mutant sequence to the wild-type polypeptide, and identify the probable types of mutations.

4. Comparisons are as follows.

   Mutant 1: This is a missense mutation in which the mutant polypeptide has one amino acid changed from Asn to Lys.

   Mutant 2: This is a nonsense mutation in which a Trp codon is changed to a stop codon.

   Mutant 3: This mutant contains alterations of five consecutive amino acids, beginning with the second amino acid (His to Met). The wild-type sequence is restored beginning with the seventh amino acid (Glu). This mutant results from two compensatory frameshift mutations. The first alters the reading frame, and the second restores it.

5. Determine the mRNA change producing the missense mutant.

5. The wild-type (Asn) codon is $AA^U/_C$, and the mutant (Lys) codon is $AA^A/_G$. This change results from either a transition or a transversion mutation.

6. Determine the mRNA change producing the nonsense mutant.

6. The wild-type Trp (UGG) codon is changed to a stop codon. The change is either UGG to UGA or UGG to UAG. In either case, this is a transition mutation.

7. Determine the mRNA change producing the frameshift mutant.

7. The appearance of Met in position 2 means the second codon of the frameshift mutant is AUG. This change requires deletion of the first C of the wild-type sequence and means that U, not C, is present as the sixth nucleotide of the wild type. Beginning with Glu, the wild-type amino acid sequence is restored. This requires insertion of G immediately after the Ala codon.

For more practice, see Problems 4, 9, and 32.
Visit the Study Area to access study tools. **Mastering**Genetics™

Spontaneous Nucleotide Base Changes

DNA nucleotide bases are organic chemical structures that can occasionally convert, in what are called tautomeric shifts, to alternative structures known as tautomers.

Tautomers are structures that have the same composition and general arrangement but a slight difference in bonding and placement of a hydrogen. The generation of a tautomer changes the three-dimensional structure of the nucleotide base from a more stable common form to a rare, less stable form. Tautomeric shifts affecting nitrogenous bases can lead to base-pair mismatch between a rare tautomer on one DNA strand and a common form on the complementary strand.

Mispairing of DNA nucleotides due to the presence of tautomers is the most common form of DNA replication error. Figure 12.7a shows standard base pairing involving the common tautomeric forms of the nucleotide bases. In comparison, base-pair mismatches that occur between a rare tautomeric nucleotide and a normal nucleotide are shown in Figure 12.7b. Notice in each case of mismatch that purine-pyrimidine pairing is maintained, but that the rare tautomer forms the wrong number of hydrogen bonds, leading to the mispairing with the common tautomeric form of the incorrect nucleotide of the opposite type. For example,

the rare tautomer of the pyrimidine thymine forms three hydrogen bonds instead of the normal two hydrogen bonds, and thus it mispairs with guanine, which is the wrong purine.

Tautomeric shifts can lead to base-pair substitution mutations. In Figure 12.8, the rare tautomer of thymine mispairs with guanine during DNA replication. A tautomeric shift of thymine switches it back to its common,

(a) Standard base pairing of common tautomers

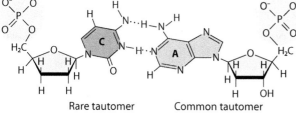

(b) Base mispairing involving rare tautomers

Figure 12.7 **Base pairing of nucleotide tautomers.**
(a) Standard base pairing of common nucleotide tautomers.
(b) Base-pair mismatches resulting from pairing of a common and an uncommon nucleotide tautomer.

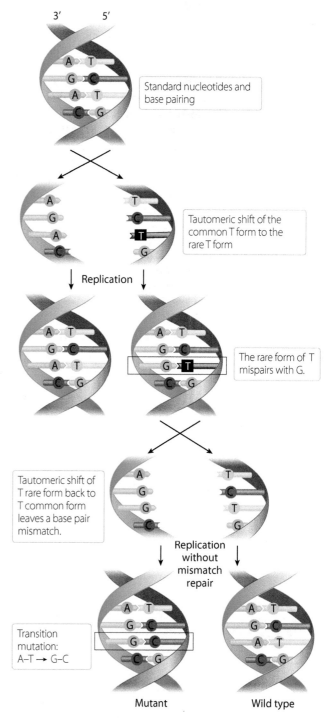

Figure 12.8 **Transition mutation arising from a tautomeric shift of the common form of thymine to the rare form.**

more stable form, leaving a base-pair mismatch of T-G. If this mismatch is not repaired, DNA replication produces one chromatid with a wild-type T-A base pair and the sister chromatid with a C-G base-pair substitution mutation. This is a transition mutation: G replaces A and T replaces C.

DNA Nucleotide Lesions

Two types of spontaneous damage to individual nucleotides are associated with subsequent mutation. **Depurination** is the loss of one of the purines, adenine or guanine, from a nucleotide by breakage of the covalent bond at the 1' carbon of deoxyribose that links the sugar to the nucleotide base (**Figure 12.9**). Living cells lose thousands of purines a day, making depurination one of the most frequent spontaneous chemical changes affecting DNA. This forms a DNA lesion known as an **apurinic (AP) site.** Fortunately, nearly all AP sites are replaced by the correct purine before the next DNA replication cycle. Repair enzymes discussed later in the chapter use the opposite strand to identify the correct complementary purine to fill the AP site. If an AP site is not repaired before the beginning of the next

replication cycle, the site does not contain a nucleotide that can act as a template base. DNA polymerase will then place a nucleotide, most commonly adenine, opposite the AP site. The strand with the inserted adenine goes on in the next replication cycle to direct the addition of thymine to its daughter strand, and the mutation has been generated. This is a transition mutation with T replacing G and A replacing C. The AP site might be repaired before the next replication cycle, but if not, then during the next DNA replication cycle it once again is likely to attract an adenine to fill the newly synthesized strand.

Deamination, the loss of an amino (NH_2) group from a nucleotide base, is a second form of spontaneous chemical modification that can lead to mutation. Each of the DNA nucleotide bases contains an amino group, but deamination of cytosine is the deamination event most often associated with mutation. When cytosine is deaminated, the amino group is replaced by an oxygen atom, forming the nucleotide base uracil (**Figure 12.10a**). DNA mismatch repair readily recognizes uracil as an RNA nucleotide base and removes it from DNA. The excised uracil is replaced by cytosine, and wild-type sequence is restored.

Figure 12.9 Depurination. (a) Breakage of the 1' carbon bond releases a purine and creates an apurinic site. **(b)** Adenine is most commonly used to fill apurinic sites during DNA replication. **(c)** This causes a G-C to T-A mutation in this case.

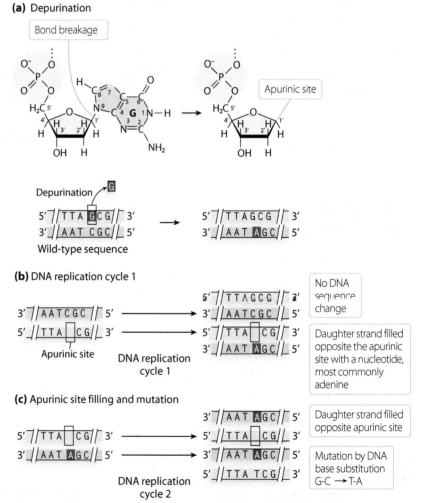

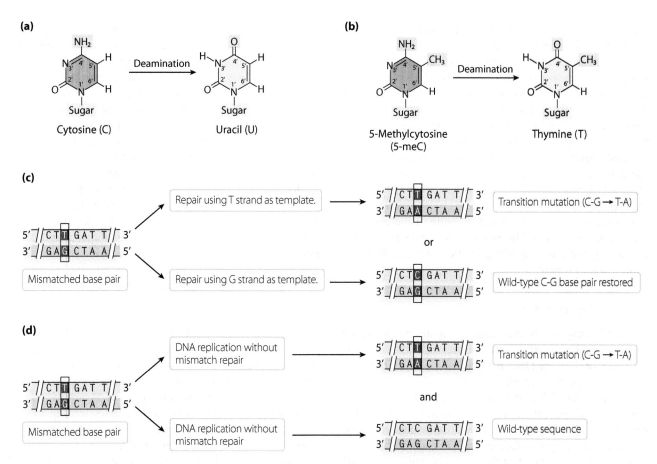

Figure 12.10   Deamination. **(a)** Unmethylated cytosine is deaminated to form uracil.
(b) Deamination of 5-methylcytosine forms thymine that is mismatched to guanine. **(c)** Mismatch
repair can create a `G-C` to `T-A` transition mutation or can remove the thymine to restore wild-type
sequence. **(d)** When unrepaired mismatches are replicated they produce one wild-type chromatid and
one transition mutation chromatid.

A different scenario occurs, however, when deamination takes place on a cytosine that has been methylated. A methylated cytosine has the hydrogen atom at the number 5 carbon replaced with a CH_3 (methyl) group. This is the most common nucleotide methylation event in most genomes. Deamination of 5-methylcytosine (5meC) creates thymine and generates a base-pair mismatch between the newly formed thymine on one strand and the previously complementary guanine on the other strand (Figure 12.10b). If mismatch repair enzymes correct the mismatch before the next DNA replication cycle, two outcomes are possible: Either (1) the repair will restore the wild-type `G-C` base pair, or (2) the repair will generate an `A-T` base-pair transition substitution (Figure 12.10c). Alternatively, if mismatch repair does not occur prior to replication, one daughter chromatid will be mutant and one will be wild-type. The guanine-containing strand will be used to produce a daughter duplex with the wild-type (`G-C`) sequence, while the thymine-containing strand will be used to synthesize a daughter duplex containing a `G-C` to `A-T` base-pair substitution (Figure 12.10d).

Cytosines that are side by side with guanines in a DNA strand are joined by a phosphodiester bond. These dinucleotides are identified as `CpG` dinucleotides (the *p* signifies the single phosphate bond of the phosphodiester bond). Cytosines of `CpG` dinucleotides are frequent targets for methylation in mammalian promoters, where methylation helps regulate transcription. Experimental evidence shows that `CpG` dinucleotides are hotspots of mutation as a result of deamination of methylated cytosine and the production of thymine.

12.4 Mutations May Be Induced by Chemicals or Ionizing Radiation

Induced mutations are mutations produced by interaction between DNA and a physical, chemical, or biological agent that generates damage resulting in mutation. The agents generating mutation-inducing DNA damage are called **mutagens.** Frequently, the term *induced mutations* is also used to describe the application of mutagens in an experimental context in order to produce mutations for direct study, to study the consequences of mutations on organisms, or to study the processes that repair the DNA damage done by mutagens. As we discuss in this section, chemical and physical mutagens interact with DNA in specific ways to create particular types of changes in sequence. A third category of mutagens, biological mutagens, are primarily mobile genetic elements. We discuss mobile genetic elements and the mutations they cause in Chapter 13. Mutagens are sometimes exotic or rare, but often they are routinely present in the everyday life of an organism. For this reason, the study of mutagenesis is as important for public health and safety as it is for advancing our understanding of the biological basis of mutation and repair.

Chemical Mutagens

Chemical compounds that induce mutations do so by specific and characteristic interactions with DNA nucleotide bases or with the DNA molecule. As a result, they can be classified by their mode of action on DNA. Chemical mutagens create DNA damage by acting as (1) nucleotide base analogs, (2) deaminating agents, (3) alkylating agents, (4) oxidizing agents, (5) hydroxylating agents, or (6) intercalating agents. Compounds in each of these categories and the types of mutations they cause are listed in Table 12.5. As we discuss mutagen–DNA interactions, remember that each mutagen reacts in a specific way with DNA and produces a consistent and particular kind of mutation as a result.

Nucleotide Base Analogs A **nucleotide base analog** is a chemical compound that has a structure similar to one of the DNA nucleotide bases and therefore can work its way into DNA, where it pairs with nucleotide base in the DNA duplex. DNA polymerases are unable to distinguish nucleotide base analogs from normal nucleotide bases due to their similarity in molecular size and shape. Consequently, base analogs are incorporated into DNA strands during replication. For example, the compound 5-bromodeoxyuridine (BrdU) is a derivative of uracil and is very similar to thymine in size and shape. In cells, it acts as an analog of thymine. After BrdU becomes incorporated during DNA replication, it pairs with adenine (Figure 12.11). Replication of the template strand containing the mispaired adenine results in a T-A to C-G transition mutation. Other base analogs produce different base-pair substitution mutations. One nucleotide base analog that is frequently used in experiments designed to produce transition mutations for study is the compound 2-aminopurine (2-AP). It is a base analog with two distinct forms. In one form, 2-AP acts as an analog of adenine that pairs with thymine. This leads to A-T to G-C transition mutations. In its other form, 2-AP is protonated. In this form it mispairs with cytosine and produces G-C to A-T transition mutations.

Deaminating Agents Nitrous acid (HNO_2) is a deaminating agent, meaning an agent that removes an amino group (NH_2). It is capable of removing amino groups from any nucleotide. In most instances, deamination produces no mutagenic effect; but deamination of 5-methylcytosine (shown in Figure 12.11) is an exception, leading to G-C to A-T base-pair substitution. In addition, when nitrous acid deaminates adenine, the product is hypoxanthine, a modified nucleotide that can mispair with cytosine and lead to an A-T to G-C base-pair substitution mutation (Figure 12.12a).

Alkylating Agents Alkylating agents add bulky side groups such as methyl (CH_3) and ethyl ($CH_3–CH_2$) groups to nucleotide bases. These added groups are known as **bulky adducts.** Ethyl methanesulfonate (EMS) is a powerful alkylating agent that adds an ethyl group to thymine, producing 4-ethylthymine, or an ethyl group to guanine, creating O^6-ethylguanine (Figure 12.12b). This and other bulky adducts interfere with normal DNA base pairing and may distort the DNA double helix.

Table 12.5	Examples of Mutagenic Agents and Their Consequences	
Mutagen	**Type of Agent**	**Mutagenic Event**
2-Aminopurine	Nucleotide base analog	Transition mutation (A-T to G-C or G-C to A-T)
5-Bromodeoxyuridine	Nucleotide base analog	Transition mutation (T-A to C-G)
Ethyl methanesulfonate	Alkylating agent	Transition mutation (G-C to A-T and A-T to G-C)
Hydroxylamine	Hydroxylating agent	Transition mutation (C-G to T-A)
Nitrous oxide	Deaminating agent	Transition mutation (G-C to A-T and A-T to G-C)
Oxygen radicals	Oxidizing agent	Transversion mutation (G-C to T-A)
Acridine orange	Intercalating agent	Frameshift mutation
Proflavin	Intercalating agent	Frameshift mutation

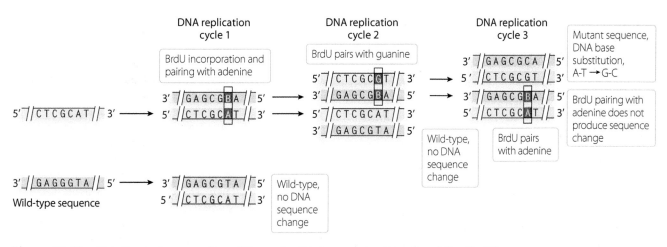

Figure 12.11   Mutation by incorporation of the nucleotide base analog 5-bromouridine (BrdU).

Hydroxylating Agents Hydroxylation is the addition of a hydroxyl (OH) group to a recipient compound by a donor called a hydroxylating agent. Hydroxylamine is a hydroxylating agent that adds a hydroxyl group to cytosine by displacing an H_2, thus creating hydroxylaminocytosine (**Figure 12.12c**). Hydroxylaminocytosine often pairs with guanine but frequently mispairs with adenine, leading to C-G to T-A base-pair transition mutations.

Oxidative Reactions Oxidation is a chemical process of electron transfer by addition of an oxygen atom or removal of an atom of hydrogen. Numerous oxidizing agents

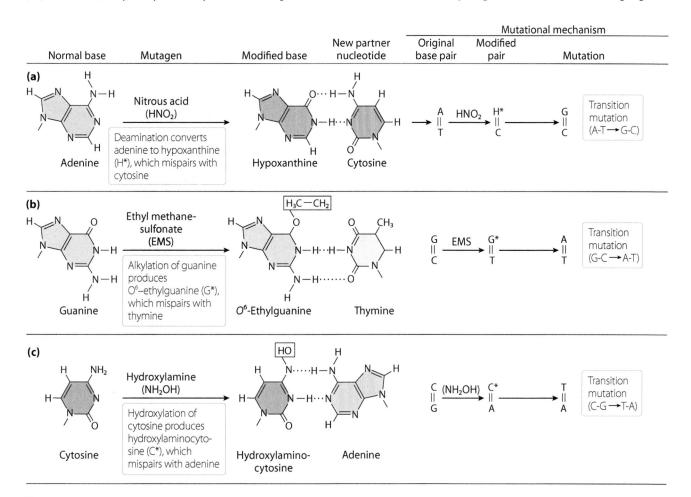

Figure 12.12   Examples of the action of chemical mutagens. In (a), H* is hypoxanthine. In (b) and (c), the asterisks (*) denote modified nucleotides.

such as bleach and hydrogen peroxide cause oxidative reactions that can lead to mutations. One example of mutation stemming from the action of an oxidizing agent is the production of 8-oxy-7,8-dihydrodeoxyguanine from guanine by the addition of an oxygen atom to the 7 carbon and transfer of a hydrogen atom from the 8 carbon to the 7 carbon of the purine ring. The oxidized form of guanine frequently mispairs with adenine, leading to a transversion mutation (G-C to T-A).

DNA Intercalating Agents Certain small molecular compounds called **DNA intercalating agents** can squeeze their way between DNA base pairs. DNA-intercalating compounds, such as proflavin, benzo(a)pyrene (a component of cigarette smoke), and aflatoxin (a toxin found in mold-contaminated peanuts) can find their way between base pairs and distort the duplex (**Figure 12.13**). These compounds can also attach to nucleotide bases to form bulky adducts that contribute to DNA distortion. These helical distortions lead to DNA strand nicking that is not efficiently repaired. Strand nicking appears to be caused by the intercalating agent interfering with the action of topoisomerase II that is active in relieving DNA supercoiling. In the following replication cycle, the nicked strands can gain or lose one or more nucleotides. As a result, intercalating agents cause frameshift mutations.

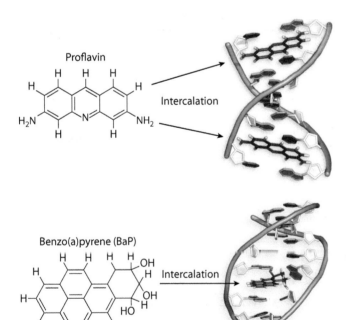

Figure 12.13   DNA intercalating agents. Proflavin and benzo(a)pyrene intercalate into the double helix and distort its shape, generating strand nicking that can produce frameshift mutations.

Radiation-Induced DNA Damage

Electromagnetic energy is conveyed in waves, or rays, and categorized by its wavelength, the distance between the equivalent points in its repeating troughs or peaks. Higher-energy radiation has shorter wavelengths than lower-energy radiation. One category of electromagnetic energy is visible light that has wavelengths between approximately 750 nm and 380 nm. All forms of radiant energy with wavelengths less than 380 nm—in other words, energy above the visible spectrum—can cause DNA damage and are mutagenic. These DNA-damaging forms of radiation are ultraviolet radiation, X-rays, gamma rays, and cosmic energy. Ultraviolet (UV) radiation, produced as a component of sunlight, is the mutagen to which we and other organisms are most often exposed, and in this section we focus on UV-induced DNA damage and mutation.

Like the effects of chemical mutagens, the mutagenicity of UV radiation derives from specific lesions it creates in DNA. UV irradiation alters DNA nucleotides by inciting the formation of additional bonds that form aberrant structures called **photoproducts.** One type of photoproduct, called a **pyrimidine dimer,** is produced by the formation of one or two additional covalent bonds between adjacent pyrimidine dinucleotides in a strand of DNA. Two prominent kinds of pyrimidine dimers occur (**Figure 12.14**). One is a **thymine dimer,** which has two covalent bonds joining the 5 and 6 carbons of thymines that are adjacent in the same DNA strand. The second, called a **6-4 photoproduct,** also joins adjacent thymines by formation of a bond between the 6 carbon of one thymine and the 4 carbon of the other thymine. Either of these dimeric complexes can also involve the other pyrimidine, cytosine, although cytosine is less commonly included than thymine. The formation of these dimers distorts DNA by pulling the dimerized nucleotide bases closer together and disrupting hydrogen bond formation with their complementary nucleotides on the opposite strand.

Organisms from bacteria to humans have DNA repair systems that identify and correct most pyrimidine dimers, but a few may escape repair; and when they do, DNA replication can be disrupted. Consider the problem posed during replication when pyrimidine dimers are encountered by DNA polymerase performing its synthesis and proofreading activities (see Section 7.4). DNA polymerase adds new nucleotides to nascent DNA strands by identifying the nucleotide complementary to the template strand and then catalyzing phosphodiester bond formation between the 5′ triphosphate of the new nucleotide and the 3′ OH of the previous nucleotide on the new strand. Hydrogen bond formation between complementary nucleotides on the old and newly synthesizing strand orients the 3′ OH of the previously added nucleotide so that it is in the correct position to react with the 5′ triphosphate of the incoming nucleotide. A mismatched base on a nascent DNA strand will fail to form normal hydrogen bonds with the nucleotide

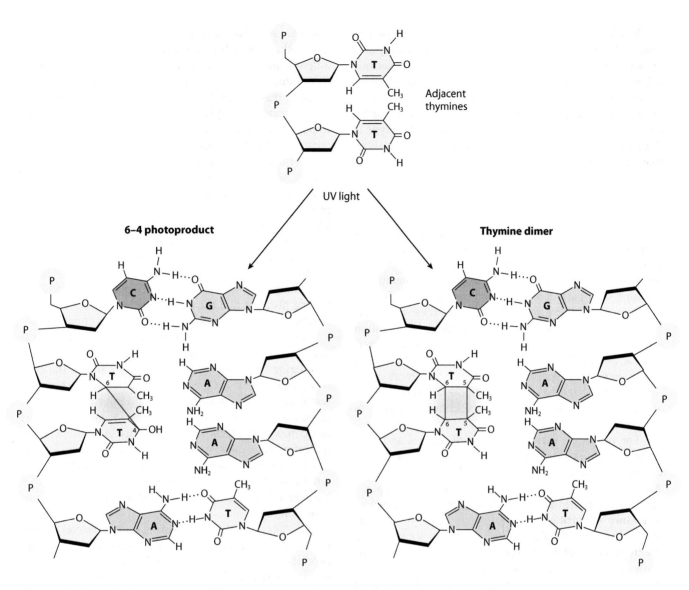

Figure 12.14   UV photoproducts. UV irradiation forms photoproducts from adjacent pyrimidines, distorting the double helix and potentially blocking replication.

on the template strand, leaving the 3′ OH out of position as DNA polymerase attempts to catalyze the next phosphodiester bond. This occurrence activates the proofreading function of the DNA polymerase.

More specifically, when it encounters thymines in a dimer on the template strand, DNA polymerase attempts to add complementary adenines to the nascent DNA strand. But the first adenine fails to form the necessary hydrogen bonds, because the placement of its complementary partner is distorted. In attempting to add the second adenine, DNA polymerase identifies the mispositioned 3′ OH of the first adenine, initiates 5′-to-3′ proofreading activity, and then attempts to resume synthesis in the thymine dimer region—but with the same negative result. Continued repetition of these unsuccessful attempts to replicate across the thymine dimer causes replication to stall at this point.

How does the replication process overcome the blockage caused by the presence of pyrimidine dimers? It circumvents the problem. Replication blockage by pyrimidine dimers induces reinitiation of DNA synthesis at an adjacent RNA primer site. This reinitiation of replication potentially leaves gaps spanning dozens to hundreds of nucleotides in newly synthesized DNA strands, but the gaps are subsequently filled by **translesion DNA synthesis,** which is carried out by specialized bypass DNA polymerases (one in bacteria and several in eukaryotes) that can replicate across the gaps. These specialized DNA polymerases are more prone to replication error, however, because they lack proofreading ability. In fact, it is the absence of proofreading activity that allows these polymerases to carry out replication across pyrimidine dimers. Replication can thus proceed, but at the risk of introducing mutations. We discuss the process further in Section 12.6.

Irradiation that has higher energy than that of UV waves—X-rays, and radioactive materials, for example—can cause DNA damage in multiple ways, the most serious being the induction of DNA single-strand or double-strand breaks. These breaks potentially block DNA replication and thus pose a significant threat to the integrity and survival of affected cells. DNA damage of this type is dealt with by specialized strand-break repair mechanisms that we discuss later in the chapter.

The Ames Test

In our day-to-day lives, we encounter scores of naturally occurring and synthetic chemicals and compounds in the food we eat, the air we breathe, the cars we drive, and even the books we read. Each year new chemical compounds are introduced as part of various commercial and industrial processes. How do we determine which of these chemicals pose a hazard to our health by increasing the mutation frequencies of genes? Occasionally, the mutagenic or carcinogenic potential of a compound is so great that evidence of its danger is relatively easy to identify. Much more often, however, the mutagenicity of a compound is more subtle, and careful analysis of experimental data is required to ascertain it.

For nearly 40 years, thousands of natural and synthetic compounds have been assayed for mutagenic potential by a simple biological test developed by Bruce Ames. This procedure, called the **Ames test,** exposes bacteria to experimental compounds in the presence of a mixture of purified enzymes produced by the mammalian liver. In animals, ingested chemicals are routed to the liver, where they are broken down by detoxifying enzymes. Using a critical subset of detoxifying liver enzymes called the S9 extract, the Ames test mimics the biological defense processes that take place in the liver of animals exposed to chemical compounds. During enzymatic breakdown in the liver, numerous intermediate products can be produced, some of which may be mutagenic, even if the original compound was not. The purpose of the Ames test is to detect whether the original compound or any of its normal breakdown products are mutagens.

The Ames test most commonly uses strains of the bacterium *Salmonella typhimurium* that carry mutations affecting their ability to synthesize the amino acid histidine. These bacteria are designated *his*⁻ to indicate their mutation prevents histidine synthesis. They will not grow unless they are provided with a medium that is supplemented with histidine. The Ames test is designed to identify the rate of *reversion mutations* (*his*⁻ to *his*⁺) that restore the ability of bacteria to synthesize their own histidine, thus eliminating the need for histidine supplementation of the growth medium.

The Ames test uses multiple *his*⁻ strains of *S. typhimurium,* each carrying different kinds of mutations of histidine-synthesizing genes. Some test strains carry base-pair substitution (transition and transversion) mutations; others carry frameshift mutations. The use of these different mutant strains allows detection of compounds that induce base-pair substitution mutations as well as of those that induce frameshift mutations, by comparing reversion rates in experimental bacterial cultures exposed to potential mutagens with spontaneous reversion rates in control bacterial cultures.

In each experimental culture, the S9 extract is added to mutant strains of *S. typhimurium* with base-pair substitution or frameshift mutations and each mixture is separately plated onto a medium lacking histidine (**Figure 12.15**). The test compound, in different concentrations, is added to a filter paper disk in the center of each test plate, and the plates are incubated. To determine the frequency of spontaneous reversion from *his*⁻ to *his*⁺, control cultures containing *his*⁻ bacteria and S9 are plated onto medium lacking histidine and the plates are incubated. Bacteria on the control plates are not exposed to the test compound.

The results of an Ames test are interpreted by counting the number of growing colonies on each plate and comparing the numbers to one another and to the control plates. These data are used to determine whether a test compound is mutagenic and to develop a growth-response curve describing how the concentration of the test compound affects its mutagenicity. A positive result, indicating that the test compound is mutagenic, is indicated by a significant increase in the reversion rate in bacterial cells that have one kind of mutation over cells that have the other kind of mutation and over the spontaneous reversion rate.

In **Figure 12.16**, the dose-response curve reveals the strong mutagenic potential of aflatoxin B_1, a toxin produced by the fungus *Aspergillus* that grows on nuts and maize (corn). This powerful mutagen induces large numbers of base-pair substitution mutations in the *his*⁻ strain designated TA 100 that contains a base-pair substitution and is highly sensitive to aflatoxin B_1. At all doses tested, the reversion rate for aflatoxin B_1 in base-pair substitution *his*⁻ strains is elevated above that of the *his*⁻ strain TA 1538, which contains a frameshift mutation. This result indicates that aflatoxin B_1 actively induces reversion of base-pair substitution mutants, but not of frameshift mutants. **Genetic Analysis 12.2** guides you through an analysis of an Ames test of potential mutagens.

12.5 Repair Systems Correct Some DNA Damage

The structural and informational integrity of DNA is under continuous assault from spontaneous chemical change and from various chemical and physical mutagens. Despite this ongoing challenge, organisms preserve the fidelity of their DNA by repairing most lesions that occur and leaving

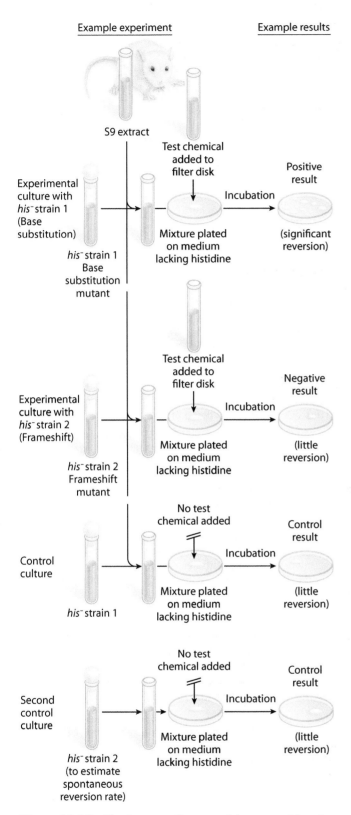

Figure 12.15 **The Ames test for potential mutagenicity of chemical compounds.**

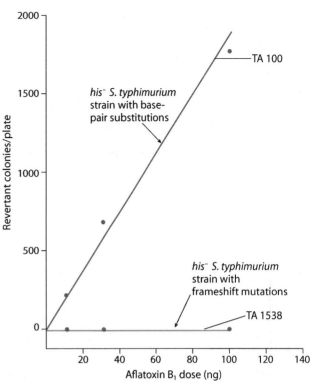

Figure 12.16 **Mutagenicity of aflatoxin B$_1$ determined by the Ames test.** Aflatoxin B$_1$ induces a high rate of reversions in *his$^-$* bacteria with base-pair substitution mutations (strain TA 100), but not in frameshift mutants (strain TA 1538).

ultimately affect survival of the species. On the other hand, too few mutations will limit the range of genetic variability and may hamper the species' ability to evolve.

Organisms must therefore strike a balance between the accumulation of mutations and repair of DNA damage before mutations accrue. To manage this balance, organisms have evolved multiple repair mechanisms, and often these are partially redundant with regard to the lesions they identify and repair. In broad terms, these damage repair processes fall into two categories: (1) those that directly repair DNA damage and restore it to its wild-type state; and (2) those that allow the organism to circumvent problems such as blocked DNA replication, which can occur when damage is not repaired but which leave the DNA damage in place.

Direct Repair of DNA Damage

We have already encountered the most direct way to repair DNA lesions and to reverse DNA damage before it causes mutation. This mechanism is proofreading by DNA polymerase (see Chapter 7), that identifies a base-pair mismatch, removes the erroneous DNA segment, and resynthesizes the sequence. Several other repair systems also carry out direct repair of DNA damage.

Mismatch Repair The proofreading that accompanies DNA replication is an efficient system that helps keep the mutation rate low. Still, some mismatched nucleotide

very few mutations to accrue. However, a species' survival depends on maintaining a delicate balance between mutation and repair. Since most mutations are deleterious to the organism, too many mutations may doom an organism and

PROBLEM Three potentially hazardous compounds, A, B, and C, are assayed by the Ames test. Two strains of *his⁻* bacteria (1 and 2) are used. Auxotrophy in strain 1 is caused by a frameshift mutation and in strain 2 by the substitution of one base pair, resulting in a nonsense mutation. Each strain is treated with the different compounds. An S9 fraction (supernatant of solubilized rat liver enzymes) was added to each mixture of auxotrophic bacteria plus one of the compounds.

After treatment, the cells were plated on minimal medium. Control plates contain each of the two strains treated with S9 alone, without A, B, or C present. The table below shows the number of prototrophic colonies observed on the plates:

> **BREAK IT DOWN:** The Ames test examines the potential mutagenicity of compounds or their breakdown products by exposing bacteria and determining the rate of reversion from mutant to wild-type phenotype (p. 408).

> **BREAK IT DOWN:** Growth of a bacterial colony on a minimal medium plate indicates it is wild-type (see Research Technique 6.1, pp. 189–190).

Compound Tested	Strain 1	Strain 2
A	904	6
B	5	4
C	3	680
Control (no compound)	6	3

a. Assess the growth results, and determine whether each compound is mutagenic.

b. Determine the type of mutation most likely induced by any mutagens.

> **BREAK IT DOWN:** See the Ames test sample data in Figure 12.17 (p. 411).

Solution Strategies	Solution Steps
Evaluate	
1. Identify the topic this problem addresses and the nature of the required answer.	1. This problem concerns interpretation of the results of an Ames test of three compounds. The answer must identify which if any of the compounds are mutagenic and describe the nature of that mutagenicity.
2. Identify the critical information given in the problem.	2. The number of revertant colonies is given for each compound. A control result is also given. The cause of auxotrophy in each mutant strain is identified.
Deduce	
3. Describe the meaning of growth results on the control plate.	3. The control plates have had no test compound added. The growing colonies on these plates are spontaneous revertants from each of the auxotrophic tester strains.
4. Deduce the meaning of growth results on each of the experimental plates.	4. Compound A produces many revertants of strain 1, but no reversion over spontaneous levels in strain 2. Compound C generates many revertants of strain 2, but does not produce revertants at a rate greater than the control in strain 1. Compound B does not increase the reversion rate above the spontaneous level in either strain.
Solve	Answer a
5. Identify the mutagenic compounds and justify your answer.	5. Compounds A and C are mutagenic, but compound B is not. The large numbers of revertant colonies on the strain 1 test of compound A and the number of revertants on the strain 2 test of compound C identify these compounds as mutagens. Compound B does not show an increased rate of reversion relative to the background numbers on the control plates.
	Answer b
6. Describe the nature of mutagenicity for each compound.	6. Compound A causes frameshift mutations by inducing a high rate of reversion of *his⁻* strain 1 auxotrophs. Compound C causes a high rate of reversions of strain 2 auxotrophs by inducing base-pair substitution reversions.

> **TIP:** Base-pair substitution mutagens generally revert base-pair substitution auxotrophs, and frameshift mutagens revert frameshift auxotrophs.

For more practice, see Problems 30, 34, and 37.

Visit the Study Area to access study tools.

MasteringGenetics™

base pairs escape proofreading. These and other base pair mismatches, such as those generated by tautomeric shifts of nucleotide bases, can be detected and repaired by **mismatch repair.** Mismatch repair has been most extensively studied in *E. coli*, but similar processes that include the action of homologous genes in eukaryotes, including humans, have also been examined in detail.

When faced with a base-pair mismatch, repair enzymes must correctly identify the nucleotide to be replaced, and this requires distinguishing between the original DNA strand, with the correct nucleotide, and the new DNA strand with the mismatched nucleotide. The identification is accomplished by the sensitivity of mismatch repair enzymes to methylation (the addition of CH_3 groups) of specific nucleotides in the original DNA strand. In *E. coli*, methylation is particularly common on the adenine of 5'-GATC-3' sequences. GATC sequences are palindromes, meaning that both strands of DNA will contain a 5'-GATC-3' sequence. The addition of methyl groups is delayed after the completion of replication, meaning that immediately after replication is complete, original strands contain methylated adenines in GATC sequences, but daughter strands do not.

Two *E. coli* genes, *mutS* and *mutL*, produce enzymes that recognize and bind to DNA containing base-pair mismatches. MutS protein binds first to the mismatch region, and then it recruits MutL protein to the site as well (**Figure 12.17**). This begins a series of enzyme-driven steps that recruits a third protein, MutH, that breaks a phosphodiester bond on the 5' side of the guanine of a GATC sequence on the unmethylated daughter strand. Broken phosphodiester bonds are known as "nicks," and the nick generated by MutH attracts an exonuclease that digests a short stretch of nucleotides extending beyond the GATC and including the mismatched base. DNA polymerase then uses the original strand as a template to fill the gap created by nuclease digestion, and DNA ligase completes the repair. A specialized methylase enzyme known as Dam methylase then methylates the adenine of the GATC sequence on the daughter strand.

After mismatch repair was described in *E. coli*, a similar repair mechanism was identified in yeast, and homologs to bacterial *mutS*, *mutL*, and *mutH* were identified. In yeast, the genes *pms1* and *mlh1* are homologs for the bacterial *MutL* gene, and *msh2* is a homolog for *mutS*. Yeast also has a homolog for bacterial *MutH*. The resulting yeast proteins are very active in the repair of insertions and deletions produced by strand slippage. Geneticists studying human cancer quickly realized that a rare type of human hereditary cancer known as hereditary nonpolyposis colorectal cancer (HNPCC) was typically caused by mutations that increased the number of DNA sequences, and they wondered if mutations of *pms1*, *mlh1*, or *mlh2* might be the cause. It was quickly determined that HNPCC can be caused by mutations of any of these genes, indicating that this condition is a cancer-prone syndrome caused by mutation of the DNA mismatch repair system. Other

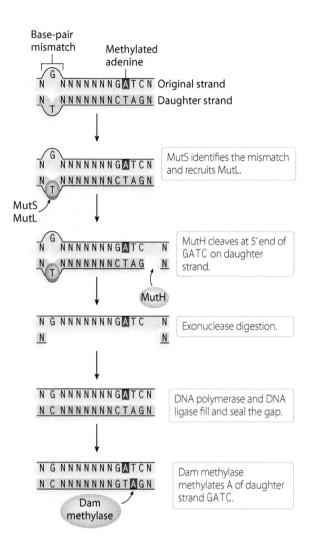

Figure 12.17 **DNA mismatch repair by MutS and MutH in *E. coli*.**

cancer-prone syndromes also result from mutations of genes that normally repair DNA damage, as we discuss at the end of this section.

Nucleotide Base Excision Repair A multistep process called **nucleotide base excision repair** identifies and removes modified bases and then replaces the entire nucleotide. Base excision repair is initiated by DNA glycosylases, which recognize modified bases such as uracil created by deamination of 5-methylcytosine, hypoxanthine, and other base modifications. In **Figure 12.18**, for example, a DNA glycosylase removes a modified base to generate an AP site. The enzyme AP endonuclease then removes the remainder of the nucleotide, after which DNA polymerase and DNA ligase fill the nucleotide gap and seal the sugar-phosphate backbone.

Nucleotide Excision Repair Another repair system, known as **nucleotide excision repair,** recognizes and removes bulky adducts that distort DNA.

DNA containing a modified nucleotide

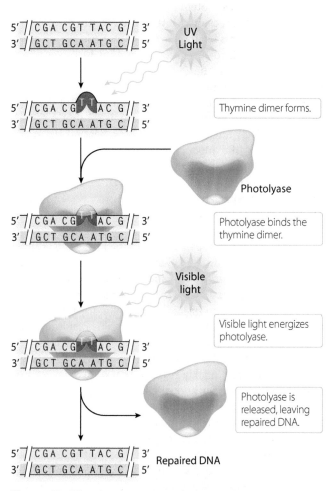

DNA glycosylase

X Modified nucleotide

① DNA glycosylase removes the modified nucleotide, leaving an AP site.

AP endonuclease

Excised AP deoxyribose

AP site

② AP endonuclease excises the AP deoxyribose.

DNA polymerase + dNTPs

③ DNA polymerase synthesizes new DNA from the 3′ OH site using the lower strand as a template.

DNA ligase

④ DNA ligase seals the single-stranded gap and reforms an intact duplex with the original sequence.

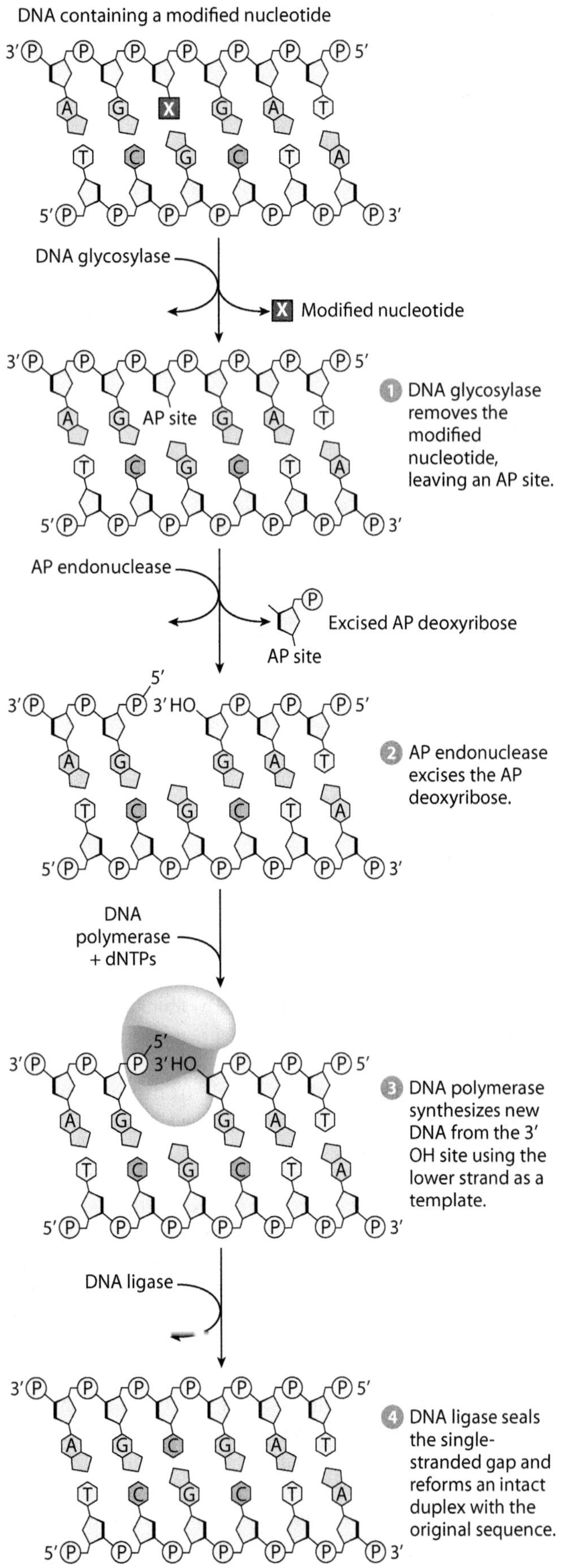

Figure 12.18 **Nucleotide base excision repair.** DNA glycosylase and AP (apurinic) endonuclease remove chemically modified nucleotides from DNA.

Bulky modifications such as O^6-ethylguanine and 4-ethylthymine generated by the action of alkylating agents like EMS and distortions created by damage done by ultraviolet light are targeted by nucleotide excision repair. Repair of the damage involves enzymes that recognize and bind to the damaged region, followed by removal of a short segment of as many as several dozen nucleotides from the damaged strand. The missing nucleotides are replaced by the activity of DNA polymerase followed by that of DNA ligase.

Direct Repair of UV-Induced Photoproducts Ultraviolet radiation is the most common mutagen humans, and most other organisms, encounter on a daily basis. As such, it may come as no surprise that organisms have a variety of ways to identify and repair UV-induced DNA damage. Pyrimidine dimers, the common photoproducts of UV-induced DNA damage, can be directly repaired by **photoreactive repair,** a DNA repair mechanism found in bacteria, single-celled eukaryotes, plants, and some animals (e.g., *Drosophila*), but not in humans. Photoreactivation utilizes the enzyme photolyase to break the bonds formed during pyrimidine dimerization. In **Figure 12.19**, a thymine dimer produced by UV irradiation is bound by photolyase. Visible light energy is absorbed by photolyase and is redirected to break the bonds forming the dimer. Photolyase is the product

5′ CGA CGT TAC G 3′
3′ GCT GCA ATG C 5′

UV Light

5′ CGA CG T T AC G 3′
3′ GCT GCA ATG C 5′

Thymine dimer forms.

Photolyase

5′ CGA CG AC G 3′
3′ GCT GCA ATG C 5′

Photolyase binds the thymine dimer.

Visible light

5′ CGA CG AC G 3′
3′ GCT GCA ATG C 5′

Visible light energizes photolyase.

Photolyase is released, leaving repaired DNA.

5′ CGA CGT TAC G 3′
3′ GCT GCA ATG C 5′

Repaired DNA

Figure 12.19 **Photoreactive repair.**

412

of the *phr* (photoreactive repair) gene of *E. coli*. *phr* gene mutations result in a substantial increase in UV-induced mutations in bacteria.

UV Repair Another system for directly repairing UV-induced damage to DNA that is widely distributed among organisms from bacteria to humans is known as **ultraviolet (UV) repair** (Figure 12.20). This is a form of nucleotide excision repair that uses certain proteins to recognize DNA damage and other proteins to remove a short region of the strand containing the photoproduct. The names of the proteins vary among organisms, but they are largely homologous. In *E. coli*, UV repair is carried out by the protein products of four UV repair genes called *uvr-A*, *uvr-B*, *uvr-C*, and *uvr-D*. Two molecules of UVR-A protein and one molecule of UVR-B protein bind on one strand of DNA opposite the site of the photoproduct. The two molecules of UVR-A dissociate from the strand, and a molecule of UVR-C joins UVR-B to form a UVR-BC complex. Each UVR-C cleaves a

bond about four or five nucleotides to the 3′ side or the 5′ side of the photoproduct. The single-stranded fragment of approximately 12 nucleotides containing the photoproduct is released UVR-D, which is a DNA helicase, binds along with DNA pol I to the exposed 3′ OH. UVR-D unwinds and releases the severed single strand segment, and pol I uses the complementary strand to synthesize a replacement for the missing segment. In the final step of the excision repair process, DNA ligase binds to the region to seal the sugar-phosphate backbone. This process removes the lesion and restores the DNA duplex.

DNA Damage Signaling Systems

The biochemical mechanisms that recognize DNA damage and mount a damage repair response are crucial to the health and survival of an organism. They consist of tightly regulated genetic processes involving numerous genes and proteins. In humans and other mammals, a multiprotein complex acts as a genomic sentry to identify damage. This damage response process is active throughout the cell cycle and is especially important in regulating the G_1-to-S transition, preventing the cell cycle from progressing to S phase until the cell has adequately repaired any mutations.

One important protein in this process is BRCA1, the product of the first gene implicated in familial breast and ovarian cancer susceptibility (see Experimental Insight 5.1, page 169). A second protein that plays a pivotal role in communicating DNA damage is called ATM. DNA damage acquired through chemical or radiation exposure is sensed using ATM as a signal transduction molecule to activate transcription of the *p53* gene that produces the protein p53. By this mechanism, ATM activates the "p53 repair pathway" that controls cellular response to mutation by deciding either (1) to pause the cell cycle at the G_1-to-S transition to allow time for mutation repair or (2) to direct the cell to the apoptotic pathway, in which it undergoes programmed cell death (Figure 12.21).

In healthy cells, p53 level is low, but ATM increases the level in response to DNA damage. Acting as a transcription factor, p53 initiates G_1 arrest of the cell cycle by inducing synthesis of the protein p21 that inhibits formation of Cdk–cyclin complexes. The p53-induced pause in the cell cycle allows time for the repair of DNA damage. The completion of DNA repair depletes p53, and the cell cycle transitions to S phase.

At the same time as it activates cell cycle arrest at the G_1–S transition, p53 also activates transcription of the *BAX* gene. The BAX protein is a slowly acting inhibitor of the BCL2 protein that represses the apoptotic pathway. In healthy cells in which p53 level is low, *BAX* transcription is not initiated. As a result, BCL2 protein remains uninhibited and represses apoptosis. In damaged cells, however, BAX inhibition of BCL2 leads to

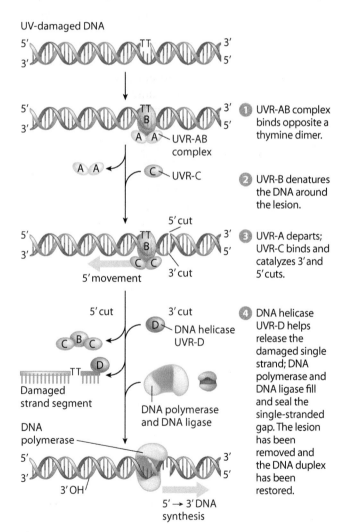

Figure 12.20 An example of nucleotide excision repair. UVR proteins remove UV-induced damage from DNA strands.

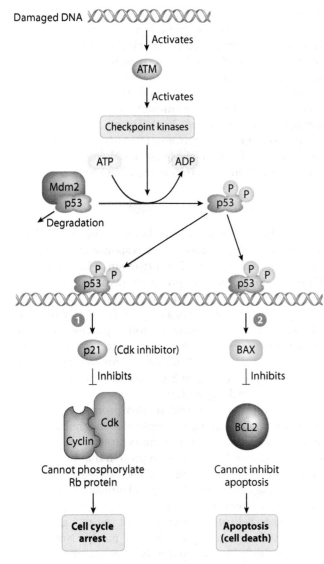

Figure 12.21 The *p53* DNA damage repair pathway.

activation of the apoptotic pathway. Thus, if the p53-induced pause in the cell cycle goes on too long, the pathway senses that there is a large amount of DNA damage that cannot be quickly repaired. The long pause allows the apoptotic pathway to go forward, and the cell undergoes programmed cell death.

DNA Damage Repair Disorders

DNA damage repair disorders, resulting from mutations in genes that participate in the repair of DNA damage or in the signaling or initiating of damage repair, cause an organism to be highly sensitive to chemical mutagens and to radiation. Such disorders greatly increase the organism's susceptibility to cancers caused by mutagen exposure. We return to this theme in the Case Study that concludes this chapter, where we discuss a connection between mutations of *p53* and the occurrence of cancer and the role of transmission of *p53* mutation in the human familial cancer syndrome known as Li-Fraumeni syndrome (OMIM 151623). **Table 12.6** lists some human mutation repair disorders that are associated with significantly elevated risks of specific types of cancer.

Research conducted since the 1990s on gene mutations in cancer has combined with cancer genomics, genome sequence analysis of cancers, to offer a new way to test for the inheritance of gene mutations that may significantly increase a person's lifetime risk of cancer. Several individual gene tests are available, but recently a group of medical researchers at the University of Washington assembled and tested a genome sequence-based breast and ovarian cancer analysis that examines 24 genes associated with the diseases. The test panel, called BROCA, promises to offer individuals at risk for breast cancer an unprecedented opportunity to assess their risk. **Experimental Insight 12.2** describes BROCA.

Table 12.6	Selected Human Mutation Repair Disorders
Disorder and OMIM Number	**Description**
Ataxia telangiectasia (208900)	Mutation of the *ATM* gene and absence of ATM protein. Poor coordination (ataxia), red marks on the face (telangiectasia), increased sensitivity to X-rays and other radiation, high cancer risk.
Breast–ovarian cancer (604370)	Mutation of *BRCA1*. Defective DNA repair and increased susceptibility to breast and ovarian cancer.
Li-Fraumeni syndrome (151623)	Mutation of *p53* and defective p53 pathway. High cancer risk.
Nonpolyposis colon cancer (120435)	Defective base-pair mismatch repair caused by mutation of any one of seven different genes. High risk of colon cancer.
Trichothiodystrophy (601675)	Mutations of any one of five gene mutations causing increased sensitivity to oxidative damage. Mental retardation, dwarfism, skin and hair abnormalities, and increased cancer risk.
Xeroderma pigmentosum (278700)	Defective excision repair resulting from the mutation of any one of seven UV damage repair genes. Extreme sensitivity to UV-induced damage and high skin cancer risk.

BROCA: Cancer Genomics: Genome Sequencing to Evaluate Cancer Risk

The average woman reading this textbook has about a 12% chance of developing breast cancer in her lifetime. Approximately 90% to 95% of the cases that develop will be so-called sporadic cases, meaning there were no known hereditary factors that increased the person's breast cancer risk. The remainder of cases, however, will occur because the woman inherited a gene mutation that predisposed her to breast cancer.

Since their discovery in the 1990s, two genes, *BRCA1* and *BRCA2*, have been at the forefront of genetic testing for inherited mutations that predispose to a woman's risk of hereditary breast and ovarian cancer. Certain mutations of *BRCA1* and *BRCA2* are very strongly associated with an almost 75% lifetime risk of breast and ovarian cancer, whereas other mutations of these genes appear to carry much lower predisposition risks. Commercial testing for mutations of these genes was, until 2013, controlled by a single company and was limited to the most common mutations linked to increased cancer risk. Many women with breast or ovarian cancer who are members of families with a high hereditary breast cancer risk test negative for the *BRCA1* or *BRCA2* mutations screened by the commercial test, suggesting that either untested *BRCA1* or *BRCA2* mutations or else mutations of other genes are responsible for increased hereditary risk. A 2013 U.S. Supreme Court decision revoked the patent held by the company on *BRCA1* and *BRCA2* testing and opened the way for wider application and use of genetic testing for mutations of genes that may increase lifetime cancer risk.

A new genome sequence–based genetic test known as the BROCA test is designed to examine the sequences of all the genes known to contribute to breast cancer risk. The test is named after the French physician, surgeon, and anatomist Pierre Paul Broca (1824–1880), whose contributions to medical science include the first descriptions of families in which there appears to be inherited susceptibility to breast cancer.

At present, mutations of 24 genes, including *BRCA1* and *BRCA2*, that are suspected to contribute to inherited susceptibility to breast cancer are examined in the BROCA test. Mutations of any one of these genes could potentially increase a woman's lifetime risk of cancer to levels ranging from a few percent higher to several times that of an average woman in the population. Tomas Walsh, Mary-Claire King, and numerous colleagues have collaborated to develop the BROCA test, which uses advanced genome sequencing to fully sequence all 24 genes implicated in increased breast cancer risk. Complete gene sequencing allows detection of all point mutations, all repeat-sequence copy number variants, and all insertion and deletion mutations.

Published reports in 2010 and 2011 and an additional preliminary report in 2013 outline the effectiveness of BROCA in detecting mutations linked to breast cancer risk in high-risk families that contain members who have previously tested negative for one of the commercially tested *BRCA1* or *BRCA2* mutations. The 2013 report identified 149 mutations of 18 genes in 191 breast cancer families. Through complete gene sequencing, BROCA identified 66 families in which there were *BRCA1* or *BRCA2* mutations that were not detected by the commercial test. In 125 additional families, mutations of one of the genes other than *BRCA1* or *BRCA2* were detected.

The comprehensive testing provided by BROCA may prove pivotal in identifying women at increased risk of breast cancer due to hereditary predisposition. Women in this situation can then be offered several options before cancer appears. BROCA is among the first of a coming wave of genome-based genetic tests that herald an era in which certain kinds of medical treatment will be personalized to take into account individual genome sequence differences.

12.6 Proteins Control Translesion DNA Synthesis and the Repair of Double-Strand Breaks

The repair mechanisms described to this point are able to repair DNA damage, but not all DNA damage is repaired in this way. Damage that escapes repair before the initiation of DNA replication has the potential to block replication. Circumventing this potential blockage requires mechanisms that can permit replication to progress despite the presence of damage that is potentially mutagenic. In addition, events that lead to the breakage of one or both DNA strands present unique challenges to organisms. The repair of certain kinds of strand breakage can take place in an error-free manner that does not introduce mutation. Other types of strand breakage, however, are "error-prone," meaning that repair of the damage may itself introduce mutations. It may not immediately be obvious why repair mechanisms that are prone to introducing additional errors have evolved. After all, the point of DNA repair systems is just that—to repair damage so as to maintain the integrity of the genome. This conundrum is explained by the fact that error-prone repair mechanisms are activated only in instances of widespread DNA damage that would otherwise prevent the completion of DNA replication andmight cause cell death.

Translesion DNA Synthesis

In response to widespread DNA damage, molecular activities in the cell may direct the cell to apoptosis. The activity of the p53 protein in eukaryotic cells can lead to this outcome. *E. coli* cells that undergo extensive damage might also die, but there is a second repair mechanism that can be activated in *E.coli* in response to massive

DNA damage. This repair system, called SOS repair, has been known for decades but has only recently been understood at the molecular level. The system takes its name from the maritime phrase "save our ship," used when sinking was imminent. In the past, SOS repair was described as a last-ditch effort on the part of a heavily damaged bacterial cell to replicate its DNA and divide before succumbing to DNA damage. Recent research demonstrates that SOS repair is accomplished by activating specialized DNA polymerases in a process known as translesion DNA synthesis. This short-lived process allows DNA replication by alternative polymerases across lesions that block the action of DNA polymerase III (pol III), the main DNA-replicating polymerase in *E. coli*.

Translesion DNA synthesis is performed by **translesion DNA polymerases,** also called **bypass polymerases.** Bypass polymerases operate differently from pol III in several respects. First, bypass polymerases are able to replicate across DNA lesions that stall pol III. This ability is accounted for by the second difference distinguishing bypass polymerases, the absence of proofreading. In other words, bypass polymerases do not have 3′-to-5′ exonuclease capacity and are unable to remove newly added nucleotides that fail to hydrogen bond with the template strand nucleotide. Due to their lack of proofreading capability, the third distinguishing feature of bypass polymerases is that they are prone to making replication errors. Finally, bypass polymerases synthesize only short segments of DNA; they fall off the template strand after synthesizing a small number of nucleotides. From these distinguishing features, molecular biologists conclude that bypass polymerases are used to complete replication that would otherwise be blocked. This comes at the price, however, of potentially introducing new mutations.

The SOS system in *E. coli* operates through a specialized bypass polymerase identified as polymerase V ("polymerase five"), or pol V. When pol III stalls at damaged DNA, RecA protein coats the template strand ahead of the lesion that is already bound by single-stranded binding protein (SSB). Recall that SSB coats the single DNA strands separated ahead of the replication fork (see Figure 7.14). The RecA protein in the DNA–RecA–SSB complex is an active form that also activates transcription of several genes, including pol V. Pol V displaces polymerase III, synthesizes a short portion of the daughter strand across the DNA lesion, and is then replaced by pol III, which resumes its normal replication activity.

Eukaryotic genomes utilize a similar mechanism for translesion DNA synthesis. In eukaryotes, however, bypass polymerases are always present in cells, so the system of regulating their access to DNA is quite different. The regulatory mechanism guiding the choice of polymerase decides which polymerase binds to PCNA, the eukaryotic sliding clamp. When eukaryotic replication stalls at a DNA lesion, a protein called Rad6 that is always present at the replication fork adds a ubiquitin (Ub) group to PCNA. This process, called ubiquitination, normally

targets a protein for destruction. On PCNA, however, ubiquitination merely causes an alteration of conformation, giving the bypass polymerase a strong affinity for ubiquitinated PCNA. In this process, bypass polymerase displaces normal DNA polymerase and carries out translesion synthesis of DNA. As in the SOS system, the use of bypass polymerases in eukaryotic cells is error prone because the enzyme lacks proofreading capability.

Double-Strand Break Repair

A common feature of the DNA repair mechanisms we have examined is the use of DNA polymerase and a template strand of DNA to guide the repair, replacement, or synthesis of DNA. These repair systems are effective as long as one strand of DNA is intact and can serve as a template. But what happens if *both strands* of DNA are damaged in a manner that does not provide a template strand for strand repair? Such damage is a frequent consequence of exposure to X-rays and certain types of oxygen radicals. The damage caused by these agents breaks both strands of DNA, leaving lesions that are known as double-strand breaks. Because they can cause chromosome instability and incomplete replication of the genome, double-strand breaks are potentially lethal to cells and elevate the risk of cancer and the chance of chromosome structural mutations.

To protect organisms from the unpleasant consequences of double-strand breaks, two mechanisms have evolved to carry out **double-strand break repair.** The first is an error-prone repair process known as *nonhomologous end joining* that repairs double-strand breaks occurring before DNA replication. The second is an error-free process called *synthesis-dependent strand annealing* that repairs double-strand breaks occurring after the completion of DNA replication.

Nonhomologous End Joining If a double-stranded break damages a eukaryotic chromosome during G_1 of the cell cycle, replication of the damaged chromosome is blocked. Considering that DNA polymerases, even bypass polymerases, require a template strand to direct synthesis of a daughter strand, it is clear that a double-strand break is incompatible with the completion of replication. One repair alternative that allows cells to reacquire their capacity to fully replicate their genome is **nonhomologous end joining (NHEJ),** although its four-step process for repairing double-strand breaks inevitably leads to mutation (**Figure 12.22**).

In the first step, double-strand breaks are recognized by a protein complex containing the proteins PKcs, Ku70, and Ku80. This complex attaches to each of the broken ends of the DNA duplex. The complex then trims back (resects) the free ends of each broken strand. Resection leaves blunt ends on each side of the break. Finally, the blunt ends are ligated by a specialized ligase called ligase IV ("ligase four").

Completion of NHEJ produces an intact DNA duplex and allows replication across the repaired region in the

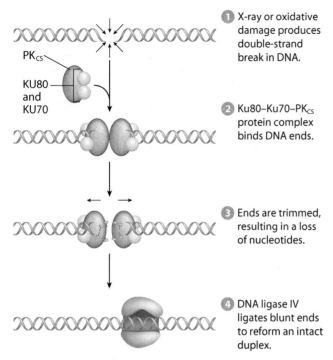

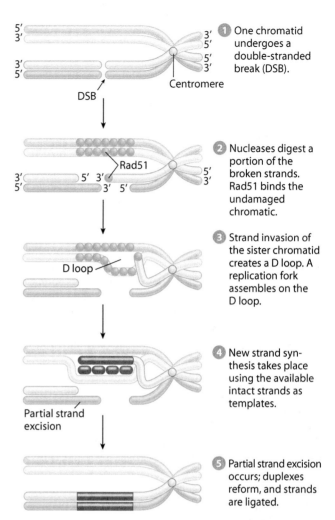

Figure 12.22   Nonhomologous end joining. NHEJ is an error-prone system that rejoins DNA strands following a double-stranded break.

Figure 12.23   Synthesis-dependent strand annealing (SDSA).

upcoming replication cycle, but the repair is often imperfect because resection removes nucleotides that cannot be replaced. For this reason, NHEJ is error prone. Yet, as potentially damaging as this process is, its outcome is superior to the alternatives suffered by cells that are unable to repair double-strand breaks, and it prevents more extensive loss from degradation of unprotected ends. Mutations can be generated, however, when nucleotides are lost from transcribed genes.

Synthesis-Dependent Strand Annealing   In eukaryotes, once DNA replication is complete, each chromosome is composed of two identical sister chromatids. Double-stranded breaks at this stage can be repaired by exploiting the intact sister chromatid to repair the damaged chromatid in an error-free repair process known as **synthesis-dependent strand annealing (SDSA).**

As shown in **Figure 12.23**, a double-stranded break (DSB) affects one sister chromatid; the other chromatid is undamaged. SDSA begins with trimming of one of the broken strands. This is followed by attachment of the protein Rad51 to the broken region to form a nucleoprotein filament. Rad51 binds to the strands and facilitates the invasion of the intact chromatid by the resected end of a strand from the sister chromatid. This **strand invasion** process displaces one strand of the duplex and creates a **displacement (D) loop.** DNA replication within the D loop synthesizes new DNA strands from intact template strands. The sister chromatids are reformed by dissociation and annealing of the nascent strand to the other side

of the break. By accomplishing the removal of DNA in the immediate vicinity of a double-stranded break and the replacement of the excised DNA with a duplex identical to that in the sister chromatid, SDSA carries out error-free repair of double-stranded breaks.

12.7 DNA Double-Strand Breaks Initiate Homologous Recombination

Homologous recombination is the exchange of genetic material between homologous molecules of DNA. All organisms undertake homologous recombination. In bacteria, homologous recombination occurs during events such as conjugation and as a consequence of the repair of double-strand breaks. Archaea undertake homologous recombination under circumstances similar to those in bacteria. In eukaryotes, whereas a limited amount of homologous recombination takes place during mitosis, recombination between homologous chromosomes is essential in prophase I of meiosis. In eukaryotes, homologous recombination during meiosis is initiated by controlled double-strand DNA breaks.

Proper chromosome segregation during meiosis depends on the occurrence of recombination between homologous chromosomes. Without it, homolog synapsis does not take place, and errors are likely to occur during chromosome segregation. This leads to nondisjunction and to gametes with the wrong number of chromosomes (we discuss the consequences of these events in Chapter 13).

Cell biologists and geneticists have interpreted and understood the genetic consequences of recombination for more than a century, but an understanding of homologous recombination and meiotic recombination at the molecular level has been more elusive. Though initially discovered in the early 20th century through the work of Thomas Hunt Morgan and his colleagues, who detected recombinant chromosomes in gametes, homologous recombination could not be studied on a molecular level until the 1950s. In the decade following the determination of the double helical structure of DNA, numerous researchers attempted to construct likely models of homologous recombination. In more than 60 years since work began in earnest to describe the molecular mechanism of homologous recombination, many models have been proposed, and modification of models has been continuous. Molecular biologists continue to adjust models of recombination to match observations, but two salient points are now clear. First, meiotic recombination is a genetically controlled process initiated by enzymes that produce double-stranded DNA breaks; and second, the molecular mechanism of homologous recombination is closely related to the processes that repair double-stranded DNA breaks.

The Holliday Model

The first viable molecular model of meiotic recombination was proposed by Robin Holliday in 1964 and was based on the study of homologous recombination in *E. coli*. Known as the **Holliday model,** it offered a plausible scheme for meiotic recombination by hypothesizing that spontaneously generated single-stranded breaks in one chromatid led to invasion of a homologous molecule. Holliday's scheme for breaking and rejoining DNA strands suggested that some encounters between homologous chromosomes would produce crossovers whereas others would not.

The original Holliday model ultimately proved to be too simplistic and has been superseded by more accurate models of meiotic recombination. The more recent models rely on some of the features of the Holliday model but incorporate new knowledge and steps. Perhaps the most important features distinguishing the current model of meiotic recombination from the original Holliday model are, first, that meiotic recombination is now known to be initiated by *double-stranded DNA breaks* and, second, that the double-stranded breaks initiating meiotic recombination are generated in a programmed manner by the activity of a specialized enzyme.

The Bacterial RecBCD Pathway

Homologous recombination in all organisms shares many features in terms of the mechanical processes involved as well as the homologies of proteins that are active in recombination. The first, and still the most detailed, molecular description of homologous recombination pertained to *E. coli*. This homologous recombination model describes the action of several proteins that are critical to initiating and completing homologous recombination.

Known as the **RecBCD pathway,** the system of homologous recombination in bacteria relies on the occurrence of DNA double-strand breaks to initiate the process. Double-strand DNA breaks attract the protein RecA. Bacterial RecA is a homolog of the eukaryotic and archaeal protein Rad51, which performs a similar function in those organisms. The multiprotein complex known as RecBCD then attaches to the region of a bacterial chromosome with bound RecA, and this complex promotes single-strand invasion and the formation of D loops. The process is highly similar in appearance to the strand invasion and D-loop formation we saw in SDSA. RecBCD activity is followed by binding of RuvAB and RuvC proteins. The Ruv complex completes homologous recombination between the bacterial DNA molecules.

The Double-Stranded Break Model of Meiotic Recombination

The bacterial RecBCD pathway of homologous recombination was the starting point for the study of meiotic recombination in eukaryotes since numerous protein homologies have been identified. The outline of the current model of meiotic recombination was proposed in 1983 by Jack Szostak, Terry Orr-Weaver, Rodney Rothstein, and Franklin Stahl. Their model was the first to predict that the creation of double-stranded breaks controlled by the activity of a specific protein was the foundation of meiotic recombination. The accumulated experimental evidence has confirmed this view, and the research has added major new details to the original proposal by Szostak and his colleagues.

Among these new findings is the determination that the double-strand breaks that precede meiotic recombination are under precise protein control. This is in contrast to a more generalized and diverse process of generating double-strand breaks in bacterial DNA.

The bacterial RecBCD pathway leading to homologous recombination is very closely related to the recombination pathway in archaea and to mitotic and meiotic recombination in eukaryotes. Table 12.7 lists several of the critical gene homologies between bacteria and eukaryotes and archaea. The eukaryotic and archaeal systems appear to have stronger homology than do the bacterial and archaeal systems. In part for this reason, the eukaryotic and archaeal recombination proteins carry the same names.

In the current model, meiotic recombination is initiated by the protein Spo11 ("Spo eleven") that was first

Table 12.7	Recombination Protein Homology	
	Recombination	
Step	**Bacterial Protein**	**Eukaryotic/Archaeal Protein**[a]
DSB introduction	Not specific	Spo11
Homologous DNA pairing and strand invasion	RecA	Rad 51 + Dmc1
Strand invasion	RecBCD	Rad52 and Rad59
Branch migration	RuvAB	Unknown
Holliday junction resolution	RuvC	Rad51 and XRCC

[a] Eukaryotic and archaeal recombination proteins have strong homology and carry the same names.

discovered in yeast and is now known to exist in homologous form in all eukaryotes (Foundation Figure 12.24, ❶). Note that bacteria lack a homolog to Spo11 (see Table 12.7), so while homologous recombination in bacteria is tied to repair of double-strand breaks, the breaks apparently occur at random or through the action of non-specific proteins.

Spo11 is a dimeric protein that generates slightly asymmetric double-strand cuts in one chromatid. The proteins Mrx and Exo1 associate with Spo11, and after Spo11 degrades, Mrx, assisted by additional proteins. Mrx and associated proteins are homologs of RecBCD helicase and nuclease, resects the single strands ❷. Mrx and associated proteins are homologs of RecBCD helicase and nuclease. Two RecA homolog proteins, Rad51 and Dmc1, join at the trimmed region ❸. Rad51 and Dmc1 are RecA homologs. This protein complex helps form a strand-exchange assemblage, facilitating strand invasion and formation of a D loop ❹, ❺.

The invading strand pairs with the complementary strand in the D loop. Outside the D loop, the two strands that appear to cross over one another form a **Holliday junction,** an interim structure proposed in the original Holliday model. Notice that there is also a **heteroduplex region,** containing two complementary strands of DNA that originated in different homologs. Also identified as **heteroduplex DNA,** these regions are a molecular signature of homologous recombination. Because the two strands of the heteroduplex DNA originate in different homologs, there may be mismatched base pairs between them. In other words, if heterozygosity is present in the DNA sequences forming a heteroduplex region, one or more base pairs will be mismatched in the heteroduplex DNA. We discuss the implications of this situation in the following section.

Extension of the invading strand and DNA synthesis within the broken strand are guided by intact template strands ❻, and are assisted by additional proteins, including Rad52 and Rad59, that are RecBCD homologs. ❼. At this point, a second heteroduplex region has formed. The 3′ end of the invading strand next connects with

the 5′ end of a strand segment that was initially part of the invading strand ❽, to form a second Holliday junction. Now the nonsister chromatids of the recombining chromosomes are interconnected to one another by the presence of **double Holliday junctions (DHJs):** The recombining chromosomes contain DHJs and two heteroduplex regions.

Holliday Junction Resolution

The recombinational steps just described take place in prophase I of meiosis, and any connections between homologous chromosomes must be resolved in prophase, long before the homologs attach to spindle fibers in metaphase. Cutting and reconnecting single strands of interconnected homologous chromosomes resolves crossing over. In bacteria, this process is accomplished by the RuvAB complex and RuvC. In eukaryotes, the Rad51c-XRCC3 complex, which is homologous to RuvC and RecAB, accomplishes resolution of Holliday junction connections between homologous chromosomes. Archaea have homologous proteins to accomplish this step of recombination. The best current evidence finds these archaeal proteins to have closer homology to the eukaryotic proteins than to the bacterial proteins.

Two Holliday junction resolution patterns, called same sense resolution and opposite sense resolution (❶ and ❷ in Foundation Figure 12.24), complete crossing over and disengage homologs so they can be separated during anaphase I. Same sense resolution involves either two **north-south (NS) resolution** cuts or two **east-west (EW) resolution** cuts of DNA strands to separate the homologs (see Foundation Figure 12.24). When the connection between homologs is resolved by two NS or EW cuts, the flanking markers (A_1 and B_1 and A_2 and B_2) *do not recombine.* As a consequence, recombination of those genes is not produced, although heteroduplex regions are present. This resolution occurs only rarely. Far more common is resolution in which one Holliday junction region is resolved by a NS cut and the other by an EW cut. The resulting chromosomes are recombinant and carry A_1 and B_2 or A_2 and B_1. These recombinations are detectable among progeny, where they are counted as recombinants between the genes.

12.8 Gene Conversion Is Directed Mismatch Repair in Heteroduplex DNA

Our final topic in this chapter is **gene conversion,** a process of so-called directed DNA sequence change that occurs by base-pair mismatch repair within heteroduplex DNA. These base-pair mismatches can occur when DNA sequence is heterozygous in a heteroduplex region created during meiotic recombination. In gene conversion, the "directed" change is base-pair mismatch repair that switches the nucleotide sequence of one allele to that of another allele that

Material Molecular Model of Meiotic Recombination

Meiotic crossing over and double Holliday junction formation

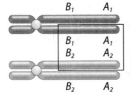

Meiotic recombination diagrammed between these nonsister chromatids of homologous chromosomes

1 Spo11 creates double-strand break in one DNA duplex.

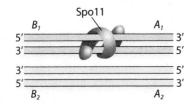

2 Enzymatic digestion 5′ → 3′ by Mrx creates single-stranded segments.

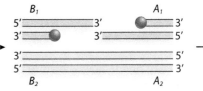

5 Strand invasion creates one D loop and the first heteroduplex region. Rad52, Rad59, and other proteins participate.

6 Strand extension by DNA polymerase displaces D loop DNA, which pairs with complementary single-stranded DNA to form the second heteroduplex region.

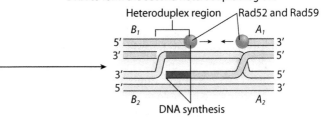

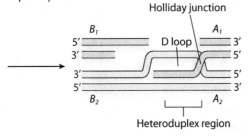

Resolution of Holliday junction crossovers

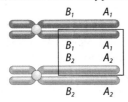

Meiotic recombination diagrammed between these nonsister chromatids of homologous chromosomes

1 Same Sense Resolution

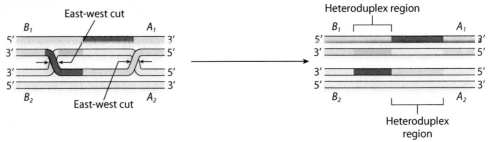

Same sense resolution produces offset heteroduplex regions but no recombination of flanking genes. This form of resolution occurs infrequently.

3 XRCC3 and Rad51c assemble strand-exchange nucleoprotein filaments.

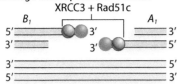

4 The strand-exchange filaments promote strand invasion.

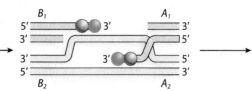

7 Strand extension and ligation fills the single-stranded gap in the strand paired with D loop DNA.

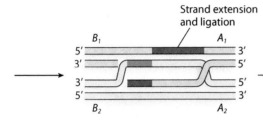

8 Double Holliday junctions form after the nick is sealed; chromatids contain offset heteroduplexes.

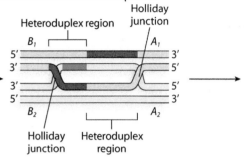

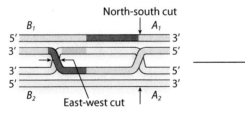

Meiotic recombination diagrammed between these nonsister chromatids of homologous chromosomes

2 Opposite Sense Resolution

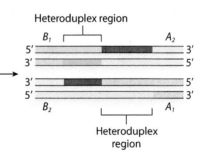

Opposite sense resolution is very common. It generates recombination of flanking genes and creates offset heteroduplex regions.

is already present because the organism is heterozygous in the portion of the genome where heteroduplex DNA forms. In contrast to mutation, which can change one allele into any other allele, gene conversion can only switch one allele to another allele already present in a heterozygous genotype.

Gene conversion is most readily detected in fungi that form an ascus, a sack of haploid spores that are the products of meiotic division. For example, we identified that for fungi with the genotype a^+a, the ratio of these alleles in spores in an eight-cell ascus is expected to be equal (4:4) (see Figure 5.23). Gene conversion changes that ratio by switching one or more alleles from one form to another: either a^+ to a, or a to a^+. The result is an **aberrant ratio** of spores in an eight-cell ascus, commonly 5:3 or 6:2 instead of 4:4. Since gene conversion is strictly limited to conversions from one allele to the alternative form in a heterozygous genotype, it is distinct from mutation, in which an allele can be altered to almost an infinite variety of forms. Similarly, in organisms producing a four-cell ascus, a 2:2 ratio is expected for a heterozygote, and any other ratio is an aberrant ratio.

Figure 12.25 illustrates the formation of heteroduplex DNA for alleles A_1 and A_2 that differ by substitution of one base pair. Allele A_1 carries a C-G base pair at the differing position, and A_2 carries an A-T base pair. Mismatches between G and A, and between C and T, are highlighted in the heteroduplex regions.

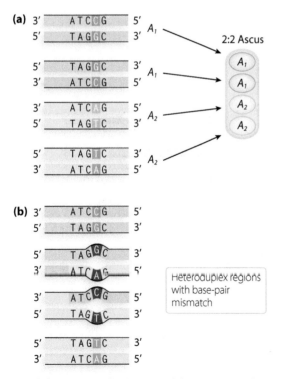

Figure 12.25 Heteroduplex DNA. (a) A segment of allele A_1 contains a C-G base pair, whereas allele A_2 contains an A-T base pair at the same location. Segregation produces a 2:2 ascus. **(b)** Crossover between homologous chromosomes generates heteroduplex DNA containing G-A and C-T base-pair mismatches (in red) between the otherwise complementary strands.

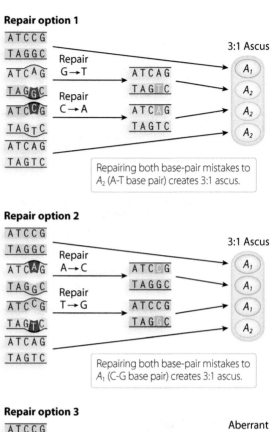

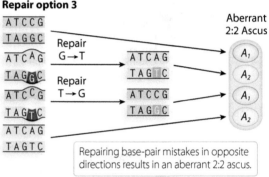

Figure 12.26 Example mismatch repair and gene conversion patterns in a four-celled ascus.

In a four-celled ascus, the repair of base-pair mismatches in heteroduplex DNA results in three aberrant ratios or patterns of spores (**Figure 12.26**). In repair option 1, both mismatches repair by converting the sequence to that of A_2. Conversely, in repair option 2, both mismatches repair to produce A_1. In each case, gene conversion has taken place, and the resulting asci contain an aberrant 3:1 ratio of alleles. In repair option 3, the pattern of mismatch repair produces an ascus with an aberrant 2:2 ratio in which A_1 and A_2 are in alternating order instead of the like alleles being side by side as expected normally.

The pattern of mismatch repair also determines the aberrant ratios in the eight-celled ascus by gene conversion. **Figure 12.27** shows three options for the repair of base-pair mismatches. In option 1, both mismatch repairs favor a single allele (A_1 in this case) and produce an ascus containing an aberrant 6:2 ratio. A similar aberrant

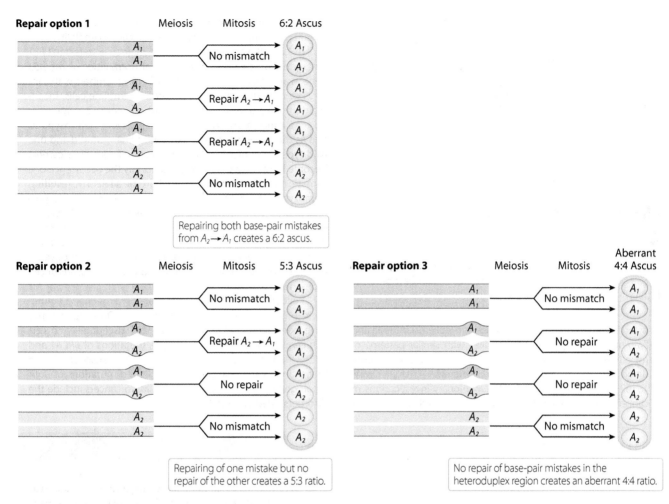

Figure 12.27 **Mismatch repair and gene conversion in an eight-celled ascus.**

6:2 ratio producing an ascus containing 6 A_2 and 2 A_1 gametes occurs if both mismatches are repaired in favor of A_2 rather than A_1. In repair option 2, just one rather than both base-pair mismatches are repaired before the DNA replication cycle, resulting in an ascus containing an aberrant 5:3 ratio. Two different aberrant 5:3 ratios, 5 A_1:3 A_2 and 5 A_2:3 A_1, are possible, depending on the favored allele in the single mismatch repair. In repair option 3, no mismatch repair takes place. The spores are arrayed in a 3:1:1:3 pattern, a distribution called an aberrant 4:4 ratio.

CASE STUDY

Li-Fraumeni Syndrome Is Caused by Inheritance of Mutations of *p53*

Numerous studies of human cancers identify *p53* as the most commonly mutated gene in cancer cells. From the pivotal role *p53* and its protein product play in cells, it is easy to see why cells lacking *p53* function are abnormal. In the absence of functional p53 protein, DNA damage goes undetected and cells progress through G_1 of the cell cycle to S phase with the DNA damage present. Similarly, homozygous inactivation of *p53* interferes with the initiation of apoptosis in cases where cells have high levels of damage. By itself, homozygous mutation of *p53* does not cause cancer. Other mutations must be present to cause the rapid cell proliferation and other abnormalities that characterize cancer. Still, homozygous *p53* mutation can play a pivotal role in the accumulation of additional mutations that lead to cancer development.

In 1969, Frederick Li and Joseph Fraumeni encountered a family in which cancer ravaged each generation (**Figure 12.28**). This family stood out for its pattern of cancer that was consistent with an autosomal dominant mode of transmission and because many of the cancer cases occurred decades earlier than are typical for these types of cancer in the general population (i.e., breast cancers appeared in the 30s in affected family members as opposed to the 60s in members of the general population). Both of these features are hallmarks of cancer-prone families in which an inherited germ-line mutation increases individual susceptibility to cancer. Interestingly, however, unlike most cancer-prone families, in which one or two types of cancers predominate, this family studied by Li and Fraumeni had many types of cancer, including soft tissue sarcomas, breast cancers, brain cancer,

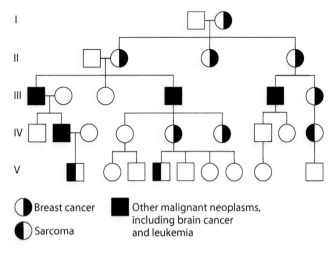

○ Breast cancer ■ Other malignant neoplasms,
including brain cancer
◐ Sarcoma and leukemia

Figure 12.28 Li-Fraumeni syndrome. Inherited mutations of *p53* greatly increase susceptibility to sarcoma, breast cancer, brain cancer, leukemia, and other cancers.

osteosarcoma, adrenocortical cancer, and leukemia. After Li and Fraumeni's description, other families with similar patterns of mixed cancers were identified. This inherited cancer-prone condition was designated Li-Fraumeni syndrome 1 (LFS1; OMIM 151623). Study of LFS1 sparked revolutionary investigations of cancer biology and genetics that identified several genes that are frequently mutated in cancer cells, as well as investigations of the inheritance of mutations that increase cancer susceptibility.

In 1997, the first evidence of the molecular defect in LFS1 emerged with the identification of abnormalities of the *p53* gene in approximately 70% of LFS1 family members with cancer. The mutations were discovered in germ-line cells, meaning that one parent passed a mutant copy of *p53* in sperm or egg. At conception, the fertilized eggs were heterozygous, and as they developed, all cells carried one mutated and one wild-type copy of *p53*. Individual cells of mutation carriers become homozygous for *p53* mutation by the occurrence of a somatic mutation that alters the wild-type allele. The resulting homozygous mutant cells do not produce normal p53 protein, and they are unable to properly regulate the cell cycle or entry into apoptosis. Cancers develop in individuals without functioning *p53* through the accumulation of somatic mutations of other genes. The specific types of cancer that develop depend on which genes are mutated and on the tissues or cell types in which the mutations occur.

Following identification of the role of germ-line *p53* mutations in LFS1, inherited mutations of other DNA repair genes have been identified as increasing the susceptibility to certain cancers in families. For example, mutations of *BRCA1* and *BRCA2* that interact with *p53* can increase susceptibility to breast and ovarian cancer. Other inherited mutations of DNA repair genes that increase susceptibility to cancers include the disorders listed in Table 12.6.

SUMMARY ❨MasteringGenetics™❩ For activities, animations, and review quizzes, go to the Study Area.

12.1 Mutations Are Rare and Occur at Random

▌ Mutations occur at random in genomes.

▌ Mutations result from damage done to DNA.

▌ Mutation frequencies are low in all organisms.

▌ Mutational hotspots are genes or regions where mutations occur much more often than average.

12.2 Gene Mutations Modify DNA Sequence

▌ Base-pair substitution mutations can be either transitions or transversions.

▌ Base-pair substitutions can change one amino acid of the polypeptide, can create a new stop codon, or can leave the polypeptide unchanged.

▌ Frameshift mutations result from the insertion or deletion of one or more base pairs that shift the mRNA reading frame during translation.

▌ Regulatory mutations alter gene transcription or pre-mRNA splicing.

▌ Forward mutation alters a wild-type allele to mutant form, and reversion changes a mutant back to wild-type or near wild-type form.

12.3 Gene Mutations May Arise from Spontaneous Events

▌ DNA replication errors can substitute base pairs, and strand slippage can modify the number of repeats of a DNA sequence.

▌ Tautomeric shifts of nucleotide base structure can induce spontaneous base-pair substitution mutations.

▌ Different kinds of spontaneous changes in nucleotide structure can result in mutation of DNA sequence by base-pair mismatching.

12.4 Mutations May Be Induced by Chemicals or Ionizing Radiation

▌ Mutagenic chemicals interact in characteristic reactions with DNA nucleotides and generate specific mutations.

▌ Chemical compounds may create mutations by acting as nucleotide base analogs, adding or removing side groups from nucleotides, or intercalating into DNA.

▌ Energy in the ultraviolet range and higher (shorter in wavelength) is mutagenic. Ultraviolet radiation induces the formation of photoproducts that lead to base-pair substitution mutations.

▌ The Ames test identifies mutagenic chemical compounds by testing for increased reversion rates in auxotrophic bacteria exposed to a test compound in the presence of detoxifying enzymes from the eukaryotic liver.

12.5 Repair Systems Correct Some DNA Damage

▌ Direct repair of DNA lesions removes damaged nucleotides and prevents mutation.

▌ Mismatched DNA nucleotides, photoproducts induced by UV radiation, and modified nucleotide side chains are removed by direct repair.

▌ Nucleotide excision repair and UV repair remove segments of DNA single strands containing damaged nucleotides and direct new synthesis to fill the resulting single-stranded gap.

▌ Genetically controlled systems monitor the genome and regulate DNA repair.

12.6 Proteins Control Translesion DNA Synthesis and the Repair of Double-Strand Breaks

▌ SOS repair, controlled by the RecA protein, is a specialized process activated during replication in bacteria in response to widespread DNA damage.

▌ Translesion DNA synthesis uses bypass polymerases to complete replication when damage is present.

▌ Nonhomologous end joining repairs double-strand DNA breaks occurring before DNA replication.

▌ Synthesis-dependent strand annealing repairs double-strand breaks occurring after the completion of replication.

12.7 DNA Double-Strand Breaks Initiate Homologous Recombination

▌ Homologous recombination is controlled by the RecBCD pathway in bacteria. In eukaryotes, meiotic recombination is initiated through the activity of Spo11 that regulates the production of double-strand breaks.

▌ In meiotic recombination, strand invasion and new DNA synthesis form heteroduplex DNA in both homologous chromosomes.

▌ Heteroduplex DNA contains base-pair mismatches if DNA sequences are heterozygous.

▌ DNA strands forming double Holliday junctions are cut and rejoined to different homologs before their separation in meiosis.

▌ Resolution of double Holliday junctions generates heteroduplex DNA and can produce recombinant or nonrecombinant chromosomes.

12.8 Gene Conversion Is Directed Mismatch Repair in Heteroduplex DNA

▌ Gene conversion occurs by the repair of base-pair mismatches in heteroduplex DNA.

▌ Gene conversion in a four-celled or eight-celled ascus generates aberrant ratios of spores that differ from the expected 2:2 or 4:4 ratios.

KEYWORDS

6-4 photoproduct *(p. 406)*
aberrant ratio *(p. 422)*
Ames test *(p. 408)*
apurinic (AP) site *(p. 402)*
base-pair substitution mutation *(p. 394)*
bulky adduct *(p. 404)*
bypass polymerase (translesion DNA polymerase) *(p. 416)*
cryptic splice site *(p. 397)*
deamination *(p. 402)*
depurination *(p. 402)*
displacement loop (D loop) *(p. 417)*
DNA intercalating agents *(p. 406)*
double Holliday junction (DHJ) *(p. 419)*
double-strand break repair *(p. 416)*
east-west (EW) resolution *(p. 419)*
forward mutation (mutation) *(p. 397)*
frameshift mutation *(p. 395)*
gene conversion *(p. 419)*
heteroduplex DNA (heteroduplex region) *(p. 419)*

Holliday junction *(p. 419)*
Holliday model *(p. 418)*
homologous recombination *(p. 417)*
hotspot of mutation *(p. 393)*
induced mutation *(p. 403)*
intragenic reversion *(p. 397)*
mismatch repair *(p. 411)*
missense mutation *(p. 394)*
mutagen *(p. 403)*
mutation rate *(p. 392)*
nonhomologous end joining (NHEJ) *(p. 416)*
nonsense mutation *(p. 394)*
north-south (NS) resolution *(p. 419)*
nucleotide base analog *(p. 404)*
nucleotide excision repair *(p. 411)*
nucleotide base excision repair *(p. 411)*
photoproduct *(p. 406)*
photoreactive repair *(p. 412)*
point mutation *(p. 394)*

promoter mutation *(p. 396)*
pyrimidine dimer (thymine dimer) *(p. 406)*
RecBCD pathway *(p. 418)*
regulatory mutation *(p. 396)*
reversion (reverse mutation) *(p. 397)*
second-site reversion *(p. 397)*
silent mutation *(p. 394)*
splicing mutation *(p. 397)*
spontaneous mutation *(p. 397)*
strand invasion *(p. 417)*
strand slippage *(p. 398)*
suppressor mutation *(p. 397)*
synthesis-dependent strand annealing (SDSA) *(p. 417)*
transition mutation *(p. 394)*
translesion DNA synthesis *(p. 407)*
transversion mutation *(p. 394)*
trinucleotide repeat disorder *(p. 398)*
true reversion *(p. 397)*
ultraviolet (UV) repair *(p. 413)*

PROBLEMS   (MasteringGenetics™) Visit for instructor-assigned tutorials and problems.

Chapter Concepts

1. Identify two general ways chemical mutagens can alter DNA. Give examples of these two mechanisms.

2. Nitrous acid and 5-BrdU alter DNA by different mechanisms. Identify each mechanism and describe how each compound creates mutation.

For answers to selected even-numbered problems, see Appendix: Answers.

3. Using the adenine-thymine base pair in this DNA sequence

    ...GCTC...

    ...CGAG...

   a. Give the sequence after a transition mutation.
   b. Give the sequence after a transversion mutation.

4. The partial amino acid sequence of a wild-type protein is

   ...Arg–Met–Tyr–Thr–Leu–Cys–Ser...

   The same portion of the protein from a mutant has the sequence

   ...Arg–Met–Leu–Tyr–Ala–Leu–Phe...

   a. Identify the type of mutation.
   b. Give the sequence of the wild-type DNA template strand. Use $^A/_G$ if the nucleotide could be either purine, $^T/_C$ if it could be either pyrimidine, N if any nucleotide could occur at a site, or the alternative nucleotides if a purine and a pyrimidine are possible.

5. Thymine is usually in its normal, common form. Diagram the base pair that would result if a tautomeric shift occurs just before DNA replication.

6. Ultraviolet (UV) radiation is mutagenic.

   a. What kind of DNA lesion does UV energy cause?
   b. How do UV-induced DNA lesions lead to mutation?
   c. Identify and describe two DNA repair mechanisms that remove UV-induced DNA lesions.

7. Researchers interested in studying mutation and mutation repair often induce mutations with various agents. What kinds of gene mutations are induced by

   a. Chemical mutagens? Give two examples.
   b. Radiation energy? Give two examples.

8. The effect of base-pair substitution mutations on protein function varies widely from no detectable effect to the complete loss of protein function (null allele). Why do the functional consequences of base-pair substitution vary so widely?

9. The two DNA and polypeptide sequences shown are for alleles at a hypothetical locus that produce different polypeptides, both five amino acids long. In each case, the lower DNA strand is the template strand:

   allele A_1:   5'...ATGCATGTAAGTGCATGA...3'

   3'...TACGTACATTCACGTACT...5'

   A_1 polypeptide   N–Met–His–Val–Ser–Ala–C

   allele A_2:   5'...ATGCAAGTAAGTGCATGA...3'

   3'...TACGTTCATTCACGTACT...5'

   A_2 polypeptide   N–Met–Gln–Val–Ser–Ala–C

   Based on DNA and polypeptide sequences alone, is there any way to determine which allele is dominant and which is recessive? Why or why not?

10. In numerous population studies of spontaneous mutation, two observations are made consistently: (1) most mutations are recessive, and (2) forward mutation is more frequent than reversion. What do you think are the likely explanations for these two observations?

11. Two different mutations are identified in a haploid strain of yeast. The first prevents the synthesis of adenine by a nonsense mutation of the *ade-1* gene. In this mutation, a base-pair substitution changes a tryptophan codon (UGG) to a stop codon (UGA). The second affects one of several duplicate tRNA genes. This base-pair substitution mutation changes the anticodon sequence of a tRNA^{Trp} from 3'-ACC-5' to 3'-ACU-5'.

   a. Do you consider the first mutation to be a forward mutation or a reversion? Why?
   b. Do you consider the second mutation to be a forward mutation or a reversion? Why?
   c. Assuming there are no other mutations in the genome, will this double-mutant yeast strain be able to grow on minimal medium? If growth will occur, characterize the nature of growth relative to wild type.

12. Many human genes are known to have homologs in the mouse genome. One approach to investigating human hereditary disease is to produce mutations of the mouse homologs of human genes by methods that can precisely target specific nucleotides for mutation.

   a. Numerous studies of mutations of the mouse homologs of human genes have yielded valuable information about how gene mutations influence the human disease process. In general terms, describe how and why creating mutations of the mouse homologs can give information about human hereditary disease processes.
   b. Despite the homologies that exist between human and mouse genes, some attempts to study human hereditary disease processes by inducing mutations in mouse genes indicate there is little to be learned about human disease in this way. In general terms, describe how and why the study of mouse gene mutations might fail to produce useful information about human disease processes.

13. Answer the following questions concerning the accuracy of DNA polymerase during replication.

   a. What general mechanism do DNA polymerases use to check the accuracy of DNA replication and identify errors during replication?
   b. If a DNA replication error is detected by DNA polymerase, how is it corrected?
   c. If a replication error escapes detection and correction, what kind of abnormality is most likely to exist at the site of replication error?
   d. Identify two mechanisms that can correct the kind of abnormality resulting from the circumstances identified in part (c).
   e. If the kind of abnormality identified in part (c) is not corrected before the next DNA replication cycle, what kind of mutation occurs?
   f. DNA mismatch repair can accurately distinguish between the template strand and the newly replicated strand of a DNA duplex. What characteristic of DNA strands is used to make this distinction?

14. Apert syndrome is a human autosomal dominant condition that affects development of the head, hands, and feet. In a survey of 322,182 consecutive births in Ireland, two new cases of Apert syndrome were identified. What is the mutation rate of this gene per gamete?

15. Polydactyly is a human autosomal dominant condition that produces extra fingers and toes. Studies of hundreds of families with polydactyly have determined that penetrance for the dominant allele is 70%. Hospital-based surveys of live births

find that 1 in 40,000 infants has a new case of polydactyly. Use this information to estimate the mutation rate of the gene.

16. The table shown lists the approximate new mutation rates for three autosomal dominant human diseases.

Trait	Mutations per 10^6 Gametes
Retinoblastoma (tumor of the retina)	20
Achondroplasia (statural dwarfism)	80
Neurofibromatosis (tumor of nervous tissue)	220

a. In a series of 50,000 consecutive live births recorded in a large metropolitan area, how many new cases of each disease are expected?
b. Identify two possible molecular reasons why the rate of new mutations causing neurofibromatosis is more than 10 times greater than the mutation rate causing retinoblastoma.

17. A 1-mL sample of the bacterium *E. coli* is exposed to ultraviolet light. The sample is used to inoculate a 500-mL flask of complete medium that allows growth of all bacterial cells. The 500-mL culture is grown on the benchtop, and two equal-size samples are removed and plated on identical complete-medium growth plates. Plate 1 is immediately wrapped in a dark cloth, but plate 2 is not covered. Both plates are left at room temperature for 36 hours and then examined. Plate 2 is seen to contain many more growing colonies than plate 1. Thinking about DNA repair processes, how do you explain this observation?

18. A strain of *E. coli* is identified as having a null mutation of the *RecA* gene. What biological property do you expect to be absent in the mutant strain? What is the molecular basis for the missing property?

19. Define *gene conversion* and contrast it with *gene mutation*.

20. Some homologous recombination events produce gene conversion. Is homologous recombination a mutational event? Explain why or why not.

21. What is heteroduplex DNA, and why does it form? What is the relationship between heteroduplex DNA and gene conversion?

22. Is heteroduplex DNA always an outcome of homologous recombination? Why or why not?

23. A strain of yeast producing a four-celled ascus is heterozygous for the wild-type allele *Ala-B* and the mutant allele *ala-b*. The wild-type allele carries an A - T base pair and the mutant allele a G - C base pair at a site that is part of a heteroduplex region. Identify the events that produce the following kinds of asci.
a. 3 *Ala-B*: 1 *ala-b*
b. 3 *ala-b*: 1 *Ala-B*
c. 2 *ala-b*: 2 *Ala-B*

24. Gene conversion is relatively easy to detect in four-cell and eight-cell asci of fungi, where ratios such as 3*A*:1*a* or 5*a*:3*A* indicate that gene conversion has taken place. Why is gene conversion much more difficult to detect in multicellular eukaryotes?

25. If homologous recombination did not occur, what consequences would result?

26. In this chapter, three features of genes or of DNA sequence that contribute to the occurrence of mutational hotspots were described. Identify those three features and briefly describe why they are associated with mutational hotspots.

27. Briefly compare the production of DNA double-strand breaks in eukaryotes versus in bacteria.

28. During mismatch repair, why is it necessary to distinguish between the template strand and the newly made daughter strand? Describe how this is accomplished.

Application and Integration

29. Following the spill of a mixture of chemicals into a small pond, bacteria from the pond are tested and show an unusually high rate of mutation. A number of mutant cultures are grown from mutant colonies and treated with known mutagens to study the rate of reversion. Most of the mutant cultures show a significantly higher reversion rate when exposed to base analogs such as proflavin and 2-aminopurine. What does this suggest about the nature of the chemicals in the spill?

30. A geneticist searching for mutations uses the restriction endonucleases *Sma*I and *Pvu*II to search for mutations that eliminate restriction sites. *Sma*I will not cleave DNA with CpG methylation. It cleaves DNA at the restriction digestion sequence

$$\downarrow$$
5'-CCC GGG-3'
3'-GGG CCC-5'
$$\uparrow$$

For answers to selected even-numbered problems, see Appendix: Answers.

*Pvu*II is not sensitive to CpG methylation. It cleaves DNA at the restriction sequence

$$\downarrow$$
5'-CAG CTG-3'
3'-GTC GAC-5'
$$\uparrow$$

a. What common feature do *Sma*I and *Pvu*II share that would be useful to a researcher searching for mutations that disrupt restriction digestion?
b. What process is the researcher intending to detect with the use of these restriction enzymes?

31. A wild-type culture of haploid yeast is exposed to ethyl methanesulfonate (EMS). Yeast cells are plated on a complete medium, and 6 colonies (colonies numbered 1 to 6) are transferred to a new complete medium plate for further study. Four replica plates are made from the complete medium plate to plates containing minimal medium or

minimal medium plus one amino acid (replica plates numbered 1 to 4) with the following results:

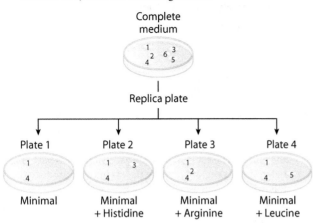

a. Identify the colonies that are prototrophic (wild type). What growth information leads to your answer?
b. Identify the colonies that are auxotrophic (mutant). What growth information leads to your answer?
c. Identify any colonies that are *his⁻*, *arg⁻*, *leu⁻*.
d. For colonies 1, 3, and 5, write "+" for the wild-type synthesis and "−" for the mutant synthesis of histidine and leucine.
e. Are there any colonies for which genotype information cannot be determined? If so, which colony or colonies?

32. A fragment of a wild-type polypeptide is sequenced for seven amino acids. The same polypeptide region is sequenced in four mutants.

Wild-type polypeptide	N...Thr–His–Ser–Gly–Leu–Lys–Ala...C
Mutant 1	N...Thr–His–Ser–Val–Leu–Lys–Ala...C
Mutant 2	N...Thr–His–Ser–C
Mutant 3	N...Thr–Thr–Leu–Asp–C
Mutant 4	N...Thr–Gln–Leu–Trp–Ile–Glu–Gly...C

a. Use the available information to characterize each mutant.
b. Determine the wild-type mRNA sequence.
c. Identify the mutation that produces each mutant polypeptide.

33. Experiments by Charles Yanofsky in the 1950s and 1960s helped characterize the nature of tryptophan synthesis in *E. coli*. In one of Yanofsky's experiments, he identified glycine (Gly) as the wild-type amino acid in position 211 of tryptophan synthetase, the product of the *trpA* gene. He identified two independent missense mutants with defective tryptophan synthetase at these positions that resulted from base-pair substitutions. One mutant encoded arginine (Arg) and another encoded glutamic acid (Glu). At position 235, wild-type tryptophan synthetase contains serine (Ser), but a base-pair substitution mutant encodes leucine (Leu). At position 243, the wild-type polypeptide contains glutamine, and a base-pair substitution mutant encodes a stop codon. Identify the most likely wild-type codons for positions 211, 235, and 243. Justify your answer in each case.

34. Common baker's yeast (*Saccharomyces cerevisiae*) is normally grown at 37°C, but it will grow actively at temperatures down to approximately 20°C. A haploid culture of wild-type yeast is mutagenized with EMS. Cells from the mutagenized culture are spread on a complete-medium plate and grown at 25°C. Six colonies (1 to 6) are selected from the original complete-medium plate and transferred to two fresh complete-medium plates. The new complete plates (shown below) are grown at 25°C and 37°C. Four replica plates are made onto minimal medium or minimal plus adenine from the 25°C complete-medium plate. The new plates are grown at either 25°C or 37°C, as indicated below.

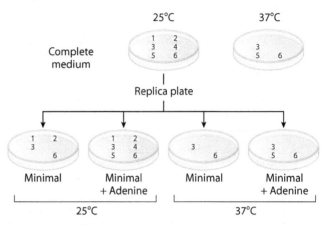

a. Which colonies are prototrophic and which are auxotrophic? What growth information is used to make these determinations?
b. Classify the nature of the mutations in colonies 1, 2, and 5.
c. What can you say about colony 4?

35. The two gels illustrated below contain dideoxynucleotide DNA-sequencing (see Section 7.5) information for a segment of wild-type and mutant DNA corresponding to the N-terminal end of the protein. The start codon and the next five codons are sequenced.

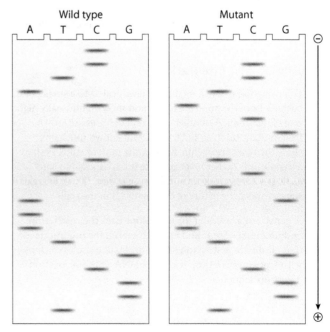

a. Write the DNA sequence of both alleles, including strand polarity.
b. Identify the template and nontemplate strands of DNA.

c. Write out the mRNA sequences encoded by each template strand, and underline the start codons.

d. Determine the amino acid sequences translated from these mRNAs.

e. What is the cause of the mutation?

36. Alkaptonuria is a human autosomal recessive disorder caused by mutation of the *HAO* gene that encodes the enzyme homogentisic acid oxidase. Restriction mapping of the *HAO* gene region reveals four *Bam*HI restriction sites (B1 to B4) in the wild-type allele and three *Bam*HI restriction sites in the mutant allele. *Bam*HI utilizes the restriction sequence 5'-GGATCC-3'. The *Bam*HI restriction sequence identified as B3 is altered to 5'-GGAACC-3' in the mutant allele. The mutation results in a Ser-to-Thr missense mutation. Restriction maps of the two alleles are shown below, and the binding sites of two molecular probes (probe A and probe B) are identified.

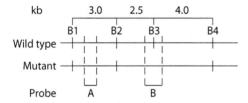

DNA samples taken from a mother (M), father (F), and two children (C1 and C2) are analyzed by Southern blotting of *Bam*HI-digested DNA. The resulting autoradiograph is illustrated below.

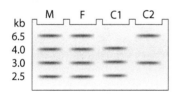

a. Using *A* to represent the wild-type allele and *a* for the mutant allele, identify the genotype of each family member. Identify any family member who is alkaptonuric.

b. In a separate figure, draw the autoradiograph patterns for all the genotypes that could be found in children of this couple.

c. Explain how the DNA sequence change results in a Ser-to-Thr missense mutation.

37. In an experiment employing the methods of the Ames test, two *his⁻* strains of *Salmonella* are used. Strain A contains a base substitution mutation, and Strain B contains a frameshift mutation. Four plates are prepared to test the mutagenicity of the compound ethyl methanesulfonate (EMS). Plate 1 is a control plate with Strain A and S9 extract but no EMS. Plate 2 is also a control plate and contains Strain B and S9 extract but no EMS. Plate 3 contains Strain A along with S9 extract and EMS, and Plate 4 contains Strain B, S9 extract, and EMS.

a. Characterize the expected distribution of colony growth on the four plates. Defend your growth prediction for each plate.

b. What event is being detected by growth of a colony on any of the four plates?

c. Why is the S9 extract added to each of the plates?

d. Suppose the compound being tested was proflavin instead of EMS. Would this change the Ames test results? Explain why or why not.

38. Using your knowledge of DNA repair pathways, choose the pathway that would be used to repair the following types of DNA damage. Explain your reasoning.

a. A change in DNA sequence caused by a mistake made by DNA polymerase during replication

b. Heavily damaged bacterial DNA

c. A thymine dimer induced as a result of UV exposure

d. A double-strand break that occurs just after replication in an actively dividing cell

e. A double-stranded break that occurs during G_1 and prevents completion of DNA replication

f. A cytosine that has been deaminated to uracil

39. Ataxia telangiectasia (OMIM 208900) is a human inherited disorder characterized by poor coordination (ataxia), red marks on the face (telangiectasia), increased sensitivity to X-rays and other radiation, and an increased susceptibility to cancer. Recent studies have shown that this disorder occurs as a result of mutation of the *ATM* gene. Propose a mechanism for how a mutation in the *ATM* gene leads to the characteristics associated with the disorder. Be sure to relate the symptoms of this disorder to functions of the ATM protein. Further, explain why DNA repair mechanisms cannot correct this problem.

40. Two haploid strains of fungus are fused to form a diploid that produces eight-celled asci. Fungus strain A has the genotype + *ade1 his2*, and strain B is *a* ++. The three genes are linked and occur in the order given.

a. The alleles at the *A* gene locus are determined in an ascus, and the order is *aaaa++++*. Write the genotype for all three genes that you expect to find most commonly.

b. One ascus from the diploid is of the following type:

+ *ade1 his2*
+ *ade1 his2*
+ *ade1 his2*
+ *ade1 his2*
a ade1 +
a + +
a + +
a + +

Explain the events that produced this ascus.

c. One ascus from the diploid is of the following type:

a + +
a + +
a + *his2*
a + *his2*
+ *ade1 his2*
+ *ade1 his2*
+ *ade1 his2*
+ *ade1 his2*

Explain the events that produced this ascus.

13

Chromosome Aberrations and Transposition

CHAPTER OUTLINE

13.1 Nondisjunction Leads to Changes in Chromosome Number

13.2 Changes in Euploidy Result in Various Kinds of Polyploidy

13.3 Chromosome Breakage Causes Mutation by Loss, Gain, and Rearrangement of Chromosomes

13.4 Chromosome Breakage Leads to Inversion and Translocation of Chromosomes

13.5 Transposable Genetic Elements Move throughout the Genome

13.6 Transposition Modifies Bacterial Genomes

13.7 Transposition Modifies Eukaryotic Genomes

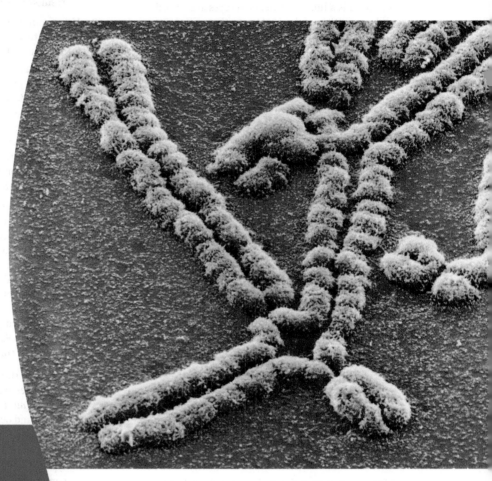

ESSENTIAL IDEAS

- Nondisjunction causes changes in the number of chromosomes and may result in gametes containing the wrong chromosome number.

- Changes in the number of sets of chromosomes alter phenotypes and can confer evolutionary advantages.

- Chromosome breakage can change chromosome structure and may lead to loss or duplication of genes.

- Chromosome breakage can lead to chromosome inversions and translocations.

- Transposable genetic elements move throughout the genome and modify genes, chromosomes, and genomes.

- Bacterial transposable genetic elements facilitate DNA transfer.

- Transposition is a source of mutation and expansion of eukaryotic genomes.

Chromosome translocations are mutations that rearrange chromosome structure. This electronmicrograph shows two pairs of homologous chromosomes that have exchanged segments and must form a tetravalent structure involving the four chromosomes in order to synapse their homologous regions during prophase I.

Something interesting is happening to the mice on Madeira, a tiny island off the western coast of Portugal: They are in the process of differentiating into two species! Madeira, about 20 miles long and 8 miles wide, has steep volcanic mountains running down the middle that form a barrier to easy mouse migration. The common house mouse (*Mus musculus*) was introduced to Madeira by sailors in the 1400s. Today, Madeira has two distinct populations of mice, one on either side of the central mountain range.

In addition to the mountain range separating these two populations, each has also undergone multiple chromosome fusions that have reduced their diploid number. The usual chromosome number for *Mus musculus* is 20 pairs ($2n = 40$). On Madeira, however, one population has $2n = 22$, and the other has $2n = 24$. Because each population has a different chromosome number, interpopulation hybrids are sterile. Such hybrids carry 23 chromosomes (11 from one parent and 12 from the other) and therefore cannot form viable gametes. This is an example of reproductive isolation that can lead to speciation based on differences in chromosome structure and chromosome number.

Variation and evolution at the chromosome level are genomic in scope—that is, they potentially alter the content of the genome, changing interactions between homologous chromosomes in meiosis and limiting the possibility of reproduction between organisms with chromosomal differences. This chapter addresses two distinct categories of chromosome change. The first consists of alterations of chromosome number and chromosome structure known collectively as **chromosome aberrations.** The second category of chromosome change is chromosome alteration by *transposition*, the movement of DNA elements within the genomes of organisms. Chromosome aberrations and transposition are examples of mutation at the chromosome level. In addition, transposition is a biological source of mutation as well as a source of additional DNA sequence that can increase the size of genomes. Both chromosome aberrations and transposition contribute to evolution and speciation by reorganizing and reshaping the content of genomes.

13.1 Nondisjunction Leads to Changes in Chromosome Number

In Section 3.2, we discussed the connection between Mendel's two laws of heredity and the disjunction of homologous chromosomes and sister chromatids during meiosis. In the discussion that follows, we focus on *non-disjunction* (mentioned briefly in Section 3.3) as a process of failed chromosome and sister chromatid disjunction that can result in abnormalities of chromosome number.

The changes in chromosome number we describe in the following paragraphs exert their effects primarily by adding or removing one or more chromosomes from the normal complement in a nucleus. Such changes are mutations that add or remove large numbers of genes. In animal species, but less so in plant species, aneuploidy almost always alters the phenotype, and can have an effect on the development and reduce fertility and viability of the aneuploid organism.

Euploidy and Aneuploidy

The number of chromosomes contained in a nucleus and the relative size and shape of each chromosome are species-specific characteristics, but neither parameter is directly associated with the complexity of the organism (**Table 13.1**). Chromosome number varies widely among species, though closely related species tend to have similar numbers.

With a few unusual exceptions, the number of chromosomes is the same for males and females of a species, and the number of chromosomes in nuclei of normal cells is a multiple of the haploid number (n), the number in a single set of chromosomes. Regardless of whether the total chromosome number is $2n$ (diploid), $3n$ (triploid), or a higher multiple of n, it is described as a **euploid** number of chromosomes if it is a whole-number multiple of the haploid number. If cells contain a number of chromosomes that is not euploid, the chromosome number is **aneuploid.** Aneuploidy occurs when one or more chromosomes are lost or gained relative to the normal euploid number. Chromosome nondisjunction is a principal cause of aneuploidy.

Chromosome Nondisjunction

The term *chromosome nondisjunction*, or simply *nondisjunction*, applies to the failure of homologous chromosomes or sister chromatids to separate as they normally do during

Table 13.1	Chromosome Number in Selected Animal Species
Species	**Diploid Chromosome Number ($2n$)**
Carp (*Cyprinus carpio*)	104
Cat (*Felis catus*)	38
Chicken (*Gallus domesticus*)	78
Chimpanzee (*Pan troglodytes*)	48
Cow (*Bos taurus*)	60
Dog (*Canis familiarus*)	78
Frog (*Rana pipiens*)	26
Fruit fly (*Drosophila melanogaster*)	8
Horse (*Equus caballus*)	64
Human (*Homo sapiens*)	46
Mouse (*Mus musculus*)	40
Rat (*Rattus norvegicus*)	42
Rhesus monkey (*Macaca mulatta*)	42

cell division. Nondisjunction can occur in somatic cells or in germ-line cells, with the result that daughter cells of the division will have the wrong number of chromosomes. If a single pair of homologous chromosomes fails to properly disjoin in a somatic cell during mitotic cell division, one of the resulting daughter cells carries an extra chromosome ($2n + 1$), and the other is missing a chromosome ($2n - 1$).

In animals, mitotic cells that contain the wrong number of chromosomes may suffer reduced viability in comparison to cells that have a normal, diploid number of chromosomes. The poor survival of these cells usually limits their number in organisms, although cells with abnormal numbers of chromosomes are common in cancer, where other genetic changes play a major role in cell survival and proliferation.

In contrast to the limited circumstances under which changes to chromosome number may be maintained in animal cells, plants apparently have substantially more tolerance for changes in chromosome number, and it is not unusual to find plant strains with more than two copies of each chromosome. We describe this situation in more detail in a later section.

Nondisjunction in germ-line cells produces aneuploid gametes—reproductive cells that have one or more extra or missing chromosomes—which can lead to the production of aneuploid fertilized eggs. Meiotic nondisjunction can occur in either meiosis I or II and most often affects just a single homologous pair or a single pair of sister chromatids. Meiosis I nondisjunction is the failure of homologous chromosomes to separate. It results in both homologs moving to a single pole. One secondary gametocyte contains both chromosomes, and the other contains neither chromosome (**Figure 13.1**). These gametocytes contain aneuploid chromosome numbers of $n + 1$ and $n - 1$ (assuming only one chromosome pair is affected). Meiosis II usually proceeds normally even when

meiosis I is aberrant, and its completion sends the sister chromatids to different gametes. The four resulting gametes each contain an aneuploid number of chromosomes. Union of an aneuploid gamete with a normal haploid gamete (shown in the figure) results in a fertilized egg with an aneuploid number of chromosomes that will be either **trisomic** ($2n + 1$), having three of one of the chromosomes rather than a homologous pair, or **monosomic** ($2n - 1$), having just a single copy of one of the chromosomes rather than a homologous pair.

If nondisjunction occurs in meiosis II, it typically follows a normal meiosis I. As a result, both secondary gametocytes contain the haploid number of chromosomes (**Figure 13.2**). Since these are separate cells, they independently divide during meiosis II; thus, if nondisjunction occurs, only one of the secondary gametocytes will be affected. Among the four resulting gametes, two are normal because normal disjunction took place during each meiotic division. The other two gametes are aneuploid: one contains $n + 1$ chromosomes and the other $n - 1$ chromosomes. Trisomic or monosomic fertilized eggs are produced when one of these aneuploid gametes unites with a normal gamete at fertilization.

Gene Dosage Alteration

In 1913, at about the same time Calvin Bridges was demonstrating the chromosome theory of heredity by examining nondisjunction in fruit flies (see Section 3.3), Albert Francis Blakeslee and John Belling reported the phenotypic consequences of aneuploidy in the diploid ($2n = 24$) jimson weed (*Datura stramonium*), in which 12 chromosome pairs are identified as A to L. Blakeslee and Belling identified 12 phenotypically distinct lines of trisomic *Datura*, one for each of the chromosome pairs (**Figure 13.3**).

Figure 13.1 Meiosis I nondisjunction. Homologous chromosomes fail to disjoin in meiosis I, and all resulting gametes are aneuploid. Fertilization by a normal haploid gamete produces fertilized eggs that are trisomic ($2n + 1$) or monosomic ($2n - 1$).

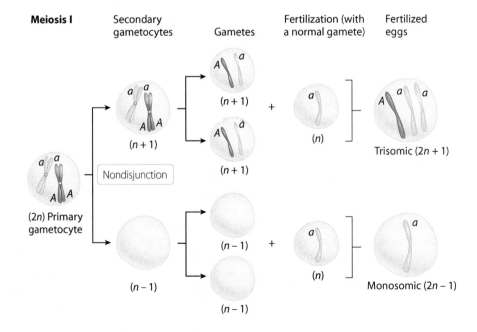

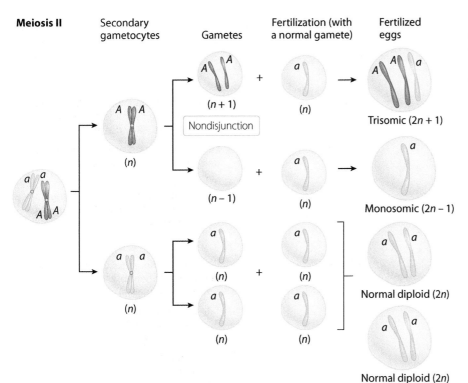

Figure 13.2   Meiosis II nondisjunction. Sister chromatid disjunction fails in meiosis II. Normal fertilization of the resulting gametes generates trisomy, monosomy, or normal diploidy at fertilization.

This result suggests that chromosome number is a factor in phenotype. In the years that followed Blakeslee and Belling's report, other studies documented that aneuploidy causes severe phenotypic consequences in nearly all animal species and that it affects the phenotype of many plant species. The abnormalities associated with aneuploidy result from changes in **gene dosage,** the number of copies of a gene in the genome. Aneuploidy changes the dosage of *all the genes* on the affected chromosome. In a diploid organism where two copies of a gene, on a homologous pair of chromosomes, generate 100% of gene dosage, a monosomic mutant has just one gene copy and just 50% of normal gene dosage for each gene on the chromosome. In contrast, a trisomic mutant has three copies and 150% of normal gene dosage for each of the genes on the chromosome.

Changes in gene dosage lead to an imbalance of gene products from the affected chromosome relative to unaffected chromosomes, and this imbalance is at the heart of alterations of normal development and the production of abnormal phenotypes. Most animals are highly sensitive to changes in gene dosage, and their developmental biology, especially within the nervous system, does not proceed normally in the presence of gene dosage imbalance. In contrast to the potential for developmental disruptions due to aneuploidy in animals, gene dosage changes are more easily tolerated in many species of plants, owing in part to their distinct developmental programs.

Aneuploidy in Humans

Humans are enormously sensitive to the changes in gene dosage and almost all human aneuploidies are incompatible with life. Theoretically, there are potentially 24 different kinds of trisomy in humans—one for each autosome, and one each for the X and Y chromosomes—and an equal number of potential monosomies. Yet only autosomal trisomies of chromosomes 13, 18, and 21, and no autosomal monosomies, are seen with any measurable frequency in newborn human infants. Multiple forms of sex-chromosome trisomy are detected with some frequency at birth, however, as is one type of sex-chromosome monosomy (Table 13.2). A wide variety of other chromosome abnormalities occur in newborn infants as well. Each of the aneuploidy conditions identified in Table 13.2, along with the other chromosome abnormalities that occur, result in significant phenotypic abnormalities in newborn infants.

Human biologists know that trisomies and monosomies other than those listed in the table occur at conception, but the resulting zygotes almost never survive to be

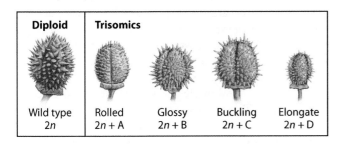

Diploid	Trisomics			
Wild type 2n	Rolled 2n + A	Glossy 2n + B	Buckling 2n + C	Elongate 2n + D

Figure 13.3   The appearance of the seed head in wild-type diploid and in four trisomic lines of jimson weed (*Datura stramonium*).

Table 13.2	Human Aneuploidies and Frequencies at Birth		
Aneuploidy	**Syndrome**	**Frequency at Birth**	**Syndrome Characteristics**
Autosomal Aneuploidy			
Trisomy 13	Patau syndrome	1 in 15,000	Mental retardation and developmental delay, possible deafness, major organ abnormalities, early death
Trisomy 18	Edward syndrome	1 in 8000	Mental retardation and developmental delay, skull and facial abnormalities, early death
Trisomy 21	Down syndrome	1 in 1500	Mental retardation and developmental delay, characteristic facial abnormalities, short stature, variable life span
Sex-Chromosome Aneuploidy			
47, XXY	Klinefelter syndrome (males)	1 in 1000	Variable secondary sexual characteristics, infertility, frequent breast swelling; no impact on mental capacity
47, XYY	Jacob syndrome (males)	1 in 1000	Tall stature common; possible reduction but not loss of fertility; no impact on mental capacity
47, XXX	Triple X syndrome (females)	1 in 1000	Tall stature common; possible reduction of fertility; menstrual irregularity; no impact on mental capacity
45, XO	Turner syndrome (females)	1 in 5000	No secondary sexual characteristics; infertility, short stature; webbed neck common; no impact on mental capacity

born alive. The explanation for this situation is that the abnormalities of development produced by these other trisomies and monosomies are so severe that they almost always lead to spontaneous abortion early in pregnancy, and sometimes the aneuploidy is so disruptive to early zygotic mitotic division that implantation in the uterine wall never occurs.

The best available data on human aneuploidy rates and survival come from studies that monitor women for hormone changes associated with conception and the earliest stages of pregnancy. These studies make two surprising observations. First, in the first trimester of pregnancy, about half of all human conceptions spontaneously abort, and second, more than half of the spontaneously terminated human pregnancies carry abnormalities of chromosome number or chromosome structure. These observations point to a surprisingly high (15% to 25%) frequency of meiotic nondisjunction in humans. Other errors producing gametes with abnormal chromosomes can occur as well.

To ascertain the biological basis for the high rate of meiotic nondisjunction in humans, trisomy 21 (Down syndrome)—the most common autosomal trisomy at birth—has been the focus of intense study. Epidemiologic studies conducted over several decades have linked the risk of a child having trisomy 21 to the age of the mother at conception. Table 13.3 illustrates the connection between maternal age and the risk of trisomy 21.

Molecular and genomic analyses of Down syndrome have determined that a small number of genes on chromosome 21 are responsible for the mental retardation and heart abnormalities that are principal symptoms of the syndrome. The critical portion of chromosome 21 for Down syndrome, known as the Down syndrome critical region (DSCR), was identified by studying people with partial trisomy of chromosome 21. These individuals carry two complete copies of chromosome 21 and a small additional segment of chromosome 21 on another chromosome. These studies identify region 21q22.2 as the DSCR. In other words, Down syndrome individuals invariably carry 21q22.2 in three copies. Among a handful of candidate genes, *DYRK*, a homolog of a gene in mice and *Drosophila* that produces dosage-sensitive learning defects, makes a major contribution to Down syndrome. In mice, increased dosage of the *DYRK* homolog reduces brain size. *DSCAM* is a second gene whose increased dosage is linked to Down syndrome. This gene also has homologs in mouse and *Drosophila*, where its protein product participates in the formation of the heart and components of the developing nervous system.

A different kind of change in gene dosage is seen in humans with Turner syndrome, a monosomy of the X chromosome in which there is one X chromosome but no second sex chromosome (see Table 13.2). Despite the occurrence of random X-inactivation in human female embryos that leads to one expressed X chromosome and one inactive X chromosome in each nucleus, two sex

Table 13.3	Risk of Down Syndrome (Trisomy 21) by Maternal Age[a]		
Maternal Age Range	Total Live Births Studied	Trisomy 21 Births	Rate per 1000 Births
15–19	30,272	18	0.49
20–24	117,593	87	0.73
25–29	108,746	96	0.90
30–34	49,487	72	1.56
35–39	19,522	73	4.19
40–44	4880	73	18.02
45–49	304	19	55.02

[a] Data adapted from E. B. Hook and A. Lindsjo, Down syndrome in live births by single year maternal age interval in a Swedish study: Comparison with results from a New York State study. *Am. J. Hum. Genet.* 30 (1978): 19–27.

chromosomes are necessary for normal early development. In female embryos that are XO (Turner syndrome), the single copy of the gene *SHOX*, located in pseudoautosomal region 2 on the short arm of the X chromosome and the Y chromosome, is insufficient to direct certain aspects of normal development. The haploinsufficiency of *SHOX* appears to play a central role in producing Turner syndrome.

Reduced Fertility in Aneuploidy

The type and extent of developmental abnormalities in an aneuploid organism are a consequence of changes in the dosage of the genes affected, but aneuploidy also disrupts normal patterns of chromosome segregation during meiosis. This results in a reduction in the number of normal haploid gametes, and it can reduce fertility.

Two patterns of homologous chromosome synapsis are possible among the three chromosomes at metaphase I in trisomy (**Figure 13.4**)—either a trivalent synaptic structure or two of the chromosomes form a bivalent synaptic structure and the other chromosome is a univalent that does not synapse with another chromosome. There is no mechanism to divide three chromosomes equally at anaphase I. Thus, two chromosomes move to one pole and one chromosome moves to the opposite pole during anaphase. On completion of meiosis, half of the gametes are haploid, having received one copy of the chromosome, but the remaining gametes contain two copies of the chromosome. These are $n + 1$ gametes. This effectively reduces the number of viable gametes by approximately one-half because the gametes with an extra chromosome will produce trisomic progeny that are unlikely to survive.

This circumstance results in a form of **semisterility,** a reduction—but not complete elimination—of fertility.

Mosaicism

Our discussion of random X-inactivation of mammalian females identified the phenomenon as an example of naturally occurring mosaicism, in which different cells of the

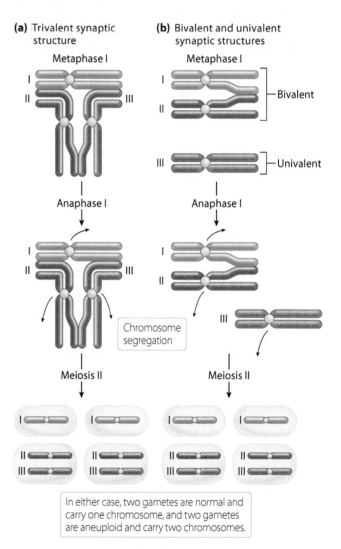

(a) Trivalent synaptic structure

(b) Bivalent and univalent synaptic structures

In either case, two gametes are normal and carry one chromosome, and two gametes are aneuploid and carry two chromosomes.

Figure 13.4 Two meiotic patterns of segregation in trisomics. (a) Three chromosomes form a trivalent structure at synapsis and produce only two normal haploid gametes among the four gametes. **(b)** A bivalent and a univalent arrangement of three chromosomes also leads to just two normal haploid gametes.

organism contain differently functioning X chromosomes (see Section 3.6). Mosaicism refers to the condition in which an individual is composed of two or more cell types having different genetic or chromosomal makeup. Mosaicism can also develop as a consequence of mitotic nondisjunction early in embryogenesis. Mosaicism derived from early mitotic nondisjunction is one of the many kinds of chromosome abnormalities that occur in newborn infants. For example, 25–30% of cases of Turner syndrome, the X-chromosome monosomy (XO), occur in females having mosaicism in which some cells are 45, XO and others are 46, XX. Some individuals with mosaic Turner syndrome carry 47, XXX cells as well. This kind of mosaicism is usually derived from mitotic nondisjunction in a 46, XX zygote (Figure 13.5).

In fruit flies, butterflies, and moths, sex-chromosome mosaicism produces a particular sexually ambiguous phenotype called a **gynandromorphy.** Gynandromorph sex morphology is female ("gyn") on one half of the body and male ("andro") on the other half. Gynandromorphy develops as a

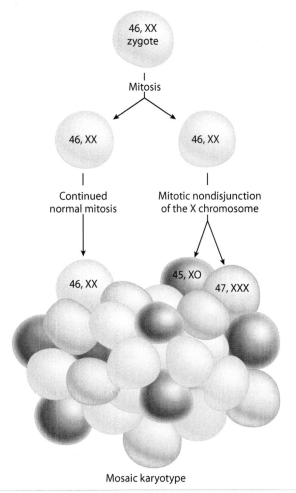

Mosaic karyotype

Turner syndrome mosaic females contain 46, XX and 45, XO cells, and they may also have cells with 47, XXX.

Figure 13.5 **Chromosome mosaicism.** Mosaicism usually begins with a normal diploid zygote. Mitotic nondisjunction produces one or more aneuploid cell lines that persist and are found in the newborn.

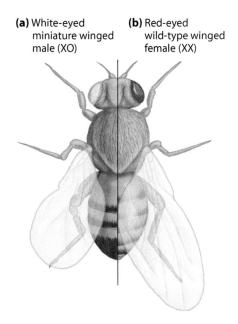

(a) White-eyed miniature winged male (XO)

(b) Red-eyed wild-type winged female (XX)

Figure 13.6 **Gynandromorphy in *Drosophila*.** White eye and miniature wing are X-linked recessive traits present in the hemizygous (XO) male half of the fly. Heterozygous genotypes for both genes are present in the wild-type (XX) female half of the fly.

consequence of mitotic X chromosome nondisjunction early in development.

In the example of gynandromorphy shown in Figure 13.6, a fly at fertilization is a wild-type female heterozygous for alleles for white eye (w) and miniature wing (m). Both genes are X-linked, and the genotype is $w^+ m^+/w\ m$. Normal mitotic division retains both X chromosomes until mitotic nondisjunction results in loss of the X chromosome bearing the wild-type alleles. As a consequence of nondisjunction and continued mitosis, about half the cells of the adult are $w^+ m^+/w\ m$, and about half are $w\ m$/O. Heterozygous cells in the right-hand half of the fly lead its structures to develop with female appearance and wild-type eye color and wing form. The left-hand half of the fly is hemizygous $w\ m$/O, having lost an X chromosome. These alleles direct development of structures that appear to be male with white eye and miniature wing.

Trisomy Rescue and Uniparental Disomy

A rare abnormality of chromosome content called **uniparental disomy** has been identified in humans. Uniparental disomy occurs when both copies of a homologous chromosome pair originate from a single parent. It was first identified in connection with two chromosomal conditions, Angelman syndrome (OMIM 105830) and Prader-Willi syndrome (OMIM 176270), that are usually the result of a partial deletion of the 15q11.12 portion of chromosome 15.

Uniparental disomy has two mechanisms of origin. The rarer mechanism requires nondisjunction of the same chromosome in both the sperm and egg, with the result that one gamete contributes two copies of the chromosome and the other does not contribute a copy of the chromosome. The second mechanism is more common. It involves nondisjunction in one parent that results in an aneuploid gamete contributing two copies of chromosome 15. The other gamete is normal and contributes a single copy of chromosome 15. Gamete union results in trisomy 15 in the fertilized egg. This is a condition that is invariably incompatible with survival. By a process known as **trisomy rescue,** however, some fertilized eggs that are initially trisomic can survive and lead to the formation of a zygote that can survive. In trisomy rescue, one of the extra copies of chromosome 15 is randomly ejected in one of the first mitotic divisions following fertilization. Which of the three chromosomes is ejected is apparently random. Thus, one result of trisomy rescue can be a cell with one chromosome from each parent. Zygotes with this result have normal chromosome content. Alternatively, trisomy rescue could result in a zygote that retains two copies of chromosome 15 from the same parent, and this is uniparental disomy.

13.2 Changes in Euploidy Result in Various Kinds of Polyploidy

Polyploidy is the presence of three or more sets of chromosomes in the nucleus of an organism. Polyploidy is common, particularly in plant species, and can result either from the duplication of euploid chromosome sets from a single species or from the combining of chromosome sets from different species. Many types of polyploidy are possible—triploids ($3n$), tetraploids ($4n$), pentaploids ($5n$), hexaploids ($6n$), octaploids ($8n$), and so on. Polyploids whose karyotype is comprised of chromosomes derived from a single species are designated **autopolyploids** (*auto* = "self"), and polyploids with chromosome sets from two or more species are called **allopolyploids** (*allo* = "different"). Terms such as *autotetraploid* ($4n$ chromosomes that all derive from a single species) and *allohexaploid* ($6n$ with chromosomes from two or more species) are used to describe a polyploid organism's genomic content.

Autopolyploidy and Allopolyploidy

Three mechanisms lead to autopolyploidy (**Figure 13.7**). The first two of these mechanisms are forms of **sexual polyploidization.** Events tied to meiosis are the basis for these polyploid outcomes. The third mechanism is **asexual polyploidization,** in which events taking place in mitosis result in polyploidy.

1. **Multiple fertilizations.**   Fertilization of an egg by more than one haploid pollen grain results in a zygote that is triploid ($3n$) or higher. This is generally a rare event because most sexually reproducing

(a) Fertilization by multiple pollen grains

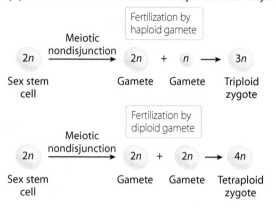

(b) Increase in chromosome number by meiotic nondisjunction

(c) Increase in chromosome number by mitotic nondisjunction

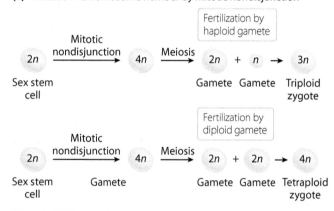

Figure 13.7   Mechanisms creating triploid and tetraploid zygotes in plants.

plants have elaborate mechanisms to prevent fertilization of an egg by more than a single pollen grain.

2. **Meiotic nondisjunction.**   Meiotic nondisjunction affecting all of the chromosomes in a nucleus can produce a diploid gamete instead of a haploid gamete. This is a common mechanism for polyploidization in sexually reproducing plants. After such a doubling of chromosomes in a gamete, the union of the resulting $2n$ gamete and a haploid gamete produces a $3n$ zygote. Similarly, the union of two diploid gametes produces $4n$ zygotes.

3. **Mitotic nondisjunction.**   Mitotic nondisjunction in sex stem cells can result in chromosome doubling, thus this process is asexual. These cells divide by mitosis before entering meiosis (thus the process is asexual), and mitotic nondisjunction doubles the

number of chromosomes from $2n$ to $4n$. The gametes that result from meiotic division of $4n$ sex stem cells are $2n$. If a $2n$ gamete unites with a haploid gamete, the resulting progeny are $3n$, and if two $2n$ gametes unite, the result is a $4n$ zygote.

In contrast, the multiple sets of chromosomes that are carried by allopolyploids originated in different species. The union of a haploid set of chromosomes from species 1 (n_1) and a haploid gamete from species 2 (n_2) produces a hybrid organism that may have either an even number or odd number of chromosomes, since related species may have different diploid numbers. For example, a new species of salt grass, *Spartina anglica*, arose along the English coastline in the late 1800s as a result of interspecific allopolyploidy. *S. anglica* has 122 chromosomes. It arose through the interspecific hybridization of native salt grass, *Spartina maritima* ($2n = 60$), with a non-native salt grass, *Spartina alterniflora* ($2n = 62$) (**Figure 13.8**). Haploid gametes from the two parental species fused to produce an interspecific hybrid with 61 chromosomes. The genome of the hybrid was stabilized, and fertility was generated by chromosome nondisjunction that doubled the chromosome number to 122. With an even number of chromosomes, balanced gametes could form. This established the new species that grew vigorously and spread its range along the English coast.

Consequences of Polyploidy

Allopolyploids of plant species frequently occur naturally and are also produced by human manipulation. When used for commercial purposes, plant polyploidy generates three main consequences. First, fruit and flower size is increased. The nuclei and cells of polyploid strains are larger than those of diploid strains, and many familiar fruit and vegetable varieties benefit from this effect. Apples ($3n = 51$), bananas ($3n = 33$), strawberries ($8n = 56$), peanuts ($4n = 40$), and potatoes ($4n = 48$) are just a few examples.

Increased fruit and flower size in polyploid plants comes at the cost of the second effect—fertility. The problem is particularly acute for odd-numbered polyploids ($3n$, $5n$, etc.), in which the odd number of chromosomes cannot be evenly divided at the first meiotic division. The result is an unequal distribution of chromosomes that makes almost all of the resulting gametes nonviable. This reproductive disadvantage is turned into commercial advantage in cultivated plants with odd-numbered polyploidy. Certain "seedless" fruits and vegetables in the produce aisle of your local grocery store are odd-numbered polyploids.

While most animals do not tolerate polyploidy, there are some exceptions among certain fishes and amphibians. One of these exceptions is the weed-eating fish the grass carp (*Ctenopharyngodon idella*) that is being employed to reduce weed growth in more than 50 countries worldwide. Triploid grass carp are created by first artificially fertilizing carp eggs and then heat-shocking the newly fertilized eggs. Heat-shock causes the diploid fertilized

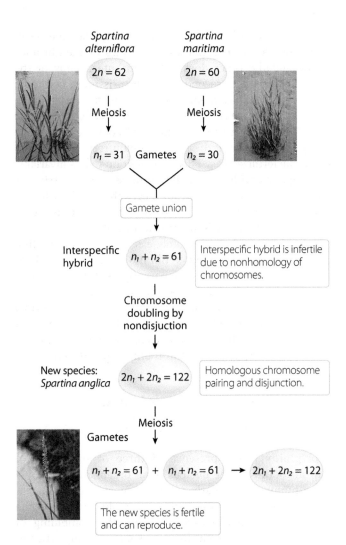

Figure 13.8 **The production of a new species by allopolyploidy.** Two salt grass species, *Spartina maritima* ($2n = 60$) and *Spartina alterniflora* ($2n = 62$) produced an interspecific hybrid ($2n = 61$) that subsequently doubled its chromosome number by nondisjunction to produce the new salt grass species *Spartina anglica*, an allotetraploid ($4n = 122$).

eggs to divide unevenly, producing a triploid cell that goes on to develop into a fish that is fully viable. The triploid grass carp eat weeds vigorously and, in doing so, help reduce weed growth in bodies of water without the use of herbicides. As a consequence of their triploidy, however, the carp are infertile, so they are unable to reproduce and don't invade the habitats into which they are introduced. The triploid grass carp must be restocked periodically if its continued presence is desired to control weed growth.

Allopolyploids exhibit a third characteristic of commercial importance—increase in heterozygosity relative to diploids that comes about when inbred lines are crossed and is the basis of additional growth vigor. This phenomenon is known as **hybrid vigor,** and it consists of more rapid growth, increased production of fruits and flowers, and improved resistance to disease among the heterozygous (hybrid) progeny of inbred lines.

Reduced Recessive Homozygosity

The pattern of single-gene inheritance in polyploids differs from that in diploids with respect to the proportions of dominant and recessive phenotypes from certain crosses. This difference is tied directly to the additional number of gene copies in polyploid genomes. A dominant phenotype is produced by any genotype containing one or more copies of the dominant allele, and the recessive phenotype is produced only by the homozygous recessive genotype. In the case of a phenotype decided by a single gene with a dominant and a recessive allele, the likelihood of producing the recessive phenotype in a tetraploid strain is decreased compared to the likelihood of producing it in a diploid.

Taking an autotetraploid with the genotype $AAaa$ as an example, let's determine the probability that progeny produced by self-fertilization would have the genotype $aaaa$. We'll use the designations A_1, A_2, a_3, and a_4 for alleles of the gene. The ratio of dominant to recessive alleles is 2:2 in the tetraploid, and six diploid gamete genotypes are produced by homologous disjunction: A_1A_2, A_1a_3, A_1a_4, A_2a_3, A_2a_4, and a_3a_4. Among these gametes, only one (one-sixth of the total) contains two recessive alleles. The probability of union of two fully recessive gametes is therefore $(1/6)(1/6) = 1/36$, much less than the 1/4 probability of producing homozygous recessive offspring from heterozygous diploids with the genotype Aa. **Genetic Analysis 13.1** guides you through an analysis of a genetic cross involving polyploids.

Polyploidy and Evolution

The disadvantages in growth and reproduction experienced by polyploid organisms can be outweighed by the evolutionary advantages of polyploidy. More than half of all contemporary flowering plant species are derived from ancestors that evolved by polyploidy, and many flowering plant genuses include species with different numbers of complete sets of chromosomes. In the genus *Chrysanthemum*, for example, a diploid species has $2n = 18$. The chromosome numbers of other *Chrysanthemum* species differ from one another by 18 chromosomes, with closely related species having 36, 54, 72, and 90 chromosomes.

Evolution by polyploidy is a sudden, dramatic event that can lead to the development of a new species over a span of just one or two generations as we discuss momentarily for modern wheat species (**Figure 13.9**). The change in chromosome number—say, by doubling of chromosomes—can be a reproductive isolation mechanism. For example, mating between related plants plant A with 18 chromosomes and plant B with 36 chromosomes could produce hybrid progeny with 27 chromosomes. A gamete with 9 chromosomes from plant A and 18 chromosomes from plant B would have an odd-numbered ploidy, which dramatically reduces fertility. Viable progeny are produced by self-fertilization of plant A or plant B or by mating of either plant with another having an identical chromosome number.

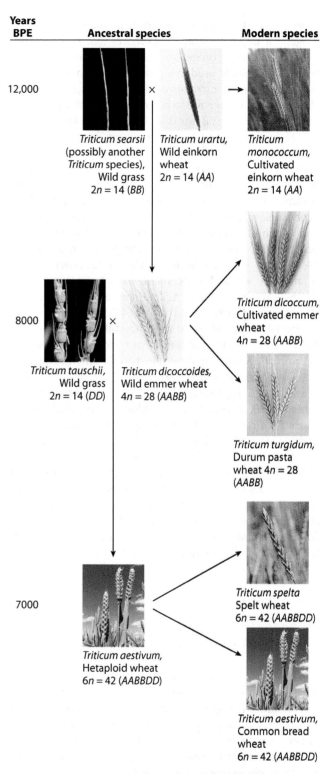

Figure 13.9   The evolution of modern wheat (*Triticum aestivum*), spelt wheat (*T. spelta*), durum pasta wheat (*T. turgidum*), and other modern species from crosses of ancestral species.

Species that have had a quiescent genetic history can experience a sudden burst of evolutionary change through the development of polyploidy by two mechanisms. First, as mentioned above, allopolyploidy can result in the evolution of a new species, owing to the fact that the newly polyploid progeny are reproductively isolated from their nonpolyploid progenitor by chromosomal differences that make hybridization between the progenitor and the new species unlikely. Second, polyploidy produces gene duplication that relaxes natural selection constraints on duplicated copies of genes, allowing them to vary and to potentially diversify to generate new functions. (We discuss these ideas in Chapter 22.)

Numerous examples of speciation by polyploidization have been documented in plants, but perhaps no common plant species embody the evolutionary impact of polyploidy more dramatically than *Triticum aestivum*, common bread wheat, and *Triticum spelta*, spelt wheat allohexaploid that developed through the union of diploid genomes of three ancestral species in two hybridization events. Modern members of the genus *Triticum* have 14, 28, and 42 chromosomes. The evolutionary history of modern wheat begins about 12,000 years ago with the hybridization of two diploid species that contain 14 chromosomes each. Einkorn wheat (*T. monococcum*) is a cultivated variety of wheat that can still be found around the world and is the modern form of wild einkorn wheat (*T. urartu*). Represented by the chromosome designation *AA*, *T. urartu* hybridized with a wild grass species, either, *T. searsii* or *T. tripsacoides*, each with chromosomes represented as *BB*, to form an allotetraploid variety called Emmer wheat (*T. dicoccoides*). Emmer wheat has 28 chromosomes and a chromosome formula *AABB* and was being cultivated approximately 8000 years ago when it underwent a second hybridization event with another wild diploid grass species, *T. tauschii* (chromosome formula *DD*), to form *T. aestivum* and *T. spelta* (chromosome formula *AABBDD*), the modern allohexaploid species, which each have 42 chromosomes. Modern forms of each of the ancestral wheat species are shown in Figure 13.9.

13.3 Chromosome Breakage Causes Mutation by Loss, Gain, and Rearrangement of Chromosomes

We have seen that particularly for animals the proper balance of gene dosage is important for promoting normal growth and development and that changes in gene dosage can have substantial phenotypic consequences. For this reason, mutations that result in the loss or gain of whole chromosomes or chromosome segments have the potential to produce severe abnormalities. In this section, we examine changes to chromosome structure that occur by chromosome breakage and other events that lead to the loss or gain of chromosomal segments.

Partial Chromosome Deletion

When a chromosome breaks, both strands of DNA are severed at a location called a **chromosome break point.** The broken chromosome ends at a break point retain their

chromatin structure, and they can adhere to one another, to other broken chromosome ends or to the ends of intact chromosomes. Any part of a broken chromosome that remains **acentric** (without a centromere), can be lost during cell division.

Chromosome breakage can result in **partial chromosome deletion,** by the loss of a portion of a chromosome. The size of the deletion and the specific genes deleted are significant factors in the degree of ensuing phenotypic abnormality. Larger chromosome deletions are detected by microscopy through the observation of altered chromosome banding patterns. In these larger deletions, many genes are affected, and the likelihood of substantial phenotypic consequences is very high. A chromosome break that detaches one arm of a chromosome leads to a **terminal deletion** (Figure 13.10a). The chromosome fragment broken off in terminal deletion contains one of the chromosome ends, or *termini,* consisting of a telomere and additional genetic material. Without a centromere, the acentric fragment lacks a kinetochore. It is unable to attach spindle fibers and cannot migrate to a pole of the cell during division. Acentric chromosome fragments are lost during cell division. Organisms carrying one wild-type chromosome and a homolog with a terminal deletion are called **partial deletion heterozygotes.** A human condition known as cri-du-chat syndrome (OMIM 123450) is an example of a chromosome syndrome caused by terminal deletion of 5p15.2–5p15.3 (Figure 13.10b). The syndrome is named

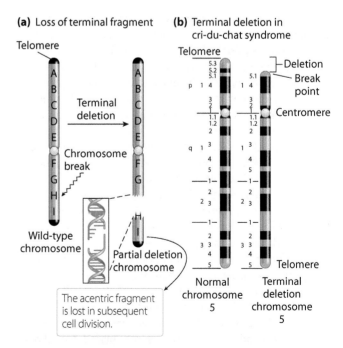

Figure 13.10 Chromosome terminal deletion. (a) A double-stranded DNA break at a chromosome break point in region H leads to terminal deletion of the acentric fragment. **(b)** Terminal deletion of chromosome 5 in cri-du-chat syndrome.

for the distinctive cat-cry-like sound emitted by infants with the condition.

In contrast to a terminal deletion, which results from a single break at one end of a chromosome, an **interstitial deletion** is the loss of an internal segment of a chromosome that results from two chromosome breaks. Interstitial deletions can be seen in many organisms, including humans. WAGR syndrome (OMIM 194072) and a closely related condition, WAGRO (OMIM 612469), both result from an interstitial deletion in humans affecting chromosome bands 11p1.3 and the adjoining band, 11p2. Studies of chromosome 11 structural abnormalities in patients with WAGR syndrome and WAGRO syndrome reveal partial chromosome deletions of various sizes, with the smallest common deletion region at 11p1.3 to 11p2. (**Figure 13.11**). The initials WAGR stand for **W**ilms tumor (a type of hereditary kidney cancer), **a**niridia (the absence of the iris in the eye), **g**enitourinary abnormalities, and mental **r**etardation. WAGRO has the same four developmental abnormalities as WAGR, with the addition of obesity. Patients with the largest deletions of 11p12–p13 have all five conditions, whereas patients with smaller deletions may have just one or two of the disorders.

WAGR syndrome and WAGRO syndrome result from gene dosage imbalance as a consequence of partial chromosome deletion. Researchers have identified two critical gene deletions in WAGR syndrome and an additional critical gene deletion in WAGRO syndrome. The gene *PAX6* produces a DNA-binding protein that is a transcription-regulating protein in development of the eye. The loss of this gene produces aniridia. The gene *WT1* produces a transcription-regulating protein that is essential for genitourinary development, and its loss is also tied to Wilms tumor and to mental disability. The third critical gene deleted in WAGRO syndrome is *BDNF*, which produces a protein expressed in the brain to protect striatal neurons from damage and destruction. When this gene is deleted, it produces obesity. Other mutant alleles of *BDNF* are associated with anorexia, bulimia, memory impairment, and obsessive-compulsive disorder. *BDNF* may play a role in the mental impairment that is part of WAGR syndrome.

Unequal Crossover

The process of reciprocal recombination achieves the recombination of alleles on homologous chromosomes without causing a gain or loss of chromosomal material that would result in mutation (see Sections 5.2 and 12.6). Occasionally, however, crossing over between homologs is inaccurate, resulting in chromosome mutations that are due to **unequal crossover.** These mutations result in the **partial duplication** and **partial deletion** of chromosome segments on the resulting recombinant chromosomes. An organism carrying one homolog with duplicated material is a **partial duplication heterozygote,** whereas one with material deleted from one chromosome is a partial deletion heterozygote. Both states change the dosage of genes carried on the duplicated or deleted chromosome segments, and phenotypic abnormalities due to dosage effects can occur.

Unequal crossover is rare and occurs most commonly when repetitive regions of homologous chromosomes misalign. The human condition known as Williams-Beuren syndrome (WBS; OMIM 194050) is frequently found in partial deletion heterozygotes for a segment of chromosome 7. In wild-type chromosome 7, this region contains duplicate copies of the gene *PMS*, designated PMS_A and PMS_B, that are located near one another and have 17 genes located in between (**Figure 13.12a**). Misalignment of the homologous chromosomes results in mispairing of PMS_A on one chromosome with PMS_B on the homologous chromosome. A copy of *PMS* on each chromosome is looped out from each homolog during misalignment (**Figure 13.12b**). Unequal crossing over between the misaligned chromosomes results in one recombinant chromosome that has a partial deletion chromosome 7 that results in WBS. This chromosome contains a nonfunctional hybrid PMS_A-PMS_B gene and is missing intact PMS_A and PMS_B genes as well as the 17 genes normally found between PMS_A and PMS_B (**Figure 13.12c**). The partial duplication chromosome (containing duplicated copies of the hybrid PMS_A-PMS_B gene and the 17 intervening genes) does not cause readily identifiable phenotypic abnormalities.

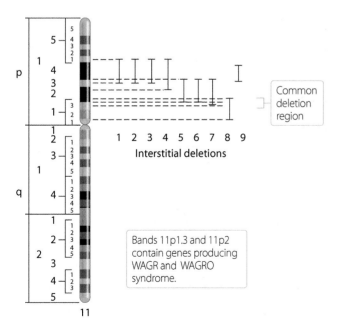

Common deletion region

1 2 3 4 5 6 7 8 9
Interstitial deletions

Bands 11p1.3 and 11p2 contain genes producing WAGR and WAGRO syndrome.

11

Figure 13.11　Interstitial deletions of chromosome 11 in WAGR and WAGRO syndromes. Deletions 5 through 8 result in WAGR, but deletions 1 through 4 and 9 do not. The smallest common deletion region 11p12–p13 affects bands 11p1.3 and 11p2.

(a) Normal chromosome 7 structure

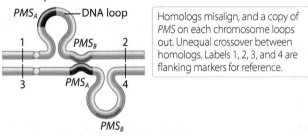

Duplicated copies of *PMS_A* and *PMS_B* with 17 genes between the copies

(b) Homologous chromosome misalignment and unequal crossover

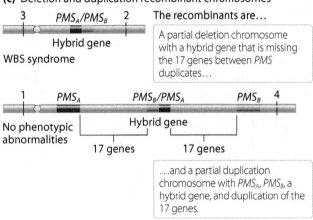

Homologs misalign, and a copy of *PMS* on each chromosome loops out. Unequal crossover between homologs. Labels 1, 2, 3, and 4 are flanking markers for reference.

(c) Deletion and duplication recombinant chromosomes

3   *PMS_A/PMS_B*   2   The recombinants are…

Hybrid gene

WBS syndrome

A partial deletion chromosome with a hybrid gene that is missing the 17 genes between *PMS* duplicates…

1   *PMS_A*   *PMS_B/PMS_A*   *PMS_B*   4

No phenotypic abnormalities

Hybrid gene

17 genes   17 genes

…and a partial duplication chromosome with *PMS_A*, *PMS_B*, a hybrid gene, and duplication of the 17 genes.

Figure 13.12 **Unequal crossover in creation of Williams-Beuren syndrome.**

Detecting Duplication and Deletion

Large deletions or duplications of chromosome segments can be detected by microscopic examination that reveals altered chromosome banding patterns resulting from the structural change to the chromosome. Such deletions and duplications are generally quite large. In human chromosomes, duplications and deletions of about 100,000 to 200,000 base pairs are at the lower limit of chromosome banding visualization. **Microdeletions** and **microduplications** are considerably smaller and are generally not easily detected by chromosome banding analysis. Instead, molecular techniques such as FISH (fluorescent in situ hybridization) can be used to detect the absence or duplication of a particular gene or chromosome sequence (**Figure 13.13**; also see Section 11.3).

Irrespective of the mechanism that produced them, prophase I homologous chromosome synapsis during meiosis produces a telltale signature of partial chromosome duplication or deletion. Homologous pairs that are mismatched

(a) Wild-type chromosome

FISH probes   *A*   *B C*

(b) Microinterstitial deletion

A   *B C*

No fluorescence detected from probe B.

(c) Microduplication

A   *B   C*

Two fluorescent spots indicate the target of probe B is duplicated.

Figure 13.13 **Detection of chromosome microdeletion and microduplication by FISH.** (a) Three FISH probes identify genes *A*, *B*, and *C*. (b) Microdeletion of a chromosome segment containing *B* prevents probe hybridization. (c) Microduplication results in hybridization of probe *B* to duplicated genes.

because one contains a large duplication or deletion will form an **unpaired loop** in synapsis (**Figure 13.14**). Along most of the length of the homologous pair, normal synaptic pairing occurs. But in regions of structural difference, the extra material present on one chromosome bulges out to allow synaptic pairing on either side. The material in the loop is normal genetic material if one chromosome carries a deletion, and it is duplicated genetic material if one homolog carries a duplication.

Deletion Mapping

Pseudodominance is a genetic phenomenon that occurs when a normally recessive allele is "unmasked" and expressed in the phenotype because the dominant allele on the homologous chromosome has been deleted. Pseudodominance is used to map genes in deleted chromosome regions by a method known as **deletion mapping.**

We discussed a version of deletion mapping in Section 6.7 in connection with Benzer's fine-structure

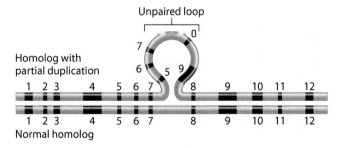

Figure 13.14 **An unpaired loop at synapsis.** The partial duplication heterozygote shown here has duplicated genetic material of bands 5 through 9. The extra material forms an unpaired loop at synapsis to allow homologous regions to align correctly.

PROBLEM Flower color in an autotetraploid plant is a single-gene character with two alleles, R_1 and R_2, at the gene locus. The R_1 allele produces color, but the R_2 allele does not. As a consequence, flower-color intensity is determined by the number of R_1 alleles in the genotype. The genotype-phenotype correspondence is as follows:

> **BREAK IT DOWN:** The plants are tetraploids (4n), not diploids (2n), thus each genotype contains four copies of the R gene, accounting for the variation in flower color (p. 438).

Genotype	Phenotype
$R_1R_1R_1R_1$	Dark red
$R_1R_1R_1R_2$	Light red
$R_1R_1R_2R_2$	Pink
$R_1R_2R_2R_2$	Light pink
$R_2R_2R_2R_2$	White

A pink-flowered plant is self-fertilized. What are the expected flower-color phenotypes, and in what proportions are they expected?

> **BREAK IT DOWN:** Chromosome segregation in meiosis generates multiple combinations of chromosomes in pollen and eggs. Each pollen of egg cell contains two copies of the chromosome (p. 439).

Solution Strategies	Solution Steps

Evaluate

1. Identify the topic this problem addresses and the nature of the required answer.

2. Identify the critical information given in the problem.

> **TIP:** The gametes of an autotetraploid are diploid. Each gamete contains two of the chromosomes in the tetraploid genotype.

1. This problem concerns self-fertilization of an autotetraploid. The answer requires determination of the phenotypes of progeny and the expected frequency of each phenotype.

2. The plant is identified as an autotetraploid, and the specific genotype–phenotype relationships are given.

> **TIP:** Autotetraploids are 4n and carry four homologous chromosomes derived from a single species.

Deduce

3. Identify the genotype of the self-fertilized plant and the possible gametes it produces.

3. The genotype of the pink-flowered plant is $R_1R_1R_2R_2$. The gametes will be diploid. Six random combinations of chromosomes can form during gametogenesis. The first R_1 chromosome can occur in a gamete with the second R_1 or with either of the R_2 chromosomes, forming three of the gametes. The second R_1 can occur with either of the R_2 chromosomes, forming two more gametes, or the two R_2 chromosomes can form a gamete, making the sixth combination.

4. Determine the genotype and expected frequency of each possible gamete.

> **TIP:** Add the predicted frequencies of the gametes to be sure their sum is 1.0.

4. Each combination of chromosomes in the gametes will form with equal frequency, meaning that the expected frequency of each gamete is 1/6. One combination contains both of the R_1 chromosomes, and one contains both of the R_2 chromosomes. The remaining gametes are different combinations with the genotype R_1R_2, for a combined frequency of 4/6.

Solve

5. Describe the possible gamete unions and the production of progeny by fertilization.

> **TIP:** Use a Punnett square to display gamete unions.

5. The results of union of the three gamete genotypes are as follows:

	R_1R_1 ($\frac{1}{6}$)	R_1R_2 ($\frac{4}{6}$)	R_2R_2 ($\frac{1}{6}$)
R_1R_1 ($\frac{1}{6}$)	$R_1R_1R_1R_1$ ($\frac{1}{36}$)	$R_1R_1R_1R_2$ ($\frac{4}{36}$)	$R_1R_1R_2R_2$ ($\frac{1}{36}$)
R_1R_2 ($\frac{4}{6}$)	$R_1R_1R_1R_2$ ($\frac{4}{36}$)	$R_1R_1R_2R_2$ ($\frac{16}{36}$)	$R_1R_2R_2R_2$ ($\frac{4}{36}$)
R_2R_2 ($\frac{1}{6}$)	$R_1R_1R_2R_2$ ($\frac{1}{36}$)	$R_1R_2R_2R_2$ ($\frac{4}{36}$)	$R_2R_2R_2R_2$ ($\frac{1}{36}$)

6. Summarize the genotypes, phenotypes, and frequencies expected from this cross.

TIP: Add the predicted frequencies to be sure their sum is 1.0.

6. Self-fertilization of a pink plant with the $R_1R_1R_2R_2$ genotype is expected to produce the following outcome:

Genotype	Phenotype	Frequency
$R_1R_1R_1R_1$	Dark red	1/36
$R_1R_1R_1R_2$	Light red	8/36
$R_1R_1R_2R_2$	Pink	18/36
$R_1R_2R_2R_2$	Light pink	8/36
$R_2R_2R_2R_2$	White	1/36

For more practice, see Problems 1, 2, and 11.

Visit the Study Area to access study tools.

MasteringGenetics™

analysis of the genes involved in bacterial lysis by bacteriophage. In that analysis, Benzer focused on whether it was possible to form a wild-type lysis recombinant between a lysis-deficient phage with a point mutation (a revertible mutation) and one with a deletion mutation (a nonrevertible mutation). In studies using deletion mutation analysis in diploid organisms, the unmasking of a recessive allele (the observation of pseudodominance) is central to gene mapping.

Figure 13.15 shows deletion mapping using pseudodominance to map the *Notch* gene (*n*) in *Drosophila*. The *Notch* gene resides on the X chromosome, and its location is revealed by the detection of pseudodominance in fruit flies that are heterozygous for partial X-chromosome deletions. Pseudodominance appears in females that are heterozygous for the partial deletion, carry the recessive allele on the intact X chromosome, and have lost the dominant allele from the other, partial deletion of the X chromosome. In the figure, the gray segments represent chromosome segments present on

the partial deletion X chromosomes of six different mutants, and color identifies segments that have been deleted from that chromosome in each mutant. The first two partial deletions (rJ1 and 258-42) do not lead to pseudodominance (in other words, the dominant wild-type phenotype is observed), indicating that the regions deleted do not contain the *Notch* gene. The other two partial deletions, 62d18 and N71a, result in pseudodominance (in other words, the recessive phenotype is observed), indicating that the *Notch* gene locus containing the dominant allele is in the region 3C5 to 3C9. To home in on the location of *Notch*, progressively smaller partial deletions are used to identify the smallest deletion segment common to all deletions resulting in pseudodominance. In this instance the smallest partial deletion common to genomes expressing pseudodominance for Notch is region 3C-7, which is missing from mutant 264-39. This is where the gene resides. **Genetic Analysis 13.2** guides you through analysis of deletion mapping.

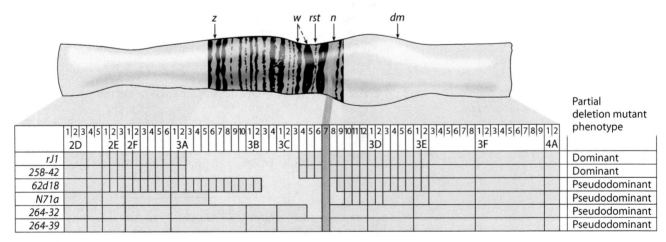

Figure 13.15 **Deletion mapping of the *Drosophila Notch* (*n*) gene.** The extent of each partial deletion of the *Drosophila* X chromosome is shown by the colored bars for six partial deletion mutants. The retention of the dominant character or the emergence of notch by pseudodominance is indicated. The smallest X-chromosome segment missing from all pseudodominant mutants is region 3C-7, indicating this as the location of the gene.

PROBLEM In *Drosophila*, the X-linked recessive mutant traits singed bristle, lozenge eye, and cut wing are encoded at linked genes. Five strains of *Drosophila*

> **BREAK IT DOWN:** Pseudo-dominance can emerge in heterozygous organisms when the dominant allele on one copy of a chromosome pair is deleted, leaving only the recessive allele on the unaltered chromosome (p. 442).

produced by the cross of pure-breeding wild-type and pure-breeding mutant flies (*SLC/SLC* × *slc/slc*) are expected to have the trihybrid genotype *SLC/slc* and express the wild-type phenotypes. Females of each strain exhibit pseudodominance for one or more of the traits, however, due to partial deletion of the X chromosome.

Comparative X-chromosome maps showing the extent of deletions in each pseudodominant strain (indicated by dashed lines) are given here along with the pseudodominant phenotypes found in each strain. Use this information to locate each gene as accurately as possible along the X chromosome.

> **BREAK IT DOWN:** Gene mapping by pseudodominace seeks to identify the smallest chromosome that might contain a particular gene (p. 444).

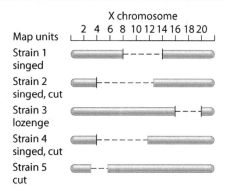

Solution Strategies	Solution Steps
Evaluate	
1. Identify the topic this problem addresses and the nature of the required answer.	1. This problem addresses deletion mapping using pseudodominance to locate the position of each gene. The answer requires construction of a map of gene locations.
2. Identify the critical information given in the problem.	2. The deletion regions on chromosomes and the corresponding pseudodomi-nant phenotypes are given.
Deduce	
3. Review the meaning of pseudodomi-nance and the connection between chromosome deletion and pseudodominance.	3. Pseudodominance is the appearance of a recessive trait in a presumed het-erozygous organism due to deletion of a chromosome segment carrying the dominant allele. In deletion mapping using pseudodominance, the location of a gene maps to the smallest common deletion region shared by all organ-isms expressing the pseudodominant trait.
Solve	
4. Interpret the meaning of the pseudo-dominant phenotype in strain 1.	4. Strain 1 is missing chromosome material from the 8th to the 14th map unit. The appearance of the pseudodominant phenotype singed indicates that the *singed* gene maps to this interval.
5. Compare strain 2 to strain 1, and interpret the meaning of the new pseudodominant phenotype cut. **TIP:** Compare deletion mutants that share pseudodominance phenotypes to see where their deletions overlap.	5. Strain 2 has a deletion from map units 4 to 13 that includes both *singed* and *cut*. This narrows the location of *singed* to the interval between 8 and 13 map units. The *cut* location is between the 4th and 8th map unit, based on its appearance with the deletion of this interval.
6. Assess pseudodominance of strain 3.	6. Co-occurrence of the deletion between map units 16 and 20 and the appearance of the pseudodominant lozenge phenotype map the *lozenge* gene to this location.
7. Assess strains 4 and 5, and refine the locations of the genes further where possible. **TIP:** Again, compare deletion mutants that share pseudodominance phenotypes to see where their deletions overlap.	7. Strain 4 contains a deletion between map units 4 and 12 and confines the location of *singed* to the interval between 8 and 12. This strain provides no additional information about the location of *cut*. The deletion between map units 3 and 6 in strain 5 includes *cut* and refines its location to between map units 4 and 6.
8. Identify gene locations based on the deletion mapping analysis.	8. Based on the data for pseudodominance in these five strains, *cut* resides in the interval between units 4 and 6, *singed* lies between 8 and 12, and *lozenge* is between 16 and 20.

13.4 Chromosome Breakage Leads to Inversion and Translocation of Chromosomes

Chromosome breakage involves double-strand DNA breaks that sever a chromosome. Breakage that is not followed by reattachment of the broken segment leads to partial chromosome deletion—but what happens if the broken chromosome reassembles but the broken segment reattaches in the wrong orientation or if the broken segment reattaches to a nonhomologous chromosome? The answers are that reattachment in the wrong orientation produces a **chromosome inversion,** whereas attachment to a nonhomologous chromosome results in **chromosome translocation.** We discuss two types of chromosome inversion events and two types of chromosome translocation in this section. A repeating theme that will emerge from this discussion is that as long as no critical genes or regulatory regions are mutated by chromosome breakage, and as long as dosage-sensitive genes are retained in their proper balance, heterozygous carriers of chromosome inversion or chromosome translocation may experience no phenotypic abnormalities. However, complications during meiosis may affect the efficiency of chromosome segregation, and fertility may be affected in those individuals.

Chromosome Inversion

Chromosome inversions occur as a result of chromosome breaks followed by reattachment of the free segment in the reverse orientation. Two kinds of chromosome inversion are observed, depending on whether the centromere is part of the inverted segment (Figure 13.16). **Paracentric inversion** results from the inversion of a chromosome segment on a single arm and *does not* involve the centromere, whereas **pericentric inversion** reorients a chromosome segment that *includes* the centromere.

Inversion most commonly affects just one member of a homologous pair, and such organisms are either paracentric or pericentric **inversion heterozygotes** in which one chromosome has normal structure and the homolog contains an inversion. Inversion heterozygotes may experience no genetic or phenotypic abnormalities, as long as no critical genes or regulatory DNA sequences are disrupted by chromosome breaks. In such cases, the 180-degree reorientation of inverted segments does not change the genetic content or gene expression of the affected chromosome.

Chromosome inversion does, however, cause a difference in linear order of genes between the homologs; thus, to bring the homologs of an inversion heterozygote into synaptic alignment during meiosis requires the formation of an unusual **inversion loop** at synapsis. Note,

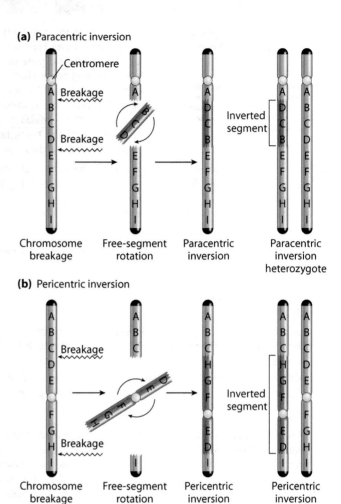

(a) Paracentric inversion

Chromosome breakage → Free-segment rotation → Paracentric inversion → Paracentric inversion heterozygote

(b) Pericentric inversion

Chromosome breakage → Free-segment rotation → Pericentric inversion → Pericentric inversion heterozygote

Figure 13.16 Paracentric and pericentric chromosome inversion. The letters represent regions of chromosomes, not single genes.

however, that an organism that is homozygous for an inversion carries the same order of genes and chromosome regions on both homologs and therefore will experience normal chromosome synapsis without the need for inversion loop formation.

In inversion heterozygotes, inversion loop formation readily occurs and does not affect subsequent chromosome segregation. Crossing over takes place between the homologs, but whereas crossing over that occurs *outside* the region spanned by the inversion loop takes place in the normal manner, crossing over *inside* the region of the inversion loop results in duplications and deletions among the recombinant chromosomes.

Figure 13.17 illustrates crossover within the inversion loop between chromosome regions B and C in a paracentric inversion heterozygote. Following crossover, one normal-order chromosome (1·ABCDEFGHI 1′) and one inverted-order chromosome (3·ADCBEFGHI 3′) are unchanged by recombination (the dot represents the

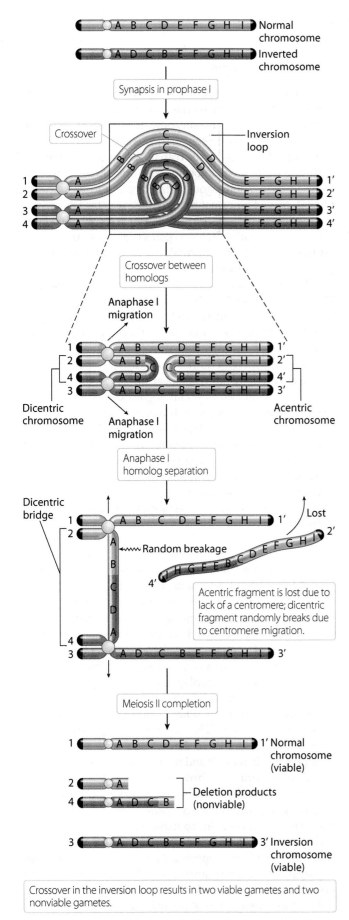

Crossover in the inversion loop results in two viable gametes and two nonviable gametes.

Figure 13.17 The consequences of crossover in the inversion loop in paracentric inversion heterozygotes.

centromere). The recombinant chromosomes, however, are abnormal: One is a **dicentric chromosome** with two centromeres (2 · ABCDA · 4), and the other is an acentric fragment that has no centromere (2' IHGFEDCBEFGHI 4'). At anaphase I, when centromeres on homologous chromosomes normally migrate toward opposite poles, a **dicentric bridge** forms as the dicentric chromosome is pulled toward both poles of the cell. Eventually the bridge snaps under the tension, at a random break point. Both products of the break have a centromere, but both are also missing genetic material. In contrast, the acentric fragment, lacking a centromere, has no mechanism by which to migrate to a pole of the cell and will be lost during meiosis. The completion of meiosis of this paracentric inversion heterozygote results in two viable gametes, one with the normal-order chromosome (1 · ABCDEFGHI 1') and one with the inverted-order chromosome (3 · ADCBEFGHI 3'), and two nonviable gametes with partial deletion chromosomes.

Crossover in the inversion loop in a pericentric inversion heterozygote yields two viable gametes and two nonviable gametes (**Figure 13.18**). One viable gamete contains the normal-order chromosome (1 ABCDE · FGHI 1') and one contains the inversion-order chromosome (3 ABCHGF · EDI 3'). Crossover also results in two nonviable gametes, each having a combination of deletions and duplications (2 ABCDE · FGHCBA 4 and (4' IDE · FGHI 2').

Three observations about recombination in inversion heterozygotes have important genetic implications:

1. **The probability of crossover within the inversion loop is linked to the size of the inversion loop.** Small inversions produce small inversion loops that have a low frequency of crossover. On the other hand, larger inversions produce loops that span more of the chromosome and correlate with a higher probability of crossover.

2. **Inversion suppresses the production of recombinant chromosomes.** The viable gametes produced by inversion heterozygotes contain either the normal-order chromosome or the inversion-order chromosome, but no recombinant chromosomes are viable, due to duplications and deletions of chromosome segments. The absence of recombinant chromosomes in progeny is identified as **crossover suppression.** In reality, crossovers do occur between homologous chromosomes carried by inversion heterozygotes, but because the recombinant chromosomes contain duplications and deletions, there is little possibility of viability for any progeny formed from the gametes that contain them. Geneticists have taken advantage of crossover suppression in research to mark homologous chromosomes with dominant alleles that aid in the interpretation of genetic crosses. **Experimental Insight 13.1** describes research by Hermann Muller, who used the so-called ClB ("See-el-bee") chromosome to identify and

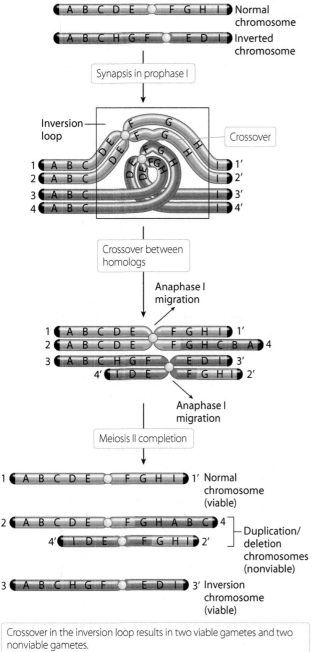

Figure 13.18 **The consequences of crossover in the inversion loop in pericentric inversion heterozygotes.**

later investigate lethal X-linked mutations induced in *Drosophila* by X-ray exposure.

3. **Fertility may be altered if an inversion heterozygote carries a very large inversion.** When an inversion spans all or nearly all the length of a chromosome, any crossover that occurs will produce two viable and two nonviable gametes. This means that approximately half the gametes will be lost in the specific case of an inversion heterozygote who carries a very large inversion. No such loss of fertility is expected for organisms with small inversions.

Chromosome Translocation

Chromosome translocation takes place following chromosome breakage and the reattachment of a broken segment to a *nonhomologous* chromosome. If no critical genes are severed or have their regulation disrupted by the breakage or translocation events, **translocation heterozygotes,** with one normal chromosome and one altered chromosome in each homologous pair, have a normal outward phenotype and a normal pattern of gene expression. Even if no phenotypic abnormalities are detected, however, certain translocation heterozygotes can experience semisterility as a result of abnormalities of chromosome segregation, as we describe below.

Three principal types of translocation are observed. **Unbalanced translocation** arises from a chromosome break and subsequent reattachment to a nonhomologous chromosome in a one-way event; that is, a piece of one chromosome is translocated to a nonhomologous chromosome and there is no reciprocal event (Figure 13.19a). **Reciprocal balanced translocation** is produced when breaks occur on two nonhomologous chromosomes and the resulting fragments switch places when they are reattached (Figure 13.19b). **Robertsonian translocation,** also known as **chromosome fusion,** involves the fusion of two nonhomologous chromosomes (Figure 13.19c). One consequence of Robertsonian translocation is the reduction of chromosome number. Our discussion in this section focuses on reciprocal balanced translocations and on Robertsonian translocations.

Reciprocal Balanced Translocation In reciprocal balanced translocation, one member of each homologous pair is altered by translocation, and none of the four chromosomes has a fully homologous partner. Instead, the translocated chromosome segments homologous to the normal member of each pair are dispersed on two other chromosomes. The absence of complete homology between chromosome pairs requires formation of an unusual tetravalent synaptic structure, a cross-like configuration made up of the four chromosomes related by the translocation, to enable homologous regions to synapse during metaphase I, as shown in Figure 13.20. The chromosomes in the figure are labeled I, II, III, and IV so that we may more easily follow their progress in meiosis and meiotic outcomes.

Two patterns of chromosome segregation emerge from the tetravalent structures found in translocation heterozygotes. *Alternate segregation* and *adjacent-1 segregation* each occur in approximately 50% of meiotic divisions, although the actual proportions vary somewhat among different species. At anaphase I in **alternate segregation,** chromosomes I and IV move to one cell pole and chromosomes II and III move to the opposite pole. At the completion of meiosis, all gametes are viable because each contains a complete set of genetic information for the two chromosomes. Fertilization of a gamete containing chromosomes I and IV will produce a normal

(a) Unbalanced translocation

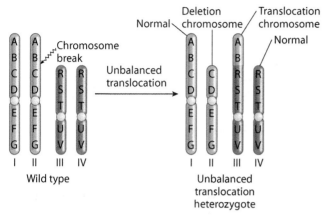

Wild type

Unbalanced translocation heterozygote

(b) Reciprocal balanced translocation

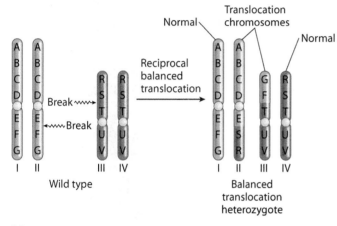

Wild type

Balanced translocation heterozygote

(c) Robertsonian translocation (chromosome fusion)

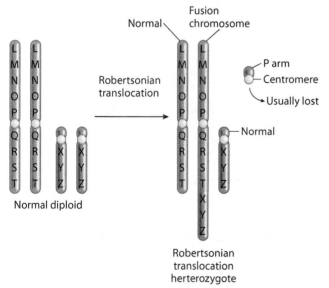

Normal diploid

Robertsonian translocation herterozygote

Figure 13.19   Unbalanced, reciprocal balanced, and Robertsonian chromosome translocations.

zygote, whereas fertilization of a gamete containing chromosomes II and III will produce a zygote with reciprocal balanced translocation heterozygosity, like the parent illustrated in the figure.

In anaphase I of **adjacent-1 segregation,** chromosomes I and III are moved to one cell pole and chromosomes II and IV go to the opposite pole. None of the gametes formed by this pattern of segregation is viable because of duplications and deletions of genetic information. Gametes containing chromosomes I and III have a duplication of the F and G regions, along with deletion of the R and S regions. Conversely, gametes containing chromosomes II and IV have a duplication of the R and S regions and a deletion of regions F and G.

Occasionally, an unusual pattern of segregation known as adjacent-2 segregation takes place. It is rare because it requires that chromosomes I and II, which share homologous centromeres, move to the same pole of the cell at anaphase I. Correspondingly, chromosomes III and IV, which also share homologous centromeres, also move to the same cell pole (opposite chromosomes I and II). This is atypical of the usual pattern at anaphase I, in which homologous chromosomes (that carry homologous centromeres) are separated in the reduction division. None of the gametes or progeny resulting from adjacent-2 segregation are viable.

In summary, cell biologists conclude that in balanced translocation heterozygotes, only alternate segregation produces viable gametes and viable progeny. This pattern accounts for just one-half of all meiotic events in these individuals; thus, the semisterility of translocation heterozygotes is due to reduction by about one-half in the number of viable gametes that can be produced.

Robertsonian Translocation In organisms with a Robertsonian translocation, also known as chromosome fusion, two nonhomologous chromosomes fuse to form a single, larger chromosome, resulting in a reduction in chromosome number. If two pairs of chromosomes fuse by Robertsonian translocation, the number of chromosomes in a genome is reduced to $2n - 2$. This is a frequently observed mechanism by which chromosome number evolves in related organisms. This mechanism accounts for the difference in chromosome number between human ($2n = 46$) and chimpanzee ($2n = 48$), as discussed in the Case Study. If multiple chromosomes undergo Robertsonian translocation, as was the case with mice on Madeira, larger reductions in chromosome number occur.

Carriers of a single Robertsonian translocation have one chromosome fusion. The homologs of the fused chromosomes remain separate chromosomes. **Figure 13.21** illustrates this pattern of Robertsonian translocation in humans in a condition called *familial Down syndrome* that is the cause of 5–10% of Down syndrome (trisomy 21) cases. Familial Down syndrome occurs when one parent is a carrier of a Robertsonian translocation of chromosome 21 to another autosome, most often chromosome 14. The translocation-heterozygous parent has a normal diploid genotype produced by a complete copy of chromosome 14, a complete copy of 21, and a 14/21 fusion chromosome. The fusion chromosome has lost the short arms of

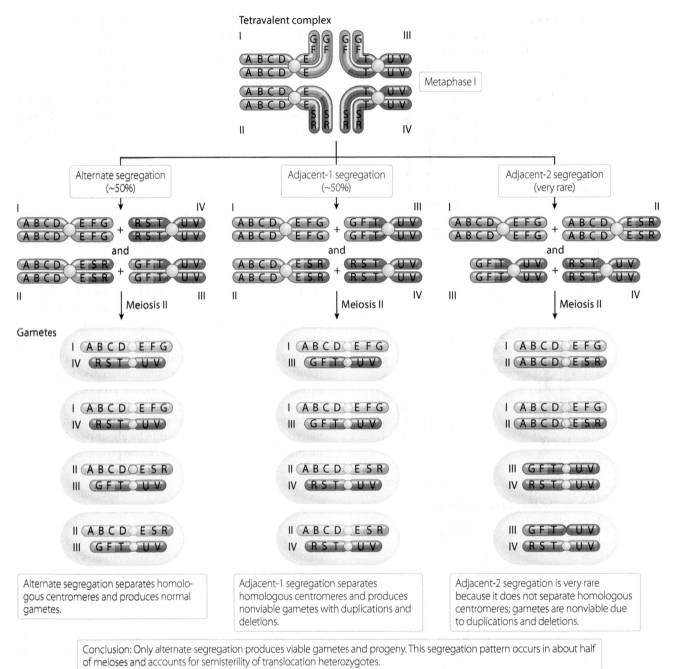

Figure 13.20 **The tetravalent synaptic structure and alternate and adjacent chromosome segregation in reciprocal balanced translocation heterozygotes.**

chromosome 14 and chromosome 21, but these contain no critical genetic information, and so the Robertsonian translocation carriers have a normal phenotype. Three possible patterns of segregation of the three chromosomes are equally likely following formation of the trivalent complex. Six possible gametes produced by these patterns are shown in the left column of the figure. When united with a normal gamete, three of the six possible gamete types result in nonviable zygotes (categories 4, 5, and 6 in the figure). The other three types of gametes produce viable zygotes (categories 1, 2, and 3). Two have normal phenotype and one, category 3, has Down syndrome. This

form of Robertsonian translocation heterozygosity leads to about a 1 in 3 chance of producing a child with trisomy 21, and this high risk is present each time a child is conceived.

13.5 Transposable Genetic Elements Move throughout the Genome

Transposable genetic elements are DNA sequences of various lengths and sequence composition that have evolved the ability to move within the genome

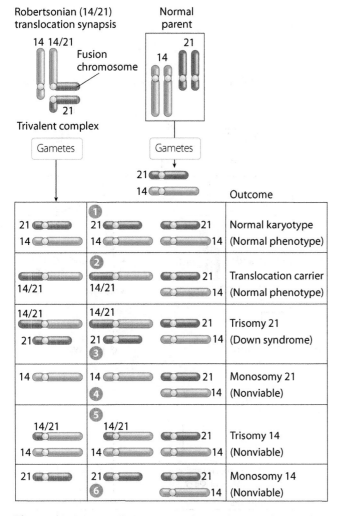

Figure 13.21 Familial Down syndrome due to Robertsonian translocation. For reproduction between a 14/21 Robertsonian translocation carrier and an individual with a normal karyotype, three nonviable zygotes (categories 4, 5, and 6) and three viable zygotes (categories 1, 2, and 3) are possible. Approximately one-third of the children from such unions (category 3) have trisomy 21 (Down syndrome).

by an enzyme-driven process known as **transposition.** Transposition is a mutational event—one that has a biological basis, as opposed to the chemical or physical bases of mutagenesis we discussed in Chapter 12. Transposable elements exist in dozens of forms that range in size from 50 bp to more than 10 kb. They vary in copy number from a few copies up to hundreds of thousands of copies.

Transposable elements typically create mutations by their insertion into wild-type alleles. The insertion of new DNA into a functional gene is the equivalent of inserting a random string of letters into a sentence. And just as the insertion of a random string of letters renders the sentence unintelligible, so too the consequence of DNA transposition is to render the wild-type allele nonfunctional by making it unable to produce a wild-type gene product. This mutational process is known as **insertional inactivation.**

Evolutionarily, transposable elements can increase genome size. Many transposable elements seem to have

the sole function of increasing their own copy number. As a consequence, organisms carrying certain transposable elements derive no useful benefit from their presence. Alternatively, some transposable elements contain expressed genes that may benefit the organism. In this and the following two sections, we discuss transposable elements in bacterial and eukaryotic genomes, and their evolutionary relationships.

The Discovery of Transposition

Barbara McClintock discovered transposition in a series of studies of a mutant phenotype of kernel color in maize (*Zea mays*) that took place in the 1930s. The *C* gene for kernel color is located on chromosome 9 in corn. At this gene a dominant wild-type allele *C* produces purple kernels and a mutant c_1 allele produces colorless kernels. One gene linked to *C* produces plump (*Sh*) or shrunken (*sh*) kernels, and a second linked gene produces shiny (*Wx*) or waxy (*wx*) kernels (**Figure 13.22a**). In experiments

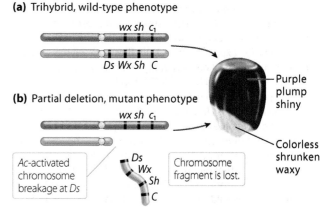

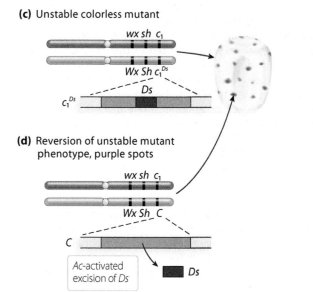

Figure 13.22 Mutation producing colorless sectors and reversion of the unstable colorless mutation in maize by the transposable genetic elements *Ds* and *Ac*.

Experimental Insight 13.1

Hermann Muller and the *Drosophila* ClB Chromosome Method

Hermann Muller, a student of Thomas Hunt Morgan, made numerous important contributions to genetics. Among Muller's accomplishments were his discovery that X-rays induce mutations by chromosome breakage and his development of a genetic method to identify lethal X-ray–induced mutations of the X chromosome in *Drosophila*.

To identify these mutations, Muller created an X chromosome called the ClB chromosome ("see-el-bee"): "C" for crossover suppression, "l" for presence of a recessive lethal mutation, and "B" for a dominant mutation producing an abnormal bar-shaped eye. Crossover suppression results from the presence of multiple inversions that prevent the appearance of recombinants between inverted and wild-type X chromosomes in females. Bar eye is a dominant mutant phenotype that permanently marks the inversion chromosome, since it cannot be reshuffled by recombination. Potentially lethal recessive mutations (*m*?) are generated on male X chromosomes by X-ray exposure.

Drosophila males that are hemizygous for ClB (ClB/Y) die as a result of the lethal mutation (*l*) on the X chromosome. Female carriers of ClB (ClB/+) survive and preserve the chromosome. Muller began his search for lethal X-ray–induced mutations by exposing male fruit flies to X-rays to induce mutations in germ-line cells. X-ray–exposed males were then crossed to a bar-eyed female (ClB/+), in Cross I. Next, bar-eyed female progeny from Cross I were individually mated to wild-type males, in Cross II. Cross II would be expected to produce a 2:1 ratio of females to males if X-ray exposure *did not* induce a lethal mutation on the X chromosome. In this case, only males inheriting the ClB chromosome would die. If on the other hand a lethal mutation was induced, only female progeny would be produced by Cross II. Males inheriting the ClB chromosome would die, but so would males inheriting the X chromosome with the induced lethal mutation.

Identifying X-ray–induced lethal mutations using the ClB method is highly accurate: It requires only a determination of whether males are produced by Cross II. Muller recognized that when X-ray exposure induced a lethal mutation, he could study it by means of the Cross II females with normal eyes, which are heterozygous carriers of the induced lethal mutation. Muller used the ClB method to demonstrate that X-ray exposure induces mutations at a rate more than 150 times greater than the spontaneous mutation rate in *Drosophila*. His work led to the characterization of numerous mutations and to the identification of the linear relationship between the level of X-ray exposure and the frequency of induced lethal mutations.

MULLER'S ClB METHOD

X-ray–exposed males are mated to bar-eyed females carrying the ClB chromosome in Cross I. Progeny bar-eyed females that potentially carry a lethal X-linked mutation [*m*(?)] are crossed to wild-type males in Cross II. The absence of male progeny from Cross II identifies the occurrence of an induced lethal mutation.

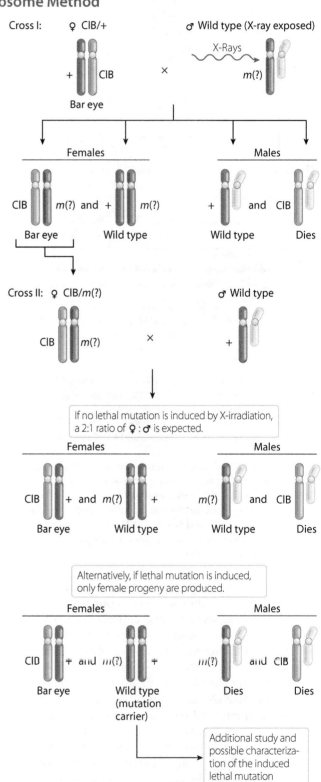

with several trihybrid strains of maize with the genotype *C Sh Wx/c₁ sh wx*, McClintock found a few unusual kernels that were mostly purple but had colorless sectors that varied among different kernels. Invariably, however, the purple regions were plump and shiny, but the colorless sectors were shrunken and waxy.

Looking at chromosome 9 in nuclei of cells from the colorless sectors of kernels, McClintock noticed a terminal deletion of one chromosome 9 homolog. In contrast, both chromosome 9 homologs were intact in cells from purple sectors. McClintock concluded that the simultaneous appearance of colorless, shrunken, and waxy resulted from pseudodominance due to deletion of the dominant alleles from one homolog (**Figure 13.22b**). Mitotic division of an original cell containing the chromosome deletion produced the abnormal sectors.

The frequency of sectored kernels was too high to be a result of spontaneous chromosome mutation, and more importantly, McClintock saw that break points of chromosome 9 occurred in the same place in all affected kernels of a given strain. Based on these observations she concluded that a genetic element, later named a **dissociation (*Ds*) element,** was located at the site of chromosome breakage. What puzzled McClintock, however, was why *Ds* generated chromosome breakage in some cells but not in others. To explain this, she suggested that *Ds* alone could not generate chromosome breakage. Instead, chromosome breakage at *Ds* was activated by an unlinked genetic element she called an **activator (*Ac*) element.**

McClintock's *Ds/Ac* proposal proved to be the explanation for another highly unusual observation she made in maize. She found occasional colorless maize mutants that had an **unstable mutant phenotype.** These unstable mutants had kernels that were mostly colorless but also had purple spots. The patterns of purple spotting differed from kernel to kernel on the same maize ear, indicating that it developed by some sort of reversion in somatic cells that was perpetuated by subsequent mitotic division (**Figure 13.22c**). Her investigation led McClintock to conclude that the unstable mutant alleles were produced by the insertion of *Ds* into the *C* allele to form the mutant c_1^{Ds} allele. This allele is mutated by the insertional inactivation process and as a result it produces no kernel color. The c_1^{Ds} allele is reverted through the action of *Ac* that activates the excision of *Ds* in individual somatic cells of developing kernels. The reversion of c_1^{Ds} to *C* in these and descendant cells leads to pigment production and purple spots.

McClintock's transposable genetic element hypothesis was that the unstable mutant phenotype was the result of a transposable genetic element (*Ds*) that created a mutation when it inserted into *C* and led to reversion when the expression of *Ac* led to its removal (**Figure 13.22d**). McClintock's hypothesis came at a time when genes were first being described, before DNA was known to be the hereditary material, and before DNA structure was described.

It was difficult for many biologists to understand how genetic elements could be mobile, and so the transposition hypothesis was much debated for years. Eventually, however, more examples of transposition emerged in maize, in other plant species, in animals, in archaea, and in bacteria. Since McClintock's discovery of transposition in maize, the process has been identified in virtually all organisms. For her discovery of transposition, McClintock was awarded the 1983 Nobel Prize in Physiology or Medicine.

McClintock's observation of the effects of transposition were important, but they were not the first example of a geneticist examining a mutant caused by transposition. In a bit of genetic irony, the first of Gregor Mendel's gene to be identified and sequenced, the gene controlling round versus wrinkled seed shape, turns out to have a recessive allele (wrinkled) that results from the insertional inactivation of the dominant wild-type (round) allele. **Experimental Insight 13.2** describes the identification and analysis of the alleles of the *R* gene in peas.

The Characteristics and Classification of Transposable Elements

The acceptance of McClintock's proposal of the existence and movement through the genome of transposable elements led to their discovery in all organisms. Transposable elements have even been found in bacteriophage genomes. There are many different types of transposable elements, ranging from the simplest, which have just the sequences required for transposition, to much more complex transposable elements that carry multiple genes; and there are several different mechanisms by which transposable elements move about the genome. Despite these differences, transposable elements have two distinctive sequence features in common that make them recognizable in genomes. The transposable element itself is flanked by **terminal inverted repeats,** and the inserted transposable element is bracketed by **flanking direct repeats** (**Figure 13.23**). The presence of terminal inverted repeats and flanking direct repeats was instrumental in permitting Cathie Martin and her colleagues to confirm

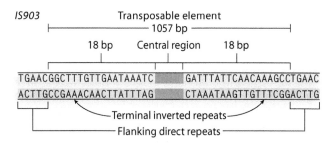

Figure 13.23   ***E. coli* insertion sequence *IS903*.** The central region and terminal inverted repeats constitute the transposable element. Flanking direct repeats are synthesized during transposition.

Experimental Insight 13.2

Mendel's Peas Are Shaped by Transposition

Gregor Mendel left good descriptions, data, and analyses of the crosses he used for establishing the law of segregation and the law of independent assortment, but he did not leave any seeds to give geneticists direct access to the genes themselves. Experimental Insight 12.1 identifies three of the genes studied by Mendel that have now been identified and analyzed. Details of the discovery in 1990 of a fourth gene are described here. It is the gene responsible for the round and wrinkled seed shapes described by Mendel, now known as *SBE1*, the starch branching enzyme 1 gene.

The gene was identified and shown to be responsible for the seed shape variation Mendel reported by a laboratory group led by Cathie Martin (Bhattacharyya et al., 1990). In its paper, the group reports western blot, northern blot, and Southern blot evidence that the recessive mutant allele, *r*, is altered by the insertion of approximately 800 bp of DNA. The insertion is of transposable DNA, and its effect is insertional inactivation of the ability to produce a starch branching enzyme that is the normal gene product. The researchers also provide a physiological explanation for the appearance of wrinkled seed shape.

WESTERN BLOT ANALYSIS

Prior to the start of this study, considerable evidence already suggested that seed shape variation was due to differences in starch synthesis. Among candidate enzymes known to be important in starch synthesis was SBE1. The researchers used *RR* (pure-breeding round) plants as a source of SBE1 to raise an antibody against the enzyme. They used protein gel electrophoresis and western blot analysis to test for reactivity between the anti-SBE1 antibody and proteins extracted from *RR* and *rr* (pure-breeding wrinkled) plants. The antibody detected the enzyme in *RR* plant protein gels but not in *rr* plant protein gels ❶. This indicates that *RR* plants produce SBE1 but that *rr* plants do not.

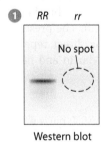

Western blot

NORTHERN BLOT ANALYSIS

The researchers next derived a molecular probe for the *SBE1* gene and tested mRNA from *RR* and *rr* plants in northern blot analysis. They found that the molecular probe hybridized with a 3300-nucleotide mRNA derived from *RR* plants and with a 4100-nucleotide mRNA from *rr* plants. They found as well that the larger transcript from *rr* plants was about tenfold less abundant than the smaller transcript from *RR* plants ❷. These results indicate that the transcript of *SBE1* in *rr* plants is longer

than in *RR* plants and that it is produced at just a fraction of the percentage present in *RR* plants.

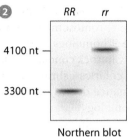

Northern blot

SOUTHERN BLOT ANALYSIS

The *SBE1* gene contains several restriction sequences, including two for the restriction enzyme *Eco*RI. The researchers took DNA isolated from *RR* and *rr* plants, digested it with *Eco*RI, and performed DNA gel electrophoresis and Southern blot analysis with the *SBE1* molecular probe. They found that the probe hybridized a DNA fragment approximately 3.5 kb in length from *RR* plants and a fragment of about 4.3 kb from *rr* plants ❸. This result could indicate either the insertion of approximately 800 bp of DNA into the *r* allele or the presence of a mutation that changes an *Eco*RI restriction sequence and alters the size of the restriction fragment (see Section 10.2). Analysis of the DNA sequence of the *r* allele revealed that the larger restriction fragment was created by insertion of DNA into one of the exons of the *SBE1* gene ❹. This event caused insertional inactivation of the *r* allele of *SBE1*. Additional examination of the DNA insert found it to be very similar to the *Ac* transposable genetic element identified by McClintock. The transposable DNA element identified by this work is named *Ips-r* (insertion *Pisum sativum-r*).

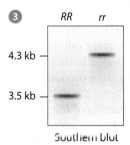

Southern blot

WRINKLED SEED DEVELOPMENT

The physiological explanation of wrinkled seed development is tied to the loss of function of SBE1. In mature round peas, almost half the dry weight is starch. About 35% of the starch is in a simple linear form known as amylose. The remainder is in complexly branched forms, most commonly a form known as amylopectin. Free molecules of sucrose make up about 5% of the dry weight. Amylose is actively converted to amylopectin by SBE1 in round seeds. In wrinkled seeds, about 30% of starch is amylopectin, and about 70% is amylose. Amylose readily

Experimental Insight **13.2** Continued

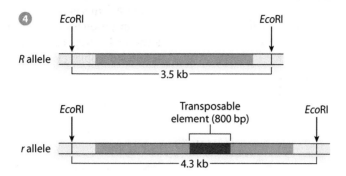

loses molecules of free sucrose, and the sugar accounts for more than 10% of the dry weight of wrinkled seeds.

During early seed development, SBE1 is active in immature seeds that will become round, but it is inactive due to mutation in immature seeds that will become wrinkled. In seeds that will be wrinkled, the high percentage of free sucrose causes cells to import large amounts of water to dilute the excess sugar. The extra water results in larger cells and larger

immature seeds that stretch the seed membrane. As all pea seeds mature, they dehydrate to the same level, and this is when wrinkling appears in *rr* seeds. The over-stretched membranes of those seeds collapse, much like an over-inflated balloon that has lost air, causing the seeds to look wrinkled. Membranes of *RR* and *Rr* seeds have not been stretched by extra water importation. They are resilient, and the seeds appear round.

---

the insertion of a transposable element as the mutational event creating the *r* allele (see Experimental Insight 13.1).

Terminal inverted repeats are part of the sequence of a transposable element, but flanking direct sequence is not. Flanking direct sequence is generated by DNA polymerase activity as part of the insertion event. Three features characterize all transposition events, and they account for the synthesis of flanking direct repeats at sites of transposition (**Figure 13.24**). First, the new target site for insertion of a transposable element has both strands of DNA cut in a staggered manner that leaves short single-stranded overhangs on each end of the cut. Second, the transposable element is inserted into its new site as double-stranded sequences that are joined to the single-strand ends at the new insertion site. Lastly, DNA is replicated at the new sites of insertion to fill the single-stranded gaps generated by cleavage. This DNA replication produces the direct repeats that flank transposable elements.

Transposable elements fall into two categories. **DNA transposons** (also called Class II transposable elements) transpose as DNA sequences. Their transposition produces flanking direct repeats at the site of insertion. At a minimum, all DNA transposons carry the **transposase** gene that produces the transposase enzyme required for the movement of the transposon, but many DNA transposons carry other genes in addition. DNA transposons are found in bacterial, archaeal, and eukaryotic genomes. Bacterial transposition is exclusively through DNA transposition.

Some DNA transposons, particularly many found in bacteria, are **simple transposons.** This term indicates that

the transposon has terminal inverted repeats surrounding the transposase gene with no other genes present. Simple transposons in bacteria are identified as *insertion sequences*. In contrast, **composite transposons** contain two insertion sequences and one or more additional genes. Composite transposons are in reality composed of two insertion sequences.

The second category of transposable elements consists of **retrotransposons** (also called Class I transposable elements), which transpose through an RNA intermediate. Retrotransposons are composed of DNA, but they are transcribed into RNA before transposition, and the RNA transcript is then copied back into DNA by the specialized enzyme **reverse transcriptase.** The reverse-transcribed DNA is then inserted into a new location, where flanking direct repeats are formed. Some, but not all, retrotransposons carry the reverse transcriptase gene, an enzyme that copies single-stranded RNA into DNA. Retrotransposons carrying the reverse transcriptase gene can initiate their own transposition, while those lacking the gene must utilize reverse transcriptase synthesized by another retrotransposon. Because retrotransposons transpose through RNA intermediates, they do not encode transcriptase. Retrotransposons are common in eukaryotes, but they are not found in bacteria. None have yet been found in archaeal genomes.

Retrotransposons always generate new copies of themselves for transposition. Thus, as transposition by retrotransposons takes place in a genome, the number of retrotransposons increases. Some DNA transposons also transpose in this manner and increase their number in a genome. This process is known as **replicative transposition,** and it

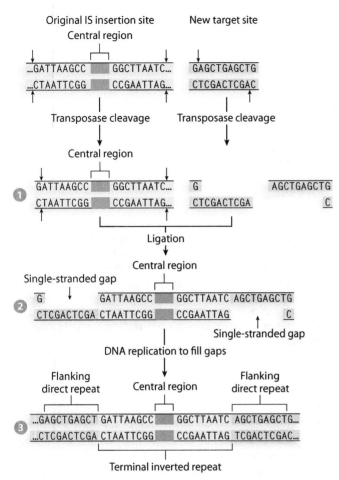

Figure 13.24 Transposition of an IS element. ❶ The IS element is removed from its original insertion site by transposase cleavage at the end of each inverted repeat. The new target site undergoes double-stranded, staggered cleavage by transposase. ❷ Ligation joins the IS element to the new target site at one end of each strand. ❸ Remaining single-stranded gaps are filled by DNA replication to create direct repeats that flank inserted IS elements.

can be thought of as a "copy-and-paste" process, whereby the original copy of the transposable element remains in place and a new copy is transposed to another location.

Alternatively, some DNA transposons undergo **nonreplicative transposition;** this can be thought of as a "cut-and-paste" mechanism. In this process, the original copy of the transposon is excised, and it is then reinserted into a new location. Nonreplicative transposition does not increase the number of copies of a transposable element in a genome.

13.6 Transposition Modifies Bacterial Genomes

Bacterial genomes, as well as plasmids and viruses, contain two types of transposable elements: (1) simple transposons known as **insertion sequences (ISs)** contain sequences encoding terminal inverted repeats surrounding a gene (sometimes two genes) encoding transposase and (2) composite transposons, designated Tn in bacteria, that contain transposase plus one or more additional genes.

Insertion Sequences

Numerous IS elements are found in bacterial, archaeal, and viral genomes and also in plasmids (**Table 13.4**). These are simple DNA sequences that contain only the genetic information necessary for their own transposition. Ranging between about 800 and 2000 bp, IS elements insert by either replicative or nonreplicative transposition. All IS elements have terminal inverted repeats surrounding the transposase gene. The inverted repeats vary in sequence. The length of inverted repeats also varies, as Table 13.4 indicates. Transposition of an IS element leads to formation of flanking direct repeats. Insertion sequences are designated by "IS" followed by a distinguishing number. Thus, *IS1, IS2, IS4,* and so on, identify insertion sequences that differ in total length and in the length and sequence of their terminal inverted repeats.

Because IS elements carry only the genetic information needed for their own transposition, they influence bacteria only in limited ways. One effect of the

Table 13.4	Characteristics of Insertion Sequence Elements in *E. coli*				
Element	Length (bp)	Inverted Repeat Length (bp)	Direct Repeat Length (bp)	Number in *E. coli*	Integration Target Sequence[a]
IS1	768	23	9	5–8	Random
IS2	1327	41	5	5	Hotspots
IS4	1428	18	11	1–2	$AAAN_{20}TTT$
IS5	1195	16	4	Variable	Hotspots
IS10R	1329	23	9	Variable	NGCTNAGCN
IS50R	1531	9	9	Variable	Hotspots
IS903	1057	18	9	Variable	Random

[a] N indicates any nucleotide.

transposition of IS elements is to produce mutation. The mutations result from insertion of an IS element into a gene or into a regulatory sequence. Typically, insertion inactivates the function of the gene or sequence. IS elements do have another role as well, as we discussed in Section 6.1: IS regions are potential sites of recombination between bacterial chromosomes and plasmids forming Hfr chromosomes. In this role, IS elements promote recombination that can lead to gene transfer between bacteria.

The transposable elements identified to date in archaeal genomes are all of the IS type, and they have sequences that show close homology with bacterial IS elements. Genetic Analysis 13.3 guides you through an assessment of potential terminal inverted repeat sequences of IS elements.

Composite Transposons

Bacterial composite transposons (Tn) are composed of two copies of an IS element, each flanked by its terminal inverted repeat sequences, and one or more additional genes. Tn elements are considerably longer than IS elements, ranging up to about 10,000 bp in length (Table 13.5). The additional genes in Tn elements are variable and are contained in a central region that is flanked by the two IS elements (Figure 13.25a). The genes in the central region confer characteristics such as antibiotic resistance and resistance to the toxic consequences of heavy metal exposure. These transposable elements can thus carry genes that may confer a growth advantage in certain environments.

Tn10 has a structure typical of most composite transposons (Figure 13.25b). It contains two copies of the *IS10* element, each with its terminal inverted repeats. These are designated *IS10R* on the right (R) side and *IS10L* on the left (L) side, and they flank the central region Each of the IS elements is about 1300 bp in length, and the *Tn10*

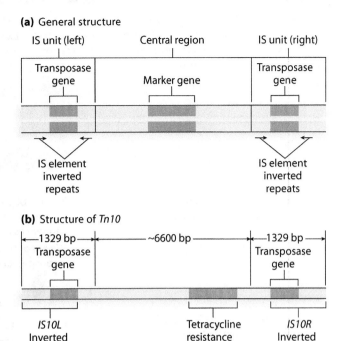

Figure 13.25   Structure of a composite transposon.

central region is about 6600 bp in length. It contains a *Tet^R* gene for resistance to the antibiotic tetracycline. The total length of *Tn10* is about 9300 bp. The *Tn10* transposon readily inserts into plasmid DNA, allowing rapid dissemination of tetracycline resistance among bacterial strains that carry the plasmid.

Bacteria can also carry a third type of DNA transposon known as a **noncomposite transposon.** These transposons do not contain insertion sequences but do carry additional genes. They transpose in the same manner as composite transposons. The noncomposite transposon *Tn3*, for example, carries two 38-bp inverted repeats flanking a 4957-bp central region that encodes three genes: transposase and resolvase, both of which are required for transposition, and β-lactamase, which provides resistance to the antibiotic ampicillin.

13.7 Transposition Modifies Eukaryotic Genomes

Transposable genetic elements are plentiful and highly varied in eukaryotic genomes. Eukaryotic genome sequence analysis finds that substantial proportions of many genomes are composed of transposable DNA. For example, nearly half of the human genome is composed of transposable DNA. Much of this DNA is repetitive in sequence, indicating that tens to thousands of copies of various transposable elements are present. Many

Table 13.5	Characteristics of Bacterial Composite Transposons			
Transposon	Insertion Sequences	Sequence Difference between IS Elements	Transposon Length (bp)	Marker Gene[a]
Tn5	IS50L	1-bp difference	5700	Kan^R
	IS50R			
Tn9	IS1	None	2500	Cam^R
Tn10	IS10L	2.5% difference	9300	Tet^R
	IS10R			
Tn903	IS903	None	3100	Kan^R

[a] *Cam* = chloramphenicol, *Kan* = kanamycin, *Tet* = tetracycline.

PROBLEM The following DNA sequences occur on the same strand of DNA and are separated by a large number of nucleotides. Which of these sequences might be found flanking an insertion sequence? Explain your answer, and identify the relevant parts of your selected sequences.

a. 5′-TTAGCAC . . . CAGGATT-3′

b. 5′-GGCCAAT . . . ATTGGCC-3′

c. 5′-CCGACCGTA . . . CCGACCGTA-3′

d. 5′-AGTATACCGC . . . GCGGTATGGC-3′

> **BREAK IT DOWN:** Inverted repeat sequences are characteristically found at the ends of insertion sequences (p. 456).

Solution Strategies	Solution Steps
Evaluate	
1. Identify the topic this problem addresses and the nature of the required answer.	1. This problem requires you to recognize DNA sequences that might flank a bacterial insertion sequence. You must identify one or more of the given sequences as a candidate flanking sequence.
2. Identify the critical information given in the problem.	2. We are given single-stranded sequences from the same strand of DNA on opposite sides of potential insertion sequences.
Deduce	

3. Determine the double-stranded sequences for each of the single-stranded sequences listed.	3. The double-stranded sequences are
	
	a. 5′-TTAGCAC . . . CAGGATT-3′
	   3′-AATCGTG . . . GTCCTAA-5′
	b. 5′-GGCCAAT . . . ATTGGCC-3′
	   3′-CCGGTTA . . . TAACCGG-5′
	c. 5′-CCGACCGTA . . . CCGACCGTA-3′
	   3′-GGCTGGCAT . . . GGCTGGCAT-5′
	d. 5′-AGTATACCGC . . . GCGGTATGGC-3′
	   3′-TCATATGGCG . . . CGCCATACCG-5′

4. Review what you know about the sequences flanking insertion elements.	4. The sequences flanking insertion elements are inverted repeat sequences.
Solve	
5. Identify any sequence that might be found flanking an insertion sequence.	5. Sequences b and d in step 3 are the ones most likely to be found flanking insertion sequences, because each sequence forms an inverted repeat sequence in double-stranded DNA.

For more practice, see Problems 30 and 31. | Visit the Study Area to access study tools. | **Mastering**Genetics™

---

eukaryotic genomes follow a similar profile, and it seems clear that transposition has been a major factor in eukaryotic genome evolution. It is equally evident that transposition continues to play an active role in the evolution of genomes and in mutation. We discuss some of this activity later in this section.

The replicative and nonreplicative mechanisms that accomplish transposition in eukaryotes are the same as those described earlier for bacteria. DNA transposons in eukaryotic genomes are of multiple types. The *Ac/Ds* elements described by McClintock are DNA transposons, for example. A prominent *Drosophila* transposable element known as a *P element* is also a DNA transposon. More commonly, however, eukaryotic transposable elements are retrotransposons, including the human genome. We begin our examination of transposition in eukaryotic genomes with a look at *Drosophila P* elements and then discuss additional eukaryotic transposable elements.

Drosophila P Elements

The genome of *Drosophila melanogaster* carries several dozen copies of a transposable genetic element called a **P element.** These DNA transposons were not part of the genome of *D. melanogaster* collected from the wild before about 1960. Today, however, all *D. melanogaster* collected in the wild carry *P* elements in their genome, suggesting that *P* elements were introduced into *D. melanogaster* about 1960, perhaps by cross-species transfer from a distantly related species. Since their introduction to the genome, *P* elements have quickly proliferated. The *Drosophila* life cycle can produce 20 to 25 generations per year; thus, *P* elements have been evolving for about 1000 generations or so in *D. melanogaster* since first being introduced into the genome.

The *P* elements exist in multiple forms. Full-length *P* elements encode transposase and are capable of autonomous transposition. These *P* elements are approximately

2900 bp in length, and they have a central region containing a gene for transposase that is encoded in four exons and three introns flanked by 31-bp inverted repeats. Transcription and translation of the transposase gene in full-length *P* elements produces an 87-kD transposase enzyme that activates *P* element transposition in germ-line cells. Several types of nonfunctional *P* elements are also found in the *D. melanogaster* genome, none producing functional transposase and all being shorter than 2900 bp.

The *P* elements were discovere *D. melanogaster* by Margaret Kidwell in 1985 when she identified **hybrid dysgenesis,** a phenomenon in which sterility occurs in the F$_1$ progeny of a cross between laboratory-bred female flies and males derived from natural populations. In these crosses, the female laboratory fly has the so-called M cytotype (*M* is for "maternal"), and the wild-type male fly has the P ("paternal") cytotype. The P-cytotype male has three to four dozen *P* elements scattered throughout its genome. In contrast, the M-cytotype female has no *P* elements. The progeny of this cross between laboratory and wild flies are hybrids that have a normal external appearance, but they are dysgenic—in other words they are biologically deficient. The term *hybrid dysgenesis* refers to the combination of sterility, a high mutation rate, and a propensity chromosomal aberrations and nondisjunction present in these flies. Importantly, the mutations found in dysgenic flies are unstable, reverting to wild-type or mutating again at a high rate. Curiously, the reciprocal cross—a P-cytotype female (this genome contains P elements) crossed to an M-cytotype male (this genome is P element-free) results in normal flies that show no evidence of hybrid dysgenesis.

The current model for hybrid dysgenesis explains why the phenotype occurs only when males have the P cytotype and females the M cytotype and not in the reciprocal cross (**Figure 13.26**). The key appears to be that the transposase genes in P elements are silenced by a suppressor protein in P-cytotype strains. This inhibits their transposition and potential for causing mutations. In matings of P-cytotype males and M-cytotype females, sperm from P-cytotype males contains chromosomes only and virtually no cytoplasmic material. The chromosomes carry P-elements, but as there is no cytoplasmic material, sperm, do not possess the transposition repressor protein. The eggs of M-cytotype females contain abundant cytoplasmic material but carry no transposition repressor protein because the chromosomes in the M cytotype are free of *P* elements. At fertilization, sperm add *P* element–laden chromosomes into an egg lacking transposition-repressing protein. Extensive transposition takes place, creating multiple mutations by insertion of *P* elements into functional genes or by inducing chromosome breaks similar to those observed by McClintock in the maize genome. Following embryonic development, the consequence of this widespread transpositional activity is widespread mutation by insertional inactivation that results in hybrid dysgenesis. In contrast, hybrid dysgenesis does not occur in the reciprocal cross between females with the P cytotype and males of either the M cytotype. In these crosses, the chromosomes derived from the P-cytotype female carry P-elements and the cytoplasm of eggs contains the transposition-repressing protein. This, blocks *P* element transposition. The F$_1$ receives chromosomes

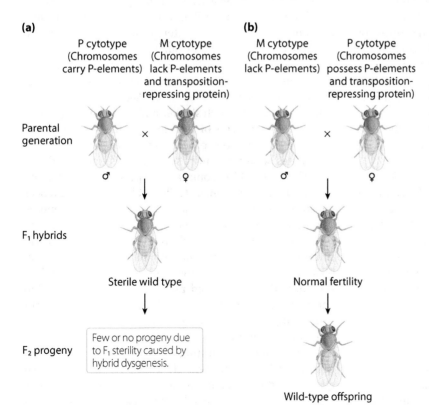

(a)

P cytotype (Chromosomes carry P-elements)   M cytotype (Chromosomes lack P-elements and transposition-repressing protein)

(b)

M cytotype (Chromosomes lack P-elements)   P cytotype (Chromosomes possess P-elements and transposition-repressing protein)

Parental generation

♂   ×   ♀   ♂   ×   ♀

F$_1$ hybrids

Sterile wild type   Normal fertility

F$_2$ progeny

Few or no progeny due to F$_1$ sterility caused by hybrid dysgenesis.

Wild-type offspring

Figure 13.26   Hybrid dysgenesis in *Drosophila*. (a) Male *Drosophila* of the P cytotype crossed to females of the M cytotype produce F$_1$ progeny that are largely infertile due to mutations resulting from *P* element transposition. (b) Crosses of P-cytotype females to males with either the P or the M cytotype yield F$_1$ progeny of normal fertility.

that are free of P-elements from the M cytotype male, and the germ line of the F_1 hybrid progeny remains stable.

The genomes of laboratory strains of fruit flies (M cytotype) are free of P-elements, whereas the genomes of natural populations of flies (P cytotype) contain scores to hundreds of P-elements. Yet the laboratory strains used today derive from natural populations collected by Thomas Hunt Morgan and others beginning in the early 1900s. Why are laboratory strains and natural flies so different? The answer appears to be the introduction and rapid evolution of P-elements in natural populations after the capture of the ancestors of today's laboratory strains. The origin of P-elements and the mechanism of their spread through the natural fruit fly genome are not yet clear, but it is known that transposable elements, once introduced into a population, can spread rapidly.

Retrotransposons

Retrotransposons are the most common transposable elements in eukaryotic genomes. They are related to RNA-containing retroviruses that reverse transcribe their genetic information into DNA in order to parasitize host cells. In a similar manner, retrotransposons use reverse transcriptase to synthesize a DNA copy of the retrotransposon transcript for insertion into new genome locations.

Retroviruses generally encode at least three genes, called *gag*, *env*, and *pol*. Gag and env encode proteins that form the retroviral particle. New retroviral particles are produced within infected cells and perpetuate the infection by invading new cells. The *pol* gene encodes the enzyme *reverse transcriptase* that directs the synthesis of double-stranded DNA from single-stranded RNA.

Figure 13.27 illustrates comparative structures of a retrovirus and three retrotransposons. Two constant features of retrotransposons are seen. First, all retrotransposons encode reverse transcriptase (*pol*) to catalyze transposition, and some contain *gag*, but none contains *env*. Second, the gene or genes carried by retrotransposons are flanked by **long terminal repeats (LTRs)** that may be up to several hundred base pairs in length.

Ty Elements of Yeast Many different forms of *Ty* retrotransposons of yeast are found, all sharing the common features of retrotransposons. In *Ty* elements, the central element is approximately 6 kb, flanked by LTRs that are each about 330 bp in length. Both LTRs contain promoters that direct the transcription of different genes in the central region. Approximately 50 to 100 copies of *Ty* elements are present in the typical *Saccharomyces cerevisiae* genome. The *Ty* elements cause mutation in yeast genes by insertion.

Copia Elements of *Drosophila* Multiple forms of the retrotransposon *copia* are found in the *Drosophila* genome. *Copia* elements have a central element of 5 to 8.5 kb that contains *pol* and *gag* genes and is flanked by LTRs of 250 to 600 bp each. The word *copia* comes from

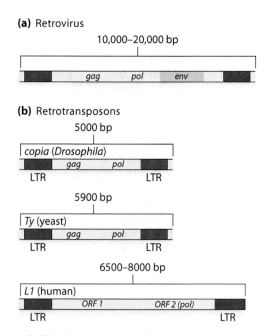

Figure 13.27 **Retrovirus structure and selected eukaryotic retrotransposons.**

the Latin for "abundance," and befitting this designation, more than 5% of the *Drosophila* genome is composed of *copia* retrotransposons. This abundance leads to many mutations throughout the genome that are usually the result of insertion of *copia* into a wild-type gene.

LINE and SINE Elements of Humans More than 45% of the human genome is composed of transposable DNA. Among the functional transposable genetic elements in the human genome, LINE (long interspersed nuclear elements) and SINE (short interspersed nuclear elements) families of elements stand out because of their relative abundance and their ability to cause spontaneous human gene mutations. LINEs are up to several thousand base pairs in length and have an average length of about 900 bp. SINEs are much shorter and have their sequences truncated at one end of the element, likely because the reverse transcription process used for their transfer terminates before the entire sequence has transposed.

Almost 1 million copies of LINE sequences are found in the human genome. Collectively, these sequences constitute a little more than 20% of the total genome sequence. Human *L1* elements are the most common members of the LINE family of elements in the human genome. The *L1* elements vary in length from about 6500 bp to 8000 bp. Full-length *L1* elements encode a protein with nuclease and reverse transcriptase function and may also encode a second RNA-binding protein, but shortening of the element affects its ability to transpose. The human genome contains approximately 600,000 copies of *L1* alone, constituting more than 17% of the total genome. *L1* elements actively transpose in the human genome and produce mutations. For example, mutations of the *F8* gene, an X-linked gene whose mutation causes an X-linked recessive version of the blood-clotting disorder hemophilia A, are traced to *L1* insertion into the gene.

SINE elements, too, are common in the human genome. Just over 10% of human genome sequence is composed of SINEs. The *Alu* element is the most common of the human SINE sequences. *Alu* elements vary in length from 100 to 300 bp and are each flanked by direct repeats of 7 to 20 bp. They are so named because each element can be cleaved into two segments by the restriction endonuclease *Alu*I (*Al-LOO-one*) that recognizes the 4-bp restriction enzyme target sequence 5′-AGCT-3′. The human genome contains more than 1 million *Alu* elements, and they actively generate mutations. A comprehensive review of the role of *Alu*

elements in human genetic disease by Prescott Deininger and Mark Batzer in 1999 found numerous examples of new gene mutations caused by *Alu* insertions. The mutational mechanisms identified are alterations of gene expression by *Alu* insertion into regulatory DNA sequences such as promoters, *Alu* insertions into exons that alter the reading frame (frameshift mutations), disruption of normal mRNA splicing following *Alu* insertion into introns, and unequal crossover events between homologous chromosomes involving *Alu* elements. Overall, *Alu* elements were estimated to transpose in about 1 in 200 people and to be directly responsible for about 0.3% of all human hereditary disease, much of it due to new mutations.

CASE STUDY

Human Chromosome Evolution

Researchers can trace the evolution of human chromosomes by comparing chromosome structure and genetic composition of humans to those of other species that share a common ancestor. We describe two such comparative approaches here: One compares syntenic clusters of genes (genes on the same chromosome) in distantly related species, and the second compares banding patterns of chromosomes in closely related species.

Figure 13.28 compares syntenic clusters of genes on 20 chromosomes (19 autosomes and the X chromosome) in the mouse genome and their relation to the same sequences on the 23 chromosomes (22 autosomes and the X chromosome) in humans. Published in 2002 by a large research group known as the Mouse Genome Sequencing Consortium, this study compares 342 syntenic chromosome segments. The average size of the syntenic segments is a little less than 10 million base pairs. Syntenic groups of genes found in the human genome are dispersed among several chromosomes in the mouse genome. Interestingly, human chromosomes 17 and 20 each correspond entirely to a portion of mouse chromosomes 11 and 2, respectively. In both cases, the human chromosome corresponds to a long cluster of contiguous syntenic groups in the respective mouse chromosome. Comparison of X chromosomes of human and mouse reveal very strong sequence and genetic similarity.

This comparison leads to two salient evolutionary conclusions. First, mouse and human share similar syntenic clusters because their common ancestor carried these clusters. Human and mouse chromosomes have diverged from those of their common ancestor by numerous rearrangements, including chromosome translocation, chromosome fusion, and chromosome inversion, that have changed many attributes of chromosome structure, but they also retain large segments of genes and sequences as syntenic clusters. Second, for X-linked genes specifically, the strong syntenic relationship has been maintained by natural selection driven by the requirements of embryonic development and the necessity to maintain a balance in dosage of X-linked genes by random X-inactivation.

Figure 13.29 illustrates the banding patterns of chromosomes 1, 2, and 3 of human (H), chimpanzee (C), gorilla (G), and

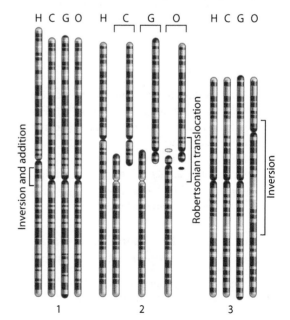

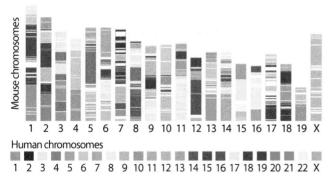

Figure 13.28 **Evolutionary conservation of chromosome synteny between mouse and human chromosomes.** Each of 23 human chromosomes is uniquely colored and its segments superimposed on 20 mouse chromosomes.

Figure 13.29 **Human and great ape chromosome evolution.** Chromosomes 1, 2, and 3 of human (H), chimpanzee (C), gorilla (G), and orangutan (O) are compared to determine the events leading to different chromosome numbers and structures.

orangutan (O). These four closely related primate species last shared a common ancestor between 30 and 35 million years ago. In each of the three chromosomes, strong similarity of banding patterns directly reflects the strong genetic similarity between the species. Structural and numerical differences between the chromosomes allow reconstruction of the evolutionary events that shaped the contemporary chromosomes of each species. Taking the events from the perspective of human chromosomes, we can reconstruct the evolution for each chromosome as follows.

- Chromosome 1 is very similar in the four primate species, with the exception of a pericentric inversion and the addition of a small segment near the centromere of the human chromosome (1q1.2 to 1q2.1).

- Chromosome 2 holds the explanation for the difference in diploid number between humans ($2n = 46$) and our close relatives ($2n = 48$). The reduction in human diploid number is the result of a Robertsonian translocation fusing two small acrocentric chromosomes that belong to separate chromosome pairs in chimp, gorilla, and orangutan.

- Chromosome 3 shows strong similarity of banding pattern in the four species with the exception of the orangutan chromosome, which has undergone a pericentric inversion that changed the relative arm lengths and altered the position of the centromere in comparison to the other primate chromosomes.

SUMMARY

(MasteringGenetics™) For activities, animations, and review quizzes, go to the Study Area.

13.1 Nondisjunction Leads to Changes in Chromosome Number

- In euploid nuclei, the number of chromosomes is equal to a multiple of the haploid number (n), whereas aneuploid nuclei have additional or missing chromosomes.

- Chromosome nondisjunction is the failure of homologous chromosomes or sister chromatids to separate and is a common cause of aneuploid gametes.

- Aneuploidy alters the phenotype of an organism by changing the balance of gene dosage of critical genes.

- Human aneuploidy manifests as trisomy of particular autosomes and as trisomy or monosomy of sex chromosomes.

- Chromosomal mosaics are organisms containing cells with two or more genetic or chromosomal constitutions.

- Uniparental disomy occurs when both homologous copies of a chromosome originate in a single parent.

13.2 Changes in Euploidy Result in Various Kinds of Polyploidy

- Polyploids carry three or more haploid sets of chromosomes.

- Allopolyploids carry chromosome sets from different species, whereas autopolyploids have multiple chromosome sets from a single species.

- Polyploidy is common in plant species, where increases in fruit and flower size alter fertility and can produce hybrid vigor.

- Polyploids have a reduced frequency of recessive homozygosity compared to diploid species.

13.3 Chromosome Breakage Causes Mutation by Loss, Gain, and Rearrangement of Chromosomes

- Chromosome breakage can result in terminal deletion or in interstitial deletion and may alter chromosome banding patterns.

- Heterozygosity for partial deletion or partial duplication produces phenotypic abnormalities through disturbances of gene dosage balance.

- Homologous chromosome synapsis involving a partial deletion or partial duplication chromosome produces a characteristic unpaired loop.

- Microdeletions and microduplications too small to be seen by banding changes are detected by molecular methods.

- The detection of pseudodominance provides important positional indicators for deletion mapping of genes.

13.4 Chromosome Breakage Leads to Inversion and Translocation of Chromosomes

- Chromosome breakage can lead to inversion or translocation of chromosome segments.

- Chromosome inversion heterozygotes have one chromosome with the normal order but have an inversion in the homolog. Homologs in these organisms form an inversion loop at synapsis.

- Paracentric inversions have two break points on one arm only, and the inversion does not include the centromeric region. Pericentric inversions have break points on each arm, and the centromeric region is included in the inverted region.

- Chromosome inversion is a crossover-suppression mechanism.

- A tetravalent synaptic structure containing chromosomes involved in reciprocal translocation leads to two patterns of chromosome segregation in meiosis.

- The reduction in the number of viable gametes produced by reciprocal balanced translocation heterozygotes results in semisterility.

- Robertsonian translocation occurs by the fusion of nonhomologous chromosomes.

13.5 Transposable Genetic Elements Move throughout the Genome

- Transposition is the process that moves transposable genetic elements in genomes and was first discovered in maize.

- Transposase is the enzyme responsible for transposition, and it is encoded by many transposable genetic elements.

- Transposition produces mutations through insertional inactivation modifying gene expression and by contributing to unequal crossing over between homologous chromosomes.
- DNA transposons encode transposase and perhaps other genes and transpose as DNA sequences.
- Retrotransposons encode reverse transcriptase and perhaps other genes and transpose through an RNA intermediate.
- Retrotransposons and some DNA transposons transpose by replicative transposition, a "copy-and-paste" mechanism.
- Some DNA transposons transpose by nonreplicative transposition, a "cut-and-paste" mechanism.

13.6 Transposition Modifies Bacterial Genomes

- Bacterial insertion sequences encode transposase and are flanked by inverted repeat sequences unique to each insertion sequence.

- Composite and noncomposite transposons carry transposase and additional genes, including those for antibiotic resistance.

13.7 Transposition Modifies Eukaryotic Genomes

- *Drosophila P* elements are common, transpose actively, and cause hybrid dysgenesis in certain crosses.
- Retrotransposons, including *Ty, copia,* LINE, SINE, and *Alu,* are common in eukaryotic genomes and produce mutations.
- Almost half the human genome is derived from transposable DNA. LINE, SINE, and *Alu* sequences are retrotransposons that predominate in human transposable DNA.

KEYWORDS

acentric (acentric chromosome) *(p. 440)*
activator (*Ac*) element *(p. 453)*
adjacent-1 segregation *(p. 449)*
alternate segregation *(p. 448)*
aneuploid *(p. 431)*
asexual polyploidization *(p. 437)*
chromosome aberration *(p. 431)*
chromosome break point *(p. 440)*
chromosome (paracentric, pericentric) inversion (inversion heterozygote) *(p. 446)*
chromosome translocation *(p. 446)*
composite transposon *(p. 455)*
crossover suppression *(p. 447)*
deletion (interstitial, microdeletion, partial deletion, partial deletion heterozygote, terminal) *(pp. 440, 441, 442)*
deletion mapping *(p. 442)*
dicentric bridge (dicentric chromosome) *(p. 447)*
dissociation (*Ds*) element *(p. 453)*
DNA transposon *(p. 455)*

duplication (partial duplication, partial duplication heterozygote) *(p. 441)*
euploid *(p. 431)*
flanking direct sequence repeat *(p. 453)*
gene dosage *(p. 433)*
gynandromorphy *(p. 436)*
hybrid dysgenesis *(p. 459)*
hybrid vigor *(p. 438)*
insertion sequence (IS) *(p. 456)*
inversion loop *(p. 446)*
insertional inactivation *(p. 451)*
long terminal repeats (LTRs) *(p. 460)*
microduplications *(p. 442)*
monosomy *(p. 432)*
noncomposite transposon *(p. 457)*
nonreplicative transposition *(p. 456)*
partial chromosome deletion *(p. 440)*
P element *(p. 458)*
polyploidy (allopolyploidy, autopolyploidy) *(p. 437)*
pseudodominance *(p. 442)*

reciprocal translocation (balanced, unbalanced) *(p. 448)*
replicative transposition *(p. 455)*
retrotransposon *(p. 455)*
reverse transcriptase *(p. 455)*
Robertsonian translocation (chromosome fusion) *(p. 448)*
semisterility *(p. 435)*
sexual polyploidization *(p. 437)*
simple transposon *(p. 455)*
terminal inverted repeat *(p. 453)*
translocation heterozygote *(p. 448)*
transposase *(p. 455)*
transposition (transposable genetic element) *(pp. 450, 451)*
trisomy *(p. 432)*
trisomy rescue *(p. 437)*
unequal crossover *(p. 441)*
unpaired loop *(p. 442)*
uniparental disomy *(p. 436)*
unstable mutant phenotype *(p. 453)*

PROBLEMS

(MasteringGenetics™) Visit for instructor-assigned tutorials and problems.

Chapter Concepts

For answers to selected even-numbered problems, see Appendix: Answers.

1. Consider synapsis in prophase I of meiosis for two plant species that each carry 36 chromosomes. Species A is diploid and species B is triploid. What characteristics of homologous chromosome synapsis can be used to distinguish these two species?

2. For one set of chromosomes carried by a triploid plant species, assume the chromosome pair as one bivalent

involving chromosomes C1 and C2, and as one univalent with chromosome C3. Show the gametes that result from this synaptic pattern, and identify the frequency and content of the genetically different gametes produced by the species.

3. If the haploid number for a plant species is 4, how many chromosomes are found in a member of the species that

has one of the following characteristics? Explain your reasoning in each case.

a. diploid
b. pentaploid
c. octaploid
d. trisomic
e. triploid
f. monosomic
g. tetraploid
h. hexaploid

In the list above, which plants are likely to be infertile or to have reduced fertility?

4. From the following list, identify the types of chromosome changes you expect to show phenotypic consequences.

a. pericentric inversion
b. interstitial deletion
c. duplication
d. terminal deletion
e. trisomy
f. reciprocal balanced translocation
g. paracentric inversion
h. monosomy
i. polyploidy

5. Mating between a male donkey ($2n = 62$) and a female horse ($2n = 64$) produces sterile mules. Recently, however, a very rare event occurred—a female mule gave birth to an offspring by mating with a horse.

a. Determine how many chromosomes are in the mule karyotype, and explain why mules are generally sterile.
b. How many chromosomes does the mule–horse offspring carry?
c. Why is it very unlikely that the offspring will have fully horse-like genetic characteristics?

6. Studies of hybrid dysgenesis in *Drosophila* indicate that the transposition repressor protein produced by *P* elements is part of a process that limits the number of *P* elements present in a genome. Why is it advantageous to limit the number of *P* elements in a genome?

7. What evidence suggests that *copia* elements of fruit flies and *Ty* elements of yeast are related to RNA-containing viruses?

8. What can we conclude about a mutational event that renders *IS1* unable to transpose?

9. In terms of the chromosome content of nuclei, what is meant by the term *mosaic*?

10. In *Drosophila*, an X-linked recessive allele produces yellow body color. The cross of a yellow female and a male with wild-type body color usually produces wild-type females and yellow males. Occasionally however, a yellow female is produced. Explain how the unusual female is produced.

Application and Integration

For answers to selected even-numbered problems, see Appendix: Answers.

11. The plants in this problem are the same as those described in Genetic Analysis 13.1, where flower color in the autotetraploid is a single-gene character determined by alleles R_1 and R_2 that have an additive relationship. The genotype–phenotype correspondence is as follows:

Genotype	Phenotype
$R_1R_1R_1R_1$	Dark red
$R_1R_1R_1R_2$	Light red
$R_1R_1R_2R_2$	Pink
$R_1R_2R_2R_2$	Light pink
$R_2R_2R_2R_2$	White

a. Predict the phenotypes and frequencies of progeny produced by self-fertilization of a light red plant.
b. A light pink and a light red plant are crossed. Predict the frequencies of phenotypes among the progeny.

12. A normal chromosome and its homolog carrying a paracentric inversion are given. The dot ($\cdot$) represents the centromere.

Normal   ABC·DEFGHIJK
Inversion   abc·djihgfek

a. Diagram the alignment of chromosomes during prophase I.
b. Assume a crossover takes place in the region between F and G. Identify the gametes that are formed following this crossover, and indicate which gametes are viable.
c. Assume a crossover takes place in the region between A and B. Identify the gametes that are formed by this crossover event, and indicate which gametes are viable.

13. A pair of homologous chromosomes in *Drosophila* has the following content (single letters represent genes):

Chromosome 1   RNMDHBGKWU
Chromosome 2   RNMDHBDHBGKWU

a. What term best describes this situation?
b. Diagram the pairing of these homologous chromosomes in prophase I.
c. What term best describes the unusual structure that forms during pairing of these chromosomes?
d. How does the pairing diagrammed in part (b) differ from the pairing of chromosomes in an inversion heterozygote?

14. An animal heterozygous for a reciprocal balanced translocation has the following chromosomes:

MN·OPQRST
MN·OPQRjkl
cdef·ghijkl
cdef·ghiST

a. Diagram the pairing of these chromosomes in prophase I.

b. Identify the gametes produced by alternate segregation. Which of these gametes are viable?

c. Identify the gametes produced by adjacent-1 segregation. Which of these gametes are viable?

d. Identify the gametes produced by adjacent-2 segregation. Which of these gametes are viable?

e. Among the three segregation patterns, which is least likely to occur? Why?

15. Dr. Ara B. Dopsis has an idea he thinks will be a boon to agriculture. He wants to create the "pomato," a hybrid between a tomato (*Lycopersicon esculentum*) that has 12 chromosomes and a potato (*Solanum tuberosum*) that has 48 chromosomes. Dr. Dopsis is hoping that his new pomato will have tuber growth like a potato and the fruit production of a tomato. He joins a haploid gamete from each species to form a hybrid and then induces doubling of chromosome number.

a. How many chromosomes will the hybrid have before chromosome doubling?

b. Will this hybrid be infertile?

c. How many chromosomes will the polyploid have after chromosome doubling?

d. Can Dr. Dopsis be sure the polyploid will have the characteristics he wants? Why or why not?

16. Suppose polymerase chain reaction (PCR) is used to amplify a single DNA marker on human chromosome 21. Further suppose that a couple who have a child with Down syndrome (trisomy 21) is examined for this marker. The mother has marker alleles of 310 and 380 bp. Her mate has marker alleles of 290 and 340 bp. What PCR bands are present in their child with Down syndrome if nondisjunction occurred in

a. maternal meiosis I

b. maternal meiosis II

c. paternal meiosis I

d. paternal meiosis II

17. Chromosome IV in *Drosophila* is a very small chromosome and carries a tiny amount of genetic material. Fruit flies that are trisomic for chromosome IV have no apparent phenotypic abnormalities, and they retain their fertility. Among the genes on chromosome IV is one for which a recessive allele *ey* produces the "eyeless" phenotype. A male that is trisomic for chromosome IV and has the genotype ++*ey* is crossed to a diploid eyeless female with the genotype *eyey*.

a. Assuming random segregation of chromosomes takes place during spermatogenesis and that all sperm are viable, what sperm genotypes are expected and in what proportions?

b. If these sperm are united with eggs from the eyeless female, what is the expected ratio of eyeless to normal-eyed flies among the progeny?

18. A healthy couple with a history of three previous spontaneous abortions has just had a child with cri-du-chat syndrome, a disorder caused by a terminal deletion of chromosome 5. Their physician orders karyotype analysis of both parents and of the child. The karyotype results for chromosomes 5 and 12 are shown here.

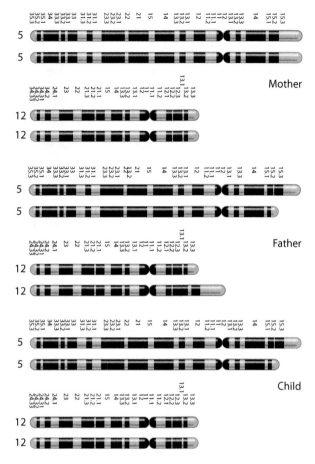

a. Are the chromosomes in the child consistent with those expected in a case of cri-du-chat syndrome? Explain your reasoning.

b. Which parent has an abnormal karyotype? How can you tell? What is the nature of the abnormality?

c. Why does this parent have a normal phenotype?

d. Diagram the pairing of the abnormal chromosomes.

e. What segregation pattern occurred to produce the gamete involved in fertilization of the child with cri-du-chat syndrome?

f. What is the approximate probability that the next child of this couple will have cri-du-chat syndrome?

g. Do the karyotypes of the parents help explain the occurrence of the three previous spontaneous abortions? Explain.

19. A boy with Down syndrome (trisomy 21) has 46 chromosomes. His parents and his two older sisters have a normal phenotype, but each has 45 chromosomes.

a. Explain how this is possible.

b. How many chromosomes do you expect to see in karyotypes of the parents?

c. What term best describes this kind of chromosome abnormality?

d. What is the probability the next child of this couple will have a normal phenotype and have 46 chromosomes? Explain your answer.

20. Human chromosome 5 and the corresponding chromosomes from chimpanzee, gorilla, and orangutan are shown on the following page. Describe any structural differences

you see in the other primate chromosomes in relation to the human chromosome, and propose a mechanism to explain each difference.

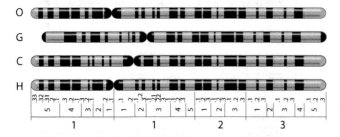

21. A small population of deer living on an isolated island are separated for many generations from a mainland deer population. The populations retain the same number of chromosomes and are interfertile, but one chromosome (shown here) has a different banding pattern.

    a. Describe how the banding pattern of the island population chromosome most likely evolved from the mainland chromosome. What term or terms describe the difference between these chromosomes?

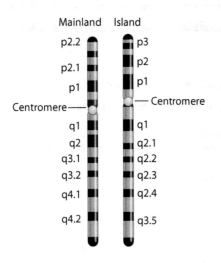

    b. Draw the synapsis of these homologs during prophase I in hybrids produced from the cross of mainland with island deer.

    c. In a mainland–island hybrid deer, recombination takes place in band q1 of the homologous chromosomes. Draw the gametes that result from this event.

    d. Suppose that 40% of all meioses in mainland–island hybrids involve recombination somewhere in the chromosome region between q2.1 and p2. What proportion of the gametes of hybrid deer are viable? What is the cause of the decreased proportion of viable gametes in hybrids relative to the parental populations?

22. In humans that are XX/XO mosaics, the phenotype is highly variable, ranging from females who have classic Turner syndrome symptoms to females who are essentially normal. Likewise, XY/XO mosaics have phenotypes that range from Turner syndrome females to essentially normal males. How can the wide range of phenotypes be explained for these sex-chromosome mosaics?

23. A plant breeder would like to develop a seedless variety of cucumber from two existing lines. Line A is a tetraploid line, and line B is a diploid line. Describe the breeding strategy that will produce a seedless line, and support your strategy by describing the results of crosses.

24. In *Drosophila*, seven partial deletions (1 to 7) shown as gaps in the following diagram have been mapped on a chromosome. This region of the chromosome contains genes that express seven recessive mutant phenotypes, identified in the following table as *a* through *g*. A researcher wants to determine the location and order of genes on the chromosome, so he sets up a series of crosses in which flies homozygous for a mutant allele are crossed with flies that are homozygous for a partial deletion. The progeny are scored to determine whether they have the mutant phenotype ("m" in the table) or the wild-type phenotype ("+" in the table). Use the partial deletion map and the table of progeny phenotypes to determine the order of genes on the chromosome.

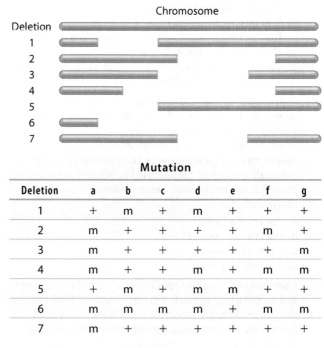

Deletion	a	b	c	d	e	f	g
1	+	m	+	m	+	+	+
2	m	+	+	+	+	m	+
3	m	+	+	+	+	+	m
4	m	+	+	m	+	m	m
5	+	m	+	m	m	+	+
6	m	m	m	m	+	m	m
7	m	+	+	+	+	+	+

25. Two experimental varieties of strawberry are produced by crossing a hexaploid line that contains 48 chromosomes and a tetraploid line that contains 32 chromosomes. Experimental variety 1 contains 40 chromosomes, and experimental variety 2 contains 56 chromosomes.

    a. Do you expect both experimental lines to be fertile? Why or why not?

    b. How many chromosomes from the hexaploid line are contributed to experimental variety 1? To experimental variety 2?

    c. How many chromosomes from the tetraploid lines are contributed to experimental variety 1? To experimental variety 2?

26. In the tomato, *Solanum esculentum*, tall (*D*–) is dominant to dwarf (*dd*) plant height, smooth fruit (*P*–) is dominant to peach fruit (*pp*), and round fruit shape (*O*–) is dominant to oblate fruit shape (*oo*). These three genes are linked on

chromosome 1 of tomato in the order *dwarf-peach-oblate*. There are 12 map units between *dwarf* and *peach* and 17 map units between *peach* and *oblate*. A trihybrid plant (*DPO/dpo*) is test-crossed to a plant that is homozygous recessive at the three loci (*dpo/dpo*). Progeny plants are grown with the results shown below. Identify the mechanism responsible for the resulting data that do not agree with the established genetic map.

Progeny Phenotype	Number
Tall, smooth, round	473
Dwarf, peach, oblate	476
Tall, smooth, oblate	12
Dwarf, peach, round	8
Tall, peach, oblate	17
Dwarf, smooth, round	13
Tall, peach, round	0
Dwarf, smooth, oblate	1
	1000

27. In *Drosophila*, the wild-type red eye color is produced by the X-linked allele w^+. Mutants for eye color often lack the ability to deposit pigment in the eye and have white eye color. For the purpose of this problem, assume that in Southern blot analysis a molecular probe hybridizes to a 5.0-kb fragment of DNA from the eye-color locus. The probe binds to DNA fragments containing either wild-type or mutant sequence.

    a. If a male *Drosophila* has white eye color as a result of inactivation of w^+ by movement of a 3-kb *P* element into the wild-type allele, diagram the expected Southern blot pattern of DNA fragments from wild-type males and white-eyed males and females that carry the mutant allele. Explain your reasoning.

    b. Several male progeny of a female carrier of the mutant allele have red sectors on their eyes. The number and size of the sectors vary among the males. Explain the origin of these red sectors, and account for the variation in number and size.

    c. If Southern blotting is used to compare DNA isolated from a white sector and a red sector of the same eye, is a difference in DNA fragment size expected? Explain.

28. A *Drosophila P* element 2.5 kb in length is modified by adding a 1.0-kb intron sequence to one of its exons. A *copia* element of 6.0 kb is modified by adding the same 1.0-kb intron to its central region.

    a. A *Drosophila* genome carrying both transposable elements is induced to undergo transposition. What is the length of the newly transposed *P* element?

    b. What is the length of the newly transposed *copia* element?

    c. Explain the results for each case of transposition.

29. A biologist studying flight mechanisms in insects wants to introduce a dominant mutant allele producing over-sized wings, called *flapper*, into the *Drosophila* genome. The biologist chooses a strain of fruit fly homozygous for a recessive mutant producing miniature wings. How will the biologist design the experiment using a *P* element to deliver the mutant allele to the genome?

30. After reading Experimental Insight 13.2 and examining the results of western, northern, and Southern blot analysis of plants with the genotypes *RR* and *rr*, describe the results you would expect to see for each of the three kinds of analysis for plants with the genotype *Rr*. Specify the number of bands or spots expected for each analysis, and give the expected position of each band or spot.

31. Two *Not*I restriction enzymes cleave DNA on opposite sides of the *Dbm* gene in a species of yeast. A molecular probe for *Dbm* detects a DNA restriction fragment of 8.5 kb in organisms that are wild type at *Dbm*. In a strain of yeast, a *Ty1* transposable genetic element mutates *dbm*. *Ty1* is 5.6 kb in length.

    a. In haploid yeast with this *dbm* mutation, what is the length of the restriction fragment detected by the probe following *Not*I digestion?

    b. What DNA-fragment sizes are detected in a diploid yeast strain that is heterozygous for wild-type and mutant alleles at *dbm*?

    c. Insertion of *Ty1* into *dbm* causes a loss-of-function mutation. Explain why this is the case.

32. For the following crosses, determine as accurately as possible the genotypes of each parent, the parent in whom nondisjunction occurs, and whether nondisjunction takes place in the first or second meiotic division. Both color blindness and hemophilia, a blood-clotting disorder, are X-linked recessive traits. In each case, assume the parents have normal karyotypes (see Table 13.2).

    a. A man and a woman who each have wild-type phenotypes have a son with Klinefelter syndrome (XXY) who has hemophilia.

    b. A man who is color blind and a woman who is wild type have a son with Jacob syndrome (XYY) who has hemophilia.

    c. A color-blind man and a woman who is wild type have a daughter with Turner syndrome (XO) who has normal color vision and blood clotting.

    d. A man who is color blind and has hemophilia and a woman who is wild type have a daughter with triple X syndrome (XXX) who has hemophilia and normal color vision.

14 Regulation of Gene Expression in Bacteria and Bacteriophage

CHAPTER OUTLINE

14.1 Transcriptional Control of Gene Expression Requires DNA–Protein Interaction

14.2 The *lac* Operon Is an Inducible Operon System under Negative and Positive Control

14.3 Mutational Analysis Deciphers Genetic Regulation of the *lac* Operon

14.4 Transcription from the Tryptophan Operon Is Repressible and Attenuated

14.5 Bacteria Regulate the Transcription of Stress Response Genes and Translation and Archaea Regulate Transcription in a Bacteria-like Manner

14.6 Antiterminators and Repressors Control Lambda Phage Infection of *E. coli*

Jacques Monod (left), André Lwoff (middle), and François Jacob (right) on October 14, 1965, following the announcement of the awarding of the Nobel Prize in Physiology or Medicine for their work describing the lactose (*lac*) operon in *E. coli*.

ESSENTIAL IDEAS

- Gene expression in bacteria is controlled primarily through transcriptional regulation, often by regulating groups of genes known as operons.

- Transcription of lactose (*lac*) operon genes is induced by lactose and is repressed in the absence of lactose.

- Transcription of the repressible tryptophan (*trp*) operon adjusts to the level of available tryptophan.

- Specialized regulatory processes control transcriptional response to environmental stress and regulate translation.

- Bacteriophage use transcriptional regulation to express the genes responsible for infecting their hosts.

- Competition between regulatory proteins determines the course of bacteriophage lambda infection in bacteria.

Take a moment to think about the ever-changing environment endured by the billions of *Escherichia coli* that populate your intestinal tract. These bacteria are accustomed to a diverse and constantly shifting set of environmental factors and nutritional conditions, as well as to competition from the many other bacterial species in your gut. In all these rapidly changing environmental conditions, bacterial survival depends on the ability to deal with whatever conditions prevail at the moment. Each individual bacterial cell is almost entirely self-reliant when it comes to producing the proteins necessary to carry out metabolism and to generate the compounds it needs to stay alive and to reproduce.

What is the best strategy for survival in a rapidly changing environment? Should the organism transcribe and translate all its genes at all times, or should gene transcription and translation be regulated in a closely monitored manner that can respond in a matter of minutes to accommodate changes in growth conditions as they arise? Answering these kinds of questions was critically important to understanding how evolution has shaped the processes of gene expression in organisms. On one hand, if bacteria transcribed and translated all their genes at all times, they could be instantly ready for almost any environmental shift that might occur. On the other hand, continuously expressing all genes would be terribly costly in metabolic terms and entail a great deal of unnecessary transcription and translation. Biologists in the 1950s and 1960s hypothesized that energetic and metabolic expenditures associated with regulated gene expression would be evolutionarily favored over the high cost of continuous gene expression. But to demonstrate the validity of that hypothesis, examples of regulated gene expression had to be identified and studied.

The first research describing the gene actions and molecular mechanism for regulated gene expression was by Francois Jacob, Jacques Monod, André Lwoff, and others, who showed how the lactose (*lac*) operon system in *E. coli* was transcriptionally regulated in response to the presence or absence of the milk sugar lactose. This research was a milestone in biology that introduced a new way of thinking about the expression of genes. It opened the door to research on mechanisms that regulate gene expression—research that is just as active today as it has ever been.

In this chapter, the regulatory systems we discuss are principally found in *E. coli*, the most widely used model bacterium. We begin with a general introduction to regulated gene expression and introduce the concept that the interaction between DNA-binding regulatory proteins and regulatory DNA sequences regulates transcription. Next we explore the organization, function, and regulation of the *E. coli* lactose (*lac*) operon system, whose gene transcription is induced (turned on) by the presence of the sugar lactose in the growth medium. This topic is followed by a discussion of mutational analysis and molecular explanation of the transcriptional control of *lac* operon genes. We then turn our attention to the genetic structure and molecular control of transcription of the tryptophan (*trp*) operon that contains the genes needed to synthesize the amino acid tryptophan. After moving on to a discussion of post-transcriptional regulation of bacterial genes and a discussion of regulated gene expression in archaeal species, we examine the regulatory process that controls infection of bacterial cells by bacteriophage λ (lambda).

14.1 Transcriptional Control of Gene Expression Requires DNA–Protein Interaction

Certain bacterial genes—specifically, those whose products are needed continuously to perform routine tasks—undergo **constitutive transcription,** a term identifying the genes as being transcribed continuously with no regulatory control. In contrast, the need for agile and calibrated responses to changing environmental conditions has resulted in the evolution of mechanisms for the **regulated transcription** of many bacterial genes.

Regulation of the transcription of bacterial genes is the predominant mode by which bacteria regulate responses to the environment, and it takes place at two levels. At both levels, control results from interactions between DNA-binding proteins and specific regulatory sequences of DNA. The first level of control regulates the *initiation of transcription,* determining whether a particular gene or group of genes is transcribed at all. The second transcriptional control level determines the *amount of transcription,* regulating either the duration of transcription or the amount of mRNA transcript produced from the gene.

Additionally, post-transcriptional regulatory mechanisms are important, controlling the level of translation of mRNA or the activity of proteins and enzymes. **Figure 14.1** provides an overview of bacterial regulatory mechanisms.

Negative and Positive Control of Transcription

Mechanisms of transcription control are described as negative or positive. **Negative control** of transcription involves the binding of a *repressor protein* to a regulatory DNA sequence, with the consequence of *preventing*

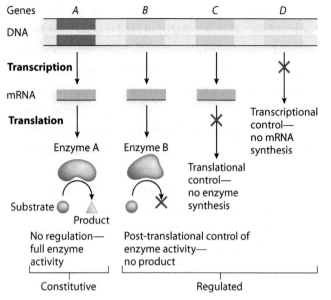

Figure 14.1 **An overview of gene expression in bacteria.** Unregulated (constitutive) expression and three patterns of regulated gene expression occur in bacteria.

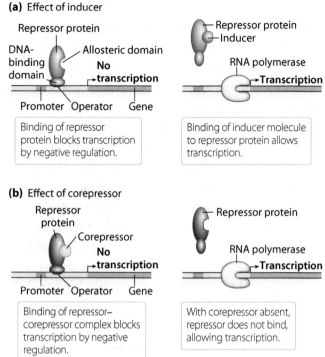

Figure 14.2 **Mechanisms of negative control of transcription.**

transcription of a gene or a cluster of genes. On the other hand, **positive control** of transcription involves the binding of an *activator protein* to regulatory DNA, with the result of *initiating* gene transcription.

Repressor proteins are a broad category of regulatory proteins that exert negative control of transcription. In their active form, repressor proteins bind to regulatory DNA sequences, including those called **operators,** as we describe below for the lactose operon. Repressor protein binding blocks transcription initiation by RNA polymerase. The repressor protein acts by occupying the space on regulatory DNA where the polymerase would otherwise bind or by preventing formation of the open promoter complex necessary for transcription initiation. Repressor proteins can be activated or inactivated by interactions with other compounds.

Repressor proteins commonly contain two active sites through which their functional role is performed. The **DNA-binding domain** is responsible for locating and binding operator DNA sequence or other target regulatory sequences. The **allosteric domain** binds a molecule or protein and, in so doing, causes a change in the conformation of the DNA-binding site. The property belonging to some enzymes of changing conformation at the active site as a result of binding a substance at a different site is known as **allostery.**

Allosteric domains operate in two modes. Certain repressor proteins undergo inactivation of their DNA-binding domain because of allosteric changes brought about by an **inducer** compound binding to the allosteric site (Figure 14.2a). If the inducer is removed from the allosteric site, the repressor's conformation is switched, the DNA-binding site is reactivated, and the protein can repress transcription. On the other hand, some repressor proteins

require binding of a **corepressor** molecule at the allosteric site to activate the DNA-binding site (Figure 14.2b). In this case, transcriptional repression is reversed when the corepressor is removed from the allosteric site.

Positive control of transcription is accomplished by **activator proteins** that bind to regulatory DNA sequences called **activator binding sites.** Activator protein binding facilitates RNA polymerase binding at promoters and helps initiate transcription. Activator proteins have a DNA-binding domain that binds the activator binding site of DNA. In one mode of action for activator proteins, the DNA-binding domain remains inactive until the allosteric domain is bound by an **allosteric effector compound.** The induced allosteric change leads to the formation of a functional DNA-binding domain, allowing the activator protein to bind to DNA (Figure 14.3a). Alternatively, certain activator proteins have a functional DNA-binding domain that is converted to an inactive conformation by binding of an **inhibitor** compound in the allosteric binding domain (Figure 14.3b).

Regulatory DNA-Binding Proteins

Most DNA-binding proteins that exert regulatory control bind DNA at specific sequences to accomplish their regulatory activity. These interactions occur by association of the amino acid side chains of the proteins with the specific nucleotide bases and the sugar-phosphate backbone of DNA. The proteins make their contact with specific base pairs located in the major groove and the minor groove of

(a) Effect of allosteric effector compound

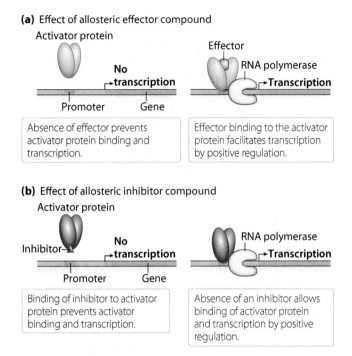

Absence of effector prevents activator protein binding and transcription.

Effector binding to the activator protein facilitates transcription by positive regulation.

(b) Effect of allosteric inhibitor compound

Binding of inhibitor to activator protein prevents activator binding and transcription.

Absence of an inhibitor allows binding of activator protein and transcription by positive regulation.

Figure 14.3   Mechanisms of positive control of transcription.

the DNA helix using the unique patterns of hydrogen, nitrogen, and oxygen atoms that characterize each base pair.

To achieve protein–DNA specificity in these interactions, the protein must simultaneously contact multiple

nucleotides. A common motif in the structures of DNA-binding regulatory proteins is the formation of protein secondary structures, most commonly α helices, that contain the amino acids that contact regulatory nucleotides. Frequently, two protein segments contact the DNA target sequence. The paired DNA-binding regions of a regulatory protein form in two ways. In one type of interaction, a single polypeptide folds to form two domains that bind specific DNA sequences. In the other type, the regulatory protein consists of two or more polypeptides joined to form a multimeric complex of two (dimeric), three (trimeric), or four (tetrameric) polypeptides. When identical polypeptides join together, the prefix *homo-* is used. A "homodimer" contains two identical polypeptides in the functional protein. When different polypeptides join together, the complex is identified by the prefix *hetero-*, as in "heterodimer."

Extensive studies of transcription-regulating proteins in bacteria have identified the characteristic structural features of DNA-binding regulatory proteins and the DNA sequence they bind. Bacterial regulatory DNA sequences frequently contain inverted repeats or direct repeats. Each polypeptide of a homodimeric regulatory protein, or each of the binding regions of a folded polypeptide, interacts with one of the inverted repeat segments. By far, the most common structural motif seen in these proteins in bacteria is the **helix-turn-helix (HTH) motif** (Figure 14.4). In the HTH motif, two α-helical

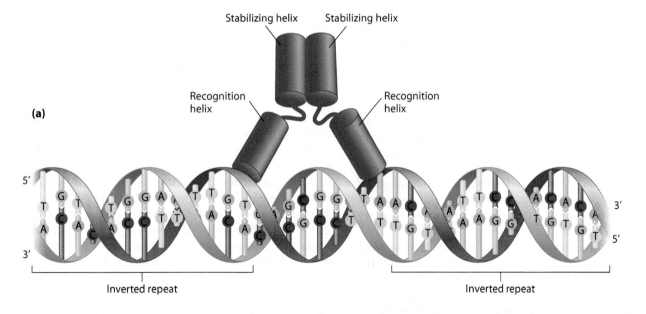

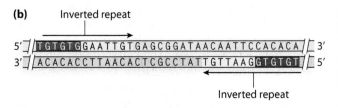

Figure 14.4   The helix-turn-helix regulatory protein motif. (a) DNA-binding proteins forming an HTH motif are usually dimeric. Two subunits of an HTH dimer are shown as shaded cylinders. The recognition helices bind to inverted repeat sequence in the major groove, and the stabilizing helices bind to the sugar-phosphate backbone. (b) Inverted repeat sequences are often targets of DNA-binding regulatory proteins, such as HTH proteins.

regions in each of two polypeptides in a homodimer interact with inverted repeat regulatory sequences in DNA. In each of the polypeptides, one of the two α-helical regions is the recognition helix that fits into the major groove of DNA and binds the inverted repeat sequences. The second helix is the stabilizing helix. It lies across the major groove and contacts the sugar-phosphate backbone, ensuring a strong DNA-protein interaction and properly orienting the recognition helix to sit in the major groove. Many different DNA-binding regulatory proteins with the HTH motif have been identified in bacteria. We will see some examples in later sections of this chapter and in discussions of regulatory protein motifs in eukaryotes in Chapter 15.

14.2 The *lac* Operon Is an Inducible Operon System under Negative and Positive Control

In comparing the genomes of different forms of life, one conclusion is that evolution has operated to restrict the total size of bacterial genomes compared to most others and to limit the percentage of repetitive (noncoding) DNA to less than 15 percent on average. These limitations are imposed by various factors, including the dependence of bacteria on their abilities to reproduce rapidly and respond quickly to environmental changes. Possession of a relatively small genome and small percentage of noncoding DNA speeds the DNA replication process and shortens the reproduction time. The need for rapid responsiveness to environmental change and for restricted genome size dictates another evolutionary adaptation in bacteria: the clustering and coordinated transcriptional regulation of genes involved in the same metabolic processes.

Clusters of genes undergoing coordinated transcriptional regulation by a shared regulatory region are called **operons.** Operons are common in bacterial genomes, and the genes that are part of a given operon almost always participate in the same metabolic or biosynthesis pathway. Besides having a single promoter, shared by the operon genes, operons contain additional regulatory DNA sequences that interact with promoters to share transcriptional control.

In this discussion, we focus on the **lactose (*lac*) operon** of *E. coli*. This operon is responsible for the production of three polypeptides that permit *E. coli* to utilize the sugar lactose as a carbon source for growth and metabolic energy. In this section, we explain how the *lac* operon works, describe the circumstances under which its genes are transcribed, and identify the regulatory mechanisms that control operon gene transcription. In the following section, we turn our attention to mutational and molecular analyses of the *lac* operon to understand the function of operon genes and to explore the molecular interactions that regulate operon gene transcription.

Lactose Metabolism

The monosaccharide sugar glucose is the preferred energy source of *E. coli*, just as it is for your cells. Glucose is metabolized by the biochemical pathway called glycolysis, a sequence of biochemical reactions that oxidizes glucose, and closely related compounds, to produce pyruvate and ATP (adenosine triphosphate), the compound used universally by cells to store and produce energy. This pathway occurs in virtually all cells as part of fermentation and cellular respiration. Glycolysis is the principal energy-producing reaction in your cells, and it is the energy-producing reaction in, *E. coli*, which, like humans and other organisms, are capable of metabolizing sugars other than glucose as well. Sugars such as galactose, lactose, fructose, and arabinose are also metabolized for energy production, but glucose is the preferred sugar because it can be directly metabolized in glycolysis. The alternative sugars require separate metabolism to first produce glucose or a glucose derivative that can then be processed by glycolysis. Thus, *E. coli* will consume all available glucose before a genetic switch is flipped that changes the metabolic pathway to one that uses an alternative sugar.

The genetic switch to lactose utilization requires that lactose be present in the cell, but the lactose is not used by the cell until after glucose has been depleted. Lactose utilization is controlled by genes and regulatory sequences that form the *lac* operon, which is an **inducible operon** system, meaning that under the specific circumstances that lactose is present in the growth medium and glucose is absent, transcription of the operon genes is activated, or induced. The inducible nature of the *lac* operon and other inducible operons also means that expression of operon genes is limited to the circumstance in which the *inducer compound* is available. Other nutritional requirements may have to be met as well for transcription induction to occur.

Lactose is a disaccharide consisting of two monosaccharides, glucose and galactose, that are joined by a covalent β-galactoside linkage (**Figure 14.5**). Bacteria that have a ***lac*⁺ phenotype** ("lack plus") are able to grow on a medium containing lactose as the only sugar. *lac*⁺ strains accomplish this growth by producing a gated channel at the cell membrane that allows lactose to enter the cell. The channel is formed by the enzyme permease. On entering the cell, lactose is processed by the enzyme β-galactosidase that processes lactose in two ways. The principal activity of β-galactosidase is to break the β-galactoside linkage to release glucose and galactose. Glucose produced by lactose breakdown can immediately enter glycolysis. The molecule of galactose can be further processed to produce glucose. In addition to producing glucose and galactose, β-galactosidase also converts some lactose to an isomer called **allolactose.** Allolactose plays a critical role in regulating the transcription of *lac* operon genes by acting as the inducer compound. Allolactose that is not used for induction can be cleaved

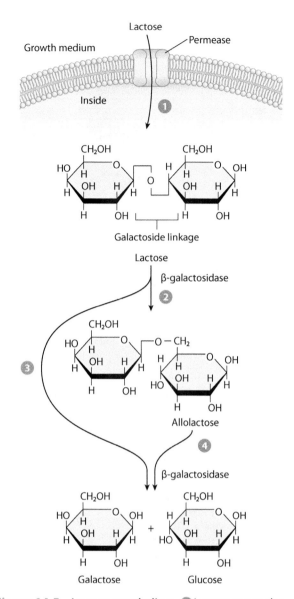

Figure 14.5   Lactose metabolism. ❶ Lactose enters the *E. coli* cell from the growth medium with the aide of permease. **❷** β-galactosidase converts some lactose to its isomeric form, allolactose. **❸** Most of the lactose has its galactoside linkage cleaved by β-galactosidase to yield galactose and glucose. **❹** Allolactose acts as the inducer. Excess allolactose is cleaved by β-galactosidase.

by β-galactosidase. Bacteria that are unable to grow on a lactose-containing medium are identified as having a ***lac⁻* phenotype** ("lack minus"). These strains are either unable to import lactose to the cell, unable to break it down once it is in the cell, or both.

lac Operon Structure

The *lac* operon consists of a multipart regulatory region and a structural gene region containing three genes (**Figure 14.6a**). The regulatory region contains three protein-binding regulatory sequences. One is the promoter that binds RNA polymerase, another is the operator

(*lacO*) sequence that binds the *lac* repressor protein, and the third is the CAP binding site. These three regions partially overlap and are immediately upstream of the start of transcription of *lac* operon genes.

The three structural genes of the *lac* operon are identified as ***lacZ***, a gene encoding the enzyme β-galactosidase; ***lacY***, which encodes the enzyme permease; and ***lacA***, which encodes transacetylase. These three genes are transcribed as a **polycistronic mRNA,** an mRNA molecule that is the transcript of all the genes in the operon. Each gene transcript that is part of a polycistronic mRNA contains a start and a stop codon sequence. The translation of a polycistronic mRNA generates a distinct polypeptide for each gene.

The β-galactosidase produced by the *lacZ* gene is responsible for cleaving the β-galactoside linkage of lactose to release molecules of glucose and galactose. As mentioned above, the enzyme also converts a small amount of lactose into allolactose, which has a chemical structure very similar to that of lactose. The permease enzyme encoded by *lacY* functions at the cell membrane to facilitate the entry of lactose into the cell. Transacetylase, the product of *lacA*, is not essential for lactose utilization, although in bacteria it protects against potentially damaging by-products of lactose metabolism. Our discussion focuses only on transcription of *lacZ* and *lacY*, and on the action of β-galactosidase and permease, since transacetylase is not essential for lactose utilization.

Adjacent to, but not part of the *lac* operon, is the regulatory gene, *lacI* ("lack eye"), that produces the *lac* repressor protein. The *lacI* gene has its own promoter that is not regulated and drives constitutive transcription. The *lac* repressor protein is a homotetramer that has two functional domains. The first is a DNA-binding domain that binds the operator regions, and the second is an allosteric domain that binds the inducer substance allolactose.

Figure 14.6b shows the DNA sequence composition of the *lac* operon promoter (*lacP*) and the *lac* operator (*lacO*), which together only span about 80 base pairs. The promoter and the operator sequences are directly adjacent, with the position of the operator sequence overlapping the +1 nucleotide that starts transcription. *LacP* contains the −10 and −35 consensus sequence sites that are critical for RNA polymerase binding (see Section 8.2). *LacO*, which binds the repressor protein produced by *lacI*, overlaps *lacP* near the start of transcription. Notice also that the CAP binding site is near the −35 and −10 regions of the promoter. We discuss this relationship in the next section.

lac Operon Function

The *lac* operon is transcriptionally silent when no lactose is available and when glucose is available to the cell (**Figure 14.7a**). In the absence of production of β-galactosidase, there is no allolactose in the cell and the

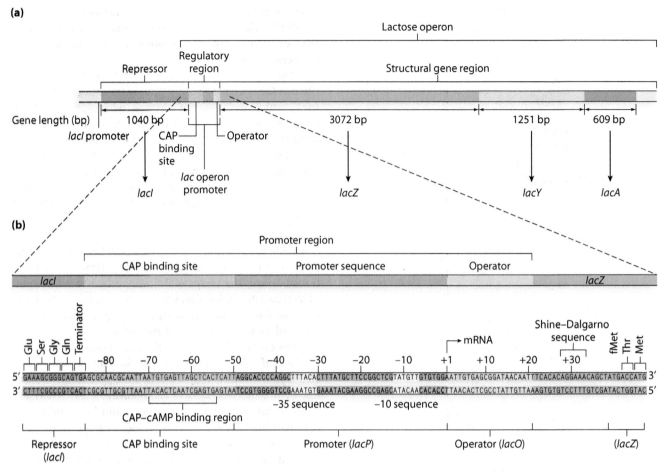

Figure 14.6 **The lactose (*lac*) operon of *E. coli*.** (a) The repressor protein (*lacI*) is encoded by a 1040-bp segment under separate transcriptional regulation. The transcription regulatory region consists of a CAP binding site, a promoter consensus sequence region, and an operator sequence. The three structural genes of the *lac* operon encode the enzymes β-galactosidase (*lacZ*), permease (*lacY*), and transacetylase (*lacA*). (b) The DNA sequence of the regulatory region of the *lac* operon, including the −10 and −35 consensus sequences, the operator, and the CAP binding site.

constitutively produced *lac* repressor protein binds to *lacO*, using its DNA-binding domain. By its presence at the operator, *lac* repressor blocks RNA polymerase from binding to *lacP* and prevents transcription initiation. This transcriptional regulatory interaction is an example of negative control of transcription that is achieved through the binding of repressor protein to the transcription-regulating operator sequence.

In contrast, the availability of lactose in the growth medium and the unavailability of glucose lead to the induction of transcription of the *lac* operon structural genes (Figure 14.7b). On this basis, the *lac* operon is identified as an inducible operon. With synthesis of β-galactosidase, the production of allolactose occurs. By binding to the allosteric domain of the repressor protein, allolactose forms the **inducer–repressor complex.** The formation of this complex induces an allosteric change that alters the conformation of the DNA-binding domain of the repressor protein to a form that does not recognize or bind the operator. An essential part of the induction of

transcription is the binding of the CAP-cAMP complex to the CAP binding site, which facilitates achievement of the highest level of transcription. The polycistronic mRNA is synthesized, and translation produces β-galactosidase, permease, and transacetylase.

When both glucose and lactose are available, *E. coli* utilize glucose. The presence of lactose, however, generates a small amount of allolactose that carries out its normal inducer function by binding to repressor protein. The inducer-repressor interaction opens the promoter region, and RNA polymerase binds.

By itself, however, RNA polymerase is very ineffective at accomplishing transcription of the *lac* operon genes. This is due to the absence of binding of the CAP-cAMP complex at the CAP binding site (more on this in a moment). RNA polymerase by itself is only able to manage **basal transcription** (Figure 14.7c)—transcription that produces only a small number of polycistronic mRNAs and leads to the translation of a few molecules of β-galactosidase, permease, and transacetylase per cell.

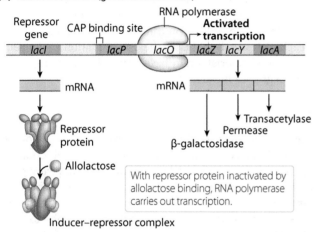

(a) Lactose unavailable (glucose available)

lac repressor protein binds to the operator (*lacO*) sequence and inhibits transcription.

(b) Lactose available (glucose unavailable)

With repressor protein inactivated by allolactose binding, RNA polymerase carries out transcription.

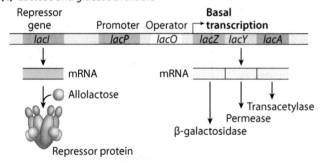

(c) Lactose and glucose available

Figure 14.7   *lac* operon transcription regulation. **(a)** When glucose is available and lactose is unavailable, *lac* operon genes are not transcribed. **(b)** Lactose availability in the absence of glucose induces activated transcription of operon genes by binding of CAP-cAMP at the CAP site. **(c)** The presence of both glucose and lactose leads to basal transcription of the operon.

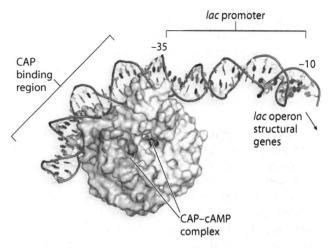

Figure 14.8   CAP–cAMP complex binding to the CAP binding region. DNA bends at an approximate 90° angle around the CAP–cAMP complex and facilitates strong RNA polymerase binding that generates activated transcription of the *lac* operon.

binding site contains the sequence that attracts the **CAP–cAMP complex,** a small molecular complex composed of a protein known as the catabolite activator protein (CAP) and the nucleotide cyclic adenosine monophosphate (cAMP). Binding of the CAP–cAMP complex to its binding site causes DNA to bend around the complex, and it increases the ability of RNA polymerase to transcribe *lac* operon genes (**Figure 14.8**). This positive regulatory effect leads to a high level of transcription—that is, to activated transcription—of *lac* operon genes that is many times greater than basal transcription. Activated transcription allows the cell to metabolize lactose and grow on a lactose-containing medium.

The positive regulatory process is itself regulated indirectly by the level of glucose, which modulates the availability of cAMP. Cyclic AMP is synthesized from ATP (adenosine triphosphate) by the enzyme adenylate cyclase. During glycolysis, the availability of adenylate cyclase is limited and cAMP synthesis is reduced. Thus, when glucose is available, cAMP is very low in concentration, almost no CAP–cAMP can form, and *lac* operon gene transcription is highly inefficient. This effect of glucose in blocking *lac* operon gene transcription, even when lactose is present, is known as **catabolite repression,** during which the presence of the preferred catabolite (glucose) represses the transcription of genes for an alternative catabolite (lactose).

With your budding understanding of *lac* operon gene transcription, perhaps the following question—a kind of chicken-and-egg conundrum—has occurred to you. Lactose must enter the cell so that allolactose can be produced to act as an inducer. Lactose cannot enter the cell without the aid of permease that helps bring lactose into the cell. But since the *lacY* gene that produces permease is part of the *lac* operon, and transcription is not induced until lactose is present inside the cell, how does lactose

Basal transcription driven solely by RNA polymerase that gains access to the *lac* promoter through the inducer–repressor complex mechanism is insufficient to generate enough copies of the polycistronic mRNA to drive active lactose metabolism. A second regulatory process featuring positive control of transcription is required to fully activate *lac* operon gene transcription. Positive control of *lac* operon transcription lies in a DNA–protein interaction that occurs at the **CAP–cAMP binding region** of the *lac* operon promoter. This site is located at approximately −60 of *lacP* (see Figure 14.6b and Figure 14.7c). The CAP

enter the cell in the first place? It does so in two ways. One stems from the reversibility of the interaction between the repressor protein and the *lac* operator. In the presence of glucose and the absence of lactose, the repressor protein is almost always bound to the operator sequence. Occasionally and spontaneously, however, the repressor protein loses contact with the operator sequence. While short-lived, this spontaneous release is just enough to allow momentary transcription of the operon and production of a few molecules of β-galactosidase and permease. This small amount of permease and β-galactosidase, amounting to no more than a few molecules per cell, is sufficient to bring the first molecules of lactose to cross the cell membrane and to generate allolactose. This trickle of lactose quickly induces more transcription, launching a transcriptional cascade that soon causes the cell to switch its metabolism to lactose utilization.

The second way also involves the production of a tiny amount of permease and β-galactosidase—in this case, through basal transcription that takes place when both glucose and lactose are available to a cell. Basal transcription becomes fully activated transcription when glucose is exhausted and only lactose is available to a cell.

14.3 Mutational Analysis Deciphers Genetic Regulation of the *lac* Operon

The identification and description of the *lac* operon began with a series of publications in the early 1960s by François Jacob, Jacques Monod, André Lwoff, and several other colleagues. Their genetic analysis of numerous *lac* operon mutants led to the identification of each gene and regulatory region, and to the functional description of the operon we provided in the previous section. Jacob, Monod, and Lwoff were awarded the Nobel Prize in Physiology or Medicine in 1965 for this work (see the chapter opener photo). Their work also laid the foundation for a description of *lac* operon transcription regulation at the DNA sequence level. We discuss several of the analyses of *lac* operon mutants and elements of the molecular analysis of *lac* operon transcriptional regulation in this section. As you read this discussion, refer to Table 14.1 and Table 14.2 for a list of *lac* operon genes and regulatory sequences, as well as example genotypes and phenotypes associated with mutations we discuss. You can also refer to Experimental Insight 6.1, which discusses the determination of the genotype of a bacterial strain based on its pattern of growth and no growth in various media.

Analysis of Structural Gene Mutations

The genetic analysis of the *lac* operon by Jacob, Monod, and colleagues was made possible by the induction of operon mutations. Several dozen *lac⁻* mutants were generated by treatment of *E. coli* with mutagens. The mutants were first subjected to genetic complementation experiments to determine whether the *lac⁻* phenotypes of different mutants resulted from mutation of the same gene or from mutations of different genes. Investigations showed that *lac⁻* mutants formed two complementation groups, indicating that two genes are responsible for the *lac⁻* phenotype. The two complementation groups are today known to correspond to *lacZ* (β-galactosidase) and *lacY* (permease).

Table 14.1	*lac* Operon Genes and Regulatory Sequences		
Gene/Sequence	**Product/Sequence Type**	**Function**	**Important Mutants**
Protein-Producing Genes			
lacI	Repressor protein	Contains two binding sites, one for the operator and one for allolactose, the inducer	I^-: Unable to bind to operator I^S: Unable to bind the inducer (allolactose)
lacZ	β-galactosidase	Cleaves lactose into two monosaccharides (glucose and galactose)	Z^-: No functional β-galactosidase
lacY	Permease	Facilitates lactose transport across the cell membrane	Y^-: No functional permease
lacA	Transacetylase	Protects against harmful by-products of lactose metabolism	A^-: No transacetylase
Regulatory Sequences			
lacO	Operator	Binds repressor protein to block transcription of operon genes	O^C: Fails to bind repressor protein
lacP	Promoter	Binds RNA polymerase	P^-: Fails to bind RNA polymerase or does so weakly

Table 14.2	Synthesis of β-Galactosidase and Permease by Haploids and Partial Diploids with Structural Gene Mutations					
Genotype	β-Galactosidase[a]		Permease[a]		Description	
	Lactose	No Lactose	Lactose	No Lactose		
1. $I^+ P^+ O^+ Z^+ Y^+$	+	−	+	−	Wild-type (*lac*[+])	
2. $I^+ P^+ O^+ Z^- Y^+$	−	−	+	−	No functional β-galactosidase (*lac*[−])	
3. $I^+ P^+ O^+ Z^+ Y^-$	+	−	−	−	No functional permease (*lac*[−])	
4. $I^+ P^+ O^+ Z^+ Y^- / I^+ P^+ O^+ Z^- Y^+$	+	−	+	−	Wild-type response by complementation (*lac*[+])	

[a] Symbols + and − indicate production and no production, respectively, of functional enzymes.

The complementation analysis was carried out using partial diploid bacterial strains that were produced by conjugation between F′ (*lac*) and F⁻ bacteria (see Section 6.3). Recall that exconjugants produced by F′ × F⁺ conjugation have two copies of a portion of the genome and are thus partially diploid. In the case of *lac* operon partial diploids, one copy of the *lac* operon information resides on the recipient bacterial chromosome, and the second copy of the operon is acquired on the F′ plasmid. The genotype of partial diploids is written with the F′ segment on the left and the recipient chromosome on the right. The homologous chromosomes are separated by a slash (/). For example, the genotype of a partial diploid demonstrating complementation of *lac* gene mutations can be written as follows:

$$F'\ I^+ P^+ O^+ Z^+ Y^- / I^+ P^+ O^+ Z^- Y^+$$

Analyzed as haploid genotypes, each portion of the partial diploid genotype above would produce the *lac*⁻ phenotype. The F′ haploid lacks the ability to produce permease (*lacY*⁻), and the bacterial haploid is unable to produce β-galactosidase (*lacZ*⁻). Genetic complementation occurs in this partial diploid, however, and the resulting phenotype is *lac*⁺ (see Table 14.2). The molecular basis of genetic complementation in this case is that the F′ portion of the partial diploid provides β-galactosidase by its *lacZ*⁺ gene, and the recipient portion of the partial diploid provides permease by its *lacY*⁺ gene. Based on the analysis of structural gene mutations, Jacob, Monod, and colleagues concluded that there are two protein-producing genes required for *lac*⁺ growth behavior and that *lacZ* and *lacY* wild-type alleles are usually dominant to mutant alleles. Recombination mapping analysis revealed close genetic linkage of the three structural genes of the *lac* operon, but the order of these structural genes (*lacZ-lacY-lacA*) was ultimately determined by mutational analysis.

Another type of structural gene mutation that proved useful for understanding the process of translation of the *lac* polycistronic mRNA was base substitution nonsense mutations that generate stop codons in inappropriate locations. If one of these mutations, known as **polar mutations,** occurs early in the *lacZ* portion of the polycistronic mRNA, it has the curious effect of significantly reducing or preventing translation of the other gene sequences in the transcript. How could this be? The answer is that there is just one Shine–Dalgarno sequence in the *lac* operon mRNA. It occurs upstream of the start codon for the *lacZ* gene (see Figure 14.6). Normally, individual ribosomes identify the Shine–Dalgarno sequence and translate the entire length of the *lac* operon polycistronic mRNA, producing three polypeptides. The presence of the polar (nonsense) mutation in the *lacZ* gene stops translation by the ribosome. As there is no other Shine–Dalgarno sequence in the transcript, the ribosome is unable to translate the *lacY* or *lacA* sequences. Thus, when a polar mutation occurs in the *lacZ* gene, no permease is produced, even if the strain is *lacY*⁺.

lac Operon Regulatory Mutations

Mutations of regulatory components of the *lac* operon alter the inducible response of the operon to the presence of lactose and allolactose in the cell. Certain mutations of the *lac* operon lead to **constitutive mutants,** which are unresponsive to the presence or absence of lactose in the growth medium. These mutants continuously transcribe the operon genes, rather than transcribing the genes in an inducible manner. Other regulatory mutations block all response to lactose and render the cell *lac*⁻. Genetic mapping of constitutive mutations would eventually identify two distinct sites of constitutive mutations of the *lac* operon: *lacO* and *lacI*. Constitutive mutations of *lacO* render the operator DNA sequence unrecognizable to the wild-type DNA-binding portion of the repressor protein. On the other hand, constitutive mutations of *lacI* result from production of a repressor protein with a mutated DNA-binding region that is unable to recognize and bind wild-type operator sequence. Both mutations prevent negative regulation of *lac* operon transcription.

It was the initial discovery of the existence of two sites of *lac* operon constitutive mutations suggested to Jacob and Monod that a negative regulatory system with two components exercises transcriptional control of the structural genes. They postulated that one constitutive mutation site is the gene producing a regulatory protein and the second is the target DNA-binding site for the regulatory protein binding.

Operator Mutations The genetic evidence indicating that the operator is the DNA sequence binding the repressor protein comes from the finding that *lac* operator (*lacO*) mutations are exclusively **cis-acting;** that is, they influence the transcription of genes only *on the same chromosome.* In the wild-type organism, *lacI*$^+$ produces repressor protein that has an allosteric (allolactose) binding domain and a functional operator binding domain. Repressor protein uses its operator binding domain to bind the regulatory sequence and block transcription (**Figure 14.9a**). Bacteria with operator mutations are constitutive for transcription of *lac* operon genes and have the genotype $I^+ P^+ O^C Z^+ Y^+$ (**Figure 14.9b**). The O^C allele designation signifies an "operator-constitutive mutation." In O^C mutants, the nucleotide sequence of the operator region is altered and is no longer recognized by wild-type repressor protein. In the absence of repressor protein bound to the operator sequence, constitutive transcription of the operon genes takes place and β-galactosidase and permease are produced continuously.

The crucial experiments revealing the cis-acting nature of *lacO* were performed with partial diploids. First it was shown that creation of partial diploids by conjugation of a constitutive *lac*$^+$ strain ($I^+ P^+ O^C Z^+ Y^+$) with a *lac*$^-$ strain producing defective β-galactosidase ($I^+ P^+ O^+ Z^- Y^+$) does not alter the constitutive transcription of β-galactosidase. Note that *lacO*^{C} in the partial diploid appears dominant to *lacO*$^+$. Dominance on the part of *lacO*^{C} arises because transcription of the wild-type *lacZ*$^+$ allele is exclusively controlled by the *lacO*^{C} mutation, since these two alleles are on the same chromosome. The wild-type operator has no effect on the *lacZ*$^+$ allele because operator DNA is a cis-acting element, not a trans-acting element.

In a second experiment, the *lacZ* alleles were on different chromosomes, and the partial diploid genotype F′ $I^+ P^+ O^C Z^- Y^+ / I^+ P^+ O^+ Z^+ Y^-$ was produced using two *lac*$^-$ strains. In this case, the F′ strain is constitutive for permease production but does not produce functional β-galactosidase due to a *lacZ* mutation. The bacterial recipient strain produces β-galactosidase by the wild-type inducible mechanism, but it does not produce functional permease, due to mutation of *lacY*. The partial diploid produces permease constitutively, but β-galactosidase is produced only when transcription is induced by lactose. This result could occur only if the operator is a cis-acting element. In this case, the operator allele in cis to Z^+ is wild type, so β-galactosidase production falls under the inducible control of the wild-type operator sequence. Notice that in this partial diploid, the wild-type operator appears to be dominant to the O^C mutant.

(a) *I*$^+$ (wild type)

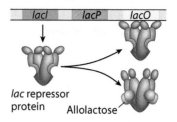

Repressor binds operator when the inducer is absent and forms an inducer–repressor complex when inducer is present.

(b) O^c (operator constitutive mutation)

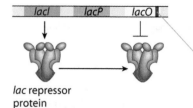

Operator-site mutation prevents repressor protein binding and leads to constitutive synthesis of the *lac* operon.

(c) *I*$^-$ (repressor mutation)

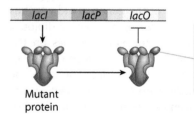

Repressor protein mutation prevents repressor binding to the operator and produces constitutive synthesis of the *lac* operon.

(d) *I*^{s} (super-repressor mutation)

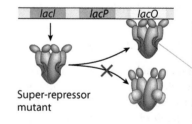

Repressor protein mutation blocks binding to the inducer, preventing formation of the inducer–repressor complex. Mutant repressor protein binds to the operator, preventing transcription.

Figure 14.9   Regulatory mutations of *lacI* and *lacO*. (a) Wild-type *lacI* and *lacO*. (b) Operator-constitutive (*lacO*^{C}) mutation. (c) *lacI*$^-$ (operator-binding domain) mutation. (d) *lacI*^{S} (super-repressor) mutation of the allosteric binding domain.

The apparent difference in the dominance relationship of O^+ and O^C alleles is understandable if the *lac* operator is a cis-acting element that only controls the transcription of genes on the same DNA molecule. Taken together, the two experiments reveal the *lac* operator to be **cis-dominant,** meaning that the only genes the operator is able to influence are genes located downstream on the same gene. For the *lac* operon, the "dominant" operator allele can differ, depending on the alleles carried by structural genes on each chromosome. If both wild-type structural genes are in cis to *lacO*^{C}, the mutant operator is dominant because it constitutively transcribes both genes. This is the case in the first experiment. On the other hand, if wild-type structural genes are on different

Table 14.3	Synthesis of β-Galactosidase and Permease by Haploids and Partial Diploids with Regulatory Mutations				
Genotype	β-Galactosidase		Permease		Description
	Lactose	No Lactose	Lactose	No Lactose	
1. $I^- P^+ O^+ Z^+ Y^+$	+	+	+	+	Constitutive transcription due to *lacI⁻* mutation.
2. $I^+ P^+ O^C Z^+ Y^+$	+	+	+	+	Constitutive transcription due to *lacO^C* mutation.
3. $I^S P^+ O^+ Z^+ Y^+$	−	−	−	−	Transcription is not inducible, due to *lacI^S* mutation.
4. $I^+ P^- O^+ Z^+ Y^+$	−	−	−	−	No effective transcription, due to *lacP⁻* mutation.

chromosomes, as in the second experiment, then the *lacO⁺* allele is dominant because it exerts inducible transcriptional control on one of the two genes required for lactose metabolism (Table 14.3).

Constitutive Repressor Protein Mutations Experimental evidence supporting the hypothesis that the repressor gene produces a regulatory protein comes from the analysis of mutants that constitutively transcribe *lac* operon genes where the mutant allele is recessive to wild-type allele.

To see the dominance relationship of these alleles, let's first consider a haploid cell with the *lac* operon genotype $I^- P^+ O^+ Z^+ Y^+$. This cell constitutively transcribes and produces both β-galactosidase and permease (Figure 14.9c). Similarly, a haploid strain with the genotype $I^- P^+ O^+ Z^+ Y^-$ produces β-galactosidase constitutively, but no permease is produced, and bacteria with the genotype $I^- P^+ O^+ Z^- Y^+$ constitutively produce permease but do not produce β-galactosidase.

In contrast, a partial diploid with the genotype F′ $I^+ P^+ O^+ Z^- Y^+$ / $I^- P^+ O^+ Z^+ Y^-$ expresses both enzymes in their normal inducible manner. The I^+ allele can be on either the F′ plasmid or the recipient chromosome and have the same effect, inevitably resulting in the dominance of I^+ over I^-. This outcome indicates that *lacI* produces a regulatory protein that is **trans-acting**—capable of influencing the expression of genes on other chromosomes. In this context, *trans* refers to a protein capable of diffusing through the cell and binding to a cis-acting target sequence.

The molecular explanation of the trans-acting ability of the *lac* repressor protein is that a *lacI⁻* mutant alters the DNA-binding domain of the protein, rendering it incapable of binding the operator sequence. In the absence of negative control, transcription is constitutive. In partial diploids that are I^+/I^-, however, repressor protein with a functional DNA-binding domain is present in the cell and responds normally to the addition or removal of lactose from the cell.

Super-Repressor Protein Mutations A second set of repressor protein mutations produces a different consequence for *lac* operon transcription. These mutants produce mutant repressor protein with an altered allosteric domain. The mutant proteins are unable to bind allolactose and are unresponsive to lactose addition or removal from cells. The DNA-binding domain is unaffected by the allosteric domain mutation, but as a result of the nonfunctional allosteric domain, mutant repressor proteins cannot release the operator even in the presence of allolactose.

Haploids and partial diploids with mutations of the allosteric domain of the repressor protein are identified as I^S mutants and are designated super-repressors. These mutants are **noninducible,** meaning that operon gene transcription cannot be induced (Figure 14.9d and Table 14.3). Haploids with the genotype $I^S P^+ O^+ Z^+ Y^+$ produce a repressor protein that binds normally to operator sequence, but lacking a functional allosteric domain, the protein is not removed from the operator by lactose in the cell. Such mutants are *lac⁻* and cannot be induced to metabolize lactose. Cultures of partial diploid bacteria with the genotype F′ $I^S P^+ O^+ Z^+ Y^+$ / $I^+ P^+ O^+ Z^+ Y^+$ may initially have some inducible responsiveness to lactose, but this ability is lost as mutant repressor protein binds to operator sequences. This partial diploid reveals the dominance of I^S over I^+.

Promoter Mutations Mutations of promoter consensus sequences significantly reduce transcription or may eliminate it entirely (see Figure 8.11). To know the specific effect of a promoter mutation usually requires direct testing of transcription in the mutant organism. Promoters, like operators, are cis-acting regulatory sequences, and most mutations of *lacP* significantly reduce, and may entirely eliminate, transcription of *lacZ* and *lacY* genes, which are located in cis. This reduces β-galactosidase and permease production to such a low point that haploid bacteria with the genotype $I^+ P^- O^+ Z^+ Y^+$ are *lac⁻*.

Table 14.4 summarizes the conditions for *lac* operon gene transcription given the presence or absence of glucose and lactose. Active transcription of operon genes

Table 14.4	Transcription Conditions for the *lac* Operon				
Glucose	Lactose	cAMP	Allolactose	*lac* Operon Transcription	Explanation
Present	Absent	Absent	Absent	None	Glucose is present to provide energy. There is no allolactose to bind repressor. There is no CAP–cAMP complex to bind CAP site.
Present	Present	Absent	Present	Basal	Glucose is present to provide energy; absence of cAMP prevents positive transcription regulation, but allolactose is present and acts as an inducer to allow a small amount of transcription.
Absent	Absent	Present	Absent	None	CAP–cAMP forms, but no allolactose is present to block repressor binding at operator.
Absent	Present	Present	Present	High	Inducer and CAP–cAMP are available to induce and positively regulate transcription.

takes place only when glucose is depleted from the cell and lactose is present. Under these conditions, the following events occur:

1. Cyclic AMP level rises as a result of the availability of adenylcyclase.

2. CAP–cAMP complex forms and binds to the CAP site of the *lac* promoter, thus activating transcription.

3. Allolactose is produced by a side reaction of the metabolism of lactose by β-galactosidase.

4. Repressor protein conformation is modified by interaction with allolactose, causing the protein to release from the operator, thus allowing operon gene transcription.

Basal transcription occurs when both glucose and lactose are present due to the presence of allolactose to bind repressor protein. When lactose is absent, no inducer–repressor complex can form, and no transcription takes place. To test your understanding of the *lac* operon, see **Genetic Analysis 14.1**, which guides you through analysis of some *lac* operon mutants.

Molecular Analysis of the *lac* Operon

In the 50 years since Jacob, Monod, and colleagues described their genetic analysis of the *lac* operon, molecular analysis and genome sequence analysis have identified the DNA sequences of its components (see Figure 14.6b). This and other accumulated molecular information weaves a virtually complete picture of *lac* operon transcription regulation, revealing it to be somewhat more complex, but wholly consistent, with the description presented above.

Experimental Insight 14.1 discusses two important pieces of experimental molecular evidence derived from DNA footprint protection analyses that pertain to transcriptional regulation of the *lac* operon. The first observation is that the repressor protein binding location at the *lac* operator overlaps with the promoter binding location of RNA polymerase. This observation supports the hypothesis that repressor protein binding blocks RNA polymerase binding and transcription initiation and, conversely, that when the repressor protein is not bound to the operator, RNA polymerase can access and initiate transcription at the promoter. The second observation identifies three distinct segments of operator DNA sequence. These operator segments, designated O_1, O_2, and O_3, interact differently with the repressor protein, and the result of the interactions provides a mechanism by which repressor protein binding can block RNA polymerase access to the promoter.

Additional molecular analysis reveals that the repressor protein is a homotetrameric protein formed by the union of four identical 360–amino acid polypeptides (**Figure 14.10**). The four polypeptides are joined together

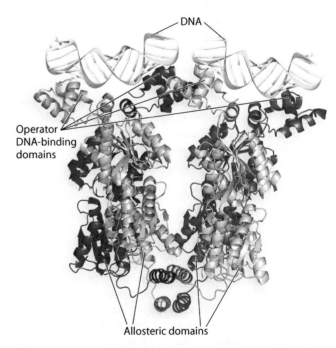

Figure 14.10   The homotetrameric structure of the *lac* repressor protein. Operator binding and allosteric domains are formed on opposite sides of the protein.

PROBLEM Evaluate the following *lac* operon partial diploids. Indicate whether the production of functional β-galactosidase from *lacZ* and of permease from *lacY* is "inducible," "constitutive," or "noninducible" for each partial diploid.

> **BREAK IT DOWN:** Partial diploids have two copies of each *lac* operon gene and regulatory sequence. Success evaluating the *lac* operon depends on knowing the function of each operon component. Study Table 14.1 thoroughly (p. 476).

a. $I^- P^+ O^+ Z^+ Y^+ / I^+ P^+ O^+ Z^- Y^-$

b. $I^+ P^+ O^C Z^+ Y^- / I^+ P^+ O^+ Z^- Y^+$

c. $I^+ P^+ O^C Z^- Y^+ / I^S P^+ O^+ Z^+ Y^+$

> **BREAK IT DOWN:** The transcription of *lac* operon genes is inducible if it is responsive to lactose presence and absence, constitutive if it is always on regardless of lactose availability, or noninducible if it cannot be activated (pp. 477–480).

Solution Strategies	Solution Steps
Evaluate	
1. Identify the topic this problem addresses and the nature of the required answer.	1. This problem concerns an analysis of patterns of transcriptional regulation and the production of functional β-galactosidase and permease by operon genotypes. The answer requires a determination of whether the enzymes are produced inducibly, constitutively, or not at all.
2. Identify the critical information given in the problem.	2. The *lac* operon genotypes of three partial diploids are given.
Deduce	
3. Describe the consequences of any mutations in genotype *a*. TIP: Assess regulatory mutations first; then consider the consequences for structural gene transcription in each partial diploid by evaluating the effect of each allele on transcription.	3. The I^- mutation produces a repressor protein that is unable to bind operator sequence. The Z^- mutation will not produce functional β-galactosidase, and the Y^- mutation will not produce functional permease. PITFALL: You must understand the wild-type function of each operon component before evaluating genotypes. Do not attempt to memorize patterns of "+" and "−" for operon components in hopes of determining *lac⁺* or *lac⁻* phenotypes.
4. Describe the consequences of any mutations in genotype *b*.	4. The O^C mutation alters the operator sequence and prevents binding and transcriptional repression by repressor protein. The Z^- and Y^- mutations block production of functional β-galactosidase and permease.
5. Describe the consequences of any mutations in genotype *c*.	5. The I^S mutation produces a super-repressor protein that has an altered allosteric domain and will not interact with allolactose. The O^C and Z^- alter function as described above.
Solve	
	Answer a
6. Determine the expression pattern of functional enzymes for partial diploid *a*.	6. Wild-type repressor protein is trans-active and binds the wild-type operator. This cis-acting operator blocks transcription of Z^+ and Y^+ when lactose is not in the cell, but permits transcription when lactose is present. Therefore, both enzymes are produced inducibly.
	Answer b
7. Determine the expression pattern of functional enzymes for partial diploid *b*.	7. O^C is cis-active on Z^+, resulting in constitutive transcription. Y^+ is under the cis-active transcriptional control of O^+. Therefore, β-galactosidase is produced constitutively, and permease is produced inducibly.
	Answer c
8. Determine the expression pattern of functional enzymes for partial diploid *c*.	8. The O^C sequence is not recognized by either the wild-type repressor or the super-repressor. Both repressors have wild-type DNA-binding sequences. Cis-active O^C constitutively transcribes Y^+. The super-repressor binds O^+, and its cis activity renders Z^+ and Y^+ noninducible. Therefore, β-galactosidase is noninducible, and permease production is constitutive.

Regulatory Proteins Binding to *lac* Operon Regulatory Sequences

DNase I footprint protection analysis of the kind described in Research Technique 8.1 has been used to precisely identify the binding locations of *lac* repressor protein relative to the location of RNA polymerase binding in the regulatory region of the *lac* operon. Recall from the earlier description of this technique that identical control and experimental DNA fragments containing regulatory sequences are end-labeled with ^{32}P. The experimental fragments are then exposed to DNA-binding proteins, but the control fragments are not. All fragments are then exposed to DNase I that randomly digests those segments not protected by bound proteins. The resulting DNase I-digested DNA fragments are separated by gel electrophoresis to reveal the "footprint" of protein protection.

The figure here shows the results of footprint analysis of a 123-bp segment of the *lac* operon regulatory region from position +39 to −84. Control DNA in the first lane ❶ is not protein protected. The gel shows that the promoter regions protected by ❷ RNA polymerase and ❸ *lac* repressor protein partially overlap one another. The relative positions of these protein-protected regions are consistent with the model that repressor protein binding can interfere with RNA polymerase binding.

Separate DNase I footprint analysis of the *lac* operator region detects three segments of DNA sequence that are protected by *lac* repressor protein : O_1, O_2, O_3. Lane a of the gel shown is control DNA not bound by protein, and is therefore unprotected DNA. The experimental analysis identifies one protected segment, designated O_1, as the principal operator sequence. The two other regions of protein-protected operator DNA sequence are designated O_2 and O_3. Lanes d through g of the DNA footprint-protection gel are protected by repressor protein, and show the footprint gaps corresponding to these operator elements.

Lanes of the gel also identify two regions, designated C_1 and C_2, that are protected from DNase I digestion by the CAP–cAMP complex. This segment contains the consensus sequences for the CAP binding site that partially overlaps operator regions O_1 and O_3. The relative positions of these protein-binding sites indicate two kinds of interactions between proteins binding the *lac* promoter and operator. First, when CAP–cAMP is bound to the CAP binding site, RNA polymerase gains enhanced access to the promoter, establishing conditions for efficient transcription of *lac* operon genes. Second, the overlap of the CAP binding region with O_1 suggests that when repressor protein is bound to DNA, the CAP–cAMP complex is unable to bind, thus preventing positive regulation of transcription.

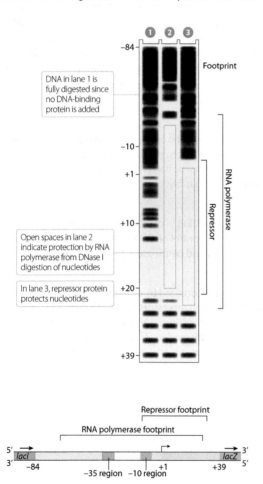

DNaseI footprint protection analysis of the *lacP* and *lacO* regions and model.

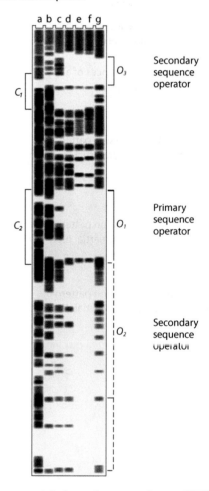

***lac* repressor protein footprint protection and DNA binding.**

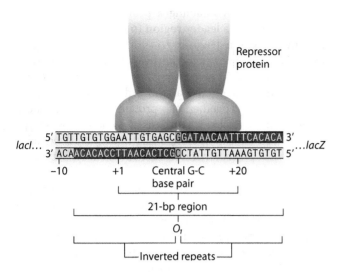

Figure 14.11 **The *lacO* region *O₁* contains an inverted repeat sequence.** The central G-C base pair is the pivot point of this region of twofold nucleotide symmetry of an inverted repeat sequence.

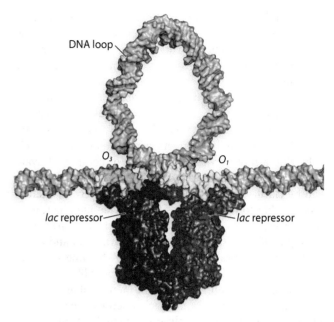

Figure 14.12 ***lac* repressor protein binding.** The crystal structural model of *lac* repressor binding at *lacO*.

at their C-terminal ends and are arranged as two identical bundles. One end of each bundle forms an operator DNA-binding domain, and the other end forms the allosteric domain. The three operator DNA segments that are the targets of repressor protein binding share a conserved, 21-bp inverted repeat sequence. In each sequence, a central G-C base pair is at the midpoint of a twofold axis of symmetry (**Figure 14.11**). On either side of the central G-C base pair are inverted repeat sequences of 10 bp each that are the specific binding location for polypeptides in each half of the repressor protein. Mitchell Lewis and his colleagues examined the crystal structure of DNA-bound repressor protein in a 1996 study and determined that the tetrameric repressor protein binds to O_1 and O_3 and induces **DNA loop** formation that draws the O_1 and O_3 regions closer together (**Figure 14.12**). This DNA loop structure contains part of the *lac* promoter and prevents transcription by blocking access of RNA polymerase.

Parallel experiments examining mutated operator DNA sequences reveal how constitutive operator mutations are caused by alterations of the DNA sequence in region O_1. **Figure 14.13** shows several base-pair substitutions that cause constitutive operator (O^C) mutations. Each of these changes disrupts the twofold symmetry of O_1, masking the sequence from recognition by repressor protein. Since O_1 is the primary binding target of the repressor protein and O_1 must be bound before binding to O_3 can occur, O_1 mutation also disrupts binding to O_3. The inability of repressor protein to bind to mutant operator sequence means that the transcription-repressing DNA loop cannot form. This in turn leaves the promoter available for binding by RNA polymerase and opens the door to continuous transcription and constitutive expression of the *lac* operon genes.

14.4 Transcription from the Tryptophan Operon Is Repressible and Attenuated

The *lac* operon is an example of an inducible operon that produces proteins responsible for the breakdown of a sugar that is an alternative energy source to glucose. Operons like *lac* that are involved in catabolism of alternative energy sources are typically inducible, since they are called upon only when glucose is depleted and the alternative sugar is available. In contrast, operons involved in anabolic pathways (pathways that synthesize

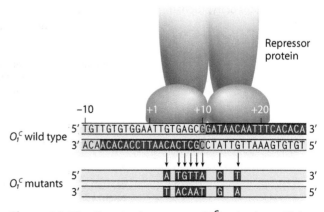

Figure 14.13 **Constitutive operator (O^C) mutations.** Eight base-substitution mutations in *lacO* region O_1 producing operator-comstitutive mutations. Each mutation disrupts the twofold symmetry of the operator inverted repeat sequences and prevents *lac* repressor protein binding.

compounds needed by the cell) can be regulated by negative feedback mechanisms that operate through activity of the end product of the pathway to block operon gene transcription. Operons of this kind are **repressible operons.**

In addition to the negative feedback mechanism, certain repressible operons have a second regulatory capability known as **attenuation** that has the ability to fine-tune transcription to match the momentary requirements of the cell, achieving a more-or-less steady state of compound availability. The difference between attenuation and inducibility can be clarified by an analogy. Inducible operons, such as *lac*, are akin to light switches that provide illumination in one setting ("on") and no illumination in the alternative setting ("off"). Inducible operons are turned on and off by molecular switches controlled by DNA-binding proteins. Attenuation, on the other hand, works more like a dimmer switch that allows illumination to be incrementally adjusted up or down. For several amino acid operons, the regulation of gene expression has evolved to maintain steady amino acid levels in cells. In such systems, feedback inhibition turns off operon gene transcription when the amino acid is readily available, and attenuation fine-tunes the amino acid level to maintain a steady-state concentration.

Feedback Inhibition of Tryptophan Synthesis

The tryptophan (*trp*) operon ("trip operon") in the *E. coli* genome contains five structural genes that share a regulatory region containing a promoter (*trpP*), an operator (*trpO*), and a **leader region (*trpL*)** that contains the **attenuator region** (Figure 14.14). The regulatory region spans 312 base pairs, and the five structural genes span approximately 6800 base pairs. The five structural genes transcribed in the operon are, in order, *trpE, trpD, trpC, trpB,* and *trpA*. Together, the protein products of these genes are responsible for synthesis of the amino acid tryptophan. Outside the operon, a sixth gene, *trpR*, encodes the repressor protein that is not activated until it pairs with tryptophan.

Transcription of *trp* operon genes is regulated by a feedback inhibition system that responds to free tryptophan in the cell. In this system, tryptophan acts as a corepressor by binding to and activating the *trp* repressor protein that is not active without its bound corepressor. Feedback inhibition is the principal mechanism turning on and turning off *trp* operon gene transcription (Figure 14.15). In the absence of tryptophan, the inactive repressor is unable to bind *trpO*, and operon gene transcription takes place. When tryptophan is present, however, it binds the repressor to activate it, and the repressor–corepressor complex binds the operator to block transcription. This is an efficient mechanism that shuts down transcription of genes whose expression is not needed at the moment. Such systems have evolved because they save metabolic energy that would otherwise be wasted transcribing unneeded mRNA and later recycling the unused transcript.

Figure 14.14 The tryptophan (*trp*) operon. Transcription is initiated from the promoter P_{trp} and progresses through the tryptophan leader (*trpL*) region to transcribe the five operon genes (*trpE* to *trpA*) into a polycistronic mRNA. The protein products of the operon genes catalyze successive steps of tryptophan synthesis.

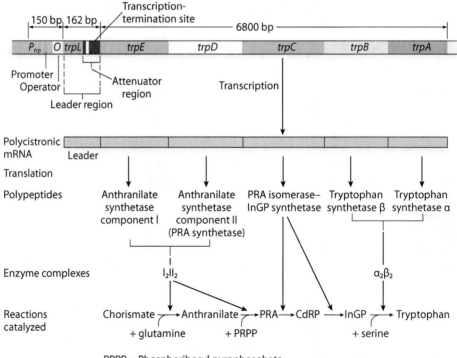

PRPP = Phosphoribosyl pyrophosphate
PRA = Phosphoribosyl anthranilate
CdRP = 1-(o-carboxyphenylamino)-1-deoxyribulose 5-phosphate
InGP = Indole-3-glycerol phosphate

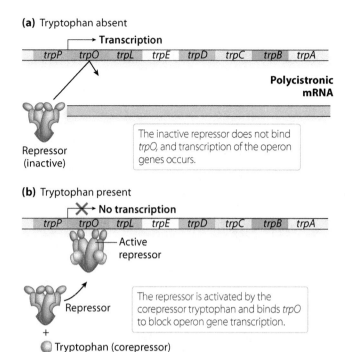

(a) Tryptophan absent

Transcription

trpP | trpO | trpL | trpE | trpD | trpC | trpB | trpA

**Polycistronic
mRNA**

Repressor
(inactive)

The inactive repressor does not bind
trpO, and transcription of the operon
genes occurs.

(b) Tryptophan present

No transcription

trpP | trpO | trpL | trpE | trpD | trpC | trpB | trpA

Active
repressor

Repressor

+

Tryptophan (corepressor)

The repressor is activated by the
corepressor tryptophan and binds trpO
to block operon gene transcription.

Figure 14.15 *Trp* operon transcription regulation by the repressor, with tryptophan absent (a) and with tryptophan present (b).

Based on this description, and knowing about the feedback inhibition of gene transcription, one might expect that *trpR⁻* bacteria that are mutant for the repressor protein would show constitutive transcription of operon genes regardless of whether tryptophan is present. Surprisingly, however, this is not the case. In wild-type bacteria (*trpR⁺*), tryptophan synthesis is very low when tryptophan is present in the cell, but while tryptophan synthesis by *trpR⁻* strains is higher under the same conditions, it is not at 100% capacity (Table 14.5). Both *trpR⁺* and *trpR⁻* strains synthesize tryptophan at 100% of capacity when tryptophan is absent. This suggests that a second regulatory mechanism is also affecting transcription of *trp* operon genes.

Attenuation of the *trp* Operon

The second mechanism regulating *trp* operon gene transcription is attenuation that is controlled by alternative folding undertaken by mRNA synthesized from the 162-bp *trpL* region. RNA polymerase binds to *trpP* and

Table 14.5	**Percentage of Full Tryptophan Expression for *trpR⁺* and *trpR⁻* Strains**	
	Tryptophan Present	**Tryptophan Absent**
trpR⁺	8%	100%
trpR⁻	33%	100%

initiates transcription of *trpL*. The *trpL* region contains four repeat DNA sequences (1 to 4), and the mRNA transcript of this region contains complementary repeats that lead to the folding of mRNA into double-stranded regions. The *trp* leader region also encodes a start codon, a short polypeptide of 14 amino acids, and a stop codon. Translation of this 14–amino acid polypeptide plays a pivotal role in attenuation (Figure 14.16a). Two features of the *trpL* region are critical to its attenuation function. First, the four repeat sequences, designated 1, 2, 3, and 4, can form different stem-loop structures (Figure 14.16b–d). (Stem-loop structures are discussed in Section 8.2 in connection with intrinsic transcription termination in bacteria; see Figure 8.7.) Second, among the codons for the 14 amino acids encoded by *trpL* mRNA, there are two back-to-back tryptophan codons (UGG) that function to sense the availability of tryptophan and are essential for attenuation.

The formation of stem loops of *trpL* mRNA is directly tied to the continuation or termination of transcription of the five *trp* operon genes. In the *trpL* region mRNA, region 1 is complementary to region 2, region 2 is complementary to region 3, and region 3 is complementary to region 4. Two of these stem-loop structures, the *3–4 stem loop* and the *2–3 stem loop*, are central to attenuation. The third type of stem loop, the *1–2 stem loop*, plays a minor role in attenuation.

The **3–4 stem loop** of mRNA, which is the **termination stem loop,** signals transcription termination. This is identified as the transcription termination site in Figure 14.14d. Formation of the 3–4 stem-loop halts RNA polymerase progress along the DNA, terminating transcription in the leader region before it reaches the structural genes of the operon (Figure 14.17a). Notice that region 4 is followed immediately by a poly-uracil sequence (a poly-U tail). This configuration—an mRNA stem loop followed by a uracil string—is the same as one described in connection with intrinsic termination of transcription in bacteria (see Figure 8.7). Formation of a 3–4 stem loop may be accompanied by formation of a 1–2 stem loop, which can induce a pause in the attenuation process. Formation of the 1–2 stem loop occurs when a ribosome does not affiliate with the nascent *trp* operon leader mRNA. In the absence of an RNA-bound ribosome, regions 1 and 2 form a double-stranded stem. This leads, in turn, to subsequent formation of a 3–4 stem loop that terminates transcription.

The alternative to the 3–4 stem loop is the **2–3 stem loop,** which is the **antitermination stem loop.** This stem loop forms when region 1 is unavailable for immediate pairing with region 2. This situation leads region 2 to pair with region 3. As a consequence, formation of the 2–3 stem loop precludes the formation of a 3–4 stem loop (Figure 14.17b). The antitermination stem loop allows RNA polymerase to continue transcription through the leader region and into the structural genes of the *trp*

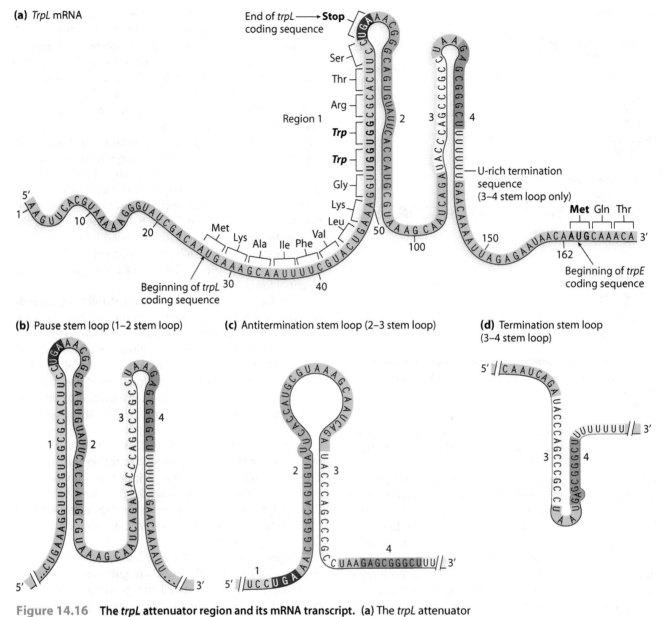

Figure 14.16   The *trpL* attenuator region and its mRNA transcript.   (a) The *trpL* attenuator contains 162 nucleotides that include a 14–amino acid coding sequence and four inverted repeat sequences that encode regions 1 through 4 in *trpL* mRNA. **(b)–(d)** Three alternative stem loops can form in mRNA. That encode region 1 to 4 and the short 14–amino acid polypeptide coding region.

operon, beginning with the transcription of *trpE*. If transcription progresses past region 4, a polycistronic mRNA spanning the five *trp* genes is produced. Translation of the five enzymes required for tryptophan synthesis follows.

Each mRNA transcribed from the *trpL* operon eventually forms either a 2–3 stem loop or a 3–4 stem loop, but what determines the type of stem loop an mRNA will form? The coupling of transcription and translation that is a prominent feature of bacterial gene expression plays a critical role in deciding this outcome. Transcription of the *trpL* region begins at the +1 nucleotide after RNA polymerase initiates transcription. Transcription across repeat

regions 1 and 2 can lead to formation of a 1–2 stem loop that temporarily pauses the progress of RNA polymerase. The pause is only momentary, however; it lasts just long enough for a ribosome to bind at the start codon in *trpL* and begin translation of the 14–amino acid polypeptide starting with the AUG codon identified in Figure 14.16. Translation initiation breaks the 1–2 stem loop, RNA polymerase resumes transcription, and the ribosome and RNA polymerase begin their coupled progression.

Notice three features of the leader mRNA depicted in Figure 14.17: (1) The polypeptide-coding sequence overlaps the entirety of leader region 1, and the stop codon is

(a) Tryptophan abundance: Termination

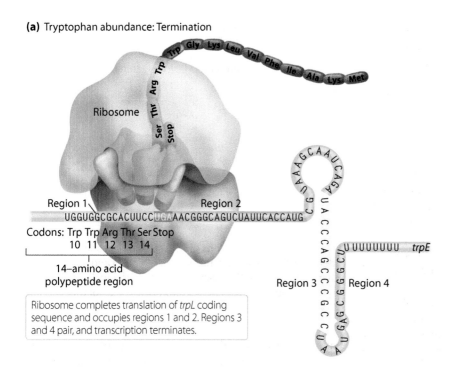

Ribosome completes translation of *trpL* coding sequence and occupies regions 1 and 2. Regions 3 and 4 pair, and transcription terminates.

(b) Tryptophan starvation: Antitermination

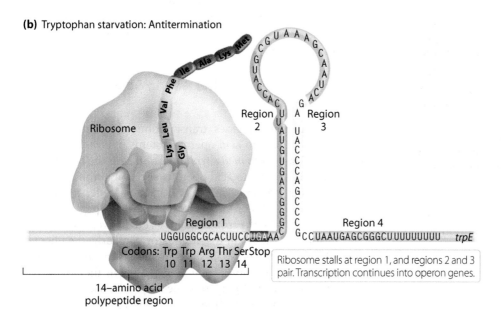

Ribosome stalls at region 1, and regions 2 and 3 pair. Transcription continues into operon genes.

Figure 14.17 *TrpL* **mRNA stem loop formation.** **(a)** In tryptophan abundance, the 3–4 (termination) stem loop terminates transcription after the poly-U string. **(b)** In tryptophan starvation, the 2–3 (antitermination) stem loop leads to polycistronic mRNA synthesis.

immediately adjacent to region 2; (2) codons 10 and 11 of the mRNA specify tryptophan, making completion of translation dependent on tryptophan availability; and (3) region 4 is followed immediately by a poly-U string, a feature associated with intrinsic termination of transcription. As coupled transcription and translation proceed, the relative positions of RNA polymerase and the ribosome are determined by how efficiently the ribosome can progress along the mRNA. This process, in turn, is tied directly to the availability of tryptophan and the rapidity with which tryptophan is inserted into the nascent polypeptide chain. When the cell has an adequate supply of tryptophan, the

ribosome makes steady progress along *trpL* mRNA, arriving at the stop codon where it partially overlays region 1 and region 2. Simultaneously, RNA polymerase is transcribing region 3, followed by region 4. With a portion of region 2 occupied by the ribosome and unavailable for pairing in a stem loop, region 3 forms a stem loop with region 4, the only available complementary segment of the mRNA. The 3–4 stem loop, being immediately followed by a poly-U string, causes transcription to spontaneously terminate at the end of region 4 by the intrinsic process. Formation of the 3–4 stem loop (the termination stem loop) stops transcription of the *trp* operon in the leader sequence before RNA polymerase reaches the beginning of the *trpE* gene. Transcription thus ceases only when the system senses that no additional tryptophan is needed to supply translation.

When the cell is starved for tryptophan, the supply of charged tRNA^{Trp} is low. The ribosome is forced to pause momentarily at codons 10 and 11 to await the arrival of a charged tryptophan tRNA that will incorporate tryptophan into the nascent polypeptide. As the ribosome pauses, its mass covers region 1. Meanwhile, RNA polymerase continues to transcribe *trpL*. As RNA polymerase transcribes region 3, the region finds a complementary partner in region 2, leading to 2–3 stem-loop formation. Region 3 is not followed by a poly-U string, making intrinsic termination impossible. Transcription continues through region 4 and on into the structural gene region of the operon to produce the polycistronic mRNA transcript of the operon. Formation of a 2–3 stem loop (the antitermination stem loop) thus permits transcription and translation of the enzymes necessary to synthesize tryptophan when the system senses that the available supply of tryptophan is insufficient to support translation.

Each *trpL* mRNA makes a molecularly based "decision" about whether to form a 3–4 or a 2–3 stem loop, depending on the availability of charged tRNA^{Trp} at the moment tRNA^{Trp} is needed by ribosomes. It is likely that at any given moment in time, a single bacterial cell contains a mixture of *trpL* mRNAs with 2–3 stem loops and *trpL* mRNAs with 3–4 stem loops. The balance shifts in the direction of more 3–4 stem loops and fewer 2–3 stem loops at higher levels of tryptophan concentration and shifts in the opposite direction—more 2–3 stem loops and fewer 3–4 stem loops—as tryptophan concentration falls. The resulting fine-tuning allows each cell to maintain a relatively steady concentration of tryptophan by turning tryptophan synthesis up or down to meet the needs of the cell.

Attenuation Mutations

The attenuation model is supported by mutagenesis experiments. For example, experiments in which one of the two adjacent tryptophan codons (in positions 10 and 11 of the *trpL* mRNA) has been altered by missense mutation to specify another amino acid have provided evidence of the importance of the back-to-back tryptophan codons in the *trpL* transcript. Mutation of one tryptophan UGG codon affects the attenuator responsiveness to tryptophan. If both tryptophan codons are altered by missense mutation, the attenuator no longer senses tryptophan concentration and instead senses the availability of the amino acid encoded by the mutated codons. Mutagenesis experiments have also targeted regions 3 and 4 of the leader sequence (Figure 14.18). Base

Remainder of
trpL mRNA
Nucleotide position 110
Poly-U string
140
Region 3
Region 4
Mutations that reduce complementarity
125

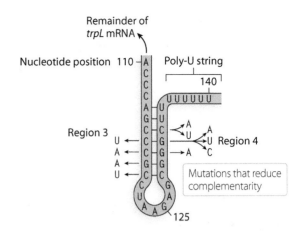

Figure 14.18 Mutations of *trpL*. Mutational analyses identify 10 base-pair substitutions in regions 3 and 4 of *trpL* that each decrease the efficiency of transcriptional regulation in the attenuator region by disrupting formation of the 3–4 stem loop.

substitutions that reduce the percentage of complementary base pairs binding these two regions destabilize the termination stem loop and reduce the efficiency of the mutated operon system in repressing structural gene transcription. Genetic Analysis 14.2 examines mutations of the *trp* operon.

Attenuation in Other Amino Acid Operon Systems

Attenuation represses transcription of structural genes in several amino acid operon systems in bacteria such as *E. coli* and *Salmonella typhimurium*. Like the *trp* operon, these other amino acid operons also contain multiple codons for the target amino acid in their leader transcripts (Figure 14.19). For example, the leader polypeptide of the *E. coli* histidine operon contains a run of seven consecutive histidine residues in the attenuator. Similarly, the phenylalanine leader polypeptide contains seven phenylalanine residues in a span of nine amino acids in the attenuator region. Like the *trp* operon, these operons use attenuation to form antitermination stem loops to regulate operon gene transcription.

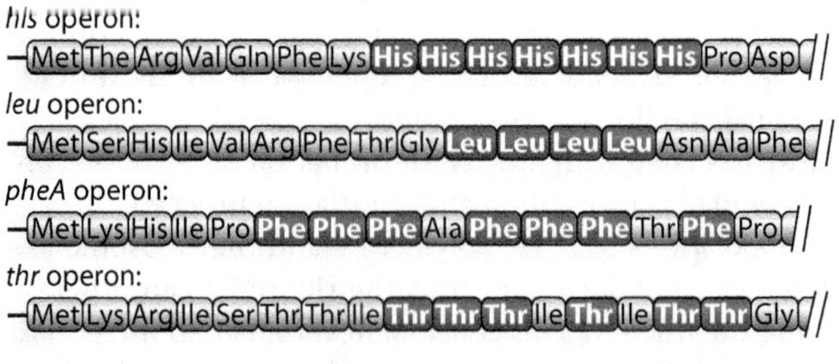

his operon:
Met The Arg Val Gln Phe Lys His His His His His His His Pro Asp
leu operon:
Met Ser His Ile Val Arg Phe Thr Gly Leu Leu Leu Leu Asn Ala Phe
pheA operon:
Met Lys His Ile Pro Phe Phe Phe Ala Phe Phe Phe Thr Phe Pro
thr operon:
Met Lys Arg Ile Ser Thr Thr Ile Thr Thr Thr Ile Thr Ile Thr Thr Gly

Figure 14.19 Four bacterial amino acid operons with attenuator control of transcription. The regulatory amino acid for each operon is shown in bold.

PROBLEM Describe the effects on attenuation and on tryptophan synthesis of the following mutations of the tryptophan codons (UGG) in the attenuator region of the operon.

a. The tryptophan codons are mutated to UAGUGG.

b. The tryptophan codons are mutated to UUGUUG.

> **BREAK IT DOWN:** You should be able to define attenuation and to describe how the presence of two tryptophan codons in the *trp* operon leader transcript participate in determining whether the termination (3–4) stem loop or the antitermination (2–3) stem loop forms in the transcript. See Figure 14.17 (p. 487).

Solution Strategies	Solution Steps
Evaluate	
1. Identify the topic this problem addresses and the nature of the required answer.	1. This problem concerns the consequences of mutations to the UGG (tryptophan) codons in the attenuator region of the *trp* operon. The answer requires a description of mutational consequences for tryptophan regulation and synthesis.
2. Identify the critical information given in the problem.	2. The mutant codon sequences are given.
Deduce	
3. Examine the nature of the mutation in part (a).	3. The base substitution in mutant (a) creates a stop codon in place of the first tryptophan codon.
4. Examine the nature of the mutation in part (b).	4. Two base substitutions are seen in mutant (b). Each creates a leucine codon in place of a tryptophan codon.
Solve	Answer a
5. Describe the consequence of the mutation in part (a).	5. UAG is a stop codon that halts translation of the polypeptide. The location of this stop codon will prevent the ribosome from covering repeat region 2. The 2–3 stem loop is the only regulatory configuration that can form, and it will lead to constitutive tryptophan synthesis.
TIP: Compare the transcription of the wild-type operon to that of this mutant operon (see Figures 14.16 to 14.18).	Answer b
6. Describe the consequence of the mutation in part (b).	6. Both mutant codons in this case encode leucine. These mutational changes will prevent attenuation of the *trp* operon in response to tryptophan level. Instead, tryptophan synthesis will attenuate in response to the level of leucine since the availability of leucine to add to the polypeptide will determine which stem loop will form.

For more practice, see Problems 7, 15, and 25. | Visit the Study Area to access study tools. | **Mastering Genetics**™

14.5 Bacteria Regulate the Transcription of Stress Response Genes and Translation and Archaea Regulate Transcription in a Bacteria-like Manner

The need on the part of bacteria to respond rapidly to changing environmental conditions suggests that transcriptional regulation must accommodate both common and rare circumstances, and also that the regulation of translation must be available under certain circumstances. This section presents examples of transcriptional regulation in bacteria under rarely encountered conditions, describes how bacteria regulate translation, and concludes with a discussion of transcription regulation mechanisms in Archaea.

Alternative Sigma Factors and Stress Response

The operon mechanisms described to this point are examples of the regulatory strategies employed by bacterial cells under conditions they encounter routinely. In response to rare or unusual environmental circumstances, however, bacteria switch gene transcription patterns to use genes that are not normally expressed. The response of *E. coli* to heat stress illustrates how expression of an *alternative sigma (σ) factor* alters gene transcription by activating the transcription of specialized heat stress response genes.

Escherichia coli grow vigorously at 37°C and can tolerate only narrow temperature variation. At low temperatures, their growth slows—an important reason refrigeration is used to preserve foods. At the other extreme, high temperatures kill the bacteria. This is the reason cooking is so efficient at reducing bacterial contamination of food. At the less dramatically elevated temperatures of 45°C, *E. coli* change their pattern of transcription by activating the expression of genes that are part of the heat shock response by the cell. The heat shock response protects *E. coli* cells from certain kinds of heat-induced damage. Similar mechanisms are common in other microorganisms as well as in fruit flies, plants, and animals, including humans.

Heat shock response in bacteria involves expression of an **alternative sigma (σ) factor** that changes the promoter-recognition capacity of the RNA polymerase core enzyme. Recall that the RNA polymerase core enzyme is bound by a sigma factor to form the holoenzyme (see Section 8.2). Under normal growth conditions, the RNA polymerase holoenzyme recognizes bacterial promoters containing an AT-rich Pribnow box at the −10 site. The common sigma factor, identified as σ^{70}, forms this holoenzyme that transcribes a wide array of bacterial genes under normal physiological conditions.

Bacteria grown at 45°C undergo several changes, including initiation of the expression of heat shock proteins, which are expressed only at high temperature, and of chaperon proteins, a class of proteins that either refold or degrade other proteins damaged by high heat. At these higher temperatures, σ^{70} is unstable, and RNA polymerase containing it functions very poorly. To explain the transcription of heat shock proteins in the presence of poorly functioning σ^{70}-containing RNA polymerase, researchers proposed and quickly found genetic evidence pointing to an alternative, high-temperature σ factor.

The evidence came from studies of mutant, temperature-sensitive *E. coli* that grow normally at 37°C but fail to grow at 45°C. This temperature sensitivity is a conditional lethal mutation affecting a gene called *rpoH*, which encodes an alternative sigma factor known as σ^{32}. When σ^{32} binds an RNA polymerase core enzyme, the holoenzyme recognizes different promoter sequences than are recognized by holoenzymes containing σ^{70} (**Figure 14.20**). In contrast to the AT richness that characterizes the Pribnow box sequence of bacterial promoters, the −10 region of promoters recognized by σ^{32}-containing RNA polymerase is rich in G-C base pairs.

The promoter for *rpoH* is recognized by σ^{70}-containing RNA polymerase when the temperature is elevated. The polypeptide translated from *rpoH* mRNA is very active in stimulating transcription of heat shock genes. In addition, transcription of a third sigma factor known as σ^{24}, which is normally present in *E. coli* cells at a very low level, is greatly elevated. The RNA polymerase holoenzyme containing σ^{24} also recognizes the *rpoH* promoter and transcribes the gene at elevated temperatures that inactivate σ^{70}.

A second transcriptional change that occurs as a consequence of high heat is a change in the chaperon

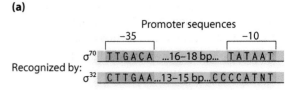

(a)

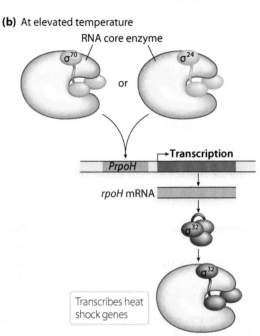

(b) At elevated temperature

Figure 14.20   Alternative sigma factors for heat shock genes. (a) Promoter sequences recognized by σ^{70}- and σ^{32}-containing RNA polymerase. (b) At elevated temperature, σ^{70} and σ^{24} transcribe *rpoH*, which encodes σ^{32} that in turn joins the RNA core enzyme to transcribe heat shock genes.

proteins. At normal growth temperatures, several chaperon proteins bind the small amount of σ^{32} present in the cell to inhibit its ability to form holoenzyme. At high temperatures, chaperone proteins release σ^{32}, leaving it free to join an RNA polymerase core enzyme and form a holoenzyme. Free chaperon proteins are redirected to bind heat-damaged cellular proteins instead. In this role, chaperon proteins either degrade the proteins they bind or assist in refolding the proteins.

Several additional examples of the use of alternative sigma factors in bacteria have been described. For example, *Bacillus subtilis* is a bacterium that normally propagates by vegetative growth, but poor growth conditions switch the growth mode to sporulation by activating the expression of alternative sigma factors. The gene transcription evidence shows that as growth conditions deteriorate, transcription of the common sigma factor is replaced by the transcription of two alternative sigma factors. The new sigma factors recognize the unique promoters and transcribe genes used in sporulation. A broad array of evidence shows that switching transcription from the normal sigma factor to alternative sigma factors induces a genome-wide change in the pattern

Table 14.6	Mechanisms of Transcription Regulation in Bacteria
Mechanism	**Actions and Outcomes**
1. Operon-specific control	Inducer substances, such as lactose, and negative feedback mechanisms, such as tryptophan availability, regulate gene transcription in coordinately controlled operons.
2. CAP–cAMP control	CAP–cAMP is utilized as a positive regulator of transcription for genes in several different operons, including the *lac* operon.
3. Alternative sigma factors	Extreme growth conditions, such as heat stress and starvation, induce transcription of alternative sigma factors.

of gene expression that silences previously active genes and initiates transcription of specialized genes that are used only under restrictive or extreme growth conditions. Table 14.6 compares and contrasts the mechanisms of gene regulation in bacterial systems.

Translational Regulation in Bacteria

Transcriptional regulation is far and away the predominant mode of controlling gene expression in bacteria, but bacteria are also capable of translational regulation. Translational regulation takes place by two mechanisms, one that binds protein to an mRNA to prevent its translation and another that pairs complementary *antisense RNA* with the mRNA to block its translation.

Translation repressor proteins regulate translation by binding mRNA in the vicinity of the Shine–Dalgarno sequence. Protein binding in this location interferes with recognition of the Shine–Dalgarno sequence by the 16S rRNA in the small ribosomal subunit and so blocks translation initiation. One of the clearest examples of this kind of regulatory protein–mRNA interaction is seen in the translational regulation of ribosomal proteins in *E. coli*. The ribosomal proteins are encoded in a series of operons that produce polycistronic mRNAs. These operons are under a certain degree of transcriptional regulation, but the most prominent control of production of ribosomal proteins is at the translational level. One of the protein products from each ribosomal protein operon can bind that operon's polycistronic mRNA near the 5′-most Shine–Dalgarno sequence, thus preventing binding of the small ribosomal subunit to the polycistronic mRNA and inhibiting synthesis of the proteins encoded by the operon.

Bacterial translation can also be inhibited by the activity of **antisense RNA,** an RNA molecule that is complementary to a portion of a specific mRNA. The binding of an mRNA by an antisense RNA prevents ribosome attachment to the mRNA and blocks translation. Several examples of bacterial translational regulation by antisense RNA have been described. One of the first-discovered mechanisms of antisense control of translation comes from the regulation of transposase production by the bacterial insertion sequence *IS10*. Transposase is the enzyme that drives the movement of transposable genetic

elements in genomes (see Section 13.6). Transposase cuts DNA for transposable element removal and insertion. A low level of transposition can be tolerated by bacterial genomes and may even be advantageous. Excessive transposase expression, however, leads to excessive transposition, which may cause lethal mutations due to transposon insertion into critical genes.

The *IS10* insertion sequence contains two promoters. One, called P_{IN}, is relatively weak and controls transcription of the DNA strand coding for active transposase. The second promoter, P_{OUT}, is much stronger. This promoter is embedded in the transposase gene and directs transcription of the noncoding strand of the gene, producing an antisense RNA that is complementary to the 5′ end of transposase mRNA and covers up the Shine–Dalgarno sequence of the mRNA, preventing its recognition by the small ribosomal subunit (Figure 14.21). As a consequence of the stronger P_{OUT} promoter, *IS10* antisense RNA is more abundant than transposase mRNA. This results in most of the transposase mRNA being bound by antisense RNA and effectively prevents translation of nearly all

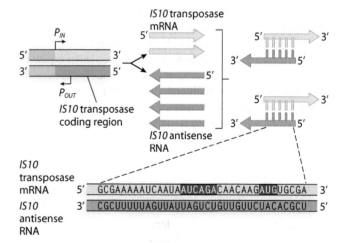

Figure 14.21 **Antisense RNA control of the expression of *IS10* transposase.** Two promoters each drive the synthesis of a transcript from the *IS10* transposon. The transposase gene mRNA transcript (from P_{IN} can hybridize with the antisense RNA transcript (from P_{OUT}) to block production of the transposase enzyme by preventing translation.

transposase mRNA. Nevertheless, an occasional transposase mRNA escapes antisense binding and undergoes translation. This generates a low level of transposase that initiates the rare event of *IS10* transposition within the bacterial genome.

Transcriptional Regulation in Archaea

In previous chapters, we have seen numerous examples of how Archaea, Bacteria, and Eukarya have diverged from their common ancestor. We have also looked with interest at patterns in the features they continue to share. Section 8.3, for example, described the basic transcription machinery of archaea, including RNA polymerase and some general transcription factors, as being clearly eukaryote-like. We will now see, however, that many of the transcription regulatory proteins in archaea are similar to bacterial transcription regulators. This suggests that archaea are likely to use bacteria-like mechanisms to regulate transcription. Indeed, research on archaeal transcription regulation has identified several instances in which a repressor protein exerts negative control of transcription. Evidence of positive control of transcription of archaeal genes has also been found.

Archaeal genomes contain many operons producing polycistronic mRNA. The preceding pages have demonstrated this pattern of gene organization to be common in bacteria, but it has not been documented in eukaryotes. In keeping with the organization of many of their genes into operons, archaea frequently use repressor proteins to bind operator sites near, or overlapping, the promoters. As in similar bacterial systems, repressor-protein binding in archaea interferes with RNA polymerase binding and transcription initiation, thus exerting negative control of transcription.

One example of this negative transcriptional control has been identified in the archaeon *Methanococcus maripaludis*, where the protein NprR operates as a repressor of the transcription of two operon genes, *nif* and *glnA*, that are required for nitrogen metabolism. Transcription of these genes is normally induced when nitrogen is present and is repressed when nitrogen is absent. Genetic analysis of *M. maripaludis* strains with mutations that

block production of NprR detect constitutive transcription of *nif* and *glnA*. This finding is analogous to the observation of constitutive transcription of *lac* operon genes in *lacI⁻* bacteria. The genetic evidence suggests that binding of NprR blocks recruitment of RNA polymerase to the operon promoter. Another example of negative control of transcription by a repressor protein has been documented in *Archaeoglobus fulgidus*, where the repressor protein Mdr1 binds to an operator site and in so doing blocks binding of RNA polymerase at an operon promoter. Table 14.7 lists these and additional examples of archaeal transcription-regulating proteins.

Positive control of transcription of archaeal operons has also been observed. The protein Ptr2 in *Methanococcus jannaschii* has been shown to act as a transcription activator. When Ptr2 binds upstream of the RNA polymerase binding site in the promoter region, the binding of the archaeal general transcription factor protein TBP (a protein homologous to eukaryotic TATA-binding protein) is enhanced. TBP helps recruit RNA polymerase to the promoter. This action is similar to the positive regulatory effect of the CAP–cAMP complex binding to the CAP binding site upstream of the bacterial *lac* operon RNA polymerase binding site in the promoter.

The archaeal domain is diverse, and research on archaeal transcription and transcription regulation is in its infancy in comparison with similar research on bacteria and eukaryotes. Yet it already seems clear that further research will reveal transcriptional systems both novel and familiar.

14.6 Antiterminators and Repressors Control Lambda Phage Infection of *E. coli*

Bacteriophage (or phage, for short) are viruses that infect bacterial cells. Like all viruses, they must infect host cells to reproduce (see Section 6.5). Their tiny genomes do not contain all the genes necessary for replication, transcription, and translation, so phage are obligate parasites that use an ingenious array of tricks to accomplish these

Table 14.7	Selected Transcriptional Regulatory Proteins in Archaea[a]		
Species	**Protein**	**Repressor or activator**	**Mode of action**
A. fulgidus	Mdr1	Repressor	Blocks RNA polymerase binding
M. maripaludis	NrpR	Repressor	Blocks RNA polymerase binding
S. solfataricus	Lrs14	Repressor	Blocks TBP binding
P. furiosus	PhrA	Repressor	Blocks RNA polymerase binding
M. jannaschii	Ptr2	Activator	Facilitates TBP binding

[a] Information adapted from S. D. Bell. 2005. Archaeal transcription regulation—variation on a bacterial theme. *Trends Microbiol.*, 13: 262–65.

molecular processes. The secret to their reproductive success lies in their ability to commandeer bacterial proteins and enzymes to preferentially express phage genes over bacterial genes.

Given the limited content of phage genomes, some of the most important genes for phage reproduction are those that redirect the activity of bacterial host genes to serve phage requirements. Successful phage infection requires (1) that genetic regulatory switches be controlled through phage gene expression to redirect the action of host genes and (2) that phage gene expression initiate a sequence of events leading the bacterium to participate in the expression of phage genetic information. In no bacteriophage is there a clearer picture of the processes that control regulatory genetic switching than in lambda (λ) phage.

Recall that all bacteriophage are capable of infecting and reproducing within the host bacterial cell. The infection ends with the lysis of the host cell, in a process called the lytic cycle (see Figure 6.15). But certain bacteriophage known as temperate phage, of which λ phage is an example, are also capable of a lysogenic cycle, or lysogeny. The lysogenic cycle is characterized by integration of the phage into the host chromosome, converting the host into a lysogen. Lysogenic integration is site specific, meaning it occurs at a sequence shared by the phage and the bacterial host (see Figure 6.19). The phage enzyme integrase is responsible for lysogenic integration. In this section, we discuss the two life cycles of λ phage, examining the regulatory proteins that control which life cycle a particular infection will undertake, as well as the actions of the proteins that control each life cycle.

The Lambda Phage Genome

The λ phage genome is composed of approximately 48 kb of linear, double-stranded DNA that encodes nearly 60 genes (**Figure 14.22a**). Its injection into a host bacterial cell leads to an immediate circularization inside the host cell that is accomplished by the joining of two single-stranded **cohesive (*cos*) ends** that are each 12 nucleotides in length (**Figure 14.22b**). A host DNA ligase seals the two gaps that are left when the cohesive ends join and produces a circularized λ phage that is ready to begin gene expression.

The λ phage genome is organized as a series of operons. The genes in each operon are expressed in a well-defined sequence. Expression of genes in certain operons begins immediately after circularization. The specific order of gene expression is critical to the ability of λ phage to carry out successful infection of its bacterial host. Consequently, **immediate early genes** are expressed shortly after circularization, **delayed early genes** are expressed next, and **late genes** are expressed later in the infection cycle. The transcription of immediate early, delayed early, and late gene regions is determined by binding of two regulatory proteins, one known as an

antiterminator, whose binding permits gene transcription by preventing transcription termination, and the other protein acting as a repressor that blocks additional transcription.

Immediately following circularization of the λ phage chromosome, **early promoters** and **early operators** control transcription of genes whose protein products interact to determine whether the phage undergoes the lytic cycle or the lysogenic cycle (see Chapter 6). The lytic cycle results in a rapidly progressing infection leading to lysis (rupture) of the host cell and release of scores of progeny phage. In the lysogenic life cycle, on the other hand, the phage chromosome integrates into the host chromosome, as noted above. Expression of genes in the integrated phage chromosome (the prophage) is minimal; only the genes necessary to maintain lysogeny are expressed. Replication of the bacterial chromosome produces daughter cells that carry a copy of the prophage. Lysogeny continues until the prophage excises itself from its integration site, reactivating phage gene expression and the lytic cycle.

Early Gene Transcription

Upon circularization of the phage chromosome, the two immediate early λ phage genes *N* and *cro* are transcribed, and the N and cro proteins are translated. Transcription and translation of these genes, as well as all of the other genes we mention, is accomplished by bacterial host proteins and ribosomes because the λ phage genome does not encode these functions. The N protein is an antiterminator protein, and the cro protein is a repressor. These two proteins engage in a molecular tug-of-war for control of a genetic switch that determines whether the infection will result in the lytic cycle or the lysogenic cycle. The early promoter P_R controls rightward transcription of immediate early genes, beginning with the *cro* gene (for *c*ontrol of *r*epressor and *o*thers) (**Foundation Figure 14.23, ❶**). The immediate early promoter P_L controls leftward transcription beginning with the *N* gene, whose protein product blocks transcription termination and allows delayed early and late genes to be transcribed ❶.

The antitermination protein N binds to three transcription-terminating DNA sequences: t_L, t_{R1}, and t_{R2} (see Foundation Figure 14.23, ❷). When not bound by N protein, termination sequence t_L acts to block leftward transcription beyond *N*. In the other direction, t_{R1} and t_{R2} prevent rightward transcription beyond *cro* or beyond three other early genes—*cII*, *O*, and *P*. When N protein binds t_L, t_{R1}, and t_{R2}, however, delayed early genes leftward of t_L and rightward of t_{R1} and t_{R2} are transcribed. One of the proteins produced by leftward transcription is integrase (the product of the *int* gene), which is required for prophage integration into the bacterial chromosome. In the other direction, rightward transcription produces protein cII, which forms a complex with protein cIII, one

Figure 14.22 The genome map of λ (lambda) phage.
(a) The λ phage genome is organized into operons that function at defined times during infection of a host cell. (b) The cohesive (*cos*) site is the region that enables the linear phage chromosome to circularize when it enters the host bacterial cell. Immediate early, delayed early, and late genes are expressed in order.

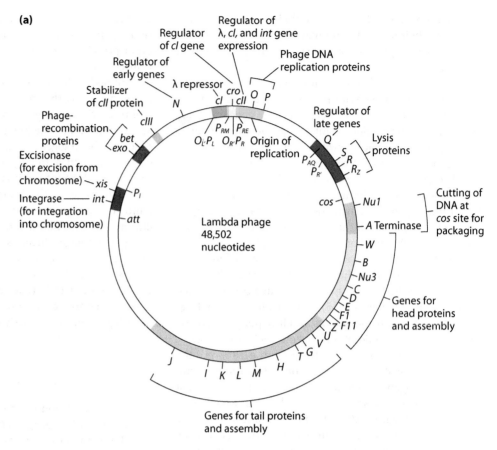

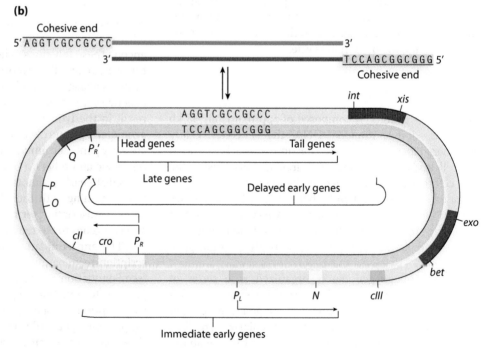

of the products of leftward transcription ❸. Together, the cII/cIII complex binds to the promoter P_{RE} (for *re*pressor *e*stablishment). This promoter initiates leftward transcription of the *cI* gene, producing the cI protein, which is also known as the λ repressor protein (Foundation Figure 14.23, ❹ and ❺).

Before the lytic cycle or the lysogenic cycle of infection can begin, two critical molecular "decisions" have to be made. The first of these decisions involves determining whether bacteria are actively growing. With active bacterial growth, lysis is favored because new progeny phage will readily find new host cells. If bacteria are growing poorly,

Regulation of Bacteriophage Entry into the Lytic or Lysogenic Cycle

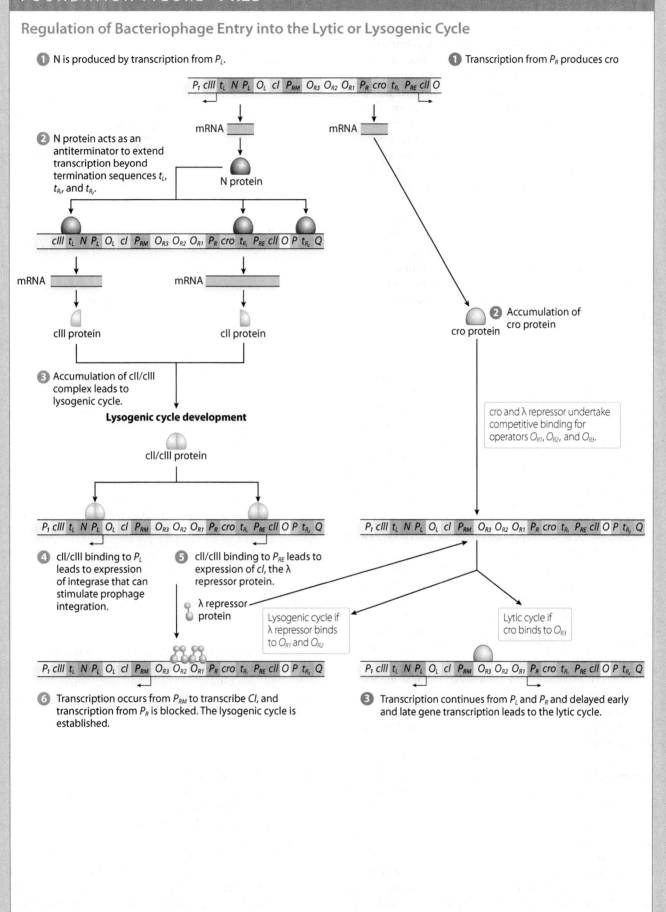

1 N is produced by transcription from P_L.

1 Transcription from P_R produces cro

mRNA

mRNA

2 N protein acts as an antiterminator to extend transcription beyond termination sequences t_L, t_{R_1}, and t_{R_2}.

N protein

mRNA

mRNA

cIII protein

cII protein

cro protein

2 Accumulation of cro protein

3 Accumulation of cII/cIII complex leads to lysogenic cycle.

Lysogenic cycle development

cII/cIII protein

cro and λ repressor undertake competitive binding for operators O_{R1}, O_{R2}, and O_{R3}.

4 cII/cIII binding to P_L leads to expression of integrase that can stimulate prophage integration.

5 cII/cIII binding to P_{RE} leads to expression of *cI*, the λ repressor protein.

λ repressor protein

Lysogenic cycle if λ repressor binds to O_{R1} and O_{R2}

Lytic cycle if cro binds to O_{R3}

6 Transcription occurs from P_{RM} to transcribe *CI*, and transcription from P_R is blocked. The lysogenic cycle is established.

3 Transcription continues from P_L and P_R and delayed early and late gene transcription leads to the lytic cycle.

however, lysogeny is favored. In this state, the prophage can remain quiescent until growth conditions improve.

The protein cII is critical to this first molecular decision. Protein cII is sensitive to bacterial proteases, enzymes that degrade proteins. Proteases are in abundance when bacterial growth conditions are favorable, but they are sparse under starvation conditions. If bacteria are actively growing in good conditions, cII is degraded, it never forms a complex with cIII, and little λ repressor protein is produced. If, on the other hand, bacterial growth conditions are poor, cII remains, it forms a complex with cIII, and λ repressor protein is produced.

The second molecular decision to be made involves direct competition between the cro protein and the λ repressor protein. They compete for binding to operator sites, with the winning molecule determining whether the lytic cycle or the lysogenic cycle is established. In the following discussion, we focus on the competitive binding between λ repressor protein and cro protein.

Cro Protein and the Lytic Cycle

Entry into the lytic cycle requires the transcription of late genes that are regulated by **late promoters** and **late operators.** These genes are rightward of P_R, and are involved in the synthesis of head and tail proteins, as well as products that lyse the host cell. The genetic switch governing whether λ phage enters the lytic or the lysogenic cycle hinges on the binding of cro protein and λ repressor protein, respectively. Both cro protein and λ repressor protein have affinity for operator sequences O_{R1}, O_{R2}, and O_{R3}, located between P_R and P_{RM}. The two proteins have opposite binding affinities. The cro protein binds O_{R3} with highest affinity but has lower affinity for O_{R2} and O_{R1}. The λ repressor, on the other hand, has highest affinity for O_{R1}. Its affinity for O_{R2} is not as high, and its affinity for O_{R3} is much lower. The three operator sequences each have a 17-bp target for binding of either cro protein or λ repressor protein. The O_{R1} sequence lies fully within P_R, and O_{R3} lies fully within P_{RM}; O_{R2} is split between the two promoters (**Figure 14.24a**).

The cro protein product is a 66-amino acid monomer that forms a globular structure. Functional cro protein is a homodimer that precisely spans the 17 bp of DNA that are its target binding sequence on the operators. Dimerized cro protein has strong binding affinity for O_{R3} and O_{R2}, but lower affinity for O_{R1}. As cro protein concentration increases, however, it binds, in order, to O_{R3}, O_{R2}, and O_{R1}.

The presence of cro protein at the operator sequences blocks the access of RNA polymerase to P_{RM}, exerting negative control of cI gene transcription and preventing production of λ repressor protein (**Figure 14.24b**). This action is analogous to the effect of the *lac* repressor protein binding to the operator sequence in the *lac* operon. At the same time, cro protein binding exerts positive control on P_R, leading to enhanced transcription of *cro* and other genes that are rightward of P_R. Among these rightward

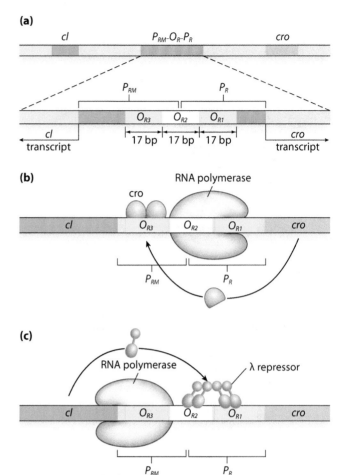

Figure 14.24 **Transcription of λ phage genes *cro* and *cl*.** (a) Promoters P_R and P_{RM} overlap three operator sites—O_{R1}, O_{R2}, and O_{R3}—that are competitively bound by regulatory proteins. (b) The *cro* gene is transcribed from P_R. Cro protein binds O_{R3} and O_{R2}, leading to transcription of genes that generate the lytic cycle. (c) The *cl* gene is transcribed from P_{RM} to produce λ repressor that binds to O_{R1} and drives additional *cl* transcription. Other gene transcription is blocked, and lysogeny is established.

genes is Q, a gene producing Q protein, which is a positive regulator of transcription of late genes that are rightward of the late promoter $P_{R'}$. These late genes include genes encoding proteins of the phage head and tail as well as genes required for lysis of the host cell.

The λ Repressor Protein and Lysogeny

Successful binding by λ repressor protein at operator sites O_{R1} and O_{R2} is cooperative. This binding is a positive regulator of transcription from the promoter P_{RM}. The effect is much like binding of the CAP–cAMP complex in the *lac* operon (**Figure 14.24c**).

Under the influence of λ repressor protein binding to the operator region, transcription from P_{RM} produces more repressor protein. Repressor binding also prevents transcription from P_R, effectively blocking *cro* transcription, and lysogeny results.

Resumption of the Lytic Cycle Following Lysogeny Induction

The λ repressor protein is the product of the *cI* gene. This protein is a 236–amino acid polypeptide containing 92 amino acids in the C-terminal domain (amino acids 1–92), 105 amino acids in the N-terminal domain (amino acids 132–236), and the remaining 39 amino acids (93–131) linking the two domains. Functional λ repressor protein is dimeric, and monomers are linked at their C-terminal ends. The resulting dimers have a dimension that spans 17 bp of DNA, precisely the size of each operator sequence (Figure 14.25a).

Lysogeny is a semipermanent state that can be maintained for an extended period of time by the ongoing binding of λ repressor protein to O_{R1}, O_{R2}, and O_{R3}. The

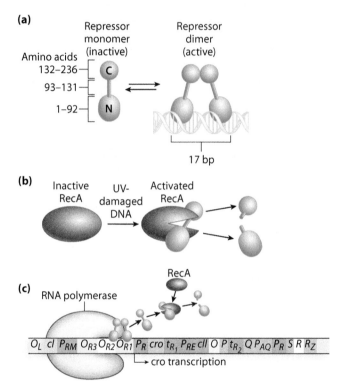

(a)

(b)

(c)

Figure 14.25 **Lysogeny maintenance and termination.** (a) A homodimeric λ repressor protein binds to 17-bp operator sequences to regulate its own transcription and maintain lysogeny. (b) UV light and other DNA-damaging agents activate RecA, which cleaves λ repressor monomers to inactivate repressor protein. (c) Lysogeny ends with the removal of λ repressor protein from operator sequences and the initiation of transcription of *cro*.

persistence over long periods of the lysogenic state raises two questions. First, what makes lysogeny come to an end, and second, how does the phage resume the lytic cycle and produce progeny phage?

Induction is the process that brings lysogeny to an end and reinitiates the lytic cycle by excising the prophage from its integrated location in the bacterial chromosome. You might think of induction as another molecular decision, this one triggered by DNA damage done by extracellular forces. The principal force causing injury to DNA is ultraviolet light, whose effects on DNA we described in Section 12.4. UV-induced DNA damage activates many proteins involved in DNA repair. Among the numerous proteins activated in the DNA repair cascade is the protein RecA, whose role in mutation repair is to activate recombination.

When bacterial DNA is damaged by UV light, however, the protease (protein-destroying) activity of RecA protein is also activated. Among other targets of this he protease activity is the amino acid segment of λ repressor monomers that join the N- and C-terminal regions of each protein (Figure 14.25b). The C terminus is clipped off each monomer, effectively breaking apart repressor dimers. This causes the N-terminal ends to fall off DNA. With λ repressor no longer bound to DNA, the O_{R1}, O_{R2}, and O_{R3} sequences are exposed, and positive regulation of *cI* transcription ends, as does the negative regulation of *cro* transcription. A consequence of the removal of λ repressor from the operator region is the renewed production of cro protein (Figure 14.25c). The cro protein binds to the operators no longer occupied by repressor protein. This leads to the expression of *Xis*, producing the enzyme excisionase that removes the lysogen from its integrated location. This event triggers the resumption of the lytic cycle and ultimately results in host cell lysis and the release of progeny phage.

In summary, λ phage is an elegant regulatory system that facilitates two molecular decisions controlling whether a genetic switch is flipped in favor of the lytic cycle or the lysogenic cycle. The crucial interaction is between the protein products of the early genes *cro* and *cI* that compete for binding to operator sequences O_{R1}, O_{R2}, and O_{R3}. If cro protein prevails by successfully binding to O_{R2} and O_{R3}, expression of *cI* is repressed, and the synthesis of late genes leading to completion of the lytic cycle is assured. On the other hand, if λ repressor protein prevails, its early occupation of O_{R1} and O_{R2} prevents transcription of late genes, ensuring that the lysogenic cycle will proceed.

CASE STUDY

Vibrio cholerae—Stress Response Leads to Serious Infection

THE INFECTIOUS DISEASE CHOLERA Cholera is a severely debilitating and potentially fatal disease caused by infection with the intestinal bacterium *Vibrio cholerae*. It is a major

public health problem in developing countries where sanitation and supplies of clean water are inadequate or following disasters that disrupt normal sanitation and supplies of clean water. The bacterium is transmitted from person to person through contact with infected fecal material. The ingestion of fecal-contaminated water is the most common way of contracting cholera. Many ingested bacteria are killed by the highly acidic environment of the stomach, but *V. cholerae* in particular can survive in greater numbers than most bacteria by undertaking a rapid switch in gene regulation that shuts down the expression of some genes and activates the expression of stress response genes. Unfortunately for infected humans, the *V. cholerae* stress response produces toxins that can rapidly lead to degradation of the mucosal cells lining the intestines and to excessive leakage of water from the damaged cells. The leakage disturbs the osmotic balance of the cells; to compensate, they secrete water, initiating a repeating cycle of ion leakage and water release that produces watery diarrhea and severe dehydration. Unless immediate antibiotic treatment and rehydration therapy are started, death can occur within hours.

VIBRIO CHOLERAE TOXINS In *V. cholerae*, three genes—*ToxS, ToxR,* and *ToxT*—exert positive control over the transcription of genes producing virulence (active bacterial growth that causes disease). The expression of *ToxS* and *ToxR* genes is stimulated by the environmental cues encountered by *V. cholerae* in the hostile environment of the stomach. A protein complex formed by the products of these genes activates transcription of *ToxT*. The polypeptide product of *ToxT* is a transcription-activating protein that binds to the promoter P_{ctx} that controls transcription of two genes, *CtxA* and *CtxB* (abbreviations for "cholera toxin A" and "cholera toxin B") that are part of an operon. The polypeptide products of *CtxA* and *CtxB* are the cholera toxins that initiate the series of actions that lead to cholera symptoms.

PREVENTING AND STUDYING THE DISEASE PROCESS Preventing cholera is an obvious public health priority. According to the World Health Organization, between 3 million and 5 million people contract cholera each year, and more than 100,000 deaths are attributed to cholera annually. Vaccines can help prevent some cholera cases, and oral antibiotics can help treat the disease once it has been acquired. Important as well is gaining understanding of how the ToxS–ToxR complex and ToxT operate in promoter recognition, and identifying the other genes they regulate. Similarly, gathering information about the stress response and virulence genes in *V. cholerae* will help medical practitioners and microbiologists understand how the bacterium produces its lethal effects. Such knowledge may suggest new strategies that can disable the bacterium before it causes disease or new treatments that can prevent the most serious consequences of infection.

SUMMARY   (MasteringGenetics™   For activities, animations, and review quizzes, go to the Study Area.

14.1 Transcriptional Control of Gene Expression Requires DNA–Protein Interaction

▌ Regulated genes are under transcriptional control, whereas constitutive genes are not regulated.

▌ In negative control of transcription, regulatory proteins bound to DNA reduce or eliminate transcription.

▌ Regulatory proteins, also called repressors, have a DNA-binding domain to bind regulatory DNA sequences and an allosteric domain to bind a regulatory molecule.

▌ An inducer molecule binds to the repressor molecule at an allosteric site to inhibit its action.

▌ In positive regulatory control, activator proteins bind DNA at promoters and other regulatory sequences and initiate or increase transcriptional efficiency.

14.2 The *lac* Operon Is an Inducible Operon System under Negative and Positive Control

▌ Bacterial operons transcribe two or more genes under the coordinated regulatory control of shared promoters, operators, and other regulatory elements.

▌ The lactose (*lac*) operon is an inducible operon system that produces three proteins—β-galactosidase (*lacZ*), permease (*lacY*), and transacetylase (*lacA*) that are required to metabolize lactose and its by-products. Its regulatory control center contains a promoter and an operator sequence (*lacO*).

▌ Negative control of *lac* operon gene transcription is exerted by a repressor protein (*lacI*) that binds to the *lacO* region to block transcription. Allolactose inactivates the repressor protein by changing its conformation and preventing it from binding to the operator.

▌ Positive control of transcription of *lac* operon genes is exerted by the CAP–cAMP complex that forms in the absence of glucose and binds to the CAP site of the *lac* promoter.

14.3 Mutational Analysis Deciphers Genetic Regulation of the *lac* Operon

▌ Mutation studies determined the order of *lac* operon genes as *lacZ-lacY-lacA*.

▌ The analysis of mutant haploid and partial diploid bacteria identified the trans-acting repressor protein that binds the operator sequence.

▌ *lac* operator mutation analysis indicates that the operator is a cis-acting element that controls transcription of immediately adjacent genes on the chromosome.

▌ The *lac* repressor binding site overlaps the RNA polymerase binding location in the *lac* promoter.

▌ *lac* repressor protein binding induces DNA loop formation that prevents RNA polymerase binding at the promoter.

▌ The CAP–cAMP complex binds to the CAP binding site of the *lac* promoter and facilitates RNA polymerase binding.

14.4 Transcription from the Tryptophan Operon Is Repressible and Attenuated

▌ The tryptophan (*trp*) operon is a repressible operon that produces five polypeptides that participate in tryptophan synthesis.

▌ *trp* operon transcription is inhibited by a feedback mechanism involving tryptophan as a corepressor.

▌ *trp* operon gene expression is attenuated to maintain the cellular concentration of tryptophan at a steady state. Many of the amino acid operons are regulated by an attenuation mechanism.

▌ The *trpL* (leader) region contains an attenuator sequence of four DNA repeats that form one of two alternative mRNA stem loops.

▌ The 2–3 (antitermination) stem loop formed by mRNA permits transcription of five *trp* operon structural genes in a polycistronic mRNA.

▌ The 3–4 (termination) stem loop of mRNA terminates transcription before RNA polymerase binds to the structural genes of the operon.

14.5 Bacteria Regulate the Transcription of Stress Response Genes and Translation and Archaea Regulate Transcription in a Bacteria-like Manner

▌ Alternative sigma factors are used to generate RNA polymerases that recognize promoters of genes not transcribed by the common bacterial RNA polymerase.

▌ Genes transcribed using alternative sigma factors are required only under specialized circumstances, such as in response to heat shock.

▌ The translation of bacterial mRNA can be blocked by RNA-binding translation repressor proteins or by antisense RNA that binds to mRNA from specific genes.

▌ Many archaeal genes are organized into operons, and several transcription repressor and transcription activator proteins controlling these operons have been identified.

14.6 Antiterminators and Repressors Control Lambda Phage Infection of *E. coli*

▌ Early genes of the bacteriophage λ genome produce proteins that compete to bind at the same regulatory region. The protein that prevails determines whether the phage infection will follow the lytic cycle or the lysogenic cycle.

▌ Completion of the lytic cycle requires the expression of late λ phage genes.

▌ Lysogen integration and maintenance requires ongoing expression of the λ repressor protein, which regulates its own transcription.

▌ Lysogen integration is reversed by environmental changes that lead to induction and to resumption of the lytic cycle.

KEYWORDS

activator binding site *(p. 470)*
activator protein *(p. 470)*
allolactose *(p. 472)*
allosteric domain (allostery) *(p. 470)*
allosteric effector compound *(p. 470)*
alternative sigma (σ) factor *(p. 490)*
antisense RNA *(p. 491)*
antiterminator *(p. 493)*
attenuation (attenuator region) *(p. 484)*
basal transcription *(p. 474)*
CAP binding region (CAP–cAMP complex) *(p. 475)*
catabolite repression *(p. 475)*
cis-acting *(p. 478)*
cis-dominant *(p. 478)*
cohesive (*cos*) ends *(p. 493)*
constitutive transcription (constitutive mutants) *(pp. 469, 477)*

corepressor *(p. 470)*
delayed early genes *(p. 493)*
DNA-binding domain *(p. 470)*
DNA loop *(p. 483)*
early operators (early promoters) *(p. 493)*
helix-turn-helix (HTH) motif *(p. 471)*
immediate early genes *(p. 493)*
inducer *(p. 470)*
inducer–repressor complex *(p. 474)*
inducible operon *(p. 472)*
induction *(p. 497)*
inhibitor *(p. 470)*
lac+ phenotype *(p. 472)*
lac− phenotype *(p. 473)*
lacA gene (*lacY* gene, *lacZ* gene) *(p. 473)*
late genes (late operators, late promoters) *(pp. 493, 496)*

leader region (*trpL*) *(p. 484)*
negative control (of transcription) *(p. 469)*
noninducible *(p. 479)*
operator *(p. 470)*
operon [lactose (*lac*), tryptophan (*trp*)] *(p. 472)*
polar mutation *(p. 477)*
polycistronic mRNA *(p. 473)*
positive control (of transcription) *(p. 470)*
regulated transcription *(p. 469)*
repressible operon *(p. 484)*
repressor protein *(p. 470)*
stem loop [3–4 (termination stem loop), 2–3 (antitermination stem loop)] *(p. 485)*
trans-acting *(p. 479)*
translation repressor protein *(p. 491)*

PROBLEMS

MasteringGenetics™ Visit for instructor-assigned tutorials and problems.

Chapter Concepts

For answers to selected even-numbered problems, see Appendix: Answers.

1. Bacterial genomes frequently contain groups of genes organized into operons. What is the biological advantage of operons to bacteria? Identify the regulatory components you would expect to find in an operon. How are the expressed genes of an operon usually arranged?

2. Transcriptional regulation of operon gene expression involves the interaction of molecules with one another and of regulatory molecules with segments of DNA. In this context, define and give an example of each of the following:
   a. operator
   b. repressor
   c. inducer
   d. corepressor
   e. promoter
   f. positive regulation
   g. allostery
   h. negative regulation
   i. attenuation

3. Why is it essential that bacterial cells be able to regulate the expression of their genes? What are the energetic and evolutionary advantages of regulated gene expression? Is the expression of all bacterial genes subject to regulated expression? Compare and contrast the difference between regulated gene expression and constitutive gene expression.

4. Identify similarities and differences between an inducible operon and a repressible operon in terms of
   a. the transcription-regulating DNA sequences.
   b. the presence and action of allosteric regulatory molecules.
   c. the organization of structural genes of the operon.

5. The transcription of β-galactosidase and permease is inducible in *lac*⁺ bacteria with a wild-type *lac* operon. Explain the mechanism by which lactose gains access to the cell to induce transcription of the genes.

6. Is attenuation the product of an allosteric effect? Is attenuation the result of a transcriptional or a translational activity? Explain your answers.

7. The *trpL* region contains four repeated DNA sequences that lead to the formation of stem-loop structures in mRNA. What are these stem-loop structures, and how do they affect transcription of the structural genes of the *trp* operon?

8. The CAP binding site in the *lac* promoter is the location of positive regulation of gene expression for the operon. Identify what binds at this site to produce positive regulation, under what circumstances binding occurs, and how binding exerts a positive effect.

9. What role does cAMP play in transcription of *lac* operon genes? What role does CAP play in transcription of *lac* operon genes?

10. How would a *cap*⁻ mutation that produces an inactive CAP protein affect transcriptional control of the *lac* operon?

11. Explain the circumstances under which attenuation of operon gene expression is advantageous to a bacterial organism. Would you expect attenuation to be found in a single-celled eukaryote? In a multicelled eukaryote?

12. Consider the transcription of genes of the *lac* operon under two conditions: (1) when both glucose and lactose are present and (2) when glucose is absent and lactose is present. Describe the comparative levels of transcription of *lac* operon genes under these conditions, and explain the molecular basis for the difference.

13. Describe the lytic and lysogenic life cycles of λ bacteriophage. What roles do λ repressor and cro protein play in controlling transcription from P_R and P_{RM}, and how are these roles linked to lysis and lysogeny?

14. Define *antisense RNA,* and describe how it affects the translation of a complementary mRNA. Why is it more advantageous to the organism to stop translation initiation than to inactivate or destroy the gene product after it is produced?

Application and Integration

For answers to selected even-numbered problems, see Appendix: Answers.

15. Attenuation of *trp* operon transcription is controlled by the formation of stem-loop structures in mRNA. The attenuation function can be disrupted by mutations that alter the sequence of repeat DNA regions 1 to 4 and prevent the formation of mRNA stem loops. Describe the likely effects on attenuation of each of the following mutations under the conditions specified.

Mutated Region	Tryptophan Level
a. Region 1	Low
b. Region 1	High
c. Region 2	Low
d. Region 2	High
e. Region 3	Low
f. Region 3	High
g. Region 4	Low
h. Region 4	High

16. In the *lac* operon, what are the likely effects on operon gene transcription of the mutations identified below?
    a. Mutation of consensus sequence in the *lac* promoter
    b. Mutation of the repressor binding site on the operator sequence
    c. Mutation of the *lacI* gene affecting the allosteric site of the protein
    d. Mutation of the *lacI* gene affecting the DNA-binding site of the protein
    e. Mutation of the CAP binding site of the *lac* promoter

17. Identify which of the following *lac* operon haploid genotypes transcribe operon genes inducibly and which transcribe genes constitutively. Indicate whether the strain is *lac*⁺ (able to grow on lactose-only medium) or *lac*⁻ (cannot grow on lactose medium).
    a. $I^+ P^+ O^+ Z^+ Y^-$
    b. $I^+ P^+ O^C Z^- Y^+$
    c. $I^- P^+ O^+ Z^+ Y^+$
    d. $I^+ P^- O^+ Z^+ Y^+$

e. $I^+ P^+ O^+ Z^- Y^+$
f. $I^+ P^+ O^C Z^+ Y^-$
g. $I^+ P^+ O^C Z^+ Y^+$

18. Complete the following table, indicating whether functionally active β-galactosidase and permease are produced in the presence and absence of lactose. Use "+" to indicate the presence of a functional enzyme and "−" to indicate its absence. Indicate whether the partial diploid strain is lac^+ (able to grow on lactose-only medium) or lac^- (cannot grow on lactose medium).

Genotype	β-Galactosidase		Permease		Phenotype
	Lactose	No Lactose	Lactose	No Lactose	
Example: $I^+ P^+ O^+ Z^+ Y^+$	+	−	+	−	lac^+
a. $I^S P^+ O^+ Z^+ Y^+/I^- P^+ O^+ Z^+ Y^+$					
b. $I^- P^+ O^+ Z^- Y^+/I^+ P^+ O^C Z^+ Y^-$					
c. $I^+ P^+ O^+ Z^- Y^+/I^+ P^- O^+ Z^+ Y^-$					
d. $I^- P^+ O^C Z^+ Y^+/I^+ P^- O^+ Z^+ Y^+$					
e. $I^+ P^+ O^C Z^+ Y^-/I^+ P^+ O^+ Z^+ Y^-$					
f. $I^+ P^+ O^+ Z^- Y^+/I^S P^+ O^+ Z^+ Y^-$					
g. $I^S P^+ O^+ Z^- Y^+/I^+ P^+ O^C Z^+ Y^-$					

19. List possible genotypes for *lac* operon haploids that have the following phenotypic characteristics:

a. The operon genes are constitutively transcribed, but the strain is unable to grow on a lactose medium. List two possible genotypes for this phenotype.

b. The operon genes are never transcribed above a basal level, and the strain is unable to grow on a lactose medium. List two possible genotypes for this phenotype.

c. The operon genes are inducibly transcribed, but the strain is unable to grow on a lactose medium. List one possible genotype for this phenotype.

d. The operon genes are constitutively transcribed, and the strain grows on lactose medium. List two possible genotypes for this phenotype.

20. Suppose each of the genotypes you listed in parts (a) and (b) in Problem 19 are placed in a partial diploid genotype along with a chromosome that has a fully wild-type *lac* operon.

a. Will the transcription of operon genes in each partial diploid be inducible or constitutive?

b. Which partial diploids will be able to grow on a lactose medium?

21. Four independent lac^- mutants (mutants A to D) are isolated in haploid strains of *E. coli*. The strains have the following phenotypic characteristics:

Mutant A is lac^-, but transcription of operon genes is induced by lactose.

Mutant B is lac^- and has uninducible transcription of operon genes.

Mutant C is lac^+ and has constitutive transcription of operon genes.

Mutant D is lac^+ and has constitutive transcription of operon genes.

A microbiologist develops donor and recipient varieties of each mutant strain and crosses them with the results shown below. The table indicates whether inducible, constitutive, or noninducible transcription occurs, along with lac^+ and lac^- growth habit for each partial diploid. Assume each strain has a single mutation.

Mating	Transcription and Growth
A × B	lac^-
A × C	lac^+, inducible
A × D	lac^+, constitutive
B × C	lac^+, inducible
B × D	lac^+, constitutive
C × D	lac^+, constitutive

Use this information to identify which *lac* operon gene is mutated in each strain.

22. Suppose the *lac* operon partial diploid $cap^- I^+ P^+ O^+ Z^- Y^+/cap^+ I^- P^+ O^+ Z^+ Y^-$ is grown.

a. Will this partial diploid strain grow on a lactose medium?

b. Is transcription of β-galactosidase and permease inducible, constitutive, or noninducible?

c. Explain how genetic complementation contributes to the growth habit of this strain.

23. A bacterial inducible operon, similar to the *lac* operon, contains three genes—*R*, *T*, and *S*—that are involved in coordinated regulation of transcription. One of these genes is an operator region, one is a regulatory protein, and the third produces a structural enzyme. In the table below, "+" indicates that the structural enzyme is synthesized and "−" indicates that it is not produced. Use the information provided to determine which gene is the operator, which produces the regulatory protein, and which produces the enzyme.

Genotype	Enzyme Synthesis	
	Inducer Present	Inducer Absent
$R^+ S^+ T^+$	+	−
$R^- S^+ T^+$	−	−
$R^+ S^- T^+$	+	+
$R^+ S^+ T^-$	+	+
$R^- S^+ T^+/R^+ S^- T^-$	+	+
$R^+ S^- T^+/R^- S^+ T^-$	+	+
$R^+ S^+ T^-/R^- S^- T^+$	+	−

24. A repressible operon system, like the *trp* operon, contains three genes, *G*, *Z*, and *W*. Operon genes are synthesized when the end product of the operon synthesis pathway is absent, but there is no synthesis when the end product is present. One of these genes is an operator, one is a regulatory protein, and the other is a structural enzyme involved in synthesis of the end product. In the table below, "+" indicates that the enzyme is synthesized by the operon, and "−" means that no enzyme synthesis occurs. Use this information to determine which gene corresponds to each operon function.

Genotype	Enzyme Synthesis	
	End Product Present	End Product Absent
$G^+ Z^+ W^+$	−	+
$G^- Z^+ W^+$	+	+
$G^+ Z^- W^+$	−	−
$G^+ Z^+ W^-$	+	+
$G^- Z^+ W^+/G^+ Z^- W^-$	+	+
$G^+ Z^- W^+/G^- Z^+ W^-$	+	+
$G^- Z^- W^-/G^+ Z^+ W^+$	−	+
$G^+ Z^+ W^-/G^- Z^- W^+$	−	+

25. What is the likely effect of each of the following mutations of the *trpL* region on attenuation control of *trp* operon gene transcription? Explain your reasoning.
    a. Region 3 is deleted.
    b. Region 4 is deleted.
    c. The entire *trpL* region is deleted.
    d. The start (AUG) codon of the *trpL* polypeptide is deleted.
    e. Two nucleotides are inserted into the *trpL* region immediately after the polypeptide stop codon.
    f. Twenty nucleotides are inserted into the *trpL* region immediately after the polypeptide stop codon.
    g. Ten nucleotides are inserted between regions 2 and 3 of *trpL*.
    h. Two nucleotides are inserted immediately following the polypeptide start codon.
    i. The entire polypeptide coding sequence of *trpL* is deleted.
    j. The eight uracil nucleotides immediately following region 4 are deleted.

26. Suppose that base substitution mutations sufficient to eliminate the function of the operator regions listed below were to occur. For each case, describe how transcription or life cycle would be affected.
    a. *lacO* mutation in *E. coli*
    b. O_{R1} mutation in λ phage
    c. O_{R3} mutation in λ phage

27. Two different mutations affect P_{RE}. Mutant 1 decreases transcription from the promoter to 10% of normal. Mutant 2 increases transcription from the promoter to tenfold greater than the wild type. How will each mutation affect the determination of the lytic or lysogenic life cycle in mutant λ phage strains? Explain your answers.

28. How would mutations that inactivate each of the following genes affect the determination of the lytic or lysogenic life cycle in mutated λ phage strains? Explain your answers.
    a. *cI*
    b. *cII*
    c. *cro*
    d. *int*
    e. *cII* and *cro*
    f. *N*

29. The bacterial insertion sequence *IS10* uses antisense RNA to regulate translation of the mRNA that produces the enzyme transposase, which is required for insertion sequence transposition. Transcription of the antisense RNA gene is controlled by P_{OUT}, which is over 10 times more efficient at transcription than the P_{IN} promoter that controls transposase gene transcription.
    a. If a mutation reduced the transcriptional efficiency of P_{OUT} so as to be equal to that of P_{IN}, what is the likely effect on the transposition of *IS10*?
    b. If a mutation of P_{IN} eliminates its ability to function in transcription, what is the likely effect on the transposition of *IS10*?

30. Northern blot analysis is performed on cellular mRNA isolated from *E. coli*. The probe used in the northern blot analysis hybridizes to a portion of the *lacY* sequence. Below is an example of the autoradiograph from northern blot analysis for a wild-type *lac*+ bacterial strain. In this gel, lane 1 is from bacteria grown in a medium containing only glucose (minimal medium). Lane 2 is from bacteria in a medium containing only lactose. Following the style of this diagram, draw the autoradiograph appearance for northern blots of the bacteria listed below. In each case, lane 1 is for mRNA isolated after growth in a glucose-containing (minimal) medium, and lane 2 is for mRNA isolated after growth in a lactose-only medium.

Lane

Autoradiograph
of northern blot

a. *lac*⁺ bacteria with the genotype $I^+ P^+ O^C Z^+ Y^+$

b. *lac*⁻ bacteria with the genotype $I^+ P^+ O^+ Z^- Y^+$

c. *lac*⁻ bacteria with the genotype $I^+ P^- O^C Z^+ Y^+$

d. *lac*⁺ bacteria with the genotype $I^- P^+ O^C Z^+ Y^+$

e. *lac*⁻ bacteria with the genotype $I^+ P^+ O^+ Z^- Y^+$ that has a polar mutation affecting the *lacZ* gene

f. *lac*⁻ bacteria with the genotype $I^+ P^+ O^C Z^- Y^-$

g. *lac*⁻ bacteria with the genotype $I^+ P^+ O^+ Z^+ Y^+$ and a mutation that prevents CAP–cAMP binding to the CAP site

31. The electrophoresis gel shown below in part (a) is from a DNase I footprint analysis of an operon transcription control region. DNA sequence analysis of a 35-bp region is shown in part (b). The control region, labeled with ³²P at one end, is shown in a map in part (c). Separate samples of control-region DNA are exposed to DNase I, and the resulting DNase I–digested DNA is run in separate lanes of the electrophoresis gel. Unprotected DNA is in lane 1, DNA protected by repressor protein is in lane 2, and RNA polymerase-protected DNA is in lane 3. The numbers along the electrophoresis gel correspond to the 35-bp sequence labeled on the map in part (c). Use the information provided to solve the following problems.

    a. Determine the DNA sequence of the 35-bp region examined.

    b. Locate the regions of the sequence protected by repressor protein and by RNA polymerase.

(a) Phase I treatment   **(b)** DNA sequencing

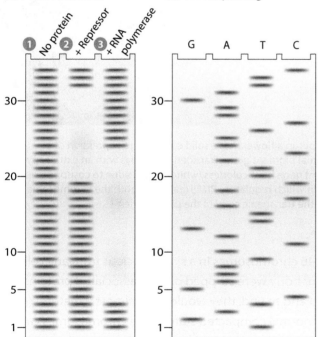

(c)

32. For the following *lac* operon partial diploids, determine whether the synthesis of *lacZ* mRNA is "constitutive," "inducible," or "uninducible," and indicate whether the merodiploid is *lac*⁺ or *lac*⁻ (able or not able to utilize lactose).

Genotype	*lacZ* mRNA Synthesis	*lac* Phenotype
a. $I^- P^+ O^+ Z^+ Y^+/I^+ P^+ O^+ Z^+ Y^+$		
b. $I^+ P^+ O^C Z^+ Y^+/I^+ P^+ O^+ Z^- Y^+$		
c. $I^S P^+ O^+ Z^+ Y^+/I^+ P^+ O^+ Z^+ Y^+$		
d. $I^+ P^+ O^+ Z^- Y^+/I^+ P^- O^+ Z^+ Y^+$		
e. $I^+ P^+ O^+ Z^+ Y^-/I^+ P^+ O^+ Z^+ Y^-$		

33. The following hypothetical genotypes have genes *A*, *B*, and *C* corresponding to *lacI*, *lacO*, and *lacZ*, but not necessarily in that order. Data in the table indicate whether β-galactosidase is produced in the presence and absence of the inducer for each genotype. Use this data to identify the correspondence between *A*, *B*, and *C* and the *lacI*, *lacO*, and *lacZ* genes. Carefully explain your reasoning for identifying each gene.

Genotype	β-Galactosidase Production	
	Inducer Present	Inducer Absent
1. $A^- B^+ C^+$	+	+
2. $A^+ B^+ C^-$	+	+
3. $A^- B^+ C^+ / A^+ B^+ C^+$	+	+
4. $A^+ B^+ C^- / A^+ B^+ C^+$	+	−

34. For an *E. coli* strain with the *lac* operon genotype $I^+ P^+ O^+ Z^+ Y^+$, identify the level of transcription of the operon genes in each growth medium listed. Specify transcription as "none," "basal," or "activated" for each medium, and provide an explanation to justify your answer.

    a. Growth medium contains lactose and glucose.

    b. Growth medium contains glucose but no lactose.

    c. Growth medium contains lactose but no glucose.

15

Regulation of Gene Expression in Eukaryotes

CHAPTER OUTLINE

15.1 Cis-Acting Regulatory Sequences Bind Trans-Acting Regulatory Proteins to Control Eukaryotic Transcription

15.2 Chromatin Remodeling and Modification Regulates Eukaryotic Transcription

15.3 RNA-Mediated Mechanisms Control Gene Expression

ESSENTIAL IDEAS

- Regulatory DNA sequences bind regulatory proteins to control the initiation or silencing of transcription in eukaryotes.

- Chromatin remodeling and modification regulates gene transcription by shifting position or changing the chemical composition of nucleosomes.

- The structure of chromatin varies among different types of cells and sets the gene-expression program for distinct cell types.

- RNA-mediated mechanisms regulate eukaryotic gene expression by post-transcriptional interactions with mRNA.

Wild-type petunia flowers have solid color due to expression of a chromosomal pigment gene. Transgenic petunias with an extra copy of the pigment gene have colorless (white) regions due to cosuppression, a process in which regulatory RNAs inactivate both the chromosomal copy and the transgenic copy of the pigment gene.

If the 46 chromosomes in a single nucleus from any cell in your body were stripped of their associated proteins and laid end to end, they would span almost 2 meters. Yet in their normal compacted state, these chromosomes can fit inside a nucleus that is about 5 microns (5 millionths of a meter) in diameter and still leave room for DNA replication, transcription, pre-mRNA processing, and numerous other activities to take place. This efficient packaging and access to DNA are made possible by the chromatin structure of the genome and the dynamic changes of which chromatin is capable throughout the cell cycle.

The genomes of eukaryotic organisms—yours included—are considerably larger on average than those of bacterial and archaeal species, and they are packaged much differently as well. One major packaging difference is the localization of chromosomes in a nucleus in eukaryotic cells. Nuclear localization sequesters the chromosomes and encapsulates DNA replication, transcription, and the various RNA-processing activities. A second difference is the incorporation of DNA into chromatin.

The process of chromatin condensation initiates at the beginning of prophase and culminates in fully condensed chromosomes in metaphase. This is an essential predecessor of efficient chromosome separation in anaphase. Chromatin condensation also plays a pivotal role in permitting or blocking transcription. No cell in your body expresses all 22,000 or so genes of the human genome. Instead, most human cell types express only a few thousand genes, while the other genes are transcriptionally silent. In recent decades, cell biologists studying the close connection between structural changes in chromatin and the transcription of eukaryotic genes have succeeded in uncovering many crucial details.

The processes that regulate gene expression in eukaryotes (see Chapters 8 and 9) are more varied and multifaceted than those governing gene expression in bacterial genomes (Figure 15.1). In the present chapter, we focus on elements that do not occur in prokaryotes and yet are central to the regulation of transcription and gene expression in eukaryotes: (1) the organization of regulatory sequences other than promoters that contribute to the regulation of transcription; (2) mechanisms that remodel chromatin or reconfigure the association between nucleosomes and DNA to regulate transcription; (3) epigenetic mechanisms that exert transcriptional regulatory control in cell lineages over the course of an organism's development; (4) the transmission of epigenetic states from one generation of cells to another to exercise long-term control of differential gene expression; and (5) RNA-based mechanisms

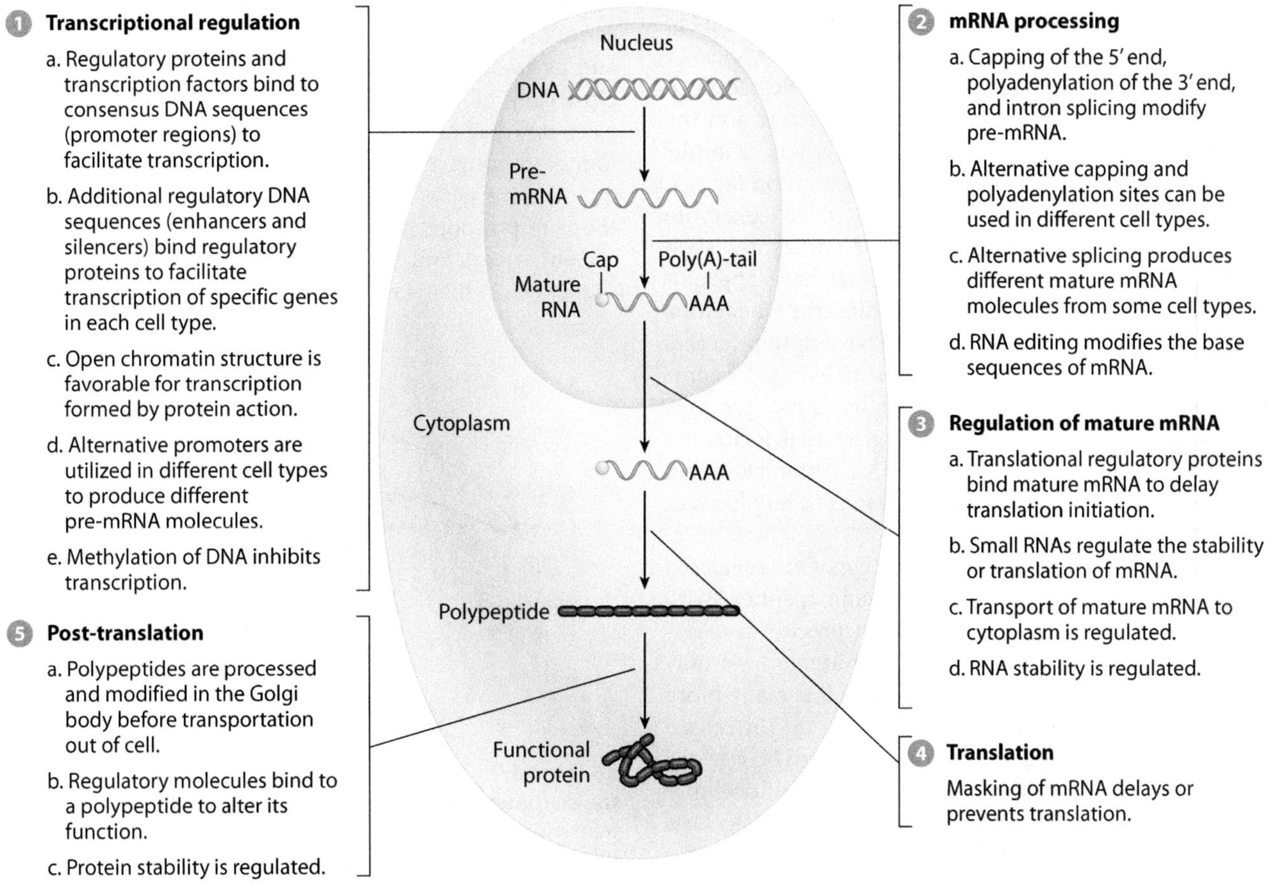
1 Transcriptional regulation
a. Regulatory proteins and transcription factors bind to consensus DNA sequences (promoter regions) to facilitate transcription.
b. Additional regulatory DNA sequences (enhancers and silencers) bind regulatory proteins to facilitate transcription of specific genes in each cell type.
c. Open chromatin structure is favorable for transcription formed by protein action.
d. Alternative promoters are utilized in different cell types to produce different pre-mRNA molecules.
e. Methylation of DNA inhibits transcription.
5 Post-translation
a. Polypeptides are processed and modified in the Golgi body before transportation out of cell.
b. Regulatory molecules bind to a polypeptide to alter its function.
c. Protein stability is regulated.
Nucleus
DNA
Pre-mRNA
Cap
Poly(A)-tail
Mature RNA
AAA
Cytoplasm
AAA
Polypeptide
Functional protein
2 mRNA processing
a. Capping of the 5′ end, polyadenylation of the 3′ end, and intron splicing modify pre-mRNA.
b. Alternative capping and polyadenylation sites can be used in different cell types.
c. Alternative splicing produces different mature mRNA molecules from some cell types.
d. RNA editing modifies the base sequences of mRNA.
3 Regulation of mature mRNA
a. Translational regulatory proteins bind mature mRNA to delay translation initiation.
b. Small RNAs regulate the stability or translation of mRNA.
c. Transport of mature mRNA to cytoplasm is regulated.
d. RNA stability is regulated.
4 Translation
Masking of mRNA delays or prevents translation.

Figure 15.1 An overview of gene regulation mechanisms in eukaryotes.

operating post-transcriptionally to regulate the availability of mature mRNA for translation and therefore the ability to produce polypeptides.

15.1 Cis-Acting Regulatory Sequences Bind Trans-Acting Regulatory Proteins to Control Eukaryotic Transcription

Despite the considerable differences between eukaryotes and bacteria, the basic mechanisms controlling transcription are broadly similar in both groups of organisms. The DNA–protein interactions in eukaryotes follow a scheme familiar from bacterial processes. *Activator proteins* bind regulatory sequences to stimulate transcription (positive regulation of transcription), and *repressor proteins* bind other regulatory sequences to hinder transcription (negative regulation of transcription). Unlike their counterparts in bacteria, however, eukaryotic transcription activators and repressors, collectively known as transcription factors, are often found in large complexes composed of a large number of distinct regulatory proteins that bind a wide and diverse array of regulatory sequences. These proteins aggregate in diverse combinations that activate or repress transcription of different patterns of genes in different tissues and at different times in the life cycle.

The complexity of gene regulation is reflected both in the numbers of different transcription factors and the diversity of the target genes they regulate. For example, the bacterium *E. coli* has about 270 transcription factors, about the same number as the single-celled eukaryote *S. cerevisiae*. In contrast, multicellular eukaryotes such as *Drosophila*, humans, and *Arabidopsis* have approximately 600, 1400, and 1900 different transcription factors, respectively. Similarly, consider the transcription factors regulating the *lac* operon in *E. coli*: the cAMP–CAP complex regulates about a dozen loci in the *E. coli* genome, and the lac repressor has only a single target locus, the *lac* operon. In contrast, individual transcription factors in multicellular eukaryotes may regulate tens to hundreds of target genes.

In multicellular eukaryotes, many genes are regulated in a developmental or cell-type specific manner, with some genes utilized multiple times in precise developmental patterns of expression. Because humans have only about five times as many genes as *E. coli* but many more times the number of distinct cell types, the increased complexity in gene regulation is considered to be responsible for the evolution and development of multicellular eukaryotes. Changes in gene regulation are held to be a significant driver in the evolution of morphological complexity. To cite a finer scale example, since the coding sequences of chimp and human genes are nearly identical,

it is likely that most differences between the two species are due to differences in gene regulation rather than functional differences in protein products.

Another major difference between bacteria and multicellular eukaryotes is the precision of gene regulatory control. *E coli*, being a single-celled organism, needs to be able to rapidly change gene expression patterns in order to respond quickly to changing environmental conditions. Thus, even for genes that are "off," a few transcripts are always present in the cell, a situation that, as we saw in the case of the *lac* operon, enabled the sensing of the presence of lactose. In contrast, in multicellular eukaryotes with hundreds to thousands of different cell types, genes encoding proteins that are required only in specific cell types need to be tightly regulated. This precise regulation, where genes that are "off" are absolutely transcriptionally silent, is mediated by the packaging of chromatin into an inactive state, a subject we will explore later in this chapter, after we first discuss the role of transcription factors in eukaryotic gene regulation.

Transcriptional Regulatory Interactions

Three sets of regulatory DNA sequences are commonly involved in eukaryotic regulation of transcription of specific genes. The first set of regulatory sequences is the *core promoter region* containing the TATA box and other sequences; it is immediately adjacent to the start of transcription and is the sequence to which RNA polymerase II and its associated transcription factors bind (**Figure 15.2**). Upstream of the core promoter are various *proximal elements* that are a second set of regulatory sequences found in some genes and which are often involved in quantitative gene regulation. At greater distances from the core promoter are **enhancer** and **silencer sequences** (or **enhancers** and **silencers**), the third set of regulatory sequences, which bind regulatory proteins and interact

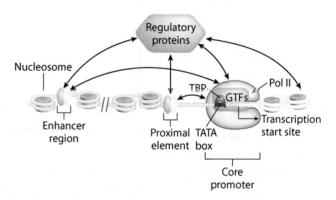

Figure 15.2 Regulatory interactions in eukaryotic transcription. TATA-binding protein (TBP), other general transcription factors (GTFs), and RNA polymerase II (Pol II) bind the core promoter. Other regulatory proteins bind proximal promoter and enhancer regions and interact with nucleosomes to activate transcription.

with proteins bound to other promoter segments, providing both quantitative and qualitative control of gene expression. Unlike core promoter and proximal promoter elements, which are invariably located upstream of and close to the genes they regulate, enhancers and silencers can be upstream or downstream of genes they regulate as well as residing in introns and occasionally even *within* coding regions. Although some enhancer and silencer sequences are close to the genes they regulate, others are great distances, thousands to tens of thousands of nucleotides, away from the genes they regulate. All three of these regulatory regions contain **cis-acting regulatory sequences,** which means they regulate transcription of genes located *on the same chromosome* as the sequences.

RNA polymerase II (pol II) and various general transcription factors (GTFs) are recruited to and bind the core promoter (see Section 8.3). Transcriptional activator proteins or transcriptional repressor proteins bind to proximal promoter elements and to enhancers. All these proteins are **trans-acting regulatory proteins:** They are able to identify and bind target regulatory sequences on *any* chromosome. RNA polymerase II, for example, is able to bind any core promoter region if the right general transcription factors are also present. Similarly, transcription activator and repressor proteins can bind any target regulatory sequence and can influence transcription with equal efficiency no matter where the sequence occurs.

Besides the regulatory proteins that bind regulatory DNA in a sequence-specific manner, many additional proteins also associate with regulatory regions of DNA by protein–protein interactions that form larger complexes. At enhancers, for example, aggregation of multiple proteins, a few binding enhancer sequences and the others binding other proteins, forms a large protein complex known as an **enhanceosome.** Enhanceosomes direct DNA bending into loops that bring the enhanceosome into contact with RNA polymerase and transcription factors bound at the core promoter and to proximal promoter elements (see Figure 8.12). The DNA loops can be small or large, in keeping with the observation that enhancers may be close to or quite distant from the genes they regulate. Repressor proteins act in a similar manner, with some proteins binding DNA in a sequence-specific manner and recruiting additional proteins into a larger repressor complex.

Enhancer and silencer sequences can be identified using the same approaches used for gene identification.

Mutant analysis can reveal sequences important for gene regulation. For example, the O^c mutants of the *lac* operon that Jacob and Monod characterized identified the *lac* operator as an important regulatory sequence. Examples of mutations in eukaryotic enhancers have similarly been identified by mutant analysis, as described in a later section. Conservation of noncoding sequences across species can also indicate functional regulatory sequences, a concept to which we will return in Chapter 18. In addition, direct testing of sequences for regulatory functions can be used to delineate regulatory sequences, an approach we will explore further in Chapter 16.

Integration and Modularity of Regulatory Sequences

Despite the diversity of the combinations through which regulatory sequences and proteins control transcription in eukaryotes, there are some commonalities in the molecular machinery that coordinates this regulatory activity. Enhancers and silencers are typically composed of binding sites for a number of transcription factors, and this allows them to integrate the activities of different sets of transcription factors in order to produce different outputs. Such a group of transcription factor binding sites is often referred to as an enhancer or silencer module. For example, studies of enhancer-sequence composition in the eukaryotic virus SV40 (simian virus 40) revealed modular sequences that have since been found to be similar to those of enhancers of other eukaryotes. The SV40 enhancer module consists of adjacent regions of conserved sequences located about 200 bp upstream of the transcription start point of regulated genes. Each of seven segments of conserved sequence binds specific regulatory proteins (**Figure 15.3**).

While we have characterized regulatory sequences as enhancers or silencers, some regulatory modules bind both activators and repressors and thus act to integrate both positive and negative signals into a single output. In such cases, repressor activity often prevails over the activity of activators. (An example of such a regulatory module is present in Figure 20.9.) As we will see in the next section, the modularity of transcriptional regulation in eukaryotes can provide the flexibility that multicellular organisms need for regulation of differential gene expression.

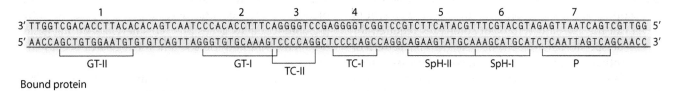

Figure 15.3   Enhancer sequences and the regulatory proteins that bind them. The SV40 enhancer sequence contains seven short sequence segments targeted by specific regulatory proteins.

Transcription Regulation by Enhancers and Silencers

In a broad sense, enhancer and silencer activity controls the timing and location of eukaryotic gene transcription to help ensure the proper function and development of organisms (for example, by making a polypeptide available at crucial times or in specific cells or tissues). The enhancers and silencers controlling transcription of a gene can be nearby or far from the gene they regulate, though DNA loop formation can bring even very distant sequences together. In yeast, enhancers and silencers are usually situated relatively close to the genes they regulate. The major enhancer controlling expression of the β-globin complex in humans is also very close to the genes it regulates. Often, however, the distance between an enhancer or silencer sequence and the gene it targets for regulation is vast.

An example of a distant enhancer is provided by the *SHH* (*Sonic hedgehog*) gene, which in humans and other mammals directs the development of limbs and in its wild-type form produces five digits (fingers and toes) on each appendage. *SHH* is expressed in a tissue-specific manner in limbs under the direction of an enhancer that is 1 million base pairs (1 megabase) away from the gene. Genomic sequencing analysis reveals that the *SHH* enhancer is actually located in an intron of a neighboring gene (see Figure 18.15).

A general model for eukaryotic transcription regulation must incorporate the action of enhancers and silencers while taking the variability of their locations and their tissue-specific patterns of regulation into account. The model depicted in Figure 15.4, for *SHH*, shows two distant enhancers controlling transcription of the same gene in a tissue-specific manner. In this example, *SHH* gene is shown expressed in the brain and in limbs. Transcription in these tissues is controlled by different regulatory proteins and transcription factors produced in each cell type. One combination of regulatory proteins binds one enhancer in brain cells, but a different combination of regulatory proteins binds an alternative enhancer in limb cells. The different regulatory proteins present in different types of cells lead to tissue-specific patterns of expression of the target gene, producing a different set of polypeptides in each case. Similar models depicting the binding of repressor proteins to silencer sequences describe how distant silencers can inhibit transcription of targeted genes.

This model illustrates an important aspect of eukaryotic transcription regulation. Only when all of the necessary transcription factors and regulatory proteins are present in a cell can the assembly of protein complexes required for the tissue-specific or development-stage–specific pattern of transcription take place. The protein complexes assembled at regulatory sequences direct patterns of gene expression by activating transcription of certain genes while blocking transcription of other genes. The polypeptides that are

(a) Limb cells

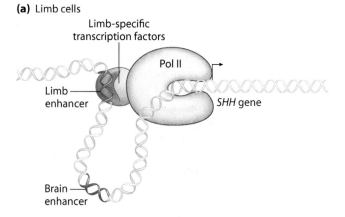

(b) Brain cells

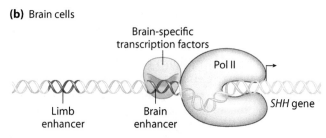

Figure 15.4 **Tissue-specific enhancer action.** **(a)** The limb-specific enhancer binds different, limb-specific transcription factors to express *SHH* differently in limb cells. **(b)** A different brain-specific enhancer is bound by brain-specific transcription factors and activates *SHH* transcription in brain cells.

ultimately produced in each cell or at each stage of development drive the processes that make cells distinctive and lead to the observed developmental changes.

Locus Control Regions

The human β-globin gene was the focus of our attention in an earlier chapter (see Chapter 10). Recall that this gene produces the β-globin polypeptide, two copies of which join with two α-globin polypeptides produced by the α-globin gene to form the heterotetrameric hemoglobin molecule. The β-globin gene is, however, only one of six very closely related globin genes forming the β-globin complex on human chromosome 11 (Figure 15.5a). Located close to the β-globin complex is a regulatory region known as a **locus control region (LCR).** LCRs are highly specialized enhancer elements that regulate the transcription of multiple genes packaged in complexes of related genes. The LCR regulating transcription of genes in the β-globin complex contains four distinct cis-acting regulatory sequences, designated HS1 to HS4. Together these elements orchestrate the sequential developmental expression of the β-globin–complex genes as a fetus develops during gestation. The LCR and the six genes it regulates occupy just over 70 kb.

Each gene of the β-globin complex produces a distinct globin polypeptide that imparts a different oxygen-carrying capacity to hemoglobin. During gestation, the

(a) β-globin–gene complex

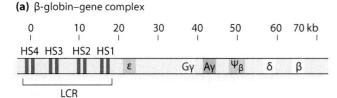

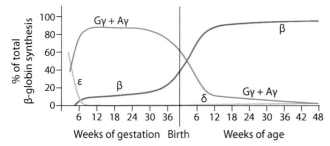

(b) Developmental expression of β-globin–complex genes

Figure 15.5   Locus control and developmental expression of human β-globin–complex genes. (a) The locus control region (LCR) of the human β-globin complex contains four regulatory segments (HS1 to HS4). **(b)** The LCR regulates the expression of five genes (ψβ is an unexpressed pseudogene) in a developmental pattern matched to gestational age.

Mechanism of transcriptional activation by LCR

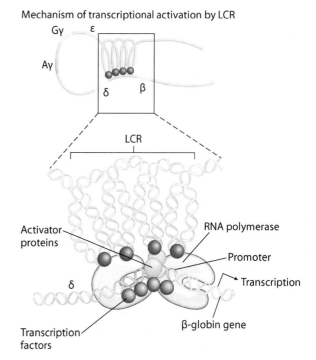

Figure 15.6   Human β-globin–complex locus control region. In combination with regulatory proteins that vary with developmental stage, the LCR forms DNA loops that also vary with developmental stage, allowing it to activate transcription of specific genes of the complex. RNA polymerase at the left transcribes the δ globin gene and the RNA polymerase at the right the β globin gene.

oxygen requirements of the developing fetus change as its size increases and its organs develop. As gestation proceeds, transcription of the genes of the β-globin complex is switched from one to the next to produce hemoglobin molecules that have the oxygen-carrying capacity required by the developing fetus. The order of expression of β-globin–complex genes during development matches the order in which they occur on the chromosome. Figure 15.5b shows the expression profile of these genes during development. The HS1 to HS4 components of the β-globin–complex LCR bind regulatory proteins that direct the formation of small DNA loops, and these serve as a bridge to the promoters of the β-globin–complex genes (Figure 15.6). The composition of enhanceosomes bound to the LCR varies during development to vary the resulting loops and thus produce the developmentally regulated pattern of gene expression from the β-globin complex. A similar LCR drives transcription of a smaller number of genes in the α-globin complex.

Mutations in Regulatory Sequences

Our previous discussions of mutations have described numerous ways in which changes in DNA can result in abnormal polypeptides or abnormal levels of polypeptide production. Recent genome-wide mapping studies in humans suggest that many disease-susceptibility alleles reside in noncoding sequences that may be regulatory. Here, we take a moment to consider examples of enhancer mutations that are the cause of hereditary disorders in humans.

   The term *thalassemia* is used to describe certain hereditary anemias in which mutation leads to an imbalance

of production of α-globin and β-globin polypeptides. This imbalance reduces the amount of functional hemoglobin, since each molecule needs an equal number of both polypeptides. Many distinct types of thalassemia result from different mutations of the α-globin or β-globin genes. In some thalassemia patients, however, no mutations of either globin gene were detected. Furthermore, the promoters of both genes were wild type, so the search for the source of the mutations in this group of patients had to be expanded. In several cases, the thalassemia mutations are due to deletion or chromosome-rearrangement mutations that alter the LCR of one of the globin gene complexes. These deletions result in enhancer mutations that alter the level of transcription of affected genes and lead to an imbalance of polypeptide production.

   Base-substitution mutations in enhancers are another source of enhancer dysfunction. The *SHH* enhancer, located 1 megabase from the *SHH* gene it regulates, is mutated in certain cases of a condition called polydactyly, in which extra fingers and toes can form during development. The extra digits result from abnormal expression of the *SHH* gene. In studies of certain human families with polydactyly, single-base substitutions in the *SHH* enhancer have been identified. In addition, studies in mice, in which a deletion of the *SHH* enhancer has occurred, reveal significant abnormalities of limb development.

Figure 15.7 Conservation of enhancer sequences. The enhancer sequence of β-interferon contains multiple sequences (colored boxes) conserved among mammalian species. Highlighted sequences are crucial to binding of specific regulatory proteins.

		ATF	Jun	IRF	IRF	IRF	IRF	NF-κB			
						Bound protein					

```
                 ATF    Jun     IRF      IRF      IRF      IRF      NF-κB
Human   AAATGTAAATGACATAGGGAAAACTGAAAGGGAGAAGTGAAAGTGGGAAATTCCTCTGAAT
Mouse   .....AAATGACATAGGGAAAACTGAAAGGGAGAACTGAAAGTGGGAAATTCCTCTGA..
Rat     .....AAATGACGTAGGGAAAAGTGAAAGGGAGAACTGAAAGTGGGAAATTCCTCTGA..
Swine   .....AAATGACATAGGGAAAACTGAAAGGGAGAACTGAAAGTGGGAAATTCCTCTGAA.
Horse   .AATGTAAATGACATAGGGAAAACAGAAAGGGAGAACTGAAAGTGGGAAATTCCTCTGAA.
Bovine2 ....TAAATGACATAGGGAAAACTGAAAGGGAGAACTGAAAGTGGGAAATCCCTCC....
Bovine  ....TAAATGACATAGGGAAAAATGAAAGCGAGAACTGAAAGTGGGAAATTCCTCT....
```

Enhancer-Sequence Conservation

Comparisons among species reveal DNA-sequence conservation in some enhancers. This implies that natural selection is operating to retain enhancer function, that is, to retain the capacity to bind specific regulatory proteins by conserving sequence composition. **Figure 15.7** shows enhancer sequences for the β-interferon gene in several mammals; the abbreviations represent the enhancer-binding proteins whose binding relies on certain sequences. The species listed in the figure share a common ancestor from which their different lineages diverged approximately 100 million years ago.

Genomic sequence analysis indicates evolutionary constraint on the diversification of some enhancer sequences. Enhancer elements that have been conserved throughout vertebrate evolution regulate key genes controlling the development of the vertebrate body plan. We will return to genomics approaches to identifying conserved regulatory sequences in Chapter 18. In contrast, enhancer module sequences have also been observed to evolve quite rapidly. In these cases, since the output from an enhancer module is a result of the integration of several inputs, different combinations of activators and repressors can still result in similar outputs.

Yeast Enhancer and Silencer Sequences

The yeast *Saccharomyces cerevisiae* provides a simple model to illustrate the principles of eukaryotic transcriptional regulation. The regulation of transcription by enhancer sequences is well understood in *Saccharomyces cerevisiae*, where transcription of genes involved in the galactose utilization pathway, among others, is carefully regulated by enhancer-like sequences. When the monosaccharide galactose is the only sugar in the growth medium, strains of *gal*+ yeast will induce the transcription of four enzyme-producing genes, *GAL1*, *GAL2*, *GAL7*, and *GAL10*, that together import extracellular galactose (*GAL2*) and then, through a short series of biochemical reactions, break down intercellular galactose into glucose-1-phosphate for glycolysis (*GAL1*, *GAL7*, and *GAL10*; **Figure 15.8**). Each of the four genes has its own promoter, but transcription of the genes is regulated by another gene, *GAL4*, which produces a regulatory protein. Gal4 protein is a transcription activator protein that binds to an enhancer element—called an **upstream activator sequence (UAS)** in yeast—located upstream of each of the four *GAL* genes. The Gal4 regulatory protein is continuously available in yeast cells and interacts with Gal80, the product of the *GAL80* gene. When Gal80 protein binds to Gal4 protein, it inactivates Gal4 and blocks its ability to activate transcription.

The UAS$_G$ sequences are cis-acting regulatory elements, and Gal4 protein is a trans-acting regulatory protein. Each UAS$_G$ element contains two 17-bp repeat sequences that are the binding sites for Gal4 protein. In its active, DNA-binding form, Gal4 is a homodimeric protein composed of two identical polypeptides that form two active domains. The DNA-binding domain, at one end of the Gal4 dimer, targets the 17-bp repeats of UAS$_G$. The activation domain, at the opposite end, is a target for binding by the protein Gal80. Since Gal4 and Gal80 are each constitutively produced, they are normally bound to one another at the activation domain of Gal4. In this configuration, the DNA-binding domain of Gal4 is inactive, and the dimer is unable to bind UAS$_G$. Without Gal4 binding to UAS$_G$, transcription of *GAL* genes is blocked

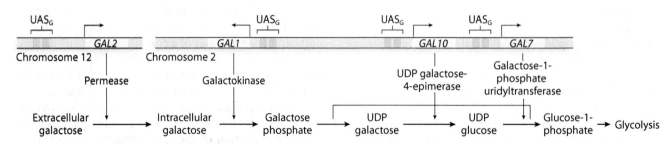

Figure 15.8 Galactose utilization in *S. cerevisiae*. Galactose utilization requires the action of products of each of four galactose-utilization (*GAL*) genes.

(a) Galactose absent

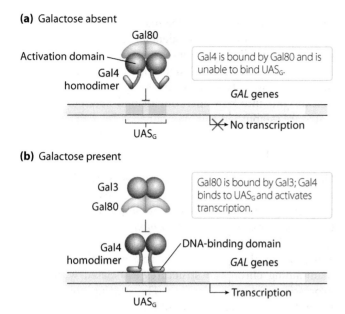

(b) Galactose present

Figure 15.9   Regulation of *GAL* gene transcription.
(a) When galactose is absent, Gal80 protein binds the activation domain of Gal4 to inactivate that protein and block *GAL* gene transcription. **(b)** When galactose is present, Gal3 protein binds Gal80 protein to prevent it from binding Gal4 protein. The DNA-binding domain of Gal4 protein is then available to bind the two 17-bp segments of UAS$_G$ to help initiate *GAL* gene transcription.

(**Figure 15.9a**). Conversely, when galactose is present, galactose and Gal3, the protein product of another *GAL* gene, bind to Gal80. Binding of the galactose–Gal3 complex alters Gal80 and causes it to release Gal4. The free Gal4 dimer then binds UAS$_G$ and activates *GAL* gene transcription (**Figure 15.9b**).

In the *GAL* gene system, Gal4 acts as an activator protein, initiating transcription. Its target DNA sequence is UAS$_G$, which acts like an enhancer sequence and is separated from *GAL* gene promoters by a large number of nucleotides. Gal4 binding leads to the formation of a multiprotein complex known as **Mediator,** which is an enhanceosome that forms after Gal4 binds UAS$_G$. When inducing the formation of a DNA loop, Mediator makes contact with the general transcription apparatus—including TFIID (transcription factor II D) and RNA polymerase II (Pol II)—at a *GAL* gene promoter (see Figure 8.12). Thus, the transcription of *GAL* genes by RNA polymerase II is dependent on transcription activation by Gal4 binding to UAS$_G$ elements and causing the formation of Mediator. Distant enhancers and silencers use the same mechanism of DNA loop formation to regulate transcription of targeted genes.

A common mode by which repressor proteins inhibit transcription in bacteria is to bind to operator sequences that overlap promoters, blocking the binding of RNA polymerase (see Chapter 14). In eukaryotes, this mechanism of transcription inhibition is not seen. Among the mechanisms by which eukaryotic repressors do inhibit

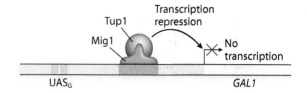

Figure 15.10   Transcription repression of the yeast *GAL1* gene. The proteins Mig1 and Tup1 bind to the Mig1 site to repress transcription when glucose is available in the growth medium.

transcription is the binding of eukaryotic repressors to silencer sequences, thus directly preventing enhancer-mediated transcription. The galactose-utilization genes in yeast offer an example of this direct mechanism of transcription repression. When glucose is present in the yeast growth medium, the protein Mig1 is produced. Mig1 binds a silencer sequence located between UAS$_G$ and the *GAL1* promoter (**Figure 15.10**). Mig1 in turn attracts the protein Tup1, and together these proteins form a repressor complex that prevents UAS$_G$ from directing the initiation of transcription.

Insulator Sequences

Considering that enhancers can be located far from the genes they regulate, what mechanisms direct enhancer action toward the intended gene and away from other nearby genes that are not regulated by the same enhancer? The answer, in part, lies in **insulator sequences,** cis-acting sequences located so as to separate enhancers from promoters of genes that are to be insulated from the effects of the enhancer. Insulators are protein-binding sequences that direct enhancers to interact with the intended promoter and that block communication between enhancers and other promoters (**Figure 15.11**). The mechanism of this activity may consist of allowing the formation of DNA loops containing enhancers and their intended promoter targets while preventing the formation of DNA loops containing an enhancer and a promoter that is not its intended target.

Up to this point our description of eukaryotic gene regulation has analogies with that of gene regulation in bacteria. First, in both lineages, specific sequences upstream of the transcription start site are required for recruitment of an RNA polymerase. Second, the transcriptional output is a result of the combinatorial activities of activator and repressor transcription factors bound to regulatory sequences that promote or facilitate RNA polymerase activity. For example, the *lac* operon in *E. coli* is positively regulated by the CAP–cAMP complex binding to upstream regulatory sequences and negatively regulated via the lac repressor protein, with repression being dominant over activation—a situation similar in concept if not molecular mechanism to a gene regulatory module in eukaryotes. The major difference in gene regulation between eukaryotes and bacteria is related to the packaging of DNA, the subject of the next section.

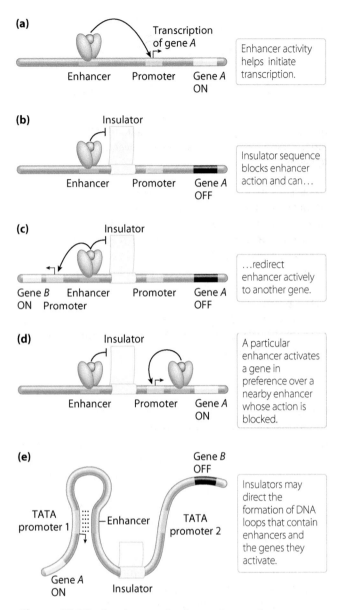

Figure 15.11   **Insulator and enhancer interactions.**

15.2 Chromatin Remodeling and Modification Regulates Eukaryotic Transcription

Recall from Chapter 11 that eukaryotic chromatin can be broadly divided into two categories based on its extent of compaction: euchromatin, which is loosely compacted and available for transcription, and heterochromatin, which is more densely compacted and is transcriptionally inert. Some regions of the genome are always heterochromatic, referred to as constitutive heterochromatin, while others switch back and forth between being euchromatic and heterochromatic. These latter regions often contain genes that are active only at specific times or in certain tissues. When DNA that is normally euchromatic is placed in the vicinity of heterochromatin,

the heterochromatic character may spread into the normally euchromatic region, silencing gene expression, a phenomenon called position effect variegation (PEV) (see Section 11.4). Analysis of mutations that affect the frequency or intensity of PEV in *Drosophila* provided the first insights into how euchromatic and heterochromatic states are established and maintained.

PEV Mutations

Genetic analysis of eukaryotic genomes reveals PEV to be a widespread phenomenon, suggesting that mechanisms controlling chromatin structure are important in the control of gene expression. In *Drosophila*, mutations modifying PEV have led to the identification of several genes and proteins that play a direct role in establishing and maintaining chromatin structures associated with gene expression and gene silencing. The starting point was a mutant line in which the eye color is variegated, wild-type red and mutant white, due to an inversion placing the white gene in the vicinity of centromeric heterochromatin (see Figure 11.18). Mutations in which the variegation is either enhanced or suppressed were then identified. Mutations known as *E(var)* **mutations,** where *E(var)* is short for *enhancers of position effect variegation, increase or enhance the appearance of the mutant white-eye phenotype by encouraging the spread of heterochromatin beyond its normal boundaries. The effect of *E(var)* mutation is to produce a greater number of eye cells lacking pigment (**Figure 15.12**). In contrast, *Su(var)* **mutations,** where *Su(var)* is short for *suppressors of position effect variegation, restrict the spread of heterochromatin or interfere with its formation. *Su(var)* mutations increase the extent of normally pigmented regions of the eye by suppressing the emergence of white patches.

Variegated eye   ***Su(var)* mutations**   ***E(var)* mutations**

| Red patches are produced by cells in which *w⁺* is transcribed, and white patches in which *w⁺* is inactivated by heterochromatin spread. | Mutations block efficient formation of heterochromatin and leave most cells with active *w⁺* transcription. | Mutations enhance heterochromatin formation and restrict *w⁺* expression to small patches. |

Figure 15.12   ***E(var)* and *Su(var)* mutations.** Mutations in genes whose protein products participate in chromatin modification are detected by enhancement or suppression of position effect variegation.

Several dozen *E(var)* and *Su(var)* mutations are known in the *Drosophila* genome, and *Su(var)* mutations have proven especially valuable in the identification of genes and proteins that modulate chromatin structure. Genetic analysis of *E(var)* and *Su(var)* mutations supports the hypothesis that chromatin structure is dynamic and is associated with gene expression. In fact, chromatin structure appears to oscillate: Sometimes it is in a highly condensed state in which gene transcription is silenced (i.e., heterochromatic), and sometimes it is in a more loosely condensed state that allows transcription (i.e., euchromatic), but it often exists in an intermediate state of condensation.

The analysis of one prominent group of *Su(var)* mutations exemplifies how the detection of defective proteins can elucidate normal functions. Some *Su(var)* mutations are caused by defective expression of heterochromatin protein-1 (HP-1), a protein found in association with centromeres, telomeres, and other heterochromatic chromosome locations in *Drosophila*. Comparison of *Su(var)* mutants with wild types reveals that HP-1 is a nucleosome-binding protein that targets lysine amino acids in position 9 of histone H3 if they carry a methyl group. Methylation of lysine 9 of H3 is one of the most common epigenetic modifications of histones in heterochromatic regions. The absence of HP-1 interferes with heterochromatin formation and suppresses variegation.

A second group of *Su(var)* mutations affects genes encoding histone methyltransferases (HMTs), enzymes responsible for catalyzing the addition of methyl groups to amino acids of histone proteins. Histone methyltransferases appear to target methylation-specific basic amino acids (e.g., arginine and lysine) in nucleosomes, attaching methyl groups to these amino acids as part of epigenetic marking of histones. As noted above, the lysine residue in position 9 of histone protein H3 is a frequent target for methylation. Upon methylation, this location is described as H3K9me, which is short for *histone 3*, lysine (one-letter abbreviation *K*), position 9, and *me*thylation. If HMTs are not functioning properly, epigenetic methylation is not established, and heterochromatin formation is inhibited.

The identification of the functions of these two groups of *Su(var)* mutations led to a simple model of HP-1 and HMT function predicting that specific methylated histone locations in nucleosomes (e.g., H3K9me) are methylated by HMTs and act as sites of HP-1 binding that helps condense chromatin structure to silence gene expression (Figure 15.13). According to this model, *Su(var)* mutants that are defective in their silencing of *w+* could carry an HMT gene mutation that leads to the failure to properly methylate nucleosomes, or they could carry a mutation of the *HP-1* gene and be rendered unable to remodel chromatin to a tightly condensed form.

Collectively, the experimental analyses of suppressors and enhancers of PEV identify genes that make epigenetic "marks" on histone proteins, causing attachment and detachment of methyl, acetyl, and phosphoryl groups to

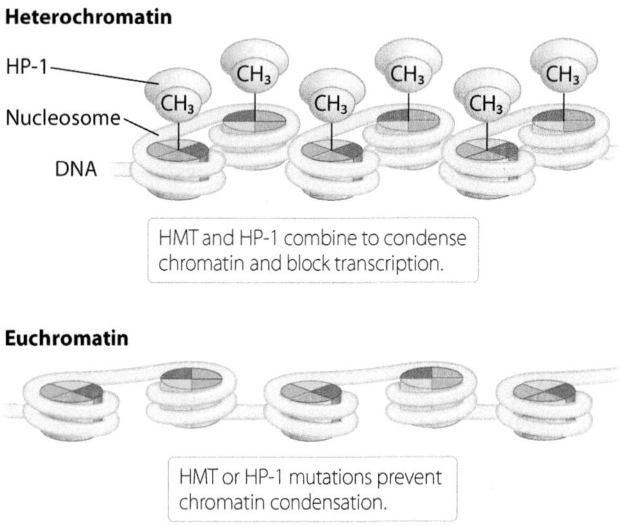

Figure 15.13   HMT and HP-1 modify chromatin. Mutation analysis identifies the proteins HMT and HP-1 as drivers of heterochromatin formation. HMT or HP-1 mutations prevent chromatin modification.

amino acids of the histones. These epigenetic marks are associated with chromatin remodeling that leads to gene transcription or gene silencing. The patterns of methylation and demethylation, acetylation and deacetylation, and phosphorylation and dephosphorylation are maintained on histones and may be passed through successive generations of cells, as we explore more closely in later pages. Five important features of epigenetic modification have been identified by researchers: (1) Epigenetic modifications alter chromatin structure, (2) they are transmissible during cell division, (3) they are reversible, (4) they are directly associated with gene transcription, and (5) they *do not* alter DNA sequence. We turn now to a discussion of how chromatin architecture is remodeled and modified and then explore examples of how changes in chromatin structure lead to activation or repression of gene expression.

Overview of Chromatin Remodeling and Chromatin Modification

The defining feature of eukaryotic DNA is its packaging into chromatin. How, then, do the activator and repressor transcription factors bind to regulatory DNA that is packaged into chromatin? There are three basic mechanisms by which trans-acting proteins access specific regulatory DNA sequences in eukaryotic chromosomes.

First, some regulatory sequences are not tightly bound by histones, which thus allow more or less direct entry to the regulatory DNA. These sequences include the "linker" sequences between nucleosomes and sequences with specific characteristics that prevent histones from binding efficiently.

Second, proteins called *chromatin remodelers* can enzymatically change the distribution or composition of histone octamers (nucleosomes). Chromatin-remodeling enzymes are recruited to specific sites in the chromatin by trans-acting factors that bind to specific DNA sequences.

As a third mechanism of access, proteins called *chromatin modifiers* can enzymatically modify histones by adding or removing methyl or acetyl groups at specific amino acid residues, most commonly lysines, of histone proteins. The addition of acetyl groups is associated with gene activation and is typically found in euchromatin. In contrast, removal of acetyl groups and addition of methyl groups to specific lysine residues are associated with gene repression and typically found in heterochromatin. As with chromatin-remodeling enzymes, chromatin-modifying enzymes are recruited to specific sites in chromatin by trans-acting factors that bind to specific DNA sequences.

This combination of activities determines the relative access of trans-acting transcription factors to cis-acting DNA sequences in particular cells, at different times of organismal development, and under certain physiological conditions. Thus, chromatin remodelers and chromatin modifiers mediate the reversible transition from inactive heterochromatic DNA to active euchromatic DNA.

Open and Covered Promoters

Two contrasting states of nucleosome association with promoter sequences, known as *open promoters* and *covered promoters*, are at opposite ends of a continuum of nucleosome association with regulatory DNA sequence. Most promoters fall somewhere between these extremes with respect to their association with nucleosomes, but an examination of open promoters and covered promoters can help us understand how chromatin structure contributes to transcription regulation.

Open promoters cause genes to be constitutively transcribed. These promoters have a **nucleosome-depleted region (NDR),** which is a 150- to 100-bp region containing few nucleosomes that lies immediately upstream of the start of transcription. These promoters do not generally contain a TATA box. Instead, a region rich in adenine and thymine, known as a poly A/T tract, is located in the NDR, near the transcription start site (**Figure 15.14a**). The poly A/T tract contains binding sequences (BS) that attract transcription activators (ACT). This binding region is usually flanked by sequences that help position two nucleosomes, one upstream and one downstream, of the NDR. The downstream nucleosome, identified as the +1 nucleosome, is placed at the transcription start site. This +1 nucleosome contains a variant histone 2A protein known as H2AZ that is readily modified for removal from the transcription start site at transcription initiation, allowing RNA polymerase II to bind and access the transcription start sequence.

Covered promoters, on the other hand, characterize genes whose transcription is regulated. Transcription of these genes is blocked until nucleosomes are displaced or

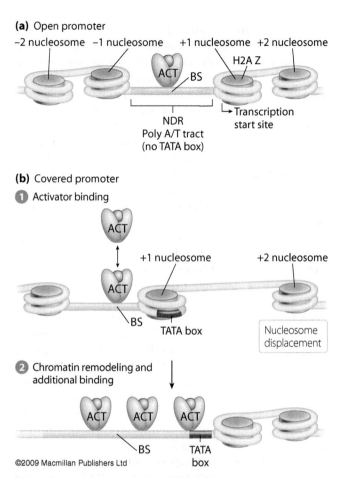

(a) Open promoter

NDR
Poly A/T tract
(no TATA box)

(b) Covered promoter

1 Activator binding

2 Chromatin remodeling and additional binding

©2009 Macmillan Publishers Ltd

Figure 15.14 **Transcription of open and covered promoters.** **(a)** Open promoters have a nucleosome-depleted region (NDR) and no TATA box. Activator proteins (ACT) are attracted to binding sequences (BS) to recruit RNA polymerase II for transcription. **(b)** With covered promoters, transcription is activated by activator-protein binding and displacement of nucleosomes.

removed from the promoter to allow transcription activators to bind to the necessary sequences, an event that leads in turn to RNA polymerase II binding and transcription initiation (**Figure 15.14b**). These promoters generally contain TATA boxes and other transcription-factor binding sequences. At covered promoters, there is active competition between nucleosomes and transcription-activating factors for binding. As a result, regulatory mechanisms are required that remodel chromatin to give activator proteins access to binding sequences in order to initiate transcription.

Mechanisms of Chromatin Remodeling

Chromatin remodeling refers to chromatin modifications that reposition nucleosomes in such a way as to open or close promoters and other regulatory sequences. Moving nucleosomes off regulatory sequences improves access to them by transcription-activating regulatory proteins. **Open chromatin** is chromatin in which the association of DNA with nucleosomes is relaxed in regions containing regulatory sequences, allowing access by regulatory proteins. Modifications that cause regulatory DNA to be covered by nucleosomes, thus restricting the access of regulatory proteins to the sequences, produce **closed chromatin.** In closed chromatin, regulatory sequences cannot be efficiently accessed by regulatory proteins, and genes are transcriptionally silent.

Molecular biologists can determine experimentally whether a region of DNA contains closed chromatin or open chromatin by assessing the sensitivity of the region to the DNA-digesting enzyme DNase I. This enzyme randomly cuts DNA in open chromatin regions but is not able to do so where chromatin is closed. Regions of open chromatin, sensitive to DNase I digestion, are known as **DNase I hypersensitive sites.** Where DNase I hypersensitivity is detected, genes are potentially transcribable. The experimental analysis of DNA for DNase I hypersensitivity is much like DNA footprint protection analysis described in Research Technique 8.1 (pages 279–280). Fragments of DNA created by exposure to DNase I are separated and analyzed by gel electrophoresis.

DNase I hypersensitivity occurs in the immediate vicinity of transcribed genes and can also appear 1000 bp or more upstream or occasionally downstream of actively transcribed genes. Hypersensitive regions surround promoters, enhancers, and other transcription-regulating sequences. The open chromatin complexes detected by DNase I hypersensitivity are the sites for binding by transcription-activating proteins and for transcription (Figure 15.15). **Genetic Analysis 15.1** guides you through an analysis for the presence of DNase I hypersensitivity in a region of DNA.

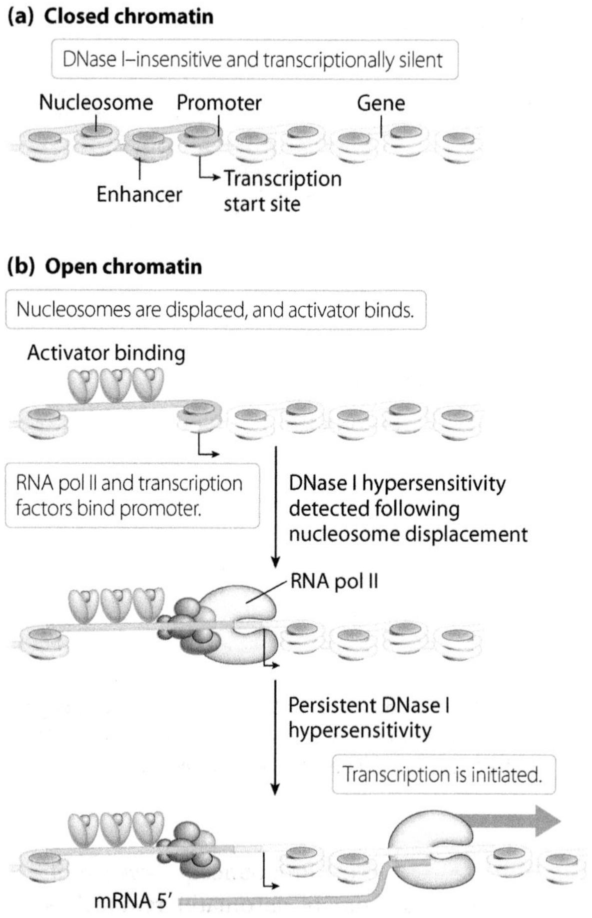

Another, more direct technique for identifying where proteins are bound to DNA is a process called chromatin immunoprecipitation (ChIP). The transcription factors, with associated chromatin and DNA, are isolated from living cells by first chemically cross-linking the proteins and DNA together and then, using an antibody specific to a transcriptional regulatory protein of interest to precipitate the DNA-chromatin combination containing that protein of interest. The DNA from the precipitated chromatin is then released by reversing the cross-linking, after which the isolated DNA is amplified by PCR (Chapter 7) and sequenced. The sequences obtained will correspond to the DNA to which the transcriptional regulatory protein of interest was bound in the cells. This approach is not only applicable to specific activator or repressor proteins but also can be performed using antibodies targeting specific chromatin modifications described later in this chapter. ChIP can be targeted to determine whether a protein of interest is bound to a specific DNA locus or can be used to determine all the sites in the genome to which a particular protein is bound, a concept that we will return to in Chapter 18.

Chromatin remodelers are the protein complexes that carry out chromatin remodeling by moving

(a) Closed chromatin

DNase I–insensitive and transcriptionally silent

Nucleosome   Promoter   Gene

Enhancer   Transcription
                  start site

(b) Open chromatin

Nucleosomes are displaced, and activator binds.

Activator binding

RNA pol II and transcription factors bind promoter.

DNase I hypersensitivity detected following nucleosome displacement

RNA pol II

Persistent DNase I hypersensitivity

Transcription is initiated.

mRNA 5′

Figure 15.15   Closed and open chromatin structure.
(a) Closed chromatin is inaccessible to transcriptional proteins and insensitive to DNase I digestion. **(b)** Open chromatin binds transcriptional proteins and is DNase I hypersensitive.

nucleosomes in three principal ways (two are seen in Figure 15.16). One type of chromatin-remodeling enzyme changes nucleosome organization by either sliding them along the chromosome or removing them from the DNA. These enzymes usually work by uncovering enhancers or promoters and thus are associated with gene activation. A second type of chromatin-remodeling enzyme reorganizes nucleosomes by inducing nucleosome movement. These enzymes usually repress transcription by moving nucleosomes. The third type of chromatin-remodeling enzyme changes the composition of histone octamers, replacing specific histone proteins with variant proteins. These changes are associated with gene activation.

A number of distinct chromatin remodelers are known. Three of the best-understood categories, classified by their main functions, are the *SWI/SNF complex,* which both slides and relocates nucleosomes; the *ISWI complex,* which helps direct the placement of nucleosomes; and the *SWR1 complex,* which substitutes the variant histone protein H2AZ in nucleosomes in place of the more common H2A protein.

(a) Nucleosome sliding

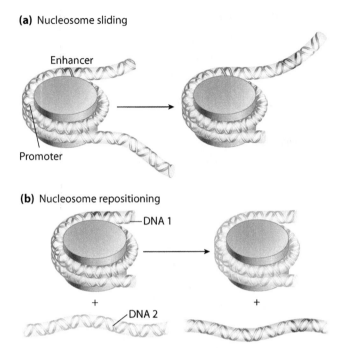

(b) Nucleosome repositioning

Figure 15.16 **Nucleosome displacement to expose regulatory sequences.** (a) Nucleosomes can be displaced by sliding or (b) can be repositioned on other DNA regions.

The SWI/SNF Complex Pronounced "swee-sniff" or "swy-sniff" this category of chromatin remodelers was first described in yeast and is now known to operate in all eukaryotes. It was discovered through analysis of mutations that affect two unconnected activities of yeast. One set of yeast mutants were unable to switch (SWI) mating type, a process tied to the ability of haploid yeast strains to fuse to form diploid strains. SWI mutations result from alterations of any of three genes, designated *SWI1, SWI2,* and *SWI3.* A second set of mutants was sucrose-nonfermenting (SNF) mutants. SNF mutants lose the ability to grow on medium containing the sugar sucrose owing to a mutation in any of three genes

designated *SNF2, SNF5,* and *SNF6.* The discovery that *SWI2* and *SNF2* are the same gene indicated that the activity blocked in *SWI* and *SNF* mutants was broader than just mating-type switching or the ability to initiate the transcription of genes needed for sucrose fermentation.

The composition of the **SWI/SNF complex** varies somewhat among eukaryotic species, but in each species the complex functions to open chromatin structure by displacing or ejecting nucleosomes. These actions expose promoter and other regulatory sequences to allow binding of transcription factors or activators that help initiate transcription (**Figure 15.17 ❶**).

The ISWI Complex Chromatin remodelers of the **ISWI** (imitation switch) **complex** primarily function to control the placement of nucleosomes into an arrangement that causes the region to be transcriptionally silent. These proteins have the ability to "measure" the length of linker DNA between bound nucleosomes in order to place the nucleosomes at regular intervals where they will cover promoters, thus preventing regulatory proteins from having access to the TATA box and other regulatory sequences. There is some evidence that certain nucleosome modifications can block ISWI activity, by a process that could be related to the opening of promoter and chromatin structure (see Figure 15.18 ❷).

The SWR1 Complex The switch remodeling 1, or **SWR1 complex,** is responsible for replacing the common histone 2A protein of nucleosomes with a variant form known as H2A.Z that differs from the more common form by amino acid differences internal to the protein and in the amino terminal (N-terminal) protein tail. The differences found in H2A.Z alter its pairing with other H2A proteins and its interactions with H3/H4 tetramers in the nucleosome.

H2A.Z is found primarily at the so-called +1 nucleosome that is affiliated with the start of transcription. Functional analyses in several species suggest that the role of H2A.Z is in the creation of unstable nucleosomes that

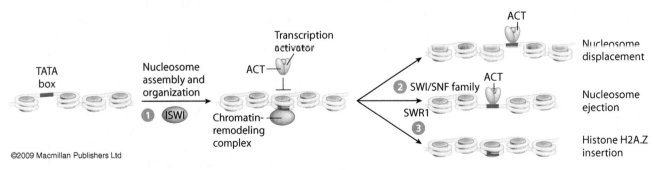

Figure 15.17 **The actions of chromatin-remodeling complexes.** ❶ISWI assembles and organizes nucleosomes in a regular pattern and contributes to transcription repression. ❷The SWI/SNF family opens chromatin structure and helps initiate transcription by either relocating nucleosomes away from regulatory sequences or ejecting nucleosomes. ❸SWR1 inserts the modified histone protein H2A.Z into nucleosomes to help facilitate displacement.

might then be displaced, ejected from DNA, or modified to regulate transcription (see Figure 15.18 ③).

Chemical Modifications of Chromatin

In contrast to chromatin remodelers that move histones, the proteins called **chromatin modifiers** chemically modify histone proteins in the nucleosomes by adding or removing specific chemical groups. These modifications alter the strength of association between nucleosomes and DNA. The changes can cause chromatin structure to relax, leading to open promoters and to transcription activation, or they can lead to closed structures that inhibit transcription. The principal chemical modifications to nucleosomes take place through the addition and removal of, primarily, acetyl and methyl groups at specific amino acids in the N-terminal (amino terminal) region of histones.

Because different patterns of modifications of histone tails lead to greater or lesser amounts of transcription by contributing to the opening and closing of chromatin structures, molecular biologists Thomas Jenuwein and C. Davis Allis suggested that a "histone code" exists. This hypothesized code consists of different combinations of chemical modifications in histone N-terminal tails, resulting in different changes to the chromatin structure. Supporting this idea, two studies examining different aspects of chromatin complexity in two evolutionarily distant eukaryotes suggest chromatin exists in only a limited number of distinct states (Table 15.1). Examining the combinatorial complexity of chromatin modifications in *Drosophila* cells in 2010, Guillaume Filion and colleagues identified five principal types of chromatin, each designated by color (the Greek word *chroma* means "color"). A similar study of chromatin in *Arabidopsis* by Francois Roudier and colleagues in 2011 examined histone modifications and DNA methylation to identify four prominent chromatin states (CS) that roughly correspond to those in *Drosophila*. Thus, despite the potential for an enormous number of different chromatin states, it appears that only a limited number exist in vivo.

Enzymes that add chemical groups are collectively known as "writers," while those that remove groups are

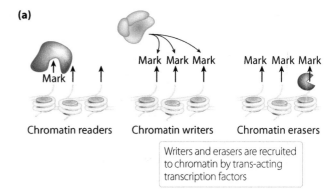

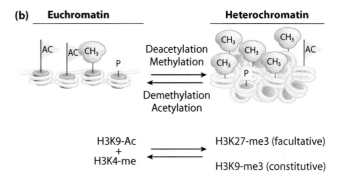

Figure 15.18   **Chromatin readers, writers, and erasers.**

known as "erasers" (Figure 15.18a). Proteins that recognize the modified histone are called readers. Writers and erasers are recruited to specific chromatin locations by sequence-specific DNA binding proteins, such as activators and repressors. The recruited writers and erasers modify the histone tails, producing an opening or condensing of chromatin structure at the locus. The two prominent chemical modifications are acetyl groups ($COCH_3$) and methyl groups (CH_3), which are added to or removed from lysine (K) residues in the N-terminal tail of histone 3. Three lysines, K4, K9, and K27, are particularly important targets for writers and erasers (Figure 15.18b).

Histone acetyltransferases (HATs) are chromatin-modifying writers that add acetyl groups, and the acetyl groups are removed by **histone deacetylases (HDACs),**

Table 15.1	Principal Chromatin States in *Drosophila* and *Arabidopsis*	
Drosophila	**Arabidopsis**	**Function of Chromatin State**
Yellow	CS1	Active gene transcription (euchromatin)
Red	CS1	Active gene transcription (euchromatin)
Blue	CS2	Polycomb repressed genes (facultative heterochromatin)
Green	CS3	Repressed repetitive sequences (constitutive heterochromatin)
Black	CS4	Repressed transcription (distinct from other heterochromatin)

Data from Filion, G. J., et al., 2010 and Roudier, F., et al., 2011.

PROBLEM The tissue enzyme TE2 is expressed in various mouse tissues at different times during the life cycle. Identical chromosome segments were isolated at different times in the cycle from a region immediately upstream of *TE2* and analyzed for DNase I hypersensitivity. The chromosome segments were collected from embryonic (E) and adult (A) mouse heart (H), kidney (K), and thymus gland (T). In the analysis, a radioactive label was attached to one end

> **BREAK IT DOWN:** DNase I cuts in regions of open chromatin but not condensed chromatin (p. 515).

of each chromosome fragment, and the samples from each tissue were exposed to DNase I to determine if the regions upstream of *TE2* were DNase I hypersensitive. The content from each sample was then separated by gel electrophoresis, and the results are as shown below.

a. Based on the gel results, is there evidence that chromatin remodeling plays a role in the expression of *TE2*? Explain your reasoning.

b. In which tissue(s) and at what times during development do the results indicate the expression of *TE2* was most likely taking place?

> **BREAK IT DOWN:** chromatin remodeling is the process by which nucleosome position or identity is altered (p. 516).

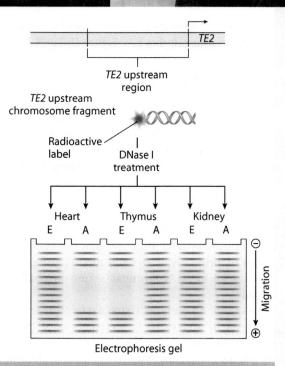

Solution Strategies	Solution Steps

Evaluate

1. Identify the topic this problem addresses and the nature of the required answer.

1. This problem concerns an experimental analysis for DNase I hypersensitivity in the region upstream (i.e., the promoter region) of *TE2*. The answers require interpretation of experimental results with respect to chromatin structure and gene expression.

2. Identify the critical information given in the problem.

> **TIP:** DNase I hypersensitivity is detected when chromatin structure is open and potentially accessible to transcription-activating proteins. Closed chromatin is not hypersensitive to DNase I.

2. Gel electrophoresis results are given for identical chromosome fragments from embryonic and adult heart, thymus, and kidney. All chromosome fragments were exposed to DNase I.

Deduce

3. Compare and contrast the meaning of a continuous series of bands in some lanes of the gel versus lanes in which gaps are seen between bands.

3. A continuous series of DNase I–digested bands indicates DNase I hypersensitivity. Hypersensitivity correlates with open chromatin that is accessible to transcription. Gaps between gel bands indicate that certain fragments of chromosomes are not generated by DNase I treatment. This result signals the absence of DNase I hypersensitivity in those regions and suggests closed chromatin structure and no transcription.

4. Evaluate the gel, and describe the patterns of DNase I–digestion bands for each sample.

4. Discontinuous band patterns are observed in adult heart and embryonic thymus gland DNA. This absence of DNase I hypersensitivity suggests closed chromatin structure. Each of the other DNA samples indicates hypersensitivity to DNase I.

Solve

5. Determine whether the gel data indicates chromatin modification near *TE2*.

Answer a

5. The DNase I hypersensitivity results indicate differential patterns of *TE2* expression in different tissues and at different times of development due to chromatin modifications. DNase I hypersensitivity resulting from open chromatin appears in embryonic and adult kidney, in embryonic heart, and in adult thymus chromosomal material. Hypersensitivity is not seen in adult heart or in embryonic thymus chromosomal material, indicating closed chromatin.

6. Name the tissues in which *TE2* is expressed, and describe the developmental timing.

Answer b

6. *TE2* expression is likely to occur at embryonic and adult stages in the kidney, in the embryonic heart, and in the adult thymus gland. *TE2* expression is unlikely to occur in adult heart or in embryonic thymus gland.

For more practice, see Problems 20 and 21. | Visit the Study Area to access study tools. | **MasteringGenetics**™

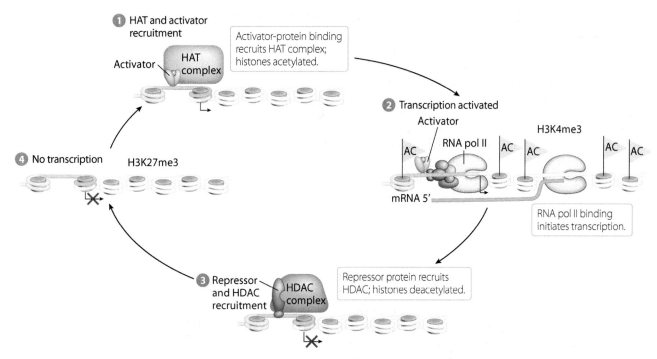

Figure 15.19   Acetylation and deacetylation in open and closed chromatin structure. Histone deacetylases (HDACs) deacetylate amino acids in N-terminal histone protein tails and close the chromatin structure. Histone acetyltransferases (HATs) acetylate N-terminal amino acids and help open the chromatin structure to activate transcription.

which act as erasers (**Figure 15.19**). In their unacetylated form, positively charged amino acids such as lysine promote nucleosome adherence to negatively charged DNA. Acetylation neutralizes the positive charge and relaxes the tight hold the nucleosomes have on DNA. Thus, acetylation of K9 of histone 3, designated H3K9Ac, is associated with an opening of the chromatin and active transcription. HATs are recruited to the chromatin by activator proteins (❶), leading to the formation of euchromatin and active transcription (❷). Conversely, HDACs are recruited by repressors (❸), resulting in the formation of transcriptionally inactive heterochromatin (❹).

A second common chemical modification of amino acids in N-terminal tails of histone proteins is methylation, the addition of methyl (CH_3) groups by chromatin-modifying **histone methyltransferases (HMTs),** which act as writers. Again, lysine is frequently targeted for methylation, and residues can be mono- (me), di- (me2), or tri-methylated (me3). Depending upon the K residue, methylation plays a role in converting open chromatin to closed chromatin in conjunction with deacetylation (as in the case of H3K9 and H3K27) or, conversely (as in the case of H3K4, in conjunction with H3K9 acetylation), forms open chromatin (see Figure 15.18b). Demethylation is carried out by **histone demethylases (HDMTs),** which act as erasers. HMTs and HDMTs are also recruited to the chromatin by activators and repressors in a manner similar to that depicted for HATs and HDACs in Figure 15.20. Thus, the chromatin state can be reversibly

converted between euchromatin (active) and heterochromatin (inactive) through the combined action of transcription factors and chromatin modifiers.

Multiple chemical modifications of N-terminal amino acids are required to remodel chromatin from a closed to an open structure and vice versa. No single acetylation or methylation event determines chromatin structure, but it is an event localized to a gene or regions of a gene. While writers and erasers must usually be recruited to chromatin by sequence-specific DNA-binding proteins, readers, as their name implies, can directly bind to the modified histones. The role of readers is to "read" the chromatin structure and act to maintain it in either an active or inactive state.

Facultative heterochromatin can alternate between an open euchromatic state and a closed heterochromatic state. Changes between these two states are driven by the recruitment of chromatin-modifying enzymes by activator or repressor proteins. In many eukaryotes, this involves an interplay between the opposing activities of writers and erasers, with a protein complex called the Polycomb group (PcG) acting in gene repression and another protein complex called Trithorax (Trx) acting to maintain gene expression. PcG and Trx complexes are recruited to specific loci by repressors and activators, respectively. The PcG complex acts to maintain a chromatin state that is marked with H3K27me3 and not acetylated; that is, it has an H3K27 HMT and an HDAC. In contrast, the Trx complex has a HAC and an H3K27 HDMT (see Figure 15.19). These states can be stable for the life of an organism, forming a cellular memory and ensuring the stable differentiation of cell types. We will revisit the role of these complexes during the development of a multicellular organism in Chapter 20.

Finally, recall from the original description of PEV in Chapter 11 that the *white* gene was relocated next to centromeric constitutive heterochromatin. In contrast to facultative heterochromatin, this type of heterochromatin is characterized by H3K9me3 and is one of the types of chromatin identified in *Drosophila* and *Arabidopsis*. We will return to the question of how constitutive heterochromatin is maintained later in this chapter.

An Example of Transcriptional Regulation in *S. cerevisiae*

To illustrate the role of chromatin modifications in transcription initiation, we turn to transcription regulation of the *PHO5* gene in the yeast species *S. cerevisiae*. Our discussion of this particular example is based on numerous studies that collectively paint a comprehensive picture of the actions associated with chromatin modification in *PHO5* transcription initiation and regulation.

PHO5 is a repressible gene encoding an acid phosphatase that removes phosphate groups from other proteins. In yeast, *PHO5* transcription is activated by phosphate starvation, but it is repressed when phosphate level is high. In the repressed state, access of transcription factors and RNA polymerase II to the promoter's TATA box is blocked by a nucleosome labeled −1 in Figure 15.20a. Similarly, access of transcription activator proteins to a UAS element labeled UASp2 is blocked by a nucleosome labeled −2. In the repressed state, the transcription activator protein Pho2 and the acetylase protein NuA4 are present upstream of the promoter at a UAS element labeled UASp1. Upstream of these are nucleosomes labeled −3 and −4. There is a low level of acetylation of nucleosomes −1 to −4 in the repressed state. Together, the presence of the nucleosomes −1 to −4 blocks access of activator protein and transcription factors to *PHO5* regulatory sequences.

Transcription of *PHO5* occurs when phosphate level falls. The Pho4 protein attaches to Pho2, forming a protein complex that begins transcription activation. Additional acetylation of the −1 to −4 nucleosomes takes place under the direction of NuA4. The Pho4–Pho2 complex then initiates chromatin modification by displacing nucleosome −2 (Figure 15.20b), making UASp2 available for binding by the Pho4 protein. The SWI/SNF protein complex assembles, and additional chromatin modification displaces nucleosomes −1 (that previously covered the TATA box), −3, and −4. With chromatin opened by nucleosome displacement, general transcription factor proteins and RNA polymerase II are able to bind the promoter and initiate transcription of the *PHO5* gene.

(a) High phosphate results in transcription repression

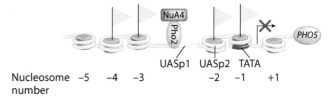

Nucleosome number −5 −4 −3 −2 −1 +1

(b) Low phosphate results in transcription activation

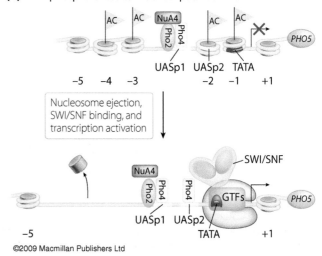

©2009 Macmillan Publishers Ltd

Figure 15.20 **Transcription control of *PHO5* in *Saccharomyces cerevisiae*.** (a) Transcription is repressed in high-phosphate conditions. (b) In low-phosphate conditions, Pho4 joins Pho2 at UASp1, and NuA4 directs acetylation of nearby nucleosomes. The SWI/SNF complex attaches, leading to the ejection of nucleosomes −1 to −4. RNA polymerase II and general transcription factors initiate *PHO5* transcription.

Epigenetic Heritability

Activating the transcription of an individual gene requires a confluence of regulatory proteins that remodel or modify chromatin to provide enhancer and promoter access to transcription factors that initiate and carry out transcript synthesis, as we saw above in the detailed description of *PHO5* transcription. Mechanisms controlling differential chromatin state formation and maintenance produce patterns of gene expression in different types of cells that are required for the growth and development of complex organisms. In a broad sense, these regulatory processes are the reason a single fertilized egg can develop and produce many distinct types of cells (liver cells, muscle cells, brain cells, and so on) that look and act differently even though they carry the same genetic information.

Among the trillions of somatic cells in your body are scores of different cell types, and yet all these cells contain the same genetic information. The differences of morphology and function between cell types are genetically controlled, as evidenced by the fact that daughter cells have the same structures and functions as parental cells, but DNA sequence variability *is not* the reason for those differences. Instead, the differences between somatic cells are **epigenetic,** resulting from the distinct chromatin states affecting gene transcription in specific types of cells.

To repeat, epigenetic patterns are often heritable through mitosis from one generation of cells to the next, causing daughter cells to have the same patterns of gene expression as their parent and sibling cells—a cellular memory. On the other hand, some epigenetic changes occur in the course of normal growth and development, in some cases resulting from different physiological conditions. These changes are potentially reversible and variable during the life cycle of an organism, during which the transcription of certain genes is turned on and later off again, or vice versa. Note that most epigenetic marks added during the lifetime of an organism are erased during meiosis, resetting the epigenetic landscape for the next generation. However, there is evidence that some epigenetic differences can be heritable through meiosis, from one generation of the organism to the next, a topic we will explore in the Case Study.

We have previously encountered examples of mitotically heritable variation of gene expression that has an epigenetic basis. For instance, position effect variegation (PEV) in *Drosophila* results from the movement of the transcriptionally active w^+ allele into the centromeric region of the fruit-fly X chromosome (see Figure 11.18). The DNA sequence of the gene is not altered. Instead, the spread of heterochromatin closes chromatin structure and blocks gene transcription by an epigenetic mechanism. The repressed transcriptional state is then maintained in daughter cells through mitotic division. The result is patches of cells descendant from original progenitor cells that share the same pattern of inactivation of w^+ expression. These cells form patches of white in the eye of the fly.

How is epigenetic control maintained in cells? For cellular memory to be maintained, any acetyl and methyl groups that are present on histones before DNA replication must be maintained or established on both the old and new histones after DNA replication. The specific molecular mechanics of this process are not entirely clear, but the partial disassembly and subsequent reassembly of nucleosomes is an essential component (see Figure 11.10). Recall that chromatin structure is broken down as the replication fork passes (see Chapter 11). Nucleosomes are separated from the parental DNA strands so the latter can serve as templates for the synthesis of daughter strands. The nucleosomes partially break apart, and old nucleosome segments along with newly synthesized nucleosome segments are reassembled on both new duplexes.

Immediately after DNA replication, the newly formed nucleosomes carry only part of their previous epigenetic information. The original epigenetic state must be quickly reestablished by epigenetic marking of the newly synthesized histones. Old histones are able to modify new histones to have the same pattern of epigenetic marks. This process takes place among adjacent nucleosomes,

thus preserving local epigenetic control of gene transcription. The interaction must also occur over long distances so as to maintain higher-order chromatin structure, such as that characterizing inactivated X chromosomes (see below). It is likely that the presence of PcG and Trx complexes is required for the continued maintenance of chromatin states through mitoses.

A Role for lncRNAs in Gene Regulation

It is becoming increasingly apparent that a class of RNA molecules in eukaryotic cells called **long noncoding RNAs (lncRNAs)** play critical roles in gene regulation. As their name implies, they are long RNAs without substantial open reading frames. A study of lncRNAs expressed in embryonic stem cells in mice suggests that many lncRNAs may act as scaffolds linking chromatin regulatory proteins to affect gene expression. Given that the genomes of mammals encode a large number of lncRNAs, this may be a critical mechanism of gene regulation in the mammalian lineage. The best-known example of a lncRNA regulating gene expression is *Xist*, which is involved in X chromosome inactivation in eutherian female mammals.

Inactivation of Eutherian Mammalian Female X Chromosomes

To achieve the correct balance of X-linked gene expression in eutherian mammalian females, the dosage compensation mechanism known as X-inactivation occurs. We discussed this problem in Chapter 3 and explained that mammalian females undergo random X inactivation in each nucleus early in gestational development. Recall that random X inactivation leaves one active X chromosome that is largely euchromatic and one inactive X chromosome that is almost entirely heterochromatic in each nucleus. The heterochromatic X chromosome is almost completely silent with respect to gene expression. This highly heterochromatic X chromosome forms a Barr body in the nucleus. All cells descending from the ones that originally underwent random X inactivation maintain the same active (euchromatic) and inactive (heterochromatic) X chromosomes, leading to the mosaic pattern of cells characteristic of eutherian mammalian females (see Figure 3.27).

Extensive studies of X inactivation in mice and humans have detected about a dozen genes on the heterochromatic (inactive) X chromosome that escape silencing. One of these genes is critically important to the establishment and maintenance of X-inactivation. The gene, called *X-i*nactivation-*s*pecific *t*ranscript (*Xist*), is *active* on the heterochromatic X chromosome and is *inactive* on the euchromatic chromosome. It is located in the X-inactivation center, or XIC, of the X chromosome (**Figure 15.21**). The *Xist* gene is transcribed only on the heterochromatic chromosome, where it is active; it is not transcribed on the euchromatic X chromosome, where it is inactive.

Heterochromatic X chromosome

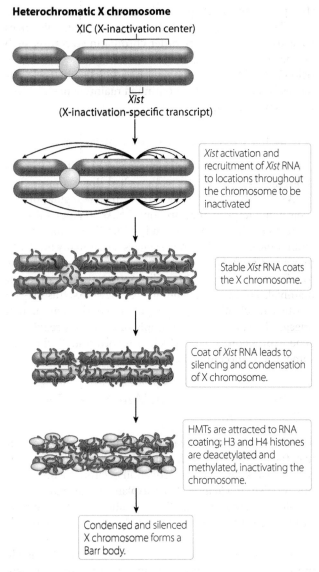

XIC (X-inactivation center)

Xist
(X-inactivation-specific transcript)

Xist activation and recruitment of *Xist* RNA to locations throughout the chromosome to be inactivated

Stable *Xist* RNA coats the X chromosome.

Coat of *Xist* RNA leads to silencing and condensation of X chromosome.

HMTs are attracted to RNA coating; H3 and H4 histones are deacetylated and methylated, inactivating the chromosome.

Condensed and silenced X chromosome forms a Barr body.

Figure 15.21 The X-inactivation center (XIC). The XIC contains *Xist*, which is transcribed to produce a specialized RNA that coats the X chromosome. This mechanism is responsible for random inactivation in eutherian mammals.

The gene transcript is a specialized RNA transcript called *Xist* RNA that never leaves the nucleus and is never translated. Instead, *Xist* RNA exclusively coats the X chromosome that produces it. The *Xist* RNA coating attracts HMTs and HDACs that methylate and deacetylate histones, respectively. These epigenetic modifications are linked directly to transcriptional silencing of genes.

The *Xist* RNA coating, subsequent methylation and deacetylation, and other protein-driven modifications inactivate one X chromosome and condense it into a heterochromatic state in each eutherian mammalian female nucleus. One idea of how the modification is accomplished is that the Xist RNA may act as a molecular bridge between the inactive chromatin and the repressive chromatin-modifying complexes such as PcG. This would ensure that the patterns of chromatin modifications

of the X chromosome established in embryogenesis are maintained throughout the lifetime of the organism. Note, however, that X-inactivation is reversible in eutherian mammalian female germ-line cells, ensuring that the process starts over each generation.

Genomic Imprinting

A specialized example of resetting of epigenetic patterns in meiosis occurs in certain mammalian and flowering plant genes in a mechanism known as **genomic imprinting.** For the small number of mammalian genes subject to genomic imprinting, both copies of the gene are functional but just one is expressed.

In mammals, two copies of each autosomal gene are inherited—one copy is on a chromosome inherited from the mother, and the other copy is on the homologous chromosome from the father, and usually both gene copies are expressed. For a small number of genes whose expression is subject to genomic imprinting, however, this pattern does not hold. Instead, one copy of the gene is actively expressed while the other copy is silent. The expressed gene copy is always inherited from a particular parent (for some genes it is the mother, for others it is the father), and the silent copy is the one inherited from the other parent.

The best-studied examples of genomic imprinting are two human genes encoded very near one another on chromosome 15. The insulin growth factor 2 (*IGF2*) gene on the paternally derived copy of the chromosome is expressed, whereas the *IGF2* gene on the maternally derived chromosome is silent. The opposite is the case for the *H19* gene, which is expressed from the maternally derived chromosome 15 but is silent on the paternal copy. These two genes are in a region of chromosome 15 containing several other genes that are also imprinted. They are among the few dozen human genes whose transcription is controlled by genomic imprinting.

Two regulatory sequences are responsible for these two instances of genomic imprinting. One is an enhancer downstream of *H19*; the other is an insulator sequence, called the **imprinting control region (ICR),** located between *H19* and *IGF2* (**Figure 15.22**). In the maternal chromosome, activator proteins bind the enhancer sequence and direct transcription of *H19* by interacting with transcription factors and RNA polymerase II at the promoter. The ICR in the maternal chromosome is bound by an insulator protein that blocks the enhancer from affecting *IGF2*. On the paternal chromosome, on the other hand, extensive methylation of the ICR and *H19* prevents insulator protein binding and blocks transcriptional protein binding at the *H19* promoter. In the absence of the insulator protein, the enhancer stimulates transcription of *IGF2*.

Genomic imprinting silences expression of paternal *H19* and maternal *IGF2* and directs transcription of paternal *IGF2* and maternal *H19* in all somatic cells. This pattern is essential for normal development, and any other pattern produces profound abnormalities. A genetic

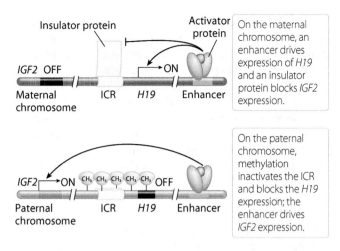

Figure 15.22 **Differential genomic imprinting of chromosome 15 in humans.**

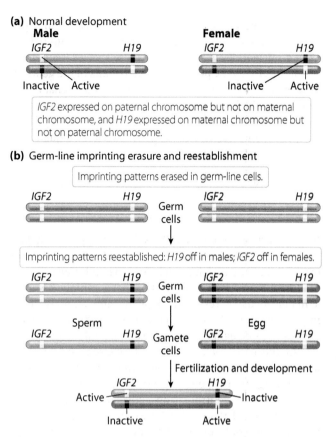

Figure 15.23 **Inheritance of genomic imprinting.** The genomic imprinting patterns on chromosome 15 are erased and reestablished in sex-specific forms early in gametogenesis to ensure reproductive success.

condition called Prader-Willi syndrome (OMIM 176270) most often results from partial deletion of the portion of the paternal copy of chromosome 15 containing *H19* and *IGF2*. The condition can also occur if the paternal chromosome 15 is not properly imprinted. A different condition called Angelman syndrome (OMIM 105830) is most often produced by partial deletion of the same portion of the maternal chromosome 15. Angelman syndrome also occurs if the maternal chromosome is not properly imprinted.

Given the importance of imprinting for certain genes and considering the different imprinting patterns of gene expression in maternally derived versus paternally derived chromosomes, how does the inheritance of correctly imprinted chromosomes occur? The answer is that in primordial germ-line cells, the inherited imprinting patterns are first erased and then are reestablished in the sex-specific pattern of the germ line early in gametogenesis (**Figure 15.23**). In the female germ line, methylation of the paternal chromosome is reversed by demethylase activity, and the insulator protein is removed from the ICR on the maternal chromosome. Both chromosomes are then re-imprinted with the female-specific pattern. In the male germ line, both chromosomes have their imprinting erased and then reestablished in the male-specific pattern. These processes ensure that each parent passes a properly imprinted chromosome during reproduction.

Nucleotide Methylation

The methylation pattern identified in genomic imprinting of the ICR and *H19* gene is a type of methylation that is associated with repression of gene expression in many plants and vertebrates, particularly mammals, that differs from methylation of amino acids in N-terminal histone protein tails. In this case, methyl (CH_3) groups are attached to specific DNA *nucleotides,* not to amino acids in histone protein tails. Nucleotide methylation is performed by specialized DNA methyltransferases that add methyl groups primarily to cytosines located in **CpG dinucleotides,**

side-by-side cytosine and guanine nucleotides in the same DNA strand. The *p* in CpG represents the single phosphoryl group in the phosphodiester bond connecting the nucleotides. Complementary strands of DNA containing CpG dinucleotides each have 5'-CG-3'. In plants, other C nucleotides may be methylated—the ones in 5'-CNG-3' and 5'-CNN-3' configurations, for example.

Much of the cytosine-methylated DNA in eukaryotic genomes is in transposable element sequences and noncoding sequences and is associated with a transcriptionally silent chromatin state. Just as with chromatin-remodeling enzymes, the DNA methyltransferases are recruited to specific loci by transcription factors when DNA methylation is being established. Also paralleling nucleosome modification, the pattern of cytosine-methylated sites is usually mitotically stable but can be reset during meiosis. A simple modification of Sanger sequencing in which the DNA is first treated with bisulfite, which converts cytosine to uracil but leaves methylcytosine untouched, allows the direct determination of the methylation status of DNA.

Recall from Section 12.4 that deamination of a methylated cytosine creates a thymine, which generates a mismatch that is repaired either to a C-G or a T-A base pair at an approximately equal frequency. Thus, in organisms with a significant amount of cytosine methylation, such as in vertebrates, where most of the cytosines in CpG dinucleotides are methylated, over time the number of CpG dinucleotides is reduced. In these species, sequences rich in CpG, called **CpG islands,** are regions of the genome in which there is strong selection for maintenance of cytosines, reflecting a functional role for such regions. As a result, CpG islands can be used to identify potentially functional genomic regions such as gene regulatory sequences.

15.3 RNA-Mediated Mechanisms Control Gene Expression

In the past several years, RNA has emerged as a key component in the regulatory control of eukaryotic gene expression. Largely unknown before the mid-1990s, RNA-mediated regulatory mechanisms have rapidly become a major focus of research in plants and animals. This important area of inquiry emerged unexpectedly from experiments designed to produce a more colorful petunia.

In the early 1990s, Richard Jorgensen and his colleagues were attempting to deepen the color of petunias by introducing into the petunia genome a pigment-producing gene under the control of an active promoter. The researchers hoped that active transcription of this recombinant gene would dramatically deepen flower color. To Jorgensen's surprise, however, rather than exhibiting more intense color overall, many of the resulting flowers were variegated (see the chapter opener photo). Some flowers had stripes of deep pigment and stripes lacking pigment, and some flowers were almost entirely white. The researchers called this phenomenon **cosuppression** because expression of both the introduced pigment gene and the petunia's natural pigment-producing gene was suppressed.

By 1995, similar gene-silencing phenomena had been documented in numerous plant species, in the fungus *Neurospora crassa*, in the nematode worm *Caenorhabditis elegans*, and in the fruit fly *Drosophila*. The fundamental mechanism behind this form of regulation was identified in 1998 by a research team led by Andrew Fire and Craig Mello. Fire and Mello found that double-stranded RNA (dsRNA) molecules were taking part in a post-transcriptional regulatory mechanism now known universally as **RNA interference (RNAi).** Fire and Mello received the Nobel Prize in Physiology or Medicine in 2006 for their work.

Gene Silencing by Double-Stranded RNA

RNA interference silences gene expression either by blocking transcription of targeted genes or by blocking gene expression post-transcriptionally. Post-transcriptional silencing occurs following binding of small regulatory RNAs to mRNA targets by complementary base pairing. The binding of these regulatory RNAs either can lead to the destruction of the target mRNAs or can block their translation. Alternatively, some regulatory RNAs enter

the nucleus where they bind DNA to block transcription of targeted genes. Any of these regulatory processes first require that small regulatory RNA molecules use complementary base pairing to bind their targets.

The regulatory RNAs in RNAi are derived from various sources that produce double-stranded RNAs. An enzyme known as **Dicer** (Figure 15.24) cuts the double-stranded RNA into 21- to 25-bp fragments. These fragments are then bound by a protein complex called the **RNA-induced silencing complex (RISC)** that denatures the double-stranded RNAs into single strands of 21 to 25 nucleotides. The RNA single strands produced by RISC are identified as the **guide strand,** which is biologically active, and the passenger strand, which is usually degraded. The guide strand remains bound to RISC, and the complex directs one of three gene-silencing processes (numbers 1 through 3 in the figure): ❶ The complex uses complementary base pairing to attach the guide strand to mRNA, and the mRNA is destroyed; ❷ the RISC–guide RNA binds to complementary mRNAs and blocks their translation; or ❸ the complex directs chromatin-modifying enzymes to the nucleus, where they silence transcription of selected genes.

What is the origin of the dsRNA? It can be produced from endogenous genes or from the transcription of other endogenous sequences (e.g., transposons), or it can come from exogenous sources. In many eukaryotes, genes encode precursors of dsRNA that are processed into 21- to 24-nucleotide **microRNAs (miRNAs)** at a Dicer complex (Figure 15.24 ❹). Most genes encoding miRNAs are transcribed by RNA polymerase II, and the resulting transcript folds back on itself into a dsRNA. The targets of miRNAs are endogenous mRNAs that are then either cleaved or have their translation blocked subsequent to activity mediated through RISC.

Another type of dsRNA is **small interfering RNA (siRNA).** In contrast to miRNAs, siRNAs are usually not derived from genes but rather come from exogenous sources or from other endogenous transcription. For example, if both strands of a genomic region happen to be transcribed, dsRNA can form. Transcription from opposite strands of repetitive elements, such as transposons, can also lead to dsRNA production ❺. In the latter case, the two strands do not have to be derived from the same genomic location. Some eukaryotes possess RNA-dependent RNA polymerases, which can produce dsRNA using single-stranded RNA as a template. The endogenous sources of dsRNAs can direct either posttranscriptional silencing, through the destruction of target mRNAs, or transcriptional silencing of target genes that takes place by chromatin modifying processes. Finally, exogenous sources of dsRNA can include RNA viruses ❻ that trigger virus-induced gene silencing.

Cleaving dsRNA The general mechanism of action by which Dicer cleaves dsRNA into fragments of the proper

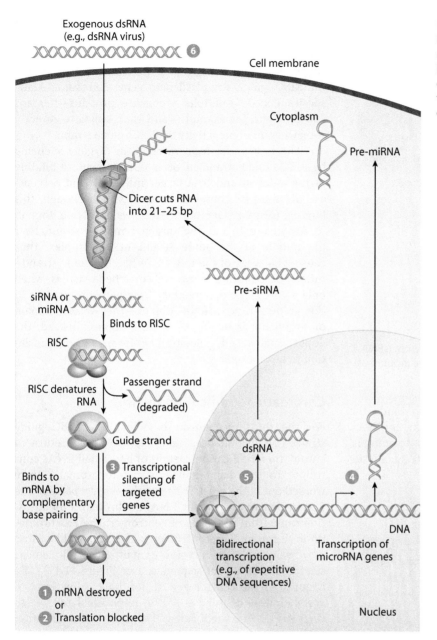

Figure 15.24 **Gene silencing by RNAi.** Dicer cuts dsRNA into 21- to 25-bp siRNA or miRNA segments that are then denatured by RISC. RISC–guide strand complexes can degrade targeted mRNAs, block translation of target mRNAs, or enter the nucleus to modify chromatin.

size was identified in 2006 when Jennifer Doudna and her colleagues determined the crystal structure of Dicer in the intestinal parasite *Giardia intestinalis*. Doudna's research group used the crystal structure to determine that the dsRNA-binding site on Dicer, called PAZ, is separated by 65 Å from the sites of two RNase domains that cut the RNA. The 65-Å space between PAZ and the RNase domains corresponds to the 24-bp length of the resulting dsRNA fragments (Figure 15.25). Dicer repeats this action, each time behaving as a molecular ruler measuring off precisely sized dsRNAs. The spacing between the PAZ site and RNase domains varies among species and appears to correlate with species-specific differences in the lengths of siRNAs produced by subsequent RISC processing of dsRNAs.

Precursor transcripts of miRNAs and siRNAs are synthesized in the nucleus of a cell and are processed into miRNAs and siRNAs by Dicer activity. In the case of miRNA, the precursor transcript is called a primary microRNA (pri-miRNA). The pri-miRNA folds to form a double-stranded stem typically containing 65 to 70 nucleotides and having free ends on one side and a single-stranded loop on the other side (Figure 15.26). In animals, the **Drosha** enzyme complex cuts pri-miRNA near the middle of the stem and produces two segments, one of which, now called precursor microRNA (pre-miRNA), contains the remainder of the upper stem, which is approximately 21 to 25 bp, and the terminal loop. The pre-miRNA is transported to the cytoplasm, where Dicer removes the terminal loop, leaving dsRNA

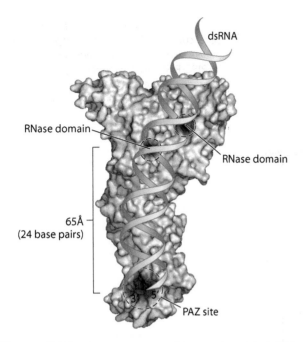

Figure 15.25 Dicer structure and interaction with dsRNA. The distance between the PAZ binding site and the location of RNases determines the length of siRNA.

of approximately 21 to 25 bp. RISC then binds the dsRNA and separates the strands to create miRNAs. The creation of siRNA is similar. In contrast to animals, plants use a single Dicer enzyme to perform all the miRNA processing activities.

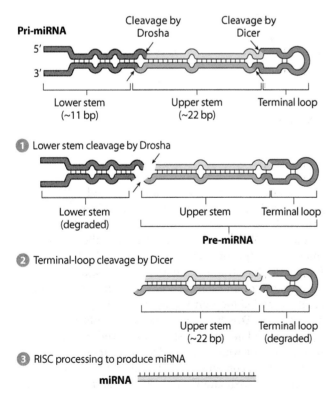

Figure 15.26 Stepwise processing of pri-miRNA to produce miRNA.

RISC and Argonaute The newly produced siRNA or miRNA remains bound by RISC to act as a guide strand. Within the RISC multiprotein complex is a protein of the **Argonaute** gene family that plays a central role in how the RISC–guide strand silences gene expression. Many species encode multiple Argonaute proteins—humans encode eight, for example—and each seems to direct a somewhat different activity by RISC–guide strand.

The best-understood mechanism of gene silencing by RISC–guide strand involves complementary binding of the guide strand to a target mRNA. If the percentage of base-pair complementation is high enough, this binding forms a structure that allows an RNase domain of Argonaute to cut the targeted mRNA strand near the middle of the guide strand–mRNA duplex, thus causing cleavage of the mRNA. When the guide strand–mRNA base pairing is less well matched—that is, when only a core of complementary base pairs are present in the guide strand–mRNA duplex—the RNase domain of Argonaute is unable to cut the duplex. Instead, the duplex retains its double-stranded form, causing translation to be blocked.

Chromatin Modification by RNAi

For the third mechanism by which the RISC–guide strand complex silences gene expression, we return to chromatin modification. Details of how small RNAs contribute to the maintenance of heterochromatin were worked out in the yeast *Schizosaccharomyces pombe*. The first evidence of a role for RNAi in chromatin modification came from the study of centromeric heterochromatin in *S. pombe*. The centromeres of *S. pombe*, like those of other complex eukaryotes, contain a central element surrounded by repeat sequences (see Figure 11.17). The histones in the centromeric region have a low level of acetylation, and lysine 9 of the N-terminal tail of H3 (that is, H3K9) is methylated. Both types of modification are consistent with the formation of a closed chromatin structure and the spread of heterochromatin to silence nearby genes.

S. pombe possesses single genes for Dicer and for Argonaute, and mutation of either gene disrupts RNAi activity in the cell. The surprising finding, however, was that *S. pombe* with Dicer or Argonaute mutations also lacks methylation of H3K9 and does not have gene silencing around the centromere. The explanation for these additional deficiencies is that in *S. pombe*, both strands of the centromeric repeat sequences are transcribed by RNA polymerase II. The resulting mRNAs are complementary and form double-stranded RNAs that Dicer cuts. The fragments produced by this process are then separated into single strands that bind to Argonaute, which then joins a protein known as Chp1 and other proteins to form a RISC-like complex called the **RNA-induced transcriptional silencing (RITS) complex** (Figure 15.27)

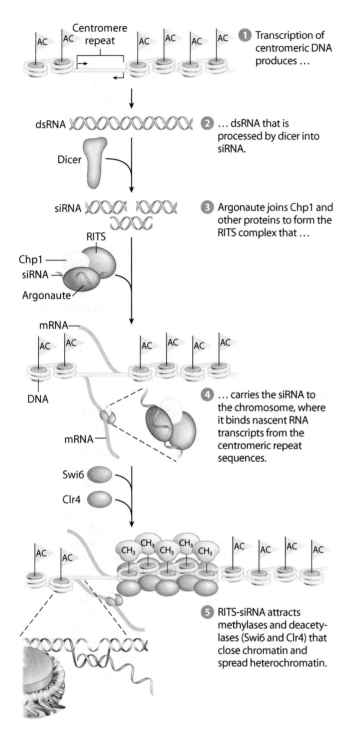

Centromere repeat

1 Transcription of centromeric DNA produces …

dsRNA

Dicer

2 … dsRNA that is processed by dicer into siRNA.

siRNA

3 Argonaute joins Chp1 and other proteins to form the RITS complex that …

RITS

Chp1
siRNA
Argonaute

mRNA

DNA

mRNA

4 … carries the siRNA to the chromosome, where it binds nascent RNA transcripts from the centromeric repeat sequences.

Swi6

Clr4

5 RITS-siRNA attracts methylases and deacetylases (Swi6 and Clr4) that close chromatin and spread heterochromatin.

Figure 15.27   RNA-induced transcriptional silencing (RITS) in yeast.

that carries the siRNA into the nucleus. The siRNA–RITS complex is attracted to the centromere, where the siRNA appears to use complementary base pairing to form a duplex with nascent transcripts of the centromeric repeat sequences. This pairing attracts other proteins that promote the deacetylation of histones and the methylation of H3K9 to close the chromatin structure and spread heterochromatin outward from the centromere.

The Evolution and Applications of RNAi

RNAi is widespread in eukaryotes, and the mechanism of transcriptional silencing in *S. pombe* is thought to be related to RNAi-mediated transcriptional silencing in other eukaryotic species. But how did RNAi evolve? The answer is still under investigation, but the operating hypothesis is that RNAi evolved by helping organisms protect their genomes against the mutational effects of transposable genetic elements (described in Chapter 13).

Transposable elements are diverse and make up large percentages of the genomes of complex eukaryotes. For example, almost half the human genome is composed of transposable elements. In the human genome and in other eukaryotic genomes, most of these transposons are located in heterochromatin and are silent; however, researchers have discovered that mutations in the RNAi machinery of an organism can reactivate normally quiescent transposons by reversing transcriptional silencing. This can lead to the movement of some transposable elements around the genome and potentially to the production of new mutations. The evidence suggests that RNAi plays a role in silencing the transcription of transposons.

RNAi also plays a protective role in response to viral infection. In plants, the infection of one leaf by a virus can generate an RNAi response that blocks viral replication and prevents the infection from spreading throughout the plant. In support of this observation, plants with Dicer or Argonaute mutations are much more susceptible to the spread of viral infections than are plants without Dicer or Argonaute mutations. These findings are consistent with the idea that RNAi evolved as a genome-protection mechanism against transposable genetic elements and viral infection. To return to Jorgensen's petunias and their cosuppression for a moment, biologists now know that RNAi is responsible for blocking expression of the chromosomal pigment-producing gene as well as the introduced copy of the pigment-producing gene.

Both plants and animal genomes encode miRNAs, but the mode of action of miRNAs differs slightly between the two taxa. In plants, miRNAs display near-complete sequence complementarity with their mRNA targets and usually cleave the target rather than block translation. In contrast, miRNAs in animals are usually only complementary to their targets at one end of the miRNA and usually repress translation rather than cleave the target. These differences suggest that miRNAs may have evolved independently in the two lineages.

RNAi is emerging as a powerful research tool that can be used in a multitude of ways. One frequent application of RNAi in research is the use of interfering RNAs to "knock down" the expression of selected genes. This is a way of discovering the gene's effect on the phenotype by examining how phenotype is altered in the absence of expression of the gene. A second area for application of RNAi is in medicine, where biomedical researchers are exploring the possible uses of RNAi to control the expression of genes that produce too much transcript or produce abnormal transcripts in disease. In certain cancers, for example, the disease process is driven in part by overexpression of certain genes. RNAi therapy would involve designing and constructing small RNA molecules that specifically bind and block the translation of the transcripts of disease-causing genes while not affecting the transcripts of other genes. We discuss other experimental applications of RNAi in Chapter 16.

CASE STUDY

Environmental Epigenetics

Here's a simple question: How are traits passed from one generation to the next? The first answer that came to your mind was probably (and not incorrectly) that traits are passed by the transmission of genes from parents to offspring. But over the past decade or so, the answer to that question has expanded in an unexpected direction. Emerging evidence suggests that in certain cases, parental nutrition and diet may lead to epigenetically controlled modifications of gene expression and that in a few select instances, the affected genes can be transmitted to offspring in their epigenetically modified form. More surprisingly, the data also indicate that the epigenetically modified state of the genes may persist in later generations. In other words, it may be possible for the nutritional experience of grandparents to affect gene expression in their grandchildren!

HONEYBEE DESTINY Three lines of evidence suggest a role for nutrition and dietary history in the epigenetic modification of gene expression. The first comes from studies in honeybees, where it has been shown that genetically identical larvae can develop into either fertile queens or sterile worker bees following differential feeding with royal jelly, the compound fed to larvae that become queens. Experimental analysis led by Ryszard Maleszka in 2008 reveals that silencing the expression of the DNA methyltransferase Dnmt3 by knocking down translation of the *Dnmt3* transcript by RNA interference leads to the development of fertile queens. In other words, blocking a major histone methylation pathway led to the expression of genes that are typically expressed only when a larva is fed royal jelly. The implication is that methylation is an important epigenetic mechanism for repressing gene expression and directing the development of worker bees. Methylation and the resulting transcriptional repression are subverted by feeding royal jelly to produce the development of fertile queen bees.

EVIDENCE IN MICE The second line of evidence comes from multiple studies of the connection between environmentally generated methylation of genes and variation in gene expression in rats and mice. In one study, genetically identical mice carry a modified *agouti* gene that produces yellow coat color and extreme obesity when the gene is expressed, whereas the normal brown coat color and normal body weight are produced if the modified gene is not expressed. The coat color and body weight of genetically identical mouse pups carrying this modified gene are determined by the diet of the mother in the weeks before impregnation and during pregnancy and lactation.

In controlled experiments, mothers that will transmit the modified *agouti* gene to their pups are fed either a diet enriched with three compounds that each act as donors of methyl groups to DNA—folic acid (vitamin B_{12}), choline chloride, and anhydrous betaine—or a diet without these compounds. The controlled dietary period begins 2 weeks before mating and continues through pregnancy and lactation. The pups produced are genetically identical, and after they are weaned, they are all fed the same diet. At 3 weeks of age, however, the appearance of the pups is dramatically different. Mice produced by mothers who were fed the enriched diet have brown coat color and normal body weight, whereas genetically identical mice produced by mothers not fed the enriched diet have yellow coat color and are obese. The difference indicates that the modified *agouti* gene is expressed when it is transmitted from mothers that were not fed the diet enriched with methyl donors. If the modified gene is transmitted from mothers receiving the enriched diet, however, the modified *agouti* gene is methylated and silenced.

INHERITANCE OF FAMINE EFFECTS The third line of evidence comes from an unfortunate event during World War II. A severe famine occurred in German-occupied Netherlands between November 1944 and May 1945. The famine reduced daily caloric intake to 500 to 800 calories per day, much less than the body needs to fuel its normal metabolic activities. Long-term studies have been performed on Dutch people who were conceived or born during the famine and on their descendants. Studies of the health effects of the famine find that so-called famine babies were often born severely underweight. As the famine babies grew into adults and aged, they suffered increased risk of cardiovascular disease, diabetes, and obesity compared to peers who had not been affected by the famine. The proposed explanation is that the restricted nutritional conditions in the womb caused alterations of gene expression, producing an energetically "thrifty" metabolism. More surprising, however, was that among the children of the famine babies, there is also an elevated risk of cardiovascular and other diseases. The explanation proposed for this second-generation effect is epigenetic modification of gene expression that is transmitted through multiple generations.

A 2008 study by Bastiaan Heijmans on the methylation pattern of the *IGF2* gene on chromosome 15 confirms the epigenetic control mechanism that we discussed previously in connection with genomic imprinting, Prader-Willi syndrome, and Angelman syndrome. Heijmans and colleagues found that *IGF2* in certain famine babies (now in their 60s) still bears the marks of famine. The *IGF2* genes of those exposed to famine during the first 10 weeks of gestation are marked by significantly fewer methyl groups than are the genes of their same-sex siblings not exposed to famine conditions. These results support the idea that prenatal conditions can impart specific epigenetic patterns to genes and that environmental factors contributing to epigenetic patterns may play an important role in modifying gene expression over multiple generations.

SUMMARY   (MasteringGenetics™)   For activities, animations, and review quizzes, go to the Study Area.

15.1 Cis-Acting Regulatory Sequences Bind Trans-Acting Regulatory Proteins to Control Eukaryotic Transcription

- Regulatory proteins in eukaryotes bind to specific nucleotides exposed in major and minor grooves of DNA.

- Promoters, proximal elements, and enhancers are cis-acting DNA sequences that bind trans-acting regulatory proteins to regulate transcription.

- Enhancer sequences are strongly conserved, indicating they perform essential functions.

- Upstream activator sequences (UAS) in yeast are enhancer-like elements that regulate the expression of genes such as those involved in galactose utilization.

- Locus control regions (LCRs) are specialized enhancers that control the sequential expression of sets of genes such as those in the developmentally regulated human β-globin gene complex.

- Silencer sequences bind repressor proteins to block transcription of targeted genes.

- Insulators block enhancer influence on certain genes and direct that influence to other genes.

15.2 Chromatin Remodeling and Modification Regulates Eukaryotic Transcription

- Open promoters are constitutively transcribed, whereas transcription from covered promoters is regulated.

- In regions of closed chromatin structure, the DNA is wound tightly around nucleosomes. These regions are transcriptionally silent.

- In regions of open chromatin structure, the association of DNA and nucleosomes is looser, allowing genes to be expressed.

- Chromatin-remodeling complexes displace nucleosomes to allow transcription initiation by RNA pol II and general transcription factors.

- Chromatin is modified by writers and erasers, and read by readers. Writers and erasers are recruited by transcription factors to open and close the chromatin by adding and removing acetyl and methyl groups at specific amino acids in the N-terminal tails of histone proteins.

- Epigenetic states of chromatin are heritable in somatic cells that divide by mitosis and may be reset in germ-line cells that divide by meiosis.

- Genomic imprinting in mammalian genomes involves nucleotide methylation and the action of enhancer and insulator sequences.

15.3 RNA-Mediated Mechanisms Control Gene Expression

- RNA interference (RNAi) is an RNA-mediated mechanism for regulating gene expression in eukaryotes.

- Small interfering RNAs (siRNAs) and microRNAs (miRNAs) are principal regulatory RNA molecules.

- The Dicer protein complex processes dsRNAs into their regulatory form.

- The RISC complex carries regulatory RNAs to RNAs targeted for destruction or for blockage of translation.

- A specific form of regulatory RNA directs mammalian X-inactivation.

KEYWORDS

Argonaute *(p. 526)*
chromatin modifier *(p. 517)*
chromatin remodeler (SWI/SNF, ISWI, SWR1) *(pp. 515, 516)*
chromatin remodeling *(p. 514)*
cis-acting regulatory sequence *(p. 507)*

closed chromatin *(p. 515)*
cosuppression *(p. 524)*
covered promoter *(p. 514)*
CpG dinucleotide (CpG island) *(pp. 523, 524)*
Dicer *(p. 524)*

DNase I hypersensitive site *(p. 515)*
Drosha *(p. 525)*
enhanceosome *(p. 507)*
enhancer (enhancer sequence) *(p. 506)*
epigenetic *(p. 521)*
E(var) mutation *(p. 512)*

genomic imprinting *(p. 522)*
guide strand *(p. 524)*
histone acetyltransferase (HAT) *(p. 517)*
histone deacetylase (HDAC) *(p. 517)*
histone demethylase (HDMT) *(p. 519)*
histone methyltransferase (HMT) *(p. 519)*
imprinting control region (ICR) *(p. 522)*
insulator sequence *(p. 511)*
ISWI complex *(p. 516)*
locus control region (LCR) *(p. 508)*

long noncoding RNA (lncRNA) *(p. 521)*
Mediator *(p. 511)*
microRNA (miRNA) *(p. 524)*
nucleosome-depleted region (NDR) *(p. 514)*
open chromatin *(p. 514)*
open promoter *(p. 514)*
RNA-induced silencing complex (RISC) *(p. 524)*
RNA-induced transcriptional silencing (RITS) complex *(p. 526)*

RNA interference (RNAi) *(p. 524)*
silencer sequence *(p. 506)*
small interfering RNA (siRNA) *(p. 524)*
Su(var) mutation *(p. 512)*
SWI/SNF complex *(p. 516)*
SWR1 complex *(p. 516)*
trans-acting regulatory protein *(p. 507)*
upstream activator sequence (UAS) *(p. 510)*

PROBLEMS

MasteringGenetics™ Visit for instructor-assigned tutorials and problems.

Chapter Concepts

For answers to selected even-numbered problems, see Appendix: Answers.

1. Devoting a few sentences to each, describe the following structures or complexes and their effects on eukaryotic gene expression:
   a. promoter
   b. enhancer
   c. silencer
   d. RISC
   e. Dicer

2. Describe and give an example (real or hypothetical) of each of the following:
   a. upstream activator sequence (UAS)
   b. insulator sequence action
   c. silencer sequence action
   d. enhanceosome action
   e. RNA interference

3. What is meant by the term *chromatin remodeling*? Describe the importance of this process to transcription.

4. What general role does acetylation of histone protein amino acids play in the transcription of eukaryotic genes?

5. Describe the roles of writers, readers, and erasers in eukaryotic gene regulation.

6. Outline the roles of RNA in eukaryotic gene regulation.

7. What are the roles of the Polycomb and Trithorax complexes in eukaryotic gene regulation?

8. Most biologists argue that the regulation of gene expression is considerably more complex in eukaryotes than in bacteria. List and describe the four factors that in your view make the largest contribution to this perception.

9. Compare and contrast the transcriptional regulation of *GAL* genes in yeast with that of the *lac* genes in bacteria.

10. The term *heterochromatin* refers to heavily condensed regions of chromosomes that are largely devoid of genes. Since few genes exist in those regions, they almost never decondense for transcription. At what point during the cell cycle would you expect to observe the decondensation of heterochromatic regions? Why?

11. Compare and contrast promoters and enhancers with respect to their location (upstream versus downstream), orientation, and distance (in base pairs) relative to a gene they regulate.

12. How are the different types of chromatin classified, and what is their relationship with gene expression?

13. Define epigenetics, and provide examples illustrating your definition.

14. What is one proposed role for lncRNAs?

Application and Integration

15. A hereditary disease is inherited as an autosomal recessive trait. The wild-type allele of the disease gene produces a mature mRNA that is 1250 nucleotides (nt) long. Molecular analysis shows that the mature mRNA consists of four exons that measure 400 nt (exon 1), 320 nt (exon 2), 230 nt (exon 3), and 300 nt (exon 4). A mother and father with two healthy children and two children with the disease have northern blot analysis performed in a medical genetics laboratory. The results of the northern blot for each family member are shown below.

For answers to selected even-numbered problems, see Appendix: Answers.

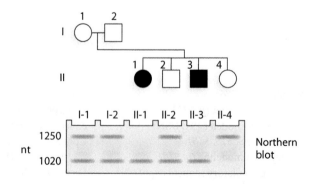

a. Identify the genotype of each family member, using the sizes of mRNAs to indicate each allele. (For example, a person who is homozygous wild type is indicated as "1250/1250.")

b. Based on your analysis, what is the most likely molecular abnormality causing the disease allele?

16. The *UG4* gene is expressed in stem tissue and leaf tissue of the plant *Arabidopsis thaliana*. To study mechanisms regulating *UG4* expression, six small deletions of DNA sequence upstream of the gene-coding sequence are made. The locations of deletions and their effect on *UG4* expression are shown below.

a. Explain the differential effects of deletions B and F on expression in the two tissues.

b. Why does deletion D raise *UG4* expression in leaf tissue but not in stem tissue?

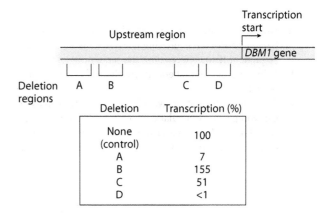

Deletion	Transcription (%)	
	Stem	Leaf
None (control)	100	100
A	100	100
B	<1	92
C	100	100
D	100	163
E	98	<1
F	100	100

c. Why does deletion E lower expression of *UG4* in leaf tissue but not in stem tissue?

17. A gene expressed in long muscle of the mouse is identified, and the regulatory region upstream of the gene is isolated. Various segments of the upstream sequence are fused to the *lacZ* gene, and each fusion is assayed to determine how efficiently it transcribes the gene. In the accompanying diagram, the dark bars indicate the upstream segments that are present in each of six different fusion genes. The transcriptional efficiency of each fusion is measured against the control fusion, that is, the full-length upstream segment fused to the *lacZ* gene.

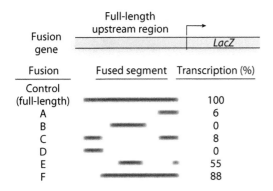

Fusion	Fused segment	Transcription (%)
Control (full-length)		100
A		6
B		0
C		8
D		0
E		55
F		88

a. Identify the upstream region that contains the enhancer.

b. Identify the upstream region containing the promoter.

c. Speculate about the reason for the different transcription rates detected in fusions E and F.

18. The consequences of four deletions from the region upstream of the yeast gene *DBM1* are studied to determine the effect on transcription. The normal rate of transcription, determined from study of transcription of genes that do not have upstream deletions, is defined as 100%. The location of each deletion and the effects of deletions on *DBM1* transcription are shown below.

a. Which mutations(s) affect an enhancer sequence? Explain your reasoning.

b. Which mutation(s) affect a silencer sequence? Explain your reasoning.

c. Which mutation(s) affect the promoter? Explain your reasoning.

Deletion	Transcription (%)
None (control)	100
A	7
B	155
C	51
D	<1

19. Provide a description of the mechanistic roles of transcription factors and chromatin-modifying and chromatin-remodeling enzymes in the control of eukaryotic gene expression.

20. A muscle enzyme called ME1 is produced by transcription and translation of the *ME1* gene in several muscles during mouse development, including heart muscle, in a highly regulated manner. Production of ME1 appears to be turned on and turned off at different times during development. To test the possible role of enhancers and silencers in *ME1* transcription, a biologist creates a recombinant genetic system that fuses the *ME1* promoter, along with DNA that is upstream of the promoter, to the bacterial *lacZ* (β-galactosidase) gene. The *lacZ* gene is chosen for the ease and simplicity of assaying production of the encoded enzyme. The diagram shows the structure of the recombinant, as well as bars that indicate the extent of six deletions the biologist makes to the *ME1* promoter and upstream sequences. The blue bar is the site of the promoter whereas the gray bars span potential enhancer/silencer modules. The table displays the percentage of β-galactosidase activity in each deletion mutant in

comparison to the recombinant gene system without any deletions.

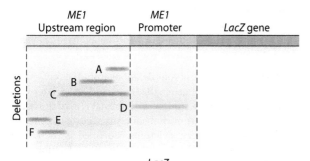

Deletion	*LacZ* activity (%)
None (control)	100
A	100
B	100
C	4
D	<1
E	170
F	5

a. Does this information indicate the presence of enhancer and/or silencer sequences in the *ME1* upstream sequence? If so, where is/are the sequences located?

b. Why does deletion D effectively eliminate transcription of *lacZ*?

c. Given the information available from deletion analysis, can you give a molecular explanation for the observation that *ME1* expression appears to turn on and turn off at various times during normal mouse development?

21. A muscle protein in mouse is produced through the use of alternative promoters in heart and skeletal muscle. A diagram of the gene region is shown below. The gene contains a total of six exons, and there are three restriction sites recognized by the restriction enzyme *Hin*dIII in the vicinity of the gene. In the diagram, the locations of heart (P_H) and skeletal (P_S) promoters are indicated, as are two molecular probes. Probe *a* hybridizes to exon 2, and probe *b* hybridizes to exon 4. Transcription of the gene in heart and skeletal muscle terminates after exon 6. The protein produced by the gene is recognized in heart and muscle samples by the same antibody.

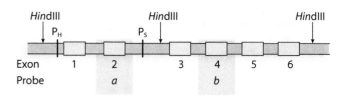

Diagram the expected results of the studies described below.

a. *Hin*dIII digestion of DNA from heart muscle and skeletal muscle followed by the use of probes *a* and *b* in Southern blot analysis, with each of the probes in a separate analysis

b. Northern blot analysis of mature mRNA extracted from heart muscle and skeletal muscle, using probes *a* and *b* in separate analyses

c. Western blot analysis of the protein from heart muscle and skeletal muscle, using the antibody as a probe

Analysis of Gene Function by Forward Genetics and Reverse Genetics

CHAPTER OUTLINE

16.1 Forward Genetic Screens Identify Genes by Their Mutant Phenotypes

16.2 Genes Identified by Mutant Phenotype Are Cloned Using Recombinant DNA Technology

16.3 Reverse Genetics Investigates Gene Action by Progressing from Gene Identification to Phenotype

16.4 Transgenes Provide a Means of Dissecting Gene Function

Thomas Hunt Morgan's fly room (he is at far right, back row) was the site of the original mutagenesis. The first screens were limited by their reliance on spontaneous mutants, but the discovery by Hermann Muller (second from right. back row) that X-rays are mutagenic turned genetic screens into routine and powerful tools to uncover gene function. Also visible in this photo are Calvin Bridges (third from left, back row), who used nondisjunction to prove the chromosome theory of heredity, and Alfred Sturtevant (middle front row), who constructed the first genetic map.

ESSENTIAL IDEAS

- Forward genetic screens induce mutations to identify genes involved in a biological process; subsequent cloning sheds light on their molecular function.

- DNA sequences of specific genes can be discovered using recombinant DNA technology.

- Reverse genetics techniques start with a gene sequence and then proceed to the identification of a mutant phenotype.

- Phenotypes of transgenic organisms can provide information on gene function.

A central goal of biology is to understand the molecular and genetic bases of physiology and development. Beginning with Mendel and resuming in the first part of the 20th century, geneticists attempted to dissect the rules of heredity by connecting phenotypes to genetic loci. The discovery of DNA as the hereditary material indicated that genes are specific DNA sequences and that allelic differences reflect differences in those sequences. In the 1970s, discoveries stemming from the study of bacteria and their phages led to the development of tools to manipulate DNA in vitro. With these tools, collectively referred to as *recombinant DNA technology*, geneticists could for the first time obtain the precise DNA sequences of specific genes and alleles, thus identifying the molecular basis of phenotypic differences.

The exploration of how genes control physiological and developmental processes is approached in two ways that attack the problem from diametrically opposite directions. These opposite approaches are known as *forward genetic analysis* and *reverse genetic analysis*. The goals of forward and reverse analysis are the same: to identify the genes responsible for hereditary variation, to determine the structure and function of wild-type alleles controlling traits, and to describe how mutant alleles generate abnormal phenotypes. However, the two strategies begin at different ends of the process of gene identification.

Forward genetic analysis starts with a **genetic screen** that identifies specific phenotypic abnormalities in a population of organisms that have been mutagenized—**mutagenesis** being the intentional introduction of mutations into the genome of an organism. The abnormal phenotype is then studied to identify the nature of the hereditary abnormality

and, by inference, the normal functions of an associated gene. Ultimately, the sequence of the gene responsible for the abnormality is determined and may suggest the molecular function of the corresponding gene product (**Figure 16.1a**). In contrast to forward genetics approaches, which begin genetic investigation with a mutant phenotype and proceed toward the identification of a gene sequence, **reverse genetics** approaches begin with a gene sequence and seek to identify the corresponding mutant phenotype (**Figure 16.1b**). In a reverse genetics experiment, loss-of-function alleles of specific genes are created by a variety of approaches, and the resulting phenotypes are examined to see how they differ from the wild type. Reverse genetic analysis has risen to prominence as a result of the enormous quantity of DNA sequence data made available since the late 1990s.

In this chapter, we discuss forward and reverse genetic analyses from a conceptual viewpoint and in Chapter 17 present details of how recombinant DNA technology can be used to manipulate DNA sequences in vitro and in vivo.

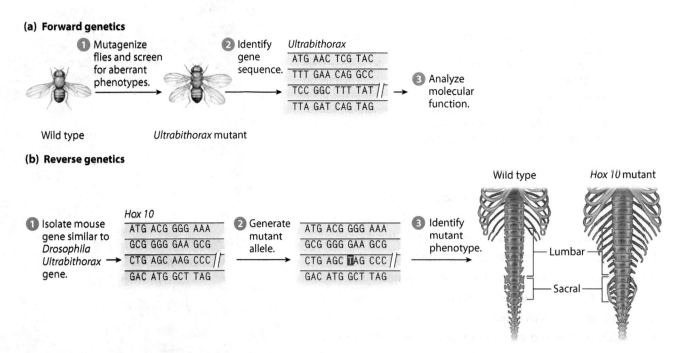

Figure 16.1 General strategies of forward and reverse genetics.

16.1 Forward Genetic Screens Identify Genes by Their Mutant Phenotypes

With the discovery by Hermann Muller that ionizing radiation induces mutations (see Section 12.3), geneticists realized that mutant organisms could be generated at will and systematically screened for phenotypes of interest. Mutant phenotypes provide information on the function of the wild-type allele and insight into biological processes. The earliest example of this logic is the work of Archibald Garrod, who in 1908 connected the human autosomal recessive hereditary condition alkaptonuria to the lack of a specific biochemical activity, the metabolism of benzene rings in homogentisic acid (see Chapter 9). He suggested that the wild-type version of the gene encodes the enzyme responsible for this biochemical activity. After Muller brought the mutagenic powers of X-rays to their attention (see Section 12.3), geneticists began to employ systematic genetic screens to dissect other biological processes, and the genetic bases for entire biochemical pathways were elucidated.

The designing of genetic screens to identify genes involved in specific biological processes is limited only by the imagination of the geneticist. An example is the research by Seymour Benzer that led to the field of behavioral genetics in the 1970s. Benzer believed mutations could be identified that specifically affect behavioral processes, such as one you are using now, the process of learning and memory. At the time, behavior was thought by many to be too complex to be dissected genetically. However, Chip Quinn, a graduate student in Benzer's lab, built on previous ideas and designed an ingenious screen to identify learning- and memory-deficient mutants in *Drosophila*. Wild-type flies could be taught that a pulse of odor would be followed by a shock; later, when the flies smelled the odor, they would take evasive action. When Quinn and Benzer subjected a mutagenized population of *Drosophila* to this genetic screen, they identified mutant strains of flies that could perceive the odor but seemed unable to associate the odor with the stimulus; either they did not learn or could not remember.

Two mutant genes identified in the study, *dunce* and *rutabaga*, were later shown to encode proteins involved in the production or degradation of the small signaling molecule cyclic adenosine monophosphate (cAMP). At the time, signaling via a cAMP pathway was known to be required for learning in the sea hare, *Aplysia*. Since both *Drosophila* mutants were defective in cAMP physiology, other genes that encoded proteins involved in cAMP signaling and response were also investigated for roles in learning. Ultimately, a transcription factor called *creb* (*cAMP* *r*esponse *e*lement–*b*inding protein), which activates or represses genes in response to cAMP signaling, was shown to be critical for storing memories in flies. Remarkably, *creb* is widely conserved in animal species,

and mouse mutants lacking *creb* activity also fail to remember. A similar gene is found in our genome.

A great strength of forward genetic screens is that they are unbiased; no prior knowledge of the molecular function of the encoded gene product is required. In a sense, by performing a mutagenesis, the geneticist is allowing the organism to reveal how its biological processes operate. Once genes in particular physiological or developmental processes have been identified by mutation, clues to the molecular function of the gene product can be obtained using recombinant DNA technology.

General Design of Forward Genetic Screens

Forward genetic screens often require the mutagenesis of thousands of individuals, followed by screening large numbers of their progeny for mutant phenotypes. Each progeny may contain multiple mutations, but only a small fraction of the progeny will have a mutant phenotype of interest. For example, in their screens to identify auxotrophs, Beadle, Tatum, and colleagues screened many thousands of individual mutant lines to find the few arginine auxotrophs that were produced. While some screens necessitate the visual inspection of all progeny, others are specifically designed to highlight certain mutants of interest against the background of all other mutants. The designing of such screens is an art.

Perhaps the most dramatic screen is one in which application of a simple selection technique allows mutants of interest to survive while those not of interest die. Examples include the isolation of bacteria resistant to antibiotics, insects resistant to insecticides, and plants resistant to herbicides. Similarly, isolation of mutants resistant to analogs of cellular chemicals or to high levels of naturally occurring hormones has proven useful in genetic screens. Often in such cases, mutations identify genes encoding proteins involved in the metabolism or signaling pathways of the respective chemicals.

Even when strong selection criteria cannot be applied, knowledge of the biological process of interest can influence the design of the screen. For example, when Wieschaus and Nüsslein-Volhard performed their screen for *Drosophila* embryogenesis mutants, they assumed that the mutations of interest were all likely to be lethal to the larva (see Section 20.2). Thus they could limit their intensive analysis to mutant lines in which larval lethality was evident.

Specific Strategies of Forward Genetic Screens

Forward genetic screens begin with a mutagenesis—an organism is treated with a mutagen to create mutations randomly throughout the genome. A typical goal is to induce mutations in every gene in a population of mutagenized individuals, by an approach called **saturation mutagenesis.** The mutagenized population is then screened for phenotypic defects in whatever biological process is being studied, and the mutants are collected and propagated for further analysis. Strategies for mutagenesis depend on the biological process of interest, which dictates the experimental organism to use, the choice of mutagen, and the screening procedure to identify mutations.

Choosing an Organism The attributes that make an organism a good genetic model also make it a good choice for a mutagenesis experiment (see back end sheets): An organism must be able to progress through its entire life cycle in the laboratory, have a short generation time (for eukaryotic models, the time it takes to produce sexually mature progeny and complete the sexual life cycle), produce a reasonable number of progeny, and be amenable to crossing. Organisms that are diploid must have a starting genotype (the genotype to be mutagenized) that is inbred—in other words, homozygous at all loci. This genotype allows newly induced mutations to be readily identified, without interference from the confounding effects of polymorphisms. Finally, it is advantageous to use the simplest organism possible for the biological process under study. Because *Saccharomyces cerevisiae* has a rapid life cycle and is easily manipulated in the laboratory, it is often used to investigate biological processes common to all eukaryotes. The principles elucidated in *S. cerevisiae* can often be extended to other eukaryotes, including humans.

Choosing a Mutagen The choice of mutagen is dictated by both the organism and the type of mutant alleles desired; different mutagens have different advantages and disadvantages (**Table 16.1**). Mutagens inducing different types of changes in DNA sequences were described in Section 12.4. Treatment with chemical mutagens can induce hundreds of mutations in a single individual, allowing saturation to be reached with only a few thousand mutagenized individuals. However, the cloning of genes identified by chemical mutagenesis can be laborious. In contrast, mutagens that result specifically in insertions of DNA, such as transposons, result in far fewer mutations per individual, making saturation difficult. But these mutagens have the advantage of being able to provide a DNA "tag" that facilitates finding and cloning the mutated genes. In all mutageneses used for forward genetic screens care must be taken to outbreed mutants of interest by crossing them with the wild-type progenitor strain, thus ensuring that the collected mutant lines have only the mutation of interest and not others that were also induced during the mutagenesis.

Strategy for Identifying Dominant and Recessive Mutations The overall goal of mutagenesis is to identify multiple independent mutant alleles of each gene involved in the biological process of interest. Let us consider the identification of dominant and recessive mutations in a typical animal example.

Most animals spend most of their life cycle in the diploid state. Their germ cells are set aside early in development and do not contribute to the somatic development of the remainder of the animal body. When animals are treated with a mutagen—for example, by feeding males ethyl methanesulfonate (EMS), a potent mutagen that causes a spectrum of alleles (see Table 16.1)—only the mutations induced in the germ cells are heritable and will be passed to the progeny of the mutagenized animals.

Newly induced dominant mutations can be identified in the F_1 generation that is produced by breeding the mutagenized males with wild-type females (**Figure 16.2a**). However, only a small fraction of the F_1 progeny will exhibit a mutant phenotype, since dominant mutations are rare. This rarity is due to the low probability that any change in the DNA sequence of a gene will produce a gain in function for the encoded gene product, either qualitatively or quantitatively.

Mutations that result in a loss of function are more common, but loss-of-function mutations are usually recessive and do not result in an observable phenotype in the F_1 generation. Therefore, further breeding must be performed to produce homozygous loss-of-function mutants. Specifically, recessive mutations are identified in an F_3

Table 16.1	**Common Mutagens Used for Mutagenesis**		
Mutagen	**Mutation Spectrum**	**Mutation Rate per Locus**	**Allele Spectrum**
Chemical Ethyl methanesulfonate (EMS)	G → A (C → T) conversion Stop codons created: TGG → TAG Splice sites destroyed: AG → AA	High	Null, hypomorphic, hypermorphic
Radiation Fast-neutron X-ray Gamma-ray	Rearrangements (deletions, inversions, translocations)	Moderate	Usually loss-of-function (often null), but can be gain-of-function
Insertional Transfer DNA Transposons	Insertions	Low	Usually loss-of-function (often null)

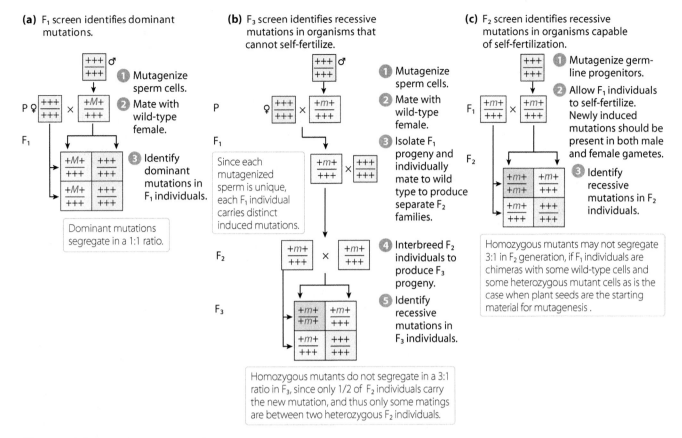

(a) F_1 screen identifies dominant mutations.

(b) F_3 screen identifies recessive mutations in organisms that cannot self-fertilize.

(c) F_2 screen identifies recessive mutations in organisms capable of self-fertilization.

Figure 16.2   Mutagenesis strategies.

screen (**Figure 16.2b**). In this screen, each F_1 individual derived from the mating of mutagenized males with wild-type females carries unique mutations. The F_1 individuals are then crossed with wild-type females, producing an F_2 generation in which 1/2 of the individuals will carry the newly induced mutations. The F_2 siblings are interbred, producing an F_3 population segregating for individuals that are homozygous for the induced mutation. The interbreeding of the F_2 to produce homozygous mutant F_3 is inefficient, since only half of the F_2 are heterozygous for the induced mutation. Nonetheless, such mutagenesis strategies are employed with many species, such as mice and zebrafish.

Identification of recessive mutations is somewhat simpler in organisms that self-fertilize, such as *Caenorhabditis elegans* and many plants (e.g., *Arabidopsis* and maize). In these organisms, F_1 individuals are self-fertilized to produce an F_2 generation from which recessive mutations can be identified. An example of an F_2 screen is shown in **Figure 16.2c**. In either an F_2 or F_3 screen, mutations resulting in homozygous lethality can be maintained in heterozygous siblings.

Use of Balancer Chromosomes for Tracking Mutations
The inefficiency of an F_3 screen can be circumvented using chromosomes that are marked so they can be followed through generations. **Balancer chromosomes** developed in *Drosophila* allow specific chromosomes to be transmitted intact and followed through multiple generations.

Balancer chromosomes have three general features: (1) one or more inverted chromosomal segments, within which meiotic recombinants are not transmitted (see Section 13.5 for a review); (2) a recessive allele that results in lethality, so an individual cannot be homozygous for the balancer chromosome; and (3) a "mark" in the form of a dominant mutation conferring a visible nonlethal phenotype, so the segregation of the chromosome can be followed through generations. An example of a balancer chromosome is the *ClB* chromosome used by Hermann Muller to demonstrate that X-rays induce mutations (see Experimental Insight 13.1).

Balancer chromosomes are available for all of the *Drosophila* chromosomes and can be used to identify mutations on specific chromosomes (**Figure 16.3**). Male flies are fed EMS to induce mutations and then are mated with females containing a balancer chromosome. Note that while mutations are induced throughout the genome, only those on the homolog of the balancer chromosome are analyzed. Male F_1 progeny are selected that inherit a mutagenized chromosome from their father and the balancer chromosome from their mother. Next, the selected males are mated to females of the balancer stock, producing F_2 progeny. The F_2 generation consists of both males and females heterozygous for the induced mutation and can be interbred to produce F_3 progeny. In the F_3 generation, 25% should be homozygous for the induced mutation and will not carry the dominant allele of the balancer

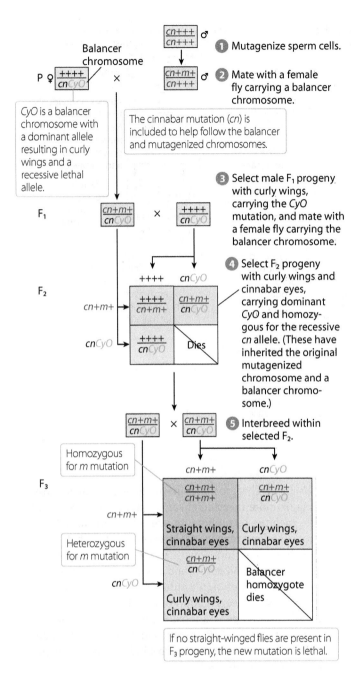

Figure 16.3 **Identifying recessive mutations in *Drosophila* using a balancer chromosome.**

colleagues in a screen to identify *Drosophila* mutations that disrupt pattern formation during embryogenesis. The research is described in detail in Section 20.2.

Screening for Conditional Alleles in Haploid Organisms

The use of haploid organisms in a forward genetic screen has the advantage of allowing both recessive loss-of-function mutations and dominant mutations to be identified directly. With single-celled organisms, a population of mitotically active cells can be mutagenized, and mutants with an altered phenotype can be selected directly in the colonies derived from the mutagenized cells. A disadvantage is that mutations disrupting essential processes in growth and physiology are often lethal, interfering with the propagation of alleles and thus complicating genetic screening. Fortunately, it is often feasible to design a screen to identify conditional mutant alleles of essential genes. In conditional mutants, the encoded gene product is either functional or not needed under one environmental condition—the **permissive condition**—but is required and either inactive or absent under another—the **restrictive condition** (see Section 4.1).

With some lethal mutations, the mutant phenotype can be rescued by addition of a needed substance to the growth medium. For example, histidine auxotrophic mutants can grow only when histidine is present in the growth medium. In a screen for conditional mutants of this type, the mutagenized population is initially grown under permissive conditions—in this case, in a medium containing histidine—so that both mutant and wild type will grow. This mutagenized population is then replica plated, and the population is screened for phenotypic defects (e.g., lethality) when grown under the restrictive condition (e.g., a lack of histidine). Such genetic screens were performed by Beadle and Tatum to identify auxotrophs in *Neurospora* in the research that established biochemical genetics and produced the one gene–one enzyme theory (see Section 4.3).

Some kinds of mutants can be rescued not by supplying a certain substance to the medium but by altering other kinds of environmental conditions instead. In temperature-sensitive mutants, the stability of the polypeptide product of a mutant allele differs with temperature (see Section 4.1), often as a result of a missense mutation.

This type of conditional lethal allele in the yeasts *S. cerevisiae* and *Schizosaccharomyces pombe* led to a molecular genetic understanding of the cell cycle, a biological process shared by all eukaryotes. Mutagenized yeast were grown at a permissive temperature to allow propagation, and then the mutant lines were exposed to a restrictive temperature, causing an arrest in growth of some of the mutant strains (**Figure 16.4a**). Surprisingly, in some mutant lines, growth was arrested at specific stages of the cell cycle, rather than randomly along the continuous spectrum of growth (the latter would be expected if the mutation had disrupted a metabolic pathway). These yeast mutants fell into discrete phenotypic categories defined by the stage of the cell cycle at which they were

chromosome; 50% will be heterozygous for the newly induced mutation and also carry the dominant allele; and the remaining 25% will die due to homozygosity for the balancer chromosome. The homozygous progeny lacking the dominant allele from the balancer chromosome can be screened for an aberrant phenotype.

What happens if the new mutation results in lethality when it is homozygous? In that case, all surviving F₃ individuals will carry the dominant allele, located on the balancer chromosome. When a lethal mutation is identified in this way, the mutant allele can be propagated from the heterozygous siblings. This mutagenesis strategy was used by Eric Wieschaus, Christiane Nüsslein-Volhard, and

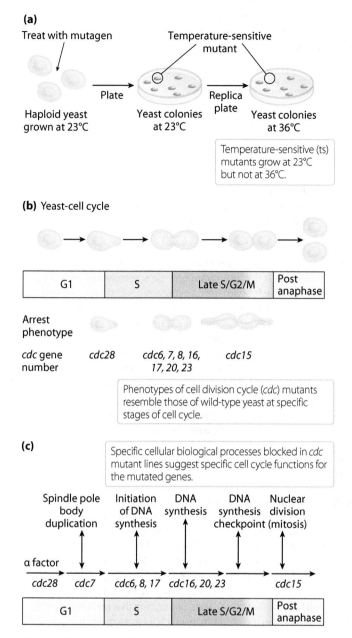

Figure 16.4 **Identification and analysis of conditional alleles.**

identified in the mutagenesis? (3) How many different mutant alleles of each gene have been identified?

Determining Dominance or Recessiveness The answer to the first question provides insight into whether the mutant allele likely represents a loss of function or a gain of function (see Sections 4.1 and 12.2 for descriptions of these categories). Dominance or recessiveness, which is assessed during the mutagenesis, is confirmed using the same approach Mendel employed. Individuals homozygous for the new mutations are crossed with the wild-type strain in which the mutagenesis was performed. The phenotype in the F_1 progeny derived from the cross allows the mutant allele to be designated as dominant or recessive.

Determining the Numbers of Genes Identified The answer to the second question—about the number of different genes revealed—provides clues to how many genes are involved in the biological process of interest. The most straightforward method of determining the number of genes represented by a new collection of mutants that produce similar mutant phenotypes is to perform complementation tests between different pairs of the mutant lines. If the progeny produced by crossing two recessive mutant lines exhibit a mutant phenotype, then the two mutations are in the same gene, whereas if the progeny exhibit a wild-type phenotype, then the two mutations are in different genes (see Section 4.4). In practice, we can limit the number of crosses by recognizing that complementation is communicative; that is, if mutation A is allelic to mutation B, and mutation B is allelic to mutation C, then mutations A and C are allelic. In some special cases, such as with mutations that are dominant or gametophytically lethal (lethal in a haploid stage of the life cycle, e.g., in pollen; see Section 4.1), complementation experiments cannot easily be performed, and other methods to ascertain allelism, such as mapping (see Section 5.2), may be employed.

Determining the Number of Mutant Alleles Identified for a Gene The answer to the third question should follow from the complementation analysis. Obtaining multiple mutant alleles of each gene is useful for two reasons. Comparing mutant phenotypes of multiple alleles allows an assessment of the range of phenotypic variation that can be obtained by mutation of the gene in question (see Section 4.1). The recovery of multiple alleles for each gene also provides information on the saturation of the genetic screen; in other words, it suggests what percentage of the genes that could be identified have in fact been identified. When a mutagenesis experiment is shown to have produced multiple independent mutations in each gene identified, most genes in the process of interest have likely been mutated.

Genetic Analysis 16.1 challenges you to design a screen that identifies genes involved in a particular biological process.

arrested. One possible explanation was the existence of specific checkpoints in the cell cycle (**Figure 16.4b**), and, indeed, some of the genes identified by these mutations were found to regulate the cell's progression through various stages of the cell cycle (**Figure 16.4c**). The studies in yeast provided the foundation for understanding the role of cell cycle regulation in cancer (see Section 3.1).

Analysis of Mutageneses

Typically, the initial analysis of mutants obtained by mutagenesis will focus on three key questions: (1) Are mutant alleles dominant or recessive with respect to the wild-type allele? (2) How many different genes have been

PROBLEM In all eukaryotic organisms, proteins to be secreted from the cell or embedded in the plasma membrane are translated at the endoplasmic reticulum and travel via the Golgi apparatus to reach the plasma membrane. Outline a genetic screen for identifying genes involved in protein secretion.

> BREAK IT DOWN: These post-translational processing steps can be reviewed in Section 9.6 (p. 330).

> BREAK IT DOWN: In planning a mutagenesis, what type of organism and mutagen are appropriate?

Solution Strategies	Solution Steps
Evaluate	
1. Identify the topic this problem addresses and the nature of the required answer.	1. This problem is about designing a genetic screen to find a certain type of gene.
2. Identify the critical information given in the problem.	2. Information is given about protein secretion in cells, a universal process among eukaryotes. The purpose of the screen is to identify mutations in genes that function in that process.
Deduce	
3. Consider any information given about genes involved in the secretory process. TIP: Consider experimental approaches that do not require prior knowledge of gene function.	3. Since we have not been given any information about the genes involved in protein secretion, a forward genetic screen would be a good approach because forward genetic mutageneses do not depend on prior knowledge about biochemical functions or gene sequences.
4. Based on the chapter discussion of forward genetic screens, choose an appropriate organism. TIP: In which organisms does the biological process occur?	4. Since secretory systems in all eukaryotes are similar, they are likely to be homologous, that is, inherited from a common ancestor. Thus we can choose any eukaryote amenable to genetic analysis. *Saccharomyces cerevisiae* would be a good choice because many genetic tools already exist for this model genetic organism.
5. Based on the chapter discussion of designing a forward genetic screen and on the phenotypic consequence of a loss of protein secretion, pick a strategy for identifying desirable mutant alleles. PITFALL: Avoid the possibility of mutations that are lethal under all growth conditions.	5. Because complete loss of a functioning secretory system is likely to be lethal to any organism, we should use a strategy to identify conditional mutant alleles. Thus we should use a mutagen that induces point mutations.
Solve	
6. Design an approach for a genetic screen based on Solution Steps 3–5.	6. A good design would be one similar to the procedure used to identify temperature-sensitive mutant alleles in genes of the cell cycle in *S. cerevisiae*. Mutagenesis of haploid cells could be performed at a permissive temperature (e.g., 25–30°C), followed by screening for mutant phenotypes at a restrictive temperature (e.g., 39°C).
7. Describe how you would identify mutations specifically affecting secretion.	7. A method to monitor secretion is required. One approach would be to select a protein known to be secreted into the growth media of wild-type *S. cerevisiae* and look for mutants that do not secrete that protein (i.e., the protein is not detected in the medium in which they are growing).

For more practice, see Problems 12, 13, 14, 18, 19, and 21. | Visit the Study Area to access study tools.

MasteringGenetics™

Identifying Interacting and Redundant Genes Using Modifier Screens

Generally, mutant phenotypes reflect the response of the organism to a loss or change of a particular gene product. However, individual genes do not act in isolation. The activity of other genes may modify, by either enhancing or suppressing, the phenotypic defects caused by the loss of a gene product. One approach to discovering genetic interactions is to carry out a genetic **modifier screen** to see if mutations in a second gene can enhance or suppress the phenotype of the first mutation. An **enhancer screen** is a modifier screen in which mutations in a second site enhance the phenotype of the initial mutant. A **suppressor screen** is a modifier screen designed to identify second-site mutations that suppress the phenotype of the initial genotype. Note that both types of screens can be performed simultaneously. Enhancer–suppressor screening strategies are almost limitless in number and sophistication and have the potential to identify genes that function in interacting genetic pathways.

Modifier screens can identify double mutants that display an unexpected phenotype, one that is not simply the combination of the phenotypes of the two single mutants. In perhaps the most dramatic form of enhancement, termed **synthetic lethality,** the two single mutants are viable but the double mutant is inviable.

Synthetic lethality, or synthetic enhancement, was first noted by *Drosophila* geneticists who observed that some pairwise combinations of mutant alleles were inviable. For example, when Alfred Sturtevant crossed *prune* (*pn*) mutant females (*pn* is on the X chromosome) with males from a stock of separate origin called S/E-S, he noted that the progeny consisted solely of *pn*⁺ females and no viable males (**Figure 16.5a**). Sturtevant determined that the S/E-S males carried an autosomal dominant mutation, which he called *Prune-killer* (*K-pn*), that in combination with *pn* results in lethality, but he noted that flies homozygous for *K-pn* mutation alone did not have an aberrant phenotype. In his cross, all male progeny inherited a *pn* allele from their mother and a *K-pn* allele from their father, and therefore these progeny died. In contrast, the female progeny were viable, since despite inheriting a *K-pn* allele from their father, they also inherited a *pn*⁺ allele from their father. In this example, both *pn* and *K-pn* mutants are viable, but the *pn, K-pn* double mutant results in lethality.

Figure 16.5b shows two possible mechanisms to explain synthetic lethality. In one mechanism, the two genes in question act in parallel complementary pathways. In this scenario, mutations resulting in the loss of either pathway can be compensated for by the activity of the remaining pathway. However, when both pathways are disrupted, a dramatic enhancement in mutant phenotype is observed. An alternative mechanism is possible when both genes are acting in the same pathway: A reduction in function of one component of the pathway results in a mild phenotype, but when two components are disrupted, the pathway no longer functions effectively. Note that in the latter scenario, hypomorphic alleles can result in synthetic enhancement, but null alleles cannot.

The first scenario, where two genes act in parallel, is an example of **genetic redundancy,** where the loss of the function of either gene alone is compensated for by the activity of the other nonmutant gene. Only when both genes are mutant would a conspicuous mutant phenotype be evident. In such a case, a 15:1 segregation ratio could be expected in the F₂ of a cross between the two recessive single mutants (see Section 4.3). In the most obvious case of genetic redundancy, two genes encode very similar proteins that can function interchangeably. In many instances, the activities of the two genes do not fully compensate for one another, such that single mutations, in either gene alone, result in a mild phenotype, while a severe phenotype is seen when both genes are mutant. Genetic redundancy caused by the presence of duplicate genes can arise through small-scale duplications or through whole-genome duplications. As we explore in detail in Chapter 18, genome sequences of eukaryotes show such duplications to be very common.

(a) Sturtevant's cross identifying synthetic lethality

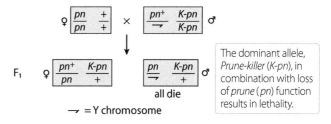

→ = Y chromosome

> The dominant allele, *Prune-killer* (*K-pn*), in combination with loss of *prune* (*pn*) function results in lethality.

(b) Possible mechanisms for synthetic enhancement

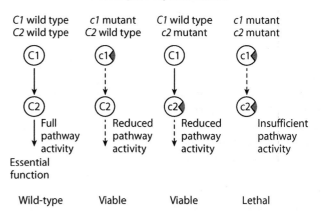

©2007 Macmillan Publishers Ltd

Figure 16.5   Synthetic enhancement.

Genetic redundancy can also arise from the compensatory action of genes that have little or no sequence similarity and encode biochemically different activities. This type of genetic redundancy is difficult to predict on the basis of the DNA sequences of the genes, but it too can be uncovered by enhancer–suppressor screens. Enhancer–suppressor screens have been performed on many organisms, including *Drosophila, C. elegans, Arabidopsis,* and mice (see Section 18.3), and are extremely successful at identifying interacting genetic pathways (see Section 20.3).

16.2 Genes Identified by Mutant Phenotype Are Cloned Using Recombinant DNA Technology

While genes can be identified by genetic screens, determination of the specific DNA sequences of the wild-type and mutant alleles requires the *cloning*, or large-scale copying, of the gene, using recombinant DNA techniques to manipulate DNA molecules in vitro and in vivo. In this section, we discuss the theoretical foundations of how cloning of specific genes is achieved.

To appreciate the magnitude of the task of cloning a specific gene, consider that the goal is to identify the particular gene responsible for the mutant phenotype from among the thousands (or tens of thousands, in the cases of many eukaryotes) in the organism's genome, the proverbial needle in a haystack. Because both the biology and the ease of manipulation vary depending on the organism, different approaches have been developed for different species. In this section, we describe four of those approaches.

Although recombinant DNA technology is discussed in detail in Chapter 17, we preview here two aspects of the technology that are required for explaining how genes are cloned. First, gene sequences created in vitro can be introduced into the genome of a living organism. Such genes are termed **transgenes,** and the resulting organism is a **transgenic organism.** As this process is similar to the transformation of bacteria—that is, the uptake of free DNA from outside the cell to inside the cell (see Chapter 6)—the creation of a transgenic organism is also referred to as transformation. The ease with which this process is accomplished varies significantly between organisms and thus influences strategies for gene cloning.

A second key aspect is the creation of libraries, collections of clones of DNA fragments, derived from the total DNA or mRNA isolated from an organism. A library is a set of recombinant DNA molecules that collectively includes clones of all the relevant DNA sequences of an organism.

Genomic libraries are collections of cloned DNA fragments that as a group represent the entire genome of an organism, including repetitive and noncoding sequences. Genomic libraries usually consist of tens to hundreds of thousands of clones, each carried within an individual **cloning vector**—usually a plasmid (see Section 6.1) or bacteriophage (see Section 6.5) that has been modified to accommodate the insertion of exogenous fragments of DNA and that can be stably maintained in a host, such as *E. coli.* Genomic libraries are often constructed in a cloning vector such as a **bacterial artificial chromosome (BAC),** which can carry large pieces, greater than 100 kb, of genomic DNA. The BACs are then propagated in bacteria. A collection of many thousands of BAC-containing bacterial colonies, each of which harbors a BAC containing a different fragment of the genome, makes up the genomic library.

In contrast, **cDNA libraries** are collections of cloned DNA fragments that represent all the mRNA produced by an organism. In other words, only that portion of the genome that is transcribed is represented in a cDNA library. The clones of a cDNA library are also placed in cloning vectors, such as specially modified plasmids, and introduced into bacteria so that the complete cDNA library is composed of a large number of bacterial colonies, each of which harbors a different cDNA clone derived from the mRNA population.

Within a library, clones containing specific DNA sequences can be identified through complementary base pairing in a manner similar to that described in Research Technique 10.2 and in more detail in Chapter 17. With awareness of these tools, we can now consider the four approaches that are the focus of this section and whose purpose is to physically identify specific genes.

- First, genes can be identified by introducing a wild-type copy of a gene to complement a recessive mutant phenotype.

- A second approach is to use a piece of DNA, such as a transposon, with a known sequence to "tag" the gene of interest. The tag can then be used to identify flanking sequences, DNA on either side of the tag, that contain the gene.

- A third approach is to map the gene of interest relative to known genetic markers (see Chapter 5), then to identify DNA clones spanning the locus, and finally to search through the DNA for the gene of interest.

- Lastly, advances in DNA sequencing technology have made it feasible to obtain genes identified in genetic screens by directly comparing the genome sequence of the mutant with that of the wild-type strain from which it was derived.

Cloning Genes by Complementation

The most direct approach to identifying specific genes is to detect genetic complementation of a mutant phenotype by an introduced wild-type gene. This approach is restricted to cases in which large numbers of transgenic organisms can be generated. Consider the yeast temperature-sensitive cell-cycle mutants described in Section 16.1. If clones of a yeast cDNA expression library are transformed into a yeast cell-cycle mutant, any clones that complement the mutant phenotype so that the cells grow normally should contain wild-type alleles of the mutated gene (**Figure 16.6**). In a procedure of this type, the yeast strain would first be transformed and grown at the permissive temperature. The resulting yeast colonies would then be transferred to an environment maintained at the restrictive temperature. Only the yeast colonies receiving a clone encoding a wild-type version of the mutant gene in question would be able to continue growth at the restrictive temperature; in those colonies, the

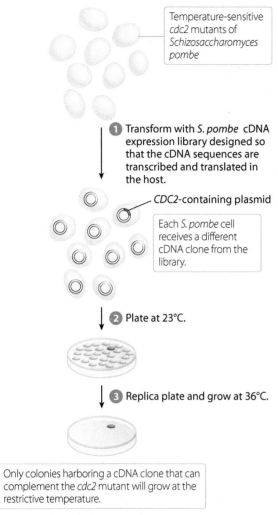

1 Transform with *S. pombe* cDNA expression library designed so that the cDNA sequences are transcribed and translated in the host.

CDC2-containing plasmid

Each *S. pombe* cell receives a different cDNA clone from the library.

2 Plate at 23°C.

3 Replica plate and grow at 36°C.

Only colonies harboring a cDNA clone that can complement the *cdc2* mutant will grow at the restrictive temperature.

Figure 16.6   Cloning by complementation.

mutant phenotype would have been complemented by the added gene.

Complementation experiments can also be used to identify similar genes from other species, if there is sufficient conservation of protein function. For example, research in which a yeast cell-cycle mutant was transformed using a human cDNA expression library (one in which the human cDNA clones were first fused with sequences allowing for their transcription and translation in yeast) has led to identification of human genes similar in function to the mutated yeast genes. The fact that both human and plant genes can complement these yeast mutants demonstrates the universality of the cell-cycle machinery and indicates that such proteins were present in the common ancestor of eukaryotes.

Using Transposons to Clone Genes

Transposons can be used as an identifying tag to clone specific genes, a technique called **transposon tagging.** Recall that transposons are mobile genetic elements that

can integrate into the genome with little if any target-sequence specificity (see Chapter 13). If the sequence of a transposon is known, the transposon sequence can be used to probe a genomic library constructed from DNA of a strain in which the same transposon has been inserted into a target gene. Sequences adjacent to the transposon should belong to the target gene.

The fact that the sequence of a transposon must first be known if the transposon is to be used as a probe is a chicken-and-egg problem similar to others we have encountered with probes. A solution in this particular case is to "trap" the transposon in a gene whose sequence is already known. Recall that allele instability is characteristic of transposon insertion (see Chapter 13). If researchers first identify unstable mutant alleles of a cloned gene—alleles likely to contain a transposon—they can then use a probe for that cloned gene to isolate the transposon sequence.

For transposon tagging to succeed in practice, the biology of transposons must be considered. Since transposons often occur in high copy numbers in the genome, techniques are necessary to distinguish the copy of the transposon in the target gene from all other copies of the transposon in the genome. The ideal situation is to begin with a genotype harboring only a single copy or a low copy number of a transposon of known sequence and then mobilize the transposon to create a mutant collection, which is then screened for phenotypes.

Also to be considered is that, since transposons are mobile, a transposon that has been inserted into the target gene may jump out again. To circumvent this problem, the transposon that is used as a tag is often separated into two components—the transposase and the inverted repeats whose sequence the transposase recognizes (see Section 13.5). The inverted repeats form the functional part of a nonautonomous element that cannot move on its own but can be mobilized if transposase is supplied in trans. Ideally, the transposase activity is produced from a mutant transposon that is not capable of moving because it lacks the inverted repeats. The new insertions of the nonautonomous transposon can be stabilized by removal of the transposase source through outcrossing.

A general protocol for using a transposon to tag a gene in a diploid eukaryote is shown in **Figure 16.7**. Two lines are initially crossed, one of which is homozygous for a stable mutant allele of the target gene and the second of which carries an active transposon system and is homozygous for the wild-type allele of the target gene. The F_1 of this cross is heterozygous for the mutant allele of the target gene in a genomic background with an active transposon. If the transposon moves into the gene of interest, thus creating a second mutant allele, the F_1 individual will display the homozygous recessive mutant phenotype. Screening of a large number of F_1 individuals is usually required to find any with new transposon-induced mutations in the target gene, since transposon movement into a specific gene is

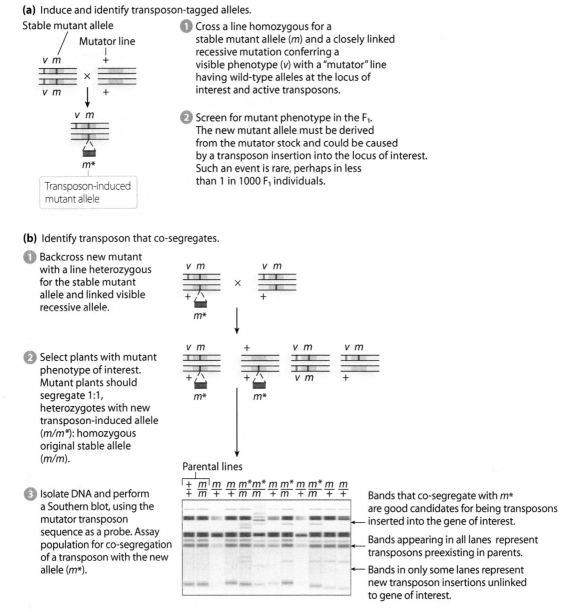

Figure 16.7 **Use of transposons for tagging genes.**

a rare event. Once a transposon-induced allele is identified, the causative transposon can be cloned and the DNA flanking the causative transposon should represent the gene of interest.

Transposon tagging is limited to organisms that harbor active transposons or into which an active transposon can be introduced from another species. However, this limitation is not often a problem since, for example, the maize Ac/Ds transposon system (see Section 13.5), when introduced on a transgene, is active in other plant species, such as *Arabidopsis* and tomato, and is even active in zebrafish. We will return to the use of transposons to mutate genes when we discuss reverse genetics.

Positional Cloning

The approaches to cloning genes we have discussed thus far are not applicable to all organisms, as they rely on either a high efficiency of transformation (available in many bacteria and some fungi) or on active transposons. When these tools are not available, how do biologists find the DNA sequence for a gene that is known only by its mutant phenotype? They do it by combining a genetic map made from recombination frequencies (Chapter 5) with a physical map of the genome based on DNA clones, or, when available, the genome sequence in order to find the DNA sequence at a specific map position. Figure 16.8 provides an overview of the relationships between genetic

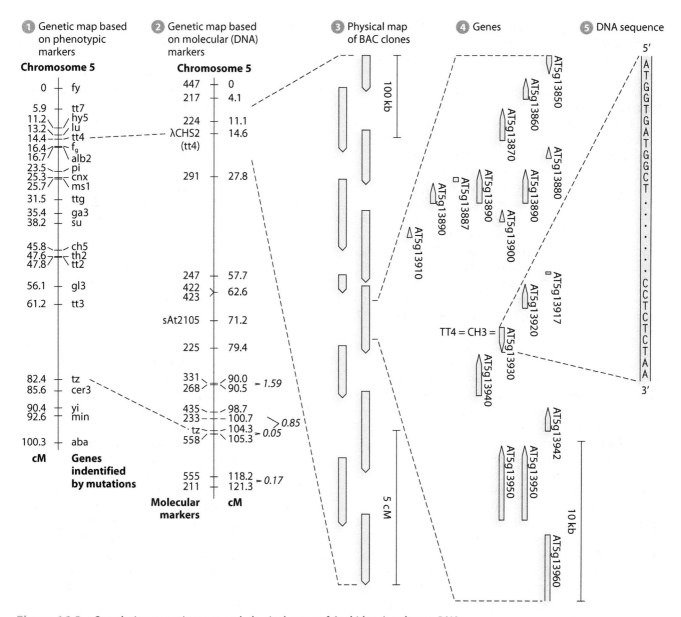

Figure 16.8 Correlating genetic maps and physical maps of *Arabidopsis* to locate DNA sequences of genes.

maps based on the segregation of genetic loci, physical maps based on sets of overlapping genomic clones, genes, and the DNA sequence of the genome. If two molecular (DNA) markers are identified that flank the gene of interest, the gene must reside in the intervening DNA. The DNA for the gene can ultimately be identified by isolating a set of DNA clones that collectively span the region between the flanking markers. This approach is referred to as **positional cloning,** or **chromosome walking,** since it consists of "walking" along the chromosome in sequential steps, from one flanking marker toward the other, by joining overlapping DNA clones (as described below).

Positional cloning is done in three steps. The first step is to construct a genetic map (map ❶ in Figure 16.8) that shows the location of the gene of interest relative to mapped DNA markers (map ❷ in Figure 16.8 consists

of markers). The second step is to identify DNA clones (map ❸ of Figure 16.8) that span the markers flanking the gene of interest. The third step is to identify the gene of interest (see examples in map ❹ of Figure 16.8) within the spanning DNA and determine its nucleotide sequence (map ❺ of Figure 16.8).

Step 1: Constructing a Genetic Map Using DNA Markers In 1980, a landmark paper by David Botstein and colleagues proposed an idea for using DNA markers as the basis of a genetic map for the purpose of performing positional cloning of human genes. In the decades that followed, the cloning of many human "disease genes" was accomplished using this protocol. Even now that the human genome has been sequenced, a similar mapping protocol continues to be used for gene identification in humans, and the general approach to positional cloning, as described here, can be applied to any organism.

The key to positional cloning is to identify molecular markers flanking the gene you wish to clone. The flanking DNA markers define the two ends of the DNA sequence within which the gene of interest is located. Any DNA sequence that varies between individuals can potentially be a DNA marker, including single-nucleotide polymorphisms (SNPs), restriction fragment length polymorphisms (RFLPs), small insertions or deletions, and various repeating DNA sequence variants (see Chapter 10). Once a collection of polymorphic DNA markers has been identified, detecting the segregation of these markers in a "mapping population" will allow placement of each marker at a particular location in the genome. Map construction with molecular markers follows the same procedure as with phenotypic markers (see Chapter 5); different DNA markers that co-segregate are physically linked, with a recombination frequency proportional to the distance in map units between them.

To examine how mapping works, let's take an example from *Arabidopsis* in which a gene is mapped in an F_2 population (Figure 16.9). The first step in the construction of a genetic map is to identify two strains that differ in DNA sequence; in this case, the strains were Landsberg (L) and Columbia (C). Each strain is highly homozygous due to inbreeding, yet they differ from each other at polymorphic loci throughout the genome.

The mapping population is generated by crossing the two homozygous lines to produce an F_1 generation that is heterozygous at all loci that differ between the two inbred lines. These F_1 individuals are then interbred or allowed to self-fertilize. At each locus in the genome, individuals in the resulting F_2 population can be either homozygous for alleles of one or the other of the original inbred lines, or they can be heterozygous. Alleles for the gene of interest, in this case *AP2*, are also segregating in the F_2 population, since one parent (L) was homozygous for a recessive *ap2* mutant allele while the other parent (C) was homozygous for the wild-type *AP2* allele.

The genotypes of each F_2 individual are determined for the DNA markers and the gene of interest. DNA markers that co-segregate with the mutation are linked to the gene of interest, and their distances from the gene is proportional to the recombination frequency; unlinked DNA markers should segregate independently of the mutation. In most cases, the alleles of DNA markers are codominant, so that examination of DNA allows direct determination of genotype. In contrast, only F_2 individuals homozygous for a recessive mutation in the gene of interest can be accurately genotyped, and the genotype of phenotypically wild-type F_2 individuals has to be determined in the F_3 or by a test cross. While this example comes from a model genetic system, genetic mapping in humans with molecular markers follows a similar protocol (see Section 5.5).

Because the number of DNA sequence differences between two strains is likely to be greater than the total number of genes in the organism, genetic maps based on DNA markers are often dense enough for flanking markers closely linked to the gene of interest to be identified. Once DNA markers are found that flank the gene of interest, the next step of identifying the DNA between the markers can proceed.

Step 2: Constructing Contiguous Sequences of DNA
Before the advent of genome sequencing projects, researchers were forced to assemble the DNA spanning two markers by constructing **contiguous sequences (contigs)** from sets of overlapping genomic clones (Figure 16.10). The DNA markers flanking the gene of interest ❶ can be used as probes on a genomic library to identify genomic clones that contain the DNA markers ❷. The ends of these genomic clones can be used to probe the genomic library again to identify clones that overlap the initial clones ❸. Reiteration of this process will identify additional overlapping genomic clones (contigs) extending in both directions from the initial two flanking DNA markers. Extension in one direction reveals sequences closer to the gene of interest, and extension in the other direction reveals sequences farther from the gene of interest.

How is the directionality of the chromosome "walk" determined? Genetic mapping of polymorphic DNA sequences in the newly isolated genomic clones can resolve the directionality of the overlapping genomic clones ❹. If the end of the genomic clone maps closer to the gene of interest than to the initial DNA marker, the directionality is toward the target gene. Conversely, if the end of the genomic clone maps farther from the gene of interest than from the initial DNA marker, the directionality is away from the target gene. Once directionality is ascertained, reiterative probing of genomic libraries in the direction approaching the gene, using the sequences at the ends of newly isolated genomic clones, allows the construction of ever-larger contigs that should eventually span the entire DNA sequence between the two flanking DNA markers ❺.

The availability of genome sequences for many model genetic organisms has simplified positional cloning. With these species, the construction of a contig is not required, so once the gene of interest has been mapped, the researcher can proceed directly to the identification of candidate genes in the genome sequence spanning the mapped interval, as described below.

Step 3: From Contig to Gene A contig spanning two markers that flank a gene of interest must, by definition, include the target gene, but how do we find the gene of interest among the other genes in the contig ❻? The answer depends to a large degree on the organism under study. If the genome sequence is known, the number and identity of candidate genes—that is, sequences

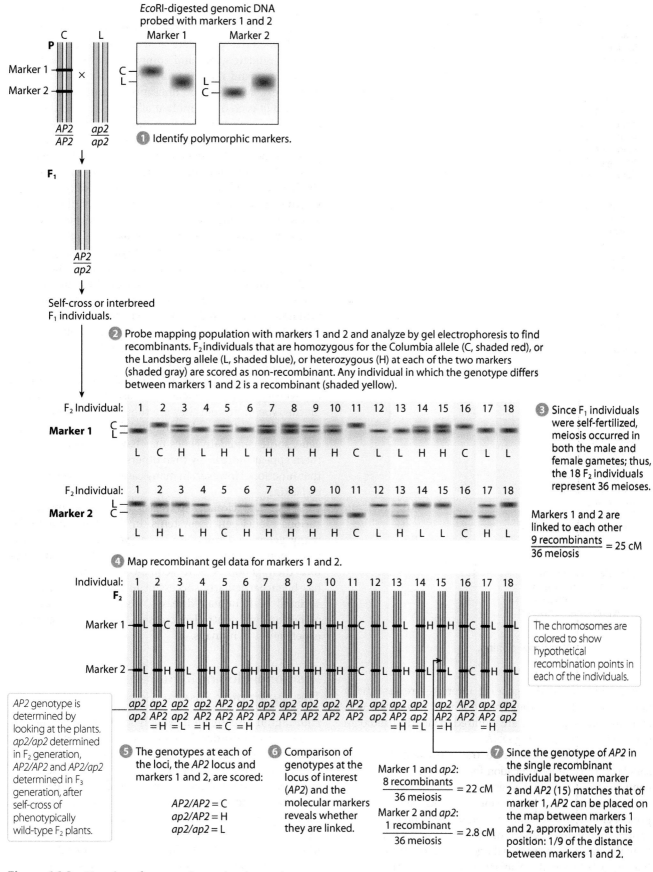

Figure 16.9   Mapping of genes using molecular markers.

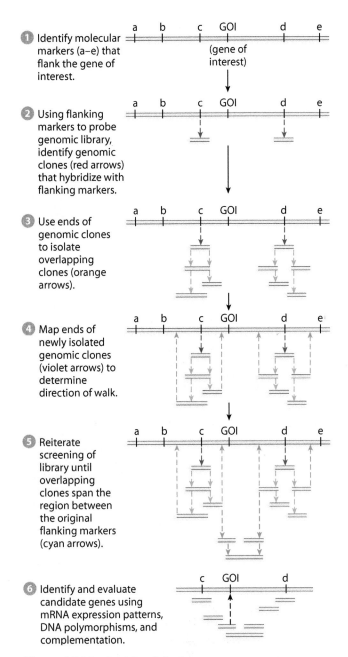

1. Identify molecular markers (a–e) that flank the gene of interest.

2. Using flanking markers to probe genomic library, identify genomic clones (red arrows) that hybridize with flanking markers.

3. Use ends of genomic clones to isolate overlapping clones (orange arrows).

4. Map ends of newly isolated genomic clones (violet arrows) to determine direction of walk.

5. Reiterate screening of library until overlapping clones span the region between the original flanking markers (cyan arrows).

6. Identify and evaluate candidate genes using mRNA expression patterns, DNA polymorphisms, and complementation.

Figure 16.10 Positional cloning.

In organisms not amenable to transformation (e.g., humans), other approaches can be used to identify and characterize candidate genes. First, direct sequencing of candidate genes and comparison of the sequences in wild-type and mutant individuals can reveal the gene of interest. Missense or nonsense mutations might be expected in each of the mutant alleles relative to the wild-type allele. However, because mutations outside of the coding region may be responsible for the altered gene expression, noncoding sequences may have to be surveyed as well. Note that for non-inbred species, if there is only a single mutant allele to examine, it may be difficult to tell whether differences in the DNA sequences of candidate genes are the cause of the mutant phenotype or simply polymorphisms existing in the population.

A second approach to identifying the target gene where transformation is not possible is to use the nature of the phenotypic defect conferred by the mutant allele as a source of clues to probable gene expression patterns. Candidate genes can then be assayed for those expression patterns in specific cells and tissues. It may also be possible to detect changes in RNA expression patterns—for example, mutations resulting in altered patterns of splicing or those resulting in mRNA that is less stable than the wild-type mRNA. Genes can also be surveyed based on the type of protein they are thought to encode. If it is possible to predict the biochemical function of the target gene, some candidate genes may have features that make them appear more likely than others to be able to perform that function. However, in many cases this knowledge will be lacking.

Positional cloning strategies have been applied to various model genetic systems. In the 1980s and 1990s, many genes in *Drosophila, C. elegans,* and *Arabidopsis* were identified by positional cloning protocols, long before their genomes were sequenced. Positional cloning has been particularly successful in identifying genes associated with human diseases, despite the infeasibility of performing controlled crosses and complementation experiments in humans.

Positional Cloning in Humans: The Huntington Disease Gene

Huntington disease, an inevitably fatal, late-onset neurodegenerative disorder, is named for George Huntington, the physician who published the classic description of the disease and its inheritance in 1872. His description specified the symptoms of movement disorder, personality change, and cognitive decline and, notably, outlined the autosomal dominant pattern of inheritance, a feature that went unappreciated until after the rediscovery of Mendel's work in 1900. Huntington recognized the pattern of inheritance thanks to the combined experience of his father and grandfather, both also physicians, who had the unique opportunity of observing several generations

that could encode the gene of interest—are essentially known. In contrast, if the genome sequence is not known, experimental approaches are required to identify candidate genes within the spanning DNA.

In organisms amenable to transformation, the "gold standard" of gene identification for positional cloning is to complement the mutant phenotype by introducing a copy of the wild-type allele into the mutant background. This approach is similar to cloning by complementation described earlier, except the number of candidate genes is reduced from the entire set of genes in the genome to only those genes that map between the flanking markers. Transformation experiments are routine in many model genetic organisms and are described in more detail in Chapter 17.

of the disease in a local family. He did not encounter the juvenile onset form of the disease, however, which presents additional symptoms, such as rigidity and seizures. In a form of inheritance termed *anticipation*, juvenile-onset Huntington is inherited through a paternal allele.

Mapping of the *HD* Gene Researchers have compiled extensive pedigrees depicting the transmission of Huntington disease in a large family in Venezuela. The pedigrees span 10 generations and include nearly 20,000 individuals, many of whom are living. In the early 1980s, James Gusella and Susan Wexler and colleagues, studying this Venezuelan kindred as well as a large Ohio family, mapped the *HD* gene to the short arm of chromosome 4 (see the Chapter 5 Case Study for a similar mapping experiment). Additional polymorphic markers linked to dominant mutant alleles of the *HD* gene further confined it to a region of 2.2 Mb on chromosome 4. Mutant *HD* alleles were known from a large number of unrelated families from diverse genetic backgrounds, suggesting that dominant mutant *HD* alleles have arisen multiple times independently. Mapping data from 75 families identified a haplotype shared by about one-third of the families and suggested that the *HD* gene was likely to reside within 500 kb of the shared haplotype (step ❶ in Figure 16.11; see Chapter 5 for a discussion of haplotypes).

Candidate Gene Identification Before 2001, the year a draft of the human genome sequence was published, identification of genes in large stretches of human genomic sequence was an arduous task. To clone the *HD* gene in the early 1990s required construction of a contig of genomic clones spanning the *HD* locus, using the techniques described in Figure 16.10 for isolating overlapping genomic clones. To identify transcribed sequences within the 500-kb genomic region, a novel exon-trapping approach was used. Fragments of the genomic DNA were cloned into a vector, where they were flanked by two exons contained in the vector sequence. When assayed in human cells in culture, if the genomic DNA did not contain an exon, the two vector exons would become spliced together in post-transcriptional processing, generating a transcript of a defined size. However, if the cloned genomic DNA contained an exon, it would be spliced to the two flanking exons, creating a transcript of a larger size. This technique revealed the presence of four transcribed genes in the region.

Two approaches were undertaken to evaluate the candidate genes. First, the mRNA expression patterns of the genes were analyzed. However, no difference in expression patterns or levels for any of the four genes was detected between normal and HD individuals. Second, the candidate genes were examined for DNA polymorphisms (steps ❷ and ❸ in Figure 16.11). One of the candidate genes was polymorphic between individuals. A striking difference in the lengths of a trinucleotide repeat sequence

in exon 1 of this gene was observed; normal individuals had 17 to 34 copies of a CAG repeat, and HD individuals had from 42 to more than 66 copies. The same correlation was seen in all 75 families, strongly suggesting that this was the *HD* gene. As further supporting evidence, the length of the repeats in the HD individuals also correlated with the age of onset of disease symptoms.

The *HD* gene spans 210 kb, encoding an mRNA of more than 10 kb, and has an open reading frame of 9432 bases encoding a protein of 3144 amino acids. In this case, there is little in the protein sequence that provides a clue to function (and possible treatment). However, knowledge of the DNA sequence has provided a way of testing for the presence of the disease allele in families in which it is segregating. This information can be used in prenatal diagnostics to eliminate the allele from the next generation if therapeutic abortion is an option. While this test may seem to be a blessing, it introduces many ethical quandaries. Should one test a child for an adult-onset disease where there is no prospect for treatment or a cure at present? Might testing in a young adult inadvertently provide information about another individual, such as a parent, who does not wish to know his or her own genetic status?

Analysis of the polymorphic CAG repeat has also provided insight into the phenomenon of anticipation. The CAG alleles whose length approaches the high end of the normal range [$(CAG)_{27-35}$] are unstable during transmission and change size from one generation to the next. Instability occurs in both maternal and paternal inheritance, but large expansions have been noted only during male transmission; this explains why juvenile patients almost always inherit the mutant allele from their father. While the molecular basis of this gender bias has become apparent, the mechanistic basis is still unknown.

Genome Sequencing to Determine Gene Identification

The most direct way to identify the molecular nature of mutations might seem to be to compare the genome sequence of the mutant line with that of the wild-type strain from which it was derived. Such an approach would obviate the need for the often time-consuming and expensive steps involved in positional cloning. In theory, comparison of wild-type and mutant sequences should be straightforward, but there are both technical and experimental obstacles. First, in organisms like humans, it is difficult to distinguish between causative mutations and widespread polymorphisms. Second, even in inbred laboratory animals, typical mutagenesis protocols produce up to several hundred new mutations in each mutagenized gamete, introducing the need to backcross new mutant lines with their wild-type parental strain, as described earlier in this chapter, in order to isolate the causative mutation from the background of other mutations induced during the mutagenesis.

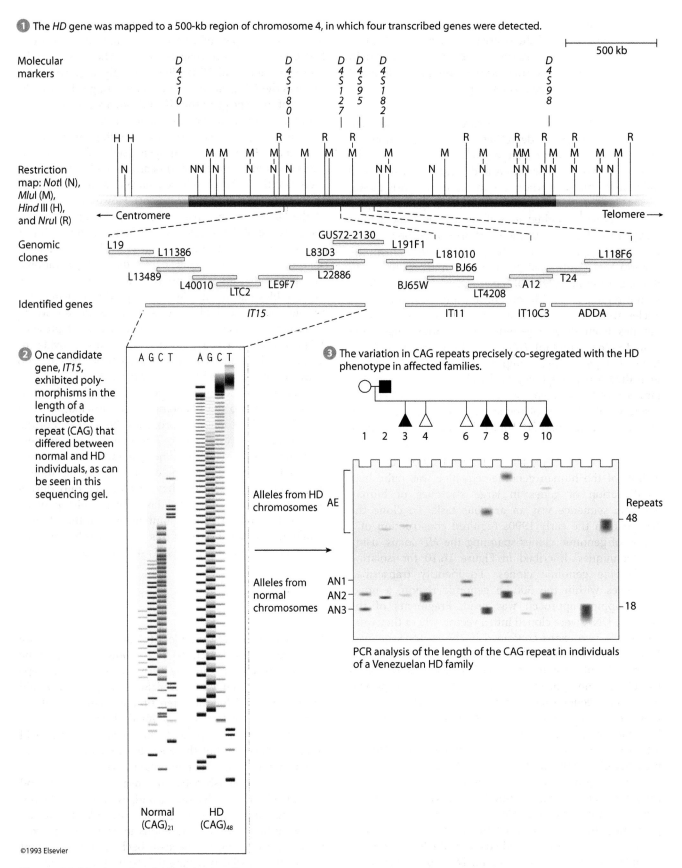

Figure 16.11   **Locating the Huntington disease gene.**

1 The *HD* gene was mapped to a 500-kb region of chromosome 4, in which four transcribed genes were detected.

2 One candidate gene, *IT15*, exhibited polymorphisms in the length of a trinucleotide repeat (CAG) that differed between normal and HD individuals, as can be seen in this sequencing gel.

3 The variation in CAG repeats precisely co-segregated with the HD phenotype in affected families.

PCR analysis of the length of the CAG repeat in individuals of a Venezuelan HD family

These obstacles can be overcome by simultaneously examining the genomes of many mutant organisms after backcrossing. The details of how genome sequencing is accomplished are described in Chapter 18, but a conceptual outline of its application to identify a gene originally defined by a mutant phenotype is presented in Figure 16.12. First, the newly identified mutant line is backcrossed

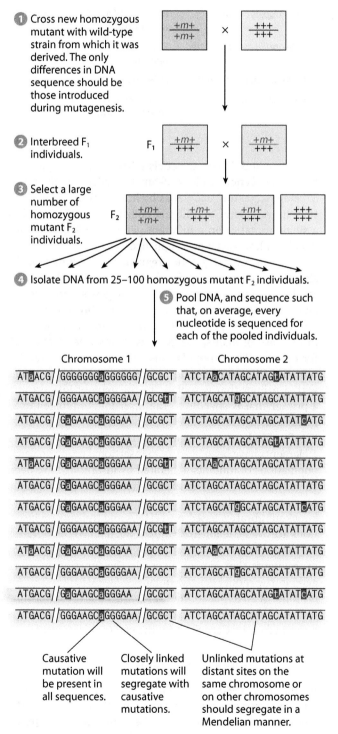

Figure 16.12   Genomics approach to gene identification following mutagenesis.

with the wild-type strain from which it was derived. The resulting F_1 individuals are interbred to produce an F_2 generation from which homozygous mutants can be selected. DNA is isolated from a number of homozygous mutants in the F_2 and is then pooled and sequenced in amounts sufficient to ensure that, on average, every nucleotide in the genome of each individual will be sequenced. The idea is that the causative mutation will be homozygous in all F_2 individuals selected, while other mutations will not. Mutations that are not linked to the causative mutation will segregate in a Mendelian fashion in the F_2, and this situation will be reflected in the genome sequences. Mutations that *are* linked will segregate according to how closely they are linked to the causative mutation.

The concept behind using a large number of F_2 progeny is that, while in a single F_2 individual the probability of recombination between the causative mutation and another, closely linked mutation will be low, in a population some level of recombination will occur between the causative mutation and most unlinked mutations. For example, if 50 homozygous mutant F_2 individuals are examined, 100 meiotic events are being assayed (since meiosis will have occurred to produce each of the gametes in the F_1 parents), providing a resolution of approximately 1 cM. Knowing the genome sizes of the model genetics organisms and their genetic map length (see back endsheets), a researcher can approximate the likelihood of identifying only a small number of candidate mutations. The process of confirming the gene identification then follows that described earlier for positional cloning. Due to inexpensive DNA-sequencing technologies, this approach for going from mutant phenotype to gene identification is becoming commonplace in *Drosophila, C. elegans*, and *Arabidopsis*.

16.3 Reverse Genetics Investigates Gene Action by Progressing from Gene Identification to Phenotype

Forward genetics was for a long time the primary—and for much of the last century, the only—approach to uncovering gene function. Now, however, the development of molecular methods for gene identification and advances in sequencing technologies are making reverse genetics approaches increasingly valuable and common.

The reasons for this shift in emphasis are twofold. First, the enormous amount of genomic sequence available has increased by orders of magnitude the number of known gene sequences, and only a fraction of them have been assigned a function by forward genetics. For example, when the *E. coli* genome was fully sequenced, 4288 protein-coding genes were identified, only 1853 of which had been previously identified through forward genetic screens. Second, genomic sequencing and reverse genetic screens have uncovered a degree of gene duplication not previously suspected. Gene duplications often result in genetic redundancy. In forward genetic screens, such duplicated genes would not be identified, since mutation of only one of the genes would not usually result in a conspicuous mutant phenotype. However, reverse genetics approaches, where the functions of both duplicates can be disrupted in an individual organism, are particularly suited in these situations to provide evidence of gene function.

Reverse genetics begins with the creation of a mutant allele for a gene identified only by its sequence (see Figure 16.1). The selection of mutational tools is largely dependent on the biology of the experimental organism. In organisms in which homologous recombination readily occurs, targeted sequence changes, such as deletions, are the method of choice. In organisms amenable to transformation and in which homologous recombination occurs at a reasonable frequency, the ideal approach is to precisely delete the gene of interest. This approach works in many bacteria and fungi and has also been used in mice. In Chapter 17 we discuss the details of how gene deletion by homologous recombination is accomplished. In organisms amenable to transformation but in which homologous recombination is rare, two approaches are widely used. The first is to generate a large collection of random mutations and then screen them for mutations in the gene of interest using PCR-based techniques (see Chapter 7 for review of PCR). The second approach is to harness a gene-silencing phenomenon known as RNA interference (RNAi), which is induced by double-stranded RNA molecules. In species not amenable to large-scale transformation experiments, nontransgenic methods of mutagenesis can be used. These basic techniques for reverse genetics are described in the rest of this section.

Use of Insertion Mutants in Reverse Genetics

Conceptually, the simplest way to construct a loss-of-function allele would be to delete the gene of interest from the genome. The deletion of a specific sequence from the genome requires techniques, such as homologous recombination, that precisely manipulate the genomes of living organisms. As we will discuss further in Chapter 17, these techniques are very efficient in many microorganisms, such as bacteria, archaea, and some simple eukaryotes, but they are much less efficient in more complex eukaryotes like plants and animals. Thus, the approaches used in reverse genetics differ between organisms (Table 16.2).

Reverse genetics approaches for most of the commonly used model genetic organisms utilize **knockout libraries,** collections of mutants in which most or all genes have been mutated by inactivating (or "knocking out") their expression. Most knockout mutants are produced by the insertion of exogenous pieces of DNA into the genome to generate loss-of-function alleles; thus, most alleles in the libraries are null alleles. *Saccharomyces*

Table 16.2	Reverse Genetics Approaches in Model Genetic Organisms
Species	**Reverse Genetics Tools**
Escherichia coli	Knockouts by homologous recombination
Saccharomyces cerevisiae	Knockouts by homologous recombination
Arabidopsis thaliana	Random T-DNA and transposon insertions; TILLING; RNAi
Drosophila melanogaster	Random *P* element insertion lines; RNAi
Caenorhabditis elegans	RNAi loss-of-function alleles
Mus musculus	Knockouts by homologous recombination; RNAi

cerevisiae and *E. coli* geneticists have, for example, systematically generated loss-of-function alleles of all known *S. cerevisiae* and *E. coli* genes by homologous recombination. In these knockout library collections, each strain has a single mutation in a different gene. See Chapter 17 for details on how this is accomplished.

In many model genetic organisms, it is not technically simple or economically feasible to systematically generate loss-of-function mutants for all genes. However, if an organism is easy to transform, populations of random mutants can be generated by transposon insertions or, in the case of plants, T-DNA insertions (see Chapter 17 for details). These populations can then be screened for mutations in specific genes, using PCR-based techniques with a primer that is specific to the gene of interest and a primer that is specific to the insertional mutagen used (Figure 16.13).

For model genetic systems such as *Drosophila*, where *P* elements have been used as an insertional mutagen, large populations of mutants generated by insertions have been characterized to such an extent that mutations in specific genes can be ordered directly from a stock center. Similar knockout libraries based on T-DNA and transposon insertions are available for *Arabidopsis.* Such knockout libraries are an invaluable resource for large-scale reverse genetics experiments that aim to elucidate the function of every gene in the model genetic organism (see Chapter 18). An example of an application of reverse genetics to determine the function of closely related genes in *Arabidopsis* is described in the Case Study at the end of this chapter.

RNA Interference in Gene Activity

In the late 1980s, researchers introduced a chalcone synthase transgene into *Petunia* in an effort to increase the amount of floral pigment. To their surprise, some transgenic lines exhibited complete loss of pigment production (Chapter 15). Not only was the chalcone synthase transgene not expressed properly in these lines, but the endogenous

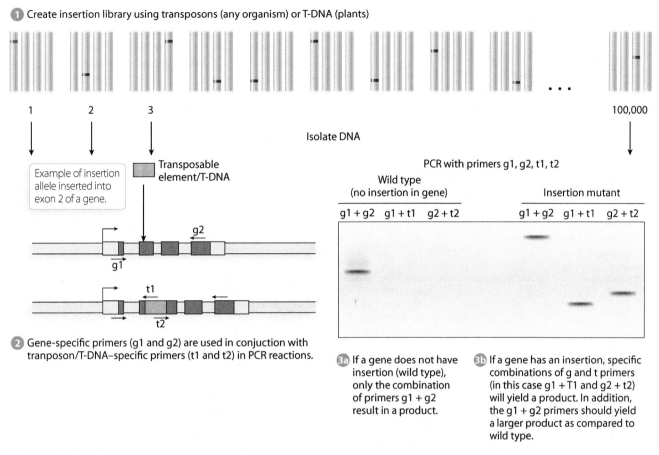

① Create insertion library using transposons (any organism) or T-DNA (plants)

1   2   3   100,000

Isolate DNA

Example of insertion allele inserted into exon 2 of a gene.

Transposable element/T-DNA

PCR with primers g1, g2, t1, t2

Wild type (no insertion in gene)

Insertion mutant

g1 + g2   g1 + t1   g2 + t2   g1 + g2   g1 + t1   g2 + t2

② Gene-specific primers (g1 and g2) are used in conjuction with tranposon/T-DNA–specific primers (t1 and t2) in PCR reactions.

③a If a gene does not have insertion (wild type), only the combination of primers g1 + g2 result in a product.

③b If a gene has an insertion, specific combinations of g and t primers (in this case g1 + T1 and g2 + t2) will yield a product. In addition, the g1 + g2 primers should yield a larger product as compared to wild type.

Figure 16.13   Reverse genetics using insertional mutagenesis.

chalcone synthase gene also was silenced, a phenomenon they termed co-suppression. A similar phenomenon was subsequently observed in both fungal and animal systems. This method of silencing genes was initially called quelling in *Neurospora* and **RNA interference (RNAi)** in animals. The phenomenon is now universally known as RNAi. In the 1990s, Andrew Fire and Craig Mello, who won the 2006 Nobel Prize in Physiology or Medicine for their work on RNAi, used a genetics approach to dissect and elucidate the biochemical mechanism for RNAi in *C. elegans*.

Double-stranded RNA (dsRNA) can act as a trigger for the degradation not only of the double-stranded RNA itself but also of any RNA molecules that are complementary to the double-stranded RNA (see Chapter 15). A primary role of this gene-silencing system is to silence repetitive DNA. Transcription from several different copies of repetitive elements often generates double-stranded RNA molecules, since collectively both strands of the repetitive DNA are often transcribed. In addition, RNAi protects cells against double-stranded RNA viruses. Thus, dsRNA-mediated gene silencing acts as a genomic immune system to silence both repetitive DNA sequences and invading nucleic acids.

To take advantage of endogenous RNAi activity as a way of silencing genes, scientists utilize double-stranded RNA that is complementary in sequence to the target gene (**Figure 16.14**). The mRNA of the target gene will then be degraded through the action of Dicer and Argonaute enzymes (described in Chapter 15), causing a loss-of-function phenotype of the target gene. The efficiency of silencing can approach that of a null allele, although often the phenotypes induced represent a range of partial loss-of-function phenotypes.

The double-stranded RNA can be introduced directly into cells or organisms by injection of double-stranded RNA or indirectly by infection with a double-stranded RNA virus. Alternatively, a transgene can be designed that results in the production of double-stranded RNA, a method that has the added advantage of being heritable. In animals, transient introduction of double-stranded RNA into cell cultures has been successful. One of the methods for introducing double-stranded RNA into *C. elegans* is surprisingly simple. *Caenorhabditis elegans* normally eats *E. coli* as food, and, remarkably enough, when *C. elegans* is fed *E. coli* that is producing double-stranded RNA, the double-stranded RNA will be taken up into *C. elegans* and will silence genes in many organs of the *C. elegans* body. While in this case the RNAi phenotype is not indefinitely heritable, the phenotypic effects can be seen in several subsequent generations produced by self-fertilization of the worm that was fed the *E. coli*.

The advantages of the RNAi approach to reverse genetics include the ease and rapidity of applying the method. It allows large-scale reverse genetic screens to be conducted

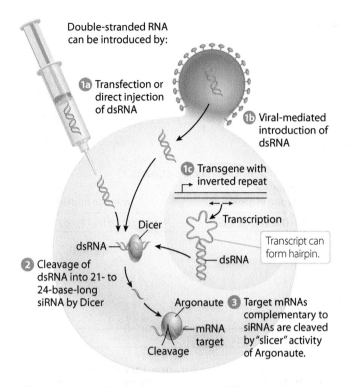

Figure 16.14 **Reverse genetics using RNAi.**

in cell cultures and whole organisms without the laborious preparatory task of creating mutagenized populations. In addition, transient RNAi-mediated gene silencing offers an alternative means of applying reverse genetics in species for which stable transformation protocols do not exist.

In a related approach, synthetic micro RNAs have been created to target the degradation of specific mRNAs. Like RNAi-mediated gene silencing, synthetic micro-RNA–mediated gene silencing takes advantage of endogenous gene-silencing machinery (see Chapter 15). The synthetic microRNAs are designed according to principles derived from known microRNAs but are customized to direct the translational repression or mRNA cleavage of the gene of interest.

Reverse Genetics by TILLING

Reverse genetics can also be performed on species that cannot be transformed easily, as long as the species is amenable to standard genetic analyses. One approach to reverse genetics that can be applied to any genome is **targeted induced local lesions in genomes (TILLING)**. In a TILLING protocol, a population of organisms of an inbred strain is randomly mutagenized throughout the genome (Figure 16.15). Enough independent lines are produced to bring the level of mutagenesis to near saturation, at which, ideally, each gene is represented by multiple mutant alleles in the mutagenized population. Often, the mutagen employed in the development of the mutagenized lines is a chemical such as EMS (Table 16.1). DNA from the mutagenized lines is screened

systematically using PCR-based methods to search for mutations in a particular gene of interest.

For each individual of the mutagenized population, both progeny and DNA are collected. The generation derived from the mutagenized population is often referred to as the M_1 generation (Figure 16.15a). DNA is isolated from M_1 individuals or from M_2 families of organisms. Any mutation induced in the mutagenesis will be either heterozygous (if the DNA was derived from an M_1 individual) or segregating (if the DNA was derived from an M_2 family). A region of the target gene is chosen for PCR-based amplification. The PCR products generated in this analysis are expected to contain both the wild-type sequence and mutant sequence. Those that consist solely of the wild-type allele can be distinguished from those consisting of a mixture of the wild-type allele and a mutant allele.

The PCR products are first denatured and allowed to reanneal, creating some homoduplex DNA, in which the strands are fully complementary if derived from the same allele, and some heteroduplex DNA (Figure 16.15b). Heteroduplex DNA is composed of strands that are largely complementary but contain one or more mismatched base pairs, indicating that the strands are derived from DNA containing different alleles. Heteroduplex DNA can be distinguished from homoduplex DNA by either a difference in migration of the products during electrophoresis or by differential susceptibility to an endonuclease that cleaves heteroduplex DNA at mismatched base pairs. Heteroduplex DNA forms only in DNA samples in which a mutation in the target gene is present. Screening progeny from several thousand mutagenized individuals often allows identification of multiple mutant alleles of the target gene. Individuals homozygous or heterozygous for the mutant allele can then be identified in the appropriate M_2 family.

When chemical mutagenesis is used to produce TILLING alleles, it results in both null alleles and partial loss-of-function alleles. The spectrum of phenotypes produced by alleles obtained through TILLING approaches is often useful for dissecting gene function, even in organisms where gene knockouts are available. While TILLING was developed for studies in model genetic species, it is suitable for any organism that can be mutagenized and genetically analyzed. It is currently being applied to several crop plants.

Genetic Analysis 16.2 tests your understanding of the reverse genetics analytical techniques discussed in this section.

16.4 Transgenes Provide a Means of Dissecting Gene Function

Transgenes have other uses in the study of gene function, in addition to the creation of loss-of-function alleles. Chimeric genes, transgenes composed of regulatory sequences from one gene and coding sequences from a

(a) Seeds are mutated to produce M₁ generation. Each M₁ plant is heterozygous for mutations in different genes (colors).

M₁ individuals

(b) Mutations in specific genes are identified by analyzing DNA isolated from each M₂ family. For example, one representative M₂ family with a mutant (red) segregating:

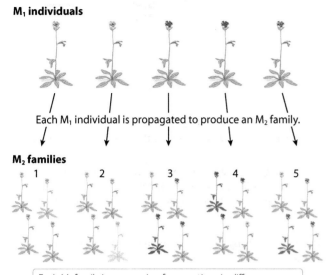

Each M₁ individual is propagated to produce an M₂ family.

M₂ families

Each M₂ family is segregating for mutations in different genes (homozygous mutants in color). Seed stock and DNA samples are collected from each M₂ family. Seed stocks represent a repository of mutants.

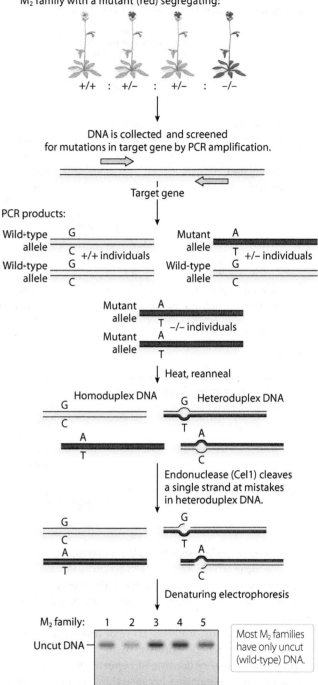

Figure 16.15   Reverse genetics by TILLING.

PROBLEM In searching the mouse genome, you identify the sequences of three genes similar to the single *hedgehog* gene of *Drosophila*: *Sonic hedgehog*, *Indian hedgehog*, and *Desert hedgehog*. Describe the research design you would use to learn the function of each of the genes and whether that gene function is unique or redundant in the mouse.

> **BREAK IT DOWN:** When genes in different species are highly similar, they are likely to have originated from a single ancestral gene in a common ancestor.

> **BREAK IT DOWN:** You are starting with gene sequences and wish to know gene functions. Which genetics approach, forward or reverse, is most appropriate?

Solution Strategies	Solution Steps
Evaluate	
1. Identify the topic this problem addresses and the nature of the required answer.	1. This problem is about designing research to identify the functions of genes known only by sequence and to discover whether those functions are unique or redundant.
2. Identify the critical information given in the problem.	2. While only one *hedgehog* gene exists in *Drosophila*, three 'hedgehog' gene sequences exist in mouse, raising the question of whether the three mouse genes have different functions or whether there is any sharing of function.
Deduce	
3. Consider possible approaches to discovering the functions of genes known only by sequence. *TIP: Reverse genetics approaches can be used for functional analysis.*	3. Functions of genes known only by sequence can be determined by reverse genetics approaches.
4. Consider possible approaches to reverse genetics available for use with mice. *TIP: Consider the methods discussed to create mutations in mice.*	4. Homologous recombination approaches can be used to produce loss-of-function mutations in mice. Other reverse genetics approaches, such as RNAi, could also be used, but homologous recombination is the preferred method, as it results in null alleles.
Solve	
5. Describe a genetics approach to determine whether the genes have unique or redundant functions.	5. First, create loss-of-function knockout alleles of each of the three genes by homologous recombination. Homozygous mutant lines can then be bred and the phenotypes of each of the three single knockouts examined. Interbreeding the single-mutant lines will lead to the creation of strains in which combinations of two or more genes are inactive. Comparison of phenotypes of single mutants with those of multiple mutants allows an assessment of whether the genes exhibit unique or redundant functions.

For more practice, see Problems 9, 10, and 22.   Visit the Study Area to access study tools.   **MasteringGenetics™**

---

second gene or coding sequences from two different genes, provide a means to create gain-of-function alleles, as well as to monitor gene expression patterns. This section describes in greater detail the ways transgenes can reveal genetic function.

While an almost limitless array of transgenes can be constructed for genetic analysis, many fall into two categories. One category consists of **reporter genes**, used to investigate gene regulation because they produce a visual output of gene expression patterns. Fusion of the regulatory sequences of a gene of interest to coding sequences of a reporter gene provides information about where, when, and how much a gene is expressed. Some reporter genes facilitate live imaging and monitoring of gene expression in real time.

The second category of transgenes useful for genetic analysis consists of gain-of-function alleles generated by placing coding regions from one gene under control of regulatory sequences derived from another gene. An allele

constructed in this way often results in ectopic expression, expression occurring at times or in places where the gene is not normally expressed. The use of either or both of these types of transgenes can complement analyses of loss-of-function alleles by providing information on how genes are normally expressed and the phenotypic consequences of changing their normal expression pattern.

Monitoring Gene Expression with Reporter Genes

A gene can act as a reporter if its product can be detected directly or is an enzyme that produces a detectable product. The regulatory sequences of the gene of interest are used to drive the expression of the reporter gene. Two types of reporter gene fusions can be constructed: transcriptional and translational (**Figure 16.16**).

In a *transcriptional fusion*, regulatory sequences directing transcription of the gene of interest are fused

Gene in eukaryotic genome

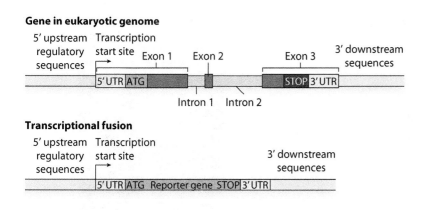

Transcriptional fusion

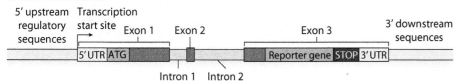

Translational fusion

Figure 16.16   Transcriptional versus translational gene fusions.

directly with the coding sequences of the reporter gene. In this case, the reporter gene will be transcribed in the pattern directed by the regulatory sequences to which it is fused. Note that the transcriptional fusion shown in Figure 16.6 is idealized and that regulatory sequences may reside in other regions in addition to the 5′ upstream sequences. In *translational fusion*, not only the regulatory sequences but also the coding sequence of the gene of interest are fused to the reporter gene in such a way that the reading frame for translation is maintained for both the gene of interest and the reporter gene. As a result, the reporter protein is translationally fused with the protein of interest, and the location of the reporter protein provides information not only on the spatial and temporal transcriptional expression pattern but also on the subcellular location of the fusion protein. In translational fusions, care must be taken to find out if the fusion protein is still functional, since the addition of the reporter protein could interfere with the proper folding or activity of the protein of interest.

Some frequently used reporter genes are represented in Figure 16.17. The choice of reporter gene depends on the biological question being addressed. With some reporter genes, the assay to monitor gene expression requires sacrificing the organism, whereas the expression of other reporter genes can be traced in a living organism. Reporter gene products sometimes require substrates that must penetrate into the tissues or cells where the reporter genes are expressed. In addition, reporter genes vary in their sensitivity.

One of the first reporter genes to be developed emerged from research on the *lac* operon in *E. coli* (see Section 14.3). To purify and study the activity of β-galactosidase, encoded by the *lacZ* gene, a number of β-galactosides were synthesized and tested as substrates.

Two β-galactosides, abbreviated X-gal and ONPG, were found to be useful. β-galactosidase cleaves the colorless substrate, ONPG, into a yellow product. This assay is typically used for in vitro measurement of β-galactosidase activity. In contrast, X-gal, also colorless, is cleaved by β-galactosidase into a blue product. This assay can be used in bacteria in vivo, since bacterial cells can take up the X-gal substrate without a reduction in viability.

The *lacZ* gene can be used in conjunction with the substrate X-gal as a reporter gene in animal systems (Figure 16.17a). However, since plants have an endogenous β-galactosidase activity, *lacZ* is not suitable for studying plant systems. An alternative option is the *E. coli* *uidA* gene encoding β-glucuronidase, which enzymatically cleaves a colorless precursor, X-gluc, into a blue product (Figure 16.17b). Conversely, since animals have endogenous β-glucuronidase activity, the *uidA* gene cannot be used as a reporter in animals. A limitation of both of these reporter genes in organisms other than bacteria is that in order for the substrate to be taken up effectively into internal tissues, the tissue to be stained must be bathed in a solution that kills the cells.

Research into reactions that cause the natural emission of light in some animals has led to the development of reporter genes that cause light to be produced in living cells. For example, luciferase, the enzyme responsible for the glow of fireflies, catalyzes a reaction between the substrate luciferin and ATP that results in the emission of light. Transgenic plants expressing the luciferase gene will emit a yellow-green glow if supplied with the substrate (Figure 16.17c). However, luciferin is not delivered to all cells of the plant in equal measure, which in many cases limits the usefulness of the luciferase gene as a reporter.

The development of **green fluorescent protein (GFP)** led to great strides both in genetics and cell

(a) *Lin-3* regulatory sequences driving *lacZ* reporter gene in *C. elegans*

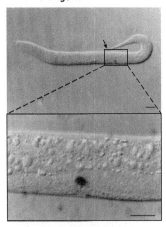

(b) *PHABULOSA* regulatory sequences driving *uidA* reporter gene in *Arabidopsis*

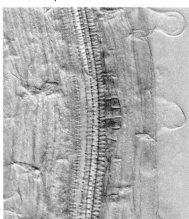

(c) *CaMV 35S* regulatory sequences driving luciferase reporter gene in tobacco

(d) *RHODOPSIN* regulatory sequences driving *GFP* reporter gene in *Mus musculus*

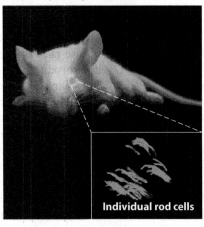

Individual rod cells

(e) *Mus musculus* neurons expressing three different fluorescent reporter genes, derived from modifying GFP

Figure 16.17   Reporter genes.

biology by providing a noninvasive means of visualizing gene and protein expression patterns in living organisms (Figure 16.17d). The *GFP* gene, derived from the jellyfish *Aequoria victoria*, is the source of the natural biolumi-nescence of this species. Its wild-type protein product, consisting of 238 amino acids, fluoresces green (a 509-nm wavelength) when illuminated with UV light (a 395-nm wavelength), which in this case is the "substrate," deliv-ered by laser.

Because UV light, with its short wavelength, can be harmful to organisms (e.g., causing thymidine dimers to form in DNA, as described in Section 12.3), the wild-type *GFP* gene was mutated to produce variants that respond to lower-energy wavelengths. A major improvement was a mutation that shifted the excitation wavelength to 488 nm, corresponding to blue light and minimizing the potential damage to cells being illuminated. Subsequent modifica-tion of the GFP protein sequence has led to the produc-tion of variants that emit other colors (e.g., yellow, cyan, blue). Genes encoding fluorescent reporter proteins have also been isolated from marine corals and other jellyfish.

The availability of multiple fluorescent reporter makes it possible to visualize the expression of several genes si-multaneously in a single organism (Figure 16.17e). Osamu Shimomura, Martin Chalfie, and Roger Y. Tsien received the 2008 Nobel Prize in Chemistry for their discovery and development of GFP.

Reporter genes can be used to dissect regulatory DNA sequences and identify specific sequences required for particular aspects of gene regulation. The general approach is to start with a clone in which all the regula-tory sequences required for proper gene expression are present and then to assay the effects of deleting or chang-ing specific portions of the clone. An example of such an analysis of the *Drosophila even-skipped* (*eve*) gene, which is expressed in seven stripes in the segmentation pattern of the embryo, is shown in **Figure 16.18**. Overlapping deletions spanning large regions are assayed first. Then regions identified as important for gene regulation are dissected with smaller deletions. The concept is simi-lar to that described earlier for deletion mapping (see Sections 6.6 and 13.3). When specific sequences required

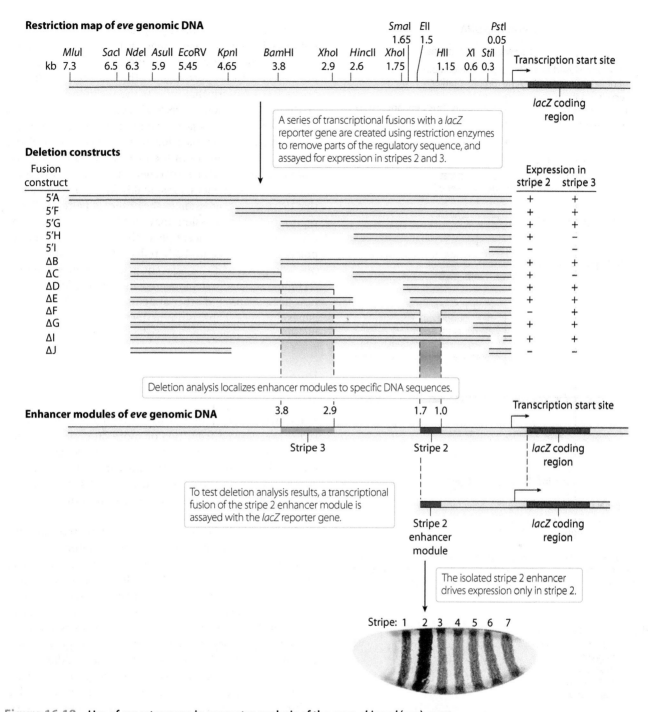

Figure 16.18   **Use of reporter gene in promoter analysis of the *even-skipped* (*eve*) gene.**

for proper gene expression are deleted, expression of the reporter gene will be correspondingly altered.

If genomic sequence is available from two or more related species, regulatory elements may be predicted by searching for sequences that are conserved between the related species, using a method known as *phylogenetic footprinting* (discussed in Chapter 18). Such initial genomic sequence analyses can direct subsequent experimental tests that use reporter genes to analyze expression in transgenic organisms.

Enhancer Trapping

Enhancer trapping uses a variation of an insertional library to identify genes based on expression patterns. This approach combines the generation of a large number of random insertion mutants with the expression of a reporter gene (**Figure 16.19**). In its simplest application, a population of transgenic organisms is generated by random insertion of a transposon (or T-DNA) containing the coding sequence of a reporter gene fused with a

(a)

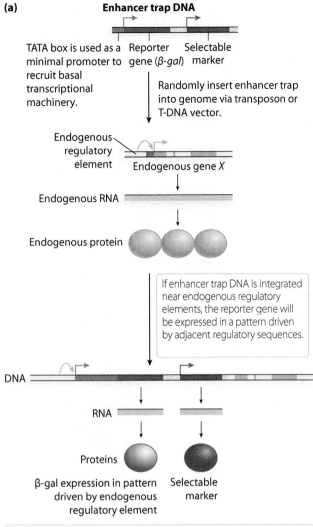

Enhancer trap DNA

TATA box is used as a minimal promoter to recruit basal transcriptional machinery.

Reporter gene (*β-gal*)

Selectable marker

Randomly insert enhancer trap into genome via transposon or T-DNA vector.

Endogenous regulatory element

Endogenous gene *X*

Endogenous RNA

Endogenous protein

If enhancer trap DNA is integrated near endogenous regulatory elements, the reporter gene will be expressed in a pattern driven by adjacent regulatory sequences.

DNA

RNA

Proteins

β-gal expression in pattern driven by endogenous regulatory element

Selectable marker

If enhancer trap disrupts coding region of gene, a loss-of-function allele is created. However, insertion of vector may occur 5' or 3' to a gene and still "trap" enhancers without causing a loss-of-function mutation.

(b)

Three patterns of gene expression in *Drosophila* embryos seen in enhancer trap lines using β-galactosidase as a reporter gene.

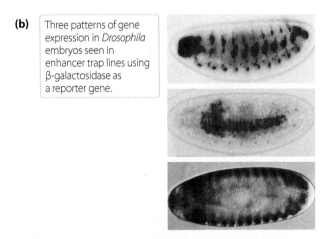

Figure 16.19 Enhancer trapping to reveal expression patterns of endogenous genes. (a) Strategy for generation of enhancer trap lines. **(b)** Examples of enhancer trap lines in *Drosophila*.

minimal promoter for RNA polymerase II transcription. If the insertion occurs near enhancer or silencer regulatory sequences that can act in conjunction with the minimal promoter of the reporter gene, the reporter can be expressed in a pattern that reflects the regulatory capability of the nearby genomic DNA sequences. The enhancers (or silencers) of the adjacent genomic DNA are co-opted, or "trapped," by the insertion to drive expression of the reporter gene. Thus, from the expression patterns of the inserted reporter gene, researchers can infer the existence of regulatory sequences, presumably from adjacent genes, that drive gene expression in the observed patterns. While reporter gene expression may not precisely reflect the expression of the adjacent gene, the expression of the reporter often at least partially reflects the normal gene expression pattern of the adjacent gene. Enhancer trapping techniques were first pioneered in *Drosophila* and have now been adapted to other systems. Because they identify genes by gene expression patterns, enhancer trapping techniques complement forward genetic screens.

Investigating Gene Function with Chimeric Genes

A **chimeric gene** is one in which regulatory and coding sequences derived from two or more different genes are recombined in a novel manner. For example, combining the regulatory sequences from one gene with the coding sequences from another gene often results in a gain-of-function allele due to ectopic expression of the gene represented by the coding sequences.

Figure 16.20 shows one way experimenters can take advantage of this potential to obtain information on gene function. Recessive loss-of-function mutations in the *eyeless* gene of *Drosophila* result in a failure of eyes to develop. The *eyeless* gene is normally expressed only in the eye imaginal discs during *Drosophila* development. Imaginal discs are groups of precursor cells that are set aside during embryonic development. These grow by mitotic proliferation during larval life and later differentiate into adult body tissues during metamorphosis. A gain-of-function *eyeless* allele can be created by constructing a chimeric gene in which expression of the *eyeless* coding sequences is driven by regulatory sequences active in all imaginal discs. If the *eyeless* gene is ectopically expressed in non-eye imaginal discs, such as those that would normally give rise to the antennae or legs, the imaginal discs will differentiate as eye tissue instead. This outcome indicates that cells in any imaginal disc are capable of differentiating into eyes and that the *eyeless* gene product can promote the development of eyes from any imaginal disc. Thus, when the *eyeless* allele is ectopically expressed as a gain-of-function mutation in inappropriate imaginal discs, the resulting phenotype is the converse of the phenotype of the loss-of-function *eyeless* allele—ectopic eyes as opposed to an absence of eyes.

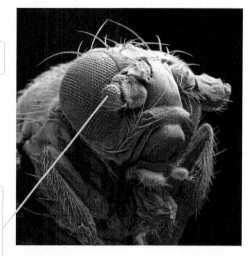

Wild-type *Drosophila* has red eyes.

Gain-of-function eyeless mutants, in which *eyeless* gene is ectopically expressed in the wrong imaginal discs, develop ectopic eyes on antennae, legs, and wings. Ectopic eyes are anatomically normal despite their ectopic locations.

Loss-of-function *eyeless* mutants lack eyes entirely.

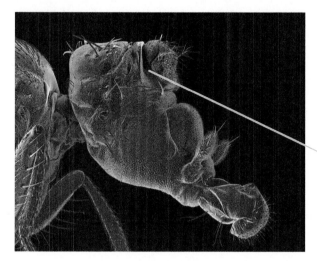

Figure 16.20   Comparison of loss- and gain-of-function alleles.

In cases where the gain-of-function and loss-of-function phenotypes are complementary, interpretation of the effects of ectopic expression is straightforward. Thus, in the preceding example, *eyeless* is revealed to be a master control gene for the differentiation of eyes in *Drosophila*. However, ectopic expression of genes can also lead to enigmatic phenotypes that are more difficult to interpret. For example, ectopic expression of *eyeless* during embryogenesis leads to embryonic lethality, a phenotype that is not easily reconciled with the loss-of-function phenotype. Therefore, when considering gain-of-function alleles generated by ectopic expression, we must remember that the phenotypes represent what the gene is capable of doing when expressed in particular contexts and may not reflect the normal function of the gene.

CASE STUDY

Reverse Genetics and Genetic Redundancy in Flower Development

In this case study, we see an example of how forward genetics and reverse genetics work together to provide a broader view of both gene function and evolution. The story begins with forward genetics—the isolation of a mutant that alters flower development and the subsequent identification of the mutant gene sequence using recombinant DNA technology. The gene is then cloned and used as a probe for cloning genes of similar sequence. Finally, reverse genetics approaches are applied to identify mutant alleles of related genes, and their biological function is inferred based on the mutant phenotypes.

FORWARD GENETICS REVEALS GENES OF INTEREST
In flowering plants, the types of floral organs that develop are decided by the expression of a set of transcription factors. (For further description of this activity, see Chapter 20.)

The identity of *Arabidopsis* reproductive organs (stamens and carpels) is determined in part by the activity of the *AGAMOUS* gene. Recessive null loss-of-function *agamous* alleles lead to the development of petals in the positions usually occupied by stamens and of an additional flower in the position usually occupied by carpels. Homozygotes are sterile and do not produce gametes (hence the name *AGAMOUS*). In forward genetic screens aimed at identifying genes involved in *Arabidopsis* flower development, *agamous* mutant alleles induced by either EMS or T-DNA have been isolated (Figure 16.21, step ①).

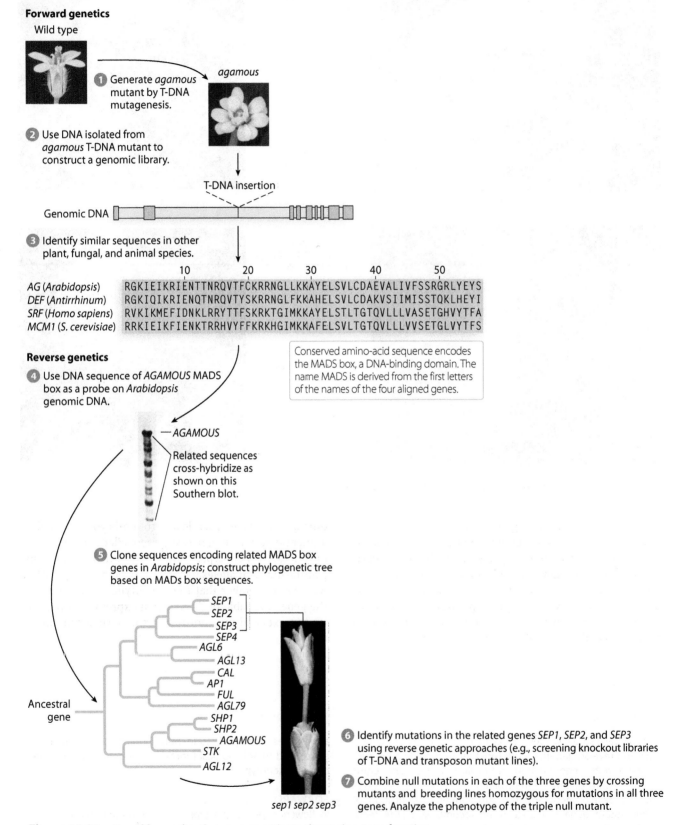

Figure 16.21   Use of forward and reverse genetics to determine gene function.

The T-DNA–induced allele proved a useful tool for cloning the *AGAMOUS* gene because the T-DNA "tagged" the gene (step ②). The approach is similar to that described for transposon tagging in Section 16.2: First, a genomic library is constructed from DNA isolated from *agamous* mutants (see Section 16.2 for construction and screening of genomic libraries). Then the genomic library is screened with a probe consisting of T-DNA sequence. The probe identifies genomic clones in the library that have T-DNA sequence. Since the T-DNA was inserted into the *AGAMOUS* gene, *Arabidopsis* DNA adjacent to the T-DNA sequences encodes the *AGAMOUS* gene.

Subsequently, the genomic clone encoding *AGAMOUS* can be used to identify an *AGAMOUS* cDNA clone from a library constructed with mRNA from wild-type flowers ③. Sequencing of the *AGAMOUS* cDNA clones reveals that the encoded protein has a similarity to known eukaryotic transcription factors. This conclusion is based on the similarity between a 60–amino acid domain of the AGAMOUS protein and DNA-binding domains in yeast and mammalian transcription factors.

IDENTIFICATION OF HOMOLOGOUS GENES When the *AGAMOUS* cDNA is used to probe a Southern blot of restriction-enzyme–digested *Arabidopsis* genomic DNA, sequences related to the *AGAMOUS* gene sequence can be identified ④ (see Section 10.2 to review Southern blotting). The same *AGAMOUS* cDNA can be used as a probe on the flower cDNA library to identify clones of related genes. Genes related to *AGAMOUS* were called *AGAMOUS-LIKE*, or *AGL*, genes. These related genes possess the same highly conserved DNA-binding domain but differ in the rest of their protein sequences. To determine how the *AGL* genes are related to *AGAMOUS* and to each other, a phylogenetic tree can be constructed ⑤ (see Section 1.4 to review phylogenetic trees).

REVERSE GENETICS REVEALS FUNCTIONS OF HOMOLOGOUS GENES Since the related genes are known by gene sequence only, a reverse genetics approach can be undertaken to determine gene function. Transposon- or T-DNA–induced mutant alleles of many of the *AGL* genes in *Arabidopsis* can be identified in available knockout libraries ⑥ (see Section 16.3). Researchers were initially surprised that plants homozygous for loss-of-function alleles of many single genes did not display an aberrant phenotype. Hypothesizing that the more closely related the genes, the more similar their functions would be, researchers crossed mutants to obtain organisms containing multiple loss-of-function alleles of closely related genes ⑦. For example, *sep1* mutants—having mutations of the *SEPALLATA1* gene—were crossed with *sep2* mutants, after which *sep1 sep2* double mutants were identified in the F$_2$ generation. Disappointingly, the *sep1 sep2* double mutants did not differ significantly from wild-type plants. However, *sep1 sep2 sep3* triple mutant plants proved to have flowers consisting solely of sepals, which indicates that these genes have a function related to floral organ specification but distinct from the role of *AGAMOUS*.

Genetic redundancy due to gene duplications is extensive in most eukaryotic genomes (see Chapter 18). Immediately following an occurrence of gene duplication, the duplicate genes often have identical DNA sequences and expression patterns, and they are therefore genetically redundant. Over time, however, the functions of the two genes may diverge due to the accumulation of mutations that lead to changes in protein sequence and expression pattern. Yet, since the genes are evolutionarily related, they often function in similar biological processes. Reverse genetics approaches can facilitate the analysis of closely related genetically redundant genes.

SUMMARY 〔 MasteringGenetics™ 〕 For activities, animations, and review quizzes, go to the Study Area.

16.1 Forward Genetic Screens Identify Genes by Their Mutant Phenotypes

▪ Forward genetic screens are designed to identify genes by creation of a mutant phenotype, often allowing researchers to infer the biological function of a gene.

▪ Complementation tests are used to discover the number of alleles and the number of genes affected in a forward genetic screen.

▪ Mutations resulting in lethality can be identified in genetic screens for conditional alleles.

▪ Enhancer and suppressor genetic screens identify genes that act in related or redundant pathways.

16.2 Genes Identified by Mutant Phenotype Are Cloned Using Recombinant DNA Technology

▪ Some genes can be cloned by complementation of a mutant phenotype.

▪ Transposons and other integrating elements can be used to tag genes, facilitating their subsequent cloning.

▪ Positional cloning, or chromosome walking, provides a means of identifying cloned genes known only from a mutant phenotype.

▪ Positional cloning approaches proceed by first mapping mutations and then constructing contigs of DNA that span the target gene. The target gene can be identified by expression analyses, DNA sequence analyses, or complementation experiments.

▪ Advances in sequencing technologies facilitate direct identification of mutant genes.

16.3 Reverse Genetics Investigates Gene Action by Progressing from Gene Identification to Phenotype

▪ Reverse genetics approaches, in which determination of biological function proceeds from gene sequence to mutant phenotype, make use of collections consisting of mutants that are each defective in a different defined gene.

▪ Collections of insertion alleles, the TILLING process, and RNAi-mediated gene silencing all contribute to the reverse genetics analysis of model organisms.

16.4 Transgenes Provide a Means of Dissecting Gene Function

▌ Reporter genes are used to monitor gene-expression patterns in transgenic organisms and for the dissection of

regulatory sequences. Some reporter genes, such as the green fluorescent protein, can be visualized in real time in living organisms.

▌ Chimeric genes represent novel alleles that provide clues to gene function.

KEYWORDS

bacterial artificial chromosome (BAC) *(p. 542)*
balancer chromosome *(p. 537)*
cDNA library *(p. 542)*
chimeric gene *(p. 560)*
cloning vector *(p. 542)*
contiguous sequence (contig) *(p. 546)*
enhancer screen *(p. 540)*
enhancer trapping *(p. 559)*
forward genetic analysis (forward genetics) *(p. 534)*

genetic redundancy *(p. 541)*
genetic screen *(p. 534)*
genomic library *(p. 542)*
green fluorescent protein (GFP) *(p. 557)*
knockout library *(p. 552)*
modifier screen *(p. 540)*
mutagenesis *(p. 534)*
permissive condition *(p. 538)*
positional cloning (chromosome walking) *(p. 545)*
reporter gene *(p. 556)*

restrictive condition *(p. 538)*
reverse genetic analysis (reverse genetics) *(p. 534)*
RNA interference (RNAi) *(p. 553)*
saturation mutagenesis *(p. 535)*
suppressor screen *(p. 540)*
synthetic lethality *(p. 541)*
targeted induced local lesions in genomes (TILLING) *(p. 554)*
transgene *(p. 542)*
transgenic organism *(p. 542)*
transposon tagging *(p. 543)*

PROBLEMS

(MasteringGenetics™) Visit for instructor-assigned tutorials and problems.

Chapter Concepts

For answers to selected even-numbered problems, see Appendix: Answers.

1. What are the advantages and disadvantages of using *GFP* versus *lacZ* as a reporter gene in mice, *C. elegans*, and *Drosophila*?

2. A transcriptional fusion of regulatory sequences of a particular gene with a reporter gene results in relatively uniform expression of the reporter gene in all cells of an organism, whereas a translational fusion with the same gene shows reporter gene expression only in the nucleus of a specific cell type. Discuss some biological causes for the difference in expression patterns of the two transgenes.

3. Genetic maps and physical maps are both representations of a genome.
   a. What are the similarities and differences between how genetic and physical maps are created?
   b. If genetic maps of a particular organism are independently constructed in two different laboratories, will

   they be identical? What about two independently constructed physical maps?
   c. How can the information in genetic and physical maps be combined?

4. Using the data inside the back cover of the book, calculate the average number of kilobase (kb) pairs per centimorgan in the six multicellular eukaryotic organisms. How would this information influence strategies to positionally clone genes in these organisms?

5. What are the advantages and disadvantages of using insertion alleles versus alleles generated by chemicals (via TILLING) in reverse genetic studies?

6. You have cloned the mouse ortholog of the gene associated with human Huntington Disease (*HD*) and wish to examine its expression in mice. Outline the approaches you might take to examine the temporal and spatial expression pattern at the cellular level.

Application and Integration

For answers to selected even-numbered problems, see Appendix: Answers.

7. The *CBF* genes of *Arabidopsis* are induced by exposure of the plants to low temperature.
   a. How would you examine the temporal and spatial patterns of expression after induction by low temperature?
   b. Can you design a method that would indicate these changes in gene expression in a way that a farmer could recognize them by observing plants growing in the field?

8. When the *S. cerevisiae* genome was sequenced, only about 40% of its predicted genes had been previously identified in forward genetic screens. This left about 60% of predicted genes with no known function, leading some to dub the genes *fun* (function unknown) genes.
   a. As an approach to understanding the function of a certain *fun* gene, you wish to create a loss-of-function allele. How will you accomplish this?

b. You wish to know the physical location of the encoded protein product. How will you ascertain such information?

9. Translational fusions between a protein of interest and a reporter protein are used to determine the subcellular location of proteins in vivo. However, fusion to a reporter protein sometimes renders the protein of interest non-functional because the addition of the reporter protein interferes with proper protein folding, enzymatic activity, or protein–protein interactions. You have constructed a fusion between your protein of interest and a reporter gene. How will you show that the fusion protein retains its normal biological function?

10. In enhancer trapping experiments, a minimal promoter and a reporter gene are placed adjacent to the end of a transposon so that genomic enhancers adjacent to the insertion site can act to drive expression of the reporter gene. In a modification of this approach, a series of enhancers and a promoter can be placed at the end of a transposon so that transcription is activated from the transposon into adjacent genomic DNA. What types of mutations do you expect to be induced by such a transposon in a mutagenesis experiment?

11. In Genetic Analysis 16.1, we designed a screen to identify conditional mutants of *S. cerevisiae* in which the secretory system was defective. Suppose we were successful in identifying 12 mutants.
    a. Describe the crosses you would perform to determine the number of different genes represented by the 12 mutations.
    b. Based on your knowledge of the genetic tools for studying baker's yeast, how would you clone the genes that are mutated in your respective yeast strains? What are two approaches to cloning the human orthologs of the yeast genes?

12. How would you design a genetic screen to find genes involved in meiosis?

13. The eyes of *Drosophila* develop from imaginal discs, groups of cells set aside in the fly embryo that differentiate into the adult structures during the pupal stage. Despite their importance in nature, eyes are dispensable for fruit-fly life in the laboratory.
    a. Devise a genetic screen to identify genes directing development of the fly eye.
    b. What complications might arise from genetic screens targeting an organ that differentiates late in development?

14. Given your knowledge of the genetic tools for studying *Drosophila*, outline two methods by which you could clone the *dunce* and *rutabaga* genes identified by Seymour Benzer's laboratory in the genetic screen described at the beginning of this chapter.

15. Mutations in the *CFTR* gene result in cystic fibrosis in humans, a condition in which abnormal secretions are present in the lungs, pancreas, and sweat glands. In the effort to positionally clone the *CFTR* gene, the gene was mapped to a region of 500 kb on chromosome 7 containing three candidate genes.
    a. Using your knowledge of the disease symptoms, how would you distinguish between the candidate genes to decide which is most likely to encode the *CFTR* gene?
    b. How would you prove that your chosen candidate is the *CFTR* gene?

16. You have cloned the cDNA for the *CFTR* gene (see Problem 15). You have used the cDNA, which is 4.5 kb in length, to identify a 250-kb BAC clone from a genomic library that fully contains the *CFTR* gene.
    a. Describe the strategies that you will use to sequence each of these clones.
    b. You assume that the vast majority of the disease-causing mutations in this gene are within exons or at intron–exon boundaries. If you are correct, how might you identify mutations in patients while using a minimum amount of sequencing?

17. How would you devise a screen to identify recessive mutations in *Drosophila* that result in embryo lethality? How would you propagate the recessive mutant alleles?

18. In land plants, there is an alternation of generations between a haploid gametophyte generation and a diploid sporophytic generation. Both generations are typically multicellular and may be free-living. The male (pollen) and female (embryo sac) gametophytes are the haploid generation of flowering plants.
    a. How would you devise a screen to identify genes required for female gametophyte development in *Arabidopsis*?
    b. How would you devise a screen to identify genes required for male gametophyte development?

19. The *Drosophila even-skipped* (*eve*) gene is expressed in seven stripes in the segmentation pattern of the embryo. A sequence segment of 8 kb 5' to the transcription start site (shown as +1 in the figure on page 559) is required to drive expression of a reporter gene (*lacZ*) in the same pattern as the endogenous *eve* gene. Remarkably, expression of each of the seven stripes appears to be specified independently, with stripe 2 expression directed by regulatory sequences in the region 1.7 kb 5' to the transcription start site. To further examine stripe 2 r egulatory sequences, you create a series of constructs, each containing different fragments of the 1.7-kb region of 5' sequence. In the lower part of the figure, the bars at left represent the sequences of DNA included in your reporter gene constructs, and the + and − signs at right indicate whether the corresponding *eve:lacZ* reporter gene directs stripe 2 expression in *Drosophila* embryos transformed through *P* element mediation. How would you interpret the results—that is, where do the regulatory sequences responsible for stripe 2 expression reside?

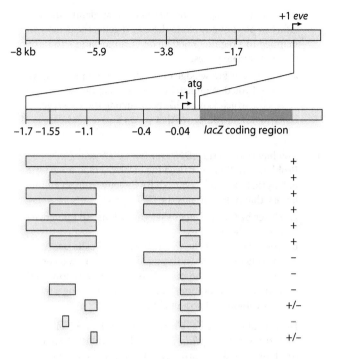

20. Most organisms display a circadian rhythm, in which biological processes are synchronized with day length (e.g., in humans, rapid movement between time zones results in jet lag, in which established circadian rhythms are out of synch with daylight hours). In *Drosophila*, pupae eclose (emerge as adults after metamorphosis) at dawn.

    a. Using this knowledge, how would you screen for *Drosophila* mutants that have an impaired circadian rhythm?

    b. In most plants, such as *Arabidopsis*, genes whose encoded products have roles related to photosynthesis have expression patterns that vary in a circadian manner. Using this knowledge, how would you screen for *Arabidopsis* mutants that have an impaired circadian rhythm?

    c. In each case, how would you clone the genes you identified by mutation?

21. As shown in Figure 16.1, mutations in the *Drosophila Ultrabithorax* (*Ubx*) gene result in wings developing from two thoracic segments rather than just one as in wild-type flies. In the mouse genome there are three *Ubx* orthologs. How would you determine whether the three mouse genes have distinct or redundant functions?

Recombinant DNA Technology and Its Applications

17

CHAPTER OUTLINE

17.1 Specific DNA Sequences Are Identified and Manipulated Using Recombinant DNA Technology

17.2 Introducing Foreign Genes into Genomes Creates Transgenic Organisms

17.3 Gene Therapy Uses Recombinant DNA Technology

17.4 Cloning of Plants and Animals Produces Genetically Identical Individuals

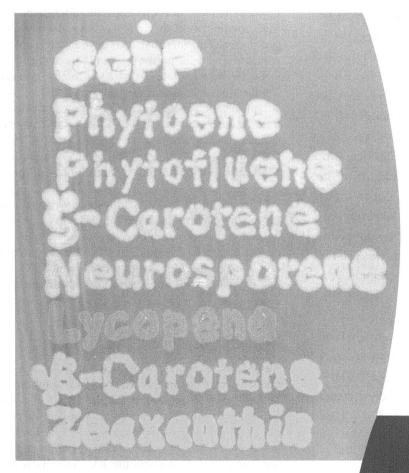

Transgenic *E. coli* expressing the genes for the carotenoid biosynthetic pathway, derived from plants. Carotenoid pigments, responsible for the red and orange colors of tomatoes, peppers, and oranges, act as a buffer system to absorb excess electrons and radicals produced during photosynthesis.

ESSENTIAL IDEAS

- DNA can be amplified by either molecular cloning or the polymerase chain reaction.

- In molecular cloning, DNA fragments are ligated into a cloning vector, which in turn is replicated in a live host.

- Libraries are collections of clones of DNA fragments, derived from the DNA or mRNA isolated from cells or an organism.

- Transgenic organisms are created by harnessing biological vectors to introduce genes into organisms.

- Recombinant DNA technology in humans is a pathway to the development of gene therapy.

- Cloning of plants and animals produces genetically identical individuals.

The advent of recombinant DNA technology for recombining, copying, and analyzing genetic sequences opened the way to studying gene function at the molecular level. This aspect of genetic exploration began with a set of basic strategies for the in vitro manipulation of DNA and for identifying the sequence of any given gene. The next step after that achievement was to invent methods for the precise manipulation of gene action in living organisms.

One of the central technical developments propelling the latter advance was development of the ability to create *transgenic organisms*—organisms that have had genes from other organisms inserted into their genomes. The methodology, now routine in genetic analysis, can be adapted to an almost limitless number of experimental approaches. It is a powerful tool for manipulating the activity of specific genes, observing the resultant phenotypes, and in this way acquiring new insight into biological processes. In addition, transgenic organisms can be fashioned for specific medical, agricultural, or industrial purposes.

Collectively, the techniques of recombinant DNA technology have permitted the sequencing of the entire genomes of many species, including our own, providing an unprecedented view of life. Increasingly sophisticated techniques have enabled both in vitro and in vivo manipulation of DNA sequences, shedding light on the molecular basis for development and physiology and for genetic variation both within and between species. If used wisely, this knowledge can be applied to better the human condition as well as that of the planet.

In this chapter, we discuss these applications of recombinant DNA technology, focusing on the methods used to create transgenic organisms and manipulate gene activity. The discussions in the present chapter furnish the nuts-and-bolts details of how reverse genetics is accomplished in different model organisms.

17.1 Specific DNA Sequences Are Identified and Manipulated Using Recombinant DNA Technology

Recombinant DNA technology is the set of techniques developed for amplifying, maintaining, and manipulating specific DNA sequences in vitro and also in vivo. This technology, which is based on advances in microbiology—particularly in understanding the life cycles of bacteria and their viruses, the bacteriophages—has revolutionized the study of genetics. With the ultimate goal of studying specific genes and their functions, biologists use recombinant DNA techniques to (1) fragment DNA into easily managed pieces and then separate and purify these fragments; (2) create many copies of DNA molecules of identical sequence; (3) combine DNA fragments to construct chimeric, or recombinant, DNA molecules; (4) determine

the exact sequence of specific DNA molecules; (5) identify fragments of DNA containing complementary sequences; (6) introduce specific DNA molecules into living organisms; and (7) assay the phenotypic effects of the introduced DNA.

The major challenges of recombinant DNA technology are the identification of specific DNA sequences and their manipulation in vitro. To see these challenges in perspective, consider that each of your cells contains two copies each of 22 autosomes and 2 sex chromosomes. Collectively, a haploid set of 23 chromosomes contains 3 billion base pairs and carry some 22,800 or so genes. A typical gene encodes an mRNA transcript consisting of a few thousand bases, although the mRNA may be transcribed from a region that spans millions of base pairs. Molecular analysis of genes and of allelic variation is possible only by distinguishing a gene of interest from others in the genome.

Recombinant DNA technology allows researchers to divide the genome into smaller segments that can then be analyzed and reassembled to provide a molecular view of genes and the genome. In the following sections we describe the development of recombinant DNA technology tools and their application to identify specific DNA sequences.

Restriction Enzymes

Restriction enzymes, which cut DNA at specific sequences, have become a basic tool of recombinant DNA technology (see Section 10.2). Each type of restriction enzyme recognizes a particular sequence at which it cuts both strands of the sugar-phosphate backbone of the DNA, cleaving the restriction sequence in the same way each time it is encountered. Restriction enzymes were originally discovered in bacterial cells, where they protect the bacteria from invasions of nucleic acids, such as the injected genomes of bacteriophages, by digesting foreign DNA. They were given the name *restriction enzymes* because they restrict the growth of the bacteriophages. Bacterial cells also contain **restriction-modification systems,** which modify the restriction sequences in the bacterial DNA by the addition of methyl groups and thus protect the bacteria's own DNA from being digested by endogenous restriction enzymes. **Experimental Insight 17.1** explains how restriction enzymes and restriction-modification systems were identified and how they became an indispensable part of molecular biology.

Restriction enzymes are common in bacteria. The names given these enzymes are generally derived from the first letter of the bacterial genus and first two letters of the species moniker, followed by a Roman numeral. For example, *Eco*RI is derived from *Escherichia coli*; the letter R denotes the strain from which the enzyme was

Experimental Insight 17.1

From Bacteriophage to Restriction Enzymes: Basic Research Spawned a Biological Revolution

Basic biological research aims to discover and understand phenomena from every part of the spectrum of life. Thousands of biologists engage in this research every day, and most have specialties that may seem obscure or trivial to nonscientists. Nevertheless, their discoveries can not only revolutionize research but affect how we view the world.

In the mid-1960s, Werner Arber was studying a bacterial phenomenon called *host-controlled restriction and modification*, which acts as a simple immune system for bacteria invaded by bacteriophages. He showed that *E. coli* produces two enzymes that affect the same short palindromic DNA sequences (see Section 10.2 for discussion of palindromic sequences). One enzyme, called a *restriction endonuclease*, cleaves DNA at that sequence, like a pair of molecular scissors. The second enzyme, called a *modification enzyme*, adds methyl groups (CH_3) to DNA, thereby preventing restriction endonucleases from binding to and cleaving the DNA.

In 1970, Hamilton Smith extended Arber's work by studying a restriction endonuclease from *Haemophilus influenzae*. Smith isolated the restriction endonuclease, now called *Hind*II, and determined that it cleaves at the sequence

$$5'\text{-GTPyPuAC-}3' \qquad\longrightarrow\qquad 5'\text{-GTPyPuAC-}3'$$
$$3'\text{-CAPuPyTG-}5' \qquad\qquad\qquad 3'\text{-CAPuPyTG-}5'$$

*Hind*II cleaves both strands of its target sequence between the central purine (Pu = A or G) and pyrimidine (Py = T or C), leaving blunt ends on either side of the cut (blunt ends are discussed on page 574).

Smith's work on *Hind*II identified some important characteristics of restriction enzymes. First, *Hind*II cleaves foreign DNA into large fragments, but it does not affect *H. influenzae* DNA. This confirmed Arber's idea that bacterial DNA is protected from the action of the bacteria's own restriction enzymes. Second, each resulting DNA fragment has the same three base pairs at its ends, indicating that cleavage occurs only at the target sequence. Smith also discovered that restriction enzymes cleave every copy they encounter of their target sequence.

In 1971, Daniel Nathans pioneered the use of restriction endonucleases to address genetic and genomic questions. Nathans used *Hind*II to digest the small genome of the Simian virus SV40 and found that 11 DNA fragments were formed. In 1973, Nathans digested SV40 with two newly discovered restriction endonucleases. He then used the three sets of restriction fragments to create the first *restriction map* of the SV40 genome, by determining the number of restriction sites for each enzyme and their order in the genome and assembling the information into a map (as demonstrated elsewhere in this chapter).

By the time Nathans completed his SV40 genome map, biologists were already looking for other restriction enzymes. Within 5 years, over 100 more restriction enzymes were discovered. Many formed "sticky" ends on digested DNA (described on this page), and Paul Berg realized that DNA fragments from different organisms could be joined together if they had complementary sticky ends. This finding led to his creating the first recombinant DNA molecule, in 1975.

Arber, Smith, and Nathans shared the Nobel Prize in Physiology or Medicine in 1978 for their work on restriction enzymes, and Berg won the prize in 1980 for the development of recombinant DNA. Since then, restriction enzymes have become a ubiquitous tool in genetic and genomic research. Arber's initial study of an obscure event in bacteria had spawned a revolution as momentous as Watson and Crick's description of DNA structure or Mendel's description of the laws of heredity.

---

obtained (RY13), and the numeral (I) indicates it was the first enzyme identified. *Eco*RI recognizes the palindromic sequence

$$5'\text{-GAATTC-}3'$$
$$3'\text{-CTTAAG-}5'$$

Recall that a palindrome has the same 5'-to-3' base sequence in both of its antiparallel DNA strands. Most restriction enzymes recognize palindromic sequences. For example, *Eco*RI cuts the sugar–phosphate bond between the G and the adjacent A residues in both strands, and the staggered cut results in two products, each ending with a four-base, single-stranded sequence:

$$5'\text{-G} \qquad\qquad \text{AATTC-}3'$$
$$3'\text{-CTTAA} \qquad\qquad \text{G-}5'$$

The single-stranded segments at the ends of each *Eco*RI fragment are referred to as **sticky ends** because they can "stick" to a complementary base-pair sequence by hydrogen bonding. Production of sticky ends facilitates the combining of DNA fragments generated with restriction enzymes, and complementary base pairing plays a role in almost all recombinant DNA techniques. The principle is that if two DNA molecules produced by restriction enzyme digestion have complementary sticky ends, they can be combined by complementary base pairing.

Another enzyme, *Eco*RI methylase, protects the *E. coli* genome from being itself digested by the *Eco*RI endonuclease. *Eco*RI methylase does this by adding a methyl group to the A adjacent to the T in both strands of the DNA. This is the "modification" performed by the *Eco*RI restriction-modification system.

Hundreds of restriction enzymes have been isolated from bacteria and are commercially available (see Table 10.1). While many restriction enzymes produce sticky ends, either with 5' overhangs (as produced by *Eco*RI) or with 3' overhangs, some restriction enzymes leave **blunt ends** that lack a single-stranded segment. Blunt-ended DNA molecules can also be recombined, by techniques discussed later in this chapter (see page 574).

Some restriction enzymes recognize 4-bp sequences, others recognize sequences of 5 bp, or 6, or 8. The length of the recognition sequence influences how frequently a given enzyme will cut DNA. If the DNA of an organism were to consist of 25% A, 25% T, 25% G, and 25% C and the bases were randomly distributed, then a restriction enzyme that had a 4-bp recognition sequence would be expected to cut the DNA once every 256 bp ($1/4 \times 1/4 \times 1/4 \times 1/4 = 1/256$). Likewise, a restriction enzyme that recognized a 6-bp sequence would cut the DNA once every 4096 bp ($1/4^6$) on average, and a restriction enzyme that recognized an 8-bp sequence would cut the DNA once every 65,536 bp ($1/4^8$) on average. In reality, genomes of most organisms do not consist of equal amounts of each of the four bases. For example, most genomes of multicellular eukaryotes are AT-rich (that is, their genomes have a higher content of A and T than of G and C), and so restriction enzymes that recognize a GC-rich sequence would cut less frequently on average than would enzymes that recognize an AT-rich sequence.

Scientists use data from restriction experiments, including the number of restriction sites and the number of base pairs between the sites, to create maps of specific DNA sequences. These **restriction maps** provide a foundation for further manipulation of the DNA fragments—for example, by suggesting where to further subdivide cloned fragments in order to clone still smaller fragments, in a process known as **subcloning.**

Let's use the genome of *E. coli* lambda phage in an example of the restriction mapping process. The DNA of the phage genome can be isolated by purifying the phage and removing its protein coat. If this is done gently, the isolated nucleic acid will be the entire lambda chromosome, which is a linear molecule 48,502 bp in length. Electrophoresis of the chromosome in an agarose gel including a fluorescent stain for DNA (see Chapter 10) would reveal a single fluorescent 48.5-kb band (first lane in **Figure 17.1**). If the purified lambda chromosome is first digested with *Apa*I, two fragments, one measuring 10.1 kb and the other 38.4 kb, are generated, indicating that *Apa*I must cut the genome once. This allows us to begin drawing the restriction map as shown below.

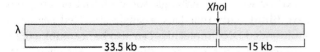

If we digest the purified lambda chromosome with *Xho*I, two fragments, one 33.5 kb and one 15 kb, are generated, indicating that *Xho*I must also cut the genome once:

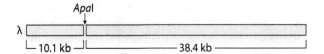

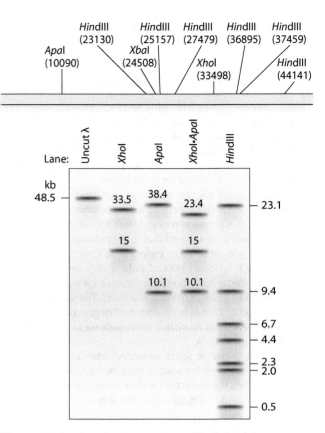

Figure 17.1 **Restriction mapping of lambda phage.**

However, two orientations are possible for the *Xho*I restriction map relative to the *Apa*I restriction map drawn above. It could also be drawn as shown below.

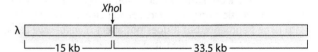

To determine which order is correct, we need to perform a double digest, in which both enzymes are used simultaneously to cut the lambda genome. This experiment generates three pieces: 10.1 kb, 15 kb, and 23.4 kb. Since the 15-kb *Xho*I fragment remained intact but the 33.5-kb *Xho*I fragment was cut into two fragments (10.1 kb and 23.4 kb) by *Apa*I, we conclude that the map must be:

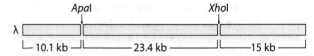

The other possible map can be eliminated as incorrect since it would generate fragments of 4.9 kb, 10.1 kb, and 33.5 kb:

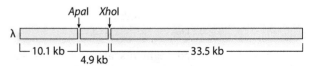

Genetic Analysis 17.1 provides additional practice at constructing a restriction map.

PROBLEM You have isolated a plasmid from *E. coli* and wish to begin your analysis of it by making a restriction map. Using three restriction enzymes, ❶ *Bam*H1, ❷ *Eco*RI, ❸ *Not*I, you perform six different digestions: single digests using each enzyme alone and double digests using each combination of two enzymes. Agarose gel electrophoresis of the resulting fragments produces the results shown here. Draw a restriction map of the plasmid.

> **BREAK IT DOWN:** A plasmid is a circular DNA molecule (Chapter 6, p. 188). Cut once, it becomes linear; cut twice, it forms two fragments; and so on.

> **BREAK IT DOWN:** Gel electrophoresis separates linear DNA fragments by their length, with the smallest fragments moving farthest from the origin of migration (Chapter 10, p. 343).

> **BREAK IT DOWN:** A restriction map (p. 570) is a depiction of the relative positions of restriction-enzyme sites (p. 568).

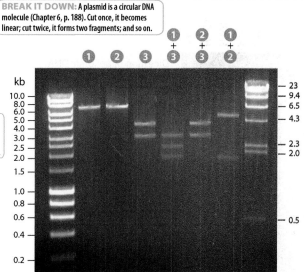

Solution Strategies	Solution Steps

Evaluate

1. Identify the topic this problem addresses and the nature of the required answer.

1. This problem is about restriction mapping and asks you to construct a restriction map of a plasmid.

2. Identify the critical information given in the problem.

2. Electrophoresis results are given for three single digests and the three possible double-digest combinations.

Deduce

3. Identify the sizes of each of the fragments of the single digests, and determine how many times each enzyme cuts the plasmid.

> **TIP:** Compare the sizes of fragments in the sample lanes with the sizes of the standards.

3. *Bam*HI—A single 7-kb fragment. Since plasmids are circular, *Bam*HI must cut the plasmid only once.

   *Eco*RI—A single 7-kb fragment. One site in the plasmid.

   *Not*I—Two fragments: 3 kb and 4 kb. *Not*I must cut the plasmid at two sites.

4. Identify the sizes of each of the fragments of the double digests.

4. *Not*I + *Bam*HI—Three fragments: 3 kb, 2.3 kb, 1.7 kb.

   *Not*I + *Eco*RI—Two fragments: 4 kb, 3 kb.

   *Bam*HI + *Eco*RI—Two fragments: 5.3 kb, 1.7 kb.

5. Compare single- and double-digest results for similarities and differences.

> **TIP:** In analyzing double digests, the relative position of restriction sites can be determined by observing which fragments remain intact and which are cut into smaller fragments.

> **PITFALL:** If two sites are very close to one another, there will be fewer fragments than expected in the double digest.

5. *Not*I + *Bam*HI—Three fragments, with the 3-kb *Not*I fragment intact, suggesting the *Bam*HI site is within the 4-kb *Not*I fragment.

   *Not*I + *Eco*RI—Two fragments, with both the 4-kb and 3-kb *Not*I fragments intact, suggesting the *Eco*RI site is adjacent to one of the *Not*I sites.

   *Bam*HI + *Eco*RI—Two fragments, indicating the two sites are separated by 1.7 kb (or 5.3 kb the long way around the plasmid).

Solve

6. (a) Draw a restriction map with *Not*I sites. (b) Add in the *Bam*HI site. (c) Add in the *Eco*RI site.

> **TIP:** Drawing of the restriction map does not require the three enzymes to be examined in any particular order.

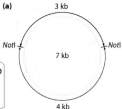

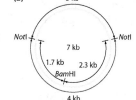

Digestion with *Bam*HI cuts the 4-kb *Not*I fragment into 2.3-kb and 1.7-kb fragments.

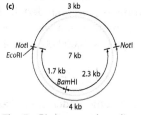

The *Eco*RI site must be adjacent to one of the *Not*I sites and is 1.7 kb from the *Bam*HI site. The relative order of the *Eco*RI and adjacent *Not*I sites cannot be determined, since the resolution of gel electrophoresis is not sufficient.

For more practice, see Problems 16, 18, 19, 20, and 21.

Visit the Study Area to access study tools.

MasteringGenetics™

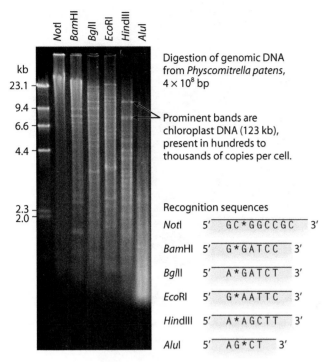

kb

23.1 —
9.4 —
6.6 —
4.4 —

2.3 —
2.0 —

Digestion of genomic DNA
from *Physcomitrella patens*,
4×10^8 bp

Prominent bands are
chloroplast DNA (123 kb),
present in hundreds to
thousands of copies per cell.

Recognition sequences

*Not*I	5′ GC*GGCCGC 3′	
*Bam*HI	5′ G*GATCC 3′	
*Bgl*II	5′ A*GATCT 3′	
*Eco*RI	5′ G*AATTC 3′	
*Hind*III	5′ A*AGCTT 3′	
*Alu*I	5′ AG*CT 3′	

Figure 17.2   Restriction-enzyme digestion of genomic DNA.

To analyze DNA from organisms with large genomes, researchers must fragment the genomes into more manageable pieces. For example, the *Physcomitrella patens* genome consists of 400 million base pairs, and when digested with a restriction enzyme like *Eco*RI that cuts on average every 4096 bp, approximately 100,000 different DNA fragments are produced. When this digested DNA is electrophoresed through an agarose gel, the fragments making up the resulting "smear" range from over 20 kb down to smaller than 100 bp (Figure 17.2). The smeared appearance results because, although the enzyme cuts every 4096 bp on average, the distances between *Eco*RI sites will vary due to variation in the genome sequence, and the resolving power of agarose gel electrophoresis is not sufficient to separate all of the different-sized fragments into discrete bands. This lack of resolution is compounded in larger genomes, such as ours, where digestion with *Eco*RI produces approximately 730,000 pieces (3,000,000,000/4096).

Molecular Cloning

After a genome under study has been reduced to smaller pieces by restriction enzymes, the individual pieces must be reproduced in large amounts—generally, either by molecular cloning or by the polymerase chain reaction (PCR)—so that each of them can be analyzed in greater detail. Molecular cloning arose from discoveries in bacterial enzymology and utilizes bacteria and their plasmids or phages to amplify and propagate specific fragments of DNA.

In molecular cloning, isolated DNA fragments are inserted into a **vector,** a carrier fragment of DNA with

attributes that will allow amplification (replication) in a biological system. Then the recombinant DNA molecule is introduced into a biological system that amplifies the DNA, making many identical copies called **DNA clones.** Molecular cloning produces a large quantity of identical DNA molecules that can be analyzed by a variety of techniques, including restriction enzyme analysis and DNA sequencing.

Molecular cloning has three general steps:

1. The joining together of the cloning vector and a donor DNA fragment to produce a **recombinant clone**

2. Selection of vectors containing copies of the DNA segment of interest

3. Amplification of the recombinant clone in a biological system

In this section, we describe how DNA fragments are combined in vitro, the attributes of some common cloning vectors, and the means of their amplification. We then describe how DNA libraries—collections of cloned DNA fragments, usually derived from a single DNA source—are constructed.

Creating Recombinant DNA Molecules One common method of producing recombinant DNA is to digest DNA from the donor source and DNA of the cloning vector with the same restriction enzyme. The resulting linear fragments from the two DNA sources can then be annealed at their complementary sticky ends. Figure 17.3 illustrates restriction digestion by *Eco*RI of both the vector DNA—a plasmid, in this case—and DNA from the human genome. Mixing the two DNAs in a test tube allows the sticky ends to hybridize to one another by complementary base pairing, after which the remaining single-stranded nicks are sealed with DNA ligase (see Chapter 7), resulting in a recombinant DNA molecule. In this case, a recombinant plasmid containing human DNA is formed.

While it is common to cut both source and vector DNA with the same enzyme, variations on this theme are frequently employed. For example, two different restriction enzymes that create complementary sticky ends are sometimes used. When different restriction enzymes are used to digest vector and donor DNA, complementary sticky ends are called **cohesive compatible ends**. For example, *Bam*HI recognizes the 6-bp sequence

$$5'-GGATCC-3'$$
$$3'-CCTAGG-5'$$

and leaves sticky ends

$$5'-G \qquad GATCC-3'$$
$$3'-CCTAG \qquad G-5'$$

*Sau*3A recognizes the 4-bp sequence

$$5'-GATC-3'$$
$$3'-CTAG-5'$$

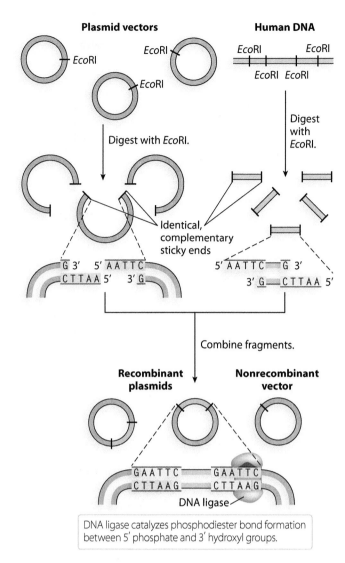

Figure 17.3   Making recombinant DNA molecules.

and leaves sticky ends

$$5'-N \qquad GATCN-3'$$
$$3'-NCTAG \qquad N-5'$$

(where N represents any nucleotide). Since the sticky ends created by the two enzymes are the same (5'-GATC-3'), the ends of a *Bam*HI- and a *Sau*3A-digested fragment can combine to create recombinant DNA molecules. However, in this case, the resulting ligated products will often lack an intact *Bam*HI site, since the 5' Ns from the *Sau*3A site may not be Gs.

Usually the goal of this process is to create recombinant DNA molecules in which a single piece of source DNA is combined with a single cloning vector molecule. However, because digested DNA from both sources is mixed together in a test tube, a variety of recombinant molecules may arise. For example, some recombinants may have a single donor-DNA insert, whereas others may have two or more donor fragments that join together and

then insert into the vector. In addition, the sticky ends of vectors can rejoin each other rather than incorporating a donor insert, producing a **nonrecombinant vector.** Because neither nonrecombinant vectors nor clones with multiple inserts are desired results, techniques to favor the production of single-insert clones have been developed. For example, the occurrence of nonrecombinant vectors can be reduced by removal of the 5' phosphates on the vector DNA, so that the vector DNA cannot ligate to itself to produce nonrecombinant clones.

A feature of experiments using a single restriction enzyme or using two enzymes with cohesive compatible ends is that the insert DNA can be ligated into the vector in either orientation. One way to ensure that insert DNA is cloned into a vector in a specific orientation is to use two restriction enzymes with different compatible ends, a process called **directional cloning** (Figure 17.4). Directional cloning has three desirable features. First, only insert-DNA fragments possessing the two different compatible ends will be efficiently inserted into the vector. Second, the

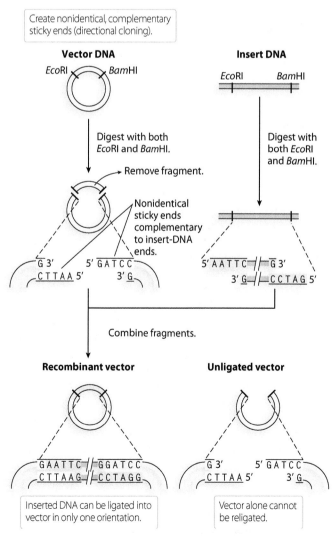

Figure 17.4   Directional cloning of DNA molecules.

inserted fragments are ligated in a particular orientation dictated by the cohesive compatible ends. And third, due to the incompatibility of the two ends of the digested vector DNA, the vector cannot re-ligate to itself, thus minimizing the creation of nonrecombinant vectors.

While hundreds of restriction enzymes are commercially available, cohesive compatible ends are not always possible to produce at the positions necessary for constructing the desired recombinant DNA molecules. One approach to creating compatible ends in such a case is to generate blunt ends—ends without any overhang—that can then be ligated to form a recombinant molecule.

Some restriction enzymes naturally create blunt ends, but any restriction enzyme site can be converted into a blunt end. There are two general strategies (**Figure 17.5**). For example, DNA polymerase (see Chapter 7) can use a 5′ overhang as a template and add dNTPs to the recessed 3′ end until a blunt end has been produced. Alternatively, 3′ overhangs can be made blunt by a DNA exonuclease (see Chapter 7) that degrades only single-stranded DNA and "chews back" the 3′ overhang. Some procedures use shearing force rather than restriction enzymes (as when DNA is passed through a fine needle), producing random DNA fragments whose ends can then be blunted by treatment with a DNA polymerase and exonuclease. Conversely, blunt ends can be converted into sticky ends by ligation of short oligonucleotides onto the blunt-ended DNA molecules. The oligonucleotides can be synthesized to have sequences for any restriction enzyme desired, thus adding any specific restriction site to the end of any DNA molecule. Oligonucleotides of this type are called **linkers**.

Plasmids as Cloning Vectors Plasmids are circular DNA molecules that replicate autonomously in bacteria and usually carry nonessential genes. The F-factor involved in *E. coli* conjugation (see Chapter 6) is a plasmid. Plasmids used as cloning vectors replicate independently of the bacterial chromosome and, unlike the F-factor, which can recombine into the *E. coli* chromosome, always remain separate from it. Most plasmids used as cloning vectors have been modified in the laboratory to possess several features that facilitate the production of recombinant DNA molecules (**Figure 17.6a**). For example, plasmids are equipped with an *origin of replication (ori)* that drives efficient replication of the plasmid within the bacterial host. They also contain a gene conferring a trait that permits bacteria harboring the plasmid to be selectively grown. Genes conferring resistance to antibiotics are commonly used as selectable markers.

Two types of plasmids, identified as pUC-based plasmids and pBR-based plasmids, are most frequently used in constructing recombinant plasmids capable of transforming competent bacteria. Both types have many different forms, developed through extensive genetic engineering in the laboratory. In these vectors, the *β-lactamase* gene, conferring resistance to ampicillin, is often used as the

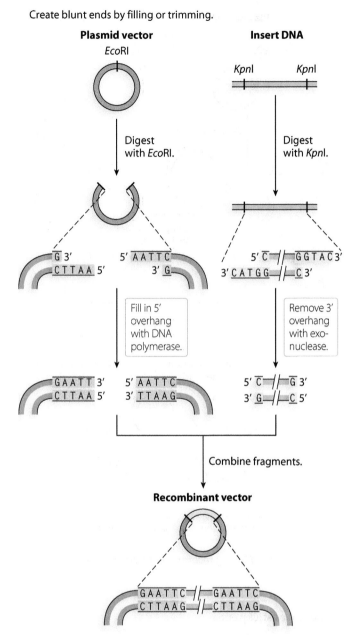

Create blunt ends by filling or trimming.

Figure 17.5 **Connecting blunt ends to create recombinant DNA molecules.**

selectable marker. The origin of replication was derived from a naturally occurring *E. coli* plasmid called the ColE1 plasmid. The ColE1 *ori* allows these plasmids to be maintained at a high copy number of 100–200 plasmids per cell.

Both pUC and pBR plasmids also contain a **multiple cloning site (MCS)** that has several different restriction enzyme sites into which DNA can be inserted These restriction enzyme sites occur only within the MCS and nowhere else in the plasmid. In pUC-based plasmid cloning vectors, the MCS is embedded in the *lacZ* gene, which encodes β-galactosidase, an arrangement that provides a colorimetric assay for determining which bacteria harbor vectors with an insertion of DNA into

(a)

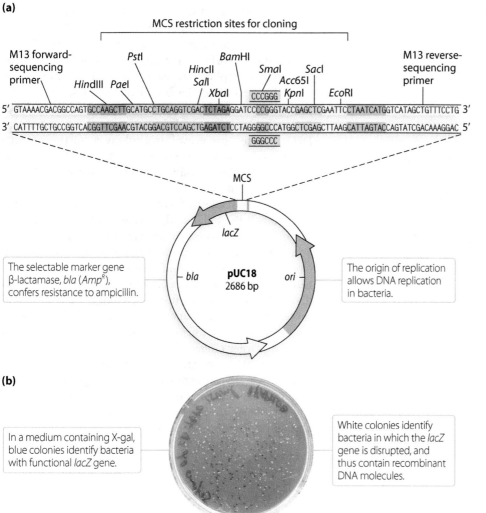

Figure 17.6   **A plasmid cloning vector.**

(b)

In a medium containing X-gal, blue colonies identify bacteria with functional *lacZ* gene.

White colonies identify bacteria in which the *lacZ* gene is disrupted, and thus contain recombinant DNA molecules.

the MCS (**Figure 17.6b**). Although the normal substrate for β-galactosidase is lactose, the enzyme can also cleave lactose analogs, such as X-gal. When the colorless substrate X-gal is added to the growth medium, bacteria with a functional *lacZ* gene producing β-galactosidase will convert X-gal to a blue product. When a fragment of DNA is inserted into the MCS, the *lacZ* gene is disrupted and rendered nonfunctional. Bacteria then will appear as white colonies, whereas bacteria harboring a cloning vector that does not contain a fragment of DNA inserted in the MCS are blue. This difference allows rapid identification of colonies harboring vectors with inserts in the MCS. Thus, selection based on antibiotic resistance allows identification of bacteria that have been transformed, and *blue versus white* screening allows identification of bacteria harboring plasmid vectors with an insertion of recombinant DNA.

Amplifying Recombinant DNA Molecules For amplification—that is, replication of the recombinant DNA molecules in large numbers—the recombinant

molecules are introduced into *E. coli* by transformation, the same process described by Griffiths and by Avery, MacLeod, and McCarty in their early investigations of the hereditary function of DNA (**Figure 17.7**; see Chapter 6). In modern laboratories, DNA is mixed with *E. coli* in a test tube. The bacteria are chemically treated with either divalent cations (such as Ca^{2+}) or an electrical shock to open pores in their membranes, thus making the bacteria "competent" to take up exogenous DNA by transformation. For safety purposes, the bacterial strains used in recombinant DNA experiments are chosen for characteristics that do not allow them to survive well outside of the laboratory.

The concentrations of DNA used to transform competent bacteria are those determined empirically to be concentrations at which individual bacterial cells are likely to take up no more than one DNA molecule. After transformation, the bacteria are allowed to recover for a short period of time and are then plated on growth medium that selects for cells containing the selectable marker gene, conferring resistance to

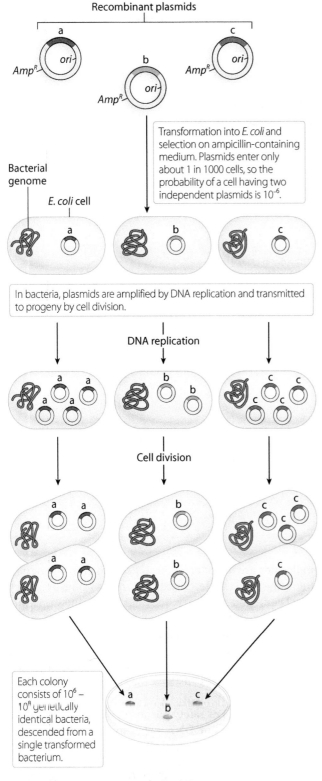

Figure 17.7 **Amplification of recombinant DNA molecules in bacteria.**

Recombinant DNA molecules introduced into microbial cells are amplified by repeated cycles of DNA replication within the bacteria. Since the recombinant vector has an origin of replication, it will amplify by autonomous replication using bacterial enzymes. After that, the next time the bacterium divides, each of its progeny will receive copies of the recombinant DNA molecule. Because a single bacterium with a recombinant DNA molecule can grow into a colony consisting of some 10^8 bacteria, each with multiple copies of the recombinant DNA molecule, billions of identical copies of DNA molecules are made.

The use of plasmid vectors for cloning large DNA fragments is limited, mainly because large plasmids (over 20 kb) are not efficiently maintained in a high copy number. This limitation restricts the usefulness of plasmids in cloning eukaryotic genomic DNA. Eukaryotic genomes can be large (the human genome is 3×10^9 bp), with individual genes that are often much longer than 20 kb and therefore cannot be cloned in a single plasmid. To overcome these limitations of plasmids, vectors capable of handling larger clones have been developed (Table 17.1). Two general approaches have been employed to propagate larger DNA fragments. In one approach, vectors based on the life cycle of bacteriophages—in particular, bacteriophage lambda—accommodate larger fragments of DNA. The second approach harnesses single-copy origins of replication to efficiently propagate even larger recombinant DNA molecules in both bacteria and yeast.

Bacteriophage Vectors Bacteriophage lambda is capable of both a lytic life cycle and a lysogenic life cycle (see Section 14.6). Phage propagation through the lysogenic life cycle requires the presence of all the genes of the lambda genome, but genes that are specifically involved in the lysogenic life cycle are dispensable for the lytic life cycle. If the genes required for lysogeny are removed, they can be replaced by up to 23 kb of DNA from another source, and the recombinant phage can then be propagated through a lytic life cycle (Figure 17.8a). In bacteriophage-based vectors, it is the replication of the phage within the bacterium that amplifies the recombinant DNA molecule.

The size of inserted DNA that can be accommodated is further increased by taking advantage of another feature of the lambda bacteriophage system: rolling circle replication (see Chapter 6). During the lytic life cycle, replication of lambda DNA by rolling circle replication results in successive concatenation of 50-kb genomes into long DNA molecules. A lambda-encoded nuclease then recognizes a specific sequence within the lambda genome and cleaves the concatenated genomes into single-genome units. Subsequently, specific sequences called **cohesive end sequence**, or *cos*, **sites** in the lambda genome will interact with lambda phage coat proteins to "package" the individual lambda genomes into discrete phage particles in vitro. The *cos*

an antibiotic, encoded on the DNA vector. When the transformed bacteria are plated on media containing the antibiotic, only those bacteria harboring vector DNA will survive.

Table 17.1	Cloning Vectors			
Vector	**Form of DNA**	**Host**	**Capacity**	**Uses**
Plasmid	Circular	*E. coli*	<15 kb	Subcloning and cDNA libraries
Lambda	Linear phage chromosome	*E. coli*	<23 kb	cDNA and genomic libraries
Cosmid	Circular	*E. coli*	30–45 kb	Genomic libraries
BAC	Bacterial chromosome	*E. coli*	100–200 kb	Genomic libraries
YAC	Yeast chromosome	*S. cerevisiae*	200–2000 kb	Genomic libraries

sites are the only lambda sequences required for packaging of DNA, so when DNA from another source is concatenated with *cos* sequences derived from lambda, the ligated DNA can be packaged into phage particles. In this case, neither the genes for lysis nor the genes for lysogeny are in the phage particles; thus, after infection of a host bacterium, the injected DNA does not enter the lambda life cycle. If an origin of replication and a selectable marker are included in the vector, however, the DNA can be replicated as a plasmid in the bacterium (**Figure 17.8b**). Vectors with these features are known as **cosmid vectors.** Since the lambda phage can hold up to 50 kb, cosmid vectors can carry up to 45 kb of insert sequence along with 5 kb of *cos*, origin of replication, and selectable marker sequence.

Artificial Chromosomes While both lambda and cosmid vectors have been historically important, vectors called artificial chromosomes, which have the capacity to carry even larger DNA fragments, are now more frequently used. These were developed through accumulated knowledge of how chromosomes propagate in bacteria and eukaryotes, and of the functions of different chromosome regions in replication.

Yeast artificial chromosomes (YACs) were the first artificial chromosomes developed and are used as cloning vectors in *S. cerevisiae*. A YAC vector contains sequences corresponding to a centromere (see Section 11.3), telomeres, a selectable marker, and a cloning site, and it can accept an insert size of 200 kb to 2 megabases (Mb). YACs carrying an insert smaller than 200 kb are often unstable and do not properly segregate at mitosis.

Bacterial artificial chromosomes (BACs) were developed shortly after YACs. Although BACs have a smaller insert-size capacity (100–200 kb) than YACs, they are the preferred artificial chromosome cloning vector, largely due to the ease of using *E. coli* rather than yeast as a host. Like plasmids, BAC vectors contain an origin of replication, a selectable marker gene, and an MCS. However, the origin of replication in BAC vectors is derived from the F-factor plasmid. Unlike replication via the ColE1 origin, replication via the F-factor origin is strictly controlled, producing only one or two copies of the F-factor per cell. This difference allows large plasmids to

be maintained, circumventing the problem encountered with plasmids that have high copy numbers.

The utility of BAC cloning vectors becomes apparent when we consider the typical sizes of eukaryotic genes. For example, while individual globin genes in the β-globin locus are about 1.4 kb in length, the regulatory sequences controlling the cluster of globin genes span about 70 kb of genomic DNA. The entire β-globin locus can be contained in a single BAC, but would not be contained in a single plasmid or cosmid clone. However, some eukaryotic genes, such as the gene for Duchenne's muscular dystrophy in humans, span more than a megabase and are unlikely to be contained within a single BAC or YAC clone.

DNA Libraries

A **DNA library** is a collection of cloned fragments of DNA, usually derived from the nucleic acids of a single source (recall our use of *library* in Chapter 16). DNA libraries come in two varieties: those derived from the genomic DNA of an organism are called **genomic libraries,** and those derived from mRNA are called **complementary DNA (cDNA) libraries.** Since the source of nucleic acids for each type of library differs, the kinds of sequences represented in each type also differ.

In theory, genomic libraries should contain all the sequences found in the genome of the source organism. For example, a human genomic library would contain all 3×10^9 bp in the haploid genome sequence. This would include the exons and introns of genes, the regulatory sequences controlling gene expression, the intergenic sequences (noncoding sequences between genes), and repetitive sequences (centromeres, telomeres, ribosomal DNA, transposons, retroelements, etc.). By contrast, cDNA libraries are derived from mRNA and thus represent the DNA sequences that are transcribed in the tissue from which the mRNA is derived. Since only a fraction of the genes present in the genome are likely to be expressed in any particular tissue, and even those are expressed at different levels, only a fraction of the genes are represented, and in different amounts, in any cDNA library. Thus, the number of times a specific sequence is represented in a library differs significantly between genomic and cDNA libraries.

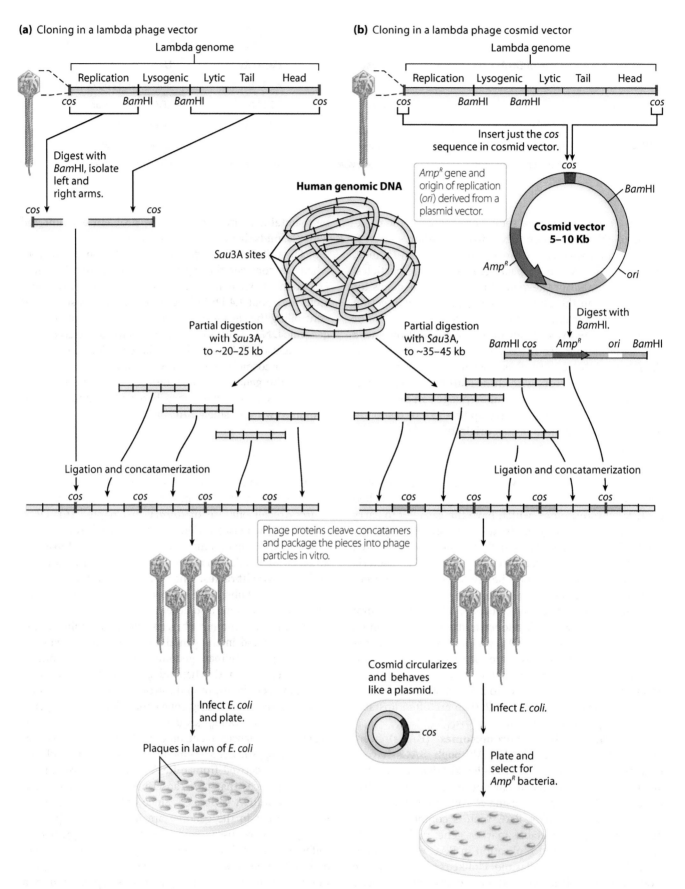

(a) Cloning in a lambda phage vector

(b) Cloning in a lambda phage cosmid vector

Figure 17.8 **Cloning in bacteriophage vectors.**

Constructing Genomic Libraries Genomic libraries are collections of individual clones derived from the genomic DNA of an organism. To construct a genomic library, genomic DNA, usually from a single individual, is isolated and fragmented into smaller pieces that are then ligated into cloning vectors (**Figure 17.9**). The recombinant vectors are transformed into bacteria (in the case of plasmid and BAC vectors) or used to infect bacteria (in the case of phage vectors) that grow into colonies or plaques that collectively contain clones representing the entire genome.

A genomic library contains each sequence in the genome at approximately the same frequency. Thus, sequences representing the exons and introns of genes, the regulatory sequences controlling their expression, and repetitive and intergenic sequences are all approximately equally represented in the genomic library. However, in practice, some sequences are not efficiently maintained in the host cells and will be underrepresented, so the entire genome is not fully represented in any typical genomic library. For example, repetitive DNA tends to be under-represented due to its propensity to undergo intragenic recombination that results in deletion of DNA sequences within clones.

Three desirable attributes for a genomic library are that (1) the genomic clones are broadly representative of DNA of the entire genome, (2) the genomic clones are large enough to be useful for sequencing and subcloning, and (3) the genomic clones are roughly similar in size. Let's look at how these attributes are achieved.

To ensure that a genomic library is broadly representative, care must be taken to fragment it into random

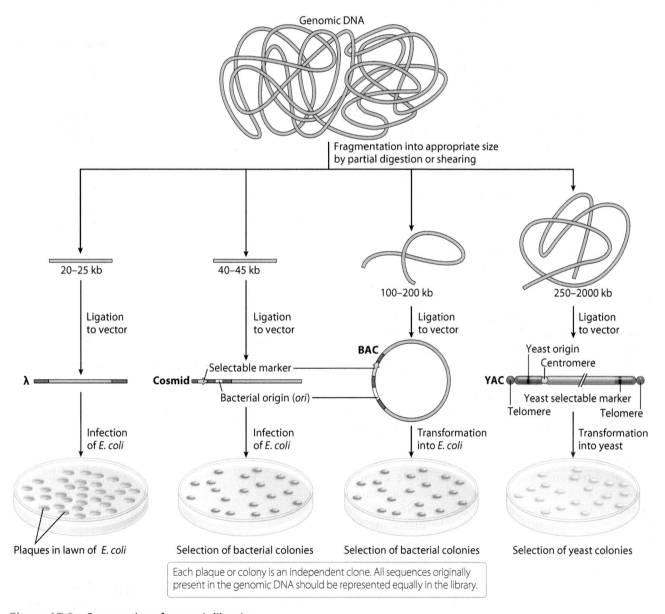

Figure 17.9   Construction of genomic libraries.

pieces of an appropriate and relatively uniform size for cloning into a vector. Random fragmentation is accomplished by two different methods. In one technique, the DNA is *partially digested* with an enzyme that cuts very frequently (e.g., a restriction enzyme that has a 4-bp recognition sequence). Partial digestion refers to the use of *less* restriction enzyme than would be needed to cut the DNA at every restriction sequence the enzyme recognizes, resulting in cuts at some of the restriction sequences but not all of them. Since a 4-bp recognition sequence should occur every 256 bp on average, partial digestion of DNA in which, on average, only one in 400 recognition sequences are cut, should result in DNA fragments of approximately 100 kb. Thus, partial digestion with an enzyme that otherwise cuts frequently will generate random, large genomic DNA fragments with sticky ends, as desired. The second technique for obtaining random fragmentation of DNA is random shearing of genomic DNA with subsequent enzymatic treatment to create blunt ends. In theory, either technique should provide random representation of genomic DNA from the entire genome.

The size of DNA clones in genomic libraries results from technical choices that seek a balance between, on the one hand, the difficulty of isolating, cloning, and propagating large molecules of DNA and, on the other hand, the greater number of smaller fragments that would have to be cloned in order to span the entire genome. As we discuss in Chapter 18, however, a set of genomic libraries that each have a different-sized insertion can be useful for determining the sequence of an entire genome.

Constructing cDNA Libraries The starting material for a cDNA library is mRNA, often derived from a specific tissue or cell type. Messenger RNA cannot be cloned directly because it is single stranded and is of course RNA, not DNA. Cloning of mRNA sequences can be accomplished by synthesizing a double-stranded cDNA copy of the mRNA and then ligating the cDNA into a vector. cDNA libraries are especially useful for working with eukaryotic organisms whose gene sequences are interrupted by many long introns.

The concept and development of cDNA libraries required advances in understanding the life cycle of retroviruses and the movement of retrotransposons (see Section 13.7). The availability of the enzyme **reverse transcriptase,** found in RNA-containing retroviruses, and of retrotransposons, which use single-stranded RNA as a template to produce a complementary strand of DNA, makes cloning from mRNA possible. Reverse transcriptase creates cDNA by first transcribing a single-stranded DNA molecule complementary to mRNA acting as a template. The poly-A tail added to RNA polymerase II transcripts of eukaryotes facilitates the construction of cDNA libraries from such mRNA, since the first strand of cDNA can be synthesized using an oligo dT primer (**Figure 17.10**). The mRNA template

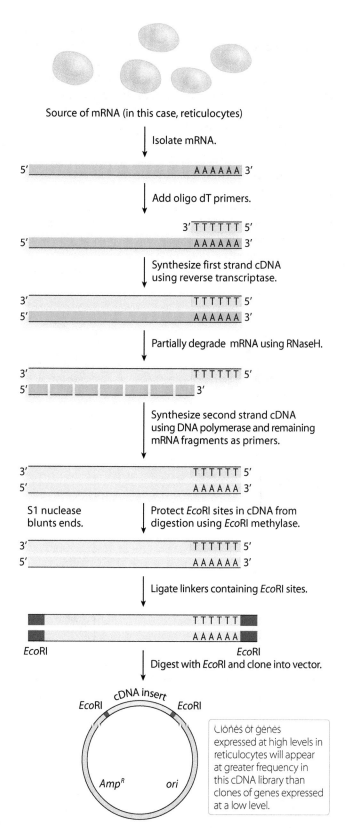

Figure 17.10 **Construction of cDNA libraries.**

is then enzymatically removed, and the second strand of DNA is synthesized by DNA polymerase, using the first cDNA strand as a template.

The composition of a cDNA library reflects the level of expression of different genes active in the tissue from which the mRNA was extracted. Genes that are highly expressed are represented in the mRNA at a higher frequency than genes expressed at a lower level, and genes not expressed in the tissue of origin are not represented. In contrast to genomic libraries, which represent all genes at approximately equal frequency, the frequency with which any particular gene will be represented in a cDNA library is difficult to estimate, since it depends on the expression level of the gene in the original mRNA population (Figure 17.11).

Since cDNA libraries are usually made from mature cytoplasmic mRNA, the only sequences included in the cDNA clones are the 5′ untranslated region (5′-UTR), the exons, and the 3′-UTR (see Section 9.1 for discussion of UTRs); the clones will lack any intronic and intergenic sequences. Since the genetic code is universal, cDNA clones derived from one organism can be expressed in any other organism as long as appropriate transcriptional (e.g., promoter) and translational signals are inserted to promote efficient gene expression in the host organism. A cDNA library constructed with such features is called an *expression library*. An example of a use for an expression library is described in Section 16.2.

The Uses of Libraries DNA libraries have many uses, especially as a resource from which genomic or cDNA

clones of specific genes can be identified and then employed in subsequent experiments. For example, clones from a library can be manipulated to create reporter genes or to produce novel alleles (e.g., chimeric genes) that can then be used in the creation of transgenic organisms (see Section 16.4). In addition, library construction is the starting point for most protocols performing next-generation sequencing of the genomes or mRNA content of organisms, which we will explore in greater detail in Chapter 18.

Once a library or other collection of clones is produced, biologists use techniques described in previous chapters—PCR and the analysis of nucleic acids by hybridization—to identify clones containing specific DNA sequences (see Research Technique 10.2 on page 354). All techniques to identify fragments containing specific nucleic acid sequences take advantage of the exquisite specificity of complementary base pairing between single-stranded molecular probes and single-stranded target-sequence regions of DNA or RNA.

Recall that in hybridization-based techniques, DNA fragments are fixed onto a membrane that is then exposed to a labeled probe. The probe hybridizes to any fragments containing a complementary sequence. When the excess probe is washed from the membrane, the DNA fragments that have hybridized with the probe can be detected.

The same concept applies when a labeled probe is applied to cloned DNA fragments from a library (Figure 17.12). A membrane is laid on top of the bacterial colonies growing on a petri dish. Each colony contains clones of a different fragment from the library, and some of the bacteria in each colony stick to the membrane. The bacteria remaining on the petri dish serve as a resource for a later step in the procedure. The membrane-bound bacteria are lysed, and their DNA is denatured. The membrane can then be probed with a labeled single-stranded nucleic acid and treated as described in Research Technique 10.2 for Southern blots. DNA that hybridizes with the probe is detected (e.g., by autoradiography), and the colonies it came from are identified by their position on the original petri dish. The same protocol is followed for phage, which form plaques in lawns of bacteria spread on petri dishes, and for yeast, which forms colonies similar to those of bacteria. Alternatively, PCR-based techniques can be used to identify and amplify clones within a library that contain specific sequences, namely, those of the primers that are used in the PCR reaction.

Sequencing Long DNA Molecules

The ultimate description of any DNA molecule is its precise sequence of bases. The process of Sanger sequencing, also known as dideoxy sequencing, was developed for this purpose in the 1970s (see Chapter 7). In dideoxy sequencing, approximately 800 to 1000 consecutive bases are sequenced in each reaction—called a sequencing "read."

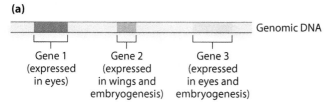

(a)

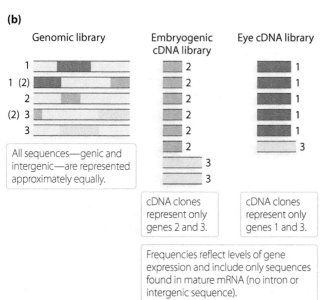

(b)

Figure 17.11   Content of genomic versus cDNA libraries.

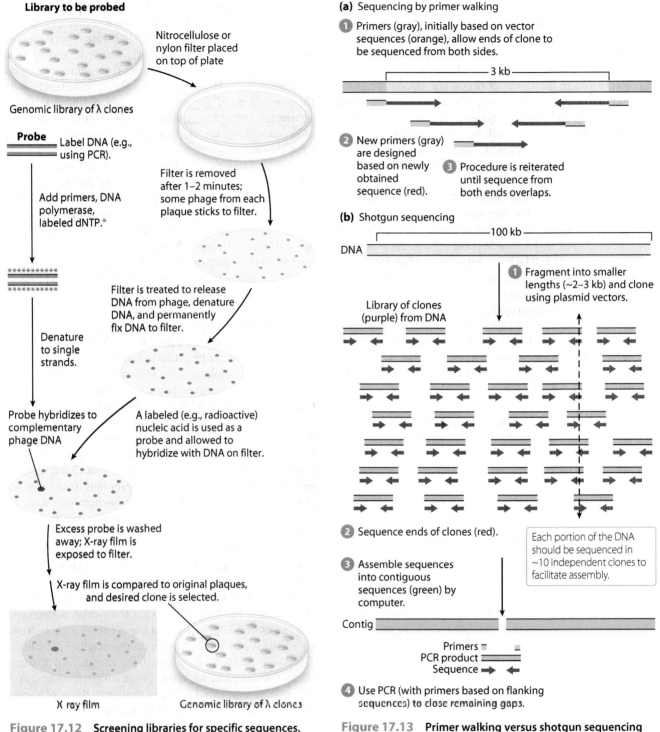

Figure 17.12 **Screening libraries for specific sequences.**

Figure 17.13 **Primer walking versus shotgun sequencing approaches.**

But most DNA regions of interest are larger than this. How are larger fragments of DNA sequenced?

There are two basic strategies for sequencing large DNA molecules. The first technique, **primer walking** (Figure 17.13a), relies on the successive synthesis of primers based on the progressive attainment of new sequence information. The DNA sequence information obtained in the first dideoxy sequencing reaction provides a foundation for the design of a second primer. If the second primer is 600 to 800 bases from the first primer, the second dideoxy sequencing reaction can extend the known sequence up to 1800 bases from the first primer. Reiterations of this process allow technicians to "walk" along a long DNA molecule, designing new primers every 600 to 800 bases. The speed with which a molecule is sequenced by this method is limited by its reiterative nature.

A second method for sequencing large molecules of DNA is **shotgun sequencing,** an approach that relies on redundant sequencing of fragmented target DNA in the hope that all regions will be sequenced at least a few times. In this technique, a large DNA molecule (e.g., a BAC clone of 100 kb) is fragmented into smaller pieces, and the fragments are ligated into cloning vectors (**Figure 17.13b**). The fragments may be generated by partial restriction enzyme digestion or by shearing the DNA. The key here is that fragmentation is done in such a way as to produce random and hence overlapping pieces. The ends of these clones can then be sequenced using a primer based on the vector sequence. The clones of these fragments can be considered a *library* of sequences from the larger DNA molecule. The strategy is to sequence enough clones to be able to assemble a complete contiguous sequence on the basis of overlaps in the sequences. Computer algorithms are available to perform much of this task, allowing data from millions of sequencing reactions to be assembled quickly (see Section 18.1). Thus, in shotgun sequencing, the sequencing of the many different fragments proceeds simultaneously ("in parallel"), allowing long DNA molecules to be sequenced rapidly.

17.2 Introducing Foreign Genes into Genomes Creates Transgenic Organisms

The introduction of a gene from one organism into the genome of another organism creates a **transgenic organism.** The introduced gene is known as a **transgene;** if the introduced gene comes from a different species, it is a heterologous transgene. The two principal challenges to creating a transgenic organism are (1) the need to introduce DNA into a cell in such a way that the DNA integrates into the genome and (2) the need to provide appropriate regulatory sequences so that the transgene will be properly expressed.

Because cells of different organisms differ in the ability to import DNA from their environment and in their propensity to recombine exogenous DNA into their genomes, protocols for introducing transgenes vary according to the organism. Nevertheless, the production of transgenic organisms is surprisingly straightforward, perhaps because naturally occurring mechanisms have evolved in most lineages of life for the uptake or delivery of DNA. Many organisms or cells will absorb DNA from their environment, and once inside the cell, one potential fate of the DNA is to recombine into the genome. Recall our discussion of certain naturally occurring versions of this process, including gene transfer by Hfr donors into recipient bacteria, transduction of genes from a bacterial donor to a recipient, and gene transfer between and within species by transformation (see Chapter 6).

Although the designing of transgenes utilizes techniques of recombinant DNA technology, the expression of transgenes is like the expression of any gene: The gene sequence must first be transcribed into mRNA and then translated into a polypeptide. The universality of the genetic code permits the expression of coding sequences even when transferred between the most distantly related organisms—even when one of them is bacterial or archaeal and the other a eukaryote. However, regulatory sequences and their molecular interactions with transcriptional and translational machinery vary significantly among organisms, and they are not interchangeable between distantly related organisms. Thus, for transgenes to be efficiently expressed, they must be combined with host regulatory sequences.

Expression of Heterologous Genes in Bacterial and Fungal Hosts

Bacterial transformation by a recombinant plasmid is the primary method for generating transgenic bacteria. As seen in Section 17.1, foreign DNA can be introduced into bacteria, such as *E. coli,* using a plasmid vector possessing sequences required for DNA replication and also possessing a selectable marker, such as antibiotic resistance, to facilitate the identification of transformants.

Expression vectors are vectors that have been furnished with sequences capable of directing efficient transcription and translation of transgenes (**Figure 17.14**). For transgenes to be properly expressed in *E. coli,* regulatory sequences compatible with the transcription and translation machinery in *E. coli* need to be present in the vector. Expression vectors for use in *E. coli* are constructed from plasmids that have been equipped with promoter sequences that bind RNA polymerase upstream of the multi-cloning site (MCS) of the plasmid. Recall that the MCS is a cluster of unique restriction sites into which the gene to be expressed is inserted in recombinant clones. Efficient translation of mRNA in *E. coli* also requires the presence of a Shine–Dalgarno sequence in the 5′ untranslated region of the mRNA, another feature that is built into *E. coli* expression vectors. In addition, since mRNA-splicing machinery does not exist in bacteria, eukaryotic transgenes must be free of introns if they are to be properly translated in bacteria. This requirement necessitates the use of cDNAs as eukaryotic transgenes in *E. coli* expression systems.

Expression of the heterologous gene carried by an expression vector can be either constitutive ("on" all the time) or regulated by the addition or removal of inducer compounds. An example of the latter approach is the use of the regulatory apparatus of the *lac* operon of *E. coli* to induce expression of transgenes: Fusion of the *lac* operator and CAP binding sites of the *lac* operon to the RNA polymerase binding site allows the transgene to be controlled in the same inducible manner as the genes of the *lac* operon (the *lac* operon is described in Chapter 14).

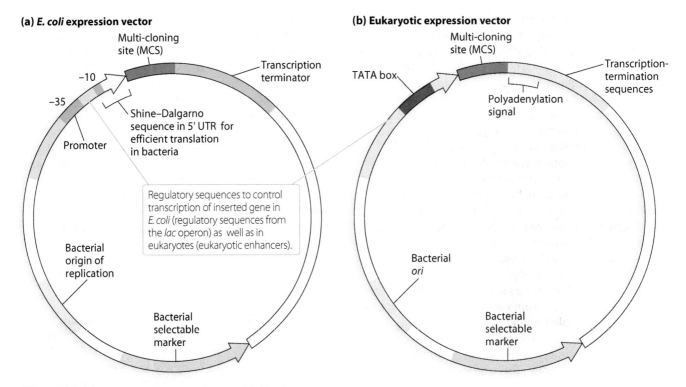

(a) *E. coli* **expression vector**

Multi-cloning site (MCS)

−10

−35

Transcription terminator

Shine–Dalgarno sequence in 5' UTR for efficient translation in bacteria

Promoter

Regulatory sequences to control transcription of inserted gene in *E. coli* (regulatory sequences from the *lac* operon) as well as in eukaryotes (eukaryotic enhancers).

Bacterial origin of replication

Bacterial selectable marker

(b) Eukaryotic expression vector

Multi-cloning site (MCS)

TATA box

Transcription-termination sequences

Polyadenylation signal

Bacterial *ori*

Bacterial selectable marker

Figure 17.14   Expression vectors for *E. coli* and eukaryotes.

Two kinds of variation in the genetic mechanisms of living organisms can hamper the efficient production of functional transgenic products. The first complication affects the efficiency of translation. While the universal genetic code does indeed allow the expression of heterologous transgenes, organisms vary in the degree to which they use specific codons when the genetic code contains more than one for a given amino acid or signal. In most species, synonymous codons are not used with equal frequency. For example, glycine is encoded by GGN, with N representing any nucleotide, but GGA and GGG are rarely used in *E. coli*, whereas these codons are commonly used in the other organisms listed in Table 17.2. The tRNAs corresponding to frequently used codons are expressed at higher levels than are the tRNAs for rarely used codons. This preferential use of codons is called **codon bias.** Thus, for efficient production of heterologous proteins in *E. coli*, the codon usage within the heterologous gene sequences may have to be altered to approximate the codon bias in *E. coli*. Note that such changes do not alter the amino

acid sequence of the encoded protein; they only alter the efficiency with which translation occurs in *E. coli*. Codon bias can affect the expression of heterologous transgenes in any case where genes are being transferred between distantly related species.

A second possible obstruction to the production of functional heterologous proteins in *E. coli* is presented by the post-translational modifications many proteins must undergo in order to function. Post-translational modifications of proteins differ between species, in particular between eukaryotes and bacteria. For example, carbohydrate and lipid groups are added to many kinds of eukaryotic proteins. In addition, the functions of proteins may be modified by phosphorylation, acetylation, or methylation of amino acid residues; other post-translational polypeptide processing; and specific protein-folding activities. Most of these processes either do not occur in bacterial cells or they occur but with significant differences. In such cases, eukaryotic cells, such as yeast or cells in tissue culture, and eukaryotic expression vectors must be used. **Eukaryotic expression vectors** have the eukaryotic features analogous to the features found in bacterial expression vectors, including sequences for the regulation of transcription (such as a TATA box for binding of RNA polymerase II), enhancer sequences for qualitative and quantitative control of transcription, and polyadenylation and transcription-termination signals (see Figure 17.14).

Production of Human Insulin in *E. coli*   A gene encoding insulin was among the first human genes to be expressed in *E. coli*, and human insulin was the first protein

Table 17.2	Preference in Different Organisms for Specific Glycine Codons			
Codon	*E. coli*	*S. cerevisiae*	*H. sapiens*	*A. thaliana*
GGA	0	23%	23%	37%
GGG	2%	12%	26%	15%
GGC	38%	20%	33%	14%
GGT	59%	45%	18%	34%

manufactured from recombinant DNA technology for therapeutic use in humans. Insulin, a protein hormone, regulates sugar metabolism in animals by stimulating liver and muscle cells to take in glucose, and fat cells to take in lipids, from the blood. Individuals who are unable to produce insulin, or whose cells cannot respond to it, have diabetes, an often debilitating disease that affects millions of people worldwide.

Insulin is cyclically produced in the pancreas by specialized cells in the islets of Langerhans and is released into circulating blood in response to the ingestion of sugar-containing carbohydrates. The pancreatic cells initially synthesize a 110–amino acid precursor protein called preproinsulin that is not secreted and does not have hormonal function until it is proteolytically processed. Twenty-four N-terminal amino acids—the "pre" amino acids of preproinsulin—are cleaved from the precursor to produce proinsulin, an event followed by the cleavage of an additional 35 amino acids—called the "pro" segment—from the middle of the protein. Further cleavage generates two amino acid chains, called the A chain and the B chain, that are 21 and 30 amino acids, respectively, in length. The A chain is joined to the B chain by disulfide bonds between cysteine residues to produce insulin.

The amino acid sequence of insulin was determined by Fred Sanger in the early 1950s (**Figure 17.15**, ❶), but the human gene encoding insulin was not identified until the late 1970s. Even before the human insulin gene was cloned, however, molecular biologists began experiments designed to produce human insulin in *E. coli* by constructing recombinant plasmids containing chemically synthesized DNA encoding human insulin. An experimental strategy called the two-chain method utilized two synthetic genes, one encoding the A chain and the other encoding the B chain. Each synthetic gene was constructed from oligonucleotides whose sequence was based on the reverse translation of the amino acid sequences of the human insulin gene chains ❷.

The synthetic genes were cloned into separate plasmid vectors. In each case the chain was fused, in the same reading frame, to the 3′ terminus of the *lacZ* gene encoding β-galactosidase. Genetic constructs like this, consisting of two or more genes or gene segments joined together to form a new, artificial gene, are called **fusion genes.** Transcription and translation of a fusion gene produce a **fusion protein,** which in each of these cases contained the polypeptide of one insulin chain fused to the carboxyl terminus of β-galactosidase (the protein product of the *lacZ* gene). To separate the insulin peptides from β-galactosidase peptides and to form functional insulin molecules, a methionine residue was engineered into the fusion protein at the junction between the N-terminal end of the insulin peptides and the C-terminal end of the β-galactosidase peptides to serve as a peptide cleavage site ❸❹.

In the recombinant plasmid, transcription is under control of the *lac* operator regulatory sequences. Gene transcription is induced by lactose in the absence of glucose ❺ and ❻ (see also Chapter 14). Under appropriate growth conditions, up to 20% of the total protein produced by the recombinant *E. coli* strains is the fusion protein. Treatment of proteins with cyanogen bromide (CNBr) cleaves peptide bonds at the carboxyl end of methionine residues ❼. Apart from the methionine that was inserted at the junction of the two peptides, there are no other methionine residues in the fusion protein, so CNBr treatment releases the insulin chains from the β-galactosidase peptides without causing any other breaks. When the A and B chains are purified from their recombinant host strains and mixed together under oxidizing conditions, disulfide bonds form to link the A and B chains and produce active insulin molecules ❽.

The recombinant human insulin molecules originally produced by this method were identical to naturally occurring human insulin. Since the implementation of this synthetic process in the 1980s, however, more-efficient methods for producing recombinant human insulin have been developed. Some of these methods have introduced amino acid changes in the recombinant human insulin, in order to create proteins that have different desired effects on the uptake of glucose by targeted cells. These various forms of recombinant human insulin are used by millions of insulin-dependent diabetics around the world every day.

The ease and economy of working with bacteria as compared to eukaryotes have made it practical to produce many eukaryotic proteins in bacteria for both medical and industrial applications. In addition to human insulin, proteins such as human growth hormone (HGH) and erythropoietin (which induces red blood cell formation) are produced in bacterial systems. The recombinant systems used to produce these and many other pharmaceutical and industrial agents are safe and effective sources of otherwise scarce material. For example, before the production of human insulin by recombinant DNA technology, insulin was extracted from pig and cow pancreases collected as a by-product of the meat industry. Pig and cow insulin are very similar to human insulin, but not identical to it; as a result, allergic reactions compromised their use by diabetics. Insulin extractions from animals also carry a risk of contamination from the source tissues. Likewise, HGH extracted from the pituitary glands of human cadavers carries a risk of transmitting neurological disease (e.g., Creutzfeldt-Jacob disease) due to the possible presence of contaminating proteins. Both recombinant human insulin and recombinant HGH have proven safe and effective over decades of use.

Many proteins used in industrial processes as well as in everyday household products are produced in bacteria. For example, proteases are protein-degrading enzymes added to laundry detergents to aid in removing stains from clothing. Isolation of genes encoding proteases from psychrophilic, or cold-loving, bacteria has allowed the industrial production of proteases that act in cold water,

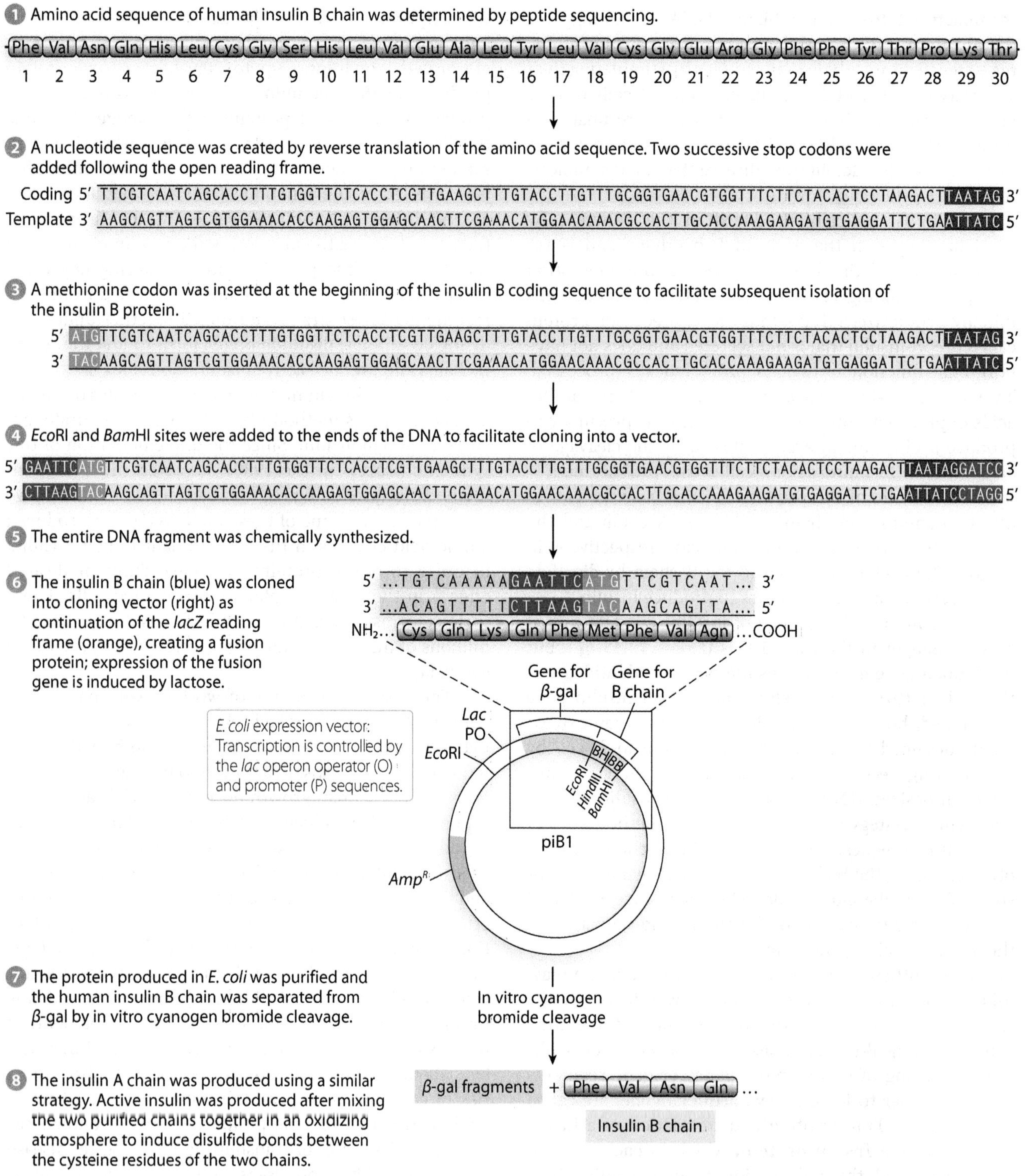

1 Amino acid sequence of human insulin B chain was determined by peptide sequencing.

-Phe Val Asn Gln His Leu Cys Gly Ser His Leu Val Glu Ala Leu Tyr Leu Val Cys Gly Glu Arg Gly Phe Phe Tyr Thr Pro Lys Thr-
 1   2   3   4   5   6   7   8   9 10 11 12 13 14 15 16 17 18 19 20 21 22 23 24 25 26 27 28 29 30

2 A nucleotide sequence was created by reverse translation of the amino acid sequence. Two successive stop codons were added following the open reading frame.

Coding 5′ TTCGTCAATCAGCACCTTTGTGGTTCTCACCTCGTTGAAGCTTTGTACCTTGTTTGCGGTGAACGTGGTTTCTTCTACACTCCTAAGACTTAATAG 3′
Template 3′ AAGCAGTTAGTCGTGGAAACACCAAGAGTGGAGCAACTTCGAAACATGGAACAAACGCCACTTGCACCAAAGAAGATGTGAGGATTCTGAATTATC 5′

3 A methionine codon was inserted at the beginning of the insulin B coding sequence to facilitate subsequent isolation of the insulin B protein.

5′ ATGTTCGTCAATCAGCACCTTTGTGGTTCTCACCTCGTTGAAGCTTTGTACCTTGTTTGCGGTGAACGTGGTTTCTTCTACACTCCTAAGACTTAATAG 3′
3′ TACAAGCAGTTAGTCGTGGAAACACCAAGAGTGGAGCAACTTCGAAACATGGAACAAACGCCACTTGCACCAAAGAAGATGTGAGGATTCTGAATTATC 5′

4 *Eco*RI and *Bam*HI sites were added to the ends of the DNA to facilitate cloning into a vector.

5′ GAATTCATGTTCGTCAATCAGCACCTTTGTGGTTCTCACCTCGTTGAAGCTTTGTACCTTGTTTGCGGTGAACGTGGTTTCTTCTACACTCCTAAGACTTAATAGGATCC 3′
3′ CTTAAGTACAAGCAGTTAGTCGTGGAAACACCAAGAGTGGAGCAACTTCGAAACATGGAACAAACGCCACTTGCACCAAAGAAGATGTGAGGATTCTGAATTATCCTAGG 5′

5 The entire DNA fragment was chemically synthesized.

6 The insulin B chain (blue) was cloned into cloning vector (right) as continuation of the *lacZ* reading frame (orange), creating a fusion protein; expression of the fusion gene is induced by lactose.

5′ ...TGTCAAAAAGAATTCATGTTCGTCAAT... 3′
3′ ...ACAGTTTTTCTTAAGTACAAGCAGTTA... 5′
NH₂...Cys Gln Lys Gln Phe Met Phe Val Agn ...COOH

E. coli expression vector: Transcription is controlled by the *lac* operon operator (O) and promoter (P) sequences.

Gene for β-gal   Gene for B chain

Lac PO

*Eco*RI

*Eco*RI
*Hin*dIII
*Bam*HI

piB1

Amp^R

7 The protein produced in *E. coli* was purified and the human insulin B chain was separated from β-gal by in vitro cyanogen bromide cleavage.

In vitro cyanogen bromide cleavage

8 The insulin A chain was produced using a similar strategy. Active insulin was produced after mixing the two purified chains together in an oxidizing atmosphere to induce disulfide bonds between the cysteine residues of the two chains.

β-gal fragments + Phe Val Asn Gln ...

Insulin B chain

Figure 17.15 Producing human insulin in *E. coli*. This strategy was used in the late 1970s by the City of Hope National Medical Center and the biotechnology company Genentech to produce human insulin in *E. coli*.

leading to substantial savings in energy costs stemming from household hot water usage. The genetic engineering of *E. coli* and other microbes to produce proteins or compounds used in industry, agriculture, and health care is an active field that will flourish in the coming years as more microbial systems are investigated at the genomic and physiological levels. An example of the transfer of an entire biochemical pathway into *E. coli* in order to produce a medically important compound is described in **Experimental Insight 17.2**.

Experimental Insight 17.2

Plant-Derived Antimalarial Drugs Produced in *E. coli*

The production of amorphadiene in *E. coli* exemplifies the use of genetic engineering to produce a high-value pharmaceutical product. Amorphadiene is the immediate precursor to artemisinin, a potent antimalarial drug. Artemisinin has been touted as the next-generation antimalarial drug because it is effective at treating multiple stages of malarial infection and exhibits no cross-resistance with existing antimalarial drugs, such as chloroquine and quinine. Chloroquine and quinine have been used to fight malarial infection for several decades, but their effectiveness is decreasing due to the evolution of resistant strains of *Plasmodium*, the malaria parasite.

OBSTACLES TO ARTEMISININ PRODUCTION

Like many modern drugs, artemisinin was originally discovered in plant extracts. Currently the drug is extracted and purified from the sweet wormwood plant, *Artemisia annua*. The logistics of growing *Artemisia* are limiting factors, however, and the cost of producing large amounts of artemisinin from its natural source is also prohibitive. Production of artemisinin in a fermentable biological system such as *E. coli* could increase drug supply, conserve natural resources, and dramatically lower production costs.

Artemisinin is a complex terpene molecule produced in several biosynthetic steps. All plants produce the precursors of the terpene pathway, isopentenyl pyrophosphate (IPP) and dimethylallyl pyrophosphate (DMAPP), but the specific terpenes produced from them by each plant species vary. The final two steps in artemisinin biosynthesis, from farnesyl pyrophosphate (FPP) to artemisinin, are catalyzed by enzymes encoded by genes specific to *Artemisia*. While *E. coli* naturally produces IPP and DMAPP, the pathway is subject to feedback inhibition, preventing large quantities of these molecules from accumulating.

SUCCESS THROUGH GENETIC ENGINEERING

This obstacle to producing large quantities of amorphadiene in *E. coli* is circumvented by use of a combination of eight genes from *Saccharomyces cerevisiae* and *E. coli* to recreate the biosynthetic pathway leading to FPP production. ❶ A mutant *E. coli* strain is used in which the normal feedback inhibition of the FPP biosynthetic pathway is lacking. ❷ Expression of the eight *S. cerevisiae* genes is coordinated by distribution of the genes into two operons—one containing three genes and one containing five—controlled by *lac* operon regulatory sequences (see Chapter 14 for a review of the *lac* operon system). In this way, gene expression is induced in the presence of either lactose or the synthetic inducer isopropyl-β-D-thiogalactopyranoside (IPTG). ❸ The amorphadiene synthetase (ADS) gene is cloned from *Artemisia* and placed under the control of *lac* operon regulatory sequences.

In initial experiments with this system, the levels of ADS protein produced in *E. coli* were disappointingly low. The reason was discovered to be differences in codon bias between *Artemisia* and *E. coli*. When codons preferred by *Artemisia* were replaced with synonymous codons preferred by *E. coli*, the production of ADS protein in *E. coli* became much more efficient. ❹ Now the bacteria produced a large quantity of amorphadiene, which could be converted into artemisinin either by chemical synthesis or in vivo by the introduction of the artemisinin synthetase gene from *Artemisia*.

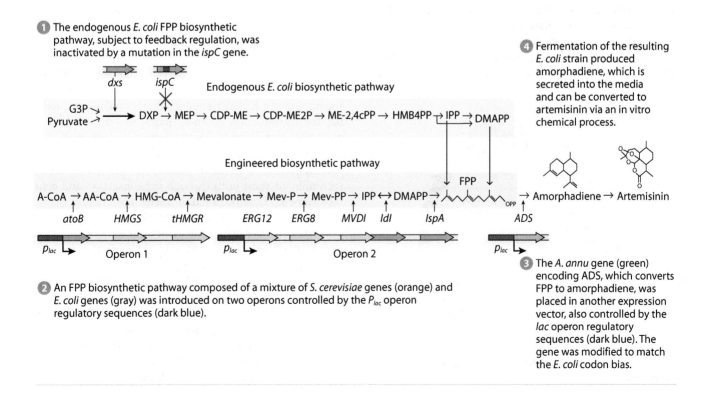

❶ The endogenous *E. coli* FPP biosynthetic pathway, subject to feedback regulation, was inactivated by a mutation in the *ispC* gene.

❹ Fermentation of the resulting *E. coli* strain produced amorphadiene, which is secreted into the media and can be converted to artemisinin via an in vitro chemical process.

❷ An FPP biosynthetic pathway composed of a mixture of *S. cerevisiae* genes (orange) and *E. coli* genes (gray) was introduced on two operons controlled by the P_{lac} operon regulatory sequences (dark blue).

❸ The *A. annu* gene (green) encoding ADS, which converts FPP to amorphadiene, was placed in another expression vector, also controlled by the *lac* operon regulatory sequences (dark blue). The gene was modified to match the *E. coli* codon bias.

Transgenes can be introduced into fungal cells in a manner similar to the techniques described for bacteria, using a plasmid system developed for the fungus *Saccharomyces cerevisiae* (baker's yeast). In addition, DNA can be readily integrated into the genome of many fungi by homologous recombination, making direct manipulation of the fungal genome feasible.

Yeast Plasmids Some strains of *S. cerevisiae* harbor a circular 6.3-kb plasmid that, because of its approximately 2-μm diameter, is known as the 2-micron plasmid. This plasmid can be modified into a recombinant plasmid by the insertion of transgenes. An *E. coli* origin of replication and appropriate selectable markers are also introduced into the 2-micron plasmid, which already contains the *S. cerevisiae* origin of replication (**Figure 17.16**). With these additions, the plasmid becomes a **Shuttle vector**, a vector that can replicate in two species—in this case, both *E. coli* and *S. cerevisiae*—and thus can be used to shuttle DNA sequences between them. With this shuttle vector, DNA sequences can be manipulated in *E. coli*, where manipulation is easier, after which the modified plasmids can be shuttled into yeast for heterologous protein expression.

Integrating DNA into the Genome of *S. cerevisiae* If DNA that is introduced into an organism has no origin of replication, it undergoes one of two fates: enzymatic degradation or integration into the host genome. Enzymatic degradation, accomplished by nucleases that are common in cells, will eliminate the introduced DNA. Integration of DNA into the host genome, in contrast, allows the introduced nucleic acid to persist in the host cell. Integration is accomplished by either of two distinct mechanisms of recombination: illegitimate recombination or homologous recombination.

Illegitimate recombination integrates introduced DNA at a random, nonhomologous location. This form of recombination does not require any homology between the introduced DNA and the genomic DNA into which the former is integrated. In contrast, the second mechanism for integration of introduced DNA, **homologous recombination** between the introduced DNA and the host genomic sequence, requires a significant length of DNA sequence in common between the two recombining molecules. The relative frequencies with which these mechanisms occur depend on the species into which the DNA is introduced. In most plant and animal species, illegitimate recombination is the most common fate, although techniques exist to select for individuals in which homologous recombination has occurred (as described later in this chapter). In bacterial and fungal species, introduced DNA is often recombined in the genome in a homologous manner.

Segments of DNA introduced into *S. cerevisiae* have a propensity to undergo homologous recombination. An introduced circular molecule of DNA can recombine by either a single crossover or a double crossover (**Figure 17.17a**). In a single crossover, the entire molecule of introduced circular DNA is integrated into the yeast genome with no loss of any genomic DNA. If recombination of a circular molecule occurs by double crossover, however, only DNA between the homologous flanking sequences is integrated into the recipient genome, and the integration is accompanied by a concomitant loss from the genome of the DNA between the homologous sequences. Thus, recombination with two crossovers results in replacement of the genomic DNA with the introduced DNA flanked by the homologous sequences.

Introducing a linear rather than circular molecule of DNA favors retrieval of recombinants produced by double crossover, since a single crossover will cause a deletion event resulting in recombinant molecules lacking a large portion of the original chromosome and therefore likely to be lethal (**Figure 17.17b**). Linearized DNA molecules recombine at a higher frequency than circular ones, making the introduction of linear molecules the method of choice for homologous recombination experiments.

Taking advantage of this tendency for homologous recombination to occur in yeast, yeast geneticists create recombinant yeast both through gene insertion and gene replacement. Loss-of-function alleles are created by replacing the target gene with heterologous DNA, often a selectable marker gene, thus eliminating the production of functional wild-type protein by the target gene. Gene insertions that result in a deletion of the entire coding region of the gene create null alleles that produce no protein product. Such insertion alleles are often called **gene knockouts** because the insertion "knocks out" the function of the gene, creating a recessive loss-of-function allele (recall the knockout libraries referred to in Section 16.3). Conversely, inserting a functional gene, often creating a gain-of-function allele, is called a knock-in.

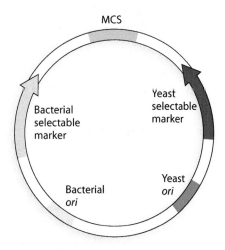

Figure 17.16 **Shuttle vector for *E. coli* and *Saccharomyces cerevisiae*.**

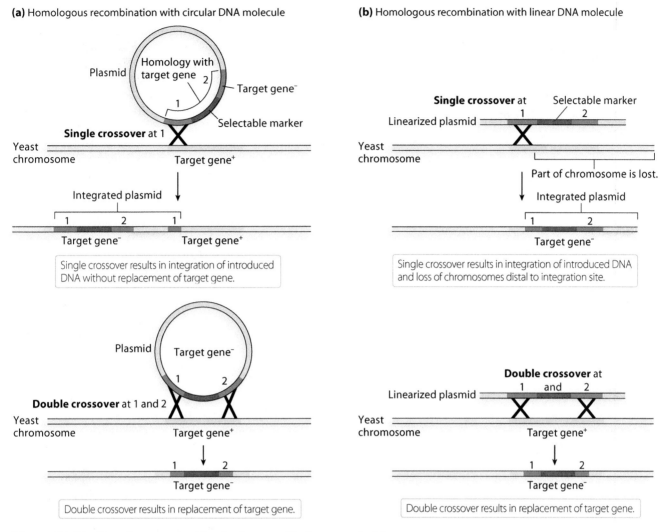

(a) Homologous recombination with circular DNA molecule

(b) Homologous recombination with linear DNA molecule

Figure 17.17   Homologous recombination in yeast: Single versus double crossovers.

The ease with which homologous recombinants are generated in *S. cerevisiae* has allowed the production of a large number of yeast strains for genetic analysis of biological processes in this organism. Loss-of-function alleles of every gene in the *S. cerevisiae* genome have been generated and can be ordered from a stock center. Such stocks have greatly facilitated genetic research by relieving scientists of the need to produce mutations in the genes of interest at the start of every new genetic experiment.

Transformation of Plant Genomes by *Agrobacterium*

Our food is mainly derived from plants, and humans have been genetically modifying plants since the beginning of agriculture, nearly 10,000 years ago. For most of this history, genetic improvement was limited to interbreeding wild and domesticated species to select for traits already present in nature. The recently developed techniques for introducing DNA from many sources into plants have added a new dimension to the genetic modification of plants for agricultural purposes. By these new means, the genetic variation available in plants has been extended to include not only genes from other plant species but also genes derived from animals, fungi, and bacteria.

The most widely used method of generating transgenic plants takes advantage of a natural plant transformation system that has evolved in the soil bacterium *Agrobacterium tumefaciens*. In nature, this bacterium is the cause of crown gall disease, an uncontrolled cell division in plant cells. This disease results in tumors (galls), typically at the crown (the base near the soil) of the plant. Wild strains of *A. tumefaciens* harbor a large plasmid (200 kb) called the tumor-inducing plasmid, or **Ti plasmid** (Figure 17.18a). A portion of the Ti plasmid, a region referred to as the **transfer DNA (T-DNA)** is transferred from the bacterium into the nucleus of a plant cell. Mary-Dell Chilton and colleagues conclusively demonstrated the nature of this remarkable cross-kingdom transfer of DNA in the late 1970s by demonstrating that

(a)

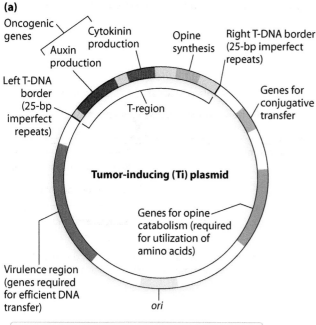

Oncogenic genes
Cytokinin production
Auxin production
Opine synthesis
Right T-DNA border (25-bp imperfect repeats)
Left T-DNA border (25-bp imperfect repeats)
T-region
Genes for conjugative transfer

Tumor-inducing (Ti) plasmid

Genes for opine catabolism (required for utilization of amino acids)

Virulence region (genes required for efficient DNA transfer)

ori

Transfer DNA (T-DNA) contains auxin and cytokinin biosynthetic genes and genes for amino acid biosynthesis.

(b) *Agrobacterium tumefaciens* (1–2 microns wide)   **Plant cell** (5–50 microns wide)

Ti plasmid
T-DNA
T-strand
Virulence proteins

A single strand of T-DNA is transferred into the plant cell and is integrated into the plant nuclear genome.

(c)

Expression of auxin and cytokinin biosynthetic genes leads to uncontrolled cell division and gall formation; gall cells produce the unusual amino acids that *Agrobacterium* uses as carbon and nitrogen sources.

Figure 17.18 Crown gall disease caused by *Agrobacterium* via plant transformation.

Agrobacterium Ti plasmid DNA can be detected inside plant cells. Once inside the plant cell, the T-DNA can recombine illegitimately with the plant nuclear genome, resulting in an insertion of the T-DNA at a random location in the plant genome (**Figure 17.18b**).

From the bacterial perspective, the outcome of this natural transformation event is the expression of genes in the T-DNA that encode proteins causing plant cells to (1) divide in an uncontrolled manner and (2) produce amino acids only the bacterium can utilize as an energy source. *Agrobacterium* essentially reprograms the plant cells into food factories for the bacteria. Bacterial genes encoding plant-hormone–biosynthesizing enzymes cause transformed plant cells to produce high levels of two plant hormones, auxin and cytokinin, which in turn cause uncontrolled division of plant cells, resulting in tumor formation (**Figure 17.18c**). The other genes on the T-DNA encode opine-biosynthesizing enzymes. Opines, such as nopaline and octopine, are amino acids that do not naturally occur in plants; therefore, plants do not produce any enzymes capable of metabolizing opines. *Agrobacterium* does have such enzymes, however; consequently, the opines produced by the plant cells can be used as carbon and nitrogen sources by the bacteria. Other genes on the Ti plasmid, but not located within the T-DNA region, encode enzymes required for the transfer of the T-DNA to the plant cell.

Sequence analysis has revealed that the genes involved in the transfer of T-DNA are evolutionarily related to those involved in the transfer of the F-factor in *E. coli* (see Chapter 6). Thus, *Agrobacterium* has evolved a mechanism to transfer DNA into plant cells by adapting genes originally involved in bacterial conjugation. A striking aspect of this cross-kingdom gene transfer is that the genes on the T-DNA have evolved to be transcribed and translated efficiently in plant cells instead of in bacterial cells. In nature, *Agrobacterium* normally transforms plants only; but in the laboratory, the bacterium has the ability to transfer DNA into almost any eukaryotic cell, including human cells.

Creating Transgenic Plants Scientists can use *Agrobacterium* to transfer any gene of interest into plants. To do so, they remove the opine- and tumor-producing genes normally found in the T-DNA and replace them with DNA encoding the gene of interest. The T-DNA then transfers the gene of interest into the plant cell, where it becomes integrated into the genomic DNA of the plant.

Figure 17.19a depicts the manner in which the Ti plasmid is modified for transformation procedures. First, the tumor-inducing and opine genes are deleted from the Ti plasmid, producing what is called a "disarmed" Ti plasmid. Then the gene of interest is inserted between the two ends of the T-DNA region, referred to as the left and right borders. These border regions contain sequences required for efficient transfer. Proteins encoded by genes of the Ti plasmid outside of the T-DNA recognize specific sequences in the left and right border and catalyze the transfer of a single strand of T-DNA from the bacterium to the plant cell; when this occurs, the gene of interest that has been inserted between the two border sequences will be transferred as well. As with any other protocol for constructing transgenic organisms, a selectable marker is included (between the left and right borders) in addition to the gene of interest to allow efficient selection of transformed plants. For experiments with plants, genes conferring resistance to either antibiotics (inhibiting translation in the chloroplast) or herbicides may be employed as selectable markers. The selectable marker genes are usually expressed using a promoter that confers constitutive expression, so that transgenic plants can be selected at any stage of their development.

Because the Ti plasmid is too large to be easily manipulated, most experimental protocols that use *Agrobacterium* construct a strain harboring two plasmids: One is a disarmed Ti plasmid, and the second is a plasmid that contains left and right border sequences flanking the DNA of interest (**Figure 17.19a**). This strategy, separating the functional elements of the Ti plasmid into two plasmids, is referred to as the binary approach. It results in the efficient transfer of the DNA of interest into the plant cell and its subsequent integration into the plant genome (**Figure 17.19b**).

Unlike bacteria and yeast, which are single-celled organisms, transformed plant cells must be regenerated into an entire plant in order to reveal the effects of transgenes on the plant phenotype. Traditionally, scientists have taken advantage of a unique feature of plant development, the **totipotency** of most plant cells: Under the appropriate environmental and hormonal conditions, an entire normal plant can be regenerated from a single isolated plant cell. Thus, after infection of plant cells with the modified *Agrobacterium* strain and selection of transformed cells on the basis of the selectable marker gene, progeny plants can be regenerated from the individual transformed cells (**Figure 17.19c**). This technique has been successfully applied to a wide variety of flowering plant species, including crop species such as rice, maize, and tomatoes.

Plant researchers using *Arabidopsis* as a model system for studying basic biological processes sought an easier method of transformation that would not require regeneration from a single transformed cell. After several different techniques were attempted, they discovered that the simple technique of dipping *Arabidopsis* flowers into a culture of *Agrobacterium* works surprisingly well. It allows the T-DNA to be transferred directly from *Agrobacterium* to the egg cell of the female gametophyte. In this protocol, transgenic plants are selected from seed produced by the plant exposed to *Agrobacterium*.

Many plant species are susceptible to *Agrobacterium*-mediated transformation. If they are not, DNA can be directly introduced into their cells. The cell walls of isolated plant cells are first removed enzymatically, after which the cells are mixed with heterologous DNA and given a heat or electrical shock to depolarize the membrane and facilitate the entry of DNA. Once in the cell, the DNA has the same fate as described above for DNA transferred into fungi. In plants, homologous recombination is rare relative to illegitimate recombination, so the most common outcome is the insertion of the heterologous DNA into a random location in the genome. In another technique, DNA is introduced into plant cells by particle gun bombardment, the use of high pressure to fire microscopic particles coated with DNA into plant cells. The particles are propelled with enough force to penetrate the cell wall and plasma membrane. Both of these techniques can be applied to any plant species.

Transgenic Plants in Agriculture The two most common traits engineered into transgenic crops grown today are herbicide resistance and insect resistance. With herbicide-resistant crops—for example, the varieties sold as Roundup Ready—farmers can apply herbicide to a field to clear the ground of weeds and other non-crop plants without damaging the crop itself. This reduces the amount of tilling done to plow weeds under at the beginning of the season. Less tilling results in less soil loss and also saves on the use of fossil fuels.

Cotton and maize crops resistant to insect herbivory are two of the most widely grown transgenic crops. Insect resistance is usually conferred by the expression of genes derived from the bacterium *Bacillus thuringiensis*. Genes encoding approximately 100 insect toxins, known as Bt toxins, have been identified in different strains of *B. thuringiensis*. The toxins work by perforating the guts of different insect species, and different toxins have different "host" specificity. Transgenic plants expressing genes encoding Bt toxins are less palatable to insects and exhibit reduced insect herbivory. As a consequence, transgenic plants expressing Bt toxin genes require significantly less application of insecticides than do non-transgenic plants, thus reducing the insecticide load in the environment.

While Bt toxins are clearly toxic to insects, other herbivores, such as humans, are impervious to the compounds. The properties of Bt toxins have been appreciated for some time. Organic farmers routinely spray *B. thuringiensis* directly on their crops to act as a "natural" insecticide. Millions of acres of transgenic maize, cotton, and potatoes expressing Bt genes and of herbicide-resistant soybeans are presently cultivated in the United States and several other countries.

Golden Rice While many transgenic crops thus far used in agriculture have primarily benefited farmers in the developed world, the humanitarian potential for crop modification in aid of subsistence farmers in developing countries is exemplified by Golden Rice. Rice

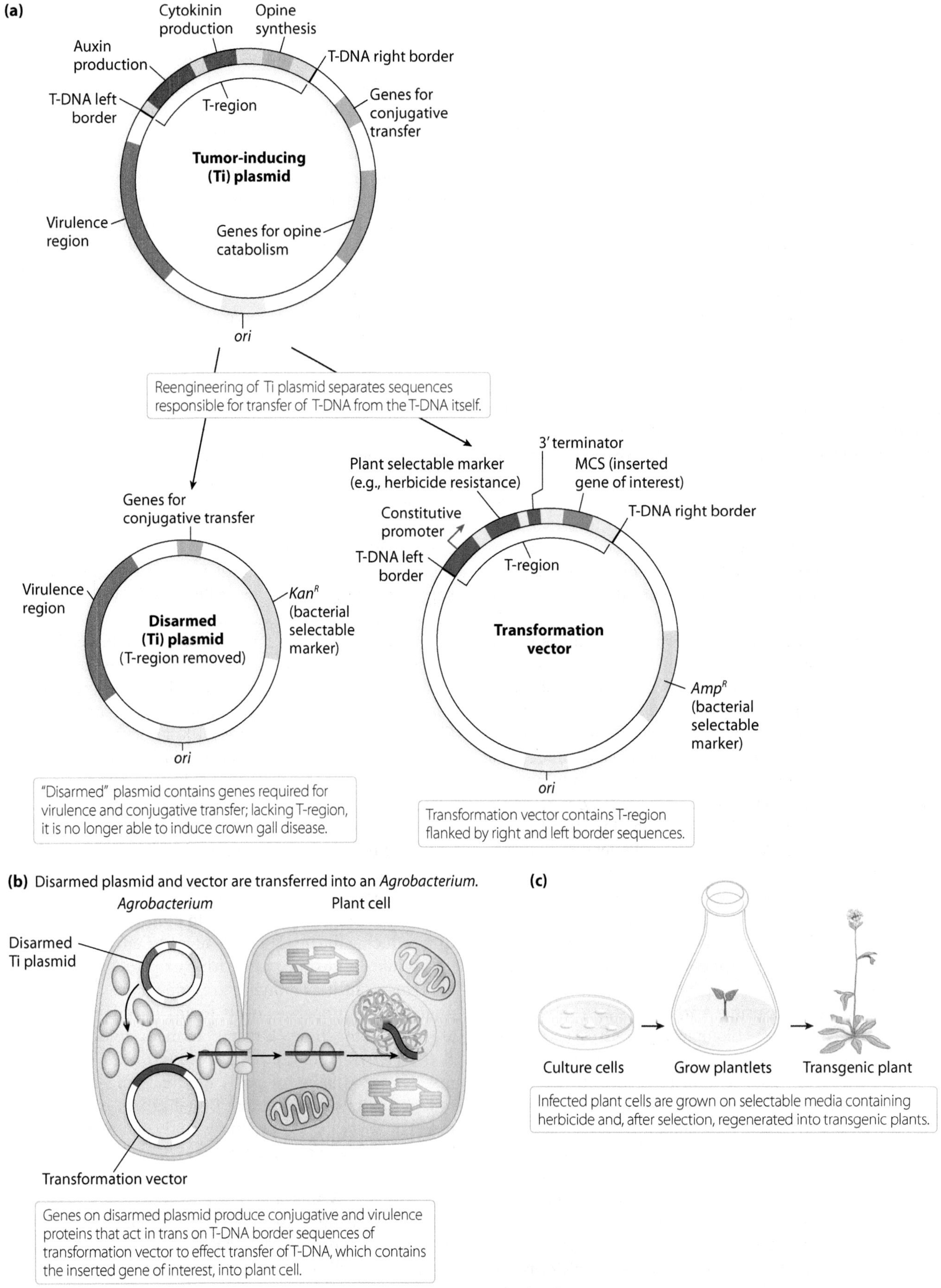
(a)
Cytokinin production
Opine synthesis
Auxin production
T-DNA right border
T-DNA left border
T-region
Genes for conjugative transfer
Tumor-inducing (Ti) plasmid
Virulence region
Genes for opine catabolism
ori
Reengineering of Ti plasmid separates sequences responsible for transfer of T-DNA from the T-DNA itself.
3′ terminator
Plant selectable marker (e.g., herbicide resistance)
MCS (inserted gene of interest)
Genes for conjugative transfer
Constitutive promoter
T-DNA right border
T-DNA left border
T-region
Virulence region
Disarmed (Ti) plasmid (T-region removed)
Kan^R (bacterial selectable marker)
Transformation vector
Amp^R (bacterial selectable marker)
ori
ori
"Disarmed" plasmid contains genes required for virulence and conjugative transfer; lacking T-region, it is no longer able to induce crown gall disease.
Transformation vector contains T-region flanked by right and left border sequences.
(b) Disarmed plasmid and vector are transferred into an Agrobacterium.
Agrobacterium
Plant cell
Disarmed Ti plasmid
Transformation vector
Genes on disarmed plasmid produce conjugative and virulence proteins that act in trans on T-DNA border sequences of transformation vector to effect transfer of T-DNA, which contains the inserted gene of interest, into plant cell.
(c)
Culture cells
Grow plantlets
Transgenic plant
Infected plant cells are grown on selectable media containing herbicide and, after selection, regenerated into transgenic plants.

Figure 17.19 **Reengineering the Ti plasmid to create transgenic plants.**

(*Oryza sativa*) is the major staple food for much of the world. Because oil tends to become rancid, especially in tropical climates, rice is often milled until its oil-rich outer layer has been removed. Unfortunately, the remaining edible grain, the endosperm, lacks several micronutrients, including provitamin A, a vitamin A precursor. (Vitamin A can be obtained directly through consumption of animal products or indirectly from plants that produce carotenoids, which are converted to vitamin A after ingestion and are therefore termed provitamin A.)

Vitamin A deficiency results in blindness and increased disease susceptibility, thus contributing to childhood mortality in many developing countries. It is estimated that vitamin A deficiency affects between 140 million and 250 million preschool children worldwide, leading to 250,000 to 500,000 cases of blindness per year. Because no wild or domesticated cultivars of rice produce provitamin A in the endosperm, recombinant technologies, rather than a conventional breeding program, are required to produce rice that has an endosperm containing provitamin A.

Scientists knew that rice endosperm synthesizes geranylgeranyl diphosphate (GGPP), a precursor in the synthesis of carotenoids. Study of the carotenoid biosynthetic pathway in plants suggested that five plant-derived enzymes are needed to convert GGPP to β-carotene. However, the discovery that a single bacterial enzyme (CRTI) could replace three of the plant enzymes (PDS, ZDS, CRTISO) simplified the genetic engineering strategy (**Figure 17.20a**). Then, in 2000, Ingo Potrykus, Peter Beyer, and colleagues reported that the addition of only two genes, a daffodil-derived gene called *PSY* and the bacterial gene called *CRTI*, resulted in the production of β-carotene in rice endosperm (**Figure 17.20b**). This outcome was surprising because a gene called *LCY* was expected to be necessary as well, but apparently the endogenous rice *LCY* gene is already expressed in endosperm.

Subsequently, work has focused on tailoring the process so that (1) the transgenes would be expressed only during endosperm formation and only in endosperm, (2) the β-carotene synthesis could be increased using different versions of the genes, (3) the selectable marker could be removed from the transgenic lines, and (4) the transgenes could be introduced into rice cultivars that are typically used by subsistence farmers in southeast and south central Asia and Africa. These improvements have led to transgenic lines that should provide a significant fraction of the required daily intake of provitamin A from a serving of Golden Rice (**Figure 17.20c**).

The funding for the research to produce Golden Rice was public, in part from the Rockefeller Foundation, but patents on many of the techniques and tools used to generate the transgenic rice are held by biotech companies. Fortunately, these companies agreed to license the inventors of Golden Rice to provide the technology free of charge for humanitarian use in developing countries.

(a) Synthesis of GGPP

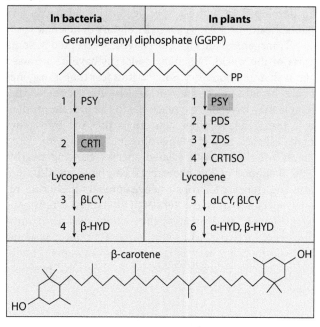

(b) Recombinant plasmids

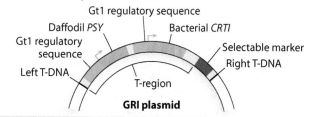

First-generation golden rice (GRI): Daffodil phytoene synthase gene (*PSY*) and bacterial gene (*CRTI*) from *Erwinia uredovora* are driven with rice glutelin-1 (Gt1) endosperm regulatory sequences (green).

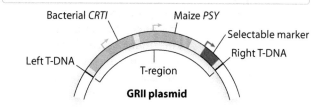

Second-generation golden rice (GRII): A maize *PSY* gene was exchanged for the daffodil *PSY* gene, boosting the production of β-carotene.

(c) Appearance of wild-type and transgenic rice

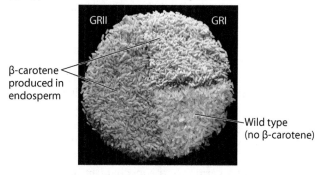

Figure 17.20   The generation of Golden Rice.

Golden Rice is an example of how customized crops can be developed to address specific nutritional needs and public health problems caused by dietary deficiencies.

Transgenic plants have been largely accepted in some parts of the world, but many concerns have been raised about their introduction. Some critics fear that transgenes could be adverse to human health—for example, that people may have allergic reactions to the protein product of a transgene. Another concern is that the transgenes may "escape" into the environment if transgenic crop plants interbreed with related species growing nearby. The likelihood of this occurrence can be reduced by not growing transgenic crops in environments harboring related species that have potential to interbreed. Transgenic crops must be tested to allay these concerns, but we must also recognize that, while the concerns about transgenic agricultural crops are valid, they are equally applicable to the cultivation of crops developed by traditional breeding methods.

Transgenic Animals

Protocols for the generation of transgenic animals are similar to those described for fungi, but as with plants, homologous recombination occurs much less frequently than illegitimate recombination (i.e., recombination not based on sequence homology). *Caenorhabditis elegans*, *Drosophila*, and *Mus musculus* (mice) are three of the most widely used genetic model animals and provide examples of the variety of methods available for creation of transgenic animals. Totipotency is not characteristic of most of their cells; thus, methods to produce transgenic animals rely on the injection of DNA into eggs, embryos, or cells that will give rise to gametes, with the hope that the injected DNA will be integrated into the genome either by homologous or illegitimate recombination.

Where injection directly into gametes is not feasible, DNA can be injected into isolated cells that are subsequently transplanted into an embryo. The embryo then develops as a **genetic chimera,** an organism in which some cells have a different genotype than others, and will transmit transgenes to progeny only if the embryonic germ cells carry a copy of the transgene. As with the protocols utilized in fungi and plants, methods for the production of transgenic animals vary depending on the biological characteristics specific to each type of organism.

C. elegans In the nematode worm *C. elegans*, one protocol for creating transgenic animals is to inject DNA directly into the gonads of hermaphrodites during oocyte development (**Figure 17.21**). The gonads are syncytial, meaning that gonadal cells each contain many nuclei and a large amount of cytoplasm. Eventually, each nucleus gives rise to a germ cell. If the injected DNA is integrated into the genome of a germ cell, the mechanism of integration is almost always illegitimate recombination.

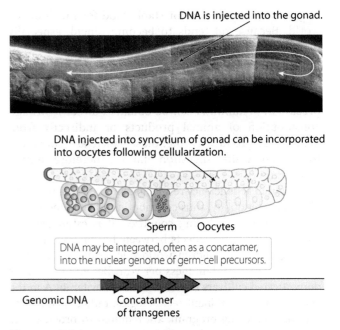

DNA is injected into the gonad.

DNA injected into syncytium of gonad can be incorporated into oocytes following cellularization.

Sperm   Oocytes

DNA may be integrated, often as a concatamer, into the nuclear genome of germ-cell precursors.

Genomic DNA   Concatamer of transgenes

Figure 17.21   Transgenic C. elegans.

The DNA is often, but not always, inserted as a concatemer, that is, as multiple tandem copies of the inserted DNA. Concatemers are undesirable because they result in abnormal levels of gene expression, either because of the additional copies producing too much gene product or because of RNA-mediated gene-silencing effects triggered by the repetitions in the concatemer (discussed in Chapter 15). Alternatively, the injected DNA may exist as extrachromosomal arrays that are not integrated into the genome and which therefore may not segregate properly during mitosis.

As with other systems for gene transfer, a selectable marker is built into the injected DNA to facilitate identification of cells that have been transformed. In *C. elegans*, a dominant mutant allele of the *roller-6* gene [specifically, *rol-6(su1006)*] can be used. Animals with this dominant mutant allele exhibit a behavioral defect: Rather than moving in the normal serpentine pattern, they tend to roll in tight circles. Because animals with several copies of the mutant allele do not survive, it serves as a "marker" that also selects against concatemers of transgenes.

Drosophila In the 1980s, Gerald Rubin and Allan Spradling demonstrated that *P* transposable elements, a class of transposons, offered an efficient means of creating transgenic *Drosophila*, in most cases inserting only one copy of the DNA being transferred (see Chapter 15 for a description of *P* elements). Their idea was to use the endogenous activity of *P* elements to transpose transgenes into the genome (**Figure 17.22**).

Based on their knowledge of **P element** transposition, Rubin and Spradling reasoned that they could replace much of the *P* element DNA with exogenous

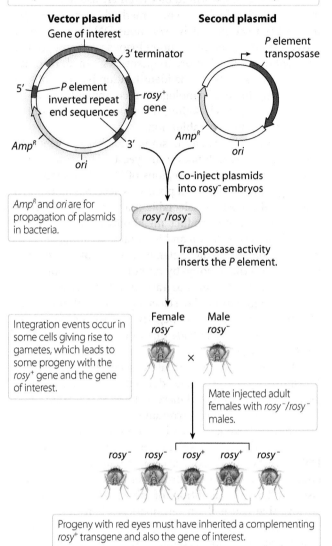

The *P* element used as a vector contains the gene of interest and also the *rosy*⁺ gene conferring wild-type eye color but lacks a functional transposase. A second plasmid supplies the transposase activity in trans.

Vector plasmid
Gene of interest
3′ terminator
5′
P element inverted repeat end sequences
rosy⁺ gene
*Amp*ᴿ
3′
ori

*Amp*ᴿ and *ori* are for propagation of plasmids in bacteria.

Second plasmid
P element transposase
*Amp*ᴿ
ori

Co-inject plasmids into rosy⁻ embryos

rosy⁻/*rosy*⁻

Transposase activity inserts the *P* element.

Integration events occur in some cells giving rise to gametes, which leads to some progeny with the *rosy*⁺ gene and the gene of interest.

Female   Male
rosy⁻   *rosy*⁻

×

Mate injected adult females with *rosy*⁻/*rosy*⁻ males.

rosy⁻   *rosy*⁻   *rosy*⁺   *rosy*⁺   *rosy*⁻

Progeny with red eyes must have inherited a complementing *rosy*⁺ transgene and also the gene of interest.

Figure 17.22   *P* element–mediated transformation in *Drosophila*.

a biological system that has evolved to recombine DNA into a host genome.

Since *P* elements transpose only in the germ-line cells of *Drosophila*, the injection is made into an early-stage embryo, targeting those cells that will give rise to the germ line. Early-stage *Drosophila* embryos are syncytial, and nuclei at the posterior end of the syncytium are most likely to give rise to the germ cells. The fly derived from the injected embryo is therefore a chimera in which most soma and some gametes are wild type, but some soma and gametes are transgenic. When the injected fly is mated with an uninjected fly of the same strain, gametes into whose genomes a *P* element was inserted will produce transgenic progeny.

A commonly used selectable marker in *Drosophila* is the *rosy* (*ry*) gene. In the procedure under discussion, the embryos to be injected are *ry*⁻/*ry*⁻ and have rosy eyes, rather than the wild-type red eyes. A wild-type, *ry*⁺, copy of the gene is included in the modified *P* element, in addition to the DNA to be transformed into the fly. While flies derived from the injected embryos will have rosy eyes, some of the progeny derived from transgenic gametes of the injected fly will have red eyes due to the action of the *ry*⁺ allele on the inserted *P* element. As is characteristic of transposons, *P* elements insert into the genome at random locations.

Vertebrates   A general approach to creating transgenic vertebrates is to inject DNA directly into the nucleus of a fertilized egg cell, in a manner similar to that described above for *C. elegans* and *Drosophila*. The injected DNA can become integrated into the genome at random positions by illegitimate recombination. Because the DNA integrates randomly into the genome, the transgene becomes inserted at different locations in the genomes of different individual animals. In organisms such as salmon, each injected egg has the potential to develop into a transgenic individual (**Figure 17.23**).

Two features of this method lead to variability in the expression of the transgene. First, due to the integration of the transgenes as multicopy concatemers, gene expression levels can be affected as described for *C. elegans*. Second, the expression of the transgene can be abnormal because of the chromosomal environment in which it is located. For example, if the transgene is inserted into heterochromatin, gene expression may be altered as described for position effect variegation in *Drosophila* (see Chapter 15). Note that the problem of transgene position effects is shared by all transgenic organisms in which the transgene is integrated into the genome by illegitimate recombination. While position effects can pose problems in *Drosophila*, *C. elegans*, and plants, they are exacerbated in mice due to the larger average size of vertebrate genes and the larger amount of heterochromatin in vertebrate genomes. To overcome this variability, methods to more precisely insert transgenes were developed for mice.

DNA as long as (1) transposase, the enzyme that controls *P* element movement, was provided; and (2) the *P* element ends were retained, since these are required for recognition by the transposase. In their method, two DNA molecules, one a modified *P* element and the other a DNA molecule encoding the transposase but lacking the sequences required for transposition, are co-injected into a *Drosophila* embryo. The modified *P* elements are induced to insert into the genome at random positions by the action of the transposase. Typically, only a single *P* element is inserted, precluding the problems associated with the concatemeric arrays seen in transgenic *C. elegans*. This strategy resembles the use of *Agrobacterium* to transform plants in that it too utilizes

Endogenous sockeye salmon growth hormone gene

Enhancer elements of sockeye salmon growth hormone gene are responsive to light and active only in spring and summer.

Sockeye salmon growth hormone gene

TATA box

5' UTR

Combine gene fragments in vitro using recombinant DNA technology.

Engineered sockeye salmon gene

Enhancer elements from sockeye salmon *metallothionein-B* gene activate gene expression throughout the year.

Sockeye salmon growth hormone gene

TATA box

5' UTR

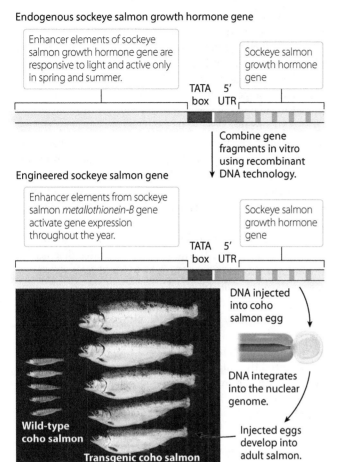

DNA injected into coho salmon egg

DNA integrates into the nuclear genome.

Wild-type coho salmon

Transgenic coho salmon

Injected eggs develop into adult salmon.

Figure 17.23 **Creation of transgenic salmon through injection of DNA into salmon eggs.**

Mus musculus Mice are important genetic models for human diseases and human physiology. The ability to create transgenic mice enables scientists to dissect not only the genetic and molecular basis of mouse development and physiology but also, by proxy, many aspects of human development and physiology. Two methods are available to create transgenic mice, a targeted approach and a nontargeted approach.

In the nontargeted approach, the transgene is randomly inserted into the genome through illegitimate recombination; in the targeted approach, the transgene is inserted into a specific locus in the genome through homologous recombination. The latter method transformed the study of mouse biology since it allows for the creation of mice with specific loss-of-function (or knockout) and gain-of-function alleles. In 2007, Mario Capecchi, Martin Evans, and Oliver Smithies shared the Nobel Prize in Medicine or Physiology for their work leading to the development of knockout mice.

Problems associated with variable genomic positions and expression of transgenes led geneticists to explore the possibility of using homologous recombination for transgene integration. Homologous recombination would

provide more consistent transgenic mouse strains and would also facilitate the creation of mutations in specific mouse genes, which would be extremely useful for studying mammalian biology. Thus, methods were developed to identify mice in which exogenous DNA had been inserted into the genome by homologous recombination as opposed to the much more frequent illegitimate recombination (Figure 17.24a). The identification is accomplished by selecting for the homologous recombinant and at the same time selectively killing the transformants resulting from illegitimate recombination.

The overall strategy is similar to that described for homologous recombination in yeast. The transformation vector contains two regions of DNA homologous to the target locus flanking a positive selectable marker. An example of a positive selectable marker is the *Neomycin* (*Neo*) gene, whose product metabolizes the drug G418, which blocks translation and is lethal to mammalian cells. A vector containing these elements is capable of being integrated into the genome by homologous recombination, but more than 99% of integrations will occur by illegitimate recombination. To select against nonhomologous recombination events, a negative selectable marker is added to the vector outside one of the regions of homology to the target gene.

A commonly used negative selectable marker is a *thymidine kinase* (*tk*) gene derived from a herpes simplex virus. Thymidine kinase catalyzes the addition of a phosphate to deoxythymidine, forming deoxythymidine monophosphate, which is eventually converted to deoxythymidine triphosphate, one of the substrates for DNA synthesis. In contrast to mammalian thymidine kinase, thymidine kinase from herpes simplex virus can also catalyze the addition of phosphate to thymidine analogs that cause chain termination when incorporated into DNA. Because the endogenous mammalian thymidine kinase does not recognize the thymidine analogs as substrates, only those cells expressing the herpes simplex virus *tk* gene are sensitive to the thymidine analogs. Thus, cells harboring the viral *tk* gene will be selected against when plated on media containing the thymidine analog ganciclovir. Such thymidine analogs are also used as potent antiviral medications, since only cells harboring the virus are sensitive to the analog.

For transformed mouse cells to survive, they must acquire the positive marker and must lose the negative marker. The occurrence of a homologous recombination event between the negative and positive markers is one possible way in which the introduced DNA can be integrated to produce a cell that possesses the positive and lacks the negative marker. Selection for this type of transformation is called **positive–negative selection.** A related protocol, negative–positive–negative selection, where negative selectable markers are positioned at each end of the introduced DNA, has been successfully used to identify homologous recombination events in plants,

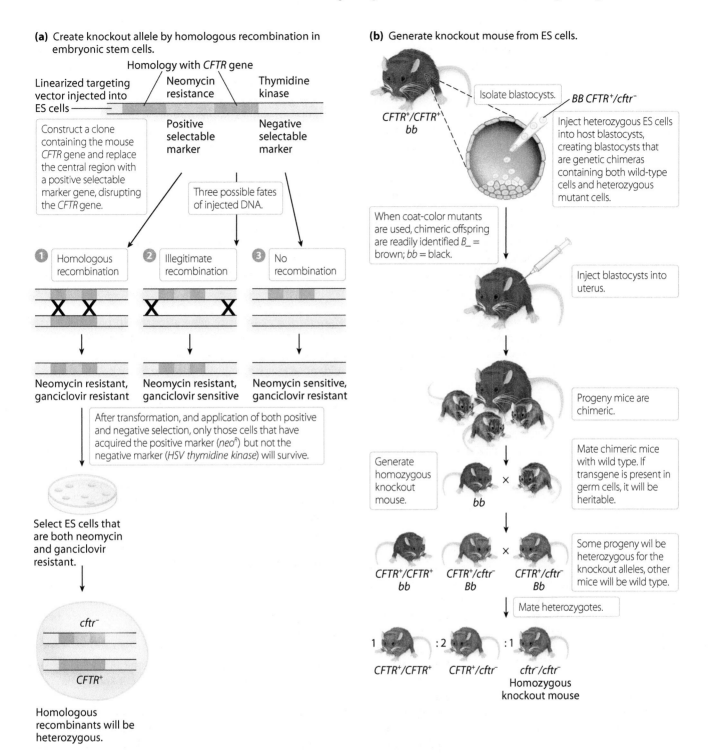

(a) Create knockout allele by homologous recombination in embryonic stem cells.

(b) Generate knockout mouse from ES cells.

Figure 17.24 **Creating a loss-of-function CFTR (cystic fibrosis transmembrane conductance regulator) allele in mice through homologous recombination.** Mutations in the human ortholog are the cause of cystic fibrosis.

such as rice, and should be generally applicable to any species.

What types of mammalian cells are typically targeted for gene transfer? The blastocyst-stage mammalian embryo consists of an outer sphere of cells and a small pool of cells inside the sphere. At the blastocyst stage, the internal cells, known as embryonic stem (ES) cells, are totipotent. The production of a transgenic mouse starts with the isolation of ES cells from the mouse strain to be transformed. The ES cells are grown in culture, and DNA is introduced into the cells, often by transiently depolarizing their membranes to make the cells permeable to

DNA. The cells are then transferred to media containing the agents for positive and negative selection, and transformed cells in which homologous recombination occurred are selected.

The selected transformed ES cells are reintroduced into a blastocyst from a mouse of a genotype different from that of the transformed cells, allowing the progeny derived from the transformed ES cells to be detected (**Figure 17.24b**). For example, alleles conferring differences in coat color are often used. The blastocyst, now carrying transformed ES cells, is implanted into a surrogate female mouse. Because only some of the ES cells in the host blastocyst are transgenic, the mouse that develops from the embryo in which the transformed cells were introduced is a genetic chimera in which some tissues are derived from the transformed ES cells and other tissues are derived from host ES cells. Chimeric animals can be readily identified by their variegated coat color.

It is hoped that at least some of the gametes of the chimeric offspring of the host mouse will be derived from the transformed ES cells, so that some mice in the subsequent generation will be heterozygous for the mutation caused by the homologous recombination event. If two heterozygous offspring of this generation are interbred, mice homozygous for the mutation can be produced. Technologies for the construction of other transgenic mammals, including sheep, cats, cows, horses, monkeys, and rats, follow a similar protocol.

Advances in Altering and Synthesizing DNA Molecules

Sometimes, the wild-type version of a gene is the one that geneticists wish to express as a transgene. But we have seen that in some cases, it is desirable to express a modified version in which specific nucleotides have been changed. One reason it is sometimes desirable to alter the sequence of an encoded protein is to render the protein either more or less active. For example, changes in the identities of specific amino acids can sometimes cause an enzyme to be constitutively active or to be more stable at high or at low temperatures. A second reason to change the nucleotide sequence of a gene is to improve its expression in a species with a different codon bias than that of the species from which the gene was derived (as noted above under "Transgenes in *Escherichia coli*").

In the past, making specific changes to a DNA sequence was a laborious process. However, technology for chemically synthesizing DNA molecules has improved significantly in recent years in terms of both accuracy and cost, making the synthesis of any DNA sequence feasible. Consider the example of human insulin genes. In the late 1970s, the construction of the B-chain gene from 18 chemically synthesized oligonucleotides 10 to 12 nucleotides long and of the A-chain gene from 12

oligonucleotides 10 to 15 nucleotides long was a monumental task. Today, however, oligonucleotides tens to hundreds of bases in length are inexpensive to construct via PCR-based approaches.

More recently, chemical syntheses of DNA molecules up to 50,000 bases in length have become feasible. Geneticists are able to design a DNA molecule from scratch and synthesize it for subsequent use in living organisms. This approach is useful when multiple changes would otherwise be required in a DNA molecule before its introduction into a transgenic organism. As with sequencing technologies, advances in chemical synthesis of large DNA molecules have the potential to transform biotechnology and biological research. In 2008, the entire 582,970-bp genome of *Mycoplasma genitalium* was chemically synthesized in vitro, cloned into a YAC vector, and propagated in *Saccharomyces cerevisiae*. The synthetic genome was then transplanted into a receptive *Mycoplasma* cytoplasm, generating a cell that would use the genetic information contained on the synthetic chromosome. This ability to synthesize genome-sized nucleic acid molecules is revolutionizing experimental biology.

Manipulation of DNA Sequences in Vivo

The ultimate technology for investigation of gene function and also for gene therapy would be the ability to precisely change DNA sequences in the genome in vivo. Such technology would facilitate the examination of gene function by the creation of specific alleles and allow the "correction" of DNA sequences in cells with deleterious alleles. While these technologies do not yet exist, recent advances, two of which are described here, have made in vivo manipulation of genome sequences possible.

Site-Specific Recombination In some cases it is desirable to manipulate transgenes after they have been introduced into an organism. For example, the ability to remove the positive selectable marker gene after selection of transformants mitigates one of the concerns raised by critics of transgenic plants (as shown below). In addition, in vivo manipulation of transgenes facilitates the production of conditional alleles of genes whose null allele is lethal. The ability to specifically recombine DNA molecules makes in vivo manipulation of transgenes feasible.

Several bacteriophages use **site-specific recombination** systems during their life cycle, either for intramolecular recombination within the bacteriophage genome or for intermolecular recombination into host genomes. These recombination systems can be harnessed for producing recombinant DNA molecules in vitro and for recombining DNA molecules in vivo. Bacteriophage site-specific recombination systems have two components: (1) DNA sequences in the bacteriophage genome that are identical to sequences in the target bacterial genome and (2) an enzyme, commonly called a recombinase or integrase, that binds to the identical DNA sequences and catalyzes their recombination. Two bacteriophage recombination systems, one in bacteriophage λ and the other in bacteriophage P1, have proven particularly valuable in the development of site-specific recombination for use in molecular biology experiments.

A site-specific recombination system derived from bacteriophage P1 utilizes Cre recombinase, a bacteriophage-encoded protein that acts to recombine DNA containing *loxP* sequences (Figure 17.25). The *loxP* sites are 34-bp sequences consisting of two 13-bp inverted repeats separated by an 8-bp spacer that provides asymmetry, and they are specifically recognized by Cre recombinase. The Cre recombinase binds to two *loxP* sites and catalyzes a recombination event between them. If the two *loxP* sites are direct repeats, the intervening DNA is deleted, whereas if the two *loxP* sites are inverted relative to one another, the intervening sequence is inverted.

The Cre–*lox* recombination system has been adapted to recombine DNA in vivo in transgenic organisms. For example, *loxP* sites are added to the ends of the DNA to be deleted or inverted and introduced as a transgene into an organism. A second transgene encoding the Cre recombinase is also introduced into the same organism. In cells where the Cre recombinase is expressed, the DNA flanked by the *loxP* sites will be deleted or inverted.

One reason a geneticist might want to delete a transgene after having introduced it into the genome is to assess the function of the gene at specific times and in specific tissues during development. For example, if a null loss-of-function allele results in embryonic lethality, the role of the gene at later developmental stages is difficult to assess. One approach to determining the post-embryonic function of such genes is to complement a loss-of-function mutant with a functional copy of the gene flanked by *loxP* sites. In cells where the Cre recombinase

is active, the transgene will be deleted, causing these cells and their descendants to have a mutant genotype. If the Cre recombinase is driven by a promoter that confers inducible expression or expression that is temporally or spatially restricted, a genetic chimera can be created, allowing an assessment of gene function in specific tissues.

A second application is the removal of selectable markers in transgenic organisms. An objection to the use of transgenic organisms in agriculture is that some transgenic strains contain a selectable marker providing resistance to antibiotics, which might spread into the natural population. The antibiotic selectable marker genes were used to select the transgenic organism but are no longer needed once the transgenic organism has been identified. One strategy for eliminating the selectable marker is to flank the unwanted transgene with *loxP* sites in a direct repeat orientation. A plant containing this transgene is then crossed with another transgenic plant expressing the Cre recombinase, and the unwanted transgene is deleted in the F$_1$. It is then possible to segregate the transgene encoding the Cre recombinase away from the desired transgene in subsequent generations.

Targeted DNA Sequence Changes One approach to inducing changes in genomic sequences in vivo is to design a DNA endonuclease to target a specific genomic location. The endonuclease creates a double-strand break at the site, which is subsequently repaired by endogenous repair mechanisms.

Two different approaches are presently being used to cause the nuclease to target a specific site in the genome. First, the nuclease can be translationally fused to a sequence-specific DNA binding domain that recognizes only the site in the genome to be targeted. Second, the nuclease can be incorporated into a complex with an RNA molecule, which then provides specificity via complementary base pairing with the target sequence of interest. This latter approach is based on reengineering a bacterial system called CRISPR-CAS that evolved as a defense mechanism against invading nucleic acids. The CAS nuclease introduces double strand breaks in DNA molecules at sites determined by an RNA molecule with which it forms a complex.

If the double-strand break is repaired by non-homologous end-joining, then small deletions often remain at the site of the break, leading to possible loss- or gain-of-function alleles, depending on what sequences are lost. Alternatively, the break may be repaired by homologous recombination, either with endogenous sequence from the homologous chromosome in a diploid cell or with exogenously supplied DNA sequences. In the latter case, if the exogenously supplied DNA has been constructed in such a way that it contains the desired change, a specific sequence change in the chromosome may be accomplished.

Genetic Analysis 17.2 asks you to put some of these ideas to work by designing a mouse model of a human disease.

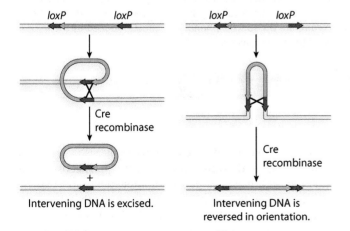

Figure 17.25   Bacteriophage site-specific recombination systems.

PROBLEM Mouse models of human diseases are valuable research tools that can be used to test therapies and drugs. How would you make a transgenic mouse model of Huntington disease, which is caused by an autosomal dominant mutation consisting of an expanded sequence of trinucleotide repeats?

> BREAK IT DOWN: Review the discussion on p. 597 of procedures for creating transgenic mice.

> BREAK IT DOWN: Review the defining features of an autosomal dominant mutation (see Section 4.1).

Solution Strategies	Solution Steps
Evaluate	
1. Identify the topic this problem addresses and the nature of the required answer.	1. This problem about recombinant DNA technology asks how to construct a specific strain of transgenic mouse.
2. Identify the critical information given in the problem.	2. The desired disease model is of Huntington disease (HD), described as an autosomal dominant mutation that consists of an expanded sequence of trinucleotide repeats. The transgenic mouse is to be used to test therapies and drugs.
Deduce	
3. Inheritance patterns are always a key consideration in genetic research designs. Identify the inheritance pattern of the HD phenotype.	3. Since HD is dominant, a phenotype should be evident if a single mutant allele is introduced into the genome.
4. Evaluate the ways in which the *HD* allele can be transferred into mice.	4. Transgenic mice can be generated by random integration of a transgene or, alternatively, by homologous recombination that replaces the endogenous gene with a mutant version.
5. Choose the method of generating a transgenic mouse that will come closest to modelling the disease of interest. PITFALL: Randomly integrated transgenes may exhibit variation in expression patterns.	5. Since we want the transgene to be expressed in the same pattern as the wild-type mouse *HD* gene, homologous recombination is the best approach, because the mutant *HD* gene will then be in the same genomic context and will be expressed in the same pattern as the wild-type gene.
Solve	
6. Design a strategy to replace the wild-type mouse *HD* gene with a mutant version of the human *HD* gene. PITFALL: Since a functional allele is desired, the positive selectable marker must not interfere with *HD* transgene function.	6. The positive–negative selection approach outlined in Figure 17.24 to produce a transgenic mouse by homologous recombination results in a loss-of-function allele. This approach must be modified to create a gain-of-function allele. a. Construct a vector in which a human mutant *HD* gene is flanked by mouse *HD* regulatory sequences (5′ and 3′ of the *HD* gene). b. The positive selective marker gene can be placed downstream of the *HD* gene, in a position not likely to interfere with HD gene expression, or could be removed using the Cre–*lox* approach outlined in Figure 17.25. c. A second type of transgenic mouse, expressing the wild-type human gene driven by the same regulatory sequences, would provide a useful control to compare the specific phenotypic effects induced by the expression of the mutant allele.

For more practice, see Problems 7, 0, 11, 27, and 30.   Visit the Study Area to access study tools.   MasteringGenetics™

17.3 Gene Therapy Uses Recombinant DNA Technology

The ability to manipulate gene expression through the introduction of a transgene raises the possibility that human genetic diseases could be treated by the introduction of a functional version of the mutant gene. The use of genes as therapeutic agents to cure or alleviate disease symptoms is termed **gene therapy**. From a genetic perspective, gene therapy is similar to a genetic complementation experiment in which the gene introduced by gene therapy compensates for a genetic abnormality in the altered cell. Two types of gene therapy, classified as somatic gene therapy and germinal gene therapy, are feasible.

Two Forms of Gene Therapy

Somatic gene therapy targets somatic cells, whose descendants will not give rise to germ cells. Any genetic alterations induced in the targeted cells will be passed to daughter cells by mitosis, but the alteration will not be inherited by progeny of the individual undergoing somatic gene therapy. The specific somatic cells to be targeted depend on the disease in question. For example, in individuals with cystic fibrosis, the epithelial cells of the lungs represent a logical target, since lungs are severely affected in cystic fibrosis. On the other hand, for diseases of the blood, cells of the various hemopoietic lineages are the target cells; they can be removed from bone marrow, treated, and returned to the same individual. Somatic gene therapy turns the treated individual into a genetic chimera that has the transgene present in the target cells but not in other somatic cells or in germ cells. Somatic gene therapy can potentially be used to treat several genetic diseases whose phenotype becomes apparent early in childhood.

The alternative strategy for gene therapy, **germinal gene therapy,** targets cells of the germ line, which give rise to gametes. Because germinal gene therapy alters germ-line cells, the therapeutic transgene is transmitted to the progeny of the treated individual. Both types of gene therapy have been successful in animal systems; but for ethical reasons, only somatic gene therapy has been attempted in humans. In the following paragraphs, we discuss somatic gene therapy in humans and describe modifications of these protocols suggested by successful somatic gene therapy experiments in mice.

Gene Therapy in Humans

The primary difficulties in human somatic gene therapy concern the delivery of the transgene to the somatic cells of interest and the proper expression of the transgene in targeted cells. The DNA encoding the gene must be delivered to the proper cells, pass through the cell membrane and into the nucleus, and, once there, be expressed at a level that is sufficient to provide normal gene function. In some cases—for example, in hemopoietic diseases—the cells to be treated can simply be extracted from the body, treated in vitro, and then injected back into the body.

However, in other cases—for example, cystic fibrosis, in which lung epithelial cells are the target—the cells must be treated in situ because they cannot be removed from the patient.

The choice of vector to deliver the DNA to the cells is pivotal. Gene therapy methods often take advantage of viruses that have evolved mechanisms to access specific cell types. Essentially, viruses are harnessed to transduce the transgene into the target cells the way the transduction of DNA between bacteria is performed by bacteriophage (see Chapter 7). The viruses can be "disarmed" so that they no longer have the ability to cause the diseases associated with their wild-type relatives. Several types of viral vectors have been used, including gammaretroviruses, lentiviruses, and adenoviruses (Table 17.3). Each has advantages and disadvantages for gene therapy protocols.

Many viral vectors deliver transgenes by integrating into the genome of the target cell. Integration provides a mechanism for stable gene transfer and thus permanent correction of the defect. Integration of the vector into the genome is not without risks, however; the insertion may cause a detrimental mutation, a problem that has plagued most human gene therapy experiments to date. The treatment of a serious immune system disease called severe combined immune deficiency syndrome (SCIDS) provides an example.

SCIDS patients lack the ability to produce a category of blood cells called T cells that are critical to the body's defense against infection. One form of SCIDS is due to mutations in the gene encoding the gamma subunit (γ chain) of the interleukin-2 receptor on T cells and is X-linked. In the mid-1990s, a gene therapy approach was designed using a retroviral vector carrying the γ chain cDNA driven by viral regulatory sequences. The retrovirus carrying the cDNA was bounded by long terminal repeats (LTRs; see Chapter 12). In one study, 9 of 10 patients were successfully treated, and they exhibited functioning, adaptive immune systems following gene therapy. In three patients, however, an uncontrolled increase of mature T cells, termed T-acute lymphoblastic leukemia, developed in the years immediately following treatment. In each of these individuals, the retrovirus became inserted into the *LMO2* gene in such a way that the retroviral LTR promoter was able to cause unregulated expression of

Table 17.3	Viruses Used as Vectors in Gene Therapy		
Virus Type	**Integration into Genome**	**Target**	**Capacity**
Retrovirus	Integrates; insertional mutagen	Infects dividing cells	8 kb
Lentivirus	Integrates; insertional mutagen	Infects nondividing cells	8 kb
Adenovirus	Nonintegrating	Infects nondividing cells	7.5 kb
Adeno-associated virus	Episomal, but can integrate	Infects nondividing cells	4.5 kb

LMO2. This gene is known to be required for the differentiation of hemopoietic cells. Its overexpression is thought to be what led these patients to develop leukemia.

This trial highlighted one of the concerns raised by the use of retroviruses as gene therapy vectors—that they may act as mutagens. Once this possibility was recognized, the SCIDS gene therapy trials just described were suspended. However, the high proportion of treated individuals whose immune defects were corrected in the study suggests that gene therapy can be a viable approach to treating such diseases.

In addition to concerns over safety and efficacy, the use of viral vectors presents technical challenges stemming from size limits on the amount of DNA that can be packaged in the viral capsid (similar limits were discussed in regard to bacterial transduction in Chapter 7). In most cases, the amount of DNA that can be packaged by a virus is much smaller than the size of a typical human gene. For example, the transcribed region of the *CFTR* gene spans approximately 170,000 bp, from which are produced a 6132-bp processed mRNA encoding a 1480–amino acid protein. Since viral vectors can accept only 5 to 10 kb of DNA, only a cDNA of the *CFTR* gene lacking all endogenous gene-expression regulatory elements can be accommodated in a viral vector. In the absence of these endogenous regulatory sequences, the expression of the *CFTR* coding sequence is driven by viral regulatory sequences, which might not regulate the transgenes in a manner appropriate for proper gene function in the target cells.

Virus-based gene therapy continues to be employed in selected experimental cases despite past failures and continuing concerns over the safety of the procedures. Successes in treating patients with cystic fibrosis, SCIDS, and several other human hereditary conditions offer hope that continued research will identify effective vectors for delivering treatment that is sustained, targeted, and safe.

The Case Study in this chapter examines an approach to gene therapy whereby mutant alleles are corrected in cultured cells that are then reintroduced into the host.

17.4 Cloning of Plants and Animals Produces Genetically Identical Individuals

Many plants have the capacity for vegetative (asexual) propagation in addition to sexual propagation. For example, poplar and aspen (*Populus* sp.) groves often consist of vegetatively propagated clones, all genetically identical.

Some of these clonal groves are estimated to be at least 10,000 years old. Humans, taking advantage of the ability of plants to reproduce vegetatively, have been clonally propagating plants for centuries in agricultural practices. In these protocols, heterozygous genotypes of agriculturally desirable specimens are propagated intact, without the segregation of alleles that occurs during sexual reproduction. Heterozygous genotypes often exhibit hybrid vigor, resulting in high yields in comparison to inbred varieties.

Perhaps the most conspicuous example of agricultural vegetative propagation is the cultivation of grapes (*Vitus vinifera*), which were domesticated 6000 to 7000 years ago. Most grape cultivars are highly heterozygous; that is, they have two different alleles at many genomic loci. Thus, when they are self-fertilized or crossed with another cultivar, extensive segregation of genotypes and phenotypes is observed in the progeny. Because this presents an obstacle to controlling the properties of grape plants through breeding, cultivars that possess favorable phenotypes are propagated by cuttings (that is, additional plants are grown from pieces of source plants). In most vineyards, the vines are chimeric: The shoots are all genetically identical and chosen on the basis of their fruit phenotype, and the roots, also identical to one another, are of a different genotype that is chosen for being well adapted to local soil conditions.

Several wine grape cultivars can be traced back to the Middle Ages, and some are likely to be even older. For example, Pinot was first described in Roman times and is thought to be at least 2000 years old. While clonal propagation allows maintenance of specific genotypes, somatic mutations—due, for example, to errors in DNA replication and transposable element activity—can accumulate over time and lead to phenotypic variation. Thus, a mutation in a gene required for pigment synthesis led to the formation of Pinot blanc, a white-berry cultivar, from Pinot noir, the ancestral black-berry cultivar.

Unlike plants, most animals do not readily propagate clonally in nature—but there are exceptions. For example, some aphid species undergo multiple parthenogenetic (clonal) generations in the spring and summer, followed by sexual reproduction in the autumn. Since most animal cells are not totipotent, animals do not readily regenerate from single cells. (An important exception is embryonic stem cells, which have the potential to differentiate into any cell type in the body.) Thus, techniques for cloning animals, and in particular mammals, from single differentiated cells are considerably more complicated than those for cloning plants.

Dolly, a sheep, was the first cloned mammal. In the protocol used to produce Dolly, a diploid nucleus is isolated from a differentiated cell of the animal to be cloned (**Figure 17.26**). This nucleus, containing all the nuclear genetic information of the animal from which it was taken, is injected into an egg cell that has had its own nucleus removed. The egg cell can be derived from the animal to be cloned (if it possesses egg cells) or from a different individual. If the nuclear transplantation is successful, the genome of the donor nucleus will direct the development of the embryo derived from the egg cell. The use of a diploid donor nucleus means that fertilization with a sperm cell is not required to produce a diploid nucleus in the embryo; thus, the genetic constitution of the embryo will be identical to that of the donor. Bear in mind, however, that while the nuclear genome is genetically identical to that of the donor, the mitochondrial genome is derived from the surrogate egg cell. The diploid egg cell is then induced to begin embryogenesis and implanted into a surrogate mother. If all goes well, it will develop into a normal embryo, and birth of a normal offspring will follow.

In most mammals, the frequency of success with this protocol has been quite low. Dolly's was the only one out of 270 implanted egg cells that resulted in the birth of a sheep. Donor cells have been derived from adult animals—Dolly's donor cell was a mammary gland cell—and are therefore highly differentiated somatic cells rather than totipotent embryonic stem cells. In differentiated somatic cells, such as those of the mammary gland, the patterns of facultative heterochromatin (see Chapter 15) are vastly different from those of embryonic stem cells. In other words, although the sequences of nucleotides in the genomes of differentiated and embryonic stem cells are identical, the epigenetic modifications of the histones and DNA methylation patterns differ. The low frequency of success in the initial attempts to clone mammals was likely due to deficiencies in reprogramming the genetic material of the injected nucleus to mimic the epigenetic modifications characteristic of an embryonic stem cell. A failure in epigenetic reprogramming has also been postulated as a possible cause of Dolly's shortened life span.

Nevertheless, advances in knowledge of ES cell biology, and their application to reprogram certain differentiated cells in vitro to behave like stem cells, suggest that the cloning of mammals will increase over time (see the chapter Case Study for more details). Despite the difficulties, many different mammals besides sheep have been successfully cloned, including mice, cows, horses, donkeys, cats, and dogs.

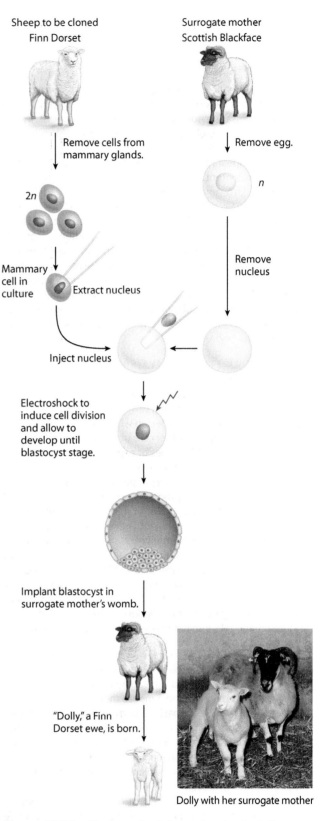

Figure 17.26   Cloning animals by nuclear implantation.

CASE STUDY

Curing Sickle Cell Disease in Mice

The ideal somatic gene therapy would be one that corrects the specific mutation causing the genetic disease rather than just compensating for the mutant allele. Advances in understanding the biology of embryonic stem (ES) cells have brought new forms of somatic gene therapy that may approach the ideal for some genetic diseases. Embryonic stem cells are totipotent, meaning they have the potential to differentiate into any cell type in the body. In addition, as discussed in Section 17.2, the genome of an ES cell can be manipulated by homologous recombination. Thus, if ES cells can be isolated from an individual, gene mutations within the cells could perhaps be corrected, and the cells could then be induced to differentiate into the appropriate cell type to treat the genetic disease. As illustrated in the mouse experiment described below, the ability to create and manipulate ES cells provides a means of isolating cells from an individual, correcting mutations in the cells, and reintroducing the "corrected" cells into the body.

CREATING ES CELLS FROM FIBROBLASTS In many cases, the diagnosis of a genetic disease is not made until early childhood, when the body no longer possesses any ES cells, because they form only during early embryogenesis. How can ES cells be obtained from a person who has none? The answer is to create ES cells from other cells of the body.

In 2006 and 2007, a series of experiments demonstrated that mouse or human fibroblasts, a type of cell occurring in connective tissue, could be reprogrammed in vitro to behave like stem cells. These reprogrammed cells have been called induced pluripotent stem cells, or iPS. (The word *pluripotent* is used because scientists do not yet know if the iPS cells are totipotent.) This reprogramming of differentiated cells was accomplished by expressing a combination of three to four transcription factors (choices included Oct4, Sox2, c-Myc, and Klf4). The transcription factors that were used are normally expressed in ES cells and appear to be sufficient to induce reprogramming of the transcriptional networks of differentiated somatic cells into networks characteristic of ES cells.

GENE THERAPY PROOF OF PRINCIPLE These advances set the stage for using iPS cells in gene therapy. Proof of principle (a phrase used by scientists to mean proof that the general idea is valid) was provided using a mouse model for sickle cell disease (Figure 17.27). The basic strategy being tested consisted of ❶ harvesting adult cells, ❷ reprogramming adult cells into iPS cells, ❸ repairing the genetic defect through homologous recombination, ❹ differentiating the iPS cells into hemopoietic precursors in vitro, and ❺ transplanting the corrected cells into bone marrow of affected mice.

The starting point for this test of somatic gene therapy was the creation of a "humanized" mouse model for sickle cell anemia by substituting human α-globin genes for the endogenous mouse α-globin genes and substituting human β^S (sickle) globin genes for the mouse β-globin genes. Mice homozygous for the β^S-globin allele (β^S/β^S) exhibited typical disease symptoms, including severe anemia and erythrocyte sickling. Fibroblasts isolated from the tail of β^S/β^S mice were infected with retroviruses encoding the Oct4, Sox2, and Klf4 transcription factors and with a lentivirus encoding the c-Myc transcription factor. Expression of these four transcription factors resulted in the reprogramming of the fibroblast cells into iPS cells. On either side of the *c-Myc* gene on the lentivirus, *lox* sites had been placed, to allow the gene to be excised from the genome when the cells were infected with an adenovirus encoding Cre recombinase. This was important because continued expression of *c-Myc* predisposes cells to become cancerous. Although the other three transgenes were not removed in this experiment, their removal by a similar mechanism is also recommended.

To correct a β^S-globin allele, a transformation vector encoding the β^A-globin allele was introduced into the iPS cells, and hygromycin- and ganciclovir-resistant homologous recombinants were created using the procedure described in Section 17.2. The corrected iPS cells were now heterozygous at the β-globin locus (β^A/β^S). The β^A/β^S iPS cells were then differentiated into hemopoietic progenitors (HPs, cells that have the potential to differentiate into any of the hemopoietic lineages) by infection with another retrovirus encoding the *HoxB4* gene, which induces the differentiation of ES cells into HPs when incubated with cytokines secreted from bone marrow cells. The β^A/β^S HPs were then transplanted back into β^S/β^S mice in which the endogenous β^S/β^S bone marrow cells had been eliminated by irradiation, so that now the β^A/β^S HPs constituted the primary source of hemopoietic cells. In this particular experiment, the *HoxB4* coding sequence was translationally fused with that of green fluorescent protein (GFP), so the activity of the β^A/β^S HPs could be monitored by the presence of *GFP*$^+$ cells in the blood. Subsequently, by all physiological tests, the mice receiving the β^A/β^S HPs were cured of sickle cell disease.

These experiments in mice suggest there is promise in the use of ES or iPS cells for gene therapy, but at least two facets of gene therapy procedures continue to cause concern. Problems associated with using retroviruses and oncogenes for reprogramming need to be resolved before implementing such a protocol in humans. In addition, whether iPS cells are truly totipotent or still contain an epigenetic memory of their origin remains to be determined. Since an individual's own cells are used as the source for genetic modification, there are no impediments due to immune system incompatibility. However, this approach is limited to those diseases, such as blood disorders, in which cells can be isolated, genetically corrected, and reintroduced into the body.

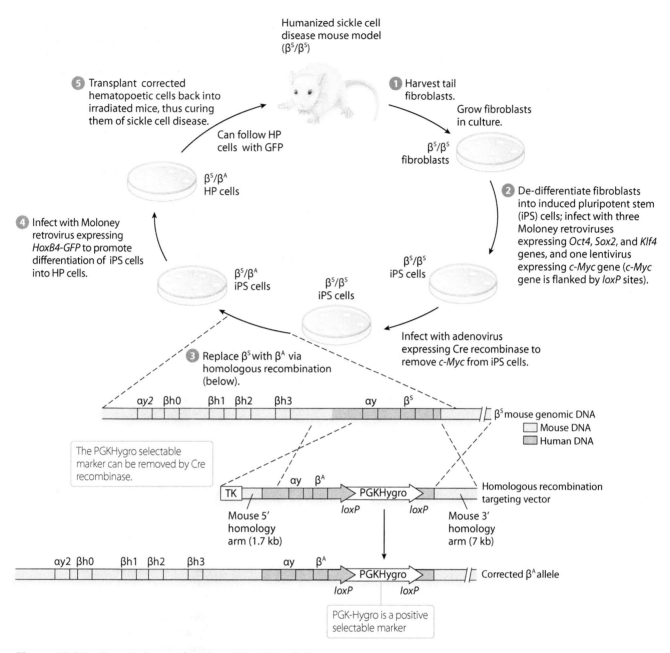

Figure 17.27 **Genetic therapy for mice with sickle cell disease.**

The figure labels include:

Humanized sickle cell disease mouse model (β^S/β^S)

5 Transplant corrected hematopoetic cells back into irradiated mice, thus curing them of sickle cell disease.

Can follow HP cells with GFP

β^S/β^A HP cells

4 Infect with Moloney retrovirus expressing *HoxB4-GFP* to promote differentiation of iPS cells into HP cells.

β^S/β^A iPS cells

β^S/β^S iPS cells

3 Replace β^S with β^A via homologous recombination (below).

1 Harvest tail fibroblasts.

Grow fibroblasts in culture.

β^S/β^S fibroblasts

2 De-differentiate fibroblasts into induced pluripotent stem (iPS) cells; infect with three Moloney retroviruses expressing *Oct4*, *Sox2*, and *Klf4* genes, and one lentivirus expressing *c-Myc* gene (*c-Myc* gene is flanked by *loxP* sites).

β^S/β^S iPS cells

Infect with adenovirus expressing Cre recombinase to remove *c-Myc* from iPS cells.

$\alpha y2$ $\beta h0$ $\beta h1$ $\beta h2$ $\beta h3$ αy β^S — β^S mouse genomic DNA

☐ Mouse DNA
▨ Human DNA

The PGKHygro selectable marker can be removed by Cre recombinase.

TK — αy β^A — PGKHygro — Homologous recombination targeting vector

Mouse 5′ homology arm (1.7 kb) — *loxP* — *loxP* — Mouse 3′ homology arm (7 kb)

$\alpha y2$ $\beta h0$ $\beta h1$ $\beta h2$ $\beta h3$ αy β^A PGKHygro — Corrected β^A allele

loxP — *loxP*

PGK-Hygro is a positive selectable marker

SUMMARY   **MasteringGenetics™**   For activities, animations, and review quizzes, go to the Study Area.

17.1 Specific DNA Sequences Are Identified and Manipulated Using Recombinant DNA Technology

▌ Restriction enzymes, which cut at specific DNA sequences, are used to fragment large DNA molecules into defined smaller pieces.

▌ A restriction map of a DNA molecule can be constructed by analyzing patterns of DNA fragments after restriction enzyme digestion.

▌ DNA fragments can be ligated to create recombinant DNA molecules, usually composed of a vector that can be

amplified in a biological system and a target DNA insert to be amplified.

▌ While cohesive compatible ends facilitate the creation of recombinant DNA molecules, any two DNA fragments can be ligated if their ends are made blunt.

▌ Amplification of recombinant DNA molecules in a biological system allows the production of DNA clones.

▌ Bacteriophage and bacterial and yeast artificial chromosomes allow the cloning of large DNA molecules.

▌ Genomic libraries are collections of cloned DNA fragments that represent the entire genome of an organism.

- cDNA libraries are collections of cloned DNA fragments that represent the mRNA population of an organism or tissue.

- DNA hybridization, which depends on complementary base pairing, is a means of identifying similar sequences in a mixture of DNA sequences.

- Long DNA molecules can be sequenced using primer walking methods or by shotgun sequencing and reassembly via computer algorithms.

17.2 Introducing Foreign Genes into Genomes Creates Transgenic Organisms

- Genes introduced into an organism are called transgenes. Genes introduced from another species are termed heterologous transgenes.

- Transgenes can be introduced into yeast on plasmids or, alternatively, by homologous recombination into the yeast chromosome.

- *Agrobacterium* and its tumor-inducing plasmid can be harnessed to create transgenic plants in which the transfer DNA carries the desired transgene.

- Transgenic *Drosophila* are created by injection into embryos of a *P* element transposon carrying the transgene.

- Transgenes are introduced into mice by direct injection of DNA into isolated cells. Detection of homologous recombination events is facilitated by positive–negative selection of embryonic stem cells. Transgenic mice are then created by injection of transgenic embryonic stem cells into an embryo that is subsequently implanted into a surrogate mother, and the resulting progeny are chimeric. Non-chimeric mice are selected in the following generation.

- Bacteriophage recombination systems can be used to manipulate DNA sequences in vitro and transgenes in vivo.

17.3 Gene Therapy Uses Recombinant DNA Technology

- Gene therapy is the application of recombinant DNA technology and transgenesis to treat human diseases.

- In somatic gene therapy, transgenes are targeted to somatic cells and are not heritable. In germinal gene therapy, transgenes are targeted to germ cells and are thus heritable.

17.4 Cloning of Plants and Animals Produces Genetically Identical Individuals

- Many plants reproduce clonally in nature, whereas clonal reproduction in animals is rare.

- Clonal reproduction in mammals requires reprogramming of differentiated somatic cells into stem cells.

KEYWORDS

bacterial artificial chromosome (BAC) (*p. 577*)
blunt end (*p. 569*)
codon bias (*p. 584*)
cohesive compatible end (*p. 572*)
cohesive end sequence (*cos*) site (*p. 576*)
complementary DNA (cDNA) library (*p. 577*)
cosmid vector (*p. 577*)
directional cloning (*p. 573*)
DNA clone (*p. 572*)
DNA library (*p. 577*)
eukaryotic expression vector (*p. 584*)
expression vector (*p. 583*)
fusion genes (*p. 585*)
fusion protein (*p. 585*)

gene knockouts (*p. 588*)
gene therapy (*p. 600*)
genetic chimera (*p. 594*)
genomic library (*p. 577*)
germinal gene therapy (*p. 601*)
homologous recombination (*p. 588*)
illegitimate recombination (*p. 588*)
linker (*p. 574*)
multiple cloning site (MCS) (*p. 574*)
nonrecombinant vector (*p. 573*)
P element (*p. 594*)
positive–negative selection (*p. 596*)
primer walking (*p. 582*)
recombinant clone (*p. 572*)
restriction map (*p. 570*)

restriction-modification system (*p. 568*)
reverse transcriptase (*p. 580*)
shotgun sequencing (*p. 583*)
shuttle vector (*p. 588*)
site-specific recombination (*p. 598*)
somatic gene therapy (*p. 601*)
sticky end (*p. 569*)
subcloning (*p. 570*)
Ti plasmid (*p. 589*)
totipotency (*p. 591*)
transfer DNA (T-DNA) (*p. 589*)
transgene (*p. 583*)
transgenic organism (*p. 583*)
vector (*p. 572*)
yeast artificial chromosome (YAC) (*p. 577*)

PROBLEMS

MasteringGenetics™ Visit for instructor-assigned tutorials and problems.

Chapter Concepts

For answers to selected even-numbered problems, see Appendix: Answers.

1. What purpose do the *β-lactamase* and *lacZ* genes serve in the plasmid vector pUC18?

2. The human genome is 3×10^9 bp in length.
   a. How many fragments would be predicted to result from the complete digestion of the human genome with the following enzymes: *Sau*3A (˘GATC), *Bam*HI (G˘GATCC), *Eco*RI (G˘AATTC), and *Not*I (GC˘GGCCGC)?
   b. How would your initial answer change if you knew that the average GC content of the human genome was 40%?

3. Ligase catalyzes a reaction between the 5′-phosphate and the 3′-hydroxyl at the ends of DNA molecules. The enzyme calf intestinal phosphatase catalyzes the removal of the 5′-phosphate from DNA molecules. What would be the consequence of treating a cloning vector, before ligation, with calf intestinal phosphatase?

4. You have constructed four different libraries: a genomic library made from DNA isolated from human brain tissue, a genomic library made from DNA isolated from human muscle tissue, a human brain cDNA library, and a human muscle cDNA library.

    a. Which of these would have the greatest diversity of sequences?

    b. Would the sequences contained in each library be expected to overlap completely, partially, or not at all with the sequences present in another of the libraries?

5. Using the genomic libraries in Problem 4, you wish to clone the human gene encoding myostatin, which is expressed only in muscle cells.

    a. Assuming the human genome is 3×10^9 bp and that the average insert size in the genomic libraries is 100 kb, how frequently will a clone representing myostatin be found in the genomic library made from muscle?

    b. How frequently will a clone representing myostatin be found in the genomic library made from brain?

    c. How frequently will a clone representing myostatin be found in the cDNA library made from muscle?

    d. How frequently will a clone representing myostatin be found in the cDNA library made from brain?

6. The human genome is 3×10^9 bp. You wish to design a primer to amplify a specific gene in the genome. In general, what length of oligonucleotide would be sufficient to amplify a single unique sequence? To simplify your calculation, assume that all bases occur with an equal frequency.

7. Using animal models of human diseases can lead to insights into the cellular and genetic bases of the diseases. Duchenne muscular dystrophy (DMD) is the consequence of an X-linked recessive allele.

    a. How would you make a mouse model of DMD?

    b. How would you make a *Drosophila* model of DMD?

8. Compare methods for constructing homologous recombinant transgenic mice and yeast.

9. Chimeric gene-fusion products can be used for medical or industrial purposes. One idea is to produce biological therapeutics for human medical use in animals from which the products can be easily harvested—in the milk of sheep or cattle, for example. Outline how you would produce human insulin in the milk of sheep.

10. Why are diseases of the blood more likely targets for treatment by gene therapy than are many other genetic diseases?

11. Injection of double-stranded RNA can lead to gene silencing by degradation of RNA molecules complementary to either strand of the dsRNA. Could RNAi (see Sections 15.3 and 16.3) be used in gene therapy for a defect caused by a recessive allele? A dominant allele? If so, what might be the major obstacle to using RNAi as a therapeutic agent?

12. Compare and contrast methods for making transgenic plants and transgenic *Drosophila*.

13. It is often desirable to insert cDNAs into a cloning vector in such a way that all the cDNA clones will have their 3′ end in one orientation in the plasmid and their 5′ end in the other orientation. This is referred to as directional cloning. Outline how you would directionally clone a cDNA library in the plasmid vector pUC18.

14. A major advance in the 1980s was the development of technology to synthesize short oligonucleotides. This work both facilitated DNA sequencing and led to the advent of the development of PCR. Recently, rapid advances have occurred in the technology to chemically synthesize DNA, and sequences up to 10 kb are now readily produced. As this process becomes more economical, how will it affect the gene-cloning approaches outlined in this chapter? In other words, what types of techniques does this new technology have potential to supplant, and what techniques will not be affected by it?

Application and Integration

For answers to selected even-numbered problems, see Appendix: Answers.

15. The bacteriophage lambda genome can exist in either a linear form (see Figures 17.1 and 17.8) or a circular form. The circular form occurs when the 20-bp cos sites (cohesive ends) anneal at their complementary base pairs and are ligated.

    a. How many fragments will be formed by restriction enzyme digestion with *Xho*I, with *Xba*I, and with both *Xho*I and *Xba*I in the linear and circular forms of the lambda genome?

    b. Diagram the resulting fragments as they would appear on an agarose gel after electrophoresis.

16. The restriction enzymes *Xho*I and *Sal*I cut their specific sequences as shown below:

*Xho*I	5′-C	TCGAG-3′	
	3′-GAGCT	C-5′	
*Sal*I	5′-G	TCGAC-3′	
	3′-CAGCT	G-5′	

    Can the sticky ends created by *Xho*I and *Sal*I sites be ligated? If yes, can the resulting sequences be cleaved by either *Xho*I or *Sal*I?

17. The bacteriophage φX174 has a single-stranded DNA genome of 5386 bases. During DNA replication, double-stranded forms of the genome are generated. In an effort to create a restriction map of φX174, you digest the double-stranded form of the genome with several restriction enzymes and obtain the following results. Draw a map of the φX174 genome.

*Pst*I	5386	*Pst*I + *Psi*I	3078, 2308
*Psi*I	5386	*Pst*I + *Dra*I	331, 1079, 3976
*Dra*I	4307, 1079	*Psi*I + *Dra*I	898, 1079, 3409

18. You have identified a 0.80-kb cDNA clone that contains the entire coding sequence of the *Arabidopsis* gene *CRABS CLAW*. In the construction of the cDNA library, linkers with *Eco*RI sites were added to each end of the cDNA, and the cDNA was cloned into the *Eco*RI site of the MCS of the vector shown below. You perform digests on the *CRABS CLAW* cDNA clone with restriction enzymes and obtain the following results. Can you determine the orientation of the cDNA clone with respect to the restriction enzyme sites in the vector? The enzymes listed in the dark blue region are found only in the MCS of the vector.

*Eco*RI	0.8, 3.0
*Hin*dIII	0.3, 3.5
*Eco*RI + *Hin*dIII	0.3, 0.5, 3.0

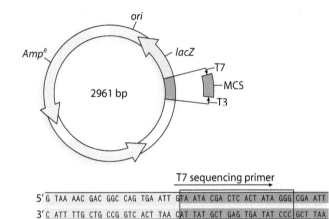

19. You have isolated a genomic clone with an *Eco*RI fragment of 11 kb that encompasses the *CRABS CLAW* gene (see Problem 18). You digest the genomic clone with *Hin*dIII and note that the 11-kb *Eco*RI fragment is split into three fragments of 9 kb, 1.5 kb, and 0.5 kb.

    a. Does this tell you anything about where the *CRABS CLAW* gene is located within the 11-kb genomic clone?

    b. Restriction enzyme sites within a cDNA clone are often also in the genomic sequence. Can you think of a reason why occasionally this is not the case? What about the converse: Are restriction enzyme sites in a genomic clone always in a cDNA clone of the same gene?

20. To further analyze the *CRABS CLAW* gene (see Problems 18 and 19), you create a map of the genomic clone. The 11-kb *Eco*RI fragment is cloned into the *Eco*RI site of the MCS of the vector shown in Problem 18.

You digest the double-stranded form of the genome with several restriction enzymes and obtain the following results. Draw, as far as possible, a map of the genomic clone of *CRABS CLAW*.

*Eco*RI	11.0, 3.0		
*Eco*RI + *Xba*I	4.5, 6.5, 3.0	*Xba*I	4.5, 9.5
*Eco*RI + *Xho*I	10.2, 3.0, 0.8	*Xho*I	13.2, 0.8
*Eco*RI + *Sal*I	6.0, 5.0, 3.0	*Sal*I	6.0, 8.0
*Eco*RI + *Hin*dIII	9.0, 3.0, 1.5, 0.5	*Hin*dIII	12.0, 1.5, 0.5

What restriction digest would help resolve any ambiguity in the map?

21. You have isolated another cDNA clone of the *CRABS CLAW* gene from a cDNA library constructed in the vector shown in Problem 18. The cDNA was directionally cloned using the *Eco*RI and *Xho*I sites. You sequence the recombinant plasmid using primers complementary to the T7 and T3 promoter sites flanking the MCS (the positions of these

sequences are shown in the figure in Problem 18). The first 30 to 60 bases of sequence are usually discarded since they tend to contain errors.

a. Which sequence represents the 5′ end of the gene? Which sequence represents the 3′ end of the gene?

b. Will the long stretch of T residues in the T3 sequence exist in the genomic sequence of the gene?

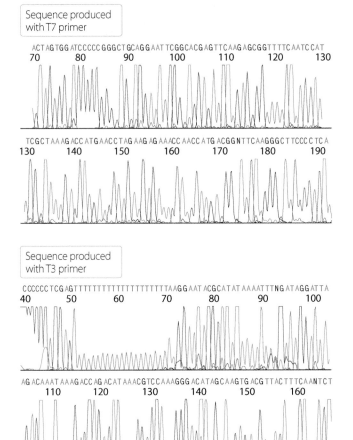

Sequence produced with T7 primer

ACT AG TGG ATC CCCC GGG CT GCAG G AAT TC GGC ACG AG TTC AAG AGC GGT T TTC AATC CAT
70   80   90   100   110   120   130

TC GCT AA AG ACC ATG A ACC TAG AAG AG A AACC A ACC A TG ACGG N TTC AAG GGGC T TCCC C TC A
130   140   150   160   170   180   190

Sequence produced with T3 primer

CCCCC C TCG AG TT T TT T T TT T TT T T TTT T T TT TTT T TAAG G AAT ACG CAT AT AAA AT TTNG AT AGG AT TA
40   50   60   70   80   90   100

AG AC AAAT AAA G ACC AG AC AT A AAC GTC C AAA GGG AC ATAG C AAG TG ACG T TTA C T TTC AAN TC T
110   120   130   140   150   160

c. Can you identify which sequences are derived from the vector (specifically the MCS) and which sequences are derived from the cDNA clone?

d. Can you identify the start of the coding region in the 5′ end of the gene? What does the sequence preceding the start codon represent?

22. You have identified five genes in *S. cerevisiae* that are induced when the yeast are grown in a high-salt (NaCl) medium. To study the potential roles of these genes in acclimation to growth in high-salt conditions, you wish to examine the phenotypes of loss- and gain-of-function alleles of each.

a. How will you do this?

b. How would your answer differ if you were working with tomato plants instead of yeast?

23. You have generated three transgenic lines of maize that are resistant to the European corn borer, a significant pest in many regions of the world. The transgenic lines (T₁ in the accompanying table) were created using *Agrobacterium*-mediated transformation with a T-DNA having two genes,

the first being a gene conferring resistance to the corn borer and the second being a gene conferring resistance to a herbicide that you used as a selectable marker to obtain your transgenic plants. You crossed each of the lines to a wild-type maize plant and also generated a T₂ population by self-fertilization of the T₁ plant. The following segregation results were observed (herbicide resistant:herbicide sensitive):

Cross	Line 1	Line 2	Line 3
Transgenic (T₁) × wild type	1:1	3:1	5:1
Self-cross (T₂)	3:1	15:1	35:1

Explain these segregation ratios.

24. Bacterial *Pseudomonas* species often possess plasmids encoding genes involved in the catabolism of organic compounds. You have discovered a strain that can metabolize crude oil and wish to identify the gene(s) responsible. Outline an experimental protocol to find the gene or genes required for crude oil metabolism.

25. Two complaints about some transgenic plants presently in commercial use are that (1) the Bt toxin gene is constitutively expressed in them, leading to fears that selection pressures will cause insects to evolve resistance to the toxin, and (2) a selectable marker gene, for example conferring kanamycin resistance, remains in the plant, leading to concerns about increased antibiotic resistance in organisms in the wild. How would you generate transgenic plants that produce Bt only in response to being fed upon by insects and without the selectable marker?

26. In *Drosophila*, loss-of-function *Ultrabithorax* mutations result in the posterior thoracic segments differentiating into body parts with an identity normally found in the anterior thoracic segments. When the *Ultrabithorax* gene was cloned, it was shown to encode a transcription factor and to be expressed only in the posterior region of the thorax. Thus, *Ultrabithorax* acts to specify the identity of the posterior thoracic segments. Similar genes were soon discovered in other animals, including mice and men. You have found that mice possess two closely related genes, *Hoxa7* and *Hoxb7*, which are orthologous to *Ultrabithorax*. You wish to know whether the two mouse genes act to specify the identity of body segments in mice.

a. How will you determine where and when the mouse genes are expressed?

b. How will you create loss-of-function alleles of the mouse genes?

c. How will you determine whether the mouse genes have redundant functions?

27. You have identified an enhancer trap line (see Figure 16.19) generated by *P* element transposition in *Drosophila* in which the marker gene from the enhancer trap is specifically expressed in the wing imaginal disc.

a. How can you identify the gene adjacent to the insertion site of the enhancer trap?

b. How would you show that the expression pattern of the enhancer trap line reflects the endogenous gene expression pattern of the adjacent gene?

28. The highlighted sequence shown below is the one originally used to produce the B chain of human insulin in *E. coli*. The sequence of the human gene encoding the B chain of insulin was later determined from a cDNA isolated from a human pancreatic cDNA library and is shown below without highlighting. Explain the differences between the two sequences.

```
ATGTTCGTCAATCAGCACCTTTGTGGTTCTCACCTCGTTGAAGC
TTTGTACCTTGTTTGCGGTGAACGTGGTTTCTTCTACACTCCT
             AAGACTTAA
GCCTTTGTGAACCAACACCTGTGCGGCTCACACCTGGTGGAAGC
TCTCTACCTAGTGTGCGGGGAACGAGGCTTCTTCTACACACCC
             AAGACCCGC
```

30. The *RAS* gene encodes a signaling protein that hydrolyzes GTP to GDP. When bound by GDP, the RAS protein is inactive, whereas when bound by GTP, RAS protein activates a target protein, resulting in stimulation of cells to actively grow and divide. A single base-pair mutation (see below) results in a mutant protein that is constitutively active, leading to continual promotion of cell proliferation. Such mutations play a role in the formation of cancer. You have cloned the wild-type version of the mouse *RAS* gene and wish to create a mutant form to study its biological activity in vitro and in transgenic mice. Outline how you would proceed.

```
                     Gly Ala Gly Gly Val Gly
Wild-type RAS DNA:  5'...GGC GCC GGC GGT GTG GGC...3'
                              ↓
Mutant RAS DNA:               GTC
                              Val
```

31. Vitamin E is the name for a set of chemically related tocopherols, which are lipid-soluble compounds with antioxidant properties. Such antioxidants protect cells against the effects of free radicals created as by-products of energy metabolism in the mitochondrion. Different tocopherols have different biological activities due to differences in their retention by binding to gut proteins during digestion. The one retained at the highest level is α-tocopherol, while γ-tocopherol is retained at less than 10% of that efficiency. In *Arabidopsis*, α-tocopherol is the most abundant tocopherol in leaves, while γ-tocopherol is the most abundant in seeds. An enzyme encoded by the *VTE4* gene can convert γ-tocopherol to α-tocopherol. How would you create an *Arabidopsis* plant that produces high levels of α-tocopherol in the seeds?

32. You have cloned a gene for an enzyme that degrades lipids in a bacterium that normally lives in cold temperatures. You wish to transfer this gene into *E. coli* to produce industrial amounts of enzyme for use in laundry detergent.
    a. How would you accomplish this?
    b. You have managed to produce transgenic *E. coli* expressing mRNA of your gene, but only a low level of protein is produced. Why might this be so? How could you overcome this problem?

Developmental Genetics

20

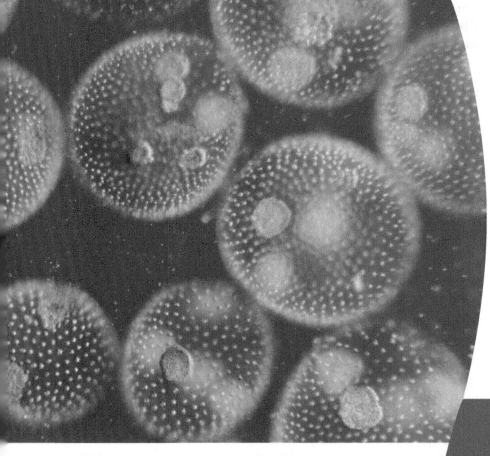

Multicellularity has evolved multiple times within the eukaryotes, as exemplified by *Volvox*, a chlorophyte green alga and member of a multicellular lineage independent of land plants and animals. In *Volvox*, the outer cells are somatic while the germ cells will be derived from the inner cells.

T he development of a multicellular organism from a single fertilized egg cell is one of the wonders of evolution. The fertilized egg undergoes an initial mitotic division to produce two genetically identical daughter cells. Those two cells divide to produce four identical cells, which divide to produce eight cells, and so on. Yet, while all cells in the growing embryo continue to carry the same genetic information, many of them acquire different identities as the embryo develops different body parts, organs, and tissues. This development is a genetically programmed process, occurring in the same way in all members of a species.

CHAPTER OUTLINE

20.1 Development Is the Building of a Multicellular Organism

20.2 *Drosophila* Development Is a Paradigm for Animal Development

20.3 Cellular Interactions Specify Cell Fate

20.4 "Evolution Behaves Like a Tinkerer"

20.5 Plants Represent an Independent Experiment in Multicellular Evolution

ESSENTIAL IDEAS

- Genes encoding transcription factors or signaling molecules direct the formation of specialized cell types.

- *Drosophila* embryos are subdivided into segments with unique identities by the sequential action of batteries of transcription factors.

- *Hox* genes specify the identity of body segments of *Drosophila* and are largely conserved throughout metazoans.

- Cells signal to either induce or inhibit neighboring cells from adopting particular developmental pathways.

- Morphological evolution can be the result of changes in gene expression patterns of a common genetic toolkit.

- Plant developmental genetics shares similarities with that of animals despite multicellularity evolving independently.

Different species exhibit both similarities and differences in development, the former because of shared evolutionary ancestry and the latter because of species-specific adaptations.

Geneticists rely on defects in development to reveal the mechanisms of normal development. As early as 1790, the German scientist and philosopher Johann Wolfgang von Goethe recognized the potential of this approach:

> From our acquaintance with…abnormal metamorphosis, we are enabled to unveil the secrets that normal metamorphosis conceals from us, and to see distinctly what, from the regular course of development, we can only infer.

Even so, the connections between developmental abnormalities, gene mutations, and the mechanisms that control normal development could not be understood in any detail until scientists began to apply the basic principles of genetics to the study of development. This process began around 1900, when the young embryologist Thomas Hunt Morgan decided to shift his research to focus on the nascent field of genetics, using the fruit fly *Drosophila* as his experimental organism. While Morgan never returned to the study of embryology, his students and his students' students blazed new trails by exploiting *Drosophila* genetics to illuminate many of the secrets of development in all metazoans (multicellular animals) and in plants as well.

In this chapter, we discuss the genetic processes that control development in complex multicellular organisms and the experimental approaches that led to their discovery.

20.1 Development Is the Building of a Multicellular Organism

An animal begins its life as a single cell, the zygote, from which all the cell types, each characterized by a specific gene expression pattern, of the adult animal ultimately are derived. The key to understanding the molecular genetic basis of development is to understand how different patterns of gene expression are established and maintained as cells differentiate and specialize.

In 1915, Calvin Bridges (a student of Thomas Hunt Morgan) identified a *Drosophila* mutation in which the small hind wings, the halteres, developed into structures resembling the forewings (**Figure 20.1a**). Mutations in which an apparently normal organ or body part develops in the wrong place are called **homeotic mutations** (from the Greek *homeos*, meaning "the same" or "similar"), and they have been central to the progress geneticists have made in understanding how complex organisms develop and evolve. Ed Lewis (a student of Morgan's student Alfred Sturtevant) later identified the *bithorax* complex of genes as being responsible for the homeotic mutation observed by Bridges. As we discuss in this chapter, mutations in *bithorax* genes change the developmental program of a portion of the fruit-fly body, resulting in the transformation of the halteres into a second set of forewings. Another example is the dominant *Antennapedia* mutation, in which relatively normal fly legs develop in the positions that should be occupied by the antennae (**Figure 20.1b**). To understand the cascades of events responsible for such developments, we must first examine the phenomenon of cell differentiation and pattern formation.

(a) In a *bithorax* mutation, halteres seen in wild-type *Drosophila* (left) develop instead into a second set of wings (right).

Halteres

A second set of wings in the position normally occupied by halteres

(b) In an *Antennapedia* mutation, antennae in wild-type *Drosophila* (left) develop instead into legs (right).

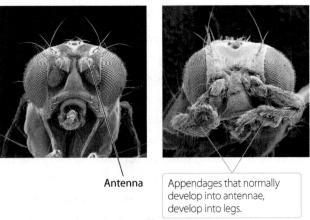

Antenna

Appendages that normally develop into antennae, develop into legs.

Figure 20.1 **Inappropriate positions of organs and body structures in homeotic mutants.**

Cell Differentiation

In an animal, fertilization of an haploid egg cell by a haploid sperm cell forms a single-celled diploid zygote, which undergoes several mitotic divisions to form a small cluster of embryonic cells that are genetically identical. These embryonic cells are **totipotent,** which means they have the potential to differentiate into any tissue or cell type the animal can produce. In vertebrates, totipotent cells of early embryos are called **embryonic stem cells.** In totipotent cells, all genes have the potential to be expressed given the appropriate cues. As development proceeds, however, cells become **differentiated,** taking on different morphologies and undertaking different physiological activities.

Differentiation is characterized by changes in patterns of gene expression that progressively limit which genes continue to be expressed by each cell type. At a certain stage in development, cells retain the potential to give rise to many different types of descendants, but not to all types—at this stage, the cells are said to be **pluripotent.** As development progresses further, however, most cells ultimately become specialized: These fully differentiated and specialized cells express only a subset of genes in the genome, and each cell type has its own characteristic pattern of gene expression. Thus development is a progressive process during which totipotent cells differentiate into specialized cell types through a series of genetically controlled steps that place ever more restrictive limits on their developmental potential.

While most cells of adult animals are fully differentiated and locked into a specific cell fate, there are some exceptions. In our bodies, various types of pluripotent stem cells—such as muscle, epidermal, epithelial, and hematopoietic (blood) cells—retain the capacity to develop into a range of further-specialized cells to replenish cells that are lost.

Pattern Formation

How do genetically identical cells acquire different fates? Two mechanisms have been identified: Cells can inherit some definitive molecule that specifies cell fate, or the fate of cells can be determined by their interaction with neighboring cells through the action of signaling molecules. Inheritance of a fate-determining molecule depends on the identity of progenitor cells, whereas development through the influence of neighboring cells depends on the identity of those neighbors.

The term *pattern formation* describes the intricately interacting events that organize differentiating cells in the developing embryo to establish the three body-plan axes of the mature organism: anterior–posterior, dorsal–ventral, and left–right (Figure 20.2). Cells have various ways of "knowing" their locations with regard to these axes. The combination of internal and external signals that a cell perceives during development provides information on the cell's location within an organism and its appropriate course of differentiation.

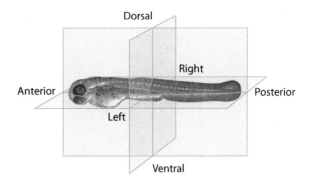

Figure 20.2   The three embryonic axes of a zebrafish.

To understand the role that the **positional information** represented by these signals plays in development, consider the French flag, which has a simple pattern of three vertical stripes in the order blue, white, and red, along a single (anterior–posterior) axis (Figure 20.3a). While French flags may come in various sizes, the proportions of the stripes within each flag remain generally constant, dividing the flag into thirds. Imagine the entire flag to consist of cells descended from a single parent cell. How do daughter cells know whether they are to differentiate as blue, white, or red? The cells could interpret their position by one or more of various mechanisms, but the simplest to envision is based on the concentration gradient of a molecule that is highly concentrated at one end of the embryonic flag and much less concentrated at the opposite end. The position of each cell on the flag's anterior–posterior axis is defined by the concentration of this molecule, in which threshold values define boundaries between discrete fates: Above a certain concentration, the result is blue cell identity; below this threshold concentration, white cells develop; and below an even lower threshold, red cells develop. Substances whose presence in different concentrations directs developmental fates are referred to as **morphogens.** If activation or repression of gene expression is dependent upon threshold concentrations of a morphogen (e.g., concentrations above which a gene is active and below which a gene is inactive), discrete boundaries of gene expression can be established.

Once a cell has acquired a specific identity, it may induce its neighbors to acquire a certain fate; this process is termed **induction.** A classic case of induction was first noted more than a century ago, when transplantation of cells from one region of a developing frog embryo to another region of a second embryo induced the surrounding cells to form a second body axis (Figure 20.3b). The region from which the transplanted cells were derived was called the **organizer** because the cells of that region possess the ability to organize cells in the surrounding tissue. Alternatively, a cell that acquires a specific fate may produce an inhibitory substance that prevents its neighbors from acquiring a certain fate, and this process is called **inhibition** (Figure 20.3c). Inhibition can be used

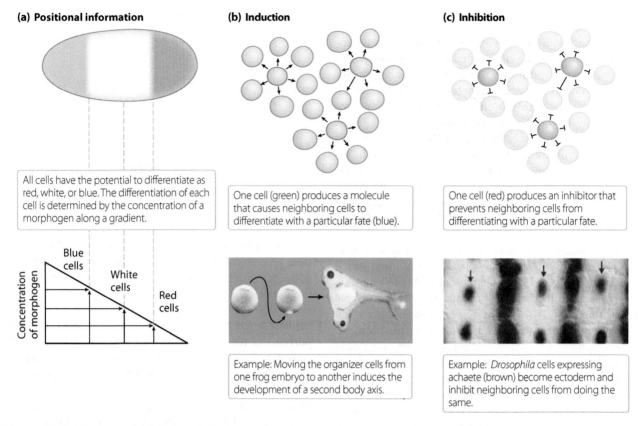

(a) Positional information

All cells have the potential to differentiate as red, white, or blue. The differentiation of each cell is determined by the concentration of a morphogen along a gradient.

Blue cells
White cells
Red cells

Concentration of morphogen

(b) Induction

One cell (green) produces a molecule that causes neighboring cells to differentiate with a particular fate (blue).

Example: Moving the organizer cells from one frog embryo to another induces the development of a second body axis.

(c) Inhibition

One cell (red) produces an inhibitor that prevents neighboring cells from differentiating with a particular fate.

Example: *Drosophila* cells expressing achaete (brown) become ectoderm and inhibit neighboring cells from doing the same.

Figure 20.3   Mechanisms of differentiation.

to produce patterns of regularly spaced cells of a particular fate within a field of cells that would otherwise all differentiate in the same manner, such as in the example of *Drosophila* shown in Figure 20.3c. Other examples of tissues with regular spacing include many epidermal features, such as bristles, feathers, hairs, and scales.

The developmental histories of cells can affect how the cells respond to cues from their neighbors. For example, for a cell to be able to respond to an inductive or inhibitory signal from neighboring cells, it must express the appropriate receptor. In addition, cells able to respond to a signal may behave differently depending on what other factors are present in the cell. When a cell divides, the daughter cells usually inherit the same set of transcription factors and chromatin states that existed in the cell they were derived from (the importance of chromatin states is discussed in Section 20.2). However, occasional asymmetric cell divisions in which the two daughter cells inherit different cellular constituents and acquire different fates underlie developmental patterning events in some species.

Positional information, induction, inhibition, and asymmetric cell divisions are common processes directing cell differentiation and pattern formation in multicellular organisms. When employed sequentially and reiteratively during embryogenesis, these processes enable a single-celled zygote to develop into a complex organism having

a multitude of cell types. Each cell division in the embryo brings about changes in the relative positional relationships between the cells, so new opportunities for cell–cell communication are constantly created. In keeping with the importance of positional information, induction, and inhibition in development, most genes identified as having prominent roles in developmental processes encode proteins that act as either transcription factors or signaling molecules.

20.2 *Drosophila* Development Is a Paradigm for Animal Development

Discoveries about the developmental processes of *Drosophila* have made it ontogenetically one of the best-understood animals on the planet. These insights have in turn profoundly influenced how geneticists perceive the development and evolution of all other animals, ourselves included. For their work in unraveling some of the mechanisms underlying pattern formation in *Drosophila*, Edward B. Lewis, Christiane Nüsslein-Volhard, and Eric Wieschaus were awarded the Nobel Prize in Physiology or Medicine in 1995.

One of the reasons that *Drosophila* is an ideal genetic experimental organism is its short, 9-day life cycle (**Figure 20.4a**). Embryogenesis spans the first 24 hours of

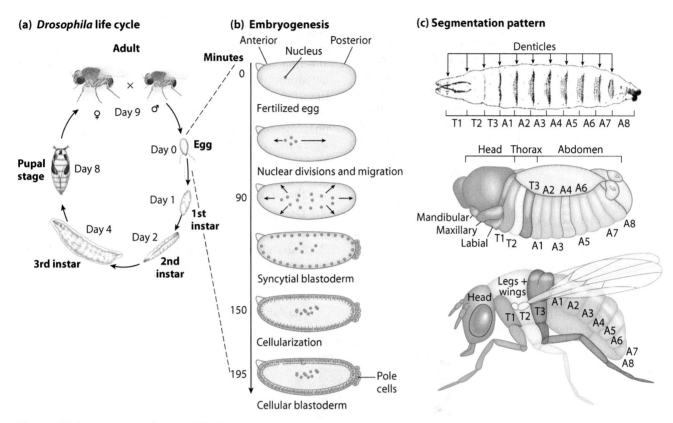

Figure 20.4 Overview of *Drosophila* development.

Drosophila development, commencing with the deposition of a fertilized egg that immediately begins a rapid series of genetically controlled changes (**Figure 20.4b**). After embryogenesis, development progresses through three distinct larval stages, called instars. Each instar stage is marked by progressive development of tissues and structures that will form the adult fly. Following the third instar stage, the larva forms a pupa in which metamorphosis will take place. At the conclusion of pupation a fully formed adult fruit fly emerges, ready to begin the cycle anew.

The *Drosophila* egg has conspicuous anterior–posterior and dorsal–ventral polarities that are acquired during its production in the female fly. In contrast to early development in many other species, early embryonic development in *Drosophila* proceeds by nuclear division without division of cytoplasm. Rather than forming blastomeres, as in mammalian development, this process forms a **syncytium,** a multinucleate cell in which the nuclei are not separated by cell membranes (see Figure 20.4b). The fertilized egg undergoes nine mitotic nuclear divisions, after which the nuclei migrate to the periphery of the embryo. At this time, about 10 pole cells, from which the germ line will be derived, are set aside at the posterior end of the embryo. The somatic cells undergo another four rounds of mitotic divisions at the periphery, forming a **syncytial blastoderm** containing about 6000 nuclei. By about 3 hours after egg laying, cellularization of the syncytium occurs by the assembly of cell membranes that separate nuclei into individual cells, thus forming a **cellular blastoderm.**

During the syncytial blastoderm and cellularization stages, cells become progressively restricted in their developmental potential. This can be demonstrated experimentally by transplanting cellular blastoderm cells from one embryo into another. Blastoderm cells implanted into an equivalent region of a host embryo are incorporated normally into host structures, but those transplanted into different regions will develop autonomously into tissues reflecting the original position of the cells in the donor embryo. Thus, at the cellular blastoderm stage, cells have already become committed to differentiate into particular tissues.

Drosophila is typical of insects in the segmentation pattern of its adult body. Eight abdominal and three thoracic segments are easily distinguished (**Figure 20.4c**). The head consists of at least three distinct developmental segments. The segments of the insect body are first visible during embryogenesis, where they are indicated by the pattern of denticles (small hooks for gripping during larval movement) on the ventral epidermis. The body plan established during embryogenesis determines the organization of tissues and organs in the adult fly.

The Developmental Toolkit of *Drosophila*

Large-scale genetic screens (see Section 16.1) were commenced by Christiane Nüsslein-Volhard, Eric Wieschaus, and others in the late 1970s and early 1980s to identify and describe the function of genes directing pattern formation in *Drosophila* embryos. It is estimated that mutations in about 5000 of the 14,000 genes in *Drosophila* will result in a lethal phenotype. Most mutations resulting in lethality affect genes that have essential cellular functions, and these genes are sometimes described as **housekeeping genes.** However, several hundred genes producing lethal phenotypes are involved directly in developmental programs of pattern formation during embryogenesis.

Nüsslein-Volhard and Wieschaus faced a significant challenge when designing genetic screens for mutations in pattern formation because flies in which segmental pattern formation is severely disrupted rarely survive beyond the larval stage. Their solution was to focus on embryos and larvae. They reasoned that mutations affecting embryonic pattern formation would not be lethal until larval formation, leaving a short window of time for observation of the effects of such mutations. From the types of spatial defect exhibited by the mutant phenotypes, mutants were grouped into four gene classes, with a fifth class identified earlier by Ed Lewis:

1. **Coordinate genes:** Defects affect an entire pole of the larva (**Figure 20.5a**).

2. **Gap genes:** Mutants are missing large, contiguous groups of segments (**Figure 20.5b**).

3. **Pair-rule genes:** Mutants are missing parts of adjacent segment pairs, in two alternating patterns (**Figure 20.5c**).

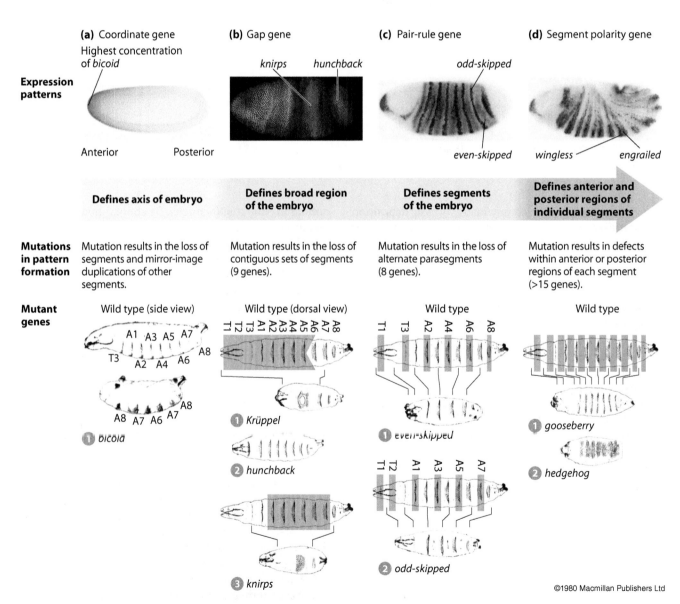

©1980 Macmillan Publishers Ltd

Figure 20.5 Mutations causing defects in pattern formation in *Drosophila*. A fifth class of mutations, homeotic gene mutations, is represented in Figure 20.10.

4. **Segment polarity genes:** Defects affect patterning within each of the 14 segments (**Figure 20.5d**).

5. **Homeotic genes:** Defects affect the identity of one or more segments.

These five gene classes are expressed sequentially during embryogenesis: The coordinate genes act first, followed by gap genes, pair-rule genes, segment polarity genes, and finally homeotic genes. The cascade of gene expression subdivides the embryo in successive steps, first into broad regions and then into progressively smaller domains, and each of the 14 resulting segments acquires a specific identity. The patterns of mRNA and protein expression of each gene correspond, both in space and in time, to its mutant phenotype (see Figure 20.5). For example, expression of the gap gene *knirps* spans a contiguous embryonic domain that is destined to become abdominal segments. These abdominal segments are missing in *knirps* mutants, as is evident in the early larva (see Figure 20.5b).

Expression of the pair-rule genes follows that of gap genes and produces 14 stripes in the embryo. Curiously, the stripes of gene expression of pair-rule genes do not correspond to the segments of the adult insect, but rather straddle the boundaries between segments, thus occupying the posterior part of one segment and the anterior part of its neighbor. The domains of gene expression controlled by the pair-rule genes are therefore called **parasegments.** Expression of the segment polarity genes occurs in 14 polar stripes (i.e., each stripe has anterior and posterior "poles"), one for each segment of the embryo. The homeotic genes are the last to be expressed and affect broad domains of contiguous parasegments along the anterior–posterior axis. The anterior expression boundaries of the homeotic genes correspond to parasegment boundaries defined by the pair-rule genes. Thus, the sequential activation of different classes of genes during early development is reflected in the sequential subdivision of the organism, from a single-celled zygote into a segmented embryo.

When the expression pattern of a gene in a wild-type embryo corresponds precisely to the cell fates that are disrupted when the gene is mutated, the activity of the gene is said to be cell autonomous. A gene whose action is cell autonomous affects only the cells in which the gene is transcribed and expressed. Four of the five classes of genes act largely cell autonomously, an observation consistent with the identity of these genes as transcription factors. The exception is the segment polarity class of genes, which often encode signaling molecules that can act non-autonomously, that is in cells other than where the gene is expressed. In the following sections, we examine how the embryo is successively subdivided by the activity of these sets of genes.

Maternal Effects on Pattern Formation

In animals, the mother often supplies critical gene products to the egg that subsequently direct embryo development. These genes are called **maternal effect genes.** Note that maternal effects are different from maternal inheritance (introduced in Chapter 19), in that maternal effects entail the maternal deposition of protein or mRNA in the egg cell, whereas maternal inheritance refers to maternal transmission of genetic material (e.g., organelle genomes).

How can the maternal effect genes that influence development be identified in mutant screens, given that for these genes, the embryonic phenotype is determined by the genotype of the mother rather than that of the embryo? An answer becomes apparent when we compare the inheritance patterns observed with maternal effect genes against those observed with **zygotic genes,** genes that are active only in the zygote or embryo. For zygotic genes, *the genotype of the embryo determines the phenotype.* The following cross illustrates this principle for an autosomal recessive mutation (*m*).

Inheritance Pattern with Zygotic Genes and Inheritance Pattern with Maternal Effect Genes

Zygotic Genes

Parents	Offspring	Phenotype
m/+ × *m/+*	*m/+, +/+*	Normal (3)
	m/m	Mutant (1)

With maternal effect genes, where *the genotype of the mother determines the phenotype of the zygote,* the same cross as above, involving an autosomal recessive mutation (*m*), would give the following outcomes:

Maternal Effect Genes

Parents (female × male)	Offspring	Phenotype
m/+ × *m/+*	*m/m, m/+, +/+*	All normal
m/+ × *m/m*	*m/m, m/+*	All normal
m/m × *+/+* or *m/+* or *m/m*	*m/m, m/+*	All mutant

These divergent patterns allow discrimination between maternal effect genes and zygotic genes. Crosses can be performed to determine whether the genes are active maternally, zygotically, or both. When such crosses were performed to test the five classes of mutants described above, the coordinate genes were found to be maternally active; their expression *in the mother* rather than in the embryo provides positional information to the egg. Most gap genes are active zygotically, but at least one, *hunchback*, also exhibits maternal activity. All pair-rule, segment polarity, and homeotic genes act strictly zygotically. These findings make sense given the developmental stage at which the different classes of gene are active and the observation that zygotic gene expression commences only in the syncytial blastoderm stage of embryogenesis.

Coordinate Gene Patterning of the Anterior–Posterior Axis

The genetic control of development is essentially a process of regulating gene expression in three-dimensional space over time. It is not surprising, then, that most of the early-acting genes establishing the anterior–posterior axis of *Drosophila* encode transcription factors. The interaction of transcription factors with cis-acting regulatory elements of target genes provides spatial control of gene expression. This spatial control is coordinated over time by continual inputs from neighboring cells. In this section, we describe examples of the spatial and temporal regulation of gene expression that results in subdivision of a developing *Drosophila* embryo into its characteristic segments.

The coordinate gene *bicoid* plays a major role in the establishment of the anterior–posterior axis in *Drosophila*. Loss-of-function *bicoid* alleles result in a loss of anterior portions of the embryo; the anterior portions are replaced instead by a mirror-image duplication of posterior regions (**Figure 20.6a**). *Bicoid* mRNA is anchored to the anterior region of the egg during oogenesis in the mother (**Figure 20.6b**). After translation, the resulting protein (Bicoid) diffuses from its site of synthesis at the anterior pole of the embryo throughout the syncytial embryo, owing to the absence of cell membranes to impede protein diffusion. The diffusion results in a gradient of Bicoid in which the highest concentration is at the anterior end and very little Bicoid is detected beyond the middle of the embryo.

Cytoplasmic transplantation experiments elegantly demonstrate that Bicoid specifies anterior identity. Anterior cytoplasm extracted from a wild-type embryo and then injected into a *bicoid* mutant embryo causes anterior structures to develop at the site of injection (see Figure 20.6a). When the *bicoid* gene was cloned, similar experiments were carried out with purified *bicoid* mRNA, which produced the same result. These findings indicate that the concentration gradient of Bicoid provides positional information along the anterior–posterior axis of the embryo, presumably by differentially regulating several genes that respond to different concentrations of Bicoid. Among the known zygotic genes whose transcription is directly regulated by Bicoid is the gap gene *hunchback*.

Surprisingly, examination of the distribution of *hunchback* mRNA revealed that *hunchback* is also maternally expressed and that its maternal expression is uniform throughout the egg (**Figure 20.7a**). The hunchback protein (Hunchback), on the other hand, is found only at the anterior end of the early embryo, implying that posterior *hunchback* mRNA is not translated. This seeming contradiction was explained by the discovery of another maternally expressed coordinate gene, *nanos*. The posterior end of the embryo is patterned by *nanos*, whose protein forms a gradient with the highest concentration at the posterior end. Rather than encoding a transcription factor, *nanos* encodes a protein that represses translation of *hunchback* mRNA. Thus, Hunchback is restricted to the anterior end of the embryo by posterior translational repression of maternal *hunchback* mRNA. In addition, zygotic *hunchback* expression in the anterior end is transcriptionally activated by anteriorly localized Bicoid.

Patterning of the posterior end of the embryo is governed by similar interactions. In addition to acting as a transcription factor, Bicoid acts as a translational repressor of the maternally supplied *caudal* mRNA, which is uniformly distributed throughout the egg. Translational repression of *caudal* mRNA by the anterior gradient of Bicoid results in a posterior gradient of *caudal* protein (Caudal). The end result is an embryo with graded distributions of three transcription factors: Bicoid and Hunchback, in which the highest concentration is at the anterior end; and Caudal, in which the highest concentration is at the posterior end. The relative concentrations of these three proteins provide positional information along the length of the embryo, which is interpreted by the subsequently acting gap genes.

Domains of Gap Gene Expression

The broad gradients of maternally supplied coordinate gene products are transformed into domains of gap gene expression with discrete boundaries. This occurs through a combination of cooperative binding of transcription factors—similar to the activation of the lambda repressor described in Chapter 14—and cross-regulatory

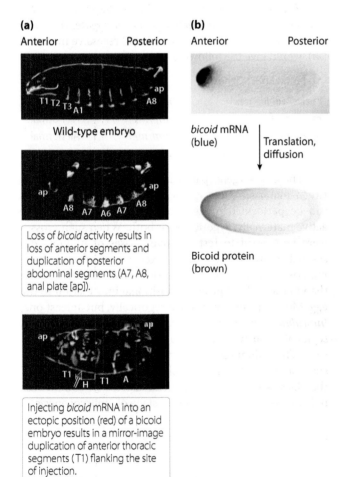

(a)

Anterior · · · · · · · · · · · · Posterior

Wild-type embryo

Loss of *bicoid* activity results in loss of anterior segments and duplication of posterior abdominal segments (A7, A8, anal plate [ap]).

Injecting *bicoid* mRNA into an ectopic position (red) of a *bicoid* embryo results in a mirror-image duplication of anterior thoracic segments (T1) flanking the site of injection.

(b)

Anterior · · · · · · · · · · · · Posterior

bicoid mRNA (blue) | Translation, diffusion

Bicoid protein (brown)

Figure 20.6 Maternal *bicoid* patterning of the embryo along the anterior–posterior axis.

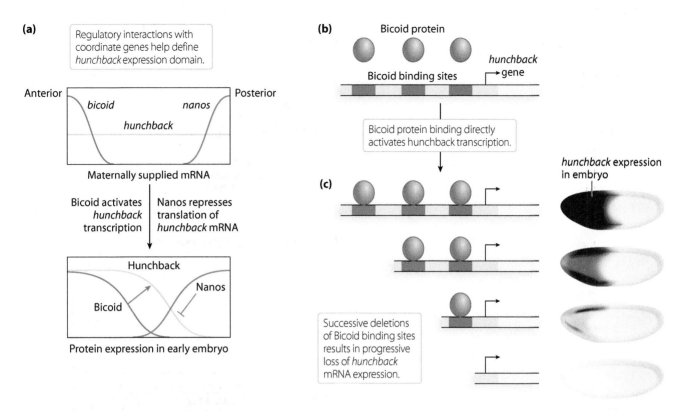

Figure 20.7 **Gap gene expression patterns are activated by coordinate genes.**

interactions among the gap genes themselves. To begin, let's consider further how the gradual concentration gradient of Bicoid is translated into the more discrete pattern of *hunchback* mRNA expression.

As noted earlier, zygotic expression of the gap gene *hunchback* is confined to the anterior region of the embryo. Unlike Bicoid, which exhibits a gradual concentration gradient, the concentration of *hunchback* mRNA declines precipitously at a particular point along the anterior–posterior axis. Transcription of *hunchback* is activated by the binding of Bicoid to cis-regulatory elements 5′ to the *hunchback* coding region (Figure 20.7b). In this location, there are multiple cis-acting sites to which Bicoid can bind, and these sites are bound in a cooperative manner, meaning that the binding of one Bicoid molecule to one site facilitates the binding of a second Bicoid molecule to a second nearby site, and so on. Mutation of the Bicoid binding sites alters the responsiveness of *hunchback* expression to Bicoid, and removal of all binding sites abolishes *hunchback* expression in the embryo (Figure 20.7c).

A threshold level of Bicoid must be present in order for *hunchback* expression to be activated. Consequently, *hunchback* expression occurs on one side of a threshold concentration with no expression on the other, and a sharp boundary is produced. In this manner, the gradual anterior concentration gradient of Bicoid is translated into a distinct anterior region of *hunchback* mRNA expression, which, after translation, produces a sharp gradient of Hunchback (see Figure 20.7a).

The gradient of hunchback protein is critical for the regulation of other gap genes, such as *Krüppel* (Figure 20.8), which is repressed by high levels of Hunchback but activated in the central region of the embryo where Bicoid levels are moderate. These interactions establish the anterior margin of *Krüppel* expression toward the posterior end of the Hunchback protein gradient. The posterior margin of *Krüppel* expression appears to be determined through negative regulation by other gap genes, *knirps* and *giant*. Similar regulatory interactions between other gap genes help establish the rest of the partially overlapping patterns of gap gene expression that subdivide the developing embryo into discrete domains.

Regulation of Pair-Rule Genes

From the domains of gap gene expression emerge 14 narrower stripes of gene expression that represent the first manifestation of segmentation of the anterior–posterior body plan. Analysis of the regulation of the pair-rule gene *even-skipped* (*eve*) revealed that each stripe is established by independent enhancer modules of cis-acting regulatory sequences of *eve*. Each enhancer module from a pair-rule gene responds to specific combinations of gap genes (Figure 20.9a). Thus, the formation of stripes of gene expression is the result of combinatorial control of gene expression through multiple cis-acting regulatory elements of the pair-rule genes. This situation is conceptually similar to the regulation of the gap genes, as described earlier for *hunchback*.

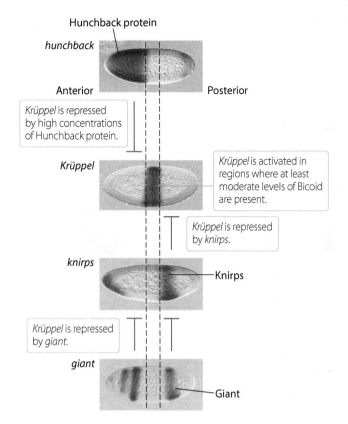

Hunchback protein

hunchback

Anterior | Posterior

Krüppel is repressed by high concentrations of Hunchback protein.

Krüppel

Krüppel is activated in regions where at least moderate levels of Bicoid are present.

Krüppel is repressed by *knirps*.

knirps

Knirps

Krüppel is repressed by *giant*.

giant

Giant

Figure 20.8 **Cross-regulatory interactions among gap genes define their expression patterns.**

(a) The pair-rule gene *even-skipped* (*eve*) and its enhancer modules

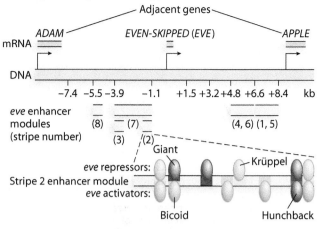

Adjacent genes

ADAM EVEN-SKIPPED (EVE) *APPLE*

mRNA

DNA

−7.4 −5.5 −3.9 −1.1 +1.5 +3.2 +4.8 +6.6 +8.4 kb

eve enhancer modules (stripe number)

(8) (7) (4, 6) (1, 5)

(3) (2)

Giant

eve repressors: Krüppel

Stripe 2 enhancer module

eve activators:

Bicoid Hunchback

(b) Distribution of gap gene expression

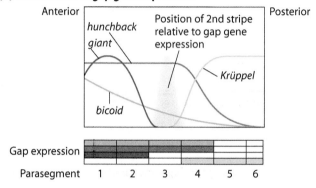

Anterior Posterior

hunchback Position of 2nd stripe relative to gap gene expression

giant

Krüppel

bicoid

Gap expression

Parasegment 1 2 3 4 5 6

Stripe 2 of *eve* provides an example of modularity in gene regulation. Gene expression within stripe 2 is controlled by a cis-regulatory element—the stripe 2 enhancer module—located about 1700 bp to 1000 bp upstream of the transcription initiation site of *eve* (see Figure 20.9a). When this regulatory element is isolated and used to drive a reporter gene (see Section 16.4) in transgenic *Drosophila* embryos, expression is observed only in stripe 2, indicating that these regulatory sequences are sufficient for stripe 2 expression. Detailed sequence analysis of this module identified binding sites for the gap proteins Hunchback, Krüppel, and Giant, as well as binding sites for Bicoid. Mutational analysis of different combinations of binding sites demonstrates that both Hunchback and Bicoid act as activators of *even-skipped* stripe 2 gene expression, while both Giant and Krüppel act as repressors.

Stripe 2 lies entirely within the *hunchback* expression domain of the embryo and is flanked on the anterior side by the *giant* expression domain and on the posterior side by the *Krüppel* expression domain (**Figure 20.9b**). It contains an intermediate level of Bicoid remaining from the maternally established gradient. Thus the position of *eve* stripe 2 along the anterior–posterior axis is a zone with a high concentration of Hunchback, low concentrations of Giant and Krüppel, and an intermediate concentration of Bicoid. Only in parasegment 3, which is the location of stripe 2, are both positive regulators present and both negative regulators absent (**Figure 20.9c**). This combination of gap and coordinate protein concentrations does not occur

(c) Occupancy of regulatory sites on *eve* stripe 2 enhancer module in different parasegments

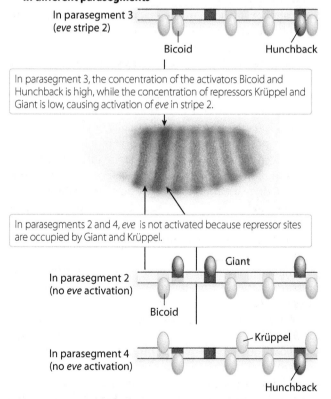

In parasegment 3 (*eve* stripe 2)

Bicoid Hunchback

In parasegment 3, the concentration of the activators Bicoid and Hunchback is high, while the concentration of repressors Krüppel and Giant is low, causing activation of *eve* in stripe 2.

In parasegments 2 and 4, *eve* is not activated because repressor sites are occupied by Giant and Krüppel.

In parasegment 2 (no *eve* activation)

Giant

Bicoid

In parasegment 4 (no *eve* activation)

Krüppel

Hunchback

Figure 20.9 **Stripes of gene expression, established by combinatorial coordinate and gap gene activities.**

anywhere else along the axis of the embryo and uniquely defines the *eve* stripe 2 position. The integration of positive and negative regulators results in the precise limiting of *even-skipped* stripe 2 to a region only a few cells in width along the anterior–posterior axis. Similar combinatorial mechanisms are thought to control the expression patterns of all of the pair-rule and segment polarity genes.

The discovery that in multicellular organisms *the control of gene expression is modular* provided important insight into the evolution of organisms. Modularity of gene regulation allows changes in specific domains of expression without catastrophic disruption of global expression patterns.

Specification of Parasegments by *Hox* Genes

Having explored the mechanisms by which gap and pair-rule genes subdivide the *Drosophila* embryo into 14 segments, we can now consider how each segment acquires a unique identity through the action of the homeotic genes. Once again, the key discoveries were made through the study of mutations, pioneered by Edward B. Lewis starting in the 1950s.

As we saw at the beginning of the chapter, a remarkable aspect of homeotic mutant phenotypes is the development of relatively normal structures in inappropriate positions.

Another general feature of homeotic mutations is that they cause identity transformations of serially repeated structures. Legs, for example, are appendages that are normally limited to the three thoracic segments in *Drosophila*, whereas antennae are appendages that normally develop only on the third cephalic (head) segment. In the case of *Antennapedia* mutants, however, a leg appears in a segment ordinarily reserved for an antenna (see Figure 20.1), suggesting that *Antennapedia* normally specifies the identity of one or more of the thoracic segments. Analyses of homeotic genes in *Drosophila* demonstrate that in fact they act in combination to specify the identity of each of the 14 body segments.

The homeotic genes of animals are also remarkable for being clustered in gene complexes. In *Drosophila* there are two homeotic clusters on the third chromosome: the **Antennapedia complex,** consisting of five genes, and the **bithorax complex,** consisting of three genes. In other organisms, the homeotic genes are usually in a single cluster. Amazingly, the order of the genes within the complexes reflects the positions along the anterior–posterior axis that are influenced by each gene (Figure 20.10).

The cloning of the homeotic genes revealed another surprise: All eight genes encode closely related proteins, suggesting that all members of the complex were derived from a

(a) Adult body segments

(b) In vivo *Hox* gene expression patterns

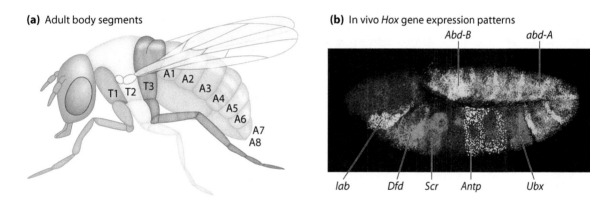

(c) *Hox* complexes on chromosome 3, and expression patterns in embryo

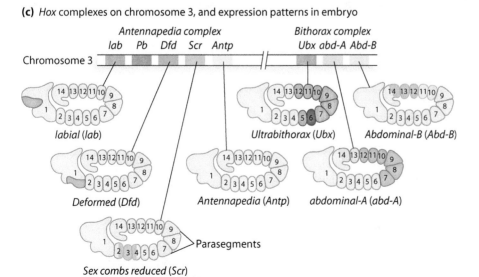

Figure 20.10 *Hox* **genes of the *Antennapedia* and *bithorax* complexes.**

common ancestor through a series of gene duplications. All of the genes share a conserved sequence of DNA of 180 nucleotides that was dubbed the **homeobox,** which encodes a 60–amino acid protein domain, termed the **homeodomain,** with a helix-turn-helix motif. Such motifs had previously been recognized in bacterial and phage transcription factors, such as the *Lac* repressor and the lambda repressor proteins. They function to bind cis-regulatory DNA sequences of target genes. Since the homeobox genes of the *Antennapedia* and *bithorax* complexes share both molecular and functional similarity as well as having a common evolutionary origin, they are known collectively as ***Hox* genes.**

The patterns of *Hox* gene expression correlate with the regions affected in the corresponding mutants. Each of the *Hox* genes has a well-defined anterior boundary of expression but in most cases a more diffuse boundary on the posterior, resulting in overlapping domains of *Hox* gene expression. The anterior boundaries of *Hox* gene expression do not correspond to segmental boundaries but rather to boundaries of segment polarity gene expression. Thus, *Hox* gene expression is out of register with the groups of cells that give rise to segments in the adult fly and instead marks the boundaries of parasegments.

Because of the parasegmental pattern of *Hox* gene expression, mutations of those genes affect cellular identity in a parasegmental manner. Each parasegment of the embryo expresses a unique combination of *Hox* gene products, giving each parasegment a specific identity. The activation of *Hox* genes is controlled by the earlier-acting gap and pair-rule genes in a combinatorial manner similar to that described for the activation of pair-rule genes by the gap and coordinate genes. In the absence of all *Hox* gene activity, segments are formed, but they all differentiate into a "default" state that resembles a head segment. This outcome indicates that *Hox* genes are not required for the formation of the segments but rather for the specification of their identity.

The *Antennapedia* Complex The *Antennapedia* complex consists of five *Hox* genes—*labial*, *Deformed*, *Sex combs reduced*, *proboscipedia (Pb)*, and *Antennapedia*—that act in combination to specify the cephalic and thoracic parasegments (see Figure 20.10c). The original *Antennapedia* mutant (see Figure 20.1) was dominant and was found to be the result of a gain-of-function allele (see Section 4.1). The *Antennapedia* gene is normally expressed only in parasegments 4 and 5 (see Figure 20.10c), which give rise to thoracic segments that each produce a pair of legs. In flies carrying the dominant *Antennapedia* mutation, however, *Antennapedia* is expressed ectopically—meaning it is expressed at an inappropriate time or place or both. One of the normal roles of *Antennapedia* expression in the thoracic segments is to promote the differentiation of thoracic appendages into legs. When expressed ectopically in the third head segment, *Antennapedia* inappropriately promotes differentiation of head appendages (antennae) into legs instead.

The *bithorax* Complex In contrast to *Antennapedia* mutations that affect anterior body segments, mutations in the three genes of the *bithorax* complex—*Ultrabithorax*, *abdominal-A*, and *Abdominal-B*—affect more-posterior segments (**Figure 20.11a**). The *bithorax* complex genes are

(a) Wild type

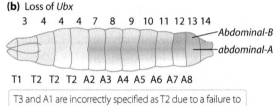

Both *Ubx* and *abd-A* have a diffuse posterior boundary of expression due to negative regulatory interactions between genes.

(b) Loss of *Ubx*

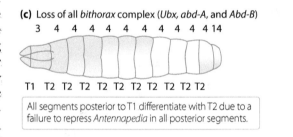

T3 and A1 are incorrectly specified as T2 due to a failure to repress *Antennapedia* in these segments.

(c) Loss of all *bithorax* complex (*Ubx*, *abd-A*, and *Abd-B*)

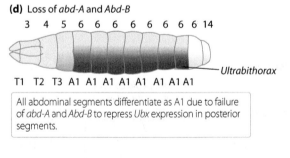

All segments posterior to T1 differentiate with T2 due to a failure to repress *Antennapedia* in all posterior segments.

(d) Loss of *abd-A* and *Abd-B*

All abdominal segments differentiate as A1 due to failure of *abd-A* and *Abd-B* to repress *Ubx* expression in posterior segments.

(e) Loss of *Abd-B*

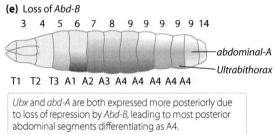

Ubx and *abd-A* are both expressed more posteriorly due to loss of repression by *Abd-B*, leading to most posterior abdominal segments differentiating as A4.

Figure 20.11   Cross-regulatory interactions between *bithorax* complex genes, specifying thoracic and abdominal segment fates.

expressed in overlapping sets of thoracic and abdominal parasegments and act in combination to specify the identity of those parasegments. How do only three genes specify the identity of nine segments, one thoracic and eight abdominal? The three genes vary not only in their spatial patterns of expression but also in expression levels between segments. Each has a sharp anterior border of expression and a more diffuse posterior boundary of expression. Thus, each segment exhibits a unique qualitative and quantitative pattern of *Hox* gene expression.

Loss of *Ultrabithorax* activity results in parasegments 5 and 6 having a combination of *Hox* gene products resembling that normally found in parasegment 4. This causes transformations of the identity of thoracic segment T3 and abdominal segment A1 into thoracic segment T2 (**Figure 20.11b**). Loss of the entire *bithorax* complex causes most abdominal segments to develop as T2, so each has legs as appendages (**Figure 20.11c**). This observation suggests that expression of *Antennapedia*, which promotes leg identity in appendages, extends posteriorly in such mutants and that genes of the *bithorax* complex normally repress posterior expression of *Antennapedia*. Such cross-regulatory interactions between *Hox* genes, whereby more posteriorly expressed *Hox* genes repress the expression of *Hox* genes normally expressed in more-anterior positions, is a common although not universal feature in the regulation of *Hox* genes (**Figure 20.11d–e**).

As you have probably noticed, there is no single *Hox* gene called *bithorax*; so what became of the original *bithorax* (*bx*) mutation that was isolated by Calvin Bridges? When Ed

Lewis recognized that mutations such as *bithorax* could provide valuable insights into the genetic mechanisms of development, he began collecting mutations with similar but distinct phenotypic defects, some of which he called *post-bithorax (pbx), Contrabithorax, Ultrabithorax,* and *bithoraxoid (bxd)*. Each of these mutations mapped to a different position in the same chromosomal region, so that they were separable by recombination events, and double-mutant combinations could be constructed. At the time Lewis performed these studies, molecular cloning was unknown, and he assumed that each mutant he identified represented a different gene. When the *bithorax* complex was eventually cloned in 1983, however, many of the mutant phenotypes were found to result from mutations in different enhancer modules controlling the expression of a single coding region that is now called the *Ultrabithorax* gene (**Figure 20.12a**).

Mutations of the regulatory elements can be either recessive, if in an enhancer module that acts to positively regulate gene expression, or dominant, if in a silencer module that acts to negatively regulate gene expression. While null loss-of-function alleles of *Ultrabithorax* result in embryo lethality, disruption of single enhancer modules results in milder defects. For example, recessive *Ultrabithorax^bithorax* mutations *(bx)* result in the transformation of the anterior part of T3 into T2, causing the anterior portion of the haltere to develop as a wing (**Figure 20.12b**). Conversely, recessive *Ultrabithorax^postbithorax* mutations *(pbx)* result in the transformation of the posterior region of T3 into T2 identity, and the posterior portion of the haltere develops as a wing. Only in the *Ultrabithorax^bithorax Ultrabithorax^postbithorax* double

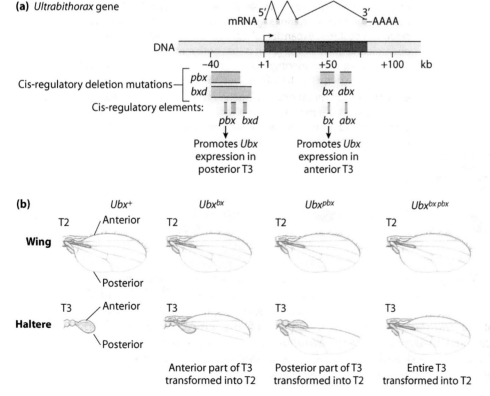

(a) *Ultrabithorax* gene

Cis-regulatory deletion mutations

Cis-regulatory elements:

pbx   bxd → Promotes *Ubx* expression in posterior T3

bx   abx → Promotes *Ubx* expression in anterior T3

(b)

Wing

Haltere

Ubx⁺ / Ubx^bx / Ubx^pbx / Ubx^bx pbx

T2 / T3 — Anterior / Posterior

Anterior part of T3 transformed into T2

Posterior part of T3 transformed into T2

Entire T3 transformed into T2

Figure 20.12 Mutations in cis-regulatory elements of *Ultrabithorax* cause homeotic transformations.

PROBLEM Why do loss-of-function mutations in *bithorax* complex genes result in homeotic transformations of parasegments into identities that correspond to more-anterior parasegments, whereas gain-of-function mutations (see Section 4.1) tend to result in identities corresponding to more-posterior parasegments?

BREAK IT DOWN: *bithorax* complex genes specify identity along the anterior-posterior axis of *Drosophila* (see p. 691).

BREAK IT DOWN: In a homeotic transformation, a normal body part is replaced by another body part normally found in another region of the body.

Solution Strategies	Solution Steps
Evaluate	
1. Identify the topic this problem addresses and the nature of the required answer.	1. The subject of this question is the effect of mutations in the *bithorax* complex on segment pattern formation. The answer requires descriptions of why loss-of-function mutations lead to segments that resemble more-anterior segments, whereas gain-of-function mutations lead to the formation of segments that resemble more-posterior segments.
2. Identify the critical information given in the problem.	2. The question suggests there is a key difference between the effects of loss-of-function mutations and gain-of-function mutations of the *bithorax* complex.
Deduce	
3. Review the general patterns of expression and segmental pattern formation resulting from the normal expression of homeotic genes. TIP: Use *Hox* genes as an example of a set of developmental genes.	3. Homeotic genes, such as the *Hox* genes, specify segment identity in a combinatorial manner through overlapping expression domains in parasegments. Each gene has a well-defined anterior boundary but a more diffuse posterior boundary. Cross-regulatory interactions refine *Hox* gene expression domains, so that more-posterior genes repress more anteriorly expressed genes.
4. Review the general pattern of expression and the normal segmental pattern formation of *bithorax* genes.	4. The *bithorax* complex consists of three genes, *Ubx*, *abd-A*, and *Abd-B*. *Ubx* is expressed in the anterior abdominal segments and posterior thoracic segments, *abd-A* is expressed in the middle abdominal segments, and *Abd-B* is expressed in the posterior abdominal segments. Segment identity is specified by the combination of *Hox* gene products and their levels of expression.
Solve	
5. Explain why loss-of-function mutations of *bithorax* genes lead parasegments to take on a more-anterior identity. TIP: Consider the cross-regulatory interactions of the *Hox* genes.	5. The loss of function of a posterior gene leads to both the absence of expression of the mutant gene and posterior expansion in the expression domains of more-anterior genes. For example, the posterior gene *Abd-B* acts to repress *abd-A* in the most-posterior segments. Loss-of-function mutations in *Abd-B* result in a posterior expansion of *abd-A* expression into more-posterior abdominal segments. The result is that both middle and posterior abdominal segments acquire an identity that is similar to that of the middle abdominal segments—a homeotic transformation to more-anterior identity.
6. Explain why gain-of-function mutations of *bithorax* genes lead parasegments to take on a more-posterior identity. TIP: Gain-of-function *Antennapedia* mutations cause legs (a posterior structure) to develop in the position normally occupied by antennae (an anterior structure)	6. Gain-of-function mutations cause gene expression at inappropriate times and locations. Gain-of-function alleles often, but not always, result in *Hox* gene expression in a more-anterior domain than in wild-type animals, thus resulting in homeotic transformations to a more-posterior identity.

For more practice, see Problems 6, 7, 22, and 26.   Visit the Study Area to access study tools.   MasteringGenetics™

mutant is the identity of the entire T3 segment transformed into a T2 identity, causing a four-winged fly to develop (see Figure 20.1).

The cis-regulatory elements of *Ultrabithorax* span over 120 kb (see Figure 20.12a), and their modularity allows the evolution of changes in gene expression without catastrophic disruption of *Ultrabithorax* function, such as those caused by nonsense mutations within the coding region. Thus, *Ultrabithorax*^{bithorax} *Ultrabithorax*^{postbithorax} double mutants survive to adulthood because the remainder of the cis-regulatory elements controlling *Ultrabithorax* expression are intact. **Genetic Analysis 20.1** asks you to evaluate cross-regulatory interactions among *Hox* genes.

Downstream Targets of *Hox* Genes

Given that combinatorial action of the *Hox* genes specifies parasegment identity and that *Hox* genes encode transcription factors, it follows that the downstream target genes activated by the *Hox* genes must differ between segments. These *Hox* target genes have been called **realizator genes,** and their expression contributes to the characteristic morphology of each segment. As an example, let's consider the formation of appendages on each segment.

Wild-type flies have antennae on the most-anterior head segment and have mandibles and maxillary and labial sense organs on other head segments. The three thoracic segments have legs; T2 and T3 also have wings and halteres, respectively. The eight abdominal segments lack appendages. Loss of all *Hox* activity is lethal to the embryo and causes all segments to resemble a head segment having antennae as appendages. This outcome indicates that all segments have the potential to form an appendage, and that expression of *Hox* genes can either specify the appendage identity or repress its formation.

The formation of an appendage is dependent upon a gene called *Distal-less*. In wild-type *Drosophila*, *Distal-less* is expressed in the head and thoracic segments but not in any abdominal segments. This pattern suggests that the abdominal segment identity genes, *Ultrabithorax*, *abdominal-A*, and *Abdominal-B*, negatively regulate *Distal-less* expression in the abdominal segments. Loss of function of all *bithorax* complex genes results in ectopic *Distal-less* expression in all abdominal segments, along with a concomitant development of appendages (legs) on all abdominal segments. Conversely, if *Ultrabithorax* is ectopically expressed at high levels throughout the embryo, *Distal-less* is not activated in any segment and no appendages are formed. Thus, action of specific *bithorax* complex Hox proteins on *Distal-less* cis-regulatory sequences represses *Distal-less* gene expression in the abdominal segments. The identity of the appendages is determined by the combinatorial activity of the *Hox* genes in conjunction with *Distal-less*. For example, the identity of the T1 leg is specified by *Distal-less* and *Sex combs reduced*, whereas the identity of the T2 leg is specified by *Distal-less* and *Antennapedia*.

Hox Genes in Metazoans

Soon after the discovery of *Hox* gene clusters in *Drosophila*, researchers began to inquire whether *Hox* genes are a peculiarity of *Drosophila* development, or whether they are found in a broader range of species. Many developmental biologists did not expect to find *Hox* genes in other animals, since there was no reason to expect that other animals would use the same genes to direct very different developmental programs. However, cross-hybridization studies using *Drosophila Hox* sequences as molecular probes revealed *Hox* gene sequences in the genomes of all animals, including insects, spiders, molluscs, and vertebrates (such as humans). This revelation suggested a common developmental mechanism among animals.

Subsequent experiments showed not only that most animals have clusters of *Hox* genes but also that they are arranged in a manner similar to that in *Drosophila* (**Figure 20.13**). Each cluster consists of genes corresponding to those in the *bithorax* and *Antennapedia* clusters of *Drosophila*, with some minor deletions and duplications. For example, as in *Drosophila*, the mouse *Hox* genes are expressed in an anterior-to-posterior pattern that corresponds to the chromosomal position of the genes within the *Hox* clusters. This pattern suggests that *Hox* genes also specify identity along the anterior–posterior axis of the mouse and, by extension, of mammals in general.

The conservation of *Hox* gene clusters among animals indicates that a common ancestor possessed a *Hox* gene cluster specifying pattern formation along its anterior–posterior axis. This cluster was duplicated during the evolution of the vertebrate genome, which has four copies. The conservation of the *Hox* complexes for more than 500 million years suggests that the spatial colinearity of *Hox* genes along the chromosome with their expression along the body axis is essential for optimal functionality.

Mice embryos with loss-of-function alleles of *Hox* genes, constructed using gene-targeting techniques described in Chapter 17, exhibit defects in the identity of serially repeated structures. For example, loss of *Hox* function results in a homeotic transformation of the lumbar and sacral vertebrae, which do not normally bear ribs, into structures resembling more-anterior thoracic vertebrae that do carry ribs (see Figure 16.1). These and additional *Hox* gene mutations suggest *Hox* genes direct the development of body plans in chordates as well as in annelids, arthropods, molluscs, nematodes, and other animals.

Studies of *Hox* complexes in other metazoans reveal that gene duplication took place before the divergence of bilaterian animals (animals that have bilateral symmetry). Thus, all bilaterian animals have essentially the same homeotic gene toolkit to pattern their anterior–posterior axis. This homology indicates that the differences between animals reflect how the toolkit is employed rather than differences in the component parts. Indeed, large-scale sequencing of cnidarian (jellyfish, sea anemone) genomes suggests that other components of the genetic toolkit are also largely shared by all metazoans. Given that all animals share fundamental developmental patterning processes and genes, much of what we learn from the study of model animals such as *Drosophila*, *Caenorhabditis elegans*, and mice can be extended to other members of the animal kingdom, including ourselves.

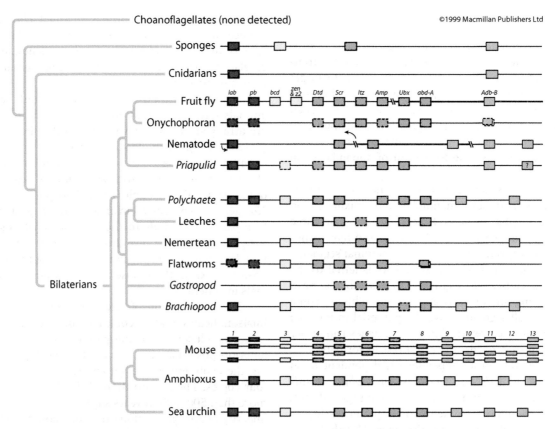

Figure 20.13 Occurrence and arrangement of *Hox* complexes in metazoans. *Hox* genes have not been detected in choanoflagellates, single-celled organisms that represent the sister clade to metazoans, but they are present in all metazoans. In the vertebrate lineage (exemplified by the mouse), the entire complex has been duplicated twice, resulting in four *Hox* complexes. Such events have produced duplicated genes that were later co-opted to new developmental functions.

Stabilization of Cellular Memory by Chromatin Architecture

The preceding sections describe how the basic body plan of *Drosophila* is established in early embryogenesis by the action of coordinate, gap, and segmentation genes and through spatially restricted patterns of *Hox* gene expression that specify segmental identity. The patterns of *Hox* gene expression are then faithfully propagated throughout the remainder of embryonic development. The proteins that activate *Hox* gene expression have an ephemeral pattern of expression; it disappears soon after *Hox* expression patterns are initiated. Thus, one challenge cells face during embryonic development is for specific lineages to maintain their identity as they proliferate.

Genetic screens for homeotic genes revealed that mutations at loci other than those encoding the *Hox* genes can also produce homeotic mutant phenotypes. In general, mutations at these other loci fall into two classes. The first class, exemplified by *trithorax* mutations, produces phenotypes reminiscent of multiple *Hox* loss-of-function mutations. In contrast, phenotypes of mutants of the second class, exemplified by *Polycomb* mutations, often resemble multiple gain-of-function alleles of *Hox* genes. At the molecular level, expression of multiple *Hox* genes is found to

be ectopic in *Polycomb* mutants and reduced in *trithorax* mutants. While *Hox* gene expression is established normally in both *Polycomb* and *trithorax* mutants, the expression either fails to be maintained (*trithorax* mutants) or is later activated in inappropriate locations (*Polycomb* mutants). Thus, rather than "remembering" what type of tissue they are destined to form, mutant *trithorax* and *Polycomb* cell lineages appear to "forget" their identity.

Both *trithorax* and *Polycomb* encode proteins that act in large protein complexes whose function is to modulate chromatin structure. Components of the complexes are encoded by genes known, respectively, as the trithorax group (trxG) genes and the Polycomb group (PcG) genes. Both the trxG and PcG protein complexes are recruited to specific DNA sequences, and each complex possesses a distinct type of histone-3-methyltransferase activity (see Section 15.2) in which the activity of the trxG complex is opposite to the activity of the PcG complex. The PcG complexes repress target gene expression by recruiting histone-modifying protein complexes capable of histone deacetylation. In contrast, trxG complexes recruit protein complexes that acetylate histone, leading to maintenance of active gene expression. These two types of modification are associated with transcriptionally inactive heterochromatin and transcriptionally active euchromatin, respectively (see Chapter 15). It is believed that trxG and PcG complexes are recruited to the cis-acting regulatory sequences of *Hox* genes to "lock" the chromatin into a particular form, allowing maintenance of either active or silent states of gene expression. In this way, these proteins provide a type of epigenetic cellular memory that is propagated through cell divisions occurring long after the initial activators of *Hox* gene expression patterns have disappeared.

Study of *trithorax* and *Polycomb* mutants has helped clarify that the establishment of euchromatic or heterochromatic chromatin at specific developmental genes is a primary mechanism by which the potential fates of cells become restricted as development proceeds from totipotent zygote to differentiated cell types. The relative rigidity or plasticity of these different chromatin states is directly responsible for a cell's ability to express some genes and not express others, thus influencing the developmental potential of particular cell types.

20.3 Cellular Interactions Specify Cell Fate

The adult *C. elegans* only contains about 1000 cells, and its development provides a model of organogenesis. For example, the development of the *Caenorhabditis elegans* vulva provides an example of how inductive and inhibitory signals between cells direct the differentiation of distinct developmental fates in a group of pluripotent cells. John Sulston, Sydney Brenner, and Robert Horvitz shared the Nobel Prize in Physiology or Medicine in 2002 for their research on the genetic regulation of organ development and programmed cell death in *C. elegans*.

Inductive Signaling between Cells

Caenorhabditis elegans is a hermaphrodite nematode worm in which external genitalia, the vulva, forms a portal to the uterus through which eggs are laid. Early in their development, hermaphroditic worms produce sperm, which they store for later use. Eggs are subsequently produced in the gonads, fertilized with the stored sperm, and then extruded through the vulva. The vulva forms during the last larval stage, from six precursor cells called vulval precursor cells (VPCs); see **Figure 20.14a–b**. Three of these larval cells give rise to structures of the vulva itself: One is called the primary (1°) cell, and the other two are called secondary (2°) cells of the vulva. The other three cells differentiate into hypodermis and are called tertiary (3°) cells. The VPC closest to a specific gonadal cell called the anchor cell differentiates as a 1° cell and forms the central part of the vulva. The two cells flanking the 1° cell differentiate as 2° cells and form the peripheral regions of the vulva. The 1° and 2° fates can be easily distinguished by their distinct cell-division patterns.

(a) Six cells, P3.p to P8.p, have potential to develop into vulva.

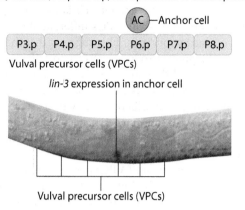

(b) The three cells closest to anchor cell—P5.p to P7.p—form the vulva; the other cells develop into hypodermis.

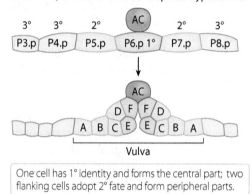

One cell has 1° identity and forms the central part; two flanking cells adopt 2° fate and form peripheral parts.

(c) Loss of the anchor cell results in loss of vulval development; all cells adopt hypodermal fate.

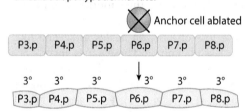

(d) Inductive signal from anchor cell induces vulval cell differentiation.

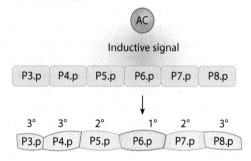

Figure 20.14 **Inductive signaling during vulval development in *C. elegans*.**

Initially, each of the six VPCs has the potential to differentiate along any of the pathways—1°, 2°, or 3°. This flexible cell-fate potential is demonstrated by laser-ablation experiments that destroy the anchor cell or one or more VPCs (Figure 20.14c). If the anchor cell is destroyed, no vulva will form, because all six VPCs differentiate with a 3° fate and become hypodermis. This suggests that the anchor cell must be present to induce VPCs to differentiate with 1° or 2° fates and thus form the vulva. Alternatively, if the VPC closest to the anchor cell is ablated, one of the cells that would normally differentiate with a 2° fate instead develops with a 1° fate and the two cells flanking this new 1° cell differentiate as 2° cells, suggesting that any of the VPCs can differentiate with a 1° or 2° fate.

What limits the number of VPCs destined to form the vulva to three? Given the loss of both the 1° and 2° fates when the anchor cell is removed, researchers hypothesized that the anchor cell might provide an **inductive signal** to induce vulval cell differentiation (Figure 20.14d). If this inductive signal is disseminated in a gradient, the cell closest to the anchor cell could acquire a different fate than cells that are more distant.

As predicted by the inductive interaction model, mutations that eliminate either the inductive signal or the ability of cells to respond to the inductive signal result in a loss of vulval development, and all VPCs differentiate as hypodermis (Figure 20.15a). This mutant phenotype is called the vulva-less phenotype. In contrast, mutations that disseminate the inductive signal to all VPCs cause all VPCs to differentiate into vulval cells, producing a multi-vulva phenotype. Multi-vulva mutants lay eggs similarly to normal worms; however, the fertilized eggs of vulva-less worms cannot be laid and instead develop and hatch inside the mother's uterus. Progeny developing in the uterus eventually consume their mother from the inside and then hatch out of the carcass.

Recessive loss-of-function alleles at several loci produce a vulva-less phenotype. These genes encode proteins that act either in the production of the inductive signal from the anchor cell or that facilitate cell response to the inductive signal (Figure 20.15b). For example, the *lin-3* gene encodes a small, secreted protein expressed only in the anchor cell and acting as the inductive signaling molecule (see Figure 20.14a and d). Mutations that result in a loss of active LIN-3 protein result in the loss of the inductive signal from the anchor cell. In contrast, the *let-23* and *let-60* genes are expressed in the VPCs and act as the receptor (LET-23) for the *lin-3*–encoded signal and as a signal transduction molecule (LET-60) that communicates the signal from the plasma membrane to the nucleus, where changes in gene expression are induced. The absence of a receptor for LIN-3, or the inability to transmit receipt of the signal, blocks the normal developmental fate of VPCs.

Epistatic analysis of developmental pathways, conducted by studying multiple mutant combinations, is used to identify groups of genes that interact to control a particular cellular process or pathway and to establish an order-of-function map for the genes in the pathway (see Section 4.3). Genetic analysis of developmental pathways can be more complicated than analysis of biochemical

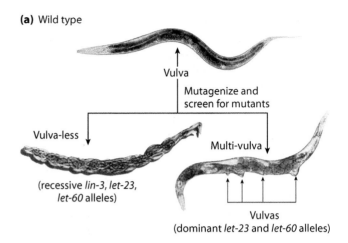

(a) Wild type

Vulva

Mutagenize and screen for mutants

Vulva-less

(recessive *lin-3, let-23, let-60* alleles)

Multi-vulva

Vulvas
(dominant *let-23* and *let-60* alleles)

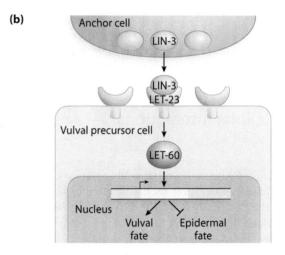

(b)

Anchor cell

LIN-3

LIN-3
LET-23

Vulval precursor cell

LET-60

Nucleus

Vulval fate   Epidermal fate

Figure 20.15   Genetic analysis of vulval development in *C. elegans*.

pathways because often there is no way of assaying intermediate steps in the developmental pathway. The analysis of double mutants and the availability of gain-of-function alleles can be crucial in these endeavors, as the studies of vulva-less and multi-vulva mutants in *C. elegans* show (Figure 20.16). In the case of recessive loss-of-function alleles of *lin-3, let-23,* and *let-60,* all single mutants have the same phenotype, suggesting all these genes might act in the same pathway. However, all double-mutant loss-of-function combinations also exhibit a vulva-less phenotype (Figure 20.16b), which complicates the effort to discover the order of genes in the pathway.

As shown in Figure 20.15, genetic screens of *C. elegans* identified dominant multi-vulva mutations in which all VPCs differentiated as 1° or 2° cells. Two of the dominant mutations mapped to the same positions as *let-23* and *let-60,* suggesting that they might be gain-of-function alleles of these genes, and both dominant mutant alleles proved to be epistatic to recessive loss-of-function alleles of *lin-3* (i.e., the double mutants have a multi-vulva phenotype like the *let-23* and *let-60* gain-of-function single mutants), as outlined in Figure 20.16e–f. The double-mutant phenotype indicates that the gain-of-function alleles of either

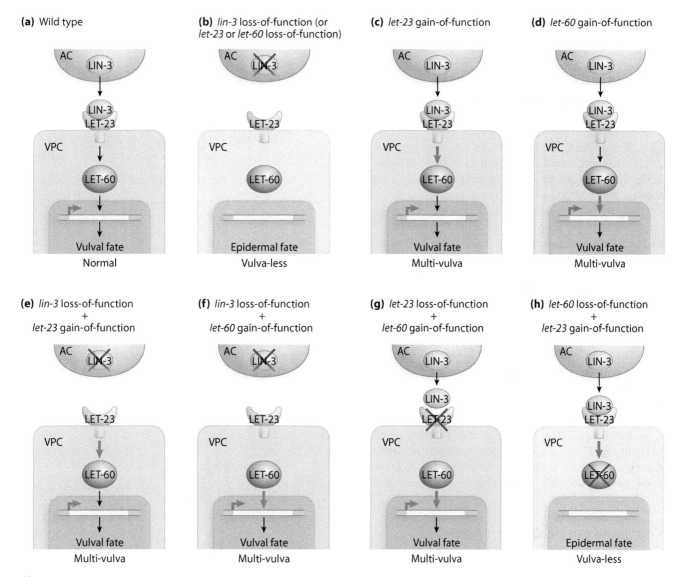

Figure 20.16 **Analysis of double-mutant phenotypes to find order of genes in developmental pathways.** **(a)** In wild-type worms, the vulva developmental pathway is active only in the presence of the signal (LIN-3). **(b)** In *lin-3* mutants, no signal is present, and worms develop with a vulva-less phenotype. **(c)** and **(d)** In either *let-23* or *let-60* gain-of-function alleles, the pathway is constitutively active, and worms develop with a multi-vulva phenotype. **(e)** and **(f)** Gain-of-function alleles of *let-23* and *let-60* are epistatic to loss-of-function *lin-3* alleles. The pathway is constitutively active regardless of whether the *lin-3* signal is present. **(g)** and **(h)** Gain-of-function alleles of *let-60* are epistatic to loss-of-function alleles of *let-23*. Conversely, loss-of-function alleles of *let-60* are epistatic to gain-of-function alleles of *let-23*. This places *let-60* downstream of *let-23*.

let-23 or *let-60* do not require the function of *lin-3* to exert their phenotypic effects, thus placing both *let-23* and *let-60* downstream of *lin-3*.

Similar analysis enables the ordering of the *let-23* and *let-60* genes in the pathway (see Figure 20.16g–h). Dominant *let-60* alleles are epistatic to recessive *let-23* alleles, indicating that *let-60* can function in the absence of functional *let-23*, a finding that places *let-60* downstream of *let-23*. This conclusion is supported by the converse experiment, where recessive *let-60* alleles are epistatic to dominant *let-23* alleles, which indicates that *let-23* requires the function of *let-60* to exert a phenotypic effect.

The genetic pathway was determined before the nature of the proteins had been analyzed. Now that we know the molecular identities of LIN-3 (signal), LET-23 (receptor), and LET-60 (signal transduction molecule), these epistatic relationships make sense. For example, dominant gain-of-function mutations of *let-60* result in constitutive activity of this protein, allowing it to transduce a signal independent of the state of the LET-23 receptor. Likewise, gain-of-function alleles of *let-23* act as if they are receiving a signal all the time, whether or not *lin-3* is functional, and thus activate the downstream signal-transduction cascade, which in turn depends on having a functional allele of *let-60*.

Lateral Inhibition

Given that they are both induced by the *lin-3*–encoded signal, how are the 1° and 2° fates specified? One possibility is a differential response of the VPCs to a graded *lin-3* signal, where the highest concentration of signal produces a 1° fate and a lower concentration of signal produces 2° cells. However, when the cell that would normally be a 1° cell is ablated, a cell that would normally have been a 2° cell differentiates into a 1° cell instead. It is thus unlikely that the absolute concentration of signal perceived is solely responsible for directing cell fate.

A possible explanation is that after reception of the *lin-3* signal, a second signal is sent from the 1° cell that inhibits the neighboring cells from becoming 1° cells (**Figure 20.17a**). This process is termed **lateral inhibition,** where an initial asymmetry is reinforced by signalling between adjacent cells (**Figure 20.17b**). All VPCs initially have the potential to express a lateral signal, encoded by the *lag-2* gene, and to express the receptor for the LAG-2 signal, encoded by the *lin-12* gene. The *lag-2* gene is activated in response to the LIN-3 signal, so it is expressed at higher levels in the 1° cell. Reception of LAG-2 results in down-regulation of the *lag-2* gene in the receiving cells and up-regulation of the gene for its receptor, LIN-12 (**Figure 20.17c**). This creates a feedback loop that reinforces the initial asymmetry between the 1° and 2° cells. Continued feedback between the signal and its perception amplifies the differences between the two cells, causing them to acquire distinct developmental fates.

Cell Death during Development

One of the striking observations made when Sulston, Brenner, and Horvitz tracked the fate of every cell during *C. elegans* development is that many cells are fated to die. Of the 1090 cells produced during the development of a hermaphrodite worm, 131 cells undergo a process called programmed cell death, or apoptosis (introduced in Sections 3.1 and 12.5).

Because the fate of every cell in *C. elegans* development is known, researchers have been able to identify mutants in which a cell fails to undergo apoptosis. Genetic analyses of such mutants have elucidated a genetic pathway that leads to cell death in response to a signaling molecule. This pathway is largely conserved across the animal kingdom (in humans, as well) and is a natural and important process that helps sculpt the development of tissues as well as maintain tissues in adult organisms. Indeed, it is estimated that 10^{11} cells are programmed to die every day in an adult human, many of them in epithelial tissues such as skin and intestine. While loss-of-function mutants for genes in the apoptosis pathway are viable in *C. elegans*, loss-of-function mutations in homologous genes in mice result in embryo death, indicating that cell death is an essential part of life in mammals.

(a)

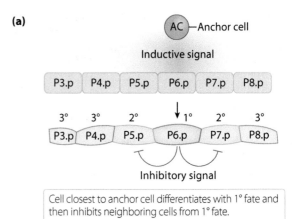

Cell closest to anchor cell differentiates with 1° fate and then inhibits neighboring cells from 1° fate.

(b)

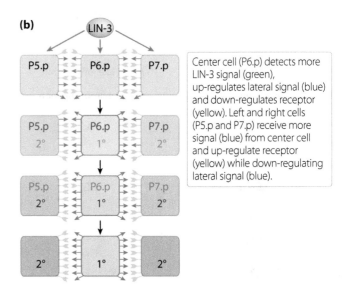

Center cell (P6.p) detects more LIN-3 signal (green), up-regulates lateral signal (blue) and down-regulates receptor (yellow). Left and right cells (P5.p and P7.p) receive more signal (blue) from center cell and up-regulate receptor (yellow) while down-regulating lateral signal (blue).

(c)

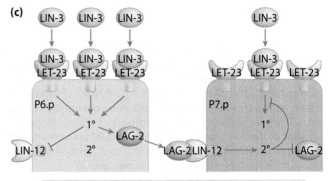

Strong activation of *lin-3/let-23* pathway promotes 1° cell fate, in turn activating the *lag-2/lin-12* pathway, which promotes a 2° cell fate in neighboring cells.

Figure 20.17 Lateral inhibition in *C. elegans* vulval differentiation.

20.4 "Evolution Behaves Like a Tinkerer"

One of the major surprises emerging from genome sequence analysis of animals is that, within a factor of about 2, most animal genomes have very similar numbers of genes. The range is from about 12,000 to about 25,000. Thus relatively simple animals such as *Drosophila* have a genome containing about 14,000 genes, whereas the human genome contains about 25,000 genes. Even organisms such as jellyfish and sea anemones possess genomes with gene numbers largely similar to those of vertebrates.

Given this consistency of gene number, what is the biological explanation of how the presumed "complexity" of vertebrates is produced from a genetic toolkit that is similar to the one possessed by comparatively "simple" animals? The answer seems to lie in the relative complexity of gene regulation rather than the invention of new genes for additional developmental processes. This proposal suggests that existing genes are recruited for new roles by means of changes in their regulation, both in space and time. Biologist Francois Jacob summed up this view of evolution when he said, "Evolution behaves like a tinkerer.... [It] does not produce novelties from scratch. It works on what already exists, either transforming a system to give it new functions or combining several systems to produce a more elaborate one."

A common theme in the evolutionary history of all genes, and particularly those influencing development, is the **co-option** of genes and genetic modules to direct the patterning or growth of novel organs. In this section, we consider an example of the co-option of genes by evolutionary "tinkering" to form newly evolved structures: digits (fingers and toes) on tetrapod limb appendages such as hands and feet. The study of the evolution of development is often referred to as **evo-devo**.

Evolution through Co-option

Limb positioning in tetrapods (four-legged vertebrates) results in large measure from the expression of *Hox* genes that direct the anterior–posterior organization of the body. Work on chickens and mice, demonstrates that expression of *Hox* genes along the anterior–posterior body axis defines the position at which a limb will develop. The anterior limit of the expression domains of two *Hox* genes, *Hoxc8* and *Hoxc6*, demarcates the position of the forelimb, and the posterior limit of expression marks the position of the hindlimb (Figure 20.18a). The expression of these two genes specifies the thoracic region of vertebrates, which is characterized by the formation of ribs from the vertebral column.

Once limb positions are specified, cells of the mesenchyme (loosely connected sub-ectodermal cells) send a signal to the overlying ectodermal cells. This signal promotes changes within a narrow band of cells that then forms the apical ectodermal ridge (AER), whose primary function is to direct limb-bud outgrowth by responding to signals produced in a group of mesenchymal cells toward the posterior side of the limb bud called the **zone of polarizing activity (ZPA**; Figure 20.18b). The ZPA acts as an organizer that promotes digit formation at the distal ends of limb buds (that is, the ends farther from

the center of the body) through the production of a morphogen, a small secreted signaling protein called Sonic hedgehog (Shh). The *Sonic hedgehog* (*Shh*) gene is orthologous to the *Drosophila* segment polarity gene *hedgehog*. *Sonic hedgehog* is expressed principally in the neural tube, where it helps organize the brain, eyes, and other structures through patterning of a group of cells known as the floor plate, and in developing limbs, where it directs the development of digits. The Case Study in this chapter discusses the consequences of different *Shh* mutations on mammal development and morphology.

All extant tetrapods are characterized by five or fewer digits in each set, and each digit in the set has a unique identity. Tetrapod digits arise along the anterior–posterior axis of the limb bud. If you allow your arms to hang straight down, you will see that your thumb (digit 1) is in the anterior position on your hand, while your pinky (digit 5) is in the posterior position. *Sonic hedgehog* expressed in the ZPA plays an important role in initiating digit formation, and loss-of-function alleles of *Shh* result in a loss of digits 2–5; only digit 1 forms independently of *Shh* function. A second role of *Shh* in limb patterning is in the specification of digit identity. Experiments where a second ZPA is transplanted to an anterior position result in a mirror-image duplication of digits, suggesting that the ZPA instructs those digits closer to the ZPA to differentiate with posterior identity (see Figure 20.18b).

The *Hox* genes that play a conserved role in patterning the anterior–posterior axis in animals were considered candidates to be the genes acting downstream of *Shh* to specify the patterning events in digits. In mice (and by inference humans), five Hox genes are expressed in the limb bud at the time and place where the digits are developing: *Hoxd9*, *Hoxd10*, *Hoxd11*, *Hoxd12*, and *Hoxd13* (Figure 20.18c). These genes are also expressed in the posteriormost regions of the mouse embryo, where they contribute to patterning along the anterior–posterior body axis, and later in the developing nervous system. Despite the difference in position of hindlimb and forelimb along the body axis, the same five *Hox* genes are expressed in the developing digits of each limb. Their expression in the limb bud follows a precise temporal and spatial pattern and is dependent on *Shh* activity. The first gene to be expressed is *Hoxd9*, followed by *Hoxd10*, then *Hoxd11*, and so on through *Hoxd13*. Spatially, all genes share the same posterior boundary, but the anterior boundary of expression is different for each gene. Consequently, the five *Hoxd* genes subdivide the limb bud into five zones, each specified by a different combination of *Hoxd* gene expression. Analogous to patterning along the anterior–posterior axis, ectopic expression of different *Hoxd* genes within the developing limb bud results in transformations of digit identity. A similar combinatorial code of *Hox* gene expression also appears to specify the proximal–distal patterning of the limb buds themselves (e.g., upper arm, forearm, hand, digits).

Mutations that expand or increase *Shh* expression result in extra digits and have been documented in mice,

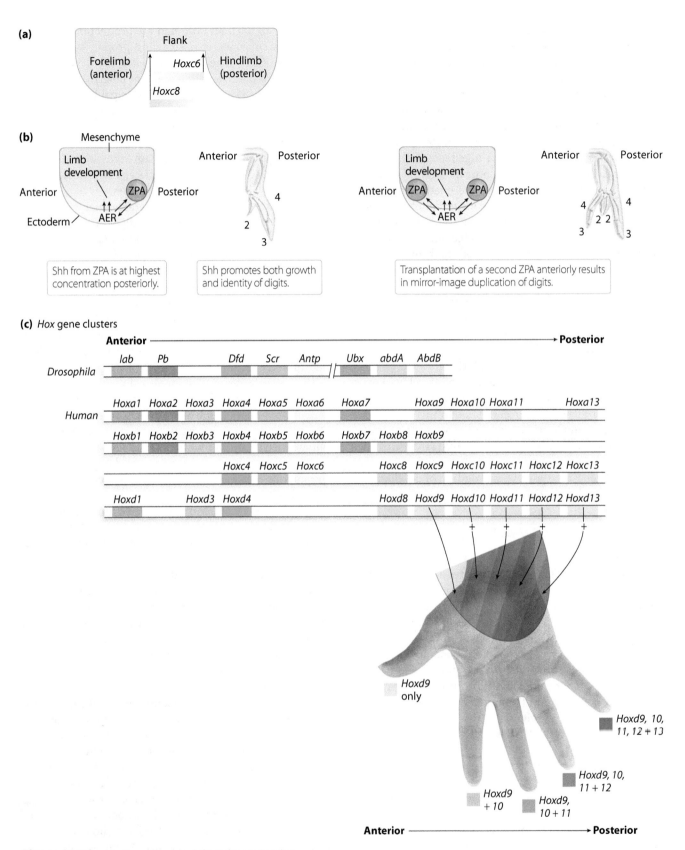

Figure 20.18   Limb-position and digit determination.

chickens, dogs, cats, and humans. However, because identity is controlled by only five *Hox* genes, the extra digits always have a morphology closely resembling that of an

adjacent digit, rather than having a unique identity (see Figure 4.13). Finally, it is worth noting that the separation of the human limb bud into individual digits requires programmed cell death (see Section 20.3) of the intervening cells—a process that has been lost in duck and bat limbs and has led to webbing in those animals.

These programs have been further modified during evolution in the secondary loss of legs in snakes and cetaceans. The loss of the front legs of snakes is due to an anterior shift in both *Hoxc6* and *Hoxc8* gene expression all the way to the base of the head. All vertebrae behind the snake head, except the first one, develop as thoracic vertebrae with ribs. In contrast, the convergent evolution of loss of hind legs in snakes and cetaceans is due to independent alterations in *Shh* activity in the developing hind limb bud.

Constraints on Co-option

The ancestral roles of *Hoxd* genes pertained to patterning along the anterior–posterior axis of the body. Therefore, the role of *Hoxd* genes in specifying digit identity represents a co-option of function of already existing genes. These same genes also acquired roles in the later differentiation of the nervous system. Likewise, the presence of the floor plate in all vertebrates is an indication that the floor plate evolved before limbs during vertebrate evolution. Limbs developed later within the tetrapod lineage, and in the course of limb evolution, *Shh* was co-opted to pattern digits, structures that did not previously exist. By what process are genes co-opted for new functions during evolution?

In the case of limb evolution, genes of the *Hoxd* cluster could have come under control of limb-specific enhancer modules leading to expression of the *Hoxd* genes in developing limbs. As long as changes in regulation did not disrupt *Hoxd* expression during anterior–posterior patterning of the body axis, the changes would not result in defects of this earlier process. The acquisition of gene expression in the developing limb could be thought of as a gain-of-function mutation. The modularity of enhancers and silencers facilitates evolution by co-option because individual enhancer modules are free to evolve independently. Thus the patterning of a novel tetrapod organ, the limb, involved the co-option of, or tinkering with, preexisting genetic programs that already had developmental roles elsewhere. As noted above, a major constraint on this type of evolutionary change is that the more ancestral functions of the gene must not be disrupted.

20.5 Plants Represent an Independent Experiment in Multicellular Evolution

Multicellularity has evolved independently many times in the history of life on Earth. The two lineages of multicellular organisms you are likely to be most familiar with are animals and land plants. Since the common ancestor of plants and animals was a single-celled organism, multicellularity evolved independently in each lineage.

Due to their independent origins, animals and plants differ in certain crucial aspects of their development. One difference is that germ-line cells in animals separate from somatic (body) cells much earlier in development than do the germ-line cells in land plants. Another difference is that animal cells are often motile during development, whereas plant cells are encased in a cell wall that essentially fixes them in the location at which they arise. Animals and land plants also differ with respect to when the basic form of the body plan takes shape. The animal body plan is established during embryogenesis, and subsequent development consists primarily of growth in size but without the addition of new organs. In contrast, throughout their lifetimes plants add new organs that are produced from pluripotent stem-cell populations. Finally, because plants often grow in a fixed location and are unable to migrate as many animals can, a plant must be able to alter its develop mental program in response to changing environmental conditions throughout its lifetime. Thus, while identical twins in animals are nearly indistinguishable, genotypically identical plants may develop to look very different depending upon their growth environment. Despite these differences, developmental processes occurring in plants are remarkably similar to those in animals, especially in their reliance upon the coordinated action of transcription factors and signaling molecules.

Development at Meristems

Plant development occurs at organized groups of pluripotent cells called **meristems.** The two functions of meristems are generation of organs and self-maintenance (to ensure that a pool of stem cells is always present). The above-ground parts of a plant are produced by shoot meristems and the below-ground parts by root meristems. The shoot meristem is divided into three functional domains— a peripheral zone from which leaves are formed, a rib zone from which part of the stem is derived, and a central zone that acts as a stem-cell reservoir to replenish cells lost to the developing leaves and stem (**Figure 20.19**). Meristems are generally indeterminate—that is, they can remain active for years, or in some cases the entire life of the plant. For example, the shoot meristem at the top of a pine tree can be active for centuries, continually producing leaves and side branches. Over time, the sizes of the central and peripheral domains remain remarkably constant. It is the continual production of new organs from meristems throughout the life of a plant that allows plants to adjust and adapt to changing local environmental conditions.

The identity of the meristem determines what types of organs are produced from its periphery. Early in the life of a flowering plant, leaves are produced from the flanks of the shoot meristem, and roots are produced from the root meristem. At the upper side of the attachment point of the leaf to the stem an axillary meristem is formed, from which a branch can arise. This reiterative formation of meristems that produce leaves that produce branches containing meristems forms the basis of most aboveground development of flowering plants. In response to appropriate environmental

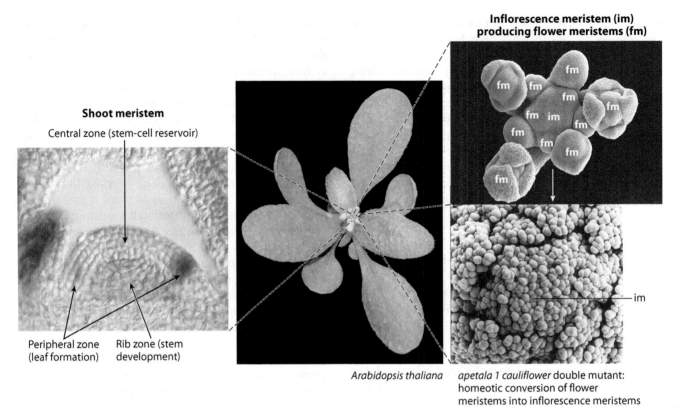

Shoot meristem
Central zone (stem-cell reservoir)

Peripheral zone (leaf formation)   Rib zone (stem development)

Inflorescence meristem (im) producing flower meristems (fm)

im

Arabidopsis thaliana   *apetala 1 cauliflower* double mutant: homeotic conversion of flower meristems into inflorescence meristems

Figure 20.19   Shoot meristems in plant growth.

conditions, the identity of meristems can change. For example, shoot meristems, which have been producing leaves, are converted in response to seasonal changes into reproductive meristems. A reproductive meristem may either develop directly into a flower meristem, or alternatively into an inflorescence meristem that produces flower meristems—an inflorescence being a group of flowers. In turn, flower meristems produce floral organs from their peripheral zones. Unlike the other meristems, flower meristems are determinate: no more stem cells are available after it has produced a fixed number of organs.

Because each type of meristem is characterized by a specific pattern of gene expression, mutations in key genes can result in homeotic transformations of meristem types. We have all eaten one such mutant, cauliflower, in which meristems that would normally be specified as flowers behave instead as inflorescence meristems (see Figure 20.19, lower right). The genetic basis of this phenotype has been identified in *Arabidopsis* as loss-of-function alleles of two closely related paralogs, *APETALA1* and *CAULIFLOWER*, encoding transcription factors.

Combinatorial Homeotic Activity in Floral-Organ Identity

Several flowering plant species have been adopted as models for the study of genetics. For example, peas (*Pisum sativum*), with which Mendel performed his experiments, and maize (*Zea mays*), in which transposons were discovered,

were introduced in earlier chapters. Due to its small size, short generation time, and fully sequenced genome, the most widely used model plant is *Arabidopsis thaliana*. Since the 1980s, study of homeotic mutants in *Arabidopsis* and another plant species, *Antirrhinum* (snapdragon), has led to insights into the genetic basis of flower development and revealed developmental parallels with animals.

Arabidopsis flowers are composed of four concentric whorls of organs (**Figure 20.20**). The outermost whorl is occupied by sepals, organs that protect the flower bud during development. The second whorl is occupied by petals, which in many species attract pollinators. Stamens, the male organs that produce pollen, are located in the third whorl, and the female organs—carpels, containing the ovules—occupy the central whorl.

Homeotic Floral Mutants of *Arabidopsis* Recessive floral homeotic mutants of *Arabidopsis* fall into three classes, each having defects in two adjacent whorls (see Figure 20.20). One class, named the A class, exhibits homeotic transformations in the outer two whorls, where carpels develop in the positions normally occupied by sepals and stamens replace petals, so that the four floral whorls consist of carpels, stamens, stamens, and carpels (see Figure 20.20). A second class, the B-class mutants, exhibit homeotic transformations in the middle two whorls, where sepals replace petals and carpels replace stamens, so that the four whorls consist of sepals, sepals, carpels, and carpels. In C-class mutants, homeotic

Wild-type Arabidopsis
- Whorl 1 sepals
- Whorl 2 petals
- Whorl 3 stamens
- Whorl 4 carpels

A-class mutant
(*apetala2*)
- Whorl 1 carpels
- Whorl 2 stamens
- Whorl 3 stamens
- Whorl 4 carpels

B-class mutant
(*apetala3* or *pistillata*)
- Whorl 1 sepals
- Whorl 2 sepals
- Whorl 3 carpels
- Whorl 4 carpels

C-class mutant
(*agamous*)
- Whorl 1 sepals
- Whorl 2 petals
- Whorl 3 petals
- Whorl 4 sepals

BC double mutant
(*apetala3 agamous*)
- Whorl 1 sepals
- Whorl 2 sepals
- Whorl 3 sepals
- Whorl 4 sepals

AC double mutant
(*apetala2 agamous*)
- Whorl 1 leaf-like carpels
- Whorl 2 petal-like stamens
- Whorl 3 petal-like stamens
- Whorl 4 leaf-like carpels

ABC triple mutant
(*apetala2 pistillata agamous*)
- Whorl 1 leaf-like carpels
- Whorl 2 leaf-like carpels
- Whorl 3 leaf-like carpels
- Whorl 4 leaf-like carpels

Figure 20.20 **Floral homeotic mutations in *Arabidopsis*.**

transformations in the third and fourth whorls result in flowers where petals develop in the positions normally occupied by stamens, and the cells that would normally

give rise to the carpels behave as if they were another flower meristem that reiterates the developmental cycle. Similar mutants can be found in a number of ornamental plant species and are often referred to as "double flowers."

In *Arabidopsis*, A-class activity is promoted by two genes, *APETALA2* and *APETALA1*, B-class activity by the *APETALA3* and *PISTILLATA* genes, and C-class activity by the *AGAMOUS* gene. Double mutants either display an additive phenotype (e.g., *apetala3 agamous* flowers consisting of only sepals) or exhibit novel phenotypes (e.g., *apetala2 agamous* flowers with novel floral organs that do not exist in wild-type flowers). Additive double-mutant phenotypes suggest that the two genes do not interact, whereas nonadditive double-mutant phenotypes suggest that the two genes interact to influence a common developmental pathway. For example, in *apetala2 agamous* flowers, the first and fourth whorls have leaf-like carpels while the second and third whorls are occupied by organs with features of both petals and stamens. The *agamous* mutation has a phenotype effect in the first and second whorls in an *apetala2* background (compare the identities of these whorls in an *apetala2* single mutant to a *apetala2 agamous* double mutant), an effect not observed in a wild-type background, where phenotypic defects of *agamous* are limited to the third and fourth whorls. This indicates that *AGAMOUS* is ectopically active in first and second whorls in *apetala2* mutants. Likewise, based on the double-mutant phenotype, *APETALA2* is active in the inner whorls of *agamous* mutants.

On the basis of single and multiple mutant phenotypes, a model was formulated in which the identity of organs developing in any whorl is determined by the combination of homeotic genes active in that whorl (**Figure 20.21**). It was presumed that each class of gene is active in those whorls affected in the respective mutants: *APETALA2* and *APETALA1* in the outer two whorls, *APETALA3* and *PISTILLATA* in the middle two whorls, and *AGAMOUS* in the inner two whorls. Thus, each whorl is characterized by a different combination of homeotic gene activity that specifies floral organ identity. The A-class activity by itself in the first whorl specifies sepals, A-class + B-class in the second whorl specifies petals, B-class + C-class in the third whorl specifies stamens, and C-class by itself in the fourth whorl specifies carpels. To account for the mutant phenotypes (specifically the *apetala2 agamous* mutant described above), a second postulate of the model is that the A-class and C-class activities are mutually antagonistic, so that in an A-class mutant background, C-class activity is found in all four whorls; and conversely, in a C-class mutant background, A-class activity is in all four whorls. The specification of identity by combinations of homeotic gene activities and cross-regulatory interactions between the floral homeotic genes is reminiscent of specification of segmental identity in *Drosophila* by *Hox* genes.

The model successfully predicts the phenotypes of multiple mutants. For example, in a double mutant in which both B-class and C-class activities are absent, only A-class genes are expressed in all four whorls, and a flower

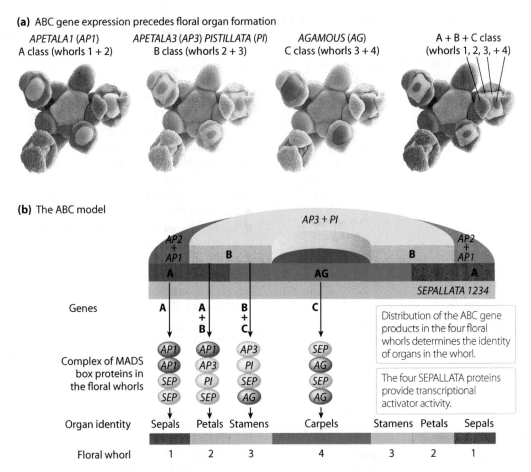

Figure 20.21 **The ABC model of flower development.**

with only sepals develops (see Figure 20.20). In ABC triple mutants, in which all floral-organ-identity gene activity is compromised, leaf-like organs are found in all whorls. These observations suggest that since floral organs are evolutionarily derived from leaves, one role of the floral homeotic genes is to modify a leaf into a specialized floral organ.

Homeotic MADS Box Transcription Factors As do animal homeotic genes, many floral homeotic genes encode closely related transcription factors. However, rather than encoding homeobox genes, the floral homeotic genes encode **MADS box** genes, named after the DNA-binding domain of the transcription factors. The name MADS box is derived from four members of the gene family: *MCM1* of *Saccharomyces cerevisiae, AGAMOUS* of *Arabidopsis, DEFICIENS* of *Antirrhinum*, and *SRF* of humans. All of the B- and C-class genes, as well as *APETALA1*, encode MADS boxes. Consistent with the model described above, the B-class genes are expressed in whorls two and three, and the C-class gene, *AGAMOUS*, is expressed in the third and fourth whorls (see Figure 20.21).

Subsequent studies have shown that the ABC classes of MADS box proteins interact with another class of MADS box protein encoded by the *SEPALLATA* (*SEP*) genes (see Chapter 16 Case Study). The SEP proteins together with the A-, B-, and C-class proteins form higher-order

complexes that regulate transcription (see Figure 20.21). The SEP proteins provide a transcriptional activation activity to the complexes, an activity that the B and C proteins lack. Conversely, the A, B, and C proteins provide specificity to the complexes, an activity the SEP proteins lack. When A-, B-, or C-class genes are ectopically expressed throughout the flower meristem, they cause homeotic transformations of floral organ identity. For example, if B-class genes are ectopically expressed throughout the flower, the result is a flower with organ identities of petal, petal, stamen, stamen, from the first to the fourth whorls. In contrast, ectopic expression of the A-, B-, and C-class genes alone is not sufficient to convert the leaves of the *Arabidopsis* plant into floral organs. However, if the *SEP* genes are ectopically expressed in addition to, for example, the A and B genes, the combination is sufficient to convert leaves into petals. In this manner, the identities of leaves and floral organs are interconvertible by the absence or presence of the expression of the floral homeotic genes, consistent with floral organs evolving by modification of an ancestral leaf.

Studies of B- and C-class genes from flowering plants and gymnosperms (e.g., conifers) suggest that for all seed plants, C-class genes alone promote female reproductive development and that B + C gene activity promotes male reproductive development. However, unlike the

PROBLEM You are interested in the development of the body plan of kelp, a common brown alga found along many coastlines. Would reverse or forward genetics approaches be more suited to identifying the genes required for early kelp development?

> **BREAK IT DOWN:** In a "forward genetics" approach, no prior knowledge of gene identity is required, while a "reverse genetic" approach starts with known gene sequences.

> **BREAK IT DOWN:** Review Figure 19.18 to find the relationship between brown algae and the other organisms you have been studying.

Solution Strategies	Solution Steps
Evaluate	
1. Identify the topic this problem addresses and the nature of the required answer.	1. This problem concerns the investigation of genes determining development of kelp. Devising an answer requires evaluating the relative potential of reverse genetic analysis versus forward genetic analysis (see Chapters 16 and 17).
2. Identify the critical information given in the problem.	2. Kelp is identified as brown algae, a form of life distinct from land plants and animals.
Deduce	
3. Determine if looking for gene homology (a reverse genetic approach) has a high probability of successfully identifying developmental genes in kelp.	3. Examination of Figure 18.11 indicates that kelp is only distantly related to either land plants or animals. Therefore, searching for brown algal genes based on the sequences of plant or animal developmental genes is something of a fishing expedition.

> **TIP:** Was the common ancestor of animals, plants, and kelp unicellular or multicellular? Review Figure 18.11

> **PITFALL:** Distantly related organisms are likely to have evolved substantially since they last shared a common ancestor, and the extent of gene homology decreases as evolutionary distance between species increases.

Solve	
4. Determine whether the use of mutagenesis (a forward genetics approach) is likely to help identify kelp developmental genes.	4. A good approach to finding developmental genes is to perform a mutagenesis experiment that will identify mutants in which pattern formation is perturbed. Mutagenesis can potentially affect any gene; thus, the forward genetics approach is not biased or restricted to genes that share homology with genes in other species. Mutants displaying abnormalities of wild-type pattern formation are likely to carry mutations of pattern-forming genes.

> **TIP:** How were genes that regulate development in *Drosophila* originally identified?

For more practice, see Problems 17, 19, 23, 25, and 28.   Visit the Study Area to access study tools.   **Mastering**Genetics™

Hox genes, which appear to have evolved at the base of the animal lineage and which control patterning in all known animals, the B- and C-class genes are unknown in earlier-diverging lineages of land plants, such as ferns, lycophytes, and bryophytes, whose reproductive structures differ substantially in morphology and development and whose leaf-like organs evolved independently.

We have seen that the specification of serially repeated structures in both *Drosophila* and *Arabidopsis* is controlled in a similar manner via the combinatorial action of closely related transcription factors. Although the mechanism of developmental patterning in plants and animals is similar, the genes involved in development in the two kingdoms are not related; this is consistent with the independent evolution of multicellularity in plants and animals.

Genetic Analysis 20.2 asks you to design an experimental strategy to genetically dissect development in another group of multicellular eukaryotes.

CASE STUDY

Cyclopia and Polydactyly—Different *Shh* Mutations with Distinctive Phenotypes

Sonic hedgehog (*Shh*), introduced in Section 20.4, is an evolutionarily conserved gene that performs multiple related but distinctive roles in developing tissues of animals. The gene's best-understood developmental roles, stemming from its expression in limb buds and in the neural tube, pertain to digit formation and to the development of the floor plate. The floor plate divides the brain into hemispheres and is required for midline separation of other anatomical features, including separating developing eye tissue into right and left eyes. Given the central role of *Shh* in development, it stands to reason that *Shh* mutations profoundly affect normal development and morphology. Here we briefly examine two abnormal conditions that are caused by changes in *Shh* activity: holoprosencephaly/cyclopia and polydactyly.

HOLOPROSENCEPHALY/CYCLOPIA Holoprosencephaly (HPE) is a genetically heterogeneous abnormality, meaning that mutations in different genes can cause the disorder. One form of holoprosencephaly, HPE3, is caused by *Shh* mutations. HPE3 is a clinically variable disorder that produces many different morphological abnormalities in patients. The most subtle phenotypic defect is a slight loss of midline separation, resulting in a single central incisor. More severe defects include characteristic brain abnormalities; abnormalities of the mid-face, such as the formation of a proboscis-like nose; or possibly, in the most extreme cases, cyclopia, the presence of a single large mass of eye tissue rather than two separate eyes.

Numerous *Shh* mutations that cause HPE3 affect the coding region of the gene and result in the production of a severely defective or nonfunctional protein product, leading to a failure to form the floor plate and thus to form brain hemispheres (Figure 20.22a). To date, there are no specific genotype–phenotype correlations that tie specific *Shh* mutations to more severe or less severe manifestations of HPE3 or cyclopia. Pedigrees exhibit variation in both penetrance and expressivity, most likely because other genes involved in brain and mid-face formation (i.e., the other genes that cause the HPE phenotype) influence the extent of morphological abnormality (Figure 20.22b). Although the HPE3 mutations in *Shh* are missense, nonsense, and frameshift loss-of-function alleles, familial cases of HPE3 are inherited in an autosomal dominant manner. This indicates that the *Shh* mutations are haploinsufficient: The presence of a single copy of a wild-type allele is not sufficient for normal activity. Thus, as with most genetic disorders that have been characterized in humans, both penetrance and expressivity of abnormal phenotypes are modified significantly by genetic background.

During the 1950s, an epidemic of cyclopia was reported among sheep in the Western United States (Figure 20.22c). The compound cyclopamine, found in the plant *Veratrum californicum*, was implicated as an environmental cause of the abnormalities. Evidence indicated that ingestion of

(a) *Sonic hedgehog* gene

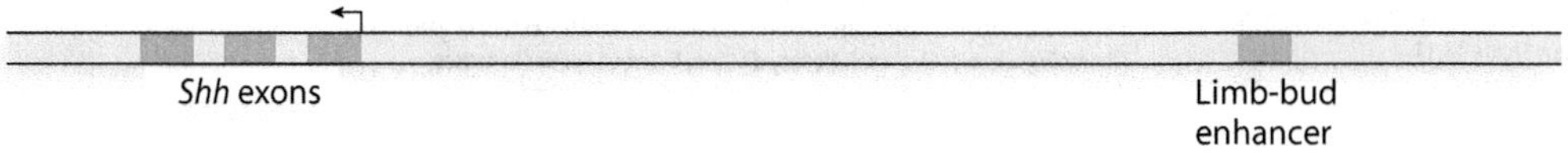

Shh exons

Limb-bud enhancer

(b) Pedigrees in which *Shh* mutations segregate

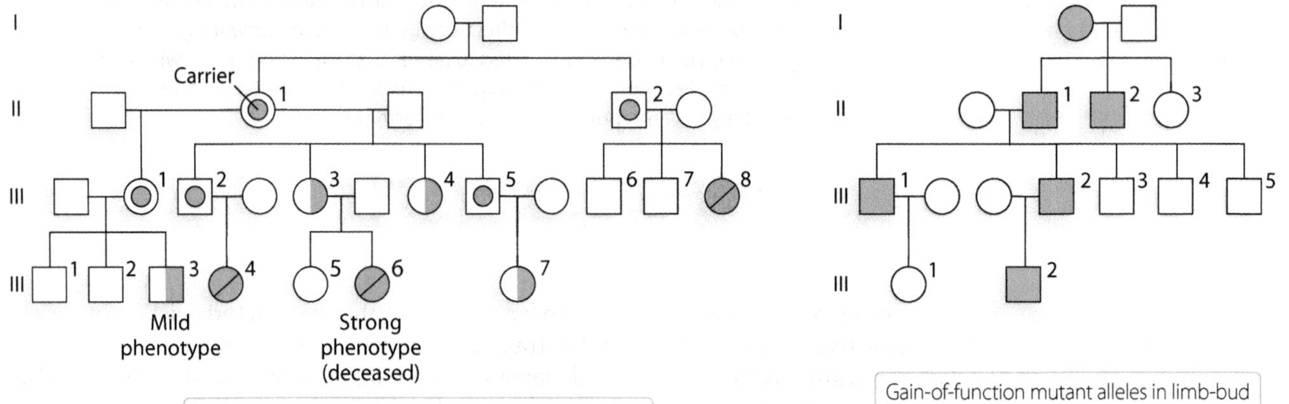

Mild phenotype

Strong phenotype (deceased)

Loss-of-function mutant alleles in *Shh* exons are haploinsufficient and inherited in a dominant manner.

Gain-of-function mutant alleles in limb-bud enhancer prolong *Shh* expression and are inherited in a dominant manner.

(c) Phenotypes associated with alterations in *Shh* activity

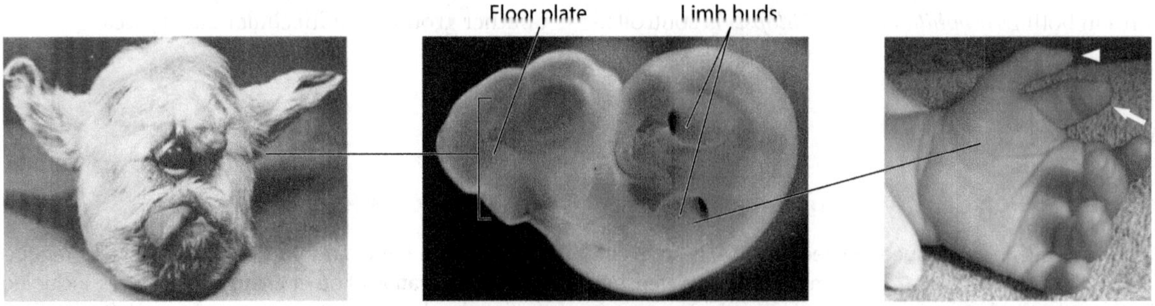

Floor plate   Limb buds

Loss of *Shh* activity in floor plate causes cyclopia.

Shh expression in developing mouse embryo

Prolonged *Shh* activity in limb bud causes extra digit development.

Figure 20.22 Effects of alterations in Shh morphogen activity in the floor plate and the limb bud.

V.californicum during gestation caused the production of lambs with cyclopia. In 2002, Philip Beachy and colleagues looked at the mechanism by which cyclopamine caused cyclopia and discovered that the compound binds directly to cells in the floor plate and blocks their response to Shh protein. This study illustrates that the action of normal proteins can be inhibited under certain environmental circumstances to produce effects similar to those seen with gene mutation. When an environmental condition induces a phenotype similar to that caused by mutation, the environmental condition is said to induce a phenocopy of the mutant phenotype.

POLYDACTYLY If *Shh* expression is eliminated from the developing limb bud by loss-of-function mutations inactivating the Shh protein, limb patterning is perturbed and digits do not form. However, if *Shh* expression is altered by mutation in the cis-regulatory region of the gene, changes in the Shh protein concentration gradient can result in polydactyly, the presence of extra digits (see Figure 20.22c). The extra digits develop because Shh protein is present in high concentration in parts of the limb bud where it is not normally found. Polydactyly in humans (discussed in Section 4.2) is an autosomal dominant disorder. Its inheritance is dominant because the ectopic expression resulting from the mutation is a gain of function. The enhancer element responsible for appropriate *Shh* expression in the developing limb buds was identified using a phylogenetic footprinting approach (see Figure 18.15).

SUMMARY   (MasteringGenetics™   For activities, animations, and review quizzes, go to the Study Area.

20.1 Development Is the Building of a Multicellular Organism

- Multicellularity has evolved independently multiple times.

- The development of a multicellular organism from a fertilized egg cell entails the formation of specialized cell types, driven by differential expression of genes.

- As animal development proceeds, cells become progressively restricted in their potential developmental fates, changing from totipotent to pluripotent to differentiated.

- Morphogens can provide positional information that is converted into differential gene expression.

- Signaling between neighboring cells can induce or inhibit developmental pathways. Genes controlling developmental processes often encode transcription factors or molecules involved in signaling between cells.

20.2 *Drosophila* Development Is a Paradigm for Animal Development

- Genetic screens in *Drosophila* identified sets of successively acting genes directing pattern formation during embryonic development.

- The *Drosophila* embryo is successively subdivided into segments, each with a unique identity, by the sequential action of batteries of transcription factors.

- Genes whose products are supplied to the egg by the mother and act to guide the development of the embryo are called maternal effect genes. The genotype of the mother, rather than that of the embryo, dictates the embryonic phenotype for the traits these genes determine.

- Gap genes are regulated by maternal effect genes and subdivide the *Drosophila* embryo into several broad regions. Pair-rule genes are regulated by both maternal effect and gap genes, and they subdivide the embryo into parasegments.

- Homeotic genes known as the *Hox* genes act in combination to specify the parasegments of *Drosophila. Hox* genes are largely conserved throughout the metazoan kingdom.

- Downstream targets of the *Hox* genes contribute to the morphogenesis of body segments.

- *Hox* gene expression patterns are maintained by regulation at the level of chromatin, providing a cellular memory of gene expression propagated through mitoses.

20.3 Cellular Interactions Specify Cell Fate

- In *C. elegans*, an inductive signal from the anchor cell determines vulval cell fates, and lateral inhibition refines cell specification in the developing vulva.

- Programmed cell death, or apoptosis, is a normal aspect of development in animals. It is required for sculpting the body plan during embryogenesis and maintaining tissues post-embryonically.

20.4 "Evolution Behaves Like a Tinkerer"

- Most animals possess the same types of genes; therefore, the differences between animals are largely due to differences in how genes are deployed during development.

- Genes can be co-opted to direct the development of new organs and tissues, often through changes in gene expression patterns. For example, the evolution of limbs and digits in tetrapods occurred through changes in *Hox* and *Sonic hedgehog* gene expression.

20.5 Plants Represent an Independent Experiment in Multicellular Evolution

- Despite differences in cellular behavior between plants and animals, the genetic control of development in plants has many similarities to that of animals.

- Plants continue to add organs throughout their life span due to the action of meristems, which are groups of pluripotent stem cells.

- Combinatorial action of homeotic genes specifies the identity of floral organs in flowering plants; the homeotic genes in plants encode MADS box transcription factors, analogous to the transcription factors encoded by the homeobox in animals.

KEYWORDS

Antennapedia complex *(p. 691)*

bithorax complex *(p. 691)*

cellular blastoderm *(p. 685)*

co-option *(p. 701)*

coordinate gene *(p. 686)*

differentiation *(p. 683)*

embryonic stem cell *(p. 683)*

evo-devo *(p. 701)*

gap gene *(p. 686)*

homeobox *(p. 692)*

homeodomain *(p. 692)*

homeotic gene *(p. 687)*

homeotic mutation *(p. 682)*

housekeeping gene *(p. 686)*

Hox gene *(p. 692)*

induction *(p. 683)*

inductive signal *(p. 698)*

inhibition *(p. 683)*

lateral inhibition *(p. 700)*

MADS box *(p. 706)*

maternal effect gene *(p. 687)*

meristem *(p. 703)*

morphogen *(p. 683)*

organizer *(p. 683)*

pair-rule gene *(p. 686)*

parasegment/segment *(p. 687)*

pluripotent *(p. 683)*

positional information *(p. 683)*

realizator gene *(p. 695)*

segment polarity gene *(p. 687)*

syncytial blastoderm *(p. 685)*

syncytium *(p. 685)*

totipotency *(p. 683)*

zone of polarizing activity (ZPA) *(p. 701)*

zygotic gene *(p. 687)*

PROBLEMS

 MasteringGenetics™ Visit for instructor-assigned tutorials and problems.

Chapter Concepts

For answers to selected even-numbered problems, see Appendix: Answers.

1. Explain why many developmental genes encode either transcription factors or signaling molecules.

2. Bird beaks develop from an embryonic group of cells called neural crest cells that are part of the neural tube that gives rise to the spinal column and related structures. Amazingly, neural crest cells can be surgically transplanted from one embryo to another, even between embryos of different species. When quail neural crest cells were transplanted into duck embryos, the beak of the host embryo developed into a shape similar to that found in quails, creating the "quck." Duck cells were recruited in addition to the quail cells to form part of the quck beak. Conversely, when duck neural crest cells were transplanted into quail embryos, the beak of the embryo resembled that of a duck, creating a "duail," and quail cells were recruited to form part of the beak. What do these experiments tell you about the autonomy or non-autonomy of the transplanted and host cells during beak development?

3. How is positional information provided along the anterior–posterior axis in *Drosophila*? What are the functions of *bicoid* and *nanos*?

4. Early development in *Drosophila* is atypical in that pattern formation takes place in a syncytial blastoderm, allowing free diffusion of transcription factors between nuclei. In many other animal species, the fertilized egg is divided by cellular cleavages into a larger and larger number of smaller and smaller cells.

   a. What constraints does this impose on the mechanisms of pattern formation?

   b. How must the model that describes *Drosophila* development be modified for describing other animal species whose early development is not syncytial?

5. Consider the *even-skipped* regulatory sequences in Figure 20.9.

   a. How are the sharp boundaries of expression of *eve* stripe 2 formed?

   b. Consider the binding sites for gap proteins and Bicoid in the stripe 2 enhancer module. What sites are occupied in parasegments 2, 3, and 4, and how does this result in expression or no expression?

   c. Explain what you expect to see happen to *even-skipped* stripe 2 if it is expressed in a *Krüppel* mutant background. A *hunchback* mutant background? A *giant* mutant background? A *bicoid* mutant background?

6. What is the difference between a parasegment and segment in *Drosophila* development? Why do developmental biologists think of parasegments as the subdivisions that are produced during development of flies?

7. Why do loss-of-function mutations in *Hox* genes usually result in embryo lethality, whereas gain-of-function mutants can be viable? Why are flies homozygous for the recessive loss-of-function alleles *Ultrabithorax*^*bithorax* and *Ultrabithorax*^*postbithorax* viable?

8. Compare and contrast the specification of segmental identity in *Drosophila* with that of floral organ specification in *Arabidopsis*. What is the same in this process, and what is different?

9. Actinomycin D is a drug that inhibits the activity of RNA polymerase II. In the presence of actinomycin D, early development in many vertebrate species, such as frogs, can proceed past the formation of a blastula, a hollow ball of cells that forms after early cleavage divisions; but development ceases before gastrulation. What does this tell you about maternal versus zygotic gene activity in early frog development?

10. Ablation of the anchor cell in wild-type *C. elegans* results in a vulva-less phenotype.

    a. What phenotype is to be expected if the anchor cell is ablated in a *let-23* loss-of-function mutant?

    b. What about if the anchor cell is ablated in a *let-23* gain-of-function mutant?

11. In gain-of-function *let-23* and *let-60 C. elegans* mutants, all of the vulval precursor cells differentiate with 1° or 2° fates.

Do you expect adjacent cells to differentiate with 1° fates or with 2° fates? Explain.

12. In mammals, identical twins arise when an embryo derived from a single fertilized egg splits into two independent embryos, producing two genetically identical individuals.

Application and Integration

13. *bicoid* is a coordinate, maternal effect gene.
    a. A female *Drosophila* heterozygous for a loss-of-function *bicoid* allele is mated to a male that is heterozygous for the same allele. What are the phenotypes of their progeny?
    b. A female that is homozygous for a loss-of-function *bicoid* allele is mated to a wild-type male. What are the phenotypes of their progeny?
    c. If loss of *bicoid* function in the egg leads to lethality during embryogenesis, how are females homozygous for *bicoid* produced? What is the phenotype of a male homozygous for *bicoid* loss-of-function alleles?

14. Given that maternal Bicoid activates the expression of *hunchback* (see Figure 20.7), what would be the consequence of adding extra copies of the *bicoid* gene by transgenic means, thus creating a female fly with two (the wild-type condition), three, or four copies of the *bicoid* gene? How would *hunchback* expression be altered? What about the expression of other gap genes and pair-rule genes?

15. What phenotypes do you expect in flies homozygous for loss-of-function mutations in the following genes: *Krüppel, odd-skipped, hedgehog, Ultrabithorax*?

16. The pair-rule gene *fushi tarazu* is expressed in the seven even-numbered parasegments during *Drosophila* embryogenesis. In contrast, the segment polarity gene *engrailed* is expressed in the anterior part of each of the 14 parasegments. Since both genes are active at similar times and places during development, it is possible that the expression of one gene is required for the expression of the other. This can be tested by examining expression of the genes in a mutant background—for example, looking at *fushi tarazu* expression in an *engrailed* mutant background, and vice versa.
    a. Given the hierarchy of gene action during *Drosophila* embryogenesis, what might you predict to be the result of these experiments?
    b. Based on your prediction, can you predict the phenotype of the *fushi tarazu* and *engrailed* double mutant?

17. In contrast to *Drosophila*, some insects (e.g., centipedes) have legs on almost every segment posterior to the head. Based on your knowledge of *Drosophila*, propose a genetic explanation for this phenotype, and describe the expected expression patterns of genes of the *Antennapedia* and *bithorax* complexes.

18. The bristles that develop from the epidermis in *Drosophila* are evenly spaced, so that two bristles never occur immediately adjacent to each other. How might this pattern be established during development?

a. What limits might there be, from a developmental genetic viewpoint, as to when this can occur?
b. The converse phenotype, fusion of two genetically distinct embryos into a single individual, is also known. What are the genetic implications of such an event?

For answers to selected even-numbered problems, see Appendix: Answers.

19. You are traveling in the Netherlands and overhear a tulip breeder describe a puzzling event. Tulips normally have two outer whorls of brightly colored petal-like organs, a third whorl of stamens, and an inner (fourth) whorl of carpels. However, the breeder found a recessive mutant in his field in which the outer two whorls were green and sepal-like, while the third and fourth whorls both contained carpels. What can you speculate about the nature of the gene that was mutated?

20. A powerful approach to identifying genes of a developmental pathway is to screen for mutations that suppress or enhance the phenotype of interest. This approach was undertaken to elucidate the genetic pathway controlling *C. elegans* vulval development.
    a. A *lin-3* loss-of-function mutant with a vulva-less phenotype was mutagenized. Based on your knowledge of the genetic pathway, what types of mutations will suppress the vulva-less phenotype?
    b. In a complementary experiment, a gain-of-function *let-23* mutant with a multi-vulva phenotype was also mutagenized. What types of mutations will suppress the multi-vulva phenotype?

21. *Zea mays* (maize, or corn) was originally domesticated in central Mexico at least 7000 years ago from an endemic grass called teosinte. Teosinte is generally unbranched, has male and female flowers on the same branch, and has few kernels per "cob," each encased in a hard, leaf-like organ called a glume. In contrast, maize is highly branched, with a male inflorescence (tassel) on its central branch and female inflorescences (cobs) on axillary branches. In addition, maize cobs have many rows of kernels and soft glumes. George Beadle crossed cultivated maize and wild teosinte, which resulted in fully fertile F_1 plants. When the F_1 plants were self-fertilized, about 1 plant in every 1000 of the F_2 progeny resembled either a modern maize plant or a wild teosinte plant. What did Beadle conclude about whether the different architectures of maize and teosinte were caused by changes with a small effect in many genes or changes with a large effect in just a few genes?

22. The *Hoxd9–13* genes are thought to specify digit identity (see Figure 20.18).
    a. What would be the consequence of ectopically expressing *Hoxd10* throughout the developing mouse limb bud? What about *Hoxd11*? What about both *Hoxd10* and *Hoxd11*?
    b. You wish to examine the effect of loss-of-function alleles in developing limbs. How would you construct a mouse in which the function of *Hoxd9–13* is retained during anterior–posterior embryonic patterning but is absent from developing limbs?

23. Three-spined stickleback fish live in lakes formed when the last ice age ended 10,000 to 15,000 years ago. In lakes where the sticklebacks are prey for larger fish, they develop 35 bony plates along their body as armor. In contrast, sticklebacks in lakes where there are no predators develop only a few or no bony plates.

    a. In crosses between fish of the two different morphologies, the lack of bony armor segregates as a recessive trait that maps to the *ectodermal dysplasin (Eda)* gene. Comparisons between the *Eda*-coding regions of the armored and non-armored fish revealed no differences. How can you explain this result?

    b. Loss-of-function mutations in the coding region of the homologous gene in humans result in loss of hair, teeth, and sweat glands, as in the toothless men of Sind (India). What does this suggest about hair, teeth, and sweat glands in humans?

24. In *C. elegans* there are two sexes: hermaphrodite and male. Sex is determined by the ratio of X chromosomes to haploid sets of autosomes (X/A). An X/A ratio of 1.0 produces a hermaphrodite (XX), and an X/A ratio of 0.5 results in a male (XO). In the 1970s, Jonathan Hodgkin and Sydney Brenner carried out genetic screens to identify mutations in three genes that result in either XX males (*tra-1*, *tra-2*) or XO hermaphrodites (*her-1*). Double-mutant strains were constructed to assess for epistatic interactions between the genes (see table). Propose a genetic model of how the *her* and *tra* genes control sex determination.

Genotype[a]	XX Phenotype	XO Phenotype
Wild-type	Hermaphrodite	Male
tra-1^{rec}	Male	Male
tra-2^{rec}	Male	Male
her-1^{rec}	Hermaphrodite	Hermaphrodite
tra-1^{dom}/+	Hermaphrodite	Hermaphrodite
tra-^{rec}1 tra-2^{rec}	Male	Male
tra-1^{rec} her-1^{rec}	Male	Male
tra-2^{rec} her-1^{rec}	Male	Male
tra-2^{rec}tra-1^{dom}/+	Hermaphrodite	Hermaphrodite

[a] *rec* = recessive mutation; *dom* = dominant mutation.

25. The flowering jungle plant *Lacandonia schismatica*, discovered in southern Mexico, has a unique floral structure. Petal-like organs are in the outer whorls surrounding a number of carpels, and stamens are in the center of the flower. Closely related species are dioecious; female plants bear flowers that resemble those of *Lacandonia*, but without the central stamens. What type of mutation could have resulted in the evolution of *Lacandonia* flowers?

26. Homeotic genes are thought to regulate each other.

    a. What aspect of the phenotype of *apetala2 agamous* double mutants indicates that these two genes act antagonistically?

    b. Are similar interactions observed between *Hox* genes? Compare the action of the floral homeotic genes in specifying floral organ identity and the *Hox* genes in specifying identity along the anterior–posterior axis of animals.

27. Dipterans (two-winged insects) are thought to have evolved from a four-winged ancestor that had wings on both T2 and T3 thoracic segments, as in extant butterflies and dragonflies. Describe an evolutionary scenario for the evolution of dipterans from four-winged ancestors. What types of mutations could lead to a butterfly developing with only two wings?

28. Basidiomycota is a monophyletic group of fungi that includes most of the common mushrooms. You are interested in the development of the body plan of mushrooms. How would you identify the genes required for patterning during mushroom development?

29. In *Drosophila*, recessive mutations in the *fruitless* gene (*fru*) result in males courting other males; and recessive mutations in the *Antennapedia* gene (*Ant$^-$*) lead to defects in the body plan, specifically in the thoracic region of the body, where mutants fail to develop legs. The two genes map 15 cM apart on chromosome 3. You have isolated a new dominant *Ant^d* mutant allele that you induced by treating your flies with X-rays. Your new mutant has legs developing instead of antennae on the head of the fly. You cross your newly induced dominant *Ant^d* mutant (a pure-breeding line) with a homozygous recessive *fru* mutant (which is homozygous wild type at the *Ant$^+$* locus), as diagrammed below:

$$\frac{Ant^d fru^+}{Ant^d fru^+} \times \frac{Ant^+ fru}{Ant^+ fru} \rightarrow F_1 \frac{Ant^d fru^+}{Ant^+ fru}$$

    a. What phenotypes, and in what proportions, do you expect in the F_2 obtained by interbreeding F_1 animals?

    b. Your cross results in the following phenotypic proportions:

Legs on head, normal courting behavior	75
Normal head, abnormal courting behavior	25
Legs on head, abnormal courting behavior	0
Normal head, normal courting behavior	0

    Provide a genetic explanation for these results and describe a test for your hypothesis.

    c. Provide a molecular explanation for the reason your new *Ant^d* mutant is dominant and for its novel phenotype.

Genetic Analysis of Quantitative Traits

21

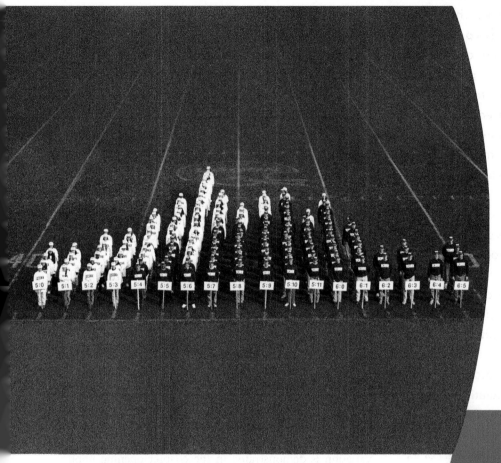

A human histogram depicting the distribution of heights among faculty and students of the University of Connecticut. The women are in white shirts and the men are in blue shirts.

CHAPTER OUTLINE

- 21.1 Quantitative Traits Display Continuous Phenotype Variation
- 21.2 Quantitative Trait Analysis Is Statistical
- 21.3 Heritability Measures the Genetic Component of Phenotypic Variation
- 21.4 Quantitative Trait Loci Are the Genes That Contribute to Quantitative Traits

ESSENTIAL IDEAS

- Quantitative traits are influenced by multiple genes and may also be influenced by the environment. They are continuously distributed along a phenotypic scale. Some quantitative traits are separated into distinct phenotypes by a threshold.

- The phenotypic distributions of quantitative traits are described by statistical measures that also estimate the genetic and environmental contributions to phenotype.

- The extent to which genetic variation contributes to phenotype variability can be estimated for quantitative traits and provides an indication of how traits may respond to artificial selection.

- The genes that influence quantitative traits are identified and mapped using genetic crosses and molecular and statistical techniques.

Explaining the connection between phenotypes and genotypes is simplest when the phenotypic variation in a trait is determined by variation in a single gene. The segregation of alleles of a single gene determining whether peas are round or wrinkled, as in Mendel's studies, is a classic example. Other genes are not involved, and there is no evidence of gene interaction (i.e., epistasis) or of interaction between the gene and specific environmental factors. Similarly, your blood type—either A, B, AB, or O—is determined exclusively by inherited variation in a single gene, and the environment in which you were raised had no effect on that outcome.

In reality, however, such direct correlations between phenotypes and genotypes are not common. Many traits display variation resulting from epistatic gene interactions (see Section 4.3). In addition, numerous traits, known as **polygenic traits,** result from the influence of multiple genes. The contributing genes generally, assort independently to produce a large number of genotypes and multiple phenotypes. The inheritance of polygenic traits is identified as **polygenic inheritance.** Further complicating the correlations between genotypes and phenotypes is the finding that the phenotypes of many traits whose inheritance is polygenic are influenced by environmental factors. Thus both genetic variation and environmental variation contribute to the phenotypic variation of certain traits, which are therefore referred to as **multifactorial traits.**

A key indication of the influence of multiple genes and of environmental factors on certain phenotypes is the assessment of variation for those traits in *quantitative* rather than *qualitative* terms. "Round seeds" versus "wrinkled seeds" or "blood type A" versus "blood type B" are examples of qualitative phenotypic differences. Qualitative phenotypes fall into discrete categories that correspond to particular genotypes and that are often distinctly different from one another. In contrast, quantitative phenotypic variation usually takes the form of continuous variation along a phenotypic scale, and the traits are frequently described using units of measure. For example, one might use kilograms to measure quantitative variation in the weight of cattle or centimeters to measure quantitative variation in the length of ears of corn. Traits of this kind are called **quantitative traits.** This term also applies to traits that vary over a phenotypic range that is non-numeric. Thus, while many measured in values such as grams or centimeters but are instead described using non-numeric terms, as with a range of color phenotypes (e.g., from black through shades of gray to white).

The genetic study and analysis of quantitative traits is the focus of the field of inquiry known as **quantitative genetics.** In this chapter, we explore how quantitative genetics examines the hereditary variation of polygenic and multifactorial traits. In the process, we address some of the ways geneticists attempt to disentangle the genetic and environmental influences on trait variation and describe genetic approaches to interpreting the relative effects of those factors on quantitative trait phenotypes.

21.1 Quantitative Traits Display Continuous Phenotype Variation

For most of the traits we discuss in earlier chapters, phenotypic variation is controlled by allelic variation at single genes. The phenotypes of these single-gene traits commonly display **discontinuous variation,** meaning differences that allow organisms to be assigned to discrete, sharply distinguishable phenotypic categories. The discontinuous patterns of variation lead to the specification of consistent phenotype ratios, such as a 3:1 ratio among the F_2 progeny of self-fertilized F_1 organisms. Even when two genes take part in epistatic interactions that affect phenotypic expression, the phenotypes are discrete and occur in predictable ratios (see Section 4.3).

In contrast, polygenic and multifactorial traits usually display **continuous variation,** which is phenotypic variation distributed across a range of values in an uninterrupted continuum. This section explores the genetic factors contributing to traits displaying continuous variation.

Genetic Potential

Human adult height is an example of a multifactorial trait that varies continuously along a scale of measurement usually marked off in centimeters or inches. This continuous variation is demonstrated in the chapter-opening photo, in which some 138 University of Connecticut students and faculty are arranged according to height. The height distribution of this sample, divided into 1-inch increments, ranges from 60 inches (5 feet) to 77 inches (6 feet 5 inches). The length of each line of individuals behind the height markers represents the frequency of each incremental category, and the sweatshirt and hat color identifies the wearer's sex (white for women and blue for men). Examining the overall distribution, you can see that it is actually composed of two different distributions, one for each sex, and you can also see that the distribution is uneven.

Adult height is influenced by multiple genes. For example, a 2011 study by Matthew Lanktree and many colleagues used the analysis of human genomic variation and statistical methods to suggest that more than 60 genes may influence adult height. While the actual number of genes influencing human height continues to be investigated, your own personal experiences, as well as population studies, most likely tell you that taller parents tend to have taller children and shorter parents tend to have shorter children.

In addition to this genetic influence, however, environmental and developmental factors can have a significant effect. If your genetics class is typical of most, a survey of your classmates would likely find that many of the men are taller than their fathers and grandfathers and that many of the women are taller than their mothers and grandmothers. These differences are due almost exclusively to improved prenatal and childhood health and nutrition and only minimally to changes in the population genetic makeup influencing adult height. Longitudinal studies confirm that much of the world's population is getting taller. During the 20th century, the height of the average American woman increased from approximately 5'2" in 1900 to almost 5'5" in 2000. An even more dramatic increase in average adult height can be observed by walking through the doors of houses and other structures built a few centuries ago. Most modern-day visitors have to stoop to enter! Such observations lead to the clear conclusion that adult height is a multifactorial trait.

To understand the role of genetics in a trait like adult height, you might think of parents as transmitting to their children a "genetic potential" for reaching a certain maximum adult height; the genetic potential will be attained if the child grows and develops under ideal conditions. Not all of the children of a particular pair of parents will have the same genetic potential, since segregation and independent assortment of the contributing genes can produce many different genotypes. These processes produce offspring with different genotypes conveying genetic potential for a range of heights, including heights that are greater or lesser than those of their parents. On average, however, progeny genetic potential for height will be at approximately the midpoint of the two parents' genetic potential. The phenotypic outcome (actual adult height) is subject to various influences on the height potential conveyed by the genotype, including prenatal and maternal health and childhood health and nutrition, as the following discussion illustrates.

Major Genes and Additive Gene Effects

The continuous phenotypic variation of polygenic traits results from the effects of multiple genes that may exert different amounts of influence. For example, the human *OCA2* gene has several alleles that strongly influence eye color. The color of the adult eye is further influenced by other genes that act less strongly than *OCA2*. A gene like *OCA2* is classified as a **major gene,** since it has a strong effect on the phenotype. Genes that have minor effects on the phenotype are classified as **modifier genes.**

On the other hand, if the continuous phenotypic distribution results from incremental contributions by multiple genes, then the genes contributing to phenotypic variation in this way are known as **additive genes.** Each allele of additive genes can be assigned a quantitative value that indicates its contribution to a polygenic trait

known as an **additive trait.** In the absence of environmental influence, phenotypes can be predicted by adding the values of the alleles together. For certain traits, each of the additive genes has an approximately equal effect, while for other traits the influence of each gene is distinct.

Grasping the notion of additive genes requires a different way of thinking about genotypes and phenotypes than we have discussed previously. Since traits controlled by additive genes have a phenotype that is the sum of allelic contributions across multiple genes, it is possible for more than one genotype to correspond to certain phenotypes. Segregation and independent assortment of additive alleles produces the various genotypes, but the phenotype corresponding to each is based on the sum of the values of the alleles at all the contributing loci.

In the early 1900s, coinciding with the verification and expansion of the then recently rediscovered hereditary principles of Mendel, geneticists began to explore the hypothesis that the segregation of alleles of multiple genes played a role in phenotypic variation of particular traits. Known as the **multiple-gene hypothesis,** the proposal was that alleles at each of the contributing genes obeyed the principles of segregation and independent assortment and had an additive effect in the production of phenotypic variation.

The multiple-gene hypothesis was the foundation of quantitative genetics, and the plant geneticist Hermann Nilsson-Ehle was one of the first to use the hypothesis in his 1909 description of genetic control of kernel color in wheat. **Figure 21.1** illustrates one of Nilsson-Ehle's genetic models, describing the determination of wheat kernel color by additive alleles of two genes. In this model, only genetic effects on phenotype are being considered. The model predicts that kernel color spans a spectrum from dark red to white. Gene *A* and gene *B* each have two alleles. Alleles A_1 and B_1 are equivalent to one another, each adding an equal unit of color to the phenotype. Alleles A_2 and B_2 are also equivalent, neither adding any units of color to the phenotype. Under the additive genetic model, the more "number 1" alleles, either A_1 or B_1, the genotype contains, the darker the color of wheat kernels. Conversely, the fewer number 1 alleles (or the more "number 2" alleles) there are in the genotype, the lighter the kernel color. The deepest red color (dark red) is present when four number 1 alleles are present ($A_1A_1B_1B_1$). Conversely, white kernels are produced when no copies of number 1 alleles are in the genotype ($A_2A_2B_2B_2$).

Figure 21.1 shows a cross between pure-breeding dark red and pure-breeding white plants. The cross produces F_1 plants that are dihybrid ($A_1A_2B_1B_2$) and have dark pink kernel color as a consequence of carrying just two number 1 alleles. Crossing the F_1 plants produces an F_2 generation with five different kernel colors, each dependent on the total number of number 1 alleles in the genotype. For these two loci, genotypes can have a maximum of four number 1 alleles and a minimum of

P

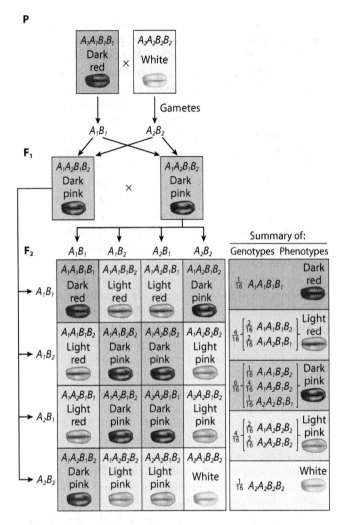

Figure 21.1 **Polygenic inheritance of wheat kernel color controlled by two additive genes.** Each 1 allele (either A_1 or B_1) adds a unit of color, but 2 alleles (A_2 or B_2) add no units of color. Pure-breeding parents (one dark red, one white) produce dihybrid F_1 with dark pink kernel color. Five phenotype classes are predicted among F_2 progeny in a ratio determined by the total number of A_1 plus B_1 alleles in the genotype.

zero number 1 alleles. The five different totals of number 1 alleles produce the five different phenotypes in the F_2 generation, in proportions determined by independent assortment. Among the F_2, 1/16 carry four number 1 alleles and produce dark red kernels like the parental plant, 4/16 carry three number 1 alleles and have light red kernels, 6/16 have two number 1 alleles and have dark pink kernels, 4/16 carry a single number 1 allele and have light pink kernels, and the final 1/16 have no number 1 alleles and have white kernels like the parental plant.

As the number of additive genes contributing to a phenotypic trait increases, the number of phenotype categories increases as well. **Figure 21.2** illustrates an additive genetic model in which wheat kernel color is determined by three genes. In this example, genes A, B, and C each have two alleles whose additive effect is computed in the same way as for the two-gene system

of Figure 21.1: Phenotype categories are determined by the number of "1" alleles contained in a genotype. A cross of pure-breeding dark red and pure-breeding white parental plants produces an F_1 of an intermediate (dark pink) color as a result of its trihybrid genotype ($A_1A_2B_1B_2C_1C_2$). Independent assortment produces an F_2 that falls into seven phenotypic categories that are determined by genotypes that have a maximum of six 1 alleles and a minimum of zero 1 alleles.

Continuous Phenotypic Variation from Multiple Additive Genes

The more phenotypes that occur along a limited scale of measurement, the narrower is the slice of the distribution each category occupies and the less obvious the demarcation between categories may become. **Figure 21.3** shows five histograms illustrating the distribution of F_2 phenotypes produced by different numbers of additive genes that each have two alleles. As in the preceding examples, each number 1 allele adds a unit of color to the phenotype, but number 2 alleles do not. The proportions for each phenotype can be determined using probability, or one can use Pascal's triangle to determine each expected proportion (see Figure 2.15). Notice the increase in the number of phenotype classes as the number of genes contributing to the phenotype increases from one to five. Moreover, the adjacent phenotype classes resemble one another more closely as the number of classes increases, blending into a continuous phenotypic distribution.

The number of distinct phenotype categories for a polygenic trait produced by the segregation of additive alleles of a given number of genes (n) is calculated as $2n + 1$. For example, for three additive genes contributing to a polygenic trait, $n = 3$, and the number of distinct phenotypic categories is $2(3) + 1 = 7$. **Table 21.1** lists the numbers of phenotypic categories for different numbers of contributing genes and gives the frequency of the most extreme phenotypes in each distribution. If more than two alleles occur for the contributing genes, the number of phenotypes can increase.

Allele Segregation in Quantitative Trait Production

In 1916, plant geneticist Edward East undertook a comprehensive examination of the multiple-gene hypothesis by testing its ability to explain patterns of inherited variation that he produced in the length of the corolla (the petal-producing part of the flower) in *Nicotiana longiflora*. In this long-flower species of tobacco, the corolla is a tube-shaped structure whose length can be measured and compared with corollas in other plants.

East began his experiments with pure-breeding parental lines, one having a short corolla approximately 40 millimeters long and the other producing a long corolla

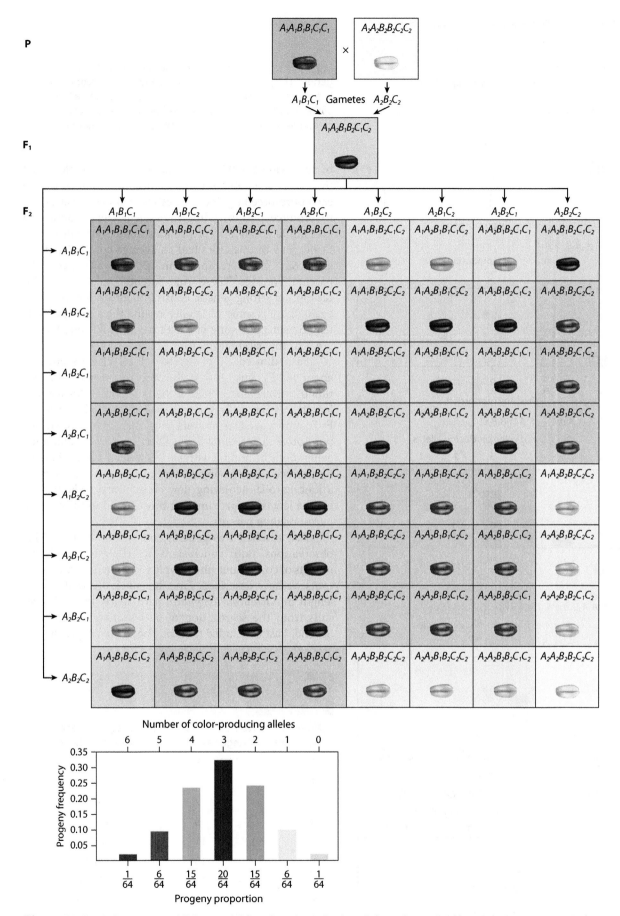

Figure 21.2 A three-gene additive model for wheat kernel color. Color is determined by total number of 1 alleles (A_1, B_1, and C_1) in the genotype. The F_2 have seven phenotypic classes in proportions generated by independent assortment at three loci.

(a) One locus: $A_1A_2 \times A_1A_2$

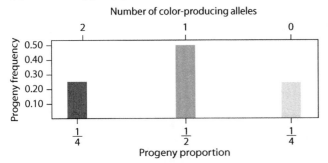

(b) Two loci: $A_1A_2B_1B_2 \times A_1A_2B_1B_2$

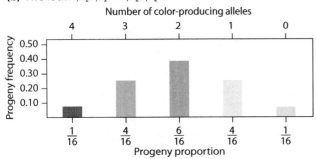

(c) Three loci: $A_1A_2B_1B_2C_1C_2 \times A_1A_2B_1B_2C_1C_2$

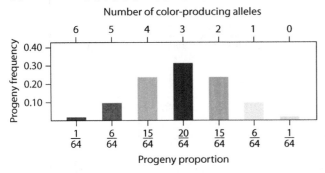

(d) Four loci: $A_1A_2B_1B_2C_1C_2D_1D_2 \times A_1A_2B_1B_2C_1C_2D_1D_2$

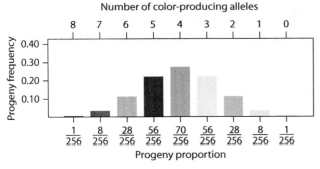

(e) Five loci: $A_1A_2B_1B_2C_1C_2D_1D_2E_1E_2 \times A_1A_2B_1B_2C_1C_2D_1D_2E_1E_2$

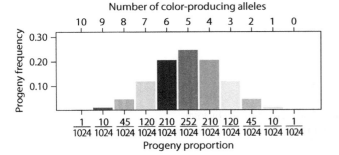

Figure 21.3 **Phenotype distributions with additive genes.** The parents producing progeny in each example are heterozygous for each gene. The color-contributing alleles are designated as 1 for each gene. The number of F_2 phenotype categories increases with the number of additive genes.

of approximately 90 millimeters (**Figure 21.4**). Note that there is a small amount of variation in corolla length in each pure-breeding line, suggesting that despite attempts to produce pure-breeding lines, gene–gene interaction or multifactorial effects produce some variability. The F_1 progeny of this cross had an average corolla length of about 65 millimeters, approximately midway between the parental averages. These "mid-parental" values are an indication of strong genetic control of corolla length. Once again, there is some variability around the average corolla length value, but none of the F_1 have corolla lengths that are near the parental values.

East allowed F_1 plants to self-fertilize to produce about 450 F_2, among which he observed a wider distribution of corolla length than in the F_1, although the average length was about the same as that of the F_1. None of the F_2 East produced had corolla lengths equal to those of the pure-breeding parental lines. Then, over three additional generations beginning with F_2, East selectively bred plants to produce a line having a short corolla and a line having a long corolla, achieving new collections of plants with corolla lengths approximating those found in the original pure-breeding parents.

East reached two general conclusions based on his observations. Both conclusions are consistent with the models of continuous phenotypic variation of quantitative traits we have described. First, he concluded that corolla length in *Nicotiana longiflora*, particularly in the F_2, results from the segregation of alleles of multiple genes. Second, East concluded that the phenotypic expression of

Table 21.1	The Effect of Polygenes on Phenotypic Variation	
Number of Genes (n)	**Number of Phenotype Categories**	**Frequency of Most Extreme Phenotypes**
1	3	1/4
2	5	1/16
3	7	1/64
4	9	1/256
5	11	1/1024
6	13	1/4096
7	15	1/16,384
8	17	1/65,536
9	19	1/262,144
10	21	1/1,048,576

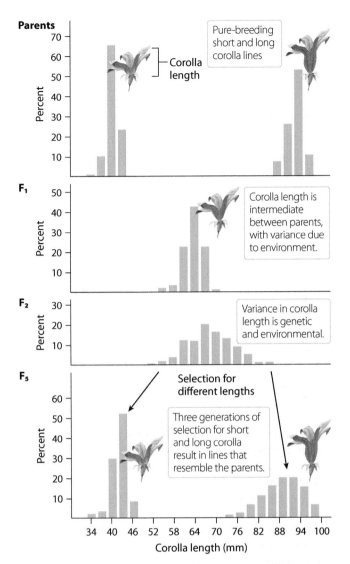

Figure 21.4   Corolla length in tobacco. Edward East determined that alleles of multiple genes control genetic variance in corolla length of tobacco (*Nicotiana longiflora*).

contributing to these diseases is the ultimate goal of research, but it must be approached in small, incremental steps that include modeling of the interactions of hereditary and nonhereditary factors.

Figure 21.5 shows a general approach taken by models of this kind. It displays the phenotypic ranges that would be associated with the genotypes A_1A_1, A_1A_2, and A_2A_2 under different assumptions of gene–environment interaction. In Figure 21.5a, no gene–environment interaction takes place, and each genotype corresponds to a distinct phenotype. Predictable correspondence of genotype and phenotype is seen in the F_2, where phenotypic distribution is discontinuous and a 1:2:1 phenotype ratio is found. Figure 21.5b shows the phenotypic ranges of parents and F_1 and F_2 progeny when moderate interaction occurs between the genotype and environmental factors. In each generation, a range of phenotypic values is associated with each genotype, and in the F_2, there is a small degree of overlap between the phenotypic ranges of different genotypes. In Figure 21.5c, substantial interaction between genes and environment takes place. A wide range of phenotypic values is associated with each genotype, and in the F_2 a significant degree of phenotypic overlap between the genotypes is seen, so that a large proportion of heterozygotes have phenotypes that overlap those of a homozygote. Gene–environment interaction of this kind is typical of multifactorial traits and can make it difficult to determine the genotype of an organism simply by looking at its phenotype. In a later chapter section, we refer to the influence of environmental factors on genotype using the term *environmental variance*. In that section, we describe a quantitative approach to determining how much of the variance in phenotype is due to environmental factors.

The use of a "phenotype scorecard" to predict the outcome of polygenic inheritance and of gene–environment interaction in determining the multifactorial trait of height in a hypothetical plant is illustrated in **Experimental Insight 21.1**.

Threshold Traits

Most polygenic and multifactorial traits exhibit a continuous phenotypic distribution, but certain of these traits, while having an underlying continuous distribution, can nevertheless be divided into distinct categories. Such traits are often called **threshold traits,** and a number of them are identified by threshold traits are often encountered in medical contexts, where attempts are made, not always successfully, to identify two clinical categories—"unaffected" (or "normal") and "affected" (or "abnormal")—and thus to distinguish individuals who have an abnormality from those that do not. For human threshold traits, the vast majority of the population will have phenotypes on the unaffected side of the threshold and will display the normal phenotype. A small proportion of the population, however, are found on the other side of the threshold and have an affected or abnormal phenotype. Cases that lie at the

each genotype is influenced by nongenetic factors, that is, genes interacting with environmental factors to blur the direct correspondence between a given genotype and a specific phenotype. The nongenetic factors partially explain the variation around average corolla length. **Genetic Analysis 21.1** guides you through your own analysis of polygenic contributions to plant height.

Effects of Environmental Factors on Phenotypic Variation

Disentangling the genetic and nongenetic factors that determine phenotypic variation is a difficult but important task in genetics. In humans, for example, common diseases such as heart disease, cancer, and diabetes are influenced by heredity, but nonhereditary factors are also critically important in disease development. Identifying the particular genes and the specific nonhereditary factors

Figure 21.5 **The effect of gene–environment interaction.** The phenotype determined by a single gene with codominant alleles can be modified by the action of environmental factors.

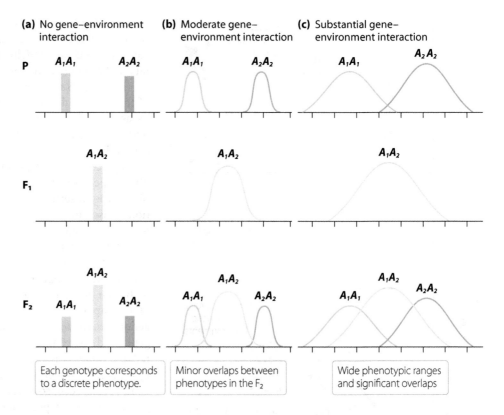

(a) No gene–environment interaction

(b) Moderate gene–environment interaction

(c) Substantial gene–environment interaction

Each genotype corresponds to a discrete phenotype.

Minor overlaps between phenotypes in the F₂

Wide phenotypic ranges and significant overlaps

borderline between the two categories can be problematic to diagnose.

The genetic hypothesis explaining threshold traits proposes that the trait is polygenic or multifactorial, so that underlying the affected and unaffected phenotype categories is a continuous distribution of **genetic liability**—a term for the organism's risk of having the affected phenotype as the result of inheriting a particular genotype. Each member of a population has a specific genotype, and different genotypes may confer a different genetic liability, making some individuals more likely to display an affected phenotype by crossing the threshold. **Figure 21.6** shows a continuous distribution of genetic liability for a population and the designation of a threshold that separates unaffected from affected individuals in the population. The portion of the population lying to the left

of the **threshold of genetic liability,** by far the majority, are identified as unaffected or normal, and the small group to the right of the threshold are considered affected or abnormal.

Models are used to test the applicability of these concepts to real-world observations at the population level. In these models, the likelihood of crossing the threshold of liability increases when more "liability alleles" are present in the genotype, that is, when the genotype confers greater genetic liability. For example, **Figure 21.7a** depicts a hypothetical three-gene model in which alleles are designated as either 1 or 2 at each locus and in which genetic liability increases with a greater number of 1 alleles. In this model, the threshold of liability is passed when at least five 1 alleles are present. A greater number of 1 alleles in parental genotypes increases the proportion of progeny that will lie to the right of the threshold of liability and thus display an affected phenotype. The model can compare the risks of having a child affected by a threshold trait for parents carrying different numbers of liability alleles.

Figure 21.7a illustrates Cross 1 between a parent with two 1 alleles and a parent with three 1 alleles. Both parents have the unaffected (normal) phenotype, and each is on the unaffected side of the threshold. Among the progeny of this cross, 1/32 (3%) are expected to carry five 1 alleles, but none can carry six 1 alleles. Thus, 1/32 of the progeny lie to the right of the threshold of liability and have the affected phenotype. **Figure 21.7b** shows Cross 2 with different parents that produce a higher level of genetic liability in their progeny. In this cross, each parent carries three liability alleles, but neither is affected because the liability threshold is 5 or more liability alleles. Among their

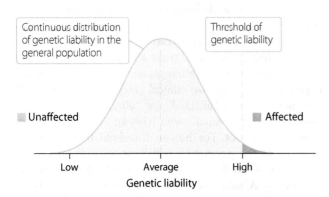

Continuous distribution of genetic liability in the general population

Threshold of genetic liability

Unaffected

Affected

Low   Average   High

Genetic liability

Figure 21.6 **Threshold traits.** A theoretical continuous phenotypic distribution and a threshold of genetic liability for a threshold trait.

(a) Cross 1: $A_1A_2B_1B_2C_2C_2$ × $A_1A_2B_1B_2C_1C_2$
(Two liability alleles)   (Three liability alleles)

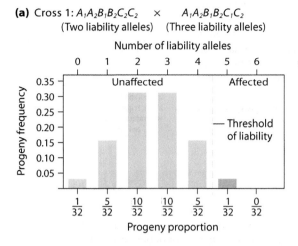

(b) Cross 2: $A_1A_2B_1B_2C_1C_2$ × $A_1A_2B_1B_2C_1C_2$
(Three liability alleles)   (Three liability alleles)

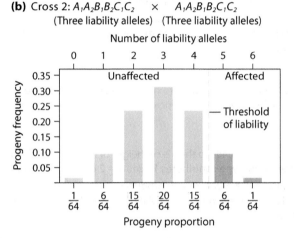

Figure 21.7   A polygenic model for a threshold trait. Any allele designated as 1 confers genetic liability, any allele designated as 2 confers no liability, and the 1 alleles are additive. **(a)** In Cross 1, the couple has a 1/32 chance of producing an affected child. **(b)** In Cross 2, the couple has a 7/64 chance of producing an affected child.

progeny, however, independent assortment predicts that 7/64 (11%) will have genotypes that contain five or more 1 alleles. These progeny lie to the right of the threshold of liability and have the affected phenotype. The genotypes in the second cross confer almost a fourfold increased risk (3% versus 11%) of producing an affected offspring compared to the first cross. This difference is analogous to the difference we might see between different families in a population. Overall, a mating in the general population has a low risk of producing a child with a threshold trait. Different families may have different risks, however, and a mating of parents that both come from families with a history of the trait will be most likely to produce children who also have the trait.

The influence of environmental and developmental factors on phenotypes of threshold traits is an important additional component. These factors can play a role in determining whether individuals whose genetic liability places them near the threshold of liability end up having the trait. The threshold model envisions organisms possessing high genetic liability (i.e., possessing a genome with many liability alleles) as having the *potential* to develop the affected phenotype. Whether the affected phenotype develops may be due to the influence of other hereditary, developmental, or environmental factors. Less often, an organism may have a genetic liability slightly below the threshold but the influence of environmental factors could push the phenotype into the affected category.

Certain threshold traits are more likely to occur in one sex than the other. Dislocated hips at birth is about four times more common in girls than in boys, for example. Thus, sex, and the developmental and hormone-based differences that distinguish the sexes, can influence whether a certain genotype produces an affected or an unaffected phenotype. This has important clinical implications. If a couple has previously had a child with dislocated hips, a physician will want to carefully examine all future children, especially if they are female, for hip dislocation.

Lastly, there is a caveat to consider with regard to defining the categories and classification of threshold traits, particularly in humans. Because these traits are quantitative and fall along a continuum, precise determination of categories and phenotypes can be inexact. For example, it is easy to classify a person's blood pressure as normal if it lies well within the normal range or as abnormal if the blood pressure is very high. Many people, however, have "borderline" high pressures that are difficult to assign to either the normal or high blood pressure category.

21.2 Quantitative Trait Analysis Is Statistical

The statistical methods most often applied today to the study of quantitative traits are a direct extension of contributions made nearly a century ago by statistician and evolutionary biologist Sir Ronald Fisher. In 1918, Fisher used statistical analysis to show that quantitative traits result from the segregation of alleles of multiple genes displaying an additive effect. Fisher also showed that interactions between genes can be detected by these methods. In addition, he explored the role of gene–environment interaction and concluded that environmental factors contribute to continuous variation by blurring the lines between phenotypic classes. The tools and approaches described here and pioneered by Fisher allow scientists to identify genetic influences on phenotypes in terms of quantitative measurement rather than qualitative appearance. In the following description and illustrations of quantitative trait analysis, we explore some concepts in statistics described in connection with chi-square analysis (see Section 2.5).

Statistical Description of Phenotypic Variation

The first step in quantifying the phenotypic variation of a trait in a population is to construct a **frequency distribution** of values of the trait on a quantitative scale.

PROBLEM Dr. Ara B. Dopsis, a famous plant geneticist, develops several pure-breeding lines of daffodils. Under ideal growth conditions, line A plants are the tallest and grow to a height of 48 centimeters, whereas line B plants are the shortest and grow to 12 centimeters. Dr. Dopsis devises a genetic model with three additive genes that contribute equally to explain polygenic inheritance of plant height. He assumes that line A has the genotype $A_1A_1B_1B_1C_1C_1$ and that line B has the genotype $A_2A_2B_2B_2C_2C_2$. In answering the following questions, assume that genotype alone determines plant height under ideal growth conditions.

> **BREAK IT DOWN:** Three additive genes have a total of six alleles that make approximately equal contributions to continuous variation in plant height (p. 715).

> **BREAK IT DOWN:** Pure-breeding plants in line A and line B are homozygous for 1 and 2 alleles, respectively. Seven progeny categories will produce continuous variation in height (p. 717 and Figure 21.3).

a. If these two pure-breeding parental plants are crossed, what will be the genotype and height of the F_1 progeny plants?

b. If F_2 are produced, what is the expected frequency of plants with different heights?

Solution Strategies	Solution Steps
Evaluate	
1. Identify the topic this problem addresses and the nature of the requested answer.	1. This problem concerns assessment of a three-gene additive model for plant height, application of the model to crosses of pure-breeding parental plants of different heights, and evaluation of the F_1 and F_2 progeny.
2. Identify the critical information given in the problem.	2. The genotypes of the pure-breeding parents are given. In applying the polygenic additive model, we are to assume that genotype alone determines variation in plant height.
Deduce	
3. Deduce the contribution of each allele of the additive genes to height in line A. TIP: Assume that each allele makes an equal contribution in this additive genetic model.	3. The 48-cm height of line A plants is determined by six alleles of additive genes. Each "1" allele in the line A genotype contributes 48 cm/6 = 8 cm to plant height.
4. Deduce the contribution of each allele of the additive genes to height in line B.	4. Six alleles also contribute equally to the 12-cm height of line B plants. Each "2" allele in the line B genotype contributes 12 cm/6 = 2 cm to plant height.
5. Deduce the gametes produced by each pure-breeding line. TIP: The laws of segregation and independent assortment apply to genes controlling polygenic traits.	5. Line 1 has the genotype $A_1A_1B_1B_1C_1C_1$ and produces gametes with the genotype $A_1B_1C_1$. Line 2 has the genotype $A_2A_2B_2B_2C_2C_2$ and produces the gamete genotype $A_2B_2C_2$.
Solve	Answer a
6. Determine the genotype and height of F_1 plants.	6. F_1 progeny of these pure-breeding parental plants will have the genotype $A_1A_2B_1B_2C_1C_2$. Based on the contribution of each 1 and 2 allele, the predicted F_1 plant height is [(3)(8 cm)] + [(3)(2 cm)] = 30 cm.
	Answer b
7. Determine the frequency and height of each category of F_2 plants. TIP: Either use Pascal's triangle (Figure 2.15) or determine the probability of genotypes containing different numbers of 1 and 2 alleles. PITFALL: Remember that for most categories there are multiple genotypes with the same total number of 1 and 2 alleles.	7. The expected F_2 progeny are

Number of Alleles		Frequency	Height (cm)
1	2		
0	6	1/64	12
1	5	6/64	18
2	4	15/64	24
3	3	20/64	30
4	2	15/64	36
5	1	6/64	42
6	0	1/64	48

For more practice, see Problems 8, 9, and 20.
Visit the Study Area to access study tools.

MasteringGenetics™

Experimental Insight 21.1

Phenotype Scorecard: A Multifactorial Quantitative Phenotype Simulation

Here's a hands-on activity that illustrates an approach to modeling a multifactorial quantitative trait. In this hypothetical example, the mature height of a plant is under the control of five additive genes designated A to E. Two alleles at each gene make different contributions to height. Each allele with the subscript 1 adds 5 centimeters to the genetic potential, and each allele with the subscript 2 adds 10 centimeters. Therefore, a plant homozygous for 1 alleles at each locus $(A_1A_1B_1C_1C_1D_1E_1E_1)$ has genetic potential for a height of $[(10 \text{ alleles})(5 \text{ cm/allele})] = 50$ cm, as compared to a plant carrying a genotype composed entirely of 2 alleles, which has a height potential of $[(10 \text{ alleles})(10 \text{ cm/allele})] = 100$ cm. Plants carrying genotypes with different numbers of 1 and 2 alleles have different genetic potentials for heights distributed at 5-cm intervals along a continuum between 50 and 100 cm.

At this point, let's ask the following question: "How many 1 and 2 alleles must be present to give a height potential of 80 cm?" Each genotype contains a total of 10 alleles, two at each of the five loci. Therefore, any genotype with six 2 alleles and four 1 alleles will produce a height potential of $[(6)(10) + (4)(5)] = 80$ cm.

Here's a follow-up question: "What proportion of the progeny of two plants, each with a height potential of 75 cm, will have a height potential of 80 cm?" This problem is more complex. Plants with a height potential of 75 cm have five 2 alleles and five 1 alleles $[(5)(10) + (5)(5) = 75]$. Progeny genotypes that contain six 2 alleles and four 1 alleles will have a height potential of 80 cm. We can use the histogram in Figure 21.3e to predict the answer: 210 of the 1024 progeny (20.5%) have six copies of 2 alleles and four copies of 1 alleles.

Having examined the relationship between genotype and potential height in this model, let's examine the effect of five environmental factors on the attainment of height:

1. Amount of water
2. Amount of sunlight
3. Soil drainage
4. Nutrient content of soil
5. Temperature

Each environmental factor can vary from optimal to poor. If all factors are optimal, we'll assume that full potential height is attained. However, if one or more of the environmental factors is less than optimal, then height is reduced. The state of each environmental factor has an effect on growth. In this exercise, we'll assume that the growth is affected according to the following scale:

Environmental Factor State	Height Lost
Optimal (O)	0 cm lost
Good (G)	4 cm lost
Fair (F)	8 cm lost
Marginal (M)	12 cm lost
Poor (P)	16 cm lost

If, for example, one environmental factor is optimal, two are good, one is fair, and one is marginal, the loss of potential height is 28 cm.

The following table illustrates how the same genotype can produce different phenotypes under differing environmental conditions and how different genotypes can produce similar phenotypes under different conditions. Notice that the first two genotypes are identical but result in different phenotypes because of environmental differences. Also note that the third genotype has lower height potential than the other genotype but, in combination with a superior environment, results in the tallest plant. You can try your own combinations of genotypes and growth conditions to see different results.

Genotype	Height Potential	Environmental Factor States					Height Attained
		1	2	3	4	5	
$A_1A_2B_1B_2C_2C_2D_1D_2E_1E_2$	80 cm	G	F	O	G	M	52 cm
$A_1A_2B_1B_2C_2C_2D_1D_2E_1E_2$	80 cm	F	M	G	G	F	44 cm
$A_1A_1B_1B_2C_1C_2D_1D_2E_1E_2$	70 cm	O	G	G	G	G	54 cm

A frequency distribution shows what proportion of the population exhibits each measured value of the trait or falls into each category defined for the trait. Figure 21.8a provides an example, showing the number and frequency of each designated height category in a sample of 1000 college-aged males.

The individuals in this study are considered a random sample. They have not been selected for any attribute related to their height, and so their height distribution is assumed to resemble that of the general population of college-aged males. Random samples are used in quantitative trait analysis for two reasons. First, it is often impossible or impractical to collect data on every individual in a population; and second, random samples can be just as accurate in the statistical sense as "samples" consisting of whole populations. As an analogy, about 10 milliliters of blood—approximately two-tenths of 1% of a person's total blood volume—is usually drawn for most routine blood tests. The amount taken is not large enough to cause physiological problems, but it is representative enough to provide dependable information concerning a person's health status.

After the frequency distribution is constructed, the first piece of information obtained from it is the average, or mean, value ($\bar{x}$) for the distribution. Recall that this is calculated by summing all the values in the sample and dividing by the total number of individuals in the sample (n; see Section 2.5). Using the actual height of each of the

(a) Number and frequency of heights in 3-cm intervals

Height (cm)	Number	Frequency (%)
155–157	4	0.4
158–160	8	0.8
161–163	26	2.6
164–166	53	5.3
167–169	89	8.9
170–172	146	14.6
173–175	188	18.8
176–178	181	18.1
179–181	125	12.5
182–184	92	9.2
185–187	60	6.0
188–190	22	2.2
191–193	4	0.4
194–196	1	0.1
197–199	1	0.1
	1000	100

(b) Number of females and males of each height

Female		Male	
Height (in)	Number	Height (in)	Number
60	5	64	2
61	5	65	5
62	7	66	2
63	7	67	6
64	9	68	7
65	9	69	7
66	12	70	9
67	6	71	6
68	3	72	10
69	2	73	7
70	1	74	2
71	1	75	3
72	1	76	1
		77	3

Total	68		70
Average	64.5 inches		70.2 inches
Standard deviation	+/– 2.7 inches		+/– 3.2 inches
Variance	+/– 7.29 inches		+/– 10.24 inches

Figure 21.8   Adult height. The frequency distribution of height in 1000 college-aged males is shown in tabular form (**a**). Height data for 138 male and female college students (**b**).

1000 men in his sample, Castle calculated a mean height value of 175.33 cm (about 68.5 inches). In contrast, the height averages for the 138 University of Connecticut students shown in the chapter-opening photo and summarized in **Figure 21.8b** are 64.5 inches for the women and 70.2 inches for the men. Both of these values are very close to the current U.S. population averages.

The shapes of frequency distributions vary depending on several factors, including the sample size and the number of classification categories for the trait. It is therefore necessary to provide a statistical description of the shape of the frequency distribution when comparing trait values. For example, it is important to report the **mode,** or **modal value,** that is, the most common value in a distribution. For the height data shown in Figure 21.8, the mode is the 173–175 cm category, containing 188 individual values. Each distribution also possesses a middle value, known as the **median,** or **median value.** In the height distribution, you

can think of the median value as entry number 500 (in order of increasing height) of the 1000 entries in the distribution. This median value also resides in the 173–175 cm category.

Data in the real world are usually skewed—that is, unevenly distributed on either side of the mean, as Figure 21.8 and the chapter-opening photo both illustrate. Therefore, to describe the frequency distribution, we must also have ways of measuring (and thus describing) the nature of the distribution around the mean. Two forms of measurement are commonly used.

The first, called the **variance (s^2),** is a numerical measure of the spread of the distribution around the mean. This measure interprets how much variation exists among individuals in the sample. The variance value depends on the relationship between the width of the distribution and the number of observations in the sample. It will be small if all the observations are close to the mean, and it will be large if the observations are widely spread around the mean (**Figure 21.9**). The variance is determined by summing the square of the difference between each individual value and the sample mean and dividing that sum by the number of degrees of freedom (df) in the sample. The

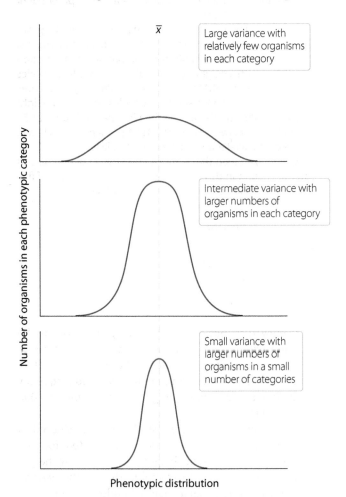

Figure 21.9   Normal distributions. The shape of curves depicting normal distributions is changed by the sample size and the number of outcome classes. Variance around the average is correspondingly large, intermediate, and small.

number of degrees of freedom is equal to the number of independent variables. Squaring the differences between individual values and the sample mean prevents positive and negative differences from canceling each other out. This is why the variance is expressed as squared units:

$$s^2 = \sum (x_i - \bar{x})^2 / df$$

In our example of variation in a quantitative phenotype, the variance is described as **phenotypic variance (V_P).** Because we are measuring height in centimeters, the variance will be expressed in centimeters squared.

The second measure that describes the distribution of data is the **standard deviation (s),** a value expressing deviation from the mean in the same units as the scale of measurement for the sample. The standard deviation (s) is calculated as $s = \sqrt{s^2}$. In our sample of the heights of 1000 college-aged males, $V_P = s^2 = 43.30$ cm^2, and the standard deviation is $s = 6.58$ cm. In the sample of 138 college students, the standard deviations and variances for height of the 68 females and 70 males are as reported in Figure 21.8c.

Partitioning Phenotypic Variance

A key part of analyzing quantitative trait variation is to analyze the factors thought to contribute to phenotypic variance, V_P. Quantitative phenotypes are the joint product of genes, environment, and gene interactions; consequently, phenotypic variance can be partitioned among those influences. As a first step, the phenotypic variance can be divided into two principal components: *genetic variance (V_G)* and *environmental variance (V_E).* Under this assumption, phenotypic variance can be expressed in terms of genetic variance plus environmental variance: $V_P = V_G + V_E$.

In this expression, **genetic variance (V_G)** is the proportion of phenotypic variance that is due to differences among genotypes. In highly inbred populations in which all individuals are homozygous for alleles controlling a quantitative phenotype, $V_G = 0$. Such populations are found only after strictly controlled laboratory inbreeding, however; they are rarely found in nature, due to the ubiquitous presence of genetic variation in natural populations. Genetic variation in natural populations generates individuals with different genotypes for quantitative traits and leads to phenotypic variability that is directly attributable to the genetic variability.

Environmental variance (V_E) is the portion of phenotypic variance that is due to variability of the environments inhabited by individual members of a population. Differences in sun exposure, in water and nutrient content of the soil, and in exposure to pests are examples of environmental variables that influence V_E in plants. Carefully controlled laboratory experiments can sometimes control all of the environmental variables and produce a situation in which V_E approximates zero. In nature, however, such circumstances rarely occur. Individual members of natural populations are almost certain to experience variability in the environmental conditions they encounter.

Some differences may be systematic and predictable. For example, members of a plant population growing below a natural spring will experience wetter growth conditions than plants living above the spring. Other environmental variables are sporadic or unpredictable. For example, a dry year might reduce the flow of water from a natural spring and affect the plants living below the spring more severely than those living above it.

Let's use an example to illustrate the dissection of V_G and V_E as components of V_P. Suppose that two different pure-breeding parental lines are established. Each line is genetically uniform, with $V_G = 0$; therefore, $V_P = V_E$ (Figure 21.10a). The pure-breeding lines are crossed to produce F_1 progeny that are genetically uniform. In the F_1, $V_G = 0$ because there is no genetic variation among the individuals, and $V_P = V_E$ (Figure 21.10b). Production of F_2 leads to genotypic variation and thus to the production of phenotypic variation that results from a combination of genetic variance and environmental variance (Figure 21.10c). Among the F_2, $V_P = V_E + V_G$. Since V_E has been determined among the parents and in the F_1, genetic variance can be calculated by subtracting environmental variance from the phenotypic variance among the F_2. In other words, $V_G = V_P - V_E$. **Genetic Analysis 21.2** provides practice in determining environmental and genetic variance.

(a)

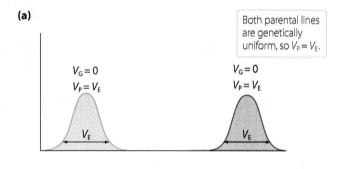

(b)

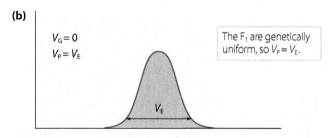

(c)

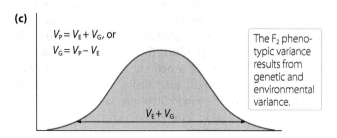

Figure 21.10   Sources of phenotypic variance.

PROBLEM Two pure-breeding lines of tomatoes, P_1 and P_2, producing fruit with different average weights, are crossed. The means and variances of their F_1 and F_2 progeny are shown in the table to the right.

Line	Average Fruit Weight (g)	V_P
P_1	6.5	1.6 g^2
P_2	14.2	3.5 g^2
F_1	10.2	2.2 g^2
F_2	9.8	4.0 g^2

a. What is the environmental variance (V_E) for this trait?

b. What is the genetic variance (V_G) determined from the F_2?

> **BREAK IT DOWN:** Phenotypic variance equals genetic variance plus environmental variance. The three values can be manipulated to isolate and quantify one value at a time (p. 725).

Solution Strategies	Solution Steps
Evaluate	
1. Identify the topic this problem addresses and the nature of the requested answer.	1. This problem concerns the determination of environmental variance and genetic variance for the tomato plant data given.
2. Identify the critical information given in the problem.	2. Fruit weight and phenotypic variance are given for the two pure-breeding parental lines and for the F_1 and F_2 progeny.
Deduce	
3. Describe the relationship between V_P, V_G, and V_E.	3. $V_P = V_G + V_E$
④ Identify the variance values that contribute to V_P in each line and generation. **TIP:** For organisms that are genetically identical, $V_P = V_E$.	4. Each of the pure-breeding parental lines (P_1 and P_2) and the F_1 progeny are genetically uniform. As a consequence, all phenotypic variance is due to environmental variance, and genetic variance makes no contribution. The F_2 contains genotypic variety, so both V_G and V_E contribute to V_P.
Solve	Answer a
5. Determine V_E for this trait.	5. In the genetically uniform P_1, P_2, and F_1, $V_G = 0$, and in each line $V_P = V_E$. The average environmental variance among these three lines is calculated as $(1.6 + 3.5 + 2.2)/3 = 2.43$ grams.
	Answer b
6. Determine V_G for this trait.	6. V_G is calculated by rearranging the expression in step 3 to $V_G = V_P - V_E$. The genetic variance for these data is $V_G = 4.0 - 2.43 = 1.57$ grams.

For more practice, see Problems 4, 10, and 12.   Visit the Study Area to access study tools.   **Mastering Genetics™**

Partitioning Genetic Variance

Each allelic difference affecting a quantitative trait contributes to genetic variance in a population, but not necessarily each in the same way. Indeed, it can be difficult to measure the specific effect of each allelic variant. Nevertheless, genetic variance can theoretically be partitioned into three different *kinds* of allelic effects. **Additive variance (V_A)** derives from the additive effects of all alleles contributing to a trait. Additive variance is the result of incomplete dominance of alleles at a locus, which causes heterozygotes to have a phenotype intermediate between the homozygous phenotypes. **Dominance variance (V_D)** is variance resulting from dominance relationships in which alleles of a heterozygote produce a phenotype that is not exactly intermediate between those of homozygotes (i.e., the nonadditive effects of alleles of contributing genes). Lastly, **interactive variance (V_I)** derives

from epistatic interactions between the alleles of different genes that influence a quantitative phenotype. Collectively these three components unite to produce the genetic variance in a model summarized by $V_G = V_A + V_D + V_I$. We use these values in the following section to discuss *heritability*.

21.3 Heritability Measures the Genetic Component of Phenotypic Variation

One goal of quantitative genetics is to estimate the extent to which genetic variation influences the phenotypic variation seen in a trait. This is a challenging task when a trait is determined by a combination of genetic variation, environmental variation, and gene–environment interaction. The concept of trait **heritability** was developed to help measure the proportion of phenotypic variation that is due to genetic variation.

Heritability differs from trait to trait. The phenotypic variation observed in a trait with high heritability is largely the result of genetic variation and thus can be strongly influenced by selection programs focused on changing the frequency of a phenotype in a population. Conversely, only a small proportion of the phenotypic variation of a trait with low heritability can be attributed to genetic variation, so the expression of the trait in a population is not effectively changed by selection processes. Heritability is an important measure of the potential responsiveness of a trait to natural selection or artificial selection. It is of special interest to evolutionary biologists and plant and animal breeders, who use it to assess the potential impact of selection on traits of agricultural or economic importance.

Two widely used measures of heritability assess different components of the contribution of genetic variation to phenotypic variation. **Broad sense heritability (H^2)** estimates the proportion of phenotypic variation that is due to total genetic variation. This form of heritability is defined by the equality $H^2 = V_G/V_P$. **Narrow sense heritability (h^2)** estimates the proportion of phenotypic variation that is due to additive genetic variation. Narrow sense heritability is defined by the equality $h^2 = V_A/V_P$. Both measures of heritability are expressed as proportions that range in magnitude from 0.0 to 1.0. In all cases, greater heritability values indicate a larger role for genetic variation in phenotypic variation.

Heritability is easily misunderstood. An erroneous understanding can lead to the mistaken idea that genetic variation makes a much larger contribution to phenotypic variation than the data actually support. Heritability is difficult to apply to humans except under limited circumstances (described later in the discussion of twin studies), but it can be used for other organisms. The following attributes of heritability are central to its meaning:

1. Heritability is a measure of the degree to which *genetic differences* contribute to *phenotypic variation* of a trait. In other words, heritability is high when much of the phenotypic variation is produced by genetic variation and little is contributed by environmental variation. Heritability *is not* an indication of the mechanism by which genes control a trait, nor is it a measure of how much of a trait is produced by gene action.

2. Heritability values are accurate only for the environment and population in which they are measured. Heritability values measured in one population cannot be transferred to another population, because both genetic and environmental factors may differ between populations.

3. Heritability for a given trait in a population can change if environmental factors change, and changes in the proportions of genotypes in a population can

alter the effect of environmental factors on phenotypic variation, thus changing heritability.

4. High heritability does not mean that a trait is not influenced by environmental factors. Traits with high heritability can be very responsive to environmental changes.

Broad Sense Heritability

We have seen that genetic variance (V_G) is a composite value that derives its magnitude from additive, dominance, and interaction variance. Unfortunately, genetic variance is not always easy to partition into these separate components. Fortunately, broad sense heritability ($H^2 = V_G/V_P$) can be used as a general measure of the magnitude of genetic influence over phenotypic variation of a trait, when V_G cannot be partitioned.

In a 1988 study of the genetics and evolution of cave fish (*Astyanax fasciatus*), Horst Wilkens used broad sense heritability analysis to describe the genetic contribution to the evolution of the organism's eye tissue. Some populations of this species live in completely dark underground cave streams in Eastern Mexico and have a dramatically reduced amount of eye tissue in comparison to closely related fish living aboveground. In these populations, the eye tissue appears to be undergoing rapid evolutionary change. The eyes in sighted fish of this species are approximately 7 cm in diameter. In comparison, blind cave fish have less than 2 cm of eye tissue diameter.

Wilkens crossed sighted cave fish to blind cave fish, measured eye tissue mean and variance in the F_1, and then produced F_2 fish and measured their eye tissue as well. Since the F_1 fish are nearly genetically uniform, the variance in the amount of eye tissue is due entirely to the environment. In these F_1, V_E was 0.057 cm^2. Among the F_2, phenotypic variance (V_P) was 0.563 cm^2 and was the result of both genetic and environmental variance ($V_G + V_E$). Broad sense heritability is derived by determining V_G and dividing it by phenotypic variation. In this case,

$$V_G = V_P - V_E = 0.563 - 0.057 = 0.506$$

$$H^2 = V_G/V_P = 0.506/0.563 = 0.899$$

This broad sense heritability of approximately 0.90 means that approximately 90% of the phenotypic variation in eye size between these populations of cave fish is due to genetic variation.

Twin Studies

Heritability can be quantified when both mating and environmental factors can be controlled. However, when mating and environmental variation are not among the controlled experimental parameters, heritability is far more difficult—some would say impossible—to measure accurately. This limitation applies to attempts to measure the heritability of traits in humans. Fortunately, studies of phenotypic variation in human twins can offer insights into broad sense heritability of human traits.

Identical twins, also known as monozygotic twins (MZ twins), are produced by a single fertilization event that is followed by a splitting of the fertilized embryo into two zygotes. Monozygotic twins share all of their alleles. Theoretically, broad sense heritability can be determined by assuming that phenotypic variance between them is fully attributable to environmental variance. Under this assumption, in MZ twin pairs, $V_P = V_E$.

Fraternal twins, on the other hand, are dizygotic (DZ twins), produced by two independent fertilization events that take place at the same time. Dizygotic twins are siblings that are born at the same time, but they are no more closely related than siblings born at different times. Like all full siblings, DZ twins have an average of 50% of their alleles in common. To control for differences between the sexes, only DZ twins of the same sex are used in twin studies. Phenotypic variance between DZ twins is the sum of environmental variance plus one-half of the genetic variance (the 50% of alleles not shared by the average DZ twin pair): In DZ twin pairs, $V_P = V_E + 1/2V_G$. On the basis of these general formulas for calculation of H^2, broad sense heritability can be estimated for human traits by methods we do not discuss here (Table 21.2).

Studies of traits in human twins usually compare MZ twins to same-sex DZ twins to make heritability estimates more accurate. Even so, heritability studies of human twins are prone to several sources of error that lead to inaccurately high values. Following are the most common sources of error:

1. *Stronger shared maternal effects in identical twins than in fraternal twins.* These effects include the sharing of embryonic membranes and other aspects of the uterine environment that lead to more similar developmental conditions for identical twins than for fraternal twins.

2. *Greater similarity of treatment of identical twins than of fraternal twins.* Parents, other adults, and peers have a tendency to treat identical twins more equally than they treat fraternal twins of the same sex. This gives identical twins a similar social and behavioral environmental experience, while fraternal twins more often are treated differently.

3. *Greater similarity of interactions between genes and environmental factors in identical twins than in fraternal twins.* Identical twins have the same genotype and are affected in similar, if not identical, ways by environmental factors. On the other hand, fraternal twins have genetic differences that can be influenced differently by environmental factors. This may result in greater variance between fraternal twins than between identical twins.

Because of the difficulties and the potential sources of error in making heritability estimates based on twin studies, the values in Table 21.2 are more likely to be too high than too low.

The study of identical twins reared together versus those reared apart is an alternative approach to estimating the influence of genes on phenotypic variation. Such studies measure the **concordance,** the percentage of twin pairs in which both members of the pair have the same phenotype for a trait, versus the **discordance,** the percentage in which the twins of a pair have dissimilar phenotypes for a trait. Concordance and discordance frequencies give a general picture of the overall influence of genes on phenotypes. If phenotypic variation for a trait is 100% genetic, MZ twins should always be concordant for their phenotypes, whether reared together or apart. In this case, concordance would be 100%. Dizygotic twins share an average of 50% of their genes in common and would have concordance of about 50% for a trait whose variation is completely genetic. When phenotypic variation of a trait is due entirely to nongenetic factors, on the other hand, concordance among MZ and DZ twins will be approximately equal. For traits with phenotypic variation that is determined to a significant extent by genetic variation, concordance among MZ twin pairs will be substantially greater than for DZ twins. A number of human diseases, malformations, and other phenotypic variants fall into the latter category. Table 21.3 shows MZ and DZ twin concordance values for common malformations and

Table 21.2	Some Broad Sense Heritability (H^2) Values from Human Twin Studies
Trait	**Heritability (H^2), %**
Biological Traits	
Total fingerprint ridge count	90
Height	85
Maximum heart rate	85
Club foot	80
Amino acid excretion	70
Weight	60
Total serum cholesterol	60
Blood pressure	60
Body mass index (BMI)	50
Longevity	29
Behavioral Traits	
Verbal ability	65
Sociability index	65
Temperament index	60
Spelling aptitude	50
Memory	50
Mathematical aptitude	30

Table 21.3	Concordance Values for Common Threshold Conditions in Humans	
Trait	**Percent Concordance**	
	MZ Twins	**DZ Twins**
Alzheimer disease	60	25
Autism	70	10
Cleft lip	40	4
Club foot	30	2
Congenital hip dislocation	35	3
Depression	70	25
Insulin-dependent diabetes	50	10
Pyloric stenosis	25	3
Reading disability	70	45
Schizophrenia	60	20

Table 21.4	Some Narrow Sense Heritability (h^2) Values for Animals and Plants	
Organism	**Trait**	**Heritability (h^2)**
Cattle	Body weight	0.65
	Milk production	0.40
Corn	Plant height	0.70
	Ear length	0.55
	Ear diameter	0.14
Horse	Racing speed	0.60
	Trotting speed	0.40
Pig	Back-fat thickness	0.70
	Weight gain	0.40
	Litter size	0.05
Poultry	Body weight (8 weeks)	0.50
	Egg production	0.20

other abnormalities that are determined to a large extent by genetic variation but are also a product of environmental triggers that play as yet undetermined roles.

Narrow Sense Heritability and Artificial Selection

Narrow sense heritability ($h^2 = V_A/V_P$) estimates the proportion of phenotypic variation that is due to additive genetic variance (V_A), variance resulting from the alleles of additive genes. These estimates are particularly useful in agriculture, where they predict the potential responsiveness of a trait in an animal or plant to artificial selection imposed through selective breeding programs or controlled growth conditions. High narrow sense heritability values are correlated with a greater degree of response to selection than low values, because additive genetic variance is responsive to selection.

Table 21.4 gives examples of h^2 values, covering a broad spectrum of magnitude, for several characteristics of plants and animals. Since higher h^2 values have the strongest correlation with selection response, biologists predict that traits such as body weight in cattle, back-fat thickness in pigs, and corn plant height will be most amenable to change through artificial selection schemes. On the other hand, litter size in pigs, egg production in poultry, and ear diameter in corn have low h^2 values and will be less responsive to selection.

Estimating the potential response to selection for a trait begins with calculation of a value known as the **selection differential (S),** which measures the difference between the population mean value for a trait and the mean trait value for the mating portion of a population.

Suppose, for example, that a goal of an artificial selection experiment is to increase plant height. Choosing taller-than-average plants to mate will be an effective way to increase the height of progeny if h^2 is high. If the population average height is 37.5 cm and the average height of plants selected for mating is 42 cm, then $S = 42$ cm $- 37.5$ cm $= 4.5$ cm.

The potential **response to selection (R)** depends on the extent to which the difference between the mating trait mean value and the population mean value can be passed on to progeny. This probability is estimated using the formula $R = S(h^2)$. For this plant height example, let's assume we examine corn plant height, $h^2 = 0.70$ (see Table 21.4). In this case, $R = (4.5$ cm$)(0.70) = 3.15$ cm. Under stable growth conditions, the progeny plants could be expected to have a height equal to the population average plus the value of R, or 37.5 cm $+$ 3.15 cm $= 40.65$ cm. Narrow sense heritability can be measured by rearranging the terms in the response-to-selection equation to $h^2 = R/S$. For the plant-height example, $h^2 = 3.15$ cm$/4.5$ cm $= 0.70$.

Estimates of heritability have important practical applications for plant and animal breeders, and for evolutionary biologists. Whether traits are subjected to artificial selection by breeders or to natural selection, the extent to which the mean value of a trait changes in a population depends on its heritability. Breeders and evolutionary biologists predict substantial change in trait mean values (i.e., large values for R) when heritability is high, but little or no change in trait mean values when heritability is low. In other words, traits evolve when a substantial proportion of the phenotypic variation is due to genetic variation.

Figure 21.11a shows three examples in which the selection differentials are the same but the response to

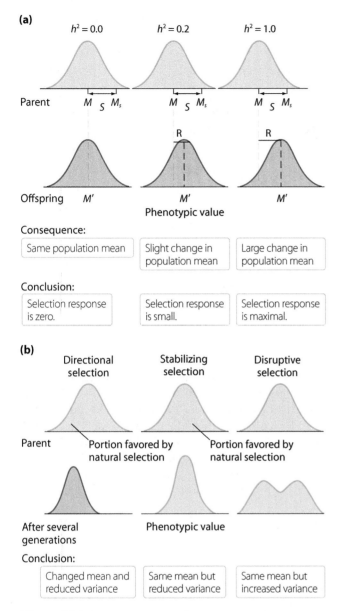

Figure 21.11 **Response to artificial and natural selection.**
(a) Response to artificial selection after one generation depends on h^2. M is mean phenotype in parental generation; M_S is the mean phenotype after selection; M' is the mean phenotype of offspring after selection; selection differential is $S = M_S - M$.
(b) Expected changes in phenotypic means and variances after several generations of natural selection.

selection differs as a result of different degrees of heritability. This comparison illustrates that selection response is expected to be maximal when heritability is $h^2 = 1.0$. Selection response is substantially less when heritability is $h^2 = 0.2$, and there is no selection response when heritability is $h^2 = 0$. Selection also affects quantitative traits in natural populations. **Figure 21.11b** shows natural selection operating over many generations in three different modes that have different effects on phenotypic means and variances. In the mode known as **directional selection,** the mean phenotypic value is shifted in one direction because

one extreme of the phenotype distribution is favored. This narrows the phenotypic range and reduces phenotypic variance. In contrast, natural selection favoring an intermediate phenotype over extreme phenotypes results in **stabilizing selection** that reduces the phenotypic variance without shifting the mean value. **Disruptive selection** occurs when both extreme phenotypes are favored over intermediate phenotypes. The result is an increase in the phenotypic variance and, potentially, a phenotypic split within the population.

21.4 Quantitative Trait Loci Are the Genes That Contribute to Quantitative Traits

The genes that contribute to the variation in a quantitative trait are collectively called **quantitative trait loci (QTLs).** Individually, a gene that contributes to a quantitative trait is referred to as a **quantitative trait locus.** QTLs were initially of interest in agricultural plants such as tomatoes and corn, where they influence important attributes including fruit sweetness, acidity, and color. QTL analysis has expanded greatly in recent decades through analysis of many distinct traits in plants and animals, including humans.

In one way, QTLs are no different from other genes we discuss. For example, they often produce polypeptides that operate in metabolic pathways producing compounds that give flavor or color to fruit. Identifying QTLs by experimental analysis is different from identifying other genes that control phenotypic variation, however, because many genes are influencing the trait, and the presence or absence of a particular allele does not correlate well with distinct phenotypes. Specialized statistical methods have been developed to detect and map QTLs. This process is called **QTL mapping,** and it involves the identification of chromosome regions that are likely to contain QTLs.

The general process of QTL mapping is similar to the methods used to determine genetic linkage between genes. A chromosome region likely to contain a QTL is identified by the frequent co-occurrence of a specific genetic marker such as a single nucleotide polymorphism (SNP) in organisms with a particular phenotype. The inherited DNA sequence variation of an SNP is usually not the molecular basis of the QTL. Instead, the SNP is usually genetically linked to the QTL. The connection between the genetic marker and the phenotype implies that a QTL exists near the genome location encoding the genetic marker.

QTL Mapping Strategies

Contemporary QTL mapping uses DNA markers that have known chromosome locations to assist with the mapping and identification of genes. SNPs are particularly useful in these analyses, as are other DNA marker variants such as restriction fragment length polymorphisms (RFLPs) and variable number tandem repeats (VNTRs), in which different numbers of repeats of specific nucleotide base pairs occur in different chromosomes.

Multiple approaches can be taken in QTL mapping experiments. At its core, however, QTL mapping is a statistical process that seeks to identify regions of genomes containing genetic markers that are linked to QTLs. The statistical analysis for QTLs is closely related to the statistical analysis of genetic linkage using logarithm of the odds (lod) score analysis (see Section 5.5). QTL analysis can lead to identification of the potential *chromosome location* of a QTL influencing phenotypic variation of a quantitative trait, but by itself it does not identify the molecular basis of action of the QTL. Other genetic methods are available for molecular description of QTL action.

QTL mapping uses the parents and progeny produced by controlled crosses as the sources of DNA for genetic marker identification and as the source of data for the quantitative trait of interest. If, for example, a researcher wants to identify QTLs that influence large fruit size in tomatoes, he or she will cross two parental lines of tomatoes that differ in fruit size. The F_1 progeny of this cross could then be used to produce F_2 progeny or, as we illustrate here, the F_1 could be used in a backcross to one of the parental lines. Genetic markers will be determined in the original parental lines and in the backcross progeny. Tomato sizes produced by backcross progeny will be weighed and the results compared to genetic markers in the individual plants.

Figure 21.12a illustrates the structure of a backcross experiment designed to collect genetic marker and tomato-weight data for QTL mapping analysis. One parental tomato strain producing large fruit that averages 100 grams (g) contains genetic markers that are identified by the letter L. There are actually many markers linked to QTLs in the line, and for each marker gene tested, the large-tomato strain will have two copies of the large-strain marker allele genotype designated LL. Similarly, a small-tomato-producing strain, with an average tomato weight of 10 grams, is characterized for the same genetic markers, and each of the loci tested in the small-strain genotype is designated SS. The F_1 progeny of the large × small cross is heterozygous for each marker locus and is designated LS. These plants in this example are shown to produce tomatoes that weigh 60 g. The backcross is made to the large-tomato strain, and the marker genotype will be either LL, if the F_1 transmits the large-strain allele, or LS, if the F_1 transmits the small-strain allele. The backcross progeny in this example produce tomatoes that vary in weight from 80 g to 88 g. Tomato weight from the backcross plants is greater than from the F_1 plants because the backcross plants are the result of a cross between the F_1 and the large-tomato strain.

Table 21.5 displays tomato-weight data for 10 backcross plants (1–10) and genetic marker data for two genes,

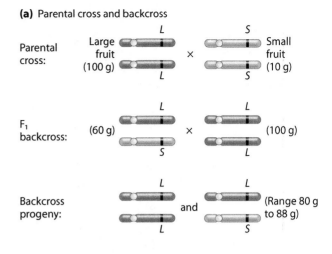

(a) Parental cross and backcross

(b) Lod score profile

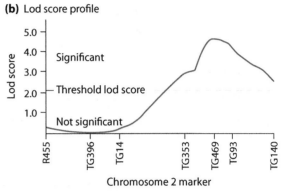

Figure 21.12   Quantitative trait locus (QTL) detection and mapping. (a) Parental tomato plants producing large (*LL*) or small (*SS*) fruit are crossed to produce F_1 (*LS*). The F_1 are then backcrossed to the large-fruit line to yield backcross progeny that are either *LL* or *LS*. **(b)** The significance of linkage between potential QTLs and genetic markers is tested among backcross progeny by lod score analysis. A lod score profile assessing fruit-weight QTLs reveals significant scores exceeding the threshold value on tomato chromosome 2.

marker A (M_A) and marker B (M_B), that are not linked to one another and are located in different parts of the genome. In an actual QTL backcross experiment, several hundred backcross plants might be examined, and each plant might be genotyped for dozens of genetic markers that ideally would be spaced about every 5 to 10 centimorgans (cM) in the genome. This number of genetic markers and their close proximity maximize the chance of identifying the location of QTLs detected by the analysis.

In Table 21.5, the average weight of tomatoes from backcross plants is 84 grams. Average tomato weight is compared for *LL* plants versus *LS* plants for each marker. There is almost no difference in average weight for M_A (*LL* = 83.8 g versus *LS* = 84.2 g), but for M_B, *LL* plants produce tomatoes that are 4 grams heavier on average than are the tomatoes from *LS* plants (*LL* = 86.0 g versus *LS* = 82.0 g). These data may indicate that a QTL influencing tomato weight is located near M_B. Conversely, there is no evidence to indicate that a QTL is located near M_A.

Table 21.5	QTL Analysis of Tomato Weight in Backcross Progeny		
Backcross Plant	**Average Fruit Weight (g)**	**Markers**	
		M_A	M_B
1	86	LS	LL
2	82	LL	LS
3	85	LL	LL
4	88	LL	LL
5	81	LS	LS
6	83	LS	LS
7	84	LL	LL
8	80	LL	LS
9	84	LS	LS
10	87	LS	LL
Total average weight	84		
LL average weight		83.8	86.0
LS average weight		84.2	82.0

To determine the statistical significance of the kind of information provided for genetic markers and tomato weight, a lod score is calculated. The lod score is an odds ratio of the probability of the data if a QTL is linked to the marker divided by the probability of the data if there is no QTL linked to the marker. The odds ratios for the backcross plants are added together, and the log (the *log* of the *odd*s) is taken to yield the lod score. Like the analysis of lod scores for genetic linkage, there is a threshold value for significance of the score (see Section 5.5). If the lod score for a genetic marker is greater than the threshold value, the lod score indicates a statistically significant probability that a QTL is linked to the marker.

In **Figure 21.12b**, a lod score profile for several genetic markers located on chromosome 2 of tomato reveals significant evidence indicating genetic linkage to a QTL. Beginning at the marker designated TG353 and spanning to the right through marker TG140, the lod score values are greater than the threshold value and give statistically significant evidence favoring linkage between these genetic markers and a QTL. On the other hand, the lod scores falling below the threshold value in the figure give no statistical evidence of linkage to a QTL. For chromosome 2 in tomato, lod scores for genetic markers to the left of TG353 are less than the threshold lod score value. By using a large number of regularly spaced genetic markers distributed every few centiMorgans along each chromosome, QTL mapping analysis can potentially detect the location of any QTL influencing a quantitative trait phenotype. Commonly, multiple QTLs in a genome are identified.

Andrew Paterson and his colleagues published a 1988 study mapping 15 QTLs in the tomato genome that influence fruit weight, fruit acidity, and the amount of soluble solids in the fruit. Each trait has agricultural importance, and together they determine the quality and yield of tomato paste from the fruit. Paterson's study used 70 DNA markers spaced an average of 20 cM apart throughout the tomato genome. Collectively, these markers span about 95% of the 12 chromosomes that constitute the tomato genome.

The parental plants were two closely related and interfertile species: a domestic tomato (*Lycopersicon esculentum*) and a wild South American green-fruited tomato (*Lycopersicon chmielewskii*). The F₁ hybrids were backcrossed to *L. esculentum,* producing 237 backcross progeny plants for analysis. All backcross plants were grown under identical conditions to minimize the influence of environmental factors on the traits of interest. Individual fruits from backcross plants were assayed for fruit weight (grams), soluble solids content (percentage), and acidity (pH). Lod score analysis was used to test whether genes influencing any of the three traits exhibited genetic linkage to genome markers. Significant lod score values traced six genes influencing fruit weight, five influencing acidity, and four influencing soluble solids content to regions of nine chromosomes in the tomato genome. The regions of tomato chromosomes 6 and 7 containing QTLs influencing all three traits are shown in **Figure 21.13**.

Identification of QTL Genes

Since QTL mapping identifies the location of genes influencing quantitative traits, but not the genes themselves; additional genetic analysis is required to identify the genes. To acquire information leading to gene identity, researchers use **near isogenic lines (NILs),** also called **introgression lines (ILs).** These lines are derived

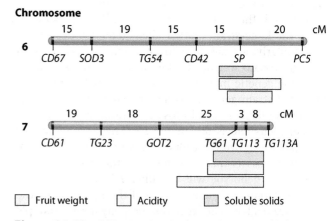

Figure 21.13 QTL mapping in domestic tomato (*Solanum lycopersicon*). Multiple QTLs influencing fruit weight, fruit acidity, and percentage of soluble solids of tomatoes are shown on chromosome 6 and chromosome 7. Many other QTLs populate the rest of the genome. Distances between genes are in cM (centiMorgans).

from backcross progeny produced as described earlier. Different backcross progeny are self-fertilized over many generations to form highly inbred lines. The resulting lines are nearly isogenic, meaning they are genetically identical at almost all genes. The lines differ from one another, however, by carrying different crossovers that have introduced different alleles near the site of a QTL. The introduced differences are called introgressions, thus giving these lines their name.

Figure 21.14a illustrates six introgression lines (IL1 to IL6) descended from a cross between two original parental lines, one a domesticated species and the other a wild species. The chromosome colors illustrate crossovers that produce differences between the introgression lines. Crossover locations are identified by analysis of genetic markers, and each introgression line is characterized for a trait phenotype. In the figure, the bars to the right of each line indicate the percentage difference between the phenotype of the IL and the domesticated parental species. Two potential QTL regions, QTL-A and QTL-B, contain variations of the crossover segments. The greatest positive percentage difference relative to the domesticated species phenotype occurs in IL2 and IL3 that carry crossover chromosomes containing domesticated DNA in the vicinity of QTL-A and wild-species DNA near QTL-B.

To identify the genes responsible for QTL variation, "candidate genes," genes that are potentially responsible for the observed variation, must be identified and investigated. Genes in the QTL-A and QTL-B regions are located by examining DNA sequences, and sequence variants in candidate genes among introgression lines are identified. The sequence differences detected are studied to determine if they correlate with phenotypic variation.

Figure 21.14b illustrates the results of experimental analysis of tomato introgression lines by Eyal Fridman and colleagues in 2004 designed to identify genes contributing

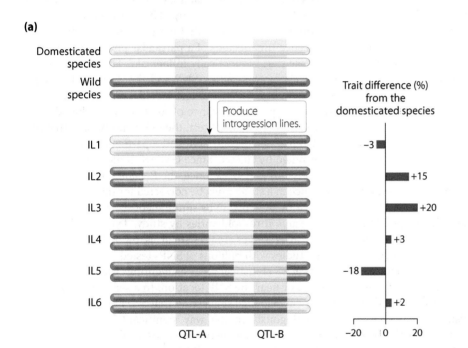

(a)

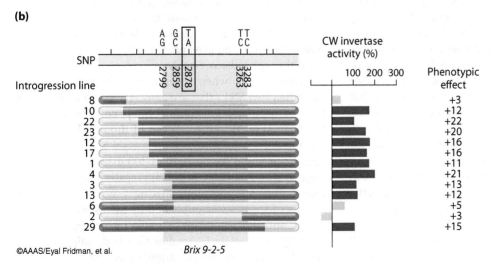

(b)

©AAAS/Eyal Fridman, et al.   *Brix 9-2-5*

Figure 21.14 QTL analysis in introgression lines. (a) Six introgression lines (IL1 to IL6) formed by mating between a domesticated species and a wild species have different patterns of recombination in the region of two QTLs. The difference in trait expression between the trait in the domesticated species and each IL is given as a percentage. **(b)** Analysis of *Brix 9-2-5* in 13 introgression lines identifies SNPs that alter CW invertase activity. The SNP at position 2878 has a substantial influence on CW invertase function.

to Brix value in tomato. The Brix value of fruit refers to the total soluble solids content, of which sugars and acids are the primary constituents. Fridman and colleagues created a large number of ILs from an initial cross between the domesticated tomato species (*Solanum lycopersicum*) and a wild relative (*Solanum pennellii*).

The parental species and each of the ILs were studied for Brix value, and a QTL found to have a high Brix value, *Brix 9-2-5*, was intensively studied. DNA sequencing of the 484 nucleotides (positions 2799 to 3283) in *Brix 9-2-5* revealed the five SNP variants shown in the figure. The *Brix 9-2-5* QTL corresponds to a segment of the tomato *LIN5* gene that produces the cell wall enzyme invertase (CW invertase). In the figure, the positions of SNPs are shown relative to 13 ILs that carry recombination in or near *Brix 9-2-5*. The bar to the right of each IL indicates its percentage difference in CW invertase activity relative to *S. lycopersicum*. The results show that when the *S. pennellii* sequence is present, CW invertase activity is significantly greater than in *S. lycopersicum*. The SNP at position 2878 (boxed) was strongly correlated with increased CW invertase activity. DNA and protein sequence analysis revealed that this SNP produced an amino acid difference that altered CW invertase activity.

Genome-Wide Association Studies

The widespread availability of genome sequencing information has opened a new avenue to the identification of QTLs in numerous species, including humans. Known as **genome-wide association studies (GWAS),** the method seeks to tie the presence of a sequence variant of a DNA marker to a QTL influencing a specific phenotype. The relationship between an inherited genetic marker variant and the phenotype is by "association," which means organisms that carry a particular variant are more likely to have a certain phenotype than are organisms that carry a different variant. The assessment of association is quantitative; that is, it expresses the percentage of organisms with a genetic marker that also display a certain phenotype versus the percentage that have the phenotype but not the genetic marker.

One advantage of GWAS over other QTL mapping approaches is that GWAS can scan the entire genome for QTLs by statistically testing for marker variants that are associated with phenotypic variation. Positive statistical results indicating association identify chromosome regions that can be more closely inspected for genes that influence the trait. A second advantage of GWAS is that organisms in random mating populations can be analyzed. Rather than requiring controlled crosses and the formation of introgression lines GWAS uses "cases," or organisms with a particular phenotype, and compares them to "controls" that lack the particular phenotype to assess the association between QTL markers and a phenotype.

This case–control approach identifies the SNP genotypes in all the individuals with the disease (cases) as well as in healthy controls. The frequency of each SNP allele in the cases is compared to the allele frequency in the controls. When the allele frequency in the case group is greater than the frequency in the control group, the odds ratio is greater than 1.0. Statistics applied to the odds ratio determine the *P* value of each odds ratio. Significant association between a SNP and a disease is found when the *P* value is less than the cutoff value. The results of each SNP examination are plotted as described momentarily.

GWAS takes advantage of the tendency of alleles of closely linked genetic markers to display linkage disequilibrium (see Section 5.6). Specific combinations of alleles in linkage disequilibrium occur at frequencies significantly greater than expected by chance. Linkage disequilibrium occurs because recombination has not reshuffled the alleles into random combinations. Groups of alleles in linkage disequilibrium form haplotypes along segments of chromosomes. If a group of closely linked SNPs form a haplotype, then identification of a particular SNP for one marker means that other SNPs that are part of the same haplotype are likely to be found nearby. The presence of SNPs in haplotypes can be correlated with the presence (affected) or absence (unaffected) of a particular phenotype, such as a disease that is genetically influenced. The statistical test of association between a SNP and the disease phenotype is similar to a chi-square test (see Section 2.5). Like chi-square analysis, significance of the outcome is based on *P* values. In this statistical test, the null hypothesis is that the occurrence of a certain SNP and a particular phenotype is determined by chance. Since GWAS studies test hundreds to thousands of SNPs at once, the *P*-value threshold for significance in a study must be corrected for multiple hypothesis testing of many SNPs simultaneously. This means that the *P*-value threshold varies by study. Typically, however, significant *P* values are very small, as low as 10^{-7} to 10^{-8} for large studies with millions of SNPs tested.

GWAS statistical analysis identifies the presence of a QTL at or near the SNP location. In a sense, this provides statistical evidence suggesting that a QTL is located close by, analogously to the way significant lod scores indicate genetic linkage between genes. Additional molecular analysis can identify candidate genes and to link specific allelic variation to the production of phenotype variation. This is, once again, analogous to the need to find the actual disease-causing gene after its location has been identified through lod score analysis.

Since 2005, when Josephine Hoh and colleagues identified two SNPs that are associated with a hereditary form of macular degeneration (an eye condition), GWAS has been applied to the analysis of thousands of human genomes. To date, approximately 4000 SNP associations have been found for more than 200 diseases or traits. A large meta-analysis (a study aggregating the results of many other studies) summarizing GWAS results from dozens of studies was published by the Wellcome Trust Case Control Consortium in 2007. It drew together data from approximately 50 studies that had collectively assessed 14,000 genomes of patient cases and 3000 control genomes for seven common diseases. In total, 24 significant associations were detected for the seven diseases.

Figure 21.15 shows seven "Manhattan plots" (so named because their high-rise profile reminds some of the Manhattan skyline) that plot *P* values on the vertical axis against the SNP location for each of the diseases. In each Manhattan plot, chromosome numbers are identified, and statistically significant *P* values are highlighted in green. The strongest significant associations are found on chromosome 2 for bipolar disorder and on chromosome 9 for coronary artery disease. Each disorder also has additional associations. Crohn's disease has nine significant associations. The other diseases have three to seven significant associations. Most tests for SNP–disease association do not produce significant *P* values. These tests are represented by the light blue and dark blue background colors for each chromosome.

For most of the chromosome regions containing significant associations, the identity of the suspect genes has been determined. These too are shown in Figure 21.15. Some of these genes and associations confirm previously known information. For example, the chromosome 6 associations for rheumatoid arthritis and for type 1 (insulin-dependent) diabetes are with the *HLA-DRB1* gene in the HLA (human leucocyte antigen) system that is involved in these and several other autoimmune diseases. Other associations pointed to genes not previously known to be associated with disease. We look at the information identifying one of these genes, *CARD15,* in association with Crohn's disease in the Case Study at the end of the chapter.

Experience with GWAS analysis of the human genome has been both positive and negative. On the positive side, hundreds of new genes contributing to disease risk have been identified. New therapies are being developed to target these genes in an attempt to prevent or to more effectively treat disease. On the negative side are unexpectedly meager results. At its inception, many researchers expected GWAS analysis to find many significant

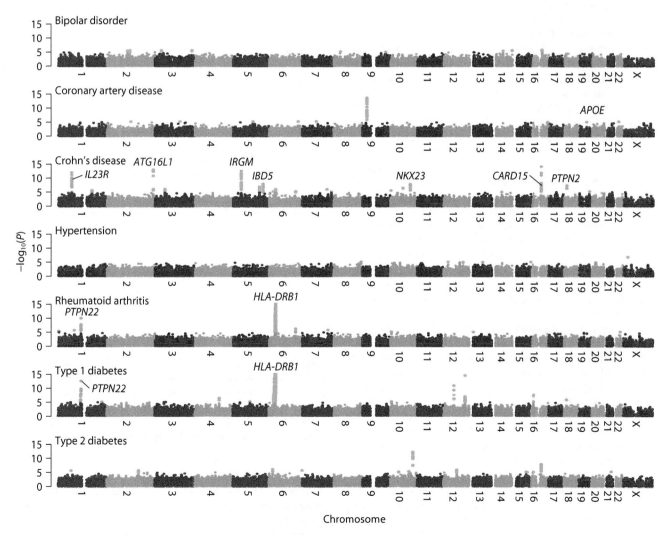

Figure 21.15 Manhattan plots of the results of a genome-wide association study of seven common diseases. The vertical axis shows *P* values for each SNP–disease association. The 22 human autosomes and the X chromosomes are represented along the horizontal axis. Green dots or bars indicate the locations of statistically significant associations. Known genes mapping to these regions are given.

associations with a large number of human diseases and traits. This has not happened, and to date only a small percentage of the inherited variation thought to exist has been detected. Several hypotheses have been proposed to account for the apparent inability of GWAS to detect the anticipated genetic variation. One of the strongest is that although the alleles causing increased disease susceptibility are numerous, each individual allele is rare. If so, then the variant allele leading to disease susceptibility may differ from family to family. This would make finding statistically significant *P* values an occasional rather than a frequent event.

CASE STUDY

GWAS and Crohn's Disease

Yasunori Ogura and colleagues used GWAS to identify several chromosome regions associated with Crohn's disease (CD), an inflammatory bowel disease that affects humans at a prevalence of 150 to 200 cases per 100,000 people. The etiology of CD is unknown, but one prominent hypothesis proposes that it is an inflammatory response to intestinal bacteria and other microflora.

CD clusters in families: Susceptibility to the disease is inherited but is influenced by multiple genes. The severity of CD is highly variable, from relatively mild to potentially fatal. Clinicians describe CD severity using a scale that captures the quantitative nature of the trait, making CD a candidate disease for QTL analysis. In the study by Ogura and colleagues, the strongest statistical evidence of association of a genetic marker with a susceptibility gene came from chromosome region 16q12. A gene initially identified as *NOD2* and subsequently renamed *CARD15* (caspase recruitment domain, member 15), is a candidate for a gene influencing susceptibility to CD.

GENE STRUCTURE AND MUTATION *CARD15* encodes 12 exons that direct the production of a 1040–amino acid protein. Ogura and colleagues sequenced the exons and introns of *CARD15* in 12 CD patients from different families having multiple cases of CD. They performed the same gene sequencing on four healthy control individuals as well. The study identified an identical C - G base pair insertion at nucleotide 3020 of exon 11 in three of the 12 CD patients. The insertion, designated *3020insC*, induces a frameshift mutation that generates a premature stop codon, shortening the mutant protein by 1007 amino acids.

Ogura and colleagues developed an allele-specific polymerase chain reaction (PCR) assay for *320insC* and tested 101 CD patients whose parents were heterozygous for the wild-type allele and the *320insC* allele. Of the 101 CD patients, 68 were homozygous for *320insC* (Figure 21.16a). Biochemical analysis shows mutant protein from the gene has only a small fraction of the activity of the wild-type protein. This diminished capacity reduces the sensitivity of the immune system to the microbial invader and, by a mechanism that remains to be elucidated, results in CD.

OTHER CONTRIBUTING MUTATIONS Mutations of *CARD15* are not the sole cause of CD; numerous CD patients do not carry *320insC* or any other known mutation of the gene. The Wellcome Trust Case Control Consortium publication in 2007 identified nine significant associations for Crohn's disease, and six of these genes have been identified, as well as *CARD15* (Figure 21.16b).

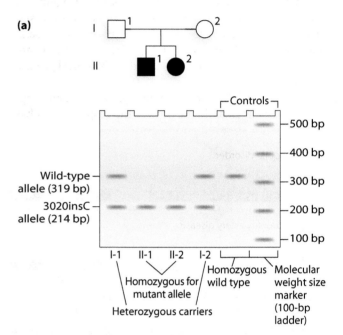

(b) SNPs significantly associated with Crohn's disease

Chromosome	Gene
1	*IL23R*
3	*ATG16LI*
5	*IRGM*
5	*IBD5*
10	*NKX2-3*
16	*CARD15*
18	*PTPN2*

Figure 21.16 **Detection of *320insC* in *CARD15* in a family with Crohn's disease.** (a) Gel electrophoresis of PCR products from four members of a family are shown in lanes 1 through 4. A wild-type control is in lane 5, and molecular weight size markers are in lane 6. (b) Seven QTLs influencing the expression of Crohn's disease, identified by GWAS.

Since the identification of *3020insC*, two additional mutations of *CARD15* have been found to increase the risk of CD. All three mutations appear to be null alleles, meaning that there is no functional protein product produced. The role of the protein product of *CARD15* is not fully known, but it appears to play a role in modulating inflammatory response. The absence of this protein may lead to an increase in the inflammatory response, a primary feature of Crohn's disease.

21.1 Quantitative Traits Display Continuous Phenotype Variation

- Quantitative phenotypic traits are polygenic and are described by scales of measure that can be assigned values having a quantitative basis.

- The phenotypes of multifactorial traits result from polygenic inheritance and the influence of environmental factors.

- Most quantitative traits have a continuous phenotypic distribution. Those influenced by larger numbers of genes are more likely to display continuous variation. Discontinuous variation in phenotype is particularly likely with threshold traits.

- Threshold traits are explained by additive alleles and have a threshold of liability that separates one phenotypic category (unaffected) from another (affected). The threshold of liability is crossed when a sufficient number of additive alleles accumulate in the genotype.

21.2 Quantitative Trait Analysis Is Statistical

- Quantitative traits are analyzed using statistical methods that evaluate the mean, median, mode, and variance of quantitative trait phenotype distribution.

- The frequency distribution for the phenotype range is described by the variance or the standard deviation in sample values. In the case of quantitative trait phenotypes, the phenotypic variance (V_P) is a useful measure of the sample distribution.

- The phenotypic variance of a trait is the sum of genetic variance (V_G) and environmental variance (V_E).

- Genetic variance is partitioned into additive variance (V_A), dominance variance (V_D), and interactive variance (V_I), the latter resulting from the epistatic interaction of genes determining a phenotype.

21.3 Heritability Measures the Genetic Component of Phenotypic Variation

- Heritability is a measure of the extent to which genetic variation contributes to total phenotypic variation.

- Broad sense heritability (H^2) measures the ratio of genetic variance to phenotypic variance (V_G/V_P). One method of applying broad sense heritability analysis to humans is through twin studies that give a general estimate of heritability.

- Narrow sense heritability (h^2) measures the contribution of additive genetic variance to phenotypic variance (V_A/V_P).

- Narrow sense heritability is used to predict the selection response (R) of a trait to artificial selection.

21.4 Quantitative Trait Loci Are the Genes That Contribute to Quantitative Traits

- QTL mapping is used to determine the location of potential QTLs in genomes using methods that closely resemble recombination mapping.

- Controlled crosses and analysis of recombinant chromosomes are required for QTL mapping.

- Specific genes influencing quantitative trait phenotypes are identified and their variation characterized through QTL candidate locus analysis.

- Genome-wide association studies (GWAS) scan the entire genome of organisms in random mating populations for statistical evidence of QTLs.

KEYWORDS

additive gene (additive trait) *(p. 715)*
additive variance (V_A) *(p. 726)*
broad sense heritability (H^2) *(p. 727)*
concordance *(p. 728)*
continuous variation *(p. 714)*
directional selection *(p. 730)*
discontinuous variation *(p. 714)*
discordance *(p. 728)*
disruptive selection *(p. 730)*
dominance variance (V_D) *(p. 726)*
environmental variance (V_E) *(p. 725)*
frequency distribution *(p. 721)*
genetic liability *(p. 720)*
genetic variance (V_G) *(p. 725)*

genome-wide association study (GWAS) *(p. 734)*
heritability *(p. 726)*
interactive variance (V_I) *(p. 726)*
introgression line (IL) (near isogenic line) (NIL) *(p. 732)*
major gene *(p. 715)*
median (median value) *(p. 724)*
mode (modal value) *(p. 724)*
modifier gene *(p. 715)*
multifactorial trait *(p. 714)*
multiple-gene hypothesis *(p. 715)*
narrow sense heritability (h^2) *(p. 727)*
phenotypic variance (V_P) *(p. 725)*

polygenic inheritance *(p. 714)*
polygenic trait *(p. 714)*
quantitative genetics *(p. 714)*
quantitative trait *(p. 714)*
quantitative trait locus (QTL) *(p. 730)*
QTL mapping *(p. 730)*
response to selection (R) *(p. 729)*
selection differential (S) *(p. 729)*
stabilizing selection *(p. 730)*
standard deviation (s) *(p. 725)*
threshold of genetic liability *(p. 720)*
threshold trait *(p. 719)*
variance (s^2) *(p. 724)*

Chapter Concepts

For answers to selected even-numbered problems, see Appendix: Answers.

1. Which of the following traits would you expect to be inherited as quantitative traits?
   a. body weight in chickens
   b. growth rate in sheep
   c. milk production in cattle
   d. fruit weight in tomatoes
   e. coat color in dogs

2. For the traits listed in the previous problem, which do you think are likely to be multifactorial traits with phenotypes that are influenced by genes and environment? Identify two environmental factors that might play a role in phenotypic variation of the traits you identified.

3. Compare and contrast broad sense heritability and narrow sense heritability, giving an example of each measurement and identifying how the measurement is used.

4. In a cross of two pure-breeding lines of tomatoes producing different fruit sizes, the variance in grams (g) of fruit weight in the F_1 is 2.25 g, and the variance among the F_2 is 5.40 g. Determine the genetic and environmental variance (V_G and V_E) for the trait and the broad sense heritability of the trait.

5. Describe the difference between continuous phenotypic variation and discontinuous variation. Explain how polygenic inheritance could be the basis of a trait showing continuous phenotypic variation. Explain how polygenic inheritance can be the basis of a threshold trait.

6. Calculate the mean, variance, and standard deviation for a sample of turkeys weighed at 8 weeks of age that have the following weights in ounces: 161, 172, 155, 173, 149, 177, 156, 174, 158, 162, 171, 181.

7. Provide a definition and an example for each of the following terms:
   a. additive genes
   b. concordance of twin pairs
   c. multifactorial inheritance
   d. polygenic inheritance
   e. quantitative trait locus
   f. threshold trait

Application and Integration

For answers to selected even-numbered problems, see Appendix: Answers.

8. Three pairs of genes with two alleles each (A_1 and A_2, B_1 and B_2, and C_1 and C_2) control the height of a plant. The alleles of these genes have an additive relationship: each copy of alleles A_1, B_1, and C_1 contributes 6 cm to plant height, and each copy of alleles A_2, B_2, and C_2 contributes 3 cm.
   a. What are the expected heights of plants with each of the homozygous genotypes $A_1A_1B_1B_1C_1C_1$ and $A_2A_2B_2B_2C_2C_2$?
   b. What height is expected in the F_1 progeny of a cross between $A_1A_1B_1B_1C_1C_1$ and $A_2A_2B_2B_2C_2C_2$?
   c. What is the expected height of a plant with the genotype $A_1A_2B_2B_2C_1C_2$?
   d. Identify all possible genotypes for plants with an expected height of 33 cm.
   e. Identify the number of different genotypes that are possible with these three genes.
   f. Identify the number of different phenotypes (expected plant heights) that are possible with these three genes.

9. For the three-gene system in the previous problem, suppose that instead of incomplete dominance among the additive alleles of each gene, the 1 allele is dominant in each case

and the 2 allele is recessive. Under this revised scheme, the dominant phenotype contributes 10 cm to expected height and the recessive phenotype contributes 4 cm.
   a. What is the expected height of a plant that is homozygous for 1 alleles?
   b. What is the expected height of a plant that is homozygous for 2 alleles?
   c. What is the height of the F_1 progeny of these homozygous plants?
   d. What are the phenotypes and proportions of each phenotype among the F_2?

10. Two inbred lines of sunflowers (P_1 and P_2) produce different total weights of seeds per flower head. The mean weight of seeds (grams) and the variance of seed weights in different generations are as follows.

Generation	Mean Weight/Head (g)	Variance
P_1	105	3.0
P_2	135	3.8
F_1	122	3.5
F_2	125	7.4

a. Use the information above to determine V_G, V_E, and V_P for this trait.

b. Determine H^2 for this trait.

11. A total of 20 men and 20 women volunteer to participate in a statistics project. The height and weight of each subject are given in the table.

Subject	Men		Women	
	Height (in.)	Weight (lb)	Height (in.)	Weight (lb)
1	65	136	60	95
2	66	146	61	103
3	67	141	62	110
4	67	148	62	109
5	68	147	62	118
6	68	166	63	137
7	69	165	63	152
8	69	173	64	134
9	69	159	64	127
10	70	188	64	166
11	70	183	65	129
12	70	179	65	130
13	70	190	66	148
14	71	169	66	152
15	71	186	67	155
16	71	190	67	149
17	72	206	68	157
18	72	210	68	138
19	73	238	69	162
20	74	267	70	169

a. Draw one histogram for height of the subjects and a separate histogram for weight. Use different colors for men and women so that you can visually compare the distributions by sex and plot weights in 10-pound intervals (i.e., 90–99 lbs, 100–109 lbs, 110–119 lbs, etc.).

b. Calculate the mean, variance, and standard deviation for height and weight in men and women.

c. Compare the numerical values with the visual distribution of heights and weights you drew in the histograms and describe whether you think your visual impression matches the numerical values.

12. In *Nicotiana*, two inbred strains produce long (P_L) and short (P_S) corollas. These lines are crossed to produce F_1, and the F_1 are crossed to produce F_2 plants in which corolla length and variance are measured. The following table summarizes mean and variance of corolla length in each generation. Calculate H^2 for corolla length in *Nicotiana*.

Generation	Mean Corolla Length (mm)	Variance
P_L	85.75	4.21
P_S	43.15	2.89
F_1	62.26	3.62
F_2	67.37	38.10

13. Suppose the length of maize ears has narrow sense heritability (h^2) of 0.70. A population produces ears that have an average length of 28 cm, and from this population a breeder selects a plant producing 34-cm ears to cross by self-fertilization. Predict the selection differential (S) and the response to selection (R) for this cross.

14. In a line of cherry tomatoes, the average fruit weight is 16 grams. A plant producing tomatoes with an average weight of 12 grams is used in one self-fertilization cross to produce a line of smaller tomatoes, and a plant producing tomatoes of 24 grams is used in a second cross to produce larger tomatoes.

a. What is the selection differential (S) for fruit weight in each cross?

b. If narrow sense heritability (h^2) for this trait is 0.80, what are the expected responses to selection (R) for fruit weight in the crosses?

15. Two pure-breeding wheat strains, one producing dark red kernels and the other producing white kernels, are crossed to produce F_1 with pink kernel color. When an F_1 plant is self-fertilized and its seed collected and planted, the resulting F_2 consist of 160 plants with kernel colors as shown in the following table.

Kernel Color	Number
White	9
Dark red	12
Red	39
Light pink	41
Pink	59

a. Based on the F_2 progeny, how many genes are involved in kernel color determination?

b. How many additive alleles are required to explain the five phenotypes seen in the F_2?

c. Using clearly defined allele symbols of your choice, give genotypes for the parental strains and the F_1. Describe the genotypes that produce the different phenotypes in the F_2.

d. If an F_1 plant is crossed to a dark red plant, what are the expected progeny phenotypes and what is the expected proportion of each phenotype?

16. In studies of human MZ and DZ twin pairs of the same sex who are reared together, the following concordance values are identified for various traits. Based on the values shown, describe the relative importance of genes versus the influence of environmental factors for each trait.

Trait	Concordance	
	MZ	DZ
Blood type	100	65
Chicken pox	89	87
Manic depression	67	13
Schizophrenia	72	12
Diabetes	62	15
Cleft lip	51	6
Club foot	40	4

17. During a visit with your grandparents, they comment on how tall you are compared to them. You tell them that in your genetics class, you learned that height in humans has high heritability, although environmental factors also influence adult height. You correctly explain the meaning of heritability, and your grandfather asks, "How can height be highly heritable and still be influenced by the environment?" What explanation do you give your grandfather?

18. An association of racehorse owners is seeking a new genetic strategy to improve the running speed of their horses. Traditional breeding of fast male and female horses has proven expensive and time-consuming, and the breeders are interested in an approach using quantitative trait loci as a basis for selecting breeding pairs of horses. Write a brief synopsis (~50 words) of QTL mapping to explain how genes influencing running speed might be identified in horses.

19. Applied to the study of the human genome, a goal of GWAS is to locate chromosome regions that are likely to contain genes influencing the risk of disease. Specific genes can be identified in these regions, and particular mutant alleles that increase disease risk can be sequenced. To date, the identification of alleles that increase disease risk has occasionally led to a new therapeutic strategy, but more often the identification of disease alleles is the only outcome.
    a. From a physician's point of view, what is the value of being able to identify alleles that increase the risk of a particular disease?
    b. What is the value of being able to identify alleles that increase disease risk for a person who is currently free of the disease but who is at risk of developing the disease due to its presence in the family?
    c. What personal or ethical issues arising from GWAS might be of concern to physicians or to those who might carry an allele that increases disease risk?

20. Suppose a polygenic system for producing color in kernels of a grain is controlled by three additive genes, G, M, and T. There are two alleles of each gene, G_1 and G_2, M_1 and M_2, and T_1 and T_2. The phenotypic effects of the three genotypes of the G gene are $G_1G_1 = 6$ units of color, $G_1G_2 = 3$ units of color, and $G_2G_2 = 1$ unit of color. The phenotypic effects for genes M and T are similar, giving the phenotype of a plant with the genotype $G_1G_1M_1M_1T_1T_1$ a total of 18 units of color and a plant with the genotype $G_2G_2M_2M_2T_2T_2$ a total of 3 units of color.
    a. How many units of color are found in trihybrid plants?
    b. Two trihybrid plants are mated. What is the expected proportion of progeny plants displaying 9 units of color? Explain your answer.
    c. Suppose that instead of an additive genetic system, kernel-color determination in this organism is a threshold system. The appearance of color in kernels requires 9 or more units of color; otherwise, kernels have no color and appear white. In other words, plants whose phenotypes contain 8 or fewer units of color are white. Based on the threshold model, what proportion of the F_2 progeny produced by the trihybrid cross in part (b) will be white? Explain your answer.
    d. Assuming the threshold model applies to this kernel-color system, what proportion of the progeny of the cross $G_1G_2M_2M_2T_2T_2 \times G_1G_2M_1M_2T_1T_2$ do you expect to display colored kernels?

21. New Zealand lamb breeders measure the following variance values for their herd.

Trait	V_P	V_G	V_A
Body mass (kg)	42.4	20.5	7.4
Body fat (%)	38.9	16.2	5.7
Body length (cm)	51.6	26.4	8.1

    a. Calculate the broad sense heritability (H^2) and the narrow sense heritability (h^2) for each trait in this lamb herd.
    b. How would you characterize the potential response to selection (R) for each trait?

22. Cattle breeders would like to improve the protein content and butterfat content of milk produced by a herd of cows. Narrow sense heritability values are 0.60 for protein content and 0.80 for butterfat content. The average percentages of these traits in the herd and the percentages of the traits in cows selected for breeding are as follows.

Trait	Herd Average	Selected Cows
Protein content	20.2%	22.7%
Butterfat content	6.5%	7.4%

    a. Determine the selection differential (S) for each trait in this herd.
    b. Which trait is likely to be the most responsive to artificial selection applied by the cattle breeders through selection of cows for mating?

23. In human gestational development, abnormalities of the closure of the lower part of the midface can result in cleft lip, if the lip alone is affected by the closure defect,

or in cleft lip and palate (the roof of the mouth), if the closure defect is more extensive. Cleft lip and cleft lip with cleft palate are multifactorial disorders that are threshold traits. A family with a history of either condition has a significantly increased chance of a recurrence of midface cleft disorder in comparison to families without such a history. However, the recurrence risk of a midface cleft disorder is higher in families with a history of cleft lip with cleft palate than in families with a history of cleft lip alone.

a. Suppose a friend of yours who has not taken genetics asks you to explain these observations. Construct a genetic explanation for the increased recurrence risk of midface clefting in families that have a history of cleft disorders versus families without a history of such disorders.

b. Construct a similar explanation of why the recurrence risk of a cleft disorder is higher in families with a history of cleft lip with cleft palate than in families with a history of cleft lip alone.

24. The children of couples in which one partner has blood type O (genotype ii) and the other partner has blood type AB (genotype $I^A I^B$) are studied.

a. What is the expected concordance rate for blood type of MZ twins in this study? Explain your answer.

b. What is the expected concordance rate for blood type of DZ twins in this study? Explain why this answer is different from the answer to part (a).

25. Answer the following in regard to multifactorial traits in human twins.

a. If the trait is substantially influenced by genes, would you expect the concordance rate to be higher in MZ twins or higher in DZ twins? Explain your reasoning.

b. If the trait is produced with little contribution from genetic variation, what would you expect to see if you compared the concordance rates of MZ twins versus DZ twins? Explain your reasoning.

22

Population Genetics and Evolution at the Population, Species, and Molecular Levels

CHAPTER OUTLINE

22.1 The Hardy-Weinberg Equilibrium Describes the Relationship of Allele and Genotype Frequencies in Populations

22.2 Natural Selection Operates through Differential Reproductive Fitness within a Population

22.3 Mutation Diversifies Gene Pools

22.4 Migration Is Movement of Organisms and Genes between Populations

22.5 Genetic Drift Causes Allele Frequency Change by Sampling Error

22.6 Inbreeding Alters Genotype Frequencies

22.7 Species and Higher Taxonomic Groups Evolve by the Interplay of Four Evolutionary Processes

22.8 Molecular Evolution Changes Genes and Genomes through Time

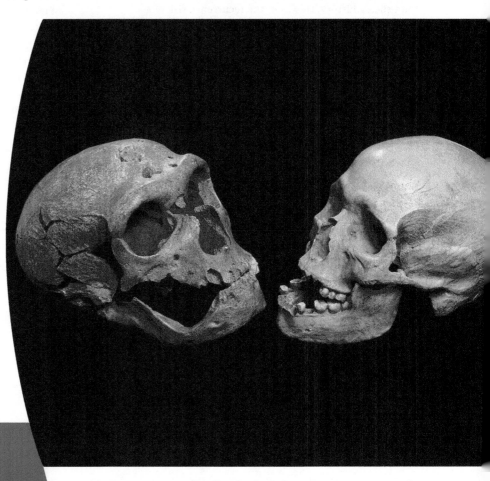

ESSENTIAL IDEAS

- The Hardy-Weinberg equilibrium predicts frequencies of genotypes in populations.

- The impact of natural selection on allele frequencies can be estimated.

- The effect of mutations on allele frequencies can be quantified.

- The effects of migration on allele frequencies in populations can be determined.

- Chance events can lead to changes in allele frequency.

- Inbreeding is a pattern of nonrandom mating that can alter genotype frequencies.

- Species evolve by processes that lead to genetic isolation.

Modern humans, represented by the skull of *Homo sapiens sapiens* at the right, evolved from a branch of the human phylogenetic tree that gave rise to Neandertals, represented by the skull of *Homo sapiens neanderthalensis* at the left. Neandertals lived in Europe and Asia until about 30,000 years ago, and recent research comparing the modern human and Neandertal genomes finds tell-tale evidence of interbreeding between the lineages.

In 1970, Theodosius Dobzhansky, one of the most influential geneticists of the 20th century, wrote:

> Nothing in biology makes sense except in the light of evolution.

Dobzhansky and the other architects of the *modern synthesis of evolution* (see Section 1.4) identified evolution and evolutionary analysis as central organizing principles of biology, necessary for understanding modern forms of life and their origins. Evolution shaped the living world we see today, just as it shaped life in the past and will continue to shape life into the future.

The modern synthesis focused on uniting two elements of evolutionary biology. One was the large-scale evolutionary change linked to speciation and to the divergence of taxonomic groups above the species level. The second element included what was known about Mendelian inheritance and the connection between inherited molecular variation (i.e., variation of DNA and protein sequences) and evolutionary change. All four of the evolutionary processes—natural selection, mutation, migration, and genetic drift—play a role in shaping the evolutionary history of genes, proteins, populations, and species (see Section 1.4).

The impact of the evolutionary processes has been a focus of population biologists, evolutionary biologists, and mathematicians since the beginning of the 20th century, several decades before DNA was identified as the hereditary molecule and its structure became known. Since those early days, the central predictions made about populations on the basis of evolutionary principles have been proven correct time and again in countless experiments and observations. In this chapter, we focus both on the evolution of populations and on evolution at the molecular level, that is, the evolution of genes, genomes, and proteins. We begin our discussion with the application of evolutionary principles to populations that forms the foundation of the field of **population genetics.** We then discuss the operation of each of the evolutionary processes, using examples that largely focus on humans. The causes of speciation are then explored, and we conclude the chapter with a discussion of the evolution of genes and genomes.

22.1 The Hardy-Weinberg Equilibrium Describes the Relationship of Allele and Genotype Frequencies in Populations

The origin of population genetics can be traced to the earliest years of the 1900s, shortly after the rediscovery of Mendel's laws of heredity, and to a time when George Udny Yule, William Castle, Karl Pearson, Godfrey Hardy, Wilhelm Weinberg, and others first debated the fate of genes in populations. In 1902, the inheritance of brachydactyly (OMIM 112500), an autosomal dominant condition characterized by shortening of fingers and toes, was described in humans as a trait paralleling a Mendelian pattern of heredity. In contemplating this observation, Yule proposed that since three-quarters of the progeny of a cross of heterozygous parents with brachydactyly will also display shortened digits, the frequency of the dominant allele might be expected to increase over time. William Castle thought Yule was wrong, and in 1903 he offered, as a partial refutation of Yule's contention, a mathematical demonstration that in the absence of natural selection, genotype frequencies remain stable in populations. Karl Pearson supported Castle's position by showing that if two alleles of a gene had equal frequency in a population, there would be a single, stable equilibrium frequency for their genotypes. Reginald Punnett (of Punnett square fame) also thought Yule was wrong, but unable to formulate a mathematical argument to refute Yule, he took the problem to his friend and regular cricket partner Godfrey Hardy.

Hardy, a mathematician rather than a biologist, quickly identified a "very simple" solution to the question of the fate of alleles in populations. He showed that with random mating and in the absence of evolutionary change in a population, the allele frequencies result in a stable equilibrium frequency. Hardy also showed that, at equilibrium, allele frequencies are stable and that genotypes occur in predictable frequencies derived directly from allele frequencies. In 1908, Hardy penned a letter to the editors of *Science* magazine that began with these self-effacing words:

> I am reluctant to intrude in a discussion concerning matters of which I have no expert knowledge, and I should have expected the very simple point which I wish to make to have been familiar to biologists. However, some remarks of Mr. Udny Yule, to which Mr. R. C. Punnett has called my attention, suggest it may be worth making.

In his letter, Hardy laid out the concept that has become known as the **Hardy-Weinberg (H-W) equilibrium.** The name recognizes Hardy's explanation of allele and genotype frequencies in populations as well as an independent explanation of the same principle by Wilhelm Weinberg (a German physician) that was also published in 1908. The H-W equilibrium is a cornerstone of population genetics and was the first of many developments in evolutionary genetics that culminated in the modern synthesis. Hardy may have been reluctant to intrude into matters of biology, but biologists for more than 100 years have been glad he did!

Populations and Gene Pools

A **population** is a group of interbreeding organisms. The collection of genes and alleles found in the members of a population is known as a **gene pool.** The gene pool is the source of genetic information from which the next generation is produced. Each population member carries a portion of the gene pool in its genome, but typically, the amount of genetic variation in a gene pool is greater than the variation carried by individual members of the population. The pattern of mating between individuals and the effect of evolutionary processes on alleles determine (1) how alleles are dispersed into genotypes and (2) their frequencies in successive generations.

The H-W equilibrium serves as a model that calculates the frequencies of alleles and genotypes in a theoretical population that is infinite in size, practices random mating, and does not experience evolutionary change. Under these conditions, the H-W equilibrium predicts that allele frequencies will be stable from generation to generation, that the frequencies of genotypes are predictable from their constituent allele frequencies, and that genotype frequencies too will remain the same in successive generations.

In nature, however, no real population meets all the criteria assumed by the H-W equilibrium. For example, all populations are finite in size and are subject to genetic drift as a consequence (a phenomenon we encounter in Section 22.5). In addition, natural selection, migration, and mutation each exert their influences on a population. Despite these circumstances, most populations adhere closely enough to the assumptions of the H-W equilibrium that alleles are distributed into genotypes in the proportions it predicts. The H-W equilibrium has proven to be a dependable arithmetic tool for assessing population genetic structure and detecting evolutionary change and nonrandom mating, and it is applied in numerous ways to the analysis of autosomal and X-linked genes in populations.

The Hardy-Weinberg Equilibrium

The predictions of the H-W equilibrium can be modeled for any number of alleles of an autosomal or an X-linked gene. The simplest model, however, is for two alleles of an autosomal gene, here designated A_1 and A_2, and we will discuss this model exclusively. The assumptions and predictions of the H-W equilibrium are given in **Table 22.1**. The assumptions of the H-W equilibrium can be thought of simply as meaning that the population is infinitely large, experiences no evolution, and contains members that mate at random. As stated previously, these assumptions are not met by real populations, but reality is often close enough to the theory to allow accurate predictions to be made based on the H-W equilibrium. For the general case of two alleles of an autosomal gene, the alleles are given frequencies of $f(A_1) = p$ and $f(A_2) = q$, with the frequencies equal in males and females. Since A_1 and A_2 are the only alleles that occur at this gene, the sum of their frequencies is $p + q = 1.0$. Rearrangements of this equality allow the frequency of one allele to be used to determine the frequency of the other allele; thus, $p = 1 - q$ and $q = 1 - p$.

Table 22.1	The Hardy-Weinberg Equilibrium

Assumptions

1. Population size is infinite, and no genetic drift occurs.
2. Random mating occurs in the population, allowing genotype frequencies to be predicted by allele frequencies.
3. Natural selection does not operate.
4. Migration does not introduce new alleles.
5. Mutation does not introduce new alleles.

Predictions

1. Allele frequencies remain stable over time.
2. Allele distribution into genotypes is predictable.
3. Stable equilibrium frequencies of alleles and genotypes are maintained.
4. Evolutionary and nonrandom mating effects are predictable.

Allelic segregation predicts the relationship between allele frequencies and genotype frequencies in populations. For the two alleles in our example, there are three genotypes: A_1A_1, A_1A_2, and A_2A_2. The genotype frequencies are computed using a binomial expansion $[(p + q)^2]$, where the two $(p + q)$ expressions represent male and female contributions to mating. Alternatively, a representation of random mating in the population that resembles a Punnett square can be used. Both methods make the same genotype frequency predictions of $f(A_1A_1) = p^2$, $f(A_1A_2) = 2pq$, and $f(A_2A_2) = q^2$ **(Figure 22.1)**. The summation of these three genotype frequencies equals unity: $p^2 + 2pq + q^2 = 1.0$.

We can demonstrate the application of the H-W equilibrium by assigning frequencies to each allele in a hypothetical population: say, $f(A_1) = p = 0.6$ and $f(A_2) = q = 0.4$. As required, the sum of the two allele frequencies is $0.6 + 0.4 = 1.0$. In this hypothetical population example, 60 percent of gametes carry A_1 and 40 percent carry A_2 **(Figure 22.2)**. If the population is in H-W equilibrium, probability predicts that an A_1-containing gamete from a male and an A_1-containing female gamete will unite to produce A_1A_1 progeny with a probability of $(0.6)(0.6) = 0.36$.

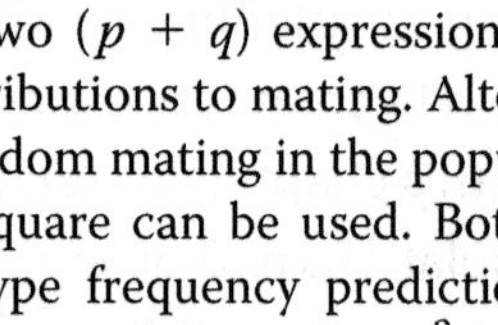

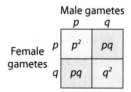

Binomial expansion
$(p + q)(p + q) = p^2 + pq + pq + q^2 = p^2 + 2pq + q^2 = 1$

Figure 22.1   The Hardy-Weinberg equilibrium for autosomal genes. The Punnett square method and the binomial expansion of alleles with frequencies p and q predict genotype frequencies under assumptions of the Hardy-Weinberg equilibrium.

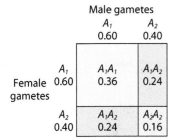

Binomial expansion:
$(0.60 + 0.40)(0.60 + 0.40) = 0.36 + 0.24 + 0.24 + 0.16 = 1.00$

Genotype frequencies:
$A_1A_1 = 0.36$
$A_1A_2 = 0.48$
$A_2A_2 = \underline{0.16}$
Total = 1.00

Figure 22.2 **Application of the Hardy-Weinberg equilibrium.** The Punnett square method and the binomial expansion method applied to a population in which $f(A_1) = 0.60$ and $f(A_2) = 0.40$.

Similarly, the production of A_2A_2 progeny, from the union of two A_2-containing gametes, has a probability of $(0.4)(0.4) = 0.16$. Heterozygous progeny are produced in two ways, with a combined frequency predicted as $(0.6)(0.4) + (0.6)(0.4) = 0.48$. The sum of frequencies of the three genotypes is $(0.36) + (0.48) + (0.16) = 1.00$. The binomial expansion method of calculating the genotype frequencies in progeny makes identical predictions.

In this example we see one of the predictions of the H-W equilibrium: Random mating for one generation produces genotype frequencies that can be predicted from allele frequencies. For any frequencies of p and q between 0.0 and 1.0, an expected equilibrium distribution of genotype frequencies can be derived (**Figure 22.3**). Notice that as the frequency of p decreases and q increases, the proportions of genotypes shift, altering the frequency of each homozygous class and the frequency of heterozygotes in

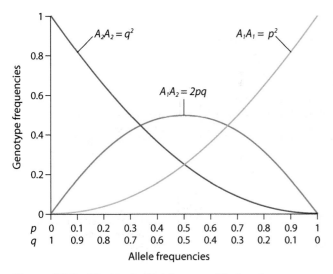

Figure 22.3 **The Hardy-Weinberg equilibrium for two autosomal alleles.** Each curve shows the frequency of the genotype for the indicated frequencies of the alleles p and q.

the population. Heterozygous frequency has a maximum of 0.50 (50 percent), when the frequencies are $p = q = 0.50$.

This example also allows us to observe the second prediction of the H-W equilibrium: With random mating and no evolution, allele frequencies do not change from one generation to the next. We see this if we count the alleles in progeny genotypes, recognizing that *all* of the alleles in A_1A_1 are alleles of a single type, and all the alleles in A_2A_2 progeny are alleles of the other type. The A_1A_1 progeny are 36 percent of the new generation, and A_2A_2 are 16 percent. Among the 48 percent of the progeny that are heterozygotes, exactly *one-half* of the alleles are A_1 and *one-half* are A_2. Consequently, the frequency of A_1 among the progeny is 36 percent plus 24 percent, or 60 percent of the alleles carried by progeny, which is the same frequency that was seen in the parental generation. The A_2 frequency is 16 percent plus 24 percent, or 40 percent of the progeny-generation alleles, also the same as the frequency found in the parental generation. Expressed as p and q, the frequency of A_1 in the progeny generation is $f(A_1) = p^2 + pq$, and the frequency of A_2 is $f(A_2) = q^2 + pq$.

The observation that random mating leads to predictable genotype frequencies and that allele frequencies are stable from one generation to the next can be portrayed in a mating-table format that shows the consequence of reproduction under the assumptions of the H-W equilibrium (**Table 22.2**). In the mating-table analysis, parental genotypes unite to reproduce at proportions predicted by their frequency. If parents have the same genotype, there is no reciprocal mating to account for, but if different genotypes occur in the parents, the reciprocal matings must be taken into account. The progeny of each mating are predicted according to Mendelian principles. The frequency or fraction of offspring with each genotype is summed once the table is filled. The term that is the sum of each genotype frequency can be simplified to show that offspring are produced in the genotype proportions p^2, $2pq$, and q^2, just as they occur in the parents. This analysis is compelling evidence that in the presence of random mating and the absence of evolutionary change, the allele frequencies in populations are stable over time.

In populations that meet the assumptions of the H-W equilibrium, a single generation of random mating will "reset" the genotype frequencies in the population into the predicted proportions p^2, $2pq$, and q^2. Moreover, if a population *is not* initially in H-W equilibrium, we can predict the consequence of one generation of random mating. As an example, **Figure 22.4** illustrates the effect of uniting two previously separate populations with different frequencies of A_1 and A_2 to form a new population. Each of the contributing populations originally contained 500 individuals, and the new population contains 1000 individuals. Immediately after forming the new population, the genotypes *are not* in Hardy-Weinberg proportions. One generation of mating in the new population under Hardy-Weinberg assumptions, however, produces

Table 22.2	Hardy-Weinberg Mating Table for Two Alleles of an Autosomal Gene			
Mating	**Mating Frequency**	**Progeny Genotypes**		
		A_1A_1	A_1A_2	A_2A_2
$A_1A_1 \times A_1A_1$	$(p^2)(p^2) = p^4$	p^4	—	—
$A_1A_1 \times A_1A_2$	$2[(p^2)(2pq)] = 4p^3q$	$2p^3q$	$2p^3q$	—
$A_1A_1 \times A_2A_2$	$2[(p^2)(q^2)] = 2p^2q^2$	—	$2p^2q^2$	—
$A_1A_2 \times A_1A_2$	$(2pq)(2pq) = 4p^2q^2$	p^2q^2	$2p^2q^2$	p^2q^2
$A_1A_2 \times A_2A_2$	$2[(2pq)(q^2)] = 4pq^3$	—	$2pq^3$	$2pq^3$
$A_2A_2 \times A_2A_2$	$(q^2)(q^2) = q^4$	—	—	q^4
Total	1.0	p^2	$2pq$	q^2

Among the progeny, a common term is factored out of each summation to produce the frequency of each genotype:

$$A_1A_1 = p^4 + 2p^3q + p^2q^2 = p^2(p^2 + 2pq + q^2) = p^2$$
$$A_1A_2 = 2p^3q + 2p^2q^2 + 2p^2q^2 + 2pq^3 = 2pq(p^2 + pq + pq + q^2) = 2pq$$
$$A_2A_2 = p^2q^2 + 2pq^3 + q^4 = q^2(p^2 + 2pq + q^2) = q^2$$

The sum of progeny genotype frequencies is $p^2 + 2pq + q^2 = 1.0$.

genotype frequencies in the next generation that *are* in H-W equilibrium. The new population has new allele frequencies as a result of the mixing of the two populations.

Determining Autosomal Allele Frequencies in Populations

Allele frequencies and genotype frequencies are commonly used measures of the genetic structure of populations. Comparison of these frequencies between populations can identify relationships and diversification of populations, and documentation of allele frequency change over time is a hallmark of population evolution.

Allele frequencies in populations can be estimated by two methods, the gene-counting method and the square root method. The gene-counting method does not require any assumptions about the population; it only requires that all genotypes can be identified. The square root method assumes the population is in H-W equilibrium. The square root method is often used when the trait of interest is the result of a recessive homozygous genotype and where the heterozygous and homozygous dominant genotypes result in identical phenotypes.

For the gene-counting method, the allele frequencies can be calculated in two ways: either by calculating the proportions of genotypes or by directly counting the number

Figure 22.4 **One generation of random mating produces Hardy-Weinberg equilibrium frequencies for genotypes of autosomal genes.**

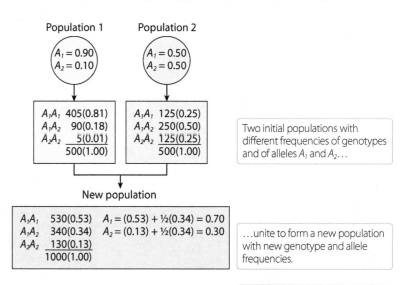

of alleles from the genotypes themselves. We describe these two approaches separately for convenience, but they are really the same. The choice of method is dictated by the type of genotype or phenotype information available and the composition of the population or of the sample data.

The Genotype Proportion Method The first approach to gene counting is called the **genotype proportion method.** This approach calculates allele frequencies (f) by adding the frequency of the homozygotes for the allele and the frequency of one-half of the heterozygotes carrying the allele. As an example, suppose that a population has the following composition: $B_1B_1 = 0.64$, $B_1B_2 = 0.32$, $B_2B_2 = 0.04$. Applying the genotype proportion method, the frequency of B_1 is the sum of the frequency of B_1B_1 plus one-half the frequency of B_1B_2 heterozygotes. In this case, $f(B_1) = p = (0.64) + [(0.5)(0.32)] = 0.80$. Similarly, for B_2, the allele frequency is calculated by adding the frequency of B_2B_2 and one-half the frequency of B_1B_2, or $f(B_2) = q = (0.04) + [(0.5)(0.32)] = 0.20$. For this example, notice that $p + q = 0.80 + 0.20 = 1.0$.

The Allele-Counting Method The second approach to the gene-counting method is called the **allele-counting method.** As an example of the allele-counting method, consider the human MN blood group system, a codominant system produced by two alleles, M and N. Both alleles are present in all human populations and produce three blood group phenotypes: type M, type MN, and type N. Each blood group has a corresponding genotype. Individuals with blood type M or blood type N have homozygous genotypes MM and NN, respectively, and the blood type MN is produced by the MN genotype. MN blood group testing of 1482 members of a Japanese population produced the following results:

Blood group	M	MN	N	
Number	406	744	332	=1482

The allele frequency calculation recognizes that each of the 1482 people in the sample carries two alleles of the gene and that there are $(2)(1482) = 2964$ alleles represented in the sample. The frequency of each allele is determined by counting the two alleles of that type from each homozygote and the single allele of that type from each heterozygote. The allele frequencies are therefore $f(M) = [(2)(406) + (744)]/2964 = 0.525$ and $f(N) = [(2)(332) + (744)]/2964 = 0.475$.

The Square Root Method The alternative approach for allele frequency determination in populations is the **square root method.** It is used only when the two alleles of a gene are dominant and recessive and when the condition or trait of interest is recessive. In the human autosomal recessive disorder cystic fibrosis, for example, one allele (cf) is recessive and therefore is evident only in the homozygous genotype. When the recessive allele is in a heterozygous genotype, it is "hidden" by the dominant allele (CF). In a circumstance like this, the dominant phenotype consists of two genotypes, $CFCF$ and $CFcf$. In contrast, the recessive phenotype is produced only by the homozygous recessive genotype $cfcf$. The correspondence of the recessive phenotype and homozygous genotype allows use of the Hardy-Weinberg principles to estimate the frequency of the recessive allele by taking the square root of the recessive homozygous genotype frequency. In the U.S. population, the frequency of cystic fibrosis among newborn infants is approximately 1 in 2000. Where $f(CF) = p$ and $f(cf) = q$, $f(cfcf) = q^2 = 0.0005$. The frequency of q is thus estimated as the square root of 0.0005, or $f(q) = 0.022$; that is, about 2.2 percent.

With $f(cf)$ determined, the frequency of CF is estimated as $f(CF) = p = 1 - q = 1.0 - 0.022 = 0.978$. The frequency of carriers of cystic fibrosis is of practical importance for determining the chance that a person is a carrier of cystic fibrosis. According to the Hardy-Weinberg principle, the population frequency of carriers is $f(CFcf) = 2pq = 2(0.978)(0.022) = 0.043$. In other words, approximately 4.3 percent of the population, or about 1 in 23 people, carry a recessive mutant allele for cystic fibrosis. Estimates like this can be particularly valuable in genetic counseling situations, where it is desirable to know the probability that a person who has a dominant phenotype might be a heterozygous carrier of a recessive allele. **Genetic Analysis 22.1** provides more practice in calculating allele frequencies and applying the H-W equilibrium.

The Hardy-Weinberg Equilibrium for More than Two Alleles

Having examined the application of the H-W equilibrium to genes with two alleles, we can now consider the more complex case of a gene that has more than two alleles. We shall limit our discussion to three alleles, whose frequencies are represented by the variables p, q, and r, where $p + q + r = 1.0$, and where the trinomial expansion $(p + q + r)^2$ represents random mating and predicts the distribution of alleles in genotypes. Six genotypes are predicted by application of H-W equilibrium for a gene with three alleles (**Table 22.3a**). The sum of genotype frequencies resulting from the trinomial expansion is $(p + q + r)^2 = p^2 + 2pq + q^2 + 2pr + r^2 + 2qr = 1.0$.

The human ABO blood group system provides an opportunity for the application of the H-W equilibrium to a gene with three alleles (see Section 4.1). Recall that among the three alleles producing ABO blood types—I^A, I^B, and i—I^A and I^B exhibit dominance over i but are codominant to one another. These allelic relationships result in four blood types from the six genotypes (see Figure 4.3). Using $f(I^A) = p$, $f(I^B) = q$, and $f(i) = r$, along with data reporting the frequencies of each blood type in a population, we can estimate the frequency of each allele by applying a version of the square root method. This approach provides an approximate estimate of ABO allele frequencies

Table 22.3 Hardy-Weinberg Equilibrium Genotype Frequencies for Three Alleles of a Gene

(a) Genotype prediction for three alleles

Genotype	Genotype Frequency
A_1A_1	p^2
A_1A_2	$2pq$
A_1A_3	$2pr$
A_2A_2	q^2
A_2A_3	$2qr$
A_3A_3	r^2

(b) Hardy-Weinberg analysis of ABO blood group data

Genotype	Genotype Frequency[a]	Blood Type
I^AI^A	$p^2 = (0.23)^2 = 0.053$	A
I^Ai	$2pr = 2[(0.23)(0.68)] = 0.314$	A
I^BI^B	$q^2 = (0.09)^2 = 0.008$	B
I^Bi	$2qr = 2[(0.09)(0.68)] = 0.122$	B
I^AI^B	$2pq = 2[(0.23)(0.09)] = 0.041$	AB
ii	$r^2 = (0.68)^2 = 0.462$	O

[a] Where $f(A_1) = p$; $f(A_2) = q$; $f(A_3) = r$; and $p + q + r = 1.0$

based on observed frequencies of each blood group in a population. The allele frequencies in the U.S. population, for example, are derived as follows:

Step 1. Blood type O is found with recessive homozygous genotypes, and the frequency of the blood type is $r^2 = 0.46$. The square root of $0.46 = r$; thus, the allele frequency is $f(i) = r = 0.68$.

Step 2. The combined frequency of blood types A and O is $p^2 + 2pr + r^2 = (p + r)^2$, so $f(I^A) = p$ is estimated by the square root of the combined frequency of A plus O minus r. The calculation is $f(I^A) = p = \sqrt{[0.37 + 0.46]} - r = 0.91 - 0.68 = 0.23$.

Step 3. Having estimated p and r, we can solve for q by $q = 1 - (p + r) = 1 - (0.23 + 0.68) = 0.09$

In this way, from the U.S. population frequencies we can estimate that the frequencies of the ABO alleles are $f(I^A) = 0.23$, $f(I^B) = 0.09$, and $f(i) = 0.68$. Based on these estimated allele frequencies, **Table 22.3b** calculates genotype frequencies for the ABO blood types in the U.S. population.

The Chi-Square Test of Hardy-Weinberg Predictions

Strictly speaking, the assumptions of the H-W equilibrium are unattainable in real populations. From a statistical perspective, however, what matters is whether the observed genotype frequencies in populations deviate *significantly* from the predictions of the H-W equilibrium. The chi-square statistic is used to compare observed and expected results in order to evaluate the validity of an estimate based on the H-W equilibrium.

If it is found that a population does not deviate significantly from H-W equilibrium predictions, the population is assumed to be exhibiting random mating and not to be experiencing significant evolutionary change in the current generation. If, on the other hand, chi-square analysis detects a significant deviation from H-W equilibrium expectations, the cause can be investigated. The reasons differ, but for human populations the sources of significant deviation are most often either small population size, substantial migration in or out of the population, or nonrandom mating. We discuss these effects in following sections.

22.2 Natural Selection Operates through Differential Reproductive Fitness within a Population

Application of the H-W equilibrium to idealized populations provides insight into the mechanism that retains equilibrium when evolution does not occur. In the sense that the allele frequencies it describes do not change from generation to generation, the H-W equilibrium describes a static situation. But what happens to allele frequencies when evolution does occur? The simple answer is that allele frequencies change, and along with them genotype frequencies are altered. The evolutionary impact can be quantified by determining the change in allele frequencies. In this section, we look at the effects of different mechanisms of natural selection on allele frequencies and H-W equilibrium. In later sections, we examine how the other evolutionary processes—mutation, migration (gene flow), and genetic drift—affect allele frequencies and H-W equilibrium in populations (see Section 1.4).

Differential Reproduction and Relative Fitness

Natural selection favors certain members of a population over others as a result of differences in anatomical, physiological, behavioral, or other traits they possess. The favored individuals survive to reproductive age at higher rates than other population members, they reproduce at higher rates, or both. This leads individuals with the most favored phenotype to be the most successful at producing offspring for the next generation. This phenomenon is called **differential reproduction.**

A common way to measure the intensity of natural selection is to determine the impact of differential reproduction on the next generation. This involves use of the **relative fitness (w)** of organisms, a value that quantifies

PROBLEM A worldwide survey of genetic variation in human populations reported the autosomal codominant MN blood group types in a sample of 1029 Chinese from Hong Kong. The sample contained 342 people with blood type M, 500 with blood type MN, and 187 with blood type N.

a. Determine the frequencies of both alleles (*M* and *N*) using the genotype proportion method and the allele-counting method.

b. Determine the expected genotype frequencies under assumptions of the Hardy-Weinberg equilibrium.

> **BREAK IT DOWN:** For this codominant trait where the number of individuals with each genotype available, the 2058 alleles can each be enumerated (p. 747).

Solution Strategies	Solution Steps

Evaluate

1. Identify the topic this problem addresses and the nature of the required answer.

1. This problem addresses the determination of allele frequencies from population data and the determination of expected genotype frequencies under assumptions of the Hardy-Weinberg equilibrium.

2. Identify the critical information given in the problem.

2. The number of individuals with each blood type is given, and the blood type is identified as an autosomal codominant trait.

Deduce

3. Determine the genotype corresponding to each blood group.

3. For this autosomal codominant trait, blood type M individuals have the genotype *MM*, those with blood type N are *NN*, and MN individuals are *MN*.

4. Calculate the frequency of each blood type in the sample.

> **TIP:** The frequency of each genotype is the number of people with the genotype over the total sample size.

4. Blood type M is 342/1029 = 0.332, MN is 500/1029 = 0.486, and N is 187/1029 = 0.186.

Solve

5. Calculate allele frequencies using the genotype proportion method.

Answer a

5. The frequencies are
$$f(M) = (0.332) + [(0.5)(0.486)] = 0.575 \text{ and}$$
$$f(N) = (0.186) + [(0.5)(0.486)] = 0.425.$$

6. Calculate the allele frequencies by the allele-counting method.

> **TIP:** If the allele frequencies are calculated correctly, their sum will be 1.0.

6. For the sample of 1029 people, there are 2058 alleles. The allele frequencies are
$$f(M) = [(2)(342)] + (500)/2058 = 0.575 \text{ and}$$
$$f(N) = [(2)(187)] + (500)/2058 = 0.425.$$

Answer b

7. Determine the expected genotype distribution under Hardy-Weinberg assumptions.

> **TIP:** Assume $f(M) = p$ and $f(N) = q$, and expand the binomial equation $(p + q)^2 = p^2 + 2pq + q^2$.

7. The expected genotype frequencies are
$$MM = (0.575)^2 = (0.33)(1029) = 339.57,$$
$$MN = 2[(0.575)(0.425)] = (0.49)(1029) = 504.21, \text{ and}$$
$$NN = (0.425)^2 = (0.18)(1,029) = 185.22.$$

For more practice, see Problems 17, 18, 21, and 25. Visit the Study Area to access study tools. **Mastering**Genetics™

the reproductive success of other genotypes relative to the most favored genotype. Since this is a relative comparison, organisms with the greatest reproductive success have a relative fitness of $w = 1.0$.

The genotypes that reproduce less successfully than the most favored genotype have a relative fitness of less than $w = 1.0$. These less fit genotypes have their relative fitness reduced by a proportion called the **selection coefficient (*s*)**. The selection coefficient identifies the proportionate difference between the fitnesses of organisms with different traits.

For example, if an organism not having the favored trait reproduces 80 percent as well as the organism with the trait, the selection coefficient is $s = 0.2$, and the relative fitness of the organism is expressed as $w = 1 - s$, or $1 - 0.2 = 0.8$. If other organisms experience yet a different level of relative fitness, a second selection coefficient, designated *t*, is used. Where an organism with one genotype is most fit and organisms with either of two other genotypes experience reduced fitness, the relative fitness values for the two less fit genotypes are expressed as $w = 1 - s$ and $w = 1 - t$.

Directional Natural Selection

The pattern of natural selection called **directional natural selection** favors one phenotype with a homozygous genotype. Organisms with this phenotype have higher relative fitness than other phenotypes in the population. Natural selection favoring one homozygous genotype produces a directional change in allele frequencies that increases the favored allele frequency and decreases others.

In the directional selection example that follows, assume alleles B_1 and B_2 are codominant. The codominant relationship of the alleles will result in one genotype that occurs in organisms with the highest relative fitness and in reduced fitness in organisms with the other genotypes. In this example, where the allele frequencies are $f(B_1) = 0.6$ and $f(B_2) = 0.4$, there are 1000 members of the population, the favored phenotype has a relative fitness of $w = 1.0$, and the other phenotypes have different relative fitness values of $w = 0.80$ and $w = 0.40$, the genetic profile of the population is as follows.

Genotype	B_1B_1	B_1B_2	B_2B_2
Frequency	0.36	0.48	0.16
Number	360	480	160
Relative fitness (w)	1.0	0.80	0.40

In this example, the B_1B_1 organisms have the highest relative fitness ($w = 1.0$). In comparison, B_1B_2 organisms have $s = 0.20$ and $w = 1 - s = 0.80$, and organisms with the B_2B_2 genotype have a selection coefficient of $t = 0.60$ and a relative fitness of $w = 1 - t = 0.40$.

The impact of natural selection is computed in two steps. First, assuming natural selection has its effect before organisms reach reproductive age, the surviving number of organisms of each genotype is calculated by multiplying the original number of each genotype by the relative fitness value of the genotype. In this case the numbers of survivors of each genotype are $B_1B_1 = (1.0)(360) = 360$, $B_1B_2 = (0.80)(480) = 384$, and $B_2B_2 = (0.40)(160) = 64$. In this hypothetical population, 808 organisms of the original 1000 remain after natural selection.

The second step is determination of the allele frequencies after natural selection and of the genotype frequencies in the next generation. In this case, the frequencies are most readily calculated using the allele-counting method, since we can identify the genotype of each survivor. There are a total of 1616 alleles in the 808 survivors, and the allele frequencies after natural selection are $f(B_1) = [(2)(360) + (384)]/1616 = 1104/1616 = 0.683$, and $f(B_2) = [(2)(64) + (384)]/(2)(808) = 512/1616 = 0.317$. If we assume that random mating takes place among the survivors, the genotype frequencies in the next generation are $f(B_1B_1) = (0.683)^2 = 0.467$, $f(B_1B_2) = 2(0.683)(0.317) = 0.433$, and $f(B_2B_2) = (0.317)^2 = 0.100$.

The changes in allele frequencies are symbolized by the Greek delta (Δ) and found by taking the absolute value of the difference between the original allele frequency and the new allele frequency. For this example in which B_1 has increased and B_2 has decreased, the values are, $\Delta B_1 = 0.683 - 0.60 = 0.083$, and $\Delta B_2 = 0.317 - 0.40 = 0.083$. If this pattern of natural selection continues for enough generations, the frequency of the B_1 allele will eventually become fixed at $f(B_1) = 1.0$, and the frequency of B_2 will be eliminated, so that its final frequency will be $f(B_2) = 0.0$. Once an allele frequency is either fixed ($f = 1.0$) or eliminated ($f = 0.0$), natural selection can no longer change the frequency. Population allele frequencies of 0.0 or 1.0 can, however, be changed by migration and mutation. **Figure 22.5** illustrates that directional selection favoring B_1 increases the frequency of that allele at a pace determined by the intensity of natural selection.

The concept of relative fitness values can be applied to populations in several ways. **Table 22.4** illustrates a case natural selection against the homozygous recessive in which frequencies $f(B) = 0.50$ and $f(b) = 0.50$ are subjected to natural selection against bb, where $w_{bb} = 0.0$ and $w_{Bb} = w_{BB} = 1.0$. No bb individuals survive to reproductive age, thus removing 25 percent of the population. When the relative genotype frequencies are determined using their new proportions in the surviving reproductive population, $f(B)$ and $f(b)$ are calculated to be $f(B) = 0.667$ and $f(b) = 0.333$. Among the progeny in generation 1, genotype frequencies are $f(BB) = 0.445$, $f(Bb) = 0.444$, and $f(bb) = 0.111$.

Directional natural selection against the homozygous recessive genotype causes the frequency of the dominant

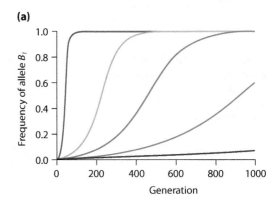

(a)

(b)

Selection strength	Relative fitness		
	B_1B_1	B_1B_2	B_2B_2
Strong	1.0	0.90	0.80
	1.0	0.98	0.96
	1.0	0.99	0.98
	1.0	0.995	0.990
Weak	1.0	0.998	0.996

Figure 22.5 **The consequences of the intensity of natural selection on allele frequency.** (a) The curves illustrate the relationship between the rate of change in $f(B_1)$ and the intensity of natural selection. (b) Relative fitness values for natural selection of different intensities.

Table 22.4	A Model of Directional Selection against a Recessive Lethal Allele		
	Genotype		
	BB	*Bb*	*bb*
Frequency	0.25	0.50	0.25
Relative fitness (*w*)	1.0	1.0	0.0
Survivors after selection (total, 0.75)	0.25	0.50	0.00
Relative genotype frequencies	0.25/0.75 = 0.333	0.50/0.75 = 0.667	0.00

Estimated allele frequencies after natural selection:

$$f(B) = (0.333) + (0.5)(0.667) = 0.667$$
$$f(b) = (0) + (0.5)(0.667) = 0.333$$

Estimated genotype frequencies after reproduction:

$$f(BB) = (0.667)^2 = 0.445$$
$$f(Bb) = 2(0.667)(0.333) = 0.444$$
$$f(bb) = (0.333)^2 = 0.111$$

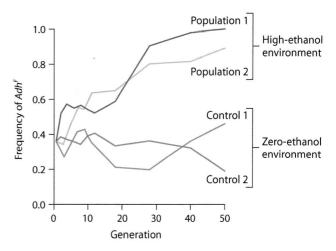

Figure 22.6   **Directional artificial selection favoring the Adh^F allele in experimental *Drosophila* populations.**   The Adh^F allele increases in frequency in both experimental populations exposed to an ethanol-rich environment. Allele frequencies in two control populations (no natural selection) drift up and down over the generations, ending up higher (control 1) and lower (control 2) than their starting frequencies.

allele to increase and the frequency of the recessive allele to decrease. Eventually, the recessive allele may be eliminated from the population gene pool. The recessive allele is not eliminated quickly, however, and its frequency changes slowly, especially as the allele gets less frequent. The slow pace of evolutionary change at low allele frequencies is due to the smaller number of recessive homozygotes in the population.

Numerous directional selection experiments, taking place over the last several decades of research, demonstrate adherence to the theoretical predictions for populations. A 1981 study by Douglas Cavener and Michael Clegg examined four subpopulations of *Drosophila melanogaster* for 50 generations to test the effectiveness of artificial directional selection at increasing the frequency of the allele Adh^F of the *alcohol dehydrogenase* (*Adh*) gene, whose enzyme product of Adh^F rapidly breaks down ethanol. An original population with an Adh^F frequency of 0.38 was divided into four subpopulations of equal size. Two subpopulations reared on ethanol-rich food (population 1 and population 2) showed progressive increases in the frequency of Adh^F over 50 generations (Figure 22.6). In contrast, control populations (control 1 and control 2), which were reared on food without ethanol, showed an overall upward (control 1) and downward (control 2) drift of Adh^F frequency.

A similar effect is seen in the action of strong directional natural selection in human populations. Two independent reports published in 2010, one by Xin Yi and colleagues and the other by Tatum Simonson and colleagues, describe the rapid evolutionary changes that have occurred in the last 5000 years in native Tibetans who have adapted to low oxygen conditions in the high-altitude environment of the Himalayan mountains. Strong directional natural selection has operated in favor of certain alleles of multiple genes that increase oxygen utilization and improve oxygen transport and metabolism.

Natural Selection Favoring Heterozygotes

A pattern of natural selection that can produce and maintain genetic diversity in populations is seen when the heterozygous genotype is favored. We described this type of natural selection in Chapter 10 in connection with the evolution of the β^S allele for β-globin. The consequence of natural selection favoring the heterozygote is a **balanced polymorphism,** in which alleles reach stable equilibrium frequencies that are maintained in a steady state, balancing the selective pressures favoring the β^S allele when it occurs in a heterozygote and acting against it when it occurs in a homozygous genotype.

Table 22.5 depicts a natural selection scheme favoring heterozygotes. In this example, the relative fitness values are based on the heterozygous genotype (*Cc*) being 1.0, the relative fitness of *CC* being 0.80, and the fitness of *cc* being 0.20, indicating that few of these homozygotes survive to reproductive age. Beginning in generation 0 with $f(C) = f(c) = 0.50$, natural selection changes allele frequencies to $f(C) = 0.60$ and $f(c) = 0.40$ in the matings that produce generation 1.

Natural selection operating in favor of heterozygotes will eventually lead to a balanced polymorphism. Once attained, the equilibrium frequencies of the alleles will be maintained in a balanced polymorphism as long as natural selection remains steady. Population geneticists can predict the stable equilibrium frequencies of alleles in a balanced polymorphism using the relative intensity of natural selection against the homozygous genotypes.

Table 22.5	A Model of Natural Selection Favoring the Heterozygous Genotype		
	Genotype		
	CC	*Cc*	*cc*
Frequency	0.25	0.50	0.25
Relative fitness	0.80	1.0	0.20
Survivors after selection	0.20	0.50	0.05
Relative genotype frequencies	0.20/0.75 = 0.267	0.50/0.75 = 0.067	0.05/0.75 = 0.667

New allele frequencies after natural selection:
$$f(C) = 0.600$$
$$f(c) = 0.400$$

Genotype frequencies after reproduction:
$$f(CC) = (0.60)^2 = 0.36$$
$$f(Cc) = 2[(0.60)(0.40)] = 0.48$$
$$f(cc) = (0.40)^2 = 0.16$$

Using the variables s and t to represent the natural selection coefficients operating against the homozygous genotypes, the relative fitness of CC is $1 - s$ and the relative fitness of cc is $1 - t$. Solving for the values of s and t,

$$s = 1.0 - 0.80 = 0.20, \text{ and } t = 1.0 - 0.20 = 0.80$$

The stable equilibrium for p and q, designated p_E and q_E, in the balanced polymorphism are calculated as ratios of selection coefficients operating against the homozygous genotypes. In this example, the equilibrium p_E and q_E values are

$$p_E = t/(s + t) = 0.80/(0.20 + 0.80) = 0.80 \text{ and}$$
$$q_E = s/(s + t) = 0.20/(0.20 + 0.80) = 0.20$$

Convergent Evolution

Natural selection favors the most fit organism in a given environment, and on occasion, mutant alleles that are identical or nearly identical can be independently generated and can be similarly favored in separate populations. When this occurs, the mutant alleles evolve independently in each population Such events produce and evolutionary phenomenon known as **convergent evolution.** One well-established example of convergent evolution of a morphological trait is the presence of wings in birds and wings in bats. Birds and mammals are distantly related, sharing the common ancestor of reptiles and mammals, but the development of wings is more recent. Wings of birds are traced to their reptilian ancestors and have an underlying anatomical structure that is distinct from what is found in bats. Bats developed wings through a series of changes that modified ancestral appendages that had five digits—the equivalent of the human hand. Despite their distinctive evolutionary histories and anatomical differences, the wings in bats and birds appear similar in form and function and are identified as convergent.

Recent human evolutionary history provides an example of convergent evolution of a molecular characteristic, the ability to digest the disaccharide milk sugar lactose into adulthood. All humans have the ability to break down lactose at birth—it is a carbohydrate component of mammalian breast milk—but most individuals lose that ability rapidly after weaning. Lactose digestion is made possible by production of the enzyme lactase-phlorizin hydroxylase, commonly known as "lactase," encoded by the *LCT* gene on chromosome 2. Lactase is functionally equivalent to β-galactosidase, the bacterial enzyme that cleaves lactose that we discussed in Section 14.2. Individuals who lose the ability to digest lactose after weaning are often identified as "lactose intolerant," whereas those who digest lactose into adulthood are termed "lactase persistent." Lactase persistence is common in individuals of European ancestry whose ancestral populations were pastoralists. The evolution of lactase persistence in these populations is tied to the domestication of cattle 7500 to 9000 years ago and to the availability of milk and other dairy products that provided a readily accessible source of protein. Lactase-persistent individuals have the evolutionary advantage, in the pastoral environment, of being able to exploit that protein source.

Lactase persistence is not limited to Europeans, however, and a 2007 study by Sarah Tishkoff and colleagues studied the evolution of lactase persistence in pastoral African populations in Tanzania, Kenya, and the Sudan to determine if lactase persistence in Europeans and Africans has the same genetic basis or is the result of different mutations and a separate evolutionary history. The study determined that European and African lactase persistence is produced by different mutations of the *LCT* gene and represents an example of convergent evolution of a molecular trait.

A SNP (single nucleotide polymorphism; see Section 10.2) in the upstream regulatory region of *LCT* is responsible for lactase persistence in Europeans. This SNP is a base-pair substitution that substitutes a cytosine with a thymine at nucleotide position 13910. The SNP is designated C/T-13910, and it occurs in nearly 100% of Europeans with lactase persistence. C/T-13910 is not found in Africans with lactase persistence. Instead, three other SNPs also located in the upstream *LCT* regulatory region are detected; G/C-14010, T/G-13915, and C/G-13907 are each associated with lactase persistence in Africans.

Given the molecular genetic data identifying distinct SNPs associated with lactase persistence in pastoral Europeans and Africans, a logical hypothesis is that natural selection favored different mutations producing lactase persistence in these populations. The demonstration of evolution producing convergence of the lactase-persistence trait comes from the examination of variants of genes that are linked to *LCT* but that do not play a role in lactase persistence. Evolutionary theory predicts that if a particular SNP is favored, it's frequency will increase, but so too will the frequency of alleles of genes that are linked to the favored SNP. Natural selection directly favors a specific allele and indirectly favors the alleles of closely linked genes on the same chromosome. The alleles of linked genes on the same chromosome as the favored SNP can have their frequencies increased by a phenomenon known as **genetic hitchhiking.** In genetic hitchhiking, the alleles of closely linked genes that happen to be on the same chromosome as the favored allele are taken along for the evolutionary ride, at least temporarily. Initially, this produces linkage disequilibrium (LD) in which the favored allele and the alleles of linked genes occur together on chromosomes significantly more often than expected by chance (see Section 5.6 for a discussion). Genetic hitchhiking produces particular combinations of alleles at linked genes on chromosomes carrying the favored allele, leading to distinctive haplotypes on those chromosomes.

Over time, homologous recombination will break up the haplotype and randomize the combinations of alleles among the linked genes. In other words, recombination gradually eliminates LD and restores linkage equilibrium. In the meantime, however, the detection of distinct haplotypes on chromosomes carrying favored alleles, such as the SNPs associated with lactase persistence, strongly suggests the operation of natural selection and the occurrence of convergent evolution. The distinct haplotypes in Europeans and Africans with *LCT* SNPs is thus a hallmark of convergent evolution.

Genetic Analysis 22.2 examines another example of the consequences of natural selection on a population.

22.3 Mutation Diversifies Gene Pools

Mutation is the ultimate source of all new genetic variation in populations, and the genetic variation it generates is an indispensable component of evolution. By itself, however, gene mutation is a very slow evolutionary process because its effect on allele frequencies in populations is small and gradual. For example, if mutation converts one in every 10,000 A_1 alleles to A_2 alleles each generation, a population containing $f(A_1) = 0.90$ and $f(A_2) = 0.10$ in generation 0 will have frequencies $f(A_1) = 0.81$ and $f(A_2) = 0.19$ after 1000 generations, assuming no effects from the other evolutionary processes.

An additional reason that mutation alone is a slow evolutionary process has to do with the two directions in which mutation can affect any given allele. The **forward mutation rate (μ)** pertains to mutations that create a new A_2 allele by mutation of A_1, whereas the **reverse mutation rate (v),** also known as the **reversion rate,** pertains to mutation of alleles in the opposite direction, A_2 to A_1. Forward and reverse mutation can create a balanced

equilibrium, given a sufficient number of generations and the absence of other evolutionary processes.

Quantifying the Effects and Reverse Mutation Rates

In the absence of other evolutionary effects, the consequences of forward and reverse mutation (reversion) on allele frequencies in a population can be quantified. If $f(A_1) = p$ and $f(A_2) = q$, the effect of forward mutation on $f(A_1)$ is described by the value μp, and the effect of reversion on $f(A_2) = vq$. These two expressions identify, respectively, the rate at which A_2 alleles are created by forward mutation and the rate at which A_2 alleles are reverted to A_1. In each generation, the change in the frequency of A_2 is quantified by the expression Δq ("delta q") that is calculated as $\Delta q = \mu p - vq$. Over an infinite number of generations in a theoretical population where μ and v are constant and no other evolutionary processes are operating, allele frequency equilibrium is established.

The equilibrium frequencies of alleles subject only to mutation and reversion are a ratio of the frequencies of the respective events. Since the equilibrium frequencies are purely a function of the ratios of the rate at which new copies of an allele are added and removed from the population gene pool, they are calculated as $p_E = v/(\mu + v)$ and $q_E = \mu/(\mu + v)$. In a theoretical population where $f(A_1) = 0.99$, $f(A_2) = 0.01$, $\mu = 2 \times 10^{-6}$, and $v = 3 \times 10^{-8}$, Δq is expressed as $\Delta q = [(2 \times 10^{-6})(0.99) - (3 \times 10^{-8})(0.01)] = 1.98 \times 10^{-6}$. This small change gradually increases $f(A_2)$ and decreases $f(A_1)$, leading eventually to equilibrium allele frequencies in this population that are

$$p_E = 3 \times 10^{-8}/(2 \times 10^{-6} + 3 \times 10^{-8}) = 0.015 \text{ and}$$
$$q_E = 2 \times 10^{-6}/(2 \times 10^{-6} + 3 \times 10^{-8}) = 0.985$$

Mutation–Selection Balance

Unlike the theoretical population just described, mutations in the real world are commonly subject to natural selection. In cases where the deleterious mutation is recessive, the mutant allele is masked by the wild-type dominant allele in heterozygous genotypes. Recessive mutant alleles are subjected to natural selection only when they occur in the homozygous recessive genotype. This results in the persistence of recessive mutant alleles in most populations at a frequency somewhat greater than the mutation frequency.

Under these circumstances, the frequency of mutant alleles in a population is a balance of the intensity of natural selection against the mutant and the frequency of mutation of the gene. This expression is called the **mutation–selection balance,** and it determines the equilibrium frequency of the mutant allele (q_E) by considering the rate of elimination of deleterious alleles by natural selection (s) and the rate at which new mutant alleles are generated (μ).

PROBLEM In a *Drosophila* species, a naturally occurring autosomal inversion is found in two forms, Arrowhead (AR) and Standard (ST). Flies of this species can be homozygous for either chromosome form (AR/AR or ST/ST), or they can be heterozygous (AR/ST). In the 1970s, researchers determined that the relative fitness values for the three genotypes differed with respect to the fruit flies' ability to resist the now banned insecticide DDT. The relative fitness values are as follows:

Genotype	Relative Fitness
AR/AR	0.65
AR/ST	1.00
ST/ST	0.50

a. Describe the pattern of natural selection operating on these chromosomes, and make a statement about the eventual fate of the two chromosome forms in this species.

b. Use the information provided to determine the equilibrium frequencies of AR and ST.

> **BREAK IT DOWN:** Natural selection can eliminate an allele (frequency 0.0), fix an allele (frequency 1.0), or establish equilibrium frequencies for two or more alleles, depending on the pattern of natural selection (p. 750).

> **BREAK IT DOWN:** The pattern of natural selection is determined by the relative fitness values that assign a fitness of 1.0 to the most fit genotype and lesser relative fitness values to the other genotypes (p. 748).

Solution Strategies	Solution Steps
Evaluate	
1. Identify the topic of this problem and the nature of the required answer.	1. This problem is about the effects of natural selection on the frequencies of two chromosome forms, AR and ST. The answer requires an explanation of the pattern of natural selection and a calculation to determine the ultimate frequencies of the chromosome forms.
2. Identify the critical information given in the problem.	2. The relative fitness values are given, and these can be used to determine the final frequencies of AR and ST.
Deduce	
3. Examine the relative fitness values for each genotype, and calculate the selection coefficients (s and t) against each genotype. TIP: Subtract the relative fitness of a genotype from 1.0 to determine the selection coefficients s and t.	3. The relative fitness value for the heterozygous genotype is 1.0, and the relative fitnesses of the homozygous genotypes are lower. The selection coefficient s operating against AR/AR is $1.0 - 0.65 = 0.35$. The selection coefficient t operating against ST/ST is $1.0 - 0.50 = 0.50$.
4. Consider how the relative fitness values can be used to calculate the final frequencies of AR and ST.	4. A ratio of relative fitness values operating against each homozygous genotype can be used to calculate the equilibrium frequency of each of the chromosome forms, with $p_E = t/(s + t)$ and $q_E = s/(s + t)$.
Solve	Answer a
5. Describe the natural selection pattern operating on these genotypes.	5. This is an example of heterozygous advantage that is expected to retain both chromosome forms in the population at equilibrium values determined by the relative strength of natural selection against each form.
	Answer b
6. Determine the equilibrium frequencies of each chromosome form. PITFALL: Double-check your arithmetic by making sure that the sum of the equilibrium frequencies you calculate is 1.0.	6. If the equilibrium frequency of AR is p_E and of ST is q_E, the equilibrium frequencies are $p_E = 0.50/(0.35 + 0.50) = 0.588$ and $q_E = 0.35/(0.35 + 0.50) = 0.412$.

For additional practice see Problems 4, 11, and 24.   Visit the Study Area to access study tools.   MasteringGenetics™

Consider the following situation for a recessive lethal mutation.

Genotype	A_1A_1	A_1A_2	A_2A_2
Relative fitness	1	1	$1 - s$

Here, the equilibrium frequency of the recessive allele (q_E) is calculated as the balance between selection against a recessive genotype (s) and the rate of mutation (μ), i.e.

$$q_E = \sqrt{\mu/s}$$

This expression predicts that when selection against the recessive genotype is complete (i.e., $s = 1.0$), the equilibrium frequency of the mutant allele is approximately the square root of the mutation rate. When the selection coefficient is less than 1.0, the equilibrium frequency is greater than the square root of the mutation frequency.

In the case of complete selection against a lethal dominant mutant allele B_2, the relative fitness values of the genotypes are as follows.

Genotype	B_1B_1	B_1B_2	B_2B_2
Relative fitness	1	$1-s$	$1-s$

In this case, $q_E = \mu$. In other words, when $s = 1.0$ against a lethal dominant mutation, the equilibrium frequency of the mutant allele is equal to the mutation frequency.

Numerous examples of mutation–selection balance have been investigated in organisms, including humans. Several studies of human hereditary disease alleles reveal that recessive mutant alleles are maintained in populations at frequencies predicted by calculating the mutation–selection balance.

22.4 Migration Is Movement of Organisms and Genes between Populations

In population genetics, **migration** refers to the movement of organisms and subsequent reproduction in new populations. Adding or subtracting alleles from a population can immediately change allele frequencies in the population, and these changes can become established through and the reproduction in the new populations. In evolutionary terms, migration is also known as **gene flow,** and the new mixed population is identified as an **admixed population.**

Effects of Gene Flow

Gene flow has two principal effects on populations. First, in the short run, gene flow can change the frequency of alleles in the admixed population, particularly if the starting allele frequencies in one of the participating populations differ from those in the other and if the number of immigrants constitutes a large proportion of the admixed population. Second, in the long run, gene flow acts to equalize frequencies of alleles between populations that remain in genetic contact by the exchange of population members back and forth between the populations. This exchange can also slow genetic divergence of populations and can block speciation. Let's look at how both of these effects are explained.

The change in allele frequencies produced in an admixed population by gene flow from population 1 into population 2 can be described by the **island model** of migration that depicts a one-way process of gene flow, that is, from a mainland population to an island population. In the example illustrated in **Figure 22.7a**, gene flow changes allele frequencies by reducing $f(A_1)$ on the island from 1.0 to 0.60 and increasing $f(A_2)$ from 0.0 to 0.40.

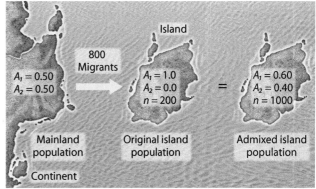

(a) The island model of migration

(b) Consequence of migration

Island population	A_1A_1	A_1A_2	A_2A_2	Genotype frequencies in admixed population
Original ($n = 200$)	200	0	0	$f(A_1) = 0.60$
Admixed ($n = 1000$)	400	400	200	$f(A_2) = 0.40$
Genotype frequencies in admixed population	0.36	0.48	0.16	

Figure 22.7   The island model of migration.

In the example shown in Figure 22.7, gene flow has produced an almost instantaneous evolutionary change (**Figure 22.7b**). The admixed population has allele frequencies of $f(A_1) = 0.60$ and $f(A_2) = 0.40$, but the genotypes are not in H-W equilibrium immediately following migration. A single generation of random mating, however, will bring the genotype frequencies into ratios consistent with the H-W equilibrium: $A_1A_1 = 0.36$, $A_1A_2 = 0.48$, and $A_2A_2 = 0.16$.

The consequence of gene flow on allele frequencies in an admixed population is expressed by a formula that calculates p_N, the new value of p, as the weighted average of the allele frequency among island residents and mainland immigrants. The expression uses p_I and p_C to represent $f(A_1)$ in the original island and mainland populations, respectively. The formula identifies the fraction of individuals or alleles from the mainland population as m, and the fraction contributed by island residents as $1 - m$. The value of p_N as a result of gene flow is $p_N = (1 - m)(p_I) + (m)(p_C)$. Applying this formula to our example in Figure 22.7, we find $p_N (0.20)(1.0) + (0.80)(0.50) = 0.60$.

Allele Frequency Equilibrium and Equalization

We have just seen that gene flow can produce rapid evolutionary change in the allele frequencies of populations. In the short term, the effect of gene flow is determined by the change in the frequency of p in the new gene pool of the island population. This value, Δp_I, is the difference in allele frequency before and after migration, and is defined as $\Delta p_I = p_N - p_I$. Substituting the formula for p_N and simplifying gives $\Delta p_I = [(1 - m)(p_I) + (m)(p_C)] - p_I = m(p_C - p_I)$. Allele frequency equilibrium occurs when $\Delta p_I = 0$; thus, at equilibrium, $m(p_C - p_I) = 0$, indicating that p remains constant either when there is no migration ($m = 0$) or when p in the island gene pool equals the allele frequency in the mainland gene pool ($p_I = p_C$).

Population and evolutionary biologists use this analysis to conclude that gene flow has a homogenizing, or equalizing, effect on allele frequencies among participating populations. By this mechanism, gene flow maintains genetic contact between populations and can thus prevent evolutionary divergence of populations. In broader evolutionary terms, gene flow hinders the establishment of the reproductive isolation that is an important component of evolutionary divergence between populations and of potential speciation.

22.5 Genetic Drift Causes Allele Frequency Change by Sampling Error

The term **genetic drift** refers to chance fluctuations of allele frequencies that result from "sampling error," a statistical term signifying that a small sample taken from a larger population is not likely to contain all alleles in exactly the same frequencies as in the larger population. Genetic drift affects all populations, but it is especially prominent in small populations in which a small number of gametes unite to produce each subsequent generation.

To appreciate the cause and consequences of genetic drift, picture a gene pool with alleles at frequencies $f(A_1) = f(A_2) = 0.50$ from which two separate samples are drawn. In sample one, 20 alleles are drawn at random, whereas in the second sample, 1000 alleles are drawn. These two separate draws represent the alleles that, in the two respective cases, unite to form the next generation. In the first sample, containing 20 alleles, each allele represents 5 percent (one allele out of 20) of the total for the next generation, whereas in the 1000-allele sample, each allele only represents 1/1000 of the alleles in the next generation. Any deviation from exactly 10 A_1 alleles and 10 A_2 alleles in the first sample will substantially change allele frequencies in the next generation. If, for example, the draw of 20 alleles contains 12 A_1 alleles and 8 A_2 alleles, the allele frequencies in the next generation will be $f(A_1) = 12/20 = 0.60$ and $f(A_2) = 8/20 = 0.40$. A change of such magnitude can easily occur by chance in the small sample, but it is very unlikely to occur in the larger sample of 1000 alleles.

Sampling errors of the kind described for the first sample can randomly raise or lower the frequency of an allele in a small population each generation. Once the allele frequencies are changed, the next generation, when it reproduces, has the new allele frequencies as a starting point.

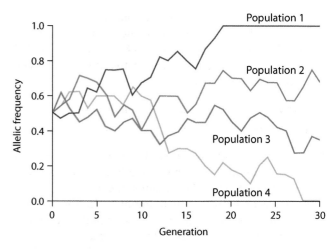

Figure 22.8   Genetic drift of an allele frequency. Four simulated populations each start with a frequency of 0.50 for a hypothetical allele whose frequency fluctuates randomly in each population over 30 generations. The allele eventually becomes fixed in population 1, is eliminated in population 4, and is still present in populations 2 and 3 at distinct frequencies.

Over multiple generations, the frequency of an allele in a small population will randomly fluctuate, or "drift," sometimes increasing and sometimes decreasing, due to nothing more than the chance deviations in small random samples.

Allele frequency changes due to genetic drift are random. In the absence of any other evolutionary influence, they may drift for a large number of generations, and one allele will ultimately reach fixation at a frequency of 1.0 and all other alleles will be eliminated. **Figure 22.8** illustrates four different simulations of genetic drift of an allele in experimental populations and shows how the result of genetic drift for 30 generations can vary among populations that are initially identical. Each experimental population begins with 20 organisms and maintains that number throughout the 30 generations. The initial starting frequency of each allele is 0.50 in each population.

The Founder Effect

Small population size provides the conditions under which sampling errors can produce significant genetic drift of allele frequency. One mechanism that can produce this outcome is called the **founder effect**, and it occurs when a new, small population branches off from a larger population. Since the new population founders are drawn from a larger original population, and the number of founders is small, the allele frequencies carried by the founders may be higher or lower from those in the original population, and some alleles may be missing altogether. These changes are due to sampling error. The founder effect can create new populations with allele frequencies that differ substantially from those found in the original population.

Small human populations whose origins can be traced to religious, social, political, or other distinctions are often established by a small number of individuals and contain few members of reproductive age. Often, the founders consist of several families. Since the family members are related and share alleles, allele frequencies among the founders likely will differ from allele frequencies in the larger population from which the founders emigrate.

One consequences of founder effect and genetic drift can be high frequencies of autosomal recessive disorders in the new population that are rare in the original population. The Old Order Amish are a religious population established by about 200 founding members in Lancaster County, Pennsylvania, between 1720 and 1770. The founding population came from English and European populations and consisted of several extended families. Other Amish communities were established by different founders in Ohio, Indiana, and elsewhere in North America. These populations tend to be small, and mating within each population is common. Due to the founder effect, Amish populations exhibit high frequencies of several autosomal and X-linked recessive disorders that are rare in their populations of origin and in surrounding non-Amish communities.

One example of a disorder found in high frequency in an Amish community is Ellis–van Creveld syndrome (EvC; OMIM 225500), an autosomal recessive disorder that produces short stature accompanied by short forearms and lower legs and by the frequent appearance of extra digits on hands or feet. In a survey of nearly 8000 Old Order Amish in Lancaster County completed several years ago, 43 cases of EvC were identified. From this information, the estimated frequency of the allele producing EvC in the population is estimated by taking the square root of the frequency of the recessive trait in the population. The calculation is $q = \sqrt{43/8000} = 0.073$, or about 7.3 percent. Among other Amish populations, and in the general (non-Amish) population, the frequency of this recessive allele is $q < 0.001$.

The genealogical history of the Old Order Amish community in Lancaster County identifies that all families with EvC trace their genealogies to Mr. and Mrs. Samuel King, who immigrated to Lancaster County in 1744. At the time, there were about 400 people in the Lancaster County population, and the evidence suggests that both Mr. King and Mrs. King were carriers of the recessive mutant allele for EvC. This information establishes the initial frequency of the mutant allele in the founding population at approximately $f(q) = 2/800 = 0.0025$, more than twice the frequency in the population of origin. Genetic drift and the tendency for the Amish to mate within the Lancaster County community subsequently contributed to the rise in the frequency of the allele in the population.

Genetic Bottlenecks

A second mechanism producing large allele frequency sampling errors in small populations is the **genetic bottleneck,** in which a relatively large population is substantially

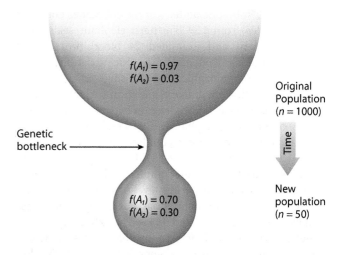

$f(A_1) = 0.97$
$f(A_2) = 0.03$

Original Population ($n = 1000$)

Genetic bottleneck

Time

$f(A_1) = 0.70$
$f(A_2) = 0.30$

New population ($n = 50$)

Figure 22.9   A genetic bottleneck. Catastrophic population reduction not due to natural selection can restrict or eliminate the alleles that pass through the bottleneck and alter allele frequencies in the surviving population.

reduced in number by a catastrophic event independent of natural selection. The survivors of the bottleneck—a small, random sample of the original population—are likely to have a very low level of genetic diversity due to the loss of alleles from the gene pool. They are likely to carry alleles in frequencies that differ radically from those in the original population (**Figure 22.9**). In the statistical sense, founder effect and genetic bottlenecks are equivalent. Indeed, the founder effect is effectively one version of a genetic bottleneck. Both establish a new breeding population from a small subset of the ancestral population.

The loss of genetic diversity from a genetic bottleneck can be quantified in two ways: first, by determining the percentage of polymorphic loci in the population, and second, by determining the percentage of loci in an average individual that are heterozygous.

Genetic bottlenecks can affect single populations, or they can affect an entire species. An example of the latter case would be a near-extinction event such as the one that affected the Northern elephant seal (*Mirounga angustirostris*). This animal was historically distributed along the western coast of North America, in numbers that exceeded 150,000 in the mid-1800s. Extensive hunting devastated the rookeries where young elephant seals were raised, and by 1884 fewer than 100 elephant seals remained. Some biologists have estimated that the surviving population may have been as small as 20 individuals. The entire remaining population bred at an isolated rookery on Guadalupe Island, about 200 miles off the western shore of Baja California. Elephant seal protection measures put in place by the U.S. and Mexican governments in the early 1900s led to population growth and the reestablishment of additional rookeries. Today, the Northern elephant seal remains a protected species that has returned to its historic population size of approximately 150,000 individuals.

In 1974, Robert Selander and his colleagues collected blood samples from 159 Northern elephant seals from five populations and examined 24 blood protein and enzyme genes for evidence of genetic variation. All 24 genes were monomorphic, and the single allele of each gene was identical in all five populations! About 20 years later, A. Rus Hoelzel and colleagues expanded the genetic survey of Northern elephant seals to include 43 genes in 61 individuals from the five populations. They also found no genetic variation. Additionally, Hoelzel and colleagues examined variation of mitochondrial DNA in Northern elephant seals and found a low level of sequence variation in two distinctive mitochondrial DNA haplotypes that had frequencies of 0.725 and 0.275. The extremely limited genetic variation in Northern elephant seals is wholly consistent with the historical genetic bottleneck that left very little genetic variation in the surviving population members.

22.6 Inbreeding Alters Genotype Frequencies

Descriptions of population genetic structure based on the Hardy-Weinberg principle assume random mating within the population. If this assumption is not met, however—if mating in the population is nonrandom—the distribution of alleles into genotypes occurs in frequencies inconsistent with the chance predictions of the Hardy-Weinberg equilibrium. *Inbreeding*, mating between related individuals, is a form of nonrandom mating that alters the distribution of alleles into genotypes.

The Coefficient of Inbreeding

Inbreeding, also known as **consanguineous mating** (consanguineous means "with blood"), is mating between related individuals who share a greater proportion of alleles with one another than with random members of a population. The principal genetic consequences of inbreeding are an increase in the frequency of homozygous genotypes in a population and a decrease in the frequency of heterozygous genotypes relative to the frequencies expected from random matings. The likelihood of homozygosity is increased because related organisms share alleles and are thus more likely to produce homozygotes, especially when the alleles involved are rare in the general population.

Inbreeding is a normal reproductive process for self-fertilizing plants and for some animals that reproduce by self-fertilization. The effect of self-fertilization on genotype proportions is shown in **Table 22.6**, where a heterozygous organism self-fertilizes and produces genotypes in generation 1 in a 1:2:1 ratio. Self-fertilization of generation 1 individuals produces a generation 2 that has an overall increase in the frequency of both homozygous

Table 22.6	Consequences of Self-Fertilization to Genotype Frequencies

P: A_1A_2 (self-fertilization)

Progeny Generation	Genotype		
	A_1A_1	A_1A_2	A_2A_2
1	0.250	0.500	0.250
2	0.375	0.250	0.375
3	0.437	0.125	0.437
4	0.468	0.063	0.468

genotypes and a decrease of one-half in the frequency of the heterozygous genotype. The decrease in heterozygous frequency of one-half occurs each generation. By generation 4, just over 6 percent of the progeny are heterozygous, and more than 93 percent are homozygous. Note, however, that the allele frequencies of A_1 and A_2 remain at $f(A_1) = f(A_2) = 0.50$ in each generation.

Among sexually reproducing organisms, the effect of inbreeding is similar, but it takes place over a larger number of generations since the proportion of organisms in a population participating in consanguineous matings is generally low. The population geneticist Sewall Wright investigated the consequences of inbreeding in sexually reproducing populations and devised the **coefficient of inbreeding (F)** as an arithmetic measure of the probability of homozygosity for an allele obtained in identical copies from an ancestor. The coefficient of inbreeding quantifies the probability that two alleles in a homozygous individual are **identical by descent (IBD),** having descended from the same copy of the allele carried by a common ancestor of the inbred individual. A common ancestor is an ancestor shared by two inbreeding organisms, and potentially the source of identical alleles that could be carried by the inbreeding organisms. If inbreeding takes place, all genes in the genome are susceptible to the same inbreeding effects. Thus F can also be used to estimate the proportion of loci that will be homozygous IBD.

The quantification of F as a measure that a particular allele is IBD is most readily accomplished through pedigree analysis. The three key elements to determining F from pedigrees are (1) the number of alleles of a gene carried by common ancestors, (2) the number of transmission events required to produce a genotype that is homozygous IBD, and (3) the probability of transmission for each event linking the allele in a common ancestor to the inbred individual. **Figures 22.10a** and **22.10b** show a mating between half-siblings having the same mother (I-2) as the common ancestor. The general solution for F is $(1/2)^n$, where 1/2 is the probability of transmission of an allele and n is the number of transmission events required to produce identity by descent. In this example, either the allele A_1 or A_2 of the mother could be transmitted to

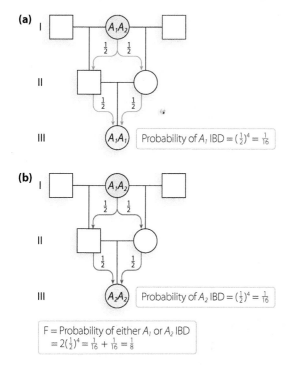

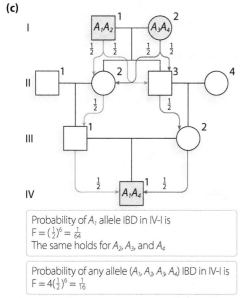

Figure 22.10   **Calculation of the inbreeding coefficient (F).**
(a) The probability of A_1 IBD equals the likelihood of four transmission events, each with a probability of 1/2. **(b)** The probability of A_2 IBD also requires four transmission events, each with a probability of 1/2. The likelihood of either allele IBD is $F = 2(1/2)^4$. **(c)** With two common ancestors, there are four alleles (A_1, A_2, A_3, and A_4) that can be IBD. For this first-cousin mating, the probability for each allele IBD is the same: $F = (1/2)^6$. For all shared alleles combined, $F = 4(1/2)^6 = 1/16$.

both II-1 and II-2 and then to their offspring III-1, so the general solution for F is $(1/2)^n + (1/2)^n$. The arrows in the figure show the four transmission steps that are required for either allele to end up in III-1 IBD. Each required

transmission event has a probability of 50 percent. Thus, the probability that either allele is found in III-1 in a homozygous IBD genotype is $(1/2)^4 = 1/16$. For this case, the inbreeding coefficient is the probability that *any* allele of a locus is homozygous IBD; thus, for each gene, $F = (1/2)^4 + (1/2)^4 = 1/8$. Notice that the arrows in the figure indicating transmission of alleles from I-2 to III-3 trace the two sides of a loop. This visual representation indicates the movement of the allele from generation to generation. If this loop were incomplete, identity by descent could not occur.

Figure 22.10c shows a first-cousin mating in a pedigree in which alleles from either I-1 or I-2 could make their way to IV-1. Here there are four alleles, any of which could be IBD in IV-1. Each allele must complete six transmission steps (indicated by arrows in the figure) to be identical by descent in IV-1, and the transmission probability for each step is 1/2. For each allele carried by I-1 and each allele carried by I-2, the probability the allele is IBD in IV-1 is $(1/2)^6 = 1/64$. For this pedigree, there are four alleles for each gene, two per common ancestor, and F is determined by adding the probability of the four complete loops (one for each allele) that could link an allele in a common ancestor to an inbred homozygous IBD descendant. In this case, $F = (1/2)^6 + (1/2)^6 + (1/2)^6 + (1/2)^6 = 1/16$. The value can also be determined as $F = 4(1/2)^6 = 1/16$. **Genetic Analysis 22.3** demonstrates another computation of an inbreeding coefficient.

First-cousin mating is a form of inbreeding that is relatively common in many human societies and is common in mammals in general. Negative genetic outcomes in the form of infants with recessive conditions due to inbreeding occur when a recessive allele is very rare in a population (i.e., $q = 0.005$ or less). In such cases there can be a 20- to 30-fold increase in the likelihood that a first-cousin mating will produce a child with a recessive phenotype compared to the risk by random mating. However, when the recessive allele frequency is as common as $q = 0.01$, for example, the chance of producing a recessive homozygote from a first-cousin mating is only a few times more likely than the chance of producing a recessive homozygote by random mating. The effect disappears as the frequency of q in the population increases further.

Inbreeding Depression

The genetic consequences of inbreeding for populations are an increase in the frequency of homozygous genotypes and a decrease in the frequency of heterozygous genotypes. One immediate impact of these consequences is seen in conservation genetics, where small, captive populations of individual organisms are bred to perpetuate a nearly extinct species. The increased frequency of homozygosity can lead to a phenomenon known as **inbreeding depression,** the reduction in fitness of inbred organisms, often as a result of the reduced level of genetic

PROBLEM The pedigree shown here depicts crosses performed as part of an antelope captive-breeding program. Use the pedigree information to calculate the coefficient of inbreeding (*F*) for the mating of IV-1 and III-3 that produces the animal identified as V-1.

> **BREAK IT DOWN:** Each allele transmission probability is 1/2. Individual V-1 has two common ancestors, either of whom could be the source of an allele that is IBD (p. 759).

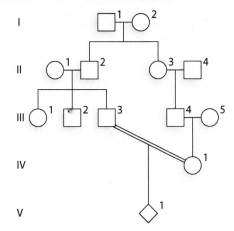

Solution Strategies	Solution Steps
Evaluate	
1. Identify the topic of this problem and the nature of the required answer.	1. This problem concerns determination of the coefficient of inbreeding (*F*) for a specific mating.
2. Identify the critical information given in the problem.	2. The pedigree depicting the common ancestry of the related animals is given.
Deduce	
3. Count the number of transmission events that must occur for an allele to be identical by descent (IBD) in V-1.	3. Counting from a common ancestor to individual V-1, there are seven transmission steps required to produce an allele that is IBD.
4. Identify the transmission probability for each step of transmission.	4. For an autosomal allele, the transmission probability is 1/2.
5. Identify the total number of alleles of an autosomal gene in the common ancestors of V-1.	5. There are two common ancestors (I-1 and I-2) for the inbred individual (V-1). There are two alleles per gene in each common ancestor, for a total of four alleles at each locus.
Solve	
6. Calculate the coefficient of inbreeding for this pedigree.	6. The coefficient of inbreeding is $F = 4(1/2)^7 = 1/32$.

For more practice, see Problems 33, 34, 35, and 36.   Visit the Study Area to access study tools.   MasteringGenetics™

heterozygosity. The reduced fitness associated with inbreeding depression can be due either to an increase in the proportion of deleterious homozygous genotypes or to the higher fitness of heterozygotes.

The magnitude of inbreeding depression depends on the organism. Among plants that naturally reproduce by self-fertilization, the amount of inbreeding depression is small. Many bird species also experience only relatively minor inbreeding depression. This lack of negative consequence has been particularly beneficial in captive breeding programs that have bred bird species such as the California condor and then reintroduced the birds into their natural environment. In contrast to birds and plants, however, mammals experience severe inbreeding depression. Consequently, captive breeding programs for mammals must be managed far more carefully, from a genetic

perspective. Multiple studies indicate that breeding programs designed to avoid inbreeding reduce the mortality of inbred mammals caused by inbreeding depression.

22.7 Species and Higher Taxonomic Groups Evolve by the Interplay of Four Evolutionary Processes

Our discussion to this point has focused on microevolution, that is, evolution operating at the population level. In this section, we turn our attention to evolution at the species level and above.

This evolutionary change is driven by **reproductive isolation** that can result from any morphological, behavioral, or geographic condition or set of conditions that prevents one population from breeding with others. Reproductively isolated populations adapt separately to their particular circumstances, and divergence is a likely consequence. In each environment, differential reproductive success driven by natural selection allows the better-adapted organisms to leave more progeny.

Processes of Speciation

Charles Darwin was the first to describe the concept that existing species evolve from preexisting species. In his famous 1859 book, *On the Origin of Species by Means of Natural Selection*, he laid out two guiding principles of species formation that are still considered fundamental aspects of macroevolution. First, Darwin proposed that hereditary variation is present in all species and controls the phenotypic variability in each species. Second, Darwin proposed that natural selection allows species members with favored phenotypic attributes to survive and reproduce in greater numbers than species members with other phenotypes. Darwin described his model combining these principles as "the theory of descent with modification through variation and natural selection." In other words, Darwin viewed inherited variation and the operation of natural selection as the elements essential to the transformation of one species into another.

Innumerable biological investigations in the last 150 years have verified and elaborated upon Darwin's original proposals as well as quantified the effects and the interplay of each of the four evolutionary processes (natural selection, mutation, migration, and genetic drift) on speciation. The clear picture of speciation that emerges from these studies is that the evolutionary lineages leading from ancestral organisms to descendant forms are almost never simple, straight lines of descent. Instead, the evolutionary history of modern species is filled with side branches that died out because a species, once developed, could not adapt to new environments or was displaced by competing species. It can be tempting to look backward into the evolutionary past and identify a linear step-by-step process leading to modern species, but this perspective minimizes the occurrence of adaptive changes that led to evolutionary "dead ends." More important, the backward-looking approach ignores a major reality of evolution: Evolutionary history is far more like a multi-branched bush rather than like a tree with a long, straight trunk connecting past and present.

The evolutionary history of modern horses and their relatives zebras and donkeys (all three being members of the genus *Equus*) is an example of the typical complexity of evolutionary history (**Figure 22.11**). One can trace a lineage leading more or less directly from *Hyracotherium* in the early Eocene (about 54 million years ago) to modern *Equus*, but this would ignore the many other branches of the evolutionary tree that did not produce modern-day organisms.

The evolutionary tree of *Equus* also illustrates two patterns by which new species evolve from preexisting species. **Anagenesis** is the divergence of a lineage from a common ancestor that produces new forms or new species over time. During anagenesis, a preexisting species experiences natural selection that leads to adaptive change of that species into a new species. In contrast, the pattern of species evolution known as **cladogenesis** is one of branching in which an ancestral species gives rise to two or more new forms or new species.

Reproductive Isolation and Speciation

Although anagenesis and cladogenesis are distinct patterns of species formation, they share two essential features: (1) inherited variation controlling critical phenotypic variation and (2) adaptation through natural selection. Reproductive isolation is also an important component for both cladogenesis and anagenesis, although the precise mechanisms of isolation may differ.

The concept of cladogenesis and reproductive isolation of species derives from work by Theodosius Dobzhansky, Ernst Mayr, and other evolutionary biologists who recognized that new species can form when reproductive barriers prevent the exchange of genes between populations. In describing the necessity of reproductive isolation in this context, two mechanisms are identified (**Table 22.7**). **Prezygotic mechanisms** of reproductive isolation are those that prevent mating between members of different species or prevent the formation of a zygote following interspecies mating. On the other hand, **postzygotic mechanisms** of reproductive isolation result in the failure of a fertilized zygote to survive, or result in sterile offspring of an interspecies mating. These mechanisms of reproductive and genetic isolation lead to patterns of speciation that are most frequently allopatric or sympatric, two patterns defined below.

Allopatric Speciation In **allopatric speciation,** populations are separated by a physical barrier. New species can develop in separate geographic locations as a consequence of their reproductive isolation. Two principal mechanisms create the separations that lead to reproductive isolation: (1) physical separation of a segment of a large population by a physical barrier that prevents gene flow and (2) colonization of new territory (**Figure 22.12**). Geographic events such as the advance of a glacier, the emergence of a mountain range, change in flow pattern of a river, or erosion of a canyon are typical of the kinds of physical changes that lead to reproductive isolation and species diversification. An example of this kind of geographic separation and species development is found in the American Southwest, where the formation of the Grand Canyon beginning 5 to 6 million years ago split an ancestral species of ground squirrel and led to its eventual diversification into two distinct species. Today, *Ammospermophilus leucurus*

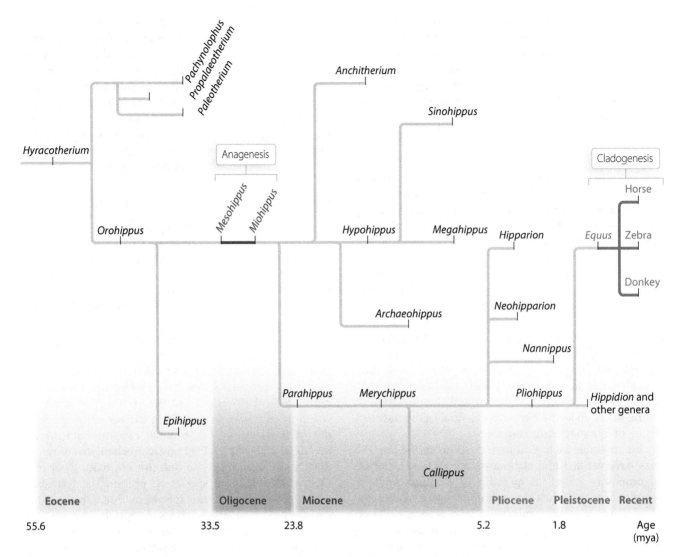

Figure 22.11 **Evolution of the genus *Equus*.** This multibranched evolutionary tree includes examples of anagenesis and cladogenesis as well as numerous examples of evolutionary branches that did not lead to modern species.

Table 22.7	Mechanisms of Reproductive Isolation

Prezygotic Mechanisms

Behavioral isolation: Patterns of sexual behavior in different species are incompatible, or sexual attraction is lacking between them.

Gametic isolation: Mating takes place between different species, but the gametes fail to unite with one another due to differences in gamete compatibility or to failure of male gametes to survive until fertilization of female gametes.

Geographic isolation: Species reside in separate geographic locations or are separated by geographic features that prevent their contact.

Habitat isolation: Species inhabit different ecosystems that prevent them from coming into contact.

Mechanical isolation: Male and female genitalia or reproductive structures of different species are anatomically incompatible.

Temporal isolation: Timing of reproductive ability or receptivity in different species is incompatible.

Postzygotic Mechanisms

Hybrid breakdown: Viable and fertile interspecies hybrids form, but after the F$_1$ generation the fitness of the progeny of hybrids is less than that of progeny from non-hybrids.

Hybrid inviability: The fertilized zygote of an interspecies mating fails to survive gestation.

Hybrid sterility: Interspecies hybrids are viable but infertile.

(a) Population bifurcation by a barrier to reproduction

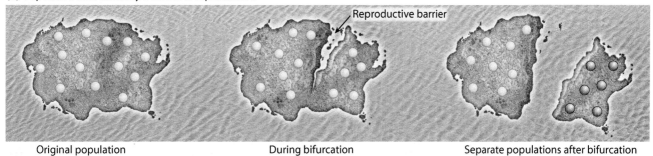

Original population   During bifurcation   Separate populations after bifurcation

(b) Colonization of new territory by migration

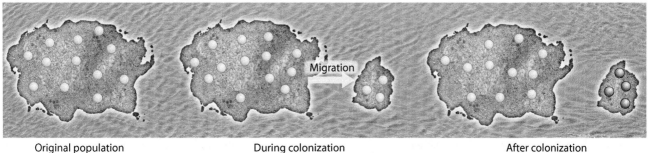

Original population   During colonization   After colonization

Figure 22.12   Processes leading to allopatric speciation.

is a gray-colored ground squirrel found on the north rim of the Grand Canyon, whereas squirrels on the south rim of the canyon are members of the chestnut-colored *Ammospermophilus harrisii*.

The colonization model of allopatric speciation predicts that new species diversify following colonization of new habitats. The diversification of *Drosophila* species on the Hawaiian Islands is a case study of this mechanism (**Figure 22.13**). The Hawaiian Islands are part of a long chain of landmasses and submarine structures that stretch in a northwest-to-southeast direction and are produced by the movement of the Pacific tectonic plate over a volcanic hotspot that lies in the earth's mantle beneath it. As the plate slides toward the west, new islands are produced by volcanic activity of the hotspot. The oldest of the islands are Nihau and Kauai to the northwest; the youngest island is Hawaii, which is still growing by volcanic eruptions of Mauna Loa and Kilauea.

In 2005, James Bonacum and his colleagues examined genetic and morphologic data in numerous Hawaiian *Drosophila* species to test the allopatric speciation model. They found that the most closely related species occur on adjacent islands and that the phylogenetic pattern of species formation corresponds to the pattern of emergence of islands. These results provide support and documentation for the model of allopatric speciation by colonization.

Sympatric Speciation   In **sympatric speciation,** populations share a single habitat but are isolated by genetic, behavioral, seasonal or ecosystem-based mechanisms that prevent gene flow. Species that diverge while occupying the same geographic area are sympatric species.

One clear example of sympatric speciation occurs in plant species that diversify from one another through the development of polyploidy. Mating between a polyploid species and one that is not polyploid can result in reduced fertility of hybrid individuals. Section 13.2 discusses the development of polyploidy through nondisjunction and

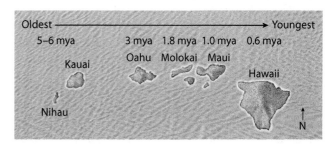

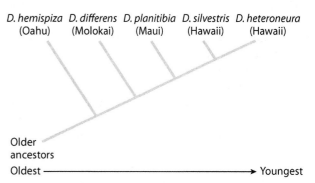

Figure 22.13   Phylogenetic relationships among Hawaiian *Drosophila* **species.** Evolutionary evidence supports the colonization of younger islands and the formation of new species following migration from older islands.

highlights the evolution of the modern bread wheat species (*Triticum aestivum*) from a wild diploid grass to its contemporary allohexaploid form (see Figure 13.9). Animals that develop nocturnal or diurnal patterns of activity that make them more likely to encounter only those other members of the population that are active at the same time are another example of potential sympatric speciation. Similarly, changes in the seasonality of reproduction can limit organisms to the ability to reproduce only during certain times of the year. Organisms living in the same geographic area that do not have the same reproductive seasonality will be unable to mate.

Contemporary Evolution in Darwin's Finches

As the Hawaiian Islands study of *Drosophila* clearly illustrates, the examination of living organisms can reveal enlightening details of evolutionary relationships. Another example comes from long-term studies of Darwin's finches on Daphne Major in the Galapagos Island chain. The studies are by Peter and Rosemary Grant, a husband-and-wife team, who have studied finches on Daphne Major since the early 1980s and have provided powerful support for Darwin's concepts of evolution and speciation.

In 2004, the Grants were part of one of two research teams that identified bone morphogenic protein (Bmp) as the protein likely to be responsible for beak shape variation in Darwin's finches and other birds. One study found that beak shape in chickens could be altered by changing the timing and level of expression of *Bmp*[4], the gene that produces Bmp, in chicken embryos. Increased Bmp production strongly correlated with larger beak size. The research group including the Grants studied Bmp in Darwin's finches and found that finches with larger beaks produced Bmp earlier in development and produced more Bmp than did finches with smaller beaks.

In 2006, the Grants reported on a shift in the shape of the beak of Daphne Major finches that was brought about by a drought and decrease in the availability of an important seed resource. They observed that finches with medium beak size survived and that those with a large beak did not. This is precisely what Darwin predicted to be the mechanism for evolution of differing characteristics among the finches he observed in the Galapagos Islands. The Grants' observation traces back to the early 1980s when a species of large ground finches with a large beak arrived on Daphne Major from a neighboring island. The newly arrived large-beaked finches were able to easily break open the large seeds of a particular herbaceous plant that the medium-beaked finches native to Daphne Major rarely utilized because they could break open only with great effort. These large seeds became the exclusive food source for the large-beaked finches. The numbers of large-beaked finches grew, but for reasons of differences in mate preference between the two types of finches, they did not interbreed. When Daphne Major was hit with a drought in 2003 and 2004, the herbaceous plant that produced the large seeds was particularly hard hit. The medium-beaked finches were able to exploit the smaller seeds available from other plants, but the large-beaked finches died out almost entirely due to their inability to switch to eating smaller seeds of other plants.

In 2004 and 2005, the Grants documented that the distribution of beak sizes on Daphne Major had changed dramatically. The Grants attributed these changes to the preferential survival of native medium ground finches that ate small seeds over finches that preferred large seeds.

In 2009, the Grants described evidence of a potential new speciation event under way on Daphne Major. Following the drought in 2003–2004, only a single mating pair of the large ground finches survived on Daphne Major. This pair mated and produced offspring, and in the ensuing years, the number of, large-beaked finches increased. Mating still does not occur between the two types of finches, thus the two forms are reproductively isolated, suggesting the possibility that the two closely related finch populations on Daphne Major could be in the early stages of a new speciation event.

22.8 Molecular Evolution Changes Genes and Genomes through Time

The heritable variation that provides the raw material of evolution begins at the molecular level, with alterations in DNA sequence and proteins. These molecular changes are part and parcel of the evolutionary process and they can be examined at several levels, from the evolution of individual genes and gene families to the evolution of entire genomes. In this final section, we describe two avenues of molecular evolutionary analysis. The first is the study of the evolution of gene families. We look specifically at genes that are members of the vertebrate steroid receptor (SR) family and discuss the evolutionary process that has generated multiple new molecular functions from an ancestral gene of limited function. Our second examination concerns the evolution of the human genome and the consequences of the introgression of Neandertal DNA by human–Neandertal interbreeding.

Vertebrate Steroid Receptor Evolution

Evolutionary theory predicts that novel molecular functions arise as consequence of the action of natural selection on favorable mutations. For complex systems with multiple active elements, however, the challenge for evolutionary biology is to identify how new protein functions arise when all the components of the complex are not initially present. The evolution of vertebrate steroid receptors (SRs) illustrates one way in which this has occurred. Dissection of this process shows how an ancestral receptor with a single original function duplicated and diversified to produce new genes and proteins with the ability to bind new compounds. The basic scenario of duplication of the ancestral gene, followed by diversification of function, is one commonly encountered in evolutionary biology.

Contemporary vertebrates possess several closely related genes that are responsible for producing SR proteins. Functionally, SR proteins are a family of cell surface proteins that have a ligand (hormone)–binding domain outside the cell to bind hormones. Hormone binding changes the SR protein conformation so as to initiate the transcription of particular genes. In this way, the hormones act as signaling molecules that work through SRs to initiate transcription. The contemporary vertebrate SR protein family includes two estrogen receptors (ERα and ERβ) and one receptor each for androgens (AR), progesterones (PR), mineralocorticoids (MR), and glucocorticoids (GR).

The SR proteins have highly conserved DNA-binding domains (DBDs) that recognize specific DNA sequences called response elements in the promoter regions of specific target genes. Hormone binding to the ligand-binding domains (LBDs) triggers conformational change of the protein into its transcription-activating forms that are capable of DNA binding to response elements. Activated ER proteins recognize the response element sequence AGGTCA; the other activated SR proteins (AR, PR, MR, and GR) recognize the response element sequence AGAACA. Differences in response element recognition enable the vertebrate SR proteins to mediate hormone-induced transcription of a range of different genes. SR proteins that are closely related to the vertebrate SRs have been found in mollusks, annelids, and the invertebrate cephalochordates. How did this closely related yet diversified family of proteins evolve?

Novel Functions from the Ancestral Steroid Receptor The first step in tracing the evolutionary pathway of SR protein diversification is to identify the clades to which contemporary SRs belong. Based on their sequences, two major SR clades have been identified. One contains the ERs, and the other contains the other SR proteins (ARs, PRs, MRs, and GRs) (**Figure 22.14**). The SR proteins of all organisms have the capacity to bind estrogen as a ligand. This is one of several clues indicating that the ancestral SR protein, called *AncSR1*, was an estrogen-binding protein. The strong sequence similarities among the other SR genes and proteins indicate that the diversification of SRs began when *AncSR1* underwent a gene-duplication event. This gave rise to the two major SR protein clades. In the ER clade, the proteins diversified to produce estrogen-binding capability in mollusks, annelids, and cephalochordates. Later gene-duplication events in this clade gave rise to the vertebrate ERα and ERβ proteins. In the clade of the other SRs, the original duplication of *AncSR1* was followed by additional gene duplication and diversification to produce the four new vertebrate SR proteins (see Section 18.2 for additional discussion of genome duplication).

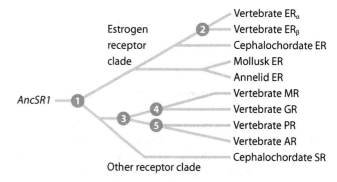

Figure 22.14   Evolution of the vertebrate SR gene family. Multiple duplications of the ancestral estrogen receptor gene *AncSR1* was followed by diversification to produce two vertebrate estrogen receptors (ERs) and other ERs. Other vertebrate steroid receptors (MR, GR, PR, and AR) evolved to use intermediates in the estrogen biosynthetic pathway as ligands.

Ancestral Gene and Protein Reconstruction Phylogenetic reconstruction based on comparisons of gene and protein sequence similarities is one way to identify the probable evolutionary history and function of the ancestral SR protein. Over more than a decade of such analysis, Joseph Thornton and his colleagues have developed several lines of evidence to demonstrate that *AncSR1* was an ER and have deciphered the process that led to the evolution of new SR functions in vertebrates. Part of Thornton's identification of *AncSR1* function is based on statistical analysis of the phylogenetic information to identify the most likely nucleotide at each location in the ancestral gene. The researchers used these data to recreate multiple versions of the inferred ancestral protein by placing a synthesized DNA copy of each putative ancestral gene into an expression system capable of transcription and translation. Each recreated version of *AncSR1* produced slightly different results, but all versions functioned as estrogen receptors.

The Evolution of Novelty Results by Thornton and others show that the inferred *AncSR1* sequence is highly similar to vertebrate ERs in both its LBD and DBD domains. This provides additional evidence that the function of *AncSR1* was estrogen binding and indicates that the ancestral protein most likely recognized an AGGTCA-containing response element as do contemporary ERs. The subsequent diversification of the SR protein occurred with a switch of the DBD to recognize AGAACA response-element sequences and with changes in the LBDs to facilitate binding of the new ligands.

Changing the LBDs to recognize new hormone ligands may seem to be a more complex evolutionary problem than switching DBD recognition. In reality, however, this may be a simple and common occurrence. Research indicates that just two nucleotide base pair changes are required to switch DBD recognition from one response element sequence to the other. Furthermore, estrogen is the end product of a multistep biochemical pathway that begins with cholesterol and

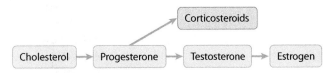

Figure 22.15   The estrogen biosynthesis pathway.

has progesterone, corticosteroids, and testosterone as intermediates (Figure 22.15). The development of new ligand targets for the diversified SR proteins is an example of an evolutionary mechanism in which the ancestral molecule recognized the end product of a multistep biosynthetic pathway, estrogen in this case, and duplication and subsequent diversification eventually produced proteins that recognize and interact with intermediate compounds in the same pathway. Computer simulation studies have found that changing just two to four amino acids in the LBD of a modern human ER is sufficient to change its LBD to one binding progesterone or testosterone. Derived copies of *AncSR1* may have undergone similar changes in ligand recognition by equally simple alterations.

Human Genetic Diversity and Evolution

The Human Genome Sequencing Project (HGSP) completed in the early 2000s was a significant milestone in biology that has paved the way for an unprecedented wave of new information about the composition, evolution, and genetic diversity of the human genome. As expected based on our known evolutionary relationships, many human genes were shown to be directly related to those of our primate and mammalian relatives. More surprising was the identification of many human genes that are homologous to distantly related organisms, including bacteria. An additional surprise was the finding that a sizeable percentage of the human genome consists of transposable genetic elements, many active, many others inactivated.

The HGSP was just the beginning, and by the start of 2014, entire genome sequences of thousands of individuals were available, representing the full array of human genetic diversity. In addition, many much older human genome samples from Neandertals and the lesser known Denisovans have recently been sequenced using DNA from bones recovered in ancient human habitation sites. These ancient samples date from 12,000 years ago to almost 45,000 years ago and, collectively, these modern and ancient human genomes provide an unprecedented view of human genetic diversity and lead to powerful insights into past events that contributed to the evolution of the modern human genome.

SNPs and Indels A sampling of single nucleotide polymorphism (SNP) variation between the genomes of two randomly chosen individuals today reveals differences at about 1 in 1000 DNA base pairs, an approximately 3 million base-pair difference in the 3×10^9 bases in

the genome. Variation accumulates over time, and the greatest variation is expected in the oldest population. The genomes of Africans contain the most variation, consistent with Africa being the place where our species originated. Mutational studies comparing SNP variation in parental genomes with that in their offspring find variation accumulates at a rate of about 30 new SNPs in each individual's germ cells in each generation.

In addition to SNP variation, human genome analysis has revealed a high frequency of insertions or deletions, called **indels,** along with small inversions. These indels and inversions are similar to those described in Sections 13.3 and 13.4, but they usually occur in noncoding regions of chromosomes and they do not cause phenotypic abnormalities.

Comparisons of the genomes of four donors of African ancestry, two Southeast Asian donors, and two Caucasian donors revealed 1565 indels and other small chromosome variants. These findings suggest that human genomes can differ by hundreds to thousands of small chromosome structural variants. As with SNP variation, African donors possessed much greater genetic diversity than did non-Africans.

Human Genetic History The distribution of polymorphic alleles among populations provides insight into the evolutionary history of humans as a species (Figure 22.16). A number of these are associated with dietary or environmental adaptation. We previously discussed SNPs that confer a dietary advantage: the SNPs affecting the *LCT* gene that lead to lactase persistence in European and African pastoral populations. The selective advantage conferred by these SNPs is to allow milk and dairy product consumption in adults.

Another example of polymorphism is the genes that determine skin color. Alleles conferring darker skin pigmentation arose in environments with high levels of UV irradiation. In such environments, dark skin pigmentation helps shield skin from UV damage. In lower UV environments, however, dark pigmentation can reduce UV penetration and interfere with the synthesis of the essential compound vitamin D_3. Thus, natural selection may have favored alleles that lightened skin pigmentation in ancient human populations that migrated to environments with low UV irradiation to promote easier vitamin D_3 production, particularly in Europe and Asia. One particular allele of interest in this regard is a mutation of the melanocortin-1 receptor (*MC1R*) gene that is particularly common in northern Europe. Specific mutant alleles of *MC1R* are associated with red hair and light skin pigmentation. Contemporary population genetic estimates indicate that approximately 40% of people whose ancestry is traced to the United Kingdom carry at least one mutant *MC1R* allele. *MC1R* mutations are found in most human populations, but the frequency is usually quite low. One hypothesis is that *MC1R* mutations are at a selective disadvantage in environments with high UV irradiation; but,

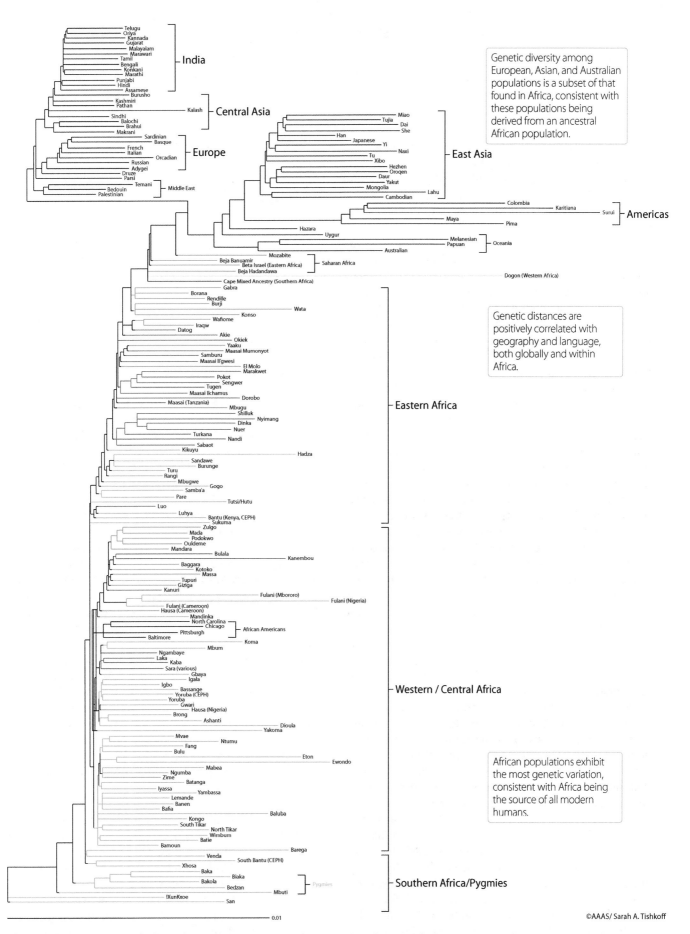

Genetic diversity among European, Asian, and Australian populations is a subset of that found in Africa, consistent with these populations being derived from an ancestral African population.

Genetic distances are positively correlated with geography and language, both globally and within Africa.

African populations exhibit the most genetic variation, consistent with Africa being the source of all modern humans.

©AAAS/ Sarah A. Tishkoff

Figure 22.16 **Cladogram showing genetic distances and relationships between human populations.** This phylogenetic tree is based on 1327 polymorphic markers, 848 repetitive sequence variants, 476 indels, and three SNPs.

in environments where UV irradiation is low, the selective disadvantage is no longer present, and the mutant allele can increase in frequency.

What It Means to Be Human While analysis and comparisons among modern human genomes provide insight into what makes us individuals, biologists and geneticists look to our closest primate relatives and to our recently extinct human relatives to understand what makes us human.

Humans and chimpanzees last shared a common ancestor about 6 million years ago. Both lineages have diverged since that time. Many phenotypic and behavioral differences between humans and chimpanzees are obvious, but what about genetic differences? Genetic and genomic analysis indicates that about 5% of each genome is lineage-specific, that is, found in one lineage exclusively but not in the other. Stated another way, the genomes of humans and chimpanzees are about 95% identical. There are about 30 million SNPs differentiating the human and chimpanzee genomes, or roughly 10 times the number that differentiate one human from another (the vast majority in noncoding regions). In addition, there are about 5 million indels accounting for an additional portion of the difference. Comparing orthologous proteins, 29% of human and chimpanzee proteins have identical amino acid sequences, and the average protein differs by about two amino acids between the two lineages. Beyond these differences are gains and losses of genes in each lineage. Complete genome tabulations show that the number of genes differs by several hundred. And, notably, humans and chimpanzees also differ in chromosome number—humans have 46 chromosomes, whereas chimpanzees have 48 chromosomes. This difference is due to the fusion (Robertsonian translocation) of two autosomes carried by the common ancestor and by chimpanzees that forms human chromosome 2 (see the Case Study in Chapter 13).

How can biologists determine which changes were functionally important in the evolution of humans as they diversified from their shared common ancestor with the chimpanzee? The first step is to identify those changes that occurred exclusively in the human lineage. This is done using the genome sequence of a third, more distantly related, species, such as *Gorilla*, for comparisons that allow researchers to separate human and chimpanzee alleles into those that are ancestral and those that are derived (**Figure 22.17**). Human alleles are considered *ancestral* if they are shared by humans and gorillas but differ in chimps. Conversely, the human allele is considered *derived* if it differs from the allele shared by chimps and gorillas. Once uniquely human alleles are identified, they can be investigated to determine what, if any, difference in phenotype is attributable to the allele. The functional and evolutionary significance of identified phenotypic variation can then be investigated.

A companion approach to exploring important human alleles has developed within the past decade with

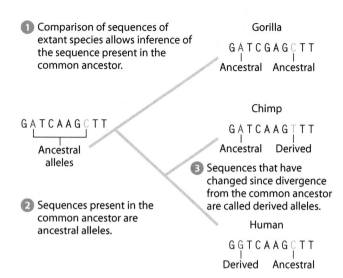

Figure 22.17 **Identifying ancestral versus derived alleles.**

the availability of high-quality genome sequences from Neandertals and a previously unknown human lineage, the Denisovans. Neandertals and Denisovans are descendants of human lineage that diverged about 400,000 years ago from what became the modern human lineage. These ancient humans migrated out of Africa and into the Middle East and Eurasia where their descendants lived until about 30,000 years ago. Modern humans stayed in Africa until about 75,000 to 85,000 years ago, when they migrated to Eurasia and coexisted with Neandertals and interbred (see the Case Study in Chapter 1).

Since modern humans and Neandertals cohabited in Eurasia for millennia, questions have persisted about whether interbreeding occurred between the lineages. The first comparisons of genome sequences revealed that about 1% to 3% of the modern human genome is of Neandertal origin. Initially, the introgression of Neandertal DNA into the modern human genome was thought to be limited to non-Africans, but recently Neandertal DNA has been identified in the genomes of the Masai who currently reside in Kenya and Tanzania. Additional analysis of high-quality Neandertal genomic sequence has determined that while the average modern human carries a few percent of Neandertal DNA in the genome, it is not the same DNA in each person. The current estimate is that 10% to 20% of the Neandertal genome is present today if all modern human genomes are considered collectively.

This analysis has also revealed that Neandertal DNA is unevenly distributed in the human genome. For example, there is virtually no Neandertal DNA on the X chromosome. Each autosome, on the other hand, carries Neandertal DNA, with the precise distribution differing among human populations (**Figure 22.18**). Benjamin Vernot and Joshua Akey, reported in early 2014 on the distribution of Neandertal DNA in the human genome. They speculated that the absence of Neandertal DNA from the human X chromosome indicates that the descendants of human–Neandertal hybrids bearing Neandertal X chromosome DNA became less fertile over time and

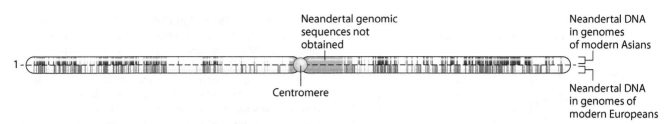

Figure 22.18   The distribution of Neandertal DNA in the modern human genome. The distribution of Neandertal DNA in European and East Asian genomes. Neandertal DNA has been detected in all 22 human autosomes. Chromosome 7 shown here is typical. Neandertal DNA is European genomes is indicated in the blue and the East Asian genomes is indicated in red. The genome region in the gray region contains data insufficient to identify its origin.

the Neandertal DNA was eventually lost. This may have been particularly the case for males, whose X chromosome genes are present in a single copy. Without a second copy of a gene to compensate, the less-fit X-linked Neandertal alleles were selected against, so that eventually most of them were lost from the human X chromosome.

Notwithstanding the fate of Neandertal genes on the X chromosome, two independent research groups reported in 2013 and 2014 on the identification of a Neandertal version of a gene that affects the skin, hair, and nail protein keratin that is found in about 60% of the genomes of Europeans and East Asians. Keratin thickens and toughens the skin, giving it elasticity and protection against water, heat, cold, and pathogens. The researchers speculate that the additional protection afforded to the skin was advantageous in the colder and wetter climates of Europe and Asia. A Neandertal gene that affects the size of the optic disc in the eye has also been identified. So have genes influencing several human disorders. Neandertal genes that make humans more susceptible to Crohn's disease, lupus, and type 2 diabetes and even

a gene influencing potential addiction to smoking have been identified. Researchers speculate that these alleles did not harm Neandertals or the humans who carried the Neandertal alleles, at least until very recently. It may be that prior to the last century or so, the average human life span was not long enough for the effects of these alleles to manifest themselves, or they may have provided some as yet unidentified advantage.

Several questions regarding the evolution of the modern human genome remain to be answered: Did the Denisovans contribute any genes or DNA sequences to the human genome? Was there another ancient human lineage that contributed to the makeup of the human genome? What does interpopulation patterning of human genetic variation tell us about the migration of modern humans out of Africa and their subsequent spread around the globe? There is much more to be told in the story of what in our genetic and evolutionary history makes us human, and undoubtedly some surprises will be revealed, as researchers study the evolution of the human genome.

CASE STUDY

CODIS—Using Population Genetics to Solve Crime and Identify Paternity

Each of us, with the exception of monozygotic multiple births, has a unique genome. Moreover, given the amount of genetic variability uncovered by human genome analysis, each of us may be genetically different from any other person who has ever lived. The concept of genetic uniqueness has practical applications in individual identification through the identification of genotypes of DNA marker genes. This analysis is commonly known as DNA fingerprinting, or DNA profiling. Individual identification uses laboratory analyses of selected genetic markers in combination with statistical analysis based on the H-W equilibrium to determine the probability that a particular individual is the source of a specific DNA sample.

The genetic markers used in DNA profiling are variable number tandem repeats (VNTRs) that contain different numbers of copies of short, repeating DNA sequences. The DNA repeats for a particular VNTR marker range in length from 2 base pairs (bp) to about 20. VNTR analysis is carried out using polymerase chain reaction (PCR) amplification of targeted

DNA sequences followed by gel electrophoresis. The DNA fragment-length variation observed for VNTRs is essentially identical to that seen for RFLPs (see Section 10.2). These methods are highly automated, and the results are highly reproducible and reliable in the hands of trained laboratory technicians.

In 1997, the U.S. Federal Bureau of Investigation (FBI) selected 13 independently assorting human STRP markers to form the core of the bureau's Combined DNA Index System (CODIS; Figure 22.19). Extensive analysis determined the number and frequencies of alleles for the 13 original CODIS VNTRs in most human populations. Studies also precisely defined laboratory methods for the analysis of CODIS VNTRs. More VNTRs were added to the original CODIS markers in later years, and more than 20 CODIS markers are in use today.

The statistical power of CODIS-based identification rests on the Hardy-Weinberg equilibrium and the product rule of probability for independently assorting genes. The VNTR allele frequencies in each population are used to predict

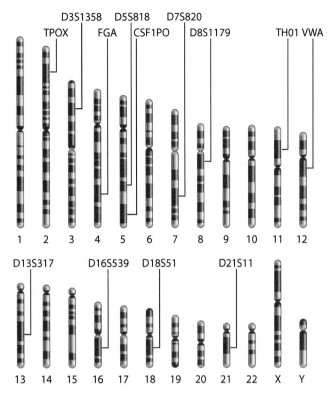

Figure 22.19 **The original 13 independently assorting CODIS VNTR genetic markers.**

and for *FGA*, f(20/25), is 2[(0.125)(0.094)] = 0.0235 (2.35%). Based on independent assortment of the three markers, the joint probability of the genotypes is determined by the product rule: (0.0180)(0.0209)(0.0235) = 8.84 × 10⁻⁶, or approximately 1 in 8.84 million. Most often, all 13 CODIS markers are used, and researchers estimate that the likelihood of two unrelated people having the same genotype is very small. According to some estimates, the theoretical probability of a random match of two unrelated people is about 10⁻¹⁵, or about one in a quadrillion!

CODIS markers have been used in countless criminal and paternity cases since 1997. In criminal cases where the DNA fingerprint of a suspect is compared to a sample from a crime scene, the genotypes for all the markers are compared to determine if any mismatches exist—that is, to see whether the suspect carries an allele not found in the crime scene sample, or vice versa. The detection of such a mismatch results in the *exclusion* of the suspect as the source of the genetic material from the crime scene. **Figure 22.20** shows an

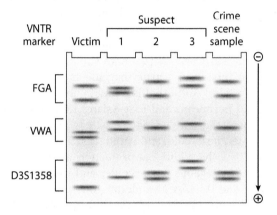

Figure 22.20 **DNA marker analysis.** CODIS VNTR data produced by PCR analysis of three loci, *FGA*, *VWA*, and *D3S1358*. Suspects 1 and 3 are excluded as the source of crime scene DNA by mismatches at each gene. Suspect 2 is not excluded by this analysis.

population genotype frequencies. **Table 22.8** lists the frequencies of alleles for three example VNTR loci, *D3S1358*, *VWA*, and *FGA*. Using these frequencies, let's determine the probability that a person selected at random from the population is homozygous for the 14 allele of D3S1358 (i.e., has the 14/14 genotype), is heterozygous 15/19 for *VWA*, and is heterozygous 20/25 for *FGA*. The frequency of the 14 allele of D3S1358 is *f*(14) = 0.134 and the homozygous frequency is *f*(14/14) = (0.134)(0.134) = 0.018 (1.8%). The genotype frequency for *VWA*, *f*(15/19), is 2[(0.119)(0.088)] = 0.0209 (2.09%)

Table 22.8	Allele Frequencies for Three VNTR Loci Used in CODIS				
D3S1358		**VWA**		**FGA**	
Allele	Frequency	Allele	Frequency	Allele	Frequency
12	0.015	12	0.015	18	0.015
13	0.015	14	0.131	19	0.061
14	0.134	15	0.119	20	0.125
15	0.270	16	0.186	21	0.180
16	0.229	17	0.257	22	0.209
17	0.162	18	0.189	23	0.131
18	0.162	19	0.088	24	0.146
19	0.015	20	0.015	25	0.094
				26	0.018
				27	0.015

example analysis of the genes *D3S1358, VWA*, and *FGA* from a crime scene sample, the crime victim, and three suspects. Mismatches between the crime scene sample and Suspects 1 and 3 exclude these two suspects as sources of the crime scene sample. On the other hand, Suspect 2 is not excluded on the basis of these three genes. Additional CODIS genes can be analyzed, and if they do not exclude Suspect 2 as the source of the crime scene sample, the probability that another person is the source of the crime scene genotype can then be calculated using the methods described.

SUMMARY   MasteringGenetics™ For activities, animations, and review quizzes, go to the study area.

22.1 The Hardy-Weinberg Equilibrium Describes the Relationship of Allele and Genotype Frequencies in Populations

- A population is a group of interbreeding organisms that share a collection of genes known as a gene pool.
- If there are two alleles at a locus, with frequencies represented by p and q, the sum of allele frequencies $p + q = 1.0$.
- The Hardy-Weinberg equilibrium predicts that two alleles will be distributed into genotypes of frequencies p^2, $2pq$, and q^2. The sum of genotype frequencies $p^2 + 2pq + q^2 = 1.0$.
- The Hardy-Weinberg equilibrium assumes that the members of a population mate at random and that the population is not altered by any of the four evolutionary processes.
- Allele frequencies in populations can be determined by the genotype proportion method, allele counting, or the square root method.
- The Hardy-Weinberg equilibrium can be used even when more than two alleles occur for a gene.
- Chi-square analysis compares the number of observed genotypes to the number expected under assumptions of the Hardy-Weinberg equilibrium.

22.2 Natural Selection Operates through Differential Reproductive Fitness within a Population

- Relative fitness is the comparative capacity of individuals with different phenotypes to make genetic contributions to the next generation due to influence of natural selection.
- A selection coefficient is the percentage decrease in reproductive success experienced by an organism possessing a relative fitness that is less than 1.0.
- Directional selection drives the frequency of the favored allele toward fixation in the population and the disfavored allele toward elimination.
- Balanced polymorphism is a stable allele frequency equilibrium resulting from natural selection that favors heterozygotes.
- Convergent evolution leads to similar or identical phenotypes in populations that have separate evolutionary histories.

22.3 Mutation Diversifies Gene Pools

- Forward and reverse mutation slowly change the frequencies of alleles in populations.
- Deleterious mutations are removed by natural selection, striking an equilibrium frequency by balancing mutation and selection rates.

22.4 Migration Is Movement of Organisms and Genes between Populations

- Gene flow is the transfer of alleles by the migration of individuals between populations.
- Gene flow can produce new allele frequencies in admixed populations.
- Gene flow homogenizes allele frequency differences among populations that exchange members.

22.5 Genetic Drift Causes Allele Frequency Change by Sampling Error

- Genetic drift is the random fluctuation of allele frequencies caused by errors in sampling.
- Genetic drift leads ultimately to allele fixation and elimination, but small populations are particularly susceptible to its effects.
- Founder effect is a special form of genetic drift that occurs when a small number of individuals from a larger population establish a new, small population.
- A genetic bottleneck is a random and substantial reduction in population size that significantly changes allele frequencies among survivors.

22.6 Inbreeding Alters Genotype Frequencies

- Inbreeding is nonrandom mating based on genotype that occurs between relatives who are more closely related to one another than to a random member of the population.
- The coefficient of inbreeding (F) is the probability that an allele is homozygous identical by descent in an inbred individual.
- Inbreeding increases the frequency of homozygosity and decreases heterozygosity.
- Inbreeding depression often develops in inbred populations due to the cumulative effects of numerous homozygous loci.

22.7 Species and Higher Taxonomic Groups Evolve by the Interplay of Four Evolutionary Processes

- New species emerge in reproductive isolation through adaptive change in response to conditions.
- Prezygotic reproductive isolation prevents mating between individuals in different populations. Postzygotic reproductive isolation reduces the ability of individuals from different populations to produce living and fertile offspring when they mate.

▋ In allopatric speciation, new species develop as a result of the physical separation of populations into different geographic areas.

▋ Sympatric speciation results from genetic differences that prevent reproduction among organisms that occupy the same habitat.

22.8 Molecular Evolution Changes Genes and Genomes through Time

▋ The evolution of gene families often occurs by one or more duplications of an ancestral gene, followed by diversification of sequence and function of the new gene copies.

▋ In keeping with the relatively short evolutionary span of modern humans, the level of genetic diversity in the modern human genome is modest in comparison to genetic diversity in other genomes.

▋ The modern human genome has undergone introgression of genes and DNA sequences from Neandertals as the result of interbreeding in regions of Eurasia where the species co-existed.

KEYWORDS

admixed population (p. 755)
allele-counting method (p. 747)
allopatric speciation (p. 761)
anagenesis (p. 761)
balanced polymorphism (p. 751)
cladogenesis (p. 761)
coefficient of inbreeding (F) (p. 758)
convergent evolution (p. 752)
differential reproduction (p. 748)
directional natural selection (p. 750)
forward mutation rate (μ) (p. 753)
founder effect (p. 756)
gene pool (p. 743)
genetic bottleneck (p. 757)

genetic drift (p. 756)
genetic hitchhiking (p. 753)
genotype proportion method (p. 747)
Hardy-Weinberg (H-W) equilibrium (p. 743)
identical by descent (IBD) (p. 758)
inbreeding (consanguineous mating) (p. 758)
inbreeding depression (p. 759)
indels (p. 766)
island model (p. 755)
migration (gene flow) (p. 755)
mutation (p. 753)

mutation–selection balance (p. 753)
population (p. 743)
population genetics (p. 743)
postzygotic mechanism (p. 761)
prezygotic mechanism (p. 761)
relative fitness (w) (p. 748)
reproductive isolation (p. 760)
reverse mutation rate (v; reversion rate) (p. 753)
selection coefficient (s; t) (p. 749)
square root method (p. 747)
sympatric speciation (p. 763)

PROBLEMS

(MasteringGenetics™) Visit for instructor-assigned tutorials and problems.

Chapter Concepts

For answers to selected even-numbered problems, see Appendix: Answers.

1. Compare and contrast the terms in each of the following pairs:
   a. population and gene pool
   b. random mating and inbreeding
   c. natural selection and genetic drift
   d. a polymorphic trait and a polymorphic gene
   e. founder effect and genetic bottleneck

2. In a population, what is the consequence of inbreeding? Does inbreeding change allele frequencies? What is the effect of inbreeding with regard to rare recessive alleles in a population?

3. Identify and describe the evolutionary forces that can cause allele frequencies to change from one generation to the next.

4. Describe how natural selection can produce balanced polymorphism of allele frequencies through selection that favors heterozygotes.

5. Thinking creatively about evolutionary mechanisms, identify at least two schemes that could generate allelic

polymorphism in a population. Do not include the processes described in the answer to Problem 4.

6. Genetic drift, an evolutionary factor affecting all populations, can have a significant effect in small populations, even though its effect is negligible in large populations. Explain why this is the case.

7. Over the course of many generations in a small population, what effect does random genetic drift have on allele frequencies?

8. Catastrophic events such as loss of habitat, famine, or overhunting can push species to the brink of extinction and result in a genetic bottleneck. What happens to allele frequencies in a species that experiences a near-extinction event, and what is expected to happen to allele frequencies if the species recovers from near extinction?

9. George Udny Yule was wrong in suggesting that an autosomal dominant trait like brachydactyly will increase in frequency in populations. Explain why Yule was incorrect.

10. The ability to taste the bitter compound phenylthiocarbamide (PTC) is an autosomal dominant trait. The inability to taste PTC is a recessive condition. In a sample of 500 people, 360 have the ability to taste PTC and 140 do not. Calculate the frequency of
   a. the recessive allele
   b. the dominant allele
   c. each genotype

11. Figure 22.6 (page 751) illustrates the effect of an ethanol-rich and an ethanol-free environment on the frequency of the *Drosophila* Adh^F allele in four populations in a 50-generation laboratory experiment. Population 1 and population 2 were reared for 50 generations in a high-ethanol environment, while control 1 and control 2 populations were reared for 50 generations in a zero-ethanol environment. Describe the effect of each environment on the populations, and state any conclusions you can reach about the role of any of the evolutionary processes in producing these effects.

12. Biologists have proposed that the use of antibiotics to treat human infectious disease has played a role in the evolution of widespread antibiotic resistance in several bacterial species, including *Staphylococcus aureus* and the bacteria causing gonorrhea, tuberculosis, and other infectious diseases. Explain how the evolutionary mechanisms mutation and natural selection may have contributed to the development of antibiotic resistance.

13. Two populations of deer, one large one living in a mainland forest and a small one inhabiting a forest on an island,

regularly exchange members who migrate across a land bridge that connects the island to the mainland.
   a. If you compared the allele frequencies in the two populations, what would you expect to find?
   b. An earthquake destroys the bridge between the island and the mainland, making migration impossible for the deer. What do you expect will happen to allele frequencies in the two populations over the following 10 generations?
   c. In which population do you expect to see the greatest allele frequency change? Why?

14. Directional selection presents an apparent paradox. By favoring one allele and disfavoring others, directional selection can lead to fixation (a frequency of 1.0) of the favored allele, after which there is no genetic variation at the locus, and its evolution stops. Explain why directional selection no longer operates in populations after the favored allele reaches fixation.

15. What is inbreeding depression? Why is inbreeding depression a serious concern for animal biologists involved in species-conservation breeding programs?

16. Certain animal species, such as the black-footed ferret, are nearly extinct and currently exist only in captive populations. Other species, such as the panda, are also threatened but exist in the wild thanks to intensive captive-breeding programs. What strategies would you suggest in the case of black-footed ferrets and in the case of pandas to monitor and minimize inbreeding depression?

Application and Integration

17. Genetic Analysis 22.1 (page 749) predicts the number of individuals expected to have the blood group genotypes *MM*, *MN*, and *NN*. Perform a chi-square analysis using the number of people observed and expected in each blood-type category, and state whether the sample is in Hardy-Weinberg equilibrium (see pages 50 and 51 for the chi-square formula and table).

18. In a population of rabbits, $f(C_1) = 0.70$ and $f(C_2) = 0.30$. The alleles exhibit an incomplete dominance relationship in which C_1C_1 produces black rabbits, C_1C_2 tan-colored rabbits, and C_2C_2 rabbits with white fur. If the assumptions of the Hardy-Weinberg principle apply to the rabbit population, what are the expected frequencies of black, tan, and white rabbits?

19. Sickle cell disease (SCD) is found in numerous populations whose ancestral homes are in the malaria belt of Africa and Asia. SCD is an autosomal recessive disorder that results from homozygosity for a mutant β-globin gene allele. Data on one affected population indicates that approximately 8 in 100 newborn infants have SCD.
   a. What are the frequencies of the wild-type ($β^A$) and mutant ($β^S$) alleles in this population?
   b. What is the frequency of carriers of SCD in the population?

20. Epidemiologic data on the population in the previous problem reveal that before the application of modern medical treatment, natural selection played a major role in shaping the frequencies of alleles. Heterozygous individuals have the highest relative fitness, and in comparison to

For answers to selected even-numbered problems, see Appendix: Answers.

heterozygotes, those who are $β^Aβ^A$ have a relative fitness of 82 percent, but only about 32 percent of those with SCD survived to reproduce. What are the estimated equilibrium frequencies of $β^A$ and $β^S$ in this population?

21. The frequency of tasters and nontasters of PTC (see Problem 10) varies among populations. In population A, 64 percent of people are tasters (an autosomal dominant trait) and 36 percent are nontasters. In population B, tasters are 75 percent and nontasters 25 percent. In population C, tasters are 91 percent and nontasters are 9 percent.
   a. Calculate the frequency of the dominant (*T*) allele for PTC tasting and the recessive (*t*) allele for nontasting in each population.
   b. Assuming that Hardy-Weinberg conditions apply, determine the genotype frequencies in each population.

22. Tay-Sachs disease is an autosomal recessive neurological disorder that is fatal in infancy. Despite its invariably lethal effect, Tay-Sachs disease occurs at very high frequency in some Central and Eastern European (Ashkenazi) Jewish populations. In certain Ashkenazi populations, 1 in 750 infants has Tay-Sachs disease. Population biologists believe the high frequency is a consequence of genetic bottlenecks caused by pogroms (genocide) that have reduced the population multiple times in the last several hundred years.
   a. What is a genetic bottleneck?
   b. Explain how a genetic bottleneck and its aftermath could result in a population that carries a lethal allele in high frequency.

c. In the population described, what is the frequency of the recessive allele that produces Tay-Sachs disease?

d. Assuming mating occurs at random in this population, what is the probability a couple are both carriers of Tay-Sachs disease?

23. Cystic fibrosis (CF) is the most common autosomal recessive disorder in certain Caucasian populations. In some populations, approximately 1 in 2000 children have CF. Determine the frequency of CF carriers in this population.

24. In the mouse, *Mus musculus*, survival in agricultural fields that are regularly sprayed with a herbicide is determined by the genotype for a detoxification enzyme encoded by a gene with two alleles, *F* and *S*. The relative fitness values for the genotypes are:

Genotype	Relative fitness
FF	0.72
FS	1.00
SS	0.45

a. Why will this pattern of natural selection result in a stable equilibrium of frequencies of *F* and *S*?

b. Calculate the equilibrium frequencies of the alleles.

25. In a population of flowers growing in a meadow, C_1 and C_2 are autosomal codominant alleles that control flower color. The alleles are polymorphic in the population, with $f(C_1) = 0.80$ and $f(C_2) = 0.20$. Flowers that are C_1C_1 are yellow, orange flowers are C_1C_2, and C_2C_2 flowers are red. A storm blows a new species of hungry insects into the meadow, and they begin to eat yellow and orange flowers but not red flowers. The predation exerts strong natural selection on the flower population, resulting in relative fitness values of $C_1C_1 = 0.30$, $C_1C_2 = 0.60$, and $C_2C_2 = 1.0$.

a. Assuming the population begins in H-W equilibrium, what are the allele frequencies after one generation of natural selection?

b. Assuming random mating takes place among survivors, what are the genotype frequencies in the second generation?

c. If predation continues, what are the allele frequencies when the second generation mates?

d. What are the equilibrium frequencies of C_1 and C_2 if predation continues?

26. Assume that the flower population described in the previous problem undergoes a different pattern of predation. Flower color determination and the starting frequencies of C_1 and C_2 are as described above, but the new insects attack yellow and red flowers, not orange flowers. As a result of the predation pattern, the relative fitness values are $C_1C_1 = 0.40$, $C_1C_2 = 1.0$, and $C_2C_2 = 0.80$.

a. What are the allele frequencies after one generation of natural selection?

b. What are the genotype frequencies among the progeny of predation survivors?

c. What are the equilibrium allele frequencies in the predation environment?

27. ABO blood type is examined in a Taiwanese population, and allele frequencies are determined. In the population, $f(I^A) = 0.30$, $f(I^B) = 0.15$, and $f(i) = 0.55$. Assuming

Hardy-Weinberg conditions apply, what are the frequencies of genotypes, and what are the blood group frequencies in this population?

28. A total of 1000 members of a Central American population are typed for the ABO blood group. In the sample, 421 have blood type A, 168 have blood type B, 336 have blood type O, and 75 have blood type AB. Use this information to determine the frequency of ABO blood group alleles in the sample.

29. A sample of 500 field mice contains 225 individuals that are D_1D_1, 175 that are D_1D_2, and 100 that are D_2D_2.

a. What are the frequencies of D_1 and D_2 in this sample?

b. Is this population in Hardy-Weinberg equilibrium? Use the chi-square test to justify your answer.

c. Is inbreeding a possible genetic explanation for the observed distribution of genotypes? Why or why not?

30. In humans the presence of chin and cheek dimples is dominant to the absence of dimples, and the ability to taste the compound PTC is dominant to the inability to taste the compound. Both traits are autosomal, and they are unlinked. The frequencies of alleles for dimples are $D = 0.62$ and $d = 0.38$. For tasting, the allele frequencies are $T = 0.76$ and $t = 0.24$.

a. Determine the frequency of genotypes for each gene and the frequency of each phenotype.

b. What are the expected frequencies of the four possible phenotype combinations: dimpled tasters, undimpled tasters, dimpled nontasters, and undimpled nontasters?

31. Albinism, an autosomal recessive trait characterized by an absence of skin pigmentation, is found in 1 in 4000 people in populations at equilibrium. Brachydactyly, an autosomal dominant trait producing shortened fingers and toes, is found in 1 in 6000 people in populations at equilibrium. For each of these traits, calculate the frequency of

a. the recessive allele at the locus

b. the dominant allele at the locus

c. heterozygotes in the population

d. For albinism only, what is the frequency of mating between heterozygotes?

32. Using the population data in Table 22.8,

a. Calculate the population frequency of individuals with the 16/18 genotype at *D3S1358*, the 14/18 genotype at *VWA*, and the 23/26 genotype at *FGA*.

b. Explain how the Hardy-Weinberg principles are used in the analysis of CODIS genotypes and other STRP-locus comparisons.

33. Evaluate the following pedigree, and answer the questions below for individual IV-1.

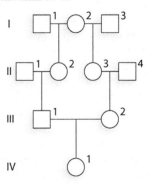

a. Is IV-1 an inbred individual? If so, who is/are the common ancestor(s)?

b. What is *F* for this individual?

34. Evaluate the following pedigree, and answer the questions below.

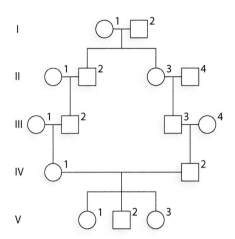

a. Which individual(s) in this family is/are inbred?
b. Who is/are the common ancestor(s) of the inbred individual(s)?
c. Calculate *F* for any inbred members of this family.

35. The following is a partial pedigree of the British royal family. The family contains several inbred individuals and a number of inbreeding pathways. Carefully evaluate the pedigree, and identify the pathways and common ancestors that produce inbred individuals A (Alice in generation IV), B (George VI in generation VI), and C (Charles in generation VIII).

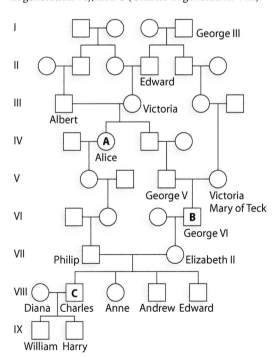

36. Draw a separate pedigree, identifying the inbred individuals and the inbreeding pathways, for each of the following inbreeding coefficients:

a. $F = 4(1/2)^6$
b. $F = 2(1/2)^5$
c. $F = 4(1/2)^8$
d. $F = 2(1/2)^7$

37. The human melanocortin 1 receptor (*MC1R*) gene plays a major role in producing eumelanin, a black-brown pigment that helps determine hair color and skin color. Jonathan Rees and several colleagues (J. L. Rees et al., *Am. J. Human Genet.* 66(2000): 1351–1361) studied multiple *MC1R* alleles in African and European populations. Although this research found several *MC1R* alleles in African populations, *MC1R* alleles that decrease the production of eumelanin were rare. In contrast, several alleles decreasing eumelanin production were found in European populations. How can these results be explained by natural selection?

38. Achromatopsia is a rare autosomal recessive form of complete color blindness that affects about 1 in 20,000 people in most populations. People with this disorder see only in black and white and have extreme sensitivity to light and poor visual acuity. On Pingelap Island, one of a cluster of coral atoll islands in the Federated States of Micronesia, approximately 10 percent of the 3000 indigenous Pingelapese inhabitants have achromatopsia.

Achromatopsia was first recorded on Pingelap in the mid-1800s, about four generations after a typhoon devastated Pingelap and reduced the island population to about 20 people. All Pingelapese with achromatopsia trace their ancestry to one male who was one of the 20 typhoon survivors. Provide a genetic explanation for the origin of achromatopsia on Pingelap, and explain the most likely evolutionary model for the high frequency there of achromatopsia.

39. New allopolyploid plant species can arise by hybridization between two species. If hybridization occurs between a diploid plant species with $2n = 14$ and a second diploid species with $2n = 22$, the new allopolyploid would have 36 chromosomes.

a. Is it likely that sexual reproduction between the allopolyploid species and either of its diploid ancestors would yield fertile progeny? Why or why not?
b. What type of isolation mechanism is most likely to prevent hybridization between the allopolyploid and the diploid species?
c. What pattern of speciation is illustrated by the development of the allopolyploid species?

References and Additional Reading

Chapter 1 The Molecular Basis of Heredity, Variation, and Evolution

Chargaff, E. 1951. Structure and function of nucleic acids as cell constituents. *Fed. Proc.* 10: 654–59.

Dronamraju, K. 1992. Profiles in genetics: Archibald E. Garrod. *Am. J. Hum. Genet.* 51: 216–19.

Dunn, L. C. 1965. *A Short History of Genetics.* New York: McGraw-Hill.

Garrod, A. E. 1902. The incidence of alkaptonuria: A study in chemical individuality. *Lancet* ii: 1616–20.

———. 1909. *Inborn Errors of Metabolism.* London: Frowde, Hodder and Stoughton.

Judson, H. F. 1978. *The Eighth Day of Creation: Makers of the Revolution in Biology.* Woodbury, NY: Cold Spring Harbor Press.

Lander, E. S., and R. A. Weinberg. 2000. Genomics: Journey to the center of biology. *Science* 287: 1777–82.

Meyer, M., M. Kircher, M-T. Gansauge, et al. 2012. A high-coverage genome sequence from an archaic Denisovan individual. *Science* 338: 222–26.

Organ, C. L., et al. 2007. Origin of avian genome size and structure in non-avian dinosaurs. *Nature* 446: 180–84.

Ridley, M. 1999. *Genome: The Autobiography of a Species in 23 Chapters.* New York: Perennial.

Schweitzer, M. H., et al. 2007. Analyses of soft tissue *Tyrannosaurus rex* suggests the presence of protein. *Science* 316: 277–80.

Sturtevant, A. H. 1965. *A History of Genetics.* New York: Harper and Row.

Vernot, B., and J. M. Akey. 2014. Resurrecting surviving Neandertal lineages from modern human genomes. *Science* 343: 1017–21.

Wacey, D., M. R. Kilburn, M. Saunders, et al. 2011. Microfossils of sulphur-metabolizing cells in 3.4 billion year old rocks of Western Australia. *Nature Genetics* 4: 698–702.

Watson, J. D. 1968. *The Double Helix.* New York: Atheneum.

Watson, J. D., and F. H. C. Crick. 1953. Genetical implications of the structure of deoxyribonucleic acid. *Nature* 171: 964–69.

———. 1953. Molecular structure of nucleic acids: A structure for deoxyribose nucleic acid. *Nature* 171: 737–38.

Chapter 2 Transmission Genetics

Armstead, I. I., et al. 2007. Cross-species identification of Mendel's *I* locus. *Science* 315: 73.

Aubry, S., J. Mani, and S. Hörtensteiner. 2008. Stay-green protein, defective in Mendel's green cotyledon mutant, acts independently and upstream of pheophorbide *a* oxidase in the chlorophyll catabolic pathway. *Plant Mol. Biol.* 67: 243–56.

Bateson, W. 1913. *Mendel's Principles of Heredity.* Cambridge: Cambridge University Press.

Bennett, R. L., et al. 1995. Recommendations for standardized human pedigree nomenclature. *Am. J. Hum. Genet.* 56: 745–52.

Bhattacharyya, M., C. Martin, and A. Smith. 1993. The importance of starch biosynthesis in the wrinkled shape character of peas studied by Mendel. *Plant Mol. Biol.* 22: 525–31.

Bhattacharyya, M., et al. 1990. The wrinkled-seed character of pea described by Mendel is caused by a transposon-like insertion in a gene coding starch-branching enzyme. *Cell* 60: 115–22.

Detlefsen, J. A. 1918. Fluctuations of sampling in a Mendelian population. *Genetics* 3: 599–607.

Fisher, R. A. 1936. Has Mendel's work been rediscovered? *Ann. Science* 1: 115–37.

Hartl, D., and V. Orel. 1992. What did Gregor Mendel think he discovered? *Genetics* 131: 245–53.

Hellens, R. P., et al. 2010. Identification of Mendel's white flower character. *PLoS ONE* 5: 1–7.

Henig, R. M. 2001. *A Monk in the Garden: The Lost and Found Genius of Gregor Mendel, the Father of Genetics.* New York: Houghton-Mifflin.

Lester, D. R., et al. 1997. Mendel's stem length gene (*Le*) encodes a gibberellin 3β-hydroxylase. *Plant Cell* 9: 1435–43.

Martin, D. N., W. M. Proebsting, and P. Hedden. 1997. Mendel's dwarfing gene: cDNAs from the *Le* alleles and function of the expressed proteins. *Proc. Natl. Acad. Sci. USA* 94: 8907–11.

Mendel, G. (1866) 1966. Experiments in plant hybridization. In *The Origins of Genetics: A Mendel Source Book,* edited by C. Stern and E. Sherwood. Translated. San Francisco: W. H. Freeman.

Olby, R. C. 1985. *Origins of Mendelism.* London: Constable.

Orel, V. 1996. *Gregor Mendel: The First Geneticist.* Oxford: Oxford University Press.

Peters, J. (ed.). 1959. *Classic Papers in Genetics.* Englewood Cliffs NJ: Prentice-Hall.

Reid, J. B., and J. J. Ross. 2011. Mendel's genes: Toward a full molecular characterization. *Genetics* 189: 3–10.

Stern, C., and E. Sherwood (eds.). 1966. *The Origins of Genetics: A Mendel Source Book.* San Francisco: W. H. Freeman.

Stubbe, H. 1972. *History of Genetics: From Prehistoric Times to the Rediscovery of Mendel's Laws.* Cambridge, MA: MIT Press.

Tschermak-Seysenegg, E. 1951. The rediscovery of Mendel's work. *J. Hered.* 42: 162–72.

Welling, F. 1991. Historical study: Johann Gregor Mendel 1822–1884. *Am. J. Med. Genet.* 40: 1–25.

White, O. E. 1917. Studies of inheritance in *Pisum.* II. The present state of knowledge of heredity and variation in peas. *Proc. Am. Phil. Soc.* 56: 487–88.

Chapter 3 Cell Division and Chromosome Heredity

Barr, M. L. 1960. Sexual dimorphism in interphase nuclei. *Am. J. Hum. Genet.* 12: 118–27.

Bridges, C. B. 1916. Nondisjunction as proof of the chromosome theory of heredity. *Genetics* 1: 1–52 and 107–63.

Gonzalez, A. N., et al. 2008. A shared enhancer controls a temporal switch between promoters during Drosophila primary sex determination. *Proc. Natl. Acad. Sci. USA* 105: 18436–41.

Gould, K. L., and P. Nurse. 1989. Tyrosine phosphorylation of the fission yeast cdc2$^+$ protein kinase regulates entry into mitosis. *Nature* 342: 39–45.

Hartwell, L. H. 1991. Twenty-five years of cell cycle genetics. *Genetics* 129: 975–80.

Hartwell, L. H., et al. 1974. Genetic control of cell division cycle in yeast. *Science* 183: 46–51.

Hartwell, L. H., J. Culotti, and B. J. Reid. 1970. Genetic control of cell division in yeast. I. Detection of mutants. *Proc. Natl. Acad. Sci. USA* 66: 352–59.

Hartwell, L. H., and M. W. Unger. 1977. Unequal division in *Saccharomyces cerevisiae* and its implications for the control of cell division. *J. Biol. Chem.* 75: 422–35.

Hodgkin, J. 1989. *Drosophila* sex determination: Cascade of regulated splicing. *Cell* 56: 905–6.

Hunt, D. M., et al. 1995. The chemistry of John Dalton's color blindness. *Science* 267: 984–88.

Hunt, T., and M. W. Kirschner. 1993. Cell manipulation. *Current Opinions in Cell Biol.* 5: 163–65.

Johnson, R. T., and P. N. Rao. 1970. Mammalian cell fusion: Induction of premature chromosome condensation in interphase nuclei. *Nature* 226: 717–22.

Koopman, P., et al. 1991. Male development of chromosomally female mice transgenic for *Sry. Nature* 351: 117–21.

Lyon, M. F. 1962. Sex chromatin and gene action in the mammalian X-chromosome. *Am. J. Hum. Genet.* 14: 135–48.

Masui, Y., and C. L. Markert. 1971. Cytoplasmic control of nuclear behavior during meiotic maturation of frog oocytes. *J. Exp. Zool.* 177: 129–45.

Morgan, T. H. 1910. Sex-limited inheritance in *Drosophila. Science* 32: 120–22.

Murray, A. W., and M. W. Kirschner. 1989. Cyclin synthesis drives the early embryonic cell cycle. *Nature* 339: 275–80.

Nathans, J., D. Thomas, and D. S. Hogness. 1986. Molecular genetics of human color vision: The genes encoding blue, green, and red pigments. *Science* 232: 193–202.

Nathans, J., et al. 1986. Molecular genetics of inherited variation in human color vision. *Science* 232: 203–10.

Page, D. C., A. de la Chapelle, and J. Weissenbach. 1985. Chromosome Y-specific DNA in human XX males. *Nature* 315: 224–26.

Page, D. C., et al. 1987. The sex-determining region of the Y chromosome encodes a finger protein. *Cell* 51: 1091–1104.

Rao, P. N., and R. T. Johnson. 1970. Mammalian cell fusion studies on the regulation of DNA synthesis and mitosis. *Nature* 225: 159–64.

Salz, H. K., and J. W. Erickson. 2010. Sex determination in *Drosophila*: The view from the top. *Fly* 4: 60–70.

Stevens, N. M. 1905. Studies in spermatogenesis with especial reference to the "accessory chromosome." Washington, DC: Carnegie Institute of Washington, Publication No. 36.

Willard, H. F. 1996. X chromosome inactivation, *XIST*, and pursuit of the X-inactivation center. *Cell* 86: 5–7.

Wilson, E. B. 1895. *An Atlas of the Fertilization and Karyokinesis of the Ovum.* New York: Columbia University Press.

Chapter 4 Inheritance Patterns of Single Genes and Gene Interaction

Beadle, G. W., and E. L. Tatum. 1941. Genetic control of biochemical reactions in *Neurospora*. *Proc. Natl. Acad. Sci. USA* 27: 499–506.

Bultman, S. J., E. J. Michaud, and R. P. Woychik. 1992. Molecular characterization of the mouse *agouti* locus. *Cell* 71: 1195–1204.

Duhl, D. M. J., et al. 1994. Pleiotropic effects of the mouse *lethal yellow* (A^Y) mutation explained by detection of a maternally expressed gene and the simultaneous production of *agouti* fusion RNAs. *Development* 120: 1695–1708.

Flatt, T., M-P. Tu, and M. Tatar. 2005. Hormonal pleiotropy and the juvenile hormone regulation of *Drosophila* development and life history. *BioEssays* 27: 999–1010.

Garrod, A. E. 1902. The incidence of alkaptonuria: A study in chemical individuality. *Lancet* 2: 1616–20.

———. (1909) 1963. *Inborn Errors of Metabolism.* London: Oxford University Press.

Garrod, S. C. 1989. Family influences on A. E. Garrod's thinking. *J. Inherit. Metabol. Dis.* 12: 2–8.

Jackson, I. J. 1994. Molecular and developmental genetics of mouse coat color. *Ann Rev. Genet.* 28: 189–217.

Lahn, B. T., and D. C. Page. 1999. Four evolutionary strata on the human X chromosome. *Science* 286: 964–67.

Landsteiner, K., and P. Levine. 1927. Further observations on individual differences of blood group. *Proc. Soc. Exp. Biol. Med.* 24: 941–42.

Michaud, E. J., et al. 1994. A molecular model for the genetic and phenotypic characteristics of the mouse lethal yellow (Ay) mutation. *Proc. Natl. Acad. Sci. USA* 91: 2562–66.

Phillips, P. C. 1998. The language of gene interaction. *Genetics* 149: 1167–71.

Race, R. R., and R. Sanger. 1975. *Blood Groups in Man.* 6th ed. Cambridge: Oxford University Press.

Sandstedt, S. A., and P. K. Tucker. 2004. Evolutionary strata on the mouse X chromosome correspond to strata on the human X chromosome. *Genome Res.* 14: 267–72.

Siracusa, L. D. 1994. The *agouti* gene: Turned on to yellow. *Trends Genet.* 10: 423–28.

Srb, A. M., and N. H. Horowitz. 1944. The ornithine cycle in *Neurospora* and its genetic control. *J. Biol. Chem.* 154: 129–39.

Yamamoto, F., et al. 1990. Molecular genetic basis of the histo-blood group ABO system. *Nature* 345: 229–33.

Chapter 5 Genetic Linkage and Mapping in Eukaryotes

Bateson, W., E. R. Saunders, and R. C. Punnett. 1905. Experimental studies in the physiology of heredity. *Rep. Evol. Committee Royal Soc.* II: 1–55, 80–99.

Bregger, T. 1918. Linkage in maize: The *C* aleurone factor and waxy endosperm. *Am. Nat.* 52: 57–61.

Bridges, C. B., and T. M. Olbrycht. 1926. The multiple stock "Xple" and its use. *Genetics* 11: 41–56.

Creighton, H. B., and B. McClintock. 1931. A correlation of cytological and genetic crossing over in *Zea mays*. *Proc. Natl. Acad. Sci. USA* 17: 492–97.

Green, M. M., and K. C. Green. 1949. Crossing-over between alleles at the Lozenge locus in *Drosophila melanogaster*. *Proc. Natl. Acad. Sci. USA* 35: 596–91.

Gusella, J. F., et al. 1983. A polymorphic DNA marker genetically linked to Huntington's disease. *Nature* 306: 234–38.

Hall, J. M., et al. 1990. Linkage of early-onset familial breast cancer to chromosome 17q21. *Science* 250: 1684–89.

———. 1992. Closing in on a breast cancer gene on chromosome 17q. *Am. J. Hum. Genet.* 50: 1235–42.

Houlahan, M. B., G. W. Beadle, and H. G. Calhoun. 1949. Linkage studies with biochemical mutants of *Neurospora crassa*. *Genetics* 34: 493–507.

Huntington's Disease Collaborative Research Group (58 authors). 1993. A novel gene containing a trinucleotide repeat that is expanded and unstable on Huntington's disease chromosomes. *Cell* 72: 971–83.

Ikeda, Y., et al. 2006. Spectrin mutations cause spinocerebellar ataxia type 5. *Nat. Genet.* 38: 184–90.

Janssens, F. A. 1909. La theorie de la chiasmatypie. *La Cellule* 25: 389–411.

Knudson, A. G. Jr. 1971. Mutation and cancer: Statistical study of retinoblastoma. *Proc. Natl. Acad. Sci. USA* 68: 820–23.

Lindegren, C. C. 1933. The genetics of *Neurospora*. III. Pure-bred stocks and crossing over in *N. crassa*. *Bull. Torrey Bot. Club* 60: 133–54.

Morgan, T. H. 1910. Sex-limited inheritance in *Drosophila*. *Science* 32: 120–22.

———. 1910. The method of inheritance of two sex-limited characters in the same animal. *Proc. Soc. Exp. Biol. Med.* 8: 17.

———. 1911. An attempt to analyze the constitution of the chromosomes on the basis of sex-limited inheritance in *Drosophila*. *J. Exp. Zool.* 11: 365–414.

———. 1911. Random segregation versus coupling in Mendelian inheritance. *Science* 34: 384.

Morgan, T. H., et al. 1915. *The Mechanism of Mendelian Heredity.* New York: Henry Holt.

Morton, N. E. 1955. Sequential tests for the detection of linkage. *Am. J. Hum. Genet.* 7: 277–318.

Stern, C. 1931. Zytologisch-genetische untersuchungen als beweise fur die Morgansche theorie des fakorenaustauchs. *Biol. Zentralbl.* 51: 547–87.

Stern, C., and D. Doan. 1936. A cytogenetic demonstration of crossing-over between X- and Y-chromosomes in the male of *Drosophila melanogaster*. *Proc. Natl. Acad. Sci. USA* 22: 649–54.

Strachan, T., and A. P. Read. 2004. *Human Molecular Genetics.* 3rd ed. London and New York: Garland Science.

Sturtevant, A. H. 1913. The linear arrangement of six sex-linked factors in *Drosophila* as shown by their mode of association. *J. Exp. Zool.* 14: 43–59.

Weber, J. L., et al. 1993. Evidence for human meiotic recombination interference obtained through construction of a short tandem repeat polymorphism linkage map of chromosome 19. *Am. J. Hum. Genet.* 53: 1079–95.

Wexler, Alice. 1995. *Mapping Fate: A Memoir of Family, Risk, and Genetic Research.* New York: Times Books, Random House.

Chapter 6 Gene Analysis and Mapping in Bacteria and Bacteriophages

Bachmann, B. J. 1990. Linkage map of *Escherichia coli* K-12, Edition 8. *Microbiol. Rev.* 54: 130–97.

Benzer, S. 1959. On the topology of the genetic fine structure. *Proc. Natl. Acad. Sci. USA* 45: 1607–20.

———. 1961. On the topology of the genetic fine structure. *Proc. Natl. Acad. Sci. USA* 47: 403–16.

Blattner, F. R., G. Plunkett III, and C. A. Bloch. 1997. The complete genome sequence of *Escherichia coli* K-12. *Science* 277: 1453–62.

Curtiss, R. 1969. Bacterial conjugation. *Ann. Rev. Microbiol.* 23: 69–123.

Davis, B. D. 1950. Nonfiltrability of the agents of recombination. *J. Bacteriol.* 60: 507–8.

Hayes, W. 1953. Observations on a transmissible agent determining sexual differentiation in Bact. Coli. *J. Gen. Microbiol.* 8: 72–88.

Hotchkiss, R. D., and M. Gabor. 1970. Bacterial transformation with special reference to recombination processes. *Ann. Rev. Genet.* 4: 193–224.

Lederberg, J. 1986. Forty years of genetic recombination in bacteria: A fortieth anniversary reminiscence. *Genetics* 28: 491–511.

Lederberg, J., and E. L. Tatum. 1946. Gene recombination in *Escherichia coli*. *Nature* 158: 558–59.

Nakamura, Y., T. Itoh, H. Matsuda, and T. Gojobori. 2004. Biased biological functions of horizontally transferred genes in prokaryotic genomes. *Nature Genet.* 36: 760–66.

Robinson, K. M., K. B. Sieber, and J. C. Dunning Hotopp. 2013. A review of bacterial-animal lateral gene transfer may inform our understanding of diseases like cancer. *PLOS Genetics* 9: 1–6.

Stent, G. S. 1963. *Molecular Biology of Bacterial Viruses.* San Francisco: W. H. Freeman.

Susman, M. 1970. General bacterial genetics. *Ann. Rev. Genet.* 4: 135–76.

Wollman, E. L., F. Jacob, and W. Hayes. 1962. Conjugation and genetic recombination in *E. coli* K-12. *Cold Spring Harbor Symp. Quant. Biol.* 21: 141–62.

Yanofsky, C., and E. S. Lennox. 1959. Transduction and recombination study of linkage relationships among the genes controlling tryptophan synthesis in *Escherichia coli*. *Virology* 8: 425–47.

Zinder, N. D. 1958. Transduction in bacteria. *Sci. Am.* 199: 38–46.

Zinder, N. D., and J. L. Lederberg. 1952. Genetic exchange in *Salmonella*. *J. Bacteriol.* 64: 679–99.

Chapter 7 DNA Structure and Replication

Avery, O. T., C. M. Macleod, and M. McCarty. 1944. Studies on the chemical nature of the substance inducing transformation of pneumococcal types: Induction of transformation by a desoxyribonucleic acid fraction isolated from pneumococcus type III. *J. Exp. Med.* 79: 137–58.

Barry, E. R., and S. D. Bell. 2006. DNA replication in Archaea. *Microbiol. Molec. Biol. Rev.* 70: 876–87.

Blackburn, E. H. 1991. Structure and function of telomeres. *Nature* 350: 569–73.

Blackwood, J. K., N. J. Rzechorzek, A. S. Abrams, et al. 2011. Structural and functional insights into DNA-end processing by the archaeal HerA helicase-NurR nuclease complex. *Nuc. Acids Res.* 39: 1–14.

Cairns, J. 1963. The bacterial chromosome and its manner of replication as seen by autoradiography. *J. Mol. Biol.* 6: 208–13.

DeLucia, P., and J. Cairns. 1969. Isolation of an *E. coli* strain with a mutation affecting DNA polymerase. *Nature* 224: 1164–66.

Garrett, R. A. and H-P. Klenk (eds.) 2007. *Archaea: Evolution, Physiology, and Molecular Biology.* Malden, MA: Blackwell Publishing.

Georgescu, R. E., et al. 2007. Structure of a sliding clamp on DNA. *Cell* 132: 43–54.

Greider, C. W., and E. H. Blackburn. 1987. The telomere terminal transferase of *Tetrahymena* is a ribonucleoprotein enzyme with two kinds of primer specificity. *Cell* 51: 887–98.

Griffith, F. 1928. The significance of pneumococcal types. *J. Hyg.* 27: 113–59.

Hanahan, D., and R. Weinberg. 2000. The hallmarks of cancer. *Cell* 100: 57–70.

Harley, C. B., A. B. Futcher, and C. W. Greider. 1990. Telomeres shorten during ageing of human fibroblasts. *Nature* 345: 458–60.

Hayflick, L., and P. S. Moorhead. 1961. The serial cultivation of human diploid cell strains. *Exp. Cell. Res.* 25: 585–621.

Hershey, A. D., and M. Chase. 1952. Independent function of viral protein and nucleic acid in growth of bacteriophage. *J. Genet. Phys.* 36: 39–56.

Huberman, J. A., and A. D. Riggs. 1968. On the mechanism of DNA replication in mammalian chromosomes. *J. Mol. Biol.* 32: 327–41.

Huberman, J. A., and A. Tsai. 1973. Direction of DNA replication in mammalian cells. *J. Mol. Biol.* 75: 5–12.

Huntington's Disease Collaborative Research Group. 1993. A novel gene containing a trinucleotide repeat that is expanded and unstable on Huntington's disease chromosomes. *Cell* 72: 971–83.

Kornberg, A. 1960. Biological synthesis of DNA. *Science* 131: 1503–8.

Lemon, K. P., and A. D. Grossman. 2000. Movement of replicating DNA through a stationary replisome. *Mol. Cell* 6: 1321–30.

Margulies, M., et al. 2005. Genome sequencing in microfabricated high-density picolitrereactors. *Nature* 437: 376–80.

Meselson, M., and F. W. Stahl. 1958. The replication of DNA in *Escherichia coli*. *Proc. Natl. Acad. Sci. USA* 44: 671–82.

O'Donnel, M., and J. Kuriyan. 2006. Clamp loaders and replication initiation. *Curr. Opin. Struct. Biol.* 16: 405–15.

Ogawa, T., and R. Okazaki. 1980. Discontinuous DNA replication. *Ann. Rev. Biochem.* 49: 421–57.

Rodriguez, R. L., M. S. Dalbey, and C. I. Davern. 1973. Autoradiographic evidence for bidirectional DNA replication in *Escherichia coli*. *J. Molec. Biol.* 74: 599–604.

Spies, M., I. Amitani, R. J. Baskin, and S. C. Kowalczykowski. 2007. RecBCD enzyme switches lead motor subunits in response to chi recognition. *Cell* 131: 694–705.

Steitz, T. A. 1998. A mechanism for all polymerases. *Nature* 391: 231–32.

———. 2006. Visualizing polynucleotide polymerase machines at work. *EMBO J.* 25: 3458–68.

Chapter 8 Molecular Biology of Transcription and RNA Processing

Berget, S. M., C. Moore, and P. Sharp. 1977. Spliced segments at the 5′ terminus of adenovirus 2 late mRNA. *Proc. Natl. Acad. Sci. USA* 74: 3171–75.

Bogenhagen, D. F., S. Sakonju, and D. D. Brown. 1980. A control region in the center of the 5S RNA gene directs specific initiation of transcription: II. the 3′ border of the region. *Cell* 19: 27–35.

Brenner, S., F. Jacob, and M. Meselson. 1961. An unstable intermediate carrying information from genes to ribosomes for protein synthesis. *Nature* 190: 575–80.

Cech, T. 1987. The chemistry of self-splicing RNA and RNA enzymes. *Science* 236: 1532–39.

Chambon, P. 1981. Split genes. *Sci. Am.* 244: 60–71.

Cramer, P., et al. 2000. Architecture of RNA polymerase II and implications for the transcription mechanism. *Science* 288: 640–49.

Darnell, J. E. 1983. The processing of RNA. *Sci. Am.* 249: 90–100.

De Carlo, S., S-C. Lin, D. J. Taatjes, and A. Hoenger. 2010. Molecular basis of transcription initiation in archaea. *Transcription* 1: 103–11.

Dugaiczyk, A., et al. 1978. The natural ovalbumin gene contains seven intervening sequences. *Nature* 274: 328–33.

Hamkalo, B. 1985. Visualizing transcription in chromosomes. *Trends. Genet.* 1: 255–60.

Kersanach, R., et al. 1994. Five identical intron positions in ancient duplicated genes of eubacterial origin. *Nature* 367: 387–89.

Kim, M., et al. 2006. Distinct pathways for snoRNA and mRNA termination. *Mol. Cell* 24: 723–34.

Lees-Miller, J. P., L. O. Goodwin, and D. M. Helfman. 1990. Three novel brain tropomyosin isoforms are expressed from the rat α-tropomyosin gene through the use of alternative promoters and alternative RNA processing. *Mol. Cell. Biol.* 10: 1729–42.

Logsdon, J. M. Jr., et al. 1995. Seven newly discovered intron positions in the triose-phosphate isomerase gene: Evidence for the intron-late theory. *Proc. Natl. Acad. Sci. USA* 92: 8507–11.

Maniatis, T., S. Goodbourn, and J. A. Fischer. 1987. Regulation of inducible and tissue-specific gene expression. *Science* 236: 1237–45.

Maniatis, T., and R. Reed 2002. An extensive network of coupling among gene expression machines. *Nature* 416: 499–506.

Myers, R. M., K. Tilly, and T. Maniatis. 1986. Fine structure genetic analysis of the β-globin promoter. *Science* 232: 613–18.

Peng, N., Y. X. Liang, and Q. She. 2011. Archaeal promoter architecture and mechanism of gene activation. *Biochem. Soc Trans.* 39: 99–103.

Pribnow, D. 1975. Nucleotide sequence of an RNA binding site at an early T7 promoter. *Proc. Natl. Acad. Sci. USA* 72: 784–88.

Reed, R. 2003. Coupling transcription, splicing, and mRNA export. *Curr. Opin. Cell Biol.* 15: 326–31.

Reed, R., and T. Maniatis. 1985. Intron sequences involved in lariat formation during pre-mRNA splicing. *Cell* 41: 95–105.

Sakonju, S., D. F. Bogenhagen, and D. D. Brown. 1980. A control region in the center of the 5S RNA gene directs specific initiation of transcription: I. the 5′ border of the region. *Cell* 19: 13–25.

Sharp, P. 1994. Nobel Lecture: Split genes and RNA splicing. *Cell* 77: 805–15.

Sudhof, T. C., et al. 1985. Cassette of eight exons shared by genes for LDL and EGF precursors. *Science* 228: 893–95.

Tilghman, S., et al. 1978. The intervening sequence of a mouse beta-globin gene is traced to the 15S beta-globin mRNA precursor. *Proc. Natl. Acad. Sci. USA* 75: 1309–13.

Tocchini-Valentini, G., P. Fruscoloni, and G. P. Tocchini-Valentini. 2011. Evolution of introns in the archaeal world. *Proc. Nat. Acad. Sci. USA* 108: 4782–87.

Chapter 9 The Molecular Biology of Translation

Blobel, G., and B. Dobberstein. 1975. Transfer of proteins across membranes. I. Presence of proteolytically processed and unprocessed nascent immunoglobulin light chains on membrane-bound ribosomes of murine myeloma. *J. Cell. Biol.* 67: 835–51.

Brenner, S., F. Jacob, and M. Meselson. 1969. An unstable intermediate carrying information from genes to ribosomes for protein synthesis. *Nature* 190: 576–81.

Carrell, R. W., and D. A. Lomas. 2002. Alpha-1 antitrypsin deficiency—a model conformational disease. *N. Engl. J. Med.*, 346: 45–53.

Cech, T. R. 2000. The ribosome is a ribozyme. *Science* 289: 878–79.

Chapeville, F. F., et al. 1962. On the role of soluble ribonucleic acid in coding for nucleic acids. *Proc. Natl. Acad. Sci. USA* 48: 1086–92.

Crick, F. 1966. Codon-anticodon pairing: The wobble hypothesis. *J. Mol. Biol.* 19: 548–55.

Crick, F., et al. 1961. General nature of the genetic code for proteins. *Nature* 192: 1227–32.

Fox, T. D. 1987. Natural variation in the genetic code. *Ann. Rev. Genet.* 21: 67–91.

Johnson, A. W., E. Lund, and J. Dahlberg. 2002. Nuclear export of ribosomal subunits. *Trends Biochem. Sci.* 27: 850–57.

Khorana, H. G., et al. 1967. Polynucleotide synthesis and the genetic code. *Cold Spring Harbor Symp.* 31: 39–49.

Kloc, M., N. R. Zearfoss, and L. D. Etkin. 2002. Mechanisms of subcellular mRNA localization. *Cell* 108: 533–44.

Kozak, M. 1978. How do eukaryotic ribosomes select initiation regions in mRNA? *Cell* 15: 1109–23.

———. 1987. An analysis of 5′-noncoding sequences from 699 vertebrate messenger RNAs. *Nuc. Acid Res.* 15: 8125–48.

Nirenberg, M. W., and P. Leder. 1964. RNA code words and protein synthesis. I. The effects of trinucleotides upon the binding of sRNA to ribosomes. *Science* 145: 1399–1407.

Nirenberg, M. W., and J. H. Matthaei. 1961. The dependence of cell-free protein synthesis in *E. coli* upon naturally occurring or synthetic polyribosome *Proc. Natl. Acad. Sci. USA* 47: 1588–1602.

Patil, C., and P. Walter. 2001. Intracellular signaling from the endoplasmic reticulum to the nucleus: The unfolding protein response in yeast and mammals. *Curr. Opin. Cell Biol.* 13: 349–55.

Sachs, A. B., P. Sarnow, and M. W. Hentz. 1997. Starting at the beginning, middle, and end: Translation initiation in eukaryotes. *Cell* 89: 831–38.

Saito, K., K. Kobayashi, M. Wada, I. Kikuno, et al. 2010. Omnipotent role of archaeal elongation factor 1 alpha (EF1α) in translation elongation and termination, and quality control of protein synthesis. *Proc. Nat. Acad. Sci. USA* 107: 19242–47.

Shine, J., and L. Dalgarno. 1974. The 3′-terminal sequence of *Escherichia coli* 16S ribosomal RNA: Complementary to nonsense triplet and ribosome binding sites. *Proc. Natl. Acad. Sci. USA* 71: 1342–46.

Tsugita, A., et al. 1962. Demonstration of the messenger role of viral RNA. *Proc. Natl. Acad. Sci. USA* 48: 846–53.

Watson, J. D. 1963. Involvement of RNA in the synthesis of proteins. *Science* 140: 17–26.

Zheng, N., and L. M. Gierasch. 1996. Signal sequences: The same yet different. *Cell* 86: 849–52.

Chapter 10 The Integration of Genetic Approaches: Understanding Sickle Cell Disease

Allison, A. C. 1954. Protection afforded by sickle cell trait against subtertian malarial infection. *Br. Med. J.* 1: 290–94.

Antonarakis, J. S., et al. 1984. Origin of sickle beta globin gene in blacks: The contribution of recurrent mutation or gene conversion or both. *Proc. Natl. Acad. Sci. USA* 81: 853–56.

Carlson, J., et al. 1994. Natural protection against severe *Plasmodium falciparum* malaria due to impaired rosette formation. *Blood* 84: 3909–14.

Cavalli-Sforza, L. L., and W. Bodmer. 1971. *The Genetics of Human Populations*. San Francisco: W. H. Freeman.

Cavalli-Sforza, L. L., and M. W. Feldman. 2003. The application of molecular genetic approaches to the study of human evolution. *Nat. Genet.* 33(suppl.): 266–75.

Cholera, R., et al. 2008. Impaired cytoadherence of *Plasmodium falciparum*-infected erythrocytes containing sickle hemoglobin. *Proc. Natl. Acad. Sci. USA* 105: 991–96.

Cooke, G. S., and A. V. S. Hill. 2001. Genetics of susceptibility to human infectious disease. *Nat. Rev. Genet.* 2: 967–77.

Desai, D. V., and H. Dhanani. 2004. Sickle cell disease: History and origin. *Internet J. Hematology* 1: 2.

Herrick, J. B. 1910. Peculiar elongated and sickle shaped red blood corpuscles in a case of severe anemia. *Arch. Intern. Med.* 6: 517–21.

Ingram, V. E. 1957. Gene mutations in human haemoglobin: The chemical difference between normal and sickle cell haemoglobin. *Nature* 180: 326–28.

Kurnit, D. M. 1979. Evolution of sickle variant gene. *Lancet* 1: 104.

Livingstone, F. B. 1958. Anthropological implications of sickle cell gene distribution in West Africa. *Am. Anthropol.* 60: 533–62.

Neel, J. V. 1949. The inheritance of sickle cell anemia. *Science* 110: 64–66.

Pauling, L., et al. 1949. Sickle cell anemia, a molecular disease. *Science* 110: 543–48.

Savitt, T. L., and M. F. Goldberg. 1989. Herrick's 1910 case report of sickle cell anemia. The rest of the story. *JAMA* 261: 266–71.

Smithies, O. 1995. Early days of electrophoresis. *Genetics* 139: 1–4.

Soloman, E., and W. F. Bodmer. 1979. Evolution of sickle variant gene. *Lancet* 1: 923.

Southern, E. M. 1975. Detection of specific sequences among DNA fragments separated by gel electrophoresis. *J. Mol. Biol.* 98: 503–17.

Wiesenfeld, S. L. 1967. Sickle cell trait in human and biological evolution. *Science* 157: 1134–40.

Chapter 11 Chromosome Structure

Bendich, A. J., and K. Drlica. 2000. Prokaryotic and eukaryotic chromosomes: What's the difference? *BioEssays* 22: 481–86.

Blackburn, E. H. 2000. Telomere states and cell fates. *Nature* 408: 53–56.

Carbon, J. 1984. Yeast centromeres: Structure and function. *Cell* 37: 352–53.

Clarke, L. 1990. Centromeres of budding and fission yeasts. *Trends Genet.* 6: 150–54.

Craig, J. M., W. C. Earnshaw, and P. Vagnarelli. 1999. Mammalian centromeres: DNA sequence, protein composition, and role in cell cycle progression. *Exp. Cell. Res.* 246: 249–62.

Cremer, T., and C. Cremer. 2001. Chromosome territories, nuclear architecture and gene regulation in mammalian cells. *Nat. Rev. Genet.* 2: 292–301.

Cross, I., and J. Wolstenholme. 2001. An introduction to human chromosomes and their analysis. In *Human Cytogenetics: Constitutional Analysis* (3rd ed.), edited by D. E. Rooney. Oxford: Oxford University Press.

Deal, R. B., J. Henikoff, and S. Henikoff. 2010. Genome-wide kinetics of nucleosome turnover determined by metabolic labeling of histones. *Science* 328: 1161–64.

DeLange, R. J., et al. 1969. Calf and pea histone IV. III. Complete amino acid sequence of pea seedling histone IV; comparison with the homologous calf thymus histone. *J. Biol. Chem.* 244: 5669–79.

Duan, Z., et al. 2010. A three-dimensional model of the yeast genome. *Nature* 465: 363–67.

Hayes, J. J., and J. C. Hansen. 2001. Nucleosomes and the chromatin fiber. *Curr. Opin. Genet. Dev.* 11: 124–29.

Heikanen, M., L. Peltonen, and A. Palotie. 1996. Visual mapping with high resolution FISH. *Trends Genet.* 12: 379–84.

Kornberg, R. D., and A. Klug. 1981. The nucleosome. *Sci. Am.* 244(2): 52–64.

Luger, K., et al. 1997. Crystal structure of the nucleosome core particle at 2.8 Å resolution. *Nature* 389: 251–60.

Luger, K., and T. J. Richmond. 1998. DNA binding within the nucleosome core. *Curr. Opin. Struct. Biol.* 8: 33–40.

———. 1998. The histone tails of the nucleosome. *Curr. Opin. Genet. Dev.* 8: 140–46.

Thanbichler, M., and L. Shapiro. 2006. Chromosome organization and segregation in bacteria. *J. Struct. Biol.* 156: 292–303.

Thanbichler, M., S. C. Wang, and L. Shapiro. 2005. The bacterial nucleoid: A highly organized and dynamic structure. *J. Cell. Biochem.* 96: 506–21.

Trask, B. J. 2002. Human chromosomes: 46 chromosomes, 46 years and counting. *Nat. Rev. Genet.* 3: 769–78.

Woodcock, C. L., and S. Dimitrov. 2001. Higher-order structure of chromatin and chromosomes. *Curr. Opin. Genet. Dev.* 11: 130–35.

Yunis, J. J. 1982. The origin of man: A chromosomal pictorial legacy. *Science* 215: 1525–30.

Chapter 12 Gene Mutation, DNA Repair, and Homologous Recombination

Bzymek, M., et al. 2010. Double Holliday junctions are intermediates of DNA break repair. *Nature* 464: 937–41.

Cox, M. M. 2001. Recombinational DNA repair of damaged replication forks in *Escherichia coli*: Ques. *Ann Rev. Genet.* 35: 53–82.

De Laat, W. L., N. G. Jaspers, and J. H. Hoeijmakers. 1999. Molecular mechanism of excision nucleotide repair. *Genes Dev.* 13: 768–85.

Eichler, E. E., and D. Sankoff. 2003. Structural dynamics of eukaryotic chromosome evolution. *Science* 301: 793–97.

Holliday, R. 1964. A mechanism for gene conversion in fungi. *Genet. Res.* 5: 282–304.

Kowalczykowski, S. C. 2000. Initiation of genetic recombination and recombination-dependent replication. *Trends Biochem. Sci.* 25: 156–64.

Kunkel, T. A., and D. A. Erie. 2005. DNA mismatch repair. *Annu. Rev. Biochem.* 76: 681–710.

Lusetti, S. L., and M. M. Cox. 2002. The bacterial RecA protein and the recombinational DNA repair of stalled replication forks. *Annu. Rev. Biochem.* 71: 71–100.

Lynch, M. 2010. Evolution of mutation rate. *Trends Genet.* 26: 345–52.

McCann, J., and B. N. Ames. 1978. The *Salmonella*/microsome mutagenicity test: Predictive value for animal carcinogenicity. In *Advances in Modern Technology* (Vol. 5: Mutagenesis), edited by W. G. Flamm and M. A. Mehlman. Washington, DC: Hemisphere Publishing.

Ossowski, S., et al. 2010. The rate and molecular spectrum of spontaneous mutations in *Arabidopsis thaliana*. *Science* 327: 92–94.

Page, S. L., and R. S. Hawley. 2003. Chromosome choreography: The meiotic ballet. *Science* 301: 785–89.

Sekiguchi, J. M., and D. O. Freguson. 2006. DNA double-strand break repair: A relentless hunt uncovers new prey. *Cell* 124: 260–62.

Szostak, J. W., et al. 1983. The double-strand break repair model for recombination. *Cell* 33: 25–35.

Walsh, T., M. K. Lee, S. Casadei, A. M. Thornton, et al. 2010. Detection of inherited mutations for breast and ovarian cancer using genomic capture and massively parallel sequencing. *Proc. Nat. Acad. Sci. USA* 107: 12629–33.

Walsh, T., S. Casadei, M. K. Lee, C. C. Pennil, et al. 2011. Mutations in 12 genes for inherited ovarian, fallopian tube, and peritoneal carcinoma identified by massively parallel sequencing. *Proc. Nat. Acad. Sci. USA* 108: 18032–37.

Chapter 13 Chromosome Aberrations and Transposition

Blakeslee, A. F. 1934. New jimson weeds from old chromosomes. *J. Hered.* 25: 80–108.

Deininger, P. L., and M. A. Batzer. 1999. Alu repeats and human disease. *Molec. Genet. Metabol.* 67: 183–93.

Drucker, R., and E. Whitelaw. 2004. Retrotransposon-derived elements in the mammalian genome: A potential source of disease. *J. Inherit. Metabol. Dis.* 27: 319–30.

Federoff, N. V. 1993. Barbara McClintock (June 16, 1902–September 2, 1992). *Genetics* 136: 1–10.

Feldman, M., and E. R. Sears. 1981. The wild gene resources of wheat. *Sci. Am.* 244: 102–12.

Gardner, R. J. M., and G. R. Sutherland. 2004. *Chromosome Abnormalities and Genetic Counseling.* 3rd ed. Oxford: Oxford University Press.

Gersh, M., et al. 1995. Evidence for a distinct region causing a catlike cry in patients with 5p deletions. *Am. J. Hum. Genet.* 56: 1404–10.

Grindley, N. D. F., and R. R. Reed. 1985. Transpositional recombination in prokaryotes. *Annu. Rev. Biochem.* 54: 863–96.

Hassold, T. J., and D. Chiu. 1985. Maternal age-specific rates of numerical chromosome abnormalities with special reference to trisomy. *Hum. Genet.* 70: 11–17.

Hassold, T. J., and P. Hunt. 2001. To err (meiotically) is human: The genesis of human aneuploidy. *Nat. Rev. Genet.* 2: 280–91.

Hassold, T. J., and P. A. Jacobs. 1984. Trisomy in man. *Annu. Rev. Genet.* 18: 69–97.

Hook, E. B., and A. Linsjo. 1978. Down syndrome by single year maternal age interval in a Swedish study: Comparison with results from a New York study. *Am. J. Hum. Genet.* 30: 19–27.

Hunt, P. A., and T. J. Hassold. 2008. Human female meiosis: What makes a good egg go bad? *Trends Genet.* 24: 86–93.

Kaiser, P. 1984. Pericentric inversions: Problems and significance for clinical genetics. *Hum. Genet.* 68: 1–47.

Madan, K. 1995. Paracentric inversions: A review. *Hum Genet.* 96: 503–15.

McClintock, B. 1939. The behavior in successive nuclear divisions of a chromosome broken at meiosis. *Proc. Natl. Acad. Sci. USA* 25: 406–16.

———. 1951. Chromosome organization and genic expression. *Cold Spring Harbor Symp. Quant. Biol.* 16: 13–47.

Medstrand, P., et al. 2005. Impact of transposable elements on the evolution of mammalian gene regulation. *Cytogenet. Genome Res.* 110: 342–52.

Miki, Y. 1998. Retrotransposal integration of mobile genetic elements in human disease. *J. Hum. Genet.* 43: 77–84.

Nelson, D. L., and R. A. Gibbs. 2004. The critical region in trisomy 21. *Science* 306: 619–21.

O'Hare, K. 1985. The mechanism and control of *P* element transposition in *Drosophila. Trends Genet.* 1: 250–54.

Patterson, D., and A. Costa. 2005. Down syndrome and genetics—A case of linked histories. *Nat. Rev. Genet.* 6: 137–45.

Warburton, D. 2005. Biological aging and the etiology of aneuploidy. *Cytogenet. Genome Res.* 111: 266–72.

Chapter 14 Regulation of Gene Expression in Bacteria and Bacteriophage

Bell, S. D. 2005. Archaeal transcription regulation—variation on a bacterial theme? *Trends Microbiol.* 13: 262–65.

Bertrand, K., and C. Yanofsky. 1976. Regulation of transcription termination in the leader region of the tryptophan operon of *Escherichia coli. J. Mol. Biol.* 103: 339–49.

Dickson, R. C., et al. 1975. Genetic regulation: The *Lac* control region. *Science* 187: 27–33.

Fisher, R. F., et al. 1985. Analysis of the requirements for transcription pausing in the tryptophan operon. *J. Mol. Biol.* 182: 397–409.

Fried, M. G. 1996. DNA looping and *Lac* repressor–CAP interaction. *Science* 274: 1930.

Jacob, F., and J. Monod. 1961. Genetic regulatory mechanisms in the synthesis of proteins. *J. Mol. Biol.* 3: 318–56.

Lee, D., and R. Schleif. 1989. In vivo loops in *araCBAD*: Size limits and helical repeats. *Proc. Natl. Acad. Sci. USA* 86: 476–80.

Lewis, M., et al. 1996. Crystal structure of the lactose operon repressor and its complexes with DNA and inducer. *Science* 271: 1247–54.

Matthews, K. S. 1996. The whole lactose repressor. *Science* 271: 1245–46.

Pardee, A. B., F. Jacob, and J. Monod. 1959. The genetic control and cytoplasmic expression of inducibility in the synthesis of β-galactosidase by *E. coli. J. Mol. Biol.* 1: 165–78.

Ptashne, M. 2005. *A Genetic Switch: Phage Lambda Revisited.* 3rd ed. Cold Spring Harbor, NY: Cold Spring Harbor Laboratory Press.

Ptashne, M., and A. Gann. 2002. *Genes and Signals.* Cold Spring Harbor, NY: Cold Spring Harbor Laboratory Press.

Schlief, R. 2000. Regulation of the L-arabinose operon of *Escherichia coli. Trends Genet.* 16: 559–66.

———. 2003. AraC protein: A love-hate relationship. *BioEssays* 25: 274–82.

Schultz, S. C., G. C. Shields, and T. A. Steitz. 1991. Crystal structure of a CAP-DNA complex: The DNA is bent 90°. *Science* 253: 1001–7.

Tijan, R. 1995. Molecular machines that control genes. *Sci. Am.* 272: 55–61.

Ullman, A. 2003. *Origins of Molecular Biology: A Tribute to Jacques Monod.* rev. ed. Washington, DC: ASM Press.

Chapter 15 Regulation of Gene Expression in Eukaryotes

Augui, S., et al. 2011. Regulation of X-chromosome inactivation by the X-inactivation centre. *Nat. Rev. Genet.* 12: 429–42.

Ambrose, V., and X. Chen. 2007. The regulation of genes and genomes by small RNAs. *Development* 134: 1635–41.

Black, D. L. 2000. Protein diversity from alternative splicing: A challenge for bioinformatics and postgenomic biology. *Cell* 103: 367–70.

Cairns, B. R. 2009. The logic of chromatin architecture and remodeling at promoters. *Nature* 461: 193–98.

Dillon, N., and P. Sabbattini. 2000. Functional gene expression domains: Defining the functional unit of eukaryotic gene regulation. *BioEssays* 22: 657–65.

Fedoriw, A. M., et al. 2004. Transgenic RNAi reveals essential function of CTCF in H19 gene imprinting. *Science* 303: 238–40.

Filion, G. J., et al. 2010. Systematic protein location mapping reveals five principal chromatin types in *Drosophila* cells. *Cell* 143: 212–24.

Flintoft, L. 2010. Complex diseases: Adding epigenetics to the mix. *Nat. Rev. Genet.* 11: 94–95.

Fuda, N. J., M. Behfar Ardehali, and J. T. Lis. 2009. Defining mechanisms that regulate RNA polymerase II transcription *in vivo. Nature* 461: 186–92.

Gregory, P. D., K. Wagner, and W. Hurz. 2001. Histone acetylation and chromatin remodeling. *Exp. Cell Res.* 265: 195–202.

Grewal, S. I. S., and S. Jia. 2008. Heterochromatin revisited. *Nat. Rev. Genet.* 8: 35–46.

Guttman, M. et al. 2011. lincRNAs act in the circuitry controlling pluripotentcy and differentiation. *Nature* 477: 295–300.

Hassan, A. H., et al. 2001. Promoter targeting of chromatin-modifying complexes. *Frontiers in Bioscience* 6: 1054–64.

Horn, P. J., and C. L. Peterson. 2002. Chromatin higher order folding: Wrapping up transcription. *Science* 297: 1824–27.

Jenuwein, T., and C. D. Allis. 2001. Translating the histone code. *Science* 293: 1074–80.

Kappeler, L., and M. J. Meaney. 2010. Epigenetics and parental effects. *BioEssays* 32: 818–27.

Kucharski, R., et al. 2008. Nutritional control of reproductive status in honeybees via DNA methylation. *Science* 319: 1827–30.

Lawrence, P. A. 1992. *How to Make a Fly.* London: Blackwell Scientific.

Lusser, A., and J. T. Kadonaga. 2003. Chromatin remodeling by ATP-dependent molecular machines. *BioEssays* 25: 1192–1200.

MacRae, I. J., et al. 2006. Structural basis for double-stranded RNA processing by Dicer. *Science* 311: 195–98.

Margueron, R., and D. Reinberg. 2010. Chromatin structure and the inheritance of epigenetic information. *Nat. Rev. Genet.* 11: 285–96.

Meister, G., and T. Tuschl. 2004. Mechanisms of gene silencing by double-stranded RNA. *Nature* 431: 343–49.

Moore, M. J. 2005. From birth to death: The complex lives of eukaryotic mRNAs. *Science* 309: 1514–18.

Roudier, F., et al. 2011. Integrative epigenomic mapping defines four main chromatin states in *Arabidopsis. EMBO J.* 30:1928–38, doi:10.1038/emboj.2011.103.

Schwarz, Y. B., and Pirrotta, V. 2007. Polycomb silencing mechanisms and the management of genomic programs. *Nat. Rev. Genet.* 8: 9–22.

Siomi, H., and M. C. Siomi. 2007. Expanding RNA physiology: MicroRNAs in unicellular organisms. *Genes Dev.* 21: 1153–56.

Small, S., et al. 1991. Transcriptional regulation of a pair-rule gene in *Drosophila. Genes Develop.* 5: 827–39.

Sudarsanam, P., and F. Winston. 2000. The SWI/SNF family of nucleosome-remodeling complexes and transcriptional control. *Trends Genet.* 16: 345–51.

Turner, B. M. 2000. Histone acetylation and the epigenetic code. *BioEssays* 22: 836–45.

Van Steensel, B. 2011. Chromatin: Constructing the big picture. *EMBO J.* 30: 1885–95, doi:10.1038/emboj.2011.135.

Visel, A., E. M. Rubin, and L. A. Pennacchio. 2009. Genomic views of distant-acting enhancers. *Nature* 461: 199–205.

Wang, H., et al. 2004. Using atomic force microscopy to study nucleosome remodeling on individual nucleosomal arrays in situ. *Biophys. J.* 87: 1964–71.

Weake, V. M., and J. L. Workman. 2010. Inducible gene expression: diverse regulatory mechanisms. *Nat. Rev. Genet.* 11: 426–37.

Chapter 16 Analysis of Gene Function by Forward Genetics and Reverse Genetics

Austin, C. P., et al. 2004. The knockout mouse project. *Nat. Genet.* 36: 921–24.

Bates, G. P. 2005. The molecular genetics of Huntington disease—a history. *Nat. Rev. Genet.* 6: 766–73.

Bellen, H. J., et al. 1989. P-element-mediated enhancer detection—A versatile method to study development in *Drosophila. Genes & Development* 3: 1288–300.

Boone, C., H. Bussey, and B. J. Andrews. 2007. Exploring genetic interactions and networks with yeast. *Nat. Rev. Genet.* 8: 437–49.

Echeverri, C. J., and N. Perrimon. 2006. High-throughput RNAi screening in cultured cells: A user's guide. *Nat. Rev. Genet.* 7: 373–84.

Forsburg, S. L. 2001. The art and design of genetic screens: Yeast. *Nat. Rev. Genet.* 2: 659–68.

Halder, G., P. Callaerts, and W. J. Gehring. 1995. Induction of ectopic eyes by targeted expression of the eyeless gene in *Drosophila. Science* 267: 1788–92.

Hannon, G. J. 2002. RNA interference. *Nature* 418: 244–51.

Hartwell, L. H., et al. 1973. Genetic control of the cell division cycle in yeast: V. genetic analysis of *cdc* mutants. *Genetics* 74: 267–86.

Huntington's Disease Collaborative Research Group. 1993. A novel gene containing a trinucleotide repeat that is expanded and unstable on Huntington's Disease chromosomes. *Cell* 72: 971–83.

Kile, B. T., and D. J. Hilton. 2005. The art and design of genetic screens: Mouse. *Nat. Rev. Genet.* 6: 557–67.

McCallum, C. M., et al. 2000. Targeting induced local lesions in genomes (TILLING) for plant functional genomics. *Plant Physiol.* 123: 439–42.

Page, D. R., and U. Grossniklaus. 2002. The art and design of genetic screens: *Arabidopsis thaliana. Nat. Rev. Genet.* 3: 124–36.

Pelaz, S., et al. 2000. B and C floral organ identity functions require *SEPALLATA* MADS-box genes. *Nature* 405: 200–203.

Poinar, H. N., et al. 2006. Metagenomics to paleogenomics: Large-scale sequencing of mammoth DNA. *Science* 311: 392–94.

Small, S., A. Blair, and M. Levine. 1992. Regulation of *even-skipped* stripe-2 in the *Drosophila* embryo. *EMBO J.* 11: 4047–57.

Shuman, H. A., and T. J. Silhavy. 2003. The art and design of genetic screens: *Escherichia coli. Nat. Rev. Genet.* 4: 419–31.

St Johnston, D. 2002. The art and design of genetic screens: *Drosophila melanogaster. Nat. Rev. Genet.* 3: 176–88.

Sturtevant, A. H. 1955. A highly specific complementary lethal system in *Drosophila melanogaster. Genetics* 40: 118–23.

Thomas, J. H. 1993. Thinking about genetic redundancy. *Trends Genet.* 9: 395–399.

Chapter 17 Recombinant DNA Technology and Its Applications

Berg, P., et al. 1974. Potential biohazards of recombinant DNA molecules. *Proc. Natl. Acad. Sci. USA* 71: 2593–94.

———. 1975. Summary Statement of the Asilomar Conference on recombinant DNA molecules. *Proc. Natl. Acad. Sci. USA* 72: 1981–84.

Berg, P., and Singer, M. A. 1995. The recombinant DNA controversy: Twenty years later. *Proc. Natl. Acad. Sci. USA* 92: 9011–13.

Chilton, M. D., et al. 1977. Stable incorporation of plasmid DNA into higher plant cells: The molecular basis of crown gall tumorigenesis. *Cell* 11: 263–71.

Cohen, S. A., et al. 1973. Construction of biologically functional plasmids in vitro. *Proc. Natl. Acad. Sci. USA* 70: 3240–44.

Danna, K., and D. Nathans. 1971. Specific cleavage of simian virus 40 DNA by restriction endonuclease of *Hemophilus influenzae. Proc. Natl. Acad. Sci. USA* 68: 2913–17.

Goeddel, D. V., et al. 1979. Expression in *Escherichia coli* of chemically synthesized genes for human insulin. *Proc. Natl. Acad. Sci.* 76: 106–10.

Grunstein, M., and D. S. Hogness. 1975. Colony hybridization—Method for isolation of cloned DNAs that contain a specific gene. *Proc. Natl. Acad. Sci. USA* 72: 3961–65.

Hanna, J., et al. 2007. Treatment of sickle cell anemia mouse model with iPS cells generated from autologous skin. *Science* 318: 1920–23.

Hershfie, V., et al. 1974. Plasmid ColE1 as a molecular vehicle for cloning and amplification of DNA. *Proc. Natl. Acad. Sci. USA* 71: 3455–59.

Jackson, D., R. Symons, and P. Berg. 1972. Biochemical methods for inserting new genetic information into DNA of simian virus 40: Circular SV40 DNA molecules containing lambda phage genes and the galactose operon of *Escherichia coli. Proc. Natl. Acad. Sci. USA* 69: 2904–9.

Kelley, T. J. Jr., and H. O. Smith. 1970. A restriction enzyme from *Hemophilus influenzae.* II. Base sequence of the recognition site. *J. Molec. Biol.* 51: 393–409.

Kimmelman, J. 2008. Science and society: The ethics of human gene transfer. *Nat. Rev. Genet.* 9: 239–44.

Linn, S., and W. Arber. 1968. Host specificity of DNA produced by *Escherichia coli.* X. In vitro restriction of phage fd replicative form. *Proc. Natl. Acad. Sci. USA* 59: 1300–6.

Martin, V. J. J., et al. 2003. Engineering a mevalonate pathway in *Escherichia coli* for production of terpenoids. *Nat. Biotechnol.* 21: 796–802.

Rubin, G. M., and A. C. Spradling. 1982. Genetic-transformation of *Drosophila* with transposable element vectors. *Science* 218: 348–53.

Sambrook, J., E. F. Fitch, and T. Maniatis. 1989. *Molecular Cloning: A Laboratory Manual.* 2nd ed. Cold Spring Harbor, NY: Cold Spring Harbor Press.

Smith, H. O., and K. W. Wilcox. 1970. A restriction enzyme from *Hemophilus influenzae.* I. Purification and general properties. *J. Molec. Biol.*, 51: 379–91.

Thomas, K. R., and M. R. Capecchi. 1987. Site-directed mutagenesis by gene targeting in mouse embryo-derived stem-cells. *Cell* 51: 503–12.

Waehler, R., S. J. Russell, and D. T. Curiel. 2007. Engineering targeted viral vectors for gene therapy. *Nat. Rev. Genet.* 8: 573–87.

Wilmut, I., et al. 1997. Viable offspring derived from fetal and adult mammalian cells. *Nature* 385: 810–13.

Wofenbarger, L. L., and P. R. Phifer. 2000. The ecological risks and benefits of genetically engineered plants. *Science* 290: 2088–93.

Ye, X., et al. 2000. Engineering the provitamin A (β-carotene) biosynthetic pathway into (carotenoid-free) rice endosperm. *Science* 287: 303–5.

Chapter 18 Genomics: Genetics from a Whole-Genome Perspective

Adams, M. D., et al. 2000. The genome sequence of *Drosophila melanogaster. Science* 287: 2185–95.

The *Arabidopsis* Genome Initiative. 2000. Analysis of the genome sequence of the flowering plant *Arabidopsis thaliana. Nature* 408: 796–814.

Blattner, F. R., et al. 1997. The complete genome sequence of *Escherichia coli* K-12. *Science* 277: 1453–61.

Boffelli, D., M. A. Nobrega, and E. M. Rubin. 2004. Comparative genomics at the vertebrate extremes. *Nat. Rev. Genet.* 5: 456–65.

Boone, C., H. Bussey, and B. J. Andrews. 2007. Exploring genetic interactions and networks with yeast. *Nat. Rev. Genet.* 8: 437–49.

Brune, A. 2007. Woodworker's digest. *Nature* 450: 487–88.

Cavalli-Sforza, L. L. 2005. The Human Genome Diversity Project: Past, present, and future. *Nat. Rev. Genet.* 6: 333–40.

The Chimpanzee Sequencing and Analysis Consortium. 2005. Initial sequence of the chimpanzee genome and comparison with the human genome. *Nature* 437: 69–87.

Chu, S., et al. 1998. The transcriptional program of sporulation in budding yeast. *Science* 282: 699–705.

DeRisi, J. L., V. R. Iyer, and P. O. Brown. 1997. Exploring the metabolic and genetic control of gene expression on a genomic scale. *Science* 278: 680–86.

Feuk, L., A. R. Carson, and S. W. Scherer. 2006. Structural variation in the human genome. *Nat. Rev. Genet.* 7: 85–97.

Fleischmann, R. D., et al. 1995. Whole genome random sequencing and assembly of *Haemophilus influenzae* Rd. *Science* 269: 496–512.

Giaever, G., et al. 2002. Functional profiling of the *Saccharomyces cerevisiae* genome. *Nature* 418: 387–91.

Geib, S. M., et al. 2008. Lignin degradation in wood-feeding insects. *Proc. Natl. Acad. Sci. USA* 105: 12932–37.

Girirajan, S. et al. 2011. Human copy number variation and complex genetic disease. *Annu. Rev. Genet.* 45: 203–26.

Goffeau, A., et al. 1996. Life with 6000 genes. *Science* 274: 562–67.

Gonzalez, A. et al. 2011. Our microbial selves: what ecology can teach us. *EMBO Reports* 12: 775–84.

Green, R. E., et al. 2010. A draft sequence of the Neanderthal genome. *Science* 328: 710–22.

Grice, E. A., and Sgre, J. A. 2011. The skin microbiome. *Nature Reviews Microbiology* 9: 244–53.

Hattori, M., et al. 2000. The DNA sequence of human chromosome 21. *Nature* 405: 311–19.

Hui, L., and D. W. Bianchi. 2013. Recent advances in the prenatal interrogation of the human fetal genome. *Trends Genet.* 29: 84–91.

International Human Genome Sequencing Consortium. 2001. Initial sequencing and analysis of the human genome. *Nature* 409: 860–921.

Keeling, P. J., et al. 2005. The tree of eukaryotes. *Trends Ecol. and Evol.* 12: 670–76.

Kellis, M., et al. 2003. Sequencing and comparison of yeast species to identify genes and regulatory elements. *Nature* 423: 241–54.

Kobayashi, K., et al. 2003. Essential *Bacillus subtilis* genes. *Proc. Natl. Acad. Sci. USA* 100: 4678–83.

Lindblad-Toh, K., et al. 2005. Genome sequence, comparative analysis and haplotype structure of the domestic dog. *Nature* 438: 803–19.

Lockhart, D. J., and E. A. Winzeler. 2000. Genomics, gene expression and DNA arrays. *Nature* 405: 827–36.

Long, M., et al. 2003. The origin of new genes: Glimpses from the young and old. *Nat. Rev. Genet.* 4, 865–75.

Mazurkiewicz, P., et al. 2006. Signature-tagged mutagenesis: Barcoding mutants for genome-wide screens. *Nat. Rev. Genet.* 7: 929–39.

Mouse Genome Sequencing Consortium. 2002. Initial sequencing and comparative analysis of the mouse genome. *Nature* 420: 520–62.

Rosenberg, N. A., et al. 2002. Genetic structure of human populations. *Science* 298: 2381–85.

Tishkoff, S. A., et al. 2009. The genetic structure and history of Africans and African Americans. *Science* 324: 1035–44.

Turnbaugh, P. J., et al. 2007. The Human Microbiome Project. *Nature* 449: 804–10.

Uetz, P., et al. 2000. A comprehensive analysis of protein-protein interactions in *Saccharomyces cerevisiae*. *Nature* 403: 623–27.

Venter, J. C., et al. 2001. The sequence of the human genome. *Science* 291: 1304–51.

———. 2004. Environmental genome shotgun sequencing of the Sargasso Sea. *Science* 304: 66–74.

Warnecke, F., et al. 2007. Metagenomic and functional analysis of hindgut microbiota of a wood-feeding higher termite. *Nature* 450: 560–69.

Warren, W. C., et al. 2008. Genome analysis of the platypus reveals unique signatures of evolution. *Nature* 453: 175–84.

Wienberg, J. 2004. The evolution of eutherian chromosomes. *Curr. Opinion in Gen. Devel.* 14: 657–66.

Yamada, K., et al. 2003. Empirical analysis of transcriptional activity in the *Arabidopsis* genome. *Science* 302: 842–46.

Chapter 19   Organelle Inheritance and the Evolution of Organelle Genomes

Brown, J. R. 2003. Ancient horizontal gene transfer. *Nat. Rev. Genet.* 4: 121–32.

Burger, G., M. W. Gray, and B. F. Lang. 2003. Mitochondrial genomes: Anything goes. *Trends Genet.* 19: 709–16.

Cann, R. L., M. Stoneking, and A. C. Wilson. 1987. Mitochondrial DNA and human evolution. *Nature* 325: 31–36.

Cavalli-Sforza, L. L., and M. W. Feldman. 2003. The application of molecular genetic approaches to the study of human evolution. *Nat. Genet.* 33(suppl.): 266–75.

Chase, C. D. 2007. Cytoplasmic male sterility: A window to the world of plant mitochondrial-nuclear interactions. *Trends Genet.* 23: 81–90.

Chen, X. J., and R. A. Butow. 2005. The organization and inheritance of the mitochondrial genome. *Nat. Rev. Genet.* 6: 815–25.

Embley, T. M., and W. Martin. 2006. Eukaryotic evolution, changes and challenges. *Nature* 440: 623–30.

Finlayson, C. 2005. Biogeography and evolution of the genus *Homo*. *Trends Ecol. Evol.* 20: 457–63.

Garrigan, D., and M. F. Hammer. 2006. Reconstructing human origins in the genomic era. *Nat. Rev. Genet.* 7: 669–80.

Gilson, P. R., et al. 2006. Complete nucleotide sequence of the chlorarachniophyte nucleomorph: Nature's smallest nucleus. *Proc. Natl. Acad. Sci. USA* 103: 9566–71.

Huang, C. Y., M. A. Ayliffe, and J. N. Timmis. 2003. Direct measurement of the transfer rate of chloroplast DNA into the nucleus. *Nature* 422: 72–76.

Kotera, E., M. Tasaka, and T. Shikanai. 2005. A pentatricopeptide repeat protein is essential for RNA editing in chloroplast. *Nature* 433: 326–30.

Lang, B. F., et al. 1997. An ancestral mitochondrial DNA resembling a eubacterial genome in miniature. *Nature* 387: 493–97.

Lehman, N., et al. 1991. Introgression of coyote mitochondrial DNA into sympatric North American gray wolf populations. *Evolution* 45: 104–19.

Leister, D. 2003. Chloroplast research in the genomic age. *Trends Genet.* 19: 47–56.

Martin, W. 2002. Evolutionary analysis of *Arabidopsis*, cyanobacterial, and chloroplast genomes reveals plastid phylogeny and thousands of cyanobacterial genes in the nucleus. *Proc. Natl. Acad. Sci. USA* 99: 12246–51.

Oda, K., et al. 1992. Gene organization deduced from the complete sequence of liverwort *Marchantia polymorpha* mitochondrial DNA. *J. Mol. Biol.* 223: 1–7.

Prezant, T. R., et al. 1993. Mitochondrial ribosomal RNA mutation associated with both antibiotic-induced and non-syndromic deafness. *Nat. Genet.* 4: 289–94.

Rivera, M. C., et al. 1998. Genomic evidence for two functionally distinct gene classes. *Proc. Natl. Acad. Sci. USA* 95: 6239–44.

Stegemann, S., and R. Bock. 2006. Experimental reconstruction of functional gene transfer from the tobacco plastid genome to the nucleus. *Plant Cell* 18: 2869–78.

Taylor, R. W., and D. M. Turnbull 2005. Mitochondrial DNA mutations in human disease. *Nat. Rev. Genet.* 6: 389–402.

Timmis, J. N., et al. 2004. Endosymbiotic gene transfer: Organelle genomes forge eukaryotic chromosomes. *Nat. Rev. Genet.* 5: 123–35.

Trifunovic, A., et al. 2004. Premature ageing in mice expressing defective mitochondrial DNA polymerase. *Nature* 429: 417–23.

Wallace, D. C., et al. 1988. Mitochondrial DNA mutation associated with Leber's hereditary optic neuropathy. *Science* 242: 1427–30.

Ward, T. J., et al. 1999. Identification of domestic cattle hybrids in wild cattle and bison species: A general approach using mtDNA markers and the parametric bootstrap. *Animal Conservation* 2: 51–57.

Chapter 20   Developmental Genetics

Bender, W., et al. 1983. Molecular-genetics of the bithorax complex in *Drosophila melanogaster*. *Science* 221: 23–29.

Binns, W., L. F. James, and J. L. Shupe. 1964. Toxicosis of *Veratrum californicum* in ewes and its relationship to a congenital deformity in lambs. *Ann. N.Y. Acad. Sci.* 111: 571–76.

Bowman, J. L., D. R. Smyth, and E. M. Meyerowitz. 1991. Genetic interactions among floral homeotic genes of *Arabidopsis*. *Development* 112: 1–20.

Chen, J. K., et al. 2002. Inhibition of hedgehog signaling by direct binding of cyclopamine to smoothened. *Genes Dev.* 16: 2743–48.

Coen, E. S., and Meyerowitz, E. M. 1991. The war of the whorls: Genetic interactions controlling flower development. *Nature* 353: 31–37.

De Robertis, E. M., and H. Kuroda. 2004. Dorsal-ventral patterning and neural induction in *Xenopus* embryos. *Annu. Rev. Cell Dev. Biol.* 20: 285–308.

de Rosa, R., et al. 1999. Hox genes in brachiopods and priapulids and protostome evolution. *Nature* 399: 772–76.

Driever, W., and C. Nusslein-Volhard. 1988. The Bicoid protein determines position in the *Drosophila* embryo in a concentration-dependent manner. *Cell* 54: 95–104.

Driever, W., V. Siegel, and C. Nusslein-Volhard. 1990. Autonomous determination of anterior structures in the early *Drosophila* embryo by the Bicoid morphogen. *Development* 109: 811–20.

Horvitz, H. R. 2003. Worms, life and death. *Bioscience Reports* 23: 239–69.

Lemons, D., and W. McGinnis. 2006. Genomic evolution of Hox gene clusters. *Science* 313: 1918–22.

Lettice, L. A., et al. 2002. Disruption of a long range *cis*-acting regulator for *Shh* causes preaxial polydactyly. *Proc. Natl. Acad. Sci. USA* 99: 7548–53.

Lewis, E. B. 1978. Gene complex controlling segmentation in *Drosophila*. *Nature* 276: 565–70.

Nanni, L., et al. 1999. The mutational spectrum of the *sonic hedgehog* gene in holoproencephaly: *Shh* mutations cause a significant proportion of autosomal dominant holoproencephaly. *Hum. Mol. Genet.* 8: 2479–88.

Nusslein-Volhard, C., and Wieschaus, E. 1980. Mutations affecting segment number and polarity in *Drosophila*. *Nature* 287: 795–801.

Shubin, N., C. Tabin, and S. Carroll. 1997. Fossils, genes, and the evolution of animal limbs. *Nature* 388: 639–48.

———. 2009. Deep homology and the origins of evolutionary novelty. *Nature* 457: 818–23.

Small, S., A. Blair, and M. Levine. 1992. Regulation of *even-skipped* stripe-2 in the *Drosophila* embryo. *EMBO J.* 11: 4047–57.

Sternberg, P. W., and M. Han. 1998. Genetics of RAS signaling in *C. elegans*. *Trends Genet.* 14: 466–72.

Chapter 21   Genetic Analysis of Quantitative Traits

Castle, W. 1916. *Genetics and Eugenics*. Cambridge, MA: Harvard University Press.

deVicente, M. C., and S. D. Tanksley. 1993. QTL analysis of transgressive segregation in an interspecific tomato cross. *Genetics* 134: 585–96.

Dudley, J. W. 1977. 76 generations of selection for oil and protein percentage in maize. In *Proc. Internat. Conf. on Quant. Gene.*, edited by E. Pollack, O. Kempthorne, and T. Bailey. Ames: Iowa State University Press.

East, E. M. 1910. A Mendelian interpretation of variation that is apparently continuous. *Am. Nat.* 44: 65–82.

———. 1916. Studies on size inheritance in *Nicotiana*. *Genetics* 1: 161–76.

Fridman, E., et al. 2004. Zooming in on a quantitative trait for tomato yield using interspecific introgressions. *Science* 305: 1786–89.

Lanktree, M. B., et al. 2011. Meta-analysis of dense gene centric association studies reveals common and uncommon variants associated with height. *Am. J. Hum. Genet.* 88: 6–18.

Laurie, C. C., et al. 2004. The genetic architecture of response to long-term selection for oil concentration in the maize kernel. *Genetics* 168: 2141–55.

Moose, S. D., J. W. Dudley, and T. R. Rocheford. 2004. Maize selection passes the century mark: A unique resource for 21st century genomics. *Trends Plant Sci.* 7: 358–64.

Nilsson-Ehle, H. 1909. Kreuzengsunter-su-chungen an hafer und weizen. *Lunds Univ. Aarskrift, N.F. Atd.*, Ser. 2, 5: 1–122.

Ogura, Y., et al. 2001. A frameshift mutation in *NOD2* associated with susceptibility to Crohn's disease. *Nature* 411: 603–6.

Tanksley, S. D. 2004. The genetic, developmental, and molecular bases of fruit size and shape variation in tomato. *Plant Cell* 16: S181–89.

Weedon, M. N., et al. 2008. Genome-wide association analysis identifies 20 loci that influence human height. *Nat. Genet.* 40: 575–83.

Wellcome Trust Case Control Consortium. 2007. Genome wide association study of 14,000 cases of seven common diseases and 3,000 shared controls. *Nature* 447: 661–78.

Chapter 22 Population Genetics and Evolution at the Population, Species, and Molecular Levels

Abzhanov, A., M. Protas, B. R. Grant, et al. 2004. *Bmp4* and morphological variation in beaks in Darwin's finches. *Science* 305: 1462–65.

Cavalli-Sforza, L. L., and W. F. Bodmer. 1971. *The Genetics of Human Populations.* San Francisco: W. H. Freeman and Co.

Cavener, D. R., and M. T. Clegg. 1981. Multigenic response to ethanol in *Drosophila melanogaster. Evolution* 35: 1–10.

Crow, J. F. 1986. *Basic Concepts in Population, Quantitative, and Evolutionary Genetics.* New York: W. H. Freeman.

Diamond, J. M., and J. I. Rotter. 1987. Observing the founder effect in human evolution. *Nature* 329: 105–6.

Dobzhansky, T. 1970. *Genetics of the Evolutionary Process.* New York: Columbia University Press.

Eick, G., and J. W. Thornton. 2011. Evolution of steroid receptors from an estrogen-sensitive ancestral receptor. *Molec. and Cell. Endocrin.* 334: 31–38.

Elena, S. F., V. S. Cooper, and R. E. Lenski. 1996. Punctuated evolution caused by selection of rare beneficial mutations. *Science* 272: 1802–4.

Freeman, S., and J. C. Herron. 2001. *Evolutionary Analysis.* Upper Saddle River, NJ: Prentice Hall.

Grant, P. R., and B. R. Grant. 2006. Evolution of character displacement in Darwin's finches. *Science* 313: 224–26.

———. 2009. The secondary contact phase of allopatric speciation in Darwin's finches. *Proc. Nat. Acad. Sci. USA* 106: 20141–48.

Green, R. E., et al. 2010. A draft sequence of the Neandertal genome. *Science* 328: 710–22.

Hardy, G. H. 1908. Mendelian proportions in a mixed population. *Science* 28: 49–50.

McKusick, V. A. 2000. Ellis-van Crevald syndrome and the Amish. *Nature Genet.* 24: 203–4.

National Institute of Standards (NIST). "Overview of STR Fact Sheets." Last updated May 20, 2011. www.cstl.nist.gov/strbase/str_fact.htm.

———. "Material Measurement Laboratory." Last updated May 25, 2011. www.cstl.nist.gov/strbase/fbicore.htm.

Ralls, K., K, Brugger, and J. Ballou. 1979. Inbreeding and juvenile mortality in small populations of ungulates. *Science* 206: 1101–3.

Simonson, T. S., et al. 2010. Genetic evidence for high-altitude adaptation in Tibet. *Science* 329: 72–75.

Slatkin, M. 1987. Gene flow and the geographic structure of natural populations. *Science* 236: 787–92.

Smith, J. M. 1989. *Evolutionary Genetics.* New York: Oxford University Press.

Thornton, J. W. 2001. Evolution of vertebrate steroid receptors from an ancestral estrogen receptor by ligand exploitation and serial genome expansions. *Proc. Nat. Acad. Sci. USA* 98: 5671–76.

Tishkoff, S. A., F. A. Reed, A. Ranciaro, et al. 2007. Convergent adaptation of human lactase persistence in Africa and Europe. *Nature Genet.* 39: 31–40.

Vernot, B., and J. M. Akey. 2014. Resurrecting surviving Neandertal lineages from modern human genomes. *Science* 343: 1017–21.

Weinberg, W. 1908. Ueber den nachweis der vererbung beim menschen. *Jahreshefte des Vereins für Vaterländische Naturkunde in Württemburg* 64: 368–82. English translation in Boyer, S. H. 1963. *Papers on Human Genetics.* Englewood Cliffs, NJ: Prentice Hall.

Yi, X., et al. 2010. Sequencing of 50 human exomes reveals adaptation to high altitude. *Science* 329: 75–78.

Yule, G. U. 1902. Mendel's laws and their probable relations to intra-racial heredity. *New Phytologist* 1: 193–207.

Appendix: Answers

Chapter 1

2. Protein, not DNA, was the focus of efforts to understand heredity before this discovery. Only after this discovery was serious attention turned to understanding DNA structure and function. Whereas the complexity of protein structure confounded thinking about mechanisms of inheritance, DNA structure provided profound insight into the mechanism of heredity, suggesting a simple, elegant mechanism for duplication (inheritance), change (mutation and evolution), and phenotype specification (coding). The finding that DNA is universal facilitated rapid progress because study results from all organisms were now directly related. This also fostered the development of recombinant DNA technologies in bacteria and bacteriophage, which led to the explosion of biological information that excites and confounds us today.

4. Evolution states that all life descended from a common ancestor, which passed its genes and the mechanisms by which those genes were used to its descendants. These mechanisms would include the structure of nucleotides, the structure of DNA, the enzymes that replicate and read DNA, the enzymes that translate mRNA into amino acid sequences, and many more. Any change to one of these components would be harmful, slowing or preventing reproduction, and would be removed by natural selection (mountains of experimental evidence demonstrate that mutations in genes encoding basic genetic machinery are lethal). Thus, once established as the genetic material, DNA would be maintained as the genetic material by natural selection and therefore would be expected to be found as the genetic material in all existing organisms.

6. *Genotype* refers to the genetic makeup of a cell or organism, whereas *phenotype* refers to observable characteristics of the cell or organism, such as appearance, physiology and behavior. The genotype of an organism is part of what determines the phenotype of the organism; however, environment also plays a role in the organism's phenotype. The genotype is heritable, and, therefore, its contribution to phenotype will be inherited. The aspects of phenotype that are due to environment are not heritable.

8. The modern synthesis of evolution is the reconciliation of Darwin's evolutionary theory with the findings of modern genetics. Darwin's theory proposed that all evolution was adaptive. Genetic studies on mutation and genetic recombination initially argued against the importance of natural selection as an agent for change because mutation and recombination were nonadaptive. The modern synthesis stated that evolution is due to the combined action of adaptive and nonadaptive evolutionary forces. In particular, the modern synthesis explained how mutation and recombination could provide the raw material (new genotypes and phenotypes) on which natural selection acts.

10a. *Transcription* is the synthesis of RNA by RNA polymerase. The RNA is complementary to the strand of DNA that was used as the template for transcription.

10b. An *allele* is a specific form of a gene or genetic locus.

10c. The *central dogma of biology* originally stated that genetic information flows from DNA to RNA (by transcription) and from RNA to protein (by translation). A point of emphasis of this dogma was that information does not flow in the reverse direction and has been modified to account for reverse transcription.

10d. *Translation* is the synthesis of a polypeptide using the information in an mRNA. *Translation* and *protein synthesis* are synonyms.

10e. *DNA replication* is the process by which DNA is copied by DNA polymerase.

10f. A *gene* is a segment of DNA that contains all the information necessary for its proper transcription, including the promoter, transcribed region, and termination signals.

10g. A *chromosome* is a heritable molecule composed of DNA and protein that typically contains genes.

10h. The term *antiparallel* refers to the orientation of the two strands of nucleic acid in a double-stranded nucleic acid (RNA or DNA). Each end of the double-stranded nucleic acid will contain the 5′ end of one strand and the 3′ end of the other.

10i. *Phenotype* refers to the observable characteristics of an organism, which include morphology, physiology, and molecular composition. The phenotype of an organism is a product of the interaction between its genotype and its environment.

10j. *Complementary base pair* refers to the two nucleotides on opposite, antiparallel strands of a double-stranded nucleic acid, which are hydrogen bonded to each other. One nucleotide contains a purine base that makes hydrogen bond to the pyrimidine base that is part of the other nucleotide.

10k. *Nucleic acid strand polarity* refers to the orientation of the nucleotides along a single strand of nucleic acid. One end of the strand terminates at the 3′ hydroxyl group of a ribose (or deoxyribose) sugar, whereas the other strand terminates at the 5′ phosphate group on the sugar. These are commonly referred to as the 3′ and 5′ ends of the strand.

10l. *Genotype* refers to the genetic makeup of an organism. The genotype can refer either to the organism's entire genetic makeup or to the genetic information at only one or a few loci.

10m. *Natural selection* is the process by which populations and species evolve and diverge through differential rates of survival and reproduction of members that are due to their inherited differences.

10n. *Mutation* is the process that generates new genetic variety through change to existing alleles.

10o. *Modern synthesis of evolution* is the term applied to the reconciliation of modern genetic analysis with Darwin's theory of evolution by natural selection.

12. The template DNA strand is complementary and antiparallel to the RNA transcript. The coding strand is parallel and identical to the mRNA transcript, except that thymidine is in place of uridine.

14. The 5′ end is a phosphate group. The 3′ end is a hydroxyl group. A phosphodiester bond is a covalent bond that joins nucleotides in a strand of nucleic acid.

16. The central dogma is a description of the flow of genetic information. The flow is unidirectional, from DNA to RNA to protein. The process by which information flows from DNA to RNA is called transcription. Transcription is the synthesis of RNA by RNA polymerase. The RNA is complementary to the strand of DNA that was used as the template for transcription. The flow of information from RNA to protein is called translation. Translation is the synthesis of a polypeptide using the information in an mRNA.

18a. The mRNA sequence is 5′-UUCCAUGUC-3′.

18b. The amino acid sequence is Phe-His-Val.

20a. 6 clades

20b. A backbone (They are all vertebrates.)

20c. The mammalian and human clades share these characteristics: have backbones and four legs, have fur and produce milk.

22. The samples are (1) double-stranded DNA, (2) single-stranded RNA, (3) double-stranded RNA, and (4) single-stranded DNA.

Evaluate: DNA will contain thymine (T) but not uracil (U), whereas RNA will contain U but not T. Double-stranded DNA will contain equal proportions of adenine (A) and T and equal proportions of guanine (G) and cytosine (C), whereas single-stranded DNA typically does not. Double-stranded RNA will contain equal proportions of A and U and equal proportions of G and C, whereas single-stranded RNA typically does not. *Deduce:* Sample 1 contains T but not U, and the percentage of A is the same as T; therefore, it is probably double-stranded DNA. Sample 2 contains U but not T, and the percentage of A is not the same as U; therefore, it is single-stranded RNA. Sample 3 contains U but not T, and the percentage of A is the same as U; therefore, it is probably double-stranded RNA. Sample 4 contains T but not U, and the percentage of A is not the same as T; therefore, it is single-stranded DNA. *Solve:* Samples 1 and 3 are double-stranded, whereas samples 2 and 4 are single-stranded.

24. Mammals

Chapter 2

2. The genotype ratio will be 1/2 *BB* and 1/2 *Bb*. The phenotype will be all B.

8a. False. The expected *phenotype* ratio is 9/16 : 3/16 : 3/16 : 1/16, assuming simple dominance and independent assortment of genetic loci (*AaBb* × *AaBb*). There are nine different genotypes, and the genotype ratio is 1/16 (*AABB*) : 2/16 (*AABb*) : 1/16 (*AAbb*) : 2/16 (*AaBB*) : 4/16 (*AaBb*) : 2/16 (*Aabb*) : 1/16 (*aaBB*) : 2/16 (*aaBb*) : 1/16 (*aabb*).

8b. True

8c. True

8d. False. The law of *independent assortment* is of primary importance in predicting the outcome of dihybrid and trihybrid crosses. The law of segregation is also necessary but not sufficient.

8e. False. Reciprocal crosses that produce identical results indicate that the traits being studied are autosomal.

8f. False. The law of segregation predicts that she will produce two gamete genotypes with respect to her albinism gene at equal frequency.

8g. True

8h(1). True

8h(2). False. There will be 1/16 *AABB*, 1/16 *AAbb*, 1/16 *aaBB*, and 1/16 *aabb*. All four genotypes will be true-breeding; therefore, 1/4 of the progeny will be true-breeding.

8h(3). False. Being "heterozygous at one or both loci" excludes only the progeny that are homozygous at both loci. In part (b) of this question, it was calculated that 1/4 will be homozygous at both loci; therefore, 3/4 will be heterozygous at one or both loci (2/16 *AaBB*, 2/16 *AaBB*, 4/16 *AaBb*, 2/16 *Aabb*, and 2/16 *aaBb*).

10a. Mottled is the dominant phenotype.

10b. The results are consistent with autosomal inheritance.

10c. 1/2 of the F₂ of both crosses are expected to be homozygous, and 1/2 are expected to be heterozygous.

10d. One cross would be a test cross, and the other would be a back-cross. The test cross would be the mottled F₂ to a true-breeding leopard individual. The backcross would be the mottled F₂ to one of its parents (both are heterozygotes).

12a. The mode of fur color inheritance in these crosses is likely to be a single gene with two alleles controlling fur color, and black will be dominant to brown.

12b. Assign the letter *B* for the black allele and *b* for the brown allele. The brown male must be *bb*. The black female in the first cross must be *Bb*. The black female in the second cross must be *BB*.

14a. The results suggest that the inheritances of color and fin shape are each due to segregation of two alleles at a single gene.

14b. The results indicate that gold is dominant to black and that split fin is dominant to single fin.

14c. The chi-square value for color is 0.061, which corresponds to a *P* value between 0.7 and 0.9. The chi-square value for fin shape is 0.05, which corresponds to a *P* value between 0.7 and 0.9. Neither *P* value is less than 0.05, which indicates that the hypothesis of one gene with two alleles for color and fin shape cannot be rejected.

16b. Of the F₂ progeny, 3/4 will have yellow seeds, 1/4 will have green seeds, 3/4 will have round seeds, and 1/4 will have wrinkled seeds.

16c. 9/16 yellow, round; 3/16 yellow, wrinkled; 3/16 green, round; 1/16 green, wrinkled

20. The χ^2 value is 4.81. There is one degree of freedom (df = 1) in this calculation, and the *P* value is less than 0.05. Therefore, the hypothesis that bicolor corn-kernel color is the result of segregation of two alleles at a single genetic locus should be rejected for this experiment.

22a. 0.132

22b. 0.178

22c. 0.822

24a. 0.422

24b. 0.0313

24c. 0.4219

24d. 0.0469

26. 1800 full wings and gray bodies, 600 full wings and ebony bodies, 600 vestigial wings and gray bodies, 200 vestigial wings and ebony bodies

28a. *Evaluate:* The Blue Persian and Spanish Dwarf varieties are assumed to be true-breeding for seed color and plant height; therefore, the resulting F₁ generation will be heterozygotes. *Deduce:* Since tall and white are expressed in the heterozygotes, they are the dominant traits. The reappearance of short and blue in the F₂ confirm that they are the recessive traits. *Solve:* Tall and white are the dominant traits, whereas short and blue are recessive.

28b. The expected phenotypic distribution in the F₂ is 9/16 tall, white; 3/16 tall, blue; 3/16 short, white; and 1/16 short, blue.

28c. The hypothesis being tested in this experiment is that the two pea plant varieties differ at two independently assorting genetic loci, and two alleles show simple dominance at each locus.

28d. The chi-square value is 0.78, which corresponds to a *P* value between 0.9 and 0.7, indicating that the hypothesis cannot be rejected (the results are consistent with the hypothesis).

30a. 9/16

30b. 3/8

30c. 3/4

32a. *Evaluate:* The total number of children in these families was 480. The number of children with CF was $(52 \times 1) + (32 \times 2) + (18 \times 3) + (2 \times 4) = 178$; therefore, $480 - 178 = 302$ were normal. *Deduce:* The expected number of children with CF is $480 \times {}^{1}/_{4} = 120$; therefore, $480 - 120 = 360$ are expected to be normal. *Solve:* The chi-square value using these numbers is 37.4. The number of degrees of freedom is (2 classes) − 1 = 1. Using Table 3.4, the chi-square of 37.4 for 1 degree of freedom corresponds to a *P* value less than 0.001, which is much lower than 0.05, indicating that observed results are inconsistent with those expected and that you must reject the hypothesis that CF is inherited as an autosomal recessive trait based on these results. *Solve:* The observed results for the total number of children with CF in families in which both parents are carriers are inconsistent with expectations (*P* value < 0.001).

32b. One expects 38 families to have no CF children, 50.6 to have 1 child with CF, 25.3 to have 2 children with CF, 5.6 to have 3 children with CF, and 0.47 to have 4 children with CF.

32c. *Evaluate:* The observed values are given in the problem, and the expected values were calculated in the answer to part b. *Deduce:* The chi-square using these numbers is 47. The number of degrees of freedom is (5 classes) − 1 = 4. Using Table 3.4, the chi-square value of 47 for

4 degrees of freedom corresponds to a *P* value less than 0.001. This indicates that the difference between the observed and expected results is highly statistically significant and therefore is not consistent with that expected under binomial probability. **Solve:** The results are not consistent with expectations based on a binomial distribution (*P* value < 0.001).

34. 0.988

36. The probability of 5 unaffected children is 0.237, of 4 unaffected and 1 affected is 0.396, of 3 unaffected and 2 affected is 0.264, of 2 unaffected and 3 affected is 0.0879, of 1 unaffected and 4 unaffected is 0.0146, and of all 5 affected is 0.000977.

38. *Experiment One:* (1) Cross the true-breeding short, brown-furred and long, white-furred guinea pigs to create an F_1 population; (2) test that they are dihybrids by crossing male F_1 with female F_1 to produce F_2 guinea pigs; (3) cross both sets of pure-breeding parents to create 24 F_1 progeny and intercross all the F_1 (12 crosses) to produce 144 F_2; (4) compare observed phenotypic distribution with expected results. *Experiment Two:* (1) Cross the F_1 with their long, white-furred parent to produce backcrossed guinea pigs; (2) cross two of the F_1 males with their long, white-haired mother, thus producing 24 progeny; and (3) cross the long, white-haired male guinea pig with all of the short, brown-haired female F_1, which would produce 144 progeny.

40. Cross the parents to produce (*FfRrTt*) trihybrids, and self-fertilize the F_1 to create an F_2 population that will include all possible phenotypes and genotypes. Among the F_2, 3/64 will produce yellow, pear-shaped tomatoes and have axial flowers (*ffrr*). To determine which of these plants are *TT*, self-fertilize them and identify the plants that breed true for axial flower position.

42a. All four adults are heterozygous carriers of alkaptonuria (*Aa*).

42b. For Sarah and James, the chance that their next child will have alkaptonuria is 1/4, not *very low*; for Mary and Frank, the chance is 1/6000, not *0*.

42c. 1/4

42d. 3/4

42e. The probability that one of their children with alkaptonuria will have a child with alkaptonuria is dependent on the genotype of their child's mate. **Deduce:** If their child's mate has no family history of alkaptonuria, then there is a 4/1000 chance that they will be a carrier. If the mate is a carrier, then there will be a 1/2 chance that a grandchild will have alkaptonuria. The overall probability is therefore (4/1000) × 1/2 = 1/500. The probability that their affected child will have a child with alkaptonuria will increase dramatically if their child's mate has a close relative with the disorder. For example, if their child's mate's grandmother had alkaptonuria, then the mate will have at least a 1/2 chance of being a carrier, and the overall probability that their first child will be affected is at least 1/2 × 1/2 = 1/4.

44. The genotypic ratios will be 4/9 *FFpp*, 4/9 *Ffpp*, and 1/9 *ffpp*. The phenotypic ratio will be 8/9 feathered legs and single comb, and 1/9 no leg feathers and single comb.

Chapter 3

2a. 48 chromosomes

2b. 48 chromosomes

2c. 24 chromosomes (23 autosomes and 1 sex chromosome)

2d. 48 chromosomes

2e. 48 chromosomes

2f. 48 chromosomes

4. Cohesion opposes the pulling forces attempting to separate sister chromatids until all pairs of sister chromatids are attached to microtubules from opposite poles of the spindle (i.e., bipolar attachment). Premature, as well as delayed, sister chromatid separation can cause sister chromatids to partition together instead of separating during anaphase and can lead to errors in chromosome segregation. Sister chromatid cohesion is due to cohesin, a protein complex that binds

to sister chromatids and attaches them to each other. When all pairs of sister chromatids are under the tension generated by bipolar attachment and sister chromatid cohesion, the protease separase is activated. Separase cleaves a component of cohesin, which simultaneously ends cohesion on all pairs of sister chromatids and allows sister chromatids to be pulled toward opposite poles of the spindle.

8. Anaphase II

10. A normal human female nucleus contains one Barr body, whereas a normal male nucleus contains no Barr bodies.

12a. *Dd*

12b. 50%

12c. There is no chance that her daughter will have OTD, but there is a 1/2 or 50% chance that her daughter will be a carrier for OTD.

12d. *dY*

12e. 1/2 of the daughters and 1/2 of the sons will have OTD.

14a. The male parent was M^+Y and P^+p^- and the female was M^+m^- and P^+p^-.

14b. Among the females with purple eyes, half are M^+m^- and p^-p^- and half are M^+M^+ and p^-p^-. Males with purple eyes and miniature wings are m^-Y and p^-p^-.

16. The unusual number of Barr bodies seen in the rare male and female infants is the result of nondisjunction during meiosis, which creates abnormal gametes containing an additional X chromosome or lacking an X chromosome.

18. **Evaluate:** The syndrome is an X-linked, recessive trait. Therefore, males inheriting this mutation must express it (hemizygous), whereas it is possible for females to be heterozygous for the mutation (carrier females). **Deduce:** Because of random X inactivation, the tissue of heterozygous females will contain some cells that express the wild-type allele and some that express the mutant allele. The problem states that most female carriers do not show symptoms; therefore, the pattern of X-inactivation normally results in sufficient wild-type gene expression to promote normal development. **Solve:** In female carriers that show symptoms, X-inactivation must have occurred such that wild-type gene expression was insufficient for normal development. The symptoms are less severe in these symptomatic female carriers because they express some level of the wild-type allele.

22. For cross A, all males are barred-feathered, 1/2 of the females are barred-feathered and 1/2 are non-barred. For cross B, 1/2 males are barred, 1/2 males are nonbarred, 1/2 females are barred, and 1/2 are nonbarred.

24a. The reciprocal crosses produced different results, which is diagnostic for sex-linked traits.

24b. The female is the heterogametic sex (ZW), whereas males are homogametic (ZZ). Black spot is dominant, and nonspotted is recessive. Using Z-linked alleles designated *B* for black-spot and *b* for nonspotted, the parents of cross I are *Bb* male and *bW* female. Their progeny are 1/4 black-spot males (*Bb*), 1/4 nonspotted males (*bb*), 1/4 black-spot females (*BW*), and 1/4 nonspotted females (*bW*). For cross II, the parents are a *bb* male and a *BW* female. Their progeny are approximately 1/2 *Bb* males and 1/2 *bW* females.

26. Rare sex-reversed males carry an altered X chromosome that contains a fragment of the Y chromosome including the *SRY* gene. Thus, they develop male sex characteristics yet lack a Y chromosome. Rare sex-reversed females carry an altered Y chromosome the lacks the *SRY* gene. Thus, they develop female sex characteristics even though they have a Y chromosome.

28a. Female is *ECec; Vv* and the male is *ecY; Vv*.

28b. The parents are *ECec; Vv Ee* female and *ECY; Vv Ee* male.

28c. The parents are *ECec; Vv ee* female and *ecY; Vv Ee* male.

30. **Evaluate:** The children of the first mating, *Cc × cY*, are expected to be 1/2 color blind and 1/2 normal, with equal proportions of male and female progeny in each class. The children of the second mating, $cc \times CY$, are expected to be 1/2 color blind and 1/2 normal, but all the color-blind individuals will be male and all the normal individuals will be female. *Deduce:* The reciprocal matings give different results, which is indicative of X-linked inheritance. *Solve:* The results suggest recessive inheritance because the mother in the first mating is not affected but has affected children. The results differ from those predicted for autosomal recessive inheritance because the second mating yields all males with one phenotype and all females with the other.

Chapter 4

2. *Evaluate:* Epistasis indicates that two or more genes interact to contribute to a particular phenotype. Pleiotropy indicates that one mutant allele contributes to two or more mutant phenotypes. *Deduce and Solve:* Epistasis and pleiotropy can be distinguished by inheritance patterns in pedigrees or from crosses. If the inheritance pattern of one phenotype indicates that more than one gene is segregating, then epistasis is occurring. If two or more phenotypes are inherited together in a pattern that indicates segregation of alleles of a single gene, then pleiotropy is occurring.

4a. The bacteria in the 12 colonies that grew on minimal medium are prototrophs, whereas those in the 3 colonies that could not grow on minimal medium were auxotrophs.

4b. The bacteria in the three colonies that could not grow on minimal medium but could grow on minimal medium plus serine are serine-requiring auxotrophs. They carry mutations in one or more genes required for the biosynthesis of serine.

4c. Mutant 1 carries a mutation in the gene coding for a component of enzyme C, mutant 2 carries a mutation in the gene coding for a component of enzyme A, and mutant 3 carries a mutation in the gene coding for enzyme B.

6. Child b's parents must be 1. Child a's parents could be 1 or 3; however, since child b's parents are 1, child a's parents must be 3. Child c's parents could be 3 or 4; however, since child a's parents are 3, child c's parents must be 4. Child d's parents could be 2, 3, or 4; however, since child a's parents are 3 and child c's parents are 4, child d's parents must be 2.

10a. At the B locus, one parent was *Bb* and the other was *bb*. At the D locus, one parent was *Dd* and the other was *dd*.

10b. One parent was *BbDd* (brown) and the other was *bbDd* (yellow).

10c. At the B locus, one parent was *BB* and the other parent could have had any genotype (*BB, Bb,* or *bb*). At the D locus, one parent was *Dd* and the other was *dd*.

12a. One parent was *BBDdCc* and the other was *DdCc*. Any genotype is possible at the B locus.

12b. The parents were *BbddCc* × *bbddCc*.

12c. Both parents were *BbDdCc*.

12d. The parents were both *Bb* at the *B* locus. Between the two parents, there was a *DD* and a *CC* locus, but these need not have been in the same parent. The other *D* and *C* loci could have any genotype.

14. The F_2 will be 1/4 red, 1/2 pink, and 1/4 ivory.

16. 2/3 short stature and short limbs and 1/3 normal stature and limbs

18a. Pure-breeding red petunias are *aaBB*.

18b. Pure-breeding blue petunias are *AAbb*.

18c. The phenotypic distribution in the F_2 will be 9/16 purple, 3/16 red, 3/16 blue, and 1/16 white.

20a. *Evaluate:* Recall that variable expressivity indicates that individuals with the same mutant genotype vary in severity of mutant phenotype. *Deduce:* Evidence of variable expressivity would be the appearance of some individuals with two thumbs affected and others with only one thumb affected. The pedigree shows both types of affected individuals. *Solve:* Yes

20b. *Evaluate:* Recall that incomplete penetrance indicates that not all individuals with a mutant genotype show the mutant phenotype. *Deduce:* Evidence of reduced penetrance would be the appearance of an affected child that had unaffected parents. IV-4 and IV-5 are affected children of unaffected parents. The nonpenetrant individuals are III-5 and III-10. *Solve:* Yes

22a. Genetic heterogeneity

22b. There are five complementation groups: Group 1 is defined by mutations 1, 3, and 7; Group 2 is defined by mutations 4 and 8; Group 3 is defined by mutations 5, 6 and 10 and Group 4 is defined by mutation 2. Mutation 9 fails to complement any of the other mutants and may represent complementation group 5.

24a. The parental strains are *AAbb* and *aaBB*.

24b. The phenotypic distribution will be 9/16 blue (*A_B_*), 6/16 purple (*A_bb + aaB_*), and 1/16 red (*aabb*).

24c. The progeny of the backcross of the F_1 to the *AAbb* parent will be 1/2 blue (*AABb* and *AaBb*) and 1/2 purple (*AAbb* and *Aabb*) progeny. The progeny of the backcross of the F_1 to the *aaBB* parent will be 1/2 blue (*AaBB* and *AaBb*) and 1/2 purple (*aaBB* and *aaBb*).

26a. $Y_1 \times G_1$ produces all yellow F_1, which produce 3/4 yellow and 1/4 green F_2. Green appears to be recessive and the 3:1 ratio suggests segregation of alleles of a single gene. $Y_2 \times G_1$ produces all green F_1, which produces 3/4 green and 1/4 yellow. Here, yellow appears recessive and, again, the 3:1 ratio suggest segregation of alleles at a single gene. $Y_1 \times Y_2$ produces all yellow F_1, which produces 13/16 yellow and 3/16 green. The sixteenths in the F_2 suggests alleles at 2 genes are segregating. The two genes segregating in the third cross correspond to the genes segregating in the first two crosses. *Solve:* The results of these crosses indicate that two genes control squash fruit color.

26b. In cross I, Y_1 is *AABB*, and G_1 is *aaBB*. Their yellow F_1 progeny are *AaBB*, and their F_2 are 3/4 yellow (*A_BB*) and 1/4 green (*aaBB*). In cross II, Y_2 is *aabb*, G_1 is *aaBB*, their green F_1 are *aaBb*, and their F_2 are 3/4 green (*aaB_*) and 1/4 yellow (*aabb*). The F_1 of $Y_1 \times Y_2$ resulting from cross III are *AaBb* and their F_2 are 9/16 yellow (*A_B_*), 3/16 yellow (*A_bb*), 3/16 green (*aaB_*), and 1/16 yellow (*aabb*).

26c. The progeny will be 1/2 yellow (*AaBB* and *AaBb*) and 1/2 green (*aaBB* and *aaBb*).

28a. All the mutants are temperature-sensitive mutants, carrying a mutant allele of a gene required for normal growth at 37°C. The typical mechanistic explanation of this is that the gene is required for growth at all temperatures, and the mutant allele is functional at 25°C but not 37°C (an alternative explanation is that the gene is required only at 37°C). This explains the five mutants that cannot grow at 37°C. For the two mutants that grow slowly at 37°C, the alleles probably retain partial function at 37°C.

28b. This study identifies three complementation groups: Group 1 is defined by A, D and F, Group 2 is defined by B and G, and Group 3 is defined by C and E.

30a. The chi-square value is

$$\frac{(22-25)^2}{25} + \frac{(23-25)^2}{25} + \frac{(55-50)^2}{50} = 1.02.$$

There are three phenotypic classes; therefore, this calculation has two degrees of freedom. A chi-square value of 1.02 with 2 df gives a P value between 0.5 and 0.7; therefore, the results are consistent with a 1:2:1 hypothesis, and that hypothesis cannot be rejected.

30b. The chi-square value is

$$\frac{(22-18.75)^2}{18.75} + \frac{(55-56)^2}{55} + \frac{(23-25)^2}{25} = 0.75.$$

There are three phenotypic classes; this calculation has two degrees of freedom. A chi-square value of 0.75 with 2 df gives a P value between 0.5 and 0.7; therefore, the results are consistent with a 9:4:3 hypothesis, and that hypothesis cannot be rejected.

30c. Neither hypothesis can be rejected based on the chi-square analysis.

30d. Self-fertilize all the purple progeny and determine the proportion that breed true. If 1:2:1 is correct, all purple plants will breed true. If 9:4:3 is correct, then 2/3 of the purple plants will not breed true (i.e., they will produce some whites).

32. Strains 1 and 2 are homozygous for mutations in the same gene, *A*, that causes albinism. Strain 3 is homozygous for a mutation in a different gene, *B*, which causes albinism. Strains 1 and 2 are *aaBB*, as are the F_1 and F_2 of cross A. Strain 3 is *AAbb*. The F_1 of cross B and cross C are *AaBb*. The F_2 of cross B and cross C are 9/16 *A_B_* (pigmented), 3/16 *A_bb* (albino), 3/16 *aaB_* (albino), and 1/16 *aabb* (albino).

Chapter 5

2a. Parental: 41% *DR*, 41% *dr*; recombinant: 9% *Dr*, 9% *dR*

2b. Parental: 41% *Dr*, 41% *dR*; recombinant: 9% *DR*, 9% *dr*

4. *E* and *H* are not genetically linked, because a single crossover in every meiosis results in production of equal proportions of *EH*, *Eh*, *eH*, and *eh* gametes. *EH* and *eh* are parental gametes, whereas *Eh* and *eH* are recombinant gametes. The percentage of parental gametes is the same as the percentage of recombinant gametes, which is 50%.

6a. Yes, the *y* and *w* genes are expected to show linkage because they are less than 50 map units (m.u.) apart.

6b. Yes, *y* is expected to assort independently of *f* because *y* and *f* are more than 50 m.u. apart. The same applies to *w* and *f*.

6c. There will be 24.625% of each of the following progeny types: gray with red eyes and forked bristles, gray with red eyes and normal bristles, yellow with white eyes and forked bristles, and yellow with white eyes and normal bristles. There will be 0.375% of each of the following types: gray with white eyes and forked bristles, gray with white eyes and normal bristles, yellow with red eyes and forked bristles, and yellow with red eyes and normal bristles.

6d. The female is heterozygous at *y*, *w*, and *f*, and the male is hemizygous recessive. Consider the linked *y* and *w* loci first. The *y* and *w* genes are 1.5 m.u. apart, so the females will make 0.4925 of each parental gamete type, which are y^+w^+ and y^-w^-. They will make 0.0075 of each recombinant gamete type, which are y^+w^- and y^-w^+. The *f* gene is unlinked to *y* and *w*, so its alleles assort independently of *y* and *w*; 0.50 of each y^-w^- genotype receives an f^+ allele and 0.50 receives an *f* allele. The fraction of $y^+w^+f^+$ is $0.4925 \times 0.5 = 0.24625$. The same is true for y^+w^+f, $y^-w^-f^+$, and $y^-w^-f^-$. The fraction of $y^+w^-f^+$ is $0.0075 \times 0.50 = 0.00375$. The same is true for $y^+w^-f^-$, $y^-w^+f^+$, and $y^-w^+f^-$.

8a. See figure.

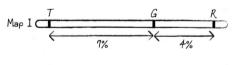

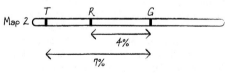

8b. A trihybrid organism with dominant alleles on one chromosome and recessive alleles on the homologous chromosome (*GRT/grt*) could be test crossed to a pure-breeding recessive (*grt/grt*). The number of test-cross progeny in each outcome category can be used to determine which genetic map is correct.

10. Syntenic genes that are separated by 50 map units or more will assort independently because there will be one or more crossovers between them per meiosis.

12a. To measure distance between *Y* and *Lz*, cross a yl/y^+l^+ female to a *yl/Y* male. The progeny should be 36% (360/1000) yellow lozenge, 36%

(360/1000) gray normal eyes, 14% (140/1000) yellow normal eyes, and 14% gray lozenge eyes. To measure the distance between *Lz* and *F*, cross an lf/l^+f^+ female to an *lf/Y* male. The progeny will be 34% (340/1000) lozenge forked bristles, 34% (340/1000) normal eyes and normal bristles, 16% (160/1000) normal eyes with forked bristles, and 16% (160/1000) with lozenge eyes and normal bristles.

12b. No cross can demonstrate genetic linkage between genes *Y* and *F* because the recombination frequency between genes *Y* and *Lz* plus that between *Lz* and *F* is greater than 50%; therefore, the percent recombination between *Y* and *F* in any cross will be 50%.

12c. Syntenic genes (genes on the same chromosome) that are separated by more than 50 map units do not display genetic linkage and, therefore, assort independently.

14a. Nail–patella syndrome is a dominant trait.

14b. Yes, NPS appears to segregate with blood type A in this pedigree, indicating genetic linkage between these traits.

14c. I-1 is I^On/I^On, I-2 is I^AN/I^On, II-2 is I^On/I^On, II-4 is I^AN/I^On, II-6 is I^AN/I^On, II-7 is I^On/I^On, and II-9 is I^AN/I^On.

14d. III-6 is I^ON/I^On and III-8 is I^On/I^On. Even though III-6 and III-8 are both *O* blood type, III-6 has nail–patella syndrome because he inherited the recombinant chromosome, I^ON, from his mother, whereas III-8 inherited the nonrecombinant I^On from her mother.

14e. The genotypes of III-11 and III-12 cannot be unambiguously determined because they have type A blood and both of their parents are I^AI^O. Thus, either or both could be I^AI^A or I^AI^O. For this reason, it is not clear whether III-11 and III-12 are parental-type or recombinant-type progeny.

16a. The order is *G T L*.

16b. The recombination frequencies are 0.139 between *G* and *T*, 0.088 between *T* and *L*, and 0.214 between *G* and *L*.

16c. The recombination frequency for *G* and *L* is less than for *G* and *T* plus *T* and *L* because the double-crossover progeny do not appear to be recombinant for *G* and *L* and, therefore, are not counted.

16d. The interference value (*I*) is 0.49.

16e. The meaning of *I* = 0.49 is that only half of the expected number of double-crossover progeny were observed. This indicates that a meiotic cell undergoing a crossover between *G* and *T* is about half as likely to also have a crossover occur between *T* and *L*. Similarly, a crossover between *T* and *L* reduces the likelihood of a crossover between *G* and *T*.

18a. Yes, the data provides strong support for linkage between Rh and elliptocytosis because the maximum lod score supporting linkage is above 3 (it's about 5.5 for linkage at a θ value just over 0.1).

18b. The maximum lod score is about 5.5 for linkage at a θ value just over 0.1.

18c. The results support linkage at θ values from just under 0.05 to about 0.30.

22. The chi-square value is 168.3. For 3 degrees of freedom, this corresponds to a *P* value of less than 0.001.

24a. The pure-breeding brown-eyed fly line is ccd^+d^+, the pure-breeding short-bristled line is c^+c^+dd, and the F_1 is cc^+dd^+.

24b. The cross should be a test cross of the F_1 dihybrid. The test-cross strain would be *ccdd*. The test cross will yield four progeny categories whose phenotypes will be determined by the dominant or recessive alleles contributed by the F_1 dihybrid.

24c. The progeny will be 36% cd^+, 36% c^+d, 14% *cd*, and 14% c^+d^+.

24d. The progeny will be 25% cd^+, 25% c^+d, 25% *cd*, and 25% c^+d^+.

28a. I-1 is either *N1/n2* or *N2/n1*. I-2 is *n2/n2*. II-1 is *N1/n2*. II-2 is *n2/n2*. III-1 is *N1/n2*. III-2 is *N1/n2*. III-3 is *n2/n2*. III-4 is *N1/n2*. III-5 is *n2/n2*. III-6 is *N2/n2*. III-7 is *N1/n2*. III-8 is *n2/n2*.

28b. III-6 is a recombinant. Her genotype indicates that the marker allele 2 is on the same chromosome as the *NF1* allele, unlike the allele arrangement in her mother (II-1).

28c. 1/8

30a. The gene order is scute, echinus, crossveinless. The allelic phase in the trihybrid is $+ e + / s + c$.

30b. The recombination frequency between scute and echinus is 0.067. The recombination frequency between echinus and crossveinless is 0.095. The recombination frequency between scute and crossveinless is 0.162.

30c. There are no discrepancies across this genetic interval.

30d. The chi-square value is 38,555, which corresponds to a P value well below 0.01, which indicates that the results of this experiment are not due to independent assortment.

32a. The chi-square values for both sets of data correspond to P values well below 0.01 and therefore indicate that the results significantly deviate from expectation based on independent assortment. This supports linkage of the colorless and waxy genes.

32b. The recombination frequency from cross 1 was 0.27, and the recombination frequency from cross 2 was 0.24.

32c. Yes, both sets of data are compatible with the hypothesis of genetic linkage, although the recombination frequencies of the two sets differed slightly.

32d. The recombination frequency using combined data is 0.27

Chapter 6

2. Link 1: Transfer of an entire F^+ plasmid from an F^+ cell converts an F^- cell to an F^+ cell. Link 2: Integration of the F plasmid into the host chromosome converts an F^+ cell to an Hfr cell. Link 3: Precise excision of the F plasmid from the chromosome of an Hfr cell converts an Hfr cell to an F^+ cell. Link 4: Excision of the F plasmid plus some host DNA from the chromosome of an Hfr cell converts an Hfr cell into an F′ cell.

4. *Evaluate:* All three mechanisms can involve homologous recombination of the transferred DNA into the recipient chromosome. In all three mechanisms, if the DNA entering the cell is linear or does not contain an origin of replication, then recombination of the DNA into the recipient cell chromosome or episome is required for the DNA to be stably maintained. If the DNA entering the recipient is circular and contains sequences required for replication and maintenance, then recombination into the recipient cell chromosome or an episome is not required.

These three mechanisms differ in how DNA is transferred from one cell to another. Only conjugation requires genetic information for transfer in the donor cell (F plasmid DNA) and physical contact between the donor and recipient cell. Transduction is characterized by infection of the donor cell by a bacteriophage. On the other hand, transformation does not require particular genes in the donor or the help of a phage: DNA is released from the "donor" cell due to cell lysis and enters the "recipient" cell via DNA transporters.

6. Lysis of an infected bacterial host cell, and the release of progeny phage particles, is the end result of the lytic cycle of bacteriophage. Lysogeny involves the integration of the phage chromosome (known as a prophage once integrated) by site-specific recombination into a specific site (DNA sequence) in the bacterial chromosome. Once integrated, the prophage can replicate along with the rest of the bacterial chromosome until conditions induce excision of the prophage and resumption of the lytic cycle.

8. A *prophage* is a bacteriophage genome that is part of the host cell chromosome. It is formed by integration of a bacteriophage chromosome into the host cell chromosome by site-specific recombination.

10. In genetic complementation, bacterial lysis occurs because the two viruses have mutations in different genes. This is analogous to complementation analysis in eukaryotes. In recombination, bacterial lysis occurs because, although the viruses have mutations in the same gene, rare homologous recombination events produce recombinant wild-type viruses. Complementation and recombination can be differentiated by the frequency of bacterial lysis after simultaneous infection with two mutant viruses: lysis is frequent in the case of complementation (many plaques are formed), whereas it is rare in the case of recombination.

20a. Selection for met^+ was done on minimal medium containing glucose and phenylalanine. The met^+ transductants were assayed for cotransduction of phe^+ using minimal medium containing glucose. The met^+ transductants were assayed for cotransduction of ara^+ using minimal medium containing arabinose. Selection of phe^+ transductants was done on minimal medium containing glucose and methionine. The phe^+ transductants were assayed for cotransduction of met^+ on minimal medium containing glucose. The phe^+ transductants were assayed for cotransduction of ara^+ on minimal medium containing arabinose. The $met^+ phe^+$ transductants were selected on minimal medium containing glucose. The $met^+ phe^+$ transductants were assayed for cotransduction of ara^+ on minimal medium containing arabinose. The ara^+ transductants were selected on minimal medium containing arabinose, phenylalanine, and methionine. The ara^+ transductants were assayed for cotransduction of met^+ on minimal medium containing arabinose and phenylalanine. The ara^+ transductants were assayed for cotransduction of phe^+ on minimal medium containing arabinose and methionine.

20b. The gene order is *phe-ara-met* or *met-ara-phe*.

22a. 4 genes

22b. Mutations 1, 5, and 8 are in one gene. Mutation 2 is in a second gene. Mutations 3 and 7 are in a third gene. Mutations 4 and 6 are in a fourth gene.

22c. Complementation resulted in the formation of many plaques on each plate (the lysis of many different bacteria) due to coinfection by bacteriophage with mutations in different genes. The vast majority of these phage are mutants that cannot by themselves infect and lyse bacteria. Recombination between mutations in the same gene results in rare plaques (very few bacteria lyse); however, all the virus particles produced are wild type and can infect and lyse bacteria.

22d. Mutation 9 is a deletion that inactivates two genes. It overlaps mutations 1 and 7 but not mutation 3, 5, or 8.

22e. Mutation 10 is a deletion mutation that inactivates two genes. It overlaps mutations 4 and 8 but not mutation 1, 5, 6, or 9.

22f. The mutation order is 3, 7, 1, 5, 8, 4, 6, and 2.

Chapter 7

2. *Evaluate:* The key results were those showing that enzymes that destroyed RNA and protein did not destroy the transforming principle, whereas enzymes that destroyed DNA did. *Solve:* The transforming principle was considered to be genetic material. The most reasonable interpretation of those results was that DNA was the only essential component of the transforming principle, and therefore, the genetic material.

4. *Evaluate:* Hershey and Chase prepared T2 particles whose protein was labeled with the radioactive sulfur, S^{35}, and whose DNA was labeled with radioactive phosphorous, P^{32}. They used the labeled T2 to infect bacteria and then separated the infected bacteria from the empty phage shells (phage ghosts) using a blender. They found that essentially all the P^{32}-labeled T2 DNA but little to none of the S^{35}-labeled T2 protein was in the infected bacterial cells. *Solve:* Since T2 genetic material must be inside the infected cells in order to direct new virus particle synthesis, these results pointed to DNA as the genetic material of phage T2.

6. *Evaluate:* The problem concerns the chemical bonds that form base pairs in double-stranded DNA. Recall that hydrogen bonds are weak, non-covalent bonds involving two atoms sharing a hydrogen nucleus. The distance between the atoms sharing the hydrogen nucleus is critical for hydrogen bonds to form. *Deduce:* The bases in the two complementary antiparallel DNA strands are aligned such that each of the atoms that share hydrogen nuclei (N and O or N and N) in each base are positioned next to each other at a distance that allows all possible hydrogen bonds to form. *Solve:* The bases in the complementary but parallel strands are not aligned in this manner; therefore, the atoms that could form hydrogen bonds do not align and are not close enough together to allow hydrogen bonding between all possible and necessary chemical groups.

8a. Phosphodiester bonds

8b. Hydrogen bonds

8c. There are 12 phosphodiester bonds in the molecule.

8d. There are 17 hydrogen bonds in the DNA molecule.

10. DNA polymerase III determines which free nucleotide triphosphate is complementary to the base being copied. DNA polymerase III catalyzes phosphodiester bond formation between the α-phosphate of the incoming nucleotide triphosphate and the 3′ hydroxyl group of the last nucleotide added to the strand.

12. RNA is synthesized and serves as a primer for elongation by DNA polymerase.

14a. DNA polymerase I is required to remove the RNA primer and fill in the gap with DNA. DNA polymerase III is responsible for the bulk of synthesis of DNA on the leading and lagging strands.

14b. The absence of DNA pol I will not prevent the bulk of DNA replication but will result in newly replicated DNA containing small segments of RNA and nicks at the junctions of polymerase III synthesized DNA and the 5′ end of the RNA primers.

14c. An *E. coli* mutant without a functional DNA polymerase III will be unable to replicate its DNA because it lacks the enzyme responsible for the bulk of DNA synthesis during replication.

16a. True

16b. False

16c. True

16d. False

16e. True

18. Helicase, SSB, primase, DNA pol III, DNA pol I, ligase

20. *Evaluate:* Recall the Meselson-Stahl experiment and consider how the results excluded the alternatives to the semiconservative model for DNA replication. Meselson and Stahl initially cultured *E. coli* in medium containing only N15 (heavy nitrogen) until all cells contained only N15/N15 DNA. They then cultured the N15/N15 *E. coli* in normal medium (N14) and collected samples after one, two, and three rounds of DNA replication. The results showed that before transfer to N14 medium, only N15/N15 DNA was present. After one round of replication in N14 medium, all of the DNA was N15/N14; after two rounds of replication, half the DNA was N15/N14 and half was N14/N14; and after the third round of replication, 1/4 of the DNA was N15/N14 and 3/4 was N14/N14. *Deduce:* The conservative model predicted that the original N15/N15 DNA would remain throughout, and therefore the results ruled out the conservative model. The dispersive model predicted that after each round of replication there would be only one form of DNA, which would become less and less dense. *Solve:* Although this model was not ruled out after one round of replication, the persistence of the N15/N14 DNA and the presence of two classes of DNA (N15/N14 and N14/N14) after rounds two and three ruled out the dispersive model.

22. *Evaluate:* Cells were incubated in medium containing 3H-thymine for a short period of time (a "pulse") and then transferred to medium containing an excess of unlabeled thymine (the "chase"). The cells were then collected and their DNA was prepared for electron microscopy, which can detect replication bubbles in DNA, and for autoradiography, which reveals the location of 3H-thymine incorporation into DNA. *Deduce:* Recall that bidirectional replication from a replication origin produces a replication bubble with DNA synthesis occurring at both ends, whereas unidirectional replication results in a replication bubble with DNA synthesis occurring at one end. The results showed that DNA replication bubbles contained regions of label on the sides of the midpoint of the bubble, which corresponds to the replication origin. *Solve:* If DNA synthesis was unidirectional, then label would be present on only one side of the origin.

24. *Evaluate:* DNA helicases unwind dsDNA during DNA replication and repair. Bloom syndrome is characterized by chromosome instability and an increased rate of cancer. Chromosome instability is evident when chromosomes are lost from cells, typically because of a failure during mitosis. Mitosis fails to occur properly if chromosomes are not completely replicated. Cancer is a disease caused by accumulation of somatic mutations, which will accumulate at an elevated rate if DNA repair by DNA replication is defective. *Solve:* Based on the information provided, it is reasonable to speculate that lack of the DNA helicase encoded by the Bloom syndrome gene results in incomplete replication during S phase and during repair of DNA damage. Failure to completely replicate chromosomes could result in a failure to pass chromosomes on to progeny cells during mitosis, which would results in chromosome instability. Failure to repair DNA damage would also lead to an increased rate of somatic mutation, which would lead to cancer.

26a. Telomeric DNA is composed of a repetitive, short DNA sequence. In many organisms, the repeated sequence is 5′-TTAGGG-3′ or a variant thereof.

26b. Telomerase uses a segment of its RNA as the template to add multiple copies of a simple sequence to the 3′ end of each strand of DNA on a linear chromosome. This strand, which corresponds to the template for lagging strand synthesis, is copied by the normal mechanism of lagging strand synthesis after it is extended by telomerase.

26c. Telomeres are thought to provide two functions, one in chromosome replication and the other in chromosome protection. Telomeres provide a mechanism for replication of the ends of linear chromosomes. Without telomeres, lagging strand synthesis would fail to extend to the chromosome ends, leaving a gap at each end after each round of replication. This would shorten the chromosome and, after many rounds of replication, would result in loss of important DNA sequences (genes). Telomeres are repetitive DNA, which prevents loss of important DNA sequences if shortening occurs. Telomeres are also the binding site for telomerase, which extends the lagging strand template to compensate for sequences lost during incomplete lagging strand synthesis. Telomeres also provide a protective "cap" on the ends of linear chromosomes; this cap distinguishes normal chromosome ends from ends generated by double-stranded chromosome breaks (DNA damage). Without telomeric DNA and the proteins that bind telomeric DNA, the ends of chromosomes are recognized as broken chromosomes and are fused together by DNA repair enzymes. Such breakage can create chromosome end-to-end fusions, which then create dicentric chromosomes that can be broken during the next cell division, creating new breaks and new fusions in an endless cycle known as the bridge-break-fusion cycle.

26d. *Evaluate:* Germ-line cells divide many times, whereas many somatic cells are capable of a limited number of cell divisions (some are unable to divide at all). *Solve:* Telomerase is required to ensure complete chromosome replication in germ cells, ensuring that every mitosis produces two daughter cells with complete chromosomes. Telomerase is not required in somatic cells because they cannot divide enough times to result in loss of important DNA at chromosome ends. It is also thought that the lack of telomerase in somatic cells prevents indefinite cell division because loss of DNA at chromosome ends will activate DNA damage responses that stop division and lead to cell death. This response would help protect the organism from the spread of cancerous cells.

28a. The reaction would have equal concentrations of deoxycytidine triphosphate, deoxythymidine triphosphate, and deoxyguanidine triphosphate. It would also have a mixture of deoxyadenosine triphosphate and dideoxyadenosine triphosphate.

28b. Dideoxysequencing uses DNA synthesis to generate labeled DNA fragments of different lengths, which are then resolved by gel electrophoresis or column chromatography. To visualize the products of DNA synthesis in traditional dideoxysequencing, relatively high levels of template were necessary. The use of PCR allows detectable levels of DNA synthesis from much lower levels of template DNA.

28c. Dideoxynucleotides contain a hydrogen group instead of a hydroxyl group on their 3′ carbon. When a dideoxynucleotide is incorporated into a growing DNA strand, there is no 3′ hydroxyl group present to allow phosphodiester bond formation with the next nucleotide to be added; therefore, no additional nucleotides are added to this DNA strand, and thus synthesis of this strand is terminated.

32. Approximately 7500 origins of replication. Five minutes = 300 seconds. Working bidirectionally, each origin generates (300 sec.) (40 nt.)(2) = 24,000 nucleotides per second, requiring $1.8 \times 10^8 / 2.4 \times 10^4$ = 0.75×10^4 origins.

Chapter 8

2. The three major modifications of mRNA are 5′ capping, intron splicing, and 3′ polyadenylation. The process of 5′ capping involves addition of a guanosine monophosphate by guanylyl transferase to the 5′ end of a pre-mRNA via a 5′-to-5′ triphosphate linkage and the subsequent methylation of the guanine and sometimes additional nucleotides on the pre-mRNA. Intron splicing involves the removal of introns from the pre-mRNA and the joining of adjacent exons by the spliceosome. The process of 3′ polyadenylation involves the cleavage of the pre-mRNA downstream of the polyadenylation sequence by cleavage factors and addition of 20 to 200 adenine nucleotides by polyadenylate polymerase.

6. DNA and RNA polymerases are similar in that both (1) catalyze phosphodiester bond formation to polymerize nucleotides into nucleic acids, (2) polymerize in a 5′-to-3′ direction, and (3) are dependent on a DNA sequence template. DNA and RNA polymerases differ in that (1) RNA polymerase can initiate strand synthesis whereas DNA polymerase can only extend an existing strand, (2) most DNA polymerases can proofread using a 3′-to-5′ exonuclease activity whereas RNA polymerases cannot, and (3) DNA polymerases use deoxyribonuclotide triphosphates as substrates whereas RNA polymerases use ribonucleotide triphosphates as substrates.

8. The primary transcripts of bacterial and eukaryotic genes differ in that bacterial transcripts often contain more than one coding sequence (they are polycistronic) whereas eukaryotic transcripts do not. Polycistronic mRNAs allow for coordinate regulation of production of several proteins by controlling initiation of transcription of only one gene. Eukaryotes accomplish this by coordinate regulation of transcription of multiple genes by gene-specific transcription factors. Prokaryotic and eukaryotic primary transcripts differ in that eukaryotic transcripts are extensively modified before translation whereas prokaryotic transcripts are not. The modification of eukaryotic transcripts includes 5′ capping and 3′ polyadenylation, which generate structures that are critical for regulation of the initiation of translation and for controlling the half-life of the mRNA. Mechanisms controlling translation initiation and mRNA half-life in bacteria do not involve these structures. The modification of eukaryotic transcripts also includes intron splicing, which is required for generating the complete open reading frame used in translation and allows for the generation of multiple, different (but related) mRNAs from a single primary transcript. This last mechanism increases the number of different proteins that are coded by a genome without increasing the number of genes present.

10. Recall that enhancers are DNA sequences that increase the level (rate) of transcription of genes in a position- and orientation-independent manner. Enhancers are binding sites for transcription factors that stimulate transcription of one or more genes. Since the expression of the transcription factors is often specific to the cell type or tissue, enhancers often provide for a mechanism to stimulate transcription of genes in a manner specific to the cell type or tissue. Possible rationales for the lack of enhancers in bacteria include (1) the lack of differentiated cell types in most bacteria; (2) little to no intergenic space on bacterial chromosomes, which makes long-range-acting enhancer sequences unnecessary; and (3) bacterial operons make coordinate regulation of protein synthesis by enhancers unnecessary.

18. *Evaluate:* This problem requires application of your understanding of the band shift assay to match each condition listed to the result shown on a gel. *Deduce:* The bands in lanes 2 and 4 have migrated the most rapidly; therefore, they correspond to naked DNA molecules. Lanes 1, 3, and 5 have migrated more slowly than naked DNA; therefore, they are DNA + protein complexes. Lane 1 showed slightly higher mobility than lane 5, which showed higher mobility than lane 3. Higher mobility indicates less protein is bound to the DNA. *Solve:* Conditions c and d should result in naked DNA because c contains DNA only, and d contains DNA plus RNA pol II, which cannot bind to DNA in the absence of general transcription factors. Therefore, c and d correspond to lanes 2 and 4 (either lane is equally possible for either condition). Condition e contains the lowest number of transcription factors, followed by condition a, and condition b has the most transcription factors. Thus, lane 1 corresponds to condition e, lane 5 corresponds to condition a, and lane 3 corresponds to condition b.

20a. The organism transcribes as a wild type.

20b. The organism transcribes slowly (i.e., is leaky).

20c. The organism does not transcribe genes.

20d. Temperature-sensitive mutant

22a. *Evaluate:* Recall that AG is the consensus sequence found at the 3′ end of introns. *Deduce and Solve:* Since this mutation is in an intron but causes a defect in β-globin, it must affect splicing efficiency. The mutation replaces A with U, changing the 3′ splice site sequence AG to UG. This change is likely to affect the efficiency with which the spliceosome recognizes the end of intron 2 and leads to either inclusion of intron 2 in the mRNA—which results in an insertion or premature termination—or causes a change in the location of the 3′ splice junction, which leads to an insertion, deletion, or frameshift mutation.

22b. This problem requires you to consider the structure of genes and identify important DNA sequences that are not part of exons. Non-exon-located mutations that could prevent gene function include mutations in the promoter or terminator sequences as well as in enhancer or silencer sequences. Mutations in the promoter would diminish or prevent transcription, which would reduce or eliminate the mRNA. Mutations in the terminator could prevent or alter termination, which would elongate the mRNA. Mutations in an enhancer would diminish transcription, which would reduce mRNA abundance. Mutations in the silencer would enhance transcription, which would increase mRNA abundance.

24a. First, the eukaryotic promoter is unlikely to be recognized by bacterial RNA polymerase holoenzyme. Second, the introns will not be removed from the pre-mRNA, which will result in production of an abnormal protein. Third, sequences required for efficient translation initiation in bacteria are not present.

24b. First, I would make a cDNA copy of the gene. The cDNA is a DNA copy of the mRNA sequence, which lacks introns. Second, I would place the cDNA sequence downstream of a known bacterial promoter, which will ensure that the gene is transcribed. Third, I would modify the coding sequence upstream of the ATG start codon to contain a Shine–Dalgarno sequence, which is important for proper initiation of translation. Fourth, I would place an intrinsic or rho-dependent termination sequence downstream of the cDNA to ensure efficient transcription termination.

26a. *Evaluate:* This problem challenges you to interpret the results of a DNA footprinting experiment. Recall that DNA footprints correspond to sites where bound protein protects an end-labeled DNA fragment from digestion by the endonuclease, DNase. *Deduce and Solve:* The DNA-only and DNA + protein lanes differ because bands are missing from the DNA + protein lanes. This result indicates that the proteins are bound to the DNA. Since the proteins are transcription factors and RNA polymerase, which bind to promoters, it is reasonable to conclude that the DNA fragment contains a promoter sequence.

26b. 200 base pairs

26c. *Evaluate:* This problem challenges you to apply your understanding of promoter structure and function to design experiments to test a DNA fragment for promoter function. ***Tip:*** The function of a promoter is to provide all the DNA sequences required for binding of transcription factors and RNA polymerase and for start of transcription. ***Deduce and Solve:*** One reasonable experiment would be to clone this DNA sequence upstream of the coding sequence for a protein whose expression is easy to assay and then introduce that chimeric construct into cells and assay for protein expression. If the result is negative, then the orientation of the fragment should be inverted to check that it was not inserted backward in the first attempt. Also, a known, control promoter should be used to confirm that the protein-coding sequence is correct and that the protein can be detected in the cells used.

Chapter 9

2a. Nirenberg and Matthaei developed an in vitro translation system that contained everything necessary for translation except for amino acids and mRNAs. Synthetic RNA composed of only U (poly-U) was added to 20 separate reactions, each containing a different radioactive amino acid as well as the other 19 nonradioactive amino acids. Only the reaction with radioactive phenylalanine produced radioactive protein. Since the RNA sequence poly-U contains only UUU codons, then UUU codes for phenylalanine.

2b. Only reaction with radioactive proline produces radioactive protein. Since poly-C contains only CCC codons, CCC codes for proline.

2c. One type of polypeptide composed of alternating Arg and Glu amino acids was produced.

2d. No detectable polypeptides would be produced.

4. I. Preinitiation complex formation: the small ribosomal subunit and IF3 bind to the mRNA, the AUG start codon is identified by 16S rRNA base-pairing with the Shine–Dalgarno sequence, and the AUG codon is in the ribosomal P site.

   II. Formation of the 30S preinitiation complex: fMet–tRNA^fMet bound to IF2–GTP binds to start codon in the P site, and IF1 binds.

   III. Formation of the 70S initiation complex: 50S ribosomal subunit binds, IF2 cleaves GTP to GDP + phosphate, and IF1, IF2–GDP, and IF3 leave the complex.

6. tRNAs that are charged with different amino acids have unique structural features that allow them to interact with their cognate aminoacyl tRNA synthetases. Unique features include the anticodon sequence as well as sequences and base modifications in the T-arm and D-arm.

8a. 5'-CUA-3' and 5'-CUG-3'

8b. 5'-UUU-3'

8c. 5'-GAG-3'

8d. 5'-CAU-3'

8e. 5'-AUC-3' and 5'-AUU-3'

10. See table.

	Bacterial Ribosome	**Eukaryotic Ribosome**
Similarities		
Composition	RNA and protein	RNA and protein
Number of subunits	two (small and large)	two (small and large)
tRNA binding sites	three (E, P, and A)	three (E, P, and A)
Differences		
Number and size of rRNAs	three (16S, 23S, and 5S)	four (18S, 28S, 5.8S, 5S)
Size of subunits	30S and 50S	40S and 60S
Numbers of proteins	21 in the small subunit and 31 in the large subunit	~35 in the small subunit and 45 to 50 in the large subunit

12a. The errors in the diagram are (1) ribosome is moving in the wrong direction along mRNA, (2) mRNA contains T's, (3) amino terminal amino acid of the peptide is incorrect, (4) ribosomal subunit sizes are incorrect, (5) anticodon sequence of the tRNA in P site is incorrect, and (6) amino acids on tRNAs in P and A sites are incorrect.

14. 31

16. See table.

DNA	Non-template (5' to 3')	AAC	A̲TA	TGT	GAA	G̲G̲C̲	GAG	AAT̲	GAA̲	CGA̲
	Template (5' to 3')	TTG	TA̲T	ACA	CTT̲	CCG	CTC	TTA	CTT	GC̲T̲
	mRNA (5' to 3')	AAC	AUA	UGU	GAA	GGC	GAG	AA̲U	GAA	C̲GA
	tRNA (5' to 3')	UUG	UAU	ACA	CUU	CCG	CUC	UUA	CUU	GCU
Amino acid abbreviations	3-letter	Asn	Ile	Cys	Glu	Gly	Glu	Asn	Glu	Arg
	1-letter	N	I	C	E	G	E	N	E	R

22. Soon after initiation of translation of an mRNA coding for a secretory protein, the amino terminus of the secretory protein is synthesized and is exposed on the surface of the ribosome. The amino terminus contains the signal sequence that marks this protein for cotranslational translocation into the endoplasmic reticulum (ER). The signal receptor particle (SRP) binds to the signal sequence and the ribosome and halts further translation. The SRP/ribosome/mRNA complex binds to the ER membrane—SRP binds to its receptor, and the ribosome binds to a protein translocation channel. SRP is released, translation resumes, and the growing polypeptide is extruded through the channel into the lumen of the ER. There, the signal sequence is cleaved by signal peptidase and the protein is glycosylated, folded with the help of chaperones, and packaged into transport vesicles destined for the Golgi apparatus. The carbohydrate on the protein is modified as the protein passes through the compartments of the Golgi, and the protein is packaged into vesicles destined for transport to the plasma membrane. Fusion of the transport vesicle membrane with the plasma membrane releases the secretory protein into the extracellular fluid.

24a. 5'-UGUGUGUGUGUGUGUG . . . -3'

24b. Cys-Val-Cys-Val-Cys-Val-Cys-Val . . .

24c. The experiment resulted in production of a polypeptide composed of alternating Val and Cys amino acids, which is what was predicted for a nonoverlapping triplet code.

24d. Two polypeptides, each composed of a single type of amino acid, would be produced if the code had been a doublet, nonoverlapping code.

24e. Translation of the RNA using an overlapping doublet or triplet code gives the same result—a single type of polypeptide with two alternating types of amino acids. This result does not differ from that predicted based on a nonoverlapping three-letter code but does differ from that predicted for a nonoverlapping two-letter code.

26. 438

32a. The start and stop codon are in bold print. 5'-*CAPCCAAGCGUU*A**CAUG**UAUGGAGAGAAUGAAACUGAGGCUUGCCACGUUUGUU**AAG**CACCUAUGCUACCG*AAAAAAAAAAAAAAAAAAAAAAAAAAAA*-3'

32b. Met-Tyr-Gly-Glu-Asn-Glu-Thr-Glu-Ala-Cys-His-Val-Cys (MYGENETEACHVC)

34. The consensus sequence is CCCGCCGCCACCAUGG. Also see table.

Position	−12	−11	−10	−9	−8	−7	−6	−5	−4	−3	−2	−1	[start]	+4
Percent A	23	26	25	23	19	23	17	18	25	61	27	15	[AUG]	23
Percent C	35	35	35	26	39	37	19	39	53	2	49	55	[AUG]	16
Percent G	23	21	22	33	23	20	44	23	15	36	13	21	[AUG]	46
Percent T	19	18	18	18	19	20	20	20	7	1	11	9	[AUG]	15
Consensus	C	C	C	G	C	C	G	C	C	A	C	C	**AUG**	G

36. GCCACCAUGG

Chapter 10

2. Evaluate: Recall that genetic diseases are those determined by genetic factors in the individual's own genome. On the other hand, infectious diseases are caused by foreign agents that have invaded the individual. **Deduce:** All genetic diseases are also molecular diseases since the genes involved encode molecules that are responsible for development of the disease. The only difference between the terms *genetic* and *molecular* is their point of emphasis: *genetic* emphasizes that a disease is not infectious, whereas *molecular* emphasizes that defects in one or more molecules are the ultimate cause of the disease. Sickle cell disease (SCD) is the first genetic disease for which the molecular mechanism was understood. SCD is seen in individuals homozygous for the β^S allele, which encodes an altered β-globin polypeptide that leads to formation of an altered hemoglobin protein, polymerization in red blood cells under low oxygen conditions, cells with a sickle shape, blockage of capillaries in peripheral tissue, and ultimately pain and tissue damage.

4. Evaluate: Recall that electrophoretic mobility is the rate at which a molecule migrates during electrophoresis. The electrophoretic mobility of a protein is determined by its charge, size, and shape, which in turn are primarily a result of its amino acid sequence. **Deduce:** Two proteins with different electrophoretic mobility typically have some difference in amino acid sequence. If different alleles of a protein-coding gene code for polypeptides that differ in sequence, even if they differ at only one amino acid position, the charge or shape of the proteins can differ and result in differences in electrophoretic mobility.

6. See "Template Strand (DNA)" column of table.

β-globin Form	Position	Amino Acid	Codon (mRNA)	Coding Strand (DNA)	Template Strand (DNA)
β^A (wild type)	7	Glu	5′-GAG-3′	5′-GAG-3′	5′-CTC-3′
Siriraj	7	Lys	5′-AAG-3′	5′-AAG-3′	5′-CTT-3′
San Jose	7	Gly	5′-GGG-3′	5′-GGG-3′	5′-CCC-3′
β^A (wild type)	58	Pro	5′-CCU-3′	5′-CCT-3′	5′-AGG-3′
ZIGUINCHOR	58	Arg	5′-CGU-3′	5′-CGT-3′	5′-ACG-3′
β^A (wild type)	145	Tyr	5′-UAU-3′	5′-TAT-3′	5′-ATA-3′
Bethesda	145	His	5′-CAU-3′	5′-CAT-3′	5′-ATG-3′
Fort Gordon	145	Asp	5′-GAU-3′	5′-GAT-3′	5′-ATC-3′

8. Evaluate: Recall that mutations that increase the length of a polypeptide either change the stop codon to a sense codon or shift the reading frame before, but close to, the stop codon. By comparing the sequences, we can determine that the wild-type and mutant sequences differ immediately after codon 144. **Deduce:** The continued change in sequence after codon 144 rules out base-substitution mutants, which would affect specific bases only, and points to a shift in the reading frame caused by the insertion of AG between codon 144 and codon 145. The two-nucleotide insertion shifts the reading frame to one that includes 13 sense codons (compared with two sense codons in the wild type) before a stop codon appears, which happens to be after codon 157.

10. The primary molecular parameter affecting the electrophoretic mobility of DNA and mRNA is size (typically expressed as length). For proteins, size (the number of amino acids), charge, and shape affect electrophoretic mobility.

12. Electrophoretic mobility is a measure of the size (length) of mRNA and DNA molecules; however, comparing them to each other is, in most cases, like comparing apples to oranges. The length of an mRNA is an inherent, biological property of the gene that encodes the mRNA and is not dependent on the method used to prepare the mRNA for gel electrophoresis. The size of the DNA molecule containing the gene is entirely dependent on the experimental method used to prepare it for electrophoresis. For example, the size of a DNA restriction fragment containing a gene is determined by which restriction enzyme is used. DNA fragment sizes will likely differ for different restriction enzymes and are unlikely to be the same length as the mRNA. The exception to this rule is the comparison of a cDNA molecule to an mRNA molecule. A cDNA molecule is a double-stranded DNA copy of the mRNA. If the DNA copy is perfect, then cDNA length in base pairs should equal the mRNA length in nucleotides.

14. Evaluate: The frequency of β^S will be determined by the evolutionary forces acting on the phenotypes of $\beta^S\beta^S$, $\beta^S\beta^A$, and $\beta^A\beta^A$ individuals. The β^S allele encodes an abnormal β-globin polypeptide that forms abnormal hemoglobin molecules that reduce the life span of red blood cells. This is most severe in $\beta^S\beta^S$ homozygotes and is detectable but less severe in $\beta^S\beta^A$ heterozygotes. The reduced life span of the red blood cells interrupts the life cycle of the malaria protists and results in a certain level of resistance to malaria. **Solve:** The severity of the anemia in $\beta^S\beta^S$ individuals decreases their reproductive fitness relative to $\beta^A\beta^A$, which selects against the β^S allele. The less severe effect in $\beta^S\beta^A$ heterozygotes does not affect fitness, except in populations where malaria is endemic, where it increases reproductive fitness relative to $\beta^A\beta^A$. Based on this, a reasonable hypothesis would be that malaria is more prevalent in western Africa than southern Africa.

16a. Yes, the fetus has a 1/4 chance of having SCD.

16b. The fetus will develop SCD because it is homozygous for the β^S allele.

18. Some restriction enzymes make a staggered double-stranded DNA cut at their recognition sequence, cutting the two DNA strands at different positions. This leaves single-stranded DNA ends, called "sticky ends" because they can form base pairs with the single-stranded ends of other restriction fragments and cause the fragments to stick together. Some restriction enzymes make a clean double-stranded DNA cut at their recognition sequence, cutting both strands at the same site. This leaves ends that are blunt in the sense that all of their nucleotides are base-paired. Blunt ends, therefore, are not sticky.

20. Evaluate: Restriction enzymes break two phosphodiester bonds between the same nucleotides in the same sequence on both strands of DNA. Two sites of action suggest two active sites in the enzyme. **Solve:** Restriction enzymes typically bind as dimers with each monomer binding to the recognition sequence on opposite strands and cutting that sequence in the same location. Thus, 5′GGTACC3′ 3′CCATGG5′ is bound by a *Bam*HI dimer, where each monomer binds to and positions its active site to break the phosphodiester bond between the G's.

24a. One type of mutation would be a deletion of 3.5 kb within the gene but not including the region corresponding to the probe. A second type of mutation would be a point mutation that creates a new restriction site 4.0 kb in from the right end of the map.

24b. For the deletion mutant, I would expect either a smaller mRNA (3500 nucleotides shorter than the wild type) or less mRNA if the mutant mRNA is unstable. For the point mutation, I would not expect the mRNA to be different in length (unless the mutation alters pre-mRNA splicing), although the abundance of the mRNA may change if the mutation changes the stability of the mRNA.

26. Evaluate: Linear DNA molecules can be considered to move through an agarose gel matrix as extended (rod-like) molecules that have the same charge-to-mass ratio regardless of length. *Deduce:* Since their shape and charge-to-mass ratio are the same, the only factor affecting their relative electrophoretic mobility is their length. The gel will slow the longer molecule to a greater extent than the shorter molecule. The same rationale applies to mRNAs, assuming electrophoresis under conditions where mRNAs are linear.

28. *Evaluate:* Recall that restriction endonucleases are components of bacterial defense systems that protect against invasion by foreign DNA. *Deduce:* You can infer from the information provided that the restriction enzyme is able to cut foreign DNA, for example, DNA from an invading bacteriophage's genome. DNA from a bacteriophage is digested by the restriction enzyme, which decreases the likelihood that the bacteriophage will successfully infect the bacterium.

30. Yes, the father could be ♂1 but not ♂2 because puppy P3 has a band that is not in the mother or in ♂2 but is in ♂1.

Chapter 11

2. Recall that the term *haploid* refers to one copy of genetic information. The terms do not conflict because a bacterium is haploid regardless of whether its genes are contained in one or more than one chromosome.

4. Approximately $2.9 \times 10^9/(146 + 50) = 1.48 \times 10^7$ nucleosomes.

6. Recall that the G-banding pattern of light and dark bands of chromosomes is characteristic for each chromosome. These distinctive band patterns allow a cytologist to unambiguously identify each chromosome in a human karyotype. This pattern allowed for the development of cytogenetics, which is the genetic analysis of an individual that is performed by microscopy. Genetic abnormalities associated with alterations in chromosome number or structure can be detected by cytogenetic analysis, allowing for the rapid diagnosis of some genetic diseases.

8. Interphase chromosomes will be less condensed than metaphase chromosomes. Chromosomes are difficult to resolve by microscopy in interphase, whereas chromosomes are easily resolved in metaphase due to their high degree of condensation.

10. *Evaluate:* This problem asks you to consider DNA sequence elements that are essential, evolutionarily conserved components of bacterial or eukaryotic chromosomes. *Deduce:* Chromosomes must be replicated and passed on to progeny cells. Bacterial chromosomes must have all the genes essential for bacterial life, an origin of replication for initiation of replication, and a site for attachment to the bacterial membrane to ensure segregation of daughter chromosomes of each cell at cell division. Eukaryotic chromosomes must contain a centromere, a telomere at each end, and multiple origins of replication. Eukaryotic chromosomes must also contain genes essential for eukaryotic life, although these genes can be dispersed among the chromosomes. Natural selection will select against chromosomes that lack sequences required for replication or segregation and the cells that contain them because they will be less fit than those that contain these sequences. The same argument applies to chromosomes that lack essential genes.

12. Bacterial chromosomes are typically circular and are attached to the bacterial cell membrane. Circular chromosomes do not require telomeres; therefore, telomeres are not present on bacterial chromosomes, and there would be no evolutionary advantage for a chromosome to have them. Bacteria do not have microtubules; therefore, bacterial chromosomes do not need a centromere to facilitate assembly of a microtubule binding site. The membrane attachment site of a bacterial chromosome serves to promote segregation of daughter bacterial chromosomes to opposite sides of a dividing cell, which is analogous to the function of eukaryotic chromosome centromeres.

14. Telomeres are composed of repetitive DNA in which the repeated sequence is a simple sequence (for example, TAAGGC repeated many times). Directly next to the telomere are telomere-associated sequences, which are also composed of repetitive DNA, but the repeated sequences are more complex and may include genes. Directly next to the telomere-associated sequences are "normal" chromosome sequences that contain

genes and intergenic regions. Note that there is variation in this sequence organization among chromosomes in the same organism and between chromosomes in different organisms.

18a. *Evaluate:* Recall that nucleosomes are spaced 200 bp apart and that after S phase there are two copies of each chromosome. The haploid genome size of *Arabidopsis* is 10^8 bp. *Deduce:* The number of nucleosomes per genome in a diploid is given by $\dfrac{10^8}{200} \times 2 = 5 \times 10^5$.

There are twice as many nucleosomes after completion of S phase.

Solve: $2\left(\dfrac{10^8}{200} \times 2\right) = 10^6$.

18b. The histone proteins that were part of nucleosomes before S phase are recycled and used to form the new nucleosomes during S phase. The additional histone proteins required to double the nucleosome number are newly synthesized. Therefore, half of the histone protein present on chromosomes after S phase is newly synthesized, and the other half was already present.

22a. Recall that the *E. coli* chromosome is 1000 times longer than an *E. coli* cell, yet it fits into a small region of the cell called the nucleoid. As with other bacterial chromosomes, the *Methanococcus jannaschii* chromosome is compacted by supercoiling and the binding of proteins that fold the chromosome. The combination of supercoiling and folding (condensation) reduces the volume occupied by the chromosome, allowing it to fit into the region of the bacterial cell known as the nucleoid.

22b. The chromosome is likely compacted in two steps. First, it is bound by nucleoid-associated proteins and SMC proteins, which loop segments of the chromosome and condense them. Second, the DNA is supercoiled by the action of topoisomerases.

22c. Recall that most bacterial chromosomes and plasmids are negatively supercoiled. Negative supercoiling folds chromosomal DNA and promotes unwinding of regions of the chromosome. This promotes access to ssDNA for enzymes such as DNA polymerase and RNA polymerase. Supercoiling of the *M. jannaschii* chromosome folds the chromosome and promotes the function of DNA and RNA polymerases.

24. *Evaluate:* Recall that histones interact with DNA in a sequence-independent manner to form nucleosome core particles that are conserved in structure and function from yeast to man. Also recall that evolutionary change of a protein's sequence is under "functional constraint," which limits or prevents changes to sequences that perform essential functions. *Deduce and Solve:* Histone H4 is one of the core histones and is part of the nucleosome core particle. Most of the amino acid residues of H4 interact with either DNA or other histone proteins; therefore, most of the H4 amino acid sequence is under functional constraint (any change to the H4 amino acid sequence will likely be deleterious and therefore will be selected against by natural selection). Thus, little change occurs in the sequence of H4 over many millions of years that separate pea plants and cows from their common ancestor.

26. *Evaluate:* Recall that all four histones are synthesized at the beginning of S phase and that, after completion of S phase, half the histone proteins present will be new and half will be left over from previous cell cycles. *Tip:* ^{35}S-containing methionine can be used in a pulse-chase experiment to radioactively mark all the histone proteins synthesized during one S phase. *Deduce and Solve:* Start with cells that contain unlabeled methionine and are in G_1 phase. Place them in medium containing ^{35}S-methionine and allow them to complete S phase. Take a sample of cells for analysis and then transfer the remaining cells to medium containing unlabeled methionine and allow them to divide and go through multiple rounds of S phase and cell division, collecting samples after each S phase. Analyze the nucleosomes of each sample by microscopy and autoradiography. If nucleosomes are a mixture of old and new histones, then most or all nucleosomes will be radiolabeled after the first S phase, about half will be radiolabeled after the second round, and 1/4 after the third round. If all nucleosomes contain either old or new histones, then about half of the nucleosomes will be radiolabeled after the first S phase, 1/4 after the second, and 1/8 after the third.

28a. *Evaluate:* Recall that DNase I degrades DNA that is not protected by protein. "Large amounts" of DNase I would be expected to digest DNA completely, leaving only those sequences bound by nucleosomes protected. *Tip:* Review the DNase footprinting technique introduced in Chapter 9. *Deduce and Solve:* The only DNA sequences protected from DNase I would be those in the nucleosome core particle. There would be one band, approximately 145 bp in size.

28b. *Evaluate, Deduce, and Solve:* Each band would represent the DNA bound by histones in the nucleosome core particle. All non-nucleosomal DNA and all linker DNA between nucleosomes would be digested.

28c. *Evaluate:* Recall that the 10-nm fiber model for chromatin states that the 10-nm fiber is a linear array of nucleosomes and that the chromatin is not folded into higher order structures. *Deduce and Solve:* The only protection against digestion by DNase I was due to histones bond to DNA in nucleosomes, indicating that no other proteins and no higher order packing of the chromatin at this region occurred. Higher order structures would have generated fragments of DNA that are larger than the nucleosome core.

Chapter 12

2. *Evaluate:* Recall that 5-BrdU is a base analog and that nitrous acid is a deaminating agent. *Deduce and Solve:* 5-BrdU is a thymidine analog that can base-pair like thymine or like cytosine. If 5-BrdU is incorporated in place of thymidine and then base-pairs like cytosine in the subsequent round of replication, it causes an A-T to G-C transition. If 5-BrdU is incorporated into DNA in place of cytidine and then base-pairs like thymine in the following round of replication, it causes a G-C to A-T transition. Nitrous acid converts cytosine to uracil, which will base-pair with adenine in the next round of replication and cause a C-G to T-A transition. Nitrous acid can also convert adenine to hypoxanthine, which will base-pair with cytosine in the next round of replication and cause an A-T to G-C transition.

4a. The mutation is a frameshift mutation (insertion or deletion).

4b. TCT/G-TAC-ATA-TGC-GAG-ACA-AGN

8. *Evaluate:* This problem concerns the relationship between the coding sequence of a gene and the function of the encoded protein. Recall that the effect of a single-nucleotide substitution depends on whether the substitution changes the meaning of the codon and, if so, whether that change has a significant impact on the structure of the protein. *Deduce:* Nucleotide substitutions can result in silent, missense, or non-sense mutations. Silent mutations do not change the amino acid sequence of the protein and therefore have no effect on protein function. Missense mutations change one amino acid in a protein. *Solve:* Therefore, the effect on the function of the protein depends on the importance of the amino acid that was replaced and the functional similarity (or lack thereof) of the R-group on the substituted amino to that of the wild-type amino acid.

10. *Evaluate:* This problem tests your understanding of the effect of spontaneous mutations on gene function. Recall that spontaneous mutations are typically nucleotide substitutions and, if detected, are not silent. *Deduce and Solve:* (1) Recessive mutations are typically loss-of-function mutations. Wild-type gene sequences have been selected during evolution for optimum function; therefore, any change (mutation) to that sequence is likely to replace a nucleotide maintained by natural selection with one that reduces the function of the gene. (2) Forward mutations include all mutations in a gene that convert it from wild type to mutant, whereas reverse mutations are only those that precisely reverse a specific mutation to wild type. Thus, the number of possible nucleotide changes corresponding to a forward mutation is much greater than those that reverse a given mutation, making forward mutations far more frequent than reversion.

12a. *Evaluate:* Consider the close evolutionary relationship between mice and humans and the experimental utility of the mouse as a model research organism. *Deduce and Solve:* The mouse (*Mus musculus*) is a widely used model organism for genetic analysis of mammalian development and physiology, specifically in relation to human disease, because many of these processes in mice and humans are evolutionarily conserved. The other advantage is that with mice, researchers can perform experimental manipulations that are not possible when studying humans or even nonhuman primates.

12b. *Evaluate:* Consider the differences between mice and humans. *Deduce:* Although the mouse (*Mus musculus*) is a mammal, there are many developmental, behavioral, and physiological differences between mice and humans. In addition, not every human gene has a homolog in the mouse genome. *Solve:* Therefore, in cases where the physiology or genetics of mice and humans differ, mutations in a mouse homolog to a human disease gene may not provide useful information on the human disease process.

14. 1 mutation per 322,182 gametes

16a. 2 births with retinoblastoma, 8 births with achondroplasia, and 22 births with neurofibromatosis

16b. Two reasons that could explain why the neurofibromatosis (NF1) mutation rate is higher than retinoblastoma (RB1) mutation rate are (1) the *NF1* gene is larger than *RB1*, and (2) a higher percentage of mutations within *NF1* affect NF1 function as compared to *RB1*.

18. *Evaluate:* This problem tests your knowledge of the function of the *E. coli RecA* gene. *Deduce and Solve:* The *RecA* gene is required for recombination repair of DNA damage. *E. coli* with a null mutation in *RecA* would lack *RecA* function and would be deficient in recombination repair. Recombination repair is used to fill in a single-stranded DNA gap created by the lack of replication of a region due to DNA damage (for example, a UV photoproduct). Several steps in recombination repair are catalyzed by *RecA*, including two-stranded invasion events and a single-stranded DNA cleavage event.

20. *Evaluate:* This problem tests your understanding of mutation and homologous recombination. *Deduce and Solve: Mutation* is defined as "a change in DNA sequence." Gene conversion resulting from recombination changes the DNA sequence of a chromosome; therefore, it fits within the definition of mutation. Recombination also combines chromosome sequences in new ways, creating new stretches of DNA sequence; therefore, recombination also is arguably a form of mutation. However, *mutation* is typically reserved to describe DNA sequence changes that are due to processes other than homologous recombination and gene conversion.

22. Yes; heteroduplex DNA is always created during homologous recombination.

24. *Evaluate:* Recall that gene conversion is rare and results in the conversion of the genotype of one gamete out of four during meiosis. *Deduce and Solve:* The four products of meiosis in multicellular eukaryotes are not identifiable as such and instead are pooled with the four products or with those of hundreds if not thousands of other meioses. Furthermore, these gametes are detected only by mating individuals and observing the phenotype of the resulting progeny. The high numbers of gametes produced and the random sampling of gametes during zygote formation make statistically significant identification of aberrant 3:1 segregation impossible.

34a. *Evaluate:* This problem tests your ability to analyze yeast mutant phenotypes. *Deduce and Solve:* Prototrophic yeast are able to grow on minimal medium, whereas auxotrophic yeast cannot. Yeast in colonies 4 and 5 grew on complete medium at 25°C but not on minimal medium at either temperature; therefore, colonies 4 and 5 correspond to auxotrophic yeast mutants. The remainder can grow on minimal medium at 25°C and therefore are prototrophic yeast.

34b. *Evaluate:* This problem tests your ability to analyze yeast mutant phenotypes. *Deduce and Solve:* The yeast in colonies 1 and 2 can grow on all media at 25°C but not on any of the media at 37°C. These yeast mutants are temperature sensitive for growth. The yeast in colony 5 cannot grow on minimal medium at either temperature but can grow on minimal plus adenine at both temperatures. This yeast mutant is an adenine auxotroph.

34c. *Evaluate:* This problem tests your ability to analyze yeast mutant phenotypes. *Deduce and Solve:* The yeast in colony 4 have two separate mutant phenotypes. This mutant cannot grow on complete medium at 37°C and therefore has a temperature-sensitive growth phenotype. This mutant also cannot grow on minimal medium at 25°C but can grow on minimal plus adenine at 25°C; therefore, it is also an adenine auxotroph. The fact that the yeast mutant corresponding to colony 4 has two different mutant phenotypes is an indication that this mutant carries two separate mutations, one affecting growth independently of adenine metabolism and a second affecting only adenine metabolism.

40a. The ascus shows 6:2 segregation of $brp^+ : brp^-$.

40b. *Evaluate:* This problem tests your understanding of the process of gene conversion and its relationship to recombination during meiosis. *Deduce and Solve:* The aberrant ratio of 6 brp^+ : 2 brp^- indicates that gene conversion in the brp locus occurred during the meiosis producing this ascus. Gene conversion is associated with recombination, which indicates that a recombination event was initiated in the region between *ala* and *cty* during this meiosis.

40c. *Evaluate:* This problem tests your understanding of the genotype of asci that show evidence of gene conversion. *Deduce and Solve:* Recombination is accompanied by formation of heteroduplex DNA between the two Holliday junctions that form. A region of the heteroduplex can contain mismatched base pairs if that region in the homolog is not identical. In this case, the heteroduplex included the region containing the sequence difference that distinguishes bry^- from bry^+ and therefore contained mismatched bases. These mismatches are repaired by mismatch repair, but the direction of the repair is not controlled, such that a homolog that should have bry^- could be repaired to contain bry^+ information. The heteroduplex occupies only a portion of the region undergoing recombination, which in this case did not include the *ala* or *cty* loci. Therefore, there was no gene conversion at *ala* or *cty*, and those alleles segregated normally—4:4.

Chapter 13

4. b. interstitial deletion; c. duplication; d. terminal deletion; e. trisomy; f. reciprocal balanced translocation; g. paracentric inversion; h. monosomy; i. polyploidy

6. Since *P* elements can cause mutations if they insert into genes, limiting their number reduces the likelihood of a new mutation.

8. Mutation of a single *IS1* sequence in *E. coli* will prevent insertion of transposable DNA into the element. Copies of *IS1* that are not mutated can undergo transposition.

10. Yellow-bodied females can be produced from this cross if nondisjunction in the female parent produces an egg with two X chromosomes and the egg is fertilized by a sperm containing the Y chromosome. The XXY zygote will develop as female and will be homozygous for the recessive yellow-body allele.

16c. Two PCR marker combinations are possible: 290, 310, 340; and 290, 340, 380.

16d. Four PCR marker combinations are possible: 290, 310; 290, 380; 310, 340; and 340, 380.

20. The human and orangutan chromosome have identical banding patterns along their entire lengths, and all four species have the same chromosome 5 banding pattern from band 5q14.1 to the q arm telomere. In comparison to human chromosome 5, the chimpanzee chromosome has undergone a pericentric inversion with breakpoints at approximately 5p13.2 and 5q13.3. The gorilla chromosome differs from the human chromosome from 5q13.3 to the telomere of 5p. It may have undergone a balanced translocation with another chromosome.

22. Mosaicism refers to the condition in which the body has cells with more than one karyotype. The range of phenotypic effects observed in these sex chromosome mosaics is dependent on the relative percentages of cells with each karyotype. Greater percentages of XO cells correspond to phenotypes that are more similar to those with Turner syndrome.

26. In this analysis, both recombination frequencies are much lower than expected: Recombination between *peach* and *oblate* is 2.1% instead of 17%, and recombination between *dwarf* and *peach* is 3.1% instead of 12%. This result is consistent with inversion of the chromosome region containing *peach* and the presence of heterozygosity for the inversion in the trihybrid line. Inversion heterozygosity is suppressing the appearance of most of the crossover chromosomes in this cross.

28a. 3.5 kb

28b. 7.0 kb

28c. The insertions of intron sequences into the *P* element and into the *copia* element are likely to disrupt gene expression from each element.

Chapter 14

2a. A DNA sequence that binds a regulatory protein, such as the *lac* operator sequence.

2b. A regulatory protein that binds DNA, such as the *lac* repressor protein.

2c. A compound that induces or activates transcription, such as lactose.

2d. A compound that interacts with another protein or compound to form an active repressor, such as the *trp* corepressor.

2e. A DNA sequence that binds RNA polymerase and regulates transcription, such as the *lac* promoter.

2f. A process of transcription regulation through which the binding of regulatory proteins to DNA activates transcription, such as the CAP binding site of the *lac* promoter.

2g. A process by which the stereochemistry of a protein is altered to change its interaction capabilities, such as the *lac* repressor protein.

2h. A process of transcriptional regulation through which binding of regulatory proteins to DNA blocks transcription, such as *lac* repressor protein binding to *lac O*.

2i. A mechanism of transcriptional regulation in which transcription level is modified (attenuated) to meet environmental requirements, such as *trp* operon attenuation.

4a. *Similarities:* Both have promoter and operator regulatory sequences. *Differences:* Inducible operons bind repressor protein to block transcription and may use positive control to help activate transcription. Inducible operons require an inducer substance to activate transcription. Repressible operons use a corepressor plus the pathway end product to repress transcription. Repressible operons often utilize attenuation.

4b. *Similarities:* Both types of regulatory systems utilize allostery in regulating transcription. *Differences:* The mechanism and consequences of allostery differ. In *lac* operon regulation, the repressor protein binds the operator, but allosteric change caused by allolactose prevents binding. In *trp* operon regulation, the corepressor protein cannot bind the operator until its allosteric shape is changed by binding to tryptophan.

4c. *Similarities:* Both types of operons contain multiple genes that share a single promoter and a single operator sequence. *Differences:* Repressible operons often use attenuation and contain a transcribed leader sequence that participates in determining structural gene transcription. This mechanism is not found in inducible operons.

6. Attenuation does not involve allosteric changes. Attenuation is the result of transcription of a leader sequence that undergoes translation. Coupling of transcription and translation dictates whether transcription continues past the leader sequence and into the structural genes.

8. The CAP binding site is part of the *lac* promoter and is located at approximately −60. It binds the CAP–cAMP complex and opens DNA slightly to allow efficient RNA polymerase binding at the *lac* promoter.

10. A *Cap⁻* mutation would alter the CAP binding site sequence and render it unrecognizable by CAP–cAMP. The required positive regulation of transcription would not occur, and *lac* operon transcription would be minimal. The strain would be *lac⁻*.

12. Transcription occurs under both conditions because allolactose, the inducer, is present. Transcription is higher in the absence of glucose because CAP-cAMP levels, which stimulate transcription, are higher.

14. Antisense RNAs are single-stranded RNAs that are complementary to a portion of specific mRNA transcripts. Bound to their mRNA targets, antisense RNAs can either block translation or lead to the destruction of mRNA. Blocking translation prevents the production of proteins that might initiate unnecessary or harmful actions.

16a. Blocks all transcription

16b. Produces constitutive transcription

16c. Blocks all transcription (this is an I^S mutation)

16d. Produces constitutive transcription (this is an I^- mutation)

16e. Only minimal transcription will occur.

18. See table.

Genotype	β-Galactosidase		Permease		Phenotype
	No		No		
	Lactose	Lactose	Lactose	Lactose	
Example: $I^+ P^+ O^+ Z^+ Y^+$	+	−	+	−	lac^+
a. $I^S P^+ O^+ Z^+ Y^+ / I^- P^+ O^+ Z^+ Y^+$	−	−	−	−	lac^-
b. $I^- P^+ O^+ Z^- Y^+ / I^+ P^+ O^C Z^+ Y^-$	+	+	+	−	lac^+
c. $I^+ P^+ O^+ Z^- Y^+ / I^+ P^- O^+ Z^+ Y^-$	−	−	+	−	lac^-
d. $I^- P^+ O^C Z^+ Y^+ / I^+ P^- O^+ Z^+ Y^+$	+	+	+	+	lac^+
e. $I^+ P^+ O^C Z^+ Y^- / I^+ P^+ O^+ Z^+ Y^-$	+	+	−	−	lac^-
f. $I^+ P^+ O^+ Z^- Y^+ / I^S P^+ O^+ Z^+ Y^-$	−	−	−	−	lac^-
g. $I^S P^+ O^+ Z^- Y^+ / I^+ P^+ O^C Z^+ Y^-$	+	+	−	−	lac^-

20a. $I^- P^+ O^+ Z^- Y^+ / I^+ P^+ O^+ Z^+ Y^+$ will have inducible transcription of both genes. $I^+ P^+ O^C Z^- Y^+ / I^+ P^+ O^+ Z^+ Y^+$ will have constitutive transcription of $lacY$ and inducible transcription of $lacZ$. $cap^+ I^+ P^- O^+ Z^+ Y^+ / I^+ P^+ O^+ Z^+ Y^+$ will have inducible transcription of both genes. $cap^- I^S P^+ O^+ Z^+ Y^+ / I^+ P^+ O^+ Z^+ Y^+$ will be noninducible.

20b. The first three partial diploids will be able to grow on a lactose medium, but the final partial diploid ($I^S P^+ O^+ Z^+ Y^+ / I^+ P^+ O^+ Z^+ Y^+$) will not.

22a. No; permease is not produced.

22b. Transcription of $lacZ$ is inducible from the $cap^+ I^- P^+ O^+ Z^+ Y^-$ chromosome. Only minimal transcription occurs from the other chromosome, so permease is noninducible.

22c. The $lacI$ gene has its own promoter and is not affected by lac operon regulation of gene mutations. The cap^- mutation minimizes transcription, but repressor protein produced from this chromosome is trans-active and binds O^+ on the other chromosome to induce $lacZ$ expression.

24. Gene Z is the enzyme, gene W is the repressor, and G is the operator.

26a. This would prevent the lac repressor from binding to the operator, which would cause constitutive transcription of the lac operon.

26b. This would prevent the repressor from binding to O_{R1}, allow cro binding to O_{R3} and O_{R2}, prevent transcription of P_{RM}, allow transcription of P_R, promoting the lytic life cycle.

26c. This would prevent cro from binding to O_{R3}, allow repressor binding to O_{R2} and O_{R1}, prevent transcription of P_R, allow transcription of P_{RM}, promoting the lysogenic life cycle.

28a. The mutant is incapable of establishing lysogeny. Lytic gene transcription from the O_R sites cannot be repressed.

28b. The mutant is incapable of establishing lysogeny.

28c. The mutant will be unable to carry out lysis. No transcription activation occurs from O_L or O_R.

28d. The mutant will be unable to establish lysogeny. The mutant cannot undertake site-specific recombination to integrate the lysogen.

28e. The mutant will be unable to carry out lysis due to the cro mutation, and it will be unable to establish lysogeny due to the cII mutation.

28f. The mutant will be unable to carry out lysogeny. The expression of the late gene that takes place through the antiterminator activity of N at t_L, t_{R1}, and t_{R2} will not occur.

30a. The same band in both lanes

30b. No band in lane 1; band in lane 2

30c. No band in either lane

30d. The same band in both lanes

30e. No band in lane 1 and a band in lane 2

30f. No band in either lane

32. See table.

Genotype	LacZ mRNA Synthesis	Lac Phenotype
a. $I^- P^+ O^+ Z^+ Y^+ / I^+ P^+ O^+ Z^+ Y^+$	inducible	lac^+
b. $I^+ P^+ O^C Z^+ Y^+ / I^+ P^+ O^+ Z^- Y^+$	constitutive	lac^+
c. $I^S P^+ O^+ Z^+ Y^+ / I^+ P^+ O^+ Z^+ Y^+$	uninducible	lac^-
d. $I^+ P^+ O^+ Z^- Y^+ / I^+ P^- O^+ Z^+ Y^+$	uninducible	lac^-
e. $I^+ P^+ O^+ Z^+ Y^- / I^+ P^+ O^+ Z^+ Y^-$	uninducible	lac^-

Chapter 15

2a. UAS elements are found in the yeast genome, where they operate as enhancer-like regulatory sequences. Gal4 protein binds yeast UAS elements to activate transcription of galactose utilization genes.

2b. Insulator sequences shield genes from enhancer effects. The mechanism of action may be through the formation of specific DNA loops that protect particular genes from enhancers.

2c. Silencer sequences prevent transcription of particular genes. The mechanism of action may be through competitive protein binding at silencer sequences that overlap with enhancer sequences. The yeast Mig1 and Tup1 proteins bind a silencer sequence during glycolysis to prevent transcription of galactose utilization genes.

2d. The protein complexes that assemble at enhancers to facilitate transcription are known as enhanceosomes. The enhanceosome complex known as Mediator assembles at yeast enhancers. It contacts promoter-bound proteins to activate transcription.

2e. RNA interference describes the posttranscriptional regulation of mRNAs by regulatory RNA molecules. RNAi is a prominent feature of the regulation of gene expression in most eukaryotic genomes.

4. Acetylation occurs when acetyl groups are added to amino acids of the histone protein by acetylase enzymes. These acetylation events are most often associated with transcription activation, though there are many exceptions.

6. mRNAs are transcribed from DNA and carry the information to be translated into protein. rRNAs provide both scaffold and enzymatic activities to ribosomes. tRNAs binds an amino acid at their 3′ ends and recognize codons in mRNA via their anticodons, thus translating nucleic acid sequence information into protein sequence information. miRNAs and siRNAs act to regulate gene expression via RISC, either to slice or inhibit translation of mRNA targets, or to facilitate recruitment of chromatin modifying enzymes to chromosomal loci. Some lncRNAs act as scaffolds to bring chromatin regulatory proteins to chromosomal loci.

8. Several factors can be cited, including the following: (1) the presence of a nucleus in eukaryotic cells, (2) the chromatin structure of eukaryotic genomes, (3) multicellularity that is frequent in eukaryotes, and (4) differential gene expression among different types of eukaryotic cells.

10. Heterochromatin regions will decondense for DNA replication during the S phase of the cell cycle to allow replisome access.

12. Chromatin is classified into euchromatin and heterochromatin based on the chemical modifications on the histone proteins. Euchromatin is characterized by H3K9-acetylation and is transcriptionally active. Heterochromatin is transcriptioanlly inactive and may be either constitutive, in which case it is marked with H3K9-methylation, or facultative, in which case it is marked with H3K27 methylation.

Facultative heteraochromatin can be converted to euchromatin, and vice versa, by chromatin modification.

14. One potential role of lncRNAs in gene regulation is to act as scaffolds to recruit chromatin modifying emzymes to the chromatin. An example is Xist, which acts to recruit the polycomb complex to the X chromosome that is destined to be inactivated.

16a. The enhancer is most likely in the region at the left-hand side that is present in mutant E and mutant F.

16b. The promoter region is most likely in the region at the right-hand side that is present in mutant E and mutant F.

16c. Mutant E likely contains all or most of the enhancer and promoter sequences, but DNA between the sequences is missing. This leads to difficulty forming the correct DNA loop and appears to interfere with efficient transcription initiation. In contrast, mutant F contains additional DNA sequence, particularly between the enhancer and the promoter. Its higher level of transcription indicates greater efficiency in transcription initiation.

18a. Mutant A has an enhancer mutation. This deletion is located well upstream of the start of transcription and substantially reduces transcription.

18b. Mutant B affects a silencer sequence. This deletion results in a substantial increase in the level of transcription.

18c. Both mutants C and D are promoter mutations. Their location immediately upstream of the transcription start and the reduced levels of transcription from these mutants are consistent with promoter mutations.

20a. Enhancer and silencer sequences are each detected in this analysis. The enhancer sequence is located in the deleted region that is common to mutant E and mutant F. The silencer sequence is located in the deletion region unique to mutant E.

20b. The deletion in mutant D deletes the *ME1* promoter sequence.

20c. It seems likely that regulation of *ME1* is developmentally controlled by the combined activity of an enhancer and a promoter that activate transcription and a silencer sequence that represses transcription at particular times during development.

Chapter 16

2. Difference suggests posttranscriptional regulation. One possibility is that the protein is stable in only one cell type and is rapidly degraded in other cell types. Another possibility is that the mRNA is translated in only one cell type.

4. *E. coli*: 4.64×10^6 bp / 100 minutes = 4.64×10^4 bp / minute

Arabidopsis: 130×10^6 bp / 600 cM = 2.17×10^5 bp / cM

Saccharomyces: 12×10^6 bp / 4500 cM = 2.67×10^3 bp / cM

C. elegans: 100×10^6 bp / 300 cM = 3.33×10^5 bp / cM

Drosophila: 180×10^6 bp / 275 cM = 6.55×10^5 bp / cM

Danio rerio: 2000×10^6 bp / 3000 cM = 6.67×10^5 bp / cM

Mus: 3000×10^6 bp / 1400 cM = 2.14×10^6 bp / cM

Homo female: 3000×10^6 bp / 4460 cM = 6.73×10^6 bp / cM

Homo male: 3000×10^6 bp / 2590 cM = 1.16×10^6 bp / cM

Homo average: 3000×10^6 bp / 4460 cM = 8.51×10^6 bp / cM

There will always be a balance between increasing the size of the mapping population and thereby having a more accurate map position and identifying the physical DNA spanning flanking mapped markers. In organisms with a large number of base pairs per cM, it is often worthwhile to increase the number of individuals in a mapping population and thereby decrease the number of base pairs of DNA potentially encoding the locus of interest.

6. While PCR or northern blotting approaches can give some perspective on expression patterns, observing them in situ provides more information. For this, either a transcriptional or translational fusion to a reporter gene (e.g., *lacZ* or *GFP*) would be best. The difficulty may be in initially identifying the sequences responsible for proper expression of the gene. These experiments are judged by the following standards: (1) How well does the observed expression pattern of the marker line match with all other data on expression patterns? and (2) Can a translational fusion gene complement a loss-of-function mutant phenotype?

8a. In yeast, I would create loss-of-function alleles by homologous recombination gene replacement.

8b. I would create a translational fusion with a reporter gene (e.g., *GFP*), preferably with all endogenous regulatory sequences.

10. If the transposon supplies additional regulatory elements, insertion of the transposon adjacent to a gene may result in ectopic or overexpression of the adjacent gene, resulting in a dominant gain-of-function allele. Alternatively, if the transposon is inserted into the coding region of a gene, it will result in a loss-of-function allele.

12. Since meiosis is not required for viability, a genetic screen searching for mutants that fail to undergo meiosis properly would work. However, the ability to cross the mutant for complementation tests would be useful, and thus a screen for conditional mutants would be desirable. Since chemical mutagenesis induces the broadest spectrum of alleles, it would be a better choice of mutagen than insertion of deletion alleles, which are often null. Finally, the simplest genetic system in which meiosis occurs would be the best system to examine this question. *S. cereviseae*, where many genetic tools are available, would be a good choice.

14. Because you have no a priori information on the nature of the gene product, homology-based techniques are not applicable. Positional cloning would work and requires only a mutant phenotype to go from map position to gene. Since the genome of *Drosophila* has been sequenced, one could take a sequence-based approach as outlind in Figure 16.12. Transposon tagging would work by starting with an organism heterozygous for a mutation in one of the genes and mobilizing the *P* element. Since identifying the mutants is the most time consuming, the sequence-based approach is the better choice.

16a. The smaller 4.5-kb cDNA could be sequenced using a primer walking technique. For the 250-kb BAC clone, fragmentation and shotgun sequencing would be a good approach.

16b. I would focus on sequencing cDNA clones from the patients in order to identify both exonic and intron–exon boundary mutations. But this approach would not identify mutations in regulatory elements that are in non-transcribed regions.

18a. Since *Arabidopsis* is a flowering plant, the female gametophyte (egg) is retained on the female parent, on the placenta. Female gametogenesis can be directly observed within the ovules. Mutations resulting in female gametophytic mutations (e.g., lethality) can be observed as a 1:1 ratio.

18b. Since the male gametophyte (pollen) is produced in excess and is not retained on the plant, to observe male gametophytic mutations, I would observe the developing pollen directly.

20a. Screen for mutants in which the pupae either eclose at a time other than dawn or eclose at random times during the day/night. While this phenotype might be detrimental in nature, in the laboratory it is likely to be completely viable.

20b. Screen for mutations in which the expression of genes encoding photosynthetic machinery is no longer synchronized with the circadian rhythm. Again, while this phenotype in nature would be detrimental, in the laboratory it is likely to be viable, though a change in the color of the plants (e.g., lighter green) might be observed.

20c. Positional cloning or since the genomes of these organisms have been sequenced, a sequence-based method (i.e., Fig. 16.12).

Chapter 17

2a. *Sau*3A, 1.17×10^7; *Bam*HI, 7.32×10^5; *Eco*RI, 7.32×10^5; *Not*I, 4.58×10^4

2b. *Sau*3A, 1.08×10^7; *Bam*HI, 4.32×10^5; *Eco*RI, 9.72×10^5; *Not*I, 7.68×10^3

4a. The genomic libraries

4b. The two genomic libraries should completely overlap. The cDNA libraries should be a subset of the genomic libraries. The two cDNA libraries should only partially overlap.

6. A 16 base-pair (bp) sequence is predicted to occur randomly once in 4.3×10^9 bp; thus, oligonucleotides should be of at least this length to have a reasonable probability of being unique in the genome.

8. The principles are identical for both species, but the techniques differ because homologous recombination occurs frequently in yeast and rarely in mice. Thus, positive–negative selection techniques are required in mice, while only positive selection is required in yeast.

10. Gene therapy often targets blood diseases because blood circulates throughout the body. Thus, replacement of mutant bone marrow cells with corrected ones allows the defect to be corrected throughout the body.

12. Both methods use "naturally" occurring biological entities. In plants, the Ti-plasmid is reengineered to have the gene of interest and then is reintroduced into *Agrobacterium*, which naturally transfers the T-DNA into the genome at random locations of plant cells. In *Drosophila*, the *P* element is reengineered to have the gene of interest and then injected into embryos, where it integrates into the genome at random locations.

14. Most recombinant DNA manipulations involving combining of DNA fragments of less than 10 kb, including changing specific base pairs in a known sequence, can be accomplished by synthesis. However, for instances where the exact sequence of the DNA in question is not known, standard recombinant DNA techniques will continue to be needed.

16. The sticky ends can be religated since the single strand overhangs can anneal, but neither enzyme can cut the resulting sequence following ligation.

18. Based on the restriction enzyme digests, the following map can be drawn:

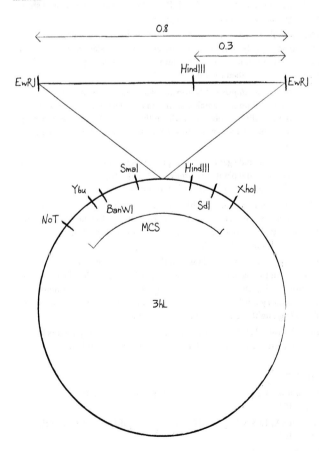

20. Based on the restriction enzyme digests, the following map can be drawn:

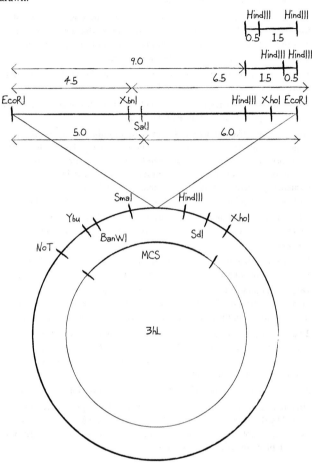

A *Xho*I + *Hin*dIII double digest would enable the two small *Hin*dIII fragments to be ordered with respect the remainder of the restriction sites.

22a. Loss-of-function alleles in *S. cerevisiae* can be produced by homologous recombination (see also Figure 17.5). Gain-of-function alleles, such as those that produce the gene product constitutively, can be constructed by making a gene fusion combining a promoter that drives transcription constitutively in *S. cerevisiae* with the coding region of the gene of interest (see also Figures 17.14 and 17.17).

22b. Since homologous recombination is not routine in tomato, loss-of-function alleles can be created by using RNAi-mediated mechanisms. In this case, a promoter that drives transcription constitutively can be transcriptionally fused with a sequence containing an inverted repeat, such that the mRNA produced can form a stem–loop including double-stranded RNA (see also Figure 17.18). The chimeric gene can be introduced into tomato using *Agrobacterium* (see also Figures 17.6 and 17.7). Gain of function alleles would be produced in a similar manner as described for *S. cerevisiae*, except the regulatory sequences need to be suited to tomato and the transgenic organisms produced by *Argobacterium*-mediated transformation.

24. There are two possible approaches: (1) Mutagenize the bacterial strain and screen for mutants that can no longer metabolize crude oil. Then clone the corresponding gene(s) using a complementation assay, as outlined in Chapter 16. (2) Alternatively, clone the gene(s) by transferring large genomic clones from the strain of interest into a related *Pseudomonas* strain that cannot metabolize crude oil. This approach often works in bacteria with specialized traits since the gene conferring the trait is often found within a single operon.

26a. There are two possible approaches: (1) perform in situ hybridization using probes made from each of the two genes or (2) construct translational or transcriptional fusion genes with a reporter gene (*LacZ*, *GFP*) via homologous recombination methods. Translational fusions may retain their functionality as long as the marker gene fusion does not disrupt function of the protein of interest. If in a gene replacement, transcriptional fusions would result in a loss-of-function allele, but if in a recessive gene, transcription fusions would still provide information about gene expression in a phenotypically wild-type mouse.

26b. Use homologous recombination techniques to replace the coding region of the gene with a selectable marker. Alternatively, you can use an RNAi-based approach to create a loss-of-function phenotype. The former approach has the advantage of heritability.

26c. Create loss-of-function alleles via homologous recombination for each of the genes and examine the mutant phenotypes. Cross the two single mutants to create an F_1 population, interbreed the F_1s to produce an F_2, and identify a double-mutant strain and examine its phenotype. If the double-mutant strain exhibits phenotypic defects beyond what is expected by the addition of the single-mutant phenotypes, then the two genes have redundant functions. Alternatively, you can use an RNAi-based approach to create a loss-of-function phenotype, but again, this approach is not heritable.

28. Because the original sequence (highlighted) was from reverse translation of the protein sequence, in nucleotide positions where there is degeneracy in potential sequences, these may differ from the actual sequence encoded in the genome.

30. The mutant sequence can be created using site-directed mutagenesis. These clones could be used to create wild-type and mutant protein to be studied in vitro. To study in vivo consequences, it would be best to introduce the mutant version of the gene into its endogenous chromosomal location. Unlike the creation of loss-of-function alleles, where a selectable marker replaces the endogenous gene, the creation of gain-of-function mutations is slightly more complicated. One solution is to create the point mutation in the genome via homologous recombination and then remove the selectable marker using a Cre-lox-based system. However, care must be taken not to leave a "footprint" of non-endogenous sequences in any coding or regulatory sequences.

Chapter 18

2a. Repetitive DNA can often be assembled in many different ways, making unambiguous assembly difficult. On a finer scale, repetitive DNA can also lead to polymerase slippage causing sequence errors.

2b. Dispersed, repetitive DNA that is longer than a single sequencing read and is found at many locations in the genome is particularly problematic.

2c. Paired-end sequencing is one approach to identify unique sequences flanking repetitive DNA.

4. cDNA sequences provide information on which genomic sequences are transcribed and processed into mature mRNAs. Different forms of full-length cDNAs from the same region of genomic DNA can indicate alternative splicing.

6. In eukaryotic genomes, one must account for the possible presence of introns; in prokaryotic genomes, open reading frames should be contiguous. Predictive algorithms must also take into account differences in promoter and enhancer elements/consensus sequences.

8. *Bioinformatic Method:* Use an algorithm to search for potential open-reading frames within the sequence. This method is only predictive and not very accurate, so experimental data are needed to confirm accuracy.

Comparative Method: BLAST the sequence against the database of known sequences. If sequences are conserved, they are likely to be functional. This method also needs experimental verification.

Experimental Method: Use the sequence as a probe against a cDNA library or other technique (e.g., microarray, rtPCR) to determine which sequences are transcribed. This is the best method, but it is also much more time- and labor-intensive than the others.

10. Human proteins are closer to fungal proteins than to plant proteins; plant proteins are equidistant from either human or fungal proteins.

12. Expression microarrays represent all the sequences of a genome that are transcribed, whereas tiling arrays represent all of the sequences in a genome. Expression or tiling microarrays can be used to obtain information on which sequences are transcribed in a specific tissue or cell type; tiling arrays can be used to identify binding sites of DNA binding proteins and to assay recombination events between polymorphic strains. For most applications, high-throughput sequencing can provide the same type of information that arrays can. The former provides more quantitative information and information on alternative splicing than the latter. At present, the cost for high-throughput sequencing is higher than for arrays, but this may change in the future.

14. This DNA sequence is the synthetic version (the nucleotide sequence inferred from reverse translation of the protein sequence) of the human insulin gene.

16a. All three genes are orthologs.

16b. *AY1* and *AY2* are paralogs; *AY1* and *BY* are orthologs; *BY* and *CY* are orthologs.

16c. *AZ1* and *AZ2* are paralogs; *BZ1* and *BZ2* are paralogs; *BZ2* and *BZ3* are paralogs; *BZ1* and *BZ3* are paralogs; *CZ1* and *CZ2* are paralogs; *AZ1* and *AZ2* are orthologous to *BZ1*, *BZ2*, and *BZ3*; *AZ1* and *AZ2* are orthologous to *CZ1* and *CZ2*; *CZ1* is orthologous to *BZ1* and *BZ2*; *CZ2* is orthologous to *BZ3*.

18. While large-scale chromosomal rearrangements appear to have been rare in primate evolution during mammalian evolution, small-scale rearrangements appear to be common and frequent.

20. Segmental duplications, resulting in large-scale gene duplication, can often lead to genetic redundancy, especially if the duplication is evolutionarily recent. Using reverse genetics (see Chapter 17), loss-of-function alleles can be created in the duplicate genes. Due to potential genetic redundancy, double mutants of the two paralogs might have to be constructed to observe an aberrant mutant phenotype.

22a. Any of these approaches are possible: (1) create a loss-of-function allele by gene replacement and examine for mutant phenotype, (2) create a gain-of-function allele by constitutive expression of the gene and examine for mutant phenotype, (3) create a reporter gene fusion allele by gene replacement to examine where and when in the cell the protein is expressed, (4) perform a synthetic enhancer screen in the loss-of-function background, (5) perform a two-hybrid screen to identify interacting proteins, (6) perform transcriptome analysis to examine the expression pattern of the gene.

22b. In a human genome, the possibilities are much more limited: only (5) and (6) from the answer to question 22a would work.

24. The first step is to organize the data to identify genes that behave similarly and those that behave differently. For example *a, c, d, e, f, g, i, j, k, n, q,* and *r* all increase in expression with both high salt and high temperature; *b, p,* and *s* all decrease in expression with both high salt and high temperature; *h* and *o* decrease in response to salt but increase in response to high temperature; *l* and *m* increase in response to salt but decrease in response to high temperature. This analysis provides information into possible roles of genes that may be involved in a general stress response versus genes that may have specific roles in response to salt or temperature stress.

28. The *PEG10* gene is likely derived form the insertion of a retrotransposon, and its protein-coding sequences have been co-opted to perform a role in placenta formation. Retrotransposons contain a gene encoding reverse transcriptase, a nucleic-acid-binding protein that could be co-opted to have a role in binding and regulating endogenous nucleic acid sequences. The presence of the gene in placental mammals only suggests that the insertion of the retrotransposon occurred in the common ancestor of therian mammals, after the divergence of the monotremes from the rest of the mammals.

Chapter 19

2. Their membrane system, chromosomal organization, replication, transcription, and translation (ribosome structure) are all similar to those in bacteria.

4. Sequencing of eukaryotic genomes has revealed evidence of transfers that are recent and transfers that are ancient. Transferred sequences that are highly similar must have been transferred recently.

6. See Table 19.1 for variations in the genetic code in mitochondria. A consequence of tRNA gene number reductions and the change in the code minimizes errors such that the two closely related codons, UGA and UGG, are both Trp.

8. There are three steps in this process: (1) Transfer of organelle DNA from organelle to nucleus and integration into the nuclear genome. (2) Acquisition of nuclear transcriptional regulatory elements such that the organellar gene is transcribed in the nucleus. Translational regulatory elements are similar (except where there are changes in the genetic code or RNA editing, both of which might inhibit production of a functional protein). (3) For the protein to be targeted back to the organelle, protein sequences facilitating efficient subcellular targeting need to be acquired from adjacent genomic sequences.

10. Transcription and/or translational and/or posttranslational regulation of the multiple components of the complexes need to be coordinated such that appropriate stoichiometries of the subunits are produced.

12. The most appropriate advice would be the following: for III-1, none of your progeny will be afflicted; for III-2, all of your progeny will be afflicted, and the extent may vary between individuals depending on levels of homo- and heteroplasy; for III-3, all of your progeny will be afflicted, though the extent may vary between individuals depending on levels of homo- and heteroplasy.

14. Maternal inheritance

16. *pet1* is a segregational (nuclear) mutation; *pet2* is a neutral mutation. The expected progeny is 2 wild type : 2 *petite*.

18. Since inheritance of this syndrome is maternal and not paternal, there is no need to worry, but if the mother exhibits symptoms, then there is a probability that their children would be affected. The extent to which their children will
be affected depends on whether the mother is homoplasmic (all offspring would be affected) or heteroplasmic (possibility that some might not be affected).

20. Sibling II-2's children will be afflicted, but II-5's children will not be afflicted because MERRF is maternally, not paternally, inherited.

22. Maternal inheritance is the most likely, but it is penetrant only in males.

24. mtDNA is found in many copies per cell, and the probability of being preserved is higher than it is for nuclear DNA. It is also highly useful for elucidating evolutionary relationships.

26. If there was no interbreeding, all coyote sequences would be more closely related to each other than to wolf sequences; this is not the case, so there must have been interbreeding.

28. Examine the genome of the sea slug and search for genes that are closely related to nuclear genes of the algae. If they are present in the nuclear genome of the sea slug, horizontal gene transfer can be assumed to have occurred. Use sequencing to confirm that these genes are not present in relatives of the sea slug.

Chapter 20

2. The neural crest cells differentiate autonomously with the identity of the species from which they are derived. However, they can recruit host cells to contribute to the beak, suggesting that the neural crest cells non-autonomously influence the developmental fate of neighboring host cells.

4a. In a syncytium proteins are free to diffuse, so mechanisms whereby factors are restricted by membranes are not functional.

4b. Gradients of morphogens such as *bicoid* and *nanos* either must not exist or the gradients must be established in another manner, such as cell–cell communication.

6. Segments correspond to the clear morphological and anatomical divisions in the larva or adult organism. Parasegments are offset from the segments, spanning the posterior part of one segment and the anterior part of its neighbor, and correspond to domains of gene expression. Developmental biologists consider parasegments as the subdivisions that are produced during fly development because they correspond to the domains of gene expression that control pattern formation and identity in the organism.

8. *Similarities:* Both segmentation in *Drosophila* and floral organ whorls in *Arabidopsis* are serially repeated structures/segments with identities controlled by related sets of transcription factors that act combinatorially and exhibit cross-regulation. ***Differences:*** In *Drosophila* the genes are *Hox* genes and are encoded in complexes in the genome, whereas in *Arabidopsis* the genes are *MADS*-box genes that are dispersed throughout the genome.

10a. In a loss-of-function mutant, the phenotype is vulva-less.

10b. In a gain-of-function mutant, the phenotype is multi-vulval.

12a. This phenomenon can occur only when cells are totipotent. Once cells are only pluripotent, the identities of possible differentiation pathways are limited and may not be able to form a complete organism.

12b. The resulting individual will be a genetic mosaic, consisting of two distinct genotypes. This probably happens more than is acknowledged, but it is detected only when multiple parts of an individual are genotyped.

14. Extra copies of *Bicoid* would increase the amount of *bicoid* mRNA that the mother puts into her eggs, thus increasing the amount of *bicoid* protein. This would result in a posterior shift in threshold levels of *bicoid* required to activate downstream targets; hunchback expression would be increased; other gap genes and pair-rule genes are also likely to be affected, with a general shift of anterior gene expression patterns (and subsequent fates) to more posterior positions—shifting the other gap gene expression patterns to more posterior positions.

16a. Pair-rule genes might be expected to influence the expression of the segment polarity genes, which act at a later time in development.

16b. The *fushi tarazu* single mutant likely has a loss of the even-numbered parasegments (*fushi tarazu* is Japanese, meaning "too few segments"), and the engrailed single mutant likely has defects in the anterior part of each parasegment. Thus, one might predict that the double mutant would be a combination of these two single-mutant phenotypes.

18. This pattern could be established by lateral inhibition.

20a. Gain-of-function alleles in *let-23* and *let-60* would result in a vulva being produced in the *lin-3* loss-of-function background.

20b. Loss-of-function alleles of *let-60* would suppress the gain-of-function *let-23* multi-vulva phenotype and result in a vulva-less worm.

22a. The consequence of ectopically expressing *Hoxd10* throughout the developing mouse limb bud would be that the "thumb" would acquire an "index finger" identity; for *Hoxd11*, the "index finger" would acquire a "middle finger" identity, and the "thumb" would have an altered identity promoted by *Hoxd9* + *Hoxd11* (but it is not clear what it might look like, since that combination is not found in any wild-type digit). For *Hoxd10* and *Hoxd11*, both the "thumb" and "index finger" would acquire a "middle finger" identity.

22b. To construct this model, you need to create a conditional allele. One approach would be to introduce *lox* sites flanking the *Hoxd9–13* cluster of genes via homologous recombination (see Chapter 17). The intervening DNA including the genes could then be excised by induction of the Cre recombinase protein, which could be controlled either by regulatory elements driving expression in the limb bud or perhaps by a heat shock.

24. *tra-1* and *tra-2* mutant alleles are epistatic to the *her-1* mutant allele, while the putative gain-of-function *tra-1* allele (*her-2*) is epistatic to recessive loss-of-function alleles of *tra-1* and *tra-2*. Since the wild-type allele of *tra-1* acts as a repressor of male development and the wild-type allele of *her-1* acts as a repressor of hermaphrodite development, the activities of the genes in a wild-type animal can be summarized as follows:

genotype	her-1	tra-2	tra-1	phenotype
XX	off	on	on	hermaphrodite
XO	on	off	off	male

Based on the observation that *tra-1* is epistatic to *her-1*, *tra-1* should be downstream of *her-1*. In addition, assuming that *her-2* is a gain-of-function allele of *tra-1* and is epistatic to *tra-2*, this places *tra-1* downstream of *tra-2*. Thus, a model for the control of sex determination can be constructed.

In one model, the X:A ratio influences the activity of a repressor, *her-1*, which represses *tra-2*, which in turn activates *tra-1*, which then promotes hermaphrodite (female) fate and represses male development:

X:A ratio	---] her-1	---] tra-2	→ tra-1	or	→
high (XX/AA)	low	high	high	→	hermaphrodite development
low (XO/AA)	high	low	low	→	male development

26a. In an otherwise wild-type background, the phenotypic effects of *agamous* mutations are confined to the third and fourth whorls, but in an *apetala2* mutant background, phenotypic effects of *agamous* mutations are also seen in the first and second whorls. This implies that in an *apetala2* mutant background, *AGAMOUS* is ectopically expressed in the first and second whorls, and the converse is true for the phenotypic effects of *apetela2* mutations.

26b. Yes; cross-regulatory interactions occur among *Hox* genes in animals. Posteriorly expressed *Hox* genes often repress the expression of *Hox* genes normally expressed in respective anterior positions. This is a common, though not universal, feature in the regulation of *Hox* genes.

28. Based on the phylogeny of eukaryotes (see Figure 18.11), the last common ancestor of Basidiomycota and animals (or plants) was likely a single-celled organism. Thus, as in the comparison of multicellular development of plants and animals, Basidiomycota are likely to utilize a unique set of genes to direct their development. While the genes might be expected to encode transcription factors and signaling molecules, they are not likely to be homologous to those directing development in plants and animals. Thus, a forward genetic screen to identify pattern formation mutants in mushrooms would likely be a more successful approach than any reverse genetic screens.

Chapter 21

2. Traits 1a through 1d are likely to be multifactorial. Dietary nutrition and temperature are two environmental conditions likely to influence each trait.

4. $V_E = 2.25$, $V_G = 5.40 - 2.25 = 3.15$.

6. The mean is 165.75, $s^2 = 1137.22/11 = 103.38$, and $s = 10.17$.

8a. $A_1A_1B_1B_1C_1C_1 = 36$ cm and $A_2A_2B_2B_2C_2C_2 = 18$ cm.

8b. 27 cm

8c. 24 cm

8d. Any genotype with five "1" alleles and one "2" allele yields $[(5)(6 \text{ cm})] + (3 \text{ cm}) = 33$ cm.

8e. There are $(3)^3 = 27$ possible genotypes.

8f. Seven different phenotypes are possible.

10a. $V_E = 3.5$ and $V_G = 7.4 - 3.5 = 3.9$.

10b. $H^2 = 3.9/7.4 = 0.527$.

12. $H^2 = 34.48/38.10 = 0.905$.

14a. For the cross involving 12-gram tomatoes, $S = -4$ g; for the cross involving 24-gram tomatoes, $S = 8$ g.

14b. For the cross involving 12-gram tomatoes, $R = (-4)(0.8) = -3.2$ g; for the cross involving 24-gram tomatoes, $R = (8)(0.8) = 6.4$ g.

16. Blood type is known (see Chapter 4) to be the result of three alleles of a single gene, and the MZ results confirm the exclusive genetic determination of blood type. Chicken pox is an infectious disease, and there is no reason to suspect gene-dependent differences in infection as the equal concordance values indicate. For the five other conditions, MZ concordance is considerably higher than DZ concordance, suggesting that genes have a pronounced effect on the appearance of the conditions.

18. QTL analysis screens a large number of SNP and other DNA sequence variants and plots the results on the phenotype of interest, running speed in this case. Any DNA markers associated with faster running speed could potentially indicate the nearby location of a gene (quantitative trait locus) influencing running speed.

22a. For protein content, $S = 22.7 - 20.2 = 2.5\%$; for butterfat content, $S = 7.4 - 6.5 = 0.9\%$.

22b. Response to selection will be greater for protein content $[(2.5)(0.60) = 1.5\%]$ than for butterfat content $[(0.9)(0.80) = 0.72\%]$.

24a. 100%. Blood type is controlled by genotype alone, and MZ twins are genetically identical.

24b. 50%. Blood types A ($I^A i$) and B ($I^B i$) are both expected, with a probability of 1/2. The chance that DZ twins will have the same blood group is 1/4 for blood type A plus 1/4 for blood type B, or 1/2. It is also possible that since DZ twins are the result of independent fertilization events, one twin could be blood type A and the other blood type B.

Chapter 22

2. Inbreeding is a genome-wide phenomenon that increases homozygosity and reduces heterozygosity. It does not change allele frequencies; rather, it nonrandomly distributes alleles into genotypes. Inbreeding can increase the probability that inbred organisms might be homozygous for a rare recessive allele.

4. Natural selection conferring the highest relative fitness on particular heterozygous organisms will eliminate the two alleles when they occur in homozygous genotypes. Equilibrium allele frequencies are established as a ratio of the selection coefficients operating against the alleles.

6. Among a very small number of population samples, each outcome contributes a large percentage to the total; in much larger samples, each individual outcome contributes a much smaller percentage to the total.

8. A genetic bottleneck substantially reduces the number of organisms in a population. Elimination and survival are random. Some alleles may be lost, and others may survive at much different frequencies than were present before the bottleneck. The overall result is less genetic diversity after the bottleneck. As populations increase in size after a bottleneck, they display a reduced level of genetic variability in comparison to diversity before the bottleneck.

10a. $\sqrt{0.28} = 0.53$.

10b. $1 - 0.53 = 0.47$.

10c. Using $p = 0.47$ for the dominant allele T and $q = 0.53$ for the recessive allele t, $TT = (0.47)^2 = 0.22$, $Tt = 2(0.47)(0.53) = 0.50$, and $tt = (0.53)^2 = 0.28$.

12. Mutation can generate new antibiotic-resistant alleles that confer improved survival on bacteria carrying the mutant alleles that are exposed to an antibiotic.

14. Evolutionary processes, including directional selection, require inherited variability for their operation. In the absence of inherited variation, there is just a single allele of a gene, and selection has no alternative alleles on which to exert selective pressure.

16. Inbreeding may be reduced by carefully managing matings to ensure that the level of relationship is minimized to the extent possible when matings take place.

18. The expected frequencies of rabbits are black $(C_1C_1) = (0.70)^2 = 0.49$, tan $(C_1C_2) = 2(0.70)(0.30) = 0.42$, and white $(C_2C_2) = (0.30)^2 = 0.09$.

20. In this problem, $s = 1 - 0.82 = 0.18$, and $t = 1 - 0.32 = 0.68$. The estimated equilibrium frequencies are $\beta^A = t/s + t = 0.68/0.86 = 0.791$ and $\beta^S = s/s + t = 0.18/0.86 = 0.209$.

22a. A genetic bottleneck is a substantial population reduction that eliminates population members at random.

22b. Since the loss of population members is random in a genetic bottleneck, the overall level of genetic diversity is reduced; certain alleles are eliminated and other alleles retained at frequencies that are higher or lower than before the bottleneck. In Ashkenazi populations, repeated bottlenecks followed by population growth generated a founder effect that brought alleles such as the recessive for Tay-Sachs disease to high frequency.

22c. In this population, the recessive allele frequency, $f(t)$, is $\sqrt{0.00133} = 0.0365$.

22d. The dominant allele frequency is $f(T) = 1 - 0.0365 = 0.9635$, and the carrier frequency is $2(0.9635)(0.0365) = 0.070$, or about 7 per 1000 people.

26a. Following one generation of natural selection, the relative genotype frequencies are $C_1C_1 = 0.421$, $C_1C_2 = 0.526$, and $C_2C_2 = 0.032$. The approximate allele frequencies are $C_1 = 0.421 + (0.5)(0.526) = 0.684$, and $C_2 = 0.053 + (0.5)(0.526) = 0.316$.

26b. Following reproduction of the survivors of predation, the genotype frequencies are $C_1C_1 = (0.684)^2 = 0.468$, $C_1C_2 = 2(0.684)(0.316) = 0.432$, and $C_2C_2 = (0.316)^2 = 0.010$.

26c. The equilibrium allele frequencies are predicted to be $C_1 = 0.2/0.6 + 0.2 = 0.25$, and $C_2 = 0.6/0.6 + 0.2 = 0.75$.

28. Assuming $f(I^A) = p$, $f(I^B) = q$, and $f(i) = r$, the frequency of

$$r = \sqrt{\frac{336}{1000}} = 0.579, \text{ the frequency of } p \text{ is } \sqrt{0.421 + 0.336} - 0.579$$

$= 0.290$, and the frequency of q is $1 - (0.579 + 0.290) = 0.131$.

30a. For dimpling, the genotype frequencies are estimated to be $DD = (0.62)^2 = 0.3844$, $Dd = 2(0.62)(0.38) = 0.4712$, and $dd = (0.38)^2 = 0.1444$. For PTC tasting ability, the genotype frequencies are estimated to be $TT = (0.76)^2 = 0.5776$, $Tt = 2(0.76)(0.24) = 0.3648$, and $tt = (0.24)^2 = 0.0576$.

30b. The expected phenotypes are dimpled taster $(D\_T\_) = (0.8556)$ $(0.9424) = 0.8063$; dimpled nontaster $(D\_tt) = (0.8556)(0.0576) = 0.0493$; undimpled taster $(ddT\_) = (0.1444)(0.9424) = 0.1361$; undimpled nontaster $(ddtt) = (0.1444)(0.0576) = 0.0083$.

32a. For *D3S1358*, the frequency of 16/18 heterozygotes is estimated to be $2(0.229)(9.162) = 0.0742$. For *VWA*, the estimated frequency of 14/18 heterozygotes is $2(0.131)(0.189) = 0.0495$. For *FGA*, the estimated frequency of 23/26 heterozygotes is $2(0.131)(0.018) = 0.0047$.

32b. Each heterozygous genotype of a CODIS gene is estimated by an expression similar to that used to determine the heterozygous class for a gene with two alleles (i.e., $2pq$). Homozygous genotypes are estimated as the square of the allele frequency (i.e., p^2). The joint probability for multiple genotype of independently assorting CODIS genes is estimated using the product rule.

34a. Individuals V-1, V-2, and V-3 are inbred.

34b. Common ancestors are I-1 and I-2.

34c. $F = 4(1/2)^8 = 0.015625$.

38. The recessive allele producing achromatopsia was present in the original (pre-typhoon) Pingelapese population, though the original allele frequency is unknown. The typhoon produced a genetic bottleneck that produced a frequency of approximately 1 copy in 40 alleles, or $q = 0.025$ for the recessive allele. Subsequent repopulation of the island was affected by genetic drift and inbreeding that may have acted to increase the frequency of the allele (genetic drift) and to increase the likelihood of individuals who are homozygous IBD (inbreeding).

Glossary

2-micron plasmid A naturally occurring *Saccharomyces cerevisae* plasmid (circumference = 20 μm) that has been engineered to work as a vector in yeast.

3′ polyadenylation (3′ poly-A tailing) During eukaryotic pre-mRNA processing, an enzyme-driven modification that removes the 3′ end of the pre-mRNA and adds numerous adenines.

3′ splice site In eukaryotic pre-mRNA processing, the location of cleavage at the 3′ end of an intron. Contains an AG dinucleotide in a consensus sequence.

3′ to 5′ exonuclease activity DNA- and RNA-digesting activity that progresses in the 3′ to 5′ direction to remove nucleotides. See also *DNA proofreading*.

3′ untranslated region (3′ UTR) The untranslated segment of mRNA between the stop codon and the 3′ end of the transcript.

5′ capping In eukaryotic pre-mRNA processing, the addition of 7-methylguanosine to the nucleotide at the 5′ end of pre-mRNA by a triphosphate bridge. Methylation of adjacent nucleotides may also occur.

5′ splice site In mRNA processing, the location of cleavage at the 5′ end of an intron. Contains a GU dinucleotide in a consensus sequence.

5′ to 3′ exonuclease activity DNA- or RNA-digesting activity that progresses in the 5′ to 3′ direction to remove nucleotides.

5′ to 3′ polymerase activity DNA synthesizing activity of DNA polymerases that progresses in the 5′ to 3′ direction to add new nucleotides to a growing DNA strand. Requires a template strand.

5′ untranslated region (5′ UTR) The untranslated segment of mRNA between the 5′ end of the transcript and the start codon.

6-4 photoproduct A DNA lesion and potential mutagenic event caused by exposure to ultraviolet (UV) irradiation.

−10 consensus sequence See *Pribnow box*.

10-nm fiber The "beads-on-a-string" form of chromatin, in which DNA is wrapped around nucleosomes.

30-nm fiber A structure of chromatin in which histone 1 (H1) partially condenses chromatin fibers into a coiled form. Also known as *solenoid* or *solenoid structure*.

30S initiation complex In bacterial translation, the complex formed by a small ribosomal subunit, mRNA, and the tRNA carrying fMet.

−35 consensus sequence A specific consensus sequence of the bacterial promoter at which RNA polymerase is bound.

70S initiation complex The fully assembled bacterial ribosome that is prepared to initiate translation.

300-nm fiber A structural state of chromatin in which chromatin fibers are looped and condensed.

α-globin gene and protein A gene belonging to a family of closely related genes that encode a globin polypeptide that is part of hemoglobin.

α-helix (alpha helix) A form of secondary protein structure in which segments of proteins form helical structures that are held together by hydrogen bonds.

α-proteobacteria Lineage of bacteria that are the closest extant relatives of the lineage that gave rise to mitochondria.

β^A allele The common (wild-type) allele of the human β-globin gene.

β-globin gene and protein A gene belonging to a family of closely related genes that encode a globin polypeptide that is part of hemoglobin.

B-pleated sheet (beta-pleated sheet) A form of secondary protein structure in which segments of proteins form n parallel arrays that are held together by hydrogen bonds.

β^S allele A specific mutant allele of the human β-globin gene that produces sickle cell disease in homozygous individuals.

θ (theta) structure In bacterial DNA replication, the name given to an intermediate structure of DNA replication of a circular molecule with a single origin of bidirectional replication.

θ (theta) value A variable indicating a recombination distance between genes. Used in lod score analysis.

aberrant ratio In fungi, a ratio of haploid spore genotypes within a single ascus indicating gene conversion.

acentric fragment (acentric chromosome) A chromosome fragment without a centromere.

acrocentric chromosome A eukaryotic chromosome in which the centromere is very near one end. Forms a chromosome with long and short arms of distinctly different lengths.

activator (*Ac*) element In transposition, a transposable genetic element containing a transposase gene.

activator binding site DNA sequence to which an activator protein binds to regulate gene expression. Term refers to regulatory sites in bacteria; in eukaryotes, the equivalent sequence would be called an enhancer element.

activator protein A transcription factor that binds to regulatory sequences associated with a gene and upregulates that gene's expression.

addition rule See *sum rule*.

additive genes Genes contributing to a polygenic trait and producing their effect by their cumulative contributions that are approximately equal for each gene.

additive variance (V_A) For quantitative traits, the component of genetic variance contributed by genes having an additive effect on phenotypic variance.

adenine (A) One of four nitrogenous nucleotide bases in DNA and RNA; one of the two types of purine nucleotides in DNA and RNA.

adjacent-1 segregation A pattern of chromosome segregation that can occur following reciprocal balanced translocation. Leads to gametes carrying gene duplications and deletions.

admixed population A population whose members are a blend of formerly distinct populations.

agarose An inert material derived from agar that is mixed with buffer and used to form gels for gel electrophoresis.

allele An alternative form of a gene.

allele-counting method A method for determining allele frequency in a sample by tabulating the number of alleles of each type.

allelic phase Describing the cis and trans arrangements of alleles of linked genes on homologous copies of a chromosome pair.

allelic series A group of alleles of a gene that display a hierarchy of dominance relationship among them.

allolactose A modified from of lactose that binds to the lac repressor protein, inducing an allosteric change that reduces the DNA binding ability of the complex.

allopatric speciation The development of new species in geographic isolation.

allopolyploidy A polyploidy organism arising through the union of chromosome sets from different species.

allosteric domain Domain of a protein that allows the protein to change shape when it binds to a specific molecule; the protein in the new shape is altered in its ability to bind to a second molecule (e.g., DNA). Also known as *allostery*.

allosteric effector compound Molecule that binds to the allosteric protein domain and subsequently induces a change in the bound protein.

allostery Reversible interactions of a small molecule with a protein that lead to changes in the shape of the protein and to a change in the interaction of the protein with a third molecule.

alternate segregation A pattern of chromosome segregation that can occur following reciprocal balanced translocation that leads to the production of viable gametes.

alternative pre-mRNA processing (alternative intron splicing, promoter, polyadenylation) In eukaryotic pre-mRNA processing, alternative processes by which different mRNAs can be produced from the same gene using different promoters or polyadenylation sites or by removal of different exon elements.

alternative sigma (σ) subunit Different forms of the sigma subunit of bacterial RNA polymerase that induce distinct conformational changes to the RNA polymerase core and to the recognition of distinct promoters.

Ames test A laboratory method commonly used to determine whether a compound or one of its breakdown products is mutagenic.

amino acid An aminocarboxylic acid that is a component of a polypeptide or protein.

aminoacyl site (A site) The site on a ribosome at which incoming charged tRNAs match their anticodon sequence with mRNA codons.

aminoacyl-tRNA synthetase (tRNA synthetase) A group of enzymes whose specific functions are to identify particular tRNAs and catalyze the attachment of the appropriate amino acid at the 3′ terminus.

amorphic mutation See *null mutation*.

anagenesis Phylogenetic evolution of a new species from an ancestral species without branching.

anaphase The phase of mitosis during which sister chromatids separate (*anaphase A*) and move to opposite poles (*anaphase B*).

aneuploid An uneven number of chromosomes. Usually the result of the gain or loss of a chromosome—that is, $2n + 1$ (trisomy) or $2n - 1$ (monosomy).

annotation (gene annotation, genome annotation) The process of attaching biological functions to DNA sequences. Genome annotation is the process of identifying the location of genes and other functional sequences within the genome sequence; gene annotation defines the biochemical, cellular, and biological function of each gene product the genome encodes.

Antennapedia complex One of two homeotic gene clusters in *Drosophila* consisting of five genes (*labial, Deformed, Sex combs reduced, proboscipedia,* and *Antennapedia*) that act in combination to specify the cephalic and thoracic parasegments.

antibiotic resistance An inherited trait of a microbe that permits it to grow in the presence of a compound that kills or prevents the growth of antibiotic-sensitive microbes.

anticodon The nucleotide triplet sequence of transfer RNA that pairs with an mRNA codon sequence in translation.

antiparallel Opposite 5′ and 3′ orientations of two complementary nucleic acid strands.

antisense RNA An RNA molecule that is complementary to a portion of a specific mRNA.

antitermination stem loop (antiterminator) A stem loop that allows RNA polymerase to continue transcription through the leader region of bacterial attenuator controlled operons and into the structural genes of an operon (e.g., the 2-3 stem loop in trp operon regulation).

apurinic (AP) site The location of a nucleotide that has lost its purine base.

arabinose (*ara*) operon An inducible operon consisting of genes encoding enzymes allowing the use of arabinose as a carbon source. The operon is controlled by a single regulatory protein, which carries out both positive and negative transcriptional regulation.

Archaea One of the three domains of life; separate from Bacteria and Eukarya.

archaeal initiation factor (aIF) The transcription initiation proteins found in archaeal cells.

Argonaute Protein subunit of RISC (RNA-induced silencing complex) that binds small RNA molecules and provides either the catalytic "slicer" activity or the translational repressor activity.

artificial cross-fertilization A controlled cross between plants made by an investigator who transfers pollen from one plant to fertilize the other plant.

ascus The spore sac formed by fungi containing four (tetrad) or eight (octad) haploid spores. Also called spores.

asexual polyploidization Chromosome duplication that is the product of nondisjunction in mitotic cell division.

aster The structure forming during cell division that contains microtubules emanating from centrosomes.

attachment site (att site) Identical or nearly identical sequences on the bacterial and bacteriophage chromosomes that are cut and used to integrate or to excise the bacteriophage chromosome from the bacterial chromosome.

attenuation A gene regulatory mechanism that fine-tunes transcription to match the momentary requirements of the cell, achieving a more or less steady state of compound availability.

attenuator region A regulatory region downstream of the promoter of repressible amino acid operons that exerts transcriptional control (in the form of *transcription termination*) based on the translation of a leader peptide, the efficiency of which is determined by the availability of specific amino acids.

autopolyploidy A pattern of polyploidy produced by the duplication of chromosomes from a single genome.

autoradiograph A photographic image obtained by exposure of X-ray film to the radioactive decay of isotopes attached to molecular probes. Used in the analysis of *gel electrophoresis*.

autosomal dominant inheritance A pattern of hereditary transmission in which the dominant allele of an autosomal gene results in the appearance of the dominant phenotype.

autosomal inheritance Hereditary transmission of genes carried on autosomes.

autosomal recessive inheritance A pattern of hereditary transmission in which the recessive allele of an autosomal gene results in the appearance of the recessive phenotype.

auxotroph A microbe with one or more mutations that prevents its growth on a minimal medium.

Bacteria One of the three domains of life; separate from Archaea and Eukarya.

bacterial artificial chromosome (BAC) Cloning vector used in bacteria that utilizes the F plasmid origin of replication; can accept DNA inserts up to 500 kb.

bacterial chromosome The main, usually singular, chromosome encoding the genome of a bacterium.

bacteriophage (phage) A virus whose host is a bacterium.

balanced polymorphism A genetic polymorphism maintained in a population because organisms with the heterozygous genotype have higher relative fitness than do organisms with either of the homozygous genotypes.

balancer chromosome A chromosome with inversions used to maintain specific allele combinations (e.g., recessive lethal alleles) in genetic stocks.

balancing selection The form of natural selection that operates in favor a heterozygous genotype and leads to stable equilibrium frequencies of the alleles in a population.

band (in electrophoresis gel) A region in an electrophoresis gel or in an autoradiograph where a protein of nucleic acid congregates. Usually visualized using a stain or molecular probe.

barcode Short DNA sequences that identify specific strains in knockout libraries.

Barr body The darkly staining inactive X chromosome visible in mammalian female nuclei. The result of random X inactivation.

basal transcription The very low level of transcription characteristic of a bacterial promoter that requires an inducer to initiate transcription.

base excision repair DNA repair that excises a damaged nucleotide base and then replaces the entire nucleotide.

base-pair substitution mutation A DNA sequence change resulting in the substitution of one base pair for another.

base stacking A phenomenon of DNA base-pair interaction that rotates the base pairs around a central axis of symmetry and imparts twisting to the double helix.

basic local alignment search tool (BLAST) A computer program designed to search for homologous sequences in databases.

bidirectional DNA replication The standard method of DNA replication that synthesizes new DNA in both directions from a replication origin.

binomial probability A probability function using two coefficients, *a* and *b*, whose sum equals 1 and whose products predict the probability of events.

bioinformatics The use of computational approaches to decipher DNA-sequence information.

biparental inheritance Condition in organellar inheritance where both parental gametes make contributions of cytoplasmic organelles to the zygote; contributions are often unequal because one gamete contributes more of the cytoplasm and the other gamete makes a smaller contribution.

bithorax **complex** One of two homeotic gene clusters in *Drosophila* consisting of three genes (*Ultrabithorax*, *abdominal-A*, and *Abdominal-B*) that act in combination to specify the thoracic and abdominal parasegments.

blending theory of heredity An obsolete theory of heredity proposing that the traits of offspring are the average of parental traits.

blotting (in gel electrophoresis) The process of transferring proteins or nucleic acids from an electrophoresis gel to a permanent membrane or filter.

blunt end 5′ or 3′ ends of double-stranded DNA lacking any single-stranded overhangs.

branch point adenine In intron splicing, an adenine nucleotide near the 3′ splice site of an intron that joins with a guanine located at the 5′ splice site by a 2′-to-5′ phosphodiester bond to form a lariat intron.

BRCA1-associated genome surveillance complex (BASC) A multiprotein complex that surveys the genome for mutations at the G_1- to S-phase cell cycle checkpoint.

broad sense heritability (H²) The proportion of total phenotypic variance that is contributed by total genetic variance.

bulky adduct Large chemical groups added to nucleotides by alkylating agents.

bypass polymerase A group of DNA polymerases that are unstable and synthesize short regions of DNA under conditions in which the main DNA polymerase is unable to function,

such as when faced with DNA lesions that block replication. Also called translesion DNA polymerase.

CAAT box A common consensus sequence component of eukaryotic promoters.

CAP (catabolite activator protein) In bacterial transcription regulation, binds cAMP (cyclic AMP) at low glucose concentrations to positively regulate the transcription of operons that allow the use of alternative carbon sources.

CAP binding site A bacterial DNA regulatory sequence to which the CAP–cAMP complex binds to positively regulate gene expression. See also *CAP–cAMP complex.*

CAP–cAMP complex Formed by joining catabolite activator protein to cAMP, the complex binds to the CAP binding site of the bacterial *lac* promoter to regulate gene expression.

capsid The protein coat of a viral particle.

catabolite repression Situation where the presence of the preferred catabolite (e.g., glucose) represses the transcription of genes for an alternative catabolite (e.g., lactose).

Cdk (cyclin-dependent kinases) A group of multimeric proteins whose levels fluctuate during the cell cycle. Composed of cyclin proteins and protein kinases, Cdks control entry and progression through mitosis.

cell cycle Consisting of interphase (*G_1 phase, S phase*, and *G_2 phase*) and *M phase* (mitosis or meiosis) in cells. The transition from one phase to the next is controlled by protein-based interactions.

cellular blastoderm Stage of *Drosophila* embryogenesis in which the nuclei are located at the periphery of the embryo and are enclosed by cell membranes.

central dogma of biology The description of the functional relationship between DNA, RNA and proteins (DNA to RNA to protein).

centromere A specialized DNA sequence on eukaryotic chromosomes that is the site of kinetochore protein and microtubule binding.

centrosome A cytoplasmic region, containing a pair of centrioles in many eukaryotic species, from which the growth of microtubules forms the spindle apparatus during cell division.

character displacement The pattern of natural selection in which one phenotypic character in a population is displaced by another form of the character confers greater relative fitness.

chaperone A category of eukaryotic proteins that assist with the folding or movement of other polypeptides. A protein that acts as a chaperone is often referred to as a chaperonin.

Chargaff's rule The observation that the percentage of adenine equals that of thymine and that guanine percentage equals cytosine percentage in DNA.

charged tRNA A tRNA to which the correct amino acid has been attached.

chiasma (plural: chiasmata) Points of contact between homologous chromosomes that are coincident with crossover locations between the homologs.

chimeric gene A gene sequence composed of sequences from two or more sources.

chi-square test (χ² test) A statistical test to compare the observed results of an experiment with the results predicted by chance.

chloroplast An organelle, bounded by a double membrane, where photosynthetic reactions convert light energy and CO_2 into fixed organic carbon.

chromatin The complex of nucleic acids and proteins that compose eukaryotic chromosomes.

chromatin modifier Proteins that chemically modify histone proteins in the nucleosomes by adding or removing specific chemical groups, thereby modifying chromatin structure and regulating gene expression.

chromatin remodeler Proteins that reposition nucleosomes within chromatin in such a way as to open or close promoters and other regulatory sequences or that change the composition of nucleosomes, altering their biological activity (e.g., SWI/SNF, ISWI, SWR1).

chromatin remodeling Processes that modify the structure or composition of chromatin. Usually associated with alterations of nucleosome binding to DNA and affecting the regulation of gene transcription.

chromatography A technique for separating the components of a molecular mixture by their similarities and differences.

chromosome A structure composed of DNA and associated proteins that in total contain the genome of an organism.

chromosome aberration An abnormality of chromosome number or structure.

chromosome arm [long arm (q arm), short arm (p arm)] The segments of eukaryotic chromosomes between the centromere and the telomeres.

chromosome banding A group of laboratory methods that stain eukaryotic chromosomes to reveal distinctive patterns of light and dark bands. Chromosome banding by Giemsa staining produced standardized patterns for different chromosome of selected species. Also known as *Giemsa (G) banding.*

chromosome break point The location of a chromosome break.

chromosome fusion See *Robertsonian translocation.*

chromosome inversion (paracentric, pericentric) A structural alteration of a chromosome in which a segment breaks away from the chromosome and subsequently reattaches after 180° rotation. See also *inversion heterozygote.*

chromosome scaffold Composed of numerous nonhistone proteins, the superstructure of eukaryotic chromosomes.

chromosome territory The region within a nucleus occupied by a particular chromosome during interphase.

chromosome theory of heredity The theory developed in the early 20th century that genes are carried on chromosomes and that the meiotic behavior of chromosomes is the physical basis of Mendel's laws.

chromosome translocation The relocation of a chromosome or chromosome segment to a non-homologous chromosome.

chromosome walking See *positional cloning.*

cis-acting Acting on the same chromosome (e.g., DNA sequences that control expression of genes encoded on the same piece of DNA).

cis-acting regulatory sequence Sequences to which proteins bind to regulate transcription of genes located on the same chromosome as the sequences.

cis-dominant The principle that the operator can influence only the transcription of adjacent downstream genes.

clade In phylogenetics, a group of organisms defined by characteristics that are unique to the group and distinguish the group from others.

cladistics The classification of organisms by characteristics that are unique to the group and distinguish it from other groups. Involves branching of new species from ancestral species. See also *clade.*

cladogenesis Phylogenetic evolution by branching of descendant species from ancestral species.

clamp loader A multiprotein complex that pairs with DNA polymerase and the sliding clamp during replication.

clone-by-clone sequencing An approach to genome sequencing where each chromosome is first broken into overlapping clones that are then arranged in linear order to produce a physical map of the genome. Each clone in the map is then sequenced separately. Contrast with *whole-genome shotgun (WGS) sequencing.*

cloning vector A piece of DNA derived from a plasmid, virus, or other biological source that can be stably maintained in an organism and into which heterologous pieces of DNA can be inserted.

closed chromatin Chromatin in which regulatory DNA is covered by nucleosomes, thus restricting the access of regulatory proteins to the sequences rendering genes in closed chromatin transcriptionally silent.

closed promoter complex The initial stage of transcription that forms when RNA polymerase loosely binds the promoter.

coding region The region of a gene that encodes the gene product.

coding strand (nontemplate strand) The nontemplate strand of DNA that has the same 5′-to-3′ polarity as its transcript and the same sequence, except for T in DNA and U in RNA.

codominance The equal and detectable expression of both alleles in a heterozygous organism.

codon The nucleotide triplet of mRNA that encodes a single amino acid.

codon bias The preferential use of specific codons where there is redundancy in encoding a specific amino acid.

coefficient of coincidence (c) The ratio of the observed number of double recombinants to the number of double recombinants expected to occur by chance.

coefficient of inbreeding (F) The probability that two alleles carried in an individual are homozygous identical by descent (IBD).

cohesive compatible end Short, single-stranded overhangs at 5′ and 3′ ends produced after digestion with certain restriction ends. The cohesive ends are termed compatible if they can base-pair with complementary single-stranded ends of another DNA molecule. Compare with *cohesive end sequence (cos) sites.*

cohesive end sequence (cos) site The single-stranded ends of phage lambda that facilitate circularization or concatamerization of lambda phage genomes and that interact with coat proteins during packaging of phage particles. Compare with *cohesive compatible ends.*

cointegrate In replicative transposition, the fusion of two circular transposable elements into a single, larger circular element.

comparative genomics See *evolutionary genomics.*

compensatory mutation A second mutation occurring at another site that fully or partially restores wild-type function lost when an initial mutation occurs.

complementary base pairs The specific pattern of purine-pyrimidine pairing of nucleic acid strands. In DNA, G with C and A with T; RNA uses U instead of T.

complementary DNA (cDNA) library Collection of DNA clones, originally derived via reverse transcription of mRNA molecules into DNA (cDNA) and cloned into a vector.

complementary gene interaction (9:7 ratio) A characteristic ratio of phenotypes produced by the interaction of two complementary genes that control a trait.

complementation group A group of mutations that affect the same gene.

complete genetic linkage The absence of crossing over between linked genes.

complete initiation complex The multisubunit complex that forms at the promoter immediately before the onset of transcription.

complete penetrance The observation that the phenotype for a trait is always produced when the corresponding genotype(s) are present (in contrast, see *incomplete penetrance*).

composite transposon In bacteria, a transposable element containing multiple genes located between terminal insertion sequences.

concordance In twin studies, the observation that both twins exhibit the trait.

conditional probability A probability prediction that is dependent on another previous event having taken place.

conjugation The short-term union of two bacterial cells for the unidirectional transfer of DNA from the "donor" to the "recipient." The transferred material may be plasmid DNA or donor bacterial chromosome DNA.

conjugation pilus The hollow filament extending from the donor bacterium to the recipient bacterium through which DNA is transferred. Also known as *conjugation tube.*

conjugation tube See *conjugation pilus.*

consanguineous mating See *inbreeding.*

consensus sequence A nucleotide sequence in a DNA segment derived by comparing sequences of similar segments from other genes or organisms. The most commonly occurring nucleotides at each position comprise the sequence.

conservative DNA replication A disproven model of DNA replication positing that one duplex produced by replication contained the two original strands and the other two daughter strands.

conserved noncoding sequence (CNS) Sequences that do not code for amino acids and are conserved across significant phylogenetic distances.

constitutive heterochromatin Chromosome regions containing chromatin that is always densely compacted. Usually containing highly repetitive DNA sequences.

constitutive mutants Mutants in which a gene is always expressed rather than being under regulatory control.

constitutive transcription State in which a gene is continuously transcribed.

contiguous sequence (contig) Overlapping DNA clones that together cover an uninterrupted continuous stretch of DNA sequence.

continuous variation In polygenic and multifactorial traits, the observation of phenotypic distribution over a continuous range.

controlled genetic cross Genetic crosses controlled by an investigator who usually knows the genotypes and/or phenotypes of the organisms being crossed.

convergent evolution Processes of independent evolution of similar structures in unrelated species. Also known as *homoplasmy.*

co-option A common theme in the evolutionary history of genes by which genes and genetic modules are reused in a new manner to direct the patterning or growth of novel organs.

coordinate gene Genes, often with maternal effects, that establish the major axes of the embryo, especially the anterior-posterior and dorsal-ventral axes; examples include *bicoid* and *nanos*.

copy number variant (CNV) A specific type of structural variant due to insertions or deletions (indels) greater than 1 kb in length.

core DNA The approximately 146 base pairs of eukaryotic DNA that wrap each nucleosome.

core element Consensus sequences in the active regions of promoters recognized by RNA polymerase I.

corepressor An accessory molecule required for a repressor protein to exert its function.

cosmid vector Cloning vector used in bacteria that utilizes phage lambda *cos* sites for packaging of phage and a bacterial origin of replication for subsequent maintenance in bacteria; can accept DNA inserts of up to 40 kb.

cosuppression The silencing, via a small RNA mediated mechanism, of an endogenous gene due to the presence of a homologous transgene or virus. Cosuppression can occur at the transcriptional or post-transcriptional level.

cotransduction The simultaneous transduction of two or more genes contained on a donor DNA fragment into a recipient cell, where it undergoes homologous recombination to be spliced into the transductant chromosome.

cotransduction frequency The frequency with which two genes are transduced.

cotransduction mapping A method of mapping donor bacterial genes based on their frequency of cotransduction.

cotransformation Simultaneous transformation of two or more genes carried on a donor DNA fragment into a recipient.

covered promoter Promoter in which nucleosomes are found adjacent to the transcription start site, preventing efficient transcription initiation. This feature is common at highly regulated genes.

CpG dinucleotide See *CpG island*.

CpG island Region in which the frequency of CpG dinucleotides is higher than the average for the genome; commonly found near the transcription start sites of animal genes. The cytosines are often methylated when the gene is inactive and demethylated when the gene is transcriptionally active.

crossing over The breakage and reunion of homologous chromosomes that results in reciprocal recombination.

crossover suppression The significant reduction, or complete absence, of progeny with recombinant chromosomes due to duplications and deletions of genetic material following crossing over within the inversion loop in organisms that are heterozygous for an inversion.

cryptic splice site A 5' or 3' splice site that is not normally used except when a mutation either inactivates an authentic splice site or creates a new splice site at the cryptic site location. See also *splicing mutation*.

cyanobacteria Lineage of photosynthetic bacteria that are the closest extant relatives of the lineage that gave rise to the plastids.

cyclin protein A family of proteins whose levels fluctuate during the cell cycle. Cyclins pair with protein kinases to form cyclin-dependent kinases (Cdks) that help regulate the cell cycle.

cytokinesis Part of telophase, the process of cytoplasmic division between daughter cells.

cytological markers Structural differences between homologous chromosomes that serve to differentiate the chromosomes when they are visualized using microscopy.

cytosine (C) One of four nitrogenous nucleotide bases in DNA and RNA; one of the two types of pyrimidine nucleotides in DNA and RNA.

daughter cell The genetically identical cells produced by mitotic cell division.

daughter strand A newly synthesized strand of DNA that is complementary to a template strand.

deamination A DNA lesion resulting in the loss of an amino group (NH_2) from a nucleotide base.

degrees of freedom (*df*) The number of independent variables in an experiment. In a chi-square test, most often the number of outcome class minus 1 $(n - 1)$.

delayed age of onset The appearance of an abnormal phenotype that is not present at birth but appears later in life and is caused by an inherited mutation.

delayed early genes A group of genes in λ (lambda) bacteriophage that are expressed following expression of the early genes that initiate the lytic cycle.

deletion The loss of genetic material. See also *interstitial, microdeletion, partial deletion, partial deletion heterozygote,* and *terminal deletion.*

deletion mapping A method for mapping genes utilizing partial chromosome deletions with known locations to expose recessive mutants by pseudodominance.

denaturation In DNA, the separation of complementary strands of nucleic acids by hydrogen bond breakage. In polypeptides and proteins, the unfolding of tertiary or quaternary structures.

densitometry A technique for passing light through an electrophoresis gel to detect the presence of a stained band of protein or nucleic acid.

deoxynucleotide 5'-monophosphate (dNMP) Monophosphate forms of deoxynucleotides.

deoxynucleotide 5'-triphosphate (dNTP) Triphosphate forms of deoxynucleotides.

deoxyribonucleic acid (DNA) The hereditary molecule of organisms. Composed of two complementary strands of nucleotides with purine bases adenine (A) and guanine (G) and pyrimidine bases thymine (T) and cytosine (C).

depurination A DNA lesion occurring when a deoxyribose molecule loses its purine nucleotide base. See *apurinic (AP) site.*

dicentric bridge In a dicentric chromosome, the portion between the two centromeres that are drawn to opposite poles of the cell during division.

dicentric chromosome A chromosome with two centromeres.

dicer Ribonuclease that acts on double-stranded RNA responsible for the generation of small regulatory RNA molecules, such as microRNAs and small interfering RNAs; typically 21–30 nucleotides in length.

dideoxy DNA sequencing A method of DNA sequencing devised by Fred Sanger that uses a mixture of deoxynucleotide and dideoxynucleotide triphosphates to selectively block DNA replication, producing a ladder of partially synthesized DNA strands of different lengths. Also known as the *Sanger method.*

dideoxynucleotide triphosphate (ddNTP) Rare DNA nucleotides absent oxygen molecules at the 2' and the 3' carbons that are most commonly used in dideoxynucleotide DNA sequencing.

differential reproduction See *relative fitness (w).*

differentiation Process by which cells become restricted in their developmental potential and take on specialized morphologies and physiological activities.

dihybrid cross A cross between organisms that are heterozygous for two loci.

diploid number The characteristic number of chromosomes (*2n*) in somatic cell nuclei during the diploid phase of the eukaryotic life cycle. Equal to twice the haploid (*n*) number of chromosomes found in the nuclei of gametes of sexually reproducing diploid species.

directed assembly A precess for the assembly of viral particles that is directed by non-capsid proteins.

directional cloning Technique whereby a DNA insert is cloned with a specific directionality with respect to sequences of the cloning vector; usually accomplished by using two different restriction enzymes.

directional natural selection See *directional selection.*

directional selection Natural or artificial selection that continuously changes the frequency of an allele in a direction toward fixation (frequency = 1.0) or toward elimination (frequency = 0.0).

discontinuous variation A phenotype distribution containing discrete or separable categories.

discordance In twin studies, the observation that the traits exhibited by the twins are different.

disjunction The normal process separation of homologous chromosomes or of sister chromatids during cell division.

dispersive DNA replication A disproven model of DNA replication positing that each strand of daughter duplexes is composed of segments of original DNA and segments of newly synthesized DNA.

displacement loop (D loop) During DNA damage repair and homologous recombination, the displacement of a single strand of DNA by strand invasion.

disruptive selection Natural or artificial selection of phenotypic extremes in a population, leading eventually to two strains with distinctive phenotypes.

dissociation (*Ds*) element In transposition, a non-autonomous genetic element that is incapable of transposing on its own.

DNA-binding protein A general term for a protein that binds to DNA; the interaction can be either DNA-sequence specific (most regulatory proteins) or DNA-sequence nonspecific (e.g., structural proteins such as histones).

DNA clone A fragment of DNA that is inserted into a vector, such as a plasmid, cosmid, or artificial chromosome.

DNA double helix (DNA duplex) The two complementary strands of DNA arranged in antiparallel orientation.

DNA gyrase (topoisomerase II) A member of the class of DNA replication enzymes known as topoisomerases that assist with the unwinding of supercoiled DNA.

DNA intercalating agents Mutagenic compounds of a size and shape that allow them to access to the space between nucleotide base pairs, thereby distorting the DNA duplex and potentially causing insertion or deletion mutations.

DNA library Collection of DNA clones in which the DNA is usually derived from a single source.

DNA ligase An enzyme active in DNA replication that joins together segments of a DNA strand by catalyzing formation of a phosphodiester bond.

DNA loop In gene regulation, a condition where the DNA sequences between regulatory elements form an extended loop that allows distant regulatory sequences with associated DNA-binding proteins to interact.

DNA microarray Collections of synthesized DNA fragments attached to a solid support and representing sequences present in a genome; can be used to assess transcription patterns,

transcription factor binding sites, and recombination patterns, among other uses.

DNA nucleotides DNA building blocks composed of deoxyribose sugar, a nitrogenous base, and one or more phosphate groups. See also *adenine (A)*, *thymine (T)*, *cytosine (C)*, and *guanine (G)*.

DNA polymerase (pol I, pol II, pol III) The large multisubunit complex responsible for the synthesis of new strands of DNA during DNA replication or DNA repair.

DNA proofreading The capacity of many types of DNA polymerase to utilize a 3′ to 5′ exonuclease activity to remove and replace mismatched or damaged nucleotides during replication. See also *3′ to 5′ exonuclease activity*.

DNA replication The synthesis of new DNA strands by complementary base pairing of nucleotides in a daughter strand to those in a template strand.

DNA supercoiling (negative supercoiling, positive supercoiling) Superhelical twisting of DNA causing overwinding (positively supercoiled) or underwound (negatively supercoiled) of the molecule. Supercoiling is most prominent in circular chromosomes where it plays a role in normal chromosome packaging in cells.

DNA transposon One type of transposable genetic element encoding a transposase and capable of transposition.

DNA triplet Three DNA nucleotides corresponding to a codon of mRNA.

DNase I hypersensitive site Regions of chromatin sensitive to cleavage by DNase I; these often represent open chromatin that is transcriptionally active.

dominance variance In polygenic and multifactorial inheritance, the portion of genetic variance attributed to the dominance effects of contributing genes.

dominant epistasis (12:3:1 ratio) A characteristic ratio of phenotypes produced by the interaction of two genes that control a trait in which a dominant allele of one gene masks or reduces the expression of alleles of a second gene.

dominant interaction (9:6:1 ratio) A characteristic ratio of phenotypes produced by the interaction of two genes that control a trait in which the presence of dominant alleles of both genes produces one phenotype, one dominant allele of either gene produces a second phenotype, and organisms with only recessive alleles for the interacting genes have a third phenotype.

dominant negative mutation A dominant mutation that behaves as a loss-of-function, often due to blocking the formation or normal function of a multimeric protein complex.

dominant phenotype The phenotype observed in a heterozygous organism that is identical to the phenotype observed in a homozygote. The phenotype produced when

an organism is homozygous for the dominant allele or carries a single copy of the dominant allele in the heterozygous genotype. Compare with *recessive phenotype*.

dominant suppression (13:3 ratio) A characteristic ratio of phenotypes produced by the interaction of two genes that control a trait in which the dominant allele of one gene suppresses the expression of the dominant allele of the second gene.

donor cell (bacterial donor) The bacterial cell that is the source of DNA transferred to a recipient cell by either conjugation, transduction, or transformation.

donor DNA DNA to be used in cloning or other recombinant DNA technologies.

dosage compensation A mechanism for equalizing the expression of X-linked genes in males and females of a species.

double Holliday junction (DHJ) An intermediate structure temporarily connecting chromatids of homologous chromosomes that forms during homologous recombination.

double recombinant (double crossover) The occurrence of two crossovers between homologous chromosomes in a particular region. May involve two, three, or all four chromatids.

double-strand break repair Following phosphodiester bond breakage on both strands of a DNA duplex, a mechanism of DNA damage repair. Related to the mechanism for homologous recombination.

downstream Referring to a gene or sequence location that is toward the 3′ direction on the *coding strand*.

drosha Ribonuclease that processes pri-microRNA molecules into pre-microRNA molecules in animals.

duplicate gene action (15:1 ratio) A characteristic ratio of phenotypes produced by the interaction of two genes that duplicate each other's action due to genetic redundancy.

duplication The gain of genetic material by the inclusion of one or more additional copies of a chromosome segment. See also *microduplication*, *partial duplication*, and *partial duplication heterozygote*.

early operators The operator sequence in the genome of bacteriophage λ (lambda) that controls transcription of early genes. See also *delayed early genes* and *late genes*.

early promoters Regulatory sequences responsible for the activation of early genes or operons in bacteriophage. See also *delayed early genes* and *late genes*.

east-west (EW) resolution One of the possible patterns for resolving a Holliday junction to separate homologous chromosomes before meiotic anaphase.

electrophoretic mobility A measurement of (1) the distance of migration or (2) the speed of migration of a nucleic acid or protein in gel electrophoresis.

elongation factor (EF) A group of proteins associated with ribosomes that contribute to the elongation of the polypeptide product.

embryonic stem cell In vertebrates, totipotent cells of early embryos that can give rise to any and all cell types of the organism.

endosymbiont An organism that lives within the body or cell of another organism.

endosymbiosis An (often) mutually beneficial relationship between organisms in which one organism, the endosymbiont, inhabits the body of the other.

endosymbiosis theory Hypothesis that the mitochondrion and chloroplast are evolutionarily derived from bacterial endosymbionts related to extant α-proteobacteria and cyanobacteria, respectively.

enhanceosome Protein complex that binds enhancer elements and directs DNA bending into loops that bring the protein complex into contact with RNA polymerase and transcription factors bound at the core promoter or with protein complexes bound to proximal promoter elements.

enhancer A eukaryotic cis-acting DNA regulatory sequence to which trans-acting factors bind and stimulate transcription. See also *enhancer sequence.*

enhancer screen A genetic screen designed to identify mutations in genes that worsen the phenotypic effects of mutations in another gene.

enhancer sequence Sets of regulatory sequences that bind specific transcriptional proteins that can elevate transcription of targeted eukaryotic genes.

enhancer trapping A transgenic construct inserted randomly into the genome that allows identification of enhancer elements controlling specific patterns of gene expression.

enveloped virus A viral particle coated with cytoplasmic material derived from the infected host organism.

environmental variance (V_E) For quantitative traits, the proportion of the total phenotypic variance contributed by differences in the environment experienced by population members.

epigenetic Heritable patterns or changes in gene expression that are not associated with any change in DNA sequence.

epigenetic marks A collection of chemical marks and modifications, such as acetylation and methylation of histone proteins, that are functional in chromatin remodeling. Also known as *epigenetic modification.*

epigenetic modification Chemical modifications of DNA or associated histones, such as acetylation and methylation, that alter chromatin structure and influence gene transcription.

episome A bacterial plasmid that is able to both replicate autonomously and integrate into the host genome.

epistasis See *epistatic interaction.*

epistatic interaction A group of specific patterns of gene interaction in which an allele of one gene modifies or prevents the expression of alleles of another gene. Also known as *epistasis.*

equilibrium frequency The stable frequency of an allele in a population attained and maintained through the action of evolutionary processes.

eraser A chromatin-modifying enzyme that removes chemical groups from chromatin (e.g., methyl or acetyl groups from the lysines of histone 3).

ethidium bromide (EtBr) A compound used to stain DNA and RNA in electrophoresis gels.

euchromatic region See *euchromatin.*

euchromatin Chromosome regions containing chromatin that is not densely compacted. Most expressed genes are located within euchromatic regions of chromosomes. Also known as *euchromatic region.*

Eukarya One of the three domains of life; separate from Archaea and Bacteria. See also *eukaryote.*

eukaryote Referring to organisms belonging to the domain Eukarya.

eukaryotic expression vector A vector that contains all the necessary cis-regulatory sequences to enable gene expression in a eukaryotic cell.

eukaryotic initiation factor (eIF) A group of eukaryotic proteins that associate with ribosomal subunits and help initiate translation.

euploid A number of chromosomes that is an exact multiple of the haploid number.

E(var) mutation Mutations that enhance position effect variegation in *Drosophila.* Mutated genes produce proteins that are active in chromatin remodeling.

evo-devo The study of the evolution of development.

evolution (1) Any change in the genetic characteristics of a population, strain, or species over time. (2) The theory that all organisms are related by common ancestry and have diversified from common ancestors over time.

evolutionary genetics The study of evolution and evolutionary processes using genetic techniques and tools.

evolutionary genomics The comparison of genomes, both within and between species. It illuminates the genetic basis of similarities and differences between individuals or species.

evolutionary processes Four processes—natural selection, migration, mutation, and random genetic drift—that can cause changes in the genetic characteristics of a population or lineage.

exconjugant cell The cell that is the product of conjugation between a donor cell and a recipient cell.

exit site (E site) On the ribosome, the site through which an uncharged tRNA exits.

exon A nonintron segment of the coding sequence of a gene. Joined together following intron splicing, exons correspond to the mRNA sequence that is translated into a polypeptide.

exonic and intronic splicing enhancers (ESE and ISE) Exon and intron sequences that play a role in stimulating intron splicing.

exonic and intronic splicing silencers (ESS and ISS) Exon and intron sequences that play a role in suppressing intron splicing

expression array DNA microarray that carries unique sequences from every annotated gene of the genome and is used to monitor gene expression patterns.

expression vector Cloning vector possessing DNA sequences required for DNA fragments inserted into the vector to be transcribed and translated. Vectors with sequences facilitating expression in eukaryotes are called *eukaryotic expression vectors.*

F (fertility) factor The plasmid containing genes that confer the ability to act as a donor cell on a bacterium. May be either an extrachromosomal plasmid or may be incorporated into the donor bacterial chromosome. Also known as *F plasmid.*

F plasmid See *F (fertility) factor.*

F$^+$ cell (F$^+$ donor) A donor bacterium containing an extrachromosomal fertility plasmid.

F$^-$ (F$^-$ cells) A bacterial recipient cell; does not contain an F (fertility) plasmid.

F′ cell (F′ donor) A bacterial donar cell harboring an F (fertility) plasmid.

F′ factor An extrachromosomal fertility plasmid into which a portion of the donor bacterial chromosome has been incorporated.

F$_1$ generation (first filial generation) The first generation of offspring. In genetic experiments, usually the offspring produced by crossing pure-breeding parents.

F$_2$ generation (second filial generation) The second generation, produced by crossing F$_1$ organisms.

F$_3$ generation (third filial generation) The third generation, produced by crossing F$_2$ organisms.

facultative heterochromatin Heterochromatic chromosome regions whose level of compaction can vary. Often contains repetitive DNA, but may also contain some expressed genes.

first-division segregation In *Neurospora* and other organisms forming an ascus, the separation of alleles at the first meiotic division due to no crossing over having occurred.

flanking direct sequence repeat Identical repetitive sequences flanking the sites of insertion of transposable genetic elements.

fluorescent in situ hybridization (FISH) A laboratory method for identifying genes or DNA sequences using molecular probes labeled with a compound that can emit fluorescent light upon excitation.

forked-line diagram A method for diagramming the probabilities of outcomes in a branching format.

forward genetic analysis The classical approach to genetic analysis whereby genes are first identified by mutant phenotypes caused by mutant alleles and the gene sequence is subsequently identified by recombinant DNA technologies. Also known as *forward genetics*.

forward genetics See *forward genetic analysis*.

forward mutation A mutation that alters a wild type and generates a mutant. Also known as *mutation*.

forward mutation rate (μ) The frequency of mutation from wild-type alleles to mutant alleles.

founder effect The random occurrence of allele and genotype frequency differences between a new population established by a small number of founders and the larger parental population.

four-strand double crossover Two crossover events between a pair of homologous chromosomes that involve all four chromatids.

frameshift mutation The insertion or deletion of DNA base pairs resulting in translation of mRNA in an incorrect reading frame.

frequency distribution A visual display or histogram of quantitative data.

functional domain A protein region with a specific function or interaction.

functional genomics Using genomic sequences and genome-wide patterns of transcripts and protein expression to understand gene function in an organism.

functional RNA Various types of transcripts that are not translated and are functional as nucleic acids. See also *tRNA, rRNA, snRNA, miRNA, siRNA,* and *ribozyme*.

fusion gene A recombinant gene composed of DNA sequences from more than one source (e.g., the codon sequences derived from one gene and the sequences responsible for expression derived from a second gene).

fusion protein A recombinant protein encoded by DNA sequences from more than one source; made by combining the open reading frames of two unrelated genes.

G_0 phase The "G zero" phase of the cell cycle, an alternative to G_1 of the cell cycle entered by mature cells that generally do not divide again until they die. Compare with *G_1 phase* and *G_2 phase*.

G_1 phase The "Gap 1" phase of the cell cycle during which genes are actively transcribed and translated and cells carry out their normal functions. Compare with *G_0 phase* and *G_2 phase*.

G_2 phase The "Gap 2" phase of the cell cycle during which the cell prepares to divide. Compare with *G_0 phase* and *G_1 phase*.

gain-of-function mutation A mutation causing a gene to be overexpressed, to be expressed at the wrong time, or to encode a constitutively acting protein. Usually inherited as a dominant mutation.

gamete The reproductive cells produced by male and female reproductive structures; sperm or pollen in male animals and plants and eggs in females.

gap gene In *Drosophila*, genes that control development in large contiguous regions along the anterior-posterior axis; examples include *hunchback, giant, Krüppel,* and *knirps*.

Gaussian distribution See *normal distribution*.

gel electrophoresis A laboratory method for separating proteins or nucleic acid molecules or fragments using electrical current in a gel matrix.

gene The physical unit of heredity, composed of a DNA sequence that is transcribed and encodes a polypeptide or another functional molecule.

gene conversion Repair of mismatched (non-complementary) DNA nucleotides in heteroduplex DNA that forms during meiotic recombination. One allele is switched for another allele already in the genotype.

gene dosage The number of copies of a gene.

gene–environment interaction Interactions taking place between particular genes and specific environmental factors.

gene family A group of genes that is evolutionarily related via successive gene duplication events that are followed by diversification.

gene flow The movement of genes into, out of, or between populations as a consequence of the movement of organisms. See also *migration*.

gene interaction Referring to genes that interact with one another due to their participation in the production of a particular product or trait.

gene knockout Loss-of-function allele of a gene usually obtained via a reverse genetic approach.

gene pool The total of all alleles present in breeding members of a population at a given moment.

gene therapy The use of genes as therapeutic agents to cure or alleviate symptoms of a genetic disease.

general transcription factors (GTFs) Eukaryotic transcription-activating proteins that bind the promoter region to form part of the apparatus that initiates basal transcription.

generalized transducing phage In transduction, a bacteriophage that carries a random segment of the chromosome of a donor cell to the recipient cell.

generalized transduction The transduction of a random segment of a donor chromosome into a recipient cell by a transducing phage. See also *generalized transducing phage*.

genetic bottleneck A period or event characterized by a substantial random reduction in population size. Loss of genetic diversity and allele frequency changes usually occur.

genetic chimera A tissue or organism composed of cells of two or more distinct genotypes.

genetic code The universal set of correspondences of mRNA codons to amino acids. Used in translation to synthesize polypeptides.

genetic complementation (1) The observation of a wild-type phenotype in an organism or cell containing two different mutations. (2) The cross of two pure-breeding mutants that yields progeny that are exclusively wild type.

genetic dissection The use of mutations and recombinants in genetic analyses to identify and assemble the genetic components of a biological property or process.

genetic drift A process of evolution referring to random changes in allele frequencies that result from sampling errors. Occurs in all populations but is strongest in small populations.

genetic fine structure The method of high-resolution analysis of intragenic recombination to map genes at the nucleotide level.

genetic heterogeneity The observation of the same phenotype produced by mutation of any one of two or more different genes.

genetic hitchhiking The phenomenon in which specific alleles of genes that are closely linked to a gene undergoing positive natural selection have their frequencies increased by virtue of their presence on the same chromosomes as the favored allele.

genetic liability See *threshold of genetic liability*.

genetic linkage The result of genes being located so near one another on a chromosome that their alleles do not assort independently. Identified by detecting certain pairs of alleles (parentals) that are transmitted together significantly more often than expected by chance and of other pairs of alleles (nonparentals or recombinants) that are transmitted together significantly less often than expected.

genetic linkage mapping Process for creating maps of genes based on their linkage relationships to other genes.

genetic markers Alleles of either expressed genes or noncoding chromosomal regions identifying a specific region of a chromosome. Can be used to trace or identify another gene, the chromosome, or a cell, organ, or individual.

genetic network Set of interacting genes identified from double mutants or other analyses indicating gene interaction.

genetic redundancy The situation where the functions of one gene are compensated for by the actions of another gene.

genetic screen A procedure whereby a population of organisms is mutagenized and their progeny are propagated and examined for mutant phenotypes. Also known as *mutagenesis*.

genetic variance (V_G) In polygenic and multifactorial inheritance, the proportion of total phenotypic variance contributed by genetic variation.

genome The entire complement of DNA sequences in a chromosome set of an organism.

genome-wide association studies (GWAS) Association analysis performed using genetic marker genes distributed throughout the genome. Designed to locate genes that may influence the variation of quantitative traits.

genomics The study of the structure, fuction, composition, and evolution of genomes.

genomic imprinting Epigenetic phenomena that create differential expression of alleles depending on whether they were maternally or paternally inherited.

genomic island Genome segments that differ in sequence makeup from the surrounding genome sequence. Often these are a consequence of lateral gene transfer.

genomic library A set of clones consisting of the DNA representing the genome of an organism.

genotype (1) The genetic composition of an organism or a cell (i.e., all the alleles of all the genes). (2) The alleles of a single gene or a specified set of genes in a cell or organism.

genotype proportion method A method for estimating allele frequencies in a population by manipulation of genotype frequencies.

genotypic ratio (1:2:1 ratio) (1) A ratio or set of relative proportions between organisms with different genotypes. (2) The ratio of $1/4 : 1/2 : 1/4$ observed among the homozygous and heterozygous F_2 progeny of a monohybrid cross.

germinal gene therapy Gene therapy aimed at correcting the genetic defect in the germ cells, such that progeny would not inherit the genetic defect.

germ-line cell See *gamete*.

Giemsa (G) banding See *chromosome banding*.

Goldberg-Hogness box See *TATA box*.

green fluorescent protein (GFP) A gene, derived from the jellyfish *Aequoria victoria*, that is the source of the natural bioluminescence of this species, fluorescing green (a 509-nm wavelength) when illuminated with UV light (a 395-nm wavelength). When used as a reporter gene, GFP allows a noninvasive means of visualizing gene and protein expression patterns in living organisms.

guanine (G) One of four nitrogenous nucleotide bases in DNA and RNA; one of the two types of purine nucleotides in DNA and RNA.

guide RNA (gRNA) In RNA editing, the nucleic acid that directs the addition or removal of nucleotides from mRNA. Also known as *guide strand*.

guide strand See *guide RNA (gRNA)*.

gynandromorphy A condition in which the body of an organism is mosaic, appearing to contain both male and female features.

hairpin structure See *stem loop*.

haploid Possessing a single set of chromosomes (*n*); a cell or organism that possesses one-half the number of chromosomes found in diploid cells of the organism.

haploid number The number of chromosomes (*n*) typically found in nuclei during the haploid phase of the eukaryotic life cycle. One-half the diploid (2*n*) number.

haploinsufficient A wild-type allele that is unable to support wild-type function in a heterozygous genotype. Classified as a recessive wild-type allele. Compare with *haplosufficient*.

haplosufficient A wild-type allele that supports wild-type function in heterozygous organisms. Classified as a dominant wild-type allele. Compare with *haploinsufficient*.

haplotype The specific array of alleles encoded by linked genes in a segment of a single chromosome.

Hardy-Weinberg equilibrium The population genetic principle that in a population practicing random mating and in the absence of natural selection, mutation, migration, or random genetic drift, allele frequencies are stable at frequencies $p + q = 1.0$ for two alleles and are distributed into genotypes at frequencies $p2$, $2pq$, and $q2$.

helicase In DNA replication, the enzyme responsible for breaking hydrogen bonds between complementary nucleotides of a DNA duplex. Unwinding of the strands occurs ahead of the advancing replication fork.

helix-turn-helix (HTH) motif A DNA-binding protein domain consisting of two alpha helices: one helix binds to a specific DNA sequence, and the second helix stabilizes the interaction.

hemizygous Referring to the genotype of males that carry a single copy of each X-linked gene.

hemoglobin (Hb) A globin protein composed of four polypeptides (two α-globin and two β-globin) found in blood that transports oxygen.

heritability See *broad sense heritability* and *narrow sense heritability*.

heterochromatin A chromosome region containing densely compacted chromatin and few, if any, expressed genes. See *constitutive heterochromatin* and *facultative heterochromatin*. Also known as heterochromatic region.

heteroduplex DNA A DNA duplex created during homologous recombination by combining complementary strands of DNA from nonsister chromatids. Also known as heteroduplex region.

heteroplasmic cell or organism A cell or organism that harbors a mixture of alleles of an organellar gene. Also known as *heteroplasmy*.

heteroplasmy See *heteroplasmic cell or organism*.

heterozygous advantage In evolution, the greater relative fitness of heterozygous organisms compared with homozygous organisms in a population. May result in a *balanced polymorphism*.

heterozygous genotype A diploid genotype characterized by the presence of two different alleles of a gene.

Hfr cell An abbreviation for "high frequency recombination," pertaining to Hfr chromosomes or to Hfr donors in bacterial conjugation.

Hfr chromosome See *Hfr donor*.

Hfr donor A donor bacterial strain containing an F factor integrated into its chromosome. Also known as *Hfr chromosome*.

histone acetyltransferase (HAT) Chromatin-modifying enzyme that adds acetyl groups to specific positively charged amino acids (e.g., lysine) in the N-terminal tails of histones.

histone deacetylase (HDAC) Chromatin-modifying enzyme that removes acetyl groups to specific positively charged amino acids (e.g., lysine) in the N-terminal tails of histones.

histone demethylase (HDMT) Chromatin-modifying enzyme that removes methyl groups to specific positively charged amino acids (e.g., lysine) in the N-terminal tails of histones.

histone methyltransferase (HMT) Chromatin-modifying enzyme that adds methyl groups to specific positively charged amino acids (e.g., lysine) in the N-terminal tails of histones.

histone protein (H1, H2A, H2B, H3, H4) Five proteins encoded by a gene family that form octameric nucleosomes (H2A, H2B, H3, and H4) and adhere to DNA to condense chromatin (H1).

Holliday junction A DNA structure that forms during meiotic recombination in which single strands are crossed over between nonsister chromatids of homologous chromosomes.

Holliday model Proposed originally by Robin Holliday; a model intended to explain meiotic recombination at a molecular level.

holoenzyme A fully functional multisubunit protein complex in bacteria, for example, the RNA polymerase holoenzyme.

homeobox A conserved sequence of DNA of 180 nucleotides encoding a *homeodomain* composed of three α-helices in a family of transcription factors found throughout eukaryotes; in metazoans some genes with homeobox genes are homeotic genes.

homeodomain A 60-amino acid DNA-binding domain.

homeotic gene Gene that controls the developmental fate of a region of the body of an organism; examples include the *Hox genes* in metazoans and the *MADS-box* genes in flowering plants.

homeotic mutation Mutation in which an apparently normal organ or body part develops in an inappropriate location.

homologous chromosomes Chromosomes that synapse (pair) during meiosis. Chromosomes with the same genes in the same order. Also known as homologous pair, *homologs*.

homologous genes Genes descended from a common ancestral gene. Also known as *homologs*.

homologous nucleotides Nucleotides descended from a common ancestral nucleotide.

homologous recombination Exchange of genetic information between homologous DNA molecules.

homologs Homologous chromosomes that have the same genes and structure and pair with one another during meiosis.

homology Evolutionarily related, having descended from a common ancestor.

homoplasmic cell or organism A cell or organism in which all copies (alleles) of a cytoplasmic organelle gene are the same. Also known as *homoplasmy*.

homoplasmy The presence of one allelic version of DNA in the organellar genomes of a cell.

homozygous genotype A diploid genotype characterized by the presence of two identical alleles of a gene.

host cell The cell containing a parasitic organism or infective particle.

hotspot of mutation A location within a gene or genome at which mutations occur much more often than average.

housekeeping gene Genes that have essential cellular or physiological functions.

***Hox* gene** Members of the homeobox gene clusters found throughout metazoans; the genes often pattern the anterior-posterior axis and are homeotic genes.

hybrid dysgenesis In *Drosophila*, the failure of F_1 progeny of P-cytotype males crossed with M-cytotype females to develop due to the presence of P elements.

hybrid vigor The greater growth, survival, and fertility of hybrids produced by crossing highly inbred lines.

hybridization (of molecular probe) In an electrophoresis gel or in gel blotting, the binding of a single-stranded nucleic acid probe to a single-stranded target nucleic acid by complementary base pairing.

hydrogen bond Weak electrostatic attraction formed by the sharing of a positively charged hydrogen atom by negatively charged oxygen and nitrogen atoms. Hydrogen bonds form between complementary nucleotides to hold nucleic acid strands together.

hypermorphic mutation A mutant whose phenotype is similar to, but greater than, the wild-type phenotype.

hypomorphic mutation See *leaky mutation*.

identical by descent (IBD) A homozygous genotype in an organism in which both copies of the allele in an individual can be traced back to a common ancestor.

illegitimate recombination Exchange of genetic information between non-homologous DNA molecules.

immediate early genes Genes expressing immediately upon infection of a host bacterial cell by bacteriophage λ (lambda). See also *delayed early genes* and *late genes*.

imprinting control region (ICR) Master regulatory cis-acting DNA sequences to which trans-acting factors bind to regulate genomic imprinting.

inbreeding Mating between relatives. Also known as *consanguineous mating*.

inbreeding depression A reduction in vigor, survival, or reproductive fitness of offspring due to inbreeding.

incomplete dominance The observation that the phenotype occurring in heterozygous organisms is intermediate between the phenotypes of homozygous organisms, but more similar to one homozygous phenotype than to the other. Also known as *partial dominance*.

incomplete genetic linkage The occurrence of crossing over between linked genes.

incomplete penetrance The occurrence of individual organisms that have a particular genotype or allele but not the corresponding phenotype.

indels A shorthand term for small insertions and small deletions that are generally too small to cause obvious phenotypic abnormalities.

induced mutation Mutations generated by exposure to physical, chemical, or biological mutagens.

inducer An accessory molecule that binds to a protein that leads to activation of gene expression. The inducer can bind to a repressor protein and prevent its function or bind to an activator protein and stimulate its function.

inducer–repressor complex A molecular complex consisting of a repressor protein and a bound inducer molecule.

inducible operon Operon that is not expressed under one set of environmental conditions, but whose transcription is activated under an alternative environmental condition (i.e., the *lac* operon).

induction Process by which one cell or tissue promotes a particular developmental fate in neighboring cells or tissues.

inductive signal A molecule that acts non-cell autonomously to influence cell fate; in *C. elegans* vulval development, the lin-3 protein secreted from the anchor cells acts as an inductive signal to influence the fate of vulval precursor cells.

informational gene Class of genes that encode protein products that perform informational processes in the cell such as DNA replication, packaging of chromosomes, transcription, and translation.

ingroup A species within a clade used to compare to other members of the clade.

inhibition Process by which one cell or tissue prevents a particular developmental fate in neighboring cells or tissues.

inhibitor An accessory molecule that converts activator proteins to an inactive conformation by binding to an allosteric binding domain of the activator protein.

initial committed complex In eukaryotic transcription, a partially completed multiprotein complex that is preparing to bind RNA polymerase II.

initiation complex In eukaryotic translation, the complex formed by the small ribosomal subunit, mRNA, and charged tRNA-carrying methionine.

initiation factor (IF) A group of proteins, associated with ribosomes, that contribute to ribosome assembly and translation initiation.

initiator tRNA The first charged tRNA associated with the ribosome.

inosine (I) A modified nucleotide found occasionally in anticodons that can base-pair with uracil, cytosine, or adenine.

insertion sequence (IS) A bacterial DNA sequence that is the target of insertion of a transposable genetic element or is the site of integration of a plasmid such as an F plasmid.

insertional inactivation A process of mutation in which the insertion of DNA into a gene renders it nonfunctional.

in situ hybridization A laboratory method for hybridizing a molecular probe to a DNA sequence or a gene on an intact chromosome.

insulator sequence Cis-acting sequences that act to prevent cross-talk between regulatory elements of an adjacent gene and are located between enhancers and promoters of genes that are to be insulated from the effects of the enhancer.

interactive variance (V_I) In polygenic and multifactorial inheritance, the proportion of total phenotypic variance that is due to the interactions of genetic and environmental factors.

interactome The sum of all of the protein–protein interactions in an organism.

interchromosomal domain Open spaces between chromosome domains in the interphase nucleus.

interference (*I*) Measured on a zero to 1.0 scale, the measurement of the independence of crossovers. Expressed as 1.0 minus the *coefficient of coincidence (c)*.

intergenic region DNA sequence between coding genes.

internal control region (ICR) Promoter consensus sequences of certain rRNA and tRNA genes that are downstream of the start of transcription (i.e., sequences that are internal to the transcriptional region of the gene).

internal promoter element Promoter consensus sequences of snRNA and tRNA genes that are downstream of the start of transcription (i.e., sequences that are internal to the transcriptional region of the gene).

interphase The multiphase period of the cell cycle between cell divisions. See also *G_1 phase*, *S phase*, and *G_2 phase*.

interrupted mating A technique used to map bacterial genes that stops conjugation at timed intervals to determine which genes have transferred from the donor cell to the recipient cell.

interspecific comparison Any comparison between different species. Compare with *intraspecific comparison*.

interstitial deletion The loss of a portion of a chromosome from within one arm.

intragenic recombination Crossing over within a gene.

intragenic reversion A reversion produced by a second site mutation within a single gene.

intraspecific comparison Any comparison between individuals of the same species. Compare with *interspecific comparison*.

intrinsic termination In bacterial transcription, the DNA sequence-dependent mechanism for *transcription termination*. Inverted repeat DNA sequences induce formation of 3′ mRNA stem loop (hairpin) structures that are followed by multiple uracils (transcribed from adenines).

introgression line Lines of experimental organisms in which genome segments from two or more other lines are present due to repeated back crosses between hybrids and organisms of one parental line.

intron Intervening sequences between the exons of many eukaryotic genes. Present in DNA and pre-mRNA, but spliced out during pre-mRNA processing.

intron self-splicing The capacity of certain RNA transcripts to undergo self-generated splicing that does not require splicing enzymes of the spliceosome complex.

intron splicing The spliceosome complex-driven process that removes introns from eukaryotic pre-mRNA and ligates exons to form mature mRNA.

inversion heterozygote Organisms whose homologous chromosomes have different structural organization. Most commonly, one has normal structure whereas the homolog carries an inversion.

inversion loop At homologous chromosome synapsis in an *inversion heterozygote*, the structure that forms by the looping of one chromosome to align homologous regions.

inverted repeat (IR) sequence Identical or nearly identical DNA sequences located on the same molecule but with opposite orientations.

IS (insertion sequence) element Mobile DNA elements in bacteria that cause mutations by inactivating the expression of genes into which they insert.

island model In evolutionary genetics, a model of species evolution in which new species are reproductively isolated from an ancestral population.

isoaccepting tRNA The group of tRNAs that carry the same amino acid but recognize synonymous codons.

ISWI complex Imitation switch complex that functions primarily to control the placement of nucleosomes into an arrangement that causes a region to be transcriptionally silent.

joint probability The likelihood of an outcome requiring the occurrence of two or more simultaneous or sequential events.

karyokinesis Part of telophase, the process of nuclear division between daughter cells.

karyotype A digital or analog photograph of chromosomes arranged by conventional chromosome numbering.

kilobase (kb) A length of nucleic acid containing 1000 nucleotides.

kinetochore The site of attachment of multiple proteins that connects a spindle fiber microtubule to the centromeric region of a chromosome. Forms during *M phase* of cell division.

knockout library Collections of mutants in which most or all genes of a particular organism have been mutated by inactivating (or "knocking out") their expression.

Kozak sequence A specific consensus sequence of eukaryotic mRNA that contains the authentic start codon (AUG) sequence.

lac⁻ phenotype Bacteria that are not able to grow on a medium containing lactose as the only sugar. Compare with *lac⁺ phenotype*.

lac⁺ phenotype Bacteria that are able to grow on a medium containing lactose as the only sugar. Compare with *lac⁻ phenotype*.

lacA gene A gene of the bacterial *lac* operon; encodes lac transacetylase. Compare with *lacY gene* and *lacZ gene*.

lactose (lac) operon An inducible operon consisting of genes (*lacA*, *lacY*, *lacZ*) encoding enzymes allowing the use of lactose as a carbon source. The operon is repressed by the lac repressor regulatory protein that binds to the lac operator sequence and is activated by the CAP–cAMP complex that binds to sequences of the CAP binding site.

lacY gene A gene of the bacterial *lac* operon; encodes lac permease, which facilitates import of lactose into the cell. Compare with *lacZ gene* and *lacA gene*.

lacZ gene A gene of the bacterial *lac* operon; encodes β-galactosidase, which breaks down lactose into glucose and galactose. Compare with *lacY gene* and *lacA gene*.

lagging strand In DNA replication, the discontinuously synthesized strand whose Okazaki fragments are ligated to complete new strand synthesis. Compare with *leading strand*.

large ribosomal subunit The larger of two subunits of the ribosome.

lariat intron structure During intron splicing, the structure formed by covalent bonding of the 5′ guanine of an intron to the branch point adenine of the intron.

late genes Bacteriophage genes expressed late in the lytic cycle. Encode protein products required for packaging of phage particles and lysis of the host cell. Late promoters and late operators are the regulatory sequences responsible for late gene activation.

lateral gene transfer (LGT) Transfer of genetic material between organisms belonging to the same or to different taxonomic groups.

lateral inhibition Process by which one cell or tissue prevents neighboring cells or tissues from acquiring a developmental fate similar its own.

law of independent assortment (Mendel's second law) The random distribution of alleles of unlinked genes into gametes.

law of segregation (Mendel's first law) The separation of alleles of a gene during gamete formation.

leader region (trpL) Transcribed region upstream of the major enzyme encoding genes of repressible amino acid biosynthesis operons (e.g., *trpL*). Region encodes a small peptide whose rate of translation reflects the concentration of the amino acid (e.g., tryptophan) in the cells and consequently regulates transcription of the operon.

leader sequence See *signal sequence*.

leading strand In DNA replication, the continuously synthesized strand. Compare with *lagging strand*.

leaky mutation A mutant whose phenotype is similar to, but less than, the wild-type phenotype. Also known as *hypomorphic mutation*.

lethal allele See *lethal mutation*.

lethal mutation An allele that results in the premature death of the organisms that carry it. Lethality most often affects homozygous organisms. Also known as *lethal allele*.

linkage disequilibrium The nonrandom distribution into gametes of alleles of linked genes.

linkage equilibrium The random distribution into gametes of alleles of linked genes achieved by crossing over between the genes.

linkage group A group of genes displaying genetic linkage.

linker A short, chemically synthesized oligonucleotide that can be ligated to DNA molecules.

linker DNA DNA between nucleosomes in the 10-nm fiber structure of chromatin.

locus control region (LCR) Specialized enhancer element that regulates the transcription of multiple genes, often complexes of closely related genes.

lod score (log of the odds ratio) Based on analysis of transmission in pedigrees, the statistic used to calculate the likelihood of genetic linkage between genes.

long noncoding RNA (lncRNA) A transcribed RNA molecule that does not possess an extended open reading frame and that does not represent a tRNA, RRNA, or miRNA.

long terminal repeats (LTRs) Arrays of scores to hundreds of nucleotides that bracket the ends of retroviruses integrated into host chromosomes.

loss-of-function mutation A mutant that prevents the production of the wild-type protein or renders it inactive. Most commonly a recessive mutation.

lysis See *lytic cycle*.

lysogenic cycle The life cycle of a bacterium infected by a temperate bacteriophage that integrates into the host chromosome and replicates along with it.

lysogeny See *lysogenic cycle*.

lytic cycle The life cycle of a bacterium infected by a bacteriophage that replicates within the host cell and lyses the host to release progeny bacteriophage.

M phase The cell division phase of the cell cycle. Follows *interphase*.

macroevolution Evolutionary processes operating at the species level and higher.

MADS-box A conserved sequence of DNA of 168–180 nucleotides encoding a 56–60 amino acid DNA-binding domain in a family of transcription factors found throughout eukaryotes; in flowering plants, some MADS-box genes are homeotic genes.

major gene A gene that has a substantial effect on phenotypic variation.

major groove The larger of two grooves formed in the DNA sugar-phosphate backbone by the helical twist of the double helix and exposing certain base pairs.

mapping function Corrective calculations used to more accurately estimate recombination frequencies between linked genes. Mapping functions differ among certain species.

map unit (m.u.), centiMorgan (cM) A theoretical unit of distance between linked genes on a chromosome.

maternal effect gene Genes that act in the mother to impart gene products (RNA or protein) into the egg and subsequently the embryo. For maternal effect genes, the embryonic phenotype is determined by the genotype of the mother rather than that of the embryo.

matrix attachment region (MAR) Portions of the chromosome scaffold to which loops of chromatin are attached.

mature mRNA The fully processed product of eukaryotic transcription that moves to the cytoplasm for translation.

mean (μ) The average value of a group of values.

median In a sample distribution, the middle most values. Also known as *median value*.

median value See *median*.

mediator An enhanceosome complex that forms a bridge between activator proteins bound to enhancer elements and the basal transcriptional machinery bound to the promoter.

megabase (Mb) Equal to 1,000,000 nucleotide bases. Refers to DNA or to RNA molecules or fragments.

meiosis The process of cell division occurring in germ-line cells. Produces four haploid gametes or spores through two successive nuclear divisions in diploid species.

meiosis I First nuclear division characterized by homologous chromosomes separating. Compare with *meiosis II*.

meiosis II Second nuclear division characterized by sister chromatids separating. Compare with *meiosis I*.

Mendelian genetics Referring to genetic applications and analyses using the law of segregation and the law of independent assortment originally described through experiments and analysis by Gregor Mendel.

meristem Organized groups of pluripotent cells at the growing tips of plants that both generate organs and self-maintain to ensure that a pool of stem cells is always present.

messenger RNA (mRNA) A form of RNA transcribed from a gene and subsequently translated to produce a polypeptide or protein.

metabolomics The study of proteins, processes, and interactions involved in the metabolism of organisms.

metacentric chromosome A chromosome with a centrally located centromere that produces long and short arms of approximately the same length.

metagenome Sequence derived from whole-genome shotgun sequencing of DNA from entire natural communities consisting of a range of organisms.

metaphase The stage of *M phase* during which chromosomes align in the middle of the cell.

metaphase plate The cell midline along which chromosomes align during metaphase.

microdeletion A small chromosome deletion detectable only by using molecular methods of analysis.

microduplication A small chromosome duplication detectable only by using molecular methods of analysis.

microevolution Evolutionary changes at the population level.

microRNA (miRNA) Small (21–24 nuts) regulatory RNAs produced by Dicer and acting in a RISC complex to either repress translational or cleave target mRNA molecules. Compare with *RNA interference (RNAi)*.

microsynteny Conservation of the order of a small number of genes in the same order in related species.

migration A process of evolution referring to the movement of organisms and genes between populations. Also known as *gene flow*.

minimal initiation complex In eukaryotic transcription, a partially completed multiprotein complex that is preparing to bind RNA polymerase II.

minor groove The smaller of two grooves formed in the sugar-phosphate backbone by the helical twist of the double helix, exposing certain base pairs.

mismatch repair The DNA repair process that repairs noncomplementary base pairs that occur through errant DNA replication or through nucleotiude base modification. The process restores normal complementary base pairing.

missense mutation A DNA base-pair substitution that leads to production of a polypeptide in which one amino acid substitutes for another.

mitochondrion An organelle, bounded by a double membrane, encoding polypeptides that interact with nuclear gene polypeptides in oxidative phosphorylation to generate ATP. In many species, mitochondria also participate in other metabolic processes and biochemical reactions, including ion homeostasis and biosynthetic pathways.

mitosis The process of cell division in somatic cells that produces genetically identical daughter cells through a single nuclear division.

mitosome Double-membrane-bound organelles that are evolutionarily derived from mitochondria but have lost all of the ancestral genome; proteins requiring an anaerobic environment to function are imported into them.

mitotic crossover Crossing over between homologous chromosomes during mitosis.

modal value See *mode.*

mode In a sample distribution, the most commonly occurring value. Also known as *modal value.*

modern synthesis of evolution Referring to the broad-based effort beginning in the middle of the 20th century to unite Mendelian genetics with Darwin's theory of evolution by natural selection.

modifier gene A gene that modifies the effect of a major gene.

modifier screen A genetic screen designed to identify mutations in genes that modify, either enhance or suppress, the phenotypic effects of mutations in another gene.

molecular cloning The process whereby a single DNA molecule is selectively cloned from a mixture of DNA molecules and then amplified to produce a large number of identical copies.

molecular genetics The subfield of genetics that studies hereditary transmission, variation, mutation, and evolution through the analysis of nucleic acids and proteins.

molecular probe (probe) A single-stranded nucleic acid or antibody protein labeled with a detectable marker that attaches to a specific target molecule, allowing target molecule detection in subsequent analysis. Single-stranded nucleic acid probes detect target nucleic acids, and antibody probes bind specific target proteins.

monohybrid cross A genetic cross between organisms that are heterozygous for one gene.

monophyletic group A group of organisms with a single common ancestor.

monosomy The presence of a single chromosome instead of a homologous pair, resulting in a chromosome number that is $2n - 1$.

morphogen Substance whose presence in different concentrations directs different developmental fates.

multifactorial inheritance The inheritance of traits whose phenotypic variation is the result of polygenic inheritance and environmental influences. See also *multifactorial trait.*

multifactorial trait Traits whose phenotypic variation is the result of polygenic inheritance and environmental influences. See also *multifactorial inheritance.*

multiple cloning site (MCS) A vector DNA sequence containing several unique restriction enzyme target sequences facilitating cloning of inserted DNA fragments.

multiple gene hypothesis The hypothesis that alleles of multiple genes contribute to the production of certain traits.

multiplication rule See *product rule.*

multipoint linkage analysis A statistical method for testing and mapping alternative orders of multiple genes linked on a chromosome. Related to lod score analysis.

mutagen A chemical, physical, or biological agent capable of damaging DNA and creating a mutation.

mutagenesis A procedure whereby a population of organisms is mutagenized and their progeny are propagated and examined for mutant specific phenotypes. See also *genetic screen.*

mutation An inherited change in DNA.

mutation rate The rate at which mutations occur per gene per unit of time. Most often expressed per gene per generation.

mutation–selection balance An arithmetic expression used to determine the equilibrium frequencies of alleles in populations as a result of allele elimination by natural selection and new allele creation by mutation.

narrow sense heritability (h^2) The proportion of total phenotypic variance that is contributed by additive genetic variance.

natural selection The evolutionary process operating through differences in survival, fecundity, and relative fitness of organisms with different genotypes and phenotypes.

negative control (of transcription) Condition where binding of a repressor protein to a regulatory DNA sequence prevents transcription of a gene or a cluster of genes.

negative interference Occurring when the *coefficient of coincidence (c)* is greater than 1.0, the observation of more double crossovers than expected between a pair of genes.

negative supercoiling Twisting of the DNA duplex in the direction opposite to the turns of the double helix.

neofunctionalization The process, following gene duplication, whereby a mutation in one of the duplicates provides a function not performed by the original gene.

neomorphic mutation A mutant expressing a new or novel function not seen in the wild type.

next-generation sequencing High throughout massively parallel DNA sequencing by synthesis.

N-formylmethionine (fMet; tRNAfMet) A modified methionine amino acid usually used as the amino acid that initiates bacterial translation. Carried by a specialized tRNA.

node An evolutionary branch point in a phylogenetic tree.

noncomposite transposon Bacterial transposable genetic elements that lack insertion sequences.

nondisjunction The failure of homolog or sister chromatid separation during cell division. Results in nuclei with the wrong number of chromosomes.

nonenveloped virus Viral particles consisting only of a protein capsid and other proteinaceous elements.

nonhistone protein Numerous nuclear proteins that are not histones associated with chromosomes.

nonhomologous end joining (NHEJ) An error-prone mechanism of double-stranded DNA break repair in eukaryotic genomes in which damaged nucleotides are removed and blunt ends of strands are joined.

noninducible Condition in which transcription of bacterial genes or operons cannot be activated.

nonparental ditype (NPD) In an ascus, the occurrence of four haploid spores that are each recombinant.

nonpenetrant An organism with a genotype corresponding to a mutant phenotype that instead displays the wild-type phenotype.

nonrecombinant vector Produced in a cloning experiment when the intended vector does not pick up a DNA insert.

nonreplicative transposon A transposable genetic element that transposes by excision from the original genome location, followed by insertion into a new location.

nonrevertible mutants Mutations caused by partial deletion of DNA nucleotides that cannot be reverted to wild type.

nonsense mutation A type of point mutation producing a stop codon in mRNA.

nonsister chromatid A chromatid belonging to a homologous chromosome. Nonsister chromatids of homologs are involved in crossing over.

nontemplate strand See *coding strand.*

normal distribution The continuous distribution of outcomes predicted by chance. Also known as *Gaussian distribution.*

northern blotting A method for transferring mRNA from an electrophoresis gel to a permanent membrane or filter.

north-south (NS) resolution One possible pattern for resolving a Holliday junction to separate homologous chromosomes before meiotic anaphase.

nuclear mitochondrial sequence (NUMTS) Mitochondrial DNA sequences found in the nucleus as a result of recent transfer from the mitochondrial genome to the nuclear genome.

nuclear plastid sequence (NUPTS) Plastid DNA sequences found in the nucleus as a result of recent transfer from the plastid genome to the nuclear genome.

nucleoid The region of bacterial and archaeal cells (or mitochondria or chloroplasts) where the main chromosome resides.

nucleolus (plural: nucleoli) Nuclear organelle containing rRNA-encoding genes.

nucleomorph In a secondary endosymbiosis, the nuclear genome of the secondary endosymbiont.

nucleosome An octameric protein complex composed of two polypeptides each of histones H2A, H2B, H3, and H4, around which DNA wraps in chromatin.

nucleosome core particle The octameric histone protein complex (two molecules each of H2A, H2B, H3 and H4) around which core DNA can wrap.

nucleosome-depleted region (NDR) A 100- to 150-bp region containing few nucleosomes, which lies immediately upstream of the start of transcription.

nucleotide base analog A compound with a size and shape that mimics a natural nucleotide base.

nucleotide excision repair A mechanism of DNA damage repair in which a segment of one strand containing damaged nucleotides is excised and replaced.

null mutation A mutant that produces no functional product. Most commonly a recessive allele. Also known as *amorphic mutation*.

Okazaki fragment A short segment of newly synthesized DNA that is part of a lagging strand and is ligated to other Okazaki fragments to complete lagging strand synthesis.

oncogene A mutated form of a proto-oncogene; frequently associated with cancer development.

one gene–one enzyme hypothesis Proposed by George Beadle and Edward Tatum in 1941, the hypothesis proposing that each gene encodes a specific protein product and controls a distinct function.

open chromatin Chromatin in which the association of DNA with nucleosomes is relaxed in regions containing regulatory sequences, allowing access by regulatory proteins and giving genes in open chromatin the potential to be transcriptionally active.

open promoter Promoters that reside in open chromatin, resulting in constitutive transcription. See also *open promoter complex*.

open promoter complex At transcription initiation, the stage at which RNA polymerase is bound and a short region of DNA opens to allow transcription from the template strand. See also *open promoter*.

operational gene Class of genes that encode proteins involved in cellular metabolic processes (e.g., amino acid biosynthesis, biosynthesis of cofactors, fatty acid and phospholipid biosynthesis, intermediary metabolism, energy metabolism, nucleotide biosynthesis).

operator Regulatory DNA sequences to which repressor or activator proteins bind. Term used in bacterial systems.

operon A set of adjacent genes that are transcribed in a polycistronic mRNA and are thus coordinately regulated; an operon is generally considered to include associated regulatory sequences (e.g., promoter, operator, etc.). Primarily found in bacteria and archaea.

ordered ascus The linear sequence in an ascus of haploid spores whose arrangement allows determination of the chromatids participating in crossing over.

organelle inheritance The transmission of genes on mitochondrial and chloroplast chromosomes.

organizer Groups of cells that possess the ability to influence the fates of cells in the surrounding tissues via non-autonomous signals.

origin of migration The starting point of nucleic acid or protein migration in gel electrophoresis.

origin of replication The specific sequence at which DNA replication begins.

origin of transfer (oriT) The site within the fertility (F) factor sequence where transfer to the recipient cell is initiated.

orthologous genes Genes in different species whose origin lies in a speciation event and that can be traced to a single gene in a common ancestor of the two species. Also known as *orthologs*.

orthologs See *orthologous genes*.

outgroup A species related to members of a *clade* but outside the clade; used to root the clade.

P element A specific type of transposable genetic element prevalent in the *Drosophila* genome.

P value (probability value) In the chi square test, the likelihood that a repeat experiment will produce a result as deviant or more deviant than expected in comparison to the experimental result being tested.

paired-end sequencing Sequence generated from both ends of a DNA clone; provides evidence of physical linkage of the two paired sequences.

pair-rule gene In *Drosophila*, genes that delimit parasegments along the anterior-posterior axis; examples include *even-skipped* and *odd-skipped*.

paracentric inversion A chromosome inversion in which the inverted segment does not include the region of the centromere.

paralogous genes Genes whose origin lies in a gene duplication event within an extant or ancestral species. Also known as *paralogs*.

paralogs See *paralogous genes*.

paraphyletic group A group of organisms that includes some but not all the members descended from a common ancestor.

parasegment In *Drosophila*, the posterior part of one segment and the anterior part of its neighbor. The stripes of gene expression of pair-rule genes correspond to parasegments, straddling the boundaries between segments.

parental (nonrecombinant) chromosome Chromosomes in gametes produced when crossing over does not take place between linked genes. Alleles marking each gene are retained in their initial (parental) configurations.

parental ditype (PD) In an ascus, the occurrence of four haploid spores that are each nonrecombinant.

parental generation (P generation) The parents of F_1 progeny. In controlled genetic crosses, the parents are pure-breeding.

parental strand The DNA strand acting as a template to direct the synthesis of a new ("daughter") strand of DNA.

partial chromosome deletion The loss of a segment of a chromosome.

partial deletion The loss of a segment of a chromosome. Results in partial monosomy for the affected chromosome segment.

partial deletion heterozygote An organism with one wild-type chromosome and a homolog that is missing a segment.

partial diploid An exconjugant bacterium that acquires a second copy of one or more genes by conjugation with an F' donor cell.

partial dominance See *incomplete dominance*.

partial duplication The duplication of a segment of a chromosome.

partial duplication heterozygote An organism with one wild-type chromosome and a homologous chromosome with a duplicated segment.

particle gun bombardment Technique of using high pressure to fire microscopic particles coated with DNA into plant cells. The particles are propelled with enough force to penetrate the cell wall and plasma membrane.

particulate inheritance Mendel's theory that genetic information is transmitted from one generation to the next as discrete units or elements of heredity.

Pascal's triangle A diagram listing the coefficients of a given binomial expansion in which the binomial expression is expanded *n* number of times.

pathogenicity island Regions of laterally transferred DNA that contain genes with pathogenic function.

pedigree A family tree composed of standard symbols that depicts relationships in successive generations and often displays individual phenotypes.

penetrant Expression of the phenotype corresponding to a particular genotype.

peptide bond A type of covalent bond that joins amino acids in polypeptide chains. Formed between the amino end of one amino acid and the carboxyl end of the adjoining amino acid.

peptide fingerprint analysis A form of chromatography in which polypeptide fragments are separated and distinctive patterns revealed.

peptidyl site (P site) The site on the ribosome where amino acids are joined by a peptide bond.

pericentric inversion A chromosome inversion in which the inverted segment includes the region of the centromere.

permissive condition Environmental condition in which environmentally sensitive (e.g., temperature sensitive) mutants exhibit the wild-type phenotype or can survive.

phenocopy A phenotype similar to a phenotype caused by mutation but that is produced instead by an environmental condition.

phenotype (1) The observable physical characteristics or traits of an organism. (2) The physical manifestation of a specific genotype.

phenotypic ratio (3:1 ratio and 9:3:3:1 ratio) A ratio or set of relative proportions between organisms with different phenotypes— for example, the ratio of progeny produced by a monohybrid cross (3:1) or a dihybrid cross (9:3:3:1).

phenotypic variance (V_P) The total variance observed for a trait.

phosphodiester bond A type of covalent bond formed between two nucleotides in a nucleic acid strain. Formed between the 5′ phosphate group of one nucleotide and the 3′ OH of the adjacent nucleotide.

photoproduct A characteristic DNA lesion produced by exposure to ultraviolet light.

photoreactive repair A mechanism of DNA damage repair in bacteria that uses light in the visible part of the spectrum to provide the energy to remove the damage done by ultraviolet irradiation.

phylogenetic footprinting Technique whereby conserved sequences are identified by searching for similar sequences in species separated by large evolutionary distances.

phylogenetic shadowing Technique whereby conserved sequences are identified by first eliminating sequences that are not conserved in closely related species.

phylogenetic tree A diagram of evolutionary relationships among organisms or genes based on morphological or molecular characteristics.

phylogenomics Method for determining phylogenetic relationships of organisms using genomic DNA sequence information. See also *evolutionary genomics*.

physical gap Sequence gap between scaffolds for which there is no clone to supply the sequence.

plasmid One of multiple types of extrachromosomal circular DNA molecules that may be found in bacterial cells.

plastid Organelle, bounded by a double membrane, descended from the cyanobacterial endosymbiont; specialized types of plastids include chloroplasts and chromoplasts.

pleiotropy A single gene mutation that affects multiple and seemingly unconnected properties of an organism.

pluripotent State of a cell when it can give rise to many but not all cell types of an organism.

point mutation A DNA lesion at a defined location. Usually either a base pair substitution or the insertion or deletion of one or a small number of base pairs.

polar mutation Mutations affecting downstream genes in an operon by reducing production or altering translation of polycistronic mRNA.

polyacrylamide A synthetic compound mixed with buffer and used to form electrophoresis gels.

polyadenylation signal sequence A hexanucleotide sequence of mRNA, usually AAUAAA, that identifies the location of 3′ pre-mRNA cleavage and polyadenylation.

polycistronic mRNA In bacteria, an mRNA containing the transcripts of two or more genes.

polygenic inheritance A quantitative trait dependent on the contributions of multiple genes. Also known as *polygenic trait*.

polygenic trait See *polygenic inheritance*.

polymerase chain reaction (PCR) A laboratory method for controlled replication of a specific target sequence of DNA in successive cycles. Using two short single-stranded primers that bind to sequences on opposite sides of the target sequence, exponential replication of the target sequence occurs.

polypeptide A chain of amino acids joined by peptide bonds. Formed at ribosomes during translation.

polyploidy The presence of more than two complete sets of chromosomes in a genome. See also *allopolyploidy* and *autopolyploidy*.

polyribosome In translation, the simultaneous translational activity of multiple ribosomes on a single mRNA.

population A group of organisms that mate with one another to establish the next generation.

population genetics The subfield of genetics that studies the genetic structure and evolution of populations.

positional cloning The process by which the DNA sequence of a gene identified only by mutant phenotype can be obtained by using genetic and physical maps. Also known as *chromosome walking*.

positional information Process by which gene expression or other chemical cues establish geographical addresses along the axes of a developing embryo or organ primordium.

position effect variegation (PEV) The observation in *Drosophila* of a specific type of mutation producing variegation of eye color due to the abnormal positioning of the *w* (white) gene for eye color.

positive control (of transcription) Condition where binding of an activator protein to a regulatory DNA sequence stimulates transcription of a gene or a cluster of genes.

positive–negative selection The use of both negative and positive selectable markers to follow the fate of introduced DNA to select for homologous recombination events.

positive supercoiling Superhelical twisting of DNA.

posttranslational polypeptide processing In eukaryotes, modifications to polypeptides in the endoplasmic reticulum and Golgi apparatus after the completion of translation.

postzygotic mechanism Mechanisms operating after mating to reduce or prevent the possibility of producing hybrids between populations or species.

precursor microRNA (pre-miRNA) The stem loop product derived from processing of pre-microRNAs. The pre-microRNA stem loop is further processed by Dicer to produce the mature single-stranded microRNA from the double-stranded region of the stem loop.

precursor mRNA (pre-mRNA) The initial transcript of a eukaryotic gene requiring mRNA processing prior to translation.

preinitiation complex (PIC) In eukaryotic transcription, a large multiprotein complex containing several general transcription factors and RNA polymerase II.

prezygotic mechanism Mechanisms operating before mating to reduce or prevent the possibility of producing hybrids between populations or species.

Pribnow box (–10 consensus sequence) A specific consensus sequence component of the bacterial promoter with a location centered at approximately −10 relative to the start of transcription.

primary microRNA (pri-miRNA) The primary transcript, with single-stranded ends and a stem loop, from which pre-microRNAs are derived by processing. The single-stranded ends of the pri-microRNA are removed, by Drosha in animals and Dicer in plants, to produce the pre-microRNA.

primase (DnaG) The specialized RNA polymerase that synthesizes the RNA primer during DNA replication.

primer annealing In PCR, the binding by complementary base pairing of a short single-stranded primer by complementary base pairing.

primer extension In PCR, the synthesis of DNA by DNA polymerase beginning at the 3′ end of a short single-stranded primer.

primer walking Technique for sequencing long DNA molecules where new sequencing primers are synthesized based on successive DNA sequence reads. Compare with *shotgun sequencing*.

product rule The probability of an event requiring the sequential or simultaneous occurrence of two or more contributing events. The probabilities of contributing events are multiplied, and their product is the event in question. Also known as the *multiplication rule*.

proliferating cell nuclear antigen (PCNA) In eukaryotic DNA replication, the functional equivalent of the bacterial sliding clamp that adheres DNA polymerase to the template strand and drives its progression.

prometaphase In *M phase* of the cell cycle, sometimes identified as a stage between prophase and metaphase.

promoter A regulatory sequence of DNA near the 5′ end of a gene that acts as the binding location of RNA polymerase and directs RNA polymerase to the start of transcription.

promoter mutation A mutation altering promoter sequence and function.

promoter-specific element (PSE) A specific promoter consensus sequence located upstream of small nuclear RNA genes.

prophage The designation for bacteriophage that has integrated into the host bacterial chromosome.

prophase The stage of *M phase* during which chromosome condensation occurs.

protein A string of amino acids encoded during translation of mRNA and linked together by peptide bonds. See also *polypeptide*.

proteome Set of the proteins in a cell, tissue, or organism.

proteomics The study of all the proteins, collectively known as the proteome, within a cell, tissue, or organism.

proto-oncogene A broad category of normal genes producing protein whose generalized functions promote cell proliferation. It is often mutated in carcinogenesis.

prototroph The wild-type strain of a microorganism. Also, any organism that can synthesize its nutrients from inorganic material.

pseudoautosomal region (PAR) Homologous regions on the X and Y chromosomes that synapse and cross over.

pseudodominance The phenotypic expression of a recessive allele on one chromosome due to deletion of a portion of the homologous chromosome containing the dominant allele.

pseudogene Sequences recognizable as mutated gene sequences often derived from gene duplication or retrotransposition events.

Punnett square Named in honor of early 20th–century geneticist Reginald Punnett, a checkerboard-like diagram that predicts the genotypes and genotype frequencies of progeny from a genetic cross.

pure-breeding strains A group of genetically identical homozygous organisms that, when self-fertilized or intercrossed, only produce offspring that have a phenotype identical to the parents. Also known as *true-breeding strains*.

pyrimidine dimer The specific type of lesion formed on DNA due to exposure to ultraviolet irradiation. Also known as *thymine dimer*.

QTL locus analysis A method for characterizing the effects of quantitative trait loci on variation.

QTL mapping A method for locating quantitative trait loci in a genome.

quantitative genetics The subfield of genetics that studies quantitative traits.

quantitative trait A trait exhibiting polygenic inheritance and displaying continuous phenotypic variation.

quantitative trait locus (QTL) A gene contributing to the phenotypic variation of a quantitative trait.

quaternary structure The state of protein function requiring the joining of two or more polypeptides to form a functional protein (e.g., hemoglobin protein).

R-group The functional groups that give each amino acid their distinctive characteristics.

R (resistance) plasmid A type of bacterial plasmid conferring resistance to one or more antibiotic compounds.

radial loop–scaffold model A model of chromatin structure that predicts rosettes of looped chromatin on a chromosome scaffold.

random X inactivation (Lyon hypothesis) Proposed by Mary Lyon in the mid-20th century, the process of randomly inactivating one copy of the X chromosome in each mammalian female nucleus early in zygotic development.

reader A chromatin modifying enzyme that binds to chemical groups of chromatin (e.g., methyl or acetyl groups on the lysines of histone 3).

reading frame The partitioning of sequential sets of mRNA trinucleotide segments (codons) that are used in translation to determine amino acid order of a polypeptide.

realizator gene In *Drosophila*, the *Hox* target genes whose expression contributes to the characteristic morphology of each segment.

RecBCD pathway A complex of three bacterial proteins that cut DNA and facilitate homologous recombination, a foundation of eukaryotic homologous recombination.

recessive epistasis (9:3:4 ratio) A characteristic ratio of phenotypes produced by the interaction of two genes that control a trait in which alleles of one gene mask or reduce the expression of alleles of a second gene.

recessive phenotype The phenotype observed in an organism that is homozygous for the recessive allele. Compare with *dominant phenotype*.

recipient cell (F⁻ cell) A bacterial cell that does not contain fertility factor DNA sequence and can conjugate with a donor bacterium.

reciprocal cross Paired crosses involving distinct parental phenotypes in which the sexes are switched (i.e., if one cross is ♂ phenotype A × ♀ phenotype B, the reciprocal cross is ♂ phenotype B × ♀ phenotype A).

reciprocal translocation (balanced, unbalanced) Exchange of chromosome segments between non-homologous chromosomes. If all genes are present, the translocation is "balanced," but if genes are missing, the translocation is "unbalanced."

recombinant (nonparental) chromosome Chromosomes in gametes produced by crossing over between linked genes. Alleles marking each gene are rearranged on chromatids by crossing over.

recombinant clone A combination of DNA molecules from different sources (e.g., vector and insert DNA) that are joined together using *recombinant DNA technology*.

recombinant DNA technology The set of laboratory techniques developed for amplifying, maintaining, and manipulating specific DNA sequences in vitro as well as in vivo.

recombination coldspot A chromosome region with a recombination rate that is lower than average for the number of nucleotide base pairs present.

recombination hotspot A chromosome region with a recombination rate that is higher than average for the number of nucleotide base pairs present.

recombination frequency (r) The rate of occurrence of recombination between a pair of linked genes. Expressed as the number of recombinants divided by the total number of meioses.

recombination nodule Protein aggregations along the synaptonemal complex that are thought to play a role in crossing over.

reference genome sequence The DNA sequence of the individual or individuals used to construct the initial complete genome sequence.

regulated transcription Condition in which gene expression is controlled at the transcriptional level in response to changing environmental conditions.

regulatory mutation A mutation altering a regulated attribute of gene expression.

relative fitness (w) In evolutionary genetics, the measurement of the reproductive fitnesses of organisms in a population relative to one another. The organism class with greatest fitness has a relative fitness of $w = 1.0$.

release factor (RF) Molecules that bind mRNA stop codons and contribute to translation termination.

repetitive DNA Sequences of DNA that are found in more than one locus in a genome.

repetitive DNA sequence DNA sequences that contain repeating nucleotides with unit lengths ranging from two base pairs (dinucleotides) to thousands of base pairs.

replicate cross Repeated crosses involving parents with the same genotypes and phenotypes.

replication bubble A region of active bidirectional DNA replication containing replication forks on each end, an origin of replication in the middle, and leading and lagging strands in each half of the bubble.

replication fork In DNA replication, the site of the replisome structure, and the site of synthesis of leading strand and lagging strand DNA.

replicative segregation Random segregation of organelles during cell division.

replicative transposition Transposition carried out by replicating a copy of a transposable element and inserting the copy in a new genome location.

replisome The large molecular machine located at the replication fork that coordinates multiple reaction steps during DNA replication.

reporter gene A gene whose expression is easy to assay phenotypically. Fusion of reporter genes with heterologous sequences allows both transcriptional and translational expression patterns to be visualized.

repressible operon Operon that is expressed under one set of environmental conditions, but whose transcription is repressed under an alternative environmental condition (i.e., the *trp* operon).

repressor protein A transcription factor that binds to regulatory sequences associated with a gene and represses that gene's expression.

reproductive isolation The absence of interbreeding between populations or species; often involves geographic, physical, or behavioral mechanisms or conditions.

response to selection (R) The amount of change in the phenotype of a trait between parental and offspring generations as a result of selection on the parents.

restriction endonuclease One of a large number of DNA-digesting enzymes, usually of bacterial origin, that cut DNA at specific recognition sites called restriction sequences. Each enzyme has its own particular *restriction sequence* and generates double-stranded cleavage of DNA at the restriction sequence. Also known as *restriction enzyme*.

restriction enzyme A DNA endonuclease that targets a specific base pair sequence for enzymatic cleavage.

restriction fragment length polymorphism (RFLP) A fragment of DNA generated by treatment with a restriction endonuclease.

restriction map A map showing the numbers and relative positions of target sites for restriction enzymes of a DNA molecule.

restriction sequence The specific base-pair sequence recognized by a particular restriction endonuclease.

restriction-modification system System of a restriction enzyme with a specific recognition sequence and a modifying enzyme that adds methyl groups to bases of the recognition sequence. The system protects the bacteria's own DNA from being digested by endogenous restriction enzymes but allows restriction of invading exogenous DNA.

restrictive condition Environmental condition in which environmentally sensitive (e.g., temperature sensitive) mutants exhibit the mutant phenotype.

retrotransposon A transposable element that uses reverse transcriptase to transpose through an RNA intermediate.

reverse genetics Genetic analysis that begins with a gene sequence, which is used to identify or introduce mutant alleles and subsequently to identify and evaluate the resulting mutant phenotype. It is the complementary approach to forward genetics.

reverse mutation rate (v) The rate at which mutant alleles are reverted to wild-type alleles. Also known as *reversion rate*.

reverse transcriptase Enzyme, derived from retroviruses or retrotransposons, that catalyzes the synthesis of a DNA strand (cDNA) from an RNA template.

reverse transcription The process of DNA synthesis from an RNA template by the enzyme reverse transcriptase.

reverse translation The process of using the genetic code to deduce the possible DNA sequences encoding a specific amino acid sequence.

reversion mutation A mutation that alters a mutant to wild-type sequence and function. Also known as *reversion*.

reversion rate The rate at which reversion (reverse) mutations occur in an organism.

revertible mutant A point mutation caused by base-pair substitution or deletion of one or a few base pairs that can be reverted to wild type.

rho-dependent termination (rho protein) The process of bacterial *transcription termination* involving rho protein.

rho utilization site (rut site) The site of attachment of rho protein that aids in rho-protein-driven bacterial *transcription termination*.

ribonucleic acid (RNA) A family of polynucleotides that are transcribed from DNA. RNAs are composed of nucleotides containing the sugar ribose, one or more phosphate atoms, and one of four nitrogenous bases (A, G, C, and U).

ribonucleotide Composed of ribose, one or more phosphate groups, and one of four nitrogenous bases, the nucleotides that make up RNA. See also *adenine (A)*, *uracil (U)*, *guanine (G)*, and *cytosine (C)*.

ribose The 5-carbon sugar molecule in ribonucleotides.

ribosomal RNA (rRNA) A group of RNA molecules that compose part of the structure of ribosomes.

ribosome Ribonucleoprotein particles, composed of rRNAs and numerous proteins, at which translation takes place.

ribozymes Catalytically active RNAs.

RNA editing The process of post-transcriptional addition or removal of nucleotide of certain mRNAs.

RNA interference (RNAi) A regulatory gene-silencing mechanism based on double-stranded RNA, which can target complementary sequences for inactivation. The machinery can be harnessed to silence gene expression in a reverse genetic approach.

RNA pol A shorthand term for *RNA polymerase*.

RNA polymerase The enzyme that catalyzes the synthesis of RNA. See also *RNA pol*, *RNA pol I*, *RNA pol II*, and *RNA pol III*.

RNA polymerase I (RNA pol I) In eukaryotic transcription, the enzyme that transcribes certain rRNA genes.

RNA polymerase II (RNA pol II) In eukaryotic transcription, the enzyme that transcribes protein-coding genes to produce mRNA.

RNA polymerase III (RNA pol III) In eukaryotic transcription, the enzyme that transcribes tRNA genes.

RNA polymerase core The five-polypeptide component of bacterial RNA polymerase that actively carries out transcription.

RNA primer In DNA replication, the short, single-stranded RNA segment synthesized by primase. The 3' end of the RNA primer is used by DNA polymerase to begin synthesis of DNA.

RNA-induced silencing complex (RISC) Complex containing Argonaute protein that binds small RNA molecules and targets complementary RNA molecules for degradation or translational repression.

RNA-induced transcription-silencing (RITS) complex RISC-like complex that mediates small RNA-induced transcriptional gene silencing.

Robertsonian translocation The fusion of two non-homologous chromosomes, often with the deletion of a small amount of nonessential genetic material. Also known as *chromosome fusion*.

rolling circle replication A unidirectional mode of DNA replication used to replicate circular plasmid molecules in which the replicating circular molecule appears to reel off its nontemplate DNA strand, using the other as the template for replication.

S phase (synthesis phase) The middle phase of interphase, during which DNA replication takes place.

Sanger method See *dideoxy DNA sequencing*.

saturation mutagenesis Mutagenesis aimed at identifying multiple mutant alleles for all loci in the genome of an experimental organism.

scaffold A set of contigs that are physically linked.

scanning In eukaryotic translation, the process used by the small ribosomal subunit to locate the authentic start codon.

secondary endosymbiosis (tertiary endosymbiosis) Endosymbiotic event where one eukaryotic, usually photosynthetic, is an endosymbiont within another eukaryote resulting in an organism with genomes derived from at least two nuclear genomes and multiple organellar genomes.

secondary structure A form of protein folding in which hydrogen bonds between amino acids of a polypeptide stabilize α-helical twists or β-sheets.

second-division segregation Patterns of haploid spores in an ascus that indicate the alleles were separated at the second meiotic division as a result of crossing over between a gene and the centromere.

second-site reversion A specific type of reversion taking place at a location separate from the site altered to generate the original mutation.

segment Division of the body along the anterior-posterior axis into a series of morphological similar units.

segment polarity genes In *Drosophila*, genes that delimit the anterior and posterior regions of individual parasegments along the anterior-posterior axis; examples include *wingless*, *engrailed*, *hedgehog*, and *gooseberry*.

selected marker screen An experimental method used to detect microorganisms with a specific genotype.

selection coefficient (s) The value of the reduction in reproductive fitness for an organism (i.e., $w = 1.0 - s$).

selection differential (S) The difference between the population mean value for a phenotype and the phenotype value of population members selected as parents for the next generation.

selective growth medium The growth medium used in a selective marker screen.

semiconservative replication The established method of DNA replication in which each strand of a parental duplex acts as a template for daughter strand synthesis and each daughter duplex is composed of one parental strand and a complementary daughter strand.

semisterility Reduced fertility, commonly the result of the occurrence of adjacent segregation during meiosis in balanced translocation heterozygotes.

sequence gap Gap between two contigs for which a clone is available for further sequencing that could close the gap.

sex chromosome Homologous chromosomes that differ between the sexes. Designated X and Y in species in which females are XX and males XY. Designated Z and W in species in which females are ZW and males are ZZ.

sex determination The genetically controlled processes that determine the sex of offspring.

sex-influenced expression The differential expression of an allele that depends on whether it occurs in a male or a female. Usually detected in heterozygous genotypes.

sex-influenced trait A gene, usually autosomal, whose expression differs between males and females of a species. Also known as *sex-influenced expression.*

sex-limited trait A gene or trait expressed exclusively in one sex. Also known as sex-limited gene.

sex-linked inheritance The inheritance of genes on the sex chromosomes.

shared derived characteristics Characteristics or traits of organisms that evolve from more ancestral characteristics or traits found in ancestral organisms.

Shine–Dalgarno sequence In bacterial translation, the 5′ UTR mRNA consensus sequence that pairs with nucleotides near the 3′ end of 16S rRNA in the small ribosomal subunit to orient the start codon on the ribosome.

shotgun sequencing Method for sequencing large molecules of DNA that relies on redundant sequencing of fragmented target DNA in the hope that all regions will be sequenced at least a few times. Contrast with *primer walking.*

shuttle vector A vector that can replicate in two species and thus can be used to shuttle DNA sequences between them.

sickle cell disease (SCD) A human autosomal recessive disorder resulting from homozygosity; a specific mutant allele (β^S) of the β-globin gene that is part of hemoglobin protein.

sigma (σ) subunit Accessory protein that changes the promoter-recognition specificity of the bacterial RNA polymerase core.

signal hypothesis The accepted hypothesis proposing that the polypeptide *leader sequence* identify post-translational processing and transport.

signal sequence A string of amino acids at the N terminal and of certain eukaryotic polypeptides containing information directing post-translational processing and the extracellular destination of the polypeptide. Also known as *leader sequence.*

silencer A eukaryotic cis-acting DNA regulatory sequence to which trans-acting factors bind to repress transcription.

silencer sequence Regulatory DNA sequences that can repress transcription of specific genes that may be located distantly from the sequence. Also known as a *silencer.*

silent mutation A base substitution mutation that changes one codon to a synonymous codon and does not alter the amino acid sequence of a polypeptide.

simple transposon In bacterial transposition, a transposon containing multiple genes between two inverted repeats.

single nucleotide polymorphism (SNP) A single base-pair difference in a specific genome location detected by comparing individual DNA sequences.

single-stranded binding protein (SSB) In DNA replication, a protein that adheres to each template strand following unwinding by helicase to prevent strand reannealing before the arrival of the replication fork.

sister chromatids The identical DNA duplexes that are produced by DNA replication and are temporarily joined to one another during the early stages of cell division.

sister chromatid cohesion The protein-based temporary attachment of sister chromatids facilitated by cohesin protein that resists the pulling forces of spindle fibers in metaphase.

site-directed mutagenesis Introduction of specific nucleotide changes in a DNA molecule in vitro.

site-specific recombination An exchange between two DNA molecules that requires specific sequences in common and that is catalyzed by an enzyme specific to that recombination (e.g., integration of phage lambda into the *E. coli* genome).

sliding clamp In bacterial DNA replication, the multisubunit protein complex that joins with DNA polymerase to hold polymerase on the template and helps drive polymerase along the template.

small interfering RNA (siRNA) Single-stranded 21- to 24-nucleotide RNA molecules derived from either endogenous or exogenous double-stranded RNA molecules that are incorporated in RISC to mediate RNAi. Endogenously produced siRNAs are most often from non-genic regions (e.g., repetitive RNA or products of an RNA-dependent RNA polymerase). Exogenously produced siRNAs are often derived from invading nucleic acids (e.g., transposons and viruses).

small nuclear RNA (snRNA) Regulatory RNAs operating in the nucleus.

small nucleoid-associated proteins In bacterial DNA, small proteins localized to the nucleoid and associated with the main chromosome.

small ribosomal subunit The smaller of two subunits of the ribosome.

solenoid structure See *30-nm fiber.*

somatic gene therapy Gene therapy aimed at correcting a genetic defect in the somatic cells.

Southern blotting A laboratory method devised by Edwin Southern for transferring DNA from an electrophoresis gel to a permanent membrane or filter.

specialized transduction (specialized transducing phage) Transduction from a donor cell to a recipient cell of a few select genes located near the site of bacteriophage integration.

spindle fiber microtubule (kinetochore, polar, and astral microtubule) Composed of tubulin proteins, the fibers emanating from centrosomes that attach to kinetochore regions (kinetochore), overlap to control cell shape (polar), or attach to the cell membrane to stabilize centrosomes (astral).

spliceosome The multiprotein complex that carries out intron splicing.

splicing mutation A mutation altering the normal splicing pattern of a pre-mRNA.

spontaneous mutation Mutations occurring due to spontaneous events or changes involving nucleotides or nucleotide bases.

square root method A method for estimating allele frequencies based on manipulation of the frequency of a homozygous genotype.

SRY The gene on the mammalian Y chromosome known as the sex-determining region of Y that initiates male sex development in mammals.

stabilizing selection A pattern of natural or artificial selection that reduces population variation by removing organisms with extreme phenotypes.

standard deviation (σ) A statistical value that measures the scatter of outcome values around the mean or average outcome value. Expressed as the square root of the sum of squared deviations of each value from the mean value.

start codon Most commonly AUG, encoding methionine, the first codon translated in polypeptide synthesis.

start of transcription The DNA location at which transcription begins.

stem loop Short double-stranded segments of RNA topped by a single-stranded loop containing unpaired nucleotides. Also known as a *hairpin structure*.

sticky end Short single-stranded overhangs created by the cleavage of DNA by specific restriction endonucleases, which can potentially base-pair with complementary single-stranded sequences.

stop codon One of three codons that bind a release factor instead of base-pairing with tRNA to initiate a series of events that stops translation.

strand invasion During synthesis-dependent strand annealing and meiotic recombination, the entry of the 3′ end of a displaced DNA into the intact sister chromatid.

strand polarity (5′ and 3′) The orientation of a nucleic acid strand indicating its 5′ phosphate and 3′ hydroxyl ends.

strand slippage During DNA replication, a mutational event leading to increased or decreased numbers of repeating nucleotides in newly synthesized DNA and caused by

slippage of DNA polymerase on the template strand or slippage of the newly synthesized strand on DNA polymerase.

structural gene A protein-producing gene whose product plays a biosynthetic, metabolic, or structural role in cells.

structural genomics The sequencing of whole genomes and the cataloging, or annotation of sequences within a given genome.

structural maintenance of chromosomes (SMC) protein A category of bacterial proteins localized to the nucleoid and associated with the main chromosome.

Su(var) **mutations** Mutations that suppress position effect variegation in *Drosophila*. Mutated genes produce proteins that are active in chromatin remodeling.

subcloning Process by which DNA clones are further subdivided in order to clone still smaller fragments for analyses.

subfunctionalization The process, following gene duplication, whereby mutations in each of the two copies can result in the two genes having complementary activities such that their combined activity is the same as the activity of the gene before duplication.

submetacentric chromosome A chromosome with a centromere located near the midpoint that produces long and short arms of different lengths.

sugar-phosphate backbone The alternating sugar (deoxyribose or ribose) and phosphate molecule pattern of nucleic acid strands formed by the formation of phosphodiester bonds linking nucleotides in the strand.

sum rule The probability of an event that can result from two or more equivalent outcomes. The probabilities of the contributing events are added, and their sum is the probability of the event in question. Also known as the *addition rule*.

supercoiled DNA The superhelical twisting of covalently closed circular DNA. See *positive supercoiling* and *negative supercoiling*.

suppressor mutation A mutation whose effect is to reverse the effect of another mutation. Acts to restore wild-type, or near wild-type, function.

suppressor screen A modifier genetic screen designed to identify mutations in genes that suppress the phenotypic effects of mutations in another gene.

SWI/SNF (switch/sucrose nonfermentable) A yeast chromatin-remodeling complex that modulates nucleosome positioning in an ATP-dependent manner.

SWR1 complex (switch remodeling 1) A chromatin-remodeling complex responsible for replacing the common histone 2A protein of nucleosomes with a variant form known as H2AZ.

sympatric speciation An evolutionary process in which new species form in overlapping

regions. Reproductive isolation mechanisms accompanying speciation are usually behavioral or mechanical.

synapsis The close approach and contact between homologous chromosomes during early prophase I in meiosis.

synaptonemal complex A specialized three-layer protein complex, consisting of a central element and two lateral elements, that forms between homologous chromosomes at synapsis.

syncytial blastoderm Stage of *Drosophila* embryogenesis in which the nuclei are located at the periphery of the embryo but are not separated by cell membranes.

syncytium A multinucleated cell in which the nuclei are not separated by cell membranes.

synonymous codon The groups of codons that specify the same amino acid.

syntenic genes Genes located on the same chromosome.

synteny The conserved order of genes together on a chromosome in species that share a common ancestor.

synthesis-dependent strand annealing (SDSA) An error-free mechanism for repair of DNA double-strand breaks occurring after the completion of DNA replication and utilizing strand invasion to provide wild-type sequences for repair.

synthetic lethality The situation where a particular double mutant results in lethality but the two respective single mutants are viable.

systems biology Prediction of biological functions of genes based on correlations between different data sets.

T strand The DNA strand of the T-DNA cleaved to initiate the transfer of plasmid DNA during rolling circle replication.

targeted induced local lesions in genomes (TILLING) A reverse genetic approach in which a population of organisms of an inbred strain is randomly mutagenized throughout the genome and this population is then screened to find mutations in a gene of interest for which the sequence is known.

TATA-binding protein (TBP) A general transcription factor protein that binds the TATA box and assists in binding other transcription factors and RNA polymerase II to promoters.

TATA box The thymine- and adenine-rich consensus sequence region found in most eukaryotic promoters. Also known as *Goldberg-Hogness box*.

TBP-associated factor (TAF) Specific general transcription factors that associate with TATA-binding protein.

telocentric chromosome A chromosome with a centromere located at one end, producing a long arm only.

GLOSSARY

telomerase The ribonucleoprotein complex whose RNA component provides a template used to synthesize repeating DNA segments that form chromosome telomeres.

telomere Repeating DNA sequences, synthesized by *telomerase*, at the ends of linear chromosomes in eukaryotes; contain dozens to hundreds of copies of specific short DNA sequence repeats that buffer the coding sequence of the chromosome from loss during successive cycles of DNA replication.

telophase The last stage of *M phase*, in which the nuclear contents are divided (*karyokinesis*) and the daughter cells are divided (*cytokinesis*).

temperate phage A bacteriophage, such as λ phage, that can integrate into the bacterial host chromosome and produce either the lytic or lysogenic life cycle.

temperature-sensitive allele A mutation evident only at or above a certain temperature due to an abnormality of the protein product that affects its stability.

template strand The DNA strand serving as a template for synthesis of a complementary nucleic acid strand.

terminal deletion The loss of a chromosome segment that includes the telomeric region.

terminal inverted repeat Identical sequences found at both ends of a transposable genetic element. The sequences are inverted relative to one another.

termination region The region of a gene containing the transcription-terminating sequence or region.

termination sequence DNA sequences that serve to stop transcription. Also known as *transcription termination*.

termination stem loop Stem loop of an mRNA transcript that signals RNA polymerase to terminate transcription in the leader region of bacterial attenuator-controlled operons (e.g., *trp* operon).

tertiary structure The state of protein folding stabilized by hydrogen bonds and covalent bonds that form the functional structure of a protein. A protein may have more than one tertiary structure.

test cross The cross of an organism with the dominant phenotype that may be heterozygous with an organism that is homozygous for a recessive allele. Also known as test-cross analysis.

tetrad An ascus containing four haploid spores.

tetrad analysis The analysis of genetic linkage by analysis of different tetrad segregation types.

tetratype (TT) In an ascus, the occurrence of both types of parentals and both types of recombinants among the spores.

thalassemias A large category of inherited anemias caused by reduced production of hemoglobin. These mutations cause an imbalance in the production of α-globin and β-globin protein.

theta value (θ value) See *θ (theta) value*.

third-base wobble The flexibility of purine-pyrimidine base pairing between the third base of a codon and the corresponding nucleotide of the anticodon.

three-point test-cross analysis A test cross designed to identify genetic linkage between three genes and to provide data for determination of recombination frequency between linked genes.

three-strand double crossover The occurrence of double crossover involving three of the four chromatids.

threshold of genetic liability In polygenic and multifactorial inheritance, a trait with different phenotypes (e.g., affected and unaffected) that are determined by whether individual organisms are above or below a particular critical value on the phenotypic scale. Also known as *threshold trait*.

threshold trait See *threshold of genetic liability*.

thymine (T) One of four nitrogenous nucleotide bases in DNA; one of the two types of pyrimidine nucleotides in DNA.

thymine dimer See *pyrimidine dimer*.

tiling array DNA array that contains all sequences of the genome or a genomic interval, including introns, exons, untranslated regions (UTRs), and intergenic regions.

time-of-entry mapping A method of donor gene mapping by conjugation that uses interrupted mating to determine the order and relative timing of gene transfer.

Ti plasmid A large (200 kb) circular plasmid of *Agrobacterium tumefaciens* that harbors genes for transfer of DNA into plants cells and genes that cause uncontrolled division of plant cells; hence, the tumor-inducing (Ti) plasmid. It has been engineered for the construction of transgenic plants.

topoisomerase Enzyme that relaxes DNA supercoiling by controlled strand nicking and rejoining.

totipotency State of a cell when it can give rise to any and all cell types of an organism.

trans-acting Acting between two molecules (e.g., DNA sequences that control expression of genes interacting with a diffusible protein product).

trans-acting regulatory protein Proteins that act in trans by binding to cis-acting regulatory sequences and consequently regulating nearby genes, either by activating or repressing transcription. Often referred to as *transcription factors (TFs)*.

transcription The cellular process that synthesizes RNA strands from a DNA template strand.

transcription factors (TFs) Proteins that bind promoters and are functional in transcription.

transcription-terminating factor I (TTFI) A specific protein that binds a termination sequence to stop transcription.

transcription termination See *termination sequence*.

transcriptome Set of transcripts present in a cell, tissue, or organism.

transcriptomics The study of all the transcripts, collectively known as the transcriptome, within a cell, tissue, or organism.

transductant The bacterium that is the product of transduction.

transduction In bacterial systems, the process of transfer of DNA from a donor bacterial cell to a recipient cell using a bacteriophage as a vector. More generally can refer to the process by which foreign DNA is introduced into another cell via a viral vector.

transfer DNA (T-DNA) The portion of the Ti plasmid that is transferred from the bacterium into the nucleus of a plant cell.

transfer RNA (tRNA) A family of small RNA molecules that each bind a specific amino acid and convey it to the ribosome, where the anticodon sequence undertakes complementary base pairing with an mRNA codon during translation.

transformant The bacterium that is the product of transformation.

transformation (1) The bacterial process of gene transfer in which donated DNA fragments originating in a dead donor cell, or plasmid DNA, are taken up across the cell wall and membrane of a recipient cell and recombined into the transformant genome. (2) More generally refers to the process by which exogenous DNA is directly taken up by a cell resulting in a genetic alteration of the cell. (3) The conversion of animal cells to an abnormal unregulated state by an oncogenic virus or by transforming DNA.

transgene A gene that has been modified in vitro by recombinant DNA technology and introduced into the genome via transformation.

transgenic organism An organism harboring a transgene.

transition mutation A type of DNA base-pair substitution in which one purine replaces the other or one pyrimidine replaces the other.

translation The process taking place at ribosomes to synthesize polypeptides. Complementary base pairing between mRNA codons and tRNA anticodons determines the order of amino acids composing the polypeptide.

translation repressor protein In bacteria, proteins that regulate translation by binding mRNA in the vicinity of the Shine–Dalgarno sequence and thereby prevent ribosome binding.

translesion DNA synthesis Utilizing a bypass polymerase, a mechanism for replicating DNA in the presence of damage that blocks replication by the common polymerase.

translocation heterozygote An organism with chromosome translocation in which chromosome pairs consist of one normal chromosome and a homolog carrying a translocation.

transmission genetics The subfield of genetics concerned with assessment and analysis of gene transfer from parents to offspring. Synonymous with *Mendelian genetics.*

transposable genetic element A class of DNA sequences that can move from one chromosome location to another, either by excision and reinsertion or by replication and reinsertion of the replicated copy.

transposase The enzyme produced by transposons that cuts DNA to allow the excision and insertion of the transposon.

transposition The process by which mobile genetic elements move from one portion of a genome to another. See also *transposable genetic element.*

transposon tagging Technique used to identify and clone genes through insertion of a transposon into the target gene.

transversion mutation A type of DNA base substitution mutation in which a purine substitutes for a pyrimidine, or vice versa.

tree of life The phylogenetic tree depicting the evolutionary relationships between organisms.

trihybrid cross A genetic cross between organisms that are heterozygous for three genes.

trinucleotide repeat disorder A hereditary disorder caused by a mutant gene containing an increased number of repeats of a DNA trinucleotide sequence.

trisomy The presence in a genome of three copies of a chromosome rather than a homologous pair of chromosomes and resulting in a number of chromosomes that is $2n - 1$.

trisomy rescue In a trisomic genome, the random loss of one extra chromosome to reduce the chromosome number to the diploid.

true-breeding strains See *pure-breeding strains.*

true reversion A type of reversion that exactly reverses the original mutation.

tumor suppressor gene A broad category of normal genes whose generalized functions slow, pause, or stop cell proliferation. It is often mutated in carcinogenesis.

two-hybrid system A method for discovering whether two proteins interact using the GAL4 protein of yeast, which is separated into a DNA-binding domain and a transcriptional activation domain. The two GAL4 domains are fused with the two proteins of interest respectively, and the resultant fusion proteins are assayed for their ability to activate transcription, which indicates interaction of the two proteins of interest.

two-point test-cross analysis A test cross designed to identify genetic linkage between two genes and to provide data for determination of recombination frequency between linked genes.

two-strand double crossover The occurrence of a double crossover involving two of the four chromatids.

ultraviolet (UV) repair A multiprotein DNA damage repair system that corrects lesions caused by exposure to ultraviolet irradiation.

uncharged tRNA A tRNA not carrying an amino acid.

unequal crossover Resulting from the improper synaptic pairing of homologous chromosomes and crossing over between the mispaired chromosomes. A source of duplication and deletion of genetic material.

uniparental disomy In a genome, the presence of a pair of homologous chromosomes that originate from a single parent.

uniparental inheritance Condition in organellar inheritance whereby just one parental gamete—often the maternal gamete—contributes all of the cytoplasmic organelles.

unordered tetrad Haploid spores in an ascus that are arranged in random order.

unpaired loop At synapsis involving partial deletion or partial duplication of one chromosome of a homologous pair, the "extra" genetic material that does not have a homolog on the paired chromosome.

unselected marker screen An experimental technique used to screen microbial genotypes. Commonly used following selected marker screening.

unstable mutant phenotype A mutation with an unusually high frequency of reversion.

upstream Referring to a gene or sequence location that is toward the 5′ direction of a *coding strand.*

upstream activator sequence (UAS) An enhancer-like sequence in yeast, located just upstream of the genes they regulate.

upstream control element An upstream consensus sequence found in certain eukaryotic gene promoters.

uracil (U) One of four nitrogenous nucleotide bases in RNA; one of the two types of pyrimidine nucleotides in RNA.

variable expressivity Variation in the degree, magnitude, or intensity of expression of a phenotype.

variance (S^2) A statistical measurement of the variation of sample values around the mean value.

vector A DNA fragment with attributes that will allow its amplification (origin of replication) in a biological system and serves as a carrier for foreign DNA inserted into it. Vectors usually also possess genes (e.g., encoding resistance to an antibiotic) that allow selection of hosts carrying the vector.

virus An infective particle that carries a rudimentary genome and is an obligate parasite on host cells.

western blotting A method for transferring protein from an electrophoresis gel to a permanent membrane or filter.

whole-genome shotgun (WGS) sequencing An approach to genome sequencing whereby DNA representing the entire genome is fragmented into smaller pieces and a large number of fragments are chosen at random and sequenced with the aim that all genomic regions will be sequenced multiple times. Compare with *clone-by-clone sequencing.*

whole-genome tiling array A microarray on which sequences representing the entire genome are present.

writer A chromatin modifying enzyme that adds chemical groups to chromatin (e.g., methyl or acetyl groups added to the lysines of histone 3).

X/autosome ratio (X/A ratio) The ratio of X chromosomes to a pair of autosomes. Used in *Drosophila* as the mechanism of sex determination.

X-linked dominant A pattern of inheritance consistent with the transmission of a dominant allele of a gene on the X chromosome. Compare with *X-linked recessive.*

X-linked inheritance The pattern of inheritance characteristic of genes located on the X chromosome.

X-linked recessive A pattern of inheritance consistent with the transmission of a recessive allele of a gene on the X chromosome. Compare with *X-linked dominant.*

yeast artificial chromosome (YAC) Cloning vector used in yeast that utilizes an endogenous yeast origin of replication, centromere, and telomere; can accept DNA inserts in excess of 1 megabase.

Y-linked inheritance The exclusively male-to-male transmission of genes on the Y chromosome.

Z_{max} The most likely recombination distance (theta [θ] value) between genes as determined by lod score analysis.

zone of polarizing activity (ZPA) The posterior side of the limb bud that acts as an organizer, secreting Sonic hedgehog (Shh) protein that acts to pattern the developing limb.

Z/W system The sex chromosome inheritance system in species in which the male is homogametic (ZZ) and the female is heterogametic (ZW).

zygotic gene Genes that are active only in the zygote or embryo. For zygotic genes, the genotype of the embryo determines the phenotype.

GLOSSARY

Credits

Photo Credits

Chapter 1 **p. 1, CO-01** Mark F. Sanders; **p. 3, 1.1a** Scala/Art Resource, NY; **p. 3, 1.1b** Andrew McRobb/DK Images; **p. 3, 1.2a** Jenifer Glynn/National Library of Medicine; **p. 3, 1.2b** Dr. G.H. Shull/Library of Congress Prints and Photographs Division; **p. 3, 1.2c** American Philosophical Society; **p. 6, 1.4a** Science Source; **p. 6, 1.4b** Jenifer Glynn/National Library of Medicine; **p. 7, 1.5** National Institutes of Health; **p. 16, 1.13** David Wacey.

Chapter 2 **p. 26, CO-02** Luis Dafos/Alamy; **p. 44, EI2.1** Denise Kappa/Shutterstock.

Chapter 3 **p. 64, CO-03** Pascal Goetgheluck/Science Source; **p. 68, 3.2a–f** Jennifer Waters/Science Source; **p. 71, 3.5a** Don W. Fawcett/Science Source; **p. 71, 3.5b** Dartmouth Electron Microscope Facility; **p. 84, 3.18a** Georg Halder; **p. 84, 3.18b** Georg Halder; **p. 90, 3.22a (left)** Richard Peterson/Shutterstock; **p. 90, 3.23a** Margo Harrison/Shutterstock; **p. 90, 3.22b** Catalin Petolea/Shutterstock; **p. 90, 3.22c** Margo Harrison/Shutterstock; **p. 90, 3.22d** Catalin Petolea/Shutterstock; **p. 90, 3.22e** Margo Harrison/Shutterstock; **p. 90, 3.22f** Richard Peterson/Shutterstock; **p. 90, 3.22g** Potapov Alexander/Shutterstock; **p. 94, 3.25** AP Images; **p. 96, 3.27** Joy Brown/Shutterstock.

Chapter 4 **p. 104, CO-04** Ken Leslie/Photolibrary/Getty Images; **p. 110, 4.3** Karen Petersen; **p. 115, 4.7** John Bowman; **p. 115, 4.8a** McPHOTO/SHU/INSADCO Photography/Alamy; **p. 115, 4.8b** Stanton K. Short/The Jackson Laboratory; **p. 119, 4.13** Biophoto Associates/Science Source; **p. 129, 4.21a, b** Eric Isselee/Shutterstock; **p. 129, 4.21c** Jagodka/Shutterstock; **p. 129, 4.21d, e** Eric Isselee/Shutterstock; **p. 129, 4.21e** Eric Isselee/Shutterstock; **p. 129, 4.21f** Marina Jay/Shutterstock.

Chapter 5 **p. 144, CO-05** Science Source.

Chapter 6 **p. 186, CO-06** David Scharf/Science Source; **p. 188, 6.1** Huntington Potter/University of South Florida College of Medicine; **p. 207, 6.13a** Eye of Science/Science Source; **p. 207, 6.13b** Dr. Michel Wurtz/Biozentrum, University of Basel/Science Source; **p. 215, 6.20** Lester V. Bergman/Encyclopedia/Corbis.

Chapter 7 **p. 227, CO-07** John L. Bowman/University of California at Davis; **p. 229, 7.1** Centers for Disease Control and Prevention (CDC); **p. 239, 7.10** Dr. Gopal Murti/Science Source; **p. 240, 7.12** R.L. Rodriguez, M.S. Dalbey, and C.I. Davern. 1973. "Autoradiographic evidence for bidirectional replication in *Escherichia coli*." *Journal of Molecular Biology* 74:599–604. © 1973 by Elsevier Science Ltd.; **p. 241, 7.13a** Cold Spring Harbour Symposia on Quantitative Biology; **p. 259, 7.30** Cancer Research Technology/Wellcome Images; **p. 262, 7.32** Dr. James Gusella.

Chapter 8 **p. 267, CO-08** Ann L. Beyer; **p. 289, 8.20** Phillip A. Sharp.

Chapter 9 **p. 310, RT9.1** Dr. Robert Traut; **p. 320, 9.11** B.A. Hamkalo and O.L. Miller. 1973. "Electronmicroscopy of genetic material." *Annual Review of Biochemistry* 42:379, Figure 6a.

Chapter 10 **p. 338, CO-10** SPL/Science Source; **p. 339, 10.1** Janice Haney Carr/Centers for Disease Control and Prevention (CDC); **p. 349, 10.10a** John L. Bowman; **p. 349, 10.10b** A.F. Azad, S. Radulovic, J.A. Higgins, B.H. Noden, and J.M. Troyer. 1997. "Flea-borne rickettsioses: ecologic considerations." *Emerging Infectious Diseases* 3(3):319–327. Review Fig. 4.

Chapter 11 **p. 365, CO-11** Reprinted by permission from *Nature Reviews Genetics* 2:292–301. © Macmillan Magazines Limited/Nature Publishing Group, S/B T. Cremer; C. Cremer; **p. 367, 11.2** R.W. Horne/Biophoto Associates/Science Source; **p. 368, 11.3** Dr. Klaus Boller/Science Source; **p. 370, 11.5** Courtesy James C. Wang; **p. 372, 11.6a** Courtesy of James C. Wang; **p. 372, 11.6b** Courtesy of Barbara Hamkalo; **p. 374, 11.8a** Courtesy of Ulrich K. Laemmli; **p. 374, 11.8b** Power and Syred/Science Source; **p. 378, 11.12** Courtesy of Hesed M. Padilla-Nash, Antonio Fargiano, and Thomas Ried, National Cancer Institute, National Institutes of Health; **p. 378, 11.13a** Wellcome Trust Medical Photographic Library; **p. 378, 11.13b** L. Willatt/Science Source; **p. 386, 11.20** Paul Edwards.

Chapter 12 **p. 391, CO-12** Frank Augstein/AP Images.

Chapter 13 **p. 430, CO-13** SPL/Science Source; **p. 438, 13.8** Miguel Sanz Alcantara; **p. 439, 13.9 (top left)** Vanessa Morgan, PSU-Center for Lakes and Reservoirs; **p. 439, 13.9 (bottom left)** FloralImages/Alamy; **p. 439, 13.9 (middle left)** W. Jon Raupp; **p. 439, 13.9 (top middle)** Western Regional Research Center, Agricultural Research Service, U.S. Department of Agriculture; **p. 439, 13.9** Dr. John Brackenbury/Science Source; **p. 439, 13.9** Dr. John Brackenbury/Science Source; **p. 439, 13.9 (top right)** James King-Holmes/Science Source; **p. 439, 13.9 (bottom right top)** Imagebroker/Alamy; **p. 439, 13.9 (middle)** Bon Appetit/Alamy; **p. 439, 13.9 (middle right bottom)** Bon Appetit/Alamy; **p. 439, 13.9 (middle right top)** O. Diez/Arco Images/AGE Fotostock; **p. 439, 13.9 (top left)** Dr. Adina Breiman PhD.

Chapter 14 **p. 468, CO-14** Bettmann/Corbis.

Chapter 15 **p. 504, CO-15 (top left)** Richard Jorgensen; **p. 504, CO-15 (top right)** C. Napoli, C. Lemieux, and R. Jorgensen; **p. 504, CO-15 (bottom)** Richard Jorgensen.

Chapter 16 **p. 533, CO-16** Courtesy of the Archives, California Institute of Technology; **p. 558, 16.17a** Paul W. Sternberg; **p. 558, 16.17b** John L. Bowman/University of California at Davis; **p. 558, 16.17c** Dr. Keith V. Wood, PhD; **p. 558, 16.17d** Courtesy of John Wilson, Baylor College of Medicine; **p. 558, 16.17e** Livet, Weissman, Sanes, and Lichtman. Harvard University; **p. 561, 16.20 (top left)** Eye of Science/Science Source; **p. 561, 16.20 (top right)** Eye of Science/Science Source; **p. 561, 16.20 (bottom left)** David Scharf/Science Source; **p. 561, 16.20 (bottom right)** Eye of Science/Science Source; **p. 562, 16.21 (bottom)** John L. Bowman/University of California at Davis; **p. 562, 16.21 (middle)** John L. Bowman/University of California at Davis; **p. 562,16.21 (top right)** John L. Bowman/University of California at Davis; **p. 562, 16.21** John L. Bowman/University of California at Davis.

Chapter 17 **p. 567, CO-17** Reproduced with permission from the *Annual Review of Plant Physiology and Plant Molecular Biology*; **p. 570, GA17.1** John L. Bowman/University of California at Davis; **p. 572, 17.2** John L. Bowman/University of California at Davis; **p. 575, 17.6b** John L. Bowman/University of California at Davis; **p. 590, 17.18c** John L. Bowman/University of California at Davis; **p. 593, 17.20** Golden Rice Institute; **p. 594, 17.21** Paul W. Sternberg; **p. 596, 17.23** Robert H. Devlin, PhD; **p. 603** The Roslin Institute, The University of Edinburgh.

Chapter 18 **p. 611, CO-18** John Bowman; **p. 615, 18.3** From Fleischmann et al. 1995. "Whole genome random sequencing and assembly of *Haemophilus influenzae* Rd." *Science*; **p. 632, 18.15a** From James Sharpe and Laura Lettice. 1999. "Identification of Sonic hedgehog as a candidate gene responsible for the polydactylous mouse mutant Sasquatch." *Current Biology* 9:97–100; **p. 632, 18.15b** Robert Hill; **p. 637, 18.20** David J. Lockhart and Elizabeth A. Winzeler; **p. 639, 18.21** From Patrick Brown. 1998. "The transcriptional program of sporulation in budding yeast." *Science* 282:699–705; **p. 640, 18.22** From Joseph R. Ecker. 2003. "Empirical analysis of transcriptional activity in the Arabidopsis genome." *Nature*.

Chapter 19 **p. 649, CO-19** Dartmouth Electron Microscope Facility; **p. 663, 19.11** Dr. David Furness/Keele University/Science Source; **p. 663, 19.12** Don W. Fawcett/Science Source; **p. 666, 19.15** Dr. Jeremy Burgess/Science Source; **p. 667, 19.16** Dr. Richard D. Kolodnar/Dana-Farber Cancer Institute.

Chapter 20 **p. 681, CO-20** FLPA/Alamy; **p. 682, 20.1a (left)** Edward B. Lewis, California Institute of Technology Archives; **p. 682, 20.1b (right)** Edward B. Lewis, California Institute of Technology Archives; **p. 682, 20.1b (left)** Edward B. Lewis, California Institute of Technology Archives; **p. 682, 20.1b (right)** Edward B. Lewis, California Institute of Technology Archives; **p. 682, 20.1c** Eye of Science/Science Source; **p. 682, 20.1d** Eye of Science/Science Source; **p. 683, 20.2** Dr. Steven J. Baskauf, PhD; **p. 684, 20.3** James B. Skeath; **p. 684, 20.3** Reproduced with permission from the Annual Review of Cell and Developmental Biology//Edward M. De Robertis and Hiroki Kuroda; **p. 686, 20.5a** Daniel St. Johnston and Wolfgang Driever; **p. 686, 20.5c** James B. Jaynes; **p. 686, 20.5** James B. Jaynes; **p. 686, 20.5b** John Reinitz; **p. 688, 20.6** Daniel St. Johnston and Wolfgang Driever; **p. 688, 20.6b (bottom)** Daniel St. Johnston and Wolfgang Driever; **p. 688, 20.6b (top)** Daniel St. Johnston and Wolfgang Driever; **p. 690, 20.8 (second from top)** Matthias Mannervik; **p. 690, 20.8 (third from top)** Matthias Mannervik; **p. 690, 20.8 (bottom)** Matthias Mannervik; **p. 690, 20.8 (top)** Matthias Mannervik; **p. 690, 20.9c** Stephan Small; **p. 691, 20.10** William McGinnis; **p. 697, 20.14a** Paul W. Sternberg;

p. 698, 20.15 Dr. Erik M. Jorgensen, PhD; **p. 698, 20.15** Paul W. Sternberg; **p. 698, 20.15** Paul W. Sternberg; **p. 702, 20.18** Tatiana Popova/Shutterstock; **p. 704, 20.19 (bottom right)** John L. Bowman/University of California at Davis; **p. 704, 20.19 (left)** John L. Bowman/University of California at Davis; **p. 704, 20.19 (middle)** John L. Bowman/University of California at Davis; **p. 704, 20.19 (top right)** John L. Bowman/University of California at Davis; **p. 705, 20.20a** John L. Bowman/University of California at Davis; **p. 705, 20.20b** John L. Bowman/University of California at Davis; **p. 705, 20.20c** John L. Bowman/University of California at Davis; **p. 705, 20.20d** John L. Bowman/University of California at Davis; **p. 705, 20.20e** John L. Bowman/University of California at Davis; **705, 20.20f** John L. Bowman/University of California at Davis; **p. 705, 20.20g** John L. Bowman/University of California at Davis; **p. 708, 20.22c (left)** Robert Hill; **p. 708, 20.22c (middle)** Robert Hill; **p. 708, 20.22c (right)** W. Binns, L.F. James, and J.L. Shupe; Credit: W. Binns, L.F. James, and J.L. Shupe (1964) "Toxicosis of *Veratrum californicum* in ewes and its relationship to a congenital deformity in lambs." *Annals of the New York Academy of Sciences.*

Chapter 21 **p. 713, CO-21** Peter Morenus.

Chapter 22 **p. 742, CO-22** Pascal Goetgheluck/Science Source.

Text and Illustration Credits

Chapter 1 **p. 3** William Bateson; **p. 19** J.D. Watson and F.H.C. Crick. "Molecular structure of nucleic acids: a structure for deoxyribose nucleic acid"; **p. 32** R. Dawkins. *River Out of Eden: A Darwinian View of Life*, New York: Basic Books; **p. 18, 1.13** Adapted by permission from N.A. Campbell and J.B. Reece, *Biology*, 8th ed., Fig 1.22, p. 17. © 2008.

Chapter 2 **p. 38** Gregor Johann Mendel. Mendel's second law, law of independent assortment.

Chapter 3 **p. 79, 3.14** M. Cummings, *Human Heredity*, 5th ed. © 2000. Brooks/Cole, a part of Cengage Learning, Inc. Reproduced by permission. www.cengage.com/permissions; **p. 94, 3.25b** Adapted by permission from Macmillan Publishers Ltd: *Nature Genetics*, vol. 10, no. 2, Luis E. Figuera, Massimo Pandolfo, Patrick W. Dunne, Jose M. Cantú, and Pragna I. Patel, "Mapping of the congenital generalized hypertrichosis locus to chromosome Xq24 -q27.1," copyright 1995. http://www.nature.com/ng/index.html.; **p. 97, 3.28** Karin Jegalian and Bruce T. Lah. 2001. "Why the YIs so weird." *Scientific American*, 56–61.

Chapter 4 **p. 122, 4.16** M.W. Strickberger. *Genetics*, 3rd ed., p. 543. © 1985. Reprinted and Electronically reproduced by permission of Pearson Education, Inc., Upper Saddle River, New Jersey.

Chapter 5 **p. 148, Table 5.1** Data from J. Hall et al. 1994; **p. 153** A.H. Sturtevant. *A History of Genetics*. Harper & Row, 1965; **p. 164, 5.13** J.L. Weber et al. 1993. "Evidence for human meiotic recombination interference obtained through construction of a short tandem repeat polymorphism linkage map of chromosome." *American Journal of Human Genetics* 19; **p. 165, 5.14** Based on Fig. 11–27, p. 373, Watson et al. *Molecular Biology of the Gene*, 7th ed. Pearson, 2014.

Chapter 6 **p. 198, 6.8a** Adapted from E.L. Wollman, F. Jacob, and W. Hayes. 1956. "Conjugation and genetic recombination in *Escherichia coli* K-12." *Cold Spring Harbor Symposia on Quantitative Biology* 21:141. Used with permission of the © holder, Cold Spring Harbor Laboratory Press and the Estate of Elie Wollman; **p. 198, 6.8a** Based on E.L. Wollman, F. Jacob, and W. Hayes. 1956. "Conjugation and genetic recombination in *Escherichia coli* K-12." *Cold Spring Harbor Symposia on Quantitative Biology* 21:141. Used with permission of the © holder, Cold Spring Harbor Laboratory Press and the Estate of Elie Wollman; **p. 201, 6.10b** Barbara J. Bachmann. 1990. "Linkage map of *Escherichia coli* K-12, Edition 8+." *Microbiological Reviews* 54(2):133. © 1990, American Society for Microbiology. Reproduced with permission from American Society for Microbiology; **p. 217 6.24** Adapted from Seymour Benzer. 1961. "On the topography of the genetic fine structure." *Proceedings of the National Academy of Sciences* 47(3):410, Fig. 6. Used with permission; **p. 218, 6.25** Adapted from Seymour Benzer. 1961. "On the topography of the genetic fine structure." *Proceedings of the National Academy of Sciences* 47(3):406, Fig. 3. Used with permission.

Chapter 7 **p. 228** Edmund Wilson in 1895; **p. 229, 7.2** F. Griffith. 1928. "The significance of pneumococcal types." *Journal of Hygiene* 27:113–159; **p. 230, 7.3** O.T. Avery, C.M. Macleod, and M. McCarty. 1944. "Studies on the chemical nature of the substance inducing transformation of pneumococcal types: induction of transformation by a deoxyribonucleic acid fraction isolated from pneumococcus type III." *Journal of Experimental Medicine* 79:137–158; **p. 231, 7.4** A.D. Hershey and M. Chase. 1952. "Independent function of viral protein and nucleic acid in growth of bacteriophage." *Journal of Genetics and Physiology* 36:39–56; **p. 236** J.D. Watson and F.H.C. Crick. 1953. "A structure for deoxyribose nucleic acid." *Nature* 171:737–738; **p. 237, 7.8** M. Meselson and F.W. Stahl. 1958. "The replication of DNA in *Escherichia coli*." *Proceedings of the National Academy of the Sciences of the USA* 44:671–682; **p. 238, 7.9** M. Meselson and F.W. Stahl. 1958. "The replication of DNA in *Escherichia coli*." *Proceedings of the National Academy of the Sciences of the USA* 44:671–682; **p. 239, 7.11** Reprinted from J.A. Huberman and A.D. Riggs. 1968. "On the mechanism of DNA replication in mammalian chromosomes." *Journal of Molecular Biology* 32:327–341. © 1968, with permission from Elsevier; **pp. 243–244, 7.14** S. Freeman, K. Quillin, and L. Allison. *Biological Science* 5th ed. © 2014. Reprinted and electronically reproduced by permission of Pearson Education, Inc. Upper Saddle River, New Jersey; **p. 250, 7.22** J.D. Watson, T.A. Baker, S.P. Bell, A. Gann, M. Levine, R. Losick, and CSHPL, Inglis. *Molecular Biology of the Gene*, 6th ed. © 2008. Reprinted and Electronically reproduced by permission of Pearson Education, Inc. Upper Saddle River, New Jersey.

Chapter 8 **p. 282, 8.11** From R.M. Myers, K. Tilly, and T. Maniatis. 1986. "Fine structure genetic analysis of a beta-globin promoter." *Science* 232:613–618. Reprinted with permission from AAAS and the author; **p. 288, 8.19** J.D. Watson, T.A. Baker, S.P. Bell, A. Gann, M. Levine, R. Losick, and CSHPL, Inglis. *Molecular Biology of the Gene*, 6th ed., © 2008. Reprinted and Electronically reproduced by permission of Pearson Education, Inc. Upper Saddle River, New Jersey; **p. 292, 8.23b** Reprinted from D.L. Black. "Protein diversity from alternative splicing." *Cell* 103:367–370. © 2000, with permission from Elsevier; **p. 293, 8.24** Adapted from J.P. Lees-Miller, L.O. Goodwin, and D.M. Helfman. 1990. "Three novel brain tropomyosin isoforms are expressed from the rat cx-tropomyosin gene through the use of alternative promoters and alternative RNA processing." *Molecular and Cellular Biology*, Fig. 8, p. 1739. Amended with permission from American Society of Microbiology.

Chapter 9 **p. 306, 9.1** Adapted from S. Freeman, L. Allison, M. Black, G. Podgorski, K. Quillin, J. Monroe, and E. Taylor. *Biological Science*, 5th ed. Pearson Education; **p. 308, Table 9.2** Data from S. Freeman, L. Allison, M. Black, G. Podgorski, K. Quillin, J. Monroe, and E. Taylor. *Biological Science*, 5th ed. Pearson Education; **p. 327, Table 9.8** Data from H.G. Khorana et al. 1967. "Polynucleotide synthesis and the genetic code." *Cold Spring Harbor Symposium on Quantitative Biology* 31:39–49.

Chapter 10 **p. 351, 10.5** J.B. Reece, L.A. Urry, M.L. Cain, S.A. Wasserman, P.V. Minorsky, and R.B. Jackson. *Campbell Biology*, 10th ed., 2013, Figure 5.19, p. 82; **p. 368, 10.17a,b** D. O'Neil. "Modern Theories of Evolution: Natural Selection." http://anthro.palomar .edu/synthetic/synth_4.htm. Accessed 4/22/14. Website created and maintained by Dr. Dennis O'Neil, Behavioral Sciences Department, Palomar College, San Marcos, California. © 1997–2014 by Dennis O'Neil. All rights reserved; **p. 368, 10.17c** Adapted by permission from Macmillan Publishers Ltd: Graham S. Cooke and Adrian V. S. Hill. 2001. "Genetics of susceptibility to human infectious disease." *Nature Reviews Genetics* 2(12). © 2001. http://www.nature.com/nrg/index.html. Data from World66.com; **p. 358, 10.32** Sanders/Bowman; **p. 358, 10.33** Sanders/Bowman; **p. 338, 10.08** Stryer, L. *Biochemistry*, 4th ed., Figure 7.46, p. 171. WH Freeman, 1995.

Chapter 11 **p. 379, 11.15** Adapted by permission from Macmillan Publishers Ltd: Zhijun Duan, Mirela Andronescu, Kevin Schutz, Sean McIlwain, Yoo Jung Kim, and Choli Lee. 2010. "A three-dimensional model of the yeast genome." *Nature* 465(7296). © 2010. ww.nature.com; **p. 380, 11.16** Figure adapted from J.J. Yunis and O. Prakash. 1982. "The origin of man: a chromosomal pictorial legacy." *Science* 215(4539):1525–1530. Reprinted with permission from AAAS. http://www.sciencemag.org/content/215/4539/1525; **p. 385, 11.19** Plate 13.1, unnumbered page following p. 158, in R.A. Garrett and H.P. Klenk (eds.) *Archaea: Evolution, Physiology and Molecular Biology*. Blackwell Publishing, 2007; **p. 386, 11.20** Figure 3, page 523, K. Sandman and J.N. Reeve. 2006. "Archaeal histones and the origin of the histone fold." *Current Opinion in Microbiology* 9(5):520–525.

Chapter 12 **p. 409, 12.16** H.H. Hiatt, J.D. Watson, and J.A. Winsten (eds.). 1977. *Origins of Human Cancer* 1431–1450. Cold Spring Harbor Laboratory Press, Cold Spring Harbor, NY. Used with permission; **p. 414, 12.21** Based on J. Hardin, G. Paul, and L.J. Kleinsmith. *Becker's World of the Cell*, 8th ed. © 2012. Printed and Electronically reproduced by permission of Pearson Education Inc. Upper Saddle River, New Jersey.

Chapter 13 **p. 435, Table 13.3** Data adapted from F.B. Hook and A. Lindsjo. 1978. "Down syndrome in live births by single year maternal age interval in a Swedish study: comparison with results from a New York State study." *American Journal of Human Genetics* 30: 19–27; **p. 460, 13.27** Adapted by permission from Macmillan Publishers Ltd: Mouse genome sequencing consortium. "Initial sequencing and comparative analysis of the mouse genome." *Nature* 420(6915). © 2002. http://www.nature.com.

Chapter 14 **p. 471, 14.4a** Based on Watson et al. *Molecular Biology of the Gene*, 7th ed. Pearson Education; **p. 471, 14.4b** Based on M.T. Madigan, J.M. Martinko, D.A. Stahl, and D.P. Clark. *Brock Biology of Microorganisms*, 13th ed., 2012, Printed and Electronically reproduced by permission of Pearson Education, Inc., Upper Saddle River, New Jersey; **p. 492, Table 14.7** Information adapted from

S.D. Bell. 2005. "Archaeal transcription regulation—variation on a bacterial theme." *Trends in Microbiology* 13:262–265.

Chapter 15 **p. 514, 15.14** Adapted by permission from Macmillan Publishers Ltd: B.R. Cairns. "The logic of chromatin architecture and remodelling at promoters." *Nature* 461(7261). © 2009; **p. 516, 15.16** Based on J.D. Watson, T.A. Baker, S.P. Bell, A. Gann, M. Levine, R. Losick, and CSHLP, Inglis. *Molecular Biology of Gene*, 6th ed. © 2008. Printed and Electronically reproduced by permission of Pearson Education Inc., Upper Saddle River, New Jersey; **p. 516, 15.17** Adapted by permission from Macmillan Publishers Ltd: B.R. Cairns. 2009. "The logic of chromatin architecture and remodelling at promoters." *Nature* 461(7261). © 2009; **p. 520, 15.20** Adapted by permission from Macmillan Publishers Ltd: N.J. Fuda, M.B. Ardehali, and J.T. Lis. 2009. "Defining mechanisms that regulate RNA polymerase II transcription in vivo." *Nature* 461:189. © 2009; **p. 523, 15.22** Based on J.D. Watson, T.A. Baker, S.P. Bell, A. Gann, M. Levine, R. Losick, and CSHLP, Inglis. *Molecular Biology of Gene*, 6th ed. © 2008. Printed and Electronically reproduced by permission of Pearson Education Inc., Upper Saddle River, New Jersey.

Chapter 16 **p. 541, 16.5** Reprinted by permission from Macmillan Publishers Ltd. *Nature Reviews Genetics* 8:437–449 (June 2007) © 2007; **p. 550, 16.11** *Cell* 72(6):971–983, 26 March 1993, © 1993 Elsevier; **p. 557, 16.16** Based on Nan Peng, Xiang Ao, Yun Xiang Liang, and Qunxin She. *Archaeal Promoter Architecture and Mechanism of Gene Activation*. Portland Press Ltd., 2011.

Chapter 18 **p. 620, 18.6a** Adapted by permission from Macmillan Publishers Ltd: The Arabidopsis Genome initiative. 2000. "Analysis of the genome sequence of the flowering plant *Arabidopsis thaliana*." *Nature* 408(6814). © 2000. www.nature.com; **p. 620, 18.06b** Data from Mark D. Adams, et al. 2000. "The Genome Sequence of Drosophila melanogaster." *Science* 287, 2185; DOI: 10.1126/science.287.5461.2185; **p. 632, 18.15** Adapted/Reprinted from J. Sharp et al. 1999. "Identification of Sonic hedgehog as a candidate gene responsible for the polydactylous mouse mutant Sasquatch." *Current Biology* 9:97–100. © 1999, with permission from Elsevier; **p. 633, 18.16** Adapted by permission from Macmillan Publishers Ltd. D. Boffelli, M.A. Nobrega and E.M. Rubin. "Comparative genomics at the vertebrate extremes." *Nature Reviews Genetics* 5. © 2004. www.nature.com/nrg/index.html; **p. 634, 18.18b** Adapted by permission from Macmillan Publishers Ltd: The Arabidopsis Genome initiative. "Analysis of the genome sequence of the flowering plant *Arabidopsis thaliana*." *Nature* 408(6814). © 2000. www.nature.com; **p. 640, 18.22** Adapted from K. Yamada et al. "Empirical analysis of transcriptional activity in the Arabidopsis genome." *Science* 302:843; **p. 640, 18.23b** Adapted by permission from Macmillan Publishers Ltd: P. Uetz, L. Giot et al. "A comprehensive analysis of protein-protein interactions in *Saccharomyces cerevisiae*." *Nature* 403(6770). © 2000. www.nature.com; **p. 641, 18.24** Adapted by permission from Macmillan Publishers

Ltd. C. Boone, H. Bussey, and B.J. Andrews. 2007. "Exploring genetic interactions and networks with yeast." *Nature Reviews Genetics* 8(6). © 2007. www.nature.com; **p. 643, 18.26** Adapted from Amy Hin Yan Tong et al. "Systematic genetic analysis with ordered arrays of yeast deletion mutants." *Science* 294:2364–2368, Fig. 3. Reprinted with permission from AAAS and the author.

Chapter 19 **p. 651, 19.1** John Bowman. Data from Genbank; **p. 651, 19.6** L. Vigilant, M. Stoneking, H. Harpending, K. Hawkes, and A.C. Wilson. 1991. "African populations and the evolution of human mitochondrial DNA." *Science* 253:1503–1507, Figure 3 on p. 1505; **p. 655, 19.6** L. Vigilant, M. Stoneking, H. Harpending, K. Hawkes, and A.C. Wilson. 1991. "African populations and the evolution of human mitochondrial DNA." *Science* 253:1503–1507, Figure 3 on p. 1505; **p. 655, 19.6** L. Vigilant, M. Stoneking, H. Harpending, K. Hawkes, and A.C. Wilson. 1991. "African populations and the evolution of human mitochondrial DNA." *Science* 253:1503–1507, Figure 3 on p. 1505; **p. 655, 19.6** L. Vigilant, M. Stoneking, H. Harpending, K. Hawkes, and A.C. Wilson. 1991. "African populations and the evolution of human mitochondrial DNA." *Science* 253:1503–1507, Figure 3 on p. 1505; **p. 655, 19.6** L. Vigilant, M. Stoneking, H. Harpending, K. Hawkes, and A.C. Wilson. 1991. "African populations and the evolution of human mitochondrial DNA." *Science* 253:1503–1507, Figure 3 on p. 1505; **p. 656, 19.7a** Reprinted from S. DiMauro et al. 1998. "Mitochondria in neuromuscular disorders." *Biochimica et Biophysica Acta* 1366:206. © 1998, with permission from Elsevier. http://www.sciencedirect.com/science/journal/00052736; **p. 658, 19.8b** © Pearson Education, Inc.; **p. 664, 19.13a** From Macmillan Publishers Ltd: R.W. Taylor and D.M. Turnbull. 2005. "Mitochondrial DNA mutations in human disease." *Nature Reviews Genetics* 6(5). © 2005. http://www.nature.com/nrg/index.html; **p. 664, 19.13a** From http://tolweb.org/Jakobida/97407. © 2000 OGMP (The Organelle Genome Megasequencing Program), 26/Feb/00: http://megasun.bch.umontreal.ca/ogmp/; **p. 664, 19.13b** Adapted from G. Burger and M.W. Gray. "Mitochondrial genomes: anything goes." *Trends in Genetics* 19:709–716. © 2003, with permission from Elsevier. http://www.sciencedirect.com/science/journal/01689525; **p. 665, 19.14** Adapted from Bonawitz et al. "Initiation and beyond: multiple functions of the human mitochondrial transcription machinery." *Molecular Cell* 24:814. © 2006, with permission from Elsevier. http://www.sciencedirect.com/science/journal/10972765; **p. 667, 19.16b** Reprinted from K. Umesono and H. Ozeki. "Chloroplast gene organization in plants." *Trends in Genetics* 3:281. © 1987, with permission from Elsevier. http://www.sciencedirect.com/science/journal/01689525; **p. 671, 19.18** L.A. Katz. 2012. "Origin and diversification of eukaryotes." *Annual Review of Microbiology* 66:411–427, Figure 3 on p. 421; doi 10.1146/anurev-micro-090110-102808; **p. 673, 19.20** Reprinted from D. Leister. "Chloroplast research in the genomic age." *Trends in Genetics* 19:47–56. © 2003, with permission from Elsevier. http://www.sciencedirect.com/science/journal/01689525; **p. 676, 19.22a** Adapted by permission

from Macmillan Publishers Ltd: T.R. Prezant et al. "Mitochondrial ribosomal RNA mutation associated with both antibiotic-induced and non-syndromic deafness." *Nature Genetics* 4. © 1993. http://www.nature.com/ng/index.html.

Chapter 20 **p. 682** Goethe's Botany. *The Metamorphosis of Plants* 1790, and *Tobler's Ode to Nature* 1782. With an Introduction and Translations by Agnes Arber; **p. 686, 20.5** Adapted by permission from Macmillan Publishers Ltd: Christiane Nusslein-Volhard and Eric Wieschaus. "Mutations affecting segment number and polarity in Drosophila." *Nature* 287. © 1980. Adapted from *Developmental Biology*, 6th ed., Fig. 9.27, p. 286. Sunderland: Sinauer Associates, 2000. Used with permission. http://www.nature.com/nature/index.html; **p. 696, 20.13** Adapted by permission from Macmillan Publishers Ltd: R. de Rosa, J.K. Grenier, T. Andreeva, C.E. Cook, A. Adoutte, et al. "Hox genes in brachiopods and priapulids and protostome evolution." *Nature* 399(6738). © 1999. http://www.nature.com/nature/index.html; **p. 696** F. Jacob. 1977. "Evolution and tinkering." *Science* New Series, 196(4295):1161–1166.

Chapter 21 **p. 719, 21.4** Adapted from *Biometrical Genetics*, ed. K. Mather, Fig. 2, p. 6. Dover Publications, 1949. Used with permission of the publisher; **p. 720, 21.6b** Data from P.R. Burton, D.G. Clayton, L.R. Cordon, N. Craddock, P. Deloukas et al. 2007. "Genomewide association study of 14000 cases of seven common diseases and 3000 shared controls." *Nature* 447; **p. 724, 21.8a** Data from William Castle. *Genetics and Eugenics*. Harvard University Press, 1916; **p. 729, Table 21.3** Data from R. Plomin et al. 1994. "The genetic basis of complex human behaviours." *Science* 264:1733–1739; **p. 733, 21.14b** Adapted from E. Fridman et al. "Zooming in on a quantitative trait for Tomato yield using interspecific introgressions." *Science* 305(5691):1787, Fig. 2. Reprinted with permission from AAAS and the author; **p. 735, 21.15** The Welcome Trust Case Control Consortium (2007). *Nature*, 447: 661–678.

Chapter 22 **p. 742** G.H. Hardy. 1908. "Mendelian proportions in a mixed population." *Science* New Series XXVIII:49–50 (letter to the editor); **p. 750, 22.5** Adapted from S. Freeman and J.C. Herron. *Evolutionary Analysis*, 4th ed. © 2007. Printed and Electronically reproduced by permission of Pearson Education Inc., Upper Saddle River, New Jersey; **p. 761** Charles Darwin, In his famous 1859 book, *On the Origin of Species by Means of Natural Selection*, J. Murray; **p. 762, 22.11** Based on Campbell, Neil A, Reece Jane B, *Biology*, 8th ed., 2008. Printed and Electronically reproduced by permission of Pearson Education Inc., Upper Saddle River, New Jersey; **p. 763, 22.13** Adapted from S. Freeman and J.C. Herron. *Evolutionary Analysis*, 4th ed. © 2007. Printed and Electronically reproduced by permission of Pearson Education Inc., Upper Saddle River, New Jersey; **p. 767, 22.16** Adapted from S.A. Tishkoff et al. "The genetic structure and the history of Africans and the African Americans." *Science* 324:1036, Figure 1. Reprinted with permission from the Author and the AAAS; **p. 769, 22.18b** Vernot and J.M. Akey. 2014. *Science* 343:1017–1021, figure 2A, page 1019; **p. 770, Table 22.8** Data from cstl.nist.gov/strbase/str_fact.htm.

Index

Note: A *b* following a page number indicates a box, an *f* indicates a figure, and a *t* indicates a table. Page numbers in **bold** indicate pages on which key terms are discussed.

"-omic" approaches, 15

2–3 stem loop, **485–486,** 487*f*
3′ polyadenylation, **285,** 286–287, 287*f*
3′ splice site, **289,** 290*f*
3′-to-5′ exonuclease activity, **251**
3′ untranslated region (3′ UTR), **307**
3–4 stem loop, **485–486,** 487*f*
5′-to-3′ exonuclease activity, **248**
5′-to-3′ polymerase activity, **248**
5′ capping, **285**
  mRNA, 285–286, 286*f*
5′ splice site, **288–289,** 290*f*
5′ untranslated region (5′ UTR), **307,** 315
6-4 photoproduct, **406,** 407*f*
10-nm fiber, **371**
−10 (Pribnow) consensus sequence, **273,** 275*b*
30-nm fiber, **373**
30S initiation complex, **313**
−35 consensus sequence, **273,** 275*b*
70S initiation complex, **313**
300-nm fiber, **374**

A

A-form DNA, 235–236
α-globin gene, **340,** 340*f*
α-globin polypeptide, **359**
α-globin protein, **340,** 340*f*
α-helix (alpha helix), **308**
α-proteobacteria, **670**
Aberrant ratio, **422**
ABO alleles, dominance relationships of, 110, 110*f*
  molecular basis of, 111–112, 111*f*
Acentric fragment, **440**
Acrocentric chromosome(s), **380**
Activator binding sites, **470**
Activator (Ac) element, **453**
Activator proteins, **470**
Adaptive evolution, 16
Addition rule of probability theory, **45**
Additive genes, **715,** 716*f,* 717*f*
  multiple, continuous phenotypic variation form, 716, 718*f,* 718*t*
Additive trait, **715**
Additive variance, **726**
Adenine (A), **7**
  branch point, **289**
Adenosine triphosphate (ATP), 3
Adjacent-1 segregation, **449**
Admixed population, **755**
Adrenal hyperplasia, gene mutation causing congenital, 89*b*
Aflatoxin B$_1$ mutagenicity, 408, 409*f*
Agarose, **342**
Age, recombination frequency and, 164
Aging, telomeres and, 254
Agouti gene, **528**
Agrobacterium tumefaciens, transformation of plant genomes by, 589–594, 590*f,* 592*f,* 593*f*
Alcohol dehydrogenase (Adh) gene, 751, 751*f*
Alkaptonuria, 305
Alkylating agents, DNA damage from, 404, 405*f*
Allele(s)
  ABO, dominance relationships of, 110, 110*f*
    molecular basis of, 111–112, 111*f*
  ancestral, definition of, 768

ancestral vs. derived, 768, 768*f*
β^A, **341**
β^S, **341**
  malaria and, 353, 357–358
  conditional, in haploid organisms, screening for, 538–539, 539*f*
  derived, definition of, 768
  genes of, **4**
  haploinsufficient, **106**
  haplosufficient, **106**
  interactions between, dominance relationships produced by, 105–118
  lethal, **113,** 113–117
    delayed age of onset of, 118, **118,** 118*f*
    loss- and gain-of-function, 560, 561*f*
    Mendel's conceptual understanding of, 33
    mutant, 262 (*see also under* Mutation(s))
      identified for gene, number of, 539, 540*b*
    on parental chromosomes, for three-point recombination mapping, 157
    temperature-sensitive, 113
    that are both dominant and recessive, 116–117
    variable expressivity of, 119, **120,** 120*f*
Allele-counting method for determining autosomal allele frequencies, 747, **747**
Allele frequencies, autosomal
  in populations, determining, 746–747
Allele frequency change by sampling error, genetic drift causing, 756–758, 756*f*
Allele frequency equilibrium and equalization, 755–756
Allele segregation, 33–34
  monohybrid crosses revealing, 31–36, 32*f*
  in quantitative trait production, 716, 718–719, 719*f*
Allelic identification, 189–190*b*
Allelic phase, **166,** 166–167, 167*f*
Allelic series, **111,** 111–115, 113*f,* 114*f*
  C-gene, molecular basis of, 113
Allis, C. Davis, on "histone code," 520
Allolactose, **472–473**
Allopatric speciation, 761, **761,** 763, 763*f*
Allopolyploids, **437**
Allopolyploidy, 437–438, 438*f*
Allosteric domain, **470**
Allosteric effector compound, **470,** 470*f*
Allostery, **470**
Alpha helix. *See* α-helix (alpha helix)
Alternate segregation, **448**
Alternative intron splicing, **292,** 292–294
Alternative mRNA processing, 293*f,* 295*b*
Alternative polyadenylation, **293**
Alternative pre-mRNA processing, **292**
Alternative promoters, **293**
Alternative sigma (σ) factor, 490, **490,** 490*f*
Alternative sigma subunits, **272–273**
Altman, Sidney, intron self-splicing and, 296
Amelogenesis imperfecta, 91*t*
Ames test, 408, **408,** 409*f,* 410*b*
Amino acid(s), **9**
  chain properties, 307*t*
  transfer RNA in the transport of, 12
Amino acid structure, 306–307
Aminoacyl site (A site), **309,** 309*f*
Aminoacyl-tRNA synthetases (tRNA synthetases), **322,** 323*f*
Amorphic mutation, **106,** 107*f*
Anabolic pathways, 189*b*
Anagenesis, **761**
Anaphase, mitotic, **66,** 67–68, 68*f*
Anaphase I, 76*f,* 77, 78*f*
Anaphase II, 77*f*

AncSR1, 765
Androgen insensitivity syndrome, gene mutation causing, 89*b*
Aneuploid, **431**
Aneuploidy
  fertility reduction in, 435, 435*f*
  in humans, 433–435, 434*t,* 435*t*
Angelman syndrome, 436
  genomic imprinting defects in, 523
Anhidrotic ectodermal dysplasia, 91*t*
Animals
  cloning of, 602–603, 603*f*
  transgenic, 594–598, 594*f,* 596*f*
Annotation, **617**
  ascribing biological functions to DNA sequences, 617–619, 620*f,* 621*f*
  computational approaches to, 618–619, 623*b*
  to describe genes, 617*f*
  experimental approaches to, 617
  genome, 631–632
Anorexia nervosa, 441
Antennapedia complex, **691,** 691*f,* 692–694
Antibiotic resistance, 220
  evolution of (Case Study), 220–221*b*
Antibiotic resistance genes, **188**
Antibiotics, translation interference and (Case Study), 332*b*
Anticodon, **12,** 13*f*
Antiparallel, **7–8**
Antisense RNA, **491,** 494*f*
Antitermination stem loop, **485–486,** 487*f*
Apolipoprotein B gene, RNA editing in, 299, 299*f*
Apurinic (AP) site, **402,** 402*f*
AR gene mutation, androgen insensitivity syndrome from, 89*b*
Arabidopsis, homeotic floral mutants of, 704–705, 705*f,* 706*f*
Arabidopsis thaliana, 115, 517, 546, 562–563*b,* 591, 670, 671
Arber, Werner, host-controlled restriction and modification studies of, 569*b*
Archaea, 3, **4,** 5*f,* 242
  reproduction of, 73
Archaeal chromosome and gene characteristics, 384–385
Archaeal chromosomes, 368*t*
  chromatin organizes, 384–385
Archaeal histones, 385
Archaeal initiation factor proteins (aIFs), 314
Archael transcription, 285
Archael translation initiation, 313–314
  implications for evolution, 313–315
Archaic genome sequences, 21
Archea promoter consensus sequences, 285*f*
Argonaute gene family, RNA-induced silencing complex and, **526**
Artemesia annua (sweet wormwood), 587*b*
Artemisinin, 587*b*
Artificial cross-fertilization, **29,** 29*f*
  Mendel's experiments using, 29–30, 29*f*
Artificial selection, narrow sense heritability and, 729–730, 729*t,* 730*f*
Ascospores, **171–172**
Ascus, **81,** 171
  ordered, **173**
    analysis of, 173–175, 175*f,* 176*f*
Asexual reproduction, 72–73
Assortment, independent. *See* Independent assortment; Independent assortment, law of (Mendel's second law)
Aster, 67

Astrachan, Lazarus, in mRNA discovery, 269
Astral microtubules, **67,** 70*f*
Ataxia, 399*t,* 414*t*
Ataxia, Friedreich, 399*t*
Ataxia telangiectasia, 414*t*
ATM, 406
Attachment (*att*) site, **212,** 212*f,* 213*f*
Attenuation, **484**
Attenuation mutations, 488, 488*f*
Attenuator region, **484,** 484*f*
Autoimmune disease, 735
Autopolyploids, **437**
Autopolyploidy, 437–438, 437*f*
Autosomal genetic linkage, test-cross analysis in
    detection of, 150–151, 151*f,* 152*b*
Autosomal inheritance, **51**
    dominant, **51,** 52*f*
    Mendel's hereditary principles and, 51–55
    recessive, **53,** 53*f*
        of sickle cell disease, 56*b*
Autotrophs, 189*b*
Avery, Oswald
    on DNA as transformation factor, 230, 230*f*
    on DNA identification, 4

B

β-globin gene, **340,** 340*f*
β-globin gene transcript, northern and western blot
    analysis of, 352–353, 353*f*
β-globin gene variation, Southern blot analysis of,
    350–352, 352*f,* 356*b*
β-globin polypeptide, **359**
β-globin protein, **340,** 340*f*
    northern and western blot analysis of, 352–353, 353*f*
β-pleated sheet (beta-pleated sheet), **308**
β^A allele, **341**
β^C allele evolution, 358, 358*f*
β^E allele evolution, 358, 358*f*
β^S allele, **341**
B-form DNA, 235
Bacteria, 3, **4,** 5*f*
    gene structure in, 12*f*
    gene transfer in
        by conjugation, 187–197
        by transduction, 206–213
        by transformation, 204, 206, 207*f*
    genetic analysis and mapping in, 188–226
    polyribosomes of, 319, 320*f*
    regulating transcription of stress response,
        489–491, 490*f*
    reproduction of, 73
    restriction enzymes in, 568–572
    translational regulation in, 491–492, 491*t*
    tRNA processing in, 298
Bacteria RNA polymerase, 272–273, 272*f*
Bacterial artificial chromosomes (BACs), **577**
Bacterial chromosome compaction, 368–369,
    369*f,* 370*f*
Bacterial chromosome organization, 368–369, 368*t,*
    369*f,* 370*f*
Bacterial chromosomes, **188,** 188*f. See also* Bacterial
    artificial chromosomes (BACs)
    bacteriophage chromosomes mapped by
        fine-structure analysis, 213–219
Bacterial DNA replication
    initiation of, 244–246, 245*f*
    origin and directionality of, 237–239
Bacterial DNA replication polymerases, 247*t,* 249
Bacterial genome(s)
    characteristics of, 188
    transposition modifying, 456–459, 456*f,* 457*f,*
        457*t,* 458*b*
    whole-genome shotgun sequencing of, 614–615, 615*f*
Bacterial genome content, 368
Bacterial hosts, expression of heterologous genes in,
    583–589
Bacterial RecBCD pathway, **418**
Bacterial transcription, 274*f*
    elongation in, 274*f,* 276
    initiation of, 273, 274*f,* 276, 276*t*

negative control of, 469–470, 470*f*
    positive control of, 470, 471*f*
    process of, 271–278
Bacterial transcription termination, 274*f,* 276
Bacterial transcription termination mechanisms,
    276–278, 277*f*
Bacterial translation, polypeptide elongation in,
    315, 316*f*
Bacterial translation initiation, 312–313
Bacteriophage(s), **231.** *See also* Gene expression: in
    bacteria and bacteriophage
    bacterial transduction mediated by, 206–213
    entry into lytic or lysogenic cycle, regulation of,
        493, 495*b,* 496
    generalized transducing, **209,** 210*f*
    life cycles of, 207–209, 208*f*
    site-specific recombination in, 598–599, 599*f*
    specialized transducing, **212,** 212*f*
    structure of, 207, 207*f*
    temperate, 493
Bacteriophage chromosomes mapped by fine-
    structure analysis, 213–219
Bacteriophage T4, 367*t*
Bacteriophage vectors, 576–577, 578*f*
Bacteriophage λ (lambda). *See* Lambda (λ) phage
    (bacteriophage λ)
Baker's yeast. *See* Yeast, baker's (*Saccharomyces
    cerevisiae*)
Balanced polymorphism, **358,** 751
Balanced selection, **358**
Balancer chromosomes, **537**
    for tracking mutations, 537, 538*f*
Band in electrophoretic gel, **344,** 344*f*
Band shift assay, to identify promoters, 279–280*b*
Barcodes, **641,** 641*f*
Barnett, Leslie, proof of triplet genetic code,
    323–324, 324*t*
Barr body, **95**
Basal transcription, **474**
Base analog, **404**
Base-pair substitution mutations, **394,** 394–395, 394*f*
Base stacking, **235**
Basic local alignment search tool (BLAST), **624,** 626*b*
Bateson, William
    and complementary gene interaction, 132
    and documentation of human hereditary
        disorder, 2
    and genetic linkage discovery, 148
Baur, Erwin, on cytoplasmic inheritance, 649–651
BDNF, 441
Beadle, George, one gene–one enzyme hypothesis of,
    124–127, 125–126*b,* 306
Beetle, yellow mealworm (*Tenebrio molitor*), 84
Belling, John, on gene dosage changes, 432
Benzer, Seymour
    behavioral genetics and, 535
    deletion-mapping analysis of, 216–217, 217*f,* 218*f*
    genetic complementation analysis of, 215, 215*f*
    on genetic fine structure, 213, 215, 442, 444
    intragenic recombination analysis of, 216
Beta-pleated sheet. *See* β-pleated sheet (beta-pleated
    sheet)
Bicoid gene in anterior-posterior axis in *Drosophila,*
    688, 688*f*
Bidirectional DNA replication, **237,** 237–239,
    239*f,* 240*f*
Binary fission, 187
Binomial expansion formula, 46–47
Binomial probability, **46**
    application to progeny phenotypes, 47–48, 47*f*
    in probability theory, 46–48
Bioinformatics, **618–619,** 623*b*
Biology
    central dogma of, **9,** 10*f*
    genetics in modern, 4–6
    systems, **15,** 644
Biosynthetic pathways, 124
    roles of individual gene mutations in, 127
Biparental inheritance, **650**
    in *Saccharomyces cerevisiae,* 661–662, 661*f*

Bithorax complex, **691,** 691*f,* 692–695, 692*f*
Bithorax mutation, discovery of, 682, 682*f*
Blackburn, Elizabeth, telomere and telomerase
    discovery and, 252–253
Blakeslee, Albert Francis, on gene dosage
    changes, 432
BLAST (basic local alignment search tool), **624,** 626*b*
Blastoderm
    cellular, **685**
    syncytial, **685**
Blau, C. Anthony, three-dimensional model of
    chromosomes in yeast nucleus, 379
Blending theory of heredity, **28,** 32–33
Blobel, Gunther, signal hypothesis and, 331
Blood group(s)
    ABO, 110–111, 110*f,* 111*f*
    MN, 112*b*
Blotting methods, 349, 354–355*b*
Blunt-end cloning, 574, 574*f*
Blunt ends, **346,** 569
Bonds, hydrogen, 7
Boveri, Theodor
    observations on chromosomes, 379
    on relation of meiosis and Mendelian hereditary
        principles, 79
    and study of chromosome movement, 2
Branch point adenine, **289**
BRCA1 (Breast Cancer 1) gene, 169, 169*b,* 413, 424*b*
    lod score analysis in mapping, 169*b*
Breast cancer, 414*t,* 415*b. See also BRCA1 (Breast
    Cancer 1)* gene
    mapping a gene for susceptibility to, 169*b*
Brenner, Sidney
    and mRNA discovery, 270
    on nonoverlapping genetic code, 323
    proof of triplet genetic code, 323–324, 324*t*
Bridges, Calvin, 85–86, 86*f*
    on sex determination in *Drosophila,* 87, 89
Broad sense heritability, 727, **727**
Brock, Louise, 255
Brock, Thomas, 255
Bulbar muscular atrophy, 399*t*
Bulimia nervosa, 441
Bulky adducts, **404**
Burkitt's lymphoma, 386*f,* 387, 387*b*
Bypass polymerases, **416**

C

*C-*gene allelic series, molecular basis of, 113
*C-*gene system, for mammalian coat color, 112–113,
    113*f,* 114*f*
CAAT box, **280–281**
Caenorhabditis elegans, 548, 553, 594, 613, 697–699
    transgenic, 594, 594*f*
Cairns, John, DNA replication in *E. coli* and, 237
Calcitonin/calcitonin gene-related peptide (CT/CGRP)
    gene, alternative splicing of, 292–293, 292*f*
Cancer, 423–424*b,* 424*f. See also* Breast cancer;
    Burkitt's lymphoma; Chronic myelogenous
    leukemia (CML); Ovarian cancer
    cell cycle mutations and, 72
    colorectal, 414*f,* 618*b*
    hereditary, 411
    mapping a gene for susceptibility to breast and
        ovarian, 169*b*
    telomeres, aging, and, 254
Cancer cells, chromosome abnormalities in, FISH
    detection of (Case Study), 386–387*b,* 387*f*
CAP binding site, **474–475**
CAP–cAMP binding region, **475**
CAP–cAMP complex, **475,** 475*f*
Capecchi, Mario, knockout mouse development
    and, 596
Capsid, **366**
Carbon, John, on centromeric DNA, 381
Carboxyl terminal domain (CTD) of RNA
    polymerase II, 289–290
CARD15, 736*b,* 736*f*
Castle, William, on genotype frequencies in
    populations, 743

Catabolic pathways, 189*b*
Catabolite activator protein (CAP), **474–475**
Catabolite repression, **475**
Cauliflower mosaic virus, 367*t*
Cavalli-Sforza, Luigi Luca, on high-frequency
    recombination (Hfr) strains, 194
Cavener, Douglas, directional selection experiments
    of, 751
Cdk (cyclin-dependent kinases), **70–71**
    in cell cycle checkpoints, 70–71, 72*f*
    regulating cell cycle, 71, 73*f*
Cech, Thomas, intron self-splicing and, 296
Cell(s)
    differentiation of, 683, **683**
    inductive signaling between, 697–700,
        697*f*–699*f*
Cell cycle, **65**
    mutations of, and cancer, 72
    stages of, 65–66, 66*f*
Cell cycle checkpoints, **70**, 72*f*
Cell death during development, 700
Cell division
    chromosome heredity and, 64–103
    completion of, 68–69
Cellular blastoderm, **685**
Cellular interactions specifying cell fate, 697–700,
        697*f*–699*f*
Cellular memory, stabilization by chromatic
        architecture, 696–697
CentiMorgan (cM), **154**
Central dogma of biology, **9**, 10*f*
Centromere, **67**
Centromere structure, 381, 382*f*
Centromeric DNA elements (CDE), 381
Centromeric heterochromatin, 382–384
Centrosome, **67**, 70*f*
Character displacement, **764**
Chargaff, Erwin, DNA structure research by, 6
Chargaff's rule, **6**
Charged tRNAs, **311**
Chase, Martha, on DNA in bacteriophage infection
        of bacterial cells, 231, 231*f*
Chemical mutagens, 404–406, 404*t*, 405*f*, 406*f*
    Ames test for, 408, **408**, 409*f*
Chi-square analysis, 48–51, 50*t*, 51*t*
    of genetic linkage data, 154
Chi-square (χ^2) test, **49**
    of Hardy-Weinberg predictions, 749
Chiasmata/chiasma, **77**
Chiba, Yasutane, on cytoplasmic inheritance, 651
Chilton, Mary-Dell, on Ti plasmid in *Agrobacterium*,
        589–590
Chimera, genetic, **594**
Chimeric genes, **560**
    in gene function investigation, 553*f*, 560–561
Chimpanzee vs. human genomes, 767*f*, 768
Chlamydomonas reinhardii, mating type
        and chloroplast segregation in, 659, 661
Chloroplast(s), **650**
    endosymbiosis theory of the evolution of,
        668–675, 671*f*
    genome structure and gene content of,
        667–668, 667*f*
    as sites of photosynthesis, 666–668, 666*f*–668*f*
Chloroplast mRNA, editing of, 668, 668*f*
Chloroplast segregation in Chlamydomonas, mating
        type and, 659, 661
Chloroplast transcription and translation, 668
Chloroplasts, 3, 4
Cholera, 497–498*b*
    stress response in *Vibrio cholerae* (Case Study),
        497–498*b*
Chromatids
    nonsister, 76, **76**, 78*f*
    sister, **67**
Chromatin, 278, 286–287, **370**
    closed, **515**, 515*f*
    composition of, 371, 371*t*, 372–373, 372*f*
    Kornberg's nucleosome-based model of, 371, 373
    open, **514–515**, 515*f*

organizes archaeal chromosomes, 384–385
principal states of, 517*f*
Chromatin architecture, stabilization of cellular
        memory by, 696–697
Chromatin compaction, 370–371
Chromatin immunoprecipitation (ChIP), 515
Chromatin modification, 513*f*. *See also under*
        Chromatin remodeling
    overview of, 513–514
    by RNAi, 526–527, 526*f*
Chromatin modifiers, **517**
    in eukaryotic transcription regulation,
        513–514, 517
Chromatin organization
    eukaryotic chromosomes organized into
        chromatin, 370–376
    higher-order, 373–374
Chromatin readers, writers, and erasers, 517*f*
Chromatin remodelers, 514–516, **515**, 515*f*
    in eukaryotic transcription regulation, 513–514
Chromatin remodeling, **514–515**
    in eukaryotic transcription regulation, 512–524
        chemical modifications of chromatin, 517, 517*f*,
            519–520, 519*f*
        epigenetic heritability in, 520–521
        genomic imprinting in, 522–524, 523*f*
        by nucleosome modification, 514–517, 515*f*,
            518*b*, 519*f*
        nucleotide methylation in, 523–524
        open and covered promoters in, 514–517, 514*f*
    mechanisms of, 514–517
    overview of, 513–514
Chromatin-remodeling proteins, 513
Chromatin states (CS), 517
Chromatin structure
    dynamic, 382–384, 384*f*
    higher-order, 375*f*, 377*f*
    influencing gene transcription, 512–514
Chromatography, **344**
Chromosomal abnormalities in cancer cells, FISH
        detection of (Case Study), 386–387*b*, 387*f*
Chromosome(s), **2**. *See also* Archaeal chromosomes;
        Bacterial artificial chromosomes (BACs);
        Bacterial chromosomes; X chromosomes
    acrocentric, **380**
    artificial, 577
    balancer, **537**
        for tracking mutations, 537, 538*f*
    condensation of
        in meiosis I, 75–77, 75*f*
        in mitosis, 67
    dicentric, **447**
    distribution of, 67–68
    DNA in, 228
    eukaryotic, organization of, 370–376
    gene order on, for three-point recombination
        mapping, 157–158
    gene recombination by exchange of, hypothesis
        of, 160
    genes carried on, chromosome theory of heredity
        proposing, 81, 84–86
    genomic imprinting of, 522–524, 523*f*
    Hfr, **194**, 195*f*
        formation of, 194–195
    homologous, **2**
    human, evolution of (Case Study), 461–462*b*
    limits of recombination along, 160–162
    metacentric, **380**
    monosomic, **432**
    movement of, early studies on, 2
    nonrecombinant, 145
    parental, 145
        alleles on, for three-point recombination
            mapping, 157
    recombinant, **145**
    recombination along, limits of, 161*f*, 162*f*
    sex, **65**
    multiple sets of, 90
    in situ hybridization of, 377–379, 378*f*
    submetacentric, **380**

telocentric, **380**
trisomic, **432**
Y, mammalian, (degenerative) evolution of,
        96–98, 97*f*
Chromosome aberrations, **431**
Chromosome arms, **376**, 377*f*
Chromosome banding, 377, **380**, 380–381, 380*f*
Chromosome break point, **440**
Chromosome breakage
    leading to inversion and translocation of
        chromosomes, 446–450
    mutations from, 439–444, 441*f*, 442*f*, 444*f*, 445*b*
Chromosome fusion, **448**, 449*f*
Chromosome heredity, cell division and, 64–103
Chromosome inversion, **446**, 446–448,
        446*f*–448*f*, 452*b*
Chromosome nondisjunction, 431–432.
        See also Nondisjunction
Chromosome number
    aneuploid, **431**
    diploid, 65
    euploid, 431
    haploid, 65
    nondisjunction leading to changes in, 431–437
    in selected animal species, 431*t*
Chromosome scaffold, **374**, 374*f*
Chromosome structure, 365–390
    higher-order chromatin organization and, 373–374
Chromosome territories
    in eukaryotic nucleus, 379*f*
    imaging, during interphase, 379–380
Chromosome territory, **379**
Chromosome theory of heredity, **65**
    genes carried on chromosomes proposed by,
        81, 84–86
    proof of, 86, 86*f*
Chromosome translocation, **446**, 448–450,
        449*f*–451*f*
Chromosome walking, **545**
Chronic myelogenous leukemia (CML), 386*f*,
        387, 387*b*
Cis-acting mutations, **478**, 478*f*
Cis-acting regulatory sequences, **507**
    in eukaryotic gene expression regulation, 506–511
Cis-dominant *lac* operator, **478**
Clades, **17**
    identification based on morphological
        characteristics, 18*f*
Cladistic approach to phylogenetic tree
        construction, **17**
Cladogenesis, **761**
Clamp loader, 249, 249*f*
Clarke, Louis, on centromeric DNA, 381
Clegg, Michael, directional selection experiments
        of, 751
Clinton, Bill, on human genome sequence
        "draft," 616
Clone(s)
    DNA, **572**
    recombinant, **572**
Clone-by-clone sequencing, **613**
Clone-by-clone sequencing approach to structural
        genomics, 612*t*, 613
Cloning
    blunt-end, 574, 574*f*
    directional, **573–574**, 573*f*
    functional, 166
    of genes
        by complementation, recombinant DNA
            technology in, 542–544, 543*f*
        positional, 544–549, **545**, 545*f*, 547*f*, 548*f*
        using transposons, recombinant DNA technol-
            ogy in, 543–544, 544*f*
    molecular, in recombinant DNA technology,
        572–577, 573*f*–575*f*, 577*t*, 578*f*
    of plants and animals, 602–603, 603*f*
Closed chromatin, **515**, 515*f*
Closed promoter complex, **273**, 274*f*
CNSs (conserved noncoding sequences), **631**,
        631–632, 632*f*

Co-option, **701**
  constraints on, 703
  evolution through, 701–703, 702*f*
Coding region, **272**
Coding sequences, conserved, in genome
    annotation, 631
Coding strand, **11**, 11*f*
CODIS (Case Study), 769–771*b*, 770*f*, 770*t*
Codominance, **109**, 109–112, 110*f*, 111*f*, 112*b*
  of ABO alleles, molecular basis of, 111–112
Codon(s), **12**, 12–13, 13*f*
  glycine, preference of organisms for, 584, 584*t*
  start, **12**, 13*f*
  stop, **12**, 13*f*
  synonymous, **321**
Codon bias, **584**
Cohesive compatible ends, **573**
Cohesive end sequence (cos) sites, **576–577**
Cohesive *(cos)* ends, **493**, 494*f*
Coincidence, coefficient of, **159**
Collins, Francis, on human genome sequence
    "draft," 616
Colonies, 189*b*
Color blindness as X-linked recessive disorder,
    91, 91*t*
Colorectal cancer, 618*b*
  nonpolyposis, 414*f*
    hereditary, 411
Complementary base pairs, **6**
  in DNA, formation of, 7, 8*f*
Complementary DNA (cDNA) libraries, **577**
  constructing, 580–581, 580*f*
Complementary gene interaction (9:7 ratio), 130*f*,
    132, **132**
Complementation
  cloning genes by, recombinant DNA technology in,
    542–544, 543*f*
  genetic, 132, **134**
Complementation analysis, 134, 136, 136*f*, 215, 215*f*
Complementation group(s), **136**
  in xeroderma pigmentosum, identification of
    (Case Study), 137*b*
Complete initiation complex, **282**, 282*f*
Composite transposons, **457**, 457*f*, 457*t*
Concordance, **728**
Conditional probability, **45**
Congenital adrenal hyperplasia, gene mutation
    causing, 89*b*
Congenital generalized hypertrichosis (CGH), 91*t*
  transmission of, 94, 94*f*
Conjugation, bacterial, **191**
  definition, 187
  with F' strains, producing partial diploids,
    203–204, 204*f*, 205–206*b*
  gene transfer by, 187–197
  Hfr, 196–197, 196*f*
  interrupted mating stopping, 197–198
  outcomes of, 194*t*
Conjugation pilus, **192**
Conjugation tube, **192**
Consanguineous mating, 758
Consensus sequences, **242**, **273**
  archaea promoter, 285*f*
  for RNA polymerase II transcription, 278–282
Conservative DNA replication model, **236**, 237*f*
Conserved noncoding sequences (CNSs), **631**,
    631–632, 632*f*
Constitutive heterochromatin, **381**
Constitutive mutants, **477**
Constitutive repressor protein mutations,
    478*f*, 479, 479*t*
Constitutive transcription, **469**
Contiguous sequences (contigs), **546**
Continuous (phenotypic) variation, **714**
  from multiple additive genes, 716, 718*f*, 718*t*
Controlled genetic cross, **30**
Convergent evolution, 18, **752**, 752–753
Coordinate gene patterning of anterior-posterior
    axis, 687–688, 688*f*, 689*f*
Coordinate genes, **686**, 686*f*

Copia elements of *Drosophila*, 460
Copy-number variants (CNVs) in human genetic
    diversity, **635**, 635*f*, 636
Core DNA, **371**
Core element, **283**, 283*f*
Core enzyme, 272, 272*f*
Core promoter region in eukaryotic transcription,
    506, 506*f*
Corepressor, **470**, 470*f*
Corn, genetics of bicolor, 44*b*
Correns, Carl
  on cytoplasmic inheritance, 649–651
  on hereditary transmission, 2, 3*f*
  research of, paralleling Mendel's, 42
Cosmid vector, **577**
Cosuppression, **524**
Cotransduction, 210, **210**, 214*b*
Cotransduction frequency, **210**, 214*b*
Cotransduction mapping, 206, **210**, 210–211, 211*f*,
    212*f*, 214*b*
Cotransformation, **206**
Covered promoters, **514**, 514–517, 514*f*
CpG dinucleotides, **523**
CpG islands, **524**
Creighton, Harriet, research on crossing over in corn,
    160, 160*f*
Cremer, Christoph, on chromosome territories, 379
Cremer, Thomas, on chromosome territories, 379
Creutzfeldt-Jakob disease (CJD), 585
Cri-du-chat syndrome, 440–441
Crick, Francis, 7*f*
  central dogma of biology and, 9, 10*f*
  proof of triplet genetic code, 323–324, 324*t*
  research on double-helical structure of DNA
    by, 4, 6
Cro protein, entry of lambda phage into lytic cycle
    and, 496, 496*f*
Crohn's disease (CD), 735
  contributing mutations, 736*b*
  gene structure and mutation, 736*b*
  GWAS and, 736*b*, 736*f*
  microbiota and, 618*b*
  Neandertal genes and, 769
Cross(es)
  to determine X-linkage of genes, 84–85, 84*f*, 85*f*
  dihybrid, 36
  monohybrid, 33
  reciprocal *(see* Reciprocal cross(es))
  replicate, 30
  segregation of alleles and, 31–36, 32*f*
  test, 31, 31*f*
  trihybrid, 41
Cross-fertilization, artificial, 29, 29*f*
  Mendel's experiments using, 29–30, 29*f*
Crossing-over hypothesis, 150, 150*f*, 160
Crossing over of genetic material, **76**
  hypothesis of recombination by, 160
  recombination results from, 160–166
Crossover
  double
    four-strand, 161, **161**, 162*f*
    results of, 161, 162*f*
    three-strand, 161, **161**, 162*f*
    two-strand, 161, **161**, 162*f*
  mitotic, 176
    producing distinctive phenotypes,
      175–176, 177*f*
  single, results of, 161, 161*f*
  unequal, 441
Crossover suppression, **447**
Crown gall disease, 589, 590*f*, 592*f*
Cryptic splice sites, **397**, 397*f*
Cyanobacteria, **670**
Cyclin D–Cdk4 complex function, 71
Cyclin D1–Cdk4 complex, retinoblastoma protein
    and, 71
  mutations altering interaction of, 72
Cyclin-dependent kinases (Cdk), **70–71**
  in cell cycle checkpoints, 70–71, 72*f*
  regulating cell cycle, 71, 73*f*

Cyclin proteins, **70**
  in cell cycle checkpoints, 70–71, 72*f*
  regulating cell cycle, 71, 73*f*
Cyclopia, *Shh* mutations in (Case Study), 707–709*b*,
    707–709*f*
CYP21 gene mutation and congenital adrenal
    hyperplasia, 89*b*
Cystic fibrosis (CF)
  alleles, genotypes, and, 747
  gene therapy for, 601, 602
  linkage data from forms with, 178*t*
  mapping the gene for (Case Study), 177–178*b*
Cystic fibrosis transmembrane conductance regula-
    tor (CTFR) allele, 597*f*
*Cystic fibrosis transmembrane conductance regulator
    (CTFR)* gene, 177–178*b*
Cytokinesis, **66**, 68*f*
  in plant and animal cells, 68, 71*f*
Cytomegalovirus (CMV), 366, 367*t*
Cytoplasmic inheritance, **4**, 649–680, **650**
  discovery of, 650–651, 651*f*
  modes of, 654–662
  transmitting genes carried on organelle
    chromosomes, 650–653
Cytoplasmic male sterility (CMS) in flowering
    plants, 669*b*
Cytosine (C), 7

D

DA-binding domain, **470**
Damage signaling systems, 414*f*
Darwin, Charles, theory of evolution of, 16–17
Darwin's finches, contemporary evolution in, 764
Daughter cells, **65**
Daughter strand in semiconservative replication,
    9, 9*f*
Davis, Bernard, on need for physical contact for
    bacterial gene transfer, 191, 192*f*
Dawkins, Richard, on molecular basis of evolution, 15
Dawson, Martin, on DNA as transformation
    factor, 230
de Vries, Hugo
  on hereditary transmission, 2, 3*f*
  research of, paralleling Mendel's, 42
Deafness. *See* Ototoxic deafness, mitochondrial
    gene-environment interaction in (Case Study)
Deaminating agents, mutations induced by, 404, 405*f*
Deamination, **402**, 403, 403*f*
Degrees of freedom *(df)*, 49–50
Delayed age of onset of lethal alleles, 118, **118**, 118*f*
Delbrück, Max, 392
Deletion(s), **440–441**
  detecting, 442, 442*f*
  partial, **441**
Deletion heterozygote, partial, **441**
Deletion mapping, **216**, **442**, 444, 444*f*, 445*b*
Deletion-mapping analysis, 216–217, 217*f*, 218*f*, 219
Densitometry of hemoglobin proteins, 344, 344*f*
Deoxynucleotide monophosphates (dNMPs),
    232, 232*f*
Deoxynucleotide triphosphates (dNTPs), **232**
Deoxyribonucleic acid (DNA). *See* DNA
Depurination, **402**, 402*f*
Derived allele(s)
  vs. ancestral allele(s), 768, 768*f*
  definition of, 768
Development. *See also specific topics*
  as building of multicellular organism, 682–684,
    683*f*, 684*f*
  evolution of, 700–701
Developmental genetics, 681–712
Developmental pathways, **124**
DHJs (double Holliday junctions), **419**
Diabetes, 585
  type 1, 735
  type 2, Neandertal genes and, 769
Diakinesis stage of prophase I, 75, 76*f*, 77, 78*f*
Dicentric bridge, **447**
Dicentric chromosome, **447**
Dicer, **524**, 525*f*

Dideoxy DNA sequencing of Huntington disease (HD) genes, 262f
Dideoxynucleotide DNA sequencing (Sanger method), 256–259, 258f, 259f, 260b
Dideoxynucleotide DNA sequencing-dideoxy sequencing, **257**
Dideoxynucleotide triphosphate (ddNTP), **257**
Differential reproduction, **748**
Differentiation, cell, 683, **683**
    mechanisms of, 683–684, 684f
Digestive microbiome, 618b
Dihybrid cross, **36**
Dihybrid-cross analysis of two genes, 36, 36f, 38–39
Dinucleotides, CpG, **523**
Diploid number of chromosomes, **65**
Diploids, **3**
    partial, **203**
        conjugation with F′ strains producing, 203–204, 204f, 205–206b
    single-celled, segregation in, 81, 82f
Diplotene stage of prophase I, 75, 75f, 78f
Direct repeats, 453, **455**
Directed assembly, **368**
Directional cloning, 573–574, 573f
Directional natural selection, **750**, 750–751, 750f, 751t
Directional selection, **730**
Discontinuous variation, **714**
Discordance, **728**
Disjunction
    chromosome, **67**
    homologous chromosome, in meiosis I, 77
Dispersed repetitive DNA, 621
Dispersive DNA replication model, **236**, 237f
Displacement (D) loop, **417**
Disruptive selection, **730**
Dissociation (Ds) element, **453**
DNA (deoxyribonucleic acid), **5**, 227–266. See also Mitochondrial DNA; Supercoiled DNA
    in chromosomes, 228
    composition, 8f
    core, **371**
    dispersed repetitive, 621
    as hereditary material of organisms, 6
    as hereditary molecule, 6, 228–232, 231f
    heteroduplex, **419**
    integration into genome of S. cerevisiae, 588–589, 589f
    linker, **371**
    restriction fragments of, 345–346, 348
    transfer (T-DNA), **589–590**
    as transformation factor, 230, 230f
    Watson and Crick's model of, 6–7, 7f, 236
DNA-binding domains (DBDs), **470**, 765
DNA-binding proteins
    regulatory, 470–472, 471f
    structural motifs of, 505f
DNA clone, **572**
DNA damage
    from alkylating agents, 404, 405f
    radiation-induced, 406–408, 407f
DNA damage repair, 408–415
    direct, 409–413, 413f
    nucleotide excision and replacement in, 411–412, 412f, 413f
DNA damage repair disorders, 414, 414t
DNA damage repair pathway, p53, 413, 414f
DNA damage signaling systems, 413–414
DNA double helix, **5**, 6, 235f. See also DNA structure: double-helical
DNA duplex, **5**. See also DNA double helix
DNA gyrase, **369**
DNA intercalating agents, mutations induced by, **406**, 406f
DNA isolation, countertop, 11b
DNA library(ies), 577, **577**, 579–581, 579f–582f
    complementary, **577**
        constructing, 580–581, 580f
    genomic, 577
        constructing, 579–580, 579f
    screening, 581, 582f

DNA ligase, **248**
DNA loop, **483**, 483f
DNA microarrays, **637**, 637f
DNA molecules
    advances in altering and synthesizing, 598
    long, sequencing, 581–583, 582f
DNA nucleotide base changes, spontaneous, 400–402, 401f
DNA nucleotide lesions, 402–403, 402f, 403f
DNA nucleotide pairing, complementary, 233f, 234, 234b
DNA nucleotides, **7**, 232, 232f, 233f, 234
    components of, 7
    excision and replacement of, 411–412, 412f, 413f
    methylation of, in gene silencing, 523–524
DNA polymerase I (pol I), **248**
DNA polymerase III (pol III) holoenzyme, **246**
DNA polymerase in DNA strand elongation, 232, 233f
DNA proofreading, 249, **249**, 251, 251f
DNA-protein interaction in transcriptional control of gene expression, 469–472, 470f, 471f
DNA replication, **5**, 8–9, 9f, 236, 236–240. See also Bacterial DNA replication
    bidirectional, evidence of, 237–239, 239f, 240f
    continuous strand, 246–247, 247f
    discontinuous strand, 246–247, 247f
    DNA loss in cycle of, 251–252
    DNA structure and mechanism of, 6–9
    Meselson-Stahl experiment on, 236–237, 237f, 238f
    models of, 236, 237f
        Kornberg/trombone, 249, 250f
    molecular genetic analytical methods using processes of, 254–261
    multiple origins in eukaryotes, 239–240, 241f
    nucleosome distribution and synthesis during, 374–376, 377f
    Okazaki fragment ligation for, 247–248, 248f
    precisely duplicating genetic material, 241–254
    principal proteins of, 248f
    RNA primer removal for, 247–248, 248f
    in S phase, 66
DNA replication errors, mutations from, 397–399, 399f
DNA sequence variations, identification of, 34, 345–346, 346f, 348, 348t
DNA sequences
    constructing contiguous, 546, 548f
    gene mutations modifying, 393–397
    recombinant DNA technology recognizing (see Recombinant DNA technology)
    at replication origins, 242
    in vivo manipulation of, 598–599
DNA sequencing technologies, 568–583, 582f
    new, 259, 261
DNA structure, 5–9, 8f
    double-helical (see also DNA double helix)
    complementary and antiparallel strands in, 232–236, 234b
    research on, 4, 6
    twisting, 234–236, 235f
DNA synthesis. See also DNA molecules
    translesion, 407
    protein control of, 407–410
DNA transfer from organelles, continual, 670–672, 672f, 673f
DNA transposons, **455**
DNase I hypersensitive sites, 515, 518b
dNMPs (deoxynucleotide monophosphates), **232**, 232f
dNTPs (deoxynucleotide triphosphates), **232**
Dobzhansky, Theodosius
    on evolution, 742
    and modern synthesis of evolution, 17
Domains of life, 4–5, 5f
Dominance
    incomplete, **108–109**, 109f
    molecular basis of, 105–106
    partial, **108–109**, 109f

Dominance relationships
    of ABO alleles, 110, 110f
        molecular basis of, 111–112, 111f
    allele interactions producing, 105–118
Dominance variance, **726**
Dominant epistasis (12:3:1), 131f, 133, **133**
Dominant gene interaction (9:6:1 ratio), 130f, **132**, 132–133
Dominant interaction. See under Epistatic (gene) interactions
Dominant mutant, determination of, 539
Dominant negative mutations, 107f, **108**
Dominant phenotype, **31**, 35
Dominant suppression (13:3 ratio), 131f, **133**, 133–134
Donor cell (F⁺), **191–192**
    conjugation between recipient cell and, 193–194, 193f
    DNA fragment from, recipient cell uptake of, 204, 206, 207f
Doppler, Christian, in Mendel's education, 26, 27
Dosage, gene, **433**
Dosage compensation, **95**, 95–96
    mechanisms of, in animals, 95t
    random X inactivation in, 95–96, 96f
Double crossovers, **157**, 157–158
    frequency of, as consistent with independence of single crossovers, 158–159
Double Holliday junctions (DHJs), **419**
Double recombinants, **157**, 157–158
Double-strand break repair, **416**, 416–417, 417f
Double-stranded DNA breaks, 417–418
    initiating meiotic recombination, 418–419
Double-stranded RNA (dsRNA), 524
    cleaving, 524–525
    gene silencing by, 524–526, 525f
Doudna, Jennifer, on cleaving dsRNA, 524
Down syndrome, 434t, 450
    familial, 449, 451f
    maternal age and risk of, 435t
    meiotic nondisjunction in, 434, 435t
Down syndrome critical region (DSCR), 434
Downstream, **272**
Drosophila, transgenic, 594–595, 595f
Drosophila melanogaster. See Fruit fly (Drosophila melanogaster)
Duchenne muscular dystrophy, 91t, 393, 577
Duplicate gene action (15:1 ratio), 130f, 132, **132**
Duplication(s), **441**
    detecting, 442, 442f
    gene, 627–629, 628f, 629f
    segmental, 634
    unequal, **441**
    whole-genome, 633–634
Duplication heterozygote, partial, **441**
Dyskeratosis congenita, 254

E

Early genes, **493**
Early operators, **493**
Early promoters, **493**
East, Edward, on multiple-gene hypothesis, 716, 718–719, 719f
East-west (EW) resolution, **419**
Edward syndrome, 434t
Electrophoresis, gel. See Gel electrophoresis
Electrophoretic mobility, 344
Ellis-van Creveld (EvC) syndrome, 757
Elongation factor (EF) proteins, **315**
Embryonic stem (ES) cells, 597–598, **683**
    creating, from fibroblasts, 604b
Emerson, Rollins, three-point test-cross analysis, 156, 156t
Endonucleases, restriction, **345**, 348t
Endosymbiont, **670**
Endosymbiosis, **668**
    secondary, 674–675, **674–675**
    tertiary, 674–675, **674–675**

Endosymbiosis theory, **670**
  of mitochondria and chloroplast evolution, 668–675
Enhancement, synthetic, 541, 541f
Enhanceosome, **507**
Enhancer screen, **540**
Enhancer sequences (enhancers), **282–283**, 283f, **506–507**
  conservation of, 510, 510f
  in eukaryotic transcription, 506–508, 508f, 510, 510f
  hereditary disorders from mutations of, 509
  insulator sequence interactions with, 511, 512f
Enhancer trapping, **559**, 559–560, 560f
Enveloped viruses, **367**, 367f
Environment
  mitochondrial gene interactions with, and human genetic disease, 675–676b
  and phenotypic variation, 719, 720f, 723b
  recombination frequency and, 164
Environment-gene interactions, **119–120**
Environmental modification to prevent hereditary disease, 120–121
Environmental variance, **725**
Enzyme(s), restriction, **345**, 345–346, 348t
  in recombinant DNA technology, 568–572, 569b, 571b, 572f
Epigenetic heritability, **520–521**
Epigenetic modifications, environmental (Case Study), 528–529b
Episome, **193**
Epistasis, **127**, **129**
  dominant (12:3:1), 131f, 133, **133**
  recessive (9:3:4 ratio), 131f, 133, **133**
  results of, 127, 129, 129f, 132–134
Epistatic (gene) interactions, **127**, 129, **129**, 129f, 132–133, 135b
  complementary (9:7 ratio), 130f, 132, **132**
  dominant (9:6:1 ratio), 130f, **132**, 132–133
  duplicate (15:1 ratio), 130, 130f, 132
  no interaction (9:3:3:1 ratio), 129, 129f, 132
Equilibrium frequency, **358**
Escherichia coli (E. coli)
  chromosome compaction, 368–369
  consolidated Hfr map of, 200–201, 201f, 203
  genome content, 368
  HfrH and F⁻ P678 strains of, genotypes of, 197–200, 197t
  human insulin production in, 584–586, 586f
  lac operon of, **472** (see also *Lac* operon)
  nucleoid of, 368, 368f
  pathogenicity islands in, 220
  plant-derived antimalarial drugs produced in, 587b
  ribosome structure, 309–311, 309f
  transgenes in, 583–588, 584f
  trp operon gene map for, 210–211, 212f
Estrogen biosynthesis pathway, 765–766, 766f
Ethidium bromide (EtBr), 348–349, 349f
Euchromatic regions, **381**
Euchromatin, **381**
Eukaryote cells, mitochondria as energy factories of, 662–666
Eukaryote chromosomes, organization of, 370–376
Eukaryotes/eukarya, **4**, **5**?
  DNA replication polymerases of, 247t, 249
  gene structure in, 12f
  genes in development of, 707b
  genetic linkage and mapping in, 144–185
    (see also Genetic linkage; Genetic linkage mapping/maps)
  multiple RNA polymerases in transcription in, 278–285
  regulation of gene expression in, 504–532
    chromatin remodeling in, 512–524
    cis-acting regulatory sequences in, 506–511
    RNA-mediated mechanisms in, 524–528, 525f, 526f
  replication origins in
    DNA sequences at, 242
    multiple, 239–240, 241f
  tRNA processing in, 298

Eukaryotic expression vectors, **584**
Eukaryotic genome(s)
  transposition modifying, 457–461, 459f, 460f
  whole-genome shotgun sequencing of, 615–616, 616f
Eukaryotic initiation factor (eIF), **313**
Eukaryotic lineage, origin of, 673–674, 674f
Eukaryotic primase, 245–246
Eukaryotic transcription termination, torpedo model of, 287, 288f
Eukaryotic translation initiation, 313, 314f, 317–318b
Euploid, **431**
Euploidy, 431
  changes in, resulting in polyploidy, 437–439
Evans, Martin, knockout mouse development and, 596
E(var) mutations, 512–513, 512f
Even-skipped (eve) gene, 689–690, 690f
Evo-devo, **701**
Evolution, **16**. See also under Migration
  adaptive, 16
  chloroplast, endosymbiosis theory of, 668–675, 671f
  convergent, 18, **752**, 752–753
  in Darwin's finches, contemporary, 764
  Darwin's theory of, 16–17
  of development, 700–701
  of eukaryotes, 673–674, 674f
  gene regulation in, 701–703
  human chromosome (Case Study), 461–462b
  mitochondrial, endosymbiosis theory of, 668–675, 671f
  modern synthesis of, 17
  molecular basis of, 15–22 (see also Molecular evolution)
  multicellular, in plants, 703–707
  by natural selection, 16
  nonadaptive, 16–17
  polyploidy and, 439, 440f
  population genetics and, 742–775
  processes of, 17, 760–764, 762f, 762t, 763f
  through co-option, 701–703, 702f
Evolution models, hominin, 21
Evolutionary genetics, **5**
Evolutionary genomics, **612**, 622, 624–636. See also Interspecific comparisons of genomes
  human genetic diversity and, 766–769, 767f, 768f
  intraspecific genome comparisons in, 634–635
  tree of life in, 624, 625f, 626b
Evolutionary relationships, tracing, 17–21
Exconjugant cell, **192**
  Hfr, 196–197, 196f
  partial diploid, production of, 203–204, 204f
Exit site (E site), **309**, 309f
Exonic splicing enhancers (ESEs), **294**, 294f
Exons, **11**, 12f
Expression arrays, **637**, 637–638, 639f
Expression vectors, **583**, 583–584, 584f
  eukaryotic, **584**?

F

F⁻ cell (recipient cell), **191–192**
  and F⁺ cell, conjugation between, 193–194, 193f
F⁺ cell (donor cell), **191–192**
  and F⁻ cell, conjugation between, 193–194, 193f
F′ (F prime) cells, **203**
F′ (F prime) donor, **203**
F (fertility) factor
  in Hfr strains, 194–195, 195f
  transfer of, 192–194, 192f
F′ (F prime) factor, **203**
F (fertility) plasmid, **188**
  structure of, 192, 192f
F₁ (first filial) generation, **30**, 30f
F₂ (second filial) generation, **30**, 30f
F₂ self-fertilization in segregation hypothesis testing, 35, 35f, 36t
F₃ (third filial) generation, **30**, 30f
Factor VIII (F8) gene mutation, hemophilia A from, 92, 92f
Facultative heterochromatin, **381**

Familial Down syndrome, 449, 451f
Family, the modern human, 21–22
Family trees, 52. See also Pedigree(s)
Fertility, reduced, in aneuploidy, 435, 435f
Fertilizations, multiple, creating autopolyploidy, 437, 437f, 438
Fibroblasts, creating embryonic stem (ES) cells from, 604b
Filion, Guillaume, on chromatin types, 517, 517f
Finches, Darwin's, contemporary evolution in, 764
Fine-structure analysis, bacteriophage chromosome mapping by, 213–219
Fire, Andrew, on RNA interference, 524, 553
First-division segregation, **175**, 175f
FISH (fluorescent in situ hybridization), **378**, 378–379, 378f
  in chromosome abnormality detection in cancer cells (Case Study), 386–387b, 387f
Fisher, Ronald
  and evolutionary genetics research, 17
  and statistical analysis of quantitative traits, 721
Flanking direct repeats, **453**, **455**
Fleming, Alexander, penicillin discovered by, 220b
Florey, Howard, penicillin production and, 220b
Fluorescent in situ hybridization (FISH), **378**, 378–379, 378f
  in chromosome abnormality detection in cancer cells (Case Study), 386–387b, 387f
Forked-line diagram, **38**, 38f
Forward genetic analysis, **534**
Forward genetic screens, designing, 535–539
Forward genetics, 533–541, **534**, 534f
Forward mutation rate (μ), **753**
Forward mutations, **397**
Fossils, earliest, 16f
Founder effect, **756**, 756–757
Four-strand double crossover, 161, **161**, 162f
Fraenkel-Conrat, Heinz, on nonoverlapping genetic code, 323
Fragile X syndrome, 91t, 399t
Frameshift mutation, **324**, **395**, 396f
Franklin, Rosalind, research on double-helical structure of DNA by, 4, 6, 6f
Frequency distribution, **721**, 724f
Friedreich ataxia, 399t
Fruit fly (*Drosophila melanogaster*), 630b, 754b
  bithorax mutation in, discovery of, 682, 682f
  development of, as paradigm for animal development, 684–697, 685f
  development toolkit of, 686–687, 686f
  eye color in
    complementation analysis of, 133, 136, 136f
    genes for, 123, 124f
  mitotic crossover in, 176, 177f
  multiple replication origins in, 240, 241f
  P element in, 459, **459**
  pleiotropy in, 121
  scam gene of, alternative splicing in, 293
  sex determination in, 87, 89
    alternative mRNA splicing and (Case Study), 299–300b, 300f
  studies of genes on chromosomes in, 81, 84–86, 84f, 85f
Functional cloning, 166
Functional genomics, **612**, 636–644
  genetic networks in, 642–644
  genomic approaches to reverse genetics in, 641, 641f
  transcriptomics in, 636–638, 637f, 639f, 640f
  yeast mutants to categorize genes in, 641–642, 642f
Functional RNAs, **270**, **271**
Fungal hosts, expression of heterologous genes in, 583–589
Fungus, generation of transgenic, 588–589, 588f, 589f
Fusion genes, **585**
Fusion protein, **585**

G

G (Giemsa) banding, **380**
G₀ ("G zero") of interphase, **66**, 66f
G₁ (Gap 1) phase of interphase, **66**, 66f, 71f

G$_2$ (Gap 2) phase of interphase, **66**, 66*f*, 68*f*
Gaertner, Carl Friedrich, genetic research of, 45*b*
Gain-of-function alleles, 560, 561*f*
Gain-of-function mutation, **106**, 107*f*, 108
Gamete(s), **4**, **33**, **65**
Gamete frequencies, determining from genetic maps, 159–160, 159*f*
Gap gene expression, domains of, 688–689, 689*f*, 690*f*
Gap genes, **686**, 686*f*
Garden pea. *See* Pea, garden (*Pisum sativum*)
Garrod, Archibald
    and documentation of human hereditary disorder, 2, 124
    on gene–protein connection, 305
    genetic screens and, 535
Gaussian (normal) distribution, **48–49**, 49*f*
GC-rich box, **280–281**
Gel electrophoresis, **342**, 342–344, 343*f*, 344*f*
    in hemoglobin peptide fingerprint analysis, 344
    in SCD analysis, 349–353
    two-dimensional, in ribosomal protein identification, 310*b*
Gender. *See* Sex
Gene(s), **2**. *See also specific topics*
    alternative transcripts of single, 290, 292–294
    annotation describing, 617–619, 617*f*
    births and deaths of, 626–627, 627*f*
    original definition of, 267
Gene conversion, 419, **419**, 422–423, 422*f*, 423*f*
Gene dosage. *See* Dosage, gene
Gene dosage alteration, 432–433
Gene expression, 10–15. *See also* Bacteria; Bacteriophage; Eukaryotes
    in bacteria and bacteriophage, regulation of, 468–503
        antiterminators and repressors in, 492–497
        inducible operon system in, 473–483
        repression and attenuation in, 483–488
        stress response and, 489–491
        translational, 491–492
    DNA-protein interaction required for transcriptional control of, 469–472, 470*f*, 471*f*
    monitoring with reporter genes, 556–559, 558*f*, 559*f*
    transcription in, 10–12
    translation in, 12–13
Gene expression machine model, for coupling transcription with pre-mRNA processing, 289–290, 294*f*
Gene families, 619, **619**
Gene flow, **755**
    effects of, 753, 755*f*
Gene identification, genome sequencing to determine, 549, 551, 551*f*
Gene interaction(s), 104–143, **121**. *See also* Epistatic (gene) interactions
    allelic series as, 111–115, 113*f*, 114*f*
    delayed age of onset of, 118, 118*f*
    in pathways, 121–124, 124*f*
    types of, 105
Gene knockouts. *See* Knockouts, gene
Gene order, 632–634, 633*f*
Gene pool, **743–744**
    mutation diversifying, 753–755
Gene reconstruction, ancestral, 765
Gene therapy, **600**
    in curing sickle cell disease in mice, 604*b*, 605*f*
    germinal, **601**
    human, 601–602, 601*t*
    somatic, **601**
    using recombinant DNA technology, 600–602, 601*t*, 605*f*
Gene therapy proof of principle, 604*b*
Gene transmission
    basic principles of, discovered by Mendel, 27–31
    in mitosis, 4
    in sexual reproduction, 4
Generalized transducing phages, **209**, 210*f*
Generalized transduction, 206, **209**, 210*f*
Genetic bottlenecks, **757**, 757–758, 757*f*

Genetic chimera. *See* Chimera, genetic
Genetic code, 321*f*
    deciphering, 326–327, 326*f*, 327*t*, 328*f*, 329*b*
        experiments in, 322–330
    displaying third-base wobble, 321–322, 322*t*
    no gaps in, 324, 326
    nonoverlapping, 323, 324*f*
    redundancy of, 321
    in translation, **12**
        of mRNA into polypeptide, 320–322
    triplet, 323–324, 324*t*
    universality of, 327–328, 328*t*
Genetic code specificity, tRNAs and, 328, 330
Genetic complementation analysis. *See* Complementation analysis
Genetic cross, controlled, **30**
Genetic dissection, **124**, **126**
    to investigate gene action, 126–127, 127*f*, 128*b*
Genetic distances and relationships between human populations, 766, 767*f*
Genetic diversity, human, 766–769, 767*f*, 768*f*
    and evolution, 766–769
Genetic drift, **756**, 756–758, 756*f*
    random, as evolutionary process, 17
Genetic fine structure, **213**
    discovery of, 213, 215
Genetic heterogeneity, **134**
Genetic hitchhiking, 753
Genetic liability, **720**
    threshold of, **720**
Genetic linkage, **145**
    autosomal, test-cross analysis in detection of, 150–151, 151*f*, 152*b*
    complete vs. incomplete, 147–148, 147*f*
    discovery of, 148–150
    in haploid eukaryotes, identified by tetrad analysis, 171–175
    vs. independent assortment, 146–147, 146*f*
    indications of, 146–148
    for three-point recombination mapping, data consistent with the proposal of, 157
Genetic linkage analysis, as tracing genome evolution, 170–171
Genetic linkage data, chi-square analysis of, 154
Genetic linkage mapping/maps, **145**. *See also* Mapping
    basis of, 153–154, 153*f*
    biological factors affecting accuracy of, 164, 164*f*
    constructing three-point recombination, 156–159
    cotransduction, **210**, 210–211, 211*f*, 212*f*
    first, 153–154, 153*f*
    gamete frequency determination from, 159–160, 159*f*
    mapping linked human genes using lod score analysis, 166–169
    by transformation, 204, 206, 207*f*
    units for, 154
    using lod score analysis, 168*f*, 168*t*, 169*b*, 170*b*
    for cystic fibrosis gene, 177–178*b*
Genetic map, using DNA markers to construct, 545–546, 547*f*
Genetic maps distances. *See also* Genetic linkage mapping/maps
    correction of, 165–166, 166*f*
Genetic networks, **642**
Genetic potential, 714–715
Genetic principles, 4
Genetic redundancy, **541**
    in flower development, reverse genetics and (Case Study), 561–563*b*
Genetic screen(s), **534**
    for conditional alleles in haploid organisms, 538–539, 539*f*
    designing, 535–539
        general design, 535
    enhancer, **540**
    forward, 535–541
    modifier, **540**
    in mutagenesis analysis, 539, 540*b*
    strategies of

    for identifying dominant and recessive mutations, 536–537, 537*f*
    mutagen selection in, 536, 536*t*
    organism selection in, 536
    use of balancer chromosomes for tracking mutations, 537–538, 538*f*
    suppressor, **540**
Genetic theorists, early-20th-century, 3*f*
Genetic variance. *See* Variance
Genetics. *See also specific topics*
    ancient applications of, 2, 3*f*
    evolutionary, **5**
    history of modern, 2–4
    in modern biology, 4–6
    notation systems in, 109
    overview of, 1–2
    from whole-genome perspective, 611–648 (*see also* Genomics)
Genome(s), **4**. *See also* Bacterial genome(s)
    chimpanzee vs. human, 767*f*, 768
    chloroplast, structure of, 667–668, 667*f*
    eukaryotic
        transposition modifying, 457–461, 459*f*, 460*f*
        whole-genome shotgun sequencing of, 615–616, 616*f*
    history of, 622, 624–636
    introducing foreign genes into, to create transgenic organisms, 583–599
    lambda phage, 493, 494*f*
    lateral gene transfer in, 220
    modern human, 21
    nucleotide-base composition of, 7*t*
    organelle
        replication of, 652, 653*f*
        replicative segregation of, 653
        variable segregation of, 654*f*
    plant, transformation by *Agrobacterium*, 589–594, 590*f*, 592*f*, 593*f*
    of *S. cerevisiae*, integrating DNA into, 588–589, 589*f*
    transposable genetic elements moving through, 450–456, 451*f*
    viral, 366, 367*t*
Genome annotation, 617–619, 617*f*, 631–632
Genome comparisons. *See also* Interspecific comparisons of genomes
    intraspecific, 634–635
Genome evolution, genetic linkage analysis as tracing, 170–171
Genome organization among species, variation in, 620–621, 621*f*, 622*f*
Genome sequence analysis, determination of mutation rate from, 393
Genome sequence draft, human, 616
Genome sequences. *See also* Whole-genome shotgun (WGS) sequencing
    archaic, 21
    examples of, 612*t*
    insights from, 621–622
    reference, **635**
Genome sequencing to determine gene identification, 549, 551
Genome structure, mitochondrial, 662–665, 663*f*, 664*f*
Genome-wide association studies (GWAS), **734**, 734–736, 736*b*
Genomic era of genetics, 4
Genomic imprinting, **522**, 522–523, 523*f*
Genomic islands, **220**
Genomic libraries, **577**
    constructing, 579–580, 579*f*
Genomic story of hominins, 21–22
Genomics, **13**, 611–648. *See also* Evolutionary genomics; Functional genomics; Structural genomics
    definition of, 611
Genomics approach to gene identification following mutagenesis, 551, 551*f*
Genotype(s), **4**
    homoplastic and heteroplastic, **651–652**, 652*f*

Genotype frequencies
  inbreeding altering, 758–760
  in populations, 743–748
Genotype proportion method, for determining auto-
  somal allele frequencies, 747, **747**
Genotypic ratio (1:2:1), 33
Genotyping, microbial growth for, 189–190*b*
Germ-line cells, **65**
Germinal gene therapy, **601**
Gilbert, Walter, DNA-sequencing protocols of, 256
Globin gene mutations, 340–341, 341*f*
Globin genes, **340**, 340*f*
Goldberg-Hogness box, **280**
Golden Rice (*Oryza sativa*), 591, 593–594, 593*f*
Goss, John, genetic research of, 45*b*
Grant, Peter, 764
Grant, Rosemary, 764
Green, Kathleen, on intragenic recombination, 162
Green, Melvin, on intragenic recombination, 162
Green fluorescent protein (GFP), **557**
Greider, Carol, telomere and telomerase discovery
  and, 252–253
Griffith, Frederick, transformation factor identified
  by, 229–230, 229*f*
Grooves, major and minor, **235**
Growth medium, selective, **195**
Guanine (G), 7
Guide RNA (gRNA), **298**, 298*f*
Guide strand, **524**
Gusella, James, studies of Huntington disease by, 549
GWAS (genome-wide association studies), **734**,
  734–736, 736*b*
Gynandromorphy, **436**, 437*f*
Gyrase, DNA, **369**

H

H19 gene, 522
Haemophilus influenzae genome, whole-genome
  shotgun sequencing of, 614–615, 615*f*
Hairpin, **277**
Haldane, J. B. S., evolutionary genetics research
  and, 17
  mapping function of, 166, 166*f*
Haploid, **3**
Haploid eukaryotes, genetic linkage in, identified by
  tetrad analysis, 171–175
Haploid number of chromosomes, **65**
Haploid organisms, screening for conditional alleles
  in, 538–539, 539*f*
Haploinsufficient allele, **106**
Haplosufficient allele, **106**
Haplotype, **171**
Hardy, Godfrey, on genotype frequencies in popula-
  tions, 743
Hardy-Weinberg (H-W) equilibrium, **743**, 744–746,
  744*f*, 744*t*, 745*f*, 749*b*
  chi-square test of predictions of, 749
  CODIS based on, 769–770*b*
  for more than two alleles, 747–748, 748*t*
HATs (histone acetyltransferases) in chromatin
  modification, **517**, **519**, 519*f*
Hayes, William
  on F factor transfer, 192
  on interrupted mating in time-of-entry
    mapping, 197
Hb. *See* Hemoglobin (Hb)
HDACs (histone deacetylases) in chromatin modification, **517**, **519**, 519*f*
HDMTs (histone demethylases) in chromatin modification, **519**
Helicase, **244**
Helix-turn-helix (HTH) motif, **471–472**, 471*f*
Hemizygous, **85**
Hemoglobin (Hb), **339**
  inherited variant of, causing sickle cell disease,
    339–341, 339*f*, 340*f*
  peptide fingerprint analysis of, in SCD, 344
  structural change in sickle cell disease, 342*f*
Hemoglobin protein peptide fragment analysis,
  344, 345*f*

Hemophilia
  F8 gene mutation causing, 92
  in royal families of Europe, 92, 92*f*
  as X-linked recessive disorder, 93
Hemophilia A, gene mutation causing, 91–93,
  91*t*, 92*f*
Hereditary disorder. *See also specific disorders*
  environmental modification for prevention of,
    120–121
  first documentation of, 2
Hereditary molecule, DNA as, 230–232, 231*f*
Hereditary nonpolyposis colorectal cancer
  (HNPCC), 411
Hereditary transmission
  early studies on, 2
  purpose of, 6
Heredity
  blending theory of, 26
  chromosome, and cell division, 64–103
  chromosome theory of, **65**
  proof of, 86, 86*f*
Heritability, **726–727**
  broad sense, **727**, **727**
  measuring genetic component of phenotypic
    variation, 726–730
  narrow sense, **727**
    artificial selection and, 729–730, 729*t*, 730*f*
  twin studies of, 727–729, 729*t*
Herpes simplex virus (HSV), 366, 367*t*, 596
Herrick, James, history of sickle cell disease and,
  339–340
Hershey, Alfred, on DNA in bacteriophage infection
  of bacterial cells, 231, 231*f*
Heterochromatic regions, **381**
Heterochromatin, **381**
  centromeric, 382–384
Heterochromatin protein-1 (HP-1), 513, 513*f*
Heteroduplex DNA, **419**
  gene conversion as directed mismatch repair in,
    419, 422–423, 422*f*, 423*f*
Heteroduplex region, **419**
Heterogeneity, genetic, **134**
Heterologous genes, expression in bacterial and
  fungal hosts, 583–589
Heteroplasmic cell/organism, **652**
Heteroplasmy, 651–652, **652**, 652*f*
  penetrance of human hereditary disease and,
    658–659, 658*f*
Heterotetramer, **308**
Heterozygote(s)
  inversion, **446**, 447*f*
  natural selection favoring, 751–752, 751*t*
  partial deletion, **441**
  partial duplication, **441**
  translocation, **448**
Heterozygous advantage, **358**
  for β^A β^S individuals, 357–358
Heterozygous genotype (heterozygote), **33**
Hfr chromosomes, **194**, 195*f*
  formation of, 194–195
Hfr gene transfer, 195–197, 196*f*
Hfr maps, consolidation of, 200–201, 201*f*, 203
High-frequency recombination (Hfr) strains, **194**
High-throughput sequencing, transcriptome analysis
  by, 638
Histone acetyltransferases (HATs) in chromatin
  modification, **517**, **519**, 519*f*
Histone deacetylases (HDACs) in chromatin
  modification, **517**, **519**, 519*f*
Histone demethylases (HDMTs) in chromatin modi-
  fication, **519**
Histone methyltransferases (HMTs) in chromatin
  modification, **512**, 513, 513*f*, **519**
Histone proteins (H1, H2A, H2B, H3, H4),
  286–287, **371**
  archaeal DNA wrapping of, 385*f*
  characteristics, 371*t*
  phylogenetic origins of, 385
Histones, archaeal, 385
HIV (human immunodeficiency virus), 366, 367*t*

HMTs (histone methyltransferases) in chromatin
  modification, **512**, 513, 513*f*, **519**
Hoelzel, A. Rus, on genetic bottlenecks, 758
Holliday, Robin, model of meiotic recombination
  of, **418**
Holliday junction, **419**, 420–421*f*
Holliday junction resolution, 419
Holliday model, **418**
  of meiotic recombination, 418
Holoenzyme, **246**
Holoprosencephaly, *Shh* mutations in (Case Study),
  708–709*f*, 708*b*
Homeobox, **692**
Homeodomain, **692**
Homeotic activity in floral-organ identity, 704–707
  combinatorial activity of, in floral-organ
    identity, 705*f*
Homeotic genes, 686*f*, **687**
  combinatorial activity of floral, in floral-organ
    identity, 706*f*
  parasegmental pattern of expression of, 691–695
Homeotic MADS box transcription factors, 706–707
Homeotic mutations, **682**
Hominin evolution models, 21
Hominins, genomic story of, 21–22
Homologous chromosomes, **2**
Homologous genes, **628**
Homologous nucleotides, **624**
Homologous recombination, **588**, 589*f*
Homologs, **2**, **628**
Homology, **17**, 19*f*
Homoplasmic cell/organism, **651**
Homoplasmy, **18**, **651**, 651–652, 652*f*
Homotetramer, **308**
Homozygosity, reduced recessive, in polyploids, 439,
  443–444*b*
Homozygous genotype (homozygote), **33**
Horowitz, Norman, genetic dissection analysis
  of, 126
Host cell, **366**
Hotspots, 261–262
  of mutations, **393**
  recombination as dominated by, 164–165
Housekeeping genes, **686**
Hox genes, 691*f*, **692**, 694*b*
  downstream targets of, 695
  in metazoans, 695, 696*f*
  parasegment specification by, 691–695
HP-1 (heterochromatin protein-1), 513, 513*f*
HTH (helix-turn-helix) motif, **471–472**, 471*f*
Huberman, Joel, pulse-chase labeling evidence of
  bidirectional DNA replication and,
  238–239, 239*f*
Human Genome Project (HGP), 13, 611, 616
Human Genome Sequencing Project (HGSP), 766
Human immunodeficiency virus (HIV), 366, 367*t*
Hunchback gene, 688, 689, 689*f*
Huntington, George, description of Huntington disease by, 548–549
Huntington disease (HD)
  delayed age of onset of dominant lethal allele in,
    118, 118*f*
  presymptomatic molecular diagnosis of, 262
  transgenic mouse model of, 600*b*
Huntington disease (HD) genes, 263*f*
  dideoxy DNA sequencing of, 262*f*
  positional cloning in identification of (Case Study),
    548–549, 550*f*
  wild-type, 262
Huntington disease mutations, PCR and DNA
  sequencing in analysis of (Case Study),
  261–262*b*
Hybrid dysgenesis, **459**, 459*f*
Hybrid vigor, **438**
Hybridization, **343**, 354*b*. *See also* In situ
  hybridization
Hydrogen bonds, **7**
Hydroxylating agents, mutations induced by,
  405, 405*f*
Hypermorphic mutations, 107*f*, **108**

Hypertrichosis, congenital generalized, 91*t*
  transmission of, 94, 94*f*
Hypomorphic mutation, 107*f*, **108**
Hypophosphatemia, 91*t*
Hypothesis testing
  by F$_2$ self-fertilization, 35, 35*f*, 36*t*
  by test-cross analysis, 34–35, 34*f*, 35*f*

I

ICR (imprinting control region), **522**
Identical by descent (IBD), **758**, 758–759
Illegitimate recombination, **588**, 589*f*
ILs (introgression lines), **732–733**
Imprinting, genomic, **522**, 522–524, 523*f*
Imprinting control region (ICR), **522**
In situ hybridization, **378**
  of chromosomes, 377–379, 378*f*
Inbreeding, coefficient of, **758**, 758–759, 758*t*,
    759*f*, 760*b*
Inbreeding altering genotype frequencies, 758–760
Inbreeding depression, **759–760**
Incomplete dominance, **108–109**, 109*f*
Incomplete penetrance, **118**, 118–119, 119*f*
Indels, **766**
Independent assortment
  vs. genetic linkage, 145–146
  genetic linkage and, 146–147, 146*f*
  meiosis and, 79–81
  testing of
    by test-cross analysis, 39, 39*f*, 41
    by trihybrid-cross analysis, 41–42, 41*f*
Independent assortment, law of (Mendel's second
    law), **38**
  meiosis and, 79–81, 80*f*
Induced mutations, **403–404**, 403–408
  by chemicals, 404–406, 404*t*, 405*f*, 406*f*
Inducer compound, **470**, 470*f*
Inducer-repressor complex, **474**
Inducible operon, **472**
Induction, **497**, **683**, 684*f*
Inductive signal, 697*f*, **698**
Inductive signaling between cells, 697–699*f*, 697–700
Influenza virus, 367*t*
Informational genes, **674**
Ingram, Vernon, hemoglobin peptide fingerprint
    analysis and, 344
Ingroup, **18**
Inheritance. *See also* Cytoplasmic inheritance
  autosomal, **51**
  autosomal dominant, **51**, 52*f*
  autosomal recessive, **53**, 53*f*, 56*b*
  biparental, **650**
    in *Saccharomyces cerevisiae*, 661–662, 661*f*
  maternal, **651**
  mitochondrial, in mammals, 654–662
  particulate, **33**, 33–34
    evidence of, 33
  polygenic, **714**
  sex-linked, **84**
  uniparental, **650**
  X-linked, 84–85, 84*f*
  X-linked dominant, **90**
  X-linked recessive, **90**
  Y-linked, **94–95**
Inherited variation
  gene mutation as source of, 392–417 (*see also*
    Mutation(s))
  meiotic recombination as source of, 418–419
Inhibition, **683–684**, 684*f*
  lateral, **700**
    in cellular differentiation, 700, 700*f*
Inhibitor compound, 424*f*, **470**
Initial committed complex, **281**, 282*f*
Initiation, **282**, **313**
  in anaphase I, 76*f*, 77
Initiation factor (IF) proteins, **312**, 312–313, 312*f*
Initiator tRNA, **311**, 312*f*
Inosine (I), **322**
Insertion mutants, use in reverse genetics, 552
Insertion or deletion (indel) in human genetic
    diversity, **766**

Insertion sequence (IS) elements, **192**
  in bacterial genomes, transposition of, 456–457,
    456*t*, 458*b*
Insertional inactivation, **451**
Insulator sequences, 511, **511**, 512*f*
Insulin growth factor 2 (*IGF2*) gene, 522, 529
Insulin production in *E. coli*, human, 584–586, 586*f*
Interacting and redundant genes, identifying,
    540–541
Interactive variance, **726**
Interactome, **641**
Intercalating agents, mutations induced by, **406**, 406*f*
Interchromosomal domain, **379**
Interference (I), **158**, 158–159
  negative, 159
Internal control regions (ICRs), **284**, 284*f*
Internal promoter elements, **284**
Interphase, **65**, 66*f*, 68*f*, 74
  imaging chromosome territory during,
    379–380, 379*f*
Interrupted mating, **197**
Interrupted mating analysis, producing time-of-entry
    maps, 197–203, 198*f*, 202*b*
Interspecific comparisons of genomes, **622**, 624
  gene content, 624–631, 625*f*, 627*f*–629*f*
  gene order in, 632–634, 633*f*
  genome annotation, 631–632, 632*f*, 633*f*
Interstitial deletion, **441**, 441*f*
Intragenic recombination, **162**, 162, 162*f*
Intragenic recombination analysis, 216
Intragenic reversion, **397**, 398*f*
Intrinsic termination, **277**, 277, 277*f*
Introgression lines (ILs), **732–733**
  QTL analysis in, 732–734, 733*f*
Intron(s), **11**, 12*f*
Intron self-splicing, **294**, 294*f*, **296**
Intron splicing, **285**
  pre-mRNA, 287–288, 289*f*, 290*f*
    alternative, 290, **292**, 292–294
Inversion, chromosome, **446**, 446–448,
    446*f*–448*f*, 452*b*
Inversion heterozygotes, **446**
Inversion loop, **446**, 447*f*
Inverted repeat (IR), **277**
Inverted repeat (IR) sequence, **456**, 456*f*
Irons, Ernest, history of sickle cell disease and, 339
Irritable bowel syndrome (IBS), 618*b*
IS (insertion sequence) elements, **192**
Island model of migration, **755**, 755*f*
Isoaccepting tRNAs, **321**, 321*f*
Isolation, reproductive, **760–761**
  mechanisms of, 762*t*
  speciation and, 761, 763–764
ISWI (imitation switch) complex in chromatin
    remodeling, 515, **516**, 519*f*

J

Jacob, François, 468*f*
  on interrupted mating in time-of-entry mapping, 197
  on *lac* operon analysis, 476, 477–478
  and mRNA discovery, 270
Jacob syndrome, 434*t*
Jacobsen syndrome, 399*t*
Jenuwein, Thomas, on "histone code," 517
Johansson, Wilhelm, introduction of the term *gene*
    by, 267
Jorgensen, Richard, on cosuppression, 524
Juvenile hormone (JH), 121

K

K-pn (*Prune-killer*), 541
Karyokinesis, **66**
  in anaphase I, 76*f*, 77
Karyotype, **377**, 377*f*
Khorana, Har Gobind, deciphering genetic code and,
    326–327
Kilobases (kb), **348**
Kinetochore, **67**
  in chromosome distribution, 67, 70*f*

Kinetochore microtubules, **67**, 70*f*
  in diakinesis, 76*f*, 77
  in metaphase I, 76*f*, 77
Klinefelter syndrome, 434*t*
Knight, Thomas Andrew, genetic research of, 45*b*
Knockout libraries, **552**, **641**, 641*f*
Knockouts, gene, **588**
Kornberg, Arthur
  model of DNA replication, 249, 250*f*
  nucleosome-based model of chromatin, 371, 373
Kosambi, Damodar, modified mapping function of,
    166, 166*f*
Kozak, Marilyn, Kozak sequence discovered by, 313
Kozak sequence, **313**
Krüppel gene, 689, 690, 690*f*

L

Lac, 189*b*, **472**
Lac operon, **472**
  function of, 473–476, 475*f*
  as inducible operon system under negative and
    positive control, 472–476
  molecular analysis of, 480–483, 480*f*, 482*b*, 483*f*
  mutational analysis deciphering genetic regulation
    of, 476–483
  regulatory mutations of, 477–480, 482*b*
  structure of, 473, 474*f*
  transcription conditions for, 480*t*
Lac operon gene, regulatory sequence for, 476*t*
Lac⁻ phenotype, **473**
Lac⁺ phenotype, **472**
LacA gene, **473**
LacI gene ("lack eye"), 473
Lactase, 752
Lactose, 752
Lactose metabolism, 472–473, 473*f*
Lactose (*lac*) operon. *See Lac* operon
LacY gene, **473**
LacZ gene, **473**
Lagging strand(s), **246**, 247*f*
  simultaneous synthesis of leading strands and,
    248–249, 249*f*, 250*f*
Lahn, Bruce, 96–97
Lambda (λ) phage (bacteriophage λ), 366, 367*t*,
    492–497
  genome of, 493, 494*f*
  lysogeny in, 493
  induction of, 497, 497*f*
Lanktree, Matthew, on genes influencing adult
    height, 714
Large ribosomal subunit, **309**
Lariat intron structure, **289**
Last universal common ancestor (LUCA), **4**, 315
Late genes, **493**
Late operators, **496**
Late promoters, **496**
Lateral gene transfer (LGT), 629, 631
  in genomes, 220
Lateral inhibition in cellular differentiation,
    700, 700*f*
Law of independent assortment. *See* Independent
    assortment, law of (Mendel's second law)
Law of segregation. *See* Segregation, law of (Mendel's
    first law)
LCR (locus control region), **508–509**, 511*f*
LCT gene, 752–753, 766
Leader region, **484**, 484*f*
Leader sequences. *See* Signal sequences (leader
    sequences)
Leading strand(s), **246**, 247*f*
  simultaneous synthesis of lagging strands and,
    248–249, 249*f*, 250*f*
Leaky mutation, 107*f*, **108**
Leber hereditary optic neuropathy (LHON), mito-
    chondrial mutations and, 656*f*, 658
Lederberg, Joshua, bacterial DNA transfer identifica-
    tion and, 188, 191, 191*f*
Leptotene stage of prophase I, 75, 75*f*
Lesch-Nyhan syndrome, 91*t*
Lethal alleles, **113**, 113–117

Lethal mutations, 113–117, 115f, 116f
Lethality, synthetic, 541, **541**, 541f
Leukemia, chronic myelogenous, 386f, 387, 387b
Lewis, Edward B
    Drosophila mutation studies of, 691
    on pattern formation in *Drosophila*, 684
LHON (Leber hereditary optic neuropathy),
    mitochondrial mutations and, 656f, 658
Li-Fraumeni syndrome, 414t
    Case Study, 423–424b
Li-Fraumeni syndrome 1 (LFS1), 424b
Life-forms, ancient, 15–16
Ligand-binding domains (LBDs), 765, 766
LINE elements of humans, 460–461
Linkage, genetic. *See* Genetic linkage
Linkage disequilibrium (LD), **171**, 753
Linkage equilibrium, **171**
Linkage groups, **166**
    of genes, 166
Linked genes, assortment of, 145–146
Linker DNA, **371**
Linkers, **574**
Locus control regions (LCRs), **508–509**, 511f
Lod score, **167**, 168t
Lod score analysis, 167–169
    mapping linked human genes using, 166–169, 168f,
        168t, 169b, 170b
    for cystic fibrosis gene, 177–178b
Lod score curves, 168f
Long arm (q arm), **377**, 377f
Long noncoding RNAs (lncRNAs), **521**
Long terminal repeats (LTRs), **460**
Loss-of-function alleles, 560, 561f
Loss-of-function mutation, **106**, 107f, 108
LTRs (long terminal repeats), **460**
LUCA (last universal common ancestor), **4**
Lupus, Neandertal genes and, 769
Luria, Salvador, 392
Lwoff, André, 468f
    on *lac* operon analysis, 476
Lymphoma, Burkitt's, 386f, 387, 387b
Lyon (random X inactivation) hypothesis, **95**
Lysis, **206**
Lysogenic cycle, 208f, **209**
Lysogeny, **209**
    in lambda phage, 493
    induction of, 497, 497f
    lambda repressor protein and, 496, 497f
Lysogeny induction, resumption of lytic cycle
    following, 497
Lytic cycle, **207**, 208f
    resumption of, following lysogeny induction, 497

M

M phase of eukaryotic cell cycle, **65**, 66f
    substages of, 66–69
MacLeod, Colin
    and deoxyribonucleic acid identification, 4
    on DNA as transformation factor, 230, 230f
MADS box, **706**
MADS box transcription factors, homeotic,
    706–707
Major, Daphne, 764
Major genes, **715**
Major groove, **235**
Malaria, 587b
    β^S allele and, 353, 357–358
    geographic distribution of, 357f
    plant-derived drugs for, produced in *E. coli*, 587b
Mammals
    coat color in, *C*-gene system for, 111–115,
        113f, 114f
    mitochondrial inheritance in, 654–662
    sex determination in, 88, 88f
Map unit (m.u.), **154**
Mapping. *See also* Genetic linkage mapping/maps;
        Quantitative trait loci (QTLs) mapping
    cotransduction, **210**, 210–211, 211f, 211t,
        212f, 214b
    deletion, **442**, 444f, 445b

interrupted mating analysis producing, 198f, 202b
    time-of-entry, 197–198
        interrupted mating analysis producing, 197–203
Mapping function, Haldane's, **166**, 166f
Maps. *See* Genetic map; Restriction maps
Marker screens, selected and unselected, **210**
MARs (matrix attachment regions), 374, 375f
Maternal effect genes, **687**
Maternal inheritance, **651**
Mating
    consanguineous, 758
    nonrandom, altering genotype frequencies,
        758–760
Mating-table analysis of genotype and allele frequen-
        cies, 745, 746f, 746t
Matrix attachment regions (MARs), 374, 375f
Matthaei, Johann Heinrich, deciphering genetic code
        and, 326
Mature mRNA, **285**
Maxam, Allan, DNA-sequencing protocols of, 256
Mayr, Ernst, modern synthesis of evolution and, 17
MC1R gene, 766
McCarty, Maclyn
    and deoxyribonucleic acid identification, 4
    on DNA as transformation factor, 230, 230f
McClintock, Barbara
    research on crossing over in corn, 160, 160f
    transposition discovered by, 451, 453
MCS (multiple cloning site), **574**
Mean (μ), **48–49**
Median, **724**
Median value, **724**
Mediator in GAL gene system transcription
        regulation, **511**
Megabases (Mb), **13**
Meiosis, **4**, 65
    Mendelian hereditary principles and, 79–81
    vs. mitosis, 73–75, 74t
    overview of, 73–75, 74f
Meiosis I, **74–75**, 76f
    nondisjunction in, 431, 432f
Meiosis II, 75, 77f, 79, 79f
    nondisjunction in, 431, 433f
Meiotic nondisjunction, creating autopolyploidy,
        437, 437f
Meiotic recombination, 420–421f
    inherited variation from, 418–419
Melanocortin-1 receptor (*MC1R*) gene, 766
Mello, Craig, on RNA interference, 524, 553
Memory impairment, 441
Mendel, Gregor (Johann), 26, 26f
    basic principles of genetic transmission discovered
        by, 27–31
    chi-square analysis of experimental data of,
        50–51, 51t
    experimental innovations of, 29–31
    genes and seed shapes described by, 453, 454–455b
    hereditary principles of, and autosomal
        inheritance, 51–55
    on hereditary transmission, 2
    modern experimental approach of, 26
    molecular genetics of traits examined by,
        54–55, 55t
    rediscovery of the research of, 42, 44
Mendelian genetics, **5**, 26. *See also* Transmission
        genetics
Mendelian ratios
    gene interactions modifying, 121–134
    mechanistic basis of, 79–81
    probability theory predicts, 44–48
Mendelism, 26. *See also* Transmission genetics
    in produce aisle (Case Study), 44b
Mendel's first law. *See* Segregation, law of (Mendel's
        first law)
Mendel's second law. *See* Independent assortment,
        law of (Mendel's second law)
Meristems, **703**
    development at, 703–704, 704f
MERRF (myoclonic epilepsy with ragged red fibers),
        mitochondrial mutations and, 658, 659

Meselson, Matthew
    DNA replication experiment of, 236–237,
        237f, 238f
    and mRNA discovery, 270
    semiconservative replication mechanism and, 8
Meselson-Stahl experiment, 236–237
Messenger RNA (mRNA), **5**, **270–271**
    5' capping of, 285–286, 286f
    alternative splicing of, sex determination in *Dro-
        sophila* and (Case Study), 299–300b, 300f
    editing chloroplast, 668, 668f
    identification of, 269–270
    mature, 285
    translation of, 12, 13f
        into polypeptide, genetic code in, 320–322
    translation of polycistronic, 320, 320f
Metabolomics, **15**
Metacentric chromosome, **377**
Metagenome, **617**
Metagenomics, 616–617
Metaphase, mitotic, **66**, 67, 68f
Metaphase I, 76f, 77, 78f
Metaphase II, 77f
Metaphase plate, **67**, 76–77f
Metazoans, *Hox* genes in, 695, 696f
Methicillin-resistant *Staphylococcus aureus* (MRSA),
        evolution and spread of, 221b
Methionine biosynthesis pathway, genetic dissection
        of, 126–127, 127f
Methylation, nucleotide, in gene silencing, 523–524
Microbial growth
    for genotyping, 189–190b
    visualizing, 189b
Microbiota, 618b
Microdeletions, **442**
MicroRNA (miRNA), **271**, **524**
Microsynteny, **633**
Microtubules
    astral, 67, 70f
    kinetochore, 67, 70f
    nonkinetochore, **67**
    polar, **67**, 70f
    spindle fiber, **67**
Miescher, Friedrich, DNA isolation by, 228
Migration, **755**, 755–756, 755f
    and evolution of humans, 22f, 655–656, 655f
    as evolutionary process, 17, 22f
    origin of, 342
Minimal initiation complex, **282**, 282f
Minimal medium, 189b
Minor groove, **235**
Mismatch repair in heteroduplex DNA, gene
        conversion as directed, 419, 422–423,
        422f, 423f
Missense mutations, 394, **394**, 394f
Mitochondria, 3, 4, **662**
    endosymbiosis theory of evolution of,
        668–675, 671f
    as energy factories of eukaryotic cells, 662–666
    structure of, 662, 663f
Mitochondrial DNA
    mother-child identity of, 654–655, 655f
    research analyzing, 657b
Mitochondrial DNA sequences and species evolution
        of, 655
Mitochondrial genome structure and gene content,
        662–665, 663f, 664f
Mitochondrial inheritance in mammals, 654–662
Mitochondrial mutations and human genetic disease,
        656, 656f, 658–659, 669b, 675–676b
Mitochondrial transcription and translation,
        665–666, 665f, 666t
Mitosis, **4**, 65
    gene transmission in, 4
    vs. meiosis, 73–75, 74t
    overview of, 69, 71f
    in somatic cell division, 65–73
Mitosomes, **673**
Mitotic crossover, **176**
    producing distinctive phenotypes, 175–176, 177f

Mitotic nondisjunction, creating autopolyploidy, 437–438, 437f
MN blood group, 112b
Modal value, **724**
Mode, **724**
Model organisms, 13
Modern synthesis of evolution, **17**
Modifier genes, **715**
Modifier screen, **540**
Mold, red bread (*Neurospora crassa*)
  growth variants of, 125–126b
  met- mutant strain of, genetic dissection analysis of, 126–127, 127f
  ordered ascus analysis of, 173–175, 175f, 176f
Molecular biology
  of transcription and RNA processing, 267–304
  of translation, 305–337
Molecular charge and electrophoretic gels, 343
Molecular cloning in recombinant DNA technology, 572–577, 573f–575f, 577t, 578f
Molecular disease, 339, 342
Molecular evolution. *See also* Evolution: molecular basis of
  changing genes and genomes through time, 764–769
Molecular genetic analysis
  gel electrophoresis in, 342–344, 343f, 344f
  of *lac* operon, 480–483, 480f, 482b, 483, 483f
  of thalassemia, 359–360, 359f
  using DNA replication processes, 254–261
    dideoxyribonucleotide DNA sequencing as, 256–259, 258f, 259f, 260b
    polymerase chain reaction as, 254–256, 255f, 257f, 260b
Molecular genetics, **5**
  inauguration of the era of, 4
  of Mendel's traits, 54–55, 55t
Molecular probes, **343**, 348–349, **349**, 354–355b
Molecular shape (molecular conformation) and electrophoretic gels, 343
Molecular weight and electrophoretic gels, 343
Monod, Jacques, 468f
  on *lac* operon analysis, 476, 477–478
Monohybrid cross(es), **33**
  segregation of alleles and, 31–36, 32f
Monophyletic group, **17**
Monosomic chromosomes, **432**
Monosomy, **432**
Morgan, Lillian, 84
Morgan, Thomas Hunt, 144f
  and discovery of recombinant chromosomes in gametes, 418
  on genetic linkage and mapping, 144, 145
  and genetic linkage discovery, 148–150, 149f
  hypothesis of recombination by crossing over, 160
  and origin of developmental genetics, 682
  studies on *Drosophila melanogaster*, 81, 84–85, 85f
Morphogens, **683**
Morphological evolution, 18f
Morton, Newton, lod score analysis and, 167
Mosaicism, 435–436, 436f
mRNA. *See* Messenger RNA (mRNA)
MRSA (methicillin-resistant *Staphylococcus aureus*), evolution and spread of, 221b
Müller, Hermann, 452b
  balancer chromosome used by, 537
  on radiation-induced mutations, 535
Multicellular organism, development as building of, 682–684, 682f–684f
Multifactorial traits, **714**
Multimeric proteins in dominant negative mutations, 108
Multimers, 308
Multiple cloning site (MCS), **574**
Multiple-gene hypothesis, **715**
Multiplication rule of probability theory, **44–45**
Multiregional (MRE) hypothesis, 21
Multiregional (MRE) model of *H. sapiens* evolution, 655–656, 655f
Mus musculus, transgenic, 596–598, 597f

Muscular dystrophy, 91t
  Duchenne, 91t, 393, 577
Mutagen(s), **403–404**
  Ames test for, 408, **408**, 409f, 410b
  chemical, 404–406, 404t, 405f, 406f
  for genetic screen, selection of, 536, 536t
Mutagenesis, 403–404, **535**
  genetic screen analysis of, 540b
  genomics approach to gene identification following, 551, 551f
  number of genes identified in, 539
  saturation, **535**
Mutagenesis analysis, genetic screen in, 539
Mutant alleles, 262
  identified for gene, number of, 539, 540b
  (*see also under* Mutation(s))
Mutants
  constitutive, **477**
  insertion, use in reverse genetics, 552
  revertible and nonrevertible, **216**
Mutation(s), 341, **753**
  altering human sex development, 89b
  amorphic, **106**, 107f
  in analysis of gene transcription, 282, 282f
  attenuation, 488, 488f
  of β-globin gene alleles, evolution of, 358, 358f
  base-pair substitution, **394**, 394–395, 394f
  bithorax, discovery of, 682, 682f
  cell cycle, and cancer, 72
  chromosome breakage causing, 439–444, 441f, 442f, 444f, 445b
  cis-acting, **478**, 478f
  constitutive repressor protein, 478f, 479, 479t
  definition of, 391
  diversifying gene pools, 753–755
  dominant negative, 107f, **108**
  enhancer, hereditary disorders from, 509
  as evolutionary process, **17**
  forward, **397**
  frameshift, **324**, **395**, 396f
  gain-of-function, **106**, 107f, 108
  in genetic screens
    balancer chromosomes for tracking, 537, 538f
    identification of dominant and recessive, 536–537, 537f, 539
  globin gene, 340–341, 341f
  homeotic, **682**
  hotspots of, **393**
  hypermorphic, 107f, **108**
  hypomorphic, 107f, **108**
  identifying types of, 400b
  induced, **403–404**, 403–408
  leaky, 107f, **108**
  lethal, 113–117, 115f, 116f
  loss-of-function, **106**, 107f, 108
  missense, 394, **394**, 394f
  mitochondrial, and human genetic disease, 656, 656f, 658–659, 669b, 675–676b
  modifying DNA sequence, 393–397
  neomorphic, 107f, **108**
  nonsense, **394**, 394f
  null, **106**, 107f
  p53 gene, causing Li-Fraumeni syndrome, 423–424b
  PEV, 512–513, 512f
  point, **394**
  promoter, **396**, 396f, 479–480
  from radiation, 406–408, 407f
  regulatory, 395–397, **396**, 396f, 398f
    of *lac* operon, 477–480, 481b
  reverse, **397**, 398f
  reversion, **324**
  in same gene, mutations in different genes distinguished from, 133–135
  silent, **394**, 394f
  splicing, 396–397, 396f, **397**
  spontaneous, **397**
  from spontaneous events, 397–403
  super-repressor protein, 478f, 479, 479t
  suppressor, **397**

  transition, **394**
  transversion, **394**
Mutation rates, **392**, 392–393, 393t
Mutation-selection balance, **753**, 753–755
Mutational analysis deciphering genetic regulation of *lac* operon, 476–483, 477t
Mycoplasma, 598
Myers, Richard, promoter mutation analysis of, 282, 282f
Myoclonic epilepsy with ragged red fibers (MERRF), mitochondrial mutations and, 658, 659
Myotonic dystrophy (type I), 399t

N

N-formylmethionine (fMet), **313**
Naegeli, Karl, 27
Narrow sense heritability, **727**
  artificial selection and, 729–730, 729t, 730f
Nathans, Daniel, restriction endonucleases and, 569b
Natural selection
  directional, **750**, 750–751, 751t
  evolution by, 16
  as evolutionary process, **17**
  favoring heterozygotes, 751–752, 751t
  operating through differential reproductive fitness within population, 748–753
Naudin, Charles, 45b
NDR (nucleosome-depleted region), **514**
Neandertal DNA in the modern human genome, 768–769
  distribution of, 769f
Neandertals, derived alleles in, 768
Near isogenic lines (NILs), **732–733**
Neel, James, transmission genetic analysis of SCD and, 342
Negative control of transcription, **469–470**
Negative interference, **159**
Negative supercoiling, **369**
Neofunctionalization, **628**
Neomorphic mutations, 107f, **108**
Neurospora crassa. See Mold, red bread (*Neurospora crassa*)
Next-generation DNA sequencing technologies, 259, 259f, 261
Next-generation sequencing, **259**
NHEJ (nonhomologous end joining), **416–417**, 417f
NILs (near isogenic lines), **732–733**
Nilsson-Ehle, Hermann, multiple-gene hypothesis and, 715
Nirenberg, Marshall, deciphering genetic code and, 326–327
Nodes, **624**
Nonadaptive evolution, 16–17
Noncoding sequences, conserved, **631**
  in genome annotation, 631–632, 632f
Noncomposite transposon, **456**
Nondisjunction, **86**
  analysis of, 85–86
  chromosome number changes from, 431–437
  meiotic, creating autopolyploidy, 437, 437f
  mitotic, creating autopolyploidy, 437–438, 437f
Nonenveloped viruses, **366–367**, 367f
Nonhistone proteins, **371**
Nonhomologous end joining (NHEJ), **416–417**, 417f
Noninducible, **479**
Nonparental ditypes (NPD), **172**
Nonparental phenotypes, 38
Nonpenetrant organisms, 118
Nonrecombinant chromosomes, **145**
Nonrecombinant vector, **573**
Nonreplicative transposition, **456**
Nonrevertible mutants, **216**
Nonsense mutations, **394**, 394f
Nonsister chromatids, **76**
  binding of, synaptonemal complex in, 76, 78f
Nontemplate strand, **271**
Normal (Gaussian) distribution, 48–49, 49f
North-south (NS) resolution, **419**

Northern blotting, **349**, 355*b*, 454*b*
in β-globin gene transcript and protein analysis, 352–353, 353*f*
Notation systems in genetics, 109
Notch gene, 444
Nuclear mitochondrial sequences (NUMTS), **671**
Nuclear plastid sequences (NUPTS), **671**
Nucleoid, **3, 368, 652**
of *E. coli*, 368*f*
Nucleolus, **283**
Nucleomorph, **675**
Nucleosome(s), **371**, 372*f*
chromatin remodeling by modification of, 514–517, 515*f*, 518*b*, 519*f*
Nucleosome core particle, **371**
Nucleosome-depleted region (NDR), **514**
Nucleosome distribution and synthesis during replication, 374–376, 377*f*
Nucleosome structure, 373, 373*f*
Nucleotide(s). *See also* DNA nucleotides
homologous, **624**
RNA, 11, 268–271
Nucleotide base analogs, **404**
mutations induced by, 404, 404*f*
Nucleotide excision repair, **411**, 412*f*
Null mutation, **106**, 107*f*
NUMTS (nuclear mitochondrial sequences), **671**
NUPTS (nuclear plastid sequences), **671**
Nüsslein-Volhard, Christiane
mutagenesis strategy used by, 538
on pattern formation in *Drosophila*, 684, 686

O

Obsessive-compulsive disorder (OCD), 441
Ogura, Yasunori, genome-wide association studies of, 736*b*
Okazaki, Reiji, research on short fragment synthesis, 246–247
Okazaki fragment(s), **247**
ligation of, for DNA replication, 247–248, 248*f*
On the Origin of Species (Darwin), 16
Oncogene, 71
One gene–one enzyme hypothesis, **124**, 124–127, 125–126*b*
Open chromatin, **514–515**, 516*f*
Open promoter complex, **273**, 274*f*, 276
Open promoters, **514**
Open reading frames (ORFs), 618–619, 625*f*, 669
Operational genes, **674**
Operator(s), **470**
early, **493**
lacO, 473
late, **496**
Operon(s), **472**. *See also Lac* operon; Tryptophan (*trp*) operon
amino acid, attenuation in, 488, 488*f*
inducible, **472**
repressible, **484**
Operon system(s)
attenuation in, 488
inducible, 473–483
lac operon as, 472–476
ORB (origin recognition box), 242, 244
Ordered ascus, **173**
Ordered ascus analysis, 173–175, 175*f*, 176*f*
Organelle genome replication, 652, 653*f*
Organelle genomes
replicative segregation of, 653
variable segregation of, 654*f*
Organelles, continual DNA transfer from, 670–672, 672*f*, 673*f*
Organelles proteins, encoding of, 672–673
Organizer in pattern formation, **683**
Origin of migration, 342
Origin of replication (ori), **237**
in bacteriophage vectors, 577
DNA sequences at, 242, 244*f*
in plasmids, 574, 575*f*
Origin of transfer (oriT), **193**

Origin recognition box (ORB), 242, 244
Ornithine transcarbamylase deficiency, 91*t*
Orr-Weaver, Terry, double-stranded break model of meiotic recombination and, 418
Orthologous genes, **628**
Orthologs, **628**
Osteogenesis imperfecta, dominant negative mutation in, 108
Ototoxic deafness, mitochondrial gene-environment interaction in (Case Study), 675–676*b*
Outgroup, **18**
Ovarian cancer, 414*t*, 415
mapping a gene for susceptibility to, 169*b*
Ovomucoid gene, intron splicing of, 289
Oxidative reactions, mutations induced by, 405–406

P

p arm, **376–377**, 377*f*
P element, **459–460, 594**
Drosophila transformation mediated by, 594–595, 595*f*
p53 DNA damage repair pathway, 413, 414*f*
p53 gene mutations, causing Li-Fraumeni syndrome, 423–424*b*
Paabo, Svante, 21
Pachytene stage of prophase I, 75, 75*f*
Page, David, 96–97
Pair-rule genes, **686**, 686*f*
regulation of, 689–691, 690*f*
Paired-end sequencing, **613**, 614*f*
PAR. *See* Pseudoautosomal region (PAR)
Paracentric inversion, **446**, 446*f*
Paralogous genes, **628**
Paralogs, **628**
Paraphyletic group, **18**
Parasegments, **687**
specification of, by *Hox* genes, 691–695
Parental chromosomes, **145**
alleles on, for three-point recombination mapping, 157
Parental ditypes (PD), **172**
Parental generation (P generation), **30**, 30*f*
Parental strand in semiconservative replication, **9**, 9*f*
Parovirus, 367*t*
Partial chromosome deletion, **440**, 440–441
Partial deletion, **441**
Partial deletion heterozygotes, **440, 441**
Partial diploid, **203**
conjugation with F′ strains producing, 203–204, 204*f*, 205–206*b*
Partial dominance, **108–109**, 109*f*
Partial duplication, **441**
Partial duplication heterozygote, **441**
Particulate inheritance, **33**, 33–34
Pascal's triangle, **47–48**, 47*f*
Patau syndrome, 434*t*
Paternity, population genetics in identifying (Case Study), 769–771*b*, 770*f*, 770*t*
Pathogenicity islands, **220**
Pattern formation in development, 683–684, 683*f*, 684*f*
maternal effects on, 687
Pauling, Linus
densitometry of hemoglobin proteins, 344, 344*f*
electrophoretic analysis of hemoglobin protein, 342–344, 343*f*, 344*f*
on sickle cell disease as molecular disease, 339, 342
PCNA (proliferating cell nuclear antigen), 249
PCR (polymerase chain reaction), **254**, 254–256, 255*f*, 257*f*, 259, 261–262*b*
detecting the number of repeats, 262
in recombinant DNA technology, 581, 582*f*
PCR primers, **255**
Pea, garden (*Pisum sativum*)
incomplete dominance in, 109, 109*f*
Mendel's research on, 27

Pearson, Karl, on genotype frequencies in populations, 743
Peas, shaped by transposition, 453, 454–455*b*
Pedigree(s), **51–52**, 53, 56, 90–96, 118–121, 166–169, 254–261, 347, 350–351*b*, 352–360, 423–424, 433–437, 439–444, 449, 528–529, 548–549, 654–662, 714, 727–729, 734–737, 758–760
symbols for, 51–52, 52*f*
Penetrance, incomplete, **118**, 118–119, 119*f*
Penetrant organisms, 118
Penicillin, discovery and use of, 220–221*b*
Peptide bond, **12**, 13*f*, **306**
Peptide bond formation, 306, 306*f*
Peptide fingerprint analysis, **344**
hemoglobin, 344, 347*b*
Peptidyl site (P site), **309**, 309*f*
Pericentric inversion, **446**, 446*f*
Permissive condition, **538**
Phages, **231**. *See also* Bacteriophage(s)
Phenotype(s), **4**
dominant, **31**, 35
genes producing variable, 118–121, 119*f*, 120*f*, 122*f*
mitotic crossover producing distinctive, 175–176, 177*f*
nonparental, 38
recessive, **31**
selection of single traits with dichotomous, 30
unstable mutant, **453**
Phenotypic ratio (3:1 and 9:3:3:1), **33**
Phenotypic variance, **725**
partitioning, 725*f*, 726*b*
sources of, 725*f*
Phenotypic variation
continuous, quantitative traits displaying, 714–721
effects of polygenes on, 716, 718*t*, 722*b*
environmental factors and, 719, 720*f*, 723*b*
heritability measuring genetic component of, 726–730
statistical description of, 721, 723–725, 724*f*
Phenylketonuria (PKU), prevention of, 120–121
PHO5 gene, 520
Phosphodiester bond, 7
Photoproducts, **406**
UV-induced, 406–408, 407*f*
repair of, 412–413, 413*f*
Photoreactive repair, **412**, 413*f*
Photosynthesis, chloroplasts as sites of, 666–668, 666*f*–668*f*
Phylogenetic footprinting, **631**, 632*f*
Phylogenetic shadowing, **631**, 633*f*
Phylogenetic tree, **17**, 18*f*
constructing
using cladistic approach, **17**
using molecular data, 19–21, 19*f*
using morphological and anatomical data, 18, 18*f*
Physical gaps, **614–615**
Pisum sativum. *See* Pea, garden (*Pisum sativum*)
PKU (phenylketonuria), prevention of, 120–121
Plants
cloning of, 602–603
multicellular evolution in, 703–707
transgenic
in agriculture, 591
creating, 589–593, 592*f*
Plasmid(s). *See also* F (fertility) plasmid
bacterial, 187–188, **188**, 188*f*
R (resistance), **188**
as cloning vectors, 574–575, 575*f*
generation of yeast, 588, 588*f*
Ti, **589–590**, 590*f*
Plastid, **666**
Pleiotropic genes, 121, 122*f*
Pleiotropy, **121**, 122*f*
Pluripotent cells, **683**
Pneumonia, 229
Point mutations, **394**
Polar microtubules, 67, 70*f*
Poliovirus, 367*t*

Poly-A tail, **285**
Polyacrylamide, **342–343**
Polyadenylation, alternative, **293**
Polyadenylation signal sequence, **286,** 287*f*
Polycistronic mRNA, **320,** 473
    bacterial, translation of, 320*f*
    translation of, 320
Polycomb group (PcG), 519
Polydactyly
    enhancer mutations causing, 509
    incomplete penetrance for, 118–119, 119*f*
    Shh mutations in (Case Study), 709*b*
Polygenes and phenotypic variation, 716, 718*t*, 722*b*
Polygenic inheritance, **714**
Polygenic traits, **714**
Polymerase(s). *See also* RNA polymerase(s)
    bypass, 416
    DNA replication
        bacterial, 247*t*, 249
        eukaryotic, 247*t*, 249
        translesion DNA, **416**
Polymerase chain reaction. *See* PCR (polymerase chain reaction)
Polymorphism(s). *See also* Single nucleotide polymorphism (SNP)
    balanced, **358,** 751
    restriction fragment length, **346,** 350–351*b*, 546
Polypeptide(s), **12, 306**
    composed of amino acid chains assembled at ribosomes, 306–311
    genetic code in translation of mRNA into, 320–322
Polypeptide and transcript structure, 307–309, 308*t*
Polypeptide elongation in translation, 315–318
Polypeptide processing, posttranslational, **330,** 330–331, 330*f*
Polyploidy, **3,** 437, **437**
    consequences of, 438
    euploidy changes resulting in, 437–439
    evolution and, 439, 440*f*
Polyribosomes, **319**
Population(s), **743**
    Darwin's principles of, 16, 17
Population genetics, 742–775, **743**
    genetic distances and relationships between human populations, 766, 767*f*
    in solving crime and identifying paternity (Case Study), 769–771*b*, 770*f*, 770*t*
Position effect variegation (PEV), **382,** 521
    mutations modifying, 512*f*
Position effect variegation (PEV) mutations, 512–513
Positional cloning, 544–549, **545,** 545*f*, 547*f*, 548*f*
Positional information, **683,** 683*f*, 684*f*
Positive control of transcription, **470**
Positive-negative selection, **596**
Positive supercoiling, **369**
Positron effect variegation (PEV), 512
Post-transcriptional RNA editing, 298–299, 298*f*, 299*f*
Posttranslational polypeptide processing, **330,** 330–331, 330*f*
Postzygotic mechanisms, **761,** 762*t*
Prader-Willi syndrome, 436
    genomic imprinting defects in, 522–523
Pre-mRNA (precursor mRNA), **285**
    polyadenylation of 3′, 286–287, 287*f*
    splicing signal sequences in, 288–289, 290*f*
Pre-mRNA processing
    3′ polyadenylation in, 286–287, 287*f*
    5′ capping in, 285, 286*f*
    alternative, **292,** 293*f*, 295*b*
    intron splicing in, 287–288, 289*f*, 290*f*
Pre-mRNA processing steps, coupling of, 289–290, 294*f*
Precursor mRNA. *See* Pre-mRNA
Preinitiation complex, **313**
Prereplication complex (preRC), 244
Prezygotic mechanisms, **761,** 762*t*
Pribnow box sequence, **273**
Primary structure of polypeptides, **308**

Primase, **245**
Primer walking, DNA sequencing by, **582,** 582*f*
Probability
    binomial, **46,** 46–48
    conditional, **45,** 45–46
Probability calculations in problem solving in genetics, 42
Probability theory
    predicts Mendelian ratios, 44–48
    product rule of, **44–45**
    sum rule of, 45
Probability (*P*) value, **49,** 50, 50*t*
Product (multiplication) rule of probability theory, **44–45**
Progenote, 5*f*
Proliferating cell nuclear antigen (PCNA), **249**
Prometaphase, mitotic, **66,** 68*f*
Promoter(s), **11,** 12*f*, **271**
    alternative, **293**
    bacterial, 272*f*, 273, 275*b*
    covered, **514,** 514–517, 514*f*
    early, **493**
    eukaryotic
        detecting promoter consensus elements, 282, 282*f*
        recognition of, 280–281, 282*f*
    lacP, 473
    late, **496**
    open, **514**
    RNA polymerase I, 283–284, 283*f*
    RNA polymerase III, 284, 284*f*
    in transcription, band shift assay to identify, 279–280*b*
Promoter consensus sequences, archaea, 285*f*
Promoter mutations, **396,** 396*f*, 479–480
Promoter-specific element (PSE), **284**
Prophage, **209**
Prophase, mitotic, **66,** 68*f*
Prophase I, 75–76*f*
Prophase II, 77*f*
Protein(s), **12**
    activator, **470**
    chromatin-remodeling, 513
    controlling double-strand break repair, 415–417
    controlling translesion DNA synthesis, 407–410
    cro, and entry of lambda phage into lytic cycle, 496, 496*f*
    cyclin, 70
        in cell cycle checkpoints, 70, 72*f*
        regulating cell cycle, 71, 73*f*
    DNA-binding, regulatory, **470–472,** 471*f*
    in DNA damage signaling systems, 413
    elongation factor, 315
    fusion, **585**
    green fluorescent, 557
    histone (H1, H2A, H2B, H3, H4), 286–287, **371,** 371*t*
    initiation factor, **312,** 312–313, 312*f*
    lambda repressor, and lysogeny, 496, 497*f*
    modularity of, 619, 621*f*
    multimeric, in dominant negative mutations, 108
    nonhistone, **371**
    organellar, encoding of, 672–673
    regulatory
        binding to *lac* operon regulatory sequences, 482*b*
        trans-acting, **507**
    repressor, **470**
    rho, 277
    small nucleoid-associated, 369
    SR, 294, 294*f*
    structural maintenance of chromosomes, **369**
    translation repressor, **491**
    two-dimensional gel electrophoresis and identification of ribosomal, 310*b*
Protein–DNA interaction in transcriptional control of gene expression, 469–472, 470*f*, 471*f*
Protein packaging, viral, 366–368
Protein reconstruction, ancestral, 765

Protein sorting, 330–331
Proteome, **15, 638**
Proteomics, **15, 638**
Proto-oncogenes, **71**
Prototrophs, 189*b*
Proximal elements in eukaryotic transcription, 506
Prune-killer (K-pn), 541
PSE (promoter-specific element), **284**
Pseudoautosomal region (PAR), **79**
    of X and Y chromosomes, 79, 79*f*, 97
Pseudodominance, **442**
Pseudogene, **626**
Pseudohermaphroditism, gene mutation causing, 89*b*
Pulse-chase labeling, evidence of bidirectional DNA replication produced by, 238–239, 239*f*
Punnett, Reginald, 33
    complementary gene interaction and, 132
    and genetic linkage discovery, 148
    on genotype frequencies in populations, 743
Punnett square, **33,** 38, 38*f*
Pure-breeding strains, **30,** 30*f*
Pyrimidine dimer, **406**

Q

q arm, **377,** 377*f*
QTLs (quantitative trait loci). *See* Quantitative trait loci (QTLs)
Quantitative genetics, **714**
Quantitative trait(s), **714**
    allele segregation in production of, 716, 718–719, 719*f*
    displaying continuous phenotype variation, 714–721
Quantitative trait analysis
    genetic analysis, 713–741
    statistical methods in, 721, 723–726
Quantitative trait loci (QTLs), **730**
    gene identification for, 732–734, 733*f*
    genome-wide association studies in identification of, 734–737, 736*f*
Quantitative trait loci (QTLs) mapping, **730**
Quantitative trait loci (QTLs) mapping strategies, 730–732, 731*f*, 732*t*
Quaternary structure of polypeptides, **308**
Quinn, Chip, genetic screen of, 535

R

R gene in peas, identification and analysis of alleles of, 453, 454–455*b*
R-group, **306–307**
R (resistance) plasmid, **188**
Radial loop-scaffold model, **374**
Radiation. *See also* Ultraviolet (UV) repair
    DNA damage induced by, 406–408, 407*f* (*see also* Ultraviolet (UV) irradiation, damage from)
Random genetic drift, as evolutionary process, **17**
Random X inactivation (Lyon) hypothesis, **95**
RB1 gene mutation and cancer, 72
Reading frame, **324**
Realizator genes, **695**
RecBCD pathway, **418**
Recent African origin (RAO) hypothesis, 21
Recent African origin (RAO) model of *H. sapiens* evolution, 655–656, 655*f*
Recessive epistasis (9:3:4 ratio), 131*f*, 133, **133**
Recessive homozygosity, reduced, in polyploids, 439, 443–444*b*
Recessive mutant, determination of, 539
Recessive phenotype, **31**
Recessiveness, molecular basis of, 105–106
Recipient cell (F⁻), **191–192**
    and donor cell, conjugation between, 193–194, 193*f*
Reciprocal cross(es), **31,** 31*f*
    to determine X-linkage of genes, 84–85, 84*f*, 85*f*
    in Z/W system, 90, 90*f*
Reciprocal translocation, **448,** 448*f*, 449*f*, 450*f*
Recombinant chromosomes, **145**
Recombinant clone, **572**

Recombinant DNA molecules
  amplifying, 575–576, 578f
  creating, 572–574, 573f, 574f
Recombinant DNA technology, 568
  applications of, 567–610
  in cloning genes by complementation,
    542–544, 543f
  in cloning genes using transposons, 543–544, 544f
  in cloning highly expressed genes, 582f
  in creation of transgenic organisms, 583–599
  DNA libraries in, 577, 579–581, 579f–582f
  DNA sequencing technologies in, 582f
  gene therapy using, 600–602, 601t, 605f
  genes identified by mutant phenotype are cloned
    using, 542–551
  molecular cloning in, 572–577, 573f–575f,
    577t, 578f
  polymerase chain reaction in, 581, 582f
  in positional cloning, 544–548, 545f, 547f, 548f
  restriction enzymes in, 568–572, 569b, 571b, 572f
Recombination
  along chromosomes, limits of, 160–162, 161f, 162f
  from crossing over, 160–166
  cytological evidence of, 160, 160f
  as dominated by hotspots, 164–165
  and evolution and genetic diversity, 170–171
  between genes, 163b
  within genes, 162, 162f
  homologous, 588, 589f
  illegitimate, 588, 589f
  intragenic, 162, 162, 162f
  meiotic, 420–421f
    inherited variation from, 418–419
  site-specific, 598, 598–599, 599f, 600b
Recombination frequency, 148
  of gene pairs, 148
    biological factors affecting, 164, 165f
    genetic linkage mapping based on,
      153–154, 153f
    limits of, 161
    linked, calculation of, 163b
    physical distance between genes and, 165, 166f
    in three-point recombination mapping, 158
  between genes, 153–165
Recombination hotspots, 164
Recombination nodules, 76, 76
Recombination protein homology, 418–419, 419t
Red blood cells, normal and sickle-shaped, 339f
Red bread mold. See Mold, red bread
  (Neurospora crassa)
Reduction division, 77. See also Meiosis I
Redundant and interacting genes, identifying,
  540–541
Redundant genes, identifying, 541
Reference genome sequence, 635
Regulated transcription, 469
Regulatory mutations, 395–397, 396, 396f, 398f
Regulatory proteins
  binding to lac operon regulatory sequences, 482b
  trans-acting, 507
Regulatory sequences
  cis-acting, 507
    in eukaryotic gene expression regulation,
      506–511
  mutations in, 509
Relative fitness, 748–749
  differential reproductive fitness and, 748–749
Release factors (RF), 318, 318–319
Reovirus, 367t
Replica plating, 189b
Replicate crosses, 30
Replication. See also DNA replication
  of organelle genomes, 652, 653f
  rolling circle, 194
  semiconservative, 8, 9f
Replication bubble, 237, 240f, 246, 247f
Replication factor C (RFC) complex, 249
Replication fork, 238, 240f
Replicative segregation, 653, 654f

Replicative transposition, 455
Replisomes, 242, 246
Reporter genes, 556
  monitoring gene expression with, 556–559,
    558f, 559f
Repressible operons, 484
Repressor protein(s), 470
  in eukaryotic transcription regulation, 506–508,
    511, 511f
  lambda, and lysogeny, 496, 497f
Reproduction
  asexual, 72–73
  sexual, 72–73
    gene transmission in, 4
  of single-celled organisms, 81, 82f
Reproductive fitness, differential, 748–749
  within population, natural selection of, 748–753
Reproductive isolation, 760–761
  mechanisms of, 762t
  speciation and, 761, 763–764
Resistance (R) plasmid, 188
Response to selection, 729
Restriction endonucleases, 345, 348t
Restriction enzymes, 345, 345–346, 348t
  in recombinant DNA technology, 568–572, 569b,
    571b, 572f
Restriction fragment length polymorphism (RFLP),
  346, 350–351b, 546
Restriction maps, 570, 570, 570f, 571b
Restriction-modification systems, 568, 569b
Restriction sequence, 345–346, 348t
Restrictive condition, 538
Retinitis pigmentosa, 91t
Retinoblastoma, RB1 gene mutation in, 72
Retinoblastoma protein (pRB), cyclin D1–Cdk4
    complex and, 71
  mutations altering interaction of, 72
Retrotransposons, 455, 455, 460–461, 460f
Rett syndrome, 91t
Reverse genetic analysis, 534
Reverse genetics, 166, 534f
  genetic redundancy in flower development and
    (Case Study), 561–563b
  genomic approaches to, 641, 641f
  insertion mutants in, 552
  investigating gene action, 551–554, 554f,
    555f, 560f
  by TILLING, 554–556, 555f
Reverse mutation rate (v), 753
  quantifying the effects of, 753
Reverse mutations, 397, 398f
Reverse transcriptase, 455
Reverse transcription, 10
Reversion mutation(s), 324
  Ames test for rate of, 408
Reversions, 397, 398f
Revertible mutants, 216
RF (release factors), 318, 318–319
RFLP (restriction fragment length polymorphism),
  346, 350–351b, 546
Rheumatoid arthritis, 735
Rho-dependent termination, 277, 277–278
Rho protein, 277
Rho utilization site (rut site), 277
Ribonucleic acid. See RNA (ribonucleic acid)
Ribonucleotides, RNA, 269, 269f
Ribose, 269
Ribosomal RNA (rRNA), 4–5, 9, 271
Ribosomal RNA processing, 296–297, 296f
Ribosomal subunits, 309
Ribosome structures, 309–311, 309f, 310b
  three-dimensional, 311, 311f
Ribosomes, 5
  in translation, 307–311
Ribozymes, 271
Rice, Golden (Oryza sativa), 591, 593–594, 593f
Riggs, Arthur, pulse-chase labeling evidence
    of bidirectional DNA replication and,
    238–239, 239f

RISC (RNA-induced silencing complex), 524
  Argonaute gene family and, 526
RITS (RNA-induced transcriptional silencing)
    complex, 526
RNA (ribonucleic acid), 5. See also Messenger RNA
    (mRNA); MicroRNA (miRNA); Ribosomal
    RNA (rRNA); tRNA (transfer RNA)
  antisense, 491, 494f
  classification of, 270–271
  double-stranded
    cleaving, 524–525
    gene silencing by, 524–525, 525f
  functional, 271
  gene expression control mediated by, 524–528,
    525f, 526f
  small interfering, 271
  small nuclear, 271
  transcription producing, 10–12
RNA editing, 298
  post-transcriptional, 298–299, 298f, 299f
RNA-induced silencing complex (RISC), 524
  Argonaute gene family and, 526
RNA-induced transcriptional silencing (RITS)
    complex, 526
RNA interference (RNAi), 524, 553
  chromatin modification by, 526–527, 526f
  evolution and applications of, 527–528
  in gene activity, 552–554, 554f
RNA polymerase(s), 269
  bacterial, 272–273, 272f
  eukaryotic, 278
    multiple, transcription using, 278–285
  protein subunits of, 277–278, 278t
RNA polymerase core, 272
RNA polymerase I (RNA pol I), 278
RNA polymerase I promoters, 283–284, 283f
RNA polymerase I transcription, termination in,
    284–285
RNA polymerase II (RNA pol II), 278
RNA polymerase II transcription, consensus
    sequences for, 278–282
RNA polymerase III (RNA pol III), 278
RNA polymerase III promoters, 284, 284f
RNA polymerase III transcription, termination in,
    284–285
RNA polymerase transcription, 12
RNA primer(s), 245
RNA primer removal for DNA replication,
    247–248, 248f
RNA processing, 267–304
  post-transcriptional, 285–299
RNA synthesis, 269–270, 270f
RNA transcripts, carrying messages of genes,
    268–271
RNAi (RNA interference), 524
Roberts, Richard, "split genes" discovery by, 288
Robertsonian translocation, 448, 449–450,
    449f, 451f
Rodriguez, Raymond, bidirectional replication
    model and, 239
Rolling circle replication, 194
Rothstein, Rodney, double-stranded break model of
    meiotic recombination and, 418
Roudier, Francois, on chromatin states, 517, 517f
rRNA (see Ribosomal RNA (rRNA))
Rubin, Gerald, creating transgenic Drosophila and,
    594–595

S
S (synthesis) phase of interphase, 66, 66f, 71f
Saccharomyces cerevisiae. See Yeast, baker's
    (Saccharomyces cerevisiae)
Sampling error, genetic drift causing allele frequency
    change by, 756–758, 756f
Sanger, Fred
  and amino acid sequence of insulin
    determination, 585
  and dideoxynucleotide DNA sequencing,
    256–259, 258f, 259f, 260b

Saturation mutagenesis, **535**
Sbe1 (starch branching enzyme 1) gene, 54
SBE1 (starch branching enzyme 1) gene, 454–455
Scaffold, **613**, 614*f*
Scanning, **313**, 314*f*
SCD. *See* Sickle cell disease (SCD)
Schizosaccharomyces pombe, 526
SCIDS (severe combined immunodeficiency syndrome), 601, 602
Scientific method, steps in, 26
Screening libraries, 581, 582*f*
SDSA (synthesis-dependent strand annealing), **417**, 417*f*
Second-division segregation, **175**, 176*f*
Second filial generation. *See* F₂ (second filial) generation
Second-site reversion, **397**, 398*f*
Secondary endosymbiotic events, **674**, 674–675
Secondary structure of polypeptides, **308**
Seed development, wrinkled, 454–455*b*
Segment polarity genes, 686*f*, **687**
Segregation
    allele, in quantitative trait production, 716, 718–719, 719*f*
    chloroplast, and mating type in *Chlamydomonas*, 659, 661
    chromosome, 448–449
    first-division, **175**, 175*f*
    second-division, **175**, 176*f*
Segregation, law of (Mendel's first law), **33–34**
    meiosis and, 79–80, 79*f*
    in single-celled diploids, 81, 82*f*
Segregation hypothesis, testing of
    F₂ self-fertilization in, 35, 35*f*, 36*t*
    test-cross analysis in, 34–35
Selander, Robert, on genetic bottlenecks, 758
Selected marker screen, **210**
Selection
    artificial, narrow sense heritability and, 729–730, 729*t*, 730*f*
    response to, **729**
Selection coefficient, **749**
Selection differential, **729**
Selective growth medium, **195**
Self-splicing, intron, **294**, 294*f*, **296**
Semiconservative DNA replication model, **236**, 237*f*
Semiconservative replication, **8**, 9*f*
Semisterility, **435**
Sequence (IS) elements in bacterial genomes, transposition of, 456*f*
Sequence gaps, **614–615**
Severe combined immunodeficiency syndrome (SCIDS), 601, 602
Sex, recombination frequency and, 164, 165, 165*f*
Sex chromosomes, **65**
    multiple sets of, 90
Sex determination, 87, 89
    diversity of, 88, 90, 90*f*
    in *Drosophila*, 87, 89
    mammalian, 88, 88*f*
Sex development, human, mutations altering, 89*b*
Sex-influenced traits, 117, **117**
    as gene interactions, 117, 118*f*
Sex-limited gene expression, **117**
Sex-limited traits, **117**
    as gene interactions, 117
Sex-linked inheritance, **84**
Sex-linked transmission, human, patterns of, 90–92, 94–95
Sexual reproduction, 72–73
    gene transmission in, 4
Shared derived characteristics, **17**
Sharp, Phillip, "split genes" discovery by, 288
Shine–Dalgarno sequence, 312*f*, **313**, 313–315
Short arm (p arm), **376–377**, 377*f*
Shotgun sequencing of DNA molecules, 582*f*, **583**

Shuttle vector, **588**
Sickle cell disease (SCD), 338–364, **339**
    electrophoretic analysis of, 349–353
    evolution by natural selection in human populations, 353, 357–358
    first patient with, 339–340
    genetic analysis of
        gel electrophoresis, 342–344, 343*f*, 344*f*
        hemoglobin peptide fingerprint analysis, 344–345, 347*b*
        identification of DNA sequence variation, 345–346, 346*f*, 348, 348*t*
    geographic distribution of, 357*f*
    hemoglobin structural change in, 342*f*
    inheritance of, 56*b*, 56*f*
    inherited hemoglobin variant causing, 339–341, 339*f*, 340*f*
    malaria resistance in, 357–358
    in mice, gene therapy curing, 604*b*, 605*f*
    pleiotropy in, 121, 122*f*
Sigma (σ) subunit(s), **272**, 272*f*
    alternative, **272–273**
    E. coli RNA polymerase, 276*t*
Signal hypothesis, **331**
Signal sequences (leader sequences), **331**
Signal-transduction pathways, **124**
Silencer sequences, **283**, **506**
    in eukaryotic transcription regulation, 506–508, 508*f*, 510–511, 511*f*
Silencing of genes
    by double-stranded DNA, 524–525, 525*f*
    by nucleotide methylation, 523–524
Silent mutations, **394**, 394*f*
Simian virus 40 (SV40), 367*t*
Simple transposons, **455**, 457*t*
SINE elements of humans, 460–461
Single-gene trait, **123–124**
Single nucleotide polymorphism (SNP), **345**, 346, 346*f*, 734, 752–753, 766
    SNP variation in human genetic diversity, 766, 768
Single-stranded binding protein (SSB), **244**
SiRNAs (small interfering RNAs), **524**
Sister chromatid cohesion, **67**, 70*f*
Sister chromatids, **67**
    creation of, in S phase, 66
Site-specific recombination, **598**, 598–599, 599*f*, 600*b*
Skin microbiome, 618*b*
Sliding clamp, **249**, 249*f*
Small interfering RNAs (siRNAs), **271**, **524**
Small nuclear RNA (snRNA), **271**
Small nucleoid-associated proteins, **369**
Small ribosomal subunit, **309**
SMC (structural maintenance of chromosomes) proteins, **369**
Smith, Hamilton, restriction endonucleases and, 569*b*
Smithies, Oliver, knockout mouse development and, 596
Smoking, 769
SNP (single nucleotide polymorphism), **345**, 346, 346*f*, 734, 752–753, 766
Solenoid structure, **373**
Somatic cells, **65**
    division of, mitosis in, 65–73
Somatic gene therapy, **601**
Sonic hedgehog (*Shh*) gene, 508, 509, 556, 632, 701, 707–709*b*
Southern blot analysis of β-globin gene variation, 350–352, 352*f*, 356*b*
Southern blotting, **349**, 354–355*b*, 454*b*, 581
Specialized transducing phages, **212**, 212*f*
Specialized transduction, **206**, 212–213, 212*f*
Speciation
    allopatric, 761, **761**, 763, 763*f*
    processes of, 761, 762*f*
    reproductive isolation and, 761, 763–764
    sympatric, **763**, 763–764

Spinal muscular atrophy, 399*t*
Spindle fiber microtubules, **67**
Spinocerebellar ataxia, 399*t*
Spliceosome, **289**
Splicing mutations, 396–397, 396*f*, **397**
Splicing signal sequences in eukaryotic pre-mRNA, 288–289, 290*f*
Spontaneous mutation, **397**
Spores in yeast reproduction, 81
Spradling, Allan, creating transgenic *Drosophila* and, 594–595
Square root method, for determining autosomal allele frequencies, **747**
SR proteins, 294, 294*f*
SRD5A2 gene mutation and pseudohermaphroditism, 89*b*
SRY gene
    evolution, 97
    in sex determination, 88, 88*f*, 90
SSB (single-stranded binding protein), **244**
Stabilizing selection, **730**
Stahl, Franklin
    DNA replication experiment of, 236–237, 237*f*, 238*f*
    double-stranded break model of meiotic recombination and, 418
    semiconservative replication mechanism and, 8
Standard deviation (σ), **49**, **725**
Start codon, **12**, 13*f*
Start of transcription, **11**, 12*f*
Statistically significant difference, 49
Stem cells. *See* Embryonic stem (ES) cells
Stem-loop structure, **277**
Stem loops, **485**, 487*f*
Sterility, cytoplasmic male, 669*b*
Stern, Curt
    mitotic crossover and, 176, 177*f*
    research on crossing over in *Drosophila*, 160
Steroid receptor (SR), novel functions from ancestral, 765
Steroid receptor (SR) evolution, vertebrate, 764–766
Steroid receptor (SR) proteins, 765
Stevens, Nettie, chromosome studies of, 84
Sticky ends, **346**, **569**
Stop codons, **12**, 13*f*
Strains
    pure-breeding, **30**
        to begin experimental crosses, 30, 30*f*
    true-breeding, **30**
Strand invasion, **417**
Strand polarity, 7
Strand slippage, **398**, 399*f*
Streisinger, George, strand slippage and, 398
Stress response
    bacteria regulating transcription of, 489–491, 490*f*
    in *Vibrio cholerae*, infection and (Case Study), 497–498*b*
Structural genes, **368**
Structural genomics, **612**, 613–622. *See also* Annotation; Genome sequences
    clone-by-clone sequencing approach to, 612*t*, 613
    human genome and, 616
    metagenomics in, 616–617
    variation in genome organization among species in, 620–621, 621*f*, 622*f*
    whole-genome shotgun sequencing approach to, 613–616, 614*f*–616*f*
Structural maintenance of chromosomes (SMC) proteins, **369**
Structural motifs of DNA-binding proteins, 505*f*
Sturtevant, Alfred
    genetic linkage map of, 153–154, 153*f*
        recombination data for, 153*f*
    synthetic lethality identified by, 541, 541*f*
Su(var) mutations, **512–513**, 512*f*
Subcloning, **570**

Subfunctionalization, **628**
Submetacentric chromosomes, **377**
Sugar-phosphate backbone, **234**, 235
Sum (addition) rule of probability theory, **45**
Super-repressor protein mutations, 478*f*, 479, 479*t*
Supercoiled DNA, **246**
  bacterial, 369, 370*f*
Supercoiling, DNA, **369**
Supplemented minimal medium, 189*b*
Suppressor mutation, **397**
Suppressor screen, **540**
Sutton, Walter
  on relation of meiosis and Mendelian hereditary principles, 79
  and study of chromosome movement, 2
SWI/SNF complex in chromatin remodeling, 515, **516**
SWR1 complex, 515, **516–517**
Sxl (sex-lethal) gene, 299–300
Sympatric speciation, **763**, 763–764
Synapsis, homologous chromosome, **75**
Synaptomorphies, **17**
Synaptonemal complex, 75–76, 78*f*
Syncytial blastoderm, **685**
Syncytium, **685**
Synonymous codons, **321**
Syntenic genes, **145**
  assortment of, 145
Synteny, **632**, 633*f*
Synthesis-dependent strand annealing (SDSA), **417**, 417*f*
Synthetic enhancement, 541, 541*f*
Synthetic lethality, 541, **541**, 541*f*
  in genetic interactions, 642–643, 643*f*
Systems biology, **15**, 644
Szostak, Jack, 252
  double-stranded break model of meiotic recombination and, 418

T

T-DNA (transfer DNA), **589–590**
T strand, **193–194**
TAF (TBP-associated factor), **281**
Targeted induced local lesions in genomes (TILLING), **554**
  reverse genetics by, 554–556, 555*f*
TATA-binding protein (TBP), **281**, 285
TATA box, **280**, 281, 282, 285
Tatum, Edward
  and bacterial DNA transfer identification, 188, 191, 191*f*
  one gene–one enzyme hypothesis of, 124–127, 125–126*b*, 306
Tautomeric shifts in DNA nucleotide bases, 400–402, 401*f*
TBP (TATA-binding protein), **281**, 285
TBP-associated factor (TAF), **281**
Telocentric chromosomes, **377**
Telomerase, **252**
Telomeres, **251**, 251–254
  aging, cancer, and, 254
Telophase, mitotic, **66**, 68, 68*f*, 71*f*
Telophase I, 77, 79
Telophase II, 77*f*
Temperate phages, **209**
Temperature-sensitive allele, **113**
Template strand, **10**, 11*f*, 271
Tenebrio molitor. See Beetle, yellow mealworm (*Tenebrio molitor*)
Terminal deletion, 440, 441*f*
Terminal inverted repeats, 453, 455
Termination region, **272**
Termination sequence, **11**, 12*f*
Termination stem loop, 485, 487*f*
TERT (telomerase reverse transcriptase) gene, 253–254
Tertiary endosymbiotic events, **674**, 674–675
Tertiary structure of polypeptides, **308**

Test-cross analysis
  in autosomal genetic linkage detection, 150–151, 151*f*, 152*b*
  hypothesis testing by, 34–35, 34*f*, 35*f*
  in independent assortment testing, 39, 39*f*, 41
  in segregation hypothesis testing, 34–35
  three-point, **154**
    in gene mapping, 154–160
  two-point, **150**
Test crosses, **31**, 31*f*
Tetrad(s), unordered, **172**
  analysis of, 172, 173*f*, 174*f*, 174*t*
Tetrad analysis, **172**
  of genetic linkage in haploid eukaryotes, 171–175
Tetrahymena, telomerase activity in, 252–253
Tetratype (TT), **172**
TF. *See* Transcription factors (TF)
Thalassemia, **359**
  enhancer mutations causing, 509
  transmission and molecular genetic analysis of (Case Study), 359–360, 359*f*
Theta (θ) value, **167**, 167–168
Third-base wobble, 298, **321**
  effects of, 322, 322*f*
  genetic code displaying, 321–322, 322*t*
  pairings causing, 322, 322*t*
Third filial generation (F₃ generation), **30**, 30*f*
Third-generation DNA sequencing technologies, 259, 261
Three-point mapping, finding the relative order of genes by, 154–156, 155*f*
Three-point recombination map, constructing a, 156–159
Three-point test-cross analysis, **154**
  in gene mapping, 154–160
Three-strand double crossover, 161, **161**, 162*f*
Threshold of genetic liability, **720**
Threshold traits, 719–721, **720**, 720*f*, 721*f*
Thymidine kinase (tk) gene, 596
Thymine (T), 7
Thymine dimer, **406**, 407*f*
Ti (tumor-inducing) plasmid, **589–590**, 590*f*
Tiling array, whole-genome, **638**, 640*f*
TILLING (targeted induced local lesions in genomes), **554**
  reverse genetics by, 554–556, 555*f*
Time-of-entry mapping, **197**
  interrupted mating analysis producing, 197–203, 198*f*, 202*b*
Tobacco mosaic virus (TMV), 323, 367, 367*f*, 367*t*
Topoisomerase I, **369**
Topoisomerase II, **369**
Topoisomerases, **246**
Torpedo model of transcription termination, 287, 288*f*
Totipotency, **591**
Totipotent cells, **683**
Trait(s). *See also* Quantitative trait(s)
  additive, **715**
  displaying incomplete penetrance, 118–119, 119*f*
  heritability of, 726–730
  Mendel's, molecular genetics of, 54–55, 55*t*
  multifactorial, **714**
  polygenic, **714**
  selection of single traits with dichotomous phenotypes, 30
  sex-influenced, 117, **117**
  sex-limited, 117, **117**
  single-gene, 123–124
  threshold, 719–721, **720**, 720*f*, 721*f*
  X-linked dominant, 91*t*
    transmission of, 94
  X-linked recessive, 91*t*
    expression of, 90–92
Trans-acting, **479**

Trans-acting regulatory proteins, **507**
Transcriptase, reverse, **455**
Transcription, **5**, 10–12. *See also* Bacterial transcription
  archaeal, 285
  chloroplast, 668
  constitutive, **469**
  eukaryotic
    chromatin remodeling regulating, 512–524
    enhancers and silencers in regulation of, 506–508, 508*f*, 510–511, 510*f*, 511*f*
    multiple RNA polymerases in, 278–285
    regulatory interactions in, 506–507, 506*f*
  of lambda phage gene, early, 493–494, 495*b*, 496
  mitochondrial, 665–666, 665*f*, 666*t*
  molecular biology of, 267–304
  post-transcriptional processing modifies RNA molecules, 285–299
  regulated, **469**
  start of, 11, 12*f*
  of stress response, bacteria regulating, 489–491, 490*f*
  from tryptophan operon, 483–488
Transcription factor B (TFB), 285
Transcription factors (TF), **281**
Transcription-terminating factor I (TTRI), **285**
Transcription termination
  bacterial, 274*f*, 276
  RNA polymerase I and III, 284–285
  torpedo model of, 287, 288*f*
Transcription termination mechanisms, bacterial, 276–278, 277*f*
Transcriptional fusion, 557*f*
Transcriptome, **15**, 636
  in high-throughput sequencing analysis, 637
Transcriptomics, **15**, **636**, 636–638, 637*f*, 639*f*, 640*f*
  in functional genomics, 636–638
Transductant, **209**
Transduction, **206**
  definition of, 187
  gene transfer by bacterial, 206–213
  generalized, **209**, 210*f*
  specialized, 212–213, 212*f*
Transfer DNA (T-DNA), **589–590**
Transfer RNA. *See* tRNA (transfer RNA)
Transformant, **206**
Transformation, **204–205**
  bacterial
    gene transfer by, 204, 206
    mapping by, 206, 207*f*
    of plant genomes by *Agrobacterium*, 589–594, 590*f*, 592*f*, 593*f*
    steps in, 206, 207*f*
  definition of, 187
Transformation factor
  DNA as, 230, 230*f*
  identification of, 229–230, 229*f*
Transgene(s), **542**, 583
  in *E. coli*, 583–588, 584*f*
  as means of dissecting gene function, 554, 556–561, 559*f*, 600*b*
Transgenic animals, 594–598, 594*f*, 596*f*
Transgenic fungi, generation of, 588–589, 588*f*, 589*f*
Transgenic *Mus musculus*, 596–598
Transgenic organisms, **542**, 567–568, **583**
  creation of, 583–599
Transgenic plants
  in agriculture, 591
  creating, 589–593, 592*f*
Transgenic vertebrates, 595, 596*f*
Transition mutation, **394**
Translation, **5**, 12–13. *See also* Posttranslational polypeptide processing
  bacterial, antibiotics interfering with (Case Study), 332*b*
  of bacterial polycistronic mRNA, 320*f*
  chloroplast, 668

elements of, 307–308, 307f
mitochondrial, 665–666, 666t
molecular biology of, 305–337
of mRNA into polypeptide, genetic code in, 320–322
phases of, 311–319
of polycistronic mRNA, 320
polypeptide elongation in, 315–318
speed and efficiency of, 319–320, 319f
Translation elongation factor homologs, 318, 318t
Translation initiation, 311–315
    bacterial, 312–313
    eukaryotic, 313, 314f, 317–318b
Translation initiation factor homologs, 315t
Translation repressor proteins, 491
Translation termination, 318–319, 319f, 325b
Translational complex, 319, 320f
Translational fusion, 557, 557f
Translational regulation in bacteria, 491–492, 491t
Translesion DNA polymerases, 416
Translesion DNA synthesis, 407
    protein control of, 407–410
Translocation, chromosome, 446, 448–450, 449f–451f
Translocation heterozygotes, 448
Transmission genetics, 5, 6, 26, 26–63
    in produce aisle (Case Study), 44b
Transposable genetic elements, 450, 450–456, 451f
    characteristics and classification of, 453–456
Transposition, 431, 451
    bacterial genomes modified by, 456–459, 456f, 456t, 457f, 457t, 458b
    discovery of, 451, 451f, 453
    eukaryotic genomes modified by, 457–461, 459f, 460f
    Mendel's peas shaped by, 453, 454–455b
Transposons, 456, 457, 457f
    to clone genes, recombinant DNA technology in, 543–544, 544f
Transversion mutations, 394
Tree of life, 624, 624, 625f, 626b
Trichothiodystrophy, 414f
Trihybrid cross, 41
Trihybrid-cross analysis in independent assortment, testing, 41–42, 41f
Trinucleotide repeat disorders, 398, 399t
Triple X syndrome, 434t
Trisomic chromosomes, 432
Trisomy, 432
Trisomy 21, meiotic nondisjunction in, 434, 435t
Trisomy rescue, 436–437, 437
Trithorax (Trx), 519
Trivalent synaptic structure, 435
tRNA (transfer RNA), 9, 271
    in amino acid transport, 12
    charged, 311
    genetic code specificity and, 328, 330
    initiator, 311, 312f
    isoaccepting, 321, 321f
    uncharged, 311
tRNA molecules, charging, 322
tRNA processing, 297–298, 297f
tRNA synthetases, 323, 323f
Trombone model of DNA replication, 249, 250f
Trp operon. See Tryptophan (trp) operon
True-breeding strains, 30. See also Pure-breeding strains
True reversion, 397, 398f
Tryptophan (trp) operon
    attenuation mutations of, 488, 488f, 489b
    attenuation of, 485–488, 486f, 487f
    feedback inhibition of, 484–485, 485t
    transcription from, 483–488
Tryptophan synthesis, feedback inhibition of, 484–485, 484f, 485f
TTFI (transcription-terminating factor I), 285
Tumor suppressor gene, 71
Turner syndrome, 434–436, 434t, 466

Twin studies of heritability, 727–729, 729t
Two-hybrid system, for protein interaction detection, 638, 638, 640f, 641
Two-point test-cross analysis, 150
Two-strand double crossover, 161, 161, 162f
Ty elements of yeast, 460

U
UAS (upstream activator sequence), 510
Ubiquitanation, 416
Ultrabithorax gene, 692–695, 692f, 693f
Ultraviolet (UV)-induced photoproducts, 406–408, 407f
    repair of, 412–413, 413f
Ultraviolet (UV) irradiation, damage from, 766, 768
Ultraviolet (UV) repair, 413, 413
Unbalanced translocation, 448, 449f
Uncharged tRNAs, 311
Unequal crossover, 441, 442f
Unger, Franz, 27
Uniparental disomy, 436, 436–437
Uniparental inheritance, 650
Unordered tetrad(s), 172
    analysis of, 172, 173f, 174f, 174t
Unpaired loop, 442, 442f
Unselected marker screen, 210
Unstable mutant phenotype, 453
Untranslated regions (UTRs). See 3' untranslated region (3' UTR); 5' untranslated region (5' UTR)
Upstream, 271
Upstream activator sequence (UAS), 510
Upstream control element, 283, 283f
Uracil (U), 11, 269
UTRs. See 3' untranslated region (3' UTR); 5' untranslated region (5' UTR)

V
Variable expressivity of allele, 119, 120f
Variance, 724–725
    additive, 726
    dominance, 726
    environmental, 725
    genetic, 725
        partitioning, 725
    interactive, 726
    phenotypic, 725
        partitioning, 725, 725f, 726b
    sources of, 725f
Variation
    continuous, 714
    discontinuous, 714
Vector(s)
    cloning, 577t
        bacteriophage, 576–577, 577t, 578f
        plasmids as, 574–575, 575f, 577t
    cosmid, 577
    expression, 583, 583–584, 584f
        eukaryotic, 584
    in gene therapy, viruses as, 601, 601t, 602
    recombinant, 573
    Shuttle, 588
Venter, J. Craig, on human genome sequence "draft," 616
Vertebrate steroid receptor evolution, 764–766
Vertebrates, transgenic, 595, 596f
Vibrio cholerae, 220
    infection and stress response in (Case Study), 497–498b
Vibrio cholerae toxins, 498
Viral genomes, 366
    composition and organization of selected, 367t
Viral protein packaging, 366–368
Viral structure and assembly, 367–368, 367f
Virus(es)
    bacterial (see Bacteriophage(s))
    as vectors in gene therapy, 601, 601t, 602

Viruses, 366
    enveloped, 367, 367f
    nonenveloped, 366–367, 367f
Volkin, Elliot, mRNA discovery and, 269
von Ettinghausen, Andreas, 26, 27
von Tschermak, Erich
    on hereditary transmission, 2, 3f
    research of, paralleling Mendel's, 42
Vulval precursor cells (VPCs), 697–700

W
Waardenburg syndrome, variable expressivity of, 119, 120f
WAGR syndrome, 441, 441f
WAGRO, 441
Watson, James, 7f
    research on double-helical structure of DNA by, 4, 6
Watts-Tobin, R. J., proof of triplet genetic code, 323–324, 324t
Weinberg, Wilhelm, genotype frequencies in populations and, 743
Western blotting, 349, 355b, 454b
    in β-globin gene transcript and protein analysis, 352–353, 353f
Wexler, Susan, studies of Huntington disease by, 549
WGS sequencing. See Whole-genome shotgun (WGS) sequencing
Whole-genome shotgun (WGS) sequencing, 613
    of bacterial genome, 614–615, 615f
    of eukaryotic genome, 615–616, 616f
    future of, 616
Whole-genome shotgun (WGS) sequencing approach to structural genomics, 613–616, 614f, 615f
Whole-genome tiling array, 638, 640f
Wieschaus, Eric
    mutagenesis strategy used by, 538
    on pattern formation in Drosophila, 684, 686
Wild-type Huntington disease (HD) genes, 262
Wilkens, Horst, heritability analysis by, 727
Wilkins, Maurice, research on double-helical structure of DNA by, 4
Williams-Beuren syndrome (WBS), 441, 442f
Wilms tumor, 441
Wilson, Edmund, on nuclein (DNA) in inheritance, 228
Woese, Carl, 4
Wollman, Ellie, on interrupted mating in time-of-entry mapping, 197
Wormwood (Artemesia annua), 587b
Wright, Sewall, evolutionary genetics research and, 17

X
X/A (X/autosome) ratio, 88
X chromosomes, random inactivation in placental mammals, 95, 95–96, 96f
X-inactivation, 521–522
X-linked inheritance, 84–85, 84f, 85
    dominant, 90
    recessive, 90
        features characterizing, 91–92, 91f
X-linked trait(s)
    dominant, 91t
        transmission of, 94
    recessive, 91t
        expression of, 90–92
X-ray diffraction imagery in study of DNA structure, 6, 6f
øX174, 367t
Xeroderma pigmentosum (XP), 414b
    complement groups identification in (Case Study), 137b
XIST RNA in random X inactivation, 96

Y
Y chromosome, (degenerative) evolution of mammalian, 96–98, 97f

Y-linked inheritance, **94–95**
Yanofsky, Charles, cotransduction mapping and, 210–211, 211*f*, 211*t*, 212*f*
Yeast, baker's (*Saccharomyces cerevisiae*)
  biparental inheritance in, 661–662, 661*f*
  in genetic screen design, 536
  integrating DNA into the genome of, 588–589, 589*f*
  life cycle of, 172*f*
  mutants of, in categorizing genes, 641–642, 642*f*

  reproduction of, 81, 82*f*
  transcription regulation in, 510–511, 510*f*, 520, 520*f*
Yeast, *Ty* elements of, 460
Yeast artificial chromosomes (YACs), **577**
Yeast plasmids, generation of, 588, 588*f*
Yellow mealworm beetle. *See* Beetle, yellow mealworm (*Tenebrio molitor*)
Yule, George Udny, on genotype frequencies in populations, 743

Z
Z-form DNA, 236
Z/W system, **88, 90**
Zebrafish (*Danio rerio*), 483
Z_{max}, **168**
Zone of polarizing activity (ZPA), **701,** 702*f*
Zygotene stage of prophase I, 75, 75*f*
Zygotic genes, **687**

Model Organisms

Life Cycle	E. coli	A. thaliana (mouse ear cress)	S. cerevisiae (baker's yeast)	C. elegans (nematode)
m, meiosis; f, fertilization				
Generation time	20–40 minutes	10 weeks	2–3 hours	3 days

Genome	E. coli	A. thaliana (mouse ear cress)	S. cerevisiae (baker's yeast)	C. elegans (nematode)
Size	4.64 Mb	130 Mb	12 Mb	100 Mb
Chromosomes	1 circular chromosome + plasmids	5 chromosomes ($2n = 10$)	16 chromosomes ($2n = 32$)	5 autosomes + X chromosome ($2n = 10 + $ XX or X0)
Number of genes	4200	28,775	6607	20,532
Genetic distance	100 minutes	600 cM	4500 cM	300 cM

Nomenclature	E. coli	A. thaliana (mouse ear cress)	S. cerevisiae (baker's yeast)	C. elegans (nematode)
Wild-type allele	*lacZ+*	*PHB*	*CDC28*	*dpy-10*
Mutant allele	*lacZ*	*phb*	*cdc28*	*dpy-10(allele#)*
Allele designation style	Superscript	Hyphenated number	Hyphenated number	Parenthetical
Specific mutant allele	*lacZ³*	*phb-6*	*cdc28-3*	*dpy-10(e128)*
Dominant mutant allele		*phb-1d*		
Protein product	LacZ	PHB	CDC28p	DPY-10
Gene name style	Genes are usually named based on their presumed wild-type function. They are three letters, sometimes followed by a fourth letter for genes with similar functions.	Genes are usually named based on the mutant phenotype. They are three letters, sometimes followed by a number for genes with similar mutant phenotypes.	Genes are usually named based on their presumed wild-type function. They are three letters, sometimes followed by numbers for genes with similar mutant phenotypes.	Genes are usually named based on the mutant phenotype. They are three letters, sometimes followed by a hyphen and number for genes with similar mutant phenotypes.

Website	E. coli	A. thaliana (mouse ear cress)	S. cerevisiae (baker's yeast)	C. elegans (nematode)
	www.ecolicommunity.org	www.arabidopsis.org	www.yeastgenome.org	www.wormbase.org

	Drosophila (fruit fly)	D. rerio (zebrafish)	Mus musculus (house mouse)	Homo sapiens (human)
Life Cycle				
...n, meiosis; ...fertilization	♀ 2n XX → m → Egg n; ♂ 2n XY → m → Sperm n; f	♀ 2n → m → Egg n; ♂ 2n → m → Sperm n; f	♀ 2n XX → m → Egg n; ♂ 2n XY → m → Sperm n; f	♀ 2n XX → m → Egg n; ♂ 2n XY → m → Sperm n; f
Generation time	2 weeks	3 months	10 weeks	20 years
Genome	Drosophila (fruit fly)	D. rerio (zebrafish)	Mus musculus (house mouse)	Homo sapiens (human)
...ize	180 Mb	2000 Mb	3000 Mb	3000 Mb
...hromosomes	3 autosomes + X and Y ($2n = 8$)	25 chromosomes ($2n = 50$)	19 autosomes + X and Y ($2n = 40$)	22 autosomes + X and Y ($2n = 46$)
...umber of genes	13,937	14,700	23,139	20,769
...enetic distance	275 cM (female)/ 0 cM (male)	3000 cM (female)	1400 cM (sex averaged)	4460 cM (female)/ 2590 cM (male)
Nomenclature	Drosophila (fruit fly)	D. rerio (zebrafish)	Mus musculus (house mouse)	Homo sapiens (human)
...ild-type allele	w^+ (recessive) Ant^+ (dominant)	chi^+	$+^{Tcp1}$	HTT
...utant allele	w (recessive) Ant (dominant)	$chi^{allele\#}$	Tcp1	HTT*allele#
...llele designation ...yle	Superscript	Superscript	Hyphenated number or superscript number	Numbers following an asterisk
...pecific mutant ...ele	w^1 (recessive) Ant^3 (dominant)	$chic^{123}$	Tcp1-3, $Tcp1^3$	HTT*1
...ominant mutant ...ele	first letter capital	chi^{dc121}		
...otein product	W ANT	Chi	Tcp1	HTT protein
...ene name style	Genes are usually named based on the mutant phenotype.	Genes are often named based on the mutant phenotype. They are three letters, sometimes followed by a number for genes with similar mutant phenotypes.	Genes are usually named based on their mutant phenotypes or the proteins they encode. They are three letters, sometimes followed by a number for genes with similar functions.	Genes are often named after the disorder or abnormality resulting from mutations in the gene. Names are three letters.
Website	Drosophila (fruit fly)	D. rerio (zebrafish)	Mus musculus (house mouse)	Homo sapiens (human)
	http://flybase.org	http://zfin.org	www.informatics.jax.org	http://genome.ucsc.edu

The content that follows was taken from
Concept of Genetics,
Eleventh Edition

by William S. Klug, Michael R. Cummings,
Charlotte A. Spencer, and Michael A. Palladino,
with contributions by Darrell Killian

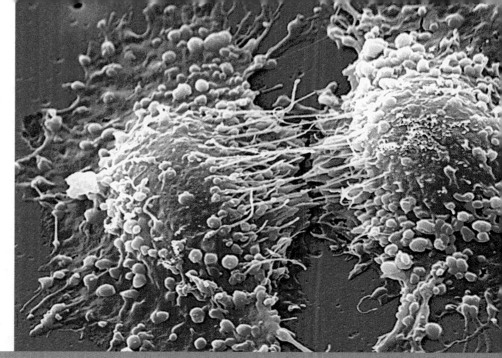

Colored scanning electron micrograph of two prostate cancer cells in the final stages of cell division (cytokinesis). The cells are still joined by strands of cytoplasm.

19 Cancer and Regulation of the Cell Cycle

CHAPTER CONCEPTS

- Cancer is characterized by genetic defects in fundamental aspects of cellular function, including DNA repair, chromatin modification, cell-cycle regulation, apoptosis, and signal transduction.

- Most cancer-causing mutations occur in somatic cells; only about 5 percent of cancers have a hereditary component.

- Mutations in cancer-related genes lead to abnormal proliferation and loss of control over how cells spread and invade surrounding tissues.

- The development of cancer is a multistep process requiring mutations in genes controlling many aspects of cell proliferation and metastasis.

- Cancer cells show high levels of genomic instability, leading to the accumulation of multiple mutations, some in cancer-related genes.

- Epigenetic effects such as DNA methylation and histone modifications play significant roles in the development of cancers.

- Mutations in proto-oncogenes and tumor-suppressor genes contribute to the development of cancers.

- Cancer-causing viruses introduce oncogenes into infected cells and stimulate cell proliferation.

- Environmental agents contribute to cancer by damaging DNA.

Cancer is the leading cause of death in Western countries. It strikes people of all ages, and one out of three people will experience a cancer diagnosis sometime in his or her lifetime. Each year, more than 1 million cases of cancer are diagnosed in the United States, and more than 500,000 people die from the disease.

Over the last 30 years, scientists have discovered that cancer is a genetic disease at the somatic cell level, characterized by the presence of gene products derived from mutated or abnormally expressed genes. The combined effects of numerous abnormal gene products lead to the uncontrolled growth and spread of cancer cells. Although some mutated cancer genes may be inherited, most are created within somatic cells that then divide and form tumors. Completion of the Human Genome Project and numerous large-scale rapid DNA sequencing studies have opened the door to a wealth of new information about the mutations that trigger a cell to become cancerous. This new understanding of cancer genetics is also leading to new gene-specific treatments, some of which are now entering clinical trials. Some scientists predict that gene-targeted therapies will replace chemotherapies within the next 25 years.

The goal of this chapter is to highlight our current understanding of the nature and causes of cancer. As we will see, cancer is a genetic disease that arises from the accumulation of mutations in genes controlling many basic aspects of cellular function. We will examine the relationship between genes and cancer, and consider how mutations, chromosomal changes, epigenetics, and environmental agents play roles in the development of cancer. Please note that some of the topics discussed in this chapter are explored in greater depth later in the text (see Special Topic Chapter 1—Epigenetics and Special Topic Chapter 4—Genomics and Personalized Medicine).

19.1 Cancer Is a Genetic Disease at the Level of Somatic Cells

Perhaps the most significant development in understanding the causes of cancer is the realization that cancer is a genetic disease. Genomic alterations that are associated with cancer range from single-nucleotide substitutions to large-scale chromosome rearrangements, amplifications, and deletions (Figure 19–1). However, unlike other genetic diseases, cancer is caused by mutations that arise predominantly in somatic cells. Only about 5 percent of cancers are associated with germ-line mutations that increase a person's susceptibility to certain types of cancer. Another important difference between cancers and other genetic diseases is that cancers rarely arise from a single mutation in a single gene, but from

the accumulation of many mutations. The mutations that lead to cancer affect multiple cellular functions, including repair of DNA damage, cell division, apoptosis, cellular differentiation, migratory behavior, and cell–cell contact.

What Is Cancer?

Clinically, cancer is defined as a large number of complex diseases, up to a hundred, that behave differently depending on the cell types from which they originate and the types of genetic alterations that occur within each cancer type. Cancers vary in their ages of onset, growth rates, invasiveness, prognoses, and responsiveness to treatments. However, at the molecular level, all cancers exhibit common characteristics that unite them as a family.

All cancer cells share two fundamental properties: (1) abnormal cell growth and division (**proliferation**), and (2) defects in the normal restraints that keep cells from spreading and colonizing other parts of the body (**metastasis**). In normal cells, these functions are tightly controlled by genes that are expressed appropriately in time and place. In cancer cells, these genes are either mutated or are expressed inappropriately.

It is this combination of uncontrolled cell proliferation and metastatic spread that makes cancer cells dangerous. When a cell simply loses genetic control over cell growth, it may grow into a multicellular mass, a **benign tumor**. Such a tumor can often be removed by surgery and may cause no serious harm. However, if cells in the tumor also have the ability to break loose, enter the bloodstream, invade other tissues, and form secondary tumors (**metastases**), they become malignant. **Malignant tumors** are often difficult to treat and may become life threatening. As we will see later in the chapter, there are multiple steps and genetic mutations that convert a benign tumor into a dangerous malignant tumor.

The Clonal Origin of Cancer Cells

Although malignant tumors may contain billions of cells, and may invade and grow in numerous parts of the body, all cancer cells in the primary and secondary tumors are clonal, meaning that they originated from a common ancestral cell that accumulated specific cancer-causing mutations. This is an important concept in understanding the molecular causes of cancer and has implications for its diagnosis.

Numerous data support the concept of cancer clonality. For example, reciprocal chromosomal translocations are characteristic of many cancers, including leukemias and lymphomas (two cancers involving white blood cells). Cancer cells from patients with **Burkitt lymphoma** show reciprocal translocations between chromosome 8 (with translocation breakpoints at or near the *c-myc* gene) and chromosomes 2, 14, or 22 (with translocation breakpoints at or near one of the immunoglobulin genes). Each Burkitt lymphoma patient exhibits unique breakpoints in his or her *c-myc* and

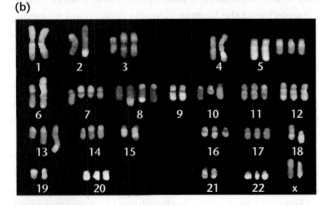

(a)

(b)

FIGURE 19–1 (a) Spectral karyotype of a normal cell. (b) Karyotype of a cancer cell showing translocations, deletions, and aneuploidy—characteristic features of cancer cells.

immunoglobulin gene DNA sequences; however, all lymphoma cells within that patient contain identical translocation breakpoints. This demonstrates that all cancer cells in each case of Burkitt lymphoma arise from a single cell, and this cell passes on its genetic aberrations to its progeny.

Another demonstration that cancer cells are clonal is their pattern of X-chromosome inactivation. As explained earlier in the text (see Chapter 7), female humans are mosaic, with some cells containing an inactivated paternal X chromosome and other cells containing an inactivated maternal X chromosome. X-chromosome inactivation occurs early in development and takes place at random. All cancer cells within a tumor, both primary and metastatic, within one female individual, contain the same inactivated X chromosome. This supports the concept that all the cancer cells in that patient arose from a common ancestral cell.

The Cancer Stem Cell Hypothesis

A concept that is related to the clonal origin of cancer cells is that of the cancer stem cell. Many scientists now believe that most of the cells within tumors do not proliferate. Those that do proliferate and give rise to all the cells within the tumor are known as **cancer stem cells**. Stem cells are undifferentiated cells that have the capacity for self-renewal—a process in which the stem cell divides unevenly, creating one daughter cell that goes on to differentiate into a mature cell type and one that remains a stem cell. Stem cells are also discussed earlier in the text (see Chapter 18). The cancer stem cell hypothesis contrasts the random or stochastic model. This model predicts that every cell within a tumor has the potential to form a new tumor.

Although scientists still actively debate the existence of cancer stem cells, evidence is accumulating that cancer stem cells do exist, at least in some tumors. Cancer stem cells have been identified in leukemias as well as in solid tumors of the brain, breast, colon, ovary, pancreas, and prostate. It is still not clear what fraction of any tumor is composed of cancer stem cells. For example, human acute myeloid leukemias contain less than 1 cancer stem cell in 10,000. In contrast, some solid tumors may contain as many as 40 percent cancer stem cells.

Scientists are also not sure about the origins of cancer stem cells. It is possible that they may arise from normal adult stem cells within a tissue, or they may be created from more differentiated somatic cells that acquire properties similar to stem cells after accumulating numerous mutations and changes to chromatin structure.

Cancer as a Multistep Process, Requiring Multiple Mutations

Although we know that cancer is a genetic disease initiated by mutations that lead to uncontrolled cell proliferation and metastasis, a single mutation is not sufficient to transform a normal cell into a tumor-forming (tumorigenic),

malignant cell. If it were sufficient, then cancer would be far more prevalent than it is. In humans, mutations occur spontaneously at a rate of about 10^{-6} mutations per gene, per cell division, mainly due to the intrinsic error rates of DNA replication. Because there are approximately 10^{16} cell divisions in a human body during a lifetime, a person might suffer up to 10^{10} mutations per gene somewhere in the body, during his or her lifetime. However, only about one person in three will suffer from cancer.

The phenomenon of age-related cancer is another indication that cancer develops from the accumulation of several mutagenic events in a single cell. The incidence of most cancers rises exponentially with age. If a single mutation were sufficient to convert a normal cell to a malignant one, then cancer incidence would appear to be independent of age. The age-related incidence of cancer suggests that many independent mutations, occurring randomly and with a low probability, are necessary before a cell is transformed into a malignant cancer cell. Another indication that cancer is a multistep process is the delay that occurs between exposure to **carcinogens** (cancer-causing agents) and the appearance of the cancer. For example, an incubation period of five to eight years separated exposure of people to the radiation of the atomic explosions at Hiroshima and Nagasaki and the onset of leukemias.

The multistep nature of cancer development is supported by the observation that cancers often develop in progressive steps, beginning with mildly aberrant cells and progressing to cells that are increasingly tumorigenic and malignant.

Each step in **tumorigenesis** (the development of a malignant tumor) appears to be the result of two or more genetic alterations that release the cells progressively from the controls that normally operate on proliferation and malignancy. This observation suggests that the progressive genetic alterations that create a cancer cell confer selective advantages to the cell and are propagated through cell divisions during the creation of tumors.

The progressive nature of cancer is illustrated by the development of colorectal cancer. Colorectal cancers are known to proceed through several clinical stages that are characterized by the stepwise accumulation of genetic defects in several genes (Figure 19–2). The first step is the conversion of a normal epithelial cell into a small cluster of cells known as an **adenoma** or **polyp**. This step requires inactivating mutations in the **adenomatous polyposis coli (APC)** gene, a gene that encodes a protein involved in the normal differentiation of intestinal cells. The APC gene is a tumor-suppressor gene, which will be discussed later in the chapter. The resulting adenoma grows slowly and is considered benign.

The second step in the development of colorectal cancer is the acquisition of a second genetic alteration in one of the cells within the small adenoma. This is usually a mutation in the *Kras* gene, a gene whose product is normally

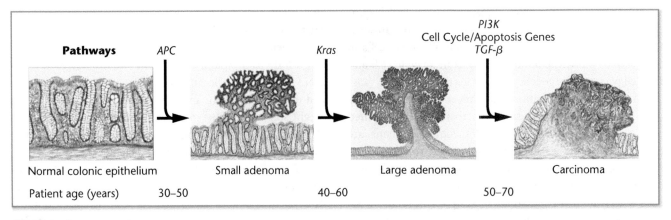

FIGURE 19–2 Steps in the development of colorectal cancers. Some of the genes that acquire driver mutations and cause the progressive development of colorectal cancer are shown at the top of the figure. These driver mutations accumulate over time and can take 40 years or more to result in the formation of a malignant tumor.

involved with regulating cell growth. The mutations in *Kras* that contribute to colorectal cancer cause the Kras protein to become constitutively active, resulting in unregulated cell division. The cell containing the *APC* and *Kras* mutations grows and expands to form a larger intermediate adenoma of approximately 1 cm in diameter—in a process known as **clonal expansion**. The cells of the original small adenoma (containing the *APC* mutation) are now vastly outnumbered by cells containing the two mutations.

The third step, which transforms a large adenoma into a malignant tumor (**carcinoma**), requires several more waves of clonal expansions triggered by the acquisition of defects in several genes, including *p53*, *PI3K*, and *TGF-β*. The products of these genes control several important aspects of normal cell growth and division, such as apoptosis, growth signaling, and cell-cycle regulation—all of which we will discuss in more detail later in the chapter. The resulting carcinoma is able to further grow and invade the underlying tissues of the colon. A few cells within the carcinoma acquire one or more new mutations that allow them to break free of the tumor, migrate to other parts of the body, and form metastases.

Driver Mutations and Passenger Mutations

Scientists are now applying some of the recent advances in DNA sequencing in order to identify all of the somatic mutations that occur during the development of a cancer cell. These studies compare the DNA sequences of genomes from cancer cells and normal cells derived from the same patient. Data from these studies are revealing that tens of thousands of somatic mutations can be present in cancer cells. Solid tumors such as those of the colon or breast may contain as many as 70 mutated genes. Some other cancers, such as lung cancer and melanomas, may contain several hundred mutations. Researchers believe that only a handful

of mutations in each tumor—called **driver mutations**—give a growth advantage to a tumor cell. The remainder of the mutations may be acquired over time, perhaps as a result of the increased levels of DNA damage that accumulate in cancer cells, but these mutations have no direct contribution to the cancer phenotype. These are known as **passenger mutations**. The total number of driver mutations that occur in any particular cancer is small—between 2 and 8.

As we will discover in subsequent sections of this chapter, the genes that acquire driver mutations that lead to cancer (called oncogenes and tumor-suppressor genes) are those that control a large number of essential cellular functions including DNA damage repair, chromatin modification, cell-cycle regulation, and programmed cell death. We will now investigate these fundamental processes, the genes that control them, and how mutations in these genes may lead to cancer.

19.2 Cancer Cells Contain Genetic Defects Affecting Genomic Stability, DNA Repair, and Chromatin Modifications

Cancer cells contain higher than normal numbers of mutations and chromosomal abnormalities. Many researchers believe that the fundamental defect in cancer cells is a derangement of the cells' normal ability to repair DNA damage. This loss of genomic integrity leads to a general increase in the mutation rate for every gene in the genome, including those whose products control aspects of cell proliferation, programmed cell death, and metastasis. The high level of genomic instability seen in cancer cells is known as the **mutator phenotype**. In addition, recent research has

(a) Double minutes

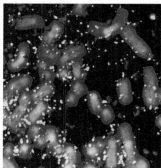

(b) Heterogeneous staining region

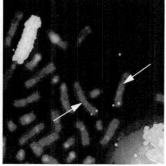

FIGURE 19–3 DNA amplifications in neuroblastoma cells. (a) Two cancer genes (*MYCN* in red and *MDM2* in green) are amplified as small DNA fragments that remain separate from chromosomal DNA within the nucleus. These units of amplified DNA are known as double minute chromosomes. Normal chromosomes are stained blue. (b) Multiple copies of the *MYCN* gene are amplified within one large region called a heterogeneous staining region (green). Single copies of the *MYCN* gene are visible as green dots at the ends of the normal parental chromosomes (white arrows). Normal chromosomes are stained red.

revealed that cancer cells contain aberrations in the types and locations of chromatin modifications, particularly DNA and histone methylation patterns.

Genomic Instability and Defective DNA Repair

Genomic instability in cancer cells is characterized by the presence of gross defects such as translocations, aneuploidy, chromosome loss, DNA amplification, and chromosome deletions (Figures 19–1 and 19–3). Cancer cells that are grown in cultures in the lab also show a great deal of genomic instability—duplicating, losing, and translocating chromosomes or parts of chromosomes. Often cancer cells show specific chromosomal defects that are used to diagnose the type and stage of the cancer. For example, leukemic white blood cells from patients with **chronic myelogenous leukemia (CML)** bear a specific translocation, in which the *C-ABL* gene on chromosome 9 is translocated into the *BCR* gene on chromosome 22. This translocation creates a structure known as the **Philadelphia chromosome** (**Figure 19–4**). The *BCR-ABL* fusion gene codes for a chimeric BCR-ABL protein. The normal ABL protein is a **protein kinase** that acts within signal transduction pathways, transferring growth factor signals from the external environment to the nucleus. The BCR-ABL protein is an abnormal signal transduction molecule in CML cells, which stimulates these cells to proliferate even in the absence of external growth signals.

In keeping with the concept of the cancer mutator phenotype, a number of inherited cancers are caused by defects in genes that control DNA repair. For example, xeroderma pigmentosum (XP) is a rare hereditary disorder that is characterized by extreme sensitivity to ultraviolet light and other carcinogens. Patients with XP often develop skin cancer. Cells from patients with XP are defective in nucleotide excision repair, with mutations appearing in any one of seven genes whose products are necessary to carry out DNA repair. XP cells are impaired in their ability to repair DNA lesions such as thymine dimers induced by UV light. The relationship between XP and genes controlling nucleotide excision repair is also described earlier in the text (see Chapter 17).

Another example is hereditary nonpolyposis colorectal cancer (HNPCC), which is caused by mutations in genes controlling DNA repair. HNPCC is an autosomal dominant syndrome, affecting about one in every 200 to 1000 people. Patients affected by HNPCC have an increased risk of developing colon, ovary, uterine, and kidney cancers. Cells from patients with HNPCC show higher than normal mutation rates and genomic instability. At least eight genes are associated with HNPCC, and four of these genes control aspects of DNA mismatch repair. Inactivation of any of these four genes—*MSH2, MSH6, MLH1,* and *MLH3*—causes a rapid accumulation of genome-wide mutations and the subsequent development of cancers.

The observation that hereditary defects in genes controlling nucleotide excision repair and DNA mismatch repair lead to high rates of cancer lends support to the idea that the mutator phenotype is a significant contributor to the development of cancer.

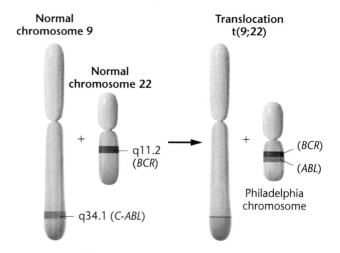

FIGURE 19–4 A reciprocal translocation involving the long arms of chromosomes 9 and 22 results in the formation of a characteristic chromosome, the Philadelphia chromosome, which is associated with chronic myelogenous leukemia (CML). The t(9;22) translocation results in the fusion of the *C-ABL* proto-oncogene on chromosome 9 with the *BCR* gene on chromosome 22. The fusion protein is a powerful hybrid molecule that allows cells to escape control of the cell cycle, contributing to the development of CML.

Chromatin Modifications and Cancer Epigenetics

The field of cancer epigenetics is providing new perspectives on the genetics of cancer. **Epigenetics** is the study of factors that affect gene expression but that do not alter the nucleotide sequence of DNA. Epigenetic effects can be inherited from one cell to its progeny cells and may be present in either somatic or germ-line cells. DNA methylation and histone modifications such as acetylation and phosphorylation are examples of epigenetic modifications. The genomic patterns and locations of these modifications can affect gene expression. For example, DNA methylation is thought to be responsible for the gene silencing associated with parental imprinting, heterochromatin gene repression, and X-chromosome inactivation. The effects of chromatin modifications and epigenetic factors on gene expression and hereditary disease are discussed in more detail later in the text (see Chapter 17 and Special Topic Chapter 1—Epigenetics).

Cancer cells contain altered DNA methylation patterns. Overall, there is much less DNA methylation in cancer cells than in normal cells. At the same time, the promoters of some genes are hypermethylated in cancer cells. These changes are thought to result in the release of transcription repression over the bulk of genes that would be silent in normal cells—including cancer-causing genes—while at the same time repressing transcription of genes that would regulate normal cellular functions such as DNA repair and cell-cycle control.

Histone modifications are also disrupted in cancer cells. Genes that encode histone acetylases, deacetylases, methyltransferases, and demethylases are often mutated or aberrantly expressed in cancer cells. The large numbers of epigenetic abnormalities in tumors have prompted some scientists to speculate that there may be more epigenetic defects in cancer cells than there are gene mutations. In addition, because epigenetic modifications are reversible, it may be possible to treat cancers using epigenetic-based therapies.

NOW SOLVE THIS

19–1 In chronic myelogenous leukemia (CML), leukemic blood cells can be distinguished from other cells of the body by the presence of a functional BCR-ABL hybrid protein. Explain how this characteristic provides an opportunity to develop a therapeutic approach to a treatment for CML.

■ **HINT:** *This problem asks you to imagine a therapy that is based on the unique genetic characteristics of CML leukemic cells. The key to its solution is to remember that the BCR-ABL fusion protein is found only in CML white blood cells and that this unusual protein has a specific function thought to directly contribute to the development of CML. To help you answer this problem, you may wish to learn more about the cancer drug Gleevec (see http://www.cancer.gov/cancertopics/druginfo/imatinibmesylate).*

19.3 Cancer Cells Contain Genetic Defects Affecting Cell-Cycle Regulation

One of the fundamental aberrations in all cancer cells is a loss of control over cell proliferation. Cell proliferation is the process of cell growth and division that is essential for all development and tissue repair in multicellular organisms. Although some cells, such as epidermal cells of the skin or blood-forming cells in the bone marrow, continue to grow and divide throughout an organism's lifetime, most cells in adult multicellular organisms remain in a nondividing, quiescent, and differentiated state. **Differentiated cells** are those that are specialized for specific functions, such as photoreceptor cells of the retina or muscle cells of the heart. The most extreme examples of nonproliferating cells are nerve cells, which divide little, if at all, even to replace damaged tissue. In contrast, many differentiated cells, such as those in the liver and kidney, are able to grow and divide when stimulated by extracellular signals and growth factors. In this way, multicellular organisms are able to replace dead and damaged tissue. However, the growth and differentiation of cells must be strictly regulated; otherwise, the integrity of organs and tissues would be compromised by the presence of inappropriate types and quantities of cells. Normal regulation over cell proliferation involves a large number of gene products that control steps in the cell cycle, programmed cell death, and the response of cells to external growth signals. In cancer cells, many of the genes that control these functions are mutated or aberrantly expressed, leading to uncontrolled cell proliferation.

In this section, we will review steps in the cell cycle, some of the genes that control the cell cycle, and how these genes, when mutated, lead to cancer.

The Cell Cycle and Signal Transduction

The cellular events that occur in sequence from one cell division to the next comprise the **cell cycle** (**Figure 19–5**). The **interphase** stage of the cell cycle is the interval between mitotic divisions. During this time, the cell grows and replicates its DNA. During **G1**, the cell prepares for DNA synthesis by accumulating the enzymes and molecules required for DNA replication. G1 is followed by **S phase**, during which the cell's chromosomal DNA is replicated. During **G2**, the cell continues to grow and prepare for division. During **M phase**, the duplicated chromosomes condense, sister chromosomes separate to opposite poles, and the cell divides in two. These phases of the cell cycle are also discussed in more detail earlier in the text (see Chapter 2).

In early to mid-G1, the cell makes a decision either to enter the next cell cycle or to withdraw from the cell cycle into quiescence. Continuously dividing cells do not exit the

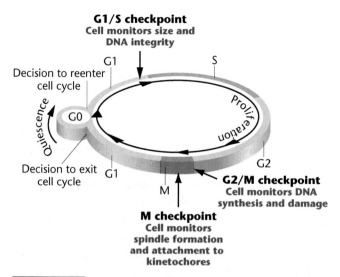

FIGURE 19–5 Checkpoints and proliferation decision points monitor the progress of the cell through the cell cycle.

cell cycle but proceed through G1, S, G2, and M phases; however, if the cell receives signals to stop growing, it enters the **G0** phase of the cell cycle. During G0, the cell remains metabolically active but does not grow or divide. Most differentiated cells in multicellular organisms can remain in this G0 phase indefinitely. Some, such as neurons, never reenter the cell cycle. In contrast, cancer cells are unable to enter G0, and instead, they continuously cycle. Their *rate* of proliferation is not necessarily any greater than that of normal proliferating cells; however, they are not able to become quiescent at the appropriate time or place.

Cells in G0 can often be stimulated to reenter the cell cycle by external growth signals. These signals are delivered to the cell by molecules such as growth factors and hormones that bind to cell-surface receptors, which then relay the signal from the plasma membrane to the cytoplasm. The process of transmitting growth signals from the external environment to the cell nucleus is known as **signal transduction**. Ultimately, signal transduction initiates a program of gene expression that propels the cell out of G0 back into the cell cycle. Cancer cells often have defects in signal transduction pathways. Sometimes, abnormal signal transduction molecules send continuous growth signals to the nucleus even in the absence of external growth signals. An example of abnormal signal transduction due to mutations in the *ras* gene is described in Section 19.4. In addition, malignant cells may not respond to external signals from surrounding cells—signals that would normally inhibit cell proliferation within a mature tissue.

Cell-Cycle Control and Checkpoints

In normal cells, progress through the cell cycle is tightly regulated, and each step must be completed before the next step can begin. There are at least three distinct points in the cell cycle at which the cell monitors external signals and internal equilibrium before proceeding to the next stage. These are the **G1/S**, the **G2/M**, and **M checkpoints** (Figure 19–5). At the G1/S checkpoint, the cell monitors its size and determines whether its DNA has been damaged. If the cell has not achieved an adequate size, or if the DNA has been damaged, further progress through the cell cycle is halted until these conditions are corrected. If cell size and DNA integrity are normal, the G1/S checkpoint is traversed, and the cell proceeds to S phase. The second important checkpoint is the G2/M checkpoint, where physiological conditions in the cell are monitored prior to mitosis. If DNA replication or repair of any DNA damage has not been completed, the cell cycle arrests until these processes are complete. The third major checkpoint occurs during mitosis and is called the M checkpoint. At this checkpoint, both the successful formation of the spindle-fiber system and the attachment of spindle fibers to the kinetochores associated with the centromeres are monitored. If spindle fibers are not properly formed or attachment is inadequate, mitosis is arrested.

In addition to regulating the cell cycle at checkpoints, the cell controls progress through the cell cycle by means of two classes of proteins: **cyclins** and **cyclin-dependent kinases** (**CDKs**). The cell accumulates and destroys cyclin proteins in a precise pattern during the cell cycle (**Figure 19–6**). When a cyclin is present, it binds to a specific CDK, triggering activity

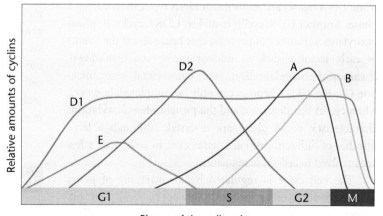

FIGURE 19–6 Relative expression times and amounts of cyclins during the cell cycle. Cyclin D1 accumulates early in G1 and is expressed at a constant level through most of the cycle. Cyclin E accumulates in G1, reaches a peak, and declines by mid-S phase. Cyclin D2 begins accumulating in the last half of G1, reaches a peak just after the beginning of S, and then declines by early G2. Cyclin A appears in late G1, accumulates through S phase, peaks at the G2/M transition, and is rapidly degraded. Cyclin B peaks at the G2/M transition and declines rapidly in M phase.

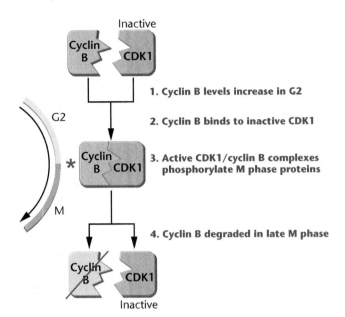

FIGURE 19–7 CDK1 and cyclin B control the transition from G2 to M phase. In late G2 phase, cyclin B accumulates and forms complexes with inactive CDK1 molecules. CDK1 is activated within the complexes and adds phosphate groups to cellular components. These phosphorylated molecules bring about the structural and biochemical changes that are necessary for M phase. In late M phase, cyclin B is degraded, CDK1 becomes inactive, and M phase phosphorylations are reversed.

of the CDK/cyclin complex. The CDK/cyclin complex then selectively phosphorylates and activates other proteins that in turn bring about the changes necessary to advance the cell through the cell cycle. For example, in G1 phase, CDK4/cyclin D complexes activate proteins that stimulate transcription of genes whose products (such as DNA polymerase δ and DNA ligase) are required for DNA replication during S phase. Another CDK/cyclin complex, CDK1/cyclin B, phosphorylates a number of proteins that bring about the events of early mitosis, such as nuclear membrane breakdown, chromosome condensation, and cytoskeletal reorganization (**Figure 19–7**). Mitosis can only be completed, however, when cyclin B is degraded and the protein phosphorylations characteristic of M phase are reversed. Although a large number of different protein kinases exist in cells, only a few are involved in cell-cycle regulation.

The cell cycle is regulated by an interplay of genes whose products either promote or suppress cell division. Mutation or misexpression of any of the genes controlling the cell cycle can contribute to the development of cancer. For example, if genes that control the G1/S or G2/M checkpoints are mutated, the cell may continue to grow and divide without repairing DNA damage. As these cells continue to divide, they accumulate mutations in genes whose products control cell proliferation or metastasis. Similarly, if genes that control progress through the cell cycle, such as those that encode the cyclins, are expressed at the wrong

time or at incorrect levels, the cell may grow and divide continuously and may be unable to exit the cell cycle into G0. The result in both cases is that the cell loses control over proliferation and is on its way to becoming cancerous.

Control of Apoptosis

As already described, if DNA replication, repair, or chromosome assembly is defective, normal cells halt their progress through the cell cycle until the condition is corrected. This reduces the number of mutations and chromosomal abnormalities that accumulate in normal proliferating cells. However, if DNA or chromosomal damage is so severe that repair is impossible, the cell may initiate a second line of defense—a process called **apoptosis**, or **programmed cell death**. Apoptosis is a genetically controlled process whereby the cell commits suicide. Besides its role in preventing cancer, apoptosis is also initiated during normal multicellular development in order to eliminate certain cells that do not contribute to the final adult organism. The steps in apoptosis are the same for damaged cells and for cells being eliminated during development: nuclear DNA becomes fragmented, internal cellular structures are disrupted, and the cell dissolves into small spherical structures known as apoptotic bodies **Figure 19–8(a)**. In the final step, the apoptotic bodies are engulfed by the immune system's phagocytic cells. A series of proteases called **caspases** are responsible for initiating apoptosis and for digesting intracellular components.

Apoptosis is genetically controlled in that regulation of the levels of specific gene products such as Bcl2 and BAX [**Figure 19–8(b)**] can trigger or prevent apoptosis. By removing damaged cells, programmed cell death reduces the number of mutations that are passed to the next generation, including those in cancer-causing genes. Some of the same genes that control cell-cycle checkpoints can trigger apoptosis. These genes are mutated in many cancers. As a result of the mutation or inactivation of these checkpoint genes, the cell is unable to repair its DNA or undergo apoptosis. This inability leads to the accumulation of even more mutations in genes that control growth, division, and metastasis.

19.4 Proto-oncogenes and Tumor-Suppressor Genes Are Altered in Cancer Cells

Two general categories of genes are mutated or misexpressed in cancer cells—the proto-oncogenes and the tumor-suppressor genes (Table 19.1). **Proto-oncogenes** encode transcription factors that stimulate expression of other genes, signal transduction molecules that stimulate cell division, and cell-cycle regulators that move the cell through

(a)

(b)

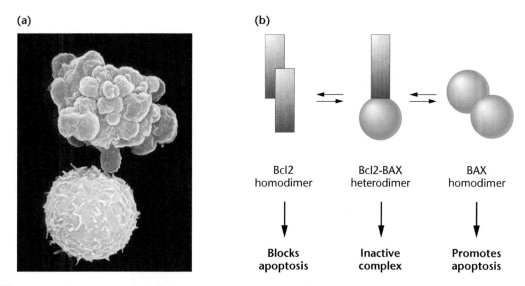

Bcl2 homodimer

Bcl2-BAX heterodimer

BAX homodimer

Blocks apoptosis

Inactive complex

Promotes apoptosis

FIGURE 19-8 (a) Normal white blood cell (bottom) and a white blood cell undergoing apoptosis (top). Apoptotic bodies appear as grape-like clusters on the cell surface. (b) The relative concentrations of the Bcl2 and BAX proteins regulate apoptosis. A normal cell contains a balance of Bcl2 and BAX, which form inactive heterodimers. A relative excess of Bcl2 results in the formation of Bcl2 homodimers, which prevent apoptosis. Cancer cells with Bcl2 overexpression are resistant to chemotherapies and radiation therapies. A relative excess of BAX results in the formation of BAX homodimers, which induce apoptosis. In normal cells, activated p53 protein induces transcription of the *BAX* gene and inhibits transcription of the *Bcl2* gene, leading to cell death. In many cancer cells, p53 is defective, preventing the apoptotic pathway from removing the cancer cells.

the cell cycle. Their products are important for normal cell functions, especially cell growth and division. When normal cells become quiescent and cease division, they repress the expression of most proto-oncogenes or modify the activities of their products. In cancer cells, one or more proto-oncogenes are altered in such a way that the activities of their products cannot be regulated in a normal fashion. This is sometimes due to mutations that result in an abnormal protein product. In other cases, proto-oncogenes may be overexpressed or expressed at an incorrect time due to mutations within gene-regulatory regions such as enhancer elements or due to alterations in chromatin structure that affect gene expression. If a proto-oncogene is continually in an "on" state, its product may constantly stimulate the cell to divide. When a proto-oncogene is mutated or abnormally expressed and contributes to the development of cancer, it is known as an **oncogene**—a cancer-causing gene. Oncogenes are proto-oncogenes that have experienced a gain-of-function alteration. As a result, only one allele of a proto-oncogene needs to be mutated or misexpressed in order to contribute to cancer. Hence, oncogenes confer a dominant cancer phenotype.

TABLE 19.1 Some Proto-oncogenes and Tumor-Suppressor Genes

Proto-oncogene	Normal Function	Alteration in Cancer	Associated Cancers
c-myc	Transcription factor, regulates cell cycle, differentiation, apoptosis	Translocation, amplification, point mutations	Lymphomas, leukemias, lung cancer, many types
c-kit	Tyrosine kinase, signal transduction	Mutation	Sarcomas
RARα	Hormone-dependent transcription factor, differentiation	Chromosomal translocations with *PML* gene, fusion product	Acute promyelocytic leukemia
E6	Human papillomavirus encoded oncogene, inactivates p53	HPV infection	Cervical cancer
Cyclins	Bind to CDKs, regulate cell cycle	Gene amplification, overexpression	Lung, esophagus, many types

Tumor-Suppressor	Normal Function	Alteration in Cancer	Associated Cancers
RB1	Cell-cycle checkpoints, binds E2F	Mutation, deletion, inactivation by viral oncogene products	Retinoblastoma, osteosarcoma, many types
APC	Cell–cell interaction	Mutation	Colorectal cancers, brain, thyroid
p53	Transcription regulation	Mutation, deletion, viruses	Many types
BRCA1, BRCA2	DNA repair	Point mutations	Breast, ovarian, prostate cancers

Tumor-suppressor genes are genes whose products normally regulate cell-cycle checkpoints or initiate the process of apoptosis. In normal cells, proteins encoded by tumor-suppressor genes halt progress through the cell cycle in response to DNA damage or growth-suppression signals from the extracellular environment. When tumor-suppressor genes are mutated or inactivated, cells are unable to respond normally to cell-cycle checkpoints, or are unable to undergo programmed cell death if DNA damage is extensive. This leads to the accumulation of more mutations and the development of cancer. When both alleles of a tumor-suppressor gene are inactivated through mutation or epigenetic modifications, and other changes in the cell keep it growing and dividing, cells may become tumorigenic.

The following are examples of proto-oncogenes and tumor-suppressor genes that contribute to cancer when mutated or abnormally expressed. Approximately 400 oncogenes and tumor-suppressor genes are now known, and more will likely be discovered as cancer research continues.

The *ras* Proto-oncogenes

Some of the most frequently mutated genes in human tumors are those in the **ras gene family**. These genes are mutated in more than 30 percent of human tumors. The *ras* gene family encodes signal transduction molecules that are associated with the cell membrane and regulate cell growth and division. Ras proteins normally transmit signals from the cell membrane to the nucleus, stimulating the cell to divide in response to external growth factors (**Figure 19–9**). Ras proteins alternate between an inactive (switched off) and an active (switched on) state by binding either guanosine diphosphate (GDP) or guanosine triphosphate (GTP). When a cell encounters a growth factor (such as platelet-derived growth factor or epidermal growth factor), growth factor receptors on the cell membrane bind to the growth factor, resulting in autophosphorylation of the cytoplasmic portion of the growth factor receptor. This causes recruitment of proteins known as nucleotide exchange factors to the plasma membrane. These nucleotide exchange factors cause Ras to release GDP and bind GTP, thereby activating Ras. The active, GTP-bound form of Ras then sends its signals through cascades of protein phosphorylations in the cytoplasm. The end-point of these cascades is activation of nuclear transcription factors that stimulate expression of genes whose products drive the cell from quiescence into the cell cycle. Once Ras has sent its signals to the nucleus, it hydrolyzes GTP to GDP and becomes inactive. Mutations that convert the *ras* proto-oncogene to an oncogene prevent the Ras protein from hydrolyzing GTP to GDP and hence freeze the Ras protein into its "on" conformation, constantly stimulating the cell to divide.

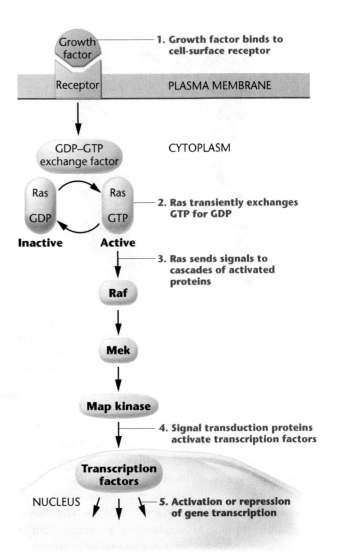

FIGURE 19–9 A signal transduction pathway mediated by Ras.

The *p53* Tumor-Suppressor Gene

The most frequently mutated gene in human cancers—mutated in more than 50 percent of all cancers—is the **p53 gene**. This gene encodes a transcription factor that represses or stimulates transcription of more than 50 different genes.

Normally, the p53 protein is continuously synthesized but is rapidly degraded and therefore is present in cells at low levels. In addition, the p53 protein is normally bound to another protein called **MDM2**, which has several effects on p53. The presence of MDM2 on the p53 protein tags p53 for degradation and sequesters the transcriptional activation domain of p53. It also prevents the phosphorylations and acetylations that convert the p53 protein from an inactive to an active form.

Several types of cellular stress events bring about rapid increases in the nuclear levels of activated p53 protein. These include chemical damage to DNA, double-stranded breaks in DNA induced by ionizing radiation, and the presence of DNA-repair intermediates generated by exposure of cells to ultraviolet light. In response to these signals, MDM2 dissociates from p53, making p53 more stable and unmasking its transcription activation domain. Increases in the levels of activated p53 protein also result from increases in protein phosphorylation, acetylation, and other posttranslational modifications (**Figure 19–10**). Activated p53 protein acts as a transcription factor that

(a) p53 in unstressed cells

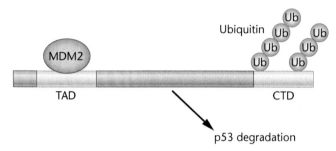

(b) After DNA damage and cell stress

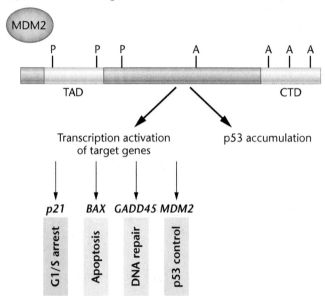

FIGURE 19–10 Steps in the regulation of p53 levels and activity. (a) In normal unstressed cells, p53 is kept inactive and at low abundance by MDM2, which binds to the transactivation domain (TAD) and stimulates the addition of ubiquitin onto lysine residues in the carboxy-terminal domain (CTD). The presence of ubiquitin promotes p53 degradation. (b) After various types of cellular stress including DNA damage, cellular kinases add phosphates (P's) to serines and threonines in the TAD, leading to dissociation of MDM2 and subsequent loss of ubiquitin. As the levels of p53 increase in the nucleus, acetyl transferases add acetyl groups (A's) to lysines in the CTD, which increases p53 stability and affinity for specific DNA sequences within the promoter regions of target genes. Examples of genes that are transcriptionally stimulated by p53 are *p21* (leading to G1/S cell cycle arrest), *BAX* (stimulating apoptosis), *GADD45* (contributing to DNA repair), and *MDM2* (returning p53 to an inactive and low abundance state).

stimulates expression of the *MDM2* gene. As the levels of MDM2 increase, p53 protein is again bound by MDM2, returned to an inactive state, and targeted for degradation, in a negative feedback loop.

The activated p53 protein initiates several different responses to DNA damage including cell-cycle arrest followed by DNA repair and apoptosis if DNA cannot be repaired. These responses are accomplished by p53 acting as a transcription factor that stimulates or represses the expression of genes involved in each response.

In normal cells, activated p53 can arrest the cell cycle at the G1/S and G2/M checkpoints, as well as retarding the progression of the cell through S phase. To arrest the cell cycle at the G1/S checkpoint, activated p53 protein stimulates transcription of a gene encoding the p21 protein. The p21 protein inhibits the CDK4/cyclin D1 complex, hence preventing the cell from moving from G1 phase into S phase. Activated p53 protein also regulates expression of genes that retard the progress of DNA replication, thus allowing time for DNA damage to be repaired during S phase. By regulating expression of other genes, activated p53 can block cells at the G2/M checkpoint, if DNA damage occurs during S phase.

Activated p53 can also instruct a damaged cell to commit suicide by apoptosis. It does so by activating the transcription of the *Bax* gene and repressing transcription of the *Bcl2* gene. In normal cells, the BAX protein is present in a heterodimer with the Bcl2 protein, and the cell remains viable (Figure 19–8). But when the levels of BAX protein increase in response to p53 stimulation of *Bax* gene transcription, BAX homodimers are formed, and these homodimers activate the cellular changes that lead to apoptosis. In cancer cells that lack functional p53, BAX protein levels do not increase in response to cell damage, and apoptosis may not occur.

Cells lacking functional p53 are unable to arrest at cell-cycle checkpoints or to enter apoptosis in response to DNA damage. As a result, they move unchecked through the cell cycle, regardless of the condition of the cell's DNA. Cells lacking p53 have high mutation rates and accumulate the types of mutations that lead to cancer. Because of the importance of the *p53* gene to genomic integrity, it is often referred to as the "guardian of the genome."

The *RB1* Tumor-Suppressor Gene

The loss or mutation of the *RB1* (**retinoblastoma 1**) tumor-suppressor gene contributes to the development of many cancers, including those of the breast, bone, lung, and bladder. The *RB1* gene was originally identified as a result of studies on **retinoblastoma**, an inherited disorder in which tumors develop in the eyes of young children. Retinoblastoma occurs with a frequency of about 1 in 15,000 individuals. In the familial form of the disease, individuals

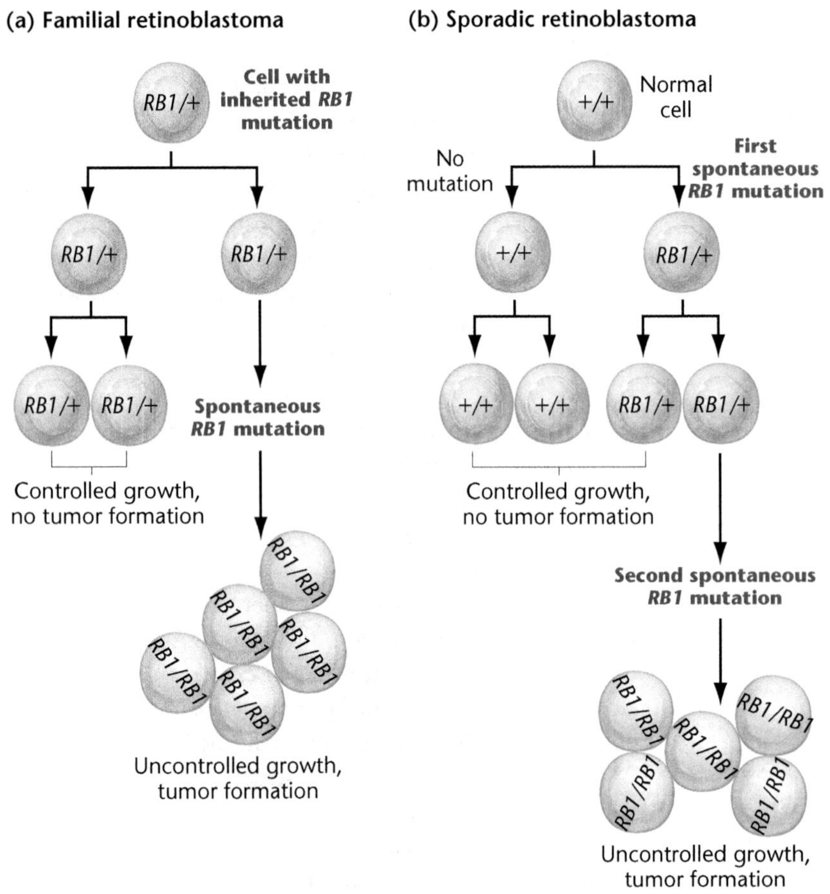

(a) Familial retinoblastoma

Cell with inherited *RB1* mutation

RB1/+

RB1/+   *RB1/+*

RB1/+   *RB1/+*   Spontaneous *RB1* mutation

Controlled growth, no tumor formation

RB1/RB1 *RB1/RB1* *RB1/RB1* *RB1/RB1* *RB1/RB1* *RB1/RB1*

Uncontrolled growth, tumor formation

(b) Sporadic retinoblastoma

Normal cell
+/+

No mutation   First spontaneous *RB1* mutation

+/+   *RB1/+*

+/+   *+/+*   *RB1/+* *RB1/+*

Controlled growth, no tumor formation

Second spontaneous *RB1* mutation

RB1/RB1 *RB1/RB1* *RB1/RB1* *RB1/RB1* *RB1/RB1*

Uncontrolled growth, tumor formation

FIGURE 19–11 (a) In familial retinoblastoma, one mutation (designated as *RB1*) is inherited and present in all cells. A second mutation at the retinoblastoma locus in any retinal cell contributes to uncontrolled cell growth and tumor formation. (b) In sporadic retinoblastoma, independent mutations in both alleles of the retinoblastoma gene within a single cell are acquired sequentially, also leading to tumor formation.

inherit one mutated allele of the *RB1* gene and have an 85 percent chance of developing retinoblastomas as well as an increased chance of developing other cancers. All somatic cells of patients with hereditary retinoblastoma contain one mutated allele of the *RB1* gene. However, it is only when the second normal allele of the *RB1* gene is lost or mutated in certain retinal cells that retinoblastoma develops. In individuals who do not have this hereditary condition, retinoblastoma is extremely rare, as it requires at least two separate somatic mutations in a retinal cell in order to inactivate both copies of the *RB1* gene (**Figure 19–11**).

The **retinoblastoma protein (pRB)** is a tumor-suppressor protein that controls the G1/S cell-cycle checkpoint. The pRB protein is found in the nuclei of all cell types at all stages of the cell cycle. However, its activity varies throughout the cell cycle, depending on its phosphorylation state. When cells are in the G0 phase of the cell cycle, the pRB protein is nonphosphorylated and binds to transcription factors such as E2F, inactivating them (**Figure 19–12**). When the cell is stimulated by growth factors, it enters G1 and approaches S phase. Throughout the G1 phase, the pRB protein becomes phosphorylated by the CDK4/cyclin D1 complex. Phosphorylated pRB releases its bound regulatory proteins. When E2F and other regulators

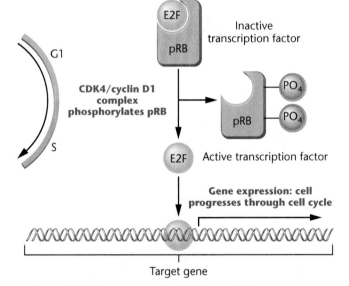

FIGURE 19–12 During G0 and early G1, pRB interacts with and inactivates transcription factor E2F. As the cell moves from G1 to S phase, a CDK4/cyclin D1 complex forms and adds phosphate groups to pRB. As pRB becomes phosphorylated, E2F is released and becomes transcriptionally active, allowing the cell to pass through S phase. Phosphorylation of pRB is transitory; as CDK/cyclin complexes are degraded and the cell moves through the cell cycle to early G1, pRB phosphorylation declines, allowing pRB to reassociate with E2F.

are released by pRB, they are free to induce the expression of over 30 genes whose products are required for the transition from G1 into S phase. After cells traverse S, G2, and M phases, pRB reverts to a nonphosphorylated state, binds to regulatory proteins such as E2F, and keeps them sequestered until required for the next cell cycle. In normal quiescent cells, the presence of the pRB protein prevents passage into S phase. In many cancer cells, including retinoblastoma cells, both copies of the *RB1* gene are defective, inactive, or absent, and progression through the cell cycle is not regulated.

NOW SOLVE THIS

19–2 People with a genetic condition known as Li–Fraumeni syndrome inherit one mutant copy of the *p53* gene. These people have a high risk of developing a number of different cancers, such as breast cancer, leukemia, bone cancer, adrenocortical tumors, and brain tumors. Explain how mutations in one cancer-related gene can give rise to such a diverse range of tumors.

■ **HINT:** *This problem involves an understanding of how tumor-suppressor genes regulate cell growth and behavior. The key to its solution is to consider which cellular functions are regulated by the p53 protein and how the absence of p53 could affect each of these functions. Also, read about loss of heterozygosity in Section 19.6.*

For more practice, see Problems 25, 26, and 27.

19.5 Cancer Cells Metastasize and Invade Other Tissues

As discussed at the beginning of this chapter, uncontrolled growth alone is insufficient to create a malignant and life-threatening cancer. Cancer cells must also become malignant, acquiring the ability to disengage from the original tumor site, to enter the blood or lymphatic system, to invade surrounding tissues, and to develop into secondary tumors. In order to leave the site of the primary tumor and invade other tissues, tumor cells must dissociate from the primary tumor and secrete proteases that digest components of the **extracellular matrix** and **basal lamina**, which normally surround and separate the body's tissues. The extracellular matrix and basal lamina are composed of proteins and carbohydrates. They surround and separate body tissues, form the scaffold for tissue growth, and inhibit the migration of cells. The ability to invade the extracellular matrix is also a property of some normal cell types. For example, implantation of the embryo in the uterine wall

during pregnancy requires cell migration across the extracellular matrix. In addition, white blood cells reach sites of infection by penetrating capillary walls. The mechanisms of invasion are probably similar in these normal cells and in cancer cells. The difference is that, in normal cells, the invasive ability is tightly regulated, whereas in tumor cells, this regulation has been lost.

Once cancer cells have disengaged from the primary tumor and traversed tissue barriers, they enter the blood or lymphatic system and may become lodged in microvessels of other tissues. At this point the cells may undergo a second round of invasion to enter the new tissue and grow into new (metastatic) tumors. Only a small percentage of circulating cancer cells—about 0.01 percent—survive to establish metastatic tumors. Other important features of metastatic cells are increased cell motility, the capacity to stimulate new blood vessel formation, and the ability to escape detection by the host's immune system.

Metastasis is controlled by a large number of gene products, including cell-adhesion molecules, cytoskeleton regulators, and proteolytic enzymes. For example, epithelial tumors have a lower than normal level of the **E-cadherin glycoprotein**, which is responsible for cell–cell adhesion in normal tissues. Also, proteolytic enzymes such as **metalloproteinases** are present at higher than normal levels in many highly malignant tumors. For example, breast cancer cells that metastasize to bone abnormally express the metalloproteinase gene *MMP1*. Those that spread to the lungs overexpress the *MMP1* and *MMP2* genes. It has been shown that the level of aggressiveness of a tumor correlates positively with the levels of proteolytic enzymes expressed by the tumor. In addition, malignant cells are not susceptible to the normal controls conferred by regulatory molecules such as **tissue inhibitors of metalloproteinases (TIMPs)**.

Like the tumor-suppressor genes that are mutated in primary cancers, **metastasis-suppressor genes** are mutated or disrupted in metastatic tumors. Less than a dozen of these metastasis-suppressor genes have been identified so far, but all appear to affect the growth and development of metastatic tumors and not the primary tumor. One example is the CD82 protein, encoded by the *CD82* gene. This protein normally inhibits functions related to metastasis such as invasiveness and cell motility. It does this by directly interacting with proteins involved in these functions. In metastatic tumors, the expression of *CD82* is reduced or lost. The expression of *CD82* and other metastasis-suppressor genes is reduced by epigenetic mechanisms rather than by mutation. This observation provides hope that researchers can develop antimetastasis therapies that target the epigenetic silencing of metastasis-suppressor genes.

19.6 Predisposition to Some Cancers Can Be Inherited

Although the vast majority of human cancers are sporadic, a small fraction (approximately 5 percent) have a hereditary or familial component. At present, about 50 forms of hereditary cancer are known (Table 19.2).

Most inherited cancer-susceptibility alleles occur in tumor-suppressor genes, and though transmitted in a Mendelian dominant fashion, are not sufficient in themselves to trigger development of a cancer. At least one other somatic mutation in the other copy of the gene must occur in order to drive a cell toward tumorigenesis. In addition, mutations in still other genes are usually necessary to fully express the cancer phenotype. As mentioned earlier, inherited mutations in the *RB1* gene predispose individuals to developing various cancers. Although the normal somatic cells of these patients are heterozygous for the *RB1* mutation, cells within their tumors contain mutations in both copies of the gene. The phenomenon whereby the second, wild-type, allele is mutated in a tumor is known as **loss of heterozygosity**. Although loss of heterozygosity is an essential first step in expression of these inherited cancers, further mutations in other proto-oncogenes, tumor-suppressor genes, or chromatin-modifying genes are necessary for the tumor cells to become fully malignant.

The development of hereditary colon cancer illustrates how inherited mutations in one allele of a gene contribute only one step in the multistep pathway leading to malignancy. In Section 19.1, we described how colorectal cancers develop through the accumulation of mutations in several genes, leading to a stepwise clonal expansion of cells and the development of carcinomas. Although the vast majority of colorectal cancers are sporadic, about 1 percent of cases result from a genetic predisposition to cancer known as **familial adenomatous polyposis (FAP)**. In FAP, individuals inherit one mutant copy of the *APC* (adenomatous polyposis) gene located on the long arm of chromosome 5. Mutations include deletions, frameshift, and point mutations. The normal function of the *APC* gene product is to act as a tumor suppressor controlling growth and differentiation. The presence of a heterozygous *APC* mutation causes the epithelial cells of the colon to partially escape cell-cycle control, and the cells divide to form small clusters of cells called **polyps** or adenomas. People who are heterozygous for this condition develop hundreds to thousands of colon and rectal polyps early in life. Although it is not necessary for the second allele of the *APC* gene to be mutated in polyps at this stage, in the majority of cases, the second *APC* allele becomes mutant in a later stage of cancer development. The remaining steps in development of colorectal carcinoma follow the same order as that shown in Figure 19–2.

NOW SOLVE THIS

19–3 Although tobacco smoking is responsible for a large number of human cancers, not all smokers develop cancer. Similarly, some people who inherit mutations in the tumor-suppressor genes *p53* or *RB1* never develop cancer. Explain these observations.

■ **HINT:** *This problem asks you to consider the reasons why only some people develop cancer as a result of environmental factors or mutations in tumor-suppressor genes. The key to its solution is to consider the steps involved in the development of cancer and the number of abnormal functions in cancer cells. Also, consider how genetics may affect DNA repair functions.*

TABLE 19.2 Some Inherited Predispositions to Cancer

Tumor Predisposition Syndrome	Chromosome	Gene Affected
Early-onset familial breast cancer	17q	BRCA1
Familial adenomatous polyposis	5q	APC
Familial melanoma	9p	CDKN2
Gorlin syndrome	9q	PTCH1
Hereditary nonpolyposis colon cancer	2p	MSH2, 6
Li-Fraumeni syndrome	17p	p53
Multiple endocrine neoplasia, type 1	11q	MEN1
Multiple endocrine neoplasia, type 2	10q	RET
Neurofibromatosis, type 1	17q	NF1
Neurofibromatosis, type 2	22q	NF2
Retinoblastoma	13q	pRb
Von Hippel-Lindau syndrome	3p	VHL
Wilms tumor	11p	WT1

19.7 Viruses Contribute to Cancer in Both Humans and Animals

Viruses that cause cancer in animals have played a significant role in the search for knowledge about the genetics of human cancer. Most cancer-causing animal viruses are RNA viruses known as **retroviruses**. In humans, most of the known cancer viruses are DNA viruses.

To understand how retroviruses cause cancer in animals, it is necessary to know how these viruses replicate in cells. When a retrovirus infects a cell, its RNA genome is copied into DNA by the **reverse transcriptase** enzyme, which is brought into the cell with the infecting virus. The DNA copy then enters the nucleus of the infected cell, where it integrates at random into the host cell's genome. The integrated DNA copy

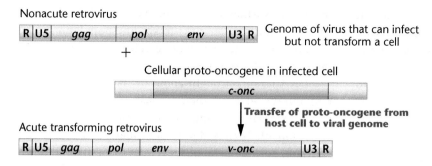

FIGURE 19–13 The genome of a typical retrovirus is shown at the top of the diagram. The genome contains repeats at the termini (R), the U5 and U3 regions that contain promoter and enhancer elements, and the three major genes that encode viral structural proteins (*gag* and *env*) and the viral reverse transcriptase (*pol*). RNA transcripts of the entire viral genome comprise the new viral genomes. If the retrovirus acquires all or part of a host-cell proto-oncogene (*c-onc*), this gene (now known as a *v-onc*) is expressed along with the viral genes, leading to overexpression or inappropriate expression of the *v-onc* gene. The *v-onc* gene may also acquire mutations that enhance its transforming ability.

of the retroviral RNA is called a **provirus**. The proviral DNA contains powerful enhancer and promoter elements in its U5 and U3 sequences at the ends of the provirus (**Figure 19–13**). The proviral promoter uses the host cell's transcription proteins, directing transcription of the viral genes (*gag, pol,* and *env*). The products of these genes are the proteins and RNA genomes that make up the new retroviral particles. Because the provirus is integrated into the host genome, it is replicated along with the host's DNA during the cell's normal cell cycle. A retrovirus may not kill a cell, but it may continue to use the cell as a factory to replicate more viruses that will then infect surrounding cells.

A retrovirus may cause cancer in three different ways. First, the proviral DNA may integrate by chance near one of the cell's normal proto-oncogenes. The strong promoters and enhancers in the provirus then stimulate high levels or inappropriate timing of transcription of the proto-oncogene, leading to stimulation of host-cell proliferation. Second, a retrovirus may pick up a copy of a host proto-oncogene and integrate it into its genome (Figure 19–13). The cellular proto-oncogene may be mutated during the process of transfer into the virus, or it may be expressed at abnormal levels because it is now under the control of viral promoters. Retroviruses that carry these cell-derived oncogenes can infect and transform normal cells into tumor cells, and are known as **acute transforming retroviruses**. Through the study of many acute transforming viruses of animals, scientists have identified dozens of proto-oncogenes. Third, a retrovirus may contain a normal viral gene whose product can either stimulate the cell cycle or act as a gene-expression regulator for both cellular and viral genes. As a result, expression of such a viral gene may lead to inappropriate cell growth or to abnormal expression of cancer-related cellular genes.

So far, no acute transforming retroviruses have been identified in humans; however, several human retroviruses, such as **human immunodeficiency virus (HIV)** and the **human T-cell leukemia virus (HTLV-1)**, are associated with human cancers. These retroviruses are thought to stimulate cancer development through the third mechanism, described in the previous paragraph.

DNA viruses also contribute to the development of human cancers in a variety of ways. Because viruses are composed solely of a nucleic acid genome surrounded by a protein coat, they must utilize the host cell's biosynthetic machinery in order to reproduce themselves. To access the host's DNA-synthesizing enzymes, viruses require the host cell to be in an actively growing state. Thus, many DNA viruses contain genes encoding products that stimulate the cell cycle. These products often interact with tumor-suppressor proteins, inactivating them. If the host cell survives the infection, it may lose control of the cell cycle and begin its journey to carcinogenesis.

It is thought that, worldwide, about 15 percent of human cancers are associated with viruses, making virus infection the second greatest risk factor for cancer, next to tobacco smoking. The most significant contributors to virus-induced cancers are listed in Table 19.3. Like other risk factors for cancer, including hereditary predisposition

TABLE 19.3 Human Viruses Associated with Cancers

Virus		Associated Cancers
DNA Viruses		
Epstein-Barr virus	EBV	Burkitt lymphoma, nasopharyngeal carcinoma, Hodgkin lymphoma
Hepatitis B virus	HBV	Hepatocellular carcinoma
Hepatitis C virus	HCV	Hepatocellular carcinoma, non-Hodgkin lymphoma
Human papilloma viruses 16, 18	HPV16, 18	Cervical cancer, anogenital cancers, oral cancers
Kaposi sarcoma-associated herpesvirus	KSHV	Kaposi sarcoma, primary effusion lymphoma
Retroviruses		
Human T-cell lymphotropic virus type 1	HTLV-1	Adult T-cell leukemia and lymphoma
Human immunodeficiency virus type-1	HIV-1	Immune suppression, leading to cancers caused by other viruses (KSHV, EBV, HPV)

to certain cancers, virus infection alone is not sufficient to trigger human cancers. Other factors, including DNA damage or the accumulation of mutations in one or more of a cell's oncogenes and tumor-suppressor genes, are required to move a cell down the multistep pathway to cancer.

19.8 Environmental Agents Contribute to Human Cancers

Any substance or event that damages DNA has the potential to be carcinogenic. Unrepaired or inaccurately repaired DNA introduces mutations, which, if they occur in proto-oncogenes or tumor-suppressor genes, can lead to abnormal regulation of the cell cycle or disruption of controls over apoptosis or metastasis.

Our environment, both natural and human-made, contains abundant carcinogens. These include chemicals, radiation, some viruses, and chronic infections. Perhaps the most significant carcinogen in our environment is tobacco smoke, which contains at least 60 chemicals that interact with DNA and cause mutations. Epidemiologists estimate that about 30 percent of human cancer deaths are associated with cigarette smoking. Smokers have a 20-fold increased risk of developing lung cancer, which kills more than one million people, worldwide, each year.

Diet is often implicated in the development of cancer. Consumption of red meat and animal fat is associated with some cancers, such as colon, prostate, and breast cancer. The mechanisms by which these substances may contribute to carcinogenesis may involve stimulation of cell division through hormones or creation of carcinogenic chemicals during cooking. Alcohol may cause inflammation of the liver and contribute to liver cancer.

Although most people perceive the human-made, industrial environment to be a highly significant contributor to cancer, it may account for only a small percentage of total cancers, and only in special situations. Some of the most mutagenic agents, and hence potentially the most carcinogenic, are natural substances and natural processes. For example, **aflatoxin**, a component of a mold that grows on peanuts and corn, is one of the most carcinogenic chemicals known. Most chemical carcinogens, such as **nitrosamines**, are components of synthetic substances and are found in some preserved meats; however, many are naturally occurring. For example, natural pesticides and antibiotics found in plants may be carcinogenic, and the human body itself creates alkylating agents in the acidic environment of the gut. Nevertheless, these observations do not diminish the serious cancer risks to specific populations who are exposed to human-made carcinogens such as synthetic pesticides or asbestos.

DNA lesions brought about by natural radiation (X rays, ultraviolet light), dietary substances, and substances in the external environment contribute the majority of environmentally caused mutations that lead to cancer. In addition, normal metabolism creates oxidative end products that can damage DNA, proteins, and lipids. It is estimated that the human body suffers about 10,000 damaging DNA lesions per day due to the actions of oxygen free radicals. DNA repair enzymes deal successfully with most of this damage; however, some damage may lead to permanent mutations. The process of DNA replication itself is mutagenic. Hence, substances such as growth factors or hormones that stimulate cell division are ultimately mutagenic and perhaps carcinogenic. Chronic inflammation due to infection also stimulates tissue repair and cell division, resulting in DNA lesions accumulating during replication. These mutations may persist, particularly if cell-cycle checkpoints are compromised due to mutations or inactivation of tumor-suppressor genes such as *p53* or *RB1*.

Both ultraviolet (UV) light and ionizing radiation (such as X rays and gamma rays) induce DNA damage. UV in sunlight is well accepted as an inducer of skin cancers. Ionizing radiation has clearly shown itself to be a carcinogen in studies of populations exposed to neutron and gamma radiation from atomic blasts such as those in Hiroshima and Nagasaki. Another significant environmental component, radon gas, may be responsible for about 50 percent of the ionizing radiation exposure of the U.S. population and could contribute to lung cancers in some populations.

NOW SOLVE THIS

19–4 Cancer can arise spontaneously, but can also be induced as a result of environmental factors such as sun exposure, infections, and tobacco smoking. If you were asked to help allocate resources to cancer research, what emphasis would you place on research to find cancer cures, compared to that placed on education about cancer prevention?

■ **HINT:** *This problem asks you to consider the outcomes of two different approaches to cancer research. The key to its solution is to think about the relative rates of environmentally induced and spontaneous cancers. (An interesting source of information on this topic is Ames, B. N. et al. 1995. The causes and prevention of cancer. Proc. Natl. Acad. Sci. USA 92: 5258–5265.)*

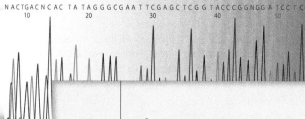

The Cancer Genome Anatomy Project (CGAP)

MasteringGenetics™ Visit the Study Area: Exploring Genomics

A research group headed by Dr. Victor Velculescu of Johns Hopkins University reported that breast and colon cancers contain about 11 gene mutations that may contribute to the cancer phenotype. The research group analyzed 13,023 of the 21,000 known genes in the human genome, comparing the DNA sequences from normal cells and cancer cells. Most of the mutations that were specific to cancer cells were not previously known to be associated with cancer.

Dr. Velculescu's study was one of the first in *The Cancer Genome Atlas* (TCGA) project, a $1.5 billion federal project designed to systematically scan the human genome to find genes that are mutated in many different cancers. In this exercise, we will explore aspects of Dr. Velculescu's

research by mining information available in the online database **Cancer Genome Anatomy Project (CGAP)**. The purpose of the CGAP is to understand the expression profiles of genes from normal, precancer, and cancer cells.

■ Exercise – Colon Cancer and the *TBX22* Gene

One gene that Dr. Velculescu's research group discovered to be mutated in colon cancers—*TBX22*—was not previously suspected to contribute to this cancer. What is *TBX22*, and how do you think a mutated *TBX22* gene would contribute to the development of colon cancer?

1. To begin your search for the answers, go to CGAP at http://cgap.nci.nih .gov/cgap.html.

2. Click the "Genes" button near the top of the page.

3. From the list of "Gene Tools" in the left-hand margin, select "Gene Finder."

4. Select "Homo sapiens" in the "Select organism" box, and type TBX22 in the "Enter a unique identifier" box. Submit the query.

5. Select "Gene Info" in the right-hand column of the table.

6. Explore the many sources of information about *TBX22* from various database links listed on this page.

Prepare a brief written or verbal report on what you learned during your explorations and which sources you used to reach your conclusions about *TBX22*.

CASE STUDY | I thought it was safe

A middle-aged woman taking the breast cancer drug Tamoxifen for ten years became concerned when she saw a news report with disturbing information. In some women, the drug made their cancer more aggressive and more likely to spread. Other women with breast cancer, the report stated, do not respond to Tamoxifen at all, and 30 to 40 percent of women who take the drug eventually become resistant to chemotherapy. The woman contacted her oncologist to ask some questions:

1. How can some people react one way to a cancer treatment and others react a different way?

2. Why do most cancers eventually become resistant to a specific chemotherapeutic drug?

3. Why does it seem that some drugs are thought to be safe one day and declared unsafe the next day?

Summary Points

MasteringGenetics™ For activities, animations, and review quizzes, go to the Study Area.

1. Cancer cells show two fundamental properties: abnormal cell proliferation and a propensity to spread and invade other parts of the body.
2. Cancers are clonal, meaning that all cells within a tumor originate from a single cell that contained a number of mutations.
3. The development of cancer is a multistep process, requiring mutations in several cancer-related genes.
4. Cancer cells contain gene mutations, chromosomal abnormalities, genomic instability, and abnormal patterns of chromatin modifications.

5. Cancer cells have defects in DNA damage repair, chromatin modifications, cell-cycle regulation, and programmed cell death.
6. Proto-oncogenes are normal genes that promote cell growth and division. When proto-oncogenes are mutated or misexpressed in cancer cells, they are known as oncogenes.
7. Tumor-suppressor genes normally regulate cell-cycle checkpoints and apoptosis. When tumor-suppressor genes are mutated or inactivated, cells cannot correct DNA damage. This leads to accumulations of mutations that may cause cancer.

8. The ability of cancer cells to metastasize requires defects in gene products that control a number of functions such as cell adhesion, proteolysis, and tissue invasion.

9. Inherited mutations in cancer-susceptibility genes are not sufficient to trigger cancer. Other somatic mutations in proto-oncogenes or tumor-suppressor genes are necessary for the development of hereditary cancers.

10. Tumor viruses contribute to cancers by introducing viral oncogenes, interfering with tumor-suppressor proteins, or altering expression of a cell's proto-oncogenes.

11. Environmental agents such as chemicals, radiation, viruses, and chronic infections contribute to the development of cancer. The most significant environmental factors that affect human cancers are tobacco smoke, chronic infections, diet, and natural radiation.

INSIGHTS AND SOLUTIONS

1. In disorders such as retinoblastoma, a mutation in one allele of the *RB1* gene can be inherited from the germ line, causing an autosomal dominant predisposition to the development of eye tumors. To develop tumors, a somatic mutation in the second copy of the *RB1* gene is necessary, indicating that the mutation itself acts as a recessive trait. Given that the first mutation can be inherited, in what ways can a second mutational event occur?

Solution: In considering how this second mutation arises, we must look at several types of mutational events, including changes in nucleotide sequence and events that involve whole chromosomes or chromosome parts. Retinoblastoma results when both copies of the *RB1* locus are lost or inactivated. With this in mind, you must first list the phenomena that can result in a mutational loss or the inactivation of a gene.

One way the second *RB1* mutation can occur is by a nucleotide alteration that converts the remaining normal *RB1* allele to a mutant form. This alteration can occur through a nucleotide substitution or through a frameshift mutation caused by the insertion or deletion of nucleotides during replication. A second mechanism involves the loss of the chromosome carrying the normal allele. This event would take place during mitosis, resulting in chromosome 13 monosomy and leaving the mutant copy of the gene as the only *RB1* allele. This mechanism does not necessarily involve loss of the entire chromosome; deletion of the long arm (*RB1* is on 13q) or an interstitial deletion involving the *RB1* locus and some surrounding material would have the same result. Alternatively, a chromosome aberration involving loss of the normal copy of the *RB1* gene might be followed by duplication of the chromosome carrying the mutant allele. Two copies of chromosome 13 would be restored to the cell, but the normal *RB1* allele would not be present. Finally, a recombination event followed by chromosome segregation could produce a homozygous combination of mutant *RB1* alleles.

2. Proto-oncogenes can be converted to oncogenes in a number of different ways. In some cases, the proto-oncogene itself becomes amplified up to hundreds of times in a cancer cell. An example is the *cyclin D1* gene, which is amplified in some cancers. In other cases, the proto-oncogene may be mutated in a limited number of specific ways, leading to alterations in the gene product's structure. The *ras* gene is an example of a proto-oncogene that becomes oncogenic after suffering point mutations in specific regions of the gene. Explain why these two proto-oncogenes (*cyclin D1* and *ras*) undergo such different alterations in order to convert them into oncogenes.

Solution: The first step in solving this question is to understand the normal functions of these proto-oncogenes and to think about how either amplification or mutation would affect each of these functions.

The cyclin D1 protein regulates progression of the cell cycle from G1 into S phase, by binding to CDK4 and activating this kinase. The cyclin D1/CDK4 complex phosphorylates a number of proteins including pRB, which in turn activate other proteins in a cascade that results in transcription of genes whose products are necessary for DNA replication in S phase. The simplest way to increase the activity of cyclin D1 would be to increase the number of cyclin D1 molecules available for binding to the cell's endogenous CDK4 molecules. This can be accomplished by several mechanisms, including amplification of the *cyclin D1* gene. In contrast, a point mutation in the *cyclin D1* gene would most likely interfere with the ability of the cyclin D1 protein to bind to CDK4; hence, mutations within the gene would probably repress cell-cycle progression rather than stimulate it.

The *ras* gene product is a signal transduction protein that operates as an on/off switch in response to external stimulation by growth factors. It does so by binding either GTP (the "on" state) or GDP (the "off" state). Oncogenic mutations in the *ras* gene occur in specific regions that alter the ability of the Ras protein to exchange GDP for GTP. Oncogenic Ras proteins are locked in the "on" conformation, bound to GTP. In this way, they constantly stimulate the cell to divide. An amplification of the *ras* gene would simply provide more molecules of normal Ras protein, which would still be capable of on/off regulation. Hence, simple amplification of *ras* would less likely be oncogenic.

Problems and Discussion Questions

MasteringGenetics™ Visit for instructor-assigned tutorials and problems.

HOW DO WE KNOW?

1. In this chapter, we focused on cancer as a genetic disease, with an emphasis on the relationship between cancer, the cell cycle, and DNA damage, as well as on the multiple steps that lead to cancer.

At the same time, we found many opportunities to consider the methods and reasoning by which much of this information was acquired. From the explanations given in the chapter,

(a) How do we know that malignant tumors arise from a single cell that contains mutations?

(b) How do we know that cancer development requires more than one mutation?

(c) How do we know that cancer cells contain defects in DNA repair?

CONCEPT QUESTION

2. Review the Chapter Concepts list on page 469. These concepts relate to the multiple ways in which genetic alterations lead to the development of cancers. The sixth concept states that epigenetic effects including DNA methylation and histone modifications contribute to the genetic alterations leading to cancer. Write a short essay describing how epigenetic changes in cancer cells contribute to the development of cancers.

3. Where are the major regulatory points in the cell cycle?

4. List the functions of kinases and cyclins, and describe how they interact to cause cells to move through the cell cycle.

5. (a) How does pRB function to keep cells at the G1 checkpoint? (b) How do cells get past the G1 checkpoint to move into S phase?

6. What is the difference between saying that cancer is inherited and saying that the predisposition to cancer is inherited?

7. As a genetic counselor, you are asked to assess the risk for a couple with a family history of retinoblastoma who are thinking about having children. Both the husband and wife are phenotypically normal, but the husband has a sister with familial retinoblastoma in both eyes. What is the probability that this couple will have a child with retinoblastoma? Are there any tests that you could recommend to help in this assessment?

8. What is apoptosis, and under what circumstances do cells undergo this process?

9. Define tumor-suppressor genes. Why is a mutated single copy of a tumor-suppressor gene expected to behave as a recessive gene?

10. A genetic variant of the retinoblastoma protein, called PSM-RB (phosphorylation site mutated RB), is not able to be phosphorylated by the action of CDK4/cyclin D1 complex. Explain why PSM-RB is said to have a constitutive growth-suppressing action on the cell cycle.

11. Part of the Ras protein is associated with the plasma membrane, and part extends into the cytoplasm. How does the Ras protein transmit a signal from outside the cell into the cytoplasm? What happens in cases where the *ras* gene is mutated?

12. If a cell suffers damage to its DNA while in S phase, how can this damage be repaired before the cell enters mitosis?

13. Distinguish between oncogenes and proto-oncogenes. In what ways can proto-oncogenes be converted to oncogenes?

14. Of the two classes of genes associated with cancer, tumor-suppressor genes and oncogenes, mutations in which group can be considered gain-of-function mutations? In which group are the loss-of-function mutations? Explain.

15. How do translocations such as the Philadelphia chromosome contribute to cancer?

16. Explain why many oncogenic viruses contain genes whose products interact with tumor-suppressor proteins.

17. DNA sequencing has provided data to indicate that cancer cells may contain tens of thousands of somatic mutations, only some of which confer a growth advantage to a cancer cell. How do scientists describe and categorize these recently discovered populations of mutations in cancer cells?

18. How do normal cells protect themselves from accumulating mutations in genes that could lead to cancer? How do cancer cells differ from normal cells in these processes?

19. Describe the difference between an acute transforming virus and a virus that does not cause tumors.

20. Epigenetics is a relatively new area of genetics with a focus on phenomena that affect gene expression but do not affect DNA sequence. Epigenetic effects are quasi-stable and may be passed to progeny somatic or germ-line cells. What are known causes of epigenetic effects, and how do they relate to cancer?

21. Radiotherapy (treatment with ionizing radiation) is one of the most effective current cancer treatments. It works by damaging DNA and other cellular components. In which ways could radiotherapy control or cure cancer, and why does radiotherapy often have significant side effects?

22. Genetic tests that detect mutations in the *BRCA1* and *BRCA2* oncogenes are widely available. These tests reveal a number of mutations in these genes—mutations that have been linked to familial breast cancer. Assume that a young woman in a suspected breast cancer family takes the *BRCA1* and *BRCA2* genetic tests and receives negative results. That is, she does not test positive for the mutant alleles of *BRCA1* or *BRCA2*. Can she consider herself free of risk for breast cancer?

23. Explain the apparent paradox that both hypermethylation and hypomethylation of DNA are often found in the same cancer cell.

24. As part of a cancer research project, you have discovered a gene that is mutated in many metastatic tumors. After determining the DNA sequence of this gene, you compare the sequence with those of other genes in the human genome sequence database. Your gene appears to code for an amino acid sequence that resembles sequences found in some serine proteases. Conjecture how your new gene might contribute to the development of highly invasive cancers.

25. Describe the steps by which the *p53* gene responds to DNA damage and/or cellular stress to promote cell-cycle arrest and apoptosis. Given that *p53* is a recessive gene and is not located on the X chromosome, why would people who inherit just one mutant copy of a recessive tumor-suppressor gene be at higher risk of developing cancer than those without the recessive gene?

Extra-Spicy Problems

MasteringGenetics™ Visit for instructor-assigned tutorials and problems.

26. Mutations in tumor-suppressor genes are associated with many types of cancers. In addition, epigenetic changes (such as DNA methylation) of tumor-suppressor genes are also associated with tumorigenesis (Otani et al., 2013. *Expert Rev Mol Diagn* 13: 445–455).

(a) How might hypermethylation of the *p53* gene promoter influence tumorigenesis?

(b) Knowing that tumors release free DNA into certain surrounding body fluids through necrosis and apoptosis (Kloten et al., 2013. *Breast Cancer Res*. 15(1): R4), outline an experimental protocol for using human blood as a biomarker for cancer and as a method for monitoring the progression of cancer in an individual.

27. Vanderbilt University Medical Center maintains a Web site (http://bioinfo.mc.vanderbilt.edu/TSGene/) that contains descriptions of tumor-suppressor genes, including 637 protein-coding genes and 79 noncoding segments of DNA. How can noncoding segments of DNA function or produce products that function as tumor suppressors?

28. A study by Bose and colleagues (1998. *Blood* 92: 3362–3367) and a previous study by Biernaux and others (1996. *Bone Marrow Transplant* 17: (Suppl. 3) S45–S47) showed that *BCR-ABL* fusion gene transcripts can be detected in 25 to 30 percent of healthy adults who do not develop chronic myelogenous leukemia (CML). Explain how these individuals can carry a fusion gene that is transcriptionally active and yet do not develop CML.

29. Those who inherit a mutant allele of the *RB1* gene are at risk for developing a bone cancer called osteosarcoma. You suspect that in these cases, osteosarcoma requires a mutation in the second *RB1* allele, and you have cultured some osteosarcoma cells and obtained a cDNA clone of a normal human *RB1* gene. A colleague sends you a research paper revealing that a strain of cancer-prone mice develop malignant tumors when injected with osteosarcoma cells, and you obtain these mice. Using these three resources, what experiments would you perform to determine (a) whether osteosarcoma cells carry two *RB1* mutations, (b) whether osteosarcoma cells produce any pRB protein, and (c) if the addition of a normal *RB1* gene will change the cancer-causing potential of osteosarcoma cells?

30. The table in this problem summarizes some of the data that have been collected on *BRCA1* mutations in families with a high incidence of both early-onset breast cancer and ovarian cancer.

Predisposing Mutations in *BRCA1*

Kindred	Codon	Nucleotide Change	Coding Effect	Frequency in Control Chromosomes
1901	24	−11 bp	Frameshift or splice	0/180
2082	1313	C → T	Gln → Stop	0/170
1910	1756	Extra C	Frameshift	0/162
2099	1775	T → G	Met → Arg	0/120
2035	NA[*]	?	Loss of transcript	NA*

Source: 1994. *Science* 266: 66–71. © AAAS.
[*]NA indicates not applicable, as the regulatory mutation is inferred, and the position has not been identified.

(a) Note the coding effect of the mutation found in kindred group 2082. This results from a single base-pair substitution. Draw the normal double-stranded DNA sequence for this codon (with the 5′ and 3′ ends labeled), and show the sequence of events that generated this mutation, assuming that it resulted from an uncorrected mismatch event during DNA replication.
(b) Examine the types of mutations that are listed in the table and determine if the *BRCA1* gene is likely to be a tumor-suppressor gene or an oncogene.

(c) Although the mutations listed in the table are clearly deleterious and cause breast cancer in women at very young ages, each of the kindred groups had at least one woman who carried the mutation but lived until age 80 without developing cancer. Name at least two different mechanisms (or variables) that could underlie variation in the expression of a mutant phenotype and propose an explanation for the incomplete penetrance of this mutation. How do these mechanisms or variables relate to this explanation?

31. The following table shows neutral polymorphisms found in control families (those with no increased frequency of breast and ovarian cancer).

Neutral Polymorphisms in *BRCA1*

Name	Codon Location	Base in Codon[†]	Frequency in Control Chromosomes[*]			
			A	C	G	T
PM1	317	2	152	0	10	0
PM6	878	2	0	55	0	100
PM7	1190	2	109	0	53	0
PM2	1443	3	0	115	0	58
PM3	1619	1	116	0	52	0

[*]The number of chromosomes with a particular base at the indicated polymorphic site (A, C, G, or T) is shown.
[†]Position 1, 2, or 3 of the codon.

Examine the data in the table and answer the following questions:
(a) What is meant by a neutral polymorphism?
(b) What is the significance of this table in the context of examining a family or population for *BRCA1* mutations that predispose an individual to cancer?
(c) Is the PM2 polymorphism likely to result in a neutral missense mutation or a silent mutation?
(d) Answer part (c) for the PM3 polymorphism.

32. Prostate cancer is a major cause of cancer-related deaths among men. Epigenetic changes that regulate gene expression are involved in both the initiation and progression of such cancers. Following is a table that lists the number of genes known to be hypermethylated in prostate cancer cells (modified from Long-Cheng, L. et al., 2005. *J. Natl. Cancer Inst.* 97: 103–115). For each category of genes, speculate on the mechanism(s) by which cancer initiation or progression might be influenced by hypermethylation.

DNA Hypermethylation of	Number of Known Genes
Hormonal response genes	5
Cell-cycle control genes	2
Tumor cell invasion genes	8
DNA damage repair genes	2
Signal transduction genes	4

```
||||||||||||||||||||||||  |  ||  |||   ||||||||||  ||||  ||||||||||  ||
TGGCTTTGGCCCTATCTTTTCTATGTCCAAGCTGTGCCCATCCAAAAAGTCCAAGA
```

Alignment comparing DNA sequence for the leptin gene from dogs (top) and humans (bottom). Vertical lines and shaded boxes indicate identical bases. *LEP* encodes a hormone that functions to suppress appetite. This type of analysis is a common application of bioinformatics and a good demonstration of comparative genomics.

```
ACCAAAACCCTCATCAAGACGATTGTCGCCAGGATCAATGACATTTCACACACGCA
||||||||||||||||||||||  ||||||  |||||||||||||||||||||||||||
ACCAAAACCCTCATCAAGACAATTGTCACCAGGATCAATGACATTTCACACACGCA

GTCCTCCAAACAGAGGGTCGCTGGTCTGGACTTCATTCCTGGGCTCCAACCAGT
||||||||||||||||   |||  |  |||  ||||||||||||||||||||||||  |  |
GTCCTCCAAACAGAAAGTCACCGGTTTGGACTTCATTCCTGGGCTCCACCCCAT

AGTTTGTCCAGGATGGACCAGACGTTGGCCATCTACCAACAGATCCTCAACAGTCT
|   ||  ||||  |||||||||||||  ||||   ||||||||||||||||||||  ||||  |
ACCTTATCCAAGATGGACCAGACACTGGCAGTCTACCAACAGATCCTCACCAGTAT

TCCAGAAATGTGGTCCAAATATCTAATGACCTGGAGAACCTCCGGGACCTTCTCCA
|||||||||  |||  ||||||||||||  ||  ||||||||||||||||||||||  |||||  ||
TCCAGAAACGTGATCCAAATATCCAACGACCTGGAGAACCTCCGGGATCTTCTTCA

CTGGCCTCCTCCAAGAGCTGCCCCTTGCCCCGGGCCAGGGGCCTGGAGACCTTTGA
|||||||  |||  |||||||||||  ||||||||  |||||||  ||||||||||||||||  ||
CTGGCCTTCTCTAAGAGCTGCCACTTGCCCTGGGCCAGTGGCCTGGAGACCTTGGA
```

Genomics, Bioinformatics, and Proteomics

CHAPTER CONCEPTS

- Genomics applies recombinant DNA, DNA sequencing methods, and bioinformatics to sequence, assemble, and analyze genomes.

- Disciplines in genomics encompass several areas of study, including structural and functional genomics, comparative genomics, and metagenomics, and have led to an "omics" revolution in modern biology.

- Bioinformatics merges information technology with biology and mathematics to store, share, compare, and analyze nucleic acid and protein sequence data.

- The Human Genome Project has greatly advanced our understanding of the organization, size, and function of the human genome.

- Ten years after completion of the Human Genome Project, a new era of genomics studies is providing deeper insights into the human genome.

- Comparative genomics analysis has revealed similarities and differences in genome size and organization.

- Metagenomics is the study of genomes from environmental samples and is valuable for identifying microbial genomes.

- Transcriptome analysis provides insight into patterns of gene expression and gene-regulatory activity of a genome.

- Proteomics focuses on the protein content of cells and on the structures, functions, and interactions of proteins.

- Systems biology approaches attempt to uncover complex interactions among genes, proteins, and other cellular components.

The term **genome**, meaning the complete set of DNA in a single cell of an organism, was coined at a time when geneticists began to turn from the study of individual genes to a focus on the larger picture. To begin to characterize all of the genes in an organism's genome, geneticists typically followed a two-part classical genetics approach: (1) identify spontaneous mutations or collect mutants produced by chemical or physical agents, and (2) generate linkage maps using mutant strains as discussed earlier in the text (see Chapter 5).

These effective strategies were used to identify genes in many of the classic model organisms discussed in this book, such as *Drosophila*, maize, mice, bacteria, and yeast, as well as in viruses, such as bacteriophages. These approaches formed the technical backbone of genetic analysis and still have their applications today; however, they have several major limitations. For instance, conventional mutational analysis and linkage requires that at least one mutation for each gene be available before all the genes in a genome can be identified. Obtaining mutants and carrying out linkage studies are very time consuming processes, and when mutations are lethal or have no clear phenotype, they can be difficult or impossible to map. In addition, although researchers can generate mutations in animal models in a laboratory, they cannot do the same with humans; thus, identifying human genes by mutational analysis is largely limited to linkage mapping of inherited or spontaneously acquired mutant genes with clear phenotypes. Another fundamental limitation of these approaches is that, although they can be used for identifying and characterizing gene loci, they do not lead to a determination of DNA sequence. Nor are they particularly useful for studying noncoding areas of the genome such as DNA regulatory sequences.

In 1977, as recombinant DNA-based techniques were developed, Fred Sanger and colleagues began the field of **genomics**, the study of genomes, by using a newly developed method of DNA sequencing to sequence the 5400-nucleotide genome of the virus ϕX174. Other viral genomes were sequenced in short order, but even this technology was slow and labor-intensive, limiting its use to small genomes. In the 1980s, geneticists interested in mapping human genes began using recombinant DNA technology to map DNA sequences to specific chromosomes. Initially, most of these sequences were not actually full-length genes but marker sequences such as restriction fragment length polymorphisms (RFLPs). Once assigned to chromosomes, these markers were used in pedigree analysis to establish linkage between the markers and disease phenotypes for genetic disorders. This approach, called **positional cloning**, was used to map, isolate, clone, and sequence the genes for cystic fibrosis, neurofibromatosis, and dozens of other disorders. Positional cloning identified one gene at a time, and yet by the mid-1980s, it had been used to assign more than 3500 genes and markers to human chromosomes.

At this time it was estimated that there were approximately 100,000 genes in the human genome, and it was readily apparent that mapping by using existing methods would be a laborious, time-consuming, and nearly insurmountable task. As you will soon learn, this estimate for gene number turned out to be inaccurate. During the next three decades, the development of computer-automated DNA sequencing methods made it possible to consider sequencing the larger and more complex genomes of eukaryotes, including the 3.1 billion nucleotides that comprise the human genome. The development of recombinant DNA technologies coupled with the advent of new, powerful DNA sequencing methods and bioinformatics is responsible for rapidly accelerating the field of genomics.

Genomic technologies have developed so quickly that modern biological research is currently experiencing a genomics revolution. In this chapter, we will examine basic technologies used in genomics and then discuss examples of genome data and different disciplines of genomics. We will also discuss *transcriptome analysis,* the study of genes expressed in a cell or tissue (the "transcriptome"), and *proteomics,* the study of proteins present in a cell or tissue.

The chapter concludes with a brief look at *systems biology,* a new area of contemporary biology that incorporates and integrates genomics, transcriptome analysis, and proteomics data. Later in the text (see Chapter 22) we will continue our discussion of genomics by describing many modern applications of recombinant DNA and genomic technologies. Please note that some of the topics discussed in this chapter are explored in greater depth in later chapters (see Special Topic Chapter 1—Epigenetics, Special Topic Chapter 2—Emerging Roles of RNA, and Special Topic Chapter 4—Genomics and Personalized Medicine).

21.1 Whole-Genome Sequencing Is a Widely Used Method for Sequencing and Assembling Entire Genomes

As discussed earlier in the text (see Chapter 20), recombinant DNA technology made it possible to generate DNA libraries that could be used to identify, clone, and sequence specific genes of interest. But a primary limitation of library screening and even of most polymerase chain reaction (PCR) approaches is that they typically can identify only relatively small numbers of genes at a time. Genomics allows the sequencing of entire genomes. **Structural genomics** focuses on sequencing genomes and analyzing nucleotide sequences to identify genes and other important sequences such as gene-regulatory regions.

The most widely used strategy for sequencing and assembling an entire genome involves variations of a method called **whole-genome sequencing (WGS)**, also known as **shotgun cloning** or shotgun sequencing. In simple terms, this technique is analogous to you and a friend taking your respective copies of this genetics textbook and randomly ripping the pages into strips about 5 to 7 inches long. Each chapter represents a chromosome, and all of the letters in the entire book are the "genome." Then you and your friend would go through the painstaking task of comparing the pieces of paper to find places that match, overlapping sentences—areas where there are similar sentences on different pieces of paper. Eventually, in theory, many of the strips containing matching sentences would overlap in ways that you could use to reconstruct the pages and assemble the order of the entire text.

Figure 21–1 shows a basic overview of WGS. First, an entire chromosome is cut into short, overlapping fragments, either by mechanically shearing the DNA in various ways (such as excessive heat treatment or sonication in which sonic energy is used to break DNA) or by using restriction enzymes to cleave the DNA at different locations. For

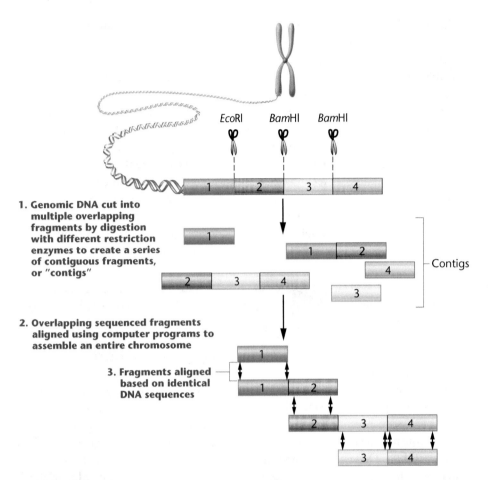

1. **Genomic DNA cut into multiple overlapping fragments by digestion with different restriction enzymes to create a series of contiguous fragments, or "contigs"**

Contigs

2. **Overlapping sequenced fragments aligned using computer programs to assemble an entire chromosome**

3. **Fragments aligned based on identical DNA sequences**

FIGURE 21–1 An overview of whole-genome sequencing (WGS) and assembly. This approach shows one strategy that involves using restriction enzymes to digest genomic DNA into contigs, which are then sequenced and aligned using bioinformatics to identify overlapping fragments based on sequence identity. Notice that *Eco*RI digestion of the portion of DNA depicted here produces two fragments (contigs 1, 2–4), whereas digestion with *Bam*HI produces three fragments (contigs 1–2, 3, 4).

use of algorithm-based software programs for creating a DNA-sequence **alignment**, in which similar sequences of bases, such as contigs, are lined up for comparison. Alignment identifies overlapping sequences, allowing scientists to reconstruct their order in a chromosome. **Figure 21–2** shows an example of contig alignment and assembly for a portion of human chromosome 2. For simplicity, this figure shows relatively short sequences for each contig, which in actuality would be much longer. The figure is also simplified in that, in actual alignments, assembled sequences do not always overlap only at their ends.

The whole-genome shotgun sequencing method was developed by J. Craig Venter and colleagues at The Institute for Genome Research (TIGR). In 1995, TIGR scientists used this approach to sequence the 1.83-million-bp genome of the bacterium *Haemophilus influenzae*. This was the first completed genome sequence from a free-living organism, and it demonstrated "proof of concept" that shotgun sequencing could be used to sequence an entire genome. Even after the genome for *H. influenzae* was sequenced, many scientists were skeptical that a shotgun approach would work on the larger genomes of eukaryotes. But improvement to shotgun approaches using next-generation sequencing technologies are now the predominant methods for sequencing genomes from nearly all species, including humans.

simplicity, here we present a basic example of DNA shearing using restriction enzymes. Increasingly, nonenzymatic approaches for shearing DNA are being used. Different restriction enzymes can be used so that chromosomes are cut at different sites; or sometimes, *partial digests* of DNA using the same restriction enzyme are used. With partial digests, DNA is incubated with restriction enzymes for only a short period of time, so that not every site in a particular sequence is cut to completion by an individual enzyme. Restriction digests of whole chromosomes generate thousands to millions of overlapping DNA fragments. For example, a 6-bp cutter such as *Eco*RI creates about 700,000 fragments when used to digest the human genome! Because these overlapping fragments are adjoining segments that collectively form one continuous DNA molecule within a chromosome, they are called **contiguous fragments**, or "**contigs**."

In the next section, we will discuss the importance of bioinformatics to genomics. One of the earliest bioinformatics applications to be developed for genomic purposes was the

High-Throughput Sequencing and Its Impact on Genomics

Cutting a genome into contigs is not particularly difficult; however, a primary hurdle that had to be overcome to advance whole-genome sequencing was the question of how to sequence millions or billions of base pairs in a timely and cost-effective way. This was a major challenge for scientists working on the Human Genome Project (Section 21.4). The Sanger sequencing method discussed earlier in the text (see Chapter 20), was the predominant sequencing technique for a long time. However, a major limitation

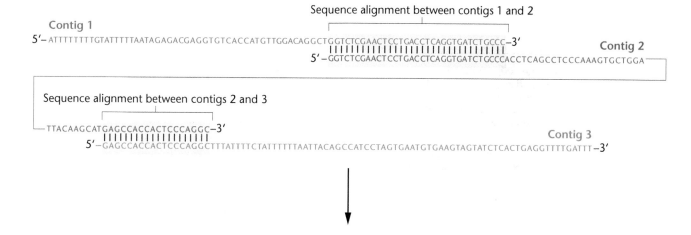

Contig 1

Sequence alignment between contigs 1 and 2

5'– ATTTTTTTTTGTATTTTTAATAGAGACGAGGTGTCACCATGTTGGACAGGCTGGTCTCGAACTCCTGACCTCAGGTGATCTGCCC–3'

Contig 2

5'–GGTCTCGAACTCCTGACCTCAGGTGATCTGCCCACCTCAGCCTCCCAAAGTGCTGGA

Sequence alignment between contigs 2 and 3

TTACAAGCATGAGCCACCACTCCCAGGC–3'

Contig 3

5'–GAGCCACCACTCCCAGGCTTTATTTTCTATTTTTTAATTACAGCCATCCTAGTGAATGTGAAGTAGTATCTCACTGAGGTTTTGATTT–3'

Assembled sequence of a partial segment of chromosome 2 based on alignment of three contigs

5'– ATTTTTTTTTGTATTTTTAATAGAGACGAGGTGTCACCATGTTGGACAGGCTGGTCTCGAACTCCTGACCTCAGGTGATCTGCCCACCTCAGCCTCCCAAAGTGCTGGA
TTACAAGCATGAGCCACCACTCCCAGGCTTTATTTTCTATTTTTTAATTACAGCCATCCTAGTGAATGTGAAGTAGTATCTCACTGAGGTTTTGATTT–3'

FIGURE 21–2 DNA-sequence alignment of contigs on human chromosome 2. Single-stranded DNA for three different contigs from human chromosome 2 is shown in blue, red, or green. The actual sequence from chromosome 2 is shown, but in reality, contig alignment involves fragments that are several thousand bases in length. Alignment of the three contigs allows a portion of chromosome 2 to be assembled. Alignment of all contigs for a particular chromosome would result in assembly of a completely sequenced chromosome.

of this technique was that even the best sequencing gels would typically yield only several hundred base pairs in each run and relatively few runs could be completed in a day. As a result, the overall production of sequence data was quite slow compared with modern techniques. Obviously, it would be very time consuming to manually sequence an entire genome by the Sanger method. The major technological breakthrough that made genomics possible was the development of computer-automated sequencers.

Many of the early computer-automated sequencers, designed for so-called **high-throughput sequencing**, could process millions of base pairs in a day. These sequencers contained multiple capillary gels that are several feet long. Some ran as many as 96 capillary gels at a time, each producing around 900 bases of sequence. Because these sequencers were computer automated, they could work around the clock, generating over 2 million bases of sequence in a day. In the past 15 years, high-throughput sequencing has increased the productivity of DNA-sequencing technology over 500-fold. The total number of bases that could be sequenced in a single reaction was doubling about every 24 months. At the same time, this increase in efficiency brought about a dramatic decrease in cost, from about $1.00 to less than $0.001 per base pair. As we will discuss in Section 21.4, without question the development of high-throughput sequencing was essential for the Human Genome Project. And as you know from earlier in the text (see Chapter 20), next- and third-generation sequencers now enable genome scientists to produce sequence nearly 50,000 times faster than sequencers in 2000 with greater output, improved accuracy, and reduced cost.

The Clone-by-Clone Approach

Prior to the widespread use of whole-genome sequencing approaches, genomes were being assembled using a **clone-by-clone** approach, also called **map-based cloning** (Figure 21–3). Initial progress on the Human Genome Project was based on this methodology, in which individual DNA fragments from restriction digests of chromosomes are aligned to create the restriction maps of a chromosome. These restriction fragments are then ligated into vectors such as bacterial artificial chromosomes (BACs) or yeast artificial chromosomes (YACs) to create libraries of contigs. Recall from earlier in the text (see Chapter 20) that BACs and YACs are good cloning vectors for replicating large fragments of DNA.

Prior to the development of high-throughput sequencing approaches, DNA fragments in BACs and YACs would often be further digested into smaller, more easily manipulated pieces that were then subcloned into cosmids or plasmids so that they could be sequenced in their entirety (Figure 21–3). After each sequenced fragment was analyzed for alignment overlaps, a chromosome could be assembled. The bioinformatics approaches we will discuss in the next section would then be used to identify possible protein-coding genes and assign them a location on the chromosome. For example, Figure 21–3 shows the use of map-based cloning to sequence part of chromosome 11, including part of the human β-globin gene.

Compared to whole-genome sequencing, the clone-by-clone approach is cumbersome and time consuming because of the time required to clone DNA fragments into different vectors, transform bacteria or yeast, select

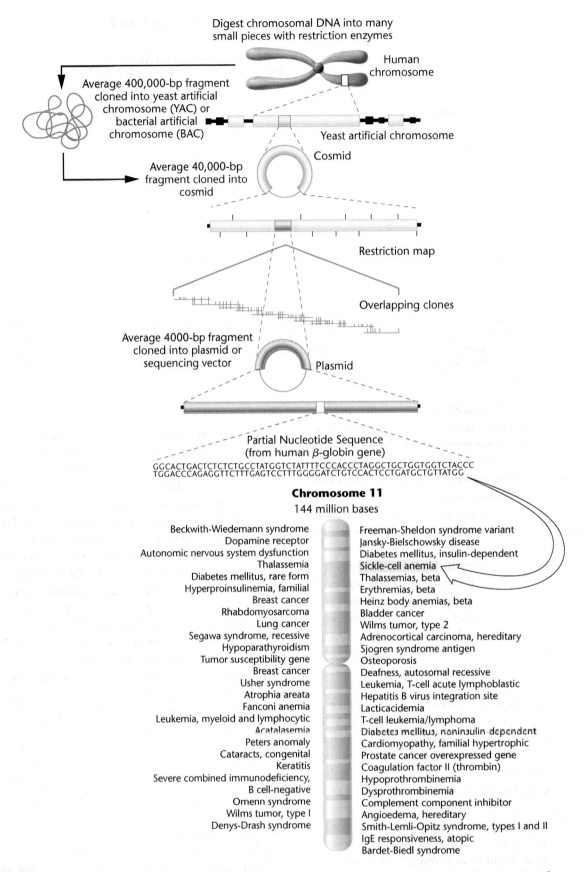

Digest chromosomal DNA into many
small pieces with restriction enzymes

Human
chromosome

Average 400,000-bp fragment
cloned into yeast artificial
chromosome (YAC) or
bacterial artificial
chromosome (BAC)

Yeast artificial chromosome

Cosmid

Average 40,000-bp
fragment cloned into
cosmid

Restriction map

Overlapping clones

Average 4000-bp fragment
cloned into plasmid or
sequencing vector

Plasmid

Partial Nucleotide Sequence
(from human β-globin gene)

GGCACTGACTCTCTCTGCCTATGGTCTATTTTCCCACCCTAGGCTGCTGGTGGTCTACCC
TGGACCCAGAGGTTCTTTGAGTCCTTTGGGGATCTGTCCACTCCTGATGCTGTTATGG

Chromosome 11
144 million bases

Beckwith-Wiedemann syndrome	Freeman-Sheldon syndrome variant
Dopamine receptor	Jansky-Bielschowsky disease
Autonomic nervous system dysfunction	Diabetes mellitus, insulin-dependent
Thalassemia	Sickle-cell anemia
Diabetes mellitus, rare form	Thalassemias, beta
Hyperproinsulinemia, familial	Erythremias, beta
Breast cancer	Heinz body anemias, beta
Rhabdomyosarcoma	Bladder cancer
Lung cancer	Wilms tumor, type 2
Segawa syndrome, recessive	Adrenocortical carcinoma, hereditary
Hypoparathyroidism	Sjogren syndrome antigen
Tumor susceptibility gene	Osteoporosis
Breast cancer	Deafness, autosomal recessive
Usher syndrome	Leukemia, T-cell acute lymphoblastic
Atrophia areata	Hepatitis B virus integration site
Fanconi anemia	Lacticacidemia
Leukemia, myeloid and lymphocytic	T-cell leukemia/lymphoma
Acatalasemia	Diabetes mellitus, noninsulin dependent
Peters anomaly	Cardiomyopathy, familial hypertrophic
Cataracts, congenital	Prostate cancer overexpressed gene
Keratitis	Coagulation factor II (thrombin)
Severe combined immunodeficiency,	Hypoprothrombinemia
B cell-negative	Dysprothrombinemia
Omenn syndrome	Complement component inhibitor
Wilms tumor, type I	Angioedema, hereditary
Denys-Drash syndrome	Smith-Lemli-Opitz syndrome, types I and II
	IgE responsiveness, atopic
	Bardet-Biedl syndrome

FIGURE 21–3 A clone-by-clone, or map-based, approach to genome sequencing involves cloning overlapping DNA fragments (contigs) into vectors. Different vectors, such as BACs, YACs, cosmids, and plasmids, are used depending on the size of each DNA fragment being analyzed. Overlapping clones are then sequenced and aligned to assemble an entire chromosome. Depicted here is a partial map of genes on chromosome 21 that are involved in human genetic disease conditions.

individual clones from the library for sequencing, and then carry out sequence analysis and assembly on relatively short sequences. Essentially, the clone-by-clone approach is the organized sequencing of contigs from a restriction map instead of random sequencing and assembly. As whole-genome sequencing approaches have become a routine method for assembling genomes, map-based cloning approaches are rarely used, and only then to resolve the problems encountered during whole-genome sequencing. For example, highly repetitive sequences in a chromosome may be difficult to align correctly in order to identify overlaps because with such sequences one cannot know for sure whether portions that are nearly identical are overlapping fragments or belong to different parts of a highly repetitive region. Frequently, there are also gaps between aligned contigs. In the textbook-ripping analogy, after you compare all your pieces of paper, you may be left with some very small ones that contain too few words to be matched with certainty to any others and with some pieces for which you just could not find matches. In these instances, a clone-by-clone approach may enable you to assemble the necessary contigs and complete the chromosome.

Draft Sequences and Checking for Errors

It is common for a draft sequence of a genome to be announced before a final sequence is eventually released. Draft sequences often contain gaps in areas that, for any number of reasons, may have been difficult to analyze. The decision to designate a sequence as "final" is dictated by the amount of error genome scientists are willing to accept as a cutoff.

Chromosome segments are typically sequenced more than once to ensure a high level of accuracy. The assembly of a final genomic sequence from multiple sequencing runs is known as **compiling**. One way to compile and error check is to sequence complementary strands of a DNA molecule separately and then use base-pairing rules to check for errors. Researchers using the shotgun method on the genome of the bacterium *Pseudomonas aeruginosa* sequenced the 6.3 million nucleotides seven times to ensure that the final sequence would be accurate. Yet even with this level of redundancy, the assembler software recognized 1604 regions that required further clarification. These regions were then reanalyzed and re-sequenced. Finally, relevant parts of the shotgun sequence were compared with the sequences of two widely separated genomic regions obtained by conventional cloning. The 81,843 nucleotides cloned and sequenced by the clone-by-clone method were in perfect agreement with the sequence obtained by the shotgun method. This level of care in checking for accuracy is not unusual; similar precautions are taken in almost every genome project.

Once compiled, a genome is analyzed to identify gene sequences, regulatory elements, and other features that reveal important information. In the next section we discuss the central role of bioinformatics in this process.

21.2 DNA Sequence Analysis Relies on Bioinformatics Applications and Genome Databases

Genomics necessitated the rapid development of **bioinformatics**, the use of computer hardware and software and mathematics applications to organize, share, and analyze data related to gene structure, gene sequence and expression, and protein structure and function. However, even before whole-genome sequencing projects had been initiated, a large amount of sequence information from a range of different organisms was accumulating as a result of gene cloning by recombinant DNA techniques. Scientists around the world needed databases that could be used to store, share, and obtain the maximum amount of information from protein and DNA sequences. Thus, bioinformatics software was already being used to compare and analyze DNA sequences and to create private and public databases. Once genomics emerged as a new approach for analyzing DNA, however, bioinformatics became even more important than before. Today, it is a dynamic area of biological research, providing new career opportunities for anyone interested in merging an understanding of biological data with information technology, mathematics, and statistical analysis.

Among the most common applications of bioinformatics are to compare DNA sequences, as in contig alignment; to identify genes in a genomic DNA sequence; to find gene-regulatory regions, such as promoters and enhancers; to identify structural sequences, such as telomeric sequences, in chromosomes; to predict the amino acid sequence of a putative polypeptide encoded by a cloned gene sequence; to analyze protein structure and predict protein functions on the basis of identified domains and motifs; and to deduce evolutionary relationships between genes and organisms on the basis of sequence information.

High-throughput DNA sequencing techniques were developed nearly simultaneously with the expansion of the Internet. As genome data accumulated, many DNA-sequence databases became freely available online. Databases are essential for archiving and sharing data with other researchers and with the public. One of the largest genomic databases, called **GenBank**, is maintained by the National Center for Biotechnology Information (NCBI) in Washington, D.C., and is the largest publicly available database of DNA sequences. GenBank shares and acquires data from databases in Japan and Europe; it contains more than 150 billion bases of sequence data from over 100,000 species; and it doubles in size roughly every 14–18 months! The Human Genome Nomenclature Committee, supported by the NIH, establishes rules for assigning names and symbols to newly cloned human genes. As sequences are identified and genes are named, each sequence deposited into Gen-Bank is provided with an **accession number** that scientists can use to access and retrieve that sequence for analysis.

The NCBI is an invaluable source of public access databases and bioinformatics tools for analyzing genome data. You have already been introduced to NCBI and GenBank through several Exploring Genomics exercises. In Exploring Genomics for this chapter, you will use NCBI and GenBank to compare and align contigs in order to assemble a chromosome segment.

Annotation to Identify Gene Sequences

One of the fundamental challenges of genomics is that, although genome projects generate tremendous amounts of DNA sequence information, these data are of little use until they have been analyzed and interpreted. Genome projects accumulate nucleotide sequences, and then scientists have to make sense of those sequences. Thus, after a genome has been sequenced and compiled, scientists are faced with the task of identifying gene-regulatory sequences and other sequences of interest in the genome so that gene maps can be developed. This process, called **annotation**, relies heavily on bioinformatics, and a wealth of different software tools are available to carry it out.

One initial approach to annotating a sequence is to compare the newly sequenced genomic DNA to the known sequences already stored in various databases. The NCBI provides access to **BLAST (Basic Local Alignment Search Tool)**, a very popular software application for searching through banks of DNA and protein sequence data. Using BLAST, we can compare a segment of genomic DNA to sequences throughout major databases such as Gen-Bank to identify portions that align with or are the same as existing sequences. **Figure 21–4** shows a representative example of a sequence alignment based on a BLAST search. Here a 280-bp chromosome 12 contig from the rat was used to search a mouse database to determine whether a sequence in the rat contig matched a known gene in mice. Notice that the rat contig (the query sequence in the

ref | NT_039455.6 | Mm8_39495_36
Mus musculus chromosome 8 genomic contig, strain C57BL/6J
Features in this part of subject sequence: insulin receptor
Score = 418 bits (226), Expect = 2e-114
Identities = 262/280 (93%), Gaps = 0/280 (0%)

```
Query   1        CAGGCCATCCCGAAAGCGAAGATCCCTTGAAGAGGTGGGCAATGTGACAGCCACTACACC   60
                 |||||||||||||||||||||||||||||||||||||||| |||||||||||| ||||
Sbjct   174891   CAGGCCATCCCGAAAGCGAAGATCCCTTGAAGAGGTGGGGAATGTGACAGCCACCACACT   174832

Query   61       CACACTTCCAGATTTTCCCAACATCTCCTCCACCATCGCGCCCACAAGCCACGAAGAGCA   120
                 ||||||||||||||| ||||||  ||||||| ||||| | |||||||||| || || |||||
Sbjct   174831   CACACTTCCAGATTTCCCCAACGTCTCCTCTACCATTGTGCCCACAAGTCAGGAGGAGCA   174772

Query   121      CAGACCATTTGAGAAAGTAGTAAACAAGGAGTCACTTGTCATCTCTGGCCTGAGACACTT   180
                 |||| |||||||||||||| || |||||||||||||||||||||||||||||||||||||
Sbjct   174771   CAGGCCATTTGAGAAAGTGGTGAACAAGGAGTCACTTGTCATCTCTGGCCTGAGACACTT   174712

Query   181      CACTGGGTACCGCATTGAGCTGCAGGCATGCAATCAGGACTCCCCAGAAGAGAGGTGCAG   240
                 |||||||||||||||||||||||||||||||||||| || ||||||| |||||||||||||
Sbjct   174711   CACTGGGTACCGCATTGAGCTGCAGGCATGCAATCAAGATTCCCCAGATGAGAGGTGCAG   174652

Query   241      CGTGGCTGCCTACGTCAGTGCCCGGACCATGCCTGAAGGT   280
                 ||||||||||| |||||||||||||||||||||||||| |||
Sbjct   174651   TGTGGCTGCCTACGTCAGTGCCCGGACCATGCCTGAAGGT   174612
```

FIGURE 21–4 BLAST results showing a 280-base sequence of a chromosome 12 contig from rats (*Rattus norvegicus*, the "query") aligned with a portion of chromosome 8 from mice (*Mus musculus*, the "subject") that contains a partial sequence for the insulin receptor gene. Vertical lines indicate exact matches. The rat contig sequence was used as a query sequence to search a mouse database in GenBank. Notice that the two sequences show 93 percent identity, strong evidence that this rat contig sequence contains a gene for the insulin receptor.

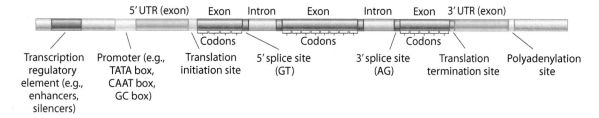

FIGURE 21–5 Characteristics of a protein-coding gene that can be used during annotation to identify a gene in an unknown sequence of genomic DNA. Most eukaryotic genes are organized into coding segments (exons) and noncoding segments (introns). When annotating a genome sequence to determine whether it contains a gene, it is necessary to distinguish between introns and exons, gene-regulatory sequences, such as promoters and enhancers, untranslated regions (UTRs), and gene termination sequences.

BLAST search) aligned with base pairs 174,612 to 174,891 of mouse chromosome 8. The accession number for the mouse chromosome sequence, NT_039455.6, is indicated at the top of the figure. BLAST searches calculate a **similarity score**—also called the **identity** value—determined by the sum of identical matches between aligned sequences divided by the total number of bases aligned. Gaps, indicating missing bases in the two sequences, are usually ignored in calculating similarity scores. The aligned rat and mouse sequences were 93 percent similar and showed no gaps in the alignment. Notice that the BLAST report also provides an "Expect" value, or **E-value**, based on the number of matching sequences in the database that would be expected by chance. E-values take into account the length of the query sequence. By chance, shorter sequences have a much greater likelihood of being present in the database than longer sequences. The lower the E-value (the closer it is to 0), the higher the significance of the match. Significant alignments, indicating that DNA sequences are significantly similar, have E-values less than 1.0.

Because this mouse sequence on chromosome 8 is known to contain an insulin receptor gene (encoding a protein that binds the hormone insulin), it is highly likely that the rat contig sequence also contains an insulin receptor gene. We will return to the topic of similarity in Sections 21.3 and 21.6, where we consider how similarity between gene sequences can be used to infer function and to identify evolutionarily related genes through comparative genomics.

Hallmark Characteristics of a Gene Sequence Can Be Recognized during Annotation

A major limitation of this approach to annotation is that it only works if similar gene sequences are already in a database. Fortunately, it is not the only way to identify genes. Whether the genome under study is from a eukaryote or a prokaryote, several hallmark characteristics of genes can be searched for using bioinformatics software (**Figure 21–5**). We discussed many of these characteristics of a

"typical" gene earlier in the text (see Chapters 13 and 17). For instance, gene-regulatory sequences found upstream of genes are marked by identifiable sequences such as promoters, enhancers, and silencers. Recall from earlier in the text (see Chapter 17) that TATA box, GC box, and CAAT box sequences are often present in the promoter region of eukaryotic genes. Recall also that splice sites between **exons** and **introns** contain a predictable sequence (most introns begin with CT and end with AG) and such splice-site sequences are important for determining intron and exon boundaries. Interestingly, current estimates indicate that only 6 percent of human genes are transcribed from a single, linear stretch of DNA that does not contain any introns.

Downstream elements, such as termination sequences and well-defined sequences at the end of a gene, where a polyadenylation sequence signals the addition of a poly-A tail to the 3′ end of a mRNA transcript, are also important for annotation (Figure 21–5). Annotation can sometimes be a little bit easier for prokaryotic genes than for eukaryotic genes because there are no introns in prokaryotic genes. Gene-prediction programs are used to annotate sequences. These programs incorporate search elements for many of the criteria mentioned above and have become invaluable applications of bioinformatics.

Yet even with bioinformatics, identifying a gene in a particular sequence of DNA is not always straightforward, particularly when one is studying genes that do not code for proteins. In fact, a reasonable question whenever one sequences a genome is "where are the genes?" In other words, how does one know what sequences of a genome are genes and which sequences are not genes or parts of a gene? Consider the sequence presented in **Figure 21–6(a)**, which shows a portion of the human genome. From a casual inspection, it is not clear whether this sequence contains any genes and, if so, how many. Analysis of the sequence, however, reveals identifiable features that provide clues to the presence of a protein-coding gene. In addition, protein-coding genes contain one or more **open reading frames (ORFs)**, sequences of triplet nucleotides

(a)

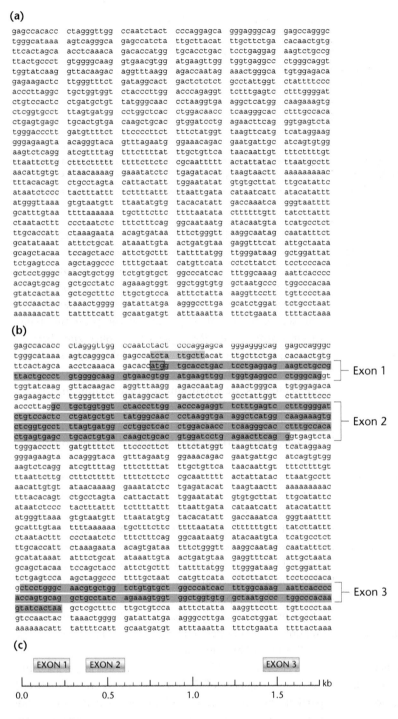

(b)

(c)

FIGURE 21–6 Annotation of a DNA sequence containing part of the human β-globin gene. By convention, the sequence is presented in groups of ten nucleotides, although in reality the sequence is continuous. (a) The location of genes, if any, in this sequence is not readily apparent from a cursory glance. (b) The analyzed sequence, showing the location of an upstream regulatory sequence (green). The red box indicates a start triplet representing a start codon in mRNA. Open reading frames for three exons of the human β-globin gene are shown in blue. (c) Diagrammatic representation of three exons for the human β-globin gene encoded by the sequence shown in (a) and (b).

start (initiation) triplet; however, ORFs can be used to identify a gene even when a promoter sequence is not apparent. Software programs can then analyze the ORFs three nucleotides at a time. The discovery of an ORF starting with an ATG followed at some distance by a termination sequence is usually a good indication that the coding region of a gene has been identified.

The way genes are organized in eukaryotic genomes (including the human genome) makes direct searching for ORFs more difficult in them than in prokaryotic genomes. First, many eukaryotic genes have introns. As a result, many, if not most, eukaryotic genes are not organized as continuous ORFs; instead, the gene sequences consist of ORFs (exons) interspersed with introns. Second, genes in humans and other eukaryotes are often widely spaced, increasing the chances of finding false ORFs in the regions between gene clusters.

Annotation of the sequence shown in Figure 21–6(a) reveals several identifiable indicators that the sequence contains a protein-coding gene: it includes a promoter sequence, an initiation codon, and three *exons* [**Figure 21–6(b)**]. The two unshaded regions between the exons represent introns that would be spliced out following transcription when the mRNA is processed [Figure 21–6(b) and (c)]. Using this sequence as the query in a search of genomic databases would reveal that it is the sequence of a single gene, the human β-globin gene.

Software designed for ORF analysis of eukaryotic genomes is highly valuable. Often such programs are used to make computational predictions of all ORFs (the ORFeome!) in a sequenced genome as a way to estimate the number of potential protein-coding genes in a genome. In addition to the features already mentioned, such software can be used to "translate" ORFs into possible polypeptide

that, after transcription and mRNA splicing, are translated into the amino acid sequence of a protein. ORFs typically begin with an initiation sequence, usually ATG, which transcribes into the AUG start codon of an mRNA molecule, and end with a termination sequence, TAA, TAG, or TGA, which corresponds to the stop codons of UAA, UAG, and UGA in mRNA. Genetic information is encoded in groups of three nucleotides (triplets), but it is not always clear whether to begin the analysis of a sequence at the first nucleotide, the second, or the third. Typically, the sequence adjacent to a promoter is examined for a sequences as a way to predict the polypeptide encoded by a gene. Shown in **Figure 21–7** is a partial sequence for the first exon of the human tubulin alpha 3c gene (*TUBA3C*). Prediction programs scan potential ORFs in the 5′ to 3′ direction on both strands of a section of genomic DNA to predict possible reading frames in each direction. Figure 21–7 shows the results for the six possible reading frames in the sequence of interest. Amino acids are shown using the single-letter code for each residue. Notice the very different results obtained for each of the six frames. For instance, the 5′ to 3′ ORF 1 contains several stop codons interspersed among amino acids but no methionine residues that are evidence of a start codon. Other ORFs would contain too many methionines to produce a functional polypeptide. For this exon of *TUBA3C*, the 5′ to 3′ ORF 2 is correct.

Prediction programs can also search for **codon bias**, the more frequent use of one or two codons to encode an amino acid that can be specified by a number of different codons. For example, alanine can be encoded by GCA, GCT, GCC, and GCG. If the codons were used randomly, each would be used about 25 percent of the time. Yet in the human genome, GCC is used 41 percent of the time, and GCG only 11 percent of the time. Codon bias is present in exons but should not be present in introns or intergenic spacers.

(a) *Homo sapiens TUBA3C* (bp 1-300)

1 ggttgaggtcaagtagtagcgttgggctgcggcagcggaggagctcaacatgcgtgagtg
61 tatctctatccacgtggggcaggcaggagtccagatcggcaatgcctgctgggaactgta
121 ctgcctggaacatggaattcagcccgatggtcagatgccaagtgataaaaccattggtgg
181 tggggacgactccttcaacacgttcttcagtgagactggagctggcaagcacgtgcccag
241 agcagtgtttgtggacctggagcccactgtggtcgatgaagtgcgcacaggaacctatag (300)

(b) Predicted polypeptides

5' to 3' Frame 1
G **Stop** G Q V V A L G C G S G G A Q H A **Stop** V Y L Y P R G A G R S P D R Q C L L G T V L P G T W N S A R W S D A K **Stop** **Stop** N H W W W G R L L Q H V L Q **Stop** D W S W Q A R A Q S S V C G P G A H C G R **Stop** S A H R N L **Stop**

5' to 3' Frame 2
V E V K **Stop** **Stop** R W A A A A E E L N **Met** R E C I S I H V G Q A G V Q I G N A C W E L Y C L E H G I Q P D G Q **Met** P S D K T I G G G D D S F N T F F S E T G A G K H V P R A V F V D L E P T V V D E V R T G T Y

5' to 3' Frame 3
L R S S S S V G L R Q R R S S T C V S V S L S T W G R Q E S R S A **Met** P A G N C T A W N **Met** E F S P **Met** V R C Q V I K P L V V G T T P S T R S S V R L E L A S T C P E Q C L W T W S P L W S **Met** K C A Q E P I

3' to 5' Frame 1
L **Stop** V P V R T S S T T V G S R S T N T A L G T C L P A P V S L K N V L K E S S P P P **Met** V L S L G I **Stop** P S G **Stop** I P C S R Q Y S S Q Q A L P I W T P A C P T W I E I H S R **Met** L S S S A A A A Q R Y Y L T S T

3' to 5' Frame 2
Y R F L C A L H R P Q W A P G P Q T L L W A R A C Q L Q S H **Stop** R T C **Stop** R S R P H H Q W F Y H L A S D H R A E F H V P G S T V P S R H C R S G L L P A P R G **Stop** R Y T H A C **Stop** A P P L P Q P N A T T **Stop** P Q

3' to 5' Frame 3
I G S C A H F I D H S G L Q V H K H C S G H V L A S S S L T E E R V E G V V P T T N G F I T W H L T I G L N S **Met** F Q A V Q F P A G I A D L D S C L P H V D R D T L T H V E L L R C R S P T L L L D L N

FIGURE 21–7 Predicted polypeptide sequences translated from potential ORFs in the human *TUBA3C* gene. (a) Nucleotides 1–300 of the first exon in the human *TUBA3C* gene. (b) A translation program predicts six possible polypeptide sequences from this exon. Which predicted sequence is correct?

Note: Methionine is highlighted using the three letter amino acid code (Met).

NOW SOLVE THIS

21–1 In a sequence encompassing 99.4 percent of the euchromatic regions of human chromosome 1, Gregory et al. (Gregory, S.G. et al., *Nature*, 441:315–321, 2006) identified 3141 genes.

(a) How does one identify a gene within a raw sequence of bases in DNA?

(b) What features of a genome are used to verify likely gene assignments?

(c) Given that chromosome 1 contains approximately 8 percent of the human genome, and assuming that there are approximately 20,000 genes, would you consider chromosome 1 to be "gene rich"?

■ **HINT:** *This problem involves a basic understanding of bioinformatics and gene annotation approaches to determine how potential gene sequences can be identified in a stretch of sequenced DNA.*

21.3 Genomics Attempts to Identify Potential Functions of Genes and Other Elements in a Genome

Reading a genome sequence is a surefire cure for insomnia. What is exciting is not the sequence of the nucleotides but the information that the sequence contains. After a genome has been annotated and ORFs have been identified, the next analytical task is to assign putative functions to all possible genes in the sequence. As the term suggests, **functional genomics** is the study of gene functions, based on the resulting RNAs or possible proteins they encode, and the functions of other components of the genome, such as gene-regulatory elements. Functional genomics can involve experimental approaches to confirm or refute computational predictions about genome functions (such as the number of protein-coding genes), and it also considers how genes are expressed and the regulation of gene expression.

Predicting Gene and Protein Functions by Sequence Analysis

One approach to assigning functions to genes is to use sequence similarity searches, as described in the previous section. Programs such as BLAST are used to search through databases to find alignments between the newly sequenced genome and genes that have already been identified, either in the same or in different species. You were introduced to this approach for predicting gene function in Figure 21–4, when we demonstrated how sequence similarity to the mouse gene was used to identify a gene in a rat contig as the insulin receptor gene. Inferring gene function from similarity searches is based on a relatively simple idea. If a genome sequence shows statistically significant similarity to the sequence of a gene whose function is known, then it is likely that the genome sequence encodes a protein with a similar or related function.

Another major benefit of similarity searches is that they are often able to identify **homologous genes**, genes that are evolutionarily related. After the human genome was sequenced, many ORFs in it were identified as protein-coding genes based on their alignment with related genes of known function in other species. As an example, Figure 21–8 compares portions of the human leptin gene (*LEP*) with its homolog in mice (*ob/Lep*). These two genes are over 85 percent identical in sequence. The leptin gene was first discovered in mice. The match between the *LEP*-containing DNA sequence in humans and the mouse homolog sequence confirms the identity and leptin-coding function of this gene in human genomic DNA.

As an interesting aside, the leptin gene (also called *ob*, for obesity, in mice) is highly expressed in fat cells (adipocytes). This gene produces the protein hormone leptin, which targets cells in the brain to suppress appetite. Knockout mice lacking a functional *ob* gene grow dramatically overweight. A similar phenotype has been observed in small numbers of humans with particular mutations in *LEP*. Although it is important to note that weight control is not regulated by a single gene, the discovery of leptin has provided significant insight into lipid metabolism and weight disorders in humans. Further studies on leptin will be important for understanding more about the genetics of weight disorders.

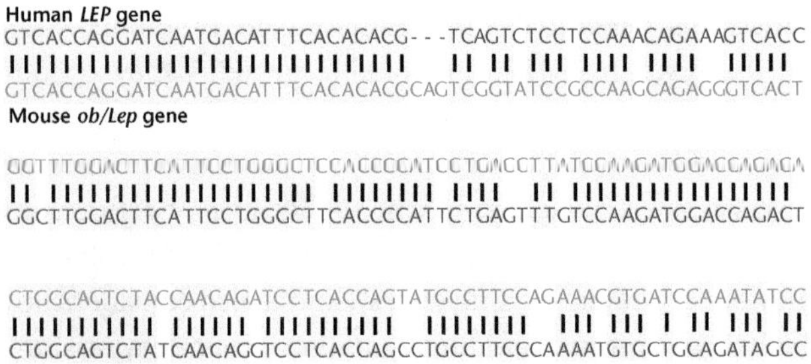

If homologous genes in different species are thought to have descended from a gene in a common ancestor, the genes are known as **orthologs**. In Section 21.6 we will consider the globin gene family. Mouse and human α-globin genes are orthologs evolved from a common ancestor. Homologous genes in the same species are called **paralogs**. The α- and β-globin subunits in humans are paralogs resulting from a gene-duplication event. Paralogs often have similar or identical functions.

Predicting Function from Structural Analysis of Protein Domains and Motifs

When a gene sequence is used to predict a polypeptide sequence, the polypeptide can be analyzed for specific structural domains and motifs. Identification of **protein domains**, such as ion channels, membrane-spanning regions, DNA-binding regions, secretion and export signals, and other structural aspects of a polypeptide that are encoded by a DNA sequence, can in turn be used to predict protein function. Recall from earlier in the text (see Chapter 17), for example, that the structures of many DNA-binding proteins have characteristic patterns, or **motifs**, such as the helix-turn-helix, leucine zipper, or zinc-finger motifs. These motifs can often easily be searched for using bioinformatics software, and their identification in a sequence is a common strategy for inferring the possible functions of a protein.

Investigators Are Using Genomics Techniques Such as Chromatin Immunoprecipitation to Investigate Aspects of Genome Function and Regulation

In this chapter and later in the text (see Chapter 22), we will consider a range of different genomic techniques that investigators are using that are valuable for functional genomics studies. One example is a technique called **chromatin immunoprecipitation (ChIP)**. Various techniques involving ChIP are designed to map protein–DNA interactions and are useful for identifying genes that are regulated by DNA-binding transcription factors.

To perform these techniques, researchers treat tissues or cultured cells with formaldehyde (Figure 21–9). Any proteins that are tightly bound to DNA will be crosslinked to the DNA by the formaldehyde. The researchers then extract DNA from the cells and shear it into small fragments. To isolate those DNA fragments that are bound to a specific protein, they add an antibody that recognizes (attaches to) the protein. These antibodies are usually attached to a bead or resin that enables the antibody to then be precipitated (by

Human *LEP* gene
```
GTCACCAGGATCAATGACATTTCACACACG- - -TCAGTCTCCTCCAAACAGAAAGTCACC
||||||||||||||||||||||||||||||   || || ||| |||| |||| |||||
GTCACCAGGATCAATGACATTTCACACACGCAGTCGGTATCCGCCAAGCAGAGGGTCACT
```
Mouse *ob/Lep* gene

```
GGTTTGGACTTCATTCCTGGGCTCCACCCCATCCTGACCTTATCCAAGATGGACCGAGACA
|| ||||||||||||||||||||| |||||||| |||| || |||||||||||||||||
GGCTTGGACTTCATTCCTGGGCTTCACCCCATTCTGAGTTTGTCCAAGATGGACCAGACT
```

```
CTGGCAGTCTACCAACAGATCCTCACCAGTATGCCTTCCAGAAACGTGATCCAAATATCC
||||||||||| |||||| ||||||||||| ||||||| ||| ||| | || ||| ||
CTGGCAGTCTATCAACAGGTCCTCACCAGCCTGCCTTCCCAAAATGTGCTGCAGATAGCC
```

FIGURE 21–8 Comparison of the human *LEP* and mouse *ob/Lep* genes. Partial sequences for these homologs are shown with the human *LEP* gene on top and the mouse *ob/Lep* gene sequence below it. Notice from the number of identical nucleotides, indicated by vertical lines, that the nucleotide sequence for these two genes is very similar. Gaps are indicated by horizontal dashes.

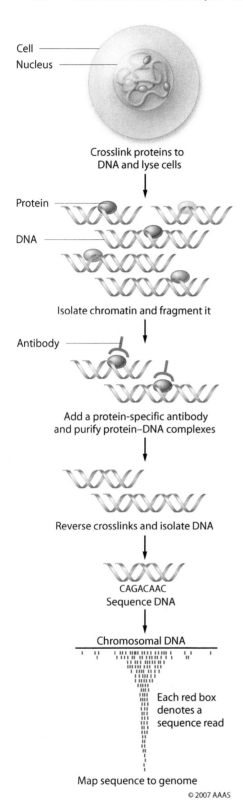

Cell

Nucleus

Crosslink proteins to
DNA and lyse cells

Protein

DNA

Isolate chromatin and fragment it

Antibody

Add a protein-specific antibody
and purify protein–DNA complexes

Reverse crosslinks and isolate DNA

CAGACAAC
Sequence DNA

Chromosomal DNA

Each red box
denotes a
sequence read

Map sequence to genome

© 2007 AAAS

FIGURE 21–9 The ChIPSeq method screens for specific transcription factor binding sites across a whole genome. In this method, formaldehyde is added to tissues or cultured cells to crosslink DNA-binding proteins currently attached to chromatin when formaldehyde was added. Then the chromatin is extracted from cells and sheared into small fragments. An antibody or antibodies that recognize specific DNA-binding proteins of interest (POI), such as a transcription factor, are added to the mixture and the antibodies attach to the POI. Then the antibody, together with its protein–DNA fragment, is pulled out of the mixture (immunoprecipitated). The immunoprecipitated DNA fragments are released from crosslinked proteins and attached antibodies and are then sequenced. Sequence data reveal the DNA-binding site for the POI and these sequences can be mapped to specific locations in the genome.

DNA complexes to the bottom of the centrifuge tube. The investigators can then purify the immunoprecipitated DNA fragments by removing them from the antibody/protein.

At this stage, there are several options for analyzing precipitated DNA fragments. **Figure 21–9** demonstrates an approach called *ChIPSeq*. Here precipitated DNA fragments are directly sequenced by high-throughput approaches. This allows researchers to study an entire genome to locate binding sites for proteins such as transcription factors, histone-related proteins, and other proteins involved in chromatin structure.

In another approach called *ChIP-chip*, the captured DNA fragments can be labeled with a fluorescent tag and hybridized to a DNA microarray (described in Section 21.9) containing synthetic oligonucleotides or cloned DNAs representing the organism's entire genome. Any spot on the microarray that hybridizes to the labeled DNA represents a DNA sequence that bound the protein. Because each spot on the DNA microarray is known, the identity of each positive signal can be determined. DNA isolated by ChIP can also be sequenced to identify DNA sequences that are bound by DNA-binding proteins.

21.4 The Human Genome Project Revealed Many Important Aspects of Genome Organization in Humans

Now that you have a general idea of the basic strategies used for analyzing a genome, let's look at the largest genomics project completed to date. The **Human Genome Project (HGP)** was a coordinated international effort to determine the sequence of the human genome and to identify all the genes it contains. It has produced a plethora of information, much of which is still being analyzed and interpreted. What is clear from all the different kinds of genomes sequenced is that humans and all other species share a common set of genes

immunoprecipitation) from the mixture, along with the protein to which it binds and any DNA fragments that are crosslinked to the protein. Immunoprecipitation is usually accomplished by centrifugation of the antibody/protein/DNA complexes. Because the antibody has a bead attached to it, the mass of the bead is used to centrifuge the antibody/protein/

essential for cellular function and reproduction, confirming that all living organisms arose from a common ancestor.

Origins of the Project

The publicly funded Human Genome Project began in 1990 under the direction of James Watson, the co-discoverer of the double-helix structure of DNA. Eventually the public project was led by Dr. Francis Collins, who had previously led a research team involved in identifying the *CFTR* gene as the cause of cystic fibrosis. In the United States, the Collins-led HGP was coordinated by the Department of Energy and the National Center of Human Genome Research, a division of the National Institutes of Health. It established a 15-year plan with a proposed budget of $3 billion to identify all human genes, originally thought to number between 80,000 and 100,000, to sequence and map them all, and to sequence the approximately 3 billion base pairs thought to comprise the 24 chromosomes (22 autosomes, plus X and Y) in humans. Other primary goals of the HGP included the following:

- To establish functional categories for all human genes

- To analyze genetic variations between humans, including the identification of **single-nucleotide polymorphisms (SNPs)**

- To map and sequence the genomes of several model organisms used in experimental genetics, including *E. coli, S. cerevisiae, C. elegans, D. melanogaster,* and *M. musculus* (mouse)

- To develop new sequencing technologies, such as high-throughput computer-automated sequencers, in order to facilitate genome analysis

- To disseminate genome information among both scientists and the general public

Lastly, to deal with the impact that genetic information would have on society, the HGP set up the **ELSI program** (standing for Ethical, Legal, and Social Implications) to consider ethical, legal, and social issues arising from the HGP and to ensure that personal genetic information would be safeguarded and not used in discriminatory ways.

As the HGP grew into an international effort, scientists in 18 countries were involved in the project. Much of the work was carried out by the International Human Genome Sequence Consortium, involving nearly 3000 scientists working at 20 centers in six countries (China, France, Germany, Great Britain, Japan, and the United States).

In 1999, a privately funded human genome project led by J. Craig Venter at **Celera Genomics** (aptly named from a word meaning "swiftness") was announced. Celera's goal was to use whole-genome shotgun sequencing and computer-automated high-throughput DNA sequencers

to sequence the human genome more rapidly than HGP. The public project had proposed using a clone-by-clone approach to sequence the genome. Recall that Venter and colleagues had proven the potential of shotgun sequencing in 1995 when they completed the genome for *H. influenzae*. Celera's announcement set off an intense competition between the two teams, which both aspired to be first with the human genome sequence. This contest eventually led to the HGP finishing ahead of schedule and under budget after scientists from the public project began to use high-throughput sequencers and whole-genome sequencing strategies as well.

Major Features of the Human Genome

In June 2000, the leaders of the public and private genome projects met at the White House with President Clinton and jointly announced the completion of a draft sequence of the human genome. In February 2001, they each published an analysis covering about 96 percent of the euchromatic region of the genome. The public project sequenced euchromatic portions of the genome 12 times and set a quality control standard of a 0.01 percent error rate for their sequence. Although this error rate may seem very low, it still allows about 600,000 errors in the human genome sequence. Celera sequenced certain areas of the genome more than 35 times when compiling the genome.

The remaining work of completing the sequence by filling in gaps clustered around centromeres, telomeres, and repetitive sequences (regions rich in GC base pairs can be particularly tough to sequence and interpret), correcting misaligned segments, and re-sequencing portions of the genome to ensure accuracy. In 2003 genome sequencing and error fixing were deemed sufficient to pass the international project's definition of completion—that it contained fewer than 1 error per 10,000 nucleotides and that it covered 95 percent of the gene-containing portions of the genome. Yet even at the time of "completion" there were still some 350 gaps in the sequence that continued to be worked on.

And of course the HGP did not sequence the genome of every person on Earth. The assembled genomes largely consist of haploid genomes pooled from different individuals so that they provide a *reference genome* representative of major, common elements of a human genome widely shared among populations of humans. Examples of major features of the human genome are summarized in Table 21.1. As you can see in this table, many unexpected observations have provided us with major new insights. The genome is not static! Genome variations, including the abundance of repetitive sequences scattered throughout the genome, verify that the genome is indeed dynamic, revealing many evolutionary examples of sequences that have changed in

TABLE 21.1 Major Features of the Human Genome

- The human genome contains 3.1 billion nucleotides, but protein-coding sequences make up only about 2 percent of the genome.

- The genome sequence is ~99.9 percent similar in individuals of all nationalities. SNPs and copy number variations (CNVs) account for genome diversity from person to person.

- The genome is dynamic. At least 50 percent of the genome is derived from transposable elements, such as LINE and *Alu* sequences, and other repetitive DNA sequences.

- The human genome contains approximately 20,000 protein-coding genes, far fewer than the originally predicted number of 80,000–100,000 genes.

- The average size of a human gene is ~25 kb, including gene-regulatory regions, introns, and exons. On average, mRNAs produced by human genes are ~3000 nt long.

- Many human genes produce more than one protein through alternative splicing, thus enabling human cells to produce a much larger number of proteins (perhaps as many as 200,000) from only ~20,000 genes.

- More than 50 percent of human genes show a high degree of sequence similarity to genes in other organisms; however, more than 40 percent of the genes identified have no known molecular function.

- Genes are not uniformly distributed on the 24 human chromosomes. Gene-rich clusters are separated by gene-poor "deserts" that account for 20 percent of the genome. These deserts correlate with G bands seen in stained chromosomes. Chromosome 19 has the highest gene density, and chromosome 13 and the Y chromosome have the lowest gene densities.

- Chromosome 1 contains the largest number of genes, and the Y chromosome contains the smallest number.

- Human genes are larger and contain more and larger introns than genes in the genomes of invertebrates, such as *Drosophila*. The largest known human gene encodes dystrophin, a muscle protein. This gene, associated in mutant form with muscular dystrophy, is 2.5 Mb in length (Chapter 14), larger than many bacterial chromosomes. Most of this gene is composed of introns.

- The number of introns in human genes ranges from 0 (in histone genes) to 234 (in the gene for *titin*, which encodes a muscle protein).

that human cells produce about 100,000 proteins. At least half of the genes show sequence similarity to genes shared by many other organisms, and as you will learn in Section 21.7, a majority of human genes are similar in sequence to genes from closely related species such as chimpanzees. There is still no consensus among scientists worldwide about the exact number of human genes. One reason is that it is unclear whether or not many of the presumed genes produce functional proteins. Genome scientists continue to annotate the genome, and as mentioned earlier, functional genomics studies have important roles in determining whether or not computational predictions about the number of protein-coding and non–protein-coding genes are accurate.

The number of genes is much lower than the number of predicted proteins in part because many genes code for multiple proteins through **alternative splicing**. Recall from earlier in the text (see Chapter 13), that alternative splicing patterns can generate multiple mRNA molecules, and thus multiple proteins, from a single gene, through different combinations of intron–exon splicing arrangements. Initial estimates suggested that over 50 percent of human genes undergo alternative splicing to produce multiple transcripts and multiple proteins. Recent studies suggest that ~94–95 percent of human pre-mRNAs contain multiple exons that are processed to produce multiple transcripts and potentially multiple different protein products. Clearly, alternative splicing produces an incredible diversity of proteins beyond simple predictions based on the number of genes in the human genome.

Functional categories have been assigned for human genes, primarily on the basis of (1) functions determined previously (for example, from recombinant DNA cloning of human genes and known mutations involved in human diseases), (2) comparison to known genes and predicted protein sequences from other species, and (3) predictions based on annotation and analysis of protein functional domains and motifs (**Figure 21–10**). Although functional categories and assignments continue to be revised, the functions of over 40 percent of human genes remain unknown. Determining human gene functions, deciphering complexities of gene-expression regulation and gene interaction, and uncovering the relationships between human genes and phenotypes are among the many challenges for genome scientists.

Individual Variations in the Human Genome

The HGP has also shown us that in all humans, regardless of racial and ethnic origins, the genomic sequence is approximately 99.9 percent the same. As we discuss in other chapters, most genetic differences between humans result from **single-nucleotide polymorphisms (SNPs)** and **copy number variations (CNVs)**. Recall that SNPs are single-base changes in the genome and variations of many

structure and location. In many ways, the HGP has revealed just how little we know about our genome.

Two of the biggest surprises discovered by the HGP were that less than 2 percent of the genome codes for proteins and that there are only around 20,000 protein-coding genes. Recall that the number of genes had originally been estimated to be about 100,000, based in part on a prediction

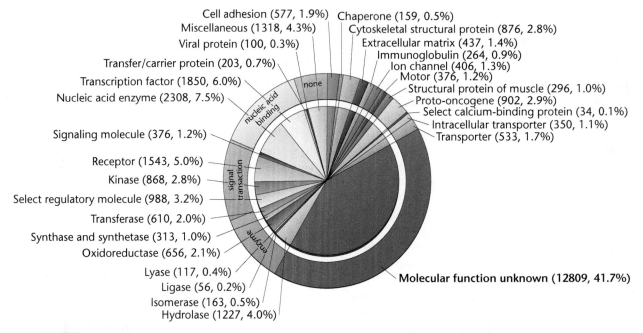

Cell adhesion (577, 1.9%)
Miscellaneous (1318, 4.3%)
Viral protein (100, 0.3%)
Transfer/carrier protein (203, 0.7%)
Transcription factor (1850, 6.0%)
Nucleic acid enzyme (2308, 7.5%)
Signaling molecule (376, 1.2%)
Receptor (1543, 5.0%)
Kinase (868, 2.8%)
Select regulatory molecule (988, 3.2%)
Transferase (610, 2.0%)
Synthase and synthetase (313, 1.0%)
Oxidoreductase (656, 2.1%)
Lyase (117, 0.4%)
Ligase (56, 0.2%)
Isomerase (163, 0.5%)
Hydrolase (1227, 4.0%)

Chaperone (159, 0.5%)
Cytoskeletal structural protein (876, 2.8%)
Extracellular matrix (437, 1.4%)
Immunoglobulin (264, 0.9%)
Ion channel (406, 1.3%)
Motor (376, 1.2%)
Structural protein of muscle (296, 1.0%)
Proto-oncogene (902, 2.9%)
Select calcium-binding protein (34, 0.1%)
Intracellular transporter (350, 1.1%)
Transporter (533, 1.7%)

Molecular function unknown (12809, 41.7%)

FIGURE 21–10 A representation of the functional categories to which genes in the human genome have been assigned on the basis of similarity to proteins of known function. Among the most common genes are those involved in nucleic acid metabolism (7.5 percent of all genes identified), transcription factors (6.0 percent), receptors (5 percent), hydrolases (4 percent), protein kinases (2.8 percent), and cytoskeletal structural proteins (2.8 percent). A total of 12,809 predicted proteins (41 percent) have unknown functions, indicative of the work that is still needed to fully decipher our genome.

SNPs are associated with disease conditions. For example, SNPs cause sickle-cell anemia and cystic fibrosis. Later in the text (see Chapter 22), we will examine how SNPs can be detected and used for diagnosis and treatment of disease.

After the draft sequence of the human genome was completed, it initially appeared that most genetic variations between individuals (the 0.1 percent differences) were due to SNPs. While SNPs are important contributing factors to genome variation, structural differences that we discussed earlier in the text (see Chapter 12) such as deletions, duplications, inversions, and CNVs, which can span millions of bp of DNA, play much more important roles in genome variation than previously thought. As we discussed earlier in the text (see Chapters 8 and 12), recall that CNVs are duplications or deletions of relatively large sections of DNA on the order of several hundred or several thousand base pairs. Many of the CNVs that vary the most among genomes appear to be at least 1 kilobase.

Although most human DNA is present in two copies per cell, one from each parent, CNVs are segments of DNA that are duplicated or deleted, resulting in variations in the number of copies of a DNA segment inherited by individuals. In some cases CNVs are major deletions removing entire genes; other deletions affect gene function by frameshifts in the reading code. CNV sequences that are duplicated can result in overexpression of a particular gene, yet many deleted and duplicated CNVs do not present clearly identifiable phenotypes.

Current estimates of the number of CNVs in an individual genome range from about 12 CNVs to perhaps 4–5 dozen per person. Some studies estimate that there may be as many as 1500 CNVs greater than 1 kb among the human genome. Other studies claim there are more than 1.5 million deletions of less than 100 bp that contribute to genome variation between individuals.

Accessing the Human Genome Project on the Internet

It is now possible to access databases and other sites on the Internet that display maps for all human chromosomes. You will visit a number of these databases in Exploring Genomics exercises. **Figure 21–11(a)** displays a partial gene map for chromosome 12 that was taken from an NCBI database called Map Viewer. You may already have used Map Viewer for the Exploring Genomics exercises ealier in the text (see Chapters 5 and 12). This image shows an ideogram, or cytogenetic map, of chromosome 12. To the right of the ideogram is a column showing the contigs (arranged lying vertically) that were aligned to sequence this chromosome. The Hs UniG column displays a histogram representation of gene density on chromosome 12. Notice that relatively few genes are located near the centromere. Gene symbols, loci, and gene names (by description) are provided for selected genes; in this figure only 20 genes are shown. When accessing these maps on the Internet, one can magnify, or zoom in on, each region of the chromosome, revealing all genes mapped to a particular area.

(a)

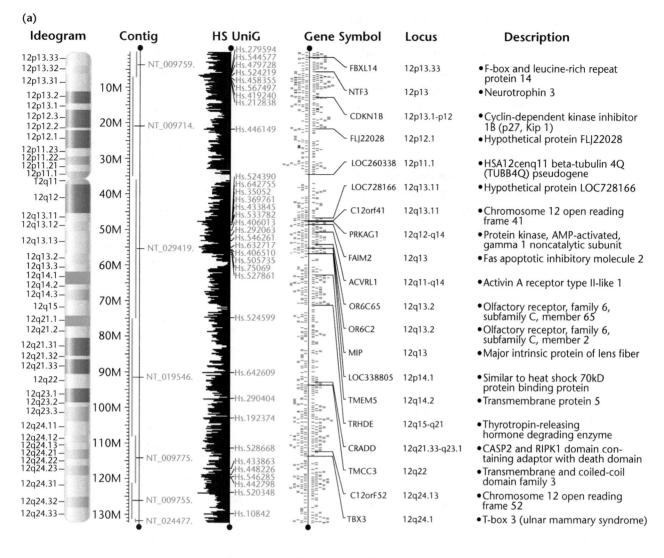

(b)

Chromosome 21
50 million bases

Coxsackie and adenovirus receptor
Amyloidosis cerebroarterial, Dutch type
Alzheimer disease, APP-related
Schizophrenia, chronic
Usher syndrome, autosomal recessive

Amyotrophic lateral sclerosis
Oligomycin sensitivity
Jervell and Lange-Nielsen syndrome
Long QT syndrome
Down syndrome cell-adhesion molecule

Homocystinuria
Cataract, congenital, autosomal dominant
Deafness, autosomal recessive
Myxovirus (influenza) resistance
Leukemia, acute myeloid

Myeloproliferative syndrome, transient
Leukemia transient of Down syndrome

Enterokinase deficiency

Multiple carboxylase deficiency

T-cell lymphoma invasion and metastasis

Mycobacterial infection, atypical
Down syndrome (critical region)
Autoimmune polyglandular disease, type 1

Bethlem myopathy
Epilepsy, progressive myoclonic
Holoprosencephaly, alobar
Knobloch syndrome
Hemolytic anemia
Breast cancer
Platelet disorder, with myeloid malignancy

FIGURE 21-11 (a) A gene map for chromosome 12 from the NCBI database Map Viewer. (b) Partial map of disease genes on human chromosome 21. Maps such as this depict genes thought to be involved in human genetic disease conditions.

You can see that most of the genes listed here have been assigned descriptions based on the functions of their products, some of which are transmembrane proteins, some enzymes such as kinases, some receptors, including several involved in olfaction, and so on. Other genes are described in terms of hypothetical products; they are presumed to be genes based on the presence of ORFs, but their function remains unknown [Figure 21–11(a)].

The HGP's most valuable contribution will perhaps be the identification of disease genes and the development of new treatment strategies as a result. Thus, extensive maps have been developed for genes implicated in human disease conditions. The disease gene map of chromosome 21 shown in Figure 21–11(b) indicates genes involved in amyotrophic lateral sclerosis (ALS), Alzheimer disease, cataracts, deafness, and several different cancers. Later in the text (see Chapter 22) we discuss implications of the HGP for the identification of genes involved in human genetic diseases, and for disease diagnosis, detection, and gene therapy applications.

21.5 The "Omics" Revolution Has Created a New Era of Biological Research

The Human Genome Project and the development of genomics techniques have been largely responsible for launching a new era of biological research—the era of "omics." It seems that every year, more areas of biological research are being described as having an omics connection. Some examples of "omics" are

- proteomics—the analysis of all the proteins in a cell or tissue

- metabolomics—the analysis of proteins and enzymatic pathways involved in cell metabolism

- glycomics—the analysis of the carbohydrates of a cell or tissue

- toxicogenomics—the analysis of the effects of toxic chemicals on genes, including mutations created by toxins and changes in gene expression caused by toxins

- metagenomics—the analysis of genomes of organisms collected from the environment

- pharmacogenomics—the development of customized medicine based on a person's genetic profile for a particular condition

- transcriptomics—the analysis of all expressed genes in a cell or tissue

We will consider several of these genomics disciplines in other parts of this chapter.

As evidence of the impact of genomics, a new field of nutritional science called nutritional genomics, or **nutrigenomics**, has emerged. Nutrigenomics focuses on understanding the interactions between diet and genes. We have all had routine medical tests for blood pressure, blood sugar levels, and heart rate. Based on these tests, your physician may recommend that you change your diet and exercise more to lose weight, or that you reduce your intake of sodium to help lower your blood pressure. Now several companies claim to provide nutrigenomics tests that analyze your genomes for genes thought to be associated with different medical conditions or aspects of nutrient metabolism. The companies then provide a customized nutrition report, recommending diet changes for improving your health and preventing illness, based on your genes! It is important to know that these tests have not been validated as accurate and they have not been approved by the U.S. Food and Drug Administration. It remains to be seen whether this approach as currently practiced is of valid scientific or nutritional value.

Stone-Age Genomics

In yet another example of how genomics has taken over areas of DNA analysis, a number of labs around the world are involved in analyzing "ancient" DNA. These so-called **stone-age genomics** studies are generating fascinating data from miniscule amounts of ancient DNA obtained from bone and other tissues such as hair that are tens of thousands to about 700,000 years old, and often involve samples from extinct species. Analysis of DNA from a 2400-year-old Egyptian mummy, bison, mosses, platypus, mammoths, Pleistocene-age cave bears and polar bears, coelacanths and Neanderthals are some of the most prominent examples of stone-age genomics. In 2013, scientists reported the oldest complete genome sequence generated to date. It came from a 700,000-year-old bone fragment from an ancient horse uncovered from the frozen ground in the Yukon Territory of Canada. This result is interesting in part because evolutionary biologists have used genomic data to estimate that ancient ancestors of modern horses branched off from other animal lineages around 4 million years ago— about twice as long ago as prior estimates.

In 2005, researchers from McMaster University in Canada and Pennsylvania State University published about 13 million bp from a 27,000-year-old woolly mammoth. This study revealed a ~98.5 percent sequence identity between mammoths and African elephants. Subsequent studies by other scientists have used whole-genome shotgun sequencing of mitochondrial and nuclear DNA from Siberian mammoths to provide data on the mammoth genome. These studies suggest that the mammoth genome differs from the African elephant by as little as 0.6 percent. These studies are also great demonstrations of how stable DNA can be under

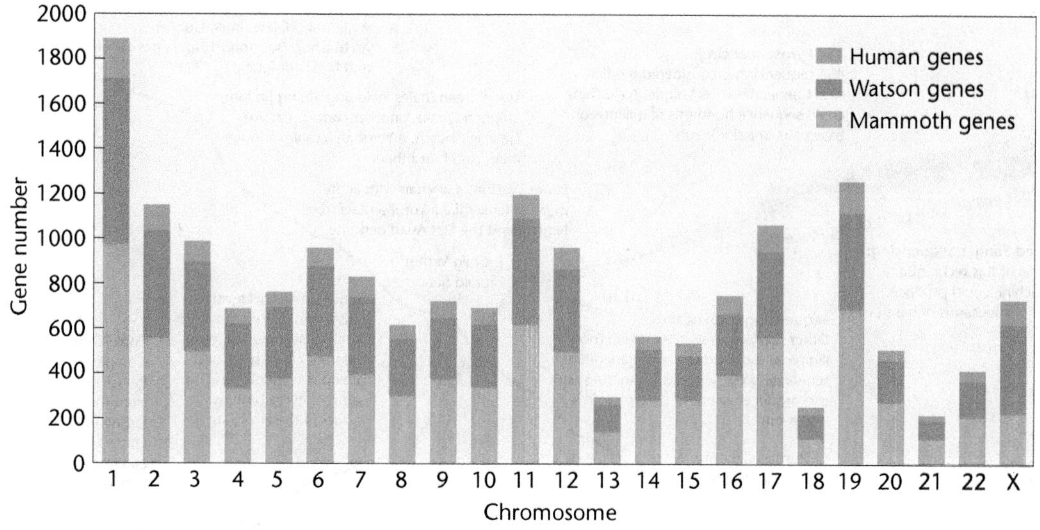

FIGURE 21–12 Plot showing the number of genes on each human chromosome (blue), the average fraction of protein-coding bases that align to Roche 454 reads from James D. Watson's genome (green), and the fraction of coding bases that align to one or more mammoth reads (orange), using predicted elephant genes that map to the human chromosome based on sequence similarity—approximately 50 percent for each autosome, but only 31 percent for the X chromosome because the mammoth used for this study was male.

the right conditions, particularly when frozen. In the future, it may be possible to produce complete genome sequences from samples that are several million years old.

Perhaps even more intriguing are similarities that have been revealed between the mammoth and human genomes. For example, as shown in **Figure 21-12**, when the gene sequences from human chromosomes were aligned with sequences from the mammoth genome, approximately 50 percent of mammoth genes showed sequence alignment with human genes on autosomes. Incidentally, notice that this figure also shows the relative number of genes from James Watson's genome (which we will discuss in the next section) compared to the human genome reference sequence.

In Section 21.6 we will discuss recent work on the Neanderthal genome. Obtaining the genome of a human ancestor this old was previously unimaginable. This work is providing new insights into our understanding of human evolution.

After the HGP: What Is Next?

Since completion of a reference sequence of the human genome, studies have continued at a very rapid pace. For example, as a result of the HGP, many other major theme areas for human genome research have emerged, including cancer genome projects, analysis of the epigenome (including a Human Epigenome Project that is creating hundreds of maps of epigenetic changes in different cell and tissue types and evaluating potential roles of epigenetics in complex diseases), characterization of SNPs (the International HapMap Project) and CNVs for their role in genome variation, disease, and pharmacogenomics applications.

We have discussed aspects of a cancer genome project (Cancer Genome Atlas Project) earlier in the text (see Chapter 19). The epigenome is covered in depth later in the text (see Special Topic Chapter 1—Epigenetics). SNPs and pharmacogenomics are discussed later as well (see Special Topic Chapter 4—Genomics and Personalized Medicine). Here we consider four examples of human genome research that are extensions of the HGP: (1) the analysis of personal genomes, (2) the ENCODE Project, (3) the Human Microbiome Project, and (4) the Genome 10K Plan.

Personal Genome Projects and Personal Genomics

As we discussed earlier in this chapter and earlier in the text (see Chapter 20), new sequencing technologies, capable of generating longer sequence reads at higher speeds with greater accuracy, have greatly reduced the cost of DNA sequencing, and expectations for continued cost reductions along with continued technological advances are high (see **Figure 21-13**). These expectations led several companies to propose WGS for individual people—a personal genomics approach. In 2006, the X Prize Foundation announced the Archon Genomics X Prize, an award of $10 million to the first private group that develops technology capable of sequencing 100 human genomes with a high degree of accuracy in 10 days for under $10,000 per genome. There were eight competitors for this prize, but none could meet the 10-day requirement. Archon subsequently canceled the X Prize in part because sequencing technology was improving in speed and decreasing in cost without the need for a

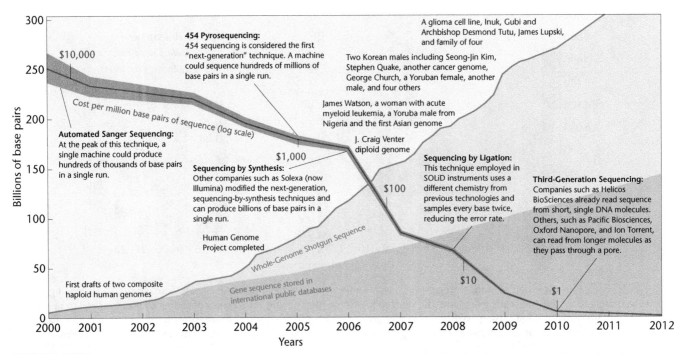

Human genome sequence explosion. Sequencing costs have steadily declined since 2000 due to innovations in sequencing technology. As a result, notice that the amount of whole-genome shotgun sequencing data stored in public databases—which include data on several individual genomes—has dramatically increased.

competition. Other groups are working on sequencing a personalized genome for a mere $1000! Two programs funded by the National Institutes of Health challenged scientists to develop sequencing technologies to complete a human genome for $1000 by 2014 (see the "Genetics, Technology, and Society" essay in Chapter 22).

In 2012, Life Technologies announced that their Ion Proton technology was used to sequence a genome for $1000. Whether the $1000 mark represents the costs of reagents to sequence a genome or actual costs when sequence preparation, labor, and analysis of the genome are taken into account can be debated. Whether the accuracy and completeness of the sequence coverage reported by Life Technologies is sufficient to definitively state that the $1000 genome threshold has been achieved has been challenged by other scientists.

As you will learn later in the text (see Chapter 22), having somebody such as a geneticist analyze genome data and consider how genome variations may affect a person's health takes a lot of time and money. So even if the cost of sequencing a person's genome is less than $1000, interpreting genome data to make sense for medical treatment may cost hundreds of thousands of dollars. Regardless of how the actual cost of sequencing a genome is calculated, the modern cost is substantially lower than the $3 billion cost of the HGP.

Pursuit of the $1000 genome was an indicator that DNA sequencing may eventually be affordable enough for individuals to consider acquiring a readout of their own genetic blueprint. The genome of James D. Watson, who together with Francis Crick discovered the structure of DNA, was the focus of "Project Jim" by the Connecticut company 454 Life Sciences, which wanted to sequence the genome of a high-profile person and decided that the co-discoverer of DNA structure and the first director of the U.S. Human Genome Project should be that person. This company used their next-generation pyrosequencing approach (see Figure 21–13) for Project Jim, and within two years it was announced that six-fold coverage of Watson's genome was complete at a rough cost of just under $1 million. James Watson was then presented with two DVDs containing his genome sequence.

Human genome pioneer J. Craig Venter, whose accomplishments we have discussed in several chapters, had his genome completed by the J. Craig Venter Institute and deposited into GenBank in May 2007. George Church of Harvard and his colleagues started a **Personal Genome Project (PGP)** and recruited volunteers to provide DNA for individual genome sequencing on the understanding that the genome data will be made publicly available. Church's genome has been completed and is available online. The concept of a personal genome project raises the obvious question: would you have your genome sequenced for $10,000, $1000, or even for free?

Since the Watson and Venter genomes were completed, in 2008 the first complete genome sequence was provided for an individual "ancient" human, a Palaeo-Eskimo, obtained from ~4000-year-old permafrost-preserved hair. This work recovered about 78 percent of the diploid genome and revealed many interesting SNPs (of which about 7 percent have not been previously reported). As of 2013, more than 30,000 individual human genomes have been sequenced.

One especially intriguing example of personal genomics involves a genetics researcher who examined his own genome for insight about a medical condition. Dr. Richard Gibbs of Baylor College of Medicine in Texas led a group that sequenced the whole genome of his colleague Dr. James Lupski, a medical geneticist who has **Charcot-Marie-Tooth (CMT) disease**. This disease is a neurological condition that causes muscle weakness. Interestingly, mutations in over 30 genes, many of which were identified by Dr. Lupski, are involved in CMT, although Lupski did not carry any of these mutations. A comparison of Lupski's genome to the HGP reference sequence revealed many SNPs and other variations, but it was unclear how many of these were simply sequencing errors or variations that were not involved in CMT.

Focusing on genes previously linked to CMT and other neurological conditions, researchers found that Lupski's genome had two different mutations in the gene *SH3TC2*, which is expressed in Schwann cells that wrap around certain neurons to form the myelin sheath essential for impulse conductions in nerves. In one *SH3TC2* allele a nonsense mutation was revealed, and in Lupski's second allele for *SH3TC2* a new missense mutation was found. When genetic tests for these alleles were carried out on Lupski's parents and seven siblings, the nonsense mutation was found in one parent and two siblings who did not have the disease. The missense mutation was found in another parent and one grandparent, neither of whom had the disorder. Only siblings who inherited both mutated alleles had CMT disease. Many consider this the first clinically relevant success for personal genome sequencing—at least for identifying disease genes.

Exome Sequencing

The focus of personal genome projects has shifted toward **exome sequencing**, sequencing the 180,000 exons in a person's genome. This can be done at a cost of less than $1000 with <100X coverage. Exome sequencing reveals mutations involved in disease by focusing only on exons as protein-coding segments of the genome. Of course, a limitation of this approach is its failure to identify mutations in gene-regulatory regions that influence gene expression. As an example, a group of scientists called the 1000 Genomes Project Consortium reported on the genomes of 1092 individuals from 14 populations representing Europe, East Asia, sub-Saharan Africa, and the Americas. Whole-genome and exome-sequencing data revealed more than 38

million SNPs and many other structural variations (CNVs). One interpretation of this work is that it reveals clear variations in individuals and associates particular diseases with geographic or ancestral background. Thus sequencing genomes of individuals from diverse populations can help us better understand the spectrum of human genetic variation and to learn the causes of genetic diseases across diverse groups. We will come back to the topic of exome sequencing later in the text (see Chapter 22), when we discuss genetic testing.

Another particularly beneficial aspect of personal genome projects is the insight they are providing into genome variation. The HGP combined samples from different individuals to create a reference genome for a *haploid genome*. Personal genome projects sequence a diploid genome; consequently, such projects indicate that haploid genome comparisons may underestimate the extent of genome variation between individuals by five-fold or more. For example, when Venter's genome was analyzed, over 4 million variations were found between his maternal and paternal chromosomes alone. From what we are learning about personal genomes, genome variation between individuals may be closer to 0.5 percent than 0.1 percent, and in a 3-billion-bp genome this is a significant difference in sequence variation. Integrating genome data from several complete individual genomes of individuals from different ethnic groups will also be of great value in evolutionary genetics to address fundamental questions about human diversity, ancestry, and migration patterns.

In a related matter, PGPs are revealing that there can be significant *mosaicism* in human somatic cells. Thus, cells in an individual person do not all contain identical genomes. Because of the sophistication of WGS methods, mosaicisms for SNPs and CNVs have been found in skin, brain, blood, and stem cells from the same individual. We are only beginning to understand the frequency and effects of genetic mosaicism on health and disease.

Later in the text (see Chapter 22), we will consider how various approaches to personal genomics can be used for genetic testing.

Encyclopedia of DNA Elements (ENCODE) Project

In 2003, a few months after the announcement that the human genome had been sequenced, a group of about three dozen research teams around the world began the **Encyclopedia of DNA Elements (ENCODE) Project**. A main goal of ENCODE was to use both experimental approaches, including ChIP-based methods as we discussed in Section 21.3, and bioinformatics to identify and analyze functional elements of the genome, such as transcriptional start sites, promoters, and enhancers, which regulate the expression of human genes.

Recall from our previous discussions that only a relatively small percentage (2 percent) of the human genome codes for proteins. ENCODE focused not on genes but on all of the sequences, commonly referred to as "junk" DNA. So what are all of the other bases in the genome doing? The term *junk DNA* has always been a misnomer. We know that such sequences are important for chromosome structure, the regulation of gene expression, and other roles. Just because these sequences themselves do not code for protein does not mean that they are unimportant. Non–protein-coding sequences are discussed in greater detail later in the text (see Special Topic Chapter 2—Emerging Roles of RNA).

ENCODE studied gene expression in 147 different cell types because genome activity differs from cell to cell. After about a decade of research and a cost of $288 million, in 2012 a group of 30 research papers were published revealing the major findings of the ENCODE project. Highlights of what ENCODE revealed include the following.

- The majority, ~80 percent, of the human genome is considered functional. This is partly because large segments of the genome are transcribed into RNA. Most of these RNAs do not encode proteins. These various RNAs include tRNA, rRNAs, and miRNAs. For example, at least 13,000 sequences specify long noncoding RNAs (lncRNAs). Other reports suggest there may be over 17,000 lncRNAs. It may turn out that the number of noncoding RNA sequences will outnumber protein-coding genes.

- The functional sequences also include gene-regulatory regions: ~70,000 promoter regions and nearly 400,000 enhancer regions.

- There are 20,687 protein-coding genes in the human genome.

- A total of 11,224 sequences are characterized as pseudogenes, previously thought to be inactive in all individuals. Some of these are inactive in most individuals but occasionally active in certain cell types of some individuals, which may eventually warrant their reclassification as active, transcribed genes and not pseudogenes.

- SNPs associated with disease are enriched within non-coding functional elements of the genome, often residing near protein-coding genes.

Clearly, it is not accurate to dismiss non–protein-coding DNA as junk. These sequences are critically important as regulatory regions. Thus one important conclusion of ENCODE is that nearly 80 percent of the genome has some functional significance. The ENCODE findings have broadly defined the functional roles of the genome to include encoding proteins or noncoding RNAs and displaying biochemical properties such as binding regulatory proteins that influence transcription or chromatin structure. Consequently, regulation of gene expression is far more complex than previously thought, with gene expression being influenced by regulatory sequences that are near and far to the gene being transcribed.

Not all scientists agree with ENCODE's definition of sequence function. And within the scientific community there has been significant debate about ENCODE and its value given the cost of the project. But research teams are already using information from ENCODE to identify risk factors for certain diseases, with the hopes of developing appropriate cures and treatments.

EVOLVING CONCEPT OF A GENE

Based on the work of the ENCODE project, we now know that DNA sequences that have previously been thought of as "junk DNA," which do not encode proteins, are nonetheless often transcribed into what we call noncoding RNA (ncRNA). Since the function of some these RNAs is now being determined, we must consider whether the concept of the gene should be expanded to include DNA sequences that encode ncRNAs. At this writing, there is no consensus, but it is important for you to be aware of these current findings as you develop your final interpretation of a gene. ■

The Human Microbiome Project

In 2007 the National Institutes of Health announced plans for the **Human Microbiome Project (HMP),** a $170 million project to complete the genomes of an estimated 600–1000 microorganisms, bacteria, viruses, and yeast that live on and inside humans. Microorganisms comprise ~1–2 percent of the human body, outnumbering human cells by about 10 to 1. Many microbes, such as *E. coli* in the digestive tract, have important roles in human health, and of course other microbes make us ill. The HMP has several major goals, including:

- Determining if individuals share a core human microbiome.

- Understanding whether changes in the microbiome can be correlated with changes in human health.

- Developing new methods, including bioinformatics tools, to support analysis of the microbiome.

- Addressing ethical, legal, and social implications raised by human microbiome research. Does this sound familiar? Recall that addressing ethical, legal, and social issues was a goal of the HGP.

The HMP has involved about 200 scientists at 80 institutions. In 2012 a series of papers were published summarizing recent findings from the HMP. The HMP analyzed 15 body sites from males and 18 sites from females from 242 healthy individuals in the United States and applied WGS of genomes for the microbes and viruses present at these sites. Each person was sampled up to three times over nearly two years. Researchers used bioinformatics to compare microbial and viral genome sequences obtained to sequences in publicly available databases. In addition to WGS analysis, sequences for 16S rRNA gene sequences in particular were used to compare bacterial samples. More than 2000 microbial sequences isolated from the human body have been sequenced to date.

The HMP has amassed more than 1000 times the sequencing data generated by the Human Genome Project. What concepts have we formulated about the human microbiome so far?

- Sequence data from the HMP have identified an estimated 81 to 99 percent of the microbes and viruses distributed among body areas in human males and females.

- As many as 1000 bacterial strains may be present in each person.

- An estimated 10,000 bacterial species may be part of the human microbiome.

- The microbiome starts at birth. Babies pick up bacteria from their mothers' microbiome.

- A surprise to HMP scientists is that the microbiome can be substantially different from person to person. Also, sequences for disease-causing bacteria are present in everyone's microbiome.

- In the human gut, for example, although the microbiome differs from person to person, it remains relatively stable over time in individuals.

There is no single "reference" human microbiome to which people can be compared. Microbial diversity varies greatly from individual to individual, and a personalization of the microbiome occurs in individuals. For instance, comparing sequences of the microbiomes from two healthy people of equivalent age reveals microbiomes that can be quite different. There are, however, similarities in certain parts of the body, with signature bacteria and characteristic genes associated with a particular location in the body.

Knowledge about the personalized nature of the microbiome will be valuable for improving human health and medicine, which in the future may include microbiome-specific therapeutic drugs. Scientists are trying to establish criteria for a healthy microbiome, which is expected to help determine, for example, how bacteria help maintain normal health, how antibiotics can disturb a person's microbiome, and why certain individuals are susceptible to certain diseases, especially chronic conditions such as psoriasis, irritable bowel syndrome, and potentially even obesity.

Related to this project, a team of researchers at the University of California, Los Angeles, analyzed DNA sequences from 101 college students, 49 of whom had acne and 52 of whom did not. Over 1000 strains of *Propionibacterium acnes* (*P. acnes*) were isolated. Using WGS and bioinformatics, researchers clustered these strains into ten strain types (related strains). Six of these types were more common among acne-prone students, and one type appeared repeatedly in skin samples from students without acne. Sequence analysis of types associated with acne indicated gene clusters that may contribute to the skin disease. Further analysis of these strain types may help dermatologists develop new drugs targeted at killing acne-causing strains of *P. acnes*.

No Genome Left Behind and the Genome 10K Plan

Without question new sequencing technologies that have been developed as a result of the HGP are an important part of the transformational effect the HGP has had on modern biology. In the late 1990s, a room full of sequencers and several million dollars were required to sequence the 97-Mb genome of *C. elegans*. As a sign of modern times in the world of genomics, recently two sequencers and $500,000 produced a reasonably complete draft of the 750-Mb cod genome—in a month!

Recent headline-grabbing genomes that have been completed include:

- the tomato, which has 31,760 genes, more genes than humans!

- the potato, a vegetable that shares 92 percent of its DNA with tomatoes, a fruit

- chickpea, the second most widely grown legume after the soybean

- the red-spotted new, which has a genome of almost 10 billion base pairs!

Modern sequencing technologies are asking some to consider the question, "What would you do if you could sequence everything?" Partners around the world, including genome scientists and museum curators, have proposed sequencing 10,000 vertebrate genomes, the **Genome 10K** plan. Shortly after the HGP finished, the National Human Genome Research Institute (NHGRI) assembled a list of mammals and other vertebrates as priorities for genome sequencing in part because of their potential benefit for learning about the human genome through comparative genomics. Genome 10K will also provide insight into genome evolution and speciation.

21.6 Comparative Genomics Analyzes and Compares Genomes from Different Organisms

As of 2013, over 4300 whole genomes have been sequenced—including many model organisms and a number of viruses. About 200 of the completed genomes are from eukaryotes. This is quite extraordinary progress in a relatively short time span! Among these organisms are yeast (*Saccharomyces cerevisiae*)—the first eukaryotic genome to be sequenced to bacteria such as *E. coli,* the nematode roundworm (*Caenorhabditis elegans),* the thale cress plant (*Arabidopsis thaliana),* mice (*Mus musculus),* zebrafish (*Danio rerio),* and of course *Drosophila.* In the past few years, genomes for chimpanzees, dogs, chickens, gorillas, sea urchins, honey bees, pigs, pufferfish, rice, and wheat have all been sequenced.

These studies have demonstrated not only significant differences in genome organization between prokaryotes and eukaryotes but also many similarities between genomes of nearly all species. In this section we discuss interesting aspects of genomes in selected organisms. Analysis of the growing number of genome sequences confirms that all living organisms are related and descended from a common ancestor. Similar gene sets are used by organisms for basic cellular functions, such as DNA replication, transcription, and translation. These genetic relationships are the rationale for using model organisms to study inherited human disorders, the effects of the environment on genes, and interactions of genes in complex diseases, such as cardiovascular disease, diabetes, neurodegenerative conditions, and behavioral disorders.

Comparative genomics compares the genomes of different organisms to answer questions about genetics and other aspects of biology. It is a field with many research and practical applications, including gene discovery and the development of model organisms to study human diseases. It also incorporates the study of gene and genome evolution and the relationship between organisms and their environment. Comparative genomics uses a wide range of techniques and resources, such as the construction and use of nucleotide and protein databases containing nucleic acid and amino acid sequences, fluorescent *in situ* hybridization (FISH), and the creation of gene knockout animals. Comparative genomics can reveal genetic differences and similarities between organisms to provide insight into how those differences contribute to differences in phenotype, life cycle, or other attributes, and to ascertain the evolutionary history of those genetic differences.

Prokaryotic and Eukaryotic Genomes Display Common Structural and Functional Features and Important Differences

Since most prokaryotes have small genomes amenable to shotgun cloning and sequencing, many early genome projects have focused on prokaryotes, and more than 900 additional projects to sequence prokaryotic genomes are now under way. Many of the prokaryotic genomes already sequenced are from organisms that cause human diseases, such as cholera, tuberculosis, and leprosy. Traditionally, the bacterial genome has been thought of as relatively small (less than 5 Mb) and contained within a single circular DNA molecule. *E. coli,* used as the prototypical bacterial model organism in genetics, has a genome with these characteristics. However, the flood of genomic information now available has challenged the validity of this viewpoint for bacteria in general. Although most prokaryotic genomes are small, their sizes vary across a surprisingly wide range. In fact, there is some overlap in size between larger bacterial genomes (30 Mb in *Bacillus megaterium*) and smaller eukaryotic genomes (12.1 Mb in yeast). Gene number in bacterial genomes also demonstrates a wide range, from less than 500 to more than 5000 genes, a ten-fold difference.

In addition, although many bacteria have a single, circular chromosome, there is substantial variation in chromosome organization and number among bacterial species. An increasing number of genomes composed of linear DNA molecules are being identified, including the genome of *Borrelia burgdorferi,* the organism that causes Lyme disease. Sequencing of the *Vibrio cholerae* genome (the organism responsible for cholera) revealed the presence of two circular chromosomes. Other bacteria that have genomes with two or more chromosomes include *Rhizobium radiobacter* (formerly *Agrobacterium tumefaciens),* *Deinococcus radiodurans,* and *Rhodobacter sphaeroides.* The finding that some bacterial species have multiple chromosomes raises questions both about how replication and segregation of their chromosomes are coordinated during cell division and about what undiscovered mechanisms of gene regulation may exist in bacteria. The answers may provide clues about the evolution of multichromosome eukaryotic genomes.

We can make two generalizations about the organization of protein-coding genes in bacteria. First, gene density is very high, averaging about one gene per kilobase of DNA. For example, the genome of *E. coli* strain K12, which was sequenced in 1997 as the second prokaryotic genome to be sequenced, is 4.6 Mb in size, and it contains 4289

TABLE 21.2 Comparison of Selected Genomes

Organism (Scientific Name)	Approximate Size of Genome (in million [megabase, Mb] or billion [gigabase, Gb] bases) (Date Completed)	Number of Genes	Approximate Percentage of Genes Shared with Humans
Bacterium (*Escherichia coli*)	4.6 Mb (1997)	4403	not determined
Chicken (*Gallus gallus*)	1 Gb (2004)	~20,000–23,000	60%
Dog (*Canis familiaris*)	2.5 Gb (2003)	~18,400	75%
Chimpanzee (*Pan troglodytes*)	~3 Gb (2005)	~20,000–24,000	98%
Fruit fly (*Drosophila melanogaster*)	165 Mb (2000)	~13,600	50%
Human (*Homo sapiens*)	3.1 Gb (2004)	~20,000	100%
Mouse (*Mus musculus*)	~2.5 Gb (2002)	~30,000	80%
Pig (*Sus scrofa*)	~3 Gb (2012)	21,640	84%
Rat (*Rattus norvegicus*)	~2.75 Gb (2004)	~22,000	80%
Rhesus macaque (*Macaca mulatta*)	2.87 Gb (2007)	~20,000	93%
Rice (*Oryza sativa*)	389 Mb (2005)	~41,000	not determined
Roundworm (*Caenorhabditis elegans*)	97 Mb (1998)	19,099	40%
Sea urchin (*Strongylocentrotus purpuratus*)	814 Mb (2006)	~23,500	60%
Thale cress (plant) (*Arabidopsis thaliana*)	140 Mb (2000)	~27,500	not determined
Yeast (*Saccharomyces cerevisiae*)	12 Mb (1996)	~5700	30%

Adapted from Palladino, M. A. *Understanding the Human Genome Project*, 2nd ed. Benjamin Cummings, 2006.
Note: Billion bp (gigabase, Gb).

protein-coding genes in its single, circular chromosome. This close packing of genes in prokaryotic genomes means that a very high proportion of the DNA (approximately 85 to 90 percent) serves as coding DNA. Typically, only a small amount of a bacterial genome is noncoding DNA, often in the form of regulatory sequences or of transposable elements that can move from one place to another in the genome.

The second generalization we can make is that bacterial genomes contain operons. Recall from an earlier chapter (see Chapter 16), that operons contain multiple genes functioning as a transcriptional unit whose protein products are part of a common biochemical pathway). In *E. coli,* 27 percent of all genes are contained in operons (almost 600 operons). In other bacterial genomes, the organization of genes into transcriptional units is challenging our ideas about the nature of operons. For example, in *Aquifex aeolicus,* one polygenic transcription unit contains six genes involved in several different cellular processes with no apparent common relationships: two genes for DNA recombination, one for lipid synthesis, one for nucleic acid synthesis, one for protein synthesis, and one that encodes a protein for cell motility. Other polygenic transcription units in this species also contain genes with widely different functions. This finding, combined with similar results from other genome projects, raises interesting questions about the consensus that operons encode products that control a single metabolic pathway in bacterial cells.

The basic features of eukaryotic genomes are similar in different species, although genome size in eukaryotes is highly variable (Table 21.2). Genome sizes range from about 10 Mb in fungi to over 100,000 Mb in some flowering plants (a ten thousand-fold range); the number of chromosomes per genome ranges from two to the hundreds (about a hundred-fold range), but the number of genes varies much less dramatically than either genome size or chromosome number.

Eukaryotic genomes have several features not found in prokaryotes:

■ **Gene density.** In prokaryotes, gene density is close to 1 gene per kilobase. In eukaryotic genomes, there is a wide range of gene density. In yeast, there is about 1 gene/2 kb, in Drosophila, about 1 gene/13 kb, and in humans, gene density varies greatly from chromosome to chromosome. Human chromosome 22 has about 1 gene/64 kb, while chromosome 13 has 1 gene/155 kb of DNA.

■ **Introns.** Most eukaryotic genes contain introns. There is wide variation among genomes in the number of introns they contain and also wide variation from gene to gene. The entire yeast genome has only 239 introns, whereas just a single gene in the human genome can contain more than 100 introns. Regarding intron size, generally the size in eukaryotes is correlated with genome size. Smaller genomes have smaller average introns, and larger genomes have larger average intron sizes. But there are exceptions. For example, the genome of the pufferfish (*Fugu rubripes*) has relatively few introns.

■ **Repetitive sequences**. The presence of introns and the existence of repetitive sequences are two major reasons for the wide range of genome sizes in eukaryotes. In some plants, such as maize, repetitive sequences are the dominant feature of the genome. The maize genome has about 2500 Mb of DNA, and more than two-thirds of that genome is composed of repetitive DNA. In the human, as discussed previously, about half of the genome is repetitive DNA.

Comparative Genomics Provides Novel Information about the Genomes of Model Organisms and the Human Genome

As mentioned earlier, the Human Genome Project sequenced genomes from a number of model nonhuman organisms too, including *E. coli, Arabidopsis thaliana, Saccharomyces cerevisiae, Drosophila melanogaster,* the nematode roundworm *Caenorhabditis elegans,* and the mouse *Mus musculus.* Complete genome sequences of such organisms have been invaluable for comparative genomics studies of gene function in these organisms and in humans. As shown in Table 21.2, the number of genes humans share with other species is very high, ranging from about 30 percent of the genes in yeast to ~80 percent in mice and ~98 percent in chimpanzees. The human genome even contains around 100 genes that are also present in many bacteria. Comparative genomics has shown us that many mutated genes involved in human disease are also present in model organisms. For instance, approximately 60 percent of genes mutated in nearly 300 human diseases are also found in *Drosophila.* These include genes involved in prostate, colon, and pancreatic cancers; cardiovascular disease; cystic fibrosis; and several other conditions. Here we consider how comparative genomics studies of several model organisms (sea urchins, dogs, chimpanzees, and Rhesus monkeys) and the Neanderthal genome have revealed interesting elements of the human genome.

The Sea Urchin Genome

In 2006, researchers from the Sea Urchin Genome Sequencing Consortium completed the 814 million bp genome of the sea urchin *Strongylocentrotus purpuratus* [pictured in Figure 21–20(a)]. Sea urchins are shallow-water marine invertebrates that have served as important model organisms, particularly for developmental biologists. One reason is that the sea urchin is a nonchordate deuterostome, and humans, with their spinal cord, are chordate deuterostomes. Fossil records indicate that sea urchins appeared during the Early Cambrian period, around 520 mya.

A combination of whole-genome shotgun sequencing and map-based cloning in BACs was used to complete the genome. Sea urchins have an estimated 23,500 genes, including representative genes for just about all major vertebrate gene families. Sequence alignment and homology searches demonstrate that the sea urchin contains many genes with important functions in humans, yet interestingly, important genes in flies and worms, such as certain cytochrome P-450 genes that play a role in the breakdown of toxic compounds, are missing from sea urchins. The sea urchin genome also has an abundance (~25 to 30 percent) of **pseudogenes**—nonfunctional relatives of protein-coding genes (we meet pseudogenes again in the next subsection). Sea urchins have a smaller average intron size than humans, supporting the general trend revealed by comparative genomics that intron size is correlated with overall genome size.

Another genome trend that urchins share with other eukaryotes is the presence of genes involved in innate immunity, the inborn defense mechanisms that provide broad-spectrum protection against many pathogens. Sea urchins have an extraordinarily rich number of genes providing innate immunity. For example, one very important category of innate immunity genes, the Toll-like receptors (TLRs), produce transmembrane proteins that are essential for pathogen recognition in nearly every cell type of vertebrates. Sea urchins have over 200 *Tlr* genes compared to 11 in humans. The abundance of these and other important innate immunity genes in sea urchins has led to categorizing these genes as the urchin "defensome." This characteristic of sea urchins may help explain how these organisms have adapted so well to the pathogen-loaded environments of seabeds.

Urchins have nearly 1000 genes for sensing light and odor, indicative of great sensory abilities. In this respect, their genome is more typical of vertebrates than invertebrates. A number of orthologs of human genes involved in hearing and balance are present in the sea urchin, as are many human-disease-associated orthologs, including protein kinases, GTPases, transcription factors, TLRs, transporters, and low-density lipoprotein receptors. Sea urchins and humans share approximately 7000 orthologs.

Another interesting aspect of the sea urchin genome project is that it has identified genes previously thought to be vertebrate-specific. One example, the *WntA* gene, important for patterning during embryonic development, as discussed earlier in the text (see Chapter 18), was thought to be absent from nonvertebrate deuterostomes. The sea urchin genome also contains genes that are not present in chordates. Further analysis of the urchin genome is expected to make important contributions to our understanding of evolutionary transitions between invertebrates and vertebrates.

The Dog Genome

In 2005 the genome for "man's best friend" was completed, and it revealed that we share about 75 percent of our genes with dogs (*Canis familiaris*), providing a useful model with which to study our own genome. Dogs have a genome that is similar in size to the human genome: about 2.5 billion base pairs with an estimated 18,400 genes. The dog offers several advantages for studying heritable human diseases. Dogs share many genetic disorders with humans, including over 400 single-gene disorders, sex-chromosome aneuploidies, multifactorial diseases (such as epilepsy), behavioral conditions (such as obsessive-compulsive disorder), and genetic predispositions to cancer, blindness, heart disease, and deafness. The molecular causes of at least 60 percent of inherited diseases in dogs, such as point mutations and deletions, are similar or identical to those found in humans. In addition, at least 50 percent of the genetic diseases in dogs are breed-specific, so that the mutant allele segregates in relatively homogeneous genetic backgrounds. Dog breeds resemble isolated human populations in having a small number of founders and a long period of relative genetic isolation. These properties make individual dog breeds useful as models of human genetic disorders.

In addition, differences in biology and behavior among dog breeds are well documented. Domestic dogs show greater variation in body size than all other living terrestrial vertebrates. The size difference between a Chihuahua and a Great Dane is an excellent example. Mapping and comparing DNA sequence differences (polymorphisms) among breeds may help identify genes that contribute to both physiological and behavioral differences. For instance, in 2007, genome-wide analysis of different large and small dog breeds revealed a locus on chromosome 15 where a single-nucleotide polymorphism in the insulin-like growth factor 1 gene (*Igf1*) is common in all small breeds of dogs but virtually absent from large dogs. It is well known that *Igf1* plays important roles in growth-hormone-regulated increases in muscle mass and bone growth during adolescence in humans. This study provides very strong evidence that mutation of *Igf1* is a primary determinant of body size in small dogs.

Dog breeders are now using genetic tests to screen dogs for inherited disease conditions, for coat color in Labrador retrievers and poodles, and for fur length in Mastiffs. Undoubtedly, we can expect many more genetic tests for dogs in the near future, including DNA analysis for size, type of tail, speed, sense of smell, and other traits deemed important by breeders and owners.

Finally, scientists have been using genomic data to determine the origin of domestic dogs. An analysis of 48,000 markers across the whole genomes of hundreds of dogs and gray wolves from different regions around the world showed that modern dogs shared more sequences in common with Middle Eastern wolves than with Asian wolves. Recent research based on sequence analysis of mitochondrial DNA (mtDNA) from the fossils of ancient dogs and wolves suggests that dogs originated in Europe from gray wolves that are now extinct. In this work, researchers compared mtDNA from samples 1000 to 36,000 years old from 77 dogs of different breeds, 49 wolves, and 4 coyotes. Based on mtDNA sequences, dogs appear to be more closely related to ancient wolves than to modern wolves. A similar conclusion was made by a team studying whole genomes. In addition, mtDNA sequences from ancient remains that most closely matched modern dogs were all from European gray wolf samples. Aging of the samples suggests that dog domestication began between 18,800 and 32,100 years ago among hunter-gatherers several thousand years before humans farmed in earnest. Scientists who believe that the domestication of dogs began in Asia have noted that the recent mtDNA study may be flawed because the researchers were unable to get DNA samples from ancient specimens from the Middle East and from East Asia. Ongoing research in this area will continue, and it will be interesting to see whether genomics can settle the debate about the origins of man's best friend.

The Chimpanzee Genome

Although the chimpanzee (*Pan troglodytes*) genome was not part of the HGP, its nucleotide sequence was completed in 2004. Overall, the chimp and human genome sequences differ by less than 2 percent, and 98 percent of the genes are the same. Comparisons between these genomes offer some interesting insights into what makes some primates humans and others chimpanzees.

The speciation events that separated humans and chimpanzees occurred less than 6.3 million years ago (mya). Genomic analysis indicates that these species initially diverged but then exchanged genes again before separating completely. Their separate evolution after this point is exhibited in such differences as that seen between the sequence of chimpanzee chromosome 22 and its human ortholog, chromosome 21 (Table 21.3; chimps have 48 chromosomes and humans have 46, so the numbering is different). These chromosomes have accumulated nucleotide substitutions that total 1.44 percent of the sequence. The most surprising difference is the discovery of 68,000 nucleotide insertions or deletions, collectively called **indels**, in the chimp and human chromosomes, a frequency of 1 indel every 470 bases. Many of these are *Alu* insertions in human chromosome 21. Although the overall difference in the nucleotide sequence is small, there are significant differences in the encoded genes. Only 17 percent of the genes analyzed encode identical proteins in both chromosomes;

TABLE 21.3   **Comparisons between Human Chromosome 21 and Chimpanzee Chromosome 22**

	Human 21	Chimpanzee 22
Size (bp)	33,127,944	32,799,845
%G + C Content	40.94	41.01
CpG Islands	950	885
SINEs (*Alu* elements)	15,137	15,048
Genes	284	272
Pseudogenes	98	89

the other 83 percent encode genes with one or more amino acid differences.

Differences in the time and place of gene expression also play a major role in differentiating the two primates. Using DNA microarrays (discussed in Section 21.9), researchers compared expression patterns of 202 genes in human and chimp cells from brain and liver. They found more species-specific differences in expression of brain genes than liver genes. To further examine these differences, Svante Pääbo and colleagues compared expression of 10,000 genes in human and chimpanzee brains and found that 10 percent of genes examined differ in expression in one or more regions of the brain. More importantly, these differences are associated with genes in regions of the human genome that have been duplicated subsequent to the divergence of chimps and humans. This finding indicates that genome evolution, speciation, and gene expression are interconnected. Further work on these segmental duplications and the genes they contain may identify genes that help make us human.

The Rhesus Monkey Genome

The Rhesus macaque monkey (*Macaca mulatta*), another primate, has served as one of the most important model organisms in biomedical research. Macaques have played central roles in our understanding of cardiovascular disease, aging, diabetes, cancer, depression, osteoporosis, and many other aspects of human health. They have been essential for research on AIDS vaccines and for the development of polio vaccines. The macaque's genome is the first monkey genome to have been sequenced. A main reason geneticists are so excited about the completion of this sequencing project is that macaques provide a more distant evolutionary window that is ideally suited for comparing and analyzing human and chimpanzee genomes. As we discussed in the preceding section, humans and chimpanzees shared a common ancestor approximately 6 mya. But macaques split from the ape lineage that led to chimpanzees and humans about 25 mya. The macaque and human genome

have thus diverged farther from one another, as evidenced by the ~93 percent sequence identity between humans and macaques compared to the ~98 percent sequence identity shared by humans and chimpanzees.

The macaque genome was published in 2007, and it was no surprise to learn that it consists of 2.87 billion bp (similar to the size of the human genome) contained in 22 chromosomes (20 autosomes, an X, and a Y) with ~20,000 protein-coding genes. Although comparative analyses of this genome are ongoing, a number of interesting features have been revealed so far. As in humans, about 50 percent of the genome consists of repeat elements (transposons, LINEs, SINEs). Gene duplications and gene families are abundant, including cancer gene families found in humans.

A number of interesting surprises have also been observed. For instance, recall from earlier in the text (see Chapter 4) and elsewhere our discussion about the genetic disorder phenylketonuria (PKU), an autosomal recessive inherited condition in which individuals cannot metabolize the amino acid phenylalanine due to mutation of the phenylalanine hydroxylase (*PAH*) gene. The histidine substitution encoded by a mutation in the *PAH* gene of humans with PKU appears as the wild-type amino acid in the protein from healthy macaques. Further analysis of the macaque genome and comparison to the human and chimpanzee genome will be invaluable for geneticists studying genetic variations that played a role in primate evolution.

The Neanderthal Genome and Modern Humans

In early 2009, a team of scientists led by Svante Pääbo at the Max Planck Institute for Evolutionary Anthropology in Germany and 454 Life Sciences reported completion of a rough draft of the Neanderthal (*Homo neanderthalensis*) genome encompassing more than 3 billion bp of Neanderthal DNA and about two-thirds of the genome. Previously, in 1997, Pääbo's lab sequenced portions of Neanderthal mitochondrial DNA from a fossil. In late 2006, Pääbo's group along with a number of scientists in the United States reported the first sequence of ~65,000 bp of nuclear DNA isolated from Neanderthal bone samples from Croatia. Bones from three females who lived in Vindija Cave in Croatia about 38,000 to 44,000 years ago were used to produce the draft sequence of the Neanderthal nuclear genome.

Because Neanderthals are members of the human family, and closer relatives to humans than chimpanzees, the Neanderthal genome is expected to provide an unprecedented opportunity to use comparative genomics to advance our understanding of evolutionary relationships between modern humans and our predecessors. In particular, scientists are interested in identifying areas in the genome where humans have undergone rapid evolution since splitting (diverging) from Neanderthals. Much of this analysis involves a comparative genomics approach to compare the Neanderthal genome to the human and chimpanzee genomes.

The human and Neanderthal genomes are 99 percent identical. Comparative genomics has identified 78 protein-coding sequences in humans that seem to have arisen since the divergence from Neanderthals and that may have helped modern humans adapt. Some of these sequences are involved in cognitive development and sperm motility. Of the many genes shared by these species, *FOXP2* is a gene that has been linked to speech and language ability. There are many genes that influence speech, so this finding does not mean that Neanderthals spoke as we do. But because Neanderthals had the same modern human *FOXP2* gene scientists have speculated that Neanderthals possessed linguistic abilities.

A 2008 study of the Neanderthal mitochondrial genome by Pääbo's team obtained 39 million sequence reads averaging 69 bp in length. Of 16,568 nucleotides present in mtDNA of modern humans, on average 206 differed from those of Neanderthals. These differences fall outside the variation among modern humans and led the research team to estimate that the most common point of ancestry, the divergence date between the two mtDNA lineages, was 660,000 years ago (±140,000). This study also provided interesting observations about rates of amino acid substitutions in key enzymes in the mitochondrial electron transport chain.

The realization that modern humans and Neanderthals lived in overlapping ranges as recently as 30,000 years ago has led to speculation about the interactions between modern humans and Neanderthals. Genome studies suggest that interbreeding took place between Neanderthals and modern humans an estimated 45,000 to 80,000 years ago in the eastern Mediterranean. In fact, the genome of non-African *H. sapiens* contains approximately 1–4 percent

of sequence inherited from Neanderthals. These exciting studies, previously thought to be impossible, are having ramifications in many areas of human evolution, and it will be interesting indeed to follow the progress of this work.

21.7 Comparative Genomics Is Useful for Studying the Evolution and Function of Multigene Families

Comparative genomics has also proven to be valuable for identifying members of **multigene families**, groups of genes that share similar but not identical DNA sequences through duplication and descent from a single ancestral gene. Their gene products frequently have similar functions, and the genes are often, but not always, found at a single chromosomal locus. A group of related multigene families is called a **superfamily**. Sequence data from genome projects are providing evidence that multigene families are present in many, if not all, genomes. One of the best-studied examples of gene family evolution is the **globin gene superfamily**, whose members encode very similar but not identical polypeptide chains with closely related functions (**Figure 21–14**). Other well-characterized

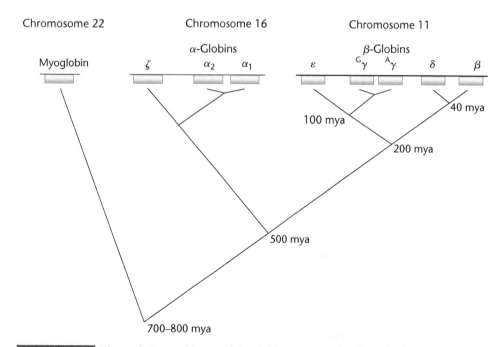

FIGURE 21–14 The evolutionary history of the globin gene superfamily. A duplication event in an ancestral gene gave rise to two lineages about 700 to 800 million years ago (mya). One line led to the myoglobin gene, which is located on chromosome 22 in humans; the other underwent a second duplication event about 500 mya, giving rise to the ancestors of the α-globin and β-globin gene subfamilies. Duplications beginning about 200 mya formed the β-globin gene subfamilies. In humans, the α-globin genes are located on chromosome 16, and the β-globin genes are on chromosome 11.

gene superfamilies include the histone, tubulin, actin, and immunoglobulin (antibody) gene superfamilies.

Recall that paralogs, which we defined in Section 21.3, are homologous genes present in the same single organism, believed to have evolved by gene duplication. The globin genes that encode the polypeptides in hemoglobin molecules are a paralogous multigene superfamily that arose by duplication and dispersal to occupy different chromosomal sites. In this family, an ancestral gene encoding an oxygen transport protein was duplicated about 800 mya, producing two sister genes, one of which evolved into the modern-day myoglobin gene. **Myoglobin** is an oxygen-carrying protein found in muscle. The other gene underwent further duplication and divergence about 500 mya and formed prototypes of the α-globin and β-globin genes. These genes encode proteins found in **hemoglobin**, the oxygen-carrying molecule in red blood cells. Additional duplications within these genes occurred within the last 200 million years. Events subsequent to each duplication dispersed these gene subfamilies to different chromosomes, and in the human genome, each now resides on a separate chromosome. Similar patterns of evolution are observed in other gene families, including the trypsin–chymotrypsin family of proteases, the homeotic selector genes of animals, and the rhodopsin family of visual pigments.

Adult hemoglobin is a tetramer containing two α- and two β-polypeptides (refer to Figure 14–20 for the structure of hemoglobin). Each polypeptide incorporates a heme group that reversibly binds oxygen. The α-globin gene cluster on chromosome 16 and the β-globin gene cluster on chromosome 11 share nucleotide- and amino acid–sequence similarity but the highest degree of sequence similarity is found within subfamilies.

The **α-globin** gene subfamily [**Figure 21–15(a)**] contains three genes: the ζ (zeta) gene, expressed only in early embryogenesis, and two copies of the α gene, expressed during the fetal (α_1) and adult stages (α_2). In addition, the cluster contains two pseudogenes (similar to ζ and α_1), which in this family are designated by the prefix Ψ (psi) followed by the symbol of the gene they most resemble. Thus, the designation $\Psi\alpha_1$ indicates a pseudogene of the fetal α_1 gene.

The organization of the α-globin subfamily members and the locations of their introns and exons demonstrate several characteristic features [**Figure 21–15(a)**]. First, the DNA encoding the three functional α genes occupies only

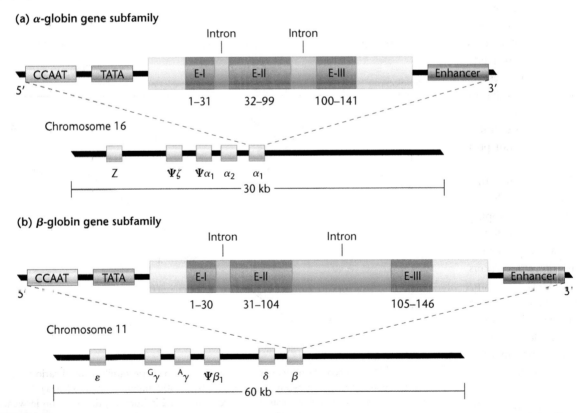

(a) α-globin gene subfamily

(b) β-globin gene subfamily

FIGURE 21–15 Organization of (a) the α-globin gene subfamily on chromosome 16 and (b) the β-globin gene subfamily on chromosome 11. Also shown in each case is the internal organization of the α_1 gene and the β gene, respectively. Both genes contain three exons (E-I, E-II, E-III) and two introns. The numbers below the exons indicate the location of amino acids in the gene product encoded by each exon.

a small portion of the 30-kb region containing the subfamily. Second, each functional gene in this subfamily contains two introns at precisely the same positions. Third, the nucleotide sequences within corresponding exons are nearly identical in the ζ and α genes. Each of these genes encodes a polypeptide chain of 141 amino acids. However, their intron sequences are highly divergent, even though the introns are about the same size. Note that much of the nucleotide sequence of each gene is contained in these noncoding introns.

The human β-globin gene cluster contains five genes spaced over 60 kb of DNA [Figure 21–15(b)]. In this and the α-globin gene subfamily, the order of genes on the chromosome parallels their order of expression during development. Three of the five genes are expressed before birth. The ε (epsilon) gene is expressed only during embryogenesis, while the two nearly identical γ genes ($^{G}\gamma$ and $^{A}\gamma$) are expressed only during fetal development. The polypeptide products of the two γ genes differ only by a single amino acid. The two remaining genes, δ and β, are expressed after birth and throughout life. A single pseudogene, $\Psi\beta_1$, is present in this subfamily. All five functional genes in this cluster encode proteins with 146 amino acids and have two similar-sized introns at exactly the same positions. The second intron in the β-globin subfamily is significantly larger than its counterpart in the functional α-globin subfamily. These features reflect the evolutionary history of each subfamily and the events such as gene duplication, nucleotide substitution, and chromosome translocations that produced the present-day globin superfamily.

21.8 Metagenomics Applies Genomics Techniques to Environmental Samples

Metagenomics, also called **environmental genomics**, is the use of whole-genome shotgun approaches to sequence genomes from entire communities of microbes in environmental samples of water, air, and soil. Oceans, glaciers, deserts, and virtually every other environment on Earth are being sampled for metagenomics projects. Human genome pioneer J. Craig Venter left Celera to form the J. Craig Venter Institute, and his group has played a central role in developing metagenomics as an emerging area of genomics research.

One of the institute's major initiatives has been a global expedition to sample marine and terrestrial microorganisms from around the world and to sequence their genomes. Through this project, called the *Sorcerer II* Global Ocean Sampling (GOS) Expedition, Venter and his

researchers traveled the globe by yacht, in a sailing voyage described as a modern-day version of Charles Darwin's famous voyage on the *H.M.S. Beagle.*

A key benefit of metagenomics is its potential for teaching us more about millions of species of bacteria, of which only a few thousand have been well characterized. Many new viruses, particularly bacteriophages, are also identified through metagenomics studies of water samples. Metagenomics is providing important new information about genetic diversity in microbes that is key to understanding complex interactions between microbial communities and their environment, as well as allowing phylogenetic classification of newly identified microbes. Metagenomics also has great potential for identifying genes with novel functions, some of which may have valuable applications in medicine and biotechnology.

The general method used in metagenomics to sequence genomes for all microbes in a given environment involves isolating DNA directly from an environmental sample without requiring cultures of the microbes or viruses. Such an approach is necessary because often it is difficult to replicate the complex array of growth conditions the microbes need to survive in culture.

For the *Sorcerer II* GOS project, samples of water from different layers in the water column were passed through high-density filters of various sizes to capture the microbes. DNA was then isolated from the microbes and subjected to shotgun sequencing and genome assembly. High-throughput sequencers on board the yacht operated nearly around the clock. One of the earliest expeditions by this group sequenced bacterial genomes from the Sargasso Sea off Bermuda. This project yielded over 1.2 million novel DNA sequences from 1800 microbial species, including 148 previously unknown bacterial species, and identified hundreds of photoreceptor genes. Many aquatic microorganisms rely on photoreceptors for capturing light energy to power photosynthesis. Scientists are interested in learning more about photoreceptors to help develop ways in which photosynthesis may be used to produce hydrogen as a fuel source. Medical researchers are also very interested in photoreceptors because in humans and many other species, photoreceptors in the retina of the eye are key proteins that detect light energy and transduce electrical signals that the brain eventually interprets to create visual images.

By early 2007, the GOS database contained approximately 6 billion bp of DNA from more than 400 uncharacterized microbial species! These sequences included 7.7 million previously uncharacterized sequences, encoding more than 6 million different potential proteins. This is almost twice the total number of previously characterized proteins in all other known databases worldwide (such

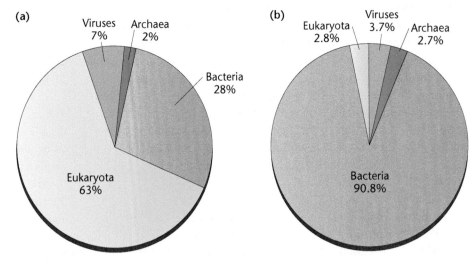

(a)

Viruses 7%

Archaea 2%

Bacteria 28%

Eukaryota 63%

(b)

Viruses 3.7%

Eukaryota 2.8%

Archaea 2.7%

Bacteria 90.8%

FIGURE 21–16 (a) Kingdom identifications for predicted proteins in NCBInr, NCBI Prokaryotic Genomes, the Institute for Genomics Research Gene Indices, and Ensembl databases. Notice that the publicly available databases of sequenced genomes and the predicted proteins they encode are dominated by eukaryotic sequences. (b) Kingdom identifications for novel predicted proteins in the Global Ocean Sampling (GOS) database. Bacterial sequences dominate this database, demonstrating the value of metagenomics for revealing new information about microbial genomes and microbial communities.

as the Swiss-Prot database discussed in the Exploring Genomics exercise for Chapter 14). **Figure 21–16(a)** shows the kingdom assignments for predicted protein sequences in publicly available databases worldwide, such as the

NCBI-nonredundant protein database (NCBInr), which accesses GenBank, Ensembl, and other well-known databases. Eukaryotic sequences comprise the majority (63 percent) of predicted proteins in these databases. Reviewing the kingdom assignments of approximately 6 million predicted proteins in the Global Ocean Sampling (GOS) dataset shows that, in contrast, the largest majority (90.8 percent) of sequences in this database are from the bacterial kingdom [**Figure 21–16(b)**].

The GOS Expedition also examined protein families corresponding to the predicted proteins encoded by the genome sequences in the GOS database: 17,067 families were medium (between 20 and 200 proteins) and large-sized (>200 proteins) clusters. A **Venn diagram**, like the image shown in **Figure 21–17**, is a common way to represent overlapping data in genomics datasets. In this figure, overlapping ovals indicate numbers of protein families belonging to certain sets of categories. Each area of the diagram is labeled with the number and percentage of families out of the 17,067 GOS medium- and large-sized clusters in each category or area of overlap. Of the 17,067 clusters in the GOS database, 3995 did not show significant homology to known protein families in prokaryotes, viruses, or eukaryotes (Figure 21–17). The results summarized in Figures 21–16 and 21–17 demonstrate the value of the GOS Expedition and of metagenomics for identifying novel microbial genes and potential proteins.

In Section 21.5 you learned about the Human Microbiome Project. This project represents an example of a metagenomics project in that it is intended to sequence the genomes of microbes and viruses present in and on humans as the "environment" being sampled. In fact, many of the techniques used in this project were based on metagenomics techniques used to sequence bacterial and viral genomes from marine water samples. Many other high-profile metagenomics applications have emerged recently, including the use of metagenomics to identify viruses and fungi thought to be involved in colony collapse disorder. One such malady has resulted in the loss of 50–90 percent of the honey bee population in beekeeping operations throughout the United States.

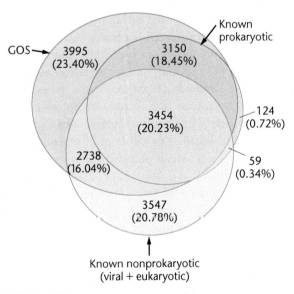

GOS

3995 (23.40%)

Known prokaryotic

3150 (18.45%)

3454 (20.23%)

124 (0.72%)

2738 (16.04%)

59 (0.34%)

3547 (20.78%)

Known nonprokaryotic (viral + eukaryotic)

FIGURE 21–17 Venn diagram representation of 17,067 medium and large clusters of protein families grouped according to three categories: GOS, known prokaryotic sequences, and known nonprokaryotic sequences. Notice that the GOS project identified 3995 medium and large clusters of gene families that are unique to the GOS database and do not show significant homology to known protein families in prokaryotes or nonprokaryotes (viral and eukaryotes).

21.9 Transcriptome Analysis Reveals Profiles of Expressed Genes in Cells and Tissues

Once any genome has been sequenced and annotated, a formidable challenge still remains: that of understanding genome function by analyzing the genes it contains and the ways the genes expressed by the genome are regulated. **Transcriptome analysis**, also called **transcriptomics** or **global analysis of gene expression**, studies the expression of genes by a genome both qualitatively—by identifying which genes are expressed and which genes are not expressed—and quantitatively—by measuring varying levels of expression for different genes.

Even though in theory all cells of an organism possess the same gene in any cell or tissue type, certain genes will be highly expressed, others expressed at low levels, and some not expressed at all. Transcriptome analysis reveals gene-expression profiles that for the same genome may vary from cell to cell or from tissue type to tissue type. Identifying genes expressed by a genome is essential for understanding how the genome functions. Transcriptome analysis provides insights into (1) normal patterns of gene expression that are important for understanding how a cell or tissue type differentiates during development, (2) how gene expression dictates and controls the physiology of differentiated cells, and (3) mechanisms of disease development that result from or cause gene-expression changes in cells. Later in the text (see Chapter 22), we will consider why gene-expression analysis is gradually becoming an important diagnostic tool in certain areas of medicine. For example, examining gene-expression profiles in a cancerous tumor can help diagnose tumor type, determine the likelihood of tumor metastasis (spreading), and develop the most effective treatment strategy.

Microarray Analysis

A number of different techniques can be used for transcriptome analysis. PCR-based methods are useful because of their ability to detect genes that are expressed at low levels. **DNA microarray analysis** is widely used because it enables researchers to analyze all of a sample's expressed genes simultaneously.

Most microarrays, also known as **gene chips**, consist of a glass microscope slide onto which single-stranded DNA molecules are attached, or "spotted," using a computer-controlled high-speed robotic arm called an arrayer. Arrayers are fitted with a number of tiny pins. Each pin is immersed in a small amount of solution containing millions of copies of a different single-stranded DNA molecule. For example, many microarrays are made with single-stranded sequences of complementary DNA (cDNA) or expressed sequenced

tags (ESTs)—short fragments of cloned DNA from expressed genes. The arrayer fixes the DNA onto the slide at specific locations (points, or spots) that are recorded by a computer. A single microarray can have over 20,000 different spots of DNA (and over 1 million for exon-specific microarrays), each containing a unique sequence for a different gene. Entire genomes are available on microarrays, including the human genome. As you will learn later in the text (see Chapter 22), researchers are also using microarrays to compare patterns of gene expression in tissues in response to different conditions, to compare gene-expression patterns in normal and diseased tissues, and to identify pathogens.

To prepare a microarray for use in transcriptome analysis, scientists typically begin by extracting mRNA from cells or tissues (**Figure 21–18**). The mRNA is usually then reverse transcribed to synthesize cDNA tagged with fluorescently labeled nucleotides. The mRNA or cDNA can be labeled in a number of ways, but most methods involve the use of fluorescent dyes. Historically, microarray studies often involve comparing gene expression in different cell or tissue samples. cDNA prepared from one tissue is usually labeled with one color dye, red for example, and cDNA from another tissue is labeled with a different-colored dye, such as green. Labeled cDNAs are then denatured and incubated overnight with the microarray so that they will hybridize to spots on the microarray that contain complementary DNA sequences. Next, the microarray is washed, and then it is scanned by a laser that causes the cDNA hybridized to the microarray to fluoresce. The patterns of fluorescent spots reveal which genes are expressed in the tissue of interest, and the intensity of spot fluorescence indicates the relative level of expression. The brighter the spot, the more the particular mRNA is expressed in that tissue.

Microarrays have dramatically changed the way gene-expression patterns are analyzed. As discussed earlier in the text (see Chapter 20), Northern blot analysis was one of the earliest methods used for analyzing gene expression. Then PCR techniques proved to be rapid and more sensitive approaches. The biggest advantage of microarrays is that they enable thousands of genes to be studied simultaneously. As a result, however, they can generate an overwhelming amount of gene-expression data. Over 1 million gene-expression datasets are now available in publicly accessible databases. Most of these datasets have been generated in the past decade largely through microarray analysis. In addition, even when properly controlled, microarrays often yield variable results. For example, one experiment under certain conditions may not always yield similar patterns of gene expression as another identical experiment. Some of these differences can be due to real differences in gene expression, but others can be the result of variability in chip preparation, cDNA synthesis, probe hybridization, or washing conditions, all of which must be carefully

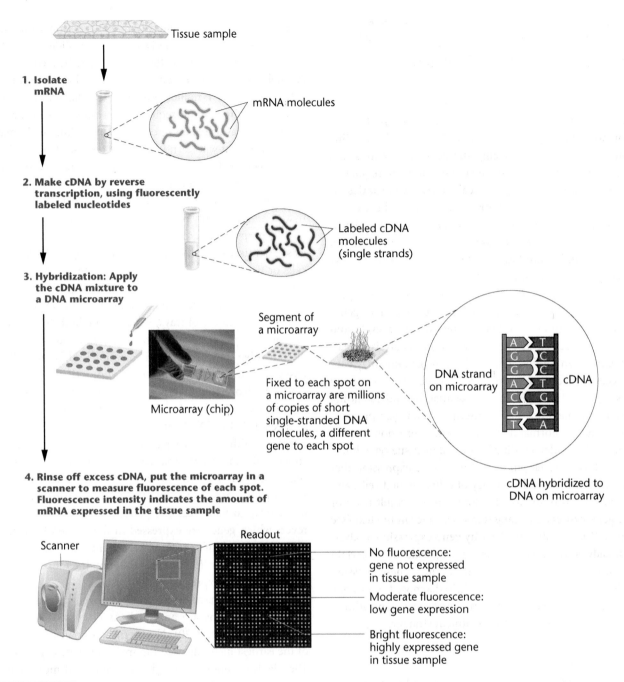

Tissue sample

1. **Isolate mRNA**

mRNA molecules

2. **Make cDNA by reverse transcription, using fluorescently labeled nucleotides**

Labeled cDNA molecules (single strands)

3. **Hybridization: Apply the cDNA mixture to a DNA microarray**

Segment of a microarray

Microarray (chip)

Fixed to each spot on a microarray are millions of copies of short single-stranded DNA molecules, a different gene to each spot

DNA strand on microarray   cDNA

cDNA hybridized to DNA on microarray

4. **Rinse off excess cDNA, put the microarray in a scanner to measure fluorescence of each spot. Fluorescence intensity indicates the amount of mRNA expressed in the tissue sample**

Scanner   Readout

No fluorescence: gene not expressed in tissue sample

Moderate fluorescence: low gene expression

Bright fluorescence: highly expressed gene in tissue sample

FIGURE 21–18 Microarray analysis for analyzing gene-expression patterns in a tissue.

controlled to limit such variability. Commercially available microarrays can reduce the variability that can result when individual researchers make their own arrays. You should also be aware that new methods for directly sequencing RNA (RNA-Seq, also called whole-transcriptome shotgun sequencing) will soon render microarrays obsolete!

Computerized microarray data analysis programs are essential for organizing gene-expression profile data from microarrays. For instance, **cluster algorithm** programs can be used to retrieve spot-intensity data from different locations on a microarray and to group

gene-expression data from one or multiple microarrays into cluster images incorporating results from many experiments. Cluster analysis groups genes according to whether they show increased (upregulated) or decreased (downregulated) expression under the experimental conditions examined.

Figure 21–19(a) shows hierarchical clusters of upregulated and downregulated gene-expression patterns for the yeast *Saccharomyces cerevisiae* grown under different experimental culture conditions. Notice that different culture times reveal different patterns of downregulation

(a)

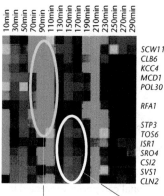

Experiments 1–15

	Genes	
		unknown
	SCW11	cell wall biogenesis glucanase (putative)
	CLB6	cell cycle B-type cyclin; S phase
	KCC4	bud growth protein kinase
	MCD1	mitosis, sister chromatid cohesion
	POL30	DNA replication DNA polymerase processivity factor
		unknown
	RFA1	DNA replication replication factor A, 69 kD subunit
		unknown
	STP3	tRNA splicing
	TOS6	unknown; similar to Mid2p
	ISR1	staurosporine resistance protein kinase
	SRO4	bud site selection, plasma membrane protein
	CSI2	cell wall biogenesis chitin synthase 3 subunit
	SVS1	vanadate resistance
	CLN2	cell cycle G1/S cyclin

Cluster of down-regulated genes

Cluster of up-regulated genes

(b)

Time (h) ⟶

FIGURE 21–19 (a) Hierarchical clusters in a microarray experiment using RNA samples from *Saccharomyces cerevisiae* grown for varying times in culture (experiments 1–15). Gene identities are labeled to the right of the array image. Red color in the array indicates upregulation in the experimental sample, and green indicates downregulation in the sample, as compared to a control culture. The intensity of the color indicates the magnitude of up- or downregulation. Brighter spots represent higher levels of expression than dimmer or black spots. The yellow oval highlights a cluster of downregulated genes, and the white oval highlights a cluster of upregulated genes. (b) High (red), intermediate (black), and low (green) levels of gene expression for *Drosophila* genes that exhibit a circadian rhythm. RNA samples from *Drosophila* were collected every four hours for six days and then used for microarray analysis. Each row shows all 36 responses of a single gene. Each column shows the gene-expression pattern for each time point sampled. Genes were arranged from top to bottom according to the time of peak activity.

(yellow oval) and upregulation (white oval). The identities of the genes in these regulated clusters indicate that many of the genes affected by the growth conditions of this experiment are genes involved in cell division.

Figure 21–19(b) reveals an interesting gene-expression profile for genes in *Drosophila* in which they display repeating patterns of expression as part of a **circadian rhythm** response. Circadian rhythms are oscillations in biological activity that occur on a regular cycle of time, such as 24 hours. Reductions in brain wave electrical activity that occur when you sleep, followed by the increased brain wave activity that occurs to wake you up, just before your alarm clock sounds in the morning, are examples of circadian responses. In the *Drosophila* microarray, each horizontal row shows expression results for a different gene. Notice how every several hours the expression for most genes is upregulated (red) and then downregulated (green) several hours later in a rhythmic pattern that repeats over the time course of this experiment (6 days). Results such as these are representative of the types of gene-expression profiles that can be revealed by microarrays. You will see similar representations of microarray data later in the text (see Chapter 24).

In Section 21.6 we briefly discussed the sea urchin genome and the importance of the sea urchin as a key model organism. Sea urchins have a relatively simple body

plan [**Figure 21–20(a)**]. They contain approximately 1500 cells with only a dozen cell types. Yet sea urchin development progresses through complex changes in gene expression that resemble vertebrate patterns of gene-expression changes during development. This is one reason urchins are a valuable model organism for developmental biology.

Scientists at NASA's Ames Genome Research Facility in Moffett, California, used microarrays to carry out a transcriptome study on sea urchin gene expression during the first two days of development (to the mid-late gastrula stage, about 48 hours postfertilization). This work revealed that approximately 52 percent of all genes in the sea urchin are active during this period of development: 11,500 of the sea urchin's 23,500 known genes were expressed in the embryo. The functional categories of genes expressed in the embryo were diverse, including genes for about 70 percent of the nearly 300 transcription factors in the sea urchin genome, along with genes involved in cell signaling, immunity, fertilization, and metabolism [**Figure 21–20(b)**]. Incredibly, 51,000 RNAs of unknown function were also expressed. Studies are underway to explain the differences between gene number and transcripts expressed, although it is already known that many sea urchin genes are extensively processed through alternative splicing. Further analysis of

(a)

(b)

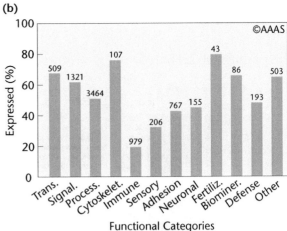

©AAAS

FIGURE 21–20 (a) The sea urchin *Strongylocentrotus purpuratus*. (b) Transcriptome analysis of genes expressed in the sea urchin embryo. The *y*-axis of the histogram displays the percentage of annotated genes in different functional categories expressed in the embryo. The number at the top of each bar represents the total number of annotated genes in the corresponding functional category. Trans., transcription factors; Signal, signaling genes; Process, basic cellular processes, such as metabolism; Cytoskelet., cytoskeletal genes; Fertiliz., fertilization; and Biominer., biomineralization.

the sea urchin genome will undoubtedly reveal interesting aspects of gene function during sea urchin development and advance our understanding of the genetics of embryonic development in both invertebrates and vertebrates.

Now that we have considered genomes and transcriptomes, we turn our attention to the ultimate end products of most genes, the proteins encoded by a genome.

21.10 Proteomics Identifies and Analyzes the Protein Composition of Cells

As more genomes have been sequenced and studied, biologists have focused increasingly on understanding the complex structures and functions of the proteins the genomes encode. This interest is not surprising given that in most of the genomes sequenced to date, many newly discovered genes and their putative proteins have no known function. Keep in mind, in the ensuing discussion, that although every cell in the body contains an equivalent set of genes, not all cells express the same genes and proteins. **Proteome** is a term that represents the complete set of proteins encoded by a genome, but it is also often used to mean the entire complement of proteins in a cell. This definition would then include proteins that a cell acquired from another cell type.

Proteomics—the complete identification, characterization, and quantitative analysis of the proteome of a cell, tissue, or organism—can be used to reconcile differences between the number of genes in a genome and the number of different proteins produced. But equally important, proteomics also provides information about a protein's struc-

ture and function; posttranslational modifications; protein–protein, protein–nucleic acid, and protein–metabolite interactions; cellular localization of proteins; protein stability and aspects of translational and posttranslational levels of gene-expression regulation; and relationships (shared domains, evolutionary history) to other proteins. Proteomics projects have been used to characterize major families of proteins for some species. For example, about two-thirds of the *Drosophila* proteome has been well catalogued using proteomics.

Proteomics is also of clinical interest because it allows comparison of proteins in normal and diseased tissues, which can lead to the identification of proteins as biomarkers for disease conditions. Proteomic analysis of mitochondrial proteins during aging, proteomic maps of atherosclerotic plaques from human coronary arteries, and protein profiles in saliva as a way to detect and diagnose diseases are examples of such work.

Reconciling the Number of Genes and the Number of Proteins Expressed by a Cell or Tissue

Recall the one-gene:one-polypeptide hypothesis of George Beadle and Edward Tatum (see Chapter 14). Genomics has revealed that the link between gene and gene product is often much more complex. Genes can have multiple transcription start sites that produce several different types of transcripts. Alternative splicing and editing of pre-mRNA molecules can generate dozens of different proteins from a single gene. Remember the current estimate that over 50 percent of human genes produce more than one protein by alternative splicing.

As a result, proteomes are substantially larger than genomes. For instance, the ~20,000 genes in the human genome encode ~100,000 proteins, although some estimates suggest that the human proteome may be as large as 150,000–200,000 proteins.

Proteomes undergo dynamic changes that are coordinated in part by regulation of gene-expression patterns—the transcriptome. However, a number of other factors affect the proteome profile of a cell, further complicating the analysis of protein function. For instance, many proteins are modified by co-translational or posttranslational events, such as cleavage of signal sequences that target a protein for an organelle pathway, propeptides, or initiator methionine residues; by linkage to carbohydrates and lipids; or by the addition of chemical groups through methylation, acetylation, and phosphorylation and other modifications. Over a hundred different mechanisms of posttranslational modification are known. In addition, many proteins work via elaborate protein–protein interactions or as part of a large molecular complex.

Well before a draft sequence of the human genome was available, scientists were already discussing the possibility of a "Human Proteome Project." One reason such a project never came to pass is that there is no single human proteome: different tissues produce different sets of proteins. But the idea of such a project led to the **Protein Structure Initiative (PSI)** by the National Institute of General Medical Sciences (NIGMS), a division of the National Institutes of Health, involving over a dozen research centers. PSI is a multiphase project designed to analyze the three-dimensional structures of more than 4000 protein families. Proteins with interesting potential therapeutic properties are a top priority for the PSI, and to date the structures of over 6,000 proteins have been determined. Developing computation protein structural prediction methods, solving unique protein structures, disseminating PSI information, and focusing on the biological relevance of the work are major goals. There also are a number of other ongoing projects dedicated to identifying proteome profiles that correlate with diseases such as cancer and diabetes.

Proteomics Technologies: Two-Dimensional Gel Electrophoresis for Separating Proteins

With proteomics technologies, scientists have the ability to study thousands of proteins simultaneously, generating enormous amounts of data quickly and dramatically changing ways of analyzing the protein content of a cell.

The early history of proteomics dates back to 1975 and the development of **two-dimensional gel electrophoresis (2DGE)** as a technique for separating hundreds to thousands of proteins with high resolution. In this technique, proteins isolated from cells or tissues of interest are loaded onto a polyacrylamide tube gel and first separated by **isoelectric focusing**, which causes proteins to migrate according to their electrical charge in a pH gradient. During isoelectric focusing, proteins migrate until they reach the location in the gel where their net charge is zero compared to the pH of the gel (**Figure 21–21**). Then in a second migration, perpendicular to the first, the proteins are separated by their molecular mass using **sodium dodecyl sulfate polyacrylamide gel electrophoresis (SDS-PAGE)**. In this step, the tube gel is rotated 90° and placed on top of an SDS polyacrylamide gel; an electrical current is applied to the gel to separate the proteins by mass.

Proteins in the 2D gel are visualized by staining with Coomassie blue, silver stain, or other dyes that reveal the separated proteins as a series of spots in the gel (Figure 21–21). It is not uncommon for a 2D gel loaded with a complex mixture of proteins to show several thousand spots in the gel, as in Figure 21–21, which displays the complex mixture of proteins in human platelets (thrombocytes). Particularly abundant protein spots in this gel have been labeled with the names of identified proteins. With thousands of different spots on the gel, how are the identities of the proteins ascertained?

NOW SOLVE THIS

21–2 Annotation of a proteome attempts to relate each protein to a function in time and space. Traditionally, protein annotation depended on an amino acid sequence comparison between a query protein and a protein with known function. If the two proteins shared a considerable portion of their sequence, the query would be assumed to share the function of the annotated protein. Following is a representation of this method of protein annotation involving a query sequence and three different human proteins. Note that the query sequence aligns to common domains within the three other proteins. What argument might you present to suggest that the function of the query is not related to the function of the other three proteins?

— Query amino acid sequence

Region of amino acid sequence match to query

■ **HINT:** *This problem asks you to think about sequence similarities between four proteins and predict functional relationships. The key to its solution is to remember that although protein domains may have related functions, proteins can contain several different interacting domains that determine protein function.*

For more practice, see Problems 24 and 26.

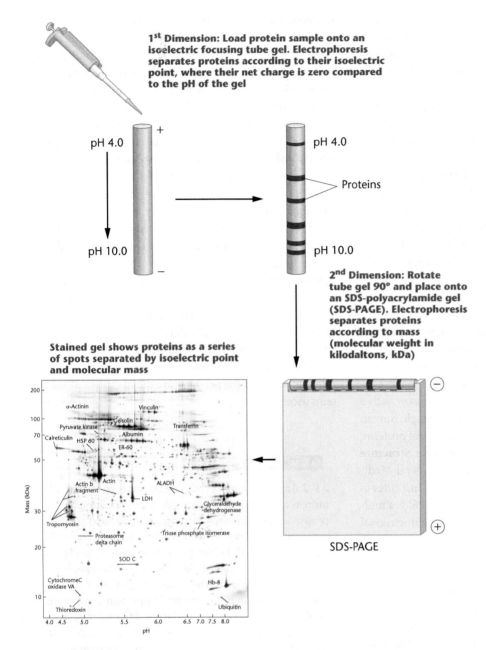

1ˢᵗ Dimension: Load protein sample onto an isoelectric focusing tube gel. Electrophoresis separates proteins according to their isoelectric point, where their net charge is zero compared to the pH of the gel

pH 4.0

pH 10.0

pH 4.0

Proteins

pH 10.0

2ⁿᵈ Dimension: Rotate tube gel 90° and place onto an SDS-polyacrylamide gel (SDS-PAGE). Electrophoresis separates proteins according to mass (molecular weight in kilodaltons, kDa)

Stained gel shows proteins as a series of spots separated by isoelectric point and molecular mass

SDS-PAGE

FIGURE 21–21 Two-dimensional gel electrophoresis (2DGE) is a useful method for separating proteins in a protein extract from cells or tissues that contains a complex mixture of proteins with different biochemical properties. The two-dimensional gel photo shows separations of human platelet proteins. Each spot represents a different polypeptide separated by molecular weight (*y*-axis) and isoelectric point, pH (*x*-axis). Known protein spots are labeled by name based on identification by comparison to a reference gel or by determination of protein sequence using mass spectrometry techniques. Notice that many spots on the gel are unlabeled, indicating proteins of unknown identity.

In some cases, 2D gel patterns from experimental samples can be compared to gels run with reference standards containing known proteins with well-characterized migration patterns. Many reference gels for different biological samples such as human plasma are available, and computer software programs can be used to align and compare the spots from different gels. In the early days of 2DGE, proteins were often identified by cutting spots out of a gel and sequencing the amino acids the spots contained. Only relatively small sequences of amino acids can typically be generated this way; rarely can an entire polypeptide be sequenced using this technique. BLAST and similar programs can be used to search protein databases containing amino acid sequences of known proteins. However, because of alternative splicing or posttranslational modifications, peptide sequences may not always match easily with the final product, and the identity of the protein may have to be confirmed by another approach. As you will learn in the next section, proteomics has incorporated other techniques to aid in protein identification, and one of these techniques is mass spectrometry.

Proteomics Technologies: Mass Spectrometry for Protein Identification

As important as 2DGE has been for protein analysis, **mass spectrometry (MS)** has been instrumental to the development of proteomics. Mass spectrometry techniques analyze ionized samples in gaseous form and measure the **mass-to-charge (*m/z*) ratio** of the different ions in a sample. Proteins analyzed by mass spectra generate *m/z* spectra that can be correlated with an *m/z* database containing known protein sequences to discover the protein's identity. Certain MS applications can provide peptide sequences directly from spectra. Some of the most valuable proteomics applications of this technology are to identify an unknown protein or proteins in a complex mix of proteins, to sequence peptides, to identify posttranslational modifications of proteins, and to characterize multiprotein complexes.

One commonly used mass spectrometry approach is **matrix-assisted laser desorption ionization (MALDI).** This approach is ideally suited for identifying proteins and is widely used for proteomic analysis of tissue samples

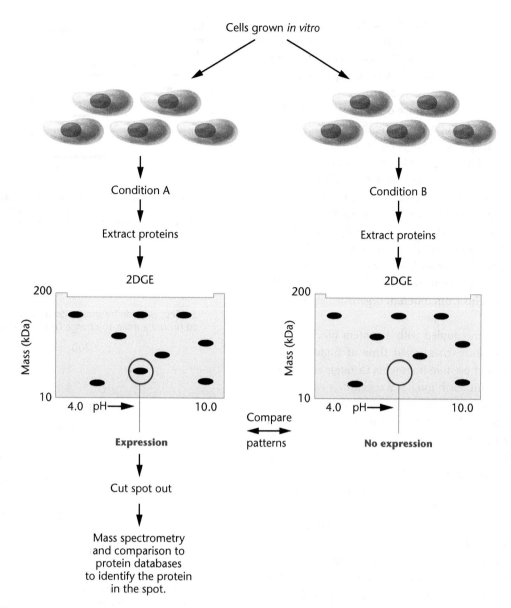

FIGURE 21-22 In a typical proteomic analysis, cells are exposed to different conditions (such as different growth conditions, drugs, or hormones). Then proteins are extracted from these cells and separated by 2DGE, and the resulting patterns of spots are compared for evidence of differential protein expression. Spots of interest are cut out from the gel, digested into peptide fragments, and analyzed by mass spectrometry to identify the protein they contain.

treated under different conditions. The proteins are first extracted from cells or tissues of interest and separated by 2DGE, after which MALDI (described below) is used to identify the proteins in the different spots. **Figure 21-22** shows an example in which two different sets of cells grown in culture are analyzed for protein differences. Just about any source providing a sufficient number of cells can be used: blood, whole tissues, and organs; tumor samples; microbes; and many other substances. Many proteins involved in cancer have been identified by the use of MALDI to compare protein profiles in normal tissue and tumor samples.

Protein spots are cut out of the 2D gel, and proteins are purified out of each gel spot. Computer-automated high-throughput instruments are available that can pick all of the spots out of a 2D gel. Isolated proteins are then enzymatically digested with a protease (a protein-digesting enzyme) such as trypsin to create a series of peptides. This proteolysis produces a complex mixture of peptides determined by the cleavage sites for the protease in the original protein. Each type of protein produces a characteristic set of peptide fragments, and these are identified by MALDI as follows.

In MALDI, peptides are mixed with a low molecular weight and ultraviolet (UV) light-absorbing acidic matrix material (such as dihydroxybenzoic acid) and the mixture is then applied to a metal plate. A UV laser, often a nitrogen laser at a wavelength of 337 nm, is fired at the sample. As the matrix absorbs energy from the laser, heat accumulating on the matrix vaporizes and ionizes the peptide fragments. Released ions are then analyzed for mass; MALDI displays the *m/z* ratio of each ionized peptide as a series of peaks representative of the molecular masses of peptides in the mixture and their relative abundance (**Figure 21–23**). Because different proteins produce different sets of peptide fragments, MALDI produces a peptide "fingerprint" that is characteristic of the protein being analyzed.

Databases of MALDI-generated *m/z* spectra for different peptides can be analyzed to look for matches between *m/z* spectra of unknown samples and those of known proteins. One limitation of this approach is database quality. An unknown protein from a 2D gel can only be identified by MALDI if proteomics databases have a MALDI spectrum for that protein. But as is occurring with genomics databases, proteomics databases with thousands of well-characterized proteins from different organisms are rapidly developing.

MALDI is often coupled with a protein biochemistry technique for mass analysis called **time of flight (TOF)**. TOF moves ionized peptide fragments through an electrical field in a vacuum. Each ion has a speed that varies with its mass. The speed with which each ion crosses the vacuum chamber can be measured, and differences in the ions' kinetic energy can be used to develop a mass-dependent velocity profile—a MALDI-TOF spectrum—that shows each ion's "time of flight." MALDI-TOF spectra can then be compared to databases of spectra for known proteins, as described above for MALDI spectra.

Many other methods involve mass spectrometry. Some incorporate liquid chromatography (LC) to separate proteins by mass and then employ **tandem mass spectrometry (MS/MS)** approaches to generate *m/z* spectra. Also emerging are new mass spectrometry techniques that do not involve the running of gels. As we mentioned when discussing genomics, high-throughput 2DGE instruments and mass spectrometers can process thousands of samples in a single day. Instruments with faster sample-processing times and increased sensitivity are under development. These instruments may soon make "shotgun proteomics" a viable approach for characterizing entire proteomes.

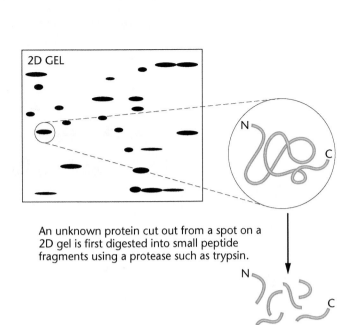

An unknown protein cut out from a spot on a 2D gel is first digested into small peptide fragments using a protease such as trypsin.

Subject peptide fragments to mass spectrometry to produce mass-to-charge (*m/z*) spectra

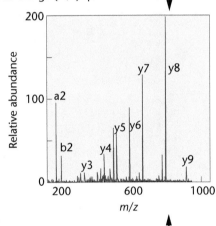

Compare *m/z* spectra for unknown protein to a proteomics database of *m/z* spectra for known peptides. A spectrum match would identify the peptide sequence of the unknown protein.

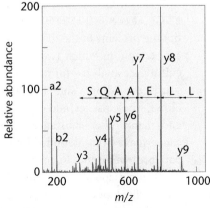

FIGURE 21–23 Mass spectrometry for identifying an unknown protein isolated from a 2D gel. The mass-to-charge spectrum (*m/z*) (determined, for example, by MALDI) for trypsin-digested peptides from the unknown protein can be compared to a proteomics database for a spectrum match to identify the unknown protein. The peptide in this example was revealed to have the amino acid sequence serine (S)-glutamine (Q)-alanine (A)-alanine (A)-glutamic acid (E)-leucine (L)-leucine (L), shown in single-letter amino acid code.

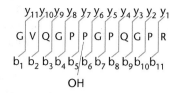

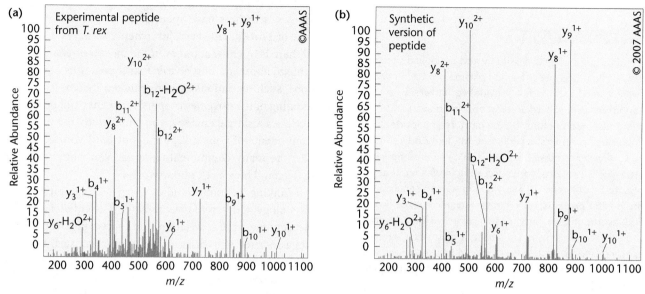

FIGURE 21–24 (a) Mass spectrometry (MS) patterns for a trypsin-digested peptide sequence—GVQPP(OH)GPQGPR—from *T. rex*. The peptide sequence, shown here in single-letter amino acid code, contains a charged hydroxyl group characteristic of collagen. (b) Mass spectrometry of a synthetic version of collagen peptide shows good alignment with the *m/z* spectra for fragmented ions from the *T. rex* peptide, thus confirming the *T. rex* sequence as collagen and demonstrating the value of MS techniques.

Protein microarrays are also becoming valuable tools for proteomics research. These are designed around the same basic concept as microarrays (gene chips) and are often constructed with antibodies that specifically recognize and bind to different proteins. These microarrays are used, among other applications, for examining protein–protein interactions, for detecting protein markers for disease diagnosis, and for studying in biosensors designed to detect pathogenic microbes and potentially infectious bioweapons.

Identification of Collagen in *Tyrannosaurus rex* and *Mammut americanum* Fossils

As mentioned earlier, DNA has been recovered from fossils, but the general assumption has been that proteins degrade in fossilized materials and cannot be recovered. Mass spectrometry analysis of bone tissue from a *Tyrannosaurus rex* skeleton excavated from the Hell Creek Formation in eastern Montana and estimated to be 68 million years old is a good demonstration that fossilization does not fully destroy all proteins in well-preserved fossils under certain conditions. This research also demonstrates the power and sensitivity of mass spectrometry as a proteomics tool.

In this work, medullary tissue was removed from the inside of the left and right femoral bones. Medullary tissue is porous, spongy bone that contains bone marrow cells, blood vessels, and nerves. *T. rex* proteins extracted from the tissue showed cross-reactivity with antibodies to chicken collagen and were digested by the collagen-specific protease collagenase. These results suggested that the *T. rex* protein samples contained collagen, a major matrix component of bone, ligaments, tendons, and skin. To definitively identify the presence of collagen, tryptic peptides from the *T. rex* samples were analyzed by liquid chromatography and mass spectrometry (LC/MS; Figure 21–23). The *m/z* spectra for one of the *T. rex* peptides was identified from a database of *m/z* spectra as corresponding to collagen. Compare the spectrum for a collagen peptide in **Figure 21–24(a)** to that of a synthetic version of a collagen peptide [**Figure 21–24(b)**], and you will notice that the m/z ratios for all major ions align almost identically, confirming that the *T. rex* sequence is collagen. The *T. rex* peptide also contained a hydroxyl group attached to a proline residue. Proline hydroxylation is a characteristic feature of collagen. Furthermore, the amino acid sequence of *T. rex* collagen peptide aligned with an isoform of chicken collagen, demonstrating sequence similarity. Such work has provided excellent experimental evidence to support the widely accepted theory that birds and dinosaurs are close relatives.

Similar results were obtained for 160,000- to 600,000-year-old mastodon (*Mammut americanum*) peptides that showed matches to collagen from extant species, including collagen isoforms from humans, chimps, dogs, cows, chickens, elephants, and mice.

21–3 Because of its accessibility and biological significance, the proteome of human plasma has been intensively studied and used to provide biomarkers for such conditions as myocardial infarction (troponin) and congestive heart failure (B-type natriuretic peptide). Polanski and Anderson (Polanski, M., and Anderson, N. L., *Biomarker Insights*, 2: 1–48, 2006) have compiled a list of 1261 proteins, some occurring in plasma, that appear to be differentially expressed in human cancers. Of these 1261 proteins, only 9 have been recognized by the FDA as tumor-associated proteins. First, what advantage should there be in using plasma as a diagnostic screen for cancer? Second, what criteria should be used to validate that a cancerous state can be assessed through the plasma proteome?

■ **HINT:** *This problem asks you to consider criteria that are valuable for using plasma proteomics as a diagnostic screen for cancer. The key to its solution is to consider proteomics data that you would want to evaluate to determine whether a particular protein is involved in cancer.*

21.11 Systems Biology Is an Integrated Approach to Studying Interactions of All Components of an Organism's Cells

We conclude this chapter by discussing **systems biology**, an emerging discipline that incorporates data from genomics, transcriptomics, proteomics, and other areas of biology, as well as engineering applications and problem solving approaches. Identifying genes and proteins by mutational analysis of genomes has been a very important and successful approach for characterizing genes when mutants showing visible phenotypes are found to be part of similar biochemical pathways. However, even extensive mutational analysis and screening will not provide a full understanding of complex cellular processes such as signal transduction pathways, metabolic pathways, and regulation of cell division, DNA replication, and gene expression. A more comprehensive, more integrated approach is needed.

As we mentioned earlier in this chapter, until relatively recently, much of what has been learned about gene and protein functions at the cellular, molecular, and biochemical levels has been acquired primarily through decades of work by scientists studying the functions of individual genes or relatively small numbers of genes and proteins. Many researchers have spent entire careers studying one gene or protein. However, just when it seems as if we know all there is to know about even the most well-characterized protein, another study reveals that it possesses novel functions. Such revelations demonstrate our incomplete understanding of the extreme complexity of genes and proteins in a cell. As a simple analogy, you could study the individual components of your cell phone, but until you focused on how the many components interact, you would not truly understand how a cell phone works.

Linking genomic studies to gene function and the physiology of different disease states is essential. For example, genome-wide association studies have uncovered many loci associated with diseases, but translating such information to make valuable and reliable diagnostic predictions and to develop drug targets of key proteins involved in disease is necessary. A major challenge in modern biology is to unravel the interactions of genes and proteins that enable complex processes such as cell division; this is what systems biology is all about. Proteins occasionally function alone, but more typically they work in complex interconnected networks under the regulation and control of other proteins or metabolites. Networks of interacting proteins form the regulatory framework controlling how cells respond to environmental signals, metabolize nutrients, move organelles, divide, and carry out many other processes. As genomics and proteomics have advanced, the discipline of systems biology has emerged as a more holistic approach to studying cell function by analyzing interactions among all of the molecular components of a biological system. Systems biology considers genes, proteins, metabolites, and other interacting molecules of a cell in order to understand molecular interactions and to integrate such information into models that can be used to better understand the biological functions of an organism.

In many ways, systems biology is interpreting genomic information in the context of the structure, function, and regulation of biological pathways. As is well known, biological systems are very complex. By studying relationships between all components in an organism, biologists are trying to build a "systems"-level understanding of how organisms function. Systems biologists typically combine recently acquired genomics and proteomics data with years of more traditional studies of gene and protein structure and function. Much of this data is retrieved from databases such as PubMed, GenBank, and other newly emerging genomics, transcriptomics, and proteomics resources. Systems models are used to diagram interactions within a cell or an entire organism, such as protein–protein interactions, protein–nucleic acid interactions, and protein–metabolite interactions (e.g., enzyme-substrate binding). These models help systems biologists understand the components of interacting pathways and the interrelationships of molecules in an interacting pathway. In recent years, the term **interactome** has arisen to describe the interacting components of a cell. Systems biologists use several different types of models to diagram protein interaction pathways. One of the most common model types is a **network map**—a sketch showing interacting proteins, genes, and other molecules. These diagrams are essentially the equivalent of an electrical wiring diagram. One disadvantage of network maps is that they are static diagrams that typically lack information about

when and where each interaction occurs. Even so, they are a useful foundation for generating computational models that allow the running of simulations to determine how signaling events occur. For example, major groups of kinases, enzymes that phosphorylate other proteins to affect their activity, have been network mapped to show their interactions with each other. Because kinases play such important roles in the regulation of most critical cellular processes, such information about the "kinome" has been very valuable for companies developing drug treatments targeted to certain metabolic pathways.

Network maps are helping scientists model intricate potential interactions of molecules involved in normal and disease processes. **Figure 21–25** shows an example of a network map. This map depicts a human disease network

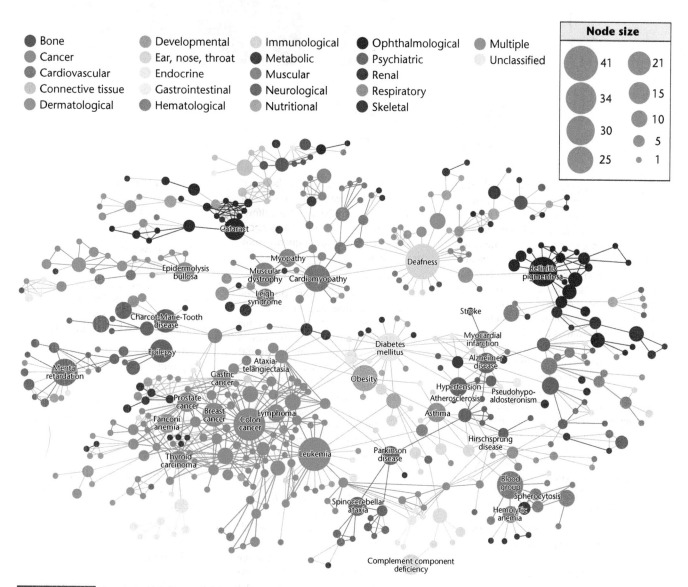

FIGURE 21-25 A systems biology model of human disease gene interactions. The model shows nodes corresponding to 22 specific disorders colored by class. Node size is proportional to the number of genes contributing to the disorder.

model illustrating the complexity of interactions between genes involved in 22 different human diseases. Look at the cluster of turquoise-colored nodes corresponding to genes involved in several different cancers. One aspect of the map that should be immediately obvious is that a number of cancers share interacting genes even though the cancers affect different organs. Knowing the genes involved and the protein interaction networks for different cancers is a major breakthrough for informing scientists about target genes and proteins to consider for therapeutic purposes.

Systems biology is becoming increasingly important in the drug discovery and development process, where its approaches can help scientists and physicians develop a conceptual framework of gene and protein interactions in human disease that can then serve as the rationale for effective drug design. Understanding disease development and progression by defining interaction networks of molecules in normal and diseased tissue will be important for detecting and treating complex diseases such as cancer. Many databases are now being developed to model interactomes for human diseases, including breast and prostate cancer, diabetes, asthma, and cardiovascular disease. Systems biology is also being used to create biofuels and to design genetically modified organisms for cleaning up the environment, among a range of other exciting applications.

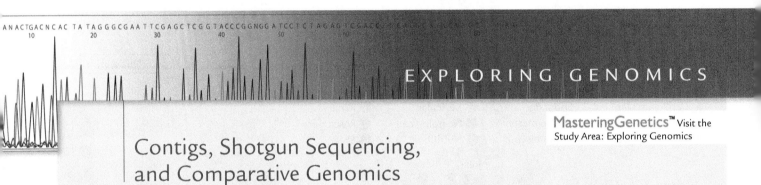

EXPLORING GENOMICS

MasteringGenetics™ Visit the
Study Area: Exploring Genomics

Contigs, Shotgun Sequencing, and Comparative Genomics

In this chapter, we discussed how whole-genome shotgun sequencing methods can be used to assemble chromosome maps. Recall that in the technique of shotgun cloning, chromosomal DNA is digested with different restriction enzymes to create a series of overlapping DNA fragments called contiguous sequences, or "contigs." The contigs are then subjected to DNA sequencing, after which bioinformatics-based programs are used to arrange the contigs in their correct order on the basis of short overlapping sequences of nucleotides.

In this Exploring Genomics exercise you will carry out a simulation of contig alignment to help you to understand the underlying logic of this approach to creating sequence maps of a chromosome. For this purpose, you will use the **National Center for Biotechnology Information BLAST** site and apply a DNA alignment program called bl2seq.

■ **Exercise I – Arranging Contigs to Create a Chromosome Map**

1. Access BLAST from the NCBI Web site at http://blast.ncbi.nlm.nih.gov/Blast.cgi. Locate and select the "Align

two sequences using BLAST (bl2seq)" category at the bottom of the BLAST homepage. The bl2seq feature allows you to compare two DNA sequences at a time to check for sequence similarity alignments.

2. Go to the Companion Web site for *Essentials of Genetics* and open the Exploring Genomics exercise for this chapter. Listed are eight contig sequences, called Sequences A through H, taken from an actual human chromosome sequence deposited in GenBank. For this exercise we have used short fragments; however, in reality contigs are usually several thousand base pairs long. To complete this exercise, copy and paste two sequences into the Align feature of BLAST and then run an alignment (by clicking on "Align"). Repeat these steps with other combinations of two sequences to determine which sequences overlap, and then use your findings to create a sequence map that places overlapping contigs in their proper order. Here are a few tips to consider:

■ Develop a strategy to be sure that you analyze alignments for all pairs of contigs.

■ Only consider alignment overlaps that show 100 percent sequence similarity.

3. On the basis of your alignment results, answer the following questions, referring to the sequences by their letter codes (A through H):

a. What is the correct order of overlapping contigs?

b. What is the length, measured in number of nucleotides, of each sequence overlap between contigs?

c. What is the total size of the chromosome segment that you assembled?

d. Did you find any contigs that do not overlap with any of the others? Explain.

4. Run a nucleotide-nucleotide BLAST search (BLASTn) on any of the overlapping contigs to determine which chromosome these contigs were taken from, and report your answer.

CASE STUDY | # Your microbiome may be a risk factor for disease

A number of genes involved in susceptibility to inflammatory bowel disorders (IBDs), including Crohn disease and ulcerative colitis, have been identified. However, it is clear that other risk factors, both genetic and nongenetic, are important in triggering the onset of these diseases. Recent research has centered on understanding the role of the gut microbiome and its interactions with the host genome in IBD. It is known that the microbiome of those with IBD is different from that of those whose IBD is in remission, and it is also different from that of people who do not have IBD. These observations suggest that transfer of microbiota from unaffected individuals via fecal microbial transplantation (FMT) might be a successful treatment for IBD. This idea is supported by the use of FMT as an effective treatment in IBD individuals for a potentially life-threatening infection caused by the bacterium *Clostridium difficile*. Currently, four clinical trials are underway to evaluate the use of FMT as a treatment for IBD.

1. If you had IBD, how would you react if your physician recommended that you enroll in one of these clinical studies to evaluate fecal transplants as a treatment?

2. Current treatment of IBD involves the use of anti-inflammatory drugs, but these drugs achieve remission only in some cases. If genetic analysis reveals that you carry susceptibility alleles for IBD that respond to periodic FMT as a therapy, would you agree to try this method?

3. Before agreeing to FMT, what would you want to know about the microbiomes of individuals who do not have IBD?

Summary Points

MasteringGenetics™ For activities, animations, and review quizzes, go to the Study Area.

1. High-throughput computer-automated DNA sequencing methods coupled with bioinformatics enable scientists to assemble sequence maps of entire genomes.

2. Bioinformatics is essential for the analysis of genomes and proteomes. Bioinformatics applies computer hardware and software together with statistical approaches to analyze biological sequence data.

3. Annotation is used to identify protein-coding DNA sequencing and noncoding sequences such as regulatory elements, while bioinformatics programs are used to identify open reading frames that predict possible polypeptides coded for by a particular sequence.

4. Functional genomics predicts gene function based on sequence analysis.

5. The Human Genome Project revealed many surprises about human genetics, including gene number, the high degree of DNA sequence similarity between individuals and between humans and other species, and showed that many genes encode multiple proteins.

6. Genomics has led to other related "omics" disciplines that are rapidly changing how modern biologists study DNA, RNA, and proteins and many aspects of cell function.

7. The genomes for many important model organisms have been completed. Genomic analysis of model prokaryotes and eukaryotes has revealed similarities and important fundamental differences in genome size, gene number, and genome organization.

8. Studies in comparative genomics are revealing fascinating similarities and differences in genomes from different organisms, including the identification and analysis of gene families.

9. Metagenomics, or environmental genomics, sequences genomes of microorganisms from environmental samples, often identifying new sequences that encode proteins with novel functions.

10. DNA chips or microarrays are valuable for transcriptome analysis in studying expression patterns for thousands of genes simultaneously.

11. Methods such as two-dimensional gel electrophoresis and mass spectrometry are valuable for analyzing proteomes—the protein content of a cell.

12. Systems biology approaches are designed to provide an integrated understanding of the interactions between genes, proteins, and other molecules that govern complex biological processes.

INSIGHTS AND SOLUTIONS

1. One of the main problems in annotation is deciding how long a putative ORF must be before it is accepted as a gene. Shown at the right are three different ORF scans of the same *E. coli* genome region—the region containing the *lacY* gene. Regions shaded in brown indicate ORFs. The top scan was set to accept ORFs of 50 nucleotides as genes. The middle and bottom scans accepted ORFs of 100 and 300 nucleotides as genes, respectively. How many putative genes are detected in each scan? The longest ORF covers 1254 bp; the next longest, 234 bp; and the shortest, 54 bp. How can we decide the actual number of genes in this region? In this type of ORF scan, is it more likely that the number of genes in the genome will be overestimated or underestimated? Why?

   Solution: Generally one can examine conserved sequences in other organisms to indicate that an ORF is likely a coding region. One can also match a sequence to previously described sequences that are known to code for proteins. The problem is not easily solved—that is, deciding which ORF is actually a gene. The shorter the ORFs scan, the more likely the overestimate of genes because ORFs longer than 200 are less likely to occur by chance. For these scans, notice that the 50-bp scans produce the highest number of possible genes, whereas the 300-bp scan produces the lowest number (1) of possible genes.

2. Sequencing of the heterochromatic regions (repeat-rich sequences concentrated in centromeric and telomeric areas) of the *Drosophila* genome indicates that within 20.7 Mb, there are 297 protein-coding genes (Bergman et al. 2002. http://genomebiology.com/2002/3/12/research/0086). Given that the euchromatic regions of the genome contain 13,379 protein-coding genes in 116.8 Mb, what general conclusion is apparent?

   Solution: Gene density in euchromatic regions of the *Drosophila* genome is about one gene per 8730 base pairs, while gene density in heterochromatic regions is one gene per 70,000 bases (20.7 Mb/297). Clearly, a given region of heterochromatin is much less likely to contain a gene than the same-sized region in euchromatin.

50

Sequenced strand

Complementary strand

100

Sequenced strand

Complementary strand

300

Sequenced strand

Complementary strand

Problems and Discussion Questions

MasteringGenetics™ Visit for instructor-assigned tutorials and problems.

HOW DO WE KNOW?

1. In this chapter, we focused on the analysis of genomes, transcriptomes, and proteomes and considered important applications and findings from these endeavors. At the same time, we found many opportunities to consider the methods and reasoning by which much of this information was acquired. From the explanations given in the chapter, what answers would you propose to the following fundamental questions:

   (a) How do we know which contigs are part of the same chromosome?

   (b) How do we know if a genomic DNA sequence contains a protein-coding gene?

   (c) What evidence supports the concept that humans share substantial sequence similarities and gene functional similarities with model organisms?

   (d) How can proteomics identify differences between the number of protein-coding genes predicted for a genome and the number of proteins expressed by a genome?

   (e) What evidence indicates that gene families result from gene duplication events?

   (f) How have microarrays demonstrated that, although all cells of an organism have the same genome, some genes are expressed in almost all cells, whereas other genes show cell- and tissue-specific expression?

CONCEPT QUESTION

2. Review the Chapter Concepts list on page 522. All of these pertain to how genomics, bioinformatics, and proteomics approaches have changed how scientists study genes and proteins. Write a short essay that explains how recombinant DNA techniques were used to identify and study genes compared

to how modern genomic techniques have revolutionized the cloning and analysis of genes.

3. What is functional genomics? How does it differ from comparative genomics?

4. Compare and contrast whole-genome shotgun sequencing to a map-based cloning approach.

5. What is bioinformatics, and why is this discipline essential for studying genomes? Provide two examples of bioinformatics applications.

6. List and describe three major goals of the Human Genome Project.

7. How do high-throughput techniques such as computer-automated and next-generation sequencing and mass spectrometry facilitate research in genomics and proteomics? Explain.

8. BLAST searches and related applications are essential for analyzing gene and protein sequences. Define BLAST, describe basic features of this bioinformatics tool, and provide an example of information provided by a BLAST search.

9. What are pseudogenes, and how are they produced?

10. Describe the human genome in terms of genome size, the percentage of the genome that codes for proteins, how much is composed of repetitive sequences, and how many genes it contains. Describe two other features of the human genome.

11. What functional information about a genome can be determined through applications of chromatin immunoprecipitation (ChIP)?

12. The Human Genome Project has demonstrated that in humans of all races and nationalities approximately 99.9 percent of the sequence is the same, yet different individuals can be identified by DNA fingerprinting techniques. What is one primary variation in the human genome that can be used to distinguish different individuals? Briefly explain your answer.

13. Annotation involves identifying genes and gene-regulatory sequences in a genome. List and describe characteristics of a genome that are hallmarks for identifying genes in an unknown sequence. What characteristics would you look for in a prokaryotic genome? A eukaryotic genome?

14. Through the Human Genome Project (HGP), a relatively accurate human genome sequence was published in 2003 from combined samples from different individuals. It serves as a reference for a haploid genome. Recently, genomes of a number of individuals have been sequenced under the auspices of the Personal Genome Project (PGP). How do results from the PGP differ from those of the HGP?

15. Describe the significance of the Genome 10K plan.

16. It can be said that modern biology is experiencing an "omics" revolution. What does this mean? Explain your answer.

17. Metagenomics studies generate very large amounts of sequence data. Provide examples of genetic insight that can be learned from metagenomics.

18. What are gene microarrays? How are microarrays used?

19. In a draft annotation and overview of the human genome sequence, F.A. Wright et al. (*Genome Biol.* 2001: 2(7): Research0025) presented a graph similar to the one shown here. The graph details the approximate number of genes from each chromosome that are expressed only in embryos. Review earlier information in the text on human chromosomal aneuploids and correlate that information with the graph. Does this graph provide insight as to why some aneuploids occur and others do not?

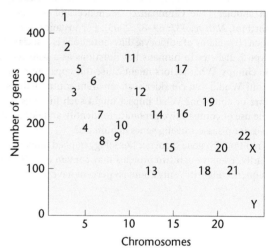

20. Annotation of the human genome sequence reveals a discrepancy between the number of protein-coding genes and the number of predicted proteins actually expressed by the genome. Proteomic analysis indicates that human cells are capable of synthesizing more than 100,000 different proteins and perhaps three times this number. What is the discrepancy, and how can it be reconciled?

Extra-Spicy Problems

21. Genomic sequencing has opened the door to numerous studies that help us understand the evolutionary forces shaping the genetic makeup of organisms. Using databases containing the sequences of 25 genomes, scientists (Kreil, D.P. and Ouzounis, C.A., *Nucl. Acids Res.* 29: 1608–1615, 2001) examined the relationship between GC content and global amino acid composition. They found that it is possible to identify thermophilic species on the basis of their amino acid composition alone, which suggests that evolution in a hot environment selects for a certain whole organism amino acid composition. In what way might evolution in extreme environments influence genome and amino acid composition? How might evolution in extreme environments influence the interpretation of genome sequence data?

22. The β-globin gene family consists of 60 kb of DNA, yet only 5 percent of the DNA encodes gene products. Account for as much of the remaining 95 percent of the DNA as you can.

23. M. Stoll and colleagues have compared candidate loci in humans and rats in search of loci in the human genome that are likely to contribute to the constellation of factors leading to hypertension. Through this research, they identified 26 chromosomal regions that they consider likely to contain hypertension genes. How can comparative genomics aid in the identification of genes responsible for such a complex human

disease? The researchers state that comparisons of rat and human candidate loci to those in the mouse may help validate their studies. Why might this be so?

24. Homology can be defined as the presence of common structures because of shared ancestry. Homology can involve genes, proteins, or anatomical structures. As a result of "descent with modification," many homologous structures have adapted different purposes.

    (a) List three anatomical structures in vertebrates that are homologous but have different functions.

    (b) Is it likely that homologous proteins from different species have the same or similar functions? Explain.

    (c) Under what circumstances might one expect proteins of similar function to not share homology? Would you expect such proteins to be homologous at the level of DNA sequences?

25. Comparisons between human and chimpanzee genomes indicate that a gene that may function as a wild type or normal gene in one primate may function as a disease-causing gene in another (The Chimpanzee Sequence and Analysis Consortium, *Nature*, 437: 69–87, 2005). For instance, the *PPARG* locus (regulator of adipocyte differentiation) is associated with type 2 diabetes in humans but functions as a wild-type gene in chimps. What factors might cause this apparent contradiction? Would you consider such apparent contradictions to be rare or common? What impact might such findings have on the use of comparative genomics to identify and design therapies for disease-causing genes in humans?

26. Traditionally, gene sequence homology implied functional similarity. Even though two proteins may contain over 60 percent sequence identity, only about 38 percent have identical func-

tions (Roy et al., 2008). In some cases, closely related homologs may engender completely different classes of proteins (enzymes). Consider the 3D structure of two proteins with 60 percent homology with entirely different functions. Explain how different functions may evolve by discussing the position of the homologous amino acid track, its relation to nonhomologous tracks, and the role that chaperones (Chapter 14) may play in determining protein function.

27. The discovery that *M. genitalium* has a genome of 0.58 Mb and only 470 protein-coding genes has sparked interest in determining the minimum number of genes needed for a living cell. In the search for organisms with smaller and smaller genomes, a new species of Archaea, *Nanoarchaeum equitans*, was discovered in a high-temperature vent on the ocean floor. This prokaryote has one of the smallest cell sizes ever discovered, and its genome is only about 0.5 Mb. However, organisms such as *M. genitalium*, *N. equitans*, and other microbes with very small genomes are either parasites or symbionts. How does this affect the search for a minimum genome? Should the definition of the minimum genome size for a living cell be redefined?

28. Whole Exome Sequencing (WES) is becoming a procedure to help physicians identify the cause of a genetic condition that has defied diagnosis by traditional means. The implication here is that exons in the nuclear genome are sequenced in the hopes that, by comparison with the genomes of nonaffected individuals, a diagnosis might be revealed.

    (a) What are the strengths and weaknesses of this approach?

    (b) If you were ordering WES for a patient, would you also include an analysis of the patient's mitochondrial genome?

DNA Forensics

Genetics is arguably the most influential science today—dramatically affecting technologies in fields as diverse as agriculture, archaeology, medical diagnosis, and disease treatment.

One of the areas that has been the most profoundly altered by modern genetics is forensic science. **Forensic science** (or *forensics*) uses technological and scientific approaches to answer questions about the facts of criminal or civil cases. Prior to 1986, forensic scientists had a limited array of tools with which to link evidence to specific individuals or suspects. These included some reliable methods such as blood typing and fingerprint analysis, but also many unreliable methods such as bite mark comparisons and hair microscopy.

Since the first forensic use of **DNA profiling** in 1986 (Box 1), **DNA forensics** (also called **forensic DNA fingerprinting** or **DNA typing**) has become an important method for police to identify sources of biological materials. DNA profiles can now be obtained from saliva left on cigarette butts or postage stamps, pet hairs found at crime scenes, or bloodspots the size of pinheads. Even biological samples that are degraded by fire or time are yielding DNA profiles that help the legal system determine identity, innocence, or guilt. Investigators now scan large databases of stored DNA profiles in order to match profiles generated from crime scene evidence. DNA profiling has proven the innocence of hundreds of people who were convicted of serious crimes and even sentenced to death. Forensic scientists have used DNA profiling to identify victims of mass disasters such as the Asian Tsunami of 2004 and the September 11, 2001 terrorist attacks in New York. They have also used forensic DNA analysis to identify endangered species and animals trafficked in the illegal wildlife trade. The power of DNA forensic analysis has captured the public imagination, and DNA forensics is featured in several popular television series.

The applications of DNA profiling extend beyond forensic investigations. These include paternity and family relationship testing, identification of plant materials, verification of military casualties, and evolutionary studies.

It is important for all of us to understand the basics of forensic DNA analysis. As informed citizens, we need to

> **"Even biological samples degraded by fire or time are yielding DNA profiles that help determine identity, innocence, or guilt."**

monitor its uses and potential abuses. Although DNA profiling is well validated as a technique and is considered the gold standard of forensic identification, it is not without controversy and the need for legislative oversight.

In this Special Topic chapter, we will explore how DNA profiling works and how the results of profiles are interpreted. We will learn about DNA databases, the potential problems associated with DNA profiling, and the future of this powerful technology.

DNA Profiling Methods

VNTR-Based DNA Fingerprinting

The era of DNA-based human identification began in 1984, with Dr. Alec Jeffreys's publication on DNA loci known as **minisatellites**, or **variable number of tandem repeats (VNTRs)**. As described earlier in the text (see Chapter 12), VNTRs are located in noncoding regions of the genome and are made up of DNA sequences of between 15 and 100 bp long, with each unit repeated a number of times. The number of repeats found at each VNTR locus varies from person to person, and hence VNTRs can be from 1 to 20 kilobases (kb) in length, depending on the person. For example, the VNTR

5′- GACTGCCTGCTAAGAT**GACTGCCTGCTAAGAT** GACTGCCTGCTAAGAT-3′

is comprised of three tandem repeats of a 16-nucleotide sequence (highlighted in bold).

VNTRs are useful for DNA profiling because there are as many as 30 different possible alleles (repeat lengths) at any VNTR in a population. This creates a large number of possible genotypes. For example, if one examined four different VNTR loci within a population, and each locus had 20 possible alleles, there would be more than 2 billion (4^{20}) possible genotypes in this four-locus profile.

To create a VNTR profile (also known as a DNA fingerprint), scientists extract DNA from a tissue sample and digest it with a restriction enzyme that cleaves on either side of the VNTR repeat region (ST Figure 3–1). The digested

BOX 1

The Pitchfork Case: The First Criminal Conviction Using DNA Profiling

In the mid-1980s, the bodies of two schoolgirls, Lynda Mann and Dawn Ashworth, were found in Leicestershire, England. Both girls had been raped, strangled, and their bodies left in the bushes. In the absence of useful clues, the police questioned a local mentally retarded porter named Richard Buckland who had a previous history of sexual offenses. During interrogation, Buckland confessed to the murder of Dawn Ashworth; however, police did not know whether he was also responsible for Lynda Mann's death. In 1986, in order to identify

the second killer, the police asked Dr. Alec Jeffreys of the University of Leicester to try a new method of DNA analysis called DNA fingerprinting. Dr. Jeffreys had developed a method of analyzing DNA regions called *variable number of tandem repeats* (VNTRs), which vary in length between members of a population. Dr. Jeffreys's VNTR analysis revealed a match between the DNA profiles from semen samples obtained from both crime scenes, suggesting that the same person was responsible for both rapes. However, neither of the DNA profiles matched those from a blood sample taken from Richard Buckland. Having eliminated their only suspect, the police embarked on the first mass DNA dragnet in history, by requesting blood samples from every adult

male in the region. Although 4000 men offered samples, one did not. Colin Pitchfork, a bakery worker, paid a friend to give a blood sample in his place, using forged identity documents. Their plan was detected when their conversation was overheard at a local pub. The conversation was reported to police, who then arrested Pitchfork, obtained his blood sample, and sent it for analysis. His DNA profile matched the profiles from the semen samples left at both crime scenes. Pitchfork confessed to the murders, pleaded guilty, and was sentenced to life in prison. The Pitchfork Case was not only the first criminal case resolved by forensic DNA profiling, but also the first case in which DNA profiling led to the exoneration of an innocent person.

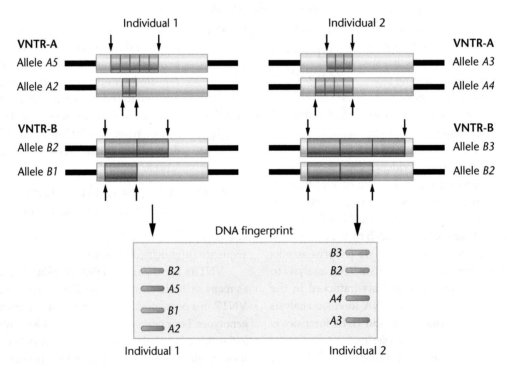

ST FIGURE 3-1 DNA fingerprint at two VNTR loci for two individuals. VNTR alleles at two loci (*A* and *B*) are shown for two different individuals. Arrows mark restriction-enzyme cutting sites that flank the VNTRs. Restriction-enzyme digestion produces a series of fragments that can be separated by gel electrophoresis and detected as bands on a Southern blot (bottom). The number of repeats at each locus is variable, so the overall pattern of bands is distinct for each individual. The DNA fingerprint profile shows that these individuals share one allele (*B2*).

DNA is separated by gel electrophoresis and subjected to Southern blot analysis (which is described in detail in Chapter 20). Briefly, separated DNA is transferred from the gel to a membrane and hybridized with a radioactive probe that recognizes DNA sequences within the VNTR region. After exposing the membrane to X-ray film, the pattern of bands is measured, with larger VNTR repeat alleles remaining near the top of the gel and smaller VNTRs, which migrate more rapidly through the gel, being closer to the bottom. The pattern of bands is the same for a given individual, no matter what tissue is used as the source of the DNA. If enough VNTRs are analyzed, each person's DNA profile will be unique (except, of course, for identical twins) because of the huge number of possible VNTRs and alleles. In practice, scientists analyze about five or six loci to create a DNA profile.

A significant limitation of VNTR profiling is that it requires a relatively large sample of DNA (10,000 cells or about 50 μg of DNA)—more than is usually found at a typical crime scene. In addition, the DNA must be relatively intact (nondegraded). As a result, VNTR profiling has been used most frequently when large tissue samples are available—such as in paternity testing. Although VNTR profiling is still used in some cases, it has mostly been replaced by more sensitive methods, as described next.

Autosomal STR DNA Profiling

The development of the polymerase chain reaction (PCR) revolutionized DNA profiling. PCR methods are described in detail earlier in the text (see Chapter 20). Using PCR-amplified DNA samples, scientists are able to generate DNA profiles from trace samples (e.g., the bulb of single hairs or a few cells from a bloodstain) and from samples that are old or degraded (such as a bone found in a field or an ancient Egyptian mummy).

The majority of human forensic DNA profiling is now done using commercial kits that amplify and analyze regions of the genome known as **microsatellites**, or **short tandem repeats (STRs)**. STRs are similar to VNTRs, but the repeated motif is shorter—between two and nine base pairs, repeated from 7 to 40 times. For example, one locus known as D8S1179 is made up of the four base-pair sequence TCTA, repeated 7 to 20 times, depending on the allele. There are 19 possible alleles of the locus that are found within a population. Although hundreds of STR loci are present in the human genome, only a subset is used for DNA profiling. At the present time, the FBI and other U.S. law enforcement agencies use 13 STR loci as a core set for forensic analysis (ST Figure 3–2). Most European countries now use 12 STR loci as a core set.

Several commercially available kits are currently used for forensic DNA analysis of STR loci. The methods vary slightly, but generally involve the following steps. As shown in ST Figure 3–3, each primer set is tagged by one of four fluorescent dyes—blue, green, yellow, or red. Each primer

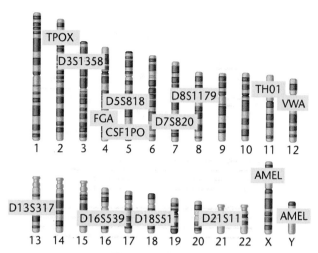

ST FIGURE 3–2 Chromosomal positions of the 13 core STR loci used for forensic DNA profiling. The AMEL (Amelogenin) locus is included with the 13 core loci and is used to determine the gender of the person providing the DNA sample. The *AMEL* locus on the X chromosome contains a 6-nucleotide deletion compared to that on the Y chromosome.

set is designed to amplify DNA fragments, the sizes of which vary depending on the number of repeats within the region amplified. For example, the primer sets that amplify the D19S433, vWA, TPOX, and D18S51 STR loci are all labeled with a yellow fluorescent tag. The sizes of the amplified DNA fragments produced allow scientists to differentiate between the yellow-labeled products. For example, the amplified products from the D19S433 locus range from about 100 to 150 bp in length, whereas those from the vWA locus range from about 150 to 200 bp, and so on.

After amplification, the DNA sample will contain a small amount of the original template DNA sample and a large amount of fluorescently labeled amplification products

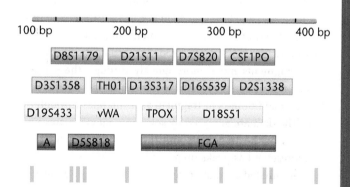

ST FIGURE 3–3 Relative size ranges and fluorescent dye labeling colors of 16 STR products generated by a commercially available DNA profiling kit. The DNA fragments shown in orange at the bottom of the diagram are DNA size markers. The AMEL locus is indicated as an A.

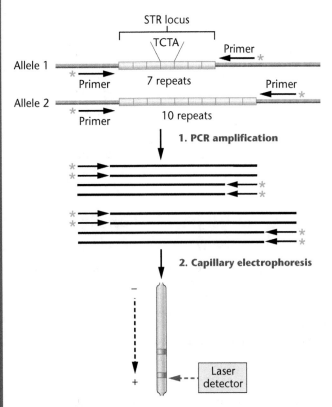

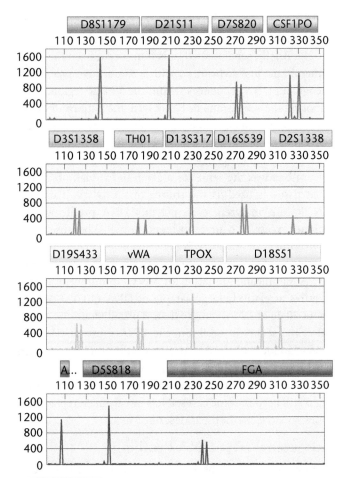

ST FIGURE 3-4 Steps in the PCR amplification and analysis of one STR locus (D8S1179). In this example, the person is heterozygous at the D8S1179 locus: One allele has 7 repeats and one has 10 repeats. Primers are specific for sequences flanking the STR locus and are labeled with a blue fluorescent dye. The double-stranded DNA is denatured, the primers are annealed, and each allele is amplified by PCR in the presence of all four dNTPs and Taq DNA polymerase. After amplification, the labeled products are separated according to size by capillary electrophoresis, followed by fluorescence detection.

ST FIGURE 3-5 An electropherogram showing the results of a DNA profile analysis using the 16-locus STR profile kit shown in ST Figure 3-3. Heterozygous loci show up as double peaks and homozygous loci as single, higher peaks. The sizes of each allele can be calculated from the peak locations relative to the size axis shown at the top of each panel. The single peak for the AMEL (A) locus indicates that this DNA profile is that of a female individual, as described in ST Figure 3-2.

(ST Figure 3–4). The sizes of the amplified fragments are measured by **capillary electrophoresis**. This method uses thin glass tubes that are filled with a polyacrylamide gel material similar to that used in slab gel electrophoresis. The amplified DNA sample is loaded onto the top of the capillary tube, and an electric current is passed through the tube. The negatively charged DNA fragments migrate through the gel toward the positive electrode, according to their sizes. Short fragments move more quickly through the gel, and larger ones more slowly. At the bottom of the tube, a laser detects each fluorescent fragment as it migrates through the tube. The data are analyzed by software that calculates both the sizes of the fragments and their quantities, and these are represented as peaks on a graph (ST Figure 3–5). Typically, automated capillary electrophoresis systems analyze as many as 16 samples at a time, and the analysis takes approximately 30 minutes.

After DNA profiling, the profile can be directly compared to a profile from another person, from crime scene evidence, or from other profiles stored in DNA profile databases (ST Figure 3–6). The STR profile genotype of an individual is expressed as the number of times the STR sequence is repeated. For example, in the profile shown in ST Figure 3–6, the person's profile would be expressed as shown in ST Table 3.1.

Scientists interpret STR profiles using statistics, probability, and population genetics, and these methods will be discussed in the section Interpreting DNA Profiles.

Y-Chromosome STR Profiling

In many forensic applications, it is important to differentiate the DNA profiles of two or more people in a mixed sample. For example, vaginal swabs from rape cases usually contain a mixture of female somatic cells and male sperm cells. In addition, some crime samples may contain evidence material from a number of male suspects. In these types of cases, STR profiling of Y-chromosome DNA is useful. There are

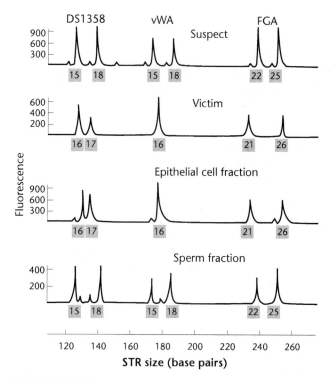

ST FIGURE 3–6 Electropherogram showing the STR profiles of four samples from a rape case. Three STR loci were examined from samples taken from a suspect, a victim, and two fractions from a vaginal swab taken from the victim. The x-axis shows the DNA size ladder, and the y-axis indicates relative fluorescence intensity. The number below each allele indicates the number of repeats in each allele, as measured against the DNA size ladder. Notice that the STR profile of the sperm sample taken from the victim matches that of the suspect.

more than 200 STR loci on the Y chromosome that are useful for DNA profiling; however, fewer than 20 of these are used routinely for forensic analysis. PCR amplification of Y-chromosome STRs uses specific primers that do not amplify DNA on the X chromosome.

One limitation of Y-chromosome DNA profiling is that it cannot differentiate between the DNA from fathers and sons, or from male siblings. This is because the Y chromosome is directly inherited from the father to his sons, as a single unit. The Y chromosome does not undergo recombination, meaning that less genetic variability exists on the Y chromosome than on autosomal chromosomes. Therefore,

all patrilineal relatives share the same Y chromosome profile. Even two apparently unrelated males may share the same Y profile, if they also shared a distant male ancestor.

Although these features of Y-chromosome profiles present limitations for some forensic applications, they are useful for identifying missing persons when a male relative's DNA is available for comparison. They also allow researchers to trace paternal lineages in genetic genealogy studies (Box 2).

Mitochondrial DNA Profiling

Another important addition to DNA profiling methods is **mitochondrial DNA (mtDNA)** analysis. Between 200 and 1700 mitochondria are present in each human somatic cell. Each mitochondrion contains one or more 16-kb circular DNA chromosomes. Mitochondria divide within cells and are distributed to daughter cells after cell division. Mitochrondria are passed from the human egg cell to the zygote during fertilization; however, as sperm cells contribute few if any mitochondria to the zygote, they do not contribute these organelles to the next generation. Therefore, all cells in an individual contain multiple copies of identical mitochondria derived from the mother. Like Y-chromosome DNA, mtDNA undergoes little if any recombination and is inherited as a single unit.

Scientists create mtDNA profiles by amplifying regions of mtDNA that show variability between unrelated individuals and populations. Two commonly used regions are known as **hypervariable segment I and II (HVSI and HVSII)** (ST Figure 3–7). After PCR amplification, the DNA sequence within these regions is determined by automated DNA sequencing. Scientists then compare the sequence with sequences from other individuals or crime samples, to determine whether or not they match.

The fact that mtDNA is present in high copy numbers in cells makes its analysis useful in cases where crime samples are small, old, or degraded. mtDNA profiling is particularly useful for identifying victims of mass murders or disasters, such as the Srebrenica massacre of 1995 and the World Trade Center attacks of 2001, where reference samples from relatives are available. The main disadvantage of mtDNA profiling is that it is not possible to differentiate between the mtDNA from maternal relatives or from siblings. Like Y-chromosome profiles, mtDNA profiles may be shared by two apparently unrelated individuals who also share a distant ancestor—in this case a maternal ancestor. Researchers use mtDNA profiles in scientific studies of genealogy, evolution, and human population migrations.

Mitochondrial DNA analyses have also been useful in wildlife forensics cases. Billions of dollars are generated from the illegal wildlife trade, throughout the world. Often, the identification of the species or origin of plant and animal

ST TABLE 3.1 STR Profile Genotypes from the Four Profiles Shown in ST Figure 3–6

STR Locus	Profile Genotype from			
	Suspect	Victim	Epithelial Cells	Sperm Fraction
DS1358	15, 18	16, 17	16, 17	15, 18
vWA	15, 18	16, 16	16, 16	15, 18
FGA	22, 25	21, 26	21, 26	22, 25

Thomas Jefferson's DNA: Paternity and Beyond

For more than two centuries, historians debated whether U.S. President Thomas Jefferson had fathered one or more children with Sally Hemings, one of his slaves. In 1997, in an attempt to resolve the controversy, scientists analyzed the Y-chromosome DNA profiles from the Jefferson and Hemings male lineages. Because Jefferson did not have any surviving male-line descendants, the researchers tested the Y chromosome from five patrilineal descendants of Jefferson's paternal uncle. They also analyzed the DNA from a patrilineal descendant of Eston Hemings, Sally Hemings's youngest son, as well as DNA from three patrilineal descendants of Jefferson's sister's sons, and five patrilineal descendants of Thomas Woodson,

who claimed to be the first child of Sally Hemings. DNA profiles were generated from 11 Y-chromosome STR loci, one larger minisatellite (MSY1), and seven SNP-like loci that differ by one nucleotide. All five of the Jefferson-line males shared identical Y-chromosome profiles, except for one individual who had a mutation at one STR locus. The profiles from the Woodson family line did not match those from the Jefferson line, excluding Thomas Woodson as a son of Thomas Jefferson. Similarly, and not unexpectedly, Jefferson's nephews did not share his Y-chromosome profile. However, the Y-chromosome profile from Eston Hemings's male descendant was identical to profiles from the Jefferson line. Although these data support the idea that Jefferson fathered at least one child of Sally Hemings, it does not exclude the possibility that another male Jefferson (such as Thomas Jefferson's brother, his brother's sons, or another male

individual sharing the Jefferson Y chromosome) could have been Eston Hemings's father.

Another interesting finding to arise from the Jefferson DNA study was that Jefferson's Y-chromosome profile pattern (haplotype K2) is extremely rare in Europeans. It occurs predominantly in men from Africa and western Eurasia. It is also found in men of Jewish ancestry from North Africa, Egypt, and the Middle East. In 2007, geneticists discovered the K2 haplotype (and matches to Jefferson's Y-chromosome profile) in 2 out of 85 men with the surname Jefferson in Britain; hence, it is likely that Jefferson's family originally came from Britain, as he claimed. However, it also suggests that sometime in the past, a Y chromosome of African or Middle Eastern origin entered the Jefferson line. To add to the Jefferson speculations, some commentators have suggested that Jefferson was the "first Jewish president" of the United States.

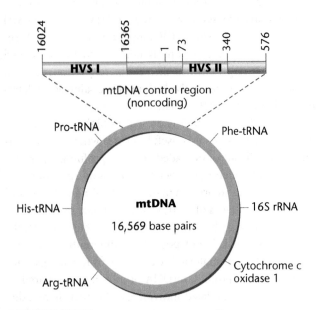

ST FIGURE 3–7 Human mtDNA molecule, showing the locations of HVS I and II regions relative to other mtDNA genes. The mtDNA control region is comprised of 1122 base pairs. Forensic DNA analysis involves sequencing the two HVS regions (610 base pairs total) and comparing sequences between individuals or samples. Sequence differences include short dinucleotide duplications as well as single base-pair changes.

material is the key to successful prosecution of wildlife trafficking cases. A case of illegal smuggling of bird eggs in Australia, solved by mitochondrial sequence analysis, is presented in Box 3.

Single-Nucleotide Polymorphism Profiling

Single-nucleotide polymorphisms (SNPs) are single-nucleotide differences between two DNA molecules. They may be base-pair changes or small insertions or deletions (ST Figure 3–8). SNPs occur randomly throughout the genome and on mtDNA, approximately every 500 to 1000 nucleotides. This means that there are potentially millions of loci in the human genome that can be used for profiling. However, as SNPs usually have only two alleles, many SNPs (50 or more) must be used to create a DNA profile that can distinguish between two individuals as efficiently as STRs.

Scientists analyze SNPs by using specific primers to amplify the regions of interest. The amplified DNA regions are then analyzed by a number of different methods such as automated DNA sequencing or hybridization to immobilized probes on DNA microarrays that distinguish between DNA molecules with single-nucleotide differences.

Forensic SNP profiling has one major advantage over STR profiling. Because a SNP involves only one nucleotide

BOX 3
The Pascal Della Zuana Case: DNA Barcodes and Wildlife Forensics

On August 2, 2006, a freelance photographer named Pascal Della Zuana was stopped by customs officers at Australia's Sydney International Airport. While questioning him about his flight from Thailand to Australia, officers noticed that he was wearing an unusual white vest under his outer clothing. Inside the vest, they discovered 23 concealed bird eggs.

Due to Australia's strict quarantine regulations, the eggs had to be treated with radiation in order to sterilize them. Unable to hatch the eggs, authorities turned to DNA typing in an attempt to identify the origin and species of the eggs.

The eggs were sent to Dr. Rebecca Johnson at the DNA Laboratory at the Australian Museum for forensic identification. Dr. Johnson took a small sample from each egg and extracted the DNA. She used PCR methods to amplify an approximately 650-bp region of the mitochondrial genome, within the cytochrome c oxidase 1 gene. She then organized these sequences into a format known as a DNA barcode. In order to identify the species, Dr. Johnson compared each DNA barcode to barcode entries in a large DNA barcode database compiled at the University of Guelph in Canada. The database contains mitochondrial DNA barcode sequences from hundreds of universities and museums throughout the world, cataloging more than 70,000 different species.

The results of Dr. Johnson's barcode sequence comparisons were dramatic. Della Zuana's vest had concealed eggs of exotic bird species such as macaws, African grey and Eclectus parrots, as well as a rare threatened species, the Moluccan cockatoo.

On January 20, 2007, Pascal Della Zuana was found guilty of contravening the Convention on International Trade in Endangered Species (CITES), as well as three Australian Customs and Quarantine Acts. He was fined $10,000 and sentenced to two years in prison.

During the court case, it was learned that, if hatched, the birds would have fetched about $250,000 on the black market. The worldwide smuggling of wildlife and wildlife parts is thought to be worth as much as US$150 billion each year—surpassed only by drugs and arms in terms of illegal profit.

---

of a DNA molecule, the theoretical size of DNA required for a PCR reaction is the size of the two primers and one more nucleotide (i.e., about 50 nucleotides). This feature makes SNP analysis suitable for analyzing DNA samples that are severely degraded. Despite this advantage, SNP profiling has not yet become routine in forensic applications. More frequently, researchers use SNP profiling of Y-chromosome and mtDNA loci for lineage and evolution studies.

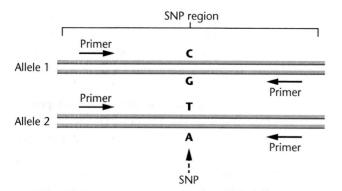

ST FIGURE 3–8 Example of a single-nucleotide polymorphism (SNP) from an individual who is heterozygous at the SNP locus. The arrows indicate the locations of PCR primers used to amplify the SNP region, prior to DNA sequence analysis. If this SNP locus only had two known alleles—the C and T alleles—there would be three possible genotypes in the population: CC, TT, and CT. The individual in this example has the CT genotype.

Interpreting DNA Profiles

After a DNA profile is generated, its significance must be determined. In a typical forensic investigation, a profile derived from a suspect is compared to a profile from an evidence sample or to profiles already present in a DNA database. If the suspect's profile does not match that of the evidence profile or database entries, investigators can conclude that the suspect is not the source of the sample(s) that generated the other profile(s). However, if the suspect's profile matches the evidence profile or a database entry, the interpretation becomes more complicated. In this case, one could conclude that the two profiles either came from the same person— or they came from two different people who share the same DNA profile by chance. To determine the significance of any DNA profile match, it is necessary to estimate the probability that the two profiles are a random match.

The **profile probability** or **random match probability** method gives a numerical probability that a person chosen at random from a population would share the same DNA profile as the evidence or suspect profiles. The following example demonstrates how to arrive at a profile probability (ST Table 3.2).

The first locus examined in this DNA profile (D5S818) has two alleles: 11 and 13. Population studies show that the 11 allele of this locus appears at a frequency of 0.361

ST TABLE 3.2   **A Profile Probability Calculation Based on Analysis of Five STR Loci**

STR Locus	Alleles from Profile	Allele Frequency from Population Database*	Genotype Frequency Calculation
D5S818	11	0.361	$2pq = 2 \times 0.361 \times 0.141 = 0.102$
	13	0.141	
TPOX	11	0.243	$p^2 = 0.243 \times 0.243 = 0.059$
	11	0.243	
D8S1179	13	0.305	$2pq = 2 \times 0.305 \times 0.031 = 0.019$
	16	0.031	
CSF1PO	10	0.217	$p^2 = 0.217 \times 0.217 \times 0.047$
	10	0.217	
D19S433	13	0.253	$2pq = 2 \times 0.253 \times 0.369 = 0.187$
	14	0.369	

Genotype frequency from this 5-locus profile $= 0.102 \times 0.059 \times 0.019 \times 0.047 \times 0.187 = 0.0000009 = 9 \times 10^{-7}$

*A U.S. Caucasian population database (Butler, J.M., et al. 2003. *J. Forensic Sci.* 48: 908–911).

© 2003 John Wiley & Sons, Inc.

in this population and the 13 allele appears at a frequency of 0.141. In population genetics, the frequencies of two different alleles at a locus are given the designation p and q, following the Hardy–Weinberg law described earlier in the text (see Chapter 25). We assume that the person having this DNA profile received the 11 and 13 alleles at random from each parent. Therefore, the probability that this person received allele 11 from the mother and allele 13 from the father is expressed as $p \times q = pq$. In addition, the probability that the person received allele 11 from the father and allele 13 from the mother is also pq. Hence, the total probability that this person would have the 11, 13 genotype at this locus, by chance, is $2pq$. As we see from ST Table 3.2, $2pq$ is 0.102 or approximately 10 percent. It is obvious from this sample that using a DNA profile of only one locus would not be very informative, as about 10 percent of the population would also have the D5S818 11, 13 genotype.

The discrimination power of the DNA profile increases when we add more loci to the analysis. The next locus of this person's DNA profile (TPOX) has two identical alleles—the 11 allele. Allele 11 appears at a frequency of 0.243 in this population. The probability of inheriting the 11 allele from each parent is $p \times p = p^2$. As we see in the table, the genotype frequency at this locus would be 0.059, which is about 6 percent of the population. If this DNA profile contained only the first two loci, we could calculate how frequently a person chosen at random from this population would have the genotype shown in the table, by multiplying the two genotype probabilities together. This would be $0.102 \times 0.059 = 0.006$. This analysis would mean that about 6 persons in 1000 (or 1 person in 166) would have this genotype. The method of multiplying all frequencies of genotypes at each locus is known as the **product rule**. It is the most frequently

used method of DNA profile interpretation and is widely accepted in U.S. courts.

By multiplying all the genotype probabilities at the five loci, we arrive at the genotype frequency for this DNA profile: 9×10^{-7}. This means that approximately 9 people in every 10 million (or about 1 person in a million), chosen at random from this population, would share this 5-locus DNA profile.

The Uniqueness of DNA Profiles

As we increase the number of loci analyzed in a DNA profile, we obtain smaller probabilities of a random match. Theoretically, if a sufficient number of loci were analyzed, we could be *almost* certain that the DNA profile was unique. At the present time, law enforcement agencies in North America use a core set of 13 STR loci to generate DNA profiles. A hypothetical genotype comprised of the most common alleles of each STR locus in the core STR profile would be expected to occur only once in a population of 10 billion people. Hence, the frequency of this profile would be 1 in 10 billion.

Although this would suggest that most DNA profiles generated by analysis of the 13 core STR loci would be unique on the planet, several situations can alter this interpretation. For example, identical twins share the same DNA, and their DNA profiles will be identical. Identical twins occur at a frequency of about 1 in 250 births. In addition, siblings can share one allele at any DNA locus in about 50 percent of cases and can share both alleles at a locus in about 25 percent of cases. Parents and children also share alleles, but are less likely than siblings to share both alleles at a locus. When DNA profiles come from two people who are closely related, the profile probabilities must be adjusted to take this into account. The allele frequencies and calculations that we describe here are based on assumptions that the population is large and has little relatedness or inbreeding. If a DNA profile is analyzed from a person in a small interrelated group, allele frequency tables and calculations may not apply.

The Prosecutor's Fallacy

It is sometimes stated, by both the legal profession and the public, that "the suspect must be guilty given that the chance of a random match to the crime scene sample is 1 in 10 billion—greater than the population of the planet." This type of statement is known as the **prosecutor's fallacy** because it equates guilt with a numerical probability derived from one piece of evidence, in the absence of other evidence. A match between a suspect's DNA profile and crime scene evidence does not necessarily prove guilt, for many reasons such as human error or contamination of samples, or even deliberate tampering. In addition, a DNA profile that does not match the evidence does not necessarily mean that the suspect is innocent. For example, a suspect's profile may not match that from a semen sample at a rape scene, but the suspect could still have been involved in the crime, perhaps by restraining the victim. For these and other reasons, DNA profiles must be interpreted in the context of all the evidence in a case. A more detailed description of problems with DNA profiles is given in the next section.

DNA Profile Databases

Many countries throughout the world maintain national DNA profile databases. The first of these databases was established in the UK in 1995 and now contains approximately 5 million profiles—representing almost 10 percent of the population. In the United States, both state and federal governments have DNA profile databases. The entire system of databases along with tools to analyze the data is known as the **Combined DNA Index System (CODIS)** and is maintained by the FBI. As of August 2013, there were more than 11 million DNA profiles stored within the CODIS system. The two main databases in CODIS are the **convicted offender database**, which contains DNA profiles from individuals convicted of certain crimes, and the **forensic database**, which contains profiles generated from crime scene evidence. In addition, some states have DNA profile databases containing profiles from suspects and from unidentified human remains and missing persons. Suspects who are not convicted can request that their profiles be removed from the databases.

DNA profile databases have proven their value in many different situations. As of August 2013, use of CODIS databases had resulted in more than 200,000 profile matches that assisted criminal investigations and missing persons searches. (Box 4). Despite the value of DNA profile databases, they remain a concern for many people who question the privacy and civil liberties of individuals versus the needs of the state.

BOX 4
The Kennedy Brewer Case: Two Bite-Mark Errors and One Hit

In 1992 in Mississippi, Kennedy Brewer was arrested and charged with the rape and murder of his girlfriend's 3-year-old daughter, Christine Jackson. Although a semen sample had been obtained from Christine's body, there was not sufficient DNA for profiling. Forensic scientists were also unable to identify the ABO blood group from the bloodstains left at the crime scene. The prosecution's only evidence came from a forensic bite-mark specialist who testified that the 19 "bite marks" found on Christine's body matched imprints made by Brewer's two top teeth. Even though the specialist had recently been discredited by the American Board of Forensic Odontology, and

the defense's expert dentistry witness testified that the marks on Christine's body were actually postmortem insect bites, the court convicted Brewer of capital murder and sexual battery and sentenced him to death.

In 2001, more sensitive DNA profiling was conducted on the 1992 semen sample. The profile excluded Brewer as the donor of the semen sample. It also excluded two of Brewer's friends, and Y-chromosome profiles excluded Brewer's male relatives. Despite these test results, Brewer remained in prison for another five years, awaiting a new trial. In 2007, the Innocence Project took on Brewer's case and retested the DNA samples. The profiles matched those of another man, Justin Albert Johnson, a man with a history of sexual assaults who had been one of the original suspects in the case. Johnson subsequently confessed

to Christine Jackson's murder, as well as to another rape and murder—that of a 3-year-old girl named Courtney Smith. Levon Brooks, the ex-boyfriend of Courtney's mother, had been convicted of murder in the Smith case, also based on bite-mark testimony by the same discredited expert witness.

On February 15, 2008, all charges against Kennedy Brewer were dropped, and he was exonerated of the crimes. Levon Brooks was subsequently exonerated of the Smith murder in March of 2008.

Since 1989, more than 250 people in the United States have been exonerated of serious crimes, based on DNA profile evidence. Seventeen of these people had served time on death row. In more than 100 of these exoneration cases, the true perpetrator has been identified, often through searches of DNA databases.

Technical and Ethical Issues Surrounding DNA Profiling

Although DNA profiling is sensitive, accurate, and powerful, it is important to be aware of its limitations. One limitation is that most criminal cases have either no DNA evidence for analysis, or DNA evidence that would not be informative to the case. In some cases, potentially valuable DNA evidence exists but remains unprocessed and backlogged. Another serious problem is that of human error. There are cases in which innocent people have been convicted of violent crimes based on DNA samples that had been inadvertently switched during processing. DNA evidence samples from crime scenes are often mixtures derived from any number of people present at the crime scene or even from people who were not present, but whose biological material (such as hair or saliva) was indirectly introduced to the site (Box 5). Crime scene evidence is often degraded, yielding partial DNA profiles that are difficult to interpret.

One of the most disturbing problems with DNA profiling is its potential for deliberate tampering. DNA profile technologies are so sensitive that profiles can be generated from only a few cells—or even from fragments of synthetic DNA. There have been cases in which criminals have introduced biological material to crime scenes, in an attempt to affect forensic DNA profiles. It is also possible to manufacture artificial DNA fragments that match STR loci of a person's DNA profile. In 2010, a research paper[1] reported methods for synthesizing DNA of a known STR profile, mixing the DNA with body fluids, and depositing the sample on crime scene items. When subjected to routine forensic analysis, these artificial samples generated perfect STR profiles. In the future, it may be necessary to develop methods to detect the presence of synthetic or cloned DNA in crime scene samples. It has been suggested that such detections could be done, based on the fact that natural DNA contains epigenetic markers such as methylation.

Many of the ethical questions related to DNA profiling involve the collection and storage of biological samples and DNA profiles. Such questions deal with who should have their DNA profiles stored on a database and whether police should be able to collect DNA samples without a suspect's knowledge or consent.

Another ethical question involves the use of DNA profiles that partially match those of a suspect. There have been cases in which a DNA profile from a crime scene gave a partial match to a profile stored in a DNA database. On the assumption that the two profiles arose from two genetically related individuals, law enforcement agencies pursued relatives of the convicted person. Testing in these cases is known

---

[1]Frumkin, D., et al. 2010. Authentication of forensic DNA samples. *Forensic Sci Int Genetics* 4: 95–103.

BOX 5

A Case of Transference: The Lukis Anderson Story

On November 30, 2012, police discovered the body of Raveesh Kumra at his home in Monte Sereno, California. Kumra's house had been ransacked, and he had suffocated from the tape used to gag him. Police collected DNA samples from the crime scene and performed DNA profiling. Several suspects were identified through matches to DNA database entries. One match, to a sample taken from Kumra's fingernails, was that of Lukis Anderson, a homeless man who was known to police. Based on the DNA profile match, Anderson was arrested, charged with murder, and jailed. He remained in jail, with a death sentence over his head, for the next five months.

The authorities believed that they had a solid case. The crime scene DNA profile was a perfect match to Anderson's DNA profile, and the lab results were accurate. Prosecutors planned to pursue the death penalty. The only problem for the prosecution was that Anderson could not have been involved in the murder, or even present at the crime scene.

On the night of the murder, Anderson had been intoxicated and barely conscious on the streets of San Jose and had been taken to the hospital, where he remained for the next 12 hours. Given his iron-clad alibi, authorities were forced to release Anderson. But they remained baffled about how an innocent person's DNA could have been found on a murder victim—one whom Anderson had never even met.

Several months after Anderson's release, prosecutors announced that they had solved the puzzle. The paramedics who had treated Anderson and taken him to the hospital had then responded to the call at Kumra's house, where they had inadvertently transferred Anderson's DNA onto Kumra's fingernails. It is not clear how the transfer had occurred, but likely Anderson's DNA had been present on equipment or clothing of the paramedics.

If Lukis Anderson had not been in the hospital with an irrefutable alibi, he may have faced the death sentence based on DNA evidence. His story illustrates how too much confidence in the power of DNA evidence can lead to false accusations. It also points to the robustness of DNA, which can remain intact, survive disinfection, and be transferred from one location to another, under unlikely circumstances.

as *familial DNA testing*. Should such searches be considered scientifically valid or even ethical?

It is now possible to accurately predict the eye and hair color of persons based on information in their DNA sample—a method known as *DNA phenotyping*. In addition, scientists are devising DNA-based tests that could provide estimates of age, height, racial ancestry, hairline, facial width, and nose size. Should this type of information be used to identify or convict a suspect?

As DNA profiling becomes more sophisticated and prevalent, we should carefully consider both the technical and ethical questions that surround this powerful new technology.

Selected Readings and Resources

Journal Articles

Brettell, T.A., et al., 2009. Forensic science. *Anal. Chem.* 81: 4695–4711.

Butler, J.M., et al., 2007. STRs vs. SNPs: Thoughts on the future of forensic DNA testing. *Forensic Sci Med Pathol* 3: 200–205.

Enserink, M. 2011. Can this DNA sleuth help catch criminals? *Science* 331: 838–840.

Frumkin, D., et al., 2010. Authentication of forensic DNA samples. *Forensic Sci International* 4: 95–103.

Garrison, N.A., et al. 2013. Forensic familial searching: Scientific and social implications. *Nature Reviews Genetics* 14: 445.

Gill, P., Jeffreys, A.J., and Werrett, D.J. 2005. Forensic applications of DNA "fingerprints." *Nature* 318: 577–579.

Jobling, M.A., and Gill, P. 2004. Encoded evidence: DNA in forensic analysis. *Nature Reviews Genetics* 5: 739–750.

Roewer, L. 2009. Y chromosome STR typing in crime casework. *Forensic Sci Med Pathol.* 5(2): 77–84.

Whittall, H. 2008. The forensic use of DNA: Scientific success story, ethical minefield. *Biotechnol J.* 3: 303–305.

Zietkiewicz, E. et al. 2012. Current genetic methodologies in the identification of disaster victims and in forensic analysis. *J. Appl. Genetics* 53: 41–60.

Web Sites

Brenner, C.H., Forensic Mathematics of DNA Matching. http://dna-view.com/profile.htm

Butler, J.M. and Reeder, D.J. Short Tandem Repeat DNA Internet DataBase. http://www.cstl.nist.gov/div831/strbase/

Obasogie, O.K. 2013. High-tech, high-risk forensics. http://www.nytimes.com/2013/07/25/opinion/high-tech-high-risk-forensics.html?_r=0

DNA initiative: advancing criminal justice through DNA technology. http://www.dna.gov

The Innocence Project. http://www.innocenceproject.org

Berson, S.B. Debating DNA collection, from Office of Justice Programs, National Institute of Justice Journal, November 2009. http://www.nij.gov/journals/264/debating-DNA.htm

CODIS-NDIS Statistics. Federal Bureau of Investigation Web site, http://www.fbi.gov/about-us/lab/biometric-analysis/codis

Review Questions

1. What is VNTR profiling, and what are the applications of this technique?
2. Why are short tandem repeats (STRs) the most commonly used loci for forensic DNA profiling?
3. Describe capillary electrophoresis. How does this technique distinguish between input DNA and amplified DNA?
4. What are the advantages and limitations of Y-chromosome STR profiling?
5. How does the AMEL gene locus allow investigators to tell whether a DNA sample comes from a male or a female?
6. Explain why mitochondrial DNA profiling is often the method of choice for identifying victims of massacres and mass disasters.
7. What is a "profile probability," and what information is required in order to calculate it?
8. Describe the database system known as CODIS. What determines whether a person's DNA profile will be entered into the CODIS system?
9. What is DNA barcoding, and what types of cases use this profiling method?
10. Why is it important to understand the prosecutor's fallacy?

Discussion Questions

1. Given the possibility that synthetic DNA could be purposely introduced to a crime scene in order to implicate an innocent person, what methods could be developed to distinguish between synthetic and natural DNA?
2. Different countries and jurisdictions have different regulations regarding the collection and storage of DNA samples and profiles. What are the regulations within your region? Do you think that these regulations sufficiently protect individual rights?
3. If you were acting as a defense lawyer in a murder case that used DNA profiling as evidence against the defendant, how would you explain to the jury the limitations that might alter their interpretation of the crime scene DNA profile?
4. The phenomena of somatic mosaicism and chimerism are more prevalent than most people realize. For example, pregnancy and bone marrow transplantation may lead to a person's genome becoming a mixture of two different genomes. Describe how DNA forensic analysis may be affected by chimerism and what measures could be used to mitigate any confusion during DNA profiling. Find out more about genetic chimerism in an article by Zimmer, C., DNA double take, *New York Times*, September 16, 2013.

Genomics and Personalized Medicine

Physicians have always practiced personalized medicine in order to make effective treatment decisions for their patients. Doctors take into account a patient's symptoms, family history, lifestyle, and data derived from many types of medical tests. However, within the last 20 years, personalized medicine has taken a new and potentially powerful direction based on genetics and genomics. Today, the phrase *personalized medicine* is used to describe the application of information from a patient's unique genetic profile in order to select effective treatments that have minimal side-effects and to detect disease susceptibility prior to development of the disease.

Despite the immense quantities of medical information and pharmaceuticals that are available, the diagnosis and treatment of human disease remain an imperfect process. It is sometimes difficult or impossible to accurately diagnose some conditions. In addition, some patients do not respond to treatments, while others may develop side-effects that can be annoying or even life-threatening. As much of the basis for disease susceptibility and the variation that patients exhibit toward drug treatments are genetically determined, progress in genetics, genomics, and molecular biology has the potential to significantly advance medical diagnosis and treatment.

The sequencing of the human genome, the cataloging of genetic sequence variants, and the linking of sequence variants with disease susceptibility form the basis of the newly emerging field of personalized medicine. In addition, a rapidly growing list of genetic tests helps physicians determine whether a patient will have an adverse drug reaction and whether a particular pharmaceutical will be effective for that patient.

Although much of the promise of personalized medicine remains in the future, significant progress is underway. As genome technologies advance and the cost of sequencing personal genomes declines, it is becoming easier to examine a patient's unique genomic profile in order to diagnose diseases and prescribe treatments. Proponents of personalized medicine foresee a future in which each person will have his or her genome sequence determined at birth and will have the sequence stored in a digital form within a personal computerized medical file. Medical practitioners will use automated methods to scan the sequence information within these files for clues to disease susceptibility and reactions to drugs. In the near future, genomic profiling and personalized medicine will allow physicians to predict which diseases you will develop, which therapeutics will work for you, and which drug dosages are appropriate.

In this Special Topic chapter, we will outline the current uses of genetic and genomic-based personalized medicine in disease diagnosis and drug selection. In addition, we will outline the future directions for personalized medicine, as well as some ethical and technical challenges associated with it.

Personalized Medicine and Pharmacogenomics

Perhaps the most developed area of personalized medicine is in the field of pharmacogenomics. **Pharmacogenomics** is the study of how an individual's entire genetic makeup determines the body's response to drugs. The term *pharmacogenomics* is used interchangeably with *pharmacogenetics*, which refers to the study of how sequence variation within specific candidate genes affects an individual's drug responses.

In pharmacogenomics, scientists take into account many aspects of drug metabolism and how genetic traits affect these aspects. When a drug enters the body, it interacts with various proteins, including carriers, cell-surface receptors, transporters, and metabolizing enzymes. These proteins affect a drug's target site of action, absorption, pharmacological response, breakdown, and excretion. Because so many interactions occur between a drug and proteins within the patient, many genes and many different genetic polymorphisms can affect a person's response to a drug.

In this subsection, we examine two ways in which genomics and personalized medicine are changing the field of

> **"In the near future, personalized medicine will allow physicians to predict which diseases you will develop, which therapeutics will work for you, and which drug dosages are appropriate."**

pharmacogenomics: by optimizing drug therapies and by reducing adverse drug reactions.

Optimizing Drug Therapies

When it comes to drug therapy, it is clear that "one size does not fit all." On average, a drug will be effective in only about 50 percent of patients who take it (ST Figure 4–1). This situation means that physicians often must switch their patients from one drug to another until they find one that is effective. Not only does this waste time and resources, but also it may be dangerous to the patient who is exposed to a variety of different pharmaceuticals and who may not receive appropriate treatment in time to combat a progressive illness.

Pharmacogenomics increases the efficacy of drugs by targeting those drugs to subpopulations of patients who will benefit. One of the most common current applications of personalized pharmacogenomics is in the diagnosis and treatment of cancers. Large-scale sequencing studies show that each tumor is genetically unique, even though it may fall into a broad category based on cytological analysis or knowledge of its tissue origin. Given this genomic variability, it is important to understand each patient's mutation profile to select an appropriate treatment—particularly those newer treatments based on the molecular characteristics of tumors (Box 1).

One of the first success stories in personalized medicine was that of the **HER-2** gene and the use of the drug **Herceptin®** in breast cancer. The human epidermal growth

Drug type		
Antidepressants (SSRIs)	38%	
Asthma drugs	40%	
Diabetes drugs	43%	
Arthritis drugs	50%	
Alzheimer drugs	70%	
Cancer drugs	75%	

© 2011 Personalized Medicine Coalition

ST FIGURE 4–1 Variations in patient response to drugs. This figure gives a general summary of the percentages of patients for which a particular class of drugs is effective.

factor receptor 2 (*HER-2*) gene is located on chromosome 17 and codes for a transmembrane tyrosine kinase receptor protein called HER-2. These receptors are located within the cell membranes of normal breast epithelial cells and, when bound to an extracellular growth factor (ligand), send signals to the cell nucleus that result in the transcription of genes involved in cell growth and division.

In about 25 percent of invasive breast cancers, the *HER-2* gene is amplified and the protein is overexpressed on the cell surface. In some breast cancers, the *HER-2* gene

SPECIAL TOPIC 4

BOX 1
The Story of Pfizer's Crizotinib

In 2007, Beverly Sotir was diagnosed with advanced non-small-cell lung cancer (NSCLC). Beverly, a 68-year-old grandmother and nonsmoker, received standard chemotherapy, but her cancer continued to proliferate. She was given six months to live. At this same time, an apparently unrelated scientific study was underway by the pharmaceutical company, Pfizer. Pfizer had developed a compound called crizotinib, which was designed to inhibit the activity of MET, a tyrosine kinase that is abnormal in a number of tumors. Although crizotinib also inhibited another kinase called ALK (anaplastic lymphoma kinase), scientists did not

consider it significant. After clinical trials for crizotinib began, an article was published[*] describing a chromosomal translocation found in a small number of NSCLCs. This translocation fused the *ALK* gene to another gene called *EML4*, leading to production of a fusion protein that stimulated cancer cell growth. Pfizer immediately changed its clinical trial to include NSCLC patients. Beverly's doctors at the Dana-Farber Cancer Institute in Boston tested her tumors, discovered that they contained the *ALK/EML4* fusion gene, and enrolled Beverly in the trials. The results were dramatic. Within six months, Beverly's tumors shrunk by more than 50 percent and some disappeared entirely. As of 2011, Beverly continued to do well.

Results of the clinical trials for crizotinib showed that tumors shrank or stabilized in 90 percent of the 82

patients whose tumors contained the *ALK* fusion gene. Those patients who responded well to treatment had positive responses for up to 15 months. Scientists report that the *ALK* fusion gene tends to occur most frequently in young NSCLC patients who have never smoked. Approximately 4 percent of patients with NSCLC have this translocation in their tumor cells. Although only a small percentage of people might benefit from crizotinib, this means that about 45,000 people a year, worldwide, may be eligible for this treatment. Crizotinib is now approved in the United States for treatment of NSCLCs.

[*]Choi, S.M., et al. 2007. Identification of the transforming EML4-ALK fusion gene in non-small-cell lung cancer. *Nature* 448: 561–566.

is present in as many as 100 copies per cell. The presence of *HER-2* overexpression is associated with increased tumor invasiveness, metastasis, and cell proliferation, as well as a poorer patient prognosis.

Using recombinant DNA technology, Genentech Corporation in California developed a monoclonal antibody known as trastuzumab (or Herceptin) that is designed to bind specifically to the extracellular region of the HER-2 receptor. When bound to the receptor, Herceptin appears to inhibit the signaling capability of HER-2 and may also flag the HER-2-expressing cell for destruction by the patient's immune system. In cancer cells that overexpress HER-2, Herceptin treatment causes cell-cycle arrest, and in some cases, death of the cancer cells.

Because Herceptin will only act on breast cancer cells that have amplified *HER-2* genes, it is important to know the HER-2 phenotype of each cancer. In addition, Herceptin has potentially serious side-effects. Hence, its use must be limited to those who could benefit from the treatment. A number of molecular assays have been developed to determine the gene and protein status of breast cancer cells. Two types of tests are used routinely to determine the amount of *HER-2* overexpression in cancer cells: immunohistochemistry (IHC) and fluorescence *in situ* hybridization (FISH). In IHC assays, an antibody that binds to the HER-2 protein is added to fixed tissue on a slide. The presence of bound antibody is then detected with a stain and observed under the microscope [ST Figure 4–2(a)]. The FISH assay (which is described in Chapter 10) assesses the number of *HER-2* genes by comparing the fluorescence signal from a HER-2 probe with a control signal from another gene that is not amplified in the cancer cells [ST Figure 4–2(b)].

Herceptin has had a major effect on the treatment of HER-2 positive breast cancers. When Herceptin is used in combination with chemotherapy, there is a 25 to 50 percent increase in survival, compared with the use of chemotherapy alone. Herceptin is now one of the biggest selling biotechnology products in the world, generating more than $5 billion in annual sales.

There are now dozens of drugs whose prescription and use depend on the genetic status of the target cells. Approximately 10 percent of FDA-approved drugs have labels that include pharmacogenomic information (ST Table 4.1). For example, about 40 percent of colon cancer patients respond to the drugs **Erbitux**® (cetuximab) and **Vectibix**® (panitumumab). These two drugs are monoclonal antibodies that bind to **epidermal growth factor receptors (EGFRs)** on the surface of cells and inhibit the EGFR signal transduction pathway. In order to work, cancer cells must express EGFR on their surfaces and must also have a wild-type *K-RAS* gene. The presence of EGFR can be assayed using a staining test and observation of cancer cells under a microscope. Mutations in the *K-RAS* gene can be detected using assays based on the polymerase chain reaction (PCR) method, which is described earlier in the text (see Chapter 20).

Another example of treatment decisions being informed by genetic tests is that of the **Oncotype DX**® Assay (Genomic Health Inc.). This assay analyzes the expression (amount of mRNA) from 21 genes in breast cancer samples, in order to help physicians select appropriate treatments and predict the course of the disease. These genes were chosen because their levels of gene expression correlate with breast cancer recurrence after initial treatment. Based on the mRNA expression levels revealed in the assay results, scientists calculate a "Recurrence Score," estimating

(a)

(b)

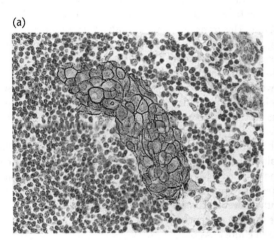
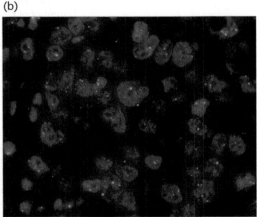

ST FIGURE 4–2   HER-2 protein and gene-amplification assays. (a) Normal and breast cancer cells within a biopsy sample, stained by HER-2 immunohistochemistry. Cell nuclei are stained blue. Cancer cells that overexpress HER-2 protein stain brown at the cell membrane. (b) Cancer cells assayed for *HER-2* gene copy number by fluorescence *in situ* hybridization. Cell nuclei are stained blue. *HER-2* gene DNA appears bright red. Chromosome 17 centromeres stain green. The degree of *HER-2* gene amplification is expressed as the ratio of red staining foci to green staining foci.

ST TABLE 4.1 Examples of Personalized Medicine Drugs and Diagnostics

Therapy	Gene Test	Description
Herceptin® (trastuzumab)	HER-2 amplification	Breast cancer test to accompany Herceptin use
Erbitux® (cetuximab)	EGFR expression, K-RAS mutations	Protein and mutation analysis prior to treatment
Gleevec® (imatinib)	BCR/ABL fusion	Gleevec used in treatment of Philadelphia chromosome-positive chronic myelogenous leukemia
Gleevec® (imatinib)	C-KIT	Gleevec used in stomach cancers expressing mutated C-KIT
Tarceva® (erlotinib)	EGFR expression	Lung cancer for EGFR-positive tumors
Drugs/surgery	MLH1, MSH2, MSH6	Gene mutations related to colon cancers
Hormone/chemotherapies	Oncotype DX® test	Selection of breast cancer patients for chemotherapy
Chemotherapies	Aviara Cancer TYPE ID®	Classifies 39 tumor types using gene-expression assays
Rituximab	PGx Predict®	Detects CD-20 variants that predict response to rituximab in non-Hodgkin lymphoma

the likelihood that the cancer will recur within a ten-year period. Those patients with a low-risk rating would likely not benefit by adding chemotherapy to their treatment regimens and so can be treated with hormones alone. Those with higher risk scores would likely benefit from more aggressive therapies.

Reducing Adverse Drug Reactions

Every year, about 2 million people in the United States have serious side-effects from pharmaceutical drugs, and approximately 100,000 people die. The costs associated with these **adverse drug reactions** (ADRs) are estimated to be $136 billion annually. Although some ADRs result from drug misuse, others result from a patient's inherent physiological reactions to a drug.

Sequence variations in a large number of genes can affect drug responsiveness (ST Table 4.2). Of particular significance are the genes that encode the cytochrome P450 families of enzymes. These family members are encoded by 57 different genes. People with some cytochrome P450 gene variants metabolize and eliminate drugs slowly, which can lead to accumulations of the drug and overdose side-effects. In contrast, other people have variants that cause drugs to be eliminated quickly, leading to reduced effectiveness. An example of gene variants that affect drug responses is that of CYP2D6 gene. This member of the cytochrome P450 family encodes the debrisoquine hydroxylase enzyme, which is involved in the metabolism of approximately 25 percent of all pharmaceutical drugs, including diazepam, acetaminophen, clozapine, beta blockers, tamoxifen, and codeine. There are more than 70 variant alleles of this gene. Some mutations in this gene reduce the activity of the encoded enzyme, and others can increase it. Approximately 80 percent of

ST TABLE 4.2 Examples of Variant Gene Products That Affect Drug Responses

Gene Product	Variant Phenotype	Drugs Affected	Response
Acetyl transferase NAT2	Slow, rapid acetylators	Isoniazid, sulfamethazine, dapsone, paraminosalicylic acid, heterocyclic amines	Slow: toxic neuritis, lupus erythematosus, bladder cancer; Rapid: colorectal cancer
Thiopurine methyltransferase	Poor TPMT methylators	6-mercaptopurine, 6-thioguanine, azathioprine	Bone marrow toxicity, liver damage
Catechol O-methyl transferase	High, low methylators	Levodopa, methyldopa	Low or increased response
CYP2C19	Poor, extensive hydroxylators	Mephenytoin, hexobarbital, proguanil, etc.	Poor or increased toxicity, poor efficacy (proguanil)
β_2 Adrenoceptor	Enhanced receptor downregulation	Albuterol, ventolin	Poor asthma control
5-HT2A serotonergic receptor	Multiple polymorphisms	Clozapine	Variable drug efficiencies
Multiple drug resistance transporter	Overexpression in cancer	Vinblastine, doxorubicin, paclitaxel, etc.	Drug resistance

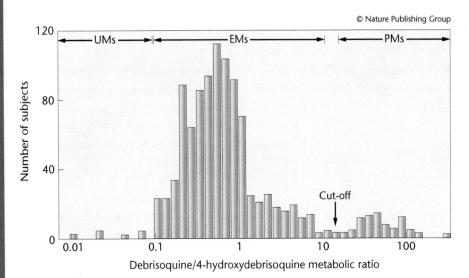

ST FIGURE 4-3 *CYP2D6* pharmacogenetic profile in a Swedish population. Individuals were tested for their ability to metabolize debrisoquine to 4-hydroxydebrisoquine, as an indication of the efficiency of debrisoquine hydroxylase enzyme activity. The population sample was divided into the categories UMs (ultra-rapid metabolizers), EMs (extensive metabolizers), and PMs (poor metabolizers). The "cut-off" label indicates the cut-off between extensive and poor metabolizers.

people are homozygous or heterozygous for the wild-type *CYP2D6* gene and are known as extensive metabolizers (ST **Figure 4–3**). Approximately 10 to 15 percent of people are homozygous for alleles that decrease activity (poor metabolizers), and the remainder of the population have duplicated genes (ultra-rapid metabolizers). Poor metabolizers are at increased risk for ADRs, whereas ultra-rapid metabolizers may not receive sufficient dosages to have an effect on their conditions.

In 2005, the FDA approved a microarray gene test called the **AmpliChip® CYP450** assay (Roche Diagnostics) that detects 29 genetic variants of two cytochrome P450 genes—*CYP2D6* and *CYP2C19*. This test detects single-nucleotide polymorphisms (SNPs) as well as gene duplications and deletions. The AmpliChip CYP450 assay is an example of a genotyping microarray, such as those described earlier in the text (see Chapter 22). After scanning with an automated scanner, the data are analyzed by computer software, and the *CYP2D6/CYP2C19* genotype of the individual is generated.

Another example of pharmacogenomics in personalized medicine is that of the *CYP2C9* and *VKORC1* genes and the drug **warfarin**. Warfarin (also known as Coumadin) is an anticoagulant drug that is prescribed to prevent blood clots after surgery and to aid people with cardiovascular conditions who are prone to clots. Warfarin inhibits the vitamin K-dependent synthesis of several clotting factors. There is an approximately ten-fold variability between patients in the doses of warfarin that have a therapeutic response. In the past, physicians attempted to adjust the doses of warfarin through a trial-and-error process during the first year of treatment. If

the dosage of warfarin is too high, the patient may experience serious hemorrhaging; if it is too low, the patient may develop life-threatening blood clots. It is estimated that 20 percent of patients are hospitalized during their first six months of treatment due to warfarin side-effects.

Variations in warfarin activity are affected by polymorphisms in several genes, particularly *CYP2C9* and *VKORC1*. Two single-nucleotide polymorphisms in *CYP2C9* lead to reduced elimination of warfarin and increased risk of hemorrhage. About 25 percent of Caucasians are heterozygous for one of these polymorphisms and 5 percent appear to be homozygous. About 5 percent of patients of Asian and African descent carry these variants. Patients who are heterozygous or homozygous for some alleles of *CYP2C9* require a 10 to 90 percent lower dose of warfarin.

The FDA recommends the use of *CYP2C9* and *VKORC1* genetic tests to predict the likelihood that a patient may have an adverse reaction to warfarin. Several companies offer tests to detect polymorphisms in these genes, using methods based on PCR amplification and allele-specific primers. It is estimated that the use of warfarin genetic tests could prevent 17,000 strokes and 85,000 serious hemorrhages per year. The savings in health care could reach $1.1 billion per year.

Pharmacogenomic tests and treatments, and the genetic information on which they are based, are rapidly advancing. A source of updated information on all aspects of pharmacogenomics can be found on the Pharmacogenomics Knowledge Base, which is described in Box 2.

Personalized Medicine and Disease Diagnostics

The ultimate goal of personalized medicine is to apply information from a patient's full genome to help physicians diagnose disease and select treatments tailored to that particular patient. Not only will this information be gleaned from genome sequencing, but it will also be informed by gene-expression information derived from transcriptomic, proteomic, metabolomic, and epigenetic tests.

SPECIAL TOPIC 4

BOX 2
The Pharmacogenomics Knowledge Base (PharmGKB): Genes, Drugs, and Diseases on the Web

The Pharmacogenomics Knowledge Base (PharmGKB) is a publicly available Internet database and information source developed by Stanford University. It is funded by the National Institutes of Health (NIH) and forms part of the NIH Pharmacogenomics Research Network, a U.S. research consortium. The goal of PharmGKB is to provide researchers and the general public with information that will increase the understanding of how genetic variation contributes to an individual's reaction to drugs. On the PharmGKB Web site (see **ST Figure 4–4**), you may search for genes and variants that affect drug reactions, information on a large number of drugs, diseases and their genetic links, pharmacogenomic pathways, gene tests, and relevant publications. Visit the PharmGKB Web site at http://www.pharmgkb.org.

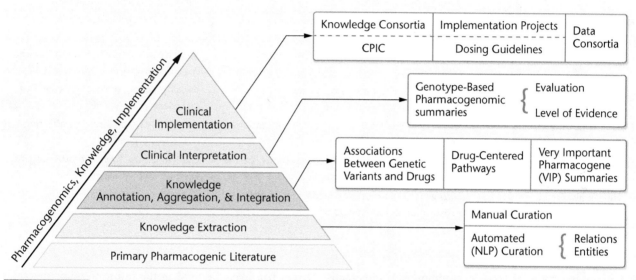

ST FIGURE 4–4 The PharmGKB Knowledge Pyramid. A visual representation of the types of information available at www.pharmgkb.org.

At the present time, the most prevalent use of genomic information for disease diagnostics is genetic testing that examines specific disease-related genes and gene variants. Most existing genetic tests detect the presence of mutations in single genes that are known to be linked to a disease (ST Table 4.3). Currently, more than 1600 such genetic tests are available. A comprehensive list of genetic tests can be viewed on the NIH Genetic Testing Registry at www.ncbi.nlm.nih.gov/gtr/. The technologies used in many of these genetic tests are presented earlier in the text (see Chapter 22).

Genetic tests are classified according to their uses, and they fall into one or more groups. *Diagnostic tests* are designed to detect the presence or absence of gene variants or mutations linked to a suspected genetic disorder in a symptomatic patient. *Predictive tests* detect mutations and variants in patients with a family history of a known genetic disorder—for example, Huntington disease or *BRCA*-linked breast cancer. *Carrier tests* help physicians identify patients who carry a gene mutation linked to a disorder that might be passed on to their offspring—such as Tay–Sachs or cystic fibrosis. *Preimplantation tests* are performed on early embryos in order to select embryos for implantation that do not carry a suspected disease. *Prenatal tests* detect potential genetic diseases in a fetus. The test for Down syndrome is a well-known example.

Over the last decade, genome sequencing methods have progressed rapidly in speed, accuracy, and cost-effectiveness. In addition, other "omics" technologies such as transcriptomics and proteomics are providing major insights into how DNA sequences lead to gene expression and, ultimately, to phenotype. (Refer to Chapter 21 for descriptions of techniques and data emerging from human "omics" technologies.) As these technologies become more rapid and cost-effective, they will begin to make important contributions to personalized medicine.

Although the application of "omics" to personalized medicine has not yet entered routine medical care, several proof-of-principle cases illustrate the way in which whole genome analysis may develop in the future. They also reveal some of the limitations that must be overcome before

ST TABLE 4.3   Some Single-Gene Defects for Which Genetic Tests Are Available

Disease	Gene Mutation	Description
Achondroplasia	*FGFR3* gene. 99% of patients have a G to A point mutation at nucleotide 1138 (G380R substitution)	Abnormal bone growth
Hereditary breast/ovarian cancer	*BRCA1* and *BRCA2* genes. Deletions, duplications, and point mutations	Predisposition to breast, ovarian, prostate, and other cancers
Duchenne muscular dystrophy	*DMD* gene. Point mutations, deletions, insertions, splicing mutations	Early-onset progressive muscular weakness, heart disease
Fragile-X syndrome	*FMR1* gene. Primarily expanded trinucleotide (CGG) repeats and loss of function	Mental retardation, developmental disorders
Friedrich ataxia	*FXN* gene. 98% of cases have expanded trinucleotide (GAA) repeats in intron 1	Ataxia, muscle weakness, spasticity, heart and other organ dysfunctions
Hemophilia A	*F8* gene. Point mutations, insertions, deletions, inversions	Factor VIII blood-clotting defects, bleeding
Huntington disease	*HTT* (*HD*) gene. Trinucleotide (CAG) repeat expansions	Midlife onset of progressive motor and cognitive disorders
Lesch-Nyhan syndrome	*HPRT1* gene. Point mutations, deletions, duplications	Developmental, motor, and cognitive disorders
Marfan syndrome	*FBN1* gene. Point mutations, splicing mutations, deletions	Connective tissue disorders affecting numerous organs
Polycystic kidney disease, dominant	*PKD1* and *PKD2* genes. Sequence variants, partial or whole-gene deletions and duplications	Cysts in kidney, liver, and other organs, vascular abnormalities
Sickle-cell disease	*HBB* gene. Point mutation leading to Glu to Val substitution at amino acid 6	Early-onset anemia

© Gene Reviews

genome-based medicine becomes commonplace and practical. In the next two sections, we will describe several of these studies as they pertain to the diagnosis of cancers and other diseases.

Personal Genomics and Cancer

As we learned earlier in the text (see Chapter 19), cancer is a genetic disease at the level of somatic cells. High-throughput sequencing of normal and cancer genomes, along with RNA sequencing and protein profiling of normal and cancer cells, has revealed more of the mutations and gene rearrangements associated with specific cancers. Studies such as the Cancer Genome Atlas project are amassing data equivalent to 20,000 genome projects on normal and tumor DNA from patients with more than 20 different types of cancer. Such studies are revealing that cancers once classified in general terms (such as "prostate cancer") are in fact many different diseases based on their genetic profiles. For example, in the past, blood cancers were categorized into two large groups: leukemias and lymphomas. Today, we know that each category can be broken down into more than 40 different types, based on gene mutation and expression characteristics. Similarly, breast cancer is now thought to be at least 10 separate diseases, based on genomic and gene-expression data. The recognition that tumors differ significantly in gene expres-

sion will likely be used in the future to tailor therapies to attack or modify specific gene-expression aberrations.

Another significant discovery from cancer genome research is that every tumor is genetically unique, even though common cellular pathways are involved. This realization indicates that each cancer may require a personalized treatment and that the genomic "net" that is cast to detect altered gene function must be wide enough to capture all relevant defects within each cancer. The potential for whole genome sequencing and gene-expression assays in cancer diagnosis and treatment is illustrated by a case described in Box 3. This story illustrates the enormous quantities of resources involved in genomic sequencing and gene-expression assays, as well as the interpretation of the resulting data. It also shows that genomic sequencing alone may not be sufficient to detect the most important defects in cancer cells, including those that would be suitable targets for therapy. The story points out that few gene-specific drugs are currently available and those that do exist are expensive and may not be covered by medical insurance. The patient in this story had been fortunate that a key defect in his cancer had been detectable using genomic techniques and could be targeted by an existing drug. As most cancers contain dozens to hundreds of genetic and gene-expression defects, and more than one gene product may drive the cells to form cancers, the goal of developing

Personalized Cancer Diagnostics and Treatments: The Lukas Wartman Story [1]

During his final year of medical school in 2002, Dr. Lukas Wartman began to experience symptoms of fatigue, fever, and bone pain. After months of tests, he was given a diagnosis of adult acute lymphoblastic leukemia (ALL). Following two years of chemotherapies, his cancer went into remission for five years. When the ALL recurred, his doctors treated him with intensive chemotherapy and a bone marrow transplant, which put him back into remission for another three years. After his second relapse, all attempts at treatment failed and he was rapidly deteriorating.

At the time of his second relapse, Dr. Wartman was working as a physician-scientist at Washington University, researching the genetics of leukemias. His colleagues, including Dr. Timothy Ley, associate director of the Washington University Genome Institute, decided to rush into a last-minute effort to save him. Making round-the-clock use of the university's sequencing facilities and supercomputers, the research team sequenced the entire genomes of his normal and cancer cells. They also analyzed his RNA types and expression levels using RNAseq technologies.

As they had expected, Dr. Wartman's cancer DNA contained many gene mutations. Unfortunately, no drugs were available that would attack the products of these mutated genes. The RNA sequence analysis, however, revealed unexpected results. It showed that the fms-related tyrosine kinase 3 (*FLT3*) gene, although having a normal DNA sequence, was overexpressed in his cancer cells—perhaps due to mutations in the gene's regulatory regions. The *FLT3* gene encodes a protein kinase that is involved in normal hematopoietic cell growth and differentiation, and its overexpression would be a potentially important contributor to Dr. Wartman's cancer. Equally interesting, and fortunate, was that the drug sunitinib, or Sutent, was known to inhibit the FLT3 kinase and had been approved for use in the treatment of advanced kidney cancers.

Dr. Wartman decided to try sunitinib. Unfortunately, the drug cost $330 per day, and Dr. Wartman's insurance company refused to pay for it. In addition, the drug company Pfizer refused to supply the drug to him under its compassionate use program. Despite these setbacks, he collected enough money to buy a week's worth of sunitinib. Within days of starting treatment, his blood counts were approaching normal. Within two weeks his bone marrow was free of cancer cells. At this point Pfizer reversed its decision and supplied Dr. Wartman with the drug. In addition, he underwent a second bone marrow transplant to help ensure that the cancer would not return. Although Dr. Wartman's long-term prognosis is still uncertain, his successful experience with personalized cancer treatment has given him hope and has spurred research into the regulation of the *FLT3* gene in other cancers.

[1]This story was reported in Kolata, G., In treatment for leukemia, glimpses of the future. *New York Times*, July 7, 2012.

drugs for each of these defects remains a challenging one. Despite these challenges, it is a story of future promise for the role of cancer diagnosis and gene-specific treatments in personalized medicine.

Personal Genomics and Disease Diagnosis: Analyzing One Genome

In 2010, the journal *Lancet* published a report illustrating the type of information that we can currently obtain from personal whole genome sequencing.[1] The personal genome sequence in this study was the first one to be sequenced using a method known as true single-molecule sequencing (tSMS™). Some high-throughput methods, such as those described earlier in the text (see Chapters 20 and 21), require cloning or PCR amplification of template DNA prior to sequencing. In contrast, the tSMS method directly sequences individual genomic DNA strands with minimum processing. The sequencing of this genome took about a week, was performed with one machine, used the services of three people, and cost $48,000. The genome sequence was that of Dr. Stephen Quake, a Stanford University professor who developed the technology and headed the research group. He was a healthy 40-year-old male who had a family history of arthritis, aortic aneurysm, coronary artery disease, and sudden cardiac death.

By comparing the patient's sequence with other human genome sequences in databases, they discovered a total of 2.6 million SNPs and 752 copy number variations. The researchers then sorted through the genome sequence data to determine which of these variants might have an effect on phenotype. This was accomplished by searching known SNPs in several large databases, manually creating their own disease-associated SNP database, and calculating likelihood ratios for various disease risks. The analysis required the combined efforts of more than two dozen scientists and clinicians over a period of about a year, and information gleaned from more than a dozen sequence databases, new and existing sequence analysis tools, and hundreds of individually accessed research papers.

[1]Ashley, E.A., et al. 2010. Clinical assessment incorporating a personal genome. *Lancet* 375: 1525–1535.

To determine how this patient may respond to pharmaceutical drugs, the researchers searched the PharmGKB database (see Box 2) for the presence of known variants within pharmacogenomically important genes. The patient was found to have 63 clinically relevant SNPs within genes associated with drug reactions. In addition, his genome contained six previously unknown SNPs that could alter amino acid sequences in drug-response genes. For example, the genome sequence revealed that the patient was heterozygous for a null mutation in the *CYP2C19* gene. This mutation could make him sensitive to a range of drugs, including those used to treat aspects of heart disease. He would also be more sensitive than normal to warfarin, based on SNPs within his *VKORC1* and *CYP4F2* genes. In contrast, the patient's sequence contained gene variants associated with good responses to statins; however, other gene variants suggested that he might require higher-than-normal statin dosages.

The search for mutations within genes that directly affect disease conditions revealed several potentially damaging variants. The patient was heterozygous for a SNP within the *CFTR* gene that would change a glycine to arginine at position 458. This mutation could lead to cystic fibrosis if it was passed on to a son or daughter who also inherited a defective *CFTR* gene from the other parent. Similarly, the patient was heterozygous for a recessive mutation in the hereditary haemochromatosis protein precursor gene (*HFE*), which is associated with the development of haemochromatosis, a serious condition leading to toxic accumulations of iron. Also, the patient was heterozygous for a recessive mutation in the solute carrier family 3 (*SLC3A1*) gene. This mutation is linked to cystinuria, an inherited disorder characterized by inadequate excretion of cysteine and development of kidney stones. The scientists discovered a heterozygous SNP within the parafibromin (*CDC73*) gene that would create a prematurely terminated protein. This gene is a tumor-suppressor gene linked to the development of hyperparathyroidism and parathyroid tumors. The presence of this SNP increased the risk that the patient might develop these types of tumors, if any of the patient's cells experienced a loss-of-heterozygosity mutation in the other copy of the gene.

The analysis of this patient's genome sequence for the purpose of predicting future development of multifactorial disease was more challenging. Genome-wide association studies have revealed large numbers of sequence variants that are associated with complex diseases; however, each of these variants most often contributes only a small part of the susceptibility to disease. Because not all variants have been discovered or characterized, it is difficult to establish a numerical risk score for each of these diseases based on the presence of one or more SNPs. As an example, the researchers discovered SNPs within three genes (*TMEM43*,

DSP, and *MYBPC3*) that may be associated with sudden cardiac death. However, the exact effects of two of these SNPs are still unclear, and the other SNP had not previously been described. The patient had five SNPs in genes associated with an increased risk of developing myocardial infarction and two SNPs associated with a lower risk. Among the SNPs associated with increased risk, a variant in the apolipoprotein A precursor (*LPA*) gene is associated with a five-fold increased plasma lipoprotein(a) concentration and a two-fold increased risk of coronary artery disease. By taking into consideration the simultaneous potential effects of many different SNPs, as well as the patient's own environmental and personal lifestyle factors, the researchers concluded that the patient's genetics contributed to a significantly increased risk for eight conditions (such as Type 2 diabetes, obesity, and coronary artery disease) and a decreased risk for seven conditions (such as Alzheimer disease). The patient was offered the services of clinical geneticists, counselors, and clinical lab directors in order to help interpret the information generated from the genome sequence. Genetic counseling covered areas such as the psychological and reproductive implications of genetic disease risk, the possibilities of discrimination based on genetic test results, and the uncertainties in risk assessments.

In 2012, another study of personal genome analysis was reported (Box 4). This study combined data from whole genome sequencing, transcriptomics, proteomics, and metabolomics profiles from a single patient at multiple time points over a 14-month period. This in-depth multilevel personal profiling allowed the patient to be monitored through both healthy and diseased states, as he contracted two virus infections and a period of Type 2 diabetes. This research points out how complex changes in gene expression may affect phenotype and shows the importance of looking beyond the raw sequence of an individual DNA. It also indicates that gene-expression profiles can be monitored by current technologies and may be applied in the future as part of personalized medical testing.

Technical, Social, and Ethical Challenges

There are still many technical hurdles to overcome before personalized medicine will become a standard part of medical care. The technologies of genome sequencing, "omics" profiling, microarray analysis, and SNP detection need to be faster, more accurate, and cheaper. Scientists expect that these challenges will be overcome in the near future; however, genome analysis needs to be used with caution until the technology becomes highly accurate and reliable. Even

BOX 4
Beyond Genomics: Personal Omics Profiling

A study published by a research team led by Dr. Michael Snyder of Stanford University provides an example of how multiple "omics" technologies can be used to examine one person's healthy and diseased states.[1]

Blood samples were taken from a healthy individual (Dr. Snyder) at 20 time points over a 14-month study period. The patient's whole genome sequence was generated at each time point using two different methods and backed up by exome sequencing using three different methods. In addition, his genome sequence was compared to that of his mother. Concurrently, whole-transcriptome sequencing, proteomic profiling, and metabolomics assays were performed.

Dr. Snyder's genome sequence revealed a number of SNPs that are known to be associated with elevated risks for coronary artery disease, basal cell carcinoma, hypertriglyceridemia,

and Type 2 diabetes. A mutation in the *TERT* gene, which is involved in telomere replication, gave an increased risk for aplastic anemia. These data were followed by a series of medical tests. Dr. Snyder had no signs of aplastic anemia, and his telomere lengths were close to normal. Similarly, his mother, who shared his mutation in the *TERT* gene, had no symptoms of aplastic anemia. Medical tests revealed he did have elevated triglyceride levels, which he subsequently controlled using medication. Blood glucose levels were initially normal but became abnormally high after he became infected with respiratory syncytial virus (RSV). In response to these data, Dr. Snyder modified his diet and exercise regime and later brought his blood glucose down to normal levels. An analysis of drug response gene variants revealed that he should have good responses to diabetic drugs.

Using RNAseq technologies, the researchers monitored the numbers and types of more than 19,000 mRNAs and miRNAs transcribed from more than 12,000 genes over

20 time points. The data showed that sets of genes were coordinately regulated in response to conditions such as RSV infection and glucose levels. The researchers also found that RNA species underwent differential splicing and editing during changes in physiological states. Editing events included changes of adenosine to inosine and cytidine to uridine, and many of these RNA edits altered the amino acid sequences of translated proteins.

The researchers also profiled the levels of more than 6000 proteins and metabolites over the time course of the study. Like the RNA data, the protein and metabolite data showed coordinated changes that occur through virus infections and glucose level changes. Some of these changes were shared between RNA, protein, and metabolites and others were unique to each category. The medical significance of these patterns will be addressed in future studies.

[1]Chen, R. et al. 2012. Personal omics profiling reveals dynamic molecular and medical phenotypes. *Cell* 148: 1293–1307.

a low rate of error in genetic sequences or test results could lead to misdiagnoses and inappropriate treatments. Perhaps an even greater challenge lies in the ability of scientists to store and interpret the vast amount of emerging sequence data. Each personal genome generates the letter-equivalent of 200 large phone books, which must be stored in databases, mined for relevant sequence variants, and meaning assigned to each sequence variant. To undertake these kinds of analyses, scientists need to gather data from large-scale population genotyping studies that will link sequence variants to phenotype, disease, or drug responses. Experts suggest that such studies will take the coordinated efforts of public and private research teams and more than a decade to complete. Scientists will also need to develop efficient automated systems and algorithms to deal with this massive amount of information. Moreover, these data analyses will have to consider that genetic variants contribute only partially to personal phenotype. Personalized medicine will also need to integrate information about environmental, personal lifestyle, and epigenetic factors.

Another technical challenge for personalized medicine is the development of automated health information

technologies. Health-care providers will need to use electronic health records to store, retrieve, and analyze each patient's genomic profile, as well as to compare this information with constantly advancing knowledge about genes and disease. Currently, fewer than 10 percent of hospitals and physicians in the United States have access to these types of information technologies.

Personalized medicine has a number of societal implications. To make personalized medicine available to everyone, the costs of genetic tests, as well as the genetic counseling that accompanies them, must be reimbursed by insurance companies, even in cases where there are no prior diseases or symptoms. Regulatory changes are required to ensure that genetic tests and genomic sequencing are accurate and that the data generated are reliably stored in databases that guarantee the patient's privacy. At the present time, less than 1 percent of genetic tests are regulated by agencies such as the FDA.

Personalized medicine also requires changes to medical education. In the future, physicians will be expected to use genomics information as part of their patient management. For this to be possible, medical schools will need to train future physicians to interpret and explain genetic data. In addition, more genetic counselors and genomics specialists will be required. These specialists will need to understand genomics and disease, as well as to manipulate bioinformatic data. As of 2010, there were only about 2500 genetic counselors and 1100 clinical geneticists in North America.

The ethical aspects of the new personalized medicine are also diverse and challenging. For example, it is sometimes argued that the costs involved in the development of genomics and personalized medicine are a misallocation of limited resources. Some argue that science should solve larger problems facing humanity, such as the distribution of food and clean water, before embarking on personalized medicine. Similarly, some critics argue that such highly specialized and expensive medical care will not be available to

everyone and represents a worsening of economic inequality. There are also concerns about how we will protect the privacy of genome information that is contained in databases and private health-care records. In addition, there need to be effective ways to prevent discrimination in employment or insurance coverage, based on information derived from genomic analysis.

Most experts agree that we are at the beginning of a personalized medicine revolution. Information from genetics and genomics research is already increasing the effectiveness of drugs and enabling health-care providers to predict diseases prior to their occurrence. In the future, personalized medicine will touch almost every aspect of medical care. By addressing the upcoming challenges of the new personalized medicine, we can guide its use for the maximum benefit to the greatest number of people.

Selected Readings and Resources

Journal Articles

Ashley, E.A., et al. 2010. Clinical assessment incorporating a personal genome. *Lancet* 375: 1525–1535.

Collins, F. 2010. Has the revolution arrived? *Nature* 464: 674–675.

McLeod, H.L. 2013. Cancer pharmacogenomics: Early promise, but concerted effort needed. *Science* 339: 1563–1566.

Ormond, K.E., et al. 2010. Challenges in the clinical application of whole-genome sequencing. *Lancet* 375: 1749–1751.

Pushkarev, D., et al. 2009. Single-molecule sequencing of an individual human genome. *Nature Biotech* 27: 847–850.

Ross, J.S. 2009. The HER-2 receptor and breast cancer: Ten years of targeted anti-HER-2 therapy and personalized medicine. *The Oncologist* 14: 320–368.

Soon, W.W., et al. 2013. High-throughput sequencing for biology and medicine. *Mol. Systems Biol.* 9: 640; doi:10.1038/msb.2012.61.

Venter, J.C. 2010. Multiple personal genomes await. *Nature* 464: 676–677.

Web Sites

Personalized Medicine Coalition, 2011. The Case for Personalized Medicine. http://www.personalizedmedicinecoalition.org/Resources/The_Case_for_Personalized_Medicine

U.S. Food and Drug Administration, 2010. Table of Valid Genomic Biomarkers in the Context of Approved Drug Labels. http://www.fda.gov/Drugs/ScienceResearch/ResearchAreas/Pharmacogenetics/ucm083378.htm

U.S. National Institutes of Health, Genetics Home Reference. What is pharmacogenomics? http://ghr.nlm.nih.gov/handbook/genomicresearch/pharmacogenomics

Review Questions

1. What is pharmacogenomics, and how does it differ from pharmacogenetics?
2. Describe how the drug Herceptin works. What types of gene tests are ordered prior to treatment with Herceptin?
3. What is the Oncotype DX Assay, and how is it used?
4. How do the cytochrome P450 proteins affect drug responses? Give two examples.
5. What types of genetic tests are currently available, and how are they classified?
6. Give two examples of how genomic studies have altered our understanding of cancers.
7. Why is it necessary to examine gene-expression profiles, in addition to genome sequencing, for effective personalized medicine?
8. Using the PharmGKB database, explain the relationship between *CYP2D6* variants and the response of patients to the breast cancer drug, tamoxifen.

Discussion Questions

1. In this chapter, we present three case studies that use personalized genomics analysis to predict and treat diseases. Although these cases have shown how personalized medicine may evolve in the future, they have triggered controversy. What are some objections to these types of studies, and how can these objections be addressed?

2. What are the biggest challenges that must be overcome before personalized medicine becomes a routine component of medical care? What do you think is the most difficult of these challenges and why?

3. How can we ensure that a patient's privacy is maintained as genome information accumulates within medical records?

How would you feel about allowing your genome sequence to be available for use in research?

4. As gene tests and genomic sequences become more commonplace, how can we prevent the emergence of "genetic discrimination" in employment and medical insurance?

Genetically Modified Foods

Throughout the ages, humans have used selective breeding techniques to create plants and animals with desirable genetic traits. By selecting organisms with naturally occurring or mutagen-induced variations and breeding them to establish the phenotype, we have evolved varieties that now feed our growing populations and support our complex civilizations.

Although we have had tremendous success shuffling genes through selective breeding, the process is a slow one. When recombinant DNA technologies emerged in the 1970s and 1980s, scientists realized that they could modify agriculturally significant organisms in a more precise and rapid way—by identifying and cloning genes that confer desirable traits, then introducing these genes into organisms. Genetic engineering of animals and plants promised an exciting new phase in scientific agriculture, with increased productivity, reduced pesticide use, and enhanced flavor and nutrition.

Beginning in the 1990s, scientists created a large number of genetically modified (GM) food varieties. The first one, approved for sale in 1994, was the Flavr Savr tomato—a tomato that stayed firm and ripe longer than non-GM tomatoes. Soon afterward, other GM foods were developed: papaya and zucchini with resistance to virus infection, canola containing the tropical oil laurate, corn and cotton plants with resistance to insects, and soybeans and sugar beets with tolerance to agricultural herbicides. By 2012, more than 200 different GM crop varieties had been created. Worldwide, GM crops are planted on 170 million hectares of arable land, with a global value of $15 billion for GM seeds.

Although many people see great potential for GM foods—to help address malnutrition in a world with a growing human population and climate change—others question the technology, oppose GM food development, and sometimes resort to violence to stop the introduction of GM varieties (ST Figure 5.1). Even Golden Rice—a variety of rice that contains the vitamin A precursor and was developed on a humanitarian nonprofit basis to help alleviate vitamin A deficiencies in the developing world—has been the target

> **"Genetic engineering of animals and plants promised an exciting new phase in scientific agriculture, with increased productivity, reduced pesticide use, and enhanced flavor and nutrition."**

of opposition and violence. On August 8, 2013, 400 protesters broke through security fences surrounding a field trial of Golden Rice in the Bicol region of the Philippines. Within 15 minutes, they had uprooted and trampled most of the GM rice plants. The attackers argued that Golden Rice was a threat to human health and biodiversity and would lead to Western corporate control of local food crops.

Opposition to GM foods is not unique to Golden Rice. In 2013, approximately two million people marched against GM foods in rallies held in 52 countries. Some countries have outright bans on all GM foods, whereas others embrace the technologies. Opponents cite safety and environmental concerns, while some scientists and commercial interests extol the almost limitless virtues of GM foods. The topic of GM food attracts hyperbole and exaggerated rhetoric, information, and misinformation—on both sides of the debate.

So, what are the truths about GM foods? In this Special Topic chapter, we will introduce the science behind GM foods and examine the promises and problems

ST FIGURE 5–1 Anti-GM protesters attacking a field of genetically-modified maize in southwestern France. In July 2004, hundreds of activists opposed to GM crops destroyed plants being tested by the US biotech company Pioneer Hi-Bred International.

of the new technologies. We will look at some of the controversies and present information to help us evaluate the complex questions that surround this topic.

What Are GM Foods?

GM foods are derived from **genetically modified organisms (GMOs)**, specifically plants and animals of agricultural importance. GMOs are defined as organisms whose genomes have been altered in ways that do not occur naturally. Although the definition of GMOs includes organisms that have been genetically modified by selective breeding, the most commonly used definition refers to organisms modified through genetic engineering or recombinant DNA technologies. Genetic engineering allows one or more genes to be cloned and transferred from one organism to another—either between individuals of the same species or between those of unrelated species. It also allows an organism's endogenous genes to be altered in ways that lead to enhanced or reduced expression levels. When genes are transferred between unrelated species, the resulting organism is called **transgenic**. The term **cisgenic** is sometimes used to describe gene transfers within a species. In contrast, the term **biotechnology** is a more general one, encompassing a wide range of methods that manipulate organisms or their components—such as isolating enzymes or producing wine, cheese, or yogurt. Genetic modification of plants or animals is one aspect of biotechnology.

In 2012, it was estimated that GM crops were grown in approximately 30 countries on 11 percent of the arable land on Earth. The majority of these GM crops (almost 90 percent) are grown in five countries—the United States, Brazil, Argentina, Canada, and India. Of these five, the United States accounts for approximately half of the acreage devoted to GM crops. According to the U.S. Department of Agriculture, 93 percent of soybeans and 88 percent of maize grown in the United States are from GM crops. In the United States, more than 70 percent of processed foods contain ingredients derived from GM crops.

Soon after the release of the Flavr Savr tomato in the 1990s, agribusinesses devoted less energy to designing GM foods to appeal directly to consumers. Instead, the market shifted toward farmers, to provide crops that increased productivity. By 2012, approximately 200 different GM crop varieties were approved for use as food or livestock feed in the United States. However, only about two dozen are widely planted. These include varieties of soybeans, corn, sugar beets, cotton, canola, papaya, and squash. ST Table 5.1 lists some of the common GM food crops available for planting in the United States. Of these GM crops, by far the most widely planted are varieties that are herbicide tolerant or insect resistant. At the time of writing this chapter, no

ST TABLE 5.1   Some GM Crops Approved for Food, Feed, or Cultivation in the United States*

Crop	Number of Varieties	GM Characteristics
Soybeans	19	Tolerance to glyphosate herbicide Tolerance to glufosinate herbicide Reduced saturated fats Enhanced oleic acid Enhanced omega-3 fatty acid
Maize	68	Tolerance to glyphosate herbicide Tolerance to glufosinate herbicide Bt insect resistance Enhanced ethanol production
Cotton	30	Tolerance to glyphosate herbicide Bt insect resistance
Potatoes	28	Bt insect resistance
Canola	23	Tolerance to glyphosate herbicide Tolerance to glufosinate herbicide Enhanced lauric acid
Papaya	4	Resistance to papaya ringspot virus
Sugar beets	3	Tolerance to glyphosate herbicide
Rice	3	Tolerance to glufosinate herbicide
Zucchini squash	2	Resistance to zucchini, watermelon, and cucumber mosaic viruses
Alfalfa	2	Tolerance to glyphosate herbicide
Plum	1	Resistance to plum pox virus

* Information from the International Service for the Acquisition of Agri-Biotech Applications, www.isaaa.org.

GM food animal was approved for consumption, although a GM salmon variety was nearing market approval in the United States (Box 1). A number of agriculturally important animals such as goats and sheep have been genetically modified to produce pharmaceutical products in their milk. The use of transgenic animals as bioreactors is discussed earlier in the text (see Chapter 22).

Herbicide-Resistant GM Crops

Weed infestations destroy about 10 percent of crops worldwide. To combat weeds, farmers often apply herbicides before seeding a crop and between rows after the crops are growing. As the most efficient broad-spectrum herbicides also kill crop plants, herbicide use may be difficult and limited. Farmers also use tillage to control weeds; however, tillage damages soil structure and increases erosion.

Herbicide-tolerant varieties are the most widely planted of GM crops, making up approximately 70 percent of all GM crops. The majority of these varieties contain a bacterial gene that confers tolerance to the broad-spectrum herbicide **glyphosate**—the active ingredient in commercial herbicides such as Roundup®. Studies have shown that

BOX 1
The Tale of GM Salmon— Downstream Effects?

t took 18 years and about $60 million, but the first GM animal to be approved as human food—the AquAdvantage salmon—may soon hit the U.S. market.

The AquAdvantage salmon is an Atlantic salmon that is genetically modified to grow twice as fast as its non-GM cousins, reaching marketable size in one and a half years rather than the usual three years. Scientists at AquaBounty Technologies in Massachusetts created the variety by transforming an Atlantic salmon with a single gene encoding the Chinook salmon growth hormone. The gene was cloned downstream of the antifreeze protein gene promoter from an eel. This promoter stimulates growth hormone synthesis in the winter, a time when the fish's own growth hormone gene is not expressed. The rapid growth of the GM salmon allows fish farmers to double their productivity.

AquaBounty intends to sell GM fish eggs to two facilities—one in the United States and one in Panama—that will raise the salmon and market them. To ensure that the fish will not escape the facilities, the company promises to sell only fertilized eggs that are female, triploid, and sterile. The facilities are to be approved only if the tanks are located inland and have sufficient filters to ensure that eggs and small fish cannot escape.

Despite these assurances, environmental groups are planning to fight the sale of GM salmon. Some grocery chains in the United States have banned GM fish, and legislators in several western U.S. states are trying to block the approval of the AquAdvantage salmon based on fears that the accidental release of these fish could contaminate wild salmon populations with transgenes and disturb normal ecosystems.

Supporters of GM fish point out that the GM salmon are very unlikely to escape their facilities, and if any did escape, they would be poorly adapted to wild conditions. Critics of the new GM salmon point out that the technique used to create sterile triploids (pressure-shocking the fertilized eggs) still allows a small percentage of fertile diploids to remain in the stock. They state that even a few fertile fish, if they escaped into the wild, could have long-term effects on

wild populations. A study published in 2013 shows that it is possible for the AquAdvantage salmon to breed successfully with a close relative, the brown trout.[*] In laboratory conditions, the hybrids grew more quickly than either the GM or non-GM varieties, and in closed stream-like systems, the hybrids outcompeted both parental fish varieties for food supplies. The authors point out that these results should be taken into account during environmental assessments, although it is still not known whether the hybrid salmon–trout variety could successfully breed in the wild. If GM salmon could escape, breed, and introduce transgenes into wild populations, there could be unknown negative downstream effects on fish ecosystems.

[*]Oke, K.B., et al. 2013. Hybridization between genetically modified Atlantic salmon and wild brown trout reveals novel ecological interactions. *Proc. R. Soc. B.* **280** (1763): 20131047.

The AquAdvantage salmon grows twice as fast as a non-GM Atlantic salmon, reaching market size in half the time.

---

glyphosate is effective at low concentrations, is degraded rapidly in soil and water, and is not toxic to humans.

Farmers who plant glyphosate-tolerant crops can treat their fields with glyphosate, even while the GM crop is growing. This approach is more efficient and economical than mechanical weeding and reduces soil damage caused by repeated tillage. It is suggested that there is less environmental impact when using glyphosate, compared with having to apply higher levels of other, more toxic, herbicides.

Recently, evidence suggests that some weeds may be developing resistance to glyphosate, thereby reducing the

effectiveness of glyphosate-tolerant crops. (This and other concerns about herbicide-tolerant GM plants are described later in this chapter.) One method used to engineer a glyphosate-tolerant plant is described in the next section.

Insect-Resistant GM Crops

The second most prevalent GM modifications are those that make plants resistant to agricultural pests. Insect damage is one of the most serious threats to worldwide food production. Farmers combat insect pests using crop rotation and predatory organisms, as well as applying insecticides.

The most widely used GM insect-resistant crops are the **Bt crops**. *Bacillus thuringiensis* (Bt) is group of soil-dwelling bacterial strains that produce crystal (Cry) proteins that are toxic to certain species of insects. These Cry proteins are encoded by the bacterial *cry* genes and form crystal structures during sporulation. The Cry proteins are toxic to Lepidoptera (moths and butterflies), Diptera (mosquitoes and flies), Coleoptera (beetles), and Hymenoptera (wasps and ants). Insects must ingest the bacterial spores or Cry proteins in order for the toxins to act. Within the high pH of the insect gut, the crystals dissolve and are cleaved by insect protease enzymes. The Cry proteins bind to receptors on the gut wall, leading to breakdown of the gut membranes and death of the insect.

Each insect species has specific types of gut receptors that will match only a few types of Bt Cry toxins. As there are more than 200 different Cry proteins, it is possible to select a Bt strain that will be specific to one pest type.

Bt spores have been used for decades as insecticides in both conventional and organic gardening, usually applied in liquid sprays. Sunlight and soil rapidly break down the Bt insecticides, which have not shown any adverse effects on groundwater, mammals, fish, or birds. Toxicity tests on humans and animals have shown that Bt causes few negative effects.

To create Bt crops, scientists introduce one or more cloned *cry* genes into plant cells using methods described in the next section. The GM crop plants will then manufacture their own Bt Cry proteins, which will kill the target pest species when it eats the plant tissues.

Although Bt crops have been successful in reducing crop damage, increasing yields, and reducing the amounts of insecticidal sprays used in agriculture, they are also controversial. Early studies suggested that Bt crops harmed Monarch butterfly populations, although more recent studies have drawn opposite conclusions (Box 2). Other concerns still exist and these will be discussed in subsequent sections of this chapter.

GM Crops for Direct Consumption

To date, most GM crops have been designed to help farmers increase yields. Also, most GM food crops are not consumed directly by humans, but are used as animal feed or as sources of processed food ingredients such as oils, starches, syrups, and sugars. For example, 98 percent of the U.S. soybean crop is used as livestock feed. The remainder is processed into a variety of food ingredients, such as lecithin, textured soy proteins, soybean oil, and soy flours. However, a few GM foods have been developed for direct consumption. Examples are rice, squash, and papaya (Box 3).

One of the most famous and controversial examples of GM foods is **Golden Rice**—a rice variety designed to synthesize beta-carotene (the precursor to **vitamin A**) in the rice grain endosperm.

Vitamin A deficiency is a serious health problem in more than 60 countries, particularly countries in Asia and Africa. The World Health Organization estimates that 190 million of the world's children and 19 million pregnant women are vitamin A deficient. Between 250,000 and 500,000 children with vitamin A deficiencies become blind each year, and half of these will die within a year of losing their sight. As vitamin A is also necessary for immune system function, deficiencies lead to increases in many other conditions, including diarrhea and virus infections. The most seriously affected people live in the poorest countries and have a basic starch-centered diet, often mainly rice. Vitamin A is normally found in dairy products and can be synthesized in the body from beta-carotene found in orange-colored fruits and vegetables and in green leafy vegetables.

Several approaches are being taken to alleviate the vitamin A deficiency status of people in developing countries. These include supplying high-dose vitamin A supplements and growing fresh fruits and vegetables in home gardens. These initiatives have had partial success, but the expense of delivering education and supplementation has impeded the effectiveness of these programs.

In the 1990s, scientists began to apply recombinant DNA technology to help solve vitamin A deficiencies in people with rice-based diets. Although the rice plant naturally produces beta-carotene in its leaves, it does not produce it in the rice grain endosperm, which is the edible part of the rice. The beta-carotene precursor, geranylgeranyl-diphosphate, is present in the endosperm, but the enzymes that convert it to beta-carotene are not synthesized (ST Figure 5–2).

In the first version of Golden Rice, scientists introduced the genes *phytoene synthase* (*psy*) cloned from the daffodil plant and *carotene desaturase* (*crtI*) cloned from the bacterium *Erwinia uredovora* into rice plants. The bacterial *crtI* gene was chosen because the enzyme encoded by this gene can perform the functions of two of the missing rice enzymes, thereby simplifying the transformation process. The resulting plant produced rice grains that were a yellow color due to the presence of beta-carotene (ST Figure 5–3). This strain synthesized modest levels of beta-carotene—but only enough to potentially supply 15–20 percent of the recommended daily allowance of vitamin A. In the second version of the GM plant, called Golden Rice 2, the daffodil *psy* gene was replaced with the *psy* gene from maize. Golden Rice 2 produced beta-carotene levels that were more than 20-fold greater than those in Golden Rice. In the next section we describe the methods used to create Golden Rice 2.

SPECIAL TOPIC 5

BOX 2
The Monarch Butterfly Story

In 1999, three years after the introduction of Bt corn in the United States, scientists published a report that ignited the anti-GM movement and triggered years of intensive research. The scientists had conducted a laboratory assay in which they fed milkweed leaves, coated with pollen from either non-GM or Bt corn, to Monarch butterfly larvae. They concluded that Bt corn pollen reduced larval survival by approximately 50 percent. Concerned about the possibility of unintended harm to nontarget organisms, the U.S. Department of Agriculture commissioned scientists from the United States and Canada to provide detailed follow-up research. In 2001, these studies culminated in a series of five published papers that examined Monarch butterfly biology and ecology and how these may be affected by different types of Bt corn and Bt proteins—in both laboratory and field conditions.

Data from these studies explained and contradicted the initial study. First, the authors of the original 1999 study had fed larvae on pollen contaminated with ground-up corn anthers, which contain 100-fold higher levels of the Cry1Ab protein than found in pollen. In the field, larvae do not eat anthers or other parts of corn plants, as larvae feed exclusively on milkweed leaves. Second, in laboratory tests, larvae were found to be sensitive to Cry1Ab and Cry1Ac proteins, but not to other Cry proteins. Third, the levels of Cry1Ab and Cry1Ac proteins present in Bt cornfields had little, if any, effects on Monarch butterfly larvae. The studies also examined the survival of larvae on Bt cornfields compared with non-Bt cornfields that are sprayed with a pyrethroid insecticide used to control cornfield pests. Larval survival on milkweed within pesticide-treated fields was between 0 and 10 percent,

whereas survival within Bt cornfields was 80 to 93 percent.

Although these studies established a low risk for Monarch butterflies, a new twist in the tale may be emerging. Since 1993, the numbers of Monarch butterflies wintering in Mexico has dropped dramatically. Numbers have dropped significantly each year since 2007—including a 30 percent drop in 2011–2012 and a 59 percent drop in 2012–2013. The reasons for these declines appear to be complex. In Mexico, butterfly reserves have suffered from logging, water diversion, and drought. In the United States and Canada, where Monarch butterflies lay their eggs each year, milkweed habitat has suffered from drought,

human development, and changes in agricultural practices. Tillage, mowing, and herbicide use have destroyed millions of acres of milkweed habitat. Along with the use of conventional herbicides that kill weeds, the growing of glyphosate-tolerant corn and soybean crops has resulted in efficient suppression of weeds in fields that used to contain small numbers of milkweed plants. By affecting milkweeds, herbicide-tolerant GM crops may be contributing to the serious decline in Monarch butterfly populations. Scientists are proposing a program to plant milkweed plants along north–south highways from Texas to Canada, to provide food for Monarch butterfly larvae.

Monarch butterfly larvae feed exclusively on milkweed.

BOX 3
The Success of Hawaiian GM Papaya

In the mid-1990s, the papaya ringspot virus (PRSV) spread rapidly throughout Hawaii's papaya fields and threatened to destroy the industry within a few years. To try to stop the destruction of Hawaiian papaya, a team of scientists from the University of Hawaii, the USDA Agricultural Research Center in Hawaii, and the Upjohn Company cloned the coat protein gene of PRSV and introduced it into cultured papaya cells using biolistic transformation. The goal was to create PRSV resistance using a mechanism known as pathogen-derived resistance. The presence of virus coat proteins within the plant is thought to interfere with the disassembly and movement of an infecting virus, slowing or preventing infection. Researchers tested resistance to PRSV in the transformed papaya plants and developed two GM varieties—SunUp and Rainbow. SunUp was homozygous for the PRSV coat protein gene, and Rainbow was an F_1 hybrid of SunUp and a non-GM variety Kapoho. After three years of field testing and two years of moving through federal regulatory processes, GM papaya was approved for use. Seeds were given for free to farmers who immediately planted them to replace their virus-devastated fields.

Within three years, papaya harvests in Hawaii doubled and consumer acceptance was positive. Virus-resistant GM papaya is credited with saving the Hawaiian papaya industry.

An interesting side-effect of the presence of GM papaya in Hawaii was the recovery of non-GM and organically grown papaya. Because PRSV levels declined due to the presence of virus-resistant fields and the abandoning of infected fields, some growers can now produce non-GM papaya, albeit on a smaller scale than before the virus spread throughout Hawaii. At the present time, more than 70 percent of Hawaiian papaya is genetically modified. GM papaya is approved for sale in the United States, Canada, and Japan.

Since the development of GM papaya in Hawaii, efforts to develop similar varieties in other parts of the world have stalled because of increasing public resistance to GM foods.

Since 2010, thousands of GM papaya trees in Hawaii have been cut down and destroyed by anonymous attackers. Efforts to introduce GM papaya in Thailand have failed, and the government recently banned GM foods. Japan has approved the sale of GM papaya, but only if it is labeled as genetically modified.

(a)   (b)

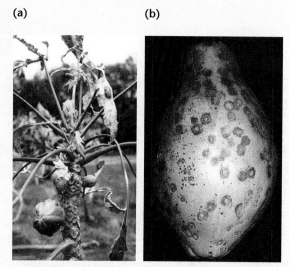

A test field of GM papaya. The "Rainbow" variety, growing in the center of the field, is unaffected by PRSV. The "Sunrise" non-GM variety surrounds the GM papaya and is severely infected.

Clinical trials have shown that the beta-carotene in Golden Rice 2 is efficiently converted into vitamin A in humans and that about 150 grams of uncooked Golden Rice 2 (which is close to the normal daily rice consumption of children aged 4–8 years) would supply all of the childhood daily requirement for vitamin A.

At the present time, Golden Rice 2 is undergoing field, biosafety, and efficacy testing in preparation for approval by government regulators in Bangladesh and the Philippines. If Golden Rice 2 proves useful in alleviating vitamin A deficiencies and is approved for use, seed will be made available at the same price as non-GM seed and farmers will be allowed to keep and replant seed from their own crops.

Despite the promise of Golden Rice 2, controversies remain. Critics of GM foods suggest that Golden Rice could make farmers too dependent on one type of food or might have long-term health or environmental effects. These and other controversies surrounding GM foods are discussed in subsequent sections of this chapter.

Methods Used to Create GM Plants

Most GM plants are created using one of two approaches: the **biolistic method** or *Agrobacterium tumefaciens-mediated transformation* technology. Both methods

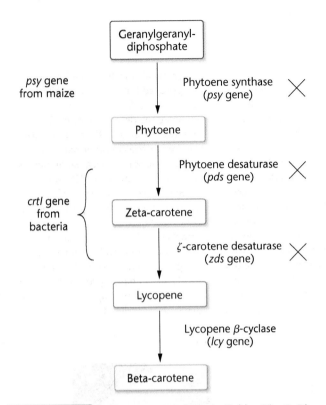

ST FIGURE 5–2 Beta-carotene pathway in Golden Rice 2. Rice plant enzymes and genes involved in beta-carotene synthesis are shown on the right. The enzymes that are not expressed in rice endosperm are indicated with an "X." The genes inserted into Golden Rice 2 are shown on the left.

ST FIGURE 5–3 Non-GM and Golden Rice 2. Golden Rice 2 contains high levels of beta-carotene, giving the rice endosperm a yellow color. The intensity of the color reflects the amount of beta-carotene in the endosperm.

target plant cells that are growing *in vitro*. Scientists can generate plant tissue cultures from various types of plant tissues, and these cultured cells will grow in either liquid cultures or on the surface of solid growth media. When grown in the presence of specific nutrients and hormones, these cultured cells will form clumps of cells called calluses, which, when transferred to other types of media, will form roots. When the rooted plantlets are mature, they are transferred to soil medium in greenhouses where they develop into normal plants.

The *biolistic method* is a physical method of introducing DNA into cells. Particles of heavy metals such as gold are coated with the DNA that will transform the cells; these particles are then fired at high speed into plant cells *in vitro*, using a device called a **gene gun**. Cells that survive the bombardment may take up the DNA-coated particles, and the DNA may migrate into the cell nucleus and integrate into a plant chromosome. Plants that grow from the bombarded cells are then selected for the desired phenotype.

Although biolistic methods are successful for a wide range of plant types, a much improved transformation rate is achieved using *Agrobacterium-mediated technology*. *Agrobacterium tumefaciens* (also called *Rhizobium radiobacter*) is a soil microbe that can infect plant cells and cause tumors.

These characteristics are conferred by a 200-kb tumor-inducing plasmid called a **Ti plasmid**. After infection with *Agrobacterium*, the Ti plasmid integrates a segment of its DNA known as transfer DNA (T-DNA) into random locations within the plant genome. (**ST Figure 5–4**). To use the Ti plasmid as a transformation vector, scientists remove the T-DNA segment and replace it with cloned DNA of the genes to be introduced into the plant cells.

In order to have the newly introduced gene expressed in the plant, the gene must be cloned next to an appropriate promoter sequence that will direct transcription in the required plant tissue. For example, the beta-carotene pathway genes introduced into Golden Rice were cloned next to a promoter that directs transcription of the genes in the rice endosperm. In addition, the transformed gene requires appropriate transcription termination signals and signal sequences that allow insertion of the encoded protein into the correct cell compartment.

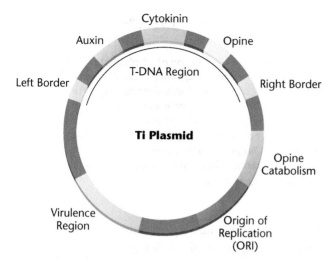

ST FIGURE 5–4 Structure of the Ti plasmid. The 250-kb Ti plasmid from *Agrobacterium tumefaciens* inserts the T-DNA portion of the plasmid into the host cell's nuclear genome and induces tumors. Genes within the virulence region code for enzymes responsible for transfer of T-DNA into the plant genome. The T-DNA region contains auxin and cytokinin genes that encode hormones responsible for cell growth and tumor formation. The opine genes encode compounds used as energy sources for the bacterium. The T-DNA region of the Ti plasmid is replaced with the gene of interest when the plasmid is used as a transformation vector.

Selectable Markers

The rates at which T-DNA successfully integrates into the plant genome and becomes appropriately expressed are low. Often, only one cell in 1000 or more will be successfully transformed. Before growing cultured plant cells into mature plants to test their phenotypes, it is important to eliminate the background of nontransformed cells. This can be done using either positive or negative selection techniques.

An example of negative selection involves use of a **marker gene** such as the hygromycin-resistance gene. This gene, together with an appropriate promoter, can be introduced into plant cells along with the gene of interest. The cells are then incubated in culture medium containing hygromycin—an antibiotic that also inhibits the growth of eukaryotic cells. Only cells that express the hygromycin-resistance gene will survive. It is then necessary to verify that the resistant cells also express the cotransformed gene. This is often done by techniques such as PCR amplification using gene-specific primers. Plants that express the gene of interest are then tested for other characteristics, including the phenotype conferred by the introduced gene of interest.

An example of positive selection involves the use of a selectable marker gene such as that encoding **phosphomannose isomerase (PMI)**. This enzyme is common in animals but is not found in most plants. It catalyzes the interconversion of mannose 6-phosphate and fructose 6-phosphate. Plant cells that express the *pmi* gene can

survive on synthetic culture medium that contains only mannose as a carbon source. Cells that are cotransformed with the *pmi* gene under control of an appropriate promoter and the gene of interest can be positively selected by growing the plant cells on a mannose-containing medium. This type of positive selection was used to create Golden Rice 2. Studies have shown that purified PMI protein is easily digested, nonallergenic, and nontoxic in mouse oral toxicity tests. A variation in positive selection involves use of a marker gene whose expression results in a visible phenotype, such as deposition of a colored pigment.

The following descriptions illustrate the methods used to engineer two GM crops: Roundup-Ready soybeans and Golden Rice 2.

Roundup-Ready® Soybeans

The Roundup-Ready soybean GM variety received market approval in the United States in 1996. It is a GM plant with resistance to the herbicide glyphosate, the active ingredient in Roundup, a commercially available broad-spectrum herbicide. Glyphosate interferes with the enzyme 5-enolpyruvylshikimate-3-phosphate synthase (EPSPS), which is present in all plants and is necessary for plant synthesis of the aromatic amino acids phenylalanine, tyrosine, and tryptophan. EPSPS is not present in mammals, which obtain aromatic amino acids from their diets.

To produce a glyphosate-resistant soybean plant, researchers cloned an *epsps* gene from the *Agrobacterium* strain CP4. This gene encodes an EPSPS enzyme that is resistant to glyphosate. They then cloned the *CP4 epsps* gene downstream of a constitutively expressed promoter from the cytomegalovirus to allow gene expression in all plant tissues. In addition, a short peptide known as a chloroplast transit peptide (in this case from petunias) was cloned onto the 5′ end of the *epsps* gene-coding sequence. This allowed newly synthesized EPSPS protein to be inserted into the soybean chloroplast (ST Figure 5–5). The final plasmid contained two *CP4 epsps* genes and, for the initial experiments, a *beta-glucuronidase (GUS)* gene from *E. coli*. The

pV-GMGT04   pV-GMGT04

ST FIGURE 5–5 Portion of plasmid pV-GMGT04 used to create Roundup-Ready soybeans. A 1365-bp fragment encoding the EPSPS enzyme from *Agrobacterium* CP4 was cloned downstream from the cauliflower mosaic virus *E35S* promoter and the petunia chloroplast transit peptide signal sequence (*ctp4*). CTP4 signal sequences direct the EPSPS protein into chloroplasts, where aromatic amino acids are synthesized. The *CP4 epsps* coding region was cloned upstream of the nopaline synthase (*nos*) transcription termination and polyadenylation sequences. The *CP4 epsps* sequences encode a 455-amino-acid 46-kDa ESPSP protein.

GUS gene acted as a positive marker, as cells that expressed the plasmid after transformation could be detected by the presence of a blue precipitate. The final cell line chosen for production of Roundup-Ready soybeans did not contain the *GUS* gene.

The plasmids were introduced into cultured soybean cells using biolistic bombardment. Afterward, cells were treated with glyphosate to eliminate any nontransformed cells. (**ST Figure 5–6**). The resulting calluses were grown into plants, which were then field tested for glyphosate resistance and a large number of other parameters, including composition, toxicity, and allergenicity.

Golden Rice 2

To create Golden Rice 2, scientists cloned three genes into the T-DNA region of a Ti plasmid. The Ti plasmid, called pSYN12424, is shown in **ST Figure 5–7**. The first gene was the *carotene desaturase* (*crtI*) gene from *Erwinia uredovora*, fused between the rice *glutelin* gene promoter (*Glu*) and

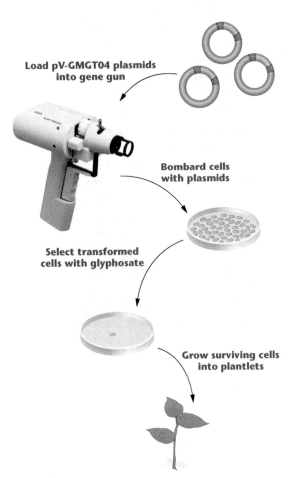

Load pV-GMGT04 plasmids into gene gun

Bombard cells with plasmids

Select transformed cells with glyphosate

Grow surviving cells into plantlets

ST FIGURE 5–6 Method for creating Roundup-Ready soybeans. Plasmids were loaded into the gene gun and fired at high pressure into cells growing in tissue cultures. Cells were grown in the presence of glyphosate to select those that had integrated and expressed the *epsps* gene. Surviving cells were stimulated to form calluses and to grow into plantlets.

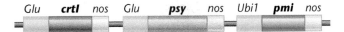

ST FIGURE 5–7 T-DNA region of T1 plasmid pSYN12424. The Ti plasmid used to create Golden Rice 2 contained the carotene desaturase (*crtI*) gene cloned from bacteria, the phytoene synthase (*psy*) gene cloned from maize, and the phosphomannose isomerase (*pmi*) gene cloned from *E. coli*. The *glutelin* (*Glu*) gene promoter directs transcription in rice endosperm, and the *polyubiquitin* (*Ubi1*) promoter directs transcription in all tissues. Transcription termination signals were provided by the nopaline synthase (*nos*) gene 3′ region.

the *nos* gene terminator region (*nos*). The *Glu* promoter directs transcription of the fusion gene specifically in the rice endosperm. The *nos* terminator was cloned from the *Agrobacterium tumefaciens nopaline synthase* gene and supplies the transcription termination and polyadenylation sequences required at the 3′ end of plant genes. The second gene was the *phytoene synthase* (*psy*) gene cloned from maize. The maize *psy* gene has approximately 90 percent sequence similarity to the rice *psy* gene and is involved in carotenoid synthesis in maize endosperm. This gene was also fused to the *Glu* promoter and the *nos* terminator sequences in order to obtain proper transcription initiation and termination in rice endosperm. The third gene was the selectable marker gene, *phosphomannose isomerase* (*pmi*), cloned from *E. coli*. In the Golden Rice 2 Ti plasmid, the *pmi* gene was fused to the maize *polyubiquitin* gene promoter (*Ubi1*) and the *nos* terminator sequences. The *Ubi1* promoter is a constitutive promoter, directing transcription of the *pmi* gene in all plant tissues.

To introduce the pSYN12424 plasmid into rice cells, researchers established embryonic rice cell cultures and infected them with *Agrobacterium tumefaciens* that contained pSYN12424 (**ST Figure 5–8**). The cells were then placed under selection, using culture medium containing only mannose as a carbon source. Surviving cells expressing the *pmi* gene were then stimulated to form calluses that were grown into plants. To confirm that all three genes were present in the transformed rice plants, samples were taken and analyzed by the polymerase chain reaction (PCR) using gene-specific primers. Plants that contained one integrated copy of the transgenic construct and synthesized beta-carotene in their seeds were selected for further testing.

GM Foods Controversies

GM foods may be the most contentious of all products of modern biotechnology. Advocates of GM foods state that the technologies have increased farm productivity, reduced pesticide use, preserved soils, and have the potential to feed

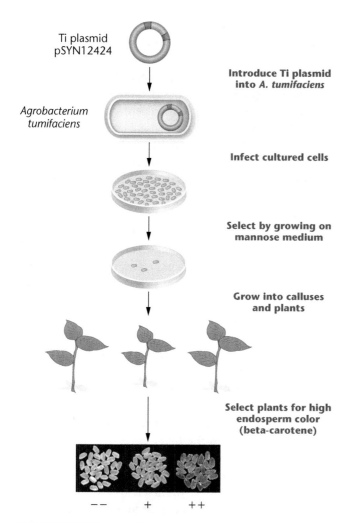

Ti plasmid
pSYN12424

Introduce Ti plasmid
into *A. tumifaciens*

*Agrobacterium
tumifaciens*

Infect cultured cells

Select by growing on
mannose medium

Grow into calluses
and plants

Select plants for high
endosperm color
(beta-carotene)

−−   +   ++

ST FIGURE 5–8 Method for creating Golden Rice 2. Rice plant cells were transformed by pSYN12424 and selected on mannose-containing medium, as described in the text. Plants that produced high levels of beta-carotene in rice grain endosperm (++), based on the intensity of the grain's yellow color, were selected for further analysis.

created for different purposes and are used in ways that are both planned and unplanned. Each construction is unique and therefore needs to be assessed separately.

We will now examine two of the main GM foods controversies: those involving human health and safety, and environmental effects.

Health and Safety

GM food advocates often state that there is no evidence that GM foods currently on the market have any adverse health effects, either from the presence of toxins or from potential allergens. These conclusions are based on two observations. First, humans have consumed several types of GM foods for more than 20 years now, and no reliable reports of adverse effects have emerged. Second, the vast majority of toxicity tests in animals, which are required by government regulators prior to approval, have shown no negative effects. A few negative studies have been published, but these have been criticized as poorly executed or nonreproducible.

Critics of GM foods counter the first observation in several ways. First, as described previously, few GM foods are eaten directly by consumers. Instead, most are used as livestock feed, and the remainder form the basis of purified food ingredients. Although no adverse effects of GM foods in livestock have been detected, the processing of many food ingredients removes most, if not all, plant proteins and DNA. Hence, ingestion of GM food-derived ingredients may not be a sufficient test for health and safety. Second, GM foods critics argue that there have been few human clinical trials to directly examine the health effects of most GM foods. One notable exception is Golden Rice 2, which has undergone two small clinical trials. They also say that the toxicity studies that have been completed are performed in animals—primarily rats and mice—and most of these are short-term toxicity studies.

Supporters of GM foods answer these criticisms with several other arguments. The first argument is that short-term toxicity studies in animals are well-established methods for detecting toxins and allergens. The regulatory processes required prior to approval of any GM food demand data from animal toxicity studies. If any negative effects are detected, approval is not given. Supporters also note that several dozen long-term toxicity studies have been published that deal with GM crops such as glyphosate-resistant soybeans and Bt corn, and none of these has shown long-term negative effects on test animals. A few studies that report negative long-term effects have been criticized as poorly designed and unreliable. GM food advocates note that human clinical trials are not required for any other food derived from other genetic modification methods such as selective breeding. During standard breeding of plants and animals, genomes may be mutagenized with radiation or chemicals to enhance the possibilities of obtaining

growing human populations. Critics claim that GM foods are unsafe for both humans and the environment; accordingly, they are applying pressure on regulatory agencies to ban or severely limit the extent of GM food use. These campaigns have affected regulators and politicians, resulting in a patchwork of regulations throughout the world. Often the debates surrounding GM foods are highly polarized and emotional, with both sides in the debate exaggerating their points of view and selectively presenting the data. So, what are the truths behind these controversies?

One point that is important to make as we try to answer this question is that *it is not possible to make general statements about all "GM foods."* Each GM crop or organism contains different genes from different sources, attached to different expression sequences, accompanied by different marker or selection genes, inserted into the genome in different ways and in different locations. GM foods are a desired phenotype. This type of manipulation has the potential to introduce mutations into genes other than the ones that are directly selected. Also, plants and animals naturally exchange and shuffle DNA in ways that cannot be anticipated. These include interspecies DNA transfers, transposon integrations, and chromosome modifications. These events may result in unintended changes to the physiology of organisms—changes that could potentially be as great as those arising in GM foods.

Environmental Effects

Critics of GM foods point out that GMOs that are released into the environment have both documented and potential consequences for the environment—and hence may indirectly affect human health and safety. GM food advocates argue that these potential environmental consequences can be identified and managed. Here, we will describe two different aspects of GM foods as they may affect the natural environment and agriculture.

1. Emerging herbicide and insecticide resistance. Many published studies report that the planting of herbicide-tolerant and insect-resistant GM crops has reduced the quantities of herbicides and insecticides that are broadly applied to agricultural crops. As a result, the effects of GM crops on the environment have been assumed to be positive. However, these positive effects may be transient, as herbicide and insecticide resistance is beginning to emerge. (**ST Figure 5–9**).

   Since glyphosate-tolerant crops were introduced in the mid-1990s, more than 24 glyphosate-resistant weed species have appeared in the United States. Resistant weeds have been found in 18 other countries, and in some

cases, the presence of these weeds is affecting crop yields. One reason for the rapid rise of resistant weeds is that farmers have abandoned other weed-management practices in favor of using a single broad-spectrum herbicide. This strong selection pressure has brought the rapid evolution of weed species bearing gene variants that confer herbicide resistance. In response, biotechnology companies are developing new GM crops with tolerance to multiple herbicides. However, scientists argue that weeds will also develop resistance to the use of multiple herbicides, unless farmers vary their weed management practices and incorporate tillage, rotation, and other herbicides along with using the GM crop. Scientists point out that herbicide resistance is not limited to the use of GM crops. Weed populations will evolve resistance to any herbicide used to control them, and the speed of evolution will be affected by the extent to which the herbicide is used.

Since 1996, more than eight different species of insect pests have evolved some level of resistance to Bt insecticidal proteins. For example, in 2011 scientists reported the first cases of resistance of the western corn rootworm to Bt maize expressing the *cry3Bb1* gene, in maize fields in Iowa. In 2010, scientists from Monsanto detected large numbers of pink bollworms with resistance to the toxin expressed from the *cry-1Ac* gene in one variety of Bt cotton. In order to slow down the development of Bt resistance, several strategies are being followed. The first is to develop varieties of GM crops that express two Bt toxins simultaneously. Several of these varieties are already on the market and are replacing varieties that express only one Bt *cry* gene. The second strategy involves the use of "refuges" surrounding fields that grow Bt crops. These refuges contain non-GM crops. Insect pests grow easily within the refuges, which place no evolutionary pressure on the insects for resistance to Bt toxins. The idea is for these nonselected insects to mate with any resistant insects that appear in the Bt crop region of the field. The resulting hybrid offspring will be heterozygous for any resistance gene variant. As long as the resistance gene variant is recessive, the hybrids will be killed by eating the Bt crop. In fields that use refuges and plant GM crops containing two Bt genes, resistance to Bt toxins has been delayed or is absent. As with emerging herbicide resistance, farmers are also encouraged to combine the use of Bt crops with conventional pest control methods.

2. The spread of GM crops into non-GM crops. There have been several documented cases of GM crop plants appearing in uncultivated areas in the United States, Canada, Australia, Japan, and Europe. For example, GM sugar beet plants have been found growing in commercial top

ST FIGURE 5–9 Herbicide-resistant weeds. Water hemp weeds, resistant to glyphosate herbicide, growing in a field of Roundup-Ready soybeans.

soils. GM canola plants have been found growing in ditches and along roadways, railway tracks, and in fill soils, far from the fields in which they were grown. A 2011 study[1] found "feral" GM canola plants growing in 288 of 634 sample sites along roadways in North Dakota. Of these plants, 41 percent contained the CP4 EPSPS protein (conferring glyphosate resistance), and 39 percent contained the PAT protein (conferring resistance to the herbicide glufosinate). In addition, two of the plants (0.7 percent of the sample) expressed both proteins (resistant to both herbicides). GM plants that express both proteins have not been created by genetic modification and were assumed to have arisen by cross-fertilization of the other two GM crops. The researchers who conducted this survey were not surprised to find GM canola along transportation routes, as seeds are often spilled during shipping. More surprising was the extent of the distribution and the presence of hybridized GM canola plants.

One of the major concerns about the escape of GM crop plants from cultivation is the possibility of **outcrossing** or **gene flow**—the transfer of transgenes from GM crops into sexually compatible non-GM crops or wild plants, conferring undesired phenotypes to the other plants. Gene flow between GM crops and adjacent non-GM crops is of particular concern for farmers who want to market their crops as "GM-free" or "organic" and for farmers who grow seed for planting.

Gene flow of GM transgenes has been documented in GM and non-GM canola as well as sugar beets, and in experiments using rice, wheat, and maize. GM critics often refer to controversial studies about GM outcrossing in Oaxaca, Mexico. In the first study in 2001, it was reported that the local maize crops contained transgenes from Monsanto's Roundup-Ready and Bt insect-resistant maize. As GM crops were not approved for use in Mexico, it was thought that the transgenes came from maize that had been imported from the United States as a foodstuff, and then had been planted by farmers who were not aware that the seeds were transgenic. Over the next ten years, subsequent studies reported mixed results. In some studies, the transgenes were not detected, and in others, the same transgenes were detected. There is still no consensus about whether gene flow has occurred between the GM and non-GM maize in Mexico.

It is thought that the presence of glyphosate-resistant transgenes in wild plant populations is not likely to be an environmental risk and would confer no positive fitness benefits to the hybrids. The presence of glyphosate-resistant genes in wild populations would, however, make it more difficult to eradicate the plants. This is illustrated in a case of escaped GM bentgrass in Oregon, where it has been difficult to get rid of the plants because it is no longer possible to use the relatively safe herbicide glyphosate. The potential for environmental damage may be greater if the GM transgenes did confer an advantage—such as insect resistance or tolerance to drought or flooding.

In an attempt to limit the spread of transgenes from GM crops to non-GM crops, regulators are considering a requirement to separate the crops so that pollen would be less likely to travel between them. Each crop plant would require different isolation distances to take into account the dynamics of pollen spreading. Several other methods are being considered. For example, one proposal is to make all GM plants sterile using RNAi technology. Another is to introduce the transgenes into chloroplasts. As chloroplasts are inherited maternally, their genomes would not be transferred via pollen. All of these containment methods are in development stages and may take years to reach the market.

The Future of GM Foods

Over the last 20 years, GM foods have revealed both promise and problems. GM advocates are confident that the next generation of GM foods will show even more promising prospects—and may also address many of the problems.

Research is continuing on ways to fortify staple crops with nutrients to address diet problems in poor countries. For example, Australian scientists are adding genes to bananas that will not only provide resistance to Panama disease—a serious fungal disease that can destroy crops—but also increase the levels of beta-carotene and other nutrients, including iron. Other GM crops in the pipeline include plants engineered to resist drought, high salinity, nitrogen starvation, and low temperatures.

Scientists hope that new genome information and more precise technologies will allow them to accurately edit a plant's endogenous genes—decreasing, increasing, or eliminating expression of one or more of the plant's genes in order to create a desirable phenotype. These approaches avoid the use of transgenes and address some of the concerns about GM foods. The current techniques that researchers use to introduce genes into plant cells result in random insertions into the genome. New techniques are being devised that will allow genes to be inserted into precise locations in the genome, avoiding some of the potential unknown effects of disrupting a plant's normal genome with random integrations.

[1]Schafter, M.G. et al. 2011. *PLoS One* 6:e25736.

Researchers are also devising more creative ways to protect plants from insects and diseases. One intriguing project involves introducing into wheat a gene that encodes a pheromone that acts as a chemical alarm signal to aphids. If successful, this approach could protect the wheat plants from aphids without using toxins. Another project involves cassava, which is a staple crop for many Africans and is afflicted by two viral diseases—cassava mosaic virus and brown streak virus—that stunt growth and cause root rot (ST Figure 5–10). Although some varieties of cassava are resistant to these viruses, the life cycle of cassava is so long that it would be difficult to introduce resistance into other varieties using conventional breeding techniques. Scientists plan to transform plants with genes from resistant cassava. This type of cisgenic gene transfer is more comparable to traditional breeding than transgenic techniques.

In the future, GM foods will likely include additional GM animals. As described in Box 1, a transgenic Atlantic salmon variety is likely to receive marketing approval in the near future. In another project, scientists have introduced a DNA sequence into chickens that protects the birds from spreading avian influenza. The sequence encodes a hairpin RNA molecule with similarity to a normal viral RNA that binds to the viral polymerase. The presence of the hairpin RNA inhibits the activity of the viral polymerase and interferes with viral propagation. If this strategy proves useful *in vivo*, the use of these GM chickens would not only reduce

ST FIGURE 5–10 Cassava tubers infected with brown streak virus. Cassava, a major food crop in sub-Saharan Africa, is threatened by infection with the mosaic virus, which stunts plant growth, and the brown streak virus, which causes root rot.

the incidence of avian influenza in poultry production, but also reduce the transmissibility of avian influenza viruses to humans.

Although these and other GM foods show promise for increasing agricultural productivity and decreasing disease, the political pressure from anti-GM critics remains a powerful force. An understanding of the science behind these technologies will help us all to evaluate the future of GM foods.

Selected Readings and Resources

Journal Articles

Butler, D. 2012. Hyped GM maize study faces growing scrutiny. *Nature* 490: 158.

Cressey, D. 2013. A new breed. *Nature* 497: 27–29.

Domingo, J.L. 2007. Toxicity studies of genetically modified plants: A review of the published literature. *Crit. Rev. Food Sci. Nutrition* 47: 721–733.

Enserink, M. 2008. Tough lessons from Golden Rice. *Science* 320: 468–471.

Gassmann, A.J., et al. 2011. Field-evolved resistance to Bt maize by western corn rootworm. *PLoS One* 6(7): e22629.

Gilbert, N. 2013. A hard look at GM crops. *Nature* 497: 21–26.

Gonsalves, D. 2004. Transgenic papaya in Hawaii and beyond. *AgBioForum* 7: 36–40.

Oke, K.B., et al. 2013. Hybridization between genetically modified Atlantic salmon and wild brown trout reveals novel ecological interactions. *Proc. R. Soc. B.*, 280: 20131047.

Paine, J.A., et al. 2005. Improving the nutritional value of Golden Rice through increased pro-vitamin A content. *Nature Biotech.* 23(4): 482–487.

Schafer, M.G., et al. 2011. The establishment of genetically engineered canola populations in the US. *PLoS One* 6(10): e25736.

Whitty, C.J.M., et al. 2013. Africa and Asia need a rational debate on GM crops. *Nature* 497: 31–33.

Web Sites

GMO Compass: EU supported GMO database. http://www.gmo-compass.org.

Adoption of Genetically Engineered Crops in the US. U.S. Department of Agriculture, Economic Research Service. http://www.ers.usda.gov/data-products/adoption-of-genetically-engineered-crops-in-the-us.aspx#.UdmLqW3fJyI

GM Approval Databases and Information. International Service for the Acquisition of Agri-Biotech Applications. http://isaaa.org

Twenty questions on genetically modified foods. World Health Organization. http://www.who.int/foodsafety/publications/biotech/20questions/en/

Golden Rice. The International Rice Research Institute. http://irri.org/golden-rice

Review Questions

1. How do genetically modified organisms compare with organisms created through selective breeding?
2. Can current GM crops be considered as transgenic or cisgenic? Why?
3. Of the approximately 200 GM crop varieties that have been developed, only a few are widely used. What are these varieties, and how prevalent are they?
4. How does glyphosate work, and how has it been used with GM crops to increase agricultural yields?
5. Describe the mechanisms by which the Cry proteins from *Bacillus thuringiensis* act as insecticides.
6. What measures have been taken to alleviate vitamin A deficiencies in developing countries? To date, how successful have these strategies been?
7. What is Golden Rice 2, and how was it created?
8. Describe how plants can be transformed using biolistic methods. How does this method compare with *Agrobacterium tumefaciens*-mediated transformation?
9. How do positive and negative selection techniques contribute to the development of GM crops?
10. Describe how the Roundup-Ready soybean variety was developed, and what genes were used to transform the soybean plants.

Discussion Questions

1. What are the laws regulating the development, approval, and use of GM foods in your region and nationally?
2. Do you think that foods containing GM ingredients should be labeled as such? What would be the advantages and disadvantages to such a strategy?
3. One of the major objections to GM foods is that they may be harmful to human health. Do you agree or disagree, and why?

Gene Therapy

Although drug treatments can be effective in controlling symptoms of genetic disorders, the ideal outcome of medical treatment is to cure a disease. This is the goal of **gene therapy**—the delivery of therapeutic genes into a patient's cells to correct genetic disease conditions caused by a faulty gene or genes. The earliest attempts at gene therapy focused on the delivery of normal, *therapeutic* copies of a gene to be expressed in such a way as to override or negate the effects of the disease gene and thus minimize or eliminate symptoms of the genetic disease. But in recent years newer methods for inhibiting or silencing defective genes, and even approaches for targeted removal of defective genes, have increasingly emerged as potential mechanisms for gene therapy. We will introduce you to each of these approaches in this Special Topic chapter.

Gene therapy is one of the ultimate goals of **translational medicine**—taking a scientific discovery, such as the identification of a disease-causing gene, and translating the finding into an effective therapy, thus moving from the laboratory bench to a patient's bedside to treat a disease. In theory, the delivery of a therapeutic gene is rather simple, but in practice, gene therapy has been very difficult to execute. In spite of over 20 years of trials, this field has not lived up to its expectations. However, gene therapy is currently experiencing a fast-paced resurgence of sorts, with several high-profile new successes and potentially exciting new technologies sitting on the horizon. It is hoped that gene therapy will soon become part of mainstream medicine. In this Special Topic chapter we will explore how gene therapy is executed, and we will highlight selected examples of successes and failures as well as discuss new approaches to gene therapy. Finally, we will consider ethical issues regarding gene therapy.

> **"The treatment of a human genetic disease by gene therapy is the ultimate application of genetic technology."**

What Genetic Conditions Are Candidates for Treatment by Gene Therapy?

Two essential criteria for gene therapy are that the gene or genes involved in causing a particular disease have been identified and that the gene can be cloned or synthesized in a laboratory. As a result of the Human Genome Project, the identification of human disease genes and their specific DNA sequences has greatly increased the number of candidate genes for gene therapy trials. Almost all of the early gene therapy trials and most gene therapy approaches have focused on treating *monogenic* diseases, conditions caused by a single gene. This has been the case because theoretically it is technically easier to affect one gene than disease conditions caused by multiple genes and potentially multiple mutations. Conceptually, this approach is simple. Identify the mutant gene responsible for the genetic condition and replace or supplement it with a normal copy of the gene. As we will see below, gene therapy has proven to be much more challenging than this.

The cells affected by the genetic condition must be readily accessible for treatment by gene therapy. For example, blood disorders such as leukemia, hemophilia, and other conditions have been major targets of gene therapy because it is relatively routine to manipulate blood cells outside of the body and return them to the body in comparison to treating cells in the brain and spinal cord, skeletal or cardiac muscle, and organs with heterogeneous populations of cells such as the pancreas. Cells of the respiratory system are another example of tissues that have also been targeted for their easy access. For example, this approach has been used to treat cystic fibrosis by gene therapy, but it has been unsuccessful for many reasons.

In the past decade, every major category of genetic diseases has been targeted by gene therapy [ST Figure 6-1(a)]. A majority of recently approved clinical trials are for cancer treatment. Gene therapy approaches are currently being investigated for the treatment of hereditary blindness, neurological (neurodegenerative) diseases including Alzheimer disease and Parkinson disease, cardiovascular disease, a variety of cancers, and infectious diseases, such as HIV, among many other conditions, including depression and drug and alcohol addiction. Over 1700 approved gene therapy clinical trials have occurred or recently been initiated for acquired and inherited diseases [ST Figure 6-1(b)].

(a)

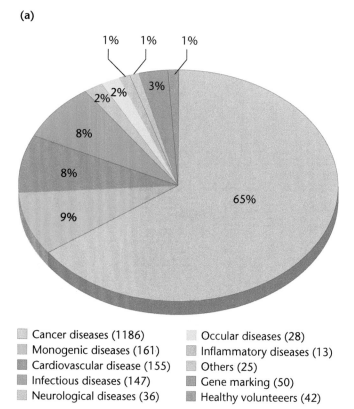

- Cancer diseases (1186)
- Monogenic diseases (161)
- Cardiovascular disease (155)
- Infectious diseases (147)
- Neurological diseases (36)
- Occular diseases (28)
- Inflammatory diseases (13)
- Others (25)
- Gene marking (50)
- Healthy volunteeers (42)

(b)

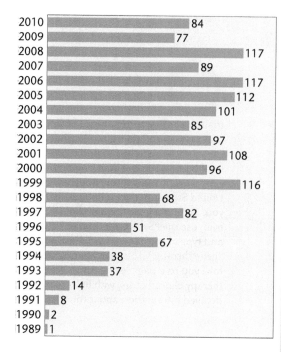

ST FIGURE 6–1   The current status of gene therapy worldwide. (a) Graphic representation of different genetic conditions being treated by gene therapy clinical trials worldwide. Notice that cancers are the major target for treatment. (b) Dozens of gene therapy clinical trials are approved by regulatory agencies around the world every year. Shown here is a partial representation of the number of approved trials initiated worldwide annually.

In the United States, proposed gene therapy clinical trials must first be approved by review boards at the institution where they will be carried out, and then the protocols must be approved by the Food and Drug Administration (FDA). Gene therapy trials that are funded by the National Institutes of Health also have to register with the NIH Recombinant DNA Advisory Committee.

How Are Therapeutic Genes Delivered?

In general, there are two broad approaches for delivering therapeutic genes to a patient being treated by gene therapy, *ex vivo gene therapy* and *in vivo gene therapy* (**ST Figure 6–3**). In *ex vivo* gene therapy, cells from a person with a particular genetic condition are removed, treated in a laboratory by adding either normal copies of a therapeutic gene or a DNA or RNA sequence that will inhibit expression of a defective gene, and then these cells are transplanted back into the person where the therapeutic gene will express normal copies of the required protein. Genetically altered cells treated in this manner can be transplanted back into the patient without

fear of immune system rejection because these cells were derived from the patient initially. As you will soon learn, this approach was used for the first successful gene therapy trial.

In vivo gene therapy does not involve removal of a person's cells. Instead, therapeutic DNA is introduced directly into affected cells of the body. One of the major challenges of *in vivo* gene therapy is restricting the delivery of therapeutic genes to only the intended tissues and not to all tissues throughout the body.

Viral Vectors for Gene Therapy

For both *in vitro* and *ex vivo* approaches, the key to successful gene therapy is having a delivery system to transfer genes into a patient's cells. Because of the relatively large molecular size and electrically charged properties of DNA, most human cells do not take up DNA easily. If they did, it would be possible to deliver genes simply by mixing DNA with cells in much the same way that transformation is achieved with bacterial cells. Therefore, delivering therapeutic DNA molecules into human cells is challenging. Since the early days of gene therapy, genetically engineered viruses as vectors have been the main tools for delivering therapeutic genes into human cells. Viral vectors for gene

SPECIAL TOPIC 6

BOX 1
ClinicalTrials.gov

One of the best resources on the Web for learning about ongoing clinical trials, including current gene therapy trials, is ClinicalTrials.gov. The site can easily be searched to find a wealth of resources about ongoing gene therapy trials throughout the United States that are of interest to you. To find a gene therapy clinical trial, use the "Search for Studies" box and type in the name of a disease and "gene therapy." This search string will take you to a page listing active gene therapy clinical trials, with links to detailed information about the trial.

ST FIGURE 6-2 The ClinicalTrials.gov Web site homepage.

therapy are engineered to carry therapeutic DNA as their payload so that the virus infects target cells and delivers the therapeutic DNA without causing damage to cells.

In a majority of gene therapy trials around the world, scientists have used genetically modified *retroviruses* as vectors. Recall from earlier in the text (see Chapter 10) that retroviruses (HIV is a retrovirus) contain an RNA genome that scientists use as a template for the synthesis of a complementary DNA molecule. The first viruses used for gene therapy were from a family of murine retroviruses called Moloney murine leukemia virus. **Retroviral vectors** are created by removing replication and disease-causing genes from the virus and replacing them with a cloned human gene. After the altered RNA has been packaged into the virus, the recombinant viral vector containing the therapeutic human gene is used to infect a patient's cells. Technically, virus particles are carrying RNA

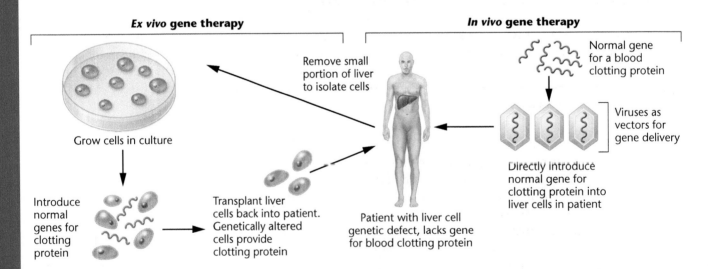

ST FIGURE 6-3 *Ex vivo* and *in vivo* gene therapy for a patient with a liver disorder. *Ex vivo* gene therapy involves isolating cells from the patient, introducing normal copies of a therapeutic gene (encoding a blood clotting protein in this example) into these cells, and then returning cells to the body where they will produce the required clotting protein. *In vivo* approaches involve introducing DNA directly into cells while they are in the body. Both approaches can also be used to deliver genes to overcome the effects of the expression of a mutant gene.

copies of the therapeutic gene. Once inside a cell, the virus cannot replicate itself, but the therapeutic RNA is reverse transcribed into DNA, which enters the nucleus of cells and *integrates* into the genome of the host cells' chromosome. If the inserted therapeutic gene is properly expressed, it produces a normal gene product that may be able to ameliorate the effects of the mutation carried by the affected individual.

One advantage of retroviral vectors is that they provide long-term expression of delivered genes because they integrate the therapeutic gene into the genome of the patient's cells. But a major problem with retroviral vectors is that they have produced severe toxicity in some cases due to *insertional mutations*. Retroviral vectors generally integrate their genome into the host-cell genome at random sites. Thus, there is the potential for retroviral integration

that randomly inactivates genes in the genome or gene-regulatory regions such as a promoter sequence. In some cases the promoter sequence of a gene therapy vector can control expression of adjacent genes in the host-cell genome—which can include activating cancer genes with devastating results, as you will soon learn.

Adenovirus vectors were used in many early gene therapy trials. An advantage of these vectors is that they are capable of carrying large therapeutic genes. But because many humans produce antibodies to adenovirus vectors they can mount immune reactions that can render the virus and its therapeutic gene ineffective or cause significant side-effects to the patient. A related virus called **adeno-associated virus (AAV)** is now widely used as a gene therapy vector [ST Figure 6–4(a)]. In its native form, AAV infects about

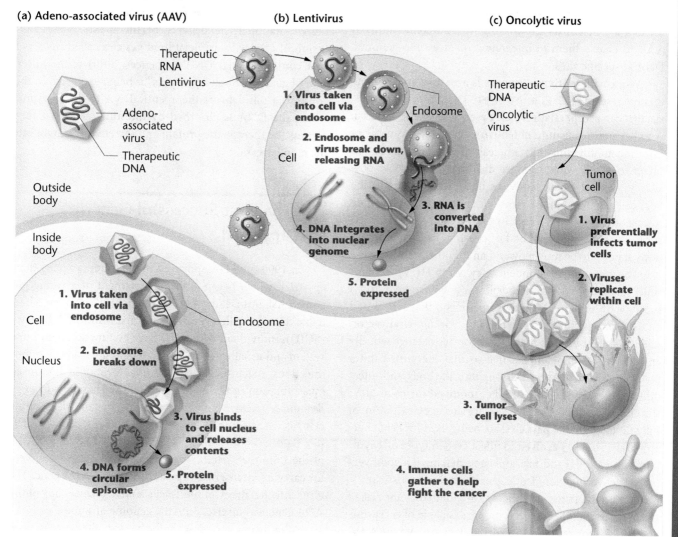

(a) Adeno-associated virus (AAV)   **(b) Lentivirus**   **(c) Oncolytic virus**

ST FIGURE 6–4   Delivering therapeutic genes. (a) Nonintegrating viruses such as modified adeno-associated virus (AAV) deliver therapeutic genes without integrating them into the genome of target cells. Delivered DNA resides as minichromosomes (episomes), but over time as cells divide, these nonintegrating hoops of DNA are gradually lost. (b) Integrating viruses include lentivirus, an RNA retrovirus that delivers therapeutic genes into the cytoplasm where reverse transcriptase converts RNA into DNA. DNA then integrates into the genome, ensuring that therapeutic DNA will be passed into daughter cells during cell division. (c) Oncolytic viruses are being used to deliver therapeutic genes to target attacks on cancer cells.

80–90 percent of humans during childhood, causing symptoms associated with the common cold. Disabled forms of AAV are popular for gene therapy because the virus is non-pathogenic, so it usually does not elicit a major response from the immune system of treated patients. AAV also does not typically integrate into the host-cell genome, so there is little risk of the insertional mutations that have plagued retroviruses, although modified forms of AAV have been used to deliver genes to specific sites on individual chromosomes. Most forms of AAV deliver genes into the host-cell nucleus where it forms small hoops of DNA called *episomes* that are expressed under the control of promoter sequences contained within the viral genome. But because therapeutic DNA delivered by AAV does not usually become incorporated into the genome, it is not replicated when host cells divide, and so the gene therapy approach may require repeated, ongoing applications to be successful [ST Figure 6–4(a)]. Scientists are working with different strains of AAV to enable them to integrate sequences into genomic DNA at specific sites.

Work with **lentivirus vectors** is an active area of gene therapy research [ST Figure 6–4(b)]. Lentivirus is a retrovirus that can accept relatively large pieces of genetic material. Another positive feature of lentivirus is that it is capable of infecting nondividing cells, whereas other viral vectors often infect cells only when they are dividing. It is still not possible to control where lentivirus integration occurs in the host-cell genome, but the virus does not appear to gravitate toward gene-regulatory regions the way that other retroviruses do. Thus the likelihood of causing insertional mutations appears to be much lower than for other vectors.

The human immunodeficiency virus (HIV) responsible for acquired immunodeficiency syndrome (AIDS) is a type of lentivirus. It may surprise you that HIV could be used as a vector for gene therapy. For any viral vector, scientists must be sure that the vector has been genetically engineered to render it inactive so that the virus cannot produce disease or spread throughout the body and infect other tissues. In the case of HIV, modified forms of HIV, strains lacking the genes necessary for reconstitution of fully functional viral particles, are being used for gene therapy trials. HIV has evolved to infect certain types of T lymphocytes (T cells) and macrophages, making it a good vector for delivering therapeutic genes into the bloodstream.

Viral vectors for gene therapy are limited by the size of the inserted therapeutic gene they are capable of accepting, about 10 kb for retroviral vectors and about 5 kb for AAV. This size presents a problem when an attempt is made to deliver very large genes or genes with complex regulatory and coding sequences. As you will learn, a major emphasis in gene therapy research is to develop safe and reliable vectors (viral and nonviral).

Researchers are even working on using *oncolytic viruses* carrying payloads of therapeutic genes [ST Figure 6–4(c)]. These viruses, such as certain forms of herpes simplex type I (HSV-1), target and destroy tumor cells and at the same time deliver therapeutic genes. Increasingly, viral vectors and nonviral vector approaches are being used to deliver therapeutic genes into *stem cells*, usually *in vitro*, and then the stem cells are either reintroduced into the patient or differentiated *in vitro* into mature cell types before being transplanted into the correct organ of a patient being treated.

Nonviral Delivery Methods

Scientists continue to experiment with various *in vivo* and *ex vivo* strategies for trying to deliver so called naked DNA into cells without the use of viral vectors. Nonviral methods that are being used to transfer genes into cells include chemically assisted transfer of genes across cell membranes, nanoparticle delivery of therapeutic genes, and fusion of cells with artificial lipid vesicles called *liposomes* that contain cloned DNA sequences. Short-term expression of genes through "gene pills" is being explored. In this concept, a pill delivers therapeutic DNA to the intestines where the DNA is absorbed by intestinal cells that then express the therapeutic protein and secrete the protein into the bloodstream.

The First Successful Gene Therapy Trial

In 1990 the FDA approved the first human gene therapy trial, which began with the treatment of a young girl named Ashanti DeSilva [ST Figure 6–5(a)], who has a heritable disorder called **severe combined immunodeficiency (SCID)**. Individuals with SCID have no functional immune system and usually die from what would normally be minor infections. Ashanti has an autosomal form of SCID caused by a mutation in the gene encoding the enzyme *adenosine deaminase (ADA)*. Her gene therapy began when clinicians isolated some of her white blood cells, called T cells [ST Figure 6–5(b)]. These cells, which are key components of the immune system, were mixed with a retroviral vector carrying an inserted copy of the normal *ADA* gene. The virus infected many of the T cells, and a normal copy of the *ADA* gene was inserted into the genome of some T cells.

After being mixed with the vector, the T cells were grown in the laboratory and analyzed to make sure that the transferred *ADA* gene was expressed (ST Figure 6–5). Then a billion or so genetically altered T cells were injected into Ashanti's bloodstream. Repeated treatments were required to produce a sufficient number of functioning T cells. In addition, Ashanti also periodically received injections of purified

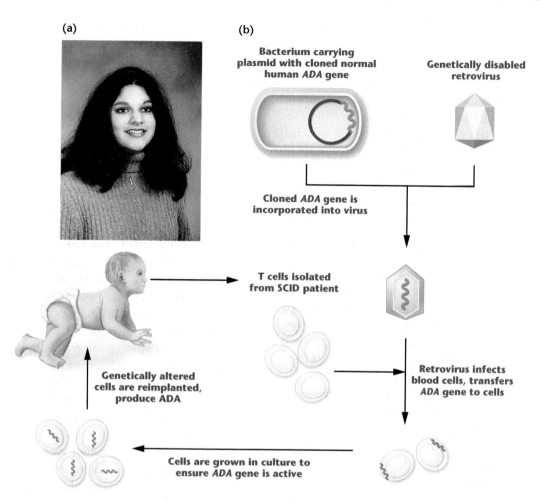

(a)

(b)

Bacterium carrying
plasmid with cloned normal
human *ADA* gene

Genetically disabled
retrovirus

Cloned *ADA* gene is
incorporated into virus

T cells isolated
from SCID patient

Retrovirus infects
blood cells, transfers
ADA gene to cells

Genetically altered
cells are reimplanted,
produce ADA

Cells are grown in culture to
ensure *ADA* gene is active

ST FIGURE 6–5 The first successful gene therapy trial. (a) Ashanti DeSilva, the first person to be successfully treated by gene therapy. (b) To treat SCID using gene therapy, a cloned human *ADA* gene is transferred into a viral vector, which is then used to infect white blood cells removed from the patient. The transferred *ADA* gene is incorporated into a chromosome and becomes active. After growth to enhance their numbers, the cells are inserted back into the patient, where they produce ADA, allowing the development of an immune response.

ADA protein throughout this process. Ashanti has ADA protein expression in 25 to 30 percent of her T cells, which was enough to allow her to lead a normal life.

Subsequent gene therapy treatments for SCID have focused on using bone marrow stem cells and *in vitro* approaches to repopulate the number of ADA-producing T cells. To date, gene therapy has successfully restored the health of about 20 children affected by SCID. SCID treatment is still considered the most successful example of gene therapy so far.

Gene Therapy Setbacks

From 1990 to 1999, more than 4000 people underwent gene therapy for a variety of genetic disorders. These trials often failed and thus led to a loss of confidence in gene therapy.

In the United States, gene therapy plummeted even further in 1999 when teenager Jesse Gelsinger died while undergoing a test for the safety of a gene therapy procedure to treat a liver disease called ornithine transcarbamylase (OTC) deficiency. Large numbers of adenovirus vectors bearing the *OTC* gene were injected into his hepatic artery. His death was triggered by a massive inflammatory response to the adenovirus vector. The virus vectors were expected to target his liver, enter liver cells, and trigger the production of OTC protein. In turn, it was hoped that the OTC protein might correct his genetic defect and cure him of his liver disease.

Researchers had previously treated 18 people with the therapeutic virus, and early results from the first 17 adult patients were promising. But as the 18th patient, Jesse Gelsinger, within hours of his first treatment, developed a massive immune reaction. He developed a high fever, his lungs filled with fluid, multiple organs shut down, and he died four days later of acute respiratory failure. It was thought that Jesse's severe response to the adenovirus may have resulted from how his body reacted to a previous exposure to the virus used as the vector for this protocol.

In the aftermath of the tragedy, several government and scientific inquiries were conducted. Investigators learned that in the clinical trial scientists had not reported other adverse reactions to gene therapy and that some of the scientists were affiliated with private companies that could benefit financially from the trials. It was determined that serious side-effects seen in animal studies were not explained to patients during informed-consent discussions. The FDA subsequently scrutinized gene therapy trials across the country, halted a number of them, and shut down several gene therapy programs. Other research groups voluntarily suspended their gene therapy studies. Tighter restrictions on clinical trial protocols were imposed to correct some of the procedural problems that emerged from the Gelsinger case. Jesse's death had dealt a severe blow to the struggling field of gene therapy—a blow from which it was still reeling when a second tragedy hit.

The outlook for gene therapy brightened momentarily in 2000, when a group of French researchers reported what was hailed as the first large-scale success in gene therapy. Children with a fatal X-linked form of SCID developed functional immune systems after being treated with a retroviral vector carrying a normal gene. But elation over this study soon turned to despair, when it became clear that 5 of the 20 patients in the trial developed leukemia as a direct result of their therapy. One of these patients died as a result of the treatment, while the other four went into remission from the leukemia. In two of the children examined, their cancer cells contained the retroviral vector, inserted near or into a gene called *LMO2*. This *insertional mutagenesis* activated the *LMO2* gene, causing uncontrolled white blood cell proliferation and development of leukemia. The FDA immediately halted 27 similar gene therapy clinical trials, and once again gene therapy underwent a profound reassessment.

On a positive note, long-term survival data from trials in the UK to treat X-SCID and SCID using hematopoietic stem cells from the patients' bone marrow for gene therapy have shown that 14 of 16 children have had their immune system restored at least 9 years after the treatment. These children formerly had life expectancies of less than 20 years. Nevertheless, the above events had major negative impacts on the progress of gene therapy.

Problems with Gene Therapy Vectors

Critics of gene therapy have berated research groups for undue haste, conflicts of interest, sloppy clinical trial management, and for promising much but delivering little. Most of the problems associated with gene therapy, including the Jesse Gelsinger case and the French X-SCID trial, have been traced to the viral vectors used to transfer therapeutic genes into cells. The use of these vectors has been shown to have several serious drawbacks.

- First, integration of retroviral genomes, including the human therapeutic gene into the host cell's genome, occurs only if the host cells are replicating their DNA. In the body, only a small number of cells in any tissue are dividing and replicating their DNA.
- Second, the injection of large amounts of most viral vectors, but particularly adenovirus vectors, is capable of causing an adverse immune response in the patient, as happened in Jesse Gelsinger's case.
- Third, insertion of viral genomes into host chromosomes can activate or mutate an essential gene, as in the case of the French patients. Viral integrase, the enzyme that allows for viral genome integration into the host genome, interacts with chromatin-associated proteins, often steering integration toward transcriptionally active genes. Unfortunately, it is not yet possible to reliably target insertion of therapeutic genes into specific locations in the genome, but as we will discuss in the next section targeted gene delivery is a major area of active research.
- Fourth, AAV vectors cannot carry DNA sequences larger than about 5 kb, and retroviruses cannot carry DNA sequences much larger than 10 kb. Many human genes exceed the 5–10 kb size range.
- Finally, there is a possibility that a fully infectious virus could be created if the inactivated vector were to recombine with another unaltered viral genome already present in the host cell.

To overcome these problems, new viral vectors and strategies for transferring genes into cells are being developed in an attempt to improve the action and safety of vectors. Researchers hope that the use of new gene delivery systems will circumvent the problems inherent in earlier vectors, as well as allow regulation of both insertion sites and the levels of gene product produced from the therapeutic genes. Thus, developing safe viral and nonviral vector systems continues to be a major area of active research, as are approaches to targeted gene therapy that we will discuss later in this chapter. Fortunately, gene therapy has experienced resurgence in part because of several promising new trials and successful treatments.

Recent Successful Trials

Treating Retinal Blindness

In recent years, patients being treated for blindness have greatly benefited from gene therapy approaches. Congenital retinal blinding conditions affect about 1 in 2000 people worldwide, many of which are the result of a wide range of genetic defects. Over 165 different genes have been implicated in various forms of retinal blindness.

Successful gene therapy has been achieved in subsets of patients with *Leber congenital amaurosis (LCA)*, a degenerative disease of the retina that affects 1 in 50,000 to 1 in 100,000 infants each year and causes severe blindness. Gene therapy treatments for LCA were originally pioneered in dogs. Based on the success of these treatments, the protocols were adapted and applied to human gene therapy trials.

LCA is caused by alterations to photoreceptor cells (rods and cones), light-sensitive cells in the retina, due to 18 or more genes. One gene in particular, *RPE65*, has been the gene therapy target of choice. The protein product of the *RPE65* gene metabolizes retinol, which is a form of vitamin A that allows the rod and cone cells of the retina to detect light and transmit electrical signals to the brain. In one of the earliest trials, young adult patients with defects in the *RPE65* gene were given injections of the normal gene. Several months after a single treatment, many adult patients, while still legally blind, could detect light, and some of them could read lines of an eye chart. This treatment approach for LCA was based on injecting AAV-carrying *RPE65* at the back of the eye directly under the retina [ST Figure 6–6(a, b)]. The therapeutic gene enters about

15 to 20 percent of cells in the retinal pigment epithelium, the layer of cells just beneath the visual cells of the retina. Adults treated by this approach have shown substantial improvements in a variety of visual functions tests, but the greatest improvement has been demonstrated in children, all of whom have gained sufficient vision to allow them to be ambulatory. Researchers think the success in children has occurred because younger patients have not lost as many photoreceptor cells as older patients.

Over two dozen gene therapy trials have been completed or are ongoing for various forms of blindness, including age-related degenerative causes of blindness. Because of the small size of the eye and the relatively small number of cells that need to be treated, the prospects for gene therapy to become routine treatment for eye disorders appears to be very good. Retinal cells are also very long-lived; thus, AAV delivery approaches can be successful for long periods of time even if the gene does not integrate.

HIV as a Vector Shows Promise in Recent Trials

Researchers at the University of Paris and Harvard Medical School reported that two years after gene therapy treatment for *β*-thalassemia, a blood disorder involving the *β*-globin gene that reduces the production of hemoglobin, a young man no longer needed transfusions and appeared to be

(a)

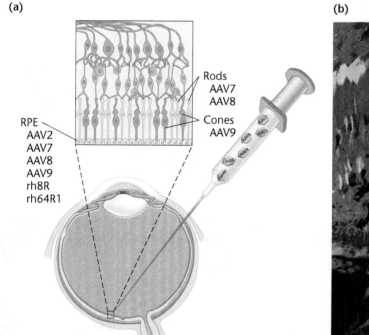

(b)

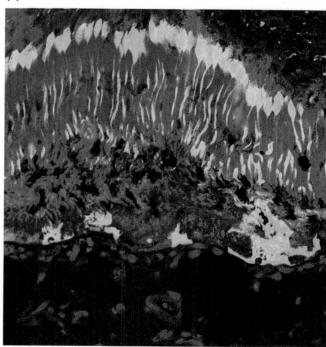

ST FIGURE 6–6 Treatment of retinal blindness. (a) Illustration of AAV delivery of specific genes targeting individual cell types of the retina, rods, cones and the layer of retinal pigment epithelial (RPE) cells. The basic approach shown here was the delivery method used to successfully treat LCA. (b) Photoreceptor layer of a monkey retina after subretinal injection of an AAV expressing green fluorescent protein (GFP; green) in rod and cone cells demonstrating successful delivery of a transgene.

Glybera Is the First Commercial Gene Therapy to Be Approved in the West

I n late 2012, a gene therapy product called Glybera (alipogene tiparvovec) made history when the European Medicines Agency of the European Union approved it as the first gene therapy trial to win commercial approval in the Western world. Glybera is an adenovirus-based vector system for delivering therapeutic copies of the *LPL* gene to treat patients with a rare disease called *lipoprotein lipase deficiency* (LPLD, also called familial hyperchylomicrone-mia). LPLD patients have high levels of triglycerides in their blood. Elevated serum triglycerides are toxic to the pancreas and cause a severe form of pancreatic inflammation called pancreatitis. Developed by Amsterdam-based company uniQure BV, it is still unclear if Glybera will be approved by the U.S. FDA. Nonetheless, the success of Glybera trials in Europe signals what many gene therapy researchers hope will be the beginning of a wave of approvals for gene therapy treatments in Europe and the United States.

---

healthy. A modified, disabled HIV was used to carry a copy of the normal *β-globin* gene. Although this trial resulted in activation of the growth factor gene called *HMGA2*, reminiscent of what occurred in the French X-SCID trials, activation of the transcription factor did not result in an overproduction of hematopoietic cells or create a condition of preleukemia.

In 2013, researchers at the San Raffaele Telethon Institute for Gene Therapy in Milan, Italy, reported two studies using lentivirus vectors derived from HIV in combination with hematopoietic stem cells (HSCs) to successfully treat children with either **metachromatic leukodystrophy (MLD)** or **Wiskott-Aldrich syndrome (WAS)**. Three years after the start of a trial involving a total of 16 patients, 10 patients with MLD and 6 with WAS, data from six patients analyzed 18 to 24 months after gene therapy indicated that the trials are safe and effective. These initial reports are based on studying three children from each study because these are the first patients for whom sufficient time has passed after gene therapy treatment to make significant conclusions regarding the safety and effectiveness of the trials. It took over 15 years of research to get to this point. These trials involved a team of over 70 people, including researchers and clinicians, which is indicative of the teamwork approach typical of gene therapy trials.

MLD is a neurodegenerative disorder affecting storage of enzymes in lysosomes and is caused by mutation in the arylsulfatase A (*ARSA*) gene that results in an accumulation of fats called sulfatides. These are toxic to neurons, causing progressive loss of the myelin sheath (demyelination) surrounding neurons in the brain, leading to a loss of cognitive functions and motor skills. There is no cure for MLD. Children with MLD appear healthy at birth but eventually develop MLD symptoms. In this trial, researchers used an *ex vivo* approach with a lentivirus vector to introduce a functional *ARSA* gene into bone marrow-derived HSCs from each patient and then infused treated HSCs back into patients.

In three children with MLD, gene therapy treatment halted disease progression for 18 to 24 months after therapy, as determined by magnetic resonance images of the brain and through tests of cognitive and motor skills (**ST Figure 6–7**). Because disease onset is predicted at 7 to 21 months, scientists are very encouraged by the outcomes of this trial. The trial was technically complicated because

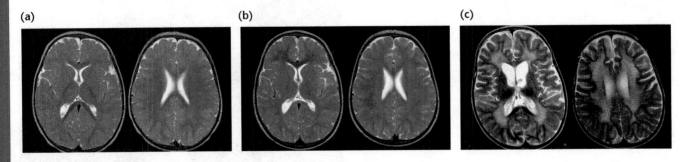

ST FIGURE 6–7   Gene therapy can prevent progression of metachromatic leukodystrophy. (a) Brain magnetic resonance images (MRIs) of a MLD patient at 16 months of age prior to gene therapy. The large white patches in the center of these images show cerebrospinal fluid in the ventricles of the brain. White spots and streaks at the periphery of the brain indicate myelin. (b) MRI images of a MLD patient two years after gene therapy. The myelin content of the brain appears relatively normal. (c) MRI image of the brain from a 39-month-old MLD patient showing severe demyelination associated with MLD-related brain atrophy.

it required that HSCs travel through the bloodstream and release the ARSA protein that is taken up into neurons. A major challenge was to create enough engineered cells to produce a sufficient quantity of therapeutic ARSA protein to counteract the neurodegenerative process.

WAS is an X-linked condition caused by a mutation in the *WASP* gene that encodes a protein that functions in the cytoskeleton of platelets. WAS results in defective platelets that make patients more vulnerable to infections, frequent bleeding, autoimmune diseases, and cancer. Patients treated for WAS showed a resolution of pretreatment eczema (inflammation of the skin) typical in WAS, improved platelet counts, and decreased frequency of infections after gene therapy treatment. Genome sequencing of MLD and WAS patients treated in these trials showed no evidence of genome integration near oncogenes. Similarly, patients showed no evidence of hematopoietic stem cell overproduction, suggesting that this lentivirus delivery protocol produced a safe and stable delivery of the therapeutic genes.

Targeted Approaches to Gene Therapy

The gene therapy approaches and examples we have highlighted thus far have focused on the addition of a therapeutic gene that functions along with the defective gene. However, the removal, correction, and/or replacement of a mutated gene and silencing expression of a defective gene are two other approaches being developed. Rapid progress is being made with these approaches.

DNA-Editing Nucleases for Gene Targeting

For nearly 20 years, scientists have been working on modifications of restriction enzymes and other nucleases to engineer proteins capable of **gene targeting** or **gene editing**—replacing specific genes in the genome. The concept is to combine a nuclease with a sequence-specific DNA binding domain that can be precisely targeted for digestion. In 1996 researchers fused DNA-binding proteins with a zinc-finger motif and DNA cutting domain from the restriction enzyme *Fok*I to create enzymes called **zinc-finger nucleases** (**ZFNs;** ST **Figure 6-8**). Recall from earlier in the text (see Chapter 17) that the zinc-finger motif is found in many transcription factors and consists of a cluster of two cysteine and two histidine residues that bind zinc atoms and interact with specific DNA sequences. By coupling zinc-finger motifs to DNA cutting portions of a polypeptide, ZFNs provide a mechanism for modifying sequences in the genome in a sequence-specific *targeted way*.

Zinc-finger arrangements in a ZFN form a loop in the polypeptide, and they dimerize to bind DNA. The DNA-binding domain of the ZFN can be engineered to attach to any sequence in the genome. Most ZFNs recognize three nucleotides in target DNA sequence. The zinc fingers bind with a spacing of 5–7 nucleotides, and the nuclease domain of the ZFN cleaves between the binding sites.

Another category of DNA-editing nucleases called **TALENs (transcription activator-like effector nucleases)** was created by adding a DNA-binding motif identified in transcription factors from plant pathogenic bacteria known as transcription activator-like effectors (TALEs) to nucleases to create TALENS. TALENS also cleave as dimers. The DNA-binding domain is a tandem array of amino acid repeats, with each TALEN repeat binding to a specific single base pair. The nuclease domain then cuts the sequence between the dimers, a stretch that spans about 13 bp.

ZFNs and TALENS have shown promise in animal models and cultured cells for gene replacement approaches that involve removing a defective gene from the genome. These enzymes can create site-specific cleavage in the genome. When coupled with certain integrases, ZFNs and TALENs may lead to gene editing by cutting out defective sequences and using recombination to introduce homologous sequences into the genome that replace defective sequences. Encouraging breakthroughs have taken place in this area using model organisms such as mice. Although this technology has not yet advanced sufficiently for reliable use in humans, there have been several promising trials.

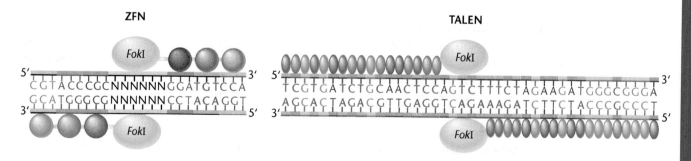

ST FIGURE 6-8   Zinc-finger nucleases and TALENs bind and cut DNA at specific sequences.

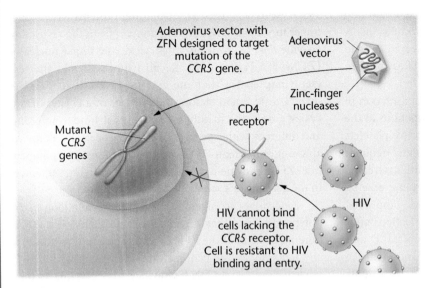

Adenovirus vector with ZFN designed to target mutation of the *CCR5* gene.

Adenovirus vector

Zinc-finger nucleases

CD4 receptor

Mutant *CCR5* genes

HIV

HIV cannot bind cells lacking the *CCR5* receptor. Cell is resistant to HIV binding and entry.

ST FIGURE 6–9 Can gene therapy be used to cure patients with HIV infections or to prevent HIV infections? One recent trial involved adenoviruses to deliver a ZFN to target disruption of the *CCR5* gene in T cells. Cells lacking the protein receptor encoded by *CCR5* are resistant to HIV binding and entry.

For example, ZFNs are actively being used in clinical trials for treating patients with HIV (ST Figure 6–9). Scientists are exploring ways to deliver immune system–stimulating genes that could make individuals resistant to HIV infection or cripple the virus in HIV-positive persons. In 2007, Timothy Brown, a 40-year-old HIV-positive American, had a relapse of acute myeloid leukemia and received a stem cell (bone-marrow) transplant. Because he was HIV-positive, Brown's physician selected a donor with a mutation in both copies of the *CCR5* gene, which encodes an HIV co-receptor carried on the surface of T cells to which HIV must bind to enter T cells (specifically CD4+ cells). People with naturally occurring mutations in both copies of the *CCR5* gene are resistant to most forms of HIV. Brown relapsed again and received another stem cell transplant from the *CCR5*-mutant donor. Eventually, the cancer was contained, and by 2010, levels of HIV in his body were still undetectable even though he was no longer receiving immune-suppressive treatment. Brown is generally considered to be the first person to have been cured of an HIV infection.

This example encouraged researchers to press forward with a gene therapy approach to modify the *CCR5* gene of HIV patients. In one promising trial, T cells were removed from HIV-positive men, and ZFNs were used to disrupt the *CCR5* gene. The modified cells were then reintroduced into patients. In five of six patients treated, immune-cell counts rose substantially following the therapy. What percentage of immune cells would have to be treated this way to significantly inhibit spread of the virus is not known, but initial results are very promising.

Recently, researchers working with human cells used TALENs to remove defective copies of the *COL7A1* gene, which causes recessive dystrophic epidermolysis bullosa (RDEB), an incurable and often fatal disease that causes excessive blistering of the skin, pain, and severely debilitating skin damage. Researchers at the University of Minnesota used a TALEN to cut DNA near a mutation in *COL7A1* gene in skin cells taken from an RDEB patient. These cells were then converted into a type of stem cell called induced pluripotent stem cells (iPSCs). The iPSCs were treated with therapeutic copies of the *COL7A1* gene and then differentiated into skin cells that expressed the correct protein. This is a promising result, and researchers now plan to transplant these skin cells into patients in an attempt to cure them of RDEB. Another group has recently taken a similar approach using TALENS to repair cultured cells in order to correct the mutation in Duchenne muscular dystrophy (DMD). Researchers are optimistic that this approach can soon be adapted to treat patients.

As another recent example of gene targeting, a system called *CRISPR* has shown great promise for replacing target gene sequences. During the first half of 2013, different groups used the CRISPR approach to target specific genes in human cells, mice, rats, bacteria, fruit flies, yeast, zebrafish, and other organisms. CRISPR is based on a single-stranded "guided" RNA sequence that is specific to the target gene and a protein called Cas9. Compared to TALEN approaches, guided RNAs are easier to design and synthesize. Cas9 delivers the guided RNA to the target DNA sequence, which enables the target DNA to be knocked out or replaced by a substitute sequence. Based on the rapid development of the CRISPR method, this approach may turn out to be a very valuable tool for gene therapy in the future.

RNA Silencing for Gene Inhibition

Attempts have been made to use **antisense oligonucleotides** to inhibit translation of mRNAs from defective genes, but this approach to gene therapy has generally not yet proven to be reliable. Nonetheless, the emergence of RNA interference as a powerful gene-silencing tool has reinvigorated gene therapy approaches by gene silencing. As you learned in earlier in the text (see Chapter 17), **RNA interference (RNAi)** is a form of gene-expression regulation (Figure 17–14). In animals short, double-stranded RNA molecules are delivered into cells where the enzyme Dicer chops them into 21- to 25-nt long pieces called **small interfering RNAs (siRNAs)**. siRNAs then join with an enyzme complex called the **RNA-inducing silencing complex (RISC)**, which shuttles the siRNAs to their target mRNA, where they bind by complementary base pairing. The RISC complex can block siRNA-bound mRNAs from being translated into protein or can lead to degradation of siRNA-bound mRNAs so that they cannot be translated into protein (**ST Figure 6–10**).

A main challenge to RNAi-based therapeutics so far has been *in vivo* delivery of double-stranded RNA or siRNA. RNAs degrade quickly in the body. It is also hard to get RNA to penetrate cells in the target tissue. For example, how does one deliver RNA-based therapies to cancer cells but not to noncancerous, healthy cells? Two common delivery approaches are to inject the siRNA directly or to deliver them via a DNA plasmid vector that is taken in by cells and transcribed to make double-stranded RNA which Dicer can cleave into siRNAs. Lentivirus, liposome, and attachment of siRNAs to cholesterol and fatty acids are other approaches being used to deliver siRNAs (ST Figure 6–10).

More than a dozen clinical trials involving RNAi are underway in the United States. Several RNAi clinical trials to treat blindness are showing promising results. One RNAi strategy to treat a form of blindness called macular degeneration targets a gene called *VEGF*. The VEGF protein promotes blood vessel growth. Overexpression of this gene, causing excessive production of blood vessels in the retina,

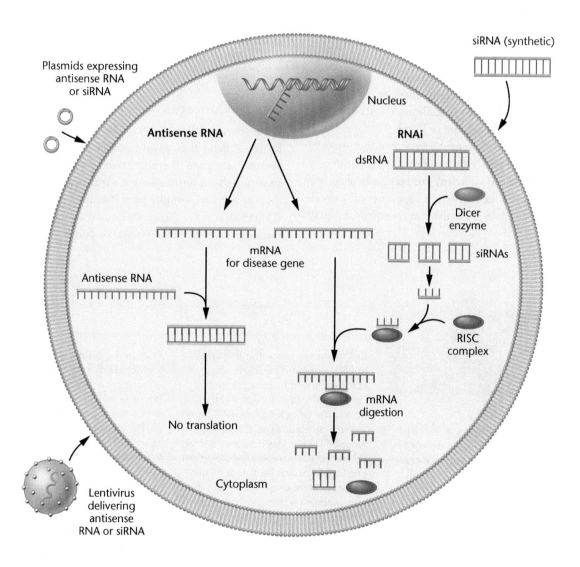

ST FIGURE 6–10 Antisense RNA and RNA interference (RNAi) approaches to silence genes for gene therapy. Antisense RNA technology and RNAi are two ways to silence gene expression and turn off disease genes. In antisense technology, an antisense RNA molecule (complementary to the sense strand of mRNA produced by a cell) binds to the mRNA expressed by the disease gene and prevents it from being translated. With RNAi technology, siRNAs are escorted by the RISC protein complex to bind to a target mRNA molecule, causing its degradation and thus preventing translation. Antisense RNA and RNAi molecules can be delivered in various ways, including direct application of synthetic RNAs, by plasmids, and via viral vectors.

leads to impaired vision and eventually blindness. Many expect that this disease will soon become the first condition to receive approval for treatment by RNAi therapy. Other disease candidates for treatment by RNAi include several different cancers, diabetes, multiple sclerosis, and arthritis.

Future Challenges and Ethical Issues

Despite the progress that we have noted thus far, many questions remain to be answered before we can hope for widespread application of the gene therapy methodology in the treatment of genetic disorders:

- What is the proper route for gene delivery in different kinds of disorders? For example, what is the best way to treat brain or muscle tissues? Tissue-specific gene delivery approaches are key.
- What percentage of cells in an organ or a tissue need to express a therapeutic gene to alleviate the effects of a genetic disorder? How can millions of cells be treated in an organ such as the brain or liver?
- What amount of a therapeutic gene product must be produced to provide lasting improvement of the condition, and how can sufficient production be ensured? Currently, many gene therapy approaches provide only short-lived delivery of the therapeutic gene and its protein.

- Will it be possible to use gene therapy to treat diseases that involve multiple genes?
- Can expression or the timing of expression of therapeutic genes be controlled in a patient so that genes can be turned on or off at a particular time or as necessary?
- Will targeted gene delivery approaches become more widely used for gene therapy trials?

For many people, the question remains whether gene therapy can ever recover from past setbacks and fulfill its promise as a cure for genetic diseases. Clinical trials for any new therapy are potentially dangerous, and often, animal studies will not accurately reflect the reaction of individual humans to the methodology leading to the delivery of new genes. However, as the history of similar struggles encountered with such life-saving developments such as the use of antibiotics and organ transplants has shown, there will be setbacks and even tragedies, but step by small step, we will move toward a technology that could—someday—provide reliable and safe treatment for severe genetic diseases.

Ethical Concerns Surrounding Gene Therapy

Gene therapy raises several ethical concerns, and many forms of gene therapy are sources of intense debate. At present, all gene therapy trials are restricted to using somatic cells as targets for gene transfer. This form of gene therapy is called **somatic gene therapy**; only one individual is affected, and the therapy is done with the permission and informed consent of the patient or family.

BOX 3
Gene Doping for Athletic Performance?

Gene therapy is intended to provide treatments or cures for genetic diseases, but the concept of gene addition or gene silencing can also apply for those seeking genetic enhancements to improve athletic performance. You are likely familiar with controversies surrounding the use of performance-enhancing drugs in amateur and professional sports. As athletes at all levels seek a competitive edge, will gene therapy as a form of "gene doping" to improve performance be far behind?

We already know that in animal models enhanced muscle function can be achieved by gene addition. For example, adding copies of the insulin-like growth factor (*IGF-1*) gene to mice improves aspects of muscle function. The kidney hormone erythropoietin (EPO) increases red blood cell production, which leads to a higher oxygen content of the blood and thus improved endurance during exercise. Synthetic forms of EPO are a banned substance in Olympic athletes. Several groups have proposed using gene therapy to deliver the *EPO* gene into athletes "naturally." As another example, transgenic mice overexpressing the peroxisome proliferator-activated receptor delta (*PPAR-δ*) gene show enhanced endurance in exercise tests.

Prior to the 2008 Olympics in Beijing, a genetics laboratory in China was offering gene-based enhancements, but it is not known if any athletes took advantage of this service.

The international community is clearly concerned, and since 2004 the World Anti-Doping Agency (WADA) has included gene doping through gene therapy as a prohibited method in sanctioned competitions. However, methods to detect gene doping are not well established. If techniques for gene therapy become more routine, many feel it is simply a matter of time before gene doping through gene therapy will be the next generation of performance-enhancement treatments. Obviously, many legal and ethical questions will arise if gene doping becomes a reality.

Two other forms of gene therapy have not been approved, primarily because of the unresolved ethical issues surrounding them. The first is called **germ-line therapy**, whereby germ cells (the cells that give rise to the gametes—i.e., sperm and eggs) or mature gametes are used as targets for gene transfer. In this approach, the transferred gene is incorporated into all the future cells of the body, including the germ cells. As a result, individuals in future generations will also be affected, without their consent. Is this kind of procedure ethical? Do we have the right to make this decision for future generations? Thus far, the concerns have outweighed the potential benefits, and such research is prohibited.

Box 3 mentioned gene doping, which is also an example of **enhancement gene therapy**, whereby people may be "enhanced" for some desired trait. This is another unapproved form of gene therapy—which is extremely controversial and is strongly opposed by many people. Should genetic technology be used to enhance human potential? For example, should it be permissible to use gene therapy to increase height, enhance athletic ability, or extend intellectual potential? Presently, the consensus is that enhancement therapy, like germ-line therapy, is an unacceptable use of gene therapy. However, there is an ongoing debate, and many issues are still unresolved. For example, the FDA now permits growth hormone produced by recombinant DNA technology to be used as a growth enhancer, in addition to its medical use for the treatment of growth-associated genetic disorders. Critics charge that the use of a gene product for enhancement will lead to the use of transferred genes for the same purpose. The outcome of these debates may affect not only the fate of individuals but the direction of our society as well.

Gene therapy is currently a fairly expensive treatment. But what is the right price for a cure? It remains to be seen how health-care insurance providers will view gene therapy. But if gene therapy treatments provide a health-care option that drastically improves the quality of life for patients for whom there are few other options, it is likely that insurance companies will reimburse patients for treatment costs.

Finally, *who* to treat by gene therapy is yet another ethically provocative consideration. In the Jesse Gelsinger case mentioned earlier, the symptoms of his OTC deficiency were minimized by a low protein diet and drug treatments. Whether it was necessary to treat Jesse by gene therapy and whether he should have ever been approved as a volunteer to test the safety of a gene therapy protocol are questions that have been widely debated.

Selected Readings and Resources

Journal Articles

Aiuti, A., et al. 2013. Lentiviral hematopoietic stem cell gene therapy in patients with Wiskott-Aldrich syndrome. *Science*, 341: 1233151.

Akst, J. 2012. Targeting DNA. *The Scientist*, 26: 36–42.

Baker, M. 2012. Gene-editing nucleases. *Nature Methods*, 9: 23–26.

Biffi, A., et al. 2013. Lentiviral hematopoietic stem cell gene therapy benefits metachromatic leukodystrophy. *Science*, 341: 1233158.

Carroll, D. 2011. Genome engineering with zinc-finger nucleases. *Genetics*, 188: 773–782.

Cartier, N., et al. 2009. Hematopoietic stem cell gene therapy with a lentiviral vector in X-linked adrenoleukodystrophy. *Science*, 326: 818–823.

Cavazzanna-Calvo, M., et al. 2010. Transfusion independence and HMGA2 activation after gene therapy of human β-thalassemia. *Nature* 467: 318–322.

Friedmann, T., Rabin, O., and Frankel, M. S. 2010. Gene doping and sport. *Science*, 327: 647–648.

Golic, K.G. 2013. RNA-guided nucleases: A new era for engineering the genomes of model and nonmodel organisms. *Genetics*, 195: 303–308.

Gorman, C., and Maron, D.F. 2014. The RNA revolution. *Scientific American*, 310:52–59.

Hacein-Bey-Abina, S., Von Kalle, C., Schmidt, M., et al. 2003. *LM02*-associated clonal T cell proliferation in two patients after gene therapy for SCID-X1. *Science*, 302: 415–419.

Jacobsen, S.G., et al. 2012. Gene therapy for Leber congenital amaurosis caused by *RPE65* mutations. *Arch. Ophthalmol.*, 130: 9–24.

Osborn, M.J., et al. 2013. TALEN-based gene correction for epidermolysis bullosa. *Molecular Therapy*, 21: 1151–1159.

Ousterout, D.G., et al. 2013. Reading frame correction by targeted genome editing restores dystrophin expression in cells from Duchene muscular dystrophy patients. *Molecular Therapy*, 4 June 2013; doi: 10.1038/mt.2013.111

Rossi, J.J., June, C.H., and Kohn, D.B. 2007. Genetic therapies against HIV. *Nature Biotechnology*, 25: 1444–1454.

Sheridan, C. 2011. Gene therapy finds its niche. *Nature Biotechnology*, 29: 121–128.

Wirth, T., Parker, N., and Ylä-Hertuttuala, S. 2013. History of gene therapy. *Gene*, 10: 162–169.

Yzer, S., et al. 2011. Gene-specific phenotypes and mechanism-based treatments in early-onset retinal dystrophies. *Retinal Physician*, July 2011.

Web Sites

All the Virology on the WWW. http://www.virology.net/garryfavwebgenether.html

American Society of Gene & Cell Therapy. http://www.asgct.org

Center for Gene Therapy – University of Iowa. http://genetherapy.genetics.uiowa.edu

ClinicalTrials.Gov. http://www.clinicaltrials.gov

Explore Research: American Cancer Society. http://www.cancer.org/research/index

Gene Therapy. http://www.nature.com/gt/index.html

Gene Therapy Clinical Trials Worldwide. http://www.abedia.com/wiley/index.html

Gene Therapy: Genetic Home Reference, National Library of Medicine. http://ghr.nlm.nih.gov/handbook/therapy

U.S. Food and Drug Administration: Cellular and Gene Therapy Research. http://www.fda.gov/BiologicsBloodVaccines/ScienceResearch/BiologicsResearchAreas/ucm124376.htm

SPECIAL TOPIC 6

Review Questions

1. What is gene therapy?
2. Compare and contrast *ex vivo* and *in vivo* gene therapy as approaches for delivering therapeutic genes.
3. When treating a person by gene therapy, is it necessary that the therapeutic gene becomes part of a chromosome (integration) when inserted into cells? Explain your answer.
4. Describe two ways that therapeutic genes can be delivered into cells.
5. Explain how viral vectors can be used for gene therapy and provide two examples of commonly used viral vectors. What are some of the major challenges that must be overcome to develop safer and more effective viral vectors for gene therapy?
6. During the first successful gene therapy trial in which Ashanti DeSilva was treated for SCID, did the therapeutic gene delivered to Ashanti replace the defective copy of the ADA gene? Why were white blood cells chosen as the targets for the therapeutic gene?
7. Explain an example of successful gene therapy trial. In your answer be sure to consider: a description of the disease condition that was treated, the mutation or disease gene affected, the therapeutic gene delivered, and the method of delivery use for the therapy.
8. What is targeted gene therapy or gene editing, and how does this approach differ from traditional gene therapy approaches?
9. How do ZFNs work?
10. Describe two gene-silencing techniques and explain how they may be used for gene therapy.

Discussion Questions

1. Discuss the challenges scientists face in making gene therapy a safe, reliable, and effective technique for treating human disease conditions.
2. Who should be treated by gene therapy? What criteria are used to determine if a person is a candidate for gene therapy? Should gene therapy be used for cosmetic purposes or to improve athletic performance?
3. Describe future challenges and ethical issues associated with gene therapy.